2014 Federal Tax Practitioner's Guide

Susan Flax Posner, J.D., LL.M. in Taxation

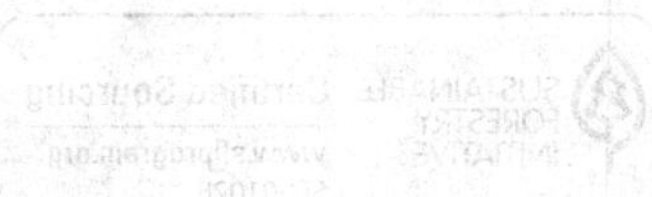

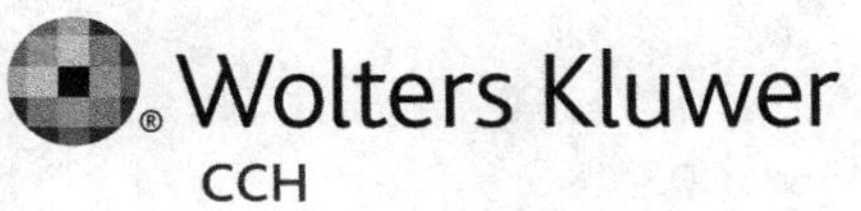

Editorial Staff

Editor .... Lynn S. Kopon, J.D., LL.M.
Production .... Linda Kalteux

ISBN: 978-0-8080-3717-0

4025 W. Peterson Ave.
Chicago, IL 60646-6085
800 248 3248
CCHGroup.com

Printed in the United States of America

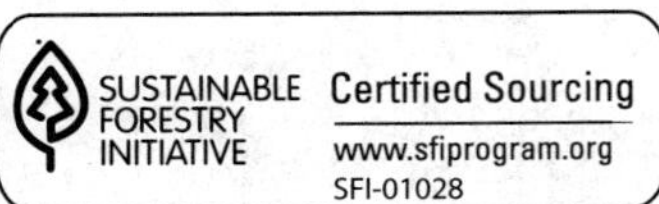

Introduction

Up-to-date tax information and decisive action are imperative when dealing with tax issues. The IRS continually makes changes affecting tax planning and tax return preparation and filing. The *2014 Federal Tax Practitioner's Guide* (formerly called the *Federal Tax Course: A Guide for the Tax Practitioner*), the most authoritative and comprehensive authority, covers all of the new changes in the federal tax structure plus all revenue and Internal Revenue Code changes, and important new IRS regulations, rulings and court decisions. This easy-to-use one-volume guide to tax preparation and planning is the equivalent of a complete educational update to all of the developments in the law. This book provides the latest guidance on how to comply with IRS rules and regulations. When you need to make a decisive action in dealing with tax issues, the *2014 Federal Tax Practitioner's Guide* will answer all your questions.

The *2014 Federal Tax Practitioner's Guide* is written in simple language with the new tax laws and regulations clearly and concisely explained for quick reading. The book is filled with hundreds of tax strategies and concrete, detailed examples with suggested solutions. This one-of-a-kind tax guide is an essential and necessary component of any tax return preparer's, business planner's, legal advisor's or business owner's library.

Highlights of the 2014 Edition

The 2014 edition of the *Federal Tax Practitioner's Guide* is updated to reflect significant case law developments as well as important IRS rulings, revenue procedures, notices, announcements, and regulations that were released in the last year. The new and revised discussions, examples, and tax planning strategies are designed to resolve the tax questions faced by tax practitioners and to help the tax return preparer complete 2013 federal income tax returns. The 2014 edition of the *Federal Tax Practitioner's Guide* reflects federal tax legislation to the date of publication.

The volume is updated to include discussion of the following tax law developments:

- Inflation adjustments for 2013.
- Updated excise tax rates.
- 2013 and 2014 income tax rate tables for individuals, corporations, and estates and trusts.
- Revised standard mileage rates for operating an auto for business, charitable, medical or moving expense purposes.
- When to use Form 1040, Form 1040A and Form 1040EZ.
- Extension of exclusion of indebtedness on principal residence.
- Reinstatement of limitation on itemized deductions for higher-income individuals.
- Reinstatement of personal exemption phaseout.

- Extension of deduction of state and local general sales taxes.
- Extension of teacher's expense deduction.
- Extension of deduction of mortgage insurance premium.
- Enhancements made to the Coverdell education savings accounts.
- Changes made to employer-provided educational assistance programs.
- Extension of federal scholarships with obligatory service requirements.
- Changes to student loan interest deduction.
- Extension of tuition and fees deduction.
- In-service rollovers from traditional to designated Roth accounts.
- Extension of qualified charitable distributions from IRAs.
- Extension of enhanced deduction for charitable contribution of real property for conservation purposes.
- Changes to earned income tax credit.
- Changes to child tax credit.
- Extension of increased child and dependent care credit.
- Changes to adoption credit and adoption assistance programs.
- Extension of American Opportunity tax credit.
- Extension of plug-in electric drive motor vehicle tax credit.
- Extension of residential energy property credit.
- Increase in Alternative Minimum Tax (AMT) exemption amounts.
- Offset of nonrefundable personal credits against regular tax and AMT liability.
- Extension of parity for exclusion limitation on van pool benefits, transit passes and qualified parking.
- Changes in capital gain tax rates for individuals, estates, and trusts.
- Extension of 100 percent gain exclusion and lower AMT preference percentage for excluded gain on qualified small business stock sales.
- Extension of reduced rates for qualified dividends.
- Extension of pass-through treatment of qualified dividend income.
- Changes to accumulated earnings tax.
- Changes to personal holding company tax rate.
- Repeal of collapsible corporation rules.
- Changes to estate, gifts, and generation-skipping transfer tax provisions.
- Increase in maximum estate and gift tax rate.
- Changes to transfer tax exclusion and exemption amounts.
- Repeal of qualified family-owned business interest deduction.
- Elimination of state death tax credit.

- Extension of state death tax deduction.
- Changes in law regarding estate tax exclusion for qualified conservation easements.
- Continuation of stepped-up basis rules for property acquired from decedent.
- Changes to deemed and retroactive allocations of GST exemption.
- Changes to law regarding severing trusts for GST purposes.
- Modification of valuation rules for GST purposes.
- Late GST elections and substantial compliance.
- Changes in law regarding estate tax installment payment for closely held business.
- Extension of availability of installment payment of estate tax for interest in lending and finance business.
- Extension of bonus depreciation to certain property.
- Changes in law regarding election to claim accelerated AMT credit in lieu of bonus depreciation.
- Increase in Code Sec. 179 expensing limits.
- Extension of 15-year straight-line cost recovery period for qualified leasehold improvements, qualified restaurant property, and qualified retail improvements.
- Extension of seven-year depreciation period for motorsports entertainment complexes.
- Extension of accelerated depreciation for business property on Indian reservations.
- Extension and modification of special allowance for cellulosic biofuel plan property.
- Extension of special expensing rules for film and television productions.
- Extension of election to expense advanced mine safety equipment.
- Extension of research tax credit.
- Changes to employer-provided child care tax credit.
- Extension of work opportunity tax credit.
- Extension of employer credit for activated military reservists.
- Extension of new markets tax credit.
- Extension of Indian employment tax credit.
- Extension of railroad track maintenance credit.
- Extension of mine rescue team training tax credit.
- Extension and expansion of cellulosic biofuel producer credit.
- Extension of production tax credit for electricity produced from renewable resource.
- Extension of credit for new energy efficient homes.
- Extension of energy efficient appliance credit for manufacturers.

- Extension of biodiesel, renewable diesel, and alternative fuels incentives.
- Extension of alternative fuel vehicle refueling property credit.
- Extension of modified rule for basis adjustment to stock of corporation making charitable contributions.
- Extension of enhanced deduction for charitable contributions of food inventory.
- Extension of reduced recognition period for S corporation built-in gains tax.
- Extension of qualified zone academy bond program.
- Extension of empowerment zone tax benefits.
- *T.J. Welle,* where sole owner of C corporation received no constructive dividend when the corporation provided construction-related services without charging profit margin.
- Practice pointers on how to avoid constructive dividend treatment.
- How to take plan loans from qualified retirement plans.
- Prohibited transactions between a disqualified person and a plan.
- *L.F. Peek,* where the court held that IRA owners' personal guarantees of loans made to a corporation owned by the IRAs constituted prohibited transactions.
- Discussion of other prohibited transactions.
- *In re Clark,* where the court concluded that a nonspousal inherited IRA was not exempt from creditor's claims in bankruptcy.
- Reg. §301.9100-3, which is used to request an extension of time to make the election to recharacterize a traditional-IRA-to-Roth-IRA conversion even if deadline passed.
- Letter Ruling 201324022 where IRS waived 60-day rollover period for wife where husband withdrew funds from wife's IRA under a power of attorney and he gambled funds away.
- When is a security "readily tradable on an established securities market."
- *R.S. Yarish,* where the court concluded that a highly-compensated employee who was fully vested in ESOP had to include in income the entire amount of his vested accrued benefit.
- Notice 2013-48, where the IRS established a *de minimis* exception to the wash sale rules of Code Sec. 1091 for redemptions of shares in a money market fund that do not maintain a constant share price under new SEC regulations.
- *W.P. Adams,* where the court held that sale by an individual of his house qualified for nonrecognition treatment as part of a like-kind exchange.
- *B.V. Belk,* where taxpayers denied charitable deduction for contributing conservation easement on real property with golf course because use restriction not granted in perpetuity.
- *C.R. Irby,* where taxpayers entitled to claim charitable contribution deductions for conservation easements because the conservation purpose protected in perpetuity despite a clause providing for remittance of the proceeds following judicial sale to the funding entities.

- Rev. Proc. 2013-13, where the IRS provided new simplified, optional method for claiming home office deduction.
- *C.A. Alphonso*, where co-op owner had sufficient property interest to claim casualty loss deduction for share of assessment needed to fix damages retaining wall collapsed.
- *R.F. Goeller*, where state criminal law statutes irrelevant in determining whether taxpayers suffered theft loss under Code Sec. 165.
- *A.R. Lantz Co.*, where the court relied on factors to determine whether the advances to the corporation gave rise to a bona fide debt as opposed to an equity investment.
- *J.C. Ramig*, where a corporate shareholder and employee not entitled to bad-debt deductions for amounts advanced to corporation because they were equity investments, rather than loans.
- *M.S. Barnes*, where S corporation shareholder's basis could be reduced by the suspended losses in the first year their basis was adequate to absorb losses even though they would not be able to deduct losses.
- Private Letter Ruling 201310002, where a trust with a distribution committee not grantor trust because grantor did not retain powers that would result in the grantor being treated as trust owner.
- *G. Thompson*, where IRS settlement officer did not abuse discretion by denying reduction of taxpayer's monthly installment payments for back taxes based on tithing obligation to church.
- *K.M. Wilson*, holding that Tax Court can consider new evidence outside the scope of the administrative record in determining whether taxpayer should receive equitable innocent spouse relief under Code Sec. 6015(f).
- *City Wide Transit, Inc.*, holding that IRS could make an employment tax assessment after expiration of three-year statute of limitations because taxpayer's accountant filed fraudulent tax returns in order to embezzle money owed to IRS.
- *R.D. Beard*, addressing whether taxpayer filed a return for purposes of tolling the three-year statute of limitations under Code Sec. 6501(a).
- Costs of materials and supplies.
- Optional election to capitalize rotable and temporary spare parts.
- Election to capitalize repair and maintenance costs.
- *De minimis* safe harbor expensing rule.
- Safe harbor for routine maintenance on property.
- Tax treatment of amounts paid to improve tangible property.
- Safe harbor for small taxpayers with buildings.
- Capitalization of betterments under Reg. § 1.263(a)-3(j)(1).
- Capitalization of restorations.
- *Metro Leasing & Dev. Corp.*, addressing the independent investor test to determine reasonableness of executive's compensation.

- Rev. Rul. 2013-17, where IRS ruled that all legal same-sex marriages will be recognized for federal tax purposes.
- *E.S. Windsor,* where the Supreme Court held that Section 3 of the Defense of Marriage Act (DOMA) was unconstitutional.
- Reg. § 301.7701-4(a) defining the meaning of the term "trust."
- Rev. Rul. 2013-14, where the IRS concluded that a Mexican Land Trust that held title to residential real property was not a trust.
- Imposition of 3.8 percent net investment income tax.
- Imposition of 3.8 percent net investment income tax on estates and trusts.
- What trusts are subject to 3.8 percent net investment income tax.
- How estates and trust can minimize exposure to 3.8 percent net investment income surtax.
- Updated discussion of grantor trusts.
- Updated discussion of tax consequences of grantor trusts.
- Sales between grantor trust and grantor.
- Income tax rules vs. estate planning rules.
- Intentionally defective grantor trusts.
- Tax planning benefits offered by IDITs.
- Obama's proposals to change tax treatment of grantor trusts.
- Factors considered by the courts in determining whether a trust actually existed for tax purposes.
- *S.E. Vlach,* where trusts established for asset protection by a doctor were found to be shams.
- What a surviving spouse must do to take advantage of a deceased spouse's spousal unused exclusion (DSUE) amount.
- New definition of DSUE amount.
- New estate, gift and generation-skipping tax rates.
- *T. Szekely,* where the IRS failed to consider the taxpayer's offer-in-compromise and proceeded too hastily in closing the case without taking it into consideration.
- *R. Cohen,* where a whistleblower's petition to order the IRS to reopen his award claim was dismissed for failure to state a claim.
- *AHG Investments, LLC,* where the court concluded that a taxpayer may not avoid application of gross valuation misstatement penalty merely by conceding on grounds unrelated to valuation or basis.
- *N. Crispin,* where the court upheld the 40 percent gross valuation misstatement penalty even though the taxpayer relied on tax professional's opinion.
- *J.A. Hatling,* where the court concluded that IRS may establish fraud by circumstantial evidence, which includes various "badges of fraud."
- Penalty imposed for fraudulent failure to file.

- How taxpayers can show reasonable cause for delay in filing or payment of tax.
- *R.W. Boyle*, where taxpayer had the burden of proving both reasonable cause and absence of willful neglect.
- Reg. § 301.6651-1(c)(1) which provides that the failure to file is due to reasonable cause if the taxpayer exercised ordinary business care and prudence and was nevertheless unable to file the return within prescribed time.
- Code Sec. 6656 penalty imposed for failure to make timely deposits of these taxes.
- *Brewery, Inc.*, where the court used bright line test and held that financial difficulties can never constitute reasonable cause to excuse penalties for failure to pay employment taxes.
- *Fran Corp.*, where the court held that a case-by-case assessment is necessary to determine whether financial difficulties excuse penalties.
- *East Wind Industries, Inc.*, and *Van Camp & Bennion*, where courts held that all facts and circumstances of taxpayers' financial situation must be examined to determine what will excuse penalties.
- Field Attorney Advice 20133101F, where taxpayer not entitled to claim an abandonment loss deduction.
- Updated discussion of tax treatment of gambling losses.
- Updated discussion of hobby losses and Reg. § 1.183-2(b) which lists nine factors to consider when determining a taxpayer's profit motive.
- *R.A. Mayo*, where taxpayer gambling on horse races held to be professional gambler.
- *J.F. Chow*, where retired physician was professional gambler because she engaged in gambling activities with continuity and regularity.
- *T.M. Le*, where taxpayers who believed in feng shui were professional gamblers.
- *L.M. Myers*, and *J. Castagnetta*, where truckers were held to be professional gamblers because they gambled in businesslike manner.
- *S.B. Whitten*, where contestant on TV's Wheel of Fortune not professional gambler because not in the trade or business of either gambling or appearing as contestant on TV game show.
- *R.L. Moore*, where individual who worked 40 hours a week as a traveling x-ray technician and gambled at slot machines in casinos when he was off work not professional gambler because he failed to conduct activities in businesslike manner.
- *D.J. Hastings*, where business owner who gambled primarily on weekends and holidays not in trade or business of gambling because showed no profit motive.
- *M.N. Merkin*, where psychiatrist's activity of playing video poker did not rise to level of trade or business activity because failed to prove profit motive.
- *M. Ferguson*, where building operator engineer who spent more than 1,000 hours of free time playing video poker not professional gambler because failed to prove profit motive.

- How trusts establish material participation for purposes of passive loss rules under Code Sec. 469.
- *Mattie K. Carter Trust*, holding that the activities of the trust's fiduciaries, employees, and agents should be considered to determine whether the trust's participation is "regular, continuous, and substantial" for passive loss purposes.
- Technical Advice Memorandum 201317010, holding that trusts establish material participation for passive loss purposes only if fiduciaries are involved in the operations of the relevant activities on "regular, continuous, and substantial basis."
- *F.J. Dirico*, where passive activity loss self-rental rule didn't apply to telecommunication tower and land rental income derived by a taxpayer from wholly owned S corporation.
- Regulations that provide "fresh start" opportunity for regrouping activities to avoid 3.8 percent net investment income tax.
- Discussion of definition of bona fide debt.
- Worthlessness defined for tax purposes in Reg. § 1.166-2(a).
- *J.M. Herrera*, addressing factors to use in determining whether bona fide debt exists.
- Updated earned income credit chart.
- Updated discussion on rules for claiming work opportunity tax credit including discussion of tax-exempt employers hiring veterans.
- *Union Carbide Corp.*, holding that consolidated group not entitled to additional research credits for supplies used to conduct research on products that were in the process of being manufactured for sale and were sold, because expenditures not qualified research expenses.
- *Hewlett-Packard Co.*, holding that a corporate taxpayer had to include nonsales income, including dividends, interest, rent, and other income in average annual gross receipts for purposes of calculating base amount used for determining amount of research tax credit.
- *B. Shami*, holding that wages paid by S corporation to shareholders/executives not qualified expenses for purposes of research credit because individuals failed to substantiate that they conducted research or engaged in direct supervision of research activities.
- Notice 2013-20, where the IRS addressed how controlled groups must allocate research credit.
- IR-2013-78 where IRS stated that all empowerment zone designations in effect on December 31, 2009, remain in effect through December 31, 2013.
- New detailed discussion on the Code Sec. 36b Premium Assistance Tax Credit.
- New discussion of credit claimed for qualified alternative fuel vehicle refueling property.
- Discussion of election to accelerate AMT credit in lieu of bonus depreciation provided for extension property.

- *In re Quality Stores, Inc.*, holding that SUB payments *not* wages and not subject to FICA withholding even though subject to income tax withholding.
- *CSX Corp.*, where the court reached a result opposite to the one reached by the court in *In re Quality Stores, Inc.*
- Supreme Court's grant of certiorari in *In re Quality Stores, Inc.* to resolve circuit split.
- Rev. Rul. 2012-18 providing guidance to taxpayers to help distinguish tips which are subject to special FICA tax rules from service charges which must be treated as wages.
- Discussion of tip reporting by large food and beverage establishments.
- Discussion of voluntary tip reporting compliance agreements.
- Discussion of what nonresident aliens must file to claim a tax treaty exemption from withholding on some or all compensation.
- Discussion of employer's 30 percent withholding rate imposed on payments to aliens.
- Discussion of 30 percent withholding and foreign agricultural workers in the United States.
- Discussion of special instructions for Form W-4.
- Announcement 2012-45, where the IRS modified VCSP.
- Announcement 2012-46, where the IRS announced that it was changing the eligibility requirements to allow more employers, particularly larger ones, to apply for the VCSP.
- IRS News Release IR-2013-23, announcing availability of a modified VCSP.
- Discussion of Conservation Reserve Program.
- *R.J. Morehouse*, holding that taxpayer who received payments under CRP was liable for self-employment tax under Code Sec. 1401.
- *F.J. Wuebker*, addressing whether CRP payments were excluded from the calculation of net earnings from self-employment as "rentals from real estate" under Code Sec. 1402(a)(1).
- Notice 2006-108, where IRS held that CRP rental payments were not payments for right to use or occupy real property.
- Discussion of deferring income on prepaid gift cards.
- Rev. Proc 2011-18, holding that taxpayer selling gift cards redeemable through other entities should be treated the same as taxpayer selling gift cards that only it redeems.
- Updated discussion on how small business corporations receive S corporation tax status.
- Rev. Proc 2013-30, providing simplified and consolidated provisions for requesting relief for late S corporation elections under Code Sec. 1362, late QSST elections, late ESBT elections, late QSub elections, and late corporate classification elections.
- Discussion of penalties imposed for failure to file S corporation.

- Discussion of Code Sec. 362(e)(2) which prevents duplication of net built-in losses in certain corporate nonrecognition transfers and applies to corporate acquisitions of property with a net built-in loss in transactions.
- Discussion of anti-loss importation limitations that apply in both Code Sec. 334(b)(1)(B) and Code Sec. 362(e)(1).
- Discussion of Code Sec. 336(e) election addressing whether certain stock sales and distributions may be treated as asset transfers.
- Discussion of tax treatment when corporation transfers property to RICs and REITs.
- Discussion of excise tax imposed under Code Sec. 4982(a) on RICs.
- Discussion of RICs exempt from the Code Sec. 4982 excise tax.
- Discussion of 4 percent excise tax imposed on undistributed REIT income under Code Sec. 4981.
- Information Letter #20130001, March 29, 2013 addressing whether tax-exempt organization can use internet fundraising platform to raise money for project without jeopardizing tax-exempt characterization.
- Technical Advice Memorandum 201320023 concluding that sales of life insurance policies by fraternal society to member's widows not substantially related to tax-exempt purpose.
- Detailed discussion of how to determine whether partnership exists as discussed in three cases: *W.O. Culbertson; A.T. Azimzadeh; W.F. Holdner*; and Letter Ruling 201323015.
- *H.M. Luna*, where the court listed eight factors to consider in determining whether partnership exists for tax purposes.
- Discussion of tax treatment of syndication expenses.
- Rev. Proc. 2013-34 updating its equitable innocent spouse relief guidance.
- Discussion of Notice 2011-70 and Prop. Reg. § 1.6015-5(b)(2) which provide that individuals who request equitable innocent spouse relief under Code Sec. 6015(f) will no longer be required to submit request within two years of IRS first collection activity against requesting spouse.
- Discussion of *K.M. Wilson* and *R.E. Neal*, where courts held that it can consider new evidence outside the scope of administrative record in determining whether taxpayer should receive equitable innocent spouse relief under Code Sec. 6015(f)
- Chief Counsel Notice 2013-011, providing that Tax Court will apply a *de novo* standard of review when reviewing requests for equitable innocent spouse relief under Code Sec. 6015(f) relief.
- Discussion of IRS *e-file* procedures as discussed in Publication 1345, *Handbook for Authorized IRS e-file Providers of Individual Income Tax Returns*.
- Discussion of short-term agreement available to pay taxpayer's delinquent tax bills.
- Discussion of IRS discretion to accept or reject installment agreements.

- *G. Thompson*, holding that IRS settlement officer did not abuse discretion by denying reduction of taxpayer's monthly installment payments for back taxes based upon tithing obligation to church.
- Discussion of Electronic Federal Tax Payment System (EFTPS) which enables individual and business taxpayers to pay federal taxes electronically 24/7 using the Internet, or by phone using the EFTPS Voice Response System.
- *PPL Corp.*, where the U.S. Supreme Court concluded that the United Kingdom's windfall profits tax on several companies that were privatized between 1984 and 1996 was creditable excess profits tax for purposes of foreign tax credit.
- *S.J. Park*, holding that nonresident alien with gambling winnings in the United States must determine gain or loss on per-session basis rather than per-bet basis.
- *C.J. LeTourneau* and *E.D. Clark*, where the courts held that U.S. taxpayer may claim foreign earned income exclusion only with respect to wages earned while in or over foreign countries and not for wages earned in international airspace or in or over the United States.
- *W.D. Rogers*, concluding that a flight attendant whose duties were performed in and out of the United States could not exclude income under foreign earned income exclusion, but only that part allocated to services performed in foreign country.
- *J.B. Harrington*, holding that taxpayer's ties to Angola were "severely limited and transitory" and that taxpayer husband's abode for purposes of Code Sec. 911 was the U.S.
- Discussion of waiver of period of stay in foreign country to qualify for foreign income exclusion.
- *A.I. Appleton*, holding that U.S. citizen who was a permanent USVI resident and who filed income tax returns with the VIBIR for three consecutive years satisfied federal income tax filing obligation.
- Detailed discussion of Foreign Account Tax Compliance Act (FATCA) which was enacted to prevent tax evasion by U.S. citizens who use offshore bank accounts to avoid paying federal income tax.
- Discussion of Form 8938, *Statement of Specified Foreign Financial Assets*.
- Discussion of difference between FBAR and FATCA requirements.
- Discussion of FATCA reporting and withholding obligations for foreign financial institutions (FFIS).
- Notice 2013-43, providing that if foreign financial institution (FFI) fails to meet the FATCA requirements, a U.S. withholding agent must deduct and withhold 30 tax percent on any payments made to FFI after June 30, 2014, unless the withholding agent can document that payment exempt from withholding under Code Sec. 1471(a) and Reg. § 1.1471-2(a).
- Discussion of how FFI satisfies reporting requirements under FATCA.
- Discussion of FATCA reporting and withholding obligations for nonfinancial foreign entities (NFFES).
- Discussion of penalties imposed for failure to disclose foreign financial assets.

- Discussion of FBAR electronic filing requirements.
- Discussion of civil penalties imposed for failure to file Form TD F 90-22.1 (Report of Foreign Bank and Financial Accounts, commonly known as an "FBAR").
- Discussion of penalty imposed for failing to file Form 3520, *Annual Return to Report Transactions With Foreign Trusts and Receipt of Certain Foreign Gifts*.
- Discussion of penalty imposed for failing to file Form 3520-A, *Information Return of Foreign Trust With a U.S. Owner*.
- Discussion of penalty imposed for failing to file Form 5471, *Information Return of U.S. Persons With Respect to Certain Foreign Corporations*.
- Discussion of penalty imposed for failing to file Form 5472, *Information Return of a 25% Foreign-Owned U.S. Corporation or a Foreign Corporation Engaged in a U.S. Trade or Business*.
- Discussion imposed for failure to file Form 926, *Return by a U.S. Transferor of Property to a Foreign Corporation*.
- Discussion of penalty imposed for failing to file Form 8865, *Return of U.S. Persons With Respect to Certain Foreign Partnerships*.
- Discussion of fraud penalties imposed under Code Sec. 6651(f) or Code Sec. 6663.
- Discussion of penalty imposed for failing to file a tax return imposed under Code Sec. 6651(a)(1).
- Discussion of penalty imposed for failing to pay the amount of tax shown on the return under Code Sec. 6651(a)(2).
- Discussion of criminal charges imposed for failure to file FBAR.
- Discussion of requirements under Offshore Voluntary Disclosure Program and eligibility to participate in program as well as possible criminal charges for failure to comply with requirements.
- Notice 2013-43 where IRS revised timelines for implementation of the FATCA requirements of Code Sec. 1471 through Code Sec. 1474.
- *J.B. Molina* holding that taxpayer cannot exclude settlement damages related to employment discrimination.
- Notice 2013-7 revising mortgage deduction safe harbor for assistance payments to financially distressed homeowners.
- Field Attorney Advice 20133901F holding that 7-year useful life applied to minor league baseball player's contract.
- Updated discussion of *Elliotts, Inc.*, holding that Tax Court erred when it analyzed corporation's bonus payment plan and failed to consider reasonableness of the compensation payments.
- *Aries Communications Inc.*, holding that compensation paid to a key employee and owner not reasonable because company had bleak financial future.

You will find that your *2014 Federal Tax Practitioner's Guide* will become an essential and necessary addition to your library as you advise your clients, draft documents, engage in tax planning and prepare tax forms.

Susan Flax Posner, J.D., LL.M. in Taxation

November 2013

About the Author

Susan Flax Posner received her LL.M. in taxation from the George Washington University National Law Center and then served as a law clerk to Judge Irene F. Scott, U.S. Tax Court. Ms. Posner co-authored *Tax Planning Strategies* as well as *Taxation of Investments*, Second Edition. Ms. Posner currently writes a monthly newsletter entitled *Federal Tax Practitioner's Newsletter* and the *Estate & Gift Tax Handbook.* She also wrote the *Taxation of Investments Handbook,* which was published by CCH. She is a graduate of McGill University and University of Baltimore Law School. She has practiced law in Washington, D.C. and in Baltimore, Maryland.

Acknowledgment

The author would like to express her sincere appreciation to Lynn S. Kopon, J.D., LL.M., and to her production editor, Linda Kalteux, whose meticulous attention to detail, high standards of excellence, dedication, patience, and hard work on this update are exemplary. Their work is truly outstanding and worthy of recognition.

Table of Contents

(A detailed Table of Contents appears on the first page of each chapter.)

Key Tax Return Filing Facts—2009-2013 . . . ¶201
Excise Tax Rates . . . ¶210
2014 Federal Tax Calendar . . . ¶301

Figuring the Individual Income Tax

1. Individuals—Filing Status, Personal Exemptions, Standard Deduction . . . ¶1001
2. Gross Income—Inclusions . . . ¶2001
3. Retirement Plans . . . ¶3001
4. Employee Fringe Benefits . . . ¶4001
5. Gross Income—Exclusions . . . ¶5001
6. Gain or Loss—Basis—Recognition . . . ¶6001
7. Gain or Loss—Sale of Residence—Casualty—Theft—Condemnation . . . ¶7001
8. Capital Gains and Losses of Individuals . . . ¶8001

Maximizing Deductions and Credits

9. Personal Deductions . . . ¶9001
10. Travel and Entertainment Deductions . . . ¶10,001
11. Depreciation . . . ¶11,001
12. Business Deductions . . . ¶12,001
13. Losses and Bad Debts . . . ¶13,001
14. Tax Credits—Estimated Tax for Individuals . . . ¶14,001

Withholding—Payroll Taxes—Minimum Tax—Tax Accounting

15. Income Tax Withholding, Employment and Net Investment Income Tax . . . ¶15,001
16. Alternative Minimum Tax . . . ¶16,001
17. Inventory . . . ¶17,001
18. Accounting . . . ¶18,001
19. Installment and Deferred Payment Sales . . . ¶19,001

Corporate Tax—S Corporations—Partnerships—Estates and Trusts

20. Corporations—Tax Rates, Income, Deductions, Gains, and Losses . . . ¶20,001
21. S Corporations . . . ¶21,001
22. Corporations—Reorganizations—Stock Redemptions . . . ¶22,001

23. Corporations—Personal Holding Companies, Etc.—Exempt Organizations . . . . ¶23,001

24. Partnerships . . . . ¶24,001

25. Estates and Trusts . . . . ¶25,001

Returns & Payments—Foreign Income & Taxpayers—Gift & Estate Taxes

26. Returns and Payment of Tax . . . . ¶26,001

27. Assessment—Collection—Refunds . . . . ¶27,001

28. Foreign Income—Foreign Taxpayers . . . . ¶28,001

29. Gift and Estate Taxes . . . . ¶29,001

30. Limited Liability Companies and Limited Liability Partnerships . . . . ¶30,001

Master Index

Index . . . . page 31,001

Key Tax Return Filing Facts—2009-2013

¶201 KEY TAX NUMBERS

Following are key tax numbers that you need to know when completing the 2013 tax return (or reviewing returns for open years):

Type of Deduction	*2013*	*2012*	*2011*	*2010*	*2009*
Personal Exemption					
Single person	$3,900	$3,800	$3,700	$3,650	$3,650
Married filing jointly	7,800	7,600	7,400	7,300	7,300
Dependency Deduction					
For each dependent	3,900	3,800	3,700	3,650	3,650
Standard Deduction					
Married filing jointly	12,200	11,900	11,600	11,400	11,400
Qualified surviving spouse	12,200	11,900	11,600	11,400	11,400
Single person	6,100	5,950	5,800	5,700	5,700
Married filing separately	6,100	5,950	5,800	5,700	5,700
Head of household	8,950	8,700	8,500	8,400	8,350
Additional Standard Deduction for Those Age 65 or Over or Blind					
Married persons	1,200	1,150	1,150	1,100	1,100
Single persons	1,500	1,450	1,450	1,400	1,400

"Kiddie tax." Tax on net unearned income of children under age 18 and that of 19 to 23 year-old students who do not provide half of his or her own support costs with earned income by the end of the year is computed at the parent's highest marginal tax rate, rather than at the child's usually lower marginal rate [Code Sec. 1(g)(2)(A)]. To arrive at net unearned income for purposes of computing the 2013 kiddie tax, you subtract from the child's unearned income (interest, capital gains and dividends) the sum of (a) $1,000 in 2013 (no change in 2014) plus (b) the greater of $1,000 in 2013 (no change in 2014) or, if the child itemizes, the amount of deductions allowed for the tax year that is directly connected with the production of unearned income (subject to the two-percent AGI limitation).

Social Security Tax

The Federal Insurance Contributions Act (FICA) imposes two taxes on employers, employees, and self-employed workers—one for Old Age, Survivors and Disability Insurance (OASDI; commonly known as the Social Security tax), and the other for Hospital Insurance (HI; commonly known as the Medicare tax).

2013 RATES

For 2013, the FICA tax rate for employers is 7.65% each—6.2% for OASDI and 1.45% for HI. For 2013, an employee pays:

(a) 6.2% Social Security tax on the first $113,700 of wages (maximum tax is $7,049.40 [6.20% of $113,700]), plus

(b) 1.45% Medicare tax on the first $200,000 of wages ($250,000 for joint returns; $125,000 for married taxpayers filing a separate return), plus

(c) 2.35% Medicare tax (regular 1.45% Medicare tax + 0.9% additional Medicare tax) on all wages in excess of $200,000 ($250,000 for joint returns; $125,000 for married taxpayers filing a separate return) [Code Sec. 3101(b)(2)].

For 2013, the self-employment tax imposed on self-employed people is:

- 12.4% OASDI on the first $113,700 of self-employment income, for a maximum tax of $14,098.80 (12.40% of $113,700), plus
- 2.90% Medicare tax on the first $200,000 of self-employment income ($250,000 of combined self-employment income on a joint return, $125,000 on a separate return) [Code Sec. 1401(a), (b)], plus
- 3.8% (2.90% regular Medicare tax + 0.9% additional Medicare tax) on all self-employment income in excess of $200,000 ($250,000 of combined self-employment income on a joint return, $125,000 for married taxpayers filing a separate return) [Code Sec. 1401(b)(2)].

2014 RATES

For 2014, the FICA tax rate for employers is 7.65% each—6.2% for OASDI and 1.45% for HI. For 2014, an employee pays:

(a) 6.2% Social Security tax on the first $117,000 of wages (maximum tax is $7,254.00 [6.2% of $117,000]), plus

(b) 1.45% Medicare tax on the first $200,000 of wages ($250,000 for joint returns; $125,000 for married taxpayers filing a separate return), plus

(c) 2.35% Medicare tax (regular 1.45% Medicare tax + 0.9% additional Medicare tax) on all wages in excess of $200,000 ($250,000 for joint returns; $125,000 for married taxpayers filing a separate return) [Code Sec. 3101(b)(2)].

For 2014, the self-employment tax imposed on self-employed people is:

- 12.4% OASDI on the first $117,000 of self-employment income, for a maximum tax of $14,508.00 (12.40% of $117,000), plus
- 2.90% Medicare tax on the first $200,000 of self-employment income ($250,000 of combined self-employment income on a joint return, $125,000 on a separate return) [Code Sec. 1401(a), (b)], plus

- 3.8% (2.90% regular Medicare tax + 0.9% additional Medicare tax) on all self-employment income in excess of $200,000 ($250,000 of combined self-employment income on a joint return, $125,000 for married taxpayers filing a separate return) [Code Sec. 1401(b)(2)].

2014 TAX RATE SCHEDULES

MARRIED INDIVIDUALS FILING JOINT RETURNS AND SURVIVING SPOUSES

If Taxable Income Is:	The Tax Is:
Not over $18,150	10% of the taxable income
Over $18,150 but not over $73,800	$1,815 plus 15% of the excess over $18,150
Over $73,800 but not over $148,850	$10,162.50 plus 25% of the excess over $73,800
Over $148,850 but not over $226,850	$28,925 plus 28% of the excess over $148,850
Over $226,850 but not over $405,100	$50,765 plus 33% of the excess over $226,850
Over $405,100 but not over $457,600	$109,587.50 plus 35% of the excess over $405,100
Over $457,600	$127,962.50 plus 39.6% of the excess over $457,600

HEADS OF HOUSEHOLDS

If Taxable Income Is:	The Tax Is:
Not over $12,950	10% of the taxable income
Over $12,950 but not over $49,400	$1,295 plus 15% of the excess over $12,950
Over $49,400 but not over $127,550	$6,762.50 plus 25% of the excess over $49,400
Over $127,550 but not over $206,600	$26,300 plus 28% of the excess over $127,550
Over $206,600 but not over $405,100	$48,434 plus 33% of the excess over $206,600
Over $405,100 not over $432,200	$113,939 plus 35% of the excess over $405,100
Over $432,200	$123,424 plus 39.6% of the excess over $432,200

UNMARRIED INDIVIDUALS (OTHER THAN SURVIVING SPOUSES AND HEADS OF HOUSEHOLDS)

If Taxable Income Is:	The Tax Is:
Not over $9,075	10% of the taxable income
Over $9,075 but not over $36,900	$907.50 plus 15% of the excess over $9,075
Over $36,900 but not over $89,350	$5,081.25 plus 25% of the excess over $36,900
Over $89,350 but not over $186,350	$18,193.75 plus 28% of the excess over $89,350
Over $186,350 but not over $405,100	$45,353.75 plus 33% of the excess over $186,350
Over $405,100 not over $406,750	$117,541.25 plus 35% of the excess over $405,100
Over $406,750	$118,118.75 plus 39.6% of the excess over $406,750

MARRIED INDIVIDUALS FILING SEPARATE RETURNS

If Taxable Income Is:	The Tax Is:
Not over $9,075	10% of the taxable income
Over $9,075 but not over $36,900	$907.50 plus 15% of the excess over $9,075

If Taxable Income Is:	The Tax Is:
Over $36,900 but not over $74,425	$5,081.25 plus 25% of the excess over $36,900
Over $74,425 but not over $113,425	$14,462.50 plus 28% of the excess over $74,425
Over $113,425 but not over $202,550	$25,382.50 plus 33% of the excess over $113,425
Over $202,550 not over $228,800	$54,793.75 plus 35% of the excess over $202,550
Over $228,800	$63,981.25 plus 39.6% of the excess over $228,800

ESTATES AND TRUSTS

If Taxable Income Is:	The Tax Is:
Not over $2,500	15% of the taxable income
Over $2,500 but not over $5,800	$375 plus 25% of the excess over $2,500
Over $5,800 but not over $8,900	$1,200 plus 28% of the excess over $5,800
Over $8,900 but not over $12,150	$2,068 plus 33% of the excess over $8,900
Over $12,150	$3,140.50 plus 39.6% of the excess over $12,150

2013 TAX RATE SCHEDULES

MARRIED INDIVIDUALS FILING JOINT RETURNS AND SURVIVING SPOUSES

If Taxable Income Is:	The Tax Is:
Not over $17,850	10% of the taxable income
Over $17,850 but not over $72,500	$1,785 plus 15% of the excess over $17,850
Over $72,500 but not over $146,400	$9,982.50 plus 25% of the excess over $72,500
Over $146,400 but not over $223,050	$28,457.50 plus 28% of the excess over $146,400
Over $223,050 but not over $398,350	$49,919.50 plus 33% of the excess over $223,050
Over $398,350 but not over $450,000	$107,768.50 plus 35% of the excess over $398,350
Over $450,000	$125,846 plus 39.6% of the excess over $450,000

HEADS OF HOUSEHOLDS

If Taxable Income Is:	The Tax Is:
Not over $12,750	10% of the taxable income
Over $12,750 but not over $48,600	$1,275 plus 15% of the excess over $12,750
Over $48,600 but not over $125,450	$6,652.50 plus 25% of the excess over $48,600
Over $125,450 but not over $203,150	$25,865 plus 28% of the excess over $125,450
Over $203,150 but not over $398,350	$47,621 plus 33% of the excess over $203,150
Over $398,350 not over $425,000	$112,037 plus 35% of the excess over $398,350
Over $425,000	$121,364.50 plus 39.6% of the excess over $425,000

UNMARRIED INDIVIDUALS (OTHER THAN SURVIVING SPOUSES AND HEADS OF HOUSEHOLDS)

If Taxable Income Is:	The Tax Is:
Not over $8,925	10% of the taxable income
Over $8,925 but not over $36,250	$892.50 plus 15% of the excess over $8,925

If Taxable Income Is:	The Tax Is:
Over $36,250 but not over $87,850	$4,991.25 plus 25% of the excess over $36,250
Over $87,850 but not over $183,250	$17,891.25 plus 28% of the excess over $87,850
Over $183,250 but not over $398,350	$44,603.25 plus 33% of the excess over $183,250
Over $398,350 not over $400,000	$115,586.25 plus 35% of the excess over $398,350
Over $400,000	$116,163.75 plus 39.6% of the excess over $400,000

MARRIED INDIVIDUALS FILING SEPARATE RETURNS

If Taxable Income Is:	The Tax Is:
Not over $8,925	10% of the taxable income
Over $8,925 but not over $36,250	$892.50 plus 15% of the excess over $8,925
Over $36,250 but not over $73,200	$4,991.25 plus 25% of the excess over $36,250
Over $73,200 but not over $111,525	$14,228.75 plus 28% of the excess over $73,200
Over $111,525 but not over $199,175	$24,959.75 plus 33% of the excess over $111,525
Over $199,175 not over $225,000	$53,884.25 plus 35% of the excess over $199,175
Over $225,000	$62,923 plus 39.6% of the excess over $225,000

ESTATES AND TRUSTS

If Taxable Income Is:	The Tax Is:
Not over $2,450	15% of the taxable income
Over $2,450 but not over $5,700	$367.50 plus 25% of the excess over $2,450
Over $5,700 but not over $8,750	$1,180 plus 28% of the excess over $5,700
Over $8,750 but not over $11,950	$2,034 plus 33% of the excess over $8,750
Over $11,950	$3,090 plus 39.6% of the excess over $11,950

2012 TAX RATE SCHEDULES

MARRIED INDIVIDUALS FILING JOINT RETURNS AND SURVIVING SPOUSES

If Taxable Income Is:	The Tax Is:
Not over $17,400	10% of the taxable income
Over $17,400 but not over $70,700	$1,740 plus 15% of the excess over $17,400
Over $70,700 but not over $142,700	$9,735 plus 25% of the excess over $70,700
Over $142,700 but not over $217,450	$27,735 plus 28% of the excess over $142,700
Over $217,450 but not over $388,350	$48,665 plus 33% of the excess over $217,450
Over $388,350	$105,062 plus 35% of the excess over $388,350

HEADS OF HOUSEHOLDS

If Taxable Income Is:	The Tax Is:
Not over $12,400	10% of the taxable income
Over $12,400 but not over $47,350	$1,120 plus 15% of the excess over $12,400
Over $47,350 but not over $122,300	$6,482.50 plus 25% of the excess over $47,350

If Taxable Income Is:	The Tax Is:
Over $122,300 but not over $198,050	$25,220 plus 28% of the excess over $122,300
Over $198,050 but not over $388,350	$46,430 plus 33% of the excess over $198,050
Over $388,350	$109,229 plus 35% of the excess over $388,350

UNMARRIED INDIVIDUALS (OTHER THAN SURVIVING SPOUSES AND HEADS OF HOUSEHOLDS)

If Taxable Income Is:	The Tax Is:
Not over $8,700	10% of the taxable income
Over $8,700 but not over $35,350	$870 plus 15% of the excess over $8,700
Over $35,350 but not over $85,650	$4,867.50 plus 25% of the excess over $35,350
Over $85,650 but not over $178,650	$17,442.50 plus 28% of the excess over $85,650
Over $178,650 but not over $388,350	$43,482.50 plus 33% of the excess over $178,650
Over $388,350	$112,683.50 plus 35% of the excess over $388,350

MARRIED INDIVIDUALS FILING SEPARATE RETURNS

If Taxable Income Is:	The Tax Is:
Not over $8,700	10% of the taxable income
Over $8,700 but not over $35,350	$870 plus 15% of the excess over $8,700
Over $35,350 but not over $71,350	$4,867.50 plus 25% of the excess over $35,350
Over $71,350 but not over $108,725	$13,867.50 plus 28% of the excess over $71,350
Over $108,725 but not over $194,175	$24,332.50 plus 33% of the excess over $108,725
Over $194,175	$52,531 plus 35% of the excess over $194,175

ESTATES AND TRUSTS

If Taxable Income Is:	The Tax Is:
Not over $2,400	15% of the taxable income
Over $2,400 but not over $5,600	$360 plus 25% of the excess over $2,400
Over $5,600 but not over $8,500	$1,160 plus 28% of the excess over $5,600
Over $8,500 but not over $11,650	$1,972 plus 33% of the excess over $8,500
Over $11,650	$3,011.50 plus 35% of the excess over $11,650

2011 TAX RATE SCHEDULES

MARRIED INDIVIDUALS FILING JOINT RETURNS AND SURVIVING SPOUSES

If Taxable Income Is:	The Tax Is:
Not over $17,000	10% of the taxable income
Over $17,000 but not over $69,000	$1,700 plus 15% of the excess over $17,000
Over $69,000 but not over $139,350	$9,500 plus 25% of the excess over $69,000
Over $139,350 but not over $212,300	$27,087.50 plus 28% of the excess over $139,350
Over $212,300 but not over $379,150	$47,513.50 plus 33% of the excess over $212,300
Over $379,150	$102,574 plus 35% of the excess over $379,150

HEADS OF HOUSEHOLDS

If Taxable Income Is:	The Tax Is:
Not over $12,150	10% of the taxable income
Over $12,150 but not over $46,250	$1,215 plus 15% of the excess over $12,150
Over $46,250 but not over $119,400	$6,330 plus 25% of the excess over $46,250
Over $119,400 but not over $193,350	$24,617.50 plus 28% of the excess over $119,400
Over $193,350 but not over $379,150	$45,323.50 plus 33% of the excess over $193,350
Over $379,150	$106,637.50 plus 35% of the excess over $379,150

UNMARRIED INDIVIDUALS (OTHER THAN SURVIVING SPOUSES AND HEADS OF HOUSEHOLDS)

If Taxable Income Is:	The Tax Is:
Not over $8,500	10% of the taxable income
Over $8,500 but not over $34,500	$850 plus 15% of the excess over $8,500
Over $34,500 but not over $83,600	$4,750 plus 25% of the excess over $34,500
Over $83,600 but not over $174,400	$17,025 plus 28% of the excess over $83,600
Over $174,400 but not over $379,150	$42,449 plus 33% of the excess over $174,400
Over $379,150	$110,016.50 plus 35% of the excess over $379,150

MARRIED INDIVIDUALS FILING SEPARATE RETURNS

If Taxable Income Is:	The Tax Is:
Not over $8,500	10% of the taxable income
Over $8,500 but not over $34,500	$850 plus 15% of the excess over $8,500
Over $34,500 but not over $69,675	$4,750 plus 25% of the excess over $34,500
Over $69,675 but not over $106,150	$13,543.75 plus 28% of the excess over $69,675
Over $106,150 but not over $189,575	$23,756.75 plus 33% of the excess over $106,150
Over $189,575	$51,287 plus 35% of the excess over $189,575

ESTATES AND TRUSTS

If Taxable Income Is:	The Tax Is:
Not over $2,300	15% of the taxable income
Over $2,300 but not over $5,450	$345 plus 25% of the excess over $2,300
Over $5,450 but not over $8,300	$1,132.50 plus 28% of the excess over $5,450
Over $8,300 but not over $11,350	$1,930.50 plus 33% of the excess over $8,300
Over $11,350	$2,937 plus 35% of the excess over $11,350

2010 TAX RATE SCHEDULES

MARRIED INDIVIDUALS FILING JOINT RETURNS AND SURVIVING SPOUSES

If Taxable Income Is:	The Tax Is:
Not over $16,750	10% of the taxable income
Over $16,750 but not over $68,000	$1,675 plus 15% of the excess over $16,750

If Taxable Income Is:	The Tax Is:
Over $68,000 but not over $137,300	$9,362.50 plus 25% of the excess over $68,000
Over $137,300 but not over $209,250	$26,687.50 plus 28% of the excess over $137,300
Over $209,250 but not over $373,650	$46,833.50 plus 33% of the excess over $209,250
Over $373,650	$101,085.50 plus 35% of the excess over $373,650

HEADS OF HOUSEHOLDS

If Taxable Income Is:	The Tax Is:
Not over $11,950	10% of the taxable income
Over $11,950 but not over $45,550	$1,195 plus 15% of the excess over $11,950
Over $45,550 but not over $117,650	$6,235 plus 25% of the excess over $45,550
Over $117,650 but not over $190,550	$24,260 plus 28% of the excess over $117,650
Over $190,550 but not over $373,650	$44,672 plus 33% of the excess over $190,550
Over $373,650	$105,095 plus 35% of the excess over $373,650

UNMARRIED INDIVIDUALS (OTHER THAN SURVIVING SPOUSE AND HEADS OF HOUSEHOLDS)

If Taxable Income Is:	The Tax Is:
Not over $8,375	10% of the taxable income
Over $8,375 but not over $34,000	$837.50 plus 15% of the excess over $8,375
Over $34,000 but not over $82,400	$4,681.25 plus 25% of the excess over $34,000
Over $82,400 but not over $171,850	$16,781.25 plus 28% of the excess over $82,400
Over $171,850 but not over $373,650	$41,827.25 plus 33% of the excess over $171,850
Over $373,650	$108,421.25 plus 35% of the excess over $373,650

MARRIED INDIVIDUALS FILING SEPARATE RETURNS

If Taxable Income Is:	The Tax Is:
Not over $8,375	10% of the taxable income
Over $8,375 but not over $34,000	$837.50 plus 15% of the excess over $8,375
Over $34,000 but not over $68,650	$4,681.25 plus 25% of the excess over $34,000
Over $68,650 but not over $104,625	$13,343.75 plus 28% of the excess over $68,650
Over $104,625 but not over $186,825	$23,416.75 plus 33% of the excess over $104,625
Over $186,825	$50,542.75 plus 35% of the excess over $186,825

ESTATES AND TRUSTS

If Taxable Income Is:	The Tax Is:
Not over $2,300	15% of the taxable income
Over $2,300 but not over $5,350	$345 plus 25% of the excess over $2,300
Over $5,350 but not over $8,200	$1,107.50 plus 28% of the excess over $5,350
Over $8,200 but not over $11,200	$1,905.50 plus 33% of the excess over $8,200
Over $11,200	$2,895.50 plus 35% of the excess over $11,200

¶210 EXCISE TAX RATES

Rates at which federal excise taxes are charged are listed below.

FUELS

Gasoline (Code Sec. 4081)	
Gasoline (per gallon)	18.4¢
Diesel fuel, biodiesel, and kerosene (Code Secs. 4041 and 4081)	
Diesel fuel (except if used on a farm for farming purposes) (per gallon)	24.4¢
Diesel fuel for use in trains (per gallon)	0.1¢
Diesel-water fuel emulsions	19.8¢
Kerosene (except if used in a farm for farming purposes) (per gallon)	24.4¢
B-100 (100 percent biodiesel) (per gallon)	24.4¢
Special fuels (Code Sec. 4041)	
Special motor fuel (per gallon)	18.4¢
Liquefied petroleum gas (LPG)	18.3¢
"P Series" fuels	18.4¢
Compressed natural gas (CNG) (per energy equivalent of a gallon of gasoline)	18.3¢
Liquefied hydrogen	18.4¢
Any liquid fuel derived from coal (including peat) through the Fischer-Tropsch process (per gallon)	24.4¢
Liquid fuel derived from biomass (per gallon)	24.4¢
Liquefied natural gas (LNG) (per gallon)	24.3¢
Liquefied gas derived from biomass (per gallon)	18.4¢
Qualified ethanol produced from coal (per gallon)	18.4¢
Qualified methanol produced from coal (per gallon)	18.4¢
Partially exempt ethanol produced from natural gas (per gallon)	11.4¢
Partially exempt methanol produced from natural gas (per gallon)	9.25¢
Fuel used on inland waterways (Code Sec. 4042)	
Inland waterways fuel use tax (per gallon)	20.1¢
Aviation fuels (Code Secs. 4081 and 4043)	

Kerosene used in commercial aviation (when removed from a refinery or terminal directly into the fuel tank of an aircraft) (per gallon)	4.4¢
Kerosene used in noncommercial aviation (when removed from a refinery or terminal directly into the fuel tank of an aircraft) (per gallon)	21.9¢
Noncommercial aviation gasoline (per gallon)	19.4¢
Fuel used in fractional aircraft ownership program flights (per gallon)	14.1¢ surtax after 3/31/2012
Fuel credits (Code Secs. 40, 40A and 6426)	
Alcohol or alcohol in fuel mixtures if 190 proof or greater (per gallon) (ethanol)	45¢ credit until 2012
Alcohol of 190 proof or greater if benefited from the small ethanol producers credit (per gallon)	55¢ credit until 2012
Alcohol and alcohol in fuel mixtures if less than 190, but at least 150 proof (per gallon) (ethanol)	33.33¢ credit until 2012
Alcohol if less than 190, but at least 150 proof if benefited from the small ethanol producers credit (per gallon)	43.33¢ credit until 2012
Alcohol if 190 proof or greater (per gallon) (methanol)	60¢ credit until 2012
Alcohol if at least 150, but less than 190 proof (per gallon) (methanol)	45¢ credit until 2012
Second generation biofuel (per gallon)	$1.01 credit until 2014
Biodiesel and biodiesel mixtures (per gallon)	$1.00 credit until 2014
Agri-biodiesel (per gallon)	$1.00 credit until 2014
Agri-biodiesel if benefited from the small agri-biodiesel producer credit (per gallon)	$1.10 credit until 2014
Renewable diesel and renewable diesel mixtures (per gallon)	$1.00 credit until 2014
Alternative fuel (as defined in Code Sec. 6426(d)(2)) (per gallon)	50¢ credit until 2014 (but until 9/30/2014 for liquefied hydrogen)
Crude oil (Code Sec. 4611)	
Crude oil (per barrel)	8¢
HEAVY TRUCKS, TRAILERS	
Trucks and trailers (Code Sec. 4051)	
Truck chassis or body (suitable for use with a vehicle in excess of 33,000 lbs. gross vehicle weight)	12% of retail price
Trailer and semitrailer chassis or body (suitable for use with a trailer or semitrailer in excess of 26,000 lbs. gross vehicle weight)	12% of retail price
Parts and accessories installed on taxable vehicles within six months after being placed in service (when cost of parts or accessories exceeds $1,000)	12% of retail price

HIGHWAY-TYPE TIRES

Tires for highway vehicles (Code Sec. 4071)

Tires with load capacity over 3,500 lbs.	9.45¢ for each 10 pounds of tire load capacity in excess of 3,500 pounds
Super single tires designed for steering	9.45¢ for each 10 pounds of tire load capacity in excess of 3,500 pounds
Super single tires not designed for steering	4.725¢ for each 10 pounds of tire load capacity in excess of 3,500 pounds
Biasply tires	4.725¢ for each 10 pounds of tire load capacity in excess of 3,500 pounds

GAS GUZZLER TAX

Fuel economy rating (Code Sec. 4064)

Mileage ratings per gallon of at least 22.5	$ 0
Mileage ratings per gallon of at least 21.5 but less than 22.5	1,000
Mileage ratings per gallon of at least 20.5 but less than 21.5	1,300
Mileage ratings per gallon of at least 19.5 but less than 20.5	1,700
Mileage ratings per gallon of at least 18.5 but less than 19.5	2,100
Mileage ratings per gallon of at least 17.5 but less than 18.5	2,600
Mileage ratings per gallon of at least 16.5 but less than 17.5	3,000
Mileage ratings per gallon of at least 15.5 but less than 16.5	3,700
Mileage ratings per gallon of at least 14.5 but less than 15.5	4,500
Mileage ratings per gallon of at least 13.5 but less than 14.5	5,400
Mileage ratings per gallon of at least 12.5 but less than 13.5	6,400
Mileage ratings per gallon of less than 12.5	7,700

FACILITIES AND SERVICES

Communications (Code Sec. 4251)

Local telephone and teletypewriter service	3% of amount paid

Transportation of persons by air (Code Secs. 4261(a) and 4261(c))

Domestic passenger tickets: from 1/1/2013 through 12/31/2013	7.5% of amount paid plus $3.90 per each flight segment (excepting segments to or from rural airports) ($8.60 per departure from Alaska or Hawaii)
International passenger tickets (per person): from 1/1/2013 through 12/31/2013	$17.20 for each arrival and departure

Transportation of property by air (Code Sec. 4271)

Air freight waybill	6.25% of amount paid

Transportation by water (Code Secs. 4461, 4462, and 4471)	
Persons	$3.00
Port use tax on imports (harbor maintenance tax)	0.125% of cargo value

ALCOHOL TAXES

Distilled spirits (Code Sec. 5001)	
Distilled spirits (per gallon)	$13.50
Beer (Code Sec. 5051)	
Beer (per barrel—31 gallons or less)	$18.00, generally
First 60,000 barrels removed during calendar year by U.S. brewer producing not more than 2 million barrels during year (per barrel)	$7.00
Wines (Code Sec. 5041)	
Not more than 14 percent alcohol (per gallon)	$1.07
More than 14 to 21 percent alcohol (per gallon)	$1.57
More than 21 to 24 percent alcohol (per gallon)	$3.15
More than 24 percent alcohol (per proof gallon)	$13.50
Artificially carbonated wines (per gallon)	$3.30
Champagne and other sparkling wines (per gallon)	$3.40
Hard cider derived from apples containing at least 1/2 of 1% and less than 7% alcohol (per gallon)	$0.226

TOBACCO TAXES (effective April 1, 2009)

Cigars (Code Sec. 5701(a))	
Cigars weighing not more than 3 lbs. (per thousand)	$50.33
Cigars weighing more than 3 lbs.	52.75% of sales price, not to exceed 40.26 cents per cigar
Cigarettes (Code Sec. 5701(b))	
Cigarettes weighing not more than 3 lbs. (per thousand)	$50.33 (over $1 per pack)
Cigarettes weighing more than 3 lbs. (per thousand)	$105.69
Cigarette papers and tubes (Code Secs. 5701(c) and 5701(d))	
Cigarette papers (per fifty)	3.15¢
Cigarette tubes (per fifty)	6.30¢
Tobacco products (Code Secs. 5701(e), 5701(f) and 5701(g))	
Snuff (per pound)	$1.51
Chewing tobacco (per pound)	50.33¢
Pipe tobacco (per pound)	$2.8311 cents
Roll-your-own tobacco (per pound)	$24.78

WAGERING TAXES

Certain wagers (Code Sec. 4401)	
State authorized wagers placed with bookmakers and lottery operators	0.25% of wager amount

Unauthorized wagers placed with bookmakers and lottery operators	2% of wager amount
Occupational taxes (Code Sec. 4411)	
License fee on state authorized persons accepting wagers (per year, per person)	$50
License fee on unauthorized persons accepting wagers (per year, per person)	$500

HIGHWAY MOTOR VEHICLE TAX

Use tax (Code Sec. 4481)	
Vehicles of less than 55,000 lbs.	No tax
Vehicles of 55,000 lbs.—75,000 lbs.	$100 per year + $22 for each 1,000 lbs. (or fraction thereof) over 55,000 lbs.
Vehicles over 75,000 lbs.	$550 per year

FIREARMS

Transfer taxes (Code Secs. 5811 and 5845(e))	
Generally (per transfer)	$200
Certain concealable weapons (per transfer)	$5
Occupational taxes (Code Sec. 5801)	
Importer	$1,000 per year
Manufacturers	$1,000 per year
Small importers and manufacturers (gross receipts under $500,000 per year)	$500 per year
Dealers	$500 per year
Regular firearms and ammunition (Code Sec. 4181)	
Pistols and revolvers	10% of sales price
Firearms other than pistols and revolvers	11% of sales price
Ammunition (shells and cartridges)	11% of sales price

RECREATIONAL EQUIPMENT

Sporting goods (Code Sec. 4161)	
Sport fishing equipment	10% of sales price
Fishing tackle boxes	3% of sales price
Electric outboard motors	3% of sales price
Bows with a peak draw weight of at least 30 lbs.	11% of sales price
Arrow shafts from 1/1/2013 through 12/31/2013	48¢ per shaft
Quivers, broadheads and points	11% of sales price

ELECTIVE COSMETIC MEDICAL PROCEDURES

Tanning services (Code Sec. 5000B)	
Indoor tanning services	10% of amount paid, starting July 1, 2010

ENVIRONMENTAL TAXES	
Oils and chemicals (Code Secs. 4611, 4661, 4681, and 4682)	
Crude oil	8¢ per barrel
Ozone-depleting chemicals	Various rates (see ¶33,725 and ¶33,945)
FOREIGN INSURANCE POLICIES	
Foreign insurance policies (Code Sec. 4371)	
Casualty insurance and indemnity, fidelity and surety bonds (per dollar of premium paid)	4¢
Life insurance, sickness and accident policies, and annuity contracts (per dollar of premium paid)	1¢
Reinsurance of taxable contracts above (per dollar of premium paid)	1¢
VACCINES	
Vaccines tax (Code Sec. 4131)	
Any vaccine containing diphtheria toxoid, tetanus toxoid, pertussis bacteria, extracted or partial cell bacteria, specific pertussis antigens, or polio virus	75¢ per dose
Any vaccine against measles, mumps, rubella, hepatitis A, hepatitis B, chicken pox, rotavirus gastroenteritis, or the human papillomavirus	75¢ per dose
Any conjugate vaccine against streptococcus pneumoniae	75¢ per dose
Any trivalent vaccine against influenza	75¢ per dose
Any HIB vaccine	75¢ per dose
Any meningococcal vaccine	75¢ per dose
COAL	
Black Lung Disability Trust Fund taxes (Code Sec. 4121)	
From underground mines (per ton sold)	$1.10, not to exceed 4.4% of selling price
From surface mines (per ton sold)	55¢, not to exceed 4.4% of selling price

2014 Federal Tax Calendar

¶301 BASIC RULES

Saturday, Sunday, or legal holiday. Generally, if a due date that is set by law falls on a Saturday, Sunday, or legal holiday, the due date is delayed until the next day that is not a Saturday, Sunday, or legal holiday.

Statewide holidays. A statewide legal holiday delays a due date only if the IRS office where the taxpayer is required to file is located in that state.

2014 Federal holidays. Federal law (5 U.S.C. 6103) establishes the following public holidays for Federal employees. Please note that most Federal employees work on a Monday through Friday schedule. For these employees, when a holiday falls on a nonworkday—Saturday or Sunday—the holiday usually is observed on Monday (if the holiday falls on Sunday) or Friday (if the holiday falls on Saturday).

Date	Holiday
Wednesday, January 1	New Year's Day
Monday, January 20	Birthday of Martin Luther King, Jr.
Monday, February 17*	Washington's Birthday
Monday, May 26	Memorial Day
Friday, July 4	Independence Day
Monday, September 1	Labor Day
Monday, October 13	Columbus Day
Tuesday, November 11	Veterans Day
Thursday, November 27	Thanksgiving Day
Thursday, December 25	Christmas Day

* This holiday is designated as "Washington's Birthday" even though other institutions such as state and local governments and private businesses may use other names.

Please refer to IRS Publication 509, *Tax Calendars* for the updated tax calendar for 2014.

Individuals—Filing Status, Personal Exemptions, Standard Deduction

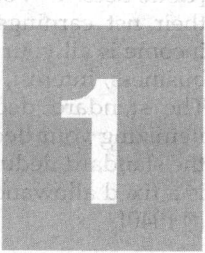

INDIVIDUAL INCOME TAX RETURNS

Who must file . . . . ¶1001

Tax return forms . . . . ¶1005

HOW TO FIGURE THE TAX

What is involved in the computation . . . . ¶1010

Steps in figuring the tax . . . . ¶1015

WHAT IS YOUR FILING STATUS?

Married couples . . . . ¶1020

Surviving spouse . . . . ¶1025

Head of household . . . . ¶1030

STANDARD DEDUCTION

Amount of standard deduction . . . . ¶1035

PERSONAL EXEMPTIONS

Amount of your personal exemptions . . . . ¶1040

Phaseout of personal exemptions . . . . ¶1045

Exemptions of married persons . . . ¶1050

EXEMPTIONS FOR DEPENDENTS

Dependency exemptions . . . . ¶1055

Support . . . . ¶1060

Relationship of dependent . . . . ¶1065

Dependent's gross income . . . . ¶1070

INDIVIDUAL INCOME TAX RETURNS

In general, if your income exceeds the total of your personal exemption and standard deduction, you must file a tax return. However, there are lower income thresholds for those who can be claimed as a dependent on someone else's return and for self-employed taxpayers. Some people who owe no tax must nevertheless file a return. Individuals who have earned less than the filing threshold, but have had tax withheld from their pay, should file a tax return to get a refund of what was withheld.

¶1001 WHO MUST FILE

To determine if you must file an income tax return, you need to know your gross income [Code Sec. 61], standard deduction [Code Sec. 63(a)] and exemption amount

[Code Secs. 151, 6012(a)]. Self-employed taxpayers are required to file a tax return if their net earnings from self-employment are at least $400 [see .05 below]. Gross income is all your income subject to tax [¶1200]. It includes salary, fees, profits from business, interest, rents, dividends gains, and social security benefits subject to tax. The standard deduction is an audit-proof amount you can write off in lieu of itemizing your deductions which require you to list your actual expenses. The size of the standard deduction varies with your filing status [¶1035]. The exemption amount is a fixed allowance in place of a deduction for personal, family, and living expenses [¶1040].

.01 Income Levels

The income levels that necessitate filing a 2013 return are listed below [Code Sec. 6012(a)(1)(A)]. To determine these levels you add together the appropriate standard deduction amount [¶1035] and the exemption amount [¶1040]:

IF your filing status is . . .	AND at the end of 2013 you were*. . .	THEN file a return if your gross income was at least . . .
Single	under 65	$10,000
	65 or older	11,500
Married filing jointly**	under 65 (both spouses)	$20,000
	65 or older (one spouse)	21,200
	65 or older (both spouses)	22,400
Married filing separately	any age	$ 3,900
Head of household	under 65	$12,850
	65 or older	14,350
Qualifying widow(er) with dependent child	under 65	$16,100
	65 or older	17,300

* If you were born on January 1, 1949, you are considered to be age 65 at the end of 2013.

** If you did not live with your spouse at the end of 2013 (or on the date your spouse died) and your gross income was at least $3,900, you must file a return regardless of your age.

.02 Filing Test for Dependents

If you can be claimed as a dependent by someone else, such as a parent or by an adult child, different rules apply depending on the amount of your earned and unearned income. Earned income includes your wages, salaries, tips and fees, as well as taxable fellowships and scholarship grants. Unearned income includes investment-type income such as taxable interest, ordinary dividends, and capital gain distributions. It also includes unemployment compensation, taxable social security benefits, pensions, annuities, and distributions of unearned income from a trust.

Consult the following chart to determine if a dependent must file a return this year.

Chart B—For Children and Other Dependents

See the instructions for line 6c to find out if someone can claim you as a dependent.

If your parent (or someone else) can claim you as a dependent, use this chart to see if you must file a return.

In this chart, **unearned income** includes taxable interest, ordinary dividends, and capital gain distributions. It also includes unemployment compensation, taxable social security benefits, pensions, annuities, and distributions of unearned income from a trust. **Earned income** includes salaries, wages, tips, professional fees, and taxable scholarship and fellowship grants. **Gross income** is the total of your unearned and earned income.

Single dependents. Were you **either** age 65 or older **or** blind?

☐ **No.** You must file a return if **any** of the following apply.

- Your **unearned income** was over $1,000.
- Your **earned income** was over $6,100.
- Your **gross income** was more than the **larger** of—
  - $1,000, or
  - Your earned income (up to $5,750) plus $350.

☐ **Yes.** You must file a return if **any** of the following apply.

- Your unearned income was over $2,500 ($4,000 if 65 or older **and** blind).
- Your earned income was over $7,600 ($9,100 if 65 or older **and** blind).
- Your gross income was more than the **larger** of—
  - $2,500 ($4,000 if 65 or older **and** blind), or
  - Your earned income (up to $5,750) plus $1,850 ($3,350 if 65 or older **and** blind).

Married dependents. Were you **either** age 65 or older **or** blind?

☐ **No.** You must file a return if **any** of the following apply.

- Your unearned income was over $1,000.
- Your earned income was over $6,100.
- Your gross income was at least $5 and your spouse files a separate return and itemizes deductions.
- Your gross income was more than the **larger** of—
  - $1,000, or
  - Your earned income (up to $5,750) plus $350.

☐ **Yes.** You must file a return if **any** of the following apply.

- Your unearned income was over $2,200 ($3,400 if 65 or older **and** blind).
- Your earned income was over $7,300 ($8,500 if 65 or older **and** blind).
- Your gross income was at least $5 and your spouse files a separate return and itemizes deductions.
- Your gross income was more than the **larger** of—
  - $2,200 ($3,400 if 65 or older **and** blind), or
  - Your earned income (up to $5,750) plus $1,550 ($2,750 if 65 or older **and** blind).

.03 Automatic Filers

You must file a return if any of the four conditions below apply for 2013.

1. You owe any special taxes, including any of the following.
   a. Alternative minimum tax.
   b. Additional tax on a qualified plan, including an individual retirement arrangement (IRA), or other tax-favored account. But if you are filing a return only because you owe this tax, you can file Form 5329, *Additional Tax on Qualified Plans (including IRAs) and Other Tax Favored Accounts,* by itself.
   c. Household employment taxes. But if you are filing a return only because you owe this tax, you can file Schedule H by itself.
   d. Social security and Medicare tax on tips you did not report to your employer or on wages you received from an employer who did not withhold these taxes.
   e. Write-in taxes, including uncollected social security and Medicare or RRTA tax on tips you reported to your employer or on group-term life insurance and additional tax on health savings account distributions.
   f. Recapture taxes including repayment of first-time homebuyer credit.
2. You and your spouse received (if filing jointly) HSA, Archer MSAs or Medicare Advantage MSA distributions.
3. You had net earnings from self-employment of at least $400.
4. You had wages of $108.28 or more from a church or qualified church-controlled organization that is exempt from employer social security and Medicare taxes.

.04 If No Tax Is Due

Even if you are entitled to claim sufficient tax deductions and credits to avoid owing any tax, if your gross income equals or exceeds the filing limit, you must still file a return.

▶ **TAX IDEA:** An employee who will owe no tax may be able to have his wages exempted from income tax withholding by filing Form W-4.

.05 Self-Employeds

If you run your own business or professional practice, you must file a return if your net earnings from the activity are $400 or more [Code Sec. 6017]. Special rules apply for self-employment income.

.06 Aliens

Individuals who are resident aliens for the entire year are subject to the same filing requirements as U.S. citizens. Nonresident aliens who are engaged in a trade or business in the U.S. must file a return regardless of their income level; other nonresident aliens can avoid filing if sufficient tax was withheld at the source of the income [Reg. § 1.6012-1(b)].

Residents of Puerto Rico are subject to the general filing requirement income thresholds. However, the gross income of a full-year resident of Puerto Rico does not include income from sources within Puerto Rico, except income received as an employee of the U.S. or any U.S. agency [Ch. 3].

¶1005 TAX RETURN FORMS

Individual taxpayers file their income tax returns on Form 1040 or, if eligible, a short form (Form 1040A or Form 1040EZ). If you cannot use either of the short forms, you must use the regular Form 1040 [Reg. § 1.6012-1(a)(6), (7)]. You must attach to your return all the withholding statements (Form W-2) received from your employers for the year. The time and place of filing and other details about returns are discussed in Chapter 26.

.01 Filing Form 1040

This is the all-purpose form for individuals. Some taxpayers must use it; others can choose to use one of the more simplified versions as their tax return. Anyone *can* use Form 1040, the so-called long form, but you *must* use Form 1040 if:

1. You received any of the following types of income:
   - Income from self-employment (business or farm income).
   - Certain tips you did not report to your employer.
   - Income received as a partner in a partnership, shareholder in an S corporation, or a beneficiary of an estate or trust.
   - Dividends on insurance policies if they exceed the total of all net premiums you paid for the contract.
2. You can exclude any of the following types of income:
   - Foreign earned income you received as a U.S. citizen or resident alien.
   - Certain income received from sources in Puerto Rico if you were a bona fide resident of Puerto Rico.
   - Certain income received from sources in American Samoa if you were a bona fide resident of American Samoa for the entire year.
3. You have an alternative minimum tax adjustment on stock you acquired from the exercise of an incentive stock option.
4. You received a distribution from a foreign trust.
5. You owe the excise tax on insider stock compensation from an expatriated corporation.
6. You owe household employment taxes.
7. You are eligible for the health coverage tax credit.
8. You are claiming the adoption credit or received employer-provided adoption benefits.
9. You are an employee and your employer did not withhold social security and Medicare tax.
10. You had a qualified health savings account funding distribution from your IRA.
11. You are a debtor in a bankruptcy case filed after October 16, 2005.
12. You must repay the first-time homebuyer credit.
13. You had foreign financial assets and must file Form 8938, *Statement of Foreign Financial Assets*.

14. You owe Additional Medicare Tax and must file Form 8959, *Additional Medicare Tax*.
15. You owe Net Investment Income Tax and must file Form 8960, *Net Investment Income Tax Individuals, Estate, and Trusts*.
16. You have adjusted gross income of more than $150,000 and must reduce the dollar amount of your exemptions.

.02 Who May Use Form 1040A

The so-called short form, Form 1040A, is a simple way for you to file your return. You can use Form 1040A if all six of the following apply.

1. You only had income from the following sources:
   a. Wages, salaries, tips.
   b. Interest and ordinary dividends.
   c. Capital gain distributions.
   d. Taxable scholarship and fellowship grants.
   e. Pensions, annuities, and IRAs.
   f. Unemployment compensation.
   g. Taxable social security and railroad retirement benefits.
   h. Alaska Permanent Fund dividends.
2. The only adjustments to income you can claim are:
   a. Educator expenses.
   b. IRA deduction.
   c. Student loan interest deduction.
   d. Tuition and fees deduction.
3. You do not itemize deductions.
4. Your taxable income is less than $100,000.
5. The only tax credits you can claim are:
   a. Child tax credit.
   b. Additional child tax credit.
   c. Education credits.
   d. Earned income credit.
   e. Credit for child and dependent care expenses.
   f. Credit for the elderly or the disabled.
   g. Retirement savings contributions credit.
6. You did not have an alternative minimum tax adjustment on stock you acquired from the exercise of an incentive stock option (see Pub. 525).

You can also use Form 1040A if you received dependent care benefits, or if you owe tax from the recapture of an education credit or the alternative minimum tax.

.03 Who May Use Form 1040EZ

The most basic tax return form is the one-page Form 1040EZ. It can be used if all of the following apply:

- Your filing status is single or married filing jointly. If you were a nonresident alien at any time during the year, your filing status must be married filing jointly.
- You do not claim any dependents.
- You do not claim any adjustments to income.
- The only tax credit you can claim is the earned income credit. The credit may result in a refund even if you do not owe any tax. You do not need a qualifying child to claim the credit.
- You (and your spouse if filing a joint return) were under age 65 and not blind at the end of the year.
- Your taxable income is less than $100,000.
- You had only wages, salaries, tips, taxable scholarship or fellowship grants, unemployment compensation, or Alaska Permanent Fund dividends, and your taxable interest was not over $1,500.
- You do not owe any household employment taxes on wages you paid to a household employee.
- You are not a debtor in a chapter 11 bankruptcy case filed after October 16, 2005.

If you do not meet all of the requirements, you must use Form 1040A or 1040.

Even if you can use Form 1040EZ, it may benefit you to use Form 1040A or 1040 instead. For example, you can claim the head of household filing status (which usually results in a lower tax than single) only on Form 1040A or 1040. Also, you can itemize deductions only on Form 1040. It would benefit you to itemize deductions if they total more than your standard deduction, which is $6,100 for most single people and $12,200 for most married people filing a joint return in 2013.

HOW TO FIGURE THE TAX

¶1010 WHAT IS INVOLVED IN THE COMPUTATION

.01 Components of the Tax Computation

To figure how much tax you owe this year, you must know your (a) gross income, (b) deductions for adjusted gross income, (c) adjusted gross income, (d) itemized deductions, (e) standard deduction, (f) personal exemptions, and (g) taxable income.

Gross Income

Gross income includes all types of income not expressly exempt from tax [Chs. 2-8] [Code Sec. 61].

Deductions from Adjusted Gross Income

You claim the following expenses as above-the-line deductions from gross income to yield your adjusted gross income [Code Sec. 62(a)]:

1. Educator expenses (Caution: Check IRS Instructions regarding educator expenses)
2. Certain business expenses of reservists, performing artists, and fee-basis government officials
3. Health savings account contributions
4. Moving expenses
5. One-half of self-employment tax
6. Self-employed SEP, SIMPLE, and qualified plan contributions
7. Self-employed health insurance expenses
8. Penalty on early withdrawal of savings
9. Alimony paid
10. IRA contributions
11. Student loan interest paid
12. Tuition and fees (Caution: Check IRS Instructions regarding tuition and fees)
13. Domestic production activities expenses

Adjusted Gross Income

Adjusted gross income is gross income less the deductions listed above [Code Sec. 62(a)].

Itemized Deductions

Itemized deductions are deductions other than deductions allowable in arriving at adjusted gross income [Code Sec. 63(d)]. Itemized deductions include, for example, property taxes and mortgage interest on your home.

Unless you elect to itemize for the tax year, no itemized deductions are allowed [Code Sec. 63(e)(1)]. You should make the election if you have itemized deductions in excess of the standard deduction.

High-Income Taxpayers

In 2013, an individual with an adjusted gross income (AGI) that exceeds an inflation-adjusted threshold amount must reduce the amount of allowable itemized deductions by the lesser of:

- Three percent of the excess of AGI over the applicable threshold amount; or
- 80 percent of the total amount of otherwise allowable itemized deductions [Code Sec. 68(a)].

In 2013, the thresholds for the itemized reduction phase-out are:

- $300,000 for married taxpayers filing joint returns and surviving spouses,
- $275,000 for heads of households,
- $250,000 for other unmarried taxpayers, and
- $150,000 for married taxpayers filing separate returns [Code Sec. 68(b)(1)].

In 2014, the thresholds for the itemized reduction phase-out are:

- $305,050 in the case of a joint return or a surviving spouse,
- $279,650 in the case of a head of household,

- $254,200 in the case of an individual who is not married and who is not a surviving spouse or head of household, and
- $152,525 in the case of a married individual filing a separate return [Code Sec. 68(b)(1)].

For further discussion, see ¶ 9001.

Standard Deduction

The standard deduction is a flat dollar allowance that can be claimed in place of itemized deductions. See ¶ 1035 for further discussion.

Personal Exemptions

There are two kinds of personal exemptions: (1) personal exemptions for you [¶ 1040]and your spouse [¶ 1050] and (2) exemptions for your dependents who are either qualifying children or qualifying relatives [¶ 1055] [Code Sec. 152]. No exemption is allowed on the return of an individual who is eligible to be claimed for a dependency exemption on another taxpayer's return [Code Sec. 151(d)(2)].

Exemption Phaseout

In 2013, higher-income taxpayers are required to reduce the amount of their exemptions when their adjusted gross income exceeds certain threshold amounts [Code Sec. 151(d)(3)(E) and (F)]. See ¶ 1045.

Taxable Income

Taxpayers who itemize their deductions should compute their taxable income by taking their adjusted gross income and subtracting both itemized deductions and the deduction for personal exemptions. Taxpayers who do not itemize their deductions should compute taxable income by taking their adjusted gross income and subtracting both the standard deduction and the deduction for personal exemptions [Code Sec. 63].

¶ 1015 STEPS IN FIGURING THE TAX

Here are nine steps to follow in computing a tax bill:

▶ **OBSERVATION:** The income and deduction facts and figures needed for each step are entered on different lines and schedules on the tax return, and in a different order than that given here. The order of steps used here is designed to make it easier to understand the tax computation structure.

.01 Step by Step Procedures

STEP 1. Start with GROSS INCOME.

This includes, for example, the following:

- Compensation for services [Ch. 2];
- Bonuses and prizes [Ch. 2];
- Pensions [Ch. 3];
- Rent and royalties [Ch. 2];

- Dividends [Ch. 2];
- Taxable interest [Ch. 2];
- Gains from sales and exchanges of property [Ch. 7; Ch. 8]; and gross receipts from business [Ch. 7; Ch. 24].

But it excludes, wholly or partially, such items as: interest on certain state or local government obligations [Ch. 5.]; annuities [Ch. 5.]; insurance proceeds [Ch. 5; gifts and bequests [Ch 5].

STEP 2. Subtract DEDUCTIONS FROM ADJUSTED GROSS INCOME from your gross income [Step 1] to get ADJUSTED GROSS INCOME. These deductions include, among others: deductions due to rent and royalty property [Ch. 12]; and losses from the sale or exchange of business or investment property [Ch. 8; Ch. 13].

STEP 3. Determine ITEMIZED DEDUCTIONS and the STANDARD DEDUCTION.

> ▶ **DEDUCTION PHASEOUT:** High-income taxpayers may have to reduce their itemized deductions. For a further discussion of this change and a worksheet for figuring the reduction, see ¶9001.

STEP 4. Select the greater of the total of ITEMIZED DEDUCTIONS or the STANDARD DEDUCTION [Step 3].

STEP 5. Determine how many PERSONAL EXEMPTIONS can be claimed. These include: one exemption each for (a) you [¶1040]; (b) each person for whom you can claim a dependency exemption [¶1055]; and (c) your spouse, if you file a joint return [¶1050]. If you are married and file separately, you get the exemption for your spouse only if your spouse had no gross income and could not be claimed as the dependent of another.

> ▶ **DEDUCTION PHASEOUT:** High-income taxpayers may lose personal and dependency exemption deductions. For a further discussion of this change and a worksheet for figuring the phaseout, see ¶1045.

STEP 6. Multiply the number of personal exemptions by $3,900 for 2013 returns.

STEP 7. To determine TAXABLE INCOME, subtract both the deduction for Step 4 and the value of the personal exemptions [Step 6] from your adjusted gross income [Step 2].

STEP 8. Find the amount of TAX from either the tax table [¶1080]or the rate schedules [¶1075]. You may have to figure tax on Schedule D if you have capital gain [¶1809].

STEP 9. Subtract CREDITS, if any, from the tax found in Step 8 to figure the net tax payable or overpayment refundable. These include the credits for: estimated tax payments or tax withheld on wages [Ch. 14; Ch. 15]; earned income [Ch. 14]; the elderly or disabled [Ch. 14]; any social security tax overpayment; foreign taxes and taxes of U.S. possessions [Ch. 28]; child care [Ch. 14].

.02 Tax Figured by Internal Revenue Service

You can have the IRS figure your tax on Form 1040EZ, Form 1040A, or Form 1040 if you file your return by April 15, 2014 [Code Sec. 6014(a); Reg. § 1.6014-2(c)]. By making the election, you need only complete your return through the line for taxable income and fill in certain other lines, such as tax withholding and estimated tax payments. The IRS cannot figure your tax for you if any of the following apply:

- You want your refund directly deposited into your accounts.
- You want any part of your refund applied to your 2014 estimated tax.
- You had income for the year from sources other than wages, salaries, tips, interest, dividends, taxable social security benefits, unemployment compensation, IRA distributions, pensions, and annuities.
- Your taxable income is $100,000 or more,
- You itemize deductions.
- You file any of the following forms: Form 2555, *Foreign Earned Income;* Form 2555-EZ, *Foreign Earned Income Exclusion;* Form 4137, *Social Security and Medicare Tax on Unreported Tip Income;* Form 4970, *Tax on Accumulation Distribution of Trusts;* Form 4972, *Tax on Lump-Sum Distributions;* Form 6198, *At-Risk Limitations;* Form 6251, *Alternative Minimum Tax-Individuals;* Form 8606, *Nondeductible IRAs;* Form 8615, *Tax for Certain Children Who Have Unearned Income;* Form 8814, *Parents' Election to Report Child's Interest and Dividends;* Form 8839, *Qualified Adoption Expenses;* Form 8853, *Archer MSAs and Long-Term Care Insurance Contracts;* Form 8915, *Qualified Hurricane Retirement Plan Distributions and Repayments;* or Form 8889, *Health Savings Accounts;* Form 8919, *Uncollected Social Security and Medicare Tax on Wages;* or Form 8930, *Qualified Disaster Recovery Assistance Retirement Plan Distributions and Repayments.*

The IRS will calculate any credit for the elderly or disabled and earned income credit to which you are entitled. What schedule you have to attach depends on what tax form you are filing.

Once the IRS figures the tax, it sends you a refund or a bill for additional tax due. There is no interest charge or late payment penalty so long as the bill is paid within 30 days from the notice mailing date (or the tax return due date, if later).[1]

WHAT IS YOUR FILING STATUS?

¶1020 MARRIED COUPLES

If you file a joint return, the tax table and tax rate schedules split your total income, and reflect the tax at a lower rate than would apply if you were a single person with the same taxable income who filed individually.

.01 Who May File a Joint Return

The rules for filing as a married couple apply regardless of how much gross income each spouse has during the tax year. Married couples, including same-sex married couples, may file jointly if, on the last day of the tax year, any one of the following applies [Code Sec. 6013(a); Reg. § 1.6013-1(a)]:

- The couple are married and living together as husband and wife. Married couples are considered for tax purposes to be living together at the end of the tax year even

[1] Treas. Dept., IRS Publication 17, "Your Federal Income Tax" (2013 Ed.), Ch. 29.

though one spouse may be away temporarily due to business, vacation, military service or other special circumstances [Reg. § 1.6012-1(a)(2)(iv)].

- For federal tax purposes, individuals of the same sex are considered married if they were lawfully married in a state whose laws authorize the marriage of two individuals of the same sex, even if the state in which they now reside does not recognize same-sex marriage. The term "spouse" includes an individual married to a person of the same sex if the couple is lawfully married under state law. However, individuals who have entered into a registered domestic partnership, civil union, or other similar relationship that is not considered a marriage under state law are not considered married for federal tax purposes.

  In *E.S. Windsor*,[2] the Supreme Court held that Section 3 of the Defense of Marriage Act (DOMA), which had required spouses to be a husband and wife of the opposite sex, violated the Fifth Amendment of the Constitution. As a result of the 5-to-4 decision in *E.S. Windsor*, the definition of marriage when applying federal law is no longer limited to a marriage of individuals of the opposite sex. In Rev. Rul. 2013-17,[3] the IRS ruled that all same-sex marriages legally entered into in one of the states (including the District of Colombia, U.S. territory or foreign country) that recognizes same-sex marriages will be recognized for federal tax purposes even if the couple reside in a state that does not recognize same-sex marriage. Note that if a couple marry by the end of the year they will be treated as married for the entire tax year for federal tax law purposes.

  Example 1-1: In 2009, Sally and Liz were married in Connecticut, a state that recognizes same-sex marriage and they lived in Connecticut until early 2013. Sally accepted a job in Illinois, a state that currently does not recognize same-sex marriage, and they moved to Illinois in March 2013. According to the IRS place of celebration approach, the Service will regard Sally and Liz as a married couple for federal tax purposes even though they reside in a state that does not recognize their same-sex marriage.

- Legally-married same-sex couples generally must file their 2013 federal income tax return using either the married filing jointly or married filing separately filing status. Individuals who were in same-sex marriages may, but are not required to, file original or amended returns choosing to be treated as married for federal tax purposes for one or more prior tax years still open under the statute of limitations. Generally, the statute of limitations for filing a refund claim is three years from the date the return was filed or two years from the date the tax was paid, whichever is later. As a result, refund claims can still be filed for tax years 2010, 2011 and 2012.
- The couple is living together in a common-law marriage recognized by the state where the marriage began.[4]
- The couple is married and living apart, but not legally separated under a decree of divorce or separate maintenance.

---

[2] *E.S. Windsor*, SCt, 2013-2 USTC ¶ 60,667, 507 US ___, 133 SCt 2675.

[3] Rev. Rul. 2013-17, IRB 2013-38, 201.

[4] Rev. Rul. 58-66, 1958-1 CB 60.

- The couple is separated under an interlocutory decree of divorce.[5]
- The couple is not considered single unless the decree is final on or before the last day of the tax year. However, if the couple filed a joint return and their marriage is later annulled, each of the former spouses must file amended returns as singles. Couple are still considered married for tax purposes if they divorce at year-end to avoid tax and then remarry early the next year.[6]

Joint Return for Year of Spouse's Death

If one spouse dies, the surviving spouse may file a joint return for the year of death [Code Sec. 6013(a)(3)]. They will be considered married for the whole year. The surviving spouse may also be entitled to continue to file as if he or she were still married for the next two years [Code Sec. 2(a)(1)(A)] [¶ 1025]. Beyond that, the surviving spouse will be treated as a head of household with a special tax-favored filing status [¶ 1030].

If the surviving spouse remarries before the end of the year that his or her spouse died, the surviving spouse can file a joint return with the new spouse. The deceased spouse's filing status is married filing separately.

U.S. Citizens Married to Nonresident Aliens

Generally, if you are married to a nonresident alien at any time during the tax year, you cannot file a joint return [Code Sec. 6013(a)(1)]. You must file as a married person filing separately[7] unless you are qualified to file as a head of household [¶ 1030]. However, if you (a U.S. citizen or resident) are married to a nonresident alien at the end of the tax year, you may file jointly if you elect to be taxed on your world-wide income. An election applies to the tax year for which made and to all subsequent years until terminated. If the election is terminated for any individuals, neither of them can make a new election [Code Sec. 6013(g), (h)]. If the election is made, certain specific allocations of community property income, as provided in the Code, will not apply [Code Sec. 879].

Regardless of any foreign community property laws, a couple, both of whom are nonresident aliens, must treat one spouse's earnings or business income as that spouse's income without income allocation [Code Sec. 879(a)].

.02 Married Persons Filing Separate Returns

Married taxpayers who choose to file two individual returns (married filing separately) rather than filing joint returns will find that the following negative tax consequences will result:

1. The child and dependent care credit is disallowed;
2. The earned income credit is disallowed;
3. The credit for the elderly and totally disabled is disallowed;
4. The credit for qualified adoption expenses is disallowed;

---

[5] *M.S. Eccles*, CA-4, 54-1 USTC ¶ 9129, 208 F2d 796; *W.G. Ostler*, CA-9, 56-2 USTC ¶ 9962, 237 F2d 501; Rev. Rul. 57-368, 1957-2 CB 896.

[6] Rev. Rul. 76-255, 1976-2 CB 40.

[7] *R.H. Hoyle*, 29 TCM 760, Dec. 30,202(M), TC Memo. 1970-172; *E. Schinasi*, 53 TC 382, Dec. 29,861 (1969); Rev. Rul. 74-370, 1974-2 CB 7.

5. The Hope scholarship and lifetime learning credits are disallowed;
6. The earned income credit is disallowed;
7. The limitation on the general business credit may be halved;
8. If the spouses live together at any time during the tax year, the threshold for including social security benefits in gross income is reduced to zero;
9. Excludable gain on the sale of a principal residence is halved, and one spouse's ownership and use are not attributed to the other spouse;
10. Excludable dependent care assistance payments are halved;
11. U.S. savings bond interest is included in income even if it is used to pay higher education expenses;
12. The amount of acquisition indebtedness and home equity indebtedness that is deductible qualified residence interest is limited;
13. The limitation on the amount of deductible losses in insolvent financial institutions that may be treated as an ordinary loss is halved;
14. For purposes of the election to expense Code Sec. 179 property, the two spouses are treated as one taxpayer in applying the dollar limitation and the reduction in the amount of the limitation;
15. The dollar limitation on the deduction and/or amortization of reforestation expenditures is halved;
16. The deduction for student loan interest is not allowed;
17. The limit on deductible IRA contributions for participants covered by pension plans is reduced;
18. The exception to the passive activity losses and credits limitation for certain real estate activities is restricted and is eliminated if the spouses live together at any time during the tax year;
19. The amount of capital losses that may be offset by ordinary income is halved;
20. Estimated tax payments and the penalty for underpayments are affected; and
21. Tax tables are adjusted for inflation by rounding to the nearest $25, rather than to the nearest $50.

Favorable Aspects of Married Taxpayers Filing Separate Returns

Despite the negative consequences listed above, separate returns can be beneficial in the following situations:

1. Because miscellaneous itemized deductions are allowed only to the extent they exceed two percent of the taxpayer's adjusted gross income, if one spouse has a large amount of miscellaneous itemized deductions and a low AGI, while the other spouse has low miscellaneous itemized deductions and a high AGI, separate returns may result in lower combined tax liability. If one spouse itemizes deductions, however, the standard deduction for the other spouse is zero.
2. Because personal casualty losses are deductible only to the extent that the excess of the losses over personal casualty gains in the same tax year is greater than 10 percent of the taxpayer's AGI, if the first spouse has a large casualty loss and the

second spouse has a large casualty gain, it may be advantageous for them to file separate returns. The loss is deducted from the first spouse's ordinary income, and the gain is taxed to the second spouse at the lower rates applicable to capital gains.

3. Because the deduction for medical expenses is allowed only to the extent the expenses exceed 10 percent of the taxpayer's AGI under Code Sec. 213(a), if one spouse has paid a large amount of qualifying medical expenses while the other spouse has not, the first spouse may get a larger deduction if they file separate returns.

4. Taxpayers treat gains and losses from the sale or exchange of property used in a trade or business, or from the involuntary conversion of capital assets held in connection with a trade or business, as long-term capital gains and losses when recognized gains in a current tax year exceed recognized losses. When the gains do not exceed the losses, the gains and losses are treated as ordinary income. Thus, if one spouse has a large gain and the other spouse has a large loss, it may be advantageous for them to file separate returns.

5. Spouses who file a joint return are jointly and severally liable for the entire tax liability that arises from that return. A taxpayer who files a separate return can generally avoid any tax liability arising from the spouse's return (though community property laws may allocate one spouse's income and deductions to both spouses even if they file separate returns). Thus, some couples may prefer to file separate returns even if doing so increases their overall tax liability if they want to avoid tax liability arising from filing a joint return with a spouse.

Community Income

If you live in Arizona, California, Idaho, Louisiana, Nevada, New Mexico, Texas, Washington, or Wisconsin, you are subject to the community property laws which address the rights of a husband and wife in property acquired by them after their marriage [see Ch. 2]. The community property laws do not deal with the taxation of the couple's income, but rather with who owns the property which produces taxable income. Each state has different laws addressing the tax treatment of income in community property states. In general, the property acquired by you and your husband after your marriage is treated as owned by both of you in community and income generated by that property is taxed equally to you and your spouse. Your deductions are similarly divided. Salaries, wages, and other compensation for the services of either or both spouses are also considered community income.

When separate returns are filed by couples who live in community property states, one-half of the community income must be reported by each spouse.

Code Sec. 66(a) provides that community income will be taxed to the spouse earning it if the couple who is married at any time during the tax year, is separated for the entire year, file separate returns and do not transfer to each other more than a *de minimis* amount of earned income. In addition, Code Sec. 66(c) provides that a spouse who files a separate return may be relieved of liability for tax on his or her share of community income earned by the other spouse if he or she did not know (or have reason to know) of community income items attributable to the other spouse. The IRS has the discretion to provide relief where failure to do so would be inequitable [Code Sec. 66(c)].

.03 Married Persons Living Apart

Both you and your spouse must consent to file a joint return. When one fails to consent, each of you generally must complete a return using the higher, married filing separately rates. However, if you and your spouse are living apart and meet certain tests, you are eligible for some tax relief. You are treated as if you were not married. As such, you can use the more favorable tax rates available to single taxpayers.

> ▶ **TAX SUGGESTION:** If you qualify, you most likely also qualify as a head of household [¶1030]. In that case, you should use the lower head of household rates, rather than the rates for singles or marrieds filing separately.

To qualify to file as head of household, all of the following conditions must be satisfied [Code Sec. 2(c)]:

- You file a separate return.
- You paid more than half the cost to keep up your home.
- Your spouse lived apart from you for the last 6 months of the tax year.
- Your home is the principal residence for more than half the year of the child for whom you can claim a dependency deduction. However, a custodial spouse can still qualify as a "married person living apart," even though the noncustodial spouse can claim the exemption for the child.

The requirements of maintaining a household for a dependent relative are substantially the same as described in ¶1030.

¶1025 SURVIVING SPOUSE

A surviving spouse can file a joint return for the year that his or her spouse dies [¶1020]. Additional split-income benefits may be available in later years. You get the same split-income benefits as on a joint return for the first two years after the year in which your spouse died, if [Code Sec. 2(a); Reg. §1.2-2]:

- You are eligible to file a joint return the year your spouse died; and
- You live with your child, stepchild or foster child for the entire tax year (except for temporary absences), and may claim a dependency exemption for such child [Code Sec. 152(a)]; and
- You pay over half the household costs (here the same tests apply as found in ¶1030 for heads of household); and
- You did not remarry by the end of the tax year.

¶1030 HEAD OF HOUSEHOLD

If you qualify as head of household, you can compute the tax by using the special head of household rate in the tax table or tax rate schedules [Code Sec. 2(b); Reg. §1.2-2(b)]. A taxpayer will qualify for head of household status if he or she is unmarried (and not a surviving spouse) on the last day of the tax year and pay more than one half of the cost of maintaining as his or her home a household that is the "principal place of abode" for more than half the year of either:

- A "qualifying child" [Code Sec. 152(c)];
- A person for whom the taxpayer may claim a dependency exemption.

Head of household status is available for a parent even if the parent does not live with the taxpayer if: (1) the taxpayer may claim a dependency exemption for the parent; (2) if the taxpayer pays over half the parent's maintenance cost for the entire year. A rest home or home for the aged qualifies as a household for this purpose.[8]

The taxpayer cannot file as head of household for a person who is a dependent only because he or she lived with the taxpayer for the whole year or because the taxpayer may claim him or her as a dependent under a multiple support agreement.

.01 Qualifying Child

A uniform definition of a *qualifying child* exists for purposes of claiming head of household status, the exemption for a dependent, the child tax credit, the child and dependent care credit, and the earned income credit. Each of these tax benefits adds some additional rules that must be followed in order to qualify for the benefit. To be a taxpayer's qualifying child for head of household filing status, a person must satisfy four tests:

- Relationship—Qualifying children include the taxpayer's children, stepchild (whether by blood or adoption) foster child, sibling or stepsibling, or a descendant of one of these [Code Sec. 152(c)(2)]. An adopted child is defined as a child legally adopted by the taxpayer or lawfully placed with the taxpayer for legal adoption by the taxpayer. A qualifying child can also be an eligible foster child, defined as a person placed with the taxpayer by an authorized placement agency or by a judgment, decree, or other court order [Code Sec. 152(f)(1)(B) and (C)]. There is no requirement that a foster child live with the taxpayer for the entire tax year.
- Residence—has the same principal residence as the taxpayer for more than half the tax year. Exceptions apply for kidnapped children, temporary absences, and for children who were born or died during the year.
- Age—must be under the age of 19 at the end of the tax year or under the age of 24 if a full-time student for at least five months of the year, or be permanently and totally disabled at any time during the year.
- Support—did not provide more than one-half of his/her own support for the year.

If a child is claimed as a qualifying child by two or more taxpayers in a given year, the child will be the qualifying child of:

- The parent;
- If more than one taxpayer is the child's parent, the one with whom the child lived for the longest time during the year, or, if the time was equal, the parent with the highest AGI;
- If no taxpayer is the child's parent, the taxpayer with the highest adjusted gross income.

---

[8] Rev. Rul. 70-279, 1970-1 CB 1; *J. Robinson*, CA-9, 70-1 USTC ¶9310, 422 F2d 873.

For purposes of claiming the head of household status, a qualifying child who is married at the end of the year must meet the following marital status and nationality tests:

- Nationality—be a U.S. citizen or national, or a resident of the United States, Canada, or Mexico. There is an exception for certain adopted children [Code Sec. 152(b)(3)].
- Marital status—if married, did not file a joint return for that year, unless the return is filed only as a claim for refund and no tax liability would exist for either spouse if they had filed separate returns.

.02 Principal Place of Abode

For purposes of claiming head of household status, the IRS maintains that the household must be the taxpayer's principal place of abode (i.e., the home the taxpayer lives in most of the time).[9] However, the 4th Circuit held that a taxpayer need only live in the household with his or her relative "for a substantial part of the time in question."[10] And the 9th Circuit held that occupancy by a taxpayer need not be actual or physical; a token or implied occupancy may be sufficient.[11] Temporary absences for vacation, sickness, or school are disregarded in determining whether a related person actually lived in the taxpayer's household [Reg. § 1.2-2(c)].

The Tax Court held that a taxpayer failed to qualify for head of household filing status for income tax returns because she did not actually live in the house she kept for her mentally disabled son.[12] To qualify for head household status, the taxpayer must also contribute over half the cost of maintaining the home. These costs include rent, mortgage interest, taxes, property insurance, upkeep and repairs, utility charges, and food consumed in the home. Not included are the costs of clothing, education, medical treatment, vacations, life insurance, transportation, the rental value of the home, or the value of services rendered by the taxpayer or members of his or her household [Reg. § 1.2-2(d)].

STANDARD DEDUCTION

¶1035 AMOUNT OF STANDARD DEDUCTION

.01 Basic Standard Deduction

The standard deduction is a flat dollar allowance that you claim in place of itemizing your personal deductions. The increase in the standard deduction, coupled with changes to the itemized deduction rules, has reduced the number of individuals who itemize.

---

[9] Rev. Rul. 72-43, 1972-1 CB 4.

[10] *J.C. Muse,* CA-4, 70-2 USTC ¶9697, 434 F2d 349.

[11] *C. Smith,* CA-9, 64-2 USTC ¶9534, 332 F2d 671.

[12] *L.B. McDonald,* 61 TCM 2764, Dec. 47,376(M), TC Memo. 1991-242.

The basic standard deduction is determined by the individual's filing status [Code Sec. 63(c)]. In 2013 and 2014, the standard deduction amounts under Code Sec. 63(c)(2) are as follows:

Filing Status	Standard Deduction in 2013	Standard Deduction in 2014
Married Individuals Filing Joint Returns and Surviving Spouses	$12,200	$12,400
Heads of Households	$8,950	$9,100
Unmarried Individuals (other than Surviving Spouses and Heads of Households)	$6,100	$6,200
Married Individuals Filing Separate Returns	$6,100	$6,200

.02 Additional Standard Deduction

Additional standard deduction amounts are allowed in the following situation:

Aged or Blind

In 2013, the additional standard deduction amount under Code Sec. 63(f) for the aged or the blind is $1,200 (no change in 2014). These amounts are increased to $1,500 in 2013 and increased to $1,550 in 2014 if the individual is also unmarried and not a surviving spouse.

For purposes of getting an additional standard deduction, you are considered to be blind if one of the following criteria is met:

1. Visual acuity does not exceed 20/200 in the better eye with corrective lenses.

2. The widest diameter of the visual field subtends an angle no greater than 20 degrees [Code Sec. 63(f)(4)].

In general, you cannot claim an additional standard deduction for a dependent (e.g., a blind child). However, there is an exception for a spouse who files a separate (rather than joint) return. If your elderly/blind spouse can be claimed as a dependent on your return, you can claim the additional standard deduction as well. For this to occur, your elderly or blind spouse must have no gross income and not be a dependent of anyone else [Code Sec. 63(f)(1)(B), (2)(B)].

.03 Dependent's Standard Deduction

Dependent

In 2013, the standard deduction amount under Code Sec. 63(c)(5) for an individual who may be claimed as a dependent by another taxpayer cannot exceed the greater of (1) $1,000 (no change in 2014), or (2) the sum of $350 (no change in 2014) and the individual's earned income.

The term "earned income" here is not defined by reference to net earnings from self-employment and thus a net loss from a business need not be subtracted from wages to determine the maximum standard deduction.[13]

[13] *A.C. Briggs*, TC Summary Op. 2004-22.

.04 Taxpayers Not Eligible for Standard Deduction

Certain individuals are not eligible to use the standard deduction. These include [Code Sec. 63(c)(6)]:

1. Married taxpayers filing separately if either spouse itemizes deductions.
2. Nonresident aliens.
3. Individuals who file returns for periods of less than 12 months because of accounting period changes.
4. Estates or trusts, common trust funds, or partnerships.

Married taxpayers who file separate returns must either both itemize or both take the standard deduction [Code Sec. 63(c)(6)(A)].

PERSONAL EXEMPTIONS

¶1040 AMOUNT OF YOUR PERSONAL EXEMPTIONS

.01 Inflation-Adjusted Amount

The personal exemption amount is $3,900 in 2013 (increasing to $3,950 in 2014). This amount is adjusted for inflation each year [Code Sec. 151(d)(3)].

.02 Number of Exemptions You Can Claim

You can claim an exemption for yourself, your spouse and each person who is your dependent [Code Sec. 151(b), (c)]. For example, in 2013, if you are married and have two dependent children and a dependent parent, you are entitled to five exemptions equal to $19,500 (five times $3,900), unless your adjusted gross income exceeds certain levels [¶1045].

There is a special rule for dependent taxpayers. No personal exemption amount is allowable on the return of an individual who is eligible to be claimed as a dependent on another taxpayer's return. For example, no exemption can be claimed on the return of your child who is eligible to be claimed for a dependency exemption on your return [Code Sec. 151(d)(2)]. Note that it doesn't matter whether you actually claim the exemption; your dependent child still loses it.

> ▶ **TAX STRATEGY:** If you have been claiming exemptions for your dependents, you should consider whether you wish to have your dependents get the tax savings of the exemptions for themselves instead. To make the shift, you must disqualify yourself from being eligible to claim the dependency exemption. This can be done by giving your former dependent income-producing assets that bring his or her income above $3,900 in 2013 (except for minor children and students under age 24) [see ¶1070] or failing to provide more than one-half support.

A nonresident alien is generally allowed only one personal exemption. He may not claim exemptions for his spouse or dependents. However, a resident of Canada or Mexico or a U.S. national may take all personal exemptions to which a citizen would be entitled [Code Sec. 873(b)(3)].

.03 Short Tax Year

The personal exemption amount is not ordinarily affected if the return covers less than 12 months. Thus, the deduction on the return for a taxpayer who dies on June 30, 2013, would be $3,900 even though the return covered only half of the year. The exemption deduction must be prorated, however, in returns for short periods made necessary by a change in accounting period (Ch. 18) [Code Sec. 443(c)].

¶1045 PHASEOUT OF PERSONAL EXEMPTIONS

In 2013, the personal exemption phases out for taxpayers with the following adjusted gross income amounts [Code Sec. 151(d)(3)]:

Filing Status	*AGI—Beginning of Phaseout*	*AGI—Completed Phaseout*
Married Individuals Filing Joint Returns and Surviving Spouses [Code Sec. 1(a)]	$300,000	$422,500
Heads of Households [Code Sec. 1(b)]	$275,000	$397,500
Unmarried Individuals (other than Surviving Spouses and Heads of Households) [Code Sec. 1(c)]	$250,000	$372,500
Married Individuals Filing Separate Returns [Code Sec. 1(d)]	$150,000	$211,250

In 2014, the personal exemption phases out for taxpayers with the following adjusted gross income amounts [Code Sec. 151(d)(3)]:

Filing Status	*AGI—Beginning of Phaseout*	*AGI—Completed Phaseout*
Married Individuals Filing Joint Returns and Surviving Spouses [Code Sec. 1(a)]	$305,050	$427,550
Heads of Households [Code Sec. 1(b)]	$279,650	$402,150
Unmarried Individuals (other than Surviving Spouses and Heads of Households) [Code Sec. 1(c)]	$254,200	$376,700
Married Individuals Filing Separate Returns [Code Sec. 1(d)]	$152,525	$213,775

¶1050 EXEMPTIONS OF MARRIED PERSONS

A married couple need not live together for the rules below to apply. They must, however, be married at the close of the tax year or, if one dies, on the date of death. If they are legally divorced or separated under a decree, they are considered single, not married [Code Sec. 7703(a)(2)]. If they are separated under an interlocutory decree of divorce, they are considered married until the decree becomes final.[14]

---

[14] Rev. Rul. 57-368, 1957-2 CB 896.

.01 If a Joint Return Is Filed

If spouses file a joint return, they may claim two exemption deductions for 2013 of $3,900 each, or a total exemption deduction of $7,800 [¶1045]. However, no exemption will be allowed to an individual who is eligible to be claimed as a dependent on another taxpayer's return [Code Sec. 151(b); Reg. § 1.151-1(b)]. If one spouse dies, the other may file a joint return for the year of death and claim an exemption deduction for the deceased spouse, unless the surviving spouse remarries during the year of the spouse's death.

.02 If Only One Spouse Files a Return

If spouses do not file a joint return and only one spouse files a separate return, that spouse may claim two exemptions (one for himself and one for his spouse), but only if the spouse, for the calendar year in which the tax year began, has no gross income and is not a dependent of another [Code Sec. 151(b); Reg. § 1.151-1(b)].

.03 If Husband and Wife File Separate Returns

If a husband and wife file separate returns, each must take his or her own exemption on their respective return. If, however, a husband or wife file separate returns and one of the spouses has no gross income and is not the dependent of another taxpayer, then the spouse with gross income may claim the personal exemption for the other spouse on his or her separate return. A married taxpayer who files a separate return may not claim two exemptions for his spouse, one as a spouse and one as a dependent [Code Sec. 152(a)(9)].

.04 If One Spouse Dies

If your spouse dies during the tax year, you can claim one exemption for yourself and one exemption for your spouse on your separate return, if your spouse had no gross income and was not a dependent of another taxpayer. But if you remarry during the same year, you cannot claim an exemption for your deceased spouse.[15] You can, however, claim an exemption for your present spouse, if he or she has no gross income and is not a dependent of another person.

If your spouse dies during the tax year and you (the surviving spouse) have no gross income and are not a dependent of another for the year, you may claim two exemptions (one for each of you) on the final separate return filed for your deceased spouse. If, however, each of you has gross income, neither of you is entitled to an exemption for the other, unless you file a joint return [Ch. 26].

> **Example 1-2:** George and Amelia are married. Amelia received $1 in interest before she died on September 30, 2013. George gets one $3,900 exemption for himself, but no exemption for Amelia on a separate return. If the conditions for filing a joint return are met, one may be filed, and the exemptions for both George and Amelia may be taken.

Although a widow who remarries in the same calendar year that her previous husband dies cannot claim both husbands on her separate return, she can be claimed twice—once on her deceased husband's separate return and again on her new husband's

[15] Rev. Rul. 71-158, 1971-1 CB 50.

separate calendar year return, but only if she has no gross income and is not a dependent of another.[16]

EXEMPTIONS FOR DEPENDENTS

¶1055 DEPENDENCY EXEMPTIONS

.01 Dependency Exemption Rules

Taxpayers may only claim an exemption for a dependent who is either a *qualifying child* or a *qualifying relative* [Code Sec. 152(a); Reg. § 1.152-4(a)].

Exceptions include:

- A taxpayer cannot claim a dependency exemption for a married individual who files a joint return unless that joint return is filed solely in an attempt to claim a refund [Code Sec. 151(c)(2); Code Sec. 152(b)(2)].
- If an individual is claimed as a dependent of another person, the dependent may not claim any dependents of his own [Code Sec. 151(d)(2)].
- As a general rule, an individual cannot be a dependent unless he or she is a citizen or national of the United States or a resident of the United States, Canada, or Mexico [Code Sec. 152(b)(3)(A)]. However, a legally adopted child or an individual who is lawfully placed by the taxpayer for legal adoption need not satisfy this rule if for the tax year the child has the same principal place of residence as the taxpayer and is a member of the taxpayer's household and the taxpayer is a citizen or national of the United States [Code Sec. 152(b)(3)(B)]. In *L. Carlebach,*[17] the Tax Court denied the taxpayers' claimed dependency exemption deductions because the taxpayer's child was not a U.S. citizen or a resident at any time during the year. The court upheld Reg. § 1.152-2(a)(1) which provides that in order for a child to qualify as a dependent, the child must be a U.S. citizen or resident.

.02 Qualifying Child Defined

To be a *qualifying child* under Code Sec. 152(c)(1), the child must satisfy the following requirements:

- *Relationship.* An individual will be a qualifying child if he or she is the taxpayer's child or stepchild (whether by blood or adoption), foster child, sibling or stepsibling, or a descendant of one of these [Code Sec. 152(c)(2)].
- *Age.* The child must be under the age of 19 at the end of the tax year, or under the age of 24 if a full-time student for at least five months of the year, or be permanently and totally disabled at any time during the year [Code Sec. 152(c)(3)]. A qualifying child must be younger than the taxpayer [Code Sec. 152(c)(3)(A)]. For instance, a taxpayer's older brother or sister cannot be the taxpayer's qualifying child. More-

[16] Rev. Rul. 71-159, 1971-1 CB 50.

[17] *L. Carlebach,* 139 TC No. 1, Dec. 59,127 (2012); *D. Stern,* 104 TCM 82, Dec. 59,128(M), TC Memo. 2012-204.

over, a qualifying child cannot file a joint return with a spouse for any tax year beginning during the calendar year in which the taxpayer's tax year begins. This test does not apply if the qualifying child files a joint return only to obtain a refund [Code Sec. 152(c)(1)(E)]. This often happens, for instance, when a taxpayer is entitled to a refund of taxes withheld from wages.

- *Principal residence.* The child must have the same principal residence as the taxpayer for more than half of the year. Exceptions apply, in certain cases, for children of divorced or separated parents, kidnapped children, temporary absences, and for children who were born or died during the year [Code Sec. 152(c)(1)(B)].
- *Not self-supporting.* The child must *not* have provided over half of his or her own support for the year [Code Sec. 152(c)(1)(D)].
- *Joint return test.* A qualifying child cannot file a joint return with a spouse for a tax year beginning in the calendar year in which the tax year of the taxpayer claiming the qualifying child begins. However, a qualifying child is allowed to file a joint return for the limited purpose of obtaining a refund [Code Sec. 152(c)(1)(E)].

.03 Children of Divorced or Separated Parents—Tie-breaker Rules

When taxpayers are divorced or legally separated under a decree of divorce or separate maintenance or are separated under a written separation agreement or are living apart at all times during the last 6 months of the year, disputes often arise regarding which parent will claim the dependency exemption.

A child cannot be claimed as a dependent on more than one tax return for any calendar year, even though the child satisfies the qualifying child tests for two or more taxpayers. The tie-breaker rules found in Code Sec. 152(c)(4) determine who may claim the dependency exemption when one child is treated as a qualifying child for more than one tax return. Code Sec. 152(c)(4)(A) provides that the child is treated as the qualifying child of (1) the taxpayer who is the child's parent, or (2) if neither taxpayer is the child's parent, the taxpayer with the highest adjusted gross income for the year.

If a child's parents do not file a joint return, the child is treated as the qualifying child of the parent with whom the child resides for a longer period of time during the year or, if the child resides with both parents for an equal period of time, of the parent with the higher adjusted gross income. However, if the custodial parent releases a claim to the exemption, the child will be treated as the qualifying child of the noncustodial parent [Reg. § 1.152-4(a)].

If the parents claiming the qualifying child do not file a joint return, the child will be treated as the qualifying child of (1) the parent with whom the child resided for the longest period of time during the year, or (2) if the child resides with both parents for the same amount of time during the year, the parent with the highest adjusted gross income [Code Sec. 152(c)(4)(B)(ii); Reg. § 1.152-4(a)].

No Parent Claiming Qualifying Child

If the parents may claim an individual as a qualifying child but neither parent does so, another taxpayer may claim the individual as a qualifying child but only if the adjusted gross income of that taxpayer is higher than the highest adjusted gross income of any parent of the individual [Code Sec. 152(c)(4)(C)].

.04 Release/Revocation of Claim by Custodial Parent

A child will be treated as the qualifying child or qualifying relative of the noncustodial parent if the custodial parent signs a "written declaration" that he or she will not claim the child as a dependent that year and the noncustodial parent attaches the declaration to his or her return for that year [Reg. § 1.152-4(b) (3) (i)].

Written Declaration

The written declaration must be an unconditional release of the custodial parent's claim to the child as a dependent for the year for which the declaration is effective. A declaration is not unconditional if the custodial parent's release requires the satisfaction of any condition, including the noncustodial parent's meeting of an obligation such as the payment of support. A written declaration must name the noncustodial parent to whom the exemption is released and specify the year or years for which it is effective [Reg. § 1.152-4(e) (1) (i)].

A release of a claim to an exemption can be executed on (1) Form 8332, *Release/Revocation of Release of Claim to Exemption for Child by Custodial Parent;* or (2) a written declaration that is not on Form 8332 but conforms to the substance of that form and must be a document executed for the sole purpose of releasing the claim. Unmarried parents may use Form 8332 to secure release of the dependency exemption from the custodial parent.[18] A court order or decree or a separation agreement may not serve as a written declaration [Reg. § 1.152-4(e) (1) (ii)]. A noncustodial parent must attach a copy of the written declaration to the parent's return for each tax year in which the child is claimed as a dependent [Reg. § 1.152-4(e) (2)].

The Tax Court has held that a noncustodial parent was not entitled to claim a dependency deduction because the noncustodial parent failed to attach a Form 8332 signed by the custodial parent to his return. The dependency deduction was denied even though a permanent order of a divorce, which the noncustodial parent attached to his return, awarded him the dependency deductions for his children.[19]

Revocation of Release

A custodial parent may revoke a written declaration by providing written notice of the revocation to the other parent. The parent revoking the written declaration must make reasonable efforts to provide actual notice to the other parent. The revocation may be effective no earlier than the year that begins in the first calendar year after the calendar year in which the parent revoking the written declaration provides, or makes reasonable efforts to provide the written notice [Reg. § 1.152-4(e) (3) (i)].

Form of Revocation

The revocation may be made on: (1) Form 8332, *Release/Revocation of Release of Claim to Exemption for Child by Custodial Parent;* or (2) written declaration that is not on Form

---

[18] *R. George*, 139 TC 508, Dec. 59,291 (2012); *J.R. King*, 121 TC 245, Dec. 55,309 (2003).

[19] *M.K. Shenk*, 140 TC No. 10, Dec. 59,528 (2013); *B.E. Armstrong*, 139 TC 468, Dec. 59,290 (2012); *C.J. Miller*, 114 TC 184, Dec. 53,811 (2000), *aff'd*, CA-10, 2002-2 USTC ¶50,473, 293 F3d 1208; *R.J. Meyer*, 85 TCM 760, Dec. 55,014(M), TC Memo. 2003-12; *J. Bramante*, 84 TCM 299, Dec. 54,869(M), TC Memo. 2002-228; *Z.S. Curello*, TC Summary Op. 2005-23; *K.A. Brettin*, TC Summary Op. 2004-95.

8332 but conforms to the substance of that form and is a document executed for the sole purpose of serving as a revocation. The revocation must specify the year or years for which the revocation is effective. A revocation that specifies all future years is treated as specifying the first year the revocation is executed and all subsequent years [Reg. § 1.152-4(e) (3) (ii)].

The parent revoking the written declaration must attach a copy of the revocation to the parent's return for each tax year for which the parent claims a child as a dependent as a result of the revocation. The parent revoking the written declaration must keep a copy of the revocation and evidence of delivery of the notice to the other parent, or of the reasonable efforts to provide actual notice [Reg. § 1.152-4(e) (3) (iii)].

Custody Defined

A child is in the custody of one or both parents for more than one-half of the calendar year if one or both parents have the right under state law to physical custody of the child for more than one-half of the calendar year [Reg. § 1.152-4(c)].

The custodial parent is defined as the parent with whom the child resides for the greater number of nights during the calendar year, and the noncustodial parent is the parent who is not the custodial parent. To be a custodial parent, the parent and the child must have shared the same principal place of abode for the greater portion of the tax year. In the event of a split custody, or if the divorce decree or agreement fails to establish who has custody, custody will be deemed to be with the parent who has physical custody of the child for the greater part of the year.[20] A child is treated as residing with neither parent if the child is emancipated under state law. A child resides with a parent for a night if the child sleeps:

- At the residence of that parent (whether or not the parent is present); or
- In the company of the parent, when the child does not sleep at a parent's residence (for example, the parent and child are on vacation together).

A night that extends over two years is allocated to the year in which the night begins. A child who does not reside with a parent for a night is treated as residing with the parent with whom the child would have resided for the night but for the absence. A child who does not reside with a parent for a night is treated as not residing with either parent for that night if it cannot be determined with which parent the child would have resided or if the child would not have resided with either parent for the night [Reg. § 1.152-4(d)].

Special Rule for Equal Number of Nights

If a child is in the custody of one or both parents for more than one-half of the calendar year and the child resides with each parent for an equal number of nights during the calendar year, the parent with the higher adjusted gross income for the calendar year is treated as the custodial parent. If, in a calendar year, due to a parent's nighttime work schedule, a child resides for a greater number of days but not nights with the parent who works at night, that parent is treated as the custodial parent. On a school day, the child is treated as residing at the primary residence registered with the school [Reg. § 1.152-4(d) (4)].

---

[20] *K.L. McCullar*, 86 TCM 384, Dec. 55,299(M), TC Memo. 2003-272.

.05 Qualifying Relative

To be a *qualifying relative* for purposes of the dependency exemption, an individual must satisfy the following tests:

1. *Relationship.* The following individuals can be classified as qualifying relatives: a child or a descendant of a child; a sibling, or step-sibling; parent and their ancestors and siblings; the taxpayer's stepparents and stepsiblings; and the taxpayer's son-in-law, daughter-in-law, father-in-law, mother-in-law, brother-in-law and sister-in-law [Code Sec. 152(d)(2)]. Qualifying relatives also include individuals, other than the taxpayer's spouse, who share an abode with the taxpayer and were members of the taxpayer's household during the year [Code Sec. 152(d)(2)(H)]. An individual is not a member of the taxpayer's household if, at any time during the taxpayer's tax year, the relationship between the individual and the taxpayer violated local law [Code Sec. 152(f)(3)]. See ¶ 1065 for further discussion;

2. *Gross income.* A dependent will be a qualifying relative if his or her gross income for the year is less than the exemption amount ($3,900 in 2013). See ¶ 1070 for further discussion.

3. *Support.* In order to claim a person as a dependent the taxpayer must prove that he or she furnished over one half of the dependent's total support for the year [Code Sec. 152(d)(1)(C); Reg. § 1.152-1]. Alimony payments are not treated as payments for the support of any dependent and, in the case of remarriage, a child's support that is provided by a parent's spouse is treated as provided by the parent [Code Sec. 152(d)(5)]. If a qualifying relative is the taxpayer's child and is a full-time student, amounts received as scholarships are not considered support [Code Sec. 152(f)(5)]. See ¶ 1060 for further discussion.

4. *Not a qualifying child.* A qualifying relative cannot be a qualifying child of the taxpayer or any other taxpayer for any tax year beginning in the calendar year in which the taxpayer's tax year begins [Code Sec. 152(d)(1)(D)].

▶ **DEPENDENT'S NUMBER:** You must provide a dependent's taxpayer identification number (TIN) in order to claim a dependency exemption for that person [Code Sec. 151(e)]. An individual's TIN is generally that individual's social security number. An incorrect TIN is treated as a mathematical or clerical error, allowing the IRS to summarily assess any additional tax due as a result of the denied exemption [Code Sec. 6213]. Any notification of additional tax is not treated as a notice of deficiency. You apply for a social security number by filing Form SS-5 with the Social Security Administration. In *Miller,*[21] the Tax Court held that parents' refusal to provide children's SSNs on religious grounds cost them dependency exemptions for the children.

---

[21] *J.W. Miller,* 114 TC 511, Dec. 53,915 (2000).

.06 Birth or Death During the Year

If all other tests or conditions are satisfied, the fact that a person was born or died during the year will not affect your right to claim the full exemption. No proration is required. But no exemption is allowed for an unborn or stillborn child.[22]

¶1060 SUPPORT

.01 Support Test Eliminated for Qualifying Child

The support test for determining whether an individual is a dependent generally does not apply to a child who satisfies the requirements of the definition of a qualifying child. The support test was eliminated except that a child who provides over one half of his own support is not a qualifying child of another taxpayer for purposes of the dependency exemption.

To claim a dependency exemption for a qualifying relative who does not satisfy the qualifying child definition, the gross income and support test, including the special rules for multiple support agreements, the special rules relating to income of handicapped dependents, and the special support test in case of students continue to apply.

.02 Support Test Unchanged for Qualifying Relative

In order to claim a person (including a parent) as a dependent under the qualifying relative test, you must supply evidence proving that you furnished over one half of the total support of the dependent for the year [Code Sec. 152(d)(1)(C); Reg. § 1.152-1]. You will satisfy this burden if you show both the total amount of a dependent's support and the one half that you supplied. There are, however, exceptions covering children of divorced parents [(b) below] and students [(c) below]. If both spouses file separate returns and both contribute to the child's support, the exemption may be claimed by the one furnishing more than half the support.

Even if a taxpayer has not actually paid for the support, you may still qualify for the deduction if you (1) take affirmative steps to provide the support, and (2) incur an unconditional obligation to pay for the items of support. But a promise to pay for the support "if and when it is possible to do so" is not enough.[23]

.03 What Is Support?

Support includes amounts spent for food, shelter, clothing, medical and dental care, education, church contributions,[24] child care expenses,[25] wedding apparel and receptions,[26] capital items such as a car or T.V. set,[27] and the like, but not the value of services performed for a dependent,[28] nor scholarships received by the dependent student [see .03 below]. Items furnished in the form of property or lodging[29] are

---

[22] Treas. Dept., IRS Publication 17, "Your Federal Income Tax" (2013 Ed.), p. 28.

[23] Rev. Rul. 58-404, 1958-2 CB 56; Rev. Rul. 67-61, 1967-1 CB 27.

[24] Rev. Rul. 58-67, 1958-1 CB 62.

[25] *P. Lustig*, CA-9, 60-1 USTC ¶9248, 274 F2d 448, *cert. denied*, 364 US 840.

[26] Rev. Rul. 76-184, 1976-1 CB 44.

[27] Rev. Rul. 77-282, 1977-2 CB 52.

[28] *F. Markarian*, CA-7, 65-2 USTC ¶9699, 352 F2d 870, *cert. denied*, 384 US 988.

[29] Rev. Rul. 58-302, 1958-1 CB 62.

measured by their fair market value [Reg. § 1.152-1(a)(2)]. Thus, if you own the house in which the dependent lives, you count the fair rental value of the lodging furnished (which includes the cost of upkeep[30]). If you live rent-free in someone's home, you must offset the fair rental value of the lodging furnished against the amounts you spent in support of the dependent.[31] If the dependent lives in his or her own home, its fair rental value is considered support the dependent provides for himself or herself.[32] Premiums for medical care insurance count toward support but not: (1) the benefits themselves; (2) payments for civil damages; (3) services in government medical facilities.[33] Neither Medicare (basic or supplemental) nor Medicaid payments are support items.[34] However, social security benefits paid to a disabled parent's child are contributions by the child to the child's own support.[35]

> ▶ **SOCIAL SECURITY BENEFITS:** Social security retirement benefits count as support to the extent they are used to pay for food, clothing, shelter, medical care and other items of support. On the other hand, Medicare benefits that provide health care do not count as support. By covering expenses that would otherwise count as support, Medicare makes it easier for you to pass the more-than-half support test for an elderly relative.

If the dependent is alive the entire year, the fact that you do not support him or her for the entire year does not affect your right to the exemption.[36]

Example 1-3: Mac Malone supports his father for 7 months of the year, at a cost of $5,800, and Mac's sister supports the father for the remaining 5 months at a cost of $5,400. Mac can claim the entire $3,900 exemption for his father's support in 2013. If his sister supported her father for 5 months at a cost of $6,000, she could claim the exemption.

If a serviceman is supporting another, the entire amount of support furnished, including any nontaxable allowances for quarter, is counted for this test.[37]

Dependent's Income

If dependents have funds of their own from any source, only the amounts they actually spend on their support are matched against the support you furnished to determine if you furnished over one-half of the support. For example, social security benefits[38] and state benefit payments based solely on need[39] are treated as contributions to the dependent's own support to the extent the benefits are so used.

Example 1-4: Mr. Gary's father gets social security of $5,400 a year. This year, the father put $1,000 into a savings account and spent the remaining $4,400 on

---

[30] Treas. Dept., IRS Publication 17, "Your Federal Income Tax" (2013 Ed.), p. 33.

[31] Treas. Dept., IRS Publication 17, "Your Federal Income Tax" (2013 Ed.), p. 33.

[32] Treas. Dept., IRS Publication 17, "Your Federal Income Tax" (2013 Ed.), p. 33.

[33] Rev. Rul. 64-223, 1964-2 CB 50.

[34] Rev. Rul. 79-173, 1979-1 CB 86; *A.H. Turecamo*, CA-2, 77-1 USTC ¶ 9415, 554 F2d 564; *M.E. Archer*, 73 TC 963, Dec. 36,798 (1980).

[35] Rev. Rul. 74-543, 1974-2 CB 39.

[36] *J.F. Scott*, 9 TCM 932, Dec. 17,920(M) (1950).

[37] Rev. Rul. 70-87, 1970-1 CB 29.

[38] Rev. Rul. 57-344, 1957-2 CB 112; Rev. Rul. 72-591, 1972-2 CB 84.

[39] Rev. Rul. 71-468, 1971-2 CB 115.

clothing, entertainment, and the like. Gary contributed $5,000 to the support of his father who had no other income. Gary meets the support test.

Parents Treated as a Unit

The total support of your parents is presumed to be spent on both equally, unless you prove otherwise.[40]

Example 1-5: Mr. Brown's parents received $14,000 total support: $8,000 from his father's social security benefits and $6,000 from Brown. Brown is not considered to have provided more than half the support of either parent, even though he may have actually provided more than half his mother's support. The parents are treated as a unit; the benefits are allocated evenly between the two.

Group Support

If you contribute a lump sum for the support of two or more dependents, it is allocated among the dependents on a pro rata basis. If a member of a household contributes more to the support of the household than his or her pro rata share, the difference counts toward the support of the other members of the household in equal amounts.[41]

Community Property States

If separate returns are filed in community property states, and the dependent is supported by community funds, either the husband or wife must take the entire exemption.[42] The following states are community property states: Arizona, California, Idaho, Louisiana, Nevada, New Mexico, Texas, Washington, and Wisconsin.

.04 Multiple Support Agreement Exception

The noncustodial parent may be able to claim the dependency exemption for a child who is a qualifying relative if a multiple support agreement provides that he or she is entitled to the dependency exemption [Code Sec. 152(d)(3)]. When two or more persons furnish more than half of the support of an individual, one of the contributing group is entitled to claim the dependency exemption if all of the following criteria are met [Code Sec. 152(d)(3)]:

- No one person contributed more than half the dependent's support.
- Each member of the group, were it not for the support test, would have been entitled to claim the individual as a dependent.
- The one claiming the deduction gave more than 10 percent of the dependent's support.
- Every person (other than the one claiming the exemption) who gave more than 10 percent of the dependent's support files a written statement on Form 2120, *Multiple*

---

40 *W. Abel*, 21 TCM 1044, Dec. 25,606(M), TC Memo. 1962-192; Rev. Rul. 72-591, 1972-2 CB 84.

41 Rev. Rul. 64-222, 1964-2 CB 47, Rev. Rul. 72-591, 1972-2 CB 84.

42 Treas. Dept., IRS Publication 555, "Community Property" (2013 Ed.), p. 5.

Support Declaration, providing that he or she will not claim the exemption in the same calendar year (or any tax year starting in the calendar year).

.05 Scholarships as Support

If a taxpayer's child, stepchild, adopted child or foster child is a student, a scholarship at an educational institution is not counted in determining if you furnished more than half the support [Code Sec. 152(f)(5); Reg. § 1.152-1(c)], unless the grant was given in return for the student's promise of future services.[43]

Example 1-6: Ben Davis gets $8,000 in support from his father and $9,000 as a scholarship granted by his university. The terms of the grant require only that he be a third-year medical student in good standing. Ben has no other income. Ben's father can claim Ben as a dependent.

▶ **LIBERAL SUPPORT RULE:** Scholarships are nontaxable to the extent they are used for tuition, books, and related expenses. Amounts received for room and board or other purposes are taxable. For purposes of the support test, though, there is no distinction. Neither taxable nor nontaxable scholarships count as support.

Who Is a Student?

Your child is a "student" if, during each of any five calendar months of the calendar year in which your tax year begins, the child (1) is in full-time attendance at an "educational institution," or (2) is taking a full-time course of institutional on-farm training [Code Sec. 152(f)(2); Reg. § 1.151-3(b)].

An educational institution is one that maintains a regular faculty and curriculum, and normally has a regularly organized body of students in attendance where the educational activities are carried out [Code Sec. 170(b)(1)(A)(ii); Reg. § 1.151-3(c)]. Thus, primary, secondary, preparatory and normal schools, colleges, universities, technical and mechanical schools are covered, but not correspondence schools and on-the-job training.

On-farm training, to qualify, must be supervised by an accredited agent of an educational institution or a state or a political subdivision of a state [Code Sec. 152(f)(2)].

Night school attendance only is generally not considered full-time attendance. But full-time attendance may include some night attendance related to a full-time course of study [Reg. § 1.151-3(b)].

¶1065 RELATIONSHIP OF DEPENDENT

.01 Qualifications

A taxpayer may claim a dependency exemption for a dependent who is categorized as either a *qualifying child* or a *qualifying relative* [Code Sec. 152(a)]. See ¶ 1055.

---

[43] Rev. Rul. 58-403, 1958-2 CB 49.

.02 Qualifying Child Relationship Test

In order to be a qualifying child, the child must satisfy the relationship test which is satisfied if the child is the taxpayer's son, daughter, stepson, stepdaughter, brother, sister, stepbrother, stepsister, or descendant of any such individual [Code Sec. 152(c)(2)]. An adopted child will qualify if the child is legally adopted by the taxpayer or the individual is lawfully placed with the taxpayer for legal adoption [Code Sec. 152(f)(1)(B)]. A foster child who is placed with the taxpayer by an authorized placement agency or by judgment, decree, or other order of any court of competent jurisdiction is treated as the taxpayer's child [Code Sec. 152(f)(1)(C)]. Prop. Reg. § 1.152-2(c)(2) provides that adoption taxpayer identification numbers can be obtained for children who are adopted in independent adoptions.

The dependency exemption is still available to an otherwise qualifying taxpayer whose child has been kidnapped by someone who is not a member of the family of the child or the taxpayer. However, this treatment ends for the tax year ending after the calendar year in which it is determined that the child is dead (or, if earlier, the year in which the child would have attained age 18).

.03 Qualifying Relative Relationship Test

The following individuals will qualify as relatives: a child or a descendant of a child; a sibling, or step-sibling; the taxpayer's parents, and their ancestors and siblings; the taxpayer's stepparents and stepsiblings; and the taxpayer's son-in-law, daughter-in-law, father-in-law, mother-in-law, brother-in-law, and sister-in-law [Code Sec. 152(d)(2)]. Qualifying relatives also include individuals, other than the taxpayer's spouse, who share an abode with the taxpayer and were members of the taxpayer's household during the year [Code Sec. 152(d)(2)(H)]. An individual is not a member of the taxpayer's household if, at any time during the taxpayer's tax year, the relationship between the individual and the taxpayer violated local law [Code Sec. 152(f)(3)].

A taxpayer may claim a parent as a dependent or a grandparent may claim a grandchild if the taxpayer furnishes more than one-half of the dependent's support and the dependent's gross income is less than the exemption amount ($3,900 in 2013).

¶1070 DEPENDENT'S GROSS INCOME

.01 General Rule

Taxpayers may only claim an exemption for a dependent who is either a qualifying child or a qualifying relative [Code Sec. 152(a)]. An individual will not be a qualifying relative for purposes of claiming a dependency exemption unless his or her gross income for the year is less than the exemption amount ($3,900 in 2013) [Code Sec. 152(d)(1)(B)]. In addition, if a dependent is permanently and totally disabled at any time during the tax year, the dependent's gross income does not include income attributable to services performed at a sheltered workshop, if the availability of medical care at the workshop is the principal reason for the dependent's presence there, and the income arises from activities that are incident to the medical care [Code Sec. 152(d)(4)].

.02 Excludable Income

In figuring a qualifying relative's gross income, exclude any type of exempt income. However, tax-exempt income is generally included in determining whether the support test is met [¶1060], if the claimed dependent has used that income for his or her support [Reg. § 1.152-1(a)(2)]. Thus, state aid benefits based solely on the dependent's needs are considered in determining support, to the extent that they are used for the dependent's support.

> **Example 1-7:** John's father earned $950 at odd jobs. He also received $5,200 during the year in social security benefits. He put $300 in the bank, but used the rest for his own support. John paid $6,000 toward his father's support and claims him as a dependent. Since the social security payments are not considered income, the $3,900 (in 2013) gross income test is met. And while the father received a total of $6,150, only $5,850 was used for his support. Therefore, John furnished more than half his father's support.

If the dependent has rental income, the gross rents are included, without deduction for taxes, repairs, etc.

Gross Income—Inclusions

2

INCOME SUBJECT TO TAX

What is gross income? . . . . ¶ 2001

COMPENSATION, PRIZES AND AWARDS, AND PENSIONS

Tax treatment of compensation . . . ¶ 2005
Compensation distinguished from gift . . . . ¶ 2010
Prizes, awards, and lotteries . . . . . ¶ 2015
Pensions and employee payments . . . . ¶ 2020
Compensation of government employees . . . . ¶ 2025
Compensation of members of armed forces . . . . ¶ 2030
Insurance as compensation . . . . . ¶ 2035
Employee stock options . . . . ¶ 2040
Nonqualified stock options (NQSOs) . . . . ¶ 2045
Qualified stock options . . . . ¶ 2050

INTEREST INCOME

Interest in general . . . . ¶ 2055
Tax treatment of loans . . . . ¶ 2060
Interest-free and low-interest loans . . . . ¶ 2065
Debt instruments—original issue discount bonds . . . . ¶ 2070

DIVIDENDS IN GENERAL

What is a dividend? . . . . ¶ 2075
How dividends are taxed . . . . ¶ 2080
Constructive dividends . . . . ¶ 2085
Tax-exempt and specially treated distributions . . . . ¶ 2090

DISTRIBUTIONS IN KIND OF SECURITIES

What is a stock dividend? . . . . ¶ 2095
Effect of nontaxable stock distributions . . . . ¶ 2100
Stock rights . . . . ¶ 2105
Effect of nontaxable stock rights . . . ¶ 2110
Taxable stock rights . . . . ¶ 2115
Rights to bonds . . . . ¶ 2120

RETURN OF CAPITAL DIVIDENDS

How a return of capital is taxed . . . ¶ 2125
What is a liquidating dividend? . . . ¶ 2130

MISCELLANEOUS INCOME

Rents and royalties . . . . ¶ 2135
Improvements by lessee . . . . ¶ 2140
Forgiveness of debt (cancellation of indebtedness) . . . . ¶ 2145
Alimony and separate maintenance . . . . ¶ 2150
Gambling income . . . . ¶ 2155
Income in respect of a decedent . . . ¶ 2160

S corporation, partnership, and limited liability company pass-through income . . . . ¶2165
Child's income—Kiddie tax . . . . . . ¶2170
Business insurance proceeds . . . . . . ¶2185
Recovery of tax benefit items . . . . . . ¶2190

INCOME SUBJECT TO TAX

Gross income is what the tax law calls the total amount of your income subject to income tax. It includes all types of income not expressly exempt from tax. This chapter covers major categories of income: compensation for services, interest, dividends, rents, and royalties. Gross income is the starting point to find the amount of income tax you owe.

¶2001 WHAT IS GROSS INCOME?

.01 General Rule

Your "gross income" includes all items of income from whatever source, except those specifically excluded from taxation by statute, such as municipal bond interest, life insurance proceeds, and gifts [Ch. 5]. It includes pay for personal and professional services, many employee fringe benefits, business income, profits from sales of your property, interest, rent, dividends and gains, profits and income derived from any source whatever unless exempt from tax by law [Code Sec. 61(a); Reg. § 1.61-1]. Your income may be realized in the form of services, meals, accommodations, stock, or other property, as well as in cash. You must report income other than cash at the fair market value of the goods or services you received. Fair market value is the price at which the property would change hands between a willing buyer and a willing seller, neither being required to buy or sell, and both having reasonable knowledge of the relevant facts.

Return of Capital

A return of capital, such as repayment of a loan or an advance, is not income unless the loan or advance had been previously deducted as a bad debt, resulting in a tax benefit. Similarly, if you receive money as a reimbursement for personal expenses incurred, you have not received taxable income.

> **Example 2-1:** Mr. Sloan owns an apartment building. He received janitorial services from Mr. Daley in return for allowing Daley to use an apartment rent-free. Sloan must include in income the fair market value of the janitorial services, and Daley must include the fair rental value of the apartment.

.02 To Whom Income Is Taxable

Salaries and other forms of pay for services generally are income to the person who performs the services. Income from property and gain from the sale of property generally are income to the property's owner. However, the income-splitting benefits on a joint return filed by a husband and wife have the effect of taxing the income as if one-half belonged to each. There are other important exceptions that are subject to special rules, such as income from partnerships and from estates and trusts.

If you receive income as an agent, it is taxable to your principal when you receive it.[1] However, if you really own the income, you cannot escape being taxed on it by having it paid or assigned to another party.[2]

.03 Title in Which Property Is Held

If you and your spouse file a joint return, the problem of who is entitled to the income from property held as tenants by the entirety (a form of joint ownership by a husband and wife) is of little importance because of the split-income benefits available on the joint return. However, if you file separate returns, applicable state law controls who is taxed on the income. In most states, you and your spouse are each treated as having received half of the income, regardless of who actually received it.

When you and another person hold property as joint tenants or as tenants in common, state law determines who is taxed on the income from the property. In most cases, the income (or proceeds from selling the property) is divided equally among you and the other joint owners. The income payor (e.g., banks paying interest and corporations paying dividends), however, records only the social security number of one joint owner. If the number is yours, report only your share on your tax return and note that the other share is reported on the other owner's return (this assumes the joint owners are not you and your spouse filing jointly). The other joint owner must, of course, report his or her share.

Community Property Income

If you and your spouse live in a state that has the community property system of ownership for marital property (Arizona, California, Idaho, Louisiana, Nevada, New Mexico, Texas, Washington and Wisconsin), you may each report one-half the community property income on separate returns.[3] Each state has its own rules for determining whether income is community income or separate income. Generally, however, income earned by you and your spouse through your efforts or investments during your marriage is community income. Likewise, income from property acquired during marriage by either you, your spouse or both (except property acquired by gift, bequest, devise, or inheritance) is generally community income. Property acquired by either of you before marriage is separate property.

For income tax purposes, the rules for community income are important only when *separate* returns are filed by you and your spouse in a community property state. If you file a joint return, you get the benefit of income splitting.

---

[1] *Maryland Casualty Co.*, SCt, 1 USTC ¶29, 251 US 342, 40 SCt 155; *J.A. Strauss*, 2 BTA 598, Dec. 754.

[2] *E.R. Porter*, CtCls, 72 CtCls 680, 52 F2d 1056.

[3] *Poe v. Seaborn*, SCt, 2 USTC ¶611, 282 US 101, 51 SCt 58; *R.K. Malcolm*, SCt, 2 USTC ¶650, 282 US 792, 51 SCt 184.

.04 Income from Illegal Activities

Income from an illegal business,[4] swindling operations,[5] or extortion[6] is taxable. Proceeds of embezzlement are taxable.[7]

COMPENSATION, PRIZES AND AWARDS, AND PENSIONS

¶2005 TAX TREATMENT OF COMPENSATION

All compensation received in return for personal services must be included in the recipient's gross income [Code Sec. 61(a); Reg. § 1.61-2]. If you are an employee, the amount of compensation you include in your gross income is generally the total amount *before payroll deductions* by your employer for such items as withheld taxes, U.S. Savings Bond purchases, and union dues. However, your gross income does not include payroll deductions that are excluded from tax, such as your pre-tax contributions to your Sec. 401(k) plan and reimbursements for business expenses that you have adequately accounted for to your employer.

What your compensation is called, how it is figured and the form of payment is immaterial. The fact that your services are merely part-time, casual, seasonal or temporary is also immaterial.

.01 Compensation Other Than Cash

If you are paid in a form other than money, the fair market value of the property or services on the date received is the amount you include in income [Reg. § § 1.61-2(d)(1), 1.83-1(a)(1)(i)].[8] If property has no fair market value, you report no income. However, you will be taxed on the full amount realized when you sell the property.[9] Certain employer-paid compensatory benefits are tax-free [see Ch. 4 for further discussion].

.02 Compensation Paid in Notes

Notes received in payment for services are income to the extent of their fair market value (usually the discount value) when received. But a note received as additional security or to cover overdue interest, rather than in payment of a debt, does not result in income.[10] If a taxpayer is paid with a note regarded as good for its face value at maturity, but not bearing interest, the taxpayer should report as income the discounted value of the note. As payments are received on the note, include in income the portion of each payment that represents the proportionate part of the discount originally taken on the entire note [Reg. § 1.61-2(d)(4)].

---

[4] *M.S. Sullivan*, SCt, 1 USTC ¶236, 274 US 259, 47 SCt 607.

[5] *Akers v. Scofield*, CA-5, 48-1 USTC ¶9249, 167 F2d 718, *cert. denied*, 335 US 823, 69 SCt 47.

[6] *J. Rutkin*, SCt, 52-1 USTC ¶9260, 343 US 130, 72 SCt 571, *reh'g denied*, 343 US 952, 72 SCt 1039.

[7] *E.C. James*, SCt, 61-1 USTC ¶9449, 366 US 213, 81 SCt 1052.

[8] Rev. Rul. 79-24, 1979-1 CB 60.

[9] *W.R. Jacques*, 5 BTA 56, Dec. 1784; *C.D. Davidson*, 34 BTA 479, Dec. 9396, *aff'd*, CA-5, 37-2 USTC ¶9414, 91 F2d 516.

[10] *C.D. Schlemmer*, CA-2, 38-1 USTC ¶9041, 94 F2d 77.

.03 Bargain Purchases by Employees

An employee or independent contractor who buys property for less than its fair market value from a person for whom he or she performs services, the difference between the price and its fair market value is included in gross income. Your basis for the property is increased by the amount of that taxable income [Reg. § 1.61-2(d) (2), Reg. § 1.83-1].

Example 2-2: R Co. sold to Mr. Conroy, an employee, shares of its stock with a fair market value of $2,000. He paid $1,700. Conroy reports $300 income. The stock's cost to him is $2,000.

.04 Types of Compensation

Taxable

Wages, salaries, commissions, and advance commissions. These include commissions on life insurance on the agent's own life[11] and on the lives of his children;[12] commissions on real estate bought for salesman's own account;[13] compensation received in the form of property (stocks, bonds, or notes); back pay awards, bonuses and awards.

Government cost-of-living allowances. These are generally included in income unless employee is a federal civilian employee or a federal court employee who is stationed in Alaska, Hawaii, or outside the United States.

Fees. Fees include marriage fees, baptismal offerings, sums received for saying masses for the dead, and other contributions received by a clergyman, evangelist or religious worker for services rendered [Reg. § 1.61-2], directors' fees, fees for serving on a jury (but not mileage reimbursement payments).[14]

Tips. If taxpayers in certain occupations, such as taxicab operators or waiters, fail to report tips, the IRS can estimate the amount based on a percentage (usually 10 to 15 percent) of the gross fares or table receipts.[15] The Supreme Court has held that the IRS may assess FICA taxes based on an estimate of aggregate unreported tips.[16] For further discussion, see Ch. 15.

Financial counseling fees. These fees are paid by corporations for the benefit of their executives.[17] The value of qualified retirement planning services can be excluded from gross income.

Golden parachute payments. Taxable compensation includes payments made, under an agreement with the corporation, to officers, shareholders and other similar "disquali-

---

[11] *S. Minzer*, CA-5, 60-2 USTC ¶9493, 279 F2d 338.

[12] *A.J. Ostheimer*, CA-3, 59-1 USTC ¶9300, 264 F2d 789, *cert. denied*, 361 US 818, 80 SCt 61.

[13] *K.W. Daehler*, CA-5, 60-2 USTC ¶9565, 281 F2d 823.

[14] *G. Jernigan*, 27 TCM 95, Dec. 28,831(M), TC Memo. 1968-18.

[15] *H.A. Roberts*, 10 TC 581, Dec. 16,324, *aff'd*, CA-9, 49-2 USTC ¶9330, 176 F2d 221; *N.D. Cesanelli*, 8 TC 776, Dec. 15,705 (1947); *M. Wexler*, 19 TCM 1486, Dec. 24,491(M), TC Memo. 1960-266.

[16] *Fior D'Italia, Inc.*, SCt, 2002-1 USTC ¶50,459, 536 US 238, 122 SCt 2117, *rem'd*, CA-9, 2002-2 USTC ¶50,528, 295 F3d 1046.

[17] Rev. Rul. 73-13, 1973-1 CB 42.

fied individuals" contingent on a change in corporate control. However, the deductibility of such payments is limited [Code Sec. 280G]. For further discussion, see Ch. 12.

Severance pay. Severance pay is taxable.

Strike benefits. Strike benefits includible in income under Code Sec. 61.[18]

Frequent flyer miles. When an employee-shareholder converts his frequent flyer miles into cash through his company, he will recognize income.[19] However, the IRS has announced that it will not assert that an individual has understated his federal tax liability because he has received or used frequent flyer miles or other promotional benefits attributable to the individual's business or official travel.[20] For further discussion of frequent flyer miles, see ¶ 4010.

Cash incentives to buy hybrid vehicles. Rebates or cash incentives offered by employers to employees to encourage them to purchase hybrid cars are taxable compensation that must be included on the employee's year-end Form W-2.[21]

Gift bags received by celebrities at Academy Awards. Gift bags given to presenters and other celebrities at the annual Academy Awards ceremony are subject to tax.[22]

Nontaxable

Adoption expenses. An employee may exclude from gross income up to $12,970 in 2013 of amounts paid or expenses incurred by his or her employer for the employee's qualified adoption expenses pursuant to a qualified adoption assistance program [Code Sec. 137(a); see ¶ 4115 for further discussion of adoption expenses].

Employer-provided transportation. Employees may exclude from income certain transportation-related fringe benefits provided by their employers. Excludable benefits include parking benefits, public transit passes, transportation to and from work in a commuter highway vehicle (such as most vans). In addition, an employer may reimburse employees for the cost of such benefits on a tax-free basis, as long as the benefits are provided in addition to, and not in lieu of, other compensation [Code Sec. 132(f)(3)]. For further discussion, see ¶ 4100.

Employee accident and health plan benefits. Amounts received by an employee from an employer-financed accident and health plan as reimbursement for medical care and payments for permanent injury or loss of bodily function are excludable from the employee's gross income [Code Sec. 105; Reg. § 1.105-1]. In addition contributions by an employer to an accident and health plan or to provide compensation for employees in the event of personal injuries or sickness are excludable from the employee's gross income [Code Sec. 106; Reg. § 1.106-1]. See also Ch. 5.

Group-term life insurance. Premiums paid by an employer for group-term life insurance coverage up to $50,000 are generally not taxable to the employee [Code Sec. 79(a); see ¶ 2035 and Ch. 4].

Reimbursement of job-related expenses. In general, employees do not report reimbursements of job-related expenses on their tax return if they are provided under an

---

[18] *R.A. Osborne*, 69 TCM 1895, Dec. 50,480(M), TC Memo. 1995-71.

[19] *P.J. Charley*, CA-9, 96-2 USTC ¶ 50,399, 91 F3d 72.

[20] Announcement 2002-18, 2002-1 CB 621.

[21] IR-2006-112.

[22] IR-2006-128.

accountable plan [Ch. 9]. If the reimbursements are not provided under an accountable plan, they must report the reimbursements on their return. Employees can claim a deduction for the job-related expenses, but it may not fully offset the reimbursement income. Employee expenses are deductible only to the extent they along with all other miscellaneous itemized deductions exceed 2 percent of adjusted gross income [Ch. 9].

Employer-provided educational assistance. Employees can exclude up to $5,250 of employer-provided education assistance for undergraduate and graduate level courses [Code Sec. 127(a)(2)]. The exclusion for employer-provided educational assistance is permanent and includes graduate-level course work which is defined as any course normally taken by an individual pursuing a program leading to a law, business, medical, or other advanced academic or professional degree [Code Sec. 127(c)(1)]; see ¶ 4055 and Ch. 12]. The term educational assistance does not include any payment for any course involving sports, games, or hobbies [Code Sec. 127(c)(1)].

Employer reimbursement of moving expenses. An employee's gross income does not include an employer's qualified reimbursement of moving expenses [Code Sec. 132(a)(6); see Ch. 4]. The expenses must be ones that the employee could have deducted on his own. In addition, the tax-free reimbursement is not available for expenses that the employee previously deducted [Code Sec. 132(g)].

Holiday gifts. Gift certificates or cash gifts must be included in income. Turkey, ham, and other items of nominal value that an employer gives an employee at Christmas or another holiday can be excluded from gross income.

Rental value of rabbi or minister's living quarters. A rabbi or minister need not include in gross income: (1) the rental value of a dwelling house, including utilities, furnished as a part of his or her compensation; or (2) the rental allowance paid to him or her as part of compensation, to the extent used to rent or provide a home and to the extent such allowance does not exceed the fair market rental value of the home, including furnishings and appurtenances such as a garage, plus the cost of utilities [Code Sec. 107].[23] For further discussion of the parsonage exclusion, see ¶ 4045.05.

Leave-sharing plan for major disasters. Employees who deposit accrued leave in an employer-sponsored leave bank for use by other employees adversely affected by a major disaster do not realize income or have wages, compensation, or rail benefits with respect to the deposited leave if certain conditions are met.[24] First, the plan must treat payments made by the employer to the leave recipient as "wages." Second, a leave donor may not claim an expense, charitable contribution, or loss deduction on account of the deposit of the leave or its use by a leave recipient. The plan must be in writing and must allow a leave donor to deposit accrued leave in an employer-sponsored leave bank for use by other employees who have been adversely affected by a major disaster.

Indian settlement payments. Settlement payments received by an individual Indian as a lump sum or periodic payment in resolution of trust fund litigation will not be included in the individual's gross income [Act Sec. 101(f) of the 2010 Claims Resolution Act]. These particular settlement payments result from a class action lawsuit filed against the

---

[23] *R.D. Warren*, 114 TC 343, Dec. 53,880 (2000), *supplemental op.*, CA-9, 2003-1 USTC ¶ 50,206, 282 F3d 1119, *mot. ruled upon*, 284 F3d 1322, *mot. denied, settled, dismissed*, CA-9, 2003-1 USTC ¶ 50,207, 302 F3d 1012.

[24] Notice 2006-59, 2006-2 CB 60.

federal government for mismanagement of individual Indian trust accounts that relate to land, oil, natural gas, mineral, timber, grazing, water, and other resources and rights on or under individual Indian lands. In addition, any payment received will not be taken into account when applying any provision of the Code that takes into account excludible income in computing adjusted gross income or modified adjusted gross income.

¶2010 COMPENSATION DISTINGUISHED FROM GIFT

The tax law specifically excludes gifts from gross income. However, it also states that amounts transferred by your employer to or for your benefit cannot come under this exclusion [Code Sec. 102(c)]. Such transfers may, however, qualify under the special exclusions for employee achievement awards or *de minimis* fringes [Ch. 4].

¶2015 PRIZES, AWARDS, AND LOTTERIES

Generally, you must pay tax on your contest winnings, whether you participated in a TV quiz show or a sales contest [Code Sec. 74]. In addition, slot machine winnings are subject to tax[25] [¶ 2155]. Every person, including the U.S. government, making any payment of winnings subject to withholding must deduct and withhold tax. The tax must be deducted and withheld upon payment of the winnings [Reg. § 31.3402(q)-1]. Winnings for these purposes include: (1) state lottery winnings in excess of $5,000 and (2) sweepstakes, wagering pool, and nonstate lottery winnings in excess of $1,000.

Code Sec. 3402(q)(5) provides an exception from the income tax withholding requirement for slot machine, keno, and bingo winnings. Slot machine winnings may be exempt from withholding, but casinos still must prepare and file with the IRS Form W-2G for any bingo or slot machine winnings in excess of $1,200 or of $1,500 or more from a keno game [Temp. Reg. § 7.6041-1]. As a result, the IRS is always aware of any big casino winnings.

If an individual using the cash receipts and disbursements method of accounting receives a qualified prize (i.e., a prize or award that is awarded as part of a contest, lottery, jackpot, game, or similar arrangement and is payable over a period of at least 10 years) and is given an option, exercisable no later than 60 days after the individual becomes entitled to the qualified prize, to receive the prize as a single cash payment, that right will not cause the individual to have to include the amount of the single cash payment in gross income even though the individual actually receives the qualified prize over a period of years [Code Sec. 451(h)].

There are three categories of prizes and awards that are excludable: qualified scholarships [Ch. 5]; employee achievement awards [Ch. 4]; and awards given in recognition of achievement in a number of broad areas (see below).

---

[25] *V. Lyszkowski*, 69 TCM 2751, Dec. 50,666(M), TC Memo. 1995-235, *aff'd without op.*, CA-3, 96-1 USTC ¶ 50,170, 79 F3d 1138.

▶ **OBSERVATION:** If you make arrangement before you receive an award or prize, it may be possible to split the proceeds among members of your family to reduce taxes.

.01 Recognition Awards

Recognition awards you receive primarily for your religious, charitable, scientific, educational, artistic, literary, or civic achievement are not taxable, if [Code Sec. 74(b); Reg. § 1.74-1(b)]:

- You were selected without action on your part to enter the contest or proceeding;
- You are not required to perform substantial future services as a condition to receiving the prize and awards; and
- You "designate," in writing, before the prize award is actually presented, that the prize or award be transferred by the payor to a governmental unit or tax-exempt charitable organization. You may not claim a charitable contribution deduction for your contribution.

Example 2-3: Dr. Dalton was awarded $10,000 for her medical research. She did not enter a contest for the award. Dalton designates that the funds are to go to the American Heart Association. Result: The $10,000 is excluded from her income.

▶ **OBSERVATION:** Dr. Dalton may be better off qualifying for the exclusion instead of taking the $10,000 into income and then claiming an offsetting charitable contribution deduction. Here's why: (1) Some personal itemized deductions (e.g., medical and miscellaneous expenses) have a percentage-of-adjusted-gross-income floor [¶ 9140]. By excluding the $10,000 from adjusted gross income, she increases her deduction for those items. (2) There are percentage-of-adjusted gross income ceilings on the charitable contribution deduction [¶ 9140]. The exclusion route helps her avoid running up against them.

.02 Tax Treatment of Lottery Winnings

The courts have consistently held that the sale by a state lottery winner of the right to receive payments due in the future will yield ordinary income rather than capital gains.[26] Courts have also held that taxpayers who win a lottery that provides for installment payments for a number of years do not constructively receive all the winnings in the first year; thus, the winnings are subject to tax in later years.[27]

.03 Tax Treatment of Whistleblower Awards

Individuals who provide valuable information to the government relating to violations of the tax laws may be entitled to receive a reward from the IRS for their efforts under the whistleblower provisions found in Code Sec. 7623.

---

[26] *S.B. Prebola*, CA-2, 2007-1 USTC ¶ 50,423, 482 F3d 610; *G. Lattera*, CA-3, 2006-1 USTC ¶ 50,165, 437 F3d 399; *J.M. Maginnis*, CA-9, 2004-1 USTC ¶ 50,149, 356 F3d 1179; *R.L. Watkins*, CA-10, 2006-1 USTC ¶ 50,329, 447 F3d 1269; *R. Womack*, 92 TCM 410, Dec. 56,672(M), TC Memo. 2006-240; *D.K. Simpson*, 85 TCM 1421, Dec. 55,170(M), TC Memo. 2003-155; *J.F. Davis*, 119 TC 1, Dec. 54,804 (2002).

[27] *A.B. Jombo*, CA-DC, 2005-1 USTC ¶ 50,197; *W.T. Kute*, CA-3, 99-2 USTC ¶ 50,853, 191 F3d 371; *R.A. Childs*, CA-11, 96-2 USTC ¶ 50,504, 89 F3d 856.

In *A.D. Campbell*,[28] the Court of Appeals for the Eleventh Circuit affirmed the Tax Court to hold that the whistleblower payment that a taxpayer received in settlement against a government contractor under the False Claims Act was taxed as ordinary income.[29] For a detailed discussion of whistleblower claims, see ¶27,071.

¶2020 PENSIONS AND EMPLOYEE PAYMENTS

Pensions and retirement allowances generally are taxable. Usually, if the taxpayer did not contribute to the cost of the pension and was not taxable on the employer's contributions, the employee must include the full amount of the pension in gross income [Code Sec. 61(a)(11); Reg. § 1.61-11]. Amounts received from employee annuity, pension or profit-sharing plans may not be fully taxable [Ch. 3; Ch. 5].

.01 Payments to Widow

Amounts paid by an employer to the survivor of a deceased employee are taxable as compensation for past services of the deceased employee if the employer was required to make the payments.[30] Voluntary payments for past services are also taxable, unless a gift was intended.[31]

.02 Nontaxable Pensions

A retired clergyman is not taxed on payments from his congregation when they were not made under an enforceable agreement, established plan, or past practice, but were based on his financial needs and the financial capacity of his congregation. These payments are considered gifts, rather than compensation.[32]

¶2025 COMPENSATION OF GOVERNMENT EMPLOYEES

The pay of all federal, state, and municipal officers and employees is taxable [Code Sec. 61].

¶2030 COMPENSATION OF MEMBERS OF ARMED FORCES

.01 Income Exclusions

Payments for Diminution in Housing Values

The Department of Defense (DOD) Homeowners Assistance Program (HAP) makes payments to employees and members of the Armed Services to offset diminution in

---

[28] *A.D. Campbell*, CA-11, 2011-2 USTC ¶50,644, *aff'g*, Dec. 58,114, 134 TC 20 (2010).

[29] *J.F. Alderson*, CA-9, 2012-2 USTC ¶50,474, 686 F3d 791.

[30] *J.C. Flarsheim*, CA-8, 46-1 USTC ¶9305, 156 F2d 105.

[31] Rev. Rul. 62-102, 1962-2 CB 37.

[32] Rev. Rul. 55-422, 1955-1 CB 14.

housing values due to military base realignment or closure. For example, if a house near a base was worth $180,000 prior to a base closure and $100,000 after a base closure, the DOD may provide the owner with a payment to offset most (but not all) of the $80,000 diminution in value. Amounts received under the HAP are excluded from income as a qualified military base realignment and closure fringe benefit. In addition, amounts received under HAP will not be considered wages for FICA tax purposes. The excludable amount is limited to the reduction in the fair market value of property.

Child-Care Benefits

Child-care benefits provided to military personnel are excludible from income [Code Sec. 129].

Penalty-Free Withdrawals

Penalty-free withdrawals may be made from Coverdell education savings accounts and qualified tuition programs (529 Plans) if the withdrawals are made on account of attendance at the United States Military Academy, the United States Naval Academy, the United States Air Force Academy, the United States Coast Guard Academy, or the United States Merchant Marine Academy. The amount of funds that can be withdrawn penalty-free is limited to the costs of advanced education at these Academies.

.02 Military Pay

Generally, the pay for service in the armed forces of the United States is fully taxable to officers as well as enlisted personnel, including students at service academies. Monthly allotments chargeable to the serviceman's pay must be included in gross income, but not monthly basic allowances for quarters to dependents.[33] Military personnel are entitled to an exemption for pay earned while on active duty even as a noncombatant in a combat zone under Code Sec. 112(a)(1) which provides: "Gross income does not include compensation received for active service as a member below the grade of commissioned officer in the Armed Forces of the United States for any month during any part of which such member . . . served in a combat zone."

"Armed Forces of the United States" is defined in Code Sec. 7701(a)(15) as including:

> all regular and reserve components of the uniformed services which are subject to the jurisdiction of the Secretary of Defense, the Secretary of the Army, the Secretary of the Navy, or the Secretary of the Air Force, and * * * includes the Coast Guard. The members of such forces include commissioned officers and personnel below the grade of commissioned officers in such forces.

The income exclusion is therefore available to enlisted personnel, warrant officers, and commissioned warrant officers [Code Sec. 112].

Commissioned officers may only exclude pay up to the highest rate of enlisted pay (plus imminent danger/hostile fire pay received) [Code Sec. 112(a)]. If a husband and wife are both enlisted personnel serving in the U.S. Armed Forces in the combat zone, they are both entitled to the income tax exclusion for military pay. The income exclusion extends to cover the period of time that the armed forces personnel was

---

[33] Treas. Dept., IRS Publication 3, "Armed Forces' Tax Guide" (2012 Ed.), p. 5.

hospitalized as a result of service in the combat zone even if the hospitalization occurred after leaving the combat zone [Code Sec. 112(a)]. If a taxpayer is injured and hospitalized while serving in the U.S. Armed Forces in the combat zone, the military pay received during this period of time will be excluded from gross income for the period of hospitalization up until two years after the date of termination of the combat zone. Commissioned officers have a similar exclusion, but it is limited to the maximum enlisted amount per month [Code Sec. 112(a)].

No Combat Pay Exclusion for Wages of Civilian Soldier

In *N.J. Holmes*,[34] the Tax Court concluded that an individual who was employed by Blackwater Security Consulting to perform security services in Iraq was not entitled to exclude his wages from gross income as combat pay under Code Sec. 112 because that provision only excludes combat pay received by members of the armed forces of the United States. Even though the taxpayer performed similar work as members of the armed forces, the court concluded that he was a civilian recruited and paid by a private company and therefore was not eligible for the exclusion.

Excluded income need not be reported on the taxpayer's Form W-2 in the box marked "wages, tips, other compensation." However, military pay for such service is subject to social security and Medicare taxes and will be reported on the taxpayer's Form W-2 in the boxes marked "Social Security wages" and "Medicare wages and tips." The following types of income can be excluded:

- Active duty pay earned in any month served in a combat zone.
- Imminent danger/hostile fire pay and military pay earned while hospitalized as a result of wounds, disease or injury incurred in the combat zone.
- A reenlistment bonus if the voluntary extension or reenlistment occurs in a month served in a combat zone.
- Pay for accrued leave earned in any month served in a combat zone. (The Department of Defense must determine that the unused leave was earned during that period.)
- Pay received for duties as a member of the Armed Forces in clubs, messes, post and station theaters and other nonappropriated fund activities earned in a month served in a combat zone.
- Awards received for suggestions, inventions, or scientific achievements because of a submission made in a month in a combat zone.

A commissioned officer (other than a commissioned warrant officer) may exclude pay according to the rules above, but the amount of the exclusion is limited to the highest rate of enlisted pay (plus imminent danger/hostile fire pay received) for each month during any part of which he or she served in a combat zone. Their exclusion is capped at the highest enlisted pay plus any hostile fire or imminent danger pay.

Annual leave payments made to enlisted members of the U.S. Armed Forces at the time of their discharge from the service are excluded from gross income to the extent the leave was accrued when the taxpayer served in the combat zone. If the taxpayer is a commissioned officer, the annual leave exclusion is limited to the amount of the

---

[34] *N.J. Holmes*, 101 TCM 1113, Dec. 58,530(M), TC Memo. 2011-26.

combat pay exclusion less the amount of military pay already excluded for that month. Those serving in the merchant marine are not members of the U.S. Armed Forces and are therefore not entitled to the combat zone military pay exclusion. The U.S. Armed Forces include all regular and reserve components of the uniformed services that are under the control of the Secretaries of Defense, Army, Navy, and Air Force, as well as the Coast Guard.

A combat zone is any area the President of the United States designates by Executive Order as an area in which the U.S. Armed Forces are engaging or have engaged in combat. Usually, an area becomes a combat zone and ceases to be a combat zone on the dates the President designates by Executive Order [Code Sec. 112(c)(2)].

¶2035 INSURANCE AS COMPENSATION

.01 Insurance Premiums

Premiums paid by an employer under policies that protect the employee, his or her family, or estate, are treated as follows:

Ordinary Life Insurance

Premiums paid by the employer on the employee's life generally are taxable to the employee if the proceeds are payable to the employee's beneficiaries [Reg. § 1.61-2(d)(2)(ii)(a)]. However, when a corporation is the beneficiary and owner of an insurance policy on the life of an employee or stockholder, premiums paid by the corporation are not income to the insured employee.[35]

Group Whole Life Insurance

If the employer pays premiums on the employee's behalf for group permanent, whole life insurance, or permanent life insurance benefits, the employee must include in income the cost of the permanent benefits minus the amount the employee paid for them.[36]

Group-Term Life Insurance

Code Sec. 79 generally requires that the cost of group-term life insurance coverage on the life of an employee that is in excess of $50,000 of coverage is included in the income of the employee. For further discussion, see ¶4030. Reg. § 1.79-3 sets forth the rules for determining the cost, for each period of coverage, of the portion of the group-term life insurance on the employee's life to be taken into account in computing the amount includible in the employee's gross income under Code Sec. 79. Table 1, which is reproduced below, determines the cost for each $1,000 of such portion of the group-term life insurance on the employee's life for each one-month period. The cost of the portion of the group-term life insurance on the employee's life for each period of coverage of one month is obtained by multiplying the number of thousand dollars of such insurance computed to the nearest tenth which is provided during such period by the appropriate amount set forth in Table 1. In any case in which

[35] *O. Casale*, CA-2 57-2 USTC ¶9920, 247 F2d 440; *H.E. Prunier*, CA-1, 57-2 USTC ¶10,015, 248 F2d 818.

[36] Treas. Dept., IRS Publication 17, "Your Federal Income Tax" (2012 Ed.), p. 47.

group-term life insurance is provided for a period of coverage of less than one month, the amount set forth in Table 1 is prorated over such period of coverage.

Any life insurance coverage provided by an employer over the first $50,000 must be reported on the employee's W-2 as taxable income.

As a result of the IRS mortality tables used to value life insurance, employees may end up paying more in taxes than they would if they bought the life insurance themselves.

Example 2-4: Mary Smith is 50 years old and her annual compensation is $200,000. She receives $550,000 of group term life insurance coverage from her employer. According to Code Sec. 79(a), she has to pay tax on the IRS-computed value of $500,000 of term insurance. (If her employer is directly or indirectly the beneficiary of the policy, she would not be taxed.) The unisex IRS tables value the insurance at $1,380, which she must include in her taxable income. If she were a healthy, nonsmoking female, she could have purchased that same term insurance for less than $1,000 a year.

Employees should determine the value of the group-term life insurance coverage provided by an employer in excess of the first $50,000 of coverage by consulting Table 1, which is reproduced below. This table provides employees with values per month for each $1,000 of face amount of group-term life insurance coverage depending on the insured's age on the basis of 5-year age brackets [Reg. § 1.79-3(d)(2)]. The age of the employee is the employee's attained age on the last day of the employee's tax year.

Table 1. Uniform Premiums for $1,000 of Group-Term Life Insurance Protection

5-year age bracket	Cost per $1,000 of protection for one month
Under 25	$.05
25 to 29	.06
30 to 34	.08
35 to 39	.09
40 to 44	.10
45 to 49	.15
50 to 54	.23
55 to 59	.43
60 to 64	.66
65 to 69	1.27
70 and above	2.06

Example 2-5: Mr. Martin, age 62, works for Fair Corporation. He has $100,000 of group-term life insurance. He pays $2 of the cost of each $1,000 of coverage and his employer pays the balance. The cost of insurance over $50,000 in Martin's age bracket is $396 (50 × .66 × 12). Martin is taxed on $196 [$396 minus employee's payment (100 × $2)].

Alert to employers. Because income imputed under Code Sec. 79 is generally subject to FICA tax which is withheld from the employee's pay, and because the withholding often is applied periodically from payrolls during the year, many employers providing employees with more than $50,000 of group-term life insurance will need to check their payroll-based withholding systems and related information collection procedures to be sure that they reflect the current Table 1.

Since the IRS table is unisex, the same valuation tables are used to value life insurance policies for both men and women. As a result group term life insurance policies beyond the $50,000 level are particularly expensive for women who would receive lower rates than men from an outside insurance company. For example, a 50-year-old male might pay $1,240 a year for a $500,000 term insurance policy from an insurance company, whereas a female might pay $1,025 for that same policy.

If you wish to opt out of some or all of the group term life insurance offered by your employer, you should try and convince your employer to drop you from coverage under the group term policy. Unfortunately, your employer may not want to be bothered with the additional bookkeeping hassles. In addition, the insurer and employer may not want to risk the possibility that someday your survivors will argue that they are entitled to a death benefit even though you have requested exemption from the group policy. Another way out is to name a charity the sole beneficiary of the taxable portion of the policy. If you choose this option, the value of the group term insurance donated to the charity will not appear on your W-2; and, if it does, you can claim a charitable deduction in the amount that the IRS tables say the insurance is worth.

.02 Split-Dollar Life Insurance

Split-dollar life insurance is a fringe benefit that employers provide for employees where employers and employees join in the purchase of a life insurance contract on the life of the employee and both parties share premium costs, cash values and death benefits. Typically, the employer pays the premiums on an employee's life insurance policy to the extent of the annual increase in the cash surrender value of the policy. The employee pays the balance. When the employee dies, the employer receives the cash surrender value. The balance is paid to the employee's beneficiaries. The employee is taxed on the value of the insurance protection as well as on cash dividends and any other benefits received under the split-dollar arrangement. Split-dollar insurance can also exist in other settings such as corporation and shareholder, partnership and partner, and between family members in conjunction with family financial planning. The employee is denied a deduction for his or her contribution to the split-dollar arrangement as would be the case with any personal insurance premium. When a corporation participates in split-dollar arrangements, the corporation cannot deduct its premium contribution or the value of the economic benefit enjoyed by the employee even though the economic benefit is taxable to the employee. The corporation will, however, receive its share of the insurance proceeds free of regular income tax (but not alternative minimum tax) when the insured dies [Code Sec. 101(a)].

Split-dollar life insurance arrangements are characterized based on who owns the policy and who pays the premium. In the endorsement plan, the employer owns the policy, is the beneficiary, and pays the premiums. The employee is given the right to designate a beneficiary for the amount by which the death benefit exceeds the employer's interest.

Collateral assignment plans provide supplemental retirement benefits in the executive compensation setting. The employee owns the policy and designates the beneficiary. The employer pays the premium but secures its premium advances by obtaining a collateral assignment of the policy.

In the reverse split dollar arrangement and equity split dollar arrangement, the premium and the insurance benefit are split differently from the methods described above. For example, in the equity split-dollar, the employer's interest in the policy's cash surrender value is generally limited to the aggregate amount of the employer's premium payments. This arrangement provides the employer with the benefit of any growth in the cash surrender value above the amount of premiums paid by the employer.

Tax Treatment of Split-Dollar Insurance Arrangements

The IRS has released final regulations that address the income, employment, and gift taxation of split-dollar life insurance arrangements. The regulations will help taxpayers compute the value of the economic benefit received when life insurance is provided in split-dollar agreements and in qualified pension and profit-sharing plans. In conjunction with the final regulations, the IRS released Rev. Rul. 2003-105,[37] which obsoletes most prior guidance on split-dollar life insurance arrangements.

The final regulations apply to any split-dollar life insurance arrangement that is entered into after September 17, 2003 and to any split-dollar life insurance arrangement entered into on or before September 17, 2003, that is materially modified after that date. As a result Notice 2002-84 will provide guidance for split-dollar arrangements entered into prior to September 18, 2004.

The regulations provide that the tax treatment of a split-dollar arrangement depends on whether the employer or the employee is treated as the owner of the life insurance policy.

Employer treated as owner—economic benefit regime. If the employer owns the policy, the economic benefit regime applies. Under this regime, when the employer pays the premiums, the employer is treated as providing current life insurance protection and other economic benefits to the employee. These benefits could include: current life insurance protection; the policy cash surrender value; compensation; distributions under Code Sec. 301; capital contributions; gifts; or other transfers [Reg. § 1.61-22]. The tax consequences will depend on the nature of the benefit. For example, if the benefit is characterized as compensation, the employee would include it in income. The value of the life insurance protection, as well as the policy cash value is determined on the last day of the nonowner's tax year, unless the parties agree to use the policy anniversary date. This provision is subject to an anti-abuse rule to prevent the parties from manipulating the values. In addition, Reg. § 1.61-22(d)(5) provides that taxpayers may change the valuation date with IRS consent.

Employee treated as owner—loan regime. The second regime, which is also called the loan regime, applies if the employee is designated as the owner of the life insurance contract under a split-dollar arrangement and the employer makes the premium pay-

[37] Rev. Rul. 2003-105, 2003-2 CB 696.

ments. This is commonly referred to as a collateral assignment split-dollar plan. The employer will be treated as a lender and the employee as a borrower if the following three conditions are satisfied: (1) The employer makes the payment directly, or indirectly, to the employee; (2) Payment is a loan under general principles of federal tax law; and (3) The loan is repaid from the proceeds of the policy or its cash surrender value. When the employee is treated as the owner, the employer's premium payments are treated as loans, causing the employee to be taxed on the difference between market-rate interest and actual interest [Reg. § 1.7872-15]. Under the loan regime, the loans are subject to the rules governing the original issue discount (OID) and the imputed interest rules of Code Sec. 7872 which deals with below market loans. If the employee is not obligated to repay the premiums paid by the employer, then these amounts are treated as compensation income to the employee at the time the premiums are paid by the employer.

.03 Salary Received in Tax-Exempt State or Local Bonds

Salary received in the form of bonds is not exempt.[38] The tax is not on the medium of payment, but on wages or salary received.

.04 Guaranteed Annual Wage Plans

Taxability of benefits under guaranteed annual wage plans depends on how the plan is set up and the nature of your interest in it. In general, supplemental unemployment benefit (SUB) payments made by your employer directly to former employees are includible in gross income.[39] SUB pay must be linked to the receipt of state unemployment compensation and must not be received in a lump sum to be excludable from the definition of wages for FICA and FUTA purposes.[40]

> **Example 2-6:** When the employee had exclusive right of ownership of an account under the plan, and also had a nonforfeitable beneficial interest in the cash benefits payable under the plan, the employer's contributions to the plan were taxable to the employee.[41]

> **Example 2-7:** When the employee's eligibility for benefits depended upon meeting prescribed conditions after termination of the employment relationship (auto industry), the employee was taxed on the benefits actually received, rather than the employer's contributions.[42]

¶2040 EMPLOYEE STOCK OPTIONS

A stock option is a written agreement which grants the holder of the option the right or privilege (not the obligation) to purchase stock from a corporation at a specific exercise

---

38 *Hitner v. Lederer*, CA-3, 3 USTC ¶ 1056, 63 F2d 877.

39 Rev. Rul. 60-330, 1960-2 CB 46; Rev. Rul. 80-124, 1980-1 CB 212.

40 Rev. Rul. 90-72, 1990-2 CB 211.

41 Rev. Rul. 57-528, 1957-2 CB 263.

42 Rev. Rul. 90-72, 1990-2 CB 211.

(strike) price at or before a certain date [Reg. § 1.421-1(a)(1)]. There are two general categories of employee stock options:

1. Nonqualified or nonstatutory stock options (NQSO) which do not satisfy the requirements imposed on qualified plans and are instead subject to rules regarding the transfer of property in exchange for services in Code Sec. 83; and
2. Qualified or statutory incentive stock options (ISO) which are governed by Code Secs. 421 through 424. Statutory stock options include incentive stock options (ISOs) and options that are granted as part of employee stock purchase plans [Reg. § 1.421-1(b)(1)].

Nonqualified stock options and qualified stock options are afforded different tax treatments as discussed below.

¶2045 NONQUALIFIED STOCK OPTIONS (NQSOs)

Nonqualified executive stock options are a popular way for corporations to compensate executives and key employees. NQSOs are used frequently in lieu of cash compensation because publicly traded companies cannot deduct more than $1 million annually in compensation paid to executives [Code Sec. 162(m); see Ch. 12]. Employers favor NQSOs because the granting of stock options to key employees gives employees an added incentive to contribute to the growth and development of the company and encourages them to "stay on board." Employees like them because NQSOs afford them an excellent risk-free opportunity to participate in the company's growth.

.01 The Mechanics of NQSOs

The executive who receives the stock options as a form of compensation has the right for a fixed period of time (usually 10 years) to buy shares in the company at a pre-set price, no matter what the fair market value (FMV) of the stock is on the stock market at the time the stock options are exercised. Typically, the options will be granted or issued with a price equal to the FMV of the stock at the date of the grant. When the price of the stock rises above the exercise price, the executive has the opportunity to purchase stock at this lower pre-set price. The situation when the option's exercise price is less than the stock's market price is called "in the money." The difference between the FMV of the stock on the exercise date and the pre-set price is called the stock option's "bargain element." If the FMV of the stock drops below the exercise price, the options are termed "under water" or "out-of-the-money" and become essentially worthless.

Nonstatutory or nonqualified stock options are the most common type of stock options offered by employers today. The executive does not recognize income when the stock options are granted, but, when the FMV of the stock increases and the stock options are exercised, the increase in value over the pre-set price is taxed as ordinary income just as compensation would be. The company gets a tax deduction equal to the increase in value at the time the employee exercises the stock options.

Stock options offer the potential for enormous appreciation because the executive is locked into purchasing the stock at a pre-set bargain price, which can become quite lucrative if the value of the stock skyrockets. The following example illustrates how the exercise of appreciated stock options can generate big profits for employees:

Example 2-8: Alan receives nonstatutory stock options from his employer, Hi-Tech, Inc. The stock options entitle Alan to purchase 10,000 shares of Hi-Tech's stock at a pre-set price of $50 a share for a total purchase price of $500,000. Four years later the stock is worth $150 a share. The street value for the 10,000 shares is $1.5 million. Alan has increased his wealth by $1 million by simply continuing to work for Hi-Tech and risking zero of his own dollars.

.02 Tax Treatment of NQSOs

Employer's Tax Treatment

The employer corporation granting the option may claim a compensation expense deduction, under Code Sec. 162, for the amount that the employee included or should have included[43] in gross income at the time the option is exercised [Code Sec. 83(h); Reg. § 1.83-6(a)(1)]. The deduction is allowed for the employee's tax year in which the amount is included in gross income [Code Sec. 83(h)]. If, however, the property transferred is substantially vested upon transfer, the deduction may be claimed under the employer corporation's method of accounting [Reg. § 1.83-6(a)(3)]. In Rev. Rul. 2003-98,[44] the IRS used four scenarios to demonstrate whether a corporate employer or a company that acquired its stock was entitled to deduct the compensation includible in an employee's gross income as a result of the employee's exercise or disposition of a nonstatutory stock option. The IRS concluded that in a situation where the corporation that granted the options was acquired by another corporation, only the employer corporation that originally granted the options could deduct the compensation includible in the employee's gross income when the employee exercised the stock option. The result changes, however, when the employer merges into the second corporation. In this situation, the surviving entity that assumed the obligations of the employer may deduct the compensation income that was includible in the employee's gross income.

Employee's Tax Treatment

The employee/executive does not recognize income when the employer corporation grants the employee NQSOs because the options typically do not have a readily ascertainable fair market value unless the stock option is actively traded on an established market [Code Sec. 83(e)(3); Reg. § 1.83-7(b)(1)]. In the absence of an established market for the stock options, a value may be ascertainable by showing that all the following conditions exist: (1) The option is transferable by the recipient; (2) The option is exercisable immediately in full by the recipient; (3) The option, or the property subject to the option, is not subject to any restriction or condition (other than a lien or other condition to secure the payment of the purchase price) which has a significant effect upon the fair market value of the option; and (4) The fair market value of the option privilege is readily ascertainable [Reg. § 1.83-7(b)(3)].

---

[43] *J.G. Robinson,* CA-FC, 2003-2 USTC ¶ 50,590, 335 F3d 1365.

[44] Rev. Rul. 2003-98, 2003-2 CB 378.

In Rev. Rul. 2007-49,[45] the IRS considered whether a transfer of substantially nonvested stock subject to Code Sec. 83 occurs in the following three situations: (1) restrictions imposed on substantially vested stock cause the stock to become substantially nonvested; (2) a service provider exchanges substantially vested stock for substantially nonvested stock in a reorganization; (3) a service provider exchanges substantially vested stock for substantially nonvested stock in a taxable stock acquisition. In the first situation, the IRS concluded that a transfer of substantially nonvested stock subject to Code Sec. 83 did not occur. In the other two situations, however, transfers of substantially nonvested stock subject to Code Sec. 83 did occur.

.03 Exercise of NQSO

Under Code Sec. 83, an employee is taxed when he exercises an NQSO if the shares have been transferred to the employee and have substantially vested [Reg. § 1.83-3(a)]. The tax equals the amount by which the fair market value of the shares exceeds the exercise price and is taxed as ordinary income just as compensation would be. Reg. § 1.83-3(a)(1) provides that "a transfer of property occurs when a person acquires a beneficial ownership interest in such property." Rights "are transferable only if the rights in such property of any transferee are not subject to a substantial risk of forfeiture," and if the transferee can sell, assign, and pledge his interest in the property [Code Sec. 83(c)(2)]. Reg. § 1.83-3(b) provides that "[p]roperty is substantially vested for such purposes when it is either transferable or not subject to a substantial risk of forfeiture." Rights are subject to a substantial risk of forfeiture "if such person's rights to full enjoyment of such property are conditioned upon the future performance of substantial services by any individual" [Code Sec. 83(c)(1)].

In *Racine*,[46] the Tax Court held that a taxable transfer occurred under Code Sec. 83 when the taxpayer exercised her stock options because the shares were transferred and she acquired beneficial ownership of the shares, even though she purchased the shares through a margin loan. When she exercised the options, the taxpayer had legal title to the shares and was entitled to all the incidents of ownership, including the right to receive dividends and to pledge the shares as collateral.

In *Cidale*,[47] the Court of Appeals for the Fifth Circuit followed *Racine* to conclude that the taxpayers owed taxes on stock options on the date the options were exercised, rather than on the date on which he repaid the margin loan. The shares were transferred and substantially vested on the date of exercise, because at that time, the taxpayer acquired beneficial ownership of the shares and had the right to receive any dividends and vote the stock. His capital was at risk under the terms of the margin agreement. Accordingly, the court concluded that a taxable event occurred when the taxpayer exercised his stock options with margin debt.

If an option has a readily ascertainable fair market value, the difference between the option's value and any lesser amount paid for it is taxable compensation when granted [Reg. § 1.61-15(b)(2)]. The amount included in the employee's income is the excess of

---

[45] Rev. Rul. 2007-49, 2007-2 CB 237.

[46] *R.C. Racine*, 92 TCM 100, Dec. 56,583(M), TC Memo. 2006-162, *aff'd*, 493 F3d 777; *J.R. Facq*, 91 TCM 1201, Dec. 56,529(M), TC Memo. 2006-111; *J.H. Tuff*, 2007-1 USTC ¶ 50,103, 469 F3d 1249; *J. Palahnuk*, FedCl, 2006-1 USTC ¶ 50,218.

[47] *R. Cidale*, CA-5, 2007-1 USTC ¶ 50,138, 475 F3d 685.

the fair market value of the property, determined at the first time that the transferee's rights in the property are either transferable or not subject to a substantial risk of forfeiture ("substantially vested"), over the amount (if any) paid for the property [Code Sec. 83(a)].[48] If the option is sold or otherwise disposed of in an arm's length transaction, the tax treatment of the transfer is determined using the same tax rules that would apply to the exercise of the option [Reg. § 1.83-7(a)]. The valuation date for stock transferred to the employee through exercise of his stock options is the date the employee signed and sent the notice to exercise the options and not the date the shares were delivered.[49]

.04 Receipt of Restricted NQSOs

Typically employees receive NQSOs that are subject to restrictions, which prevent them from selling the stock, or require them to return the shares to the employer if some event occurs. For example, they could be required to return the stock options, if they quit their job before a specific date. When a taxpayer receives restricted property for services rendered, he or she does not include its fair market value in income until the year the property is either not subject to a "substantial risk of forfeiture" or is transferable free of the risk, whichever occurs first.

A substantial risk of forfeiture exists only where rights in property that are transferred are conditioned, directly or indirectly, upon the future performance (or refraining from performance) of substantial services by any person, or upon the occurrence of a condition related to a purpose of the transfer if the possibility of forfeiture is substantial. Property is not transferred subject to a substantial risk of forfeiture to the extent that the employer is required to pay the fair market value of a portion of the property to the employee upon the return of the property. The risk that the value of property will decline during a certain period of time does not constitute a substantial risk of forfeiture [Prop. Reg. § 1.83-3(c)(1)].

The example below illustrates that a substantial risk of forfeiture is not created solely as a result of a lock-up agreement.

Example 2-9: On January 3, 2013, Y Corp. grants Q, an officer of Y, a nonstatutory option to purchase 100 shares of Y common stock for $10 per share, which is the fair market value of a Y share on the date of grant of the option. Although the option is immediately exercisable, it has no readily ascertainable fair market value when it is granted. On May 1, 2013, Y sells its common stock in an initial public offering. Pursuant to an underwriting agreement entered into in connection with the initial public offering, Q agrees not to sell, otherwise dispose of, or hedge any Y common stock from May 1 through November 1 of 2013 ("the lock-up period"). Q exercises the option and Y shares are transferred to Q on August 15, 2013, during the lock-up period. The underwriting agreement does not impose a substantial risk of forfeiture on the Y shares acquired by Q because the provisions of the agreement do not condition Q's rights in the shares upon anyone's future performance (or refraining from performance) of substantial services or on the occurrence of a condition related to the purpose of

---

[48] *R.A. Cramer*, CA-9, 95-2 USTC ¶ 50,491, 64 F3d 1406, *cert. denied*, 517 US 1244, 116 SCt 2499.

[49] *E.L. Walter*, 93 TCM 644, Dec. 56,803(M), TC Memo. 2007-2.

the transfer of shares to Q. Accordingly, neither Code Sec. 83(c)(3) nor the imposition of the lock-up period by the underwriting agreement preclude taxation under Code Sec. 83 when the shares resulting from exercise of the option are transferred to Q [Prop. Reg. § 1.83-3(c)(4), Ex. 6].

Property transferred to an employee that is subject to (a) the "insider profit" restriction of the Securities Exchange Act or (b) a restriction on transfer required to comply with the "Pooling of Interest Accounting" rules set forth in Accounting Series Releases Numbered 130 (10/5/72) and 135 (1/18/73), is considered subject to a "substantial risk of forfeiture." The transfer is not taxable until the restrictions are removed [Code Sec. 83(c)(3)].

Tax Treatment of Options Received in Connection with the Performance of Services

Code Sec. 83 provides rules for the taxation of property transferred to an individual in connection with the performance of services. Under Code Sec. 83(a), if property is transferred to any person in connection with the performance of services, the excess of the fair market value of such property (determined without regard to any restriction other than a restriction which by its terms will never lapse) at the first time the rights of the person having the beneficial interest in such property are transferable or are not subject to a substantial risk of forfeiture, whichever occurs earlier, over the amount (if any) paid for such property, is included in the gross income of the service provider in the first tax year in which the rights of the person having the beneficial interest in such property are transferrable or not subject to a substantial risk of forfeiture.

In *O. Gudmundsson*,[50] the Court of Appeals for the Second Circuit held that an employee recognized income when he received stock from his employer in connection with the performance of services because the stock was transferable even though he could transfer it only to permitted transferees and was not subject to the risk of forfeiture on the date of the distribution.

In *A.L. Davis*,[51] the Court of Appeals for the Eleventh Circuit held that a taxpayer must include in income the value of stock options that the company granted him in order to secure his participation in the company's day-to-day management after he had threatened to leave the company. The court found that the options were granted "in connection with the performance of services" because they were granted to induce him to continue working for the closely held company.

Code Sec. 83(b) Election

Code Sec. 83(b) provides that any person who has performed services in connection with the transfer of property to him may elect to include in gross income, for the year in which such property is transferred, the excess of the fair market value of such property at the time of transfer (determined without regard to any restriction other than a

---

[50] *O. Gudmundssun*, CA-2, 2011-1 USTC ¶ 50,218, 634 F3d 212.

[51] *A.L. Davis*, 102 TCM 575, Dec. 58,831(M), TC Memo. 2011-286, *aff'd*, CA-11, 2013-1 USTC ¶ 50,330.

restriction which will never lapse) over the amount paid for such property. The IRS has approved an arrangement under which an employer timely filed valid Section 83(b) elections on behalf of its employees.[52]

The effect of this election is: (1) to convert any future appreciation into lower-taxed capital gain; and (2) to result in the payment of the tax sooner—in the year of the transfer rather than in the later year when the restrictions lapse. The taxpayer's ordinary income equals the excess of the property's fair market value without regard to the restrictions (other than those that will never lapse; see 3. below) over any amount paid for the property. Any later appreciation of the property is treated as capital gains.

However, if the election is made and the property is later forfeited, the taxpayer may claim neither a refund nor a deduction [Code Sec. 83(b); Reg. § 1.83-2]. They could, however, claim a loss deduction for any excess of cost over any amount realized at the time of forfeiture or premature sale.

> ▶ **TAX STRATEGY:** If the taxpayer paid the full fair market value for shares of the company's stock, the taxpayer should make the election. Reason: They owe no current tax on account of the election. However, any appreciation after that date is taxed as preferential capital gains, provided the stock is held for more than 12 months [Ch. 8]. On the other hand, if they pay less than full fair market value for the shares, the choice isn't that simple. While the taxpayer may enjoy the capital gains tax break down the road when they sell the shares, they owe tax on the bargain element of the property transfer right away. Without the election, tax on this income is deferred.

The election must be made within 30 days after the restricted property is transferred to you. (The election may be made before the transfer actually occurs.) The election is made by signing a statement that contains the following information: (1) your name, address and taxpayer identification number, (2) a description of the property for which the election is made, (3) the date of transfer and the tax year for which the election is made, (4) the nature of the restrictions to which the property is subject, (5) the property's fair market value when transferred (determined without regard to any lapse restriction), (6) the amount (if any) paid for the property, and (7) a statement that copies have been given to other persons as required by regulations. Those copies must be supplied to the IRS office where you file your return and to the party for whom the services giving rise to the property transfer were performed. You must also attach a copy of the statement to your income tax return for the year of the property transfer [Reg. § 1.83-2(e)].

In Rev. Proc. 2012-29,[53] the IRS provided sample language to be used by taxpayers making an election under Code Sec. 83(b) and provided examples of the income tax consequences of making such an election. For the election to be valid, the taxpayer must also satisfy all the other applicable requirements, including timely filing the election with the IRS, attaching a copy of the election to the tax return, and providing a copy to the service recipient. A Code Sec. 83(b) election must contain all the information required by Reg. § 1.83-2(e), but need not use the exact format or language of the sample election.

---

[52] CCA 200203018 (Oct. 15, 2001).

[53] Rev. Proc. 2012-29, IRB 2012-28, 49.

How To Revoke Code Sec. 83(b) Election

In Rev. Proc. 2006-31,[54] the IRS provides guidance to taxpayers who wish to revoke an election under Code Sec. 83(b). Revocation of the election requires IRS consent and consent will only be granted where the person filing the election is under a "mistake of fact" as to the underlying transaction and the request is made within 60 days of the date on which he or she first discovers this mistake.

A request for consent to revoke the election will generally be granted if the request is filed on or before the due date for making the election, which is 30 days after the property is transferred to the employee or service provider. This means that the IRS will grant a taxpayer's consent to revoke the election regardless of its reason, if the request is made within the 30-day period during which the Code Sec. 83(b) election should have been made.

A request to revoke an Code Sec. 83(b) election must contain: (1) the date the election was made, (2) a copy of the election, (3) a description of the mistake of fact as to the underlying transaction, and (4) the date on which the mistake of fact first became known to the person making the election. If the request to revoke an election is being made on or before the due date for making the election, this fact must be included in the request for revocation.

Mistake of Fact Exception

The mistake of fact exception is narrow in its scope. A mistake of fact is an unconscious ignorance of a fact that is material to the transaction. Contrast this with the failure of a service provider to understand the substantial risk of forfeiture associated with the transferred property, which will not be considered a mistake of fact under Reg. § 1.83-2(f). Similarly, the failure of a service provider to understand the tax consequences of making an election under Code Sec. 83(b) is not considered a mistake of fact under Reg. § 1.83-2(f). Neither a mistake regarding the value (or decline in the value) of the property for which the election was made nor the failure of anyone to perform an act that was contemplated at the time of transfer of the property constitute a mistake of fact [Code Sec. 83(b)(2); Reg. § 1.83-2(f)].

Restrictions That Never Lapse

Special rules apply to those restrictions that will never lapse (for example, a requirement that you or your estate must sell your stock back to your employer at its then-existing book value). They are the only ones considered in determining the property's fair market value. If, under such a restriction, the restricted property can only be sold at a formula price, then the formula price is treated as the property's fair market value unless the IRS proves a higher value. If the restriction is later canceled, you have compensation income when the cancellation occurs on the excess of the full value over the sum of the restricted value at that time and any consideration paid for cancellation. However, this does not apply if you can show that the cancellation was not compensatory and not treated as such by your employer [Code Sec. 83(d); Reg. § 1.83-5].

---

[54] Rev. Proc. 2006-31, 2006-2 CB 32.

What Triggers Taxation When Property Is Transferred in Connection with the Performance of Services?

A promise to pay money in the future that is either secured or funded must be included in income under Code Sec. 83 [Reg. § 1.83-3(e)]. An unfunded or unsecured promise to pay money or property in the future will not constitute a property transfer for purposes of Code Sec. 83 and therefore will not be included in income. For example, the fair market value of several attorneys' rights to receive future annuity payments of fees pursuant to a structured settlement agreement will not be included in the attorneys' income if the promises to pay are unfunded and unsecured because these promises do not constitute property for purposes of Code Sec. 83.[55]

Reduction in Employee's Debt Is Compensation

In Rev. Rul. 2004-37,[56] the IRS concluded that in a situation where an employee issued a recourse note to an employer in satisfaction of the exercise price of an option to acquire the employer's stock and the employer and employee subsequently agree to reduce the stated principal amount of the note, the employee must recognize compensation income at the time of the reduction. Reg. § 1.83-4(c) provides that if indebtedness if treated as paid, cancelled or satisfied for less than the original debt amount, the amount of debt not paid is included in the employee's income for that year. Under Reg. § 1.1001-3(e)(2), a significant modification to a note may have tax consequences for both the issuer and the holder. If a modification to the note's principal amount produces a significant change in the note's yield, the modification is deemed significant.

¶2050 QUALIFIED STOCK OPTIONS

The following two varieties of statutory or qualified stock options exist:

1. ESPPs—Options granted under employee stock purchase plans (ESPPs), and
2. ISOs—Incentive stock options (ISOs) [Code Secs. 421, 422, 423].

An employee stock option is essentially an offer by a corporation to sell stock to an employee at what may in the future be a bargain price. The employee does not become obligated to pay the purchase price until he or she elects to exercise the option. However, if the employee receives statutory options, special rules generally postpone the tax until the employee sells the stock. For discussion of the reporting requirements imposed on companies under Code Sec. 6039 when employees exercise statutory stock options, see Ch. 26.

Employee stock options are frequently used by corporations in the following ways: (1) as incentives to attract new management, (2) to convert their officers into "partners" by giving them a stake in the business, (3) to retain the services of executives who might otherwise leave or (4) to give their employees generally a more direct interest in the success of the corporation.

---

[55] *R.A. Childs*, CA-11, 96-2 USTC ¶ 50,504, 89 F3d 856, *aff'g*, 103 TC 634, Dec. 50,239 (1994).

[56] Rev. Rul. 2004-37, 2004-1 CB 583.

.01 Employee Stock Purchase Plans (ESPPs)

ESPPs are designed to allow employees to buy stock of the employer corporation, usually at a discount. The plan must be nondiscriminatory and include all employees. Only employees owning less than 5 percent of the stock can participate in an ESPP. Stockholder approval of the ESPP is required. The plan must not discriminate in favor of officers or highly compensated personnel, but the amount of optioned stock may be proportionate to salary. All employees must be included under the plan, except highly compensated personnel, certain part-time workers and those employed fewer than two years. The price must be at least 85 percent of the value of the stock at the time of grant or exercise, whichever is less. If the plan provides that the option price is at least 85 percent of the stock's value at the time of exercise, the option may run for five years; otherwise, the option cannot run for more than 27 months. Finally, no more than $25,000 (valued at time of grant) of stock may accrue for purchase in any one year [Code Sec. 423(b)(8)(B); Reg. § 1.423-2]. The employee receiving the option must be an employee of the granting corporation, its parent or subsidiary continuously from the grant to three months before the option is exercised [Code Sec. 423(a)(2)].

Tax Treatment of ESPPs

You realize no income when you receive or exercise an option granted under an ESPP. You must hold the stock for more than 2 years from the time the stock option was granted to you and for more than 1 year from the time that the stock was transferred to you. If the shares are sold before then, any gain is taxed as compensation which is taxed as ordinary income.

.02 Incentive Stock Options (ISOs)

An employee has no taxable income when an incentive stock option is granted or when exercised [Code Secs. 421(a), 422(a)]. Instead, the employee generally has capital gain when the stock is sold. If the sale results in a loss, the loss will be a capital loss, whether or not the holding periods have been met. [For further discussion of capital gain and loss, see Ch. 8].

The ISO must be granted under a plan approved by the shareholders. The plan must specify the number of shares to be issued and the class of employee who will be eligible to receive them. Stock acquired by exercising an ISO must be held for at least two years after the option is granted and one year after the ISO is exercised in order for the difference between the pre-set "exercise price" and the stock selling price to be taxed as capital gain. The bad news, however, is that this amount, which is called the "bargain element," is considered an adjustment for alternative minimum tax purposes [Code Sec. 56(b)(3)].

To qualify as an ISO and be eligible for tax-favored capital gain treatment on any gains realized from the sale of the stock, the terms of the option must satisfy the following conditions [Code Sec. 422(b)]:

- The option must be granted under a plan that specifies the number of shares of stock to be issued and the employees or class of employees eligible to receive options. Also, the corporation's stockholders must approve the plan within 12 months before or after the plan is adopted. A corporation in this situation includes an S corporation, a foreign corporation, and a limited liability corporation that is treated as a corporation for all federal tax purposes [Reg. § 1.421-7(i)(1)]. Stock includes ownership interests other than capital stock [Reg. § 1.421-7(d)(3)]. This means that any entity that is classified as a corporation for federal tax purposes under Reg. § 301.7701-2(b) could grant statutory stock options for its ownership interests.

- The term "option" includes warrants [Reg. § 1.421-1(a)(1)].
- An option must be evidenced in paper or in an electronic form and must be enforceable under applicable law [Reg. § 1.421-1(a)(3)].
- The plan must be in paper or electronic form and must be enforceable [Reg. § 1.421-1(a)(3)]. The form must be one that provides adequate substantiation of the applicable requirements, such as the date on which the option is granted, the number of shares subject to the option, and the option price. In addition, the taxpayer must retain records relating to the option.
- The option must be granted within ten years of the date that the plan is adopted, or the date that the plan is approved by the shareholders, whichever is earlier.
- The option must be exercisable only within ten years of the date that it is granted.
- The option price must equal or exceed the fair market value of the stock when the option is granted. However, a good faith effort to accurately value the stock will excuse a failure to meet this requirement [Code Sec. 422(c)(1)].
- A statutory option may include an option transferred to a trust, if, the individual to whom the option was granted remains the beneficial owner [Reg. § 1.421-1(b)(2)].
- A transfer of a statutory option incident to a divorce will result in the option failing to qualify as a statutory option as of the date of transfer [Reg. § 1.421-1(b)(2)].
- The option must not be transferable other than on death and, during the employee's lifetime, must be exercisable only by the employee.
- The employee must not, immediately before the option is granted, own stock representing more than 10 percent of the voting power of all classes of stock of the employer corporation or its parent or subsidiary. Stock owned by others can be attributed to the employee [Code Sec. 424(d)(2)]. The 10-percent limitation is waived if the option price is at least 110 percent of the stock's fair market value when the option is granted and the option must be exercised within five years of the date it is granted [Code Sec. 422(c)(5)].
- An employee should not have more than $100,000 worth of ISOs that are exercisable for the first time during any one calendar year. If the $100,000 ceiling is exceeded, the excess of the more recently issued options will lose their ISO status [Code Sec. 422(d); Reg. § 1.422-4(a)].

.03 Modification of Options

Any modification, renewal, or extension of an option is treated as the grant of a new option. A modification is any change in the terms of an option that gives the optionee additional benefits [Code Sec. 424(h)(3)]. An additional benefit under the option at the future discretion of the granting corporation is a modification at the time the discretion is provided. Furthermore, the exercise of such discretion is a modification of the option. If the offer to change the terms of the option remains outstanding for 30 days or more, the option is treated as modified as of the date the offer to change the terms is made. There is no grant of a new option if the change results from a substitution or assumption that is due to a "corporation transaction" where a new statutory option is substituted for an outstanding statutory option or an old option is assumed. "Corporate transaction" includes the following: (1) a corporate merger, consolidation, acquisition of property or stock, separation, reorganization, or liquidation; (2) a distribution (excluding an ordinary dividend, or a stock split or stock dividend) or change in the terms or number of outstanding shares of the corporation; (3) a change in the name of the corporation whose stock is purchasable under the old option; and (4) any other corporate event designated by the IRS [Reg. § 1.424-1(a)(3)].

Generally, the stock's fair market value is determined without regard to any restrictions except those that will never lapse [Code Sec. 422(c)(7)]. Also, a change in an option's terms to make it nontransferable so that it qualifies as an incentive stock option will be treated as the granting of a new option [Code Sec. 424(h)].

Incentive stock options may be subject to any condition not inconsistent with the qualification requirements of the options [Code Sec. 422(c)(4)].

When you exercise an option, you can pay for it with a stock of the corporation granting the option [Code Sec. 422(c)(4)(A)].

> ▶ **TAX TIP: Pros and Cons on ISOs.** When your employer offers you an incentive stock option, you should typically take it because the ISO will give you the right to purchase stock of your employer, often at a discount, without recognizing income until the stock is sold.

.04 AMT Exposure

There are some risks associated with ISOs. Although no taxable income is recognized when an option is granted or exercised, the difference between the fair market value and the exercise price is an item of AMT tax preference and can trigger a significant AMT liability in the year of exercise if a large amount of appreciated stock is involved. Reason: When your rights in the stock are transferable and no longer subject to a substantial risk of forfeiture, you must include as an adjustment in figuring AMT income the amount by which the fair market value of the stock exceeds the option price. This is referred to as the "bargain element" and it is considered an adjustment for purposes of calculating the AMT. Generally, most of the AMT liability will be recovered in the year the stock is sold as an AMT credit against regular tax if the value of the stock has not decreased after the exercise of the option. Reason: When you compute your alternative minimum taxable income in the year of the sale, the AMT gain is the difference between the fair market value of the stock at the time of the sale and the fair market value of the stock at the time of the exercise. Regular tax gain, however, is the difference between the fair market value at the time of the sale and the exercise price. Because your regular tax liability will exceed the AMT tentative minimum tax in this situation, most or all of the credit for the previously paid AMT is typically claimed against your regular tax in the year of the sale [see ¶ 16,005].

> ▶ **TAX CONSIDERATIONS:** Corporations get no deduction for the issuance and exercise of ISOs. However, if the employee violates the holding period rule and disqualifies the ISO under Code Sec. 422, the company can deduct the difference between the market price at the time of exercise and the exercise price. This deduction is allowed in the year of the disqualifying sale of the stock (i.e., when the employee is taxed).

NOTE: An employer can designate at the time of grant that an option is not an ISO—even though the option otherwise meets all the requirements of being an ISO [Code Sec. 422(b)]. The employer thereby makes sure it gets a deduction when the option is exercised.

INTEREST INCOME

¶2055 INTEREST IN GENERAL

All interest is included in a taxpayer's taxable income unless it is specifically exempt from tax (for example, interest on municipal government bonds; see Ch. 5). In general, you owe tax when the interest is actually received or credited to your account because individuals usually are cash-basis taxpayers.

.01 Taxable Interest

Taxable income includes interest on corporate bonds, mortgage bonds, notes, and bank deposits and interest received from tax-exempt organizations, such as charitable, religious, or educational institutions [Code Sec. 61(a)(4); Reg. § 1.61-7]. Interest is defined as compensation for the use or forbearance of money.[57] When payment on a transaction is deferred, the tax law may deem the seller to have charged interest. Thus, a portion of a deferred payment sales price can be recharacterized as interest, even though the sales contract treats the entire price as payment for the underlying property or services.

Inclusions in Taxable Interest

The following are included in taxable interest:

- Interest on award paid for loss of life or for condemnation awards[58] (even though award itself is not income); interest on refund of federal tax; interest on legacies (not property received by gift, but income from such property);[59]
- Interest on life insurance policies paid by reason of the death of the insured;
- Usurious interest[60] unless under state law it is a payment of principal [Reg. § 1.61-7(a)].

Bonds Bought "Flat"

If you buy bonds "flat" (price covers unpaid interest as well as principal), the entire amount is a capital investment. Any accrued interest that is in arrears at the time of purchase is not income and is not taxable when paid later. These payments are returns of capital that reduce the remaining cost basis [Reg. § 1.61-7(c)].

Example 2-10: On June 15, Mr. Brown bought for $800 "flat" a bond of Apex Corp. with a face value of $1,000. The bond bore interest at 8 percent, payable each November 1. At the time of the purchase, $160 of unpaid interest had

---

[57] *Deputy v. duPont*, SCt, 40-1 USTC ¶ 9161, 308 US 488, 60 SCt 363.

[58] *H.A. Kieselbach*, SCt, 43-1 USTC ¶ 9220, 317 US 399, 63 SCt 303.

[59] Rev. Rul. 73-322, 1973-2 CB 44.

[60] *E.B. Terrell*, 7 BTA 773, Dec. 2643, acq. 1928-1 CB 31.

accrued. On November 1, Apex Corp. paid Brown $240 interest on the bond. The $160 accrued interest that was in arrears is considered to be a return of capital. Thus, Brown reports only $80 of interest on his tax return. The basis of the bond is $640 ($800 less $160).

When payments of the accrued interest exceed your basis in the bonds (as could happen when there is a high risk of the bond issuer defaulting), any further interest payments are capital gains.[61] Capital gains treatment applies, even if it appears certain that the bonds ultimately will be paid in full.[62] However, capital gains treatment does not apply to interest that accrues after the bonds are purchased.[63]

Interest Accrued on Bonds Sold Between Interest Dates

If taxable bonds are sold between interest dates, the accrued interest *to* the date of sale is taxable to the seller; the accrued interest *from* the date of sale is taxable to the buyer.

.02 Exempt Income

Interest on state and municipal bonds and obligations of U.S. possessions is generally exempt from federal income taxation. However, there are two notable exceptions. First, the interest on private activity bonds (i.e., bonds issued to provide conduit financing for activities other than general governmental operations or governmental owned-and-operated facilities) is usually taxable unless the bond qualifies as an exempt facility, qualified mortgage, qualified veterans' mortgage, qualified small issue or qualified student loan bond [Code Secs. 103(b)(1), 141(e)]. See ¶ 5005. Second, even if the bond meets these special classifications, it may be subject to the alternative minimum tax [Ch. 16] [Code Sec. 57(a)(5)].

▶ **INVESTMENT OPPORTUNITY:** If you are not hit by the alternative minimum tax, you can receive fully tax-exempt interest income by investing in so-called AMT bonds. These bonds tend to offer a higher yield than other municipals since they are not tax-free to investors who are subject to the alternative minimum tax.

NOTE: Interest paid on indebtedness incurred to buy tax-exempt certificates is not deductible [Ch. 9] [Code Sec. 265(a)(2)].

¶2060 TAX TREATMENT OF LOANS

Code Sec. 61(a) provides the following broad definition of "gross income:" "Except as otherwise provided in this subtitle, gross income means all income from whatever source derived." It is well established that exclusions from gross income must be narrowly construed. One such exclusion excepts the receipt of loan proceeds from gross income because whatever temporary economic benefit the borrower derives from the use of the funds is offset by the corresponding obligation to repay them.[64] However, for genuine indebtedness to be present there must be both good-faith

[61] *W.H. Noll*, 43 BTA 496, Dec. 11,637; *Campbell v. Sailer*, CA-5, 55-2 USTC ¶ 9544, 224 F2d 641.

[62] *Rickaby Est.*, 27 TC 886, Dec. 22,272, *acq.* 1960-2 CB 6; Rev. Rul. 60-284, 1960-2 CB 464.

[63] *S. Jaglom*, CA-2, 62-2 USTC ¶ 9519, 303 F2d 847.

[64] *H. Moore*, CA-5, 69-2 USTC ¶ 9489, 412 F.2d 974.

intent on the part of the borrower to repay the debt and good-faith intent by the lender to enforce payment of the debt. The central inquiry therefore when determining if a transaction is a bona fide loan for tax purposes is whether it is the intention of the parties that the money advanced be repaid.

.01 Distinguishing Debt from Equity

Whether a transaction constitutes a loan for income tax purposes is a factual question involving several considerations; a distinguishing characteristic of a loan is the intention of the parties that the money advanced be repaid. Important factors considered by courts to distinguish debt from equity are:[65]

1. Whether the promise to repay is evidenced by a note or other instrument;
2. Whether interest was charged;
3. Whether a fixed schedule for repayments was established;
4. Whether collateral was given to secure repayment;
5. Whether repayments were made;
6. Whether the borrower had a reasonable prospect of repaying the loan and whether the lender had sufficient funds to advance the loan; and
7. Whether the parties conducted themselves as if the transaction were a loan.

In *F.D. Todd*,[66] the Court of Appeals for the Fifth Circuit affirmed the Tax Court to conclude that an advance on a life insurance policy to a taxpayer was taxable as a distribution rather than as a tax-free bona fide loan. The parties failed to persuade the court that they intended to repay the loan.

.02 Whether Promise to Repay Was Evidenced by Note

A note or other instrument is indicative of a debtor-creditor relationship.[67] However, an instrument will be given little weight when the form of the instrument fails to correspond with the substance of the transaction.[68]

.03 Whether Interest Was Charged

The payment of interest indicates the existence of a bona fide loan.[69]

.04 Whether Fixed Schedule for Repayment Established

A fixed schedule for repayment is indicative of a bona fide loan. Evidence that a creditor did not intend to enforce payment or was indifferent to the exact time an advance was repaid indicates a bona fide loan did not exist.[70]

---

[65] *B.E. Welch*, CA-9, 2000-1 USTC ¶50,258, 204 F3d 1228; *A.R. Goldstein*, 40 TCM 752, Dec. 37,099(M), TC Memo. 1980-273; *The Vancouver Clinic*, DC Wash., 2003-1 USTC ¶50,273.

[66] *F.D. Todd*, CA-5, 2012-2 USTC ¶50,525, *aff'g per curiam*, 101 TCM 1603, Dec. 58,648(M), TC Memo. 2011-123.

[67] *N. Teymourian*, 90 TCM 352, Dec. 56,160(M), TC Memo. 2005-232.

[68] *E.L. Provost*, 79 TCM 2098, Dec. 53,904(M), TC Memo. 2000-177.

[69] *B.E. Welch*, CA-9, 2000-1 USTC ¶50,258, 204 F.3d 1228; *B.K. Morrison*, 89 TCM 864, Dec. 55,962(M), TC Memo. 2005-53.

[70] *Gooding Amusement Co.*, CA-6, 52-2 USTC ¶9808, 236 F.2d 159, *aff'g*, 23 TC 408, Dec. 20,681 (1954), *cert. denied*, 352 US 1031, 77 SCt 595.

.05 Whether Repayments Made

Repayment is an indication that a bona fide loan exists. In order for a valid debt to exist for tax purposes, an unconditional obligation to repay must exist because indebtedness is an existing, unconditional, and legally enforceable obligation for the payment of a principal sum.[71] If an alternate repayment mechanism is too contingent and indefinite, that alternative payment method will not be recognized.[72]

.06 Whether Borrower Had Reasonable Prospect of Repaying the Loan

Whether the borrower had a reasonable prospect of repaying the loan is best determined by looking to whether there was "a reasonable expectation of repayment in light of the economic realities of the situation" at the time the funds were advanced.[73] A reasonable prospect of repayment at the time the funds were advanced indicates the existence of a bona fide loan.

.07 Whether Parties Conducted Themselves as if Transaction Were a Loan

The conduct of the parties may be sufficient to indicate the existence of a loan.[74]

¶2065 INTEREST-FREE AND LOW-INTEREST LOANS

Special tax rules apply when you make a loan and charge less than the prevailing federal rate of interest (which varies with the length of the loan [Ch. 2070]). The tax law recharacterizes the loan as a two-step transaction: (1) First, the lender is considered to have transferred an amount equal to the foregone interest (the prevailing federal rate of interest less the loan's actual interest rate) to the borrower; (2) the borrower is then treated as retransferring that amount back to the lender as interest. Bottom line: There is phantom income (the amount of the foregone interest) passing from the lender to the borrower and back again [Code Sec. 7872].

Code Sec. 7872 recharacterizes a below-market loan as an arm's-length transaction in which the lender makes a loan to the borrower in exchange for a note requiring the payment of interest at a statutory rate. As a result, the parties are treated as if the lender made a transfer of fund to the borrower and the borrowed used these funds to pay interest to the lender. The transfer to the borrower is treated as a gift, dividend, contribution of capital, payment of compensation, or other payment depending on the substance of the transaction. The interest payment is included in the lender's income and generally may be deducted by the borrower.

.01 Tax Consequences

The income tax consequences to both the lender and the borrower regarding interest-free and low-interest loans depend on the type of loan transaction.

Gift Loans

Gift loans involve gratuitous transfers of the type subject to gift taxes. For example, parents typically do not charge interest when they lend money to their children. They

[71] *R.R. Midkiff*, 96 TC 724, Dec. 47,353 (1991).

[72] *A. Zappo*, 81 TC 77, Dec. 40,325 (1983).

[73] *I.D. Fisher*, 54 TC 905, Dec. 30,084 (1970).

[74] *W.C. Baird*, 25 TC 387, Dec. 21,363 (1955).

are deemed to make a gift to their child in the amount of the foregone interest and to receive an equivalent amount of interest income. The child is treated as having received a gift and used it to pay the phantom interest income to the parents. Income tax result: The parents owe tax on the phantom income received from the child. The child, on the other hand, owes no income tax on his or her phantom income; it's an income tax-free gift that is subject to gift tax. In addition, the child may be able to claim an interest deduction equal to the amount of the parent's phantom income [Ch. 9]. Note that there are important exceptions to the gift loan rules [see .02 below].

Compensation Loans

Compensation loans are made in connection with the performance of services between an employer and employee, independent contractor or contracting party or partnership and partner. For example, assume a company loans an employee money to purchase a home. Tax result: The employer is treated as (1) paying the employee deductible compensation equal to the foregone interest, and (2) receiving an equal amount of taxable interest payments from the employee for the use of the funds. So the transaction is a tax wash for the employer. As for the employee, the phantom compensation is taxable to the employee (but is not subject to withholding). The employee, in turn, may be able to claim an offsetting deduction for phantom interest payments made to the employer [Ch. 9].

Dividend Loans

In this type of transaction, a corporation lends funds to a shareholder at below-market rates. Code Sec. 7872(c)(1)(C) provides that "below-market loan" includes a below-market loan directly or indirectly between a corporation and any shareholder of such corporation. Note the use in the statute of the word "any." The shareholder need not be a controlling shareholder of the corporation in order for the IRS to impute interest on below-market loans made to any shareholders.[75] The statute is unambiguous and does not include a requirement that a shareholder control the corporation in order for the imputed interest rules to apply. Similarly, the imputed interest rules apply to indirect loans made to entities in which none of the shareholders individually hold a controlling interest because Code Sec. 7872 imputes interest to "any below-market loan made directly or indirectly between a corporation and any shareholders of the corporation." Even though no shareholder held a controlling interest, the court noted that all shareholders were part of the same family and collectively agreed to make the loans to themselves and to their family-controlled entities.

> ▶ **PLANNING TIP:** The IRS and the courts seem predisposed to impute interest under Code Sec. 7872 to all below-market loans between a corporation and its shareholders to direct and indirect loans and without regard to the extent of the shareholder's ownership interest in the corporation. In light of this warning, play it safe and avoid the expense and aggravation of an audit. Be certain that all loans from corporations to shareholders carry the market interest rate. Make sure that all documents reflect compliance with the Section 7872 requirements.

---

75 *Rountree Cotton Co.*, CA-10, 2001-1 USTC ¶50,316.

In a situation where a below-market loan has been made, the corporation is deemed to distribute dividends to the shareholder equal to the interest it failed to charge. The corporation then gets the funds back from the shareholder in the form of a phantom interest payment. Tax result: The corporation cannot deduct the dividend it paid the shareholder. Therefore, the corporation gets no deduction to offset the phantom interest income it receives from the shareholder. Again, the shareholder is taxed on the phantom dividends, but may be able to claim an offsetting deduction for phantom interest payments.

When the IRS reviews shareholder loans from corporations, the first issue will be whether the loan from the corporation to the shareholder is a bona fide debt. The answer to that question hinges on when the loan was made and whether there was a genuine intent that the borrowed funds be repaid? In answering these questions the following factors will be considered by the IRS agent.

Whether shareholder controls corporation. If a shareholder controls the majority of a corporation's stock, he or she can exercise direct control over the corporation's earnings and profits. That condition tends to suggest a constructive dividend. For example, if shareholder controls exactly 50 percent of a corporation's stock, and if an equal distribution is not made to the other 50-percent shareholder, and the other shareholder did not object to the loan treatment of the distribution, that suggests that a loan was made. The probability of an arm's length transaction is far greater if the shareholder receiving the loan does not own a majority (directly or through attribution) of the corporate stock. However, the critical element is the extent to which the shareholder is able to control the affairs of the corporation, irrespective of whether that control derives from stock ownership, family relationship, or some other source. In some situations, a shareholder may exert nearly total control of a corporation but directly own only a small percentage of the stock.

Whether security for loan provided. In most circumstances, the failure to provide security may be an indication that a distribution was intended. However, if a corporation's articles of incorporation provide that the corporation has a lien on its shares of stock for any debt or liability incurred to it by a stockholder, the fact that no security is given for the advances made to a shareholder does not preclude a finding that the advances constituted bona fide loans, even though the shareholders were unaware of the provision in the articles at the time the advances were made.[76]

Is the shareholder able to repay loan? The shareholder's salary, other income, and net worth are relevant in determining the shareholder's ability to repay. If the shareholder is in a position to repay the advances based on his current financial status, that supports a bona fide loan. The mere fact, however, that the shareholder had a good credit rating will not be conclusive to establish that the shareholder was in a position to repay the advances.[77]

Adequate earnings and profits. If there are no current or accumulated earnings and profits (E&P) at the time of distribution, the distribution will not be treated as a constructive dividend under Code Sec. 301 [Code Sec. 316 (Dividend Defined)]. That does not mean that because a corporation has a deficit or no E&P, a distribution is a

---

[76] *R.J. Shea*, DC-AL, 83-1 USTC ¶9115.

[77] *R.W. Smith*, 39 TCM 900, Dec. 36,732(M), TC Memo. 1980-15.

bona fide loan. It simply means that the distribution cannot be classified as a dividend, but could be a return of capital or capital gain [Code Sec. 301(c)(2), (3)]. Thus, before an agent challenges the validity of a loan, the issue of adequate E&P must be considered.

Certificate of indebtedness provided to corporation. The fact that no note of indebtedness was issued to the corporation is not a determinative factor. There are numerous court cases where no note was issued for advances, but, based on other factors, the advances were accepted as bona fide loans. The lack of a certificate of indebtedness has been considered an indication of a constructive dividend.

Repayment schedule or attempt to repay. Even if the repayments are made, if the amount advanced continues to increase over a sustained period of years, that would tend to support constructive dividend treatment. Repayments made either by direct payments or by such means as bonus credits would support a debtor-creditor relationship. If a regular repayment schedule is being followed for the payment of interest and reduction of principal, that would be a factor favoring a bona fide loan.

Evidence of set maturity date. Generally, a fixed maturity date is significant.[78] However, even in the absence of a fixed maturity date, a loan will be respected as such if it is repaid within a reasonable period of time.

Whether interest charged. Generally, a failure to charge interest supports constructive dividend treatment or imputed dividends under Code Sec. 7872.

Whether corporation has tried to obtain repayment. What action has the corporation taken to obtain repayment? The shareholder's failure to make payments, or only minimal payments, indicates a constructive dividend, particularly if the corporation is not taking steps to enforce the loan. If a closely held corporation does not apply pressure on a borrowing shareholder for repayment, the transaction may not be at arm's length. However, the fact that a shareholder is making reasonable payments is not one that is considered in this analysis.

Magnitude of advances. Another indication of a constructive dividend is if a corporation makes large advances to a controlling shareholder, and the shareholder's ability to repay is essentially contingent on future events.

Ceiling on amount of advance. A numerical ceiling on the amount that can be advanced to a shareholder would tend to support bona fide debt. The courts have also held that if a corporation is required to obtain the consent of an equal controlling block of stock to make an advance, that action imposes a *de facto* ceiling on the amounts which can be advanced. This is seldom a key factor, but advances in cases of a ceiling may be treated as constructive dividends in some instances.

Dividend history of corporation. Adequate earnings and profits with respect to the advances made, coupled with no history of paying dividends, favors constructive dividend treatment.

Advances to Closely Held Corporations

Cash advances made by shareholders to closely held corporations are subject to special scrutiny from the IRS and the courts to determine if the cash advances are

[78] *F.R. Hoffman Est.*, 78 TCM 898, Dec. 53,644(M), TC Memo. 1999-395, *aff'd per curiam*, CA-4 (unpublished opinion), 2001-1 USTC ¶50,401.

really below-market loans.[4] Once the advances are characterized as below-market loans, they become nondeductible and will be subject to Section 7872 recharacterization. In making this determination, the IRS will examine the repayment terms and whether the shareholders have unfettered discretion to determine when the loans will be repaid. In addition, Code Sec. 7872 operates to recharacterize below-market loans as arm's length transactions. When a loan is made interest-free, it is classified as a below market loan and interest income is imputed to the lender. Foregone interest is imputed to the lender. Foregone interest is treated as transferred by the lender to the borrower and this amount is deemed repaid by the borrower as interest to the lender. In this situation, the shareholder is treated as the lender and the corporation is treated as the borrower. The shareholder is deemed to have received phantom taxable interest payments from the corporation—and is then treated as having contributed that amount of money to the corporation. Tax result: The shareholder is taxed on the phantom interest payments, but the shareholder cannot deduct the phantom contributions of capital made to the corporation. However, the shareholder's basis in the stock is increased by the amount of the phantom capital contribution. The corporation gets more favorable tax treatment. It can deduct its phantom interest payments, and it is not taxed on the shareholder's phantom capital contributions.

.02 Exempted Loans

The below-market loan rules generally do not apply to any day the outstanding loan balance between two parties is $10,000 or less. However, this *de minimis* break does not apply to: (1) gift loans between individuals if the loans are directly attributable to the acquisition or carrying of income-producing assets; or (2) compensation and shareholder loans where one of the principal purposes of the loans is tax avoidance [Code Sec. 7872(c)(2), (3)]. There is a special ceiling for any day the amount of a gift loan's outstanding balance does not exceed $100,000. The amount of interest that is deemed to have been transferred between you and the borrower is limited to the borrower's net investment income for the year. But if the net investment income is $1,000 or less, the net investment income is deemed to be zero. In other words, there are no tax consequences to the gift loan. The $100,000 special ceiling does not apply if tax avoidance is one of the principal purposes of the loan [Code Sec. 7872(c), (d); Reg. § 1.7872-8, 9].

NOTE: Husbands and wives are treated as one person for purposes of these loan rules. All loans to or from the husband are combined with all loans to or from the wife [Prop. Reg. § 1.7872-11(c)].

Continuing Care Facilities

A loan made by a lender or lender's spouse age 62 or older to a "qualified continuing care facility" pursuant to a "continuing care contract" is exempt from the below-market interest loan rules [Code Sec. 7872(h)(1)]. This is a tax break afforded seniors who move into assisted living facilities and must pay a refundable entry fee (characterized as a loan) which will be returned, in whole or in part when they die or move out of the residence. If not for the continuing care interest exemption, the seniors would have been required to recognize phantom interest income under the below market loan rules.

Inflation-adjusted limit on loan amount no longer exists. A loan *in any amount* can be made to a qualified continuing care facility and qualify for the exclusion from the imputed interest rules if the loan is made pursuant to a "continuing care contract" and the age requirements of the lender or the lender's spouse are satisfied. Note the absence of the inflation-adjusted limitation on the amount of the loan.

Age 62 or older. The exemption is triggered beginning with the calendar year in which the lender or the lender's spouse reaches age 62. Thus, where a lender makes a loan to a qualified continuing care facility before the calendar year in which he or she reaches age 62, the loan will be subject to imputed interest rules. But for the calendar year in which the individual reaches age 62, and for each calendar year thereafter, the exemption will apply to the loan if it satisfies the other exemption requirements [Code Sec. 7872(h)(1)]. A taxpayer is treated as attaining age 62 on the day before his or her birthday.

Qualified continuing care facility. A "qualified continuing care facility" means one or more facilities: (1) which are designed to provide services under continuing care contracts, (2) which include an independent living unit, plus an assisted living or nursing facility, or both, and (3) substantially all of the independent living unit residents of which are covered by continuing care contracts [Code Sec. 7872(h)(3)(A)].

Qualified continuing care contract. A "qualified continuing care contract" is a written contract between an individual and a qualifying continuing care facility under which: (1) the lender or lender's spouse may use a qualified continuing care facility for their life or lives; (2) the lender or lender's spouse will be provided with housing, as appropriate for their health in an independent living unit (which has additional facilities outside such unit for meals and personal care) and in an assisted living facility nursing facility; and (3) the lender or lender's spouse will be provided assisted living or nursing care as their health requires and as is available in the continuing care facility [Code Sec. 7872(h)(2)].

.03 Timing of Interest Transfers

For gift term loans and demand loans of any type, the transfer and retransfer of interest are determined one year at a time [Prop. Reg. § 1.7872-6(b)]. Thus, phantom funds are deemed to flow back and forth between the lender and the borrower in equal amounts on the last day of the calendar year.

There are timing imbalances in the case of term loans other than gift loans. Basic reason: The imputed amount for the entire term of the loan is deemed to have been transferred from the lender to the borrower at the time the loan begins. For example, suppose your employer makes an interest-free loan to you. Repayment is due in the form of a lump-sum payment five years later. The difference between the present value of all payments required under the loan and the balloon payment would be the full imputed amount that is treated as having been transferred from the lender to the borrower at the time of the loan. Thus, your company gets a big up-front compensation deduction, and you have an equally large amount of compensation on which to pay tax.

The timing is different on the other side of the tax equation. The retransfer back from the borrower to the lender is treated as original issue discount [¶ 2070] and deemed to occur annually. So with your employer's interest-free loan, your phantom interest payments—that can provide you with offsetting deductions—are spread out over five years. And your company's interest income is also (fortunately for it) spread out.

Only employees who receive below-market compensation term loans get relief from the timing inequities of the nongift term loan rules. Employer loans that have a stated term but are also contingent on your future performance of services are treated as demand loans [Code Sec. 7872(f)(5)]. That means you do not have a bunching of taxable compensation if the loan from your employer is conditioned on future employment. It's conditioned on future employment if you must pay interest of at least the federal rate upon leaving the company for any reason before the term of the loan expires.

¶2070 DEBT INSTRUMENTS—ORIGINAL ISSUE DISCOUNT BONDS

There are complex tax rules for reporting income from debt instruments (e.g., bonds, debentures, notes and bank CDs) you purchase at less than their face value (i.e., at a discount). You may have to report "interest" income from these bonds, even though you don't actually receive the actual income until the instrument matures. Whether you must report income—and if so, the amount you must report—depends on the type of discount, the type of debt instrument and when the instrument was issued.

Original issue discount (OID) is the discount that is built into a debt instrument on its issue date. It occurs when the bond's "stated redemption price at maturity" (usually its face value) exceeds the bond's issue price. The issue price is: (1) the initial offering price for a publicly offered debt instrument not issued for property, (2) the price paid by the first buyer for debt instruments that are not publicly offered and not issued for property, (3) the fair market value of publicly traded debt instruments issued for property, or (4) in the case of nontraded instruments issued for property (e.g., seller financed sales of property), the stated principal amount if the stated interest is adequate, or the imputed principal amount if the stated interest is not adequate—see .07 below [Code Secs. 1273(b), 1274(a)].

The OID is a form of interest that is spread over the term of the instrument. A portion of the OID is taxed to you as interest income each year, even though no payment is actually received [(a) below]. This tough tax rule applies whether the debt instrument holder is on the cash or accrual method of accounting. You increase your basis in the debt instrument each year by the portion of the discount included in gross income [Code Sec. 1272(d)(2)]. So the OID affects the amount of gain or loss if the bond is sold before maturity.

> **Example 2-11:** XYZ Corp. issues publicly offered bonds for $3,000 that pay no current interest, but have a redemption price of $10,000 in 15 years. The $7,000 difference is original issue discount. Bondholders are taxed on a portion of it during each of the 15 years of the bond's term.

With a market discount: You may buy a bond on the resale market at less than its face value due to an increase in interest rates or a decrease in the creditworthiness of the issuer. This discount is called market discount. You do not have to pay tax on market discount until you dispose of the bond. At that time, gain realized equal to "accrued market discount" is taxed as ordinary interest income if the bond was issued after July 18, 1984 [(c) below].

.01 When Property Is Publicly Traded

For purposes of determining the issue price of a debt instrument it is often important to determine when property is publicly traded. Property (including a debt instrument) is traded on an established market if, at any time during the 31-day period ending 15 days after the issue date:

1. There is a sales price for the property,
2. There are one or more firm quotes for the property,
3. There are one or more indicative quotes for the property [Reg. § 1.1273-2(f)].

.02 OID Corporate Bonds

The amount of corporate bond OID you must include in income each year—and also add to your basis, thereby affecting the gain or loss on sale or redemption—depends on the type of bond and when it was issued.

Debt Instruments Issued After July 1, 1982

If you hold such a debt instrument with OID, you must include in income the sum of the "daily portions" of the OID for each day you held the bond during the tax year [Code Sec. 1272(a)(1)]. The daily portion is determined by allocating to each day its ratable portion of the increase in the "adjusted issue price" during the "accrual period." This is known as the constant interest method. To find the adjusted price increase:

- Multiply the bond's adjusted issue price at the start of the accrual period by the yield to maturity (determined on the basis of compounding at the close of each accrual period and adjusted for the length of the period) and
- Subtract the sum of the amounts payable as interest during that period. The adjusted issue price at the start of any accrual period is the sum of the bond's issue price plus the increases in the adjusted issue price for all preceding accrual periods. Generally, the accrual period is each six-month period determined by reference to the maturity date and the date six months before maturity (or shorter period from the issue date).

> **Example 2-12:** Mr. Prince purchases a newly issued ten-year bond for $4,146 that pays no current interest, but has a $10,000 redemption price. Assume the bond's yield to maturity is 9 percent, using semi-annual compounding (i.e., a six-month accrual period). Thus, Prince is deemed to receive $187 for the first six months ($4,146 issue price × .09 × 6/12). His adjusted issue price then becomes $4,333, and his OID for the last six months of the first year is $195. Prince's adjusted issue price for determining interest accrued during the next period is $4,528.

If the OID bond is sold before maturity at a price that exceeds the issue price plus the daily portions of the OID, the buyer gets an offset. Thus, the daily portion that he must include in income is reduced by the daily portion of such excess purchase price, computed by dividing it by the total number of days beginning with the purchase date through the day before the date of maturity [Code Sec. 1272(a)]. As a result, the purchasing taxpayer has less interest income to report than the original holder.

Example 2-13: Same facts as above. Assume, though, that Prince sells the bond after eight years for $8,500. His adjusted basis at that time would be $8,386. Result: Prince would have a $114 gain. And the buyer would reduce the amount of interest he is deemed to receive (using the 9-percent interest rate) by $57 in each of the two years remaining until maturity.

De Minimis Rule

You do not necessarily have to report OID on your income tax return. You can disregard the discount if it is less than one-fourth of 1 percent (0.0025) of the stated redemption price (i.e., $2.50 per $1,000 of redemption price) at maturity, multiplied by the number of complete years to maturity [Code Sec. 1273(a)(3)].

Example 2-14: Mr. Carter bought a ten-year bond with a stated redemption price at maturity of $1,000 at its issue price of $980. The OID was therefore $20. One-fourth of 1 percent of $1,000 (the stated redemption price) times ten (number of full years from the date of original issue to maturity) equals $25. Since the $20 discount is less than $25, Carter can disregard the OID.

.03 Exceptions to OID Rules

There are a number of debt instruments that are specifically exempt from the OID rules. The OID inclusion rules do not apply to holders of: tax-exempt obligations [(b) below]; short-term obligations (fixed maturity date not more than one year from date of issue) [(d) below]; U.S. savings bonds [(h) below]; obligations issued by natural persons before March 2, 1984; and loans between natural persons not made in the course of the lender's trade or business, not in excess of $10,000 when combined with prior loans, and without tax avoidance as one of its principal purposes [Code Sec. 1272(a)(2)].

Tax-Exempt OID Bonds

The OID on obligations issued by a state or municipality is generally exempt from tax. But OID must still be computed to determine the bondholder's basis in the bond; each year's OID is an upward adjustment in basis for figuring gain or loss on a sale or redemption. OID is figured on tax-exempt instruments using the constant interest method (which reflects true economic accrual).

Market Discount

The price of bonds on the secondary or resale market varies with interest rate shifts and the creditworthiness of the issuer. When you acquire a debt instrument for less than its issue price (adjusted for any OID allocable for prior periods), the difference is known as "market discount." Unlike OID, you do not pay tax on the market discount until you dispose of the bond. Your gain is taxed as ordinary interest income to the extent of accrued market discount.

A market discount bond is any bond, debenture, note, certificate, or evidence of indebtedness that has been traded at such a discount [Code Sec. 1278(a)]. These discount rules do not apply to obligations of less than one year [see .04 below], U.S. savings bonds, or certain installment obligations.

***De minimis* rule.** You can disregard the discount and treat it as zero if it is less than one-fourth of 1 percent (.0025) of the stated redemption price at maturity multiplied by the number of full years to maturity [Code Sec. 1278(a)(2)(C)].

Current income election. You can elect to pay tax on market discount as it accrues. In other words, you can choose to have market discount taxed as OID and increase your basis in the bond by the amount included in gross income. The election is binding on all market discount bonds acquired on or after the beginning of the election year and also applies to all subsequent years. The election cannot be revoked without IRS approval [Code Sec. 1278(b)(3)].

Loss of corresponding interest deduction. If you incur debt to purchase or hold market discount bonds, you may lose a portion of your current deduction for interest payments. If the interest expense exceeds any current taxable income from the bond (including OID), the deduction for excess is not currently deductible to the extent of the current market discount accrual. In other words, you can deduct interest only up to the sum of (a) the taxable income from the bond and (b) the amount by which the remaining interest expense exceeds the current market discount accrual.

You can make an election to carry forward the nondeductible portion of the interest payments and write it off to the extent the taxable income from the bond in a subsequent year exceeds the interest expense for that year. Any remaining interest is treated as having been paid or accrued in the year the bond is disposed of [Code Sec. 1277(b)].

> **NOTE:** Interest deductions are not deferred under the above rules if you elect to include market discount in income as it accrues [Code Sec. 1278(b)(1)(A)].

> **Example 2-15:** Mr. Baron takes out a $45,000 loan to purchase a bond with a $50,000 redemption price. He pays $4,200 of interest to the lender this year. The bond pays him $3,000 of interest this year, and the accrued market discount for the portion of the year he owned the bond is $1,000. Result: Baron gets a $3,200 interest deduction (subject to the deduction limitations for investment-related interest expense—see Ch. 9). The deduction is the sum of the taxable interest income he received on the bond plus the excess of the $1,200 additional interest he paid over the $1,000 accrued market discount. If Baron sells the bond next year, for instance, he can deduct the remaining $1,000.

.04 Discount on Short-Term Obligations

In general, individuals who invest in short-term obligations (bonds, debentures, notes, certificates or other evidences of indebtedness with a fixed maturity not over a year) can defer tax on their discount until they dispose of the obligation. However, their deduction for interest incurred with respect to the obligation is limited in the same manner as it is for long-term market discount instruments—unless they elect to include the "acquisition discount" in income currently [Code Sec. 1282(b)].

On the other hand, acquisition discount on short-term obligations must be included in income on a daily basis, if the obligation is: (1) held by an accrual basis taxpayer, or (2) held primarily for sale to customers in the ordinary course of business, or (3) held by a bank, regulated investment company or common trust fund, or (4) identified by the taxpayer as being part of a hedging transaction, or (5) a stripped bond or coupon that the holder (or someone whose basis the holder carries over) stripped [Code Sec. 1281(b)(1)]. The mandatory accrual rule also applies to certain partnerships, S corporations, trusts or other pass-through entities formed to avoid this rule [Code Sec. 1281(b)(2)].

.05 Stripped Bonds

The interest and principal elements of a bond may be separated by a process known as "stripping" the bond. For instance, as the owner of a $10,000 coupon bond, you can strip and sell the coupons while keeping the right to receive the $10,000 face value at maturity. Or you can sell the right to principal and retain the coupons; or transfer ownership of both parts to separate parties.

For dispositions after July 1, 1982, the stripped bond and detached coupon are each treated as original issue discount instruments for tax purposes [Code Sec. 1286(a)].

Exception: Certain mortgage loans that are stripped bonds are to be treated as market discount bonds rather than OID instruments.[79] Suppose that a taxpayer sells mortgages and, at the same time, enters into a contract to service them for an amount received from the initial mortgage payments. The mortgage is a "stripped bond" if, under the contract, the taxpayer can receive amounts that exceed reasonable compensation for the services performed. Buyers of these bonds must account for any discount on the bond as market discount rather than original issue discount [Reg. § 1.1286-1(b)].

Treatment of Seller

If you sell a stripped bond, you are taxed on any income that accrued between the last interest payment (or issue date, if no interest had yet been paid) and the date of disposition. This raises your basis in the bond. That basis must then be allocated between the principal element and the interest element in relation to their respective fair market values. You compute your capital gains or losses on the segment you sold using this allocated basis.

Stripped Tax-Exempt Bonds

The OID on regular tax-exempt bonds is generally exempt from tax [(b) above]. However, the OID on stripped tax-exempt bonds may be taxable. A portion of OID exceeding the "tax-exempt" portion is treated as taxable OID.

> ▶ **OBSERVATION:** In effect, the holder of the stripped bond or coupon is being taxed on market discount. The taxable OID arises from the fact that the yield on the stripped bond when it is purchased is higher than the yield on the bond when it was originally purchased.

The tax-exempt portion of the OID is the amount by which the stated redemption price at maturity (or the amount payable on the due date of a coupon) exceeds an issue price that would produce a yield to maturity as of the purchase date of the stripped bond or coupon equal to the lower of: the coupon rate on the tax-exempt obligation from which the coupons were separated, or the yield to maturity based on

---

[79] Rev. Rul. 91-46, 1991-2 CB 358.

the purchase price of the stripped bond or coupon. The taxpayer can elect to use the original yield to maturity instead of the coupon rate for these purposes.

Stripped Preferred Stock

Preferred stock can be stripped of its dividend rights in the same way bonds are stripped of interest coupons. One investor owns the right to dividend payments, and another owns the rest of the shares' value (e.g., growth in the market value of the shares). The stripped preferred stock may, in effect, be redeemed at a fixed price in the future. Under prior law, the purchaser of the stripped shares could get capital gains treatment at redemption.

The difference between the stated redemption price and the amount paid for the stripped preferred stock is actually OID interest income. This part of the investment return is taxed like stripped bonds—as it accrues each year and as ordinary income.

.06 Deferred Payment Transactions

The OID rules also apply to sales with debt instruments calling for deferred payments. If the debt instrument does not require sufficient interest to be paid currently at a constant rate over the term of the debt, the seller must include an OID amount in income each year—in addition to any interest actually received. In general, the buyer also gets a deduction for the OID—in addition to any interest actually paid. The OID rules also apply to deferred payment sales where there is adequately stated interest but the interest is not paid currently. The total amount of OID is the difference between the debt's redemption price at maturity and its principal amount (if there is adequate stated interest) or its imputed principal amount (if the stated interest is not adequate).

> ▶ **OID RULES AND IMPUTED INTEREST:** There are major exceptions to the application of the OID rules to deferred payment sales (see below). And the stated interest may be considered inadequate even if a transaction is specifically excepted from the OID rules. In other words, if debt payments are timely made but the stated interest is too low, a portion of the deferred payments may be recharacterized and imputed to the seller as interest income (see .07 below). And if a debt instrument calls for an excessively high rate of interest, the government can recharacterize part of the stated interest as a portion of the purchase price. That could cause the buyer to lose interest deductions [Reg. § 1.1274-2(b)(1)].

Transactions to Which the OID Rules Apply

Debt instruments given for the sale or exchange of property are generally covered by the OID rules if some or all of the payments are due more than six months after the date of the sale or exchange. However, the OID rules do not apply in the following transactions (but interest may be imputed nevertheless) [Code Sec. 1274(c)(3)]:

- Sales for $1 million or less of farms by individuals, estates, testamentary trusts, or small businesses.
- Sales of principal residences.
- Sales involving total payments of $250,000 or less.
- Debt instruments which are publicly traded or are issued for publicly traded property (the original issue discount rules apply instead; see .01 above).

- Certain sales of patents with payment contingent on the productivity, use, or disposition of the property transferred.
- Certain land transfers between related persons (see .07 below).
- Buyers of personal use property [Code Sec. 1275(b)]. The buyer of property that is used substantially for purposes other than business or investment cannot deduct OID interest on the debt owed to the seller. In other words, the buyer of personal use property can only deduct interest actually paid to the seller.

Adequate Stated Interest

The first question to answer in analyzing a deferred payment transaction is whether there is adequate stated interest. And there is adequate stated interest if the stated principal amount of the loan does not exceed the loan's imputed principal amount. Rationale for the rule: The imputed principal amount is the present value (using the applicable federal rate, compounded semiannually [see below]) of the total principal and interest payments called for in the instrument. That value is a liberal estimate of the principal amount of the loan and thus the true purchase price of the property. If the stated principal amount exceeds the true purchase price (i.e., the imputed principal amount), the buyer and the seller have converted some purchase price into interest—and the stated interest is inadequate [Code Sec. 1274(b); Reg. § 1.1274-2(b)(1)].

Discount Rate

The discount rate is generally the "applicable federal rate" (AFR) based on semiannual compounding (or an equivalent rate based on another compounding period). The AFR relates to the term of the debt instrument. If the term is no longer than three years, the AFR is the federal short-term rate; for instruments with terms of over three years but not over nine years, the AFR is the federal mid-term rate; for instruments with terms of over nine years, the AFR is the federal long-term rate. The buyer and seller use the lowest applicable monthly rate in the three-month period ending with the month during which a binding written sales contract was made [Code Sec. 1274(d)].

The discount rate for debt instruments not exceeding $5,339,300 in 2012 (the amount is adjusted annually for inflation) is the lower of the AFR or 9 percent, compounded semiannually. This lower rate applies only to instruments issued on account of a sale or exchange of assets other than tangible personal property used in a business [Code Secs. 1274(b)(2)(B), 1274A(a)]. A special rule applies to sale-leasebacks. The discount rate must be 110 percent of the AFR, even if the transaction involves less than $5,339,300 in 2012 [Code Sec. 1274(e)].

Deferred Payment Sales Requiring OID Interest

The seller must declare OID interest and the buyer can deduct it in the following two situations:

- The stated interest rate is adequate, but the stated redemption price at maturity exceeds the principal amount stated in the debt instrument [Code Sec. 1274(c)].
- The stated interest is inadequate. The OID is the difference between the amount due at maturity and the imputed principal amount of the debt obligation [Code Sec. 1274(c)].

Potentially Abusive Situations

For a tax shelter whose principal purpose is tax evasion or some other potentially abusive situation, the imputed principal amount of a debt instrument received in exchange for property is the property's fair market value [Code Sec. 1274(b)(3)(A)].

Variable or Contingent Interest

In general, if a debt instrument calls for a variable rate of interest based on an index, the adequacy of interest test is based on the rate of interest determined under the index as of the time of the sale or exchange. Contingent payments of interest usually are disregarded in determining whether a debt instrument calls for adequate stated interest. The IRS has published regulations under Code Sec. 1275 and other code sections relating to debt instruments with OID [Reg. § 1.1274-4]. The regulations contain rules for the treatment of contingent payment debt instruments. They provide separate rules for debt instruments that are issued for cash or publicly traded property and for debt instruments that are issued for nonpublicly traded property. The regulations provide a rule to determine the imputed principal amount of a contingent payment debt instrument issued for nonpublicly traded property. They also provide rules for the integration of certain debt instruments with related hedges. In addition, the regulations amend the rules for variable rate debt instruments in Reg. § 1.1275-5 of the final OID regulations.

Cash Basis Election

In general, both parties to a seller-financed transaction have to account for the OID annually as it accrues (i.e., seller has income and buyer has deductions). However, if both parties are cash basis taxpayers, they can elect jointly to account for the OID on a cash basis—as interest is paid and received. To qualify for this tax break, the total principal payments on the debt may not exceed $3,905,900[80] in 2013 [Code Sec. 1274A(c)].

.07 Imputed Interest Without OID

There can be imputed interest even if a transaction meets one of the exceptions to the rules explained above (e.g., the sale of a principal residence). Since the OID rules do not apply, however, there is no change in the timing of interest income or expense. In other words, cash basis buyers do not have deductible interest nor do sellers recognize income, until payments are paid and received. What does happen is that a portion of the sales price is recharacterized as interest charges.

These imputed interest rules apply if the contract calls for some or all the payments to be made more than *one year* after the date of the sale or exchange. If there is unstated interest, then interest is imputed to all payments that are due more than *six months* after the date of the sale or exchange [Code Sec. 483(c)(1)].[81]

Unstated Interest

There is unstated interest if the principal payments due more than six months after the sale or exchange exceed the sum of the present values of the interest and principal payments due under the contract. That unstated interest is imputed to each of the

---

[80] Rev. Rul. 2012-33, IRB 2012-51, 710.

[81] *Colorcon, Inc.*, FedCl 2013-1 USTC ¶ 50,310, 110 FedCl 650.

payments using the "daily portions" method that applies to OID debt instruments issued after July 1, 1982 (see .01 above) [Code Sec. 483(a), (b)].

The present value is determined by discounting the payments by the applicable federal rate—the same as under the OID rules explained above for deferred payment sales. However, special rates apply to certain types of sales [Code Sec. 483(b), (d)].

- Sale or exchange of land between family members: The discount rate for unstated interest cannot exceed 6 percent compounded semiannually for up to $500,000 of such indebtedness (including prior such sales). Note that this special rate applies to land only, and not to houses on it [Reg. § 1.483-3(b)(2)].
- Sale-leasebacks: The discount rate is 110 percent of the AFR [Code Sec. 1274(e)].
- For a debt with a stated principal amount of no more than $5,468,200[82] in 2013 (as adjusted annually for inflation), the discount rate is the lower of the AFR or 9 percent, compounded semiannually [Code Sec. 1274A(b)]. The lower rate applies only to instruments issued on account of a sale or exchange of assets other than tangible property used in a business [Code Secs. 483(g)(2), 1274A(a)].

Exceptions. The imputed interest rules do not apply to the following transactions:

- Sales prices of $3,000 or less.
- Imputing of interest to buyers when personal use property is bought. A portion of a buyer's payments becomes interest only if the property is used as business or investment property at the time of sale [Code Sec. 1275(b)(1)].
- Sales of patents with contingent payments [Code Sec. 483(d); Reg. § 1.483-2(b)].

.08 Series EE U.S. Savings Bonds

EE U.S. savings bonds are low-risk government-backed savings products that have been available for purchase since January 1, 1980 when they replaced the Series E bonds. Beginning on January 1, 2012, paper savings bonds were no longer sold at financial institutions and could only be purchased through TreasuryDirect®, a web-based system operated by the U.S. Office of Public Debt.

Yields on Series EE/E bonds purchased between May 1997 and April 30, 2005 were based on 5-year Treasury security yields and earned a variable market-based rate of return. In contrast, Series EE Bonds purchased on or after May 1, 2005 earn a fixed rate of return. Taxpayers can purchase, manage, and redeem electronic EE Bonds safely through a personal TreasuryDirect account. A program called SmartExchange allows TreasuryDirect account owners to convert their Series E, EE and I paper savings bonds to electronic securities in a special Conversion Linked Account in their online account.

Individuals, corporations, associations, public or private organizations, and fiduciaries can own paper Series EE Bonds. Effective April 2009, individuals and various types of entities including trusts, estates, corporations, partnerships, etc. can have TreasuryDirect accounts and own electronic savings bonds. Taxpayers can own U.S. Savings Bonds if they have a Social Security Number and they are a:

- Resident of the United States.
- Citizen of the United States living abroad (must have U.S. address of record).

---

82 Rev. Rul. 2012-33, IRB 2012-51, 710.

- Civilian employee of the United States regardless of residence.
- Minor. Unlike other securities, minors may own U.S. Savings Bonds.

Series EE bonds are issued at a 50-percent discount from face value. This means that taxpayers may buy a $100 face value Series EE bond for $50. The bond will increase in value as it matures and can be redeemed 6 months after the issue date. Series EE savings bonds issued on or after May 1, 2005 earn a fixed rate of interest that applies for the 30-year life of the bond. Rates for new issues are adjusted each May 1 and November 1. Taxpayers who redeem Series EE Bonds in the first 5 years of ownership will forfeit the 3 most-recent months' interest. If the redemption occurs after owning the bonds for 5 years, interest earned will not be affected.

At one time, Series EE bonds could be reinvested in Series HH bonds to defer recognition of accumulated interest. However, as of September 1, 2004, investors have not been able to exchange Series EE bonds for Series HH bonds (or to reinvest Series HH bonds).

Series EE United States savings bonds offer a number of tax advantages as follows:

- The income earned from the bond will not be subject to state or local income taxes. Note, however, that the income is subject to Federal income tax.
- Taxpayers may be able to avoid Federal income tax on the interest earned on Series EE savings bonds if they redeem the bond and use the bond proceeds on higher education for themselves, a spouse or dependents (discussed further below) [Code Sec. 135(b)].
- Taxpayers can defer Federal income taxes on the interest earned on the Series EE savings bonds until the certificates are redeemed, mature or are disposed of (whichever happens first), or they may elect to report the annual increase as taxable income [Code Sec. 454(a); Reg. § 1.454-1(a)].

To switch from the postponed tax method to reporting the interest annually, taxpayers should simply report the current interest accrual plus the prior untaxed accrual. However, once the current tax method is elected, it is binding for all subsequent tax years (and subsequent bond purchases). A switch back to the postponed tax method is considered a change in accounting and cannot be done without IRS approval [Reg. § 1.454-1(a)]. However, taxpayers can get approval automatically by attaching a completed Form 3115, *Change in the Method of Accounting*, with their tax return for the year of the switch back to the postponed tax method. They should attach a statement providing that they agree to report all untaxed interest when the bonds are redeemed, mature or are disposed of, whichever is earlier.

> **NOTE:** This expedited method for getting IRS approval can be used no more often than once every five years.

.09 Series I U.S. Savings Bonds

Series I U.S. savings bonds are a low-risk, liquid savings product. During the time that a taxpayers owns the bonds they earn interest and protect the taxpayer from inflation. These bonds are only available through the taxpayer's IRS tax refund. The bonds are sold at face value and the taxpayer pays $50 for a $50 bond. If the bond is redeemed within the first 5 years, the taxpayer will forfeit the three most recent months' interest; after 5 years, no penalty is assessed.

.10 Exclusion for Interest from Education Savings Bonds

You may be able to avoid federal income tax on interest earned on Series EE or I U.S. savings bonds entirely if, in the year you redeem the bonds, you spend an amount equal to or greater than the bond proceeds on higher education for yourself, your spouse, or your dependents [Code Sec. 135(b)]. Use Form 8815, *Exclusive of Interest from Series EE and I. U.S. Savings Bond Issued After 1989*, to compute the exclusion.

A taxpayer may exclude the interest earned on EE or I U.S. savings bonds if all of the following conditions apply:

1. The bonds were issued after December 31, 1989 [Code Sec. 135(c)(1)(A)];
2. The taxpayer purchased the bonds after attaining age 24 [Code Sec. 135(c)(2)(B)];
3. The taxpayer owns the bonds solely or jointly with his or her spouse. Thus, the exclusion is not available if a parent purchases the bonds and puts them in the name of a child. Bonds purchased by grandparents are ineligible unless the child is a dependent of the bond owner at the time of the redemption.
4. The taxpayer paid qualified higher education expenses which means tuition and fees net of scholarships, fellowships, employer-provided educational assistance, and other tuition reduction amounts required for the enrollment or attendance of the taxpayer, the taxpayer's spouse, or any dependent of the taxpayer for whom the taxpayer is allowed a deduction [Code Sec. 135(c)(2)(A)]. Tuition and fees do not include expenses related to any course or other education involving sports, games, or hobbies other than as part of a degree program [Code Sec. 135(c)(2)(B)]. They do not include expenses for room and board.
5. The tuition and fees must be for a college, university, or a vocational school that meets federal financial aid standards.
6. The taxpayer cannot be filing as a married person filing separately;
7. The taxpayer's MAGI for the year is less than specified amounts which are adjusted annually for inflation. For purposes of the phaseout, modified adjusted gross income is adjusted gross income after applying:
   a. The partial exclusion for social security and tier 1 railroad retirement benefits;
   b. Amounts deducted for contributions to IRAs; and
   c. Adjustments for limitations on passive activity losses and credits and without regard to:
      a. The Code Sec. 135 interest exclusion;
      b. The exclusion for adoption expenses;
      c. The deduction for qualified U.S. production activities income under Code Sec. 199;
      d. The exclusion for interest on qualified student loans under Code Sec. 221;
      e. The deduction for qualified tuition and related expenses under Code Sec. 222;
      f. The foreign income exclusion under Sec. 911; and
      g. The exclusion for income from sources within Guam, American Samoa, the Northern Mariana Islands, and Puerto Rico under Code Sec. 931 [Code Sec. 135(c)(4)].

Consult the chart below to see if your interest exclusion will be phased out in 2013. [Code Sec. 135(b)(2)]:

Type of Taxpayer	Threshold phaseout amount	Complete phaseout amount
Joint Filers	$112,050 MAGI	$142,050 MAGI
All Others	$74,700 MAGI	$89,700 MAGI

In 2014, the exclusion under Code Sec. 135, regarding income from United States savings bonds for taxpayers who pay qualified higher education expenses, begins to phase out for modified adjusted gross income above $113,950 for joint returns and $76,000 for all other returns. The exclusion is completely phased out for modified adjusted gross income of $143,950 or more for joint returns and $91,000 or more for all other returns.

Example 2-16: In 2013, Mom redeems $16,000 worth of Series EE savings bonds to pay for Son's college tuition. The redeemed amount includes $8,000 principal and $8,000 accrued interest. Mom files as head of household and her MAGI that year is $105,000. She cannot exclude from income $8,000 of the accrued interest because her income exceeds the threshold phaseout amount of $74,700 for taxpayers filing as head of household [Code Sec. 135(b)(2)].

If the proceeds (principal plus interest) of the bonds redeemed during the tax year are more than the year's qualified higher education expenses (i.e., tuition and fees), only a proportionate part of the interest on the bonds is excludable [Code Sec. 135(b)(1)].

Example 2-17: John and Mary Simpson redeem qualified bonds in 2013 and receive $5,000 of principal and $5,000 of accrued interest. Their modified adjusted gross income on their joint return is $70,000. In the same year, they pay $8,000 in tuition and fees for their 18-year-old daughter's first year of college. John and Mary can exclude from tax $4,000 of the accrued interest generated by the bonds—$5,000 interest × ($8,000 qualified expenses divided by the $10,000 redemption amount).

After figuring the amount of the interest exclusion without limitation, determine actual excludable savings bond interest as follows:

1. Enter MAGI.
2. Subtract the threshold amount based on your filing status ($74,700 if single, head of household or surviving spouse; $112,050 if married filing jointly).
3. Divide the amount determined in (2) above by $15,000 ($30,000 if married filing jointly).
4. Apply the percentage found in (3) above to the otherwise allowable interest exclusion.
5. Subtract the amount in (4) from the otherwise allowable interest exclusion. This is your excludable savings bond interest.

Example 2-18: Same facts as Example 2-17 except that the Simpsons' MAGI is $130,000. The Simpsons can exclude $1606.80 of the interest on the redeemed bonds figured as follows:

1. Otherwise allowable interest		$4,000
2. Modified adjusted gross income	$130,000	
3. Less: Threshold amount	112,050	
4. Balance	$17,950	
5. Applicable percentage ($17,950/$30,000)		59.83%
6. Multiply line 1 by line 5		2393.20
7. Excludable savings bond interest ($4,000 minus $2393.20)		$1606.80

DIVIDENDS IN GENERAL

¶2075 WHAT IS A DIVIDEND?

In general, a dividend is a distribution of a corporation's current or accumulated earnings and profits to the shareholders. Distributions in excess of earnings and profits are not ordinary dividends. Instead, they represent a return of capital. As such, they can be either tax-free or capital gains. Dividends can be made in the form of cash payments, shares of the payer's stock or property distributions. (NOTE There are special tax rules for distributions by S corporations; see Chapter 21 for details.)

NOTES: (1) A dividend paid in company stock is taxable if: (a) you have the option to receive cash or other property in place of stock; (b) a disproportionate share of stock is received by one class of shareholders; (c) stock you receive is not the same class of stock as you previously owned; (d) there is a disproportionate distribution of convertible preferred stock. See ¶2095.

(2) The amount distributed is taxable only to the extent that it exceeds your adjusted basis in the stock. It is then taxed as capital gains. See ¶2080.

.01 What Are Earnings and Profits

A corporation's earnings and profits (E&P) are often not the same as its taxable income. A corporation's earnings and profits (E&P) represent its retained profits from its operations. A number of items that are excludable in figuring taxable income serve to increase a corporation's retained earnings. For example, big up-front accelerated depreciation deductions cannot be used to reduce E&P; special straight-line depreciation rules apply instead. In addition, certain deductions, not allowed for tax purposes, affect the retained earnings. The amount of a corporation's accumulated earnings and profits available for dividend payments is the annual earnings and profits less losses and prior dividends paid over the corporation's life. In the case of long-established corporations, only E&P accumulated since March 1, 1913 is taken into account.

.02 The Source of the Distribution

The tax treatment of a distribution hinges on its source. Distributions are conclusively presumed to come from: (1) current E&P and then, (2) accumulated E&P to the extent E&P exists [Code Sec. 316(a); Reg. § 1.316-2(a)].

Example 2-19: At the beginning of the year, Bellar Corp. had $12,000 of accumulated earnings and profits. Its earnings for the year amounted to $30,000. Assume that it paid a single annual dividend as follows:

1. Dividend of $20,000.

The entire dividend would be taxable since it did not exceed the $30,000 earnings of the tax year.

2. Dividend of $40,000.

The entire dividend would be taxable since it did not exceed the $30,000 earnings of the tax year, plus the $12,000 accumulated E&P ($30,000 plus $12,000, for a total of $42,000).

3. Dividend of $60,000.

The dividend would be taxable to the extent of $42,000 ($30,000 earning for the year plus $12,000 accumulated E&P). The remaining $18,000 is a nontaxable return of capital (unless an allocable part exceeds your original investment in Bellar stock).

Current E&P are computed at the end of the tax year, without reduction for accumulated deficits from prior years. Thus, a distribution made during the early part of a year when your corporation has no earnings and profits could turn out to be a dividend if your corporation ends the year with a profit.

Example 2-20: Astor Corp.'s E&P account shows a deficit balance of $5,000 at the beginning of the year. However, it turns a profit—ending up with $5,000 of E&P from the current year's operations. Astor makes a $5,000 distribution that year. Result: The distribution is a taxable dividend since there was sufficient current E&P. Astor does not net its current and accumulated E&P accounts first.

▶ **SUGGESTED MOVE:** Astor could have considered holding off on declaring the distribution until the following year if it appeared Astor would have no current E&P that year. That distribution would be a return of capital—instead of a taxable ordinary dividend. Reason: The prior year's $5,000 E&P would have been netted with the $5,000 accumulated deficit to determine the new year's accumulated E&P. That net amount being zero, any distributions made in the following year would not be taxable dividends.

.03 Matching Cash Dividends and Distribution Source

Companies often make distributions more than once during the course of a year. Suppose the total distributions exceed your corporation's current and accumulated E&P and occur both before and after the shares change hands. It can make a big tax difference to former, ongoing and new shareholders how the E&P is allocated with respect to each of the distributions. For example, if you receive distributions for which no E&P are allocated, you get a return of capital.

Current Earnings

First, allocate the earnings of the tax year to each individual dividend. The proportion of each dividend which the total of the earnings or profits of the year bears to the total dividends paid during the year is regarded as out of the earnings of that year.

> **Example 2-21:** Current earnings and profits are $30,000. Four dividends of $15,000 were paid, for a total of $60,000. The proportion which the current earnings and profits ($30,000) bears to the total dividends ($60,000) is 30,000/60,000 or 50 percent. Thus, 50 percent, or $7,500, of each dividend is regarded as out of current earnings and profits and taxable to that extent.

If current earnings and profits exceed the current year's distributions, the excess either reduces prior deficits, if any, or is added to accumulated earnings and profits at the beginning of the following year.

Accumulated Earnings and Profits

Allocate the earnings and profits accumulated since February 28, 1913, in sequence to the portion of each individual dividend not out of current earnings and profits. The allocation is made to the extent of such earnings and profits available on the date of each distribution.

.04 Reporting Dividends When Earnings Are Unknown

You may have to report the entire distribution as taxable if your corporation's earnings and profits are unknown when you file your return. A situation of this kind might occur, for example, if your corporation had a fiscal year ending June 30 and you used the calendar year.[83] If necessary, you can file a refund claim later.

> ▶ **OBSERVATION:** Shareholders should receive a copy of Form 1099-DIV from the corporation showing the payments made to them.

¶2080 HOW DIVIDENDS ARE TAXED

.01 Qualified Dividends

Qualified dividends received by an individual shareholder from either a domestic corporation or a *qualified foreign corporation* are taxed at the same tax rates imposed on capital gains in tax years beginning after December 31, 2012 [see ¶8001.01 for a chart illustrating the capital gains tax rates].

Holding Period Requirement

To qualify for the lower capital gains tax rates, the taxpayer must hold the dividend-paying stock for at least 61 days during the 121-day period beginning 60 days before the ex-dividend date (the first day that the buyer will not be entitled to receive that dividend) [Code Sec. 1(h)(11)(B)(iii)]. According to the holding-period changes, a stock bought on the last day before the ex-dividend date, i.e., the latest purchase date for collecting a dividend, could still meet the holding period test for that dividend

[83] *V.U. Young*, 6 TC 357, Dec. 15,009 (1946).

because there would have been 61 days left in the 121-day period. A stock sold on the ex-dividend date (the earliest selling date after entitlement to a dividend) can also meet the test because this is the 61st day in the period. As long as the taxpayer holds the stock for at least 61 continuous days, the holding period test will be met for any dividend received (unless another restriction applied, such as a diminished risk of loss).

> ▶ **PLANNING POINTER:** As a result of this rate reduction for dividends, investors should consider reallocating their investment portfolio so that they are more heavily invested in stocks paying qualified dividends, which will be taxed at favorable capital gains tax rates. Investors should move assets out of taxable bonds where the interest will continue to be taxed at the higher ordinary income rates. Investors should shift savings out of interest-earning accounts into money market accounts where earnings will be cast as dividends. This shift will save taxes because dividends earned on money market accounts will be taxed as capital gains whereas interest income earned by savings accounts in banks will still be taxed at ordinary income rates.

Qualified Foreign Corporation

Dividends received from a "qualified foreign corporation" are classified as "qualified dividend income" and are taxed at the capital gains tax rate. See ¶8001. Qualified dividend income is defined as dividends received during the tax year from domestic corporations and qualified foreign corporations [Code Sec. 1(h)(11)(B)(i)]. *Qualified foreign corporation* means any foreign corporation that is either:

- Incorporated in a possession of the United States [Code Sec. 1(h)(11)(C)(i)(I)]; or
- Eligible for benefits under a comprehensive income tax treaty with the United States [Code Sec. 1(h)(11)(C)(i)(II)].

A foreign corporation that does not satisfy either of these two tests is treated as a qualified foreign corporation with respect to any dividend paid by such corporation if the stock with respect to which the dividend was paid is readily tradable on an established United States security market [Code Sec. 1(h)(11)(C)(ii)].

Foreign dividends will not qualify for the reduced tax rate if the distributing corporation is a passive foreign investment company (as defined in Code Sec. 1297).

A *comprehensive income tax treaty* must satisfy three requirements: (1) be comprehensive; (2) be deemed satisfactory in the eyes of the IRS; and (3) provide for the exchange of tax information [Code Sec. 1(h)(11)(c)(i)(II)].

The following countries have a qualifying treaty with the United States which allow for dividends paid by qualified foreign corporations in such countries to be taxed as capital gains:[84]

Australia	Germany	Luxembourg	South Africa
Austria	Greece	Malta	Spain
Bangladesh	Hungary	Mexico	Sri Lanka
Bulgaria	Iceland	Morocco	Sweden
Barbados	India	Netherlands	Switzerland

[84] Notice 2011-64, IRB 2011-37, 231.

Belgium	Indonesia	New Zealand	Thailand
Canada	Ireland	Norway	Trinidad and Tobago
China	Israel	Pakistan	Tunisia
Cyprus	Italy	Philippines	Turkey
Czech Republic	Jamaica	Poland	Ukraine
Denmark	Japan	Portugal	United Kingdom
Egypt	Kazakhstan	Romania	Venezuela
Estonia	Korea	Russian Federation	
Finland	Latvia	Slovak Republic	
France	Lithuania	Slovenia	

Readily Tradable Defined

Dividends paid to individual shareholders from foreign corporations that fail to qualify under the treaty rule discussed above may nevertheless qualify for taxation at capital gains tax rates if the foreign corporation's stock is "readily tradable on an established securities market in the United States" [Code Sec. 1(h)(11)(C)(ii)].[85]

Payments in Lieu of Dividends

When the tax rate imposed on *qualified dividends* paid to individual shareholders was reduced to the same tax rate imposed on capital gains, *payments in lieu of dividends* (sometimes called *substitute payments* or *manufactured dividends*) were excluded and therefore do not qualify for taxation at reduced capital gains rates. Payments in lieu of dividends are most frequently associated with short sales where the taxpayer borrows stock from a broker to sell. After this initial sale, the short seller hopes the price of the stock goes down so he can replace the borrowed stock with identical shares purchased at a lower price, pocketing the difference. In this situation, the broker delivers shares that it was holding for another customer in "street name." Any subsequent dividends paid on the stock will go to the buyer but the account of the customer whose shares were borrowed must be credited with a payment in lieu of dividend equal to the amount of the dividend.

Brokers may report payments in lieu of dividends to individuals on in Box 8 of Form 1099-MISC, *Miscellaneous Income*, whether the recipient is a corporation, an individual, or some other type of taxpayer. Brokers may furnish composite substitute payee statements for Forms 1099-DIV, *Dividends and Distributions*, and Forms 1099-MISC, reporting payments in lieu of dividends, as well as other information returns.

Excluded Dividends

The following types of dividend income are specifically excluded from the definition of "qualified dividend income" and are therefore ineligible for the reduced tax rate:

- Dividends paid by a credit union;
- Dividends paid by mutual insurance companies or regulated investment companies (RICs) will be taxed at the maximum tax rate imposed on individuals. Dividends passed through RICs from corporations will qualify for the reduced tax rate on dividends provided that the gross-income test under the RIC rules is met as

---

[85] Notice 2003-71, 2003-2 CB 922.

discussed in Ch. 23. Interest earned on money market mutual funds and bond mutual funds, although labeled dividend distributions by RICs, will not qualify for the reduced rates on qualified dividend income when passed through to mutual fund investors;

- Dividends paid by farmers' cooperatives;
- Dividends paid by tax-exempt cemetery companies;
- Dividends paid by nonprofit voluntary employee benefit associations (VEBAs);
- Dividends paid by employer securities owned by an employee stock ownership plan (ESOP) to the extent the dividends are deductible;
- Dividends paid by tax-exempt corporations;
- Dividends paid by any mutual savings bank, savings and loan, domestic building and loan, cooperative bank, or other type of bank eligible for the dividends paid deduction;
- Dividends paid by stock owned for less than 60 days in the 121-day period surrounding the ex-dividend date which is a few days before the official date of record on which shareholders receiving dividends are officially registered;
- Dividends paid by stock purchased with borrowed funds if the dividend was included in investment income in claiming an interest deduction;
- Dividends paid when the taxpayer is obligated to make related payments with respect to positions in substantially similar or related property;
- Substitute payments made in lieu of a dividend with respect to stock on loan in a short sale; and
- Dividends paid into a tax-free fund, such as a 401(k) plan, are ineligible for the reduced tax rate.

▶ **TAX RETURN TIP:** If your dividend income exceeds $1,500, you must fill out Schedule B (Form 1040) or Schedule 1 (Form 1040A) and attach it to your return. See also ¶ 2055.

Procedures for Reporting Dividends from Foreign Corporations

Under simplified procedures, the amount of dividends eligible for the reduced rate will be identified in a separate box on Form 1099-DIV. Taxpayers receiving Form 1099-DIV with respect to a foreign dividend may generally rely on that form, unless they have reason to know that the dividend does not satisfy the special rules.

.02 Property Distributions

The rules for property distributions are analogous to those for cash distributions by a corporation to its shareholders. The portion of a distribution that is taxed as a dividend cannot exceed the distributing corporation's E&P [Reg. § 1.316-1(a)(2)].

You are deemed to have received a distribution equal to the fair market value of the property on the distribution date, reduced (but not below zero) by any liability you assume or to which the property remains subject [Code Sec. 301(b); Reg. § 1.301-1(g)]. Similarly, your basis for the property is its fair market value on the date of distribution [Code Sec. 301(d); Reg. § 1.301-1(h)(1)].

Example 2-22: Adelphi Corp. has earnings and profits of $10,000. It distributes property worth $16,000 to its shareholders. The shareholders have taxable dividend income of $10,000 and reduce their basis in Adelphi stock by $6,000. Their basis in the property distributed is $16,000. Note that Adelphi's basis in the distributed property is not relevant when determining the shareholders' basis for the property.

▶ **IMPORTANT:** Adelphi may owe tax on account of the property distribution. Tax is generally due when the property's fair market value exceeds its basis in the hands of the corporation [Ch. 20].

.03 Dividends Passed Through Mutual and Money Market Funds

Corporate stock dividends that are passed through to investors by a mutual fund or other regulated investment company, partnership, real estate investment trust, or held by a common trust fund qualify for the lower tax rates, assuming the distribution would otherwise be classified as qualified dividend income as defined below.

Distributions by mutual funds that are also known as regulated investment companies (RICs) and money market funds are both classified as dividends, even though money market funds invest in interest-bearing investments. If you choose to have your dividends automatically reinvested by the fund, you are taxed on the dividends, the same as if you had received cash. See Ch. 6. Dividends passed through RICs from corporations will qualify for the reduced tax rate on dividends provided that the gross-income test under the RIC rules is satisfied as discussed in Ch. 23. Interest earned on money market mutual funds and bond mutual funds, although traditionally labeled dividend distributions by RICs when passed through to mutual fund investors, do not qualify for the lower rates available for qualified dividends.

.04 Capital Gains Dividends

Mutual funds, regulated investment companies, and real estate investment trusts may designate part of a distribution as a capital gains dividend. For discussion of tax treatment, see Ch. 8.

▶ **TAX RETURN IMPACT:** Capital gains dividends are eligible for favorable capital gains tax treatment in tax years beginning after December 31, 2012 [see ¶8001.02]. You report the capital gains on Schedule D. For further discussion of Schedule D, see Ch. 8.

A capital gain dividend is a distribution by an investment company (such as a mutual fund or real estate investment trust (REIT) or regulated investment company (RIC)) of capital gains it realizes on the sale of its investments. It is designated as such by the investment company in a written notice to its shareholders on Form 1099-DIV. Capital gain dividends are reported on Schedule D as long-term capital gains regardless of how long you owned the stock in the investment company [Code Sec. 852(b)(3)]. Any loss from the sale of regulated investment company or real estate investment trust stock (RIC or REIT stock) held for six months or less is treated as a long-term capital loss, to the extent of any long-term capital gain from a capital dividend [Code Secs. 852(b)(4), 857(b)(7)]. An exception is made for dispositions under a periodic redemption plan.

If a mutual fund or real estate investment trust retains long-term capital gains and pays tax on them, these dividends are called undistributed capital gain dividends.

You must treat your share of these gains as taxable distributions even though you did not actually receive them. They will not be included on Form 1099-DIV. Instead, you will find your share of the mutual fund's or REIT's undistributed capital gains and the amount of tax that the investment company paid on Form 2439, *Notice to Shareholder of Undistributed Long-Term Capital Gains.* You must report undistributed capital gains as long-term capital gains on Schedule D (Form 1040) [see Ch. 23]. However, you are entitled to a credit for the tax paid by the mutual fund or REIT. You may claim the credit by checking the appropriate box on Form 1040. Attach Copy B of Form 2439 to your return and keep Copy C for your records.

.05 Consent Dividends

Corporations are subject to a special tax if they accumulate too much earnings. Personal holding companies also need to distribute their income in order to avoid owing another special tax. A consent dividend, which represents a phantom distribution to shareholders, avoids both special taxes. The shareholders agree to treat corporate income as if it had been distributed to them in cash and then immediately reinvested in the corporation. They are taxed on the consent dividend, and it increases the basis of their stock as a capital contribution. See also Ch. 23.

¶2085 CONSTRUCTIVE DIVIDENDS

Some transactions between shareholders of a closely held corporation and the corporation that are not in the form of dividends may nevertheless be taxed as dividends because their effect is the same as a dividend. They are taxed even though a dividend was not formally declared[86] and payment was not made to all the shareholders in proportion to stock ownership. These transactions are viewed as constructive dividends. Shareholders can run into problems if they become lax in dealing with their closely held corporation. All dealings with a corporation should be at arm's length (totally legitimate), and the corporation should be treated at all times as a separate legal entity rather than a personal bank account. The IRS has the authority to treat withdrawals of cash from a corporation, and other transactions, as taxable constructive dividends, if transactions have not been handled with the requisite level of formality.

For example, suppose that you are a shareholder/employee and that your employer pays an unreasonably high salary to you. The IRS could treat the excessive portion of your compensation as a nondeductible dividend. Similarly, payments made in the following circumstances can be recharacterized as dividends:

- Excessive royalties[87] and rents paid to a shareholder or a member of his or her family.[88]

---

[86] *L.G. Hadley*, CA-DC, 1 USTC ¶443, 36 F2d 543.

[87] Rev. Rul. 69-513, 1969-2 CB 29.

[88] *Limericks, Inc.*, CA-5, 48-1 USTC ¶9146, 165 F2d 483.

- "Interest" on notes held to be an equity investment (stock)[89] rather than evidence of a corporate debt.
- Bargain sales of securities and other property to shareholders [¶2040] or sales by shareholders to the corporation at an inflated price.
- Cancellation of shareholder's debt to corporation.
- Corporation's purchase of shareholder's property for more than its value.[90]
- Bargain sales of inventory items to shareholders.[91]
- Life insurance proceeds paid to a shareholder if the corporation paid the premiums and held incidents of ownership [¶2035].
- Interest-free and below market rate loans made by a corporation to its shareholders. For interest-free and below market term loans made after June 6, 1984, and demand loans outstanding after that date, the corporation is treated as having made a dividend distribution to the shareholder in the amount of the foregone interest [Code Sec. 7872(a)(1)]. For loans made earlier, there had been some dispute, particularly between the Tax Court and the Claims Court, whether such a loan would constitute an actual loan or a constructive dividend.[92]
- Excessive withdrawals from the corporations with no intent to repay the withdrawn amounts.[93] You cannot use the closely held corporate account as a private bank account.
- Corporation's payment for stadium seat license.[94]
- Services such as electrical work provided by the corporation to a shareholder without expectation of repayment.[95]
- *But see T.J. Welle,*[96] where the Tax Court held that the sole owner of a C corporation did not receive a constructive dividend in the amount of forgone profit when the corporation provided construction-related services to him without charging its standard profit margin.

▶ **PRACTICE POINTER:** *How to avoid constructive dividend treatment.* The IRS and the courts can be expected to scrutinize transactions between closely held corporations and their shareholders (especially sole shareholders). In order to avoid having money received by a shareholder from a closely-held corporation taxed as a constructive dividend, follow the following simple formalities:

1. All business dealings between the shareholder and the closely held corporation should be treated as business transactions with a third-party. This means that there should be adequate recordation and documentation of all business agreements, dealings, conversations and transactions.

---

[89] *Peco Co.*, 26 TCM 207, Dec. 28,362(M), TC Memo. 1967-41.

[90] *R.W. Pope*, CA-1, 57-1 USTC ¶9291, 239 F2d 881.

[91] *L.E. Dellinger*, 32 TC 1178, Dec. 23,749 (1959).

[92] *J.S. Dean*, 35 TC 1083, Dec. 24,742 (1961), *nonacq.*, 1973-2 CB 4; *H.H. Parks*, CA-6, 82-2 USTC ¶9584, 686 F2d 408; *W.L. Hardee*, CA-FC, 83-1 USTC ¶9353, 708 F2d 661.

[93] *J. Epps*, 70 TCM 1, Dec. 50,732(M), TC Memo. 1995-297.

[94] *S.M. Kerns*, 87 TCM 1082, Dec. 55,573(M), TC Memo. 2004-63.

[95] *R. Magnon*, 73 TC 980, Dec. 36,799 (1980).

[96] *T.J. Welle*, 140 TC No. 19, Dec. 59,576 (2013).

2. Shareholders should be charged fair market value for all services, merchandise, equipment or products purchased, leased or otherwise received from their closely held business.
3. All money withdrawn by a shareholder from their closely held corporation should be recorded as loans on all corporate records and financial statements for accounting purposes. Therefore, shareholders should give the business a legally enforceable promissory note, payable either on demand, on a specified maturity date or on the dates that installment payment are due. The closely held corporation should not be viewed, referred to as, or treated as the shareholder's personal bank account.
4. The interest paid on the loan should be stated in the promissory note. The rate should equal or exceed the applicable federal rate (AFR).
5. The corporation should be given a security interest to secure the loan and the loan should have a set repayment schedule. All payments made by the shareholder should be made in accordance with the repayment schedule.
6. All loan repayments should be kept separate from other financial dealings with the closely held corporation.

.01 How to Distinguish Loans from Dividends

To distinguish a shareholder's withdrawals from a closely held corporation as tax-free loans or taxable dividend distributions, the IRS and the courts will look at whether, at the time of the withdrawal, the shareholder intended to repay the amounts received and whether the corporation intended to enforce repayment. A mere statement by the shareholder that he or she intended a withdrawal to constitute a loan is insufficient if the transaction fails to look like a loan. The following factors will be considered:

- The extent to which the shareholder controls the corporation; unfettered control of a corporation by a shareholder weighs in favor of a constructive dividend determination.
- The earnings and dividend history of the corporation; a corporate history of not declaring and paying dividends in spite of the existence of substantial earnings and profits weighs on the side of a constructive dividend determination.
- The magnitude of the advances and whether a ceiling existed to limit the amount that the corporation advanced.
- How the parties recorded the advances on their books and records; the fact that the advances were not recorded as loans indicates that they were constructive dividends.
- Whether the parties executed notes; the absence of written agreements or notes evidencing the loan weighs on the side of a constructive dividend determination.
- Whether interest was paid or accrued; the absence of interest being charged on the amounts withdrawn weighs on the side of a constructive dividend determination.
- Whether or not security was given for the loan; the absence of security for the loan indicates the existence of a constructive dividend.
- Whether there was a set maturity date for the loan; the absence of a set maturity date for the loan indicates the existence of a constructive dividend.

- Whether the corporation ever undertook to force repayment; the failure of the closely held corporation to take any action to enforce repayment makes the advance look more like a constructive dividend.
- Whether the shareholder was in a position to repay the advance.
- Whether there was any indication the shareholder attempted to repay the advance. Courts are not impressed by attempts to repay the purported loan after an IRS audit has commenced.

¶2090 TAX-EXEMPT AND SPECIALLY TREATED DISTRIBUTIONS

Dividends paid to policyholders on unmatured life or endowment insurance policies are not dividends. They are a return of premium and therefore, tax-free (until they exceed the total premium payments). However, dividends paid to the shareholders of these insurance companies are taxable [Code Sec. 316(b)(1); Reg. § 1.316-1(a)(1)].

"Dividends" from savings banks, savings and loan associations, and credit unions are not dividends. They are payments of interest and are taxed as such.

The fact that the earnings of your C Corporation are derived from tax-exempt sources does not make the dividend exempt to you. For example, a dividend received from your C Corporation is not exempt merely because part or all of the corporate earnings consisted of interest on municipal bonds.

Some stock dividends and rights, dividends paid in corporate liquidations and reorganizations, and dividends paid by certain personal holding companies [Code Sec. 316(b)(2)] are tax-exempt or subject to special tax rules.

DISTRIBUTIONS IN KIND OF SECURITIES

¶2095 WHAT IS A STOCK DIVIDEND?

.01 Stock Dividend Defined

A *stock dividend* is a distribution by a corporation to its shareholders in its *own* stock. These dividends can be used either to split a shareholder's existing interest in the company into more parts or to alter that interest. *Stock*, as used in this area, includes stock rights.

.02 How Stock Dividends Are Taxed

Stock dividends that merely divide a shareholder's interest into more parts generally are nontaxable. Reason: The shareholder's ownership rights in the corporation remain subject to the same risks; the receipt of a stock dividend is part of a continuing investment position, not a separate investment. Since the stock dividend presents no opportunity for severing the shareholder's investment ties, there is no occasion for imposing tax.

Not all stock dividends, however, are tax-free. The exceptions, listed below, are designed to tax the shareholder if the shareholder chooses to receive additional shares rather than cash. The rules treat the shareholder much the same as if the shareholder had received cash and reinvested it in the corporation. Thus, a stock dividend is taxable if:

1. The shareholder has a choice of receiving cash or other property in place of stock [Code Sec. 305(b)(1); Reg. § 1.305-2].
2. The distribution is disproportionate (some shareholders get cash or other property and the others have an increase in their proportionate interests) [Code Sec. 305(b)(2); Reg. § 1.305-3].

   ▶ **FRACTIONAL SHARE EXCEPTION:** Stock dividend formulas often entitle some shareholders to fractional shares of stock. In these instances, the tax law permits the corporation to ease its recordkeeping and registration chores by paying cash in lieu of the fractional shares—without turning the stock dividend plan into a disproportionate distribution. The actual amount of cash distributed must not exceed 5 percent of the total stock distributed [Reg. § 1.305-3(c)].

Example 2-23: Y Corporation has two classes of common, A and B, having equal rights, except that A pays only cash dividends and B only equivalent stock dividends. Since the stock dividend increases the B shareholders' proportionate interest, it is taxable.

Example 2-24: X Corporation has outstanding class A common and class B nonconvertible preferred. If dividends are declared, payable in additional shares of class A on the common and cash on the preferred, the distribution of stock is nontaxable because there is no increase in the class A shareholders' proportionate interest. However, taxability results if the dividend on class A is payable in class B stock.

Example 2-25: PY Corporation has outstanding common stock and convertible debentures. It pays cash interest on the debentures and distributes a stock dividend on the common stock. On these facts, the debentures are treated as a second class of stock. Therefore, the stock dividend and interest payment are taxable since the shareholders' equity increases.

3. The distribution involves preferred stock to some common shareholders and common stock to other common shareholders [Code Sec. 305(b)(3); Reg. § 1.305-4].
4. The distribution is with respect to preferred stock, other than an increase in the conversion ratio of convertible preferred stock to reflect a stock dividend or split with respect to which the convertible stock is convertible [Code Sec. 305(b)(4); Reg. § 1.305-5].
5. The distribution involves convertible preferred stock unless it is established to the satisfaction of the IRS that the distribution does not have the result of some shareholders receiving property and other shareholders increasing their proportionate interests in the assets or earnings and profits of the corporation. A distribu-

tion of convertible preferred stock is likely to result in such a disproportionate distribution if the conversion rights must be exercised within a relatively short period of time after the distribution and, taking into account such factors as the dividend rate, the redemption provisions, the marketability of the convertible stock, and the conversion price, it may be anticipated that some shareholders will exercise their conversion rights and some will not. [Code Sec. 305(b)(5); Reg. § 1.305-6].

Example 2-26: NT Corporation distributes convertible preferred stock on common, the only prior outstanding issue. The dividend rates are normal in light of existing market conditions, and the conversion period is four months only. Since those who wish to increase their investment will convert and those who wish cash will sell, it is likely that the result will be a disproportionate distribution. So the distribution is taxable. But suppose the conversion period is long, say 20 years. And it is likely that by the end of the conversion period substantially all the preferred would be converted. The distribution would not be disproportionate and is not taxable.

In general, when a stock dividend is a taxable distribution, the shareholder is taxed on the fair market value of the stock on the distribution date. That also becomes the shareholder's basis in the new shares. The basis in the old shares is unchanged [Reg. § 1.305-1(b)(1), Reg. § 1.301-1(h)(1)]. The holding period of the new stock begins on the date the shareholder receives the stock dividend.

Example 2-27: Mr. Kenny bought 100 shares of Joyce Co. stock for $12,000. Joyce Co. paid a taxable stock dividend and Kenny received 50 shares having a fair market value of $5,000. Kenny must include the $5,000 in income as a dividend in the year of receipt. Thirteen months after the date of original purchase Kenny sold the 100 old shares for $11,000. Less than 12 months after receipt of the 50 shares, he sold the 50 new shares for $5,300. On his return, he will show a long-term capital loss of $1,000 and a short-term capital gain of $300.

Basis of 100 old shares	$12,000
Selling price of 100 old shares	11,000
Long-term capital losses (since the old shares had been held for more than one year)	$ 1,000
Selling price of 50 new shares	$ 5,300
Basis of new shares (fair market value when received)	5,000
Short-term capital gains (since the new shares had been held for not more than one year)	$ 300

.03 Special Rule for Stock Value Counted as Dividend

If a regulated investment company offers its shareholders a choice of cash or stock of equal value, the taxable dividend will be equal to the amount of cash the shareholder could have received—even if the stock is worth a different amount when actually distributed [Reg. § 1.305-1(b)(2)].

¶2100 EFFECT OF NONTAXABLE STOCK DISTRIBUTIONS

The receipt of a nontaxable stock distribution does not, of course, result in taxable income. However, the sale or exchange of those shares is a taxable event. To calculate the amount of gain or loss, the shareholder's basis in the stock must first be determined.

.01 Basis of Old and New Stock

The basis of the stock depends on whether the old and new stocks are identical.

When Old and New Stocks Are Identical

Examples include stock splits and dividends of common on common. To find the basis of each share (old and new), divide the basis of the old stock by the total number of old and new shares [Code Sec. 307(a); Reg. § 1.307-1].

> **Example 2-28:** Mr. Harrison owned 100 shares of Haron Corporation common stock bought for $12,000 ($120 a share). Several years later, Haron Corporation declared a 50-percent stock dividend and Harrison received 50 new common shares. After the stock dividend, the basis of each share is $80 ($12,000/150).

If the shareholder bought the old stock at different times and prices, the shareholder's basis is found by allocating to each lot of the old stock the proportionate amount of dividend stock attributable to it.[97] This could raise an identification problem [Ch. 6].

> **Example 2-29:** Mr. Cleveland owned 150 shares of Haron Corporation common stock. He paid $12,000 for 100 of those shares ($120 a share) and $7,500 for the other 50 shares ($150 a share). Cleveland received 75 new common shares as a result of the 50-percent stock dividend. Fifty of those shares are allocated to the first block of stock, and 25 allocated to the shares he purchased for $150 a share. His new basis in each share is then allocated in the same manner as in Example 2-31: $80 for 150 shares and $100 for the other 75 shares.

When Old and New Stocks Are Not Identical

An example of this would be preferred stock received for common. The shareholder's basis in the old stock is allocated to the old and new stocks in proportion to their relative market values on the distribution date.

> **Example 2-30:** Ms. Jackson bought 100 shares of Redy Corp. common stock for $12,000. She received a nontaxable stock dividend of 50 shares of Redy preferred stock having a fair market value of $5,000. The value of the old stock when the dividend was received was $15,000. After the stock dividend, the bases of the old and new stock are determined as follows:

---

[97] Rev. Rul. 71-350, 1971-2 CB 176.

Basis of 100 shares of old stock		$12,000
Fair market value of old stock	$15,000	
Fair market value of new stock	5,000	
Total	$20,000	

Basis of 100 shares of old stock after dividend: $12,000 × 15,000/20,000 = $9,000

Basis of 50 shares of new stock after dividend: $12,000 × 5,000/20,000 = $3,000

.02 Holding Period of New Stock

The holding period of the new shares starts on the same date as the holding period of the old [Code Sec. 1223(5); Reg. § 1.1223-1].

Example 2-31: Assume the same facts as in Example 2-32, except that 4 months after receipt of the stock dividend, Ms. Jackson sold the 50 new shares for $4,800. Because the holding period of her old shares began in 1991, her holding period is more than 12 months. She realizes a long-term capital gains of $1,800 taxed at 15 percent (5 percent if she is in the 10 or 15 percent tax bracket), figured as follows:

Selling price	$4,800
Basis	3,000
Long-term capital gains	$1,800

¶2105 STOCK RIGHTS

Shareholders may receive rights to subscribe to a new issue of stock. The rights are issued to the shareholder, usually at less than the stock's quoted price, by the corporation in which the shareholder holds the stock. The shareholder can sell his or her rights, exercise them, or let them expire. The rules for finding if a stock right is taxed to the shareholder are the same as those for stock dividends [Code Sec. 305(d)(1); Reg. § 1.305-1(d)(1)].

Bond rights are discussed at ¶ 2120.

¶2110 EFFECT OF NONTAXABLE STOCK RIGHTS

As with the nontaxable stock distributions, the receipt of nontaxable stock rights has no effect on the shareholder's income when received. It is necessary, however, to find the basis of the stock and rights and the holding period of the rights.

.01 Basis of Stock and Rights

If the rights have a market value of less than 15 percent of the stock's value at the time they are distributed, the shareholder can either treat the rights as having a zero basis or elect to allocate part of your stock basis to the rights. If the value is 15 percent or more, the shareholder must allocate basis to the rights [Code Sec. 307(b)(1), (2); Reg. §§1.307-1, 1.307-2].

How to Allocate Basis

Stock basis is allocated between the stock and rights in proportion to their relative market values on the distribution date [Reg. §1.307-1].

Example 2-32: On June 1, Ms. Hanson, a calendar-year taxpayer, bought 100 shares of Carr Corp. stock at $100 per share. One month later, she received 100 rights entitling her to subscribe to an additional 100 shares at $95 per share. On the day the rights were issued, the fair market value of the stock was $110 a share and that of the rights was $15 each. The bases of the rights and the common stock to determine the gain or loss on a later sale are computed as follows, if the election is made:

Original cost of stock (100 × $100)	$10,000
Value of old stock when rights issued (100 × $110)	$11,000
Value of rights when issued (100 × $15)	1,500
Value of both old stock and rights when rights issued	$12,500
Basis of old stock after rights issued ($11,000/$12,500) × $10,000	$8,800
Basis of rights ($1,500/$12,500) × $10,000	$1,200
Basis of one share of old stock after rights issued ($8,800 ÷ 100)	$88
Basis of one right ($1,200 ÷ 100)	$12

If the rights are sold, the basis for determining gain or loss will be $12 per right. If the rights are exercised, the basis of the new stock acquired will be $107—the subscription price paid for it ($95) plus the basis of the rights exercised ($12). In both cases, the basis of the old stock will be set at $88 per share.

NOTE: The rights in Example 2-32 are worth less than 15 percent of the stock's value at the time of distribution. Therefore, Hanson could either assign a zero basis to the rights or allocate the cost of the original stock between that stock and the new right. This choice leaves room for tax maneuvering. To illustrate, assume Hanson sold her rights for $15 each.

- If her other capital transactions for the year result in capital gains, she could keep her gain on the sale of the rights to a minimum by electing to allocate basis. Thus, her gain would be $3 per right ($15 – $12, basis of one right), instead of $15, and the basis of her old stock would change from $100 to $88 per share.
- If her other capital transactions for the year result in a net loss, she could elect a zero basis and use more of the loss to shelter a bigger gain. The gain would be $15 per right instead of $3, and the basis of her old stock would remain at $100 per share.

How to Elect Allocation

The election above applies to all rights received in any one distribution on the same class of stock owned when the rights were distributed. The election is made in a statement attached to the taxpayer's return for the year the taxpayer receives the rights. The taxpayer should keep a copy of the election and tax return to support the allocated basis when the stock is sold [Reg. § 1.307-2].

.02 Holding Period of Stock and Rights

If the rights are sold, the taxpayer's holding period runs from the date the stock was acquired. If the taxpayer exercises the rights, the new stock's holding period starts on the date of exercise [Code Sec. 1223(5), (6); Reg. § 1.1223-1].

> **Example 2-33:** Mr. Rice bought 100 shares of Delphi Corporation stock. Seven years later, he received 100 nontaxable rights entitling him to subscribe to 25 additional shares at $120 a share. Assume the basis of each right is $4. He sold 60 of the rights for $6 each. Rice has a long-term capital gains of $120 taxed at a maximum rate of 15 percent ($360 sales price less $240 basis), since the rights were held for more than one year.

> **Example 2-34:** Assume that Mr. Rice of Example 2-33 exercised the remaining 40. He turned in the 40 rights with $1,200 for 10 new shares. Six months later, he sold the new shares for $1,500. He has a short-term capital gains of $140, figured as follows:

Selling price	$1,500
Basis of 10 new shares ($160 + $1,200)	1,360
Short-term capital gain	$ 140

¶2115 TAXABLE STOCK RIGHTS

A distribution of taxable stock rights is considered a property distribution treated as explained at ¶ 2080. The amount of the taxable distribution, and the basis of the rights, is generally the fair market value of the rights on the distribution date, whether the shareholder is an individual or a corporation. If the shareholder exercises the rights, the shareholder's basis in the new shares is the shareholder's basis in the rights plus the subscription price. The shareholder's basis in the old stock remains the same [Code Sec. 305(b), (d)(1); Reg. § 1.305-1(b)].

.01 Holding Period of Stock and Rights

If taxable rights are exercised, the holding period for the new shares begins on the date the rights were exercised. The holding period for the old shares remains unchanged [Code Sec. 1223(6); Reg. § 1.1223-1].

¶2120 RIGHTS TO BONDS

.01 Nontaxable Bond Rights

Rights to subscribe to bonds are treated in a manner similar to nontaxable stock rights if (1) the bonds are convertible into stock that, if distributed, would not result in a taxable dividend, and (2) the value of the rights arises from the conversion privilege. The taxpayer's basis in the original stock is allocated between the stock and the rights in proportion to their relative market values. The taxpayer's basis in the bonds is his or her basis in the rights plus the subscription price. If the taxpayer converts the bonds into stock, the taxpayer's basis in such stock is his or her basis in the bonds plus any consideration paid at the time of the conversion.

.02 Taxable Bond Rights

If the bonds are not convertible into stock, the rights are property dividends. The taxpayer's basis in the shares remains unchanged, and basis in the bonds is determined as if they were new stock [¶ 2080 and ¶ 2115].

RETURN OF CAPITAL DIVIDENDS

¶2125 HOW A RETURN OF CAPTAL IS TAXED

A return of capital distribution reduces the shareholder's basis or investment in the stock. So long as the shareholder has basis remaining, the distribution is tax-free. However, once the shareholder's basis becomes zero, additional returns of capital are taxed to the shareholder as capital gain. The stock's holding period determines if the stock is a long-term or short-term capital gain [Ch. 8].

> **Example 2-35:** Mr. Ames bought stock in the Ace Corp. for $500. Two years later, he received a return of capital of $480 (nontaxable). Ames reduced his basis in the stock by the amount received, to an adjusted basis of $20. If Ames received a return of capital of $30 one year later, his basis would be reduced to zero, and he would report the $10 excess as a long-term capital gain for the year.

¶2130 WHAT IS A LIQUIDATING DIVIDEND?

In general, a liquidating distribution made in complete redemption of the stock of a corporate or noncorporate shareholder is treated as the sale or exchange of the distribution for the stock. The same rule applies to the partial liquidation of stock held by a corporate taxpayer. However, a distribution in partial liquidation of a noncorporate shareholder's stock may be fully taxed to the shareholder as a dividend. Payment for the redeemed shares can take the form of cash or other corporate assets. The tax effect on the liquidating corporation is discussed at Ch. 22.

.01 Partial Liquidations to Noncorporate Shareholders

A partial liquidation distribution qualifies for capital gains or loss tax treatment only if the following requirements are met:

- The distribution is not essentially equivalent to a dividend (e.g., the distribution represents a substantially disproportionate redemption of stock).

- The distribution is made pursuant to a plan which was adopted in either the same or the year immediately preceding the year the distribution is made.

  ▶ **SAFE HARBOR:** The tax law provides that a distribution automatically meets the above requirement if the corporation distributes assets attributable to a segment of its operations that it has ceased to run. To qualify under this safe harbor, the corporation must, after the partial liquidation distribution, continue to be actively engaged in any business which it had been pursuing for the prior five-year period [Code Sec. 302(b), (e)].

.02 Complete Liquidations

The tax code does not define this term. However, it generally refers to a winding up of your corporation's affairs, payment of its debts and distribution of corporate assets to you and the other shareholders.

.03 How Liquidating Dividends Are Treated

The amount received in a: (1) complete liquidation, (2) a partial liquidation to a corporate shareholder, or (3) a qualifying partial liquidation to a noncorporate shareholder is treated as the proceeds from the sale of the redeemed stock by the shareholder. In computing the amount received, any property received is taken into account at its fair market value [Code Sec. 331(a); Reg. § 1.331-1].

Amount and Character of Gain or Loss

The amount of gain or loss is the difference between the cost or other basis of the redeemed stock and the amount received in liquidation.

> **Example 2-36:** Mr. Barnett bought 100 shares of Rocket Corp. stock for $10,000. Five years later, the Corp. dissolved and Barnett received a final liquidating dividend of $4,000. His recognized loss is $6,000.

> **Example 2-37:** Ms. Dickens bought 100 shares of Storm Corp. stock for $10,000. Five years later, the Corp. dissolved and Dickens received a final liquidating dividend of $12,000. Her recognized gain is $2,000.

Since stock is usually characterized as a capital asset, you will have capital gain or loss. If the shares were acquired at different times and prices, you compute the gain or loss separately on each block for a single distribution.[98] The distribution is allocated among the various blocks in the same proportion that the number of shares in each block bears to the total number of shares outstanding[99] [Reg. § 1.331-1(e)].

> **Example 2-38:** Mr. Able bought 40 percent of the 200 shares outstanding of the Black Corporation for $800. He acquired the remaining 60 percent of Black stock the following year for $3,600. Two years later, Able receives a final liquidating dividend of $10,000 from the Black Corporation. Able has $3,200 in capital gains

[98] *N. Cooledge*, 40 BTA 110, Dec. 10,957.

[99] Rev. Rul. 68-348, 1968-2 CB 141, *acq.* 1940-1 CB 2; Rev. Rul. 85-48, 1985-1 CB 126.

on the 40-percent purchase [(40 percent × $10,000) less $800] and $2,400 in gain on the 60-percent stock purchase [(60 percent × $10,000) less $3,600].

If you report capital gains on a liquidating dividend, you are sometimes called on as transferees to pay the corporation's tax deficiencies. These payments are treated as capital losses.[100]

.04 Reporting Gain or Loss

If liquidating dividends are distributed in installments, you need not report gain until the cost or other basis of the stock is recovered.[101] Ordinarily, you can deduct a loss through liquidation in the year the final distribution is made. However, if your corporation distributes all of its assets, except a small amount of cash reserved for expenses of dissolution, there is, in effect, a final distribution. You may take a loss to you in that year, instead of being postponed until later when the remaining cash is distributed.[102]

Information Filed with Return

If you transfer stock to the issuing corporation in exchange for property, you should report all the facts and circumstances on your return, unless the dividend is paid under a corporate resolution reciting that it is made in liquidation of the corporation, and the corporation is completely liquidated and dissolved within one year after the distribution. The distributing corporation must file Form 966 within 30 days after adopting the plan of liquidation, but liquidating distributions will be treated as such whether or not the corporation filed Form 966[103] [Ch. 22] [Reg. § 1.331-1(d)].

MISCELLANEOUS INCOME

¶2135 RENTS AND ROYALTIES

Although rents and royalties that lessors receive from lessees are includible in gross income [Code Sec. 61; Reg. § 1.61-8], lessors may also be entitled to a variety of offsetting deductions that can shelter all or some of the income from tax. These deductions include depreciation, or depletion, taxes and other ordinary and necessary expenses of operating the property. They are discussed in later chapters.

.01 Rents

Rents include more than just cash payments you receive from a tenant.

Payment to Third Parties

If, instead of straightforward rent, the tenant pays the interest on bonds that were issued by the lessors[104] or dividends on stock that was issued by the lessor,[105] the payments are rental income to the lessor and treated as rental payments by the tenant.

---

[100] *F.D. Arrowsmith*, SCt, 52-2 USTC ¶9527, 344 US 6, 73 SCt 71, *reh'g denied*, 344 US 900.

[101] *A. Ludorff*, 40 BTA 32, Dec. 10,740.

[102] *B. Winthrop*, CA-2, 38-2 USTC ¶9426, 98 F2d 74.

[103] Rev. Rul. 65-80, 1965-1 CB 154.

[104] *E.S. Amey*, 22 TC 756, Dec. 20,431 (1954).

[105] *Joliet & Chicago R.R. Co.*, SCt, 42-1 USTC ¶9222, 315 US 44, 62 SCt 442.

Amounts received by the stockholders and bondholders are dividends and interest to them.

Taxes Paid by a Tenant

Taxes paid by a tenant to or for you for business property generally are additional rent taxable to you [Reg. § 1.162-11].

Cancellation of Lease

If a tenant pays the landlord to cancel, amend, or modify a lease, the payment is taxable to the landlord as ordinary income.[106] However, an amount paid to a tenant to cancel a lease is treated as proceeds from the lease's sale or exchange [Code Sec. 1241; Reg. § 1.1241-1]. A capital gain results if the lease is of nondepreciable property [Ch. 8] [Code Sec. 1221(2); Reg. § 1.1221-1].

Example 2-39: Mr. Jones rents an apartment to Mr. Keltner. If Jones gives Keltner $1,000 to cancel the lease, Keltner has a capital gain of $1,000. The gain will be short- or long-term depending on the length of time Keltner had the leasehold.

The sale of inventory results in ordinary income, not capital gain. Therefore, lease cancellation payments received by a tenant who is in the business of entering into and marketing leases results in ordinary gain.

.02 Royalties

include payments to the owner of a mine for permitting another to extract minerals from it, payments to an owner of a patent or private formula[107] for the use of it or the right to act under it, and payments to an author of a book. For coal and iron ore royalties, see Ch. 8. For details of the offsetting depletion deduction of mine owners who receive royalties, see Ch. 12.

¶2140 IMPROVEMENTS BY LESSEE

Improvements made by a tenant that increase the value of the leased property are not income to the landlord provided the improvements were not made in lieu of rent [Code Sec. 109; Reg. § 1.109-1(a)]. The landlord recognizes gain or loss only when he or she disposes of the property.

Example 2-40: Mr. Evans leased a parcel of land to Mr. Dugal for a 20-year term, with an annual rental of $800. The land had cost Evans $5,000. During the term of the lease, Dugal erected a building at a cost of $40,000. When the lease expired, Evans repossessed the property. On the next day, Evans sold the land and building for $60,000. The annual rent was income. Evans realized no income from the improvement when it was originally made. Nor did he realize income from the improvement when the lease expired and he repossessed the

[106] *W.M. Hort*, SCt, 41-1 USTC ¶ 9354, 313 US 28, 61 SCt 757.

[107] *J.R. Hopkins*, CtCls, 49-1 USTC ¶ 9199, 82 FSupp 1015, 113 CtCls 217.

land and improvement. But when he sold the land and building for $60,000, his gain on the sale was $55,000 ($60,000 – $5,000).

.01 Adjustments to Basis

No adjustment to the landlord's basis in the property is made for improvements by the tenant [Code Sec. 1019].

.02 Improvements Instead of Rent

The fair market value of improvements that a tenant makes instead of paying rent is income to the landlord when they are placed on the property [Code Sec. 109; Reg. § 1.109-1].

Example 2-41: Mr. Evans leased another piece of land to Mr. Dugal for a period of five years. Under the lease terms, Dugal was not required to pay rent; but, in lieu of rent, he was to install an irrigation system before the end of the 5th year. Dugal installed the system in the fall of the fifth year, at which time it had a fair market value of $5,000. Evans realized $5,000 income that year.

.03 Treatment of Abandonment of Lessor Improvements at Termination of Lease

When a lessor makes an improvement of leased property for the lessee of the property and the improvement is irrevocably disposed of or abandoned at the termination of the lease, the lessor may take the adjusted basis of the improvement into account for purposes of determining gain or loss [Code Sec. 168(i)(8)].

.04 Lessee Construction Allowance Exclusion

Code Sec. 110 provides an income exclusion for lessees who receive cash or rent reductions from a lessor under a short-term lease of retail space if the amounts are used to construct or improve qualified long-term property used in the lessee's business. Qualified long-term real property is defined as nonresidential real property that is part of or present at the retail space and that reverts to the lessor when the lease terminates. A short-term lease is defined as one that is 15 years or less. Retail space is real property used in the lessee's business of selling tangible personal property or services to the general public.

Code Sec. 110(a) provides that the exclusion cannot exceed the amount spent by the lessee for construction or improvement. Expenditures made by a lessee up until 8½ months after the close of the tax year in which the construction allowance was received count towards the exclusion limit [Reg. § 1.110-1(b)(4)(ii)(A)].

Reg. § 1.110-1(b)(3) required that the lease agreement expressly provide that the construction allowance is for constructing or improving qualified long-term real property used in the lessee's business. In addition, the lease must specify the amount of the construction allowance. The IRS has explained in Rev. Rul. 2001-20[108] that it is okay for the lessee to spend less than the allowance on qualified construction, but the difference will be taxed as income. For example, if only 80 percent of the allowance was used to

---

[108] Rev. Rul. 2001-20, 2001-1 CB 1143.

improve qualified real property, only 80 percent of the allowance could be excluded from the lessee's income as a qualified construction allowance. The remaining 20 percent must be included in income by the lessee.

¶2145 FORGIVENESS OF DEBT (CANCELLATION OF INDEBTEDNESS)

.01 Discharge of Indebtedness

Taxpayers who have a commercial, private lender or employer[109] discharge part or all of their debt must include the amount that was discharged in income as cancellation of debt (COD) income unless an exception or exclusion applies. COD arises when a creditor releases a debtor from an obligation incurred at the outset of a debtor-creditor relationship. COD is taxable even though the debt forgiveness does not technically put any money in the hands of the taxpayer [Code Sec. 61(a)(12); Reg. § 1.61-12]. Exceptions to this rule are found in Code Sec. 108 and are discussed in ¶ 2145.02.

Example 2-42: Mr. Anderson, a carpenter, owes Mr. Billson $1,000. Anderson repairs Billson's house. In return, Billson forgives the debt. Anderson must include the $1,000 in his income, as compensation for services.

Reporting Requirements

Executive, judicial, and legislative agencies are required to report to the IRS on Form 1099-C, *Cancellation of Debt*, the full or partial discharge of any borrower's debt, if the discharge is $600 or more regardless of whether or not the discharge is taxable to the borrower [Code Sec. 6050P; Reg. § 1.6050 P-I]. The information return must identify the borrower and set forth the date and the amount of the discharge. A copy of the information return must be provided to the borrower by January 31 of the year following the discharge. Form 1099-C must be filed with the IRS on or before February 28 (or March 3) for electronic returns of the year following the calendar year in which the indebtedness was discharged [Reg. § 1.6050 P-1(f)(3)]. Penalties apply for failing to file the required report or provide the required statement.

Purchase Price Reduction

When a debt arises out of a property purchase, the cancellation or reduction of the amount due may be treated as a reduction of the purchase price, rather than as income. If the discharge is treated as a purchase price reduction, the debtor generally reduces basis in the purchased property and does not recognize COD income if the following six requirements are satisfied: (1) the debt is a debt of the purchaser of the property; (2) the debt is owed to the seller of the property; (3) the debt arose out of the purchase of property; (4) the debt is reduced; (5) the reduction does not occur in a title 11 case or when the debtor is insolvent; and (6) but for this provision, such decrease would be treated as income to the purchaser from COD [Code Sec. 108(e)(5)]. In Rev. Rul.

---

[109] *J.E. McAllister*, Dec. 48,021(M), TC Memo. 59,503(M).

2004-37,[110] the IRS concluded that a debt reduction would not be treated as a purchase price reduction rather than as COD under Code Sec. 108(e)(5) because the debt reduction was a significant modification under Reg. § 1.1001-3 triggering compensation income.

.02 Exceptions to Income Recognition Rule

In general, Code Sec. 108 excludes from gross income discharges (or cancellations) of indebtedness (also known as "COD" or "DOI" income) if:

1. The debt has been discharged in a Title 11 bankruptcy proceeding [Code Sec. 108(a)(1)(A)].
2. The discharge occurs when the taxpayer is insolvent[111] [Code Sec. 108(a)(1)(B)]. Code Sec. 108(d)(3) defines insolvency as the excess of liabilities over the fair market value of assets. Whether the taxpayer is insolvent and the amount of the insolvency is determined immediately prior to the discharge.[112]
3. The indebtedness is "qualified farm indebtedness," which means that the debt is due to a qualified farm expense or farm property [Code Sec. 108(a)(1)(C)], or
4. The indebtedness is "qualified real property business indebtedness," which means it is due to certain real property used in a trade or business [Code Sec. 108(a)(1)(D)].
5. Married taxpayers may be able to exclude up to $2 million of discharged qualified principal residence indebtedness[113] discharged on or after January 1, 2013, and before January 1, 2014 [Code Sec. 108(a)(1)(E)]. See further discussion at ¶ 2145.05.
6. Taxpayers whose student loans are forgiven because they worked for a certain time period in a designated profession for any of a broad class of employers generally do not have to include the discharged amount in income [Code Sec. 108(f)].
7. If a debt is cancelled by a relative or friend and the debt cancellation is intended as a gift, there are no income tax consequences as a result of the debt cancellation.
8. A debt cancelled in a lender's Last Will & Testament will not result in taxable income.
9. No income will be realized from the discharge of indebtedness to the extent that payment of the liability would have given rise to a deduction [Code Sec. 108(e)(2)].

Priority of Exclusions

Exclusions from income are allowed under Code Sec. 108 in the following order of priority:

1. Discharges of debt in a title 11 bankruptcy reorganization;
2. Discharges of debt of insolvent taxpayers;

---

[110] Rev. Rul. 2004-37, 2004-1 CB 583.

[111] *B.R. Shepherd*, 104 TCM 108, Dec. 59,136(M), TC Memo. 2012-212 (taxpayer unable to establish his insolvency and therefore failed to qualify for exception).

[112] *D.B. Merkel*, CA-9, 99-2 USTC ¶ 50,848, 192 F3d 844.

[113] LTR 201328023 (Apr. 9, 2013).

3. Discharges of qualified farm indebtedness;
4. Discharges of qualified real property business indebtedness.

For example, if a taxpayer is both in bankruptcy and insolvent, the bankruptcy exclusion applies [Code Sec. 108(a)(2)]. The bankruptcy exclusion also takes precedence over the Code Sec. 108(a)(1)(E) exclusion of discharged qualified principal residence indebtedness.

Normally, if you are insolvent and a creditor reduces or cancels a debt you owe, the cancellation would not be taxable to the extent that you are insolvent. However, this rule does not apply if you transfer appreciated property to satisfy any part of your debt. A debtor will realize taxable gain to the extent the fair market value of property transferred to a creditor to satisfy a recourse note exceeds his basis in the land.[114] Even though the debtor was insolvent both before and after the transaction and did not realize economic gain as a result of the transfer, the court concluded that the excess constituted "gains derived from dealings in property" rather than "income from discharge of indebtedness" and, therefore, was includable in the debtor's gross income. The transfer was treated as a taxable sale rather than as discharge of indebtedness which would have been nontaxable to the insolvent debtors.

Reducing Tax Attributes

This income exclusion for discharged indebtedness is not necessarily cost-free. As a bankrupt and insolvent taxpayer, you must reduce the amount of certain potentially tax-saving attributes you possess. Reducing these tax attributes serves to postpone, rather than entirely eliminate, tax on the canceled indebtedness. This prevents an excessive tax benefit (e.g., duplicative tax breaks for the same expense) from the debt cancellation. For example, if you have $10,000 of debt canceled, you avoid owing tax on that $10,000. However, you must reduce your tax attributes by $10,000. For insolvent persons who don't elect to reduce basis under Code Sec. 108(b)(5), as discussed further below, your basis reduction is limited to the excess of your aggregate bases in property held immediately after the discharge over the aggregate of your liabilities immediately after the discharge [Reg. § 1.108-6].

The debt discharge amount is applied to reduce your tax attributes in the following order [Code Sec. 108(b)]:

1. Net operating losses or net operating loss carryovers, reduced dollar for dollar;
2. General business credit carryovers, reduced 33$^1/_3$ cents for each dollar excluded;
3. Minimum tax credit carryovers, reduced 33$^1/_3$ cents for each dollar excluded;
4. Net capital losses or capital loss carryovers, reduced dollar for dollar;
5. Basis of the taxpayer's property (depreciable and nondepreciable), reduced dollar for dollar;

---

[114] *J.J. Gehl*, 102 TC 784, Dec. 49,924 (1994), *aff'd*, CA-8, 95-1 USTC ¶ 50,191; *J.S. Danenberg*, 73 TC 370, Dec. 36,459, *acq*. 1980-2 CB 1.

6. Passive activity loss and credit carryovers, reduced $33^{1}/_{3}$ cents for each dollar excluded; and
7. Foreign tax credit carryovers, reduced $33^{1}/_{3}$ cents for each dollar excluded.

After that, any remaining debt discharge amount is permanently excluded from the taxpayer's gross income [Code Sec. 108(b)]. You must first reduce the adjusted basis of the property secured by the discharged debt before reducing the bases of other property. This is referred to as a *tracing approach.* You reduce the basis of property secured by the discharged debt in the following order [Reg. § 1.1017-1(a)]:

1. The basis of real property used in your trade or business or held for investment (other than Section 1221(l) real property) that secured the discharged indebtedness immediately before the discharge;
2. The basis of personal property used in your trade or business or held for investment (other than inventory, accounts receivable, and notes receivable) that secured the discharged debt immediately before the discharge;
3. The basis of remaining property used in a trade or business or held for investment, other than inventory, accounts receivable, notes receivable, and real property described in Code Sec. 1221(l);
4. Inventory, accounts receivable, notes receivable and real property described in Code Sec. 1221(l).
5. Property not used in a trade or business or held for investment.

Election to Reduce Basis

You can make an election under Code Sec. 108(b)(5) whenever you exclude discharge of indebtedness income from gross income to apply all or part of the debt discharge amount to reduce the basis (but not below zero) of certain property instead of or before reducing other tax attributes [Code Sec. 108(b)(5); Reg. § 1.108-4(a)]. The election is made on Form 982, *Reduction of Tax Attributes Due to Discharge of Indebtedness and (Section 1082 Basis Adjustment).* Property subject to this election must be depreciable property or real property held primarily for sale to customers in the ordinary course of a trade or business [Reg. § 1.108-6]. An election under this section may be revoked only with the consent of the IRS [Reg. § 1.108-4(b)].

> ▶ **TAX STRATEGY:** If you are an insolvent taxpayer who expects to earn a profit in subsequent years, you can benefit from this election. You would be able to hold on to operating loss carryovers that could be fully applied to shelter income as soon as it is earned. In return, you would be giving up depreciation deductions of equal amount in total—but spread out over several years. On the other hand, if you expect that the net operating loss carryover will expire before it could be used, you should choose not to make the election.

The treatment of a debt discharged outside of bankruptcy depends on whether you are solvent or insolvent when the discharge is made.

Insolvent Debtors

The amount of debt discharged will be excluded from a taxpayer's gross income if the discharge occurs when the taxpayer is insolvent [Code Sec. 108(a)(1)(B)]. The amount of income excluded under Sec.108 (a)(1)(B) is limited to the amount of the taxpayer's insolvency [Code Sec. 108(a)(3)]. The term "insolvent" is defined as the excess of liabilities over the fair market value of assets [Code Sec. 108(d)(3)]. Whether a taxpayer is insolvent, and the amount by which the taxpayer is insolvent, is determined on the basis of the taxpayer's assets and liabilities immediately before the discharge. Indebtedness of the taxpayer means any indebtedness for which the taxpayer is liable, or subject to which the taxpayer holds property [Code Sec. 108(d)(1)]. In Rev. Rul. 92-53,[115] the IRS provides that the amount by which a nonrecourse debt exceeds the fair market value of the property securing the debt (excess nonrecourse debt) is treated as a liability in determining insolvency for purposes of Code Sec. 108 to the extent that the excess nonrecourse debt is discharged.

Amount of Partner Insolvency Determined When Excess Nonrecourse Debt Discharged

In Rev. Rul. 2012-14,[116] the IRS concluded that for purposes of measuring a partner's insolvency under Code Sec. 108(d)(3), each partner treats as a liability an amount of the partnership's discharged excess nonrecourse debt that is based upon the allocation of cancellation of debt (COD) income to such partner under Code Sec. 704(b). Thus, when applying Rev. Rul. 92-53 in a partnership context, the partnership's discharged excess nonrecourse debt should be associated with the partner who, in the absence of the insolvency or other Code Sec. 108 exclusion, would be required to pay the tax liability arising from the discharge of that debt.

The IRS reasoned that in order to properly apply Rev. Rul. 92-53 in a partnership context, the partnership's discharged excess nonrecourse debt should be associated with the partner who in the absence of the insolvency or other Code Sec.108 exclusion would be required to pay the tax liability arising from the debt discharge. Therefore, a partnership's discharged excess nonrecourse debt is treated as a liability of the partners for purposes of measuring the partners' insolvency under Code Sec.108 (d)(3) based upon how the COD income with respect to that portion of the debt is allocated among the partners under Code Sec. 704(b).

Example 2-43: Bank cancelled $175,000 of PRS's $200,000 excess nonrecourse debt, generating $175,000 of COD income. PRS's $175,000 COD income was allocated equally between X and Holdco under Code Sec. 704(b) and its regulations. When measuring the insolvency of the partners, PRS's discharged excess nonrecourse debt is treated as a liability of its partners based upon the COD income allocation. Thus, X treats $87,500 of PRS's debt as a liability of X, and Holdco treats $87,500 of PRS's debt as a liability of Holdco. X and Holdco treat their shares of the cancelled PRS excess nonrecourse debt as their own liabilities in determining whether, and to what extent, each is insolvent under Code Sec. 108(d)(3).

Immediately before Bank discharges the indebtedness, X's liability exceeds the value of X's partnership interest by $87,500, and similarly Holdco's liability exceeds the value of Holdco's partnership interest by $87,500. Therefore, the IRS held that X and Holdco are each insolvent to the extent of $87,500 under Code Sec. 108(d)(3) and X and Holdco may each exclude their $87,500 amount of COD income under Code Sec. 108(a)(1)(B).

---

[115] Rev. Rul. 92-53, 1992-2 CB 48.

[116] Rev. Rul. 2012-14, IRB 2012-24, 1012.

Tax Attribute Reductions in Certain Reorganizations and Liquidations

If a reorganization or other transaction described in Code Sec. 381(a) ends a year in which the distributor or transferor corporation excludes cancellation of debt (COD) income under Code Sec. 108(a), any tax attributes to which the acquiring corporation succeeds and the basis of property acquired by the acquiring corporation must reflect the reductions required by Code Sec. 108 and Code Sec. 1017 [Reg. §§1.108-7(c), 1.1017-1(b)(4)].

.03 Corporation Transferred Stock to Cancel Debt

All corporations are treated as having income from the cancellation of indebtedness on a stock-for-debt exchange. In other words, if a corporation transfers its own stock in canceling its debt, it realizes income [Code Sec. 108(e)(10)(A)]. Thus, the debtor corporation has income equal to the excess of the debt's principal amount over the stock's fair market value. Note that insolvent and bankrupt corporations may still exclude the income if they reduce tax attributes.

.04 Settlement of Mortgage for Less Than Face Value

If settlement of a mortgage for less than its face value is gratuitous, no income results to the mortgagor. Otherwise, the discount is generally considered a taxable discharge of indebtedness.

> ▶ **SELLER FINANCING EXCEPTION:** If the seller of specific property reduces the buyer's debt that arose out of the purchase, and the reduction to the buyer does not occur in a bankruptcy case or when the buyer is insolvent, then the reduction to the buyer of the purchase-money is to be treated for both the seller and the buyer as a purchase price adjustment on the property [Code Sec. 108(e)(5)]. Thus, the buyer reduces his basis in the property and the seller adjusts his gain or loss on the transaction.

> **Example 2-44:** Mr. Able sells a house to Mr. Baker for $250,000. Able receives $50,000 in cash at the time of sale and takes back a $200,000 mortgage on the home. Assume the price of real estate in the area has declined, and Able agrees to reduce Baker's indebtedness by $10,000. Result: The sales price of the house is now deemed to be $240,000.

Another alternative: Instead of reducing the indebtedness, the borrower and lender can restructure the debt—by charging less interest—without discharge of indebtedness income.[117]

.05 Forgiven Mortgage Debt Tax Relief

Code Sec. 108(a)(1)(E) provides that a taxpayer may exclude from gross income up to $2 million ($1 million for a married taxpayer filing a separate return) of forgiven mortgage debts discharged from January 1, 2013, to December 31, 2014.[118] Therefore, any debtor would not have to pay federal income tax on up to $2 million of debt forgiven

---

[117] Rev. Rul. 91-31, 1991-1 CB 19; as distinguished by Rev. Rul. 92-53, 1992-2 CB 48.

[118] *See also* Rev. Proc. 2013-16, 2013-7 IRB 488 (guidance provided to mortgage borrowers on tax treatment of mortgage assistance payments and reductions of mortgage principal under the Federal Home Affordable Modification Program (HAMP)).

for a qualifying loan secured by a qualifying principal residence if the debt is forgiven from January 1, 2013, to December 31, 2014.

An individual's acquisition debt is defined as debt relating to that individual's principal residence if it is incurred in the acquisition, construction, or substantial improvement of that residence and is secured by the residence. Qualified principal residence interest also includes refinancing of debt to the extent that the amount of the refinancing does not exceed the amount of the refinanced debt.

Principal Residence Defined

A principal residence is defined in Code Sec. 108(h)(5) as having the same meaning as used in Code Sec. 121. See ¶ 7005.

When the taxpayer has more than one property that he or she uses as a residence, the property that the taxpayer uses the majority of the time during the year will be treated as the taxpayer's principal residence for that year for purposes of the mortgage debt relief law. Other factors taken into account in determining the taxpayer's principal residence include:

- The taxpayer's place of employment;
- The principal place where the taxpayer's family lives;
- The address used by the taxpayer on tax returns, driver's license, automobile registration, and voter registration;
- The mailing address used by the taxpayer for bills and correspondence;
- The location of the taxpayer's banks; and
- The location of religious organizations and recreational clubs with which the taxpayer is affiliated [Reg. § 1.121-1(b)].

Exceptions: The discharge of a loan will not be excluded from gross income if it results from services performed for the lender or other factors unrelated to either the financial condition of the taxpayer or a decline in value of the residence. In addition, if only a portion of discharged indebtedness is qualified principal residence indebtedness, the exclusion applies only to so much of the amount discharged as exceeds the portion of the debt that is not qualified principal residence indebtedness. The basis of the taxpayer's principal residence is reduced (but not below zero) by the amount of qualified principal residence interest that is excluded from income [Code Sec. 108(h)(1)].

The exclusion does not apply to a debtor in a bankruptcy case. Instead, the exclusion under Code Sec. 108(a)(1)(A) (exclusion due to bankruptcy) applies. However, the exclusion of debt discharged on a principal residence applies to insolvent taxpayers not involved in Title 11 bankruptcy cases unless the taxpayer elects to have the exclusion of Code Sec. 108(a)(1)(B) (exclusion due to insolvency) apply [Code Sec. 108(a)(2)(C)(2)].

.06 Cancellation of Business Real Property Debt

Financially solvent owners (other than C corporations) have a way to avoid tax on income from the cancellation of mortgage debt if they use the mortgaged property in their businesses [Code Sec. 108(c)]. The amount of the exclusion reduces the basis of depreciable real property [Code Sec. 1017(b)(3)(F)]. The property owner may elect to exclude from income no more than the lesser of: (1) the owner's total adjusted bases in depreciable real property he or she owned immediately before the discharge (less basis reductions from certain debt forgiveness provisions); or (2) the amount by which the outstanding debt exceeds the fair market value of the property (reduced by the amount of any other outstanding debt secured by the property).

> **Example 2-45:** Mr. Beach owns business real estate with a tax basis of $1,000,000. One of his buildings has dropped in value from $350,000 to $275,000. The building is subject to two outstanding mortgages—a first mortgage of $220,000 and a second mortgage of $100,000. Beach is neither bankrupt nor insolvent. The second mortgage holder reduces the second mortgage debt from $100,000 to $30,000. Beach elects to avoid current tax on $45,000 of the $70,000 forgiven debt. The $45,000 limit is the difference between the outstanding debt ($100,000) and the value of the property minus the first mortgage ($275,000 less $220,000, or $55,000). The basis of the property is reduced by $45,000 for depreciation and gain or loss purposes. Any gain from the sale of the property is treated as ordinary income up to the amount of tax-free forgiven debt.

A business property owner may make the election for any mortgage taken out before 1993 and discharged after 1992. An owner may make the election for a mortgage taken out after 1992 only if (1) the mortgage was taken out to buy, build, or improve the property, or (2) the mortgage refinances a qualifying mortgage taken out before 1993.

.07 Cancellation of Certain Student Loans

In order to ensure professional participation in public service activities, many educational organizations sponsor programs that offer students an opportunity to partially or completely discharge their student loans by working for a period of time in a public service organization. However, taxpayers whose student loans are forgiven (in whole or in part) because they worked in a designated profession for any of a broad class of employers generally need not include the discharged debt in income [Code Sec. 108(f)(1)].

For purposes of the exclusion, a student loan is any loan to an individual designed to assist the student in attending an educational organization that qualifies for a tax exemption. Specifically, the loan must be made by one of the following lenders:

- The United States or one of its instrumentalities or agencies;
- A state, territory, or possession of the United States, or the District of Columbia, or any political subdivision;
- A state, county, or municipal hospital that is controlled by an exempt public benefit corporation and whose employees are deemed public employees under state law;
- Any exempt educational organization that receives the funds from which the loans are made from one of the entities listed above; or
- An exempt educational organization under a program that is designed to encourage its students to serve in occupations with unmet needs or in areas with unmet needs and under which the services provided by the students or former students are for or

under the direction of a governmental unit or a tax-exempt organization [Code Sec. 108(f)(2)].

The exclusion applies to forgiveness of loans made by educational organizations and tax-exempt organizations to refinance any existing student loans, and not just loans made by educational organizations, but only if made under a program of the refinancing organization that requires the student to fulfill a public service requirement under the direction of a governmental entity or tax-exempt organization.

Participants in the National Health Service Corps (NHSC) Loan Program may receive repayment of part of their education loans and tax assistance. Participants are required to provide medical service in a geographic area identified by the Public Health Service as having a shortage of health care professionals. States may also provide for education loan repayment programs for persons who agree to provide primary health services in health professional shortage areas. Under the Public Health Service Act, such programs may receive federal grants with respect to such repayment programs if certain requirements are met. Any amounts received by participants in the NHSC loan repayment program and state programs eligible for funds under the Public Health Service Act are excluded from gross income [Code Sec. 108(f)(4)].

Repayments Under State Loan Programs for Health Care Professionals Excluded from Gross Income

In addition to repayments under the National Health Service Corps Loan Program and state repayment programs under the Public Health Service Act, repayments under other state loan repayment or forgiveness programs that are intended to provide for the increased availability of health care services in underserved or health professional shortage areas (as determined by the state) are also excluded from gross income for tax years [Code Sec. 108(f)(4)].

Exception

No exclusion is available if the discharge was made by an educational organization on account of services performed for the organization [Code Sec. 108(f)(3)].

In Rev. Rul. 2008-34,[119] the IRS concluded that a taxpayer's forgiven student loan debt was not discharge of indebtedness income where the student had completed a period of service following graduation under a repayment assistance program that qualified under Code Sec. 108(f). A Loan Repayment Assistance Program operated by the taxpayer's school refinanced his student loans with new loans that forgave part or all of his loans if he agreed to work for minimum periods of time in qualifying public-service positions. The IRS concluded that the refinanced loans did not lose their status as tax-exempt loans because the terms of the refinanced loan required a minimum period of employment in a qualifying public service position and therefore satisfied the requirements of Code Sec. 108(f)(1).

.08 Deferral of COD Income from Reacquisition of Debt Instruments

At the election of the taxpayer, income from the discharge of indebtedness in connection with the reacquisition after December 31, 2008, and before January 1, 2011, of an

---

[119] Rev. Rul. 2008-34, 2008-2 CB 76.

applicable debt instrument is includible in gross income ratably over the five-tax-year period beginning with:

- The fifth tax year following the tax year in which the reacquisition occurs for a reacquisition occurring in 2009, and
- The fourth tax year following the tax year in which the reacquisition occurs for a reacquisition occurring in 2010 [Code Sec. 108(i)(1)].

> ▶ **TAX POINTER:** A taxpayer who elects to defer reporting cancellation of indebtedness income under Code Sec. 108(i)(1) will benefit from the deferral of federal income tax and from not having to reduce any of his or her tax attributes.

Example 2-46: In 2010, Taxpayer reacquires for $6 million notes that it issued with an adjusted issue price of $10 million. Taxpayer elects under Code Sec. 108(i) to include that income over a five-year period. Taxpayer realizes $4 million of debt discharge income, but doesn't recognize all that income in 2010. Instead, it recognizes $800,000 of debt discharge income ($4 million ÷ 5) in each of the five tax years from 2014 to 2018, inclusive.

Applicable Debt Instrument

An "applicable debt instrument" for purpose of the election under Code Sec. 108(i) is any debt instrument issued by a C corporation or by any other person in connection with the conduct of a trade or business by that person [Code Sec. 108(i)(3)(A)]. Debt instrument is broadly defined to include any bond, debenture, note, certificate, or any other instrument or contractual arrangement constituting indebtedness under Code Sec. 1275(a) [Code Sec. 108(i)(3)(B)].

A debt instrument issued by a partnership or an S corporation is an applicable debt instrument if the passthrough entity shows that it meets one of the five safe harbors under Reg. § 1.108(i)-2(d)(1) as follows:

1. The gross fair market value of the trade or business assets of the partnership or S corporation that issued the debt instrument represented at least 80 percent of the gross fair market value of that partnership's or S corporation's total assets on the date of issuance;
2. The trade or business expenditures of the partnership or S corporation that issued the debt instrument represented at least 80 percent of the partnership's or S corporation's total expenditures for the tax year of issuance;
3. At least 95 percent of interest paid or accrued on the debt instrument issued by the partnership or S corporation was allocated to one or more trade or business expenditures under Temp. Reg. § 1.163-8T for the tax year of issuance;
4. At least 95 percent of the proceeds from the debt instrument issued by the partnership or S corporation were used by the partnership or S corporation to acquire one or more trades or businesses within six months from the date of issuance; or
5. The partnership or S corporation issued the debt instrument to a seller of a trade or business to acquire the trade or business.

Reacquisition

A reacquisition means any direct or indirect acquisition of a debt instrument by the debtor or a related person [Code Sec. 108(i)(4)(A)]. Acquisition includes:

- An acquisition of the debt instrument for cash or other property,
- The exchange of the debt instrument for another debt instrument (including a modification of the debt instrument),
- An exchange of the debt instrument for corporate stock or a partnership interest,
- The contribution of the debt instrument to capital, and
- The complete forgiveness of the indebtedness by the holder of the debt instrument [Code Sec. 108(i)(4)(B)].

Mandatory Acceleration Events

An electing corporation's deferred cancellation of indebtedness income is accelerated under Code Sec. 108(i)(5)(D) only if it:

1. Changes in tax status. For example a corporation that makes the election under Code Sec. 108(i) to become an S corporation must take into account its deferred COD income immediately before the S corporation election is effective. Similarly, an electing corporation that elects to be treated as a regulated investment company (RIC) or real estate investment trust (REIT) must take into account its remaining deferred COD income immediately before the election is effective [Reg. § 1.108(i)-1(b)(2)(i)];
2. Cessation of corporation existence in a transaction to which Code Sec. 381(a) does not apply [Reg. § 1.108(i)-1(b)(2)(ii)]; or
3. Engages in a transaction that impairs its ability to pay the tax liability associated with its deferred COD income (the net value acceleration rule) [Reg. § 1.108(i)-1(b)(2)(iii)]. Under the net value acceleration rule, an electing corporation must accelerate its remaining deferred COD income if immediately after an impairment transaction, the gross value of its assets is less than 110 percent of the sum of its total liabilities and the tax on the net amount of its deferred items (the net value floor). Solely for computing the net value floor, the tax on the net amount of the electing corporation's deferred items is determined by applying the highest rate of tax specified for the tax year even though the corporation's actual tax rate of the tax year may differ [Reg. § 1.108(i)-1(b)(2)(iii)(A)].

An electing partnership or S corporation's deferred cancellation of indebtedness income is accelerated if the entity does any of the following:

- Liquidates;
- Sells, exchanges, transfers, or gifts substantially all its assets. "Substantially all" means at least 90 percent of the fair market value of the entity's net assets and at least 70 percent of the fair market value of its gross assets as measured immediately before the sale, exchange, transfer, or gift;
- Ceases doing business;
- Files a bankruptcy petition; or

- In the case of an S corporation, its S corporation election is terminated [Reg. § 1.108(i)-2(c)(3)(i)(A)].

The following events at the partner or S corporation shareholder level trigger acceleration:

- The death or liquidation of the partner, or the death of the shareholder;
- A sale, exchange (including redemption), transfer, or gift of part or all of a separate interest; or
- Abandonment of the interest [Reg. § 1.108-2(c)(3)(ii)].

Election Procedures

A taxpayer makes the Code Sec. 108(i) election to defer debt discharge income from a reacquisition of an applicable debt instrument by including with the income tax return for the tax year in which the debt instrument is reacquired a statement that clearly identifies the instrument and includes the amount of deferred income and any other information required by the IRS [Code Sec. 108(i)(5)(B)(i)]. The election is made on an instrument-by-instrument basis. Once made, the election is irrevocable and generally may not be modified [Code Sec. 108(i)(5)(B)(ii)].

In the case of COD income realized by a partnership, S corporation or other pass-through entity from the reacquisition of an applicable debt instrument, the pass-through entity makes the election [Code Sec. 108(i)(5)(B)(iii)].

▶ **PRACTICE POINTER:** *Benefits of election.* The Code Sec. 108(i) election provides a debtor the ability to elect to recognize COD income on a deferred basis ratably over a five-tax year period. The election is made on a debt-by-debt basis and, once made, is irrevocable. After the election is made, none of the taxpayer's tax attributes have to be reduced as is normally the rule in cases involving discharges of indebtedness that are excluded from gross income. Code Sec. 108(b) requires that the debtor reduce certain tax attributes, including net operating losses, general business credits, minimum tax credits, capital loss carryovers, and basis in property, by the amount of the discharge of indebtedness. In certain reductions of property tax basis, Code Sec. 1017(b)(2) provides that any basis reduction cannot be more than the excess of the total adjusted basis of property over the total liabilities of the debtor immediately after the debt discharge.

IRS Releases Guidance on Election Procedures

In Rev. Proc. 2009-37,[120] the IRS provides the exclusive procedures for electing to defer recognizing cancellation of debt income (COD) under Code Sec. 108(i), including the time and manner for making the election and specific procedures for partnerships, S corporations, and tiered pass-through and foreign entities.

Rev. Proc. 2009-37 provides that a taxpayer makes the Code Sec. 108(i) election by attaching a statement meeting the requirements of Rev. Proc. 2009-37 to its timely filed (including extensions) original federal income tax return for the tax year in which the reacquisition of the applicable debt instrument occurs. The statement must identify information for: the issuer of the debt instruments, the debt instruments

---

120 Rev. Proc. 2009-37, IRB 2009-36, 309.

themselves, the reacquisition transactions, the total COD income for each instrument, and the amount being deferred. The common parent of a consolidated group makes the election on behalf of all members of the group.

A taxpayer may treat two or more applicable debt instruments that are part of the same issue and that are reacquired during the same tax year as one applicable debt instrument for purposes of Rev. Proc. 2009-37. However, a pass-through entity may not treat two or more applicable debt instruments as one instrument if the owners and their ownerships interests in the pass-through entity immediately before the reacquisition of each instrument are not identical.

A taxpayer may make an election to defer only a portion of COD income realized from the reacquisition of any applicable debt instrument. For example, if a taxpayer realizes $100 of COD income from the reacquisition of an applicable debt instrument, the taxpayer may elect to defer only $40 of the $100 of COD income.

¶2150 ALIMONY AND SEPARATE MAINTENANCE

.01 Tax Ramifications

Divorce is such a traumatic experience that taxes are often the last thing people think about. This is a big mistake. The tax consequences of divorce should be considered because failure to do so can be expensive and result in a squandering of much-needed family assets. The three big issues are the tax ramifications of the following three divorce-related transfers: alimony, child support and property settlements. Other important considerations are whether to file separately or jointly until the divorce is final, how to divide retirement savings accounts, and whether the family residence should be sold.

Alimony and separate maintenance payments received from an ex-spouse are includible in the recipient spouse's income and deductible above-the-line by the ex-spouse [Code Secs. 215(a) and 71(b)]. (On the other hand, property settlements are not taxable to the recipient spouse nor deductible by the ex-spouse.) To qualify as deductible alimony or separate maintenance, the payments must meet the following conditions [Code Sec. 71(b)(1); Temp. Reg. § 1.71-1T]:

- The payment must be received by a spouse under a "divorce or separation instrument"[121] which is one of the following:

  a. A final decree of divorce or separate maintenance or a written instrument incident to such a decree;

  b. A written separation agreement (oral separation agreement will not qualify);[122] or,

  c. A temporary (in legal terminology, *pendente lite*) support order requiring one spouse to make alimony or separate maintenance payments to the other spouse

---

[121] *J.J. Faylor*, 105 TCM 1844, Dec. 59,558(M), TC Memo. 2013-143.

[122] *K.P. Larievy*, 104 TCM 241, Dec. 59,174(M), TC Memo. 2012-247.

[Code Sec. 71(c)]. Payments made before the existence of a written divorce or separation instrument are not considered alimony for tax purposes.[123]

- The divorce or separation instrument cannot designate a payment as excludable from the recipient spouse's gross income or nondeductible by the payor spouse.
- The payment must be made in cash to the ex-spouse or to a third party on behalf of the ex-spouse. For example, mortgage payments, taxes, and tuition payments paid on behalf of the payee spouse will qualify as alimony [Temp. Reg. § 1.71-1T(a), Q&A-5 through 7]. The cash requirement is met if the payment is made by check or money order. The Court of Appeals for the Third Circuit held that *pendente lite* support payments deposited into a joint checking account shared by a divorcing couple were alimony includible in the wife's income.[124] Transfers of services or property (including a note of a third party or an annuity contract) or the use of property of the paying spouse do not qualify as alimony payments.
- The payments must end when the recipient spouse dies. This rule exists so alimony payments will not be child support or property settlements in disguise. If the divorce decree fails to state that the payments cease when the payee spouse dies neither the payments made before or after the death of the payee spouse will qualify as deductible alimony.[125]

Example 2-47: Alan must pay Betty $10,000 in cash each year under a divorce decree which states that the payments will terminate when Betty dies. In addition, Alan must pay Betty or her estate $20,000 in cash each year for a period of ten years. Because the $20,000 annual payments will not terminate when Betty dies, these payments will not qualify as deductible alimony payments. However, the annual $10,000 payments will be deductible as alimony.

- The payment cannot be child support in disguise. Child support payments are not deductible. To avoid running afoul of this rule, be sure that the supposed alimony payments don't stop after a key event in a child's life, such as the child's 18th birthday, graduation from school, marriage or death. The IRS would view payments keyed to these pivotal events as nondeductible child support payments.
- Spouses who are legally separated under a decree of divorce or separate maintenance cannot be members of the same household at the time the payments are made [Code Sec. 71(b)(1)(C); Temp. Reg. § 1.71-1T(b), Q&A 9].

  ▶ **EXCEPTIONS:** If you and your ex-spouse are living together, you are not considered members of the same household if one of you is preparing to move out and does, in fact, do so within one month after the payment is made. Also, the living-apart condition does not apply to payments made under a written separation agreement or decree between you if you are not legally separated

---

[123] *M.A. Ali*, 88 TCM 622, Dec. 55,829(M), TC Memo. 2004-284.

[124] *P.P. Kean*, CA-3, 2005-1 USTC ¶ 50,397, 407 F3d 186.

[125] *J.R. Okerson*, 123 TC 258, Dec. 55,742 (2004); *A.M. Sperling*, 97 TCM 1804, Dec. 57,859(M), TC Memo. 2009-141; *J.R. Stedman*, 96 TCM 273, Dec. 57,566(M), TC Memo. 2008-239; *D.W. Rood*, 103 TCM 1668, Dec. 59,038(M), TC Memo. 2012-122; *D. La Point*, 103 TCM 1591, Dec. 59,023(M), TC Memo. 2012-107; *J.D. Nye*, Dec. 59,585(M), TC Memo. 2013-166.

under a divorce or separate maintenance decree [Temp. Reg. §1.71-1T(b), Q&A-9].

- Payments can't violate the excess front-loading rules (below) [Code Sec. 71(f)].

  NOTE: For divorce or separation instruments executed before 1985 that have not been modified the above requirements do not apply. To qualify as alimony under the rules prior to that time, the payments must: (1) be made under a final decree of divorce or separation or a separation agreement, (2) be based on the marital or family relationship, (3) be periodic and (4) not be for child support.

Return Treatment

Alimony is deductible by the paying ex-spouse and includible in the income of the ex-spouse who receives it. Alimony is an above-the-line deduction that is subtracted directly from the payor's gross income [Code Sec. 62(a)(10)]. This means that the payor can deduct it all without any adjusted gross income limitations. Code Sec. 215 authorizes the deduction for "alimony or separate maintenance payments" [Code Sec. 215(a)]. In this situation, "alimony or separate maintenance payments" are defined in Code Sec. 71 [Code Sec. 215(b)]. Under Code Sec. 71, a cash payment will qualify as alimony if: (a) such payment is received by (or on behalf of) a spouse under a divorce or separation instrument; (b) the divorce or separate instrument does not designate the tax treatment of the payments; (c) in the case of an individual legally separated from his spouse under a decree of divorce or of separate maintenance, the payee spouse and the payor spouse are not members of the same household at the time payment is made; and (d) there is no liability to make payments for any period after the death of the payee spouse and there is no liability to substitute payments (in cash or property) after the death of the payee spouse.

The Tax Court has found that temporary support payments made on a second mortgage for a house the former spouse lived in were not deductible as alimony to the extent that they represented nondeductible child support.[126] In another case, the court found that payment of the former spouse's attorney's fee for services rendered in connection with the couple's divorce were not deductible alimony payments because the payor's liability would not have terminated if the payor's spouse had died before the final divorce decree was entered.[127]

In *D.E. Lofstrom*,[128] the Tax Court concluded that an individual who transferred a contract for deed to his former wife in partial satisfaction of accrued and future alimony obligations could not deduct its value as an alimony payment. The contract for deed represented a debt obligation of the couple's son to pay for property that the husband had transferred to him. Since the contract for deed was a third-party debt instrument, it did not qualify as a cash payment and, thus, was not deductible as alimony.

---

[126] *A.R. Zinsmeister*, 80 TCM 774, Dec. 54,137(M), TC Memo. 2000-364, *aff'd per curiam*, CA-8 (unpublished opinion), 2001-2 USTC ¶50,717.

[127] *T.D. Berry*, 80 TCM 825, Dec. 54,147(M), TC Memo. 2000-373, *aff'd per curiam*, CA-10 (unpublished opinion), 2002-1 USTC ¶50,453.

[128] *D.E. Lofstrom*, 125 TC 271, Dec. 56,204 (2005).

Tax Planning Opportunity

The tax rules governing alimony payments provide tax planning opportunities for spouses in different tax brackets. This will occur when the payor spouse is in a higher tax bracket than the recipient spouse. The tax bracket differential allows for larger alimony payments when the after-tax consequences are factored in.

Example 2-48: Ann and Bob divorce. Ann pays Bob alimony. Ann is in the highest income tax bracket while her ex-husband Bob is in the lowest income tax bracket. By deducting the alimony payment, Alice will have a substantial income tax deduction which should be factored in when the amount of the alimony is negotiated.

.02 Excess Front-Loaded Recapture Rules

If the alimony payments decrease substantially or terminate during the first three calendar years of payment beware of the recapture rules [Code Sec. 71(f)]. The IRS may view these as nondeductible property settlements disguised as alimony. In general, a decrease of more than $15,000 from the prior year will trigger the recapture rules. Amounts that have previously been deemed alimony can be recharacterized retroactively. The exact rules depend on whether the divorce or separation instrument was executed after 1986. In either case, though, the paying spouse would have to include in income funds that were previously deducted as alimony. The recipient, on the other hand, may claim a corresponding deduction.

Under the rules for post-1986 divorce or separation instruments, recapture occurs (if at all) in the third year payments are made. That recapture relates to both the first and second year payments. If payments made in the second year exceed third year payments by more than $15,000, the excess must be recaptured. That recaptured amount is then subtracted from the second year's payment. If the first year payment exceeds that averaged sum by more than $15,000, the first year excess is recaptured as well [Code Sec. 71(f)].

Example 2-49: Under a divorce decree, Blake pays Crystal $50,000. He makes no payments in the next two years. Result: $35,000 is recaptured in the third year ($50,000 less $15,000) (assuming no exceptions discussed below apply).

Example 2-50: Assume that Blake in Example 2-49 pays $50,000 in the first year, $20,000 in the second year and $0 in the third year. Result: The recapture amount is $32,500 figured as follows:

1. Alimony paid in 2nd year	$20,000
2. Alimony paid in 3rd year	0
3. Floor	15,000
4. Add lines 2 and 3	15,000
5. Subtract lines 4 from line 1	5,000
6. Alimony paid in 1st year	50,000
7. Adjusted alimony paid in 2nd year (line 1 less line 5)	15,000

8. Alimony paid in 3rd year	0
9. Add lines 7 and 8	15,000
10. Divide line 9 by 2	7,500
11. Floor	15,000
12. Add lines 10 and 11	22,500
13. Subtract line 12 from line 6	27,500
14. Recaptured alimony (add lines 5 and 13)	$32,500

Different recapture rules apply to payments made pursuant to 1985 or 1986 divorce or separation instruments. The payments must be made for at least six consecutive years. If payments made during any of those years were more than $10,000 less than payments made in any prior years during the six-year period, the excess was recaptured as income to the payor—and deducted by the payee. Recaptures reduced the amount deemed to have been paid for calculating recaptures in later years [Temp. Reg. § 1.71-1T(d)].

There is no recapture for alimony paid under pre-1985 divorce and separation instruments.

Exceptions

The recapture rules do not apply if: (1) the payments are made under a support order, (2) the payments stop because you remarry before the end of the third post-separation year, (3) the payments stop because either of you dies before the end of the third post-separation year or (4) the payments are made under a liability (over a period of no fewer than three years) to pay a fixed portion of income from a business or property or from compensation for employment or self-employment [Code Sec. 71(f)(5)].

▶ **TAX PLANNING TIP:** The recapture rules can be avoided by making sure that the alimony payments in the early years are made in three equal installments, thus avoiding the big differentials in payments that trigger the expensive recapture rules.

.03 Property Transfers Incident to Divorce

The transfer of property between spouses incident to a divorce or separation is a nontaxable transaction [Code Sec. 1041(a)]. The transferring spouse (transferor spouse) has no gain or loss when he or she transfers the property to the transferee spouse and the transferee spouse carries over the transferor spouse's basis in the property [Code Sec. 1041(b)]. Thus, if the property has appreciated in value, the gain is not included in income upon the initial transfer and that appreciation will avoid taxation until the transferee spouse disposes of the property. This nontaxable treatment extends to transfers of cash or other property, the assumption of liabilities in excess of basis, and to transfers of installment obligations.

The tax-free rule does not apply if:

- A spouse or former spouse is a nonresident alien [Code Sec. 1041(d)];
- A spouse has transferred an installment obligation to a trust [Code Sec. 453B(g)]; or
- A spouse made transfers to a trust where liability exceeds basis [Code Sec. 1041(e)].

Property Defined

The term *property* has a broad meaning in this context and includes real or personal property, tangible or intangible, or community property. It even includes property acquired after the end of a marriage and transferred to a former spouse. It does not, however, include services.

Transfers to Third Parties Sanctioned

The three situations in which the transfer of property by one spouse to a third party will be considered transfers "incident to a divorce" are as follows:

- The transfer is required by the divorce or separation instrument,
- The transfer to the third party is based on a written request from the nontransferor spouse, or
- The transferor spouse receives from the transferee spouse written consent or ratification of the transfer to the third party [Temp. Reg. § 1.1041-1T(c), Q&A-9].

A transfer between spouses or former spouses will be "incident to a divorce" if it occurs within one year of the divorce or is "related to the cessation of the marriage." A property transfer will be related to the ending of a marriage if it is made under an original or modified divorce or separation instrument or occurs within six years after the date the marriage ends [Code Sec. 1041(c); Temp. Reg. § 1.1041-1T(b)]. The transfer of property by an individual to his former wife pursuant to an agreement in settlement of a judgment obtained by the wife with respect to the husband's violation of their original property and divorce settlement was a transfer "incident to their divorce."[129] In Letter Ruling 200709014, the IRS ruled that a proposed transfer of stock from a former husband to his former wife pursuant to an agreement modifying the original property settlement agreement did not result in either taxable income or a taxable gift to either party.

Transfers of Nonstatutory Stock Options/Nonqualified Deferred Compensation

Transfers of nonstatutory stock options and nonqualified deferred compensation to a former spouse incident to a divorce will not be taxed. In addition, payroll taxes need not be paid at the time of the transfer but may have to be paid at a later time.[130] When the stock option is finally exercised, or the deferred compensation distributed, it is the spouse who received the transfer in divorce who pays the income tax. The transfer of interests in nonstatutory stock options and in nonqualified deferred compensation from the employee spouse to the nonemployee spouse incident to a divorce will not result in a payment of wages for FICA and FUTA tax purposes. Rather, the nonstatutory stock options are subject to FICA and FUTA taxes when the nonemployee spouses exercises the options to the same extent they would be had the employee spouse retained the options and exercised them himself. The exercise results in FICA wages to the extent that the fair market value of the stock received pursuant to the exercise of the option exceeds the option exercise price.

.04 Divorce-Related Stock Redemptions

A common issue for divorcing couples who jointly own a business operated in corporate form is the tax treatment of the transfer of stock incident to a divorce.

---

[129] *L.F. Young*, CA-4, 2001-1 USTC ¶ 50,244, 240 F3d 369, *aff'g*, 113 TC 152, Dec. 53,509.

[130] Rev. Rul. 2002-22, 2002-1 CB 849; Rev. Rul. 2004-60, 2004-1 CB 1051.

When couples transfer stock incident to a divorce, it is often structured as a stock redemption whereby the transferor spouse transfers stock directly to, and receives payment for the redeemed shares from, the corporation. The tax consequences of each deemed transfer are determined under applicable Code provisions as if the spouses had actually made the transfers. Accordingly, Code Sec. 1041 applies to any deemed transfer of the stock and redemption proceeds between the transferor spouse and the nontransferor spouse, provided its requirements are otherwise satisfied for the deemed transfer. It does not apply to any deemed transfer of stock by the nontransferor spouse to the redeeming corporation in exchange for the redemption proceeds. Rather, such a deemed transfer is governed by the regular rules for redemption [Reg. § 1.1041-2(b)(2)].

Redemptions of Stock Not Resulting in Constructive Distributions

If a corporation redeems stock owned by a transferor spouse and that spouse's receipt of property in exchange for such redeemed stock is not treated as resulting in a constructive distribution to the nontransferor spouse, then the transferor spouse will be treated as having received a distribution from the corporation in redemption of stock [Reg. § 1.1041-2(a)(1)].

Redemptions of Stock Resulting in Constructive Distributions

If a corporation redeems stock owned by a transferor spouse, and the transferor spouse's receipt of property in respect of such redeemed stock is treated, under applicable tax law, as resulting in a constructive distribution to the nontransferor spouse, then the redeemed stock shall be deemed first to be transferred by the transferor spouse to the nontransferor spouse and then transferred by the nontransferor spouse to the redeeming corporation. Any property actually received by the transferor spouse from the redeeming corporation in respect of the redeemed stock shall be deemed first to be transferred by the corporation to the nontransferor spouse in redemption of such spouse's stock and then transferred by the nontransferor spouse to the transferor spouse [Reg. § 1.1041-2(a)(2)].

Agreements Causing Transferor Spouse to Be Taxed

A transferor spouse's receipt of property for redeemed stock is treated as a distribution to the transferor spouse in redemption of the stock and is not treated as resulting in a constructive distribution to the nontransferor spouse, if a divorce or separation instrument, or a valid written agreement between the transferor spouse and the nontransferor spouse, expressly provides that:

- Both spouses or former spouses intend for the redemption to be treated, for Federal income tax purposes, as a redemption distribution to the transferor spouse; and
- Such instrument or agreement supersedes any other instrument or agreement concerning the purchase, sale, redemption, or other disposition of the stock that is the subject of the redemption [Reg. § 1.1041-2(c)(1)].

Agreement Causing Nontransferor Spouse to Be Taxed

A transferor spouse's receipt of property for redeemed stock is treated as resulting in a constructive distribution to the nontransferor spouse, and is not treated as a distribution to the transferor spouse in redemption of the stock, if a divorce or separation instrument, or a valid written agreement between the transferor spouse and the nontransferor spouse, expressly provides that:

- Both spouses or former spouses intend for the redemption to be treated as resulting in a constructive distribution to the nontransferor spouse; and
- The instrument or agreement supersedes any other instrument or agreement concerning the purchase, sale, redemption, or other disposition of the stock that is the subject of the redemption [Reg. § 1.1041-2(c)(2)].

Example 2-51: Corporation X has 100 shares outstanding. A and B each own 50 shares. A and B divorce. The divorce instrument requires B to purchase A's shares, and A to sell A's shares to B, in exchange for $100x. Corporation X redeems A's shares for $100x. B has a primary and unconditional obligation to purchase A's stock, and therefore the stock redemption results in a constructive distribution to B. A will be treated as transferring A's stock of Corporation X to B in a transfer to which Code Sec. 1041 applies. B shall be treated as transferring the Corporation X stock B is deemed to have received from A to Corporation X in exchange for $100x in a transfer to which Code Sec. 1041 does not apply, but Code Secs. 302(d) and 301 apply. Finally, B shall be treated as transferring the $100x to A in a transfer to which Code Sec. 1041 applies.

Example 2-52: Assume the same facts as Example 2-51, except that the divorce instrument provides as follows: "A and B agree that the redemption will be treated for Federal income tax purposes as a redemption distribution to A." The divorce instrument further provides that it "supersedes all other instruments or agreements concerning the purchase, sale, redemption, or other disposition of the stock that is the subject of the redemption." The tax consequences of the redemption shall be determined in accordance with its form as a redemption of A's shares by Corporation X and shall not be treated as resulting in a constructive distribution to B.

Example 2-53: Assume the same facts as Example 2-51, except that the divorce instrument requires A to sell A's shares to Corporation X in exchange for a note. B guarantees Corporation X's payment of the note. Assume that B does not have a primary and unconditional obligation to purchase A's stock, and therefore the stock redemption does not result in a constructive distribution to B. The tax consequences of the redemption will be determined in accordance with its form as a redemption of A's shares by Corporation X under Code Sec. 302.

Example 2-54: Assume the same facts as Example 2-53, except that the divorce instrument provides as follows: "A and B agree the redemption shall be treated, for Federal income tax purposes, as resulting in a constructive distribution to B." The divorce instrument further provides that it "supersedes any other instrument or agreement concerning the purchase, sale, redemption, or other disposition of the stock that is the subject of the redemption." The redemption is treated as resulting in a constructive distribution to B and A shall be treated as transferring A's stock of Corporation X to B in a transfer to which Code Sec.

1041 applies. B shall be treated as transferring the Corporation X stock B is deemed to have received from A to Corporation X in exchange for a note in an exchange to which Code Sec. 1041 does not apply and Code Secs. 302(d) and 301 apply, and B shall be treated as transferring the note to A in a transfer to which Code Sec. 1041 applies.

▶ **PRACTICE POINTER:** In situations where divorce-related stock redemption are likely to occur, tax practitioners should make certain that the potential tax consequences of the stock transfers are adequately addressed in the divorce settlement agreement. In a situation where the terms of the divorce agreement required a spouse to transfer the stock to the corporation, the court found that the stock transfer was made "on behalf of" the other spouse because it relieved him of the obligation to purchase the stock. Accordingly, the stock transfer was treated as if the transferring spouse had transferred the stock directly to her former spouse, thereby qualifying for nonrecognition of gain under Code Sec. 1041.[131]

.05 Child Support Payments

A child support payment is one that the terms of the divorce or separation instrument fix as a sum payable for the support of children of the payor spouse. Child support payments will not be treated as alimony and are therefore not deductible by the payor spouse and will not be treated as income by the recipient spouse [Code Sec. 71(c)(1)].[132]

An amount specified in a divorce or separation instrument will be treated as a fixed payment made for child support (and therefore will not be deductible as alimony) to the extent the amount is to be reduced either:

- When a contingency, specified in the instrument, relating to a child or payor occurs; or
- At a time that can clearly be associated with such a contingency [Code Sec. 71(c)(2)(B)].

A contingency relates to a child if it depends on any event relating to that child, regardless of the likelihood that the event may occur. Events that relate to a child include the following: the child's attaining a specified age or income level, dying, marrying, leaving school, leaving the spouse's household, or gaining employment [Temp. Reg. § 1.71-1T(c), Q&A 17].

Example 2-55: Alan and Barbara are divorced when their son Dan is 14 years old. Under the divorce decree, Alan is required to make alimony payments to Barbara of $2,000 per month. The payments meet all the requirements to qualify as deductible alimony. However, the decree also provides that the payments are to be reduced to $1,500 per month after their son turns 21. As a result of this contingency, $500 per month will be treated as fixed for the support of Dan and

---

131 *L.K.B. Craven*, CA-11, 2000-2 USTC ¶ 50,541, 215 F3d 1201; *C.M. Read*, 114 TC 14, Dec. 53,736 (2000). *See also M.R. Hayes*, 101 TC 593, Dec. 49,514 (1993); *J.A. Arnes*, 102 TC 522, Dec. 49,765 (1994); *G.T. Blatt*, 102 TC 77, Dec. 49,641 (1994).

132 *J. Gilbert*, 85 TCM 1087, Dec. 55,100(M), TC Memo. 2003-92, *aff'd*, CA-3 (unpublished opinion), 2004-1 USTC ¶ 50,227.

therefore will not qualify as alimony or separate maintenance payments. Instead, $500 per month will be treated as nondeductible child support and only $1,500 per month will be deductible as alimony [Temp. Reg. 1.71-1T].

Fixed child support is an amount designated as such, specifically for a child only, in the divorce or separation agreement. The payment may be a fixed amount or a fixed portion of a payment. In *J.D. Lawton*,[133] where support was designated in a court order as "for support of spouse and one child," the Tax Court concluded that the support payments were not child support because the payment was not a designated fixed amount only for the child.

If an ex-spouse makes a payment for less than the full amount called for under the agreement, the amounts are allocated first to child support and then to alimony [Code Sec. 71(c)(3)].

Example 2-56: Joe Brown's divorce decree requires that he pay $500 a month alimony to his wife and $500 in child support for their son, Billy. Because of strained finances, Joe pays a total of $9,000 to his wife in 2000. Of this amount, Joe can deduct only $3,000 because the first $6,000 is allocated to child support ($500 × 12 months).

¶2155 GAMBLING INCOME

Taxpayers must include in income their total gambling winnings regardless of the amount and regardless of whether or not they receive a Form W-2G, *Certain Gambling Winnings*, or any other information return from the payor of the gambling winnings. The winnings can include the proceeds from lotteries, raffles, horse races, casinos, sweepstakes, and the like. In addition, slot machine winnings are subject to tax.[134]

The payer must give the gambler a Form W-2G if he or she receives:

- $1,200 or more in gambling winnings from bingo or slot machines;
- $1,500 or more in proceeds (the amount of winnings minus the amount of the wager) from keno;
- More than $5,000 in winnings (reduced by the wager or buy-in) from a poker tournament;
- $600 or more in gambling winnings (except winnings from bingo, keno, slot machines, and poker tournaments) and the payout is at least 300 times the amount of the wager; or
- Any other gambling winnings subject to federal income tax withholding.

---

[133] *J.D. Lawton*, 78 TCM 153, Dec. 53,469(M), TC Memo. 1999-243.

[134] *V. Lyszkowski*, 69 TCM 2751, Dec. 50,666(M), TC Memo. 1995-235, *aff'd*, CA-3 (unpublished order), 96-1 USTC ¶50,170, 79 F3d 1138.

Under Code Sec. 3402(q)(3)(C)(i), payors must withhold proceeds of more than $5,000 from a sweepstakes, wagering pool or lottery (other than a state-conducted lottery, covered by another withholding rule). The withholding rate is equal to the third lowest rate applicable to single filers under Code Sec. 1(c). Proceeds from a wager are determined by reducing the amount received by the amount of the wager [Code Sec. 3402(q)(4)(A)].

Poker tournament sponsors (including casinos) paying amounts to winners must report under Code Sec. 3402(q) winnings of more than $5,000 on Form W-2G, *Certain Gambling Winnings*. Tournament sponsors that comply with the new reporting requirement will not be required to withhold federal income tax at the end of the tournament. However, if a sponsor fails to report the winnings, the IRS will not only enforce the reporting requirement, it will also require the sponsor to pay any tax that would have been withheld from the winner if the withholding requirement had been followed. Tournament winners are required to supply their taxpayer identification numbers (usually their Social Security numbers) to the tournament sponsor. In the event that the winner fails to provide this information, the sponsor must withhold federal income tax at the rate of 28 percent.[135]

Taxpayers may deduct their gambling losses on Schedule A, *Itemized Deductions*. The deduction is limited to the amount of the taxpayer's winnings. The taxpayer must report his or her winnings as income and claim any allowable losses separately. The taxpayer cannot reduce winnings by the amount of total losses and report the difference. For further discussion of the tax treatment of gambling losses, see ¶ 13,080.

If an individual using the cash receipts and disbursements method of accounting receives lottery, gambling, or sweepstakes winnings payable over a period of at least 10 years and is given an option, exercisable no later than 60 days after the individual becomes entitled to the winnings, to receive the winnings as a single cash payment, that right will not cause the individual to have to include the amount of the single cash payment in gross income even though the individual actually receives the qualified prize over a period of years [Code Sec. 451(h)(1)].

¶2160 INCOME IN RESPECT OF A DECEDENT

Amounts that the decedent had the right to receive, and could have received had death not occurred, are treated as *income in respect of a decedent.* This includes income that a cash basis taxpayer had accrued at the time of death (i.e., accounts receivable or interest on a discount bond) and claims to income that were contingent at death. These items are taxed as income to the decedent's successor upon receipt [Code Sec. 691(a); Reg. § 1.691(a)-1, 2].

Example 2-57: Mr. Stone, a cash basis taxpayer, purchased a U.S. Savings Bond five years before his death. He paid no tax on the interest accruing on it during his lifetime. Mrs. Stone inherited the bond. When she cashes it in, Mrs. Stone

[135] Rev. Proc. 2007-57, IRB 2007-36, 547.

will be taxed on all interest that accrued on the bond during Mr. Stone's lifetime—as well as earnings allocable to her period of ownership.

For further discussion of income in respect of a decedent, see Estate and Gift Tax Handbook ¶ 720.

¶2165 S CORPORATION, PARTNERSHIP, AND LIMITED LIABILITY COMPANY PASSTHROUGH INCOME

S corporations, partnerships, and limited liability companies are so-called passthrough entities. Generally, they pay no tax because their income is passed through to (and taxed to) their shareholders or partners.

.01 S Corporations

Each shareholder must report his or her pro rata share of the S corporation's income—regardless of whether any of that income is actually distributed to the shareholder. The shareholder's basis is increased by that share of income. If a distribution is made, it is generally tax-free to the extent of the shareholder's basis, with the excess being treated as capital gain. However, a distribution from accumulated earnings and profits (for example, E&P accumulated prior to the corporation switching from C to S status) is taxable as a dividend.

Example 2-58: S corporation distributes $50,000 cash to shareholder Smith. S corp has $10,000 accumulated E&P and no "accumulated adjustments account." Smith's stock basis is $25,000. Result: $10,000 of the distribution is taxable to Smith as a dividend from E&P. As for the remaining $40,000, $25,000 is a tax-free return of Smith's stock basis and $15,000 is taxable capital gain.

For more information on S corporation passthrough income, see Chapter 21.

.02 Partnerships

A partner's income includes his or her distributive share of "separately stated items" and the partnership's taxable income, even if the partner does not actually receive any distribution. (A partner's distributive share is usually fixed by the partnership agreement.) A partner does not generally recognize gain on a distribution of partnership property (until the partner sells the property). But a partner does recognize gain to the extent a cash distribution exceeds the adjusted basis of his or her partnership interest.

Example 2-59: XYZ Partnership distributes $8,000 in cash and property worth $3,000 to Mr. Brady, who has a $10,000 basis in his partnership interest. Result: Brady recognizes no gain. However, if Brady had received $11,000 in cash, he would have recognized $1,000 of capital gains.

For more information on partnership passthrough income, see Chapter 24.

.03 Limited Liability Companies

The limited liability company (LLC) is a relatively new entity form which is often the entity of choice because it offers the best of both the corporate and partnership world. The LLC, which is a statutory creation, combines the limited liability benefit of corporations with the major tax benefit of doing business as a partnership—the ability to pass through taxable income, losses and credits to the partner level.

Like a partnership the LLC avoids tax at the entity level and passes through taxable income, losses and credits to the "member" level. In the LLC context, "member" means a person who owns an interest in the LLC and is the functional equivalent of a partner or shareholder. The members of an LLC have the discretion to decide how they want to share profit and losses provided the agreement is reflected in the LLC's operating agreement. If the members fail to agree (or don't execute an operating agreement), they will share profits and losses based on the percentage of value that the contribution of each member bears to the total contribution made to the LLC by all of the members.

For more information on taxation of limited liability companies, see Chapter 30.

¶2170 CHILD'S INCOME—KIDDIE TAX

Wages that a child receives for services performed and any other income (not gifts) are included in his or her gross income and not in the parent's gross income, even if, under state law, the parent is entitled to and receives that income [Code Sec. 73(a); Reg. § 1.73-1(a)].[136] Keep in mind however, before a kid is put on the payroll, that the employment must be bona fide and the salary must be reasonable in relation to the services performed by the child. Payments for board and lodging received by a parent from an employed child are income to the parent only to the extent they exceed the cost of household expenses attributable to the child.

.01 Kiddie Tax

The kiddie tax was created by Congress to eliminate the transfer by wealthy parents of income-producing investment property from the parents' high marginal tax rate to the child's generally lower tax bracket, thereby reducing the family's overall income tax liability. The kiddie tax put the kibosh on this scheme by applying the parents' highest tax rates on the child's unearned income.

It is important to note that only a child's "unearned income" is subject to the kiddie tax. Earned income includes wages, tips, contract service income, self-employment net income, and other payments for personal services performed. Unearned income is generally a taxpayer's investment income, e.g., interest, dividends, capital gains, rents, royalties, Social Security, and beneficiary distributions. Thus, even if a child has unearned income subject to the kiddie tax, any earned income from part-time employment or summer jobs will be taxed at the child's own tax bracket which is usually lower than his parents' tax bracket.

---

[136] *M. Marinaccio*, 8 TCM 335, Dec. 16,910(M) (1949).

In 2013, the kiddie tax applies to all children under the age of 18 and to children aged 19-23 if: (1) the child is a full-time student before the close of the tax year, and (2) the child's earned income does not exceed one-half of his or her support [Code Sec. 1(g)(2)(A)(ii)(II)]. When determining the amount of support that a qualifying student provides, scholarships are not taken into account [Code Sec. 152(f)(5)]. The exception to the kiddie tax based on earned income will not apply to a child under age 18, regardless of the amount of support provided through his or her own earned income [Code Sec. 1(g)(2)(A)(ii)(I)]. Thus, a child will not be subject to the kiddie tax if he works and earns enough income to cover half of the amount of support he receives from his parents. When this occurs, however, the parents cannot claim a dependency deduction for him.

If a parent has more than one child subject to the kiddie tax, the net unearned income of all children is combined, and a single kiddie tax is calculated. Each child is then allocated a proportionate share of the hypothetical increase, based upon the child's net unearned income relative to the aggregate net unearned income of all of the parent's children subject to the tax.

The following list summarizes when the net investment income of a child will be subject to the kiddie tax in 2013, assuming that he or she has a living parent and does not file a joint return:

- 17 years old or younger—will continue to be subject to the kiddie tax regardless of the amount of his or her own support provided with earned income;
- 18 year-old—subject to the kiddie tax unless the child provides more than one-half of his or her own support with earned income;
- 19 to 23 year-old—subject to the kiddie tax unless the child is a student and provides more than half of his or her own support with earned income.

▶ **PRACTICE POINTERS:** The child must file a separate return on Form 8615, *Tax for Certain Children Who Have Investment Income of More Than $2,000,* to report his or her income unless the parent elects to include the child's income on the parent's return.

Parents should file Form 8814, *Parent's Election to Report Child's Interest and Dividends,* if the parent elects to report the child's unearned income on the parent's return. If the election is made, the child is treated as having no income and does not have to file a return for the tax year.

To avoid kiddie tax exposure on a child's investments, parents should consider investments for children that will appreciate in value but generate little or no taxable income. Candidates would include the following: undeveloped or vacant land with growth potential but generating no rental income; high-growth, low-dividend stocks and funds that pay few dividends; stocks in closely held family businesses; tax-free municipal bonds; and U.S. series EE savings bonds where the interest is deferred until the bond is cashed in.

Parents should consider employing their children in a family trade or business and paying them a reasonable wage so that the income received by the children is earned income and not subject to the kiddie tax. A child's wages are always taxed at the child's tax rate. This strategy may also help children towards earning one-half of their support and thus not be subject to the kiddie tax under

Code Sec. 1(g)(2)(A)(ii)(II). In addition, the business could claim deductions for the amount of ordinary and necessary wages paid to children who are working in the business. Moreover, self-employed individuals can employ their own children under age 18 and do not have to pay FICA [Code Sec. 3121(b)(3)(A)]. If the child is under 21, they do not have to pay FUTA taxes [Code Sec. 3306(C)(5)].

Consider making contributions to alternative tax-deferred investments, such as traditional/Roth IRAs, Coverdell ESAs, or college savings plans because these nest eggs do not generate taxable investment income. Although a child must have earned income to contribute to a traditional or Roth IRA, there is nothing to stop a parent from supplying a portion of the amount contributed to the retirement plan.

Standard Deduction Claimed by Dependent Child

Although a dependent child is not entitled to a personal exemption on his or her tax return, the dependent child is entitled to claim a $1,000 standard deduction in 2013. A dependent child with earned income over $1,000 may claim a deduction limited to the lesser of: (1) the basic standard deduction for a single taxpayer ($6,100 in 2013) or (2) the greater of $1,000 (in 2013) or the dependent's earned income plus $300 [Code Sec. 631(c)(5)(B); ¶ 1035]. If your rate is not known when your child's return is filed, a reasonable estimate should be made and an amended return filed when the correct information is ascertained. The kiddie tax, which applies to unearned income totaling $2,000 in 2013 by children under age 18 (under 24 if full-time student in 2013) years, divides a child's unearned income into three pieces as listed in Table 2.

Table 2. Tax Rates on Unearned Income of Children with No Earned Income

Amount of Unearned Income	Tax Rate
0-$1,000	No tax—sheltered by child's minimum standard deduction
$1,001-$2,000	Taxed at 10%
Over $2,000	Taxed at parent's rate

[Code Sec. 1(g); Temp. Reg. § 1.1(i)-1T]. Use Form 8615 when computing tax on a child's 2013 investment income of more than $2,000.

.02 Parent's Election to Report Child's Unearned Income

If you are a parent of a child under age 18 who must file a return, you may be able to elect to include the child's interest and dividend income (including capital gain distributions from mutual funds) on your own federal income tax return. In order to make this election, you must attach a separate Form 8814 or Form 1040NR for each child for whom the election has been made. You may make the election for one or more of your children and not for others. Note, however that you cannot make this election if you file Form 1040A or 1040EZ. Alternatively, your child may file his or her own return on Form 8615.

In 2013, you are eligible to make the election to include your child's interest and dividend income on your tax return file by attaching Form 8814 to your return only if all the following conditions are met:

- The child was under age 19 (or under age 24 if a full-time student) at the end of 2013.

- The child's only income was from interest and dividends, including capital gain distributions and Alaska Permanent Fund dividends.
- The child's gross income for 2013 was less than $10,000.
- The child is required to file a 2013 return.
- The child does not file a joint return for 2013.
- There were no estimated tax payments for the child for 2013 (including any overpayment of tax from his or her 2012 return applied to 2013 estimated tax).
- There was no federal income tax withheld from the child's income.

.03 Consequences of Election to Include Child's Unearned Income on Parent's Return

The tax consequences of making the election on Form 8814 and including the child's unearned income on the parent's return are as follows:

- *AGI-related tax breaks affected.* The parent's adjusted gross income will be increased and could therefore reduce deductions or other tax breaks of the parent's that are related to adjusted gross income. Affected items could include deductions for medical expenses, casualty losses, traditional IRA and Roth IRA contributions; student loan interest; miscellaneous itemized deductions; itemized deductions; personal exemptions; the credit for child and dependent care expenses; the child credit; the earned income credit; the adoption credit; education credits; the exclusion for employer-provided adoption assistance; and the exclusion for interest on savings bonds used for education.
- *Capital losses.* If the child has dividends from capital gain distributions these amounts will now be included on the parent's tax return. This could reduce the family's overall tax bill if the parents have excess net capital losses that they are unable to claim because they do not have enough offsetting capital gain. Code Sec. 1211(b) provides that an individual may deduct capital losses only to the extent of capital gains plus (if the losses exceed the gains) the lower of (1) $3,000 ($1,500 for married individual filing separate returns), or (2) the excess of the losses over the gains.

  Example 2-60: Husband and Wife sold stock which resulted in a capital loss of $25,000. In the year of the sale, they had no other capital gains or capital losses. They have no children. Their taxable income that year was $235,000. On Schedule D attached to their joint federal income tax return, they can deduct only $3,000 of the capital loss against their ordinary income (salary and interest income). The unused portion of the capital loss must be carried over to the next year where it will be treated as if it had been incurred in that year. Any remaining unused capital loss can be carried over to later years until it is completely used up. Assume, however, that they have a son aged 10 who had $10,000 capital gain distributions and his parents make the election to include the child's unearned on their federal income tax return. In this situation, the parent's capital loss deduction would be increased by $10,000 because capital losses are deductible to the extent of any capital gain. They could still deduct $3,000 against ordinary income and carry over the remaining balance to the next tax year. Thus the parent's total capital loss deductions would be increased to $13,000 as a result of the election.

- *Estimated taxes.* In determining the amount of estimated tax that the parents must pay, the child's income must be considered.
- *Alternative minimum tax.* If the child has substantial interest income from tax exempt private activity bonds, that income would be subject to the AMT in the child's hands. If the parents make an election to include the child's unearned income on their own return, that income will not be subject to the AMT as a result of the parent's higher AMT exemption. See ¶ 16,015.
- *Increased investment interest deduction.* As a result of including the child's unearned income on the parent's income tax return, the parents may be able to claim a greater investment interest deduction. This will occur because the deduction for investment interest is limited to the amount of the taxpayer's net investment income. Investment income will include your child's interest and dividend income that you choose to report on your return.
- *Increased charitable deduction.* As a result of including the child's unearned income on the parent's income tax return, the parents may be able to claim a greater charitable deduction. Your deduction for charitable contributions is generally limited to 50 percent of your adjusted gross income.

.04 Child Files Own Return

Instead of including your child's interest and dividend income (including capital gain distributions from mutual funds) on your own tax return, your child may file his or her own return and calculate the "kiddie tax" using Form 8615, *Tax for Certain Children Who Have Investment Income of More Than $2,000,* if all of the following conditions are met:

- The child had more than $2,000 of investment income.
- The child is required to file a tax return.
- The child was either (a) under age 18 at the end of 2012, (b) age 18 at the end of 2013 and did not have earned income that was more than half of the child's support, or (c) a full-time student over age 18 and under age 24 at the end of 2013 and did not have earned income that was more than half of the child's support.
- At least one of the child's parents was alive at the end of 2013.
- The child does not file a joint return for 2013.

If you and your spouse file separate tax returns, the larger of your taxable income goes on Form 8615. If you are separated or divorced, the income of the parent who has custody of the child for the greater part of the year is used on the form.

Consequences of Child Filing Own Return

Alternative minimum tax exposure. Watch out for alternative minimum tax (AMT) exposure if your child claims accelerated depreciation, has interest income from a specified private activity, has a passive activity, or receives distributions from estates or trusts. Before you can complete your child's Form 8615, you must determine your own taxable income. See Ch. 3.

Parent's tax computation unaffected. The kiddie tax computation on Form 8615 does not affect the child's parent's tax liability or tax computation in any way. For this reason, it may be a better choice for the child to file his or her own return rather than the parents making the election to include the child's investment income on their return. For a child who has itemized deductions of more than $1,000 that are directly connected with the production of investment income, the $2,000 exemption is increased. Thus, if a child files his or her own tax return and the kiddie tax is computed on Form 8615, the parent's top rate applies to net investment income, i.e., gross investment income (all taxable income except compensation for personal services) minus $2,000 if the child does not have itemized deductions. However, if the child itemizes deductions and has more than $1,000 of deductions directly connected to the production of investment income, the floor for the exemption amount equals $1,000 plus directly connected itemized deductions (i.e., expenses paid to produce or collect income or to manage, conserve, or maintain income-producing property) in excess of 2 percent of the child's adjusted gross income. If after you subtract the directly connected itemized deductions, your child's net investment income exceeds her taxable income, you apply the tax to the lower taxable income, not to the net investment income. [Code Sec. 1(g)(4)]. If the directly connected itemized deductions are $1,000 or less, the regular $2,000 exemption applies.

> **Example 2-61:** Sally Johnson, 13 years old, has $4,100 of investment income, $1,500 of itemized deductions (net of the 2-percent floor) related to producing that income and no earned income. Thus, Sally has $1,600 of income ($4,100 – $1,500 – $1,000 (standard deduction)) subject to "kiddie tax." The first $1,000 will be taxed at 10 percent and the balance taxed at her parents' tax rate.

> **Example 2-62:** Joe Jones, age 13, has $2,500 of interest income. He has $800 of itemized deductions (e.g., state income tax and charitable contributions) and no earned income. These deductions are not related to the production of unearned income. Therefore, no more than $800 of them may be used to shelter that income. Thus, his net unearned income taxed at his parents' tax rate is $1,500 ($2,500 – $1,000). As in Example 2-61, $1,000 is also taxed in the child's own bracket.

¶2185 BUSINESS INSURANCE PROCEEDS

The tax treatment of business insurance proceeds depends on the nature of the loss. Insurance payments for business property destroyed by a casualty are treated much like proceeds from the sale of the property. Only the amount by which they exceed the property's basis is included in income—not the gross insurance payment. And it is possible to avoid having to report even that excess by rolling over the full proceeds into the purchase of similar property [Ch. 7]. If the proceeds are less than the property's basis, they reduce the deductible loss. See Ch. 13.

Ordinarily, proceeds of insurance against loss of profits because of a fire or other casualty are income—as the profits themselves would have been. Use and occupancy insurance and business interruption insurance proceeds are examples [Ch. 7].[137]

.01 Treatment of Death Benefits from Employer-Owned Life Insurance (EOLI)

The proceeds from a life insurance contract that are paid by reason of the death of the insured are generally excluded from gross income [Code Sec. 101(a)]. The exclusion applies regardless of who the beneficiary is, whether a family member or other individual, a corporation or a partnership. An exception to this general rule exists when employers buy life insurance policies on the lives of employees. These arrangements are known as employer-owned life insurance (EOLI) policies and Code Sec. 101(j) makes taxable the death benefits paid with respect to many EOLI policies. Code Sec. 101(j)(1) limits the the amount excluded from gross income of an *applicable policyholder* with respect to an employer-owned life insurance contract so that it may not exceed the premiums and other amounts paid by the policyholder for the life insurance policy [Code Sec. 101(j)(1)]. Thus, the excess death benefit is included in income.

Applicable Policyholder Defined

An applicable policyholder is the person engaged in commonly-controlled trades or businesses that owns the contract, if the person is engaged in a trade or business, and if the person is a beneficiary of the contract [Code Sec. 101(j)(3)(B)].

EOLI Contract Defined

An EOLI contract is defined as a life insurance contract that: (1) is owned by a person engaged in a trade or business and that person (or a related person) is a beneficiary under the contract and (2) covers the life of the individual who is an employee of the trade or business of the applicable policyholder on the date the contract was issued [Code Sec. 101(j)(3)(A)]. If coverage for each insured under a master contract is treated as a separate contract, coverage for each insured will also be treated as a separate contract.

Exceptions

The income inclusion rule does not apply to an amount received by reason of the death of an insured individual who, with respect to the applicable policyholder, was an employee at any time during the 12-month period before the insured's death, or who, at the time the contract was issued, was:

1. A director,
2. A highly compensated employee (determined without regard to the election regarding the top-paid 20 percent of employees), or

---

[137] *Oppenheim's Inc.*, DC-MI, 50-1 USTC ¶ 9249, 90 FSupp 107; Rev. Rul. 55-264, 1955-1 CB 11.

3. A highly compensated individual as defined by the rules relating to self-insured medical reimbursement plans, who is in a group of the highest paid 35 percent of employees [Code Sec. 101(j)(2)].

Information Returns

Applicable policyholders are required to report to the IRS on an annual basis:

1. The number of employees of the applicable policyholder at the end of the year;
2. The number of employees insured under employer-owned life insurance contracts at the end of the year;
3. The total amount of insurance in force at the end of the year under such contracts;
4. The name, address, and taxpayer identification number of the applicable policyholder and the type of business in which it is engaged; and
5. A statement that the applicable policyholder has a valid consent for each insured employee or, if not all consents were obtained, the total number of insured employees who did not provide a valid consent [Code Sec. 6039I].

The *applicable policyholder* must maintain all records necessary to determine whether the requirements of the reporting rule and the income inclusion rule are met.

Notice and Consent Requirement

Notice 2009-24[138] provides that the notice and consent requirements of Code Sec. 101(j)(4) are met if, before the issuance of the policy, the employee:

1. Is notified in writing that the applicable policyholder intends to insure the employee's life and of the maximum face amount for which the employee could be insured at the time the contract was issued,
2. Provides written consent to being insured under the contract and that such coverage may continue after the insured terminates employment, and
3. Is informed in writing that an applicable policyholder will be a beneficiary of any proceeds payable upon the death of the employee.

¶2190 RECOVERY OF TAX BENEFIT ITEMS

When you recover an amount attributable to a prior year's deduction, the amount is included in your income only to the extent it reduced your tax liability in the earlier year [Code Sec. 111(a)]. Here are some of the more common items to which this rule applies:

.01 State and Local Income Tax Refunds

These refunds are taxable (1) if you claimed the refunded taxes as an itemized deduction and (2) only to the extent your itemized deductions exceeded your standard deduction for the year those taxes were previously deducted.

---

[138] Notice 2009-48, IRB 2009-24, 1085.

Example 2-63: Mr. Benson had $500 of state income taxes withheld from his paychecks for the year and claimed the standard deduction on his tax return. During the following year, Benson received a $200 refund of those state tax payments. The refund is excluded from gross income since it did not reduce Benson's taxable income in the year that the deduction was claimed.

Example 2-64: Assume the same facts as in Example 2-63, except that Benson itemized his deductions and they totaled $150 more than the standard deduction. Now Benson must report $150 of the refund on his return since his taxable income was previously reduced by that amount on account of the recovered funds.

.02 Real Estate Tax Rebate

The same rules apply here as to state and local income tax refunds.

.03 Medical Insurance Reimbursements

There is often a time lag between when you pay a medical bill and when you receive a reimbursement from an insurance company or employer. If the lag straddles the end of a year, the cost is a deductible medical expense (subject to the 10 percent of adjusted gross income deduction floor under Code Sec. 213(a)) in the year you pay it. When (and if) you later receive a reimbursement, that reimbursement is taxable to the extent of any prior deduction in excess of the standard deduction.

Example 2-65: Ms. Carter paid $6,000 of unreimbursed medical expenses. Her adjusted gross income was $35,000 that year. Therefore, she claimed a medical expense deduction of $2,500 ($6,000 less $3,500, which is 10 percent of $35,000). One year later, Carter received a $2,000 reimbursement for some of those medical expenses from her insurance company. Result: Carter must report the entire reimbursement as income.

.04 Theft or Casualty Losses

These are subject to a 10 percent of adjusted gross income deduction floor. The mechanics for determining how much of a recovery is taxable involves the same process as for medical expense reimbursements.

.05 Multiple Recoveries

When you recover more than one item that was previously deducted as an itemized deduction, the income inclusion is calculated as follows: (1) If a recovery is attributable to an item that is subject to a percentage of gross income deduction floor, subtract the recovery from the total deductible expenses for which it was received. Then figure out how much less the deduction would have been. (2) Add together the amounts in (1) plus the amount of any recovery for items not subject to deduction floors. (3) Compare that sum to the excess of actual deductions over the standard deduction for the year to which the recoveries are attributable. (4) The smaller of the two is the taxable recovery to be included in income.

.06 Tax Credits

If an amount is recovered in a tax year and a credit was based on that amount in a prior tax year, your tax is increased by the amount of the credit attributable to the recovered amount to the extent the credit reduced the amount of tax. This rule does not apply to amounts for which a credit was allowed under the foreign tax credit [Code Sec. 111(b)].

.07 Special Situations

When a deduction reduces taxable income, but does not reduce the tax (because, for example, you are subject to the alternative minimum tax), recovery of the amount giving rise to the deduction can be excluded from income [Code Sec. 111(d)].

3 Retirement Plans

PENSION AND PROFIT-SHARING PLANS

Qualified plans in general . . . . ¶3001
Types of qualified plans . . . . ¶3005
Basic requirements for plan qualification . . . . ¶3015
Qualified plans—key terms . . . . ¶3020
Coverage . . . . ¶3025
Minimum participation standards . . . . ¶3030
Vesting requirements . . . . ¶3035
Limits on benefits and contributions . . . . ¶3040
Top-heavy plans . . . . ¶3045
Commonly controlled business . . . ¶3050
Defined benefit plans—benefit accrual . . . . ¶3055
Employer tax consequences . . . . . . ¶3060
Integration of qualified plans with social security . . . . ¶3065
Trust must prove exemption . . . . . . ¶3070
Distributions from qualified plans . . . . ¶3075
Taxation of distributions . . . . ¶3080
Distribution taxes and penalties . . . ¶3085
Qualified domestic relations orders (QDROs) . . . . ¶3090
Plan loans . . . . ¶3095
Prohibited transactions . . . . ¶3100

INDIVIDUAL RETIREMENT ACCOUNTS

Who is eligible to contribute to a traditional IRA? . . . . ¶3105
Spousal IRAs for stay-at-home spouses . . . . ¶3110
Excess contributions . . . . ¶3115
Distributions from IRAs . . . . ¶3120
Rollovers of retirement plan and IRA distributions . . . . ¶3125
IRA investment opportunities . . . . . ¶3130
Tax on IRA distributions . . . . ¶3135
Roth IRAs . . . . ¶3140

OTHER RETIREMENT ARRANGEMENTS

Simplified employee pensions (SEPs) . . . . ¶3145
Cash or deferred arrangements—401(k) plans . . . . ¶3150
Keogh plans . . . . ¶3155
Employee stock ownership plans (ESOPs) . . . . ¶3160
Tax-sheltered annuities—Code Sec. 403(b) plans . . . . ¶3165
Nonqualified deferred compensation . . . . ¶3170
SIMPLE retirement plans for small business owners . . . . ¶3175

PENSION AND PROFIT-SHARING PLANS

¶3001 QUALIFIED PLANS IN GENERAL

Retirement plans that satisfy specific Internal Revenue Code requirements for special tax-favored treatment are called "qualified plans." Qualified plans offer significant tax benefits to both employers and employees. Retirement plans that fail to satisfy the statutory requirements are called nonqualified plans and they are ineligible for the tax benefits that favor qualified plans.

Qualified plans are "funded." That means the money is accumulated in trust. Some plans are also "contributory" plans. They either permit or require an employee to contribute to the plan and get larger benefits or reduce employer costs.

The tax benefits of a typical employer-funded qualified plan include the following:

- Employers may deduct contributions to qualified pension plans in the tax year during which the contribution is actually paid, regardless of whether the employer uses an accrual or a cash-basis method of accounting [Code Sec. 404(a)]. Code Sec. 404(a)(6) allows for a grace period which provides that an employer will be deemed to have made a payment on the last day of the preceding tax year if the payment is on account of such tax year and is made no later than the time prescribed by law for filing the return for that tax year (including extensions). See ¶3060 for further discussion.
- The employee owes no tax on his share of employer contributions and remains untaxed until he receives a distribution, usually upon retirement.
- The employee is allowed to contribute to the plan but generally cannot deduct what he contributes. (But see discussion of Code Sec. 401(k) plans [¶3150].)
- Both employer and employee contributions are held in a tax-exempt trust and accumulate tax-free.
- When a distribution is made, the employee may be eligible to roll the distribution over into a traditional IRA or into another qualified plan or calculate the tax that may be due on the distribution using a favorable income averaging formula.

.01 Source Taxing Prohibited

The states are prohibited from taxing the qualified retirement benefits of former residents who move to states with lower or no income taxes. This is good news for retirees who move and find that the home state still subjects their retirement income to state income tax. This practice, known as *source taxing*, is prohibited. As a result, states where pensions were earned can no longer reach beyond their borders to tax retirees who have moved out of state.

The source tax act provides that no state may impose an income tax on any "retirement income" of an individual who is not a resident of the state. The term retirement income is defined to include any income earned from qualified plans maintained by employers for all their retirees.

Specifically, the states are prohibited from taxing nonresidents on payouts from the following types of retirement arrangements:

- 401(k) plans;
- Workforce-wide pension plans and other funded retirement plans;
- Simplified employee pensions;
- Annuity plans or annuity contract;
- IRAs;
- Deferred compensation plans that are set up by state and local governments and tax-exempt organizations;
- Any federal government retirement program;
- A trust created before June 15, 1959, that is part of a pension plan meeting specified requirements and funded only by contributions of employees;
- Executive retirement plans providing benefits greater than the amounts payable under the workforce-wide qualified retirement plans, such as 401(k) plans and funded pension plans; and
- Any plan, program, or arrangement where the income is part of a series of substantially equal periodic payments made for the life or life expectancy of the recipient or designated beneficiary, or for a period of not less than 10 years.

¶3005 TYPES OF QUALIFIED PLANS

Only qualified plans are eligible for the tax-favored treatment offered by the Internal Revenue Code. These benefits include a tax exemption for the fund that is established to provide the retirement benefits, a deduction by the employer for contributions made on the employee's behalf to the retirement fund, deferral of tax on earnings produced by the retirement account, and tax-favored treatment on distributions and rollovers of amounts in the retirement account. The varieties of qualified plans available for the employer include the following:

.01 Defined Benefit Plans

One of the two basic types of qualified plans is the defined benefit plan (also referred to as a "pension plan") [¶3055]. Defined benefit plans are designed to provide "definitely determinable" benefits to employees over a period of years after retirement. For example, a plan might provide that an employee who retires at age 65, with ten years of service, will receive a pension equal to 50 percent of his salary. With a defined benefit plan, the amount of benefit payable upon retirement is determinable at the outset. The contribution needed to produce that benefit is determined actuarially. Factors such as the employee's age, length of service, employee turnover and plan earnings will determine the size of the contribution needed to produce that benefit.

.02 Defined Contribution Plans

The other basic type of qualified plan is the defined contribution plan. With a defined contribution plan, contributions are made on behalf of a plan beneficiary. The amount of the benefit that a beneficiary receives depends on the amount of contributions made and how well those contributions are invested. Two types of defined contributions plans are the money purchase pension plan and profit-sharing plan.

Money-Purchase Plans

Each participant in a money-purchase plan has an individual account that will hold annual contributions and earnings generated by the investment. Money purchase pension plans provide for a fixed annual percentage rate of employer contributions to the plan up to a maximum 25 percent of the employee's eligible compensation regardless of profits generated in a particular year [Reg. § 1.401-1(b)(1)(i)]. For example, under a money purchase plan, the plan may require that the employer contribute 5 percent of each participating employee's wages, regardless of whether the employer shows a profit for the year. Employee contributions are not mandatory and usually are not permitted. Failure to make the annual contribution will subject the employer to an excise tax under Code Sec. 4971. In addition, money purchase pension plans are subject to minimum funding requirements under Code Sec. 412. These rules provide that once the funding level is established, it must be maintained at the same percentage level each year. A decrease or discontinuation of the funding amount must be accompanied by formal ERISA approval.

The contributions are divided up among individual accounts maintained for each employee and look much like individual savings accounts. That account reflects that participant's share of contributions, expenses, investment return, and forfeitures. When the employee retires he is eligible to receive benefits based on whatever has been contributed to his or her account plus accumulations of income and appreciation or depreciation of assets. Keep in mind that the amount actually handed over to the employee at retirement would depend entirely on profits and losses realized by the assets in the plan.

.03 Profit-Sharing Plans

A profit-sharing plan affords the employer the ability to determine the amount of contributions made to the plan each year. The amount of the contributions can vary from year to year based on the employer's discretion. Like other qualified plans, the plan may not discriminate in favor of highly compensated employees. A profit-sharing plan is not subject to minimum funding rules, as is the money purchase plan. The deductible contribution limit for profit-sharing plans is 25 percent of compensation (which is limited to the lesser of 100 percent of the first $255,000 of compensation or $63,750 in 2013). There is no minimum amount that must be contributed each year to profit sharing plans. Consequently, in the lean years, contributions to profit-sharing plans are not mandatory. In addition, the minimum-funding requirement does not apply to profit-sharing plans.

A profit-sharing plan must provide a definite predetermined formula for allocating the contributions made to the plan among the participants and for distributing the funds accumulated under the plan after a fixed number of years, the attainment of a stated age, or upon the prior occurrence of some event such as layoff, illness, disability, retirement, death, or severance of employment. An allocation formula is definite, for example, if it provides for an allocation in proportion to the basic compensation of each participant [Reg. § 1.401-1(b)(4)(ii)]. A profit-sharing plan is a type of defined contribution plan that differs from a pension plan in several key respects. First, the employer is not locked into an annual contribution; contributions can be reduced or avoided entirely during lean years [Reg. § 1.401-1(b)(2)]. There is great flexibility since the employer can assess its situation on a year-by-year basis and adjust the level of contributions accordingly. (With a pension plan, contributions must be sufficient to fund promised benefits [Reg. § 1.401-1(b)(1)(i)].) Note: Employers—including tax-exempt entities—can make contributions to a profit-sharing plan irrespective of profits [Code Sec. 401(a)(27)].

Another key difference concerns the allocation of contributions. While the contribution limit for profit-sharing plans is 25 percent of compensation, it refers to the employer's aggregate payroll and not each participant's compensation. While the allocation cannot discriminate in favor of highly compensated employees, there is some latitude [Code Sec. 404(a)(3)]. [For a definition of highly compensated employees, see ¶ 3020].

A third key difference concerns the type of benefits that can be paid and the events triggering distributions. While pension plans can pay incidental benefits, they are generally unable to provide benefits not usually associated with pensions [¶ 3010]. Profit-sharing plans, on the other hand, can provide for distributions on account of illness, disability or layoff [Reg. § 1.401-1(b)(1)(ii)].

.04 Stock Bonus Plans

Stock bonus plans are like profit-sharing plans except that benefits are distributable in employer stock [Reg. § 1.401-1(b)(1)(iii)]. As with profit-sharing plans, contributions can be contingent on profits, and the plan must provide a definite predetermined formula for allocating contributions among participants and for distributing funds after a fixed number of years and attaining a certain age.

The most popular form of stock bonus plan is an employee stock ownership plan (ESOP) [¶ 3160]. A cash or deferred arrangement, also known as a 401(k) plan can also be part of a stock bonus plan. See ¶ 3150.

.05 Other Types of Qualified Plans

Target Benefit Plan

A target benefit plan is a hybrid of a defined benefit and defined contribution plan. The benefit at retirement is projected and the annual contributions necessary to meet the projection are then fixed. But the ultimate benefit depends on the actual investment performance of the contributions. In a target benefit plan, the contributions are allocated to separate accounts for each of the participants.

Thrift or Savings Plans

These plans can take a variety of forms but the common feature is that the participants' contributions generally are matched, either dollar for dollar or according to some set formula, by employer contributions. The distinct advantage these plans offer is that the employee contributions can easily be made through payroll deductions.

Cash or deferred arrangements (401(k) plans) are discussed at ¶ 3150.

Cash Balance Plan

A cash balance plan is a defined benefit plan that, rather than expressing its benefit as a life annuity starting at retirement, defines its benefits using a lump sum and the actuarial benefit of a hypothetical account. The account balance is the sum of pay credits plus an interest component.

¶3015 BASIC REQUIREMENTS FOR PLAN QUALIFICATION

Qualified plan assets are generally held in trust established by the employer for the exclusive benefit of employees or their beneficiaries. The trust is exempt from tax if it meets special requirements. A qualified plan must be written, communicated to employees, and maintained for the exclusive benefit of employees and their beneficiaries. It must be impossible for trust assets to be diverted for any other purpose [Code Sec. 401(a)(2); Reg. § 1.401-1(a)(3)(iv)].

The requirements for qualification are outlined in Code Sec. 401(a). Virtually every aspect of a qualified plan's operation and administration is regulated by the Code and Treasury regulations. In addition, the Department of Labor has jurisdiction over certain matters under ERISA.[1] For example, the form and content of notices to employees regarding their benefits under the plan and ERISA rights are under the jurisdiction of the Department of Labor.[2]

If a plan fails to satisfy the requirements for qualification, the IRS can revoke its qualified status, even retroactively. A plan must meet those requirements both in its written terms and in how it operates. So a plan that is operated in compliance with all the rules can still have problems if the plan document has not been amended to reflect tax law changes.[3]

The resulting tax consequences of a plan disqualification are severe to both employers and employees. Employer deductions can be disallowed. Employees may have additional taxable income in years contributions were made, to the extent the employees' interest in the plan was nonforfeitable. In addition, the trust can be taxed on its earnings over the years because of the loss of its tax-exempt status. These harsh results can apply with respect to tax years for which the applicable statute of limitations has not run [Code Sec. 6501].

The major qualification requirements addressed here are rules that require the plan to:

1. Permit employees to participate in the plan in accordance with minimum eligibility and participation rules [Code Sec. 401(a)(3)];
2. Benefit a broad class of employees and not discriminate in favor of highly compensated employees [Code Sec. 401(a)(4)]. See ¶3020 and Code Sec. 414(q) for definition of highly compensated employee. The regulations interpreting Code Sec. 401(a)(4) provide that a plan can demonstrate that either the contributions or the benefits provided under the plan are nondiscriminatory in amount [Reg. § 1.401(a)(4)-8].

   Defined contribution plans generally satisfy the regulations by showing that contributions are nondiscriminatory in amount, through certain safe harbors provided for under the regulations or through general testing [Reg. § 1.401(a)(4)-8].

---

[1] P.L. 93-406.

[2] DOL Regs at 29 CFR 2510 *et seq.*

[3] *Hamlin Dev. Co.*, 65 TCM 2071, Dec. 48,901(M), TC Memo. 1993-89.

3. Provide that a participant's right to his benefits under the plan are nonforfeitable (vested) after specified periods of time [Code Sec. 401(a)(7)];
4. Distribute a participant's interest upon retirement in accordance with rules regulating the time and manner of benefit commencement [Code Sec. 401(a)(9)];
5. Comply with the maximum benefit and contribution limits [Code Sec. 415];
6. Only take a certain amount of a participant's compensation into account for determining the employer's deduction for contributions to the plan as well as for determining the amount of the participant's benefits [Code Sec. 401(a)(17)].
7. The plan must be maintained by the employer for the exclusive benefit of its employees or their beneficiaries. This so-called exclusive benefit rule exists to provide for the livelihood of employees or their beneficiaries after the retirement of the employees as provided in Reg. § 1.401-1(a)(2)(i). In Rev. Rul. 2008-45,[4] the IRS concluded that the exclusive benefit rule of Code Sec. 401(a) was violated when the sponsorship of a qualified retirement plan was transferred from an employer to an unrelated taxpayer and the transfer was not connected with the transfer of business assets, operations, or employees from the employer to the unrelated taxpayer.

Special qualification requirements regarding minimum funding standards and actuarial assumptions affect defined benefit plans.

¶3020 QUALIFIED PLANS—KEY TERMS

Certain concepts are central to an understanding of the design and operation of qualified plans. Here are some important terms used in discussions of qualified plans:

.01 Year of Service

An employee's tenure with the employer, both as an employee and plan participant, is important to determine his eligibility to participate in the plan, his right to plan benefits and the amount of benefits. "Year of service" is the measuring rod for counting these periods of time. A year of service is a consecutive 12-month period, designated by the plan, during which 1,000 or more hours of service are performed [Code Sec. 411(a)(5)]. Unlike tax years, a plan year need not end on the last day of a month.[5]

.02 Break in Service

If a plan participant works fewer than 500 hours during a 12-month period, it is considered a one-year break in service [Code Sec. 411(a)(6)]. Sometimes when a break in service occurs, an employee's years of service before the break can be disregarded when determining his rights to benefits. This concept is also important in calculating the effect of a leave of absence.

---

[4] Rev. Rul. 2008-45, IRB 2008-34, 403.

[5] Rev. Rul. 89-13, 1989-1 CB 112, supplemented by Rev. Rul. 93-10, 1993-1 CB 177.

.03 Accrued Benefits

Once an employee becomes a plan participant, he begins to earn benefits in accordance with the plan's benefit formula. The employee's "accrued benefit" is the amount he has earned, including employer contributions and his share of earnings or forfeitures.

.04 Vesting

Although an employee begins to accrue benefits when he becomes a plan participant, his absolute entitlement to the benefits depends on his vested interest. In other words, vesting determines what portion of accrued benefits an employee gets if he leaves service. A participant must always be fully vested in his own employee contributions. His nonforfeitable share of employer contributions and earnings depends on the plan's vesting schedule.

Amendment of Qualified Plans to Eliminate Optional Benefit Forms

A qualified plan fails to satisfy the minimum vesting standards if a participant's accrued benefit is decreased by a plan amendment (the "anti-cutback rule") [Code Sec. 411(d)(6)]. The IRS has added special rules that permit amendment of qualified defined contribution plans to eliminate some alternative forms in which an account balance can be paid under certain circumstances and allow certain transfers between defined contribution plans that previously were not permitted [Reg. § 1.411(d)-4]. A plan may not be amended, however, in a way that affects protected features of optional forms of benefit other than the medium of distribution. A defined contribution plan does not violate the Code Sec. 411(d)(6) requirements merely because the plan is amended to eliminate a participant's ability to receive payment of accrued benefits under a particular optional form of benefit if one of the alternative forms of payment available to the participant is a single-sum distribution that is identical to the optional form of benefit that is being eliminated except with respect to the timing of payments after commencement [Reg. § 1.411(d)-4, Q&A-2(e)].

All qualified plans, including single and multi-employer plans must provide that a participant's accrued benefits are fully vested under either a five year vesting schedule or over a period of three to seven year vesting schedule [Code Sec. 411(a)(2)]. For example, a plan would satisfy the five-year rule if an employee who has completed at least five years of service has a nonforfeitable right to 100 percent of the accrued benefits in the retirement account. A plan would satisfy the three-to-seven-year vesting rule if an employee has a nonforfeitable right to a percentage of the accrued benefits in the retirement account using a graduated vesting schedule which provides that he or she is 20 percent vested after three years of service, 40 percent vested after four years of service, 60 percent vested after five years of service, 80 percent vested after six years of service and 100 percent vested after seven years of service [Code Sec. 411(a)(2)].

.05 Highly Compensated Employees

Qualified plans are prohibited from favoring "highly compensated" employees. An employee is considered highly compensated if he or she (a) was more than a 5 percent owner at any time during the current year or the preceding year; or (b) had compensation from the employer in excess of $115,000 in 2013 and, if the employer so elects for the preceding year, was in the top 20 percent of employees ranked on the basis of compensation paid, for the preceding year [Code Sec. 414(q)(1); Reg. § 1.414(q)-1]. For purposes of determining the number of employees in the top-paid group, the following employees are excluded:

- Employees who have not completed six months of service;
- Employees who normally work less than 17$^{1}/_{2}$ hours per week;
- Employees who normally work not more than six months during any year;
- Employees who have not attained age 21; and
- Employees who are included in a unit of employees covered by an agreement which the Secretary of Labor finds to be a collective bargaining agreement between employee representatives and the employer [Code Sec. 414(q)(5)].

Compensation paid to (or plan contributions or benefits made on behalf of) family members of certain highly compensated employees will not be treated as paid to or on behalf of the highly compensated employee for purposes of the nondiscrimination testing rules.

¶3025 COVERAGE

To qualify for tax benefits under the Internal Revenue Code, the qualified plan must provide broad coverage for all employees. It cannot pick and choose which employees will be covered.

A plan must satisfy one of the following tests:

.01 Percentage Test

A plan must cover at least 70 percent of all employees who are not highly compensated. These employees are also called the rank-and-file employees [Code Sec. 410(b)(1)(A); Reg. § 1.410(b)-2(b)(1)].

> **Example 3-1:** ABC Corp. employs 275 people, 25 of whom are highly compensated. No employee is excluded by reason of age, service, or by coverage in a collective bargaining unit. 200 of the non-highly compensated employees accrue benefits under the plan (80 percent). The plan meets the percentage test.

.02 Employees Benefiting Under a Plan

In general, an employee "benefits" under a plan for testing purposes only if the employee accrues a benefit under the plan for that year. However, for cash or deferred plans (401(k) plans) [¶ 3150], employees who are eligible to make deferrals are treated as benefiting even if they do not make elective contributions for the year [Reg. § 1.410(b)-3(a)(2)(i)].

> **Example 3-2:** An employer maintains a 401(k) plan. Only employees who are at least age 21 and who complete one year of service are eligible employees under the plan within the meaning of Reg. § 1.401(k)-6. Only employees who have satisfied these age and service conditions are treated as benefiting under the plan [Reg. § 1.410(b)-3(a)(3), Ex. 3].

.03 Average Benefit Percentage Test

The plan benefits employees under a classification that does not discriminate in favor of highly compensated employees, and the average benefit provided to non-highly compensated employees (as a percentage of compensation) is at least 70 percent of the average benefit provided to highly compensated employees (as a percentage of compensation) [Code Sec. 410(b)(2)]. In general, all employer provided benefits, contributions and employee contributions under all employer plans are taken into account to determine if this test is satisfied.

A plan satisfies the nondiscriminatory classification test if, for the plan year, the following requirements are satisfied [Reg. § 1.401(b)-4(a)]:

1. Based on all of the facts and circumstances, the classification is reasonable and is established under objective business criteria that identify the category of employees who benefit under the plan. Reasonable classifications include specified job categories, nature of compensation (i.e., salaried or hourly), geographic location, and similar bona fide business criteria. Reg. § 1.401(b)-4(b).

2. Either (A) the plan's ratio percentage (i.e., the percentage of nonhighly compensated employees who benefit under the plan divided by the percentage of highly compensated employees who benefit under the plan) is greater than or equal to the safe harbor percentage (50 percent, reduced by three-fourth of a percentage point for each whole percentage point by which the nonhighly compensated employee concentration percentage—the percentage of all employees who are nonhighly compensated employees) or (B) the plan's ratio percentage exceeds the unsafe harbor percentage (40 percent, reduced by three-fourth of a percentage point for each whole percentage point by which the nonhighly compensated employee concentration percentage exceeds 60 percent) and, based on all the relevant facts and circumstances, the IRS finds that the classification is nondiscriminatory. Reg. § 1.401(b)-4(c).

In making a factual determination whether a classification is nondiscriminatory, no one particular fact is determinative. Included among the facts and circumstances relevant in determining whether a classification is nondiscriminatory are [Reg. § 1.401(b)-4(c)(3)(ii)]:

1. The underlying business reason for the classification. The greater the business reason for the classification, the more likely the classification is to be nondiscriminatory. Reducing the employer's cost of providing retirement benefits is not a relevant business reason.

2. The percentage of the employees benefiting under the plan. The higher the percentage, the more likely the classification is to be nondiscriminatory.

3. Whether the number of employees benefiting under the plan in each salary range is representative of the number of employees in each salary range of the employer's workforce. The more representative the percentages, the more likely the classification is to be nondiscriminatory.

4. The difference between the plan's ratio percentage and employer's safe harbor percentage. The smaller the difference, the more likely the classification is to be nondiscriminatory.
5. The extent to which the plan's average benefit percentage exceeds 70 percent.

A trust that is part of a defined benefit plan is not a qualified trust unless on each day of the plan year, the trust benefits at least the lesser of:

1. 50 employees, or
2. The greater of 40 percent of all employees, or 2 employees (or if there is only 1 employee, such employee) [Code Sec. 401(a)(26)(A)].

Plans cannot be aggregated to satisfy this requirement but an employer may elect to apply this requirement separately with respect to each different line of business of the employer [Code Sec. 401(a)(26)(F)].

The IRS has simplified the process for substantiating compliance with the nondiscrimination rules in four key areas: (1) Employers do not have to have precise data, but can use the best data available at a reasonable cost. (2) An employer can substantiate compliance based on testing a single typical day during the plan year. (3) For purposes of this so-called snap-shot testing, an employer can use a simplified test for identifying highly compensated employees. (4) Testing is required only every three years, if there are no significant changes (e.g., in compensation practices, workforce composition, or plan provisions) during the three-year period.[6]

¶3030 MINIMUM PARTICIPATION STANDARDS

The plan may condition an employee's participation in a plan on his having completed one year of service or having attained age 21, whichever is later [Code Sec. 410(a)(1)(A)].

.01 Exceptions

Generally, a plan can defer participation until two years of service have been completed provided that the employee becomes fully vested at that time [Code Sec. 410(a)(1)(B)(i)].

The measuring rod for participation is completion of a year of service. For this purpose, a year of service means at least 1,000 hours of work during a 12-month period [Code Sec. 410(a)(3)]. Thus, part-time employees who work fewer than 1,000 hours need not be included in the plan.

Once an employee meets the minimum participation requirements, he must be brought into the plan no later than the earlier of: (1) the first day of the plan year beginning after the date on which the employee first satisfied the requirements, or (2) the 6 month anniversary date of the day he first satisfied the requirements [Code Sec. 410(a)(4)]. Plans frequently have two semiannual entry dates to accommodate this.

---

[6] Rev. Proc. 95-34, 1995-2 CB 385.

Example 3-3: A calendar-year plan provides that an employee may enter the plan only on the first semiannual entry date, January 1 or July 1, after he has satisfied the applicable minimum age and service requirements. The plan satisfies the requirements because regardless of when an employee becomes eligible to participate, an entry date will be no longer than six months away. In addition, the first day of the plan year is one of those entry dates.

Example 3-4: A plan provides that an employee is not eligible to participate until the first day of the first plan year beginning after he has satisfied the minimum age and service requirements. In this case, an employee who satisfies the "6-month" rule will not be eligible to participate in the plan. Therefore, the plan does not satisfy the requirements.

Special rules come into play where a break in service has occurred. If an employee incurs a break in service (works fewer than 500 hours) at a time when he is vested in the qualified plan, he must be admitted to the plan immediately on his return. There is an exception if the consecutive one-year breaks in service equal or exceed the greater of: (1) five years or (2) years of service before the break [Code Sec. 410(a)(5)(D)]. Then he is not required to be admitted until the next entry date.

Example 3-5: A calendar-year plan provides that an employee may enter the plan only on the first semiannual entry date, January 1 or July 1, after he has satisfied the applicable minimum age and service requirements. After ten years of service, Mr. Jones separated from service with a vested benefit. Three years later, he returns to employment covered by the plan. Assuming that he completes a year of service after his return, Jones must participate immediately on his return, February 1. His prior service cannot be disregarded, and the plan may not postpone his participation until July 1.

Example 3-6: If Jones had five years of service but no vested benefit when he incurred five consecutive one-year breaks, his prior service can be disregarded. His participation in the plan may be postponed.

.02 Minimum Participation Requirements for Defined Benefit Plans

A trust that is part of a defined benefit plan is not a qualified trust unless on each day of the plan year, it benefits at least the lesser of: (a) 50 employees, or (b) the greater of 40 percent of all employees, or 2 employees (or if there is only 1 employee, such employee) [Code Sec. 401(a)(26)(A)]. Plans cannot be aggregated to satisfy this requirement but an employer may elect to apply this requirement separately with respect to each different line of business of the employer [Code Sec. 401(a)(26)(F)].

¶3035 VESTING REQUIREMENTS

A single or multi-employer qualified plan must provide that plan participants vest in their accrued benefits (i.e., have a nonforfeitable right to them) at least as rapidly as one of the following schedules:

.01 Five-Year Vesting

The employee is completely vested, which means he or she has a nonforfeitable right to 100 percent of the accrued benefits under the plan, after five years of service, but not at all vested until then.

.02 Three-to-Seven-Year Rule

Under the three-to-seven-year rule, an employee must have a nonforfeitable right to a percentage of the accrued benefits in the retirement account using a graduated vesting schedule which provides that he or she is 20 percent vested after three years of service and 100 percent vested after seven years of service [Code Sec. 411(a)(2)(A)(iii); Temp. Reg. § 1.411(a)-3T(c)].

.03 Cost-Cutting Impact

The choice of vesting schedules has a direct impact on the cost of operating the plan. For example, forfeitures result when an employee terminates employment and he is not fully vested in his accrued benefits. With respect to a defined benefit plan, forfeitures reduce future employer contributions. They cannot increase the benefits any participant would otherwise receive under the plan [Code Sec. 401(a), (b)]. In a defined contribution plan, forfeitures can reduce the employer contribution or be allocated to the accounts of remaining participants. Depending on the nature of the workforce and rate of turnover, the choice of a five-year schedule or seven-year graded schedule may be critical.

There are several other important vesting rules to consider:

- For vesting purposes, all of an employee's years of service with the employer, after he has attained age 18, must be counted [Code Sec. 411(a)(4)]. In other words, in determining a participant's vested interest in his accrued benefit, years of service before he became a plan participant are counted if he was at least 18.
- The break-in-service rules permit certain years of service to be disregarded for vesting purposes. As is true for the minimum participation standards [¶ 3030], a nonvested participant's work-time preceding breaks in service of longer than the greater of: (1) five years or (2) the aggregate years of service before the breaks may be disregarded for vesting purposes [Code Sec. 411(a)(6)].

Example 3-7: Smith separates from service in year two after completing two years of service. Because of the plan's seven-year graded vesting schedule (an employee earns the first 20 percent after three years of service), Smith has no vested benefits. Smith is rehired in year five, after incurring three one-year breaks in service. Since the three consecutive service breaks don't equal or exceed the greater of five or the two pre-break years, the two years before the break must be counted.

- Leaves of absence occasioned by maternity or paternity (including childbirth, adoption or child-care immediately after the events) are disregarded in determining compliance with the vesting schedule. The affected participant will be credited for the hours of service that he or she would have worked, but for the leave [Code Sec. 411(a)(6)(E)]. This rule applies to determine if a break in service has occurred (i.e., the participant has fewer than 500 hours of service during the year).

- An employee must at all times be fully vested in accrued benefits derived from his own contributions [Code Sec. 411(a)(1)].
- Employees must be 100 percent vested in their retirement benefits when they reach "normal retirement age" as defined by the plan [Code Sec. 411(a)]. The normal retirement age under a plan must be an age that is not earlier than the earliest age that is reasonably representative of the typical retirement age for the industry in which the covered workforce is employed. A safe harbor is provided under which a normal retirement age of at least age 62 is deemed to satisfy this requirement [Reg. § 1.401(a)-1(b)(2)].

  If a plan's normal retirement age is earlier than age 62, all relevant facts and circumstances must be considered in determining whether the age is not earlier than the earliest age that is reasonably representative of the typical retirement age for the industry in which the covered workforce is employed. If the normal retirement age is between ages 55 and 62, a good faith determination by the employer of the typical retirement age for the industry in which the covered workforce is employed is given deference. However, a normal retirement age that is lower than age 55 is presumed to be earlier than the earliest age that is reasonably representative of the typical retirement age for the industry of the relevant covered workforce absent facts and circumstances that demonstrate otherwise [Reg. § 1.401(a)-1(b)(2)].

  If all plan participants are qualified public safety employees (e.g., police officers, firefighters, and emergency medical service workers), a normal retirement age of age 50 or later is deemed not to be appropriate [Reg. § 1.401(a)-1(b)(2)(v)].

- Under Code Sec. 411(d)(3), in the event of a partial plan termination, all of the participants in a qualified plan become immediately vested or entitled to amounts credited to their accounts, regardless of whether or not they were vested before the plan termination. In one case, a company layoff of a large block of employees was treated as a partial termination, and all laid-off employees become fully vested[7] Reg. § 1.411(d)-2(b)(1) provides that whether a plan termination has occurred should be based on all the facts and circumstances of a particular case. In *Matz*,[8] the Court of Appeals for the Seventh Circuit concluded that a partial termination of a qualified plan occurred when there was a 20 percent or greater reduction in plan participants. The court ruled further that if the reduction was below 10 percent no partial termination occurred; above 40 percent, partial termination is conclusively presumed to occur. Table 1 summarizes the court's holding.

---

[7] *W. Weil*, CA-2, 91-1 USTC ¶ 50,247, 933 F2d 106.

[8] *R.J. Matz*, CA-7, 2004-2 USTC ¶ 50,403, 388 F3d 570.

Table 1. Determining Plan Termination Status

If the reduction is:	Then there is:
Below 10%	No partial termination
Above 10% but less than 20%	A rebuttable presumption of no partial termination
20% to 40%	A rebuttable presumption of partial termination
Above 40% to less than 100%	Partial termination
100%	Complete termination

The IRS concluded in Rev. Rul. 2007-43[9] that a partial termination of its qualified defined contribution plan occurred under Code Sec. 411(d)(3) when an employer ceased operations at one of its four business locations. Thus the rights of affected employees to their account balances became fully vested and nonforfeitable as of the date of the partial termination. A partial termination was presumed to have occurred because the employee turnover rate, computed by dividing the number of participating employees who had an employer-initiated severance from employment by the sum of all participating employees and employees who became participants during the applicable period, was 20 percent or more. The facts and circumstances supported the finding of a partial termination because the severances of employment occurred as a result of the employer closing one of its business locations, not as a result of routine turnover.

- In the event of a plan merger, participants are required to receive at least what they would have received under the prior plan [Code Sec. 401(a)(12)].
- In addition, an *anticutback rule* prevents an employer from amending a plan in a manner that reduces previously accrued benefits. Each participant with at least three years of service must be given the right to elect to have his nonforfeitable percentage determined under the prior vesting schedule [Code Sec. 411(a)(10)(B); Reg. § 1.411(a)-8(b)].
- For purposes of vesting and benefit accrual, an employee can be given credit for past service for another related employer. All similarly situated employees must be treated in a uniform manner.

¶3040 LIMITS ON BENEFITS AND CONTRIBUTIONS

Code Sec. 415 limits benefits under qualified defined benefit plans and contributions under qualified defined contribution plans. These limits also apply to other arrangements, such as Code Sec. 403(b) annuity contracts and simplified employee pension plans (SEPs). Under Code Sec. 404(j), Code Sec. 415 also limits the employer's deduction for plan contributions. Further, the definition of compensation that is used for Code Sec. 415 purposes is used for other statutory purposes, such as determining whether an employee is a highly compensated employee under Code Sec. 414(q) and satisfying the minimum benefits requirements for top-heavy plans.

---

[9] Rev. Rul. 2007-43, 2007-2 CB 45.

Thus, the Code Sec. 415 limits affect qualified plans in two ways. First, a plan may not base contributions or benefits on compensation in excess of the annual limit. Second, the limit also affects the amount of an employee's annual compensation that may be taken into account in applying certain nondiscrimination rules.

The annual compensation limit that may be used to determine a participant's benefit accruals under a defined benefit plan or a participant's allocations under a defined contribution plan is $255,000 in 2013 [Code Sec. 401(a)(17)]. The compensation limit is important for purposes of: (a) applying the employer deduction rules under Code Sec. 404(l); (b) nondiscrimination testing for Code Sec. 408(k) salary reduction SEPs; (c) nondiscrimination testing for voluntary employee benefit associations (VEBAs) and supplemental unemployment compensation benefit trusts (SUBs) under Code Sec. 505(b)(7); and (d) determining benefits under qualified plans. The limit is restricted, however, if the amount of benefits provided to former employees discriminates in favor of those former employees who are highly compensated employees. Employers may amend plans, however, to apply the higher limits retroactively to former employees by effectively raising the facts-and-circumstances bar needed to fail the discrimination test in such cases.[10]

Compensation for purposes of all qualified plans and IRAs (including SIMPLE arrangements) includes earned income of self-employed taxpayers. Net earnings from a business may be treated as earned income only if the personal services of the taxpayer are a material income-producing factor in that business. Typically, a limited partner's share of the net earnings of a partnership is not considered to be earned income (although guaranteed payments by a partnership to a limited partner for services actually rendered are considered to be earned income). Compensation is defined so that the self-employed persons who have elected out of the self-employment system (SECA) based on religious grounds (Code Sec. 1402(g)) may treat their exempt self-employment income as compensation from a trade or business for purposes of establishing and contributing to all qualified retirement plans and IRAs (including SIMPLE arrangements) [Code Secs. 401(c)(2)(A), 408(p)(6)(A)]. Members of the clergy, Ministers, members of religious orders and Christian Science practitioners may apply for an exemption from self-employment tax (SECA). Notwithstanding such an exemption, the net earnings of these taxpayers are still treated as earned income for retirement planning purposes.

.01 Defined Benefit Plan Maximum Benefits

The annual benefit limit under a defined benefit plan is $205,000 in 2013 [Code Sec. 415(b)(1)(A)]. The annual benefit limit is decreased if benefits begin before age 62 and increased if benefits begin after 65. Special rules will apply to plans for airline pilots.

The maximum benefit limitation for a defined benefit plan is expressed in terms of the benefit that will be paid out upon retirement. Generally, the plan cannot provide an annual retirement benefit, in the form of a single life annuity beginning at age 65, that exceeds the lesser of: (1) $205,000 in 2013, or (2) 100 percent of compensation for a participant's average compensation for his three highest consecutive years of service [Code Sec. 415(b)(1)]. The maximum is lowered to half of the maximum annual benefit

[10] Rev. Rul. 2003-11, 2003-1 CB 285.

($102,500 for 2013) for participants in certain union-negotiated plans [Code Sec. 417(b)(7)]. If a participant retires before age 62 (with certain exceptions for commercial airline pilots) or after age 65, the maximum annual benefit will be increased or decreased, respectively [Code Sec. 415(b) and (d)].

Benefit Limits for Governmental and Multiemployer Defined Benefit Plans

The rule limiting defined benefit plan distributions to 100 percent of a participant's average compensation for the participant's high three years is inapplicable to governmental plans and multiemployer plans. Thus, the benefits are limited to the annual dollar limit that is adjusted annually for cost-of-living increases ($205,000 for 2013) [Code Sec. 415(b)(1)]. Multiemployer plans cannot be combined or aggregated with nonmultiemployer plans for purposes of applying the 100 percent of compensation limit to the non-multiemployer plan, or with any other multiemployer plan for the purpose of applying other limits under Code Sec. 415.

Survivor and Disability Benefits

The early retirement reduction does not apply to: (1) disability and survivor benefits provided under governmental plans, (2) income received from a governmental plan as a pension, annuity, or similar allowance as the result of the recipient becoming disabled by personal injuries or sickness, or (3) amounts received from a governmental plan by the beneficiaries, survivors, or the estate of an employee as a result of the employee's death [Code Sec. 415(b)(2)(I)].

Police Officers, Firefighters, and Members of the Armed Forces

The early retirement reduction does not apply to certain participants in plans of state and local governmental units who are police officers, firefighters, or former members of the U.S. Armed Forces [Code Sec. 415(b)(2)(G)]. Thus, police officers and firefighters who retire at age 62 in 2013 will be entitled to a benefit of up to $205,000. This rule applies to any participant in a plan maintained by a state or political subdivision of a state, who is credited, for benefit accrual purposes, with at least 15 years of service as either (1) a full-time employee of any police department or fire department of the state or political subdivision, providing police protection, firefighting services, or emergency medical services, or (2) a member of the Armed Forces of the United States.

Commercial Airline Pilots

The annual dollar limit is reduced for benefits beginning before age 62 and increased for benefits beginning after age 65 (rather than the social security retirement age) [Code Sec. 415(b)(2)]. However, if the Federal Aviation Administration (FAA) requires a pilot to retire between age 60 and age 62, the FAA required age will be substituted for age 62 [Code Sec. 415(b)(9)(A)].

Participants with Fewer Than 10 Years of Service or Participation

A reduction in the dollar limit is also mandated where a participant retires with fewer than ten years of service or plan participation. The 100 percent of compensation limit is reduced. It becomes 10 percent of compensation times the number of years of service, and the dollar limit ($205,000 in 2013) is cut to 10 percent of the dollar limit for each year of participation. However, the reductions may not reduce the ceilings to less than 1/10 of the ceilings [Code Sec. 415(b)(5)].

Example 3-8: Ms. Singer has completed three years of participation under a plan. In 2013, the maximum annual benefit that could be provided by the plan would be the lesser of: 30 percent of compensation or $61,500 (30 percent of $205,000).

.02 Defined Contribution Plan Caps

The maximum benefit that can be provided by a defined contribution plan is expressed in terms of limits on the amount of "annual additions." Annual additions include employer and employee contributions, plus forfeitures, if any. For any year, the annual additions cannot exceed the lesser of: $51,000 or 100 percent of compensation in 2013 [Code Sec. 415(c)(1)(A)]. Although money purchase pension plans and target benefit plans are pension plans, they are tested under the defined contribution plan limits [Code Sec. 415(c)]. Salary reduction amounts used for qualified transportation benefits (employer-provided transit passes, vanpooling, and qualified parking) will not reduce qualified retirement plan contributions or benefits if an employer so chooses [Code Sec. 415(c)(1)].

.03 Combined Plan Limits

In applying the benefit, contribution, and overall limitations, all qualified defined benefit plans ever maintained by the employer are treated as one defined benefit plan and all qualified defined contribution plans ever maintained by the employer are treated as one defined contribution plan. The fact that a plan has been terminated does not prevent it from being taken into account [Code Sec. 415(f)(1); Reg. § 1.415-8(a)]. A multiemployer plan will not be aggregated with non-multiemployer plans for purposes of applying the 100-percent-of-compensation benefit limit to non-multiemployer plans [Code Sec. 415(f)(3)(A)]. In addition, a multiemployer plan will not be aggregated with any other multiemployer plan for purposes of determining any Section 415 limitation [Code Sec. 415(f)(3)(B)].

¶3045 TOP-HEAVY PLANS

A defined benefit plan is top-heavy if, as of the determination date, the present value of the cumulative accrued benefits under the plan for "key employees" exceeds 60 percent of the present value of the cumulative accrued benefits under the plan for all employees. A defined contribution plan is top-heavy if the aggregate of the accounts of key employees under the plan exceeds 60 percent of the aggregate of the accounts of all employees under the plan. Tougher eligibility and vesting rules apply to top-heavy plans [Code Sec. 416(a), (g)(1)(A)]. These requirements are not applicable to SIMPLE 401(k) or SIMPLE IRA plans. See ¶ 3175.

.01 Who Are Key Employees?

An employee will be considered a key employee if, during the prior year, the employee was (1) an officer with compensation in excess of $165,000 in 2013, (2) a more than five-percent owner, or (3) a more than one-percent owner with compensation in excess of $165,000 (not subject to an inflation adjustment) [Code Sec. 416(i)(1)(A)].

The family ownership attribution rule no longer applies in determining whether an individual is a five-percent owner of the employer for purposes of the top-heavy rules only. The family ownership attribution rule continues to apply to other provisions that cross reference the top-heavy rules, such as the definition of highly compensated employee and the definition of one-percent owner under the top-heavy rules.

.02 Faster Vesting

Plans that are top-heavy are required to vest participants more rapidly. They must satisfy one of the following schedules: (1) Full vesting in employer-derived accrued benefits after three years of service or (2) 20 percent vesting each year, after the first year, so that a participant is 100 percent vested at the end of six years [Code Sec. 416(b)].

> **Example 3-9:** Dr. Able M.D.P.C. maintains a profit-sharing plan. An annual contribution of 15 percent is made for each employee. A nurse employed by the professional corporation has an accrued benefit of $12,000 after four years of plan participation. If the plan is top-heavy, her vested accrued benefit must be at least $7,200 (60 percent). Compare: Under the regular vesting rules, her vested accrued benefit could be less. Under the five-year vesting rule, she is not required to be fully vested until completion of five years. Accordingly, she would not be required to have any vested benefit after four years of plan participation. Under the three-to-seven-year graduated vesting schedule she must be 40 percent vested after four years, so her vested accrued benefit would be $4,800.

Top-heavy status is determined on a year-by-year basis. Accordingly, it would be possible to change to a slower vesting schedule during a year when the plan was not top-heavy. However, any employee with three or more years of service could elect to retain the top-heavy vesting schedule. Accrued benefits could not be decreased by virtue of a change in the vesting schedule [Reg. § 1.416-1, Q&A V-7].

.03 Minimum Benefits or Contributions

All nonkey employees in a top-heavy plan must be provided with a minimum benefit. Certain so-called "integrated plans" are generally permitted to provide smaller benefits, taking into account the employee benefit derived by the employer payments of Social Security tax. However, if a plan is top-heavy, employees cannot be excluded from coverage because their compensation is less than the social security wage base. In addition, employees cannot be excluded because they refuse to make employee contributions [Code Sec. 416(c)]. Employer matching contributions are taken into account in determining whether the minimum benefit requirement has been satisfied for a defined contribution plan. In determining whether a defined benefit plan meets the minimum benefit requirements, any year in which a plan is frozen is not considered a year of service for purposes of determining an employee's years of service. A plan is frozen for a year when no key employee or former key-employee receives benefits under the plan [Code Sec. 416(c)(1)(C)].

In a plan year in which a defined benefit plan is top-heavy, a nonkey employee must accrue a benefit that is not less than the smaller of 20 percent of pay, or 2 percent of pay for each year of service. With respect to a top-heavy defined contribution plan, contributions for nonkey employees cannot be less than 3 percent of compensation, unless the contribution for key employees is less than 3 percent. For purposes of computing this minimum benefit, reallocated forfeitures and salary reduction contributions are taken into account.

If a nonkey employee is eligible to participate in both a defined benefit and defined contribution plan maintained by the same employer, the minimum benefit is only required to be provided in one plan [Code Sec. 416(f)]. Also for a key employee who does participate in two top-heavy plans, the combined plan minimum benefit and contribution limit is reduced [¶ 3040].

¶3050 COMMONLY CONTROLLED BUSINESS

Special rules apply to plans maintained by groups of businesses or corporations that are related through some form of common ownership. In short, for purposes of the qualification requirements including minimum participation and vesting, limits on benefits and contributions and the top-heavy rules, all employees of members of a controlled group of corporations or an "affiliated service group" [(b) below] are treated as employed by a single employer.

.01 Controlled Group of Corporations

Corporations are considered related for purposes of the qualification rules if (1) a parent corporation owns 80 percent of subsidiary stock; (2) 80 percent of the stock in brother-sister corporations is owned by the same five or fewer individuals (who also own over 50 percent of the stock of each corporation); or (3) a combined group of three or more corporations if at least one is a member of both classifications described above [Code Sec. 1563(a)].

.02 Affiliated Service Groups

An affiliated service group consists of at least one organization that is created to provide services to a related organization [Code Sec. 414(m)].

Before the enactment of these rules, it was possible to avoid the nondiscrimination rules by creating multiple entities that were not related. For example, a group of service professionals such as doctors or lawyers would separately incorporate. They would then form a partnership of their professional corporations (P.C.s) that would hire the support staff employees and maintain qualified plans for the employees. The qualified plans for the employees would be separately tested from the P.C. plans maintained by the doctors themselves. By maintaining separate service organizations, the professionals could provide generous benefits for themselves and little or no plan coverage for rank and file employees.

Under the affiliated service group rules, all organizations involved in such an arrangement are treated as one employer to test the plan coverage and nondiscrimination requirements. The rules are very technical and the subject of extensive regulations [Reg. § 1.414(l)-1].

¶3055 DEFINED BENEFIT PLANS—BENEFIT ACCRUAL

.01 Benefit Accrual Tests

Defined benefit plans must satisfy one of three benefit accrual rules. These rules insure that a vesting schedule is not undercut by the timing of benefit accrual. For example, the following practice (called backloading) is prevented by the accrual rules: A defined benefit plan provides that at normal retirement age, an employee retires on 30 percent of final pay. The plan provides that participants will accrue a benefit of 0.2 percent of compensation times years of service, for the first 25 years of service. Thereafter, the benefits will accrue at the rate of 5 percent of compensation times years of service. If the employee stays for 30 years, he receives the full benefit (0.2 percent × 25 = 5 percent plus 5 percent × 5 = 25 percent). However, if the employee left after 25 years of service, he would receive only a 5 percent (0.2 percent × 25 years) of service retirement benefit.

To avoid this result, defined benefit plans must satisfy one of the following benefit accrual tests [Code Sec. 411(b)]:

- *Three percent rule.* As of the close of a plan year, the participant must be entitled to a benefit for each year of his participation equal to three percent of the normal retirement benefit that he would be entitled to, had he begun participation at the earliest possible age and continued until the earlier of age 65 or the plan's normal retirement age [Code Sec. 411(b)(1)(A); Reg. § 1.411(b)-1(b)(1)].
- *133⅓ percent rule.* The rate of accrual for a subsequent plan year cannot be greater than 133⅓ percent of the rate for a prior year [Code Sec. 411(b)(1)(B); Reg. § 1.411(b)-1(b)(2)]. For example, if a defined benefit plan provides that a participant's benefits will accrue at 1.5 percent of compensation up to age 55, and at 2 percent thereafter, the plan qualifies under the 133⅓ percent test.
- *Fractional rule.* The accrued benefit must equal a fraction of the benefit that would accrue at normal retirement age, assuming continuing compensation at the rate the plan would use if the participant retired on the date he separated from service. The fraction is the participant's total number of years of participation, over the total years he would have participated if he separated from service at normal retirement age [Code Sec. 411(b)(1)(C); Reg. § 1.411(b)-1(b)(3)].

.02 Phased Retirement

In order for a pension plan to be a qualified plan, the plan must be established and maintained by an employer primarily to provide systematically for the payment of definitely determinable benefits to its employees over a period of years, usually for life, after retirement or attainment of "normal retirement age." A plan does not fail to satisfy this paragraph merely because the plan provides, in accordance with Code Sec. 401(a)(36), that a distribution may be made from the plan to an employee who has attained age 62 and who is not separated from employment at the time of the distribution [Reg. § 1.401(a)-1(b)(1)].

.03 Normal Retirement Age

The normal retirement age under a plan must be an age that is not earlier than the earliest age that is reasonably representative of the typical retirement age for the industry in which the covered workforce is employed. Thus, the plan sponsor has the freedom to set the normal retirement age provided it is not earlier than the "typical retirement age" for the industry in which participants work.

Age 62 Safe Harbor

A normal retirement age under a plan that is age 62 or later is deemed to be not earlier than the earliest age that is reasonably representative of the typical retirement age for the industry in which the covered workforce is employed.

Age 55 to Age 62

Ages between 55 and 61 must be reasonable under the facts and circumstances but the IRS will generally defer to the sponsor's good-faith determination.

Under Age 55

An age lower than 55 (50 for public service employees) is presumed to be unreasonably early absent facts and circumstances that demonstrate otherwise to the IRS [Reg. § 1.401(a)-1(b)(2)].

¶3060 EMPLOYER TAX CONSEQUENCES

.01 Deductions

The general rule is that employers can deduct contributions made to a qualified pension, annuity, stock bonus or profit-sharing plan in the tax year when they are paid even though the employees or beneficiaries receive benefits at a later time [Code Sec. 404(a)].

Timing of Deductions—The Grace Period Rule

Regardless of the employer's method of accounting, a contribution to a qualified plan is considered to have been made on the last day of the preceding tax year if the payment is for that year and is made not later than the return due date for that tax year (including any extended due date). This grace period rule applies, even if the taxpayer's return is not filed by that due date [Code Sec. 404(a)(6)]. Accordingly, a calendar year corporation has until September 15 to make its retirement plan contributions for the prior year, if it files an extension.

In *Vons Companies*,[11] a corporation's contributions to qualified retirement plans made after the close of two tax years but before the extended due date for filing its returns for those years were deductible in the year made, and not in the previous tax year. The taxpayer claimed deductions on its returns for plan contributions based on the number of hours worked during the months between the last day of the tax year and the return's

---

[11] *Vons Companies*, FedCl, 2003-1 USTC ¶50,356. *Lucky Stores, Inc.*, CA-9, 98-2 USTC ¶50,662, 153 F3d 964, *cert. denied*, 526 US 1111; *American Stores Co.*, CA-10, 99-1 USTC ¶50,326, 170 F3d 1267, *cert. denied*, 528 US 875.

extended due date. However, those contributions were not made on account of the tax year at issue and, thus, were not subject to the grace period for deductibility of payments made "on account of "the preceding tax year."

The IRS had similarly concluded in Rev. Rul. 90-105,[12] that contributions are not deductible for an employer's tax year if they are attributable to compensation earned by plan participants after the end of that tax year. The fact that the plan was amended and the board of directors set a minimum contribution for the plan year does not change that result, according to Rev. Rul. 2002-46[13], in which the IRS held that grace period contributions to a qualified cash or deferred arrangement or to a defined contribution plan as matching contributions are not deductible by the employer for a tax year if the contributions are attributable to compensation earned by plan participants after the end of that tax year.

Despite the liberal contribution deadline, employers must prepay their contributions to defined benefit pension plans in quarterly installments much like estimated tax payments. Otherwise, an interest penalty is imposed. For calendar year plans, the first installment is due by April 15 [Code Sec. 412(m)(3)(B)].

.02 Limitations on Amounts Deductible

Employers may deduct annual contributions to a profit sharing or stock bonus plans up to the greater of:

1. 25 percent of the compensation paid to all participants in the stock bonus or profit sharing plan, or
2. The amount the employer is required to contribute to a simple 401(k) plan [Code Sec. 404(a)(3)(A)(i)]. The total compensation for this purpose cannot include compensation to any plan participant in 2013 in excess of $255,000 [Code Sec. 404(l)]. The definition of compensation for purposes of computing the available deduction to stock bonus and profit sharing plans includes "elective deferrals" (e.g., an employee's 401(k) contributions) [Code Sec. 404(a)(12)].

The maximum deduction for contributions to defined benefit pension plans cannot exceed the amount of the full funding limitation for the year [Code Sec. 404(a)(1)]. In general, the full funding limitation is the amount necessary to bring the plan balance up to the amount of the present value of what the employees are projected to receive at retirement.

.03 Pension Funding Rules

In order to ensure that single-employer defined benefit pension plans are adequately funded, minimum and full-funding limits are imposed by Code Sec. 430.

Minimum Funding Standards for Single-Employer Defined Benefit Pension Plans

Employers maintaining single-employer defined benefit plans are subject to funding rules requiring them to make a minimum contribution to the plan each year based on

[12] Rev. Rul. 90-105, 1990-2 CB 69.

[13] Rev. Rul. 2002-46, 2002-2 CB 117, as modified by Rev. Proc. 2011-14, IRB 2011-4, Rev. Rul. 2002-73, 2002-2 CB 805 regarding automatic accounting period change.

the (1) plan's assets (reduced by credit balances), (2) funding target, and (3) target normal cost [Code Sec. 430(a)(1)]. Full funding of the plans is required and funding shortfalls must be eliminated over seven years. An employer with a plan that fails to satisfy these minimum funding requirements or to correct shortfalls will be subject to an excise tax under Code Sec. 4971. A temporary waiver of the minimum funding requirement may be available to an employer that is unable to satisfy the minimum funding standard for a plan year without "substantial business hardship" [Code Sec. 412(c)(1)(A)]. The employer may be required to provide security to the plan as a condition for the waiver [Code Sec. 412(c)(4)]. In addition, no plan amendment that has the effect of increasing plan liabilities may generally be adopted during the waiver period.

A plan is treated as satisfying the minimum funding standard for the year if:

- In the case of a single-employer defined benefit plan, the employer makes aggregate contributions to or under the plan that are not less than the minimum required contribution under Code Sec. 430 for the plan for the plan year;
- In the case of a single-employer money purchase plan, the employer makes contributions to or under the plan for the plan year that are required under the terms of the plan; and
- In the case of a multiemployer plan, the employers make aggregate contributions to or under the plan that are sufficient to ensure that the plan does not have an accumulated funding deficiency under Code Sec. 431 as of the end of the plan year [Code Sec. 412(a)].

The minimum required funding contribution must be paid by the employer sponsor responsible for making contributions to the plan [Code Sec. 412(B)(1)]. In the event the employer is a member of a controlled group, each member of the group is jointly and severally liable for the payment [Code Sec. 412(b)(2) and (d)(3)]. Joint and several liability also applies in the funding contribution due under a multiemployer plan.

Waiver of Minimum Funding Requirements

A temporary waiver of the minimum funding requirements may be provided to an employer that is unable to satisfy the minimum funding standard for a plan year without substantial business hardship.

The IRS is authorized to waive the minimum funding requirements applicable to all or any portion of the minimum funding standard for an employer that is unable to satisfy the minimum funding standard for a plan year without temporary substantial business hardship. The IRS is similarly empowered to waive all or any portion of the minimum funding requirements applicable to a multiemployer plan in which 10 percent or more of the participating employers to the participating employer are unable to meet the minimum funding standards for a plan year without substantial business hardship [Code Sec. 412(c)(1)(A)(i)].

An employer under a single-employer plan or a multiemployer plan will not be able to justify a waiver of the minimum funding standard solely on the basis of business hardship. Application of the minimum funding standard must also be adverse to the interests of plan participants in the aggregate [Code Sec. 412(C)(1)(A)(ii)]. A special rule applies for purposes of determining whether an employer that is a member of a controlled group is experiencing temporary substantial business hardship sufficient to warrant a waiver of the minimum funding requirements for its single-employer plan. Under such circumstances, the temporary substantial business hardship condition must be met by not only the employer, but by the controlled group to which the employer belongs, treating all members of the group as a single employer [Code Sec. 412(c)(5)(B)].

The factors that define temporary substantial business hardship (or substantial business hardship) include whether: (1) the employer is operating at an economic loss; (2) there is substantial unemployment or underemployment in the employer's industry; (3) sales and profits in the industry are depressed or declining; and (4) it is reasonable to expect that the plan will be continued only if the waiver is granted [Code Sec. 412(c)(2)].

Security for Waivers

An employer maintaining a single-employer defined benefit plan may be required to provide security to the plan as a condition for a waiver of the minimum funding standards [Code Sec. 412(c)(4)(A)]. Any security provided as a condition for a waiver may be perfected and enforced only by the Pension Benefit Guaranty Corporation (PBGC) or, at the direction of the PBGC, by a contributing sponsor or member of the sponsor's controlled group [Code Sec. 412(c)(4)(A)(ii)].

An exception to the security requirement is authorized for a waiver involving a plan with respect to which the sum of: (1) the aggregate unpaid minimum required contributions for the plan year (including any increase that would result from a denial of a pending waiver request) and all preceding plan years; and (2) the present value of all waiver amortization installments determined for the plan year and all succeeding plan years, is less than $1 million Code Sec. 412(c)(4)(C)(i)].

.04 Type of Contributions

Contributions of property other than cash ("in-kind" contributions), to satisfy funding requirements to qualified retirement plans are generally not allowed.[14] These contributions are treated as a prohibited sale to the plan and are subject to 5 percent excise taxes on the "amount involved" for each year that the "in-kind" contribution remains in the plan, beginning with the year it was made through the year it is corrected [¶ 3100].

During lean years, an employer may have difficulty coming up with cash to make the year's contributions. Contributions of employer securities may be considered as an option.

Generally, a plan may not acquire employer securities to satisfy its contribution obligations. However, a limited exception exists if immediately after the acquisition, the fair market value of the securities does not exceed 10 percent of the fair market value of plan assets [Code Sec. 401(a)(22)].

---

[14] *Keystone Consolidated Industries, Inc.*, SCt, 93-1 USTC ¶ 50,298, 508 US 152, 113 SCt 2006, *on remand*, CA-5, 93-2 USTC ¶ 50,533, 1 F3d 287.

.05 Form 5500, *Annual Return/Report of Employee Benefit Plan*

In general, most qualified retirement plans must file Form 5500, *Annual Return/Report of Employee Benefit Plan,* each tax year to report detailed information concerning various aspects of employee benefit plans [Code Sec. 6058]. Some plans may be able to file the simpler Form 5500-EZ, *Annual Return of One-Participant (Owners and Their Spouse) Retirement Plan,* if the plan's only participants are an individual and spouse who together own the business (whether or not incorporated) for which the plan is established. Form 5500-EZ may also be used by the plan of a partnership if the only participants are partners and their spouses. Form 5500-EZ need not be filed if the plan, and any other plan of the employer, had total assets of $250,000 or less at the end of every plan year.

Form 5500 or Form 5500-EZ must be filed no later than the last day of the seventh month after the plan year ends (e.g., July 31 for calendar year plans). A one-time extension of 2½ months may be obtained by filing Form 5558, *Application for Extension of Time to File Certain Employee Plan Returns.* An automatic extension will be granted if the plan year and the employer's tax year are the same and the employer has been granted an extension to file its tax return. Penalties may be imposed for failure to file the required annual information return or, in the case of defined benefit plans, the actuarial report [Code Sec. 6652].

¶3065 INTEGRATION OF QUALIFIED PLANS WITH SOCIAL SECURITY

Integration of a qualified plan with social security means that a private retirement plan is treated as part of an overall retirement system that includes social security. An integrated retirement plan may provide additional benefits or contributions based on compensation above the "integration level" (usually the social security wage base, which is $113,700 in 2013) without violating the nondiscrimination rules.

Under an integrated plan, each employee's total benefits under both the private retirement plan and social security must be part of an integrated system that is not discriminatory. Lower-paid employees receive preferential treatment under social security—they derive a greater share of retirement benefits, as a percent of compensation, from employer payments of social security tax than do the higher-paid. Reason: Higher-paid employees have only part of their compensation covered by social security—no social security taxes are paid, nor are benefits earned under the system, for salary in excess of the social security wage base. Integrated plans are permitted to counterbalance this social security preference for lower-paid employees, by favoring the higher-paid (with bigger contributions or benefits).

Minimum benefits must be provided for employees in integrated plans. This limits the disparity between contributions or benefits allocable to income above and below the wage base. For defined contribution plans, the permitted disparity cannot exceed the lesser of (1) twice the percentage of earnings put aside for earnings below the integration level, or (2) the sum of (a) the percentage for lower earners, plus (b) the OASDI tax rate. For further discussion of the payroll tax and rates, see ¶ 15,050.

For defined benefit plans, the disparity rules are more complicated. Basically, benefits for earnings above the integration level cannot be greater than (1) twice the benefit rate for earnings below the integration level, or (2) three-fourths of 1 percent, multiplied by the participant's years of service (up to 35 years), more than the benefit attributable to lesser earnings [Code Sec. 401(l); Reg. § 1.401(l)-2, -3]. It should be noted that the "integration level"—or break point at which contribution levels change—can be lower than the Social Security wage base, but it cannot be greater.

NOTE: A uniform retirement age, specifically, the social security retirement age, should be used when testing for discrimination under Code Sec. 401(a)(4) [Code Sec. 401(a)(5)(F)(i)]. In addition, subsidized early retirement benefits and joint and survivor annuities are not treated as being unavailable to employees on the same terms merely because such benefits or annuities are based in whole or part on an employee's social security retirement age [Code Sec. 401(a)(5)(F)(ii)]. Thus, the use of the social security retirement age as the basis for determining benefits will not violate the nondiscrimination rules [¶ 3025].

¶3070 TRUST MUST PROVE EXEMPTION

The employer who establishes or amends a pension, profit-sharing or stock bonus plan or trust will want to know in advance if the proposed plan or trust qualifies for exemption from tax. The IRS will issue a so-called "determination letter," which is essentially an advance letter ruling as to the plan's qualified status. Requests for such letters are filed with the district director on Form 5300 *Application for Determination Employee Benefit Plan*. Advance approval can also be obtained for master and prototype employee plans upon proper application on Form 4461, *Application for Approval of Master or Prototype Defined Contribution Plan*, by the sponsoring employer group.

¶3075 DISTRIBUTIONS FROM QUALIFIED PLANS

If you have money stashed away in your employers' retirement plan and you will be retiring or changing jobs in the near future, you have some important decisions to make. What you decide to do with your nest egg will have a tremendous impact on you and your family's overall financial picture. Your decision should be based on a number of factors, including your age, your health, your immediate needs for cash, your anticipated living expenses, and what other sources of income you can expect in the future. Be sure to fully evaluate all aspects of your distribution options. Keep in mind that you will be asked to make some irrevocable decisions about a large chunk of money, possibly more than you have ever managed in your life.

While the main function of retirement plans is to pay benefits, the time and manner of payment varies. Most defined benefit plans provide benefits in the form of an annuity, beginning at age 65. Defined contribution plans usually provide a lump-sum payout of the participant's individual account.

.01 Types of Distributions

Aside from a straight life annuity, the most common forms of benefit distribution are as follows:

Qualified Joint and Survivor Annuity (QJSA)

In general, a qualified plan must provide that the normal form of benefit for a married participant is a so-called "qualified joint and survivor annuity" [Code Sec. 401(a)(11)]. It is an annuity for the life of the participant with payments continuing for the surviving spouse. Payments to the surviving spouse must equal at least 50 percent of the amount paid to the participant [Code Sec. 417]. In Rev. Rul. 2012-3,[15] the IRS provided guidance on the spousal consent requirements when a plan participant purchases a deferred annuity contract under a profit-sharing plan, such as a 401(k) arrangement.

> ▶ **IMPORTANT:** The qualified joint and survivor annuity can only be waived by written spousal consent no less than 30 days and no more than 180 days before the date distribution commences [Code Sec. 417(a)(6)(A); Reg. § 1.417(e)-1(b)(2)].

For distributions involving a QJSA, a plan may permit a participant and his or her spouse to elect to waive the 30-day minimum waiting period between the time the written explanation of the terms and conditions of a qualified joint and survivor annuity is provided and the annuity starting date. A waiver is allowed only if the distribution commences more than 7 days after the written explanation is provided [Code Sec. 417(a)(7)(A)]. If you don't make a waiver, the usual waiting period will apply.

Requirement for Additional Survivor Annuity Option

The minimum survivor annuity requirements mandate that, at the election of a participant, benefits will be paid in the form of a *qualified optional survivor annuity (QOSA)* [Code Sec. 417(g)]. This law is designed to afford participants the opportunity to tailor their benefits to their specific needs. A QOSA is defined as: (1) an annuity for the life of the participant with a survivor annuity for the life of the spouse that is equal to the applicable percentage of the amount of the annuity that is payable during the joint lives of the participant and the spouse, and (2) the actuarial equivalent to a single annuity for the life of the participant [Code Sec. 417(g)(1)].

Level of Spouse Survivor Annuity Provided Under QJSA

The level of spouse survivor annuity that must be provided under a QJSA depends upon the level of spouse survivor annuity provided under a plan's QJSA (that is, the QJSA form of benefit that is provided to a married participant in the absence of a waiver of such form of benefit). If the QJSA for a married participant provides a survivor annuity for the life of the participant's spouse that is less than 75 percent of the amount of the annuity that is payable during the joint lives of the participant and the participant's spouse, the QOSA must provide a survivor annuity percentage of 75 percent. If the QJSA for a married participant provides a survivor annuity for the life of the participant's spouse that is greater than or equal to 75 percent of the amount of the annuity that is payable during the joint lives of the participant and the partici-

[15] Rev. Rul. 2012-3, IRB 2012-8, 383.

pant's spouse, the QOSA must provide a spouse survivor annuity percentage of 50 percent [Code Sec. 417(g)(2)(A)].[16]

The written explanation required to be provided to participants explaining the terms and conditions of the qualified joint and survivor annuity must also include the terms and conditions of the qualified optional survivor annuity [Code Sec. 417(a)(3)(A)(i)].

Lump-Sum Distribution

The usual benefit from a defined contribution plan is the individual's account balance paid out all at once in a "lump-sum." Also, for plans that pay benefits in the form of an annuity, the annuity can sometimes be converted into a lump-sum. Many plans require this form of payout where a plan participant terminates employment for reasons other than retirement. However, if a participant's annuity benefit has a value above $5,000, he cannot be compelled to receive the benefit as a lump-sum until the later of age 62 or the plan's normal retirement age [Reg. § 1.411(a)-11].

Life Annuity with Term Certain

Under this form of benefit, the participant receives an annuity for a term certain. Usually the payout period is structured so that benefits (in the same amount) will continue to another beneficiary, for the balance of the guaranteed period, subsequent to the participant's death.

.02 When Payments Must Start

For a trust to constitute a qualified trust, the trust plan must provide that, unless the participant elects otherwise, the payment of benefits to a participant must commence no later than 60 days after the close of the plan year in which the latest of the following occurs: (a) participant turns 65, or the plan's normal retirement age (if earlier); or (b) the tenth anniversary of the year in which the participant began participating in the plan; or (c) the termination of employment [Code Sec. 401(a)(14)].

Example 3-10: Jones has been in the Widget Corp. pension plan for 15 years. He terminates employment in 2003 at age 50. The plan would not be required to pay Jones his benefits until 60 days after the close of the plan year in which Jones turns 60. If Jones will turn 60 in 2013, the plan must commence benefits by March 1, 2014. That date is later than his tenth anniversary in the plan and his year of termination.

Death Prior to Retirement

Defined benefit plans must provide a so-called preretirement survivor annuity to married vested participants who die before they begin to receive benefits under the plan [Code Sec. 401(a)(11)]. The benefit must at least equal the benefit the spouse would have received had the participant begun to receive benefits before he died, in the form of a qualified joint and survivor annuity [Code Sec. 417(c)].

---

[16] Notice 2008-30, IRB 2008-12, 638, Q&A-8, as amplified and clarified by Notice 2009-75, IRB 2009-39, 436.

If a participant dies prior to retirement, defined contribution plans usually pay over the participant's account balance to the surviving spouse or other beneficiary. The distribution must be completed within five years after the year of death.

Exception. The five-year rule does not apply if an individual beneficiary is designated to receive benefit installments over his life. In that case, the distribution must begin by the end of the calendar year following the year of death.

Special break for surviving spouse. The five-year rule also is not binding on a surviving spouse. What's more, payments to the surviving spouse can begin later than usual. The surviving spouse is permitted to defer receipt of benefits until what would have been the required commencement date had the participant survived [Reg. § 1.401(a)(9)-1 Q&A C-5(b)].

.03 In-Service Withdrawals

In-service withdrawals are prohibited in a defined benefit plan prior to the plan's normal retirement age. The same rule applies to money purchase pension plans.[17] The rules are different for profit-sharing and stock bonus plans. These plans can permit in-service withdrawals only if they are permitted by the plan document. However, such withdrawals may be subject to a premature withdrawal penalty [¶ 3085]. Employer contributions that have been in the plan for more than two years can be made available for withdrawals.[18] All employer contributions (not limited by the two-year rule) can be made available to employees who have participated in the plan for more than five years.[19]

In a 401(k) plan, discussed at ¶ 3150, employee contributions made pursuant to a cash or deferred election cannot be withdrawn prior to age 59½ unless there is a hardship. Income earned on 401(k) contributions cannot be withdrawn on account of hardship [Code Sec. 401(k)(2)(B); Reg. § 1. 401(k)-1(d)(2)].

.04 Amount of Distribution

When a distribution is made in a lump sum, or in installments, there are no legal constraints on the minimum amount to be distributed (before age 70½). However, complex rules govern required minimum distributions (RMDs) from qualified plans, Code Sec. 403(b) tax-deferred annuities, Code Sec. 457(b) eligible deferred compensation plans maintained by state and local government and IRAs [Code Sec. 401(a)(9)]. The rules are aimed at limiting the tax deferral, and tax-free accumulation, of plan benefits.

The key year here is the year when the participant turns 70½. The RMD is based on the participant's balance as of December 31 of the prior year. For further discussion of RMDs, see ¶ 3120.

---

[17] Rev. Rul. 74-417, 1974-2 CB 131.

[18] Rev. Rul. 71-295, 1971-2 CB 184.

[19] Rev. Rul. 68-24, 1968-1 CB 150.

¶3080 TAXATION OF DISTRIBUTIONS

In general, an employee is taxed on amounts received from a qualified plan, unless the distribution qualifies for special tax treatment or as a tax-free rollover which is discussed in ¶ 3125 [Code Sec. 402(a)].

.01 Taxation of Annuities

Unless participants have a basis in the plan as a result of making after-tax employee contributions, the entire amount of each annuity distribution is taxed as ordinary income in the year of receipt. If participants make nondeductible, after-tax contributions to a plan, they have an investment or basis in the plan. Accordingly, a portion of each distribution is considered a return of capital and is nontaxable. This nontaxable portion is determined by applying an exclusionary shield equal to the your total investment in the contract divided by the total expected payments over the term of the annuity For this purpose, amounts contributed to a cash or deferred plan that were made in pre-tax dollars (i.e., were not subject to income tax) are not treated as employee contributions. They are subject to tax upon distribution. The tax treatment of annuities is discussed further at Ch. 5. The courts have held that a taxpayer was unable to adjust the basis in his retirement annuity by an inflation factor, to take account of inflation between the date of his contributions to the retirement plan and the annuity starting date.[20] Therefore, he could not increase his basis in the annuity in an attempt to reduce the amount of his pension annuity subject to tax.

A simplified method exists for determining the portion of an annuity distribution from a qualified retirement plan, qualified annuity, or tax-sheltered annuity that represents the nontaxable recovery of basis [Code Sec. 72(d)]. According to Table 2, the portion of each annuity payment that represents nontaxable return of basis is equal to the employee's total investment in the contract as of the annuity starting date, divided by the number of anticipated payments, which you determine by referring to the age of the participant as listed in the table below (unless the number of payments is fixed under the terms of the annuity in which case you use that number) [Code Sec. 72(d)(1)(B)(iii)]:

Table 2. Return of Basis in Annuity Payments

Age of primary annuitant on the annuity starting date	Number of anticipated payments
55 and under	360
56-60	310
61-65	260
66-70	210
71 and older	160

[20] *K.L. Nordtvedt*, 116 TC 165, Dec. 54,273 (2001), *aff'd*, CA-9 (unpublished memorandum), 2001-2 USTC ¶ 50,772.

The investment in the contract equals the amount of premiums and other considerations (basically, the after-tax contributions to the plan) less the amount received before the annuity starting date that was excluded from gross income.

> **Example 3-11:** You are 57 and receive a $200 per month annuity from your pension plan. Your contributions to the plan totaled $31,000. According to the simplified method, the nontaxable part of the annuity payment is $100. This is determined by dividing $31,000, your investment in the contract, by 310, which is the number of anticipated payments as determined from the chart above.

You cannot use the simplified method if you are over age 75 on the annuity starting date unless there are fewer than 5 years of guaranteed payments under the annuity [Code Sec. 72(d)(1)(E)].

Table 3 shows the number of payments to expect if the benefits are based on the life of more than one annuitant [Code Sec. 72(d)(1)(B)(iv)]:

Table 3. Payments Based on Life of Multiple Annuitants

Combined ages of annuitants	Number of payments
Not more than 110	410
More than 110 but not more than 120	360
More than 120 but not more than 130	310
More than 130 but not more than 140	260
More than 140	210

.02 Lump-Sum Distributions

If the employee was born before January 1, 1936, the employee may elect 10-year averaging of the total taxable amount of the distribution; or elect 10-year averaging of the ordinary income portion of the taxable amount of the distribution and pay a flat 20 percent tax on the capital gains portion. Ten-year averaging is reported on Form 4972, *Tax on Lump-Sum Distributions.* The term "lump sum distribution" means the distribution or payment within one tax year of the recipient of the balance to the credit of an employee (other than a self-employed person) which becomes payable to the recipient

- On account of the employee's death,
- After the employee attains age 59½,
- On account of the employee's separation from service, or
- After the employee has become disabled [Code Sec. 402(e)(4)(D)(i)].

In the case of a self-employed person, the distribution must be made because of the individual's death, or it must be made after age 59½ [Code Sec. 402(e)(4)(D)(i)].

Computing the Taxable Amount

You compute the taxable amount using 10-year averaging as follows:

1. From the total taxable amount of the distribution, subtract the minimum distribution allowance (MDA). The MDA is the lesser of $10,000 or 50 percent of the total taxable amount of the lump-sum distribution, reduced by 20 percent of the taxable

amount of the lump-sum distribution that exceeds $20,000. This means that the allowance is completely phased out for distributions of $70,000 or more.

2. Find the tax on one-tenth of the amount in Step 1, using the tax rates in the table below:
3. Multiply the result in Step 2 by 10. The result is the 10-year averaging tax

Table 4. Ten-Year Averaging Rate Table

Over—	But Not Over—	The Tax Is	of the Amount Over—
$ –0–	$1,190	11%	$–0–
1,190	2,270	$130.90 + 12%	1,190
2,270	4,530	260.50 + 14%	2,270
4,530	6,690	576.90 + 15%	4,530
6,690	9,170	900.90 + 16%	6,690
9,170	11,440	1,297.70 + 18%	9,170
11,440	13,710	1,706.30 + 20%	11,440
13,710	17,160	2,160.30 + 23%	13,710
17,160	22,880	2,953.80 + 26%	17,160
22,880	28,600	4,441.00 + 30%	22,880
28,600	34,320	6,157.00 + 34%	28,600
34,320	42,300	8,101.80 + 38%	34,320
42,300	57,190	11,134.20 + 42%	42,300
57,190	85,790	17,388.00 + 48%	57,190
85,790	...	31,116.00 + 50%	...

Consequences of election. Your adjusted gross income will not increase as a result of the election to take advantage of lump-sum averaging.

Distributions including employer securities. Special rules apply if employer securities are included as part of a lump-sum distribution. The gain attributable to the period the securities were held by the plan, so-called "unrealized appreciation," is not taxed until the securities are sold [Code Sec. 402(e)(4)(B)]. Then it is taxed as capital gain. The value of the securities at the time they were contributed to the plan (plan's basis) is ordinary income.

Deferral of tax on unrealized appreciation. The unrealized appreciation is not included in the value of a lump-sum distribution. However, a participant can elect to be taxed on the appreciation at the time the distribution is made [Code Sec. 402(e)(4)(B)].

.03 Other Forms of Plan Distributions

Distributions Used to Pay Insurance Premiums for Public Safety Officers

A retired public safety officer (law enforcement officer, firefighter, chaplain, or member of a rescue squad or ambulance crew) may elect to exclude from income distributions from an eligible retirement plan to the extent that the distributions do not exceed the amount paid for premiums for accident or health insurance or long-term care insurance for the officer, the officer's spouse, or dependents for the tax year [Code Sec. 402(l)]. The maximum annual exclusion is capped at $3,000 [Code Sec. 402(l)(2)]. The distribution must be made directly from the plan to the insurance provider [Code Sec. 402(l)(5)(A)].

An eligible retirement plan is a governmental plan that is:

- A qualified trust
- A section 403(b) plan,
- A section 403(b) annuity, or
- A section 457(b) plan.

Qualified Disaster Distributions

Unless the recipient elects otherwise, up to $100,000 in "qualified disaster recovery assistance distributions" and "qualified hurricane distributions" received by a qualified individual from an eligible retirement plan (including an IRA) are included in the recipient's income ratably over three years, beginning with the year the distribution is received. If the distributee dies during the first or second year, the amount that has not been taxed is included in income in the year of the distributee's death [Code Sec. 1400Q(a)]. An individual who received any qualified distribution may recontribute the amount of those distributions to an eligible retirement plan at any time during the three-year period beginning on the day after the distribution was received. To the extent that such a recontribution is made, the original distribution will not be taxed [Code Sec. 1400Q(a)(3)]. The individual can file an amended return or returns to claim a refund of the tax attributable to the amount recontributed.

¶3085 DISTRIBUTION TAXES AND PENALTIES

.01 Premature Distributions

A 10 percent additional tax will be imposed if, before you reach age 59½, you receive distributions from your qualified retirement plan (unless you qualify for one of the exceptions discussed below). [See ¶ 3135 for the discussion of IRA-only distributions and the exceptions.] Qualified retirement plan is defined in this situation to include an Code Sec. 403(b) tax-deferred annuity plan or IRA or annuities described in Code Sec. 408(a) and (b). Code Sec. 403(b) tax-sheltered annuities are retirement arrangements primarily for employees of public schools and certain tax-exempt organizations. The 10 percent penalty will apply even if the distribution is made on account of separation from service or retirement.

.02 Exceptions to 10-Percent Penalty for Premature Distributions

You can only avoid the 10 percent premature withdrawal penalty if the distribution qualifies under one of the following exceptions:

- *Retirement distributions to active duty military reservists.* Active duty military reservists may receive early distributions from certain retirement plans without triggering the 10-percent penalty tax generally imposed on such distributions under Code Sec. 72(t) [Code Sec. 72(t)(2)(G)]. For further discussion see ¶ 3135.

- *Public safety employees after age 50.* The 10-percent early withdrawal penalty tax does not apply to distributions from a government plan made to qualified public safety employees who separate from service after age 50 [Code Sec. 72(t)(10)(A)]. A "qualified public safety employee" means any employee of a state or political subdivision of a state who provides police protection, fire-fighting services, or emergency medical services for any area within the jurisdiction of the state or political subdivision [Code Sec. 72(t)(10)(B)].
- *Medical expenses.* The 10-percent penalty tax on early distributions from qualified retirement plans (including IRAs [¶ 3135]) does not apply to distributions that are used to pay medical expenses in excess of 10 percent of your adjusted gross income [Code Sec. 72(t)(2)(B)].

Example 3-12: Bill, age 55, participates in his employer's qualified retirement plan and has an adjusted gross income of $100,000. That year he had medical expenses in the amount of $20,000. Since these expenses exceed 10 percent of his adjusted gross income, he may withdraw up to $10,000 from his qualified retirement plan to pay his medical bill without paying the 10 percent penalty tax. He will, however, have to pay income tax on the amount of the withdrawal.

- *Health insurance premiums.* The 10 percent penalty tax does not apply to distributions from a qualified retirement plan (including IRAs [¶ 3135]) for payment of health insurance after separation from employment [Code Sec. 72(t)(2)(D)]. In order to escape the 10 percent tax, the individual must have received unemployment compensation for 12 consecutive weeks under federal or state law and the distributions must be made during any tax year in which the unemployment compensation is paid or during the next tax year. This exception to the 10 percent penalty tax does not apply to distributions made after an individual's reemployment, if he or she has been employed for at least 60 days after the initial separation from service.
- *Disability.* If you are younger than age 59½, you may withdraw money from your qualified retirement accounts (including IRAs [¶ 3135]) without paying the 10 percent penalty if the distributions are made because you are totally or permanently disabled [Code Sec. 72(t)(2)(A)(iii)]. A plan participant is considered "disabled" for these purposes if he is unable to engage in any substantial gainful activity because of a medically determinable physical or mental impairment which can be expected to result in death or be of a long-continued and indefinite duration [Code Sec. 72(m)(7)]. The term "substantial gainful activity" refers to the activity or a comparable activity in which the plan participant customarily engaged prior to the impairment [Reg. § 1.72-17A(f)(1)]. Examples approved by the IRS include the following: loss of use of two limbs; certain progressive diseases, which result in the physical loss or atrophy of a limb, such as diabetes, multiple sclerosis, or Buerger's disease; diseases of the heart, lungs, or blood vessels; inoperative and progressive cancer; brain damage; mental diseases such as psychosis; nearly total vision loss; permanent and total loss of speech; and total deafness uncorrectable by a hearing aid [Reg. § 1.72-17A(f)(2)(i)-(ix)].

  The example in Reg. § 1.72-17A(F)(2)(vi) makes it clear that a mental impairment that would prevent substantial gainful activity consists of psychosis or severe psychoneurosis requiring continued institutionalization or constant supervision of the individual.[21]

- *Leaving your job.* No penalty is imposed on distributions from your qualified retirement plan (not your IRA) if you receive the distributions after leaving your job and if the distribution is received during or after the year in which you reach age 55 [Code Sec. 72(t)(2)(A)(v)]. Keep in mind that withdrawals from your IRA are ineligible for this exception to the 10 percent penalty rule [Code Sec. 72(t)(3)(A)].[22]
- *Series of periodic payments after leaving your job.* If you are younger than age 59½, you may avoid the 10 percent penalty if after you leave your job you receive distributions from your qualified retirement plan including an Code Sec. 403(b) tax-deferred annuity or an IRA [¶ 3135] if the distributions are part of a series of "substantially equal periodic payments" made (not less frequently than annually) over your life or the joint life expectancies of you and a designated beneficiary [Code Sec. 72(t)(2)(A)(iv)]. The periodic payments must begin after the employee terminates his employment [Code Sec. 72(t)(3)(B)]. The IRS will permit individuals receiving fixed periodic IRA payments to switch, without penalty, to the required minimum distribution method, which calculates payments according to account balance and life expectancy.[23]

To calculate the amount of the distribution, the account balance at the end of the prior year is divided by the participant's life expectancy, or the joint life expectancies found in the tables under Reg. § 1.72-9. If the series of substantially equal periodic payments is subsequently modified within 5 years of the date of the first payment (or prior to age 59½, the exception to the 10 percent tax under Code Sec. 72(t)(2)(A)(iv) does not apply, and the taxpayer's tax for the year of modification is increased by an amount equal to the tax which, but for the exception under Code Sec. 72(t)(2)(A)(iv), would have been imposed, plus interest for the deferral period [Code Sec. 72(t)(4)].

- *Divorce or separation.* Distributions from your qualified retirement plans (not your IRA) will not be subject to the 10 percent penalty if the distribution is made under a qualified domestic relations order (QDRO) [¶ 3090] [Code Sec. 72(t)(2)(C)]. Note that this exception is not available for IRAs [Code Sec. 72(t)(3)(A)].
- *Death.* No 10 percent penalty is imposed on distributions from a qualified plan or IRA [¶ 3135] if the distribution is made because the employee or owner has died [Code Sec. 72(t)(2)(A)(ii)].
- *ESOP exemption.* An employee stock ownership plan (ESOP) [¶ 3160] is a defined contribution plan that invests primarily in employer securities that are readily traded on an established market. Dividends paid from stock owned by an ESOP are also exempt from the 10 percent penalty [Code Sec. 72(t)(2)(A)(vi)][¶ 3160].
- *IRS levies on employer-sponsored retirement plans or IRAs.* The 10 percent penalty will not apply to amounts withdrawn from any employer-sponsored retirement plan or IRA [¶ 3135]that is subject to levy by the IRS [Code Sec. 72(t)(2)(A)(vii)]. This

[21] *E. Dollander,* 98 TCM 107, Dec. 57,907(M), TC Memo. 2009-187, *motion to review TC denied, per curiam,* CA-11, 2010-1 USTC ¶ 50,478, 383 Fed. Appx. 932.

[22] *Young Kim,* CA-7, 2012-1 USTC ¶ 50,340, 679 F3d 623.

[23] Rev. Rul. 2002-62, 2002-2 CB 710.

exception applies only if the plan or the IRA is levied by the IRS. It does not apply, for example, if the taxpayer withdraws funds to pay taxes in the absence of a levy, in order to release a levy on other interests, or in any other situation.

.03 Reporting Requirements

Taxpayers must report tax-free rollovers as well as taxable distributions on Form 1040. The 10 percent tax or entitlement to one of the exceptions to the penalty are entered on Form 5329, *Additional Taxes on Qualified Plans (Including IRAs) and Other Tax-Favored Accounts,* and any resulting penalty is carried over to Form 1040. Taxpayers may also report rollovers on Form 1040A, but they must use Form 1040 if the 10 percent penalty applies to the distribution. Important tax information will be reported to taxpayers by plan administrators on Form 1099-R. This form will show the distribution amount, the taxable portion, any tax withheld, and a distribution code related to the 10 percent tax. However, Form 5329 need not be filed if the distribution code 1 (i.e., early distribution) is correctly shown in Box 7 of the Form 1099-R received by the individual. In this situation, the penalty is reported directly on the individual's Form 1040. Form 5329 may also be filed by individuals who believe that the penalty does not apply to the distributions they received.

.04 Excise Tax Imposed on Transfer from Terminated Plan to Qualified Replacement Plan

An employer's transfer of excess assets from a terminated defined benefit plan to a defined contribution plan is treated as a reversion of assets to the employer followed by a contribution to the defined contribution plan. The surplus is included in the employer's income and is deductible as a contribution to the defined contribution plan. Where a defined benefit pension plan terminates with a surplus, a 20 percent excise tax applies to the amount of the employer reversion [Code Sec. 4980(a)]. An employer reversion is the cash and fair market value of other property received from the plan [Code Sec. 4980(c)(2)]. The excise tax increases to 50 percent unless the employer establishes or maintains a "qualified replacement plan," or the plan provides pro rata benefit increases [Code Sec. 4980(d)(1)].

> **NOTE:** The excise tax is in addition to any income tax the employer may owe on the reversion.

There is an exception to the excise tax for amounts transferred to an employee stock ownership plan or tax credit employee stock ownership plan [Code Sec. 4980(c)(3)]. Transfers made from a qualified future retiree health benefit account in order to meet the pension plan's minimum funding requirements is not treated as an employer reversion, therefore, the transfer is not subject to the excise tax on reversion of plan assets to an employer [Code Sec. 4980(c)(2)(B)(iii)].

20 Percent Excise Tax

A *qualified replacement plan* established or maintained by the employer in connection with a qualified plan termination will only be subject to the 20 percent excise tax on employer reversions and the amount transferred will not be included in the employer's gross income [Code Sec. 4980(d)(2)(B)(iii)]. A plan qualifies as a qualified replacement plan when:

- At least 95 percent of active participants in the terminated plan who remain employed by the employer are active participants in the replacement plan;
- A direct transfer from terminated plan to replacement plan is made before any employer reversion of a 25 percent cushion which is the excess of (a) 25 percent of the maximum amount that the employer could receive as a reversion, over the present value of the aggregate increases in the accrued benefits under the terminated plan via a plan amendment adopted within 60 days before the plan termination and which takes effect immediately upon termination; and
- Certain allocation requirements are met [Code Sec. 4980(d)(2)].[24]

▶ **DOUBLE TAX WINNER:** Amounts that are transferred to a replacement plan or used to increase plan benefits not only escape the excise tax, they are also not included in the company's taxable income. On the other hand, these amounts are not deductible by the company.

50 Percent Excise Tax

The company must pay a 50 percent excise tax unless the employer establishes or maintains a qualified replacement plan, or the plan provides pro rata benefit increases [Code Sec. 4980(d)(1)].

Example 3-13: Phelps Corp. terminates its defined benefit pension plan. There was $100,000 remaining in the plan after all the pension plan liabilities were satisfied. If Phelps transfers $25,000 into a replacement plan, the $25,000 is not includible in the corporation's income. Also, it is not subject to the 50 percent excise tax. However, Phelps is liable for an excise tax of $15,000 [20 percent of $75,000 ($100,000 less $25,000 transferred to the replacement plan)], and $75,000 is subject to the corporate income tax of 34 percent, or $25,500. Thus, it retains a balance of $34,500 [$75,000 less $40,500 ($15,000 excise tax + $25,500 income tax)]. Note that if Phelps did nothing with the surplus, it would owe $34,000 in income taxes and $50,000 in excise tax.

¶3090 QUALIFIED DOMESTIC RELATIONS ORDERS (QDROs)

The ability to receive benefits from your qualified retirement plan is an extremely important and valuable right. If your marriage ends in divorce, determining who will end up with the retirement benefits is likewise an important issue. In order to transfer qualified pension or profit-sharing plan benefits incident to a divorce or separation to someone other than the employee, it is mandatory to use a *qualified domestics relations order (QDRO)* [Code Sec. 414(p)]. A QDRO is a court ordered assignment of benefits of a qualified defined benefit or defined contribution plan to a nonemployee alternate payee such as a spouse, former spouse or child. Without a QDRO, the assignment will not be valid or enforceable.

---

[24] Rev. Rul. 2003-85, 2003-2 CB 291.

.01 Benefits of a QDRO

Alternate Payees

A QDRO can provide for more than one alternate payee and is not limited to benefits that are vested as of the date the order is entered. A QDRO can provide for benefits earned and vested in the future.

Payment Forms

A QDRO could provide for a payment form that was not elected by the employee. For example, the QDRO could provide for lump-sum payments even though the actual participant in the retirement plan had elected to receive installment payments. The QDRO cannot, however, provide for a payment form that was not originally available under the plan.

Income Tax Benefits

When retirement benefits are distributed to a participant's spouse or former spouse pursuant to a QDRO, the spouse rather than the participant is taxed on the distribution.[25] The original owner's basis is allocated, pro rata, between the present value of the benefits payable to the alternate payee and the present value of those payable to the participant. If the alternate payee is someone other than the participant's spouse, or former spouse, such as the participant's child, the entire amount of the distribution is taxable to the participant. The participant's basis is retained by the participant rather than being allocated between the participant and the alternate payee.

Rollover Option Available

An alternate payee who receives benefits under a QDRO can roll over the benefits to a traditional individual retirement account (IRA) or an individual retirement annuity. The transfer will be tax-free if the alternate payee receives the entire amount to which he or she is entitled under the QDRO and that amount is transferred to a traditional IRA or individual retirement annuity within 60 days of the distribution. If the distribution is not rolled over to a traditional IRA, it will be taxed as ordinary income in the year of distribution.

Penalty Tax on Distributions from QDRO

The 10 percent penalty tax that is normally imposed on distributions from a qualified retirement plan to a participant who is less than age 59½ does not apply to distributions made to an alternate payee pursuant to a QDRO. The penalty will apply, however, if a QDRO distribution is rolled over into a traditional IRA and distributions are then made from the traditional IRA to a participant under age 59½.

.02 Requirements for QDROs

In order for a QDRO to be valid, the order must clearly state the following [Code Sec. 414(p)(2)]:

- The name and last known mailing address of the participant and name and address of each alternate payee (any spouse, former spouse, child or other dependent of a plan participant);

---

[25] *L.G. Mitchell,* 131 TC 215, Dec. 57,611 (2008).

- The amount or percentage of benefits to be paid by the plan to each alternate payee or how to calculate such amount or percentage;
- When payments to the alternate payee are to begin and the number of payments or the payment period to which the order applies;
- The name of each plan to which the order applies must be clearly specified. For example, the plan details will be different for a defined contribution plan and a defined benefit plan. Sample or form QDROs should be avoided if your attorney fails to alter them to apply to the specific retirement plan at issue.
- The state domestic relations law pursuant to which the order was issued must be adequately specified.
- The QDRO must create or recognize the existence of an alternate payee's right to receive all or a portion of the benefits payable under the qualified pension plan and must assign those rights to the alternate payee.
- The QDRO cannot provide for any type or form of benefit or any option not otherwise provided under the plan. For example, if the plan does not provide for annual payments, the QDRO cannot direct the plan to make annual payments to an alternate payee;
- The QDRO cannot provide increased benefits which are determined on the basis of actuarial value, or pay benefits to an alternate payee that are required to be paid to another alternate payee under a previous QDRO.
- The QDRO must provide that the latest date on which benefits to the alternate payee will commence is the participant's own required distribution date.

Strict Compliance with the Law as Critical

It is important to strictly comply with the law when drafting QDROs. The following example illustrates why this is so important. In one case, a taxpayer complied with his divorce decree and paid his ex-wife half of the pre-tax distributions he received from his employer's retirement plans.[26] He was taxed on the full amount, however, because sloppy drafting of the final judgment of divorce kept it from qualifying as a QDRO, which would have taxed the ex-wife on her half of the proceeds. The QDRO failed to exist because: (1) the document did not mention the term "alternate payee;" (2) the document did not specify the number of payments or periods to which the order applied; (3) the document did not identify the name and address of the plan participant and alternate payee; and (4) language in the final judgment reserving jurisdiction for a possible future QDRO indicated that the judgment itself was not intended to be a QDRO.

IRS Model Language for QDRO

The IRS has provided sample language that you may use to draft a QDRO.[27] Drafters who use the sample language will need to conform it to the terms of the retirement plan to which the QDRO applies and to specify the amounts assigned and other terms of the QDRO in order to achieve an appropriate division of marital property or level of family support. A domestic relations order is not required to incorporate the sample language

---

[26] *In re Boudreau*, BC-DC-FL, 95-1 USTC ¶ 50,115.

[27] Notice 97-11, 1997-1 CB 379.

in order to satisfy the requirements for a QDRO, and a domestic relations order that incorporates part of the sample language may omit or modify other parts.

¶3095 PLAN LOANS

.01 General Rules

Participants in qualified retirement plans who are experiencing financial difficulties can access their retirement funds before actually retiring by obtaining a loan from their retirement plan. Although not required to do so, many retirement plans offer plans loans to participants. The employee should be sure to check his or her retirement plan documents to see if the plan allows plan loans.

A plan loan is an amount employees can borrow from their retirement plan accounts and then pay back with interest. As long as the employee repays the borrowed amount, it is not taxed and the employee's retirement plan account balance is restored by the amount borrowed. Employees are not required to prove financial hardship to obtain a plan loan.

Permitted Plan Loans

Plan participants may not borrow against all retirement plans. Loans are only available from the following types of retirement plans:

- Qualified plans that satisfy the requirements of Code Sec. 401(a),
- Annuity plans that satisfy the requirements of § 403(a) or 403(b), and
- Governmental plans [Code § 72(p)(4); Reg. § 1.72(p)-1, Q&A-2].

No Plan Loans from IRAs

Loans are *not* permitted from IRAs or from IRA-based plans such as SEPs, SARSEPs and SIMPLE IRA plans. If the owner of an IRA borrows from the IRA, the IRA is no longer considered an IRA, and the value of the entire IRA is included in the owner's income [Code Sec. 408(e)(2)].

Procedures to Follow to Obtain Plan Loan

If the employee's plan allows plan loans, the employee must complete loan forms and sign a repayment agreement outlining the number, the amount, and the due dates of repayment. The employees must pay interest on the amount borrowed and, depending upon the terms for loans as stated in the plan, may have to agree to repay the loan using automatic deductions from their future wages. If a participant failed to make payments on a plan loan, the missed payments can still be made even after a deemed distribution has occurred. In that case, the participant's or beneficiary's tax basis under the plan is increased by the amount of the late repayments [Reg. § 1.72(p)-1, Q&A-21]. If the retirement plan is subject to survivor annuity requirements, spousal consent may be required for any plan loan to a married participant if more than $5,000 of the account balance is used as security for the plan loan [Reg. § 1.401(a)-20].

.02 Tax Treatment of Plan Loan

A loan from a qualified plan to a participant or beneficiary is treated as a distribution that is generally taxable and possibly subject to the 10 percent penalty tax. To avoid treatment as a taxable distribution, the loan must satisfy the following requirements found in Code Sec. 72(p)(2):

1. The plan loan must be repaid within five years. If the terms of the loan call for a payment period of more than five years, the entire loan is considered a taxable distribution, even if the loan is actually paid off within five years. If, on the other hand, a five-year loan is not paid off within the required period, only the outstanding balance at that time is considered a taxable distribution. The five-year repayment requirement does not apply to loans used to acquire the plan participant's principal residence [Code Sec. 72(p)(2)(B)(ii)]. A loan that is taken for the purpose of purchasing the employee's principal residence may be paid back over a period of more than five years [Code Sec. 72(p)(2)(B)(ii); Reg. § 1.72(p)-1, Q&A-5, -6, -7, and -8]. Refinancing does not qualify as principal residence plan loans [Reg. § 1.72(p)-1, Q&A-8(a)]. A plan may suspend loan repayments for employees performing military service [Reg. § 1.72(p)-1, Q&A-9(b)]. A plan also may suspend loan repayments during a leave of absence of up to one year. However, upon return, the participant must make up the missed payments either by increasing the amount of each monthly payment or by paying a lump sum at the end, so that the term of the loan does not exceed the original five-year term [Reg. § 1.72(p)-1, Q&A-9(a)].
2. The payments must be substantially equal and made at least quarterly. The terms of repayment must be level amortization with payments due at least quarterly. In other words, the loan cannot call for a balloon payment at the end of five years [Code Sec. 72(p)(2)(B), (C)].
3. The total outstanding balance of all of the combined plans of the employer, including any plans under common control cannot exceed the lesser of:
    a. The greater of 50 percent of the present value of the employee's vested benefits or $10,000, or
    b. $50,000, reduced by the difference between the highest outstanding loan balance in the preceding 12 months and the current balance (12-month rule).
        i. For example, if a participant has an account balance of $40,000, the maximum amount that he or she can borrow from the account is $20,000.
        ii. A participant may have more than one outstanding loan from the plan at a time. However, any new loan, when added to the outstanding balance of all of the participant's loans from the plan, cannot be more than the plan maximum amount. In determining the plan maximum amount in that case, the $50,000 is reduced by the difference between the highest outstanding balance of all of the participant's loans during the 12-month period ending on the day before the new loan and the outstanding balance of the participant's loans from the plan on the date of the new loan.
        iii. For example, assume Participant A has a vested account balance of $100,000 and took a plan loan of $40,000 on January 1, 2013, to be paid in 20 quarterly installments of $2,491. On January 1, 2014, when the outstanding balance is $33,322, Participant A wants to take another plan loan. The difference between the highest outstanding loan balance for the preceding year ($40,000) and the outstanding balance on the day of the loan ($33,322)

is $6,678. Since the new loan plus the outstanding loan cannot be more than $43,322 ($50,000 – $6,678), the maximum amount that the new loan can be is $10,000 ($43,322 – $33,322).

If the plan loan fails to satisfy all three requirements outlined above regarding the amount, duration and repayment of the loan, the loan proceeds will be treated as a deemed distribution includible in taxable income and potentially subject to the Code Sec. 72(t) 10 percent premature distribution penalty [Code Sec. 72(p); Reg. § 1.72(p)-1, Q&A-1].

In addition, the following requirements must be satisfied to avoid taxation:

1. Loans must be available to all plan participants, including both active and inactive employees, on a reasonably equivalent basis. (A plan can make distinctions based on creditworthiness and financial need.)
2. Loans can't be made to highly compensated employees in an amount greater than what is available to other employees. Permissible borrowers include sole proprietors, partners owning more than 10 percent of the capital or profits interest in a partnership, and an employee or officer of a subchapter C corporation owning more than 5 percent of the outstanding stock of the corporation. The owner of an IRA, however, continues to be prohibited from borrowing from his or her IRA.
3. The plan must specifically set forth the terms under which loans will be made.
4. The debt must be adequately secured; and
5. The plan must charge a reasonable rate of interest.[28] The plan must be able to foreclose on the collateral in the event of a default, and the value of the collateral must be sufficient so that the plan will not suffer any loss of principal or interest between the date of default and the date of the foreclosure on the collateral.

   NOTE: Even though a plan loan is permitted, Code Sec. 72(p)(1)(B) treats assignments or pledges of an employee's interest in a plan as a taxable distribution from the plan.[29]

.03 Legally Enforceable Loan Required

A loan must be evidenced by a legally enforceable agreement. However, the agreement need not be signed in jurisdictions where a signature is not required for the loan to be enforceable [Reg. § 1.72(p)-1, Q&A 3(b)]. Loan agreement may be set forth in an electronic medium that is reasonably accessible to the participant or beneficiary and reasonably secure, and that provides a reasonable opportunity to review the loan terms and confirm, modify, or rescind the loan before it is made. The system also must confirm the loan terms to the participant or beneficiary either in writing or electronically, and advise the borrower of the right to receive the confirmation in writing without charge [Reg. § 1.72(p)-1, Q&A 3(b)(2)].

A plan can use a portion of a participant's vested plan benefits as security for the loan. However, no more than 50 percent of a participant's vested benefits can be used for this purpose. As a result, if a company were to permit participants to borrow up

[28] Rev. Rul. 89-14, 1989-1 CB 111.

[29] *L.D. Armstrong*, 2004-1 USTC ¶ 50,238, 366 F3d 622.

to the limits allowed by the tax law (the lesser of $50,000 or the greater of $10,000 or 50 percent of the present value of the participant's vested benefit), a participant with less than $20,000 in vested benefits would be able to borrow an amount in excess of 50 percent of vested benefits. The Labor Department regulations supersede those imposed by the tax law.[30]

Example 3-14: Ms. Brown's nonforfeitable accrued balance in her company's profit-sharing plan is $150,000. In general, she is limited to $50,000 of loans. If Brown has a $10,000 loan outstanding, she cannot borrow more than an additional $40,000. If she has no loan outstanding at present, but paid off $50,000 of indebtedness to the plan, say, ten months ago (and she made no loan payments during the prior two months), Brown could not take out another plan loan for an additional two months (i.e., until 12 months had elapsed).

Example 3-15: Mr. Green's nonforfeitable accrued balance is $90,000. Thus, his loan ceiling is $45,000—one-half of his benefits. Suppose, though, he paid off $30,000 of indebtedness eleven months ago (and made no repayments during the prior month). In that case, he would be subject to the limitation computed as follows: $50,000 less highest outstanding loan balance during the preceding year. Result: He could not borrow more than $20,000 at this time.

.04 Interest Deduction

Interest paid on plan loans is generally subject to the same deduction rules as interest on other loans [Ch. 9] [Code Sec. 163]. However, there is a special restriction that applies to company owners and other top-level employees. "Key employees" [¶ 3045]cannot claim deductions for interest paid on retirement plan loans, regardless of how the loan proceeds are used [Code Sec. 72(p)(3)]. Also interest on loans secured by an employee's Code Sec. 401(k) or 403(b) contributions is also nondeductible.

¶3100 PROHIBITED TRANSACTIONS

Certain transactions between a qualified plan and persons with authority over the plan (so-called disqualified persons) are generally prohibited and will be subject to a two-tiered excise tax if conducted [Code Sec. 4975]. The excise tax is imposed on the disqualified person who participated in the prohibited transaction for each year in the taxable period [Code Sec. 4975(a)]. The additional second-tier excise tax is equal to 100 percent of the "amount involved" and is imposed if the transaction is not corrected within the taxable period [Code Sec. 4975(a); Reg. § 54.4975-1]. Neither the first-tier excise tax nor the 100-percent tax is deductible. Moreover, the payment of the tax does not relieve disqualified persons of their duty to the plan or of their obligation to correct the transaction. If more than one person is liable for the excise tax on the prohibited transaction, the liability is joint and several [Code Sec. 4975(f)(1)].

---

[30] See DOL Regs at 29 CFR 2550.408b.

Disqualified persons include the following [Code Sec. 4975(e)(2)]:

- A fiduciary;
- A person providing services to the plan;
- An employer any of whose employees are covered by the plan;
- An employee organization any of whose members are covered by the plan;
- An owner, direct or indirect, of 50 percent or more of: (i) the combined voting power of all classes of stock entitled to vote or the total value of shares of all classes of stock of a corporation, (ii) the capital interest or the profits interest of a partnership, or (iii) the beneficial interest of a trust or unincorporated enterprise, which is an employer or an employee organization;
- A member of the family of any previously described individual (other than an employee organization). The family of an individual is defined in Code Sec. 4975(e)(6) as an individual's spouse, ancestor, lineal descendant, and any spouse of a lineal descendant;
- A corporation, partnership, or trust or estate of which (or in which) 50 percent or more of (i) the combined voting power of all classes of stock entitled to vote or the total value of shares of all classes of stock of such corporation, (ii) the capital interest or profits interest of such partnership, or (iii) the beneficial interest of such trust or estate, is owned directly or indirectly, or held by a fiduciary, a person providing services to the plan, an employer with employees covered by the plan, an employee organization with members covered by the plan, or an owner of the plan;
- An officer, director (or an individual having powers or responsibilities similar to those of officers or directors), a 10 percent or more shareholder, or a highly compensated employee (earning 10 percent or more of the yearly wages of an employer) of an employer with employees covered by the plan, an employee organization with members covered by the plan, a direct or indirect 50 percent owner, or a corporation, partnership, trust or estate with at least 50 percent ownership interest; and
- A 10 percent or more (in capital or profits) partner of an employer any of whose employees are covered by the plan, an employee organization any of whose members are covered by the plan, a direct or indirect 50 percent owner, or a corporation, partnership, trust, or estate with at least 50 percent ownership interest.

.01 Prohibited Transactions

The types of transactions that are prohibited and subject to tax are:

- Sale, exchange or lease of property;
- Loan or extension of credit;
- Furnishing of goods, services or facilities;
- Transfer to or use by or for the benefit of the disqualified person of the income or assets of the plan;
- Use of plan income or assets by a fiduciary for his own benefit or account; or
- Receipt by a plan fiduciary of consideration for his own account from a party who is dealing with the plan in connection with plan income or assets [Code Sec. 4975(c)].

NOTE: The U.S. Supreme Court has closed off an opportunity employers might have had to fund pension plans without using cash.[31] Code Sec. 4975(f)(3) provides that the transfer of mortgaged property to a retirement plan is a prohibited sale or exchange. The U.S. Supreme Court has held that a contribution of any property other than cash by an employer to a defined benefit pension plan in satisfaction of the employer's minimum funding obligation is also a prohibited sale or exchange. But while a contribution of mortgaged property is a prohibited transaction for both involuntary (i.e., those required to meet funding obligations) and voluntary purposes, a contribution of nonmortgaged property is prohibited only for involuntary contributions. If an employer makes a voluntary contribution of nonmortgaged property—say, to reward employees for a particularly productive year—that would not be a prohibited transaction.

Guarantees of Loans to Company Owned by IRAs—Prohibited Transactions

In *L.F. Peek*,[32] the court held that IRA owners' personal guarantees of loans made to a corporation owned by the IRAs constituted prohibited transactions under Code Sec. 4975(c)(1)(B) which prohibits any direct or indirect * * * lending of money or other extension of credit between a qualified plan and a disqualified person. The court considered a loan guarantee to be an indirect extension of credit.

.02 Exemptions

The following transactions are exempt from the prohibited transaction rules under Code Sec. 4975(d):

1. Loans from a plan to a disqualified person/participant or beneficiary [ERISA Reg. § 2550.408b-1 (Title 29)];
2. Loans from a disqualified person to a leveraged Employee Stock Ownership Plan (ESOP), as defined by Code Sec. 4975(e)(7) [Reg. § § 54.4975-7, 54.4975-11; ERISA Reg. § 2550.408b-3 (Title 29)];
3. Contracts and arrangements for office space, legal and accounting services [Reg. § 54.4975-6; ERISA Reg. § 2550.408b-2 (Title 29)];
4. Reasonable compensation and reimbursement of expenses to a disqualified person [ERISA Reg. § 2550.408c-2 (Title 29)];
5. Investment of plan funds in interest-bearing accounts of fiduciary banks [ERISA Reg. § 2550.408b-4 (Title 29)];
6. Purchase of insurance from an employer/insurance company;
7. Ancillary services provided by a fiduciary/bank [ERISA Reg. § 2550.408b-6 (Title 29)];
8. Exercise of a privilege to convert securities;
9. Participation in a common trust fund maintained by a supervised bank or trust company or in a pooled investment fund maintained by an insurance company;
10. Receipt of benefits by a disqualified person who is entitled to the benefits as a participant or beneficiary;

---

[31] *Keystone Consolidated Industries, Inc.*, SCt, 93-1 USTC ¶ 50,298, 508 US 152, 113 SCt 2006, *on remand*, CA-5, 93-2 USTC ¶ 50,533, 1 F3d 287.

[32] *L.F. Peek*, Dec. 59,535, 140 TC No. 12 (2013).

11. Dual service by an individual as a fiduciary and as an officer, employee, agent, or other representative of a disqualified person;
12. Allocation of assets upon plan termination as required by Section 4044 of ERISA;
13. Acquisition or sale of qualifying employer securities or real property exempt from the prohibited transaction rules of Title I of ERISA [Reg. § 54.4975-12; ERISA Reg. § 2550.408e (Title 29)];
14. Any transaction under the withdrawal liability provisions of Section 4223 of ERISA;
15. A merger of multiemployer plans or the transfer of assets and liabilities between the plans determined by the Pension Benefit Guaranty Corporation (PBGC) to meet the requirements of Section 4231 of ERISA [Code Sec. 4975(d)(15)];
16. A sale by an IRA to an IRA beneficiary of bank stock held by the IRA;
17. The provision of investment advice by a fiduciary advisor to a participant or beneficiary in a plan that permits the participant or beneficiary to direct the investment of plan assets in an individual account [Code Sec. 4975(d)(17)];
18. Certain block trades [Code Sec. 4975(d)(18)];
19. Certain transactions between a plan and a disqualified person using an electronic communications network, alternative trading systems, or similar execution system trading or venue subject to federal regulation and oversight [Code Sec. 4975(d)(19)];
20. Transactions between a plan and a person that is a disqualified person other than a fiduciary (or an affiliate) who has or exercises any discretionary authority or control with respect to the investment of the plan assets involved in the transaction or renders investment advice with respect to those assets, solely by reason of providing services to the plan or solely by reason of a relationship to such a service provider or both, but only if, in connection with such transaction, the plan receives only adequate consideration [Code Sec. 4975(d)(20)];
21. Certain foreign exchange transactions [Code Sec. 4975(d)(21)];
22. Certain cross-trading transactions involving the purchase or sale of a security between a plan and any other account managed by the same investment manager [Code Sec. 4975(d)(22)];
23. Otherwise prohibited transactions that are corrected before the end of the correction period [Code Sec. 4975(d)(23)].

.03 Tax Liability

The initial level excise tax imposed on disqualified persons participating in a prohibited transaction with a qualified plan is 15 percent of the amount involved in the transaction [Code Sec. 4975(a)]. If the transaction is not corrected within the taxable period, the law imposes an additional tax of 100 percent of the amount involved. If more than one person takes part in the transaction, each person may be liable for the entire amount of the tax.

The amount involved in a prohibited transaction is the greater of the following:

- The amount of money and the fair market value of the other property you gave.
- The amount of money and the fair market value of any property you received.

If services are performed, the amount involved is any excess compensation given or received.

The tax is based on the amount involved as of transaction date [Code Sec. 4975(a)]. It is charged for each year in the taxable period, which starts on the transaction date and ends on the earliest day when:

- IRS mails a notice of deficiency for the tax,
- The tax is assessed, or
- You finish correcting the transaction.

The 100 percent tax is charged if the transaction is not corrected during the taxable period [Code Sec. 4975(b)]. It is based on the highest fair market value, during the taxable period, of the amount involved.

INDIVIDUAL RETIREMENT ACCOUNTS

¶3105 WHO IS ELIGIBLE TO CONTRIBUTE TO A TRADITIONAL IRA?

An individual retirement account (IRA) is a retirement savings account that permits you to put a certain amount of your compensation away each year in a tax-deferred account. Do not confuse the traditional IRA discussed here with the other types of IRAs, such as the Roth IRA [¶3140] and Coverdell education savings accounts (formerly known as education IRAs) [Ch. 5] which are subject to different tax rules.

Anybody (including a working child) will be able to set up and make contributions to a traditional IRA if they satisfy the following requirements:

- They must earn compensation at some time during the year [Code Sec. 219(b)(1)(B)]; and
- They must be under age 70$^1/_2$ at the end of the year [Code Sec. 219(d)(1)].

Compensation for these purposes includes wages, salaries, professional fees, other amounts derived or received for personal services rendered, alimony, and earnings from self-employment (reduced by any deduction claimed for a self-employment retirement plan), including earned income that is not subject to self-employment tax because of the religious beliefs of the individual. Compensation does not include income from pensions, annuities, deferred compensation, interest, dividends, or other amounts received as earnings or profits from property [Code Sec. 219(f)(1)].

You can set up an IRA and make contributions to it up to the date for filing your income tax return (not including extensions) for the previous calendar year. In other words, you can make contributions as late as April 15 and attribute them to the preceding calendar year [Code Sec. 219(f)(3)].

Roth IRAs are discussed in detail in ¶3140. In 2013 the maximum amount that a taxpayer may contribute to an IRA is $5,500 (no change in 2014) [Code Sec. 219(b)(5)(B)].

You may establish an IRA whether or not you are covered by any other retirement plan. However, if you were covered by your employer's retirement plan, your deduction may be reduced or eliminated depending on your income and filing status.

.01 Catch-Up Contributions

Additional catch-up contributions to IRAs for taxpayers age 50 may be made by the end of the tax year [Code Secs. 219(b)(5)(B), 414(v)(5)]. An employer is not required to provide for catch-up contributions in any of its plans [Reg. § 1.414(v)-1(a)(1)]. However, if any plan of an employer provides for catch-up contributions, all of its plans that provide for elective deferrals must comply with the universal availability requirement.

The maximum contribution limit (before application of the phase-out limits) for an individual who has reached age 50 before the end of the tax year is $1,000 for 2013. Thus the total contribution for this individual will be $6,500 in 2013.

.02 Tax-Free Combat Pay Counted for IRA Contribution Purposes

Members of the armed forces serving in Iraq, Afghanistan, and other combat-designated localities may count tax-free combat pay as earned income in determining the contribution amount to a traditional or Roth IRA.

.03 Married Individuals

If both you and your spouse earn income, you are each eligible to set up an IRA. This rule applies without regard to any community property laws. If both of you have compensation, one of you may elect to be treated as having no compensation [Code Sec. 219(c)(1)]. This allows the other spouse to make a contribution that exceeds his or her compensation. IRAs may also be established by stay-at-home spouses as discussed in ¶ 3150.

.04 Deductibility of Contributions

If you are covered by a retirement plan at work, your deduction in 2013 for contributions to a traditional IRA is reduced (phased out) if your modified adjusted gross income (MAGI) is [Code Sec. 219(g)(3)(B)]:

- More than $95,000 but less than $115,000 for a married couple filing a joint return or a qualifying widow(er),
- More than $59,000 but less than $69,000 for a single individual or head of household, or
- Less than $10,000 for a married individual filing a separate return.

Who Is Considered an Active Participant

You will not be considered an "active participant" in an employer-sponsored retirement plan merely because your spouse is considered one [Code Sec. 219(g)(1)]. As a result, the spouse who is not an "active participant" may be able to make a fully or partial deductible IRA contribution. If an individual is not an active participant in an employer-sponsored plan, but the spouse is, the maximum deductible IRA contribution will phase out in 2013 for taxpayers with AGI between $178,000 and $188,000 [Code Sec. 219(g)(7)].

No Reduction Below $200 Until Complete Phaseout

Your IRA deduction cannot go below $200 if your adjusted gross income has not reached the phaseout levels [Code Sec. 219(g)(2)(b)].

.05 IRA Deduction Limit for Social Security Recipients

Some Social Security benefits may be included in your adjusted gross income, depending on your gross income, as adjusted by certain items including the IRA deduction. On the other hand, your maximum IRA deduction depends on your adjusted gross income, which includes the taxable portion of Social Security benefits. To get around this circular chain of calculations, the maximum deductible IRA contribution should be determined as follows: (1) Figure the amount of your Social Security benefits that would be taxable if no IRA contribution is made; (2) Use that amount in determining the maximum IRA deduction; (3) When figuring the amount of Social Security benefits that are actually subject to tax, use the modified adjusted gross income after subtracting the applicable IRA deduction.[33]

.06 Nondeductible IRA Contributions

Generally, you can make designated nondeductible contributions to an IRA to the extent that deductible contributions are not allowed (because of reduced IRA deduction limit). You can make nondeductible contributions to an IRA up to the excess of (1) $5,500 in 2013 plus any catch-up contribution or 100 percent of compensation, whichever is less, minus, (2) the amount of your allowable IRA deduction. You are permitted to elect to treat deductible IRA contributions as nondeductible [Code Sec. 408(o)(2)(B)(ii)].

> ▶ **OBSERVATION:** An individual might make this election, for example, if the individual had no taxable income for the year after taking into account other deductions.

As with deductible contributions, designated nondeductible contributions can be made up to the due date of your tax return for the tax year (without extensions).

Since nondeductible IRA contributions do not reduce your gross income in the year they are made, you do not report them on Form 1040. However, you are required to file Form 8606 with your tax return for each year you make a nondeductible contribution or receive an IRA distribution and have ever made a nondeductible contribution. This form is used to keep track of the total nondeductible contributions you have made over the years. It is also used to determine the taxable portion of distributions received from an IRA. You do not pay tax on the distribution of your nondeductible contributions.

There is a $50 penalty for failing to file Form 8606 [Code Sec. 6693(b)(2)].

.07 Deemed IRAs Under Employer Plans

Qualified retirement plans may permit employees to make voluntary contributions to a separate account or annuity established under the plan that meets the requirements of either a traditional IRA or Roth IRA [Code Sec. 408(q)(2)]. The following types of plans are considered to be "qualified employer plans" and therefore can provide for deemed IRAs: Code Sec. 401(a) qualified plans, Code Sec. 403(a) qualified annuities,

---

[33] Announcement 88-38, IRB 1988-10, 60.

Code Sec. 403(b) tax-sheltered annuities, and Code Sec. 457(b) governmental plans. A deemed IRA can be a traditional IRA or a Roth IRA, but simplified employee pensions (SEPs) under Code Sec. 408(p) may not be used as deemed IRAs [Reg. § 1.408(q)-1(a), (b), (h)]. Keep in mind that qualified plans and deemed IRAs are separate entities even if the assets are commingled.

The separate account or annuity will be deemed to be either a traditional or Roth IRA for all tax purposes, including IRA reporting requirements. A deemed IRA will not be subject to the qualified retirement plan rules, and contributions to a deemed IRA will not be taken into account in applying contribution limits under the plan. Deemed IRAs will not be subject to ERISA reporting and disclosure, participation, vesting, funding, or enforcement requirements. However, ERISA's exclusive benefit and fiduciary rules will apply to a deemed IRA in the same manner they apply to the qualified plan [Code Secs. 219, 408, and 408a].

Documentation

If plan sponsors want to provide for deemed IRAs, then by no later than the date that deemed IRA contributions are first accepted from employees: (1) plan documents must include language authorizing a deemed IRA feature, and (2) the plan sponsor must actually have deemed IRAs in effect for employees. In addition, a plan that features deemed IRAs must contain language that satisfies the traditional IRA or Roth IRA rules found in Code Sec. 408 and Code Sec. 408A, respectively [Reg. § 1.408(q)-1(d)(1)].

.08 Distribution Rules

The minimum distribution rules found in Code Sec. 401(a)(9) must be met separately for a qualified plan and a deemed IRA. Thus, whether a qualified plan satisfies the minimum distribution rules is determined without regard to whether a participant satisfies the distribution requirements for the deemed IRA [Reg. § 1.408(q)-1(e)(2)]. The IRA distribution rules apply to distributions from deemed IRAs. Any restrictions that a trustee, custodian, or insurance company may impose on distributions from traditional and Roth IRAs may be imposed on distributions from deemed IRAs (e.g., early withdrawal penalties on annuities) [Reg. § 1.408(q)-1(e)(2)].

.09 Direct Payment of Tax Refunds to IRAs

Taxpayers can request that the IRS deposit their tax refund into an IRA. The program will allow taxpayers who use direct deposit to divide their refunds in up to three financial accounts, such as checking, savings, and retirement accounts. Form 8888 will give all individual filers the ability to split their refunds. Taxpayers will attach the new form to their returns indicating amounts of each allocation and providing account information. Refunds may be deposited with any U.S. financial institution so long as taxpayers provide valid routing and account numbers. Taxpayers who want their entire refund deposited directly into one account can still use the appropriate line on the Form 1040 series.

.10 IRAs and Bankruptcy

The U.S. Supreme Court concluded that debtors who file for bankruptcy protection may preserve the funds in their traditional IRAs from the reach of their creditors under the federal exemption statute.[34] Congress subsequently enacted legislation that excludes both traditional and Roth IRA balances of up to $1 million from the reach of creditors when the debtor has filed for bankruptcy protection. The Court of Appeals for the Seventh Circuit has concluded that a non-spousal inherited IRA was not exempt from creditor's claims in bankruptcy because the funds transferred from the beneficiary's deceased mother's IRA were not retirement funds in the hands of the beneficiary.[35]

¶3110 SPOUSAL IRAS FOR STAY-AT-HOME SPOUSES

Each spouse, including a homemaker who does not work outside the home, can make a deductible IRA contribution of up to $5,500 (if under age 50) in 2013 (no change in 2014) if the combined compensation of both spouses is at least equal to the contributed amount (for a total of $10,000) and the spouses file joint returns [Code Sec. 219(c)].

The spousal IRA rules apply to any individual if: (1) he or she files a joint tax return for the tax year, and (2) if the amount of compensation, if any, includible in the individual's gross income is less than the compensation includible in the gross income of his or her spouse. The aggregate contribution for both spouses cannot exceed the combined contribution of both spouses.

The maximum permitted IRA contribution to a deductible or nondeductible IRA for a nonworking spouse or a spouse with the lesser income cannot exceed the combined earned income of both spouses. The purpose of this rule is to prevent a nonworking (or lesser earning) spouse from making IRA contributions that exceed a couple's combined earned income. In addition, the new law provides that tax-free distributions from Roth IRAs are not subject to withholding requirements [Code Sec. 3405(e)(1)(B)].

¶3115 EXCESS CONTRIBUTIONS

Contributions to an IRA that exceed either the deductible or nondeductible limit, whichever applies, are subject to an annual 6 percent excise tax on excess contributions. You must pay the 6 percent excise tax each year on the excess amounts that remain in your IRA [Code Sec. 4973(a); Reg. § 1.408-1(c)(1)].[36] The excess is taxed for the year you make the excess contribution and each year after that until you correct it. You will not have to pay the excise tax if you withdraw the excess before your return is due. Any amount of the excess contribution that resulted in a deduction will create income that must be reported. You can carry over excess contributions to and deduct them in a year in which less than the maximum contribution has been made. The

[34] *Rousey v. Jacoway*, SCt, 2005-1 USTC ¶ 50,258, 125 SCt 1561. *See also In re Daley*, CA-6, 2013-1 USTC ¶ 50,385, 717 F3d 506.

[35] *In re Clark*, CA-7, 2013-1 USTC ¶ 50,389, 714 F3d 559. *See also In re Chilton*, CA-5, 2012-1 USTC ¶ 50,275, 674 F3d 486.

[36] *R.K. Paschall*, 137 TC 8, Dec. 58,686 (2011).

penalty tax is figured on Form 5329, *Additional Taxes on Qualified Plans (including IRAs) and Other Tax-Favored Accounts.*

¶3120 DISTRIBUTIONS FROM IRAs

.01 Automatic Rollovers of Certain Mandatory Distributions

If a qualified retirement plan participant ceases to be employed by the employer that maintains the plan, the plan may distribute the participant's nonforfeitable accrued benefit without the consent of the participant and, if applicable, the participant's spouse, if the present value of the benefit does not exceed $5,000 [Code Sec. 411(a)(11)(A)]. If this involuntary distribution occurs and the participant subsequently returns to work, the plan is not required to restore the employee's previous service unless the employee repays the benefit [Code Sec. 411(a)(7)(C)]. Generally, a participant may roll over an involuntary distribution from a qualified plan to a traditional IRA or to another qualified plan. Before making a distribution that is eligible for rollover, a plan administrator must provide the participant with a written explanation of the ability to have the distribution rolled over directly to an IRA or another qualified plan and the related tax consequences.

.02 Automatic (Default) Rollover Rule for Qualified Retirement Plans

Code Sec. 401(a)(31)(B) requires mandatory distributions of more than $1,000 from a qualified plan to be paid in a direct rollover to a designated IRA unless the participant makes an affirmative election to have the amount paid in a direct rollover to an eligible retirement plan or to receive the distribution directly [Reg. § 1.401(a)(31)-1].[37] The departing participant must make an affirmative election to (1) have the funds transferred to a different IRA or qualified plan or (2) receive the funds directly in the manner provided by the plan administrator and within the deadline established by the plan administrator [Code Sec. 401(a)(31)(A)].

> **Example 3-16:** A and B resign from ABCo. on June 30. A's qualified plan requires that any nonforfeitable accrued benefit that does not exceed $5,000 must be distributed immediately. The present value of A's vested account balance is $2,500; B's is $995. Neither A nor B make any election concerning the transfer of their accrued balance. The plan administrator utilizes the default option and properly rolls over A's account balance of $2,500 to the designated IRA. For B, the administrator properly provides a check for $796 ($995 less 20-percent withholding).

The written explanation that the plan administrator is required to provide must explain that an automatic distribution by direct transfer applies to the distribution [Code Sec. 402(f)(1)(A)]. As part of the written explanation or in a separate written notice, the plan administrator is also required to notify the participant that the distribution may be transferred to another IRA [Code Sec. 401(a)(31)(B)].

---

[37] Notice 2005-5, IRB 2005-3, 337, as modified by Notice 2005-95, 2005-2 CB 1172.

In the case of an automatic direct rollover, the participant is treated as exercising control over the assets in the IRA upon the earlier of (1) the rollover of any portion of the assets to another IRA, or (2) one year after the automatic rollover [ERISA Sec. 404(c)(3)]. This provision is important because once a participant is treated as exercising control over his or her retirement account, the plan sponsor and trustees no longer have fiduciary responsibility for any loss suffered by the participant. Thus, participants must exercise greater care in monitoring the performance of the account.

.03 Required Minimum Distributions (RMDs) at Age 70½

Money invested in tax-deferred qualified plans can not remain tax-deferred forever. Qualified plans must make required minimum distributions (RMDs) under Code Sec. 401(a)(9). Under this requirement, distribution of the employee's interest in the plan, (other than that of a five percent owner) must begin by April 1 of the calendar year following the later of (1) the calendar year in which the participant attains age 70½ or (2) the calendar year in which the participant retires [Code Sec. 401(a)(9)(C)]. This means that RMDs are not required if employees are still working and would prefer to leave their retirement savings in the tax-deferred plan.

The distribution for the first year can be postponed until April 1 of the following year. For other years, the required distribution must be made during the calendar year that the owner attains 70½.

If an individual owns multiple IRAs, RMDs must be calculated separately for each. However, it is not necessary to make distributions from every account. The required distributions from all IRAs held by the IRA owner and from all IRAs inherited from a particular decedent may be aggregated and made from any of the accounts in the group.

If the participant dies before RMDs have begun, and the entire remaining interest must be distributed within five years of the participant's death. If the five year rule applies to an account with respect to any decedent, the five-year period is determined without regard to calendar year 2009. Thus, for example, if an IRA holder died in 2008, the five-year period ends in 2014 instead of 2013.

An excise tax is imposed on an employee or beneficiary who fails to take an RMD. The tax is 50 percent of the amount by which the RMD exceeds the distribution actually made [Code Sec. 4974(a)]. The tax may be waived if the taxpayer falls to take RMD because of a reasonable error and if steps are taken to correct if. The penalty is reported on Form 5329, *Addition Taxes on Qualified Plans (Including IRAs) and Other Tax Favored Accounts*. If the taxpayer believes that the tax should not apply due to reasonable error, the tax should be paid and a letter of explanation attached to Form 5329. If the IRS agrees with the taxpayer, it will waive the tax and issue a refund.

How Distributions Are Taxed

Withdrawals from tax-deferred retirement accounts, including money from investment gains, are taxed as ordinary income rather than long-term capital gain. This rule applies to traditional IRAs, rollover IRAs, SEP, SAR-SEP, SIMPLE IRAs, as well as all qualified employer-sponsored plans including 401(k), 403(b), profit sharing, money purchase plans and defined benefit plans.

Roth IRAs as Exempt

Note that the popular Roth IRA is not subject to the mandatory distribution rules. This is one of the reasons that the Roth IRA is often favored by investors. In addition, Coverdell education savings accounts which are tax-deferred education savings vehicles, are not subject to RMDs [See ¶ 3140 for further discussion of Roth IRA].

Required Minimum Distribution Rules

The following rules provide guidance for IRA owners to calculate the RMDs that must be made from their traditional IRA.

1. *Uniform lifetime table.* The amount of the RMD is determined by dividing the account balance by the distribution period. For lifetime RMDs, there is a uniform distribution period for almost all IRA owners of the same age. The uniform lifetime distribution period table is based on the joint life and last survivor expectancy of an individual and a hypothetical beneficiary 10 years younger. However, if the IRA owner's sole beneficiary is the owner's spouse and the spouse is more than 10 years younger than the employee, a longer distribution period measured by the joint life and last survivor life expectancy of the employee and spouse is permitted to be used [Reg. § 1.401 (a) (9)-2].

   For years after the year of the IRA owner's death, the distribution period is generally the remaining life expectancy of the designated beneficiary. The beneficiary's remaining life expectancy is calculated using the age of the beneficiary in the year following the year of the IRA owner's death, reduced by one for each subsequent year. If the IRA owner's spouse is the owner's sole beneficiary, and the surviving spouse has not elected to treat the IRA as his or her own, no distribution is required until the year that the decedent would have reached age 70½. Once distributions are required, the surviving spouse's distribution period is determined as of the surviving spouse's birthday during the year distributions must be made (and is redetermined each year, not merely reduced by one each year). If the surviving spouse elects to treat the IRA as his or her own, distributions are not required until the surviving spouse attains age 70½ and are calculated as though the surviving spouse were the owner. If there is no designated beneficiary, the distribution period is the IRA owner's life expectancy calculated in the year of death, reduced by one for each subsequent year.

2. *Mortality tables.* The mortality tables use a fixed 50 percent male, 50 percent female blended rate.

   The tables also may be used to determine an IRA owner's life expectancy, or the joint life and last survivor expectancy of an IRA owner and designated beneficiary, for purposes of calculating the amount of substantially equal periodic payments under Code Sec. 72(t) (2) (A) (iv).

3. *Determination of the designated beneficiary.* The designated beneficiary is determined as of September 30 of the year following the year of the IRA owner's death. Thus, any beneficiary eliminated by distribution of the beneficiary's benefit or through disclaimer during the period between the IRA owner's death and the end of the year following the year of death is disregarded in determining the IRA owner's designated beneficiary for purposes of calculating required minimum distributions.

If, as of the end of the year following the year of the IRA owner's death, the IRA owner has more than one designated beneficiary and the account or benefit has not been divided into separate accounts or shares for each beneficiary, the beneficiary with the shortest life expectancy is the designated beneficiary. Further, if a person other than an individual is a beneficiary as of that date, the IRA owner is treated as not having a beneficiary (except as provided below with respect to trusts).

If a designated beneficiary dies during the period between the IRA owner's date of death and September 30 of the year following the year of the IRA owner's death, the individual continues to be treated as the designated beneficiary for purposes of determining the distribution period rather than the successor beneficiary. In order for an individual to be a designated beneficiary, any beneficiary must be designated under the plan or named by the IRA owner as of the date of death.

In determining an IRA owner's beneficiaries for purposes of applying the multiple beneficiary rule or determining if the IRA owner's spouse is the IRA owner's sole beneficiary, all beneficiaries of the IRA owner's interest in the plan, including contingent beneficiaries, are generally taken into account.

4. *Default rule for postdeath distributions.* If an IRA owner dies before the IRA owner's required beginning date and the IRA owner has a designated beneficiary, then the life expectancy rule in Code Sec. 401(a)(9)(B)(iii) (rather than the 5-year rule in Code Sec. 401(a)(9)(B)(ii)) is the default distribution rule. Thus, absent a plan provision or election of the 5-year rule, the life expectancy rule applies in all cases in which the IRA owner has a designated beneficiary, and the 5-year rule applies if the IRA owner does not have a designated beneficiary.
5. *Trust as beneficiary.* A trust beneficiary may be the beneficiary of an IRA for purposes of determining RMDs when the trust is named as the beneficiary of an IRA, provided that certain requirements are met. One of these requirements is that documentation of the underlying beneficiaries of the trust be provided to the IRA trustee, custodian, or issuer. In the case of individual accounts, unless the lifetime distribution period for an IRA owner is measured by the joint life expectancy of the IRA owner and the owner's spouse, the deadline under these regulations for providing the beneficiary documentation is October 31 of the year following the year of the IRA owner's death. This deadline for providing the trust documentation is coordinated with the deadline for determining the IRA owner's designated beneficiary. A revocable trust will not fail to be a trust for purposes of Code Sec. 401(a)(9) merely because the trust elects to be treated as an estate under Code Sec. 645, as long as the trust continues to be a trust under state law.
6. *Separate accounts.* Separate accounts with different beneficiaries under the plan can be established at any time, either before or after the IRA owner's required beginning date. However, the separate accounts are recognized for purposes of determining RMDs only after the later of the year of the IRA owner's death (whether before or after the required beginning date) and the year the separate accounts are established. The separate accounting must allocate all post-death investment gains and losses for the period prior to the establishment of the separate accounts on a pro rata basis in a reasonable and consistent basis among the separate accounts for the different beneficiaries. The separate accounting must also allocate any post-

death distribution to the separate account of the beneficiary receiving that distribution. Once the separate accounts are established, the final regulations permit the separate accounting to provide for separate investments for each separate account.

7. *Election of surviving spouse to treat an inherited IRA as spouse's own IRA.* A surviving spouse of a deceased IRA owner can elect to treat an inherited IRA as the spouse's own IRA at any time after the IRA owner's date of death. The RMD for the calendar year of the IRA's owner's death is determined assuming the IRA owner lived throughout the year. The surviving spouse is required to receive a minimum distribution for the year of the IRA owner's death only to the extent that the amount required was not distributed to the owner before death. If the spouse actually receives a distribution from the IRA, the spouse is permitted to roll that distribution over within 60 days into an IRA in the spouse's own name to the extent that the distribution is not a required distribution, regardless of whether or not the spouse is the sole beneficiary of the IRA owner. Further, if the distribution is received by the spouse before the year that the IRA owner would have been 70½, no portion of the distribution is a RMD for purposes of determining whether it is eligible to be rolled over by the surviving spouse.
8. *Reporting of required minimum distributions.* Trustees, custodians, and issuers must identify on Form 5498, each IRA for which a minimum distribution is required to be made to an IRA owner. The amount of the required distribution need not be reported. However, the trustee, custodian, or issuer of such an IRA, must provide the following additional information to the IRA owner: the amount of the RMD, or a minimum distribution is required for the year and a calculation of the amount of the RMD upon request.
9. *Simplifying the calculation.* For lifetime distributions, the marital status of the IRA owner is determined on January 1 each year. Divorce or death after that date is disregarded until the next year. Further, a change in beneficiary due to the spouse's death is not recognized until the following year. Contributions and distributions made after December 31 of a calendar year are disregarded for purposes of determining the minimum distribution for the following year. An IRA owner's account balance for the valuation calendar year that is also the IRA owner's first distribution calendar year is no longer reduced for a distribution on April 1 to satisfy the minimum distribution requirement for the first distribution calendar year. Contributions made after the calendar year that are allocated as of a date in the prior calendar year are no longer required to be added back. The only exceptions are rollover amounts, and recharacterized conversion contributions, that are not in any account on December 31 of a year. These changes apply to all audited plans.

.04 Phased Retirement Plan Distributions

In a phased retirement, older, more experienced employees who are at or near retirement take on a reduced schedule or workload, thereby providing a smoother transition from full-time employment to retirement.

During such a transition arrangement, employees may wish to supplement their part-time income with a portion of their retirement savings. However, phased retirement can also increase the risk of outliving retirement savings for employees who begin drawing upon their retirement savings before normal retirement age. Even though the annuity distribution options offered by defined benefit plans preclude outliving benefits, early distribution of a portion of the employee's benefit will reduce the benefits available after full retirement. On the other hand, phased retirement also can provide employees additional time to save for retirement because employees continue working while they are able to do so, and can accrue additional benefits and reduce or forgo early spending of their retirement savings.

¶3125 ROLLOVERS OF RETIREMENT PLAN AND IRA DISTRIBUTIONS

There is no immediate tax if distributions from an IRA are rolled over to an IRA or other eligible retirement plan (i.e., qualified trust, governmental Code Sec. 457 plan, Code Sec. 403(a) annuity and Code Sec. 403(b) tax-shelter annuity). For the rollover to be tax-free, the distributed amount must be recontributed to the new retirement plan within 60 days after the date that the taxpayer received the withdrawal [Code Sec. 408(d)(3)]. A distribution rolled over after the 60-day period generally will be taxed and also may be subject to a 10 percent premature withdrawal penalty tax [Code Sec. 72(t)]. Only one tax-free IRA-to-IRA rollover per IRA account can be made within a one-year period [Code Sec. 408(d)(3)(B)].

A distribution from an inherited IRA (i.e., an IRA obtained by an individual other than the IRA owner's spouse as a result of the death of the IRA owner) may not be rolled over tax-free [Code Sec. 408(d)(3)(C)]. However, if an IRA owner designates her spouse as beneficiary of her IRA, the surviving spouse may roll over the decedent's IRA into the spouse's own IRA, or elect to treat the decedent's IRA as the spouse's own IRA [Code Sec. 408(d)(3)(C)]. In order to make this election, the surviving spouse must be the sole beneficiary of the IRA and have an unlimited right to withdraw amounts from it. Additionally, a surviving spouse who actually receives a distribution from a deceased spouse's IRA is permitted to roll that distribution over into his own IRA, even if he or she is not the sole beneficiary and even if the IRA assets pass through a trust and/or estate, so long as the rollover is accomplished within the requisite 60-day period.

In general, if the proceeds of a decedent's IRA pass through a third party (i.e., trust or estate) and then are distributed to the decedent's surviving spouse, the spouse is treated as having received the proceeds from the third party and is not eligible to roll over the distributed IRA proceeds into his own IRA. However, if the surviving spouse is executor of the estate and has sole authority and discretion to pay IRA proceeds to himself then the surviving spouse can roll over the amounts into an IRA in his own name.

.01 Waiver of 60-Day Rollover Period

The IRS has the authority to waive the 60-day rollover requirement where the failure to waive the requirement would be against "equity or good conscience," including "casualty, disaster, or other events beyond the reasonable control" of the taxpayer [Code Sec. 408(d)(3)(I)]. In Rev. Proc. 2003-16,[38] the IRS set forth the factors that the IRS would

[38] Rev. Proc. 2003-16, 2003-1 CB 359.

review in determining the appropriateness of a waiver of the 60-day rollover requirement. The IRS will consider the following factors in determining whether to waive the requirement:

- Errors or wrong advice given by financial institution, bank, or investment manager;[39]
- Inability to complete a rollover due to family illness, diminished capacity, death, disability, hospitalization; incarceration, restrictions imposed by a foreign country, natural disaster or postal error;
- Use of the amount distributed;
- Time elapsed since distribution occurred.

The following additional situations would justify waiver of the 60-day rollover requirement [Code Secs. 402, 408]:

- The distribution check was not cashed;
- The widowed spouse was in mourning during that period and had to take charge of her husband's estate and decide how to handle the IRA;[40]
- The rollover could not be completed because of service in a combat zone or because of a federally declared disaster or a terrorist or military action [Reg. § 301.7508-1];[41]
- The taxpayer suffered from an irreversible neurological disease that impaired her ability to make sound financial decisions;[42]
- Deceased spouse died before correcting the beneficiary designation forms that listed her estate as the beneficiary;[43]
- Taxpayer neglected to rollover funds withdrawn from his IRA because he spent all his time caring for his ailing spouse;[44] and
- Husband withdrew funds from wife's IRA under a power of attorney that was intended to be limited to incapacity and then husband gambled the funds away. The wife didn't learn of the withdrawal until after the 60-day period had expired.[45]

When Approval Is Automatic

The 60-day rollover requirement will be waived automatically without IRS approval if failure to complete the rollover within the 60-day time frame was solely due to an error

[39] LTR 200415012 (Jan. 15, 2004), LTR 200415011 (Jan. 16, 2004); LTR 200402028 (Oct. 14, 2003); LTR 200411047 (Dec. 15, 2003); LTR 200406052 (Nov. 12, 2003); LTR 200426024 (Mar. 31, 2004); LTR 200417033 (Jan. 30, 2004); LTR 200426022 (Apr. 2, 2004); LTR 200426021 (June 25, 2004); LTR 200421008 (Feb. 27, 2004); LTR 200429012 (Apr. 22, 2004); LTR 200407023 (Nov. 17, 2003); LTR 200504037 (Nov. 4, 2004); LTR 200504041 (Nov. 2, 2004); LTR 200504042 (Nov. 1, 2004); LTR 200443034 (July 29, 2004).

[40] LTR 200401020 (Oct. 8, 2003), LTR 200401023 (Oct. 9, 2003), LTR 200401024 (Nov. 4, 2003), LTR 200401025 (Nov. 5, 2003), LTR 200402028 (Oct. 14, 2003).

[41] Rev. Proc. 2005-17, 2005-1 CB 797; *See* LTR 200502052 (Oct. 15, 2004) (60-day rollover requirement waived because taxpayer working in war zone). *But see*, LTR 200751032 (Sept. 25, 2007) where the taxpayer failed to present evidence sufficient to warrant granting a waiver and therefore the IRS denied a waiver.

[42] LTR 200814029 (Jan. 9, 2008).

[43] LTR 201212021 (Dec. 27, 2011).

[44] LTR 201210046 (Dec. 15, 2011).

[45] LTR 201324022 (March 22, 2013).

on the part of the financial institution. Automatic approval will be granted only in the following situations:

- The funds are deposited into an eligible retirement plan within one year from the beginning of the 60-day rollover period; and
- The financial institution had deposited the funds as instructed it would have been a valid rollover.

When Private Letter Ruling Required

A taxpayer must request a private letter ruling in order to apply for a hardship exception to the 60-day rollover requirement. The IRS will issue a ruling waiving the 60-day rollover requirement in cases where the failure to waive such requirement would be against equity or good conscience, including casualty, disaster or other events beyond the reasonable control of the taxpayer.

.02 Rollover Procedures

Employees who roll over employer plan distributions into an IRA no longer have to keep that IRA separate in order to execute a future rollover plan. However, taxpayers born before 1936 who want to keep special capital gains and ten-year averaging benefits will need a conduit IRA to move assets from one employer plan to another. Rollovers from IRAs to employer plans may not include any after-tax contributions. Distributions are considered to consist first of the taxable IRA portion, thus maximizing the amount eligible for rollover. Rollovers from employer plans may include after-tax contributions to those plans if the rollover is a direct trustee-to-trustee transfer. A receiving employer plan—but not an IRA trustee—must separately track such contributions and related earnings.

All distributions from qualified plans and 403(b) annuities to an employee or to the employee's surviving spouse are eligible rollover distributions to the extent that they are includible in gross income, except:

- Substantially equal periodic payments, and
- Required minimum distributions under Code Sec. 401(a)(9) [Code Sec. 402(c)(4); Reg. § 1.401(a)(31)-1].

Once you have made a tax-free rollover, you must wait at least one year from the date you receive the withdrawn money before you are eligible to initiate another tax-free rollover of the money in that account [Code Sec. 408(d)(3)(B)]. The one-year limitation applies to each separate IRA you own. This means that you can roll over the distribution received from one IRA even though you rolled over a distribution from another IRA less than a year ago. A trustee-to-trustee transfer is not considered a rollover, and there is no limit on the number of these transfers that can take place in one year.[46] Money distributed from a taxpayer's IRAs must be transferred directly into the new IRA account in order for the new contribution to be a tax-free rollover [Code Sec. 408(d)(3)]. The law specifically provides that the "same money or property" must be rolled over

[46] *M.H. Martin*, 63 TCM 3122, Dec. 48,275(M), TC Memo. 1992-331, *aff'd*, 987 F2d 770, *cert. denied*, 508 US 920.

into the new IRA in order for the rollover to be tax-free. This means that the old IRA proceeds cannot change form on the way to the new IRA account. A taxpayer who reinvested cash distributions from IRAs into other property before depositing the property into a rollover IRA, even within the 60-day rollover contribution, will still have to pay tax on the entire amount of the distribution.[47]

An employer is permitted to accomplish an employee's direct rollover by any reasonable means of delivery to the eligible retirement plan. A reasonable means of delivery includes delivery of a check to the eligible retirement plan by the employee, provided that the payee line on the check is made out in such a manner as to ensure that the check will be negotiable solely by the recipient plan's trustee. Plan administrators are not permitted to require information or documentation or to establish procedures that substantially impair the availability of a direct rollover. A safe harbor designed to encourage plans to accept rollovers has been provided for receiving plans that reasonably determine that the distributing plan is qualified. No withholding liability will be imposed on an administrator that reasonably relies on "adequate information" furnished by the distributee.

In order for a contribution of an eligible rollover distribution to an individual retirement plan to qualify for an exclusion from gross income, the participant must irrevocably elect to treat the contribution as a rollover contribution when the contribution is made to the individual plan. A direct rollover election is an irrevocable election.

▶ **PRACTICE TIP:** Transfer the money withdrawn from your IRA accounts directly from one IRA trustee to another IRA trustee. In the eyes of the IRS a trustee-to-trustee transfer is not a rollover and therefore you do not have to satisfy the onerous rollover requirements. As long as you do not touch the money and let the trustees do all the work you avoid the following requirements that apply to rollovers from one IRA account to another: (1) the 20 percent withholding requirement, (2) the 60-day rollover period, (3) the one-year waiting period between rollovers from one IRA to another, and (4) the 10 percent penalty tax on before-age-59$^1/_2$ distributions.

Withholding Requirement

Retirement distributions paid directly to you will be subject to a 20 percent tax withholding, even if the rollover is tax-free [Code Sec. 3405]. Withholding is mandatory unless the rollover is a direct transfer to an IRA or another qualified retirement plan. To avoid this withholding, authorize your employer to make a direct rollover of the funds to an IRA or other qualified plan. Distributions of stock are not subject to withholding. This withholding requirement negates the benefit of the 60-day tax-free loan for employees who take their IRA in a lump sum when they change jobs, retire or are laid off [Ch. 15].

If you do end up paying the withholding tax, however, you can get a refund for the withheld amount when you file your income tax return for the year of the withdrawal.

---

[47] *A. Lemishow*, 110 TC 110, Dec. 52,574 (1998), later proceeding, 110 TC 346, Dec. 52,724 (1998).

Example 3-17: Your 401(k) plan contains $10,000. You change jobs and rollover the $10,000 into your new employer's tax-deferred retirement plan. Rather than having the check made out directly to the new employer's plan administrator, the check is made out directly to you. The check will only be for $8,000 because of the mandatory 20 percent withholding tax. If you deposit the $8,000 plus another $2,000 from your own pocket into the new plan within 60 days, you can get a refund of the $2,000 when you file your tax return for the year of the rollover. If you only deposit $8,000 you will report and pay tax on the withheld 20 percent as a taxable distribution plus a 10 percent penalty if you are under age 59½.

Note that the mandatory 20 percent withholding tax does not apply to rollovers from a nonemployer sponsored IRA to another IRA. The 20 percent mandatory withholding tax only applies to rollovers from employer-sponsored plans to IRAs.

Also, the taxable portion of plan distributions you receive before age 59½ that is not rolled over may be subject to a 10 percent premature withdrawal penalty as well.

Any amount of plan distribution can qualify for tax-free rollover treatment if it is an eligible rollover distribution which is defined as any distribution except those that are: (1) part of a series of substantially equal periodic payments; (2) required upon the participant reaching age 70½; (3) returns of the participant's investment in the plan; (4) returns of 401(k) elective deferrals; (5) corrective distributions of excess 401(k) contributions; (6) taxable plan loans; (7) dividends paid on stock held by an ESOP; (8) costs of employer-provided group-term life insurance.

Notice of Rollovers of Retirement Plan and IRA Distributions Required

The plan administrator of a qualified plan or a 403(b) annuity is required to provide a written explanation of rollover rules to individuals who receive a distribution eligible for rollover. In general, the notice is to be provided within a reasonable period of time before making the distribution and is to include an explanation of: (1) the law providing that individuals may have the distribution directly rolled over to another eligible retirement plan, (2) the law requiring withholding if the distribution is not directly rolled over, (3) the law providing that the distribution may be rolled over within 60 days of receipt, (4) if applicable, certain other rules that may apply to the distribution, and (5) a description of the law providing that distributions from the plan receiving the distribution may be subject to restrictions and tax consequences different than those applicable to distributions from the distributing plan. [Code Sec. 402(f)(1)(E)].

.03 Election of Surviving Spouse to Treat an Inherited IRA as Spouse's Own IRA

Surviving spouses are permitted to roll over distributions from the deceased spouse's plan into either a qualified plan, 403(b) annuity, or a 457 plan in which the surviving spouse participates or into a traditional IRA [Code Secs. 402(c)(9), 408(d)]. In addition, a surviving spouse of a deceased IRA owner can elect to treat an inherited IRA as the spouse's own IRA at any time after the IRA owner's date of death. The RMD for the calendar year of the IRA's owner's death is determined assuming the IRA owner lived throughout the calendar year. The surviving spouse is required to receive a minimum distribution for the year of the IRA owner's death only to the extent that the amount required was not distributed to the owner before death. If the spouse actually receives a distribution from the IRA, the spouse is permitted to roll that distribution over within 60 days into an IRA in the spouse's own name to the extent that the distribution is not a required distribution, regardless of whether or not the spouse is the sole beneficiary of the IRA owner. Further, if the distribution is received by the spouse before the year that the IRA owner would have been 70½, no portion of the distribution is a required minimum distribution for purposes of determining whether it is eligible to be rolled over by the surviving spouse [Reg. § § 1.401(a)(9)-3, Q&A-3(b), 1.408-8, Q&A-5].

The surviving spouse also has the option to retain the inherited IRA in the deceased spouse's name. This option will be suitable if the surviving spouse thinks he or she will need the cash from the IRA because distributions made to a beneficiary or an estate on or after the death of the IRA owner will not be subject to the 10 percent penalty tax which is imposed on most pre-age 59½ withdrawals from a rollover IRA account [Code Sec. 72(t)(2)(A)(ii)].

In *C.T. Gee*,[48] a taxpayer who rolled over a distribution from her deceased husband's IRA into her separate IRA, and subsequently received an early distribution from her IRA, was liable for the 10-percent penalty tax because the amount received by the taxpayer from her deceased husband's IRA lost its character as a distribution to a beneficiary upon a decedent's death and the source of the funds became irrelevant when she rolled over the funds into her separate IRA. Therefore, the 10-percent additional tax applied.

.04 Rollovers by Nonspouse Beneficiaries

Distributions from a deceased person's "eligible retirement plan" (includes qualified retirement plan, governmental Code Sec. 457 plan, or a tax-sheltered annuity) may be rolled over tax-free into an IRA established to receive the distribution on behalf of a nonspouse beneficiary via a trustee-to-trustee transfer [Code Sec. 402(c)(11)]. If this type of transfer is made: (1) the transfer is treated as an eligible rollover distribution, (2) the transferee IRA is treated as an inherited account, and (3) the required minimum distribution rules applicable where the participant/owner dies before the entire interest is distributed apply to the transferee IRA.

Identification Requirement

The IRA must be established in a manner that identifies it as an IRA with respect to a deceased individual and also identifies the deceased individual and the beneficiary, for example, "Tom Smith as beneficiary of John Smith."[49]

Trust as IRA Beneficiary

A qualified plan may make a direct rollover to an IRA on behalf of a trust where the trust is the named beneficiary of a decedent, provided the beneficiaries of the trust meet the requirements to be designated beneficiaries within the meaning of Code Sec. 401(a)(9)(E). The IRA must be established so that the trust is identified as the beneficiary. In this case, the beneficiaries of the trust are treated as having been

[48] *C.T. Gee*, 127 TC 1, Dec. 56,568 (2006); *P.A. Sears*, 100 TCM 6, Dec. 58,261(M), TC Memo. 2010-146.

[49] Notice 2007-7, 2007-1 CB 395, as modified by Notice 2007-99, IRB 2007-52, 1243 and Notice 2009-82, IRB 2009-41.

designated as beneficiaries of the decedent for purposes of determining the distribution period.[50]

Five-Year Rule

Under the five-year rule described in Code Sec. 401(a)(9)(B)(ii), no amount must be distributed until the fifth calendar year following the year of the employee's death. In that year, the entire amount to which the beneficiary is entitled under the plan must be distributed. Thus, if the five-year rule applies with respect to a nonspouse beneficiary who is a designated beneficiary, for the first four years after the year the employee dies, no amount payable to the beneficiary is ineligible for direct rollover as an RMD. Accordingly, the beneficiary is permitted to directly roll over the beneficiary's entire benefit until the end of the fourth year. On or after January 1 of the fifth year following the year in which the employee died, no amount payable to the beneficiary is eligible for rollover.[51]

Life Expectancy Rule

If the life expectancy rule described in Code Sec. 401(a)(9)(B)(iii) applies in the year following the year of death and each subsequent year, there is an RMD. The amount not eligible for rollover includes all undistributed RMDs for the year in which the direct rollover occurs and any prior year (even if the excise tax under Code Sec. 4974 has been paid with respect to the failure in the prior years).

If the five-year rule applies, the nonspouse designated beneficiary may determine the RMD under the plan using the life expectancy rule in the case of a distribution made prior to the end of the year following the year of death. However, in order to use this rule, the RMDs under the IRA to which the direct rollover is made must be determined under the life expectancy rule using the same designated beneficiary.

If an employee dies on or after his or her required beginning date, for the year of the employee's death, the RMD not eligible for rollover is the same as the amount that would have applied if the employee were still alive and elected the direct rollover. As in the case of death before the employee's required beginning date, the amount not eligible for rollover includes all undistributed RMDs for the year in which the direct rollover occurs and any prior year, including years before the employee's death.

After a direct rollover by a nonspouse designated beneficiary, the RMD with respect to the IRA to which the rollover contribution is made is treated as an inherited IRA within the meaning of Code Sec. 408(d)(3)(C). The RMDs set forth in Code Sec. 401(a)(9)(B) and the accompanying regulations apply to the inherited IRA. The rules for determining the RMDs under the plan with respect to the nonspouse beneficiary also apply under the IRA. Thus, if the employee dies before his or her required beginning date and the five-year rule applied to the nonspouse designated beneficiary under the plan making the direct rollover, the five-year rule applies for purposes of determining RMDs under the IRA. If the life expectancy rule applied to the nonspouse designated beneficiary under the plan, the RMD under the IRA must be determined using the same applicable distribution period as would have been used under the plan if the direct rollover had not

---

[50] Notice 2007-7, 2007-1 CB 395, as modified by Notice 2007-99, IRB 2007-52, 1243 and Notice 2009-82, 2009-41 IRB.

[51] Notice 2007-7, 2007-1 CB 395, as modified by Notice 2007-99, IRB 2007-52, 1243 and Notice 2009-82, IRB 2009-41.

occurred. Similarly, if the employee dies on or after his or her required beginning date, the RMD under the IRA for any year after the year of death must be determined using the same applicable distribution period as would have been used under the plan if the direct rollover had not occurred.[52]

.05 Qualified Charitable Distributions from IRAs to Charities

In 2012 and 2013, individuals aged 70½ or older can make qualified charitable distributions (QCD) of up to $100,000 from their IRA accounts (excluding SEP or SIMPLE IRAs) to qualified public charities and have that QCD count as their required minimum distribution (RMD) [Code Sec. 408(d)(8)(F)].

If the taxpayer's IRA includes nondeductible contributions, the QCD is first considered to be paid out of otherwise taxable income. However, a special ordering rule applies to separate taxable distributions from nontaxable IRA distributions for charitable distribution purposes. Under the rule, a distribution is treated first as income up to the aggregate amount that would otherwise be includible in the owner's gross income if all amounts in all the owner's IRAs were distributed during the tax year, and all such plans were treated as one contract for purposes of determining the aggregate amount includible as gross income. To qualify, the funds must be contributed directly by the IRA trustee to an eligible charity. This means that any distributions, including any RMDs, which the IRA owner actually receives cannot qualify as QCDs. Likewise, any tax withholdings on behalf of the owner from an IRA distribution cannot qualify as QCDs. Taxpayers will not be able to claim a charitable deduction for the QCD.

Eligible Recipients

Qualified charitable distributions may be from a traditional or a Roth IRA. Ineligible recipients are donor-advised funds, and supporting organizations are not eligible recipients. The recipient of the IRA funds must be a "50 percent organization" or public charity described in Code Sec. 170(b)(1)(A) (so named because they can be deducted up to 50 percent of the taxpayer's contributions base in the contribution year). A public charity specifically includes a church or a convention or association of churches in its list of eligible charitable organizations. Other eligible charitable organizations include: educational institutions, hospitals, medical research organizations, organizations supporting governmental schools, governmental units, publicly supported organizations, common fund organizations, private operating foundations, and conduit foundations [Code Sec. 408(d)(8)].

Ineligible Recipients

Distributions from employer-sponsored retirement plans, including SIMPLE IRAs and simplified employee pension (SEP) plans, are not eligible to be treated as QCDs. In addition, distributions to supporting organizations described in Code Sec. 509(a)(3) (i.e., organizations that support churches, educational institutions, hospitals, medical research organizations, organizations supporting government schools, and publicly supported organizations) are not QCDs.

---

[52] Notice 2007-7, 2007-1 CB 395, as modified by Notice 2007-99, IRB 2007-52, 1243 and Notice 2009-82, IRB 2009-41.

No Withholding Requirements

A QCD is not subject to withholding under Code Sec. 3405 because an IRA owner that requests such a distribution is deemed to have elected out of withholding under Code Sec. 3405(a)(2). For purposes of determining whether a distribution requested by an IRA satisfies the requirements under Code Sec. 408(d)(8), the IRA trustee, custodian, or issuer may rely upon reasonable representations made by the IRA owner.

Direct Payment to Charity

A check from an IRA made payable to a charitable organization described in Code Sec. 408(d)(8) and delivered by the IRA owner to the charitable organization will be considered a direct payment by the IRA trustee to the charitable organization for purposes of Code Sec. 408(d)(8)(B)(i).

Consequences of Failed Distribution

If an amount intended to be a QCD is paid to a charitable organization but fails to satisfy the requirements of Code Sec. 408(d)(8), the amount paid is treated as: (1) a distribution from the IRA to the IRA owner that is includible in gross income, and (2) a contribution from the IRA owner to the charitable organization.

¶3130 IRA INVESTMENT OPPORTUNITIES

Contributions can be made to either a traditional IRA or individual retirement annuity plan. Use Form 5306, *Application for Approval of Prototype or Employer Sponsored Individual Retirement Arrangement (IRA)*, to adopt an officially prescribed model IRA under Code Sec. 408(a). You need not file Form 5306 with the IRS; it is only used to apply for approval of a prototype or employer sponsored individual retirement account.

.01 Individual Retirement Accounts

IRAs are domestic trusts organized for the exclusive benefit of an individual or his beneficiaries [Code Sec. 408(a)]. Normally the trustee is a bank, savings and loan association, or federal credit union. The plan must include these terms: (1) no contribution (which must be in cash) on behalf of any individual may exceed $5,500 (plus catch-up contributions) in 2013 (no change in 2014), not including tax-free rollovers; (2) the trust assets must be kept separately from other property except a common or trust investment fund; (3) the account must be nonforfeitable.

> **NOTE:** Banks are allowed to offer free checking, free checks or other free services based on the balance in an IRA. For example, assume Mr. Smith banks at First National Bank. He has $2,000 in his checking account and $10,000 in his IRA. First National offers free checking to all customers with at least $5,500 in the bank. Smith can count his IRA toward the $5,500 limit and he easily qualifies for the bank's money-saving offer.

.02 Individual Retirement Annuities

Individual retirement annuities are annuity or endowment contracts issued by an insurance company to individual participants [Code Sec. 408(b)]. The contract must be nonforfeitable and must contain no life insurance element. The annual premium on behalf of an individual may not exceed $5,500 (plus catch-up contributions) in 2013 (no change in 2014). Also, payout provisions similar to those above apply here.

.03 Investment in Collectibles

You can invest your IRA savings in platinum coins as well as gold, silver, platinum or palladium bullion of a specified minimum fineness [Code Sec. 408(m)(3)]. Investments in "collectibles" are, however, generally not permitted [Code Sec. 408(m)]. In fact, the acquisition by an IRA of any collectible will be treated as a distribution from the account in an amount equal to the cost of the collectible. The term "collectible" means any work of art, any rug or antiques, any metal or gem, any stamp or coin, any alcoholic beverage, any musical instrument, any historical objects such as documents or clothes [Prop. Reg. § 1.408-10(b)].

IRA Can Buy Shares of Trusts with Gold/Silver Investments

In Letter Ruling 200732026 and Letter Ruling 200732027, the IRS concluded that an IRA custodian could purchase shares of an investment trust formed to hold gold or silver bullion without that purchase being treated as the acquisition of a collectible under Code Sec. 408(m). Therefore the investment was not treated as a taxable distribution under Code Sec. 408(m)(1).

.04 IRA Providers May Offer Personalized Investment Advice

Qualified fiduciary advisers can offer personally tailored professional investment advice to help beneficiaries of IRAs [Code Sec. 4975(f)(8)]. "Fiduciary adviser" is defined as a person who is a fiduciary of the plan by reason of the provision of investment advice to a participant or beneficiary and who is also:

1. Registered as an investment adviser under the Investment Advisers Act of 1940 or under laws of the state in which the fiduciary maintains its principal office and place of business;
2. A bank, or a similar financial institution supervised by the United States or a state, or a savings association (as defined under the Federal Deposit Insurance Act), but only if the advice is provided through a trust department that is subject to periodic examination and review by federal or state banking authorities;
3. An insurance company qualified to do business under state law;
4. Registered as a broker or dealer under the Securities Exchange Act of 1934;
5. An affiliate of any of the preceding; or
6. An employee, agent, or registered representative of any of the preceding who satisfies the requirements of applicable insurance, banking, and securities laws relating to the provision of advice [Code Sec. 4975(f)(8)(J)].

¶3135 TAX ON IRA DISTRIBUTIONS

Generally, you are taxed on traditional IRA payouts as ordinary income in the year you actually receive the cash payments [Code Sec. 408(d)]. No tax is due on withdrawals to the extent they are allocable to your original nondeductible contributions [¶3105]. The allocation is based on a ratio of your nondeductible contributions to the total balance in all of your traditional IRAs. As discussed in ¶3140, distributions from Roth IRAs generally are tax free.

You can withdraw nondeductible contributions completely tax-free (i.e., no allocation between deductible and nondeductible contributions) at any time up to the tax return deadline, including extensions, for the year the contribution was made. However, you must withdraw all earnings attributable to the contributions as well [Code Sec. 408(d)(4)].

NOTE: An IRA distribution is income eligible for the credit for the elderly and disabled [Ch. 14].

.01 Premature IRA Distributions Subject to 10-Percent Penalty Tax

Premature distributions are amounts you withdraw from your IRA before you reach age 59½ [Code Sec. 72(t)(2)(A)(i)]. To discourage individuals from taking premature distributions from retirement plans Congress enacted Code Sec. 72(t) which imposes an additional tax of "10% of the portion of such amount which is includible in gross income" [Code Sec. 72(t)(1)]. This penalty tax may not be deducted by the taxpayer. The 10-percent early withdrawal penalty tax applies to actual as well as "deemed" distributions [Code Sec. 72(t)(1); Reg. §1.408-10(f)]. Thus, if you benefit from a "prohibited transaction" with the money in the IRA account which could include borrowing money from the IRA or using the IRA as a security for a loan, the 10-percent penalty tax can apply to the amount of the benefit [Code Sec. 408(e)(2)(A)]. An investment by an IRA or any other qualified plan in collectibles (art, rugs, antiques, gems, stamps, coins, alcoholic beverage or other item of tangible personal property specified in Code Sec. 408(m)) will be treated as a distribution of the cost of the item and will result in the 10-percent penalty tax. You can invest your IRA savings in platinum coins as well as gold, silver, platinum or palladium bullion of a specified minimum fineness without paying the 10-percent penalty [Code Sec. 408(m)]. See ¶3130.

.02 Exceptions to 10-Percent Penalty Tax for IRA Distributions

Congress enacted Code Sec. 72(t)(2) to grant relief in certain circumstances from the 10 percent additional tax. Taxpayers can only avoid the 10-percent premature withdrawal penalty if the distribution qualifies under one of the following exceptions:

- *Post-age 59½ distributions.* Distributions made after reaching age 59½ are not subject to the 10-percent penalty tax [Code Sec. 72(t)(2)(A)(i)].
- *Taxpayer death.* Distributions made because the taxpayer establishing the IRA has died [Code Sec. 72(t)(A)(ii)].
- *Taxpayer disability.* Distributions made because the taxpayer establishing the IRA is totally or permanently disabled [Code Sec. 72(t)(2)(A)(iii)]. *Disabled* is defined as the inability to engage in any substantial gainful activity because of a medically determinable physical or mental impairment which can be expected to result in death or be of a long-continued and indefinite duration [Code Sec. 72(m)(7)]. The term *substantial gainful activity* refers to the activity, or a comparable activity in which the plan participant customarily engaged prior to the impairment [Reg. §1.72-17A(f)(1)]. Examples approved by the IRS include: loss of use of two limbs; certain progressive diseases, which result in physical loss or atrophy of a limb, such as diabetes, multiple sclerosis, or Buerger's disease; diseases of the heart,

lungs, or blood vessels; inoperative and progressive cancer; brain damage; mental diseases such as psychosis; nearly total vision loss; permanent and total loss of speech; and, total deafness uncorrectable by a hearing aid [Reg. § 1.72-17A(f)(2)(i)-(ix)]. Clinical depression is not a disability that will excuse a premature IRA withdrawal where a stockbroker continued stock trading activities while being treated for his severe clinical depression.[53] A mental disease is one that requires continued institutionalization or constant supervision. Failure to prove mental disease will render a premature distribution for alleged depression subject to the 10-percent premature distribution penalty. Periodic visits with a psychiatrist are insufficient. Without proof that a mental illness requires constant supervision, it will not qualify as a disability for purposes of eliminating the 10-percent premature penalty imposed on premature IRA withdrawals [Reg. § 1.72-17A(f)(2)(vi)]. A taxpayer's depression will qualify as a disability eligible for retirement plan penalty exception if it is expected to be indefinite in duration.[54]

Example 3-18: Betty is age 45 but after a car accident is totally and permanently disabled. She can withdraw her IRA savings without paying the 10-percent early withdrawal penalty because she is totally or permanently disabled [Code Sec. 72(t)(2)(A)(iii)].[55]

- *Medical expenses.* Distributions from an IRA if proceeds used to pay for medical expenses in excess of 10 percent of adjusted gross income [Code Secs. 72(t) (2) (B), 213(a)].
- *Health insurance for unemployed.* Distributions from an IRA if proceeds used to pay health insurance premiums for unemployed individuals [Code Sec. 72(t) (2) (D)]. To avoid the penalty tax in this situation, the taxpayer must have received unemployment compensation for 12 consecutive weeks under federal or state law and the distributions must be made during any tax year in which the unemployment compensation is paid or during the next tax year. This exception does not apply to distributions made after an individual's reemployment if he or she has been employed for at least sixty days after the initial separation from service [Code Sec. 72(t) (2) (D) (ii)].
- *Series of periodic payments (SEPPs).* Distributions structured as part of a series of "substantially equally periodic payments" (SEPPs) will be penalty-free if the distributions are made (not less frequently than annually) for the life (or life expectancy) of the taxpayer or the joint lives (or joint life expectancy) of the taxpayer and beneficiary [Code Sec. 72(t) (2) (A) (iv)]. If the series of substantially equal periodic payments is subsequently modified, however, (other than by reason of death or disability) within five years from the start date, the exception to the 10-percent tax no longer applies. If this occurs, the tax for the year of modification is increased by the additional amount of income tax that the taxpayer would have paid under Code Sec. 72(t) (4). To calculate the distribution, the account balance at the end of the prior year is divided by the participant's life expectancy, or the joint life expectancies found in

[53] *R.J. Dwyer*, 106 TC 337, Dec. 51,340 (1996); *B. Johnson*, TC Summary Op. 2006-62.

[54] *M.L. Coleman-Stephens*, TC Summary Op. 2003-91.

[55] *J.M. Brown*, 72 TCM 651, Dec. 51,556(M), TC Memo. 1996-421.

the tables under Reg. § 1.72-9. If the SEPPs are subsequently modified within 5 years of the date of the first payment, the tax for the year of modification is increased by an amount equal to the tax which, but for the exception under Code Sec. 72(t)(2)(A)(iv), would have been imposed, plus interest for the deferral period [Code Sec. 72(t)(4)].

In order to qualify for the SEPP exception to the 10 percent early distribution penalty, taxpayers must withdraw amounts calculated under one of the three methods outlined in Notice 89-25[56] as follows:

1. The required minimum distribution method,
2. The fixed amortization method, or
3. The fixed annuitization method.

Taxpayers who fail to base their distributions on one of the methods in Notice 89-25 will fail to establish that the distributions qualify for the substantially equal periodic payments exception to the 10-percent additional tax.[57]

▶ **PRACTICE POINTER:** *Relief for taxpayers with depleted accounts.* In Rev. Rul. 2002-62,[58] the IRS provides that those taxpayers can switch, without incurring penalties, to a method of determining the amount of their payments based on the changing value of the accounts. The IRS provides the following two relief measures for retirement plans participants who have experienced a steep decline in the value of their retirement accounts and who need to recalculate the amount of their periodic payments based on the current value of the plan rather than the value when distributions began:

1. *One-time change to required minimum distribution method.* Taxpayers will be allowed a one-time opportunity after distributions have begun to switch to the required minimum distribution method which calculates each annual payment based on the current value of the plan account and by dividing the account balance for that year by the number from the chosen life expectancy table for that year. Under this method, the account balance, the number from the chosen life expectancy table and the resulting annual payments are redetermined each year. If this method is chosen, it will not constitute a modification in the series of substantially equal periodic payments, and will thus not trigger the 10 percent penalty under Code Sec. 72(t)(4) even if the amount of payments changes from year to year, provided there is no change to any other method of determining the payments. Once a change is made under this paragraph, the required minimum distribution method must be followed in all subsequent years. Any subsequent change will, however, be treated as a modification for purposes of Code Sec. 72(t)(4).
2. *Complete depletion of assets.* If the taxpayer sticks with a method of calculating periodic payments that will result in a complete depletion of the taxpayer's retirement account before the end of the payout period, the

---

[56] Notice 89-25, 1989-1 CB 662, as modified by Rev. Rul. 2002-62, 2002-2 CB 710.

[57] *G.A. Prough,* 99 TCM 1093, Dec. 58,124(M), TC Memo. 2010-20.

[58] Rev. Rul. 2002-62, 2002-2 CB 710.

resulting cessation of payments will not be treated as a modification of the series of payments triggering the 10 percent penalty under Code Sec. 72(t)(5).

Distribution for Higher Education Expense Not Modification of SEPP Election

In *G.T. Benz*,[59] the Tax Court held that a distribution for qualified higher education expenses from an IRA was not an impermissible modification of a series of equal periodic payments and, therefore, the distribution did not trigger the recapture tax under Code Sec. 72(t)(4). Although the additional distributions for higher education expenses were made within five years of the first annual periodic payment and before the taxpayer had attained age 59$^1/_2$, they did not result in a change in the method of calculating the annual periodic payments. Thus, the five-year rule prohibiting modifications was not violated and the substantially equal periodic payment exception continued to apply.

- *Distributions to pay for higher education.* Distributions to pay for "qualified higher education expenses" (QHEE) will be penalty-free. QHEE includes tuition at a college, university, vocational school, graduate school, or any other post-secondary educational institution as well as fees, books, supplies, and equipment required for enrollment or attendance at a postsecondary educational institutional or vocational education school [Code Sec. 72(t)(7)(A)]. QHEE also include room and board if the student is enrolled at least half-time and they are incurred by the taxpayer, his or her spouse, child, grandchild, spouse's child or spouse's grandchild [Code Sec. 72(t)(7)(A)]. The beneficiary of distributions made from the IRA and used for QHEE need not be a dependent. Taxpayers were liable for the 10-percent early withdrawal penalty tax because they used the IRA distribution to buy a computer, housewares, appliances, furniture, and bedding, which failed to qualify as QHEEs because they were not required by the university in order for the taxpayer to enroll and attend classes there.[60] IRA distributions that were used to pay credit card charges for college expenses incurred in years prior to the year of the distribution were subject to the 10-percent additional tax on early distributions because IRA distributions for QHEE costs must be used to pay current year expenses.[61]

  Even though the amount withdrawn for QHEEs is not subject to the 10-percent penalty, it must still be included in taxable income. In order to prevent taxpayers from claiming a double benefit, Code Sec. 72(t)(7)(B) provides that the amount of QHEE that may be paid for with penalty-free IRA proceeds will be reduced by the amounts of any qualified scholarship, education assistance allowance, or any other excludable payments for education expenses (but not gifts or inheritances). Report pre-age 59$^1/_2$ distributions on Form 5329 unless the entire amount was rolled over or the payer has indicated on Form 1099-R that one of the exceptions applies.

- *IRS levies on IRAs.* Amounts withdrawn from any employer-sponsored retirement plan or IRA that is subject to IRS levy will be penalty-free [Code Sec. 72(t)(2)(A)(vii)]. This exception applies only if the plan or IRA is levied by the IRS. It does not apply, for example, if the taxpayer withdraws funds to pay taxes in the

---

[59] *G.T. Benz*, 132 TC 330, Dec. 57,810 (2009).

[60] *J.M. Gorski*, TC Summary Op. 2005-112.

[61] *L.L. Lodder-Beckert*, 90 TCM 4, Dec. 56,082(M), TC Memo. 2005-162.

absence of a levy, in order to release a levy on other interests, or in any other situation.

- *Retirement distributions to active duty military reservists.* Active duty military reservists may receive early distributions from certain retirement plans without triggering the 10-percent penalty tax [Code Sec. 72(t)(2)(G)].

  ▶ **REFUND OPPORTUNITY:** The relief is retroactive so eligible reservists who have already paid the 10-percent penalty tax under Code Sec. 72(t) may claim a refund using IRS Form 1040X, Amended U.S. Individual Income Tax Return. An eligible reservist filing for a refund should write "active duty reservist" on the top of the Form 1040X and provide the following details: (1) date of the reservist's military call up, (2) amount of the distribution in question, and (3) the amount of early distribution tax paid.

- *Amount withdrawn can be recontributed.* The reservist can recontribute (in one or more contributions) part or all of the distribution to an IRA at any time during the two-year period after the end of the active duty period. The dollar limitations that would otherwise apply to IRA contributions do not apply to repayment contributions during the applicable two-year period. However, no deduction is allowed for any contribution made under this provision [Code Sec. 72(t)(2)(G)(ii)].

- *Public safety employees after age 50.* The 10-percent early withdrawal penalty tax does not apply to distributions from a government plan made to qualified public safety employees who separate from service after age 50 [Code Sec. 72(t)(10)(A)]. A "qualified public safety employee" means any employee of a state or political subdivision of a state who provides police protection, fire-fighting services, or emergency medical services for any area within the jurisdiction of the state or political subdivision [[Code Sec. 72(t)(10)(B)].

- *First-time homebuyers.* Distributions from an IRA used to pay for first-time homebuyer expenses (up to $10,000 lifetime limit) will be penalty-free if the IRA distribution is used within 120 days to pay costs of acquiring, constructing, or reconstructing, the first-time homebuyer's principal residence. A first-time homebuyer is anybody who has not had an ownership interest in a principal residence within the 2-year period ending on the date of the acquisition [Code Sec. 72(t)(2)(F)]. To qualify for the exception under Code Sec. 72(t)(8), taxpayers must be able to prove that they have legal title to the property or are the equitable owner.[62] The withdrawn money can be used to reconstruct a principal residence for the taxpayer, his or her spouse, child, grandchild, or ancestor of the taxpayer or the taxpayer's spouse. Note that the $10,000 figure is a lifetime cap and not an annual amount that can be withdrawn each year [Code Sec. 72(t)(8)(B)].

.03 Application of Wash Sale Rule to IRA

Under the wash sale rule of Code Sec. 1091(a), a loss claimed to have been sustained from the disposition of shares of stock or securities is not deductible under Code Sec. 165 if the taxpayer purchases substantially identical stock or securities during the 61-day period beginning 30 days before the sale and ending 30 days after the sale. Code Sec. 1091(d) provides rules for determining the basis of stock or securities that

[62] *L. Ung*, 105 TCM 1751, Dec. 59, 538(M), TC Memo. 2013-126.

are acquired in transactions that violate the wash-sale rules. The basis adjustment rules provide that the taxpayer's basis in the new stock is increased to reflect the disallowed loss and that the taxpayer's gain is accordingly reduced when that stock is sold.

In Rev. Rul. 2008-5,[63] the IRS addressed the deductibility of losses from wash sales of stocks and securities when an individual, who is not a dealer in stocks or securities, purchases the substantially identical stock or securities through an IRA or Roth IRA within 30 days before or after having sold the shares individually.

The IRS concluded that the taxpayer violated the wash sale rules of Code Sec. 1091(a) when he sold 100 shares of ABCo stock on day 1 and then repurchased the identical shares the very next day through his IRA because the taxpayer sold and repurchased the same shares in a two-day period. The IRS reasoned that the first sale was by the taxpayer personally and that the repurchase was by the tax-exempt trust that was his IRA. The court noted that "the difference between acquisition by [the taxpayer] personally and acquisition by the trusts amounts only to a refinement of title and may be disregarded . . . " Therefore, the court concluded that the taxpayer's sale and the repurchase of the same shares by the IRA violated the wash-sale rules. Consequently the loss on the sale of the stock was disallowed under Code Sec. 1091. In essence the IRA functioned as the taxpayer's alter-ego in the eyes of the IRS for purposes of the wash sale rules. The taxpayer's basis in the IRA could not be increased by virtue of Code Sec. 1091(d).

¶3140 ROTH IRAs

The Roth IRA is an attractive retirement and estate planning tool that appeals to taxpayers of all ages for several reasons. The deadline for making Roth IRA contributions for 2013 is April 15, 2014, even if the taxpayer has a filing extension. There are no mandatory distributions from Roth IRAs during the owner's lifetime, unlike required minimum distributions from the traditional IRA [¶3105]. A taxpayer can make contributions to a Roth IRA for a spouse provided the income requirements are satisfied.

.01 Comparison of Roth and Traditional IRA

The significant differences between traditional IRAs and Roth IRAs include the following:

1. Eligibility to contribute to a Roth IRA is subject to special modified AGI limits that begin to phase out as described below:
   a. For single taxpayers with modified adjusted gross income (MAGI) of $112,000 in 2013 and is completely phased out if MAGI is $127,000 or more,
   b. For joint filers with MAGI of $178,000 in 2013 and is completely phased out if MAGI is $188,000 or more, and
   c. For married individuals filing separate returns with MAGI between $0 and $10,000 [Code Sec. 408A(c)(3)].

---

[63] Rev. Rul. 2008-5, IRB 2008-3, 271.

For the income limits that apply to the deductibility of traditional IRAs, see ¶3105.

As with a traditional IRA, a taxpayer can make contributions to a Roth IRA for a spouse provided the income requirements are satisfied.

2. Contributions to a Roth IRA are never deductible, whereas contributions to a traditional IRA may be deductible; although taxpayers may not claim a tax deduction for contributions made to the Roth IRA, retirement savings will accumulate tax-free.
3. Qualified distributions from a Roth IRA are tax-free and penalty-free provided the account has been open for at least 5 years and the taxpayer is over age 59½, or has died, become disabled, or is using the withdrawals (up to $10,000) to purchase a first home [Code Sec. 408A(d)(2)].
4. Roth IRAs are not subject to the required minimum distribution (RMD) rules during the owner's lifetime. By contrast a traditional IRA is subject to RMDs. Therefore, a Roth IRA accountholder who reaches age 70½ does not need to begin taking the RMDs during their lifetime; instead the funds can continue to grow tax free until they are needed or are passed on to heirs. The RMD rules do, however, apply to Roth IRAs after the owner's death, but the RMDs can be made free of income tax to the beneficiaries [Code Sec. 408A(c)(5)]. An exception is available for a spouse who rolls over a deceased spouse's Roth IRA to his or her own IRA. No RMDs are required in this situation.
5. Contributions may be made to a Roth IRA at any age even after the owner has attained age 70 [Code Sec. 408A(c); Reg. § 1.408A-1, Q&A-2]. Note that a taxpayer cannot contribute to a traditional IRA if he or she has attained age 70½.
6. Roth IRAs are funded with after-tax dollars, so that beneficiaries who inherit Roth IRA receive the assets tax-free. With a traditional IRA, income tax is due on the inherited money because the IRA is funded with pretax dollars.

.02 Contribution Limits

The maximum total yearly contribution that can be made for 2013 by an individual to all IRAs (traditional and Roth) is the greater of $5,500 or the taxpayer's "compensation" for that year (no change in 2014) [Reg. § 1.408A-3, Q&A-3(c)]. Individuals who are age 50 by the end of the tax year may be able to make additional $1,000 *catch-up contributions* to Roth IRAs for a total 2013 contribution of $6,500 (no change in 2014) [Code Secs. 219(b)(5)(B), 414(v)(5)]. An employer isn't required to provide for catch-up contributions in any of its plans [Reg. § 1.414(v)-1(a)(1)]. However, if any plan of an employer provides for catch-up contributions, all of its plans that provide for elective deferrals must comply with the universal availability requirement [Code Sec. 408A(c)(3)(A); Reg. § 1.408A-3, Q&A-3].

Compensation includes wages, commissions, professional fees, tips and other amounts received for personal services, as well as taxable alimony and separate maintenance payment received under a decree of divorce or separate maintenance. Compensation does not include any amount received as a pension or annuity or as deferred compensation. In addition, a married individual filing a joint return is permitted to make an IRA contribution by treating his or her spouse's higher compensation as his or her own, but only to the extent that the spouse's compensation is not being used for purposes of the spouse making a contribution to a Roth IRA or a deductible contribution to a traditional IRA [Reg. § 1.408A-3, Q&A-4].

A contribution to a Roth IRA above the statutory limits generates a 6 percent excise tax that is imposed each year until the excess contribution is eliminated [Code Sec. 4973].

Example 3-19: Alice is not married and has an AGI of $100,000. She contributes $2,000 to her employer's 401(k) plan. Because she is an active participant in her employer's qualified plan and her AGI exceeds $60,000, she is not entitled to make any contributions to a Roth IRA.

.03 Income Limits

An individual will be able to make contributions to a Roth IRA if the individual's modified AGI is below a certain threshold that varies with the taxpayer's filing status. For 2013, your Roth IRA contribution limit is reduced (phased out) in the following situations:

- Your filing status is married filing jointly or qualifying widow(er) and your modified AGI (MAGI) is at least $178,000. You cannot make a Roth IRA contribution if your MAGI is $188,000 or more.
- Your filing status is married filing separately, you lived with your spouse at any time during the year, and your MAGI is more than 0. You cannot make a Roth IRA contribution if your MAGI is $10,000 or more.
- Your filing situation is single and your MAGI is at least $112,000. You cannot make a Roth IRA contribution in 2013 if your MAGI is $127,000 or more.

Spouses who file separate returns for a tax year and who live apart at all times during that year are treated as unmarried for income limitation purposes [Reg. § 1.408A-3, Q&A-3(b)].

If your income is too high to make you eligible to make contributions to a traditional deductible IRA or a Roth IRA, you can still make contributions to a nondeductible traditional IRA. The earnings on moneys invested will still grow tax-free until you take the money out. No more than $5,500 ($11,000 in 2013 per couple), plus catch-up contributions, per year can be contributed to all of your IRAs combined whether or not you claim a deduction.

Example 3-20: Bob White is a single taxpayer with modified AGI of $225,000. He is ineligible to contribute to a Roth IRA because his income exceeds the legal threshold. He may, however, contribute to a nondeductible traditional IRA.

Computing the Contribution Limit

The contribution limit for Roth IRAs is computed as follows:

1. Start with modified adjusted gross income (defined below).
2. Subtract the following:
   a. $178,000 if filing a joint return;
   b. $0 if married filing separately, unless the spouses lived apart at all times during the year;
   c. $112,000 for all other individuals.

3. Divide the result by $15,000 ($10,000 if filing a joint return or married filing a separate return).
4. Multiply the contribution limit (before reduction by this adjustment but after reduction for any contributions to traditional IRAs) by the result in (3).
5. Subtract this result from the contribution limit before this reduction. The result is the reduced contribution limit. If the final phaseout result is below $200 but above zero, the contribution limit will be $200. When applying the phase-out, the maximum contribution limit is rounded up to the next higher multiple of $10 [Reg. § 1.408A-3, Q&A 3(b)].

.04 Computation of AGI for Roth IRA Purposes

For purposes of the income limitation on Roth IRA contributions, MAGI includes taxable social security and railroad retirement benefits under Code Sec. 86 and the application of the passive activity rules under Code Sec. 469. Income resulting from a conversion of a non-Roth IRA to a Roth IRA is excluded [Code Sec. 408A(c)(3)(C); Reg. § 1.408A-3, Q&A 5].

The following deductions and exclusions are added back to AGI when computing MAGI:

- The traditional IRA deduction;
- The student loan interest deduction;
- The foreign earned income exclusion and the foreign housing exclusion or deduction;
- The exclusion of qualified bond interest used to pay higher education expenses shown on Form 8815;
- The exclusion of employer-paid adoption expenses shown on Form 8839.

.05 Rollovers/Conversions

For tax years beginning after December 31, 2009, there is no income limit on the conversion of a traditional IRA to a Roth IRA. Nor is there a requirement that married taxpayers file jointly in order to make the conversion [Code Sec. 408A(c)(3)].

Any amount that is converted from a traditional IRA to a Roth IRA is treated as a taxable distribution and is includible in gross income in the tax year in which the amount is distributed or transferred from the traditional IRA. The distribution amount is not however subject to the 10 percent early withdrawal penalty [Code Sec. 408A(d)(3)(A)(ii); Reg. § 1.408A-4, Q&A-7]. Any portion of the distribution or transfer that is treated as a return of basis is not includible in gross income [Code Sec. 408(d)(1); Reg. § 1.408A-4, Q&A-7(a)].

How to Convert a Traditional IRA to a Roth IRA

A qualifying taxpayer may convert existing non-Roth IRA retirement savings to a Roth IRA in one of the following manners:

- A distribution from a non-Roth IRA may be rolled over to a Roth IRA within 60 days [Code Sec. 408(d)(3)(A)(i)];
- An amount in a non-Roth IRA may be transferred to a Roth IRA, trustee-to-trustee, from one financial institution to another; or

- An amount in a non-Roth IRA may be transferred to a Roth IRA of the same financial institution [Reg. § 1.408A-4, Q&A 1].

 ▶ **PRACTICE NOTE:** Conversions and recharacterization made with the same trustee may be accomplished by simply redesignating the account or annuity contract as a Roth IRA. There is no need to open a new account or go through the hassle of the issuance of a new annuity contract for each conversion or recharacterization [Reg. § 1.408A-4, Q&A-1(b)(3)].

Required minimum distributions. A taxpayer who has attained at least age 70$^1/_2$ by the end of a calendar year cannot convert an amount distributed from a traditional IRA during that year to a Roth IRA before receiving his or her required minimum distribution with respect to the traditional IRA for the year of conversion. When a taxpayer is required to make a required minimum distribution with respect to his or her IRA, the first dollars distributed during that year are treated as consisting of the required minimum distribution until an amount equal to the required minimum distribution for that year has been distributed [Reg. § 1.408A-4, Q&A-6]. After receiving the minimum distribution, the taxpayer will be able to rollover the remaining amount in his or her traditional IRA to a Roth IRA. The minimum distribution amount cannot be rolled over tax-free [Reg. § 1.408A-4, Q&A 6(c)].

Substantially equal periodic payments (SEPPs). A taxpayer who is receiving SEPPs as discussed in ¶3135 can convert a traditional IRA to a Roth IRA [Code Sec. 72(t)(2)(A)(iv)]. The conversion amount will not be subject to the early distribution tax under Code Sec. 72(t)(4) and generally will not be treated as a distribution for purposes of determining whether a modification in the payments has occurred that would trigger the recapture tax under Code Sec. 72(t)(4)(A)].

Conversion of Coverdell Education Savings Account

Amounts may not be transferred directly from a Coverdell education savings account [Ch. 5] to a Roth IRA. A transfer of funds from a Coverdell education savings account (ESA) to a Roth IRA will be treated as a distribution from the Coverdell ESA and a regular contribution to the Roth IRA rather than a qualified rollover contribution to the Roth IRA [Reg. § 1.408A-6, Q&A 18].

Rollovers by Spouse, Former Spouse, or Surviving Spouse

A surviving spouse may roll over amounts from the decedent spouse's Roth account to a his or her own Roth IRA to the same extent the decedent could during his or her lifetime [Code Secs. 402(c)(9), 403(b)(8)(B)]. A spouse or former spouse who is an alternate payee under a qualified domestic relations order (QDRO) may roll over amounts received from the retiree's Roth account to the spouse's own Roth IRA [Code Sec. 402(e)(a)(B)].

After a rollover to a spouse's Roth account, subsequent qualified distributions from the Roth account must satisfy the age, disability, or death requirement with respect to the spouse rather than the retiree. For a direct rollover to a spouse's Roth IRA, the five-year period begins with the first tax year the spouse contributed to the recipient account or, if earlier, the first tax year the retiree contributed to the transferring account [Code Sec. 402A(d)(2)(B)(ii)]. After a rollover to a spouse's Roth IRA, subsequent qualified distributions must also satisfy the age, disability, death, etc. requirements with respect to the spouse rather than the retiree. The five years of participation requirements for a qualified distribution begins with the first tax year the spouse made any contribution or rollover to a Roth IRA [Code Sec. 408A(a)].

Tax Consequences of Rolling Over Qualified Plan to Roth IRA

In Notice 2009-75,[64] the IRS clarifies the consequences of rollovers from eligible employer plans (i.e., a Code Sec. 401(a) qualified plan, a Code Sec. 403(a) annuity plan, a Code Sec. 403(b) plan, or a Code Sec. 457(b) governmental plan) to a Roth IRA.

The guidance provides that, the amount included in income as a result of a distribution from an eligible employer plan and a rollover to a Roth IRA depends on whether or not the distribution is made from a designated Roth account.

If the distribution is not made from a designated Roth account, then the amount that would be includible in gross income were it not part of a qualified rollover contribution is included in income for the year of the distribution. The amount included in gross income is equal to the amount rolled over, reduced by the amount of any after-tax contributions that are included in the amount rolled over, in the same manner as if the distribution had been rolled over to a non-Roth IRA that was the participant's only non-Roth IRA and that non-Roth IRA had then been immediately converted to a Roth IRA.

If an eligible rollover distribution made from a designated Roth account is rolled over to a Roth IRA, the amount rolled over is not includible in gross income, whether or not the distribution is a qualified distribution from the designated Roth account.

The Notice also clarifies that if an eligible rollover distribution made before 2010 is ineligible to be rolled over to a Roth IRA either because MAGI exceeds $100,000 or because a married distribute does not file a joint return, the distribution can be rolled over into a non-Roth IRA and then the non-Roth IRA can be converted, on or after January 1, 2010, into a Roth IRA.

There are no restrictions based on the MAGI limitations and joint filing requirements that apply to a rollover of an eligible rollover distribution made from a designated Roth account under an eligible employer plan to a Roth IRA.

Converting Non-Roth Individual Retirement Annuity to Roth IRA

When a non-Roth individual retirement annuity is converted to a Roth IRA, the amount that is treated as distributed is the fair market value of the annuity contract on the date the annuity contract is converted. Similarly, when a traditional IRA holds an annuity contract as an account asset and the account is converted to a Roth IRA, the amount that is treated as distributed with respect to the annuity contract is the fair market value of the annuity contract on the date the annuity contract is converted [Reg. § 1.408A-4, Q&A-14(A)(1)].

To the extent an individual retirement annuity or an annuity contract held by an IRA is surrendered with no retained or transferred rights, the amount treated as a

[64] Notice 2009-75, IRB 2009-39, 436.

distribution is limited to the surrendered cash value (the actual proceeds available to be deposited into the Roth IRA) [Reg. § 1.408A-4, Q&A-14(A)(2)].

Determining Fair Market Value

The following three methods are available to help taxpayers determine the fair market value of the annuities for purposes of determining the amount includible in gross income as a distribution [Reg. § 1.408A-4, Q&A-14(b)]:

1. The gift tax method is based upon comparable contracts issued by the company which sold the annuity.
2. Where there is no comparable contract, fair market value can be established through an approximation based upon the interpolated terminal reserve at the date of conversion, plus the proportionate part of the premium paid before conversion covering a period after the date of conversion. For example, assume a taxpayer who is age 60 at the time of the conversion had purchased from an insurance company a contract at an earlier age which will pay him $500 per month for life beginning at age 70. If the insurance company is selling contracts that will provide a taxpayer who is age 60 $500 per month for life at age 70, then the fair market value of the taxpayer's contract, for purposes of determining the amount converted, is the current price of the similar contract.
3. A third method establishes the fair market value through a method that uses the accumulation of premiums as previously addressed in Rev. Proc. 2006-13.[65] Under the accumulation method, the fair market value of an annuity contract is determined using the methodology provided in Reg. § 1.401(a)(9)-6,A-12, with the following modifications. First, all front-end loads and other non-recurring charges assessed in the twelve months immediately preceding the conversion must be added to the account value. Second, future distributions are not to be assumed in the determination of the actuarial present value of additional benefits. Finally, the exclusions provided under Reg. § 1.401(a)(9)-6, A-12(c)(1) and (c)(2), are not to be taken into account.

Imposition of 10-Percent Penalty Tax

The 10 percent additional penalty tax imposed under Code Sec. 72(t) generally does not apply to the taxable conversion amount unless it later is withdrawn before the Roth IRA's five-year anniversary [Reg. § 1.408A-4, Q&A-7(b)]. This five-year period begins on the first day that the Roth IRA contribution or conversion was made and ends on the last day of the owner's fifth consecutive tax year [Reg. § 1.408A-6, Q&A-2]. Keep in mind that the beginning of the five-year period does not begin again when the Roth IRA owner dies. This means that the period the Roth IRA is held in the name of a beneficiary, or, in the name of a surviving spouse who treats the Roth IRA as his or her own, includes the period it was owned by the decedent [Reg. § 1.408A-6, Q&A 7(a)].

IRA Conversions and Reconversions

An IRA owner who converts an amount from a traditional IRA to a Roth IRA during any tax year and then transfers the converted amount back to a traditional IRA in a recharacterization may not reconvert that amount to a Roth IRA before: (1) the

[65] Rev. Proc. 2006-13, 2006-1 CB 315.

beginning of the tax year following the tax year in which the amount was converted to the Roth IRA; or (2) if later, the end of the 30-day period beginning on the day on which the IRA owner transfers the amount from the Roth IRA back to a traditional IRA by means of a recharacterization (regardless of whether the recharacterization occurs during the tax year in which the amount was converted to a Roth IRA or the following tax year) [Reg. § 1.408A-5, Q&A-9(a)(1)].

Taxpayers may rely on Reg. § 301.9100-3 to request an extension of time to make the election to recharacterize a traditional-IRA-to-Roth-IRA conversion even though the deadline for doing so has passed if the taxpayer can prove that he or she acted reasonably and in good faith and granting relief will not prejudice the interests of the government. Reg. § 301.9100-3(b)(1) provides that a taxpayer will be deemed to have acted reasonably and in good faith if he:

- Requests relief before the failure to make the regulatory election is discovered by IRS;
- Inadvertently failed to make the election because of intervening events beyond the taxpayer's control;
- Failed to make the election because, after exercising due diligence, the taxpayer was unaware of the necessity for the election;
- Reasonably relied on IRS's written advice; or
- Reasonably relied on a qualified tax professional, and the tax professional failed to make, or advise the taxpayer to make, the election.[66]

Ordering rules. Ordering rules must be considered when amounts that are withdrawn contain both conversion amounts and other contributions. According to these rules, any amount distributed from an individual's Roth IRA is treated as made in the following order (determined as of the end of a tax year and exhausting each category before moving to the next category):

1. From regular Roth IRA contributions;
2. From conversion contributions on a first-in, first-out basis; and
3. From earnings [Code Sec. 408A(d)(4); Reg. § 1.408A-6, Q&A 8(a)].

.06 In-Plan Roth Rollovers

A 401(k), 403(b), or Code Sec. 457(b) plan that includes a qualified Roth contribution program may rollover distributions from a participant's non-Roth account to the participant's designated Roth account within the same plan [Code Sec. 402A(c)(4)(B)]. This type of rollover is called an in-plan Roth rollover (IPRR). Employers should have amended their Code Sec. 401(k) or Code Sec. 403(b) plans to permit participants to transfer an eligible rollover distribution into a designated Roth account within the plan.

In Notice 2010-84,[67] the IRS provided detailed guidance on IPRRs. The IRS provides that an IPRR may be accomplished by a direct rollover or by a distribution of funds to the individual who then rolls over the funds into his or her designated Roth account in the plan within 60 days. An IPRR may be made by a plan beneficiary, a surviving

[66] LTR 201320022 (Feb. 19, 2013).

[67] Notice 2010-84, IRB 2010-51, 872.

spouse beneficiary, or by an alternate payee who is a spouse or former spouse of the plan participant.

The IRS makes it clear that the IPRR is not subject to 20 percent mandatory withholding under Code Sec. 3405(c). However, a participant electing an in-plan Roth rollover may have to increase his or her withholding or make estimated tax payments to avoid an underpayment penalty.

The converted amount is includible in gross income as a distribution for the tax year in which the amount is distributed or transferred. This amount is reduced by any after-tax contributions included in the amount rolled over [Code Sec. 402A(c)(4)(A)(i)].

If the owner dies before all amounts are included in income and the owner's surviving spouse does not acquire the entire interest in the Roth account, the entire amount remaining must be included in the decedent's income in the tax year of the decedent's death. If the entire interest in the Roth account goes to the spouse, the spouse must include the income under the original schedule [Code Sec. 402A(c)(4)(D)].

Additional tax. The 10-percent additional tax under Code Sec. 72(t) does not apply to rollover distributions under these rules [Code Sec. 402A(c)(4)(A)(ii)]. However, the 10-percent additional tax does apply if the amount rolled over is subsequently distributed from the Roth account within the five-tax-year period beginning with the tax year in which the contribution was made [Code Sec. 402A(c)(4)(D)].

A distribution to a Roth account under these rules is not treated as a designated Roth contribution and therefore has no effect on elective deferral limits for the tax year in which the rollover occurs.

In-service rollovers from traditional to designated Roth accounts available for employees under age 59½. Employers may amend a 401(k), 403(b), or 457(b) governmental plan to allow in-service rollovers by a current employee from a traditional account to his or her designated Roth account within the same plan without violating the distribution restrictions for the plan [Code Sec. 402A(c)(4)(E)]. For example, a 401(k) plan may allow a plan participant to make the rollover contribution even if the distribution does not result from the employee's severance from employment, death, disability, attainment of age 59, or hardship.

.07 Tax Treatment of Distributions

Under Code Sec. 408A(d), "qualified distributions" from a Roth IRA will be tax-free if withdrawn more than 5 years after a Roth IRA was established provided the distribution is either:

- Made on or after the individual attains 59½,
- Made to a beneficiary or the estate of the owner following the owner's death
- Attributable to the owner being disabled; or
- Used for first-time homebuyer expenses (up to a lifetime cap of $10,000). A first-time homebuyer is anybody who has not had an ownership interest in a principal residence within the 2-year period ending on the date of the acquisition. Any amount withdrawn for first-time homebuyer expenses, but not used for this purpose within the 120-day limitation period, may be recontributed to a Roth IRA [Reg. § 1.408A-6, Q&A-1].

When Five-Year Period Begins

The five-year period begins with the first day of the first tax year the participant contributed to any Roth account in the same plan [Code Sec. 402A(d)(2)(B)(i); Reg. § 1.402A-1, Q&A 2(b)(1)]. The beginning date for the five-year period may change only if the distributing plan receives a direct trustee-to-trustee rollover from a Roth account established under another plan. In that situation, the five-year period begins on the first date of the first tax year the retiree contributed to a Roth account in the other plan, if that date is earlier [Code Sec. 402A(d)(2)(B)(ii); Reg. § 1.402A-1, Q&A 4(b)].

Definition of Disability

A taxpayer will be considered disabled for purposes of the tax-free Roth IRA distribution, if he or she is incapable of doing substantial work because of a physical or mental medical condition that will last for a long and indefinite period or from which the taxpayer will likely die [Code Sec. 72(m)(7); Reg. § 1.402A-1, Q&A 2(b)(2)]. For this purpose, a taxpayer can do substantial work if the taxpayer is capable of working at his or her predisability or pre-retirement occupation, or a comparable occupation [Reg. § 1.72-17A(f)(1)].

Taxation of Nonqualified Distributions

If a taxpayer fails the "qualified distribution test," the Roth IRA distribution will be a nonqualified Roth IRA distribution and will be subject to income tax [Code Sec. 408A(d)(4)]. However, the Roth IRA will only be taxable to the extent there are previously undistributed current and/or accumulated earnings within the Roth IRA.

.08 How to Establish a Roth IRA

A taxpayer can establish a Roth IRA with any bank, insurance company, or other person authorized to serve as a trustee with respect to IRAs. The IRA must be clearly designated as a Roth IRA in the documents that establish it [Code Sec. 408A(b)]. The Roth IRA designation cannot later be changed. This means that a taxpayer may not designate an IRA as a Roth IRA and later redesignate the Roth IRA as a traditional IRA or otherwise treat the Roth IRA as though it were a traditional IRA for federal tax purposes [Reg. § 1.408A-2, Q&A 2]. The Roth IRA must be established for an individual. However, an employer or an association of employees can establish a trust to hold contributions of employees or members made under a Roth IRA. Each employee's or member's account in the trust is treated as a separate Roth IRA that is subject to all the Roth IRA rules [Reg. § 1.408A-2, Q&A 3]. Individuals may make contributions to a Roth IRA up to the due date (not including extensions) for filing a federal income tax return for that tax year [Reg. § 1.408A-3, Q&A-2].

State and Local Government Plans May Adopt Designated Roth Contribution Programs

Retirement savings plans sponsored by state and local government employers (457 plans) may allow participants to designate elective deferrals as Roth contributions [Code Sec. 402A(e)(1)(C)]. The Roth program must be part of an existing cash or deferred arrangement within the state or local government plan.

Establishing a Roth IRA for a Minor Child

Taxpayers can establish a Roth IRA for the benefit of a minor child or anyone else lacking legal capacity provided the child or person lacking legal capacity has earned income or compensation for the tax year that the contribution is made [Code Sec. 408A(c); Reg. § 1.408A-3].

.09 Model Forms

The IRS has released model agreements containing pre-approved language for trustees and custodians to use in setting up Roth IRAs. Use Form 5305-R, *Roth Individual Retirement Trust Account*, and/or Form 5305-RA, *Roth Individual Retirement Custodial Account*. Neither of these forms should be filed with the IRS, but you should sign them and keep them with your important tax records.

.10 IRS Targets Abusive Roth IRA Schemes

The IRS has issued guidance to halt abusive Roth IRA transactions where individuals shift income into their Roth IRAs by transferring property from a pre-existing business into a Roth IRA for less than fair market value to avoid the Code Sec. 408A contribution limits.[68]

The IRS has promised several avenues of attack including: (1) challenging the abusive transactions on several grounds, (2) recharacterizing the transactions for tax purposes, (3) asserting that the transactions are prohibited under Code Sec. 408A(e)(2)(A) thus subjecting them to a six percent excise tax under Code Sec. 4973,[69] and identifying the abusive Roth IRAs as tax avoidance transactions and listed transactions thus subjecting them to the onerous tax shelter disclosure requirements.

.11 Reporting Requirements

The amount transferred in a recharacterization (contribution plus earnings) occurring in the same year as the year for which the contributions being recharacterized were made ("same year recharacterizations") will be reported on Box 7 of Form 1099-R and identified with the code N. Recharacterizations occurring after the year for which the contributions being recharacterized were made ("prior year recharacterizations") will be reported in Box 7, Form 1099-R and identified with pre-existing code R. Prior and same-year recharacterizations can't be reported together on the same Form 1099-R, and recharacterizations can't be reported together with another reportable distribution on the same Form 1099-R. All same-year recharacterizations from the same IRA must be reported together on a single Form 1099-R, and all prior-year recharacterizations must be similarly aggregated. Recharacterizations will be reported in a box on Form 5498 titled "Recharacterized contributions."

Trustees will be allowed to (1) total and report all recharacterized contributions received by an IRA in the same year on one Form 5498, or (2) use a separate form for each recharacterized contribution. They also will be allowed to (a) use a single Form 5498 to report all contributions (including recharacterized contributions) made to an IRA in a year, or (b) report each contribution on a separate Form 5498.[70]

---

[68] Notice 2004-8, 2004-1 CB 333.

[69] *S.W. Repetto*, 103 TCM 1895, Dec. 59,090(M), TC Memo. 2012-168.

[70] Notice 2004-8, 2004-1 CB 333.

OTHER RETIREMENT ARRANGEMENTS

¶3145 SIMPLIFIED EMPLOYEE PENSIONS (SEPs)

Simplified employee pensions (SEPs) are tax-favored retirement plans that allow an employer to make deductible contributions to an employee's IRA. Self-employed individuals can also make deductible contributions to a SEP for his or her own account if they have *net earnings from self-employment* [Code Sec. 408(k)].[71] The determination of whether an individual is an employee or independent contractor will be made based on the common law tests which basically ask whether the person for whom services are performed controls the worker and the manner in which the work is performed. See ¶15,070.

Amounts in a SEP are excludable from income until distributed [Code Sec. 408(k)]. They must meet participation, nondiscrimination, and other special rules that apply to other qualified plans. SEPs are favored because they allow you to put more away for retirement than allowed under regular IRA rules. Taxpayers should consider a SEP plan if they operate their business as a:

- Sole proprietorship
- Partnership
- Subchapter S corporation
- Limited liability corporation
- Corporation

A SEP plan is a good vehicle for building retirement savings because earnings will be tax-free.

.01 Why Set Up a SEP?

When employers or self-employed individuals want to establish a tax-favored retirement account but want to avoid the overly complex rules surrounding qualified retirements plans such as Keoghs, they often set up simplified employee pensions (SEPs). Under a SEP, the employer or the self-employed individual makes contributions to individual retirement accounts or individual retirement annuities (called SEP IRAs) that have been set up by or for each employee with a bank, insurance company or other qualified financial institution [Code Sec. 408(k)(1)]. SEPs offer flexibility because contributions need not be made each year. To qualify for these tax benefits, SEPs must meet participation, nondiscrimination and other special rules that apply to other qualified plans and will be discussed in detail below.

.02 How to Set Up a SEP

Employers who want to provide SEPs must have a written plan. They may use an individually designed plan or use an IRS model SEP agreement. Sole proprietors may qualify to use IRS Form 5305-SEP, *Simplified Employee Pension-Individual Retirement Accounts Contribution Agreement* to establish their SEP. Form 5305-SEP is a model SEP

---

[71] *L.B. Levine*, 89 TCM 1063, Dec. 55,997(M), TC Memo. 2005-86.

plan and all the taxpayer has to do is check some boxes and fill in some blanks. The form may not be used by taxpayers who:

- Currently maintain any other qualified retirement plan,
- Have maintained a defined benefit plan in the past,
- Have any eligible employees for whom IRAs have not been established,
- Use the services of leased employees,
- Are a member of an affiliated group [Code Sec. 414(m)], or
- Do not pay the cost of the SEP contributions.

An alternate form is the Form 5305-A-SEP, *Salary Reduction and Other Elective SEP-IRAs Contribution Agreement.*

Most financial institutions have forms to assist taxpayers in setting up a SEP. Once the SEP is established, the employer or self-employed taxpayer makes tax-deductible contributions to his own IRA or to the IRAs of each qualifying employee. Typically the employer will establish a group IRA with each employee having an individual IRA account in his or her name.

.03 SEP Contribution (and Deduction) Limits

For 2013, annual contributions by an employer to a SEP are excluded from the employee's gross income to the extent that the contributions do not exceed the lesser of: (1) 25 percent of the participant's compensation ($255,000 maximum for 2013) or (2) $51,000 [Code Sec. 402(h)]. Note that when determining *compensation* for purposes of computing the allowable deduction to SEP plans, the definition of compensation will include *elective deferrals* (e.g., an employee's 401(k) contributions) [Code Sec. 404(a)(12)]. To the extent that the contribution exceeds the limitation, it is includible in the employee's income and the excess would be subject to the penalty tax on excess contributions [Code Sec. 4973(a)]. In addition, contributions that fit into the guidelines outlined above will be deductible by the employer [Code Sec. 404(h)]. The employer's contributions must be made not later than the due date of the employer's return for that tax year (including any extended due date). A deduction that exceeds the limitation may be carried over to succeeding years, but the excess plus the contributions for the carryover year may not exceed the 25-percent limit applicable to the carryover year [Code Sec. 404(h)(1)(C)].

SEP contributions are not included on Form W-2, *Wage and Tax Statement,* unless there are contributions in excess of the applicable limit, or there are contributions under a salary reduction arrangement discussed further below.

.04 SEP Requirements

Although contributions need not be made each year to a SEP, when you do make contributions, the following requirements must be strictly observed.

Employer Contributions

The employer contributions must be determined under a definite written formula, which specifies the requirements that an employee must satisfy to share in an allocation, and the manner in which the amount allocated is computed [Code Sec. 408(k)(5)].

The employer must contribute each year to the SEP of each employee who has:

- Attained age 21,
- Performed service for the employer during at least 3 of the last 5 years, and
- Received at least $550 in 2013 in compensation from the employer [Code Sec. 408(k)(2)(C)].

Employers need not provide SEP benefits for the following two types of employees: (1) employees who are covered by a union agreement and whose retirement benefits were bargained for in good faith by their union and their employer, and (2) nonresident alien employees who have no U.S.-source earned income. These are *excluded employees* [Code Sec. 408(k)(2)].

If an employer has leased employees who are treated as employees and who satisfy the three requirements listed in 3(a) through 3(c) above, the employer must include these employees in the SEP.

The employer's contributions are not conditioned on the retention in the plan of any portion of the amounts contributed [Code Sec. 408(k)(4)(A)].

Nondiscrimination

Contributions may not discriminate in favor of the *highly compensated* [Code Secs. 408(k)(3), 414(q)]. An employee is considered to be highly compensated if he or she:

- Was a 5 percent owner at any time during the current year or the preceding year; or
- Had compensation from the employer in excess of $115,000 (in 2013) during the preceding year and, if the employer so elects, was in the top-paid group (i.e., top 20 percent of employees by compensation) of the employer [Code Sec. 414(q)(1)].

For purposes of determining the number of employees in the top-paid group, the following employees are excluded: (1) employees who have not completed six months of service, (2) employees who normally work less than 17$^1/_2$ hours per week, (3) employees who normally work during not more than 6 months during any year, (4) employees who have not attained age 21, and (5) employees who are included in a unit of employees covered by an agreement which the Secretary of Labor finds to be a collective bargaining agreement between employee representatives and the employer [Code Sec. 414(q)(5)].

As a result of the repeal of the family aggregation rules, compensation paid to (or plan contributions or benefits made on behalf of) family members of certain highly compensated employees will not be treated as paid to or on behalf of the highly compensated employee for purposes of the nondiscrimination testing rules. This means that qualified plans can be created so that benefits to highly compensated family members are increased.

Withdrawals

The employer cannot impose any restrictions on withdrawals from the SEP.

.05 Computation of SEP Deduction

If you are self-employed (a partner or a sole proprietor), before you can compute the amount of your deductible contribution to a SEP, you must first figure your self-employment tax liability on Schedule SE and the 50 percent deduction for self-employment tax claimed on Form 1040. You compute your deductible plan contribution by taking your net profit from Schedule C and reducing it by the deduction for 50 percent of your self-employment tax and then multiplying it by your plan rate. You cannot, however, simply apply the contribution rate stated in your plan. You must first express the plan contribution rate as a decimal as illustrated in the following example where the plan contribution rate was 10.5 percent.

Self-employed person's rate:	
1. Plan contribution rate of 10.5% as a decimal	0.105
2. Rate in line 1 plus one	1.105
3. Divide line 1 by line 2 to get self-employed rate	0.0950

Your annual deductions for contributions to this plan cannot exceed 9.5 percent of your compensation from the business that has the plan. In another example, if your plan rate is 15 percent, the adjusted decimal rate is .130435 and your deduction for annual contributions to a SEP cannot exceed 13.0435 percent of your compensation from the business that has set up the SEP. If your plan's contribution rate for allocating employer contributions to employees is a whole number rather than a fraction, you can use the table provided in IRS Publication 560 (Retirement Plans for the Self-Employed) to find the rate that applies to you and to compute your deduction. Otherwise, use the rate example above.

.06 Prohibited Transaction

Borrowing money from a SEP constitutes a prohibited transaction and will disqualify the SEP from tax-favored status as discussed further in ¶3100.

.07 Contribution Requirements

Contributions to a SEP must be in the form of money such as cash, check or money order. However, you may be able to transfer or rollover certain property from one account to another. You need not make contributions each year.

.08 Distribution Rules

Distributions from SEPs are subject to the same tax treatment on distribution tax-free rollovers, required distributions and income tax withholding as any other IRA [¶3135].

¶3150 CASH OR DEFERRED ARRANGEMENTS—401(k) PLANS

A qualified cash or deferred arrangement (Code Sec. 401(k) plan) or a tax-sheltered annuity (Code Sec. 403(b) annuity) may permit a participant to elect to have the employer make payments as contributions to the plan or to the participant directly in cash. Contributions made to the plan at the election of a participant are elective deferrals. Elective deferrals must be nonforfeitable and are subject to an annual dollar limitation and distribution restrictions. In addition, elective deferrals under an Code Sec. 401(k) plan are subject to special nondiscrimination rules. Elective deferrals (and earnings attributable thereto) are not includible in a participant's gross income until distributed from the plan.

Elective deferrals for a tax year in excess of the annual dollar limitation (excess deferrals) are includible in gross income for the tax year. If an employee makes elective deferrals under a plan (or plans) of a single employer that exceed the annual dollar limitation (excess deferrals), then the plan may provide for the distribution of the excess deferrals, with earnings thereon. If the excess deferrals are made to more than one plan of unrelated employers, then the plan may permit the individual to allocate excess deferrals among the various plans, no later than the March 1 (April 15 under the applicable regulations) following the end of the tax year. If excess deferrals are distributed not later than April 15 following the end of the tax year, along with earnings attributable to the excess deferrals, then the excess deferrals are not again includible in income when distributed. The earnings are includible in income in the year distributed. If excess deferrals (and income thereon) are not distributed by the applicable April 15, then the excess deferrals (and income thereon) are includible in income when received by the participant. Thus, excess deferrals that are not distributed by the applicable April 15th are taxable both in the tax year when the deferral was made and in the year the participant receives a distribution of the excess deferral.

Section 401(k) salary reduction plans provide an effective way to shelter compensation and accumulated interest income from taxation. They are one of the few remaining tax shelters. These arrangements often take the form of a salary reduction agreement whereby the employer contributions are conditioned on the employee's election to reduce compensation or forego a raise or bonus. While such plans are conveniently administered through payroll deduction, contributions by employees are granted an added benefit: They are not subject to income tax in the year the contribution is made [Code Sec. 401(k); Reg. § 1.401(k)-1(a)(3)(iv)].

Tax-exempt organizations are also eligible to establish 401(k) plans for their employees [Code Sec. 401(k)(4)(B)]. State and local governments (or political subdivisions, agencies, or instrumentalities) continue to be barred from establishing 401(k) plans. An exception exists, however, for rural cooperatives and Indian tribal governments which are eligible to establish 401(k) plans for their employees.

.01 Contribution Limits

In 2013, employees can elect to contribute up to the lesser of: 25 percent of compensation, or $17,500 to a 401(k) plan. This limit will be adjusted for inflation thereafter [Code Sec. 402(g)(1)].

Catch-Up Contributions

Participants age 50 by the end of the tax year may make additional catch-up contributions to Code Sec. 401(k) plans for that tax year [Code Sec. 414(v)(5)]. An employer isn't required to provide for catch-up contributions in any of its plans [Reg. § 1.414(v)-1(a)(1)]. However, if any plan of an employer provides for catch-up contributions, all of its plans that provide for elective deferrals must comply with the universal availability requirement. The maximum additional contribution is the lesser of (1) a set dollar amount for the year, or (2) the participant's compensation for the year reduced by any other elective deferrals for the year. The catch-up contribution limits for Code Sec. 401(k) plans are as shown in Table 5 [Code Sec. 414(v)].

Table 5. 401(k) Plan Catch-Up Contributions

Tax Year	Catch-Up Contribution Limit
2013 (and 2014)	$5,500

Catch-up contributions will not be taken into account in applying the regular contribution limits. In addition, catch-up contributions will not be subject to the nondiscrimination rules. However, a plan will fail to meet the nondiscrimination requirements unless it allows all eligible participants to make catch-up contributions. An employer may make matching contributions with respect to catch-up contributions.

.02 Nondiscrimination Rules

The tax law contains stiff nondiscrimination rules for 401(k) plans. The percentage of compensation that eligible highly compensated employees are eligible to defer cannot exceed the greater of: (1) 125 percent of the deferral of all other nonhighly compensated employees eligible to defer under the arrangement, or (2) 200 percent of the deferral percentage of other employees but not more than 2 percentage points more than what other eligible employees defer [Code Sec. 401(k)(3)]. Net effect: Unless rank-and-file employees elect to defer an adequate amount, your company's executives cannot put as much aside for themselves on a tax-deferred basis."Highly compensated in 2013 is defined as an employee earning $115,000" No employee's 401(k) contribution can be based on compensation higher than $255,000 in 2013.

.03 Design-Based Safe Harbor

In an effort to encourage more small employers to set up 401(k) plans for their employees, Congress has simplified the nondiscrimination test for 401(k) plans. The IRS has provided guidance designed to help taxpayers apply the design-based safe harbor method.[72] A special nondiscrimination test for elective deferrals under a 401(k) arrangement is satisfied if the actual deferral percentage (ADP) for highly compensated employees for a plan year does not exceed the ADP of all other eligible employees by more than a specified percentage. The law provides that a 401(k) plan satisfies this special nondiscrimination test if the plan satisfies a safe harbor which requires compliance with one of two contribution requirements and with a notice requirement.

The contribution requirement is met under the safe harbor if either: (1) a matching contribution requirement is satisfied (in one of two ways as discussed further below), or (2) the employer makes a nonelective contribution of at least three percent of an employee's compensation to a defined contribution plan on behalf of each nonhighly compensated employee who is eligible to participate in the plan, regardless of whether the employee makes elective contributions under the plan.

The nondiscrimination safe harbor provides certainty for employers and plan participants. By meeting this test, an employer knows at the beginning of a plan year whether or not a 401(k) plan satisfies the nondiscrimination requirements for the year. Adopting a nondiscrimination safe harbor that eliminates the testing of actual

[72] Notice 98-52, 1998-2 CB 634, modified by Rev. Proc. 99-23, 1999-1 CB 920; Notice 2000-3, 2001-1 CB 413; Notice 2001-56, 2001-2 CB 277.

plan contributions removes a significant administrative burden otherwise imposed on employers.

> ▶ **OBSERVATION:** Employers are not required to use a nondiscrimination safe harbor. If an employer uses any one of them, no requirement exists that the safe harbor be used for any minimum number of years.

The notice requirement is met if each employee eligible to participate in the plan is given written notice, within a reasonable period before any year, of his or her rights and obligations under the plan. This notice must be accurate and comprehensive and written in a manner calculated to be understood by the average employee eligible to participate [Code Sec. 401(k)(12)(D)].

Matching Contribution Requirement

A plan satisfies the matching contribution requirement portion of the safe harbor if the employer makes a matching contribution on behalf of each nonhighly compensated employee of: (1) 100 percent of the employee's elective contributions up to three percent of compensation, and (2) 50 percent of the employee's elective contributions to the extent that they exceed three percent, but not 5 percent, of the employee's compensation [Code Sec. 401(k)(12)(B)(i)]. Under this matching contribution rule, the match rate for highly compensated employees cannot be greater than the match rate for non-highly compensated employees at any level of compensation [Code Sec. 401(k)(12)(B)(ii)].

Alternate method of meeting the requirement. An alternate method of meeting the contribution requirement is available. Under this alternative, the requirement is deemed to be met if: (1) the rate of an employer's matching contribution does not increase as an employee's rate of elective contributions increases, and (2) the total amount of matching contributions with regard to elective contributions up to that level of compensation that at least equals the amount of matching contributions that would be made if matching contributions satisfied the percentage rules (i.e., 100 percent of contributions up to three percent of employee compensation and 50 percent of contributions for between three and 5 percent of compensation) [Code Sec. 401(k)(12)(B)(iii)].

Alternate nondiscrimination test for matching contributions. An alternate safe harbor method for satisfying the nondiscrimination test for employer matching contributions is also available. A 401(k) arrangement satisfies the actual contribution percentage (ACP) test for defined contribution plans if the ACP (i.e., the ratio of matching contributions and employee contributions to compensation) for eligible highly compensated employees does not exceed the ACP for all other eligible employees by more than a specified percentage.

Under this alternate safe harbor, a 401(k) plan meets the nondiscrimination rules provided the plan: (1) meets the general safe harbor nondiscrimination rules discussed above [Code Sec. 401(m)(11)(A)]; and (2) satisfies a special limit on matching contributions [Code Sec. 401(m)(11)(B)]. The special limit on matching contributions is met if: (1) matching contributions on behalf of any employee with respect to employee contributions or elective deferrals is not in excess of 6 percent of compensation; (2) the rate of an employer's matching contribution does not increase as the rate of an employee's contributions or elective deferrals increases; and (3) the matching contributions for highly compensated employees at any rate of employee contribution or elective deferral is not greater than that for non-highly compensated employees.

> **NOTE:** Although this design-based safe harbor for matching contributions may help to simplify plan administration for some employers, plans permitting contributions must satisfy the ACP set forth in Code Sec. 401(m)(2).

Alternate nondiscrimination test for 401(k) plan allowing for early participation. The special nondiscrimination test for elective deferrals under a 401(k) plan is satisfied if the actual deferral percentage (ADP) for eligible highly compensated employees for a plan year does not exceed the ADP of all eligible nonhighly compensated employees by more than a specified percentage. A similar test, namely, the actual contribution percentage (ACP) test, exists for employer matching and after-tax employee contributions.

In performing the ADP and ACP tests, the plan administrator generally takes into consideration all employees eligible under the terms of the plan. However, if a plan provides that employees are eligible before they have completed: (1) the minimum age (attainment of age 21) and (2) the service requirements (completion of one year of service), those employees who have not completed the minimum age and service requirements can be tested separately. The plan administrator must perform two ADP and ACP tests for employees who have completed the minimum age and service requirements and employees who have not completed these requirements.

An alternative approach is available for employers aiming to satisfy the ADP and ACP tests for plans in which employees are eligible to participate before they have completed the age and service requirements. Under this alternative approach, if the employer satisfies the minimum coverage test (generally when the percentage of nonhighly compensated employees who benefit under a plan equals at least 70 percent of the percentage of highly compensated employees who benefit under the plan) separately with regard to those employees who have not completed the age and service requirements, the ADP and ACP tests can be applied by taking into consideration only those employees who have completed the age and service requirements as well as those employees who have not met such requirements and are highly compensated [Code Sec. 401(k)(3)(F), (m)(5)(c)].

Contribution tests may be based on prior year's deferrals. A 401(k) plan must satisfy two tests, namely, the actual deferral percentage (ADP) test and the actual contribution percentage (ACP) test for employer matching contributions and after-tax employee contributions. The ADP and ACP tests are performed using the actual deferral percentage and the actual contribution percentage of nonhighly compensated employees for the plan year preceding (not the plan year being tested, as under prior law) the plan year being tested. An employer may elect to use the current plan year (not the preceding plan year); however, this election, once made, may only be changed as provided by the IRS [Code Sec. 401(k)(3)(A), (m)(2)(A)].

> ▶ **OBSERVATION:** Permitting ADP and ACP tests to be based on the prior year's deferrals and contributions simplifies plan administration because the percentage of elective deferrals and matching contributions that can be made by and on behalf of highly compensated employees can be determined early in the plan year.

For a plan's first year, the ADP of nonhighly compensated employees for the preceding plan year is deemed to equal 3 percent, unless the employer elects to use their ADP for the initial plan year [Code Sec. 401(k)(3)(E)]. Similar rules apply with respect to determining the ACP of nonhighly compensated employees in the first plan year [Code Sec. 401(m)(3)].

Excess Deferrals

A 401(k) arrangement must meet the actual deferral percentage (ADP) test and a deferral contribution 401(k) plan allowing employee contributions must satisfy the actual contribution percentage (ACP) test each year. A plan can satisfy the ADP and ACP tests by the timely return of excess contributions to highly compensated employees.

All amounts contributed by a highly compensated employee in 2013 in excess of the $17,500 cap are currently taxable to him. However, the taxable amount does not increase his basis in the funds (i.e., he pays tax a second time on those same dollars when they are withdrawn).

Escape hatch. Employees have until March 1 of the following year to designate excess deferrals. If an employee participates in more than one plan, he should allocate the excess deferrals among the plans. Then the plan(s) can distribute the excess deferrals (plus earnings on them) by April 15. Result: The excess deferral is taxable in the year to which the deferral relates. On the other hand, income on excess deferrals is taxed in the year it is distributed. These distributions are subject to neither the 10 percent penalty tax on early distributions [Code Sec. 402(g)(2)].

The return of excess contributions (and excess aggregate contributions) to satisfy the ADP or ACP tests must be made on the basis of the amount contributed by (or on behalf of) each highly compensated employee. Thus, excess contributions (and excess aggregate contributions) are attributable first to those highly compensated employees who have the greatest dollar amount of elective deferrals, not those who have the highest deferral percentages [Code Sec. 401(k)(8)(C), (m)(6)(C)]. The new leveling provision by deferral amount is mandatory. The prior leveling method by deferral percentage is no longer available.

Matching contributions of self-employed individuals. A matching contribution made on behalf of a self-employed individual is not treated as an elective employer contribution under a qualified 401(k) plan [Code Sec. 402(g)(9)]. Thus, matching contributions on behalf of self-employed individuals are not subject to the elective contribution limit. However, qualified matching contributions that a self-employed individual treats as elective contribution for purposes of satisfying the ADP test are treated as elective contributions and are subject to the elective contribution limits [Code Sec. 402(g)(9)].

.04 Hardship Withdrawals

Employees can withdraw amounts contributed to a 401(k) plan upon severance from employment, disability, or death, hardship or the attainment of age 59½ if the plan is part of a profit-sharing or stock bonus plan, or termination of the plan [Code Sec. 401(k)(2)(B)(i)]. Employees who are experiencing a financial emergency may be able to make a hardship withdrawal of amounts stashed away in their 401(k) or 403(b) plans if the following requirements are satisfied: (1) the employer's plan permits such withdrawals; (2) the distribution is "necessary" to satisfy the employee's "immediate and heavy financial need;" and (3) other resources are not reasonably available to satisfy that need [Reg. § 1.401(k)-1(d)(3)(i)].

A retirement plan is not required to provide for hardship distributions and if it does, the specific criteria used to make a determination of hardship must be spelled out explicitly in the plan. Before considering a hardship distribution, employees must first determine (1) whether their plan allows hardship distributions, (2) the procedures the employee must follow to request a hardship distribution, (3) the plan's definition of a hardship; and (4) any limits on the amount and type of funds that can be distributed as a hardship distribution from an employee's account.

When is a Distribution Necessary?

A distribution will be considered "necessary" if all of the following requirements are satisfied:

1. The distribution does not exceed the amount of the immediate and heavy financial need of the employee including any federal, state, or local income taxes or penalties reasonably anticipated to result from the distribution;
2. The employee must have obtained all distributions (other than hardship distributions) and nontaxable loans available under all plans maintained by the employer;
3. The employee must be prohibited from making elective and employee contributions to the plan (and other employer plans) for at least 6 months after receipt of the hardship distribution; and
4. The plan (and all other employer plans) must provide that the employee's elective contributions for the tax year following the distribution may not exceed the applicable limit on elective deferrals minus the employee's elective contributions for the tax year of the distribution [Reg. § 1.401(k)-1(d)(2)(iv)(B)].

"Immediate and heavy financial need" safe harbors. The following expenses are deemed by the IRS to be of an "immediate and heavy financial need":

- Expenses for medical care incurred by the employee, the employee's spouse, or any dependent of the employee or any beneficiary of the employee under the plan;
- Costs directly related to the purchase of a principal residence for the employee (excluding mortgage payment);
- Payment of tuition, related educational fees, and room and board expenses, for the next 12 months of post-secondary education for the employee, or the employee's spouse, children, or dependents;
- Payments necessary to prevent the eviction of the employee from the employee's principal residence or foreclosure on the mortgage on that residence;
- Payment of the burial or funeral expenses of the employee's parent, spouse, children or dependents; and
- Expenses for the repair of damage to the employee's principal residence that would qualify for the casualty deduction under Code Sec. 165 [Reg. § 1.401(k)-1(d)(3)(iii)(B)].

The IRS explained in Reg. § 1.401(k)-1(d)(3)(iii)(A) that the need to pay the funeral expenses of a family member would constitute an immediate and heavy financial need but that a distribution for the purchase of a boat or television would not. A financial need may be immediate and heavy even if it was reasonably foreseeable or voluntarily incurred by the employee.

Distribution may not exceed amount of need. A distribution is treated as necessary to satisfy an employee's immediate and heavy financial need only to the extent the amount of the distribution is not in excess of the amount required to satisfy the financial need and may include any amounts necessary to pay any federal, state, or local income taxes or penalties reasonably anticipated to result from the distribution [Reg. § 1.401-1(d)(3)(iv)(A)].

Documentation of need required. It is critical that any determination of need be adequately documented by the 401(k) plan administrator. The employee should attach to the written application for a hardship distribution, a copy of the document establishing the reason for the need such as the medical or tuition bill or a copy of the eviction notice.

Employer reliance on employee representation. An "immediate and heavy financial need" generally may be treated as not capable of being relieved from other resources that are reasonably available to the employee if the employer relies upon the employee's representation that the need cannot reasonably be relieved:

1. Through reimbursement or compensation by insurance;
2. By liquidating the employee's assets;
3. By ceasing elective and employee contributions under the plan; or
4. By other currently available distributions and nontaxable loans under plans maintained by the employer or by any other employer; or
5. By borrowing from commercial sources on reasonable commercial terms in an amount sufficient to satisfy the need [Reg. § 1.401(k)-1(d)(3)(iv)(C)].

Distribution deemed necessary to satisfy immediate and heavy financial need. A distribution is deemed necessary to satisfy an employee's immediate and heavy financial need if each of the following requirements is satisfied:

1. The employee has obtained all other currently available distributions and loans under the plan and all other plans maintained by the employer; and
2. The employee is prohibited, under the terms of the plan or an otherwise legally enforceable agreement from making elective contributions and employee contributions to the plan and all other plans maintained by the employer for at least 6 months after receipt of the hardship distribution [Reg. § 1.401(k)-1(d)(3)(iv)(E)].

Limit on distributable amounts. Hardship distributions are limited to the employee's total elective contributions as of the date of distribution, reduced by the amount of previous hardship distributions. The total amount available to the employee does not include earnings, qualified nonelective contributions or qualified matching contributions, unless the plan provides that certain grandfathered amounts are included [Reg. § 1.401(k)-1(d)(3)(ii)].

.05 Tax Treatment of Hardship Distribution

A hardship distribution is included in the employee's gross income and is subject to withholding tax. In addition, participants under age 59½ are subject to an additional 10 percent penalty tax for an early distribution unless the distribution is for payment of certain medical expenses in excess of 10 percent of the taxpayer's adjusted gross income in 2013. A hardship distribution generally may not be rolled over into an IRA or other type of retirement plan [Code Sec. 402(c)(4)(C)]. However, a hardship distribution that is a "qualified recovery assistance distribution" can be recontributed and treated as a rollover.

Example 3-21: ABCo maintains a 401(k) plan for employees. The plan provides that distributions from an employee's 401(k) plan can be made to the employee on account of hardship if the employee can show immediate and heavy financial need. Emily is an eligible employee in the plan with an account balance of $50,000. The total amount of elective contributions made by Emily, who has not previously received a distribution from the plan, is $20,000. Emily requests a $15,000 hardship distribution of her elective contributions to pay 6 months of college tuition and room and board expenses for her son. At the time of the distribution request, her sole asset is a savings account with an available balance of $10,000. A distribution for payment of up to the next 12 months of post-secondary education and room and board expenses for Emily's dependent is deemed to be on account of an immediate and heavy financial need. Emily's $10,000 savings account is a resource that is reasonably available to the employee and must be taken into account in determining the amount necessary to satisfy her financial need. Thus, Emily may receive a distribution of only $5,000 of her elective contributions on account of this hardship, plus an amount necessary to pay any federal, state, or local income taxes or penalties reasonably anticipated to result from the distribution [Reg. § 1.401(k)-1(d)(6), Ex. 3].

▶ **TAX PLANNING TIP:** *Think twice before withdrawing*. Even though your 401(k) plan may seem like a handy source for cash, think twice before raiding your 401(k) plan for immediate cash needs. Consider the consequences. The funds, which grow at a tax-deferred rate, will not grow as fast if you are constantly withdrawing money. In addition, if you are terminated or quit, and are still repaying the loan from your 401(k), realize that some plans require immediate repayment upon your severance from employment. If you are unable to repay the outstanding loan, it may be treated as a distribution and be subject to income tax and a 10 percent penalty if you are not yet 59½ years old.[73]

.06 Roth 401(k) Plans

Employers may offer employees the opportunity to save for their retirement with a Roth 401(k) [Code Sec. 402A]. Like its cousin, the Roth IRA, contributions to a Roth 401(k) are made with after-tax dollars. Moreover, earnings and qualified distributions from a Roth 401(k) are tax-free. Another attractive feature of the Roth 401(k) is that any employee who is a participant in a 401(k) or 403(b) plan that allows Roth 401(k) contributions may contribute up to $17,500 in 2013 ($23,000 in 2013 for those who are 50 or older) compared with only $5,500 in 2013 for the Roth IRA ($6,500 for those 50 or older). See ¶ 3140 for a discussion of Roth IRAs.

[73] Notice 2000-32, 2000-1 CB 1274.

457 Plans May Adopt Designated Roth Contribution Programs

Eligible state and local government Code Sec. 457(b) plans (but not plans of nonprofit organizations) are permitted to allow participants to contribute deferred amounts to designated Roth accounts [Code Sec. 402A(e)(1)(C)].

Features of Roth 401(k)

Not subject to income limits. The most attractive aspect of the Roth 401(k) is that unlike Roth IRAs, Roth 401(k)s are not subject to any income limitations or restrictions. This means that an employee regardless of his or her income level may make maximum annual contributions to a Roth 401(k) (also called designated Roth accounts).

Larger contributions available. Another attractive feature of the Roth 401(k) is that Roth 401(k) contributions are keyed to a participant's elective deferrals rather than the annual limitations imposed on the Roth IRA. In 2013, Roth IRA contributions are limited to $5,500 per year, or $6,500 for those who are 50 or older (no change in 2014) [Code Sec. 408A(c)]. In contrast, Roth 401(k) contributions are subject to the 401(k) contribution ceiling, which in 2013 is $17,500 ($23,000 if the employee is at least age 50) (no change in 2014) [Code Sec. 402A(c)(2)]. Thus an employee has the option to make the larger pre-tax Roth 401(k) contributions in lieu of the traditional past-tax 401(k) contribution limit [Code Sec. 402A(b)(1)]. Therefore, an employee who has the cash to maximize his or her retirement savings contributions in 2013 could contribute $17,500 ($23,000 if age 50 or older) pre-tax to a traditional 401(k) plan or $17,500 ($23,000 if age 50 or older) post-tax to the Roth 401(k) retirement account (no change in 2014) [Code Sec. 402A(c)(2)].

Annual limit applicable to all plans. The amount of an individual's designated Roth contributions will be subject to the annual limit on elective deferrals, reduced by the amount of the participant's other elective deferrals under a 401(k) or 403(b) plan [Code Sec. 402A(c)(2)]. The annual limit applies to the total of all of the employee's pre-tax elective deferrals (including contributions to a SEP and elective employer contributions to a SIMPLE plan) and after-tax Roth contributions. The limits on elective deferrals applies to individual plan participants and not to the plan. Thus, an individual taxpayer may not defer more than the applicable limit for the tax year by participating in separate plans maintained by separate employers.

> **Example 3-22:** In 2013, Employee could not defer $8,000 in the 401(k) plan of Employer A, while also designating $10,000 in elective deferrals as Roth 401(k) contributions under the plan of Employer B, because the combined total would exceed the $17,500 limit on elective deferrals effective that year.

> **Example 3-23:** Employee participates in a 401(k) plan maintained by his employer. In 2013, he may designate up to $17,500 of his authorized elective deferrals as an after-tax Roth 401(k) contribution. If he makes pre-tax elective deferrals of $11,500 to his 401(k) plan, he may designate only $6,000 as a Roth 401(k) contribution.

Not subject to RMDs. Roth 401(k) contributions, like Roth IRAs, are not subject to the required minimum distribution requirements imposed by Code Sec. 401(a)(9) on participants age 70½ and older. Thus, no distributions of amounts attributable to Roth contributions would be required during the lifetime of the participant.

Qualified distributions not taxed. A Roth 401(k) treats any elective deferrals as being from after-tax dollars instead of pre-tax dollars. This means that "qualified distributions" from a Roth 401(k) will be tax-free. A qualified Roth 401(k) distribution is defined as a distribution that is made after a five-year participation period and that is:

1. Made on or after the date the employee attains age 59½,
2. Made to a beneficiary or the estate of the employee on or after the death of the employee, or
3. Attributable to the employee becoming disabled [Code Sec. 402A(d)(2)].

Note that a qualified distribution from a Roth 401(k) would not include a first-time homebuyer distribution as it would from a Roth IRA.

A distribution that is not a qualified distribution is included in the distributee's gross income to the extent allocable to income on the contract and excluded to the extent allocable to investment in the contract (basis).

Five-year nonexclusion period. In addition to satisfying the three requirements listed above, qualified distributions may not be made before the end of a five-year "nonexclusion period." This means that a payment or distribution from a Roth 401(k) will not escape tax as a qualified distribution if it is made within the five-tax-year period beginning with the first tax year for which the participant made a Roth 401(k) contribution to any designated account [Code Sec. 402A(d)(2)(B)(i)]. The five-tax-year periods will apply separately to separate plans [Reg. § 1.402A-1, Q-4(b)]. If a taxpayer withdraws his or her savings before termination of the five-year period, the distribution is not a "qualified" distribution and is subject to tax to the extent of earning, plus penalties. The five-year period ends when five consecutive tax years have been completed.

Plan Requirements

A company should adopt a Roth 401(k) plan only if the benefit of additional flexibility for participants is outweighed by the added administrative complexity associated with establishing a plan. Employers must keep in mind that they must first establish a regular 401(k) plan because a Roth-only-401(k) plan is not permitted by Code Sec. 402A(b)(1) because the statutory language requires taxpayers to choose between Roth and regular elective deferrals. Administrative costs associated with establishing a Roth 401(k) including the following:

Reporting and recordkeeping. Contributions and distributions from a Roth 401(k) plan must be reported on Form W-2 and Form 1099-R. Plan administrators are responsible for keeping track of the amounts of Roth 401(k) contributions and the five tax year periods for employees. Plan administrators of a recipient plan that accepts a rollover are required to notify the IRS [Reg. § 1.402A-2, Q-1].

Irrevocable designation required. The employee must make an irrevocable designation of a contribution as a Roth 401(k) contribution. As a result, taxpayers may not switch the money to a traditional 401(k) plan within the year if the employee determines that he or she needs a current-year tax deduction which is unavailable with a Roth 401(k) contribution.

Separate accounting. Contributions and withdrawals of designated Roth contributions must be credited and debited to a separate Roth 401(k) account that is maintained for the employee who made the contribution [Code Sec. 402A(b)(2)]. The account and the plan must maintain a record of the employee's investment. Gains, losses, and other credits or charges are separately allocated on a reasonable and consistent basis to the Roth 401(k) account. No contributions other than designated Roth contributions and rollover contributions may be allocated to a designated Roth 401(k) account. The separate accounting requirement applies at the time the Roth 401(k) contribution is contributed to the plan and must continue to apply until amounts in the Roth 401(k) account are completely distributed [Reg. § 1.401(k)-1(f)(2)].

Rollover rules. Amounts withdrawn from a Roth 401(k) may be rolled over tax-free into: (1) another Roth 401(k) maintained for the employee or (2) a Roth IRA in which the taxpayer participates [Code Sec. 402A(c)(3)(A); Reg. § 1.402A-1, Q-5]. Note that distributions from a Roth 401(k) account may not be rolled over to a traditional IRA or SIMPLE IRA or to a 401(k) or 403(b) plan that has not established a Roth contribution program. Reason: Roth 401(k) contributions are after-tax elective deferrals, whereas, elective deferrals to a traditional 401(k) plan have already been excluded from income.

60-day rollover required. Amounts withdrawn from a Roth 401(k) may be rolled over tax-free only if the entire withdrawn amount is rolled over within 60 days. The rollover may be accomplished by means of a direct rollover of the entire distribution by the plan administrator. If a distribution from a Roth 401(k) account is made to the employee, the employee must roll over the entire amount (or any portion thereof) into a Roth IRA within the 60-day period in order for the rollover to be tax-free [Code Sec. 402A(c)(3); Reg. § 1.402A-1, Q-5].

Tax treatment of distribution from Roth 401(k) plan that is rolled over. In the case of a rollover distribution from a Roth 401(k) account that is not a qualified distribution, if the entire amount of the distribution is not rolled over, the part that is rolled over is deemed to consist first of the portion of the distribution that is attributable to income under Code Sec. 72(e)(8). That provision provides that the portion of a distribution that is excludable from the participant's gross income is the percentage that the participant's basis in the plan is of the value of the vested portion of his interest in the plan. The remainder of the distribution is includible in income. If an employee receives a distribution from a Roth 401(k) account, the portion of the distribution that would be includible in gross income may be rolled over into a Roth 401(k) account under another plan. In this situation, Reg. §§ 1.402A-2, A-3 provides for additional reporting by the recipient plan. In addition, the employee's period of participation under the distributing plan is not carried over to the recipient plan for purposes of satisfying the five-tax-year period of participation requirement under the recipient plan.

Example 3-24: Employee receives a $14,000 eligible rollover distribution that is not a qualified distribution from his Roth 401(k) account, consisting of $11,000 of investment in the contract and $3,000 of income. Within 60 days of receipt, Employee rolls over $7,000 of the distribution into a Roth IRA. The $7,000 is deemed to consist of $3,000 of income and $4,000 of investment in the contract. Because the only portion of the distribution that could be includible in gross income (the income) is rolled over, none of the distribution is includible in Employee B's gross income [Reg. § 1.402A-1, Q-5(d)].

Ineligible contributions. Employer-matching contributions and nonelective contributions may not be designated as Roth 401(k) contributions because these are not elective deferrals of a participant.

Treatment of distributions of excess deferrals. Roth contributions that exceed the applicable limit in a year will subject the participant to double tax unless the contributions and allocable earnings are returned to the participant by a specified date. Excess deferrals (including earnings) that are attributable to designated Roth contributions and that are not returned to the participant on or before April 15 of the year following the tax year in which the excess deferral was made will be included in the participant's gross income for the tax year in which the excess deferral is distributed, as well as for the tax year of deferral [Code Sec. 402A(d)(3)]. By contrast, if excess deferrals (including earnings) that are attributable to designated Roth contributions are returned to the participant on or before April 15 of the year following the tax year in which the excess deferral was made, the participant will not be taxed on the excess deferral upon distribution. However, earnings on the excess deferral would be includible in the participant's gross income upon distribution. An excess deferral may only be corrected by a distribution of the excess amount, plus allocable earnings (or losses). However, corrective distributions of excess deferrals must be authorized by the plan. A plan may use any reasonable method for computing the income allocable to excess deferrals, provided that the method (1) does not violate the general nondiscrimination rules of Code Sec. 401(a)(4), (2) is used consistently for all participants and for all corrective distributions under the plan for the plan year, and (3) is used by the plan for allocating income to participant accounts.

Tax treatment of employer securities distributed from a Roth 401(k). If a qualified distribution includes employer securities, the distribution is not includible in gross income and the basis of each security in the hands of the distributee is the fair market value of the security on the date of distribution. The distributee will receive capital gains treatment at the time of future disposition of the security, to the extent of any post-distribution appreciation [Code Sec. 402(e)(4); Reg. § 1.042A-1, Q&A 10].

Determining remaining investment in the contract after qualified distribution from Roth 401(k). The portion of any qualified distribution that is treated as a recovery of investment in the contract is determined in the same manner as if the distribution were not a qualified distribution. Thus, the remaining investment in the contract in a Roth 401(k) after a qualified distribution is determined in the same manner after a qualified distribution as it would be determined if the distribution were not a qualified distribution.

Example 3-25: Employee receives a $12,000 distribution, which is a qualified distribution that is attributable to the employee being disabled, from his Roth 401(k) account. Immediately prior to the distribution, the account consisted of $21,850 of investment in the contract (i.e., designated Roth 401(k) contributions) and $1,150 of income. For purposes of determining recovery of investment in the contract under Code Sec. 72, the distribution is deemed to consist of $11,400 of investment in the contract [$12,000 × 21,850/(1,150 + 21,850)] and $600 of income [$12,000 × 1,150/(1,150 + 21,850)]. Immediately after the distribution, Employee's designated Roth 401(k) account consists of $10,450 of investment in the contract and $550 of income. This determination of the remaining investment in the contract will be needed if Employee subsequently is no longer disabled and takes a nonqualified distribution from the designated Roth account [Reg. § 1.402A-1, Q-7].

▶ **PLANNING POINTER:** The Roth 401(k) is an ideal retirement savings tool for the high income employee who wants to take full advantage of his retirement savings opportunities. It is particularly well suited to employees who expect to be in higher tax brackets during retirement when amounts can be withdrawn from a Roth 401(k) tax-free.

.07 401(k) Providers May Offer Personalized Investment Advice

Qualified *fiduciary advisers* can offer personally tailored professional investment advice to help participants and beneficiaries of 401(k) plans [Code Sec. 4975(f)(8)]. For 401(k) plans, fiduciary advisers may provide investment advice pursuant to an *eligible investment advice arrangement* under which (1) portfolio recommendations are generated for a participant based on an unbiased computer model that has been certified and audited by an independent third party, or (2) fiduciary advisers provide their investment advice services by charging a flat fee that does not vary depending on the investment option chosen by the participant [Code Sec. 4975(f)(8); Code Sec. 4975(d)(15)]. *Fiduciary adviser* is defined as a person who is a fiduciary of the plan by reason of the provision of investment advice to a participant or beneficiary and who is also:

1. Registered as an investment adviser under the Investment Advisers Act of 1940 or under laws of the state in which the fiduciary maintains its principal office and place of business;
2. A bank, or a similar financial institution supervised by the United States or a state, or a savings association (as defined under the Federal Deposit Insurance Act), but only if the advice is provided through a trust department that is subject to periodic examination and review by federal or state banking authorities;
3. An insurance company qualified to do business under state law;
4. Registered as a broker or dealer under the Securities Exchange Act of 1934;
5. An affiliate of any of the preceding; or
6. An employee, agent, or registered representative of any of the preceding who satisfies the requirements of applicable insurance, banking, and securities laws relating to the provision of advice [Code Sec. 4975(f)(8)(J)].

¶3155 KEOGH PLANS

If you are self-employed, as either a sole proprietor or a partner, you can set up qualified plans for yourself and your employees [Code Sec. 401(c). These plans are sometimes referred to as Keogh or H.R. 10 plans. Keogh plans come in two varieties: defined-benefit plans and defined-contribution plans. A defined-benefit plan provides for a specific retirement benefit funded by contributions based on an IRS formula and actuarial assumptions. A defined-contribution plan does not guarantee a specific retirement benefit, but instead sets the amount of annual contributions so that the amount of retirement benefits depends on contributions and income earned on those contributions. Self-employed individuals who want a defined contribution plan usually establish a profit-sharing plan, where contributions are geared to profits, or a money-purchase plan, where contributions must be made to the plan regardless of profits.

.01 How to Set Up a Keogh Plan

To establish your Keogh plan, you can adopt an IRS-approved prototype or standard master plan offered by a bank, financial institution, insurance company, or mutual fund. Alternatively, you could write your own plan meeting your specific needs. Although you are not required to secure prior IRS approval of your plan, you can apply for approval by requesting a determination letter from the IRS.[74]

Contribution Deadline

As long as your Keogh plan is set up by year-end, you have until you file your tax return, including extensions, to make the contribution.

Now that the Keogh is established, you must establish a trust or custodial account for investment of funds or buy an annuity contract or face amount certificates from an insurance company.

Maximums You Can Contribute

Following are descriptions of the contribution maximums for each type of plan found in Keoghs.

Defined benefit plans. If you have a defined benefit plan, you can deduct a maximum annual retirement benefit of the lesser of: 100 percent of compensation for your highest three consecutive years or $205,000 (for 2013) (increasing to $210,000 in 2014). See ¶ 3005 for a discussion of the plan.

Defined contribution plans. A defined contribution plan used by self-employed individuals typically is either a profit-sharing or a money purchase pension plan. For these purposes compensation is defined as the lesser of (1) a flat dollar amount ($255,000 in 2013) ($260,000 in 2014), or (2) your net earnings from self-employment (as discussed further in ¶ 3155), adjusted to take into account the deduction for contributions you made on your own behalf. Use the worksheet in IRS Publication 560 to figure your contribution limit. See ¶ 3005 for discussion of plan.

Money-purchase plan. If you are an employee, the maximum you can contribute is 25 percent of your net earnings from self-employment up to $51,000 (for 2013) ($52,000 in 2014). See ¶ 3005 for a discussion of the plan.

Profit-sharing plan. The maximum contribution that can be made to a profit sharing plan is the lesser of $51,000 (for 2013) ($52,000 in 2014) or 100 percent of compensation. There is no minimum amount you have to contribute each year to profit sharing plans. Consequently, in the lean years, you will not be forced to make contributions to profit-sharing plans. In addition, the minimum-funding requirements [¶ 3060] do not apply to profit-sharing plans. See ¶ 3005 for a discussion of the plan.

---

74 Rev. Proc. 2009-4, IRB 2009-1, 118.

Practice pointer for taxpayers with paired plans. As a result of changes in the law enacted by EGTRRA, taxpayers no longer need to create or maintain money-purchase pension plans in order to maximize contributions. [See ¶3005 for a discussion of the plan]. Therefore, taxpayers who established a paired money purchase and profit sharing plan in order to maximize contributions should consider merging or converting their money purchase plans into their profit sharing plans. Eliminating the money-purchase plan will reduce the administrative and financial burdens associated with maintaining two separate plans and will eliminate the need to comply with the rigid funding requirements associated with money purchase pension plans.

To facilitate conversion of a money purchase plan into a profit sharing plan, the IRS released Rev. Rul. 2002-42,[75] which provides that the conversion or merger of a money purchase pension plan into a profit sharing plan won't be treated as a partial termination of the plan and therefore won't cause the participants' accounts to become fully vested. According to Rev. Rul. 2002-42, if the money purchase plan is merged or converted into the profit sharing plan, the employees who were covered by the money purchase plan will remain covered under the continuing profit-sharing plan. Even though there is no partial termination when the money purchase plan is converted or merged into the profit sharing plan, employees must be given formal notice of the change or face an excise tax under Code Sec. 4980F.

▶ **PLANNING TIP:** Taxpayers wishing to eliminate their money purchase plans should chose to either merge or convert the plan into a profit sharing rather than simply terminate it. Why? When a plan terminates, plan participants become fully vested in the plan assets and can take an immediate distribution from the plan with the distribution taxed as ordinary income.

.02 Who Are Owner-Employees?

Owner-employees are (1) sole proprietors and (2) partners who own over 10 percent ownership of either the capital or profits interest in a partnership [Code Sec. 401(c)(3)]. Businesses owned by owner-employees must be aggregated to determine whether the qualification requirements are satisfied.

.03 Earnings from Self-Employment

Compensation for purposes of computing your contribution is based on your *net earnings from self-employment.* Any business income you received, including income from consulting work and director's fees, will be considered income for purposes of the figuring out how much you can contribute to the Keogh account. In fact, if you have more than one business, you may establish a Keogh plan for each of your businesses. Even if are employed elsewhere and participate in your employer's retirement plan, you can still contribute to your Keogh account provided you still have some earnings from your self-employment. But keep in mind that for purposes of the Keogh contribution limits, the income from your employment, as opposed to your self-employment income, will not be counted.

In determining net earnings from self-employment, you take your net earnings, and reduce them by (1) the deduction allowed to you for one-half of the self-employment tax, and (2) the deduction for contributions the self-employed taxpayer makes to a qualified plan or SEP [Code Sec. 401(c)(2)].

---

[75] Rev. Rul. 2002-42, 2002-2 CB 76.

.04 Multiple Plan Limits

For purposes of these deduction limits, all of your defined contribution plans are treated as a single plan, and all of your defined benefit plans are treated as a single plan, but the deductions limits are changed for combination plans as discussed above.

.05 Limited Use of Forfeitures

Forfeitures cannot be used to increase your benefits. They may only be used to reduce future employer contributions [Reg. § 1.401-7].

.06 Limit on Ancillary Benefits

Plan contributions on behalf of you that are allocable to life, accident or health insurance remain nondeductible even if they are within the overall Section 415 contribution limits. Such benefits do not count as your Keogh contribution [Code Sec. 404(e)].

.07 Plan Loan Restrictions

Plan participants are generally permitted to borrow money from qualified plans, as described in ¶ 3095. You, as owner-employee, however, are subject to special rules because of the unusual nature of your status as both owner and employee. Loans to you are considered prohibited transactions and are subject to special rules [¶ 3100].

.08 Source of Earned Income Must Be from Business

A qualified pension or profit-sharing plan that provides contributions or benefits for any owner-employer must provide that contributions on behalf of any owner-employer may be made only with respect to the earned income of the owner-employer derived from the business with respect to which the plan is established.

¶3160 EMPLOYEE STOCK OWNERSHIP PLANS (ESOPs)

An employee stock ownership plan (ESOP) is a defined contribution plan that is qualified under Code Sec. 401(a). Therefore, in addition to satisfying all ESOP requirements, an ESOP must meet the general requirements applicable to qualified plans. See ¶ 3001. An ESOP invests primarily in employer securities [Code Sec. 4975(e)(7)]. The ESOP provides shareholders of closely-held corporations with a market for their stock, resolves liquidity problems, and provides them with an opportunity to sell some or all of their shares to ESOPs without paying capital gains taxes. An ESOP can take the form of a money purchase or stock bonus plan or a combination stock bonus and money purchase plan that also meets the special requirements imposed by Code Sec. 409. Employer securities generally must be common stock "readily tradable" on an established market. If none exists, the highest class of common stock with voting power and dividend rights is acceptable. Securities of a related employer in the same "controlled group" are also okay [Code Sec. 1563(a)]. Tax on long-term capital gain from the sale of stock to the corporation's ESOP can be deferred if the seller reinvests the proceeds in other securities. A security is "readily tradable on an established securities market" if (1) the security is traded on a national securities exchange that is registered under section 6 of the Securities Exchange Act of 1934; or (2) the security is traded on a foreign national securities exchange that is officially recognized, sanctioned, or supervised by a governmental authority and the security is deemed by the SEC as having a "ready market" under SEC Rule 15c3-1 [Reg. § 401(a)(35)-1(f)(5)].[76]

.01 Voting Rights

Each participant or beneficiary must be able to direct the voting of the securities allocated to his account. They must be given the right to vote on important corporate matters, such as mergers, dissolution, liquidations or sale of substantially all the assets.

.02 Put Option

Participants must be given the right to receive distributions in employer securities. If the securities are not readily tradable, the employer must give participants a "put option;" that is, the right to require the employer to repurchase the securities under a fair valuation formula made by an independent appraiser [Code Sec. 409(h)].

.03 Employer Tax Benefits

In addition to the tax benefits of qualified plans, an ESOP offers several unique opportunities for an employer. Its principal feature, as compared with other qualified plans, is the ability to generate capital through tax-deductible loans. In effect, the ESOP is a conduit. The employer's deductible cash contributions to the ESOP are used by the ESOP to repay loans whose proceeds were used to buy employer stock. The other advantages of ESOPs, from the employer perspective, are:

Leveraged Investment in Employer Stock

An ESOP can borrow funds to purchase stock contributed to the plan even if the stock or securities are purchased from the employer corporation or its shareholders. Moreover, the loan can be used to purchase more stock than is actually needed for contributions to the plan. The balance can be used for annual expenses, discussed below.

Expense Reimbursements

If the employer borrows more than it needs to cover the securities contributed to the plan, the excess funds can be used to cover the amount paid or incurred to set up the plan, up to 10 percent of the first $100,000 transferred to the plan plus 5 percent of the excess. As reimbursement for administrative expenses, an employer may withhold up to the lesser of (1) 10 percent of the first $100,000 of dividends paid to the plan during the plan year ending with or within the employer's tax year plus 5 percent of the amount of such dividends in excess of $100,000, or (2) $100,000 [Code Sec. 409(i)].

Capital Gains Tax Deferral

Tax on long-term capital gain from the sale of stock to the corporation's ESOP can be deferred if the seller reinvests the proceeds in other securities and makes a valid election under Code Sec. 1042 for deferred recognition treatment.[77]

---

[76] Notice 2011-19, IRB 2011-11, 550.

[77] *J.W. Clause Est.*, 122 TC 115, Dec. 55,537 (2004).

It is critical that the IRS be notified of the taxpayer's intent to make the election in order for the election to be valid. The election must be made by the due date, including extensions, for filing the return. To qualify for this deferral, the employer stock must have been held for three years before the sale to the ESOP, and immediately after the sale the ESOP must own at least 30 percent of each class of the corporation's outstanding stock or of the total value of all outstanding stock [Code Sec. 1042(b)(2)]. A taxpayer or executor may defer recognition of long-term capital gain on the sale of "qualified securities" to an ESOP if qualified replacement property is purchased within the period beginning 3 months before and ending 12 months after the sale. [Code Sec. 1042(c)(3); Temp. Reg. § 1.1042-1T]. Taxpayers may notarize a statement of purchase for the qualified replacement property as late as the time the taxpayer's income tax return is filed for the tax year of the purchase [Temp. Reg. § 1.1042-1T, Q&A3].

Relief from Prohibited Transaction Rules

The prohibited transaction rules that apply in the case of loans made by disqualified persons to qualified plans will not apply to a loan to an ESOP [Code Sec. 4975(d)(3) and (e)(7)].

Deduction Ceilings Eased

Contributions made to an ESOP to enable the ESOP to repay loans incurred to purchase employer securities may be deducted to the extent that they do not exceed 25 percent of the compensation paid to participants [Code Sec. 404(a)(9)]. The normal deduction limits that apply to contributions to qualified plans do not apply in this instance. Contributions made to repay interest on a loan incurred to acquire qualifying employer securities may be deducted for the tax year with respect to which such contributions are made [Code Sec. 404(a)(9)(B)].

Deduction for Dividends Paid [Code Sec. 404(k)]

A C corporation may deduct the amount of applicable dividends paid on its stock held by an ESOP [Code Sec. 404(k)(1)]. Dividends on employer securities distributed from an ESOP under Code Sec. 404(k) must be reported on a Form 1099-R that does not report any other distributions according to that form's instructions. A dividend is an "applicable dividend" if the following requirements are met [Code Sec. 404(k)(2)]:

- The dividend is paid in cash directly to participants in the ESOP or their beneficiaries,
- The dividend is paid to the ESOP and subsequently distributed to the participants or their beneficiaries in cash no later than 90 days after the end of the plan year in which the dividends are paid to the ESOP,
- At the election of the plan participants or their beneficiaries, the dividend is payable in cash to the participants or their beneficiaries or to the plan and distributed in cash to participants or is paid to the plan and reinvested in qualifying employer securities,
- The dividends are used to repay a loan the proceeds of which were used to acquire the employer's securities (whether or not allocated to participants).

Circuit Split

In *Boise Cascade Corp.*,[78] the Court of Appeals for the Ninth Circuit held that a corporation could deduct amounts paid to redeem shares of stock held by its ESOP when participants terminated employment under Code Sec. 404(k).

Disagreeing with the Ninth Circuit on a very similar set of facts, the Court of Appeals for the Eighth Circuit affirmed the Tax Court in *Nestle Purina Petcare Co.*,[79] to hold that a corporation could not deduct payments to redeem stock held in its ESOP under Code Sec. 404(k). The Court relied on the precedent established by the Eighth Circuit in *General Mills.*[80] The Third Circuit has similarly held in *Conopco, Inc.*,[81] that payments to redeem stock held in its ESOP were not deductible under Code Sec. 162(k).

.04 Employee Tax Benefits

The following advantages are available to participants in ESOPs:

- If the ESOP is qualified and therefore satisfies all requirements imposed on qualified plans, the ESOP will be tax-exempt and all income earned by the ESOP will be tax-exempt. See ¶3001 for discussion of qualified plans. In *R.S. Yarish*,[82] the Tax Court concluded that a highly-compensated employee who was fully vested in an ESOP that was disqualified had to include in income the entire amount of his vested accrued benefit. The court interpreted Code Sec. 402(b)(4)(A) as requiring the inclusion of the vested accrued benefit to the extent it has not been previously taxed to the employee. The rule requiring the inclusion excepted the employee's "investment in the contract."
- *Diversification*: Employees who have attained age 55 and completed 10 years of service are not forced to have all their funds in a single investment (i.e., employer stock). Within 90 days after the close of each year in the qualified election period (the six-plan year period beginning with the first plan year in which an individual first becomes a qualified participant) the participant must be given the option to diversify up to 25 percent of his or her account balance [Code Sec. 401(a)(28)(B)]. During the last year of the election period, the participant may diversify up to 50 percent of the account.
- *Distributions*: Distributions can be made in stock or cash and are taxed as described in ¶3080. The ESOP must permit distributions to employees who separate from service before the plan's normal retirement age. The distribution of the entire account balance must begin no later than the later of the plan year: (1) when the participant retires, becomes disabled or dies, or (2) which is the fifth plan year after separation from service [Code Sec. 409(o)(1)(A)].

  NOTE: These rules are intended to accelerate the usual payment rules. If the general rules provide an earlier payment date, the participant may elect that date [Code Sec. 401(a)(14)].
- Dividends paid from stock owned by an ESOP are exempt from the 10 percent penalty imposed on premature (pre-age $59^1/_2$) distributions from a qualified retire-

---

[78] *Boise Cascade Corp.*, CA-9, 2003-1 USTC ¶50,472, 329 F3d 751.

[79] *Nestle Purina Petcare Co.*, CA-8, 2010-1 USTC ¶50,213, 594 F3d 968, *cert. denied*, SCt, 10/04/2010.

[80] *General Mills, Inc.*, CA-8, 2009-1 USTC ¶50,117, 554 F3d 727.

[81] *Conopco, Inc.*, CA-3, 2009-2 USTC ¶50,492.

[82] *R.S. Yarish*, 139 TC 290, Dec. 59,216 (2012).

ment plan [Code Sec. 72(t)(2)(A)(vi)] [¶3085]. Unless the ESOP provides that a participant may elect a longer distribution period, the ESOP must provide for distributions of the participant's account balance in substantially equal periodic payments (not less frequently than annually) over a period not longer than five years. However, if the participant's account balance exceeds $1,035,000 in 2013, the distribution period is extended by one year, up to an additional five years, for each $205,000 (or fraction thereof) by which the account exceeds $1,035,000 [Code Sec. 409(o)(1)(C)(ii)].

.05 Prohibited Allocations of Stock in S Corporation ESOP

Code Sec. 1361(c)(6) allows ESOPs to own stock in an S corporation thereby encouraging employee ownership of closely held businesses. Code Sec. 409(p) provides that an ESOP that holds employer securities consisting of S corporation stock must provide that no portion of the plan assets attributable to employer securities may, during a *nonallocation year* accrue (or be allocated, directly or indirectly, under any of the employer's Code Sec. 401(a) qualified plans) for the benefit of any "disqualified person."

Definition of Nonallocation Year

A *nonallocation year* means any plan year of an ESOP holding shares in an S corporation if, at any time during the plan year, disqualified persons own at least 50 percent of the number of outstanding shares of the S corporation [Code Sec. 409(p)(3)(A)]. If there is a "nonallocation year": (1) the amount allocated in a prohibited allocation to an individual who is a *disqualified person* is treated as distributed to such individual, and, the value of the prohibited allocation is included in gross income [Code Sec. 409(p)]; and (2) a 50 percent excise tax is imposed on the S corporation with respect to the amount of the prohibited allocation or any *synthetic equity* owned by a disqualified person [Code Sec. 4979A].

For purposes of determining whether there is a nonallocation year, ownership of stock generally is attributed under the attribution rules of Code Sec. 318, except that: (1) the family attribution rules are modified to include certain other family members, as described below, (2) option attribution would not apply (but instead special rules relating to synthetic equity described below would apply), and (3) "deemed-owned shares" held by the ESOP are treated as held by the individual with respect to whom they are deemed owned. Family members of an individual include (1) a spouse, (2) an ancestor or lineal descendant of the individual or his or her spouse, (3) a sibling of the individual (or the individual's spouse) and any lineal descendant of the brother or sister, and (4) the spouse of any person described in (2) or (3) [Code Sec. 409(p)(4)(D)].

Disqualified Person Defined

Under Code Sec. 409(p)(4) and Reg. §1.409(p)-1(d)(1), a *disqualified person* means any person for whom:

- The number of such person's deemed-owned ESOP shares of the S corporation is at least 10 percent of the number of the deemed-owned ESOP shares of the S corporation;
- The aggregate number of such person's deemed-owned ESOP shares and synthetic equity shares of the S corporation is at least 10 percent of the sum of: (a) The total

number of deemed-owned ESOP shares, and (b) the person's synthetic equity shares of the S corporation;

- The aggregate number of the S corporation's deemed-owned ESOP shares of such person and of the members of such person's family is at least 20 percent of the number of deemed-owned ESOP shares of the S corporation; or
- The aggregate number of the S corporation's deemed-owned ESOP shares and synthetic equity shares of such person and of the members of such person's family is at least 20 percent of the sum of: (a) The total number of deemed-owned ESOP shares, and (b) the synthetic equity shares of the S corporation owned by such person and the members of such person's family.

Deemed-Owned ESOP Shares

Code Sec. 409(p)(4)(C) and Reg. § 1.409(p)-1(e)(a) and (2) provide that a person is treated as owning his or her deemed-owned ESOP shares if:

- Any shares of stock in the S corporation constituting employer securities that are allocated to such person's account under the ESOP; and
- Such person's share of the stock in the S corporation that is held by the ESOP but is not allocated to the account of any participant or beneficiary, with such person's share to be determined in the same proportion as the shares released and allocated from a suspense account under the ESOP for the most recently ended plan year for which there were shares released and allocated from a suspense account, or if there has been no such prior release and allocation from a suspense account, then determined in proportion to a reasonable estimate of the shares that would be released and allocated in the first year of loan repayment.

Synthetic Equity Defined

Synthetic equity is treated as owned by a person in the same manner as stock is treated as owned by a person, directly or under the attribution rules. Code Sec. 409(p)(6)(C) defines "synthetic equity" to include any stock option, warrant, restricted stock, deferred issuance stock right, stock appreciation right payable in stock, or similar interest or right that gives the holder the right to acquire or receive stock of the S corporation in the future [Reg. § 1.409(p)-1(f)(2)]. Synthetic equity also includes a right to a future payment (payable in cash or any other form other than stock of the S corporation) from an S corporation that is based on the value of the stock of the S corporation or appreciation in such value, such as a stock appreciation right with respect to stock of an S corporation that is payable in cash or a phantom stock unit with respect to stock of an S corporation that is payable in cash.

The stock on which a synthetic equity interest is based is treated as outstanding stock of the S corporation and as deemed-owned shares of the person holding the synthetic equity interest if this treatment would result in the treatment of any person as a disqualified person or the treatment of any year as a nonallocation year [Code Sec. 409(p)(5)]. Thus, for example, disqualified persons for a year include those individuals who are disqualified persons under the general rule (i.e., treating only those shares held by the ESOP as deemed-owned shares) and those individuals who are disqualified individuals if synthetic equity interests are treated as deemed-owned shares.

Tax Imposed

A 50 percent excise tax is imposed under each of the following circumstances [Code Sec. 4979A(a)]:

- There is an allocation of employer securities that is prohibited by Code Sec. 409(p),
- Ownership of synthetic equity by a disqualified person during a nonallocation year, and
- Occurrence of an ESOP's first nonallocation year [Code Sec. 409(p)(2)].

.06 Abusive S ESOPs Targeted

In an effort to curb abusive tax avoidance transactions, the IRS announced in Rev. Rul. 2004-4,[83] that transactions involving S corporation ESOPs that do not substantially benefit rank-and-file employees will be characterized as patently abusive transactions. The targeted transactions will also be considered "listed transactions" thus subjecting them to stringent tax-shelter disclosure and list maintenance rules as discussed in Ch. 26.

Rev. Rul. 2004-4 prohibits use of a subsidiary's stock options to drain value from an ESOP for the benefit of the S corporation's former owners or key employees. A 50 percent excise tax is imposed on the option holders in cases where rank-and-file ESOP participants are deprived of the business profits. Rev. Rul. 2004-4 is an attempt by the IRS to put a stop to abusive transactions that shuffle business profits of the S corporation away from an ESOP and reduce benefits for rank-and-file employees. The IRS explains that the ownership structure of the S corporation is designed to allow one or more individuals or entities to take advantage of the tax-exempt status of the S corporation resulting from its ownership by an ESOP thereby avoiding tax. Consequently, Rev. Rul. 2004-4 prohibits using stock options of a subsidiary to drain value out of the ESOP for the benefit of the S corporation's former owners or key employees. Option holders would face a 50 percent excise tax under Code Sec. 4979A.

¶3165 TAX-SHELTERED ANNUITIES—CODE SEC. 403(b) PLANS

Code Sec. 403(b) tax-sheltered annuities are retirement arrangements primarily for employees of public universities and certain tax-exempt organizations. Code Sec. 403(b) also applies to contributions made for certain ministers.

Contributions to a Code Sec. 403(b) plan are excluded from gross income under Code Sec. 403(b) only if made to the following funding arrangements: (1) contracts issued by an insurance company qualified to issue annuities in a state that includes payment in the form of an annuity; (2) custodial accounts that are exclusively invested in stock of a mutual fund; or (3) a retirement income account for employees of a church-related organization.

The main tax benefit of a tax-sheltered annuity, sometimes called a 403(b) annuity plan, is that employees are not taxed on contributions made by the employer to the plan until payments under the annuity are received. Many tax-sheltered annuity

---

[83] Rev. Rul. 2004-4, 2004-1 CB 406.

plans also offer participants the opportunity to make deductible contributions through salary reduction. The advantage 403(b) plans have over 401(k) plans is that employees with 403(b) plans can transfer the accumulated savings in their plans to another investment vehicle, without employer approval, provided their employer has not contributed money to the plan. They need not wait until they change jobs or retire to make a transfer.

Contributions made by an employer on behalf of an employee to a trust which is a part of a salary reduction agreement under Code Sec. 403(b) will not be treated as distributed or made available to the employee nor as contributions made to the trust by the employee merely because the arrangement includes provisions under which the employee has an election whether the contribution will be made to the trust or received by the employee in cash [Code Sec. 402(e)(3)].

.01 Written Plan Requirement

A 403(b) contract must be issued under a written plan [Reg. § 1.403(b)-3(b)(3)]. Having a written plan allocates responsibilities among the employer, the issuer of the contract, and other parties and facilitates the enforcement of plan requirements concerning loans, hardship withdrawal, and limitations on deferrals. The plan does not have to be contained in one document but may incorporate material provisions by reference from the annuity contract or other documents.

.02 Contract Exchanges

The regulations permit three specific types of tax-free exchanges or transfers of amounts in 403(b) contracts. A nontaxable exchange or transfer is permitted for a 403(b) contract if either: (1) it is a mere change of investment within the same plan (contract exchange); (2) it constitutes a plan-to-plan transfer, so that there is another employer plan receiving the exchange; or (3) it is a transfer to purchase permissive service credit (or a repayment to a defined benefit governmental plan). An employee can transfer a plan interest to the plan of another employer for whom the employee works or worked. The transfer can only be to a 403(b) plan. Similarly, a 403(b) plan can only accept a transfer from another 403(b) plan [Reg. § 1.403(b)-10(b)].

.03 Distributions

Distributions can be made upon termination of employment, hardship, disability, or after age 59½. Employer contributions can be made upon a stated event, such as a term of years, a stated age, or the occurrence of financial need. The final regulations allow after-tax employee contributions to be paid without any in-service restrictions. Distributions must satisfy the required minimum distribution and incidental benefit rules of Code Sec. 401(a)(9). Thus nonretirement benefits such as life insurance or health benefits must be incidental to the annuity benefit [Reg. § 1.403(b)-6].

.04 Qualifying Employers

Tax-sheltered annuity programs may be established only by a qualified employer. These include state or local governments or their agencies or instrumentalities, public schools, libraries and certain tax-exempt organizations. Generally a qualified tax-exempt organization qualifies if it is formed and operated exclusively for religious, charitable, scientific or educational purposes [Reg. § 1.403(b)-1(b)(1)(i)].

.05 Exclusion from Gross Income

Generally, if an employee participates in a tax-sheltered annuity plan, the employee can exclude from income the employer's contribution made on his or her behalf equal to the employer contribution limit. It should also be noted that regardless of whether the employer contribution is excludable under the rules discussed here, they would not be immediately subject to tax if the employee's rights in the contributions are nonvested or subject to a substantial risk of forfeiture [Code Sec. 403(b)(1)(C); Reg. §§1.83-3(b), 1.403(c)-1(a)].

.06 Contribution Limit

Employee salary reduction contributions of up to $17,500 in 2013 (no change in 2014) are permitted [Code Sec. 402(g)(4)]. Each 403(b) tax-sheltered annuity contract (and not the plan) must provide that elective deferrals made under the contract may not exceed the annual limit on elective deferrals which in 2013 is $17,500 (no change in 2014) [Code Sec. 403(b)(1)(E)].

Employer may make deductible contributions to an employee's 403(b) plan up to a limit, that, when combined with the employee's elective deferrals, do not exceed $51,000 ($52,000 in 2014) or 100 percent of the employee's compensation ($255,000 in 2013) ($260,000 in 2014) [Code Sec. 415(c)].

Catch-Up Contributions

Participants age 50 by the end of the tax year may make additional catch-up contributions to 403(b) annuities for that tax year [Code Sec. 414(v)(5)]. An employer isn't required to provide for catch-up contributions in any of its plans [Reg. §1.414(v)-1(a)(1)]. However, if any plan of an employer provides for catch-up contributions, all of its plans that provide for elective deferrals must comply with the universal availability requirement. The maximum additional contribution is the lesser of (1) a set dollar amount for the year, or (2) the participant's compensation for the year reduced by any other elective deferrals for the year. The catch-up contribution limits for Code Sec. 403(b) annuities are as shown in Table 6 [Code Sec. 414(v)].

Table 6. Maximum Catch-Up Contributions for Sec. 403(b) Annuities

Tax Year	Catch-up Contribution Limit
2013 and 2014	$5,500

Automatic Salary-Reduction Election

The IRS has ruled that 403(b) plans can provide for automatic salary deferral contributions at a specified level as the default mechanism where a new or existing employee hasn't affirmatively elected to receive cash or to specify a different level of salary deferral.[84] This is called an automatic salary-reduction election feature. Under this feature, each employee's compensation would automatically be reduced by a fixed percentage and that amount would be contributed to the purchase of an annuity contract, unless he affirmatively elected to receive cash or have a different percentage contributed to the plan. An election not to make salary-reduction contributions or to contribute a different percentage could be made at any time.

---

[84] Rev. Rul. 2000-35, 2000-2 CB 138. *See* Rev. Rul. 2000-33, 2000-2 CB 142, for ability of 457 plans of a state or local employer to implement an automatic salary deferral election procedure.

.07 Other Rules

Contributions toward a tax-sheltered annuity under a salary reduction agreement are considered wages for purposes of the social security tax (FICA). This is the rule even though the contributions may be wholly or partially excluded for income tax purposes. To the extent employer contributions are excludable from gross income, they are not subject to income tax withholding. However, any part of the contribution that is in excess of the exclusion allowance, or is used to purchase current life insurance protection, is subject to withholding.[85]

.08 Distributions and Rollovers

Distributions received from a tax-sheltered annuity may be rolled over into an IRA or IRA annuity, another tax-sheltered annuity, or a qualified trust. The general rollover rules, including the 60-day requirement (except for deposits frozen in insolvent institutions), would apply [Code Sec. 402(c)(3); ¶3125]. In most cases, payments you receive or that are made available to you are taxable as ordinary income. However, if you have a basis on your contract, because amounts contributed by your employer were taxable to you, then these amounts would be recovered tax-free.

An employee participating in an Code Sec. 403(b) annuity may roll over an eligible rollover distribution tax free to another eligible retirement account, which could include an Code Sec. 401(k) plan or a governmental Code Sec. 457 plan, an IRA or another Code Sec. 403(b) annuity. In addition, eligible rollover distributions from a qualified plan, an IRA, or a governmental Code Sec. 457 plan may be rolled over tax free to a 403(b) annuity [Code Sec. 402(c)(8)(B)(vi); Reg. § 402(b)(8)(A)(ii)].

The payor must provide a written explanation of the rollover rules to individuals receiving a distribution eligible for rollover [Code Sec. 402(f)]. The rollover notice must include a description of the restrictions that may be imposed on distributions from the plan to which the distribution is rolled over and a description of any tax consequences that would be different from the rules applicable to distributions from the distributing plan [Code Sec. 402(f)(1)].

Minimum Distributions

Section 403(b) contracts are subject to the distribution rules provided by Code Sec. 401(a)(9). For purposes of applying those rules, section 403(b) contracts are treated as traditional IRAs [distribution rules applicable to traditional IRAs are discussed in ¶3120][Reg. § 1.403(b)-3]. However, there are certain differences [Reg. § 1.403(b)-3(c)]. For example: (1) the required beginning date for distributions is April 1 of the calendar year following the later of the calendar year in which the employee attains age 70$^{1}/_{2}$ or the calendar year in which the employee retires from employment with the employer maintaining the plan; (2) the surviving spouse of an employee may not treat a section 403(b) contract as the spouse's own section 403(b) contract; and (3) if the issuer of the 403(b) annuity has a record of the December 31, 1986 balance, the minimum distribution rules only apply to benefits accruing after 1986 (including post-1986 earnings on pre-1987 contributions).

.09 Nondiscrimination Requirements

There are two sets of nondiscrimination rules for 403(b) plans.

---

85 Rev. Rul. 70-453, 1970-2 CB 287.

Salary Reductions

In general, the nondiscrimination requirement here mandates that all employees be permitted to make a salary reduction contribution of more than $200. Contributions pursuant to a one-time irrevocable election made at the time of initial plan eligibility are not treated as salary reduction contributions [Code Sec. 403(b)(12)(A)(ii)].

Other 403(b) Plans

These rules are more complicated. Basically, they limit the permitted disparity between contributions for highly compensated and other employees [Code Sec. 403(b)(12)(A)(i)]. The IRS provides safe harbor disparities. The greater the percentage of non-highly compensated employees who are accruing benefits under the program, the larger is the permissible disparity. For example, the percentage of compensation contributed for highly compensated employees may be as much as 180 percent of contributions for other employees if (1) at least 50 percent of the non-highly compensated employees are currently accruing benefits under the plan, and (2) at least 70 percent of the employees who are currently accruing benefits are not highly compensated.[86]

.10 Investment Choices

The IRS will treat a contract as an annuity contract described in Code Sec. 403(a) or (b) [Code Sec. 408(b)] even though contract premiums are invested at the direction of the contract holder in publicly available securities under certain circumstances.[87] This is a significant change in light of the hard line that the IRS has taken in the past against annuities which gave the annuity holder the ability to self-direct their investments. The ability of the annuity holder to invest in publicly available securities won't result in treatment as the owner of the tax-deferred annuity contract assets, if the following requirements are satisfied:

- For a contract that is intended to qualify as an annuity contract for purposes of an Code Sec. 403(a) or 403(b) contract, no additional federal tax liability would have been incurred if the contract holder's employer had instead paid amounts into a trust or custodial account in an arrangement that satisfied the requirements of Code Sec. 401(a) or under Code Sec. 403(b)(7)(A); or
- For a contract that is intended to qualify as an individual retirement annuity for purposes of Code Sec. 408(b), no additional federal tax liability would have been incurred if the consideration for the contract had instead been held as part of a trust that would satisfy the requirements of Code Sec. 408(a) except that the general account of an insurance company shall be treated as a common investment fund for purposes of satisfying Code Sec. 408(a)(5).

Planning Implications

In the past the downside to maintaining an Code Sec. 403(b) retirement plans was the inferior investment opportunities offered by such plans. As a result of this significant change implemented by the IRS, employees with Code Sec. 403 annuities and individual retirement annuities under Code Sec. 408(b) enjoy the same investment

[86] Notice 89-23, 1989-1 CB 654, as modified by Notice 90-73, 1990-2 CB 353 and Notice 96-64 1996-2 CB 229.

[87] Rev. Proc. 99-44, 1999-2 CB 598.

opportunities available to other retirement savings plans including self-directed qualified plan individual accounts and IRA custodial accounts. Specifically the annuity holders can determine for themselves how they want to invest their retirement savings. They can now invest in either publicly available securities or mutual funds, as they see fit, within their tax-deferred accounts.

.11 Termination of 403(b) Plan

An employer is permitted to amend a Code Sec. 403(b) plan to eliminate future contributions for existing participants or to limit participation to existing participants and employees. A Code Sec. 403(b) plan is permitted to contain provisions that provide for plan termination and that allow accumulated benefits to be distributed on termination [Reg. § 1.403(b)-10(a)].

In order for a Code Sec. 403(b) plan to be considered terminated, all accumulated benefits under the plan must be distributed to all participants and beneficiaries as soon as practicable after termination of the plan. The employer cannot make any contributions to another Code Sec. 403(b) plan within 12 months after the termination of the existing plan. However, another plan is disregarded if fewer than two percent of employees in the existing plan are eligible in the other plan, during the period from 12 months before termination to 12 months after termination. A contract is not a Code Sec. 403(b) contract if it fails to satisfy the nonforfeitability requirements on plan termination.

In Rev. Rul. 2011-7,[88] the IRS explained how the plan termination provisions apply to tax sheltered annuity contracts. The regulations provide that a Code Sec. 403(b) plan may contain provisions that provide for plan termination and that allow accumulated benefits to be distributed on termination. In Rev. Rul. 2011-7, the IRS used four examples to clarify whether a plan has been terminated under Reg. § 1.403(b)-10(a) and whether distributions made to participants or beneficiaries in connection with the termination of the plan are included in gross income.

¶3170 NONQUALIFIED DEFERRED COMPENSATION

Nonqualified deferred compensation plans are benefit arrangements which do not offer to taxpayers all of the tax-favored benefits available with qualified plans. As a result, these plans are not subject to the onerous restrictive funding, vesting, distribution, and reporting requirements that are typically associated with qualified plans. Nonqualified plans are established to supplement the retirement benefits that are provided to a select group of management or highly compensated employees under their qualified deferred compensation plans. The employer promises key employees that they will receive some future benefit for services performed today. The special tax treatment that is not afforded deferred compensation plans includes a current deduction for the employer for its contributions and rollover opportunities.

.01 Document Correction Programs

Code Sec. 409A was enacted by Congress to implement rules and regulations on nonqualified deferred compensation plans. Code Sec. 409A imposes timing restric-

[88] Rev. Rul. 2011-7, IRB 2011-10, 534.

tions on how the deferred compensation is funded, and when the deferred compensation may be distributed to the service provider. The Code Sec. 409A plan must be a detailed written document. Failure to comply with the Code Sec. 409A rules in operation or in written form results in all vested compensation deferred under the plan for the year and all preceding tax years being includable in the employee's gross income. Moreover, a 20 percent additional income tax will be imposed as well as a premium interest tax.

In order to avoid these penalties, the IRS has established two separate programs that allow taxpayers to correct failures to comply with Code Sec. 409A—one for operational failures and one for written plan document failures. Notice 2008-113[89] allows for the correction of certain Code Sec. 409A failures that occur during the operation of a nonqualified deferred compensation plan. Notice 2010-6[90] allows taxpayers to voluntarily correct many types of failures to comply with the document requirements applicable to nonqualified deferred compensation plans.

To take advantage of the document correction program, the plan must satisfy certain threshold requirements, comply with the correction method and relief for the particular document failure, and meet certain information and reporting requirements for the correction.

Notice 2010-6 addresses a variety of violations, such as impermissible initial deferral elections, impermissible definitions of payment events, impermissible payment events, failure to delay payments six months to specified employees, and impermissible payment periods. Some violations require the inclusion of income if the impermissible provision triggers payment within one year of the date of correction. Inclusion generally amounts to 25 percent or 50 percent of the amount deferred.

.02 How to Designate a Compliant Time and Form of Payment

A plan will only provide for a compliant time and form of payment for a deferred amount if the plan provides for an objectively determinable form of payment payable upon: (1) a separation from service, (2) a change in control event, (3) an unforeseeable emergency, (4) a specified date or fixed schedule of payments, (5) death, or (6) disability.

For example, a plan may provide that an amount deferred under the plan will be paid in the form of a life annuity commencing on the later of the service provider's separation from service or attaining age 65. However, a plan may not provide that an amount deferred under the plan will be paid during the three years following the service provider's separation from service (with the exact timing of the payment during the three-year period determined at the discretion of the service recipient), because that plan term would not provide a compliant time and form of payment. The plan may specify any combination of payment events that is permissible under the final regulations, including that a deferred amount is to be paid upon the earliest of the events listed above or the latest of these events.

.03 Why Deferred Compensation Arrangements Are Popular

The popularity of deferred compensation plans arises from the following features:

---

[89] Notice 2008-113, IRB 2008-51, 1305, as modified by Notice 2010-80, IRB 2010-51.

[90] Notice 2010-6, IRB 2010-3, 275, as modified by Notice 2010-80, IRB 2010-51.

- Nonqualified plans need not comply with the ever more restrictive discrimination and participation rules imposed on qualified plans. This enables an employer to pick and choose the employees it would like to benefit.
- Nonqualified deferred compensation plans are not subject to the dollar limitations imposed on contributions to and benefits payable from qualified retirement plans. Employers can thus provide additional benefits to key executives with nonqualified deferred compensation plans and not be restricted by a dollar cap.
- They can be a useful tool in helping an employer attract and retain top talent.
- Unlike qualified plans, nonqualified plans need not be funded. Nonqualified deferred compensation plans are essentially contractual arrangements between the employer and the employee, where the employer promises a benefit in return for the employee's services. In fact, a single unfunded promise to pay the deferred compensation avoids the constructive receipt problem. Using an unfunded plan, however, would not prevent the employer from actually setting aside funds or segregating the plan's funds on the company's books. Compare this with the funds held in a qualified plan. They are generally segregated in trust and cannot be used by the employer for general business purposes.
- Employers can use the deferred compensation as an inexpensive source of working capital during the time that employees agree to wait before receiving their bonuses, salaries, or director's fees.

.04 Employer Tax Consequences

Employers who have set up deferred compensation plans should be aware of the following tax consequences:

- The employer must maintain a separate account for each employee in order to claim a deduction. A plan is not considered to be established until the latest: of the date on which it is adopted, the date on which it is effective, or the date on which the plan's material terms are set forth in writing [Reg. § 31.3121(v)(2)-1(b)(3)]. Phantom stock plans are nonqualified compensation plans, while certain stock appreciation rights and stock option plans are generally not nonqualified deferred compensation plans and are therefore not subject to FICA withholding until there is no substantial risk of forfeiture of the rights to such amounts.
- Employers may not claim a current deduction for interest accrued on employee's deferred compensation accounts.[91]
- In order for a plan to be characterized as a nonqualified deferred compensation plan, it must provide for the deferral of compensation. A plan provides for the deferral of compensation if the service provider has a legally binding right to compensation that is or may be payable to the service provider in a later tax year. A legally binding right to an amount that will be excluded from income when and if received does not constitute a deferral of compensation, unless the service provider has received the right in exchange for an amount that will be includible in income (other than due to participation in a cafeteria plan). A service provider does not have a legally binding right to compensation to the extent that compensa-

---

[91] *Albertson's, Inc.*, CA-9, 94-2 USTC ¶ 50,619, 42 F3d 537, *cert. denied*, 516 US 807; Notice 94-38, 1994-1 CB 350.

tion may be reduced unilaterally or eliminated by the service recipient or other person after the services creating the right to the compensation have been performed. A service provider does not fail to have a legally binding right to compensation merely because the amount of compensation is determined under a formula that provides for benefits to be offset by benefits provided under another plan or because benefits are reduced due to actual or notional investment losses, or, in a final average pay plan, subsequent decreases in compensation [Reg. § 1.409A-1(b)(1)].

- A plan will be treated as providing for a payment in a later year whether the plan explicitly provides so or the deferral condition is inherent in the terms of the contract. Where the parties have agreed that a payment will be made upon an event that could occur after the year in which the legally binding right to the payment arises, the plan generally will provide for a deferral of compensation. Thus, if a plan provides a service provider a right to a payment upon separation from service, the plan generally will result in a deferral of compensation regardless of whether the service provider separates from service and receives the payment in the same year as the grant, because under the plan, the payment is conditioned upon an event that may occur after the year in which the legally binding right to the payment arises [Reg. § 1.409A-1(b)(4)].
- If a stock option or stock appreciation right (SAR) provides a right to a payment for a term of years where the payment could be received during the short-term deferral period or a later period but is not otherwise includible in income until paid, the arrangement will provide for deferred compensation even though the service provider could receive the payment during the short-term deferral period. However, where a plan doesn't specify a payment date, payment event, or term of years, the plan generally will not provide for the deferral of compensation if the service provider actually or constructively receives the payment within the short-term deferral period [Reg. § 1.409A-1(b)(5)].
- Employers maintaining nonqualified deferred compensation plans on behalf of employees must withhold FICA on deferred amounts as of the later of when the contribution is earned or when it is no longer subject to a substantial risk of forfeiture [Code Sec. 3121(v)].

Services creating the right to deferred compensation and therefore subject to FICA withholding are considered to be performed as of the date on which, under the plan, the employee has performed all of the services necessary to obtain a legally binding right to the amount deferred. However, for services that would be treated as performed periodically during a year, an employer may treat them as performed on December 31 of that year.

> **Example 3-26:** ABC establishes a nonqualified deferred compensation account balance plan for a key employee on Nov. 1, 2013. Under the plan, the employee has a legally binding right on the last day of each calendar year to be credited with a principal amount equal to 5 percent of his compensation for the year. In addition, a reasonable rate of interest is credited quarterly. The account balance is nonforfeitable and payable to the employee on termination of employment. For 2014, a principal amount of $25,000 is credited to the employee.

Result: The services creating the right are considered performed on Dec. 31, 2013, and $25,000 must be taken into account as FICA wages on that date, which is the later of the date the services are performed or the date on which the right to the amount deferred is no longer subject to a substantial risk of forfeiture.

You determine the amount deferred under a nonqualified deferred compensation plan that is an account balance plan by taking the principal amount credited to the employee's account for the period and increase or decrease it by any income attributable to the principal amount through the date it becomes wages for FICA and FUTA purposes [Reg. § 31.3121(v)(2)-1(c)(1)]. An account balance plan exists if under the terms of the plan, a principal amount is credited to an individual account for an employee, the income attributable to each principal amount is credited to the account and the benefits payable to the employee are based solely on the balance credited to the individual account.

Example 3-27: ABC establishes a nonqualified deferred compensation plan for an employee. Under the plan, 10 percent of annual compensation is credited on behalf of the employee on December 31 of each year. In addition, a reasonable rate of interest is credited quarterly on the balance credited to the employee as of the last day of the preceding quarter. All amounts credited under the plan are 100 percent vested, and the benefits payable to the employee are based solely on the balance credited to the employee's account.

Result: The plan is an account balance plan. Thus, the amount deferred for a calendar year for FICA and FUTA purposes is equal to 10 percent of annual compensation. Note however, that the interest credited to the employee's account escapes FICA tax under Reg. § 31.3121(v)(2)-1(c) even though the total payout on termination of employment will be includible in the employee's gross income as compensation.

Once an amount has been "taken into account" for FICA purposes, it need not be counted again when the amount is distributed. Also, any earnings attributable to an amount taken into account for FICA purposes need not be counted for FICA purposes on distribution. Thus, if the FICA amount (which is often only the Medicare portion, because many taxpayers receiving nonqualified deferred compensation are above the OASDI Social Security limit) has been timely taken into account, no FICA taxes will be due on the distribution.

Employers have some degree of latitude in determining when to pay FICA taxes on deferred compensation. For example, for purposes of calculating the present value of a benefit earned in a given year, employers are allowed to determine present value using any reasonable actuarial assumptions and methods. In some cases, uncertainties pertaining to future benefits make it difficult to determine the present value of a benefit (for example, where a benefit can fluctuate depending on the varying amount of a qualified plan benefit). In such cases, the present value of the benefit need not be included in FICA wages until it becomes reasonably ascertainable.

▶ **PRACTICE TIP:** If you have paid FICA in earlier tax years based on unfavorable formulas, you should recompute how much FICA tax you owe under the reasonably ascertainable rule in the regulations. You may be able to file a refund claim for FICA tax paid in previous tax years.

Employers are also permitted to delay the inclusion of any deferred compensation in wages until the end of the year. In addition, where amounts deferred cannot be readily calculated by year-end, the employer may either estimate the amounts (and make later adjustments without interest or penalties) or postpone the inclusion in wages until the first quarter of the following year.

To prevent double taxation of deferred compensation, a special exclusion called the nonduplication rule exists. According to this rule, a benefit that was subject to FICA tax at an earlier date when the benefit was earned will not be subject to tax again when the employee actually receives the benefit.

Example 3-28: On December 15, 2013, ABC, Inc. tells its employee that, if specified goals are satisfied for 2014, he will receive a bonus on July 1, 2014, equal to a specified percentage of 2014 compensation. Because the employee meets the specified goals, ABC pays the bonus to him on July 1, 2015, consistent with the oral commitment.

Result: This arrangement is not a nonqualified deferred compensation plan for FICA and FUTA purposes because its terms were not set forth in writing and, therefore, it was not legally binding. However, the amount received as a bonus in 2008 will be subject to FICA and FUTA taxes.

Example 3-29: ABC from the example above establishes a plan under which bonuses based on performance in one year may be paid on February 1 of the following year at the discretion of the board of directors. The board of directors meets in January of each year to determine the amount, if any, of the bonuses to be paid based on performance in the prior year.

Result: Because the employee does not have a legally binding right to a bonus until January of the year in which the bonus is paid, any bonus paid under the plan in that year will not be considered deferred from the preceding calendar year and the plan will not be treated as providing for the deferral of compensation for FICA and FUTA purposes as required in Reg. § 31.3121(v)(2)-1(b)(3). However, the bonuses paid on February 1 will be subject to FICA and FUTA taxes.

.05 Employee Tax Consequences

Inclusion of Deferred Amounts in Employee's Gross Income

Under Code Sec. 409A(a)(1)(A), all amounts deferred under a nonqualified deferred compensation plan for all tax years must be included in the employee's gross income to the extent not subject to a "substantial risk of forfeiture" and not previously included in gross income if the nonqualified deferred compensation plan does not satisfy the distribution, acceleration of benefits, and election requirements of Code Sec. 409A(a)(2), (3), and (4) or is not operated in accordance with those requirements. If a taxpayer is required to include these amounts in gross income, the taxpayer's tax for the tax year will be increased by an amount equal to 20 percent of the amount required to be included in gross income plus interest at the underpayment rate plus one percentage point on the underpayments that would have occurred if the compensation had been included in income when first deferred, or if later, when not subject to a substantial risk of forfeiture [Code Sec. 409A(a)(1)(B)(i)].

Deferred Compensation from Tax Indifferent Corporations and Partnerships

Any compensation which is deferred under a nonqualified deferred compensation plan of a nonqualified entity is includible in gross income when there is no substantial risk of forfeiture of the rights to such compensation [Code Sec. 457A(a)]. For these purposes, the term "nonqualified entity" means

1. Any foreign corporation unless substantially all of its income is:
   a. Effectively connected with the conduct of a trade or business in the United States, or
   b. Subject to a comprehensive foreign income tax [Code Sec. 457A(b)(1), and
2. Any partnership unless substantially all of its income is allocated to persons other than:
   a. Foreign persons with respect to whom such income is not subject to a comprehensive foreign income tax and
   b. Organizations which are tax-exempt under the Internal Revenue Code [Code Sec. 457A(b)(2)].

The rights of a person to compensation shall be treated as subject to a substantial risk of forfeiture only if the person's rights to such compensation are conditioned upon the future performance of substantial services by any individual [Code Sec. 457A(d)(1)(A)]. Notice 2009-8[92] provides that the rights of a person to compensation (including a stock right) are not subject to a substantial risk of forfeiture merely because those rights are subject to the occurrence of a condition related to a purpose of the compensation, or are conditioned, directly or indirectly, upon the refraining from the performance of services. The addition of any risk of forfeiture after the legally binding right to compensation arises, or any extension of a period during which compensation is subject to a risk of forfeiture is disregarded for purposes of determining whether such compensation is subject to a substantial risk of forfeiture.

Earnings are includible in income when they are no subject to a substantial risk of forfeiture. Amounts included in income are not again taxable when they are paid. If an amount included in income is forfeited before it is paid, the employee is entitled to a loss. Amounts that are not determinable are taxable when the deferred amount becomes determinable. The tax due is increased by 20 percent of the compensation plus the premium interest tax (underpayment plus one percent) on the compensation.[93]

Anti-Abuse Provision

The regulations include an anti-abuse rule to address corporate structures, transactions, or stock right grants that exist principally to avoid the application of Code Sec. 409A to an arrangement otherwise providing deferred compensation [Reg.

[92] Notice 2009-8, IRB 2009-4, 347.

[93] Notice 2009-8, IRB 2009-4, 347.

§ 1.409A-1(b)(5)(iii)(E)]. Abuse occurs where the structure, transaction, or grant is intended to provide enhanced security for the value of the stock right as a means of providing deferred compensation, rather than as compensation related to an increase in the true enterprise value of the service recipient.

Written Plan Requirements

The material terms of the plan must be in writing and must specify:

1. The time an amount is deferred,
2. The amount to which the employee has a right to be paid, and
3. The payment schedule that results in payment of such amount [Reg. § 1.409A-1(c)(3)(i)].
4. The plan must provide that distribution to a specified employee cannot be made before the date that is six months after separation from service or, if earlier, death. The six-month delay rule must be specified in the plan [Reg. § 1.409A-1(c)(3)(v)].

Nonqualified deferred compensation plan defined. A *nonqualified deferred compensation plan* is any plan that provides for the deferral of compensation except the following [Code Sec. 409A(d)(1); Reg. § 1.409A-1(a)(2)]:

- A qualified employer plan including a qualified retirement plan, IRAs, tax-deferred annuity, simplified employee pension, SIMPLE plan, a qualified governmental excess benefit arrangement and a deferred compensation plan is also a qualified employer plan[Code Sec. 409A(d)(2)].
- Code Sec. 457(b) tax-exempt or governmental deferred compensation plans.
- Bona fide vacation leave, sick leave, compensatory time, disability plan, or death benefit plan, or certain medical expense reimbursement arrangements [Code Sec. 409A(d)(1); Reg. § 1.409A-1(a)(4)].
- Statutory stock options which include incentive stock options under Code Sec. 422 and options granted under an employee stock purchase plan (ESPP) under Code Sec. 423. For example, an ESPP that offers a discounted purchase price isn't subject to Code Sec. 409A [Reg. § 1.409A-1(b)(5)(ii)].
- Nondiscounted stock options and stock appreciation rights issued on service recipient (employee) stock that don't include any additional deferral feature. Service recipient stock means a class of common stock that qualifies as common stock under Code Sec. 305. In addition, the stock must not have any preferences as to distributions, other than distributions of service recipient stock and distributions in liquidations [Reg. § 1.409A-1(B)(5)(iii)(A)]. Service recipient stock may include stock of the corporation for which the service provider was providing services at the date of the grant. In addition, it may include stock of any corporation in a chain of organizations all of which have a controlling interest in another organization, beginning with the parent organization and ending with the organization for which the service provider was providing services at the date of the grant of the stock right. The term "controlling interest" means a 50-percent interest unless use of the stock in a stock right is based on legitimate business criteria, in which case only a 20-percent interest is required.

- Amounts deferred under an arrangement between a service provider and an unrelated service provider if during the service provider's tax year in which the service provider obtains a legally binding right to the deferred amount, the service provider (1) is actively engaged in the trade or business of providing services (other than as an employee or as a director of a corporation), and (2) provides significant services to two or more unrelated service recipients [Reg. § 1.409A-1(f)(2)(i)]. A service provider is deemed to be providing significant services to two or more such service recipients for this purpose if the revenues generated from the services provided to any service recipient or group of related service recipients during the tax year do not exceed 70 percent of the total revenues generated by the service provider from the trade or business. The IRS added an additional safe harbor that provides that a service provider that has actually met the 70-percent threshold in the three immediately previous years is deemed to meet the 70-percent threshold for the current year, but only if, at the time the amount is deferred, the service provider does not know or have reason to anticipate that the service provider will fail to meet the threshold in the current year [Reg. § 1.409A-1(f)(2)(iii)].
- Non-U.S. citizens who are not lawful permanent residents of the United States, amounts deferred under certain broad-based foreign retirement plans. The exclusion covers participation by a U.S. citizen or lawful permanent resident who works overseas during only part of a year, and, therefore, is not a bona fide resident of a foreign country for an uninterrupted period that includes an entire tax year, or is not present in the foreign country at least 330 days during a period of 12 consecutive months.
- Tax equalization arrangements that provide for payments intended to compensate the service provider for the excess of taxes actually imposed by a foreign jurisdiction on the compensation paid over the taxes that would be imposed if the compensation were subject solely to U.S. federal income tax are not subject to Code Sec. 409A. This exclusion applies to reimbursements of U.S. taxes that exceed foreign taxes, and by providing that the payment must be made by the end of the second tax year of the service provider following the latest filing deadline for a U.S. federal tax return or the deadline for filing foreign tax returns reflecting the compensation for which the tax equalization is provided.
- Payment for a noncompetition agreement because such a payment occurs in connection with the performance or nonperformance of services and a covenant not to compete does not create a substantial risk of forfeiture for Code Sec. 409A purposes. However, a legally binding right obtained in one year to a payment in a later year in connection with a noncompetition agreement generally constitutes deferred compensation [Reg. § 1.409A-1(d)].
- Nonqualified employer stock options with an exercise price that is not less than the fair market value of the underlying stock on the date of grant if the arrangement does not include a deferral feature other than the feature that the option holder has the right to exercise the option in the future;
- Employee stock purchase plans; and
- Amounts paid within 2½ months after the end of the tax year in which vesting occurs, using the later of the plan sponsor's tax year or the participant's tax year.

Permissible Distributions

To avoid immediate inclusion in income, distributions from a nonqualified deferred compensation plan may only be made on one of six specified events as follows: separation from service, death, a time specified by the plan, change in control of a corporation, occurrence of an unforeseeable emergency, or the disability of a participant [Code Sec. 409A(a)(2)(A)(i)-(vi); Reg. §1.409A-3(a)]. A nonqualified deferred compensation plan may not allow distributions other than upon the permissible distribution events and may not permit acceleration of a distribution.

- *Separation from service.* In the case of key employees of publicly traded corporations who separate from service, distributions may not be made earlier than six months after the date of the separation from service or upon death [Code Sec. 409A(a)(2)(B)(i); Reg. §1.409A-1(h)(i)].
- *Payments at specified time.* Amounts payable at a specified time or pursuant to a fixed schedules must be specified under the plan at the time of deferral [Code Sec. 409A(a)(2)(A)(iv)]. Amounts payable upon the occurrence of an event are not treated as amounts payable at a specified time. For example, amounts payable when an individual attains age 65 are payable at a specified time, whereas amounts payable when an individual's child begins college are payable upon the occurrence of an event.
- *Unforeseeable emergency.* An *unforeseeable emergency* is a severe financial hardship to the participant:

  — Resulting from an illness or accident of the participant, the participant's spouse, or a dependent;

  — Loss of the participant's property due to casualty; or

  — Other similar extraordinary and unforeseeable circumstances arising as a result of events beyond the participant's control [Code Sec. 409A(a)(2)(B)(ii); Reg. §1.409A-3(i)(3)].

  The amount of the distribution must be limited to the amount needed to satisfy the emergency plus taxes reasonably anticipated as a result of the distribution. Distributions may not be allowed to the extent that the hardship may be relieved through reimbursement or compensation by insurance or otherwise, or by liquidation of the participant's assets (to the extent such liquidation would not itself cause a severe financial hardship).

  In Rev. Rul. 2010-27,[94] the IRS addressed what constitutes an unforeseeable emergency distribution and concluded that the need to repair a principal residence because of significant water damage that is not covered by insurance is an extraordinary and unforeseeable circumstance that arises as a result of events beyond the control of the participant. The IRS also concluded that the need to pay for the funeral expenses of a non-dependent adult son is an extraordinary and unforeseeable circumstance that arises as a result of events beyond the participant's control. Finally, the IRS concluded that the desire to pay accumulated credit card debt, which is not due

---

[94] Rev. Rul. 2010-27, IRB 2010-45, 620.

to any extraordinary and unforeseeable circumstances from events beyond the participant's control do not present facts indicating that an unforeseeable emergency circumstance has arisen as a result of events beyond the control of the participant.

- *Disability.* A participant is considered *disabled* if he or she:
   1. Is unable to engage in any substantial gainful activity by reason of any medically determinable physical or mental impairment which can be expected to result in death or can be expected to last for a continuous period of not less than 12 months; or
   2. Is, by reason of any medically determinable physical or mental impairment which can be expected to result in death or can be expected to last for a continuous period of not less than 12 months, receiving income replacement benefits for a period of not less than three months under an accident and health plan covering employees of the participant's employer [Code Sec. 409A(a)(2)(C); Reg. § 1.409A-3(i)(4)].

Prohibition on acceleration of distributions. No accelerations of distributions may be allowed. In general, changes in the form of distribution that accelerate payments are subject to the rule prohibiting acceleration of distributions. However, the rule against accelerations is not violated merely because a plan provides a choice between cash and taxable property if the timing and amount of income inclusion is the same regardless of the medium of distribution. For example, the choice between a fully taxable annuity contract and a lump-sum payment may be permitted.

Requirements with respect to elections. A plan must provide that compensation for services performed may be deferred at the participant's election only if the election to defer is made no later than the close of the preceding year. Note the absence of a 2½ month rule in this situation. The IRS will not honor elections made in the same year the amounts are earned. In the case of any performance-based compensation based on services performed over a period of at least 12 months, the election may be made no later than six months before the end of the service period. *Performance-based compensation* includes compensation to the extent that its payment or amount is:

- Contingent on the satisfaction of preestablished organizational or individual performance criteria and
- The performance criteria are not substantially certain to be met at the time a deferral election is permitted.

A plan may allow changes in the time and form of distributions. A nonqualified deferred compensation plan may allow a subsequent election to delay the timing or form of distributions only if:

- The plan requires that such election cannot be effective for at least 12 months after the date on which the election is made;
- Except in the case of elections relating to distributions on account of death, disability or unforeseeable emergency, the plan requires that the additional deferral with respect to which such election is made is for a period of not less than five years from the date the payment would otherwise have been made; and

• The plan requires that an election related to a distribution to be made upon a specified time may not be made less than 12 months prior to the date of the first scheduled payment.

Off-shore "rabbi" trusts. Code Sec. 409A(b) also includes provisions designed to curb abuses of off-shore "rabbi" trusts (where creditors are unable to reach assets) and plans with financial health triggers where deferred compensation can be withdrawn when bankruptcy threatens the solvency of the company.

Under the off-shore rabbi trust rules, assets directly or indirectly set aside in a trust for purposes of paying nonqualified deferred compensation are treated as property transferred in connection with the performance of services for Code Sec. 83 purposes (whether or not the assets are available to satisfy the claims of general creditors): (1) at the time set aside if the assets are located outside of the United States or (2) at the time transferred if such assets are subsequently transferred outside of the United States [Code Sec. 409A(b)(1)]. Any subsequent increases in the value of, or any earnings with respect to, such assets are treated as additional transfers of property. Interest at the underpayment rate plus one percentage point is imposed on the underpayments that would have occurred had the amounts set aside been includible in income for the year in which first deferred or, if later, the first tax year not subject to a substantial risk of forfeiture. The amount required to be included in income is also subject to interest and an additional 20-percent tax [Code Sec. 409A(b)(5)].

Employer's financial health triggers. A transfer of property in connection with the performance of services for Code Sec. 83 purposes also occurs with respect to compensation deferred under a nonqualified deferred compensation plan as of: (1) the earlier of the date that the plan first provides that upon a change in the employer's financial health, assets will be restricted to providing benefits under the plan; or (2) the date on which assets are so restricted. [Code Sec. 409A(b)(2)]. An amount is treated as restricted even if the assets are available to satisfy the claims of general creditors. Interest and a 20-percent penalty also apply with regard to these financial trigger rules [Code Sec. 409A(b)(5)].

For example, in the case of a plan providing that upon a change in the employer's financial health, a trust will become funded to the extent of all deferrals, all amounts deferred under the plan are treated as property transferred under Code Sec. 83. If a plan provides that deferrals of individuals will be funded upon a change in financial health, the transfer of property would occur with respect to compensation deferred by such individuals. Any subsequent increases in the value of restricted assets are treated as additional transfers of property. Interest at the underpayment rate plus one percentage point is imposed on the underpayments that would have occurred had the amounts been includible in income when first deferred or, if later, the first year not subject to a substantial risk of forfeiture. The amount required to be included in income is also subject to an additional 20-percent tax.

Other rules. Interest imposed under the new law is treated as interest on an underpayment of tax. Income (whether actual or notional) attributable to nonqualified deferred compensation is treated as additional deferred compensation.

Aggregation rules. Employer aggregation rules apply in the case of separation from service so that the separation from service from one entity within a controlled group, but continued service for another entity within the group, would not be a permissible distribution event. Aggregation rules do not apply in the case of change in control so that the change in control of one member of a controlled group would not be a permissible distribution event for participants of a deferred compensation plan of another member of the group.

Reporting requirements. Amounts included in income are subject to reporting and federal income tax withholding requirements and must be reported on an individual's Form W-2 (or Form 1099) for the year of inclusion. Annual reporting to the IRS of amounts deferred is also required. These amounts must be reported on an individual's Form W-2 (or Form 1099) for the year deferred even if the amount is not includible in income that year.

Inclusion in FICA wage base. Under Code Sec. 3121(v)(2)(A), nonqualified deferred compensation is included in the employee's FICA wage base at the later of:

1. When the services are performed and the contribution is earned, or
2. When there is no substantial risk of forfeiture of the employee's right to the deferred amount [Ch. 15].

A deferred compensation plan will not be subject to a *substantial risk of forfeiture* and, thus will be included in the employee's FICA wage base, when the employee can take the money out of the account with no strings attached. In other words the money is his without the need to prove that he or she is performing substantial services for the employer. How do you know if an employee is performing substantial services? Look at how regularly he performs the services and how much time he spends performing them. If the numbers are high, the services probably are substantial. If the employee can decide not to perform the services without losing any rights to the retirement savings, the services are probably insubstantial.

Employees need not include deferred compensation in income until they actually or constructively receive the money. When their rights are substantially vested, either transferable or not subject to a substantial risk of forfeiture,[95] then they must include the compensation in income [Ch. 2] [Code Sec. 83; Reg. § 1.83-3(b)]. Deferred compensation plans are generally designed to shift the employee's income, and accompanying tax burden, into future retirement years, when the employee's income tax bracket may be lower.

Death Payments

Payments made under a nonqualified deferred compensation plan in the event of death are death payments not subject to FICA taxes to the extent the total benefits payable under the plan exceed the lifetime benefits payable under the plan. This excess is calculated by taking the present value of all benefits under the plan (other than disability payments) less the present value of the benefits payable to an employee, using the largest present value of the available options. A similar rule applies to disability benefits.

---

[95] Rev. Rul. 60-31, 1960-1 CB 174, as modified by Rev. Rul. 64-279, 1964-2 CB 121, and Rev. Rul. 70-435, 1970-2 CB 100.

Restrictions on Funding of Nonqualified Deferred Compensation Plans

Code Sec. 409A(b) (3) provides that during any *restricted period* with respect to a single-employer defined benefit plan, if assets are set aside or reserved in a trust in order to pay deferred compensation of an *applicable covered employee* under a nonqualified deferred compensation plan, then those assets will be treated as property transferred in connection with the performance of services for purposes of Code Sec. 83. This rule applies whether or not such assets are available to satisfy claims of general creditors. Note that this rule does not apply to any assets that are set aside before the restricted period with respect to the defined benefit plan.

A similar rule applies to a nonqualified deferred compensation plan of the plan sponsor providing that assets will be restricted to the provision of benefits under the plan in connection with a restricted period of any defined benefit plan of the employer, then such assets will be treated as property transferred in connection with the performance of services for purposes of Code Sec. 83 (whether or not such assets are available to satisfy claims of general creditors) [Code Sec. 409A(3) (A) (ii)].

A *restricted period* with respect to a single-employer defined benefit plan is: (1) any period during which the plan is in at-risk status as defined in Code Sec. 430(i); (2) any period that the plan sponsor is in bankruptcy; and (3) in the case of a plan that terminates, the 12-month period beginning on the date which is six months before the termination date of the defined benefit pension plan if, as of the termination date, the plan is not sufficient for benefit liabilities.

Special rule for payment of taxes on deferred compensation included in income. If an employer provides for the payment of any federal, state, or local income taxes with respect to any compensation required to be included in gross income, (1) interest and additional tax under Code Sec. 409A(a) (1) (B) (i) (I) and will be imposed on the amount of such payment in the same manner as if such payment was part of the deferred compensation to which it relates and (2) no deduction will be allowed with respect to such payment.

Covered employees include a corporation's chief executive officer (or an individual acting in such capacity) as of the close of the tax year, the four highest compensated officers for the tax year (other than its chief executive officer), or an individual subject to Section 16(a) of the Securities Exchange Act of 1934. An applicable covered employee means any (1) covered employee of the plan sponsor, (2) covered employee of a member of a controlled group which includes the plan sponsor, and (3) former employee who was a covered employee at the time of termination of employment with the plan sponsor or a member of the controlled group which includes the plan sponsor [Code Sec. 409A(b) (3) (D)].

Amounts included in income, additional tax, and interest. If the funding restriction applies, the assets are treated as property transferred for the performance of services under Code Sec. 83. In general, under Code Sec. 83, an employee is taxed on compensation at the time of the transfer (i.e., the fair market vale of the property less the amount paid). The amount will be taxed later, if there is a substantial risk of forfeiture on the property. If the funding restriction applies, for each year the assets remain set aside, any increase in the value of, or earnings on, the assets will be treated as an additional transfer of property [Code Sec. 409A(b) (4)]. Additionally, the tax on any amount required to be included in income is increased for interest, and by an amount equal to 20 percent of the amount to be included. The interest is the amount of interest at the underpayment rate, plus one percentage point on underpayments that would have occurred had the amount been includible in gross income for the tax year in which it was first deferred, or if later, the first tax year in which the amount was not subject to a substantial risk of forfeiture [Code Sec. 409A(b) (5)].

.06 Rabbi Trusts

Frequently, employees want the security of knowing that the promised deferred compensation will actually be there upon their retirement. This can be especially important when they are concerned about the whims of changing management or changes in corporate structure, particularly in this era of corporate takeovers. One popular vehicle for greater security in deferred compensation is the *rabbi trust*, so named because the first IRS ruling that approved the arrangement involved a rabbi.[96] The employer deducts contributions to the trust only when the payments are made to the employee.

Under a rabbi trust, which is irrevocable, funds for the employee's benefit can be placed in trust and the employee's control of the funds is subject to substantial limitations. The employee will not be in constructive receipt of the funds, just because the trust has been set up, provided: (1) the company remains the owner of the funds, and all deductions and income are reported on the company's tax return, and (2) the assets of the trust are available to the employer's general creditors, in the event of the employer's insolvency or bankruptcy.

The IRS has released a rabbi trust model for guidance when drafting rabbi trusts.[97]

¶3175 SIMPLE RETIREMENT PLANS FOR SMALL BUSINESS OWNERS

Small business owners may establish a Savings Incentive Match Plan for Employees (SIMPLE) retirement plan for their employees. The idea behind these plans is to provide an opportunity for all businesses, large and small, to have the opportunity to provide pensions for their employees. Previously, the tax laws governing qualification of pension and profit sharing plans were so complex that many small business owners were discouraged from establishing much-needed qualified retirement plans for their employees.

.01 What Is a SIMPLE Plan?

A SIMPLE plan an elective salary-reduction arrangement established under Code Sec. 408(p) that provides a simplified tax-favored retirement plan for small employers. If an employer establishes a SIMPLE plan, each employee may choose whether to have the employer make salary-reduction contributions of up to $12,000 in 2013 (no change in 2014) (if under age 50) under the SIMPLE plan or to receive these payments directly in

---

[96] LTR 8113107 (Dec. 31, 1980).

[97] Rev. Proc. 92-64, 1992-2 CB 422, modified by Notice 2000-56, 2000-2 CB 393.

cash. An employer that chooses to establish a SIMPLE plan must make either matching contributions or nonelective contributions. A SIMPLE plan can be established as either a SIMPLE IRA or a SIMPLE 401(k) plan. Salary-reduction contributions will not be reported as compensation on the employee's W-2 and are not subject to Federal income tax withholding. They are, however, subject to FICA withholding for Social Security and Medicare tax [Code Sec. 408(p)(2)].

.02 Catch-Up Contributions

Participants age 50 by the end of 2013 may make an additional catch-up contributions in the amount of $2,500 (no change in 2014) to SIMPLE plans for that tax year [Code Sec. 414(v)(5)]. An employer isn't required to provide for catch-up contributions in any of its plans [Reg. § 1.414(v)-1(a)(1)]. However, if any plan of an employer provides for catch-up contributions, all of its plans that provide for elective deferrals must comply with the universal availability requirement. The maximum additional contribution is the lesser of (1) a set dollar amount for the year, or (2) the participant's compensation for the year reduced by any other elective deferrals for the year.

Catch-up contributions will not be taken into account in applying the regular contribution limits. In addition, catch-up contributions will not be subject to the nondiscrimination rules. However, a plan will fail to meet the nondiscrimination requirements unless it allows all eligible participants to make catch-up contributions.

.03 Plan Eligibility

SIMPLE plans can be established by any small business owner who meets the following requirements:

- Employs 100 or fewer employees earning at least $5,000 in compensation for the preceding year [Code Sec. 408(p)(2)(C)(i)(I)], and
- Provides no other qualified retirement plan (including a SEP-IRA) to which contributions are made, or benefits are accrued for service in the calendar year that the SIMPLE plan is maintained.

Requirements

The 100-employee limitation. For purposes of the 100 employee limitation, all employees employed at any time during the calendar year are taken into account, regardless of whether they are eligible to participate in the SIMPLE plan. As a result, union employees who are excludable because they are included in a collective bargaining agreement [Code Sec. 410(b)(3)] or employees who fail to met the plan's minimum eligibility requirements because they are nonresident aliens who have no U.S.-source earned income that must be taken into account [Code Sec. 410 (b)(3)]. The term "employees" also includes self-employed individuals who received earned income from the employer during the year, and leased employees who are treated as employed by the employer [Code Sec. 414(n)(3)(B)].

Employers that later exceed 100-employee limitation. If an employer who initially meets the 100-employee limitation sets up a SIMPLE plan, and later grows to the point where it exceeds the permissible size, it may continue to maintain the SIMPLE plan for the two calendar years following the calendar year for which it last satisfied the 100-employee limit [Code Sec. 408(p)(2)(C)(i)(II)].

Eligibility determined on a calendar year basis. Whether an employer is eligible to establish a SIMPLE plan is determined on a calendar year basis. This means that the IRS will look at whether or not a business owner employed 100 or fewer employees during an entire calendar year. If the employer exceeds the 100-employee limitation at any time during the year, it has failed the 100-employee limitation for the entire year.

Employer aggregation rules. Simple plans may be established only by employers that had no more than 100 employees who received $5,000 or more in compensation during the preceding calendar year. For purposes of applying these and other SIMPLE rules under Code Sec. 408(p), related employers (trade or businesses under common control) are treated as a single employer. These employers include controlled groups of corporations under Code Sec. 414(b).

> **Example 3-30:** You own ABC, a computer rental agency, that has 80 employees who received more than $5,000 in compensation. You also own XYZ, which repairs computers and has 60 employees who received more than $5,000 in compensation. You are the sole proprietor of both businesses. Code Sec. 414(c) provides that the employees of partnerships and sole proprietorships that are under common control are treated as employees of a single employer. Thus, for purposes of the SIMPLE plan rules, all 140 employees are treated as employed by you. Therefore, neither ABC nor XYZ is eligible to establish a SIMPLE plan.[98]

Employees eligible to participate. All employees who received at least $5,000 in compensation from the employer during any 2 preceding calendar years (whether or not consecutive) and who are reasonably expected to receive at least $5,000 in compensation during the calendar year, must be eligible to participate in the SIMPLE plan that year.[99]

When to Establish the Plan

An existing employer may establish a SIMPLE IRA plan effective on any date between January 1 and October 1 of the year, provided that the employer (or any predecessor employer) did not previously maintain a SIMPLE plan. This requirement does not apply to a new employer who comes into existence after October 1 of the year the SIMPLE plan is established if the employer establishes the SIMPLE plan as soon as administratively feasible after the business is established.[100]

.04 Which Employees Can Be Excluded

An employer has the option to exclude from eligibility the following employees: (1) employees who are included in a unit of employees covered by an agreement that the Secretary of Labor finds to be collective bargaining agreement between employee representatives and one or more employers, if there is evidence that retirement benefits were the subject of good faith bargaining between the employee representatives and the employer; (2) employees who are nonresident aliens and who received no earned income (within the meaning of Code Sec. 911(d)(2)) from the employer that constitutes

[98] Notice 98-4, 1998-1 CB 269.

[99] Notice 98-4, 1998-1 CB 269.

[100] Notice 98-4, 1998-1 CB 269.

income from sources within the United States (within the meaning of Code Sec. 861(a)(3)) [Code Sec. 410(b)(3)].

A salary reduction arrangement may be qualified under the SIMPLE plan rules despite the existence of an employer's qualified plan for which contributions are made or benefits accrued if: (1) the employees eligible to participate in that qualified plan are covered by a collective bargaining agreement for which retirement benefits were the subject of good faith bargaining and (2) the only individuals who are eligible to participate in the salary reduction arrangement are those employees who are not covered by a collective bargaining agreement for which retirement benefits were the subject of good faith bargaining [Code Sec. 408(p)(2)(D)(i)]. In other words, employees in the collective bargaining unit who are not covered under the collectively bargained plan are not eligible to participate in the SIMPLE plan.

Participation and Contributions

Participation in multiple plans. An employee may participate in a SIMPLE plan even if he also participates in another employer's plan for the same year, but his salary reduction contributions for the year are subject to the aggregate Code Sec. 402(g) limit on exclusion for elective deferrals, which is $17,500 for 2013 (no change in 2014). Similarly, an employee who participates in a SIMPLE plan and an Code Sec. 457(b) deferred compensation plan is subject to the Code Sec. 457(c) overall limit of $17,500 in 2013 (no change in 2014). Employers are not, however, responsible for monitoring compliance with either of these limits.

Timing of employee elections. Eligible employees must be given the right to elect to participate in a SIMPLE plan during the 60-day period immediately preceding January 1 of the year (i.e., November 2 to December 31 of the preceding calendar year). However, for the first year an employee becomes eligible to make salary reduction contributions, the election can be made during the 60-day period that includes either the date he becomes eligible or the day before that date.

Contribution guidelines. Contributions to a SIMPLE plan must be made under a *qualified salary reduction arrangement* [Code Sec. 408(p)(2)(A)]. This is a written arrangement under which:

1. Eligible employees must have the right to make salary reduction contributions of up to $12,000 in 2013 (no change in 2014) in lieu of receiving cash wages, which the employer must contribute to the SIMPLE account on the electing employee's behalf. The $12,000 employee deferral may be matched by the employer, resulting in a maximum deferral to the SIMPLE IRA of $24,000; and
2. The employer must either:
    a. Match each participant's contributions on a dollar-for-dollar basis up to a maximum of between 1 percent and 3 percent of the employee's compensation up to $12,000 in 2013 (no change in 2014) [Code Sec. 408(p)(2)(A)(III)], (Note: The 1 percent matching is only available for SIMPLE IRA plans. It is not available for SIMPLE 401(k) plans.) or
    b. Make annual nonelective contributions equal to 2 percent of each eligible employee's compensation regardless of whether the employee contributes to

the plan or not. The compensation on which the 2 percent nonelective contributions are made may not exceed the annual limit on compensation under Code Sec. 401(a)(17) in effect for the year [Code Sec. 408(p)(2)(B)(ii]. The compensation limit for 2013 is $255,000 (increasing to $260,000 in 2014). As a result, the maximum nonelective contribution that can be made in 2013 is $5,100 ($255,000 × 2 percent). The maximum nonelective contribution that can be made in 2014 will increase to $5,200 ($260,000 × 2 percent).

Any matching contribution made to a SIMPLE IRA on behalf of a self-employed individual is not treated as an elective employer contribution [Code Sec. 408(p)(8)].

Dollar limitations. Employee contributions must be expressed as a percentage of the employee's compensation and cannot exceed $12,000 in 2013 (no change in 2014) [Code Sec. 408 (p)(2)(E)].

How much can the employee contribute? A SIMPLE plan participant may elect to have the employer make up to $12,000 of *salary reduction contributions* per calendar year instead of receiving the compensation as cash wages [Code Sec. 408(p)(2)(A)(i)]. The amount of salary reduction contributions may be expressed as a percentage of compensation or if the employer permits, as a specific dollar amount. The amount of SIMPLE plan contributions is determined on a calendar year basis. An employer may not place any restrictions on the amount of an employee's salary reduction contributions, such as by limiting the contribution percentage, except to the extent needed to comply with the annual limit on salary reduction contributions.

Employee access to funds. If an employer establishes a SIMPLE IRA, employees can withdraw from the plan at any time. If the employee is under age 59½, however, the withdrawals will be subject to a 25 percent penalty if taken within a two-year period beginning on the date the employee first participated in the plan. A 10 percent penalty may apply after the two-year time period has expired.

Plan Options

There are two types of SIMPLE plans. You can either establish your SIMPLE plan as a SIMPLE IRA or as a SIMPLE 401(k).

SIMPLE 401(k) guidelines. A SIMPLE 401(k) plan will be treated as meeting the nondiscrimination tests that apply to employee elective deferrals if: (1) the employer makes required SIMPLE contributions; (2) no contributions other than SIMPLE retirement plan contributions are made, or benefits accrued, for services during the year under any qualified plan of the employer, for an employee eligible to participate in the SIMPLE 401(k) plan; and (3) contributions are immediately 100 percent vested [Code Sec. 401(k)(11)(A)].

Tax strategy. Should you set up a SIMPLE-IRA or SIMPLE-401(k)? If you are debating whether to establish a SIMPLE IRA or a SIMPLE 401(k), you should be aware of the following important differences between the two plan types:

- With a SIMPLE 401(k) the employer is not allowed to reduce matching contributions below 3 percent. With a SIMPLE IRA, employers can match as little as 1 percent of each participant's compensation for any two years in a five-year period;

- Withdrawals from a SIMPLE 401(k) plan may be limited to specific hardship situations. With a SIMPLE IRA access to funds is easier. Employees can make withdrawals from the plan at any time. If the employee is below age 59½, however, penalties may apply;
- Loans from a SIMPLE 401(k) plan may be available subject to the limitations that apply to other qualified plan loans. Loans from a SIMPLE IRA plan are unavailable;
- Remember that SIMPLE 401(k) plans are qualified plans which can be costly to maintain. Plan sponsors must write an initial determination letter, which has to be rewritten every time there are changes to the qualified plan rules;
- Simplified reporting requirements apply to SIMPLE IRAs. For example, the employer need not complete any annual tax filings with the SIMPLE IRA;
- SIMPLE IRA plans are not subject to the nondiscrimination rules generally applicable to qualified plans;
- SIMPLE IRA plans can exclude union employees if they participate in a collective bargaining arrangement. SIMPLE 401(k) plans can only exclude union employees if the exclusion complies with the qualified plan nondiscriminatory coverage rules; and
- SIMPLE 401(k) plans are exempt from the top heavy rules applicable to other qualified plans maintained by an employer [¶ 3045].

Who Should Establish a SIMPLE Plan

A SIMPLE plan will be attractive to employers who employ no more than 100 employees and want employees to share the financial responsibility of saving for their own retirement by means of salary reduction contributions. In addition, a SIMPLE plan will be just the thing for employers who want to contribute something financially towards their employees' retirement plan and want to avoid the complex administrative requirements imposed on other types of qualified retirement plans, such as 401(k) plans. A SIMPLE-IRA does not require discrimination testing and is well-suited for businesses such as restaurants, retailers, accounting firms, law firms, and small manufacturing companies.

Calendar year basis. A SIMPLE IRA plan can only be maintained on a calendar year basis.

Tax treatment of contributions by employer. Contributions to a SIMPLE account are deductible by the small business owner in the tax year within which the calendar year for which contributions were made ends [Code Sec. 404(m)(2)(A)].

> **Example 3-31:** An employer's tax years ends on June 30. Contributions under the SIMPLE plan for calendar year 2013 (including contributions made in 2013 before June 30, 2013) are deductible in the tax year ending June 30, 2014.

In the case of matching contributions, the small business owner is allowed a deduction for a year only if the contributions are made by the due date (including extensions) for the small business owner's tax return. The employer's salary reduction contributions to the SIMPLE IRA are subject to FICA, FUTA, and the Railroad Retirement Tax (RRTA) and must be reported on Form W-2. Matching and nonelective contributions made by an employer to a SIMPLE IRA are not subject to FICA, FUTA, or RRTA taxes, and need not be reported on Form W-2.

Tax treatment of contributions by employee. Contributions made by an employee to a SIMPLE IRA plan are excludable from federal income tax and are not subject to income tax withholding.

The SIMPLE IRA

SIMPLE IRAs, like IRAs, are not subject to tax.

Distributions from SIMPLE IRAs. Distributions from the account are taxed under the rules applicable to IRAs [¶ 3120]. Distributions are included in income when withdrawn. However, a special rule applies to a payment or distribution received from a SIMPLE IRA during the two-year period after an individual first participates in a SIMPLE plan. Under this special rule, if the additional income tax on early distributions under Code Sec. 72(t) applies to a distribution within this two-year period, the rate of additional tax is increased from 10 percent to 25 percent. Any rollovers or transfers from a SIMPLE IRA within this two-year period, unless to another SIMPLE IRA are also subject to the 25-percent additional tax on early distributions. Certain distributions are exempt from any additional tax on early distributions and include the following distributions made:

- After the participant is 59½ years old:
- For unreimbursed medical expenses that are more than 10 percent of adjusted gross income [Code Sec. 213(a)];
- In an amount not more than the cost of medical insurance.
- After the participant is disabled:
- In the form of an annuity;
- To pay qualified higher education expenses; and
- To buy, build, or rebuild a first home.

Terminations. If the employer terminates a SIMPLE IRA plan before the two-year period, the 25-percent additional tax on early distributions still applies. Participants who want to avoid this additional tax have the option of: leaving the money in their SIMPLE IRA until the end of the two-year period, or leaving the money in their SIMPLE IRA until they meet an exception to the additional tax. Participants can roll over the balance in their SIMPLE IRA to another SIMPLE IRA, but the 25-percent additional tax on early distributions will still apply for distributions from the new SIMPLE IRA within the original two-year period. After the two-year period has been met, SIMPLE IRA assets can be rolled over or transferred to other types of retirement plans, including Code Sec. 401(k) plans, Code Sec. 403(b) plans, Code Sec. 457(b), and traditional and Roth IRAs without being subject to the 25-percent additional tax on early distributions.

Rollovers. Tax-free rollovers can be made from one SIMPLE account to another. Generally, the same tax rules apply to distributions from a SIMPLE IRA that apply to distributions from a regular IRA. However, during the two-year period after an individual first participates in a SIMPLE plan, distributions from it are treated as tax-free rollovers only if they are paid into another SIMPLE IRA and are completed within a 60-day period. After the expiration of this two-year period, tax-free rollovers can be made to regular IRAs. If an employee is no longer participating in a SIMPLE plan because the employee has terminated his employment and two years have expired since the employee first participated in the SIMPLE plan, the employee's SIMPLE account is treated as an IRA. Early withdrawals from a SIMPLE account generally are subject to the 10 percent penalty applicable to early withdrawals from IRAs [Code Sec. 72(t)(6)].

Timing of employer contributions. Employers must make salary reduction contributions to the financial institutional maintaining the SIMPLE IRA no later than the close of the 30-day period following the last day of the month in which the amounts would otherwise have been payable to the employee in cash. An employer must make its matching and nonelective contributions to the financial institution maintaining the SIMPLE IRA no later than the due date for filing the employer's income tax return, including extensions, for the tax year that includes the last day of the calendar year for which the contributions are made.

.05 Notice and Reporting Requirements

Employers who establish SIMPLE plans are required to inform employees of their rights under the SIMPLE plan immediately before the employee becomes eligible to make the salary reduction election [Code Sec. 408(l)(2)(C)]. Employers who fail to provide employees with the required notice must pay a penalty of $50 for each day on which such failure continues [Code Sec. 6693(c)(1)].

Annual Summary Description

The trustee of a SIMPLE account must, on an annual basis, provide the employer maintaining the plan with a summary description containing the following information:

1. The name and address of the employer and trustee;
2. The requirements for participation eligibility;
3. The benefits provided under the plan;
4. The time and method of making salary reduction elections; and
5. The procedures for, and effect of, withdrawals (including rollovers) from the plan account [Code Sec. 408(l)(2)(B)].

Employees also must be notified of their right to select the financial institution that will serve as the trustee of their SIMPLE plan if the employer doesn't require all contributions to be made to one designated financial institution.

The trustee also has the responsibility of providing an account statement to each individual for whom the SIMPLE account is maintained within 30 days after each calendar year.

This statement must reflect the account balance and account activity during the year. Trustees who fail to provide the summary description, the account statement, or the annual report are subject to a penalty of $50 per day until the reporting failure is corrected [Code Sec. 6693(c)(2)]. The penalty may, however, be waived if the reporting failure is due to reasonable cause [Code Sec. 6693(c)(3)].

Model Forms and Model Amendments

The IRS has released model forms and amendments[101] that make it convenient and inexpensive for employers to establish SIMPLE plans for employees and to comply with IRS reporting requirements.

Form 5305-SIMPLE contains a sample notification, which employers may use to meet SIMPLE plan notice requirements to eligible employees. In addition it contains a model salary reduction agreement. The form must be signed by the employer and the financial institution that will receive the contributions and deposit them into the SIMPLE IRA of each participating employee. The form need not be filed with the IRS. It should be retained by the employer.

Form 5304-SIMPLE (*Savings Incentive Match Plan for Employees of Small Employers (SIMPLE)-Not Subject to the Designated Financial Institution Rules*) provides small employers with an easy way to adopt a SIMPLE Plan by using a model plan document, notification to employees, and salary reduction agreement. It is meant for use by employers who permit plan participants to select the financial institutions when their SIMPLE IRAs are established.

The IRS has released two model SIMPLE IRAs for use by trustees and custodians to hold contributions for employees under SIMPLE plans. The model SIMPLE IRAs are Form 5305-S, *SIMPLE Individual Retirement Trust Account,* and Form 5305-SA, *SIMPLE Individual Retirement Custodial Account.* These forms need not be filed with the IRS.

The IRS has also provided a model amendment that can be used by employers in adopting a SIMPLE 401(k) plan. The model amendment allows plan sponsors to incorporate the SIMPLE provisions in existing plans. The alternative method of satisfying the nondiscrimination tests applicable to the plans under Code Sec. 401(k)(11) and Code Sec. 401(m)(10) is incorporated into the model amendment.

---

[101] Rev. Proc. 97-9, 1997-1 CB 624; IRS News Release, IR-96-55, December 30, 1996.

Employee Fringe Benefits

4

COMPANY CARS AND AIRPLANES

Company cars in general . . . . ¶ 4001
Valuation of personal use . . . . ¶ 4005
Automobile salespersons . . . . ¶ 4010
Company-owned aircraft . . . . ¶ 4015
Frequent flyer miles . . . . ¶ 4020

INSURANCE BENEFITS

Employer-provided accident and health plans . . . . ¶ 4025
Group-term life insurance . . . . ¶ 4030
Split-dollar insurance . . . . ¶ 4035
Long-term care insurance . . . . ¶ 4040

MEALS AND LODGING FURNISHED BY EMPLOYER

Meals and lodging . . . . ¶ 4045
Employer-subsidized cafeterias . . . ¶ 4050

OTHER EMPLOYEE BENEFITS

Education reimbursement . . . . ¶ 4055
Dependent care assistance plans . . . ¶ 4060
Services provided at no additional cost . . . . ¶ 4065
Employee discounts . . . . ¶ 4070
Employee achievement awards . . . ¶ 4075
Athletic facilities . . . . ¶ 4080
Financial counseling . . . . ¶ 4085
Working condition fringe benefits . . . . ¶ 4090
Small fringe benefits . . . . ¶ 4095
Qualified transportation fringe benefits . . . . ¶ 4100
Moving expense fringe . . . . ¶ 4105
Cafeteria employee benefit plans . . . . ¶ 4110
Adoption expense exclusion . . . . . . ¶ 4115
Employer-provided group health plans . . . . ¶ 4120

Businesses frequently provide fringe benefits to their valued employees and corporate executives as a means of rewarding their loyalty, dedication, and hard work. Benefits can range from free employee use of athletic facility skyboxes, entertainment suites, and company-owned aircraft to no-cost or low-cost loans and employer-paid vacations. Most fringe benefits are afforded favored tax treatment, which makes them valuable to companies and employees alike. However, there are often special rules and restrictions that must be met in order to qualify for the tax breaks. The IRS has found that employers may classify a taxable fringe benefit under expense accounts other than compensation, resulting in a failure to subject the fringe benefit to income and employment taxes.

COMPANY CARS AND AIRPLANES

¶4001 COMPANY CARS IN GENERAL

Many employers provide their employees with company-owned cars. If this occurs, the portion of the value of the car use attributable to business-related driving is excludable from the employee's gross income. Only the value of the personal use is taxable compensation to the employee [Reg. § 1.132-5(b)(1)(i)].

Example 4-1: Mr. Blake is provided a company car by XYZ Inc., his employer. The percentage of business use of the car is 80 percent. His taxable compensation on his personal use is 20 percent of his total use. If the total value of the company-provided car is $4,000, then $3,200 (80 percent of $4,000) is excludable from Blake's gross income as a working condition fringe benefit. Only $800 (20 percent) is taxable and included in his gross income.

.01 Records Needed

In order for an allocation to be made between business and personal use of a car, the employee must keep a diary or similar record that has detailed entries for business use (e.g., time, place, mileage, and business purpose of the trip). If the employer is determining the vehicle's nonbusiness use, the employee turns the records over to the employer. In other cases, the employee retains the records. The employee should enter the beginning and ending odometer readings for the period covered by the diary. The difference between total business miles and the sum of all mileage is the employee's personal mileage, which is taxable to him or her. If the employee deducts actual car expenses, the employee must maintain records of out-of-pocket costs (i.e., gas, tolls, parking, etc.) in order to substantiate the deduction.

There is an exception to the recordkeeping rule for certain vehicles that by their very design are not susceptible to personal use. The value of using so-called "qualified" nonpersonal use vehicles (e.g., ambulances, police or fire vehicles, tractors and other special purpose farm vehicles, flatbed trucks, or trucks customized to hold equipment) is excluded from income. Absent adequate records, farming vehicles available for personal use are presumed to be used 75 percent for business; only the remaining 25 percent is deemed as taxable personal use [Reg. § 1.132-5(g)].

.02 100 Percent Personal Use

The employer can choose to treat the car as being used 100 percent for the employee's personal use. The employer does not have the chore of finding out the breakdown (and making an allocation) between business and personal usage. As a result, the employee must report the entire value of the car as compensation [Temp. Reg. § 1.274-6T(c)]. [See Ch. 15 for tax withholding rules.] To avoid paying tax on the business use, the employee claims an offsetting deduction for the value of business mileage.

NOTE: The value of that business use must be deducted as a miscellaneous itemized deduction subject to the 2 percent of adjusted gross income floor [Ch. 9] [Temp. Reg. § 1.162-25T]. Thus, unless the employee has sufficient other miscellaneous expenses, using the 100 percent personal use method will result in a higher income tax bill.

Example 4-2: Mr. Shaul is provided a company car that he uses 75 percent for business. His employer uses the 100 percent personal use method and includes $8,000 in Shaul's gross income. This represents the full value of Shaul's car use. Shaul's adjusted gross income is $75,000. To avoid paying tax on the complete value of the car, Shaul reports a $6,000 expense (75 percent of $8,000) for the business use on Form 2106. However, he actually deducts only $4,500 of this because of the 2 percent floor (assuming Shaul has no other deductible miscellaneous expenses).

.03 Chauffeur Services

If the employer provides a car and driver for the employee's personal use, the amount excludable as a working condition fringe is the amount that would be allowable as a deduction under Code Sec. 162 or 167 if the employee paid for the chauffeur services. The working condition fringe with respect to a chauffeur is determined separately from the working condition fringe with respect to the vehicle. An employee may exclude from gross income the excess of the value of the chauffeur services over the value of the chauffeur services for personal purposes (such as commuting) as determined under Reg. § 1.61-21(b)(5) [Reg. § 1.132-5(b)(3)(i)]. The fair market value of the chauffeur services is the amount an individual would have to pay to obtain comparable chauffeur services in the same geographic area during the same period of time [Reg. § 1.61-21(b)(5)].

When determining whether miles placed on the vehicle are for the employer's business, miles placed on the vehicle by a chauffeur between the chauffeur's residence and the place where the chauffeur picks up (or drops off) the employee are considered to be eligible for the working condition fringe exclusion because they are miles placed on the vehicle for the employer's business [Reg. § 1.132-5(b)(3)(i)].

Example 4-3: Assume that an employer makes available to an employee an automobile and a chauffeur. Assume further that the value of the chauffeur services is $30,000 and that the chauffeur spends 30 percent of each workday driving the employee for personal purposes. There may be excluded from the employee's income 70 percent of $30,000, or $21,000, leaving an income inclusion with respect to the chauffeur services of $9,000 [Reg. § 1.132-5(b)(3)(ii), Ex. 1].

Example 4-4: Assume that the value of the availability of an employer-provided vehicle for a year is $4,850 and that the value of employer-provided chauffeur services with respect to the vehicle for the year is $20,000. Assume further that 40 percent of the miles placed on the vehicle are for the employer's business and that 60 percent are for other purposes. In addition, assume that the chauffeur spends 25 percent of each workday driving the employee for personal purposes (i.e., 2 hours). The value of the chauffeur services includible in the employee's income is 25 percent of $20,000, or $5,000. The excess of $20,000 over $5,000 or $15,000 is excluded from the employee's income as a working condition fringe. The amount excludable as a working condition fringe with respect to the vehicle is 40 percent of $4,850, or $1,940 and the amount includible is $4,850 – $1,940, or $2,910 [Reg. § 1.132-5(b)(3)(ii), Ex. 2].

¶4005 VALUATION OF PERSONAL USE

If an employer provides an employee with a vehicle that is available to the employee for personal use, the value of the personal use must generally be included in the employee's income and wages [Code Sec. 61; Reg. § 1.61-21]. Thus, employers must value an employee's use of a company-owned car, which must be reported on the employee's tax return as compensation. Although the valuation method affects how much the employee owes in taxes, it does not affect the employer's deductions for the car. Employers write off the car's purchase price by means of depreciation deductions.

Personal use of a company car can be valued using one of the following methods:

- Vehicle cents-per-mile valuation rule of Reg. § 1.61-21(e) can be used if the maximum value of the passenger automobile is $16,000 or $17,000 for a truck or van in 2013;[1]
- If the fair market value of the passenger automobile exceeds $16,000 or $17,000 if the vehicle is a truck or van in 2013, the employer may determine the value of the personal use under one of the following methods:
  1. The general valuation rules of Reg. § 1.21-21(b), or
  2. The automobile lease valuation rules of Reg. § 1.61-21(d) or
  3. The commuting valuation rules of Reg. § 1.61-21(f) if additional requirements are satisfied.

.01 Adopting Valuation Method

In general, the employee is locked into the valuation method that is selected by the employer when the car was first made available to the employee for personal use (except that the commuting valuation rule [(d) below] may still be used) [Reg. § 1.61-21(d)(7), (e)(5)]. An employer need not give an employee notice of a special valuation method [Reg. § 1.61-21(c)].

Neither the employee nor the employer can use a special valuation method unless at least one of the following conditions is met:

- The employer reports the benefits as wages within the time (including extensions) for filing returns for the tax year you received the benefit.
- The employee includes the benefit in income within the time (including extensions) for filing returns for the tax year that the employee received the benefit;
- The employee is not a "control" employee. A "control employee" of a nongovernmental employer is an employee who is a director of the employer, an owner of a 1 percent or greater equity, capital, or profits interest in the employer, an officer

[1] Notice 2013-27, IRB 2013-18, 985.

earning more than $100,000 in 2013, or an employee earning more than $205,000 in 2013.[2] Instead of applying this definition, an employer may treat all, and only, employees who are "highly compensated" employees (as defined by Reg. § 1.132-8(f)) as control employees [Reg. § 1.61-21(f)(5)].

- The employer makes a good faith effort to report the benefit correctly [Reg. § 1.61-21(c)(3)(ii)].

NOTE: As a general rule, the employee must value the car use on his or her tax return by using either (1) the same valuation method as the employer has used or (2) the fair market value approach (even if your employer has used a different method). However, the employee can take advantage of a special valuation method that the employer does not use, if the employer fails to report the benefit on the employee's W-2 [Reg. § 1.61-21(c)].

.02 Fair Market Value Approach

The employee may use the fair market value approach, regardless of which method the employer uses. The starting point with this method is the cost of leasing a similar car on comparable terms, in the same geographic area [Reg. § 1.61-21(b)(4)]. Then that figure is allocated between business and personal use. The personal use portion is included in the employee's gross income.

▶ **TAX STRATEGY:** If the employer gets price quotes from several leasing companies, it can select the lowest rate to figure the value of the fringe benefit. This results in a smaller taxable fringe benefit to employees—without reducing the employer's deduction. Reason: The employer's write-offs are not based on lease costs; they come from depreciation deductions—which are calculated on the employer's basis in the car.

Example 4-5: Ms. Taylor is provided a company car by her employer, ABC Corp., which values the personal use of the vehicle under the fair market value approach. ABC Corp. contacts various leasing companies and determines that it would cost $3,600 to lease a similar car on comparable terms. Taylor's business use of the car is 60 percent of her mileage. As a result, $1,440, which represents her 40 percent personal use of the car, is included in her gross income. ABC's depreciation deduction exceeds $3,600.

.03 IRS Tables

This method is, in essence, a safe-harbor shortcut of the fair market value approach. Instead of obtaining price quotes from leasing companies, your employer can consult an IRS table—contained in Reg. § 1.61-21(d)(2) (and reproduced below)—that lists annual lease values based on the fair market value of the car. This value includes all costs that would be incurred to buy the car in an arm's-length transaction, including sales tax and title fees. The employer may use the IRS table (shown in Table 1) even if it leases the car. Instead of using the actual lease charge, the employer may use the table amount for a car that is worth the manufacturer's suggested retail price less 8 percent, or the car

[2] Notice 2012-67, IRB 2012-50, 671.

value obtained from a nationally recognized pricing source that regularly reports automobile retail values (i.e., a "Blue Book") [Reg. § 1.61-21(d)(5)(ii)(C), (iii)].

NOTE: For employer-leased vehicles, the employer may use the manufacturer's invoice price (including options) plus 4 percent as the fair market value.

▶ **OBSERVATION:** The fair market value being used in the IRS table method is the fair market value for purchasing the car. The fair market value discussed above is what it would cost to lease the car.

When using the IRS tables, the car's fair market value is determined as of the first day the car was made available to any employee for personal use. That value is used for four years. After that, your employer revalues the car and uses the new value for the next four years [Reg. § 1.61-21(d)(2)(iv)].

In calculating the car's fair market value, the employer may exclude the value of a telephone or other specialized equipment in the car that is attributable to the employer's business needs. However, the exclusion is not available if the equipment is used by the employee in a business other than that of his employment by the employer providing the car [Reg. § 1.61-21(d)(5)(iv)].

Table 1. Annual Lease Value Table*

Automobile Fair Market Value (1)		Annual Lease Value (2)
$ 0 to	999	$ 600
1,000 to	1,999	850
2,000 to	2,999	1,100
3,000 to	3,999	1,350
4,000 to	4,999	1,600
5,000 to	5,999	1,850
6,000 to	6,999	2,100
7,000 to	7,999	2,350
8,000 to	8,999	2,600
9,000 to	9,999	2,850
10,000 to	10,999	3,100
11,000 to	11,999	3,350
12,000 to	12,999	3,600
13,000 to	13,999	3,850
14,000 to	14,999	4,100
15,000 to	15,999	4,350
16,000 to	16,999	4,600
17,000 to	17,999	4,850
18,000 to	18,999	5,100
19,000 to	19,999	5,350
20,000 to	20,999	5,600
21,000 to	21,999	5,850
22,000 to	22,999	6,100

Automobile Fair Market Value (1)		Annual Lease Value (2)
23,000 to	23,999	6,350
24,000 to	24,999	6,600
25,000 to	25,999	6,850
26,000 to	27,999	7,250
28,000 to	29,999	7,750
30,000 to	31,999	8,250
32,000 to	33,999	8,750
34,000 to	35,999	9,250
36,000 to	37,999	9,750
38,000 to	39,999	10,250
40,000 to	41,999	10,750
42,000 to	43,999	11,250
44,000 to	45,999	11,750
46,000 to	47,999	12,250
48,000 to	49,999	12,750
50,000 to	51,999	13,250
52,000 to	53,999	13,750
54,000 to	55,999	14,250
56,000 to	57,999	14,750
58,000 to	59,999	15,250

* Treas. Dept., IRS Publication 15-B, "Employer's Tax Guide to Fringe Benefits" (For use in 2013), p. 25.

For vehicles having a fair market value in excess of $59,999, the Annual Lease Value is equal to 25 percent of the automobile's fair market value, plus $500 [Reg. § 1.61-21(d)(2)(iii)].

To compute the amount of the employee's taxable benefit, the employer multiplies the employee's personal use percentage by the appropriate table figure. If the car has just been purchased, the employer can value the car at cost. If a car is being shifted from one employee to another, its fair market value may generally be recomputed as of January 1 of the year of transfer (assuming tax savings is not the primary reason for the transfer). At that time, the employer can use a "Blue Book" value.

▶ **TAX STRATEGY:** Suppose that the employer wants to purchase a car that has a $12,000 selling price. It should try to bargain the dealer down to the next lower thousand dollar bracket (i.e., $11,999). Reason: The car values in the IRS table are organized in thousand dollar increments. And a drop of just a few dollars in the value of a car can reduce an employee's taxable income by several hundred dollars per year.

Example 4-6: Enterprise, Inc. purchased a company car for $12,000 that will be provided to a salesperson. The annual lease value is $3,600. If Enterprise had paid $11,999, the annual lease value would be only $3,350. Assuming that 30 percent of the employee's car use is personal mileage, the employee would have $75 less taxable compensation per year if the company had paid $1 less for the car.

Special Rule for Part-Year Use

The IRS table provides values for a full year's car use. Your employer may prorate these values for a car made available to any employee for less than a full year. There are two proration formulas, depending on whether the car is available for less than 30 days or a greater portion of the year.

- If the car was made available for 30 days or more, the prorated lease value is determined by multiplying the applicable annual lease value by the number of days the car was available divided by 365.
- If the car was made available for less than 30 days, the daily lease value is determined by multiplying the annual lease value by four times the number of days the car was available divided by 365. However, the car may be treated as having been made available for exactly 30 days if doing so would result in a lower valuation [Reg. § 1.61-21(d)(4)].

Example 4-7: A $12,000 car is provided to an employee for 30 days. The $3,600 annual lease value is prorated. Thus, the value of the car's availability to the employee is $296 ($3,600 × 30/365).

Example 4-8: Same facts as Example 4-3, except that the car is made available for only 25 days. The lease value is $986 [$3,600 × (4 × 25)/365]. However, by electing to treat the car as having been made available to the employee for 30 days, the figure can be reduced to $296.

NOTE: The prorated annual lease value cannot be used if the unavailability of the car is solely due to personal reasons of the employee (e.g., the employee is away on vacation) or is designed to reduce taxes [Reg. § 1.61-21(d)(4)(iv)].

Employer-Provided Fuel

The car use values listed in the IRS table do not include fuel. If the fuel is provided by your employer—either at a company-owned gas pump or by means of a reimbursement—the fuel can be valued either at its fair market value or at 5.5 cents per mile for all miles driven by the employee within the United States (and its territories), Canada and Mexico. The value of the fuel must be added to the annual lease value of the car to determine the fair market value of the benefit provided [Reg. § 1.61-21(d)(3)(ii)].

Automobile Value Using Fleet-Average Valuation Rule for Large Car Fleets

An employer with a fleet of 20 or more automobiles providing an automobile for the first time for an employee's personal use for the entire year may determine the value of the personal use by using the fleet-average valuation rule in Reg. § 1.61-21(d)(5)(v) to calculate the annual lease values of the automobiles in the fleet. The fleet-average valuation rule may not be used to determine the annual lease value of any automobile if its fair market value on the date it is first made available exceeds $21,200 for a passenger automobile or $22,300 for a truck or van in 2013.[3]

If all other applicable requirements are met, an employer with a fleet of 20 or more vehicles consisting of passenger automobiles as well as trucks or vans may use the fleet-average valuation rule as long as none exceeds $21,200 for a passenger automobile or $22,300 for a truck or van. If the fair market value of any passenger automobile in the fleet exceeds these amounts, the employer may determine the value of the personal use under the commuting valuation method described in Reg. § 1.61-21(f) or the general valuation rules of Reg. § 1.61-21(b), or may determine the annual lease value of the automobile separately under the automobile lease valuation rule of Reg. § 1.61-21(d)(2).

Valuation under the fleet-average rule. The valuation is determined as follows:

1. Find the fair market value of each car in the fleet as of the date it was made available to employees for personal use.
2. Divide total fair market value of all cars by the number of cars to find the average fair market value for each car in the fleet.
3. Find the fleet average dollar figure in the IRS table of lease values.

The fleet average valuation rule can be applied only to cars that are regularly used for company business. Infrequent use, such as trips to the airport or between the employer's multiple business premises, is not regular use [Reg. § 1.61-21(d)(5)(v)(D), (e)(1)(iv)]. The fleet average must be recomputed every two years. When a new car is added, it is assigned the fleet average then in effect. And when a company's car fleet drops below 20 for more than 50 percent of the days in a year, the company must discontinue using the fleet average valuation rule as of January 1 of that year. In this case, the annual lease value must be determined separately for each remaining automobile in the fleet [Reg. § 1.61-21(d)(5)(v)(B)].

> **NOTE:** Employers need not include all eligible cars in the fleet; instead, employers can use the fleet valuation method for only those qualifying cars they wish. Also, employers can divide their cars up into more than one fleet [Reg. § 1.61-21(d)(5)(v)(C)].

Finally, a company that uses the fleet average valuation rule gets a special break when it comes to valuing gas used for personal driving. If the company reimburses gas costs, or supplies a company credit card, it can (1) establish its average gas cost per mile for the fleet and (2) multiply this average cost by the employee's personal mileage. Average gas cost per mile can be found by averaging per-gallon fuel costs and miles-per-gallon rates of a representative sample of the fleet for a representative period of time (for example, two months). A representative sample is the greater of 10 percent of the number of cars in the fleet, or 20 cars [Reg. § 1.61-21(d)(3)(ii)(D)].

.04 Cents-Per-Mile Valuation Method

An employer providing a passenger automobile for the first time for any employee's personal use may determine the value of the personal use by using the vehicle cents-per mile valuation rule in Reg. § 1.61-21(e) if its fair market value on the date it is first made available does not exceed $16,000 for a passenger automobile or $17,000 for a

[3] Notice 2013-27, IRB 2013-18, 985.

truck or van in 2013.[4] If the fair market value of the passenger automobile exceeds this amount, the employer may determine the value of the personal use under the general valuation rules of Reg. § 1.61-21(b) or under the special valuation rules of Reg. § 1.61-21(d) (automobile lease valuation) or Reg. § 1.61-21(f) (commuting valuation).

The 2013 optional standard mileage rates are used for computing the deductible costs of operating an automobile for business, medical or moving expense purposes and for determining the reimbursed amount of those expenses that is deemed substantiated effective for deductible transportation expenses paid or incurred on or after January 1, 2013. In addition, they are used for mileage allowances or reimbursements paid to, or transportation expenses paid or incurred by, an employee on or after January 1, 2013.

Beginning on January 1, 2013, the standard mileage rates for the use of a car (also vans, pickups or panel trucks) will be:

- 56.5 cents per mile for business miles driven
- 24 cents per mile driven for medical or moving purposes
- 14 cents per mile driven in service of charitable organizations[5]

The standard mileage rate may only be used for employer-provided vehicles that are either (1) regularly used in the employer's business or (2) actually driven primarily by employees at least 10,000 miles during a calendar year [Reg. § 1.61-21(e)(1)(iii)]. The mileage test is met if the vehicle is driven at least 10,000 miles for the year and that use is primarily by employees—even if it is mostly for their personal purposes. If your employer does not own or lease the car for the entire year, the 10,000-mile threshold is reduced proportionately. The employer determines the value of a vehicle provided to an employee for personal use by multiplying the standard mileage rate by the total miles that the employee drives the vehicle for personal purposes. Personal use is any use of the vehicle other than use in the employer's trade or business. The amount must be included in the employee's wages or reimbursed by the employee. There is no limit on the number of miles for which this rate can be used. Whether a vehicle is regularly used in an employer's trade or business is determined on the basis of all facts and circumstances. A vehicle is considered regularly used in an employer's trade or business if at least one of the following safe harbor conditions is met:

- At least 50 percent of the vehicle's total annual mileage is for the employer's trade or business;
- The employer sponsors a commuting pool that generally uses the vehicle each workday to drive at least three employees to and from work; or
- The vehicle is regularly used in the employer's trade or business on the basis of all of the facts and circumstances. Infrequent business use of the vehicle, such as occasional trips to the airport or between the employer's multiple business premises, is not regular use of the vehicle in a trade or business.

If your employer does not supply gas for your personal driving, the mileage allowance is reduced by up to 5.5 cents per mile [Reg. § 1.61-21(e)(3)(ii)].

---

[4] Notice 2013-27, IRB 2013-18, 985.

[5] Notice 2012-72, IRB 2012-50, 673.

The cents-per-mile method is available only for valuing actual personal use. It cannot be used when an employer is treating 100 percent of the car use as personal mileage [¶4001] [Reg. § 1.61-21(e)(4)].

.05 Commuting Use Method

The value of the commuting use of an employer-provided vehicle is $1.50 per one-way commute (i.e., from home to work and from work to home) for each employee who commutes in the vehicle [Reg. § 1.61-21(f)(3)]. Thus, the amount includible for each round-trip commute is $3.00 per employee. This method only can be used if (1) the vehicle is owned or leased by the employer and is provided to the employee for use in connection with the employer's trade or business and is used in the employer's trade or business; (2) the employer has a bona fide noncompensatory business reason that requires the employee to commute to and/or from work in the car (e.g., there is no secure place to park the vehicle overnight near the business premises); (3) the employer has a written policy prohibiting the employee (and anyone whose use would be taxable to the employee) from using the car for other personal use (except *de minimis* use, such as stopping on a personal errand); (4) except for *de minimis* personal use, the employee does not use the vehicle for any personal purpose other than commuting; and (5) the employee is not a "control employee" of the employer. A "control employee" of a non-government employer is a director; an owner of 1 percent or more of the equity, capital, or profit interest in the employer; an employee receiving compensation of at least $205,000; or an officer receiving compensation of at least $100,000 in 2013 (as adjusted for inflation) [Reg. § 1.61-21(f)(5)].[6] Instead of applying this definition, an employer may treat all, and only, employees who are "highly compensated" employees (as defined by Reg. § 1.132-8(f)) as control employees [Reg. § 1.61-21(f)(5)]. A "control employee" of a government employer is any elected official or employee whose compensation equals or exceeds the compensation paid to federal government employees at Executive Level V [Reg. § 1.61-21(f)(6)].

> **Example 4-9:** Mr. Brown is provided a company-owned vehicle for business use only. A written policy exists forbidding any personal use of the vehicle by Brown. Brown is required to commute to and from work in the vehicle, since there is no secure place for overnight parking at the work-site. The employer uses the commuting method. If Brown makes 150 commuting round-trips in the vehicle during the year, he is deemed to have received a $450 (150 days × $3) taxable fringe benefit.

¶4010 AUTOMOBILE SALESPERSONS

If you are a full-time automobile salesperson, special, more liberal exclusion rules apply to your use of a company car. You can exclude the value of your use of a demonstration car in the dealership's geographic sales area. This car must be in the inventory of the car dealership and available for test drives by prospective buyers. Your employer must

---

[6] Notice 2012-67, IRB 2012-50, 671.

prohibit the car's use outside of business hours. For example, the car cannot be driven by your family or used for vacation trips [Code Sec. 132(h)(3); Reg. § 1.132-5(o)].

To qualify for the exclusion, you must (1) be employed by a car dealer, (2) spend your business day on the sales floor selling cars, (3) work full-time (not less than 1,000 hours per year), and (4) derive 25 percent or more of your gross income from the dealership as a direct result of your sales activities [Reg. § 1.132-5(o)(2)].

¶4015 COMPANY-OWNED AIRCRAFT

Employees who travel on a company-owned plane primarily for business purposes, can exclude the entire value of the flight from gross income as a working condition fringe benefit. The exclusion applies even if they combine business and pleasure on the trip—as long as the trip is primarily for business purposes [Reg. § 1.61-21(g)(4)].

Example 4-10: Mr. Lee travels on the company plane from Chicago to Tampa for business reasons. After conducting the business, Lee vacations in Tampa for a couple of days. Result: The round trip flight is tax-free to Lee, despite the vacation, because the trip was made primarily for business purposes.

If, for example, Lee chose to fly on to Palm Beach in the company plane for a vacation before flying back to Chicago, the value of the round-trip between Tampa and Chicago remains a tax-free working condition fringe benefit. However, Lee is taxed on the difference between the (1) value of his total flights (Chicago-Tampa-Palm Beach-Chicago) and (2) the value of the flights he would have taken if the trip was for business only (Chicago-Tampa-Chicago) [Reg. § 1.61-21(g)(4)].

.01 Use of Company Planes by Key Employees for Entertainment

Code Sec. 274(a)(1)(A) bars deductions for entertainment, recreation, or amusement unless the taxpayer can establish that the expense was directly related to or associated with the active conduct of its trade or business. The term "entertainment" for purposes of Code Sec. 274(a)(1)(A) includes amusement or recreation facilities such airplanes, night clubs, cocktail lounges, theaters, country clubs, golf and athletic clubs, sporting events, hunting trips and fishing trips [Reg. § 1.274-2(b)(1)]. Employers who provide the company plane to executives for entertainment are subject to deduction limitations and employees who take advantage of her employer's generosity will be subject to income tax consequences because they are making personal use of a company-owned asset.

.02 Deduction Limitations Imposed on Employers

Under Code Sec. 274(e)(2)(b), an employer's deduction for the cost of providing an aircraft for entertainment use by "specified individuals" (owners and officers) is disallowed, except to the extent that the cost of providing the aircraft is treated as compensation to that individual.

Code Sec. 274(e) was enacted by Congress to close the loophole created by the courts in *Sutherland Lumber-Southwest, Inc.*,[7] where the Court of Appeals of the Eighth Circuit affirmed the Tax Court to conclude that deductions claimed by an employer who provided an aircraft to executives for nonbusiness (e.g., vacation) flights were not limited to the amount of compensation reported to executives who took the flights. Thus, employers could deduct the entire cost of providing the flight, which was often much higher than the amount that the employee took into income, as calculated under the Standard Industry Fare Levels (SIFL) formula outlined in Reg. § 1.61-21(g). Thus, a loophole was created which enabled companies to claim deductions that far exceeded the amount executives were required to include in income. Code Sec. 274(e)(2) limits the amount that a business can deduct when a company officer, director, or more-than-10 percent owner uses the company's aircraft for entertainment travel to the amount that the employee/recipient actually takes into income for use of the aircraft. The amount disallowed is reduced by any amount that the specified individual reimburses the company for the flight.

Specified individuals. The limitation on the deduction of expenses for entertainment use of an aircraft applies to use by a *specified individual,* who is defined as:

1. The direct or indirect beneficial owner of more than 10 percent of any class of any registered equity (other than an exempted security), or would be the owner if the taxpayer were an issuer of equity securities;
2. A director or officer of the issuer of the security, or who is comparable to an officer or director of an issuer of equity securities;
3. A partner that holds more than a 10 percent equity interest in the partnership, or any general partner, officer, or managing partner of a partnership;
4. A director or officer of a tax-exempt entity; and
5. A specified individual of a party related to the taxpayer within the meaning of Code Sec. 267(b) or Code Sec. 707(b) [Reg. § 1.274-9(b)].

Which expenses to allocate. In determining the nondeductible portion of airplane expenses relating to entertainment use by a specified individual, all fixed and variable expenses of maintaining and operating a plane must be taken into account. This includes fuel, take-off, landing and hangar fees, insurance, depreciation or lease payments, pilot salaries and interest on debt secured by or properly allocated to an aircraft [Reg. § 1.274-10(c), (d)]. Expenses allocable to the lease or charter of an aircraft to an unrelated third party in a bona-fide business transaction for adequate and full consideration are not taken into account [Reg. 1.274-10(b)(2)]. A taxpayer may elect to compute depreciation expenses on a straight-line basis for all of the taxpayer's aircraft and all tax years for purposes of calculating expenses subject to disallowance, even if the taxpayer uses another method to compute depreciation for other purposes [Reg. § 1.274-10(d)(3)(i)].

[7] *Sutherland Lumber-Southwest, Inc.*, 114 TC 197 (2000), *aff'd*, CA-8, 2001-2 USTC ¶ 50,503, 255 F3d 495, *acq.* AOD 2002-02 (Feb. 11, 2002).

Method of allocating expenses to flights. Taxpayers can allocate expenses associated with the use of an aircraft to provide entertainment to specified individuals using either the occupied seat hours or occupied seat miles allocation method or the flight-by-flight method. The occupied seat hours or miles method requires multiplying the total expenses for the year by the number of occupied seat hours or occupied seat miles to determine a per seat or per mile rate. Then the rate is applied to the number of hours or miles of entertainment use. The flight-by-flight method allocates expenses to a flight and then to the passengers on the flight according to whether or not the travel was entertainment-related [Reg. § 1.274-10(e)].

Trips involving business and pleasure. Where a specified individual's flight includes a business segment and entertainment segment, the entertainment cost is the excess of the total cost of the flights (by occupied seat hours or miles or the flight-by-flight method) over the cost of the flights that would have been taken without the entertainment segment [Reg. § 1.274-10(e)(2)(iii)].

Business travel not subject to limitation. Business entertainment air travel which is air travel directly related to the active conduct of the taxpayer's trade or business or related to an expense directly preceding or following a substantial and bona fide business discussion and associated with the active conduct of a taxpayer's trade or business is not subject to the Code Sec. 274(e)(2)(B) deduction limitation. In addition, entertainment does not include personal travel that is not for entertainment purposes. For example, travel to attend a family member's funeral is not considered entertainment and would therefore not be subject to the Code Sec. 274(e)(2)(B) deduction limitation [Reg. § 1.274-10(b)(1)].

.03 Value of Employee's Use of Company Plane

As a general rule, a flight's value for income taxes and withholding is the cost of chartering a similar plane for a similar flight. And if more than one employee is on board, the cost of chartering must be allocated among the employees.

> ▶ **SPECIAL VALUATION METHOD:** The government provides a shortcut for determining the value of personal use of a company plane for any flight—domestic or international. The use of this method is optional. Neither employee nor your employer is bound by the valuation method selected by the other. But if this formula is chosen, it must be used to value all flights for the calendar year [Reg. § 1.61-21(g)(5)].

The value of a flight is determined under the base aircraft valuation formula (also known as the "Standard Industry Fare Level" formula (SIFL)) by multiplying the SIFL cents-per-mile rates applicable for the period during which the flight was taken by the appropriate aircraft multiple and then adding the applicable terminal charge. The formula is: Valuation = (Aircraft multiple × SIFL figure) + Terminal charge.

Here's how it works:

Step 1

The starting point is the Standard Industry Fare Level (SIFL) rates revised by the Department of Transportation. These are per-mile rates, which are revised twice during the year and apply retroactively. For 2013, the SIFL rates are:[8]

Period During Which the Flight Is Taken	Terminal Charge	SIFL Mileage Rates
1/1/13 - 6/30/13	$48.54	Up to 500 miles = $.2655 per mile
		501-1500 miles = $.2024 per mile
		Over 1500 miles = $.1946 per mile
7/1/13 - 12/31/13	$48.53	Up to 500 miles = $.2654 per mile
		501-1500 miles = $.2024 per mile
		Over 1500 miles = $.1946 per mile

Step 2

The SIFL figure for the employee's flight is multiplied by an "aircraft multiple"—a percentage that varies depending on the maximum certified takeoff weight of the plane and the employee's position with the company. They are listed in Table 2.

Table 2. Aircraft Charter Rate Values

Maximum Certified Takeoff Weight of the Aircraft	Aircraft Multiple for a Control Employee	Aircraft Multiple for a Noncontrol Employee
6,000 lbs. or less	62.5 percent	15.6 percent
6,001-10,000 lbs.	125 percent	23.4 percent
10,001-25,000 lbs.	300 percent	31.3 percent
25,001 lbs. or more	400 percent	31.3 percent

For the purposes of this rule, a "control employee" of a nongovernmental employer is an employee who is an officer of the employer (limited to the lesser of 10 employees or one percent of all employees); an employee who is among the top one percent most highly paid employees of the employers; an employee who owns a five percent or greater equity, capital, or profits interest in the employer; or a director of the employer. An employee who is a spouse, descendant, ancestor, or sibling of a control employee is deemed to be a control employee as well. Instead of applying this definition, an employer may treat all (and only) employees who are "highly compensated" employees (as defined in Reg. § 1.132-8(f)) as control employees [Reg. § 1.61-21(g)(8)].

Step 3

A terminal charge—$48.54 for the first half of 2013—is added to the result to arrive at the valuation. This value is determined by the Department of Transportation and

[8] Rev. Rul. 2013-8, IRB 2013-15, 763; Rev. Rul. 2013-20, IRB 2013-40.

issued by the IRS.[9] For flights taken during the period from July 1, 2013 through December 31, 2013, the terminal charge is $48.53.[10]

Example 4-11: Mr. Smith is a middle management employee of XYZ, Inc. On February 1, 2013, Smith takes a 2,000 mile round-trip flight on the company's eight-seat plane for personal reasons. The plane has a certified take-off weight of 11,000 pounds. The taxable amount under the formula is $183.90. The calculation is as follows: (.313 × [(500 × .2655) + (1,000 × .2024) + (500 × .1946)]) + $48.54 terminal charge [Reg. § 1.61-21(g)(5)].

▶ **TAX-FREE PERSONAL TRIP:** In general, where 50 percent or more of the aircraft seats are occupied by employees flying primarily for business purposes, other employees (not company directors) may fill the remaining seats tax-free. Your nonemployee spouse and dependent children may also qualify for tax-free trips under this rule. Seats occupied by working members of the flight crew are not counted [Reg. § 1.61.21(g)(12)].

If friends or relatives come along on the flight the value of their flights is taxable to the employee. If control employees take friends or relatives (other than their spouses and dependent children) along on flights where the 50 percent test is met, the value of the friends' or relatives' flight is taxable to the control employee at the lower valuation rates for noncontrol employees [Reg. § 1.61.21(g)(12)(i)(B)(2)].

Example 4-12: Mr. Brown, President of XYZ, takes a 2,000 mile flight on the eight-seat company plane for personal reasons on February 1, 2013. The plane has a certified take-off weight of 11,000 pounds. Two other employees also take the flight for business purposes. Result: Brown owes tax on $1,345.89 (3 × [(500 × .2655) + (1,000 × .2024) + (500 × .1946)]) + $48.54 terminal charge. The aircraft multiple is 300 percent because Brown is a key employee.

Example 4-13: Same facts as in Example 4-12, except four other employees take the trip for business reasons. Result: No tax is owed by Brown. Reason: 50 percent of the plane's seats were used by the employees traveling on business.

¶4020 FREQUENT FLYER MILES

Most major airlines offer frequent flyer miles to frequent travelers who can accumulate miles for each flight taken on a particular airline. Individuals may also earn frequent flyer miles or other promotional benefits when they rent cars, or use a credit card affiliated with one of the airlines. These promotional benefits are often exchanged for benefits such as upgraded seating, free airline tickets, discounted travel, travel-related services, or other services or benefits. A question that has vexed taxpayers for years has been whether the frequent flyer miles or other promotional items that are received as the result of business travel are subject to tax when they are converted to personal use.

---

[9] Rev. Rul. 2013-8, IRB 2013-15, 763.

[10] Rev. Rul. 2013-20, IRB 2013-40.

The IRS has finally made it clear that frequent flyer miles or other in-kind promotional benefits attributable to the taxpayer's business or official travel will not be subject to tax when converted to personal use.[11]

The tax-free rule does not extend to:

- Frequent flyer miles that are converted to cash;
- Compensation that is paid in the form of travel or other promotional benefits; or
- Situations in which overly creative taxpayers dream up schemes to use frequent flyer miles to avoid paying taxes.

INSURANCE BENEFITS

¶4025 EMPLOYER-PROVIDED ACCIDENT AND HEALTH PLANS

Contributions by an employer to accident and health plans to provide coverage for an employee in the event of personal injury or sickness to the employee, the employee's spouse, the employee's dependents, or the employee's children under age 27 are not taxable to the employee [Code Sec. 106(a); Reg. § 1.106-1].[12] Special rules apply to contributions to Archer medical savings accounts (MSAs) and Health Savings Accounts (HSAs) [Code Sec. 106(d)]. For further discussion of Archer MSAs, see ¶ 9120. For further discussion of HSAs, see ¶ 9115.

The exclusion is applicable whether the employer's contribution is made by payment of insurance premiums or by means of a contribution to an independent fund. Moreover, retired as well as active employees are covered. The exclusion will apply if group health and accident insurance or individual insurance is involved. However, if the policy purchased provides other benefits besides health and accident benefits, then only that portion of the employer's contribution allocable to the accident and health benefits is excludable under Code Sec. 106. Employers who provide health insurance to their employees are subject to information reporting rules [¶ 26,135].

The tax treatment of any amounts received from the health insurance coverage depends on who paid for it, the purpose of the insurance payments and whether the insurance plans pass certain nondiscrimination rules [Code Sec. 105(a); Reg. § 1.105-1(a)]. Code Sec. 105 provides that amounts received as reimbursements for medical care are excludable from an employee's gross income [Code Sec. 105(b)]. Similarly, payments for permanent injury or loss of bodily function are excludable from gross income, provided the amount of the payments is determined with reference to the nature of the illness or injury and not determined with reference to the recipient's period of service or wages lost through absence from work [Code Sec. 105(c)].

---

[11] Announcement 2002-18, 2002-1 CB 621.

[12] Notice 2010-38, IRB 2010-20, 682. *See also* IRS News Release, IR-2010-53, April 27, 2010.

By contrast, amounts received by an employee through accident and health insurance that are not reimbursements of medical expenses, but are instead payments for personal injuries or sickness, generally are includible in gross income if the amounts:

1. Are attributable to contributions by the employer that were not includible in the employee's gross income, or
2. Are paid directly by the employer [Code Sec. 104(a)(3)].

.01 Long-Term Disability Benefits

The tax consequences of long-term disability benefits received by an employee depend on whether the contributions are attributable to after-tax employee contributions or before-tax employer contributions with the following result:

- Long-term or short-term disability benefits will be excluded from the employee's gross income under Code Sec. 104(a)(3) if the employee has made an irrevocable election, prior to the beginning of the plan year, to have the coverage paid by the employer on an after-tax basis;
- Long-term or short-term disability benefits will be included in the employee's gross income if the benefits are attributable solely to pre-tax employer contributions.[13]

.02 Nondiscrimination Rules

Whether benefits received under a company health plan are tax-free to all employees depends on how coverage is provided: through an employer-paid policy issued by an insurance company or through an employer's self-insured medical reimbursement plan.

Fully insured plans (e.g., plans issued by insurance companies) are generally not subject to nondiscrimination rules. As a result, there is no prohibition against a company setting up an insured health plan (as opposed to a self-insured plan) that covers executives only. Benefits received under the plan, as well as the insurance premiums the company pays out, are tax-free to covered employees (and their dependents if the company chooses) [Reg. § 1.105-1(d)(1)].

On the other hand, self-insured health plans must pass two nondiscrimination tests [Code Sec. 105(h); Reg. § 1.105-11(c)(2)]:

1. Nondiscriminatory eligibility test. The plan must meet one of three requirements: (a) the plan benefits 70 percent or more of all employees; or (b) 70 percent of all employees are eligible to be covered under the plan and 80 percent of eligible employees actually are covered under the plan; or (c) the classification of which employees benefit under the plan does not discriminate in favor of the highly compensated.
2. Nondiscriminatory benefits test. All benefits provided to highly compensated employees (and their dependents) must be provided to all other participants in the plan. In addition, a plan may not discriminate in favor of the highly compensated in terms of its operation as well as in terms of benefits offered.

---

[13] Rev. Rul. 2004-55, 2004-1 CB 1081.

Highly Compensated Employees

For purposes of these nondiscrimination tests, highly compensated employees are the five highest paid officers, 10 percent shareholders and the top 25 percent highest paid employees.

Effect of Being Discriminatory

The penalty for failing the nondiscrimination tests is that income is imputed to the highly compensated based on the amounts reimbursed by the health plan, to the extent the plan or benefit under the plan is discriminatory [Reg. § 1.105-11(e)].

Example 4-14: XYZ Inc. maintains a self-insured medical reimbursement plan that covers all employees. However, there is a reimbursement cap of $5,000 for Mr. Brown, the owner of XYZ, and $1,000 for each of the other employees. If Brown receives reimbursements for $2,500 of medical expenses, $1,500 ($2,500 minus $1,000) is taxable to him as a discriminatory benefit.

Example 4-15: LMN Inc.'s self-insured plan provides equal medical coverage to each employee. It also provides dental coverage to its president, Ms. Green. Whatever dental reimbursement Green receives is taxable as a discriminatory benefit.

Discrimination Against Individuals Based on Health Status Prohibited

A group health plan may not discriminate in eligibility for coverage, eligibility for continued coverage, or premiums based solely on the following factors relating to the individual seeking coverage or a dependent for whom coverage is sought: (1) health status, (2) medical condition (physical or mental), (3) claims experience, (4) receipt of health care, (5) medical history, (6) genetic information, (7) evidence of insurability (including conditions caused by domestic violence), or (8) disability [Code Sec. 9802(a)].

Employers of more than 50 employees who fail to meet these anti-discrimination rules will be subject to the basic penalty of $100 for each affected individual for every day in the noncompliance period. This period begins on the day the failure first occurs and ends on the date of correction [Code Sec. 4980D]. No tax is imposed, however, where the failure is not discovered in the exercise of reasonable diligence, or if the failure is due to reasonable cause and not willful neglect and the failure is corrected within 30 days after it is discovered or should have been discovered [Code Sec. 4980D(c)(2)].

.03 Employer Pays for Coverage

Employees are not taxed on premiums that an employer pays for their coverage. However, the tax treatment of the plan payouts (i.e., benefit claims) depends on the type of coverage provided by the employer. Employees are taxed on disability benefits that are based on the duration of the employee's absence from work. However, employees are entitled to exclude from gross income accident and health plan reimbursements for their medical expenses and those incurred by a spouse, or dependents. The exclusion does not apply to amounts attributable to medical expenses deducted in any prior tax year [Code Sec. 105(b), (c); Reg. § 1.105-2, -3].

Example 4-16: Northstar Corp. provides accident and health plan coverage for its employees on a nondiscriminatory basis. Mr. Black, an employee, incurs medical expenses for his dependent child and is reimbursed by the plan. The health care reimbursement is excluded from Black's gross income.

Example 4-17: Northstar Corp. has another nondiscriminatory plan that pays employees 60 percent of their salary once they are out of work for over a week because of a disability. Ms. Brown, an employee, misses six weeks of work after hip surgery. The benefits that she receives from the plan are taxable income.

Employees are also entitled to exclude payments from employer-provided plans where they are received on account of permanent loss or loss of the use of a body part or function, or for permanent disfigurement. Loss of use or disfigurement is considered permanent if it is expected to continue throughout the injured person's lifetime. The exclusion is available to the employee, his or her spouse as well as dependents [Code Sec. 105(c)(1); Reg. § 1.105-3]. See Ch. 5.

.04 Employee Pays for Coverage

In some companies, the employer and the employees share the cost of premium payments. If that is your situation and the insurance provides reimbursements for medical bills, the payouts are entirely tax-free to you, even though premium payments are shared. However, if the premiums are for disability income coverage, the portion attributable to your employer's premium payments is a taxable benefit to you. Payments made under a disability plan are allocated in proportion to the premium funding arrangement. Only the amount attributable to employee contributions is tax-free [Code Sec. 105(a); Reg. § 1.105-1(c)].

Example 4-18: Weststar Corp. maintains a plan where the company and the employees split the premium costs on disability income insurance. The company pays two-thirds of the premiums. Employer contributions are not included in the employees' gross income. The employee pays one-third of the cost by means of a payroll deduction from the employee's wages. Colby, an employee, received a payment of $150 on account of a disability that caused him to miss work. Colby excludes $50 (1/3 of the payment) and includes $100 (2/3 of the payment) in gross income.

NOTE: You are treated as having paid for coverage where your employer actually pays the premiums, but the cost is included in your gross income [Code Sec. 105(a); Reg. § 1.105-1(a)].

.05 Continuing Coverage Under COBRA

Employers are required to offer continuing group health and accident coverage to employees who leave the company and to their spouses and dependent children who would lose coverage in the case of divorce or the employee's death [Code Sec. 4980B]. This benefit is often referred to as "COBRA coverage," since the tax rule was originally enacted as part of the Consolidated Omnibus Budget Reconciliation Act of 1985.

An excise tax is imposed if a group health plan fails to satisfy the health care continuation rules. The amount of tax is $100 per day during the noncompliance period for each qualified beneficiary for whom there has been a failure to satisfy the rules (maximum of $200 per family) [Code Sec. 4980B(c)(3)].

The excise tax takes into account:

1. The number of beneficiaries with respect to whom there is a failure,
2. The period of time during a tax year in which the failure occurred,
3. An employer's knowledge of the failure, and
4. Whether the failure is corrected during the tax year [Code Sec. 4980B(b)-(c)].

The noncompliance period generally begins on the date a failure first occurs and ends on the earlier of the date the failure is corrected or the date that is six months after the last date on which the employer could have been required to provide continuation of coverage to the qualified beneficiary (without regard to payment of premiums) [Code Sec. 4980B(b)(2)]. However, inadvertent failure delays the beginning of the period. Also, the tax generally does not apply to failure due to reasonable cause, if corrected within the first 30 days of the noncompliance period [Code Sec. 4980B(c)(2)]. A minimum tax is imposed if a failure is not corrected by the date a notice of examination of income tax liability is sent to the employer and if the failure occurred or continued during the period under examination [Code Sec. 4980B(b)(3)].

The maximum liability is the lesser of (1) 10 percent of the total amount paid or incurred by the employer or predecessor employer (or, in the case of multiemployer plans, by the trust) during the preceding tax year for the employer's group health plans, or (2) $500,000 [Code Sec. 4980B(c)(4)]. However, this limit does not apply to failures attributable to willful neglect. The maximum excise tax for failures due to willful neglect during a tax year by a person other than an employer (or multiemployer plan, in case of coverage under such a plan) is limited to $2 million [Code Sec. 4980B(c)(4)(C)]. The excise tax may be waived, in whole or in part, for failures due to reasonable cause, and not to willful neglect, if payment of the tax would be excessive relative to the failure involved [Code Sec. 4980B(c)(5)].

A group health plan satisfies the health care continuation requirements only if:

1. The coverage of the costs of pediatric vaccines is not reduced below the coverage provided by the plan as of May 1, 1993; and
2. Each qualified beneficiary who would lose coverage under the plan as a result of a qualifying event is entitled to elect, within an election period, continuation coverage under the plan [Code Sec. 4980B(f)(1)].

A "qualified beneficiary" is any individual who is covered under a group health plan on the day before a qualifying event by virtue of being, on that day, a covered employee, the spouse or the dependent child of a covered employee [Reg. § 54.4980B-3, Q&A-1].

A "covered employee" is generally any individual who is or was provided coverage under a group health plan by virtue of the performance of services for the employer maintaining the plan or by virtue of membership in the employee organization maintaining the plan [Reg. § 54.4980B-3, Q&A-2].

The term "qualifying event" means, with respect to a covered employee, any of the following events that would otherwise result in a qualified beneficiary losing coverage:

1. Death of the covered employee;
2. Termination (other than by reason of gross misconduct) or reduction of hours of the covered employee's employment;
3. Divorce or legal separation of the covered employee;
4. The covered employee's becoming entitled to Medicare benefits under title XVIII of the Social Security Act;
5. A dependent child's ceasing to be a dependent under the plan's requirements; and
6. A bankruptcy proceeding in a case under title 11, United States Code, commencing on or after July 1, 1986, with respect to the employer from which the covered employee retired at any time [Code Sec. 4980B(f)(3)].

To "lose coverage" means to cease to be covered under the same terms and conditions as in effect immediately before the qualifying event. Loss of coverage may include increases in premiums or contributions and, in the case of the bankruptcy of the employer, substantial elimination of coverage under the plan [Reg. § 54.4980B-4, Q&A-1]. Apart from facts constituting gross misconduct, the facts surrounding the termination or reduction of the covered employee's hours are irrelevant in determining whether a qualifying event has occurred. Thus, it does not matter whether the employee voluntarily terminated or was discharged [Reg. § 54.4980B-4, Q&A-2].

Change of coverage status is allowed upon the birth or adoption of a child in the same way that such changes are allowed in a group health plan [Code Sec. 4980(g)(1)(A); Code Sec. 9801(f)(2)]. A newborn or adopted child may be covered immediately during a parent's period of continuation coverage.

A "covered employee" includes any individual who is provided coverage under a group health plan by virtue of the performance of service and may include someone who is not in an employer-employee relationship, such as an independent contractor [Code Sec. 4980B(f)(7); Reg. § 54.4980B-3, Q&A-2].

Payment of Premiums

The premium for any period of continuation coverage cannot exceed 102 percent of the applicable premium for that period and may, at the election of the payor, be made in monthly installments [Code Sec. 4980B(f)(2)(C)]. If a qualified beneficiary elects continuation coverage, the plan must permit payment to be made within 45 days of the date of election. A plan may not require payment before 45 days after the day of the original election for continuation coverage [Code Sec. 4980(f)(2)(C)]. A group health plan does not fail to meet the continuation coverage rules solely because the plan provides that (a) the period of extended coverage begins with the date of the coverage loss and (b) the applicable notice period begins with the date of the coverage loss [Code Sec. 4980B(f)(8)].

Notice Requirements

The employer in a multiemployer plan may notify the plan administrator of a qualifying event more than 30 days after the qualifying event, if this longer time period is provided for under the terms of the plan. The plan administrator may notify the qualified beneficiary of his rights more than 14 days after the administrator has been notified of the qualifying event, if this longer time period is provided for in the plan. The requirement that an employer notify the plan administrator of an employee's termination of employment (as a qualifying event) is considered satisfied, for multiemployer plans, if the plan provides that the determination of the occurrence of the qualifying event is to be made by the plan administrator [Code Sec. 4980B(f)(6)]. Covered employees or qualified beneficiaries must notify the plan administrator of a change in marital or dependent status and of a relevant disability.

Penalty for Failure to Notify Health Plan of Cessation of COBRA Premium Assistance Eligibility

An "assistance eligible individual" paying a reduced premium for COBRA continuation coverage is required to provide written notice to the group health plan of eligibility for coverage under another group health plan or Medicare. The notification by the assistance eligible individual must be provided to the group health plan. If an assistance eligible individual fails to provide this notification at the required time and in the required manner, and as a result the individual pays reduced COBRA continuation coverage premiums after the termination of the individual's eligibility for the reduction, a penalty is imposed on the individual equal to 110 percent of the premium reduction after termination of eligibility [Code Sec. 6720C(a)]. There will be no penalty imposed for any failure to notify if it is shown that the failure is due to reasonable cause and not to willful neglect [Code Sec. 6720C(b)].

.06 Renewability Guaranteed in Multiemployer Plans

Employers in a group health plan that is a multiemployer plan (Code Sec. 414(f)) or a multiple employer welfare arrangement cannot be denied coverage except in the following limited situations [Code Sec. 9803]:

1. For nonpayment of contributions;
2. For fraud or intentional misrepresentation;
3. For noncompliance with material plan provisions;
4. In the case where a plan ceases to offer any coverage in the geographical area;
5. In the case of a plan that offers benefits through a network plan, because no covered employee lives in the service area of the network (and the rule is applied uniformly without regard to claims experience of employers or the health status factors of the employers and their dependents); or
6. For failure to meet the terms of a collective bargaining agreement or to renew such agreement or other agreement requiring or authorizing contributions, or for failure to employ employees covered by the agreement [Code Sec. 9803].

¶4030 GROUP-TERM LIFE INSURANCE

Premiums paid by the employer for up to $50,000 of group-term life insurance coverage are not taxable to the employee. [Code Sec. 79(a); see Ch. 2.]. To qualify for this tax break, the group-term insurance plan must meet nondiscrimination rules as discussed below. The cost of coverage exceeding $50,000 provided by one or more employers is taxable to the employee in the tax year in which the premiums are paid. The cost of insurance over $50,000 is taxed to the benefited employees under the so-called Table 1 rates in Reg. § 1.79-3(d)(2). The imputed Table 1 cost is also extended to retired employees. However, if a covered employee is disabled within the meaning of Code Sec. 72(m)(7), it is not imputed to him or her for post-termination coverage under Code Sec. 79(b)(1). The employee cannot escape this taxable income by assigning his or her rights in the policy to someone else.

.01 Requirements

In order for the group-term life insurance to qualify for the income exclusion, the following requirements must be satisfied [Reg. § 1.79-1(a)]:

1. The insurance must provide a general death benefit that is not included in income; and
2. The employer must provide it to a *group of employees.* In general, life insurance is not group-term life insurance unless, at some time during the year, it is provided to at least 10 full-time employees who are members of the group of employees. For purposes of this rule, all life insurance provided under policies carried directly or indirectly by the employer is taken into account in determining the number of employees to whom life insurance is provided [Reg. § 1.79-1(c)].

"Group of Employees" Defined

A *group of employees* is all employees of an employer, or less than all employees if membership in the group is determined solely on the basis of age, marital status, or factors related to employment. Examples of factors related to employment are membership in a union some or all of whose members are employed by the employer, duties performed, compensation received, and length of service. Ordinarily the purchase of something other than group-term life insurance is not a factor related to employment. For example, if an employer provides credit life insurance to all employees who purchase automobiles, these employees are not a group of employees because membership is not determined solely on the basis of age, marital status, or factors related to employment. On the other hand, participation in an employer's pension, profit-sharing, or accident and health plan is considered a factor related to employment even if employees are required to contribute to the cost of the plan. Ownership of stock in the employer corporation is not a factor related to employment. However, participation in an employer's stock bonus plan may be a factor related to employment and a group of employees" may include employees who own stock in the employer corporation [Reg. § 1.79-0].

3. The insurance must provide an amount of insurance to each employee based on a formula that prevents individual selection. This formula must use factors such as the employee's age, years of service, pay, or position.
4. The employer must provide it under a policy carried "directly or indirectly." A life insurance policy is "carried directly or indirectly" by an employer if—
   a. The employer pays any part of the cost of the life insurance directly or through another person; or
   b. The employer or two or more employers arrange for payment of the cost of the life insurance by their employees and charge at least one employee less than the cost of his or her insurance, as determined under Table 1 of Reg.

§ 1.79-3(d)(2), and at least one other employee more than the cost of his or her insurance, determined in the same way [Reg. § 1.79-0].

Employee Defined

An *employee* for purposes of the group-term life insurance exclusion is defined as:

- A person who performs services if his or her relationship to the person for whom services are performed is the legal relationship of employer and employee described in Reg. § 31.3401(c)-1;
- A full-time life insurance salesperson described in Code Sec. 7701(a)(20); or
- A person who formerly performed services as an employee.

  A person who formerly performed services as an employee and currently performs services for the same employer as an independent contractor is considered an employee only with respect to insurance provided because of the person's former services as an employee [Reg. § 1.79-0].

Exception for S corporation shareholders. Do not treat a 2 percent shareholder of an S corporation as an employee of the corporation. An employee is someone who directly or indirectly owns at any time during the year more than 2 percent of the corporation's stock or stock with more than 2 percent of the voting power. The employee determines the value of the group-term life insurance coverage provided by his or her employer in excess of the first $50,000 of coverage by consulting the uniform premium table which is known as *Table 1* and can be found in Reg. § 1.79-3(d)(2). Contributions to the cost of insurance reduce the taxable amount [Code Sec. 79(a)(2); Reg. §§ 1.79-1(d), 1.79-3(e)]. Generally, the same rules that apply to active employees apply to retired employees.

Table 1 provides you with values per month for each $1,000 of face amount of coverage depending on the insured's age. Table 3, which is reproduced below, shows the uniform premium table amounts.

Table 3. Uniform Premiums for $1,000 of Group-Term Life Insurance Protection*

Five-Year Age Bracket	Cost per $1,000 of Protection for One Month
Under 25	$.05
25 to 29	.06
30 to 34	.08
35 to 39	.09
40 to 44	.10
45 to 49	.15
50 to 54	.23
55 to 59	.43
60 to 64	.66
65 to 69	1.27
70 and above	2.06

* Treas. Dept., IRS Publication 15-B, "Employer's Tax Guide to Fringe Benefits" (2013 Ed.), p. 13.

Example 4-19: Mr. Martin, age 62, works for Fair Corporation. He has $100,000 of group-term life insurance. He pays $2 of the cost of each $1,000 of coverage and his employee pays the balance. The cost of insurance over $50,000 in Martin's age bracket is $396 (50 × .66 × 12). Martin is taxed on $196 [$396 minus employee's payment (100 × $2)].

Employer-paid premiums for coverage over $50,000 are not taxable to the employee if the employer is the direct or indirect beneficiary of the policy, or the sole beneficiary is an organization for which a charitable deduction could be taken [Code Sec. 79(b)(2); Reg. § 1.79-2(c)(1)].

With the exception of the first $50,000 of coverage, the value of life insurance paid for by an employer must be reported on the employee's W-2 as taxable income.

Since the IRS tables are unisex, the IRS uses the same valuation tables to value life insurance policies for men and women. As a result, group term life insurance policies beyond the $50,000 level are particularly expensive for women who would have lower premiums with an outside insurance company. For example, a 50-year-old male might pay $1,240 a year for a $500,000 term insurance policy from an insurance company, whereas a female might pay only $1,025 for that same policy.

If an employee wants to opt out of some or all of the group term life insurance offered by his or her employer, the employee should try to convince his or her employer that he wants to be dropped from coverage under the group term policy. Unfortunately, the employer may not want to be bothered with the additional bookkeeping hassles. In addition, the insurer and employer may not want to risk the possibility that someday your survivors will argue that they are entitled to a death benefit even though the employee had requested exemption from the group policy. Another way out is to name a charity the sole beneficiary of the taxable portion of the policy. If this option is chosen, the value of the group term life insurance donated to the charity will not appear on the employee's W-2. In the event the employee is taxed on the charity, he or she would be able to claim a charitable deduction in the amount the IRS tables say the insurance is worth.

.02 Nondiscrimination Rules

Group-term life insurance plans must meet two basic nondiscrimination tests as follows [Code Sec. 79(d); Temp. Reg. § 1.79-4T]:

1. The *participation test.* A group-term life plan must pass any one of four requirements to pass the participation test:

   a. The plan must benefit at least 70 percent of a company's employees; or

   b. At least 85 percent of the plan's participants must not be "key employees" (see definition below); or

   c. The plan must benefit employees who qualify under a set of rules that do not favor key employees. When applying this test do not consider employees who: (1) have not completed 3 years of service; (2) are part time or seasonal employees; (3) are nonresident aliens who receive no U.S. source earned income from the employer; (4) are not included in the plan but are in a unit of employees covered by a collective bargaining agreement, if the benefits provided under the plan were the subject of good-faith bargaining between the employer and employee representatives; or

d. In the case of a plan that is part of a cafeteria plan [¶ 4110], the plan meets the nondiscrimination requirements of Code Sec. 125.

2. The *benefits test.* Benefits available to key employees must be available to all plan participants. However, a plan that offers the same multiple of compensation to key and non-key employees is considered to pass the benefits test (for example, three times annual salary)—even though higher-paid employees get more valuable benefits.

Exception for Key Employees

If the employer's group-term life insurance plan favors *key employees* in either the participation or eligibility tests listed above, the employer must include the entire cost of the insurance in the key employee's wages subject to social security and Medicare taxes. The entire cost of the insurance must also be included in the employee's wages shown in boxes 1, 3, and 5 of Form W-2. The employer may, however, exclude the cost of the insurance from the employee's wages subject to federal income tax withholding and federal unemployment tax.

Key employee defined. A *key employee* is an employee who is: (1) an officer with annual pay of more than $165,000 in 2013, (2) a more-than-5 percent owner, or (3) a more-than-1 percent owner who received more than $165,000 in compensation[14] [Code Sec. 416(i)(1)(A)]. Individuals are key employees if they meet the definition any time during the plan year.

A former employee who was a key employee upon retirement or separation from service is also a key employee.

The penalty for failing the nondiscrimination tests is that all key employees have imputed income on the entire employer-provided portion of their group-life coverage. The imputed amount includes any nondiscriminatory coverage as well as the first $50,000 of coverage that would otherwise be excluded.

Pension Trust

Premiums paid for term life insurance protection out of your employer's contributions under a pension trust plan are taxable to you (the insured employee) [Reg. § 1.72-16].

.03 Group-Term Life Insurance Combined with Permanent Benefits

Code Sec. 79 generally requires that the cost of group-term life insurance coverage on the life of an employee that is in excess of $50,000 of coverage be included in the income of the employee. Pursuant to Reg. § 1.79-1(b), under specified circumstances, group-term life insurance may be combined with other benefits, referred to as *permanent benefits* because they have an economic value extending beyond one policy year. Policies that provide for paid-up insurance and cash-surrender values constitute permanent benefits.

Under Reg. § 1.79-1(d), the employee's income includes the cost of those permanent benefits, reduced by the amount the employee paid for the benefits. The cost of the

---

14 Notice 2012-67, IRB 2012-50, 671.

permanent benefits is determined under a formula provided in the regulations that is based in part on the increase in the employee's deemed death benefit during the year. One of the factors used for determining the deemed death benefit is "the net level premium reserve at the end of that policy year for all benefits provided to the employee by the policy or, if greater, the fair market value of the policy at the end of that policy year." In Rev. Proc. 2005-25,[15] the IRS provides guidance on how to determine the fair market value of a life insurance contract for purposes of applying the rules of Code Sec. 79.

¶4035 SPLIT-DOLLAR INSURANCE

In conjunction with or as an alternative to group-term life insurance, an employer can provide life insurance protection to selected employees through a split-dollar arrangement. With *split-dollar insurance,* the employer and employee contractually share the cost and benefits of a cash-value life insurance contract. The employer typically pays premiums on the employee's life insurance policy to the extent of the annual increase in the cash surrender value. The employee pays the balance. Upon the employee's death, the employer is entitled to the cash surrender value of the life insurance policy, and the rest of the policy proceeds are distributed as the employee has directed. The tax treatment of split-dollar insurance arrangements is discussed further at Ch. 2.

¶4040 LONG-TERM CARE INSURANCE

Amounts (other than policy holder dividends or premium refunds) received by employees from employer-provided long-term care insurance will generally be treated as an accident and health insurance contract and will be tax-free subject to limitations [Code Sec. 7702B(a)].

.01 Long-Term Care Insurance Contract

In order to qualify for the income exclusion, the employer's long-term care insurance contract must provide only coverage of "qualified long-term care services" and meet the following requirements:

1. The contract must be guaranteed renewable.
2. The contract must not provide for a cash surrender value or other money that can be paid, assigned, pledged as collateral for a loan, or borrowed.
3. Refunds, other than refunds paid upon the death of the insured or complete surrender or cancellation of the contract, and dividends may only be used to reduce future premiums or to increase future benefits.
4. The contract may not pay or reimburse expenses which are reimbursable under Medicare, except when Medicare is a secondary payor or when the contract makes payments per diem or on another periodic basis without regard to actual expense.

[15] Rev. Proc. 2005-25, 2005-1 CB 962.

5. The consumer protection requirements of Code Sec. 7702B(g) are satisfied [Code Sec. 7702B(b)]. These requirements relate to guaranteed renewal or noncancellability, prohibitions on limitations and exclusion, extension of benefits, continuation or conversion of coverage, discontinuance and replacement of policies, unintentional lapse, disclosure, prohibitions against post-claims underwriting, minimum standards, inflation protection, prohibition against pre-existing conditions exclusions and probationary periods, and prior hospitalization.

.02 What Expenses Are Covered

Only benefits from a long-term care contract which pays or reimburses actual long-term care expenses will be tax-free. This includes necessary diagnostic, preventive, therapeutic, curing, treating, mitigating, and rehabilitative services, and maintenance or personal care services, which are required by a chronically ill individual and are provided pursuant to a plan of care prescribed by a licensed health care practitioner such as a physician, registered nurse and licensed social worker [Code Sec. 7702B(c)(1)].

.03 Definition of *Chronically Ill*

The term *chronically ill individual* means any individual who has been certified by a licensed health care practitioner as:

1. Being unable to perform (without substantial assistance from another individual) at least two activities of daily living (ADLs) for a period of at least 90 days because of a loss of functional capacity, (the ADL trigger) or

2. Requiring substantial supervision to protect such individual from threats to health and safety because of severe cognitive impairment (the cognitive impairment trigger) [Code Sec. 7702B(c)(2)].

For these purposes, ADLs include eating, toileting, transferring, bathing, dressing, and continence [Code Sec. 7702B(c)(2)(B)]. With respect to the ADL trigger (but not the cognitive impairment trigger) contract will not be considered a qualified long-term care insurance contract unless the determination of whether an individual is chronically ill takes into account at least five of these activities. Thus, a contract that defines a chronically ill individual as an individual who requires substantial supervision to protect him from threats to health and safety due to severe cognitive impairment is a qualified long-term care contract even if the individual can perform all of the activities of daily living.

Forms

The IRS has forms for employers paying long-term care expenses. The IRS developed Form 1099-LTC, *Long-Term Care and Accelerated Death Benefits,* so employers paying long-term care benefits or accelerated death benefits paid under a life insurance contract or paid by a viatical settlement provider can report the aggregate benefits paid and other information required under Code Sec. 6050Q.

.04 Per Diem Limitation

Per diem benefits from long-term care contracts that pay a set dollar benefit for each day of long-term care services generally are tax-free only up to $320 a day in 2013 or

$116,800 annually [Code Sec. 7702B(d)(4)].[16] However, per diem benefits above $320 a day in 2013 are also tax-free to the extent that unreimbursed long-term care expenses actually exceed that amount. The daily exclusion limit is indexed for health care inflation. Amounts treated as paid by reason of the insured's death are not taken into account if the insured is terminally ill at the time the payment is received.

See ¶ 9100 for discussion of the deduction available for long-term care insurance premiums and services.

MEALS AND LODGING FURNISHED BY EMPLOYER

¶4045 MEALS AND LODGING

Employees are not taxed on the value of meals or lodging furnished by an employer to an employee, an employee's spouse or dependents if: (1) the meals are furnished "for the convenience of the employer;" and (2) the meals are furnished on the employer's business premises or in the case of lodging, the employee is required to accept the lodging on the business premises of the employer as a condition of employment [Code Sec. 119(a); Reg. § 1.119-1]. See ¶ 4050 for discussion of employer-subsidized cafeterias.

.01 Meals

The exclusion is limited to meals furnished by an employer on the business premises for substantial noncompensatory business reasons. The reasons could include any of the following: (1) the employee must be on duty during the meal period, or (2) the employee is restricted to a very short meal period so he or she cannot be expected to eat elsewhere, or (3) eating facilities in the vicinity of the work site are not adequate, or (4) it is safer for the employee to remain in the employer's building during meal time.

Generally, the meal must be furnished during your working hours. However, if your job duties prevent you from consuming an excludable meal during business hours, the meal can be taken immediately after work with the same tax-free result.

Meals are furnished for the "convenience of the employer," if more than half of the employees must eat the free meals in order to properly perform their job responsibilities in the manner required by the employer. In other words, if *more than half* of the employees must eat the free meals on the job site because of employer demands, then *all* meals provided by the employer will be considered to be furnished for the "convenience of the employer" for tax purposes and will therefore be fully deductible [Code Sec. 119(b)(4)].[17]

> ▶ **PRACTICE POINTER:** This means that business owners such as hospitals, hotels, and restaurants operating on-site cafeterias for employees may deduct 100 percent of the cost of providing meals to all employees in the cafeteria if more than half of the employees are required to eat in the cafeteria as a condition

[16] Rev. Proc. 2012-41, IRB 2012-45.

[17] *Boyd Gaming Corp.*, CA-9, 99-1 USTC ¶ 50,530, 177 F3d 1096, *acq.* IRB 1999-32, 324.

of their employment. Not only are all the meals deductible by the employers, but they are all tax-free to the employees under Code Sec. 119(b)(4).

▶ **TAX STRATEGY:** The employer can satisfy the business premises requirement by renting space in a restaurant or hotel. The Tax Court has held employer-provided meals tax-free under such an arrangement. The company rented a hotel suite for daily luncheon conferences, which company officers were required to attend. The substantial business reason for the luncheon conferences was that meeting during regular business hours would interrupt the work of the company and consume too much time.[18]

If the nature of the job requires that you must reside on the premises, then the value of all meals taken there qualifies for the exclusion. This applies even if taking meals on the job is not a condition of employment and the meals are not taken on a working day [Reg. § 1.119-1(a)(2)(i)].

.02 Lodging

The value of lodging furnished to an employee, his or her spouse, and their dependents by the employer can be excluded from income if: (1) the employee is required to accept such lodging as a condition of employment; (2) the lodging is furnished for the convenience of the employer; and (3) the lodging is on the business premises of the employer [Code Sec. 119(a); Reg. § 1.119-1(b)]. An example of excludable lodging furnished to an employee would be an apartment building manager who is required to live in an apartment in the building in order to retain an apartment managerial job.

Convenience of Employer Test

In determining whether meals or lodging are furnished for the convenience of the employer, the provisions of an employment contract or of a state statute fixing terms of employment is not determinative of whether the meals or lodging are intended as compensation [Code Sec. 119(b)(1); Reg. § 1.119-1(b)].

Example 4-20: An employee of an institution, who must be on duty from 8 a.m. until 4 p.m., is given the choice of residing at the institution free of charge, or residing elsewhere and receiving an allowance of $30 per month in addition to his regular salary. If he elects to reside at the institution, the value of meals and lodging to the employee is taxable, because residence there is not a condition of employment necessary to properly performing his duties.

For an individual who is furnished lodging in a camp located in a foreign country by his employer, a camp is considered to be part of the business premises of the employer [Code Sec. 119(c)(2)]. A *camp* is lodging that is:

- Provided by or on behalf of the employer for the convenience of the employer because the place where the individual renders services is in a remote area where satisfactory housing is not available on the open market;
- Located, as near as practicable, in the vicinity of the place at which the individual renders services; and

[18] *C.R. Mabley, Jr.*, 24 TCM 1794, Dec. 27,666(M), TC Memo. 1965-323.

- Furnished in a common area (or enclave) which is not available to the public and which normally accommodates 10 or more employees [Code Sec. 119(c) (2)].

In *C.K. Abeyta,*[19] the Tax Court held that a taxpayer on an overseas assignment couldn't exclude the value of a home in a suburban neighborhood as lodging furnished to him by his employer. The lodging in a residential suburb, among similar housing available to the general public, failed to qualify as a foreign camp for purpose of the Code Sec. 119 exclusion, even though it was a remote location.

.03 Examples of Excludable Lodging

The following are examples of the types of lodging that are excluded:

- Value of utilities unless employee buys them directly from suppliers;[20]
- Hotel manager required to live at hotel so as to be constantly available;[21]
- Hospital employees on constant call at state hospital;[22]
- Building manager whose presence at site is required at a moment's call;[23]
- Construction workers at remote job site;[24]
- Funeral home employees needed to be available for work on 24-hour basis;[25] and
- Military quarters rental value of quarters occupied by military personnel.

Faculty Lodging Furnished by Educational Institutions to Employees

You must pay tax on the value of qualified campus housing (i.e., housing located on or near the campus, which is provided to you and used as your residence) to the extent the rent paid is less than the lesser of 5 percent of the lodging's appraised value or the average of rentals paid (other than by employees or students) to the school during the calendar year for comparable housing [Code Sec. 119(d)].

> **Example 4-21:** You are a teacher at a private boarding school. As part of your benefits, you live in a school-owned apartment on campus and pay $600 per month in rent. Comparable apartments rent for $750 per month. The appraised value of the apartment is $100,000. You may exclude the $150 monthly rent subsidy because the annual rent you pay is more than five percent of the apartment's fair market value.

Housing for Medical Research Institution Employees

Employees of certain medical research institutions or teaching hospitals may exclude from income the value of subsidized campus housing as long as the employees pay annual rent that is at least five percent of the fair market value of the housing or, if less the average rental paid by individuals (other than employees or students) for comparable housing provided by the employer. If the rent paid by the employee is less than this

---

[19] *C.K. Abeyta,* TC Summary Op. 2005-44.

[20] Rev. Rul. 68-579, 1968-2 CB 61.

[21] *J.B. Lindeman,* 60 TC 609, Dec. 32,063, *acq.* 1973-2 CB 2.

[22] *O.K. Diamond,* CA-2, 55-1 USTC ¶9323, 221 F2d 264; Rev. Rul. 68-354, 1968-2 CB 60.

[23] *H.T. Giesinger,* 66 TC 6, Dec. 33,747, *acq.* 1976-2 CB 2.

[24] *W.I. Olkjer,* 32 TC 464, Dec. 23,618, *acq.* 1960-1 CB 5.

[25] *H. Schwartz,* 22 TCM 835, Dec. 26,197(M), TC Memo. 1963-175.

safe harbor, he or she must include in income the difference between the actual rent paid and the safe harbor amount. In order for the employees to qualify for this housing exclusion, the medical research institution must satisfy the following requirements:

- Be eligible to receive charitable contributions as a hospital or medical research organization as described in Code Sec. 170(b) (1) (A) (iii)];
- Receive payments under the Social Security Act relating to graduate medical training, such as residency and fellowship programs; and
- Have as one of its principal purposes or functions the providing and teaching of basic and clinical medical science and research with the entity's own faculty [Code Sec. 119(d) (4) (B)]. Qualified campus housing must be located on the campus of the employer or, in the case of a state university system, comprised of many institutions with separate campuses, on the campus of one of the component institutions [Code Sec. 119(d) (4) (A)].

.04 Property Occupied Rent-Free by Stockholder

The exclusion has been allowed for the officer-shareholders of a ranching corporation who were required to perform caretaker-type duties in an isolated location.[26] S corporation owners were denied a deduction for lodging and meals incurred when operating a cattle and sheep ranch. The taxpayers had claimed that living on the ranch was a condition of their employment but there was no written requirement attesting to that fact and they failed to show that they used the ranch exclusively for business purposes.[27] In a situation where there was no evidence that the rental value was compensation, the Fifth Circuit held that it was a nontaxable gift from the corporation to its stockholders.[28]

.05 Parsonage Exclusion—Lodging Furnished to Clergy

The parsonage allowance permits members of clergy to exclude from taxable income a portion of their salary that is equal to the fair rental value of their home including utilities furnished to them as part of their compensation [Reg. § 1.107-1(a)]. To benefit from the parsonage exclusion, the taxpayer must be a "member of the clergy," which includes duly ordained ministers, rabbis, priests, and cantors but not church school teachers. Those employed only to teach, or as administrators by an agency that's not an integral part of a religious organization may not claim the exclusion.[29] After the Tax Court's decision in *R.D. Warren*,[30] where the Tax Court followed pre-2002 law and held that a pastor was entitled to exclude his entire salary even though it exceeded the fair rental value of his home, Congress amended Code Sec. 107 so that it provides that the gross income of a minister of the gospel doesn't include:

---

[26] *F.R. McDowell*, 33 TCM 372, Dec. 32,512(M), TC Memo. 1974-72.

[27] *J. Dilts*, DC-WY, 94-1 USTC ¶50,162, 845 FSupp 1505.

[28] *E.V. Richards*, CA-5, 40-1 USTC ¶9373, 111 F2d 376; *H.B. Peacock*, CA-5, 58-2 USTC ¶9603, 256 F2d 160.

[29] TAM 200318002 (Jan. 7, 2003).

[30] *R.D. Warren*, 114 TC 343, Dec. 53,880, *appeal dismissed*, CA-9, 2003-1 USTC ¶50,207, 302 F3d 1012.

- The rental value of a home furnished to him as part of his compensation [Code Sec. 107(1)]; or
- The rental allowance paid to him as part of his compensation, to the extent used by him to rent or provide a home, and to the extent such allowance does not exceed the *fair rental value* of the home, including furnishings and appurtenances such as a garage, plus the cost of utilities [Code Sec. 107(2) (emphasis added)].

Rental allowance includes amounts spent for rent, utilities, and for buying a home and furnishings. It can also include mortgage payments, taxes, insurance, and repairs on homes owned by members of the clergy.

What Is Included in the Rental Allowance

Rental allowance includes amounts spent for rent, utilities and for buying a home and furnishings. It can also include payment for a home (mortgage payments, interest, taxes, repairs) owned by a member of the clergy.[31]

Parsonage Allowance Available for Two Homes

In *P.A. Driscoll*,[32] the Court of Appeals for the Eleventh Circuit concluded that an ordained minister and his wife were not entitled to exclude from their gross income the portion of a parsonage allowance they used to support their second home. The appellate court found that the Tax Court erred when it concluded that the word "home" in Code Sec. 107 included both the singular and plural forms of the word. The court reasoned that the consistent use of the singular in the legislative history of Code Sec. 107 demonstrated that Congress intended for the parsonage allowance exclusion to apply to only one clergy member's home.

Who May Claim Parsonage Exclusion?

The taxpayer must be a minister of the gospel, which includes ministers, priests, rabbis, and anyone else who has been ordained, commissioned, or licensed by a church. The IRS will apply a facts and circumstances test to determine whether a person is acting as a minister of the gospel as required by law. This includes the performance of sacerdotal functions, the conduct of religious worship, the administration of a religious organization or its agencies, or the performance of teaching and administrative duties at theological seminaries. Those employed only to teach, or as administrators by an agency that's not an integral part of a religious organization, may not claim the exclusion. However, those employed to teach, or as administrators by an agency that is an integral part of a religious organization, are entitled to the exclusion.[33]

The parsonage exclusion will be unavailable to taxpayers who are simply ordained but do not act in a ministerial capacity. For example, a minister who acts as head of nursing home is not acting as a minister of the gospel and is not entitled to claim the parsonage exclusion.[34] Theological students are ineligible for the parsonage exclusion because they have not yet been ordained or received a license. Retired ministers, however, may be able to qualify if they show that any of the income they receive is for past service.

---

[31] Rev. Rul. 59-350, 1959-2 CB 45.

[32] *P.A. Driscoll*, CA-11, 2012-1 USTC ¶50,187, *rev'g and rem'g per curiam*, 135 TC 557, Dec. 58,415 (2010), *cert. denied*, 10/1/12.

[33] Rev. Rul. 62-171, 1962-2 CB 39; Rev. Rul. 63-90, 1963-1 CB 27.

[34] Rev. Rul. 72-606, 1972-2 CB 78.

Cantors may claim the housing allowance even though they may not be ordained rabbis, as long as they have a commission and are employed on a full-time basis by a congregation to perform religious functions in the observance of the Jewish faith. Traveling ministers can exclude a housing allowance received from out-of-town churches during evangelist travels, as long as it is used to maintain a permanent residence. Military chaplains who are considered to be commissioned officers may not claim a parsonage allowance. However, they may be able to exclude a basic allowance for quarters, as would any other military officer.

▶ **PRACTICE POINTER:** It is advisable for the religious organization to designate in writing the portion of payments to the clergy member that represents the housing allowance. The terms of the designation should be spelled out in a written employment contract or in organizational meeting minutes, or both. The designation should include the amount of the housing allowance and when it will be paid. If adjustments are made later, they should be formally documented by an amendment to the employment contract or in meeting minutes. In the absence of these formalities, the payments will be includible in income and ineligible for the parsonage exclusion.

.06 Meals and Lodging Furnished to Partner

Most courts have concluded that a partner is not considered to be an employee and therefore cannot exclude the value of meals and lodging from income.[35] An exception exists in the Court of Appeals for the Fifth Circuit where the court found that a partner was considered to be an employee for this purpose and therefore could exclude the value of meals and lodging provided by the partnership.[36]

¶4050 EMPLOYER-SUBSIDIZED CAFETERIAS

Many employers subsidize dining room/cafeteria facilities for their employees. If certain conditions are met, the value of the subsidy is not taxable to the employees.

To remain a tax-free fringe benefit to employees, the facility must be located on or near the employer's business premises. The employer can either lease or own the facility. The tax-free status is retained even if others run the food operations for the employer.

Employers who provide meals for their workers at the job location will be able to deduct those meals if the meals are furnished to the employees at a place of business that is convenient for the employer and if more than one-half of employees to whom such meals are furnished on the premises are also furnished the meals for the convenience of the employer [Code Sec. 119(b)(4)]. In addition, if these conditions are satisfied, the value of these meals would also be excludable from the employee's income.

---

[35] *T. Robinson*, CA-3, 60-1 USTC ¶9152, 273 F2d 503, *cert denied*, SCt, 363 US 810, 80 SCt 1246; *W.T. Briggs*, CA-10, 56-2 USTC ¶10,020, 238 F2d 53; *R.E. Moran*, CA-8, 56-2 USTC ¶9879, 236 F2d 595; *E. Doak*, CA-4, 56-2 USTC ¶9708, 234 F2d 704.

[36] *A.L. Armstrong*, CA-5, 68-1 USTC ¶9355, 394 F2d 661.

Example 4-22: We Crunch Numbers, Inc., an accounting firm, provides lunch to 125 of its 200 employees on the business premises. The food is provided to encourage the employees to spend their lunch break working and eating rather than venturing outside the firm's building. Since all these meals are treated under the tax laws as being furnished for the convenience of the accounting firm, We Crunch may deduct the cost of the meals and the employees need not include the value of the meals in their gross income.

.01 Convenience of Employer Test

The Court of Appeals for the Ninth Circuit has held that a Las Vegas casino operator could deduct 100 percent of the meals provided to its employees because its "stay-on-premises" policy was a substantial, noncompensatory business reason for furnishing meals to its employees.[37] The hotel and casino operators required their employees to stay on the business premises throughout the work shift for reasons of security and logistics. The casinos are open to the public 24 hours a day, seven days a week. Each property operates an on-site cafeteria facility, separate from the public restaurants. In these cafeterias employees are entitled to obtain free meals during their work shifts. The court concluded that the casino could deduct 100 percent of the expenses associated with its employee cafeteria because of its "stay-on-premises" requirement which resulted in "more than half" of the employees receiving free meals for the "convenience of the employer" as required in Code Sec. 119(b) (4).

▶ **PRACTICE POINTER:** Although *Boyd Gaming* dealt with security concerns relating to casino employees, its significance extends to hospital workers, stock brokers, bank employees, and any other employees whose physical presence may be required by their employers at all times.

The value of meals provided by a cafeteria operated by an employer on or near the employer's premises may be excluded from gross income as a de minimis fringe benefit if the revenue derived from the facility normally equals or exceeds the direct operating costs of the facility. This rule applies with respect to a highly compensated employee only if access to the facility is available on substantially the same terms to each member of a group of employees that is defined under a reasonable classification that does not discriminate in favor of highly compensated employees. An employee entitled under Code Sec. 119 to exclude the value of a meal provided at the facility is treated as having paid an amount for the meal equal to the direct operating costs of the facility attributable to the meal. Meals must be furnished during, immediately before, or after the workday. Thus, for example, the tax-free benefit is lost if night shift workers use the facility for their midday meal. The direct costs of the facility include food, beverage and labor costs of the operation. Employers with multiple dining facilities may choose to aggregate them when applying the direct operating costs test [Code Sec. 132(e)(2); Reg. § 1.132-7(a)(2), (b)].

Example 4-23: ABC Inc. operates a company-subsidized cafeteria on its premises for the exclusive use of its employees. The full cost of operating the facility, including rental for the space, is $300,000; the direct cost of operation is

---

[37] *Boyd Gaming Corp.*, CA-9, 99-1 USTC ¶ 50,530, 177 F3d 1096, *acq. in result*, IRB 1999-35, 314.

$190,000. The employees spend $200,000 in the cafeteria. If the employees ate elsewhere, they would spend $400,000. Since revenues exceed direct costs, the employees do not have to pay tax on the subsidy.

Suppose that you must pay tax on the company subsidy. The taxable amount is the difference between the fair market value of the meals and what you actually pay (plus any amount specifically excluded by another income tax provision) [Reg. § 1.132-7(c)]. Companies may set the fair market value at 150 percent of the eating facility's direct operating costs. The taxable excess may be allocated among employees in proportion to amounts actually spent in the cafeteria or in any other reasonable manner [Reg. § 1.61-21(j)(2)].

Example 4-24: Assume the same facts as example above. However, the direct operating costs (i.e., food, beverage, and labor) are $220,000. As a result, the ABC Inc. employees owe tax on meals because the cost exceeds the revenues. The taxable amount is the difference between the fair market value of the meals and what the employees actually pay. If ABC Inc. uses the 150 percent-of-cost measure, the fair market value is $330,000. The taxable fringe benefit is $130,000 ($330,000 – $200,000). If ABC Inc. uses the actual fair market value of $400,000, the taxable benefit is $200,000.

▶ **NONDISCRIMINATION REQUIREMENT:** The cafeteria subsidy is tax-free to highly-compensated employees only if access to the cafeteria is available to rank and file employees as well [Code Sec. 132(e)(2); Reg. § 1.132-8]. Thus, this exclusion does not apply to executive dining rooms.

OTHER EMPLOYEE BENEFITS

¶4055 EDUCATION REIMBURSEMENT

Amounts paid or incurred by an employer for educational assistance to an employee may be excluded from the employee's gross income if the amounts are paid or incurred pursuant to an educational assistance program or if the amounts qualify as a working condition fringe benefit.

.01 Employer-Provided Educational Assistance

An employee's gross income and wages does not include amounts paid by the employer for educational assistance provided to the employee if the amounts were paid pursuant to an "educational assistance" program meeting certain requirements. This exclusion is limited to $5,250 of educational assistance provided on behalf of an employee [Code Sec. 127(a)(2)]. This provision was made permanent beginning in 2013. The courses taken by the employee need not be job-related, but cannot include education involving sports, games or hobbies, unless such education involves the business of the employer or is required as part of a degree program. [Code Sec. 127(c); Reg. § 1.127-2(c)(3)(iii)].

To qualify for tax benefits, the employer's plan must be in writing [Reg. § 1.127-2(b)]. The employer may pay the expenses directly, reimburse the employees for their expenses, or provide the education directly. The plan need not be funded and prior approval of the plan by the IRS is not required, but the plan must not discriminate in favor of employees who are officers, owners, or highly compensated and not more than five percent of the total amount of benefits provided may be paid to or for employees who are shareholders or owners who own at least five percent of the business [Code Sec. 127(b); Reg. § 1.127-2(e)]. An employer maintaining an educational assistance plan must maintain records and file a return for the plan [Code Sec. 6039D].

The exclusion for employer-provided educational assistance includes graduate level courses [Code Sec. 127(c)(1)]. The term "educational assistance" includes undergraduate tuition, fees, books, supplies, and equipment [Code Sec. 127(c)(1)]. It does not include payment for, or the provision of, tools or supplies which may be retained by the employee after completion of a course of instruction, or meals, lodging, or transportation.

An employer's payment of an employee's educational expenses may be tax-free if the payments qualify as a working condition fringe benefit [Code Sec. 132(a)(3)]. To qualify, the expenses must be required by the employer for the employee to keep the employee's present salary, status, or job or maintain or improve skills needed in the employee's present work, must not qualify the employee for a new profession, and must not be required to satisfy the employer's minimum education standards.

.02 Educational Assistance to Terminated Employee

The IRS has concluded that two plans qualified as educational assistance programs under Code Sec. 127(b) even though they provided benefits to individuals after their employment had terminated, regardless of the reason for the termination.[38] Reg. § 1.127-2(h)(1) provides that the term employee includes a retired, disabled or laid-off employee. The IRS has broadened the definition even further to include former employees, without consideration of the reason for the termination.

¶4060 DEPENDENT CARE ASSISTANCE PLANS

An employee may exclude from gross income up to $5,000 ($2,500 for married couples filing separately) of employer-provided dependent care assistance as a tax-free fringe benefit [Code Sec. 129(a)(2)(A)]. Any excess benefit is taxable to the employee in the year the dependent care services were provided, even if payment for them is made in the following year. Also, the exclusion cannot exceed the employee's (or spouse's, if lower) earned income. Dependent care assistance covers the same type of expenses that qualify for the dependent care tax credit [¶ 14,001]. In general, these are expenses for household and dependent care services which are necessary for your gainful employment [Code Sec. 129(e)(1)]. They include the costs of child care help or a caretaker.

NOTE: The plan can provide cash to pay for the assistance, furnish the actual care, or take the form of a reimbursement account [¶ 4110].

---

[38] Rev. Rul. 96-41, 1996-2 CB 8.

To be considered a tax-free fringe benefit, the dependent care assistance plan must be in writing and be for the exclusive benefit of the employees. At year-end, your employer must provide, to those employees benefiting from this program, a written statement reflecting the expenses paid on the employee's behalf. The plan also must comply with special nondiscrimination tests [Code Sec. 129(d)(2)].

.01 Exception for Highly Compensated Employees

Employers cannot exclude dependent care assistance from the wages of a highly compensated employee unless the benefits provided under the program do not favor highly compensated employees and the program meets the requirements described in Code Sec. 129(d) as follows:

1. It must benefit employees who qualify under a classification set up by the employer and found by the IRS not to discriminate in favor of highly compensated employees (within the meaning of Code Sec. 414(q)) (namely, officers, owners, and highly paid employees, see discussion below) or their dependents [Code Sec. 129(d)(2)]. However, employees may be excluded from the discrimination determination if they have not reached the age of 21 and completed one year of service. Employees may also be excluded from the discrimination determination if they are covered by a collective bargaining agreement between the employer and employee representatives if there is evidence that dependent care benefits were the subject of good-faith bargaining [Code Sec. 129(d)(9)];
2. Not more than 25 percent of the amounts paid or incurred by the employer during the year may be provided for individuals who are shareholders or owners (or their spouses or dependents), each of whom owns more than five percent of the stock or of the capital or profits interest in the employer [Code Sec. 129(d)(4)];
3. Reasonable notification of the availability and terms of the plan must be provided to eligible employees [Code Sec. 129(d)(6)]; and
4. Each year, on or before January 31, the plan must furnish to each employee a written statement showing the amounts paid or expenses incurred by the employer in providing dependent care assistance to such employee during the previous calendar year.

For purposes of the dependent care assistance exclusion, in 2013, a highly compensated employee under Code Sec. 414(q)(1)(B) is an employee who meets either of the following tests:

1. The employee was a 5 percent owner at any time during the year or the preceding year; and
2. The employee received more than a specified amount ($115,000 for 2013) in pay for the preceding year. At the employer's election, the employee also must have been among the top 20 percent employees when ranked by compensation for that preceding year.

Dependent Care Assistance Reported in Box 10 of Form W-2

If a dependent care assistance program fails to meet the Code Sec. 129(d) rules, only highly compensated employees must include benefits provided under the plan in gross income [Code Sec. 129(d)(1)]. For rules relating to dependent care assistance programs offered under a cafeteria plan, see Reg. § 1.125-1, Q&A-18.

Benefits received from a dependent care plan reduce the maximum amount of expenses eligible for the dependent care tax credit [Ch. 14].

¶4065 SERVICES PROVIDED AT NO ADDITIONAL COST

Some employers give the same services to employees that they sell to customers. Employees pay no tax on the value of the services if the employer does not incur substantial additional cost to provide them. The employer's costs include lost revenue as well as out-of-pocket expenditures. This exclusion applies to price discounts and cash rebates as well as no-charge services. Examples of these types of services include telephone services provided free or at reduced price to employees working in the transportation industry, hotel accommodations and transportation by air, train, bus, subway or cruise line [Code Sec. 132(a); Reg. § 1.132-2]. (The rules for employee discounts on services for which substantial additional cost is incurred by the employer are explained in [¶ 4070].)

A retiree, a former employee who is disabled, and a former employee's surviving spouse, are all eligible for the tax-free treatment of these benefits. And so are the employee's spouse and dependent children. In the case of air transportation, parents of active employees can qualify for the tax exclusion [Code Sec. 132(h)].

> **Example 4-25:** Ace Airlines provides free tickets to its employees, their parents and their immediate families on a stand-by basis (i.e., only if seats remain unsold at flight time). Its customers are not displaced, and the airline incurs no substantial extra cost in providing this benefit. The exclusion applies because the employees and their family members occupy seats that would otherwise remain unused by customers. On the other hand, suppose Ace Airlines offered reserved seating to its employees. The airline could have to turn away paying customers, thus losing revenue. As a result, the exclusion does not apply in this case. The employees would owe tax on the value of the flight.

There is a special rule for employers engaged in more than one line of business. To be tax-free, the benefit must be derived from the business for which the employee performs substantial services. If you are directly involved in more than one line of your employer's business (e.g., central payroll department staff), you are entitled to exclude the value of the benefits received from any one of those lines of business [Reg. § 1.132-4(a)].

> **Example 4-26:** Mr. Addison works for Lilton Inc., which owns Lilton Hotels and Lilton Airlines. Addison is employed as a hotel manager for one of the Lilton's hotels. Addison, because he is employed by Lilton Hotels, can exclude the value of his hotel room from his gross income. However, because he does not perform services for Lilton Airlines, he must include the value of the air travel in his gross income.

Example 4-27: Same facts as example above, except Addison is an executive in Lilton Inc. working for all segments of the company. Because he is directly involved in both the air travel and hotel portions of the business, he is eligible to exclude the value of the hotel room and the air travel from his gross income.

.01 Reciprocal Agreements

If the employee also performs services in the same line of business for an unrelated employer, the employee may exclude fringe benefits received from other employers if all the following tests apply:

- The service must be the same type of service generally provided to customers in both the line of business in which the employee works and the line of business in which the service is provided.
- The employer and the unrelated employer providing the no-addition-cost service must have a reciprocal written agreement under which a group of employees of each employer, all of whom perform substantial services in the same line of business, may receive no-additional cost services from the other employer.
- Neither the employer nor the unrelated employer may incur any substantial additional cost either in providing the service or because of the written agreement [Code Sec. 132(i); Reg. § 1.132-2(b)].

Example 4-28: Ace Airlines has a written reciprocal agreement with other airlines. As a result, all the employees who work for the airlines covered by the agreement are considered to be working in the same line of business for all the employers. Employees of Ace Airlines may exclude from their gross income the value of free stand-by seating which they received from these other airline companies.

.02 Exception for Highly Compensated Employees

In order for employers to exclude from the wages of a highly compensated employee the value of a no-additional-cost service it must also be available on the same terms or substantially the same terms to one of the following groups:

- All employees; or
- A group of employees defined under a reasonable classification that does not favor highly compensated employees. [Code Sec. 132(j) (1); Reg. § 1.132-8].

For purposes of the exclusion for no-additional-cost services, a highly compensated employee under Code Sec. 414(q) (1) (B) for 2012 is an employee who meets either of the following tests:

- The employee was a 5 percent owner at any time during the year or the preceding year.
- The employee received more than a specified amount ($115,000 for 2013) in pay for the preceding year. At the employer's election, the employee also must have been among the top 20 percent employees when ranked by compensation for that preceding year.

¶4070 EMPLOYEE DISCOUNTS

Employees may exclude from gross income certain discounts on purchases of their employer's goods and services [Code Sec. 132(c), (f); Reg. § 1.132-3].

For purposes of this exclusion, the following individuals will qualify as employees:

- A current employee;
- A former employee who retired or left on disability;
- A widow or widower of an individual who died while an employee;
- A widow or widower of an employee who retired or left on disability;
- A leased employee who has provided services on a substantially full-time basis for at least a year if the services are performed under the employer's direction or control; and
- A partner who performs services for a partnership.

.01 Amount Excluded from Wages

The maximum tax-free discount on services bought from your employer cannot exceed 20 percent of the price offered to the public. In the case of goods, the discount cannot exceed the gross profit percentage of the price at which the property is being offered to the public. The gross profit percentage is: (1) the total sales price of the property sold to customers (including employees) less your employer's total cost of the property, (2) divided by the total sales price [Code Sec. 132(c)(2); Reg. § 1.132-3(c)].

Employee discounts available through third parties, such as a manufacturer's representative, are also entitled to the exclusion from gross income. If the actual discount is larger than the allowable exclusion (e.g., 20 percent maximum for services), the difference is taxable to you [Reg. § 1.132-3(a)(5), (e)].

> ▶**OBSERVATION:** If your employer provides goods at no charge to you, you are taxed on the regular selling price less the gross profit percentage; for services, the taxable benefit is 80 percent of the regular price.

Example 4-29: Ms. Smith, an employee of Appliance Inc., receives a 10 percent employee discount on her employer's appliances purchased at Goody's, a retail store that offers the appliances for sale to customers. Smith may exclude from gross income the amount of her employee discount on the purchased appliance if that discount does not exceed her employer's gross profit percentage.

Example 4-30: During the year, United Department Store has total merchandise sales of $1,000,000. United's cost for this property was $600,000. The gross profit percentage is 40 percent [($1,000,000 – $600,000) ÷ $1,000,000]. As a result, the employee discount as to property sold by United cannot exceed 40 percent of the selling price of the merchandise to nonemployee customers. If United offers its employees a 50 percent discount, the extra 10 percent is taxable.

The tax-free discount rule does not extend to real property of any kind or personal property held for investment [Reg. § 1.132-3(a)(2)(ii)]. As a result, you must pay tax on a discount for the purchase of residential or commercial real estate, securities, commodities, or currency. The exclusion for a qualified employee discount does not apply to property or services provided by another employer pursuant to a written reciprocal agreement that exists between employers to provide discounts on property and services to employees of the other employer [Reg. § 1.132-3(a)(3)].

.02 Exception for Highly Compensated Employees

An employer cannot exclude from the wages of a highly compensated employee any part of the value of a discount that is not available on the same terms to one of the following groups:

1. All employees; or
2. A group of employees defined under a reasonable classification that does not favor highly compensated employees.

For purposes of the exclusion for employee discounts, a highly compensated employee under Code Sec. 414(q)(1)(B) is an employee who meets either of the following tests:

- The employee was a 5 percent owner at any time during the year or the preceding year; or
- The employee received more than a specified amount ($115,000 for 2013) in pay for the preceding year. At the employer's election, the employee also must have been among the top 20 percent employees when ranked by compensation for that preceding year.

¶4075 EMPLOYEE ACHIEVEMENT AWARDS

An employee's gross income does not include the value of certain awards received for length of service or safety achievement [Code Sec. 74(c)(1); Prop. Reg. § 1.274-8(c)]. The award must be tangible personal property—not cash or a gift certificate. The exclusion does not apply to other intangible property such as vacations, meals, lodging, tickets to theatre or sporting events, stocks, bonds, and other securities.

.01 Employee Defined

For purposes of this exclusion, the following individuals qualify as employees:

- A current employee;
- A former common law employee that the employer provided coverage for in consideration of or based on an agreement relating to prior services as an employee; and
- A leased employee who has provided services to the employer on a substantially full-time basis for at least a year if the services are performed under the employer's primary direction or control.

Exception. Do not treat a 2 percent shareholder of an S corporation as an employee of the corporation. A 2 percent shareholder is someone who directly or indirectly owns (at any time during the year) more than 2 percent of the corporation's stock or stock with more than 2 percent voting power.

.02 Amount of Exclusion

The exclusion is generally limited to awards that cost your employer $400 per employee per year. However, the ceiling is $1,600 per employee per year for a qualified plan award. A qualified plan award is one made under an established written plan that does not discriminate in favor of highly paid employees [Code Sec. 274(j)(2), (3)]. A highly compensated employee within the meaning of Code Sec. 414(q)(1)(B) is an employee (1) who was a 5 percent owner at any time during the year or the preceding year or (2) who was paid more than a specified amount for the preceding year ($110,000 in 2010).

.03 Aggregation Rule

The $1,600 ceiling is the overall limit when an employee is given both qualified and nonqualified plan awards during the year. As a result, the $400 and the $1,600 maximums cannot be added together in one year [Prop. Reg. § 1.274-8(b)].

> **NOTE:** Your employer's deduction for your achievement award is limited by these same dollar caps [Code Sec. 274(j)].

An excludable employee achievement award must be received either on account of length of service or for safety achievement. It must also be awarded as part of a meaningful presentation, emphasizing your achievement. The award must not represent disguised compensation (e.g., given in the place of a prior cash bonus program) [Prop. Reg. § 1.274-8(c)].

.04 Limitation on Awards

A length of service award does not qualify for the exclusion from gross income if received during your first five years of service with the company, or if awards are given to you more frequently than five years apart. No exclusion is permitted for safety achievement awards if your employer previously gave safety achievement awards (other than ones that qualify as *de minimis* fringe benefits [¶ 4095]) during the tax year to more than 10 percent of the employees, or if safety awards were given to a manager, administrator, clerical, or professional employee [Code Sec. 274(j)(4)(C)].

¶4080 ATHLETIC FACILITIES

Employers may exclude from employee wages the value of an employee's use of an on-premises gym or other athletic facility operated by the employer if substantially all use of the facility during the calendar year is by employees, their spouses, and their dependent children. [Code Sec. 132(j)(4)(A)].

.01 Employee Defined

For purposes of the athletic facilities exclusion, the following individuals will qualify as employees:

- A current employee;
- A former employee who retired or left on disability;
- A widow or widower of an individual who died while an employee;
- A widow or widower of an employee who retired or left on disability;

- A leased employee who has provided services on a substantially full-time basis for at least a year if the services are performed under the employer's direction or control; and
- A partner who performs services for a partnership.

To qualify for the exclusion from employees' wages, the athletic facility must be located on premises leased or owned by the employer. It need not, however, be located at the employer's regular business premises. It must be operated by the employer, although your employer can hire someone to manage the facility. And the employer can join together with other companies to cut costs by collectively operating the facility. In addition, substantially all of its use must be by employees, employee spouses and dependent children or retired employees, widows and widowers of employees and their dependent children. [Code Sec. 132(j)(4)(B)(iii)].

The on-premise facility can be a gym, a pool, tennis courts, or a golf course. The exclusion does not apply to any athletic facility if access to the facility is made available to the general public through the sale of memberships or the rental of the facility [Reg. § 1.132-1(e)(1)].

.02 Discrimination Permitted

The nondiscrimination rules do not apply to the athletic facilities. As a result, an employer may use the facility as an executives-only tax-free perk [Code Sec. 132(j)(4); Reg. § 1.132-1(e)(5)].

¶4085 FINANCIAL COUNSELING

An employer may pay for financial counseling for its employees. If the planning qualifies as qualified retirement planning services, the value of those services can be excluded from the employee's gross income [Code Sec. 132(a)(7)]. "Qualified retirement planning services" means any retirement planning advice or information provided to an employee and the employee's spouse by an employer who maintains a qualified employer-sponsored retirement plan [Code Sec. 132(m)]. A highly compensated employee may qualify for this exclusion only if the services are available on substantially the same terms to each member of the group of employees normally provided education and information regarding the employer's qualified plan [Code Sec. 132(m)(2)].

There is no special tax exclusion for other types of employer-provided financial counseling. The value of the counseling is included in the employee's gross income. The same amount, though, may be claimed as a miscellaneous itemized deduction [Ch. 9]. As such, it is deductible to the extent the total of such miscellaneous expenses exceeds 2 percent of adjusted gross income [Code Sec. 67(a), (b)]. The IRS has concluded that a company planning to offer financial counseling to (1) family members or terminally ill employees, and (2) survivors of deceased employees would have to treat the fair market value of the services as income to employees and survivors under Code Sec. 61 [Reg. § 1.61-21(a)(4)].[39]

---

[39] LTR 199929043 (Apr. 22, 1999).

¶4090 WORKING CONDITION FRINGE BENEFITS

An employee may exclude working condition fringe benefits provided by an employer from taxable wages. A *working condition fringe* is any property or service provided to an employee to the extent that, the cost would be deductible as an ordinary and necessary business expense under Code Sec. 162 or through depreciation deductions under Code Sec. 167 if the employee had paid for the property or service himself [Code Sec. 132(d)]. An expense can qualify as a working condition fringe benefit even if the employee could not have actually claimed an employee expense deduction because of the 2 percent floor on deducting miscellaneous expenses [Code Sec. 132(d); Reg. § 1.132-5(a)(1)]. Business-related use of a company car or airplane [Ch. 4; Ch. 10] and employer-paid travel and entertainment [Ch. 10] fit this description. Employer-provided parking is a "qualified transportation fringe." This means that employer-provided parking is only excludable up to a dollar amount which is adjusted each year [Reg. § 1.132-9, Q&A-4] [¶4100]. The IRS has ruled that airline tickets an employer furnished to an employee for travel to a remote but nontemporary work site are subject to income and payroll tax withholding because the tickets did not qualify as a tax-free working condition fringe benefit under Code Sec. 132(d) because the expense was a nondeductible commuting expense.[40]

.01 Outplacement Assistance

The IRS has approved employer-provided outplacement assistance as a tax-free working condition fringe benefit. However, to be tax-free, the assistance must be to find new employment in a laid-off employee's same line of work. Assistance in finding a job in another field is taxable.[41]

.02 Laundry Allowances

The IRS has ruled that laundry allowances provided for security guards will not qualify as an excludable working condition fringe benefit under Code Sec. 132(d) because the employer did not require the guards to verify that the allowances were actually used for uniform maintenance.[42] The employer simply paid the guards an allowance to be used exclusively to clean and maintain the uniforms based on the number of hours worked and the local costs of dry cleaners and coin-operated machines. Due to the lack of receipts substantiating cleaning expenses, all amounts paid to the security guards were includable in the guards' income and were subject to the withholding and payment of income and withholding taxes.

▶ **TAX TIP:** If you provide a cleaning allowance to your employees who are required to wear uniforms, be sure to require all employees to verify that the cleaning allowances were actually used for uniform maintenance. Requiring employees to submit cleaning receipts should qualify the allowance as a working condition fringe benefit excludable from your employees' income.

---

[40] LTR 9641003 (June 21, 1996).

[41] Rev. Rul. 92-69, 1992-2 CB 51.

[42] LTR 9443025 (July 27, 1994).

.03 Company-Sponsored Fishing Trip Not Considered Employee Wages

The costs of a company's annual employee fishing trip may be excluded from the employees' income as a tax-free working condition fringe benefit if the trip is directly related to the active conduct of the company's business.[43]

To be certain that your company's trips to luxury vacation spots are excludable from employee wages, take the following measures:

1. Make attendance on the trip a mandatory event for all employees.
2. Don't invite spouses and children of employees.
3. Have a written agenda for the event with scheduled events that employees must attend.
4. Be sure to document in detail the nature of all discussions that occurred on the trip.
5. Be prepared to show how the discussions improved business operations and affected the company's productivity.

.04 Employer-Provided Cell Phones

Many employers provide their employees with cell phones primarily for noncompensatory business reasons. An employer will be considered to have provided an employee with a cell phone primarily for noncompensatory business purposes if there are substantial reasons relating to the employer's business, other than providing compensation to the employee, for providing the employee with a cell phone. For example, the employer's need to contact the employee at all times for work-related emergencies, the employer's requirement that the employee be available to speak with clients at times when the employee is away from the office, and the employee's need to speak with clients located in other time zones at times outside of the employee's normal work day are possible substantial noncompensatory business reasons. A cell phone provided to promote the morale or good will of an employee, to attract a prospective employee or as a means of furnishing additional compensation to an employee is not provided primarily for noncompensatory business purposes.

The IRS has provided that when an employer provides an employee with a cell phone primarily for noncompensatory business reasons, the employee's use of the cell phone for reasons related to the employer's trade or business will be treated as a working condition fringe benefit. Therefore, the value of the cell phone will be excludable from the employee's income and the substantiation requirements that the employee would otherwise have to fulfill in order to qualify for a business deduction are deemed to be satisfied. In addition, the IRS will treat the value of any personal use of a cell phone provided by the employer primarily for noncompensatory business purposes as excludable from the employee's income as a *de minimis* fringe benefit.[44]

---

[43] *Townsend Industries, Inc.*, CA-8, 2003-2 USTC ¶50,666, 342 F3d 890.

[44] Notice 2011-72, IRB 2011-38, 407.

¶4095 SMALL FRINGE BENEFITS

The value of so-called small or *de minimis* fringe benefits provided by an employer will be tax-free to the employee [Code Sec. 132(a)(4)]. In addition, they are not treated as wages and are therefore not subject to federal income tax withholding or FICA withholding. These are benefits that are of such small value that accounting for them would be administratively impracticable and unreasonable. In determining value, the frequency with which the benefit is furnished should be taken into account; the less frequently the benefit is given, the more likely it is to be tax-free [Code Sec. 132(e)(1); Reg. § 1.132-6]. The following are examples of tax-free *de minimis* fringe benefits:

- Occasional typing of personal letters by a company secretary;
- Occasional personal use of the company photocopy machine (provided at least 85 percent of the machine's use is for business purposes);
- Occasional cocktail parties or picnics for employees and their guests;
- Traditional holiday gifts of property (not cash) with a low fair market value (i.e., a Thanksgiving turkey);
- Occasional theater or sporting tickets; and
- Flowers, fruit, books or similar items provided under special circumstances (e.g., on account of illness or outstanding performance).

The following items provided by employers to employees are not excludable as *de minimis* fringes:

- Free use of company's products provided to highly paid executives when not for product evaluation;[45]
- Season tickets to sporting or theatrical events;
- Commuting use of an employer-owned car for more than one day a month;
- Membership in a private country club or athletic facility;
- Use of an employer-owned or leased facility (e.g., an apartment, hunting lodge or boat) for a weekend [Reg. § 1.132-6(e)];
- Non-monetary recognition awards having a fair market value of $100;[46] and
- Holiday gift coupon with a $35 face value redeemable at several local grocery stores.[47]

In order for a company to give products to employees on a tax-free basis (as a working condition fringe benefit), the company should impose significant limitations on the employee's use of the products in order to reduce the value of the personal benefit to the employee. In addition, the program should require employees to submit detailed testing and evaluation reports [Reg. § 1.132-5(n)(1)].

> **NOTE:** Companies can choose to reward only their highly compensated employees with a de minimis fringe benefit. The nondiscrimination rules do not affect the tax-free status of these small benefits [Code Sec. 132(e); Reg. § 1.132-6(f)].

---

[45] LTR 9401002 (Sept. 24, 1993).

[46] ILM 200108042 (Legal memorandum from IRS Office of Assistant Chief).

[47] TAM 200437030 (Apr. 30, 2004).

.01 Overtime Expenses

You do not have to pay tax on employer payments of meal money (or the value of employer-provided meals) or local transportation fare home when you work overtime. The payments are not tax-free if they are provided on a regular basis. In addition, the amount of the payment must not be based on the number of hours worked (e.g., $1.00 per hour for each hour of overtime).

A special rule applies to some employer-provided commuting. If there is a bona fide, noncompensatory reason for you to travel in an employer-provided vehicle, you are taxed on only $1.50 per trip. This tax break is not available to "control" employees [¶4005].

Safety First

A similar exception applies for certain employees who would otherwise walk or take mass transportation under unsafe (e.g., high crime) conditions. These employees would be taxed on just $1.50 for each qualified commute in an employer-provided car or bus, rather than the full fair market value of the ride [Reg. § 1.61-21(k)(3)(i)]. The break is available only to employees paid on an hourly basis and eligible for overtime. To be eligible for the exclusion the employee must perform services during the year, be paid on an hourly basis, not be claimed as exempt from the minimum wage and maximum hour provisions of the Fair Labor Standards Act, be within a classification for which the employer will pay overtime pay of at least one and one-half times the regular rate, and not receive compensation from the employer in excess of the amount permitted by Code Sec. 414(q)(1)(C) ($115,000 in 2013) [Reg. § 1.61-21(k)(6)(i)(B)].

.02 Cash Equivalents—Meal Payments and Credit Card Vouchers

Cash equivalents do not constitute tax-free *de minimis* fringes under Code Sec. 132 even though they seem so small as to make accounting for it unreasonable or administratively impracticable. Reg. § 1.132-6(c) specifically provides that a cash equivalent fringe benefit such as a gift certificate, or use of a charge account or charge card, generally is not excludable as a *de minimis* fringe, even if the same property or service, if provided in kind, would be excludable as a *de minimis* fringe. Employers will get a different result if they provide a party or group meal for their employees. Reg. § 1.132-6(e)(1) provides that value of occasional cocktail parties, group meals or picnics for employees and their guests will be excluded from the employee's income because they qualify as a *de minimis* fringe benefit.

.03 Emergency Responder's Safety Vehicles Qualify for Tax-Free Working Condition Fringe Benefit

Emergency responders who take home clearly marked public safety vehicles are eligible to treat public safety officer vehicles as tax-free working condition fringe benefits under Reg. § 1.132-5(h)(1). As such, they would be excepted from the strict substantiation requirements of Code Sec. 274(d)(4) that apply to listed property under Reg. § 1.274-5(k)(2)(ii)(A) which adds clearly marked public safety officer vehicles to the list of qualified nonpersonal use vehicles that are treated as tax-free working condition fringe benefits.

Clearly Marked Public Safety Officer Vehicles Defined

A public safety officer vehicle is defined in Reg. § 1.274-5(k)(3) as a vehicle owned or leased by a governmental unit, or any agency or instrumentality that is required to be used for commuting by a police officer, fire fighter, or public safety officer who, when not on a regular shift, is on call at all times. Personal use (other than commuting) of the vehicle outside the limit of the police officer's arrest powers or the fire fighter's or public safety officer's obligation to respond to an emergency must be prohibited by the governmental unit. A public safety officer vehicle is clearly marked if, through painted insignia or words, it is readily apparent that the vehicle is a public safety officer vehicle. A marking on a license plate is not considered a clear marking.

> **Example 4-31:** Director C is employed by City M as the director of the City's rescue squad and is provided with a vehicle for use in responding to emergencies. The city's rescue squad is not a part of City M's police or fire departments. The director's vehicle is a sedan which is painted with an insignia and words identifying the vehicle as a being owned by the City's rescue squad. C, when not on a regular shift, is on call at all times. The City's official policy regarding clearly marked public safety officer vehicles prohibits personal use (other than for commuting) of the vehicle outside of the limits of the public safety officer's obligation to respond to an emergency. When not using the vehicle to respond to emergencies, City M authorizes C to use the vehicle only for commuting, personal errands on the way between work and home, and personal errands within the limits of C's obligation to respond to emergencies. With respect to these authorized uses, the vehicle is not subject to the substantiation requirements of Code Sec. 274(d) and the value of these uses is not includable in C's gross income [Reg. § 1.274-5(k)(8), Ex. 3].

¶4100 QUALIFIED TRANSPORTATION FRINGE BENEFITS

The qualified transportation fringe allows employees to escape tax on three types of employer-provided transportation benefits:

1. Transportation in a commuter highway vehicle (vanpool) for travel between the employee's residence and place of employment;
2. Transit passes for use on a mass transit facility (e.g., subway, commuter trains, rail, bus, or ferry) or a commuter highway vehicle; and
3. Qualified parking at or near the employer's business premises or a location from which the employee commutes to work by mass transit or hired commuter vehicle. Any parking at or near the employee's residence isn't qualified parking [Code Sec. 132(f)(1), (5); Reg. § 1.132-9(b)].
4. Any qualified bicycle commuting reimbursement [Code Sec. 132(f)(1)(D)].

▶ **OVERALL DOLLAR CAPS:** In 2013, a $245 monthly exclusion amount is available for transit passes and van pool benefits provided by an employer to an employee. This amount matches the monthly exclusion amount available for qualified parking benefits. Therefore, employees may also exclude $245 for qualified parking at or near the employer's business premises [Code Sec. 132(f)(2)].

A qualified transportation fringe benefit plan need not be in writing [Reg. § 1.132-9, Q&A-6].

The exclusion for a qualified transportation fringe is available only to *employees*, who could include household employees such as nannies, housekeepers and gardeners [Reg. § 1.132-9, Q&A-5]. Self-employeds do not qualify [Code Sec. 132(f)(5)(E); Reg. § 1.132-9, Q&A-24]. Therefore, individuals who are partners, sole proprietors, or other independent contractors are not employees for purposes of Code Sec. 132(f). In addition, 2 percent shareholders of S corporations are treated as partners for fringe benefits purposes. Thus, an individual who is both a 2 percent shareholder of an S corporation and a common law employee of that S corporation is not considered an employee for purposes of Code Sec. 132(f). Note, however, that other exclusions for working condition fringe benefits under Code Sec. 132(a)(3) and *de minimis* fringes under Code Sec. 132(a)(4) may be available for these taxpayer who fail to qualify as employees and are therefore ineligible to benefit from qualified transportation fringe benefits under Code Sec. 132(f) as described in Reg. § 1.132-1(b)(2) and Reg. § 1.132-1(b)(4) [Reg. § 1.132-9, Q&A-24].

An employee may receive qualified transportation fringes from more than one employer. Keep in mind, however, that certain entities under common control will be treated as a single employer for purposes of transportation fringes [Reg. § 1.132-9, Q&A-10].

.01 Transit Passes

The provision of tax-free transit passes is beneficial to both employers and employees. Employers favor transit passes because they will not have to pay Social Security, unemployment or other taxes on the transportation benefits offered to employees. Employees favor transit passes because these vouchers will not be subject to Federal, state or local taxes.

A transit pass can be defined as any pass, token, farecard, voucher, or similar item (including an item exchangeable for fare media) entitling a person to transportation: (1) on mass transit facilities (whether or not publicly owned); or (2) provided in a highway vehicle seating at least six adults (excluding the driver) for compensation or hire [Code Sec. 132(f)(5)(A); Reg. § 1.132-9, Q&A-3]. The IRS has concluded that a mass transit voucher given to commuting employees is not wages to the extent that the value does not exceed the statutory exclusion limit.[48]

Cash reimbursement for a transit pass is a qualified transportation fringe only if a transit voucher or similar item is not "readily available" for direct distribution by the employer to the employee. Thus if vouchers are readily available, cash reimbursement of mass transit expenses is not a qualified transportation fringe benefit [Code Sec. 132(f)(3)]. IRS regulations clarify when vouchers are considered to be readily available. Reg. § 1.132-9(b), Q&A-16(b)(6) provides that vouchers may not be considered readily available where they are not (a) available for purchase at reasonable intervals, (b) offered in quantities that are reasonably appropriate to the number of

[48] LTR 9548017 (Aug. 30, 1995).

the employer's employees who use mass transportation, and (c) offered in denominations appropriate for distribution to the employer's employees. Employers are allowed to distribute tax-free transit passes in advance for more than one month (e.g., for a calendar quarter). The applicable statutory monthly on the combined amount of transit passes and transportation in a commuter highway vehicle may be calculated taking into account the monthly limits for all months for which the transit passes are distributed.

If, however, advance transit passes are provided to an employee, and the employee's employment terminates, the value of the transit passes covering the month(s) that begins after the employee's termination must be included in the employee's wages for income tax and employment tax purposes, to the extent that the employer does not recover those transit passes or their value.

Smartcards and Debit Cards

In Rev. Rul. 2006-57,[49] the IRS issued guidance on how employer-issued smartcards and debit cards can qualify as nontaxable transportation fringe benefits. Even though Rev. Rul. 2006-57 was effective January 1, 2012, employers could rely on its guidance for transactions occurring before that date.[50] Smartcards or debit cards will qualify as transportation fringe benefits in the following three situations:

1. Smartcards (a plastic card with an imbedded memory chip) purchased from a transit company if the card is usable only as fare media;
2. Terminal-restricted debit cards purchased from a third party if the card may only be used at points of sale where nothing other than fare media for a transit system is sold; and
3. Terminal-restricted debit cards that may be used by employees to purchase items other than fare media only if the card is used in connection with a bona fide reimbursement arrangement that meets specified substantiation requirements.

Transportation benefits provided through multi-use debit cards are taxable if the employee does not have to substantiate transportation expenses.

.02 Commuter Vehicles

Your employer can set up (or pay someone to operate) commuting pools for you and the other employees. A commuter highway vehicle is defined as any vehicle that: (1) seats at least six adults (not including the driver); (2) is used at least 80 percent of the time for transporting employees to and from work; and (3) is occupied on these trips by at least three adults (again, not including the driver). There is no requirement that your employer own and operate the vehicle; a third party can provide both the vehicle and the driver [Reg. § 1.132-9, Q&A-2].

.03 Parking

Code Sec. 132(a)(5) provides that employees may exclude from gross income employer-provided transportation fringe benefits, which include among other things "qualified parking." The amount excludable for qualified parking may not exceed $245 per month in 2013, or $12.25 a day ($245 divided by 20 work days a month) [Code Sec. 132(f)]. This means that reimbursement paid to an employee for parking at

---

[49] Rev. Rul. 2006-57, 2006-2 CB 911.

[50] Notice 2010-94, IRB 2010-52.

a work location away from the employee's permanent work location will be excludible from the employee's wages as a qualified transportation fringe benefit [Code Sec. 132(f)(2)(B)]. If the value of a qualified transportation fringe exceeds the dollar limits the excess cannot be claimed as either a working condition fringe or a *de minimis* fringe [Code Sec. 132(f)(7)]. Employees can, however, combine the parking reimbursement with employer-provided transit passes for a double benefit [Code Sec. 132(f)(2)(B)].

"Qualified parking" is defined as parking provided to an employee by an employer: (1) on or near the employer's business premises;[51] or (2) at a location from which the employee commutes to work by carpool, commuter highway vehicle, mass transit facilities, transportation provided by any person in the business of transporting persons for compensation or hire, or by any other means [Code Sec. 132(f)(5)(C)]. Parking on or near property used by the employee for residential purposes is not considered "qualified parking."

Park-and-Ride Break

"Park-and-ride" lots also qualify for the $245-per-month exclusion in 2013 [Code Sec. 132(f)(5)(C)]. These are defined as lots from which you commute to work by mass transit, carpool or in a commuter highway vehicle.

Parking is considered to be provided by an employer if: (1) the employer pays for the parking; (2) the employer reimburses the employee for parking expenses; or (3) the parking is on property that the employer owns or leases [Reg. § 1.132-9, Q&A-4]. Qualified parking does not include parking expenses that would otherwise be excludible as a reimbursement for an employment-related expense under an accountable plan, or that are provided in-kind as a working condition fringe [Reg. § 1.132-9(b), Q&A-4(b)].

To qualify as a tax-free transportation fringe benefit, the employee must be provided with the opportunity to elect either a fixed amount of cash compensation at a specified future date or a fixed amount of benefits to be provided for a specified future period (such as qualified parking to be used during a future calendar month) [Reg. § 1.132-9(b), Q&A-12(a)]. Additionally, the employee's election must be in writing or another form, such as electronic, that includes, in permanent and verifiable form, the information required in the election. The election must contain the date of the election, the amount of the compensation to be reduced, and the period for which the benefit will be provided. The election must relate to a fixed dollar amount or fixed percentage of compensation reduction. The election may be automatically renewed provided the employee has the opportunity to revoke the election. The compensation reduction election must be made before the employee is able to receive cash or other taxable amount at the employee's discretion. Finally, the employee may not receive a refund of the amounts by which the employee's compensation reductions exceed the actual amounts expended for qualified transportation fringes.

Who Is Eligible to Benefit

The exclusion for a qualified transportation fringe is available only to "employees," who include household employees such as nannies, housekeepers, and gardeners. Self-employed taxpayers may not take advantage of this fringe benefit [Code Sec.

[51] LTR 200347003 (July 11, 2003).

132(f)(5)(E)]. Thus, partners, sole proprietors, 2-percent shareholders of S corporations, or other independent contractors are not employees for purposes of the qualified transportation fringe benefit and may not take advantage of this tax break.

Reporting and Employment Tax Requirements

Qualified transportation fringes not exceeding the applicable statutory monthly limit are not wages for FICA, FUTA, and income tax withholding purposes. Thus, any amount by which an employee elects to reduce compensation is not subject to FICA, FUTA, or income tax withholding. Qualified transportation fringes exceeding the applicable statutory monthly limit are wages for FICA, FUTA, and income tax withholding purposes and are reported on the employee's Form W-2 [Reg. § 1.132-9, Q&A-22].

Abusive "Double-Dip" Employee Parking Arrangements Disallowed

In Rev. Rul. 2004-98[52] the IRS disallowed an abusive fringe benefit arrangement. In the targeted arrangement, an employer implemented payroll arrangement in which employees' cash compensation was reduced in return for employer provided parking, but that amount was then reimbursed by the employer, resulted in taxable income to the employees. The parking was provided by the employer at or near the employer's place of business and the cost of the parking was incurred by the employer. Thus, the value of the benefit was excludable by the employees under Code Sec. 132(a)(5). Since the employees did not actually incur any reimburseable expense, the "reimbursement" payments they received were not excludable from their gross income and were subject to federal income, FICA, and FUTA withholding.

▶ **PRACTICE NOTE:** This ruling is not limited to abusive double-dip parking arrangements. It would apply to similar double-dip arrangements involving employers reimbursing employees for transit passes and use of commuter vans.

.04 Transportation Fringe Benefit for Bicycle Commuters

An employer may provide qualified bike commuting reimbursements as a tax-free qualified transportation fringe benefit to any employee who commutes to work using a bike [Code Sec. 132(f)(1)(D)].

The applicable annual limitation in case of any qualified bicycle commuting reimbursement is $20 for every qualified bicycle commuting month for any calendar year [Code Sec. 132(f)(5)(F)(ii)]. "Qualified bicycle commuting month" refers to any month during which an employee regularly uses a bike for a substantial portion of travel between the employee's residence and place of employment and the employee did not receive any other transportation fringe benefit [Code Sec. 132(f)(5)(F)(iii)].

A "qualified bicycle commuting reimbursement" refers to any employer reimbursement during the 15-month period starting with the first day of a calendar year to an employee for reasonable expenses incurred by the employee during the calendar year for the purchase of a bike and bike accessories, repair and storage of a bike that is regularly used to ride to and from work [Code Sec. 132(f)(5)(F)(i)]. However, unlike other qualified transportation fringe benefits, the bike commuting fringe may not be provided pursuant to an elective salary reduction agreement [Code Sec. 132(f)(4)]. Under such an agreement, no amount is included in an employee's gross income

---

[52] Rev. Rul. 2004-98, 2004-2 CB 664.

solely because the employee may choose between any qualified transportation fringe benefit and compensation that would otherwise be includable in the gross income of the employee.

¶4105 MOVING EXPENSE FRINGE

Many employers reimburse employees for the costs of moving to a new job location [see Ch. 9]. Qualified moving expense reimbursements are a tax-free fringe benefit [Code Sec. 132(a)(6)]. Employer-paid deductible moving expenses are tax-free to employees (both payroll and income tax-free). The employee must substantiate his or her moving expenses to the employer. And to be tax-free, the reimbursement cannot be attributable to expenses that were deducted in an earlier year.

This means that on a Form W-2, employers don't have to report a moving expense reimbursement as wages or other compensation. So employers won't have to withhold taxes from the reimbursement—assuming the expenses are reasonable and meet the definition of deductible moving expenses.

The IRS has indicated that the amounts paid or incurred by a real estate relocation management firm after its purchase of the principal residence of a relocated employee were not includable in the employee's income as compensation for services because the costs became the firm's obligation once it acquired ownership of the residence.[53]

¶4110 CAFETERIA EMPLOYEE BENEFIT PLANS

A *cafeteria plan* is a written benefit plan maintained by an employer for the benefit of its employees. All participants must be employees and each participant must have the opportunity to select from a menu of benefits offered by the employer [Code Sec. 125(d)]. A cafeteria plan may offer participants the opportunity to select among various taxable benefits (generally cash) and qualified nontaxable benefits, but a plan must offer at least one taxable benefit and at least one nontaxable qualified benefit. For example, if participants are given the opportunity to elect only among two or more qualified nontaxable benefits, the plan is not a cafeteria plan and may not produce the desired tax result typically afforded cafeteria plans [Code Sec. 125(a)].

Cash benefits will be includible in the employee's gross income as compensation but qualified benefits will typically be excluded from gross income. An employee in a cafeteria plan will not have an amount included in gross income solely because the employee may choose among two or more benefits consisting of cash and qualified benefits [Code Sec. 125(a)]. If an employee chooses to receive a qualified benefit under the plan, the fact that the employee could have received cash or a taxable benefit instead will not make the qualified benefit taxable. Contributions used to purchase group health coverage are not included in the gross income of the employee solely because the plan uses an automatic enrollment process whereby the em-

[53] LTR 9447002 (July 11, 1994).

ployee's salary is reduced each year to pay for a portion of the group health coverage under the plan.[54]

A cafeteria plan may not include any plan that offers a benefit that defers the receipt of compensation [Code Sec. 125(d)(2)(A)]. There are three exceptions to the rule that a cafeteria plan cannot include any plan which provides for deferred compensation as follows:

1. Profit-sharing or stock bonus plan or rural cooperative plan (within the meaning of Code Sec. 401(k)(7) which includes a qualified cash or deferred arrangement to the extent of amounts which a covered employee may elect to have the employer pay as contributions to a trust under such plan on behalf of the employee [Code Sec. 125(d)(2)(B)];
2. Certain plans maintained by educational institutions to the extent of amounts which a covered employee may elect to have the employer pay as contributions for post-retirement group life insurance if all contributions for such insurance must be made before retirement, and such life insurance does not have a cash surrender value at any time [Code Sec. 125(d)(2)(C)]; and
3. Health savings accounts to the extent of amounts which a covered employee may elect to have the employer pay as contributions to a health savings account established on behalf of the employee [Code Sec. 125(d)(2)(D)].

In addition, a cafeteria plan may not operate in a manner that enables employees to defer compensation. For example, a plan that permits employees to carry over unused elective contributions or plan benefits from one plan year to another operates to defer compensation [Prop. Reg. § 1.125-1(o)(1)]. This is the case regardless of how the contributions or benefits are used by the employee in the subsequent plan year (e.g., whether they are automatically or electively converted into another taxable or nontaxable benefit in the subsequent plan year or used to provide additional benefits of the same type). Similarly, a cafeteria plan operates to permit the deferral of compensation if the plan permits participants to use contributions for one plan year to purchase a benefit that will be provided in a subsequent plan year (e.g., life, health, disability, or long-term care insurance coverage with a savings or investment feature, such as whole life insurance).

.01 Why Cafeteria Plan May Fail to Qualify for Tax-Free Treatment

Unless a plan satisfies the requirements of Code Sec. 125 and the regulations, the plan is not a cafeteria plan. A plan could fail to qualify for the following reasons: offering nonqualified benefits, not offering an election between at least one permitted taxable benefit and at least one qualified benefit, deferring compensation, failing to comply with the uniform coverage rule or use-or-lose rule, allowing employees to revoke elections or make new elections during a plan year, failing to comply with substantiation requirements, paying or reimbursing expenses incurred for qualified benefits before the effective date of the cafeteria plan or before a period of coverage, allocating experience gains (forfeitures) other than as expressly allowed in the regulations, and failing to comply with grace period rules.

---

[54] Rev. Rul. 2002-27, 2002-1 CB 925.

.02 Written Requirement

Code Sec. 125(d)(1) requires that a cafeteria plan be in writing and must be operated in accordance with the terms of the written plan. The written plan must specifically describe all benefits, set forth the rules for eligibility to participate and the procedure for making elections, provide that all elections are irrevocable and state how employer contributions may be made under the plan (for example, salary reduction or nonelective employer contributions), the maximum amount of elective contributions, and the plan year. If the plan includes a flexible spending arrangement (FSA), the written plan must include provisions complying with the uniform coverage rule and the use-or-lose rule [Prop. Reg. § 1.125-1(c)]. Because Code Sec. 125(d)(1)(A) states that a cafeteria plan is a written plan under which "all participants are employees," the written cafeteria plan must specify that only employees may participate in the cafeteria plan. In addition, all provisions of the written plan must apply uniformly to all participants.

.03 Who May Participate in Cafeteria Plan

All participants in a cafeteria plan must be employees [Code Sec. 125(d)(1)(A)]. Employees include common law employees, leased employees, and full-time life insurance salesmen [Prop. Reg. § 1.125-1(g)(1)]. Former employees (including laid-off employees and retired employees) may participate in a plan, but a plan may not be maintained predominantly for former employees [Prop. Reg. § 1.125-1(g)(1)(iv)]. A participant's spouse or dependents may receive benefits through a cafeteria plan although they cannot participate in the cafeteria plan.

The following taxpayers may not participate in a cafeteria plan: self-employed individuals [Prop. Reg. § 1.125-1(g)(2)], sole proprietors, partners, directors of corporations, and 2-percent shareholders of an S corporation [Prop. Reg. § 1.125-1(g)(2)(ii)]. A self-employed individual may, however, sponsor a cafeteria plan for his or her employees.

.04 Election between Taxable and Nontaxable Benefits

A cafeteria plan must offer employees an election among only permitted taxable benefits (including cash) and qualified nontaxable benefits [Code Sec. 125(d)(1)(B)]. For cafeteria plan purposes, cash means cash from current compensation (including salary reduction), payment for annual leave, sick leave, or other paid time off, severance pay, property, and certain after-tax employee contributions [Prop. Reg. § 1.125-1(a)(2)]. Distributions from qualified retirement plans are not considered cash.

.05 Qualified Benefits

In general, in order for a benefit to be a qualified benefit for cafeteria plan purposes, the benefit must be excludible from employees' gross income under a specific provision of the Code and must not defer compensation, except as specifically allowed in Code Sec. 125(d)(2)(B), (C) or (D). Examples of qualified benefits include the following [Prop. Reg. § 1.125-1(a)(3)]:

- Group-term life insurance on the life of an employee [Code Sec. 79];
- Employer-provided accident and health plans, including health flexible spending arrangements, and accidental death and dismemberment policies [Code Secs. 106 and 105(b)];

- A dependent care assistance program [Code Sec. 129];
- An adoption assistance program [Code Sec. 137] (for further discussion see ¶4115);
- Contributions to a Code Sec. 401(k) plan;
- Contributions to certain plans maintained by educational organizations;
- Contributions to HSAs;
- Long-term and short-term disability coverage.

.06 Nonqualified Benefits

A cafeteria plan may not offer any of the following benefits:

- Scholarships [Code Sec. 117];
- Employer-provided meals and lodging [Code Sec. 119];
- Educational assistance [Code Sec. 127];
- Fringe benefits [Code Sec. 132];
- Long-term care insurance;
- Archer Medical Savings Accounts [Code Secs. 220 and 106(b)];
- Group term life insurance for an employee's spouse, child, or dependent;
- Elective deferrals to Code Sec. 403(b) plans;
- A health FSA that provides for the carryover of unused benefits;
- A plan offering an election solely between paid time off and taxable benefits.

.07 Grace Period

A written cafeteria plan may provide an optional grace period extending the period for incurring expenses for qualified benefits up to two months and 15 days immediately following the end of a plan year [Prop. Reg. § 1.125-1(e)]. A grace period may apply to one or more qualified benefits (for example, health FSA or dependent care assistance program) but in no event does it apply to paid time off or contributions to Code Sec. 401(k) plans. Unused benefits or contributions for one qualified benefit may only be used to reimburse expenses incurred during the grace period for that same qualified benefit. The amount of unused benefits and contributions available during the grace period may be limited by the employer. A grace period may extend to the fifteenth day of the third month after the end of the plan year (but may be for a shorter period). Benefits or contributions not used as of the end of the grace period are forfeited under the use-or-lose rule. The grace period applies to all employees who are participants (including through COBRA), as of the last day of the plan year. Grace period rules must apply uniformly to all participants.

▶ **NEW TAX LAW ALERT:** *IRS Relaxes "Use-It-Or-Lose-It" Rule.* In Notice 2013-71,[55] the IRS relaxed the use-or-lose rule applicable to health FSAs. This change will enable employers, for the first time, to amend Code Sec. 125 cafeteria plan documents to provide that up to $500 of unused amounts remaining at year-end in a health FSA may be paid or reimbursed to plan participants for qualified medical expenses incurred during the following plan year, instead of forfeiting the unused amounts. Sponsors of health FSAs now have the choice of

[55] Notice 2013-71, IRB 2013-47.

either allowing employees a carryover of up to $500 or allowing them a grace period of up to two and a half months. Under the grace period rule, a Code Sec. 125 cafeteria plan may permit an employee to use amounts remaining from the previous year (including amounts remaining in a health FSA) to pay expenses incurred for certain qualified benefits during the period of up to two months and 15 days immediately following the end of the plan year [Prop. Reg. § 1.125-1(e)]. A health FSA cannot, however, offer both a carryover and a grace period.

If an employer amends its plan to adopt a carryover, the same carryover limit must apply to all plan participants. A Code Sec. 125 cafeteria plan is not permitted to allow unused amounts relating to a health FSA to be cashed out or converted to any other taxable or nontaxable benefit. Unused amounts relating to a health FSA may be used only to pay or reimburse certain medical expenses (excluding health insurance, long-term care services or insurance) [Prop. Reg. § 1.125-1(q)]. The amount that may be carried over to the following plan year is equal to the lesser of (1) any unused amounts from the immediately preceding plan year or (2) $500 (or a lower amount specified in the plan). Any unused amount in excess of $500 (or a lower amount specified in the plan) that remains unused as of the end of the plan year will be forfeited. Any unused amount remaining in an employee's health FSA as of termination of employment also is forfeited (unless, if applicable, the employee elects COBRA continuation coverage with respect to the health FSA).

Cafeteria Plan Amendment Required

To take advantage of the carryover option permitted under Notice 2013-71, a cafeteria plan offering a health FSA must be amended to include the carryover provision. The amendment must be adopted on or before the last day of the plan year from which amounts may be carried over and may be effective retroactively to the first day of that plan year. The cafeteria plan sponsors have an obligation to inform participants of the new carryover provision. A plan may be amended to adopt the carryover provision for a plan year that begins in 2013 at any time on or before the last day of the plan year that begins in 2014.

A Code Sec. 125 cafeteria plan that incorporates a carryover provision providing that unused amounts in a plan year may be carried over to the following plan year, may not also provide for a grace period in the same plan year. If a plan has provided for a grace period and is being amended to add a carryover provision, the plan must also be amended to eliminate the grace period provision by no later than the end of the plan year from which amounts may be carried over.

Impact of New Rule

The IRS notes that eliminating the use-or-lose rule, in accordance with the guidance provided in Notice 2013-17, will reduce wasteful year-end FSA healthcare spending by limiting the risk of forfeiture, and in turn, reduce the incentive to spend down as year-end approaches in order to avoid losing unused funds. Some plan sponsors may be eligible to take advantage of the option to adopt a carryover provision as early as plan year 2013.

.08 Discriminatory Benefits

A cafeteria plan that discriminates in favor of highly compensated individuals and key employees must include those discriminatory benefits in income. The nondiscrimination rules provide that a cafeteria plan may not provide highly compensated individuals more favorable rules regarding eligibility, contributions, and benefits [Prop. Reg. § 1.125-7]. A cafeteria plan does not discriminate in favor of highly compensated individuals if the plan benefits a group of employees who qualify under a reasonable classification established by the employer, and the group of employees included in the classification satisfies the safe harbor percentage test or the unsafe harbor percentage component of the facts and circumstances test of Reg. § 410(b)-4(c) [Prop. Reg. § 1.125-7(b)].

For purposes of these two safe harbors, if the cafeteria plan provides that only employees who have completed three years of employment are permitted to participate in the plan, employees who have not completed three years of employment may be excluded from consideration. However, if the cafeteria plan provides that employees are allowed to participate before completing three years of employment, all employees with less than three years of employment must be included in applying the safe harbor percentage test and the unsafe harbor percentage component of the facts and circumstances test. In addition, for purposes of the safe harbor percentage test and the unsafe harbor percentage component of the facts and circumstances test, the following employees are excluded from consideration:

- Employees (except key employees) covered by a collectively bargained plan,
- Employees who are nonresident aliens and receive no earned income from the employer which constitutes income from sources within the United States, and
- Employees participating in the cafeteria plan under a COBRA continuation provision.

A cafeteria plan does not discriminate with respect to contributions and benefits if either qualified benefits and total benefits, or employer contributions allocable to statutory nontaxable benefits and employer contributions allocable to total benefits, do not discriminate in favor of highly compensated participants. A cafeteria plan must satisfy this requirement with respect to both benefit availability and benefit utilization. Thus, a plan must give each similarly situated participant a uniform opportunity to elect qualified benefits, and the actual election of qualified benefits through the plan must not be disproportionate by highly compensated participants (while other participants elect permitted taxable benefits) [Prop. Reg. § 1.125-7(c)].

If for any plan year, the statutory nontaxable benefits provided to key employees exceed 25 percent of the aggregate of statutory nontaxable benefits provided for all employees through the cafeteria plan, each key employee includes in gross income an amount equaling the maximum taxable benefits that he or she could have elected for the plan year [Prop. Reg. § 1.125-7(d)].

Safe Harbor for Plans Providing Health Benefits

A cafeteria plan that provides health benefits is not treated as discriminatory as to benefits and contributions if:

1. Contributions under the plan on behalf of each participant include an amount which equals 100 percent of the cost of the health benefit coverage under the plan of the majority of the highly compensated participants similarly situated, or equals or exceeds 75 percent of the cost of the health benefit coverage of the

participant (similarly situated) having the highest cost health benefit coverage under the plan, and

2. Excess contributions or benefits under the plan bear a uniform relationship to compensation.

.09 Making, Revoking, and Changing Elections

Generally, a cafeteria plan must require employees to elect annually between taxable benefits and qualified benefits. Elections must be made before the earlier of the first day of the period of coverage or when benefits are first currently available. The determination of whether a taxable benefit is currently available does not depend on whether it has been constructively received by the employee. Annual elections generally must be irrevocable and may not be changed during the plan year [Prop. Reg. § 1.125-2(a)]. However, Reg. § 1.125-4 permits a cafeteria plan to provide for changes in elections based on certain changes in status such as the birth of a child. New employees are allowed to make an election within 30 days of being hired. In addition, new hires may claim benefits back to the date of hire.

A cafeteria plan may allow an employee to revoke an election for coverage and to make a new election in the situations described below. These rules apply to group health or accident plans, group-term life insurance coverage, dependent care assistance and adoption assistance. They also apply to coverage for permanent loss or loss of use of a member or function of the body [Reg. § 1.125-4(i)(4)].

Change Corresponding with Special Enrollment Rights Under HIPPA

A cafeteria plan may permit an employee to revoke an election for coverage under a group health plan during a period of coverage and make a new election that corresponds with the special enrollment rights under Code Sec. 9801(f). It generally requires group health plans to permit individuals to be enrolled for coverage following the loss of other health coverage or if a person becomes the spouse or dependent of the employee through marriage, birth, adoption (or placement for adoption). If an employee has a right to enroll in an employer's group plan or to add a family member, the employee can make a conforming election for the cafeteria plan [Reg. § 1.125-4(b)].

Example 4-32: ABCo offers health coverage to its employees under a plan that is covered under Code Sec. 9801(f). Under the plan, employees may elect either employee only coverage or family coverage. ABCo also maintains a cafeteria plan under which qualified benefits, including health coverage, are funded through salary reduction. ABCo's employee, Melvin Rose, is married and they have one child. Rose elected employee only coverage. During the year, Melvin and his wife adopt a child. Shortly after, but within 30 days of the adoption, Melvin wants to change his election from employee only to family coverage under his employer's accident or health plan. This change satisfies the conditions for special enrollment of an employee with a new dependent under Code Sec. 9801(f)(2). Melvin may enroll in family coverage in order to provide coverage effective as of the date of the child's adoption. In addition, Melvin may change his salary reduction election to family coverage for salary not currently available.

An election change can be funded through salary reduction under a cafeteria plan only on a prospective basis, except for the HIPPA enrollment right established in the case of an election made within 30 days of birth, adoption, or placement for adoption. Thus, in the case of the marriage of an employee where no retroactive coverage is required under HIPPA, a salary reduction election change is prospective only [Reg. § 1.125-4(b)(2), Ex. 2(ii)].

Changes in Status

A cafeteria plan may allow an employee to make an election change or to revoke an election during a coverage period with respect to an accident or health plan or a group-term life insurance plan and make a new election for the remaining coverage period under the following circumstances:

- Change in the employee's legal marital status [Reg. § 1.125-4(c)-2(i)];
- Change in the number of an employee's dependents (i.e., birth, death, adoption or adoption placement) [Reg. § 1.125-4(c) -2(ii)];
- Change in employment status of the employee, the employee's spouse or the employee's dependent [Reg. § 1.125-4(c) -2(iii)] (a change in employment status in this situation includes a strike or lockout and going back to work after an unpaid leave of absence);
- Change in the status of a dependent that causes the dependent to satisfy, or cease to satisfy, eligibility requirements for coverage [Reg. § 1.125-4(c) -2(iv)];
- Change in residence of the employee, spouse or dependent [Reg. § 1.125-4(c)-2(v)]; and
- Change in the case of adoption assistance, that is, the commencement or termination of an adoption proceeding [Reg. § 1.125-4(c)(2)(vi)].

▶ **PRACTICE POINTER:** Note that change in status rules cover almost all changes that affect eligibility under accident, health and group-term life insurance plans [Reg. § 1.125-4(c)(2)(iii)].

Example 4-33: Eligibility to participate in DEFCo's cafeteria plan is limited to salaried employees. Ron James, who was a salaried employee of DEFCo on January 1, elects employee-only heath coverage. In June, Ron switches from being a salary-paid employee to an hourly paid employee. This is considered a change in status and the cafeteria plan may permit Ron to revoke his election for health coverage in mid-year.

The change in status rules covers not only a change in the employee's marital status but also the employment status of the employee's spouse or dependent.

Consistency rule. An election change is permitted only if the election change is on account of and corresponds with a change in status that affects eligibility for coverage under an employer's plan. This includes a change in status that results in an increase or decrease in the number of an employee's family members or dependents who may benefit from coverage under the plan [Reg. § 1.125-4(c)(3)(i)].

Application of consistency rule. If a change in status is the employee's divorce, annulment, or legal separation from a spouse, the death of a spouse or dependent, or a dependent ceasing to satisfy the eligibility requirements for coverage, an employee's election to cancel accident or health insurance under the cafeteria plan for any individual other than the spouse involved in the divorce, annulment or legal separation, the deceased spouse or dependent, or the dependent that ceased to satisfy the eligibility for coverage, will not be covered under the change of status rules. Such an election is not consistent with the change in status. Thus, an individual whose spouse dies during the year cannot cancel coverage for his dependents when he cancels the insurance for his deceased spouse [Reg. § 1.125-4(c)(3)(iii)]. However, if the employee had one child and before his divorce had elected family coverage, the employee could change from family coverage to employee-plus-one coverage after his divorce. If one divorced spouse makes an election to cover the child under his or her employer's health plan, then the other spouse may elect employee-only coverage under his or her health plan. This change in coverage would correspond to the change in status [Reg. § 1.125-4(c)(4), Ex. (3)].

The consistency rule does not apply for COBRA changes. Thus, if the employee, spouse or dependent becomes eligible for continuation coverage under the group health plan of the employee's employer under Code Sec. 4980B or any similar state coverage, a cafeteria plan may allow the employee to elect to increase payments under the employee's cafeteria plan in order to pay for the continuation coverage.

In a case where an employee terminates employment with the employer and is subsequently rehired, the regulations adopt a safe harbor rule if the employee terminates and resumes employment within 30 days and the cafeteria plan provides that the employee's election is automatically reinstated. In such a case, the employer is not required to determine whether a bona fide change in status has occurred [Reg. § 1.125-4(c)(4), Ex. (8)]. If termination and rehiring occur *outside of the 30-day parameter,* the cafeteria plan may permit the employee the option of reinstating the election in effect prior to the termination, or making a new election under the plan. Or, the cafeteria plan may prohibit the employee from returning to the plan during that plan year.

In addition, conforming changes are permitted if they result from a judgment, decree or order resulting from divorce, legal separation, annulment or change in legal custody that requires accident or health coverage for an employee's child or foster child who is a dependent of the employee [Reg. § 1.125-4(d)]. If an employee, spouse, or dependent who is enrolled in the accident or health plan of the employer becomes entitled to Medicare or Medicaid coverage, a cafeteria plan may permit the employee to make a prospective election to change or reduce coverage of the employee, spouse, or dependent [Reg. § 1.125-4(e)].

¶4115 ADOPTION EXPENSE EXCLUSION

The Internal Revenue Code offers the following two tax breaks for individuals who pay or incur expenses to adopt a child: (1) Employees who incur adoption-related expenses may be able to exclude from income a certain annually adjusted portion of their expenses if their employer has an adoption assistance program in place and either pays or reimburses the employee's qualified adoption expenses; (2) the adoptive parent may also be able to claim an adoption credit for an annually adjusted amount of qualified adoption expenses paid or incurred by the taxpayer. The employer-provided adoption assistance program is discussed in detail below. For further discussion of the adoption credit, see ¶ 14,015.

.01 Employer-Provided Adoption Assistance Programs

Employer-provided adoption benefits are amounts an employer pays directly to either the employee or a third party for qualified adoption expenses under a qualified adoption assistance program. Code Sec. 137(a)(1) provides that an employee's gross income does not include amounts that an employer pays directly either to the employee or to a third party for qualified adoption expenses under a qualified adoption assistance program.

In 2013, the amount that can be excluded from an employee's gross income for the adoption of a child with special needs is $12,970 [Code Sec. 137(a)(2)]. The maximum amount that can be excluded from an employee's gross income for the amounts paid or expenses incurred by an employer for qualified adoption expenses furnished pursuant to an adoption assistance program for other adoptions by the employee is $12,970. In the case of an adoption of a child with special needs, the exclusion applies regardless of whether the employee has qualified adoption expenses [Code Sec. 137(a)(2)].

If the adopted child is a U.S. citizen or resident, the income exclusion is available in the year in which the employer pays the qualified adoption or special needs adoption expenses even if the adoption does not become final that year. However, if the adoptive child is not a U.S. citizen or resident, the exclusion is available only when the adoption becomes final. Amounts paid or expenses incurred by an employer in a tax year prior to a final adoption are includible in the employee's gross income for the year paid or incurred but when the adoption becomes final, the employee deduct the amounts previously included in income.

Employer-provided adoption benefits will be shown in box 12 of Form W-2 with code T. A taxpayer's salary may have to be reduced to pay these benefits. A taxpayer may also be able to exclude amounts not shown in box 12 of Form W-2 if:

1. The taxpayer adopted a child with special needs,
2. The adoption became final in 2013, and
3. The employer had a qualified adoption assistance program in place in the year the expenses were incurred.

.02 Income Phaseout Rules

The amount excludable from an employee's gross income begins to phase out under Code Sec. 137(b)(2)(A) for taxpayers with modified adjusted gross income (MAGI) in excess of $194,580 and is completely phased out for taxpayers with MAGI of $234,580 or more.

.03 Computation of MAGI for Exclusion Purposes

A taxpayer computes MAGI for the year in which the exclusion is claimed by taking adjusted gross income for the year and subtracting the following items [Code Sec. 137(b)(3)]:

- The deduction for income attributable to domestic production activities [Code Sec. 199];

- The deduction for interest paid on qualified education loans [Code Sec. 221];
- The deduction for higher education expenses [Code Sec. 222];
- Foreign earned income [Code Sec. 911]; and
- Income derived from sources within Guam, American Samoa, the Northern Mariana Islands, or Puerto Rico [Code Secs. 931 and 933].

Then the taxpayer adds back the following items:

- Social Security and tier one railroad retirement benefits [Code Sec. 86];
- Income from educational U.S. savings bonds [Code Sec. 135];
- Deduction for individual retirement account contributions [Code Sec. 219]; and
- Passive activity losses [Code Sec. 469].

NOTE: MAGI is defined differently for purposes of the adoption expense exclusion and the adoption credit which is discussed further below.

.04 Adoption Assistance Program

An adoption assistance program is a separate written plan established by an employer to provide adoption assistance to its employees. The program must satisfy the following requirements [Code Sec. 137(c)]:

- The program must benefit employees who qualify under classifications set up by the employer and may not discriminate in favor of highly compensated employees or their dependents,
- Not more than five percent of the amounts paid or incurred by the employer for adoption assistance during the year may be provided to shareholders or owners (or their spouses or dependents) who own more than five percent of the stock or of the capital or profits interest in the employer,
- The adoption assistance program need not be funded, and
- All employees who are eligible to participate in the program must be given reasonable notice of the terms and availability of the program.

Adoption reimbursement programs of the armed forces and of the Coast Guard also qualify as adoption assistance programs under Code Sec. 137(c).

.05 Qualified Adoption Expenses

Qualified adoption expenses include reasonable and necessary adoption fees, court costs, attorney fees, travel expenses (including meals and lodging) while away from home, and adoption expenses relating to the adoption of a foreign child [Code Secs. 32C(d)(1) and 137(d)]. All reasonable and necessary expenses required by a state as a condition of adoption are qualified adoption expenses including the cost of construction, renovations, alterations, or purchases specifically required by the state to meet the needs of the adopted child.

Qualified adoption expenses *do not* include the following:

- Expenses received under any federal, state, or local program;
- Expenses that violate federal or state law;
- Costs associated with a surrogate parenting arrangement;

- Expenses incurred in connection with the adoption of the child of the taxpayer's spouse; and
- Expenses allowed as a credit or deduction under any other provision of federal income tax laws [Code Secs. 137(d) and 32C(d)(1)].

.06 Eligible Child

An eligible child is defined for purposes of both the adoption expense exclusion and the adoption credit [see ¶ 14,015] as:

- Any child under age 18. If the child turned 18 during the year, the child is an eligible child for the part of the year he or she was under age 18.
- Any disabled person who is physically or mentally incapable of caring for himself or herself [Code Sec. 36C(d)(2)].

Special Needs Child

A child is a child with special needs if:

1. The child is a citizen or resident of the United States or its possessions at the time the adoption process begins;
2. A state (including the District of Columbia) has determined that the child cannot or should not be returned to his or her parent's home;
3. The state has determined that the child will not be adopted unless assistance is provided to the adoptive parents. Factors used by states to make this determination include: (a) a child's ethnic background and age, (b) the child's membership in a minority or sibling group, and (c) whether the child has a medical condition, or a physical, mental, or emotional handicap [Code Sec. 36C(d)(3)].

.07 Adopted Child Needs Identification Number

The adopted child must have some official form of identification in order for the adoptive parents to claim tax benefits with respect to the adoption of that child on their tax return [Code Sec. 36C(f)(2)]. Any of the following will suffice:

- A social security number (SSN). If the child needs an SSN, apply on Form SS-5;
- An individual taxpayer identification number (ITIN) if the child is a resident or nonresident alien and not eligible for an SSN. If the child needs an ITIN, apply on Form W-7; or
- An adoption taxpayer identification number (ATIN), which is a temporary TIN for children who are placed for adoption and an SSN is unavailable or cannot be secured. File Form W-7A with the IRS to obtain an ATIN. In order for the ATIN to be assigned, the child must be placed for adoption by an authorized placement agency that includes (in addition to governmental and private placement organizations) biological parents and other persons authorized by state law to place children for legal adoption. In addition, parents in the process of a domestic U.S. adoption are advised to write "U.S. adoption pending" in the exemption section of their tax return in place of the child's social security number and attach a copy of documentation from the adoption agency or other authority to show that the child was placed in the home for legal adoption.

.08 Double Dipping Prohibited

Although an adopting parent may claim both a credit and an exclusion in connection with the adoption of an eligible child, both may not be claimed for the same adoption-related expenses [Code Sec. 36C(b)(3)].

.09 How to Claim Adoption Exclusion

Use Form 8839, *Qualified Adoption Expenses,* to claim an adoption expense exclusion or adoption credit. For further discussion of the adoption credit, see ¶14,015. The adoption credit and income exclusion for employer-provided adoption benefits cannot be claimed on Form 1040A. They may only be claimed on Form 1040 or Form 1040NR. Taxpayers may claim the credit or exclusion if their filing status is single, head of household, qualifying widow(er), or married filing jointly. If, however, the adoptive parents are legally separated under a decree of divorce or separate maintenance agreement, or if they lived apart for the last six months of the tax year, they may claim the credit or exclusion on a separate return, provided the parent's home is the child's home for more than half the year and the parent pays more than half the cost of keeping up the home for the year.

.10 Income Tax Withholding

Amounts paid or expenses incurred by an employer for qualified adoption expenses under an adoption assistance program are not subject to income tax withholding. Amounts paid or expenses incurred by an employer for qualified adoption expenses are however subject to social security and Medicare taxes (FICA) and federal unemployment tax (FUTA). Employers must report amounts paid or expenses incurred for qualified adoption expenses on the employee's Form W-2. In addition, every employer maintaining a specified fringe benefit plan, including an adoption assistance program, must file an annual information return with the IRS [Code Sec. 6039D(d)(1)].

¶4120 EMPLOYER-PROVIDED GROUP HEALTH PLANS

Most employers provide group health coverage for employees and premiums for such coverage may be paid by the employer, by the employee, or partially by each. Generally, the amount of premiums paid by the employer is deductible by the employer. Amounts paid directly or indirectly to the employee to reimburse him for medical care expenses for himself, his spouse, or dependents are excludable from the employee's gross income [Code Sec. 105(b)].

A flexible spending account (FSA) or health reimbursement arrangement (HRA) is an employer-established benefit plan that may be offered in conjunction with other employer-provided benefits as part of a cafeteria plan. The plans provide a reimbursement account or other arrangement under which an employee is reimbursed for qualified medical expenses that are not covered by insurance.

.01 Health FSAs

Health FSAs are generally funded through voluntary salary reduction agreements between employees and their employers. Contributions to a health FSA and all distributions to pay qualified medical expenses may be excluded from the employee's income. Generally, amounts in the account at the end of the plan year cannot be carried over to the next year. However, the plan can provide for a grace period of up to 2 1/2 months after the end of the plan year.

Under Code Sec. 125(j), beginning in 2013, in order for a health FSA to be a qualified benefit under a cafeteria plan, the maximum amount available for reimbursement of incurred medical expenses of an employee, the employee's dependents, and any other eligible beneficiaries, under the health FSA for a plan year (or other 12-month coverage period) cannot exceed $2,500 which will be indexed for inflation beginning in 2014.[56] In the case of a plan providing a grace period (which may be up to two months and 15 days), unused salary reduction contributions to the health FSA for plan years beginning in 2012 or later that are carried over into the grace period for that plan year will not count against the $2,500 limit for the subsequent plan year. In addition, the IRS provides relief for certain salary-reduction contributions exceeding the $2,500 limit that are due to a reasonable mistake and not willful neglect and that are corrected by the employer.

.02 Health Reimbursement Arrangements

Health reimbursement arrangements (HRAs) are funded solely through employer contributions and distributions from an HRA are used to reimburse employees for medical care expenses and that allow unused amounts to be carried forward to the next year. In order to qualify for favorable tax treatment, the HRA must be funded solely by employer contributions, and cannot be funded through salary reduction contributions under a Code Sec. 125 cafeteria plan or by any other form of employee contribution.

Employer contributions for the plan and reimbursements made from the plan are generally excludable from the employee's gross income under Code Secs. 105 and 106.

.03 Benefits of an HRA

HRAs offer the following benefits:

- Contributions made by the employer can be excluded from the employee's gross income.
- Reimbursements may be tax free if the employee pays qualified medical expenses.
- Any unused amounts in the HRA can be carried forward for reimbursements in later years.

HRAs may only reimburse substantiated medical expenses that are incurred by the employee, by the employee's spouse, or by dependents.

Also included are former (including terminated) and retired employees, even if the employee did not elect COBRA continuation coverage. The reimbursements can be made only up to a predetermined maximum dollar amount for a coverage period and any unused portion of the reimbursements can be carried forward to increase the maximum reimbursement amount in subsequent coverage periods.

---

[56] Notice 2012-40, IRB 2012-25.

.04 Reimbursements

Amounts received as reimbursements from an accident or health plan for the medical care of an employee, an employee's spouse or an employee's dependents are excluded from income [Code Sec. 105(b); Reg. § 1.105-2]. If the amounts reimbursed are attributable to expenses incurred before the establishment of the plan they will not qualify for the exclusion under Code Sec. 105(b).[57]

Similarly, amounts paid to employees as "advance reimbursements" or "loans," without regard to whether they had suffered a personal injury or sickness or incurred medical expenses, are not excludable from gross income, regardless of whether the employees incurred medical costs during the year.[58]

In addition, the exclusion does not apply to amounts for which the medical expense deduction was claimed in a prior year.

Only amounts that are paid specifically to reimburse eligible medical care expenses as defined in Code Sec. 213(d) receive tax-favored treatment. Therefore, to provide certainty that a particular expense is for "medical care," all claims for expense reimbursements must be substantiated.

.05 Employee Defined

For purposes of this exclusion, the following individuals are treated as employees:

- A current common-law employee;
- Any child of an employee who has not attained age 27 as of the end of the year [Code Sec. 105(b)]. A child includes a son; daughter; the taxpayer's stepson or stepdaughter; a foster child placed with the taxpayer by an authorized agency or by judgment, decree, or other order of any court of competent jurisdiction; and the taxpayer's legally adopted child.
- A full-time life insurance agent who is a current statutory employee;
- A retired employee;
- A former employee for whom coverage is maintained based on the employment relationship;
- A widow or widower of an individual who died while an employee;
- A widow or widower of a retired employee; and
- For the exclusion of contributions to an accident or health plan, a leased employee who has provided services on a substantially full-time basis for at least a year if the services are performed under the employer's primary direction and control.

Exception for S Corporation Shareholder

A 2-percent shareholder of an S corporation is not an employee of the corporation for this purpose.

.06 Reimbursement of Over-the-Counter Drugs

Under Code Sec. 106(f), the gross income of an employee does not include expenses reimbursed or paid by an employer-provided plan including a health FSA or HRA, if the expenses were incurred for a medicine or drug that (1) requires a prescription, (2)

---

57 Rev. Rul. 2002-58, 2002-2 CB 541.

58 Rev. Rul. 2002-80, 2002-2 CB 925.

is available without a prescription (an over-the-counter medicine or drug) and the individual obtains a prescription, or (3) is insulin. This rule applies to medical expenses for over-the-counter drugs for all employer-provided accident and health plans, including health FSAs, HRAs, Health Savings Accounts (HSAs), and Archer Medical Savings Accounts (Archer MSAs).

Thus, purchases of over-the-counter medicine and drugs made without a prescription will no longer be reimbursed tax-free from health FSAs or HRAs. No prescription is required, however, for the tax-free reimbursement of items that are not medicines or drugs, including equipment and supplies such as crutches, bandages, glasses, contacts, or blood sugar test kits. Expenses for items such as shampoo and toothpaste, that are merely beneficial to the general health of an individual are not considered expenses for medical care and will not be reimbursed even if the employee has a prescription [Reg. § 1.213-1(e)(1)(ii)]. The IRS provides guidance on Code Sec. 106(f) in Notice 2010-59, Notice 2011-5, and Rev. Rul. 2010-23.[59]

.07 Debit Cards

Employers may use debit cards or stored-value cards to reimburse participants in their health reimbursement arrangements.

Requirements for Use of Debit Cards at Drug Stores, Pharmacies, Mail-Order and Web-Based Vendors

Health FSA and HRA debit cards may be used to purchase over-the-counter medicines or drugs at drug stores and pharmacies, at non-health care merchants that have pharmacies, and at mail order and web-based vendors that sell prescription drugs, if: (1) prior to purchase, (i) the prescription for the over-the-counter medicine or drug is presented (in any format) to the pharmacist; (ii) the over-the-counter medicine or drug is dispensed by the pharmacist in accordance with applicable law and regulations pertaining to the practice of pharmacy; and (iii) an Rx number is assigned; (2) the pharmacy or other vendor retains a record of the Rx number, the name of the purchaser (or the name of the person for whom the prescription applies), and the date and amount of the purchase in a manner that meets IRS recordkeeping requirements; (3) all of these records are available to the employer or its agent upon request; (4) the debit card system will not accept a charge for an over-the-counter medicine or drug unless an Rx number has been assigned; and (5) all legal requirements are satisfied. If these requirements are met, the debit card transaction will be considered fully substantiated at the time and point-of-sale.

Requirements for Use of Debit Cards at Other Vendors

Health FSA and HRA debit cards may also be used to purchase over-the-counter medicines or drugs from vendors (other than drug stores and pharmacies, non-health care merchants that have pharmacies, and mail order and web-based vendors that sell prescription drugs) having health care related Merchant Codes, if all requirements in the preceding paragraph are satisfied, other than the requirements in clause (1) and clause (4) of the preceding paragraph and the requirement in clause (2) of the preceding paragraph that a record of the Rx number be retained. If these require-

[59] Notice 2010-59, IRB 2010-39, 396, as modified by Notice 2011-5, IRB 2011-3, 314; Rev. Rul. 2010-23, IRB 2010-39, 388.

ments are satisfied, these debit card transactions will be considered fully substantiated at the time and point-of-sale.[60]

Basic Debit Card Requirements

In Rev. Rul. 2003-43,[61] the IRS provided guidance on the use of debit cards in health reimbursement arrangements. The purpose of the guidance was to make certain the debit cards are only used for qualified medical expenses at merchants that sell goods other than those for which a reimbursement plan may cover (e.g., grocery stores, large pharmacy chains). The IRS imposed substantiation requirements on both the employee and the vendor.

Merchant Category Code

In Notice 2006-69,[62] the IRS provided guidance on how vendors that do not have a "health care related merchant category code" can still qualify to sell products purchased using the debit cards. These stores must have implemented an inventory information system. The IRS also has issued Notice 2007-2,[63] which provides that stores with the Drug Stores and Pharmacies merchant category code can only accept the debit cards if the store has implemented the inventory information system or if, on a store-by-store basis, 90 percent of the store's receipts were for items that would qualify as qualified medical care expenses under Code Sec. 213.

.08 Transfers and Distributions

An employer can make a one-time transfer of funds from an FSA or HRA to the employee's health savings account (HSA). The comparable contribution rules are modified for the rollover contributions. For purposes of the permitted insurance rules for HSA eligibility, FSAs with no account balance are disregarded. Further, the distribution must be made after December 20, 2006, and before January 1, 2012. The IRS has provided additional guidance on this one-time transfer in Notice 2007-22.[64]

.09 COBRA Coverage

HRAs are subject to COBRA continuation coverage requirements. Additionally, an HRA may allow for continuing reimbursements after a COBRA qualifying event (e.g., termination of employment) even if the qualified beneficiary does not elect COBRA coverage.

.10 Payments Unrelated to Absence from Work

Amounts received for an injury to the employee, or his or her spouse or dependent that resulted in permanent disfigurement, loss or loss of the use of a body part (i.e., loss of a leg), or a function of the body (i.e., loss of hearing) are excluded from gross income to the extent they are computed with reference to the nature of the injury without regard to the amount of time the injured taxpayer is absent from work [Code Sec. 105(c)]. Loss of use or disfigurement is considered permanent when it may reasonably be expected to continue for the life of the individual. Loss or loss of use of a member or function of the body includes the loss or loss of use of an appendage of

---

[60] Notice 2011-5, IRB 2011-3, 314.

[61] Rev. Rul. 2003-43, 2003-1 CB 935 as amplified by Notice 2006-69, IRB 2006-31, and modified by Notice 2007-2, IRB 2007-2.

[62] Notice 2006-69, 2006-2 CB 107.

[63] Notice 2007-2, 2007-1 CB 254.

[64] Notice 2007-22, 2007-22 CB 670, as amplified by Notice 2008-59, IRB 2008-39.

the body, the loss of an eye, the loss of substantially all of the vision of an eye, and the loss of substantially all of the hearing in one or both ears. The exclusion is unavailable if the amount of the benefits is determined by reference to the period the employee is absent from work.[65] For example, if an employee is absent from work as a result of the loss of an arm, and under the accident and health plan established by his employer, he is to receive $125 a week so long as he is absent from work for a period not in excess of 52 weeks, the Code Sec. 105(c) exclusion is not applicable to such payments. In addition, the Code Sec. 105(c) exclusion does not apply to amounts which are treated as workmen's compensation or to amounts paid by reason of the death of the employee [Reg. § 1.105-3].

Example 4-34: XYZ, Inc. provides its employees with health insurance. Ms. Clark, an XYZ employee, receives a $300 reimbursement for medical bills incurred by herself and her dependent daughter. The reimbursement is excludable even though XYZ paid the insurance premiums.

Example 4-35: Construction Corp. maintains an accident plan which provides that an employee who loses a limb (i.e., arm, hand, or leg) is entitled to receive $10,000. Mr. Russell, an employee who lost an arm, receives payment from Construction Corp.'s plan. The $10,000 is excludable from his gross income.

Example 4-36: Same facts as above, except the plan provides for payment of $250 for each week the employee misses work on account of an injury, up to a maximum period of 32 weeks. Payment is made regardless of the nature of the injury. In this case, the amounts received by Russell are included in his gross income.

.11 When Employers and Employees Split Accident and Health Plan Premiums

The employee may exclude accident and health plan benefits that are attributable to the employee's own contributions [Code Sec. 104(a)(3)]. The tax treatment of the benefits attributable to the employer's portion of the plan premiums depends on the tax rules discussed above (taxable unless a medical reimbursement or made for reasons unrelated to work missed) [Code Sec. 105(a); Reg. § 1.105-1(a), (c)].

Example 4-37: Eaststar Corp. maintains a plan that pays regular wages to employees who are absent from work due to sickness or personal injury. Employees contribute 25 percent of the premium cost through payroll deductions. Mr. Taylor, an employee, received $2,000 from the plan for the four weeks of work he missed due to personal injury. Taylor may exclude 25 percent of that amount—or $500—allocable to his own premium payments. However, he must

[65] *S. Hayden*, 85 TCM 1540, Dec. 55,199(M), TC Memo. 2003-184, *aff'd in unpublished op.*, CA-9, 2005-1 USTC ¶ 50,293.

include the other 75 percent—or $1,500—since those benefits are attributable to employer contributions and don't qualify for special tax treatment.

.12 Nondiscrimination Rules

To qualify for tax-free reimbursement, an accident or health plan including HRAs must meet nondiscrimination rules discussed in detail in ¶ 4025 [Code Sec. 105(h); Reg. § 1.105-11].

Gross Income— Exclusions

TAX-FREE INCOME IN GENERAL

Basic rules ¶ 5001

General welfare and assistance payments ¶ 5002

INCOME ON GOVERNMENT OBLIGATIONS

Interest on state and municipal obligations ¶ 5005

Interest on obligations of the United States ¶ 5010

LIFE INSURANCE

Cash value build-up ¶ 5015

Life insurance proceeds ¶ 5020

Surrender of life insurance policy ¶ 5025

Life insurance endowment contracts ¶ 5030

Dividends on life insurance and endowment policies ¶ 5035

Group-term life insurance premiums ¶ 5040

DISABILITY BENEFITS

Medical and disability benefits ¶ 5045

GIFTS, INHERITANCES, AND DAMAGES

Gifts ¶ 5055

Inheritances ¶ 5060

Damages ¶ 5065

ANNUITIES

Annuities in general ¶ 5070

Joint and survivor annuities ¶ 5075

Employee annuities ¶ 5080

SPECIAL RULES

Scholarships ¶ 5085

Social security, unemployment insurance benefits and similar payments ¶ 5090

Energy conservation subsidies ¶ 5095

Exclusion of disaster relief ¶ 5100

Exclusion for long-term care insurance ¶ 5105

Qualified tuition programs (Section 529 plans) ¶ 5110

Coverdell education savings accounts ¶ 5115

Income exclusion for restitution payments to victims of Nazi persecution ¶ 5120

Foster care payments ¶ 5125

Restitution payments to human trafficking victims ¶ 5130

TAX-FREE INCOME IN GENERAL

¶5001 BASIC RULES

All items of income "from whatever source derived" are subject to income tax [Code Sec. 61; Reg. § 1.61-1]. However, despite what the Code says, not all income is subject to tax. Some items are not considered to be income at all or the tax law specifically excludes them from taxation.

For instance, loan proceeds are generally not considered taxable income. The return of invested capital is also tax-free. Example: The part of sale proceeds that equals your tax basis in the property sold or the part of an annuity payment that represents premiums you previously paid is not taxable. Thus, rules exist to separate the part that is tax-free (return of capital) from the taxable portion (appreciation).

Other items are tax-free because, by law, they are excluded from gross income subject to tax. Examples: Gifts, inherited property and life insurance proceeds that you receive are free from income tax. [Life insurance is, however, subject to estate taxes as discussed in Ch. 29.] The exclusion for life insurance proceeds is intended to achieve certain socially desirable goals. Note that income flowing from a gift or inheritance is, however, taxable. You can also exclude utility company subsidies (both rate reductions and cash payments) to residential customers who install energy-saving devices [Code Sec. 136]. See ¶ 5095 for details.

This chapter covers the following types of tax-free income:

- Municipal bond interest
- Insurance proceeds
- Medical and disability benefits
- Gifts and inheritances
- Damages
- Scholarships
- Disaster relief
- Payments to victims of Nazi persecution
- Annuities
- Foster care payments
- Restitution of payments to human trafficking victims

Other items of excludable income are covered elsewhere in the text. They are:

- Corporation stock distribution [Ch. 2]
- Employee fringe benefits [Ch.4]
- The once-every-two-year $250,000 ($500,000 if married filing joint return) exclusion available when taxpayers sell their principal residence [Code Sec. 121(a); See Ch. 7]

¶5002 GENERAL WELFARE AND ASSISTANCE PAYMENTS

.01 Types of Payments That Qualify Under General Welfare Exclusion

Code Sec. 61(a) provides that, except as otherwise provided by law, gross income means all income from whatever source derived. The IRS has consistently held, however, that under the general welfare exclusion, payments made by state and federal governments pursuant to legislation adopting social benefit programs designed to promote the general welfare are not includable in gross income.[1] In order to qualify under the administrative general welfare exclusion the payments must be made from a governmental fund, be for the promotion of general welfare (based on need), and must not represent compensation for services.[2] These payments include payments for the relief of needy persons, housing assistance, benefits under specified employment and training laws, benefits under the federal Railroad Retirement Act, veterans' benefits, certain payments from foreign governments, and miscellaneous welfare-type payments.

.02 Supplemental Security Income

Supplemental security income (SSI) payments provide assistance to certain individuals who are at least age 65 or are blind or disabled and are not taxable to the recipient. SSI payments are not considered to be social security benefits that are subject to the rule that treats up to 85 percent of social security benefits as gross income if the recipient's modified adjusted gross income exceeds certain levels.

.03 Payments to Homeowners

When a homeowner receives Pay-for-Performance Success Payments under the U.S. government's Home Affordable Modification Program (HAMP), the payments are excludable from income under the general welfare exclusion. The Pay-for-Performance Success Payments promote the general welfare by helping homeowners who are at risk of losing their homes pay the mortgage loans on their primary residence. They do not involve the performance of services.[3]

Similarly, payments made under the State Programs with funds from the Housing Finance Agency Hardest Hit Fund, payments made under the Emergency Homeowners' Loan Program (EHLP), and payments under substantially similar state programs (SSSPs) promote the general welfare by helping homeowners who are at risk of losing their homes either pay their mortgage loans or transition to more affordable housing and do not involve the performance of services. Therefore, payments made through 2015 (through 2013 for mortgage insurance premiums) under the State Programs, the EHLP, and the SSSPs to or on behalf of a homeowner are excluded from gross income under the general welfare exclusion.[4]

---

[1] Rev. Rul. 74-205, 1974-1 CB 20.

[2] Rev. Rul. 75-246, 1975-1 CB 24, Rev. Rul. 82-106, 1982-1 CB 103.

[3] Rev. Rul. 2009-19, IRB 2009-28, 112.

[4] Notice 2011-14, IRB 2011-11, 544, as modified by Rev. Proc. 2011-55, IRB 2011-47, as amplified by, Notice 2013-7, IRB 2013-64, 477.

INCOME ON GOVERNMENT OBLIGATIONS

¶5005 INTEREST ON STATE AND MUNICIPAL OBLIGATIONS

Generally, interest earned on bonds or other debt obligations issued by states or political subdivisions of states (local governments) is excluded from gross income and therefore not subject to federal income tax [Code Sec. 103(a); Reg. § 1.103-1(a)]. In addition, the interest is usually exempt from state and local income taxes to bondholders who reside in the state issuing the bond. This rule aims to bolster the ability of state and local governments to borrow money. Municipal bond investors receive their interest free of federal income tax under Code Sec. 103 in exchange for a lower rate of interest than would be offered on other types of investments.

> **NOTE:** (1) Social security recipients may be indirectly subject to tax on interest from municipals. Tax-exempt interest income can increase the portion of your social security benefits subject to tax [¶ 5090]. (2) Recipients of tax-exempt must report tax-exempt interest on Form 1040, even though it is not actually taxed.

Interest paid by state. Interest on a state obligation is tax-free because to conclude otherwise would affect the state's ability to borrow money. An "obligation" of a state does not include, however, interest upon indebtedness not incurred under the state's borrowing power. When a state's obligation to pay interest arises by operation of law, it doesn't involve the state's borrowing power. Therefore, when a state pays interest at a fixed rate pursuant to a statutory or judicial command, it is not excludable under Code Sec. 103. Conversely, when a state's obligation to pay interest arises out of voluntary bargaining, the Code Sec. 103 interest exclusion applies. In *DeNaples*,[5] the Court of Appeals for the Third Circuit reversed the Tax Court to conclude that interest paid by a state under a formal settlement agreement on installment payments to taxpayers (installment interest) in a suit arising out of the state's condemnation of their property was exempt from federal tax under Code Sec. 103. The court reasoned that the obligation was a debt incurred under the state's borrowing power.

.01 Exceptions to Tax Exemption

Bond interest is tax-free unless it is derived from (1) private activity bonds that are not exempt as qualified bonds [Code Sec. 103(b)(1)]; (2) arbitrage bonds [Code Sec. 103(b)(3)]; (3) state or local bonds that have not been issued in registered form [Code Sec. 103(b)(3)]; and (4) state or local bonds that are "federally guaranteed" [Code Sec. 149(b)(1)].

A bond is considered to be federally guaranteed if:

- The payment of any part of principal or interest on the bond is guaranteed by the federal government or any of its agencies or instrumentalities;
- The bond is part of an issue where five percent or more of the proceeds of the issue are to be either used in making loans guaranteed by the federal government (or

[5] *DeNaples*, CA-3, 2012-1 USTC ¶ 50,249, 674 F3d 172.

any of its agencies or instrumentalities) or invested in federally insured deposits or accounts; or

- The bond is otherwise indirectly guaranteed by the federal government [Code Sec. 149(b)(2)]. The exception for a guarantee by a Federal Home Loan Bank does not apply unless such bank meets safety and soundness collateral requirements [Code Sec. 149(b)(3)(E)].

.02 Private Activity Bonds

A bond is a "private activity bond" if (1) either more than 10 percent of the proceeds from the bond issue are to be used for any private business use [Code Sec. 141(b)(1)]; and (2) more than 5 percent of the proceeds from the bond issue or $5 million (whichever is less) is used (directly or indirectly) to make or finance loans to nongovernmental entities [Code Secs. 103(b)(1), 141(c)(1)].

Corporate-sponsored research agreement will not ruin tax-exempt bond status. In Rev. Proc. 2007-47,[6] the IRS explained when research agreements will not result in private business use under Code Sec. 141(b) for purposes of having state or local bonds used to fund them qualify as tax exempt. The IRS also expanded the safe harbor for industry or federal sponsored research agreements to include agreements with either a single sponsor or multiple sponsors, and by providing that the rights of the federal government and its agencies under the Bayh-Dole Act do not result in private business use.

Tax-free qualified private activity bonds. A private activity bond is a tax-free "qualified bond" if it satisfies the following requirements [Code Sec. 141(e)].

- It is an exempt facility bond, qualified mortgage bond, qualified veterans' mortgage bond, qualified small issue bond, qualified student loan bond, qualified redevelopment bond, or qualified 501(c)(3) bond [Code Sec. 141(e)]. The Code Sec. 146 volume caps apply to issuers of these tax-exempt bonds as discussed below.

- The bond is part of an issue that meets the volume caps prescribed by Code Sec. 146. The volume of bonds that state and local governments (including the District of Columbia) can issue during a calendar year is limited by a ceiling, which is the greater of an amount equal to $95 (for 2013) multiplied by the state population or $291,875,000 (for 2013) [Code Sec. 146(d)]. A carryforward election is available to governmental agencies that have unused issuing authority at the end of a year. The agency may make an irrevocable election to carry forward all or a portion of that authority, for up to three years, by identifying the purpose for which the election has been made on Form 8328, *Carryforward Election of Unused Private Activity Bond Volume Cap* [Code Sec. 146(f)(3)].

- The bond is not a qualified bond for any period during which it is held by a person who is a substantial user of the facilities or by someone related to that person [Code Sec. 147(a)(1)].

- A bond is not a qualified bond if it is issued as part of an issue and the average maturity of the bonds issued exceed 120 percent of the average reasonably expected economic life of the facilities being financed [Code Sec. 147(b)].

[6] Rev. Proc. 2007-47, 2007-2 CB 108.

- A bond is not a qualified bond if any portion of the proceeds is to be used to provide any airplane, skybox, or other private luxury box, health club facility, facility primarily used for gambling, or a store selling alcoholic beverages for consumption off premises [Code Sec. 147(e)]. Effective for obligations issued after February 14, 2012, the preceding sentence shall not apply to any fixed-wing aircraft equipped for, and exclusively dedicated to providing, acute care emergency medical services [Code Sec. 147(e)].
- A private activity bond will not be a qualified bond unless the issue has received public approval [Code Sec. 147(f)].
- A private activity bond will not qualify as tax exempt where 25 percent or more of the net bond proceeds are used directly or indirectly for the acquisition of land or an interest in land. However, where land is not being significantly used, land may be acquired by an issuing authority in connection with an airport, mass commuting facility, high-speed intercity rail facility, dock, or wharf where such land is acquired for noise abatement, wetland preservation, or for a future use as an airport, mass commuting facility, dock, or wharf [Code Sec. 147(c)]. The land acquisition limitation does not apply to mortgage revenue bonds, qualified student loan bonds, and qualified Code Sec. 501(c)(3) bonds. There is also a special exception for first time-farmers, as discussed below.
- Bonds issued after December 31, 2012 to provide qualified public educational facilities can be treated as exempt facility bonds [Code Sec. 142(a)(13)]. Private activities for which tax-exempt bonds may be issued include elementary and secondary public school facilities which are owned by private, for-profit corporations pursuant to public-private partnership agreements with a state or local educational agency [Code Sec. 142(k)(1)].
- Qualified small issue bonds are tax-exempt bonds issued by state and local governments to finance the acquisition of land and equipment by certain first-time farmers. First-time farmers may finance up to $501,100 in 2013 [Code Sec. 147(c)(2)(A)].[7] A first-time farmer is any individual who has not at any time had any direct or indirect ownership interest in substantial farmland. The definition includes those who have previously owned but disposed of farmland while insolvent. Any ownership or material participation by an individual's spouse or minor child is treated as ownership and material participation by the individual. The term *substantial farmland* means any parcel of land unless the parcel is smaller than 30 percent of the median size of farms in the county in which the parcel is located [Code Sec. 147(c)(2)(E)].
- Private activity bonds will not qualify as tax exempt if the bond proceeds are used to acquire existing property [Code Sec. 147(d)(1)]. There is an exception to this general rule for rehabilitations meeting certain expenditure requirements [Code Sec. 147(d)(2)].

Examples of private activity bonds include:

- Interest on private activity bonds issued in small amounts ($1 million or less) are tax-free but only if at least 95 percent of the proceeds go to finance manufacturing facilities or first-time farmers [Code Sec. 144(a)(12)(B)];

---

[7] Rev. Proc. 2012-41, IRB 2012-45.

- State and local governments issue qualified mortgage bonds to provide subsidized mortgages to low- and middle-income individuals who want to buy their first home. Interest on these bonds is tax-free [Code Sec. 143(a)]; and
- Interest on municipal bonds issued to finance private business expansion in "enterprise zones" is tax-free. To qualify, at least 95 percent of the proceeds must be used by businesses in these zones to acquire qualified "enterprise zone property." This includes equipment as well as land and buildings located within the zone. These bonds are fully subject to state private activity volume caps. In general, there's a $3 million dollar face-value limit on how much can be issued for each business within the zone [Code Sec. 1394(c)]. Qualifying businesses operating in empowerment zones are able to obtain tax-exempt bond financing under Code Sec. 1394 through the end of 2013 [Code Sec. 1391(d)(1)(A)(i)].

The U.S. government has designated economically distressed areas as "enterprise zones." Some of these areas are dubbed "empowerment zones," but the majority are called "enterprise communities" [Code Secs. 1391-1393]. These areas receive special tax breaks that generally will be available for the ten-year period following designation [Ch. 14]. One of these breaks is the authority to issue tax-free bonds to finance the expansion of enterprise zone businesses. To be eligible for enterprise zone designation, an area must meet certain criteria, such as an overall poverty rate of at least 20 percent. And the area must be in "general economic distress," a term that takes into account crime rates, unemployment, vacancy rates and drug use or trafficking. An empowerment zone is one that's just a little worse off economically than an enterprise community. For instance, an area can qualify as an enterprise community if, among other things, the poverty rate in its central business district is 30 percent or higher. If this figure were 35 percent, the area could qualify as an empowerment zone. See ¶ 14,100 for further discussion.

A "new empowerment zone facility bond" is not treated as a private activity bond and the limitation on bond amounts does not apply [Code Sec. 1394(f)(1)]. These bonds are not subject to the state private activity bond volume caps. *New empowerment zone facility bond* means any bond described in Code Sec. 1394(a) (relating to bonds issued as part of an issue 95 percent or more of the net proceeds of which are used to provide any enterprise zone facility if only empowerment zones designated under Code Sec. 1391(g) were taken into account under Code Sec. 1397B or 1397C). The aggregate face amount of bonds which may be designated with respect to any empowerment zone cannot exceed: $60 million if the zone is in a rural area; $130 million if the zone is in an urban area and the zone has a population of less than 100,000; $230 million if the zone is in an urban area and the zone has a population of at least 100,000 [Code Sec. 1394(f)(2)(B)].

Another type of tax-exempt bond is one issued by local hydroelectric power plants. To qualify for tax-free treatment, at least 80 percent of the money raised by the bonds must be used to promote fisheries or other wildlife resources [Code Sec. 142(j)(2)].

.03 Arbitrage Bonds

Interest earned on state and local government bonds will be tax-exempt unless the bonds are "arbitrage bonds," which are defined as bonds where the proceeds are "reasonably expected" to be used to acquire higher yielding investments. These are taxable bonds issued to raise funds that the issuer, in turn, uses to acquire higher yielding investments [Code Sec. 148]. The Tax Court[8] has held that income generated by municipal bonds issued by a county housing authority was subject to tax because the bonds were arbitrage bonds that failed to qualify for the coveted tax-exempt status.

▶ **PRACTICE TIP:** This case will serve as precedent for the resolution of other municipal bond tax issues. You should never invest tax-exempt bond proceeds in higher yielding investments if you want bond proceeds to be tax-free. In addition, if you plan to invest in municipal bonds, be sure to ascertain whether the bonds qualify for tax-exempt status and never invest in arbitrage bonds if you want the income to be tax-free.

.04 Bonds Not in Registered Form

To be tax-exempt, bonds must be in registered form [Code Secs. 103(b)(3), 149(a)(1), 163(f)(2)]. The U.S. Supreme Court has upheld this requirement.[9] In other words, tax-exempt unregistered bonds are no longer being issued. Such bonds issued prior to that date are still available on the resale market and pay tax-exempt interest.

.05 Stripped Tax-Exempt Bonds

With bonds whose interest-bearing coupons have been stripped, all that you own is the right to principal at maturity. Thus, they are sold at a deep discount on their face value [Ch. 2]. In general, your income from the bond is taxed to the extent it exceeds the stated interest rate [Code Sec. 1286(d)].

▶ **WORD TO THE WISE:** Before investing in a particular state or municipal obligation, you should check with a broker to verify the tax status of the bond.

.06 Ways to Invest in Tax-Free Municipals

You have a choice of investment opportunities when it comes to municipals.

Municipal Bond Trust

A municipal bond trust pays a fixed rate of tax-free interest and the investor receives his or her entire investment back at maturity. A trust is well-suited to investors who seek a steady stream of tax-free income and plan on holding to maturity. Investors buy into a trust by purchasing units from a securities broker or bond dealer, who charges a one-time sales charge. The maturities of the bonds range from three to 30 years.

Municipal Bond Funds

These are more suitable for an investor who likes to take advantage of changing market conditions. Generally, the yield from a municipal bond fund will fluctuate with the interest rate. The fund is tailored to those investors who believe that interest rates will drop or who are unsure of the length of their investment. You can invest in these funds through fund sponsors, who charge sales fees and management fees. Unlike a trust investor, as a fund investor you have no assurance that your original investment will be returned.

---

[8] *Harbor Bancorp,* 105 TC 260, Dec. 50,948, *aff'd,* CA-9, 97-2 USTC ¶50,532, 115 F3d 722, *cert. denied,* 522 US 1108.

[9] *South Carolina v. Baker,* SCt, 88-1 USTC ¶9284, 485 US 505, 108 SCt 1355.

▶ **INVESTOR TIP:** It is critical to check the ratings of the bonds in which a trust or a fund is investing. For example, Moody's top rating is Aaa. If the fund or trust includes lower-rated bonds (e.g., lower than A rated bonds), you may wish to invest in an insured fund or trust.

Insured Municipal Bonds

By purchasing insured municipal bonds, you have an extra layer of protection against the issuer's default. Here an insurance company backs a specific bond issue of a state or a municipality. In the event of the issuer's default, the insurance company will step into the shoes of the state. It will continue to make interest payments during the remaining life of the bond and redeem the bonds at par (face value) on the stated redemption date.

Generally, these privately insured issues are given the highest ratings but carry slightly lower yields because of the cost of the insurance.

▶ **INVESTOR TIP:** The insurance protects only against default. It does not protect against declines in the value of the bond due to rising interest rates. Thus, if you invest in insured municipals you can have a loss on the sale of a bond before maturity.

Municipal Leases

With this type of investment, your money, in effect, goes to purchase equipment that the municipality leases from you. Municipal leases pay tax-free interest at higher rates than bonds—since they are riskier investments.

Example 5-1: A town needs equipment (e.g., police cars, fire trucks, and computers) but it does not want to lay out cash or float a bond issue. Instead, the government agrees to buy the equipment under a short-term installment sales contract. The installment contract is called a municipal lease. However, the government actually purchases the equipment and ends up with clear title at the end of the lease period.

Tax-free income. You receive tax-free interest paid on the municipal obligation—whether it is a bond or an installment contract. A municipal lease arrangement, unlike a municipal bond, is not backed by the municipality's taxing authority. It is based on annual appropriations, which the state and local government must vote to approve. If the government chooses not to spend the money necessary to make the lease payments, then it defaults on the deal. As a result, you should choose a lease arrangement carefully. Remember, they are not rated nor are they privately insured.

Alternative Minimum Tax Bonds

Specified private activity bonds, which are private activity bonds issued after August 7, 1986, that are free of regular income tax, are subject to alternative minimum tax [Ch. 16]. They bear a higher rate of return than comparable bonds that produce interest free of both regular income tax and alternative minimum tax.

▶ **INVESTOR STRATEGY:** If you are subject to the alternative minimum tax, you should investigate whether the bonds you are thinking of buying are still completely tax-free.

On the other hand, if you do not have an alternative minimum tax problem, you can get a higher tax-free return by investing in private activity bonds that are subject to alternative minimum tax, but free of regular income tax.

¶5010 INTEREST ON OBLIGATIONS OF THE UNITED STATES

Interest on United States obligations, such as United States bills, notes, and bonds is includible in gross income and subject to federal income taxation [Reg. § 1.103-4(b)]. However, interest on U.S. savings bonds is exempt from state and local taxes.

▶ **INVESTMENT STRATEGY:** Interest on obligations of U.S. possessions (e.g., Puerto Rico, U.S. Virgin Islands, and Guam) is free of federal, state, and local income tax.

NOTE: Interest on some U.S. Savings Bonds (Series EE) used for qualified higher education expenses is tax-free if certain requirements are met [Ch. 2.]. Otherwise, interest on U.S. Savings Bonds can be tax-deferred until disposed of or until maturity [Ch. 18]. Interest on short-term U.S. Treasury Bills is not taxed until the year they mature.

LIFE INSURANCE

¶5015 CASH VALUE BUILD-UP

Increases in the cash value buildup of a whole life insurance policy are tax-free. In addition, dividends from participating whole life insurance policies are also tax-free (whether used to reduce premiums or purchase additional paid-up insurance).

To qualify for this special tax treatment (as well as the other tax breaks discussed later in this chapter), policies issued after 1984 must satisfy one of the following two tests.

.01 Cash Value Accumulation Test

This allows traditional whole life policies, with cash values that accumulate at reasonable interest rates, to continue to qualify as life insurance. Under this test, the cash surrender value provided under the contract at any time cannot exceed the net single premium needed at that time to fund the contract's future benefits [Code Sec. 7702(a)(1)].

.02 Guideline Premium and Cash Value Corridor Test

This test limits the definition of life insurance to contracts that allow relatively modest investments and investment returns. The two prongs of this test are designed to curb two different potential abuses. The guideline premium portion pinpoints contracts where the policyholder makes greater than usual investments in the policy. The cash value corridor pinpoints contracts with excessive cash value buildup [Code Sec. 7702(a)(2)].

¶5020 LIFE INSURANCE PROCEEDS

Life insurance policies come in a variety of forms—term, cash value and combinations of the two. However, they all call for the insurer to make payments upon the insured's death to his estate or to his beneficiaries. Those proceeds, whether paid in a lump sum or as a series of payments, are generally excluded from the beneficiary's gross income. Some other death benefit payments have the characteristics of life insurance proceeds. They are payable under the terms of a contract by reason of death, and likewise qualify for this exclusion. Examples: Workers' compensation insurance contracts, endowment contracts, and accidental death policies [Code Sec. 101(a)(1); Reg. § 1.101-1(a)(1)].

Example 5-2: Mr. Washington takes out a life insurance policy for $100,000 with his wife as beneficiary. When Mr. Washington dies, the $100,000 received by his widow is not subject to income tax under Code Sec. 101(a)(1).

▶ **OBSERVATION:** Life insurance proceeds may be subject to estate tax. You can, however, escape this tax by having someone other than the insured (e.g., the beneficiary or a trust) be the owner of the policy and not retaining any "incidents of ownership." See ¶ 29,075.

.01 Transfer for Valuable Consideration

Code Sec. 101(a)(1) provides, generally, that gross income does not include amounts received (whether in a single sum or otherwise) under a life insurance contract, if such amounts are paid by reason of the death of the insured. In the case of a transfer for valuable consideration, however, Code Sec. 101(a)(2) provides that the amount excluded from gross income shall not exceed an amount equal to the sum of the actual value of the consideration paid and the premiums and other amounts subsequently paid by the transferee. This so-called "transfer for value" rule does not apply in the following situations:

- Where the recipient's basis is determined by reference to the transferor's basis (a transfer involving a carryover basis) [Code Sec. 101(a)(2)(A); Reg. 1.101-1(b)(1)];
- Where the policy is transferred to the insured, a partner of the insured, a partnership in which the insured is a partner, or to a corporation in which the insured is a shareholder or office [Code Sec. 101(a)(2)(B); Reg. § 1.101-1(b)(1)].

Example 5-3: *B* purchased from *A* for $20,000 a "life insurance contract" on the life of *A*. The contract was originally issued by *IC*, a domestic insurance corporation. The contract was a level premium fifteen-year term life insurance contract without cash surrender value. At the time of purchase, the remaining term of the contract was 7 years, 6 months, and 15 days. The monthly premium for the contract was $500, due and payable on the first day of each month. As owner of the contract, *B* had the right to change the beneficiary and, pursuant to that right, named itself beneficiary under the contract immediately after acquiring the contract.

B had no insurable interest in *A*'s life and, except for the purchase of the contract, *B* had no relationship to *A* and would suffer no economic loss upon

> *A*'s death. *B* purchased the contract with a view to profit. When *A* died, *IC* paid $100,000 under the life insurance contract to *B*. Through that date, *B* had paid monthly premiums totaling $9,000 to keep the contract in force.

In Rev. Rul. 2009-14,[10] the IRS concluded that *B*'s acquisition of the contract was a "transfer for a valuable consideration" within the meaning of Code Sec. 101(a)(2). Neither the carryover basis exception of Code Sec. 101(a)(2)(A) nor the exception for transfers involving parties related to the insured under Code Sec. 101(A)(2)(B). Thus, Code Sec. 101(a)(1) excludes from *B*'s gross income the amount received by reason of *A*'s death, but Code Sec. 101(a)(2) limits the exclusion to the sum of the actual value of the consideration paid for the transfer ($20,000) and other amounts paid by *B* ($9,000), or $29,000. *B* therefore must include in gross income $71,000, which is the difference between the total death benefit received ($100,000) and the amount excluded under Code Sec. 101 ($29,000).

> **Example 5-4:** ABC, Inc. purchases a $20,000 policy on the life of an employee for a single premium of $5,000. ABC is the beneficiary. ABC transfers the policy to XYZ Corp. in a tax-free reorganization (XYZ carries over ABC's basis). XYZ Corp receives the proceeds of $20,000 upon the death of the employee. The entire $20,000 is excludable from the gross income of XYZ Corp.

Gratuitous Transfers

If you receive a gratuitous transfer of a life insurance policy (e.g., a gift), you may exclude from gross income (1) the amount which would have been excludable by your transferor had no transfer taken place, *plus* (2) any premiums you pay after receiving the policy. However, the full proceeds are excludable when the policy is transferred by or to the insured, his or her partner, partnership or a corporation in which the insured is a shareholder or officer [Reg. § 1.101-1(b)(2)].

> **Example 5-5:** Mr. Taylor purchased a single premium life insurance policy for $20,000 with a face value of $100,000. Taylor transferred the policy to his daughter, Amy, as a gift. Upon her father's death, Amy can exclude the entire $100,000 from her gross income. Reason: This is the amount her father's estate would have excluded for income tax purposes had no transfer occurred.

.02 Life Insurance Proceeds Held Under Agreement to Pay Interest

If the proceeds are held by the insurer under an agreement to pay interest, the interest payments must be included in the beneficiary's gross income [Code Sec. 101(c); Reg. § 1.101-3].

> **Example 5-6:** A $100,000 life insurance policy calls for payment of proceeds five years after the insured's death. The insurer does, however, make payments of $8,000 during each of those five years and then pays the $100,000 in a lump sum. Result: The beneficiary receives $8,000 of taxable interest income each year. The $100,000 policy proceeds are tax-free.

---

10 Rev. Rul. 2009-14, IRB 2009-21, 1031.

.03 Payments of Proceeds Over a Period of Time

Suppose there is an agreement or option in a life insurance contract to pay the proceeds at a time later than death. In this case, the beneficiary may be taxed on the interest element of the proceeds held by the insurer. This interest element is found by prorating the present value of the life insurance proceeds as of the date of death over the period of the payments. The prorated amount is excluded from the beneficiary's income. Amounts over that are taxable as interest [Code Sec. 101(d); Reg. § 1.101-4(a)].

> **Example 5-7:** A life insurance policy is worth $100,000 at the insured's death, but the beneficiary elects under the policy to take $12,000 a year for 10 years instead of the lump sum. He gets $10,000 a year tax-free, but the remaining $2,000 a year is taxable interest.

.04 Proceeds Payable to Shareholders

Life insurance proceeds paid to a corporation's shareholders will be taxed as dividends if the corporation uses its earnings to pay the premiums and owns the policy. This applies even if the corporation is not the beneficiary and so does not receive the proceeds.[11] However, the Sixth Circuit (which includes Ohio, Kentucky, Tennessee and Michigan) held that the proceeds are not taxable as dividends if they were neither a corporation's assets nor distributed by the corporation.[12]

.05 Viatical Settlements for the Terminally or Chronically Ill

Tax relief is available to terminally and chronically ill taxpayers who are forced to sell their life insurance policies to viatical settlement companies in order to obtain cash to pay their mounting medical bills and living expenses. A viatical settlement company buys life insurance contracts from persons who are either terminally ill or who have a dramatically limited life span due to a life-threatening disease. The company gives the insured a percentage (usually 50-80 percent depending on life expectancy) of the life insurance policy's face value before death and when the insured dies, the viatical settlement company owns the policy and collects the full death benefit from the insurance company.

What Is a Viatical Settlement?

A viatical settlement is the transfer of ownership of a life insurance policy by a person who is terminally or chronically ill, also known as the viator, to a viatical settlement company in exchange for a percentage of the insurance policy's face value. After the transfer, the viatical settlement company becomes the life insurance policy's beneficiary, paying the premiums and collecting the benefits after the original policyholder dies.

The law provides that:

1. Accelerated death benefits received from life insurance contracts on behalf of a "terminally or chronically ill" insured before the death of the insured are tax-free [Code Sec. 101(g)(1)].

---

[11] Rev. Rul. 61-134, 1961-2 CB 250.

[12] *F.H.W. Ducros*, CA-6, 59-2 USTC ¶ 9785, 272 F2d 49.

2. Amounts received when a "terminally or chronically ill" insured sells his or her life insurance contract (or assigns the death benefit) to a viatical settlement company are also tax-free [Code Sec. 101(g)(2)].

When a Viatical Settlement Is Provider Licensed

The IRS has explained in Rev. Rul. 2002-82,[13] when a viatical settlement provider will be treated as state-licensed so that a sale or assignment of a life insurance contract by a terminally or chronically ill taxpayer qualifies for the income exclusion under Code Sec. 101(g). The following providers will be treated as state-licensed:

- A viatical provider will be treated as licensed if the insurance company has received temporary authority to engage in business while the state reviews it pending licensing application;
- A viatical provider will be treated as licensed if blanket authority to engage in business was granted to all viatical settlement providers, pending further guidance; and
- A viatical provider will not be treated as licensed if there is not yet a procedure for licensing providers.

Example 5-8: An AIDS patient assigns the death benefits on his whole life insurance policy to a viatical settlement company in exchange for cash up front equal to 65 percent of the contract's face value. The assignment of the insurance contract and receipt of the life insurance proceeds will be a tax-free event [Code Sec. 101(g)(2)]. When the AIDS patient dies, the viatical settlement company collects the life insurance pay-out.

In general, outside of the viatical context, an insured individual pays premiums on a life insurance policy to an insurance company and when the insured dies, the insurance proceeds are paid to the policy beneficiaries. Typically, these life insurance proceeds received after the insured has died are not subject to income tax [Code Sec. 101(a)(1)]. This tax result changes, however, when the insurance proceeds are paid out prior to the death of the insured. This may occur when the insured needs money and cashes in the policy to get the cash. When this happens, the proceeds are taxed to the extent that they exceed the taxpayer's basis or investment in the life insurance policy. This means that anything received over and above the premiums paid will be subject to income tax.

Example 5-9: A healthy Dad cashes in his life insurance policy so he can pay his son's college tuition. The proceeds will be taxed to the extent they exceed Dad's investment in the policy. As a result of Code Sec. 101(g), the receipt of the insurance proceeds only will be tax-free if Dad is terminally ill.

Who Qualifies for a Viatical Settlement?

Terminally ill and chronically ill individuals qualify for the settlement under the following criteria:

---

[13] Rev. Rul. 2002-82, 2002-2 CB 978.

- A *terminally ill individual* is a person for whom the insurer has obtained a certificate from a physician stating that the individual has an illness or a physical condition that is reasonably expected to result in death within 24 months from the date of certification [Code Secs. 101(g)(4)(A), 7702B(c)(2) and (d)(4)(B)].

- A *chronically ill individual* is any person certified within the preceding 12-month period by a licensed health care practitioner as (1) being unable to perform at least two activities of daily living for a period of at least 90 days due to a loss of functional capacity, (2) as having a level of disability similar (as designated by regulations) to the level of disability described in (1), or (3) requiring substantial supervision to protect the person from threats to health and safety because of severe cognitive impairment [Code Secs. 101(g)(4)(B)], 7702B(c)(2)]. A terminally ill individual is not considered chronically ill.

When proceeds will be tax-free. Accelerated life insurance proceeds paid to a chronically ill insured are excludable if [Code Secs. 101(g)(3)(A), 7702B(b)(1)(B), 7702B(g)]:

- The payment is for actual costs of qualified long-term care incurred by the payee;

- The contract does not pay or reimburse expenses that are reimbursable under Medicare except when Medicare is a secondary payor or when the contracts makes payments on a per diem or another periodic basis without regard to actual expenses;

- The terms of the life insurance contract satisfy the consumer protection provisions of Code Sec. 7702B(g), standards adopted by the National Association of Insurance Commissions that specifically apply to chronically ill individuals, and standards adopted by the state in which the policyholder resides.

- Payments made on a per-diem or other periodic basis without regard to actual expenses are excludable from gross income subject to a maximum of $320 per day in 2013 [$116,800 total in 2013 (365 × $320)] or the equivalent amount in the case of payments made on a different periodic basis [Code Sec. 7702B].

Exception for business-related policies. The exclusion for accelerated death benefits is not applicable to any amounts paid to any person other than the insured if such person has an insurable interest with respect to the insured because the insured is an employee, officer or director of the person or because the insured has a financial interest in the person [Code Sec. 101(g)(5)].

> **Example 5-10:** Alan and Bill own a tax return preparation business. Bill learns that he has a fatal brain tumor and becomes too sick to work. Alan and Bill bought key man insurance on each other's lives. Alan sells Bill's life insurance policy to a viatical settlement company to get cash to pay business expenses. The life insurance proceeds are subject to income tax in Alan's hands because Alan has a financial interest in Bill's business.

¶5025 SURRENDER OF LIFE INSURANCE POLICY

If a taxpayer surrenders (whether or not voluntarily surrenders) a life insurance policy to the insurance company for a lump sum, the taxpayer has taxable income to the extent the amount received exceeds the net premiums paid (i.e., investment in the contract) [Code Sec. 72(e)(5)(A)].[14] Thus it is taxed on an income-first basis [Code Sec. 72(e)(2)]. The surrender of an insurance policy is not a "sale or exchange" of a capital asset and thus does not result in capital gain and is taxable as ordinary income.[15]

Code Sec. 72(e)(5) provides an exception to the income-first rule in the case of:

1. Certain contracts including, under life insurance contracts other than a "modified endowment contract"; and
2. Any non-annuity amount received under a contract on its complete surrender, redemption, or maturity.

If a non-annuity amount is received under a life insurance contract other than a modified endowment contract before the annuity starting date, or is received under a life insurance contract on the complete surrender, redemption, or maturity of the contract, Code Sec. 72(e)(5)(A) requires that the amount be included in gross income but only to the extent it exceeds investment in the contract. For this purpose, Code Sec. 72(e)(6) defines "investment in the contract" as of any date as the aggregate amount of premiums or other consideration paid for the contract before that date, less the aggregate amount received under the contract before that date to the extent that amount was excludable from gross income.

> **Example 5-11:** A received $78,000 on the complete surrender of a life insurance contract. *A*'s income upon surrender of the contract is determined under Code Sec. 72(e)(5). Under Code Sec. 72(e)(5)(A), the amount received is included in gross income to the extent it exceeds the investment in the contract. In Rev. Rul. 2009-13,[16] addressed this situation and explained that as *A* paid aggregate premiums of $64,000 with regard to the contract, and neither received any distributions under the contract nor borrowed against the contract's cash surrender value prior to surrender, *A*'s "investment in the contract" was $64,000. Consequently, pursuant to Code Sec. 72(e)(5)(A), A recognized $14,000 of income on surrender of the contract, which is the excess of $78,000 received over $64,000.

If a life insurance policy is surrendered before maturity, premiums paid for life insurance protection (as opposed to premiums that build up cash value) are not treated as part of the investment in the contract for purposes of determining whether any loss has been sustained.[17]

---

[14] *B.A. Brown*, CA-7, 2012-2 USTC ¶50,555, 693 F3d 765, *aff'g*, 101 TCM 1374, Dec. 58,598(M), TC Memo. 2011-83.

[15] *H.S. Barr*, 98 TCM 406, Dec. 57,981(M), TC Memo. 2009-250. *See also Wolff*, CA-2, 98-2 USTC ¶50,830, 148 F3d 186.

[16] Rev. Rul. 2009-13, IRB 2009-21, 1029.

[17] *London Shoe Co.*, CA-2, 35-2 USTC ¶9664, 80 F2d 230, *cert. denied*, SCt, 298 US 663, 56 SCt 747.

¶5030 LIFE INSURANCE ENDOWMENT CONTRACTS

An endowment policy is an insurance policy under which the insurer agrees to pay a stated sum of money at the end of a definite period. The sum can be paid all at once or in installments.

A portion of the proceeds is excluded from gross income. If you receive the proceeds in a lump sum (on maturity or surrender), the exclusion is equal to the premiums paid less any dividends or other amounts previously received under the contract. Proceeds in excess of the aggregate premiums are included in gross income [Code Sec. 72(e)(2); Reg. § 1.72-11(d)]. Suppose the proceeds are payable in installments for a fixed number of years. Each year's exclusion is found by dividing the total premiums paid by the number of years over which installments are to be paid [Code Sec. 72(c)(3)(B)].

As a beneficiary of an endowment contract, you may have the option of electing to receive payments as an annuity, rather than a lump-sum payment. If you make a timely election, the tax rules for annuities will apply [¶ 5070]. In other words, the tax will be spread out along with the payments, and part of each payment will be tax-free.

> ▶ **ELECTION DEADLINE:** Beneficiaries have only 60 days from the time a lump sum becomes payable to elect to receive an annuity and qualify for annuity tax treatment. If you wait longer than 60 days, you will be taxed as though you received a lump sum—even though the distribution is actually made in the form of an annuity [Reg. § 1.72-12].

¶5035 DIVIDENDS ON LIFE INSURANCE AND ENDOWMENT POLICIES

Dividends on unmatured life or endowment insurance policies are a partial return of premiums paid. They are tax-free until they exceed the accumulated net premiums paid for the contract. However, interest paid or credited by the insurance company on dividends left with the company is taxable.

Veterans' insurance proceeds and dividends are not taxable to veterans or their beneficiaries. The proceeds of a veteran's endowment policy paid before his or her death are also exempt. The Internal Revenue Service has ruled that interest on dividends left on deposit with the Veterans' Administration is also exempt from tax.[18] The Veterans' Benefit Act of 1957, currently in force, continues the tax exemption of benefits under previous veterans' laws.[19]

¶5040 GROUP-TERM LIFE INSURANCE PREMIUMS

Premiums paid by employers to provide group-term life insurance coverage of up to $50,000 for employees are excludable from the employee's gross income [Code Sec.

---

[18] Rev. Rul. 91-14, 1991-1 CB 18.

[19] P.L. 85-56, 71 Stat. 122.

79]. Any cost above the $50,000 coverage must be included in income. To qualify for the exclusion, the group-term life insurance plan must meet nondiscrimination tests. For detailed discussion of group-term life insurance, see Ch. 2 and Ch. 4. Group-permanent life insurance premiums paid by your employer are ordinary income to you and must be reported as wages [Reg. § 1.79-1].

DISABILITY BENEFITS

¶5045 MEDICAL AND DISABILITY BENEFITS

Taxpayers can exclude from gross income a variety of benefits received on account of injuries or sickness.

.01 Exception to Disability Benefit Exclusion Rule

Code Sec. 104(a)(3) provides that gross income generally does not include amounts received through accident and health insurance for personal injuries or sickness.[20] An exception to this exclusion applies, however, for amounts received by an employee, to the extent the amounts are either:

1. Attributable to contributions by the employer that were not includable in the employee's gross income.
2. Paid by the employer.

NOTE: For the tax treatment of employer-provided accident and health insurance policies, see ¶4120.

Under Code Sec. 105(a), the amounts received by an employee through accident or health insurance are excludable if they are attributable to after-tax contributions by the employee. Therefore, disability benefits are generally excludible to the extent attributable to premiums the employee paid with after-tax contributions. The Tax Court concluded that disability payments received by a taxpayer pursuant to a disability plan hammered out in collective bargaining between the taxpayer's union and former employer were not excluded from gross income because Code Sec. 104(a)(3) cannot be read so broadly as to exclude accident or health insurance benefits attributable to wage concessions made in a negotiated bargaining process.[21]

.02 Income Replacement Policies

An income replacement policy or a disability policy protects the insured against loss of income due to physical incapability of working. If you purchase such policies, you are entitled to exclude amounts you receive [Code Sec. 104(a)(3); Reg. § 1.104-1(d)].

.03 Workers' Compensation

Code Sec. 104(a)(1) excludes from gross income amounts which are received by an employee under a workmen's compensation act which provides compensation to employees for personal injuries or sickness incurred in the course of employment.

---

[20] *R.S. Cotler*, 94 TCM 305, Dec. 57,108(M), TC Memo. 2007-283.

[21] *T.D. Tuka*, 120 TC 1, Dec. 55,001 (2003).

Also excluded from gross income are amounts paid under a workmen's compensation act to the survivor or survivors of a deceased employee [Reg. § 1.104-1(b)].

Exception

Disability benefits will not be excludable, however, if they are based on an employee's age or length of service or the employee's prior contributions, even though the payments may be caused by an occupational injury or sickness [Reg. § 1.104-1(b)]. The reason: When the payments are keyed to the employee's age and/or length of service they look a lot more like a taxable retirement pension than tax-free disability payments that are paid regardless of how old you are or how long you have worked for the employer. The Ninth Circuit has concluded that payments received by a policeman under a workers' compensation act as compensation for personal injuries were excludable from income under Code Sec. 104(a)(1) because none of the benefits were determined by reference to the taxpayer's age or length of service.[22] But the Tax Court concluded in *J. Sewards*,[23] that the portion of the taxpayer's disability retirement payments determined by reference to a member of the sheriff's department's length of service with his employer was not excludable from the taxpayer's taxable income.

.04 Lawsuit Damages Award

There is an exclusion from gross income for any damages (other than punitive damages) received (whether by suit or agreement and whether as lump sum or as periodic payments) on account of personal physical injury or physical sickness of the taxpayer [Code Sec. 104(a)(2); Reg. § 1.104-1(c)]. However, certain types of damages are includible in gross income [¶ 5065]. In general, business-related damages, as opposed to those related to personal injury or sickness, are taxed. In addition, emotional distress will not be treated as a physical injury or physical sickness. Similarly, damages received on account of nonphysical injury or sickness (e.g., age discrimination, employment discrimination,[24] or injury to reputation) are not excludable from gross income under Code Sec. 104(a)(2).

.05 Government Disability Payments

Employees may exclude amounts received from a pension, annuity, or similar allowance for personal injury or sickness attributable to active service in the armed forces of any country, or in the Coast Guard and Geodetic Survey, or Public Health Service, or as a disability annuity payable under the Foreign Service Act of 1980 [Code Sec. 104(a)(4); Reg. § 1.104-1(e)].

Similarly, there's an exclusion for disability income received by individuals, who, as employees of the United States engaged in the performance of official duties outside the United States, are injured as a direct result of a terrorist attack or military action [Code Sec. 104(a)(5)].

In *W.D. Reimels*,[25] the court held that Social Security disability benefits paid to a war veteran could not be excluded from his gross income under Code Sec. 104(a)(4), even though his disability resulted from exposure to Agent Orange while in the military

[22] *J.A. Picard*, CA-9, 99-1 USTC ¶ 50,218, 165 F3d 744.

[23] *J. Sewards*, 138 TC 320, Dec. 59,010 (2012).

[24] *J.B. Molina*, 106 TCM 371, Dec. 59,652(M), TC Memo. 2013-226.

[25] *W.D. Reimels*, 123 TC 245, Dec. 55,727, *aff'd*, CA-2, 2006-1 USTC ¶ 50,147, 436 F3d 344.

service. Although disability benefits can be excluded from gross income if they are compensation for military injuries, Social Security disability benefits are not payments "for" such injuries but, rather, are payments for the inability to work.

.06 Qualified Domestic Relations Order

In *S.L. Fernandez,*[26] an ex-wife was not allowed to exclude her portion of her former husband's disability pay from her gross income. The benefits were taxable to her as a distributee or alternate payee under a qualified domestic relations order for purposes of Code Secs. 72 and 402(a). Her alternate argument, which was rejected by the court, was that she should be able to exclude the disability benefits by stepping into her former husband's shoes. The court explained that she could not step into her husband's shoes because the payment that she received was for her husband's personal injury and not hers.

GIFTS, INHERITANCES, AND DAMAGES

¶5055 GIFTS

A *gift* is a gratuitous transfer from a donor to a donee [See Ch. 29]. Generally, to be considered a gift, the donor must be under no legal obligation to make the transfer. Gifts that you receive are not included in your gross income. However, once the gift takes place, future earnings attributable to assets are taxable to you. (Furthermore, when you sell the asset, you could have income attributable to appreciation in its value prior to the date the gift was made. The donor's basis in the asset is generally carried over to the donee [Ch. 6]. For in depth discussion of the tax treatment of gifts, see the *Estate and Gift Tax Handbook* (CCH).

Example 5-12: Amy received stock as a gift in January. The value of the stock is $10,000. The yearly dividend received from the stock is $600. Although the $10,000 value of the stock is excluded from Amy's gross income, the $600 dividend is subject to tax.

▶ **ANOTHER TAX:** Gratuitous transfers may be subject to gift tax. This tax is imposed on the donor. However, there is an exclusion that can shelter in 2013 the first $14,000 of gifts given by a donor to a donee [Ch. 29].

.01 Employee Gifts

Transfers from an employer to employees are automatically deemed not to be gifts. As a result, the tax-free treatment does not apply to such transfers—even if the employer characterizes a transfer a "gift" [Code Sec. 102(c)]. However, the item may be tax-free on account of some other tax rule, such as the exclusion for employee achievement awards [Ch. 4]. The IRS has concluded that gift cards, certificates, or coupons distributed to employees at the holidays were equivalent to cash and were therefore taxable are such.[27]

---

[26] *S.L. Fernandez,* 138 TC 378, Dec. 59,053 (2012).

[27] TAM 200437030 (Apr. 30, 2004).

.02 Gifts to Minors

The Uniform Transfers to Minors Act has been adopted by most states as a means for minors to own property (e.g., bank accounts, stocks and bonds) without the formalities and expense of a special guardianship or a trust [Ch. 29]. The designated custodian of the property has the legal right to act on behalf of the minor. Income earned from the property generally is taxed to the minor. Income from the gift used to satisfy an individual's legal obligation to support a minor is taxable to the person whose support obligation is satisfied, no matter who made the gift.

> ▶ **PRACTICE WARNING:** Keep in mind before using the Uniform Transfers to Minors Act to save money for a child that once he or she attains the age of majority (18 or 21 depending on state law), the child becomes entitled to the property.

¶5060 INHERITANCES

The value of property acquired by inheritance is not subject to income tax although it may be subject to inheritance or estate tax. See ¶29,040 and ¶29,105. Income earned on the property after the transfer is taxable to the owner of the property and included in gross income. For in depth discussion of inheritance tax, see the Estate and Gift Tax Handbook (CCH).

¶5065 DAMAGES

.01 Damages Received for Personal Physical or Physical Sickness Injuries

Code Sec. 104(a) generally excludes the following amounts from gross income:

1. Compensation received under workers' compensation for compensation for personal injury or sickness;
2. Damages (other than punitive damages) received in a suit or settlement of a claim on account of personal physical injuries or sickness;
3. Amounts received through accident or health insurance for personal injuries or sickness, except for certain amounts that are attributable to employer contributions or paid directly by the employer;
4. Amounts received as a pension, annuity or similar allowance for personal injuries or sickness resulting from active service in the armed forces, Foreign Service or Public Health Service; and
5. Amounts received as disability income attributable to injuries incurred as a direct result of a terrorist or military action.

Gross income generally does not include the amount of any damages (other than punitive damages) received (whether by suit or agreement and whether as lump sums or as periodic payments) by individuals on account of "personal physical injuries or physical sickness" [Code Sec. 104(a)(2); Reg. § 1.104-1(c)(1)]. Emotional distress is not considered a physical injury or physical sickness. However, damages for emotional distress attributable to a physical injury or physical sickness are excluded from taxable income under Code Sec. 104(a)(2) [Reg. § 1.104-1(c)(1)].

In interpreting Code Sec. 104(a)(2), the Supreme Court in *Schleier*[28] held that damages may be excluded from the taxpayer's gross income only if the taxpayer can prove that (1) the underlying cause of action giving rise to the recovery is based on tort or tort type rights, and (2) the damages were received on account of personal injuries or sickness. The second prong of the *Schleier* test requires that a taxpayer prove that the damages were received on account of personal physical injuries or physical illness.[29] Moreover, satisfaction of the second prong requires the taxpayer to show "a direct causal link" between the damages received and the physical injury or sickness sustained. If the taxpayer fails to prove the existence of a direct causal link between the damages received and the physical injury or sickness, the damages must be included in the taxpayer's taxable income.[30]

In *J.L. Domeny*,[31] the Tax Court held that the portion of a payment the taxpayer received from her former employer in a settlement agreement that was compensation for physical illness caused by a stressful work environment was excludable from gross income under Code Sec. 104(a)(2).

The Code Sec. 104(a)(2) exclusion may apply to damages recovered for a physical personal injury or sickness under a statute, even if that statute does not provide for a broad range of remedies. The injury need not be defined as a tort under state or common law [Reg. § 1.104-1(c)(2)].

Wrongful Death Damages

The IRS has ruled consistently that survivors of individuals killed in accidents can exclude from gross income the amount received from that entity responsible for the wrongful deaths.[32]

A corporation cannot suffer personal injury because it is a business entity rather than a human being. Consequently, the corporation cannot avail itself of the income exclusion granted by Code Sec. 104(a)(2) for personal injury even if it has only one shareholder. A corporation cannot exclude from income the proceeds it receives from settlement of a lawsuit by arguing that personal injury awards are not taxable, because a corporation cannot suffer personal injury.[33]

In order for damages received for personal injuries to be tax-free, the lawsuit must be brought by an individual such as a shareholder or group of shareholders rather than by the corporate entity. The individual or shareholder must be able to prove that he or she was personally injured as a result of the actions of the wrongdoer.

---

[28] *E.E. Schleier*, SCt, 95-1 USTC ¶ 50,309, 515 US 323, 115 SCt 2159.

[29] *P.S. Lindey*, 87 TCM 1295, Dec. 55,632(M), TC Memo. 2004-113; *J. Goode*, 91 TCM 901, Dec. 56,454(M), TC Memo. 2006-48, *S.G. Shaltz*, 85 TCM 1489, Dec. 55,188(M), TC Memo. 2003-173; *R. Henderson*, 85 TCM 1469, Dec. 55,183(M), TC Memo. 2003-168.

[30] *D.H. O'Connor*, 104 TCM 571, Dec. 59,256(M), TC Memo. 2012-317.

[31] *J.L. Domeny*, 99 TCM 1047, Dec. 58,110(M), TC Memo. 2010-9.

[32] LTR 201022009 (Feb. 24, 2010), 201022010 (Feb. 19, 2010), 201022011 (Feb. 25, 2010), 201019005 (Feb. 2, 2010).

[33] *P&X Markets, Inc.*, 106 TC 441, Dec. 51,400 (1996), *aff'd*, CA-9, 98-2 USTC ¶ 50,613, 139 F3d 907.

.02 Expenses Incurred to Recover Damages

Damage awards are a form of reimbursement, whether you receive them under a judgment or in compromise of a claim. To determine whether damages constitute taxable income, you must first look at the nature of the injury for which the damages were received and how the payments are structured (e.g., punitive damages, loss of income, personal injury, or discrimination).[34]

The related expenses incurred to recover the damages, including attorneys' fees, are generally deductible as expenses for the production of income subject to the 2-percent floor on itemized deductions. Thus, such expenses are deductible only to the extent the taxpayer's total miscellaneous itemized deductions exceed 2 percent of adjusted gross income. For purposes of the alternative minimum tax, no deduction is allowed for any miscellaneous itemized deduction.

When calculating adjusted gross income (AGI), attorneys' fees and court costs incurred by or on behalf of an individual in connection with most discrimination or civil rights actions may be deducted directly from gross income, and do not need to be claimed as itemized deductions [Code Sec. 62(a)(2)]. The above-the-line deduction is limited to the amount includible in the individual's gross income for the tax year (whether paid in a lump sum or in periodic payments) on account of a judgment or settlement (whether by suit or agreement) resulting from the claim.

The deduction for litigation-related costs is available for costs related to any action involving: (1) a claim of unlawful discrimination; (2) claims against the federal government; or (3) a private cause of action under the Medicare Secondary Payer statute.

.03 Damages Received for Nonphysical Injuries (Emotional Distress)

Damages received on account of a nonphysical injury (e.g., age discrimination, emotional distress, employment discrimination, injury to reputation) are generally *not* excludable from gross income because they are not received on account of personal physical injuries or physical sickness [Code Sec. 104(a)(2)].[35] To determine the correct tax treatment of damages, the appropriate question to ask is: "In lieu of *what* were the damages awarded?"[36] If the damages were substitutes for lost compensation it is likely that the damages will be subject to tax and not excludable as personal injury damages under Code Sec. 104(a).

In *D.J. Stadnyk,*[37] the appellate court concluded that a taxpayer could not exclude from income a settlement payment for false imprisonment under Code Sec. 104(a)(2).

Code Sec. 104(a) provides specifically that "emotional distress shall not be treated as a physical injury or physical sickness. The preceding sentence shall not apply to an amount of damages not in excess of the amount paid for medical care . . . attributable to emotional distress." Thus, damages for emotional distress (including the physical symptoms of emotional distress) may not be treated as damages on account

[34] *Farmers' & Merchants Bk.*, CA-6, 3 USTC ¶972, 59 F2d 912.

[35] *I.E. Espinoza*, CA-5, 2011-1 USTC ¶50,306, 636 F3d 747.

[36] *C. Gerstenbluth*, CA-2, 2013-2 USTC ¶50,494; *S.R. Milenbach*, CA-9, 2003-1 USTC ¶50,229, 318 F3d 924; *C. Francisco*, CA-3, 2001-2 USTC ¶50,662, 267 F3d 303.

[37] *D.J. Stadnyk*, CA-6, 2010-1 USTC ¶50,252, 367 FedAppx 586.

of a personal physical injury or sickness, except to the extent of an amount paid for medical care attributable to emotional distress [Reg. § 1.104-1(c)(1)]. For example, in *M. Murphy*,[38] the Court of Appeals for the District of Columbia Circuit, concluded that a whistle-blower who suffered emotional distress and loss of professional reputation because of mistreatment by her employer could not exclude the compensatory damages she received because they were not received on account of personal physical injuries, bruxism and other physical manifestations of stress and, thus, were not excludable from gross income under Code Sec. 104(a)(2).

.04 Damages for Injury to Capital

Damages for tortious interference with contracts cannot be excluded from gross income because they were received for an economic injury, not on account of personal injury or physical sickness.[39]

Damages for loss of or injury to capital can be excluded, to the extent they do not exceed your basis in the capital.[40] However, damages for loss of profits[41] must be included in gross income.

.05 Punitive Damages

Punitive damages are awarded to punish an offender's outrageous conduct and to deter others from engaging in similar activities in the future. They are usually awarded in addition to actual or compensatory damages which only replace an injured party's loss and are therefore not intended to compensate the aggrieved party for injuries sustained. Code Sec. 104(a)(2) provides that gross income does not include compensatory damages received because of physical personal injury or sickness. Punitive damages received on account of personal injury or sickness, regardless of whether they are related to a physical injury or physical sickness, are included in taxable income [Code Sec. 104(a)(2)].[42]

The IRS has always taken the position that punitive damages, such as treble damages under antitrust laws and exemplary damages for fraud, must be included in gross income [Reg. § 1.61-14].

> ▶ **CASE STUDY:** In *K.M. O'Gilvie*,[43] the U.S. Supreme Court held that punitive damages received by the family of a woman who died from toxic shock syndrome were taxable. The Court concluded that Code Sec. 104(a)(2), which excludes from gross income "damages received on account of personal injuries," does not apply to punitive damages, which are awarded by a court to punish the wrongdoer. The case involved Code Sec. 104(a)(2) as it read in 1988 prior to its August 20, 1996 amendment which explicitly provided that punitive damages are subject to tax.

> ▶ **PRACTICE TIP:** *Allocation of Damage Awards.* Keep in mind that the tax consequences of your damage award depend on your characterization of the

[38] *M. Murphy*, DC-DC, 2007-2 USTC ¶ 50,531, 493 F3d 170, *cert. denied*, 4/21/2008. *See also M. Blackwood*, Dec. 59,113(M), TC Memo. 2012-190.

[39] *P.S. Lindsey*, 87 TCM 1295, Dec. 55,632(M), TC Memo. 2004-113.

[40] *Raytheon Prod. Corp.*, CA-1, 44-2 USTC ¶ 9424, 144 F2d 110, *cert. denied*, 323 US 779, 65 SCt 192.

[41] *H.J. Sternberg*, 32 BTA 1039, Dec. 9032, *acq.* 1935-2 CB 21.

[42] *L.R. Benavides*, CA-5, 2007-2 USTC ¶ 50,638, 497 F3d 526.

[43] *K.M. O'Gilvie*, SCt, 96-2 USTC ¶ 50,664, 519 US 79, 117 SCt 452.

proceeds in your settlement agreement. Plaintiffs involved in personal injury lawsuits should seek to structure their settlement agreements so that a realistic portion of the award is allocated to damages received on account of physical injuries or physical sickness. Only damages allocated in this fashion will be tax-free.

.06 Interest Portion of Damage Award

Part of an otherwise tax-free damage award may be taxable to the recipient as interest. For example, the recipient would owe tax on interest assessed in addition to damages paid to compensate for the delay in receiving payment of the damages.[44] Likewise, the recipient would owe tax on income received from investing a lump-sum personal injury award that represents the present value of projected costs over his or her life expectancy.[45] In *M. Brabson,*[46] the appellate court concluded that prejudgment interest awarded to a mother and her children in a personal injury lawsuit was subject to tax. The Court of Appeals for the First Circuit has held that prejudgment interest will be includable in income even if the parties explicitly agree in writing to "no interest" and the settlement agreement apportions no amount of the settlement amount between prejudgment interest and compensatory damages.[47] The court looked beyond the language used by the parties to find that 39 percent of the settlement proceeds should be allocated to prejudgment interest based on the fact that 39 percent of the state court judgment was for prejudgment interest. Similarly, in another case where no amount of the damage award was allocated to interest, the court looked at all the details surrounding the litigation to find that allocating 30 percent of the damage award to prejudgment interest was appropriate.[48]

Delay Damages Comparable to Interest Portion of Damage Award

In *C. Francisco,*[49] the Court of Appeals for the Third Circuit held that damages awarded in a personal injury case for delay did not constitute additional compensation for injuries suffered by the taxpayer, but could be compared to interest and were therefore subject to tax. Some state laws permit a jury to award delay damages when a great deal of time has passed from the date of injury to the date a settlement is reached and the taxpayer receives the monetary award. Delay damages are thought to compensate the taxpayer for what he could have earned on the award if he had received it more promptly. Time becomes the relevant factor, not the injury itself—the longer the procedural delay, the higher the award for delay damages. Since delay damages are not received "on account of" a personal injury or sickness, as required under Code Sec. 104(a)(2), they fail to qualify for the income exclusion and are therefore subject to tax.

---

44 *R.S. Kovacs,* 100 TC 124, Dec. 48,871, *aff'd,* 25 F3d 1048, *cert. denied,* 513 US 963; *A.B. Aames,* 94 TC 189, Dec. 46,410; *R. Pagliarulo,* 68 TCM 917, Dec. 50,171(M), TC Memo. 1994-506; *J.L. Meyer,* 68 TCM 1037, Dec. 50,203(M), TC Memo. 1994-536.

45 Rev. Rul. 65-29, 1965-1 CB 59.

46 *M. Brabson,* CA-10, 96-1 USTC ¶50,038, 73 F3d 1040, *cert. denied,* 519 US 1039.

47 *J.J. Delaney,* CA-1, 96-2 USTC ¶50,576, 99 F3d 20.

48 *L.A. Forest,* CA-1, 97-1 USTC ¶50,118, 104 F3d 348.

49 *C. Francisco,* CA-3, 2001-2 USTC ¶50,662, 267 F3d 303.

.07 Allocation of Damage Settlements

Taxpayers often receive monetary awards in cases involving both untaxed personal damages as well as taxable damages for business injury, such as a contract violation. Taxpayers are, therefore, motivated to allocate as much of the damages as possible to the tax-free personal injuries awards rather than the taxable contract violations awards. In several recent cases, the courts have subjected damage allocations to a high level of scrutiny. The following strategies developed from the case law in the area may help ensure the exclusion of the maximum amount of damages awards:

- When a payment compensates for physical injury as well as breach of contract, be sure to have evidence justifying your allocation of the award;
- Be sure your attorney sets the stage for excluding the appropriate damages in all aspects of your case. For example, your attorney should be sure to draft your complaint so that it clearly demands a recovery for both physical injury and the contract breach. All pleadings, evidence and arguments should clearly distinguish between physical harm and the contract breach;[50]
- Spell out how the award is divided between the two in the settlement agreement. Earmark a certain percentage or dollar amount for each type of damage awarded. The IRS has established a formula to use to determine how to allocate a settlement that includes both compensatory damages (damages received for physical injuries) and punitive damages.[51] The IRS approved allocating only 25 percent of the award to compensatory damages that can be excluded from gross income. The remaining 75 percent allocated to punitive damages will be included in taxable gross income;
- If a jury trial is involved, the jury should make a separate finding as to the amount of damages attributable to each; and
- Be able to show that bona fide arm's length, adversarial negotiations were entered into in making the allocation.

.08 Structured Settlements

Structured settlements are very popular as a method of satisfying large damages awards. Typically, the negligent party will purchase an annuity policy from an insurance company which will make periodic payments to the damaged party. This option is preferable to a lump sum payment for a number of reasons. First, it will be cheaper for the negligent party to purchase an annuity policy rather than make a lump sum settlement payment. Second, individuals receiving large damages awards are often reluctant to accept a lump sum payment because they want a guaranteed future cash flow and are fearful that they may not be able to manage a large lump sum. A structured settlement will provide an injured party with a fixed income stream for a period of years over his or her lifetime.

The negligent party cannot deduct the entire cost of funding a structured settlement in the year that the settlement was reached but can only deduct the amount paid out to the injured party each year according to the "economic performance" test contained in Code Sec. 461(h).

---

[50] Rev. Rul. 85-98, 1985-2 CB 51.

[51] *E.E. Robinson,* 102 TC 116, Dec. 49,648, *aff'd,* CA-5, 95-2 USTC ¶50,644, 70 F3d 34, *cert. denied,* 519 US 824.

From the perspective of the injured party, structured settlements offer some clever tax planning opportunities. The *entire* amount of each annuity payment (even the interest component) is excluded from the injured party's gross income even though a portion of each annuity payment represents what would otherwise be taxable interest [Code Sec. 104(a)(2)].[52] If the injured party had received a lump-sum payment and had invested the money in a savings account or had used the money to purchase an annuity on his or her own, the interest earnings would be fully taxable whenever they were earned.

ANNUITIES

¶5070 ANNUITIES IN GENERAL

An annuity ordinarily is insurance that provides for regular payments to the purchaser designed to begin at a fixed date and continue through the purchaser's life or for a term of years. Each regular payment consists of earnings on the amount paid for the annuity plus enough of the cost to complete the guaranteed payment. This liquidation of principal is calculated to extend over the purchaser's life expectancy or the term of the annuity. The part of each payment that represents a return of the annuity's cost is tax-free. The part representing investment earnings is tax-deferred; they are not taxed until the owner takes distributions from the contract [Code Sec. 72]. For discussion of the tax treatment of exchange of annuity contracts, see ¶6105.

.01 Types of Annuities

Annuity payments are amounts received under a life insurance, endowment, or annuity contract. Generally, the contract is bought from an insurance company. However, an annuity may be issued by an individual or other party as well. Most common types of annuities are:

- Fixed—paying a fixed amount at regular intervals for a fixed term;
- Single-life—paying a fixed amount at regular intervals for the life of one individual;
- Joint and survivor—paying a fixed amount at regular intervals to one person for life and, on his or her death, paying the same or different amount at the same or different intervals to a second individual for life;
- Variable—payments vary in amount depending on the insurer's investment experience, cost-of-living indices, or similar factors; payments may be made over a fixed term or for the life of one or more persons; and
- Private annuity transaction—transferring complete ownership of property to a transferee (the "obligor") in exchange for the obligor's unsecured promise to make periodic payments to the annuitant for the rest of the annuitant's lifetime. Typically, the private annuity sale is an estate planning or wealth transfer device that involves the transfer of appreciated property such as undeveloped real estate or small business stock from a parent or grandparent to a third party (an insurance

[52] Rev. Rul. 79-220, 1979-2 CB 74.

company or a child) in exchange for the third party's promise to pay the senior family member a specified sum for the remainder of his or her life. The size of the payments is determined by the value of the property transferred, current interest rates, and the life expectancy of the annuitant. For discussion of tax treatment of private annuity arrangements, see ¶ 5070.09.

Amounts Received as an Annuity

Payments constitute annuity amounts—and thus receive favorable annuity tax treatment only if (1) they are received on or after the annuity starting date; (2) they're payable at regular intervals over a period of more than one year from the annuity starting date; and (3) the total amount received can be determined from the terms of the contract or by the use of mortality tables, compound interest tables, or both [Code Sec. 72(c)(4); Reg. § 1.72-4(b)]. All other payments are "amounts not received as annuities" and receive special, but less favorable, tax treatment [(g) below].

▶ **CASH VALUE BUILD-UP:** Ordinarily, the cash value build-up of annuity contracts (much like the cash value build-up of life insurance policies) is not subject to current tax. However, an exception applies to corporate-owned annuity contracts. Corporations are taxed on the excess of (1) the net surrender value plus distributions during the tax year, over (2) the net premiums paid on the annuity contract plus amounts previously includible in gross income [Code Sec. 72(u)].

.02 Annuity Starting Date

The annuity starting date is the later of (1) the date obligations under the contract become fixed or (2) the first day of the annuity pay period (e.g., monthly, quarterly) that ends on the date of the first payment [Code Sec. 72(c)(4); Reg. § 1.72-4(b)].

.03 Tax Treatment of Annuity Benefits

Annuity benefits are taxed under the general rule which is used to compute the portion of periodic payments that is taxable. The taxpayer needs to know the following information when applying the general rule:

- The investment in the annuity is the total premiums paid, reduced by any premiums refunded, and rebates or dividends received before the annuity starting date. The investment in the contract is also reduced by the value of a refund feature which exists if the annuity provides for payments to a beneficiary or the annuitant's estate after the annuitant's death, based on the amount paid for the annuity [Code Sec. 72(c)].
- The expected return from the annuity is the total payments expected to be received. If payments are set for a term of years, the expected return is simply the annual payments times the number of years in the term. If payments are set for the life of the annuitant or the joint lives of the annuitant and spouse, the expected return is figured by multiplying the amount of the annual payment by life expectancy which can be found in actuarial tables published by the IRS in Reg. § 1.72-9. A sample table is reproduced in ¶ 5070.06.

The taxable portion is computed by [Code Sec. 72(b); Reg. § 1.72-4]:

1. Dividing the investment in the contract by the expected return and then
2. Multiplying the result by the total annual payments to find the nontaxable portion and then
3. Subtracting the nontaxable portion from the total annual payments.

Example 5-13: Taxpayer A purchased an annuity contract providing for payments of $100 per month for $12,650. Assuming that the expected return under this contract is $16,000 the exclusion ratio to be used by A is $12,650 ÷ $16,000; or 79.1 percent (79.06 rounded to the nearest tenth). If these 12 monthly payments are received by A during the year, the total amount he may exclude from his gross income that year is $949.20 ($1,200 × 79.1 percent). The balance of $250.80 ($1,200 less $949.20) is the amount to be included in gross income. If A instead received only five payments during the year, he should exclude $395.50 ($500 × 79.1 percent) of the total amounts received.

Exclusion Limited to Investment

The total exclusion is limited to the contributed amount. If the annuity owner dies before recovery of the full basis amount, the unrecovered amount may be claimed as a deduction in the final year. This deduction is not subject to the 2 percent floor on miscellaneous itemized deductions [Code Sec. 67(b)(10)]. Once the investment is recovered, 100 percent of each subsequent annuity payment is taxable [Code Sec. 72(b)(2), (3)].

.04 Investment in the Contract

The investment in the contract is the total amount of premiums paid less: (1) any premiums refunded, rebates, or dividends received on or before the annuity starting date; and (2) the value of any refund feature [Code Sec. 72(c); Reg. § 1.72-6, 1.72-7]. The refund feature reduces the amount of the investment in the contract. This comes into play if the expected return depends on life expectancy, and the contract provides either for refunds of the consideration or payment of a guaranteed amount.

.05 Expected Return

To find the expected return under a contract involving life expectancy, actuarial tables from the IRS are used [Code Sec. 72(c)(3)(A); Reg. § 1.72-9]. They provide a multiple that takes life expectancy into account in terms of total annual payments. Multiplying the amount of the annual payment by the multiple gives the expected return under the contracts [Reg. § 1.72-5]. For a fixed annuity, the expected return is easily calculated by figuring out how much will be paid after the annuity starting date. For example, the expected return on an annuity of $200 a month for 10 years is $24,000 ($200 × 120 months).

▶ **OBSERVATION:** These actuarial tables no longer make any distinction between male and female life expectancies.

If the annuitant lives longer than the date of her projected life expectancy, she realizes more on the annuity contract than expected. Once the annuitant's basis has been recovered, for individuals with an annuity starting date after December 31, 1986, subsequent payments are fully taxable [Code Sec. 72(b)(2)].

.06 Actuarial Tables

Actuarial tables have been published by the IRS [Reg. § 1.72-9], a sample of which (Table V) is reproduced here.

TABLE V—ORDINARY LIFE ANNUITIES ONE LIFE -EXPECTED RETURN MULTIPLES

AGE	MULTIPLE	AGE	MULTIPLE	AGE	MULTIPLE
5	76.6	42	40.6	79	10.0
6	75.6	43	39.6	80	9.5
7	74.7	44	38.7	81	8.9
8	73.7	45	37.7	82	8.4
9	72.7	46	36.8	83	7.9
10	71.7	47	35.9	84	7.4
11	70.7	48	34.9	85	6.9
12	69.7	49	34.0	86	6.5
13	68.8	50	33.1	87	6.1
14	67.8	51	32.2	88	5.7
15	66.8	52	31.3	89	5.3
16	65.8	53	30.4	90	5.0
17	64.8	54	29.5	91	4.7
18	63.9	55	28.6	92	4.4
19	62.9	56	27.7	93	4.1
20	61.9	57	26.8	94	3.9
21	60.9	58	25.9	95	3.7
22	59.9	59	25.0	96	3.4
23	59.0	60	24.2	97	3.2
24	58.0	61	23.3	98	3.0
25	57.0	62	22.5	99	2.8
26	56.0	63	21.6	100	2.7
27	55.1	64	20.8	101	2.5
28	54.1	65	20.0	102	2.3
29	53.1	66	19.2	103	2.1
30	52.2	67	18.4	104	1.9
31	51.2	68	17.6	105	1.8
32	50.2	69	16.8	106	1.6
33	49.3	70	16.0	107	1.4
34	48.3	71	15.3	108	1.3
35	47.3	72	14.6	109	1.1
36	46.4	73	13.9	110	1.0
37	45.4	74	13.2	111	.9
38	44.4	75	12.5	112	.8
39	43.5	76	11.9	113	.7

AGE	MULTIPLE	AGE	MULTIPLE	AGE	MULTIPLE
40	42.5	77	11.2	114	.6
41	41.5	78	10.6	115	.5

Example 5-14: Mrs. Haskins, age 65 on the annuity starting date, bought an annuity for $12,000 that will pay her $80 a month for her lifetime. Her expected return is determined as follows:

Annual payment ($80 × 12)	$960
Multiple shown in Table V, male or female, age 65	20
Expected return ($960 × 20)	$19,200

Her annual exclusion ratio is $12,000/$19,200, or 62.5%. She would exclude annually from gross income $600 ($960 × 62.5%).

.07 Amounts Not Received as an Annuity

Not all funds you receive from an annuity contract qualify as an annuity [see .01 above]. If they do not qualify, they do not get favorable annuity tax treatment. This applies to withdrawals, loans, pledges and assignments, dividends and partial surrenders. Amounts you receive before the annuity starting date are also, by definition, not amounts received as an annuity. However, they are taxable only to the extent the contract's *cash surrender value* exceeds your investment in the contract [Code Sec. 72(e)(2), (3)].

Example 5-15: Ms. Brown owns an annuity that is scheduled to start payments at age 65. She is now age 55 and will be borrowing on the policy this year. Brown has paid in $50,000, but the contract has a cash value of $70,000. If Brown borrows $30,000, she will owe tax on $20,000 of the loan proceeds ($70,000 less $50,000). The other $10,000 is a tax-free return of Brown's investment.

.08 Penalty Tax

The tax law imposes a 10 percent early distribution penalty for withdrawals from an annuity before age 59½ [Code Sec. 72(q)]. The penalty will be waived in the following circumstances:

- The annuitant is totally disabled.
- The distribution is part of a series of substantially equal periodic payments made at least annually over the life expectancy of the annuitant or joint life expectancies of the annuitant and beneficiary.
- The payment is received by a beneficiary or estate after the policyholder's death.
- The payment is allocable to investments in the contract made before August 14, 1982.
- The payment is from an annuity contract under a qualified personal injury settlement.
- The payment is from a single-premium annuity where the starting date is no more than one year from the date of purchase.

An annuity owner may choose to receive benefits from a portion of the annuity, while allowing the other portion to continue to grow on a tax-deferred basis.

Liberal Exception to Penalty

The penalty does not apply to payouts in the form of a lifetime annuity calling for payments at least annually. This is true regardless of your age [Code Sec. 72(q)(2)(D)].

The tax law also exempts distributions (1) from single premium contracts that start making substantially equal payments no more than one year after the contract is purchased, provided that those payments are made at least annually during the annuity period (so-called immediate annuities) [Code Sec. 72(q)(2)(I)] or (2) made to an employee upon separation from service from an annuity purchased by an employer on account of a qualified retirement plan's having been terminated [Code Sec. 72(q)(2)(J)].

.09 Private Annuities

The IRS has released proposed regulations that change the tax treatment of a popular tax-deferral transaction known as the private annuity arrangement in which the seller exchanges real estate or other appreciated property for an annuity contract and receives payments for the rest of his or her life. The IRS explained that the rules are designed to combat the avoidance or deferral of gain on the exchange of highly appreciated property for the issuance of annuity contracts. Under the proposed regulations, the transferor of the property in exchange for the annuity is taxed on any appreciation in the property as if that transferor had sold the property for cash and then used the proceeds to purchase the annuity [Prop. Reg. § 1.72-6(e)(1)]. As a result of this significant reversal in tax treatment, the proposed regulations are essentially the death knell of private annuity arrangements involving transfers of appreciated property.

In a private annuity transaction, a person (the "annuitant") transfers complete ownership of property to a transferee (the "obligor") in exchange for the obligor's unsecured promise to make periodic payments to the annuitant for the rest of the annuitant's lifetime. Typically, the private annuity sale is an estate planning or wealth transfer device that involves the transfer of appreciated property such as undeveloped real estate or small business stock from a parent or grandparent to a third party (an insurance company or a child) in exchange for the third party's promise to pay the senior family member a specified sum for the remainder of his or her life. The size of the payments is determined by the value of the property transferred, current interest rates, and the life expectancy of the annuitant. Taxpayers enter into these exchanges in order to avoid paying the upfront capital gains that the seller would owe if the property were sold outright. By establishing the private annuity trust, the taxpayer only pays tax on the annuity payments when they are distributed from the trust, thus deferring the payment of tax over a longer period of time.

Tax Treatment Under Proposed Regulations

In response to the use of private annuities to shelter taxable gain on appreciated assets, which the IRS characterizes as "abusive" and "inappropriate," the IRS has completely reversed its prior tax treatment of private annuity trusts. If an annuity contract is received in exchange for property other than money:

- The amount realized attributable to the annuity contract is the fair market value (as determined under the valuation tables issued under Code Sec. 7520) of the annuity contract at the time of the exchange;
- The entire amount of the gain or loss, if any, is recognized at the time of the exchange, regardless of the taxpayer's method of accounting; and
- For purposes of determining the initial investment in the annuity contract, the aggregate amount of premiums or other consideration paid for the annuity contract equals the amount realized attributable to the annuity contract (the fair market value of the annuity contract) [Prop. Reg. § § 1.72-6(e)(1), 1.1001-1(j)(1)].

.10 Partial Annuitization of Single Annuity Contract

Code Sec. 72(a)(2) provides that, if any amount is received as an annuity for 10 years or more or during one or more lives under any portion of an annuity, endowment, or life insurance contract, (a) that portion is treated as a separate contract for purposes of Code Sec. 72; (b) the investment in the contract generally is allocated pro rata between each portion of the contract from which amounts are received as an annuity and the portion from which amounts are not so received; and (c) a separate annuity starting date is determined with respect to each portion of the contract from which amounts are received as an annuity.

¶5075 JOINT AND SURVIVOR ANNUITIES

Under this arrangement, the first annuitant receives periodic payments for life and, after death, a second annuitant receives periodic payment in the same or different amounts for life. Generally, in finding the annual exclusion for a uniform payment joint and survivor annuity, the rules in ¶ 5070 apply. However, the combined life expectancy of the annuitants must be used in determining expected return [Reg. § 1.72-5(b)]. The rule for determining the survivor's income depends on when the first annuitant died. The ratio at which amounts received under the contract will be taxed may be determined at the outset of the contract by using the appropriate actuarial table.

For distribution involving a qualified joint and survivor annuity, a plan may permit a participant (and if applicable, a participant's spouse) to elect to waive the 30-day minimum waiting period between the written explanation of the terms and conditions of a qualified joint and survivor annuity and the annuity starting date. A waiver is allowed only if the distribution commences more than seven days after the written explanation is provided [Code Sec. 417(a)(7)]. The IRS has provided sample language designed to make it easier for spouses of plan participants to understand their rights to survivor annuities under qualified plans.[53] The sample language can be included in a form used for a spouse to consent to a participant's waiver of a qualified joint and survivor annuity. The language is designed to assist plan administrators in preparing spousal consent forms. No one is required to use the sample language and plan administrators that choose to use it are free to incorporate all or any part of it in their spousal consent forms.

[53] Notice 97-10, 1997-1 CB 370.

¶5080 EMPLOYEE ANNUITIES

.01 Annuity Taxation in General

If an employer buys an annuity contract under a qualified annuity plan (commonly referred to as a *pension*), or pays for any part of it, the employee is not taxed on the employer's payments when they are made. Using the annuity rules, benefits are taxed when the employee receives them [Code Sec. 403(a)]. In applying these rules, an employee's contributions are considered your investment in the contract. This reduces the portion of each annuity payment that counts as gross income. The total exclusion, though, is limited to the employee's actual investment. When the employee reaches his or her life expectancy, the exclusion ratio lapses; and, subsequent annuity payments are fully taxable [Code Sec. 72(b)(2)].

.02 Simplified Way to Figure Tax on Employee Annuities

Employees must use a simplified method to figure the taxable and tax-free portions of each annuity payment received from qualified plans, employee annuities and annuity contracts [Code Sec. 72(d)].

The simplified method must be used by distributees to comply with Code Sec. 72 and by payors to report the taxable portion of annuity distributions on Form 1099-R. Under the simplified method, the distributee recovers his or her investment in the contract in level amounts over the expected number of monthly payments determined from the tables reproduced below. The portion of each annuity payment that is excluded from gross income by a distributee for income tax purposes is a level dollar amount determined by dividing the investment in the contract by the set number of annuity payments from these tables.

The table used to determine the expected number of payments depends on whether the payments are based on the life of more than one individual [Reg. § 1.72(d)(1)(B)]. In the case of an annuity payable based on the life of only one individual, the total number of monthly annuity payments expected to be received is based on the annuitant's age at the annuity starting date. An annuity which is payable over the life of one annuitant with a term certain feature is an annuity based on the life of that individual. Similarly, an annuity which is payable over the life of one annuitant with a temporary annuity payable to the annuitant's child until the child reaches an age specified in the plan (not more than age 25) is an annuity based on the life of that individual. The expected number of payments for an annuity based on the life of one individual is set forth in Table 1 found in Reg. § 1.72(d)(1)(B)(iii).

Table 1. Annuity Payments Based on One Individual's Life

Age of Annuitant	Expected Number of Payments
55 and under	360
56-60	310
61-65	260

Age of Annuitant	Expected Number of Payments
66-70	210
71 and older	160

In the case of an annuity payable based on the life of more than one individual, the total number of monthly annuity payments expected to be received is based on the combined ages of the annuitants at the annuity starting date. If the annuity is payable to a primary annuitant and more than one survivor annuitant, the combined ages of the annuitants is the sum of the age of the primary annuitant and the youngest survivor annuitant. If the annuity is payable to more than one survivor annuitant but there is no primary annuitant, the combined ages of the annuitants is the sum of the age of the oldest survivor annuitant and the youngest survivor annuitant. In addition, any survivor annuitant whose entitlement to payments is contingent on an event other than the death of the primary annuitant is disregarded. The expected number of payments is set forth in the following table found in Reg. § 1.72(d)(1)(B)(iv):

Table 2. Annuity Payments Contingent on Combined Ages of Annuitants

Combined Ages of Annuitant s	Expected Number of Payments
110 and under	410
111-120	360
121-130	310
131-140	260
141 and older	210

Term Certain Annuities without Life Contingencies

In the case of an annuity that does not depend in whole or in part on the life expectancy of one or more individuals, the expected number of payments is the number of monthly annuity payments under the contract.

.03 Annuities Purchased by Certain Tax-Exempt Organizations

Public schools, hospitals, churches and certain other exempt organizations may offer their employees special tax deferred annuities. Contributions in the annuity are tax-free to the employee to the extent that they do not exceed $42,000 (for 2005) or the employee's compensation.

.04 Investment in the Contract Where Employer Contributes

Your investment in the contract includes amounts contributed by your employer only if the amounts (1) were includible in your income when contributed, or (2) would have been includible when contributed if they had been directly paid to you at that time [Code Sec. 72(f)]. Amounts constructively received by you are included under (1) above. Exempt income is included under (2).

.05 Amounts Received Before Annuity Starting Date

In general, the same rules apply to employee annuities as to other annuities [Code Sec. 72(e)(8)(A)]. In other words, you are taxed on early withdrawals or loans to the extent the cash value exceeds your investment in the contract.

SPECIAL RULES

¶5085 SCHOLARSHIPS

Code Sec. 117 excludes from gross income amounts received as a qualified scholarship by an individual who is a candidate for a degree and used for tuition and fees required for the enrollment or attendance (or for fees, books, supplies, and equipment required for courses of instruction) at a primary, secondary, or postsecondary educational institution. The tax-free treatment provided by Code Sec. 117 does not extend to scholarship amounts covering regular living expenses, such as room and board. In addition to the exclusion for qualified scholarships, Code Sec. 117 provides an exclusion from gross income for qualified tuition reductions for certain education provided to employees (and their spouses and dependents) of certain educational organizations. Amounts excludable from gross income under Code Sec. 117 are also excludable from wages for payroll tax purposes [Code Sec. 3121(a)(20)].

.01 Qualified Scholarships

The term "qualified scholarship" means any amount received by an individual as a scholarship or fellowship grant to the extent the individual establishes that the proceeds were used for qualified tuition and related expenses which are defined as:

- Tuition and fees required for the enrollment or attendance of a student at a primary, secondary or postsecondary educational institution, and
- Fees, books, supplies, and equipment required for courses of instruction at the educational organization [Code Sec. 117(b)(2)(B)].

.02 Exceptions

The exclusion does not apply to any portion of amounts received as a grant or tuition reduction that represent payment for teaching, research, or other services required as a condition of receiving the scholarship or tuition reduction [Code Sec. 117(c)]. However, the exclusion will still apply for amounts received by medical, dental, nursing, and physician assistant students under the National Health Service Corps (NHSC) Scholar ship Program and the Armed Forces Health Professions Scholarship and Financial Assistance Program [Code Sec. 117(c)(2)].

Recipients of these scholarships are required to serve in either an underserved community or an Army hospital. An income exclusion is available for scholarships with obligatory service requirements received by degree candidates at qualified educational organizations from the NHSC Scholarship Program or the F. Edward Hebert Armed Forces Health Professions Scholarship and Financial Assistance Program. Thus, amounts received by degree candidates at qualified educational organizations from these programs will be excluded from gross income [Code Sec. 117(c)]. This provision is permanent for tax years beginning after December 31, 2012.

The amount of an otherwise qualified grant awarded to a degree candidate is excludable (after considering the amount of any other grant also eligible for exclusion) up to the combined amount incurred for tuition and course-related expenses during the period to which the grant applies. Any excess amount of the grant is includible in income. No amount of a grant is excludable if the grant's terms earmark its use for other than tuition or course-related expenses (like room and board or meal allowances) or specify that the grant cannot be used for tuition or course-related expenses, even if the amount of the grant is less than the amount payable by the student for tuition or course-related expenses.

.03 Qualified Tuition Reductions

Qualified tuition reductions provided to an employee of an educational institution are also excluded from gross income [Code Sec. 117(d)]. The tuition reduction can be for education provided by the employer or by another qualified educational organization. The tax-free tuition reduction can be enjoyed not only by the employee, but also by the employee's spouse[54] or dependent child, as long as it is used for education below the graduate level. An exception for the "below graduate level" limitation exists for the education of an employee who is a graduate student and who is engaged in teaching or research activities for the employer including a teaching and research assistant. The income exclusion only applies if the tuition reduction is available on substantially the same terms to each member of a group of employees and does not discriminate in favor of "highly compensated employees," as defined in Code Sec. 414(q) [Code Sec. 117(d)(3)].

¶5090 SOCIAL SECURITY, UNEMPLOYMENT INSURANCE BENEFITS AND SIMILAR PAYMENTS

.01 Social Security Benefits

Social security benefits are generally not subject to tax unless your income exceeds certain levels. The maximum amount subject to tax is 50 percent of benefits at one level of income and 85 percent at the higher level.

Because social security retirement benefits are intended to replace income that the retired person will no longer receive, the amount of benefits that a retiree receives must be reduced if he or she works and earns money after retirement. An annual earnings test (see chart below) is applied to determine to what extent outside earnings of a retiree will reduce his or her social security benefits. The earnings test applies only to retired individuals who are under age 70.

Retirement Earnings Test

The Retirement Earnings Test has been eliminated for individuals ages 65-69. It remains in effect for those ages 62 through 64. A modified test applies for the year an individual reaches age 65.[55]

---

54 *T.M. Wolpaw,* CA-6, 95-1 USTC ¶50,104, 47 F3d 787.

55 Social Security Administration "Exempt Amounts Under the Earnings Test," October 16, 2012; Social Security Administration Fact Sheet, October 30, 2013.

Table 3. Retirement Earnings Test Exempt Amounts

	2013	2014
Year individual reaches 65*	$40,080/yr. ($3,340/mo.)	$41,400/yr. ($3,450/mo.)
Under age 65	$15,120/yr. ($1,260/mo.)	$15,480/yr. ($1,290/mo.)

* Applies only to earnings for months prior to attaining age 65. One dollar in benefits will be withheld for every $3 in earnings above the limit. There is no limit on earnings beginning the month an individual attains age 65.

According to this test, if you are younger than age 65 you can earn up to $15,120 a year in 2013 or $1,260 a month before facing a reduction of your Social Security benefits. For every $2 in earnings over this limit, you will lose $1 of benefits.

Age 70 and Older

If you are age 70 and older, you can earn any amount without having your Social Security benefits reduced.

Continued payment of Social Security and Medicare taxes. Keep in mind, that regardless of age, if you continue to work part-time or full-time you will have to pay social security and Medicare taxes on the earnings. If you are age 65 or over, your social security benefits will not be reduced by your earnings.

Withholding from Social Security benefits. Retirees have the option of voluntarily electing to have federal income tax withheld from their social security benefits. Withholding will eliminate the need to pay quarterly estimated taxes. You can begin withholding federal income taxes from your social security payments by completing Form W-4V, *Voluntary Withholding Request.* After checking the box on the form reflecting the desired tax rate, send the Form to the Social Security Administration and withholding will continue indefinitely unless you file a new Form W-4V requesting a new tax rate or a termination of withholding.

Tax Treatment of Social Security Benefits

Only the social security benefits of married taxpayers with *provisional income* less than $32,000 and unmarried taxpayers with provisional income less than $25,000 will escape tax [Code. Sec. 86(c)]. If your provisional income is above these amounts, you will have to compute how much of your social security benefits are taxable. Table 4 lists tax rates for provisional income by filing status.

Provisional income is:

- *Modified adjusted gross income,* which is a taxpayer's AGI (a) determined without regard to the social security benefits, the exclusion or deduction for foreign earned income and housing costs, the exclusion for interest on U.S. savings bonds redeemed to pay the exclusion for employer-provided adoption assistance, the deduction for interest on education loans, the deduction for qualified tuition and related expenses, the deduction for income attributable to domestic production activities, and the exclusion of income from sources within U.S. possessions and Puerto Rico and (b) increased by the amount of tax-exempt interest received or accrued by the taxpayer during the tax year [Code Sec. 86(b)(2)]; *plus*

- One-half of the social security benefits received for a tax year [Code Sec. 86(b)(1)(A)(ii)].

The following table shows what percentage of your social security benefits will be taxed depending on the amount of your provisional income and your filing status:

Table 4. Tax Rates for Provisional Income of Single and Married Joint-Filing Taxpayers

Provisional Income	Single
$1-$24,999	none taxed
$25,000-$33,999	the lesser of 50 percent of social security benefits or 50 percent of the excess of provisional income over $25,000
$34,000 and above	the lesser of (a) 85 percent of social security benefits or (b) 85 percent of the excess of provisional income over $34,000 plus the smaller of the amount included under the 50 percent taxable formula above or $4,500
Provisional Income	**Married (Filing Joint Return)**
$1-$31,999	none taxed
$32,000-$43,999	the lesser of 50 percent of social security benefits or 50 percent of the excess of provisional income over $32,000
$44,000 and above	the lesser of (a) 85 percent of social security benefits or (b) 85 percent of the excess of provisional income over $34,000 plus the smaller of the amount included under the 50 percent taxable formula above or $6,000

Married taxpayers filing a joint return must combine their incomes (even if one spouse received no benefits) and social security benefits to determine if any of the combined benefits are taxable.

Married Taxpayers Living Apart Defined

The Tax Court concluded that a taxpayer and his spouse, who claimed *married filing separately* as their filing status and who used that status to compute the tax owed on their social security benefits, were required to actually live in separate residences to claim that their filing status was "married filing separately."[56] The fact that they maintained separate bedrooms but lived in the same house, did not mean that they were living apart for purposes of determining the tax treatment of social security benefits. As a result of this case, taxpayers will be required to actually live in separate residences in order to claim married filing separately as their tax status.

First Tier

The portion of your first tier social security benefits that are included in gross income is equal to the lesser of (1) one-half of the benefits you receive during the tax year, or (2) one-half of the excess of the sum of (a) your modified adjusted gross income plus (b) one-half of the social security benefits you receive over the base amount [Code Sec. 86(a), (b)]. In general, your modified adjusted gross income is your adjusted gross

[56] *T.W. McAdams,* 118 TC 373, Dec. 54,743 (2002).

income plus any tax-exempt interest you receive. In the first tier, the base amount is $32,000 for married persons filing jointly, zero for married persons filing separately, and $25,000 for singles.

Second Tier

There are a second, higher set of base amounts: $44,000 for married persons filing jointly, zero for married persons filing separately and $34,000 for singles. Social security recipients with modified adjusted gross incomes (defined the same as for the first tier) above these amounts pay tax on 85 percent of their total benefits.

Planning Suggestions

If a retiree's base income is close to the threshold or base amount ($44,000 for married filing jointly or $34,000 for single filers), he or she should consider the following planning techniques:

- Avoid unnecessary withdrawals from traditional IRAs and other deferred income accounts which would increase income to exceed the base amount;
- Switch from taxable certificates of deposit to tax-exempt municipal bonds; Even though tax-exempt interest is included, the yield would be lower;
- Give children or grandchildren some income-producing assets;
- Buy a tax-deferred annuity that accumulates income rather than distributes it;
- Using some cash to buy cash-value life insurance; or
- Make an election to treat any lump-sum payment of social security benefits as received in a prior year to which the benefits are attributable rather than the current year [Code Sec. 86(e)].

.02 Unemployment Compensation

In general, unemployment compensation benefits are includible in gross income in the same manner as wages and other ordinary income for federal income tax purposes [Code Sec. 85(a)]. Unemployment benefits include payments under federal or state law, disability payments received as a substitute for unemployment benefits, and payments under certain legislative acts and other benefit programs [Code Sec. 85(b); Reg. § 1.85-1(b)]. State unemployment agencies are required to permit a recipient an election to have federal income tax withheld from their benefit payment at a 10 percent rate by filing Form W-4V, *Voluntary Withholding Request* [Code Sec. 3402(p)(2)]. States may also (but are not required to) allow individuals who apply for unemployment benefits to elect to have state and local income tax withheld from their benefits.

Although unemployment benefits are fully includible in income, in limited situations a taxpayer may reduce the amount that must be included in gross income. For example, if the taxpayer contributed to a governmental unemployment compensation program, and the contributions are not deductible, then amounts received under that unemployment compensation program are not included in income until the taxpayer recovers his contribution. Similarly, unemployment benefits from a private fund to which the taxpayer voluntarily contributes are taxable only to the extent that the amounts received exceed the taxpayer's total payments into the fund.

.03 Medicare Benefits

Basic Medicare benefits you receive under the Social Security Act are excluded from your gross income. Supplementary benefits (covering costs of doctors' services and other items not covered under basic Medicare) are also excluded since they are in the nature of medical insurance payments.[57] Employer-paid Medicare premiums are not income to an employee since these are considered contributions to employer accident or health plans.[58]

.04 Public Assistance Payments

Benefit payments from a general welfare fund in the interest of the general public, such as payments because of blindness or payments to crime victims, are excluded from gross income. In Rev. Rul. 71-425,[59] the IRS held that payments made by a state welfare agency in lieu of (and in amounts no greater than) the normal relief allowance, to participants in work-training programs under title V of the Economic Opportunity Act of 1964, were not includible in the gross income of the recipient and were not wages for employment tax purposes, since the payments were measured by the personal or family need of the recipient rather than the value of any services performed.

¶5095 ENERGY CONSERVATION SUBSIDIES

Gross income does not include the value of any subsidy provided (directly or indirectly) by a public utility to a customer for the purchase or installation of any energy conservation measure [Code Sec. 136(a)]. An "energy conservation measure" can be almost anything installed or designed primarily to (1) reduce the consumption of electricity or natural gas, or (2) reduce the demand for energy in a home [Code Sec. 136(c)(1)]. Examples include installing storm windows or buying equipment that uses fuel more efficiently.

¶5100 EXCLUSION OF DISASTER RELIEF

.01 Exclusion of Qualified Disaster Relief Payments

Code Sec. 139 provides a specific exclusion from the income of disaster victims for *qualified disaster relief payments,* which are any amount paid to or for the benefit of an individual [Code Sec. 139(b)]:

- To reimburse or pay reasonable and necessary personal, family, living, or funeral expenses incurred as a result of a qualified disaster;
- To reimburse or pay reasonable and necessary expenses incurred for the repair or rehabilitation of a personal residence or repair or replacement of its contents to the extent that the need for such repair, rehabilitation, or replacement is attributable to a qualified disaster. For purposes of determining the tax basis of a rehabilitated

[57] Rev. Rul. 79-173, 1979-1 CB 86.

[58] Rev. Rul. 67-360, 1967-2 CB 71.

[59] Rev. Rul. 71-425, 1971-2 CB 76.

residence, it is intended that qualified disaster relief payments be treated in the same manner as amounts received on an involuntary conversion of a principal residence under Code Sec. 121(d)(5) and Code Sec. 1033(b) and (h). A residence is not precluded from being a personal residence solely because the taxpayer does not own the residence. This means that a rented residence can qualify as a personal residence;

- By a person engaged in the furnishing or sale of transportation as a common carrier by reason of the death or personal physical injuries incurred as a result of a qualified disaster. Thus, for example, payments made by commercial airlines to families of passengers killed as a result of a qualified disaster would be excluded from gross income; and
- If the amounts are paid by a federal, state, or local government in connection with a qualified disaster in order to promote the general welfare. The exclusion does not apply, however, to payments in the nature of income replacement, such as payments to individuals of lost wages, unemployment compensation, or payments in the nature of business income replacement.

The exclusion does not apply, however, to payments in the nature of income replacement, such as payments to individuals of lost wages, unemployment compensation, or payments in the nature of business income replacement. Qualified disaster relief payments do not include payments for any expenses compensated for by insurance or otherwise.

Qualified Disaster Defined

A *qualified disaster* is defined as [Code Sec. 139(c)]:

- A disaster which results from a terrorist or military action (as defined in Code Sec. 692(c)(2));
- A federally declared disaster (as defined in Code Sec. 165(h)(3)(C)(i));
- A disaster which results from an accident involving a common carrier, or from any other event, which is determined to be catastrophic; or
- For purposes of payments made by a federal, state or local government, a disaster designated by federal, state, or local authorities to warrant assistance.

Deductibility of Qualified Disaster Relief Payments

Qualified disaster relief payments are deductible to the same extent they would be if they were includable in income. In addition, in light of the extraordinary circumstances surrounding a qualified disaster, it is anticipated that individuals will not be required to account for actual expenses in order to qualify for the exclusion, provided that the amount of the payments can be reasonably expected to be commensurate with the expenses incurred.

No Withholding Required

Qualified disaster relief payments also are excludable for purposes of self-employment taxes and employment taxes. Thus, no withholding applies to qualified disaster relief payments [Code Sec. 139(d)].

Terrorists Not Eligible for Relief

The income exclusion available under Code Sec. 139 does not apply to any individual identified by the attorney general to have been a participant or conspirator in any terrorist action or a representative of such individual [Code Sec. 139(e)].

Disaster Mitigation Payments

Code Sec. 139(g) provides that gross income does not include any amount received as a qualified disaster mitigation payment. It defines those payments to include any amount paid under the Robert T. Stafford Disaster Relief and Emergency Assistance Act or the National Flood Insurance Act to or for the benefit of the owner of any property for hazard mitigation with respect to that property. Thus, disaster mitigation payments made under the Federal Emergency Management Agency (FEMA) are tax-free.

Windfall prevention provisions. To prevent a windfall for taxpayers who receive FEMA grants, Code Sec. 139(g)(3) provides that any amount excluded with respect to property does not increase the adjusted basis of that property. Similarly, Code Sec. 139(h) provides that no deduction or credit is allowed to the person for whose benefit a qualified disaster relief payment or qualified disaster mitigation payment is made. Code Sec. 139(g)(3) adds that a taxpayer may not use any excluded qualified disaster mitigation payment for any property to increase his basis or adjusted basis in that property.

> **Example 5-16:** Homeowners live in an area of the country frequently destroyed by forest fires. They apply for a grant under FEMA's Pre-Disaster Mitigation Program to add fireproofing materials to their home prior to the forest fire season. They come up with $50,000 by taking out a second mortgage on their home and FEMA provides the remaining $100,000 needed to complete the fireproofing job. The $100,000 that they receive from FEMA will not be taxed under the new law. If they sell their home later at a taxable gain, however, they may not increase their home's tax basis by the amount of the $100,000 FEMA grant.

.02 Tax Treatment of Amounts Received Under Insurance Contracts for Certain Living Expenses

If a taxpayer's principal residence was damaged or destroyed by a fire, storm, or other casualty, or the taxpayer was denied access to the residence by governmental authorities because of the occurrence or threat of occurrence of such a casualty, gross income does not include amounts received under an insurance contract that provide compensation or reimbursement for living expenses incurred by the taxpayer or members of his or her household resulting from the loss of use or occupancy of the residence [Code Sec. 123(a); Reg. § 1.123-1].

.03 Victims of Terrorism Tax Relief Act of 2001

Following the September 11, 2001, attacks in New York and Washington, DC, Congress enacted the Victims of Terrorism Tax Relief Act of 2001 to provide tax relief for families of victims of the terrorist attacks.[60] Payments from the 9/11 victim fund are tax-free whether they are periodic or lump-sum.[61]

.04 Exclusion of Payments to Survivors of Public Safety Officers

Payments made to survivors of a *public safety officer* who died in the line of duty are not included in income [Code Sec. 101(h)(1)]. For purposes of this exclusion, public safety officer includes police and law enforcement officers, firefighters, and rescue squad and ambulance crews. Payments eligible for the exclusion include the death benefit paid to survivors by the Bureau of Justice Assistance, and payments under a government plan annuity which are typically based on the officer's service as a public safety officer.

.05 Exclusion of Scholarship

Scholarship grants awarded by an employer's tax-exempt, private foundation to employees, or to the children of employees seriously injured or killed due to a qualified disaster will not be taxable as compensation or as a fringe benefit.[62] Under Code Sec. 139(c), qualified disaster generally includes a disaster from a terrorist or military action, a federally declared disaster, or a disaster resulting from an accident involving a common carrier, or from any other event, determined by the IRS to be of a catastrophic nature. An employee or child of an employee is eligible to get an educational grant only if the employee is seriously injured or killed due to a qualified disaster.

.06 Federally Declared Disaster Area

Assistance provided to affected taxpayers in federally declared disaster areas by state programs, charitable organizations, or employers to cover medical, transportation, or temporary housing expenses is tax-free.[63] An affected taxpayer in a federally declared disaster areas is:

- Any individual whose principal residence is located in a covered disaster area;
- Any business entity or sole proprietor whose principal place of business is located in a covered disaster area;
- Any individual who is a relief worker affiliated with a recognized government or philanthropic organization and who is assisting in a covered disaster area;
- Any individual whose principal residence or any business entity or sole proprietor whose principal place of business is not located in a covered disaster area but whose records are necessary to meet a deadline for an act for which the time may be extended are maintained in a covered disaster area;
- Any estate or trust that has tax records necessary to meet a deadline for an act for which the time may be extended which are maintained in a covered disaster area;
- The spouse of an affected taxpayer, solely for a joint return of the husband and wife; or
- Any other person determined by the IRS to be affected by a federally declared disaster [Reg. § 301.7508A-1(d)(1)].

---

[60] Treas. Dept., IRS Publication 3920, "Tax Relief for Victims of Terrorist Attacks" (2002 Ed.).

[61] Rev. Rul. 2003-115, 2003-2 CB 1052.

[62] Rev. Rul. 2003-32, 2003-1 CB 698.

[63] Rev. Rul. 2003-12, 2003-1 CB 283.

Casualty losses are generally deductible in the year the casualty occurs unless the taxpayer is in a presidentially-declared disaster area. In this case, the taxpayer may treat the loss as having occurred in the year immediately prior to the tax year in which the disaster happened thus enabling the taxpayer to deduct the loss on his or her return or amended return for that preceding tax year [Code Sec. 165(i)]. This opportunity means that taxpayers will have the benefit of an immediate tax refund, rather than having to wait to receive the cash until they file their return for the year of the loss. Taxpayers should be aware of the basic tax rules regarding casualty losses: (1) if a taxpayer is claiming a personal casualty loss, the loss is subject to a $100 floor per casualty and to an overall 10 percent of adjusted gross income limitation [Code Sec. 165(h)(1), (2)]; (2) the total loss must be reduced by any insurance payment received for the property; and (3) the $100 floor and 10 percent of AGI limitations do not apply to a business or income-producing property casualty loss.

The election to deduct the disaster loss for the preceding year must be made by filing a return, an amended return or a refund claim on or before the later of (1) the due date of the return, without extensions, for the tax year in which the disaster actually occurred, or (2) the due date of the return, with extensions, for the tax year immediately preceding the tax year in which the disaster actually occurred [Reg. § 1.165-11(e)]. An individual taxpayer may deduct losses if they are incurred in a trade or business, if they are incurred in a transaction entered into for profit, or if they are casualty losses under Code Sec. 165(c)(3). For further discussion of casualty losses, see ¶ 13,020.

.07 List of Federally Declared Disaster Areas

The government provides a list of areas that were declared disaster areas during the year. Amendments expanding the area declared a disaster area are frequently issued. The most recent federally declared disaster areas can be found at the Federal Emergency Management Agency (FEMA) website at www.fema.gov or CCH Standard Federal Income Tax Reporter ¶ 590 and ¶ 591.

¶5105 EXCLUSION FOR LONG-TERM CARE INSURANCE

Long-term care insurance is a guaranteed renewable insurance contract that pays for long-term nursing and personal care services that many older adults and some younger individuals might require either in a nursing home or at home. The insurance is designed to cover assistance that older adults may require in performing activities of daily living (ADL). These activities could include eating, bathing, dressing, and walking. The assistance could be provided by skilled nursing care provided 24 hours a day, intermediate nursing care provided less than 24 hours a day or custodial care. Long-term care insurance picks up where Medicare, Medigap and Medicaid (which do not cover these expenses) leaves off.

Benefits (other than policy holder dividends or premium refunds) paid by a qualified long-term care insurance policy are tax-free up to the greater of $320 a day or $116,800 ($320 × 365 days) in 2013 or the costs incurred for qualified long-term care services provided the insured [Code Sec. 7702B(a), (d)]. In addition, to make long-term care insurance even more appealing for lower-income taxpayers, premiums paid on this insurance are deductible as a medical expense subject to the floor of 10 percent of adjusted gross income [Code Sec. 213(d)(1)(D); see ¶ 9100].

.01 Long-Term Care Insurance Contract

In order to qualify for the income exclusion, your employer's long-term care insurance contract must provide only coverage of "qualified long-term care services" and meet the following requirements:

- The contract must be guaranteed renewable.
- The contract must not provide for a cash surrender value or other money that can be paid, assigned, pledged as collateral for a loan, or borrowed.
- Refunds, other than refunds paid upon the death of the insured or complete surrender or cancellation of the contract, and dividends may only be used to reduce future premiums or to increase future benefits.
- The contract may not pay or reimburse expenses which are reimbursable under Medicare, except when Medicare is a secondary payor or when the contract makes payments per diem or on another periodic basis without regard to actual expense.
- The consumer protection provisions of Code Sec. 7702B(g) are satisfied [Code Sec. 7702B(b)].

Be certain to get a disclosure statement from the insurance company stating that the policy is a qualified long-term care contract.

.02 What Expenses Are Covered

Only benefits from a long-term care contract which pays or reimburses actual long-term care expenses will be tax-free. This includes necessary diagnostic, preventive, therapeutic, curing, treating, mitigating, and rehabilitative services, and maintenance or personal care services, which are required by a chronically ill individual and are provided pursuant to a plan of care prescribed by a licensed health care practitioner such as a physician, registered nurse, and licensed social worker [Code Sec. 7702B(c)(1)].

.03 Definition of *Chronically Ill*

The term *chronically ill individual* means any individual who has been certified by a licensed health care practitioner as:

- Being unable to perform (without substantial assistance from another individual) at least two activities of daily living (ADLs) for a period of at least 90 days because of a loss of functional capacity (the ADL trigger), or
- Requiring substantial supervision to protect such individual from threats to health and safety because of severe cognitive impairment (the cognitive impairment trigger) [Code Sec. 7702B(c)(2)].

For these purposes, ADLs include eating, toileting, transferring, bathing, dressing, and continence [Code Sec. 7702B(c)(2)(B)]. A contract will not be considered a qualified long-term care insurance contract under the ADL trigger unless the determination of whether an individual is chronically ill takes into account at least 5 of these activities.

Thus, a contract that defines a chronically ill individual under the cognitive impairment trigger qualifies even if the individual can perform all the activities of daily living.

ADL Trigger

For purposes of the ADL triggers, you may rely on the following safe-harbor definitions:

- *Substantial assistance* means hands-on assistance and standby assistance;
- *Hands-on assistance* means the physical assistance of another person without which the individual would be unable to perform the ADL; and
- *Standby assistance* means the presence of another person within arm's reach to prevent, by physical intervention, injury to the ill individual while the individual is performing the ADL (e.g., being ready to catch the individual in case of a fall while bathing).

Cognitive Impairment Trigger

For purposes of the cognitive impairment trigger, you may rely on either or both of the following safe-harbor definitions:

- *Severe cognitive impairment* means a loss or deterioration in intellectual capacity that is (a) comparable to (and includes) Alzheimer's disease and similar forms of irreversible dementia, and (b) measured by clinical evidence and standardized tests that reliably measure impairment in the individual's memory, orientation, and reasoning;
- *Substantial supervision* means continual supervision that is necessary to protect the severely cognitively impaired individual from threats to his or her safety from wandering; and

Employers paying long-term care benefits should use Form 1099-LTC, *Long-Term Care and Accelerated Death Benefits,* to report the aggregate benefits paid and other information required under Code Sec. 6050Q.

.04 Per Diem Limitation

Per diem benefits from long-term care contracts that pay a set dollar benefit for each day of long-term care services generally are tax-free only up to $320 a day or $116,800 in 2013 [Code Sec. 7702B(d)(4)]. However, per diem benefits above $320 are also tax-free to the extent that unreimbursed long-term care expenses actually exceed that amount. [See also ¶ 4040 and ¶ 9105].

.05 Long-Term Coverage Under Employer Plans

In addition, employees are not taxed on employer-provided coverage under a qualifying long-term care insurance contract unless the coverage is provided through a cafeteria plan [Ch. 4]. Tax-free reimbursements cannot be made for long-term care expenses under a flexible spending arrangement (employee reimbursement account).

¶5110 QUALIFIED TUITION PROGRAMS (SECTION 529 PLANS)

A qualified tuition program is a popular tax-advantaged college savings program available to investors under Code Sec. 529. These plans are established and maintained by a state instrumentality (such as a brokerage house) under which an individual may make cash contributions to an account established solely to pay the "qualified higher education expenses" of the designated beneficiary of the account.

The popularity of college savings plans or "529 plans" (named after the tax code section creating them in 1996) skyrocketed after tax law changes made withdrawals tax-free when the proceeds are used solely to fund the "qualified higher education expenses" of the designated beneficiary of the account.

The 529 plan is available to all taxpayers regardless of how much money they report on their income tax return. Unlike all other education-related tax incentives, no income limit or phaseout applies to 529 plans.

.01 Two Types of 529 Plans Available

The two types of 529 plans available to investors are the college savings plan and the prepaid tuition plan.

College Savings Plan

The more popular college funding option is the 529 college savings plan. With this plan, taxpayers make contributions to an account which is established to meet the *qualified higher education expenses* of a designated beneficiary. Contributions are invested by the selected brokerage house pursuant to any investment option you choose and the account balance is available to pay tuition and other educational expenses of the beneficiary when needed. Your investment choice may be changed once per calendar year as well as when the designated beneficiary of the account changes. Funds in the plan can be used to pay for qualified higher education expenses at any eligible college, university, or vocational school in the United States [Code Sec. 529(b)(1); Prop. Reg. § 1.529-2(a)].

Contributions to college savings plans are not deductible for federal income tax purposes although they may be deductible for state income tax purposes depending on state law. All distributions including the earnings are tax-free provided they are used to pay for qualified higher education expenses [Code Sec. 529(c)(1)]. Distributions not used for qualified higher education expenses for reasons other than the death or disability of the designated beneficiary or to the extent that the distribution exceeds amounts not covered by scholarships are subject to tax as well as an additional 10-percent penalty.

Prepaid Tuition Plans

Prepaid tuition plans provide incentives for residents to attend in-state colleges and universities. They permit taxpayers to purchase tuition credits or certificates that entitle a designated beneficiary to the waiver of tuition or payment of qualified higher education expenses [Code Sec. 529(b)(1)(A)(i)]. With this plan, a parent or grandparent purchases a specific amount of future tuition (e.g., 12 credit hours) at today's prices. A prepaid tuition plan often requires that either the parent or child reside in the state that sponsors the plan and many plans even impose a penalty if the student uses the credits to attend a private or out-of-state college. The advantage of prepaid tuition plans is that they are relatively safe investments. They give families a steady, safe, and modest return on their investment and are typically backed up by the full faith and credit of the state sponsoring the plan. They will only be attractive to parents who want to avoid the risk of market volatility and whose children are near college age and hope to attend an in-state school. Parents seeking a more attractive return on their investment and who don't want to limit college choices to in-state schools, should invest in a college savings plan. A prepaid tuition plan may be established and maintained by one or more "eligible education institutions," including private colleges and universities [Code Sec. 529(b)(1)(A)]. The income exclusion applies for distributions from qualified private plans to the extent the amounts distributed are used for qualified higher education expenses.

.02 How 529 Plans Compare to Other Savings Vehicles

When compared with the other college savings vehicles available to parents and grandparents searching for a tax-deferred way to save for college tuition, the clear winner is the 529 plan. Here's why:

- If you invest in mutual funds or stocks in your own name you will be taxed on investment income at your own tax rate;
- If you invest in custodial accounts under the Uniform Gifts/Transfers to Minor's Act, you enjoy the benefits of tax deferral, but will eventually have to hand over control of the money to your children at either age 18 or 21 depending on "the age of majority" in your state;
- If you invest in a Coverdell Education Savings Account (formerly called the Education IRA), your college dollars will grow tax-free, but you will only be able to contribute $2,000 in 2013 [Code Sec. 530(b)(1)]. See ¶ 5115 for further discussion. In addition, only joint filers with modified adjusted gross incomes between $190,000 and $220,000 ($95,000 and $110,000 for single filers) are eligible to contribute [Code Sec. 530(c)(1)(A)];
- With custodial accounts, the kiddie tax will apply to children who are under age 18 or, if the child's earned income does not exceed half of the child's own support for the year, the child is either under 19 or, if a full time student is under 24 [Code Sec. 1(g)(2)(A)]. Net unearned income of a child is the portion of adjusted gross income for the year that is not attributable to earned income, reduced by $950 in 2012), and by either (1) the standard deduction amount, which is ($950 in 2012), or (2) the child's itemized deductions relating to the production of the unearned income. For further discussion, see ¶ 2170; and
- If college funds are invested in a trust, the top tax rate of 39.6 percent will apply to trust income over $11,950 in 2013. In addition, with a trust, you will have the added cost of operating the trust and filing an annual tax return.

.03 Tax Treatment

The 529 plan is an entity that will not be subject to tax provided it does not engage in any unrelated business activities [Code Sec. 529(a)]. Earnings on amounts invested in 529 plans grow tax-free. Distributions are generally tax-free to the extent the distributed amounts are used for "qualified higher education expenses." Any excess amount will be subject to tax at the student's income tax rate, which typically will be lower than the parent or grandparent's tax rate thus offering investors an opportunity to shift income to taxpayers in lower tax brackets [Code Sec. 529(c)(3)(B)(iii)].

.04 *Qualified Higher Education Expenses* Defined

Money invested in a 529 plan may be used to pay a student's *qualified higher education expenses,* which include tuition, fees, books, supplies, and equipment required for enrollment or attendance at a college or university (or certain vocational schools) [Code Sec. 529(e)(3)(A)(i); Prop. Reg. § 1.529-1(c)]. Room and board are considered qualified higher education expenses if the student is:

1. Enrolled in a degree, certificate, or other program leading to a recognized educational credential at an eligible educational institution; and
2. The student is carrying at least half of the normal full-time work load for the course of study that the student is pursuing. If the student lives at home with his or her parents, room and board costs are the amount determined by the institution. If the student resides in housing owned or operated by the school, room and board costs will be a standard allowance based on the amount that most of the school's residents are normally charged for room and board. For all other students, room and board costs will be the amount of expenses reasonably incurred by the student for room and board.

Special Needs Beneficiary

In the case of special needs beneficiary, qualified higher education expenses include other expenses necessary for the student to complete his or her college attendance or enrollment [Code Sec. 529(e)(3)(A)(ii); Prop. Reg. § 1.529-1(c)].

Room and Board

The amount of room and board treated as qualified higher education expenses cannot exceed the greater of (1) the allowance for room and board included in the eligible educational institution's cost of attendance or (2) the actual invoice amount the student residing in housing owned or operated by the eligible educational institution is charged by the institution for room and board. [Code Sec. 529(e)(3)(B)(ii)].

.05 *Eligible Educational Institution* Defined

Money invested in a 529 plan can be used to cover qualified expenses at an eligible educational institution which is generally an accredited postsecondary educational institution offering credit toward a bachelor's degree, an associate's degree, a graduate-level or professional degree, or other recognized postsecondary credential [Code Sec. 529(3)(5); Prop Reg. § 1.529-1(c)]. Certain proprietary institutions and postsecondary vocational institutions also are eligible institutions provided the institution is eligible to participate in Department of Education student aid programs.

.06 Coordination with Other Education Benefits

To the extent that a distribution from a 529 plan is used to pay for qualified tuition and fees at an eligible postsecondary institution, the student (or her parent) may still be able to claim the HOPE credit or the Lifetime Learning credit with respect to tuition and fees not paid with distributions from the 529 plan. Taxpayers will also be able to contribute to both the Coverdell Education Savings Accounts and 529 plans in the same year for the same beneficiary provided the taxpayers' income satisfies the Coverdell limits.

Order of Reduction

Qualified expenses are first reduced for scholarships or fellowship grants excludable from gross income under Code Sec. 117 and any other tax-free education benefits, as required by Code Sec. 25A(g)(2). Expenses are then reduced for amounts taken into account in determining the education credits under Code Sec. 25A (HOPE and Lifetime Learning credits). Where a student receives distributions from both a Coverdell education savings plan and a qualified tuition program that together exceed these reduced expenses, then expenses must be allocated between the distributions [Code Sec. 529(c)(3)(B)].

.07 Rollovers

Amounts in one 529 plan may be transferred tax-free from one plan for the benefit of a designated beneficiary to another qualified tuition program for the same beneficiary. This rollover will not be considered a distribution [Code Sec. 529(c)(3)(c)]. However, the tax-free rollover treatment only applies to one transfer within any 12-month period with respect to the same beneficiary [Code Sec. 529(c)(3)(c)(iii)]. Amounts in a college savings plan may be rolled over tax-free to an account for another beneficiary who must be: (1) of the same (or higher) generation as the original beneficiary; and (2) a member of the same family [Code Sec. 529(c)(5)(B)]. The tax code provides a lengthy list of family members who qualify, including the original beneficiary's spouse, parents, children, stepchildren, grandchildren, siblings, first cousins, nieces and nephews, aunts and uncles, and all in-laws [Code Sec. 529(e)(2)(A)].

.08 State Tax Benefits

States may offer special tax benefits to investors in 529 plans. These will differ from state to state and could include an exclusion from state income tax of amounts earned by college savings plans or a deduction for contributions made to the plans.

.09 Investment Options for 529 Plans

Code Sec. 529(b)(4) states that a 529 plan will not be treated as a qualified tuition program unless it provides that any contributor or designated beneficiary may not directly or indirectly direct the investment of any contributions to the plan. Prop. Reg. §1.529-2(g) provides that a 529 plan does not violate this requirement if it permits a person who establishes a 529 account to select among different investment strategies designed exclusively by the program only at the time when the initial contribution is made establishing the account.

In Notice 2001-55,[64] the IRS acknowledged that there are a number of situations that might warrant a change in the investment strategy for a 529 account and therefore the IRS provides that a change in the investment strategy selected for a 529 account may be changed in two situations:

- Once per calendar year, and
- Upon a change in the designated beneficiary of the account.

Notice 2001-55 conditioned the applicability of this special rule on the program's compliance with a requirement that the program must (1) allow participants to select only from among broad-based investment strategies designed exclusively by the program, and (2) establish procedures and maintain appropriate records to prevent a change in investment options from occurring more frequently than once per calendar year or upon a change in the designated beneficiary of the account.

IRS Relaxes 529 Investment Restrictions

In an attempt to provide flexibility to 529 plan investors, the IRS provides in Notice 2009-1[65] that 529 plan investors will be able to change the investment strategy in their 529 plans twice a year. In Notice 2009-1 the IRS amended Notice 2001-55 to provide that a 529 plan will not violate the investment restriction under Code Sec. 529(b)(4) if it permits a change in the investment strategy selected for a 529 plan twice a year, as well as upon a change in the designated beneficiary of the account. Participants in 529 plans may rely on Notice 2009-1 pending the issuance of the final regulations.

.10 Estate Planning With 529 Plans

In 2013, taxpayers may contribute up to $14,000 to a 529 account for a beneficiary in a single year with no federal gift tax or generation skipping transfer tax implications [Prop. Reg. § 1.529-5(b)]. For married couples the limit doubles to $28,000 [Code Sec. 529(c)(2)]. If contributions exceed $14,000 in 2013 ($28,000, if a married couple), taxpayers may to treat it as if made ratably over five years beginning in the year that the contribution is made. This means that taxpayers may contribute in 2013 up to $70,000 ($140,000, if a married filing a joint return) to a 529 plan if the 5-year election is made. Note that if this election is made, any additional gifts made to the same beneficiary during the year of the contribution or the following four years in excess of the annual exclusion amount will be subject to gift tax [Code Sec. 529(c)(2)(B)].

> **Example 5-17:** In Year 1, when the annual exclusion under Code Sec. 2503(b) is $14,000, Mom and Dad make a contribution of $78,000 to a 529 plan for the benefit of their child. They elect under Code Sec. 529(c)(2)(B) to account for the gift ratably over a five-year period beginning with the year of contribution. They are treated as making an excludible gift of $14,000 in each of Years 1 through 5 and a taxable gift of $8,000 in Year 6 [Prop. Reg. § 1.529-5(b)(2)(v), Ex.].

A gift tax return (Form 709) must be filed for any contribution in excess of the annual gift-tax exclusion limit, and the election for five-year averaging must be made on the

[64] Notice 2001-55, 2001-2 CB 299.

[65] Notice 2009-1, IRB 2009-2, 250.

contributor's gift tax return. You will see a box to check on Schedule A, Line B of Form 709. Funds invested in a qualified tuition program will be excluded from the donor's and beneficiary's estate unless the donor dies during the special five-year averaging period. If this occurs, only a prorated portion of the gift will be removed from the donor's estate.

.11 Disadvantages to 529 Plans

- Contributions to the program must be made with after-tax dollars. Contributions of property other than money are prohibited [Code Sec. 529(b)(2); Prop. Reg. § 1.529-2(d)]. This means that taxpayers must sell any stocks or bonds before investing their net worth in a 529 plan.
- The qualified tuition program must maintain a separate account for each designated beneficiary who must be identified when contributions are first made to purchase an interest in a college savings plan. A transfer of credits (or other amounts) from one account benefiting one designated beneficiary to another account benefiting a different beneficiary will be considered a taxable distribution unless the beneficiaries are members of the same family as defined in Code Sec. 529(e)(2)(B). No interest in a qualified tuition program can be used as security for a loan.
- If a donor has contributed over $14,000 a year for 5 years (total investment $70,000) to a qualified tuition program and then dies during the five-year averaging period, the portion of the contribution that has not been allocated to the years prior to death is includible in the donor's taxable estate.

.12 Bankruptcy Exclusion

The Bankruptcy Abuse Prevention and Consumer Protection Act of 2004 provides bankruptcy protection, for funds that the debtor paid or contributed to a qualified tuition program before filing for bankruptcy [Bankruptcy Code Sec. 541(b)(6)]. Bankruptcy protection is available for funds the debtor used to:

- Buy tuition credits or certificates on behalf of a designated beneficiary which entitle the beneficiary to a waiver or payment of qualified education expenses; and
- Contribute to an account set up to meet the designated beneficiary's qualified education expenses, before filing for bankruptcy.

The amount of qualified tuition funds that can qualify for the bankruptcy exclusion is subject to two separate limits. First, the bankruptcy exclusion can't exceed the amount needed to provide for the designated beneficiary's qualified education expenses; Second, for funds paid or contributed to the qualified tuition program having the same designated beneficiary not earlier than 720 days, or later then 365 days, before the bankruptcy filing date, only up to $5,000 is protected.

¶5115 COVERDELL EDUCATION SAVINGS ACCOUNTS

A taxpayer may establish a *Coverdell education savings account (Coverdell ESA)* to pay the qualified education expenses of an individual who is a designated beneficiary [Code Sec. 530(b)(1)]. Covered expenses include qualified higher education expenses as well as qualified elementary and secondary education expenses (i.e., kindergarten through 12th grade tuition and certain related expenses) [Code Sec. 530(b)(2)]. Annual cash contributions to Coverdell ESAs, which take the form of trusts or custodial accounts, are set up in any bank, are not deductible and cannot exceed $2,000 per beneficiary, and may not be made after the designated beneficiary reaches age 18 [Code Sec. 530(b)(1)]. The $2,000 contribution limits for Coverdell education savings accounts is available for tax years beginning after December 31, 2012. The provision is now permanent.

You may open a Coverdell ESA with any bank, or other entity that has been approved to serve as a nonbank trustee or custodian of an IRA and the bank or entity is offering the Coverdell ESA. Keep in mind that only cash contributions may be made to a Coverdell ESA [Code Sec. 530(b)(1)(A)(i)].

.01 Military Death Gratuities and SGLI Payments Contributed to Coverdell ESAs

An individual who receives a military death gratuity or payment under the Servicemembers' Group Life Insurance (SGLI) program may now contribute an amount up to the sum of the gratuity and SGLI payments received to a Coverdell education savings account, notwithstanding the other contribution limits that may apply (e.g., the $2,000 annual contribution limit and the income phase-out of the contribution dollar limit) [Code Sec. 530(d)].

Amounts in the Coverdell ESA must be withdrawn within 30 days after the date that the beneficiary attains age 30. An exception is provided if the beneficiary dies before attaining age 30 [Code Sec. 530(b)(1)(E)]. The age limitation does not apply in the case of special needs beneficiaries. A special needs beneficiary includes an "individual who because of a physical, mental, or emotional condition (including learning disability) requires additional time to complete his or her education."

Amounts contributed to Coverdell ESAs accumulate tax-free until withdrawn. Contributions may not be made after the designated beneficiary reaches age 18 [Code Sec. 530(b)(1)(A)(ii)]. There is no limit to the number of Coverdell ESAs that can be established designating a child as the beneficiary, but total contributions for the child during a tax year cannot exceed $2,000 [Code Sec. 530(b)(1)(A)(iii)].

.02 Who Is Eligible

A Coverdell ESA can be established by any individual taxpayer (including the child) provided the contributor's modified adjusted gross income ("MAGI") is between $95,000 and $110,000 ($190,000 and $220,000 for joint returns) [Code Sec. 530(c)(1)]. Individuals with modified AGI above the phase-out range cannot make contributions to a Coverdell ESA. Code Sec. 530(c) provides that the maximum contribution that an individual can make to a Coverdell education savings account is equal to $2,000 less any reduction due to modified AGI (MAGI). The reduction is equal to:

For Single Taxpayers:

$2,000 × (MAGI – $95,000)/$15,000 = Amount of reduction
(only if positive)

For Married Taxpayers Filing Jointly:

$2,000 × (MAGI – $190,000)/$30,000 = Amount of reduction

(only if positive). *Modified AGI (MAGI)* is defined in Code Sec. 530(c)(2) as adjusted gross income of the taxpayer increased by any amount excluded from gross income under Code Sec. 911 (foreign earned income and foreign housing costs), Code Sec. 931 (income exclusion for the residents of Guam, American Samoa, and the Northern Mariana Islands), or Code Sec. 933 (income exclusion for residents of Puerto Rico) [Code Sec. 530(c)(2)].

The committee report provides that "corporations and other entities (including tax-exempt organizations) are permitted to make contributions to education IRAs, regardless of the income of the corporation or entity during the year of the contribution." This language is still effective after December 31, 2012. Therefore, corporations and other entities will continue to be able to make contributions to Coverdell accounts, and no phaseout or income limitations will apply to such contributions.

.03 No Deduction Available

No tax deduction is allowed for contributions made to Coverdell ESAs.

.04 Forms to Use for Reporting Contributions

Use Form 5498-ESA, *Coverdell ESA Contribution Information,* to report contributions to Coverdell ESAs. Use Form 1099-Q, *Payments From Qualified Education Programs (Under Sections 529 and 530),* to report distributions from the account. The IRS has eased reporting requirements for trustees and custodians of Coverdell ESAs to give them more time to implement recordkeeping procedures that will enable them to report basis and earnings information and to identify trustee-to-trustee transfers.

.05 Distributions

Until a distribution is made from a Coverdell ESA, earnings on contributions to the account grow tax-free. Distributions from a Coverdell ESA are tax-free to the extent that the distribution does not exceed the child's qualified education expenses during the year the distribution is made, regardless of whether the student is enrolled in classes on a full-time, half-time, or less than half-time basis [Code Sec. 530(d)(2)(A)]. If a student withdraws an amount from a Coverdell ESA and the amount exceeds his or her qualified education expenses during the year, he or she must include the excess in gross income and also be subject to a 10 percent additional penalty tax [Code Sec. 530(d)(4)(A)]. The penalty tax will be waived if the distribution is made because of the designated beneficiary's death or disability, which is defined as being unable to engage in any substantial gainful activity by reason of any medically determinable physical or mental impairment that can be expected to result in death or be of a long-continued and indefinite duration.

Deadline for Corrective Withdrawals

A 10 percent penalty tax, as well as a 6 percent excise tax on excess contributions, will not be imposed on certain distributions of excess contributions that are made before the first day of the sixth month following the tax year of the contribution. If the beneficiary does not have to file a return, then the distribution must be made by the 15th day of the fourth month of the tax year following the tax year in which the contribution was made. The distribution must be accompanied by the net earnings on the excess contribution [Code Sec. 530(d)(4)(C)(i)].

If the student does not need the money for postsecondary education, the account balance can be rolled over tax-free (and penalty-free) to a Coverdell education savings account benefiting another family member who can use it for their higher education.

.06 What Expenses Are Covered

A taxpayer will be able to use the proceeds from a Coverdell ESA to pay his or her qualified education expenses which include the following:

- *Qualified education expenses.* Qualified education expenses include expenses incurred while the beneficiary is in attendance or enrolled at an elementary or secondary school (i.e., kindergarten through grade 12) beginning in 2013 [Code Sec. 530(b)(4)]. Therefore, beginning in 2013 expenses can be paid tax-free from a Coverdell account for expenses such as: (1) tuition, fees, academic tutoring, special needs services, books, supplies, computer equipment (including related software and services), and other equipment incurred in connection with the enrollment or attendance of the beneficiary at a public, private, or religious school providing elementary or secondary education (kindergarten through grade 12) as determined under state law, or (2) room and board, uniforms, transportation, and supplementary items or services (including extended day programs) required or provided by such a school in connection with such enrollment or attendance of the beneficiary.
- *Special needs children.* Contributions can still be made to a Coverdell account even after the date when a beneficiary reaches age 18 for certain special needs individuals who, due to a physical, mental, or emotional condition (including learning disability), require additional time to complete their education [Code Sec. 530(b)(1)]. The special needs beneficiary exception also applies to: (1) the 30-year-old age limit used to determine when the remaining balances in an Coverdell account must be distributed, and (2) whether rollover contributions can be received and beneficiaries changed [Code Sec. 530(b)(1)].

The amount of a student's *qualified education expenses* must be adjusted for certain scholarships. This means that you reduce the amount of your qualified higher education expenses by the sum of:

- A qualified scholarship that is excludable from gross income under Code Sec. 117;
- The amount of the education assistance allowance available as veteran's benefits; and
- Any other excludable payments for education expenses (but not gifts or inheritances).

.07 Coordination with Other Education-Related Tax Benefits

A taxpayer may take advantage of the Coverdell ESA as well as the HOPE and Lifetime Learning credit and the qualified tuition program in the same year. In addition, the taxpayer will not be charged an excise tax on contributions made by any person to a Coverdell ESA on behalf of a beneficiary during any tax year in which any contributions are made by anyone to a 529 plan [¶ 5110] on behalf of the same beneficiary. If distributions from Coverdell education savings accounts and qualified tuition programs exceed the beneficiary's qualified higher education expenses for the year (after reduction by amounts used in claiming the HOPE or Lifetime Learning credit), the beneficiary is required to allocate the expenses between the distributions to determine the amount includible in income.

.08 What to Do with Assets Remaining in Account

There are two ways of dealing with the assets remaining in a Coverdell ESA after the child finishes his or her postsecondary education. The remaining balance may be withdrawn for the benefit of the child. The beneficiary will be subject to both income tax and the additional 10 percent tax on the portion of the amount withdrawn that represents earnings if the child does not have any qualified education expenses in the same year that the withdrawal is made. Alternatively, if the amount is withdrawn and rolled over to another Coverdell ESA for the benefit of another family member, the amount rolled over will not be taxed.

Any balance left in the account will be deemed distributed within 30 days after a named beneficiary reaches age 30 (or within 30 days of the beneficiary's death, if earlier), with the earnings portion included in the beneficiary's gross income and subject to a 10 percent penalty [Code Sec. 530(d)(1)]. In order to avoid being taxed on account balances, spend down the account for higher education costs or roll over the amount to another account benefiting another under age-30 family member [Code Sec. 530(d)(5)].

A "member of the family," for purposes of the Code Sec. 530 Coverdell education savings account, is defined by reference to Code Sec. 529(e)(2) and Code Sec. 152(a) and includes ancestors, descendants, brothers, sisters, nephews, nieces, cousins, certain in-laws, and the spouses of these relatives. Stepparents, stepsiblings, and stepchildren are also considered members of the family.

.09 Tax on Excess Contributions

Code Sec. 4973(a)(4) imposes a 6-percent excise tax on excess contributions to Coverdell ESAs. The first item treated as an excess contribution is any excess over the maximum annual contribution amount per beneficiary. If the contributor's allowable contribution for the year is reduced based on the modified AGI phaseout, then the amount treated as an excess contribution is the sum of the allowable reduced contributions if less than the excess over the annual contribution limit [Code Sec. 4973(e)(1)(A)]. Excess contributions are contributions to a Coverdell ESA that are greater than $2,000 per year. Rollovers from a Coverdell ESA into a member of the beneficiary family's Coverdell ESA are not considered in the calculation of excess contributions.

.10 Bankruptcy Exclusion

The Bankruptcy Abuse Prevention and Consumer Protection Act of 2004 provides bankruptcy protection, subject to a $5,000 limit for certain contributions for funds that the debtor placed in a Coverdell ESA before filing for bankruptcy. Under the bankruptcy exclusion, funds the debtor placed in a Coverdell ESA won't be included in the debtor's bankruptcy estate if four requirements are met:

- The funds are placed in the Coverdell ESA not later than 365 days before the date of the filing of the bankruptcy petition [Bankruptcy Code Sec. 541(b)(5)].

- The designated beneficiary of the account is the debtor's child, stepchild, grandchild, or step-grand-child for the tax year in which the funds were placed in the account [Bankruptcy Code Sec. 541(b)(5)(A)].
- The funds aren't pledged or promised to an entity in connection with any extension of credit [Bankruptcy Code Sec. 541(b)(5)(B)].
- The funds aren't "excess contributions" i.e., in excess of the annual per-child maximum amount permitted under Code Sec. 530(b)(1).

There is a dollar limit on the amount of certain contributions to Coverdell ESAs that can be excluded from the debtor's bankruptcy estate. For funds placed in all Coverdell ESAs having the same designated beneficiary not earlier than 720 days, or later than 365 days, before the bankruptcy filing date, only so much of the funds as do not exceed $5,000 is protected. This means that funds deposited in a Coverdell ESA between 720 and 365 days before the bankruptcy filing date are excluded from the bankruptcy estate to the extent they exceed $5,000 [Bankruptcy Code Sec. 541(b)(5)(C)].

¶5120 INCOME EXCLUSION FOR RESTITUTION PAYMENTS TO VICTIMS OF NAZI PERSECUTION

.01 Income Exclusion for Victims of Nazi Persecution

Excludable restitution payments made to an *eligible individual* or their heirs or estate are not included in gross income for federal income tax purposes. In addition, these amounts are not taken into account for any provision of the Code that takes into account excludable gross income in computing adjusted gross income (e.g., the taxation of Social Security benefits).

.02 Basis of Property Received

The basis of any property received by eligible individuals or their heirs or estate is the fair market value of such property at the time of receipt.

.03 Eligible Restitution Payment Defined

Eligible restitution payments are defined as any payment or distribution made to eligible individuals or their heirs or estate which: (1) is payable by reason of the individual's status as an eligible individual (including any amount payable by any foreign country, the United States, or any foreign or domestic entity or fund established by any such country or entity, any amount payable as a result of a final resolution of legal action, and any amount payable under a law providing for payments or restitution of property); (2) constitutes the direct or indirect return of, or compensation or reparation for, assets stolen or hidden, or otherwise lost to, the individual before, during, or immediately after World War II by reason of the individual's status as an eligible individual (including any proceeds of insurance under policies issued on eligible individuals by European insurance companies immediately before and during World War II); or (3) interest payable as part of any payment or distribution described in (1) or (2), above.

.04 Eligible Individual Defined

An eligible individual is defined as a person who was persecuted on the basis of race, religion, physical or mental disability, or sexual orientation by Nazi Germany, any other Axis regime, or any other Nazi-controlled or Nazi-allied country.[66]

¶5125 FOSTER CARE PAYMENTS

.01 Foster Care Payments Excluded From Taxation

Code Sec. 131 provides for an exclusion from income of qualified foster care payments if the payments were (1) made pursuant to a foster care program of a state; (2) paid by a state or political subdivision of the state, or a qualified foster care placement agency; and (3) paid to a foster care provider for the care of a qualified foster individual in the foster care provider's home. The exclusion for foster care payments applies to amounts paid for the provision of foster care, rather than amounts paid as reimbursements of qualified foster care expenses [Code Sec. 131(b)(1)(B)(i)].

.02 Foster Individual Defined

There are two categories of "qualified foster individuals:" (1) a person who is living in a foster place in which he or she was placed by a state agency; and (2) recipients receiving "difficulty of care payments" from the state [Code Sec. 131(b)(2)(B)].

Difficulty-of-care payments are payments representing compensation for providing additional care for "qualified foster individuals" in the home of the foster care provider if the payments are required because of the physical, mental or emotional handicap of the individual and the state has determined that there is a need for the additional compensation [Code Sec. 131(c)(1)]. If a payment qualifies as a payment for foster care, it is not considered a difficulty-of-care payment [Code Sec. 131(c)].

The exclusion for difficulty-of-care payments is limited to payments for the care of ten qualified foster individuals who are under 19 years of age and five who are over 18 years of age [Code Sec. 131(c)(2)].

.03 Foster Care Payments Defined

"Qualified foster care payments" include payments made (1) by either state or local governmental agencies, (2) by *any* "qualified foster care placement agency" that is licensed or certified by a state or local government, or (3) by an entity designated by a state or local government to make payments to foster care providers [Code Sec. 131(b)(1), (3)].

.04 Foster Care Must be Provided in Taxpayer's Residence

The Code Sec. 131 exclusion applies to providers who care within their homes for individuals who have been placed in the foster home by an agency of the state or a political subdivision. The exclusion is only applicable to care within the provider's

---

[66] Act Sec. 803(b) of the Economic Growth and Tax Relief Reconciliation Act of 2001 (P.L. 107-16).

home; care in any other facility does not qualify. In *P. Dobra*,[67] the court concluded that to qualify for the exclusion under Code Sec. 131, a foster care provider's home must be a house or other residential structure where the foster care provider actually resides. In *Dobra*, the taxpayers owned four houses where they cared for developmentally disabled people, but only one house was their personal family residence. The taxpayers unsuccessfully claimed they could exclude payments for individuals cared for in all four homes. The court disagreed and held that under Code Sec. 131 a person's "home" is where he resides.

In *J.E. Stromme*,[68] the Tax Court concluded that the taxpayer could not exclude the foster care payments received to provide foster care under Code Sec. 131 because they did not live in the house in which they provided the lodging for the developmentally disabled adults. The foster care providers merely owned the home in which the foster care was provided and the court found this to be insufficient because the foster care provider does not also reside in the home where the foster care was provided.

¶5130 RESTITUTION PAYMENTS TO HUMAN TRAFFICKING VICTIMS

.01 Nature of Tax Exclusion

Mandatory restitution payments received by individuals under the Trafficking Victims Protection Act of 2000 (TVPA) are excluded from gross income for federal income tax purposes. The TVPA requires a defendant convicted of a human trafficking offense to make payments to the victim to compensate for costs for medical services, physical and occupational therapy or rehabilitation, transportation, temporary housing, child care expenses, lost income, attorneys' fees and other costs, and other losses the victim suffers as a proximate result of the offense.[69]

.02 Purpose of Exclusion

Congress enacted the TVPA "to combat trafficking of persons, a contemporary manifestation of slavery whose victims are predominantly women and children, to ensure just and effective punishment of traffickers, and to protect their victims." Congress found that "[v]ictims are often forced through physical violence to engage in sex acts or perform slavery-like labor" and that "[s]uch force includes rape and other forms of sexual abuse, torture, starvation, imprisonment, threats, psychological abuse, and coercion." [Section 102(b)(6) of the Trafficking Victims Protection Act of 2000].

.03 Victim's Losses Defined

A victim's losses includes costs for medical services relating to physical, psychiatric, or psychological care; costs for physical and occupational therapy or rehabilitation; necessary transportation, temporary housing, and child care expenses; lost income; attorneys' fees and other costs; and other losses the victim suffers as a proximate result of the

---

[67] *P. Dobra*, 111 TC 339, Dec. 53,008 (1998).

[68] *J.E. Stromme*, 138 TC No. 9, Dec. 58,976 (2012).

[69] Notice 2012-12, IRB 2012-6.

offense.[70] A victim's losses also include the greater of the gross income or value to the defendant of the victim's services or labor or the value of the victim's labor as guaranteed under the minimum wage and overtime guarantees of the Fair Labor Standards Act.

[70] 18 USC § § 1593(b)(3) and 2259(b)(3).

Gain or Loss—Basis—Recognition

GAIN OR LOSS IN GENERAL

Factors in figuring gain or loss . . . ¶ 6001

Recognition of gain or loss . . . . ¶ 6005

COST BASIS

Property acquired by purchase . . . ¶ 6010

Taxable exchanges . . . . ¶ 6015

Property received as payment for services . . . . ¶ 6020

Property acquired before March 1, 1913 . . . . ¶ 6025

OTHER TAX BASIS

Property acquired by gift . . . . ¶ 6030

Property transfers between spouses . . . . ¶ 6035

Property acquired from a decedent . . . . ¶ 6040

TAX-FREE EXCHANGES

Nontaxable exchanges in general . . . . ¶ 6045

Like-kind exchanges . . . . ¶ 6050

"Boot" and depreciation recapture in like-kind exchange . . . . ¶ 6055

Exchange of mortgaged property in like-kind exchange . . . . ¶ 6060

Exchange of insurance policies . . . ¶ 6065

Securities for securities of same corporation . . . . ¶ 6070

Transfer of property to corporation . . . . ¶ 6075

IDENTIFICATION OF BASIS

Allocating basis . . . . ¶ 6080

Shares of stock purchased at different prices . . . . ¶ 6085

Mutual fund shares . . . . ¶ 6090

SPECIAL RULES

Property converted to business use . . . . ¶ 6095

Inventory . . . . ¶ 6100

Sale or exchange of annuity contracts . . . . ¶ 6105

Patents and copyrights . . . . ¶ 6110

Partnership interest . . . . ¶ 6115

GAIN OR LOSS IN GENERAL

Gain or loss is the difference between what a taxpayer receives from a sale or exchange and the adjusted basis of the property that he or she relinquished. In general, the starting point for calculating basis is the property's purchase price. In some acquisitions, though, it may be the property's fair market value or the basis of the person from whom the property was acquired. That figure is then adjusted if subsequent improvements have been made or depreciation deductions claimed. The difference between the final adjusted basis and what is received for the property determines gain or loss. The next step is to determine whether the gain is taxable or the loss is deductible. Our tax system is premised on the concept of "realization." Without realization there is no gain or loss. Therefore, individuals are not taxed until they actually sell property and realize gain. This chapter discusses the factors that determine a taxpayer's basis for various types of property and the conditions under which gain or loss does—or does not—have immediate tax consequences. Chapter 7 explains the special rules that apply to involuntary conversions and the sale of a personal residence.

¶6001 FACTORS IN FIGURING GAIN OR LOSS

When an asset is sold or exchanged, gain or loss is based upon the difference between the "amount realized" on the sale or exchange and the "adjusted basis" of the property. If the "amount realized" exceeds the "adjusted basis," the difference is gain; if the opposite is true, a loss is realized [Code Sec. 1001].

.01 Basis

A taxpayer's basis in any asset will depend upon how that asset was acquired. Code Sec. 1012 provides that the original basis of any property is its cost. A different rule applies when property is acquired from a decedent as discussed in ¶6040 or is acquired by gift as discussed in ¶6030.

.02 Adjusted Basis

Before computing gain or loss when property is sold, or otherwise disposed of, the seller must make adjustments to his or her basis in the property. The resulting figure is his or her adjusted basis. To figure adjusted basis, the original cost or other basis is increased by improvements and/or decreased by expenditures or tax write-offs attributable to the property described in detail as follows:

1. *Add expenditures or items chargeable to the capital account.* These include improvements, purchase commissions, sales tax, freight charges to obtain the property, installation charges, legal costs for defending or perfecting title (including title insurance), surveying expenses, and recording fees. On the other hand, expenses that are written off currently are not added to basis.
2. *Subtract returns of capital.* These include depreciation, the elected Code Sec. 179 expense deduction which is claimed in lieu of a depreciation deduction [Ch. 11], depletion, obsolescence, recognized losses on involuntary conversions, deductible casualty and theft losses, the deduction for clean-fuel vehicles and clean-air vehicle refueling property, easements, insurance reimbursements [Code Sec. 1016; Reg. §§1.1016-1–10]. Important: You are never permitted to reduce the basis below zero.[1]

Example 6-1: Ms. King bought rental real estate for $400,000. She paid title and legal fees of $8,000. King has claimed $100,000 of depreciation deductions since she owned the property. King installed new walls in order to subdivide an

[1] Rev. Rul. 75-451, 1975-2 CB 330.

office suite in the building at a cost of $12,000. The property's adjusted basis is $320,000 ($400,000 + $8,000 – $100,000 + $12,000).

.03 Amount Realized

In most transactions, this is simply the cash price received or the sum of the cash plus the face amount of a note taken back as seller financing. If other property is taken as payment, the amount realized is the fair market value of the property received. Where cash changes hands in addition to other property, the amount realized is the fair market value of the property received, increased by any money received and decreased by any money given up in the exchange.[2]

If the amount realized on the sale exceeds adjusted basis, a gain results; if it is less, a loss results [Reg. § 1.1001-1(a)].

> **Example 6-2:** Lincoln had a tractor with an adjusted basis of $2,000 and a fair market value of $8,000. Clyde had a car with a fair market value of $10,000. They exchanged vehicles, and Lincoln gave Clyde $2,000 in cash. Lincoln's amount realized on the exchange is $8,000 (the $10,000 fair market value received less the $2,000 cash given up). His gain is $6,000 (the $8,000 amount realized less his adjusted basis of $2,000).

The buyer may agree to pay the seller's personal obligations or assume or satisfy any outstanding encumbrances against the property. This is treated like an exchange of cash. Thus, the amount realized is decreased by the amount of any liabilities assumed on the property received and increased by the amount of any liabilities on the property given up [Reg. § 1.1001-2].[3]

> **Example 6-3:** Same facts as Example 6-2 except that Clyde's car is subject to an outstanding auto loan of $1,000, and Lincoln assumes the loan and pays only $1,000 in cash. Lincoln's amount realized is again $8,000—$10,000 property received, less both the $1,000 cash given up and the $1,000 debt assumed. His gain is again $6,000, computed as in Example 6-2.

Real estate taxes owed on the date of sale and assumed or satisfied by the buyer are included in the amount realized [Reg. § 1.1001-1(b)]. The cost of transferring property, such as selling expenses, reduces the amount realized and reduces your gain.

An employer paying for services with property realizes a gain to the extent that the fair market value of the property exceeds its adjusted basis on the date of the transfer. The value of the services the employer receives (amount realized) is considered equal to the fair market value of the property transferred.

.04 Capital Gains and Losses

If the property is a *capital asset* in your hands, the gain or loss is a capital gain or loss. Capital gains and losses of individuals are discussed in greater detail in Ch. 8. The

---

[2] Rev. Rul. 57-535, 1957-2 CB 513.

[3] *B.B. Crane*, SCt, 47-1 USTC ¶ 9217, 331 US 1, 67 SCt 1047.

capital asset requirement for capital gains treatment is examined in Ch. 8. Depending upon the length of time the property has been held by the investor prior to the taxable event, which is called the holding period (as discussed further in Ch. 8), the capital gain or loss may be characterized as either short-term or long-term. The holding period for short-term capital gains and losses is one year or less. The holding period for long-term capital gains and losses is more than one year. Special restrictions apply to capital losses. No more than $3,000 of a capital loss in excess of capital gain may be written off against ordinary income in a single year by noncorporate taxpayers.

Table 1 illustrates the capital gains tax rates that apply in 2013.

Table 1. Capital Gains Rate for Individuals—2013

Beginning in 2013, the capital gains rates for individuals are as follows:

- A capital gains rate of 0 percent applies to the adjusted net capital gains of *individuals* if the gain would otherwise be subject to the 10- or 15-percent ordinary income tax rate [Code Secs. 1(h)(1)(B), 55(b)(3)(B)].
- A capital gains rate of 15 percent applies to adjusted net capital gains of *individuals* if the gain would otherwise be subject to the 25-, 28-, 33-, or 35-percent ordinary income tax rate [Code Secs. 1(h)(1)(C), 55(b)(3)(C)].
- A capital gains rate of 20 percent applies to adjusted net capital gains of *individuals* if the gain would otherwise be subject to the 39.6-percent ordinary income tax rate beginning on January 1, 2013 [Code Sec. 1(h)(1)(D)]. Individuals are subject to the 39.6-percent ordinary income tax rate in 2013 to the extent their taxable income exceeds the applicable threshold amount of $450,000 for married individuals filing joint returns and surviving spouses, $425,000 for heads of households, $400,000 for single individuals, and $225,000 for married individuals filing separate returns.

These rates apply for sales or exchanges of capital assets that are held for more than 12 months, and apply for both regular income tax and alternative minimum tax (AMT) purposes. For discussion of capital gains rates for estates and trusts, see ¶ 25,045.

▶ **NEW IN 2013—3.8 Percent Net Investment Income Tax:** In 2013, higher income taxpayers must also start paying a 3.8-percent additional tax on net investment income (NII) to the extent certain threshold amounts of income are exceeded ($200,000 for single filers, $250,000 for joint returns and surviving spouses, $125,000 for married taxpayers filing separately) [Code Sec. 1411]. Therefore, taxpayers within the NII surtax range must pay the additional 3.8 percent on capital gain, whether long-term or short-term. The effective top rate for net capital gains for many higher-income taxpayers thus becomes 23.8 percent for long-term gain, and 43.4 percent for short-term capital gains starting in 2013. For further discussion, see ¶ 15,050.

¶6005 RECOGNITION OF GAIN OR LOSS

.01 What Recognition of a Gain or Loss Is

Recognition means that the gain or loss realized is included in gross income. If a realized gain is fully recognized, the entire gain is taxable. A recognized loss is deductible, but capital losses are subject to annual deduction caps [Ch. 8]. Gain or loss from a sale or exchange is recognized unless a provision of the tax law exempts the transaction. These nonrecognition transactions are covered in ¶ 6030 et seq. and Chapter 7.

.02 Recognized Gain—Nondeductible Loss

In some situations, a gain is taxable, but a loss is not deductible. This rule applies to sales of personal property, such as the sale of a family car or residence; *wash sales* (where identical securities are bought within 30 days of the sale) [Ch. 13]; and sales between related taxpayers [Ch. 13].

COST BASIS

¶6010 PROPERTY ACQUIRED BY PURCHASE

A taxpayer's original basis in property is generally the purchase price or cost. The property's cost is the amount paid for it, either in cash or other property, plus commissions and other expenses connected with the purchase [Code Sec. 1012; Reg. § 1.1012-1(a)]. A taxpayer's basis in mortgaged property is the amount paid plus the amount of the indebtedness. The mortgage is part of the buyer's basis and the amount the seller realizes whether or not the buyer assumes it, and regardless of whether the mortgage is recourse or nonrecourse debt. Thus, basis is not adjusted when a mortgage is paid off.

Example 6-4: Smith bought a house worth $260,000. She took the house subject to a $120,000 mortgage and paid $140,000 in cash. Smith's basis is $260,000.

Example 6-5: Same facts as Example 6-4, except that Smith has paid $20,000 of the mortgage. She then sells the house subject to the remaining mortgage and receives $200,000 in cash. The amount Smith realizes is $300,000 ($200,000 cash plus $100,000 mortgage). So she realizes a gain of $40,000 ($300,000 amount realized less $260,000 basis).

If a taxpayer purchases an option to buy property and exercise the option, his or her basis in the property is the sum of the option's exercise price and the cost (or other basis) of the option.

Capitalized expenditures in buying, building, or developing an asset are included in the asset's cost basis. (See the uniform capitalization rules at Ch. 17.) Real estate taxes are figured as part of the property's cost if you assume the seller's obligation to pay them [Code Sec. 1012; Reg. § 1.1012-1]. When the "price" paid for property includes payments made for reasons other than acquisition (such as giving a gift to a family member, making a capital contribution to a related business, or shifting deductions), the amount in excess of fair market value is not part of your cost.[4]

[4] *D. McDonald*, 28 BTA 64, Dec. 8053; *Mountain Wholesale Co.*, 17 TC 870, Dec. 18,645.

NOTE: If property is bought under a deferred payment contract with interest deferred, not stated or at a low rate, a part of the price may be treated as interest. This "imputed" interest is not included in the property's basis [Ch. 2].

¶6015 TAXABLE EXCHANGES

There are two methods for finding the basis of property received in exchange for other property:

- The property's fair market value when received;[5] or
- The fair market value of the property given up, increased by payments made or decreased by payments received.[6]

Example 6-6: Ames traded his $7,200 car for a boat with a fair market value of $7,200. If the car's adjusted basis was $7,000, Ames has realized a $200 taxable gain on the exchange. His basis in the boat is $7,200. If Ames later sold the boat for $7,500, he would have a $300 gain.

▶ **OBSERVATION:** The result will generally be the same under both methods. However, the result may be different if there is a nontaxable aspect to the transaction. In a part gift, part exchange, the property plus cash received is not equal to the value of the property given up.

.01 Fair Market Value

Fair market value is the price a willing buyer and a willing seller would probably reach after bargaining, when neither is acting under compulsion and both have reasonable knowledge of relevant facts.[7] Property may have a fair market value even though no buyers presently exist.[8] However, there must be some assurance that the value is what a market would establish;[9] the value must be based on something more concrete than speculative assumptions.[10] And fair market value is not the price that would result from a forced sale.[11]

Actual sales of similar property on the open market provide reliable evidence of value. Stock exchange quotations are a prime example of this. Adjustments in value, though, may be required for large blocks of stock. Thus, the trading price for small transactions would not be conclusive in valuing very large interests.[12] The value of a closely held corporation depends on such factors as the corporation's financial condition, earnings capacity and the stock prices of companies that are traded on an

[5] *Phila. Pk. Amusement Co.*, CtCls, 54-2 USTC ¶9697, 126 FSupp 184, 130 CtCls 166; *H.L. Williams*, 37 TC 1099, Dec. 25,402, *acq.* 1963-2 CB 5; Rev. Rul. 57-535, 1957-2 CB 513; Rev. Rul. 55-27, 1955-1 CB 350.

[6] *F.A. Countway*, CA-1, 42-1 USTC ¶9401, 127 F2d 69.

[7] *G.N. Williams Est.*, CA-9, 58-1 USTC ¶9252, 256 F2d 217.

[8] *L. Alvary*, CA-2, 62-1 USTC ¶9493, 302 F2d 790.

[9] *A.E. Walbridge*, CA-2, 4 USTC ¶1284, 70 F2d 683, *cert. denied*, 293 US 594.

[10] *H. Roe*, 24 TCM 528, Dec. 27,343(M), TC Memo. 1965-100.

[11] *Acme Mills, Inc.*, 6 BTA 1065, Dec. 2399, *acq.* 1927-2 CB 1; *J.L. Harris*, 14 BTA 1259, Dec. 4761.

[12] *General Securities Co.*, 38 BTA 330, Dec. 10,400, *nonacq.* 1938-2 CB 44.

exchange and are engaged in the same line of business.[13] Expert appraisers are often used to arrive at an asset's value.

.02 Property Acquired in Trade-in

A dealer who sells new property and accepts used property in part payment has the option to include the used property in inventory. If placed into inventory, the basis of the traded-in property is equal to its bona fide selling price less direct selling costs [Reg. § 1.471-2(c)]. If the trade-in is not put into inventory, its basis is equal to the fair market value given to it in the exchange for the new property.[14]

Automobile dealers may value used cars received as trade-ins at valuations listed in an official used car guide as the average wholesale prices for comparable cars.[15]

¶6020 PROPERTY RECEIVED AS PAYMENT FOR SERVICES

An individual's basis in property obtained in exchange for rendering services is the property's fair market value (less any amounts which were paid for such property) at the time of the exchange. This amount is also included in gross income, the same as if the payment had been in cash [Reg. § 1.61-2(d)(1)]. Basis in restricted property received as payment for services is the sum of any amount paid for the property plus any amount included in gross income when the property is no longer transferable or subject to a substantial risk of forfeiture [Ch. 2] [Reg. § 1.83-4(b)].

If property is transferred in connection with the performance of services, the taxpayer will be required to include in income the fair market value of such property (less any amounts which were paid for such property) in the first tax year in which such property becomes transferable or is not subject to a substantial risk of forfeiture, whichever comes first [Code Sec. 83]. See further discussion in ¶ 2045.

¶6025 PROPERTY ACQUIRED BEFORE MARCH 1, 1913

Appreciation in value before March 1, 1913, is not taxed. Thus, the basis for determining gain can be different from the basis for figuring loss. The basis for gain is the greater of the: (1) property's fair market value on March 1, 1913 (with appropriate adjustments attributable to subsequent years) or (2) the basis determined under the general rules. The fair market value on March 1, 1913 is not used to determine the basis if doing so would result in a loss [Code Sec. 1053; Reg. § 1.1053-1].

---

[13] Rev. Rul. 59-60, 1959-1 CB 237, amplified by Rev. Rul. 77-287, 1977-2 CB 319; Rev. Rul. 80-213, 1980-2 CB 101; Rev. Rul. 83-120, 1983-2 CB 170.

[14] *A&A Tool & Supply Co.*, CA-10, 50-1 USTC ¶ 9309, 182 F2d 300.

[15] Rev. Rul. 67-107, 1967-1 CB 115.

Example 6-7: Property bought for $2,000 in 1912 was valued at $1,200 on March 1, 1913. The basis for gain or loss is $2,000. If the value on March 1, 1913, was $2,500, the basis for gain would be $2,500, but the basis for calculating loss would be $2,000.

OTHER TAX BASIS

¶6030 PROPERTY ACQUIRED BY GIFT

The basis of property received as a gift depends on whether the taxpayer has a gain or loss when the property is sold. The taxpayer has gain if the amount realized exceeds the donor's basis. The taxpayer has a loss if the amount realized is less than both the donor's basis and the property's fair market value at the time of the gift. There are times when the taxpayer will have neither a taxable gain nor a deductible loss when the property is sold [(c) below]. These rules also apply to property acquired by a transfer to a trust. For gifts between spouses, see ¶ 6035.

.01 Figuring Basis for Gain

For purposes of determining gain, the basis to be used is that of the last preceding owner who did not acquire the property by gift. This rule also applies for determining the depreciable or depletable basis of property acquired by gift. In the usual situation, the donee's basis for computing gain will be the same as the basis of the donor [Code Sec. 1015(a); Reg. § 1.1015-1(a)(1)]. This is called *carry-over basis.* In the case of successive gifts, the donee's basis is the same as the basis of the last preceding owner by whom the property was not acquired by gift. However, the donee's basis may be increased by the amount of gift tax paid by the donor [see Adjustment for Gift Tax below].

▶ **IMPORTANT:** In general, the donor's basis is also used for computing depreciation, amortization and depletion, regardless of the property's fair market value at the time of the gift [Reg. § § 1.167(g)-1, 1.612-1].

Example 6-8: Mason bought bonds for $1,000. He gave them to Doran when their fair market value was $800. No gift tax was payable. If Doran sells the bonds for $1,200, his basis for calculating gain is $1,000. So he has a $200 gain.

.02 Figuring Basis for Loss

The donee's basis is the lesser of (1) the donor's basis (or the basis of the last previous person by whom the property was not acquired by gift) or (2) the property's fair market value at the time the gift is made [Code Sec. 1015(a); Reg. § 1.1015-1(a)(1)]. However, the basis may be increased for gift tax paid by the donor [see .04 below].

Example 6-9: Same facts as in Example 6-8, except that Doran sells the bonds for $700. His basis is the property's fair market value at the time of the gift: $800. That results in a $100 loss.

▶ **OBSERVATION:** If the loss in value occurred in the donor's hands, the donee will not be permitted to take advantage of that loss for loss purposes. Yet it does decrease any gain the donee would otherwise realize on the property's disposition.

.03 Neither Gain Nor Loss

Suppose the property's value at the time of the gift is less than the donor's basis, and the donee sells the property for an amount between those two amounts. Using the basis for finding a gain results in a loss, and using the basis for loss results in a gain. In that case, the donee has neither a gain nor a loss [Reg. § 1.1015-1(a)].

Example 6-10: Assume the same facts as in Example 6-8, except that Doran sells the bonds for $900. His basis for gain is $1,000, which results in a loss. His basis for loss is $800, which results in a gain. Thus, Doran has neither gain nor loss.

▶ **OBSERVATION:** If the figures in Example 6-8 had been reversed ($800 donor's basis and $1,000 value at the time of the gift), Doran would have had a $100 gain. Reason: His basis would have been $800.

.04 Adjustment for Gift Tax

In most cases, the basis for gift property is increased for gift taxes paid by the donor. The amount of the increase depends on when the gift was made.

Gifts After 1976

The donee's basis is increased by the portion of the gift tax attributable to the net appreciation in the value of the gift. Net appreciation is the excess of the fair market value over the donor's adjusted basis immediately before the gift [Code Sec. 1015(d)(6)]. The formula for computing the increase is as follows:

$$\text{Gift tax paid} \times \frac{\text{Fair market value} - \text{Adjusted basis}}{\text{Fair market value}}$$

Gifts After September 1, 1958, and before 1977

The donee's basis is increased by the amount of gift tax paid, but not above the fair market value of the property at the time of the gift [Code Sec. 1015(d)(1)(A); Reg. § 1.1015-5(a)].

Gifts Before September 2, 1958

The donee's basis is increased by the amount of gift tax paid. However, the increase cannot be greater than the difference between the property's fair market value and the donor's basis at the time the gift was made [Code Sec. 1015(d)(1)(B); Reg. § 1.1015-5(a)].

¶6035 PROPERTY TRANSFERS BETWEEN SPOUSES

No gain or loss is recognized on a property transfer between spouses or between former spouses incident to their divorce under any circumstances. The transfer is treated as a gift and the basis of the property in the hands of the donor carries over to the donee spouse. [For detailed discussion of property transfers incident to divorce, see Ch. 2.]

¶6040 PROPERTY ACQUIRED FROM A DECEDENT

.01 Step-Up Basis Rules

Generally, if a taxpayer inherits property, his or her basis in the property is its fair market value on the date of the decedent's death. This is called a step-up in basis. As a result of this step-up in basis the taxpayer will not owe income tax if he or she sells property that appreciated in value when owned by the decedent. That appreciation permanently escapes tax under current law. Similarly, if the property declined in value in the decedent's hands, the basis is stepped-down to the fair market value at the date of the decedent's death, thus eliminating any tax benefit from the loss.

.02 Exceptions to Basis Step-up Rule

There are two exceptions to the step-up in basis rule as follows: (1) If the executor elects the alternate valuation date for estate tax purposes, the taxpayer's basis is the property's value as of that date [see ¶29,110]; or (2) If the executor elects for estate tax purposes the special use valuation method of valuing farm or closely held business real property [see ¶29,110], the taxpayer's basis is the property's special use value [Code Sec. 1014(a); Reg. §1.1014-1(a)].

If the taxpayer inherits mortgaged property and doesn't assume the mortgage, there is no reduction in the property's fair market value for the debt.[16] But if the taxpayer sells the property, the amount of the outstanding mortgage assumed by the purchaser is included in calculating your amount realized.

In general, a property's fair market value is the valuation placed on it for the federal estate tax. Or if the estate is not subject to estate tax, the value for the state inheritance tax [Reg. §1.1014-3(a)]. However, a higher value may be used, if it can be proven.[17]

> ▶ **OBSERVATION:** If you inherit property through an estate that did not need to file an estate or inheritance tax return, take steps to substantiate the property's date-of-death value right away. For example, if the property is publicly traded stock, record the market quotation for the day; if it's real estate, get a professional appraisal. That will make it easier to calculate your taxable gain when you sell the property years in the future—when it would otherwise be difficult to reconstruct what the value had been at the decedent's death.

The basis of property received in settlement of a cash legacy is its fair market value on the date of receipt instead of the date of decedent's death. Such property is not acquired from the decedent. It is received in a transaction treated as a sale or other disposition by the executor [Reg. §1.1014-4(a)(3)].

---

[16] *Barkley Co. of Ariz.*, 55 TCM 1347, Dec. 44,924(M), TC Memo. 1988-324; *B.B. Crane*, SCt, 47-1 USTC ¶9217, 331 US 1, 67 SCt 1047; *J.F. Tufts*, SCt, 83-1 USTC ¶9328, 461 US 300, 103 SCt 1826.

[17] *A. Evans*, 29 BTA 710, Dec. 8352, *acq.* 1934-1 CB 6.

.03 Carryover Basis Rule in 2010

In conjunction with the repeal of the estate tax with respect to the estates of decedents dying in 2010 [Code Sec. 2210], the EGTRRA replaced the long-standing "stepped-up" basis at death rules with a carryover basis regime [Code Secs. 1014(f), 1022(a)]. Thus, effective for property acquired from a decedent dying in 2010, the recipient of the property received a basis equal to the lesser of the adjusted basis of the property in the hands of the decedent, or the fair market value of the property on the date of the decedent's death. For further discussion of the carryover basis rules in 2010, see ¶29,005.

.04 Joint Ownership

When property is owned jointly, the surviving owner automatically gets ownership of the decedent's interest in it. In general, the surviving spouse's basis in the part of the property that has been included in the decedent's estate is its fair market value at the date of the death (or alternate valuation date). The surviving spouse's basis in the part of the property that the spouse owned all along is unaffected by the decedent's death.

Estate Tax Rule

For joint tenancies, other than between spouses, the full value of the property is included in the decedent's estate, except to the extent that the survivor can show that he or she paid part of the property's cost [Code Sec. 2040(a)]. If the decedent paid the entire cost, the entire value is included in the decedent's estate, and the survivor's entire basis in the property is based on the date of death value.

Example 6-11: Mr. Frank and Mr. George bought real estate as joint tenants with right of survivorship for $10,000. Each paid one-half of the cost. When Frank died, the property was worth $15,000. George's basis in the property after Frank's death is $12,500 (his $5,000 cost basis for one-half of the property plus the $7,500 value of the portion included in Frank's estate).

Example 6-12: Same facts as Example 6-11, except Mr. Frank paid the entire cost. Thus, the property's full value is included in his estate. Mr. George's basis is $15,000.

Property owned jointly by a married couple (with no other joint owners) is treated differently. One-half of the property is included in the decedent-spouse's estate—without any inquiry into who paid for it [Code Sec. 2040(b)].

Example 6-13: Same facts as Example 6-11, except Mr. Frank bought the property with himself and his wife as the only joint owners. Upon Frank's death, his widow's basis would be $12,500—the same as in Example 6-12.

TAX-FREE EXCHANGES

¶6045 NONTAXABLE EXCHANGES IN GENERAL

Taxpayers can defer paying tax on gain or getting a tax write-off for loss with a nontaxable exchange. The most common type of nontaxable exchange is an exchange of like-kind business or investment properties [¶ 6050]. In addition, taxpayers can defer tax when they exchange life insurance policies [¶ 6065], securities for securities of the same corporation [¶ 6070], and transfer property to a controlled corporation [¶ 6075]. For tax purposes, the exchange is simply a change of form. The recognition of gain is deferred until they sell the property received in the exchange.

In an even tax-free exchange of properties, the taxpayer's basis in the new property is the same as his or her basis had been in the property given up for it, not the new property's fair market value. When cash or dissimilar property (referred to as "boot") changes hands as part of the exchange, the taxpayer may have to recognize a gain or loss. In that case, an adjustment must be made to the property's basis [¶ 6080] [Code Sec. 1031].

> ▶ **OBSERVATION:** To qualify for nonrecognition treatment as an exchange, there must be a direct transfer of properties. (The transfers do not have to be simultaneous; deferred transfers are allowed if identification requirements are met and the transfer is completed within certain time limits [¶ 6050].) Receiving cash in exchange for the old property and then using the funds to buy new property does not qualify. However, in two instances—involuntary conversions and sales of a residence—you can defer tax on gain by purchasing new property [Ch. 7].

¶6050 LIKE-KIND EXCHANGES

A like-kind exchange is a valuable tax deferral technique that taxpayers should consider when they exchange property held for investment or business use for similar property. When they engage in a like-kind exchange they have the opportunity to defer the recognition of (not elimination of) gain when they exchange unwanted property for other similar or like-kind property [Code Sec. 1031(a)(1)]. Generally, gain or loss realized from the sale or exchange of property is recognized under Code Sec. 1001(c). Code Sec. 1031 provides, however, that no gain or loss is recognized on the exchange of property held for productive use in a trade or business or for investment if the property is exchanged solely for property of a like kind that is to be held either for productive use in a trade or business or for investment [Reg. § 1.1031(a)(1)]. When money or unqualified property is received in an otherwise qualifying like-kind exchange, a taxpayer's realized gain is recognized to the extent of the sum of such money and the fair market value of such unqualified property [Code Sec. 1031(b); Reg. § 1.1031(a)-1(a)(2)].

The rationale for nonrecognition of gain or loss on the exchange of like-kind property is that the taxpayer's economic situation after the exchange is fundamentally the same as it was before the transaction occurred.[18] As a House report explained: "[I]f the taxpayer's money is still tied up in the same kind of property as that in which it was originally invested, he is not allowed to compute and deduct his theoretical loss on the exchange, nor is he charged with a tax upon his theoretical profit."[19]

Example 6-14: A taxpayer purchases for investment an antique painting for $50,000. It turns out to be worth $750,000. He exchanges it for another antique painting worth $750,000 in a like-kind exchange and has no taxable gain. If he had sold the painting a taxable gain of $700,000 would have resulted.

The gain that is not recognized at the time of the exchange is not permanently exempted from tax. The basis rules provide that the gain or loss will be accounted for on subsequent disposition of the new property by substituting the basis of the old property into the new property. In addition, the holding period of the property exchanged is added on to the holding period of the property received. [Code Sec. 1223(1)].

.01 How to Qualify for Like-Kind Exchange

Code Sec. 1031(a)(1) provides: "No gain or loss shall be recognized on the exchange of property held for productive use in a trade or business or for investment if such property is exchanged solely for property of like kind which is to be held either for productive use in a trade or business or for investment." If, however, money or unqualified property is received in an otherwise qualifying like-kind exchange, a taxpayer's realized gain is recognized to the extent of the sum of such money and the fair market value of such unqualified property (boot) [Code Sec. 1031(b); Reg. § 1.1031(a)-1(a)(2)].

In order to qualify for tax deferral under the like-kind exchange provisions of Code Sec. 1031 the following requirements must exist:

- There must be an exchange of property [Code Sec. 1031(a)(1)];
- The properties exchanged must be property held for productive use in a trade or business or held for investment [Reg. § 1.1031(a)-1(a)(1)];
- The properties exchanged must be of a "like-kind" in nature or character [Reg. § 1.1031(a)-1(b)];
- The replacement property must be identified and the exchange completed within the statutory period [Code Sec. 1031(a)(3)]; and
- The properties exchanged must be eligible for like-kind exchange treatment. Certain types of property are specifically excluded from the definition of "property" for purposes of Code Sec. 1031.

When Is Like-Kind Exchange Deferral Unavailable?

The like-kind exchange provisions are unavailable to defer the recognition of gain in the following situations:

---

[18] *See Jordan Marsh Co.*, CA-2, 59-2 USTC ¶ 9641, 269 F2d 453; *C.E. Koch*, 71 TC 54, Dec. 35,480 (1978), acq. 1979-1 CB 1.

[19] H.R. Rep. No. 73-704 (1934), 1939-1 CB (Part 2) 554, 564.

- Exchanges of property held for personal use including a personal residence;
- Stock-in-trade or other property held primarily for sale to others such as inventory;
- Stocks, bonds, notes, evidences of indebtedness;
- Certificates of trust or beneficial interests;
- Partnership interests regardless of whether the interests exchanged are general or limited partnership interests or are interests in the same partnership or in different partnerships [Code Sec. 1031(a)(2)];
- Goodwill and going concern value of one business is never like-kind to that of another business [Reg. § 1.1031(a)-2(c)(2)];
- Choses in action [Code Sec. 1031(a)(2)(F)].

The U.S. Supreme Court has defined *choses in action* as the "infinite variety of contracts, covenants, and promises, which confer on one party a right to recover . . . a sum of money from another."[20] The IRS has concluded that trade names are not choses in action.[21] In addition, patents and copyrights are not treated as choses in action. Thus, these types of intangible personal property may qualify for like-kind exchange treatment [Reg. § 1.1031(a)-2(c)(1)]. Further, not all contracts are choses in action.[22] For example, certain player contracts may be treated as property used in a trade or business and, thus, would be eligible for like-kind treatment.

Example 6-15: Wally Watson owned a restaurant called Wally's Wonderful Waffles. He transferred it (including his rights to the name "Wally's Wonderful Waffles") to Sam Sunshine for his restaurant called Sam's Sunnyside Ups (and the rights to the name "Sam's Sunnyside Ups"). The trade names are not choses in action. This is because trade names, simply by being held, do not confer upon the holder the right to recover any money or property in a lawsuit. Trade names are intangible property held for productive use in a trade or business.

Example 6-16: The Richmond Runners, a minor league baseball team, traded the contract of one player for that of another. The transaction is an exchange of like-kind property under Code Sec. 1031 and gain is recognized only to the extent of boot received.

Holding Period for Home Sale Exclusion Rule

Effective for sales or exchanges after October 22, 2004, an individual who acquires a principal residence in a like-kind exchange must own the property for at least five years prior to its sale or exchange in order to take advantage of the home sale exclusion rules [Code Sec. 121(d)]. For further discussion see ¶ 7001.

In Rev. Proc. 2005-14,[23] the IRS explained how a homeowner can exclude gain on the sale or exchange of a home and also benefit from a deferral of gain from a like-kind

---

[20] *Sheldon v. Sill*, 49 US 441 (1850).

[21] LTR 8453034 (Sept. 28, 1984).

[22] Rev. Rul. 67-380, 1967-2 CB 291; Rev. Rul. 71-137, 1971-1 CB 104.

[23] Rev Proc. 2005-14, 2005-1 CB 528.

exchange on the same property. A homeowner may benefit from both the home sale exclusion and the like-kind deferral only if both the residence exchanged and the property acquired have been used consecutively or concurrently as a home and a business (e.g., rental residence). Thus, the tax relief is only available to taxpayers who satisfy the "held for productive use in a trade or business or for investment" requirement of Code Sec. 1031(a)(1) with respect to the relinquished business property and the replacement business property.

Order of application of two provisions. Taxpayers qualifying for relief under Rev. Proc. 2005-14 may apply both the exclusion of gain from the exchange of a principal residence under Code Sec. 121 and the nonrecognition of gain from the exchange of like-kind properties under Code Sec. 1031 but Code Sec. 121 should be applied first.

Application of Code Sec. 1031 to gain attributable to depreciation. Under Code Sec. 121(d)(6), the home sale exclusion does not apply to gain attributable to depreciation deductions for periods after May 6, 1997, claimed with respect to the business or investment portion of a residence. However, Code Sec. 1031 may apply to such gain.

Treatment of boot. In applying Code Sec. 1031, cash or other nonlike-kind property (boot) received in exchange for property used in the taxpayer's trade or business or held for investment (the relinquished business property), is taken into account only to the extent the boot exceeds the gain excluded under Code Sec. 121 with respect to the relinquished business property.

Computation of basis. In determining the basis of the property received in the exchange to be used in the taxpayer's trade or business or held for investment (the replacement business property), any gain excluded under Code Sec. 121 is treated as gain recognized by the taxpayer. Thus, under Code Sec. 1031(d), the basis of the replacement business property is increased by any gain attributable to the relinquished business property that is excluded under the home sale exclusion rules.

In each example below, the taxpayer is an unmarried individual and the property or a portion of the property has been used in the taxpayer's trade or business or held for investment as well as used as a principal residence.

> **Example 6-17:** Taxpayer A buys a house for $210,000 that he uses as a principal residence from 2006 to 2010. From 2010 until 2012, A rents the house to tenants and claims depreciation deductions of $20,000. In 2012, A exchanges the house for $10,000 and a townhouse with a fair market value of $460,000 that A intends to rent to tenants. A realizes gain of $280,000 on the exchange. Because A owns and uses the house as his principal residence for at least two years during the five-year period prior to the exchange, A may exclude gain under Code Sec. 121. Because the house is investment property at the time of the exchange, A may defer gain under Code Sec. 1031. A excludes $250,000 of the $280,000 gain before applying the like-kind nonrecognition rules. A may defer the remaining gain of $30,000, including the $20,000 gain attributable to depreciation. Although A receives $10,000 of cash (boot) in the exchange, A is not required to recognize gain because the boot is taken into account only to the extent the boot exceeds the amount of excluded gain. A's basis in the replacement property is $430,000, which is equal to the basis of the relinquished property at the time of

the exchange ($190,000) increased by the gain excluded under Code Sec. 121 ($250,000), and reduced by the cash A receives ($10,000).

.02 Character of Property

In order for a like-kind exchange to qualify for a deferral of income, the property must be:

- "Held for productive use in trade or business or for investment;" and
- Not be "stock-in-trade or other property held primarily for sale" [Code Sec. 1031(a)(1)].

The term "productive uses" includes all uses "essential to commerce or manufacture." The term includes the performance of services as well as the creation of material things. Investment property includes otherwise unproductive property that is held at the time of the exchange for future use or with an eye to appreciation and not primarily for sale [Reg. § 1.1031(a)-1(b)].

Property "held primarily for sale" is not eligible for Code Sec. 1031 tax deferral treatment [Code Sec. 1031(a)(2)(A)]. In determining whether property has been held for resale or as business or investment property, your purpose for acquiring and holding the property is controlling. Thus, holding property for rental indicates that it is business or investment property. Much of the litigation in this area concerns the treatment of dealers who claim that the particular property involved in the exchange is not held for sale but rather for investment. This does not mean that taxpayers who are dealers are necessarily disqualified in such cases, but the burden falls on the taxpayer to prove that the property is not "held primarily for sale."

Property eligible for a like-kind exchange includes machinery, buildings, land, trucks, rental houses and other property, and commercial property. It does not include raw materials, personal residences, the family car, stocks, bonds, notes, accounts receivable, partnership interests, merchandise, or inventory which you hold out for sale to the public.

The character of the property is determined generally at the time of the exchange, although there is some precedent for analyzing the taxpayer's purpose during the entire holding period.

The like-kind exchange provisions are typically unavailable to defer the recognition of gain for exchanges of property held for personal use including a personal residence because the "productive use in trade or business or for investment" requirement eliminates property held for purely personal uses. Thus, a personal residence cannot be exchanged tax-free for rental property. Similarly, a vacation home used purely for personal purposes cannot be exchanged for another vacation home used purely for personal purposes.

In *W.P. Adams*,[24] the court held that sale by an individual of his house qualified for nonrecognition treatment as part of a like-kind exchange. The taxpayer sold a house that he had rented to an unrelated party and purchased another house that he rented to

---

[24] *W.P. Adams*, 105 TCM 1029, Dec. 59,408(M), TC Memo. 2013-7.

his son. The IRS argued that one house was purchased as an investment, because it was rented out, while the other was a residence for his son. However, the court found that the rent paid by the taxpayer's son was at fair market value in light of the home improvements that he made on the house while living there. Therefore, the sale of one house and purchase of another constituted a valid Code Sec. 1031 exchange. The taxpayer was liable for tax on the boot he received in the exchange, which was the difference between the price received from selling the first house and the price paid for the second, minus costs.

In *B.E. Moore,*[25] the Tax Court held that taxpayers who sold their vacation home and purchased another had not engaged in a like-kind exchange because the properties were not held primarily for use in a trade or business or for investment. The Tax Court held that the properties were held for personal use and that the "mere hope or expectation that property may be sold at a gain cannot establish an investment intent if the taxpayer uses the property as a residence." The evidence established that the taxpayers used the property as a vacation retreat, did not rent it out or claim depreciation or investment interest expenses on it, and stopped maintaining the first property when they no longer used it for personal purposes.

In *T.R. Goolsby,*[26] the Tax Court concluded that taxpayers could not defer the recognition of the gain they realized upon the sale of real property, because they did not hold the replacement property for productive use in a trade or business or for investment. They made their purchase of the property contingent on the sale of their personal residence, and they made only minimal attempts to rent the property before they moved into it themselves two months after they acquired it.

IRS Provides Safe Harbor for Dwelling Units in Like-Kind Exchanges

In Rev. Proc. 2008-16,[27] the IRS provided a safe harbor under which it will not challenge whether a dwelling unit qualifies as "property held for productive use in a trade or business or for investment" for like-kind exchange treatment under Code Sec. 1031, even though the taxpayer occasionally uses the dwelling unit for personal purposes. The ruling was necessary to clarify some confusion regarding what constitutes a personal residence for purposes of like-kind exchanges of vacation homes and other rental property after the Tax Court decision in *B.E. Moore* where the court denied like-kind exchange treatment to two vacation homes because in the courts' view personal use of a residence contravened the fact that it is investment property.

Under the safe harbor established in Rev. Rul. 2008-16, a "dwelling unit" is real property improved with a house, apartment, condominium, or similar improvement that provides basic living accommodations, including sleeping space, bathroom, and cooking facilities. The taxpayer must satisfy the following qualifying use standards for the dwelling units to qualify for the IRS safe harbor:

1. The taxpayer must own the dwelling unit to be relinquished for a period of at least 24 months immediately before the exchange.

---

[25] *B.E. Moore,* 93 TCM 1275, Dec. 56,950(M), TC Memo. 2007-134.

[26] *T.R. Goolsby,* 99 TCM 1249, Dec. 58,171(M), TC Memo. 2010-64.

[27] Rev. Proc. 2008-16, IRB 2008-10, 547.

2. In each of the two 12-month periods immediately before the exchange, the taxpayer must rent the relinquished unit to another person(s) at a fair rental for 14 days or more, and the taxpayer's personal use of the unit cannot exceed the greater of 14 days or 10 percent of the days during that 12-month period.
3. The taxpayer must own the replacement dwelling unit for a period of at least 24 months immediately after the exchange.
4. In each of the two 12-month periods immediately after the exchange, the taxpayer must rent the replacement unit to another person(s) at a fair rental for 14 days or more, and the taxpayer's personal use of the unit cannot exceed the greater of 14 days or 10 percent of the days during that 12-month period.

.03 Like-Kind Requirement

In determining whether property is exchanged for property of a like kind within the meaning of Code Sec. 1031(a), taxpayers must compare the exchanged properties to ascertain whether the nature and character of the transferred property rights are substantially alike [Reg. § 1.1031(a)-1(b)].[28] In making this comparison, taxpayer should consider the respective interests in the physical properties, the nature of the title conveyed, the rights of the parties, the duration of the interests, and any other factor bearing on the nature or character of the properties rather than their grade or quality [Reg. § 1.1031(a)-1(b)]. In order for exchanges of real property to qualify as a like-kind exchange, the properties exchanged must be held for productive use in a trade or business or for investment. Property used for personal purposes such as a taxpayer's own residence is ineligible for like-kind exchange treatment. For purposes of determining whether the like-kind requirement is met, property can be divided into three types:

1. Depreciable tangible personal property;
2. Other personal property (intangible personal property, nondepreciable personal property, and personal property held for investment); and
3. Real property.

Depreciable tangible personal property is of a like class to other depreciable tangible personal property if the exchanged properties are in either the same General Asset Class or the same Product Class. The determination of a property's class is made as of the date of the exchange [Reg. § 1.1031(a)-2(b)(1)].

General Asset Classes

The General Asset Classes are taken from asset classes 00.11 through 00.28 and 00.4 of Rev. Proc. 87-56.[29] These classes are as follows [Reg. § 1.1031(a)-2(b)(2)]:

1. Office furniture, fixtures, and equipment (asset class 00.11);
2. Information systems (computers and peripheral equipment) (asset class 00.12);
3. Data handling equipment, except computers (asset class 00.13);

[28] *Peabody Natural Res. Co.*, 126 TC 261, Dec. 56,508 (2006).

[29] Rev. Proc. 87-56, 1987-2 CB 674.

4. Airplanes (airframes and engines), except those used in commercial or contract carrying of passengers or freight, and all helicopters (airframes and engines) (asset class 00.21);
5. Automobiles and taxis (asset class 00.22);
6. Buses (asset class 00.23);
7. Light general purpose trucks (asset class 00.241);
8. Heavy general purpose trucks (asset class 00.242);
9. Railroad cars and locomotives, except those owned by railroad transportation companies (asset class 00.25);
10. Tractor units for use over-the-road (asset class 00.26);
11. Trailers and trailer-mounted containers (asset class 00.27);
12. Vessels, barges, tugs and similar water-transportation equipment, except those used in marine construction (asset class 00.28); and
13. Industrial steam and electric generation and/or distribution systems (asset class 00.4).

If neither of the exchanged properties falls into a General Asset Class, the taxpayer should look further to determine whether they fall in the same Product Class.

Product classes. The Product Classes are derived from the North American Industry Classification System (NAICS) set up by the Office of Management and Budget; they are not listed in IRS regulations [Reg. § 1.1031(a)-2(b)(3)]. A product class consists of depreciable tangible personal property that is described in a 6-digit product class within Sectors 31, 32, and 33 of NAICS [Reg. § 1.1031(a)-2(b)(3)]. Whenever the NAICS Manual is modified, the like-kind exchange Product Classes follow the modification. The Manual is generally modified every five years, in the years ending in a "2" or a "7" (e.g., 2012 and 2017). Taxpayers may rely on the modifications as they become effective (generally, January 1 of the year the Manual is modified). Alternatively, taxpayers may rely on the unmodified version of the NAICS Manual during the one-year period following the effective date of the modification [Reg. § 1.1031(a)-2(b)(4)].

If neither of the properties falls in an asset class or in a product class, the determination of whether they are like-class is based on all the facts or circumstances. In addition, state law treatment of the property may be controlling for purposes of determining whether property will be treated as like-kind. For example, in TAM 200424001,[30] the IRS concluded that components of railroad track that are assembled and attached to the land are considered real property for state law purposes are not like-kind to unassembled railroad track components that are considered personal property for state law purposes.

The following real property exchanges will qualify as a like-kind exchange:

- City real estate for a ranch or farm;
- Improved real estate for unimproved real estate [Reg. § 1.1031(a)-1(b)];
- A 30-year or more leasehold for a fee interest in real estate [Reg. § 1.1031(a)-1(c)];

[30] LTR 200424001 (Dec. 8, 2003).

- An apartment house for building lots;
- An apartment building for a store;
- A perpetual conservation easement for a fee interest in real property that was subject to a perpetual conservation easement;[31]
- Passenger cars, general purpose trucks and sport utility vehicles (SUVs) or minivans;[32] and
- Nitrogen oxide (NOx) credits for volatile organic compounds (VOCs) credits issued by a regional authority to businesses that took certain measures to reduce their emissions of pollutants character.[33]

The following exchanges do *not* qualify as like-kind exchanges:

- Apartment building for a piece of machinery;
- Short-term leasehold of real property for fee interest;
- Real estate for personal property;
- Livestock of one sex for livestock of a different sex [Code Sec. 1031(e); Reg. § 1.1031(e)-1];
- U.S. currency for foreign currency;[34]
- Gold bullion for silver bullion (assuming that each held for investment);[35]
- One vacation home for another when one home is used solely as a vacation retreat rather than investment property;[36]
- Real property located in the United States and real property located outside the United States [Code Sec. 1031(h)(1)];
- Personal property "predominantly used" within the United States for personal property predominantly used outside the United States [Code Sec. 1031(h)(2)];
- Foreign personal property for U.S. personal property because the depreciation rules applicable to foreign use property and domestic use property are so dissimilar;
- A limited partnership's exchange of water rights for farmland;[37]
- Goodwill or going concern value of a business for goodwill or going concern value of another business [Reg. § 1.1031(a)-2(c)(2)]; and
- Leasehold interest in real property improved by a motel with a remaining term of 21 years and 4 months for two real property fee interests, one containing a motel and the other an office building.[38]

.04 Code Sec. 1031 and Fractional Property Interests

Taxpayers can use the like-exchange rules to exchange real property for separate, fractional property interests in real property. In a fractional property interest (tenancy in

---

[31] LTR 200201007 (Oct. 2, 2001).

[32] LTR 200912004 (Dec. 2, 2008); LTR 200450005 (Aug. 30, 2004).

[33] LTR 201024036 (Feb. 23, 2010).

[34] Rev. Rul. 74-7, 1974-1 CB 198.

[35] Rev. Rul. 82-166, 1982-2 CB 190.

[36] *B.E. Moore*, 93 TCM 1275, Dec. 56,950(M), TC Memo. 2007-134.

[37] *D. Wiechens*, DC-AZ, 2002-2 USTC ¶ 50,708, 228 FSupp2d 1080.

[38] *VIP's Industries, Inc.*, 105 TCM 1890, Dec. 59,574(M), TC Memo. 2013-157.

common), each owner is deemed to own an undivided part of the entire parcel and is therefore entitled to a share of the whole parcel and the rights to a portion of the rents or profits generated by the property. A potential problem in this type of exchange is making sure that the fractional interest is not a partnership because under Code Sec. 1031(a)(2)(D), partnership interests do not qualify for a like-kind exchange. Reg. § 301.7701-1(a)(2) provides that a joint venture or contractual arrangement creates a separate tax entity, or a partnership if the participants carry on a trade, business, financial operation, or venture and divide the profits from the partnership. Mere co-ownership of property that is maintained, kept in repair, and rented or leased, however, does not constitute a separate entity for federal tax purposes.

IRS Sets Conditions for Ruling on Undivided Fractional Real Estate

In Rev. Proc. 2002-22,[39] the IRS specifies certain conditions under which it would consider a request for a ruling that an undivided fractional interest in rental real property is not an interest in a business entity for federal tax purposes. The IRS concluded that fractional property interests should not be considered partnerships as long as they satisfy the following conditions:

- *Tenancy in common ownership.* Each of the co-owners must hold title to the property as a tenant in common under local law.
- *Number of co-owners.* There can be no more than 35 co-owners.
- *No treatment of co-ownership as an entity.* The co-owners may not file a partnership or corporate tax return, conduct business under a common name, execute an agreement identifying any or all of the co-owners as partners, shareholders, or members of a business entity, or otherwise hold itself out as a partnership or other form of business entity.
- *Voting.* The co-owners must retain the right to approve the hiring of any manager, the sale or other disposition of the property, any leases of the property, or the creation or modification of a blanket lien.
- *Restrictions on alienation.* Each co-owner must have the rights to transfer, partition, and encumber the co-owner's undivided interest in the property without the agreement or approval of any person.
- *Sharing proceeds and liabilities upon sale of property.* If the property is sold, any debt secured by a blanket lien must be satisfied and the remaining sales proceeds must be distributed to the co-owners.
- *Proportionate sharing of profits and losses.* Each co-owner must share in all revenues generated by the property and all costs associated with the property in proportion to the co-owner's undivided interest in the property.
- *Proportionate sharing of debt.* The co-owners must share in any indebtedness secured by a blanket lien in proportion to their undivided interests.

---

[39] Rev. Proc. 2002-22, 2002-1 CB 733, as modified by Rev. Proc. 2003-3, 2003-1 CB 113.

- *Options.* A co-owner may issue an option to purchase the co-owner's undivided interest (call option), provided that the exercise price for the call option reflects the fair market value of the property determined as of the time the option is exercised.
- *No business activities.* The co-owners' activities must be limited to those customarily performed in connection with the maintenance and repair of rental real property (customary activities).
- *Management and brokerage agreements.* The co-owners may enter into management or brokerage agreements, which must be renewable no less frequently than annually, with an agent, who may be the sponsor or a co-owner (or any person related to the sponsor or a co-owner), but who may not be a lessee. The management agreement may authorize the manager to maintain a common bank account for the collection and deposit of rents and to offset expenses associated with the property against any revenues before disbursing each co-owner's share of net revenues. In all events, however, the manager must disburse to the co-owners their shares of net revenues within 3 months from the date of receipt of those revenues. The management agreement may also authorize the manager to prepare statements for the co-owners showing their shares of revenue and costs from the property. In addition, the management agreement may authorize the manager to obtain or modify insurance on the property, and to negotiate modifications of the terms of any lease or any indebtedness encumbering the property, subject to the approval of the co-owners.
- *Leasing agreements.* All leasing arrangements must be bona fide leases for federal tax purposes. Rents paid by a lessee must reflect the fair market value for the use of the property. The determination of the amount of the rent must not depend on the income or profits derived by any person from the property leased (other than an amount based on a fixed percentage or percentages of receipts or sales).
- *Loan agreements.* The lender with respect to any debt that encumbers the property or with respect to any debt incurred to acquire an undivided interest in the property may not be a related person to any co-owner, the sponsor, the manager, or any lessee of the property.
- *Payments to sponsor.* The amount of any payment to the sponsor for the acquisition of the co-ownership interest (and the amount of any fees paid to the sponsor for services) must reflect the fair market value of the acquired co-ownership interest (or the services rendered) and may not depend, in whole or in part, on the income or profits derived by any person from the property.

Letter Rulings Holding Fractional Interests Not Partnerships

In Letter Rulings 200625009[40] and 200625010,[41] the IRS concluded that undivided fractional interests in property were not interests in a business entity under Reg. §301.7701-2(a) for purposes of qualification of the undivided fractional interest (UFI) as eligible replacement property under the like-kind exchange rules of Code Sec. 1031(a). In each ruling, the taxpayer, a company, and an unrelated business entity each owned 50 percent of a property as tenants in common. Their co-ownership agreement satisfied all of the conditions of Rev. Proc. 2002-22. For example, the co-owner seeking to sell was

[40] LTR 200625009 (March 1, 2006).

[41] LTR 200625010 (March 1, 2006).

required to (1) give the other co-owner a pre-offer notice, which would include an initial due diligence disclosure; and (2) provide written notice of the intent to sell the property interest.

.05 Time Limit Requirement

A like-kind exchange is a valuable tax deferral technique for taxpayers who want to exchange appreciated property held for investment or business use for similar or like-kind property [Code Sec. 1031(a)(1)]. However, a time limit affects when property can be identified and received in an exchange to qualify for nonrecognition treatment as like-kind property:

45-Day Identification Requirement

In a like-kind exchange, the property to be received by the taxpayer must be identified within 45 days after the date on which the taxpayer transfers the relinquished property. The 45-day grace period is designed to give taxpayers sufficient time to locate suitable exchange properties.

180-Day Receipt Requirement

The identified property must be received within the earlier of: 180 days after the transfer of the property relinquished in the exchange, or the due date, including extensions, for filing the transferor's federal income tax return for the year in which the transfer of the relinquished property occurred [Code Sec. 1031(a)(3)].

The 180-day exchange requirement forces you to determine shortly after the initial transfer (and prior to the filing of your tax return) whether to receive property and qualify for tax-free treatment under the like-kind exchange provisions or to receive cash and defer the tax consequences by using, for example, the installment sale method discussed in Ch. 19.

Like-Kind Exchange Deadlines Automatically Extended for Disasters

The IRS will allow a blanket automatic 120-day extension for meeting Code Sec. 1031 like-kind exchange deadlines in the event of a federally declared disaster.[42] See ¶ 5100 for list of disaster areas. A similar extension is available for taxpayers affected by a terrorist or military action or serving in a combat zone. An additional 120 days may be tacked onto the 45-day identification period deadline and the 180-day exchange period deadline for deferred like-kind exchanges under Reg. § 1.1031(k)-1(b)(2). The postponement period also applies to the five-day business period to enter into a qualification exchange accommodation agreement (QEAA), the 45-day identification period, the 180-day exchange period, and the 180-day combined period set forth in Rev. Proc. 2000-37.[43]

If the last date day of any of these time periods falls on or after the date of a federally declared disaster, the taxpayer may qualify for the 120-day postponement for that period. The postponement only applies, however, if the relinquished property or qualified indicia of ownership were transferred on or before the date of the declared disaster.

---

[42] Rev. Proc. 2007-56, 2007-2 CB 388.

[43] Rev. Proc. 2000-37, 2000-2 CB 308, as modified by Rev. Proc. 2004-51, 2004-2 CB 294.

.06 Exchange Requirement

In order for the transaction to qualify as a tax-deferred like-kind exchange, an actual exchange must take place. This means that you must exchange property for property rather than exchange property for money. In addition, you must exchange property held for productive use in a trade or business or for investment and receive in return, property held for productive use in a trade or business or for investment. You recognize no gain or loss at the time of the exchange unless you receive boot which typically is cash or a mortgage assumed. The basis of replacement property received in a like-kind exchange equals the basis of the property relinquished, decreased by the amount of money received, plus or minus any gain or loss recognized on the exchange [Code Sec. 1031(d); Reg. § 1.1031(d)-1(e)].

> **Example 6-18:** You exchange farm property with an adjusted basis of $100,000 and a fair market value of $150,000 for farm property with a fair market value of $150,000. Although you ordinarily would realize a gain of $50,000, the like-kind tax provisions apply and allow you to defer recognition of the gain. Your basis in the new property, however, remains $100,000. If you exchange your property for farm property worth $130,000 plus $20,000 in cash in order to equalize the sale, you will only pay tax on the $20,000 (boot) [Code Sec. 1031(b)]. Your basis in the property will be $120,000 ($100,000 plus the $20,000 of gain recognized).

There are three types of exchanges:

- A "simultaneous" exchange (taxpayer conveys relinquished property and simultaneously acquires replacement property);
- A "deferred" exchange (taxpayer conveys relinquished property and subsequently acquires replacement property); and
- A "reverse" exchange (taxpayer acquires replacement property and thereafter conveys relinquished property).

.07 Multiple Property Exchanges

A typical like-kind exchange requires a "property-by-property" comparison for computing gain recognized in the transaction [Reg. § 1.1031(j)-1(a)(1)]. An exchange is considered an exchange of multiple properties if the properties transferred are separable into more than one "exchange group" consisting of all the properties transferred and received in the exchange that are of like-kind [Reg. § 1.1031(j)-1(a)(1)]. Thus, all the properties within the same General Asset Class would be in the same exchange group. For example, money and boot are placed in a separate "residual group" [Reg. § 1.1031(j)-1(b)(2)(iii)]. Taxpayers must also net any liabilities assumed as part of the exchange with any liabilities relieved as part of the exchange [Reg. § 1.1031(j)-1(a)(2)]. If the amount of liabilities for which the taxpayer is relieved in the exchange exceeds the amount of liabilities he assumes, the excess is allocated to the "residual group" as well [Reg. § 1.1031(j)-1(b)(2)(ii)(C)].[44] Thereafter, the fair market values of the proper-

[44] *J.G. Yates*, 105 TCM 1205, Dec. 59,429(M), TC Memo. 2013-28.

ties received and the properties exchanged in each exchange group are compared [Reg. § 1.1031 (j)-1 (b) (2) (iv)]. If the aggregate fair market value of the properties received in an exchange group exceeds the aggregate fair market value of the properties transferred in the same exchange group, the excess is considered an "exchange group surplus." Conversely, if the aggregate fair market value of the properties transferred in an exchange groups exceeds the aggregate fair market value of the properties received in the same exchange group, the excess is considered an "exchange group deficiency."

A taxpayer's amount of gain or loss realized with respect to each exchange group and the residual group is the difference between the aggregate fair market value of the properties transferred in that exchange or residual group and the properties' aggregate adjusted basis [Reg. § 1.1031 (j)-1 (b) (3) (i)]. Any gain realized for each exchange group is recognized to the extent of the lesser of the gain realized and the amount of the "exchange group deficiency," if any.

Safe Harbors for LKE Programs Involving Ongoing Exchanges of Tangible Personal Property Using Single Intermediary

Three safe harbors are available for programs involving ongoing exchanges of tangible personal property using a single, unrelated intermediary to accomplish the exchanges (under *LKE Programs*).[45] These safe harbors facilitate, by means of netting treatment, deferred like-kind exchange of properties with liabilities that span two tax years, especially in the partnership setting. LKE programs typically are used by the companies that dispose of and acquire hundreds of similar vehicles or pieces of machinery such as automotive leasing companies and medical equipment leasing companies. An LKE Program must have the following characteristics to qualify for the safe harbors:

- The taxpayer must regularly enter into agreements to buy/sell tangible personal property;
- The taxpayer must use a single, unrelated intermediary to accomplish the exchanges;
- The taxpayer and the intermediary must enter into a written master exchange agreement;
- The master exchange agreement must limit rights to benefit from money held by the intermediary;
- In the master exchange agreement, the taxpayer must assign to the intermediary the taxpayer's rights in existing and future agreements to sell and/or purchase relinquished property;
- The taxpayer must provide written notice of the agreement to sell and/or purchase relinquished property;
- The taxpayer must (a) implement a process that identifies potential replacement properties before the end of the identification period, (b) comply with the identification requirement by receiving replacement properties before the end of the 45-day identification period;
- The taxpayer must implement a process for collecting, holding and disbursing funds ensuring that the intermediary controls all proceeds;

---

[45] Rev. Proc. 2003-39, 2003-1 CB 971.

- Relinquished properties must be matched with replacement properties to determine the gain and basis of the replacement property; and
- The taxpayer must recognize gain or loss on the disposition of relinquished properties that are not matched with replacement properties, and the taxpayer must take a cost basis in replacement properties that are received but not matched with relinquished properties.

Following are descriptions of the three safe harbors.

Replacement property. Replacement property that is received or identified within the 45-day identification period must be treated as satisfying the requirement of Code Sec. 1031(a)(3) even if it is not matched with relinquished property until after the end of the 45-day identification period. The replacement property must, however, be matched no later than the extended due date of the taxpayer's return.

No endorsement. The check or other negotiable instrument must not be endorsed by the person to whom the check or other negotiable instrument is made payable. In addition, the person to whom the check or other negotiable instrument is made payable is not a disqualified person; and the check or other negotiable instrument must be forwarded to or for the benefit of a "qualified intermediary" (defined below) or deposited into an account in the name of the qualified intermediary, a joint account, or an account in the name of a third party for the benefit of both the taxpayer and qualified intermediary.

Qualified intermediary. For purposes of determining whether an intermediary is a disqualified person in the context of an LKE Program, the intermediary will not fail to be a qualified intermediary merely because the intermediary:

- Is assigned the taxpayer's rights in its agreements to sell relinquished properties that ultimately are not matched with replacement properties under the taxpayer's LKE Program;
- Is assigned the taxpayer's rights in its agreements to buy replacement properties that ultimately are not matched with relinquished properties under the taxpayer's LKE Program;
- Receives funds with respect to the transfer of relinquished property that ultimately is not matched with replacement property under the taxpayer's LKE Program; or
- Pays funds with respect to the acquisition of replacement property that ultimately is not matched with relinquished property under the taxpayer's LKE Program.

Safe Harbor Available for Defaulting QI in Deferred Like-Kind Exchanges

In Rev. Proc. 2010-14,[46] the IRS provides a safe harbor method of reporting gain or loss for taxpayers who undertake deferred like-kind exchanges using a qualified intermediary (QI) that defaults on its obligation to transfer replacement property to the taxpayer. The IRS created this safe harbor after becoming aware of situations in which taxpayers initiated like-kind exchanges by transferring relinquished property to a QI and were unable to complete these exchanges within the exchange period solely due to the QI's default. As a result of the default, the QI was unable to acquire and transfer replacement

---

[46] Rev. Proc. 2010-14, IRB 2010-12, 456.

property to the taxpayer because the QI's assets were frozen in bankruptcy or receivership, thus preventing the taxpayer from obtaining immediate access to the proceeds of the sale of the relinquished property.

Scope of Rev. Proc. 2010-14. The safe harbor provided in Rev. Proc. 2010-14 applies to taxpayers who:

1. Transferred relinquished property to a QI;
2. Properly identified replacement property within the identification period (unless the QI default occurs during that period);
3. Did not complete the like-kind exchange solely because of a QI default involving a QI that becomes subject to a bankruptcy proceeding or a receivership; and
4. Did not, without regard to any actual or constructive receipt by the QI, have actual or constructive receipt of the proceeds from the disposition of the relinquished property or any property of the QI prior to the time the QI entered bankruptcy or receivership.

According to the safe harbor, if a QI defaults on its obligation to acquire and transfer replacement property to the taxpayer and becomes subject to a bankruptcy proceeding, the taxpayer may not seek to enforce its rights under the exchange agreement with the QI or otherwise access the sale proceeds from the relinquished property outside of the bankruptcy proceeding while the proceeding is pending. Consequently, the IRS will treat the taxpayer as not having actual or constructive receipt of the proceeds during that period if the taxpayer reports gain under the safe harbor. Thus, the taxpayer only has to recognize gain on the disposition of the relinquished property as required under the safe harbor gross profit ratio method.

Under the safe harbor gross profit ratio method, a taxpayer may report gain realized on the disposition of the relinquished property as the taxpayer receives payments attributable to the relinquished property. Under this method, the portion of any payment attributable to the relinquished property that is recognized as gain is determined by multiplying the payment by a fraction, the numerator of which is the taxpayer's gross profit and the denominator of which is the taxpayer's contract price.

Gross profit means the selling price of the relinquished property, minus the taxpayer's adjusted basis in the relinquished property (increased by any selling expenses not paid by the QI using proceeds from the sale of the relinquished property). The selling price of the relinquished property is generally the amount realized on the sale of the relinquished property, without reduction for selling expenses. The contract price is the selling price of the relinquished property minus the amount of any satisfied indebtedness not in excess of the adjusted basis of the relinquished property.

A taxpayer may claim a loss deduction under Code Sec. 165 for the amount, if any, by which the adjusted basis of the relinquished property exceeds the sum of (1) the payments attributable to the relinquished property (including satisfied indebtedness in excess of basis), plus (2) the amount of any satisfied indebtedness not in excess of basis. A taxpayer who may claim a loss deduction may also claim a loss deduction for the amount of any gain recognized as a result of the application of the safe harbor method in a prior tax year.

Imputed interest. For purposes of applying the safe harbor gross profit ratio method to a transaction, the selling price and contract price must be reduced by the amount of any imputed interest allocable to the payment as determined under Code Secs. 483 or 1274. The taxpayer is treated as selling the relinquished property on the date of the confirmation of the bankruptcy plan. As a result, if the only payment in full satisfaction of the taxpayer's claim is received by the taxpayer on or before the date that is six months after the safe harbor sale date, then no interest is imputed on this payment. In addition, the selling price is used to determine whether Code Sec. 483 (in general, sales for $250,000 or less) or Code Sec. 1274 (in general, sales for more than $250,000) applies to a transaction.

Example 6-19: A owns investment property (Property 1) with a fair market value of $150x and an adjusted basis of $50x. A enters into an agreement with QI to facilitate a deferred like-kind exchange. On May 6, Year 1, A transfers Property 1 to QI and QI transfers Property 1 to a third party in exchange for $150x. On June 1, Year 1, A identifies Property 2 as replacement property. On June 15, Year 1, QI notifies A that it has filed for bankruptcy protection and cannot acquire replacement property. Consequently, A fails to acquire Property 2 or any other replacement property within the exchange period. As of December 31, Year 1, QI's bankruptcy proceedings are on-going and A has received none of the $150x proceeds from QI or any other source. On July 1, Year 2, QI exits from bankruptcy and pays A $130x in full satisfaction of QI's obligation under the exchange agreement on August 4, Year 2.

A is within the scope of the safe harbor in Rev. Proc. 2010-14 and thus is not required to recognize gain in Year 1 because he did not receive any payments attributable to the relinquished property that year. A recognizes gain in Year 2. A's selling price is $130x and A's contract price also is $130x because there is no satisfied or assumed indebtedness. A's gross profit is $80x (the selling price ($130x) minus the adjusted basis ($50x)). A's gross profit ratio is 80/130 (the gross profit over the contract price). A must recognize gain in Year 2 of $80x (the payment attributable to the relinquished property ($130x) multiplied by A's gross profit ratio (80/130)). Even though the payment attributable to the relinquished property ($130x) is less than the $150x proceeds received by the QI, A is not entitled to a Code Sec. 165 loss deduction because the payment attributable to the relinquished property exceeds A's adjusted basis in the relinquished property ($50x).

A taxpayer who is within the scope of this revenue procedure may file an original or amended return to report a deferred like-kind exchange that failed due to a QI default in a tax year ending before January 1, 2009.

.08 Deferred Like-Kind Exchanges Sanctioned in *Starker*

Reg. § 1.1031(k)-1(a) defines a deferred exchange as an exchange in which, pursuant to an exchange agreement, the taxpayer transfers relinquished property and subsequently receives replacement property. Under Code Sec. 1031(a)(3), a taxpayer must first identify the replacement property within 45 days of the transfer of the relinquished property and then acquire the replacement property within 180 days of the transfer of the relinquished property, or by the due date of the taxpayer's return for the year of the transfer of the relinquished property, if sooner.

Reg. § 1.1031(k)-1(g)(4) allows a taxpayer to use a QI to facilitate a deferred like-kind exchange. The QI acquires the relinquished property from the taxpayer, transfers the relinquished property, acquires the replacement property, and transfers the replacement property to the taxpayer.

Nonsimultaneous or deferred like-kind exchanges are often called *Starker* transactions and were sanctioned in a case from the Court of Appeals for the Ninth Circuit by that name.[47] In that case, a taxpayer deeded land to a corporation in exchange for an agreement by the corporation to provide the taxpayer with either suitable real property or cash within five years after the transaction. The court sanctioned this deal, which was unorthodox at the time, and held that like-kind exchanges do not mandate a simultaneous exchange of like-kind properties or an identification of these properties.

After *Starker*, a 45-day identification requirement and a 180-day receipt requirement were added to Code Sec. 1031(a)(3) in order to give taxpayers sufficient time to locate suitable exchange properties.

Starker Exchanges Limited to Property Acquired After Property Was Relinquished

After *Starker*, a like-kind exchange qualified for deferral only if the replacement property was received after the relinquished property had already been transferred by the investor, provided various identification and receipt safe harbors were satisfied as provided in Reg. § 1.1031(k)-1(a).

When the IRS issued final regulations for deferred exchanges, they specifically excluded so-called reverse-*Starker* exchanges where the replacement property was acquired *before* the relinquished property was transferred. As a result of this omission, the big question troubling practitioners was whether a deferred like-kind exchange was possible even though the replacement property was acquired *before* selling the property to be exchanged. The IRS recognized the need to provide some clarity in this situation and has released Rev. Proc. 2000-37,[48] which is a safe harbor sanctioning reverse-*Starker* like-kind exchanges.

Rev. Proc. 2000-37 Sanctions Reverse Like-Kind Exchanges

In Rev. Proc. 2000-37, the IRS provides a much-needed safe harbor for reverse like-kind exchanges or reverse *Starker* transactions where the replacement property is acquired before the relinquished property is transferred. Rev. Proc. 2000-37 allows the use of an accommodation party in a parking transaction to facilitate a reverse like-kind exchange. Rev. Proc. 2000-37 addresses transactions where the replacement property is parked with an accommodation party until the taxpayer can arrange for the transfer of the relinquished property to the ultimate transferee. If you rely on this safe harbor, your reverse-*Starker* transaction can qualify under Code Sec. 1031 as a tax-deferred like-kind exchange and the IRS won't challenge either: (a) the qualification of the property as either *replacement property* or *relinquished property* (as defined in Reg. § 1.1031(k)-1(a));

---

[47] *T.J. Starker*, CA-9, 79-2 USTC ¶9541, 602 F2d 1341.

[48] Rev. Proc. 2000-37, 2000-2 CB 308, as modified by Rev. Proc. 2004-51, 2004-2 CB 294.

or (b) the treatment of the *exchange accommodation titleholder* (EAT) as the beneficial owner of the property provided the property is held in a *qualified exchange accommodation arrangement* (QEAA), as defined below.[49] Keep in mind, however, that failure to strictly satisfy the following safe harbor rules will turn the like-kind exchange into a sale.

Restrictions on Parking for Reverse Like-Kind Exchanges with Property Already Owned by Taxpayer[50]

In Rev. Proc. 2004-51,[51] the IRS narrowed the scope of the safe harbor in Rev. Proc. 2000-37 by providing that property owned by the taxpayer before the transfer of relinquished property through the accommodation party will no longer qualify as replacement property in a parking transaction. This ruling restricts taxpayers from using parking transactions to take proceeds from the sale of real estate to pay for improvements to other real estate owned by the same taxpayer or a related party.

Qualified Exchange Accommodation Arrangements (QEAA)

Rev. Proc. 2000-37 sets forth the following safe-harbor requirements for establishing a QEAA:

1. The exchange accommodation titleholder (EAT) (not the taxpayer or a disqualified person) which is subject to federal income tax, must acquire a qualified indicia of ownership (QIO) in the parked property. To satisfy the Q10 requirement, title or some other qualified indicia of ownership to the property must be held by the exchange accommodation titleholder who is not the taxpayer and is subject to federal income tax, at all times from the date of acquisition until the property is transferred. If the person is treated as a partnership or S corporation, more than 90 percent of its interests or stock must be owned by partners or shareholders who are subject to federal income tax. Other qualified indicia of ownership include a contract, a deed, or interests in an entity that is disregarded as an entity separate from its owner for federal income tax purposes such as a single limited liability company.
2. At the time that the EAT acquires a QIO, the taxpayer has a bona fide intent that the parked property be either replacement or relinquished property in an exchange intended to qualify for deferral of gain or loss under Code Sec. 1031.
3. The EAT and the taxpayer enter into a written qualified exchange accommodation agreement no later than five business days after the EAT acquires a QIO in the parked property, providing that the EAT is holding the property for the benefit of the taxpayer in order to facilitate an exchange under Code Sec. 1031 and Rev. Proc. 2000-37. The agreement must specify that the EAT will be treated as the beneficial owner of the parked property for federal income tax purposes and that both the EAT and the taxpayer must report federal income tax attributes on their respective income tax returns in a manner consistent with this agreement.
4. No later than 45 days after the transfer of a QIO of the replacement property to the EAT, the taxpayer must properly identify the relinquished property in a manner

[49] LTR 201242003 (July 12, 2012).

[50] Rev. Proc. 2004-51, 2004-2 CB 294.

[51] Rev. Proc. 2004-51, 2004-2 CB 294.

consistent with the principles described in Reg. § 1.1031(k)-1(c). The taxpayer may also identify alternative or multiple properties as provided in Reg. § 1.1031(k)-1(c)(4). Property will be considered properly identified if: (1) all parties sign written agreement covering the exchange before end of identification period, or (2) written document identifying the replacement property is signed and delivered before end of identification period to a person involved in the exchange or an intermediary, escrow agent, title company or "virtual" qualified intermediary operated electronically through the internet. The replacement property must be unambiguously described which means a legal description or street address. The taxpayer can change the replacement property provided the change is completed before the end of the identification period by amending the original agreement or by signing an additional written document.

When taxpayers identify alternative and multiple replacement properties the following restrictions are imposed: (1) three properties may be identified regardless of fair market value (FMV); or (2) any number of properties may be identified provided their aggregate FMV as of the end of the identification period does not exceed 200% of the aggregate FMV of all relinquished properties; (3) if more than three properties are identified, any property identified within 45 days and received within 180 days will satisfy the identification requirements, if the taxpayer receives (before the end of the exchange period) at least 95% of the FMV of all identified property. The FMV of each identified property is determined as of the earlier of the date the property is received by the taxpayer or the last day of the exchange period [Reg. § 1.1031(k)-1(c)(4)(i)].

Example 6-20: Seller transfers real property to Buyer for $500,000. The sales proceeds are placed in escrow. Seller assigns the sales contract to qualified intermediary. Before the end of the identification period, Seller may identify either (1) any three replacement properties, or (2) any number of replacement properties if their aggregate FMV determined at the end of the identification period) does not exceed $1 million.

Example 6-21: The facts are the same as the example above, except before the end of the identification period, buyer acquires property from seller, following a property assignment of rights to the qualified intermediary, for $300,000. The acquired property is deemed to be identified. Buyer may identify (1) up to 2 other properties, or (2) any number of properties with an aggregate FMV not exceeding $700,000.

The identification requirement may also be satisfied if the contract specifies that the particular property to be transferred will be determined by contingencies beyond the control of the parties.

Example 6-22: Assume that X transferred real property in exchange for a promise by Y to transfer parcel A to X if certain zoning changes are approved and parcel B if the changes are not approved. The transaction qualifies as a like-kind exchange provided the contract covers these points and the exchange is made within the specified time limits for non-simultaneous transfers.

5. No later than 180 days after the transfer of a QIO of the property to the EAT, the property is transferred either directly or indirectly through a qualified intermediary to the taxpayer as replacement property (or as relinquished property to a third party buyer who is not a disqualified person). If the taxpayer receives money or other property from the first settlement before receiving the like-kind replacement property, the taxpayer has "sold" the first property rather than exchanged it and will have to pay tax on the resulting gain or loss unless the taxpayer receives one of the following safe harbors which will not constitute taxable "cash":
    - A mortgage, deed of trust, or other security interest in property, provided it does not involve cash or a cash equivalent;
    - A standby letter of credit that does not allow the taxpayer to draw on such letter of credit except in the event of a default of the seller's obligation to transfer the like-kind property. Any cash or cash equivalent must be held in a escrow account or trust and the taxpayer's rights to access the money or other property must be limited;
    - A guarantee of a third party or intermediary; or
    - Payment of interest or a growth factor provided the right to receive the interest or growth factor is limited to certain specified circumstances [Reg. § 1.1031(k)-1(g)].
6. The combined time that the QEAA may hold replacement and relinquished property may not exceed 180 days.

Transfer of title. No later than 180 days after the transfer of title to the exchange accommodation titleholder, the property is transferred (either directly or indirectly) through a qualified intermediary to the taxpayer as either replacement or relinquished property. A *qualified intermediary* is a person who is not the taxpayer or a disqualified person and who enters into a written agreement with the taxpayer and acquires the relinquished property from the taxpayer, transfers the relinquished property, acquires the replacement property and transfers the replacement property to the taxpayer [Reg. § 1.1031(k)-1(g)(4)(iii)(B)]. A *virtual qualified intermediary* may be operated electronically through an Internet site.

A *disqualified person* includes:

- An "agent" of the seller at the time of the transaction such as an employee, attorney, accountant, investment banker or broker, or real estate agent or broker within the two-year period ending on the date the seller relinquishes the property (however, services provided with respect to Section 1031 exchanges and routine financial, title, insurance, escrow, or trust services provided by a financial institution, title insurance company, or escrow company aren't taken into account); or
- Anyone related to the disqualified person under the Section 267(b) and Section 707(b) attribution rules using a 10-percent test also is treated as a disqualified person [Reg. § 1.1031(k)-1(k)(4)].

Under Reg. § 1.1031(k)-1(k)(4), a bank or bank affiliate isn't a disqualified person merely because it is a member of the same controlled group (as determined in Code Sec. 267(f)(1), using a 10-percent test) as a person that has provided investment banking or brokerage services to the taxpayer within the two year look-back period. A bank affiliate is a corporation whose principal activity is rendering services to facilitate like-kind exchanges and all of whose stock is owned by a bank or a bank holding company.

180 day limit. The combined time period that the relinquished property and the replacement property are held in a QEAA does not exceed 180 days.

Rev. Proc. 2000-37 is effective for QEAAs entered into with an accommodation title holder that acquires ownership of property after September 14, 2000.

Planning Consequences

Rev. Proc. 2000-37 (as modified by Rev. Proc. 2004-51) eases significantly the rules for reverse-*Starker* like-kind exchanges where the replacement property is purchased no more than 180 days prior to the sale. If the sale is carefully structured in accordance with the specific requirements set forth by the IRS in Rev. Proc. 2000-37, the IRS will not challenge the tax treatment of the transaction. Specifically, the property must be held in a "qualified exchange accommodation arrangement" or QEAA. After years of creative planning by practitioners, reverse-*Starker* exchanges are now sanctioned by the IRS provided you carefully structure the exchange in accordance with Rev. Proc. 2000-37.

.09 Three-Party Exchanges

Like-kind exchanges will often require the involvement of more than two parties, especially when the transaction involves investment real estate. In multi-party like-like exchanges, the third party will receive property from the seller and cash from the buyer. Then the third party will purchase replacement property and transfer it to the seller and finally transfer the seller's relinquished property to the buyer.

> **Example 6-23:** Arthur wants to sell an apartment house that has appreciated in value and Baker offers to purchase it for cash. Arthur plans to reinvest the sale proceeds in commercial property, and wants to structure the transaction as a like-kind exchange. However, the chance of finding suitable commercial property whose owner is willing to trade for Arthur's property is remote.
>
> The simplest solution is to arrange for a three-party exchange, consisting of Arthur (seller), Baker (buyer), and Chase (the seller of replacement commercial property suitable to Arthur). Baker purchases Chase's property, and then exchanges it for Arthur's property. If the transaction takes this form, Arthur converts a taxable sale into a tax-deferred like-kind exchange.

A like-kind exchange can also involve more than three parties as well as the use of escrow accounts, or some form of security or guarantee. For example, in the example above, Baker (the buyer) may not want to purchase suitable replacement property and exchange it for Arthur's (the seller's) property. In that event, the transaction would be handled through an intermediary. Arthur also may want assurances that Baker will perform as required under the agreement. Finally, Arthur may want to provide that the transaction be consummated as a sale if suitable replacement property cannot be found and an exchange cannot be arranged within the statutory time limits on identification and receipt.

Taxpayers can enjoy tax-free treatment by using a qualified escrow account, trust or intermediary, as long as their agreement with that party limits their right to receive, pledge, borrow or otherwise benefit from the money being held. The IRS has approved the use of a virtual qualified intermediary that operated electronically through an Internet site.[52]

Taxpayers who use qualified escrow arrangements and meet the requirements of the regulations will be entitled to report gain recognized on the deferred exchange under the installment method accounting rules [Reg. § 1.1031(k)-1(g)]. The regulations coordinate the installment sale rules with those pertaining to deferred like-kind exchanges. In general, if a transaction otherwise meets the like-kind exchange rules concerning the types of property that may be exchanged, and the taxpayer complies with the rules for setting up a qualified escrow or trust or uses a qualified intermediate, the transaction will not be treated as an immediate sale. In addition, if the exchange ultimately fails and the taxpayer receives cash, he would be entitled to report any gain recognized under the installment method if, at the beginning of the exchange period, the taxpayer has a bona fide intent to make a deferred exchange. The regulations provide that a taxpayer will be treated as having a bona fide intent only if it is reasonable to believe, based on all the facts and circumstances as of the beginning of the exchange period, that like-kind replacement property will be acquired before the end of the exchange period [Reg. § 1.1031(k)-1(j)(2)(iv)]. Income held in escrow or trust or held by an agent is taxable when the replacement period ends. The taxpayer has the immediate right to receive the funds at that time or at the end of the statutory exchange period.

.10 Exchanges Between Related Persons

To facilitate a deferred like-kind exchange, the taxpayer may use a qualified intermediary (QI) who is not related to the taxpayer. The QI enters into a written exchange agreement with the taxpayer and acquires property from the taxpayer, transfers this property, acquires like-kind replacement property, and transfers this replacement property to the taxpayer [Reg. § 1.1031 (k)-1(g)(4)(iii)].

Code Sec. 1031(f) provides special rules for property exchanged between related persons and states that an exchange of properties with a related party is not tax-free if, less than two years after the exchange, either:

- The relinquished property is sold by the related party, or
- The taxpayer sells the acquired property.

The realized gain or loss on the like-kind exchange is then recognized in the year of the disposition. A transaction won't trigger the related party bar and will therefore be tax-free if the taxpayer establishes to the IRS's satisfaction that neither the exchange nor the later sale had federal tax avoidance as one of its principal purposes [Code Sec. 1031(f)(2)(C)].

---

[52] LTR 200236026 (June 3, 2002).

Both the House Ways and Means Committee and the Senate Finance Committee disclosed the policy concern that led to the enactment of Code Sec. 1031(f):

> Because a like-kind exchange results in the substitution of the basis of the exchanged property for the property received, related parties have engaged in like-kind exchanges of high basis property for low basis property in anticipation of the sale of the low basis property in order to reduce or avoid the recognition of gain on the subsequent sale. Basis shifting also can be used to accelerate a loss on the retained property. The committee believes that if a related party exchange is followed shortly thereafter by a disposition of the property, the related parties have, in effect, cashed out of the investment, and the original exchange should not be accorded nonrecognition treatment.

In Private Letter Ruling 201216007[53] the IRS concluded that a real estate investment trust (REIT) may claim nonrecognition treatment under Code Sec. 1031 in a series of like-kind exchanges involving related parties. Moreover, the receipt of limited amounts of non-like-kind property by the related parties did not disqualify the exchanges under Code Sec. 1031(f). The IRS concluded that, so long as each party held its respective replacement property for at least two years following the date of acquisition, Code Sec. 1031(f) will not disqualify the taxpayer from receiving Code Sec. 1031(a) nonrecognition treatment. After closely reviewing the legislative history underlying Code Sec. 1031(f), IRS found that the abuses which the code section was created to combat—namely, tax avoidance resulting from a taxpayer's cashing out of its investment in the relinquished property without recognizing gain—were not presented by the facts in the letter ruling. The taxpayers did not show any cashing out by any of the related parties within two years of the last transfer in the series of transactions, and neither the taxpayer or any other party to the transaction were expected to receive non-like-kind replacement property in excess of 5 percent of the gain realized on its disposition of relinquished property. Instead, the IRS noted that the only acquisitions of replacement property from related parties were part of subsequent like-kind exchanges by the related parties, which will substantially constitute nonrecognition transactions. Upon completion of all transactions, all related parties would own property that was of like-kind to the properties exchanged for at least two years after the date of the last transfer in the series.

Related Parties

For purposes of Code Sec. 1031(f), "related parties" refers to, among other relationships:

- Certain family members including siblings, spouse, ancestors, and lineal descendants,
- An individual and corporation in which more than 50 percent of the value of the stock is effectively owned by such individual,
- Two corporations that are part of the same controlled group,

[53] LTR 201216007 (Jan. 9, 2012).

- A corporation and a partnership, if the same persons own more than 50 percent of the value of the corporation and more than 50 percent of the capital or profits interest in the partnership,
- An S corporation and C corporation, if the same persons own more than 50 percent of the value of outstanding stock in each corporation.
- An individual and a partnership in which the individual effectively owns more than 50 percent of the capital or profits interest in the partnership,
- Two partnerships in which more than 50 percent of the capital and profits interest are effectively owned by the same persons [Code Secs. 1031(f)(3), 267(b), 707(b)(1)].

Exceptions to the Two-Year Rule

The two-year disposition period does not apply, and therefore nonrecognition is allowed, in the three following situations:

- The disposition occurs after the earlier of the death of the taxpayer or death of the related person.
- The disposition occurs in a compulsory or involuntary conversion if the like-kind exchange occurred before the threat of such conversion.
- Neither the exchange nor the disposition had avoidance of federal income tax as a principal purpose [Code Sec. 1031(f)(2)].

The related party rules were drafted in order to deny nonrecognition treatment for transactions in which related parties make like-kind exchanges of high basis property for low basis property in anticipation of the sale of the low basis property. The legislative history underlying the provision states that "if a related party exchange is followed shortly thereafter by a disposition of the property, the related parties have, in effect, cashed out of the investment, and the original exchange should not be accorded nonrecognition treatment."[54]

The IRS has concluded that a sale more than two years after related parties exchanged like-kind properties tax-free under Code Sec. 1031 will not trigger gain recognition under the related party rule of Code Sec. 1031(f) because the rule only reaches sales within two years.[55]

> **Example 6-24:** Robert owned a factory building worth $1 million in Newfield County, with a basis of $250,000. His brother, Gene, owned a factory in Greene County. Gene's factory was also worth $1 million, but its basis was $700,000. Robert and Gene exchanged factories in a tax-free exchange. Thirteen months later, Gene sold his factory for $1 million. Gene is taxed on his $300,00 gain. Robert also must pay tax on $750,000 gain. Robert's basis in the factory he owns becomes $1 million.

Both the IRS and the Tax Court have invoked the Code Sec. 1031(f)(4) anti-abuse rule to disallow an indirect exchange between related parties, in which a third-party qualified intermediary (QI) is used in a series of steps to avoid a direct exchange between related

[54] H.R. Rep. No. 247, 101st Cong. 1st Sess. 1341 (1989).

[55] FSA 200137003 (May 10, 2001).

parties that would result in gain recognition under Code Sec. 1031(f)(1). In Rev. Rul. 2002-83,[56] the IRS concluded that a taxpayer who transferred relinquished property to a qualified intermediary in exchange for replacement property formerly owned by a related party was not entitled to nonrecognition treatment under Code Sec. 1031(a) because, as part of the transaction, the related party received cash or other nonlike-kind property for the replacement property.

The transaction was structured to allow the related parties to, in effect, sell the property transferred to the third party and receive cash, while minimizing their gain by first transferring it to the related party with a higher basis.

Courts Rule Against Deferred Related Party Like-Kind Exchanges

In several situations that involve related-party like-kind exchanges, the IRS and the courts concluded that the exchanges did not qualify for nonrecognition treatment because the taxpayers failed to prove that tax avoidance was not the principal purpose of the exchanges under Code Sec. 1031(f).

In Chief Counsel Advice 201013038,[57] the IRS concluded that a taxpayer's transactions, which were structured to avoid Code Sec. 1031(f)'s restrictions on exchanges between related parties interposed a QI to structure the transaction as an exchange between unrelated parties. In reality, however, the taxpayer had a tax avoidance purpose, which was to shift tax basis between two properties.

In *Ocmulgee Fields, Inc.*,[58] the Tax Court concluded that a deferred like-kind exchange of real property involving a corporation, a qualified intermediary and a limited liability company (LLC) that were related to the corporation did not qualify for nonrecognition of gain treatment under Code Sec. 1031 because the corporation failed to prove that tax avoidance was not the principal purpose of the exchange under Code Sec. 1031(f). The Tax Court found that although the corporation may not have had a prearranged plan to involve a related party, it failed to prove the absence of a tax-avoidance purpose since the corporation's deemed exchange with the related LLC resulted in a reduction of taxable gain and a lower applicable tax rate on the gain.

In *Teruya Brothers Ltd.*,[59] the Court of Appeals for the Ninth Circuit concluded that a taxpayer could not defer gain on its exchange of properties through a qualified intermediary that sold the properties and bought replacement properties from a related party. The taxpayer's interposition of a qualified intermediary was designed, said the court, to circumvent the Code Sec. 1031(f)(1) limitations. According to the court, the economic substance of the transactions was to engage in a tax-free cashout of the taxpayer's investments in the replacement properties with a related person ending up with the cash proceeds. In the absence of any explanation by the taxpayer for structuring the transactions as it did, the court concluded that the taxpayer did so only to avoid the related party rules found in Code Sec. 1031(f) rules. Consequently, the taxpayer could not defer the gains that it realized on the exchanges.

---

[56] Rev. Rul. 2002-83, 2002-2 CB 927.

[57] LTR 201013038 (Jan. 28, 2010).

[58] *Ocmulgee Fields, Inc.*, 132 TC 105, Dec. 57,777 (2009), *aff'd*, CA-11, 2010-2 USTC ¶50,565.

[59] *Teruya Bros. Ltd.*, 124 TC 45, Dec. 55,924 (2005), *aff'd*, CA-9, 2009-2 USTC ¶50,624, *cert. denied*, 2/22/10.

▶ **PRACTICE POINTER:** Taxpayers can avoid the consequence that occurred in *Teruya* by maintaining detailed records and memoranda documenting the business reasons for engaging in a multiparty exchange involving related parties. Taxpayers need to be able to prove the absence of federal tax avoidance motives. This can only be accomplished by valuations of the property involved in the businesses exchanged. In addition, taxpayers should be careful not to dispose of the property within the two-year period.

Form 8824 Questions Taxpayers About Related Party Exchange

Form 8824, *Like-Kind Exchanges,* which is used to report like-kind exchanges, asks taxpayers whether the exchange of property "involved a related party, either directly or indirectly (such as through an intermediary)?" If so, taxpayers are required to answer whether either party disposed of the exchanged property within two years. If there is a disposition within two years both related parties must forfeit any benefits of Code Sec. 1031 unless the disposition occurs after death of either of the related parties, was a Code Sec. 1033 involuntary conversion, or the taxpayer can establish to the satisfaction of the IRS that neither the exchange nor the disposition had a principal purpose of tax avoidance.

.11 Basis Implication of Like-Kind Exchange

Your basis in the property received in a like-kind exchange is generally determined by the basis in the property you transferred.

Example 6-25: You exchanged a parking garage having an adjusted basis of $100,000 for another parking garage. The fair market value of both properties is $200,000. The basis of your new parking garage is the same as your basis in the old parking garage ($100,000).

If you also receive unlike property or money in addition to like-kind property, you have taxable gain, but only up to the sum of the money and the fair market value of the other property received. No loss can ever be deducted under these circumstances.

Example 6-26: You exchanged a vacant lot which cost you $100,000, for $40,000 and another vacant lot with a fair market value of $120,000. Since the $60,000 gain is recognized only to the extent of the cash received, you will recognize only $40,000 as taxable income. Your basis for the new lot will be $100,000 (the cost of the old lot ($100,000), minus the cash received ($40,000) plus recognized gain of $40,000.

You can subtract exchange expenses from the consideration you receive to figure the amount you realized on the exchange. You can also add them to the basis of the like-kind property you receive. Exchange expenses include your closing costs, such as brokerage commissions, attorney fees, and deed preparation fees. If you receive cash or unlike property in addition to the like-kind property and realize a gain on the exchange, subtract the expenses from the cash or fair market value of the unlike property. You can then use the net result to figure your gain.

.12 Tax Treatment of Income Earned on Funds Used During Deferred Like-Kind Exchanges

Taxpayers engaging in deferred like-kind exchanges and escrow holders, trustees, qualified intermediaries, and others that hold the funds during like-kind exchanges need to be aware of the tax treatment of income earned on escrow accounts, trusts, and other funds used during these exchanges.

In general, the exchange funds are treated as a demand loan from a taxpayer to an exchange facilitator (as defined below) unless all earnings attributable to the taxpayer's exchange funds are paid to him under the terms of the agreement. Reg. § 1.468B-6(c) provides that money held by an exchange facilitator in a deferred exchange is treated as loaned by the taxpayer to the exchange facilitator and the exchange facilitator must take into account all items of income, deduction, and credit (including capital gains and losses) attributable to the exchange funds.

The regulations define exchange funds as any relinquished property, cash, or cash equivalent that secure an obligation of the transferee to transfer replacement property, or proceeds from a transfer of relinquished property held in a qualified escrow account, qualified trust, or other escrow account, trust, or fund in a deferred exchange [Reg. § 1.468B-6(b)(2)]. An exchange facilitator is a qualified intermediary (QI), transferee, escrow holder, trustee, or other party that holds exchange funds for a taxpayer in a deferred exchange pursuant to an escrow, trust, or exchange agreement [Reg. § 1.468B-6(3)].

If the exchange funds are treated as loaned by the taxpayer to the exchange facilitator, interest is generally imputed to the taxpayer under Code Sec. 7872, unless the exchange facilitator pays sufficient interest. The exchange facilitator has income from the imputed interest and offsetting deductions for the deemed paid interest.

Exemption for Small Facilitators

Reg. § 1.7872-5(b)(16) provides an exemption from Code Sec. 7872 for exchange facilitator loans that do not exceed $2 million and the duration of the loan is six months or less.

Interest Rate

Reg. § 1.7872-16(d) provides a special annual federal rate (AFR) that is the investment rate on a 13-week (generally 91-day) Treasury bill. Because the short-term AFR may be lower than the 91-day rate, taxpayers may apply the lower of the two when testing for sufficient interest under Code Sec. 7872. A transition period is also provided to allow exchange facilitators time to make required changes to accounting, control and reporting systems and to revise exchange agreements.

.13 Reporting Requirements

The like-kind exchange must be reported in the year in which the like-kind property is transferred. If you have exchanged capital assets, you report the exchange on Schedule D, Form 1040. If you have exchanged business property, you report the exchange on Form 4797, *Sales of Business Property.* You must also file Form 8824, *Like-Kind Exchanges* as a supporting statement for both Schedule D and Form 4797.

.14 Practice Pointer for Like-Kind Exchanges

Nonrecognition treatment for like-kind exchanges occurs automatically. You do not elect like-kind exchange deferral treatment. It is mandatory if the requirements are satisfied. The IRS watches these like-kind exchanges carefully to ensure that they are not merely disguised sales or tax avoidance schemes dreamed up by clever taxpayers. To qualify for tax deferral, the sale and repurchase must look and feel like an exchange. If the transaction becomes the subject of IRS scrutiny and ends up being litigated, the courts generally look for the following characteristics in order to determine whether a like-kind exchange occurred:

- You must show that you intended to execute a like-kind exchange and that you had no intent to sell property transferred in exchange;
- Your actions must be consistent with your expressed intent;
- You must show that you satisfied all conditions required for a like-kind exchange;
- The contracts providing for the necessary series of transfers must be interdependent;
- You must receive no cash proceeds from the sale of the first property; and
- The court must be convinced that an integrated plan for an exchange of like-kind property was conceived and implemented.
- Because no extensions are granted to taxpayers who are unable to identify replacement property within 45 days of the first settlement or to taxpayers who are unable to settle within 180 days, you should have located the replacement property before you close on the relinquished property.
- The seller of the relinquished property should not receive cash or other property that would cause the transaction to lose its tax-free characterization. Be sure that the form of security arrangement qualifies under one of the IRS safe harbors. In addition, consider the use of an intermediary to hold any unlike money or property you receive. The intermediary may cost you more but is the only way to be sure that the deal passes muster.
- If you engage in a like-kind exchange with a related party be sure that both of you refrain from selling or otherwise disposing of the properties you acquired in the exchange for at least 2 years from the date of the last transfer of property that was part of the like-kind exchange.

¶6055 "BOOT" AND DEPRECIATION RECAPTURE IN LIKE-KIND EXCHANGE

Boot is money or non-like-kind property that is transferred along with an exchange. Relief from a mortgage obligation on the property transferred can also constitute boot [¶ 6060]. The giving or receiving of boot can result in the recognition of gain (and tax to pay) in an otherwise nontaxable exchange [Reg. § 1.1031(b)-1(a)]. Boot also affects the basis of the property acquired.

In a deferred exchange, the party who first relinquishes property will receive interest or a growth factor that represents appreciation in the relinquished property. This interest is taxable income. It is not, however, considered boot and, therefore, does not affect basis.

.01 Exchange with Boot Given

If a taxpayer gives boot, the basis in the acquired property is the same as the basis of the property given (adjusted to the exchange date), increased by (1) basis in any boot given, and (2) gain recognized. The taxpayer's basis in the acquired property is decreased by any money received and any loss recognized on property not qualifying for exchange treatment that is transferred as part of the exchange [Reg. § 1.1031(d)-1].

Example 6-27: Mr. Henry exchanged a delivery truck with a $6,000 adjusted basis plus $8,000 cash for a newer truck worth $16,000. Henry has a realized gain of $2,000. However, none of it is recognized because the transaction qualifies as a like-kind exchange of business property. His basis in the new truck is $14,000 ($6,000 + $8,000).

Suppose the boot you give is non-like-kind property, rather than cash. In that case, you recognize gain or loss to the extent the non-like-kind property's fair market value differs from its basis.

NOTE: Only loss attributable to the non-like-kind property is recognized. Loss on the like-kind property exchanged is not deductible.

Example 6-28: Same facts as Example 6-28, except Mr. Henry gives up stock worth $8,000 instead of cash. If his basis in the stock is $7,000, he recognizes a gain of $1,000. His basis in the new truck is still $14,000 ($6,000 + $7,000 + $1,000). Now assume Henry's basis in the stock is $9,000. He has a recognized loss of $1,000, but his basis in the new truck remains $14,000 ($6,000 + $9,000 – $1,000).

.02 Exchange with Boot Received

A taxpayer recognizes gain to the extent he or she receives boot. On the other hand, the taxpayer doesn't recognize loss in a like-kind exchange on property exchanged for like-kind property [Code Sec. 1031(b), (c); Reg. § 1.1031(b)-1(a), -1(c)].

Cash Boot

If the boot received is entirely money, the taxpayer's basis in the property acquired is his or her basis in the property transferred (adjusted to the exchange date) decreased by the money received and increased by the amount of gain recognized.

Example 6-29: Ms. Graham exchanges investment real estate with an adjusted basis of $40,000 for similar property with a fair market value of $60,000 plus $10,000 cash. She recognizes $10,000 of the gain. Graham's basis in the new property is $40,000 ($40,000 – $10,000 + $10,000).

Example 6-30: Same facts as Example 6-30, except Graham's adjusted basis in the property she is giving up is $75,000. She realizes a nondeductible $5,000 loss. Her basis in the new property is $65,000 ($75,000 – $10,000).

Noncash Boot

If a taxpayer receives non-like-kind property as boot, the taxpayer's basis must be apportioned between the various properties acquired. Each non-like-kind property's basis is equal to its fair market value.

> **Example 6-31:** Ms. Merkel exchanges a machine she uses in her business with an adjusted basis of $8,000 for a similar machine having a fair market value of $9,000, $1,000 in cash and a television set for her home. The television has a fair market value of $500. Merkel has a realized gain of $2,500. She recognizes $1,500 of it—the cash and value of the television. Her combined basis in the machine and television is $8,500 ($8,000 – $1,000 + $1,500). The television is assigned a basis of $500, its fair market value. That leaves $8,000 to be apportioned as the machine's basis.

Boot as Liabilities Assumed

Taxable boot includes relief from liabilities. Reg. § 1.1031(d)-2 permits a taxpayer to use a netting concept to determine whether liabilities have been relieved. The taxpayer's liabilities that are assumed or taken "subject to" by the other party to the exchange may be offset against liabilities encumbering the replacement property or taken subject to by the taxpayer. Liabilities of the taxpayer encumbering the relinquished property also may be offset by cash given by the taxpayer to the other party. If the debt secured by the property is nonrecourse liability, the taxpayer will recognize gain on a foreclosure to the extent that the taxpayer's adjusted basis in the property is less than the outstanding principal amount of the debt. If the debt is a recourse liability, however, the amount of recognized gain is limited by the fair market value of the property. In this case, gain is equal to fair market value minus the tax basis of the property foreclosed on. To the extent that the principal amount of the debt exceeds the fair market value of the property, the excess is treated as cancellation of debt (COD) income.

.03 Depreciation Recapture in Like-Kind Exchanges

Exchange of Code Sec. 1245 Property

Section 1245 property is often exchanged in a like-kind exchange and the tax consequences of a transfer of this type of property must be carefully considered. Code Sec. 1245 property is defined as depreciable property that is either : (a) personal property; (b) certain tangible property with an adjusted basis in which there are reflected adjustments for depreciation or amortization for a period in which the property was used in connection with the manufacturing, production or extraction or of furnishing transportation, communications, electrical energy, gas, water, or sewage disposal services; (c) so much of real property that has an adjusted basis in which there are reflected adjustments for amortization; (d) a single purpose agricultural or horticultural structure; (e) a storage facility used in connection with the distribution of petroleum or any primary product of petroleum; or any railroad grading or tunnel bore [Code Sec. 1245(a)(3)].

If Section 1245 property is exchanged for Section 1245 like-kind property and boot, the amount of the ordinary income realized by the taxpayer will not exceed the sum of the amount of gain otherwise recognized on the like-kind exchange (because money or other property is received), plus the fair market value of any property received in the exchange which is not Code Sec. 1245 property and which is not taken into account in determining the amount of gain recognized [Code Sec. 1245(b)(4)(B)].

Example 6-32: J acquired an office building and depreciates it under the accelerated cost recovery system. The office building has an adjusted basis of $30,000 and a fair market value of $50,000. J exchanges this office building for another office building worth $50,000 in a transaction qualifying as a like-kind exchange. Ordinary income is not recaptured under Code Sec. 1245 because no boot is received.

Any gain recognized in addition to the portion characterized as ordinary income is characterized according to the property transferred.

Example 6-33: K acquired an office building and depreciates it under the accelerated cost recovery system. The building has an adjusted basis of $30,000 and a fair market value of $50,000. K exchanges the office building for $10,000 in cash and another office building worth $40,000. If K had taken $10,000 in cost recovery deductions, the $10,000 gain he would have recognized would be treated as ordinary income. If he had taken $5,000 in cost recovery deductions, $5,000 of the gain would be ordinary income and 5,000 would receive quasi-capital gain treatment under Code Sec. 1231.

The basis of the acquired Section 1245 property equals the basis of the exchanged Section 1245 property. However, if a taxpayer receives Section 1245 property and non-Section 1245 property in a like-kind exchange, the basis, adjusted for gain (or loss), is first allocated to the non-Section 1245 property received to the extent of its fair market value and the balance is allocated to the Section 1245 property received [Reg. § 1.1245-5(a)].

Example 6-34: A exchanges Section 1245 property with an adjusted basis of $100,000 for like-kind Section 1245 property with a fair market value of $90,000 and unlike property with a fair market value of $35,000. Gain of $25,000 is recognized since unlike property was received. The basis of the property acquired by A in the exchange is $125,000 ($100,000 adjusted basis of the transferred property plus $25,000 gain recognized), of which $35,000 (fair market value) is allocated to the unlike property and the remaining $90,000 is allocated to the acquired like-kind property [Reg. § 1.1245-5(a)(2), Ex.].

Exchange of Section 1250 Property

Section 1250 property is defined as any depreciable real property other than Section 1245 property. This includes all intangible real property (such as leases of land), buildings and their structural components, and all tangible real property except Section 1245 property [Code Sec. 1250(c)]. Section 1250 property is often exchanged in a like-kind exchange and the tax consequences of a transfer of this type of property must be carefully considered.

When Section 1250 properties are exchanged in a like-kind exchange, any gain recognized is characterized as ordinary income to the extent of the greater of:

- The amount of gain recognized on the disposition as a result of the receipt of money or other property (determined without regard to Code Sec. 1250); or
- The amount of gain which, if not for Code Sec. 1250(d)(4) would have been taken into account under Code Sec. 1250(a), over the fair market value (or cost, in the case of a transaction described in Code Sec. 1033(a)(2)) of the Section 1250 property received [Code Sec. 1250(d)(4)(A)].

Basis adjustments must also be considered in an exchange of Section 1250 properties. These basis rules are identical to those discussed above for Section 1245 property.

.04 MACRS Property Acquired in Like-Kind Exchange

The modified accelerated cost recovery system (MACRS) is mandatory for most tangible depreciable property placed in service after December 31, 1986, unless transitional rules apply or the property is otherwise excluded [Code Sec. 168]. Under MACRS, the cost of eligible property is recovered over a 3-, 5-, 7-, 10-, 15-, 20-, 27.5-, 31.5-, or 39 years period, depending upon the type of property by using statutory recovery methods and conventions [Code Sec. 168(d) and (e)]. For detailed discussion of MACRS, see Ch. 11.

When MACRS property is acquired in a like-kind exchange and the recovery period has not yet been exhausted, the taxpayer acquiring the MACRS property must continue depreciating the property over the remaining recovery period of the relinquished MACRS property using the same depreciation method and convention as the exchanged property. This rule only applies if the recovery period and the depreciation method are the same for both the replacement and relinquished property. Different rules apply where the recovery period and/or depreciation methods are different [Reg. § 1.168(i)-6(c)(4)]. When applying the IRS table percentages to the depreciable exchanged basis, the recovery year for the year of replacement is the same as the recovery year of the disposition year. If the replacement MACRS property has a longer recovery period, or a less-accelerated depreciation method, the general rule will not apply. In that case, the replacement property is treated as placed in service when the relinquished property was placed in service. To the extent basis in the acquired property exceeds the basis in the property given up, the acquired property is treated as newly purchased MACRS property. Any excess basis in the new MACRS property over the adjusted basis in the old MACRS property is treated as newly purchased MACRS property [Reg. § 1.168(i)-6(d)(1)].

Deferred Exchanges

If a taxpayer disposes of MACRS property before acquiring replacement property, the taxpayer may not claim depreciation deductions on the relinquished MACRS property for the period between disposal and acquisition [Reg. § 1.168(i)-6(c)(5)(iv)(A)].

Replacement Prior to Disposition

If replacement property is acquired and placed in service before the MACRS property is disposed of, the taxpayer may depreciate the unadjusted depreciable basis of the replacement property until the original MACRS property is relinquished [Reg. § 1.168(i)-6(d)(4)].

Transactions Involving Land

Land is never depreciated, even if acquired in a like-kind exchange or involuntary conversion where the relinquished property was depreciable [Reg. § 1.168(i)-6(d)(2)].

Automobiles

If the replacement vehicle is a passenger automobile subject to Section 280F(a) depreciation limits, the depreciation limitation is based on the date the replacement vehicle is put in service by the acquiring taxpayer. In allocating the depreciation limitation, the depreciation allowance for the exchanged basis in the replacement vehicle generally is limited to the amount that would have been allowed under Code Sec. 280F(a) for the relinquished vehicle if the transaction had not occurred.

Bonus First-Year Depreciation

In general, the exchanged basis (carryover basis) and the excess basis (if any) of the replacement property are eligible for the additional first-year depreciation deduction under Code Sections 168(k) and 1400L(b). However, for 50-percent bonus depreciation property and certain Liberty Zone property placed in service, then disposed of in a like-kind exchange or involuntary conversion in the same tax year, the exchanged MACRS property is ineligible for additional first-year depreciation.

Election Out

Taxpayers may elect not to apply the regulations if the rules are too burdensome or depreciation components are too difficult to track. However, if a taxpayer elects not to apply the regulations, the taxpayer must treat the entire basis (both the exchanged and excess basis) of the replacement MACRS property as being placed in service by the acquiring taxpayer at the time of replacement and the adjusted depreciable basis of the relinquished MACRS property as being disposed of at the time of disposition. The election is made separately for each like-kind exchange or involuntary conversion by the due date (including extensions) of the taxpayer's return for the year of replacement.

¶6060 EXCHANGE OF MORTGAGED PROPERTY IN LIKE-KIND EXCHANGE

.01 Relieved Debt Treated as Cash

The taxpayer recognizes gain only to the extent of money or other property received in a like-kind exchange. Reg. § 1.1031(b)-1(c) provides that consideration in the form of an assumption of liabilities (or a transfer subject to a liability) is to be treated as "other property or money." Where each party either assumes a liability of the other party or acquires property subject to a liability, then, in determining the amount of other property or money, consideration given in the form of an assumption of liabilities (or the receipt of property subject to a liability) is offset against consideration received in the form of an assumption of liability (or transfer subject to a liability).

If you transfer mortgaged property in a tax-free exchange, the mortgage debt you are relieved from paying is treated as cash received in figuring your recognized gain. This is true whether the transferee takes the property subject to a mortgage or assumes personal liability for it.

The amount of boot you give on the exchange, whether it be money, property or a receipt by you of property subject to liabilities or mortgages, reduces the amount of liabilities or mortgages that are treated as boot you receive on the exchange. However, if you assume or take subject to a mortgage that exceeds the mortgage the other party assumes or takes subject to, the excess does not reduce any other boot received by you [Code Sec. 1031(d); Reg. § 1.1031(d)-2].

Example 6-35: Mr. Roe owns a ranch with an adjusted basis of $50,000 and subject to a $10,000 mortgage. He exchanges it for a farm worth $65,000, the transferee assuming the mortgage. Roe realizes a gain of $25,000, but only $10,000 of the gain is recognized (the mortgage is treated as cash):

Value of property received	$65,000
Mortgage on property exchanged	10,000
Total consideration received	$75,000
Less: Adjusted basis of property transferred	50,000
Gain realized	$25,000

Example 6-36: The facts are the same as in Example 6-36, except that the farm Mr. Roe received is subject to a mortgage of $6,000 which he assumed. Roe realized a gain of $19,000 on the exchange, but only $4,000 of that gain is recognized. The gain is computed as follows:

Value of property received	$65,000
Mortgage on property exchanged, assumed by transferee	10,000
	$75,000
Less: Mortgage on property received	$6,000
Total consideration received	$69,000
Less: Adjusted basis of property transferred	$50,000
Gain realized	$19,000

The gain is recognized to the extent of $4,000 ($10,000 mortgage assumed by transferee less $6,000 mortgage assumed by transferor Roe).

Example 6-37: B has an adjusted basis in real property X of $40,000. On May 17, 2008, B transfers real property X, which is encumbered by a mortgage of $ 30,000 and has a fair market value of $100,000, to C with C assuming the $30,000 mortgage on real property X. On July 5, 2008, C transfers real property V, which is encumbered by a $20,000 mortgage and has a fair market value of $ 90,000, to B with B assuming the mortgage. The consideration received by B in the form of the liability assumed by C ($30,000) is offset by the consideration given by B in the form of the liability assumed by B ($20,000), and the net amount, $ 10,000, is treated as "money or other property." Thus, B recognizes gain under Code Sec. 1031(b) in the amount of $10,000 [Reg. § 1.1031(k)-1(j)(3), Ex.5].

If the transfer is to a controlled corporation, the mortgage is not considered boot received by the transferor in determining his recognized gain, unless the transaction lacks a real business purpose or is merely to avoid tax [Code Sec. 357(b); Reg. § 1.357-1(c)]. See also ¶ 6075.

.02 Properties with Liabilities Netted in Partnership Like-Kind Exchange

In Rev. Rul. 2003-56,[60] the IRS concluded that liabilities should be netted when a partnership enters into a like-kind exchange in which properties with liabilities are transferred in one year and received in the next.

¶6065 EXCHANGE OF INSURANCE POLICIES

Individuals carry over their basis and recognize no gain or loss on the exchange of:

- A life insurance contract for another life insurance contract or for an endowment or annuity contract;
- An endowment insurance contract for another endowment insurance contract providing regular payments starting at a date not later than the starting date under the old contract, or for an annuity contract; and
- One annuity contract for another, whether or not the issuer of the contract received in exchange is the same as the issuer of the original contract [Code Sec. 1035(a); Reg. § 1.1035-1]. See Ch. 5 and ¶ 6105 for further discussion of annuity contracts.

NOTE: If you receive cash or other property in addition to the new contract, the rules in ¶ 6055 apply.

You recognize gain or loss, and adjust your basis accordingly, on an exchange of (1) an endowment or annuity contract for a life insurance contract and (2) an annuity contract for an endowment contract [Reg. § 1.1035-1(c)].

.01 Exchange of Second-to-Die and Single Life Policies

Tax-free exchange treatment is not available if the life insurance policies exchanged do not relate to the same insured [Code Sec. 1035(a); Reg. § 1.1035-1]. The IRS has concluded that the exchange of single life policies for second-to-die policies will not be tax-free because the policies received in the exchange do not relate to the same insured, as required in the Regulations.[61] In addition, new reporting requirements are imposed by the IRS on the insurance companies when exchanges do not relate to the same insured. The IRS states that the life insurance company must report the exchanges to the policyowner, the IRS, and the issuer of the insurance policy received in the exchange.

A recent trend in life insurance planning is the second-to-die or survivorship life insurance policy. Here's how it works. Instead of buying individual life insurance for

---

[60] Rev. Rul. 2003-56, 2003-1 CB 985.

[61] LTR 9542037 (July 21, 1995).

either a husband or wife, for example, you purchase life insurance covering both spouses with the policy only paying a benefit after the second spouse dies. The premiums payable for second-to-die policies are often lower than they would be for single life insurance policies because the death benefit on the second-to-die policy is delayed until after the second spouse dies, thus affording the insurance company more time to invest the premiums. The downside, however, is that even though the annual premiums may be smaller, they may be payable for a much longer time. Consider the following example: A 50-year old man wants to purchase a $1 million individual universal life insurance policy. His annual premium from one insurance company is $10,150. If however, he purchased a second-to-die policy covering him and his 50-year-old wife, his annual premium would be reduced to $5,070. See Ch. 29 for further discussion of second-to-die life insurance policies.

¶6070 SECURITIES FOR SECURITIES OF SAME CORPORATION

You do not recognize gain or loss on an exchange of common for common or preferred for preferred stock in the same corporation. It does not matter whether the stock is voting or nonvoting. The exchange is nontaxable whether it is between a stockholder and the corporation or between two individual stockholders [Code Sec. 1036; Reg. § 1.1036-1]. Certain exchanges between a shareholder and the corporation are treated as a reorganization [Ch. 22].

.01 Nontaxable Exchanges

Nontaxable exchanges include:

- Restricted stock for unrestricted stock in the same corporation;[62]
- Exercising the right found in corporate bond to convert it into shares of that corporation's stock;[63] However, exercising the right to convert into stock of another corporation is a taxable exchange;[64]
- Voting trust certificates turned in for common stock;[65] and
- Converting joint tenancy in corporate stock to tenancy in common; severing joint tenancy in corporate stock under partition action.[66]

.02 Taxable Exchanges

Common taxable exchanges include:

- Stock exchanged for bonds,
- Preferred stock exchanged for common, and
- Common stock of one corporation exchanged for common stock in another.

---

[62] *F.E. Clark*, CA-3, 35-1 USTC ¶ 9247, 77 F2d 89, *acq.* XIV-2 CB 266.

[63] Rev. Rul. 72-265, 1972-1 CB 222.

[64] Rev. Rul. 79-155, 1979-1 CB 153.

[65] Rev. Rul. 72-319, 1972-1 CB 224.

[66] Rev. Rul. 56-437, 1956-2 CB 507; Rev. Rul. 90-7, 1990-1 CB 153.

¶6075 TRANSFER OF PROPERTY TO CORPORATION

If a taxpayer transfers property (or money and property) to a corporation in exchange for stock in that corporation (other than nonqualified preferred stock as discussed in Code Sec. 351(g)(2) and Ch. 22), and immediately afterwards the taxpayer is in control of the corporation, the exchange is usually not taxable. This rule applies to both individuals and to groups who transfer property to a corporation. In addition, this nonrecognition rule applies to corporations being formed and to those already in existence where property is transferred solely in exchange for stock of that corporation and immediately after the exchange, the transferor(s) are in control of the corporation [Code Sec. 351(a); Reg. § 1.351-1]. If the taxpayer received any property other than stock of the corporation (i.e., boot), the taxpayer will be taxed on the boot received. See Ch. 20.

.01 Control

To be in control of a corporation, the group of investors must own, immediately after the exchange, at least 80 percent of the total combined voting power of all classes of stock entitled to vote and at least 80 percent of the outstanding shares of each class of nonvoting stock outstanding [Code Sec. 368(c); Reg. § 1.351-1(a)].

Example 6-38: Mr. Hunter owned 2,000 of the 3,000 shares of voting common stock of Homer Corporation, and 85 of the 100 shares of nonvoting preferred stock. Hunter transfers property to the corporation, in return for which the corporation gives him 7,000 shares of newly issued common stock. No gain is recognized because Hunter is now in control of the corporation. He owns 90 percent of the voting stock (9,000 of 10,000) and 85 percent of the other class of stock (85 of 100).

Example 6-39: When starting up a corporation, Mr. Whitman contributed a building worth $200,000 (his basis in it is $50,000) in exchange for 200 shares of stock, and Mr. Bloom contributed equipment worth $100,000 in exchange for 100 shares. The corporation issued no other stock at that time. No gain or loss is recognized on the transaction since Whitman and Bloom are controlling shareholders after the exchange.

The nonrecognition provision applies only to contributed "property."[67] This does not include services rendered to the corporation. Nor does it include unsecured debts and claims against the corporation for accrued but unpaid interest on a debt [Code Sec. 351(d)].

Example 6-40: Mr. Smith contributed property worth $4,000 and services worth $6,000 in exchange for 10 shares of stock with a fair market value of $10,000. If he is a controlling shareholder, Smith would owe tax on the $6,000 of stock received in exchange for services, but not on the stock he got for the property.

---

[67] Rev. Rul. 64-56, 1964-1 CB 133, as amplified by Rev. Rul. 71-564, 1971-2 CB 179.

.02 Disproportionate Exchanges

When more than one person transfers property, the stock they receive need not be in the same proportion as the property they contribute. However, the transaction will be recharacterized, according to its true nature, as though (1) the exchanges had been proportionate and (2) the shareholder who received stock of lesser value than the property transferred made a gift or paid compensation or extinguished a debt to the shareholder who received the larger amount [Reg. § 1.351-1(b)].

Example 6-41: Mr. Alexander and Mr. Benton organize a corporation with 1,000 shares of common stock. Alexander transfers property worth $10,000 in exchange for 200 shares of stock while Benton transfers property worth $10,000 to the corporation in exchange for 800 shares of stock. No gain or loss is recognized. However, Alexander is deemed to have transferred 300 shares (worth $6,000) to Benton. If Benton had worked for Alexander, the disproportionate exchange would be taxed as compensation. If, say, Benton were Alexander's son and the deemed transfer was gratuitous, it would be treated as a gift.

.03 Corporation Assumes Shareholder's Liability

The exchange is still tax-free even if the corporation assumes a liability of the transferor [Code Sec. 357(a)]. However, there are some exceptions. If the assumption of liabilities has no real business purpose or if the main purpose in the exchange is tax avoidance, the total liability is treated as a cash payment by the corporation to the transferor [Code Sec. 357(b)(1)]. In addition, if the total liabilities assumed exceeds the total of the adjusted basis of the property transferred, then the excess will be treated as a gain from the sale of the property (capital or not as the case may be) [Code Sec. 357(c)(1); Reg. §§ 1.357-1, -2]. Reason: Code Sec. 357(c) provides that contributing property with liabilities in excess of basis can trigger immediate recognition of gain in the amount of the excess is simple. The Code treats discharging a liability the same as receiving money because the taxpayer improves his economic position when he gets rid of property that is encumbered by debt.

Example 6-42: Mr. Baker transfers property with a $5,000 adjusted basis to his controlled corporation in exchange for stock worth $6,000. The corporation agrees to assume a $3,000 liability on the property and gives Baker $1,000 of cash. Thus, Baker received consideration worth $10,000. His realized gain is $5,000. But his recognized gain is $1,000 (cash received). If the exchange is tax-motivated, though, Baker's recognized gain is $4,000 (cash plus liability assumed). All or part of a recourse liability is deemed to be assumed if the transferee has agreed to, and is expected to, satisfy the liability whether or not the transferor is relieved of the liability [Code Sec. 357(d)(1)(A)]. This determination is made based on the facts and circumstances [Code Sec. 357(d)(1)(A)]. Nonrecourse liabilities are treated as assumed by the transferee of the property to which the nonrecourse liability is subject [Code Sec. 357(d)(1)(B)]. If the liability is subject to other assets not transferred, then the liability deemed assumed is reduced by the lesser of the amount of the liability that the transferred asset or the fair market value of the nontransferred assets (determined without regard to Code Sec. 7701(g)) [Code Sec. 357(d)(2)(B)].

Example 6-43: Donald Peracchi needed to contribute additional capital to his closely held corporation (NAC) to comply with local law. He therefore contributed two parcels of real that were encumbered with liabilities which exceeded Peracchi's total basis in the properties by more than half a million dollars. In an effort to avoid a tax problem under Code Sec. 357(c), Peracchi also executed a promissory note, promising to pay NAC over a million over a term of ten years at 11 percent interest. Peracchi therefore thought that the aggregate liabilities no longer exceeded the aggregate basis, and that Code Sec. 357(c) no longer triggered any gain. The court agreed with Peracchi and concluded that he had a basis of over a million dollars in the note, which was its face value. As such, the aggregate liabilities of the property contributed to NAC do not exceed its basis, and Peracchi did not recognize any gain under Code Sec. 357(c).[68] The court found that the transfer of Peracchi's note to NAC had substantial economic effect because of the possibility that the business might go into bankruptcy and have to be enforced.

.04 Exchange with Investment Company

Gain or loss is recognized if an individual diversifies his or her interests by transferring property to an investment company. An investment company is a regulated investment company, a real estate investment trust or a corporation with substantial investment property [Code Sec. 351(e); Reg. § 1.351-1(c)(1)].

.05 Basis Determination

The taxpayer's basis in the stock received is the same as the basis of the property exchanged, increased by any gain recognized on the transaction and any amount treated as a dividend, and decreased by the fair market value of any other property or money received in the exchange and any loss recognized on the exchange [Code Sec. 358(a); Reg. § 1.358-1].

Example 6-44: Mr. Trent transfers property to Sutton Corp. in exchange for its controlling stock worth $150,000. Trent's adjusted basis in the property was $100,000. His basis in the Sutton Corp. stock is $100,000.

Example 6-45: Same facts as Example 6-44, except that Sutton gives Trent $5,000 in addition to the stock. Trent has a recognized gain of $5,000 (since the money is not covered by the nonrecognition provision). His basis in the stock is still $100,000 ($100,000 basis in stock less $5,000 cash received plus $5,000 recognized gain).

If the corporation assumes a liability of the transferor, the person who transferred the property is considered to have received taxable gain up to the fair market value of the liability that was assumed. Thus, he subtracts the liability in figuring his basis [Code Sec. 358(d)(1); Reg. § 1.358-3]. Transfers of liabilities that would be deductible by the shareholder when paid (e.g., accounts payable) or of certain liquidating payments to a

---

[68] *D.J. Peracchi,* CA-9, 98-1 USTC ¶ 50,374, 143 F3d 487.

retiring partner [Ch. 24] are not counted as liabilities [Code Secs. 357(c)(3), 358(d)(2)]. If Code Sec. 357(c) gain is realized when a nonrecourse liability is assumed by the transferee corporation and all of the property to which the debt is subject is not transferred by the transferor, then the basis step-up is limited to the amount of gain that would have been recognized if only a pro rata portion of the liability were assumed [Code Sec. 362(d)(2)].

Example 6-46: Mr. Smith transferred property with an adjusted basis of $500,000 and subject to a mortgage of $100,000 to a controlled corporation in a nontaxable exchange. He received stock worth $550,000. His basis for the stock is $400,000 (the $500,000 adjusted basis of the property transferred less the $100,000 mortgage).

.06 Corporation's Basis

The corporation's basis in the property acquired from a controlling shareholder is the shareholder's basis in the property, increased by any gain recognized by the shareholder on the exchange [Code Sec. 362(a)].

.07 Filing Requirement

Both the shareholder and controlled corporation taking part in the exchange must file a statement describing the pertinent facts with their income tax returns for the year of the exchange [Reg. § 1.351-3].

IDENTIFICATION OF BASIS

¶6080 ALLOCATING BASIS

Generally, when an individual purchases various kinds of property for a lump sum, his or her cost or other basis must be allocated among the assets in order to calculate depreciation deductions and gain or loss upon the disposition of each asset. The gain or loss on each part is the difference between the selling price and the basis allocated to that part [Reg. § 1.61-6]. The allocation is usually made according to the relative value of each part in relation to the value of the whole.[69] If allocation is impractical, no gain or loss is realized until the cost of the entire property is recovered.[70]

[69] *C.D. Johnson Lumber Corp.*, 12 TC 348, Dec. 16,853 (1949), *acq.* 1950-2 CB 3.

[70] *W. Atwell*, 17 TC 1374, Dec. 18,801 (1952), *acq.* 1953-1 CB 6.

.01 Corporate Securities Bought as a Unit

If a taxpayer purchases different classes of stock for a single lump-sum price, the lump sum is allocated in proportion to each security's respective value at the time of acquisition.[71] For a block of the same securities, the allocation is pro rata.[72]

If no reasonably accurate method of allocation exists, the purchased securities are treated as a unit for computing gain or loss. In particular, this would tend to occur with securities that are required to be resold as a unit.[73]

.02 Mixed-Use Property

When property is put to both personal and business/investment use, a basis allocation is required upon the disposition of the property. If property is sold or traded, the amount received for it is also allocated in the same manner. Thus, the disposition is treated as two separate transactions. As a result, the taxpayer may have a gain on the depreciable business/investment portion with an adjusted basis, and a loss on the nondepreciable personal part of the property with a cost basis. This occurs most commonly when a taxpayer uses a car for both business and personal driving, uses part of a home as a business office or owns a multifamily home (part of which is used as a personal residence and the remainder as rental property).

> **NOTE:** In the case of a trade-in, a special rule applies in figuring the basis in the new car. You must recalculate your basis in the old car as if it had been used 100 percent for business—and depreciated accordingly. This increases the unrecognized gain on the trade-in and lowers the basis for your new car. The new car's basis is the purchase price less your unrecognized gain on the trade-in.

A gain recognized on the personal part is taxable, but a loss on that part is not deductible [Code Sec. 165(c)].

> **Example 6-47:** Ms. Robinson purchased a car for $10,000. She used it 75 percent for business driving. Thus, her cost basis in the business portion of the car is $7,500, and her cost basis in the personal portion is $2,500. She has claimed $7,500 of depreciation deductions on account of business use. Therefore, her adjusted basis in the business portion is zero. Robinson sells the car for $2,000—$1,500 allocable to the business portion of the car and $500 to the personal portion. She has a $1,500 taxable gain on the disposition of the business part of the car and a $2,000 nondeductible loss ($2,500 basis less $500 sales proceeds) on the personal part.

> **Example 6-48:** Same facts as Example 6-47, except that Robinson trades in the car towards a new one selling for $12,000. She receives a $2,000 trade-in allowance and pays $10,000 in cash. New result: Assuming Robinson uses the

---

[71] *Meredith Broadcasting Co.*, CtCls, 69-1 USTC ¶9126, 186 CtCls 1, 405 F2d 1214; *C. Hemphill*, 25 BTA 1351, Dec. 7553.

[72] *Bancitaly Corp.*, 34 BTA 494, Dec. 9398, *nonacq.* 1943 CB 27; *Santa Maria Glass Co.*, 10 BTA 142.

[73] *H.E. Collin*, CA-6, 1 USTC ¶401, 32 F2d 753.

new car at least 75 percent for business, the trade-in is a tax-free exchange of like-kind business property. Thus, she is not taxed on the gain. However, her basis in the new car is $10,000 ($12,000 less $2,000, since depreciation on the old car is computed as if it had a 100 percent business use). The $2,000 nondeductible loss has no effect on her basis in the new car.

Example 6-49: Same facts as Example 6-47, except that Robinson uses the new car only 65 percent for business, instead of the 75 percent business use of the car she has traded in. Thus, 10 percent of the trade-in allowance is traceable to business property that is not being exchanged for like-kind property. Robinson is taxed on that portion of the gain—or $200. Her basis in the new car is $10,200 ($12,000 less $1,800 unrecognized gain).

.03 Bargain Sale to Charity

A basis allocation is required if you sell or exchange property to a qualified charitable organization for less than its fair market value. The allocation determines the amount of gain or loss on the transaction and the deductible charitable contribution [Ch. 9].

.04 Stock Splits and Dividends

The additional shares of stock you receive on account of a stock split or dividend is not a taxable event. It generally does, though, require an allocation of your basis in the original shares among all the shares you come to own [Ch. 2] [Code Sec. 307].

.05 Term Interests and Remainders

In general, when you sell a term interest (term of years, life interest, or income interest in a trust) acquired by a gift or from a decedent, your basis for determining gain or loss is zero. Thus, the entire amount you realize from selling such an interest is a gain. However, the general rules for calculating basis apply to a term interest purchased for value or sold in the same transaction as the rest of the interests in the property (e.g., you inherit real estate and sell the right to use it for a term of years and the remainder interest to two separate individuals, but at the same time). In other words, both interests get a share of your basis [Code Sec. 1001(e); Reg. § 1.1001-1].

When a property's total basis is divided between term and remainder interests, the allocation is based on the relative values of each. IRS tables [Reg. § 20.2031-7(f)] that take into account the length of the term (using life expectancies for life interests) or the passage of time until the remainder becomes a present interest are used. Purchased term interests undergo basis reductions on account of the passage of time. The cost basis is amortized over the length of the term [Reg. § 1.1014-5]. The amortization deductions can offset taxable income from the property.

Example 6-50: Ms. Patrick inherits a lifetime income interest. She sells it to Mr. Brandt for $100,000. Patrick's gain is the full $100,000 since her basis had been zero. Brandt's basis is $100,000. He recovers that basis through amortization deductions over Patrick's life expectancy. These amortization deductions offset income Brandt receives from the property. The deductions also reduce his basis.

.06 Goodwill

A special rule applies when you buy a group of assets, constituting a business, and your basis in the assets is determined by reference to the purchase price. Your basis in the goodwill—and the amount the seller is deemed to receive for it—is the excess of the purchase price over the fair market value of all the assets other than goodwill [Code Sec. 1060]. Goodwill is the value of a trade or business attributable to the expectancy of continued customer patronage. This expectancy may be due to the name or reputation of a trade or business or any other intangible factor [Reg. § 1.1060-1(b)(2)(ii)].

.07 Easements

An easement is a limited right to use property (e.g., a right of way). The amount you receive for granting an easement reduces your basis in the property. If the amount you receive for the easement is more than your basis in the property, the gain is taxable.[74] If you lose all beneficial interest in the property, granting the easement is treated as a sale of the entire property.[75]

.08 Sports Franchises

The amount the buyer allocates to player contracts on a sale or exchange of a franchise cannot exceed what the seller allocates to the contracts. However, the Code presumes that this is no more than 50 percent of the total purchase price, unless a greater allocation is proven [Code Sec. 1056(d)].

¶6085 SHARES OF STOCK PURCHASED AT DIFFERENT PRICES

If you acquired shares of the same stock (including mutual funds) at different prices, and dispose of some of your holdings, you must identify which of the shares you have given up in order to determine your gain or loss. You can avoid the problem by keeping records that identify the stock sold.

If the stock is registered in your name, it can be identified by keeping a record of dates and prices by certificate numbers. If the stock certificate is in a broker's custody, or if you hold a single certificate representing stock from different lots, identification may be made by giving the broker instructions (confirmed by him or her in writing) as to which particular stock to sell [Reg. § 1.1012-1(c)]. Stock identified in this manner is deemed to be stock sold, even though the broker delivers stock certificates from a different lot.[76] When the broker is authorized to sell without your prior approval, you may identify the particular shares sold before the settlement date (usually four business days after the trade date).[77] Special rules apply to identify Treasury bonds and notes[78] [Reg. § 1.1012-1(c)(7)].

---

74 Rev. Rul. 70-510, 1970-2 CB 159.

75 *H.L. Scales*, Dec. 3614, 10 BTA 1024, *acq.* 1928-2 CB 35; Rev. Rul. 70-510, 1970-2 CB 159.

76 Rev. Rul. 61-97, 1961-1 CB 394.

77 Rev. Rul. 67-436, 1967-2 CB 266.

78 Rev. Rul. 71-21, 1971-1 CB 221; Rev. Rul. 73-37, 1973-1 CB 374.

.01 First-In, First-Out Rule

When shares of stock are sold from lots bought at different dates or prices, and the identity of lots cannot be determined, the stock sold must be charged against the earliest purchase. The first-in, first-out rule also applies to bonds [Reg. § 1.1012-1(c)].

Example 6-51: Mr. Simms bought 100 shares of Phillips Co. stock on April 30, 2003 for $10 per share and another 100 shares of Phillips Co. stock on March 1, 2013, for $20 per share. On August 1, 2013, he sold 100 shares of the stock for $21 per share. It is assumed that the sale was from the earlier purchase. Thus, he recognizes a gain of $1,100 ($21 less $10, multiplied by 100 shares).

Example 6-52: Same facts as Example 6-51, except that Simms identifies the stock he sells as the March 1, 2013 shares. He reduces his taxable gain to $100.

▶ **OBSERVATION:** Identifying the shares at the time of disposition lets you do tax maneuvering. For example, you can defer tax on a big gain by selling the shares with a higher basis first. And you can reduce the tax on that gain by giving them to a relative in a low tax bracket (e.g., a child with college tuition bills) instead of selling the shares yourself and giving them the after-tax cash. The recipient of the gift takes over your basis in the shares [¶ 6030].

.02 Stock Received in Reorganization

The first-in, first-out rule does not apply to shares of stock received in a tax-free reorganization. Here the "average cost" rule is used.[79] The basis of each new share of stock you receive in exchange is determined by dividing your total cost of the old stock by the number of new shares received. However, if the new shares you receive in a reorganization can be traced to specific old shares, the "average cost" rule does not apply. So the cost of your new shares is the adjusted cost of your old shares with which they are identified. If you receive new stock in a split-up, the first-in, first-out rule applies, unless you identify the new shares with purchases made before the split-up.[80] A split-up is defined in Ch. 22.

¶6090 MUTUAL FUND SHARES

The tax consequences of investing in mutual funds, which are also know as regulated investment companies (RICs), may be surprisingly more complex and more expensive than investing directly in individual stocks as a result of management fees and the high tax burden imposed on mutual fund shareholders. Many investors fail to realize that net investment income and realized short-term gains generated by the mutual fund and passed through to investors are taxed at the investor's ordinary income rates. For further discussion of the tax treatment of RICs, see ¶ 23,075–¶ 23,090.

---

[79] Rev. Rul. 55-355, 1955-1 CB 418.

[80] *A.D. Bloch*, CA-9, 45-1 USTC ¶ 9230, 148 F2d 452.

.01 Tax Treatment of Mutual Fund Distributions

Dividends passed through to mutual fund investors may be an ordinary dividend, a qualified dividend, a capital gain dividend, an exempt-interest dividend, or a nontaxable return of capital (nondividend distribution). The mutual fund will send the investor a Form 1099-DIV or similar statement explaining the kind of distribution received by the taxpayer.

▶ **PRACTICE POINTER:** Note that the tax rules applicable to mutual funds, which are discussed in this chapter, do not apply to mutual fund shares held in tax-deferred retirement arrangements such as IRAs, Keogh plans, 401(k) plans and other retirement plans. These retirement savings remain tax-free until they are withdrawn. If you sell, exchange or redeem mutual fund shares you will have to calculate gain or loss on the transactions. In fact, every time you write a check on your mutual fund account or withdraw cash, you are redeeming shares and must calculate a capital gain or loss reportable on your tax return. The amount of your gain or loss is equal to the amount realized from the transaction less the adjusted basis of the fund shares that you sold.

Ordinary Dividends Distributed by Mutual Funds

An ordinary dividend distributed by a mutual fund is a distribution out of its earnings and profits. Ordinary dividends received from a mutual fund must be included on the taxpayer's individual income tax return. They will typically be reported in box 1a of Form 1099-DIV or on a similar statement received from the mutual fund.

Qualified Dividends Distributed by Mutual Funds

Qualified dividends received from mutual funds will be taxed at the same lower tax rates that apply to net capital gain. For further discussion, see ¶ 6001.04 and ¶ 2080.03. To be taxed as a qualified dividend, a dividend must satisfy the following three requirements [¶ 2080]:

- The dividend must be paid by an U.S. corporation or a qualified foreign corporation;
- The dividend must not be of a type excluded by law from the definition of qualified dividend; and
- The holding period requirement must be satisfied.

Code Sec. 854(b)(1)(C) provides that the aggregate amount that may be designated by a RIC as qualified dividend income generally may not exceed the RIC's qualified dividend income for the tax year. Code Sec. 854 does not require that expenses reduce this amount. The reduced rate for distributions of qualified dividends applies to individuals who are U.S. taxpayers; it does not apply to nonresident alien individuals (unless the income is effectively connected with an U.S. trade or business).

In Rev. Rul. 2005-31,[81] the IRS addresses the designation of distributions by mutual funds and provides that the amount that may be designated as a qualified dividend does not have to be reduced by expenses. In addition, the ruling allows mutual funds to designate distributions as consisting of capital gain dividends, interest-related dividends, and short-term capital gain dividends in percentages that in the aggregate

[81] Rev. Rul. 2005-31, 2005-1 CB 1084.

exceed the total amount of the mutual fund's dividend distributions. The following example from the ruling illustrates these points.

> **Example 6-53:** RIC's taxable income for the tax year consists of $10 million of dividend income (all of which is qualified dividend income), $10 million of interest income (all of which is qualified interest income), $5 million in short-term capital gain, and $5 million of long-term capital gain. It spent $10 million in general and administrative expenses, and distributed $20 million to shareholders for that tax year. Shareholder X, a U.S. person receives $20,000, as does Shareholder Y, a nonresident alien with no income effectively connected to U.S. business. Of the $20 million distributions, no expense may be allocated to reduce net capital gains. That leaves $25 million taxable income to which $10 million in expenses are to be allocated, or 0.4 percent expense allocated to each distribution. For interest-related dividends, that computes to a $6 million distribution allocation. Under Code Secs. 854 and 871, however, the other components of the RIC's taxable income cannot be reduced by expenses for allocation purposes. As a result, the allocations for purposes of determining downstream shareholder treatment of the distribution are:
>
> - 25 percent for capital gains dividends ($5 million of $20 million)
> - 50 percent for qualified dividend income ($10 million of $20 million)
> - 30 percent for interest-related dividends ($6 million of $20 million)
> - 25 percent for short-term capital gain dividends ($5 million of $20 million)
>
> Shareholders X and Y would use different income designations, based upon the single RIC allocations. To maximize favorable tax rates, X would chose to treat 25 percent ($5,000) as capital gain, 50 percent ($10,000) as qualified dividend income (taxable at a maximum rate of 15 percent), and the remaining 25 percent ($5,000) as dividend income that is not qualified.
>
> To maximize the withholding exemption for nonresident aliens, Y would treat 25 percent ($5,000) as capital gain dividend, 30 percent ($6,000) as interest-related dividend, and 25 percent ($5,000) as short-term capital gain dividend. The 20 percent leftover ($4,000) is dividend income that is not qualified income due to the shareholder's nonresident alien status.

Capital Gain Distributions

Capital gain distributions are paid by mutual funds from their realized long-term capital gains. They are taxed as long-term capital gain regardless of how long the taxpayer has owned the shares in the mutual fund. They are therefore taxed at favorable capital gains tax rates. Code Sec. 852(b)(3) provides rules for determining the amount distributed by a RIC to its shareholders that may be treated by the shareholders as a capital gain dividend. Code Sec. 852(b)(3)(C) limits the amount a RIC may designate as a capital gain dividend to the RIC's net capital gain for the tax year, generally determined without regard to any net capital loss or net long-term capital loss attributable to transactions after October 31 of such year. Code Sec. 1222(11) defines net capital gain as the excess of the net long-term capital gain for the tax year over the net short-term capital loss for such year.

Undistributed Capital Gain

Mutual funds may allocate capital gain to shareholders but not actually pay amounts out as dividends. The mutual fund is taxed on that income. The investors must also include an allocable portion of the capital gain in his or her income. The investor's share of the undistributed capital gains will be reported on Form 2439, *Notice to Shareholder of Undistributed Long-Term Capital Gain.* Report undistributed capital gains as long-term capital gain on Schedule D (Form 1040) even though the distribution was not actually received. However, a credit may be claimed for the tax paid by the fund. The investor should attach a copy of Form 2439 to his or her return and must increase his or her basis in the mutual fund stock by the difference between the gain reported and the credit claimed for taxes paid.

Tax-Exempt-Interest Dividends

A mutual fund may pay exempt-interest dividends to its shareholders if it meets certain requirements. These dividends are paid from tax-exempt interest earned by the mutual fund. These amounts need not be included in the investor's taxable income because exempt-interest dividends retain their tax-exempt character, but may have to be reported on the tax return and may be a tax preference item subjecting the investor to the alternative minimum tax.

Nondividend Distributions

A nondividend distribution is a distribution that is not out of earnings and profits and is a return of the investor's investment or capital. A nondividend distribution reduces the investor's basis in the shares, but not below zero.

.02 Sale of Mutual Fund Shares

When an investor disposes of mutual fund shares, the gain or loss will be capital in nature and will be long-term if the investor held the shares for more than the 12 months or short-term if the shares are held for one year or less. The investor's holding period for the shares begins on the day after the date the investor purchased the shares and includes the day that the investor disposed of the shares. See Ch. 8 for discussion of tax treatment.

Long-term capital gain will be taxed at the favorable capital gains tax rates, while short-term capital gain will be taxed at ordinary income tax rates. The investor must separate out your long-term capital gains and determine the amount of tax owed on Schedule D in order to take advantage of the lower capital gains tax rates. Net capital loss from the sale of the mutual fund shares may be used to offset the investor's ordinary income, dollar-for-dollar, up to $3,000 per year with the unused capital losses carried forward to future years [Code Secs. 1211, 1212(b)].

If, at the time of the sale of the mutual fund shares, you specify to the mutual fund company which shares you want to sell, you can use your adjusted basis (cost plus add-on amounts) of those particular shares to figure taxable gain or loss. Important: You must get written confirmation of the specification from your mutual fund. If an investor fails to specify which shares are being sold, he or she can select from one of the IRS methods of determining mutual fund basis. This choice must be made on the tax return for the year of sale.

.03 Computing Basis in Mutual Fund Shares

Figuring the investor's basis in mutual fund shares can be complicated. To begin with, the investor's basis in any share is more than just the share's quoted price at the time of purchase. The investor must add in several indirect payments that are not normally considered part of the purchase price. These include load and redemption fees, reinvested dividends, and undistributed capital gains. In addition, if the investor bought shares at different times and did not sell all shares owned in a fund at one time, the investor's basis depends on identification of the exact mutual funds shares that were sold.

Determining basis becomes more complicated when you purchase and redeem shares at different times throughout the year or if you reinvest fund distributions to purchase additional fund shares. In these situations each share sold may have a different basis. In Reg. § 1.1012-1, the IRS has authorized four methods for calculating the adjusted basis of mutual fund shares.

Average Basis or Cost, Single Category Method

With this method, to figure out your average basis you divide the total amount spent on all shares held in the fund by the number of shares owned, regardless how long you have held the shares. The first-in, first-out method is used for purposes of determining the holding period only. In other words, any shares that are sold are considered to be those held the longest. You must make an election to use this method and must have acquired the shares at various times and prices. Once elected, the average basis method must be used for all accounts in the same fund. The election is made on the return for the first tax year for which the election will apply and IRS approval is required to revoke the election.

Example 6-54: You buy 100 shares of a fund on Feb. 1, 2013, at $10 per share at a total cost of $1,000. On Dec. 31, 2013, when the price of the fund is $15 per share, the fund pays a dividend of $1 per share. You reinvest the entire $100 dividend, purchasing 6.66 shares at $15 per share. On March 1, 2014, you redeem 50 shares at $18 per share. The basis of each share sold is computed by taking the total cost of all shares purchased divided by the number of shares purchased and equals $10.31 [($1,000 + $100) divided by (100 + 6.66)]. You would compute your long-term capital gain from a capital asset held for more than 12 months (taxable at a maximum rate of 15 percent) as follows:

Redemption proceeds (50 shares at $18 a share)	$900.00
Basis (50 shares at $10.31)	$515.50
Long-term capital gain	$384.50

NOTE: Capital gain distributions are distributions of the net long-term capital gains generated by the fund's sale of its assets. Capital gain distributions to fund investors are taxed as long-term capital gains, regardless of how long the investors have owned their shares in the fund. Be sure to distinguish this type of capital gain distribution from the capital gain or loss that an investor realizes when he or she sells shares in the mutual fund [Code Sec. 852(b)(3); Reg. § 1.852-4(b)(1)].

Average Basis or Cost, Double Category Method

According to this method, you divide all shares in your account at the time of each disposition and divide them into either short-term or long-term. The average basis of a share in each category is the total basis of the shares in that category divided by the number of those shares. You have the option of specifying to your agent the category from which the shares are to be sold, and the agent must confirm your specifications in writing. In the absence of your specific instructions, the oldest shares in the category will be treated as sold first. You must make an election on your return to use this method for the first tax year to which it is to apply and once made it applies to all shares in the same fund and cannot be revoked without IRS permission.

Example 6-55: Applying the same facts from the example above, using the average basis, double-category method, the 6.66 shares purchased on Dec. 31, 2013, would be the only shares in the short-term category and each of those shares would have a $15 basis, the amount paid for each share. The rest of your shares have a basis of $10. If you designate that the 50 redeemed shares come from the long-term category, your gain would be computed as follows:

Redemption proceeds (50 shares at $18)	$900
Basis (50 shares at $10)	$500
Long-term capital gain from a capital asset held for more than 12 months	$400

Specific Share Identification Method

Under this method, you can specify which particular shares you are redeeming. You therefore have the opportunity to achieve a real tax savings because you can elect to redeem the shares with the highest basis first, regardless of the order in which the shares were purchased. For example, if you bought 100 shares of ABCo at $79 a share in February and 100 shares at $100 in November, you could decide to sell the shares purchased at $100 and avoid any tax exposure. In order to use this method, the IRS says you must (1) specify in writing to the broker at the time of the sale which shares are being sold and (2) receive written confirmation of your specification from the broker within a reasonable time. Remember that this method is only for those of you who have meticulously recorded when you bought your mutual fund shares and how much you paid for them.

Example 6-56: Applying the same facts from the example above, using the specific share identification method, you would calculate your gain as follows if you told your broker to sell the most expensive shares first:

Redemption proceeds (6.66 shares at $18)	$119.88
Basis (6.66 shares at $15)	$ 99.90
Short-term capital gain	$ 19.98
Redemption proceeds (43.34 shares at $18)	$780.12
Basis (43.34 shares at $10 a share)	$433.40
Long-term capital gain	$346.72

You would have a total gain of $366.70 with $19.98 of the gain short-term (taxable as ordinary income) and $346.72 long-term capital gain from a capital asset held for more than 12 months (taxable at a maximum rate of 15 percent).

First-in, First-out (FIFO) Method

If you elect neither the average cost nor the specific identification method, you must use the FIFO method to calculate the adjusted basis of your mutual fund stock [¶ 6085]. Under the FIFO method, the shares sold are deemed to be those that you have held the longest. The FIFO method may be the simplest method to use but will result in the greatest capital gain if the shares have appreciated in value.

Example 6-57: Applying the same facts from the example above, using the FIFO method, you would treat the first shares purchased at $10 a share as the first ones sold at $18 a shares for a long-term capital gain from a capital asset taxable at a maximum rate of 20 percent as follows:

Redemption proceeds (50 shares at $18)	$900
Basis (50 shares at $10)	$500
Long-term capital gain	$400

If you compare all four methods discussed above for calculating the basis of mutual fund shares you sell, you will see that the FIFO method is the easiest method because it simply assumes that the first shares you bought are the first ones you sell. The FIFO should be avoided, however, if shares have appreciated in value because the FIFO method results in the biggest tax bill.

The specific-share method offers you the greatest flexibility and possibly the biggest tax savings because it allows you to select which shares you want to treat as being sold first. If the shares have appreciated in value, you can always specify that the shares being sold are those with the highest basis. The specific identification method provides more opportunity for tax planning provided the shares to be sold were purchased for different amounts. The investor is able to reduce or increase gain or loss by controlling the basis of the shares sold.

The mutual fund companies typically use the single category average cost method because it is easier for them to throw all the shares that you purchased into one pot and to give each share an averaged basis. This method may not, however, be the one the produces the lowest tax bill for the investor.

Keep in mind, however, that all the methods, except the FIFO method, require you to instruct brokers in writing which shares are being sold and also require the broker to confirm the sell order in writing.

Although it may initially be time-consuming to figure out which method will produce the greatest tax savings for you, we recommend that you take the time and do the math because it will pay off at tax time. If mutual fund shares have greatly appreciated in value, you can minimize your taxable gain by electing to sell your high-basis shares before selling low-basis shares. If you want to maximize taxable gain this year because you expect rates to rise or because you expect to be in higher brackets next year, reverse your strategy and elect to sell low-basis stocks before unloading the high-basis ones. In an inflationary market, the FIFO method will yield the biggest tax bill because it assumes that you sold the first shares that you bought.

The specific identification and FIFO methods both use the actual cost or other basis of the particular shares that were deemed sold in determining the gain or loss to be reported on the investor's tax return. By comparison, the single category and the double-category methods lump the actual cost or other basis of shares together to determine their average basis. The double-category method offers some choice in determining basis and holding period where the investor has some mutual fund shares held for more than a year and others for a year or less.

.04 Dividend Reinvestment

Mutual funds commonly provide an automatic dividend reinvestment option for shareholders. If you elect this option, you do not receive cash dividends. Instead, the cash you normally would have received is used to purchase additional shares of the fund. The amount of cash that you could have received is includible in taxable income. And that same amount is your basis in the new shares.

> **Example 6-58:** Ms. Dalton owns 100 shares of Growth Fund. Her basis is $21 per share. Assume Growth Fund declares a dividend of $2 per share, and Dalton had chosen automatic dividend reinvestment. The fund purchases eight additional shares for Dalton. Her basis in the 100 original shares is still $21 per share. Her basis in the eight new shares is $200 ($2 dividend × 100 shares) or $25 per share.

If you decide to automatically reinvest mutual fund dividends in more shares in the mutual fund, in lieu of receiving cash, you are not relieved of your reporting requirements. You must report the reinvested amounts in the same manner that you would report the distribution if it were received in cash.

.05 Year-End Tax Tips for Mutual Fund Investors

Before investing in a mutual fund at year-end, you ask whether the fund is about to pay a year-end capital gains or dividend distribution which will be fully taxable to the new investor as if he or she had owned shares in the mutual fund for the entire year. Mutual funds are required to distribute their net capital gains to shareholders each year. Fund managers therefore declare an annual distribution in December based on who owns shares on the *record date,* which is usually in late December. If you buy shares just before or on a fund's record date—the date that establishes you as the person to receive the upcoming distribution—you will receive a portion of the money you just invested in the form of a taxable distribution (unless your account is tax-deferred, such as an IRA). This is not wise. It is more prudent for you to avoid buying shares of a mutual fund on or before the record date because you will be taxed on the distribution even though you only owned shares in the fund a short time. Before investing call the mutual fund manager to determine the record date and then invest with confidence after that date.

.06 Frequently Asked Questions Asked by Mutual Fund Investors

Q. What is a mutual fund distribution?

A. The portfolio manager of a mutual fund buys and sells securities to satisfy the fund's investment objectives. Each time the portfolio manager sells a security from the fund's portfolio, a taxable transaction for the fund results. In addition, certain investments made by the mutual fund may generate taxable dividends. The law requires mutual funds to distribute to shareholders at least once a year, substantially all of their net investment income and net realized capital gains. These distributions are called mutual fund distributions and shareholders must pay tax on the distributions if they receive them in cash or reinvest them in additional mutual fund shares. A distribution received from a mutual fund may be an ordinary dividend, a qualified dividend, a capital gain distribution, an exempt-interest dividend, or a nontaxable return of capital.

An ordinary dividend is a distribution by a mutual fund out of earnings and profits. They are the most common type of dividend and will be taxed as ordinary income on the investor's tax return. Qualified dividends are taxed at the lower rates that apply to a net capital gain. To be a qualified dividend: (1) the dividend must have been paid by a U.S. corporation or a qualified foreign corporation; (2) the dividend must not be of a type excluded from the definition of a qualified dividend; (3) the taxpayer must hold the dividend-paying stock for at least 61 days during the 121-day period beginning 60 days before the ex-dividend date (the first day that the buyer will not be entitled to receive that dividend) [Code Sec. 1(h)(11)(B)(iii)]. When counting the number of days you held the stock, include the day you disposed of the stock, but not the day you acquired it.

Q. If I reinvest the distributions generated by my mutual fund back into my account, do I still have to pay taxes on the distribution?

A. Yes. You will have to pay tax on the distributions whether you take them as cash or reinvest them unless: (1) the dividends are from municipal bond funds which are typically exempt from federal tax and all or a portion of the income may be exempt from state and local taxation; (2) the dividends are distributions to an IRA or other tax-sheltered retirement account where income earned is not subject to tax until the money is withdrawn. Keep in mind, however, that reinvested dividends and capital gain distributions increase your original cost basis in all nonretirement accounts and therefore reduce taxes down the road.

Q. If I switch mutual fund shares from one fund to another, is this a taxable event and do I have to report any gain or loss?

A. Yes. Unless your shares are in a tax-deferred investment, exchanging or switching from one mutual fund to another mutual fund in the same or different family has tax implications. Why? Because you are essentially selling the shares from the first fund and buying shares in the second one. An exception only exists if the exchange occurred between two tax-sheltered retirement plans. When you exchange funds from one nonretirement mutual fund for those in another mutual fund, it is the same as if you sold mutual fund shares and purchased new ones. This is a taxable event.

Q. What happens when I write a check on money invested in a mutual fund?

A. When you write a check against a mutual fund, you are selling shares in the mutual fund and have created a taxable event. You must keep meticulous records of the cost basis of the shares sold as well as the fair market value of the shares on the date the check was written. This information is critical for purposes of determining your taxable gain or loss on the transaction. For this reason, you should avoid treating your mutual fund as a money market fund and therefore avoid making frequent withdrawals.

Q. How will my gain realized on the sale of mutual fund shares be taxed?

A. The tax treatment will depend on how long you held the shares in the mutual fund. In the case of a mutual fund distribution, the tax treatment depends on how long the mutual fund held the shares. Short-term gains for securities held one year or less are reported as ordinary income and are taxed at your ordinary income rate. If the securities are held more than one year, the gain will be treated as long-term capital gain.

Q. What happens if I realize a capital loss on shares held less than six months?

A. According to a special rule found in Code Sec. 852(b)(4), if a taxpayer receives a capital loss on shares held less than six months and also receive a long-term capital gain distribution from that fund while holding those shares, only the portion of the loss that exceeds the amount of the distribution can be reported as a short-term loss. The portion that is equal to or less than the distribution will be treated as a long-term capital loss. Thus, the amount of the loss that can be used to offset ordinary income is limited. Since capital gain distributions from a mutual fund are treated as long-term under Code Sec. 852(b)(3)(B), this limit in effect converts any long-term gains to short-term gain, by requiring the long-term gains to absorb the converted short-term capital loss.

Q. Do the wash-sale rules apply to the sale and purchase of my mutual fund shares?

A. Yes. The wash-sale provisions also apply to the sale and purchase of mutual fund shares. These rules were designed to prevent investors holding stock that has depreciated in value from realizing a loss for tax purposes by selling it, while at the same time maintaining the investment by immediately repurchasing the same or substantially identical stock. A wash sale occurs when you buy substantially identical stock or securities within 30 days before or after the sale of such securities. You cannot currently deduct losses on wash sales. Instead, you add the disallowed loss to your basis in the newly acquired securities, which increases your loss or reduces your gain when you eventually sell them [Code Sec. 1091; Reg. §§1.1091-1, -2]. In Notice 2013-48,[82] the IRS established a *de minimis* exception to the wash sale rules of Code Sec. 1091 for redemptions of shares in a money market fund that do not maintain a constant share price under new Securities and Exchange Commission (SEC) regulations. This safe harbor provides that if a taxpayer realizes a loss upon redemption of certain money market fund shares and the amount of the loss is not more than .5 percent of the taxpayer's basis in the shares, the IRS will not treat the loss as part of a wash sale for purposes of Code Sec. 1091.

Q. If the mutual fund realizes capital losses during the tax year, can I deduct any portion of the losses?

A. No. The capital losses realized by the mutual fund when shares are sold during the year at a loss are used to offset capital gains realized by the mutual fund during the year. Any unused capital losses are carried forward by the fund to offset future capital gains. The only capital losses that may be used by individual mutual fund investors are

[82] Notice 2013-48, IRB 2013-31.

those incurred when the investor sells shares of a mutual fund at a loss. Capital losses incurred by an investor during the year are deductible to the extent of capital gains incurred by the investor that year [Code Sec. 1211(b)(1)]. If the investor's capital losses for the year exceed his capital gains, $3,000 ($1,500 in the case of a married individual filing a separate return) of the unused capital losses may be used by the taxpayer to offset his or her ordinary income. Capital losses not used to reduce capital gains or ordinary income in the tax year in which they are sustained are carried forward indefinitely until the investor uses up the losses or dies.

Q. Do I have to pay state income tax on income earned by a mutual fund holding U.S. government securities?

A. No. States do not tax income earned on direct U.S. government obligations.

Q. What IRS forms should I expect to receive from the mutual fund company?

A. The mutual fund is obligated to send you the following forms:

- Form 1099-DIV—reports taxable income and capital gain distributions over $10; provides general reporting instructions and supplemental information, such as the percentage of a fund's income from U.S. governmental securities and, for international funds, the percentage of income and foreign tax by country of origin;
- Form 1099-B—reports gross proceeds from any sales (redemptions) of mutual fund shares, excluding money market funds, IRAs, and certain qualified retirement accounts. Form 1099-B also includes your cost basis and capital gain or loss information for shares sold in accounts opened (other than by transfer) after December 31, 1983. This information is not given to the IRS;
- Form 1099-R—reports distributions you took from any IRA or any other retirement plan you have at the mutual fund company;
- Form 5498—reports contributions made to Coverdell ESAs (formerly education IRAs) during the year. See Ch. 5 for further discussion of Coverdell ESAs;
- 1042-S—reports taxable dividends and income tax withheld on accounts owned by nonresident aliens; and
- Form 5498—reports all IRA, SEP, and SIMPLE rollover and regular contributions for the preceding tax year.

Q. How long should I keep records of my mutual fund transactions?

A. Be sure to retain all records of mutual fund purchases and reinvestments until you sell the shares and report the transaction on your federal income tax return. You will need these records to substantiate basis and purchase price of the mutual fund shares.

Q. If I sell a large number of mutual fund shares, should I be concerned about withholding or making estimated tax payments?

A. To avoid penalties, be sure to adjust your withholding or estimated tax if you sell a large number of mutual fund shares and will have a big gain to report.

SPECIAL RULES

¶6095 PROPERTY CONVERTED TO BUSINESS USE

.01 Calculating Basis

A taxpayer may deduct a loss on the disposition of personal-use property that has been converted to business or income-producing property. However, the property's basis for determining loss is the lesser of (1) the taxpayer's adjusted basis at the time of conversion or (2) the property's fair market value at the time of conversion. Appropriate adjustments are made in either case for the period after conversion to business or investment use [Reg. § 1.165-9(b)]. The lower of fair market value or adjusted basis at the time of conversion is also the basis to be used for calculating depreciation deductions [Reg. § 1.167(g)-1].

Example 6-59: Mr. Robertson purchased a house for $250,000. He used the house as his residence for five years after which time, he turned the building into an office for his accounting practice. The house was worth $235,000 at that time. Since then, he has spent $30,000 on capital improvements and claimed depreciation deductions of $33,000. Robertson's basis for calculating loss on the sale of the house is $232,000 ($235,000 + $30,000 – $33,000).

.02 Basis for Gain

The basis for figuring gain on the sale of property converted from personal use is the taxpayer's adjusted basis at the time of conversion, adjusted from the date of conversion to the date of sale. If the taxpayer realizes a gain when using the basis for loss and a loss when using the basis for gain, the taxpayer realizes neither gain nor loss.

Example 6-60: Same facts as Example 6-59. Robertson's basis for calculating gain is $247,000 ($250,000 + $30,000 – $33,000). If Robertson sells for between $232,000 and $247,000, he doesn' t have a gain or a loss.

¶6100 INVENTORY

Manufacturers and large resellers must follow the so-called uniform capitalization rules to determine their basis in inventory. This means that the basis includes direct costs and many indirect costs of bringing the property to its sellable state [Ch. 17] [Code Sec. 263A].

¶6105 SALE OR EXCHANGE OF ANNUITY CONTRACTS

.01 Taxation of Annuity Payments

Code Sec. 72(e) governs the federal tax treatment of any amount received under an annuity contract that is not received as an annuity and Code Sec. 72(e)(2) provides that such distributions generally are taxed on an income-first basis. [See ¶ 5070–¶ 5080 for further discussion of the tax treatment of annuity contracts.]

.02 Exchange of Annuity Contracts

There is no gain or loss when one annuity contract is exchanged for another annuity contract [Code Sec. 1035(a)(e)]. The legislative history of Code Sec. 1035 states that exchange treatment is appropriate for "individuals who have merely exchanged one insurance policy for another better suited to their needs." H.R. Rep. No. 1337, 83d Cong., 2d Sess. 81 (1954). The contracts exchanged must therefore relate to the same insured, and the obligee(s) under the contract received in the exchange must be the same as under the original contract [Reg. § 1.1035-1]. If, in addition to an annuity contract, a taxpayer receives other property or money in exchange for a second annuity contract, then gain is recognized to the extent of the sum of money and the fair market value of other property received, but loss is not recognized [Code Sec. 1035(d)(1)]. The IRS concluded in Rev. Rul. 72-358,[83] that a Code Sec. 1035 tax-free exchange occurred where a taxpayer who owned a life insurance contract issued by one insurance company assigned the contract before its maturity to a second insurance company in exchange for a variable annuity contract issued by the second company.

.03 Endorsing Annuity Check to Another Issuer for Second Annuity Taxable

In Rev. Rul. 2007-24,[84] the IRS concluded that tax-free exchange treatment under Code Sec. 1035(a) will not apply if a taxpayer gets a check from a life insurance company under a nonqualified annuity contract and then endorses the check to a second company as consideration for a second annuity contract. Instead, the amount received is taxed under Code Sec. 72(e). The taxpayer did not assign the contract with the first insurance company to the second insurance company, nor was there a direct transfer of the cash value from one insurance company to the other; therefore, the transaction did not qualify for nonrecognition treatment.

When an annuity contract is sold, the amounts recovered tax-free as a return of investment are subtracted from the cost basis of the annuity contract. However, the basis of the contract may not be reduced below zero [Code Sec. 1021; Reg. § 1.1021-1]. On the transfer of appreciated property for a private annuity (i.e., the buyer's unsecured promise to make specific periodic payments to the seller—annuitant for the rest of the seller's life) the investment in the contract is the transferor's basis in the property transferred; the gain (excess of the value of the annuity over the basis of the property

[83] Rev. Rul. 72-358, 1972-2 CB 473.

[84] Rev. Rul. 2007-24, 2007-1 CB 1282.

transferred) is reported ratably over the annuitant's life expectancy.[85] For a secured private annuity, the Tax Court has held that the excess of the annuity's value, as determined under the actuarial tables, over the transferor's basis in the property exchanged is includible in income in the year of exchange.[86]

NOTE: To obtain the deferral of gain benefits of a private annuity the annuity should be unsecured.

.04 Consolidation of Annuity Contracts Tax-Free Exchange

In Rev. Rul. 2002-75,[87] the IRS concluded that the consolidation of two annuity contracts issued by two different insurance companies is a tax-free Section 1035 exchange. The consolidation is accomplished by the taxpayer's assignment of one entire annuity contract to a second insurance company, which then deposits the cash surrender value of the assigned annuity contract into a pre-exiting annuity contract owned by the same taxpayer, and issued by the second insurance company.

.05 Partial Annuity Exchanges Tax-Free

In Rev. Proc. 2011-38,[88] the IRS provided that the direct transfer of a portion of the cash surrender value of an existing annuity contract for a second annuity contract will be treated as a tax-free exchange under Code Sec. 1035 if no amount (other than an amount received as an annuity for a period of 10 years or more or during one or more lives) is received during the 180 days beginning on the date of the transfer. A subsequent direct transfer of all or a portion of either contract involved in an exchange is not taken into account for purposes of determining if the subsequent transfer qualifies as a tax-free exchange under Code Sec. 1035.

In *D.E. Conway*,[89] the Tax Court held that the direct exchange by an insurance company of a portion of an existing annuity contract to an unrelated insurance company for a new annuity contract was a tax-free exchange under Code Sec. 1035. In that case, the transfer was made directly from the first insurance company to the unrelated insurance company, and none of the assets transferred in the transaction were received by the taxpayer.

In late 1999, the IRS acquiesced to the *Conway* decision holding that the direct transfer of a portion of funds from one annuity contract to another qualifies as a nontaxable exchange under Code Sec. 1035. In Rev. Rul. 2003-76,[90] the IRS provided additional details on the tax consequences of partial annuity exchanges. Under the facts in the ruling, A owns Contract B, an annuity contract issued by Company B. A is the obligee under Contract B. A contracts with Insurance Company C to issue Contract C, a new annuity contract. A assigns 60 percent of the cash surrender value of Contract B to Company C to be used to purchase Contract C. At no time during the transaction does A have access to the cash surrender value of Contract B that is transferred by Company B to Company C and used to purchase Contract C. No consideration other than the cash surrender value of Contract B that is transferred from Company B to Company C will be paid in this transaction. The terms of

---

[85] Rev. Rul. 69-74, 1969-1 CB 43.

[86] *L.G. Bell Est.*, 60 TC 469, Dec. 32,025 (1973).

[87] Rev. Rul. 2002-75, 2002-2 CB 812.

[88] Rev. Proc. 2011-38, IRB 2011-30, 66.

[89] *D.E. Conway*, 111 TC 350, Dec. 53,010 (1998), *acq.* 1999-2 CB xvi.

[90] Rev. Rul. 2003-76, 2003-2 CB 355.

Contract B are unchanged by this transaction, and Contract B is not treated as newly issued. The IRS concluded that:

1. The direct transfer by A of a portion of the cash surrender value of Contract B to Company C for Contract C is a tax-free exchange under Code Sec. 1035.
2. After the transaction, A's basis in Contract C equals 60 percent of A's basis in Contract B immediately before the exchange. After the transaction, A's basis in Contract B equals 40 percent of A's basis in Contract B immediately before the exchange.
3. After the transaction, pursuant to Code Sec. 72, A's investment in Contract C equals 60 percent of A's investment in Contract B immediately before the exchange. After the transaction, A's investment in Contract B equals 40 percent of A's investment in Contract B immediately before the exchange.

¶6110 PATENTS AND COPYRIGHTS

A taxpayer's basis in a patent or copyright includes the purchase price (if purchased), governmental fees, cost of drawings, experimental models, attorneys' fees and development or experimental expenses [Reg. § 1.167(a)-6(a)]. If research and experimental expenditures have been deducted [Ch. 12], they are not included in your basis. The time that the taxpayer spent during the inventing process is not an element of cost.

¶6115 PARTNERSHIP INTEREST

In general, a taxpayer's basis in a partnership is the amount of money plus the adjusted basis of property that the taxpayer transferred to the partnership. Adjustments are then made to take into account the partner's share of partnership income, distributions, losses and certain expenditures [Ch. 24] [Code Sec. 705].

Gain or Loss—Sale of Residence—Casualty—Theft—Condemnation

7

SALE OF RESIDENCE

General rule for sale and replacement .... ¶7001

Definition of principal residence ... ¶7005

Ownership and use requirements .... ¶7010

Rules for married homeowners ... ¶7015

Mixed-use property .... ¶7020

Reduced exclusion in special situations .... ¶7025

Involuntary conversion of principal residence .... ¶7030

CASUALTY—THEFT—CONDEMNATION

General rule for involuntary conversions .... ¶7035

Gain or loss on involuntary conversion—general rules .... ¶7040

What qualifies as replacement property .... ¶7045

Time limit on replacement .... ¶7050

How to figure gain or loss on an involuntary conversion .... ¶7055

Basis of replacement property acquired in involuntary conversion .... ¶7060

How to make the replacement and election .... ¶7065

Special benefit assessments .... ¶7070

Severance damages .... ¶7075

SALE OF RESIDENCE

If an individual sells or exchanges his or her principal residence, regardless of his or her age, the individual can exclude up to $250,000 ($500,000 if married filing a joint return) of the profit realized. This exclusion is available once every two years and is not predicated on the reinvestment of the sales proceeds in a new home. A number of requirements must be satisfied to qualify for this valuable tax break.

¶7001 GENERAL RULE FOR SALE AND REPLACEMENT

.01 Home Sale Exclusion Amount

The home sale exclusion rules provide that after May 6, 1997, an individual can exclude up to $250,000 ($500,000 if married filing a joint return) of gain realized on the sale or exchange of a principal residence (not vacation home) if the property was owned and used as the taxpayer's principal residence for at least two years during the five-year period ending on the date of the sale or exchange. This exclusion is allowed once every two years when individuals sell or exchange a principal residence [Code Sec. 121(a); Reg. § 1.121-1(a)].

> ▶ **PRACTICE POINTER:** The home sale exclusion tax break only applies to sales of a taxpayer's primary residence, not to sales of a taxpayer's vacation or second home [see ¶ 7005.01].

.02 Reporting Requirements

Taxpayers have no reporting requirements if the gain from the sale or exchange of their principal residence is entirely excludable under Code Sec. 121. Any profit in excess of the exclusion amount should be reported as a capital gain on Schedule D. Losses from the sale of a principal residence cannot be deducted.

.03 How to Exempt Sale of Residence from Information Reporting

In general, real estate brokers must report real estate transactions to the IRS on Form 1099-S, *Proceeds From Real Estate Transactions,* and provide a payee statement to the seller [Code Sec. 6045]. These reporting requirements may be avoided if the seller provides written assurances to the real estate reporting person [Code Sec. 6045(e)(5)]. To be excepted from the information reporting requirements on the sale or exchange of a principal residence (including stock in a cooperative housing corporation), Rev. Proc. 2007-12[1] provides that the real estate reporting person must obtain from the seller a written certification, signed by the seller under penalties of perjury, providing that the assurances listed below are true. The real estate reporting person may obtain a certification at any time on or before January 31 of the year following the year of the sale or exchange of the residence. The certification must be retained by the real estate reporting person for four years after the year of the sale or exchange of the residence to which the certification applies. For purposes of this certification, the term "seller" includes each owner of the residence that is sold or exchanged. Thus, if a residence has more than one owner, a real estate reporting person must either obtain a certification from each owner (whether married or not) or file an information return and furnish a payee statement for any owner that does not make the certification. The assurances are:

1. The seller owned and used the residence as a principal residence for periods aggregating two years or more during the five-year period ending on the date of the sale or exchange.
2. The seller has not sold or exchanged another principal residence during the two-year period ending on the date of the sale or exchange.
3. No portion of the residence has been used for business or rental purposes after May 6, 1997, by the seller (or by the seller's spouse or former spouse, if the seller was married at any time after May 6, 1997).
4. At least one of the following three statements applies: (a) The sale or exchange is of the entire residence for $250,000 or less; or (b) The seller is married, the sale or exchange is of the entire residence for $500,000 or less, and the gain on the sale or

[1] Rev. Proc. 2007-12, 2007-1 CB 354.

exchange of the entire residence is $250,000 or less; or (c) The seller is married, the sale or exchange is of the entire residence for $500,000 or less, and (i) the seller intends to file a joint return for the year of the sale or exchange, (ii) the seller's spouse also used the residence as his or her principal residence for periods aggregating two years or more during the five-year period ending on the date of the sale or exchange, and (iii) the seller's spouse also has not sold or exchanged another principal residence during the two-year period ending on the date of the sale or exchange.

- During the five-year period ending on the date of the sale or exchange, the seller did not acquire the residence in a like-kind exchange;
- In cases where the seller's basis in the residence is determined by reference to the basis in the hands of a person who acquired the residence in a like-kind exchange, the like-kind exchange occurred more than five years prior to the date of the seller's sale or exchange.

.04 How to Qualify for the $500,000/$250,000 Home Sale Exclusion

To be eligible for the $500,000 ($250,000 if single) exclusion, a taxpayer must have:

- Owned the home for at least 2 years (the ownership test), and
- Lived in the home as a principal residence (not vacation home) for at least two of the five years prior to the sale or exchange (the use test).

Effective for sales and exchanges after December 31, 2008, the homesale exclusion won't apply to the extent gain from the sale or exchange of a principal residence is allocated to periods of "nonqualified use" [Code Sec. 121(b)(4)[5](A)]. For further discussion, see ¶7001.01.

A taxpayer who lived and used the property as his or her main home for fewer than two years, may be able to claim a reduced exclusion, as discussed in ¶7025. Note that the exclusion is no longer predicated on the reinvestment of the seller's gain in another home as it was under old law [Code Sec. 121].

The $500,000 maximum exclusion of gain from sales or exchanges of principal residences that applies to joint return filers will also apply to qualifying sales or exchanges by surviving spouses [Code Sec. 121(b)(4)]. See ¶7015.

> ▶ **PRACTICE TIP:** The once-every-two-years rule presents an opportunity if the taxpayer does not mind "flipping" houses every two years. For example, assume taxpayers buy a fixer-upper at a great price in a great location and live in it as their principal residence for two years, during which time they renovate the place. If they sell it at a profit of less than $500,000, they will pay zero tax if joint filers. Better yet, they can repeat this scheme every two years and never pay a dime of federal income tax on up to $500,000 of the profit earned every two years. This tactic can present a great investment opportunity for the right person with real estate clairvoyance and a willingness to renovate. Keep in mind, however, that state transfer and recording taxes and real estate commissions will be due every time the properties are sold.

Example 7-1: The married taxpayers are 80 years old. They bought a beach house 15 years ago while they still owned a home in town. They paid $12,000 for the beach house. After living in their primary residence in town for 30 years, they sold it and pocketed $500,000 of profit tax-free. They then moved into the beach house and made it their permanent residence. They lived in it for 5 years. They have tired of the upkeep and are ready to move into an assisted living condo in Florida. The beach house is now worth $750,000. Because the beach house now qualifies as their personal residence, they can sell it and again exclude up to $500,000 of the profit with a zero tax bill. Any gain over that amount will be taxed as capital gains. They have pocketed $1 million tax-free as a result of the sales of their two homes.

Expatriates

Expatriates are unable to claim the benefits of the home sale exclusion rules [Reg. § 1.121-4(f)].

Tenant-Stockholder in Cooperative Housing Corporation

A taxpayer who holds stock as a tenant-stockholder in a cooperative housing corporation may be eligible to exclude gain under Code Sec. 121 on the sale or exchange of the stock. In determining whether the taxpayer meets the requirements of Code Sec. 121, the ownership requirements are applied to stock held and the use requirements are applied to the house or apartment that the taxpayer is entitled to occupy by reason of the taxpayer's stock ownership [Reg. § 1.121-4(c)].

Bankruptcy Estate

The bankruptcy estate of an individual in a Chapter 7 or 11 bankruptcy case under Title 11 of the United States Code succeeds to and takes into account the individual's home sale exclusion if the individual satisfies the requirements of Code Sec. 121 [Reg. § 1.1398-3(a)]. The IRS will not challenge a position that a bankruptcy estate may use the home sale exclusion if the debtor would otherwise satisfy the statutory requirements.

Exclusion of Gain on Sale of Principal Residence Extended to Estates, Heirs, and Qualified Revocable Trusts

The home sale exclusion is available to a decedent's principal residence that is sold by any of the following: (1) the decedent's estate; (2) any individual who acquired the residence from the decedent as a result of his or her death; or (3) a trust established by the decedent that was a qualified revocable trust (as defined in Code Sec. 645(b)(1)) immediately prior to the decedent's death [Code Sec. 121(d)(11)]. In order for the estate to qualify for the income exclusion, the decedent must have owned and occupied the property as his or her principal residence for a total of two years during the five-year period prior to the sale.

However, if a decedent's residence is sold by an heir who occupied the property as his or her principal residence after acquiring it from the decedent, the decedent's ownership and occupancy will be added to that of the heir's in determining whether the two-year ownership and use requirements are met [Senate Finance Committee Report (S. Rep. No. 107-30)]. In addition, the decedent's period of occupancy can be combined with that of the heir's regardless of whether a qualified revocable trust owned the residence during such time (Conference Committee Report H.R. Rep. No. 107-84)).

.05 Profits in Excess of $500,000

Any profit in excess of the $500,000 limit will be taxed at long-term capital gain tax rates, which are listed below.

Capital Gains Rate for Individuals—2013

Beginning in 2013, the capital gains rates for individuals are as follows:

- A capital gains rate of 0 percent applies to the adjusted net capital gains of *individuals* if the gain would otherwise be subject to the 10- or 15-percent ordinary income tax rate [Code Secs. 1(h)(1)(B), 55(b)(3)(B)].
- A capital gains rate of 15 percent applies to adjusted net capital gains of *individuals* if the gain would otherwise be subject to the 25-, 28-, 33-, or 35-percent ordinary income tax rate [Code Secs. 1(h)(1)(C), 55(b)(3)(C)].
- A capital gains rate of 20 percent applies to adjusted net capital gains of *individuals* if the gain would otherwise be subject to the 39.6-percent ordinary income tax rate beginning on January 1, 2013 [Code Sec. 1(h)(1)(D)]. Individuals are subject to the 39.6-percent ordinary income tax rate in 2013 to the extent their taxable income exceeds the applicable threshold amount of $450,000 for married individuals filing joint returns and surviving spouses, $425,000 for heads of households, $400,000 for single individuals, and $225,000 for married individuals filing separate returns.

These rates apply for sales or exchanges of capital assets that are held for more than 12 months, and apply for both regular income tax and alternative minimum tax (AMT) purposes. For discussion of capital gains rates for estates and trusts, see ¶ 25,045.

> ▶ **NEW IN 2013—3.8 Percent Net Investment Income Tax:** In 2013, higher income taxpayers must also start paying a 3.8-percent additional tax on net investment income (NII) to the extent certain threshold amounts of income are exceeded ($200,000 for single filers, $250,000 for joint returns and surviving spouses, $125,000 for married taxpayers filing separately) [Code Sec. 1411]. Therefore, taxpayers within the NII surtax range must pay the additional 3.8 percent on capital gain, whether long-term or short-term. The effective top rate for net capital gains for many higher-income taxpayers thus becomes 23.8 percent for long-term gain, and 43.4 percent for short-term capital gains starting in 2013. For further discussion, see ¶ 15,050.

These rates apply for sales or exchanges of capital assets that are held for more than 12 months, and apply for both regular income tax and alternative minimum tax (AMT) purposes. For discussion of capital gains rates for estates and trusts, see ¶ 25,045.

> **Example 7-2:** A single taxpayer purchased a home 10 years ago for $500,000. In 2013, he sells the home for $2 million, realizing a gain of $1,500,000. Assuming that he can exclude $250,000 of gain realized under the exclusion for the sale of a principal residence, the taxpayer must pay tax on capital gains of $1,250,000.

Good Records Essential to Document Basis in Home

Home sellers will only be able to minimize or avoid gain on any home sale proceeds that exceed the $500,000/$250,000 exclusion amounts if they can document their home's tax basis. The starting point for determining a taxpayer's basis in his or her home is the purchase price plus certain closing costs. The basis is then increased for improvements made to the residence. When the residence is sold, the amount of capital gain is determined by subtracting the adjusted basis from the amount realized. By increasing basis, the homeowner will decrease the amount of his or her taxable gain. All improvements, however, will not increase a taxpayer's basis in a persona residence. For example, improvements that have been replaced and are no longer considered part of the taxpayer's home will not increase basis. In addition, repairs that maintain a home in good condition but do not add to its value or prolong its life cannot be added to the basis of the property. For example, repainting the house inside or outside, fixing the gutters or floors, repairing leaks or plastering, and replacing broken window panes are examples of repairs that do not affect basis unless the repairs are done in conjunction with an extensive home remodeling or restoration project.[2]

The $500,000/$250,000 exclusion rule only eliminates the need to keep records of capital improvements made to the home if homeowners expect their profit in the home to be less than the exclusion amount. If, however, they expect the gain to be greater than $500,000 on a joint return and $250,000 on a single return, they will need good records of the capital improvements made to the home and grounds to prove an increase in basis which will in turn reduce the amount of taxable gain. Examples of improvements include but are not limited to adding a bedroom or bathroom, putting up a new fence, adding a swimming pool, new appliances, renovating a kitchen or bathroom, installing new plumbing or wiring, and putting on a new roof. Even the cost of putting in shrubs and trees qualifies as improvements and will raise a taxpayer's cost basis. In Publication 523, *Selling Your Home*, the IRS provides the following examples of improvements that increase the homeowner's basis in a personal residence:

Additions—Bedroom, bathroom, deck, garage, porch, patio;

Lawn & Grounds—Landscaping, driveway, walkway, fence, retaining wall, sprinkler system, swimming pool;

Miscellaneous—Storm windows, doors, new roof, central vacuum, wiring upgrades, satellite dish, security system;

Heating & Air Conditioning—Heating system, central air conditioning, furnace, duct work, central humidifier, filtration system;

Plumbing—Septic system, water heater, soft water system, filtration system;

Interior Improvements—Built-in appliances, kitchen modernization, flooring, wall-to-wall carpeting; and

Insulation—Attic, walls, floors, pipes and duct work.[3]

Other reasons to retain records of capital improvements include the following:

- You do not expect to live in the home for the two-year period and you will therefore not qualify to take advantage of the exclusion;

---

[2] IRS Pub. 523, at 9 (2013).

[3] IRS Pub. 523, at 9 (2013).

- There is a possibility that you may use part of the home as your home office and will therefore claim a depreciation deduction for that part of the home, which will require you to know the basis of the home;
- There is a possibility that you may rent out part of the home and will therefore claim a depreciation deduction for the rental portion of your home; or
- You expect to live in the home for a long time and it may actually appreciate so much in value that your gain may exceed the $500,000/$250,000 exclusion amount.

The bottom line is that you should keep a file in your home where you stash any records of capital improvements you make to your principal residence. The need to compute your tax bill on profits in excess of the $500,000 exclusion amount means that compulsive record-keeping remains essential for homeowners who make improvements to their residences. The improvements will increase the homeowner's basis in the home and reduce the capital gains tax they would have to pay on profits in excess of $500,000 when they sell their home.

.06 Election Out

In certain situations, it may make sense for a taxpayer to elect out of the home sale exclusion rules for certain sales or exchanges or property [Code Sec. 121(f)]. For example, assume you own two vacation homes and both homes qualify as principal residences. You decide to sell them within a two-year period. Assume further that the sale of the first home would yield only a small taxable gain but the sale of the second home would generate a substantially greater gain. You should consider electing out of the home sale exclusion for the sale of the first home in order to preserve the entire exclusion for the second sale where it will reduce your tax bill.

The taxpayer makes the election by filing a return for the tax year of the sale or exchange that includes the gain from the sale or exchange of the taxpayer's principal residence in the taxpayer's gross income. A taxpayer may make an election out or revoke an existing election out at any time before the expiration of the three-year period beginning on the last date prescribed by law (determined without regard to extensions) for the filing of the return for the tax year in which the sale or exchange occurred [Reg. § 1.121-4(g)].

¶7005 DEFINITION OF PRINCIPAL RESIDENCE

The residence used by the taxpayer a majority of the time during the year will ordinarily be considered the taxpayer's principal residence [Reg. § 1.121-1(b)(1)]. A taxpayer's principal residence could be a houseboat, mobile home, a house trailer, or the house or apartment that the taxpayer is entitled to occupy as a tenant-stockholder in a cooperative housing corporation. Property used by the taxpayer as the taxpayer's residence does not include personal property that is not a fixture under local law [Reg. § 1.121-1(b)(1)].

If a taxpayer has more than one residence, and alternates between the properties, using each as a residence for successive periods of time, the taxpayer's principal residence will be the property that the taxpayer uses a majority of the time during the year (on a year-by-year basis). Residing the most days during the five-year period in one of multiple residences is not determinative of whether that residence is a taxpayer's principal residence. Reg. § 1.121-1(b)(2), instead, looks at whether a home is a principal residence on a year-by-year basis.[4]

In addition to the taxpayer's use of the property for the requisite number of days, the following factors are relevant in identifying a taxpayer's principal residence [Reg. § 1.121-1(b)(2)]:

1. The taxpayer's place of employment;
2. The principal place where the taxpayer's family members live;
3. The address listed on the taxpayer's federal and state tax returns, driver's license, automobile registration, and voter registration card;
4. The taxpayer's mailing address for bills and correspondence;
5. The location of the taxpayer's banks; and
6. The location of religious organizations and recreational clubs with which the taxpayer is affiliated.

Example 7-3: Taxpayer A owns two residences, one in New York and one in Florida. For a five-year period, he lives in the New York residence for seven months of the year and the Florida residence for five months of each year. The New York residence is A's principal residence and A may exclude gain from the sale or exchange of the New York residence, but not the Florida residence [Reg. § 1.121-1(b)(4), Ex. 1].

Example 7-4: Taxpayer B owns two residences, one in Virginia and one in Maine. During Years 1 and 2, she lives in the Virginia residence. During Years 3 and 4, she lives in the Maine residence. During Year 5, she lives in the Virginia residence. B's principal residence during Years 1, 2, and 5 is the Virginia residence. B's principal residence during Years 3 and 4 is the Maine residence. B may exclude gain from the sale or exchange of either residence (but not both) during Year 5 [Reg. § 1.121-1(b)(4), Ex. 2].

► **PLANNING POINTER:** Taxpayers who own more than one home and who plan to sell one of them at a profit will only be able to take advantage of the Code Sec. 121 home sale exclusion on that sale if they can show on a year-by-year basis that the home sold was their principal residence. To establish this fact, they will have to show that they treated the home and the state where it was located as their primary residence for all purposes. With this in mind, taxpayers who own several homes and who plan to sell one should arrange their affairs to establish that the home to be sold will qualify as their principal residence under the law.

---

[4] *J.M. Guinan*, DC-AZ, 2003-1 USTC ¶ 50,475.

.01 Vacation Homes

Profits realized from the sale of a vacation home will be fully taxable, because a second home does not qualify as a "principal residence" under the law. If a taxpayer sells land on which he or she had hoped to build a vacation home, he or she may not exclude any part of the gain realized on the sale, because the land does not qualify as a principal residence. A mobile home, houseboat or large yacht would, however, qualify for the exclusion if the taxpayer uses one of them as his or her main residence [Temp. Reg. § 1.163-10T(p)(3)(ii)]. Losses from the sale of a residence may not be deducted unless the former residence had been converted to income-producing property, in which case the loss will be deductible [Reg. § 1.165-1(e)].

.02 Vacant Land

Vacant land does not normally qualify as a taxpayer's principal residence [Reg. § 1.121-1(b)(3)]. Vacant land, however, may be included as part of the principal residence if these requirements are satisfied:

- The land is adjacent to land containing the dwelling unit;
- The taxpayer owned and used the vacant land as part of the principal residence;
- The taxpayer sells the dwelling unit in a transaction qualifying for Code Sec. 121 treatment within two years before, or two years after, sale of the vacant land.
- The requirements of Code Sec. 121 have otherwise been met with respect to the vacant land [Reg. § 1.121-1(b)(3)].

Only one maximum limitation amount of $250,000 ($500,000 for certain joint returns) applies to the combined sales or exchanges of the vacant land and dwelling unit. If sales or exchanges of the dwelling unit and adjacent vacant land occur in separate transactions, the home sale exclusion can only be used for one sale or exchange every two years [Reg. § 1.121-1(b)(3)(ii)(B)].

Sale or Exchange of Vacant Land Before Dwelling Unit

If the sale or exchange of the dwelling unit occurs after the sale or exchange of the vacant land and after the due date (including extensions) for filing the return for the tax year of the sale or exchange of the vacant land, any gain from the sale or exchange of the vacant land must be reported on the taxpayer's return for the year of the sale or exchange of the vacant land. If the taxpayer has reported gain from the sale or exchange of the vacant land as taxable, an amended return may be filed to exclude the gain from the sale or exchange of the vacant land.

Example 7-5: In 2000, Taxpayer C buys property consisting of a house and 10 acres that she uses as her principal residence. In May 2013, C sells 8 acres of the land and realizes a gain of $110,000. C does not sell the dwelling unit before the due date for filing her 2013 tax return; therefore, she is not eligible to exclude the $110,000 of gain. In March 2015, C sells the house and remaining 2 acres realizing a gain of $180,000 from the sale of the house. She may exclude the $180,000 of gain. Because the sale of the 8 acres occurred within 2 years from the date of the sale of the dwelling unit, the sale of the 8 acres is treated as a sale of the taxpayer's principal residence and she may file an amended return to claim an exclusion for $70,000 ($250,000 – $180,000 gain previously excluded) of the $110,000 gain from the sale of the 8 acres [Reg. § 1.121-1(b)(4), Ex. 3].

Example 7-6: In 2008, Taxpayer D buys a house and 1 acre that he uses as his principal residence. In 2008, D buys 29 acres adjacent to his house and uses the vacant land as part of his principal residence. In 2013, D sells the house and 1 acre and the 29 acres in two separate transactions. D sells the house and 1 acre at a loss of $25,000. D realizes $270,000 of gain from the sale of the 29 acres. D may exclude the $245,000 gain from the two sales [Reg. § 1.121-1(b)(4), Ex. 4].

¶7010 OWNERSHIP AND USE REQUIREMENTS

A taxpayer can satisfy the ownership and use requirement by establishing ownership and use for 24 full months or for 730 days (365 × 2) during the five-year period before the sale. The required two years need not be continuous and may be satisfied during nonconcurrent periods if both the ownership and use tests are met during the 5-year period ending on the date of the sale or exchange [Reg. § 1.121-1(c)(1)].

.01 Satisfying the Use Requirement

In establishing whether a taxpayer has satisfied the two-year use requirement, occupancy of the residence is required. However, short temporary absences, such as for vacation or other seasonal absences (although accompanied with rental of the residence), are counted as periods of use [Reg. § 1.121-1(c)(2)].

Homesale Exclusion Denied for Never-Occupied New House Constructed on Old Home Site

In *D.A. Gates*,[5] the Tax Court held that taxpayers who had never lived in a new house that was constructed on property where their previous house had been located could not exclude from income gain realized on the sale of the new house. Although they lived in the first house for two of the five years immediately preceding the sale before they demolished the original house and constructed a new house on the same property, they had never resided in the second house, thus failing to satisfy the two-of-five-years test. Because the court concluded that the terms "property" and "principal residence" refer to "a house or other dwelling unit in which the taxpayer actually resided," the couple did not meet the requirement of living in the principal residence for at least two out of the five years immediately preceding the sale of the second house and the land.

Determination of Use During Periods of Out-of-Residence Care

If a taxpayer has become physically or mentally incapable of self-care and sells or exchanges a principal residence that the taxpayer owned and used as a principal residence for periods totaling at least 1 year during the 5-year period preceding the sale or exchange, the taxpayer is treated as using the property as a principal residence for any period of time during the 5-year period in which he or she resides in any facility (including a nursing home) licensed by a State or political subdivision to care for an individual in the taxpayer's condition [Reg. § 1.121-1(c)(2)(ii)].

---

[5] *D.A. Gates*, 135 TC 1, Dec. 58,259 (2010).

Residence Owned by Trust

If a residence is owned by a trust, the taxpayer is treated as the owner and the seller of the residence during the period that the taxpayer is treated as the owner of the trust or the portion of the trust that includes the residence [Reg. § 1.121-1(c)(3)(i)]. Similar rules apply to single-owner entities (i.e., entities, such as an LLC, that have a single owner and are disregarded for federal tax purposes as an entity separate from their owner) [Reg. § 1.121-1(c)(3)(ii)].

Example 7-7: Taxpayer A has owned and used his house as his principal residence for 10 years. On January 31, 2011, A moves to another state. A rents his house to tenants from that date until April 18, 2013, when he sells it. A is eligible for the home sale exclusion because he has owned and used the house as his principal residence for at least two of the five years preceding the sale [Reg. § 1.121-1(c)(4), Ex. 1].

Example 7-8: Taxpayer B, a college professor, purchases and moves into a house on May 1, 2011. He uses the house as his principal residence continuously until September 1, 2013 when he goes abroad for a 1-year sabbatical leave. On October 1, 2014, 1 month after returning from the leave, B sells the house. Because his leave is not considered to be a short temporary absence, the period of the sabbatical leave may not be included in determining whether he used the house for periods aggregating 2 years during the 5-year period ending on the date of the sale. Consequently, he is not entitled to exclude gain under the home sale exclusion rules, because he did not use the residence for the requisite period [Reg. § 1.121-1(c)(4), Ex. 4]. If, however, he had only left his residence to teach during 2 months of the summer, the home sale exclusion will apply to exclude his gain from the sale of the residence because 2 months is considered a short temporary absence [Reg. § 1.121-1(c)(4), Ex. 5].

.02 Gain from Sale of Principal Residence Allocated to Nonqualified Use Ineligible for Exclusion

The homesale exclusion will not apply to the extent gain from the sale or exchange of a principal residence is allocated to periods of "nonqualified use" [Code Sec. 121(b)(4)[5](A)]. A period of nonqualified use is any period during which the property is not used as the principal residence of the taxpayer, his or her spouse, or former spouse [Code Sec. 121(b)(4)[5](C)(i)]. Gain is allocated to periods of nonqualified use based on the ratio which the aggregate periods of nonqualified use during the period the property was owned by the taxpayer bears to the total period of time the property was owned by the taxpayer [Code Sec. 121(b)(4)[5](B)].

Exceptions. There are several exceptions to the general definition of "period of nonqualified use" as follows:

- Any portion of the five-year period ending on the date the property is sold that is after the last date that the property is used as the principal residence of the taxpayer or his or her spouse is not considered a period of nonqualified use [Code Sec. 121(b)(4)[5](C)(ii)(I)];

- Any period (not exceeding an aggregate period of 10 years) during which the taxpayer or his or her spouse is serving on "qualified official extended duty" as a member of the armed forces, as a Foreign Service officer, or as an employee of the intelligence community [Code Sec. 121(b)(4)[5](C)(ii)(II)]. A period of qualified official extended duty is any extended duty undertaken by a taxpayer while serving at a duty station at least 50 miles from the taxpayer's principal residence [Code Sec. 121(d)(9)(c)(i)];
- Any other period of temporary absence from the taxpayer's principal residence that does not exceed two years in total because of a change of employment, health conditions, or other unforeseen circumstances [Code Sec. 121(b)(4)[5](C)(ii)(III)].

Example 7-9: Assume that an individual buys a property on January 1, 2013, for $400,000 and uses it as rental property for two years, claiming $20,000 of depreciation deductions. On January 1, 2015, the taxpayer converts the property to his principal residence. The taxpayer moves out on January 13, 2017, and sells the property for $700,000 on January 1, 2018. Gain in the amount of $20,000 that is attributable to the depreciation deductions is included in income. Of the remaining $300,000 gain, 40 percent (two years divided by five years), or $120,000, is allocated to nonqualified use and is not eligible for the exclusion. Since the remaining gain of $180,000 is less than the maximum gain of $250,000 that may be excluded, the remaining gain of $180,000 is excluded from gross income (Joint Committee on Taxation, Technical Explanation of the Housing Assistance Tax Act of 2008 (JCS-63-08), July 23, 2008).

.03 Suspension of Five-Year Period for Members of Uniformed Services, Foreign Service, and Intelligence Community

Individuals serving in the uniformed services, Foreign Service of the United States, or as an employee of the intelligence community may elect to suspend the five-year period during which the two-year ownership and use requirements must be satisfied [Code Sec. 121(d)(9)(B)]. The suspension applies for the period that the individual or the individual's spouse is serving on *qualified official extended duty* [Code Sec. 121(d)(9)].[6] The maximum period of suspension is 10 years [Code Sec. 121(d)(9)(B)].

How To Make the Election

The taxpayer makes the election by filing a return for the tax year in which the sale or exchange of the taxpayer's principal residence occurred and not including gain from the sale or exchange in gross income [Code Sec. 121(d)(9); Reg. § 1.121-5(b)].

Qualified Official Extended Duty Defined

The election to suspend the five-year use and ownership period can only be made if the taxpayer or the taxpayer's spouse is on *qualified official extended duty* as a member of the uniformed services, the Foreign Service, or as an employee of the intelligence community [Code Sec. 121(d)(9)(A)].

The term "employee of the intelligence community" means an employee of the Office of the Director of National Intelligence, the Central Intelligence Agency, the National

6 LTR 200630015 (Feb. 16, 2006).

Security Agency, the Defense Intelligence Agency, the National Geospatial-Intelligence Agency, or the National Reconnaissance Office. The term also includes employment with: (1) any other office within the Department of Defense for the collection of specialized national intelligence through reconnaissance programs; (2) any of the intelligence elements of the Army, the Navy, the Air Force, the Marine Corps, the Federal Bureau of Investigation, the Department of the Treasury, the Department of Energy, and the Coast Guard; (3) the Bureau of Intelligence and Research of the Department of State; and (4) the elements of the Department of Homeland Security concerned with the analyses of foreign intelligence information [Code Sec. 121(d)(9)(C)(iv)]. To qualify, a specified employee must move from one duty station to another and the new duty station must be located outside of the United States [Code Sec. 121(d)(9)(C)(vi)].

Qualified official extended duty is defined to mean: (1) any extended duty while serving at a duty station that is at least 50 miles from the property for which the election is being made, or (2) any extended duty while serving under government orders in government quarters [Code Sec. 121(d)(9)(C)(i)]. Extended duty is any period of active duty pursuant to a call or order to duty for a period in excess of 90 days or for an indefinite period [Code Sec. 121(d)(9)(C)(iv)].

Only One at a Time

Only one suspension election may be in effect at a time. Thus, if an election is in effect for one property, it may not be made for another property [Code Sec. 121(d)(9)(C)(i)]. However, an election may be revoked at any time [Code Sec. 121(d)(9)(D)(ii)]. Thus, a taxpayer may cancel an election with respect to one property and then make it with respect to a second property. The new law does not explain the time or manner for making or canceling the election.

Uniformed Services Defined

The term *uniformed services* is defined to mean: (1) the armed forces (Army, Navy, Air Force, Marine Corps, and Coast Guard); (2) the commissioned corps of the National Oceanic and Atmospheric Administration; and (3) the commissioned corps of the Public Health Service.

Foreign Service Defined

The term member of the *Foreign Service of the United States* means (1) Chiefs of mission; (2) Ambassadors at large; (3) Members of the Senior Foreign Service, who are the corps of leaders and experts for the management of the Service and the performance of its functions; (4) Foreign Service officers, who have general responsibility for carrying out the functions of the Service; and (5) Foreign Service personnel, who provide skills and services required for effective performance by the Service.

> **Example 7-10:** B purchases a house in Virginia in 2004 that he uses as his principal residence for three years. For eight years, from 2007 through 2015, B serves on qualified official extended duty as a member of the Foreign Service of the United States in Brazil. In 2016 B sells the house. B did not use the house as his principal residence for two of the five years preceding the sale. Under Code Sec. 121(d)(9), however, B may elect to suspend the running of the five-year

period of ownership and use during his eight-year period of service with the Foreign Service in Brazil. If B makes the election, the eight-year period is not counted in determining whether B used the house for two of the five years preceding the sale. Therefore, B may exclude the gain from the sale of the house under Code Sec. 121 [Reg. § 1.121-5(d)].

.04 Five-Year Testing Period Suspended During Peace Corps Service

For purposes of the Code Sec. 121 exclusion of gain from the sale of gain from the sale of a principal residence, an individual can elect to suspend the running of the five-year ownership and use testing period during any period that the individual or the individual's spouse is serving outside the United States as part of the Peace Corps [Code Sec. 121(d)(12)]. Assuming that rules similar to the rules for members of the uniformed services, members of the U.S. Foreign Service, and specified employees of the intelligence community apply, then, the five-year testing period for ownership and use cannot be suspended for more than 10 years due to Peace Corps service. In addition, the election cannot be made if another election to suspend the five-year testing period is in effect with respect to any other property. For purposes of the election, qualifying Peace Corps service includes service outside the United States:

- On qualified official extended duty as a Peace Corps employee, or
- As an enrolled volunteer or volunteer leader under section 5 or 6 of the Peace Corps Act [Code Sec. 121(d)(12)(A)].

.05 Principal Residence Acquired in Like-Kind Exchange

An individual who acquires a principal residence in a like-kind exchange must own the property for at least five years prior to its sale or exchange in order to take advantage of the home sale exclusion rules [Code Sec. 121(d)]. For further discussion of like-kind exchanges, see ¶ 6050. In Rev. Proc. 2005-14,[7] the IRS explained that a homeowner can exclude gain on the sale or exchange of a home and also benefit from a deferral of gain from a like-kind exchange on the same property if both the residence exchanged and the property acquired have been used consecutively or concurrently as a home and a business (e.g., rental residence). Thus, the tax relief is only available to taxpayers who satisfy the "held for productive use in a trade or business or for investment" requirement of Code Sec. 1031(a)(1) with respect to the relinquished business property and the replacement business property.

The IRS has provided a safe harbor providing that it will not challenge whether a dwelling unit qualifies as "property held for productive use in a trade or business or for investment" for like-kind exchange treatment under Code Sec. 1031, even though the taxpayer occasionally uses the dwelling unit for personal purposes. The taxpayer must satisfy qualifying use standards affecting ownership, fair rental and personal use of the dwelling unit to be relinquished during the 24-month period before the exchange. The taxpayer must also meet similar standards for the replacement dwelling unit during the 24-month period after the exchange.[8] For detailed discussion, see ¶ 6050.02.

---

[7] Rev. Proc. 2005-14, 2005-1 CB 528.

[8] Rev. Proc. 2008-16, IRB 2008-10, 547.

Treatment of Boot

In applying Code Sec. 1031, cash or other non-like kind property (boot) received in exchange for property used in the taxpayer's trade or business or held for investment (the relinquished business property), is taken into account only to the extent the boot exceeds the gain excluded under Code Sec. 121 with respect to the relinquished business property.

Computation of Basis

In determining the basis of the property received in the exchange to be used in the taxpayer's trade or business or held for investment (the replacement business property), any gain excluded under Code Sec. 121 is treated as gain recognized by the taxpayer. Thus, under Code Sec. 1031(d), the basis of the replacement business property is increased by any gain attributable to the relinquished business property that is excluded under the home sale exclusion rules.

Examples

In each example below, the taxpayer is an unmarried individual and the property or a portion of the property has been used in the taxpayer's trade or business or held for investment as well as used as a principal residence.

> **Example 7-11:** Taxpayer A buys a house for $210,000 that he uses as a principal residence from 2007 to 2012. From 2011 until 2013, A rents the house to tenants and claims depreciation deductions of $20,000. In 2013, A exchanges the house for $10,000 and a townhouse with a fair market value of $460,000 that A intends to rent to tenants. A realizes gain of $280,000 on the exchange. Because A owns and uses the house as his principal residence for at least two years during the five-year period prior to the exchange, A may exclude gain under Code Sec. 121. Because the house is investment property at the time of the exchange, A may defer gain under Code Sec. 1031. A excludes $250,000 of the $280,000 gain before applying the like-kind nonrecognition rules. A may defer the remaining gain of $30,000, including the $20,000 gain attributable to depreciation. Although A receives $10,000 of cash (boot) in the exchange, A is not required to recognize gain because the boot is taken into account only to the extent the boot exceeds the amount of excluded gain. A's basis in the replacement property is $430,000, which is equal to the basis of the relinquished property at the time of the exchange ($190,000) increased by the gain excluded under Code Sec. 121 ($250,000), and reduced by the cash A receives ($10,000).

> **Example 7-12:** Taxpayer B buys a property for $210,000. The property consists of two separate dwelling units, a house and a guesthouse. From 2008 until 2013, B uses the house as his principal residence and uses the guesthouse as an office, allocating two-thirds of the basis of the property to the house and one-third to the guesthouse. In 2013, B exchanges the entire property for a residence and a separate property that B intends to use as an office. The total fair market value of B's replacement properties is $360,000. The fair market value of the replacement residence is $240,000 and the fair market value of the replacement business property is $120,000, which is equal to the fair market value of the

relinquished business property. From 2008 to 2013, B claims depreciation deductions of $30,000 for the business use. B realizes gain of $180,000 on the exchange. B may exclude gain of $100,000 allocable to the residential portion of the house (2/3 × $360,000 amount realized, or $240,000, – 2/3 of $210,000 basis, or $140,000) because B meets the ownership and use requirements for that portion of the property. Because the guesthouse is business property separate from the dwelling unit and B has not met the use requirements for the guesthouse, B may not exclude the gain allocable to the guesthouse. However, because the fair market value of the replacement business property is equal to the fair market value of the relinquished business property and B receives no boot, B may defer the remaining gain of $80,000 (1/3 of $ 360,000 amount realized, or $120,000, minus $40,000 adjusted basis, which is 1/3 of $210,000 basis, or $70,000, adjusted by $30,000 depreciation). Because no portion of the gain attributable to the relinquished business property is excluded under the home sale exclusion rules and B receives no boot and recognizes no gain or loss in the exchange, B's basis in the replacement business property is equal to B's basis in the relinquished business property at the time of the exchange ($40,000). B's basis in the replacement residential property is the fair market value of the replacement residential property at the time of the exchange ($240,000).

¶7015 RULES FOR MARRIED HOMEOWNERS

.01 Married Homeowners

For purposes of satisfying the ownership and use requirements, a taxpayer is treated as owning and using property as the taxpayer's principal residence during any period that the taxpayer's deceased spouse owned and used the property as a principal residence before death if:

- The taxpayer's spouse is deceased on the date of the sale or exchange of the property; and
- The taxpayer has not remarried at the time of the sale or exchange of the property [Reg. § 1.121-4(a)(1)].

Example 7-13: Taxpayer H has owned and used a house as his principal residence since 2005. H and W marry on July 1, 2012 and from that date they use H's house as their principal residence. H dies on August 15, 2013, and W inherits the property. W sells the property on September 1, 2013, at which time she has not remarried. Although W has owned and used the house for less than two years, W will be considered to have satisfied the ownership and use requirements of Code Sec. 121 because W's period of ownership and use includes the period that H owned and used the property before death which satisfied the statutory requirement [Reg. § 1.121-4(a)(2)].

.02 Property Transferred to Homeseller by Spouse or Former Spouse

If a taxpayer obtains property from a spouse or former spouse in a transaction described in tax-free property transfer incident to Code Sec. 1041(a), the period that the taxpayer owns the property will include the period that the spouse or former spouse owned the property [Reg. § 1.121-4(b)(1)].

.03 Property Used by Spouse or Former Spouse

A taxpayer is treated as using property as the taxpayer's principal residence for any period that the taxpayer has an ownership interest in the property and the taxpayer's spouse or former spouse is granted use of the property under a divorce or separation instrument provided that the spouse or former spouse uses the property as his or her principal residence.

.04 Sales by Surviving Spouses

The $500,000 maximum exclusion of gain from sales or exchanges of principal residences that applies to joint return filers also applies to qualifying sales or exchanges by surviving spouses [Code Sec. 121(b)(4)]. The increased exclusion amount applies to a sale or exchange of property by an unmarried individual whose spouse is deceased on the date of the sale if:

- The sale occurs no later than two years after the date of death of such spouse, and
- Immediately before the date of death, either spouse met the two-out-of-five year ownership requirement, both spouses met the two-out-of-five year use requirement, and neither spouse was ineligible to claim the exclusion because of another sale or exchange within the prior two years that qualified for the exclusion [Code Sec. 121(b)(4)].

Thus, for the ownership and use requirements, only one spouse must have owned the property for periods aggregating two years or more during the five-year period immediately before the date of death. However, both spouses must have met the use requirement by using the property as a principal residence for periods aggregating two years or more during the five-year period immediately before the date of death [Code Sec. 121(b)(2)(A)(i) and (ii)]. The exclusion only applies to an unmarried taxpayer whose spouse is deceased on the date of sale of the principal residence. Thus, if the taxpayer remarries and sells the home within two years after the date of death of the first spouse, the taxpayer would not be entitled to the new $500,000 maximum exclusion amount for surviving spouses.

¶7020 MIXED-USE PROPERTY

A taxpayer who uses a portion of a property for both residential and business may take advantage of the home exclusion rules if the residential and business portions of the property are within the same dwelling unit [Reg. § 1.121-1(e)(1)]. The term *same dwelling unit* does not include appurtenant structures or other property. Thus, an allocation of the gain between personal use and business use is only required if the business portion of the property is not within the same building [Reg. § 1.121-1(e)(1)]. If the business portion of the property is separate from the dwelling unit used for residential purposes, the gain allocable to the business portion is not excludable under Code Sec. 121. For purposes of determining the amount of gain allocable to the residential and business portions of the property, the taxpayer must allocate the basis and the amount realized based on the square footage of the residential and business portions of the property.

The home sale exclusion is not available for any portion of the gain that is attributable to post-May 6, 1997, depreciation deductions claimed for business use of the home [Code Sec. 121(d)(6)]. Gain equal to the total depreciation claimed after May 6, 1997 is treated as unrecaptured Section 1250 gain and is taxed at 25 percent [Reg. § 1.121-1(d)(1)].

Example 7-14: *Nonresidential use of property not within the dwelling unit.* Taxpayer A owns a property that consists of a house, a stable, and 35 acres. A uses the stable and 28 acres for nonresidential purposes for more than three years during the five-year period preceding the sale. A uses the entire house and the remaining 7 acres as his principal residence for at least two years during the five-year period preceding the sale. A claims depreciation deductions of $9,000 for the nonresidential use of the stable. A sells the entire property, realizing a gain of $24,000. Because the stable and the 28 acres used in the business are separate from the dwelling unit, A must allocate the basis and amount realized between the portion of the property that he used as his principal residence and the portion of the property that he used for non-residential purposes. A determines that $14,000 of the gain is allocable to the non-residential-use portion of the property and that $10,000 of the gain is allocable to the portion of the property used as his residence. A must recognize the $14,000 of gain allocable to the non-residential-use portion of the property ($9,000 of which is unrecaptured Code Sec. 1250 gain, and $5,000 of which is adjusted net capital gain). A may exclude $10,000 of the gain from the sale of the property.

Example 7-15: *Nonresidential use of property not within the dwelling unit and rental of the entire property.* In 2006, Taxpayer B buys a property that includes a house, a barn, and two acres. B uses the house and land as her principal residence and the barn for an antiques business. In 2011, B moves out of the house and rents it to tenants. B sells the property in 2013, realizing a gain of $21,000. Between 2007 and 2013 B claims depreciation deductions of $4,800 attributable to the antiques business. Between 2011 and 2013 B claims depreciation deductions of $3,000 attributable to the house. Because the portion of the property used in the antiques business is separate from the dwelling unit, B must allocate basis and amount realized between the portion of the property that she used as her principal residence and the portion of the property that she used for nonresidential purposes. B determines that $4,000 of the gain is allocable to the nonresidential portion of the property and that $17,000 of the gain is allocable to the portion of the property that she used as her principal residence. B must recognize the $4,000 of gain allocable to the nonresidential portion of the property (all of which is unrecaptured Code Sec. 1250 gain). The Code Sec. 121 exclusion does not apply to the gain allocable to the residential portion of the property to the extent of the depreciation adjustments attributable to the residential portion of the property for periods after May 6, 1997 ($3,000). Therefore, B may exclude $14,000 of the gain from the sale of the property.

Example 7-16: *Nonresidential use of a separate dwelling unit.* In 2009 Taxpayer C buys a three-story townhouse and converts the basement level, which has a separate entrance, into a separate apartment by installing a kitchen and bathroom and removing the interior stairway that leads from the basement to the upper floors. After the conversion, the property constitutes two dwelling units. C uses the first and second floors of the townhouse as his principal residence and rents the basement level to tenants from 2010 to 2014. C claims depreciation deductions of $2,000 for that period with respect to the basement apartment. C sells the entire property in 2014, realizing gain of $18,000. Because the basement apartment and the upper floors of the townhouse are separate dwelling units, C must allocate the gain between the portion of the property that he used as his principal residence and the portion of the property that he used for nonresidential purposes. After allocating the basis and the amount realized between the residential and nonresidential portions of the property, C determines that $6,000 of the gain is allocable to the nonresidential portion of the property and that $12,000 of the gain is allocable to the portion of the property used as his residence. C must recognize the $6,000 of gain allocable to the nonresidential portion of the property ($2,000 of which is unrecaptured Code Sec. 1250 gain and $4,000 of which is adjusted net capital gain). C may exclude $12,000 of the gain from the sale of the property.

¶7025 REDUCED EXCLUSION IN SPECIAL SITUATIONS

A reduced maximum exclusion is available for taxpayers who fail to satisfy the ownership and use tests or the limit of one sale every two years because of a change in place of employment, health, or "unforeseen circumstances" affecting a qualified individual [Code Sec. 121(c)]. In a forced sale situation, an otherwise qualifying taxpayer who fails to satisfy the two-year ownership and use requirements can exclude the portion of the $250,000 amount ($500,000 if married filing a joint return), not the portion of the realized gain, which is equal to the fraction of the two years that the ownership and use requirements are met. The reduced maximum exclusion is computed by multiplying the maximum dollar limitation of $250,000 ($500,000 for certain joint filers) by a fraction. For purposes of the reduced maximum exclusion by reason of unforeseen circumstances, a *qualified* individual includes the taxpayer, the taxpayer's spouse, a co-owner of the residence, and a person whose principal place of abode is in the same household as the taxpayer [Reg. § 1.121-3(f)].

.01 Unforeseen Circumstances

A sale or exchange results from *unforeseen circumstances* if the primary reason for the sale or exchange is the occurrence of an event that the taxpayer could not reasonably have anticipated before purchasing and occupying the residence. Preference for a different residence or an improvement in financial circumstances does not qualify as unforeseen circumstances [Reg. § 1.121-3(e)(1)]. A taxpayer's primary reason for the sale or exchange is deemed to be unforeseen circumstances if one of the safe harbor events listed below occurs during the period of the taxpayer's ownership and use of the residence as a principal residence [Reg. § 1.121-3(e)(2)]. A taxpayer who does not qualify for a safe harbor may demonstrate that the primary reason for the sale or exchange is unforeseen circumstances, under a facts and circumstances test. The safe harbor events include the following [Reg. § 1.121-3(e)(2)(III)]:

1. Condemnation, seizure, or the involuntary conversion of the residence;
2. Damage to the principal residence resulting from a natural or man-made disaster or act of war or terrorism (without regard to whether, under the taxpayer's circumstances, the taxpayer is entitled to a casualty loss deduction under Code Sec. 165(h));
3. Death of a qualified individual including the taxpayer's spouse, home co-owner, or person living with the taxpayer;
4. Loss of a job and becoming eligible for unemployment compensation;
5. Change in employment or self-employment status resulting in an inability to pay housing costs and reasonable basic living expenses for the taxpayer's household (including amounts for food, clothing, medical expenses, taxes, transportation, court-ordered payments, and expenses reasonably necessary to production of income, but not for the maintenance of an affluent or luxurious standard of living);
6. Divorce or legal separation under a decree of divorce or separate maintenance;
7. Multiple births resulting from the same pregnancy of a qualified individual;
8. Neighbor's hostility, forcing sale of taxpayer's residence;[9]
9. Man-made disasters and acts of war including being a victim of the 9/11 terrorist attacks;[10]
10. Being forced to move because homeowners' association did not permit residents to maintain kennel and taxpayer was promoted to be a K-9 officer required to care for a dog and maintain a 6-foot by 9-foot kennel at the officer's residence;[11]
11. Adopting a child and being forced to sell one's home after living there for less than two years in order to comply with state adoption law which required couples who want to adopt a girl to provide her with her own sizable private bedroom;[12]
12. Being a victim of a violent crime at home that caused the taxpayer to move and never return to the residence;[13]
13. A police officer's sale of his home after using it as his principal residence for less than two years because the sale was prompted by a death threat the officer received after he arrested an alleged drug dealer;[14]
14. Exposure to unexpected excessive airplane noise necessitating a move;[15]

---

[9] LTR 200403049 (Sept. 26, 2003).
[10] Notice 2002-60, 2002-2 CB 482.
[11] LTR 200504012 (Oct. 14, 2004).
[12] LTR 200613009 (Apr. 4, 2006).
[13] LTR 200630004 (Apr. 28, 2006).
[14] LTR 200615011 (Dec. 8, 2005).
[15] LTR 200702032 (Sept. 29, 2006).

15. Second marriage and blended family necessitating purchase of a larger new home;[16]
16. Pregnancy and split-up necessitating purchase of a larger new home because the residence was not large enough to accommodate two adults and a child;[17]
17. Homeowner's daughter being subjected to verbal abuse and sexual assault while riding the school bus prompting parents to sell their home in order to move daughter away from the problems.[18]

Example 7-17: A buys a house in California. After A begins to use the house as her principal residence, an earthquake causes damage to her house. She sells the house the same year. The sale is within the safe harbor and she is entitled to claim a reduced maximum exclusion [Reg. § 1.121-3(e)(4), Ex. 1].

Example 7-18: B buys a house that he uses as his principal residence. The property is located on a heavily trafficked road. He sells the property the same year because the traffic is more disturbing than he expected. He is not entitled to claim a reduced maximum exclusion because the increased traffic and noise is not an unforeseen circumstance [Reg. § 1.121-3(e)(4), Ex. 5].

Example 7-19: D and her fiancé E buy a house and live in it as their principal residence. The following year, D and E cancel their wedding plans and E moves out of the house. Because D cannot afford to make the monthly mortgage payments alone, D and E sell the house. Even though these particular facts do not fit exactly within the parameters of one of the safe harbors, D and E are each entitled to claim a reduced maximum exclusion because the primary reason for the sale is an unforeseen circumstance [Reg. § 1.121-3(e)(4), Ex. 6].

.02 Employment Safe Harbor

A sale or exchange will result from a *change in place of employment* if the taxpayer's (or a qualified individual's) primary reason for the sale or exchange is a change in the location of the individual's employment [Reg. § 1.121-3(c) (1)]. Employment is defined as the commencement of employment with a new employer, the continuation of employment with the same employer, or the commencement or continuation of self-employment [Reg. § 1.121-3(c) (3)]. A qualified individual is defined as the taxpayer, the taxpayer's spouse, a co-owner of the residence, or a person whose principal place of abode is in the same household as the taxpayer.

The primary reason for the sale or exchange is deemed to be a change in place of employment if the new place of employment of a qualified individual is at least 50 miles farther from the residence sold or exchanged than was the former place of employment [Reg. § 1.121-3(c) (2) (ii)]. This is the same distance rule that applies for the moving expense deduction. If the individual was unemployed, the distance between the new place of employment and the residence sold or exchanged must be at least 50 miles.

---

[16] LTR 200725018 (Mar. 15, 2007).

[17] LTR 200652041 (Sept. 30, 2005), LTR 200745011 (Aug. 13, 2007).

[18] LTR 200820016 (Feb. 7, 2008).

The safe harbor applies only if the change in place of employment occurs during the period of the taxpayer's ownership and use of the property as the taxpayer's principal residence.

Example 7-20: A is unemployed and owns a townhouse that she has owned and used as her principal residence. The year after she moved in, A obtains a job that is 54 miles from her townhouse, and she sells her townhouse. Because the distance between A's new place of employment and the townhouse is at least 50 miles, the sale is within the safe harbor and she is entitled to claim a reduced maximum exclusion [Reg. § 1.121-3(c)(4), Ex. 1].

.03 Health Safe Harbor

The health condition will be satisfied if the primary purpose for the sale or exchange is (1) to obtain, provide, or facilitate the diagnosis, cure, mitigation, or treatment of disease, illness, or injury of a qualified individual, or (2) to obtain or provide medical or personal care for a qualified individual suffering from a disease, illness, or injury [Reg. § 1.121-3(d)(1)]. A sale or exchange that is merely beneficial to the general health or well being of the individual will not qualify as a sale or exchange for health reasons. A sale or exchange is deemed to be by reason by health if a physician recommends a change of residence for reasons of health [Reg. § 1.121-3(d)(2)]. For purposes of the reduced maximum exclusion for health reasons, the term *qualified individual* includes the taxpayer, the taxpayer's spouse, a co-owner of the residence, a person whose principal place of abode is in the same household as the taxpayer, and certain family members of these individuals [Reg. § 1.121-3(f)(5)]. The definition also encompasses taxpayers who sell or exchange their residence in order to care for sick family members.[19]

Example 7-21: Alice buys a house that she uses as her principal residence. She is injured in an accident and is unable to care for herself. As a result, she sells her house the following year and moves in with her daughter so her daughter can provide the care she needs. Because the primary reason for the sale of her house is her health, she is entitled to claim a reduced maximum exclusion [Reg. § 1.121-3(d)(3), Ex. 1].

Example 7-22: Brian, who has chronic asthma, purchases a house in Minnesota that he uses as his principal residence. His doctor tells him that moving to a warm, dry climate would mitigate his asthma symptoms. The following year, he sells his house and moves to Arizona to relieve his asthma symptoms. The sale is within the safe harbor and he is entitled to claim a reduced maximum exclusion [Reg. § 1.121-3(d)(3), Ex. 4]. If, however, he had not been diagnosed with chronic asthma, but merely wanted to move to a warmer climate because his doctor told him to get more exercise, the sale of the house would merely be beneficial to his general health and well being rather than because of his health

---

[19] LTR 200604013 (Oct. 18, 2005), LTR 200626024 (Mar. 23, 2006).

and he would not be entitled to claim a reduced maximum exclusion [Reg. § 1.121-3(d)(3), Ex. 5].

.04 Computation of Reduced Maximum Exclusion

For qualifying sellers, the maximum exclusion amount of $250,000 ($500,000 for a married couple filing jointly) is limited to the percentage of the two years that the person fulfilled the requirements. Thus, a qualifying seller who owns and occupies a home for one year (half of two years)—and who has not excluded gain on another home in that time—may exclude half the regular maximum amount, or up to $125,000 of gain ($250,000 for most joint returns). In more complicated situations, the reduced maximum exclusion is computed by multiplying the maximum dollar limitation of $250,000 ($500,000 for married couples filing joint returns) by a fraction. The numerator of the fraction is the shortest of the following periods: (1) the period of time that the taxpayer owned the property during the five-year period ending on the date of the sale or exchange, (2) the period of time that the taxpayer used the property as the taxpayer's principal residence during the five-year period ending on the date of the sale or exchange, or (3) the period of time between the date of a prior sale or exchange of property for which the taxpayer excluded gain and the date of the current sale or exchange. The numerator of the fraction may be expressed in days or months. The denominator of the fraction is 730 days or 24 months (depending on the measure of time used in the numerator) [Reg. § 1.121-3(g)].

Example 7-23: Taxpayer H owns a house that he has used as his principal residence since 2009. On January 15, 2012, H and W marry and W begins to use H's house as her principal residence. On January 15, 2013, H sells the house due to a change in W's place of employment. Neither H nor W has excluded gain on a prior sale or exchange of property within the last two years. Because H and W have not each used the house as their principal residence for at least two years during the five-year period preceding its sale, the maximum dollar limitation amount that may be claimed by H and W will not be $500,000, but the sum of each spouse's limitation amount determined on a separate basis as if they had not been married. H is eligible to exclude up to $250,000 of gain because he meets the requirements of Code Sec. 121. W is not eligible to exclude the maximum dollar limitation amount. Instead, because the sale of the house is due to a change in place of employment, W is eligible to claim a reduced maximum exclusion of up to $125,000 of the gain (365/730 × $250,000). H and W may exclude up to $375,000 of gain ($250,000 + $125,000) from the sale of the house [Reg. § 1.121-3(g), Ex. 2].

If taxpayers jointly own a principal residence but file separate returns, each taxpayer may exclude from gross income up to $250,000 of gain that is attributable to each taxpayer's interest in the property, if the requirements of Code Sec. 121 have otherwise been met [Reg. § 1.121-2(a)(2)].

.05 Sales or Exchanges of Partial Interests

A taxpayer may apply the home sale exclusion rules to gain from the sale or exchange of an interest in the taxpayer's principal residence that is less than the taxpayer's entire interest if the interest sold or exchanged includes an interest in the dwelling unit [Reg. § 1.121-4(e)]. Sales or exchanges of partial interests in the same principal residence are treated as one sale or exchange. Therefore, only one maximum limitation amount of $250,000 ($500,000 for certain joint returns) applies to the combined sales or exchanges of the partial interests. In applying the maximum limitation amount to sales or exchanges that occur in different tax years, a taxpayer may exclude gain from the first sale or exchange of a partial interest up to the taxpayer's full maximum limitation amount and may exclude gain from the sale or exchange of any other partial interest in the same principal residence to the extent of any remaining maximum limitation amount, and each spouse is treated as excluding one-half of the gain from the sale or exchange.

.06 Sales or Exchanges of Remainder Interests

A taxpayer may elect to apply the home sale exclusion rule to gain from the sale or exchange of a remainder interest in the taxpayer's principal residence [Reg. § 1.121-4(e)(2)]. If a taxpayer elects to exclude gain from the sale or exchange of a remainder interest in the taxpayer's principal residence, the exclusion will not apply to a sale or exchange of any other interest in the residence that is sold or exchanged separately. The taxpayer makes this election by filing a return for the tax year of the sale or exchange that does not include the gain from the sale or exchange of the remainder interest in the taxpayer's gross income. A taxpayer may make or revoke the election at any time before the expiration of a three-year period beginning on the last date prescribed by law (determined without regard to extensions) for the filing of the return for the tax year in which the sale or exchange occurred.

Example 7-24: In 1997, Taxpayer A buys a house that A uses as his principal residence. In 2012, A's friend B moves into A's house and A sells B a 50 percent interest in the house, realizing a gain of $136,000. A may exclude the $136,000 of gain. In 2013, A sells his remaining 50 percent interest in the home to B, realizing a gain of $138,000. A may exclude $114,000 ($250,000 – $136,000 gain previously excluded) of the $138,000 gain from the sale of the remaining interest [Reg. § 1.121-4(e)(3)].

¶7030 INVOLUNTARY CONVERSION OF PRINCIPAL RESIDENCE

If a taxpayer's principal residence is seized, condemned, completely destroyed,[20] or sold under the threat or imminence of condemnation, up to $250,000 ($500,000 if married filing a joint return) of the gain recognized on the involuntary conversion may be excluded from income [Code Sec. 121(d)(5)(A)]. If, however, the involuntarily converted principal residence is replaced, the tax picture becomes more complicated. The law requires you to apply the exclusion rules of Code Sec. 121 before the deferral

[20] A taxpayer's principal residence must be completely destroyed by a natural disaster for the home sale exclusion rule to apply to any gain realized from insurance proceeds [CCA 200734021].

provisions if the amount of the gain realized because of the involuntary conversion was less than $250,000 if single, or $500,000 if filing jointly. If the profits do, however, exceed these amounts, the taxpayer can avoid tax on the gain from the involuntary conversion only if he or she buys another home that exceeds the amount of the condemnation award [Code Sec. 1033(a)]. See discussion of Code Sec. 1033 at ¶ 7035.

Example 7-25: Bob and Ann Case own a home with a basis of $50,000, which was destroyed by fire. They receive insurance proceeds of $700,000. They purchase a new home that cost only $160,000. They can exclude $500,000 of the gain because they file a joint return and meet the ownership and use tests of Code Sec. 121 [¶ 7001]. They would then apply the involuntary conversion rules and would have to pay tax on $40,000 of the gain. They compute this by taking the $700,000 and subtracting the $500,000 exclusion amount to yield $200,000. They have rolled this over into a home costing $160,000 leaving $40,000 taxable gain. The new home would have a basis of $50,000, which is the $160,000 cost of the replacement residence minus the $110,000 gain [$160,000 minus the $50,000 original basis of the house] that was not recognized under the Code Sec. 1033 rules.

The taxpayer's basis in the new principal residence is determined by referring to the basis of the old principal residence. The taxpayer is treated as having owned and used the new principal residence for a period that includes the period that taxpayer owned and used the old principal residence [Code Sec. 121(d)(5)(C)].

For purposes of the home sale exclusion rules, the destruction, theft, seizure, requisition, or condemnation of property is treated as a sale of the property. In applying the Code Sec. 1033 involuntary conversion rules, the amount realized from the sale or exchange of property used as the taxpayer's principal residence is treated as being the amount determined without regard to Code Sec. 121, reduced by the amount of gain excluded from the taxpayer's gross income under Code Sec. 121 [Reg. § 1.121-4(d)(2)]. If the basis of the property acquired as a result of an involuntary conversion is determined (in whole or in part) under Code Sec. 1033(b), for purposes of satisfying the requirements of Code Sec. 121, the taxpayer will be treated as owning and using the acquired property as the taxpayer's principal residence during any period of time that the taxpayer owned and used the converted property as the taxpayer's principal residence.

Example 7-26: Fire destroys Taxpayer A's house which has an adjusted basis of $80,000. A had owned and used this property as her principal residence for 20 years prior to its destruction. A's insurance company pays A $400,000 for the house. A realizes a gain of $320,000 ($400,000 – $80,000). Later that year, A purchases a new house at a cost of $100,000. Because the destruction of the house is treated as a sale for purposes of Code Sec. 121, A will exclude $250,000 of the realized gain from A's gross income. For purposes of Code Sec. 1033, the amount realized is then treated as being $150,000 ($400,000 – $250,000) and the gain realized is $70,000 ($150,000 amount realized – $80,000 basis). A elects under Code Sec. 1033 to recognize only $50,000 of the gain ($150,000 amount realized – $100,000 cost of new house). The remaining $20,000 of gain is deferred and A's basis in the new house is $80,000 ($100,000 cost – $20,000 gain not recognized). A will be treated as owning and using the new house as A's principal residence during the 20-year period that A owned and used the destroyed house [Reg. § 1.121-4(d)].

CASUALTY—THEFT—CONDEMNATION

You may not have to pay tax when your property is completely destroyed,[21] stolen, seized or condemned in whole or in part, and you are compensated by insurance or other reimbursement. You ordinarily must report the difference between the value of what you receive and your adjusted basis in the property lost as taxable gain. The gain may not be currently taxable if you reinvest the proceeds. Gains or losses from a casualty or theft are figured on Form 4684, *Casualties and Thefts*, while Form 4797, *Sale of Business Property* is used for condemnations.

¶7035 GENERAL RULE FOR INVOLUNTARY CONVERSIONS

An *involuntary conversion* occurs when the taxpayer's property is stolen, condemned, destroyed, or disposed of under threat of condemnation, and the taxpayer receives an insurance payment or condemnation award of money or other property as compensation. To the extent the compensation exceeds the basis of the converted property, the taxpayer realizes gain. The taxpayer can elect to defer the gain from an involuntary conversion if he or she reinvests the payment or award in "similar or related" property within a certain period of time—generally, two years after the date of the conversion [Code Sec. 1033(a)(2)(B)]. The two-year time period is extended to four years in federally declared disaster areas [Code Sec. 1033(h)(1)(B)]. For list of federally declared disaster areas, see ¶ 5100.08.

In order for the involuntary conversion to be eligible for nonrecognition of gain, the following conditions must be met:

1. Property must be compulsorily or involuntarily converted in a qualifying event.

2. Eligible replacement property that is similar or related in service or use to the compulsorily or involuntarily converted property must be acquired [Code Sec. 1033(a)(1)]. See ¶ 7045.

3. The applicable time limits for replacing the converted property with eligible replacement property must be satisfied [Code Sec. 1033(a)(1); Reg. § 1.1033(a)-1(a)]. See ¶ 7050.

---

[21] CCA 200734021 (complete destruction required).

.01 Qualifying Event

Any gain realized on an involuntary conversion is eligible for deferral if property is compulsorily or involuntarily disposed of, and timely converted into, eligible property as a result of the following events:

1. Destruction in whole or in part by a casualty;
2. Fire, storm, accident, or theft;
3. Seizure of the property;
4. Requisition or condemnation of the property;
5. Sale under threat or imminence of the property's condemnation or requisition;
6. Certain dispositions of livestock;
7. Property sold pursuant to reclamation laws;
8. Property sold under FCC/SEC order authority.

.02 Fire or Theft

When a property owner receives cash or other compensation for property that has been destroyed by fire, storm, accident or some other sudden, unexpected, or unusual event, Code Sec. 1033 permits the property owner to defer recognizing any gain if the taxpayer reinvests the proceeds in similar property. *Sudden* has been defined quite liberally, and includes losses due to progressive deterioration. For example, the gain from having to cut and sell trees killed or infested by fungi or wood-destroying beetles may qualify as gain from involuntary conversion of property.[22]

Similarly, in a situation where a hurricane destroyed a taxpayer's trees and the taxpayer was forced to sell the trees prematurely, the IRS treated the transaction as an involuntary conversion under Code Sec. 1033.[23] The Tax Court has also held that a timber company could defer part of its gain on partially damaged trees under Code Sec. 1033 even though it processed them into finished products in the same way it did undamaged timber. The deferrable portion of the gain was equal to the timber's value when salvaged, less the taxpayer's basis in the trees.[24] The Tax Court ruled that the taxpayer met the general elements necessary to defer gain under Code Sec. 1033. The taxpayer's property was (1) involuntarily damaged, and (2) no longer available for the intended business purpose.

Theft includes larceny, embezzlement, and robbery [Ch. 13] [Reg. § 1.165-8(d)].

> **Example 7-27:** Brown's accountant, Smith, pledges Brown's common stock as collateral for Smith's personal loan without Brown's permission. This is theft under the involuntary conversion rules.

.03 Governmental Seizure and Condemnation

A seizure or condemnation occurs when a governmental body, in the exercise of its legal power, takes privately owned property for public use and pays a reasonable price

---

[22] LTR 8544001 (July 12, 1985).

[23] Rev. Rul. 80-175, 1980-2 CB 67.

[24] *Williamette Industries, Inc.*, 118 TC 126, Dec. 54,647 (2002).

for it. The taking of property for a limited time, however, is not an eligible conversion of property. Any compensation received is rent.[25]

Example 7-28: Gotham City, to install a new sewer system, digs up two acres of Mr. Wayne's land and replaces it one year later. This is not an involuntary conversion, and if Mr. Wayne received any money from the city, it would be taxable as rental income.

State's Taking of Stock Constituted Involuntary Conversion

In Letter Ruling 200946006,[26] the IRS ruled that a state's taking of stock under the state's escheat laws constituted an involuntary conversion under Code Sec. 1033. The two-year replacement period began when the taxpayer got hold of the proceeds of the stock sale from the state.

Sale or Exchange Under "Threat or Imminence" of Condemnation Entitled to Involuntary Conversion Treatment

A sale or exchange can qualify for tax-free treatment as an involuntary conversion if a sale or exchange takes place on account of a threat or imminence of condemnation. A threat or imminence of condemnation exists when a taxpayer is informed by a public official who has the power to condemn the property, that a decision has been made to acquire the property, and the taxpayer has reasonable grounds to believe that it will be condemned. A news media report that a condemnation is being considered is not a "threat or imminence." This occurs only when the condemning authority confirms that a decision has been made to condemn.[27]

Example 7-29: On Monday, Herman is informed by his neighbor that Herman's barn will soon be condemned. On Tuesday, Herman reads in the newspaper that the city is considering condemning his barn. On Thursday, Herman receives a visit from the mayor who tells Herman that his barn will be condemned to make way for a highway. Herman's barn was not under the "threat or imminence" of condemnation until he was informed by the mayor on Thursday.

A sale to someone other than the threatening authority qualifies as an involuntary conversion if the property owner reasonably believes that steps would be taken to condemn the property.[28] The IRS has held that a taxpayer's sale of property to a developer qualified for tax deferred treatment as an involuntary conversion since the property was under threat of condemnation that was judged by the court to be "sufficiently imminent."[29]

---

[25] Rev. Rul. 57-261, 1957-1 CB 262.

[26] LTR 200946006 (July 29, 2009).

[27] Rev. Rul. 74-8, 1974-1 CB 200, modifying Rev. Rul. 63-221, 1963-2 CB 332. *See also* LTR 200518066 (formal notification that taxpayer's property to be included in city's redevelopment plan not necessary because threat of condemnation existed).

[28] Rev. Rul. 81-180, 1981-2 CB 161.

[29] LTR 200145001 (Feb. 15, 2000); LTR 200219006 (Jan. 17, 2002).

.04 Destruction of Livestock—Disease and Drought

The destruction of livestock because of disease is treated as an involuntary conversion [Code Sec. 1033(d); Reg. § 1.1033(d)-1].

The sale or exchange of livestock (other than poultry) held for draft, breeding, or dairy purposes, in excess of the number that would normally be sold, is treated as an involuntary conversion if sold or exchanged solely on account of drought and flood or other weather-related conditions [Code Sec. 1033(e); Reg. § 1.1033(e)-1].

Involuntary Conversion of Livestock

If, because of drought, flood, or other weather-related conditions or soil contamination or other environmental contamination, it is not feasible for the taxpayer to reinvest the proceeds from compulsorily or involuntarily converted livestock in property similar or related in use to the livestock so converted, other property (including real property in the case of soil contamination or other environmental contamination) used for farming purposes will be treated as property similar or related in service or use to the livestock so converted [Code Sec. 1033(f)]. In addition, the replacement period is extended to four years (up from two years) when a taxpayer sells livestock (other than poultry) in excess of the number the taxpayer would sell if the taxpayer followed the taxpayer's usual business practices solely on account of drought, flood, or other weather-related conditions [Code Sec. 1033(e)(2)(A)]. If such weather-related conditions continue for more than three years, the IRS has authority to extend the time allowed for replacement on a regional basis for such additional time as it deems appropriate [Code Sec. 1033(e)(2)(B)].

Extension of Replacement Period for Persistent Drought

If a sale or exchange of livestock is treated as an involuntary conversion on account of drought and the taxpayer's replacement period is determined under Code Sec. 1033(e)(2)(A), the replacement period will be extended until the end of the taxpayer's first tax year ending after the first drought-free year for the applicable region. For this purpose, the first drought-free year for the applicable region is the first 12-month period that:

1. Ends on August 31;
2. Ends in or after the last year of the taxpayer's four-year replacement period; and
3. Does not include any weekly period for which exceptional, extreme, or severe drought is reported for any location in the applicable region.[30]

> **Example 7-30:** Calendar year Farmer's four-year replacement period ends on December 31, 2012. For the 12-month period ending on August 31, 2012, severe drought conditions are reported on U.S. Drought Monitor maps for all counties in the applicable region, and all of those counties are included on the list published by the IRS. For the 12-month period ending on August 31, 2013, the only drought conditions reported for the applicable region on U.S. Drought Monitor maps are severe drought conditions for one county in the applicable region for the first week in September 2011 and that county is included on the

[30] Notice 2006-82, 2006-2 CB 529.

IRS list. For the 12-month period ending August 31, 2014, U.S. Drought Monitor maps do not report drought conditions for any county in the applicable region and none of the counties are included on the list published by the IRS. Farmer's replacement period is extended through December 31, 2014 (the last day of A's first tax year ending after the first drought-free year for the applicable region). Neither the 12-month period ending on August 31, 2012, nor the one ending on August 31, 2013, is a drought-free year for the applicable region; in each of these 12-month periods, severe drought conditions have been reported for at least one county in the applicable region for a part of the 12-month period. The first drought-free year for the applicable region is the 12-month period ending on August 31, 2014.

An election to defer reporting of gain from the forced sale of livestock in the year after the sale (under Code Sec. 451(e)) is considered valid if made during the extended replacement period [Code Sec. 451(e)(3)].

.05 Use and Occupancy (Business Interruption) Insurance Proceeds

If an insurance policy by its terms insures against loss of profits due to an involuntary conversion, the recovery is treated as income, equivalent to the earnings it replaced. If, however, the policy is of the valued type (i.e., it pays a fixed amount per week), the recovery under the policy is treated as proceeds of involuntary conversion.

.06 Sales Under Reclamation Laws

The sale or exchange or other disposition of property in an irrigation project qualifies as an involuntary conversion [Code Sec. 1033(c); Reg. § 1.1033(c)-1].

¶7040 GAIN OR LOSS ON INVOLUNTARY CONVERSION—GENERAL RULES

If property is involuntarily converted directly into other similar or related property, no gain or loss is recognized [Code Sec. 1033(a)(1)]. This may happen if a condemning governmental authority gives the taxpayer property instead of a monetary award.

If you receive payment for property involuntarily converted and replace it with property that is similar or related in service or use, the following three rules apply [Code Sec. 1033(a)(2); Reg. § 1.1033(a)-1(a)]:

1. If the amount realized equals or is less than the cost of the replacement property, no gain is recognized.

   Example 7-31: Mr. Drake receives $100,000 in insurance proceeds for property destroyed and buys similar replacement property for $200,000. No gain is recognized.

2. If the amount realized exceeds the cost of replacement, gain is recognized to the extent of the excess.

Example 7-32: Mr. Drake receives $100,000 in insurance proceeds and spends only $20,000 on replacement property. Depending on Drake's basis in the old property, he may have to recognize up to $80,000 of the gain. (See ¶ 7055 for a detailed explanation of gain computations.) Important: This special relief is available to both owners and renters of principal residences [Code Sec. 1033(h)(4)].

3. A loss on an involuntary conversion is generally recognized (i.e., deductible) [¶ 7055].

The rules for nonrecognition of gain do not apply unless (a) the replacement is made within a certain period of time (generally, two years) [¶ 7050], and (b) you elect to have the rules apply [Code Sec. 1033(a)(2); Reg. § 1.1033(a)-2(c)].

NOTE: Expenses that you incur in connection with the conversion (e.g., legal, engineering and appraisal fees) reduce your amount realized and thereby reduce your involuntary conversion gain.[31]

Example 7-33: You receive a condemnation award and severance damages. One-fourth of the total was designated as severance damages in your agreement with the condemning authority. You had legal expenses for the entire condemnation proceeding. You cannot determine how much of your legal expenses are for each part of the condemnation proceeds. You must allocate one-fourth of your legal expenses to the severance damages and the other three-fourths to the condemnation award.

.01 Relief Available

Any tangible property acquired and held for productive use in a business is treated as similar or related in service or use to property that (1) was held for investment or for productive use in a business and (2) was involuntarily converted as a result of a federally declared disaster [Code Sec. 1033(h)(2)].

This involuntary conversion rule provides relief to businesses forced to close their doors for a long period of time as a result of a federally declared disaster that damaged their property. They may be forced to reinvest their money in a new or different business venture. With respect to federally declared disasters, taxpayers can elect not to recognize gain with respect to the involuntarily converted property that is replaced by any other tangible business or investment property acquired within the appropriate time period.

Example 7-34: You run a beach-front sandwich shop that was destroyed in a federally declared disaster. You receive insurance proceeds within two months of the destruction of the sandwich shop. You immediately use all of the proceeds to purchase a computer, fax machine, and printer to open a mail-order natural foods business from your home. You may elect not to recognize gain with respect to the involuntarily converted sandwich shop.

---

[31] Treas. Dept., IRS Publication 544, "Sales and Other Dispositions of Assets" (2012 Ed.), p. 7.

In Technical Advice Memorandum 201111004, the IRS concluded that inventory that was involuntarily converted in a presidentially declared disaster was "property held for productive use in a trade or business" under Code Sec. 1033(h)(2). The taxpayer suffered losses due to hurricanes, more than half of which consisted of lost or damaged inventory. The taxpayer planned to invest insurance proceeds in replacement property. Gain would be recognized only to the extent that the realized amount exceeded the cost of the replacement property. The IRS concluded that Code Sec. 1033(h)(2) applied to inventory.

Involuntary Conversions Include Dispositions Under Hazard Mitigation Programs

Code Sec. 1033(k) provides that sales or transfers to the federal, state, or local government, or an Indian tribal government to implement hazard mitigation under the Robert T. Stafford Disaster Relief and Emergency Assistance Act of the National Flood Insurance Act qualify as tax-free involuntary conversions. This means that taxpayers who sell or transfer their property under these programs may defer tax on any realized gain by timely reinvesting the proceeds into property similar or related in service or use to the damaged or destroyed property.

.02 Residence and Land Treated as One

The IRS has concluded that the sale of land that contained a principal residence destroyed by a tornado that qualified as a federally declared disaster, should be treated as part of a single involuntary conversion of the residence on the date it was destroyed.[32] Consequently gain realized on the sale of the land could be deferred for four years. Because the taxpayer's principal residence before the disaster consisted of both the dwelling and the land, the sale of that land was treated as part of a single involuntary conversion of the principal residence that occurred on the date the dwelling was destroyed.

The IRS also concluded that property continued to be eligible for mortgage interest deductions until the taxpayer sold the land, even though the principal residence that once stood on the land had been destroyed by an earthquake.[33]

.03 Principal Residence Damaged in Federally Declared Disaster

A taxpayer whose principal residence was damaged in a federally declared disaster can take advantage of the following special tax relief:[34]

- The replacement period for property involuntarily converted as a result of a federally declared disaster is four years after the close of the first tax year in which any part of the gain upon conversion is realized [Code Sec. 1033(h)(1)(A)].
- The late identification of replacement property after a principal residence has been destroyed as a result of a federally declared disaster won't disqualify a taxpayer from claiming nonrecognition of gain under the involuntary conversion rules of Code Sec. 1033.[35]

---

[32] Rev. Rul. 96-32, 1996-1 CB 177.

[33] Rev. Rul. 96-32, 1996-1 CB 177.

[34] Rev. Rul. 95-22, 1995-1 CB 145.

[35] LTR 201240006 (June 5, 2012).

- Insurance proceeds for unscheduled personal property (miscellaneous items not specifically listed in the policy) that was part of the home's contents are automatically tax-free regardless of what you do with the money [Code Sec. 1033(h)(1)(A)(i)]. There is no need to calculate whether the insurance recovery represents gain; and
- Other insurance proceeds for the home and its contents can be lumped together and treated as a "common pool of funds" for purposes of the replacement break. Thus, if you buy a replacement home (or replacement personal property), you can elect to recognize gain only to the extent the insurance proceeds for all of these items exceed replacement costs [Code Sec. 1033(h)(1)(A)(ii)]. You do not have to calculate gain on individual items. You can therefore defer paying tax on insurance proceeds only to the extent that you spend an amount equal to your "common pool of funds," which are the insurance proceeds received for the residence plus the separately scheduled contents.

¶7045 WHAT QUALIFIES AS REPLACEMENT PROPERTY

To avoid recognizing gain on an involuntary conversion, a taxpayer must generally reinvest the proceeds in property that is similar or related in service or use to the converted property [Code Sec. 1033(a)(2)].

.01 "Similar or Related in Service or Use" Test of Owner-Users

To qualify as *similar or related* property, the nature of the replacement property's service or use must be similar or related in use to the converted property.[36] The replacement property does not have to be identical to the converted property as long as it has the same general characteristics. That is, the replacement property must be functionally the same as the converted property. Thus, a business vehicle must be replaced with another, and it must perform the same function. Under this test, property is not considered similar or related in service or use to the converted property unless the physical characteristics and end uses of the converted and replacement properties are similar. For example, under the close functional similarity test, a corporation that lost its headquarters office building to fire could replace it with another office building. However, the close functional similarity test is not met if a company replaced its destroyed parking garage with a warehouse.

Example 7-35: Johnson's farmland is destroyed in a fire. If Johnson takes the insurance proceeds and purchases a vacation home, Johnson must recognize any gain from the proceeds. If Johnson uses the proceeds to purchase more farmland, the gain will not be recognized.[37]

---

[36] Rev. Rul. 64-237, 1964-2 CB 319; *F. Maloof*, 65 TC 263, Dec. 33,499 (1975).

[37] Rev. Rul. 69-240, 1969-1 CB 199.

.02 Owner-Lessors

When determining whether replacement property acquired by an owner-lessor is similar in service or use to converted property that was leased to others, focus on the similarity of the relationship of the services or uses that the original and replacement property have to the taxpayer-owner. Thus, new rental property can qualify to replace old, even though the tenant's functional uses differ.[38] In determining whether the relationship to the use of the original and replacement properties is similar, the following questions should be asked: (1) Are the properties of a similar nature? (2) What is the nature of the business risks connected with the properties? (3) What types of demands do the properties place on the taxpayer in terms of management, services and relations to his tenants?

> **Example 7-36:** Adams leased part of his old building to lessees who used it as a movie theater, and part to other lessees who sold groceries. If he leases the replacement building as a department store, it will qualify for the rollover. If he uses the new building as his personal residence, however, the replacement will not qualify.[39]

.03 Acquiring Control of a Corporation

Qualified replacement property can be bought, built, obtained directly or by acquiring control of a corporation owning similar property. Control of a corporation means you own at least 80 percent of the total combined voting power of all classes of stock and at least 80 percent of the total number of shares of all other classes of stock [Code Sec. 1033(a)(2)(E)(i); Reg. § 1.1033(a)-2(c)].

> **Example 7-37:** Glass owned a card shop that was destroyed by fire. Using the insurance proceeds, she acquired 80 percent of the stock of Ajax Company which owns a card shop similar to the one that burned down. Because she meets the "control" requirements, her gain from the proceeds will not be recognized.

.04 Like-Kind Test—Condemnation of Real Property

A special and more liberal rule applies to the replacement of real property that is held for investment or used in a trade or business (not including stock in trade or other property held primarily for sale). When such property is condemned (or is sold under its threat or imminence), gain is not recognized if you replace it with "like-kind" property [Code Sec. 1033(g); Reg. § 1.1033(g)-1].

For this purpose, *like-kind* has the same meaning as it has in the rule for nontaxable exchanges of property held for productive use or investment [¶ 6050]. Thus improved and unimproved property would be of a like-kind in condemnation cases. This special rule does not apply to acquiring a controlling interest in a corporation, or to stock in

---

[38] *Liant Record, Inc.*, CA-2, 62-1 USTC ¶ 9494, 303 F2d 326; Rev. Rul. 71-41, 1971-1 CB 223; Rev. Rul. 76-391, 1976-2 CB 243.

[39] Rev. Rul. 70-466, 1970-2 CB 165; amplified by Rev. Rul. 76-84, 1976-1 CB 219.

trade or other property held primarily for sale. You can also elect to treat outdoor advertising displays as real property [Code Sec. 1033(g)(3); Reg. § 1.1033(g)-1(b)].

¶7050 TIME LIMIT ON REPLACEMENT

.01 Two Years

The period within which you must replace the converted property starts with the date of the disposition, or the date the threat or imminence of its condemnation began, whichever is earlier. The period ends two years after the conversion is realized [Code Sec. 1033(a)(2)(B)(i)].[40]

> ▶ **SPECIAL DISASTER AREA RELIEF:** The replacement period for a taxpayer whose principal residence was damaged in a federally declared disaster area is four years [Code Sec. 1033(h)(1)(B)]. Both owners and renters are entitled to this longer replacement period. For list of federally declared disaster areas, see ¶5100.08.

Nonrecognition Replacement Period Extended for Hurricane Katrina Victims

If an individual with a principal residence damaged by Hurricane Katrina receives insurance reimbursement, the normal 4-year tax-free replacement period is extended to five years for victims of Hurricane Katrina. Businesses generally must invest in replacement property within two years to qualify for the gain exclusion. The Katrina Emergency Tax Relief Act extended that reinvestment timeframe to five years. In order for both individuals and businesses to qualify for the extended replacement period, the replacement property must be located in the disaster area.

Replacement Period for Converted Property in Midwestern Disaster Area Extended

The replacement period for property in the Midwestern disaster area that is compulsorily or involuntarily converted on or after the applicable disaster date due to the storms that hit the Midwestern United States in the summer of 2008 is extended from two years to five years.

.02 Extension

The standard two-year time period may be extended upon request [Reg. § 1.1033(a)-2(c)(3)].

.03 Prior Acquisition

If you make the replacement before the disposition of the converted property, the replacement property or stock must be held by you on the disposition.

.04 Three Years for Certain Real Property

For real property held for productive use in a trade or business or for investment, the time period for replacement is three years [Code Sec. 1033(g)(4); Reg. § 1.1033(g)-1(c)].

---

[40] *J.F. Latimer*, 55 TC 515, Dec. 30,468 (1970).

.05 Advance Payment to Contractor

A payment prior to construction of the replacement property may be timely even if the construction is not completed before the end of the replacement period. The fact that a contract to construct replacement property is entered into has fulfilled the time requirements where the taxpayer requested an extension of time for reinvestment of involuntary conversion proceeds.[41]

¶7055 HOW TO FIGURE GAIN OR LOSS ON AN INVOLUNTARY CONVERSION

The following discussion shows how to apply the rules outlined in ¶7040 governing recognition of gain or loss on involuntary conversion [Code Sec. 1033(a)(2)(A); Reg. § 1.1033(a)-2(c)]:

.01 If There Is a Direct Conversion Into Other Property

In situations of direct conversions, you do not recognize gain or loss.

Related Party Rule

As a general rule, taxpayers may not take advantage of the tax-free involuntary conversion rules if they acquire replacement property from a related party, as defined in Code Sec. 267(b). An exception to this rule exists if the taxpayer (other than a C corporation or a partnership in which one or more C corporations own, directly or indirectly, more than 50 percent of the capital interest or profits interest in the partnership at the time of the involuntary conversion) has aggregate realized gain of $100,000 or less from the converted property for the tax year. The general rule also will not apply if the related person acquired the replacement property from an unrelated person during the replacement period [Code Sec. 1033(i)(2)].

.02 If the Basis of the Converted Asset Exceeds the Amount Realized

In this case, you recognize a loss if it is a (1) casualty or theft loss [Ch. 13] or (2) incurred in a trade, business or transaction entered into for profit [Ch. 13]. Thus, an involuntary conversion loss from a fire in a residence or business building is deductible. However, an involuntary loss from condemnation is deductible only for the business building. No loss is allowed for the residence [¶7001; Ch. 13].

.03 If There Is Gain on the Conversion and the Amount Realized Exceeds the Cost of Replacement

Here you must recognize gain to the extent of the excess. You may elect nonrecognition for the remainder of the gain [Code Sec. 1033(a)(2)(A)].

Special Disaster Area Relief

It is easier for taxpayers whose principal residences are damaged in federally declared disaster areas to avoid tax on insurance proceeds [see ¶7040]. For list of federally declared disaster areas, see ¶5100.08.

---

[41] *T.M. Lemly*, 32 TCM 697, Dec. 32,040(M), TC Memo. 1973-147.

.04 If the Cost of Replacement Exceeds the Amount Realized

If there is gain and the cost of the replacement exceeds the amount realized, you may elect nonrecognition of gain. You cannot take the excess of the cost of replacement over the amount received as a loss. It is treated as a capital expenditure [Ch. 12].

¶7060 BASIS OF REPLACEMENT PROPERTY ACQUIRED IN INVOLUNTARY CONVERSION

The taxpayer's basis in replacement property in an involuntary conversion depends on a number of factors, such as whether there is a direct conversion and whether or not a gain or loss is recognized [Code Sec. 1033(b); Reg. § 1.1033(b)-1].

.01 Direct Conversion

When the taxpayer does not recognize gain because property is directly converted into other property similar or related in service or use, the taxpayer's basis in the new asset is the same as his or her adjusted basis in the old asset.

Example 7-38: Land owned by Betty that had an adjusted basis of $50,000, was condemned by the county, and Betty received similar land from the county to replace her condemned land. The basis of the new land is $50,000.

.02 When Loss Is Recognized

In this situation, the taxpayer's basis in the new property is its replacement cost.

Example 7-39: Chester's factory with an adjusted basis of $1,000,000 was destroyed by fire. The insurance proceeds were $850,000. He bought a new plant for $1,200,000. A loss of $150,000 is recognized and the new factory's basis is $1,200,000.

.03 When No Gain Is Recognized Because Cost of Replacement Exceeds Amount Realized

In this situation, the taxpayer's basis in the replacement property is its cost less gain not recognized [¶ 7040; ¶ 7055].

Example 7-40: Wilma's plant with a $1,100,000 adjusted basis was destroyed by fire. The insurance proceeds were $1,220,000. Wilma bought a new plant for $1,300,000. No gain is recognized. The basis of the new plant is $1,180,000, figured as follows:

Realized gain	$ 120,000
Recognized gain	0
Gain not recognized	$ 120,000
Cost of new plant	$1,300,000
Less: Gain not recognized	120,000
Basis of new plant	$1,180,000

.04 When Gain Is Recognized Because the Amount Realized Exceeds the Cost of Replacement

In this situation, the taxpayer's basis in the replacement property is its cost less any gain not recognized [¶ 7040; ¶ 7055].

Example 7-41: Gordon owned a garage with an adjusted basis of $65,000 which the state condemned. He received a $75,000 award and bought a new garage for $70,000. His realized gain is $10,000 but only $5,000 of it is recognized (excess of condemnation proceeds over cost of new property). The new garage's basis is $65,000, figured as follows:

Realized gain	$10,000
Recognized gain	5,000
Gain not recognized	$ 5,000
Cost of new garage	$70,000
Less: Gain not recognized	5,000
Basis of new garage	$65,000

.05 If More Than One Property Is Bought

In this situation, the taxpayer's basis is allocated to the properties in proportion to their respective costs.[42] The taxpayer's basis in improved real property must be similarly allocated between the land and improvements, according to the value of each.[43]

Example 7-42: Wilbur owned a farm with an adjusted basis of $370,000 which the state condemned. He received a $420,000 award and bought two adjoining farms totaling about the same acreage as the condemned land. He paid $180,000 for farm 1 and $220,000 for farm 2. His realized gain is $50,000, but only $20,000 of it is recognized (excess of condemnation proceeds over new properties' total cost). The basis of each of the new properties is figured as follows:

Realized gain	$ 50,000
Recognized gain	20,000
Gain not recognized	$ 30,000
Cost of new property (both farms)	$400,000
Less: Gain not recognized	30,000
Basis of new property (both farms)	$370,000

Allocation: Basis of farm #1: $180,000/400,000 × $370,000 = $166,500

Basis of farm #2: $220,000/400,000 × $370,000 = $203,500

[42] Rev. Rul. 73-18, 1973-1 CB 368.

[43] Rev. Rul. 79-402, 1972-2 CB 297.

.06 Basis in Partial Condemnation

If part of a property is condemned, the taxpayer's basis in the condemned part and his or her basis in the part retained must each be determined in order to compute gain or loss from the condemnation. It is important to determine basis in the retained part in case it is later sold or condemned. Allocating the taxpayer's basis presents a problem if the property is improved real estate that was purchased for a lump sum. In such a situation, the local tax authority's assessed valuation may be used to allocate basis.

Example 7-43: Land and building were bought for $60,000. Assessed valuations are: land—$18,000; building—$12,000. The land's basis is $36,000:

$$\frac{\$18{,}000}{\$18{,}000 + \$12{,}000} \times \$60{,}000 = \$36{,}000$$

The building's basis is $24,000 ($60,000 - $36,000). If one-third of the land was condemned, the basis of the condemned portion would be $12,000 ($36,000 ÷ 3).

.07 Basis Adjustment When Stock in Corporation Is Acquired as Replacement Property

When you satisfy the replacement property requirement of Code Sec. 1033 by acquiring stock in a corporation, the corporation generally will reduce its adjusted bases in its assets by the amount by which you reduce your basis in the stock. The corporation's adjusted bases in its assets will not be reduced, in the aggregate, below your basis in its stock (determined after the appropriate basis adjustment for the stock). In addition, the basis of any individual assets will not be reduced below zero. The basis reduction first is applied to (1) property that is similar or related in service or use to the converted property, then (2) to other depreciable property, then (3) to other property [Code Sec. 1033(b)]. The corporation is required to reduce the bases of its assets in order to prevent you from having more aggregate depreciable basis after the acquisition of replacement property than before the involuntary conversion.

▶ **WARNING:** As a result of this provision regarding basis adjustments, you may be better off acquiring replacement property directly from the corporation rather than acquiring control of a corporation that owns replacement property. There is a potential for double taxation when you acquire control of the corporation because the gain deferred as a result of the involuntary conversion is reflected in your stock basis reduction and is then duplicated when the corporation's basis in its assets is also reduced.

Example 7-44: Alex owns a strip shopping mall with an adjusted basis of $250,000 that was involuntarily converted. Alex receives $1 million in insurance proceeds and then acquires all the stock of a commercial developer who has a single asset. This asset, a shopping mall has an adjusted basis of $1,000,000. Since this stock acquisition qualifies as the acquisition of replacement property, Alex must reduce the basis in the acquired stock to $250,000 to reflect the $750,000 gain that is not recognized and the developer must reduce the adjusted basis in the mall to $250,000.

¶7065 HOW TO MAKE THE REPLACEMENT AND ELECTION

Taxpayers elect nonrecognition of gain treatment by reporting on their return only the portion of gain that is taxable after applying the involuntary conversion rules. If taxpayers don't replace the property within the time limit, or do so at a lower cost than anticipated, they must file an amended return recomputing the tax liability for the year of election.

.01 Who Must Make the Replacement?

Generally, the taxpayer or his or her agent must make the replacement. Tenants may replace leased property when they have to return it in the same condition as they receive it.[44] Replacement by a taxpayer's controlled corporation does not qualify.[45] Replacement of partnership property must be made by the partnership, not the individual partner.[46] A court has allowed a decedent's executor to make the replacement,[47] but the IRS disagrees.[48]

.02 Who Must Make the Election?

Generally, the election is made by the taxpayer. The grantor of a reversionary trust must make the election if he is taxable on the income of the trust.[49] Partnerships must make the election, not the individual partners.[50]

.03 Information on the Return

When there is a gain on an involuntary conversion, you must report the details in a statement submitted with your return for the year the gain was realized. These details relate to the replacement of the converted property, the decision not to replace or the end of the replacement period. If you actually acquire replacement property in a later year, details of the replacement are reported on the return for that year [Reg. § 1.1033(a)-2(c)(2)].

¶7070 SPECIAL BENEFIT ASSESSMENTS

In a situation where only part of your property is condemned, a special assessment levied against the remaining property may be taken out of your condemnation award. An assessment may be levied if the remaining part of your property benefited by the improvement resulting from the condemnation. Examples of such improvements that may result in a special assessment often include the widening of streets or the installation of sewers. To figure your net condemnation award the assessments first

---

[44] *W.P. Adams*, 16 BTA 497, Dec. 5153, *nonacq.* 1930-1 CB 60.

[45] *A.K. Feinberg*, CA-8, 67-1 USTC ¶9413, 377 F2d 21.

[46] Rev. Rul. 66-191, 1966-2 CB 300.

[47] *J. Goodman Est.*, CA-3, 52-2 USTC ¶9556, 199 F2d 895.

[48] Rev. Rul. 64-161, 1964-1 CB 298.

[49] Rev. Rul. 88-103, 1988-2 CB 304.

[50] Rev. Rul. 66-191, 1966-2 CB 300.

reduce any severance damages and any excess reduces the condemnation award. Anything remaining is added to the property's basis. The reductions apply only if the assessment was actually withheld from the condemnation award.[51]

Example 7-45: The city condemned a 25-foot deep strip of land when widening the street in front of your house. You were awarded $5,000 for this and spent $300 to obtain the award. Before paying the award, the city levied a special assessment of $700 for the street improvement against your remaining property. The city then paid you only $4,300. Your net award is $4,000 ($5,000 total award minus $300 expenses in obtaining the award and $700 for the special assessment). If the $700 special assessment were not taken out of the award and you were paid $5,000, your net award would be $4,700 ($5,000 – $300). The net award would not change, even if you later paid the assessment from the amount you received.

¶7075 SEVERANCE DAMAGES

.01 Severance Damages Defined

Severance damages are amounts paid to taxpayers in addition to the award they receive when their property is condemned. Severance damages are paid to taxpayers if part of their property is condemned and the value of the property retained is decreased as a result of the condemnation. For example, a taxpayer may receive severance damages if his or her property is condemned for a highway, but as a result of the condemnation the taxpayer must replace fences, dig new wells or ditches, or plant trees to restore the remaining property to the same usefulness it had before the condemnation.[52] Where it is not clearly shown that a condemnation award includes a specific amount for severance damages, it will be presumed that the proceeds were given in consideration of the property condemned only.[53] There have been cases, however, where the Tax Court allowed allocations of condemnation awards to severance damages.[54]

.02 Nonrecognition Treatment of Severance Damages

Severance damages, if used to restore retained property (e.g., rebuilding of stone wall or fence) or purchase like property, can be accorded nonrecognition treatment.[55]

Severance damages received must first be reduced by: (1) the expenses incurred in securing the severance damages and (2) the amount of any special assessment [¶ 7070] levied against the part of the property retained and withheld from the award by the condemning authority. Any balance of the proceeds you use to restore the retained

[51] Treas. Dept., IRS Publication 544, "Sales and Other Dispositions of Assets" (2012 Ed.), p. 8.

[52] Treas. Dept., IRS Publication 544, "Sales and Other Dispositions of Assets" (2012 Ed.), pp. 7-8.

[53] Rev. Rul. 59-173, 1959-1 CB 201; *A.D. Lapham*, CA-2, 50-1 USTC ¶9153, 178 F2d 994.

[54] *L.A. Beeghly*, 36 TC 154, Dec. 24,797, *acq.* 1962-1 CB 3.

[55] Rev. Rul. 83-49, 1983-1 CB 191.

property to its former use or to purchase similar use property is gain, eligible for nonrecognition treatment.

Any gain remaining after you have purchased the replacement property is recognized to the extent it exceeds the basis of the retained property.[56]

Example 7-46: Lori Smith receives a $10,000 condemnation award for part of her property taken by the state and uses the proceeds to purchase like property. She also receives $4,000 in severance damages for the decrease in value to the portion of the retained property. There is no special assessment, and Lori's basis in the retained property had been $1,000. She spends $1,500 to dig a new well on the retained property to replace the one on the condemned property, and incurs $1,000 in legal fees to obtain the severance damages. Result: Lori has $500 recognized gain ($4,000 severance damages less $1,000 legal fees incurred, less $1,500 cost of new well, less $1,000 basis in retained property) and a zero basis in the retained property.

[56] Rev. Rul. 68-37, 1968-1 CB 359. Treas. Dept., IRS Publication 544, "Sales and Other Dispositions of Assets" (2012 Ed.), p. 8.

Capital Gains and Losses of Individuals

8

CAPITAL GAINS AND LOSSES

Capital gains and losses in general . . . . . ¶ 8001
Anticonversion transactions . . . . . ¶ 8005
What is a capital asset? . . . . . ¶ 8010
A sale or exchange required . . . . . ¶ 8015

HOLDING PERIOD

Figuring the holding period . . . . . ¶ 8020
First-in, first-out rule . . . . . ¶ 8025
Short sales . . . . . ¶ 8030
"Put" and "call" options . . . . . ¶ 8035
Mark-to-market method . . . . . ¶ 8040

FIGURING CAPITAL GAIN OR LOSS

How to report capital gain or loss . . . . . ¶ 8045
Capital loss deduction . . . . . ¶ 8050
Capital loss carryforward . . . . . ¶ 8051

DISPOSING OF BUSINESS PROPERTY

Sale or exchange of Sec. 1231 assets . . . . . ¶ 8055
Recapture of depreciation . . . . . ¶ 8060
Involuntary conversions . . . . . ¶ 8065
Timber . . . . . ¶ 8070
Farmers' Code Sec. 1231 transactions . . . . . ¶ 8075
Disposal of coal and iron ore . . . . . ¶ 8080
Sale of depreciable property between related parties . . . . . ¶ 8085

SPECIAL RULES

Collapsible corporation rules repealed . . . . . ¶ 8090
Loss on Section 1244 small business stock . . . . . ¶ 8095
Subdividing realty for sale . . . . . ¶ 8100
Exclusion for qualified small business stock (QSBS) gain . . . . . ¶ 8105
Tax breaks for investing in minority businesses . . . . . ¶ 8110

CAPITAL GAINS AND LOSSES

It is important for taxpayers to identify their capital gains and losses. To begin with, they should net capital gains and losses together to figure taxable capital gain or deductible capital loss. Keep in mind that capital gain or loss is treated differently from ordinary gain or loss. There are special limits on the amount of deductible capital loss. In addition, long-term capital gain is afforded tax-favored treatment not available for other income.

¶8001 CAPITAL GAINS AND LOSSES IN GENERAL

Generally, a capital gain or loss results from disposing of a capital asset [¶8005] by a sale or exchange [¶8015]. When the property sold or exchanged is a capital asset, or treated like one, the next step is to determine how long the property has been held [¶8020-¶8035]. If the property is held for more than various holding periods described below, a sale or exchange results in a long-term capital gain or loss. Capital assets must be held for more than 12 months prior to the sale in order for the gain to be classified as long-term capital gain [Code Sec. 1222]. If the property is held for one year or less, its sale or exchange results in a short-term capital gain or loss. Both net short-term and net long-term capital losses are combined for purposes of offsetting ordinary income

> **Example 8-1:** Taxpayer has $50,000 of ordinary income, a net short-term capital loss of $700 and a net long-term capital loss of $500. Taxpayer's capital loss deduction is $1,200, the full sum of both losses.

Capital gains and losses can offset each other in full—regardless of whether they are short-term or long-term. If the taxpayer has a net capital loss for the year (capital loss exceeds capital gain), he or she can currently deduct only up to $3,000 of this loss against ordinary income (e.g., salary, interest, dividends). On the other hand, if their capital gains exceed capital losses for the year, the tax treatment of gain depends on whether the gain is long-term or short-term [¶ 8045].

Short-term capital gain is taxed at the same rates as ordinary income. That was also true for so-called "net capital gain"—the excess of net long-term capital gain over net short-term capital loss.

.01 Tax Treatment of Capital Gains

Table 1. Capital Gains Rate for Individuals—2013

Beginning in 2013, the capital gains rates for individuals are as follows:

- A capital gains rate of 0 percent applies to the adjusted net capital gains of individuals if the gain would otherwise be subject to the 10- or 15-percent ordinary income tax rate [Code Secs. 1(h)(1)(B), 55(b)(3)(B)].
- A capital gains rate of 15 percent applies to adjusted net capital gains of individuals if the gain would otherwise be subject to the 25-, 28-, 33-, or 35-percent ordinary income tax rate [Code Secs. 1(h)(1)(C), 55(b)(3)(C)].
- A capital gains rate of 20 percent applies to adjusted net capital gains of individuals if the gain would otherwise be subject to the 39.6-percent ordinary income tax rate beginning on January 1, 2013 [Code Sec. 1(h)(1)(D)]. Individuals are subject to the 39.6-percent ordinary income tax rate in 2013 to the extent their taxable income exceeds the applicable threshold amount of $450,000 for married individuals filing joint returns and surviving spouses, $425,000 for heads of households, $400,000 for single individuals, and $225,000 for married individuals filing separate returns.

These rates apply for sales or exchanges of capital assets that are held for more than 12 months, and apply for both regular income tax and alternative minimum tax (AMT) purposes. For discussion of capital gains rates for estates and trusts, see ¶ 25,045.

> ▶ **NEW IN 2013—3.8 Percent Net Investment Income Tax:** In 2013, higher income taxpayers must also start paying a 3.8-percent additional tax on net investment income (NII) to the extent certain threshold amounts of income are exceeded ($200,000 for single filers, $250,000 for joint returns and surviving spouses, $125,000 for married taxpayers filing separately) [Code Sec. 1411]. Therefore, taxpayers within the NII surtax range must pay the additional 3.8 percent on capital gain, whether long-term or short-term. The effective top rate for net capital gains for many higher-income taxpayers thus becomes 23.8 percent for long-term gain, and 43.4 percent for short-term capital gains starting in 2013. For further discussion see ¶ 15,050.

Regardless of the individual's tax rate, two additional tax rates apply to long term capital gains as follows:

- *Collectibles gain*. A 28 percent tax rate is imposed on long-term capital gain which is defined as works of art, rugs, antiques, metals, gems, coins, stamps, alcoholic beverages, and any other tangible personal property specified by the IRS. For capital gains purposes, collectibles also include certain coins and bullion [Code Secs. 1(h)(5)(A), 408(m)(3)]. Under a look-through rule, gain from the sale of an interest in a partnership, S corporation, or trust that is attributable to unrealized appreciation of collectibles is treated as gain from the sale of a collectible [Code Sec. 1(h)(5)(B)]; and
- *QSBS gain*. A 28 percent tax rate is imposed on qualified small business stock (QSBS) if the stock acquired after September 27, 2010 and before January 1, 2014; Noncorporate investors may be able to exclude up to 100 percent of the gain they realize on the sale or exchange of small business stock that has been held for more than five years [Code Sec. 1202(a)(1)]. For detailed discussion, see ¶ 8105. Gain excluded under the small business stock provision is not used in computing the taxpayer's long-term capital gain or loss, and it is not investment income for purposes of the investment interest limitation. If a sale of stock qualifies for the 100-percent gain exclusion, the remaining gain is taxed at a maximum rate of 28 percent. However, if the exclusion does not apply because the stock is sold prior to the expiration of the required five-year holding period, the entire gain qualifies for taxation at the lower capital gains rates; or
- *25-percent rate gain*. Long-term capital gain attributable to certain prior depreciation that had been claimed on real property is taxed at a rate of 25 percent. This depreciation is known as "unrecaptured Section 1250 gain" and is defined as the excess of:
  - — The amount of long-term capital gain (not otherwise treated as ordinary income) that would be treated as ordinary income if Code Sec. 1250(b)(1) included all depreciation and the applicable percentage that applied under Code Sec. 1250(a) were 100 percent over
  - — The excess of 28-percent rate loss over 28-percent rate gain [Code Sec. 1(h)(6)].

Any net 28-percent rate loss first offsets unrecaptured Code Sec. 1250 gain, and any excess loss is then applied to offset capital gains that are taxed at the maximum

20-percent rate. There are no losses in the 25-percent rate group. Code Sec. 1250 property is real property that is depreciable under Code Sec. 167, but is not subject to the recapture rule under Code Sec. 1245 [Code Sec. 1250(c)]. This includes all intangible real property (e.g., leases of land or section 1250 property and buildings and their structural components) and all other tangible real property except property that is used as an integral part of manufacturing, production or extraction, or of furnishing transportation, communications, electrical energy, gas, water or sewage disposal services or research or storage facilities used in connection with these activities. Unrecaptured depreciation taken into account in computing unrecaptured Code Sec. 1250 gain cannot exceed the amount of gain recognized on the property after the gain is reduced by any ordinary income depreciation recapture.

Pass-Through Entities

When applying the capital gains tax rates to pass-through entities, including regulated investment companies (RICs or mutual funds) and real estate investment trusts (REITs), the determination of when gains and losses are properly taken into account is made at the entity level as discussed below and at Ch. 6 and Ch. 23.

▶ **PLANNING POINTERS:** Because the difference between the highest individual income tax bracket rate (39.6 percent) and the highest capital gains rate bracket is just under 20 percent, it makes sense for investors in the higher tax brackets to strive to realize long-term capital gain instead of either short-term gain or ordinary income.

To generate tax-favored capital gains, taxpayers must hold stocks for more than 12 months and should avoid frequent trading, which will generate short-term capital gains taxed at ordinary income rates. Investors in mutual funds should favor funds run by managers who have a history of holding shares long-term rather than those who buy and sell in search of a quick trading profit. Why? A fund's short-term gains are also taxable as ordinary income and are passed through to mutual fund investors as such. Unmanaged index mutual funds typically have extremely low turnover. Investors may also consider tax-managed mutual funds, for which one of the principal goals is to limit annual distributions by matching any gains realized with offsetting losses.

Consider giving highly appreciated stock to children (or other relatives) who are in the lowest income tax bracket. These low-bracket taxpayers enjoy a 0 percent tax rate on capital assets held for more than 12 months in 2013. Parents need to beware of the kiddie tax rules which apply to children who are either age 18 by the end of the year or to children who are ages 19 to 23 by the end of the tax year where the following three situations apply:

1. The child's earned income does not exceed one-half of the child's support.
2. Either parent of the child is alive at the close of the tax year.
3. The child does not file a joint return for the tax year.

Children who are subject to the kiddie tax pay tax on unearned income above $2,000 in 2013 at their parent's top tax rate. Parents can minimize the impact of the kiddie tax if they select wisely when making gifts to their children. For example, a parent should consider giving a child an investment that is exempt from federal income tax such as a municipal bond or giving the child appreciated securities which will not be taxed until sold or exchanged. Another strategy would be to give the child EE bonds or market discount bonds where taxation is deferred. For further discussion of the kiddie tax rules, see ¶2170.

.02 Tax Treatment of Qualified Dividends

Qualified dividends received by an individual shareholder from either a domestic corporation or a *qualified foreign corporation* are taxed at the same tax rates imposed on capital gains beginning after December 31, 2012, in accordance with Table 1 in ¶8001.01. [See ¶2080 for further discussion of dividends.]

Holding Periods

To qualify for the lower tax rates, the taxpayer must hold the dividend-paying stock for at least 61 days during the 121-day period beginning 60 days before the ex-dividend date (the first day that the buyer will not be entitled to receive that dividend) [Code Sec. 1(h)(11)(B)(iii)]. According to the holding-period rules, a stock bought on the last day before the ex-dividend date, i.e., the latest purchase date for collecting a dividend, could still meet the holding period test for that dividend, because there would have been 61 days left in the 121-day period. A stock sold on the ex-dividend date (the earliest selling date after entitlement to a dividend) can also meet the test, since this is the 61st day in the period. As long as the taxpayer holds the stock for at least 61 continuous days, the holding period test will be met for any dividend received (unless another restriction applied, such as a diminished risk of loss).

Qualified Dividend Income Paid by Mutual Funds

A shareholder in a mutual fund can treat qualified dividend income passed through the fund as qualified dividend income subject to the reduced capital gains after 2012. For further discussion of capital gains tax rates, see ¶8001.01. For this purpose, the mutual fund can designate dividends paid to its shareholders as qualified dividend income if less than 95 percent of its income is derived from qualified dividend income [Code Sec. 854(b)(1)(B)].

In addition, the amount designated as qualifying dividend income may not exceed the sum of:

- The qualified dividend income of the RIC for the tax year; and
- The amount of any earnings and profits distributed for the tax year accumulated in a tax year in which the RIC rules did not apply [Code Sec. 854(b)(1)(C)].

A RIC is required to provide notice to shareholders of the amount to be treated as qualified dividend income within 60 days after the close of its tax year [Code Sec. 854(b)(2)]. See Ch. 23 for further discussion of the tax treatment of mutual funds.

In applying the reduced capital gains rates to pass-through entities, including RICs and REITs, the determination of when gains and losses are properly taken into account is made at the entity level. For further discussion of tax treatment of dividends, see Ch. 2.

.03 RIC/REIT Capital Gain Distributions

Regulated investment companies (RICs) or real estate investment trusts (REITs) should designate different classes of capital gains dividends to reflect the three-tier rate structure (15/25/28 percent). See Ch. 6 and Ch. 23 for further discussion of the tax treatment of mutual funds. The dividend will either be designated as a 15 percent rate gain distribution, an unrecaptured Code Sec. 1250 gain distribution not otherwise treated as ordinary income (taxed in the 25 percent group), or a 28 percent rate gain distribution. If no rate designation is made, the shareholders will be deemed to receive a 28 percent rate gain distribution.

.04 Constructive Ownership Transactions

Code Sec. 1260 limits the amount of long-term capital gains a taxpayer can recognize from derivative transactions called constructive ownership contracts, with respect to certain pass-through entities to the amount of gain the taxpayer would have had if the taxpayer owned a direct interest in the pass-through entity rather than through a derivative contract during the term of the derivative contract. Any gain in excess of this amount is treated as ordinary income [Code Sec. 1260(a)]. In addition, because these types of contracts often cover multiple tax years, an interest charge is imposed on the amount of gain that is treated as ordinary income [Code Sec. 1260(b)].

A taxpayer is treated as having entered into a constructive ownership transaction if the taxpayer:

1. Holds a long position under a notional principal contract with respect to the financial asset;
2. Enters into a forward contract to acquire the financial asset;
3. Is the holder of a call option, and the grantor of a put option, with respect to a financial asset, and the options have substantially equal strike prices and substantially contemporaneous maturity dates; or
4. Enters into one or more transactions, or acquires one or more other positions, that have substantially the same effect as any of the transactions described in (1) through (3), above] Code Sec. 1260(d)].

A taxpayer is treated as holding a long position under a notional principal contract with respect to any financial asset if that person (1) has the right to be paid or receive credit for all or substantially all of the investment yield, including appreciation, on the financial asset for a specified period, and (2) is obligated to reimburse or provide credit for all or substantially all of any decline in the value of such financial asset [Code Sec. 1260(d)(3)]. A forward contract is a contract to acquire in the future (or provide or receive credit for the future value of) any financial asset [Code Sec. 1260(d)(4)].

¶8005 ANTICONVERSION TRANSACTIONS

.01 In General

Code Sec. 1258 prevents investors from manipulating the tax laws to convert ordinary income into capital gains and thereby benefiting from the favorable tax rates afforded capital gains. As a result, all or part of the capital gain from the disposition or termination of a position that is part of a *conversion transaction* may be recharacterized as ordinary income. The anticonversion rules are directed at investors who have engaged in *conversion transactions,* in which the investor holds two or more positions with respect to the same or similar property and substantially all of the gain is attributable to the time value of the net investment rather than economic risk in the investment. In a prohibited conversion transaction, the taxpayer is in the economic position of a lender—he or she has an expectation of a return from the transaction which in substance is in the nature of interest and he undertakes no significant risks other than those typical of a lender. For example, conversion transactions include contracts for the sale of property that call for sales of a portion of the property at different time intervals, at increasing prices, rather than an installment sale with a stated rate of interest. If you have engaged in a conversion transaction the portion that otherwise would be capital gain is converted into ordinary income by using the applicable federal interest rate or "AFR."

.02 Requirements

A transaction is a conversion transaction if it meets both of these following tests [Code Sec. 1258(c)]:

- Substantially all of your expected return from the transaction is due to the time value of your net investment. In other words, the return on your investment is, in substance, like interest on a loan.
- The transaction is one of the following:

  1. A straddle as defined by Code Sec. 1092(c) (offsetting positions in personal property), but for purposes of the anticonversion rules any set of offsetting positions on stock;
  2. Any transaction in which you acquire property (whether or not actively traded) and on a substantially contemporaneous basis enter into a contract to sell the same property, or substantially identical property, at a price determined in the contract;
  3. Any other transaction that is marketed or sold as producing capital gains from the time value of the taxpayer's net investment. A characteristic or earmark of a prohibited transaction would be one that is sold to you on the basis that the transaction has the characteristics of a loan but that the interest-like return would be taxed as capital gain; or
  4. Any other transaction specified in IRS regulation [Code Sec. 1258(c)].

Not all transactions involving the simultaneous purchase of a property and the making of a contract to sell will be characterized as "conversion transactions." For example, a stock purchase and the grant of an option is not a conversion transaction. The stock buyer/option seller is not in any sense a lender because the option may not be exercised and investor's profit is uncertain.

> **Example 8-2:** Mr. Taylor buys shares of XYZ stock at 50 and on the same day sells an XYZ call option (it gives the holder the right to buy XYZ at 60 within the next 12 months) to Mr. Green for $5. Twelve months later, the stock price is 55, and the call option expires unexercised. This is not a conversion transaction because at the time of the stock purchase and option grant, there is no substantial certainty that the call would be exercised by Green. If it isn't exercised, the ultimate return on Taylor's investment is uncertain.

On the other hand, buying stock and buying a put option (it gives the taxpayer the right to sell the stock at a set price) will be characterized as a "conversion transaction." The taxpayer profits if the stock price rises (he sells the stock) or falls (he exercises the put at a price higher than the market price).

.03 Tax Treatment

If you are involved in a conversion transaction and the anticonversion rules apply, the gain from the transaction will be treated as ordinary income (not capital gain) for all purposes of the Internal Revenue Code [Code Sec. 1258(a)]. In addition, the income will continue to be treated as gain from the sale of property for such purposes as the unrelated business income tax (UBIT) for tax-exempt organizations and the gross income requirement for regulated investment companies.

.04 Amount of Ordinary Income

The amount of your profit from a conversion transaction that is treated as ordinary income cannot exceed the "applicable imputed income amount" [Code Sec. 1258(b)]. This amount is equal to (1) the amount of interest that would have accrued on your "net investment" for the conversion period (which ends on the date of a disposition or termination, such as the lapse of an option), reduced by (2) the amount of ordinary income that was recognized under the anticonversion rules with respect to any prior dispositions of property that was held as part of the conversion transaction [Code Sec. 1258(b)].

The "applicable federal rate" is either: (1) for transactions with a definite term, the rate from Code Sec. 1274(d) [Ch. 2]; or (2) for transactions with an indefinite term, the federal short-term rate under Code Sec. 6621(b).

Example 8-3: Mr. Sumner invests $10,000 and buys shares of ZAP stock and buys a put option on ZAP stock that will expire in two years. Sumner makes $1,500 from the exercise of the option after two years. Suppose that 120 percent of the applicable federal rate results in a return of $1,200 on his $10,000 investment. Result: Sumner treats $1,200 as ordinary income and $300 as long-term capital gain.

In determining your ***net investment*** in a conversion transaction, you include the fair market value of any position that becomes part of the transaction. Special rules apply if a position with a built-in loss—a loss would have been realized if the position had been disposed of at its fair market value—becomes part of a conversion transaction. For purposes of the conversion rules, the property is taken into account at its fair market value at the time it became part of the transaction. However, when the position is later disposed of or terminated, the built-in loss is recognized and it is a capital loss.

Example 8-4: Ms. Danner bought XYZ stock on February 1, for $150 and uses that stock as part of a conversion transaction entered into one month later. At the time of the transaction, XYZ's value had dropped to $130. The stock is treated as having a basis of $130 for purposes of recharacterizing gain as ordinary income. If Danner later sells XYZ for $140, she will have $10 of gain, some or all of which may be converted to ordinary income. At the same time, Danner will have a $20 capital loss.

Netting Rule for Certain Conversion Transactions

Taxpayers can net certain gains and losses from positions of the same conversion transaction for purposes of determining the amount of gain that is recharacterized as ordinary income under Code Sec. 1258(a) [Reg. § 1.1258-1(a)]. To be eligible, the taxpayer must identify each position of the conversion transaction before the close of the day on which the position becomes part of the conversion transaction [Reg. § 1.1258-1(b)(2)]. No particular form of identification is necessary. In addition, the taxpayer must dispose of all the positions within a 14-day period that is within a single tax year. Taxpayers are prohibited from netting built-in losses against gain in conversion transactions [Reg. § 1.1258-1(c)]. In addition, the rules treat certain losses that arise during the term of a conversion transaction as built-in losses [Reg. § 1.1258-1(c)(2)].

Example 8-5: On December 1, 2011, Mr. Frank purchased 1,000 shares of XYZ stock for $100,000 and entered into a forward contract to sell the shares on November 30, 2013 for $110,000. The stock is actively traded and is a capital asset in Mr. Frank's hands. He maintains books and records on which, on December 1, 2011, he identifies the two positions as all the positions of a single conversion transaction. On December 1, 2012, Mr. Frank sells the $1,000 shares for $95,000. On the same day, he terminates his forward contract by entering into an offsetting position, receiving $10,200. Mr. Frank terminated all positions of the conversion transaction within 14 days as required by Reg. § 1.1258-1(b)(2). Solely for purposes of Code Sec. 1258(a), the $5,000 loss realized ($100,000 basis less $95,000 amount realized) on the disposition of the stock is netted against the $10,200 gain recognized on the disposition of the forward contract. Thus the net gain from the conversion transaction is $5,200 ($10,200 gain less $5,000 loss). Only the $5,200 net gain is recharacterized as ordinary income. Mr. Frank recognized a $10,200 gain on the disposition of the forward contract ($5,200 of which is treated as ordinary income) and recognized a separate $5,000 loss on the sale of the stock [Reg. § 1.1258-1(d), Ex. 1].

.05 How to Determine Interest Amount

In order to determine the amount of interest you would have received during the time the property was held, 120 percent of the applicable federal rate (AFR), compounded semiannually, is used. The applicable federal rate to use is determined under Code Sec. 1274(d) and depends upon the length of time the property was held [Code Sec. 1258(d)(2)]. For example, if the property was not held over three years, 120 percent of the federal short-term rate is used. If the property was held over three years but not over nine years, 120 percent of the federal mid-term rate is used. If the property was held over nine years, 120 percent of the federal long-term rate is used. If the conversion transaction has an indefinite term, the federal short-term rate as determined under Code Sec. 6621(b), compounded daily, is used.

Example 8-6: You purchased stock for $100 on January 1, 2011, and on the same day agreed to sell it to Bob on January 1, 2013, for $115. Assume the applicable federal rate is 5 percent and is only compounded on an annual basis. On January 1, 2013, you deliver the stock to Bob and receive the $115. If the transaction were not a conversion transaction, you would have recognized a capital gain of $15. However, because the arrangement constitutes a Code Sec. 1258 conversion transaction, $12.36 of your gain is classified as ordinary income (*i.e.*, 120 percent of 5 percent equals 6 percent, compounded for two years, applied to your $100 investment). The remaining $2.64 in gain ($15 minus $12.36) is classified as a long-term capital gain.

.06 Source of Funds

The source of funds is generally not a consideration when determining your investment in property involved in a conversion transaction. However, if you borrow money to buy the property and are required to capitalize interest under the straddle rules of Code Sec. 263(g), the capitalized interest must be taken into consideration when computing the amount of your ordinary income.

Example 8-7: Assume the same facts as example above, above, except that you borrowed $90 from a bank to buy the stock. Assume the interest that you were required to capitalize under Code Sec. 263(g) was $10. Your investment in the stock is still $100 even though your basis is $110 after taking into account the $10 in capitalized interest. However, of your gain of $5 ($115- $110), only $2.36 is characterized as ordinary income under the anticonversion rules. This is because the $12.36 in ordinary income must be reduced by the $10 in capitalized interest.

.07 Property with a Built-in Loss

A special rule applies when property that has a *built-in loss* becomes a part of a conversion transaction. The term "built-in-loss" is defined to mean the loss (if any) that would have been realized if the position had been disposed of or otherwise terminated at its fair market value at the time the position became part of the conversion transaction [Code Sec. 1258(d)(3)(B)].

As a general rule, if conversion transaction property has a built-in loss, and the property is disposed of in a transaction in which gain or loss is recognized, the built-in loss is required to be recognized. The character of such recognized loss is determined without regard to the anticonversion provisions.

Example 8-8: Assume the same facts as example above except that you purchased the shares on December 1 for $150. On January 1, of the following year, when the value of the stock had declined to $100, you entered into the contract with Bob. Based on these facts, you would still recognize $12.36 in ordinary income, when you deliver the stock to Bob. However, under the built-in rules, you would also recognize the $50 built-in loss. The character of the loss would not be changed by the anticonversion rules and would generally be classified as a capital loss.

.08 Future Commitment of Funds

Amounts that you may be committed to provide in the future will not be treated as an investment until those amounts are committed to the transaction and are unavailable to you to invest in other ways. In determining your net investment in a conversion transaction, the fair market value of any property that becomes part of the transaction is included. Fair market value is determined on the date the property becomes part of the transaction [Code Sec. 1258(d)(4)]. Generally, the net investment will be computed by adding the aggregate amount invested in the transaction, less any amount received as consideration for entering into any position held as part of the conversion transaction, such as when the taxpayer is the grantor of an option.

.09 Special Rules for Options Dealers and Commodities Traders

Transactions of options dealers in the normal course of dealing in options, and of commodities traders in the normal course of trading Code Sec. 1256 contracts will generally not be treated as conversion transactions [Code Sec. 1258(d)(5)]. There are several kinds of Code Sec. 1256 contracts, including:

- Regulated futures contracts;
- Foreign currency contracts;
- Non-equity options;
- Dealer equity options; and
- Dealer securities futures contract.

All Code Sec. 1256 contracts are treated as if they were sold for their fair market value on the last business day of the tax year. The gains or losses thus recognized in any tax year are considered 40 percent short term and 60 percent long-term capital gain or loss without regard to the holding period [Code Sec. 1256(a)].

.10 Reporting Requirements

Use Form 6781, *Gains and Losses From Section 1256 Contracts and Straddles,* to report a conversion transaction.

¶8010 WHAT IS A CAPITAL ASSET?

The Internal Revenue Code does not provide a definition of a *capital asset* beyond stating that the term refers to "property held by the taxpayer (whether or not connected with a trade or business)" [Code Sec. 1221]. Rather, the Code defines a capital asset by stating what it is not. Capital assets are property held by a taxpayer (whether or not connected with a trade or business) *other than* property falling into one of the following categories [Code Sec. 1221; Reg. § 1.1221-1]:

- An inventoriable asset [Code Sec. 1221(a)(1)];
- Property held primarily for sale to customers in the ordinary course of the taxpayer's trade or business [Code Sec. 1221(a)(1)]. *Primarily* means "of first importance" or "principally"[1] rather than merely "substantially." Property held principally to realize appreciation in value over a substantial period of time is classified as a capital asset even where similar property could be used in a trade or business;

---

[1] *W. Malat*, SCt, 66-1 USTC ¶ 9317, 383 US 569, 86 SCt 1030.

- Depreciable property used in a trade or business even if it is fully depreciated [Code Sec. 1221(a)(2)] [but see ¶ 8055 *et seq.*];
- Real property used in a taxpayer's trade or business [but see ¶ 8055; ¶ 8060];
- A copyright, a literary, musical or artistic composition, a letter or memorandum or similar property (but not a patent or invention) held by a taxpayer who created it, or by one whose basis in the property is determined by reference to the basis of the one who created it, or in the case of a letter, memorandum or similar property, a taxpayer for whom such property was prepared or produced [Code Sec. 1221(a)(3)];
- Accounts or notes receivable acquired in the ordinary course of trade or business for services rendered or from the sale of stock in trade or property held for sale to customers [Code Sec. 1221(a)(4)];
- A U.S. Government publication (including the Congressional Record) held by a taxpayer who received it (or by another taxpayer in whose hands the publication would have a basis determined in whole or in part by reference to the taxpayer's basis) other than by purchase at the price at which the publication is offered to the public [Code Sec. 1221(a)(5); Reg. § 1.1221-1];
- Certain commodities derivative financial instruments held by commodities derivatives dealers unless the instrument has no relationship to the dealer's activities as a dealer and the instrument is shown in the records of the dealer on the date of acquisition as not being held by the dealer as part of the dealer's ordinary business activities [Code Sec. 1221(a)(6)];
- Hedging transactions clearly identified as such before the close of the day on which they were acquired, originated, or entered into [Code Sec. 1221(a)(7)]; and
- Supplies of a type regularly consumed by the taxpayer in the ordinary course of a trade or business [Code Sec. 1221(a)(8)].

.01 Capital Assets Include Property Held for Taxpayer's Personal Use

Capital assets typically include investment property (stocks and bonds held by an investor) and property held for the taxpayer's personal use, pleasure, or investment, such as the taxpayer's personal jewelry, boat, airplanes, household furnishings, personal residence, or automobile. Land and depreciable property used in a business are not capital assests, but if they are sold or exchanged, it is possible for the gain to be treated as gain from capital assets under Code Sec. 1231. See ¶ 8055. Gain from a transaction involving property held for personal use is a capital gain, but losses are never deductible unless the loss is a casualty or theft loss [¶ 8065] or if the property was held for the production of income.

.02 Stocks, Bonds, Notes, Debentures, and Similar Securities

Stocks, bonds, notes, debentures, and similar securities are capital assets, unless they fall under one of the exceptions in Code Sec. 1221.[2] Thus, stock will not be a capital asset where it is held in the hands of a dealer as inventory for sale to customers [Code Sec. 1221(a)]. Special rules used to apply to collapsible corporation stock [¶ 8090].

---

[2] *Arkansas Best*, SCt, 88-1 USTC 9210, 485 US 212, 108 SCt 971.

Small business stock and stock in a small business investment company are not considered capital assets if sold at a loss under certain conditions [¶ 8095]. Gain on transfers of stock in controlled foreign corporations may be ordinary income [Ch. 28].

.03 Real Property

Real property not used in a trade or business is a capital asset—for example, a taxpayer's private residence is a capital asset. If property is used in a trade or business, it is not a capital asset. But homes purchased under a home-buying plan by a corporation to assist relocating employees in the sale of their personal residences are capital assets when later sold by the corporations. Thus, if there is a loss on the later sale, it is a capital loss.[3]

Whether land is held primarily for sale to customers in the ordinary course of a taxpayer's trade or business is purely a factual determination. The following factors are considered by the courts in making this determination: (1) the purpose for which the property was acquired, (2) the purpose for which the property was held, (3) the improvements made to the property, (4) the frequency of sales, (5) the nature and substantiality of the transactions, (6) the nature and extent of the taxpayer's dealings in similar property, (7) the extent of advertising to promote sales, and (8) whether or not the property was listed for sale either directly or through brokers.

This list of factors grew out of the large real estate subdivision cases. There, real estate developers purchased large tracts of raw land, improved the land with utility lines, roads, and curbs, subdivided the land into building lots, and sold those lots to their customers in the ordinary course of their business. However, even such a real estate dealer could hold a particular parcel of land for investment purposes and be entitled to capital gains treatment when selling a parcel of land.[4] Also, even if a parcel of land was originally acquired for the purpose of selling it to customers, that purpose is not conclusive; the purpose could change before the sale occurred, and it is the purpose for which the land is held at the time of sale that is determinative.

.04 Property Held for the Production of Income

If property held for the production of income is not used in your trade or business, it is a capital asset [Reg. § 1.1221-1(b)].

.05 Allocation of Purchase Price for Certain Assets

Taxpayers that buy or sell multiple assets as part of a single transaction must allocate the consideration paid among the assets. The seller must make the allocation to determine the amount and character of any recognized gain or loss. The buyer must allocate the consideration paid to determine its basis in the purchased assets, which in turn will determine how much, if any, of the purchase price is depreciable or amortizable. Code Sec. 1060 prescribes special allocation rules for determining a transferee's basis and a transferor's gain or loss in an applicable asset acquisition. An applicable

---

[3] *Azar Nut Co.*, 94 TC 455, Dec. 46,470 (1990), *aff'd*, CA-5, 91-1 USTC ¶ 50,257, 931 F2d 314.

[4] *T.H. Case*, CA-6, 80-2 USTC ¶ 9764, 633 F2d 1240; *W.B. Daugherty*, 78 TC 623, Dec. 38,943 (1982); *R.H. Pritchett*, 63 TC 149, Dec. 32,840 (1974); *T.J. Phelan*, 88 TCM 223, Dec. 55,745(M), TC Memo. 2004-206; LTR 200510029 (Dec. 16, 2004), LTR 200530029 (May 5, 2005), LTR 200242041 (July 9, 2002).

asset acquisition is any transfer of assets that constitutes a trade or business and with respect to which the purchaser's basis in such assets is determined wholly by reference to the consideration paid for them [Code Sec. 1060(c)].

Code Sec. 1060 requires both the buyer and the seller of a trade or business to allocate the consideration paid or received among assets using the residual method prescribed by regulations issued under Code Sec. 338. Under this method individual assets are assigned to an "asset class." The consideration attributable to the class is split proportionately among the assets in the class to determine the basis or gain or loss.

Where the parties to an applicable asset acquisition agree in writing about the allocation of any amount of consideration, or about the fair market value of any of the assets transferred, that agreement is "binding" on the transferee and the transferor unless the IRS determines that the allocation (or fair market value) is not appropriate. But where the parties do not allocate the consideration entirely, the residual method of purchase price allocation may apply to determine both the purchaser's basis in and the seller's gain or loss from the transferred assets [Code Sec. 1060(a)(2)]. In *Peco Foods, Inc.*,[5] the Tax Court concluded that a taxpayer could not modify purchase price allocations that it agreed to in connection with asset acquisitions.

For assets acquired after January 5, 2000 there are seven asset classes. Under the residual method, the purchase price is first reduced by the amount of cash and general deposit accounts (including savings and checking accounts) other than certificates of deposit held in bank and other depository institutions transferred by the seller. These assets are referred to as Class I assets. Then the remaining amount is allocated in the following order:

Class II assets. These include actively traded personal property and certificates of deposit and foreign currency.

Class III assets. These include assets that the taxpayer marks to market at least annually for federal income tax purposes and debt instruments.

Class IV assets. These include stock in trade of the taxpayer or other property of a kind that would properly be included in the taxpayer's inventory if on hand at the close of the tax year and property held by the taxpayer primarily for sale to customers in the ordinary course of the taxpayer's trade or business.

Class V assets. These include all assets other than Class I, II, III, IV, VI, and VII assets.

Class VI assets. These include all Code Sec. 197 intangibles except goodwill and going concern value. For further discussion of Code Sec. 197, see ¶ 11,005.

Class VII assets. These include goodwill and going concern value [Reg. § 1.338-6(b)(2)].

Valuation of Assets

Generally, each asset in a class is valued at its fair market value (FMV). No asset in any class except the seventh class may be allocated more than its fair market value

[5] *Peco Foods, Inc.*, 103 TCM 1120, Dec. 58,920(M), TC Memo. 2012-18, *aff'd*, CA-11, 2013-2 USTC ¶ 50,412.

(determined at the beginning of the day after the acquisition date) [Reg. § 1.338-6(c)(1)].

If the consideration allocable to a particular asset class is less than the aggregate FMV of all the assets in the class, each asset is allocated an amount in proportion to its FMV.

The seller and purchaser each adjust the amount allocated to an individual asset to take into account the specific identifiable costs incurred in transferring that asset in connection with the asset acquisition (e.g., real estate transfer costs or security interest perfection costs). Thus, the total amount the seller allocates to an asset for which it incurs specifically identifiable costs would be less than its FMV, and for the buyer, greater than its FMV. No adjustment is made for the general costs of the asset acquisition as a whole or groups of transferred assets (e.g., non-specific appraisal fees or accounting fees). These latter groups are taken into account only through their effect on the total consideration allocated.

Information Reporting by 10-percent Owner or Transferee

The owner of a 10-percent interest in an entity who transfers any interest in the entity and the transferee are required to furnish information regarding the transaction if the owner or a related person also enters into an employment contract, covenant not to compete, royalty or lease agreement, or other agreement with the transferee in connection with the transaction [Code Sec. 1060(e)]. A 10-percent owner is defined as a person who holds 10 percent or more (by value) of the interests in the entity immediately before the transfer. For purposes of determining the ownership of stock in a corporation, the constructive ownership rules of Code Sec. 318 apply.

Both the buyer and seller involved in the sale of business assets must report the consideration's allocation among goodwill and the other business assets on Form 8594, *Asset Acquisition Statement.*

The form should be attached to the tax return for the year during which the first date assets are sold as part of the transaction. The form is a summary of how the purchase price is allocated to the assets of the business. Form 8594 is required when:

- The sale involves a group of assets that make up a trade or business; and
- The purchaser's basis in the assets will be determined solely by the amount paid for the assets.

Form 8594 is not required when:

- The assets are acquired in a like-kind exchange under Code Sec. 1031. If not all of the assets transferred qualify for like-kind exchange treatment, the assets that do not qualify must be reported on Form 8594.
- A partnership interest is transferred (in which case separate reporting requirements apply and Form 8308 should be filed).

Form 8594 requires the buyer and seller to supply the following information:

1. General information about the taxpayer, the date of sale, and the total purchase price for the assets;
2. The allocation of the purchase price among the seven asset classes identified by the IRS; and

3. Information about subsequent upward or downward adjustments to the purchase price and how these adjustments will be allocated among the seven asset classes.

.06 Partnership Interest

The portion of an individual partner's partnership interest that is attributable to certain partnership noncapital assets (primarily unrealized receivable and inventory) is an ordinary asset, whereas the remainder of his interest is a single capital asset.[6] Transfer of a partnership interest is discussed in Ch. 24.

> **NOTE:** In some partnership distributions or transfers of interests, the allocation rules summarized above apply in valuing Code Sec. 197 intangibles [Code Sec. 1060(d)]. See ¶ 11,005 for further discussion of Code Sec. 197.

.07 Copyrights, Literary or Artistic Compositions, Letters or Memoranda, and Similar Property

Code Sec. 1221(a)(3) excludes from capital asset treatment copyrights; literary, musical or artistic compositions; letters or memoranda; and similar property created by the taxpayer's personal efforts. These items are not capital assets if held by the taxpayer whose personal efforts created the property, the taxpayer for whom such property was prepared or produced (in the case of a letter, memorandum, or similar property), or the taxpayer in whose hands the basis of such property is determined for purposes of determining gain from a sale or exchange by reference to the basis of the property in the hands of a taxpayer previously described. *Similar property* includes a radio program created by a taxpayer's personal efforts, a theatrical production, a newspaper cartoon strip, or other property eligible for copyright protection. It does not include a patent, invention, or a design protected only under the patent law and not under the copyright law [Reg. § 1.1221-1(c)(1)]. Letters and memoranda include manuscripts and any other writings or recordings of a business or personal nature. A letter or memorandum addressed to a person is considered as prepared or produced for him [Reg. § 1.1221-1(c)(2)].

.08 Capital Gains for Self-Created Musical Work

Code Sec. 1221(b)(3) provides that a taxpayer who owns a musical composition or copyright in a musical work created by the taxpayer (or transferred to the taxpayer by the composition or work's creator in a transferred basis transaction) may elect to treat gain or loss from the sale or exchange of the musical composition or copyright as capital gain or loss.

Election to Treat Musical Compositions as Capital Assets

The taxpayer must make a separate election for each musical composition (or copyright in a musical work) sold or exchanged during the tax year. An election must be made on or before the due date (including extensions) of the income tax return for the tax year of the sale or exchange. The election is made on Schedule D, *Capital Gains and Losses,* of the appropriate income tax form (for example, Form 1040, *U.S. Individual Income Tax Return;* Form 1065, *U.S. Return of Partnership Income;* Form 1120, *U.S. Corporation Income Tax Return*) by treating the sale or exchange as the sale or exchange of a capital asset, in accordance with the form and its instructions [Reg. § 1.1221-3(b)].

---

[6] *M. Shapiro,* CA-6, 42-1 USTC ¶ 9260, 125 F2d 532.

Revocability of Election

An election is revocable with IRS consent. To revoke an election, a taxpayer must submit a request for a letter ruling under the applicable administrative procedures. Alternatively, the regulations provide for an automatic extension of six months from the due date of the taxpayer's income tax return (excluding extensions) to revoke the election, provided the taxpayer timely filed the taxpayer's income tax return and, within this six-month extension period, the taxpayer files an amended income tax return that treats the sale or exchange as the sale or exchange of property that is not a capital asset [Reg. § 1.1221-3(b)].

.09 Leases and Distribution Agreements

Amounts received by a lessee for the cancellation of a lease, or by a distributor of goods for the cancellation of a distributor agreement—i.e., the termination of all contractual rights other than by the expiration under the contract's terms—in which the distributor has a substantial capital investment are amounts received in exchange for such lease or agreement [Code Sec. 1241]. This rule applies to a distribution agreement only if: (1) it is for marketing or marketing and servicing of goods, (2) the distributor has made a substantial capital investment in the distributorship, and (3) the capital investment is reflected in physical assets such as inventories of tangible goods, equipment, machinery, storage facilities, or similar property [Reg. § 1.1241-1(c)]. Reg. § 1.1241-1(b) defines "cancellation" of a distributor agreement as a termination of all the contractual rights of a distributor with respect to a particular distributorship, other than by the expiration of the agreement in accordance with its terms.

In *L.W. Ray*,[7] the Court of Appeals for the Fifth Circuit affirmed the Tax Court to conclude that consideration received by the lessee for relinquishment of the restrictive covenant in the lease prohibiting the lessor from renting any part of the building to any other variety store is capital gain on the ground that the restrictive covenant constituted property in the hands of the lessee and the relinquishment by him of a right.

The type of gain or loss depends on the lease's character. A nondepreciable leasehold is a capital asset. Part of a gain from the sale or exchange of the depreciable leasehold may be ordinary income to the extent the recapture rules apply [¶ 8060]. An amount received by the landlord for canceling[8] or amending[9] a lease is ordinary income.

In Rev. Rul. 2007-37,[10] the IRS concluded that the cancellation of a distributor agreement between a manufacturer and a distributor of the manufacturer's products is a sale or exchange of property if the distributor made a substantial capital investment in the distributorship and the investment is reflected in physical assets. Any resulting gain to the distributor is capital gain if the agreement is a capital asset. The gain is Code Sec. 1231 gain and may be treated as capital if the agreement is property that is subject to the allowance for depreciation under Code Sec. 167. For this purpose, property is treated as such if it is amortizable under Code Sec. 197 or Code Sec. 1253. Any Code Sec. 1231 gain may be subject to recapture under Code Sec. 1245.

---

[7] *L.W. Ray*, CA-5, 54-1 USTC ¶ 9235, 210 F2d 390, *cert. denied*, 348 US 829, 75 SCt 53.

[8] *W.M. Hort*, SCt, 41-1 USTC ¶ 9354, 313 US 28, 61 SCt 757.

[9] *S. Thorpe*, 42 BTA 654, Dec. 11,296, *aff'd*, 121 F2d 458.

[10] Rev. Rul. 2007-37, 2007-1 CB 1390.

.10 Options

Gain or loss from the sale or exchange of an option to buy or sell property is treated the same as gain or loss from the sale or exchange of the property underlying the option. If the property that is the subject of the option is a capital asset, so is the option. If the loss results from failure to exercise the option, the option is considered to have been sold or exchanged on the day it expired [Code Sec. 1234(a)(2); Reg. § 1.1234-1(b)]. The rule does not apply to the following [Reg. § 1.1234-1(e)]:

- An option that is part of your inventory or stock in trade;
- Gain from the sale of an option if income derived from the option would be treated as ordinary income without regard to the rule. For example, if gain on the sale of an employee stock option is in the nature of compensation, the gain is not treated as a capital gain merely because the stock, if acquired, would be a capital asset in the employee's hands; and
- Loss from failure to exercise a "put" bought on the same day as the stock used to fulfill the contract [¶ 8035].

Conversion Transaction

Some or all of your profit from an option that is part of a conversion transaction is treated as ordinary income and not capital gain [¶ 8005].

A special rule applies to actively traded personal property which is property that would be a capital asset in the taxpayer's hands. Terminating rights or obligations in this property is treated as a sale or exchange from a capital asset [Code Sec. 1234A]. Common examples of these transactions include canceling forward contracts for currency or securities and regulated futures contracts (Section 1256 contracts).

> **NOTE:** The capital gain or loss treatment from certain contract terminations does not apply to the retirement of any debt instrument whether or not through a trust or participation arrangement [Code Sec. 1234A].

.11 Patents

Gain on the transfer (other than by gift, inheritance, or devise) of *all substantial rights* to a patent or of an undivided interest in patent rights by any holder qualifies for long-term capital gain treatment [Code Sec. 1235]. A patent need not be held for more than one year to qualify for long term capital gains tax rates, because the transfer by a holder of a patent is considered a sale or exchange of a capital asset held for more than one year regardless of how long the patent was actually held. A patent transferor may render ancillary and subsidiary services in connection with the sale and transfer of a patent without affecting the capital nature of the total sale proceeds.[11] Ancillary and subsidiary services include providing the transferee with technical knowledge and consulting services that are an integral part of the patent transfer. A patent transferor will be deemed to have received ordinary income, however, when the transferor receives compensation for services that are unrelated or

---

[11] *A.C. Ruge*, 26 TC 138, Dec. 21,688 (1956), *acq.* 1958-2 CB 7; *H.S. Gable*, 33 TCM 1427, Dec. 32,882(M), TC Memo. 1974-312.

tangential to the patent transfer. In *B.L. Farris*,[12] the Tax Court concluded that payments to an inventor by the purchaser of the patent were not in connection with or ancillary to the transfer of the patents. Instead, the court found that they were compensation for the inventor's services and were therefore taxed as ordinary compensation income.

Holder Defined

A *holder* is defined as: (1) the person whose efforts created the property and (2) not the creator's employer or a person who is related to the creator [Code Sec. 1235(d)].

All Substantial Rights Defined

The term *all substantial rights* is defined as "all rights (whether or not then held by the grantor) which are of value at the time the rights to the patent are transferred" [Reg. § 1.1235-2(b)]. This includes that right to make, sell, and use the patent. A contract that fails the *all substantial rights* test is deemed a license instead of a sale or exchange of a capital asset. In *Vision Information Services*,[13] the taxpayer was denied capital gain treatment for the sale of the exclusive right to use, copy, or modify its inventory management software. Because the taxpayer did not assign all substantial rights to the purchase, the income received was deemed a license fee rather than a sale of exclusive rights and know how and the taxpayer was denied capital gain treatment under Code Sec. 1235. Apparently, the purchaser could not fully exercise its rights without satisfying the terms of the conditional license.

Geographically Limited Transfers of Patent Rights

The transferor must assign the rights to make, use, and sell the patent in order for the sale or exchange to qualify for long-term capital gain treatment under Code Sec. 1235. This requirement will not be satisfied when the seller limits use of the rights to a patent by geography, field of use, length of use, or the inventions covered by patent. Reg. § 1.1235-2(b)(1)(i) provides that the transfer of patent rights within a specified geographical area is not a transfer of "all substantial rights" to a patent within the meaning of Code Sec. 1235 and will not qualify for capital gains treatment. Thus there may not be limitations as to duration of use (shorter than the patent's remaining useful life) or fields of use to qualify for capital gain treatment of the patent transfer [Reg. § 1.1235-2(b)(1)(ii)].

.12 Other Items

Capital Assets

The following have been held to be capital assets and therefore generating capital gain to the seller when sold: life estates;[14] cotton acreage allotments;[15] proceeds from sale of a subdivision lot because lot held for investment purposes, not held primarily for sale to customers in the ordinary course of business.[16]

---

[12] *B.L. Farris*, 100 TCM 325, Dec. 58,356(M), TC Memo. 2010-222.

[13] *Vision Information Services, LLC*, CA-6, 2005-2 USTC ¶ 50,534, 419 F3d 554.

[14] *F.S. Bell Est.*, CA-8, 43-2 USTC ¶ 9565, 137 F2d 454.

[15] Rev. Rul. 66-58, 1966-1 CB 186.

[16] *B.A. Rice*, 97 TCM 1807, Dec. 57,860(M), TC Memo 2009-142.

An amount received by an investor in settlement of a dispute over a mishandled brokerage account was taxable as long-term capital gain in the year of receipt. The taxpayers established a taxable investment account with a stockbroker. The taxpayers sustained losses which the taxpayers believed resulted when the stockbroker mishandled the account. The taxpayers signed a settlement agreement under which the stockbroker paid them a settlement amount which the IRS characterized the settlement as a long-term capital gain, rather than ordinary income.[17]

Noncapital Assets

The following have been held *not* to be capital assets therefore generating ordinary income to the seller when sold: right to future dividend sold by stockholder;[18] employment contract sold by an employee;[19] trade acceptance received as incident to the sale of merchandise;[20] an exclusive or perpetual right to exploit and use one's name;[21] covenant not to compete;[22] a franchise, trademark, or trade name, if the transferor retains any significant power, right or continuing interest [Code Sec. 1253]; sale of a right to receive lottery winnings;[23] termination payments received by a retiring insurance agent.[24]

.13 Dealer vs. Investor

When you determine whether your gains or losses are ordinary or capital in nature, it is necessary to determine whether you are an "investor" and held the property merely for investment or were a "dealer" and held the property for sale to customers in the ordinary course of a trade or business. If a taxpayer holds property as an investor, the property is a capital asset. If the taxpayer holds the property as a dealer, the property is not a capital asset. The following factors are applied to determine whether taxpayers hold property for investment or for sale to customers in the ordinary course of a trade or business:[25]

- *Frequency and regularity of sales.* Courts view frequency and regularity of sales as important factors in determining whether an asset is held for investment or as inventory. Frequent sales indicate that the assets are being held for sale, whereas infrequent sales indicate that the assets are being held for investment;
- *Substantiality of sales.* Courts generally view frequent sales generating substantial income as an indication that the property was held for sale to customers in the ordinary course of a trade or business rather than held for investment. Where substantial profits result from capital appreciation, however, and not from the taxpayer's efforts, infrequent sales generating large profits tend to show that the property was held for investment;

---

[17] LTR 200724012 (Mar. 1, 2007).

[18] *H.W. Rhodes Est.*, CA-6, 42-2 USTC ¶9691, 131 F2d 50.

[19] *W.G.H. Finch,* 1 TCM 191, Dec. 12,908-K (1942).

[20] *Hercules Motor Corp.*, 40 BTA 999, Dec. 10,905 *(Nonacq.).*

[21] Rev. Rul. 65-261, 1965-2 CB 281.

[22] *J.D. Beals Est.*, CA-2, 36-1 USTC ¶9117, 82 F2d 268.

[23] *G. Lattera*, 88 TCM 293, Dec. 55,756(M), TC Memo. 2004-216, *aff'd*, CA-3, 2006-1 USTC ¶50,165, 437 F3d 399.

[24] *C.E. Trantina*, CA-9, 2008-1 USTC ¶50,138, 512 F3d 567; *W.L. Baker*, 118 TC 452, Dec. 54,756 (2002), *aff'd*, 338 F3d 789.

[25] *Taylor Enterprises, Inc.*, 89 TCM 1369, Dec. 56,044(M), TC Memo. 2005-127; *G.D. Williford*, 64 TCM 422, Dec. 48,408(M), TC Memo. 1992-450.

- *Duration of ownership.* Longer holding periods suggest an asset is held for investment;
- *Nature of the taxpayer's business and the extent to which the taxpayer segregated property from regular business inventory.* Property held for sale and property held for investment must be separately identified;
- *Purpose for acquiring and holding the property before sale.* This factor relates to whether the taxpayer intended to hold the property for sale or to hold the property for investment;
- *Sales and advertising effort.* A taxpayer's extensive sales and advertising efforts indicate that the assets are held as inventory for sale, rather than for investment. Time and effort the taxpayer dedicated to the sales; and
- *Time devoted to sales activities.* Dealers will typically devote substantial time to the sales activities.

¶8015 A SALE OR EXCHANGE REQUIRED

There is no capital gain or loss unless the asset disposed of was *sold or exchanged.* Some transactions that are not actually sales or exchanges are treated as such because their effect is similar. These include:

- Involuntary conversion [¶8065];
- Cutting of timber [¶8070];
- Liquidating dividends [Ch. 2];
- Securities becoming worthless during the tax year [Ch. 13];
- Nonbusiness debts becoming worthless in the tax year [Ch. 13].

.01 Pledge of Stock for Cash Avoids Tax as Immediate or Constructive Sale

A shareholder's pledge of stock for cash to an investment bank will not constitute a taxable event, provided certain attributes are present.[26] The following three elements must exist in order for the pledge-for-cash agreement to avoid tax:

- The shareholder must not be economically compelled to deliver the shares pledged;
- The number of shares promised to be delivered at the future date must vary significantly depending on the value of the shares on that date; and
- The taxpayer must retain voting and dividend rights during the term of the pledge agreement.

If these three elements are present, neither a true taxable sale nor exchange of the stock under Code Sec. 1001 nor a constructive sale of an appreciated financial position (AFP) taxable under Code Sec. 1259 will result. See ¶8030.02 for further discussion of the constructive sales rules.

---

[26] Rev. Rul. 2003-7, 2003-1 CB 363.

A sale or exchange will not occur even though the shareholder gives up possession of the stock and may intend to transfer ownership to satisfy the future obligation because transfer of legal title of the securities to the brokerage firm will not be sufficient to constitute a transfer of real ownership when the transferor retains the unrestricted right to reacquire the securities. Further, although the interest in the stock pledged constitutes an AFP, the taxpayer has not made a constructive sale under Code Sec. 1259. A constructive sale would have occurred only if the taxpayer agreed to provide the same or substantially identical property to the investment bank. In this situation, the number of shares to be delivered under the agreement varied significantly and therefore was not a contract to deliver a substantially fixed amount of property for purposes of Code Sec. 1259(d)(1).

In *L.W. Calloway,*[27] the Court of Appeals for the Eleventh Circuit affirmed the Tax Court to hold that a transaction styled by the parties as a transfer of stock as collateral for a loan was in reality a sale of the stock. The court considered the following factors in determining that the transaction was a taxable sale in the year the stock was transferred rather than a loan:

1. The transaction looked like a sale because legal title to the stock passed to the corporation when it was authorized to sell the stock without notice.
2. The taxpayer retained no property interest in the stock; at best, he had an option to purchase an equivalent number of shares.
3. The parties failed to treat the transaction as a loan, since taxpayer made no payments.
4. The taxpayer failed to report the sale or any cancellation of indebtedness when the transaction terminated.
5. The taxpayer bore no risk of loss if the stock value declined, since he could keep the loan proceeds and forfeit the stock.
6. He had no right to the profits if the stock was sold.

.02 Forward Contract/Share Lending Arrangement Constituted Taxable Sales

In *Anschutz Co.,*[28] the Court of Appeals for the Tenth Circuit affirmed the Tax Court to conclude that a forward contract to deliver stock and a simultaneous share-lending agreement involving the same shares was a single transaction that was a taxable sale of the shares. Because the court considered the two contracts to be linked since one part could not occur without the other, the court concluded that when the taxpayer transferred the contracts, he transferred the benefits and burdens of ownership of the stock, including: legal title to the shares, all risk of loss, a major portion of any gain, voting rights, and possession. Therefore, the integrated transactions were current taxable sales of the underlying stock rather than a tax-free lending arrangement under Code Sec. 1058.

.03 Tax-Free Securities Lending Arrangements

Code Sec. 1058 prescribes rules for the tax-free treatment of certain transfers of securities whereby no gain or loss will be recognized on the exchange of the securities

---

[27] *L.W. Calloway,* 135 TC 26, Dec. 58,264 (2010), *aff'd,* CA-11, 2012-2 USTC ¶50,533.

[28] *Anschutz Co.,* 135 TC 78, Dec. 58,275 (2010), *aff'd,* CA-10, 2012-1 USTC ¶50,117, 664 F3d 313.

covered by the transfer. Congress enacted Code Sec. 1058 to encourage owners of securities to engage in securities lending transactions with brokers to enable them to make deliveries of securities to purchasers within the time required by the relevant market rules. The provision specifically provides that the transactions are tax-free.

In order for the transfer to be tax-free, Code Sec. 1058(b) requires that there be an agreement between the parties covering the transfer of securities (stock, certificate of interest, note, bond, debenture, evidence of indebtedness, or any evidence of an interest in or right to subscribe to or purchase any of the foregoing), and the agreement must:

1. Provide for the return to the transferor of identical securities;
2. Require that payments be made to the transferor in amounts equivalent to the interest, dividends, and other distributions that the owner of the securities is entitled to receive because of ownership during the period that the loan is outstanding; and
3. Not reduce the transferor's risk of loss or opportunity for gain as to the transferred securities.

As stated above, no gain or loss is recognized on the initial exchange. The lender takes a basis in the contractual obligation equal to his basis in the exchanged securities and his holding period in the obligation includes the period that he held the exchanged securities. Likewise, when the securities are returned to the lender, no gain or loss is recognized on the return, and the lender again carries over his holding period and basis.

In Rev. Proc. 2008-63,[29] the IRS provided guidance regarding the application of Code Sec. 1058 to situations involving securities loan agreements where the borrower subsequently defaults under the agreement as a direct or indirect result of its bankruptcy. If the securities loan agreement otherwise satisfies the requirements of Code Sec. 1058(b) and the lender uses collateral provided pursuant to the agreement, or cash generated by the sale of such collateral, to purchase identical securities as soon as it is commercially practicable (but in no event more than 30 days following the default), the purchase will be treated as a tax-free exchange of rights under the agreement for identical securities.

In *H. Samueli*,[30] the Court of Appeals for the Ninth Circuit affirmed the Tax Court to conclude that a complex tax-motivated transaction did not qualify for nonrecognition as a securities lending arrangement under Code Sec. 1058(b)(3) because it reduced the risk of loss or opportunity for gain of the transferor. The transaction's structure only allowed the lender access to reclaim and sell its securities on three different days during the entire term of the deal. This limited the lender's ability to sell the securities any time that a possibility of a profitable sale arose. The transaction was recharacterized as a taxable sale of the securities and a repurchase of the securities pursuant to a forward contract.

---

[29] Rev. Proc. 2008-63, 2008-2 CB 946.

[30] *H. Samueli*, 132 TC 336, Dec. 57,759 (2009), *aff'd*, CA-9, 2011-2 USTC ¶50,697. *See also K. Sollberger*, 101 TCM 1353, Dec. 58,591(M), TC Memo. 2011-78, *aff'd* CA-9, 2012-2 USTC ¶50,527.

HOLDING PERIOD

¶8020 FIGURING THE HOLDING PERIOD

It is critical for a taxpayer to determine the exact holding period of a capital asset in order to know whether capital gain or loss on its sale or exchange is long-term or short-term. The taxpayer's records should show the exact date property was acquired and disposed of. The holding period begins on the day after acquisition of the property and ends on the date the property is disposed of or transferred. Thus, in figuring the period held, exclude the date the property was acquired but include the day it was disposed of.[31] The reverse is true when figuring a prescribed period *before* a designated event (as in timber and coal transactions [¶8070; ¶8080]).[32]

▶**PRACTICE POINTER:** Taxpayers who hold property for exactly one year will be unable to claim the reduced capital gains tax rate on the disposition of that property because the holding period needs to be at least one year and a day in order for the sale to qualify as long-term capital gain.

.01 Calculating the Holding Period

The holding period is figured by calendar months and fractions of months, not by days.[33] In other words, the day after the property was acquired is the start of the holding period and this same date in each succeeding calendar month is the start of a new month regardless of the number of days in the preceding month.[34]

The holding period of various types of property is outlined below:

.02 Property or Type of Transaction Holding Period

Stock or Securities

For securities traded on an established securities market, the holding period begins the date after the trade date when the securities were bought and ends on the trade date when the securities were sold—not the settlement date.

For stock purchases in which the parties contracted for the sale, the date on which title is transferred, not the earlier contract date, governs.[35]

Real Property

The holding period begins on the day after title passes or on the day after delivery of possession is made and the buyer assumes ownership privileges, whichever occurs first. A delivery of possession under an option agreement is without significance until a contract of sale takes place through exercise of the option.[36]

---

[31] Rev. Rul. 66-5, 1966-1 CB 91; Rev. Rul. 70-598, 1970-2 CB 168.

[32] Rev. Rul. 66-6, 1966-1 CB 160.

[33] Rev. Rul. 66-5, 1966-1 CB 91.

[34] Rev. Rul. 66-7, 1966-1 CB 188; *L. Caspe*, CA-8, 82-2 USTC ¶9714, 694 F2d 1116; *M.L. Middleton*, CA-11, 82-2 USTC ¶9713, 693 F2d 124.

[35] *E.L. Armstrong*, 6 TC 1166, Dec. 15,172 (1946), *aff'd*, CA-3, 47-1 USTC ¶9259, 162 F2d 199; *A. Theophilous*, CA-9, 96-1 USTC ¶50,293, 85 F3d 440.

[36] Rev. Rul. 54-607, 1954-2 CB 177.

Newly Erected Building

Parts of a new building may be considered as having been completed before the entire building. Their holding period starts at their completion.[37]

Patents

The special rule under Code Sec. 1235 [¶ 8010] for long-term capital gain treatment on transfer of a patent applies regardless of the period held. If capital gain is sought under general capital gains rules, a patent's holding period runs from the earlier of either the date the invention is reduced to actual practice or the patent is issued.[38]

Community Property

The holding period of a surviving spouse's share generally runs from the date the property was acquired by the deceased spouse.

Optioned Property

The period during which you hold an option cannot be added to the period you own property acquired under the option.[39]

Commodity Futures

A commodity future is a contract for the sale of some fixed amount of a commodity at a future date for a fixed price. If you accept delivery of a commodity in satisfaction of a commodity futures contract, the holding period of the commodity includes the period for which you held the futures contract if such commodity futures contract was a capital asset in your hands [Code Sec. 1223(8); Reg. § 1.1223-1(h)]. For short sale rules, see ¶ 8030.

Stock Dividends and Stock Rights

See Ch. 2.

Wash Sales

See Ch. 13.

Worthless Securities

See Ch. 13.

Gifts

The holding period begins with the date the property was acquired by the donor. However, if the property had a value at the date of the gift lower than cost, and the sale results in a loss, the holding period begins on the date of the gift [Code Sec. 1223(2); Reg. § 1.1223-1(b)].

Property Acquired by Bequest, Devise, or Inheritance

Gains and losses from the sale or exchange of inherited property receive long-term capital gain or loss regardless of how long the property was held [Code Sec. 1223(11)].

---

[37] *M.A. Paul*, CA-3, 53-2 USTC ¶ 9527, 206 F2d 763; Rev. Rul. 75-524, 1975-2 CB 342.

[38] *W.O. Kronner*, CtCls, 53-1 USTC ¶ 9235, 110 FSupp 730, 126 CtCls 156.

[39] *San Joaquin Fruit and Investment Co.*, SCt, 36-1 USTC ¶ 9144, 297 US 496, 56 SCt 569, *reh'g denied*, 297 US 728.

Tax-Free Exchanges

The holding period of property you receive in a nontaxable exchange includes the holding period of the property given in exchange, if the property exchanged was either a capital asset or depreciable property used in your trade or business and if the basis of the property you receive has the same basis, in whole or in part, as the property exchanged [Code Sec. 1223(1); Reg. § 1.1223-1(a)].

> **Example 8-9:** On December 13, 2013, Mr. Frank, a calendar year taxpayer, exchanged shares of Class A stock, bought July 12, 2013, for $1,200, for shares of Class B stock in a tax-free exchange. The holding period of the Class B shares began on July 13, 2013. He sells the Class B shares on August 3, 2015, for $1,000. Since his holding period of the Class B stock is more than 12 months, his $200 loss is a long-term loss.

Partnership Interest

The holding period runs from the date the interest is acquired. A partner's death does not interrupt the holding period of the other partners' interest, as long as the business continues.[40]

¶8025 FIRST-IN, FIRST-OUT RULE

Reg. § 1.1012-1(c) provides that the first-in-first-out (FIFO) method must be used to compute basis (i.e., the sold shares are charges against the earliest acquired shares) when shares of stock are sold or transferred on different dates or at different prices, and the lot from which the stock was sold or transferred cannot be adequately identified. An exception is available if the stock can be adequately identified. An adequate identification is made if (1) certificates representing stock from a particular lot are delivered to the taxpayer's transferee, or (2) when the stock is left in the custody of the broker, the taxpayer specifies to the broker, the particular stock to be sold, and within a reasonable period afterwards, the broker confirms the specifications in writing.

In *Rendall*,[41] the Court of Appeals for the Tenth Circuit affirmed the Tax Court to hold that a taxpayer's basis on shares sold must be determined using the FIFO method, which produced a much larger gain, because the taxpayer failed to prove that he adequately identified any portion of the pledged shares sold on a last-in-first-out (LIFO) basis. The taxpayer did not identify at the time of the stock sale that the stock purchased at the higher price should be sold. As a result, gain was computed using the FIFO method.

---

[40] *D.T. Humphrey*, 32 BTA 280, Dec. 8913, *nonacq.* 1935-2 CB 34; *A.S. Lehman*, 7 TC 1088, Dec. 15,457 (1946), *aff'd*, CA-2, 48-1 USTC ¶9121, 165 F2d 383, *cert. denied*, 334 US 819, 68 SCt 1085.

[41] *J.S. Rendall*, CA-10, 2008-2 USTC ¶50,480, 535 F3d 1221, *aff'g*, Dec. 56,595(M), 92 TCM 157, TC Memo. 2006-174.

¶8030 SHORT SALES

Basically, short sales occur when speculators, believing that the price of certain stocks will fall, sell borrowed stocks with the expectation that they will be able to buy the stock back at a lower price. To effect the short sale, the taxpayer delivers securities or other property to the buyer that he has borrowed. The seller will either: (1) borrow the shares from a broker for delivery to the buyer, even if they already own an equivalent number of shares of the stock that were sold short, or (2) borrow the shares from their inventory of stock. At a later date, the sale is "closed" or covered when the same or substantially identical stock is delivered to the lender by the taxpayer. Herein lies the short seller's potential for profit: if the price of the stock declines after the short sale, he does not need all the funds to make his covering purchase; the short seller then pockets the difference. On the other hand, there is no limit to the short seller's potential loss: if the price of the stock rises, so too does the short seller's loss, and since there is no cap to a stock's price, there is no limitation on the short seller's risk. There is no time limit on this obligation to cover. A short sale is not closed where a taxpayer who is obligated to transfer stock to a broker as a result of a short sale satisfies the obligation by having another broker deliver the stock to the broker.[42]

Short sales involve two kinds of property: (1) stocks and securities, and (2) commodity futures. The taxpayer engaging in a short sale expects the stock price will fall, so that the shares purchased to replace the borrowed shares will be purchased at a lower price yielding a profit. If the stocks sold short decline in price, short sellers make a profit; if the price goes up, they have a loss. If the date for measuring the holding period is simply the date the short sale is closed, a short sale might allow you to convert what is essentially a short-term holding period into a long-term holding period. Gains or losses from short sales of property are considered gains or losses from sales or exchanges of capital assets to the extent that the property used to close out the short sale (the property returned to the lender) is a capital asset in your hands [Code Sec. 1233(a); Reg. § 1.1233-1(a)]. For "put" and "call" options, see ¶ 8035. Gain or loss is recognized when the short sale is closed, measured by the difference between the short sale price and the cost (or other basis) of the property used to close the short sale. Even though a taxpayer may move to close out a short sale on the same day that the borrowed shares are initially sold, the sale is considered complete for tax purposes on the trade date if a taxable gain results and is considered complete for tax purposes on delivery of the stock if the investor realizes a loss [Reg. § 1.1233-1(a)(1)].[43]

Example 8-10: In January, the taxpayer directs his or her broker to borrow 100 shares of ABCo stock. The taxpayer does not own any shares of that stock. On December 31 of that same year, when the value of the stock has increased (the value of the taxpayer's short position has depreciated), the taxpayer directs his or her broker to buy 100 shares of stock to close the short sale. The shares are delivered to the lender of the stock on January 4 of the following year. According to Rev. Rul. 2002-44, the short sale is not complete until the ABCo stock is delivered to close the sale. Even though the taxpayer is treated as

---

[42] Rev. Rul. 2004-15, 2004-1 CB 515.

[43] Rev. Rul. 2002-44, 2002-2 CB 84.

having acquired the stock on the trade date, the stock will not be delivered to close the sale until January of the following year.

Example 8-11: The facts are the same as in Example 8-10, except that the stock has depreciated in value and the short sale is closed out at a gain. The IRS concluded in Rev. Rul. 2002-44, the taxpayer is treated as having acquired the stock on the trade date of December 31 of the first year. However, at that time, the price of the stock decreased. The value of the short sale has increased and the taxpayer now holds an appreciated short position. The acquisition of the same or substantially identical stock is a constructive sale transaction. The taxpayer is considered to have entered into a constructive sale transaction and the taxpayer realizes a gain on the short sale on December 31 of the first year.

The wash sale rule disallows a loss deduction on the sale or disposition of certain stock or securities (including contracts or options to acquire or sell stock or securities) [Ch. 13]. The wash sale also applies to losses on a short sale if, within 30 days before or after the closing, the taxpayer sold or entered into another short sale of substantially identical securities [Code Sec. 1091(e)]. Such short-sale losses are not deductible.

.01 Special Rules for Short Sales

In general, the holding period on a short sale is figured by the length of time the seller holds the property that is eventually delivered to the lender to close the short sale. The following rules are aimed at closing what would otherwise be loophole situations:

1. If, on the date of the short sale, property substantially identical to that sold has been held for not more than one year or if such substantially identical property is acquired between the short sale and closing dates, any gain on the closing of a short sale is a short-term capital gain.

   NOTE: This rule applies regardless of when the property actually used to close the short sale was acquired, but it doesn't apply to that part of the property sold short that exceeds the substantially identical property.

   Example 8-12: On February 15, 2012, Mr. Latimer bought 100 shares of Jay stock for $1,000. On November 15, 2012, he sold short 100 shares of Jay stock for $1,500. On February 28, 2013, he closes the short sale by delivering the 100 shares of Jay stock bought on February 15, 2012. The gain of $500 ($1,500 less $1,000) is a short-term capital gain because on the date of the short sale (November 15, 2012) property substantially identical to that sold had not been held for more than a year.

2. If, as in Rule 1 above, on the date of the short sale, property substantially identical to the property sold short has been held for no more than one year or property substantially identical to the property sold short was acquired between the date of the short sale and the date the sale was closed, the holding period of such substantially identical property begins on the earlier of (a) the date the short sale was closed or (b) the date the substantially identical property was either sold, gifted or otherwise disposed of.

NOTE: This rule does not apply to that part of the substantially identical property that exceeds the amount sold short nor does it apply to short sales open no more than 20 days or to certain capital asset stock held by dealers.

Example 8-13: On February 15, 2012, Mr. Latimer bought 100 shares of Jay stock for $1,000. On November 15, 2012, he sold short 100 shares of stock for $1,500. On February 20, 2013, he closes the short sale by delivering 100 shares of Jay stock that he had bought several days before for $1,500. On February 28, 2013, he sells the 100 shares he had bought on February 15, 2012, for $1,500. The $500 gain on the last sale ($1,500 less $1,000) is a short-term gain since the holding period of this substantially identical property, bought on February 15, 2012, didn't begin until the date of the short sale (November 15, 2012).

3. If substantially identical property has been held for more than one year as of the date of the short sale, any loss on the closing of the short sale is a long-term capital loss.

NOTE: As in the case of Rule 1, this rule applies regardless of when the property actually used to close the short sale was acquired and doesn' t apply to the part of the property sold short that exceeds the substantially identical property.

Example 8-14: On February 15, 2012, Mr. Latimer bought 100 shares of Jay stock for $1,000. On February 28, 2013, he sells short 100 shares of Jay stock for $1,600. On March 16, 2013, he sells the 100 shares of Jay stock he had purchased on February 15, 2012, for $1,700. On the same day, he purchases 100 shares of Jay stock for $1,700 and uses this stock to cover the short sale. The gain of $700 on the sale of the stock originally purchased on February 15, 2012 ($1,700 less $1,000) is long-term gain because none of the above rules applied. The $100 loss on the closing of the short sale ($1,700 less $1,600) is a long-term loss because property substantially identical to the property sold short had been held for more than one year (February 15, 2012 to February 28, 2013), so Rule 3 applies.

Substantially Identical Property Defined

What is substantially identical property depends on the circumstances of each case. Generally, preferred stocks or bonds are not identical to common stock of the same corporation. Securities of one corporation are not substantially identical to securities of another (except in special situations as, for example, securities of a corporation in reorganization).

When preferred stocks or bonds are convertible into common stock of the same corporation, the relative values and price changes may be so similar as to make them substantially identical to the common stock [Reg. § 1.1233-1(d)].

Spouses Included with Taxpayer

The term *taxpayer* means the "taxpayer or spouse." Consequently, if your spouse (not legally separated or divorced) holds stock substantially identical to that sold short by you, the three rules listed above apply as if you owned the property [Code Sec. 1233(e)(2)(C); Reg. § 1.1233-1(d)(3)].

Short Sale of Small Business Investment Company (SBIC) Stock

A small business investment company (SBIC) is authorized to provide small businesses with equity capital. SBICs are private corporations that are licensed under the Small Business Investment Act of 1958 and are subject to the regulations issued by the Small Business Administration. SBICs are subject to minimum capitalization requirements. If you are an investor in small business investment company stock, generally gains from the sale of such stock are capital gains but losses from such sale can be treated as ordinary losses. However, if you acquired the stock merely to close a short sale, you are not entitled to ordinary loss treatment; a capital loss results.

.02 Constructive Sales Rules

Generally, a constructive sale occurs when a taxpayer with an appreciated financial position (for example, stock) sells short-against-the-box or takes some other offsetting position substantially eliminating the taxpayer's risk of loss and opportunity for gain on the appreciated position. Code Sec. 1259 provides that a taxpayer who enters into a short sale of the same or substantially identical property makes what is termed a *constructive sale* of an *appreciated financial position (AFP)*, and will therefore recognize gain as if such position were actually sold, assigned, or otherwise terminated at its fair market value on the date of such constructive sale. In addition, Code Sec. 1259(a)(2) provides that a proper adjustment must be made in the amount of any gain or loss subsequently taken into account on that position and a new holding period begins for that position starting on the date of the constructive sale.

A taxpayer is treated as having made a constructive sale of an AFP if the taxpayer (or a related person):

- Enters into a short sale of the same or substantially identical property;
- Enters into an offsetting notional principal contract with respect to the sale of identical property;
- Enters into a futures or forward contract to deliver the same or substantially identical property;
- In the case of an AFP that is a short sale, offsetting notional principal contract or futures or forward contract as to any property, acquires the same or substantially identical property; or
- Enters into one or more other transactions (or acquires one or more positions) that have substantially the same effect as a transaction described above.

Exceptions to Constructive Sales Rule

It is still possible to enjoy the benefits of the short sale against the box in certain limited situations. The exceptions to the constructive sales rules are as follow:

- *Nonmarketable securities.* A taxpayer will not be treated as having made a constructive sale of an AFP solely because the taxpayer entered into a contract for the sale of any stock, debt instrument, or partnership interest which is not a marketable security, as defined by Code Sec. 453(f), if the contract settles within one year after the date the contract is entered into [Code Sec. 1259(c)(2)];

- *Closed transactions.* A transaction will not be treated as a constructive sale if: (1) the taxpayer closes the transaction on or before the 30th day after the close of the tax year; (2) the taxpayer held the AFP throughout the 60-day period beginning on the date the transaction was closed; and (3) at no time during that 60-day period was the taxpayer's risk of loss with respect to the position reduced by reason of a circumstance which would be described in Code Sec. 246(c)(4) (rules relating to suspension of the holding period where the risk of loss is diminished for purposes of the dividends received deduction) [Code Sec. 1259(c)(3)(A)].

Successive Short Sales Meet Closed Transaction Exception

In Rev. Rul. 2003-1,[44] the IRS issued guidance indicating that successive short sales of stock fall within the exception to the Code Sec. 1259(a)(1) constructive sale rule under which gain must otherwise be recognized as of the date of the constructive sale. Under this exception, the taxpayer essentially must hold the appreciated financial position unhedged for a 60-day period on the date of the closing of the transaction that would otherwise be treated as a constructive sale. If a transaction that is closed is reestablished in a substantially similar position, the exception under Code Sec. 1259(a) still applies, provided that the reestablished position is closed prior to the end of the 30th day after the close of the tax year in which the original transaction occurred and the taxpayer satisfies several of the conditions found in Code Sec. 1259(c)(3).

The following example illustrates the operation of this rule:

On January 1, A owns 100 shares of X Corp. On February 1, A enters into a short sale of 100 shares of X stock (Short Sale 1). In March, A purchases an additional 100 shares of X stock and delivers those shares to close Short Sale 1. On April 1, A enters into a second short sale of 100 X shares (Short Sale 2). In May, A purchases an additional 100 shares of X stock and delivers those shares to close Short Sale 2.

On June 3, A enters into a third short sale of 100 shares of X stock (Short Sale 3). On January 15 of the following year, A purchases an additional 100 shares of X stock. Prior to the 30 days after the close of the taxpayer's tax year, A delivers those shares to close Short Sale 3. A continues to hold the 100 shares of X stock during the 60-day period beginning on the date Short Sale 3 is closed. During that 60-day period, the 100 shares of X stock are appreciated and held "unhedged."

The IRS reviewed whether all three scenarios met the Code Sec. 1259(c)(3) closed transaction exception to Code Sec. 1259(a)(1). The IRS concluded that Short Sale 1 failed the exception unless the reestablished position exception caused Short Sale 2 to be disregarded. The same analysis is applied for each successive short sale to determine if each sale is considered a constructive sale or whether each sale is disregarded on the grounds that it constitutes a closed transaction.

The IRS determined that Short Sale 3 should be treated as a reestablished position with respect to Short Sale 2. In turn, Short Sale 2 is disregarded as a reestablished position with respect to Short Sale 1. Therefore, Short Sale 1 was treated as a closed transaction under Code Sec. 1259(c)(3)(A). Using the same rationale, the IRS concluded that all three short sales were closed transactions.

---

[44] Rev. Rul. 2003-1, 2003-1 CB 291.

The IRS also indicated that changes in value of the appreciated financial position of the shares after the initial transaction occurs should be ignored. This would avoid unwarranted and differential application of the closed transaction exception. In addition, it would also avoid a potential circularity problem in the interpretation of the exception.

.03 "When-Issued" Transaction

Securities to be issued as a stock dividend, or in a reorganization or recapitalization, may be bought and sold on a "when-issued" basis. A contract to sell stock or other securities on a when-issued basis is a short sale, and the performance or assignment for value of the contract is a closing of the short sale [Code Sec. 1233(e)(2)(A); Reg. § 1.1233-1(c)(1)].

.04 Commodity Futures and Hedging Transactions

The short sale rules discussed above apply to transactions in commodity futures that are capital assets [Code Sec. 1233(b)]. A commodity future is a standard form contract to deliver a fixed quantity of a commodity (wheat, cotton, hides, etc.) in a future month for a fixed price. The purchase and sale of a commodity future results in capital gain or loss, unless the transaction is a hedge [Code Sec. 1233(a), (g); Reg. § 1.1233-1(b)]. A hedge generally is a form of price insurance to avoid the risk of change in the market price of commodities used in a business. The Supreme Court has ruled that hedging transactions that were an integral part of a business's inventory-purchase system were a noncapital asset because they were inventory.[45] Thus gains and losses from business hedges entered into in order to reduce risk or price changes are treated as ordinary gains and losses. However, the IRS does not apply this to a short sale of currency to hedge against devaluation.[46]

In applying the short sale rules to capital transactions, futures that cover different commodities (corn and wheat), or that call for different delivery months (May wheat and July wheat) are not substantially identical. Futures obtained in different markets may be treated as substantially identical in particular cases. When a taxpayer engages in two futures transactions, one to deliver and the other to receive a substantially identical commodity in two different markets, only the excess quantity in either market is considered a short sale if both transactions are made the same day and closed the same day [Code Sec. 1233(e)(3); Reg. § 1.1233-1(d)(2)(ii)].

.05 Commodity Tax Straddles

Straddles are financial transactions involving an investor who holds offsetting positions in personal property. Personal property is defined as any personal property that is actively traded [Code Sec. 1092(d)(1)]. The objective of straddle investing is to reduce the investor's risk of loss. A position is an interest in personal property, including a futures contract, a forward contract, or an option. A simple commodity straddle could be created by taking equal long (buy) and short (sell) positions in a futures contract of a commodity with different delivery dates. Some or all of the gain you have from a

---

[45] *Corn Products Refining Co.*, SCt, 55-2 USTC ¶ 9746, 350 US 46, 76 SCt 20; *Fed'l Nat'l Mortagage Ass'n*, 100 TC 541, Dec. 49,102 (1993).

[46] *International Flavors & Fragrances, Inc.*, CA-2, 75-2 USTC ¶ 9770, 524 F2d 357.

straddle (including straddles involving stock) is converted from capital gain to ordinary income [Code Sec. 1258(a)].

Generally, you cannot currently deduct losses on straddle positions to the extent that you have unrecognized gains in offsetting straddle positions. Put another way, you can currently deduct only the amount of loss in excess of unrecognized gain in offsetting positions [Code Sec. 1092(a)(3)]. There are different rules involving property on the mark to market system. See ¶ 8040 and Ch. 17.

Deferred losses carry over to the next year. They are subject to the application of the deferral rules in the later year. The losses on unidentified straddles are deferred until their offsetting positions are closed [Code Sec. 1092(a)(B); Temp. Reg. § 1.1092(b)-1T(b)].

The loss deferral rules do not apply to losses on positions and straddles that you have clearly identified as straddles on your records on the day they were acquired. However, gain and loss on these identified positions must be netted. The positions must all have been acquired on the same day and either all closed on the same day or none closed by the end of the tax year.

Straddles composed entirely of futures contracts are not subject to the loss deferral rules, but they will be taxed under the mark-to-market system [Code Sec. 1092(a)(3)(B)(ii)]. For mixed straddles, however, where the position consists partly of Sec. 1256 contracts (below), a taxpayer may elect to exclude all of those positions from mark-to-market treatment. Once the exclusion is elected, the positions are eligible for the prescribed loss deferral, wash sale and short-term rules.

No deduction is allowed for interest and carrying charges allocable to property or positions belonging to straddles. They are treated as capital expenditures [Ch. 12] [Code Sec. 263(g)(1)].

The capitalization rule does not apply to any identified hedging transactions, any positions not part of a straddle, or qualified covered call options and optioned stock [Code Sec. 1092(c)(4)(A)].

¶8035 "PUT" AND "CALL" OPTIONS

Gain or loss from the sale of an option to buy or sell property is a capital gain or loss if the property optioned is a capital asset. Options to buy and sell stock are characterized as either "put" or "call" options. A *put* is an option that gives an investor (holder of the option) the right to sell stock to the maker of the option at a stated price within a limited time. If you fail to exercise the put before its expiration date, the privilege is worthless. A *call* is an option that gives the holder the right to buy stock from the maker of the option at a stated price within a limited time. The option's maker (seller) is paid a premium for his obligation to buy or sell the stock.

.01 Background and Purpose of Put and Call Options

Investors buy puts when they expect the value of the stock to fall. They then can sell the stock at the higher option price. If the market price goes up, they can sell the stock at the higher market price rather than exercise their option. Conversely, investors buy calls if they expect the value of the stock to rise. They can buy the stock at the lesser option price. If the market goes down, they can buy the stock at the market price rather than use the option. It is not unusual for one person to write or to acquire a *straddle* (i.e., offsetting put and call options on the same stock) at the same time.

> ▶ **CONVERSION TRANSACTION:** Straddles and stock purchases combined with put options may be affected by the anticonversion rules, which provide that some or all of the gains from such transactions will be recharacterized as ordinary income rather than capital gain [¶8005].

.02 When Option Is Sold

Generally, capital gain or loss results from the sale or exchange of the option unless the taxpayer is a dealer (¶8010) [Reg. §1.1234-1(a)(3)]. A dealer is one who trades in puts and calls written by others, but not someone who writes puts and calls for a premium.[47] The maker or writer of the put or call is not affected by the sale or exchange.

.03 When Option Is Exercised

The maker of a call option includes the premium received for the option with the option price to find the amount he realized on the exercise. The holder of the call adds the premium he paid to the property's cost in determining his basis for the stock.[48] When the holder sells a 30-day call option and reacquires it before the exercise period expires, the excess cost to reacquire over the option's selling price is added to the stock's basis.[49]

When a put option is exercised, the maker subtracts the premium he received for the option from the price paid for the stock to find his basis for the acquired stock.[50] The holder subtracts the premium he paid from the stock's price to determine the amount he realized on the sale.[51]

Gain or loss on the option's exercise is determined when the sale is closed. It is a capital gain or loss if the stock is a capital asset. The holding period runs from the time the option is exercised.

Short Sales

Because a put is an option to sell, the holder generally is making a short sale when he or she acquires the put. The seller has a short-term capital gain when he or she exercises the option. The acquisition of a put is not a short sale if the holder owns substantially identical stock for more than one year before the holder buys the put. Accordingly, the holder can cover the put with this stock for a long-term capital gain or loss or cover it by other stock held less than a year for a short-term gain or loss. Also, the short sale rules do not apply when the put and the stock to be used to cover it are bought on the same day. A call is not *substantially identical* to the stock subject to the call [Code Sec. 1233(c); Reg. §1.1233-1(c)].[52] Note: Buying a put option on stock you own may bring you under the conversion transaction rules [¶8005].

---

[47] Rev. Rul. 68-151, 1968-1 CB 363.

[48] Rev. Rul. 68-151, 1968-1 CB 363.

[49] Rev. Rul. 78-182, 1978-1 CB 265.

[50] Rev. Rul. 68-151, 1968-1 CB 363.

[51] Rev. Rul. 71-521, 1971-2 CB 313.

[52] Rev. Rul. 58-384, 1958-2 CB 410.

.04 When Option Lapses

The option grantor realizes short-term capital gain or loss on a "closing transaction" or lapse of the option without exercise. A *closing transaction* means any end to the grantor's obligation other than by exercise or lapse of the option. This rule does not apply to dealers [Code Sec. 1234(b)(3)].

If the holder of a put or call lets the option expire without exercising it, he or she has a loss for the amount the holder paid for it. However, there is no loss if the put and the stock to cover it are bought at the same time. In that case, the amount paid for the put is added to the stock's cost [Code Sec. 1233(c)]. A capital loss is a long-term loss if the put or call option was held more than one year; otherwise it is short-term.

¶8040 MARK-TO-MARKET METHOD

.01 Making the Election

Mandatory Election

To more clearly reflect income, dealers in securities are required to use the mark-to-market (MTM) rules to value securities they hold in inventory [Code Sec. 475(a)]. The mark-to-market regime requires that unrealized gains and losses on a contract held at the end of each year be recognized, even though the contract has not been sold or disposed of and nothing has been realized. As a result, taxpayers' net gains or losses are approximately equal to the aggregate net amounts which are credited to their margin accounts, or which they have had to pay into their accounts during the tax year.

The term "dealer in securities" is defined in Code Sec. 475(c)(1)(A) as a taxpayer who regularly purchases securities from or sells securities to customers in the ordinary course of a trade or business; or regularly offers to enter into, assume, offset, assign or otherwise terminate positions in securities with customers in the ordinary course of a trade or business [Code Sec. 475(c)(1)(B)].

Discretionary Election

The following taxpayers have the option to elect to use the MTM rules to value their inventory:

- A dealer in commodities under Code Sec. 475(e);
- A trader in securities (e.g., day traders of stocks and bonds);
- A trader in commodities under Code Sec. 475(f) [see also Ch. 17].

Code Sec. 475(e) and (f) allows dealers in commodities and traders in securities or commodities to make an election to report all gains and losses from securities or commodities as ordinary income (or loss) rather than capital gain or loss [Code Sec. 475(d)(3)(A)(i), (f)(1)(D)]. Note that ordinary losses are fully deductible to offset ordinary income. As a result of this election, securities and commodities held at the end of the year are *marked to market* by treating them as if they had been sold (and reacquired) for fair market value on the last business day of the year [Code Sec. 475(d)(3)(A)(i)]. When the security is subsequently sold, the gain or loss that is realized is adjusted for the gain or loss that was recognized earlier as a result of the

MTM rules. Once elected, the mark-to-market treatment will be effective for the tax year for which it is made and all subsequent tax years, unless revoked with the consent of the IRS. See ¶8040.05 for further discussion of revocation rules.

> **Example 8-15:** A securities dealer bought a security for $100. Eighteen months later, the fair market value of the security is $200. The dealer must recognize $100 as ordinary income. The dealer sells the security six months later for $150. The dealer must adjust the amount of gain he recognizes to reflect the gain already recognized. Thus he has a $50 loss ($150 (the amount realized) minus $100 (his basis in the stock) minus $50 (gain already included).

Valuation Safe Harbor

The IRS has a safe harbor for valuing securities and commodities under Code Sec. 475. The valuation safe harbor generally permits eligible taxpayers to elect to have the values that are reported for eligible positions on certain financial statements treated as the fair market values of those eligible positions for purposes of Code Sec. 475, if certain conditions are met [Reg. § 1.475(a)-4(a)(1)].

Eligible taxpayers and eligible positions. The safe harbor is available to any taxpayer subject to the MTM regime under Code Sec. 475, whether the taxpayer is a dealer in securities under Code Sec. 475(a), a dealer in commodities under Code Sec. 475(e), or a trader in either securities or commodities under Code Sec. 475(f) [Reg. § 1.475(a)-4(c)]. The valuation methodology under the safe harbor applies only for positions that are properly marked under Code Sec. 475. The safe harbor only addresses valuation and does not expand or contract the scope of application of Code Sec. 475. For example, if a security is not marked under Code Sec. 475 because it has been identified as held for investment, then under the safe harbor it may not be marked for federal income tax purposes even though it is properly marked on the financial statement.

Eligible method. To qualify for the safe harbor, a financial accounting method must satisfy four basic requirements, as follows [Reg. § 1.475(a)-4(d)(2)]:

- *Frequency.* The method mark eligible positions to market through valuations made as of the last business day of each tax year.
- *Recognition at the mark.* The method must recognize into income on the income statement any gain or loss from marking eligible positions to market.
- *Recognition on disposition.* The method must recognize into income on the income statement any gain or loss on disposition of an eligible position as if a year-end mark occurred immediately before the disposition.
- *Fair value standard.* The method must arrive at fair value in accordance with U.S. GAAP.

Limitations. In addition to the basic requirements, the safe harbor also imposes three additional limitations that ensure minimal divergence from fair market value as follows [Reg. § 1.475(a)-4(d)(3)]:

- *Bid-ask method.* Except for eligible positions that are traded on a qualified board or exchange, the financial accounting method that applies to securities and commodities dealers must not result in values at or near the bid or ask values, even if the use of bid or ask values is permissible in accordance with U.S. GAAP;

- *Valuations based on present values of projected cash flows.* If the method of valuation consists of determining the present value of projected cash flows from an eligible position or positions, then the method must not take into account any cash flows of income or expense that are attributable to a period or time before the valuation date. This limitation ensures that items of income or expense will not be accounted for twice, first through current realization and then again in the mark; and
- *Accounting for costs and risks.* No cost or risk is accounted for more than once, either directly or indirectly. For example, a financial accounting method that allows a special adjustment for credit risk generally satisfies this limitation. It would not satisfy this limitation, however, if it computed the present value of projected cash flows using a discount rate that takes into account any amount of credit risk that is also taken into account by the special adjustment.

.02 Definition of Security

For purposes of the MTM rules, a *security* is defined in Code Sec. 475(c)(2) as any: (1) share of stock in a corporation; (2) partnership or beneficial ownership interest in a widely held or publicly traded partnership or trust; (3) note, bond, debenture, or other evidence of indebtedness; (4) interest rate, currency, or equity notional principal contract; (5) evidence of an interest in, or a derivative financial instrument in, any of the securities described above; or any currency, including any option, forward contract, short position, and any similar financial instrument in such a security or currency; and (6) position which is not one of the foregoing securities, but that is a hedge with respect to one of those securities that is clearly identified in the dealer's records as a hedge before the close of the day on which it is acquired or entered into or at other times, as regulations may prescribe [Code Sec. 475(c)(2)].

A hedge is defined as any position that manages the dealer's risk of interest rate or price changes or currency fluctuations, including any position that is reasonably expected to become a hedge within 60 days after the acquisition of the position [Code Sec. 475(c)(3)].

Exceptions

Reg. § 1.475(c)-2(a) provides the following three exceptions to the definition of security for purposes of the MTM rules: (1) a security if Code Sec. 1032 prevents the taxpayer from recognizing gain or loss with respect to the security; (2) a debt instrument issued by the taxpayer; or (3) a REMIC residual interest, or an interest or arrangement that has substantially the same economic effect.

A dealer will not be required to apply the MTM rules to the following three types of securities [Code Sec. 475(b)(1); Reg. § 1.475(b)-1(a)]:

- Any security held for investment, which means it is not held by you primarily for sale to customers in the ordinary course of your trade or business [Reg. § 1.475(b)-1(a)]. *Exception does not apply to notional principal contracts.* A dealer in notional principal contracts or derivative financial instruments will not be permitted to treat those securities as securities held for investment. Reg. § 1.475(b)-1(c) provides that a notional principal contract or derivative financial instrument held by a dealer in such securities is not treated as held for investment unless the taxpayer "establishes unambiguously" that the security in question was not acquired in the taxpayer's capacity as a dealer in such securities;

- Any note, bond, debenture, or other evidence of indebtedness that is acquired (including originated) by the taxpayer in the ordinary course of a trade or business of the taxpayer and not held for sale; and any obligation to acquire a note, bond, debenture, or other evidence of indebtedness if the obligation is entered into in the ordinary course of the taxpayer's trade or business and not held for sale; or
- Any security that is a hedge with respect to a security that is not subject to the MTM rules, or that is a position, right to income, or a liability that is not a security in the dealer's hands. A hedge for this purpose is any position that reduces the dealer's risk of changes in price or interest or currency exchange rates. It includes any position that is reasonably expected to become a hedge within 60 days after it is acquired.

A dealer will only be able to qualify for one of the foregoing exceptions to the MTM rules if the dealer can clearly identify the securities in its records as falling within the exceptions before the close of the day on which they were acquired, originated or entered into [Code Sec. 475(b)(2)]. In addition, you must specify the particular subparagraph of Code Sec. 475(b)(1) under which the security is exempt and identify which securities are exempt from the MTM rules [Code Sec. 475(b)(2); Reg. §1.475(b)-2(a)].[53] A dealer clearly identifies a security for these purposes if the dealer clearly identifies all its *other* securities as securities to which the MTM rules apply.

.03 Mark-to-Market (Code Sec. 1256 Contracts)

The mark-to-market regime requires that unrealized gains and losses on a contract held at the end of each year must be recognized, even though the contract has not been sold or disposed of and nothing has been realized. As a result, taxpayers' net gains or losses are approximately equal to the aggregate net amounts which are credited to their margin accounts, or which they have had to pay into their accounts during the tax year.

However, if a taxpayer holds Section 1256 contracts at the beginning of a tax year, any gain or loss subsequently realized on these contracts must be adjusted to reflect any gain or loss taken into account with respect to these contracts in a prior year.

Any capital gain or loss on a Section 1256 contract under the mark-to-market tax system is treated as if (1) 40 percent of the gain or loss is short-term capital gain or loss and (2) 60 percent of the gain or loss is long-term capital gain or loss. Ordinary income or loss items are excluded from this rule and are taxed at the regular income tax rates.

Section 1256 Contract Defined

The term Section 1256 contract includes the following types of contracts:

1. Regulated futures contracts,
2. Foreign currency contracts,[54]

---

[53] Rev. Rul. 97-39, 1997-2 CB 62.

[54] *M.D. Summitt*, 134 TC 248, Dec. 58,223 (2010) (Code Sec. 1256(g)(1) refers to a contract that requires delivery of the foreign currency, not to a contract in which delivery is left to the holder's discretion).

3. Nonequity options,
4. Dealer equity options, and
5. Dealer securities futures contracts.

Exception: Any securities futures contract or option on such a contract does not qualify as a Section 1256 contract and is, therefore, not subject to the MTM rules unless such contract or option is a dealer securities futures contract, or any interest rate swap, currency swap, basis swap, interest rate cap, interest rate floor, commodity swap, equity swap, equity index swap, credit default swap, or similar agreement [Code Sec. 1256(b)(2)].

When gains or losses from Code Sec. 1256 contracts are reported on a MTM basis, 60 percent of the gain or loss that you would have had on a sale at that time is treated as a long-term capital gain or loss; the remaining 40 percent is treated as a short-term capital gain or loss. This is true regardless of the actual character of the property and how long you held it. [Code Sec. 1256(a)(3).]When you later dispose of your Code Sec. 1256 property, you have to increase the gain or loss at that time by the gain or loss formerly recognized. The MTM rules do not apply to hedging transactions unless the transactions were entered into by a syndicate. The wash sale rules do not apply to any loss arising from a Code Sec. 1256 contract. This rule is similar to the rule in present-law Code Sec. 475 applicable to securities that are marked-to-market under that section [Code Sec. 1256(f)(5)].

You can elect to carry back commodity futures capital losses (called *net Sec. 1256 contract losses*) for three years and apply them against net commodity futures capital gains (*net Sec. 1256 contract gains*) during that period. This carryback is available only after netting regulated futures contracts (and other positions subject to the MTM rules) with capital gains and losses from other sources. The carryback is then available only if there is a net capital loss for the tax year, which, but for the election, would be a capital loss in the succeeding year [Code Sec. 1212(c)].

.04 Commodities Dealer/Traders and Securities Traders

Commodities dealers, securities traders, and commodities traders are eligible (not required) to make an election to use the MTM accounting method [Code Sec. 475(e), (f); Prop. Reg. § 1.475(f)-2(c)]. The IRS has outlined the procedures that commodities dealers, securities traders and commodities traders must follow to make a MTM election under Code Sec. 475(e) or Code Sec. 475(f) in Rev. Proc. 99-17.[55] After the election has been made, the commodities dealers, securities traders and commodities traders will use the MTM accounting method to mark securities to their market value at tax time and to deduct any losses as ordinary losses against other sources of income [Prop. Reg. § 1.475(f)-2]. This is beneficial because ordinary losses are deductible in full against ordinary income from sources such as wages, salary and dividends. Once you have made the election, it will apply to the tax year for which made and to all subsequent years unless revoked with the consent of the IRS.

▶ **PLANNING NOTE:** The MTM accounting rules are mandatory for securities dealers but may be elected by securities traders and commodities traders and dealers. Rev. Proc. 99-17 addresses in detail the procedures to follow in making

[55] Rev. Proc. 99-17, 1999-1 CB 503.

this election. Once the election has been made, however, the election may not be revoked without the consent of the IRS.

How to Distinguish Traders from Dealers

The distinction between a trader of securities and a dealer in securities is an important one. *Traders* are in the business of actively selling, buying or exchanging securities or commodities in the market for their own personal account. *Dealers* in securities, on the other hand, deal directly with their own customers when they regularly buy or sell securities or commodities in the course of their business and make their money on the difference between the cost of buying and selling the stock [Code Sec. 475(c)(1); Reg. § 1.475(c)-1(a)(2)]. Persons engaged in the trade or business of trading securities may elect to have the MTM rules apply. Whether a taxpayer's investment activities rise to the level of carrying on a trade or business is based on, among other things, the taxpayer's investment intent; the nature of income to be derived from the activity; and the frequency, extent, and regularity of the taxpayer's securities transactions.[56]

Investment Security Exception

Investment securities are exempt from MTM accounting but in order to be exempt, the exempt investment securities would have to be identified on the same day the electing trader acquires, originates, or enters into the security [Prop. Reg. § 1.475(f)-2(d)]. In addition, the trader would have to demonstrate by clear and convincing evidence that a security has no connection to the trader's trading activities [Prop. Reg. § 1.475(f)-2(a)(2)]. When an electing trader holds fungible securities for investment and also trades the same or substantially similar securities, the investment securities would have to be held in a separate, nontrading account maintained with a third party [Prop. Reg. § 1.475(f)-2(a)(3)].

.05 Mark-to-Market Election

A commodities dealer or a trader in securities or commodities may make the MTM election by filing a statement with the IRS describing the election being made, the first tax year for which the election is effective, and, in certain cases, the trade or business for which the election is made. The statement should be attached to the original return (or a request for an extension of time to file) and filed no later than the due date (without extensions) of the original return for the tax year immediately preceding the election year. Once the election has been made, however, the election may not be revoked without the consent of the IRS. A commodities dealer or trader in securities or commodities that has elected to use the MTM method of accounting under Code Sec. 475(e) or Code Sec. 475(f) may obtain automatic consent for a change in accounting method. Beginning with the first tax year for which the election is effective, MTM is the only permissible method of accounting for securities or commodities subject to the election.

A statement should be attached to either the taxpayer's timely filed federal income tax return for the tax year for which the election is first effective or with a request for an extension of time to file that return. The statement must include the following

[56] *J. Moller*, CA-FC, 83-2 USTC ¶ 9698, 721 F2d 810, *cert. denied*, 467 US 1251; *F. Chen*, 87 TCM 1388, Dec. 55,653(M), TC Memo. 2004-132; *W.G. Holsinger*, TC Memo. 2008-191, 96 TCM 85, Dec. 57,512(M).

information: (1) A statement that the MTM election is made under Code Sec. 475(f); (2) The first tax year for which the election is effective; (3) The trade or business for which you are making the election; and (4) A copy of your completed Form 3115, *Application for Change in Accounting Method.* The resulting Code Sec. 481(a) adjustment must be taken into account ratably over four tax years beginning with the year of change. Once you have made the election, it will apply to that year and all later tax years, unless you obtain permission from the IRS to revoke it.

A taxpayer cannot revoke the election without IRS consent. The IRS, however, can revoke the election if: (1) the taxpayer fails to comply with any of the recordkeeping and production requirements and cannot show reasonable cause for the failure, (2) the taxpayer ceases to use an eligible method, (3) the taxpayer ceases to have an applicable financial statement, or (4) the taxpayer holds a *de minimis* quantity of eligible positions that are subject to the safe harbor [Reg. § 1.475(a)-4(f)(3)].

Extension of Time To Make Election

Relief is available under Code Sec. 9100 to extend the time to make the election if the taxpayer provides that: (1) he acted reasonably and in good faith and (2) that the government's interests will not be prejudiced if relief is granted [Reg. § 301.9100-3(a)]. A taxpayer will be deemed to have acted reasonably and in good faith if he:

1. Requests relief before the IRS discovered the taxpayer's failure to make the election;
2. Failed to make the election because of intervening events beyond the taxpayer's control;
3. Failed to make the election because, after exercising due diligence, the taxpayer was unaware of its necessity;
4. Reasonably relied on IRS's written advice; or
5. Reasonably relied on a qualified tax professional, and the tax professional failed to make or advise the taxpayer to make the election [Reg. § 301.9100-3(b)(1)].

The purpose of relief under Reg. § 301.9000-3 is to permit taxpayers "that are in reasonable compliance with the tax laws to minimize their tax liability by collecting from them only the amount of tax they would have paid if they had been fully informed and well advised." In formulating the standards for this relief, the following two policies must be balanced:

1. The policy of promoting efficient tax administration by providing limited time periods for taxpayers to choose among alternative tax treatments and encouraging prompt tax reporting; and
2. The policy of permitting taxpayers that are in reasonable compliance with the tax laws to minimize their tax liability by collecting from them only the amount of tax they would have paid if they had been fully informed and well advised.

In *Vines*,[57] the Tax Court concluded that a taxpayer who was engaged in the trade or business of trading securities was entitled to an extension of time to file a Code Sec. 475(f) MTM election pursuant to Reg. § 301.9100-3 because he had acted reasonably and in good faith and because the interests of the government were not prejudiced by

---

57 *L.S. Vines*, 126 TC 279, Dec. 56,512 (2006).

granting him time to take the late extension. The taxpayer, who had sustained considerable short term trading losses, did not make a timely MTM election because his long-time accountant was unaware of this safe harbor procedure.

.06 Securities Futures Contracts

A securities futures contract is a new financial product that is a contract of sale for future delivery of a single security or of a narrow-based security index. The termination of a securities contract is treated in a manner similar to a sale or exchange of a securities futures contract for purposes of determining the character of any gain or loss from a termination of a securities futures contract [Code Sec. 1234A(2)]. Any gain or loss from the termination of a securities futures contract (other than a dealer securities futures contract) is treated as gain or loss from the sale or exchange of property that has the same character as the property to which the contract relates has (or would have) in the hands of the taxpayer. Losses from the sale, exchange, or termination of a securities futures contract (other than a dealer securities futures contract) generally are treated in the same manner as losses from the closing of a short sale for purposes of applying the wash sale rules. Thus, the wash sale rules apply to any loss from the sale, exchange, or termination of a securities futures contract (other than dealer securities futures contract) if, within a period beginning 30 days before the date of such sale, exchange, or termination and ending 30 days after such date: (1) stock that is substantially identical to the stock to which the contract relates is sold; (2) a short sale of substantially identical stock is entered into; or (3) another securities futures contract to sell substantially identical stock is entered into.

A securities futures contract to sell generally is treated in a manner similar to a short sale for purposes of the special holding period rules in Code Sec. 1233. Thus, subsections (b) and (d) of Code Sec. 1233 may apply to characterize certain capital gains as short-term capital gain and certain capital losses as long-term capital loss, and to determine holding periods where certain securities futures contracts to sell are entered into while holding the substantially identical stock [Code Sec. 1233(e)(2)].

FIGURING CAPITAL GAIN OR LOSS

¶8045 HOW TO REPORT CAPITAL GAIN OR LOSS

.01 Short-Term and Long-Term Transactions

As you are completing Schedule D, you will have to separate your capital gains and losses according to how long you held or owned the property. The holding period for long-term capital gains and losses is more than one year. See ¶8020 for discussion of how to compute a taxpayer's holding period. The holding period for short-term capital gains and losses is one year or less. To figure the holding period, begin counting on the day after you received the property and include the day you disposed of it. If you disposed of property that you acquired by inheritance report the disposition as long-term gain or loss, regardless of how long you actually held the property.

A nonbusiness bad debt must be treated as short-term capital loss.

.02 Netting of Capital Gains and Losses

To calculate capital gain or loss for the tax year, taxpayers must first net long-term capital gains and losses from each of the rate groups, sometimes referred to as "rate group baskets,"

Up to four different rates can apply to long term capital gains:

- 28 percent for collectible gain and gain on qualified small business stock equal to the exclusion under Code Sec. 1201,
- 25 percent for unrecaptured Code Sec. 1250 gain,
- 20 percent for individuals with income taxed in the 39.6-percent tax bracket,
- 15 percent for individuals with income taxed in the 25-percent, 28-percent, 33-percent, or 35-percent tax brackets, or
- 0-percent capital gains tax rate for taxpayers in the 10-percent or 15 percent income tax brackets in 2013. See ¶ 8001.01 for further discussion.

Noncorporate taxpayers have to follow specific netting procedures in calculating their recognized capital gain or loss for the tax year [Code Sec. 1(h)(1)]. The basic netting procedures provide that within each tax rate group (e.g., 15 percent group), gains and losses are netted in order to arrive at a net gain or loss for the group. After this basic process has been completed, the following netting and ordering rules must be applied.[58]

1. *Short-term capital gains and losses.* Short-term capital losses (including short-term loss carryovers from a prior year) are applied first to reduce short-term capital gains, if any, that would otherwise be taxable at ordinary income tax rates. A net short-term loss is used first to reduce any net long-term capital gain from the 28 percent group [Code Sec. 1(h)(5)]. Any remaining short-term loss is then used to reduce gain from the 25 percent group and then groups taxed at the lower capital gains rates.

2. *Long-term capital gains and losses.* A net loss from the 28 percent group (including long-term capital loss carryovers) is used first to reduce gain from the 25 percent group, then to reduce net gain from the 20 percent group. A net loss from the 15 percent group is used first to reduce net gain from the 28 percent group, and then to reduce gain from the 25 percent group.

   Any resulting net capital gain that is attributable to a particular rate group is taxed at that group's marginal tax rate [Code Sec. 1(h)(1)].

.03 Net Gain or Loss on the Return

Net gain from capital asset transactions is added to other income in figuring adjusted gross income. There may be special tax calculations for your long-term capital gains. If there's a net loss from capital asset transactions, the excess is deductible from ordinary income up to $3,000 with the excess carried over to succeeding tax years until used up [¶ 8050].

[58] Notice 97-59, 1997-2 CB 309.

.04 Form 8949

Taxpayers are required to use Form 8949, "Sales and Other Dispositions of Capital Assets," to report many transactions that were reported on Schedule D or D-1 in prior years. Taxpayers should complete Form 8949 before completing Schedule D. Use Form 8949 to report:

- The sale or exchange of a capital asset not reported on another form or schedule,
- Gains from involuntary conversions (other than from casualty or theft) of capital assets not held for business or profit, and
- Nonbusiness bad debts.

Schedule D should be used:

- To figure the overall gain or loss from transactions reported on Form 8949,
- To report a gain from Form 2439 or 6252, or Part I of Form 4797,
- To report a gain or loss from Form 4684, 6781, or 8824,
- To report a gain or loss from a partnership, S corporation, estate or trust,
- To report capital gain distributions not reported directly on Form 1040 (or effectively connected capital gain distributions not reported directly on Form 1040NR), and
- To report a capital loss carryover.

On Form 8949, the taxpayer must enter all sales and exchanges of capital assets, including stocks, bonds, etc. and real estate (if not reported on Form 4684, 4797, 6252, 6781, or 8824). These transactions must be included even if the decedent did not receive a Form 1099-B or 1099-S (or substitute statement) for the transaction. Short-term gains or losses are reported in Part 1 and long-term gains and losses are reported in Part 11. The details of each transaction should be entered on a separate line of Form 8949.

¶8050 CAPITAL LOSS DEDUCTION

A net loss from capital asset transactions is partially or fully deductible from other income in computing adjusted gross income [Code Sec. 1211(b); Reg. §1.1211-1(b)]. Losses from transactions of personal-use property are never deductible unless a casualty loss is involved [¶8065].

.01 Amount of Loss Deductible

Capital losses fully offset capital gains. However, to the extent a noncorporate taxpayer's capital losses exceed the taxpayer's capital gains, the net loss can only be deducted against $3,000 of ordinary income in any one year. (The limit is $1,500, for married taxpayers filing separately.) Both long-and short-term capital losses offset ordinary income, dollar-for-dollar [Code Sec. 1211(b)]. Corporations can deduct losses only to the extent of their gains [Code Sec. 1211(a)].

.02 Husband and Wife

A husband or wife filing separately is allowed to offset the excess of capital losses against only $1,500 of ordinary income. Neither spouse may use the other's loss in this case. On a joint return, they combine their capital gains and losses [Reg. § 1.1211-1(b)(6)].

¶8051 CAPITAL LOSS CARRYFORWARD

.01 Individuals

If an individual taxpayer's capital losses in the current year exceed the limits, the taxpayer may carry over the excess indefinitely until completely exhausted [Code Sec. 1212]. Taxpayers are subject to limits on their use of capital losses. For individuals, capital losses may be used to offset any capital gains (without regard to holding periods) plus the lesser of (1) $3,000 ($1,500 for married individuals filing separate returns) or (2) the excess of the capital losses over the capital gains [Code Sec. 1211(b)]. Therefore individuals can always use capital losses to shelter capital gains. However, if the taxpayer's capital losses for a year exceed his capital gains, the excess is deductible only up to a maximum of $3,000.

.02 Corporations

Corporate taxpayers can carry capital losses back three tax years preceding the loss year and forward for up to five years following the loss [Code Sec. 1212(a)].

.03 How to Compute Carryover

If taxable income is sufficient to utilize the full $3,000/$1,500 loss deduction allowance described above, the carryover is the excess of the capital loss over capital gain for that year plus the allowance amount.

Example 8-16: Sally Drake had $10,000 of long-term capital loss and $2,000 of long-term capital gain. Thus her net capital loss was $8,000 that year. She used $3,000 of it to shelter other income. Drake's carryover to the following year is $5,000.

On the other hand, if taxable income is a negative figure, the capital loss carryover is the amount of net capital loss in excess of the smaller of (1) the $3,000/$1,500 allowance or (2) taxable income increased by the $3,000/$1,500 allowance and the deduction for personal and dependency exemptions. In instances where deductions for the year exceed gross income, taxpayers should use negative taxable income to compute the amount in (2) [Code Sec. 1212(b)(2)]. The purpose of this calculation is to prevent taxpayers with negative taxable incomes from losing some of the tax benefit of their capital loss.

Example 8-17: Lou and Cecile Winston, a married couple without dependents, had $10,000 of long-term capital losses and $2,000 of long-term capital gains all in the same year, an $8,000 net capital loss. That same year, they also had $5,000 of deductions in excess of income giving them negative taxable income of $5,000. The Winstons' capital loss deduction that year was limited to $3,000. Their capital loss carryover to the following year is $8,000 minus the lesser of (a) $3,000 or (b) (-$5,000) + $3,000 + their exemptions or $8,000 – $3,000 = $5,000.

Capital loss carryovers from separate returns must be combined if a joint return is filed for the current year. However, a capital loss carryover from any joint return can be deducted only on the separate return of the person who actually sustained the loss [Reg. § 1.1212-1(c)(1)].

DISPOSING OF BUSINESS PROPERTY

Certain assets qualify for an annual deduction related to their becoming worn out, exhausted or obsolete (depreciation). The idea is to spread their cost over the period of expected usefulness. These assets, called depreciable property, are specifically excluded from the capital asset category. Thus, their disposal would not normally result in capital gain or capital loss. However, under a special rule, a portion of the gain on the disposition of depreciable business property may be capital gain—while a loss on the same property would be an ordinary loss. Sales of business property are reported on Form 4797.

¶8055 SALE OR EXCHANGE OF SEC. 1231 ASSETS

Under a special rule found in Code Sec. 1231, taxpayers can get the best of both worlds. Gains and losses on certain property used in their trade or business, which typically don' t qualify for capital gains tax treatment, may be characterized as long-term capital gains and be taxed at preferential capital gains tax rates and their losses will be treated as ordinary losses which are more desirable than capital losses because ordinary losses offset higher-taxed ordinary income without the limitations imposed on the deductibility of capital losses. Essentially, Code Sec. 1231 is designed to bestow long-term capital gain treatment on gains attributable to appreciation in value from noncapital assets and on gains from capital assets that fail to satisfy the technical "sale or exchange" requirement. Note that Code Sec. 1231 only determines the character of already recognized gains and losses. Before the characterization question is reached, you must determine whether the gain is recognized or whether the loss will be allowed. Only after this recognition determination is made do you need to determine the character of a gain or loss. For example, where Code Sec. 267 disallows losses incurred on transactions between related taxpayers, there is no need to determine the character of that loss.

.01 Transactions Qualifying for Code Sec. 1231 Treatment

Code Sec. 1231 applies to property used in the trade or business of the taxpayer, thus limiting its applicability for investors to certain capital assets that are held for more than one year in connection with a trade or business or a transaction entered into for profit [Code Sec. 1231(a)(3)(A)]. The special tax treatment applies to *Code Sec. 1231 assets*:

- Depreciable personal property used in a trade or business and held for more than one year;
- Real property used in a trade or business and held for more than one year;
- Cut and/or disposed timber treated as sold or exchanged;
- Unharvested crops sold or exchanged with land [¶ 8075];

- Disposed coal or domestic iron ore treated as sold or exchanged [¶ 8080];
- Cattle and horses acquired for draft, breeding, dairy or sporting purposes and held for 24 months or more [¶ 8075];
- Livestock (except cattle, horses and poultry) acquired for draft, breeding, dairy or sporting purposes and held 12 months or more [¶ 8075];
- Capital assets held for more than one year in connection with a trade or business or transaction entered into for profit that have been involuntarily converted [¶ 8065]; and
- Property used in a trade or business for more than one year that has been involuntarily converted [¶ 8065].

Inventory; property held for sale to customers; certain copyrights; artistic, musical, or literary compositions; letters or memoranda or similar property is not Code Sec. 1231 assets. Also, certain U.S. government publications received free or at a reduced price are not Code Sec. 1231 assets [Code Sec. 1231(b)(1)].

.02 How to Figure the Computation

To qualify for Code Sec. 1231 treatment, gain or loss must have been realized on a sale or exchange or upon the "compulsory or involuntary conversion" of Code Sec. 1231 assets. The phrase "compulsory or involuntary conversion" means conversion of property into money or other property as a result of its complete or partial destruction, theft, seizure, requisition or condemnation, or treatment of imminent requisition or condemnation [Reg. § 1.1231-1(e)]. Losses of property and money are treated as compulsory or involuntary conversions [Reg. § 1.1231-1(e)]. Code Sec. 1231 may apply even if the property destroyed was uninsured or inadequately insured, or if an inadequate condemnation award or no condemnation award at all was received by the taxpayer.

Once you determine that your recognized gains and losses fall within the application of the Code Sec. 1231 characterization rules, the next step is to determine your aggregate net gain or net loss from all Code Sec. 1231 transactions. To summarize, Code Sec. 1231 computations are made as follows:

1. Determine the amount of realized gain to be recaptured as ordinary income [¶ 8060];
2. Net the business (or nonpersonal) casualty and theft gains or losses [¶ 8065];
3. Net the Code Sec. 1231 gains and losses as follows: Code Sec. 1231 assets are segregated and netted: (a) If net gains exceed net losses, *all* the gains and losses are treated as long-term capital gains and losses; (b) If net losses exceed net gains, *all* the gains and losses are treated as ordinary. Net Code Sec. 1231 gain is treated as ordinary income to the extent of the taxpayer's unrecaptured net Code Sec. 1231 losses for the five most recent prior years starting after 1981. Losses are recaptured in the chronological order they arose [Code Sec. 1231(c)].

Personal casualty or theft gains or losses are not subject to Code Sec. 1231. Therefore, they are not netted with Code Sec. 1231 if personal casualty or theft gains exceed personal casualty or theft losses.

Example 8-18: Taxpayer is in the landscaping business. She made a $20,000 profit from the sale of a lot she used to store equipment. Taxpayer bought the lot 20 years ago. She has no other Code Sec. 1231 transactions and no Code Sec. 1231 losses for the previous five years. Her net Code Sec. 1231 gain of $20,000 is taxed at the 20 percent rate because she held the vacant lot for more than 12 months.

Example 8-19: Mr. West is a calendar-year accountant with the following taxable events this year:

$20,000 in professional fees;

$2,000 gain from the sale of stock held 24 months;

$2,700 from sale of car with an adjusted basis of $2,200 and $400 depreciation;

$3,000 in royalties (in excess of his depletion basis) from coal lands he owned for six years;

$1,000 gain from sale of a vacant lot held for four months as an investment;

$500 loss from sale of other depreciable investment property owned for three years; and

$200 loss from sale of an office machine three months after purchase.

Here is how he would account for these transactions:

Net professional fees			$20,000
Other business income (recapture of depreciation on car)			400
Less: Loss on office machine			(200)
Code Sec. 1231 transactions:			
	Gain	*Loss*	
Sale of car used in business	$ 100		
Coal royalties	3,000		
Sale of investment property		$500	
Total gains	$3,100		
Total losses		$500	
Excess of gains over losses	$2,600		
Capital gain or loss:			
1. Net long-term capital gain ($2,600 + $2,000)			$4,600
2. Net short-term capital gain		1,000	
3. Total			5,600
Adjusted gross income			$25,800

The net professional fees and $400 of the gain on the car sale are ordinary income. Because the stock was held for more than 12 months, the gain on the stock sale is a long-term capital gain taxed at 15 percent. The rest of the gain on the sale of the car, the coal royalties and the loss from the depreciable investment property are all Code Sec. 1231 gains and losses, resulting in a net Code

Sec. 1231 gain of $2,600 (if the result were a net loss, the gains and losses would be ordinary gains and losses). The gain on the sale of the lot is a short-term capital gain. The loss on the office machine is an ordinary loss deductible in full from ordinary income. It is not a Code Sec. 1231 asset because it was held less than the holding period for long-term treatment [¶ 8020].

¶8060 RECAPTURE OF DEPRECIATION

Depreciation deductions for capital assets offset ordinary income. However, when you sell these assets, special recapture rules apply to the part of gain attributable to recaptured depreciation.

.01 Gain from Dispositions of Certain Depreciable Property

A taxpayer who realizes capital gain on the disposition of certain depreciable property must recapture all or part of the gain as ordinary income to reflect the amount of depreciation, cost recovery, or other amortization deductions allowed with respect to the property [Code Sec. 1245(a)]. Depreciation is deducted against ordinary income and also reduces the basis of an asset. However, gain realized when a depreciated asset is disposed of could be a capital gain under Code Sec. 1231 even though the depreciation deductions reduced ordinary income. This recapture rule is designed to prevent the conversion of ordinary income into capital gain.

The amount that must be recaptured as ordinary income is the lesser of:

1. The total of the depreciation, cost recovery or other amortization deductions allowed or allowable with respect to the property; or
2. The total gain realized.

If the total gain realized is more than the amount that must be recaptured, the excess may be reported as capital gain. If the total of the depreciation, cost recovery and other amortization deductions is greater than the gain realized (as would be the case, for example, if the property is sold for less than it originally cost), only the actual amount of gain realized need be reported.[59] The entire amount of such gain, however, is ordinary income.

This recapture rule applies notwithstanding any other Code provision [Code Sec. 1245(a)(1); Reg. § 1.1245-6(a) and (b)]. Unless an exception or limitation specified in Code Sec. 1245 applies, gain is recognized despite any contrary nonrecognition provision or income characterizing provision. For property used in a trade or business and in the case of an involuntary conversion, Code Sec. 1231 gains are reduced by the amount of ordinary income recognized under Code Sec. 1245. The fact that only part of the gain may be recognized under Code Sec. 1245 does not prevent the balance of such gain from being considered ordinary income under another Code provision [Reg. § 1.1245-6(f)].

---

[59] *D.A. Armstrong,* 36 TCM 137, Dec. 34,244(M), TC Memo. 1977-30.

Where Code Sec. 1245 assets are sold together with other assets, allocations may be required to compute the recaptured depreciation. To overcome contractual allocations, taxpayers must offer strong proof that such allocations lack business or economic reality or that they are not the product of arm's-length negotiations.

Recomputed Basis

The recomputed basis is the key factor. "Recomputed basis" is a property's adjusted basis, recomputed by adding all adjustments reflected in the adjusted basis on account of deductions (whether in respect of the same or other property) allowed or allowable to the taxpayer or to any other person for depreciation or amortization. The deductions you add back must include any taken by another person if you have a carryover basis (such as gift property). Any gain up to the recomputed basis is Code Sec. 1245 ordinary income. Gain above recomputed basis is included in Code Sec. 1231 computations. Ordinary income is limited to actual gain on a sale or exchange for less than the full recomputed basis. If you can prove that the depreciation you took was lower than the maximum allowable, you can use the lower figure. But remember to keep permanent records to determine the recomputed basis [Code Sec. 1245(a)(2); Reg. § 1.1245-2].

.02 Special Rules: Section 197 Intangibles

The recapture rule is modified to treat more than one amortizable Code Sec. 197 intangible (as defined in Code Sec. 197(c)) disposed in a transaction or a series of related transactions as one section 1245 property [Code Sec. 1245(b)(8)(A)]. If multiple Code Sec. 197 intangibles are sold, or otherwise disposed of, in a single transaction or series of transactions, the seller must calculate recapture as if all of the Code Sec. 197 intangibles were a single asset. Thus, any gain on the sale or other disposition of the intangibles is recaptured as ordinary income to the extent of ordinary depreciation deductions previously claimed on any of the Code Sec. 197 intangibles. This rule does not apply to any Code Sec. 197 intangible with respect to which the adjusted basis exceeds the fair market value [Code Sec. 1245(b)(8)(B)]. For further discussion of Code Sec. 197, see ¶ 11,005.

.03 Code Sec. 1245 Property Defined

Property used in a trade or business or held for investment, which is subject to depreciation under Code Sec. 167 (or treated as subject to depreciation) and that, upon disposition, results in ordinary income under Code Sec. 1245 is called "section 1245 property" [Code Sec. 1245(a)(3)]. In addition, the property must be:

1. Personal property (tangible or intangible);
2. Other tangible property, but not including a building or its structural components and provided that the adjusted basis of such property reflects depreciation and amortization deductions indicated in Code Sec. 1245(a)(2), used in manufacturing, production, extraction, or in furnishing transportation, communications, electrical energy, gas, water, or sewage disposal services; a research facility used in connection with any of these activities; or a storage facility for the bulk storage of fungible commodities (including commodities in a liquid or gaseous state) if used in connection with one of these activities;
3. Elevators and escalators (placed in service before 1987);

4. That part of any real property (other than property mentioned in (2), above) that has an adjusted basis reflecting amortization deductions indicated in Code Sec. 1245(a)(3)(C);
5. Single-purpose agricultural or horticultural structures;
6. Storage facilities (not including a building or its structural components) used in the distribution of petroleum or any primary product of petroleum; or
7. Any railroad grading or tunnel bore.

Livestock is included in the definition of "Code Sec. 1245 property" and refers mainly to the sale of draft, breeding, dairy, or sporting live stock which was *purchased* and not included in inventory. Gain on the sale of livestock in excess of the amount of recaptured depreciation may qualify as a Code Sec. 1231 transaction. *Raised* livestock would generally have no basis for depreciation (raising costs are currently expensed on the cash basis), but, to the extent the livestock has a basis and is depreciated, the recapture rules would apply.

Code Sec. 1245 property need not be subject to the allowance for depreciation in the hands of the taxpayer, but will still fit the definition of Code Sec. 1245 property if it was subject to the allowance in the hands of a prior holder and such allowance was taken into account in determining the adjusted basis in the hands of the taxpayer [Reg. § 1.1245-3(a)(3)].

In order to be a Code Sec. 1245 property, tangible "other property" must be used as an integral part of manufacturing, production and extraction activity described above. Thus, Code Sec. 1245 property would not ordinarily include such assets as pavements, parking areas, advertising displays, outdoor lighting facilities, or swimming pools which are not used directly in the specified activities even though they may be used as a part of the overall business activity. Property which normally would be used as an integral part of the specified activities, for example, would include blast furnaces, oil and gas pipelines, and railroad tracks and signals. Fences would qualify where used as an integral part of a specified activity such as where used in connection with raising livestock [Reg. § 1.1245-3(c); Reg. § 1.48-1(d)].

.04 Computing the Recapture Amount

Gain on the disposition of Code Sec. 1245 property is recaptured as ordinary income to the extent of previously allowed depreciation or amortization deductions. The amount of gain is determined by subtracting the adjusted basis of the property from the smallest of the following:

1. The recomputed basis of the property, or
2. The amount realized upon a sale, exchange, or involuntary conversion of the property, or
3. The fair market value of the property in the case of any other disposition [Code Sec. 1245(a)(1)]. "Any other disposition" includes Code Sec. 1245 property transferred by a corporation to a shareholder for less than its fair market value in a sale or exchange [Reg. § 1.1245-1(c)(1)].

Example 8-20: Code Sec. 1245 property is disposed of by sale for the sum of $3,100. The adjusted basis of the property is $2,000. The recomputed basis of the property is $2,600. For recapture purposes, the amount of gain is $600 (recomputed basis minus adjusted basis).

If there is a sale, exchange, or involuntary conversion of both Code Sec. 1245 property and non-section 1245 property in one transaction, the total amount realized upon the disposition must be allocated among them in proportion to their respective fair market values [Reg. § 1.1245-1(a)(5)]. A disposition includes a sale in a sale-leaseback transaction and a transfer upon the foreclosure of a security interest. It does not include a mere transfer of title to a creditor upon creation of a security interest or to a debtor upon termination of a security interest [Reg. § 1.1245-1(a)(3)]. Thus, a disposition occurs upon a sale of property under a conditional sales contract even though the seller retains legal title to the property for security, but a disposition does not occur when the seller ultimately gives up the security interest following payment by the purchaser.

Multiple Asset Account

Recognition of gain upon normal retirements of Code Sec. 1245 property from a multiple asset account is not required if the taxpayer's method of accounting does not require recognition of such gain [Reg. § 1.1245-6(c); Reg. 1.167(a)-8(e)(2)].

General Asset Account

The recapture treatment for gain on a disposition from a general asset account is usually subject to the rules provided for general asset accounts [Reg. § 1.168(i)-1(e)(2)]. The full amount of proceeds realized on the disposition of property from a general asset account is usually treated as ordinary income. However, recapture under Code Sec. 1245 applies to a gain on a disposition where general asset account treatment is terminated or an election is made to terminate such treatment.

.05 Recomputed Basis

The recomputed basis of Code Sec. 1245 property is the adjusted basis plus all adjustments reflected in the adjusted basis for deductions (whether regarding the same or other property) allowed or allowable to the taxpayer (or any other person) for depreciation or amortization [Code Sec. 1245(a)(2)(A)]. If it can be proved that the amount allowed is less than the amount allowable, then only the amount allowed is added back to adjusted basis [Reg. § 1.1245-2(a)(7)]. In establishing recomputed basis, records must show:

1. The date and manner in which the property was acquired;
2. Basis on the date that the property was acquired;
3. The amount and date of all adjustments to the basis of the property allowed or allowable for depreciation or amortization; and
4. Adjustments to other property or allowed to other persons that are necessary in determining the adjustments to Code Sec. 1245 property presently owned [Reg. § 1.1245-2(b)].

This rule applies only in determining what part of the gain is treated as ordinary income under the recapture rules of Code Sec. 1245.

.06 Deductions Recaptured

Deductions treated as amortization for recapture purposes include the following:

- Deduction for expensing certain depreciable business property under Code Sec. 179 election [Code Sec. 179(a)];
- Deduction for clean-fuel vehicles and certain refueling property [Code Sec. 179A(a)];
- Deduction for capital costs incurred in complying with Environmental Protection Agency sulfur regulations [Code Sec. 179B(a)];
- Deduction for qualified liquid fuel refineries placed in service after August 8, 2005 [Code Sec. 179C(a);
- Deduction for energy efficient commercial buildings placed in service after December 31, 2005, and before January 1, 2014 [Code Sec. 179D(a);
- Deduction for 50 percent of the cost of qualified advanced mine safety equipment paid or incurred after December 20, 2006, and placed in service before January 1, 2014 [Code Sec. 179E];
- Deduction for qualified film and television production costs [Code Sec. 181(a)];
- Expenditures to remove architectural and transportation barriers to the handicapped and elderly [Code Sec. 190(a)];
- Deductions for qualified tertiary injectant expenses [Code Sec. 193(a); and
- Expensed reforestation expenditures [Code Sec. 194(a).

The following deductions are depreciation or are treated as depreciation and should be recaptured:

- Code Sec. 30 credit for depreciable qualified electric vehicles [Reg. § 1.30-1(b)(1);
- Code Sec. 50 investment credit which reduced the basis of an investment property [Code Sec. 50(c)(4)];
- Code Sec. 197 deduction for amortizable Code Sec. 197 intangibles generally acquired after August 10, 1993 [Code Sec. 197(f)(7)];
- Code Sec. 263A deductions of certain farmers who elected to deduct preproductive period costs of certain plants instead of capitalizing them [Code Sec. 263A(d)(3)];
- Code Sec. 611 allowance for depletion and for depreciation of improvements of mines, oil and gas wells, other natural deposits, and timber [Code Sec. 611(a)];
- Professional sports franchises, and any item acquired in connection with such a franchise, acquired after October 22, 2004 are subject to a 15-year amortization under Code Sec. 197(a). The recapture of gain on player contracts transferred in connection with the sale or exchange of the franchise is calculated under the general recapture rules, just like any Code Sec. 197 intangible.

.07 Recapture of Depreciation on Dispositions of Depreciable Realty

Gain realized on the disposition of Code Sec. 1250 property is taxed as ordinary income, rather than as capital gain, to the extent of the excess of post-1975 depreciation allowances over the depreciation that would have been available under the straight-line method [Code Sec. 1250(a)]. This excess amount is additional depreciation. The amount recaptured cannot exceed the gain on the disposition and should be included in income in the year of disposition. In general, the amount recaptured depends on: (1) the use of the property, (2) when it was acquired, and (3) on the depreciation method used.

Recapture of MACRS Deductions

Code Sec. 1250 recapture provisions do not apply to real property depreciated under the Modified Accelerated Cost Recovery System (MACRS) (i.e, residential rental property and nonresidential real property) held for more than one year because this property must be depreciated using the straight-line method MACRS method [Code Sec. 168(b)(3)]. In case of a disposition of depreciable realty (depreciated under MACRS) held one year or less, all depreciation claimed (not just the excess over straight-line) is recaptured as ordinary income to the extent of gain [Code Sec. 1250(b)(1)].

Residential Rental Property

Gain on the disposition of residential rental recovery property, is recaptured to the extent of the excess of accelerated depreciation over straight-line depreciation. There is no recapture if the straight-line ACRS method is elected.

Nonresidential Real Property

If the cost of nonresidential real recovery property held for more than one year is recovered under Accelerated Cost Recovery System (ACRS), gain on disposition is recaptured as ordinary income to the extent of all ACRS deductions. There is no recapture if the straight-line ACRS method is elected.

Recapture of ACRS Deductions

Residential rental property depreciated under ACRS is recaptured to the extent of the excess of accelerated depreciation claimed over straight-line depreciation. However, ACRS nonresidential real property is treated as Code Sec. 1245 property if it is not depreciated using the straight-line method. All accelerated depreciation claimed on such property would be subject to recapture.

.08 Code Sec. 1250 Property Defined

Code Sec. 1250 property is any real property, other than Code Sec. 1245 property, that either is or has been depreciable property. Real property is all property other than personal property [Code Sec. 1250(c)]. Code Sec. 1250 property is real property that is depreciable under Code Sec. 167, but is not subject to the recapture rule under Code Sec. 1245 [Code Sec. 1250(c)]. This includes all intangible real property, such as leases of land or Code Sec. 1250 property, buildings and their structural components, and all other tangible real property except those which used as an integral part of manufacturing, production or extraction, or of furnishing transportation, communications, electrical energy, gas, water or sewage disposal services or research or storage facilities used in connection with these activities [Reg. § 1.1250-1(e)].

.09 Special Holding Period Rule

Special holding period rules apply in determining the recapture percentage of Code Sec. 1250 property. If the taxpayer acquires Code Sec. 1250 property, the taxpayer's holding period begins on the day after the date of acquisition. But if the taxpayer constructs, erects, or reconstructs the property, the holding period begins on the first day of the month in which the property is placed in service [Code Sec. 1250(e)(1)]. The latter property is placed in service when it is first used, whether in a trade or business, in the production of income, or in a personal activity. It is immaterial when the depreciation period begins [Reg. § 1.1250-4(b)(2)].

A full month is the period that begins on a date in one month and ends on the date before the corresponding date in the next succeeding month or the last date of the succeeding month if there is no corresponding date [Reg. § 1.1250-1(d)(4)].

.10 Property Sold with Separate Elements

If real property disposed of has separate elements, the amount of gain is the total of the gain figured for each element. A separate element can be: (1) a separate improvement; (2) units placed in service before the depreciable real property was completed; (3) depreciable real property plus improvements not considered as a separate improvement [Code Sec. 1250(f)(3); Reg. § 1.1250-5].

A *separate improvement* is each improvement added to the property's capital account if the cost during a three-year period ending on the last day of any one tax year exceeds the greater of: (a) $5,000; (b) 25 percent of adjusted basis; or (c) 10 percent of unadjusted basis (i.e., basis not reduced by depreciation or amortization deductions). The basis for (b) and (c) is figured as of the first day of the 36-month period, or the first day of the property's holding period, whichever is later. In applying the three-year period test, improvements in any of the three years are omitted entirely if for such year their total does not amount to the greater of: (a) $2,000, or (b) 1 percent of the property's unadjusted basis figured as of the start of the year or the property's holding period, whichever is later [Code Sec. 1250(f)(4); Reg. § 1.1250-5(d)(1)].

.11 Exceptions to Recapture Rules

The recapture rule applies to most dispositions of depreciable personal or real property used in a trade or business, even if they would otherwise be without immediate tax consequences. Exceptions to this include gifts, charitable contributions, and transfers at death [Code Secs. 1245(b), 1250(d); Reg. §§ 1.1245-4, 1.1245-6(b), 1.1250-1(a)(4), 1.1250-3].

Gifts

Gratuitous transfers of depreciable property do not give rise to depreciation recapture [Reg. § 1.1245-4(a)]. However, the Code Sec. 1245 or 1250 potential is passed on to the person receiving the property. Thus, when the donee sells the property, he or she must take into account the donor's depreciation deductions that are subject to the recapture rules.

Charitable Contributions

If depreciable business property is given to a charity, the donor realizes no income. However, the charitable contribution deduction [Ch. 9] is reduced by Code Sec. 1245 or 1250 income that would have resulted had the property been sold for its fair market value [Code Sec. 170(e); Reg. § 1.170A-4(b)(4)].

Transfers at Death

Both the decedent and his successor are completely free from the recapture rules once the property is transferred at death, except that the successor is subject to the rules for those amounts that would have been taxed to the decedent if he had remained alive and received them. Generally, this applies only to installment obligations [Code Secs. 691, 1245(b)(2), 1250(d)(2); Reg. §§1.1245-4(b), 1.1250-3(b)]. For basis of inherited property, see Ch. 6.

.12 Nontaxable Exchanges

Generally, a like-kind exchange [¶6050] does not result in ordinary income when Code Sec. 1245 or 1250 property is disposed of unless "boot" is received. The Code Sec. 1245 gain is limited to the lesser of: (1) gain to the extent of depreciation taken since 1961, or (2) the gain recognized in a like kind exchange, plus the fair market value of the qualified property received that is not Code Sec. 1245 property. Code Sec. 1250 gain cannot exceed the greater of two limitations: (1) the total amount of the "boot," or (2) the amount of Code Sec. 1250 gain that would be recognized if the exchange was fully taxable, less the fair market value of the Code Sec. 1250 property received [Code Secs. 1245(b)(4), 1250(d)(4); Reg. §§1.1245-4(d), 1.1250-3(d)].

> **Example 8-21:** Old machine has an $8,000 adjusted basis and Code Sec. 1245 potential of $4,000. It is swapped for a new machine worth $10,000 and $1,000 cash. Although gain is $3,000, only $1,000 is recognized. It is all Code Sec. 1245 gain since it is less than the Code Sec. 1245 potential. If the taxpayer sells the new machine for $10,000 before taking further depreciation deductions, she will then recognize an additional $2,000 of Code Sec. 1245 income.

Sale or Exchange of Code Sec. 1250 Property Received in Exchange

The unrecognized Code Sec. 1250 gain of property disposed of in a like kind exchange is carried over to the Code Sec. 1250 property received in the trade-in. This carryover is added to the "excess" depreciation taken after the exchange when the property is later disposed of. To find the recognized gain on the resale, multiply the carryover gain and the "excess" depreciation by the applicable percentage [discussed above] [Code Sec. 1250(d)(4)(E); Reg. §1.1250-3(d)].

.13 Involuntary Conversions

Gain that is generally not recognized in an involuntary conversion [Ch. 7] may be affected by the depreciation recapture rules when Code Sec. 1245 or 1250 property is disposed of. However, the amount taxed as ordinary income is limited to the unreinvested conversion proceeds [Code Secs. 1245(b)(4), 1250(d)(4); Reg. §§1.1245-4(d), 1.1250-3(d)].

Code Sec. 1245 gain cannot exceed the gain recognized in an involuntary conversion, plus the fair market value of qualified replacement property that is not Code Sec. 1245 property [Code Sec. 1245(b)(4); Reg. §1.1245-4(d)]. Code Sec. 1250 gain cannot exceed the greater of two limitations: (1) the total amount of the unreinvested conversion proceeds increased by the value of controlling shares acquired in a corporation to get replacement property [Ch. 7]; or (2) the amount of Code Sec. 1250 gain that would be recognized if the proceeds were fully taxable less the cost of Code Sec. 1250 property acquired [Code Sec. 1250(d)(4); Reg. §1.1250-3(d)].

The Basis of Replacement Property

Basis for such acquired property is cost reduced by the Code Sec. 1245 or 1250 gain not recognized on the conversion. If more than one piece of Code Sec. 1245 or 1250 replacement property is bought, the bases allocated to the properties are in proportion to their respective costs [see also Ch. 7]. If other replacement property also is bought, all the bases are combined to find the total cost of the replacement property. This amount is reduced by the gain not recognized under replacement rules [Ch. 7] and the Code Sec. 1245 or 1250 gain not taken into account. The total is then allotted in proportion to their respective costs [Code Secs. 1245(b)(4), 1250(d)(4)(D); Reg. §§1.1245-5(a), 1.1250-3(d)(2)].

Example 8-22: Mr. Bailey's warehouse was condemned and he received an award of $90,000. He spent $10,500 to buy a storage shed and $31,500 for a garage. The land for the storage shed cost $12,000, and for the garage, $36,000. Assume that the unrecognized gain on the condemnation is $60,000 of which $10,000 is Code Sec. 1250 gain. The tentative total basis of the shed and the garage is therefore $32,000 ($42,000 property cost less $10,000 nonrecognized Code Sec. 1250 gain). The tentative basis of the shed is $8,000 ($32,000 × $10,500/$42,000), and the tentative garage basis is $24,000 ($32,000 × $31,500/$42,000). The basis of all the properties replaced is $30,000 figured as follows:

Cost (tentative basis) of shed		$ 8,000
Cost (tentative basis) of garage		24,000
Cost of land for shed		12,000
Cost of land for garage		36,000
Cost of properties bought		$80,000
Less: gain not recognized under replacement rules	$60,000	
Minus Code Sec. 1250 unrecognized gain	10,000	
	$50,000	
Total basis of properties bought		$30,000

The total basis of $30,000 is allocated to each property:

Shed: $30,000 × ($8,000/$80,000)	$ 3,000
Garage: $30,000 × ($24,000/$80,000)	9,000
Land for shed: $30,000 × ($12,000/$80,000)	4,500
Land for garage: $30,000 × ($36,000/$80,000)	13,500
Total	$30,000

Sale or Exchange of Code Sec. 1250 Replacement Property

These rules are similar to the sale or exchange of property received in a nontaxable exchange discussed above.

¶8065 INVOLUNTARY CONVERSIONS

A recognized gain or deductible loss from the condemnation or involuntary conversion of property may be subject to Code Sec. 1231 [¶ 8055]. Qualified property involves both business property and capital assets held over one year.

.01 Special Netting for Business Casualties or Thefts

Recognized gains and deductible losses from fire, storm, shipwreck or other casualty or theft of the qualified business property are treated separately before the Code Sec. 1231 computation is made. A condemnation does not enter into the special netting of casualty or thefts. Unreinvested conversion proceeds for Code Sec. 1245 or 1250 property are ordinary income to the extent the recapture rules apply. These recapture rules apply to the assets before the separate netting of the casualty and theft gains and losses.

This special netting process involves property used in your trade or business or any long-term capital asset held in connection with a trade or business or a transaction entered into for profit. The separate "netting computation" applies whether or not the property is insured. It is made to find how all the business casualty or theft gains and losses will be treated on the return:

- Casualty or theft *gains* exceed casualty or theft losses: Make a further netting with Code Sec. 1231 gains or losses.
- Casualty or theft *losses* exceed casualty or theft gains: All the casualty or theft gains and losses are treated separately as ordinary income or deductible losses.

.02 Netting of Personal Casualties or Thefts

Personal casualty or theft gains and losses are not netted with Code Sec. 1231 gains and losses. Thus, Code Sec. 1231 is applied without regard to these gains or losses. See Ch. 13 for separate netting of gains and losses from personal casualties or thefts.

The rules for personal casualties or thefts apply to capital assets held for personal purposes, such as a residence or automobile, but not a condemnation loss on a personal residence. Losses from condemnations of property held for personal use are not deductible. A personal casualty or theft loss that exceeds 10 percent of adjusted gross income and the $100 floor [Ch. 13], and that is deductible as an ordinary loss, is an itemized deduction.

¶8070 TIMBER

The cutting of standing timber, or disposal of timber under certain contracts, may be treated as a sale of the timber under certain circumstances. Gains or losses from these fictional sales come under Code Sec. 1231. [Code Sec. 1231(b)(2).] Timber includes evergreen trees over six years old when cut down, and sold for ornamental purposes (for example, Christmas trees).

The cutting of timber is treated as a sale if: (1) you owned the timber or had a contract right to cut it and you owned the timber or held the contract right for more than one year before the cutting; (2) it was cut for sale or for use in your trade or business; and (3) you so elect on your return [Code Sec. 631(a)].

In figuring gain or loss on this assumed sale, the basis is the adjusted basis for depletion. The fictional selling price is the fair market value of the timber as of the first day of the tax year. This market value also becomes the cost of the cut timber for future transactions.

.01 How to Elect Sale Treatment

An eligible taxpayer can elect to treat the cutting of timber as a sale or exchange of a capital asset under Code Sec. 1231 [Code Sec. 631]. Gain for this purpose is the excess of the fair market value of the cut timber over its adjusted basis for depletion in the hands of the taxpayer. An eligible taxpayer is a taxpayer who has the right to sell the timber on his or her own account, or a taxpayer who has the right to use the cut timber in his or her trade or business.

.02 Effect of Election

The effect of the election is that the difference between the adjusted basis of the timber and its fair market value as of the first day of the tax year in which it is cut is treated as a gain or loss from a sale or trade of business property under the capital gain/ordinary loss rule [Reg. § 1.631-1(a)(1)]. The fair market value then becomes the cost basis of the timber [Reg. § 1.631-1(e)(1)].

The election to treat the cutting of timber as a sale or exchange applies to all timber that the taxpayer owns or has a contract right to cut. The election must be made on the taxpayer's original return, and cannot be made on an amended return. It is made in the form of a computation showing the treatment of the cut timber under the Code Sec. 1231 capital gain/ordinary loss rule [Reg. § 1.631-1(c)].

The election is binding upon the taxpayer for the tax year for which it is made and for all subsequent years unless the IRS, on showing of undue hardship, permits the taxpayer to revoke the election. Revocation precludes any subsequent election except with IRS consent [Reg. § 1.631-1(a)(3)].

¶8075 FARMERS' CODE SEC. 1231 TRANSACTIONS

Gain or loss from the sale of livestock or unharvested crops may qualify for Code Sec. 1231 treatment.

.01 Livestock

The provisions of Code Sec. 1231 apply to livestock held for draft, breeding, dairy, or sporting purposes; but the animals must be held for at least 12 months, except cattle and horses which must be held for 24 months or more. The holding period starts from the date of acquisition, not the date the animal was put to draft, breeding, dairy or sporting purposes. Livestock includes hogs, mules, donkeys, sheep, goats, fur-bearing animals, and other mammals, as well as cattle and horses. It does not include chickens, turkeys, pigeons, geese, other birds, fish, frogs, or reptiles, etc. [Code Sec. 1231(b)(3); Reg. § 1.1231-2].

Livestock Held for Draft, Breeding, Dairy, or Sporting Purpose

Whether or not livestock is held by the taxpayer for draft, breeding, dairy, or sporting purposes depends upon all of the facts and circumstances in each case. The purpose for which the animal is held is ordinarily shown by the taxpayer's actual use of the animal. However, a draft, breeding, dairy, or sporting purpose may still be present even if an animal is disposed of within a reasonable time after its intended use if the intended use is prevented or made undesirable because of accident, disease, drought, unfitness of the animal. However, an animal is not held by the taxpayer for draft, breeding, dairy, or sporting purposes merely because it is suitable for such purposes or merely because it is held by the taxpayer for sale to other persons for use by them for such purposes. Furthermore, an animal held by the taxpayer for other purposes is not considered as held for draft, breeding, dairy, or sporting purposes merely because of a negligible use of the animal for such purposes or merely because of the use of the animal for such purposes as an ordinary or necessary incident to the other purposes for which the animal is held [Reg. § 1.1231-2(b)(1)]. The following examples illustrate application of these rules:

- An animal to be used for breeding is discovered to be sterile or unfit for the breeding and is disposed of within a reasonable time thereafter. This animal is considered as held for breeding purposes [Reg. § 1.1231-2(b)(2), Ex. 1];
- The taxpayer retires from the breeding or dairy business and sells his entire herd, including young animals which would have been used by him for breeding or dairy purposes if he had remained in business. These young animals are considered as held for breeding or dairy purposes. The same would be true with respect to young animals which would have been used by the taxpayer for breeding or dairy purposes but which are sold to reduce his breeding or dairy herd, because of drought [Reg. § 1.1231-2(b)(2), Ex. 2];
- A taxpayer in the business of raising hogs for slaughter customarily breeds sows to obtain a single litter to be raised by him for sale, and sells these brood sows after obtaining the litter. Even though these brood sows are held for ultimate sale to customers in the ordinary course of the taxpayer's trade or business, they are considered to be held for breeding purposes [Reg. § 1.1231-2(b)(2), Ex. 3];
- A horse held for racing at a public track is used for sporting purposes.

Livestock Not Held for Draft, Breeding, Dairy, or Sporting Purpose

The following lists examples of livestock not held for draft, breeding, dairy, or sporting purposes.

- A person raises horses for sale to others, to be used by them for draft purposes. He uses the horses as draft animals on his own farm to train them. Since this use is incidental to his purpose of selling the horses, they are not held by him for draft purposes [Reg. § 1.1231-2(b)(2), Ex. 4];
- A taxpayer is in the business of raising registered cattle for sale to be used by the buyers for breeding. Business practice calls for such cattle to be bred before the sale to show their fitness for breeding. The test breeding does not, of itself, establish that

the animal was held for breeding. (But any animal bred to add the calves to the taxpayer's herd would be held for breeding.) [Reg. § 1.1231-2(b)(2), Ex. 5];

- The taxpayer's business is buying cattle and fattening them for slaughter. He buys cows with calf, and the calves are born while owned by him. These cows are not held for breeding [Reg. § 1.1231-2(b)(2), Ex. 6].

.02 Unharvested Crops

Crops get Code Sec. 1231 treatment if (1) raised on land used in the trade or business and held for more than one year; (2) crop and land are sold (or exchanged or involuntarily converted) to the same person at the same time; and (3) no right or option is kept by the taxpayer, at the time of the sale, exchange, or conversion to acquire the land, directly or indirectly. (This does not bar rights under a mortgage or other security transaction.) The time the crop, as distinguished from the land, has been held does not matter [Code Sec. 1231(b)(4); Reg. § 1.1231-1(f)].

¶8080 DISPOSAL OF COAL AND IRON ORE

Coal and iron ore royalties are eligible for capital gain treatment provided by Code Sec. 1231 [Code Sec. 1231(b)(2)]. Thus, income from royalties can be taxed at capital gains rates. The disposition of coal or iron ore can be treated as the disposition of property used in the taxpayer's trade or business, regardless of whether the ore is property held by the taxpayer primarily for sale to customers in the ordinary course of a trade or business [Code Sec. 631(c); Reg. § 1.631-3(a)]. This capital-gain treatment can apply when the following requirements are met:

1. The owner must dispose of coal (including lignite) or iron ore (any ore that is used as a source of iron, including but not limited to taconite and jaspilite) mined in the United States;
2. The owner must have held the coal or ore for more than one year prior to the date of disposal with the date of disposal deemed to be the date the coal or ore was mined [Reg. § 1.631-3(b)(1)]; and
3. The owner must dispose of coal or ore under any form or type of contract where the owner retains an economic interest in the coal or ore [Reg. § 1.631-3(a)(1)].

When these requirements are met, advance payments and minimum royalties paid before mining begins are considered as amounts realized under the contract for purposes of determining gain or loss, as long as they are to be applied to subsequently mined coal or iron ore [Reg. § 1.631-3(c)(1)]. Thus, the payee may be able to treat these payments as capital gain. However, if the right to mine under the contract expires, terminates or is abandoned before the royalty is absorbed by actual mining, the royalty is treated as ordinary income [Reg. § 1.631-3(c)(2)]. Similarly, any bonus that the taxpayer receives in connection with the grant of a contract of disposal may be offset against the taxpayer's basis in the coal or iron ore, in the proportion that the bonus bears to the total expected royalties. This net bonus income is then apportioned between gain subject to the capital gain/ordinary loss rule and ordinary income, in the ratio that long-term mining bears to short-term mining [Reg. § 1.631-3(c)(2); Reg. 1.631-2(d)(3)].

For recapture of mine exploration expenses, see Chapter 12.

¶8085 SALE OF DEPRECIABLE PROPERTY BETWEEN RELATED PARTIES

Any gain recognized by the transferor on the sale or exchange of property directly or indirectly between related persons is treated as ordinary income if the property is depreciable by the transferee. For this rule, related parties include: (a) a taxpayer and all entities that are controlled entities with respect to the taxpayer, (b) a taxpayer and a trust in which the taxpayer (or the taxpayer's spouse) is a beneficiary, unless the beneficiary's interest in the trust is a remote contingent interest, and (c) except in the case of a sale or exchange in satisfaction of a pecuniary bequest, an executor of an estate and a beneficiary of the estate. A "controlled entity" with respect to a person is a corporation if more than 50 percent of the value of its outstanding stock is owned (directly or indirectly) by or for that person, a partnership if more than 50 percent of its capital interests or profits interest are owned (directly or indirectly) by or for that person, and any entity that is a related person under Code Sec. 267(b)(3), (10), (11), or (12) [Code Sec. 1239].

SPECIAL RULES

¶8090 COLLAPSIBLE CORPORATION RULES REPEALED

Prior to 2003, a collapsible corporation was a corporation with assets that had appreciated in value. The collapsible corporation rules prevented the use of a temporary (collapsible) corporation to convert what would be ordinary income to the corporation into capital gains for the stockholders. Gain from the sale of a collapsible corporation stock was generally taxed as ordinary income, rather than capital gain. [Code Sec. 341(a); Reg. § 1.341-1].

The collapsible corporation rules of Code Sec. 341 have been permanently repealed for tax years beginning after December 31, 2012.

¶8095 LOSS ON SECTION 1244 SMALL BUSINESS STOCK

Congress enacted Code Sec. 1244 to encourage taxpayers to invest money in small businesses. A special rule allows ordinary (rather than capital) loss treatment for the sale, exchange or worthlessness of qualifying small business stock (called "Code Sec. 1244 stock"). This applies even if the loss would be a capital loss under the general rules

[Code Sec. 1244]. Any amount not absorbed in the year sustained becomes part of the stockholder's net operating loss carryback and carryover [Ch. 13]. An ordinary loss is reported in Part II of Form 4797.

The rule applies to an individual, who must be the original buyer, either directly or through a partnership [Code Sec. 1244(a); Reg. § 1.1244(a)-1]. The maximum allowable as an ordinary loss in one tax year is $50,000. On a joint return, it is $100,000, whether the stock is owned by one or both spouses. Any excess loss is subject to capital-loss limitations [Code Sec. 1244(b); Reg. § 1.1244(b)-1].

.01 Qualification Requirements

In order for stock to be considered Code Sec. 1244 stock, the following requirements must be satisfied as of the date of stock issuance:

1. The corporation must be a small business corporation when the stock is issued [Code Sec. 1244(c)(1)(A) and (3)(A)];
2. The stock must be issued for money or property other than stock or securities [Code Sec. 1244(c)(1)(B)];
3. The stock must be issued directly to the original owner, who is the only one entitled to claim a Code Sec. 1244 loss [Reg. § 1.1244(a)-1(b)].
4. Both common and preferred stock (voting or nonvoting) issued after July 18, 1984, can qualify as Code Sec. 1244 stock;
5. Over 50 percent of the corporation's gross receipts for the five most recent tax years preceding the year of the loss must have come from sources other than royalties, rent, dividends, interests, annuities and sales or exchanges of stock or securities [Code Sec. 1244(c); Reg. § 1.1244(c)-1].

.02 What Is a Small Business Corporation?

A domestic corporation (including an S corporation) will be treated as a small business corporation if the aggregate amount of money and other property received by the corporation for stock, as a contribution to capital, and as paid-in surplus, as of the time the stock is issued, does not exceed $1 million. The value of the "other property" is its adjusted basis to the corporation for figuring gain, reduced by any liability which the property is subject to, or was assumed by the corporation [Code Sec. 1244(c)(3); Reg. § 1.1244(c)-2].

The determination of whether a corporation is a small business corporation is made each time stock is issued and includes the amount received by the corporation when issuing that specific stock. In the year the $1 million threshold is exceeded, the corporation may designate the shares to be treated as Code Sec. 1244 stock. If the corporation does not make a designation, the remaining Code Sec. 1244 benefit is allocated among all shares issued that year [Reg. § 1.1244(c)-2(b)].

For contributions of property other than money, the amount considered when computing a Code Sec. 1244 loss is the property's adjusted basis reduced by liabilities to which the property is subject or that the corporation assumed. However, if the property's fair market value is less than its adjusted basis when it is transferred to the corporation, any Code Sec. 1244 (ordinary) loss is limited to the property's fair market value at the time of that transfer date [Code Sec. 1244(d)(1)(A); Reg. § 1.1244(d)-1].

.03 Gross Receipts Test

The corporation must also meet a gross receipts test during the five-year period prior to the sale of the stock by the investor (or a shorter period, if the corporation has been in existence for less than five years) at the time that the shareholder sells the stock [Code Sec. 1244(c)(1)(C)]. Under the gross receipts test, more than 50 percent of the corporation's gross receipts for the five most recent tax years ending before the date the loss on the stock was sustained, must have come from sources other than royalties, rents, dividends, interest, annuities, or gains from the sales or exchanges of stocks or securities [Code Sec. 1244(c)(1)(C); Reg. § 1.1244(c)-1]. This limitation does not apply if deductions (excluding those for operating loss, partially tax-free interest, and dividends received) exceed cumulative gross income during the five-year test period [Code Sec. 1244(c)(1); Reg. § 1.1244(c)-1]. However, the corporation must be largely an operating company [Reg. § 1.1244(c)-1(e)(2)]. In general, stock received in a reorganization does not qualify. However, a stock dividend or stock received in a recapitalization or change of name, identity, etc., reorganization may qualify [Code Sec. 1244(d)(2); Reg. § 1.1244(d)-3].

This gross receipts test operates to require the corporation to be an active company for the five-year testing period. In other words, the gross receipts test bars Code Sec. 1244 treatment for corporations with primarily passive income. The company cannot be a holding or investment company that acquires and holds nonincome-producing property. Because of the existence of the gross receipts test, a shareholder cannot be certain that he will receive an ordinary loss deduction until the date he disposes of the stock, at which time he can view, in retrospect, the income of the corporation over the shorter of five years or the life of the corporation.

The gross receipts test is inapplicable when, for the period evaluated (the shorter of five years or the life of the corporation) the amount of certain allowable deductions exceeds the amount of the corporation's gross income [Code Sec. 1244(c)(2)(C)]. This exception is subject to certain limitations. The Tax Court has agreed with the IRS that although the exception protects shareholders of active (but unsuccessful) corporations, it may not be utilized by shareholders of corporations that are set up primarily to earn passive income.[60]

If the stock was issued in exchange for property, the basis of that stock in the hands of the taxpayer is determined by reference to the taxpayer's basis in the property, and the adjusted basis (for determining loss) of the property immediately before the exchange exceeded its fair market value, then in computing the amount of loss on the stock, the basis of the stock has to be reduced by the amount by which the adjusted basis of the property exceeded its fair market value. Code Sec. 1244(d)(1)(A).

Example 8-23: Property valued at $1,000 and with a $3,000 basis is transferred tax-free to a small business corporation for all its stock. The stock becomes worthless. There is an ordinary loss to the extent of $1,000 and a capital loss of $1,000.

---

[60] *H.L. Davenport,* 70 TC 922, Dec. 35,408 (1978).

If, after acquiring Code Sec. 1244 stock, a stockholder's basis for his stock is increased (for example, by additional capital contribution), any increase in basis and subsequent loss on the stock is allocated to non-Code Sec. 1244 stock [Code Sec. 1244(d)(1)(B); Reg. § 1.1244(d)-2(a)].

Example 8-24: Ms. Smith paid $10,000 for shares of stock. Later on, she made a capital contribution of $2,000, thus increasing the basis to $12,000. She sold the stock for $9,000. Of the $3,000 loss, 10/12 or $2,500, will be an ordinary loss. The remaining $500 loss must be treated as a capital loss [Reg. § 1.1244(d)-2(b)].

▶ **PLANNING TIPS:** To prevent you from exceeding the dollar limit each year, consider stretching the sales of Code Sec. 1244 stock over a period of years. This tactic will, however, be of limited value for increasing tax benefits in the case of a "large" block of worthless Code Sec. 1244 stock (*e.g.*, several hundred thousand dollars). If the stock becomes worthless,[61] you lose the benefit of utilizing the ordinary loss deduction under Code Sec. 1244 more than once because, pursuant to Code Sec. 165(g)(1), the entire loss must be taken in the year in which the stock becomes worthless. Attempting to sell a portion of the stock each year for a nominal price in order to spread the loss over several years, thereby gaining repeated use and benefit of the ordinary loss deduction under Code Sec. 1244, would likely be construed as a sham transaction. Furthermore, creditors are unlikely to postpone bankruptcy proceedings long enough to allow shareholders to stretch their Code Sec. 1244 ordinary loss deductions over a long period of time.

¶8100 SUBDIVIDING REALTY FOR SALE

Generally, a taxpayer is considered to be a dealer in land if the taxpayer subdivided real property. A dealer's sales profits are taxed as ordinary income rather than capital gain [¶ 8010].

▶ **CAPITAL GAIN BREAK:** The tax law provides a way for taxpayers to subdivide, sell off lots and still get tax-sheltered capital gain for any profit [Code Sec. 1237]. If the taxpayer satisfies Code Sec. 1237 and there is no other substantial evidence that the real property was held primarily for sale to customers in the ordinary course of business, the taxpayer is not considered to be a real estate dealer even though the tract of land was subdivided, advertised or used sales agents. This capital gains break also applies to land held by an S corporation, but not C corporations.

.01 Key Requirements

To qualify for this special tax treatment, the taxpayer must satisfy all three of the following requirements.

- The taxpayer must not otherwise be a dealer in real estate in the year of the sale and have never held the subdivided tract as a dealer [Reg. § 1.1237-1(b)(1)];

[61] *C. Cerbone*, 65 TCM 2425, Dec. 48,989(M), TC Memo. 1993-167.

- The taxpayer must have held the property at least five years—unless it was inherited, in which case this rule does not apply [Code Sec. 1.1237-1(d)(1)]; and
- The taxpayer must not have made "substantial improvements" (such as buildings, hard surface roads, sewers and water, gas and electricity, utilities) that increased the value of the property [Reg. § 1.1237-1(c)(4)].

A temporary structure used as a field office to conduct surveying, filling, draining, leveling and clearing operations and the construction of minimum all-weather access roads, including gravel roads where required by the climate, are not substantial improvements [Reg. § 1.1237-1(c)(4)].

As a rule of thumb, if improvements increase the value of the lots by 10 percent or less over the market value, the improvements are not considered substantial. But even if the increase in value is more than 10 percent, capital gain treatment is not automatically ruled out. All relevant facts will be examined to determine whether the improvements were substantial.

Ten-Year Rule

Improvements that might otherwise be substantial enough to rule out capital gain treatment can be safely made for Sec. 1237 purposes if they are "necessary." To be considered necessary, all of the following conditions must be met:

- The property must be held for at least 10 years and the improvement is either a water, sewer or drainage facility, or a road.
- The taxpayer must prove that the property could not otherwise be sold at the prevailing price for similar property.
- The taxpayer must not elect to deduct the improvement expense or add it to basis in any lot sold for purposes of determining gain [Reg. § 1.1237-1(a)(5)].

Qualifying for the 100 Percent Capital Gain Treatment

Meeting the capital gain requirements nails down 100 percent capital gain treatment only if the taxpayer sells no more than five lots in a five-year period. However, all sales made during or after the year the sixth lot is sold come under a special rule: The profit is taxed at ordinary income rates to the extent of 5 percent of the selling price; the rest of any profit is taxed as capital gain [Code Sec. 1237(b)(1)]. (Two or more contiguous lots sold to the same buyer in a single sale are counted as one parcel for this purpose.)

If, after selling any lot, the taxpayer makes no other sales from the same tract of property until at least five years later, the taxpayer can start counting the sales of the first five lots again before the 5 percent rule goes into operation.

Offsetting Ordinary Income

Selling expenses (broker's fees, legal fees and so forth) are first applied against ordinary income. In many cases, those expenses will completely offset ordinary income, leaving you with nothing but capital gain to report.

¶8105 EXCLUSION FOR QUALIFIED SMALL BUSINESS STOCK (QSBS) GAIN

The tax code provides an incentive to encourage taxpayers to invest in small businesses in Code Sec. 1202. Noncorporate investors (individuals and passthrough entities such as S corporations and partnerships) who hold "qualified small business stock" (QSBS) for more than five years can exclude up to 100 percent of their gain realized on the sale or exchange of the stock depending on the date of the stock acquisition [Code Sec. 1202(a)].

Qualified small business stock acquired after September 27, 2010, and before January 1, 2014, and held for more than five years is eligible for the 100-percent gain exclusion [Code Sec 1202(a)(4)]. Eligible gain from any single issuer is subject to a cumulative limit for any given tax year to the greater of: (1) $10 million reduced by the aggregate amount of eligible gain taken in prior years ($5 million for married individuals filing separately), or (2) 10 times the taxpayer's adjusted basis of all qualified stock of the issuer disposed of during the tax year.

For alternative minimum tax (AMT) purposes, seven percent of the excluded gain is a tax preference item [Code Sec. 57(a)]. However, none of the excluded gain is a tax preference item if the stock was acquired after September 27, 2010, and before January 1, 2014 [Code Sec. 1202(a)(4)].

.01 Exclusion for Empowerment Zone Stock Sales

Noncorporate taxpayers who sell stock of qualified small businesses operating in an empowerment zone are entitled to exclude up to 60 percent of the gain from the sale if the following conditions are satisfied [Code Sec. 1202(a)(2)]:

- The stock is acquired after December 21, 2000;
- The stock is in a corporation that is a qualified business entity during substantially all of the taxpayer's holding period for such stock; and
- The stock is held for more than five years.

A "qualified business entity" means a corporation that satisfies the requirements of a qualifying business under the empowerment zone rules during substantially all of the taxpayer's holding period. The most important of these requirements are that the corporation conduct all its businesses within an empowerment zone, that it derive at least 50 percent of its total gross income from such businesses, and that at least 35 percent of its employees are residents of an empowerment zone [Code Sec. 1397C(b)].

This increased exclusion does not apply to gain attributable to periods after December 31, 2018 [Code Sec. 1202(a)(2)(C)]. Also, this increased exclusion does not apply to stock in a D.C. Enterprise Zone (D.C. Zone), because the D.C. Zone is not treated as an empowerment zone [Code Sec. 1202(a)(2)(D)].

If a corporation ceases to be a qualifying business after the five-year holding period for the stock has ended, the exclusion only applies to the gain that accrued up to the point that the corporation ceased to be a qualifying business [Code Sec. 1202(a)(2)(B)].

Empowerment Zone Gain Rollover

Through the end of 2013, taxpayers can elect to roll over, or defer the recognition of capital gain realized from the sale or exchange of qualified empowerment zone assets that were held for more than one year if the taxpayer used the proceeds to purchase other qualifying empowerment zone assets in the same zone within 60 days of the initial sale [Code Secs. 1391(d)(1)(A)(i) and 1397B].

.02 Qualified Small Business Stock (QSBS) Defined

Only the stock of a qualified small business that is engaged in an *active business* can qualify as QSBS eligible for the exclusion. QSBS must meet all of the following five tests to qualify for the exclusion:

1. It must be stock in a C corporation (not an S corporation);
2. It must have been originally issued after August 10, 1993;
3. As of the date the stock was issued, the corporation was a qualified small business with total gross assets of $50 million or less (1) at all times after August 9, 1993, and before the stock was issued, and (2) immediately after the stock was issued. Gross assets include those of any predecessor of the corporation [Code Sec. 1202(d)]. All corporations that are members of the same parent-subsidiary controlled group are treated as one corporation;
4. The shareholder may have purchased the stock at its original issue (either directly or through an underwriter), either in exchange for money or other property or as compensation for services [Code Sec. 1202(c)]. In certain cases, the shareholder will satisfy the test if the stock was acquired from another person who satisfied the test (such as by gift or inheritance) or through conversion or exchange of QSB stock; and
5. During substantially all the time that the stock was held:
   a. The corporation was a C corporation
   b. At least 80 percent of the value of the corporation's assets were used in the "active conduct of one or more qualified businesses," and
   c. The corporation was not a foreign corporation, DISC, former DISC, regulated investment company, real estate investment trust, REMIC, FASIT, cooperative, or a corporation that has made (or that has a subsidiary that has made) a Code Sec. 936 election.

Stock will *not* be considered QSBS in the following situations:

- If the issuing corporation buys (directly or indirectly) more than a *de minimis* amount of its own stock from a taxpayer, or persons related to the taxpayer within the 4 years beginning 2 years before the issue date [Code Sec. 1202(c)(3)(A); Reg. § 1.1202-2(a)(1)]; or
- If the corporation, within the 2-year period beginning one year before the issue date, redeems more than 5 percent of the aggregate value of all of its stock as of the beginning of the 2-year period [Code Sec. 1202(c)(3)(B)].

De Minimis Amount

Stock exceeds a *de minimis* amount if the aggregate amount paid for the stock is more than $10,000 and more than 2 percent of the stock held by a taxpayer and persons related to the taxpayer is acquired. The percentage of stock acquired in any single purchase is determined by dividing the stock's value (as of the time of purchase) by the value (as of the time of purchase) of all stock held (directly or indirectly) by a taxpayer and persons related to the taxpayer immediately before the purchase. The percentage of stock acquired in multiple purchases is the sum of the percentages determined for each separate purchase [Reg. § 1.1201-2(a)(2)].

Exceptions for Termination of Services, Death, Disability or Mental Incompetence, or Divorce

A stock purchase will be disregarded if the stock is acquired in the following circumstances [Reg. § 1.1202-2(d)]:

- *Termination of services—Employees and directors.* The stock was acquired by the seller in connection with the performance of services as an employee or director and the stock is purchased from the seller incident to the seller's retirement or other bona fide termination of such services;
- *Death.* Prior to the decedent's death, the stock (or an option to acquire the stock) was held by the decedent or the decedent's spouse (or both) by the decedent and joint tenant, or by a trust revocable by the decedent or the decedent's spouse (or by both) and the stock is purchased from the decedent's estate, beneficiary, heir, surviving joint tenant, or surviving spouse, or from a trust established by the decedent or decedent's spouse and the stock is purchased within 3 years and 9 months from the date of the decedent's death;
- *Disability or mental incompetence.* The stock is purchased incident to the disability or mental incompetence of the selling shareholder, or
- *Divorce.* The stock is purchased incident to the divorce of the selling shareholder.

.03 Qualified Small Business Defined

For purposes of Code Sec. 1202, a "qualified small business" is defined as a C corporation with total gross assets of $50 million or less on the date the stock is issued and at all times on or after December 21, 2000 [Code Sec. 1202(d)]. The corporation's gross assets include cash and the adjusted bases of property held by the corporation. (For this purpose, the adjusted basis of property contributed to the corporation is figured as if the basis when contributed equaled its fair market value.) Parent and subsidiary corporations are treated as a single corporation for purposes of the $50 million cap on gross assets [Code Sec. 1202(d)(3)].

Exceeding the Maximum Assets

The exclusion break is not lost even though the corporation's assets increase to $50 million or more after the stock was issued. But once a corporation does exceed the cap, it can never again issue stock that can qualify for the exclusion.

All corporations that are members of the same parent-subsidiary controlled group are treated as one corporation.

.04 Ineligible Small Business

A "qualified small business" is a C corporation other than the following [Code Sec. 1202(e)(4)]:

- A Domestic International Sales Corporation (DISC) or former DISC;
- A regulated investment company (RIC);

- A real estate investment trust (REIT);
- A real estate mortgage investment conduit (REMIC);
- A cooperative; or
- A corporation electing under Code Sec. 936, the Puerto Rico and possessions tax credit or having a direct or indirect subsidiary so electing.

.05 Active Business Requirement

Stock can qualify for the exclusion only if the corporation is engaged in an active business for substantially all the time you hold the stock [Code Sec. 1202(c)(2)(A)]. A corporation satisfies the active business requirement if it uses 80 percent or more of its assets (determined by value) in one or more qualified trades or business. A qualified trade or business is a trade or business other than the following [Code Sec. 1202(e)(1), (3)]:

- A business involving services performed in the fields of health, law, engineering, architecture, accounting, actuarial science, performing arts, consulting, athletics, financial services, or brokerage services;
- A business whose principal asset is the reputation or skill of one or more employees;
- Any banking, insurance, financing, leasing, investing, or similar business;
- Any farming business (including the raising or harvesting of trees);
- Any business involving the production of products for which percentage depletion can be claimed; and
- Any business of operating a hotel, motel, restaurant, or similar business.

Assets help satisfy the 80 percent requirement if they are held to meet the working capital needs of the corporation, or are held for investment and are reasonably expected to be used within two years to finance research in a qualified business. In addition, the rights to computer software that produces active business computer software royalties count toward the 80 percent figure.

A corporation can satisfy the active business requirement even though it has not yet begun the business. Assets are treated as being used in the active conduct of business if, in connection with a future qualified business, they are used in certain start-up activities, research and experimental or in-house research [Code Sec. 1202(e)(2)].

On the other hand, a corporation cannot satisfy the active business requirement if it owns significant real estate or securities. The value of real estate not used in its business cannot exceed 10 percent of its *total* assets [Code Sec. 1202(e)(7)]. And the value of securities it holds in other corporations cannot exceed 10 percent of its *net* assets [Code Sec. 1202(e)(5)(B)].

.06 Tax Treatment of Qualified Small Business Stock (QSBS)

An annual dollar limit is imposed on the amount of gain excludable by a taxpayer who sells or exchanges qualified small business stock. The exclusion may not exceed the greater of:

1. $10 million ($5 million for married persons filing separately) less the total amount of eligible gain (i.e., gain on the sale or exchange of QSBS held for more than five

years) taken into account under the Code Sec. 1202(a) rules by the taxpayer with respect to dispositions of stock issued by the corporation in all earlier tax years, or

2. 10 times the taxpayer's total adjusted basis in QSBS of the corporation disposed of by the taxpayer in the tax year [Code Sec. 1202(b)(1)].

Example 8-25: A single taxpayer acquires 10,000 shares of QSBS in ABCo at $10 per share, for a total cost of $100,000. These are the only QSBS shares that he has ever owned. He sells all 10,000 shares seven years later for $20 million ($2,000 per share). The maximum gain eligible for exclusion is the greater of (1) $10 million; or (2) $1 million, i.e., 10 times his $100,000 total basis in the 10,000 shares. On the taxpayer's tax return, he can exclude $10 million of the gain.

If the taxpayer exchanges QSBS for nonqualified stock as part of an incorporation or reorganization, gain on the subsequent sale of the nonqualified stock is eligible for the exclusion. However, the gain eligible for the exclusion is limited to gain accrued on the original qualified stock as of the date of incorporation or reorganization. The holding period for the qualified stock can be tacked onto the holding period for the nonqualified stock [Code Sec. 1202(h)(4)].

If the qualified small business stock (QSBS) is held for six months or less, the gain will be short-term capital gain. If the QSBS is held for more than 6 months, but not more than one year, the gain is short-term capital gain and gain can be deferred through reinvestment of the sales proceeds in other QSBS. If the QSBS stock is held for more than one year, the gain is long-term capital gain, and gain can be deferred through appropriate reinvestment of the sales proceeds.

.07 SSBIC Exception

The active business requirement is waived for specialized small business investment companies (SSBICs), which are corporations or partnerships licensed by the Small Business Administration under Sec. 301(d) of the Small Business Investment Act of 1958 [Code Sec. 1202(c)(2)(b)] [¶ 8110].

.08 Basis Rules

When qualified stock is issued in exchange for property other than money or stock, the stock is treated as having a basis at least equal to the property's fair market value and as having been acquired on the date of the exchange [Code Sec. 1202(i)(1)]. If the basis of qualified stock is later adjusted by reason of the holder's contributions to the corporation's capital, the basis of the contributed property is treated as being at least equal to its fair market value at that time [Code Sec. 1202(i)(2)].

.09 Alternative Minimum Tax Considerations

Only 7 percent of the amount excluded must be treated as a tax preference item when computing alternative minimum taxable income (AMTI) [Code Sec. 57(a)(7)]. Thus, 3.5 percent (50 percent × 7 percent) of the investor's total realized gain from the sale or exchange of small business stock will be used in the computation of AMTI. See ¶ 16,010 for further discussion. However, none of the excluded gain is a tax preference item if the stock was acquired after September 27, 2010, and before January 1, 2014 [Code Sec. 1202(a)(4)].

.10 Rollover of Gain on QSBS

Gain from the sale or exchange of qualified small business stock held for more than six months by a noncorporate taxpayer may be rolled over tax-free by the taxpayer where the proceeds are used to purchase other qualified small business stock within 60 days of the sale [Code Sec. 1045(a)].

The election is not available to defer gain on a sale that is treated as ordinary income [Code Sec. 1045(a)].

If the election is made, gain is recognized only to the extent that the amount realized on the sale exceeds: (1) the cost of the replacement small business stock purchased during the 60-day period beginning on the date of sale, reduced by: (2) any part of the cost of the replacement QSB stock that was previously taken into account to defer recognition of gain under Code Sec. 1045 on the sale of other QSB stock [Code Sec. 1045(a)].

To the extent that capital gain is not recognized, that amount will be applied to reduce the basis of the replacement small business stock which you have purchased during the 60-day replacement period. The basis adjustment is applied to the replacement stock in the order such stock is acquired [Code Sec. 1045(b)(3)]. Generally, the holding period of the stock purchased includes the holding period of the stock sold [Code Secs. 1045(b)(4), 1223(15)]. The replacement stock must satisfy the active business requirement for the first 6-months after its purchase [Code Sec. 1045(b)(4)(B)].

.11 How Partnerships Defer Gain on QSBS

An eligible partner of a partnership that sells QSB stock may elect to apply Code Sec. 1045 if the eligible partner purchases replacement QSB stock directly or through a purchasing partnership. A taxpayer (other than a C corporation) that holds QSB stock for more than 6 months, sells such QSB stock and purchases replacement QSB stock through a purchasing partnership may elect to apply Code Sec. 1045. A Code Sec. 1045 election is revocable only with the prior written consent of the IRS. To obtain prior written consent, the person who made the Code Sec. 1045 election must submit a request for a private letter ruling.

If the partnership elects to apply Code Sec. 1045, then, each eligible partner will not recognize its distributive share of any partnership Code Sec. 1045 gain. Instead, partnership Code Sec. 1045 gain equals the partnership's gain from the sale of the QSB stock reduced by the greater of:

1. The amount of the gain from the sale of the QSB stock that is treated as ordinary income; or
2. The excess of the amount realized by the partnership on the sale over the total cost of all replacement QSB stock purchased by the partnership (excluding the cost of any replacement QSB stock purchased by the partnership that is otherwise taken into account under section 1045) [Reg. § 1.1045-1(b)(1)].

A partner's distributive share of partnership Code Sec. 1045 gain shall be in the same proportion as the partner's distributive share of the partnership's gain from the sale of the QSB stock.

The adjusted basis of an eligible partner's interest in a partnership shall not be increased under Code Sec. 705(a)(1) by gain from a partnership's sale of QSB stock that is not recognized by the partner as the result of a partnership election under Reg. § 1.1045-1(b)(1). The basis of a partnership's replacement QSB stock is reduced (in the order acquired) by the amount of gain from the partnership's sale of QSB stock that is not recognized by an eligible partner as a result of the partnership's election under Code Sec. 1045 [Reg. § 1.1045-1(b)(3)].

An eligible partner may opt out of the partnership's Code Sec. 1045 election with respect to QSB stock either by recognizing the partner's distributive share of the partnership Code Sec. 1045 gain, or by making a partner Code Sec. 1045 election under with respect to the partner's distributive share of the partnership Code Sec. 1045 gain. Opting out of a partnership's Code Sec. 1045 election does not constitute a revocation of the partnership's election, and the election will continue to apply to other partners of the partnership [Reg. § 1.1045-1(b)(4)].

.12 How to Make Election

A partnership making an election under Code Sec. 1045 must do so on the partnership's timely filed (including extensions) Federal income tax return for the tax year during which the sale of QSB stock occurs. A partner making an election under Code Sec. 1045 must do so on the partner's timely filed (including extensions) Federal income tax return for the tax year during which the partner's distributive share of the partnership's gain from the sale of the QSB stock is taken into account under Code Sec. 706 [Reg. § 1.1045-1(h)].

In Letter Ruling 200906009[62] the IRS denied a taxpayer's request for an extension of the usual 60-day window to make a Code Sec. 1045 election to defer recognition of gain on QSB stock. The taxpayer failed to report gains from some of the sales and misreported certain gain sales as losses instead. The IRS concluded that granting the request would be prejudicial to the interests of the government under Reg. § 301.9100-3 because it would encourage taxpayers to play the audit lottery.

¶8110 TAX BREAKS FOR INVESTING IN MINORITY BUSINESSES

.01 Specialized Small Business Investment Company (SSBIC)

Individuals and C corporations can sell publicly traded securities (those traded on an established securities market) at a profit and make an election to avoid current tax. To benefit from this tax deferral, the sales proceeds must be invested within 60 days of the sale in a *specialized small business investment company (SSBIC)*. A SSBIC is a corporation or partnership that is licensed by the Small Business Administration to provide financing to minority-owned small businesses [Code Sec. 1044(c)(3)]. The deferral is available whether you buy SSBIC common stock or a SSBIC partnership interest [Code

[62] LTR 200906009 (Oct. 24, 2008).

Sec. 1044(a)]. Tax is owed, however, on any gain to the extent the proceeds are not reinvested in a SSBIC.

The amount of gain not currently taxed reduces the taxpayer's tax basis in the SSBIC interest for purposes of figuring gain or loss on the later sale of the SSBIC interest [Code Sec. 1044(d)].

Example 8-26: Ms. Maples bought 200 shares of XYZ, Inc. common stock (a publicly traded stock) for $40,000. She sold the stock 10 months later for $60,000, which meant she had a $20,000 short-term capital gain. One month later, Maples invests $56,000 in newly issued SSBIC stock and elects to defer tax on $16,000 of the $20,000 gain. Maples must pay tax on $4,000 of short-term gain ($60,000 proceeds less $56,000 reinvestment) that year. Her basis in the SSBIC stock is $40,000 ($56,000 cost less $16,000 unrecognized gain). So if Maples sells it early the next year for, $62,000, she pays tax on a $22,000 long-term gain. In effect, she has deferred the tax on $16,000 of the XYZ gain for three years and has converted it from highly taxed short gain to tax-favored long-term gain.

.02 Dollar Limits

An individual may defer tax on no more than $50,000 ($25,000 if married filing separately) of gain in any one year and no more than $500,000 ($250,000 if married filing separately) over a lifetime. A corporation may defer no more than $250,000 of gain in a year, capped at $1 million over all tax years [Code Sec. 1044(b)(1), (2)].

.03 Capital Gain Exclusion

If the taxpayer's SSBIC stock satisfies the eligibility requirements to be characterized as *qualified small business stock,* the taxpayer can also elect to exclude from tax up to 100 percent gain from the sale of the stock [Code Sec. 1202(a); see ¶ 8105 for further discussion]. Important: One eligibility requirement is, in effect, waived for SSBIC stock. SSBIC stock automatically satisfies the active business requirement [Code Sec. 1202(c)(2)(B)(ii)].

Basis Not Affected

The taxpayer's basis in SSBIC stock is not reduced by your deferred gain for purposes of the 50 percent (100 percent if the QSBS is in a qualified business entity) exclusion [Code Sec. 1044(d)]. In other words, the portion of your SSBIC stock gain that is attributable to tax deferral from the sale of publicly traded securities is ineligible for the exclusion.

Example 8-27: Same facts as in the previous example, except that Ms. Maples sells the SSBIC more than five years after it was bought. The SSBIC stock is eligible to be treated as qualified small business stock. Of the $22,000 taxable gain, $6,000 is eligible for the 50 percent exclusion ($62,000 proceeds less the $56,000 investment in the SSBIC, without reduction by the $16,000 deferred XYZ gain).

Eligibility

Only individual investors can enjoy both the tax deferral break and the 50 percent (100 percent if the QSBS is in a qualified business entity) exclusion. Reason: The tax deferral offered through an SSBIC is available to individuals and C corporations, but not estates, trusts, partnerships or S corporations [Code Sec. 1044(c)(4)]. By contrast, the 50 percent qualified small business stock exclusion is available to individuals, partnerships and S corporations, but not to C corporations [Code Sec. 1202(a)].

9

Personal Deductions

Itemized deductions in general . . . ¶9001

INTEREST

Interest expense deduction in general . . . ¶9005
Personal interest . . . ¶9010
Qualified residence interest . . . ¶9015
Investment interest . . . ¶9020
Nondeductible interest . . . ¶9025

TAXES

Deductible taxes in general . . . ¶9030
Taxes deductible as expenses of producing income . . . ¶9035
Who claims the deduction . . . ¶9040
Nondeductible taxes . . . ¶9045

CHARITABLE CONTRIBUTIONS

Charitable contributions in general . . . ¶9050
Cash contributions . . . ¶9051
Noncash contributions . . . ¶9052
Benefits received for contributions . . . ¶9055
Out-of-pocket expenses . . . ¶9060
Contributions of partial interests . . . ¶9065
Contributions of fractional interests in tangible personal property . . . ¶9070
Transfers for conservation purposes . . . ¶9071
Facade easement contributions . . . ¶9072
Valuation of conservation easement . . . ¶9073
Transfers in trust . . . ¶9074
Limitations on charitable contributions . . . ¶9075
Calculating the charitable deduction . . . ¶9080
When to claim a deduction . . . ¶9085
Penalties related to charities . . . ¶9090
Tax tips for fundraisers . . . ¶9095

MEDICAL EXPENSES

Medical expense deduction in general . . . ¶9100
What medical expenses are deductible . . . ¶9105
Eligible recipient of deductible medical care . . . ¶9110
Health Savings Accounts . . . ¶9115
Medical Savings Accounts (Archer MSAs) . . . ¶9120

MOVING EXPENSES

Moving expense deduction . . . ¶9125
The distance test . . . ¶9130
The time test . . . ¶9135

DEDUCTION FOR MISCELLANEOUS EXPENSES

Miscellaneous itemized deductions . . . ¶9140

Common types of miscellaneous expenses . . . . ¶9145
Penalty for premature withdrawal from bank certificate of deposit . . . . ¶9150
Bond premiums . . . . ¶9155
Tuition and fees deduction . . . . ¶9165

¶9001 ITEMIZED DEDUCTIONS IN GENERAL

Deductions play a critical part in slashing your tax bill since they reduce the amount of income subject to tax. The expenses that individuals subtract from their adjusted gross income are called itemized deductions. They are claimed in lieu of the standard deduction. The most common itemized deductions are qualified residence interest, state and local taxes, unreimbursed medical expenses, and miscellaneous expenses.

Certain itemized deductions are allowed only to the extent that the expense amount you incurred during the tax year exceeds a specified percentage of your adjusted gross income. For example, medical expenses are deductible only to the extent that they exceed 10 percent of your adjusted gross income [¶9100].

.01 Deduction Limits Based on Adjusted Gross Income

In 2013, an individual with an AGI that exceeds an inflation-adjusted threshold amount must reduce the amount of allowable itemized deductions by the lesser of:

- Three percent of the excess of AGI over the applicable threshold amount; or
- 80 percent of the total amount of otherwise allowable itemized deductions [Code Sec. 68(a)].

For 2013, the thresholds for the itemized deduction phase-out are:

- $300,000 for married taxpayers filing joint returns and surviving spouses,
- $275,000 for heads of households,
- $250,000 for other unmarried taxpayers, and
- $150,000 for married taxpayers filing separate returns [Code Sec. 68(b)(1)].

In 2014, the thresholds for the itemized reduction phase-out are:

- $305,050 for married taxpayers filing joint returns and surviving spouses,
- $279,650 for heads of households,
- $254,200 for other unmarried taxpayers, and
- $152,525 in the case of a married individual filing a separate return [Code Sec. 68(b)(1)].

For purposes of the phase-out, the following deductions are not included in the taxpayer's total itemized deductions and, therefore, are not affected by any phase-out of the taxpayer's allowable itemized deductions:

- Investment interest expenses [Code Sec. 163(d)],
- Casualty and theft losses [Code Sec. 165(c)],

- Allowable wagering losses [Code Sec. 165(d)], and
- Medical expenses [Code Secs. 213, 68(c)].

All other limitations on itemized deductions, such as the two-percent floor for miscellaneous itemized deductions, are applied first, and then the otherwise allowable total amount of itemized deductions is reduced [Code Sec. 68(d)]. The phase-out is limited to individual taxpayers; it does not apply to estates and trusts [Code Sec. 68(a)].

.02 Where to Claim Itemized Deductions

Itemized deductions are entered on Schedule A of Form 1040.

INTEREST

¶9005 INTEREST EXPENSE DEDUCTION IN GENERAL

Interest is the amount paid for the use of money that is borrowed.[1] Interest paid by the taxpayer may be deducted, subject to special limitations, as explained in the following paragraphs.

To be a deductible interest expense, a true debtor-creditor relationship must exist between the borrower and the lender.[2] Both parties must intend that the loan be repaid. In addition, no deduction is permitted unless you are legally responsible for the debt [Code Sec. 163(a); Reg. § 1.163-1].

Mortgage interest attributable to real estate may be deducted by the legal or equitable owner, even if the taxpayer is not directly liable on the note [Reg. § 1.163-1(b)]. Tenant-shareholders of a cooperative housing corporation can deduct amounts paid to the corporation that represent interest on the corporation's mortgage [Code Sec. 216; Reg. § 1.216-1(d)].

.01 Interest and Dividends Distinguished

Payments by a corporation on its stock are nondeductible dividends. Payments made on its debt (e.g., bonds or promissory notes) are deductible interest.

The IRS can prescribe rules to determine if an interest in a corporation is debt or equity. Among the factors that can be considered are: (1) if there is a written unconditional promise to pay on demand or on a specified date a certain amount in return for an adequate consideration, and with fixed interest; (2) if there is subordination to or preference over any of the corporation's indebtedness; (3) the ratio of debt to the equity of the corporation; (4) if there is convertibility into the corporation's stock; and (5) the relationship between stock holdings in the corporation and the holdings of the interest in question [Code Sec. 385].

---

[1] *Old Colony R.R. Co.*, SCt, 3 USTC ¶880, 284 US 552, 52 SCt 211; *Deputy v. DuPont*, SCt, 40-1 USTC ¶9161, 308 US 488.

[2] *K.F. Knetsch*, SCt, 60-2 USTC ¶9785, 364 US 361, 81 SCt 132.

Classifying by Issuer

Classifying a corporate instrument, when issued, as stock or debt by the corporate issuer is binding on the issuer and on all holders. However, the IRS is not bound by this classification [Code Sec. 385(c)].

.02 Interest Expense Classifications

There are five categories of interest for tax purposes and the type of interest determines the amount of the deduction that will be allowed. You must trace the loan proceeds to specific expenditures in order to categorize the interest. Exception: For qualified residence interest, the loan collateral determines the tax treatment. The categories of interest are: personal interest [¶9010]; qualified residence interest [¶9015]; investment interest [¶9020]; trade or business interest [Ch. 12]; and passive activity interest [Ch. 13].

Allocation of Interest Expense

For a debt (other than qualified residence loans) that has been applied to mixed uses, an allocation must be made to determine the amount of interest falling into each category. The allocation is made by tracing the loan to the specific expenses [See Ch. 18].

> **Example 9-1:** Mr. Parker borrows $140,000 at a 10 percent interest rate. He uses $40,000 to purchase office equipment. He uses $75,000 to purchase a car. The remaining $25,000 is invested in stock. Because the loan was put to mixed uses, Parker must trace the loan proceeds to the specific expense to determine his interest expense deduction. Parker's yearly interest expense is $14,000 ($140,000 × 10 percent). His interest allocation is as follows: business interest $4,000 ($40,000/$140,000 × $14,000); personal interest $7,500 ($75,000/$140,000 × $14,000); investment interest $2,500 ($25,000/$140,000 × $14,000). The amount of his deduction is determined by the interest rules for each of the respective categories.

> ▶ **OBSERVATION:** To facilitate allocating interest among the various categories, you can (1) maintain separate loans or loan accounts for separate expenditures, (2) avoid commingling borrowed funds with funds from another source (e.g., savings), and (3) try not to finance several expenditures with one loan.

Where to Report Interest Deduction

Report investment interest expenses and qualified residence interest on Schedule A, Form 1040 [¶9001]. Personal interest paid on consumer debt is not deductible (see below).

.03 Deduction for Interest Owed on Tax Deficiencies

Generally individuals are not entitled to a deduction for interest paid on delinquent federal individual income tax deficiencies because the interest is nondeductible personal interest under Section 163(h) [see ¶9010] [Temp. Reg. §1.163-9T(b)(2)(i)(A)]. On the other hand, corporate taxpayers are entitled to deduct interest paid on delinquent tax deficiencies as ordinary and necessary business expenses. The confusion begins when an individual wants to deduct interest paid on delinquent federal tax owed for his or her unincorporated business. Despite a temporary regulation that specifically provides that such interest is not deductible [Temp. Reg. § 1.163-9T(b)(2)(i)(A)], the question has dogged the courts for years.

In fact, five circuit courts have addressed this issue previously, and all have held that interest paid on tax deficiencies was nondeductible personal interest even though the source of the income giving rise to the tax liability was business-related. The courts have consistently upheld the validity of the Temporary Regulation, which supports this view. The Court of Appeals for the Fifth Circuit concluded in *D.V. Alfaro*,[3] that interest on a couple's individual tax liability that arose from the husband's sole proprietorship was nondeductible personal interest. In *N. Kikalos*,[4] the Court of Appeals for the Seventh Circuit has joined four other circuit courts and held that interest a couple paid on tax deficiencies was nondeductible personal interest even though the income giving rise to the tax liability came from the taxpayer's unincorporated business. In *J.E. Redlark*,[5] the Court of Appeals for the Ninth Circuit reversed the Tax Court and held similarly that an individual taxpayer could not deduct interest on a tax deficiency even though the source of the expense was business-related. The court upheld Temp. Reg. § 1.163-9T(b)(2)(i)(A), which supports this view and agreed with decisions of the Sixth and Eighth Circuits where the identical issues were addressed.[6]

In *E.A. Robinson III*,[7] an attorney and his wife were not entitled to allocate interest on the business-related personal income tax deficiencies to the husband's unincorporated law practice in order to claim an ordinary and necessary business expense deduction. The Tax Court held that the interest was nondeductible personal interest. The Tax Court specifically noted that its holding was opposite to its holding in *Redlark* and that it would no longer follow its previous decision in that case in light of the fact that the Tax Court's decision in that case was reversed by the Court of Appeals for the Ninth Circuit.

.04 Student Loan Interest Deduction

Students who pay interest on a qualified higher education loan to enable them to pay qualified higher education expenses and attend an eligible educational institution may claim an above-the-line deduction for up to $2,500 of interest paid each year on their qualified student loans regardless of the age of the loans [Code Sec. 221]. The loans must be incurred to pay tuition for the taxpayer, the taxpayer's spouse, and the taxpayer's dependents. A loan extended to a nonresident alien will not fulfill the criteria for a qualified educational loan under Code Sec. 221(d)(1) because the borrower is not considered a taxpayer under federal tax laws.[8]

Beginning in 2013, the $2,500 maximum deduction for interest paid on qualified education loans under Code Sec. 221 begins to phase out under Code Sec. 221(b)(2)(B) for taxpayers with modified adjusted gross income (MAGI) in excess of $60,000

---

[3] *D.V. Alfaro*, CA-5, 2003-2 USTC ¶ 50,715, 349 F3d 225.

[4] *N. Kikalos*, CA-7, 99-2 USTC ¶ 50,823, 190 F3d 791.

[5] *J.E. Redlark*, CA-9, 98-1 USTC ¶ 50,322, 141 F3d 936, *rev'g*, 106 TC 31, Dec. 51,104 (1996). *See also R.R. Allen*, CA-4, 99-1 USTC ¶ 50,470, 173 F3d 533.

[6] *M. McDonnell*, CA-6, 99-1 USTC ¶ 50,556, 180 F3d 721; *D. Miller*, CA-8, 95-2 USTC ¶ 50,485, 65 F3d 687.

[7] *E.A. Robinson III*, 119 TC 44, Dec. 54,863 (2002).

[8] *W.G. LeBlanc*, BC-DC-PA, 2009-2 USTC ¶ 50,498, 404 BR 793.

($125,000 for joint returns), and is completely phased out for taxpayers with modified adjusted gross income of $75,000 or more ($155,000 or more for joint returns).

Beginning in 2014, the $2,500 maximum deduction for interest paid on qualified education loans under Code Sec. 221 begins to phase out under Code Sec. 221(b)(2)(B) for taxpayers with modified adjusted gross income in excess of $65,000 ($130,000 for joint returns), and is completely phased out for taxpayers with MAGI of $80,000 or more ($160,000 or more for joint returns).

MAGI for these purposes means adjusted gross income figured before the deduction for student loan interest and modified by adding back any of the following items that were excluded or deducted from income [Reg. § 1.221-1(d)(2)]:

1. U.S. savings bond interest that is nontaxable because you paid qualified higher educational expenses;
2. Nontaxable employer-provided adoption assistance benefits;
3. Foreign earned income exclusion;
4. Foreign housing exclusion or deduction;
5. Exclusion of income for bona fide residents of American Samoa;
6. Exclusion of income from Puerto Rico, Guam, the Northern Mariana Islands; and
7. Deduction for income from domestic production activities.

If the taxpayer's MAGI falls within the phaseout ranges listed above, the taxpayer should compute the deduction by multiplying deductible interest by a fraction, the numerator of which is MAGI less $60,000 if single, or $125,000 if filing a joint return. The denominator of the fraction is $15,000. Then subtract the result from the interest payment. The result is the amount of the deduction.

> **Example 9-2:** The taxpayer is single and incurs $2,500 of interest on a qualified education loan in 2013. Her modified AGI for the year is $68,000. The maximum deductible amount of interest for 2013 is $2,500, which must be reduced to account for the taxpayer's excess modified AGI over $60,000. Thus, the amount of her reduction is equal to $2,500 × (($68,000 – $60,000) ÷ $15,000), or $533.

Eligibility

A student will be eligible to claim the interest deduction if the student is: (1) Enrolled in a degree, certificate or other program (including a program of study abroad that is approved for credit by the institution where enrolled) leading to a recognized educational credential at an eligible educational institution, and (2) Carrying at least one-half the normal full-time work load [Code Sec. 221(d)(3); Reg. § 1.221-1(e)(3)(i)].

Interest Paid by Someone Other Than the Taxpayer

The deduction is only available for interest paid by the *taxpayer* on a *qualified education loan* [Reg. § 1.221-1(a)(1)]. Taxpayers may not claim a deduction for interest paid in conjunction with money borrowed from a relative or friend to pay tuition and related expenses. Related persons include parents, grandparents, brothers and sisters, half-brothers and half-sisters, spouse, children and grandchildren [Reg. § 1.221-1(e)(3)(iii)]. The student loan interest deduction may only be claimed by a taxpayer legally obligated to make the interest payments according to the terms of the loan [Code Sec. 221(e)(1)].

If a third party who is not legally obligated to make the payment pays the interest, the taxpayer is treated as receiving the payment from the third party and, in turn, as making the payment [Reg. § 1.221-1(b)(4)(i)]. However, the deduction is not available to an individual who for that year is claimed as a dependent by another person or by a married taxpayer filing a separate return [Reg. § 1.221-1(b)(2)(i)].

Example 9-3: *Student not claimed as dependent.* Student B pays $750 interest on qualified education loans. Student B's parents are not allowed a deduction for her as a dependent that year. Assuming fulfillment of all other relevant requirements, Student B may deduct the $750 of interest paid that year [Reg. § 1.221-1(b)(2)(ii), Ex. 1].

Example 9-4: *Student claimed as dependent.* Student C pays $750 interest on qualified education loans during the year. Only Student C has the legal obligation to make the payments. Student C's parent claims him as a dependent and is allowed a deduction with respect to Student C in computing the parent's federal income tax for that year. Student C is not entitled to deduct the $750 of interest paid that year. Because Student C's parent was not legally obligated to make the payments, Student C's parent also is not entitled to a deduction for the interest [Reg. § 1.221-1(b)(2)(ii), Ex. 2].

Example 9-5: *Payment by parent.* Student E obtains a qualified education loan to attend college. Upon graduation from college, Student E makes legally required monthly payments of principal and interest. Student E's mother makes a required monthly payment of interest as a gift to Student E. A deduction for Student E as a dependent is not allowed on another taxpayer's tax return for that tax year. Assuming fulfillment of all other requirements, Student E may deduct this payment of interest for federal income tax purposes [Reg. § 1.221-1(b)(4)(ii), Ex. 2].

Interest and Fees

Capitalized interest is deductible as qualified education loan interest [Reg. § 1.221-1(f)(1)(ii)]. Generally, fees—such as loan origination fees or late fees—are interest if the fees represent a charge for the use or forbearance of money. Therefore, if the fees represent compensation to the lender for the cost of specific services performed in connection with the borrower's account, the fees are not interest for federal income tax purposes.

Example 9-6: *Capitalized interest.* Interest on Student K's loan accrues while Student K is in school, but Student K is not required to make any payments on the loan until six months after he graduates or otherwise leaves school. At that time, the lender capitalizes all accrued but unpaid interest and adds it to the outstanding principal amount of the loan. Thereafter, Student K is required to make monthly payments of interest and principal on the loan. The interest payable on the loan, including the capitalized interest, is original issue discount. Therefore, in determining the total amount of interest paid on the loan each tax year, Student K may deduct any payments that Reg. § 1.1275-2(a) treats as payments of interest, including any principal payments that are treated as payments of capitalized interest [Reg. § 1.221-1(f)(4), Ex. 1].

Time Limits Imposed

The expenses must be paid or incurred within a reasonable period of time before or after the taxpayer incurs the indebtedness. [Reg. § 1.221-1(e)(3)(i)(C)]. Expenses are treated as paid or incurred within a *reasonable period of time* under the following circumstances: (1) The expenses are paid with loan proceeds that are part of a federal postsecondary education loan program; or (2) The expenses relate to a particular academic period and the loan proceeds used to pay the expenses are disbursed within 90 days before the start of, and 90 days after the end of, the academic period to which the expenses relate [Reg. § 1.221-1(e)(3)(ii)].

Eligible Educational Institution

The loan proceeds must be used to pay tuition and related expenses incurred to attend an eligible educational institution for a student enrolled at least half-time in a program leading to a degree, certificate, or other recognized educational credential. An eligible educational institution is any college, university, vocational school, or other postsecondary educational institution eligible to participate in the student aid program administered by the Department of Education. This includes all accredited public, nonprofit, and proprietary postsecondary institutions including those that conduct an internship or residency programs leading to a degree or certificate awarded by an institution of higher education, a hospital, or a health care facility that offers postgraduate training [Reg. § 1.221-1(e)(1)]. The deductibility of interest paid on a qualified education loan is not affected if the educational institution loses its status as an eligible educational institution after the end of the academic period for which the loan was incurred.

Qualified Expenses

Qualified higher education expenses are a student's cost of attendance as determined by the eligible educational institution and include:

- Tuition and fees;
- Room and board; and
- Books, supplies, transportation, and miscellaneous expenses of the student [Reg. § 1.221-1(e)(2)(i)].

The cost of room and board qualifies only to the extent that it is not more than the greater of:

- The allowance for room and board, as determined by the eligible educational institution, that was included in the cost of attendance (for federal financial aid purposes) for a particular academic period and living arrangement of the student, or
- The actual amount charged if the student is residing in housing owned or operated by the eligible educational institution.

Qualified expenses are reduced by certain educational benefits excludable from gross income, such as tax-free distributions from a Coverdell education savings account, a tax-free scholarship, or tax-free employer-provided educational assistance [Reg.

§ 1.221-1(e)(2)(ii)]. The qualifying expenses must be attributable to a period when the student is at least a half-time student [Reg. § 1.221-1(e)(3)(i)].

Information Reporting Requirements

Financial institutions, lenders and other entities that receive payments of interest that aggregate $600 or more for any calendar year on one or more qualified education loans are subject to information reporting requirements [Code Sec. 6050S; Reg. § 1.6050S-3(a)]. The institutions must file the information returns with the IRS and provide a corresponding statement to the individuals named on the information return showing the information that has been reported [Reg. § 1.6050S-1(a)(1)]. Lenders and other entities that receive payments of interest on education loans should file Form 1098-E, *Student Loan Interest Statement.*

Financial institutions and lenders that receive payments of interest on education loans during the tax year, must file Form 1098-E, with the IRS by February 28 of the following year if filed on paper or by magnetic media. If the filing is electronic, the filing deadline is extended until April 1. A statement containing the same information as on the Form 1098-E that was filed with the IRS must be furnished to the person paying the interest by January 31. No penalties will be imposed for failure to file correct information returns or correct statements if the failure was due to reasonable cause [Reg. § 1.6050S-1(e)(3)].

¶9010 PERSONAL INTEREST

Taxpayers may not claim a deduction for their personal interest expenses [Code Sec. 163(h)]. What is personal interest? This is a catchall category for interest that does not fit into another category.

.01 Sources of Personal Interest

The most common sources of personal interest include:

- Credit card finance charges;
- Automobile loans;
- Installment plan interest;
- Finance charges;
- Mortgage on a third home; and
- Deferred payment transactions.

▶ **TAX STRATEGY:** Within generous limits, you can deduct interest on loans secured by your primary residence plus one other home [¶9015]. Therefore, take out a home equity loan to pay for that new car, boat, and vacation or college education. Provided you are within the qualified residence limitations, you end up with a full deduction and you will probably pay interest at a lower rate.

.02 Special Rule for Long-Term Payments

Sellers can mask interest charges as part of the sales price in deferred payment transactions. When payment is due long after the purchased goods or services are delivered, interest may be imputed unless the contract calls for adequate interest to be paid currently [see Ch. 2] [Code Sec. 483; Reg. § 1.483-1].

¶9015 QUALIFIED RESIDENCE INTEREST

Individuals are generally prohibited from claiming a deduction for personal interest but exceptions are provided under Code Sec. 163(h)(1) for two categories of qualified residence interest (home mortgage interest) secured by a qualified residence: acquisition debt and home equity debt [Code Sec. 163(h)(3)(A)]. A "qualified residence" is a taxpayer's principal residence and only one other residence selected and used by the taxpayer as a residence [Code Sec. 163(h)(4)(A)].

.01 Acquisition Debt

Acquisition debt is any debt incurred to acquire, construct, or substantially improve an individual's qualified residence that is secured by the residence. The term also includes debt secured by a taxpayer's qualified residence and incurred to refinance acquisition debt; however, such debt is limited to the amount of debt refinanced at the time of the loan [Code Sec. 163(h)(3)(B)]. Individuals are entitled to deduct interest actually "paid"[9] on up to $1 million ($500,000 for a married taxpayer filing separately) of "acquisition" debt [Code Sec. 163(h)(3)(B)(ii)]. In *F. Bronstein*,[10] the Tax Court held that a taxpayer who elected the "married filing separately" status on her federal tax return and who had obtained a $1 million mortgage, was limited under Code Sec. 163(h)(3) to a deduction for interest paid on $500,000 of home acquisition indebtedness plus interest paid on $50,000 of home equity indebtedness because of her filing status. The court said that the plain language of the statute controlled.

NOTE: Homebuyers may deduct interest paid on a builder's construction loan.[11]

.02 Home Equity Debt

Home equity debt is any debt (other than acquisition debt) secured by a qualified residence, to the extent it does not exceed the residence's fair market value reduced by any outstanding acquisition debt the residence secures [Code Sec. 163(h)(3)(C)(i)]. The aggregate home equity debt for any period may not exceed $100,000 ($50,000 for a married taxpayer filing separately) [Code Sec. 163(h)(3)(C)]. Any interest over and above the home equity debt limit will be treated as personal interest and will not be deductible.

Example 9-7: Ms. Johnson purchased a home for cash 10 years ago. She did not have a mortgage on the home until last year when she took out a $25,000 loan, secured by the home, to pay for her daughter's wedding. This loan is home equity debt.

NOTE: Part of a loan may qualify as acquisition debt and part home equity debt.

---

[9] *P.C. Smoker*, 105 TCM 1389, Dec. 59,458(M), TC Memo. 2013-56 (no deduction for mortgage interest capitalized into the principal of a mortgage note and not actually paid).

[10] *F. Bronstein*, 138 TC No. 21, Dec. 59,060 (2012).

[11] *W.D. Belden*, 70 TCM 274, Dec. 50,802(M), TC Memo. 1995-360.

.03 Home Mortgage Debt Deduction Limitations

In *P.S. Pau*,[12] and *P.E. Catalano*,[13] the Tax Court addressed whether taxpayers could claim a deduction for qualified residence interest on the purchase of a residence in excess of $1 million and in effect combine the $1 million acquisition debt and $100,000 of home equity debt. In both cases, the Tax Court decided that they could not, stating that Code Sec. 163(h) restricts home mortgage interest deductions to interest paid on $1 million of acquisition debt and $100,000 of home equity debt. The court concluded that no deduction in excess of the $1 million acquisition limit was available where the taxpayers failed to show that they had home equity debt.

In Rev. Rul. 2010-25,[14] the IRS rejected these two Tax Court decisions and ruled that acquisition debt incurred by a taxpayer to acquire, construct, or substantially improve a qualified residence (i.e., the taxpayer's principal residence and one other residence selected and used by the taxpayer as a residence) could constitute home equity indebtedness to the extent it exceeded $1 million but was subject to the $100,000 and fair market value limitations of Code Sec. 163(h)(3)(c). Therefore, the taxpayer could deduct interest paid on up to $1.1 million of such debt as qualified residence interest under Code Sec. 163(h)(3), but any interest paid on debt above that amount was nondeductible personal interest.

The IRS stated that it will not follow the Tax Court decisions in *P.S. Pau* and *P.E. Catalano*, which were based on the incorrect assertion that taxpayers must demonstrate that home equity debt was not incurred in acquiring, constructing, or substantially improving their residence. According to the IRS, the definition of home equity indebtedness in Code Sec. 163(h)(3)(C) contains no such restrictions.

A similar result was reached by the IRS in Letter Ruling 200940030 where the IRS also concluded that debt that is incurred by a taxpayer to acquire, construct, or substantially improve a qualified residence can constitute "home equity indebtedness" to the extent it exceeds $1 million.

In CCA 200911007, the IRS Office of Chief Counsel explained how partial owners of a principal residence with a mortgage larger than $1 million should handle their mortgage deduction. The IRS concluded that the amount of interest that the taxpayer may deduct is determined by multiplying the amount of interest actually paid by the taxpayer on his or her qualified residence by a fraction the numerator of which is $1 million and the denominator of which is $X, the average balance of the outstanding acquisition indebtedness during the years in question.

Unmarried Co-Owners Limits on Per-Residence Basis

In *C.J. Sophy*,[15] the Tax Court held that the Code Sec. 163(h)(3) limits on the amount of indebtedness that qualifies as acquisition or home equity indebtedness does not apply separately to unmarried co-owners of two residences. The taxpayers were therefore only able to deduct interest on $1 million of acquisition indebtedness and

---

[12] *P.S. Pau*, 73 TCM 1819, Dec. 51,845(M), TC Memo. 1997-43.

[13] *P.E. Catalano*, 79 TCM 1632, Dec. 53,792(M), TC Memo. 2000-82, *rev'd on other grounds*, CA-9, 2002-1 USTC ¶50,203, 279 F3d 682. *See also J.J. Norman*, 104 TCM 837, Dec. 59,302(M), TC Memo. 2012-360.

[14] Rev. Rul. 2010-25, IRB 2010-44, 571.

[15] *C.J. Sophy*, 138 TC 204, Dec. 58,965 (2012).

$100,000 of home equity indebtedness. The taxpayers unsuccessfully argued that where co-owners are not married to each other, the limitations apply separately to each taxpayer who is a co-owner of up to two residences. The Court concluded that the indebtedness limitation should be applied on a per-residence basis, rather than a per-taxpayer basis when the taxpayers are not married to each other. The court explained that the definitions of "acquisition indebtedness" and "home equity indebtedness" in Code Sec. 163(h)(3) repeatedly focus on the word "residence" rather than the word "taxpayer."

.04 Election Not to Treat Debt as Secured by Qualified Residence

A taxpayer may elect to treat home equity debt as not secured by a residence so that the interest will no longer be subject to the qualified residence interest limitations and can be deductible as another type of interest [Temp. Reg. § 1.163-10T(o)(5)]. The election will be effective for the tax year when made and for all subsequent tax years, unless revoked with IRS consent. The election should be made in a separate statement attached to the return.

> **Example 9-8:** The taxpayer has two debts secured by a qualified residence. The amount of the first debt is $80,000 and the proceeds were used to purchase business equipment. The amount of the second debt is $60,000 and the proceeds were used to pay for her daughter's wedding. Both debts qualify as home equity debt, but their total amount ($140,000) exceeds the $100,000 cap. Therefore, interest on only the first $100,000 of the two debts would be deductible qualified residence interest. If the taxpayer makes an election under Temp. Reg. § 1.163-10T(o)(5) to treat the $80,000 debt as not secured by a qualified residence, the interest remains fully deductible as business interest and all of the $60,000 loan used to pay for the wedding, which is otherwise not deductible, becomes fully deductible as home equity debt.

.05 Requirements for Deduction

Home mortgage interest, which is interest paid or accrued on debt secured by the borrower's home and/or a second home is deductible if the following requirements are satisfied [Code Sec. 163(h)(3)]:

1. The borrower must file Form 1040 (not available on Form 1040EZ) and itemize deductions on Schedule A (Form 1040).
2. The borrower must be legally liable to repay the loan.[16] This means that the taxpayer may not claim a deduction for payments made on behalf of someone else if the taxpayer was not legally obligated to make the payments. Reg. § 1.163-1(b) provides that the taxpayer must be the legal or equitable owner of the property in order to claim a deduction for mortgage interest.

---

[16] *L.W. Golder, Jr.*, CA-9, 79-2 USTC ¶9451, 604 F2d 34; *G.F. Smith, Jr.*, 84 TC 889, Dec. 42,096, *aff'd without published op.*, 805 F2d 1073; *J.B. Hynes, Jr.*, 74 TC 1266, Dec. 37,232; *S. Uslu*, 74 TCM 1376, Dec. 52,397(M), TC Memo. 1997-551; *G.M. Daya*, 80 TCM 743, Dec. 54,131(M), TC Memo. 2000-360.

In *A.J. Adams*,[17] a trust beneficiary assumed the benefits and burdens of ownership for property held by the trust and was therefore entitled to claim mortgage interest deductions with respect to the property. The following factors indicated to the court that the trust beneficiary had assumed the benefits and burdens of ownership: the individual had a duty to repair or maintain the property; was responsible for insuring the property; had a duty to pay the property's taxes, assessments, or charges; had a right to the property's proceeds from rents, mortgages, or sales; had the right to obtain legal title at any time by paying the balance of the purchase price; bore some risk of loss; and agreed to pay the mortgage principal and interest under the occupancy and beneficiary agreements.

In *T.R. Jones*,[18] the Tax Court concluded that a taxpayer was not entitled to deduct mortgage interest and real property taxes that he paid under a lease-option agreement. Under state law, the agreement was merely an option to purchase real property, not a sales contract for the following reasons:

a. The lessee was not obligated to exercise the option and was not otherwise liable for the purchase price;

b. The lessor had no legal right to compel the lessee to purchase the property;

c. Correspondence between the parties referred to the lessor as the property's owner; and

d. The lessor remained liable for the mortgage.

3. Both the lender and the borrower must intend that the loan be repaid.
4. There must be a true debtor-creditor relationship between the borrower and the lender.
5. The mortgage must be a "secured debt" on a "qualified residence" [Code Sec. 163(h)(3)(B)(i)(II)].
6. The total interest that may be deducted on total acquisition and home equity indebtedness on the principal and second residences of joint filers may not exceed $1,000,000.

.06 *Secured Debt* Defined

A secured debt is one in which the borrower signs a mortgage providing that:

1. The borrower's ownership in a qualified home is security for payment of the debt,
2. In case of default, the home could be subjected to the satisfaction of the debt with the same priority as a mortgage or deed of trust in the jurisdiction in which the property is situated, and
3. The mortgage is recorded under any state or local law that applies [Temp. Reg. § 1.163-10T(o)(1)].

What Is Not Secured Debt

A mortgage will not be considered a secured debt and the borrower will not be entitled to the mortgage interest deduction if the loan is not secured by the borrower's home

---

[17] *A.J. Adams*, 99 TCM 1305, Dec. 58,180(M), TC Memo. 2010-72.

[18] *T.R. Jones*, 92 TCM 168, Dec. 56,597(M), TC Memo. 2006-176.

[Code Sec. 163(h)(3)(B)(i)(II)]. For example, a loan secured only by a lien on the borrower's general assets or a security interest that attaches to the property without the borrower's consent (such as a mechanic's lien or judgment lien) will not be considered "secured debt" for purposes of the mortgage interest deduction [Temp. Reg. § 1.163-10T(o)]. Typically, a wraparound mortgage will not be considered "secured debt" for these purposes unless it is recorded under state law. In addition, a mortgage that was once secured by the borrower's home, but no longer is, will no longer qualify as a secured debt for purposes of the mortgage interest deduction.

.07 *Qualified Residence* Defined

A *qualified residence* includes a taxpayer's principal or secondary residence (e.g., vacation home) [Code Sec. 163(h)(4)(A)(i)(I); Temp. Reg. § 1.163-10T(p)(1)]. The home may be a house, cooperative apartment, condominium, mobile home, boat, or a house trailer. A boat will qualify as a second home provided it has sleeping space, toilet, cooking facilities and basic living accommodations [Code Sec. 163(h)(4)(B); Temp. Reg. § 163-10T(p)(3)(ii)]. A second home may be one that is not occupied, a home that is occupied part of the year, or a home that is rented out.

Home Under Construction

A home under construction may be treated as a qualified residence for a period of up to 24 months but only if the borrower moves into the home when it is ready for occupancy and it therefore becomes a qualified residence. The 24-month period begins any time on or after the day construction on the home begins [Temp. Reg. § 163-10T(p)(5)(i)].

In *T.G. Rose*,[19] the Tax Court held that taxpayers could deduct qualified residence interest on a vacation home that was never built because they couldn't get construction financing due to a crisis in the credit markets. The court held that construction began for purposes of the qualified residence interest rules when the pre-existing home on the property was demolished by the sellers as required by the sales contract. It also concluded that the fact that the home was never built didn't prevent the taxpayers from deducting residence interest incurred during the 24-month "under construction period" sanctioned by Temp. Reg. § 1.163-10T(p)(5).

Home Destroyed in Casualty

A home or second home destroyed in a fire, storm, tornado, earthquake, or other casualty will still constitute a "qualified residence" for purposes of the mortgage interest deduction if the borrower continues to pay mortgage principal and interest after the residence has been destroyed by a disaster. The borrower will not lose the mortgage interest deduction after the casualty if the borrower rebuilds the destroyed home and moves into it or sells the land on which the home was located within a reasonable period of time after the home was destroyed.[20]

Time-Shares and Coops

A home owned under a time-share arrangement or in a cooperative housing corporation will constitute a qualified home for purposes of the home mortgage interest deduction [Temp. Reg. § 1.163-10T(p)(6) and (q)].

---

[19] *T.G. Rose*, TC Summary Op. 2011-117 (2011).

[20] Rev. Rul. 96-32, 1996-1 CB 177.

Rental of Home

If the borrower rents out a portion of his or her principal residence or second home to another person, that portion may be treated as used for residential purposes and thus qualify for the mortgage interest deduction, only if:

- Such rented portion if used by the tenant primarily for residential purposes,
- The rented portion is not a self-contained residential unit containing sleeping space and toilet and cooking facilities, and
- The total number of tenants renting the same or different portions of the residence at any time during the tax year does not exceed two. For this purpose, if two persons share the same sleeping quarters, they shall be treated as a single tenant [Temp. Reg. § 1.163-10T(p) (4) (ii)].

Second Residence

To be a qualified residence for purposes of the home mortgage interest deduction, a second home must be used as a residence rather than a rental property (subject to the limited exception discussed below) [Code Sec. 163(h) (4) (A) (i) (II)]. If the second home is rented out, it must be used as a personal residence for at least the greater of 14 days or 10 percent of the days it is rented to others [Code Sec. 280A(d) (1)]. Otherwise, it is deemed to be rental property, subject to the passive loss rules and is ineligible for the mortgage interest deduction. See ¶ 13,105 for further discussion.

Home Office

If the borrower uses part of the home for a home office, the cost of the home and the fair market value of the home must be allocated between the part used as a qualified home and the part used for the home office [Ch. 12]. The portion of interest that is attributable to the home office is deducted on Schedule C (Form 1040), *Profit or Loss From Business.*

> **NOTE:** To be a qualified residence, a home that is rented out must be used as a personal residence for at least the greater of 14 days or 10 percent of the days it is rented out. Otherwise, it is deemed to be rental property, subject to the passive loss rules [Ch. 13] [Code Sec. 163(h)(4)(A)].

Deduction Available for Only Two Homes

The interest deduction is only available for two homes. If the borrower owns more than two homes, once a year the taxpayer may change the property to be considered the second qualified home [Temp. Reg. § 1.163-10T(p)(3)(iv)].

> **Example 9-9:** Mr. Smith owns three homes—Whiteacre, Blackacre, and Greyacre, with outstanding mortgages on all of these properties. Smith lives in Whiteacre, his main home. Smith chooses to designate Greyacre as his qualified second home in year one. Provided the rules on deductible home mortgage interest are met, Smith may deduct all of the mortgage interest he pays on Whiteacre and Greyacre. The interest paid on Blackacre is nondeductible personal interest [¶ 9010]. The following year, Smith designates Blackacre as his second home. As a result, he may deduct mortgage interest on Blackacre that year. The interest paid on Greyacre does not come under the qualified residence interest rules.

The IRS has analyzed the question of what is a principal residence for purposes of the mortgage interest deduction for a taxpayer who owns two residences and also has a third residence furnished to him by his employer in connection with his job. The IRS says that the determination of which of the three residences is the principal residence depends upon the following facts and circumstances, where:

- The taxpayer filed a resident income tax return;
- The driver's license was issued;
- The taxpayer was registered to vote;
- The taxpayer's family and social connections were located;
- The taxpayer's children attended school;
- The taxpayer's job or business was located;
- The taxpayer's mailing address used for most purposes (e.g., tax returns, driver's licenses) is;
- The taxpayer maintained bank accounts; and
- The taxpayer maintained memberships (e.g., places of worship, clubs).[21]

.08 Types of Qualified Residence Interest

The following types of payments may qualify as deductible interest on a taxpayer's residence: mortgage interest (including second mortgages), "points" (see below), mortgage prepayment penalties, home equity line of credit interest, home equity loan interest, and charges on late mortgage payments (unless for a specific service).

Raw Land

In some cases, the interest paid on debt to purchase raw land can qualify for the residence interest deduction. In a ruling, the IRS allowed homeowners to treat a loan to purchase five acres of land adjacent to the home site as residential acquisition indebtedness—and the interest payments were fully deductible. Reason: The homeowners intended to clear the acreage and landscape it as part of their residence.[22]

.09 Deduction of Points

Points are a form of prepaid interest that homebuyers often pay lenders up front when buying a home or refinancing an existing mortgage. Points are also called loan origination fees, processing fees, maximum loan charges, or premium charges. One point equals 1 percent of the loan amount. The rules for deducting points differ for buying a home and refinancing the mortgage on a home. In general, buyers may deduct all points paid in the year the debt was incurred. When a homeowner refinances, the points must typically be spread over the life of the loan.

For taxpayers itemizing their deductions on Form 1040, Schedule A, loan origination fees or "points" paid to obtain an original home mortgage may be fully deductible in the year paid if all the following requirements are met:

- The loan is used to buy, build, or improve the taxpayer's principal home and the loan is secured by that home;

---

[21] FSA 200137033 (June 18, 2001).

[22] LTR 8940061 (July 12, 1989).

- The payment of points is an established business practice in the area where the loan is made; and
- The points paid do not exceed the number of points generally charged in the area [Code Sec. 461(g)(2)].[23]

In addition, the points will be deductible if:

- The buyer is legally liable for the debt;
- The loan is secured by the buyer's home where the buyer lives most of the time;
- The taxpayer uses the cash method of accounting, which means that income is reported in the year that it is received and expenses are deducted in the year that they are paid;
- The points were not paid for items that usually are separately stated on the settlement sheet such as appraisal fees, notary fees, inspection fees, title fees, document preparation fees for the mortgage note or deed or trust, VA funding fees, loan placement fees, attorney fees, and property taxes;
- At or before closing the buyer provided funds that were at least as much as the points charged, not counting points paid by the seller. To be deductible, the points may be borrowed from the lender or mortgage broker;
- The points were computed as a percentage of the principal amount of the mortgage; and
- The amount of the points paid is clearly shown on the settlement statement.

Refinancing—Treatment of Points

Points paid solely to refinance a home mortgage usually must be deducted over the life of the loan. For a refinanced mortgage, the interest deduction for points is determined by dividing the points paid by the number of payments to be made over the life of the loan. Usually, this information is available from lenders. Taxpayers may deduct points only for those payments made in the tax year.

> **Example 9-10:** Taxpayer pays $10,000 in points to refinance his home with a 30-year mortgage. The homeowner is required to make 12 payments a year or 360 total payments on the 30-year mortgage. The taxpayer can deduct $27.78 per monthly payment, or a $333.36 in one year.

If part of the refinanced mortgage money was used to finance improvements to the home and if the taxpayer meets certain other requirements, the points associated with the home improvements may be fully deductible in the year the points were paid.

If a homeowner is refinancing a mortgage for a second time, the balance of points paid for the first refinanced mortgage may be fully deductible at pay off.

> **Example 9-11:** The homeowner refinanced his house with a 30-year mortgage and paid $1,230 in points. On Schedule A, the taxpayer deducted $41 ($1,230 divided by 30) each year for 6 years. At this point, when the homeowner had

[23] IRS New Release IR-2003-127, November 3, 2003.

deducted $246 of the total points paid, he refinanced again and paid off the entire previous loan including the points. The homeowner would be able to deduct $984 in the year the mortgage ended.

Even though the IRS says that points paid by a borrower to refinance an existing home mortgage must be deducted over the loan period, the Court of Appeals for the Eighth Circuit has allowed a current deduction for points paid to refinance a short-term balloon that has been taken out to purchase a principal residence.[24] The decision will only be followed, however, in the following seven states that make up the Eighth Circuit: Arkansas, Iowa, Minnesota, Missouri, Nebraska, North Dakota, and South Dakota. Under the IRS position, each year, you can either (1) deduct the portion of the points allocable to the use of the mortgage balance for that year, or (2) write off a ratable portion of the points.[25]

Points May Be Amortized

The IRS has allowed a homebuyer to amortize points paid on a mortgage to finance the purchase of a principal residence, rather than deducting them in full in the year the home was purchased and the debt was incurred.[26] Because nothing in the legislative history of Code Sec. 461(g) precludes prepaid points from being amortized over the life of the loan, the IRS concluded that the taxpayers could amortize the points paid to the lender beginning with the second year of the loan. By sanctioning the taxpayer's ability to amortize the pre-paid points rather than deducting them all in the year of purchase, the taxpayers were able to spread out the deduction of the points rather than deducting them in full in a year when they would afford the taxpayer no tax savings. The ruling encourages taxpayers to be more flexible in timing their deductions.

.10 Seller-Paid Points Deductible by Buyer

The buyer can claim a deduction for points paid in connection with the purchase of a principal residence even if the points were paid by the seller.[27] The amount of the seller-paid points which have been deducted are subtracted from the purchase price to compute the buyer's basis in the new home.

Example 9-12: The buyer pays $400,000 for a new home and obtains a loan in the amount of $320,000. The mortgage lender charges 2 points, or $6,400. Because of cash flow problem, the buyer would rather not pay all the points upfront at settlement, so he negotiates with the seller to split the points equally. Accordingly, the seller will raise the price of the house in the amount of $3,200 which is one-half of the $6,400 and represents what he will have to pay out of his proceeds at settlement. Buyer can deduct the full $6,400 in points paid—including the points paid by the seller at settlement.

---

[24] Rev. Proc. 87-15, 1987-1 CB 624; *J.R. Huntsman*, CA-8, 90-2 USTC ¶ 50,340, 905 F2d 1182.

[25] Rev. Rul. 87-22, 1987-1 CB 146.

[26] LTR 199905033 (Nov. 10, 1998).

[27] Rev. Proc. 94-27, 1994-1 CB 613.

In order for the points paid by the seller to be deductible by the buyer, the points must be:

- Designated clearly on Uniform Settlement Statement (HUD-1) as points payable in connection with the loan;
- Computed as a percentage of the stated principal amount of the indebtedness;
- Charged under established business practice in the geographic area in which the home is located and the amount of points paid must not exceed the amount generally charged in that area. Appraisal fees, inspection fees, title fees, attorney fees, and real property taxes are not deductible points;
- Paid in connection with the purchase of a home, and the loan must be secured by that home. This means that a deed of trust (mortgage) must be recorded in local land records; and
- Points cannot be paid from borrowed funds. If the seller pays the points, the buyer must prove that he or she has paid cash in the transaction at least equal to the points deducted. If the buyer pays the points, he or she must also establish that the points have not been borrowed. This rule applies to any payments which may later constitute points, such as down payments, escrow deposits, earnest money applied at closing and other funds actually paid over by the buyer at the closing.

The seller may not, however, deduct these fees as interest. Instead, they are a selling expense that reduces the amount realized by the seller. The amount of the seller-paid points is then subtracted from the purchase price to compute basis in the home. Interest recipients must report the seller-paid points according to the Code Sec. 6050H reporting requirements.

The basis of the home must be reduced by any amount of seller-paid points deducted, even on amended returns. The long-term effects of this basis reduction should be balanced with the immediate tax deduction. Decreasing the basis in a home will increase gain when it is later sold.

In order for the points paid by the seller to be deductible by the buyer, the points must be satisfy the same requirements listed above that apply to the deduction of points by the buyer.

.11 Mortgage Insurance Premiums

Mortgage insurance may be required if a taxpayer purchasing a home doesn't have sufficient funds to make a full down payment and the lending institution requires the homebuyer to obtain mortgage insurance to guarantee repayment of the loan amount.

Premiums paid or accrued for qualified mortgage insurance by a taxpayer during the tax year in connection with acquisition indebtedness on a taxpayer's qualified residence are treated as qualified residence interest and are deductible subject to a phase-out based on the taxpayer's adjusted gross income [Code Sec. 163(h)(3)(E)]. The amount allowable as a deduction is phased out ratably by 10 percent for each $1,000 by which the taxpayer's adjusted gross income exceeds $100,000 ($500 and $50,000, respectively, in the case of a married individual filing a separate return). Thus, the deduction is not allowed if the taxpayer's adjusted gross income exceeds $110,000 ($55,000 in the case of a married individual filing a separate return). The mortgage insurance premium deduction is available through December 31, 2013 [Code Sec. 163(h)(3)(E)(iv)].

Qualified Mortgage Insurance Defined

For purposes of this deduction, qualified mortgage insurance means mortgage insurance provided by the Veterans Administration, the Federal Housing Administration, or the Rural Housing Administration, and private mortgage insurance [Code Sec. 163(h)(4)(E)].

Amounts paid for qualified mortgage insurance that are properly allocable to periods after the close of the tax year are treated as paid in the period to which they are allocated. No deduction is allowed for the unamortized balance if the mortgage is paid before its term (except in the case of qualified mortgage insurance provided by the Department of Veterans Affairs or Rural Housing Administration).

¶9020 INVESTMENT INTEREST

Investment interest is interest paid on loans where the loan proceeds are used to purchase or carry property held for investment purposes (e.g., interest on margin accounts) [Code Sec. 163(d)(3)(A)]. A taxpayer's deduction for investment interest is limited to the amount of his or her *net investment income*. Exception: Interest paid to produce tax-exempt income may not be deducted [¶ 9025]. Investment interest does not include the following:

- Home mortgage interest;
- Interest from a passive activity [Code Sec. 163(d)(3)(B)];
- Any interest expense that is capitalized, such as construction interest subject to Code Sec. 263A;
- Interest expense, disallowed under Code Sec. 264, on indebtedness, with respect to life insurance endowments, or annuity contracts issued after June 8, 1997, even if the proceeds were used to purchase any property held for investment.

.01 Limitation on Deduction of Investment Interest

Taxpayers other than corporations may only deduct investment interest to the extent of "net investment income" [Code Sec. 163(d)(1)]. This limitation exists to prevent taxpayers from sheltering or reducing tax on wages and dividends with an unrelated interest deduction. Code Sec. 163(d)(3) defines *investment interest* as any interest paid on indebtedness properly allocable to *property held for investment,* which includes any property that produces income such as "interest, dividends, annuities, or royalties not derived in the ordinary course of a trade or business," sometimes known as portfolio income [Code Sec. 469(e)(1)]. Investment interest does not include Alaska Permanent Fund dividends.

> ▶ **PRACTICE POINTER:** Choice of entity may determine deductibility of investment interest. How the business is structured may affect the ability to deduct investment interest. Consider the situation where an individual is borrowing money to purchase the stock of a corporation. For a noncorporate debtor

purchasing the stock of a corporation, the interest deduction would be limited to the debtor's net investment or portfolio income. If, however, the business were purchased by a C corporation, the corporation would be entitled to deduct the interest, without limitation, on the debt incurred to purchase the business.

Borrowers Subject to Deduction Limitation in Code Sec. 163(d)(1)

In *S.C. Russon*,[28] an individual who borrowed money to purchase stock in the C corporation that operated the family business where he was employed incurred investment interest that was not deductible in excess of investment income. The stock was property held for investment even though the corporation had never paid a dividend because it was the type of property that normally produces interest, dividend, or royalty income and the stock purchase agreement explicitly recognized that the taxpayer and other buyers would be entitled to all dividends from the stock. Since the C corporation owned the family business, the taxpayer was not its direct owner; thus, the court held that he was not entitled to deduct the interest as trade or business interest.

In Rev. Rul. 2008-12,[29] a noncorporate limited partner's distributive share of the interest expense on debt allocable to the partnership's trade or business of trading securities was investment interest and was not deductible in excess of investment income. The limitation applied because the limited partner did not materially participate in the trading activity within the meaning of Code Sec. 469. In addition, because the degree of participation by each noncorporate partner of the partnership could limit the deductibility of the interest expense allocable to its trading business, the partnership must separately state this expense.

In Rev. Rul. 2008-38,[30] the IRS amplified Rev. Rul. 2008-12 to rule that, in the case of an individual limited partner, interest paid or accrued on debt allocable to property held for investment is a trade or business deduction that is deductible in determining the individual's adjusted gross income under Code Sec. 62(a)(1). Where the individual has both investment interest expense attributable to debt allocable to property held as a passive activity and investment interest expense attributable to debt allocable to property held in an activity involving the conduct of a trade or business, and his aggregate investment interest expense is greater than his net investment income, the taxpayer must allocate his net investment income between the two categories using a reasonable method of allocation. According to the IRS, one reasonable method is the *pro-rata* method.

.02 *Net Investment Income* Defined

Net investment income is equal to the amount of investment income derived from property held for investment and includes interest, dividends, annuities, rents, royalties, and short-term capital gains from the sale of investment property, as well as interest on a refund of federal taxes,[31] less *investment expenses* [Code Sec. 163(d)(4)]. To be deductible, investment expenses must exceed 2 percent of adjusted gross income [¶9140]. Other sources of investment income include property that produces gain or loss (not derived in the ordinary course of a trade or business) from the sale or trade or property held for investment (other than an interest in a passive activity). Invest-

[28] *S.C. Russon*, 107 TC 263, Dec. 51,639 (1996).

[29] Rev. Rul. 2008-12, IRB 2008-10, 520, as amplified by Rev. Rul. 2008-38, IRB 2008-31, 249.

[30] Rev. Rul. 2008-38, IRB 2008-31, 249.

[31] LTR 9307005 (Oct. 27, 1992).

ment property also includes an interest in a trade or business activity in which the investor did not materially participate (other than a passive activity). Investment income also includes a child's interest and dividend income that is reported on the parent's tax return [Ch. 2]. Investment income does not include Alaska Permanent Fund dividends. It also does not include net capital gain from disposing of investment property (including capital gains distributions from mutual funds) or qualified dividends unless you choose to include all or part of them in investment income. You make this choice by completing Form 4562.

.03 Allocation of Interest Expense Required

When borrowed money is used for business or personal purposes as well as for investment purposes, the debt must be allocated among the different types of expenditures. Reason: Only the interest expense on the part of the debt used for investment purposes is treated as investment interest and is subject to the deduction limitation imposed on investment interest.

> **Example 9-13:** Taxpayer borrows $20,000 and uses 40 percent ($8,000) to buy stock. Taxpayer uses the other $12,000 to buy furniture for the home and to take a vacation. Since 60 percent of the debt is used for personal purposes and is therefore not deductible, 40 percent of that debt is termed investment interest and is subject to the investment interest deduction rules.

If you borrow money and deposit the funds in your bank account, the interest on that loan is considered an investment expense. If a portion or all of the loan proceeds are taken from the account and used for some other purpose, that amount must be reallocated.

.04 Election to Treat Net Capital Gain as Investment Income

An investor may elect to include in investment income all or part of the amount of qualified dividends or net capital gain received from the disposition of property held for investment [Code Sec. 163(d)(4)(B); Reg. § 1.163(d)-1]. If the investor chooses to include any amount of qualified dividends or capital gain in investment income, he or she must similarly reduce the amounts of these items that are eligible for the lower capital gains tax rate by the amount included in investment income [Code Sec. 163(d)(4)(B)(iii)]. If this election is made, the qualified dividends and net capital gain will be ineligible for taxation at capital gains tax rates. Once made, IRS consent is needed to revoke the election.

As a result of this election, the portion of qualified dividends and net capital gain used to increase the investment interest deduction will be taxed as ordinary income. The remainder of the investor's gain will be taxed as long-term capital gain, which is 15 percent for most taxpayers and 5 percent for those in a 10 percent tax bracket. Net short-term capital gain is treated as investment income in all cases.

The election is necessary because noncorporate taxpayers (individuals, partnerships, and S corporations) may only deduct investment interest to the extent of *net investment income* [Code Sec. 163(d)(1)]. This limitation exists to prevent taxpayers from sheltering or reducing tax on wages and dividends with an unrelated interest deduction. Code Sec. 163(d)(3) defines *investment interest* as any interest paid on indebtedness properly allocable to *property held for investment,* which includes any property that produces income such as "interest, dividends, annuities, or royalties not derived in the ordinary course of a trade or business," sometimes known as *portfolio income* [Code Sec. 469(e)(1)]. Investment interest does not include Alaska Permanent Fund dividends.

▶**IMPORTANT:** (1) Only the portion of qualified dividends and net capital gain used to increase your investment interest deduction will be taxed as ordinary income; the remainder of your gain is still entitled to tax-favored treatment afforded long-term capital gain which is taxed as high as 15 percent and as low as 5 percent for those in a 10 percent tax bracket. (2) Net short-term capital gain is treated as investment income in all cases.

Example 9-14: Investor R has $10,000 of investment interest expenses. He also has $20,000 of investment income: $6,000 of ordinary income from bonds and $14,000 of net long-term capital gain from the sale of stock. In order for the investor to deduct the $10,000 investment interest expense in full, he must be able to show on his return $10,000 investment income. R will not be able to satisfy this requirement without claiming the Code Sec. 163(d)(4)(B) election. He can either: (1) forego $4,000 of his interest deduction—the portion of interest in excess of his $6,000 earned from bonds that is noncapital gain investment income; or (2) make an election under Code Sec. 163(d)(4)(B) to pay tax on $4,000 of the net long-term capital gain at ordinary income rates and then deduct the $10,000 interest expense in full. This election will not affect the tax treatment of the remaining $10,000 of net long-term capital gain which will continue to qualify for taxation at favorable capital gain tax rates.

The election to reclassify long-term capital gain as investment income will reduce tax in the election year because of the ability to claim the interest expense deduction as illustrated in the following example.

Example 9-15: A married couple filing a joint return, had a net long-term capital gain of $20,000, investment interest expense of $10,000 (after applying the 2% limit on miscellaneous itemized deductions), and taxable income of $110,000. If they forego the election, their $90,000 in ordinary income would be taxed at 25% and the $20,000 long-term capital gain would be subject to the maximum 15% capital gains rate. Thus, their total federal tax liability would be $25,500 ($22,500 on ordinary income and $3,000 on capital gain). If they elect to reclassify $10,000 of long-term capital gain as investment income, their taxable income remains at $90,000 (the increased itemized deduction of $10,000 offsets the $10,000 of long-term capital gain, which is now subject to ordinary income rates). However, only the remaining $10,000 of long-term capital gain is taxed at 15%. Thus, their total income tax is $24,000 ($22,500 on ordinary income and $1,500 on capital gain). Tax savings is $1,500 resulting from the election to classify $10,000 as investment income.

	Election	*No Election*
Ordinary income	$100,000	$90,000
Investment interest expense	$10,000	$0
Tax due	22,500	22,500
Long-term capital gain	10,000	20,000
Additional tax on capital gain	1,500	3,000
Total tax liability	$24,000	$25,500

.05 *Investment Expenses* Defined

Investment expenses are costs directly related to the production of investment income (other than interest expense). Investment expenses include depreciation, depletion, attorney fees and accounting fees [Code Sec. 163(d)(4)(C)]. Keep in mind that investment expenses include all income-producing expenses relating to the investment property that are allowable deductions after applying the 2 percent limit that applies to miscellaneous itemized deductions [¶9140]. In figuring the amount over the 2 percent limit, expenses that are not investment expenses are disallowed before any investment expenses are disallowed.

Example 9-16: Alice Bard's income this year includes $3,000 in dividends (not qualified dividend income) and a net capital gain of $9,000 on the sale of investment property. Alice's investment expenses (other than interest), which were directly connected with the production of this income, amounted to $980 after taking into account the 2 percent limit on miscellaneous itemized deductions. Alice also incurred $12,500 of investment interest expense (after taking into account the 2 percent limit on miscellaneous itemized deductions). She chooses to include all of her net capital gain in investment income. Her total investment income is $12,000 ($3,000 dividends + $9,000 net capital gain). She figures her net investment income and the limit on the amount of her investment interest expense deduction for as follows:

Total investment income	$12,000
Minus investment expenses (other than interest)	980
Net investment income	$11,020
Deductible investment interest expense	$11,020

Alice's investment interest expense deduction is limited to $11,020, the amount of her net investment income. Her disallowed investment interest expense in the amount of $1,480 ($12,500 – $11,020) is carried forward to next year.

.06 Carryforward Allowed

Investment interest that is not currently deductible is carried forward [Code Sec. 163(d)(2)]. Five different courts have allowed taxpayers to deduct carryover investment interest in later years even if it exceeded taxable income in the year it was paid or incurred.[32] The IRS announced that it will follow these decisions and allow investors to deduct carryover interest paid on loans carrying investment property to a succeeding tax year even though it exceeds taxable income in the year paid or incurred.[33] As a

[32] *J.L. Allbritton*, CA-5, 94-2 USTC ¶50,550, 37 F3d 183; *J.J. Flood*, CA-9, 94-2 USTC ¶50,454, 33 F3d 1174; *J.G. Sharp*, CA-FC, 94-1 USTC ¶50,001, 14 F3d 583, *aff'd*, CA-FC, 94-1 USTC ¶50,203, 20 F3d 1153; *A. Beyer*, CA-4, 90-2 USTC ¶50,536, 916 F2d 153; *R.W. Lenz*, 101 TC 260, Dec. 49,315 (1993). The courts in these cases allowed taxpayers to deduct carryover investment interest in later years even if it exceeded taxable income in those years.

[33] Rev. Rul. 95-16, 1995-1 CB 9 (revoking Rev. Rul. 86-70, 1986-1 CB 83).

result, your ability to deduct investment interest carryovers will not be limited by your taxable income in the year the interest was paid or incurred.

.07 Rules for Making the Election

The election to pay tax on net capital gain and qualified dividend income as though it were investment income and therefore taxed at rates imposed on ordinary income must be made by the due date (including extensions) of the income tax return for the tax year in which the capital gain is recognized or the qualified dividend income is received. The elections must be made on Form 4952, *Investment Interest Expense Deduction,* and may only be revoked with IRS consent. However, you do not have to complete Form 4952 or attach it to your return if all of the following apply:

- Your investment interest is not more than your investment income from interest and ordinary dividends minus any qualified dividends.
- You do not have any other deductible investment expenses.
- You have no carryover of investment interest expense from last year.

Good news: If you meet all of these tests, you can deduct all of your investment interest without limitation.

¶9025 NONDEDUCTIBLE INTEREST

There are special provisions that disallow or limit your allowable interest deduction. These disallowances serve to eliminate unintended double tax benefits and to prevent abuses. As noted earlier, personal interest is no longer deductible.

.01 Interest Related to Tax-Exempt Income

You cannot deduct interest charges on indebtedness to purchase or "carry" tax-exempt investments [Code Sec. 265(a)(2); Reg. §1.265-2(a)]. This means that interest on debt incurred to purchase municipal bonds, tax-exempt securities, Panama Canal loan 3 percent bonds, tax-free United States obligations, and tax-exempt zero-coupon bonds will not be deductible [Reg. §1.265-2(a)]. In addition, you cannot deduct interest on money you borrow to buy tax-exempt securities or shares in a regulated investment company (mutual fund) that distributes only dividends that are exempt from interest. The IRS has broadly interpreted the meaning of carrying tax-exempt obligations. In their view, loans can be treated as carrying tax-exempts even where there is no direct link between the loan and the obligation.[34]

Reason for rule: If you received tax-exempt income and were entitled to deduct interest paid to carry the tax-exempt securities you would receive a prohibited double tax benefit.

[34] Rev. Proc. 72-18, 1972 CB 740, as modified by Rev. Proc. 87-53 1987-2 CB 669.

Example 9-17: Mr. Jones held taxable and tax-free securities in separate brokerage accounts. He financed some of the taxable securities with a margin account. Jones loses his deduction even though the loan proceeds went directly to purchase taxable securities. Reason: Jones chose to incur debt instead of liquidating his investment in the tax-free obligations. As a result, the loan helped Jones carry tax-exempt investments.

Example 9-18: Ms. Hall owns municipal bonds. She borrows money for her business expansion. Hall's interest is deductible if she can demonstrate that business reasons, unrelated to owning tax-exempt bonds, dominated the transaction.

The IRS has said that you cannot deduct interest if you could have foreseen, at the time you purchased the tax-exempts, that a business loan would be needed in the future to meet business demands.[35] On the other hand, it allowed the deduction where money that was borrowed for working capital needs was temporarily invested in tax-exempt securities.[36]

Example 9-19: ABC Corp. issues long-term bonds to finance new plant construction. The construction will take two years. The proceeds from the bond sale, in excess of immediate cash needs, are invested in short-term tax-exempt securities. ABC Corp. is entitled to an interest expense deduction.

Suppose only a portion of the loan proceeds is attributable to uses for which the interest deduction is disallowed. In that case, the interest is allocated on a proportionate basis—and the interest deduction is disallowed accordingly.

Housing Allowance

Members of the clergy or Armed Forces who receive tax-free housing allowances are still entitled to deduct mortgage interest and property taxes on the property [Code Sec. 265(a)(6)]. For further discussion of the parsonage exclusion, see ¶ 4045.

.02 Loan to Buy or Carry Single Premium Insurance Contract

You cannot deduct interest on a debt to finance a single premium life insurance or endowment contract, or a single premium annuity contract. This includes a contract on which (1) you pay substantially all the premiums within four years from the purchase date or (2) you deposit an amount with the insurer for paying a substantial number of future premiums [Code Sec. 264; Reg. § 1.264-2].

.03 Loan to Buy or Carry Insurance

You also cannot claim interest deductions when you systematically borrow from the insurance policy's cash value in order to pay the premiums.

---

[35] LTR 8624017 (Mar. 10, 1986).

[36] LTR 8632037 (May 13, 1986).

Exceptions

The deduction is allowed if:

- The annual interest is $100 or less;
- You incur the loan due to unforeseen financial difficulties;
- The loan is for business purposes; or
- You pay no part of four of the first seven annual premiums with funds borrowed under the plan [Code Sec. 264].

You can take interest deductions until four of the first seven premiums are paid by debt (i.e., borrowing of the policy's cash value). The deductions will then be disallowed for the earlier years, if open [Reg. § 1.264-4(b)].

Applying Loan Proceeds

You first apply borrowed funds used to pay more than one annual premium payment to the premium for the current policy year. You then apply the remaining loan amount to premiums for previous policy years (beginning with the most recent year). However, the loan is not applied to any previous year when you already have borrowed for the premium payment. When the borrowed amounts exceed the premiums for the current and prior years and you have already paid your current premium (i.e., in advance of the due date), the borrowing is debt used to carry the contract. The excess loan amount is applied to succeeding premium years (beginning with the next year). This rule does not apply to single premium contracts since they are paid for up-front [Reg. § 1.264-4(d)(1)(ii)].

.04 Loans to Key Employees

Company owners and certain other employees cannot deduct interest paid on loans borrowed from company retirement plans [Ch. 3].

.05 Miscellaneous Disallowances

Special rules deny or limit an interest deduction for certain: (1) carrying charges chargeable to a capital account; (2) corporate acquisition indebtedness [Code Sec. 279]; (3) related party transactions (deduction postponed) [Ch. 18]; (4) debt incurred to carry market discount bonds (deduction limited) [Ch. 2]; and (5) interest attributable to deferred payment agreements [Ch. 2].

.06 Other Nondeductible Interest Expenses

The following items are not deductible as interest: fines and penalties for violations of law regardless of their nature; appraisal fees, notary fees, preparation costs for the mortgage note or deed of trust, service charges; credit investigation fees; FHA mortgage premiums and VA funding fees; and interest paid to purchase tax-exempt securities.

TAXES

¶9030 DEDUCTIBLE TAXES IN GENERAL

A tax is imposed by an authorized government body to raise revenue. Certain state, local and foreign taxes are deductible if you itemize your deductions. To be deductible, the tax must be specifically named as deductible in the tax law, imposed on you, and paid during the tax year.

.01 Where to Report the Deduction

You report most tax payments on Schedule A, Form 1040. Taxes attributable to property producing rent or royalty, are deducted on Schedule E. State nonresident income taxes paid on net royalty income are not deductible on Schedule E. These taxes may only be claimed below-the-line as itemized deductions subject to the Section 68 limitation on itemized deductions.[37]

> **NOTE:** High-income taxpayers may lose part of their itemized deductions, including taxes.

.02 State and Local Income Taxes

State and local income taxes you pay during the tax year are deductible. These include amounts withheld from paychecks, estimated taxes and any funds you paid when you filed your tax return [Code Sec. 164(a)(3); Reg. § 1.164-1]. Purchasers of transferable state tax credits will also be allowed a state tax deduction for state income taxes paid with the purchased credits.[38]

State and local income taxes are the taxes imposed by each of the 50 states, the District of Columbia, U.S. possessions, or any of their political subdivisions (e.g., a school district or city) [Code Sec. 164(b)(2); Reg. § 1.164-3(a)].

In addition, mandatory contributions you made to state disability benefit funds that provide against loss of wages are deductible. Currently several states have such funds.

> **NOTE:** Employee contributions to private or voluntary disability plans are not deductible. In addition, you cannot deduct state and local income taxes you pay on income that is exempt from federal income tax, unless the exempt income is interest income. For example, you cannot deduct the part of a state's income tax on a cost-of-living allowance that is exempt from federal income tax.

.03 State and Local General Sales Taxes

Effective through December 31, 2013, individuals have the option to elect to claim an itemized deduction for state and local general sales taxes in lieu of claiming a deduction for state and local income taxes [Code Sec. 164(b)(5)(I)]. A taxpayer may claim a deduction for state and local general sales taxes in the amount of either:

- The actual amount of general state and local sales taxes paid or accrued during the tax year; or

---

[37] *C.E. Strange*, CA-9, 2001-2 USTC ¶ 50,753, 270 F3d 786.

[38] LTR 200348002 (Aug. 28, 2003).

- The amount prescribed in IRS tables taking into account the taxpayer's state of residence, filing status, adjusted gross income, number of dependents, and the rates of state and local general sales taxes, as well as any general sales taxes paid by the taxpayer on the purchase of a motor vehicle, boat, or other items specified by the IRS.

Taxpayers should retain their sales receipts in order to substantiate the amount of taxes paid during the year. The term "general sales tax" includes any tax imposed at one rate on the retail sales of a broad range of classes of items [Code Sec. 164(b)(5)(B)]. In the case of food, clothing, medical supplies and motor vehicles, if the applicable sales tax rate for some or all items is lower than the general sales tax rate, it is not a factor in determining whether the tax is imposed at one rate, and if the tax does not apply to some or all items, the taxes are still considered a "general sales tax" for the broad range of classes of items [Code Sec. 164(b)(5)(C)]. If the sales tax rate for motor vehicles exceeds the general sales tax rate, only the amount of the general sales tax rate is allowed as a deduction. Any excess motor vehicle sales taxes are disregarded [Code Sec. 164(b)(5)(F)].

.04 Foreign Income Taxes

Taxpayers may claim either a credit or a deduction for income taxes that are imposed by a foreign country or a U.S. possession [Code Sec. 164(b)(3); Reg. § 1.164-3(d)]. However, they cannot claim a deduction or credit for foreign income taxes paid on income that is exempt from U.S. tax under the foreign earned income exclusion or the foreign housing exclusion. [For further discussion of foreign tax credit, see Ch. 28].

.05 Personal Property Taxes

Taxpayers can deduct personal property taxes if the tax is based on the value of the personal property. They cannot deduct a tax that is based on criteria other than value (for example, the weight of a car). If a tax is based on both value and another measure, they can deduct the portion of the tax calculated as to value; they cannot deduct the remainder. In addition, the tax must be assessed on a yearly basis. However, it may be collected more or less often [Code Sec. 164(b)(1); Reg. § 1.164-3(c)].

Example 9-20: A state charges a yearly motor vehicle registration tax of 1 percent of value of the car plus 50 cents per hundred weight. Mr. Taylor, a resident of State XYZ, paid $300 personal property tax based on the value of his car ($30,000), and $10 based on the 2,000 pound weight of the car. Mr. Taylor may deduct the $300 as personal property tax, since it is based on value. However, he may not deduct the $10 paid on the weight of the vehicle.

.06 Real Estate Taxes

Real estate taxes are taxes imposed on a taxpayer's interests held in real property [Reg. § 1.164-3(b)]. Some of the characteristics of a tax imposed on real property or on an interest in real property are: (1) the tax is generally imposed or triggered by the ownership of real property and not the exercise of one or more of the incidents of property ownership, such as use or disposition, (2) the tax is measured by the value of real property, and (3) liability for the tax is not solely personal.[39]

Local, state, and foreign real estate taxes are deductible as an itemized deduction if the taxes are based on the assessed value of the taxpayer's property and are charged uniformly against all property under the jurisdiction of the taxing authority. The taxpayer cannot deduct taxes charged for local benefits and improvements that increase the value of the property. For example, assessments for sidewalks and other improvements directly traceable to the particular piece of property do not qualify as deductible real property taxes. [Reg. § § 1.164-3(b), 1.164-4(a)]. In addition, regulatory fees such as fire protection or prevention fees,[40] periodic charges for residential services such as trash removal, water delivery, or lawn care are not deductible as a real estate tax.

.07 Tenant-Shareholders in a Cooperative Housing Corporation

A tenant-shareholder can deduct his or her portion of the real estate taxes that the corporation paid or incurred on the property [Code Sec. 216(a); Temp. Reg. § 1.163-10T(q)(3)].[41] However, if the corporation leases the land and building and pays the real estate taxes under the terms of a lease agreement, you are not entitled to a real estate tax deduction. The cooperative should provide you with a statement notifying you of your portion of the tax bill.

Example 9-21: Taxpayer is a 2 percent tenant-shareholder in a cooperative housing corporation. Each year the cooperative pays $100,000 of real estate taxes. Each year the taxpayer can deduct his or her $2,000 share of the corporation's tax bill.

¶9035 TAXES DEDUCTIBLE AS EXPENSES OF PRODUCING INCOME

Taxpayers may still be able to deduct certain state and local taxes not included in those listed in ¶ 9030 if the expenses are trade or business expenses or expenses for the production of income. However, they must capitalize state and local taxes usually deductible as an expense of business or producing income if they incur them in the acquisition or disposition of property. These taxes are treated as part of the property's cost on acquisition or as a reduction in the amount realized on disposition [Code Sec. 164(a)].

---

[39] Rev. Rul. 80-121, 1980-1 CB 43; Rev. Rul. 75-558, 1975-2 CB 67; Rev. Rul. 73-600, 1973-2 CB 47.

[40] CCA 201310029 (Jan. 14, 2013).

[41] Rev. Rul. 73-15, 1973-1 CB 141.

¶9040 WHO CLAIMS THE DEDUCTION

In general, taxes are deductible only by the person upon whom they are imposed [Reg. § 1.164-1(a)]. In some situations, an allocation must be made to determine the identity of that individual.

.01 Apportionment of Taxes When Real Estate is Sold

When there is a change in the ownership of real estate, the deduction for taxes is divided between the buyer and seller according to the number of days each owned the property during the real property tax year. As a general rule, the seller pays the taxes up to the day before the date of sale, and the buyer pays the taxes beginning with the date of the sale [Code Sec. 164(d)(1); Reg. § 1.164-6(a), (b)].

NOTE: Cash-basis taxpayers are deemed to pay their share of taxes when they sell the property, provided the buyers are liable for the tax. Thus, sellers can deduct taxes they do not actually pay because they are considered to have paid their part of the tax at the time of the sale [Code Sec. 164(d)(2); Reg. § 1.164-6(b)].

Example 9-22: Mr. and Mrs. Thurston's real property tax year is the calendar year, with payment due August 1. The tax on their old home, sold May 6 of the same year, was $2,000 and the tax on their new home, bought May 4 of the same year, was $2,500. They are entitled to the following real estate tax deductions: Old property: Property was held for 125 days (January 1 to May 5—the day before the sale). Deduction = $685 (125/365 × $2,000). New property: Property was held for 242 days (May 4 to December 31—including the date of purchase). Deduction = $1,658 (242/365 × $2,500). Total real estate tax deduction: $685 + $1,658 = $2,343.

NOTE: The attorney or other person handling the closing must report on Form 1099-S the portion of property taxes for the year that is allocated to the buyer [Code Sec. 6045(e)]. See also Ch. 26.

.02 Adjustment of Amount Realized by Seller and Basis to Buyer

When the tax deduction is divided between buyer and seller, regardless of who pays the tax, adjustments may have to be made to the amount realized by the seller and the cost basis to the buyer.

If Buyer Pays the Tax

The tax treated as imposed on the buyer is not considered part of cost [Code Sec. 1012; Reg. § 1.1012-1(b)]. But the part of the tax paid by the buyer and treated as imposed on the seller is considered part of the amount realized by the seller and is an additional cost of the property to the buyer [Code Sec. 1001(b)(2); Reg. § 1.1001-1(b)].

Example 9-23: On April 4, Mr. Seller sells Mr. Buyer real property. The price is $100,000. Annual property taxes of $3,650 had become a lien on the property for that calendar year. The tax, however, is not due until year-end. Buyer pays the entire tax when it is due. Seller can deduct $900 (90/365 × $3,650) and Buyer, $2,750 (275/365 × $3,650) for taxes. The amount realized by Seller and the purchase price of Buyer is $100,900 ($100,000 + $900).

If Seller Pays the Tax

The tax treated as imposed on the seller is not considered part of the amount realized. However, the part of the tax paid by the seller and treated as imposed on the buyer reduces both the amount realized by the seller and the basis of the property to the buyer.

> **Example 9-24:** Assume the same facts as in Example 9-23 except that the tax was due on January 15 before the sale occurred and Seller paid the tax when it was due. The tax deduction for Seller is $900, and the amount realized by Seller (and the cost to Buyer) is $97,250 ($100,000 less $2,750).

However, if the buyer reimburses the seller for the taxes paid by the seller but deductible by the buyer, the amount realized by the seller and the cost to the buyer is the unadjusted sale price [Code Sec. 1001(b)(1); Reg. § 1.1001-1(b)].

> **Example 9-25:** Assume in Example 9-24 Buyer reimburses Seller for $2,750, representing the portion of the tax paid by Seller and deductible by Buyer. Seller still deducts $900 and Buyer, $2,750 for taxes. However, the amount realized by Seller and the cost to Buyer is $100,000.

There is one exception to this rule. If the seller paid the tax before the year of the sale and elected to capitalize it, then he must increase the amount realized by the reimbursement [Reg. § 1.1001-1(b)].

¶9045 NONDEDUCTIBLE TAXES

The following taxes are not deductible as itemized deductions [Code Sec. 275]:

- Federal income taxes, including amounts withheld from wages (although a self-employed individual may deduct one-half of the self-employment taxes imposed for the year under Code Sec. 164(f);
- Social Security and railroad retirement taxes imposed on employees;
- Federal war profits and excess profits taxes;
- Estate, inheritance, succession, and gift taxes;
- Taxes on real property that must be treated as imposed on another taxpayer because of apportionment between buyer and seller [Code Sec. 164(d)];
- Excise taxes on private foundations, public charities, pension plans, real estate investment trusts, and greenmail payments, and
- Excise taxes imposed by Code Sec. 4985 on the stock compensation of certain insiders of expatriated corporations;
- Income, war profits, and excess profits taxes imposed by a foreign country or U.S. possession if the taxpayer chooses to take a foreign tax credit for such taxes [Code Sec. 275(a)(4)].

CHARITABLE CONTRIBUTIONS

¶9050 CHARITABLE CONTRIBUTIONS IN GENERAL

A deduction is available for any "charitable contribution" made by the taxpayer [Code Sec. 170(a)]. A "charitable contribution" is defined as "a contribution or gift to or for the use of" a charitable organization [Code Sec. 170(c)]. A typical charitable contribution is donating money or property directly to a charitable organization.

A second type of charitable contribution is placing money or property in trust for a charitable organization. Such a transfer is a contribution "for the use of" a charitable organization.

A third type of charitable contribution occurs when a taxpayer performing services for a charitable organization incurs unreimbursed expenses. As Reg. § 1.170A–1(g) states: "[n]o deduction is allowable under Code Sec. 170 for a contribution of services. However, unreimbursed expenditures made incident to the rendition of services to an organization contributions to which are deductible may constitute a deductible contribution." In Reg. § 1.170A-1(g) the IRS lists the following specific examples of expenses that will be deductible: (1) the cost of a uniform without general utility which must be worn when performing donated services; (2) out-of-pocket transportation expenses necessarily incurred in performing donated services; and (3) reasonable expenditures for meals and lodging necessarily incurred while away from home in the course of performing donated services. For the definition of the phrase "while away from home" see ¶ 10,001.

In *Van Dusen*,[42] the Tax Court concluded that a taxpayer could deduct out-of-pocket expenses incurred with respect to the care of wild cats in her residence on behalf of a charity that neutered and spayed them, and then released them back into the wild. Although the taxpayer did not contribute money or property directly to the charity, the court held that the taxpayer's expenses were deductible as unreimbursed expenditures incident to the rendition of services to a charity under Reg. § 1.170A-1(g) because her services were directed by the charitable organization.

> ▶**PLANNING POINTER:** The Tax Court's decision in *Van Dusen* is a boon for taxpayers who affiliate themselves with a charitable organization or religious group and incur unreimbursed expenses that further the organization's mission or purpose. The case is particularly helpful to taxpayers who use their homes to sponsor charitable fundraisers and other events furthering their objectives. According to *Van Dusen*, which is appealable to the Court of the Appeals for the Ninth Circuit, now those taxpayers can deduct those unreimbursed expenses if they have meticulous records of expenses and a contemporaneous written acknowledgment from the charitable organization acknowledging the gift.

---

[42] *J.E. Van Dusen*, 136 TC 515, Dec. 58,642 (2011).

.01 Qualified Organizations

You may deduct a contribution to an organization only if the organization meets the following qualifications and, in some cases, if the gift is used for a stated purpose [Code Sec. 170(c)]:

- *Community chest, corporation, trust fund, or foundation.* These organizations must be created under federal or state laws or laws of U.S. possessions and operated exclusively for religious, charitable, scientific, literary or educational purposes, or to prevent cruelty to children or animals;
- *Veterans' organizations.* A post, group, or a trust or foundation for war or "non-war" veterans' organizations must be organized in the U.S. or its possessions [Code Sec. 501(c)(19)];
- *Fraternal organizations.* Only contributions used for the same religious, charitable, etc., purposes as community chests or funds (above) qualify as deductible contributions. The society, order or association must be a domestic organization operating under the lodge system;
- *Cemetery organizations.* This must be company owned and operated solely for the benefit of its members or a nonprofit corporation chartered solely for burial purposes and no other business; and
- *Governmental units.* Only contributions made exclusively for a public purpose (i.e., not to influence legislation and not campaign contributions) may be deducted. They may be made to a state, U.S. possession, or any political subdivision, of the United States or District of Columbia.

  NOTE: You can deduct donations you make to foster national or international amateur sport competition, whether or not the organization furnished athletic facilities or equipment. An organization would generally lose its exemption for trying to influence legislation or by taking part in getting involved in a political campaign for any candidate [Code Secs. 170(a), (c), 501(h), (j); Reg. § 1.170A-1(h)]. But special elective rules permit a limited amount of lobbying activities [Ch. 23].

The following organizations are recognized as qualified charitable organizations [Reg. § 1.70A-9]:

- Churches and synagogues;
- Salvation Army;
- Red Cross;
- CARE;
- Goodwill Industries;
- United Way; Girl Scouts of America and Boy Scouts of America;
- Boys Club of America;
- American Heart Association;
- Juvenile Diabetes Association;
- Cancer associations;
- Veterans' organizations; and Public parks.

To be certain of the deductibility of a contribution, contact the organization directly to determine whether it is qualified. To determine whether an organization is a qualifying charity, taxpayers should consult IRS Publication 78, *Cumulative List of Organizations Described in Section 170(c) of the Internal Revenue Code of 1986*. Taxpayers should keep in mind, however, that the publication does not list all qualifying organizations.

No Charitable Deduction for Contributions to Foreign Church

In *Anonymous*,[43] taxpayers could not claim charitable deductions for amounts sent to the Catholic Church of a foreign country and airfare expenses incurred while rendering services to Catholic churches in the foreign country. The deduction was denied because the wire transfer was not made to or for the use of an organization created or organized in the United States or under the laws of the United States.

Nondeductible Contributions

You cannot deduct contributions to communist organizations, foreign organizations, social clubs, civic leagues and political parties or candidates. Funds paid directly to your children to support their work as unpaid, full-time missionaries for a qualified church are nondeductible.[44] Also, donations of time, personal services and blood, as well as gifts given directly to needy individuals who do not qualify as Code Sec. 501(c)(3) organizations, do not qualify as deductible charitable contributions.

No Charitable Deduction for Transfer to Donor Advised Fund

In *S.G. Viralam*,[45] the Tax Court concluded that an individual who transferred appreciated stock to a donor advised fund failed to make a charitable contribution, and therefore could not deduct the contribution or avoid paying tax on the subsequent sale of the stock by the foundation. The taxpayer did not relinquish dominion and control over the assets because he made the transfer with the expectation that the foundation would make educational loans to his children. He also understood that the foundation would allow members of his family to earn compensation by performing charitable services for the foundation.

.02 Where to Deduct

You report charitable contributions on Schedule A, Form 1040 [¶ 9001].

.03 Charitable Contribution Deduction Denied for Transfers Associated with Split-Dollar Insurance Arrangements

Code Sec. 170(f)(10) provides that no charitable contribution deduction will be allowed for a transfer to or for the benefit of a charitable organization if in connection with the transfer:

- The organization directly or indirectly pays, or has previously paid, any premium on any "personal benefit contract" with respect to the transferor; or
- There is an understanding or expectation that any person will directly or indirectly pay any premium on any "personal benefit contract" with respect to the transferor. It is intended that an organization be considered as indirectly paying premiums if, for example, another person pays premiums on its behalf.

---

[43] *Anonymous*, 99 TCM 1359, Dec. 58,195(M), TC Memo. 2010-87.

[44] *H. Davis*, SCt, 90-1 USTC ¶ 50,270, 495 US 472.

[45] *S.G. Viralam*, 136 TC 151, Dec. 58,547 (2011).

A *personal benefit contract* is a life insurance annuity, or endowment contract, if any direct or indirect beneficiary under the contract is the transferor, any member of the transferor's family, or any other person (other than a Code Sec. 170(c) organization) designated by the transferor [Code Sec. 170(f)(10)(B)]. For example, such a beneficiary would include a trust having a direct or indirect beneficiary who is the transferor or any member of the transferor's family, and would include an entity that is controlled by the transferor or any member of the transferor's family.

Deductions for charitable contributions associated with a charitable split-dollar insurance arrangement will be denied if goods or services (such as death benefits under a life insurance policy) are provided in exchange for the contributions.[46]

In addition, an excise tax is imposed on a charitable organization that engages in a newly-prohibited type of transaction [Code Sec. 170(f)(10)(F)]. The excise tax will be equal to the amount of the premiums paid by the organization on any life insurance, annuity, or endowment contract, if the premiums are paid in connection with a transfer for which a deduction is not allowable under the deduction denial rule of Code Sec. 170(f)(10).

The charitable organization must annually report the following:

- The amount of premiums paid during the year;
- The fact that it is subject to the excise tax imposed under the provision; and
- The name and taxpayer identification number of each beneficiary under the life insurance, annuity or endowment contract to which the premiums relate.

¶9051 CASH CONTRIBUTIONS

.01 Substantiation Required for Cash, Check, or Other Monetary Charitable Contributions

No charitable deduction is allowed for any contribution of a cash, check, or other monetary gift unless the donor maintains as a record of such contribution a bank record or a written communication from the donee showing the name of the donee organization, the date of the contribution, and the amount of the contribution [Code Sec. 170(f)(17)]; Prop. Reg. §1.170A-15(a)(1)]. Where a bank statement does not include the name of the donee, a monthly bank statement and a photocopy or image obtained from the bank of the front of the check indicating the name of the donee is satisfactory.

The term *monetary gift* includes a transfer of a gift card redeemable for cash, and a payment made by credit card, electronic fund transfer, an online payment service, or payroll deduction. The term *bank record* includes a statement from a financial institution, an electronic fund transfer receipt, a canceled check, a scanned image of both sides of a canceled check obtained from a bank website, or a credit card statement. The term *written communication* includes electronic mail correspondence [Prop. Reg. §1.170A-15(b)].

---

[46] *C.H. Addis*, 118 TC 528, Dec. 54,774 (2002), *aff'd*, CA-9, 2004-2 USTC ¶50,291, 374 F3d 881, *cert. denied*, 125 SCt 1334.

Deadline for Receipt of Substantiation

The substantiation must be received by the donor on or before the earlier of:

1. The date the donor files the original return for the tax year in which the contribution was made, or
2. The due date (including extensions) for filing the donor's original return for that year [Prop. Reg. § 1.170A-15(c)].

.02 Substantiation Required for Contributions of $250 or More

No charitable deduction is allowed for any (cash or noncash) contribution of $250 or more unless the donor substantiates the contribution with a *contemporaneous written acknowledgment* which must include the following information:

1. The amount of cash and a description (but not value) of any property other than cash contributed.
2. Whether the donee organization provided any goods or services in consideration, in whole or in part, for any property received.[47]
3. A description and good faith estimate of the value of any goods or services received or, if such goods or services consist solely of intangible religious benefits, a statement to that effect. The term *intangible religious benefit* means any intangible religious benefit which is provided by an organization organized exclusively for religious purposes and which generally is not sold in a commercial transaction outside the donative context [Code Sec. 170(f)(8); Reg. § 1.170A-13(f); Prop. Reg. § 1.170A-15(a)(2)].

An acknowledgment is contemporaneous if the taxpayer obtains the acknowledgment on or before the earlier of:

1. The date on which the taxpayer files a return for the tax year in which the contribution was made, or
2. The due date (including extensions) for filing such return.

In *D.P. Durden*,[48] taxpayers were denied deductions for charitable contributions of more than $250 made to their church because they failed to comply with strict substantiation requirements. The church's contemporaneous, written acknowledgment of the contributions did not indicate whether it provided any goods or services in consideration for the contributions. The acknowledgment was not in substantial compliance with the substantiation requirement and was not sufficient to establish that the couple did not receive any goods or services in consideration of their contributions because the express terms of Code Sec. 170(f)(8)(B) require an affirmative statement. A second acknowledgment that did indicate that no goods or services were provided in consideration for the contributions was not considered because it was not contemporaneous.

---

[47] *Boone Operations Co.*, 105 TCM 1610, Dec. 59,508(M), TC Memo. 2013-101.

[48] *D.P. Durden*, 103 TCM 1762, Dec. 59,061(M), TC Memo. 2012-140; *RP Golf, LLC*, 104 TCM 413, Dec. 59,215(M), TC Memo. 2012-282.

.03 Contributions Made by Payroll Deduction

In the case of a charitable contribution made by payroll deduction, a donor is treated as meeting the substantiation requirements if the donor obtains:

1. A pay stub, Form W-2, *Wage and Tax Statement,* or other employer-furnished document that sets forth the amount withheld during the tax year for payment to a donee; and
2. A pledge card or other document prepared by or at the direction of the donee that shows the name of the donee [Prop. Reg. § 1.170A(d)(2)].

.04 Charitable Contributions Made by Partnership or S Corporation

If a partnership or an S corporation makes a charitable contribution, the partnership or S corporation is treated as the donor and therefore must comply with the substantiation requirements of Code Sec. 170(f)(17) and Prop. Reg. § 1.170A-15(a).

.05 Transfers to Certain Trusts

The substantiation requirements do not apply to a transfer of cash, check, or other monetary gift to a charitable remainder annuity trust or a charitable remainder unitrust. The substantiation requirements do apply, however, to a transfer to a pooled income fund [Prop. Reg. § 1.170A-15(g)].

¶9052 NONCASH CONTRIBUTIONS

When taxpayers make charitable contributions of property other than cash (e.g., stocks, bonds, paintings, or furniture) the amount of the deduction generally equals the fair market value of the contributed property on the date of the contribution [Reg. § 1.170A-1(c)(1)]. The fair market value of the contributed property is the price that a willing buyer and seller would set for the property on the open market [Reg. § 1.170A-1(c)(2)].

.01 Substantiation and Reporting Requirements for Noncash Contributions

Noncash Contributions Less Than $250

Individuals, partnerships, and certain corporate donors who claim deductions for noncash contributions of less than $250 are required to obtain a receipt from the donee or keep reliable records. Affected corporations are S corporations, closely held corporations, and C corporations that are personal service corporations [Prop. Reg. § 1.170A-16]. A donor that fails to substantiate a charitable deduction of property will be denied the deduction. The receipt that must be supplied by the donor must show the following information:

1. The name and address of the donee;
2. The date of the contribution;
3. A description of the property in sufficient detail for a person not generally familiar with the type of property to ascertain that the described property is the contributed property; and

4. In the case of securities, the name of the issuer, the type of security, and whether the securities are publicly traded securities [Prop. Reg. § 1.170A-16(a)].

If the donor is a partnership or S corporation, the reporting requirements are applied at the entity level, but the deduction is denied at the partnership or shareholder level.

Noncash Contributions Over $250 But Less Than $500

No charitable deduction is allowed for any (cash or noncash) contribution of $250 or more unless the donor substantiates the contribution with a *contemporaneous written acknowledgment* which must include the following information but need not be on any special form (could be a postcard, letter, or computer-generated form):

1. The amount of cash and a description (but not value) of any property other than cash contributed.
2. Whether the donee organization provided any goods or services in consideration, in whole or in part, for any property received [see ¶ 9055].
3. A description and good faith estimate of the value of any goods or services received or, if such goods or services consist solely of intangible religious benefits, a statement to that effect. The term *intangible religious benefit* means any intangible religious benefit which is provided by an organization organized exclusively for religious purposes and which generally is not sold in a commercial transaction outside the donative context [Code Sec. 170(f)(8); Reg. § 1.170A-13(f); Prop. Reg. § 1.170A-15(a)(2)].

The charity is not responsible for valuing the property it receives, but is responsible for valuing the goods and services it provides to the donor. The receipt given by the charity to the donor must specify all goods or services received (or expected to be received) in exchange for the donation in order to provide an accurate value of the contribution. Goods and services that have insubstantial value and certain annual membership benefits are disregarded for reporting purposes and need not required be documented [Reg. § 1.170A-13(f)(8)].

An acknowledgment shall be considered to be contemporaneous if the taxpayer obtains the acknowledgment on or before the earlier of:

1. The date on which the taxpayer files a return for the tax year in which the contribution was made, or
2. The due date (including extensions) for filing such return.

Noncash Contributions Over $500 But Less Than $5,000

Donors who make noncash charitable contributions and claim a deduction over $500 but not more than $5,000 must obtain a *contemporaneous written acknowledgment* and file a completed Form 8283, *Noncash Charitable Contributions,* with the return on which the deduction is first claimed. On Form 8283, the taxpayer will identify the property that was donated to the charity, give the name and address of the charity and explain how the value of the property was determined.

Noncash Contributions Over $5,000

For claimed contributions of more than $5,000, in addition to a *contemporaneous written acknowledgment,* a *qualified appraisal* is generally required, and either Section A or Section B of Form 8283, depending upon the type of property contributed, must be completed and filed with the return on which the deduction is claimed [Code Sec. 170(f)(11)(C); Reg. § 1.170A-13(c)(2)].

Noncash Contributions Over $500,000

Donors who make noncash charitable contributions and claim a deduction of more than $500,000 must attach a copy of the qualified appraisal to the return [Code Sec. 170(f)(11)(D)]. In addition, the substantiation requirements also apply to the return for any carryover year under Code Sec. 170(d).

.02 Reasonable Cause Exception

An exception in Code Sec. 170(f)(11)(A)(ii)(II) excuses the failure to attach a qualified appraisal for noncash contributions over $500,000. To qualify for the exception, the donor must show that the failure to meet these requirements is due to "reasonable cause and not willful neglect."[49] To satisfy the exception, the donor must submit a detailed explanation with his or her return, stating why the failure to comply was due to reasonable cause and not willful neglect, and he or she must have timely obtained a contemporaneous, written acknowledgment and a qualified appraisal, if applicable [Prop. Reg. § 1.170A-13(c)]. Consistent with congressional intent of reducing valuation abuses, the "reasonable cause" exception will most likely be strictly construed.

.03 Qualified Appraisal

A qualified appraisal is required for a charitable contribution of property for which a deduction of more than $5,000 is claimed by an individual, partnership, or corporation [Code Sec. 170(f)(11)(C)]. A taxpayer's charitable deduction will be denied if the taxpayer fails to strictly comply with the requirements for substantiation of charitable deductions under Code Sec. 170(f)(11)(C) and Reg. § 1.170A-13(c). The Tax Court has held that taxpayers' self-appraisals of donated properties were not qualified appraisals for purposes of Reg. § 1.170A-13(c)(2) because they were not completed by a qualified appraiser. In addition, the taxpayers failed to attach a proper appraisal summary to the returns on which the deductions for their contributions were claimed.[50] A qualified appraisal must include the following information:

1. A description of the property in sufficient detail for a person who is not generally familiar with the type of property to ascertain that the property that was appraised is the property that was (or will be) contributed;
2. In the case of tangible property, the physical condition of the property;
3. The date (or expected date) of contribution to the donee;
4. The terms of any agreement or understanding entered into (or expected to be entered into) by or on behalf of the donor or donee that relates to the use, sale, or other disposition of the property contributed, including, for example, the terms of any agreement or understanding that:
    a. Restricts temporarily or permanently a donee's right to use or dispose of the donated property,

---

[49] *J. Crimi*, 105 TCM 1330, Dec. 59,453(M), TC Memo. 2013-51.

[50] *J. Mohamed*, 103 TCM 1814, Dec. 59,074(M), TC Memo. 2012-152.

b. Reserves to, or confers upon, anyone (other than a donee organization or an organization participating with a donee organization in cooperative fund-raising) any right to the income from the contributed property or to the possession of the property, including the right to vote donated securities, to acquire the property by purchase or otherwise, or to designate the person having such income, possession, or right to acquire, or

c. Earmarks donated property for a particular use.

5. The name, address, and the identifying number of the qualified appraiser; and, if the qualified appraiser is acting in his or her capacity as a partner in a partnership, an employee of any person (whether an individual, corporation, or partnership), or an independent contractor engaged by a person other than the donor, the name, address, and taxpayer identification number of the partnership or the person who employs or engages the qualified appraiser;
6. The qualifications of the qualified appraiser who signs the appraisal, including the appraiser's background, experience, education, and membership, if any, in professional appraisal associations;
7. A statement that the appraisal was prepared for income tax purposes;
8. The date (or dates) on which the property was appraised;
9. The appraised fair market value of contribution;
10. The method of valuation used to determine the fair market value, such as the income approach, the market-data approach, and the replacement-cost-less-depreciation approach; and
11. The specific basis for the valuation, such as specific comparable sales transactions or statistical sampling, including a justification for using sampling and an explanation of the sampling procedure employed [Reg. § 1.170A-13(c)(5)].

In addition, the appraisal must to be made no earlier than 60 days before the contribution date. The valuation effective date, which is the date to which the value opinion applies, generally must be the date of the contribution. Where the appraisal is prepared before the contribution date, the valuation effective date must be no earlier than 60 days before and no later than the contribution date [Prop. Reg. § 1.170A-17(a)(4)].

Qualified Appraiser Defined

A *qualified appraiser* is defined in Code Sec. 170(f)(11)(E)(ii) as an individual who: (1) has earned an appraisal designation from a recognized professional appraiser organization, or has otherwise met minimum education and experience requirements; (2) regularly performs appraisals for pay. However, an individual cannot be a qualified appraiser with respect to any specific appraisal unless he or she: (1) demonstrates verifiable education and experience in valuing the property type being appraised; and (2) has not been prohibited from practicing before the IRS at any time during the three-year period ending on the appraisal date [Code Sec. 170(f)(11)(E)(iii)].

An individual is treated as having education and experience in valuing the relevant type of property if the date the individual signs the appraisal, the individual has successfully completed professional or college-level coursework in valuing the relevant type of property and has two or more years of experience in valuing the relevant type of property, or has earned a recognized appraisal designation [Prop. Reg. § 1.170A-17(b)].

Example 9-26: It is not customary for professional antique appraisers to appraise new furniture. Appraiser A has experience in appraising antiques but generally has no experience in appraising new furniture. Appraiser A is asked to appraise new furniture. Appraiser A does not have experience in valuing the relevant type of property [Prop. Reg. § 1.170A-17(b)(3)(ii), Ex. 3].

.04 Contributions of Art Worth More Than $20,000

If you are donating art or antiques worth more than $20,000, you must include with the tax return on which you claim the deduction, both the Form 8283 and the signed appraisal. If you fall into the over-$20,000 contribution category, you should also be familiar with the IRS's Art Advisory Panel. The Panel includes outstanding curators, museum directors, art scholars, art historians, and representatives from the nation's most esteemed auction houses. The Art Advisory Panel exists to review appraisals submitted by taxpayers in order to determine the authenticity and fair market value of works of art in income tax or estate and gift tax audits. If a return is audited and the return reported an item of artwork valued at more than $20,000, the Panel must review the appraisal of the item. This review is mandatory, even if the appraisal of the artwork was not the subject of the audit.

The Panel will review your item in a "blind" matter in order to ensure impartiality. After your item has been discussed and a consensus has been reached regarding its fair market value on the relevant valuation date, the Panel chairperson will prepare a valuation report, which will be sent to the IRS office requesting the Panel's input. You will also receive a copy of that report along with a list of the Panel members. The valuation will be considered conclusive unless you present additional evidence that was unavailable at the time of the original Panel meeting.

Gifts of Art Worth $50,000 or More

You can obtain from the IRS a "Statement of Value" for valuable artwork contributed to a qualified charitable organization. The valuation can also be used for estate and gift tax purposes. For a $2,500 fee, the IRS will tell you *before* you file your income tax return exactly how big your charitable deduction should be. Your request for a Statement of Value must include the following:

- A copy of an appraisal of the item of art;
- A check in the amount of $2,500 for one, two, or three items of art, plus $250 for each additional item of art;
- A completed appraisal summary which is Section B of Form 8283, *Noncash Charitable Contributions;* and
- The location of the District Office that has or will have examination jurisdiction over the return (not the Service Center where the return is filed).

For purposes of the revenue procedure, "art" includes painting, sculpture, watercolors, prints, drawings, ceramics, antique furniture, decorative arts, textiles, carpets, silver, rare manuscripts, historical memorabilia, and other similar objects. You must submit your request for the Statement of Value to the IRS before the filing of the tax return where you first report the contribution of the item. You must include a qualified appraisal of the artwork and the appraisal must be made no earlier than 60 days prior to the date of the contribution of the item. You must attach the Statement of Value you receive from the IRS to a completed Form 8283 and file it with the federal income tax return that first reports your contribution of the works of art.[51]

.05 Contributions of Used Clothing and Household Items

Individuals, partnerships, or corporations may only claim a deduction for contributions of household items and clothing if the items are in "good used condition or better at the time of the contribution" [Code Sec. 170(f)(16)(A); Prop. Reg. § 1.170A-18(a)(1)]. This rule ensures that donated clothing and household items will be "of meaningful use to charitable organizations." However, there is an exception for a contribution of a single item of clothing or a household item for which a donor claims a deduction of more than $500, provided the donor submits a qualified appraisal of the property prepared by a qualified appraiser and a completed Form 8283 (Section B) with the return on which the deduction is claimed [Code Sec. 170(f)(16)(C); Prop. Reg. § 1.170A-18(b)].

"Household items" include furniture, furnishings, electronics, appliances, linens, and other similar items [Code Sec. 170(f)(16)(D); Prop. Reg. § 1.170A-18(c)]. The term does not include food, paintings, antiques, other objects of art, jewelry, gems, or collections [Code Sec. 170(f)(16)(D)(ii)]. In the case of a partnership or S corporation making such contributions, these restrictions apply at the entity level, and the deduction is denied at the partner or shareholder level [Code Sec. 170(f)(16)(E)].

The fair market value of used clothing and household goods (e.g., used furniture) is the price that buyers actually pay in used clothing stores or consignment or thrift shops. Keep in mind that the fair market value of used household clothing and goods such as furniture and appliances is usually far less than the price you paid for them.

> **Example 9-27:** Dawn donated a coat to a thrift store operated by her church. She paid $300 for the coat three years ago. Similar coats in the thrift store sell for $50. The fair market value of the coat is reasonably determined to be $50. Dawn's donation is limited to $50 because the price that buyers of used items actually pay in used clothing stores is viewed as an indication of value.

There is no a fixed formula or methods for finding the value of items of clothing. If the articles are valuable because they are old or unique, support your valuation with photographs, canceled checks, receipts from your purchase of the items, or other evidence. Magazine or newspaper articles and photographs that describe the items and statements by the recipients of the items will be helpful in supporting your deduction. But remember, if you give away more than $500 worth of goods, you will need to fill out Form 8283 and attach it to your tax return. If you are really generous and give away items worth more than $5,000, you must have the donated items appraised in addition to

[51] Rev. Proc. 96-15, 1996-1 CB 627, as modified by Announcement 2001-22, 2001-1 CB 895 (regarding change of address).

completing Form 8283. See IRS Publication 561, *Determining the Value of Donated Property,* for guidelines on determining the fair market value of donated property.

.06 Cars, Boats, and Aircraft

Reporting Requirements Imposed on Charity

If a charity receives a contribution of a qualified vehicle (e.g., car, truck, boat, aircraft, but not inventory property) with a claimed value of more than $500, the charity must provide the donor with a contemporaneous written acknowledgment. The donee organization may use a completed Form 1098-C, *Contributions of Motor Vehicles, Boats and Airplanes,* for the contemporaneous written acknowledgment. The Form 1098-C along with Form 1096, *Annual Summary and Transmittal of U.S. Information Returns,* must be filed with the Internal Revenue Service Center [Code Sec. 170(f)(12)(D)].

Reporting Requirements Imposed on Donor

A taxpayer making a charitable contribution of a qualified vehicle valued at over $500 must obtain from the charity and attach to his or her federal income tax return either a Form 1098-C, *Contributions of Motor Vehicles, Boats, Airplanes,* or a similar contemporaneous written acknowledgment of the contribution [Code Sec. 170(f)(12)(A)].

Contemporaneous Written Acknowledgment

The acknowledgment must identify the donor taxpayer, list the taxpayer's and the vehicle's identification numbers, and include a description and good faith estimate of the value of any goods or services provided by the charity in exchange for the vehicle. If the goods or services consist solely of intangible religious benefits, the acknowledgment must say so. If the charity sells the vehicle without significant intervening use or material improvement, the acknowledgment must also certify that the vehicle was sold in an arm's length transaction between unrelated parties, list the gross proceeds, and state that the deduction may not exceed the gross proceeds. If the charity retains the vehicle for its significant use or makes a material improvement, the acknowledgment must certify the use or improvement, the time frame the charity will use the vehicle, and that the vehicle will not be transferred before the use or improvement is completed. The taxpayer will then be allowed to claim the fair market value of the vehicle as a charitable donation [Code Sec. 170(f)(12)].

Whether a use is a significant intervening use depends on its nature, extent, frequency, and duration. For this purpose, use by the charity includes use of the vehicle to provide transportation on a regular basis for a significant period of time or significant use directly related to instruction in vehicle repair. However, use by the charity does not include use of the vehicle to provide training in general business skills, such as marketing and sales.

Example 9-28: Evan contributes a car to the local Meals on Wheels center. As part of its regularly conducted activities, Meals on Wheels delivers meals to needy individuals. The organization used the car only a few times to deliver meals and then sold it. Because the use is infrequent and incidental, there was no significant intervening use.

Example 9-29: The facts are the same as in the example above, except that Meals on Wheels uses the car to deliver meals every day for one year. Because the use is significant and substantially furthers one of their regularly conducted activities, there is a significant intervening use.

Example 9-30: The facts are the same as in Example 9-29, except that Meals on Wheels does not use the car to deliver meals every day. However, the charity drives the car a total of 10,000 miles over a one-year period while delivering meals. Because this use is significant and substantially furthers a regularly conducted activity, there is a significant intervening use.

Material improvement includes a major repair or improvement that improves the condition of the vehicle in a manner that significantly increases the value. Cleaning, minor repairs, and routine maintenance are not considered material improvements. To be a material improvement, the improvement may not be funded by an additional payment to the charity from the donor of the vehicle. Services that are not considered material improvements include: application of paint or other types of finishes (such as rustproofing or wax); removal of dents and scratches; cleaning or repair of upholstery; and installation of theft deterrent devices.

Sale or Gratuitous Transfer to Needy Individual

If the charity sells the vehicle for a significantly low fair market value (or gratuitously transfers the vehicle) to a needy individual, the taxpayer can claim the donated vehicle's fair market value only if the sale or transfer directly furthers the charity's purpose.[52] However, if a charity sells the vehicle at auction, the IRS will not accept as substantiation an acknowledgment stating that the vehicle is to be transferred to a needy individual at a price that is significantly below fair market value. In that case, the donor taxpayer may claim a deduction greater than $500, but only to the extent that the gross sale proceeds exceed that amount and the donor substantiates the contribution with an acknowledgment listing the gross proceeds.

Determining FMV of Vehicles

A donor claiming a deduction for the FMV of a vehicle must be able to substantiate the FMV. Reg. § 1.170A-1(c)(2) provides that FMV is the price at which the property would change hands between a willing buyer and a willing seller, neither being under any compulsion to buy or sell, and each having reasonable knowledge of relevant facts. A reasonable method of determining the FMV is by reference to an established used vehicle-pricing guide. However, the dealer retail value listed for a particular vehicle in such a guide is not an acceptable measure of the FMV of a similar vehicle. Many factors must be taken into account when you consult a used vehicle-pricing guide to determine FMV. A used vehicle pricing guide establishes FMV only if the guide lists a sales price for a vehicle that is the same make, model, and year, sold in the same area, in the same condition, with the same or substantially similar options or accessories, and with the same or substantially similar warranties or guarantees, as the vehicle in question.

[52] Notice 2005-44, 2005-1 CB 1287; Notice 2006-1, 2006-1 CB 347.

The acceptable measure of the FMV of a vehicle is limited to amounts not in excess of the price listed in a used vehicle-pricing guide for private party sales of similar vehicles. If the deduction is not limited to the gross proceeds from the sale of the vehicle, the donor is required to provide a qualified appraisal as substantiation for any deductions in excess of $5,000.

.07 Gifts of Appreciated Property

If you donate appreciated property (i.e., its fair market value is more than your basis in the property), you generally will receive two benefits: (1) You will receive an income tax deduction based on the full fair market value of the property, and (2) You will avoid tax on the built-up capital gain which would have resulted if you had sold the appreciated property [Code Sec. 170(e)(1); Reg. § 1.170A-4].

Appreciated capital gain property is property that, if sold at fair market value on the contribution date, would yield a long-term capital gain. This includes such collectibles as antique furniture, rare books, rugs, paintings, and sculptures. Your deduction for contributions of appreciated property is limited to 30 percent of your adjusted gross income if the charity is one to which the 50 percent limitation applies (20 percent if the charity is one to which the 30 percent limitation applies). Any excess can be carried over for five years subject to the same percentage limit in future years. You also have the option to elect to use the 50 percent of adjusted gross income ceiling applicable to most other charitable contributions for contributions of appreciated property to a 50-percent limit organization, but this method requires that the contribution be reduced by the amount of gain that would have been long-term gain had the contributed property been sold. This method will be advantageous only if you expect your adjusted gross income to decrease in the near future and if the appreciation in the property is only moderately substantial.

> **Example 9-31:** Ann Able bought an antique clock for $50,000 and it is now worth $115,000. She donates the clock to a museum at a time when her adjusted gross income (AGI) is $100,000. If she chooses to value the clock at its fair market value of $115,000, she can claim a $30,000 deduction in the year of the contribution (30 percent × her AGI of $100,000) and carry over the $85,000 balance to future years subject to the 30 percent limitation in those later years. If instead, she elects the 50 percent option, she can claim a one-time deduction of $50,000 (50 percent of her AGI of $100,000) in the year of the contribution. This may be a smarter move for Able if she knows that she will be retiring next year and will experience a drop in adjusted gross income next year and would not have sufficient income in future years to take advantage of the carryovers.

Ordinary Income Property

The first limitation applies if you contributed appreciated property that would produce ordinary income or short-term capital gain rather than long-term capital gain if you had sold it. Your deduction is limited to the fair market value of the property less the amount of profit that would not be long-term capital gain [Reg. § 1.170A-4(a)(1)]. The following types of property fall into this category: inventory, depreciated property, a work of art created by the donor, and capital assets held for less than one year.

Example 9-32: Mr. Meyer donates, to a qualified charity, shares of stock that he purchased five months ago for $1,000. The stock is worth $1,200 at the time the contribution is made. Meyer's deduction is limited to $1,000. That's the $1,200 fair market value less the $200 that would be short-term capital gain had he sold the shares.

Long-Term Capital Gain Property

In general, you can deduct the fair market value of donations of property that would produce long-term capital gain if you had sold the item instead of donating it. Two requirements must be met in order to claim a deduction for long-term capital gain:

1. A taxpayer must prove he has owned the donated property for more than one year.
2. The donated property must meet the statutory definition of a capital asset as explained in Code Sec. 1221. See ¶ 8010 for discussion of the definition of capital asset.

However, an exception applies to donations (1) of tangible personal property that are put to use unrelated to the purpose or function of the charitable organization, (2) donations to or for the use of a private foundation (other than a private foundation described in Code Sec. 170(b)(1)(E)), or (3) a donation of any patent, copyright (other than a copyright not characterized as a capital asset), trademark, trade name, trade secret, know-how, or software (other than software not acquired in an acquisition involving assets constituting a trade or business). The donor's charitable deduction, in these cases, is limited to his or her basis in the property.

Example 9-33: Mr. Nelson donated to his college a painting worth $22,000 that he bought years ago for $2,000. The college immediately sold the painting at an auction for $22,000. Because the use was unrelated to education, Nelson's deduction is limited to $2,000, his basis.

Example 9-34: Suppose in Example 9-33 Nelson required the college to use the painting in art classes where students could study it. His charitable deduction is $22,000 (assuming it's within the percentage limitation explained at ¶ 9075).

Example 9-35: Suppose in Example 9-33 Nelson gave the painting to a private foundation (other than a private foundation described in Code Sec. 170(b)(1)(E)). His deduction is limited to $2,000, regardless of how the foundation uses it.

▶ **OBSERVATION:** The deduction allowed may be further limited by the percentage of adjusted gross income caps on charitable deductions [¶ 9075].

In *Jones*,[53] the lead defense attorney for Timothy McVeigh in the Oklahoma City bombing trial could not claim a charitable contribution deduction for the donation of discovery material from the trial. The deduction was denied because the

[53] *S. Jones*, CA-10, 2009-1 USTC ¶ 50,316, 560 F3d 1196, *aff'g*, 129 TC 146, Dec. 57,160 (2007).

Tenth Circuit Court of Appeals determined that the discovery material was excluded from the definition of capital asset as a "letter, memorandum or similar property" prepared or produced for the taxpayer thereby limiting the charitable deduction to the taxpayer's basis in the property. Because the taxpayer had no basis in the discovery material, the court held that he was precluded from claiming any income tax deduction for his charitable deduction.

Deduction for Contribution of Appreciated Property

Table 1 summarizes deductions allowed for the various types of donated property described above.

Table 1. Allowable Charitable Deductions for Various Types of Property

Type of property contributed	Type of charity	Amount of deduction
1. Property, if sold, would result in ordinary income only (e.g., inventory and short-term capital assets).	Any qualified organization	Basis
2. Property, if sold, would result in portion of ordinary income (e.g., Sec. 1245 assets)	Any qualified organization	Fair market value less amount recaptured if sold
3. Certain appreciated stock, if held over one year.	Qualified organizations, including private nonoperating foundations	Fair market value
4. Tangible personal property put to unrelated use by donee and, if sold, would result in long-term capital gain (e.g., work of art contributed by donor not creator).	Any qualified organization	Basis
5. Property, if sold, would result in long-term capital gain if 50 percent limit elected [¶9075].	Any qualified organization	Basis
6. Other property, if sold, would result in long-term capital gain and not described in numbers 4 or 5 above.	Any qualified organization	Fair market value

.08 Gifts of Property That Has Declined in Value

When business or investment property has declined in value below the amount that you paid for it, you may not claim a deductible loss when you give the property away to charity. Your deduction is limited to the fair market value of the property. The only way for you to claim both the loss and the charitable deduction is to first sell the property, claim the loss, and then contribute the cash proceeds of the sale of the charity. If, for example, you own stock for which you paid $40,000 four years ago but that has declined in value to $10,000 and donate the stock to charity, you can claim a charitable deduction of only $10,000. If you first sell the stock and then contribute the sale proceeds to charity the result is much different. If you sell the stock for $10,000, you can claim a long-term capital loss of $30,000. If you then contribute the $10,000 to charity, you can also claim a charitable deduction of $10,000.

.09 Bargain Sales to Charity

A *bargain sale* is a sale or exchange of property to a qualified charitable organization for less than its fair market value. The transaction is treated as partly a sale or exchange and partly a charitable contribution. If the transaction qualifies for a charitable contribution deduction, you must allocate the property's basis between the part of the property that was sold and the part contributed. This is necessary to calculate the gain from the sale and the deductible donation [Code Secs. 170(e)(2), 1011(b)].

You calculate your basis and appreciation allocable to the sold and contributed portions of the property as follows:

- Allocation to the part of the property sold. Multiply the item involved (adjusted basis, ordinary gain or long-term capital gain) by this fraction: proceeds from sale divided by the fair market value of the entire property at the time of sale; and
- Allocation to the part of the property contributed. Multiply the basis or gain by the following fraction: fair market value of the entire property at the time of the sale less the proceeds from the bargain sale, divided by the fair market value [Reg. § 1.170A-4(c)].

▶ **OBSERVATION:** Your deduction may be further limited by the percentage-of-adjusted-gross-income caps on charitable deductions [¶ 9075].

Example 9-36: Mr. Dobbs bought stock two years ago for $4,000. He sold it to the United Way this year for $4,000. The stock was worth $10,000 at the time of the bargain sale. Dobbs' deductible contribution is $6,000 ($10,000 FMV less $4,000 sales price). So 60 percent of the stock's FMV is allocated to the donation and 40 percent is allocated to the sale. Dobbs' taxable profit on the sale portion is $2,400—$4,000 sales price less $1,600 basis allocable to the sale ($4,000 total basis × 40 percent allocation to the sale).

.10 Reduction for Certain Interest

A special rule prevents a double deduction—interest expense and charitable donation—if you donate property on which there is an outstanding loan. You must reduce the amount of your charitable deduction by the amount of interest you pay (or will be paying) on the loan that is attributable to the post-contribution period. In addition, if the property is a bond or other debt instrument and you incurred or continued indebtedness to purchase or carry the bond, the value is further reduced by any interest paid (or to be paid) that is attributable to the pre-contribution period [Code Sec. 170(f) (5); Reg. § 1.170A-3].

.11 Contributions of Stock to Private Foundations

As a general rule, if a taxpayer contributes property to or for the use of a private foundation, the taxpayer's charitable deduction is limited to the taxpayer's adjusted basis in the property. However, if the property is of stock of a corporation that is capital gain property and for which (as of the contribution date) market quotations are readily available on an established securities market ("qualified appreciated stock"), the donor is allowed a full fair market value deduction, provided the donor and certain family members contribute no more than 10 percent of the outstanding stock of the corporation [Code Sec. 170(e)(5)].

Contributions of stock have to satisfy the substantiation requirements applied to other contributions of property. Failure to satisfy these substantiation requirements will result in a disallowance of the taxpayer's charitable contribution deduction.[54]

The deduction for "qualified appreciated stock" contributions made to private foundations applies only to the extent that total contributions made to private foundations of the stock in the corporation did not exceed 10 percent of the outstanding stock of that corporation.

A private nonoperating foundation is a nonprofit organization that is funded solely by an individual, family, or corporation and therefore does not engage in public solicitation of funds. Private foundations typically make grants to tax-exempt organizations. The tax laws impose a number of requirements on private foundations including the obligation to distribute at least 5 percent of foundation assets each year to charities [Ch. 23].

> **Example 9-37:** Joe Brilliant, a wealthy philanthropic executive in the 35 percent tax bracket this year, has done extremely well in the stock market in the last two years. Reluctant to sell any stock and pay capital gains tax, he is looking for a big deduction to shelter his income. This year he decided to contribute $500,000 of stock (with a basis of $100,000) to a private foundation. As a result he will claim a $500,000 deduction on his tax return for a tax savings of $175,000 (35 percent × $500,000) and avoid capital gains tax of $15,000 (15 percent × $100,000). His total tax savings was $190,000.

.12 Contributions of Intellectual Property

If a taxpayer contributes qualified intellectual property including a patent or other intellectual property (other than certain copyrights or inventory) to a charity, the taxpayer's initial charitable deduction is limited to the lesser of the taxpayer's basis in the contributed property or the fair market value of the property [Code Sec. 170(e)(1)(B)]. This limitation applies to patents, certain copyrights, trademarks, trade names, trade secrets, know-how, certain software, and similar property [Code Sec. 170(e)(1)(B)(iii)].

The donor may also deduct certain additional amounts in the year of contribution or in subsequent tax years based on a specified percentage of the qualified donee income received or accrued by the charity with respect to the contributed property [Code Sec. 170(m)]. For this purpose, *qualified donee income* includes net income received or accrued by the donee that is allocable to the intellectual property itself (as opposed to the activity in which the intellectual property is used) [Code Sec. 170(m)(3)].

The amount of any additional charitable deduction is calculated as a sliding-scale percentage of qualified donee income received by the charity that is allocable to the contributed property as shown in Table 2.

---

[54] *J.C. Todd,* 118 TC 334, Dec. 54,721 (2002).

Table 2. Deduction for Donee Income from Contributed Property

Tax Year of Donor Ending On or After Date of Contribution	Deduction Permitted
1st year	100 percent of qualified donee income
2nd year	100 percent of qualified donee income
3rd year	90 percent of qualified donee income
4th year	80 percent of qualified donee income
5th year	70 percent of qualified donee income
6th year	60 percent of qualified donee income
7th year	50 percent of qualified donee income
8th year	40 percent of qualified donee income
9th year	30 percent of qualified donee income
10th year	20 percent of qualified donee income
11th year	10 percent of qualified donee income
12th year	10 percent of qualified donee income
Tax years thereafter	No deduction permitted

An additional charitable deduction is allowed only to the extent that the aggregate of the amounts that are calculated pursuant to the sliding-scale exceed the amount of the deduction claimed upon the contribution of the patent or intellectual property. No charitable deduction is permitted for any revenues or income received or accrued by the charity after the expiration of the legal life of the patent or intellectual property, or after the tenth anniversary of the date the contribution was made by the donor.

Notification Requirements

The taxpayer is required to inform the donee at the time of the contribution that the taxpayer intends to treat the contribution as a contribution subject to the additional charitable deduction provisions of Code Sec. 170(m). In addition, the taxpayer must obtain written substantiation from the donee of the amount of any qualified donee income properly allocable to the contributed property during the year. A donor will satisfy the notification requirement if the donor delivers or mails to the donee, at the time of the contribution, a written statement containing the following information:

- The name, address, and taxpayer identification number of the donor;
- A description of the qualified intellectual property in sufficient detail to identify the qualified intellectual property received by the donee;
- The date of the contribution to the donee; and
- A statement that the donor intends to treat the contribution as a qualified intellectual property contribution.

Reporting Requirements

Each donee organization that receives or accrues net income during a tax year from any qualified intellectual property contribution must file an information return on Form 8899, *Notice of Income from Donated Intellectual Property* [Code Sec. 6050L]. An information return is required for any tax year of the donee that includes any portion of the

10-year period beginning on the date of the contribution. However, an information return is not required for tax years beginning after the expiration of the legal life of the qualified intellectual property.

The IRS will disallow improper deductions for charitable contributions of patents and other intellectual property and will impose penalties on those claiming improper deductions as well as on taxpayers promoting the contributions and appraising the intellectual property.[55]

¶9055 BENEFITS RECEIVED FOR CONTRIBUTIONS

In *American Bar Endowment*,[56] the Supreme Court established the basic rule that donated property generally cannot constitute a charitable contribution if the contributor expects a substantial benefit in return. The test established by the Supreme Court in *American Bar Endowment* requires an examination of whether the fair market value of contributed property exceeds the fair market value of the benefit received by the donor. However, the Court also recognized that a taxpayer's payment to a charitable organization that is accompanied by the receipt of a benefit may have a "'dual character' of a purchase and a contribution" if the payment exceeds the value of the benefit received in return. The Court consequently adopted a two-part test for determining when part of a dual payment is deductible. "First, the payment is deductible only if and to the extent it exceeds the market value of the benefit received. Second, the excess payment must be made with the intention of making a gift." The *American Bar Endowment* test has since been incorporated into Reg. § 1.170A-1(h) which provides that no part of a payment that a taxpayer makes to a charity that is in consideration for goods or services is deductible unless the taxpayer:

1. Intends to make a payment in an amount that exceeds the fair market value of the goods or services, and
2. Makes a payment in an amount that exceeds the fair market value of the goods or services [Reg. § 1.170A-1(h)].

> **Example 9-38:** Mr. Gillian paid $20 for a picnic box lunch at a Juvenile Diabetes Association picnic. The Association gives Gillian a receipt indicating that the lunch plus the entertainment has a fair market value of $6. The excess paid ($14) is a deductible contribution to the charity provided all the proceeds of the picnic go to the organization.

If you contribute to your alma mater's athletic programs, you may receive, in exchange, the right to purchase season tickets, or purchase advance tickets to athletic events. Although the price of the ticket is not deductible, 80 percent of the contribution is deductible and 20 percent is treated as the nondeductible cost of the right to purchase the tickets [Code Sec. 170(l)]. For example, if you paid $312.50 for the right to purchase

---

[55] Notice 2004-7, 2004-1 CB 310.

[56] *American Bar Endowment*, SCt, 98-1 USTC ¶9482, 477 US 105 (1986).

tickets to a college athletic event, the right to purchase the tickets is treated as having a value of $62.50 and is not deductible and the remaining $250 is treated as a deductible charitable contribution you must substantiate as required under Code Sec. 170(f)(8) [Reg. § 1.170A-13(f)(14)].

Example 9-39: Mr. Jobe contributes $300 to his alma mater's athletic scholarship program. In exchange, he becomes a "member" of the program. The membership fee is paid annually. Jobe is entitled to purchase a season ticket to the university's home football games in a desirable area of the stadium (i.e., excellent seats) for $120. Only 80 percent of the $300 is eligible for deduction as a charitable contribution.

Example 9-40: Assume same facts as above, except the $300 contribution includes the price of the ticket. Jobe is allowed a deduction of $144 [($300 – $120) × 80%].

Determining the amount of the deduction becomes more complicated when the right to purchase tickets at stadium events entitled the donor to purchase skybox or luxury seats at the stadium. The IRS has ruled that a taxpayer could deduct 80 percent of a donation to a university in return for priority rights to buy or lease skybox seats at athletic events in the university's stadium.[57] The IRS noted, however, that amounts used for actual ticket purchase, passes to visit the skybox, and parking privileges are not deductible.

In *T.R. Rolfs*,[58] the Court of Appeals for the Seventh Circuit affirmed the Tax Court to conclude that taxpayers who donated their lake house to a volunteer fire department to be used for controlled burn practice exercises failed to make a charitable contribution because they received a substantial benefit in exchange for the donation in the form of demolition services, and they failed to prove that the value of the donated residence exceeded the value of the benefit received. The appellate court found that the taxpayers incorrectly valued their gift of the house to the fire department when they valued the house as if were given away intact and without conditions. The court noted further that when a gift is made with conditions, the conditions must be taken into account in determining the fair market value of the donated property. The taxpayer must consider the economic effect of the condition that the house be destroyed because it reduces the fair market value of the gift so much that no net value is ever likely to be available for a deduction. According to the court, the taxpayers, by deciding to destroy the house and making the demolition a condition of their gift, became responsible for the decrease in value, even if the fire department provided the mechanism to accomplish it. The court found that the taxpayers received a benefit of at least $10,000 because it would have cost at least that much to demolish the house themselves. Therefore, the court held that when property is donated to a charity on the condition that it be destroyed, that condition must be taken into account when valuing the gift.

---

[57] LTR 200004001 (July 7, 1999).

[58] *T.R. Rolfs*, 135 TC No. 24, Dec. 58,381 (2010), *aff'd*, CA-7, 2012-1 USTC ¶ 50,186.

.01 Refusal of Benefits

If you refuse benefits such as theater tickets offered by a charitable organization your deduction is limited to the amount paid in excess of the value of the tickets that you refused. You cannot increase your deduction by the amount of the benefit you refused. A deduction in the full amount of your payment may be allowed, however, if you properly reject the right to the tickets at the time of contribution by checking off a box on a form provided by the charity. If you have properly rejected a benefit offered by a charitable organization in this fashion, you may claim a deduction in the full amount of the payment to the charitable organization, and the contemporaneous acknowledgment need not reflect the value of the rejected benefit.

.02 Insubstantial Benefits

When cash or noncash contributions of $250 or more are made, the deduction is allowed only if the donor obtains a *contemporaneous written acknowledgment* from the donee organization on or before the date the donor files the return reporting the contribution or on or before the due date (including extensions) of the return, whichever comes first [Code Sec. 170(f)(8); Reg. § 1.170A-13(f)(1)]. For further discussion of contemporaneous written acknowledgment, see ¶ 9051 and ¶ 9052.

Any benefits received by the donor in exchange for his contribution will reduce the amount of the charitable deduction unless the benefit is inconsequential or insubstantial [Reg. § 1.170A-13(f)(8)].

The meaning of the term "insubstantial" is adjusted annually. In 2013, an object will be considered insubstantial if: (1) its fair market value is no more than the lesser of 2 percent of the contribution or $102, or (2) if the contribution is worth $51 or more and in connection with it the donor receives only token benefits (bookmarks, calendars, mugs, posters, tee shirts, etc.) generally costing less than $10.20 in 2013; or (3) the charity mails or otherwise distributes free, unordered items to patrons. Under these guidelines, if you make a payment to a charitable organization in the context of a fundraising campaign, and receive benefits with a fair market value of not more than 2 percent of the amount of the payment (up to a maximum of $102, for 2013), the benefits received are considered to have insubstantial value for purposes of determining the amount of your deduction [Reg. § 1.170A-1(h)(3)].[59]

In addition, if you made a payment in 2013 of $51 or more to a charity and receive only token items in return, the items are considered to have insubstantial value if they:

- Bear the charity's name or logo, and
- Have an aggregate cost to the charity in 2013 of $10.20 or less.

In addition, newsletters not of commercial quality and low-cost items provided for free without an advance order are considered to have insubstantial value.

Quid pro Quo Contributions

A *quid pro quo* contribution is a payment made partly as a contribution and partly as payment for goods or services provided by the charitable organization [Code Sec. 6115(a)]. You cannot deduct the entire amount of your *quid pro quo* contribution. You

[59] Rev. Proc. 2012-41, 2012-45 IRB 539.

can only deduct the amount that exceeds the value of goods or services you received in exchange for your contribution.

When a charitable organization receives a *quid pro quo* contribution in excess of $75, the organization must provide the donor with a written statement informing the donor that the amount of the deductible contribution is limited to the excess of the donation over the value of the goods or services provided by the organization. In addition the charity must provide the donor with an estimate of the value of such goods or services [Code Sec. 6115(a)].

> **Example 9-41:** Ms. Brown contributes $100 to the ABC Charity in exchange for a $60 dinner. As required, ABC gives Brown a written statement stating that the dinner is worth $60 and the deduction is $40. Written substantiation of the contribution is not required because the donation is less than $250.

Failure by the charity to provide the necessary statement results in a fine imposed on the charity of $10 per contribution and up to $5,000 per fundraising event or mailing [Code Sec. 6714].

The charity's disclosure must be made so that it will readily catch the attention of the donor. A one-liner buried in a large document is not good enough. The charity need not comply with the disclosure requirements if it is only supplying insubstantial or *de minimis*, token goods or services to the donor in exchange for the contribution. For example, a charity providing the donor with a bookmark, calendar, key chain, mug, poster, or T-shirt bearing the charity's name or logo will not be subject to the disclosure requirement.

No disclosure is necessary if the donor only receives intangible religious benefits in exchange for his contribution. Examples of contributions for which the donor receives only intangible religious benefits include annual membership dues in a church or synagogue, building fund assessments, church pew rents, and High Holiday seats. If however, you pay for tuition at your church or synagogue's religious school, buy something from the gift shop, or go on vacation with your church or synagogue's travel club, these activities do not constitute intangible religious benefits. You would not be entitled to a deduction for the full amount of your check written to cover these expenses and the religious organization has an obligation to send you a statement informing you of the amount of your charitable donation by subtracting the value of the goods and services you received from the amount of the contribution you made.

No Deduction for Religious Day School Tuition

Parents may not claim a charitable deduction under Code Sec. 170 for tuition payments made to a religious day school or a parochial school because the parents clearly derive an identifiable substantial benefit in exchange for the tuition payments, which entitle their children to attend a facility where they benefit from a religious as well as a secular education.[60]

---

[60] *M. Sklar*, CA-9, 2002-1 USTC ¶50,210, 279 F3d 697, *aff'g*, 79 TCM 1815, Dec. 53,834(M), TC Memo. 2000-118; *M. Sklar*, CA-9, USTC ¶50,106, 549 F3d 1252, *aff'g*, 125 TC 281, Dec. 56,225 (2005).

▶ **PLANNING POINTER:** The IRS specifically states that the Service has not published any ruling and has no position regarding the deductibility of payments made by taxpayers for tithes, High Holiday tickets, torah readings, and synagogue dues. It appears, however, based on the regulations that these payments would be deductible because the benefit received by the donor is purely religious in nature.

In meeting the $75 figure, separate checks written to different charities made at different times of the year will not be combined. The only time checks will be aggregated is if multiple checks are written on the same date. This rule exists to prevent abuse of the no-aggregation rule by creative taxpayers.

Certain Goods or Services Disregarded

Certain goods and services you receive in exchange for a charitable contribution will be disregarded and will not reduce the amount of your charitable contribution. These include membership benefits that you receive in exchange for a payment of $75 or less per year. The membership benefits include rights or privileges that are not limited as to use, such as free or discounted admission or parking, and gift shop discounts [Reg. § 1.170A-13(f)(8)(B)].

Additional membership benefits that will be disregarded include admission to events that are open only to members and for which the charitable organization reasonably projects that the cost per person (excluding allocable overhead) for each event will be less than or equal to the standard for low cost articles ($8.30 in). For example, a modest reception including light refreshments served to members of a charitable organization before an event will not reduce the value of a charitable contribution.

In addition, rights or privileges that members can exercise frequently during the membership period, such as free admission to a museum, are benefits that can be disregarded when computing the amount of a charitable contribution.

Example 9-42: You pay $50 to become a member of the local art museum. As a member you are entitled to unlimited entry into the museum and a 10 percent discount in the museum shop. You have made a charitable contribution to the museum of $50. You do not have to subtract the value of your free-entry pass or your museum shop discounts from the $50 in computing the amount of your charitable contribution.

Goods or Services Provided to Donor's Employees

The IRS also provides relief where charities provide goods or services to your employees. Goods or services that may be disregarded when provided directly to a donor may also be disregarded for the same purposes when provided to a donor's employees [Reg. § 1.170A-13 (f) (9) (i)].

Reliance on Estimates

You may treat a good faith estimate of the value of goods or services as the fair market value if the estimate is in a contemporaneous written acknowledgment or a written disclosure statement [Reg. § 1.170A-13 (f) (9) (ii)]. Thus, a taxpayer that makes a payment to an organization and receives an item in return generally may rely on the organization's good faith estimate of the value of the item in calculating its charitable contribution deduction if the estimate is included in a contemporaneous written acknowledgment or a written disclosure statement. However, an estimate may not be treated as the fair market value of the goods or services if you know or have reason to know that the treatment is unreasonable.

Example 9-43: A local charity offers to provide a one-hour tennis lesson with a tennis pro in return for your $500 contribution. The pro normally charges $100 for a one-hour tennis lesson. A good faith estimate of the fair market value of the lesson provided in exchange for your contribution is $100 [Reg. § 1.6115-1(a), Ex. 2]. Your charitable deduction is $400.

Contributions Made by a Partnership or an S Corporation

If a partnership or an S corporation makes a charitable contribution of $250 or more, the partnership or S corporation will be treated as the taxpayer and thus is required to obtain a contemporaneous written acknowledgment for each charitable contribution of $250 or more that it reports on its income tax return (regardless of whether any partner's or shareholder's distributive share of the contribution is less than $250). Because the partnership or S corporation must satisfy the substantiation requirements in order to list charitable contributions of $250 or more on the schedules provided to its partners or shareholders, the partners and shareholders are not required to obtain any additional contemporaneous written acknowledgments before taking a deduction for their allocable shares of the partnership's or S corporation's charitable contribution [Reg. § 1.170A-13(f)(15)].

¶9060 OUT-OF-POCKET EXPENSES

Although you cannot deduct the value of your donated service to a qualified organization, you can claim a deduction for unreimbursed expenditures made incident to the rendition of services to a qualified charitable organization [¶ 9095]. These include such items as the cost and upkeep of uniforms, out-of-pocket expenses (not depreciation) and travel costs [Reg. § 1.170A-1(g)]. For the incidental expenditures to be deductible, however, they must be made in connection with your own performance of services.[61] Volunteers who incur unreimbursed out-of-pocket expenses while performing services for a charity are allowed to substantiate their contributions with a statement describing the services and the date they were performed. Volunteers claiming a charitable contribution deduction for an unreimbursed expense of $250 or more are still required to obtain substantiation confirming the type of services they performed for the charity [Reg. § 1.170A-13(f)(10)].

NOTE: You may use a standard rate of 14 cents per mile in 2013 to determine your deduction for the expense of using your car (including van, pickup, or panel truck) for charitable purposes [Code Sec. 170(i); Reg. § 1.170A-1(g)].

---

[61] *H. Davis*, SCt, 90-1 USTC ¶ 50,270, 495 US 472.

.01 Travel Expense Restrictions

It is common for individuals to incur significant travel expenses in connection with their charitable work. Generally, taxpayers can claim a charitable contribution deduction for unreimbursed travel expenses (including amounts expended for meals and lodging) necessarily incurred by the taxpayer while away from home unless there is a significant element of "personal pleasure, recreation, or vacation" involved in the charitable travel [Code Sec. 170(j)]. Deductibility of these charity-related travel expenses will depend on the necessity of the travel in relation to the performance of the charitable services. For instance, a deduction for travel expenses will be denied to a taxpayer who performs only nominal services for a charity while traveling or who is not required to render services to the charity for significant portions of the trip.

Even if the charitable travel away from home involves a significant element of personal enjoyment, recreation, or vacation, the travel expenses may still be deductible if the taxpayer is on duty for the charity in a genuine and substantial sense throughout the trip. If, however, the taxpayer has only nominal duties during the trip or if for significant parts of the trip he or she has no duties that involve the charity, the travel expenses may not be deducted.

Example 9-44: Taxpayer is a leader of a tax-exempt youth group and takes the group on a camping trip. Taxpayer organizes setup and breakup of the campsite, provides adult supervision for all activities and transports the group home. The taxpayer has been volunteering in this manner all his life and derives a significant amount of personal pleasure from the activity. The taxpayer can deduct all of his or her travel expenses.

Example 9-45: Taxpayer works for four hours each morning on an archeological dig sponsored by a charitable organization but spends the rest of the day on recreational and sightseeing activities. Taxpayer may not claim a charitable contribution deduction even though he works very hard during the morning hours.

Example 9-46: Taxpayer travels out-of-town to attend a charitable organization's regional meeting as a chosen representative. In the evening the taxpayer is on his own and goes out to the theater. Taxpayer can deduct his travel expenses as a charitable contribution but cannot claim the cost of the theatre tickets.

Example 9-47: A mother tries to deduct expenses incurred on behalf of her son who participated in a church- sponsored foreign work project for teenagers. The son went to Europe, worked in a kibbutz-like project, worked on an archaeological dig in the Holy Land, and went on various sight-seeing tours. The Tax Court denied the deduction in *G.B. Tate*,[62] after concluding that the trip was, in essence, a vacation.

---

[62] *G.B. Tate*, 59 TC 543, Dec. 31,810 (1973).

Example 9-48: Unreimbursed expenses incurred by a lay member of a church when attending a church convention as a delegate are deductible.[63]

Example 9-49: Unreimbursed expenses incurred by an American Legion member when attending an American Legion Convention, as a delegate are deductible.[64]

Example 9-50: Unreimbursed expenses incurred by a taxpayer as a participant in a "study mission" to Europe and Asia authorized by a charity are not deductible as charitable contributions because the participants in the study mission were not directly carrying out a specific function of the local organization and the taxpayers were not rendering services to the local charity or to the domestic national organization during the trip.[65]

The IRS has offered the following guidelines to help taxpayers determine whether their charity-related travel is deductible:[66]

1. Taxpayers must be volunteering to work for a qualified organization with a tax-exempt status. Without this status, the expenses will not be deductible no matter how honorable the charitable travel is.
2. Only unreimbursed travel expenses incurred by a taxpayer serving as a volunteer are deductible. The volunteer cannot deduct the value of his or her time or services.
3. The expenses will be deductible only if there is no significant element of personal pleasure, recreation or vacation in the travel. However, even if the taxpayer actually enjoys the trip, the taxpayer may still be able to deduct the expenses.
4. The taxpayer can deduct his or her travel expenses only if his work is real and substantial throughout the trip. Expenses incurred for taxpayers who only have nominal duties or who do not have any duties for significant parts of the trip are not deductible.
5. Taxpayers may deduct the following travel expenses related to their charitable work:
   a. Air, rail and bus transportation expenses.
   b. Car expenses including out-of-pocket expenses incurred while traveling to perform charitable services. The standard mileage rate used to determine the deduction is 14 cents per mile in 2013. The standard mileage rate is an alternative to use of the actual expense method. Under either method, a taxpayer may also deduct parking fees and tolls but may not deduct general repair or maintenance expenses, depreciation, insurance or registration fees.
   c. Lodging costs.
   d. The cost of meals.
   e. Taxi fares or other transportation costs between the airport or station and hotel.

[63] Rev. Rul. 58-240, 1958-1 CB 141.

[64] Rev. Rul. 58-240, 1958-1 CB 141.

[65] Rev. Rul. 71-135, 1971-1 CB 94.

[66] IRS Summertime Tax Tip 2013-05.

Taxpayer may only deduct expenses relating to travel by the taxpayer or by a person associated with the taxpayer (e.g., a family member). Therefore they may not deduct expenses for travel by third parties who are participants in the charitable activity. For example, a leader for a tax-exempt youth group who takes children belonging to the group on a camping trip may not deduct expenses personally incurred for the children's travel because the children are unrelated to the taxpayer. Also nondeductible are expenses incurred in any arrangement where two unrelated taxpayers pay each other's travel expenses, or members of a group contribute to a fund that pays for all of their travel expenses.

Substantiation of Out-of-Pocket Expenses

Where you have unreimbursed expenditures made incident to the rendition of services and of an amount requiring substantiation, the expenditures may be substantiated by the donor's normal records and an abbreviated written acknowledgment provided by the charitable organization. The written acknowledgment must contain a description of the services provided by the donor, the date the services were provided, whether or not the donee organization provided any goods or services, and a description and good faith estimate of the fair market value of those goods or services. This written acknowledgment must be obtained by you on or before the earlier of the date you file your original return for the year in which the contribution was made, or the due date (including extensions) for filing your original return for that year [Reg. § 1.170A-13(f)(10)].

.02 Deduct Expenses Paid for Unrelated Student Living with Taxpayer

A taxpayer may deduct the expense of having a foreign or American student live in the taxpayer's home [Code Sec. 170(g)(1)]. The person must be a full-time student in the 12th or lower grade of a school located in the United States. The deduction is limited to a maximum of $50 for each calendar month the student is attending school for 15 or more days [Code Sec. 170(g)(2)(A)]. The student may be foreign or American, but may not be the taxpayer's dependent or relative. The student must be a member of the taxpayer's household, under a written agreement between the taxpayer and a qualified organization. The purpose of the agreement must be to provide educational opportunities for the student. Expenses that qualify for the deduction include books, food, clothing, entertainment and medical or dental care.

No deduction is permitted if the taxpayer is compensated or reimbursed for any portion of the costs of having a student live with him [Code Sec. 170(g); Reg. § 1.170A-2]. For example, if you receive $30 a month for student costs, any additional costs incurred by you on account of the student are not deductible.

The following expenses do not qualify for the deduction: depreciation on your home, the fair market value of lodging, general household expenses such as taxes, insurance, and repairs. In addition, you cannot deduct the costs of a foreign student living in your home under a mutual exchange program that allows your child to live with another family in a foreign country.

¶9065 CONTRIBUTIONS OF PARTIAL INTERESTS

With certain major exceptions, taxpayers may not deduct donations of less than their entire interest in property (e.g., an income or remainder interest) [Code Sec. 170(f)(3)].[67] However, the following situations are exceptions to the general rule disallowing a deduction for the contribution of a partial interest [Code Sec. 170(f)(3)(B); Reg. § 1.170A-7(a)(1)]:

- A charitable deduction is allowed for a contribution of a partial interest that is an undivided portion of the donor's entire interest in property, consisting of a fraction or percentage of each and every substantial interest or right owned by the donor in the property and extending over the entire term of the donor's interest in the property [Code Sec. 170(f)(3)(B)(ii); Reg. § 1.170A-7(b)(1)]. Thus, a deduction is allowed if the donee charity is given the right, as a tenant in common with the donor, to possession, dominion, and control of the property for the portion of each year corresponding to its interest in the property.
- A charitable deduction is allowed for contributions of remainder interests in real property consisting of personal residences or farms;
- A charitable deduction is allowed if a charitable deduction would have been allowed if the interest had been transferred in trust; and
- A charitable deduction is allowed for a qualified conservation contribution which is a contribution of qualified real property interest to a qualified organization exclusively for "conservation purposes" [Code Sec. 170(h)(2); Reg. § 1.170A-14(a)].

Example 9-51: Husband gives securities to his wife for life, with the remainder interest to his son. The son makes a charitable contribution of his remainder interest to a qualified organization. The son may claim a deduction for the present value of his remainder interest in the securities because he has donated the entire interest he has in the property.

Example 9-52: A owns a 10-story office building and donates the rent-free use of the top floor of the building for the year to a charity. Since the contribution consists of a partial interest, he is not entitled to a charitable contribution deduction for the contribution of the partial interest [Reg. § 1.170A-7(d), Ex. 1].

Example 9-53: B contributes to a charity an undivided one-half interest in 100 acres of land, whereby as tenants in common they share in the economic benefits from the property. The present value of the contributed property is $50,000. Because B's contribution consists of an undivided portion of his entire interest in the property, he is allowed a deduction for his charitable contributions of $50,000 [Reg. § 1.170A-7(d), Ex. 2].

---

[67] *J.L. Winokur*, 90 TC 733, Dec. 44,712 (1988), *acq.* 1989-1 CB 1; *D.M. Bennett*, 62 TCM 1400, Dec. 47,791(M), TC Memo. 1991-604.

Example 9-54: C loans $10,000 in cash to a charitable organization and does not require the organization to pay any interest for the use of the money. Because C's contribution consists of a partial interest, she is not entitled to a charitable contribution deduction for the contribution of the partial interest [Reg. § 1.170A-7(d), Ex. 3].

In *U.G. Patel*,[68] the Tax Court held that taxpayers were not entitled to claim a charitable contribution deduction for a house donated to the local fire department so the house could be burned to the ground in conjunction with the department's training exercises. The Court found that the taxpayers' grant to the fire department of the right to destroy the building while conducting training exercises on the property wasn't a conveyance of ownership, title, or possession, but was rather a "mere license" to use the property. Although the fire department had the right to destroy a building on the property, the taxpayer retained the benefits and burdens of home ownership. The fire department did not have the right to keep and use the building, to sell the building with all the rights attached, or to construct a new building on the site of the destroyed building. The taxpayers retained those substantial indicia of ownership. Therefore, the court concluded that their purported contribution consisted of only a partial interest. The court further found that none of the exceptions under Code Sec. 170(f)(3) applied to save the charitable contribution deduction. The court went to say that the donation did not include the taxpayers' entire interest in the property, which would have included the land in addition to the house.

¶9070 CONTRIBUTIONS OF FRACTIONAL INTERESTS IN TANGIBLE PERSONAL PROPERTY

No deduction is allowed for contributions of fractional interests in tangible personal property for income or gift tax purposes, unless immediately before a contribution of a fractional interest in property by the donor, all the interests in the property are owned either (1) by the donor (in the case prior to an initial contribution) or (2) by the donor and the donee organization (in the case following the initial contribution) [Code Secs. 170(o)(1)(A) and 2522(E)(1)(a)]. Thus, if any party other than the donor and the donee organization holds an interest in the property, a contribution of a fractional interest by the donor will be disallowed.

.01 Valuation of Subsequent Gifts

The amount of the income tax charitable deduction for additional contributions of tangible personal property (such as artwork) in which the donor has previously made a contribution of an undivided fractional interest (an initial fractional contribution) is restricted to the lesser of: (1) the fair market value of the property used to determine the charitable deduction for the initial fractional contribution or (2) the fair market value of the property at the time of the additional contribution [Code Sec. 170(o)(2)].

---

[68] *U.G. Patel*, 138 TC No. 23, Dec. 59,100 (2012), nonacq., AOD-2012-05 (Jan. 17, 2013) (on accuracy related penalty issue).

Example 9-55: Taxpayer contributed a 25-percent interest in a painting to an art museum in June 2012 that entitles the museum to possession of the painting for three months of each year. A charitable deduction of up to $250,000 is allowable based on the sculpture's fair market value of $1,000,000 at the time of contribution. Taxpayer makes similar contributions of a 25-percent interest in both June of 2013 and June of 2014, giving the museum an undivided 75-percent interest in the sculpture. If at the time of the additional gifts the value of the property has risen to $1,125,000 in 2013 and $1,150,000 in 2014, the charitable deduction for both 2013 and 2014 will be determined using the lower value at the time of the initial fractional contribution.

.02 Recapture Rules

Any income tax or gift tax charitable deduction allowed for contributions of undivided interests in tangible personal property will be recaptured (with interest) if: (1) the donor fails to contribute all of the remaining interests in the property to the donee (or another charitable organization if the donee is no longer in existence) before the earlier of the tenth anniversary of the initial fractional contribution or the donor's date of death, or (2) the donee fails to take substantial physical possession of the property or fails to use the property in a manner related to the donee's exempt purpose during the period beginning after the initial fractional contribution and ending on the earlier of the tenth anniversary of the initial contribution or the donor's date of death [Code Secs. 170(o)(3) and 2522(e)(2)].

If an income tax or a gift tax charitable deduction is recaptured, as described above, an additional tax will be imposed in an amount equal to 10 percent of the amount recaptured [Code Secs. 170(o)(3)(B) and 2522(e)(2)(B)].

¶9071 TRANSFERS FOR CONSERVATION PURPOSES

Taxpayers are generally not entitled to claim a deduction for gifts of property that consist of less than the taxpayers' entire interest in that property. An exception is made for qualified conservation contributions, which are only partial interests in property, because legislative history reveals that Congress recognized the important role that conservation easements play in preserving the country's natural resources and cultural heritage [Code Sec. 170(f)(3)(A)].

A taxpayer may claim a charitable deduction for a *qualified conservation contribution* if the taxpayer satisfies the following three requirements and proves that: (1) the real property contributed is a *qualified real property interest,* (2) the contributee is a *qualified organization,* and (3) the contribution is *exclusively for conservation purposes* [Code Sec. 170(h)(1); Reg. § 1.170A-14(a)].[69]

These interests could include: (1) the taxpayer's entire interest other than subsurface mineral interests, (2) a remainder interest and (3) certain permanent restrictions on the

[69] *C.F. Glass,* 124 TC 258, Dec. 56,037 (2005), *aff'd,* CA-6, 2007-1 USTC ¶50,111, 471 F3d 698.

use of real property such as easements or restrictive covenants [Code Sec. 170(f)(3)(B)(iii), (h)(2)].

.01 Qualified Real Property Interest

An interest in real property is a *qualified real property interest* if the interest is: (a) the donor's entire interest in that real property (other than a qualified mineral interest); (b) a remainder interest; or (c) a restriction granted in perpetuity on the use which may be made of the real property [Code Sec. 170(h)(2)]. A restriction granted in perpetuity on the use which may be made of the real property must be legally enforceable to limit any use of the real property that is inconsistent with the conservation purpose of the contribution. This requirement may be met by recording the restriction in the land records of the jurisdiction in which the real property is located [Reg. § 1.170A-14(g)(1)].

In *B.V. Belk*,[70] taxpayers were denied a charitable deduction for contributing a conservation easement on real property that contained a golf course because the use restriction was not granted in perpetuity as required in Code Sec. 170(h)(2)(C). The conservation easement agreement permitted the parties to substitute what property would be subject to the conservation easement and thus violated the requirements of Reg. § 1.170A-14(b)(2) which requires that a restriction be granted by the donor in perpetuity on the use made of the contributed real property.

In *C.R. Irby*,[71] taxpayers were entitled to claim charitable contribution deductions for conservation easements because the conservation purpose of two conservation easements was protected in perpetuity despite a clause providing for remittance of the proceeds following a judicial sale to the funding entities. The court pointed out that pursuant to the deeds, the donor unconditionally agreed that in the event of a change in conditions giving rise to the extinguishment of the conservation easements, the donee would be entitled to an amount at least equal to its proportionate share of the proceeds arising from the extinguishment of the conservation easement.

.02 Qualified Organization

A *qualified organization* is (1) a governmental unit; (2) a corporation, trust, or community chest, fund, or foundation; (3) a charitable organization that meets the public support test of Code Sec. 509(a)(2); or (4) a charitable organization that meets the requirements of Code Sec. 509(a)(3) and is controlled by an organization described in (1), (2), or (3) [Reg. § 1.170A-14(c)(1)]. The organization must be committed to protecting the conservation purposes of the contribution and have the resources necessary to enforce the restrictions granted in perpetuity [Reg. § 1.170A-14(c)(1)].

.03 Conservation Purposes

A contribution is made "exclusively for conservation purposes" if it satisfies one of the following four purposes:

1. Preserves land for outdoor recreation by, or the education of, the general public,
2. Protects a relatively natural habitat of fish, wildlife, or plants, or similar ecosystem,

---

[70] *B.V. Belk*, 140 TC 1, Dec. 59,401 (2013), reconsideration denied, 105 TCM 1878, Dec. 59,570(M), TC Memo. 2013-154.

[71] *C.R. Irby*, 139 TC 371, Dec. 59,235 (2012).

3. Preserves open space (including farmland and forest land) for the scenic enjoyment of the general public or pursuant to a federal, state, or local governmental conservation policy that will yield a significant public benefit, or
4. Preserves a "historically important land area" or a "certified historic structure" [Code Sec. 170(h)(4)(A)]. See also Reg. § 1.170A-14(d)(1).

Historically Important Land Area Defined

The term "historically important land area" includes independently significant land areas (for example, a Civil War battlefield) and historic sites and related land areas whose physical or environmental features contribute to the historic or cultural importance and continuing integrity of historic structures or districts [Reg. § 1.170A-14(d)(5)].

Code Sec. 170(h)(4)(C) provides that certified historic structures is defined to include:

- Buildings if located in a registered historic district; *and*
- Structures, buildings, or land areas if listed on the National Register.

In *J.M. Herman*,[72] a conservation easement that restricted the development of air space over a certified historic structure did not preserve a "historically important land area" or a "certified historic structure" because the terms of the covenant granting the easement did not oblige the taxpayer, or subsequent purchasers, to preserve the building or underlying land. In addition, the easement did not protect the building underlying the air space easement.

Certified Historic Structure Defined

A certified historic structure is defined as any building, structure, or land area which is listed on the National Register of Historic Places [Code Sec. 170(h)(4)(C)].

"Exclusively for Conservation Purposes"

Code Sec. 170(h)(5)(A) provides that a contribution of a qualified real property interest will be treated as exclusively for conservation purposes only if it is protected in perpetuity. In order for a conservation easement to be enforceable in perpetuity, the interest in the property retained by the donor must be subject to legally enforceable restrictions that will prevent uses of the retained interest inconsistent with the conservation purposes of the donation [Reg. § 1.170A-14(g)(1)]. An example of a legally enforceable restriction is recordation in the land records of the jurisdiction in which the property is located.

The regulations provide in Reg. § 1.170A-14(g)(3) that a deduction for a qualified conservation contribution will not be disallowed merely because the interest which passes to the charity may be defeated by the performance of some act or the happening of some event, if on the date of the gift it appears that the possibility that such act or event will occur is so remote as to be negligible.

If a subsequent unexpected change in the conditions surrounding the donated conservation property can make continued use of the property impossible or impractical for

[72] *J.M. Herman*, 98 TCM 197, Dec. 57,931(M), TC Memo. 2009-205.

conservation purposes, the conservation purpose can nonetheless be treated as protected in perpetuity if the restrictions are extinguished by judicial proceeding and all of the donee's proceeds from a subsequent sale or exchange of the property are used by the charity in a manner consistent with the conservation purposes of the original contribution [Reg. § 1.170A-14(g)(6)(i)].

Reg. § 1.170A-14(g)(6)(ii) provides that in order for a conservation easement deduction to be allowed:

> at the time of the gift the donor must agree that the donation of the perpetual conservation restriction gives rise to a property right, immediately vested in the donee organization, with a fair market value that is at least equal to the proportionate value that the perpetual conservation restriction at the time of the gift bears to the value of the property as a whole at that time. *** Accordingly, when a change in conditions gives rise to the extinguishment of a perpetual conservation restriction . . ., the donee organization, on a subsequent sale, exchange, or involuntary conversion of the subject property, must be entitled to a portion of the proceeds at least equal to that proportionate value of the perpetual conservation restriction ***.

In *R.L. Mitchell*,[73] the Tax Court held that the grant of a conservation easement failed to qualify for a charitable deduction because it was not enforceable in perpetuity. At the time interest was conveyed, the deed of trust securing a mortgage on the property was not subordinated to the land conservancy. The "so-remote-as-to-be-negligible" standard, with respect to the probability of the donor defaulting on the mortgage on the property prior to the subordination of the deed of trust to the donee organization, did not apply in determining whether the subordination requirement was met. An oral agreement with the mortgagee that the property would not be subdivided or developed did not protect the conservation easement purpose in perpetuity because the mortgagee still could have foreclosed on the property.

In the case of a contribution of any interest where there is a retention of a qualified mineral interest, the exclusive conservation purpose will only be satisfied if any extraction or removal of minerals by any surface mining method (unless the ownership of the surface estate and mineral interest has been separated and the probability of surface mining occurring on the property is so remote as to be negligible) is prohibited, and any use that would conflict with the purpose of the easement is also prohibited [Code Sec. 170(h)(5)(B); Reg. § 1.170A-14(g)(4)].

.04 Proof of Preservation Efforts Required

In *J.D. Turner*,[74] the Tax Court concluded that a taxpayer was not entitled to a charitable deduction for a qualified conservation easement under Code Sec. 170(h) because the taxpayers failed to prove that granting the easement furthered conservation purposes or preserved a historically important land area or a certified historic structure. The deed

[73] *R.L. Mitchell*, 138 TC No. 6, Dec. 59,013 (2012). *See also K.M. Carpenter*, 103 TCM 1001, Dec. 58,902(M), TC Memo. 2012-1, reconsideration denied, Dec. 59,591(M), TC Memo. 2013-172.

[74] *J.D. Turner*, 126 TC 299, Dec. 56,522 (2006).

failed to preserve open space or a historically important land area or certified historical structure [Code Sec. 170(h)(4)(A)]. In *C.F. Glass*,[75] the taxpayer's charitable contributions of conservation easements on undeveloped lake-front property to a nonprofit nature conservancy satisfied the conservation purposes test because they presented credible evidence that the donated easement would protect and preserve the bald eagles' habitat and communities of threatened plant species on the land.

.05 How a Conservation Easement Operates

With a conservation easement in place, the original landowner still owns and controls the land even after the contribution and title to the land has been transferred to the qualified charitable conservation organization. The easement merely limits what activities can be conducted—activities such as clearing, development and construction. The original owner of the property retains the right to sell, mortgage, lease, or fully dispose of the property to his or her family either by gift or by will despite the grant of the conservation easement.

Assume a taxpayer owns undeveloped farmland but also wants to preserve the environment and claim a charitable deduction. The county can purchase development rights from the taxpayer and hold those rights in perpetuity. The county will permit the land to be used only for agricultural purposes. Rather than pay full fair market value for the development rights, the county pays much less and the taxpayer calls it a bargain sale and claims a charitable deduction based on the fair market value of the donated easement.

> ▶ **PRACTICE POINTER:** The IRS has targeted donors that claim improper deductions for conservation easements transferred to a charity in connection with the taxpayers' purchase of real property.[76] The IRS is focusing on inflated valuation claims and on taxpayers who deduct part of their purchase price for property obtained from a charity. The IRS intends to disallow deductions for easements that are not substantiated; assess donors with penalties of 20 or 40 percent for substantially overstating the value of an easement; assess intermediate sanctions on disqualified persons who purchase property from a charity and improperly claim an easement; impose intermediate sanctions on organization managers participating in the purchase; and bring penalties against promoters, appraisers, and others involved in abusive transactions.

.06 Charitable Contribution of Real Property for Conservation Purposes

In order to encourage corporate and individual farmers and ranchers to donate appreciated capital gain real property to qualified charities for conservation purposes, Code Sec. 170(b)(1)(E)(vi) and Code Sec. 170(b)(2)(B)(iii) provide for increased deduction percentage limits and enhanced carry forward rules for charitable contributions of property for conservation purposes made through December 31, 2013.

Qualified Conservation Contributions

Although a charitable deduction is not usually allowed for a contribution of a partial interest in real property, an exception is made for a donation of property that is considered a "qualified conservation contribution" [Code Sec. 170(f)(3)(B)(iii)]. A

---

[75] *C.F. Glass*, 124 TC 258, Dec. 56,037 (2005), *aff'd*, CA-6, 2007-1 USTC ¶50,111, 471 F3d 698.

[76] Notice 2004-41, 2004-2 CB 31.

"qualified conservation contribution" is a contribution of a qualified real property interest to a qualified organization, exclusively for conservation purposes [Code Sec. 170(h)(1)(C)]. The contribution may consist of all of the owner's interests in the property or a remainder interest, provided that the property is subject to a perpetual easement or restrictive covenant that prevents the development of the property and safeguards its natural character or historical significance [Code Sec. 170(h)(2), (4)].

Limitations on Deductions

The deduction for charitable contributions of appreciated capital gain real property is limited to a percentage of the donor's contribution base. The limitation is generally either 20 percent or 30 percent depending on the type of charitable organization receiving the donation [Code Sec. 170(b)(1)]. The deduction limitation is increased, however, to 50 percent for qualified conservation contributions [Code Sec. 170(b)(1)(E)(i)].

Individual Farmers and Ranchers

If an individual is a qualified farmer or rancher for the tax year in which a charitable contribution of appreciated capital gain real property is made, the individual's contribution base for that year is raised from 50 percent to 100 percent [Code Sec. 170(b)(1)(E)(iv)(I)]. A qualified farmer or rancher is an individual whose gross income from the trade or business of farming is greater than 50 percent of the taxpayer's gross income for the tax year [Code Sec. 170(b)(1)(E)(v)]. The property donated must be subject to a restriction that ensures it will remain available for agriculture or livestock production [Code Sec. 170(b)(1)(E)(iv)(II)].

Corporations

A corporation's charitable contribution deduction for the tax year generally may not exceed 10 percent of its taxable income. However, a corporation that is a qualified farmer or rancher during the contribution year is allowed to deduct qualified conservation contributions to the extent that the aggregate of such contributions is not more than the excess of the corporation's taxable income over the amount of allowable charitable deductions for the tax year (which cannot exceed 10 percent of its taxable income) [Code Sec. 170(b)(2)(B)(i)(I) and (II)].

¶9072 FACADE EASEMENT CONTRIBUTIONS

Taxpayers may claim a charitable deduction if they contribute a façade easement which is a qualified real property interest that restricts any change in the exterior of a historically significant building located in a registered historic district [Code Sec. 170(h)(4)(B)].

.01 Exclusively for Conservation Purposes

In order for the contribution of a facade easement in a registered historic district to be deductible, the contribution must be "exclusively for conservation purposes." This requirement will be satisfied if the following conditions in Code Sec. 170(h)(4)(B)(i) are satisfied:

- The interest must include a restriction which preserves the entire exterior of the building (including the front, sides, rear, and height of the building),

- The interest must prohibit any change in the exterior of the building which is inconsistent with the historical character of such exterior, and
- The donor and donee enter into a written agreement certifying, under penalty of perjury, that the donee is a qualified organization with a purpose of environmental protection, land conservation, open space preservation, or historic preservation, and has the resources to manage and enforce the restriction and a commitment to do so [Code Sec. 170(h)(4)(B)].

In addition, the taxpayer must include with the taxpayer's return for the year of the contribution: (1) a qualified appraisal of the qualified property interest, (2) photographs of the entire exterior of the building, and (3) a description of all restrictions on the development of the building, including, for example, zoning laws, ordinances, neighborhood association rules, restrictive covenants, and other similar restrictions. Failure to obtain and attach an appraisal or to include the required information results in disallowance of the deduction [Code Sec. 170(h)(4)(B)(iii)].

Taxpayers who seek deductions over $10,000 for such contributions must submit a $500 filing fee with their return [Code Sec. 170(f)(13)(A)].

.02 Access Required

In order for the contribution of the easement to be deductible and to be considered as having been granted for a conservation purpose, Reg. § 1.170A-14(d)(5)(iv) provides that some visual public access to the donated property is required. Further, if the donated property is not visible from a public way, for example, the subject of the easement is the interior of a building, then the terms of the easement must provide that the general public is given the opportunity on a regular basis to view the characteristics and features of the donated property consistent with the nature and condition of the property.

.03 Conservation Purpose Protected in Perpetuity

In order for a contribution to be considered "exclusively for conservation purposes," Code Sec. 170(h)(5)(A) provides that the conservation purpose must be protected in perpetuity. Any interest in the property retained by the donor (and the donor's successors in interest) must be subject to legally enforceable restrictions that will prevent uses of the retained interest inconsistent with the conservation purposes of the donation. The regulations establish further substantive requirements that conservation contributions must satisfy in order to be deductible (independent of the appraisal requirements). Four provisions relevant here are:

- Reg. § 1.170A-14(g)(1) provides that the "[e]nforceable in perpetuity" requirement, states that "any interest in the property retained by the donor . . . must be subject to legally enforceable restrictions . . . that will prevent uses of the retained interest inconsistent with the conservation purposes of the donation."
- Reg. § 1.170A-14(g)(2) provides that the mortgage subordination requirement, states that "no deduction will be permitted under this section for an interest in property which is subject to a mortgage unless the mortgagee subordinates its rights in the property to the right of the [donee] organization to enforce the conservation purposes of the gift in perpetuity."
- Reg. § 1.170A-14(g)(3) provides that a deduction will not be disallowed merely because the interest which passes to, or is vested in, the donee organization may be

defeated by the performance of some act or the happening of some event, if on the date of the gift it appears that the possibility that such act or event will occur is so remote as to be negligible [Reg. § 1.170A-14(g)(3)].

- Reg. § 1.170A-14(g)(6)(ii) explains that "when a change in conditions give rise to the extinguishment of a perpetual conservation restriction [by judicial proceeding], the donee organization, on a subsequent sale, exchange, or involuntary conversion of the subject property, must be entitled to a portion of the proceeds at least equal to that proportionate value of the perpetual conservation restriction, unless state law provides that the donor is entitled to the full proceeds from the conversion."[77]

In *L.G. Graev*,[78] the Tax Court disallowed charitable contributions of a façade conservation easement that were donated to a charitable organization because the court found that the donations were conditional gifts. A gift of a façade conservation easement is considered conditional if: (1) the charitable contribution is not considered made because the possibility that the receiving organization's interest in the contribution would be defeated by a subsequent event is "not so remote as to be negligible"; (2) the donor contributed less than his entire interest in property and there is a likelihood that the receiving organization's interest in the contribution would be defeated by a subsequent event is "not so remote as to be negligible"; or (3) the possibility that the receiving organization may be divested of its interest in the easement by a subsequent event is "not so remote as to be negligible" [Reg. §§ 1.170A-1(e), 1.170A-7(a)(3) and 1.170A-14(g)(3)].

¶9073 VALUATION OF CONSERVATION EASEMENT

Under Reg. § 1.170A-14(h)(3)(i), the value of a perpetual conservation restriction is the fair market value of the restriction at the time of the contribution. If there is a substantial record of sales of easements comparable to the donated easement, the fair market value of the donated easement is based on the sales prices of those comparable easements. If, however, there is no substantial record of market-place sales of comparable easements, generally the fair market value of a perpetual conservation restriction is equal to the difference between the fair market value of the property before the granting of the restriction and the fair market value of the property after the granting of the restriction. This is generally referred to as the "before and after" approach and is used in most cases involving the valuation of charitable donations of facade and conservation easements.[79] The taxpayer would need to obtain an appraisal

[77] *G. Kaufman*, CA-1, 2012-2 USTC ¶ 50,472, 687 F3d 21.

[78] *L.G. Graev*, 140 TC No. 17, Dec. 59,573 (2013).

[79] *H.T. Scheidelman*, CA-2, 2012-1 USTC ¶ 50,402, *vac'g and rem'g*, 100 TCM 24, Dec. 58,269(M), TC Memo. 2010-151; *D.J. Simmons*, 98 TCM 211, Dec. 57,934(M), TC Memo. 2009-208, *aff'd*, CA-DC, 2011-2 USTC ¶ 50,469; *Trout Ranch*, CA-10, 2012-2 USTC ¶ 50,524, *aff'g*, 100 TCM 581, Dec. 58,427(M), TC Memo. 2010-283; *M.G. Hilborn*, 85 TC 677, Dec. 42,464; Rev. Rul. 73-339, 1973-2 CB 68, clarified in Rev. Rul. 76-376, 1976-2 CB 53; *H.T. Stotler*, 53 TCM 973, Dec. 43,956(M), TC Memo. 1987-275; *F. Nicoladis*, 55 TCM 624, Dec. 44,709(M), TC Memo. 1988-163; *G.P. Dorsey*, 59 TCM 592, Dec. 46,585(M), TC Memo. 1990-242; *J.E. Griffin*, 56 TCM 1560, Dec. 45,568(M), TC Memo. 1989-130, *aff'd per curiam*, CA-5, 90-2 USTC ¶ 50,507, 911 F2d 1124; *Kiva Dunes Conservation, LLC*, 97 TCM 1818, Dec. 57,863(M), TC Memo. 2009-145; *S. Rothman*, 104 TCM 126, Dec. 59,142(M), TC Memo. 2012-218; CCA 200738013 (Aug. 9, 2007).

of the property based on its highest and best use immediately before the donation of the restriction and then immediately after the restriction takes place [Reg. § 1.170A-14(h)(3)(ii)].

The use of the before-and-after approach to value conservation easements results in a larger valuation and is therefore good news for taxpayers hoping to preserve undeveloped land and also claim a charitable deduction. Taxpayers will be entitled to larger charitable deductions because the after-value of the property will be dramatically lower once the land is held by the public agency and it is this value that will be subtracted from the before-value to obtain the fair market value.[80]

¶9074 TRANSFERS IN TRUST

.01 Transfers of Income Interest

A taxpayer can deduct the present value of an income interest donated to a charity. With this arrangement, the taxpayer transfers assets to a trust that makes distributions to a charity for a term of years or an individual's lifetime. After the expiration of the designated time period, the property is returned to the donor. The charity must receive either a guaranteed annuity interest (the right to a specified sum payable at least annually) or a unitrust interest (payment, at least annually, of a specified percentage of the fair market value of the trust assets, determined annually) [Reg. § 1.170A-6(c)]. The amount of the donor's deduction is determined by using tables in Reg. § § 1.664-4 and 20.2031-7 (and IRS Publication 1457) and interest rates that are revised monthly by the IRS [Reg. § 25.2512-5(d)].

> **Example 9-56:** Mr. Green has been contributing $5,000 to his favorite charity each year. Instead of making these annual gifts, suppose he contributes funds to a trust that produce $5,000 of income each year. The trust is designated to pay the $5,000 to the charity annually for ten years. After that, the assets revert to Green. Result: Green gets an upfront deduction equal to the present value of the ten $5,000 payments to the charity.

.02 Transfer in Trust of Remainder Interest

The holder of a remainder interest does not get possession of the property until another interest terminates. You cannot claim an income tax deduction for the transfer in trust of a charitable remainder unless the trust is a charitable remainder annuity trust, a charitable remainder unitrust or a pooled income fund [Code Sec. 170(f)(2)(A); Reg. § 1.170A-6(b)].

With a charitable remainder annuity trust, the charity gets what is left after a specified amount is paid at least annually to someone for life or a term of years. The amount paid to the noncharitable organization must be at least 5 percent of the value of the property put in trust, measured at the time it is put in the trust [Code Sec. 664(d)(1)].

---

80 *Whitehouse Hotel Ltd.*, 139 TC 304, Dec. 59,231 (2012).

When a charitable remainder unitrust is used, the amount paid out at least annually is a fixed percentage (at least 5 percent) of the value of the trust assets, valued annually. Thus, the payout varies with the investment experience of the unitrust. As with the annuity trust, the charity gets what is left after these payments have been made for a term of years or the other party's life [Code Sec. 664(d)(2)].

With a pooled income fund, you transfer assets to a trust and retain an income interest for life. The trust can accept assets only under an arrangement whereby they go to a charity upon the termination of the income interest [Code Sec. 642(c)(5)].

.03 Right to Use Property

A taxpayer cannot claim a deduction for a contribution of the right to use property for a period of time because it is treated as a contribution of less than the taxpayer's entire interest in property (unless the contribution is made through a transfer in trust) [Code Sec. 170(f)(3)(A); Reg. § 1.170A-7(a)(1)].

¶9075 LIMITATIONS ON CHARITABLE CONTRIBUTIONS

A taxpayer's charitable contributions deduction may be limited by three ceilings: 20 percent, 30 percent, or 50 percent of the taxpayer's adjusted gross income. The particular ceiling depends on the type of property donated and the type of organization receiving the donation. Amounts in excess of the 20 percent, 30 percent, or 50 percent ceilings may be carried forward for five years [Code Sec. 170(b); Reg. § 1.170A-8].

> **NOTE:** If all a taxpayer's qualified charitable contributions for the year do not add up to more than 20 percent of adjusted gross income, the taxpayer is not affected by these limits. Thus, you need not do the calculations in ¶9080; your contributions are fully deductible.

.01 50 Percent Limit

Your annual deduction for contributions to certain charities is limited to 50 percent of your adjusted gross income. The following charities qualify as *50 percent charities* [Code Sec. 170(b)(1); Reg. § 1.170A-8(b)]:

- A church, or a convention or association of churches;
- An educational organization that maintains a regular faculty and curriculum, and has a regularly enrolled student body;
- An organization providing medical or hospital care;
- A medical research organization directly engaged in the continuous active conduct of medical research in conjunction with a hospital, if certain conditions are met;
- A governmental unit;
- A state university fund;
- A corporation, trust, fund, community chest or foundation that gets a substantial part of its support, directly or indirectly, from a governmental unit or from the general public;

- Certain private foundations, including: (1) private operating foundations [Code Sec. 4942(j); Reg. § 53.4942(b)-l]; (2) private nonoperating foundations that distribute contributions within $2^1/_2$ months after the year of receipt, provided the distribution is treated as a distribution of corpus [Reg. § 1.170A-9(g)]; and (3) a pooled income fund [Code Sec. 170(b)(1)(E)];
- Exempt charitable organizations that normally receive more than $^1/_3$ their support from the general public and $^1/_3$ or less from gross investment income. Other charitable organizations set up for and controlled by "$^1/_3$ charitable organizations" are also allowed the 50 percent limitation [Code Sec. 509(a)(2), (3); Reg. § 1.509(c)-2]; and
- Certain community trusts if they meet the tests specified in the regulations [Reg. § 1.170A-9(e)(10)].

Example 9-57: Dr. Small, a retired physician, donates $60,000 to the kidney research center in the hospital where he used to practice. His adjusted gross income for this year is $100,000. His current charitable deduction is limited to $50,000 ($100,000 × 50 percent). The $10,000 ($60,000 – $50,000) Small cannot deduct this year may be carried over to future years [¶ 9080].

On a joint return, the percentage limits apply to the total adjusted gross income of you and your spouse [Reg. § 1.170-2(a), 1.170A-8(a)].

.02 30 Percent Limit

The 30 percent limit applies in either of two situations:

- Contributions to 30 percent charities. All qualified charities other than 50 percent charities are 30 percent charities [Code Sec. 170(b)(1)(B)]. Examples of 30 percent charities include veterans' organizations, fraternal societies, and private nonoperating foundations. Your current deduction for contributions to 30 percent charities (other than contributions of long-term capital gain property) is limited to 30 percent of your adjusted gross income.

Example 9-58: Same facts as Example 9-57, except the doctor gives the $60,000 to a local veteran's organization. Now his current charitable deduction is limited to $30,000 ($100,000 × 30 percent). The $30,000 he cannot deduct currently may be carried over to future years [¶ 9080].

- Contributions of appreciated property. Your current deduction for contributions of appreciated long-term capital gain property to 50 percent charities is limited to 30 percent of your adjusted gross income. However, the 30 percent ceiling will not apply if your deduction is limited to your basis in the property [Code Sec. 170(b)(1)(C)].

Example 9-59: Same facts as Example 9-58, except the doctor gives his alma mater a painting worth $60,000 to display in its art museum. He bought the painting 15 years ago, and his basis in it is $40,000. Since the college uses the painting for a purpose related to its tax-exempt function, the full fair market value is deductible. However, the deduction is subject to the 30 percent ceiling. In this case, he can currently deduct $30,000 ($100,000 × 30 percent). He can carry over the remaining $30,000 and deduct it next year, subject to the 30 percent ceiling.

Example 9-60: Same as Example 9-59, except Small gives the college the painting to sell in order to raise money for a scholarship fund. Only Small's basis in the painting is deductible, but the more generous 50 percent ceiling applies. In this case, Small can currently deduct $40,000 (his basis in the painting) because the 50 percent ceiling ($50,000) was not reached.

Special Election to Take 50 Percent Limit

Even if your deduction for long-term capital gain property donated to a 50 percent charity is not automatically limited to your basis in the property you may still be able to use the 50 percent ceiling instead of the 30 percent ceiling. How to do it: You elect to use your basis rather than the property's fair market value as the amount of your contributions of appreciated long-term capital gain property for the year [Code Sec. 170(b)(1)(C)(iii)].

Example 9-61: Same as Example 9-59, except Small elects to have his donations valued at his basis. Now, he can deduct his basis in the donated property ($40,000) currently since the 50 percent ceiling ($50,000) was not reached. Of course, he does not get any carryover deduction next year.

You make the election by filing a statement with your tax return for the year of the election [Reg. § 1.170A-8(d)(2)].

.03 20 Percent Limit

Your current deduction for contributions of long-term capital gain property to 30 percent charities is limited to 20 percent of your adjusted gross income. There is no election out of the 20 percent ceiling corresponding to the election out of the 30 percent ceiling. Still, the value of your contributions that exceeds the 20 percent ceiling may be carried over to future years [¶ 9080] [Code Sec. 170(b)(1)(D)].

¶9080 CALCULATING THE CHARITABLE DEDUCTION

The way you figure your charitable deduction for the year depends on the kind of property you donated, the kind of charity to whom you made your donations and, if you have excess contributions from the prior five years, the kind of contributions to which they relate.

.01 Current Contributions

Your maximum charitable deduction is limited to 50 percent of your adjusted gross income [Code Sec. 170(b)(1)(A), (B)(ii)]. If the value of all your contributions does not exceed this limit, and you have not exceeded the 50 percent, 30 percent, or 20 percent limits on specific types of contributions [¶ 9075], you may deduct the full value of all your contributions. If your contributions exceed any of these limits, however, you deduct your contributions—up to 50 percent of your adjusted gross income—in the following order:

1. Contributions qualifying for the 50 percent limit.
2. Contributions (other than long-term capital gain property) qualifying for the 30 percent limit to the extent of the lesser of:
   - 30 percent of adjusted gross income or
   - 50 percent of adjusted gross income minus contributions to 50 percent limit organizations (including contributions of long-term capital gain property donated to 50 percent charities).
3. Contributions of long-term capital gain property donated to 50 percent charities (up to 30 percent of adjusted gross income).
4. Contributions qualifying for the 20 percent limit to the extent of the lesser of:
   - 20 percent of adjusted gross income or
   - 30 percent of adjusted gross income minus contributions of long-term capital gain property to which the 30 percent limit applies.

Example 9-62: Mr. Smith's AGI is $50,000. During the year, he gave his church $2,000 cash and land with a fair market value of $30,000. He purchased the land ten years ago and its basis is $22,000. He held the land for investment purposes. The deduction for the gift of land does not have to be reduced by the appreciation in value. He also gives $5,000 cash to a private foundation to which the 30 percent limit applies.

The $2,000 cash donated to the church is considered first and is fully deductible. Smith's contribution to the private foundation is considered next. However, because his contributions to 50 percent limit organizations ($2,000 + $30,000) are more than $25,000 (50 percent of $50,000), his contribution to the private foundation is not deductible. It may be carried over to later years. The deduction for the gift of land is limited to $15,000 (30 percent × $50,000). The unused part ($15,000) may be carried over. Therefore, Smith's charitable deduction this year is $17,000 ($2,000 + $15,000).

.02 Carryover Amounts

You can carry over for up to five years the amount you could not deduct currently because of the percentage of adjusted gross income deduction limits.

50 Percent Property

You may treat the amount of your carryover contributions that exceeded the 50 percent limit in a prior year as contributed this year to the extent your actual contributions for this year are less than 50 percent of your adjusted gross income [Code Sec. 170(d)(1)(A); Reg. § 1.170A-10(b)(2)].

Example 9-63: Mr. Jones has an adjusted gross income of $40,000 in 2013 and $60,000 in 2014. In 2013, Jones gave $24,000 in cash to the American Society for the Prevention of Cruelty to Animals (a 50 percent charity). In 2014, he gave the

ASPCA $28,000. Jones can claim a $20,000 ($40,000 × 50 percent) charitable deduction in 2013. The remaining $4,000 he can carry over for the next five years. In 2014, Jones can claim a deduction of $30,000 ($60,000 × 50 percent). The deduction includes his $28,000 contribution for 2014 and $2,000 ($30,000 less $28,000) of his excess from 2013. He can carry over the remaining $2,000 ($4,000 less $2,000) for the next four years.

Other Property

If the maximum deduction has not been reached after considering excess contributions of property to which the 50 percent limit applies, you may consider excess contributions of other property donated in the five preceding years. For example, excess contributions of long-term capital gain property to 50 percent charities that exceeded the 30 percent limit in the year they were donated may be treated as contributed that year, up to the extent that your contributions of such property that year are less than 30 percent of your adjusted gross income and to the extent that the total deduction does not exceed the maximum allowable deduction (i.e., 50 percent of your adjusted gross income) [Reg. § 1.170A-10(c)(2)].

Your excess contributions are also carried over and deducted subject to analogous rules [Code Sec. 170(b)(1)(C)(ii), (D)(ii)].

Change to Joint Returns in Carryover Years

If you have a contribution carryover and change to a joint return (or a spouse changes from a joint to a separate return) in a later year, you must specially compute the carryover deduction. An unused carryover of a deceased spouse can be applied only on a return (separate or joint) of the year the spouse dies [Reg. § 1.170A-10(d)(4)]. After that, the carryover is lost.

.03 Special Election Property

Suppose you elect to reduce your deductions for all of your contributions of capital gain property in a tax year and apply the 50 percent instead of the 30 percent limitation [¶ 9075]. Then you must continue to apply the 50 percent limit to any excess in carryover years. If you carry over contributions of long-term capital gain property from a year the election was not in effect to a year the election is in effect, you must use the property's basis as the value of the contribution and recalculate your carryover using the higher 50 percent limit [Code Sec. 170(b)(1)(C)(iii); Reg. § 1.170A-8(d)(2)(B)].

Example 9-64: Your AGI this year is $50,000 and you contributed capital gain property valued at $30,000 to a 50 percent limit organization and did not choose to use the 50 percent limit. Your basis in the property was $20,000. Your deduction was limited to $15,000 and $15,000 was carried over to next year. Next year, your AGI is $80,000 and you contribute capital gain property valued at $25,000 to a 50 percent limit organization. Your basis in the property is $20,000 and you choose to use the 50 percent limit. You must refigure your carryover as if you not had taken the appreciation into account this year as well as next year. Because your deduction this year would have been $20,000 instead of the $15,000 you actually deducted, your refigured carryover is $5,000 ($20,000 less $15,000). Your total deduction next year is $25,000 (your $20,000 current contribution plus your $5,000 carryover). If you do not itemize deductions in any of the carryover years, you must reduce the carryover by the amount that would have been deductible had you itemized your deductions.

Example 9-65: You have a contributions carryover of $500 from this year to next year. Next year your AGI is $10,000, your deductible contributions are $300, and you do not itemize deductions. If you had itemized your deductions, the total of your contributions paid next year plus the carryover from last year would have fallen below 50 percent of your AGI and would have been deductible.

.04 Net Operating Loss Carryover

Once you make an excess contribution, a net operating loss carryback [Ch. 13] from later years does not change the contribution carryover amount; but a net operating loss carryover to the contribution year reduces the contribution carryover to the extent it increases the net operating loss carryover to later years [Reg. §§ 1.170-2(g), 1.170A-10(d)(2), (3)].

¶9085 WHEN TO CLAIM A DEDUCTION

You can deduct contributions only in the year you actually pay for them. In general, this applies whether you use a cash or accrual method of accounting. However, an accrual corporation may claim a deduction for a charitable contribution even if payment is made as late as two months and 15 days after the close of the year, provided the board of directors had authorized the contribution before the end of the year [Code Sec. 170(a)(2)].

NOTE: You are deemed to have made payment on the date a check is mailed if it clears the bank in due course.

Example 9-66: On December 31, 2013, Mr. Smith mails a check for $100 to the American Heart Association, a qualified organization. The check is received on January 2, 2014, and clears Smith's bank soon afterwards. Smith can deduct the contribution on his 2013 tax return.

NOTE: You are deemed to have paid qualified contributions in trust when you transfer the assets to the irrevocable trust.

A taxpayer who pledges a stock option to a private foundation, may claim a charitable contribution deduction for the year that the option is exercised.[81]

---

[81] LTR 200202034 (Sept. 4, 2001).

¶9090 PENALTIES RELATED TO CHARITIES

.01 Penalties for Overstating Value of Contributed Property

Donors who overstate the fair market value of property contributed to charity will be subject to penalties of either 20 percent or 40 percent depending on the degree of their valuation misstatement. The 20 percent penalty is imposed on the portion of any underpayment of tax caused by a substantial valuation misstatement [Code Sec. 6662(e)]. A substantial valuation misstatement occurs if the understatement of tax attributable to the valuation misstatements exceeds $5,000 ($10,000 in the case of a corporation other than an S corporation or a personal holding company) and the value of any property claimed on the return is 150 percent or more of the correct amount [Code Sec. 6662(e)(1)(A)].

The valuation misstatement penalty is increased to 40 percent in the case of a gross valuation misstatement [Code Sec. 6662(h)(1)]. A gross valuation misstatement occurs if the understatement of tax attributable to valuation misstatement exceeds $5,000 ($10,000 in the case of a corporation other than an S corporation or a personal holding company) and the value of any property claimed on the return is 200 percent or more of the amount determined to be the correct valuation or adjusted basis [Code Sec. 6662(h)(2)(A)].[82] There is a reasonable cause exception to the penalty discussed below.

Reasonable Cause Exception

The valuation misstatement penalties will not apply to any portion of an underpayment if the taxpayer establishes that there was reasonable cause for such portion and that the taxpayer acted in good faith [Code Sec. 6664(c)(1)]. However, the exception under Code Sec. 6664(c)(1) can apply to a charitable deduction only if (1) the claimed value of the property was based on a "qualified appraisal" made by a "qualified appraiser," and (2) the taxpayer made a good faith investigation of the value of the contributed property [Code Sec. 6664(c)(2)].

.02 Penalties for False or Fraudulent Acknowledgments and Knowing Failure to Furnish Proper Acknowledgment

Code Sec. 6720 imposes penalties on a charity that receives a contribution of a *qualified vehicle* and knowingly furnishes a false or fraudulent acknowledgment of the contribution to the donor, or knowingly fails to furnish the acknowledgment as required under Code Sec. 170(f)(12). An acknowledgment is presumed to be false or fraudulent and therefore subject to a penalty if the car is sold to a buyer, other than a needy individual, without a significant intervening use or material improvement within six months of the donation. The penalty imposed on the charity for knowingly furnishing a false or fraudulent acknowledgment with respect to a qualified vehicle sold without a significant use or material improvement is greater of:

- The product of the highest rate of tax (currently 39.6 percent) and the sales price stated on the acknowledgment if the vehicle is sold without a significant intervening use or material improvement; or
- The gross proceeds from the sale of the vehicle.

---

[82] *B.J. Bergquist,* 131 TC 8, Dec. 57,492 (2008).

The penalty applicable to an acknowledgment relating to any other vehicle the claimed value of which is more than $500 is the greater of:

- The product of the highest rate of tax and the claimed value of the vehicle, or
- $5,000.

A qualified vehicle is any: (1) motor vehicle manufactured primarily for use on public streets, roads, and highways, (2) boat, or (3) airplane, but the term does not include any property held primarily for sale to customers [Code Sec. 170(f)(12)(E)].

Example 9-67: A charity receives a contribution of a subcompact car that has been driven more than 100,000 miles. The charity typically delivers food and other needed goods to the rural poor at remote locations. For this purpose, the charity needs three large vehicles suitable for delivering heavy loads across rugged terrain. Among many contributed vehicles, the charity has identified three suitable vehicles that they intend to use for this purpose. The subcompact car is not suitable. The charity provides an acknowledgment to the donor of the subcompact car in which the charity knowingly makes a false certification of the intended use of the vehicle and the duration of such intended use. The donor claims a deduction of $2,300. The charity is subject to a penalty under for knowingly furnishing a false or fraudulent acknowledgment to the donor. The amount of the penalty is $5,000, because that amount is greater than $911, the product of the claimed value ($2,300) and 39.6 percent.

Example 9-68: A charity receives a contribution of a car that is sold without any significant intervening use or material improvement. Gross proceeds from the sale are $300. The charity provides an acknowledgment to the donor in which the charity knowingly includes a false or fraudulent statement that the gross proceeds from the sale of the vehicle were $1,000. The charity is subject to a penalty for knowingly furnishing a false or fraudulent acknowledgment to the donor. The amount of the penalty is $396, the product of the sales price stated in the acknowledgment ($1,000) and 39.6 percent, because that amount is greater than the gross proceeds from the sale of the vehicle ($300).

Recapture of Tax Benefit for Charitable Contributions of Exempt Use Property Not Used for Exempt Purpose

If a donee organization disposes of "applicable property" within three years of when the property was contributed and the donee hasn't made a "certification," then the donor's tax benefit is subject to adjustment [Code Sec. 170(e)(7)]. Thus, the tax benefit of contributing appreciated capital gain property, rather than being a deduction equal to its fair market value at the time of contribution, may be limited to the taxpayer's basis in the donated property [Code Sec. 170(e)(7)(A)(ii)]. "Applicable property" is defined as tangible personal property identified by the donee organization as related to the purpose or function constituting the donee's basis for tax exemption and for which a deduction in excess of the donor's basis is claimed.

Certification Requirements

If an officer of the donee organization certifies upon disposition of the donated property that the use of the property was related to the purpose or function constituting the basis of the donee's tax-exempt status, the donor may claim a charitable deduction in the amount of the fair market value (not the donor's basis) of the property. A qualifying certification must be a written statement which is signed under penalty of perjury by an officer of the donee organization and which certifies that the use of the property by the donee was substantial and related to the purpose or function constituting the basis for the donee's exemption.

The certification must also describe how the property was used and how such use furthered the charity's purpose or function, or state the intended use of the property by the donee at the time of the contribution and certify that such intended use has become impossible or infeasible to implement [Code Sec. 170(e)(7)(D)].

¶9095 TAX TIPS FOR FUNDRAISERS

If you have attended or volunteered your time to support your favorite charitable organization, you may have wondered how much of your philanthropy qualifies for a charitable deduction. The federal government rewards you with a deduction for some of your expenses if you itemize your deductions. The tax consequences of your participation, assistance, and/or purchases at these events can be confusing. Review the following questions and answers to determine the tax consequences of your participation.[83]

Question: I am involved with a charitable organization sponsoring a fundraising event. What are the organization's tax responsibilities?

Answer: If your organization is sponsoring a fundraising event where something of value will be received in return for a contribution, you are required to provide a written disclosure statement informing the donor of the fair market value of the specific items or services being purchased. Before the event you should determine the fair market value of the benefit received and state that amount in your fundraising materials such as invitations, tickets, and receipts so the donor can determine in advance exactly how much is deductible. Your disclosure statement should be made by the time payment is received. These disclosure responsibilities apply to any fundraising situations where each complete payment, including the contribution portion, exceeds $75. In addition, donors must have contemporaneous written acknowledgment from you for any charitable contribution of $250 or more. This written receipt must contain: (1) a description of the volunteer's services; (2) a statement whether the charity provided any goods or services in exchange for the unreimbursed expenses; and (3) a description and good faith estimate of the fair market value of any goods or services provided [Code Sec. 170(f)(8); Reg. § 1.170A-13(f)(7).

---

[83] Rev. Rul. 67-246, 1967-2 CB 104, amplified by, Rev. Proc. 90-12, 1990-1 CB 471, amplified by, Rev. Proc. 92-49, 1992-1 CB 987.

Example 9-69: A charity will provide a one-hour golf lesson with a pro in return for your $250 contribution. The pro normally charges $50 for a one-hour lesson. A good faith estimate of the fair market value of the lesson provided in exchange for your contribution is $50 [Reg. § 1.6115-1(a), Ex. 2]. Your charitable deduction is $200.

Question: Can I claim a charitable deduction for the entire cost of what I purchased at an auction fundraiser?

Answer: No! You can only deduct the amount that exceeds the value of the goods or services you receive in return for your payment. If you will receive any benefit (such as free tuition or use of a vacation home or a free dinner) in return, you can deduct only the amount that exceeds the value of the benefit you will receive. When you pay more than fair market value for merchandise, goods, or services, only that excess will be your charitable contribution.

Example 9-70: At a charity auction you purchase dinner for two at a local restaurant for $150. The restaurant gift certificate is worth only $50. You can claim a charitable deduction in the amount of $100. You cannot claim a deduction for the $50 dinner you bought. Only the $100 you paid over and above the value of your dinner constitutes your charitable contribution.

Question: At a charity auction, I paid $600 to purchase a weekend stay at someone's donated vacation home. What can I deduct?

Answer: The answer depends on what the fair market value of a weekend stay at the home would be worth. If the place would rent for $600 a weekend you have **not** made a deductible charitable contribution. If the rent would only be $200, however, you have made a charitable contribution of $400.

Question: If I don't intend to use the item I purchase at a charity auction can I claim a deduction for the full purchase amount?

Answer: No. Whether or not you actually use what you purchase has no effect on the amount you can deduct. You can only deduct the excess of what you paid over the fair market value of the item.

Question: What if I purchase an item at a charity auction and immediately turn around and contribute it back to be auctioned again, can I then claim a deduction for the full purchase price?

Answer: Yes. If after purchasing the item, you return it for re-auction, you can deduct the entire amount you paid for the item.

Question: I volunteered to help out with the fundraiser. Can I deduct the value of my time?

Answer: No. You cannot deduct the value of your time spent helping with the fundraiser. For example, if you volunteer your accounting skills to the auction and you are normally paid $50 an hour for these services, you cannot claim a deduction for the value of your labor [Reg. § 1.170A-1(g)].[84]

Question: I volunteered to help out with the fundraising activity and have driven all over town making arrangements. What can I deduct for the use of my car and what kind of records must I keep?

Answer: You can deduct your unreimbursed out-of-pocket expenses, such as the cost of gas and oil, that are directly related to the use of your car while doing volunteer work. You cannot deduct general repair and maintenance expenses, depreciation, registration fees or the cost of tires or insurance. If you do not want to deduct your actual expenses, you can use a standard rate of 14 cents a mile driven in service of charitable organizations to figure the amount of your charitable deduction.

If you are claiming a charitable contribution deduction for an unreimbursed expense of $250 or more, you must obtain written substantiation from the charity confirming the type of services you performed [Reg. § 1.170A-13(f)(10)].

Question: I had to travel out of town and be away from home overnight in connection with the fundraiser. What can I deduct?

Answer: You can deduct reasonable payments for meals and lodging as well as your transportation costs. Your out-of-pocket costs at a convention connected with your volunteer work are deductible only if they are properly substantiated non-lobbying expenses, they are reasonable in amounts, and there is no significant element of personal pleasure, recreation, or vacation in the travel [Code Sec. 170(f)(6), (j); Reg. § 1.170A-1(g)]. Deductible expenses include the taxpayer's out-of-pocket round-trip travel cost, taxi fares, and other costs of transportation between the airport or station and the hotel, lodging, and meals.

Question: I purchased first class accommodations and first class airfare in connection with travel to a charity event out-of-town. What can I deduct?

Answer: The Tax Court has held that such costs are deductible if they are "reasonable" under the facts and circumstances, using criteria similar to those that would apply if the traveler were on a business trip. Thus, the court allowed a traveler who held relatively prestigious positions in large charitable organizations to deduct the cost of staying at posh hotels because staying in qualify lodging was an acceptable practice for someone in his position.[85]

Question: I had a big catered dinner dance at my home for 250 people to benefit my favorite charity. What can I deduct?

Answer: You may deduct the cost of entertaining others on behalf of a charity (e.g., wining and dining potential large contributors), but the cost of your own entertainment or dining expenses are not deductible.[86] The IRS has allowed taxpayers to claim charitable deductions for charity events hosted by the taxpayers at their homes.[87]

---

[84] *W.W. Grant*, 84 TC 809, Dec. 42,067 (1985), *aff'd w/o op.*, 800 F2d 260; *S.M. Levine*, 54 TCM 209, Dec. 44,132(M), TC Memo. 1987-413.

[85] *H.T. Cavalaris*, 72 TCM 46, Dec. 51,435(M), TC Memo. 1996-308.

[86] *F. Louis*, 25 TCM 1047, Dec. 28,107(M), TC Memo. 1966-204.

[87] LTR 8121070 (Feb. 25, 1982); Rev. Rul. 69-473, 1969-2, as modified by Rev. Rul. 84-61, 1984-1 CB 39.

Question: I purchased uniforms for all volunteers at the latest charity event. What can I deduct?

Answer: The cost of uniforms required to be worn when providing services to a charity are deductible as long as the uniforms have no general use [Reg. § 1.170A-1(g)]. The cost of cleaning the uniform is also deductible.

Question: What are my substantiation and recordkeeping responsibilities?

Answer: In order to claim a charitable deduction for a contribution of $250 or more, the contribution must be substantiated by a contemporaneous written acknowledgment. In general, the written acknowledgment must state: (1) the amount of cash and a description (but not the value) of any property other than cash contributed; (2) whether the donee provided any goods or services in consideration for the contribution; (3) a description and good-faith estimate of the value of those goods or services; and (4) if the goods or services consist entirely of intangible religious benefits (admission to a religious ceremony), a statement to that effect [Code Sec. 170(f)(8)(B)(i); Reg. § 1.170A-13(f)(2)].

Question: Can I deduct the cost of a babysitter for my children while I work on or attend the charity function?

Answer: No. You cannot claim a charitable deduction for child care expenses even though it is necessary to pay a sitter so you can volunteer.

Question: Can I claim a deduction for something I contributed to be auctioned at a charity fundraiser?

Answer: Yes. You can claim a deduction for the fair market value of the items or services you contribute to be auctioned at a fundraiser. Fair market value is what someone would pay for the item if they were under no pressure to buy and knew all facts relating to the item.

Question: The private school my son attends is conducting a tuition raffle at their fundraiser. The winner gets free tuition next year. If I win the tuition raffle, will I have to pay tax on it?

Answer: Yes. You will have to include whatever the tuition is worth in your taxable income. You can deduct from that amount whatever you spent to purchase the raffle tickets.

Question: Can I deduct the entire cost of the tickets I purchased to attend a charity event which included dinner and a show.

Answer: No. You cannot deduct the value of the dinner and show. The value of these items must be subtracted from the ticket price to determine the amount of your charitable deduction. In order for your payment to be fully deductible you must receive no benefit in return. Where you receive dinner and entertainment in connection with your payments to a charity fundraising event, only the amount that exceeds the value of these items is deductible.

Question: I gave $102 to my favorite charity this year and received in return a water bottle and T-shirt imprinted with the charity's logo and a sun-visor. How much may I deduct?

Answer: You could deduct $102 in 2013 because you made a contribution to a charitable organization in the context of a fundraising campaign and received benefits with a fair market value of not more than two percent of the amount of the payment. These benefits received are considered to have insubstantial value for purposes of determining the amount of your deduction [Reg. § 1.170A-1(h)(3)]. In addition, since you made a payment in 2013 of $51 or more to a charity and received only token items in return, the items are considered to have insubstantial value because they: (1) bear the charity's name or logo, and (2) cost the charity $10.20 or less in 2013. In addition, newsletters not of commercial quality and low-cost items provided for free without an advance order are considered to have insubstantial value. See ¶ 9055.02.

MEDICAL EXPENSES

¶9100 MEDICAL EXPENSE DEDUCTION IN GENERAL

Individuals may claim unreimbursed medical expenses as itemized deductions if they paid them during the tax year. The medical care must be for the taxpayer, the taxpayer's spouse or one of the taxpayer's dependents. It does not matter when the injury occurred, so long as the taxpayer actually paid the medical expenses during the tax year [Code Sec. 213(a); Reg. § 1.213-1(a)].

.01 Deduction Floor

Individuals can deduct unreimbursed medical expenses only to the extent that they exceed 10 percent of adjusted gross income beginning in 2013 [Code Sec. 213(a)]. The threshold for the itemized deduction for unreimbursed medical expenses increased from 7.5 percent of AGI to 10 percent of AGI for regular income tax purposes beginning in 2013. However, for the years 2013, 2014, 2015, and 2016, if either the taxpayer or the taxpayer's spouse turns 65 before the end of the tax year, the increased threshold does not apply and the threshold remains at 7.5 percent of AGI. For discussion of medical expenses and the AMT, see ¶ 16,005.

> **Example 9-71:** Mr. Frank has an adjusted gross income of $60,000 in 2013. He spent $10,000 on medical care during the year. He received $1,000 from his insurance company on account of some of those costs. Thus, Frank has $9,000 of unreimbursed medical expenses. And he gets a medical deduction of $3,000 [$9,000 – $6,000 (which is 10 percent of $60,000)].

If taxpayers file a joint tax return, the 10 percent floor is applied to the combined incomes of both the taxpayer and his or her spouse. Therefore, if a taxpayer or a spouse has high medical bills this year, they may come out ahead by filing separately rather than jointly.

> **Example 9-72:** Mr. Cooper has an adjusted gross income (AGI) of $115,000, and Mrs. Cooper has an AGI of $35,000, for a combined total of $150,000. Mrs. Cooper has $10,000 of unreimbursed medical bills resulting from back surgery. If the Coopers file a joint return, Mrs. Cooper's medical expenses will be

deductible only to the extent they exceed $15,000 (10 percent of $150,000 combined AGI). Based on these facts, the Coopers will get no deduction for the $10,000 of medical expenses. By filing separate returns, Mrs. Cooper can deduct $6,500 of her medical expenses. That's because the 10 percent floor on her separate AGI of $35,000 is only $3,500. And $10,000 – $3,500 = $6,500.

.02 Health Insurance Premiums

Taxpayers can deduct as a medical expense the cost of insurance premiums paid for medical care policies that provide reimbursement for medical care and prescription drugs for the taxpayer, the taxpayer's spouse, and the taxpayer's dependents [Code Sec. 213(d)(1)(D); Reg. § 1.213-1(e)(4)].

Caution: If a policy covers both medical care and something else (e.g., accidental loss of life), the taxpayer cannot deduct any part of the premium unless the policy specifies the amount attributable for medical coverage. No deduction is allowed if the charge for medical insurance is unreasonably large in relation to the total charges under the contract [Code Sec. 213(d)(6); Reg. § 1.213-1(e)(4)]. Amounts paid for insurance coverage for unnecessary cosmetic surgery are not deductible [Code Sec. 213(d)(9)].

Premiums paid for the following types of health insurance are deductible:

- Hospitalization, surgical fees, X-rays;
- Prescription drugs;
- Replacement of lost or damaged contact lenses;
- Membership in an association that gives cooperative or "free-choice" medical service, or group hospitalization and clinical care;
- Qualified long-term care insurance contracts;
- Medicare Part A if taxpayer enrolls voluntarily; or
- Medicare Part B because Medicare B is a supplemental medical insurance.

Employer-Sponsored Health Insurance Plan

Taxpayers may not deduct any insurance premiums paid by an employer-sponsored health insurance plan unless the premiums are included in box 1 of Form W-2. Similarly, taxpayers may not deduct any other medical and dental expenses paid by the plan unless the amount paid is included in box 1 of Form W-2.

.03 Health Insurance for Self-Employed

If you are self-employed, a general partner (or a limited partner receiving guaranteed payments) in a partnership, or a 2 percent S corporation shareholder [Ch. 21], in 2013 you can deduct from your gross income 100 percent of amounts paid during the year for health insurance premiums paid for yourself, your spouse and your dependents [Code Sec. 162(l)(1)(B)]. Children under the age of 27 will be considered dependents of a taxpayer for purposes of the deduction for health insurance premiums [Code Sec. 162(l)(1)(D)]. A child includes: a son, daughter, stepson, or stepdaughter of the taxpayer; a foster child placed with the taxpayer by an authorized placement agency or by judgment, decree, or other order of any court of competent jurisdiction; and legally adopted child of the taxpayer or a child who has been lawfully placed with the taxpayer for legal adoption [Code Sec. 152(f)(1)].

The deduction cannot exceed the taxpayer's net earned income derived from the trade or business for which the insurance plan was established, minus deductions for 50 percent of the self-employment tax and/or the deduction for contributions to qualified retirement plans, self-employment SEP, or SIMPLE plans. See Chapter 3.

The insurance plan must be established under the taxpayer's business and the taxpayer must fit into one of the following categories:

- A self-employed individual with a net profit reported on Schedule C (Form 1040), *Profit or Loss From Business,* Schedule C-EZ (Form 1040), *Net Profit From Business,* or Schedule F (Form 1040), *Profit or Loss From Farming.*
- A partner with net earnings from self-employment reported on Schedule K-1 (Form 1065), *Partner's Share of Income, Deductions, Credits, etc.,* box 14, code A.
- A shareholder owning more than 2 percent of the outstanding stock of an S corporation with wages from the corporation reported on Form W-2, *Wage and Tax Statement.*

How to title the insurance policy:

- For self-employed individuals filing a Schedule C, C-EZ, or F, the policy can be either in the name of the business or in the name of the individual.
- For partners, the policy can be either in the name of the partnership or in the name of the partner. The partner can either pay the premiums or the partnership can pay them and report the premium amounts on Schedule K-1 (Form 1065) as guaranteed payments to be included in gross income. However, if the policy is in the partner's name and the partner pays the premiums, the partnership must reimburse the partner and report the premium amounts on Schedule K-1 (Form 1065) as guaranteed payments to be included in the partner's gross income. Failure to do so will result in the insurance plan not being considered to be established through the business.
- For more-than-two percent shareholders, the policy can be either in the name of the S corporation or in the name of the shareholder. The shareholder can either pay the premiums directly or the S corporation can pay the premium and report the premium amounts on Form W-2 as wages to be included in the shareholder's gross income. However, if the policy is in the shareholder's name and the shareholder pays the premiums, the S corporation must reimburse the shareholder and report the premium amounts on Form W-2 as wages to be included in gross income. Failure to do so will result in the insurance plan not being considered to be established through the business.

Premium Prepayments

If you are below age 65, you may deduct certain medical premium prepayments. The insurance must cover you, your spouse, or your dependents and must take effect after you reach age 65. To be eligible for this deduction, the premiums must be payable on a level basis for a period of at least the lesser of 10 years or until you attain age 65. However, in no case may the period be less than 5 years [Code Sec. 213(d)(7)].

.04 Premiums for Long-Term Care Insurance

Premiums paid on qualified long-term care policies will be included as deductible medical expenses for itemized deduction purposes, subject to the 10 percent adjusted gross income floor. To qualify, these policies must provide for long-term care services for the chronically ill. For further discussion, see ¶ 4040 and ¶ 5105. Code Sec. 213(d)(10)(A) limits the annual amount of premiums that are deductible depending upon the insured's age before the close of the tax year, as illustrated in Table 3 (as indexed for inflation).

For tax years beginning in 2013, the limitations under Code Sec. 213(d)(10), regarding eligible long-term care premiums includible in the term "medical care," are as follows:

Table 3. Long-Term Care Insurance Premium Deduction Limits—2013

Attained Age Before the Close of the Tax Year	*Limitation on Premiums*
40 or less	$360
More than 40 but not more than 50	$680
More than 50 but not more than 60	$1,360
More than 60 but not more than 70	$3,640
More than 70	$4,550

For tax years beginning in 2014, the limitations under Code Sec. 213(d)(10), regarding eligible long-term care premiums includible in the term "medical care," are as follows:

Table 4. Long-Term Care Insurance Premium Deduction Limits—2014

Attained Age Before the Close of the Tax Year	*Limitation on Premiums*
40 or less	$370
More than 40 but not more than 50	$700
More than 50 but not more than 60	$1,400
More than 60 but not more than 70	$3,720
More than 70	$4,660

Similarly, unreimbursed expenses for qualifying long-term care services provided to a taxpayer, or his or her spouse or dependents because one of them is chronically ill are also treated as medical care for purposes of the medical expense itemized deduction [Code Sec. 213(d)(1)(C)].[88] *Chronically ill individual* means any individual who has been certified by a licensed health care practitioner as:

- Being unable to perform (without substantial assistance from another individual) at least two activities of daily living for a period of at least 90 days due to a loss of functional capacity, or
- Requiring substantial supervision to protect such individual from threats to health and safety because of severe cognitive impairment [Code Sec. 7702B(c)(2)].

For these purposes, activities of daily living include eating, going to the toilet, transferring, bathing, dressing and continence [Code Sec. 7702B(c)(B)]. With respect to item (1) above (being unable to perform at least two activities of daily living), a contract will

---

[88] *L. Baral Est.*, 137 TC 1, Dec. 58,685 (2011).

not be considered a qualified long-term care insurance contract unless the determination of whether an individual is chronically ill takes into account at least five of these activities. A contract that defines a chronically ill individual as an individual who requires substantial supervision to protect him from threats to health and safety due to severe cognitive impairment is a qualified long-term health contract even if the individual can perform all the activities of daily living.

Qualifying long-term care services for a chronically ill individual are broadly defined as necessary diagnostic, preventive, therapeutic, curing, treating, mitigating, and rehabilitative services, and maintenance or personal care services, which are required by a chronically ill individual and are provided pursuant to a plan of care prescribed by a licensed health care practitioner.

Amounts paid for qualified long-term care services are not treated as medical care if provided by a relative, either directly or through another entity, unless the relative is a licensed professional with respect to the service [Code Sec. 213(d)(11)]. This also includes services rendered by a corporation or partnership that is related to the individual receiving care [Code Sec. 267(b)]. Relative includes stepparents, stepchildren, in-laws, and children of a sibling [Code Sec. 152(a)(1)-(8)].

¶9105 WHAT MEDICAL EXPENSES ARE DEDUCTIBLE

Code Sec. 213(a) allows a deduction for uncompensated expenses for medical care of a taxpayer, the taxpayer's spouse, or a dependent, to the extent the expenses exceed 10 percent of adjusted gross income. Section 213(d)(1) defines expenses for medical care as amounts paid for the diagnosis, cure, mitigation, treatment, or prevention of disease, or for the purpose of affecting any structure or function of the body. Reg. § 1.213-1(e)(1)(ii) provides that the deduction for medical care expenses is confined strictly to expenses incurred primarily for the prevention or alleviation of a physical or mental defect or illness. An expense that is merely beneficial to the general health of an individual is not considered an expense for medical care.

Medical expenses include more than just doctor bills. Medical expenses include a wide variety of costs associated with diagnosing, curing, mitigating, treating, or preventing disease. The medical expense deduction is also available for the cost of related transportation and health insurance [Code Sec. 213(d)(1)].

.01 Effect of Reimbursement

When calculating the medical expense deduction, expenses are reduced by reimbursements received during the year. Thus, there is no deduction if reimbursements exceed expenses. Generally, though, this excess is not included in gross income [Code Sec. 213(a)].

Exception

If medical insurance premiums are paid in part by your employer, you must include in gross income the pro rata share of the excess reimbursement [Ch. 5].

NOTE: Reimbursements for medically unnecessary cosmetic surgery under an employer-provided health plan (including a flexible spending arrangement) are taxable income.

If you receive insurance reimbursements in a year after a medical expense deduction was claimed (e.g., deduction claimed this year; reimbursement received next year), you must include all or part of the reimbursement in gross income next year [Reg. § 1.213-1(g)]. The amount taxable is the lesser of the reimbursement or the deduction allowed [Ch. 2].

.02 Fees for Services

In determining if fees paid for health-related services are deductible, you must look to the nature of the service provided. The deductibility of these expenses is not based on the experience, qualifications, or the title of the person performing those services.[89] The following is a sampling of what are—and are not—deductible fees and services:

Deductible Fees for Services

Fees for doctors, dentists and other services are deductible and include fees of surgeons, dentists, podiatrists, acupuncturists, psycho-analysts, eye doctors, authorized Christian Science practitioners, chiropodists, chiropractors, osteopaths, qualified psychologists;[90] practical or registered nurses (including cost of nurses' board and social security taxes[91] where paid by taxpayer); cost of clerk in family business to let wife perform nursing services;[92] fees for healing services, laboratory, x-ray, fees to health institutes if prescribed by physician as necessary to health;[93] membership fees in association furnishing medical services, hospitalization, and clinical care; part of monthly fees or lump-sum amounts paid to a continuing care retirement hotel community that are allocable to medical care if breakdown is provided or is readily obtainable;[94] a portion of housekeeper's salary where duties include medical care;[95] obstetrical expenses; therapy treatment; cost of operation, including legal abortion or vasectomy;[96] legal fees paid in guardianship proceeding to commit an incompetent;[97] cost of acupuncture,[98] self-initiated medical diagnostic tests administered without a referral or prescription including an annual physical even though the taxpayer is experiencing no signs of illness prior to the test, the costs of a full body scan even though no signs of illness are present prior to the test, and the cost of a pregnancy test kit.[99]

---

89 *M.P. Dodge Est.*, 20 TCM 1811, Dec. 25,192(M), TC Memo. 1961-346.

90 *C.F. Fischer*, 50 TC 164, Dec. 28,935 (1968), *acq.* 1969-2 CB xxiv; *D.E. Starrett*, 41 TC 877, Dec. 26,715 (1964), *acq.* 1970-2 CB xxi; *H.J. Hendrick*, 35 TC 1223, Dec. 24,772 (1961), *acq.* 1962-2 CB 4.

91 Rev. Rul. 57-489, 1957-2 CB 207.

92 *S.J. Ungar*, 22 TCM 766, Dec. 26,169(M), TC Memo. 1963-159.

93 Rev. Rul. 78-221, 1978-1 CB 75; Rev. Rul. 62-189, 1962-2 CB 88.

94 *D.L. Baker*, 122 TC 143, Dec. 55,548 (2004); Rev. Rul. 54-457, 1954-2 CB 100; Rev. Rul. 67-185, 1967-1 CB 70.

95 Rev. Rul. 58-339, 1958-2 CB 106; *Ochs*, 195 F2d 692, *cert. denied*, 344 US 827.

96 Rev. Rul. 73-201, 1973-1 CB 140; Rev. Rul. 73-603, 1973-2 CB 76; Rev. Rul. 97-9 1997-1 CB 77.

97 Rev. Rul. 71-281, 1971-2 CB 165; Rev. Rul. 78-266, 1978-2 CB 123.

98 Rev. Rul. 72-593, 1972-2 CB 180.

99 Rev. Rul. 2007-72, IRB 2007-50, 1154.

Hospitalization and institutional costs. These include hospital fees; cost of renting and equipping an apartment in lieu of hospitalization;[100] cost of special schools or institutions for mentally or physically handicapped (including board, lodging and ordinary education incidental to special services) if medical resources of institution are primary reasons for being there[101] [Reg. § 1.213-1(e)]; and also the cost of keeping a mentally retarded patient in a specially selected home to aid in his adjustment to community life after institutional care.[102] The Tax Court has held that tuition for special training (including tuition at a school providing a dyslexia program) may be deductible, although not the cost of board and lodging.[103] The IRS concluded that parents of a medically handicapped dependent child could deduct, as a medical expense, tuition payments for the child to attend a special school that would help her be able to attend college someday.[104] Treatment for drug or alcohol abuse including the cost of traveling to a specialized clinic such as the Betty Ford Clinic is deductible. In Rev. Rul. 2003-58,[105] the IRS concluded that an individual's payments for certain nonprescription equipment, supplies, or diagnostic devices such as crutches and bandages may be deductible medical care expenses, but that amounts paid for nonprescription drugs are not.

Nondeductible Medical Expenses

Examples of services whose costs are not deductible include those of:

- Illegal operations;
- Personal analysis required by students in psychoanalytic training schools;[106]
- Fees for practical nurses hired to care for motherless but healthy child[107] (but see below);
- Cost of dancing lessons even though recommended by doctors;[108]
- Funeral, burial and cremation expenses;[109] and expenses for ear piercing or tattoos.[110]
- Expenses attributable to providing medical marijuana to individuals suffering from AIDS and other debilitating diseases are not deductible because Code Sec. 280E prohibits the deduction of expenses incurred in connection with the trafficking of a controlled substance.[111]

Child Care Expenses as Medical Expense

If an expense (such as a nurse's fee) qualifies both as a credit-eligible child care expense [Ch. 14] and as a medical expense, you cannot claim both tax benefits for the same dollars spent. In other words: (1) you cannot also treat that part allowed as a

---

[100] *S.J. Ungar*, 22 TCM 766, Dec. 26,169(M), TC Memo. 1963-159.

[101] Rev. Rul. 58-280, 1958-1 CB 157; LTR 200704001 (Sept. 29, 2006).

[102] Rev. Rul. 69-499, 1969-2 CB 39.

[103] *R.A. Baer Est.*, 26 TCM 170, TC Memo. 1967-34; LTR 200521003 (Mar. 1, 2005).

[104] LTR 200729019.

[105] Rev. Rul. 2003-58, 2003-1 CB 959.

[106] Rev. Rul. 56-263, 1956-1 CB 135.

[107] *G.B. Wendell*, 12 TC 161, Dec. 16,788 (1949).

[108] *J.J. Thoene*, 33 TC 62, Dec. 23,802 (1959).

[109] *K.P. Carr*, 39 TCM 253, Dec. 36,352(M), TC Memo. 1979-400; *C.W. Libby Est.*, 14 TCM 699, Dec. 21,110(M), TC Memo. 1955-180.

[110] Rev. Rul. 82-111, 1982-1 CB 48.

[111] *M. Olive*, 139 TC No. 2, Dec. 59,146 (2012); *Californians Helping to Alleviate Medical Problems, Inc.*, 128 TC 173, Dec. 56,935 (2007).

child care expense as a medical expense; and (2) the amount you treat as a medical expense for determining the medical expense deduction cannot also be allowed as a child care expense [Code Sec. 213(e)].

.03 Special Aids and Supplies

You can include facilities and supplies purchased to alleviate a physical defect or provide relief for an ailment with other medical expenses.

Deductible Expenses

Expenses that may be deducted include artificial limbs and teeth; braces and crutches; dental supplies (but not toothpaste or toothbrushes),[112] eyeglasses (or contact lenses), including examination fees; hearing aids including hearing aid animal;[113] oxygen and oxygen equipment;[114] iron lung and operating expenses;[115] special mattress and plywood boards for arthritic condition,[116] air conditioning units (less resale or salvage value) and operating expenses, if primarily for illness and they do not become a permanent part of dwelling;[117] cost of "seeing eye" dog and its maintenance;[118] wheel chair [Reg. § 1.213-1(e)] or "autoette" and its costs to operate and maintain if used primarily to alleviate sickness or disability and not merely as transportation to work;[119] cost of special equipment for physically handicapped to enter and operate automobile;[120] excess cost of auto specially designed to accommodate wheelchair passengers;[121] special aids (special typewriter, tape recorder, etc.) to assist in educating child becoming progressively blind;[122] clarinet and lessons recommended by orthodontist to help correct teeth;[123] fees for note-taker for deaf child at college;[124] and the cost and repair of special equipment for deaf person to communicate effectively over a regular telephone.[125]

Breast pumps and supplies that assist lactation qualify as medical care under Code Sec. 213(d) because, like obstetric care, they affect a structure or function of the body of the lactating woman. Therefore, expenses paid for breast pumps and supplies that assist lactation are deductible medical expenses.[126]

Nondeductible Expenses

Personal expenses such as maternity clothing, diaper service, and health club memberships are not deductible as medical expenses. In general, the cost of purchasing a wig, unless ordered by a doctor as essential to health will not be deductible.[127]

.04 Smoking Cessation Programs

The IRS has ruled that smokers may deduct as medical expenses the unreimbursed cost of smoking-cessation programs, as well as the cost of prescription drugs that are

---

112 *O.G. Russell*, 12 TCM 1276, Dec. 19,973(M) (1953); LTR 8042075 (July 25, 1980).

113 Rev. Rul. 57-461, 1957-2 CB 116; Rev. Rul. 68-295, 1968-1 CB 92; LTR 8033038 (May 20, 1980) (cat registered as hearing aid).

114 *Zipkin*, 86 AFTR2d ¶ 2000-5571.

115 Rev. Rul. 55-261, 1956-1 CB 307.

116 Rev. Rul. 55-261, 1956-1 CB 307.

117 Rev. Rul. 55-261, 1956-1 CB 307.

118 Rev. Rul. 87-106, 1987-2 CB 67; Rev. Rul. 68-295, 1968-1 CB 92.

119 Rev. Rul. 67-76, 1967-1 CB 70.

120 Rev. Rul. 66-80, 1966-1 CB 57.

121 Rev. Rul. 70-606, 1970-2 CB 66.

122 Rev. Rul. 58-223, 1958-1 CB 156.

123 Rev. Rul. 62-210, 1962-2 CB 89.

124 *R.A. Baer Est.*, 26 TCM 170, Dec. 28,352(M), TC Memo. 1967-34.

125 Rev. Rul. 73-53, 1973-1 CB 139.

126 Announcement 2011-4, IRB 2011-9.

127 Rev. Rul. 62-189, 1962-2 CB 88.

designed to alleviate nicotine withdrawal.[128] Expenses incurred to purchase nonprescription anti-smoking drugs, such as nicotine gum and nicotine patches are not deductible.

.05 Infertility-Related Expenses Deductible

An infertile taxpayer can deduct all unreimbursed expenses incurred to obtain a donated egg for implantation, become pregnant, and overcome infertility.[129]

The following fees will be deductible:

- The donor's fee for her time and expense in following proper procedures to ensure a successful egg retrieval;
- The agency fee for procuring the donor and coordinating the transaction between the donor and recipient;
- Expenses for medical and psychological testing of the donor prior to the procedure and insurance for any medical or psychological assistance that the donor may require after the procedure; and
- Legal fees for preparing a contract with the egg donor if there is a direct or proximate relationship between the legal expenses and the provision of medical care to a taxpayer. For example, legal expenses incurred to create a guardianship in order to involuntarily hospitalize a mentally ill taxpayer will be deductible medical expenses because the medical treatment could not otherwise have occurred.[130] In contrast, legal expenses related to obtaining a divorce that the taxpayer claimed was necessary for his mental health were not deductible because the divorce would have occurred regardless of the petitioner's depression.[131]

A taxpayer will be denied a medical expense deduction for *in vitro* fertilization (IVF) expenses incurred in fathering children if the taxpayer is a fertile man who uses IVF for non-medical reasons and has no physical or mental condition that prevents him from procreating without the use of IVF technologies. To be deductible the expenses must be incurred for the treatment of a medical condition or for the purpose of affecting any structure or function of the body.[132]

.06 Cosmetic Surgery

The cost of most cosmetic surgery is not a deductible medical expense. *Cosmetic surgery* for tax purposes is any procedure that: (1) is directed at improving the patient's appearance; and (2) does not meaningfully promote the proper function of the body or prevent or treat illness or disease [Code Sec. 213(d)(9)].

Exceptions

The cost of cosmetic surgery is deductible if the surgery or procedure corrects a (1) deformity related to a congenital abnormality, (2) personal injury from an accident or trauma, or (3) disfiguring disease. For this purpose, cosmetic surgery is any procedure to improve the patient's appearance without promoting the proper function of the body or prevent or treat illness or disease [Code Sec. 213(d)(9)]. This means that

---

[128] Rev. Rul. 99-28, IRB 1999-25, 6.

[129] LTR 200318017 (Jan. 9, 2003).

[130] *C.A. Gerstacker*, CA-6, 69-2 USTC ¶9580, 414 F2d 448.

[131] *J.H. Jacobs*, 62 TC 813, Dec. 32,773 (1974).

[132] *W. Magdalin*, 96 TCM 491, Dec. 57,629(M), TC Memo. 2008-293, *aff'd*, CA-1, 2010-1 USTC ¶50,150, *cert. denied*, 4/26/10.

you will not be able to deduct medical expenses that are basically cosmetic in nature, such as hair removal, electrolysis, hair transplants, liposuction and face lifts unless they are medically necessary to promote the proper function of your body and only incidentally affect your appearance. For example, reconstructive surgery following removal of a malignancy will be a deductible medical expense, but elective surgery to enlarge the size of a woman's breast will not be deductible.

Deduction for Reconstructive Surgery After Weight Loss

The Tax Court held that an obese person was entitled to a medical expense deduction for surgeries performed to remove a loose-hanging skin mass left after a substantial weight loss even though the surgeries were cosmetic in nature.[133]

If the cosmetic surgery expenses are not deductible, then the premiums for insurance coverage for such expenses are also not deductible medical expenses. In addition, any reimbursement from a health plan for nondeductible cosmetic surgery is taxable income. The IRS has concluded that the collection and storage of DNA is not a deductible medical expense in the absence of a showing of how the DNA will be used for medical diagnosis.[134] A taxpayer might have DNA collected and stored for use later when genetic tests are developed for conditions such as breast cancer, Alzheimer's disease, and Parkinson's disease.

> ▶ **PRACTICE POINTER:** DNA collection and storage could be deductible as a medical care expense if the taxpayer can show that he or she has an identifiable disease or defect which DNA can show a likelihood of contracting or provide an effective diagnosis.

In Rev. Rul. 2003-57,[135] the IRS concluded that expenses incurred by a taxpayer for breast reconstruction surgery following a mastectomy and vision correction surgery are deductible as medical expenses under Code Sec. 213, whereas teeth whitening costs are nondeductible.

Weight Loss Programs Deductible as Medical Expense

In Rev. Rul. 2002-19,[136] the IRS concluded that the uncompensated amounts paid by taxpayer to participate in weight-loss programs to treat physician-diagnosed obesity qualify as deductible medical expenses under Code Sec. 213. Even the fees charged to join the weight-loss program and to attend the periodic meetings were deductible medical expenses. If a taxpayer is not suffering from any specific disease or ailment, but participates in a weight-loss program merely to improve his or her general health and appearance, the cost of joining a weight loss program would not be deductible.

Special Foods and Beverages Not Deductible

The cost of purchasing special food and beverages, including infant formula,[137] diet food, meal replacements, and diet supplements is not deductible as a medical expense.[138] The cost of purchasing special food, snacks and beverages will only be deductible if: (1) the food alleviates or treats an illness, (2) it is not part of the normal nutritional needs of the taxpayer, and (3) the need for the food is substantiated by a

---

133 *C.S. Al-Murshidi*, TC Summary Op. 2001-185.

134 LTR 200140017 (June 25, 2001).

135 Rev. Rul. 2003-57, 2003-1 CB 959.

136 Rev. Rul. 2002-19, 2002-1 CB 778.

137 LTR 200941003 (July 1, 2009).

138 Information Letter 2007-0037, 9/28/2007.

physician.[139] Special foods, diet snacks and diet beverages that are a substitute for the food the taxpayer normally consumes and that satisfy the taxpayer's nutritional needs are not considered medical care and are therefore not deductible.[140] As such, they are not deductible medical expenses, even for taxpayers with a disease (such as hypertension) that qualifies them to deduct weight loss program costs.

.07 Cost of Medicines or Drugs

Amounts you pay for prescription medicines or drugs (including insulin) are deductible as a medical expense [Code Sec. 213(b); Reg. § 1.213-1(e)(2)]. The cost of special foods and beverages prescribed by doctors for medicinal purposes in addition to the normal diet is also counted as a medicine and drug expense.[141] *Medicine and drugs* includes only items that are legally procured [Reg. § 1.213-1(e)(2)]. Amounts you spend for illegal operations or treatments are never deductible. The IRS concluded that amounts taxpayers spent to purchase a substance controlled by the Drug Enforcement Administration (such as marijuana) for medical purposes is not a deductible medical expense.[142] The cost of purchasing a controlled substance will not be deductible as a medical expense even if a physician recommended purchasing the drug to help relieve internal eye pressure in patients with glaucoma, control nausea in cancer patients on chemotherapy and reduce weight loss associated with AIDS.

The IRS also concluded that amounts paid to obtain laetrile were no longer deductible as a medical expense despite a prior ruling to the contrary.[143] Laetrile is a substance derived from apricot pits and is used to treat certain types of cancer.

.08 Transportation Expenses

You can deduct the cost of getting to and from a deductible medical treatment. In contrast, you cannot deduct the cost of operating an automobile to transport a disabled individual to and from work because the automobile expenses are not incurred primarily to alleviate a physical defect or illness. An indirect medical benefit does not make a personal expense deductible.[144]

Deductible transportation-related medical expenses include payments for:

- Bus, taxi, plane fare, or ambulance service;
- Out-of-pocket expenses of driving (e.g., gas, oil, parking fees, tolls); you cannot, however, take a deduction for depreciation, insurance, general repair, and maintenance expenses. Instead of deducting the actual amount of out-of-pocket expenses, you can claim a deduction based on simply the number of medically connected miles you drive. In 2013, the standard mileage rates for use of a car (including vans, pickups, or panel trucks) is 24 cents per mile driven for medical purposes.[145]
- Transportation expenses of a parent accompanying a child who is traveling to receive medical care, if the parent's presence is necessary.[146]

---

[139] Rev. Rul. 55-261, 1955-1 CB 307; *J.P. Massu*, 77 TCM 1484, Dec. 53,270(M), TC Memo. 1999-63, *aff'd in unpublished order*, CA-10, 2000-1 USTC ¶ 50,245, 208 F3d 226.

[140] Rev. Rul. 2002-19, 2002-1 CB 778.

[141] Rev. Rul. 78-221, 1978-1 CB 75; Rev. Rul. 62-189, 1962-2 CB 88.

[142] Rev. Rul. 97-9, 1997-1 CB 77; *Californians Helping to Alleviate Medical Problems, Inc.*, 128 TC 173, Dec. 56,935 (2007).

[143] Rev. Rul. 97-9, 1997-1 CB 77.

[144] *J.A. Alderman*, TC Summary Op. 2004-74.

[145] Notice 2012-72, IRB 2012-50, 673.

[146] *L.K. Stringham*, CA-6, 50-2 USTC ¶ 9367, 183 F2d 579; Rev. Rul. 65-255, 1965-2 CB 76.

Transportation for Care of Chronic Ailments

If you travel to a more healthful climate on a doctor's advice to alleviate a specific chronic ailment, you can deduct the transportation expenses incurred. In addition, you can deduct the transportation expense for your spouse, if the spouse's presence is necessary in order for you to receive medical treatment. However, there is no deduction for lodging expenses or the cost of meals [Reg. § 1.213-1(e)(1)(iv)]. The IRS has concluded that amounts paid by a father for a dependent son's expenses (limited to transportation costs and registration fee) of attending a medical conference relating to the chronic disease of the father's dependent son are deductible as a medical expense.[147]

> **Example 9-73:** Son suffers from a chronic disease and his doctor recommends that Dad travel out-of-town to attend a conference related to Son's disease. Dad spends the majority of his time at the conference attending sessions that disseminate medical information concerning Son's disease. Amounts paid by Dad to attend and travel to a medical conference relating to the chronic disease of dependent Son are deductible as medical expenses because the costs are primarily for and essential to the medical care of the dependent son. The cost of meals and lodging incurred while attending the conference, however, are not deductible as medical expenses because Dad, his spouse, or a dependent was not receiving medical care from a physician at a licensed hospital or similar institution.

.09 Lodging Away from Home

You can deduct lodging expenses you incur while away from home receiving care. The lodging expenses of a person who accompanies the person seeking medical care are also deductible. The medical care must be provided by a physician in a licensed hospital or equivalent medical care facility. The lodging cannot be lavish or extravagant, and there must be no significant element of personal pleasure, recreation or vacation in the travel away from home.

Ceiling on Lodging Deduction for Medical Care

The medical care lodging expense deduction is limited to $50 per person per night [Code Sec. 213(d)(2)]. Deductions for food may not be claimed.

.10 Home Improvement as Medical Expense

Expenses incurred for the permanent improvement of property may qualify as a medical expense if the expense is directly related to medical care. In general, the deduction is limited to the improvement's cost less the property's increase in value on account of it (if any).

The cost of operating and maintaining the improvement will also qualify for the deduction if the capital expense qualifies as a medical expense. The entire amount of the operation and maintenance is deductible even if none or only part of the capital asset's original cost qualifies for the deduction.

---

[147] Rev. Rul. 2000-24, 2000-1 CB 963.

Example 9-74: This year, Mr. Jones installed an elevator in his home because his wife, who has a heart condition, had difficulty climbing the stairs. The cost of installing the elevator was $3,500. Maintenance and operation cost (electricity and maintenance checkup) was $150 this year. The increase in the value of their residence was determined to be $2,500. The difference of $1,000, which is the amount in excess of the value enhancement, is deductible as a medical expense—as well as the entire amount of the operation and maintenance ($150).

Improvements Not Affecting Property Value

You can fully deduct some improvements regardless of the effect their installation has on the underlying property's market value. In other words, they are treated as adding no value to the home.[148]

Fully Deductible Improvements

Constructing entrance or exit ramps to home; widening doorways at entrances or exits to the home; widening or otherwise modifying halls and interior doorways; installing railings, support bars or other modifications to bathrooms; lowering of or making other modifications to kitchen cabinets and equipment; altering the location of or otherwise modifying electrical outlets and fixtures; installing porch lifts and other forms of lifts (this does not include elevators since they may increase the value of your home); modifying fire alarms, smoke detectors and other warning systems; modifying stairs; adding handrails and grab bars, whether or not in bathrooms; modifying hardware on doors; modifying areas in front of entrance and exit doorways. A District Court has even approved as a medical deduction, amounts incurred to build a home made of steel, concrete, and other special components, including special ventilation and filtering system to address the taxpayer's multiple chemical sensitivity syndrome.[149]

.11 Sex Change Surgery Deductible as Medical Expenses

In *R. O'Donnabhain*,[150] an individual's gender identity disorder (GID) was characterized as a disease within the meaning of Code Sec. 213(d)(1)(A) and Code Sec. 213(d)(9)(B) after considering the following factors: (1) GID is widely recognized in diagnostic and psychiatric reference texts as a legitimate diagnosis, (2) GID is psychologically debilitating and is a condition of a serious nature as described in learned treatises in evidence and as acknowledged by experts; (3) the severity of the taxpayer's impairment; (4) the consensus in the appellate courts that GID constitutes a serious medical need for purposes of the Eighth Amendment.

Therefore, the costs of hormone therapy and sex-reassignment surgery were deductible medical expenses. However, the cost of breast augmentation surgery was not deductible because it constituted cosmetic surgery under Code Sec. 213(d)(9)(B) and, therefore, was not promoting the proper function of the body or treating a disease.

---

[148] Conference Report 99-841, p. 21, 99th Cong. 2nd Sess.; Rev. Rul. 67-76, 1967-1 CB 70.

[149] Rev. Rul. 66-216, 1966-2 CB 100; Rev. Rul. 79-175, 1979-1 CB 117.

[150] *R. O'Donnabhain*, 134 TC No. 4, Dec. 58,122 (2010), *acq.* AOD-2011-03.

.12 Penalty-Free IRA Withdrawals Permitted for Medical Expenses

The 10 percent penalty tax for withdrawals before age 59½ from an IRA does not apply to distributions for (1) your unreimbursed medical expenses, if they are in excess of the 7.5 percent floor for deductible medical expenses, or (2) your medical insurance premiums after you have been separated from service provided you have received at least 12 consecutive weeks of unemployment compensation and the distributions from the IRA are made during the year in which the unemployment compensation is paid or the next tax year [Code Secs. 72(t)(3)(A), 213(d)(1)(D)]. Self-employed taxpayers not eligible for unemployment compensation can qualify for this tax break if they would have received unemployment compensation if they were not self-employed. [For further discussion, see Ch. 3].

¶9110 ELIGIBLE RECIPIENT OF DEDUCTIBLE MEDICAL CARE

You may deduct those medical expenses you incur for yourself, your spouse, or your dependents. The status of an individual as a spouse or a dependent may be met either at the time the services were rendered or when you pay the expenses [Code Sec. 213(a); Reg. § 1.213-1(e)(3)].

.01 Effect of Legal Separation

No deduction is permitted for medical expenses paid by you for medical care your spouse received after you were legally separated under a decree of separate maintenance [Reg. § 1.213-1(e)(3)].

Example 9-75: Barry and Nancy Hall were married on January 1, 2013. Barry may deduct payments he made in 2013 for medical treatment Nancy received in 2012. On November 30, 2015, Barry and Nancy were legally separated. Barry may deduct the medical bills he pays for Nancy in December only if they are attributable to care she received before December 2014.

.02 Who Is a Dependent?

Your *dependent* for medical expense deduction purposes is any qualifying child or qualifying relative (as those terms are defined by Code Sec. 152, but with the following exceptions: someone who is a dependent of another taxpayer can have a dependent; a married individual who files a joint return can be a dependent; and there is no gross income test for qualifying relatives).

Example 9-76: Mr. Block provides more than half of his parents' support—including the payment of their medical bills. However, he cannot claim them as dependents on his tax return because their income exceeds the exemption amount. Nonetheless, he may claim the medical expenses he pays for them.

Divorced Parents with a Child

Medical expenses of a child paid by a divorced or legally separated parent are deductible by that parent, whether or not he or she is entitled to the dependency exemption [Code Sec. 213(d)(5)].

Medical Expenses of a Parent

If you pay medical expenses on behalf of a parent who qualifies as your dependent, you may be able to claim these unreimbursed medical expenses as itemized deductions to the extent that they exceed 10 percent of your adjusted gross income [Code Sec. 213(a); Reg. § 1.213-1(a)]. Note that the reduction in allowable itemized deductions for high-income taxpayers does not apply to medical expenses [Code Sec. 68(c)(1)]. The status of a parent as a dependent may be met either at the time the services were rendered or when you pay the medical expenses [Code Sec. 213(a); Reg. § 1.213-1(e)(3)]. A parent will qualify as your dependent for medical expense deduction purposes if you provide more than half of the parent's support and your parent is a U.S. citizen or national or a resident of the U.S., Canada, or Mexico.

Deductible medical expenses for the dependent include a wide variety of costs associated with diagnosing, curing, mitigating, treating, or preventing disease. In addition, the medical expense deduction is also available for the cost of related transportation and health insurance premiums [Code Sec. 213(d)(1); Reg. § 1.213-1(e)(1)].

¶9115 HEALTH SAVINGS ACCOUNTS

.01 Establishing an HSA

A Health Savings Account (HSA) is a tax-exempt trust or custodial account established exclusively for the purpose of paying qualified medical expenses of the account beneficiary [Code Sec. 223]. HSAs can be established by employees through their employer's cafeteria plans. These accounts permit eligible individuals to save for, and pay, health care expenses on a tax-free basis. The HSA must satisfy certain requirements with respect to minimum annual deductibles and maximum annual out-of-pocket expenses and may be set up with a U.S. financial institution such as a bank or insurance company. Taxpayer may claim an above-the-line tax deduction for contributions made to an HSA even if they do not itemize their deductions. In addition, contributions made by the taxpayer's employer (including contributions made through a cafeteria plan) will not be included in gross income and distributions will be tax-free if used to pay for qualified medical expenses. Contributions to HSAs are accumulated or distributed on a tax-free basis and may be used to pay or reimburse qualified medical expenses.

Eligibility

Code Sec. 223(c)(1)(A) defines *eligible individual* with respect to any month, as an individual who:

1. Is covered under a high-deductible health plan (HDHP) on the first day of such month;

2. Is not also covered by any other health plan that is not an HDHP (with certain exceptions for plans providing certain limited types of coverage);
3. Is not entitled to benefits under Medicare (generally, has not yet reached age 65); and
4. May not be claimed as a dependent on another person's tax return.

How to Establish an HSA

Any eligible individual can establish an HSA with a qualified HSA trustee or custodian, in much the same way that individuals establish IRAs or Archer MSAs. No permission or authorization from the IRS is necessary to establish an HSA. An eligible individual who is an employee may establish an HSA with or without involvement of the employer.

Who Is a Qualified HSA Trustee or Custodian?

Any insurance company or any bank can be an HSA trustee or custodian. In addition, any other person already approved by the IRS to be a trustee or custodian of IRAs or Archer MSAs is automatically approved to be an HSA trustee or custodian. The HSA can be established through a qualified trustee or custodian who is different from the HDHP provider. Where a trustee or custodian does not sponsor the HDHP, the trustee or custodian may require proof or certification that the account beneficiary is an eligible individual, including that the individual is covered by a health plan that meets all of the requirements of an HDHP.

Contributions to HSAs

The amount that the taxpayer, the taxpayer's family members, or the taxpayer's employer may contribute to a HSA depends on the type of HDHP coverage the taxpayer has and his or her age. For an HSA established by an employee, the employee, the employee's employer or both may contribute to the HSA. For an HSA established by a self-employed (or unemployed) individual, the individual may contribute to the HSA. Family members may also make contributions to an HSA on behalf of another family member as long as that other family member is an eligible individual.

The maximum annual contribution to an HSA is the sum of the limits determined separately for each month, based on status, eligibility, and health plan coverage as of the first day of the month. Special rules are provided for married individuals in Code Sec. 223(b)(5). In general, if either spouse has family coverage, both spouses are treated as having such coverage. If both spouses are treated as having family coverage, both spouses are treated as having the family coverage with the lowest deductible.

An individual with a high-deductible health plan may contribute to a HSA even if his or her spouse has nonqualifying family coverage.[151] So long as the spouse's non-HDHP does not cover the individual, that individual is eligible to contribute to an HSA, and the special rules for married individuals found in Code Sec. 223(b)(5) do not apply. The maximum amount that the eligible individual may contribute is based on whether the individual has self-only or family HDHP coverage. The individual may also make a catch-up HSA contribution, assuming he or she is an otherwise eligible individual who has attained age 55 before the close of the calendar year.

---

[151] Notice 2008-59, IRB 2008-30.

2013 Annual contribution limitation. For calendar year 2013, the annual limitation on deductions under Code Sec. 223(b)(2)(A) for an individual with self-only coverage under a high deductible health plan is $3,250. For calendar year 2013, the annual limitation on deductions under Code Sec. 223(b)(2)(B) for an individual with family coverage under a high deductible health plan is $6,450.

2013 High deductible health plan. For calendar year 2013, a "high deductible health plan" is defined under Code Sec. 223(c)(2)(A) as a health plan with an annual deductible that is not less than $1,250 for self-only coverage or $2,500 for family coverage, and the annual out-of-pocket expenses (deductibles, co-payments, and other amounts, but not premiums) do not exceed $6,250 for self-only coverage or $12,500 for family coverage.[152]

2014 Annual contribution limitation. For calendar year 2014, the annual limitation on deductions under Code Sec. 223(b)(2)(A) for an individual with self-only coverage under a high deductible health plan is $3,300. For calendar year 2014, the annual limitation on deductions under Code Sec. 223(b)(2)(B) for an individual with family coverage under a high deductible health plan is $6,550.

2014 High deductible health plan. For calendar year 2014, a "high deductible health plan" is defined under Code Sec. 223(c)(2)(A) as a health plan with an annual deductible that is not less than $1,250 for self-only coverage or $2,500 for family coverage, and the annual out-of-pocket expenses (deductibles, co-payments, and other amounts, but not premiums) do not exceed $6,350 for self-only coverage or $12,700 for family coverage.[153]

After an individual has attained age 65 (the Medicare eligibility age), contributions, including catch-up contributions, cannot be made to an individual's HSA [Code Sec. 223(b)(3)].

All HSA contributions made by or on behalf of an eligible individual to an HSA are aggregated for purposes of applying the limit. The annual limit is decreased by the aggregate contributions to an Archer MSA. The same annual contribution limit applies whether the contributions are made by an employee, an employer, a self-employed person, or a family member. Unlike Archer MSAs, contributions may be made by or on behalf of eligible individuals even if the individuals have no compensation or if the contributions exceed their compensation. If an individual has more than one HSA, the aggregate annual contributions to all the HSAs are subject to the limit.

Prescription Drug Coverage

A taxpayer may not contribute to an HSA if the taxpayer is covered by both a HDHP that does not cover prescription drug benefits and by a separate prescription drug plan that does not qualify as an HDHP because the plan provides benefits before the taxpayer has satisfied the minimum annual deductible required by Code Sec. 223(C)(2)(A).[154]

---

[152] Rev. Proc. 2012-26, IRB 2012-20, 933.

[153] Rev. Proc. 2013-25, IRB 2013-21, 1110.

[154] Rev. Rul. 2004-38, 2004-1 CB 717.

Preventive Care HSAs

Preventive care HSAs can be established only by eligible individuals covered by a HDHP.[155]

In general, the HDHP is barred from providing benefits prior to satisfaction of the deductible; however, an exception applies to benefits for preventive care. Thus, an HDHP may provide preventive care benefits without a deductible or with a deductible below the minimum annual deductible. A safe harbor list of benefits that may be provided by an HDHP clarifies that such traditional preventive care benefits as annual physicals, immunizations, and screening services qualify as preventive care for HSA purposes. Preventive care, which also covers routine prenatal and well-child care, tobacco cessation programs, and obesity weight-loss programs, does not include the treatment of existing conditions. The determination of whether health care that is mandated under state law to be provided by an HDHP without regard to a deductible is preventive is to be based on IRS guidelines, rather than how that care is characterized by state law.

Qualified Medical Expenses Defined

Qualified medical expenses are expenses paid by the account beneficiary, his or her spouse, or dependents for medical care but only to the extent the expenses are not covered by insurance or otherwise. The qualified medical expenses must be incurred only after the HSA has been established. For purposes of determining the itemized deduction for medical expenses, medical expenses paid or reimbursed by distributions from an HSA are not treated as deductible medical care expenses.[156]

Health insurance premiums are not qualified medical expenses except for the following: qualified long-term care insurance, COBRA health care continuation coverage, and health care coverage while an individual is receiving unemployment compensation. In addition, for individuals over age 65, premiums for Medicare Part A or B, Medicare HMO, and the employee share of premiums for employer-sponsored health insurance, including premiums for employer- sponsored retiree health insurance, can be paid from an HSA. Premiums for Medigap policies are not qualified medical expenses.

If the account beneficiary is no longer an eligible individual (e.g., the individual is over age 65 and entitled to Medicare benefits, or no longer has an HDHP), distributions used exclusively to pay for qualified medical expenses continue to be excludable from the account beneficiary's gross income.

Contribution Computation When Both Spouses Have Family Coverage

If one or both spouses have family coverage, the contribution limit for the spouses is the lowest deductible amount, divided equally between the spouses unless they agree on a different division. The family coverage limit is reduced further by any contribution to an Archer MSA. However, both spouses may make the catch-up contributions for individuals age 55 or over without exceeding the family coverage limit.

---

155 Notice 2004-23, 2004-1 CB 725.

156 Notice 2004-25, 2004-1 CB 727.

Form of HSA Contributions

Contributions to an HSA must be made in cash. For example, contributions may not be made in the form of stock or other property. Payments for the HDHP and contributions to the HSA can be made through a cafeteria plan.

Tax Treatment of HSAs

The following features of HSAs affect their deductibility:

- Contributions to an HSA are deductible by the eligible individual in determining adjusted gross income (i.e., "above-the-line"). The contributions are deductible whether or not the eligible individual itemizes deductions. However, the individual cannot also deduct the contributions as medical expense deductions under Code Sec. 213;
- Contributions made by a family member on behalf of an eligible individual to an HSA are deductible by the eligible individual in computing adjusted gross income. The contributions are deductible whether or not the eligible individual itemizes deductions. An individual who may be claimed as a dependent on another person's tax return is not an eligible individual and may not deduct contributions to an HSA;
- Employer contributions to the employee's HSA are treated as employer-provided coverage for medical expenses under an accident or health plan and are excludable from the employee's gross income. The employer contributions are not subject to withholding from wages for income tax and are not subject to FICA, FUTA, or the Railroad Retirement Tax Act. Contributions to an employee's HSA through a cafeteria plan are treated as employer contributions. The employee cannot deduct employer contributions on his or her federal income tax return as HSA contributions or as medical expense deductions under Code Sec. 213;
- An HSA is generally exempt from tax (like an IRA or Archer MSA), unless it has ceased to be an HSA. Earnings on amounts in an HSA are not includable in gross income while held in the HSA (i.e., inside buildup is not taxable);
- Upon death, any balance remaining in the account beneficiary's HSA becomes the property of the individual named in the HSA instrument as the beneficiary of the account. If the account beneficiary's surviving spouse is the named beneficiary of the HSA, the HSA becomes the HSA of the surviving spouse. The surviving spouse is subject to income tax only to the extent distributions from the HSA are not used for qualified medical expenses. If, by reason of the death of the account beneficiary, the HSA passes to a person other than the account beneficiary's surviving spouse, the HSA ceases to be an HSA as of the date of the account beneficiary's death, and the person is required to include in gross income the fair market value of the HSA assets as of the date of death. For such a person (except the decedent's estate), the includable amount is reduced by any payments from the HSA made for the decedent's qualified medical expenses, if paid within one year after death; and
- Distributions from an HSA used exclusively to pay for qualified medical expenses of the account beneficiary, his or her spouse, or dependents are excludable from gross income. In general, amounts in an HSA can be used for qualified medical expenses and will be excludable from gross income even if the individual is not currently eligible for contributions to the HSA. However, any amount of the distribution not

used exclusively to pay for qualified medical expenses of the account beneficiary, spouse or dependents is includable in gross income of the account beneficiary and is subject to an additional 10-percent tax on the amount includable, except in the case of distributions made after the account beneficiary's death, disability, or attaining age 65.

Timing of Contributions and Distributions

Contributions can be made in one or more payments, prior to the time prescribed by law (without extensions) for filing the eligible individual's federal income tax return for that year, but not before the beginning of that year. For calendar year taxpayers, the deadline for contributions to an HSA is generally April 15 following the year for which the contributions are made. Although the annual contribution is determined monthly, the maximum contribution may be made on the first day of the year. An individual may receive distributions from an HSA at any time.

Excess Contributions

Contributions to an HSA are not deductible to the extent they exceed statutory limits. Contributions by an employer to an HSA for an employee are included in the gross income of the employee to the extent that they exceed these limits or if they are made on behalf of an employee who is not an eligible individual. In addition, an excise tax of 6 percent for each tax year is imposed on the account beneficiary for excess individual and employer contributions. However, if the excess contributions for a tax year and the net income attributable to such excess contributions are paid to the account beneficiary before the last day prescribed by law (including extensions) for filing the account beneficiary's federal income tax return for the tax year, then the net income attributable to the excess contributions is included in the account beneficiary's gross income for the tax year in which the distribution is received but the excise tax is not imposed on the excess contribution and the distribution of the excess contributions is not taxed.

Rollover Contributions

Prior to 2012, employees could transfer funds tax-free from their flexible spending account (FSA) or health reimbursement arrangement (HRA) to their HSA. An individual is permitted only one qualified distribution with respect to each FSA or HRA and the distribution must occur before 2012.[157]

One-Time Rollovers from IRAs into HSAs Permitted

Taxpayers may make a one-time tax-free transfer of funds from an IRA (other than a simplified employer pension plan or SIMPLE retirement account) to an HSA [Code Sec. 408(d)].[158] The amount transferred cannot exceed the HSA contribution limit for the year. The contribution must be made in a direct trustee-to-trustee transfer. Amounts distributed from an IRA are not includible in income to the extent that the distribution would otherwise be includible in income. In addition, such distributions are not subject to the 10-percent additional tax on early distributions.

The amount that can be distributed from the IRA and contributed to an HSA is limited to the otherwise maximum deductible contribution amount to the HSA computed on the

---

[157] Notice 2007-22, IRB 2007-10, 670, as amplified by Notice 2008-59, IRB 2008-30, 1.

[158] Notice 2008-51, IRB 2008-25.

basis of the type of coverage under the high deductible health plan at the time of the contribution. The amount that can otherwise be contributed to the HSA for the year of the contribution from the IRA is reduced by the amount contributed from the IRA. No deduction is allowed for the amount contributed from an IRA to an HSA.

If the individual does not remain an eligible individual during the testing period, the amount of the distribution and contribution is includible in gross income of the individual. An exception applies if the employee ceases to be an eligible individual because of death or disability. The testing period is the period beginning with the month of the contribution and ending on the last day of the 12th month following such month. The amount is includible for the year of the first day during the testing period that the individual is not an eligible individual. A 10-percent additional tax also applies to the amount includible.

Responsibility of HSA Trustees or Custodians

HSA trustees or custodians are not required to determine whether HSA distributions are used for qualified medical expenses. Individuals who establish HSAs make that determination and should maintain records of their medical expenses sufficient to show that the distributions have been made exclusively for qualified medical expenses and are therefore excludable from gross income.

Comparability Rules

Unlike other employer-provided tax-favored benefits, HSAs aren't subject to nondiscrimination rules restricting the amount of benefits provided to highly compensated employees. Instead, if an employer decides to fund HSAs, the employer must make "comparable" contributions to all comparable participating employees' HSAs.

Contributions are considered comparable if they are either the same amount or same percentage of the deductible under the HDHP. The comparability rule is applied separately to part-time employees (i.e., employees who are customarily employed for fewer than 30 hours per week). The comparability rule does not apply to amounts rolled over from an employee's HSA or Archer MSA, or to contributions made through a cafeteria plan. If employer contributions do not satisfy the comparability rule during a period, the employer is subject to an excise tax equal to 35 percent of the aggregate amount contributed by the employer to HSAs for that period [Code Sec. 4980G].

Employers may make larger HSA contributions for nonhighly compensated employees than for highly compensated employees [Code Sec. 4980G(d)]. Highly compensated employees are defined as under Code Sec. 414(q) and include any employee who was:

1. A five-percent owner at any time during the year or the preceding year; or
2. For the preceding year, (a) had compensation from the employer in excess of $115,000 in 2012 and (b) if elected by the employer, was in the group consisting of the top 20 percent of employees when ranked based on compensation. Nonhighly compensated employees are employees not included in the definition of highly compensated employee under Code Sec. 414(q).

The comparable contribution rules continue to apply to contributions made to nonhighly compensated employees so that the employer must make available comparable contributions on behalf of all nonhighly compensated employees with comparable coverage during the same period.

For example, an employer is permitted to make a $1,000 contribution to the HSA of each nonhighly compensated employee for a year without making contributions to the HSA of each highly compensated employee.

HSA not established by December 31. An employer must satisfy the notice and contribution requirements with respect to: (1) employees who have not set up an HSA by year-end; and (2) employees who have not notified their employers that they have set up an HAS. Notice must be provided to employees by January 15 of the new calendar year [Prop. Reg. § 54.4980G-4, Q&A 14]. If these employees then establish an HSA and inform their employer of that fact by the last day of February, they must be included in the employee group that receives comparable contributions. The employer must contribute to their HSAs by April 15, comparable amounts (taking into account each month that the employee was a comparable participating employee) plus reasonable interest. The notice may be delivered electronically. The proposed regulations provide sample language that employers may use as a basis in preparing the notices.

Acceleration of employer contributions. An employer may accelerate part or all of its contributions for the entire year to the HSAs of employees who have incurred qualified medical expenses exceeding the employer's cumulative HSA contributions at that time. If an employer accelerates contributions for this reason, these contributions must be available on an equal and uniform basis to all eligible employees throughout the year and employers must establish reasonable uniform methods and requirements for acceleration of contributions and the determination of medical expenses. An employer is not required to contribute reasonable interest on either accelerated or non-accelerated HSA contributions [Reg. § 54.4980G-4, Q&A 15].

Eligibility for Inclusion in Cafeteria Plan

Both an HSA and an HDHP may be offered as options under a cafeteria plan. Thus, an employee may elect to have amounts contributed as employer contributions to an HSA and an HDHP on a salary-reduction basis.

Reporting Requirements

Employer contributions to an HSA must be reported on the employee's Form W-2. The IRS has released model forms (Form 5305-C, *Health Savings Custodial Account* and Form 5305-B, *Health Savings Trust Account*) to serve as safe harbors for banks, financial institutions and other custodians or trustees that manage HSA accounts.

¶9120 MEDICAL SAVINGS ACCOUNTS (Archer MSAs)

Eligible taxpayers could establish Archer Medical Savings Accounts (MSAs) through December 31, 2007 [Code Sec. 220(i)(2)]. After 2007 no new MSAs could be established, but contributions to existing Archer MSAs may continue (nonactive employees of participating employers would also be eligible to make an Archer MSA contribution).

.01 Who Is Eligible?

Taxpayers may only open an Archer MSA if they are self-employed or if they work for a small business with 50 or fewer employees. In addition, participation in an Archer MSA is conditioned upon coverage under a high deductible or catastrophic health plan [Code Sec. 220(c)(2)]. You cannot be covered under any other health plan, with the exception of Medicare supplemental insurance coverage for accidents, disability, dental care, vision care or long-term care insurance, and still qualify to open an Archer MSA [Code Sec. 220(c)(1)(B)].

Both the employer and employee can make contributions, but an individual is not eligible to make contributions for a year in which the employer has already made contributions. If a small employer ceases to be a small employer, it remains an eligible employer until it has more than 200 employees. After that, only employees of the employers who already have an Archer MSA can continue to make contributions to the Archer MSA as long as they remain employed by the employer. An employer will be considered a small employer if the employer employs, on average of any business day during the two preceding calendar years, no more than 50 employees [Code Sec. 220(c)(4)(A)].

Health Savings Accounts (HSAs) provide tax-favored treatment for amounts that are contributed and used to pay the account beneficiary's medical expenses [Code Sec. 223]. HSAs are basically Archer MSAs with the existing eligibility restrictions removed. For further discussion of HSAs see ¶ 9115. Distributions from an Archer MSA are not treated as taxable distributions if they are rolled over into an HSA within 60 days [Code Sec. 220(f)(5)(A)].

.02 Contribution Limits

The maximum amount that can be contributed to an Archer MSA annually is 65 percent of the deductible under the high deductible plan in the case of individual coverage and 75 percent of the deductible in the case of family coverage [Code Sec. 220(b)(2)]. If one spouse has family coverage, they both come under the 75 percent limit, but they must split it between themselves. For self-employed individuals, contributions are limited by income earned from the business. For an employee, by compensation earned from the employer.

.03 What Is a High-Deductible Plan?

Table 5 shows the limits for annual deductibles and the maximum out-of-pocket expenses for high deductible plans [Code Sec. 220(c)(2)(A)].[159]

Table 5. Limits for High Deductible Health Plans in 2013

Type of coverage	Minimum annual deductible	Maximum annual deductible	Maximum annual out-of-pocket expenses
Self-only	$2,150	$3,200	$4,300
Family	$4,300	$6,450	$7,850

[159] Rev. Proc. 2012-41, IRB 2012-45, 539 (2013); Rev. Proc. 2013-35, IRB 2013-47 (2014).

In 2014, the term "high deductible health plan" as defined Code Sec. 220(c)(2)(A) means, for self-only coverage, a health plan that has an annual deductible that is not less than $2,200 and not more than $3,250, and under which the annual out-of-pocket expenses required to be paid (other than for premiums) for covered benefits do not exceed $4,350.

For family coverage, a health plan that has an annual deductible that is not less than $4,350 and not more than $6,550, and under which the annual out-of-pocket expenses required to be paid (other than for premiums) for covered benefits do not exceed $8,000.

.04 Tax Treatment of Archer MSAs

Archer MSAs are afforded the following tax benefits:

- The contributions made by employees and the self-employed will be deductible above-the-line [Code Sec. 220(a)]. If the employer makes the contributions, they are excluded from the employee's income and will not be subject to payroll tax.
- Earnings on amounts in an Archer MSA are tax-free.
- Withdrawals from an Archer MSA to pay medical bills for the benefit of you, your spouse, or your dependents are not taxed. Withdrawals for nonmedical bills are taxed and are subject to an extra 15 percent penalty if you are under age 65. If you are over age 65 or disabled, withdrawals for nonmedical expenses are taxed but not penalized.
- Upon death, any remaining Archer MSA balance would be included in the decedent's gross estate, under rules similar to those applicable to IRAs.

  NOTE: Married Archer MSA participants who intend to pass assets to their surviving spouse should name their spouse as the beneficiary to avoid inclusion of the account value in their gross estate.

What Coverage Is Provided?

Archer MSAs provide medical insurance coverage in two parts. First they offer a high-deductible insurance plan that pays for catastrophic medical expenses. Second, they offer a medical savings account that operates like a medical IRA and is used to accumulate funds to pay routine medical expenses. At the end of the year, if the money deposited in the Archer MSA has not been spent on medical care expenses, the funds can remain in the account tax-free or be rolled over tax-free into your IRA.

Contributions to an Archer MSA Must Be Made in Cash

For example, contributions may not be made in the form of stock or other property.[160]

.05 Filing Requirements

Taxpayers making contributions to their Archer MSA should report these contributions on Form 8853 and attach it to their Form 1040. Trustees and custodians of Archer MSAs must file the following forms:

- Form 1099-SA, *Distributions from an HAS, Archer MSA, or Medicare Advantage MSA,* should be used by trustees to report gross distributions from an Archer MSA to an account holder. The payer is not required to compute the taxable amount of the

---

[160] Notice 96-53, 1996-2, CB 219; LTR 9821016.

distributions. An Archer MSA distribution is not taxable if used to pay for qualified medical expenses or if rolled over into another Archer MSA. If the distribution was not used for a qualified medical expense or was not rolled over into another Archer MSA, it must be included in the recipient's income and may also be subject to a 15-percent penalty.

- Form 5498-SA, *HSA, Archer MSA, or Medicare Advantage MSA Information,* should be used by trustees to report contributions to an Archer MSA. Trustees are to file the form to report regular or rollover contributions made to an individual's account, in addition to reporting the account's value.
- Form 8851, *Summary of Archer MSAs,* will be used by trustees to report the number of Archer MSAs established. Form 8851 may be filed magnetically or electronically. Trustees reporting 250 or more Archer MSAs are required to file magnetically or electronically. However, the IRS encourages all trustees to file Form 8851 magnetically/electronically.[161]

.06 Medicare Advantage MSA

The Medicare Advantage MSA is an Archer MSA designated by Medicare to be used solely to pay the qualified medical expenses of the account holder. To be eligible for a Medicare Advantage MSA, you must be eligible for Medicare and have a high-deductible health plan that meets the Medicare guidelines [Code Sec. 138]. Medicare Advantage MSAs must be used in conjunction with an Archer MSA plan.

Individuals suffering from end-stage renal disease are ineligible to establish a Medicare Advantage MSA. If an individual develops end-stage renal disease while enrolled in an Archer MSA plan, he may still continue to participate in the plan. Individuals must reside in the United States for at least 183 days during any year of enrollment in an Archer MSA plan.

Medicare Advantage MSAs must meet the following statutory requirements [Code Sec. 138(b)]:

- The Archer MSA must be designated as a Medicare Advantage MSA;
- Contributions must be made by the Secretary of Health and Human Services or by the Trustee of another Medicare Advantage MSA through a trustee-to-trustee transfer;
- The trust document must authorize trustee-to-trustee transfers;
- The Archer MSA must be established in conjunction with an Archer MSA plan; and
- An account holder may only withdraw money from the Medicare Advantage MSA to pay the account holder's qualified medical expenses.

Distributions may not be used to pay for medical expenses of the account holder's spouse, children, or other dependents [Code Sec. 138(c)(1)(A)]. *Qualified medical expenses* include amounts paid for the diagnosis, cure, mitigation, treatment, or prevention of disease [Code Sec. 213(d)].

---

[161] Rev. Proc. 2007-29, 2007-1 CB 1004.

The tax consequences of establishing a Medicare Advantage MSA include the following:

- Contributions made to the Medicare Advantage MSA by the Secretary of Health and Human Services will be excluded from the account holder's annual gross income;
- Any earnings on amounts held in an Archer MSA will not be included in the account holder's taxable income;
- Distributions for the account holder's qualified medical expenses will be excluded from income;
- Funds may be transferred tax-free from one Medicare Advantage MSA of an account holder to another Medicare Advantage MSA of the same account holder;
- After-death distributions for the qualified medical expenses of a surviving spouse of spouse's dependents are not taxable where the surviving spouse is the named beneficiary;
- The value of the Medicare Advantage MSA will be included in the account holder's gross estate for estate tax purposes; and
- After the account holder dies, a surviving spouse named as a beneficiary may continue the Archer MSA for himself or herself, but no new contributions may be made. Distributions from the account for the qualified medical expenses of the surviving spouse or the spouse's dependents are not includible in income. In addition, earnings on the account balance are not includible in income. Finally, distributions that are not used for medical expenses are includible in income and are subject to an additional 15 percent tax unless made after age 65, or due to death or disability.

MOVING EXPENSES

¶9125 MOVING EXPENSE DEDUCTION

If taxpayers make a work-related move, they may be able to deduct some of the costs associated with the move. The expenses will only be deductible if the taxpayer moves to start a new job or to work at the same job in a new job location. The taxpayer's move-related expenses must be incurred within one year of the date that the taxpayer first reports to work at the new job location. The deduction is available to both employees and self-employed taxpayers [Code Sec. 217(a); Reg. § 1.217-2(a)(3)]. Self-employed individuals are treated as having obtained employment when they make substantial arrangements to commence work in the new location (e.g., lease or purchase workspace and equipment, make arrangements to purchase inventory and make arrangements to contact customers) [Reg. § 1.217-2(f)(2)]. To qualify for the moving deduction, they must satisfy both the distance test [¶ 9130] and the time test [¶ 9135].

.01 What Expenses Qualify?

Only the following direct moving expenses are deductible:

- The cost of moving household goods and personal effects from the former residence to the new residence,
- The cost of connecting and disconnecting utilities, and
- The cost of traveling from the former residence to the new residence [Code Sec. 217(b)(1)(A), (B)].

The moving expenses of a member of the taxpayer's household can also be deducted if that person resided with the taxpayer before and after the move. None of the moving expenses of a tenant in the residence, or an individual such as a servant, governess, chauffeur, nurse, valet, or personal attendant are deductible [Code Sec. 217(b); Reg. § 1.217-2(b)(10)].

No moving expense deduction will be allowed for amounts paid for the following moving-related expenses:

- Meals eaten while moving from the old residence to your new residence;
- Travel expenses, meals, and lodging for pre-move house-hunting trips;
- Meals and lodging while occupying temporary quarters;
- Home sale, purchase, and lease expenses;
- Temporary living expenses;
- Storage charges except those incurred in-transit and for foreign moves;
- Driver's license;
- Refitting carpets and draperies;
- Car tags;
- Mortgage penalties;
- Any part of the purchase price of the new home;
- Losses from disposing of memberships in clubs;
- Losses on the sale of the home;
- Expenses of buying or selling a home;
- Expenses of obtaining and signing or breaking a lease;
- Security deposits (including any lost as a result of the move);
- Home improvements made to help sell the old home; and
- Real estate taxes.

Sale-related expenses that are no longer deductible as moving expenses can be offset against the amount realized on the sale of your residence [Ch. 7]. These include the real estate agent's commission, escrow fees, expenses of advertising the property for sale, the cost of preparing the deed and other legal expenses related to the sale, "points" paid to obtain an FHA mortgage for the buyer, and state transfer taxes paid or incurred in the sale or exchange. Taxpayers may not deduct the expense of fixing up their home or any loss sustained on the sale. The cost of a loan can be added to the basis of the new residence. These expenses include legal fees, title costs and appraisal fees. They cannot deduct payments or prepayments of rent on a lease for the new residence [Code Sec. 217(b)(2); Reg. § 1.217-2(b)(7)].

.02 Standard Mileage Rate for Moving Expenses

The standard mileage rates for use of a car (including vans, pickups, or panel trucks) is 24 cents per mile driven for moving purposes for 2013.[162]

.03 Reimbursements

Employer reimbursements under an accountable plan [Ch. 10] for deductible moving expenses are tax-free to employees—both payroll and income tax-free [Code Sec. 132(a)(6)]. They are, of course, taxable if they reimburse expenses that were deducted in a prior year.

.04 When to Claim the Deduction

Taxpayers may claim the moving expense deduction either (1) on an original tax return for the year they incurred the expenses, or (2) on an amended return for that year, filed when the time test is actually satisfied. For example, if the taxpayer starts work too late in the year to have worked 39 weeks by the tax return filing deadline, but expects to meet the time test later on the taxpayer can claim the moving expense deduction right away. Recapture rules apply if they later stop working in the locale and fail to meet the time test. They take into income the amount previously deducted in the year they fail the test [Code Sec. 217(d)(2), (3); Reg. § 1.217-2(d)(2), (3)].

.05 Where to Deduct and Report Moving Expenses

The deduction for moving expenses is no longer an itemized deduction, but rather is an "above the line" deduction which reduces gross income directly without consideration of income limits or floors [Code Sec. 62(a)(15)]. Employer reimbursements for qualified moving expenses must be reported on Form W-2, *Wage and Tax Statement.* Qualified moving expenses include transportation and storage of household goods and personal effects, plus travel and lodging expenses, but not meals, in moving from your old home to your new home. Use Form 3903, *Moving Expenses,* to report expenses for both domestic and foreign moves. Taxpayers who change their mailing address after a move should be sure to notify the IRS using Form 8822, *Change of Address.* They should mail the form to the Internal Revenue Service Center from their old address.

¶9130 THE DISTANCE TEST

Taxpayers are divided into two groups for satisfying the minimum distance requirement: (1) those changing job locations and (2) those beginning work for the first time or returning to full-time employment (e.g., college graduate or mother returning to work).

You will pass the distance test and be able to deduct your moving expenses if you moved in connection with your job or business and the distance between your new primary job and your former home is at least 50 miles greater than your old commute [Code Sec. 217(c)(1)]. There is no requirement that your old and new homes be at least 50 miles apart. For example, if your old job was 3 miles from your former home, your new job must be at least 53 miles from that former home.

162 Notice 2012-72, IRB 2012-50, 673.

Example 9-77: You moved to a new home because you found a new job. Your old job was only 5 miles from your old home. Your new job is 60 miles from that home. Because your new job is 55 miles farther from your former home than the distance from your former home to your old job, you meet the 50-mile distance test.

NOTE: The distance between two points is the shortest of the more commonly traveled routes between the two points, regardless of the route selected by you [Code Sec. 217(c); Reg. § 1.217-2(c)(2)(iii)].

Example 9-78: Ms. Taylor moved to a new home after receiving a job transfer by her employer. Taylor's old job was three miles from her former home. Because her new job is 60 miles from the former home, she satisfies the 50 mile distance requirement. Assuming the other criteria are established, she is entitled to a moving expense deduction for the expenses incurred.

.01 Exception for Members of U.S. Armed Forces

Armed forces personnel who must move because of a permanent change of station are not required to satisfy the distance test [Code Sec. 217(g)].

.02 Principal Place of Work

Your *principal* place of work is the place where you spend most of your time—at the plant, office, shop, store or other property. Your principal place of work can also be where your business activities are centered (a home base) if there is no one place where you spend a substantial portion of your working time (e.g., a railroad terminal for a train conductor) [Reg. § 1.217-2(c) (3) (i)].

▶ **DOUBLE DEDUCTION DENIED:** You cannot take a moving and business expense deduction for the same expense. A deduction is permitted under only one category [Reg. § 1.217-2(c)(3)(iii)].

¶9135 THE TIME TEST

In order for you to deduct your moving expenses, you must also meet the so-called time test. This test was created so the IRS will be sure that you really moved for your work and aren't simply trying to get the IRS to foot the bill for a mere change in scenery. You must work in the new locale for a specific length of time to qualify for the moving expense deduction. Different time requirements apply to employees and self-employeds.

.01 Time Test for Employees

To be eligible for a deduction, employees must work full-time for at least 39 weeks during the first year after arriving in the area of the new job [Code Sec. 217(c)(2)(A); Reg. § 1.217-2(c)(4)(a)]. The time is measured from the arrival date in the new job's general location.

You do not have to remain in the employ of the same employer for the 39-week period. You must, however, count only full-time employment. To be eligible for the moving expense deduction, you only must be employed in the same general location of the new job [Reg. § 1.217-2(c)(4)(iii)]

.02 Time Test for the Self-Employed

A self-employed taxpayer must work full time for at least 39 weeks during the first year and for a total of at least 78 weeks during the first two years after arriving in the area of the new workplace [Code Sec. 217(c)(2)(B)]. If spouses that file a joint return both work full time, either of the spouses can satisfy the full-time work test. If either of the spouses fails to satisfy the time test, the couple cannot combine the weeks that they each individually worked to satisfy it.

NOTE: If you are both an employee and self-employed, your principal activity will determine if the 39- or 78-week test is applicable [Reg. § 1.217-2(c)(4)(a)].

.03 Seasonal Employees

If your work is seasonal, you are considered to be working full-time during the off season, if the employment contract covers an off-season period of less than six months [Reg. § 1.217-2(c)(4)(b)(iv)].

Example 9-79: A school teacher on a 12-month contract, who teaches full-time for more than six months, is considered a full-time employee for 12 months.

Example 9-80: A self-employed motel owner in a resort area that closes down for five months of the year is deemed to work all year even though the motel is closed during the off-season.

Time Test for Spouses

Either you or your spouse may satisfy the minimum period of employment, if you file a joint tax return. Let's say you are an employee and your spouse is self-employed. You must satisfy the time test applicable to your employee status, or your spouse must satisfy the test applicable to her own situation [Reg. § 1.217-2 (c) (4) (b) (v)].

Example 9-81: Mr. Albert is an electrician residing in New York City. He moves himself, his family, and his household goods and personal effects, at his own expense, to Denver. He commences work with ABC Aircraft Inc. After working 30 weeks, Albert leaves the job. He moves to and commences work in Los Angeles. Employment lasts for more than 39 weeks. No moving expense deduction is permitted for expenses incurred from New York City to Denver because Albert was not employed in the general location of ABC Aircraft in Denver for at least 39 weeks. A moving expense deduction is permitted (if all other conditions are met) for the expenses incurred in relocating from Denver to California.

Example 9-82: Same facts as Example 9-81. Assume Albert and his wife, Mary, file a joint tax return. Mary began working in Denver at the same time as Mr. Albert. Mary continued working in Denver for 10 weeks after he left for California. The moving expenses incurred in the move from New York City to Denver are deductible (assuming all criteria are met) because Mary has satisfied the 39 week requirement in Denver. If they filed separate tax returns, only Mary would be entitled to the moving expense deduction based on the New York to Denver move.

.04 Exceptions to the Time Test Requirement

The time test requirement is waived if the taxpayer dies, becomes disabled or is involuntarily separated from service, other than for willful misconduct [Code Sec. 217(d)(1)(B)].

Retirees

If you retire from a workplace outside of the United States and had maintained a foreign residence as well, you may treat the cost of moving to the United States in connection with retirement as job-related moving expenses. No post-move time test applies. Similarly, a spouse or dependent of a decedent who had worked outside of the United States may deduct the cost of moving to the United States within six months after the decedent's death [Code Sec. 217(i)].

Military Personnel

Members of the United States armed forces are not required to meet the 39-week time test if a subsequent move is on account of a military order or permanent change of station [Code Sec. 217(g)].

DEDUCTION FOR MISCELLANEOUS EXPENSES

¶9140 MISCELLANEOUS ITEMIZED DEDUCTIONS

You can claim expenses that are reported as miscellaneous deductions on Schedule A of Form 1040 [¶ 9001]only if you itemize your deductions. You can deduct most of these expenses only to the extent that they exceed 2 percent of your adjusted gross income [Code Sec. 67(a)].

Your deduction is equal to the total of all allowable miscellaneous expenses reduced by 2 percent of your adjusted gross income. Generally, you apply the 2 percent limit after any other deduction limitation (for example, the percentage limit on meals and entertainment [Ch. 10]) is figured.

.01 Miscellaneous Expenses Subject to 2 Percent Deduction Limit

The following expenses are subject to the 2 percent deduction limit:

- Expenses for the production or collection of income which are deductible anyway such as investment advisory fees, certain attorneys' fees, service fees paid to a custodian (for example, a bank) of investment property, administrative fees in connection with an IRA or Keogh plan, subscriptions to investment advisory publications, and the cost of a safe deposit box used for investment purposes [Temp. Reg. § 1.67-1T(a)(1)(ii)];
- Expenses for tax preparation and other tax-related services such as tax counsel fees and appraisal fees [Temp. Reg. § 1.67-1T(a)(1)(iii)];

- Nonreimbursed employee business such as expenses for transportation, travel fares and lodging while away from home, business meals and entertainment, continuing education courses, subscriptions to professional journals, union or professional dues, professional uniforms, job hunting, and the business use of the employee's home [Temp. Reg. § 1.67-1T(a)(1)(i)];
- Dues to unions or professional societies;
- Safe deposit box rental;
- Employment-related education [Ch. 12];
- Certain appraisal fees;
- Certain legal fees (e.g., those incurred in connection with employment or to recover unpaid alimony);
- Clerical help and office rent in caring for investments, including the cost of a computer;
- Expenses incurred for management of undeveloped land and other property held for appreciation;
- Fees to collect interest and dividends;
- Hobby expenses, but generally not more than hobby income [Temp. Reg. § 1.67-1T(a)(1)(iv)]. Note that the hobby income limitation is applied before the 2 percent rule [Ch. 13];
- Investment counsel and seminar fees;
- Liquidated damages paid to former employer for breach of employment contract;
- Looking for a new job (including fees paid to employment agencies and resume printing and mailing costs);
- Employee's malpractice insurance premiums;
- Medical examinations required by employer;
- Occupational taxes;
- Part of home used regularly and exclusively in work [Ch. 12];
- Research expenses of a college professor;
- Small tools and supplies used in the taxpayer's work;
- Subscriptions to professional journals and trade magazines related to work;
- Tax professionals' fees to prepare IRS ruling requests;[163]
- User fee paid to IRS for ruling requests;[164]
- Travel and entertainment expenses directly related to or associated with an employee's job [Ch. 10];
- Travel expenses in connection with the management of investments;
- Union dues and expenses;
- Work clothes and uniforms; and
- Wrap fees paid on brokerage accounts that charge a flat percentage fee instead of a commission.[165]

---

[163] Rev. Rul. 89-68, 1989-1 CB 82.

[164] Rev. Rul. 89-68, 1989-1 CB 82.

[165] CCA 200721015 (Jan. 16, 2007).

▶ **OBSERVATION:** If you or your spouse have a lot of miscellaneous expenses subject to the 2 percent floor, you may be better off filing separately rather than jointly this year. That way the 2 percent floor is applied separately to each spouse's adjusted gross income (AGI).

.02 Deductible Miscellaneous Expenses Not Subject to 2 Percent Limit

The following miscellaneous expenses are not subject to the 2 percent limit:

- Interest deductions under Code Sec. 163;
- Any deduction allowable in connection with personal property used in a short sale;
- Deduction for amortizable bond premiums under Code Sec. 171 [¶9155];
- Tax deductions under Code Sec. 164;
- Personal casualty and theft losses in excess of 10 percent of adjusted gross income and a $100 floor for each loss described in Code Secs. 165(a)(c)(3) or (d);
- Deduction for charitable contributions under Code Sec. 170;
- Gambling losses to the extent of gambling winnings [Ch. 13];
- Deduction if annuity payments cease before the investment is recovered;
- Deduction for impairment-related work expenses as defined in Code Sec. 67(d)];
- Deduction allowed to trusts and estates for amounts paid or permanently set aside for charitable purposes;
- Deductions in connection with personal property used in a short sale;
- Deductions in connection with cooperative housing corporations by a tenant-shareholder under Code Sec. 216;
- Deduction for moving expenses under Code Sec. 217;
- Deductions for estate tax in the case of income in respect of a decedent under Code Sec. 691(c); and
- Tax adjustments where the taxpayers restore a substantial amount held under a claim of right under Code Sec. 1341.

.03 How the 2 Percent Floor Applies to Pass-Through Entities

The 2 percent floor does not apply to the investment expenses of pass-through entities such as partnerships, S corporations, a common trust fund, real estate mortgage investment companies (REMICs), or nonpublicly traded regulated investment companies (RICs) at the entity level [Code Sec. 67(c); Temp. Reg. §§1.67-2T(g)(1), -2T(e), -3T]. Instead, the miscellaneous itemized deductions of these entities are segregated from other expenses and an allocable portion is passed through as gross dividends to each investor based on his or her ownership interest.

This means that for pass-through entities (i.e., partnerships, S corporations and grantor trusts), the 2 percent floor is applied at the investor level. Thus, as an investor, you are deemed to have incurred an allocable share of these types of expenses—which are subject to your 2 percent-of-adjusted-gross-income floor [Temp. Reg. §1.67-2T].

The 2 percent limitation then applies when the investor claims the expense as a miscellaneous itemized deduction on Schedule A [Temp. Reg. § 1.67-1T]. Note that the 2 percent floor does not apply to the following pass-through entities: estates, trusts (other than grantor trusts), cooperatives, or real estate investment trusts (REITs) [Code Sec. 67(c)]. For discussion of whether a trust's investment advice fees are subject to the 2 percent floor, see ¶ 25,055.03.

Mutual Fund Investments

Investors in a publicly offered regulated investment company (mutual fund) are exempt from the application of the 2 percent floor [Code Sec. 67(c)(2)]. The mutual fund will report this expense to you on Form 1099-DIV, in box 1 by means of a net figure which represents your net dividend income (gross ordinary dividends minus investment expense). You in turn will report this net figure in your taxable income for the year.

How to Avoid 2 Percent Floor

One way to avoid the 2 percent floor is to avoid classification for tax purposes as an "investor." Reason: Professional "traders" and "dealers," as opposed to investors, may claim their investment-related expenses as ordinary and necessary trade or business expenses under Code Sec. 162 without being subject to the 2 percent floor on miscellaneous itemized deductions that is imposed on investors.

¶9145 COMMON TYPES OF MISCELLANEOUS EXPENSES

What are probably the most common types of deductible miscellaneous expenses fall into three groups: Employee business expenses, investment expenses and expenses of determining tax liability.

.01 Employee Business Expenses

Employee business expenses are generally miscellaneous expenses that are subject to the 2 percent of adjusted gross income floor. However, special rules apply when you are reimbursed by your employer for these costs. The tax treatment of your reimbursed employee business expenses depends on how your employer treated the reimbursement and if you adequately accounted to your employer (i.e., submitted records substantiating expenses) under a so-called accountable plan.

Accountable Plans

An accountable plan [Ch. 10] is any expense arrangement that satisfies three requirements: (1) payments cover only job-related expenses you could have otherwise deducted, (2) you must substantiate to the company the expense's date, time, place, amount and business purpose, and (3) you must return any excess reimbursement amount within a reasonable time period.

Automatic Allowances

If you use one of the so-called automatic allowances, you meet the substantiation requirement as long as the allowance is within IRS-approved limits. These allowances include a mileage allowance (equal to or less than the standard mileage rate for business travel) for employees who use their cars for business travel [Ch. 10] and a per-diem allowance for meals and/or lodging for employees traveling away from home on business [Ch. 10]. If you meet the accountable plan requirements, and the reimbursement is not included on Form W-2, you need not report the expenses and reimbursement on your tax return—unless you want to deduct your employee business expenses in excess of the reimbursement.

Otherwise, you report the expenses and reimbursements on Form 2106 [Ch. 10]. You transfer any expenses in excess of reimbursements to Schedule A of Form 1040 [¶9001]. You subtract reimbursements that were not included on Form W-2 from the expenses on Form 2106. You can deduct expenses up to the amount of reimbursements that were included on Form W-2 as an adjustment to your gross income (they offset the additional reimbursement income). You may claim unreimbursed expenses as a miscellaneous itemized deduction, subject to the 2 percent of adjusted gross income floor.

> **NOTE:** The rules for deducting business travel and entertainment expenses are discussed in Chapter 10. Other business expenses are covered in Chapter 12.

.02 Investment Expenses

The miscellaneous itemized deduction category includes expenses you incur to produce, or collect income, and to manage or maintain property held for the production of income. The income must be taxable (e.g., expenses associated with investments in tax-exempt municipal bonds are not deductible) [Code Sec. 212; Reg. § 1.212-1(a),(d)].

> **NOTE:** You report expenses incurred in the rental of property or in the production of royalty income (including depreciation, repairs, taxes and interest) on Schedule E, Form 1040. These expenses are deductions for adjusted gross income.

.03 Expenses of Determining Tax Liability

You can claim the cost of determining the amount of tax due, seeking a refund or contesting an assessment as a miscellaneous itemized deduction. The taxing authority may be federal, state, or municipal.

> **NOTE:** The cost of tax return preparation and tax litigation connected with a sole proprietorship or rental income can be written off as a deduction to arrive at adjusted gross income. In other words, these expenses are not considered miscellaneous itemized expenses. Thus, the deduction for these expenses is not subject to the 2 percent-of-AGI floor.[166]

---

[166] Rev. Rul. 92-29, 1992-1 CB 20.

¶9150 PENALTY FOR PREMATURE WITHDRAWAL FROM BANK CERTIFICATE OF DEPOSIT

Banks generally impose a penalty if you withdraw funds from a certificate of deposit or other time savings account before the maturity date. You deduct this penalty, or forfeiture of interest, as an adjustment to gross income [Code Sec. 62(a)(9)]. Thus, you can claim it regardless of whether or not you itemize your deductions.

¶9155 BOND PREMIUMS

When your purchase price (or other basis for purposes of determining loss on sale or exchange) for a bond is more than the bond's face value, the difference between the purchase price and the face value is called the bond premium [Code Sec. 171(b)(1)]. For example, a bond with a face value of $1,000 would have a $50 premium if it sells for $1,050. Bonds usually are issued at a premium when the rate of interest payable on the bond exceeds the market rate of interest. Receipt of the bond premium reduces your basis in the bond and, if you include interest from the bond in income, you may write off the amount of the bond premium.

Normally, you treat bond premiums as received in the year the bond matures. However, certain bond premiums may be "amortized," that is, treated as an offset against the interest received each year over the life of the bond. The amount of the bond premium allocated to each year is called the amortizable bond premium [Code Sec. 171(b)(2)].

.01 Taxable Bonds

You are allowed to write off an amount representing your amortizable bond premium for each year you receive interest from a taxable bond [Code Sec. 171(a)(1)]. Because the amortizable bond premium is a return of your investment, you must also reduce your basis in the bond by the amount you deduct [Code Sec. 1016(a)(5)]. How you handle the deduction and basis reduction depends on the year you acquired the bond.

Bonds Acquired After 1987

Bonds acquired during this period are handled in one of two ways:

- You may elect to amortize the bond premium by offsetting your interest income from the bond with a proportional deduction (reducing your basis by the amount of the deduction) in each year you hold the bond [Code Sec. 171(c)(1), (e)]. If an election is made for any particular bond issue, it applies to all bonds owned at the date of election and all bonds later acquired. The election must be made by claiming the offset on your return. It is binding for all future years, unless it is revoked on application to the IRS [Code Sec. 171(c)(2)]. Elections made in a refund claim after the return is filed are not recognized.[167]

---

[167] *W.B. Barnhill*, CA-5, 57-1 USTC ¶9436, 241 F2d 496.

- You can forgo your opportunity to elect amortization [Reg. § 1.171(a)(2)]. You will be allowed a deductible loss for the amount of the bond premium in the year you redeem or dispose of the bond, pursuant to the regular rules for capital losses.

.02 Tax-Exempt Bonds

If you invest in a bond that produces tax-exempt interest, you must amortize any premium you paid to buy the bond. Because the interest is tax exempt, no deduction will be allowed for the amount of the amortizable bond premium. Still, you must reduce your basis in the bond by the amount of the premium you would have otherwise deducted [Code Secs. 171(a)(2), 1016(a)(5); Reg. § § 1.171-1(b), 1.1016-5(b)].

.03 Figuring the Amortizable Bond Premium

You have a choice of methods for calculating your amortizable bond premium for the year. Under the general rule, you use your yield to maturity with semiannual compounding. The amortizable premium is the difference between the interest actually paid on the bond and the earnings based on the yield to maturity [Code Sec. 171(b)].

> **Example 9-83:** Ms. Burger bought a $10,000 bond that pays 11 percent interest—or $550 every six months—for $12,000. Thus, she paid a $2,000 premium. Since Burger will receive only $10,000 when the bond matures, her yield to maturity is less than 11 percent—the exact yield depends on the remaining term of the bond. Assume the actual yield comes to 8 percent compounded semiannually. For the first six months, an 8 percent yield on the $12,000 basis is $480. The $70 difference between this and the $550 interest payment she receives is the amortizable bond premium. For the next six months, her basis is $11,930. An 8 percent annual yield on that for six months is $477. Thus, Burger's amortizable bond premium and basis reduction for this period is $73 ($550 – $477).

Alternatively, you can use a straight-line type of amortization method. You divide the number of months you owned the bond during the year by the number of months from your acquisition date until the maturity date. Then you multiply the result by the premium you had as of the acquisition date. Fractional parts of a month are disregarded, unless they are more than half a month. In that case, they are treated as full months [Reg. § 1.171-2(f) (2)].

> **Example 9-84:** Mr. Crown buys a $10,000 bond on March 20, 2008, for $11,000. The bond will mature on July 31, 2014. Thus, the bond has 100 months until maturity (not counting the fractional month of March). Crown's amortizable bond premium for 2008 is $90 (9 months ÷ 100 months × $1,000). If Crown holds the bond throughout 2008, his amortizable bond premium for that year is $120 (12 months ÷ 100 × $1,000).

.04 Special Situations

The situations described here use special rules.

Callable Bonds

A taxable bond that is subject to a call before it matures can be redeemed by the issuer before the scheduled maturity date. The premium on taxable bonds is amortized to either the maturity date or an earlier call date, whichever results in a smaller deduction [Code Sec. 171(b)(1)(B)]. If a bond is called before a premium is fully amortized, you can deduct the portion not yet amortized in the year of the call [Code Sec. 171(b)(2)].

Convertible Bonds

Convertible bonds may be amortized if the bondholder has the right to decide whether to convert the bond on a specified date. However, the extra amount paid for the conversion privilege cannot be amortized. The amount of the premium that represents the conversion feature may be found by getting the yield on similar bonds without conversion features selling on the open market, and adjusting the price of the convertible bond to this yield. This adjustment may be made by using standard bond tables [Reg. § 1.171-2(c)].

Capitalized Expenses

You generally may amortize capitalized expenses (such as buying commissions) as part of the bond premium, unless the premium is made up entirely of capitalized expenses. In that case, you may choose to amortize your capitalized expenses, but you are not required to do so [Reg. § 1.171-2(d)].

¶9165 TUITION AND FEES DEDUCTION

Taxpayers may claim an above-the-line deduction for "qualified tuition and related expenses" that were paid before January 1, 2014 [Code Sec. 222(e)].

.01 Qualified Tuition and Related Expenses Defined

Qualified tuition and related expenses are defined as tuition and fees required for the enrollment or attendance of the taxpayer, the taxpayer's spouse, or any dependent for whom the taxpayer is entitled to deduct a dependency exemption, at an eligible educational institution for courses of instruction. Special rules apply for individuals claimed as dependents by another taxpayer, married individuals filing separately, and nonresident aliens. Generally, any accredited public, nonprofit, or proprietary post-secondary institution is an eligible educational institution as defined for purposes of the education credits under Code Sec. 25A [Code Sec. 222(d)(1)]. The deduction is allowed for expenses paid during a tax year in connection with enrollment during the year or in connection with an academic term beginning during the year or the first three months of the following year [Code Sec. 222(d)(3)].

Taxpayers may not use the deduction for qualified tuition and related expenses to claim a double benefit. If a qualified tuition and related expense is deductible under any other provision, it is not deductible under Code Sec. 222 [Code Sec. 222(c)(1)]. The taxpayer must reduce the total amount of qualified tuition and related expenses by the amount excluded for: (1) interest on U.S. savings bonds used to pay for higher education [Code Sec. 135], (2) distributions from a qualified tuition program (or qualified tuition plan (QTP) or 529 plan) [Code Sec. 529(c)(1)], or (3) distributions from a Coverdell education savings account (formerly, an education IRA) [Code Sec. 530(d)(2)]. Finally, in determining the amount to exclude from qualified tuition and related expenses for distributions from a qualified tuition plan, the amount excluded does not include the portion of that distribution that represents a return on contributions to the plan [Code Sec. 222(c)(2)(B)].

.02 Amount of Deduction

The amount of the tuition and fees deduction is limited to $4,000, and is only available to taxpayers with AGI not exceeding $65,000 ($130,000 for joint filers) for the year [Code Sec. 222(b)(2)(A)]. Taxpayers whose income exceeds that limit but does not exceed $80,000 ($160,000 for joint filers) may deduct up to $2,000 in qualified expenses [Code Sec. 222(b)(2)(B)].

.03 What Form to File

Taxpayers should file Form 8917, *Tuition and Fees Deduction,* to claim this deduction and attach the Form to either Form 1040 or Form 1040A. The taxpayer must include the name and taxpayer identification number (TIN) of the student for whom the expenses were paid on the taxpayer's return in order to claim the deduction [Code Sec. 222(d)(2)]. As an above-the-line deduction, it may even be claimed by taxpayers who do not itemize their deductions. Taxpayers cannot claim both an education credit and the tuition and fees deduction or the same student in the same tax year.

Travel and Entertainment Deductions

TRANSPORTATION AND TRAVEL EXPENSES

Travel and transportation expenses . . . . ¶ 10,001
Special restriction on travel deductions . . . . ¶ 10,005
Substantiation and reporting of travel expenses . . . . ¶ 10,010
Travel allowances and reimbursements . . . . ¶ 10,015

DEDUCTIONS FOR BUSINESS CARS

Auto expenses in general . . . . ¶ 10,020
Depreciation deductions for cars . . ¶ 10,025
Leased cars . . . . ¶ 10,030
Reporting and substantiation of auto expenses . . . . ¶ 10,035

BUSINESS ENTERTAINMENT DEDUCTIONS

Entertainment deductions in general . . . . ¶ 10,040
Special entertainment deduction rules . . . . ¶ 10,045
Business gifts . . . . ¶ 10,050
Reporting and substantiation . . . . ¶ 10,055

TRANSPORTATION AND TRAVEL EXPENSES

This chapter deals with the deductibility of transportation and travel expenses you pay in connection with your trade or business or for the production of income. The examples present ideas that can help you increase your travel deductions.

¶10,001 TRAVEL AND TRANSPORTATION EXPENSES

Taxpayers can deduct transportation costs if they are ordinary and necessary expenses incurred in connection with a trade or business or for the production of income. Travel expenses are also deductible if they satisfy an additional requirement: Taxpayers incur them while they are away from their tax home [Code Sec. 162(a)(2)].

Transportation expenses are the direct cost of going from one place to another (e.g., cab fares, car expenses). Travel expenses include transportation costs and living expenses incurred when taxpayers are away from home. Travel expenses cover the following:

- Air, rail and business fares;
- The cost of operating and maintaining a car or an airplane;
- Taxi fares or other transportation costs between an airport or station and a hotel, between business meetings, and from a business meeting to a hotel or restaurant;
- Meals at restaurants;
- Hotel charges or other lodging costs;
- Cleaning and laundry services;
- Telephone and telegraph expenses;
- Public stenographers' fees; and
- Tips incidental to any of the above expenses.

NOTE: You cannot deduct membership dues paid to a hotel or airline club that provides special services to travelers [See ¶ 10,045].

The deduction for transportation and travel expenses is available to corporations, partnerships, sole proprietors and to employees who incur these expenses in connection with their employment. For example, if an employer reimburses an employee for expenses incurred while away from home on business, the employer can deduct the reimbursement as a travel expense. And the reimbursement is tax-free to the employee so long as a proper record of the expenses is submitted to the employer [¶ 10,015].

.01 Travel Away From Home—Sleep-or-Rest Rule

Taxpayers may deduct the cost of meal and incidental expenses (M&IE) when "away from home" in the pursuit of a trade or business [Code Sec. 162(a)(2)]. Traveling expenses include travel fares, meals, lodging, and other expenses incident to travel [Reg. § 1.162-2].

The standard used to determine whether a taxpayer is "away from home" was developed through a series of cases including *Williams v. Patterson*.[1] In *Williams*, the taxpayer, a railroad engineer, worked a 16-hour work day every other day. On a turnaround run between Montgomery, Alabama, his home terminal, and Atlanta, Georgia, he had a 6-hour layover in Atlanta before his return to Montgomery the same day. Although the taxpayer was not required by his employer to do so, during the layover period he felt it was necessary to sleep and rest and therefore rented a hotel room where he had lunch and dinner as well as rested and slept before returning to work. The Court of Appeals for the Fifth Circuit concluded that on account of the length of the taxpayer's workday (16 hours), the duration of his layover (6 hours), and the responsibility of his position, it was necessary for the taxpayer to rest during his layover in order to carry out his assignment, even though no statute, regulation, or railroad rule required him to sleep or rest before his return trip. Furthermore, the court reasoned that the phrase "away from home" does not require a person to actually be away overnight. The court held that the costs of meals, lodging, and tips during the 6-hour layover were deductible. As stated in *Williams*, as applied to a traveler whose work does not require him to be "away from home" overnight, the standard is:

---

[1] *F.M. Williams v. Patterson,* CA-5, 61-1 USTC ¶ 9183, 286 F2d 333, 340.

> If the nature of the taxpayer's employment is such that when away from home, during released time, it is reasonable for him to need and to obtain sleep or rest in order to meet the exigencies of his employment or the business demands of his employment, his expenditures (including incidental expenses, such as tips) for the purpose of obtaining sleep or rest are deductible traveling expenses * * *. [Id.]

This standard is commonly referred to as the "sleep or rest rule." Thus, taxpayers can deduct the cost of meals, lodging and other travel expenses when they are away from their tax home on business overnight or for a period long enough to require sleep or rest to meet the demands of their work. Napping in the car does not satisfy the rest requirement. If they do not satisfy the sleep-or-rest requirement, they may not claim a travel deduction.[2] On the other hand, they can deduct business transportation expenses whether or not they are away from home.

Example 10-1: Mr. Baker lives and works in Los Angeles. He flies to San Francisco on business and returns the same day. Results: (1) He can deduct the cost of his airfare as a transportation expense. (2) He cannot deduct the cost of his meals in San Francisco because meals are a travel expense, and Baker was not away from home overnight. However, if Baker stays in San Francisco overnight and returns the next day, his hotel and meal expenses in San Francisco are deductible.

A taxpayer's tax home is the location of his or her place of business or employment, regardless of where the taxpayer lives.[3] The entire city or general area in which the business or employment is located is his or her tax home. In *M.G. Bissonnette*,[4] the Tax Court concluded that a ferryboat captain who worked 15- to 17-hour days with a six-hour layover during off-season voyages was entitled to deduct 50 percent of the full-day per diem amount for meal and incidental expenses (M&IEs). The court concluded that it was reasonable for the captain to rest during the six-hour layover to meet his responsibilities to his crew and for the safety of up to 1,200 passengers. Therefore the court held that the taxpayer was "away from home" for purposes of the Code Sec. 162(a)(2) deduction for meal and incidental expenses incurred while away from home in the pursuit of a trade or business. The court considered the following factors in determining that the taxpayer needed sleep or rest: (1) the taxpayer's age; (2) physical condition; (3) the length of the taxpayer's workday; and (4) the importance of being alert so the taxpayer can carry out his job's responsibilities without fear of injury to others. These factors must be applied against the background of the taxpayer's experience in his employment and the practices and customs of similarly situated individuals.

Two Places of Business

If the taxpayer has two or more regular work locations, his or her main place of work is considered his or her tax home. In determining which location is the main place of work, the taxpayer has to take into account such factors as the total time spent at each

---

[2] *H.O. Correll*, SCt, 68-1 USTC ¶9101, 389 US 299, 88 SCt 445; Rev. Rul. 75-170, 1975-1 CB 60.

[3] Rev. Rul 71-247, 1971-1 CB 54; *G.W. Newman*, 58 TCM 1024, Dec. 46,225(M), TC Memo. 1989-672; *L.A. Bjornstad*, 83 TCM 1256, Dec. 54,657(M), TC Memo. 2002-47.

[4] *M.G. Bissonnette*, 127 TC 124, Dec. 56,648 (2006).

location, the degree of business activity there and the amount of income derived there. The taxpayer can deduct the cost of business travel from his or her primary work location to a secondary location, even if the family residence is in the area of the secondary location. The taxpayer can also deduct a portion of his or her family living expenses to the extent they are attributable to the taxpayer's presence while conducting business at the secondary location.[5]

Example 10-2: Mr. Mason works three weeks a month in Detroit and one week in Chicago. Mason's family lives in Chicago. Mason can deduct his travel expenses to and from Chicago because he is away from home (Detroit) on business. And, for the same reason, he can also deduct an allocable portion of his family's meal and lodging expenses while in Chicago. He cannot, however, deduct his living expenses in Detroit; that is his tax home.

Local Business-Related Lodging Expenses Deductible

Reg. § 1.262-1(b)(5) provides that an employee's lodging expenses that are incurred in the same town as the employer will be deductible provided the lodging is necessary for the employee to participate in a meeting or function sponsored by the employer.[6] The IRS will no longer challenge an employer's deduction of the cost of employee lodging that is located in the same town as the employer under the following conditions:

1. The lodging is on a temporary basis;
2. The lodging is necessary for the employee to participate in or be available for a bona fide business meeting or function of the employer; and
3. The expenses are otherwise deductible by the employee, or would be deductible if paid by the employee, under Code Sec. 162(a).

Expenses paid or incurred by an employee for local lodging may be deductible as ordinary and necessary expenses of a taxpayer's trade or business if the employee satisfies the following safe harbor created in Prop. Reg. § 1.162-31(b):

1. The lodging is necessary for the individual to participate fully in or be available for a bona fide business meeting, conference, training activity, or other business function;
2. The lodging is for a period that does not exceed five calendar days and does not recur more frequently than once per calendar quarter;
3. If the individual is an employee, the employee's employer requires the employee to remain at the activity or function overnight; and
4. The lodging is not lavish or extravagant under the circumstances and does not provide any significant element of personal pleasure, recreation, or benefit.

Example 10-3: Employer conducts training for its employees at a hotel near Employer's main office. Some employees attending the training are traveling away from home and some employees are not traveling away from home.

[5] *E.W. Andrews,* CA-1, 91-1 USTC ¶ 50,211, 931 F2d 132.

[6] Notice 2007-47, 2007-1 CB 1393.

Employer requires all employees attending the training to remain at the hotel overnight for the *bona fide* purpose of facilitating the training. Employer pays the costs of the lodging at the hotel directly to the hotel and does not treat the value as compensation to the employees. Employer has a noncompensatory business purpose for paying the lodging expenses. Employer is not paying the expenses primarily to provide a social or personal benefit to the employees. If the employees who are not traveling away from home had paid for their own lodging, the expenses would have been deductible as ordinary and necessary business expenses. Therefore, the value of the lodging is excluded from the employees' income as a working condition fringe under Code Sec. 132(a) and (d). Employer may deduct the lodging expenses, including lodging for employees who are not traveling away from home, as ordinary and necessary business expenses [Prop. Reg. § 1.162-31(c), Ex. 1].

Example 10-4: Employer is a professional sports team. Employer requires its players and coaches to stay at a local hotel the night before a home game to conduct last minute training and ensure the physical preparedness of the players. Employer pays the lodging expenses directly to the hotel and does not treat the value as compensation to the employees. Employer has a noncompensatory business purpose for paying the lodging expenses. Employer is not paying the lodging expenses primarily to provide a social or personal benefit to the employees. If the employees had paid for their own lodging, the expenses would have been deductible by the employees as ordinary and necessary business expenses. Therefore, the value of the lodging is excluded from the employees' income as a working condition fringe. Employer may deduct the expenses for lodging the players and coaches at the hotel as ordinary and necessary business expenses [Prop. Reg. § 1.162-31(c), Ex. 3].

Travel Between Home Office and Work Deductible

If the taxpayer legitimately maintains a home office in the eyes of the IRS, the taxpayer is entitled to a special perk [See Ch. 12]. Once the taxpayer has established a part of his or her home as a home office, the taxpayer can deduct the daily transportation expenses incurred when traveling between an office in his or her home, which now becomes one of the taxpayer's work locations, and other work locations, regardless of whether the location is regular or temporary, or is within or outside of the metropolitan area. The daily transportation expenses incurred in going between the home office and other work locations must be incurred in the same trade or business. The Tax Court sanctioned this deduction in 1980.[7]

Example 10-5: Bob is an architect who uses the basement in his home as his principal place of business. When he is working he drives from his home to client's homes, job sites, the interior designer's office, and various showrooms and fabricators. His transportation costs for all these trips are deductible because he is traveling from one work site (his home) to another work location.

[7] *E.R. Curphey*, 73 TC 766, Dec. 36,753 (1980).

Home Office Required to Be Principal Place of Business

To qualify for the deduction, however, the office your home must satisfy the principal place of business requirement of Code Sec. 280A(c)(1)(A) [See ¶ 12,125]. You can claim a deduction on Form 8829 for the business use of your home only when the strict home office deduction rules are satisfied. This means that you must have set aside a specific part of your home as your home office and use it exclusively and regularly as your principal place of business, or as a place to meet with patients, clients or customers. There can be no other fixed location where you conduct these activities.

Your home office qualifies as your principal place business even if you perform administrative or management activities in the office and see no patients, clients, or customers there. You must, however, have no other fixed location where you are allowed to conduct these substantial administrative or management activities. Some of the activities considered to be administrative or managerial in nature include billing customers, clients or patients, keeping books and records, setting up appointments and forwarding orders or writing reports.

The home office can be in separate structure not attached to your dwelling, which may include a house, apartment, condominium, mobile home, boat, or similar property that provides basic living accommodations such as sleeping space, toilet, and cooking facilities. All other structures next to or near your dwelling unit, such as separate garage or shed in your back yard, could qualify as your home office. Keep in mind that hotels, motels, or inns will not qualify as a home office.

Temporary v. Permanent Place of Work

If your work location is temporary, you can deduct: (1) transportation expenses between your residence to a "temporary" work or business location outside the metropolitan area where you live and normally work; (2) transportation expenses between your residence to a "temporary work location in the same trade or business within the metropolitan area where you live and normally work only if: (a) you have one or more regular work locations away from your residence or (b) if your residence is your principal place of business under Code Sec. 280A(c)(1)(A) [See Ch. 12].

In Rev. Rul. 99-7,[8] the IRS established that a work location will be considered "temporary," in the absence of facts and circumstances indicating otherwise, if employment at that location is realistically expected to last (and does in fact last) for one year or less. If employment at a work location is realistically expected to last for more than one year or there is no realistic expectation that it will last for one year or less, the employment isn't temporary, whether or not it actually exceeds one year. If employment at a work location initially is realistically expected to last one year or less, but at some later date the employment is realistically expected to exceed one year, that employment is temporary until the date that the taxpayer's realistic expectation changes, and is treated as not temporary after that date.

Example 10-6: Sam, who lives in Wilmington, Delaware is a self-employed computer specialist. He finds an assignment to work for a bank in Baltimore,

[8] Rev. Rul. 99-7, 1999-1 CB 361; *J. Balla*, 95 TCM 1090, Dec. 57,319 (M), TC Memo. 2008-18; *R.M. Brockman*, 85 TCM 733, Dec. 55,004(M), TC Memo. 2003-3.

Maryland. His task is to upgrade all the bank computers. The job is expected to last for 9 months. Sam drives from Wilmington to his job in Baltimore every day for 9 months. This assignment is defined as temporary and he can either deduct his transportation expenses or exclude from income any reimbursement he receives from the bank for his travel expenses. If Sam is informed that they will need him for 18 months rather than just 9 months, his employment no longer is classified as temporary as of the date he is informed of the change. At that point his transportation expenses become nondeductible commuting expenses.

Example 10-7: Kim is a decorative painter who commutes every day for six months from her home in Baltimore to a commercial job site in Philadelphia, which is 2 hours away. She is entitled to deduct her travel expenses for this six month period when she is working outside the Baltimore metropolitan area where she normally lives and works.

In determining whether a work assignment is temporary, a two-to-three week break will be deemed to be inconsequential, but a seven-month break will restart the clock.[9] Thus, two offsite work assignments separated by a seven-month continuous break would be treated as two separate period of employment for purposes of the one-year temporary workplace limit.

In *K.R. Saunders*,[10] the Tax Court concluded that a construction worker's expenses for travel to five temporary work sites were nondeductible personal expenses because the taxpayer failed to prove that he met any of the exceptions to the general rule treating commuting expenses as nondeductible personal expenses.

.02 Commuting

The costs incurred by a taxpayer to commute between his or her residence and place of business are generally nondeductible personal expenses because, as the Supreme Court explained in *J.N. Flowers*,[11] the taxpayer makes a personal choice about where to live [Code Sec. 262(a); Reg. §§1.162-2(e), 1.262-1(b)(5)]. In Rev. Rul. 99-7,[12] the IRS recognized the following three exceptions to the general rule that commuting expenses are nondeductible personal expenses:

1. Transportation between the taxpayer's residence and a temporary work location outside the metropolitan area where the taxpayer lives and normally works is deductible ("temporary distant workplace exception");
2. If the taxpayer has one or more "regular work locations away from the taxpayer's residence," transportation between the taxpayer's residence and a temporary work location is deductible ("regular work location exception"); and

---

[9] Chief Counsel Advice 200025052 (Apr. 26, 2000), 200026025 (May 31, 2000).

[10] *K.R. Saunders*, 104 TCM 74, Dec. 59,123(M), TC Memo. 2012-200.

[11] *J.N. Flowers*, SCt, 46-1 USTC ¶9127, 326 US 465, 66 SCt 250, *reh'g denied*, 326 US 816.

[12] Rev. Rul. 99-7, 1999-1 CB 361. *See G.P. Bogue*, CA-3, 2013-1 USTC ¶50,354, unpublished op. *aff'g per curiam*, 102 TCM 41, Dec. 58,697(M), TC Memo. 2011-164.

3. Transportation between the taxpayer's residence (if the residence serves as the taxpayer's principal place of business) and a regular or temporary work location is deductible ("home office exception"). But the deduction cannot exceed what it would have cost the taxpayer to remain at the temporary work assignment location rather than travel between the two locations.[13]

Example 10-8: Ms. Parker is away from home for two weeks on business. On Friday of the first week, she travels back home. On Sunday she returns to her temporary assignment location. Her airfare to and from home is $780. If Parker had stayed at her temporary assignment location for the weekend, her meal, and lodging costs would have been $500. Result: Parker can only deduct $500 of her airfare.

.03 Business Exigencies Rule

In *Wilbert*,[14] the Court of Appeals for the Seventh Circuit applied the "business exigencies" rule established by the Supreme Court in *Flowers*,[15] to conclude that an airline mechanic was not entitled to deductions for vehicle, meal and lodging expenses because he was not "away from home" when the expenses were incurred. In *Flowers*, the Supreme Court said that "the exigencies of business rather than the personal conveniences and necessities of the traveler must be the motivating factors" in the decision to travel.

In *Flowers*, the Supreme Court went on to say that in order to claim a travel expense deduction, a taxpayer must show that:

1. His expenses are ordinary and necessary,
2. He was away from home when he incurred the expense, and
3. The expense was incurred in pursuit of a trade or business.

Whether a particular expense fulfills these three conditions is generally a question of fact and all three conditions must be satisfied to claim the deduction.

Although the taxpayer's jobs in the three other cities lasted for very short periods of time, each of those stays was indefinite in nature; thus, the taxpayer did not have a business reason to be living in two places. The taxpayer was expected to locate his home for tax purposes at his major post of duty so as to minimize the amount of business travel away from home. His decision to do otherwise was not motivated by business necessity but purely personal reasons. The taxpayer failed to prove that he had a tax home for the year in issue. Therefore, the court in *Wilbert* concluded that the taxpayer was not away from home in the three other cities and the expenses he incurred while there were not deductible.

In *Minick*,[16] the Tax Court concluded that a couple who primarily lived in a camper could not deduct travel expenses for the husband's employment, because the expenses

---

[13] Rev. Rul. 99-7, 1999-1 CB 361.

[14] *D.A. Wilbert*, CA-7, 2009-1 USTC ¶50,171, 553 F3d 544; *M. Abdassian*, 97 TCM 1165, Dec. 40,312(M), TC Memo. 1983-442; *Burley*, TC Summary Op. 2009-65.

[15] *J.N. Flowers*, SCt, 46-1 USTC ¶9127, 326 US 465, 66 SCt 250, *reh'g denied*, 326 US 816.

[16] *J.M. Minick*, 99 TCM 1054, Dec. 58,115(M), TC Memo. 2010-12.

were not incurred "away from home," and were not ordinary and necessary. Although the couple maintained a personal residence in one state, neither of the spouses was employed in that state. Moreover, the couple maintained their driver's licenses and registered and titled their cars in a neighboring state. The husband was assigned to construction job sites in two completely different states, and the couple primarily resided in a camper near those job sites. Maintenance of the personal residence in a state where neither spouse worked was their personal decision and the court found that it did not have a business purpose.

.04 Mixing Business and Personal Travel

If you travel to a destination for both business and personal reasons, you can deduct travel expenses to and from the destination only if the primary purpose of your trip is business [Reg. § 1.162-2(b)(1)]. But even if the trip is not primarily business-connected, you can still deduct business expenses at the destination.

Whether a trip is primarily related to business depends on the facts and circumstances of each situation. The amount of time you spend on business activities compared with the time you spend on personal activities is an important determining factor [Reg. § 1.162-2(b)(2)].

Example 10-9: Mr. Brown travels from New York to Florida for a two-week vacation. On day two, he interrupts his vacation to meet with customers of his company. Result: Brown cannot deduct his travel expenses between New York and Florida because the trip is primarily personal. However, he can deduct expenses allocable to the two-day business portion of the trip.

Example 10-10: Ms. Smith travels to Los Angeles on business for her company. She spends one week in Los Angeles meeting with her company's customers. She then decides to stay on another three days to go sightseeing. Result: Smith's trip is primarily for business. So she can deduct 100 percent of her expenses en route to and from Los Angeles and her expenses during the one-week business portion of her stay. What she spends during the other three days is personal and nondeductible.

A special tax rule says that weekends count as business days for purposes of claiming a travel deduction. Result: If your business trip flanks a weekend, you can claim a travel deduction for the cost of your hotel room, meals, and other living expenses during the weekend. You get the deduction even if you spend the weekend sightseeing, visiting friends, or pursuing other leisure activities. However, your out-of-pocket cost for leisure activities is not deductible.

Similarly, you can get a deduction break when you conclude your business discussions on Friday, but you stay over an extra day to take advantage of low weekend airfares. You can claim a travel deduction for your hotel room, meals and other living expenses for that extra day, provided your extra expenses are at least offset by your savings on the airfare.

The cost of traveling to a convention or other meeting may constitute an ordinary and necessary business expense. You are entitled to a deduction if there is a sufficient relationship between your business and the convention so that your attendance benefits your business [Reg. § 1.162-2(d)].

Spouse's Travel Expenses

When your spouse accompanies you on a business trip, your spouse's expenses are usually considered personal and nondeductible unless:

- Your spouse's presence on the trip serves a legitimate business purpose;
- Your spouse is either:

  a. An employee of your company if it is reimbursing you for the travel expenses, or

  b. Your employee if you are paying the expenses out of your own pocket; and

- The expenses are otherwise deductible (e.g., you and your spouse are not away from home for more than a year).

The rules for your spouse's expenses also apply if you are traveling with your child or anyone else [Code Sec. 274(m)(3)].

> ▶ **OBSERVATION:** Even where your spouse is not an employee, you can still deduct the entire cost of traveling as if you were alone. In other words, you are not necessarily limited to a deduction of 50 percent of the combined travel expenses of you and your spouse.

> **Example 10-11:** Mr. Nolan drives from Denver to San Francisco solely for business reasons. Mrs. Nolan goes with him. Result: Nolan can deduct all of the auto expenses of the trip because the expenses would have been the same whether Mrs. Nolan accompanied him or not. And if the hotel rooms in San Francisco are $175 a day for singles, and $200 for doubles, Nolan can deduct $175.

.05 Federal Crime Investigations

If you are a federal employee participating in a federal crime investigation, you are not subject to the one-year rule for deducting temporary travel expenses [Code Sec. 162(a)]. You may therefore be able to deduct travel expenses even if you are away from your tax home for more than one year. In order to qualify the Attorney General must certify that you are traveling:

- For the federal government;
- In a temporary duty status; and
- To investigate or provide support services for the investigation of a federal crime [Code Sec. 162(a)].

.06 Education-Related Travel

You can deduct the cost of education that maintains or improves skills needed in your business or employment or that is required to retain your current job or pay rate [Ch. 12] [Reg. § 1.162-5(a)]. If you travel away from home overnight to obtain education that is deductible, then your travel expenses (including meals and lodging) are also deductible [Reg. § 1.162-5(e)]. However, travel itself is not deductible as a form of education [Code Sec. 274(m)(2)]. For example, a high school French teacher cannot deduct the cost of a trip to France so the teacher can be exposed to the language. Similarly, an architect cannot deduct the cost of a trip through Italy to view the architect. But there are situations where a teacher's traveling expenses may be deductible if he or she can prove that the travel was an ordinary and necessary business expense under Reg. § 1.162-5(a)]. For example, the Tax Court has allowed a teacher to deduct all travel and tuition costs for overseas courses because the courses maintained or improved skills required in the teacher's employment under Reg. § 1.162-5(a).[17]

Example 10-12: Ms. Graham is a Spanish teacher who takes a sabbatical leave to travel to Spain to improve her understanding of the language and culture. Graham's travel costs are not deductible.

Example 10-13: Mr. Blaine is a history teacher. He goes to Paris to do research on an article he is writing on French history for a periodical. Assuming his nontravel research expenses are deductible, his travel expenses are deductible too.

.07 Investment-Related Travel

You can deduct ordinary and necessary expenses related to the production of income or for the management and conservation of property held for the production of income [Code Sec. 212]. Deductible "nonbusiness" expenses include travel and transportation expenses you incur in looking after your investments. You cannot, however, deduct the cost of attending conventions, seminars or similar meetings in connection with investments, financial planning or other activities related to the production of income [Code Sec. 274(h)(7)]. This disallowance covers transportation costs, registration fees and meals and lodging expenses.[18] Additionally, you cannot claim a deduction for travel expenses incurred to investigate new investments.

Investment-Related Travel Deductions Allowed

Following are examples of travel pertaining to management of investments for which you can claim a deduction:

- Aircraft rental incurred by a taxpayer to attend board and shareholder meetings of corporation in which he was a major stockholder;[19]
- Travel expenses incurred by a taxpayer in going from St. Louis to Charlotte twice a year to maintain three unimproved lots owned by taxpayer;[20]
- Trips by a taxpayer to manage rental property located 30 miles from the taxpayer's home.[21]

---

[17] *A. Jorgensen*, 79 TCM 1926, Dec. 53,855(M), TC Memo. 2000-138.

[18] *C.H. Jones III*, 131 TC 25, Dec. 57,496 (2008).

[19] *D.S. Weinstein*, CtCls, 70-1 USTC ¶9190, 420 F2d 700, 190 CtCls 437.

[20] *D. Stranahan*, 43 TCM 883, Dec. 38,882(M), TC Memo. 1982-151.

[21] *O.E. Harris*, 37 TCM 1370, Dec. 35,360(M), TC Memo. 1978-332.

Investment-Related Travel Deductions Disallowed

Following are examples of investment-related travel that have been disallowed:

- A taxpayer's travel expenses incurred for inspecting rental property when the main purpose of trip was to visit relatives;[22]
- Trips to plants of corporations in which a taxpayer held stock when the costs involved did not bear a reasonable relationship to investments;[23]
- Transportation costs incurred to attend stockholder meetings when a taxpayer is attending to get useful information for future investments.[24]

▶ **OBSERVATION:** There is often a fine line between nondeductible investment travel and deductible business travel. For example, a taxpayer, who owned 21 rental apartments, went to Palm Springs to investigate the purchase of additional real estate. The taxpayer was allowed to deduct the trip to Palm Springs because he was in the business of owning rental real estate.

¶10,005 SPECIAL RESTRICTION ON TRAVEL DEDUCTIONS

Even when your travel away from home is an ordinary and necessary business expense, the tax law may impose limits on deductions for certain kinds of travel expenses and the deduction may be limited or denied in its entirety [Code Sec. 274].

.01 Meals

A taxpayer's deduction for expenses incurred for food, beverages, entertainment activities, or entertainment facilities while away from home on business is limited to 50 percent of the amount otherwise allowable [Code Sec. 274(n)(1)]. Taxes and tips related to the meals are subject to the percentage limit, but transportation to and from the meal location is not.

Special Rule for Transportation Workers

The deduction percentage of the cost of meals consumed while away from home by individuals subject to Department of Transportation hours of service rules (e.g., interstate truck drivers) is 80 percent for years 2008 and thereafter [Code Sec. 274(n)(3)].

If you incur charges for goods and services while traveling and part of the charges are attributable to meals, you must make a reasonable allocation between the meal and nonmeal portion. For example, if the room rate at a hotel includes one or more meals, then you must segregate the meal costs from the lodging costs. The lodging costs are fully deductible, but the percentage limit applies to the meal costs.

If you are reimbursed for the cost of business meals by your employer, only the company is subject to the percentage limit; its deduction is limited to 50 percent of the reimbursement [Code Sec. 274(n)(1)(A)]. The reimbursement is tax-free to you, provided recordkeeping requirements are met [¶10,015].

---

[22] *L.H. Mayer*, 10 TCM 559, Dec. 18,377(M) (1951).

[23] *L.I. Holmes*, 46 TCM 872, Dec. 40,312(M), TC Memo. 1983-442.

[24] *W.R. Kinney*, 66 TC 122, Dec. 33,778 (1976).

If the reimbursement is in the form of a per diem allowance for lodging and incidental expenses, your employer is required to separate out the meal portion on a "reasonable basis" to apply the percentage limit.

Safe Harbor for Travel Allowance

The IRS has authorized a mechanical way for your employer to separate out the meal portion of a per-diem travel allowance: (1) It can allocate 40 percent of the allowance to meals if the allowance is less than the per diem travel rate paid to federal employees for that locality [¶ 10,015]. (2) It can allocate an amount equal to the federal meals and incidental expense rate to meals if the allowance equals or exceeds the per diem travel rate paid to federal employees.[25]

> ▶ **OBSERVATION:** If an employer intends to pay a travel allowance at a rate less than or equal to the federal lodging rate, the employer should pay an allowance for lodging only. Additionally, if a travel allowance is higher than the federal lodging rate but less than the combined lodging and meals rate, the employer may want to pay two allowances: a lodging allowance at the maximum federal lodging rate and a separate meals allowance to cover the additional cost of eating away from home. That way, the employer reduces the impact of the percentage limit for meals.

> **NOTE:** The percentage limit also applies when you are reimbursed by a third party who is not your employer (e.g., a business colleague). The party who reimburses you is subject to the disallowance [Code Sec. 274(e)(3)].

.02 Foreign Business Travel

When you travel outside the United States for both business and personal reasons, you may not be able to deduct full travel costs to and from the foreign destination, even though the trip is primarily business related [Code Sec. 274(c)(1)]. (If the trip is primarily personal, no deduction is allowed for travel costs en route to and from the destination, under the same rule that applies to domestic travel.)

Except as provided below, when you travel to a foreign destination primarily for business and you engage in both personal and business activities, you must allocate your travel expenses to and from the destination between the days spent on personal activities and the days spent on business activities. You can deduct only the portion attributable to business days. For this purpose, the actual days spent traveling to and from the foreign destination are considered business days [Reg. § 1.274-4(d)(2)(i)].

> **Example 10-14:** Ms. Claiborne travels from New York to London by plane. She spends the next five days on business matters and then spends the following three days sightseeing. On the tenth day, she returns to New York. Her round-trip airfare is $1,000. Result: Seventy percent of Claiborne's travel expense is allocable to business (seven days out of ten). So Claiborne can deduct $700 of her airfare.

> ▶ **OBSERVATION:** Suppose Claiborne is an employee and her employer reimburses her $1,000 for the airfare. Then the employer may deduct the entire $1,000. And assuming the reimbursement is provided under an accountable plan

---

[25] Rev. Proc. 90-15, 1990-1 CB 476.

[¶ 10,015], the employer need only report $300 as income on Claiborne's W-2 form.

If your principal activity during working hours is business-related, the day is considered a business day [Reg. § 1.274-4(d)(2)(iii)]. Weekends and holidays are considered business days if they fall between regular business days. However, if you have completed your business activities and remain at the foreign location for personal reasons, weekends and holidays are treated as personal days [Reg. § 1.274-4(d)(2)(v)].

Foreign travel includes any travel outside of the 50 states and the District of Columbia (for example, a business trip to Puerto Rico or Canada would be considered foreign travel) [Reg. § 1.274-4(a)]. However, if one leg of the trip involves travel between two points in the U.S., that portion of the travel expenses does not have to be allocated between business and personal days [Reg. § 1.274-4(e)].

Example 10-15: Mr. Robinson travels by plane from Chicago to Puerto Rico on business. If the plane flies nonstop, the entire airfare is considered a foreign travel expense. But if the plane makes a stop in Miami, only the cost of the Miami-Puerto Rico leg is considered a foreign travel expense.

If the nonbusiness activity on your foreign trip takes place at or beyond your business destination, the travel expenses subject to allocation are the round-trip expenses to your business destination. If the nonbusiness activity takes place en route to or from your business destination, then the expenses subject to allocation are only the round-trip expenses to your nonbusiness destination [Reg. § 1.274-4(f)].

Example 10-16: Ms. Carson travels from New York to Rome on business. She spends two weeks in Rome and then takes a one week vacation before returning to New York. If she spends the vacation week in Greece, she must allocate the round trip cost from New York to Rome (two-thirds business, one-third personal). The trip from Rome to Greece is entirely personal and nondeductible. However, if she spends the vacation week in Paris, the allocation applies to a round trip fare from New York to Paris. The added cost of going to Rome is a fully deductible business expense.

Exceptions

Not all foreign business trips are subject to the allocation rule. You do not have to allocate your travel expenses to and from a foreign destination if:

- You are not traveling outside the United States for more than one week [Code Sec. 274(c)(2)(A); Reg. § 1.274-4(c)]. For this purpose, one week means seven consecutive days. The day in which the trip outside the U.S. begins does not count, but the day you return to the U.S. does count. For example, if you leave the U.S. on Wednesday morning and return in the evening of the following Wednesday, you are considered to have been outside the U.S. for seven days, and no allocation is necessary;
- Your nonbusiness activities outside of the U.S. constitute less than 25 percent of the total travel time [Code Sec. 274(c)(2)(B); Reg. § 1.274-4(d)]. This determination is

made in the same way you allocate travel expenses when an allocation is required (i.e., business days versus nonbusiness days);

Example 10-17: Mr. Gregory flies from Los Angeles to Mexico City on Wednesday. On Thursday and Friday, he has business meetings. He spends the weekend on nonbusiness activities and on Monday and Tuesday, he has more business meetings. On Wednesday and Thursday, he again has nonbusiness activities and flies back to Los Angeles on Friday. Result: No allocation is required. Of his ten travel days, eight are considered business days (four days of business meetings, two days of the intervening weekend, and two days en route). So less than 25 percent of his total travel time is spent on nonbusiness activities.

- You do not have substantial control over arranging the trip [Reg. § 1.274-4(f)(5)(i)]. For this purpose, you are not treated as having substantial control over the arrangements simply because you have control over the timing of the trip. If you travel as an employee under a reimbursement or expense account arrangement with your employer, you are considered not to have substantial control unless you (1) are a managing executive who can authorize the trip without effective veto procedures or (2) have a more-than-10 percent ownership interest in the employer; and
- You did not have a vacation as a major consideration in making the trip [Reg. § 1.274-4(f)(5)(ii)]. This is determined on the basis of the facts and circumstances of your individual situation. For example, suppose you have no intention of doing any vacationing when you make your foreign travel plans. But your business at the foreign destination is unexpectedly cut short for some reason. So you stay on for a few extra days of sightseeing. The IRS may determine that your vacation was not a major consideration in making the trip.

Accompanying Family Members

Code Sec. 274(m)(3) disallows a deduction for travel expenses paid or incurred for a family member accompanying the business traveler, unless the following circumstances exist:

- The family member is an employee of the taxpayer.
- The family member's travel is for a bona fide business purpose.
- Travel expenses would otherwise be deductible by the accompanying family member.

The family member's performance of some incidental service does not cause the travel expenses to be deductible. If the accompanying family member's expenses are not deductible, the deductible costs are only those that would have been incurred for a single traveler.

Example 10-18: The Browns live in New York City. Mrs. Brown plan on taking a business trip to San Diego, California, accompanied by her husband who works for another firm. They fly from New York to California and stay for three nights at the Hilton. The deductible costs are as follows:

- Cost of Mrs. Brown's plane ticket;
- Cost of a single room at the Hilton;
- Mrs. Brown's meals subject to a 50 percent limitation;
- Taxi fares for business local transportation costs; and
- Other incidentals, such as tips.

If the Browns decide to drive instead of fly, the full cost of transportation to and from California would be deductible since the cost would the same whether there was one person or two.

.03 Foreign Conventions

You cannot claim any deduction for the expenses of attending a convention, seminar or similar meeting held outside the "North American area" unless (1) the meeting is directly related to the active conduct of your trade or business and (2) it is as reasonable to hold the meeting outside of the North American area as it is to hold it within the North American area [Code Sec. 274(h)(1)].

In determining the reasonableness of holding the meeting outside North America, the following factors are taken into account: (1) the purpose of the meeting and the activities taking place at the meeting; (2) the purposes and activities of the sponsoring organization or groups; (3) the residences of the organization's active members and the places at which their other meetings have been or will be held; and (4) other relevant factors.

The locations considered to be in the "North American area" and thus not subject to the rules for foreign conventions are:[26]

1. The fifty states of the United States and the District of Columbia;
2. The possessions of the United States, which for this purpose are American Samoa, Baker Island, the Commonwealth of Puerto Rico, the Commonwealth of the Northern Mariana Islands, Guam, Howland Island, Jarvis Island, Johnston Island, Kingman Reef, the Midway Islands, Palmyra Atoll, the United States Virgin Islands, Wake Island, and other United States islands, cays, and reefs not part of the fifty states or the District of Columbia;
3. Canada;
4. Mexico;
5. The Republic of the Marshall Islands;
6. The Federated States of Micronesia;
7. The Republic of Palau;

For expenses incurred in attending a convention that began after:

8. Antigua and Barbuda (February 9, 2003)
9. Aruba (September 12, 2004)
10. Bahamas (December 31, 2005)

[26] Rev. Rul. 2011-26, IRB 2011-48.

11. Barbados (November 2, 1984)
12. Bermuda (December 1, 1988)
13. Costa Rica (February 11, 1991)
14. Dominica (May 8, 1988)
15. Dominican Republic (October 11, 1989)
16. Grenada (July 12, 1987)
17. Guyana (August 26, 1992)
18. Honduras (October 9, 1991)
19. Jamaica (December 17, 1986)
20. Netherlands Antilles (March 21, 2007)
21. Panama (April 18, 2011)
22. Trinidad and Tobago (February 8, 1990)

The IRS will continue to treat Saint Lucia as not included in the North American area with respect to conventions that begin after April 4, 2007, except with respect to expenses for which the taxpayer demonstrates a nonrefundable contractual obligation existing as of April 4, 2007.

If your employer reimburses you for foreign convention expenses, your employer's deduction for the reimbursement will also be subject to the disallowance rule unless the reimbursement is reported on your Form W-2 as income [Code Sec. 274(h)(4)(B)].

.04 Conventions on Cruise Ships

Generally, you cannot claim a deduction for expenses you incur in connection with a business convention, seminar, or similar meeting held on a cruise ship. However, you can claim a deduction for up to $2,000 of cruise expenses per year if:

- The ship is a U.S. flag ship;
- All ports of call are located in the U.S., its possessions, or Puerto Rico;
- You attach to your return a written statement signed by you that includes:
  a. The total days of the trip, excluding the days of transportation to and from the cruise ship port,
  b. The number of hours each day that you devoted to scheduled business activities, and
  c. A program of the scheduled business activities of the meeting [Code Sec. 274(h)(2)];
- You attach to your return a written statement signed by an officer of the organization or group sponsoring the meetings that includes:
  a. A schedule of the business activities of each day of the meeting, and
  b. The number of hours you attended the scheduled business activities; and
- The convention, seminar or meeting is directly related to your trade or business.

.05 Luxury Water Transportation

There is a limit on the amount of expenses you can deduct when using an ocean liner, cruise ship, or other "luxury water transportation" to reach a business destination. Your deduction for each day on the boat cannot exceed twice the highest per diem amount paid by the U.S. government to employees of the executive branch of the federal government while they are away from home but traveling in the U.S. [Code Sec. 274(m)(1)(A)]. You are not subject to this limit if you attend a convention, seminar, or other business meeting while on a cruise ship (see .04 above for special limits). Also, if you are reimbursed by your employer or client, you are not subject to the per diem limit. But the employer or client's deduction for the reimbursement is limited to twice the U.S. government per diem rate [Code Sec. 274(m)(1)(B)].

.06 State Legislators' Travel Expenses

Under Code Sec. 162(a), a state legislator may be entitled to deduct expenses paid or incurred in conducting legislative business (e.g., living, transportation, and miscellaneous expenses) while travelling away from home. In addition, Code Sec. 162(h) allows a state legislator to elect to treat their principal place of residence within their legislative district as their "tax home." Under Code Sec. 162(h), a state legislator who makes the election can only deduct deemed living expenses during specified legislative days. The election deems a state legislator to be away from home during each legislative day in pursuit of a trade or business, therefore expending living expenses on each day.

A state legislator is deemed to be "away from home" for purposes of the deduction in pursuit of a trade or business on each legislative day. Reg. § 1.162-24(b) provides that a "legislative day is any day on which the taxpayer is a state legislator and:

1. The legislature is in session;
2. The legislature is not in session for a period that is not longer than four consecutive days, without extension for Saturdays, Sundays, or holidays;
3. The taxpayer's attendance at a meeting of a committee of the legislature is formally recorded; or
4. The taxpayer's attendance at any session of the legislature that only a limited number of members are expected to attend (such as a pro forma session) is formally recorded."

¶10,010 SUBSTANTIATION AND REPORTING OF TRAVEL EXPENSES

There are special substantiation requirements if you deduct expenses for travel away from home [Code Sec. 274(d)]. However, your expenses for local transportation are not subject to the special substantiation requirements, unless your auto is used.

.01 Substantiation of Expenses

In general, you must substantiate the following elements of each expense:

- *Amount.* You must show the amount of each separate travel expense. At your option, you can aggregate the total daily amount of certain expenses like meals and taxi fares if the expenses are repetitious or concurrent. You can also aggregate tips with the underlying expenses [Temp. Reg. § 1.274-5T(b)(2)(i), (b)(3)(i), (c)(6)(i)];
- *Time and place.* You must show the date of departure and return for each trip, the number of days away from home and the travel destination [Temp. Reg. § 1.274-5T(b)(3)(ii)]; and
- *Business purpose.* You must show the business reason for the travel away from home.

.02 How to Prove the Elements

You must substantiate each element of an expense either by adequate records or by sufficient evidence corroborating your own statement. However, written evidence has more value as proof than oral evidence. In addition, the value of written evidence is greater the closer in time the writing is to the time you incur the expense [Temp. Reg. § 1.274-5T(c)(1)].

Adequate Records

To meet the *adequate records* requirement, you must maintain (1) an account book, diary, log, statement of expense, trip sheets or similar records and (2) documentary evidence that, in combination, proves each required element [Reg. § 1.274-5(c)(2)]. You must make the record in the account book, diary, etc. at or near the time you incur the expense so that you have present knowledge of each of the required elements [Reg. § 1.274-5(c)(2)(ii)].

Fax and e-mail as Adequate Proof of Travel Expenses

The IRS has concluded that fax and e-mail copies of travel itineraries and other documents qualify as *documentary evidence* for purposes of substantiating travel expenses when claiming deductions for business expenses.[27] Reg. § 1.274-5(c) does not require that documentary evidence consist of "original" documents. In addition, there is no prohibition against documentary evidence in the form of facsimile or photocopies.

You must have documentary evidence (e.g., receipts or paid bills) for (1) any lodging expense and (2) any other business, travel and entertainment expense of $75 or more [Reg. § 1.274-5(c)(2)(iii)(B)]. This means that you must have adequate records to prove the expenses you incur for business travel, entertainment, or gifts in excess of $75 in order to claim a deduction for these expenses. However, no documentary evidence is required for transportation charges away from home if it is not readily available. Documentary evidence may, by itself, be sufficient to prove the required elements. For example, a hotel receipt is sufficient to substantiate travel expenses if it contains the name, date, location and separate amounts for charges such as lodging, meals and telephone [Reg. § 1.274-5(c)(2)(ii)].

---

[27] LTR 9805007 (Oct. 24, 1997).

In unforeseen instances, such as the loss or destruction of records due to a fire, you can substantiate expenses by reasonable reconstruction of the records [Reg. § 1.274-5(c)(5)]. Credit card statements or records of credit card charges do not qualify as adequate substantiation of lodging expenses because they do not segregate lodging from partially deductible expenses such as meals and entertainment or from nondeductible personal expenses such as personal phone calls and personal gift purchases. The IRS will, however, accept electronic ticket statements as adequate substantiation of business travel expenses [Reg. § 1.274-5(c)(2)(iii)].

.03 How to Report Travel Expenses on the Return

Business travel and transportation expenses incurred by self-employed individuals are deducted from adjusted gross income and are reported on Schedule C of Form 1040 [Ch. 12]. Travel and transportation expenses incurred by employees are miscellaneous itemized deductions [Ch. 9]deductible from adjusted gross income on Form 2106 and Schedule A of Form 1040.

You generally can deduct travel expenses you incur in connection with investments as a miscellaneous itemized expense. Miscellaneous itemized expenses are deductible to the extent that they exceed 2 percent of your adjusted gross income. Travel expenses related to rental or royalty property are deductions from adjusted gross income [Ch. 1].

¶10,015 TRAVEL ALLOWANCES AND REIMBURSEMENTS

An employee doesn't pay tax on an advance, reimbursement, or other expense allowance received from an employer or from a third part under an accountable plan [Code Sec. 62(a)(2)(A), (c); Reg. § 1.62-2(c)(4)]. This means that employees who receive a travel allowance or reimbursement under an *accountable plan*" need not report the employer's payment as income on their tax return or claim an offsetting deduction for the business travel expenses.

In contrast, a travel allowance provided under something other than an accountable plan is considered taxable wages. Your employer must withhold on the payments and report them as income on your Form W-2. You treat the payments as income on your tax return and claim an offsetting deduction for the actual travel expenses [Reg. § 1.62-2(c)(5)].

▶ **OBSERVATION:** Your expenses under a nonaccountable plan must be treated as a miscellaneous itemized deduction. You can deduct miscellaneous expenses only to the extent their total for the year exceeds 2 percent of your adjusted gross income [Ch. 9]. Net result: If your miscellaneous expenses don't reach the 2 percent mark, you end up with no deduction to offset the taxable allowance.

.01 Accountable Plan Requirements

A travel allowance is provided under an accountable plan if it satisfies the following four key requirements which are discussed in detail below: (1) business connection, (2) substantiation, (3) return of unspent amounts, and (4) timeliness. An advance that fails to satisfy these conditions is treated as paid under a nonaccountable plan, taxed to the employee, and subject to FICA and income tax withholding [Code Sec. 62(c); Reg. § 1.62-2(c)(5)].

NOTE: Reimbursements for deductible job-related moving expenses [Ch. 9] are no longer reported on Form W-2 as long as the accountable plan requirements are complied with.

Business Connection

The allowance must be limited to job-related expenses that could be claimed as an employee deduction if paid for out of pocket. An advance payment qualifies only if it is for reasonably expected business expenses. For example, a "travel" advance to an employee who never travels is subject to withholding when it is paid, even though the employee later returns the entire amount [Reg. § 1.62-2(d)].

If a single plan covers deductible business expenses as well as other bona fide business expenses that are not deductible, the advance is considered to be paid under two separate plans: one that satisfies the business connection requirement and is tax-free, and one that does not and is taxable [Reg. § 1.62-2(d)(2)].

Example 10-19: Ms. Lane is an employee of Acme, Inc. She frequently travels out of town on company business. Sometimes, she stays away overnight. At other times, Lane returns home on the same day. Acme provides her with an advance for all her anticipated meal and lodging expenses, even though Lane could not deduct the day trip travel expenses if she had paid them out of her own pocket. Result: The portion of each advance that covers overnight meals and lodging expenses (the "business" portion) is tax-free. However, the portion covering the day trips ("personal" portion) is taxable.

▶ **OBSERVATION:** Even the personal portion of a reimbursement or advance must be paid for expenses that are, in some way, business-related. An employer payment that covers strictly personal expenses could render the whole plan nonaccountable. What is more, a payment can be provided only for expenses your employer reasonably expects you and other employees to incur. Suppose your employer provides travel advances to a group of employees, and even a few of the group's members are not likely to travel on business. Then the entire plan fails the business connection requirement [Reg. § 1.62-2(d)].

In Rev. Rul. 2004-1,[28] a courier company hired employee drivers to deliver packages locally using vehicles that they owned or leased. The drivers' mileage allowances satisfied the business connection requirements and were paid with respect to deductible employee business expenses reasonably expected to be incurred by the drivers. The IRS concluded that those allowances could be treated as paid under an accountable plan. In the second situation, the employer paid its drivers a commission equal to a percentage of the tag rate reduced by a mileage allowance equal to the number of miles traveled multiplied by the business standard mileage rate. The variable allocation between commission and mileage allowance failed to satisfy the business connection requirements, and the reimbursement arrangement was treated as a nonaccountable plan.

In Rev. Rul. 2012-25,[29] IRS clarifies when arrangements that recharacterizes taxable wages as nontaxable reimbursements fail to satisfy the business connection requirement of the accountable plan rules under Code Sec. 62(c). Therefore, the reimburse-

---

[28] Rev. Rul. 2004-1, 2004-1 CB 325. [29] Rev. Rul. 2012-25, IRB 2012-37, 337.

ments are treated as made under a nonaccountable plan and are taxable. The guidance includes four situations, three of which illustrate arrangements that impermissibly recharacterize wages so that the arrangements are not accountable plans. A fourth situation illustrates an arrangement that does not impermissibly recharacterize wages. In this arrangement, an employer prospectively altered its compensation structure to include a reimbursement arrangement.

Substantiation

The employer must require the employee to turn over the same detailed expense records that would be required if the employee had to substantiate deductions on his or her own return [Reg. § 1.62-2(e)]. However, the employer does not have to require you and other employees to substantiate miscellaneous expenses, provided the payments covering miscellaneous expenses are separated from payments made under your employer's accountable plan. In this case, the payment covering the miscellaneous expenses is treated as paid under a nonaccountable plan, but the payments covering substantiated expenses are tax-free.

If you use one of the so-called automatic allowances, you do not have to substantiate amounts. The allowances automatically are tax-free to the extent they are within IRS-approved limits. The allowances include a mileage allowance for employees who use their cars for business travel [¶ 10,035] and a per diem allowance for meals and/or lodging for employees traveling away from home on business ((c) below).

Return of Unspent Amounts

The employer must require the employees to return any advance payments over your substantiated amounts. If the employee is required to return excess amounts, but fails to do so, the arrangement is still an accountable plan to the extent of the substantiated amount. Only the excess amount is taxable [Reg. § 1.62-2(f)].

Exception. The employee's allowance may often be based on the number of days away from home or miles driven. In this situation, the employer can let the employee keep any amount that exceeds actual expenses as long as the employee actually travels the number of days or drives the number of miles that the allowance specifies.

> **Example 10-20:** Mr. Mason drives his luxury car about 3,000 business miles per month. His company pays him 65 cents for each of those miles (his approximate cost of driving the car). This gives Mason a total monthly advance of $1,950. The IRS-approved mileage allowance is 56.5 cents per mile for business travel in 2013 [¶ 10,020]. Mason can get a tax-free car allowance of $1,695 per month. In addition, he does not have to return the remaining $255 since his company pays him in the form of a mileage allowance (although he is taxed on it). Suppose, however, Mason drives only 2,000 business miles in one month. Here, he must return the monthly advance that represents business miles not actually driven.

Timeliness

The employee must substantiate expenses and return unsubstantiated amounts within a reasonable period of time after the expenses are incurred. What constitutes a "reasonable" period of time depends on the individual facts and circumstances of each situation

[Reg. § 1.62-2(g)]. For example, if the employee is on a month-long assignment out of town, he will have more time to substantiate expenses than if on an overnight trip.

The IRS does provide two safe harbors. Under the first, the employee will automatically meet the timeliness requirement if he or she:

- Gets an advance payment no more than 30 days before the expenses are incurred;
- Substantiates the expenses to the employer no more than 60 days after the expenses are incurred; and
- Returns the unsubstantiated amount no more than 120 days after the expenses are incurred. The second safe harbor requires the employer to provide statements (at least once a quarter) to employees that detail the advances that have not yet been substantiated. The employee has up to 120 days following the receipt of the statement to either substantiate expenses or return the unsubstantiated amount.

A sample of an employee travel expense voucher appears on the following page. The employee can use his or her own records and receipts to fill out the voucher and submit it to the employer at the end of each trip. By requiring employees to use this type of arrangement, the employer can make sure its travel allowances and reimbursements satisfy the tough accountable plan requirements.

Travel Expense Voucher

Name ______________________ Department ______________________

For Period Beginning __________ Ending __________

										Total
Date										
Destination		From								
		To								
Purpose of Business Trip:										
Transportation	Car Travel	Mileage								
		Rate × Miles								
		Car Rental								
		Parking								
		Tolls								
	Air Fare									
	Rail Fare									
	Carfare & Bus									
	Limousine/Taxi									
	Tips									
Hotel	Room Charge									
	Hotel Tips									
Meals (inc. Tips)	Personal Meals	Breakfast								
		Lunch								
		Dinner								
	Business Meals (receipts on reverse)	Breakfast								
		Lunch								
		Dinner								
Misc.	Postage									
	Telephone/Telegrams									
	Laundry									
	Other, Attach Statement									
		Total								

I certify these travel expenses were incurred by me in the transaction of authorized company business	Less Amount Advanced	
Signature	Balance Due	

Electronic Expense Reimbursement Approved as Accountable Plan

The IRS has approved the use by an employer of an electronic reimbursement arrangement for travel and entertainment expenses that mostly eliminates the need for paper receipts and expense reports.[30]

Under this arrangement, the credit card company provides the employer daily with an electronic receipt for all expenses billed to the employee's business credit card. The electronic receipt contains the date of the charge, the amount of the charge, the merchant's name, the merchant's location, and if available, an itemization from the merchant of each expense included in the charge. The employer transfers the electronic receipts to a database, which the employees can access to create an expense report containing details about each expense and the business purpose served.

.02 Actual Expenses Exceed Allowance

If you receive an allowance or reimbursement that does not fully compensate you for your actual expenses, you may claim a deduction on your tax return. To get the deduction, however, you must (1) report any allowance you receive as income and (2) deduct all your actual expenses. You cannot simply claim a deduction for the excess amount that is not covered by the allowance.

Example 10-21: Ms. Eller is a salesperson with an adjusted gross income of $80,000 per year. She drives 30,000 business miles during the year and receives 7 1/2 cents from her employer for each business mile she drives. Her total mileage allowance comes to $2,250. Eller keeps a record of all her auto expenses and calculates that her actual expenses (including depreciation) run about 30 cents per mile or $9,000. *Result:* Ms. Eller has a choice. She can ride along with the tax-free allowance and report nothing on her tax return. Or she can report the $2,250 allowance as income and claim the $9,000 of actual expenses as a miscellaneous itemized deduction. As such, the actual expenses are deductible to the extent her total miscellaneous deductions exceed $1,600 (2 percent of her adjusted gross income).

NOTE: If Eller wants to deduct her actual auto expenses, she must report any other allowance she receives (e.g., meals and lodging, entertainment, etc.) and deduct her actual expenses for these as well.

.03 Per Diem Methods for Substantiating Meals and Lodging Expenses

Employees and self-employed taxpayers must substantiate the amount, time, place, and business purpose of expenses paid or incurred in traveling away from home if they expect to deduct these expenses. In lieu of forcing taxpayers to keep actual records of travel expenses, the IRS has provided per diem allowances under which the *amount* of away-from-home meals and incidental expenses (M&IE) will be deemed to be substantiated. Thus the need to substantiate actual costs is eliminated. However, even if per diem allowances are used to calculate the deductible amount, taxpayers must still substantiate the time, place, and business purpose of the travel with adequate records or other evidence.

---

30 Rev. Rul. 2003-106, 2003-2 CB 936.

Although most frequently used in the employer-employee relationship, per diem allowances may be used in connection with arrangements between any payor and payee, such as between independent contractors and those contracting with them. However, the per diem substantiation method is unavailable if the employee is related to the employer. This will occur if:

1. The employer is the taxpayer's brother, sister, half-brother, or half-sister, spouse, ancestor, or lineal descendent;
2. The employer is a corporation in which the taxpayer owns, directly, indirectly, more than 10 percent in value of the outstanding stock, or
3. Certain fiduciary relationships exist between the taxpayer and his or her employer involving grantors, trusts, and beneficiaries.

Types of Per Diem Allowances

There are three types of per diem allowances: (1) M&IE only, which provides a per diem allowance for meals and incidental expenses only, (2) lodging plus M&IE, which provides a per diem allowance to cover lodging as well as meals and incidental expenses, and (3) incidental expenses only, to be used when no meal or lodging expenses are incurred.

Incidental Expenses

Incidental expenses include the following expenses:

- Fees and tips given to porters, baggage carriers, bellhops, hotel maids, stewards or stewardesses and others on ships, and hotel servants in foreign countries;
- Transportation between places of lodging or business and places where meals are taken, if suitable meals cannot be obtained at the temporary duty site; and
- Mailing cost associated with filing travel vouchers and payment of Government sponsored charge card billings.

Incidental expenses do not include expenses for laundry, cleaning and pressing of clothes, lodging taxes, or the costs of telegrams or telephone calls.[31]

Optional Incidental Expense Only Method

Instead of using actual expenses in computing deductions for ordinary and necessary incidental expenses of away-from-home business travel, employees and self-employed individuals who don't incur meal expenses for a calendar year (or partial day) of travel away from home may for post-September 30, 2013, travel, deduct $5 per day for each day (or partial day) that the taxpayer is away from home.[32] The amount of incidental expense incurred is deemed substantiated for purposes of Reg.§ 1.274-5T(b)(2)(i) and (c), provided the employee or self-employed individual substantiates the elements of time, place, and business purpose of the travel for that day or partial day. The incidental expense only method cannot be used by payors that use a per diem or M&IE only per diem, or by employees or self-employed individuals who use the M&IE only per diem method.

---

[31] Treas. Dept. IRS Publication 463, "Travel, Entertainment, Gift and Car Expenses" (2013 Ed.) p. 5.

[32] Notice 2013-64, IRB 2013-42.

M&IE Only Per Diem

If a payor pays a per diem allowance only for M&IE in lieu of reimbursing actual M&IE incurred by an employee for travel away from home, the amount of the expenses that is deemed substantiated for each calendar day is equal to the lesser of the per diem allowance for that day or the amount computed at the federal M&IE rate for the locality of travel for that day or partial day. A per diem allowance is treated as paid for M&IE only if (1) the payor pays the employee for actual expenses for lodging based on receipts submitted to the payor, (2) the payor provides the lodging in kind, (3) the payor pays the actual expenses for lodging directly to the provider of the lodging, (4) the payor does not have a reasonable belief that the employee will or did incur lodging expenses, or (5) the allowance is computed on a basis similar to that used in computing an employee's wages or other compensation (such as the number of hours worked, miles traveled, or pieces produced).

Transition Rule

For travel in the last three months of a calendar year: (1) a payor must continue to use the same method for an employee as the payor used during the first nine months of the calendar year; (2) a payor may use either the rates and high-cost localities in effect for the first nine months of the calendar year of the updates rates and high-cost localities in effect for the last three months of the calendar year if the payor uses the same rates and localities consistently for all employees reimbursed under the high-low method.

Lodging Plus M&IE Per Diem

Under the lodging plus M&IE per diem method, the amount of an employee's (or other payee's) reimbursed expenses that is deemed substantiated (for purposes of the employer's return) is equal to the lesser of the employer's per diem allowance or the federal per diem amount for the locality of travel for the period in which the employee is away from home.[33] The employer is not required to produce lodging receipts if per diem allowances are used to substantiate such expenses. The locality of travel is the place where the employee stops for sleep or rest. Employees and self-employed individuals may determine their allowable deductions for *unreimbursed* meals and incidental expenses while away from home by using the following federal M&IE rate.

Per Diem Rates

The federal per diem rate is equal to the sum of the applicable federal lodging expense rate and the applicable federal M&IE rate for the day and locality of travel. If a payor pays a per diem allowance in lieu of reimbursing actual lodging, meal, and incidental expenses incurred by an employee for travel away from home, the amount of the expenses that is deemed substantiated for each calendar day is equal to the lesser of the per diem allowance for that day or the amount computed at the federal per diem rate for the locality of travel for that day. The term "per diem allowance" means a payment under a reimbursement or other expense allowance arrangement that is:

---

[33] Rev. Proc. 2011-47, IRB 2011-42, 520.

1. Paid for ordinary and necessary business expenses incurred, or that the payor reasonably anticipates will be incurred, by an employee for lodging, meal, and incidental expenses, or for meal and incidental expenses, for travel away from home performing services as an employee of the employer,
2. Reasonably calculated not to exceed the amount of the expenses or the anticipated expenses, and
3. Paid at or below the applicable federal per diem rate.[34]

The federal per diem rate for lodging plus M&IE depends upon the locality of travel.

The General Services Administration (GSA) publishes the rates for localities in the continental United States (CONUS). The GSA rates are available on the internet at *www.gsa.gov*. The rates for localities outside the continental United States (OCONUS) are established by the Secretary of Defense (rates for non-foreign localities, including Alaska, Hawaii, Puerto Rico, the Northern Mariana Islands, and the possessions of the United States) and by the Secretary of State (rates for foreign localities). These rates are published in the Per Diem Supplement to the Standardized Regulations (Government Civilians, Foreign Areas) (updated on a monthly basis) and are available on the internet at *www.defensetravel.dod.mil* and *www.state.gov*.

Effective October 1, 2013 for travel after that date, the special M&IE rates for taxpayers in the transportation industry are $52 for any locality of travel in the continental United States (CONUS) and $65 for any locality of travel outside the continental United States (OCONUS).[35]

High-Low Substantiation Method

IRS established the high-low substantiation method in order to simplify the administrative burden imposed on the employer for an employee who travels extensively for business during the year. Under the high-low method, the IRS published a list of localities that are classified as high-cost areas. All other areas within the continental U.S. (CONUS) were classified as low-cost areas. The IRS then established a per diem rate for the two types of localities. Certain areas were designated as high-cost areas for only a portion of the year, e.g., peak tourist season, and as low-cost areas for the rest of the year.

For purposes of the high-low substantiation method, the *per diem* rates under the *per diem* substantiation method are $251 for travel to any high-cost locality and $170 for travel to any other locality within CONUS. The amount of the $251 high rate and $170 low rate that is treated as paid for meals for purposes of Code Sec. 274(n) is $65 for travel to any high-cost locality and $52 for travel to any other locality within CONUS. The *per diem* rates under the meal and incidental expenses only substantiation method are $65 for travel to any high-cost locality and $52 for travel to any other locality within CONUS.[36]

High-cost localities. The following localities have a federal *per diem* rate of $210 or more, and are high-cost localities for all of the calendar year or the portion of the calendar year specified in parentheses under the key city name.[37]

---

[34] Rev. Proc. 2011-47, IRB 2011-42, 520.

[35] Notice 2013-65, IRB 2013-42.

[36] Notice 2013-65, IRB 2013-42.

[37] Notice 2013-65, IRB 2013-42.

	Key city	*County or other defined location*
Arizona		
	Sedona (March 1-April 30)	City limits of Sedona
California		
	Monterey (July 1-August 31)	Monterey
	Napa (October 1-November 30 and April 1-September 30)	Napa
	San Diego	San Diego
	San Francisco	San Francisco
	Santa Barbara	Santa Barbara
	Santa Cruz (June 1-August 31)	Santa Cruz
	Santa Monica	City limits of Santa Monica
	Yosemite National Park (June 1-August 31)	Mariposa
Colorado		
	Aspen (December 1-March 31 and June 1-August 31)	Pitkin
	Denver/Aurora	Denver, Adams, Arapahoe, and Jefferson
	Steamboat Springs (December 1-March 31)	Routt
	Telluride (December 1-March 31 and June 1-September 30)	San Miguel
	Vail (December 1-August 31)	Eagle
District of Columbia		
	Washington D.C. (also the cities of Alexandria, Falls Church, and Fairfax, and the counties of Arlington and Fairfax, in Virginia; and the counties of Montgomery and Prince George's in Maryland) (See also Maryland and Virginia)	
Florida		
	Boca Raton/Delray Beach/Jupiter (January 1-April 30)	Palm Beach/Hendry
	Fort Lauderdale (January 1-May 31)	Broward
	Fort Walton Beach/De Funiak Springs (June 1-July 31)	Okaloosa and Walton
	Key West	Monroe
	Miami (January 1-March 31)	Miami-Dade

Key city	County or other defined location
Naples	Collier
(January 1-April 30)	
Illinois	
Chicago	Cook and Lake
(October 1-November 30 and March 1-September 30)	
Louisiana	
New Orleans	Orleans, St. Bernard, Jefferson and Plaquemine Parishes
(October 1-June 30)	
Maine	
Bar Harbor	Hancock
(July 1-August 31)	
Maryland	
Baltimore City	Baltimore City
(October 1-November 30 and March 1-September 30)	
Cambridge/St. Michaels	Dorchester and Talbot
(June 1-August 31)	
Ocean City	Worcester
(June 1-August 31)	
Washington, DC Metro Area	Montgomery and Prince George's
Massachusetts	
Boston/Cambridge	Suffolk, City of Cambridge
Falmouth	City limits of Falmouth
(July 1-August 31)	
Martha's Vineyard	Dukes
(July 1-August 31)	
Nantucket	Nantucket
(June 1-September 30)	
New Hampshire	
Conway	Carroll
(July 1-August 31)	
New York	
Floral Park/Garden City/Great Neck	Nassau
Glens Falls	Warren
(July 1-August 31)	
Lake Placid	Essex
(July 1-August 31)	
Manhattan (includes the boroughs of Manhattan, Brooklyn, the Bronx, Queens and Staten Island)	Bronx, Kings, New York, Queens, Richmond

Key city	*County or other defined location*
Saratoga Springs/Schenectady	Saratoga and Schenectady
(July 1-August 31)	
Tarrytown/White Plains/New Rochelle	Westchester
North Carolina	
Kill Devil	Dare
(June 1-August 31)	
Pennsylvania	
Philadelphia	Philadelphia
Rhode Island	
Jamestown/Middletown/Newport	Newport
(October 1-October 31 and May 1-September 30)	
South Carolina	
Charleston	Charleston, Berkeley and Dorchester
(March 1-May 31)	
Texas	
Midland	Midland
Utah	
Park City	Summit
(December 1-March 31)	
Virginia	
Washington, DC Metro Area	Cities of Alexandria, Fairfax, and Falls Church; counties of Arlington and Fairfax
Virginia Beach	City of Virginia Beach
(June 1-August 31)	
Washington	
Seattle	King
Wyoming	Teton and Sublette
Jackson/Pinedale	
(July 1-August 31)	

Deduction for Meals by Crew Members of Commercial Vessels

Code Sec. 274(n)(2)(E) provides an exception to the 50-percent limitation on the deductibility of meal expenses when the expense is for meals required by a federal law to be provided to crew members of a commercial vessel which is operating on the Great Lakes, the Saint Lawrence Seaway, or any inland waterway of the United States, and which is of a kind which would be required by federal law to provide food and beverages to crew members if it were operated at sea, provided on an oil or gas platform or drilling rig if the platform or rig is located offshore, or provided on an oil or gas platform or drilling rig, or at a support camp which is in proximity and integral to such platform or rig, if the platform or rig is located in the United States north of 54 degrees north latitude.

In *M. Kurtz,*[38] the Court of Appeals for the Eleventh Circuit affirmed the Tax Court to conclude that an individual who worked as an engineer on commercial fishing vessels was not entitled to deduct full federal per diem rates for meals and incidental expenses. The deduction was limited to 50 percent of the applicable M&IE rates for the years in issue. The exception to the 50-percent limitation under Code Sec. 274(n)(2)(E) did not apply because the meals provided by the companies that the taxpayer worked for were not required by federal law. The provision for full deductibility does not apply to fishing boats.

50-Percent Cap on Business-Related Meals While Away from Home on Business

A taxpayer's deduction for meal and entertainment expenses is limited to 50 percent by Code Sec. 274(n)(1). An exception to this limitation is provided in Code Sec. 274(e)(3) for expenses a taxpayer pays or incurs in performing services for another person under a "reimbursement or other expense allowance arrangement." The exception applies if the taxpayer is an employee performing services for an employer and the employer does not treat the reimbursement for the expenses as compensation and wages paid to the employee. Under this type of arrangement, the employee is not treated as having additional compensation and has no deduction for the expense. Instead, the employer deducts the expense and is subject to the 50 percent deduction limitations imposed by Code Sec. 274(n)(1) [Reg. § 1.274-2(f)(2)(iv)(*b*)].

The exception under Code Sec. 274(e)(3) also applies if the taxpayer performs services for a person other than an employer and the taxpayer accounts or substantiates the expense [Code Sec. 274(e)(3)(B)]. In a reimbursement or other expense allowance arrangement in which a client or customer reimburses the expenses of an independent contractor, the deduction limitations do not apply to the independent contractor to the extent the independent contractor accounts to the client by substantiating the expenses as required by Code Sec. 274(d). If the independent contractor is subject to the deduction limitations, the limitations do not apply to the client.

The Tax Court has uniformly held that a trucking company could not avoid the 50-percent limitation on per diem allowances for meal deductions by leasing employees from a related company and paying them a per diem allowance. Thus, the Tax Court has limited the employer's deduction to 50 percent of the total per diem payments.[39]

In *Transport Labor Contract/Leasing, Inc.,*[40] the court addressed the deductibility of expenses in a three-party transaction. Transport Labor was a company in the business of leasing truck drivers to independent trucking companies. The truck drivers were paid wages and a per diem meals allowance by Transport Labor who in turn leased the drivers to an independent trucking company. Transport Labor billed the independent trucking company for the drivers' wages and per diem allowances and the

---

[38] *M. Kurtz,* 95 TCM 1411, Dec. 57,416(M), TC Memo. 2008-111, *aff'd,* CA-11, 2009-2 USTC ¶ 50,517.

[39] *Beech Trucking Co.,* 118 TC 428, Dec. 54,753 (2002); *C.A. Boyd,* 122 TC 305, Dec. 55,625 (2004); *see also* Chief Counsel Advice 200317016.

[40] *Transport Labor Contract/Leasing, Inc.,* CA-8, 2006-2 USTC ¶ 50,478, 461 F3d 1030, *acq.,* Rev. Rul. 2008-23, IRB 2008-18, 852.

independent trucking company paid Transport Labor for these expenses. Thereafter the parties deducted their respective expenses. The Tax Court applied the 50 percent deduction limitation found in Code Sec. 274(n) to Transport Labor's deductions because they were the drivers' common law employer. The Court of Appeals for the Eighth Circuit reversed the Tax Court to conclude that Transport Labor wasn't subject to the 50-percent deduction limitation found in Code Sec. 274(n) because of the reimbursement arrangement between the parties. Instead, the appellate court held that Transport Labor qualified for the reimbursement exception found in Code Sec. 274(e)(3)(B) because Transport Labor was not the party that ultimately paid the per diem expenses because they were reimbursed by the independent trucking companies. The independent companies ultimately bore the burden of the expense and were therefore subject to the 50 percent limitation.

In Rev. Rul. 2008-23,[41] the IRS acquiesced to the result in *Transport Labor* and therefore agrees with the appellate court's opinion that the Code Sec. 274(n) 50 percent limitation should apply only to the party that ultimately pays the per diem expense in a three-party reimbursement arrangement regardless of which party is the employer under the common law rules. The IRS did not agree with the opinion to the extent that it could be read to imply that status as a common law employer is relevant to the Code Sec. 274(n) analysis.

Definition of Reimbursement. A "reimbursement or other expense allowance arrangement" involving employees is defined as an arrangement under which an employee receives an advance, allowance or reimbursement from a payor (the employer, its agent, or a third party) for expenses the employee pays in performing services as an employee [Reg. § 1.274-2(f)(2)(iv)(D)(1)]. A reimbursement or other expense allowance arrangement involving persons that are not employees is an arrangement under which an independent contractor receives an advance, allowance, or reimbursement from a client or customer for expenses the independent contractor pays or incurs in performing services if either (1) a written agreement between the parties expressly provides that the client or customer will reimburse the independent contractor for expenses that are subject to the deduction limitations, or (2) a written agreement between the parties expressly identifies the party that is subject to the limitations under Code Sec. 274(n) and Reg. § 1.274-2(a)-(e) [Reg. § 1.274-2(f)(2)(iv)(D)(2)].

Two-Party Reimbursement Arrangements. The rules for applying the exceptions to the Code Sec. 274(a) and Code Sec. 274(n) deduction limitations apply to reimbursement or other expense allowance arrangements with employees, whether or not a payor is an employer [Reg. § 1.274-2(f)(2)(iv)(A)]. A payor includes an employer, an agent of the employer, or a third party. For example, either an independent contractor or a client or customer may be a payor of a reimbursement arrangement. Thus, any party that reimburses an employee is a payor and bears the expense if the payment is not treated as compensation and wages to the employee [Reg. § 1.274-2(f)(2)(iv)(B)].

If a reimbursement or other expense allowance arrangement between an independent contractor and a client or customer includes an agreement expressly providing that the client or customer will reimburse the independent contractor for expenses that are subject to the deduction limitations, the deduction limitations do not apply to an independent contractor that accounts to the client under Code Sec. 274(d). However,

---

[41] Rev. Rul. 2008-23, IRB 2008-18, 852.

the deduction limits do apply to the independent contractor and not to the client if the independent contractor fails to account to the client [Reg. § 1.274-2(f)(2)(iv)(C)]. Alternatively, the parties may enter into an express agreement identifying the party that is subject to the deduction limitations [Reg. § 1.274-2(f)(2)(iv)(D)].

Multiple-Party Reimbursement Arrangements. Multiple-party reimbursement arrangements are separately analyzed as a series of two-party reimbursement arrangements. Thus, an arrangement in which (1) an employee pays or incurs an expense subject to limitation, (2) the employee is reimbursed for that expense by another party (the initial payor), and (3) a third party reimburses the initial payor's payment to the employee, is analyzed as two two-party reimbursement arrangements: one arrangement between the employee and the initial payor, and another arrangement between the initial payor and the third party. Examples illustrate that the limitations apply to the party that receives an accounting and that ultimately bears the expense [Reg. § 1.274-2(f)(2)(iv)(E)].

Example 10-22: Eliot, an employee, performs services under an arrangement in which LLCo, an employee leasing company, pays Eliot a per diem allowance of $10 for each day that Eliot performs services for LLCo's client, CCo, while traveling away from home. The per diem allowance is a reimbursement of travel expenses for food and beverages that Eliot pays in performing services as an employee. Eliot enters into a written agreement with CCo, under which CCo agrees to reimburse Eliot for any substantiated reimbursements for travel expenses, including meals that LLCo pays to Eliot. The agreement does not expressly identify the party that is subject to the deduction limitations. Eliot performs services for CCo while traveling away from home for 10 days and provides LLCo with substantiation of $100 of meal expenses incurred by Eliot while traveling away from home. LLCo pays Eliot $100 to reimburse those expenses pursuant to their arrangement. LLCo delivers a copy of Eliot's substantiation to CCo. CCo pays Eliot $300, which includes $200 compensation for services and $100 as reimbursement of LLCo's payment of Eliot's travel expenses for meals. Neither LLCo nor CCo treats the $100 paid to Eliot as compensation or wages.

Eliot and LLCo have established a reimbursement or other expense allowance arrangement. Because the reimbursement payment is not treated as compensation and wages paid to Eliot, he is not subject to the Code Sec. 274 deduction limitations. Instead, LLCo, the payor, is subject to the deduction limitations. Because the agreement between LLCo and CCo expressly states that CCo will reimburse LLCo for expenses for meals incurred by employees while traveling away from home, LLCo and CCo have established a reimbursement or other expense allowance arrangement. LLCo accounts to CCo for its reimbursement by delivering to CCo a copy of the substantiation LLCo received from Eliot. Therefore, CCo and not LLCo is subject to the Code Sec. 274 deduction limitations [Reg. § 1.274-2(f)(2)(iv)(E), Ex. 1].

Meals Provided to Employees Subject to DOT Hours of Service Limitations

The deductible percentage of the cost of meals consumed by individuals subject to Department of Transportation (DOT) hours of service rules is 80 percent after 2008 or thereafter [Code Sec 274(n)(3)(B)]. The increased meal deduction is available for meals consumed while away from home by an individual during, or incident to, a period of duty subject to the DOT's hours of service limitations. Individuals subject to the hours of service limitations include:

- Air transportation employees, such as pilots, crew, dispatchers, mechanics, and control tower operators;
- Interstate truck operators and interstate bus drivers;
- Railroad employees, such as engineers, conductors, train crews, dispatchers, and control operations personnel; and
- Merchant mariners.

Lodging-Only Rate

Employers can provide an allowance for lodging only. The allowance is tax-free to employees to the extent it does not exceed the federal travel rate for the locality less the meal and incidental expense rate for that locality.

.04 Employer-Designed Travel Allowances

Employers may use travel allowances that are tailored to its individual travel circumstances. The allowances can be based on a flat rate or on a stated schedule set by the employer. For example, your employer could provide a cents-per-mile meal allowance for employees who spend most of their travel time on the road.

The rate or schedule must be "reasonably calculated" not to exceed your actual expenses. It must also be "consistently applied" and "in accordance with reasonable business practice."

.05 Excess Per-Diem Allowances

If a taxpayer's expenses are substantiated using a per diem amount, regardless of whether it covers lodging plus M&IE or only M&IE, and the reimbursement exceeds the relevant federal per diem rates for that type of allowance, then the employee (or independent contractor) is required to include the excess in gross income. The excess portion is treated as paid under a nonaccountable plan; thus, it must be reported on the employee's W-2 and is subject to withholding. In Rev. Rul. 2006-56,[42] the IRS held that in situations where an expense allowance arrangement has no mechanism or process to determine when an allowance exceeds the amount that may be deemed substantiated and the arrangement routinely pays allowances in excess of the amount that may be deemed substantiated without requiring actual substantiation of all the expenses or repayment of the excess amount, the failure of the arrangement to treat the excess allowances as wages for employment tax purposes causes all payments made under the arrangement to be treated as made under a nonaccountable plan (and thus taxed as wages).

---

[42] Rev. Rul. 2006-56, 2006-2 CB 874.

DEDUCTIONS FOR BUSINESS CARS

The most common mode of local business transportation is the automobile. It is also frequently used for business travel away from home. This section explains your deductions for the business use of your automobile.

¶10,020 AUTO EXPENSES IN GENERAL

You can deduct your automobile expenses to the extent the auto is used for ordinary and necessary business purposes. The deduction is available to self-employeds, employees who use their cars in their jobs and employers who provide their employees with cars.

If you use your car solely for business purposes, you can write off 100 percent of your automobile expenses. If you are like most taxpayers, however, you put some business miles and some personal miles on the car. In this situation, you can deduct only the portion of your auto expenses allocable to the business use. When you use a car solely for personal transportation, no business deduction generally is allowed.

The 2013 optional standard mileage rates are used for computing the deductible costs of operating an automobile for business, medical or moving expense purposes. In addition, they are used to determine the reimbursed amount of those expenses that will be deemed substantiated. They are also used for mileage allowances or reimbursements paid to, or transportation expenses paid or incurred by, an employee on or after January 1, 2013.

Beginning on January 1, 2013, the standard mileage rates for the use of a car (also vans, pickups or panel trucks) will be:

- 56.5 cents per mile for business miles driven
- 24 cents per mile driven for medical or moving purposes
- 14 cents per mile driven in service of charitable organizations[43]

Deductible car expenses generally are computed in one of two ways: You can deduct (1) the actual costs for operating and maintaining a business car or (2) the standard mileage rate.

.01 Actual Expenses

Actual expenses that can be deducted for the business (not personal) use of a car include the costs of gas, oil, tires, repairs, insurance, registration, depreciation [¶ 10,025], interest to buy the car, property taxes, licenses, tags, garage rent (including state and local taxes), parking fees and tolls. If you lease a business car, your lease payments can be deducted to the extent allocable to business use. For discussion of depreciation deductions, see ¶ 10,025. If you select the actual expense method, you must maintain a detailed diary chronicling business use of your car. This means you will have to maintain a record of your business trips including the number of miles traveled, date, customers or clients visited and business purpose of your trip. When you select

[43] Notice 2012-72, IRB 2012-50, 673.

the IRS mileage method you save yourself from this recordkeeping burden. You may only claim a deduction for the business use of your car. No deduction is available for personal use or for nonbusiness income-producing activities such as driving around to inspect your investment real estate.

Interest and Taxes Paid

If you use a car in your job as an employee, interest you pay on a car loan is not considered deductible business interest. Instead, it is treated as nondeductible personal interest [Code Sec. 163(h)(2)].

Sales taxes paid on the purchase of a business car must be capitalized and recovered through depreciation [Code Sec. 164(a)].

When a car is used for both business and personal reasons, the car's expenses must generally be allocated on the basis of mileage [Reg. § 1.280F-6(e)(2)]. The deductible portion of the expenses is determined by dividing business mileage for the year by total mileage. However, parking fees and tolls must be allocated on a per trip basis.

> **Example 10-23:** Mr. Hardy drives 10,000 miles on business-connected trips during the year and 5,000 miles on personal trips. He incurs $800 in parking and toll expenses on his business trips and $200 on his personal trips. His other car expenses come to $6,000. Result: Hardy can deduct $800 for the business parking and tolls plus two-thirds (10,000 ÷ 15,000) of his other expenses. Total deduction: $4,800.

For purposes of making the allocation between business and personal mileage, use the same rules that apply to the deductibility of transportation costs in general [¶ 10,001]. For example, if you drive from home to work, that is not considered business mileage. But driving between two work locations or between home and a temporary workplace is considered business-related.

Employer-Provided Cars

If an employer provides an employee with a car, the employer ordinarily can deduct the entire cost of the car, including an allowance for depreciation. Even if the car is used for both business and personal driving, use is considered entirely business connected, insofar as the employer's deductions are concerned. [See ¶ 10,035 for discussion of tax consequences of employee's person use of business car.]

The employer's cost attributable to business use is deductible as a business expense. And the employer's cost attributable to personal use can be written off as compensation, as long as the employer reports the value of the personal use as income paid to the employee [Ch. 4].

Employee-Owned Cars

An employee can write off business auto expenses as a miscellaneous itemized deduction. That means the employee can deduct the expenses to the extent your total miscellaneous expenses exceed 2 percent of adjusted gross income.

> **Example 10-24:** Ms. Steed is an employee of Texxon Corporation who earns $100,000 per year. She drives 15,000 business miles per year, and her business

auto expenses (including depreciation) come to about $3,000. Steed has no other miscellaneous expenses eligible for a deduction. Result: Steed can deduct only $1,000 of her business auto expenses. The first $2,000 of the expenses is counted in meeting the deduction threshold.

NOTE: If the taxpayer is self-employed, he or she is not subject to the 2 percent floor. Therefore, the taxpayer can deduct 100 percent of his or her business auto expenses.

Investment Use of Auto

You can deduct auto expenses incurred while managing and maintaining property held for the production of income [Code Sec. 212].

Example 10-25: Bob Hackett drives 12,000 business miles during the year. He drives an additional 3,000 miles to oversee the upkeep and management of an apartment building he owns. He also drives 5,000 personal miles. Bob's car expenses for the year total $10,000. Result: Bob can deduct $6,000 as a business auto expense (12,000 business miles ÷ 20,000 total miles × $10,000). Additionally, he can deduct $1,500 as an investment expense (3,000 investment miles ÷ 20,000 total miles × $10,000).

.02 Standard Mileage Rate

In lieu of deducting actual expenses, you may deduct an IRS-approved amount based on the number of miles you drive.

Beginning on January 1, 2013, the standard mileage rates for the use of a car (also vans, pickups or panel trucks) will be:

- 56.5 cents per mile for business miles driven
- 24 cents per mile driven for medical or moving purposes
- 14 cents per mile driven in service of charitable organizations[44]

Add to that figure business-related parking fees and tolls, interest on loans attributable to the business use of the car (other than interest paid or accrued on indebtedness allocable to the trade or business of performing services as an employee) as well as state and local taxes (other than those included in the cost of gasoline. The standard mileage rate option applies to business use of a car, van, pick-up, or panel truck.

▶ **OBSERVATION:** If you use the standard mileage rate as discussed above, your deduction will probably be higher than it would be under the actual expense method which allows you to deduct such items as gas and oil, insurance, interest on auto loans, repairs, licenses, parking fees, tolls, tires, and depreciation. Why? Strict dollar caps have been placed on the amount of depreciation that you can claim under the actual expense method.

When you use the IRS allowance, you may not claim a separate depreciation deduction. The standard mileage rate contains a depreciation element that must be taken into account when determining your taxable profit or loss when the car is eventually sold [Ch. 6]. For example, depreciation is allowed at a rate of 23 cents per

[44] Notice 2012-72, IRB 2012-50, 673.

business mile in 2013.[45] So you must reduce your adjusted basis in the car by 23 cents for each business mile you drove in those years.

Eligibility

To use the standard mileage rate, you must (1) own the car, (2) not use the car for hire (e.g., as a taxi), and (3) not operate two or more cars simultaneously in the same business.

If you want to use the standard mileage rate, you must elect it in the first year you use the car for business. You cannot deduct your actual expenses plus depreciation for two years and then decide to switch to the standard mileage allowance method. It's too late at that point.

On the other hand, you can use the IRS standard mileage allowance for two years and then decide to switch to deducting your actual expenses plus depreciation. But be careful because you will be limited to the straight-line depreciation method for the remaining estimated useful life of the car. You are stuck with this result because by choosing to use the standard mileage rate, you are considered to have made an election not to use the depreciation methods under the modified accelerated cost recovery system (MACRS) [¶ 10,025].

When deciding which option to use, you should project whether your deduction will be bigger using the standard mileage allowance or deducting your actual costs plus depreciation. You will have to estimate your business-related mileage, operating expenses and depreciation expenses over the years you intend to use the car. Also factor in your record-keeping responsibilities.

If you use the actual expense method in the first year the car is placed in service, you must continue using it for all future years.

> ▶ **OBSERVATION:** The useful life of your car may be shorter than the five-year depreciation period allowed under MACRS. So, in some cases, it may be beneficial for you to use the actual expense method. You could write off the car's cost over a shorter period of time.

Choose Method Early

If you want to use the IRS standard allowance method, you must decide to do so in the first year you place the car in service for business use. You cannot deduct your actual expenses plus depreciation for two years and then decide to switch to the standard mileage allowance method. It's too late at that point.

On the other hand, you can use the IRS standard mileage allowance for two years and then decide to switch to deducting your actual expenses plus depreciation. But be careful because you will be limited to the straight-line depreciation method for the remaining estimated useful life of the car. You are stuck with this result because by choosing to use the standard mileage rate, you are considered to have made an election not to use the depreciation methods under the modified accelerated cost recovery system (MACRS).

When deciding which option to use, you should project whether your deduction will be bigger using the standard mileage allowance or deducting your actual costs plus depreciation. You will have to estimate your business-related mileage, operating

---

45 Notice 2012-72, IRB 2012-50, 673.

expenses and depreciation expenses over the years you intend to use the car. Also factor in your record-keeping responsibilities.

▶ **PLANNING TIP:** If you are compulsive about keeping good detailed records you are probably better off claiming your actual expenses rather than using the IRS standard mileage allowance.

.03 FAVR Allowance

Rather than using the allowance at the standard mileage rate, an employer has the option of reimbursing employees for the business use of their personally owned car by way of a *fixed or variable rate allowance (FAVR)*. This method gives employees a cents-per-mile rate to cover gas and other costs incurred in operating the car including depreciation, insurance, and registration. Use of the FAVR allowance method affords employers the opportunity to set reimbursements at a rate that more closely approximates employee expenses. When an employer establishes a FAVR, employees must provide records that substantiate mileage and car ownership information. Employees will be happy to learn that FAVR reimbursements up to the FAVR limits will not be reported as taxable wages on their W-2 Forms.

With a FAVR allowance, you do not keep track of your actual expenses; you can get by with a minimum record of the date, business purpose, and mileage of each trip. Unlike the mileage allowance, however, you are not limited to a set figure.

A FAVR allowance is made up of two parts: (1) a periodic flat payment covering fixed costs for depreciation, insurance, registration, and license fees and (2) a periodic variable payment covering operating costs for gas, oil, tires, and routine maintenance and repairs.

There are restrictions on who can receive a FAVR allowance:

- A FAVR allowance may be paid only to an employee who substantiates to the employer for a calendar year at least 5,000 miles driven in connection with the performance of services as an employee or, if greater, 80 percent of the annual business mileage of that FAVR allowance. If the employee is covered by the FAVR allowance for less than the entire calendar year, these limits must be prorated on a monthly basis;
- A FAVR allowance many not be paid to a control employee. This means that for nongovernmental employers, officers earning more than $100,000 in 2013, and directors cannot receive FAVR allowances, nor can employees who own at least 1 percent of the employer;
- At no time during a calendar year may a majority of the employees covered by a FAVR allowance be management employees;
- At all times during a calendar year at least five employees of an employer must covered by one of more FAVR allowances;
- A FAVR allowance may be paid only with respect to an automobile, (a) owned or leased by the employee receiving the payment, (b) the cost of which, when new, is at least 90 percent of the standard automobile cost taken into account for purposes of determining the FAVR allowance for the first calendar year the employee receives the allowance with respect to that automobile, and (c) the model year of which does not differ from the current calendar year by more than the number of years in the retention period;

- A FAVR allowance may not be paid with respect to an automobile leased by an employee for which the employee has used actual expenses to compute the deductible business expenses of the automobile for any year during the entire lease period;
- The insurance cost component of a FAVR allowance must be based on the rates charged in the base locality for insurance coverage on the standard automobile during the current calendar year without taking into account such rate-increasing factors as poor driving records or young drivers; and
- A FAVR allowance may be paid only to an employee whose insurance coverage limits on the automobile with respect to which the FAVR allowance is paid are at least equal to the insurance coverage limits used to compute the periodic fixed payment under that FAVR allowance.

FAVR allowances are too complicated for most employers to set up and administer by themselves; they will need outside help—which can be costly.

For 2013, the FAVR allowance can be based on the costs associated with a standard auto that costs no more than $28,100 (excluding trucks and vans) or $29,900 for trucks and vans.[46]

¶10,025 DEPRECIATION DEDUCTIONS FOR CARS

If you purchase a new or used auto for use in your business you may elect to depreciate the cost of that car [Code Sec. 168(b)(3)]. Cars placed in service after 1986 are depreciated using the Modified Accelerated Cost Recovery Systems (MACRS) [For further discussion, see Ch. 11].

.01 General Rules

Under MACRS, you can write off the adjusted basis (generally cost less prior depreciation deductions) of your car by claiming annual depreciation deductions. The amount of your annual deduction is based on three factors: (1) the applicable recovery period (i.e., the number of years required to fully depreciate the car), (2) the applicable depreciation method (i.e., accelerated or straight line), and (3) the applicable convention (i.e., when you are deemed to place the car in service) [Code Sec. 168(a)].

- *Recovery period.* Under MACRS, you generally write off cars over a five-year cost recovery period [Code Sec. 168(e)(3)(B)(i)]. However, the five-year period is not based on tax years. Instead, it straddles six tax years.
- *Depreciation method.* The usual way you write off your car's cost is to claim accelerated depreciation using the 200 percent declining balance method and switching to the straight-line method when that yields a bigger deduction [Code Sec. 168(b)(1)(A)]. Under the 200 percent declining balance method, your annual depreciation deduction is 40 percent of the car's adjusted basis (200 percent divided by five years).

46 Notice 2012-72, IRB 2012-50, 673.

In the fifth year of the recovery period, straight-line depreciation will yield a larger deduction than the 200 percent declining balance method. Therefore, you should switch over to straight line at this point. To calculate your depreciation deduction under the straight-line method, you multiply your applicable depreciation percentage by the car's adjusted basis. The applicable depreciation percentage is: 1 ÷ (remaining years in the recovery period + 0.5).

NOTE: You can elect to use straight-line depreciation during the entire recovery period. Of course, this will produce smaller write-offs than the declining balance method in early years and larger write-offs later on [Code Sec. 168(b)(5)].

- *Applicable convention.* You generally use the half-year convention to determine when you are deemed to place the car in service. Under this convention, a car put in service at any time during the year is treated as being placed in service at the midpoint of the year. So your depreciation deduction for the first year is one-half of what would be allowed for a full year [Code Sec. 168(d)(1), (4)].

▶ **OBSERVATION:** The half-year convention means you normally write off the car over six tax years: a half year of depreciation in the year you start using it, a full year of depreciation in each of years two through five, and a half year of depreciation in the sixth year (after which the car is fully depreciated).

Depreciation Tables

In most situations, you can determine your depreciation deduction without going through the arithmetic calculations described above. An IRS table expresses the annual write-offs as a percentage of the car's basis. You can write off 20 percent of your car's original basis in the first year you place it in service, 32 percent of the car's original basis in the second year, 19.2 percent in the third year, 11.52 percent each in the fourth and fifth years and 5.76 percent in the sixth year. If you elect to use straight-line depreciation for the entire recovery period, you generally can write off 10 percent of the original basis in the first year, 20 percent each in years two through five and 10 percent in the sixth year.

Example 10-26: Mr. Nolan sells his old car and buys a new one for $13,000 that he uses exclusively for business. His basis in the car is $13,000, and his first-year depreciation deduction is 20 percent of that basis or $2,600, whether he puts the car in service on January 1 or December 31. His second-year depreciation deduction is 32 percent of his original basis or $4,160.

If your car is used for both business and personal travel, your depreciation deduction is figured only on the portion of your adjusted basis allocable to your business travel. But in computing subsequent deductions, you must reduce your adjusted basis by what you could have deducted had the car been used 100 percent for business [Code Sec. 280F(d) (2)].

Example 10-27: Same facts as before, except that Nolan's business mileage each year is 60 percent of his total mileage. Result: His first-year depreciation deduction is 60 percent of $2,600 or $1,560. However, his adjusted basis in the car is reduced by the full $2,600.

If you make a capital improvement to your car, the improvement is depreciated separately from the car. But you must use the same recovery period, depreciation method and convention as you would if the car itself had been placed in service at that time.[47] So you generally use a five-year recovery period for the improvement, regardless of what kind it is.

.02 Special Depreciation Rules

There are a number of exceptions to the general depreciation rules that can affect the amount of your automobile write-offs.

Midquarter Convention

The most important exception comes into play when you place more than 40 percent of your business property (excluding real estate) in service during the last quarter of the tax year [Code Sec. 168(d)(3)]. Under this rule, you must use a mid-quarter convention to calculate your depreciation write-offs instead of the usual half-year convention. This rule prevents you from placing the bulk of your business property in service at the end of the year and then claiming a half-year of depreciation.

With the mid-quarter convention, a car placed in service during any quarter of the year is treated as if it was placed in service at the midpoint of that quarter [Code Sec 168(d)(4)(C)]. Instead of getting a half-year of depreciation, you get 10½ months worth if you place the car in service in the first quarter, 7½ months if you place the car in service in the second quarter, 4½ months if you place the car in service in the third quarter and only 1½ months if you place the car in service in the last quarter. For a complete discussion of the mid-quarter convention, see Ch. 11.

> **Example 10-28:** Ms. Kirk buys a business car for $11,000 in October. She uses the car exclusively for business and buys no other business property during the year. Result: Kirk must use the mid-quarter convention to compute her automobile depreciation deduction. Since she placed the car in service during the fourth quarter of the year, her depreciation percentage is 5 percent [40 percent full year's depreciation × (1.5 ÷ 12 months)]. So she can claim a depreciation deduction of $550 (5 percent of her $11,000 cost).
>
> ▶ **OBSERVATION:** October 1 is a key date for calendar-year business car buyers. If you buy before October 1, you can get a much larger first-year depreciation deduction than if you buy on or after October 1. For example, if Kirk had put her new car in service in September instead of October, her deduction for the year would have been $2,200.

Calculating the Adjusted Basis

Your depreciation deduction each year is a percentage of your adjusted basis in the car. Under the usual rule, your adjusted basis in the year you buy the car is its cost (plus tax and registration). For depreciation purposes, your adjusted basis in subsequent years is your original cost less the depreciation you could have claimed in prior years had you used the car 100 percent for business [Code Sec. 280F(d)(2)].

---

47 Rev. Proc. 89-15, 1989-1 CB 816.

In some situations, however, you must modify the original cost figure to determine your adjusted basis. If you trade in your existing car, your adjusted basis in the old car is carried over to your new car. So if you have a loss on the trade-in, this loss is added on to your basis in the new car and can increase the size of your depreciation deductions. You have a loss if your adjusted basis in the old car exceeds the amount the dealer credits you for it. Similarly, you have a profit if the amount the dealer credits you exceeds your adjusted basis. A profit reduces your basis in the new car and can decrease your depreciation deductions.

Using the Family Car on Business

If you start using a personal car for business driving, you can claim a depreciation deduction for that car. However, your adjusted basis for the deduction is the lesser of (1) the adjusted basis on the date of conversion or (2) the fair market value on the date of conversion [Reg. § 1.167(g)-(1)].

> **Example 10-29:** Ms. Smith gets a new job that requires her to use her personal car for business driving. Smith bought the car several years ago for $15,000 and until now, she only used it for personal driving. The car is now worth about $5,000. Result: Smith can claim a depreciation deduction for the car this year. but her deduction is computed on the car's current $5,000 value.

.03 Dollar Caps on Depreciation

Owners of passenger automobiles used in the taxpayer's trade or business are subject to dollar limitations on depreciation deductions as well as the lease income inclusion rules discussed in ¶ 10,030 for the year the cars are first placed in service and for each subsequent year [Code Sec. 280F(a)]. The term "passenger automobiles" includes any four-wheeled vehicle which is manufactured primarily for use on public streets, roads, highways, and is rated at an unloaded gross vehicle weight of 6,000 pounds or less [Code Sec. 280F(d)(5)(A); Reg. § 1.280F-6(c)(1)]. Trucks and nonpersonal use vans with a gross vehicle weight rating (GVWR) greater than 6,000 pounds are not subject to the annual depreciation caps. Sport utility vehicles ("SUVs") that weigh more than 6,000 pounds are not subject to the luxury auto depreciation limitations in Code Sec. 280F even though they are really oversized passenger cars.

Gross Vehicle Weight Rating Defined

Gross vehicle weight rating (GVWR) is the maximum allowable weight of a fully loaded vehicle (i.e., weight of vehicle, including vehicle options, passengers, cargo, gas, oil, coolant, etc.). Generally, the GVWR is equal to the sum of the vehicle's curb weight and payload capacity. The GVWR of a particular vehicle is usually located on the vehicle's Safety Compliance Certification Label, which is attached to the left front door lock facing or the door latch post pillar.

Luxury Car Limitations

The maximum Code Sec. 179 expense allowance that may be claimed on an SUV is limited to $25,000 regardless of the year [Code Sec. 179(b)(5)]. See ¶ 11,045 for further discussion. This rule also applies to trucks with a cargo bed less than six feet long and also to certain vans. It simply prevents a taxpayer from expensing the maximum amount otherwise allowable under Code Sec. 179 ($500,000 in 2013). Consequently, owners of heavy sport utility vehicles will still be able to claim a significantly higher first-year depreciation deduction than owners of lighter vehicles. Alternatively, a taxpayer may still purchase a pick-up truck with a bed at least six feet long and with a GVWR in excess of 6,000 pounds and expense the entire cost, if the truck is used 100 percent for business.

SUV defined. An SUV is any four-wheeled vehicle: (1) primarily designed or which can be used to carry passengers over public streets, roads, or highways (except any vehicle operated exclusively on a rail or rails); (2) which is not subject to the Code Sec. 280F depreciation caps (i.e., the vehicle has a GVWR in excess of 6,000 pounds or is otherwise exempt); and (3) which has a GVWR of not more than 14,000 pounds [Code Sec. 179(b)(5)(B)(i)].

Because this definition is broad enough to encompass most trucks, an exception is made for vehicles which have an open cargo area of at least 6 feet in interior length or a capped cargo area of that length if the cargo area was designed for use as an open area and is not readily accessible directly from the passenger compartment. The definition of an SUV also encompasses certain heavy vans. Exceptions, however, are made for a vehicle (1) designed to have a seating capacity of more than 9 passengers behind the driver's seat (e.g., certain large commuter vans) or (2) which has an integral enclosure, fully enclosing the driver compartment, does not have seating behind the driver's seat, and has no body section protruding more than 30 inches ahead of the leading edge of the windshield (e.g., certain cargo vans) [Code Sec. 179(b)(5)(B)(ii)].

Limitations on Depreciation Deductions for Certain Automobiles

The IRS has issued the tables indicating the depreciation deductions for owners of passenger automobiles, trucks and vans first placed in service during calendar year 2013.[48]

Table 1. Depreciation Limitations for Passenger Automobiles (That Are Not Trucks or Vans) Placed in Service in 2013—Bonus Depreciation Deduction Applies

Tax Year	*Amount*
1st Tax Year	$11,160
2nd Tax Year	$5,100
3rd Tax Year	$3,050
Each Succeeding Year	$1,875

Table 2. Depreciation Limitations for Trucks and Vans Placed in Service in 2013—Bonus Depreciation Applies

Tax Year	*Amount*
1st Tax Year	$11,360
2nd Tax Year	$5,400
3rd Tax Year	$3,250
Each Succeeding Year	$1,975

[48] Rev. Proc. 2013-21, IRB 2013-12, 660.

Table 3. Depreciation Limitations for Passenger Automobiles (That Are Not Trucks or Vans) Placed in Service in 2013—No Bonus Depreciation Applies

Tax Year	*Amount*
1st Tax Year	$3,160
2nd Tax Year	$5,100
3rd Tax Year	$3,050
Each Succeeding Year	$1,875

Table 4. Depreciation Limitations for Trucks and Vans Placed in Service in 2013—No Bonus Depreciation Applies

Tax Year	*Amount*
1st Tax Year	$3,360
2nd Tax Year	$5,400
3rd Tax Year	$3,250
Each Succeeding Year	$1,975

.04 Expensing Deduction

In lieu of depreciation, you may elect to "expense" (i.e., currently deduct) the cost of machinery and equipment in the year it is placed in service in your business [Code Sec. 179]. See also ¶ 11,045 for further discussion of the expensing deduction and the increased expensing deduction available in Liberty Zone property.

.05 Mixed Use

If your "qualified business use" of a car does not exceed 50 percent of the total use, there are special restrictions: (1) You must use straight line depreciation and (2) you cannot claim an expensing deduction [Code Sec. 280F(b)(2), (d)(1)].

Qualified business use is any use of the car in your trade or business. It does not include investment use [Reg. § 1.280F-6(d)(2)(i)].

Example 10-30: Ms. Barker, an employee of XYZ, Inc. buys a new car for $12,000 in August. During the rest of the year, she drives 4,000 miles for business reasons, 2,000 miles for investment reasons and 4,000 miles for personal reasons. Result: Since Barker's qualified business use did not exceed 50 percent of her total use, she must use straight line depreciation. The car's adjusted basis allocable to her combined business/investment use is $7,200. She can write off $720 ($7,200 × 10 percent).

Employer-Provided Cars

Qualified business use generally includes all use by employees of employer-owned cars. Your use of your employer's car for personal trips is treated as qualified business use for purposes of computing your employer's depreciation, as long as the value of the personal use is reported on your Form W-2 [Reg. § 1.280F-6(d)(2)(ii)(3)].

Exception. If you own a 5 percent or greater interest in your employer, your personal use is not considered qualified business use, even though your employer treats your personal use as taxable compensation [Reg. § 1.280F-6(d)(2)(ii)(2)].

Example 10-31: Same facts as in Example 10-30, except that XYZ owns the car that Barker is using and she is a 5 percent shareholder of XYZ. Result: XYZ's adjusted basis for computing depreciation includes both the portion allocable to business use and the portion allocable to nonbusiness use. So its depreciable basis is $12,000. However, only 40 percent of Barker's use is connected with her job at XYZ; the other 60 percent is personal use excluded for purposes of the 50 percent test. So XYZ must use straight line depreciation to write off the $12,000 adjusted basis.

▶ **OBSERVATION:** Getting over the 50 percent business use mark is important, particularly in the year you place the car in service. The first-year deduction under straight line depreciation is only half of what you would get under MACRS. So, at year-end, if you find out you are a few miles short of 50 percent, it may be worthwhile to accelerate a business trip you had been planning.

Recapture

If your business use exceeds 50 percent in the year the car is placed in service, but falls to 50 percent or less in a subsequent recovery year, a special recapture rule applies. In the subsequent year, you must include in income the difference between (1) the expensing and depreciation deductions you claimed in prior years and (2) the depreciation deductions that you could have claimed had you used straight line depreciation.

Example 10-32: Mr. Latimer purchased a $12,000 car in June. He used the car 75 percent for business that year and claimed a depreciation deduction of $1,800 ($12,000 × 20 percent × 75 percent). The following year, his business use drops to 40 percent and he is subject to the recapture rule. If Latimer had used straight-line depreciation the first year, his deduction would have been $900 ($12,000 × 10 percent × 75 percent). Therefore, he has to include $900 ($1,800 less $900) in income the second year.

.06 Employee Use

As an employee, your own use of your car is not considered depreciable business use unless the use is for the convenience of your employer and required as a condition of employment [Code Sec. 280F(d)(3)]. That means your use of the car must be required in order for you to perform the duties of your employment properly. The presence or absence of your employer's statement requiring the use of the car is not decisive [Reg. § 1.280F-6(a)(2)(ii)].

¶10,030 LEASED CARS

.01 Inclusions in Income of Lessees of Passenger Automobiles

A taxpayer first leasing a passenger automobile during the year must determine the inclusion amount that is added to gross income using the tables that are updated annually by the IRS.[49] See Table 5 for latest update. The amount included each tax year that the automobile is leased is a percentage of part of the fair market value of the leased passenger automobile on the first day of the lease term (or the capitalized cost specified in the lease agreement) multiplied by the percentage of business/investment use of the automobile for the tax year. The inclusion amount varies according to the date on which the vehicle was originally leased and is prorated over the number of days of the lease term included in the tax year.

The following factors may affect inclusion amounts:

1. Less than 100 percent business (or investment) use,
2. Reduction of business use to 50 percent or less, and
3. Lease terms covering less than the full tax year.

You use a four-step process to figure your inclusion amount for any given tax year:

Step 1: Finding FMV

Find the fair market value of your leased car on the first day of the lease in the first column. Make sure you are using the correct table. Remember that a separate table is provided for leased passenger automobiles and trucks and vans.

Step 2: Finding Tax Year

Then go to the right to the appropriate column for the tax year of the lease. If you are computing your inclusion amount for the last tax year of the lease and that year does not begin and end in the same tax year, use the column for the preceding year.

Step 3: Prorate Inclusion Amount

Prorate the inclusion amount listed in the table by the number of days of the lease term included in the tax year. For example, if you lease a car for only 180 days, the inclusion amount would be only 49.3 percent of the amount found in the "1st" column.

Step 4: Figure Percentage of Business/Investment Use

If you do not use the leased car exclusively for business and investment purposes, multiply the result in Step 3 by the percentage of business and investment use.

Example 10-33: On April 1, 2013, Ms. Franklin, a calendar year taxpayer, leases and places in service a passenger automobile with a fair market value of $79,000. The lease is for a three-year period. During tax years 2013 and 2014, Franklin uses the automobile exclusively in a trade or business. During 2015 and 2016, her business/investment use is 45 percent. The appropriate dollar amounts from the table are $34 for 2013 (first tax year during the lease), $75 for 2014 (second tax year during the lease), $111 for 2015 (third tax year during the lease), and $133 for 2016. Since 2016 is the last tax year during the lease, the dollar amount for the preceding year (the third year) is used, rather than the dollar amount for the fourth year. For tax years 2013 through 2016, Franklin's inclusion amounts are determined as follows:

[49] Rev. Proc. 2013-21, IRB 2013-12, 660.

Tax Year	Dollar Amount	Proration	Business Use	Inclusion Amount
2013	$34	275/365	100%	$25.62
2014	$75	365/365	100%	$75
2015	$111	365/365	45%	$49.95
2016	$111	90/365	45%	$12.32

Table 5. Dollar Amounts for Passenger Automobiles (That Are Not Trucks or Vans) with a Lease Term Beginning in 2013

Fair Market Value of Passenger Automobile		Tax Year During Lease				
Over	Not Over	1st	2nd	3rd	4th	5th & later
$19,000	$19,500	2	4	6	7	8
19,500	20,000	2	5	6	9	9
20,000	20,500	2	5	8	9	11
20,500	21,000	3	6	8	10	12
21,000	21,500	3	6	10	11	13
21,500	22,000	3	7	10	13	14
22,000	23,000	4	8	11	14	16
23,000	24,000	4	9	14	16	18
24,000	25,000	5	10	15	18	21
25,000	26,000	5	12	16	21	23
26,000	27,000	6	12	19	23	25
27,000	28,000	6	14	20	25	28
28,000	29,000	7	15	22	27	30
29,000	30,000	7	16	24	29	33
30,000	31,000	8	17	26	31	35
31,000	32,000	8	19	27	33	38
32,000	33,000	9	20	29	35	40
33,000	34,000	10	21	31	37	43
34,000	35,000	10	22	33	39	45
35,000	36,000	11	23	35	41	48
36,000	37,000	11	25	36	43	50
37,000	38,000	12	26	38	45	53
38,000	39,000	12	27	40	47	55
39,000	40,000	13	28	42	49	58
40,000	41,000	13	29	44	52	59
41,000	42,000	14	30	45	54	63
42,000	43,000	14	32	47	56	64
43,000	44,000	15	33	48	59	67
44,000	45,000	15	34	51	60	69
45,000	46,000	16	35	52	63	72
46,000	47,000	17	36	54	65	74

Fair Market Value of Passenger Automobile		Tax Year During Lease				
Over	Not Over	1st	2nd	3rd	4th	5th & later
47,000	48,000	17	38	55	67	77
48,000	49,000	18	39	57	69	79
49,000	50,000	18	40	59	71	82
50,000	51,000	19	41	61	73	84
51,000	52,000	19	42	63	75	87
52,000	53,000	20	43	65	77	89
53,000	54,000	20	45	66	79	92
54,000	55,000	21	46	68	81	94
55,000	56,000	21	47	70	84	96
56,000	57,000	22	48	72	85	99
57,000	58,000	22	50	73	88	101
58,000	59,000	23	51	75	90	103
59,000	60,000	24	52	76	92	106
60,000	62,000	24	54	79	95	110
62,000	64,000	25	56	83	99	115
64,000	66,000	27	58	87	103	120
66,000	68,000	28	60	90	108	125
68,000	70,000	29	63	93	112	130
70,000	72,000	30	65	97	117	134
72,000	74,000	31	68	100	121	139
74,000	76,000	32	70	104	125	144
76,000	78,000	33	73	107	129	149
78,000	80,000	34	75	111	133	154
80,000	85,000	36	79	117	141	162
85,000	90,000	39	85	126	151	174
90,000	95,000	41	91	135	162	186
95,000	100,000	44	97	144	172	199
100,000	110,000	48	106	157	188	217
110,000	120,000	53	118	174	210	241
120,000	130,000	59	129	193	230	266
130,000	140,000	64	141	210	252	290
140,000	150,000	70	153	227	273	315
150,000	160,000	75	165	245	294	339
160,000	170,000	80	177	263	315	363
170,000	180,000	86	189	280	336	388
180,000	190,000	91	201	298	357	412
190,000	200,000	97	212	316	378	436
200,000	210,000	102	224	333	400	461
210,000	220,000	107	236	351	420	486

Fair Market Value of Passenger Automobile		Tax Year During Lease				
Over	Not Over	1st	2nd	3rd	4th	5th & later
220,000	230,000	113	248	368	442	509
230,000	240,000	118	260	386	463	534
240,000	And up	124	272	403	484	558

Table 6. Dollar Amounts for Trucks and Vans with a Lease Term Beginning in 2013

Fair Market Value of Truck or Van		Tax Year During Lease				
Over	Not Over	1st	2nd	3rd	4th	5th & later
19,000	19,500	1	3	4	5	6
19,500	20,000	2	3	5	6	7
20,000	20,500	2	4	6	7	8
20,500	21,000	2	5	7	8	9
21,000	21,500	2	5	8	9	11
21,500	22,000	3	6	8	10	12
22,000	23,000	3	7	10	11	14
23,000	24,000	4	8	11	14	16
24,000	25,000	4	9	14	16	18
25,000	26,000	5	10	15	18	21
26,000	27,000	5	12	17	20	23
27,000	28,000	6	13	18	23	25
28,000	29,000	6	14	20	25	28
29,000	30,000	7	15	22	27	30
30,000	31,000	7	16	24	29	33
31,000	32,000	8	17	26	31	35
32,000	33,000	8	19	27	33	38
33,000	34,000	9	20	29	35	41
34,000	35,000	10	21	31	37	43
35,000	36,000	10	22	33	39	46
36,000	37,000	11	23	35	41	48
37,000	38,000	11	25	36	43	51
38,000	39,000	12	26	38	45	53
39,000	40,000	12	27	40	48	55
40,000	41,000	13	28	42	49	58
41,000	42,000	13	29	44	52	60
42,000	43,000	14	30	46	54	62
43,000	44,000	14	32	47	56	65
44,000	45,000	15	33	48	59	67
45,000	46,000	15	34	51	60	70

Fair Market Value of Truck or Van		Tax Year During Lease				
Over	Not Over	1st	2nd	3rd	4th	5th & later
46,000	47,000	16	35	52	63	72
47,000	48,000	17	36	54	65	74
48,000	49,000	17	38	55	67	77
49,000	50,000	18	39	57	69	79
50,000	51,000	18	40	59	71	82
51,000	52,000	19	41	61	73	84
52,000	53,000	19	42	63	75	87
53,000	54,000	20	43	65	77	89
54,000	55,000	20	45	66	80	91
55,000	56,000	21	46	68	81	94
56,000	57,000	21	47	70	84	96
57,000	58,000	22	48	72	86	98
58,000	59,000	22	50	73	88	101
59,000	60,000	23	51	75	90	103
60,000	62,000	24	52	78	93	108
62,000	64,000	25	55	81	97	113
64,000	66,000	26	57	85	101	118
66,000	68,000	27	60	88	106	122
68,000	70,000	28	62	92	110	127
70,000	72,000	29	64	96	114	132
72,000	74,000	30	67	99	118	137
74,000	76,000	31	69	103	122	142
76,000	78,000	32	72	105	127	147
78,000	80,000	34	73	110	131	151
80,000	85,000	35	78	116	138	160
85,000	90,000	38	84	124	149	172
90,000	95,000	41	90	133	160	184
95,000	100,000	44	95	142	171	196
100,000	110,000	48	104	156	186	214
110,000	120,000	53	116	173	207	240
120,000	130,000	58	128	191	228	264
130,000	140,000	64	140	208	249	288
140,000	150,000	69	152	226	270	313
150,000	160,000	75	164	243	292	336
160,000	170,000	80	176	261	312	361
170,000	180,000	85	188	278	334	386
180,000	190,000	91	199	296	355	410
190,000	200,000	96	211	314	376	434
200,000	210,000	101	223	332	397	459

Fair Market Value of Truck or Van		Tax Year During Lease				
Over	Not Over	1st	2nd	3rd	4th	5th & later
210,000	220,000	107	235	349	418	483
220,000	230,000	112	247	367	439	507
230,000	240,000	118	259	384	460	532
240,000	And up	123	271	401	482	556

¶10,035 REPORTING AND SUBSTANTIATION OF AUTO EXPENSES

No deduction is allowed for a business car unless you meet special substantiation requirements [Reg. § 1.274-5].

.01 What to Substantiate

If you are deducting your actual auto expenses, you must be able to prove:

- The amount of each expense;
- The mileage for each business or investment use of the car, plus the total mileage for the car during the year;
- The date each business/investment use occurred or expense was incurred; and
- The business/investment purpose of each use or expense [Temp. Reg. § 1.274-5T(b)(6)].

If you use the standard mileage rate, you do not have to prove your expenses. But you do have to prove the date and purpose of your driving, as well as the amount of your mileage.

.02 How to Prove Expenses

You must generally substantiate each car expense or use of the car by adequate records or by sufficient evidence corroborating your own statement [Reg. § 1.274-5(c)(1)]. You are not required to keep a contemporaneous log of each use or expense. But a record made at or near the time of the use or expense has a much higher value as proof than one made weeks or months later.

You can aggregate separate uses of a car if part of an overall, uninterrupted business use. For example, if you make a sales trip out of town to see customers, a single record of the miles traveled is sufficient [Reg. § 1.274-5(c)(6)(C)]. Likewise, you can aggregate expenses such as gasoline and repairs. You have to keep a record of the amount and date of each expense, but you do not have to record the business purpose. Instead, you can simply prorate the expenses based on business mileage [¶ 10,020].

A sample of a page from a diary of auto use that you might keep is shown below.

List all auto expenses:				List all business trips:			
DATE	DESCRIPTION	AMOUNT		DATE	TRIP BETWEEN—	BUSINESS PURPOSE	MILES
11/18	gasoline	26	50	11/18	Phila. & NYC	conference with	
	tolls	7	50		& back	client XYZ Inc.	180
11/18	parking	24	00	11/19	office & ad agency	review ad	
11/20	oil change filter	20	00		& back	campaign	16
11/21	gas	19	25	11/20	office & factory	check product	
11/22	gas	10	00		& back	packaging	66
	tolls	5	60	11/22	Phila. & Baltimore	company's annual	
	parking BALT.	15	00		& back	marketing conference	192
Total parking and tolls		52	10				
Total other expenses		75	75			TOTAL	454

Sampling

You can maintain an adequate record of your business/investment use for only part of the year if you can show that part is representative of the year as a whole [Reg. § 1.274-5(c)(3)(ii)].

Example 10-34: Ms. Bowen runs a business out of her home. She uses the automobile for trips around town to visit customers and suppliers. She maintains adequate records for the first three months of the year indicating that 75 percent of the use of the car was in her business. Her business records (e.g., invoices, billings, etc.) show that the level of her business activity was fairly uniform throughout the year. So she will be considered to have adequate records to support a 75 percent business use rate for the entire year.

.03 Employer-Provided Cars

An employer should require employees who drive company-owned cars to submit a record of your automobile use. The record should satisfy the accountable plan rules [¶ 10,015]. Specifically, each employee's record must state the date, business purpose, and mileage of each trip, and it must be submitted to the employer in a timely manner.

In lieu of receiving a detailed record the employer can accept a statement summarizing use. But, in this case, the employee must retain adequate records supporting the statement [Temp. Reg. § 1.274-5T(e) (2) (ii)].

If the accountable plan requirements are satisfied, the employer generally can write off 100 percent of its automobile expenses, and the employee is not taxed on business use of the automobiles. Only the value of your personal use, if any, is treated by the employee as compensation.

Cents-per-Mile Valuation Rule

When an employer allows an employee to use a company car exclusively for business purposes, the use of the car is considered a tax-free working condition fringe. Use of company car is no longer considered a tax-free benefit when an employee drives the car for his or her personal use. Reg. § 1.61-21(a) (1) provides that the value of an employee's personal use of a company car is a taxable fringe benefit that will be treated as noncash compensation paid to the employee.

When an employee uses the company car for personal use, the employer must issue the employee a W-2 which includes the number derived when you multiply the number of miles driven for personal use times the standard mileage rate. This is known as the "vehicle cents-per-mile valuation rule" and it only applies to passenger automobiles first made available to any employee for personal use, if the fair market value of the auto on the date it is first made available to the employee is less than $16,000 in 2013 or if the fair market value of a truck or van, which includes automobiles built on a truck chassis, such as minivans and sport-utility vehicles (SUVs) built on a truck chassis, is $17,000 for 2013 [Code Sec. 280F(d)(7); Reg. § 1.62-21(e)].[50]

The employee must include in taxable income the value of the benefit as stated on the W-2 issued by his or her employer.

> **Example 10-35:** In July 2013, Alan's employer provides him with a car with a fair market value of $25,400. During the second half of the year, Alan drives the car 2,000 personal miles and 3,000 business miles during that period. The standard mileage rate for business use of an automobile is 56.5 cents per mile in 2013. The value of the personal use of the car is $1,130 (2,000 personal miles × 56.5 cents). Alan must include this amount in his taxable income that year because he used the company-provided car for his own personal use.

If the accountable plan rules are not satisfied, your employer must report 100 percent of the car use as taxable compensation on your Form W-2. You can claim an offsetting deduction for the business use, but only to the extent the auto deduction, when combined with your other employee business expenses and miscellaneous deductions, exceeds 2 percent of your adjusted gross income [Ch. 9].

Cars Not Used for Personal Travel

An employer does not have to meet the substantiation requirements for cars that are not used for personal driving [Temp. Reg. § 1.274-6T(a)(2)]. The following conditions have to be met:

- The employer must have a policy statement in writing that specifically prohibits employees from using the car for personal driving (other than incidental personal use, such as stops for lunch);
- The employer reasonably believes that its written policy statement is being honored by employees;
- The cars are kept on the employees' premises when not in use; and
- No employee using a vehicle lives on the employer's business premises.

Cars Not Used for Personal Travel Other Than Commuting

An employer is exempt from the substantiation requirements for cars used only for business and commuting purposes if the following conditions are met:

---

[50] Notice 2013-27, IRB 2013-18, 985.

- For bona fide noncompensatory reasons, the employer requires an employee to commute to and from work in the car;
- The employer has a written policy statement prohibiting personal use other than commuting or de minimis personal use, and the employer reasonably believes that this policy is being carried out;
- The employer reports the value of the commute in the employee's wage statement; and
- The employee is not an officer or director of the employer or does not own a 1 percent-or-more interest in the employer required to use an automobile [Temp. Reg. § 1.274-6T(a)(3)].

.04 Automobile Allowances and Reimbursements

You may receive an automobile allowance or reimbursement under an accountable plan [¶ 10,015]. If so, you need not report the employer payment as income on your tax return or claim a deduction for your offsetting expenses [Reg. § 1.62-2(c)(4)].

If, however, your expenses exceed the reimbursement and you have an adequate record of your expenses, you can report the reimbursement as income and deduct the excess auto expenses. The expenses are combined with your other employee business expenses and miscellaneous deductions, and the total is deductible to the extent it exceeds 2 percent of your adjusted gross income [Ch. 9].

Mileage Allowance

You do not have to substantiate your actual automobile expenses to your employer to the extent you receive a mileage allowance of no more than the standard mileage rate. You can get by with a record of the date, business purpose, and mileage of each trip. The IRS has said that an employer can use the automatic mileage allowance to figure the tax-free portion of a reimbursement—even if the employer uses another method (e.g., fixed costs of maintaining a car) to calculate the reimbursement itself.[51]

> ▶ **CAUTION:** If you receive an allowance or reimbursement below the standard mileage rate, you may report the reimbursement on your return and deduct your actual expenses or the standard mileage rate. However, your automobile deduction is grouped with your other employee business expenses and miscellaneous deductions, and the total is deductible only to the extent it exceeds 2 percent of your adjusted gross income.

BUSINESS ENTERTAINMENT DEDUCTIONS

This section covers the deductibility of expenses incurred when you entertain customers, clients, employees, and associates in connection with your trade or business.

---

[51] LTR 9117052 (Jan. 30, 1991).

¶10,040 ENTERTAINMENT DEDUCTIONS IN GENERAL

You may be able to deduct 50 percent of your business-related entertainment expenses if the expenses are both ordinary and necessary and the expenses are either directly-related or associated with your trade or business [Code Sec. 274(n)].

.01 What Is Entertainment?

Entertainment comprises more than amusement or recreation. It includes entertaining at night clubs, social, athletic, and sporting clubs, at theaters, at sporting events, on yachts, or on hunting, fishing, vacation, and similar trips. Entertainment can also cover meeting the personal, living or family needs of individuals, such as providing a hotel room or car for customers or their families [Reg. § 1.274-2(b)(1)]. However, in general, no deduction is allowed for the cost of providing meals to someone else unless you (or your employee) are present [Code Sec. 274(k)(1)(B)].

Keep in mind that club dues, initiation fees, and membership fees are not deductible if the purpose of the club is to entertain members or their guests or to provide members or their guests with access to entertainment facilities. Look at the purpose of the club not its name in making this determination. This means that you cannot deduct dues paid to country clubs, golf and athletic clubs, airline clubs, hotel clubs, and any clubs operated to provide meals under circumstances generally considered to be conducive to business discussions.

Your trade or business is taken into account when determining if an activity is entertainment. For example, going to a theater is not entertainment to a theater critic. And if a dress designer puts on a fashion show to introduce a new line, it would not be treated as entertaining customers.

.02 Ordinary and Necessary

You cannot deduct an entertainment expense unless it's incurred with an intent to obtain a specific business benefit, is directly related to the conduct of your business[52] and is customary in your trade or business. The expense can not be lavish or extravagant. For example, if you are a self-employed professional who depends on referrals from other professionals, the cost of entertaining them is usually considered an ordinary and necessary expense. The same applies to your employer's reimbursements to you for the cost of entertaining customers. However, no deduction is generally allowed for entertainment designed to expand your circle of acquaintances in the hope that some extra business might result.

Entertaining employees through picnics, holiday parties and the like is usually considered an ordinary and necessary expense because the employer benefits through improved employee morale. But including a few employees in a large social gathering does not convert personal expenses into business expenses.

Entertainment Expenses of Employees

If you, as an employee, claim deductions for unreimbursed business entertainment, you must do more than show that the expenses are ordinary and necessary business

[52] *R.G. Moore*, DC-VA, 96-2 USTC ¶ 50,413, 943 FSupp 603.

expenses. You must show the expenses are ordinary and necessary in your business as an employee. You must be expected to incur these expenses as part of your duty or position. Or your income must be dependent on the entertainment. For example, if a salesperson on commission entertains a customer of the company, that would generally be considered an ordinary and necessary expense. But if the personnel director of the same company entertains the customer, it probably is not treated as an ordinary and necessary expense.

The fact that your employer does not reimburse you may indicate that it is not an ordinary and necessary expense. On the other hand, if you can be reimbursed for entertainment expenses, but choose not to be, the expenses are considered nondeductible personal expenses.

Personal Expenses

As a general rule, when you incur ordinary personal living expenses in your business, you can only deduct the portion in excess of what you would normally pay. For example, according to this rule, if your lunch expenses usually run around $10, but your meal costs $25 when you entertain a customer, only $15 would be an ordinary and necessary business expense. But the IRS says this rule will not be enforced except in abusive situations.[53] So the full cost of your meal, as well as your customer's, is treated as an ordinary and necessary expense (subject, of course, to the percentage limitation on your deduction).

Personal Guests

When you entertain both business guests and nonbusiness guests, you must allocate your expenses between the business portion and the personal portion. For example, if you entertain three customers and three social acquaintances at a restaurant, only 4/7 of the restaurant tab is considered an ordinary and necessary expense the portion allocable to your meal and the meals of your three customers.

When your spouse and a customer or client's spouse attend the entertainment activity, their expenses are considered ordinary and necessary if you have a clear business purpose for the entertainment.

> **Example 10-36:** Mr. Soden, a good customer of XYZ Company, is in town for business discussions. Mrs. Soden is with him. Mr. Brown, an employee of XYZ, invites Soden to dinner at a restaurant. Because it would be impractical for Soden to dine without his wife, Mrs. Soden also comes to the restaurant. And because Mrs. Soden is there, Brown asks his wife to come too. XYZ picks up the tab. Result: XYZ's entire cost is considered an ordinary and necessary expense.

.03 50 Percent Deduction Limit

You can deduct only 50 percent of the cost of an otherwise allowable entertainment, amusement, or recreation expense [Code Sec. 274(n)(1)]. This 50 percent deduction limitation applies to food, beverages, and any item related to an activity which is of a type generally considered to constitute entertainment, amusement, or recreation. This means that the limit applies not only to the actual cost of your entertainment activity,

---

[53] Rev. Rul. 63-144, 1963-2 CB 129.

but to taxes, tips and other related charges (e.g., nightclub cover charges, parking fee at the entertainment site, etc.). However, it does not include transportation to and from the location of the entertainment; that cost is fully deductible.

Example 10-37: Mr. Burke pays a $10 cab fare to meet a client for dinner. The dinner bill comes to $80, plus $5 tax and a $15 tip. Result: Assuming the expenses qualify as deductible, Burke can write off $60 (50 percent of the total restaurant charges, plus the $10 cab ride).

If your employer reimburses you for entertainment expenses, only your employer is subject to the percentage deduction limit [Code Sec. 274(e)(3)].

For example, if the taxpayer in Example 10-37 above is reimbursed in full by his employer, the employer can only deduct $60 of the reimbursement. And Burke excludes 100 percent of the reimbursement from his taxable income as long as the reimbursement is provided under an accountable plan [¶ 10,015]. If you are not fully reimbursed for entertainment expenses, the percentage deduction limit applies at your employer's level to the extent of any reimbursement. But the limit applies at your level to determine how much of the excess entertainment expenses you can write off. Unless you're self-employed, your deduction is then subject to the 2 percent-of-adjusted-gross-income deduction floor [Ch. 9].

Exceptions

Certain types of expenses are not subject to the percentage limit and are deductible in full [Code Sec. 274(n)(2)]. These include:

- *Amounts treated as compensation.* If an employer reports an entertainment reimbursement as imputed income or compensation on the employee's W-2, the reimbursement is fully deductible by the employer and included in the employee's income. Code Sec. 274(e) limits the amount that a business can deduct when a company officer, director, or more-than-10 percent owner uses the company's aircraft for entertainment travel to the amount that the employee/recipient actually takes into income for use of the aircraft. Code Sec. 274(e) essentially overturns *Sutherland-Lumber-Southwest, Inc.*,[54] where the Court of Appeals for the Eighth Circuit concluded that an employer's deduction for vacation-related usage of the corporate jet by company executives was not limited to the compensation imputed to the employees on account of the flight. This loophole enabled companies to claim deductions that far exceeded the amounts that executives were required to include in income. For further discussion, see Ch. 4.
- *De minimis fringe benefits.* These are perks that are graciously provided to an employee by his or her employer and excluded from the employee's income (e.g., subsidized company cafeteria, holiday gifts of turkeys, etc.) [Code Sec. 132(a)];[3]
- *Employer-provided recreation.* This covers holiday parties, summer picnics, and similar recreational and social activities for employees.

---

[54] *Sutherland Lumber-Southwest, Inc.*, 114 TC 197, Dec. 53,817 (2000), *aff'd*, CA-8, 2001-2 USTC ¶ 50,503, 255 F3d 495, *acq.* IRB 2002-6.

- *Items such as goods, services, and facilities made available by the taxpayer to the general public.* In *Churchill Downs,*[55] the Court of Appeals for the Sixth Circuit held that a race track operator could deduct only 50 percent of the cost of hosting special entertainment events at its facilities. This exception to the 50 percent limit didn't apply because the events weren't part of the racetrack's core entertainment product and were attended by a selected audience rather than the general public;
- *Entertainment sold to customers.* If you charge a customer the full fair market value for an entertainment-type activity, your expenses are fully deductible. For example, a nightclub can write off 100 percent of the cost of its floor show; and
- *Charitable sporting events.* The cost of business entertainment at a sporting event is not subject to the percentage limit; it's fully deductible if (1) the event's primary purpose is to benefit a charity, (2) the entire net proceeds go to the charity, and (3) the event uses volunteers to perform substantially all of the work needed for the event. Golf tournaments for charity are a prime example of this kind of business entertainment activity.

Tickets

If you buy tickets to an entertainment event (e.g., Broadway show, baseball game), your deduction cannot exceed 50 percent of the face value of the ticket [Code Sec. 274(l) (1) (A)]. No deduction is allowed for the premium paid a "scalper," nor is any deduction permitted for the fee paid a ticket agency.

Skybox Rentals

A special limit applies to deductions for using skyboxes or other private luxury boxes for business entertainment. If you rent the box for more than one event, your deduction cannot exceed 50 percent of the face value of the same number of nonluxury box seats [Code Sec. 274(1) (2)].

¶10,045 SPECIAL ENTERTAINMENT DEDUCTION RULES

Code Sec. 274(a) (1) (A) bars deductions for entertainment, recreation, or amusement unless the taxpayer can establish that the expense was directly related to or associated with the active conduct of its trade or business.

.01 Entertainment Directly Related to Business

Entertainment is generally directly related to the taxpayer's business if, during the entertainment period, the taxpayer holds active discussions or negotiations with an eye on a specific business benefit. To qualify an expense as directly related to business, the taxpayer must meet three basic conditions [Reg. § 1.274-2(c) (3)]:

---

[55] *Churchill Downs,* 115 TC 279, Dec. 54,059 (2000), *aff'd,* CA-6, 2002-2 USTC ¶ 50,691, 307 F3d 423.

- There is more than a general expectation of deriving income or other business benefit from providing the entertainment. For example, a discussion at dinner about the general state of the economy is not considered directly related to business. However, you are not required to show that new income or a specific benefit actually resulted from each and every expense. If the business discussion is fruitless, a deduction is still allowed;
- The taxpayer actively engaged in a discussion, negotiations, or a transaction during the entertainment. However, expenses may still be deductible if the taxpayer expected to discuss business, but no business was actually discussed for reasons beyond his or her control; and
- The principal character of the combined entertainment/business activity was the active conduct of the taxpayer's business. This doesn't mean, for example, that the taxpayer and a customer have to talk business all the way through lunch. But an incidental business discussion isn't sufficient.

An expense automatically qualifies as directly related to business if it occurs in a clear business setting and is designed to further the taxpayer's business [Reg. § 1.274-2(c)(4)]. A clear business setting is one in which the recipient of the entertainment could reasonably conclude that the taxpayer has no motive for providing the entertainment other than business. For example, if a company operates a hospitality room at a convention to display its products, that would be considered a clear business setting.

Entertainment is presumed to fail the "directly related" test if the taxpayer holds it under circumstances where there is little or no possibility that business can be discussed, such as in a nightclub, theater, or sporting event [Reg. § 1.274-2(c)(7)]. However, in some cases, taxpayers have been allowed deductions for these types of expenses.[56]

In order to sustain a business deduction for entertaining clients, the Tax Court requires the taxpayer to do more than introduce yourself and shake hands. The law contemplates a more direct, primary relationship to the production of business income in order to establish the existence of a business meeting. The Tax Court has denied the business expense deductions of a part-time insurance salesman,[57] who deducted the expenses he allegedly incurred while attempting to build his insurance client base by golfing and socializing in a resort area. The taxpayer could not claim a business deduction for such activities as playing golf or having dinner with persons he considered potential clients, even if he occasionally would ask them if they needed insurance. Since the taxpayer failed to prove that his trips to the resort were more business than personal in nature, the claimed costs associated with these trips were not deductible.

.02 Entertainment Associated with Business

Entertainment is associated with your business if (1) there is a clear business purpose to the expenditure, such as soliciting business or improving an existing business

---

[56] *G. Detko*, 53 TCM 186, Dec. 43,719(M), TC Memo. 1987-99.

[57] *S.J. Miller*, 70 TCM 1120, Dec. 50,974(M), TC Memo. 1995-518.

relationship, and (2) it directly precedes or follows a substantial and bona fide business discussion [Reg. § 1.274-2(d)(1)].

Whether or not a discussion is substantial or bona fide depends on the facts and circumstances of each situation. Generally, you must show that you are engaged in a business discussion, conference meeting, or negotiation that had a business or income-producing goal. The meeting does not have to last any specific length of time, and it does not have to last longer than the entertainment that precedes or follows it. But you must show that the principal character of the combined business/entertainment activity is business [Reg. § 1.274-2(d)(3)(i)(a)].

> **Example 10-38:** Dr. Gilbert, a family practitioner, refers patients to Dr. Moss, a surgeon. One morning, Gilbert and Moss discuss patients' cases. Then Moss takes Gilbert out to lunch at a restaurant. After that they go for a round of golf, and Moss pays the greens fees. Result: The meal and golfing are generally considered associated with the active conduct of Moss's practice.

A business, professional conference, or convention qualifies as a substantial business discussion, assuming you can deduct the cost of attending the conference or convention [Reg. § 1.274-2(d)(3)(i)(b)]. For example, if you entertain a customer following a convention session, you can deduct your cost (subject to the percentage limit), even though it's strictly for goodwill and no business is discussed.

Generally speaking, a business discussion directly precedes or follows an entertainment activity if both occur on the same date. If they occur on different days, the entertaining may be considered associated with business if the facts and circumstances warrant it [Reg. § 1.274-2(d)(3)(ii)].

> **Example 10-39:** Mr. Morton, a customer of XYZ, and Mrs. Morton fly in from out of town. Mr. Pickford, a sales executive with XYZ, has the Mortons over to his home for dinner. Afterwards, they go to the theater. The following day Morton and Pickford spend several hours at XYZ's office negotiating a sales contract. Result: The cost of the dinner and theater tickets is considered associated with Pickford's business.

.03 Entertainment Facilities

In general, you cannot deduct expenses with respect to a facility used for entertainment [Code Sec. 274(a)(1)(B)]. An entertainment facility includes yachts, hunting lodges, fishing camps, swimming pools, automobiles and other items of personal or real property owned, rented or used in connection with business entertainment [Reg. § 1.274-2(e)(2)]. Disallowed deductions include those for depreciation, rents, repair expenses, utility charges, and salaries or expenses paid to caretakers or watchmen. In addition the phrase includes losses on the sale or other disposition of the facility [Reg. § 1.274-2(e)(3)(i)].

The disallowance rule does not apply to the expenses that could be deducted even if the facility were not used for business entertainment [Reg. § 1.274-2(e)(3)(iii)(c)]. So property taxes, mortgage interest and casualty losses on an entertainment facility may be deductible. And you can also deduct expenses attributable to the business use of a facility for other than entertainment [Reg. § 1.274-2(e)(3)(iii)(b)]. For example, if you let a customer use your business car for entertainment purposes, you can still claim deductions for other nonentertainment business use of the car. In addition, you can write off out-of-pocket entertainment expenses at a facility, as long as they are otherwise deductible [Reg. § 1.274-2(e)(3)(iii)(a)]. For example, if you take a client fishing on your boat following a business discussion, what you spend for gas and bait is considered a deductible expense.

.04 Entertaining at Clubs

You can deduct 50 percent of your out-of-pocket cost of entertaining a customer or client at your country, social or athletic club, provided the entertainment activity is directly related to or associated with your business. For example, after a morning business meeting, you treat a client to lunch and golf at your club. Result: You can deduct a percentage of what you spend on meals and drinks in the club dining room as well as a percentage of the greens fees and golf cart rental.

You cannot deduct membership dues, fees (including initiation fees), or any amounts paid to any type of club, even if the club is used exclusively for business purposes [Code Sec. 274(a)(3)]. This disallowance applies to business, social, athletic, recreational and luncheon clubs and clubs operated by hotels and airlines to provide special services to travelers. And it applies whether the club is used for entertaining customers or clients or for providing recreation to employees.

The dues disallowance rules do not apply to: (1) civic or public service organizations such as Kiwanis, Lions, Rotary, Civitan, and similar organizations; (2) professional organizations such as bar associations and medical associations; and (3) certain organizations similar to professional organizations, specifically, business leagues, trade associations, chambers of commerce, boards of trade, and real estate boards.

If, however, amounts paid to any of the three exceptions mentioned above are for the principal purpose of conducting entertainment activities for members or their guests or providing members or their guests with access to entertainment facilities, then the amounts will not be deductible [Reg. § 1.274-2(e)(3)(iii)(b)].

Example 10-40: Mr. Morley uses his country club solely to hold business discussions with customers and for goodwill entertaining. His annual dues are $5,000. His out-of-pocket expenses for the year come to $4,000. Result: Morley gets no deduction for the $5,000 dues. But he can deduct the $4,000 to the extent it is directly related or associated with business (and, of course subject to the 50 percent limit).

If your employer reimburses you for your dues to the extent of your business use of the club, the disallowance generally does not apply to you [Code Sec. 274(e)(3)]. Instead, your employer loses a deduction for the reimbursement. But this treatment applies only if (1) your employer does not report the reimbursement as compensation and (2) you make an accounting to your employer.

.05 Exceptions

The complicated restrictions do not apply for some business entertainment expenses [Code Sec. 274(e); Reg. § 1.274-2]. Some expenses can be deducted, whether or not they are directly related or associated with business. These include the following:

- Food and beverages furnished to employees on the employer's premises (subject to the 50 percent limitation). This includes executive dining rooms and company cafeterias and applies even though business guests may occasionally be served.
- Amounts treated as compensation. The cost of the entertainment activity or facility must be deducted as compensation on the employer's original tax return, and the value must be included in the employee's wages for withholding and reporting purposes. In other words, you cannot go back and change an entertainment expense to compensation on an amended return.
- Reimbursed expenses. The purpose here is to apply the disallowance rule to either the employee incurring the expense or the employer on whose behalf the expense is incurred—but not both. If the amount received is treated as a reimbursement and the employee substantiates the expenses under an accountable plan [¶ 10,015], the employer is subject to the disallowance rules (i.e., the employee may offset the expense against the reimbursement); if a payment to the employee is treated as compensation, the employee suffers the loss of deductions (i.e., the compensation is deductible by the employer, but the employee cannot claim a deduction to offset the taxable compensation).
- Recreational activities or facilities primarily for the benefit of employees. This exception does not apply to expenditures made mainly for the benefit of officers, other highly compensated employees, shareholders, or business owners. And it does not apply to the disallowance of the deduction for club dues (see above) [Code Sec. 274(e)(4)].

  ▶ **PLANNING POINTER:** Once it is established that a facility is used primarily (more than 50 percent) for the benefit of employees, then all of the use of the facility is exempt from the disallowance rules (including the percentage deduction limit). So if you also entertain customers at the facility, you can write off all the expenses attributable to that use as well.[58]

- Shareholder or employee business meetings. Here the primary purpose of the meeting must be to transact business.
- Expenses of attending business meetings or conventions of tax-exempt organizations. This includes business organizations and chambers of commerce.
- Items made available to the general public. This covers the distribution of samples to the public and maintenance of recreational facilities for public use.
- Entertainment sold to customers in bona fide transactions.
- Entertainment provided as compensation or a prize to someone who is not an employee.

---

[58] LTR 8321003 (Jan. 20, 1983).

¶10,050 BUSINESS GIFTS

Gifts to customers, clients, or even the general public may be both a deductible goodwill expense for the donor and excludable from the recipient's income as a tax-free gift. In such a case, you can deduct no more than $25 for business gifts you give to any one person during your tax year [Code Sec. 274(b)(1)]. But you can deduct any amount up to $25 in full; there is no 50 percent disallowance as there is with entertainment.

> **Example 10-41:** XYZ, Inc. sends out hams at Christmas to its customers. The cost of each ham is $40. XYZ can deduct $25. If the hams cost $20, XYZ could deduct the $20 in full.

For purposes of the deduction limit, a business gift does not include:

- Amounts other than gifts that are excludable from income (e.g., scholarships);
- An item having a cost of $4 or less on which your name or company name is clearly and permanently imprinted, and which is one of a number of identical items you distribute generally; or
- A sign, display rack, or other promotional material to be used on the business premises of the recipient [Reg. § 1.274-3(b)(2)].

In figuring the amount subject to the $25 limit, you do not have to include incidental costs, such as engraving, packaging, or mailing [Reg. § 1.274-3(c)]. A gift to the spouse of a customer or client is considered an indirect gift to the customer or client (unless you have independent business dealings with the spouse). So if you give the spouse a $25 gift, you cannot deduct any additional gifts to the customer for the year [Reg. § 1.274-3(d)(i)]. By the same token, you and your spouse are treated as one taxpayer for purposes of the deduction limit. If you and your spouse each give a $25 gift to a customer or client, your total deduction is limited to $25 [Code Sec. 274(b)(2)(B)]. If you give gifts to a partnership and to individual partners, you can deduct up to $25 for each gift to each of the partners and for the gift to the partnership. [Code Sec. 274(b)(2)(A)].

A gift of tickets to an event is considered entertainment if you accompany the recipient. However, if you don't attend, you may treat the tickets as either entertainment or a gift [Reg. § 1.274(b)(1)(iii)(b)(2)].

> ▶ **OBSERVATION:** If the event does not qualify as associated with or directly related entertainment [¶10,045], you obviously want to treat the tickets as gifts; otherwise you get no deduction. On the other hand, if the event does qualify as directly related or associated with entertainment, you should elect to treat the tickets as entertainment if they cost more than $50. Above the $50 level, your 50 percent deduction as entertainment exceeds the $25 limit on gifts.

¶10,055 REPORTING AND SUBSTANTIATION

.01 Substantiation

To claim a deduction for an entertainment expense that is directly related to business, you must be able to prove the following:

- The amount of each expense for entertainment;
- The date of the entertainment;
- The name, address or location of the site of the entertainment (including a designation of the type of entertainment if not readily apparent from the name of the place);
- The business reason for the entertainment or the nature of the business benefit to be derived and the nature of any business discussion or activity; and
- The name, title or other designation of the person being entertained, sufficient to establish his or her business relationship to you [Temp. Reg. § 1.274-5T(b)(3)].

For entertainment deducted as an expense associated with your business (i.e., a substantial business discussion precedes or follows it), you must prove all of the items above, plus the following:

- The date and duration of the business discussion;
- The place of the business discussion;
- The nature of the discussion; and
- The identification of the participants in the discussion [Temp. Reg. § 1.274-5T(b)(4)].

The following items that must be proved in the case of deductions for business gifts:

- The cost of the gift;
- The date of the gift;
- A description of the gift;
- The business reason for the gift or the business benefit expected to be derived; and
- The name, title or other designation of the recipient sufficient to establish your business relationship with the recipient [Temp. Reg. § 1.274-5T(b)(5)].

You must substantiate the items above by adequate written records or by sufficient evidence corroborating your own statement. "Adequate records" include an account book, diary, log, or similar record, prepared at or near the time each expense is incurred, that is sufficient to establish each required item of proof [Temp. Reg. § 1.274-5T(c)(2)]. A sample diary page of entertainment expenses appears below.

DATE	MEALS AND ENTERTAINMENT				
TOTAL					

In addition to the adequate records requirement, you must keep receipts or other documentary evidence for entertainment expenses in excess of $75 [Reg. § 1.274-5(c)(2)(D)(ii)].

.02 Allowances and Reimbursements

If you are an employee who receives an entertainment allowance or reimbursement, you must keep records that satisfy .01 above plus you must be required to submit a record of your expenses to your employer under an accountable plan [¶ 10,015]. This is the only way for you to avoid the 2-percent-of-adjusted-gross-income deduction floor [Ch. 9]. The IRS has approved the use of electronic receipts and expense reports under an accountable plan [¶ 10,015].

.03 Statistical Sampling

The IRS allows the use of statistical sampling methods to establish the amount of substantiated expenses paid or incurred for meals and entertainment that are not subject to the 50-percent limitation on deductibility.[59] Generally, business-related entertainment and meal expenses are deductible if they are ordinary and necessary expenses incurred in the operation of the taxpayer's business. In addition, these expenses must be adequately substantiated in order to be deductible. The deductibility of ordinary and necessary business-related entertainment and meal expenses that are adequately substantiated is generally limited to 50 percent of the expense. However, there are specific exceptions to the 50-percent limitation on deductibility to which the statistical sampling methodology may be applied. A taxpayer filing an original return, under examination, in litigation, or making a refund claim, may use statistical sampling in connection with establishing the amount of the taxpayer's substantiated expenses paid or incurred for meals and entertainment excepted from the 50-percent deduction disallowance rule.

[59] Rev. Proc. 2004-29, 2004-21 CB 918, as modified and amplified by Rev. Proc. 2011-42, IRB 2011-37.

Depreciation

DEPRECIATION IN GENERAL

General rules . . . . ¶ 11,001

What property can be depreciated . . . . ¶ 11,005

Who can deduct depreciation . . . . ¶ 11,010

How much can be depreciated . . ¶ 11,015

When you can depreciate . . . . ¶ 11,020

Tax returns and recordkeeping . . ¶ 11,025

MODIFIED ACCELERATED COST RECOVERY SYSTEM

MACRS in general . . . . ¶ 11,030

What property is eligible . . . . ¶ 11,035

MACRS and personal property . . ¶ 11,040

Code Sec. 179 expensing deduction . . . . ¶ 11,045

MACRS and real estate . . . . ¶ 11,050

OTHER DEPRECIATION SYSTEMS

Accelerated Cost Recovery System . . . . ¶ 11,055

Useful life depreciation system . . ¶ 11,060

Depreciation methods not based on years . . . . ¶ 11,065

DEPRECIATION IN GENERAL

A deduction for depreciation may be claimed each year for property with a limited useful life that's used in a trade or business or held for the production of income. The depreciation deduction allows taxpayers to recover the costs of business or income-producing property over a period of years.

¶11,001 GENERAL RULES

A taxpayer is allowed to recover, through annual depreciation deductions, the cost of certain property used in a trade or business or for the production of income.

A taxpayer's annual depreciation deduction is generally a fraction or percentage of his or her depreciable basis, computed according to the method of depreciation used. Property cannot be depreciated below a reasonable salvage value. For this reason it is important to accurately determine the correct salvage value of the property to be depreciated. *Salvage value* is the estimated value of property at the end of its useful life. It is what a taxpayer expects to receive for the property if he or she sold it after it could no longer be used productively. Salvage value is affected both by how the property is used and how long it is used. If it is the taxpayer's policy to dispose of property that is still in good operating condition, the salvage value can be relatively large. However, if the taxpayer's policy is to use property until it is no longer usable, its salvage value can be its junk value.

Once the salvage value for property is determined, it should not be changed merely because prices have changed.

Depreciation deductions are computed under one of the following methods or systems:

- The Modified Accelerated Cost Recovery System (MACRS) for property placed in service after 1986 [¶ 11,030];
- The Accelerated Cost Recovery System (ACRS) for property placed in service after 1980 and before 1987 [¶ 11,040];
- The useful-life (or facts-and-circumstances) system for property placed in service before 1981; or
- A method not based on a prescribed period of years including the unit-of-production method, the operating-day method and the income forecast method [¶ 11,065].

Which system controls depreciation on a particular property depends on when the property was placed in service.

Depreciation for most property placed in service after 1980 is governed by a strict statutory scheme, controlling the rate and period over which the specific property can be depreciated. The depreciation deduction allowed under MACRS and ACRS is also known as a cost recovery deduction.

The depreciation system for property placed in service before 1981 is less specific than MACRS or ACRS. It permits a reasonable allowance for depreciation based on the particular facts and circumstances [¶ 11,060]. This system can also be used to figure depreciation on certain property placed in service after 1980 that is ineligible for MACRS or ACRS.

.01 Bonus Depreciation

The Code Sec. 168(k) 50-percent bonus depreciation allowance is extended to apply to qualifying property acquired by a taxpayer after December 31, 2007, and before January 1, 2014 (or pursuant to a written binding contract entered into after December 31, 2007, and before January 1, 2014), and placed in service before January 1, 2014 (or before January 1, 2015, in the case of property with a longer production period and certain noncommercial aircraft) [Code Sec. 168(k)(2)].

The additional first-year depreciation deduction is allowed for both regular tax and alternative minimum tax purposes, but is not allowed for purposes of computing earnings and profits.

The basis of the property and the depreciation allowances in the year of purchase and later years must be adjusted to reflect the additional first-year depreciation deduction. In addition, there are no adjustments to the allowable amount of depreciation for purposes of computing a taxpayer's alternative minimum taxable income. The amount of the additional first-year depreciation deduction is not affected by a short tax year.

The taxpayer may elect out of additional first-year depreciation for any class of property for any tax year. The election out applies to all assets in the property class that are placed in service in the tax year regardless of whether the 50-percent or 100-percent bonus depreciation applies.

.02 Qualifying Property—In General

Property qualifying for the additional first-year depreciation deduction must meet all of the following requirements [Code Sec. 168(k)(2)].

1. The property must fit into one of the following four categories:
   a. Tangible property with a MACRS recovery period of 20 years or less;
   b. Water utility property with a MACRS recovery period of 20 years;
   c. Computer software depreciable over a 36-month period, whether developed internally or purchased; or
   d. MACRS qualified leasehold improvement property.
2. The taxpayer acquires the qualified property after December 31, 2007, and before January 1, 2014 (before January 1, 2015, in the case of transportation property with a longer production period). A taxpayer acquires the qualified property when the taxpayer pays or incurs the cost of the property. Qualified property that a taxpayer manufactures, constructs, or produces for use in its trade or business or for its production of income is acquired when the taxpayer begins constructing, manufacturing, or producing that property. If a taxpayer enters into a written binding contract to acquire, manufacture, construct, or produce qualified property, the property will be treated as having met the acquisition requirement.
3. The taxpayer places the qualified property in service before January 1, 2014 (before January 1, 2015, in the case of transportation property with a longer production period.
4. The original use of the qualified property commences with the taxpayer. Original use refers to the first use to which the property is put [Reg. § 1.168(k)-1(b)(3)]. An item of new inventory, such as a new car held by a dealer, however, is considered originally used by the purchaser. A taxpayer who purchases an unfinished asset that is under construction, such as a building, is considered the original user if the taxpayer completes construction and places the asset in service for the taxpayer's own use.

The following property cannot qualify for bonus depreciation:

- Nonresidential real property such as commercial buildings depreciable over 39 years;
- Residential rental property such as apartment buildings, depreciable over 27.5 years [Code Sec. 168(c), (e)(2)];
- Used property; any property that must be depreciated using the MACRS ADS;
  - — MACRS ADS property includes property used predominately outside of the United States (other than airplanes, vessels, containers, and vehicles used in transportation activities between the United States and foreign countries); tangible property leased to a tax-exempt entity or to the extent financed with

tax-exempt bonds; and listed property used 50 percent or less for business purposes during the tax year.

- Any property, except for computer software, that is not depreciated using MACRS (for example, intangible property, property depreciated using the sum-of-the-years'-digits method, income-forecast method, or work hours method); or
- An asset placed in service and disposed of in the same tax year.

.03 What Property Qualifies for Bonus Depreciation

Taxpayers are entitled to claim bonus depreciation for the following types of property:

Qualified Restaurant Property and Qualified Retail Improvement Property

In Rev. Proc. 2011-26,[1] the IRS provides that qualified property that meets the definition of both qualified leasehold improvement property (see definition below) and qualified restaurant property (as defined in Code Sec. 168(e)(7)) or qualified retail improvement property (as defined in Code Sec. 168(e)(8)) is eligible for the 50-percent or 100-percent additional first year depreciation deduction if all other requirements in Code Sec. 168(k) are met.

Qualified Leasehold Improvement Property

For purposes of qualifying for bonus depreciation under Code Sec. 168(k), qualified leasehold improvement property means any improvement, which is Code Sec. 1250 property, to an interior portion of a building that is nonresidential real property if:

- The improvement is made under or pursuant to a lease by the lessee (or any sublessee) of the interior portion, or by the lessor of that interior portion;
- The interior portion of the building is to be occupied exclusively by the lessee (or any sublessee) of that interior portion; and
- The improvement is placed in service more than 3 years after the date the building was first placed in service by any person [Code Sec. 168(k)(3)(A); Reg. §1.168(k)-1(c)(1)].

Qualified leasehold improvement property does not include any improvement for which the expenditure is attributable to:

- The enlargement of the building;
- Any elevator or escalator;
- Any structural component benefiting a common area; or
- The internal structural framework of the building [Code Sec. 168(k)(3)(C)(i); Reg. §1.168(k)-1(c)(2)].

Property with a Longer Production Period

Property with a longer production period will qualify for bonus depreciation if it is acquired after December 31, 2007, and before January 1, 2014, and placed in service before January 1, 2015 [Code Sec. 168(k)(2)(A)(iv)]. Longer-production property acquired pursuant to a written binding contract entered into after December 31, 2007,

[1] Rev. Proc. 2011-26, IRB 2011-16, 664.

and before January 1, 2014, is deemed acquired after December 31, 2007, and before January 1, 2014.

Progress expenditures. Although the placed-in-service deadline for 50-percent bonus depreciation property with a longer production period is extended one year through December 31, 2014, only pre-January 1, 2014, progress expenditures are taken into account in computing the bonus depreciation allowance. Thus, progress expenditures that increase the adjusted basis of such property during 2014 do not qualify for bonus depreciation [Code Sec. 168(k)(2)(B)(ii)].

> **Example 11-1:** A taxpayer enters into a contract for the purchase of a new commercial passenger plane (i.e., property with a longer production period) on February 1, 2010. The plane is delivered and placed in service on November 1, 2014. The plane qualifies for bonus depreciation at the 50-percent rate because it was acquired pursuant to a contract entered into after December 31, 2007, and before January 1, 2014, and was placed in service before January 1, 2015. However, progress expenditures attributable to 2014 construction do not qualify for the bonus deduction.

Noncommercial aircraft. Noncommercial aircraft must be acquired after December 31, 2007, and before January 1, 2014, and placed in service before January 1, 2015, in order to qualify for bonus depreciation at the 50-percent rate [Code Sec. 168(k)(2)(A)(iv)]. A noncommercial aircraft acquired pursuant to a written binding contract entered into after December 31, 2007, and before January 1, 2014, is deemed acquired after December 31, 2007, and before January 1, 2014.

Self-constructed property. If a taxpayer manufactures, constructs, or produces property for the taxpayer's own use, the requirement that the property be acquired after December 31, 2007, and placed in service before January 1, 2014, is deemed satisfied if the taxpayer begins manufacturing, constructing, or producing the property after December 31, 2007, and before January 1, 2014 [Code Sec. 168(k)(2)(E)(i)]. The property, however, still needs to be placed into service before January 1, 2014 (or before January 1, 2015, in the case of property with a longer production period). In addition, the property must meet the following additional requirements:

- The property must have a recovery period of at least 10 years or is transportation property,
- It is subject to the uniform capitalization rules under Code Sec. 263A, and
- It must have an estimated production period exceeding one year and an estimated cost exceeding $1 million as set forth in Code Sec. 263A(f)(1)(B)(iii).

Cellulosic Biofuel Plant Property

Code Sec. 168(l) provides a separate 50-percent bonus depreciation allowance for cellulosic biofuel plant property placed in service before January 1, 2014 [Code Sec. 168(l)]. Cellulosic biofuel is any liquid fuel which is produced from any lignocellulosic or hemicellulosic matter that is available on a renewable or recurring basis. Examples include bagasse (from sugar cane), corn stalks, and switchgrass.

Qualified Disaster Property

Taxpayers may claim 50-percent bonus depreciation for the tax year in which qualified disaster assistance property is placed in service [Code Sec. 168(n). The additional first-year depreciation deduction is equal to 50 percent of the adjusted basis of the qualified disaster assistance property. The adjusted basis of the property is reduced by the amount of the additional deduction before computing the amount otherwise allowable as a depreciation deduction for the tax year [Code Sec. 168(n)(1)]. Qualified disaster assistance roperty must satisfy the following requirements:

1. The property must be described in Code Sec. 168(k)(2)(A)(i) and be MACRS recovery property with a recovery period of 20 years or less, computer software that is depreciable over three years, water utility property, qualified leasehold improvement property, or residential rental property.
2. Substantially all of the use of the property must be in a disaster area with respect to a federally declared disaster occurring before January 1, 2014 and in the active conduct of the taxpayer's trade or business in that disaster area [Code Sec. 168(n)(2)(C)].
3. The property must rehabilitate property damaged or replace property destroyed or condemned as a result of the disaster.
4. The original use of the property in the disaster area must commence with an eligible taxpayer on or after the applicable disaster date.
5. The property must be acquired by the eligible taxpayer by purchase on or after the applicable disaster date, but only if no written binding contract for the acquisition was in effect before that date.
6. The property must be placed in service by the eligible taxpayer on or before the date that is the last day of the third calendar year following the applicable disaster date (or the fourth calendar year in the case of nonresidential rental property and residential rental property) [Code Sec. 168(n)(2)(A)].

An eligible taxpayer is one who has suffered an economic loss attributable to a federally declared disaster [Code Sec. 168(n)(3)(D)].

"Luxury" Car Depreciation Cap

Although the heading of Code Sec. 280F provides depreciation limits for so-called "luxury" automobile, the term "luxury" is very misleading. In fact, the annual depreciation limitations apply to most all passenger automobiles not just passenger automobiles that are very expensive and considered luxury cars.

Code Sec. 168(k)(2)(F)(i) provides that the first-year depreciation cap on a "luxury" vehicle is increased by an additional $8,000 in 2013 if the vehicle qualifies for bonus depreciation and the taxpayer makes no election out of bonus depreciation. In general, a vehicle will qualify for bonus depreciation if it is new, acquired after December 31, 2007 (no pre-January 1, 2008 binding contract for acquisition may be in effect), and placed in service before January 1, 2014.

The maximum depreciation limits under Code Sec. 280F for "luxury" passenger automobiles that qualify for bonus depreciation and that are first placed in service by the taxpayer during 2013 are: $11,160 for the first tax year ($3,160 plus $8,000); $5,100 for the second tax year; $3,050 for the third tax year; and $1,875 for each tax year thereafter.[2] If the vehicle does not qualify for bonus depreciation because it is a used vehicle or an election out of bonus depreciation is made, the first year cap is limited to $3,160 for passenger automobiles, other than trucks and vans.

The maximum depreciation limits under Code Sec. 280F for trucks and vans first placed in 2013 are $11,360 for the first tax year ($3,360 plus $8,000); $5,400 for the second tax year; $3,250 for the third tax year; and $1,975 for each tax year thereafter.

Sport Utility Vehicles (SUVs) and pickup trucks with a gross vehicle weight rating in excess of 6,000 pounds are exempt from the luxury vehicle depreciation caps because SUVs are excluded from the definition of a passenger automobile to which the depreciation caps apply. If the vehicle does not qualify for bonus depreciation, the first year cap is $3,360 for qualifying trucks and vans.

Alternative minimum tax. The bonus depreciation deduction, as well as regular depreciation deductions on bonus depreciation property, are allowed in full for AMT tax purposes (i.e., this rule continues to apply to bonus depreciation claimed on property placed in service in 2013 or in 2014 for long production property) [Code Sec. 168(k)(2)(G)].

¶11,005 WHAT PROPERTY CAN BE DEPRECIATED

In general, you can claim depreciation deduction for property only if the property meets all the following requirements:

1. The property must have a determinable useful life of more than one year; see exception below.
2. The property must be used your trade or business (which includes most so-called Code Sec. 1231 assets; see Ch. 8); or be held for the production of income (which falls into the category of capital assets). However, if economically recoverable precious metals are physically or chemically fabricated into an item of property used in a taxpayer's trade or business and the cost of those metals represents more than half of the cost of the object, the costs of the precious metals are nondepreciable and are accounted for separately from the item into which they are fabricated.[3] You can depreciate property available for use in your business, even though it's not actually used in the business [¶ 11,020]. By the same token, you may be able to claim depreciation deduction for property you hold for the production of income, although income is never produced. For example, you can depreciate a residence advertised and maintained for rental use, despite the fact that it is not rented.[4]
3. The property must wear out, decay, get used up, become obsolete or lose its value from natural causes. Common examples of depreciable property include business machinery, patents, office furniture, autos used in business and commercial buildings. Note: The IRS has said that when recyclable materials (which aren't deprecia-

[2] Rev. Proc. 2013-21, IRB 2013-12, 660.

[3] Rev. Rul. 90-65, 1990-2 CB 41, as corrected by Announcement 91-15, IRB 1991-5, 49.

[4] *M.L. Robinson*, 2 TC 305, Dec. 13,349 (1943), *acq.* 1944 CB 23; LTR 8030017.

ble) represent more than 50 percent of the cost of property, they must be accounted for separately. The remaining cost of the property can be depreciated. The IRS concluded that the buyer of a professional sports franchise couldn't depreciate the cost of the media rights that the team was entitled to purchase as a member of its league because the rights had no determinable expiration.[5]

.01 Exception to Determinable Useful Life Requirement

A number of cases have held that professional musicians can claim depreciation deductions on their rare early-19th century musical instruments including violin bows even though the musicians could not prove that the antique equipment had a useful life.[6] These decisions directly contradict a long-standing tax principle providing that you cannot depreciate valuable and treasured works of art because they do not have a determinable useful life capable of being set or fixed with certainty. The depreciation deductions were allowed because the instruments were used in the musician's trade or business and would suffer substantial wear and tear as a result of frequent use and therefore qualified for depreciation.

In another case,[7] a taxpayer was able to depreciate deductions under MACRS for state-of-the-art, high-tech cars that he used only for exhibit purposes in car shows and promotional photography because the cars were subject to exhaustion, wear and tear, or obsolescence.

As a result of the taxpayer victories in these cases, the gate is now open for depreciation of dual-purpose collectibles that are used in your trade or business, but which you expect to appreciate in real economic value. For example, executives who fill their offices with valuable antique furniture are now able to depreciate the antiques as office furniture over seven years even though the antiques will outlast the depreciation period and probably appreciate in value over time.

> ▶ **PRACTICE TIP:** In order for the depreciation deductions you claim on the valuable collectibles used in your trade or business to be upheld, you will have to show that the property suffered wear and tear or obsolescence as a result of being used in your trade or business. In the absence of such proof, your depreciation deductions will likely be denied by the IRS.

.02 Land

In general, a taxpayer cannot claim depreciation deductions for land because land does not wear out or become obsolete and it cannot be used up. So, for example, the cost of enclosing and filling in part of a lake to create additional land for industrial facilities is considered a land acquisition cost and is not depreciable.[8] Similarly, the cost of planting trees and bushes to serve as "windbreaks" on commercial land to prevent soil erosion and conserve moisture in the fields cannot be depreciated.[9]

---

[5] FSA 200142007.

[6] *R.L. Simon*, 103 TC 247, Dec. 50,059 (1994), *aff'd*, CA-2, 95-2 USTC ¶50,552, 68 F3d 41, *nonacq.* 1996-2 CB 2 and *nonacq.* IRB 1997-1, 6; *B.P. Liddle*, 103 TC 285, Dec. 50,060 (1994), *aff'd*, CA-3, 95-2 USTC ¶50,488, 65 F3d 329.

[7] *B. Selig*, 70 TCM 1125, Dec. 50,975(M), TC Memo. 1995-519.

[8] Rev. Rul. 77-270, 1977-2 CB 79.

[9] *G. Everson*, CA-9, 97-1 USTC ¶50,258, 108 F3d 234.

You can, however, depreciate some improvements to land if the costs you incur prepare the land for business use and if the improvement has a predictably limited useful life or when you can prove that the land improvement becomes obsolete or exhausted over time. Here are some examples of depreciable improvements:

- Excavation, grading and removal costs directly associated with construction of buildings and paved roadways;[10]
- Tunnels between buildings;[11]
- Sidewalks, gutters and drains added to a mill;[12]
- Construction costs of earthen dam;[13] and
- Irrigation system for citrus grove.[14]

Term Interest Buyer May Depreciate Basis Allocable to Land

In Letter Ruling 200852013, the IRS ruled that the business buyer of a term interest in buildings and land may depreciate the portion of his basis in the interest that's allocable to the land over the period of the term. A depreciation deduction for a term interest in land is sanctioned in Reg. § 1.167(a)-3(a) which provides that if an intangible asset is known from experience or other factors to be of use in the business or in the production of income for only a limited period, the length of which can be estimated with reasonable accuracy, such an intangible asset may be the subject of a depreciation allowance. Thus the IRS concluded that the portion of the taxpayer's basis in the lead interest allocable to the land is subject to the allowance for depreciation under Code Sec. 167(a) because it was an intangible asset that could be depreciated ratably over the term of the lead interest.

.03 Inventories and Other Property Held for Sale

You cannot depreciate inventory or any property you hold primarily for sale to customers in the ordinary course of your business.[15] You must account for decreases in the value of inventory items through inventory valuation [Ch. 17]. For example, the IRS has concluded that furniture displayed by a manufacturer in its showroom was inventory and not depreciable property used in its trade or business.[16] The IRS also denied depreciation deductions to car dealer who sought to depreciate demonstrator autos because the demonstrator autos did not become property used in a business merely because the autos were used for demonstration purposes or temporarily withdrawn from stock or inventory for business use.[17] Similarly, the IRS has held that homebuilders may not depreciate houses used as models or sales offices. Those houses were held primarily for sale to customers in the ordinary course of the builder's business, and their temporary use as models or sales offices didn't change that status.[18]

---

[10] Rev. Rul. 68-193, 1968-1 CB 79.

[11] *E.W. Edwards*, DC-NY, 39-2 USTC ¶ 9712, 29 FSupp 671.

[12] *Clinton Cotton Mills, Inc.*, CA-4, 35-2 USTC ¶ 9449, 78 F2d 292.

[13] *R. Fancher*, DC-SD, 62-2 USTC ¶ 9819.

[14] Rev. Rul. 80-25, 1980-1 CB 65; Rev. Rul. 83-67, 1983-1 CB 74; Rev. Rul. 83-128, 1983-2 CB 57.

[15] Chief Counsel Advice 201025049 (no depreciation deductions for equipment held for rent or sale).

[16] FSA 199949031.

[17] Rev. Rul. 75-538, 1975-2 CB 34.

[18] Rev. Rul. 89-25, 1989-1 CB 79.

You generally cannot depreciate containers because they are viewed as part of your inventory. Contrast that result with the rule regarding durable containers which can be depreciated if: (1) they have a life longer than one year, (2) qualify as property used in your business, and (3) title to the container does not pass to the buyer. To deduct your durable containers you will have to show that: (1) your sales contract, sales invoice, or other type of order acknowledgment indicates that you have retained title to the containers; (2) your invoice treats the containers as separate items; (3) your records state your basis in the containers.

.04 Rent-to-own Property

You can depreciate over 3 years qualified rent-to-own property under the General Depreciation System (GDS) [Code Sec. 168(e)(3)(A)(iii)]. Qualified rent-to-own property is assigned a four-year class life for purposes of the ADS [Code Sec. 168(g)(3)(B)]. See ¶11,040.

Qualified rent-to-own property is property held by a rent-to-own dealer for purposes of being subject to a rent-to-own contract [Code Sec. 168(i)(14)(A)]. A qualified rent-to-own dealer is a person who, in the ordinary course of business, regularly provides customers with consumer property subject to the terms of a rent-to-own contract, but only where a substantial portion of those contracts terminate resulting in the return of the goods before receipt of all payments required to transfer ownership of the property from the dealer to the customer. Consumer property is tangible personal property generally used in the home, such as televisions, camcorders, stereos, and furniture [Code Sec. 169(i)(14)(B)].

A rent-to-own contract means any lease for the use of consumer property between a rent-to-own dealer and a customer who is an individual provided the contract meets the following requirements [Code Sec. 168(i)(14)(D)]:

- Is titled "Rent-to-Own Agreement" or "Lease Agreement with Ownership Option," or uses other, similar language;
- Provides a beginning date and a maximum period of time (not to exceed 156 weeks or 36 months from the beginning date), for which the contract can be in effect (including renewals or options to extend);
- Provides for regular periodic weekly or monthly payments that can be either level or decreasing. If the payments are decreasing, then no payment can be less than 40 percent of the largest payment;
- Provides for total payments to generally exceed the normal retail price of the property plus interest;
- Provides for total payments that do not exceed $10,000 for each item of property;
- Provides that the customer has no legal obligation to make all payments outlined in the contract and that at the end of each weekly or monthly payment period, the customer may either continue to use the property by making the next payment or return the property in good working order and be free of any further obligations and not be entitled to a return of any prior payments;
- Provides that legal title to the property remains with the rent-to-own dealer until the customer makes either all the required payments or the early purchase payments required under the contract to acquire legal title; or

- Provides that the customer has no right to sell, sub-lease, mortgage, pawn, pledge, or otherwise dispose of the property until all contract payments have been made.

.05 Code Sec. 197 Intangibles

A taxpayer is entitled to an amortization deduction if the taxpayer acquires amortizable Code Sec. 197 intangible assets.

Intangibles can be defined as assets that cannot be seen or touched; they include goodwill, trademark and trade names. Taxpayers may elect to amortize the cost of these intangibles, which are called "Section 197 intangibles" over 15 years [Code Sec. 197(c)(1); Reg. § 1.197-1].

To qualify for the 15-year amortization, taxpayers must acquire the intangibles in connection with the conduct of their trade or business or in an activity engaged in for the production of income [Code Sec. 197(c)(1)].[19] Classification as a Code Sec. 197 intangible is beneficial only if the cost of the asset cannot be written off using any other provision more rapidly.

A taxpayer's basis in the intangible will be written off ratably over a 15-year period, starting on the later of the first day of the month in which either the intangible is acquired or the active trade business or the Code Sec. 212 investment activity that uses the intangible begins. The taxpayer may not claim amortization for the month of disposition. Disregard the salvage value when determining the basis of the intangible for depreciation purposes. No other depreciation, amortization or business expense deduction may be claimed on the intangible that is amortized under Code Sec. 197 [Reg. § 1.197-2(a)(1)].

> **Example 11-2:** XYZ, Inc., a calendar-year corporation, acquires a Code Sec. 197 intangible on September 1, 2013, for $90,000. XYZ can claim an amortization deduction of $2,000 on its 2013 return (4 months out of 180), $6,000 annually for 2014 through 2026 (12 months each year out of 180), and $4,000 in 2024 (8 months out of 180).

The following assets qualify as Code Sec. 197 intangibles assets and are therefore eligible for the 15-year write-off [Code Sec. 197(d)(1); Reg. § 1.197-2(b)]:

- Goodwill or going concern value of a business [Code Sec. 197(d)(1)(A) and (B)];
- Workforce in place, including its composition and the terms and conditions of its employment (e.g., employment contracts) [Code Sec. 197(d)(1)(C)(i)];
- Business books and records, operating systems, customer lists, training manuals and other information bases;
- Formulas, processes, designs, patterns, knowhow, and formats;
- Subscription contracts and other customer-based intangibles;
- Favorable contracts with suppliers and other supplier-based intangibles;
- Licenses, permits and other rights granted by government agencies [Code Sec. 197(d)(1)(D);

[19] *D.R. Fitch*, 104 TCM 828, Dec. 59,300(M), TC Memo. 2012-358 (purchase price of accounting practice could be amortized under Code Sec. 197).

- Franchises (including professional sports franchises acquired after October 22, 2004) [Code Sec. 197(d)(1)(F)];
- Trademarks and trade names;
- Contracts for the use of, and term interests in, other Code Sec. 197 intangibles [Code Sec. 197(e)(4)(D)];

a. Covenants not to compete and other similar arrangements regardless of duration only if entered into in connection with an acquisition of an interest in a trade or business [Code Sec. 197(d)(1)(E)];[20]

b. Computer software only if entered into in connection with an acquisition of an interest in a trade or business;

c. Interests in film, sound recordings, videotapes, books or other similar property only if entered into in connection with an acquisition of an interest in a trade or business;

d. Rights to receive tangible property or services only if entered into in connection with an acquisition of an interest in a trade or business;

e. Interests in patents or copyrights only if entered into in connection with an acquisition of an interest in a trade or business;

f. Mortgage servicing rights only if entered into in connection with an acquisition of an interest in a trade or business; and

g. Certain rights under a contract or licenses, permits or other rights only if entered into in connection with an acquisition of an interest in a trade or business and if granted by a governmental unit that have a duration of less than 15 years or that are fixed in amount and would, without regard to Code Sec. 197, be recoverable under a method similar to the unit-of-production method.

If an amortizable Code Sec 197 intangible is transferred as part of a "nonrecognition" transaction (e.g., an exchange of like-kind properties under Code Sec. 1031 [see Ch. 6] or a tax-free incorporation under Code Sec. 351 [see Ch. 6], the transferee is treated as the transferor [Code Sec. 197(f)(2)(A); Reg §1.197-2(g)(2)(i)]. This means that the transferee will adopt the transferor's amortization schedule to the extent of his or her basis in the intangible [Code Sec. 197(f)(2); Reg. §1.197-2(g)].

> **Example 11-3:** Alice owns an amortizable Code Sec. 197 intangible with 10 years to run on the amortization period and an unamortized basis of $300,000. Alice and Bob agree to a like-kind exchange in which Alice transfers her property and $100,000 in cash for Bob's qualified intangible. Alice takes the new Code Sec. 197 intangible with a basis of $400,000. Three hundred thousand dollars ($300,000) is amortized over the remaining 10 years of the original amortization period, and $100,000 is amortized over the 15 years beginning at the date of transfer.

---

[20] *Frontier Chevrolet*, 116 TC 289, Dec. 54,336 (2001), *aff'd*, CA-9, 2003-1 USTC ¶50,490, 329 F3d 1131; *Recovery Group, Inc.*, 99 TCM 1324, Dec. 58,184(M), TC Memo. 2010-76, *aff'd*, CA-1, 2011-2 USTC ¶50,541.

▶ **IMPORTANT:** The 15-year amortization period applies only to costs that must be capitalized. For example, suppose a taxpayer acquires a business that has a service contract with a vendor on very favorable terms. That contract has a value and part of the purchase price of the business must be allocated to the contract. This cost must be written off over 15 years. But payments made to the vendor under the contract would not be subject to the 15-year amortization period. (Exceptions: Most payments made under covenants not to compete and franchise, trademark and trade name agreements must be capitalized.)

Assets That Are Not Code Sec. 197 Intangibles

Some intangibles are ineligible for amortization under Code Sec. 197 because they are subject to cost recovery under other depreciation methods or because these items are not capital in nature and the related expenses may be deductible currently. In addition, Code Sec. 197 cannot be applied to an intangible created by the taxpayer unless the intangible is created in connection with the acquisition of assets constituting a trade or business or a substantial part of a trade or business [Reg. § 1.197-2(d)(2)].

Example 11-4: Dotty forms a cookie dough business and after 20 years of success, a substantial portion of the value of the business is attributable to her goodwill. Dotty may never amortize the value of that goodwill, but someone who buys that business from Dotty could amortize the portion of the purchase price that is attributable to the goodwill over 15 years under Code Sec. 197.

The following intangibles are specifically excluded from the definition of a Code Sec. 197 intangible and therefore cannot be amortized over 15 years [Code Sec. 197(e)(1); Reg. § 1.197-2(c)]:

- Interests in a corporation, partnership, trust or estate;
- Interests under certain financial contracts including futures contracts, foreign currency contracts, notional principal contracts, interest rate swaps and other similar financial contracts whether or not the interest is regularly traded on an established market;
- Interests in land such as easements, mineral rights, fee interests, life estates, remainder interests, farm allotments, farm commodity quotas, zoning variances, crop acreage bases, riparian rights, timber grazing and air rights;
- Computer software that is:
  - — Otherwise deductible;
  - — Not acquired as part of the acquisition of assets constituting a trade or business or a substantial portion of a trade or business;
  - — Readily available for purchase by the general public under a nonexclusive license and that has not been substantially modified (even if acquired as part of the acquisition of a business);
  - — Part of the cost of property that is not a Code Sec. 197 intangible.

- The following, if not acquired as part of the acquisition of the assets constituting a trade or business or a substantial portion of a trade or business:
  - — Interests in films, sound recordings, videotapes, books or similar property;
  - — Rights to receive tangible property or services under a contract or from a governmental unit;
  - — Interest (including interests as a licensee) in a patent, patent application or copyright;
  - — Rights to service indebtedness secured by residential real property.
- Interest as a lessors or lessees under an existing lease or sublease of tangible real or personal property;
- Creditor or debtors interests under an indebtedness in existence when the interest was acquired; (e.g., assumption of a below-market rate mortgage);
- A franchise to engage in professional football, basketball, baseball, or any other professional sport, as well as any item acquired in connection with such a franchise, is not a Code Sec. 197 intangible if it was acquired on or before October 22, 2004. Consequently, if a professional sports franchise was acquired on or before October 22, 2004, the cost of acquiring the franchise and related assets should be allocated among the assets without regard to Code Sec. 197. For franchises acquired after October 22, 2004, the rules of Code Sec. 197 apply.
- Transaction costs and fees for professional services incurred in a transaction in which gain or loss is not recognized in a corporate organization or reorganization.
- For intangibles not subject to the 15-year write-off period, you may claim amortization deductions over their useful lives if they are limited in duration and can be estimated with reasonable accuracy [Reg. § 1.167(a)(3)].

Computer software. Reg. § 1.167(a)-14(a) provides special rules for amortizing computer software and other separately acquired rights, such as rights to receive tangible property or services, patents and copyrights, certain mortgage servicing rights and rights of fixed duration or amount that are excluded from Code Sec. 197. The amortization period for computer software is 36 months beginning on the first day of the month that the computer software is placed in service [Reg. § 1.167(a)-14(b)(1)]. Keep in mind, however, that bundled software that is included without being separately stated in the cost of computer hardware is treated as part of the cost of the hardware and thus is depreciated as part of the hardware [Reg. § 1.167(a)-14(b)(2)]. The amortization period for mortgage servicing rights is 108 months beginning on the first day of the month that the rights are placed in service [Reg. § 1.167-14(d)(1)].

Disposition of Code Sec. 197 intangibles. If you dispose of Code Sec. 197 property held for more than one year, any gain on the disposition, up to the amount of allowable amortization, will be taxed as ordinary income (Code Sec. 1245 gain). Any remaining gain, or loss, is treated as a Code Sec. 1231 gain or loss [See Ch. 8]. This means that any net gain will be treated as a long-term capital gain and any net loss will be treated as an ordinary loss. If you held the property one year or less, any gain or loss on its disposition is an ordinary gain or loss.

If you acquire more than one Code Sec. 197 intangible in a transaction or series of transactions and later dispose of one of them or if one of them becomes worthless, you cannot recognize any loss on the intangible. Instead, increase the adjusted basis of each remaining amortizable Code Sec. 197 intangible by the part of the loss not recognized [Code Sec. 197(f)(1)(A)]. Figure the increase by multiplying the loss not recognized on the disposition by the following fraction:

- The numerator is the adjusted basis of that remaining intangible as of the date of its disposition.
- The denominator is the total adjusted basis of all retained amortizable Code Sec. 197 intangibles as of the date of the disposition [Reg. § 1.197-2(g)(1)(i)].

All members of the same controlled corporation are treated as a single taxpayer when Code Sec. 197 intangibles are sold or otherwise disposed of [Code Sec. 197(f)(1)(C)]. Therefore, a member of a controlled group of corporations may not claim a loss when it sells a Code Sec. 197 intangible if another member of the group retains other Code Sec. 197 intangibles that were acquired in the same transaction or a series of related transactions [Reg. § 1.197-2(g)(1)(iv)].

Recapture of Code Sec. 197 amortization modified. If multiple Code Sec. 197 intangibles are sold, or otherwise disposed of, in a single transaction or series of transactions, the seller must calculate recapture as if all of the Code Sec. 197 intangibles were a single asset [Code Sec. 1245(b)(9)(A)]. Thus, any gain on the sale or other disposition of the intangibles is recaptured as ordinary income to the extent of ordinary depreciation deductions previously claimed on any of the Code Sec. 197 intangibles.

Antichurning Rules

The antichurning rules prevent you from converting Code Sec. 197 intangibles, such as existing goodwill or going concern value, that do not qualify for amortization into property that would qualify for 15-year amortization under Code Sec. 197 [Code Sec. 197(f)(9); Reg. § 1.197-2(h)]. Specifically the antichurning rules provide that you may not treat an otherwise ineligible intangible as a Code Sec. 197 intangible if:

- You or a related person held or used the intangible prior to the Code Sec. 197 effective date,
- You acquired the intangible from a person who held or used the intangible at any time during the effective date and as part of the transaction, the user does not change, or
- You grant the right to use the intangible to a person (or a person related to that person) who held or used the intangible at any time during the effective date [Reg. § 1.197-2(h)(2)].

In addition, the IRS has provided rules for determining the amount of a basis adjustment that would be subject to the anti-churning rules under Code Sec. 732(b) and Code Sec. 743(b) [Reg. § 1.197-2(h)(12)].

¶11,010 WHO CAN DEDUCT DEPRECIATION

Taxpayers who own the property (e.g., individuals, corporations, trusts and estates) are entitled to claim depreciation deductions if they use the property in their trade or business or for producing income and if they will suffer the economic loss when the property depreciates in value. Ordinarily, owners meet this requirement and their deduction will not be challenged. However, bare legal title does not, by itself, guarantee the deduction. For example, a mortgagee who holds title merely for security purposes and does not own the property cannot depreciate it. But if you assume a previous owner's mortgage, you own the property and can depreciate it.

.01 Purchased Property

If you are buying depreciable property but do not yet have title, you can claim depreciation if you have assumed the benefits and burdens of ownership. Whether that assumption has occurred depends on various factors, such as: (1) how you and the seller treat the transaction; (2) whether you have acquired any equity in the property; (3) the extent of your control over the property; (4) whether you bear the risk of damage to the property; (5) whether you will receive any benefit from the operation or disposition of the property.[21]

.02 Leased Property

You cannot claim depreciation deductions on property you are leasing from someone else. However, you can depreciate any capital improvements that you make to the leased property. For example, if you construct a building on land you lease, you may claim depreciation on just the building.

.03 Life Estates and Remainders

You may have the right to use depreciable property during your lifetime (i.e., life estate). After you die, the property goes outright to someone else. This is known as the remainder interest.

As the holder of the life estate, you can depreciate the property as if you were the absolute owner. After your death, the holder of the remainder interest can write off any unrecovered amount [Code Sec. 167(d)].

If you buy a life estate in nondepreciable property (e.g., land), you can amortize your cost over your remaining life expectancy. However, no amortization deduction is allowed for life estates if the remainder interest is held directly or indirectly by a person related to you [Code Sec. 167(e)]. A person related to you includes your spouse, child, parent, brother, sister, half-brother, half-sister, ancestor, or lineal descendant.

In addition, you cannot claim a deduction if you acquire a life estate by gift or inheritance [Code Sec. 273].

---

[21] *M.O. Houchins*, 79 TC 570, Dec. 39,387 (1982).

¶11,015 HOW MUCH CAN BE DEPRECIATED

Your annual depreciation deduction is a fraction or percentage of your "depreciable basis." Your depreciable basis, in turn, depends on which depreciation system you are using. For example, under MACRS [¶ 11,030], your depreciable basis is generally the same as your basis for figuring gain or loss on a sale [Ch. 6], unadjusted for prior depreciation.

.01 Conversion of Personal Property to Business Property

A special rule applies when you convert property from personal-use property to business-use property. Your basis for figuring depreciation is the lower of (1) the property's fair market value at the time of conversion or (2) its adjusted basis [Ch. 6] when converted [Reg. § 1.167(g)-1].

Example 11-5: Mr. Brown purchased a personal residence for $100,000 last year. This year, he vacates the residence and rents it out. At that time, the house is worth $110,000. Result: Since Brown's adjusted basis at the time of conversion is lower than the fair market value, his basis for depreciation is $100,000.

Example 11-6: Same facts as before, except the value of the home has declined to $90,000 this year. Result: Brown's basis for depreciation is $90,000.

.02 Allocation of Basis

If you purchase both depreciable and nondepreciable property for a lump sum, you must allocate your basis (cost) between the two to figure your depreciation. The depreciable part must bear the same ratio to the lump sum that the fair market value of the depreciable property bears to the entire property [Reg. § 1.167(a)-5].

Example 11-7: Ms. Johnson purchases a small apartment house. The fair market value of the building is $200,000 and the land is worth $50,000. But Johnson is able to purchase the property for only $225,000. Result: Since 20 percent of the total fair market value of the property is allocable to the land, Johnson must allocate 20 percent of her cost—$45,000—to the land. So her basis for figuring depreciation on the building is $180,000 ($225,000 – $45,000).

How to Determine Allocation

Get an expert appraisal of the separate properties when you buy. Then spell out in the sales contract exactly how much of the purchase price is allocable to the depreciable property and how much to the nondepreciable.

You must make a similar allocation when you use property for both business and personal purposes. For example, when you use an auto for both personal and business travel during the year, you compute depreciation on the basis of mileage, i.e., what portion of total annual mileage is business-connected [Ch. 10]. When you use a house both as a personal residence and business office, your allocation is based on the number of rooms or floor space [Ch. 12].

Code Sec. 167(c)(2) prohibits taxpayers from allocating a portion of the cost of acquiring tangible property to any leases or subleases to which the property is subject immediately prior to the sale. In *Union Carbide Foreign Sales Corp.*,[22] a taxpayer that purchased a ship in order to terminate a burdensome lease on it could not allocate a portion of the cost of acquiring the vessel to the termination of the lease. The Tax Court held that Code Sec. 167(c)(2) required the entire cost to be allocated to the basis of the vessel.

.03 Allocating Basis of Commercial Real Estate

A purchaser of commercial real estate must keep in mind when allocating cost basis that commercial buildings and their structural components are depreciated as one unit via straight line over a 39 year recovery period. Structural components are typically those components used for building maintenance or operation and would include, for example, electrical or plumbing facilities including a sprinkler system.[23] A general rule of thumb is that anything assisting in the overall operation of a building will be considered a structural component and must be depreciated straight line over a 39 year recovery period. But special electrical or plumbing connections that are necessary for and used directly with or between particular machines or equipment will be classified personal property rather than structural components.[24] For example, plumbing connections will not be considered structural components if they (a) don't relate to general building plumbing; (2) carry water and steam directly to specific pieces of equipment such as dishwashers, coffee urns and x-ray equipment; and (3) were necessary for the operation of that equipment.[25]

> ▶ **PRACTICE POINTER:** The commercial buyer should be aware, however, that not all components are subject to the 39-year depreciation schedule. For example, commercial property often contains elements that are not structural components and therefore are depreciated separately over a shorter recovery period via accelerated depreciation. The buyer should therefore allocate as much of the purchase price as possible to the depreciable improvements rather than to the nondepreciable land.

Noncomponent Portion of Building May Be Personal Property

In *Hospital Corp. of America*,[26] the Tax Court held that a non-component portion of a building that was treated by the courts as personal property (rather than slowly recoverable building or a structural component) under prior law's repealed investment tax credit also is tangible personal property for MACRS depreciation purposes. Note that the following items have been held to be personal property rather than structural components for purposes of the investment tax credit. This means that you

---

[22] *Union Carbide Foreign Sales Corp.*, 115 TC 423, Dec. 54,111 (2000).

[23] Rev. Rul. 66-299, 1966-2 CB 14; *Scott Paper*, 74 TC 137, Dec. 36,920 (1980); *Central Citrus Co.*, 58 TC 365, Dec. 31,403 (1972).

[24] Rev. Rul. 66-299, 1966-2 CB 14; Rev. Rul. 70-160, 1070-1 CB 7.

[25] *Hospital Corp. of America*, 109 TC 21, Dec. 52,163 (1997), *aff'd*, CA-6, 2003-2 USTC ¶50,702, 348 F3d 136, *cert. denied*, 125 SCt 48, *acq. and nonacq.* IRB 1999-35, 314, as corrected by Announcement 99-116, 1999-2 CB 763.

[26] *Hospital Corp. of America*, 109 TC 21, Dec. 52,163 (1997), *aff'd*, CA-6, 2003-2 USTC ¶50,702, 348 F3d 136, *cert. denied*, 125 SCt 48, *acq. and nonacq.* IRB 1999-35, 314, as corrected by Announcement 99-116, 1999-2 CB 763.

should be able to allocate a portion of the purchase price to the items listed below and depreciate them separately over a shorter recovery period.

▶ **CAUTION:** You will, however, need a formal appraisal to achieve the proper allocation of purchase price.

- Movable and removable partitions are personal property[27] if (1) they can be readily and economically removed and reused without doing more than minor damage to the partition or the building; (2) it is more economical to remove and reuse the partitions than to destroy them and put in new ones; and (3) it is reasonable to expect that partitions will in fact be moved to suit tenants or their changing business needs.[28]
- Exterior ornamentation such as false balconies and a restaurant chain's décor finishes, decorative canopy system including the concrete foundation, concrete piers, lumber and signs belong in the Asset Class 57.0 for MACRS and therefore are 5-year property.[29]
- Carpeting installed by fastening the carpet to wood strips along the wall is personal property rather than a structural component.[30] Carpeting attached to the floor by means of a general purpose latex adhesive also qualifies as tangible personal property because it can be removed without requiring resurfacing or restorative work to the floor and can be reused and/or reinstalled if desired at another location.[31] Based on this reasoning, even vinyl floor covering will be classified as tangible personal property.
- Solar water-heating equipment integrated with, but not replacing the conventional system is tangible personal property where it can be easily and cheaply removed without damage to the building.[32]

How to Allocate Basis

The regulations provide that: (1) the purchase price allocation must be based on the ratio of the depreciable improvements' value at acquisition to the entire property's value at that time, and (2) if the purchase is part of an applicable asset acquisition under Code Sec. 1060, the allocation can't exceed the consideration allotted to the property under the Code Sec. 1060 regulations [Reg. § 1.167(a)-5; Temp. Reg. § 1.167(a)-5T].

Appraisal Critical

A tax assessor's valuation or a mortgage appraisal may be used to allocate the purchase price between the land and buildings.[33] However, you cannot allocate cost basis in land and buildings solely according to their assessed values for property tax

---

[27] Rev. Rul. 75-178, 1975-1 CB 9.

[28] *Metro National Co.*, 52 TCM 1440, Dec. 43,649(M), TC Memo. 1987-38.

[29] *Walgreen Co. & Subsidiaries*, 72 TCM 382, Dec. 51,503(M), TC Memo. 1996-374.

[30] Rev. Rul. 67-349, 1967-2 CB 48.

[31] LTR 7752075 (Sept. 30, 1997); *Hospital Corp. of America*, 109 TC 21, Dec. 52,163 (1997), *aff'd*, CA-6, 2003-2 USTC ¶ 50,702, 348 F3d 136, *cert. denied*, 125 SCt. 48, *acq. and nonacq.* IRB 1999-35, 314, as corrected by Announcement 99-116, 1999-2 CB 763.

[32] *M.H. Wood*, 61 TCM 2571, Dec. 47,334(M), TC Memo. 1991-205.

[33] *J.W. Peterson*, 54 TCM 808, Dec. 44,246(M), TC Memo. 1987-508; *M.M. Dillon* 42 TCM 1364, Dec. 38,329(M), TC Memo. 1981-583, *aff'd*, CA-10, 83-1 USTC ¶ 9177.

purposes where better evidence, such as an engineering report, exists to establish fair market value.[34]

Allocating Basis to Land Related Improvements

It may be possible to allocate a significant part of the property's acquisition, construction or reconstruction cost to land-related improvements such as landscaping, shrubbery, sidewalks, roads within the property, and fences. These assets are placed in Class 00.3 and are assigned a 20-year class life according to Rev. Proc. 87-56.[35] As a result of this classification, the land improvements may be depreciated over 15 years using 150 percent declining balance depreciation under MACRS [Code Sec. 168(b)(2)(B), (e)(1)]. But the IRS limits the depreciation of land improvements to only that part of the landscaping that is immediately adjacent to buildings because only this portion would be destroyed if the buildings themselves were destroyed or replaced. The balance of the landscaping must be capitalized and added to the basis of the land.[36] It thus behooves taxpayer to obtain a detailed appraisal when purchasing commercial real estate. Be sure that the appraisal allocates costs to land-related items and breaks down the landscaping into depreciable and nondepreciable elements.

How to Depreciate Nonstructural Components

How the nonstructural components are depreciated depends upon which class the assets are placed. For example, Section 1245 property with no class life will be depreciated over seven years using 200-percent declining balance depreciation [Code Sec. 168(e)(3)(C)]. Alternatively, the asset may be placed in a special class by Rev. Proc. 87-56.[37] Rev. Proc. 87-56 sets forth class lives of property subject to depreciation and establishes two broad categories of depreciable assets: (1) asset classes for assets used in all business activities (the "asset" group); and (2) other asset classes used in specific business activities (the "activity" group). For example, tangible personal property in Asset Class 57.0, "Distributive Trades or Services" which includes "assets used in wholesale or retail trade and personal and professional services" will be classified as 5-year property under MACRS.

.04 Self-Constructed Property

If you are building depreciable property for use in your business, your basis for the property is the cost of construction, including depreciation on the equipment used to build it. To the extent the depreciation on that equipment is allocable to the construction of the new property, you cannot deduct it currently. Instead, it must be added to the basis of the new property and depreciated along with it.[38]

¶11,020 WHEN YOU CAN DEPRECIATE

Depreciation begins when an asset is "placed in service" for use in your trade or business or for the production of income [Reg. § 1.167(a)-10(b)]. Property is consid-

---

[34] LTR 9110001 (Nov. 7, 1990).

[35] Rev. Proc. 87-56, 1987-2 CB 674, as clarified and modified by Rev. Proc. 88-22, 1988-1 CB 785.

[36] Rev. Rul. 74-265, 1974-1 CB 56.

[37] Rev. Proc. 87-56, 1987-2 CB 674, as clarified and modified by Rev. Proc. 88-22, 1988-1 CB 785.

[38] *Idaho Power Co.*, SCt, 74-2 USTC ¶ 9521, 418 US 1, 94 SCt 2757.

ered to be placed in service in the year it is ready and available to perform the function it was designed to do [Reg. § 1.167(a)(11)(e)(1)]. For example, the IRS found that a newspaper publisher forced to mothball a new plant because of a union dispute could not begin depreciating the machinery and equipment in the plant until it actually began printing newspapers at the facility. That was true even though the plant was operable in an earlier year and had actually produced a test run of newspaper.[39] (Special "conventions" usually apply in determining at what point during the year the property is placed in service. See Ch. 11.)

Example 11-8: XYZ, Inc. begins construction of a manufacturing building in November 2013. The building is completed in August 2014. Equipment used in the production line process is installed during September and October 2014. It is tested in November 2014. Equipment used in the finishing line process is installed in December 2014 and January 2015. All of the equipment is tested during February 2015. Production actually begins in April 2015. Result: The building is considered placed in service in August 2014, when it becomes available for the installation of equipment. So XYZ can claim a depreciation deduction for the building in 2014. None of the equipment, however, is considered placed in service until 2015, when the equipment first became available to produce an acceptable product.[40]

Example 11-9: In October 2013, Mr. Crane installs new equipment in four retail stores he owns. Two of the stores are being remodeled, but remain open during the remodeling. The other stores are newly constructed and do not open for business until early 2014. Result: Crane can deduct depreciation in 2013 on the equipment installed in the remodeled stores. That's because the equipment became available for use immediately upon installation. But no depreciation can be claimed on the equipment put in the new stores until 2014. Until the stores open for business, the equipment cannot be used.[41]

When depreciation ends depends on which depreciation system you use, the type of property, the depreciation method, etc. (see below). But in no case can you claim a deduction after the property has been retired from service or has been fully depreciated. Once you write off your cost for the property, depreciation ceases—even though the property may still be in use [Reg. § § 1.167(a)-1(a), (a)-10(b)].

▶ **OBSERVATION:** You should always be sure that the correct deduction is claimed in the proper year. Once property is placed in service, you cannot accumulate depreciation and then deduct the accumulated amount in later years. Your basis in the property will be reduced each year by your allowable depreciation, even though you never actually deduct it [Reg. § 1.167(a)-10(a)].

---

[39] FSA 1997-6.

[40] Rev. Rul. 76-238, 1976-1 CB 55.

[41] *Piggly Wiggly Southern, Inc.*, CA-11, 86-2 USTC ¶ 9789, 803 F2d 1572, *aff'g*, 84 TC 739, Dec. 42,039 (1985), *nonacq.* 1988-2 CB 1.

¶11,025 TAX RETURNS AND RECORDKEEPING

In general, depreciation deductions are computed on Form 4562. (Exception: Employees claiming depreciation on a car used in their job compute depreciation on Form 2106.) You then enter the total on the appropriate expense line of the return. Individuals and fiduciaries claiming depreciation on rental property enter their Form 4562 amount on Schedule E of Form 1040. Self-employed business and professional people and fiduciaries claiming depreciation on business property report their Form 4562 amount on Schedule C of Form 1040. Unreimbursed employees claim depreciation as a miscellaneous itemized expense on Schedule A of Form 1040. A Code Sec. 179 deduction is also claimed on Form 4562.

Records should be complete and detailed enough to support and permit verification of the claimed depreciation deductions. A taxpayer's regular accounting books need not reflect the same depreciation as depreciation claimed for tax purposes—so long as permanent auxiliary records are maintained to reconcile the differences.[42]

.01 How to Correct Depreciation Mistakes

In Rev. Proc. 2007-16,[43] IRS released an automatic consent procedure that allows taxpayers to change accounting method for certain depreciable or amortizable property after its disposition. Application of the two-year rule set forth in Rev. Rul. 90-38,[44] is waived, and transition rules for previously filed Forms 3115 for automatic consent are provided. The guidance applies to taxpayers changing from an impermissible method of accounting for depreciation of property that has been disposed of by the taxpayer during the year of change, and for which the taxpayer did not take into account any depreciation allowance, or took into account some depreciation but less than that allowable in the year of change or any prior tax year. The change does not apply to certain property held by tax-exempt organizations, a property for which a taxpayer is revoking a timely valid depreciation election or making a late depreciation election, a property for which the taxpayer deducted the cost or other basis of the property as an expense, and any property disposed of by a taxpayer under a nonrecognition provision of the Internal Revenue Code.

MODIFIED ACCELERATED COST RECOVERY SYSTEM

¶11,030 MACRS IN GENERAL

A taxpayer generally must capitalize the cost of property used in a trade or business and recover such cost over time through annual deductions for depreciation or amortization. Tangible property generally is depreciated under the modified accelerated cost recovery system (MACRS), which determines depreciation by applying

[42] Rev. Rul. 59-389, 1959-2 CB 89.

[43] Rev. Proc. 2007-16, IRB 2007-4, 358.

[44] Rev. Rul. 90-38, 1990-1 CB 57.

specific recovery periods, placed-in-service conventions, and depreciation methods to the cost of various types of depreciable property [Code Sec. 168].

The Modified Accelerated Cost Recovery System (MACRS) basically applies to most tangible depreciable property placed in service in your trade or business after 1986 [Code Sec. 168]. With limited exceptions, the use of MACRS is mandatory. MACRS consists of two systems that determine how you depreciate your property. The main system is called the General Depreciation System (GDS) and the second system is called the Alternative Depreciation System (ADS) [¶11,040, ¶11,050]. You generally will use GDS unless you are required by law to use the ADS which provides for a longer recovery period and uses only the straight-line method of depreciation to figure the deduction. Both GDS and ADS have pre-determined class lives for most property. Under GDS, most property is assigned to eight property classes based on these class lives. These property classes provide the recovery periods to be used. This means that the number of years over which you recover the cost of an item is pre-established.

Eligible property generally must be written off in accordance with the following rules:

- *Applicable recovery period:* Depreciable assets are divided into several classes, based on how long it takes to write off an asset. For example, the "applicable recovery period" for automobiles is five years.
- *Applicable convention:* Under depreciation conventions, all property you place in service during a period is treated as placed in service at a specified point in the period. And depreciation is allowed only from that point on. MACRS real estate, for example, uses the mid-month convention. For purposes of figuring your deduction, real estate you place in service any time during a month is depreciable starting at the middle of the month. Thus, the owner of a factory building actually placed in service on November 1 is entitled to a depreciation deduction for only 1 months on a calendar-year return.
- *Applicable depreciation method:* This is the rate at which a property is depreciated. If more than half of the cost is written off during the first half of the recovery period, the depreciation is said to be "accelerated." MACRS generally provides for accelerated methods of depreciation.

.01 MACRS Reclassification

In *Brookshire Brothers Holding Inc.,*[45] the court held that a taxpayer that reclassified property for MACRS depreciation purposes by placing it in a shorter recovery class did not make an accounting method change requiring prior IRS consent under Code Sec. 446. The court compared the reclassification to a change in useful life, which is not considered an accounting method change requiring prior IRS consent [Reg. § 1.446-1(e)(2)(ii)(b)]. Similarly, in *R. O'Shaughnessy,*[46] the court held that reallocation of depreciable property to another MACRS category isn't a change in accounting method under Code Sec. 446 and, as a result, the taxpayer did not need to make a

[45] *Brookshire Bros. Holding, Inc.*, CA-5, 2003-1 USTC ¶50,214, 320 F3d 507; *Green Forest Mfg., Inc.*, 85 TCM 1020, Dec. 55,083(M), TC Memo. 2003-75.

[46] *R. O'Shaughnessy*, CA-8, 2003-1 USTC ¶50,522, 332 F3d 1125.

Code Sec. 481 adjustment. In light of these cases, for tax years ending before December 30, 2003, the IRS will not challenge a change in calculating depreciation as a "change in accounting method," which must have prior IRS approval under Code Sec. 446(e).[47]

For further discussion of accounting method changes, see Ch. 18.

> **Example 11-10:** If a taxpayer reclassifies MACRS property, based on a cost segregation study, from nonresidential property to a 15-year property under Code Sec. 168(e), the IRS will not assert that the change in computing depreciation is a change in method of accounting under Code Sec. 446(e). If some of the MACRS property was actually placed in service in 2012, rather than 2013 as reported by the taxpayer, the IRS will not litigate whether the change in computing depreciation was a result from the change in service date.

.02 Change in Use

Special rules explain how to depreciate property under the MACRS system when a taxpayer's use of the property changes. A change is use that requires a change in the computation of MACRS depreciation occurs if the property's primary use in one year differs from the primary use in the previous year. A change in the use of MACRS property also occurs:

- When the taxpayer begins or ceases to use MACRS property predominantly outside the United States,
- When the taxpayer's use results in a reclassification of the property under Code Sec. 168(e), or
- When the property begins or ceases to be tax-exempt use property.

If a change in the use of MACRS property has occurred, the depreciation allowance for the MACRS property for the year of change is determined as though the change in the use of the MACRS property occurred on the first day of the year of change [Reg. § 1.168(i)-4(d)(2)(iii)].

Conversion to Business or Personal Use

When personal use property is converted to business or investment use, the property is treated as placed in service on the date of the conversion. The property is then depreciated using the applicable depreciation method, recovery period, and convention beginning in the tax year of the conversion [Reg. § 1.168(i)-4(b)(1)].

> **Example 11-11:** Owner A purchases a house that she occupies as her principal residence. Ten years later, she stops living in the house and converts it to residential rental property. At the time of the conversion to residential rental property, the house's fair market value (excluding land) is $130,000 and adjusted depreciable basis attributable to the house (excluding land) is $150,000. A is considered to have placed in service residential rental property on the day she converted the house to a residential rental property with a depreciable basis of $130,000. A depreciates the residential rental property under the general

[47] Chief Counsel Notice 2004-7.

depreciation system by using the straight-line method, a 27.5-year recovery period, and the mid-month convention. Thus, the depreciation allowance for the house for year one is $4,136, after taking into account the mid-month convention (($130,000 adjusted depreciable basis multiplied by the applicable depreciation rate of 3.636 percent (1/27.5)) multiplied by the midmonth convention fraction of 10.5/12) [Reg. § 1.168(i)-4(b)(1), Ex. 2].

Conversion to personal use. A conversion of MACRS property from business or income-producing use to personal use is treated as a disposition of the property in that tax year. Depreciation for the year of change is computed by taking into account the applicable convention. No gain, loss, or depreciation recapture is recognized upon the conversion [Reg. § 1.168(i)-4(c)].

Change in use after placed-in-service year. If use of MACRS property changes during the same tax year that it is placed in service, then depreciation deductions are computed using a method and recovery period determined by reference to the primary use during that tax year.

Change in recovery period or depreciation method. If change in use results in a shorter recovery period and/or a more accelerated depreciation method, the property's remaining basis at the beginning of the year of change is depreciated using the more accelerated method or the shorter recovery period. However, the taxpayer may elect to disregard the change in use and continue to compute depreciation in the same manner as before [Reg. § 1.168(i)-4(d)(3)].

If a change in the use of MACRS property results in a longer recovery period and/or slower depreciation method, the basis of the property is depreciated over the longer recovery period and/or by the slower depreciation method as though the taxpayer originally placed the MACRS property in service with the longer recovery period and/or slower depreciation method.

Change in use during placed-in-service year. If use of a property changes during the same tax year that it is placed in service, then depreciation deductions are computed using a method and recovery period determined by reference to the primary use during that tax year [Reg. § 1.168(i)-4(e)(1)]. In determining whether MACRS property is used within or outside the United States during the placed-in-service year, the predominant use, instead of the primary use, of the MACRS property governs [Reg. § 1.168(i)-4(e)(2)(i)]. Further, in determining whether MACRS property is tax-exempt use property or imported property covered by an Executive order during the placed-in-service year, the use of the property at the end of the placed-in-service year governs. Moreover, MACRS property is tax-exempt bond financed property during the placed-in-service year if a tax-exempt bond for the MACRS property is issued during that year.

¶11,035 WHAT PROPERTY IS ELIGIBLE

MACRS applies to most tangible depreciable property, new and used, personal and real property, placed in service after 1986. MACRS does not apply to an automobile if you use the standard mileage rate to compute your deductions for business-connected transportation [Ch. 10], intangibles [¶ 11,005], and films and video tapes. You cannot use MACRS to depreciate the following property: (1) intangible property; (2) any motion picture film or videotape; (3) any sound recording; (4) certain real and personal property placed in service before 1987; and, (5) property you elect to exclude from MACRS that is properly depreciated under a method of depreciation that is not based on a term of years.

.01 Antichurning Provisions

There are special rules designed to prevent you from "churning" property you placed in service before 1987—engaging in transactions that would place the property in service after 1986 simply to make it eligible for MACRS [Code Sec. 168(f)(5)]. MACRS does not apply to equipment and other personal property if: (1) it was owned or used at any time during 1986, (2) the property is acquired from a person who owned it at any time during 1986, and (3) as part of the transaction, the user of the property did not change, or the taxpayer leased the property to a person who owned or used the property during 1986. You are not subject to the antichurning rules if they would give you a bigger deduction than you would get under MACRS [Code Sec. 168(f)(5)(B)]. There are no MACRS antichurning rules for real estate.

.02 Tax-Free Transactions

The antichurning rules do not fully apply to all transactions. If the transferor put the property into service before 1987, you are not eligible to use MACRS on the property to the extent of the transferor's under-depreciated basis. However, to the extent your basis exceeds the transferor's basis, you are eligible for MACRS.

Transactions subject to the antichurning rule are the type where no gain or loss is recognized because of a special provision. They include: (1) transfers to controlled corporations [Ch. 6], (2) liquidations of subsidiary corporations [Ch. 22], (3) contributions to partnership by partners [Ch. 24], and (4) distributions by partnerships to partners [Ch. 24]. Note: Tax-free exchanges of like-kind property [Ch. 6] are not included in this list. If you acquire property after 1986 in a like-kind exchange, you must use MACRS, even though the transferor put the property into service before 1987. For further discussion of depreciating MACRS property acquired in a like-kind exchange, see Ch. 6.

.03 Electing Out of MACRS

MACRS does not apply if:

- The taxpayer makes proper, timely elections to exclude property from MACRS.
- For the first year depreciation is allowable, the taxpayer uses the unit-of-production method or any depreciation method not expressed in a term of years [Code Sec. 168(f)(1)]. Temp. Reg. § 301.9100-7T(a)(3) provides that the attached statement used for making the election must provide the following information:
  a. The electing taxpayer's name, address, and the taxpayer identification number.
  b. The identification of the election.
  c. The Internal Revenue Code section under which the election is made.
  d. The period for which the election is being made and the property to which the election is to apply.

e. Any other information required by the Code and necessary to show the taxpayer is entitled to make the election.

Failure to comply or even substantially comply with the requirements of Code Sec. 168(f) will mean that you have failed to properly opt out of MACRS and will be unable to claim quicker depreciation deductions.[48]

You must make this election for the year the property is placed in service [Temp. Reg. § 301.9100-7T(a)(3)].

Under the unit-of-production method, an asset is depreciated in accordance with the product units or other output which can be produced before the asset is worn out. For the unit-of-production method to apply, the usefulness or life of the property must be limited by its production, or by a source of supply, or some other similar factor. The unit-of-production or similar depreciation method results in cost recovery that more closely matches an asset's economic depreciation than MACRS. Depending on an asset's useful life and how intensively it is used, the unit-of-production or similar method may result in faster depreciation deductions than MACRS. For further discussion of depreciation systems not based on a prescribed number of years, see ¶ 11,065.

.04 Public Utility Property

MACRS is not available to public utility property unless the benefits of MACRS are "normalized" in setting rates charged customers [Code Sec. 168(f)(2)]. This means that the tax savings from MACRS' accelerated depreciation cannot flow to customers. Instead, they must be put in a reserve account. The reserve account is drawn upon when MACRS produces smaller deductions than a slower depreciation method. If the tax savings are not normalized, then a public utility must use the same depreciation method used in its regulated books of account.

.05 Indian Reservation Property Recovery Periods

To encourage the purchase of depreciable property used on Indian reservations, Code Sec. 168(j) substitutes shortened MACRS recovery period for the recovery periods that normally apply. In addition, the MACRS depreciation deduction allowed for regular tax purposes using these shortened recovery periods also applies for AMT purposes [Code Sec. 168(j)(3)]. As a result, no AMT adjustment is required. This incentive applies to qualified Indian reservation property that is MACRS 3-, 5-, 7-, 10-, 15-, 20-year property and 39-year nonresidential real property that meets all of these requirement:

- The property must be used predominantly in the active conduct of a trade or business within an Indian reservation;
- The property may not be used or located outside an Indian reservation on a regular basis;
- The property may not be acquired (directly or indirectly) from a related person; and
- The property may not be used for certain gaming purposes.

48 *New Gaming Systems, Inc.*, 82 TCM 794, Dec. 54,520(M), TC Memo. 2001-277.

- The alternative depreciation system does not apply to the property (determined without regard to the election to use ADS and after application of the rule relating to listed property with limited business use).

The shortened recovery periods apply to qualified Indian reservation property placed in service before January 1, 2014 [Code Sec. 168(j)(8)]. Table 1 shows the shortened recovery periods [Code Sec. 168(j)(2)].

Table 1. Shortened Recovery Periods for Indian Reservation Property

PROPERTY CLASS	RECOVERY PERIOD
3-year property	2 years
5-year property	3 years
7-year property	4 years
10-year property	6 years
15-year property	9 years
20-year property	12 years
Nonresidential real property	22 years

Note that there is no shortened recovery period for MACRS 27.5-year residential rental property used on an Indian reservation.

¶11,040 MACRS AND PERSONAL PROPERTY

The applicable recovery period for equipment, machinery and other personal property ranges from 3 years to 20 years, depending on the type of property [Code Sec. 168(b)(1)]. The applicable depreciation convention is the half-year (or midyear) convention ((b) below) [Code Sec. 168(d)(1), (4)(A)]. The applicable depreciation method is a combination of the declining balance method and the straight-line method [Code Sec. 168(b)(1), (2)]. You have a choice of computing your allowable depreciation deduction yourself or using optional tables issued by the IRS [(e) below].

.01 Recovery Period

How quickly you can write off property depends on what the MACRS recovery period is for the property. MACRS contains six different recovery periods for personal property: 3, 5, 7, 10, 15, and 20 years. Which recovery period applies to a particular item depends on what its class life was under the Asset Depreciation Range (ADR) system.

The ADR system was an optional depreciation system used before 1981. Under ADR, the Revenue Service separated tangible property into classes and gave a range of allowable useful lives for each class.

For example, with ADR, equipment used in the manufacture of glass products could be depreciated in as little as 11 years or as long as 17 years, with 14 years being the midpoint.

MACRS generally keys its recovery periods into the midpoint class lives under ADR.

Under GDS, which is the main depreciation system under MACRS, most tangible property is assigned to one of eight main property classes. Table 2 shows the nine property classes with examples of what property would be included in each.

Table 2. Property Classes and Types of Property

Type of Property	Examples of Property Included
3-Year Property	Tractor units for over-the-road use [Code Sec. 168(e)(3)(A)]
	Any race horse placed in service after December 31, 2008, and before January 1, 2014, that is over 2 years old when placed in service
	Any other horse (other than a race horse over 12 years old when placed in service
	Qualified rent-to-own property. See ¶11,005 for further discussion of rent-to-own property
5-Year Property	Automobiles, taxis, buses, trucks [Code Sec. 168(e)(3)(B)]
	Semi-conductor manufacturing equipment
	Any qualified technological equipment
	Computers and peripheral equipment including computer-based telephone central office switching equipment
	Office machinery (such as typewriters, calculators, and copiers)
	Any property used in research and experimentation
	Breeding cattle and dairy cattle
	Rental tuxedos
	Appliances (such as stoves and refrigerators), carpet, furniture, etc., used in a residential rental real estate activity
	Stand alone gasoline pump canopies that are not permanent structures[49] (any supporting concrete footings are permanent structures and are land improvements classified as 15-year property)
	Building components such as electrical distribution systems, television wiring, telephone equipment, water piping, room partitions, patient corridor handrails, and vinyl wall coverings[50]
	Heavy petroleum storage tanks[51]
	Commercial building canopies and awnings; concrete foundations or footings; doors and window accessories; decorative light fixtures; exterior lighting; exterior pole mounted lighting; floor covering such as carpet; kitchen HVAC; decorative millwork; music and PA system; poles and pylons; nonstructural theme elements in restaurants; signs; site grading drainage; sidewalks; machinery or equipment (other than a grain bin, cotton ginning asset, fence or land improvement) which is used in a farming business, where the original use commences with the taxpayer

[49] Rev. Rul. 2003-54, IRB 2003-23, 982.

[50] *Hospital Corp. of America*, 109 TC 21, Dec. 52,163 (1997) *acq. and nonacq.* IRB 1999-35, 314, as corrected by Announcement 99-116, IRB 1999-52, 763.

[51] *PDV Am., Inc.*, 87 TCM 1330, Dec. 55,638(M), TC Memo. 2004-118.

Type of Property	Examples of Property Included
	Certain geothermal, solar, and wind energy property
	Cell phone switch[52]
7-Year Property	Any motorsports entertainment complex and related ancillary and support facilities placed in service on or before December 31, 2013 [Code Sec. 168(i)(15)(D)]
	Any Alaska natural gas pipeline [Code Sec. 168(e)(3)(C)]
	Office furniture (not used in rental real estate which is eligible for a five-year recovery period)
	Office fixtures such as desks, files, safes, etc.
	Agricultural machinery and equipment
	Railroad track and single-purpose agricultural or horticultural structures placed in service before 1989
	Any property that does not have a class life and has not been designated by law as being in any class
	Returnable containers used in food manufacturing[53]
	Air pollution control facility used in connection with a plan or other property that began operation after January 1, 1976 [Code Sec. 169(d)]
	Air pollution control facility used in connection with an electric generation plant or other property that is primarily coal-fired [Code Sec. 169(d)(4)(B)]
	Any natural gas gathering line, placed in service after April 11, 2005 [Code Sec. 168(e)(3)(C)(iv)]
	Assets used to convert corn to ethanol[54]
	Street lights[55]
	Minor league baseball player contracts[56]
10-Year Property	Barges, tugs and similar water transportation vessels
	Any single purpose agricultural or horticultural structure placed in service after 1988 [Code Sec. 168(e)(3)(D)]
	Any tree or vine bearing fruits and nuts[57]
	Any petroleum refining equipment and property used in manufacturing tobacco and certain food products
	Qualified small electric meter and qualified smart electric grid system placed in service on or after October 3, 2008

[52] *R. Broz*, 137 TC 25, Dec. 58,693 (2011).

[53] FSA 200144031 (July 17, 2001).

[54] Notice 2009-64, IRB 2009-36, 307.

[55] *P.P.L. Corp.*, 135 TC 176, Dec. 58,286 (2010); *Entergy Corp.*, 100 TCM 79, Dec. 58,288(M), TC Memo. 2010-166.

[56] Field Attorney Advice 20133901F (Aug. 26, 2013).

[57] *L. Trentadue*, 128 TC 91, Dec. 56,886 (2007).

Type of Property	Examples of Property Included
	Cell phone equipment, leased cell phone digital equipment, and all telephone central office equipment.[58]
15-Year Property	Retail motor fuels outlet, such as a convenience store; Real property is a "retail motor fuels outlet" if used to a substantial extent in the retail marketing of petroleum or petroleum products (whether or nor it is also used to sell food or other convenience items) and meets any of the following three tests: (1) it is not larger than 1,400 square feet; (2) 50% of more of the gross revenues generated from the property are derived from petroleum sales; The 50 percent or more gross revenue test must be applied on a building-by-building basis.[59] (3) 50% or more of the floor space in the property is devoted to petroleum marketing sales. A retail motor fuels outlet does not include any facility related to petroleum and natural gas trunk pipelines;
	Municipal wastewater treatment plant [Code Sec. 168(e)(3)(E)];
	Any telephone distribution plant and comparable equipment used for 2-way exchange of voice and data communication [Code Sec. 168(e)(3)(E)(ii)]
	General land improvements (such as shrubbery, bridges, roads and fences)
	Cost of building or rebuilding "modern greens" of a golf course (the cost of creating "push-up" greens and the cost of general earth-moving, grading or initial shaping of a golf course is not depreciable)[60]
	Initial clearing and grading land improvements for gas utility property;
	Any qualified restaurant property that is an improvement to a restaurant placed in service before January 1, 2014 [Code Sec. 168(e)(3)(E)(v)].
	Qualified leasehold improvement property placed in service before January 1, 2014 [Code Sec. 168(e)(3)(E)(iv)].
	Any Code Sec. 1245 property used in the transmission at 69 or more kilovolts of electricity placed in service after April 11, 2005 [Code Sec. 168(e)(3)(E)(vii) and (g)(3)(B)]
	New natural gas distribution lines placed in service after April 11, 2005 [Code Sec. 168(e)(3)(E)(viii) and (G)(3)(B)]
	Qualified retail improvement property if placed in service before January 1, 2014 [Code Sec. 168(e)(3)(E)(ix)]
	Cell phone antenna support structures[61]
20-Year Property	Farm buildings (other than single purpose agricultural or horticultural structures)
	Irrigation systems and wells[62]
	Municipal sewers not classified as 25-year property

[58] *R. Broz*, 137 TC 25, Dec. 58,693 (2011).

[59] *Iowa 80 Group, Inc.*, CA-8, 2005-1 USTC ¶50,343, 406 F3d 950.

[60] Rev. Rul. 2001-60, IRB 2001-51, 587.

[61] *R. Broz*, 137 TC 25, Dec. 58,693 (2011).

[62] *L. Trentadue*, 128 TC 91, Dec. 56,886 (2007).

Type of Property	Examples of Property Included
	Initial clearing and grading improvements with respect to gas utility property [Code Sec. 168(e)(3)(E)(vi)]
	Certain electric transmission property originally placed in service after April 11, 2005 will be MACRS 15-year property [Code Sec. 168(e)(3)(E)(vii)]. A 30-year recovery period is assigned for purposes of the MACRS alternative depreciation system (ADS) [Code Sec. 168(g)(3)(B)]. Thus, the regular recovery period for qualifying property is reduced from 20 years to 15 years and the ADS recovery period is unchanged. The provision applies to any Code Sec. 1245 property used in the transmission at 69 or more kilovolts of electricity for sale. The original use of the electrical transmission assets must begin with the taxpayer after April 11, 2005. Thus, used property, such as property acquired as part of the purchase of a business, will not qualify [Code Sec. 168(e)(3)(E)(vii)].
25-Year Property	Property that is an integral part of the gathering, treatment, or commercial distribution of water, and that, without regard to this provision, would be 20-year property
	Municipal sewers placed in service after June 12, 1996, other than property placed in service under a binding contract in effect at all times since June 6, 1996
Residential Rental Property—27.5 Years	Any building or structure, such as a rental home or structure (including a mobile home) if 80 percent or more of its gross rental income for the tax year is from dwelling units which include a house or apartment used to provide living accommodations in a building or structure [Code Sec. 168(e)(2)]. A dwelling unit is a house or apartment used to provide living accommodations in a building or structure. It does not include a unit in a hotel, motel, inn, or other establishment where more than half the units are used on a transient basis. If you occupy any part of the building or structure for personal use, its gross rental income includes the fair rental value of the part you occupy. A building housing a hotel condo and a rental apartment condo can be treated as one unit for depreciation purposes.[63] See ¶11,050 for further discussion of MACRS and real estate.

[63] LTR 201243003 (July 24, 2012).

Type of Property	Examples of Property Included
Nonresidential Real Property—39 Years	Code Sec. 1250 property such as an office building, store, or warehouse, that is not residential rental property or property with a class life less than 27.5 years [Code Sec. 168(e)(2)(B)]. This class includes property that either has no ADR class life or whose class life is 27.5 years or more, including elevators and escalators. Code Sec. 1250 property is defined as any real property other than Code Sec. 1245 property, which is or has been of a character subject to the allowance for depreciation [Code Sec. 1250(c)]. The recovery period for nonresidential real property is *39 years* for property you placed in service **after** May 12, 1993, or *31.5 years* for property you placed in service **before** May 13, 1993. A home office placed in service after May 12, 1993 will be classified as nonresidential real property and can therefore be depreciated over 39 years. See ¶11,050 for further discussion of MACRS and real estate. See Ch. 12 for further discussion of home offices. Another example of nonresidential real property is an entertainment facility built on a barge.[64] Heating, ventilation, and air conditioning (HVAC) unit installed outside a building, either located on the roof of a building or located on a concrete pad adjacent to the building.[65]

The IRS generally has the power to change the ADR life—and thus possibly the MACRS recovery period—of any property [Code Sec. 168(i)(1)]. Likewise, it can assign an ADR life to property that currently does not have one.

.02 Half-Year Convention

MACRS uses the half-year convention for personal property [Code Sec. 168(d)(1)]. This treats all property placed in service or disposed of during a year as placed in service or disposed of at the year's midpoint. This means that you can claim a half-year's worth of depreciation in the first year you place property in service, regardless of when during the year you actually placed the property in service. Likewise, if you dispose of property before the end of the recovery period, you can claim a half-year of depreciation for the disposition year.

One practical effect of the half-year convention is that you must wait until the year after the end of the recovery period to fully depreciate the property. The half year of depreciation not allowed in the first year is tacked on after the end of the recovery period.

For example, if you place an item of three-year property into service on April 1 of year one, you can claim only a half-year of depreciation that year (even though the property is used for three-fourths of the year). In year two and year three, you can claim a full year of depreciation. The remaining half-year is written off in year four.

If you have a short tax year, the depreciation allowed under the half-year convention is correspondingly reduced. For example, if your tax year is only four months long, any

[64] FSA 199919683.

[65] CCA 201310028 (Oct. 9, 2012).

personal property placed in service during the year would be allowed two months of depreciation.[66]

.03 Depreciation Method

MACRS property is initially depreciated under the declining balance method. For all but 15-year and 20-year property, the 200 percent declining balance method is used; for 15-year and 20-year property, the 150 percent declining balance method is used.

These methods have the effect of allowing you to recover the bulk of your cost in the first half of the recovery period. However, if you continue to use the declining balance methods over the entire recovery period, you would still have unrecovered basis at the end of the period. So, under MACRS, you switch to the straight-line depreciation method at the point where it produces a larger deduction than the declining balance method.

Straight-line Method

Under straight-line depreciation, you deduct an equal amount in each of the remaining years of the recovery period. But your rate of depreciation changes each year. Your rate is one divided by the number of years left in the recovery period. For example, if you have four years left, your depreciation deduction is one-fourth of your adjusted basis for the current year, one-third of your adjusted basis for the following year and so on.

Declining Balance Method

With the declining balance, your rate stays the same each year, but the amount of your deduction changes. Your rate is (1) one divided by the number of years in the recovery period, multiplied by (2) either 200 percent or 150 percent, depending on which declining balance method is allowed. For example, if you have a five-year asset, your depreciation rate is 40 percent—one-fifth multiplied by 200 percent. This same rate is applied each year to your adjusted basis for that year.

Special Elections

You can choose less accelerated methods of depreciation if you wish. You may elect to use either (1) straight-line depreciation over the regular MACRS recovery periods or (2) 150 percent declining balance switching to straight line over the recovery periods provided in the Alternative Depreciation System [discussed below]. An election is made separately for each recovery class and covers all property in the class you put in service during the year. You must make the election by the tax return due date (including extensions) for the years.

.04 How to Figure MACRS Deduction

Assuming that you are not electing one of the slower methods of depreciation, here is how you figure your MACRS deduction on personal property:

- Divide the declining balance percentage (changed to a decimal) by the recovery period. The result is the declining balance rate;
- Multiply the property's adjusted basis by the declining balance rate;
- Apply the half-year convention to figure the first year's depreciation;

[66] Rev. Proc. 89-15, 1989-1 CB 816.

- In the second year, adjust the basis for the depreciation taken for the first year;
- Multiply the adjusted basis by the same declining balance rate used in the first year;
- Continue the process until your deduction for a year figured under the declining balance method falls to that allowed under the straight-line method;
- At that point switch to the straight-line method until the end of the recovery period;
- In the year following the end of the recovery period, deduct your remaining adjusted basis (i.e., a half year of depreciation).

Example 11-12: Mr. Nolan buys office furniture (7-year property) on August 11 of year one for $10,000. Here is how Nolan computes his depreciation deductions:

1. Nolan divides 2.0 (200 percent) by 7 to get his basic declining balance rate of 28.57 percent.
2. He then multiplies his $10,000 adjusted basis by 28.57 percent to get $2,857, the amount of a full year's depreciation.
3. Since the half-year convention applies for the year the furniture is placed in service, his deduction for the year the office furniture is placed in use is half of $2,857—or $1,428.50.
4. In year two, his depreciation deduction is $2,448.88—his $8,571.50 adjusted basis ($10,000 less $1,428.50) multiplied by 28.57 percent.
5. For year three, his deduction is $1,749.23 ($6,122.62 adjusted basis × 28.57 percent).
6. For year four, his deduction is $1,249.48 (4,373.39 adjusted basis × 28.57 percent).
7. For year five, his deduction is $892.50 ($3,123.91 adjusted basis × 28.57 percent).
8. For year six, his deduction under the 200 percent declining balance method would be $637.51 ($2,231.41 adjusted basis × 28.57 percent). Under the straight-line method, his rate would be 40 percent (1 divided by 2.5 remaining years of depreciation) and his deduction would be $892.56 ($2,231.41 × 40 percent). So Nolan switches to the straight-line method and deducts $892.56.
9. For year seven, his straight-line rate is 66.67 percent (1 divided by 1.5 years) and he deducts $892.61 (66.67 percent × $1,338.85).
10. For the final year, he deducts his remaining adjusted basis—$446.24—to recover the total $10,000 cost of the furniture.

.05 Optional MACRS Table

Instead of figuring your MACRS deduction as described above, you have the option of using a table issued by the IRS.

The table gives you the percentage depreciation rate to be used each year for each class of property and reflects half-year convention and the switch from the declining balance method to the straight-line method. The rate is to be applied to the property's basis unadjusted for prior depreciation. However, you reduce the basis by any Code Sec. 179 expensing deduction [¶ 11,045] you claim for the property.

You can use the table for some items of personal property and not others, even within the same class. But once you begin using the table for an item, you must continue to use the table for the entire recovery period. However, if there is a reduction in an item's basis because of a casualty, you can no longer use the table. Beginning with the year of the casualty adjustment, you must figure your deduction the long way.

The optional table (Table A-1) is reproduced below as Table 3.[67]

Table 3. IRS Optional MACRS Table A-1 (Half Year Convention)

If the Recovery Year Is:	*and the Recovery Period Is:*					
	3-year	*5-year*	*7-year*	*10-year*	*15-year*	*20-year*
	the Depreciation Rate Is:					
1	33.33	20.00	14.29	10.00	5.00	3.750
2	44.45	32.00	24.49	18.00	9.50	7.219
3	14.81	19.20	17.49	14.40	8.55	6.667
4	7.41	11.52	12.49	11.52	7.70	6.177
5		11.52	8.93	9.22	6.93	5.713
6		5.76	8.92	7.37	6.23	5.285
7			8.93	6.55	5.90	4.888
8			4.46	6.55	5.90	4.522
9				6.56	5.91	4.462
10				6.55	5.90	4.461
11				3.28	5.91	4.462
12					5.90	4.461
13					5.91	4.462
14					5.90	4.461
15					5.91	4.462
16					2.95	4.461
17						4.462
18						4.461
19						4.462
20						4.461
21						2.231

.06 Alternate Depreciation System (ADS)

You may elect an Alternative Depreciation System (ADS) for most property [Code Sec. 168(g)(7)]. ADS is a less accelerated depreciation system than regular MACRS, and might be elected, for example, by a new company that wants to conserve depreciation deductions for future use—when its income is more highly taxed. Under ADS, you use straight-line depreciation and, in many cases, longer recovery periods than the standard

[67] Rev. Proc. 89-15, 1989-1 CB 816; Treas. Dept., IRS Publication 946, "How to Depreciate Property" (2013 Ed.), Appendix A (Table A-1), p. 71.

MACRS periods. The regular depreciation conventions apply—either half-year or mid-quarter [discussed below] for the year the property is placed in service and disposed of. The recovery periods for ADS are:

- The class life of the property;
- 12 years for personal property with no class life;
- 50 years for water utility property.

For example, the recovery period is:

- 4 years for qualified rent-to-own property;
- 5 years for cars, light trucks, qualified technological equipment and semiconductor manufacturing equipment;
- 9.5 years for computer-based telephone central-office switching equipment;
- 10 years for railroad track;
- 12 years for personal property with no class life;
- 15 years for single-purpose agricultural and horticultural structures;
- 20 years for any tree or vine bearing fruit or nuts;
- 24 years for municipal waste water treatment plants and telephone distribution plants and other equipment used for 2-way exchange of voice and data communications;
- 50 years for municipal sewers; and

You make a separate ADS election for each class of recovery property. And you can make an ADS election for a particular class one year and not the next. But once an election is made it is irrevocable.[68]

ADS Required

In some situations, the use of ADS is mandatory, not elective. For discussion of ADS to depreciate real estate see ¶ 11,050.03. You must use ADS for (1) certain "listed" property [discussed below], (2) tangible property used predominantly outside of the U.S., (3) property leased, used, or financed by a tax-exempt organization, (4) tax-exempt bond-financed property, (5) property imported from a foreign country that maintains discriminatory trade practices, and (6) any property used predominantly in a farming business and placed in service during any tax year in which you make an election not to apply the uniform capitalization rules to certain farming costs. [Code Sec. 168(g)(1)]. You also use ADS for computing earnings and profits in determining how much of a corporate distribution is a taxable dividend [Ch. 2].

ADS is also used for computing the alternative minimum tax [Ch. 16]. But, for personal property, the 150 percent declining balance method is used instead of straight-line depreciation [Code Sec. 56(g)(4)(A)].

---

[68] Rev. Proc. 89-15, 1989-1 CB 816; Treas Dept., IRS Publication 946, "How to Depreciate Property" (2013 Ed.), p. 36.

.07 Special Mid-Quarter Convention

In general, most business assets that you purchase (other than real estate) are depreciated using the half-year convention no matter when in the year the assets were acquired and placed in service. As a result, assets placed in service at any time during the year are treated as placed in service in the middle of the year and you are entitled to claim only one half of the normal first year's depreciation deduction [Code Sec. 168(d)(2)]. The half-year convention applies unless you are unfortunate enough to have the mid-quarter convention apply. Taxpayers often want to avoid the mid-quarter convention because when used, assets are depreciated beginning in the middle of the quarter when placed in service and the amount of the depreciation deduction is vastly reduced. As a result, taxpayers often time the acquisition of property to avoid application of the mid-quarter convention.

If a large portion of the depreciable personal property you place in service during a year is placed in service in the last calendar quarter, you may not be permitted to use the half-year convention [discussed above]. You must use a "mid-quarter" convention if the combined bases of property placed in service during the last three months of the tax year exceed 40 percent of the combined bases of personal property put in service during the entire year [Code Sec. 168(d)(3)] Property that you do not depreciate under MACRS (for example, certain public utility property, films and video tapes, and sound recordings) should not be counted when applying the 40 percent test. On the other hand, you should take into account "listed property" (for example, cars, entertainment property, computers and cellular phones) [Reg. § 1.168(d)-1(b)(2)]. Reduce the basis of property placed in service during the year by any expensing deduction claimed for the property.

Under the mid-quarter convention, all property you place in service or sell or otherwise dispose of during any quarter of a tax year is treated as placed in service or disposed of at the quarter's midpoint. This has the effect of increasing your depreciation deduction for property placed in service in the first two quarters of the year and decreasing your deduction for property placed in service in the last quarter. Instead of deducting 50 percent of a full year's depreciation for all property placed in service during the year, the mid-quarter convention gives you an 87.5 percent deduction for property placed in service in the first quarter, 62.5 percent deduction for second quarter property, 37.5 percent for third quarter property and 12.5 percent for fourth quarter property.

Whether the mid-quarter convention benefits you or hurts you depends on how much property you place in service in each quarter.

> **Example 11-13:** Alpha Corp., a calendar-year taxpayer, placed two items of property into service during the year—both five-year properties. The first item cost $40,000 and was placed in service in February. The other item cost $30,000 and was placed in service in December. Result: Since more than 40 percent of total bases of property put in service was put in service during the fourth quarter ($30,000 of $70,000 total), Alpha must use the mid-quarter convention. For the $40,000 item, a full year's depreciation would be $16,000 (40 percent rate for five-year property × $40,000), assuming Alpha doesn' t use ADS. So Alpha can deduct $14,000 (87.5 percent of $16,000). For the $30,000 item, the full year deduction would be $12,000, so Alpha can deduct $1,500 (12.5 percent of

$12,000). Total depreciation deduction that year: $15,500. By comparison, with the half-year convention, Alpha's total deduction would be only $14,000.

Example 11-14: Beta Corp., also a calendar-year taxpayer, makes the same purchases as Alpha Corp., except that it puts the $40,000 item in service in July. Result: Beta also is subject to the mid-quarter convention. But it only gets a deduction of $6,000 for the $40,000 item (37.5% of $16,000). So its total depreciation for the two items for the year is $7,500—$8,000 less than Alpha's and $6,500 less than with the half-year convention.

▶ **OBSERVATION:** Timing your equipment and machinery purchases is crucial if you are dealing with the mid-quarter convention. For example, if Beta had simply waited until January of the following year to place the $30,000 item into service, it would not have been subject to the mid-quarter convention and its depreciation deduction for the year the items were placed in service would have been $500 higher. Or if it had accelerated the purchase—putting the $30,000 item into service before the fourth quarter—its deduction would have been $6,500 higher.

To avoid having the mid-quarter convention apply, be sure that the aggregate bases of property placed in service in the last quarter do not exceed 40 percent of the aggregate bases of all property placed in service during the first nine months of the year. The following example illustrates why you should avoid the mid-quarter convention.

Example 11-15: You buy and place in service equipment costing $10,000 in the first quarter, equipment costing $10,000 in the second quarter, and equipment costing $100,000 in the third quarter. Now you want to buy and place in service additional equipment costing $85,000 in the fourth quarter. Since $85,000 exceeds 40 percent of the aggregate bases of all equipment placed in service during the year, the mid-quarter convention applies and you would have to use the mid-quarter tables to compute your depreciation deduction. If all the equipment is five-year property your depreciation deduction would total $25,250 computed as follows: $3,500 ($10,000 × 40 percent × 87.5 percent) for 1st quarter purchases, $2,500 ($10,000 × 40 percent × 62.5 percent) for 2nd quarter purchases, $15,000 ($100,000 × 40 percent × 37.5 percent) for 3rd quarter purchases and $4,250 ($85,000 × 40 percent × 12.5 percent) for 4th quarter purchases. If however, the 4th quarter equipment had been $80,000 rather than $85,000, the mid-quarter convention would not have applied and the half-year convention would have yielded a total first year depreciation deduction of $40,000 (20 percent of total $200,000)—a $14,750 increase.

Before buying a car, equipment, or other depreciable property for use in your business before the end of the year, take out a calculator to be sure that you will not be trapped by the mid-quarter convention.

Example 11-16: You buy and place in service equipment costing $10,000 in the first quarter, equipment costing $10,000 in the second quarter, and equipment costing $100,000 in the third quarter. Now you want to buy and place in service additional equipment costing $85,000 in the fourth quarter. Since $85,000 exceeds 40 percent of the aggregate bases of all equipment placed in service during the year, the mid-quarter convention applies and you would have to use the mid-quarter tables to compute your depreciation deduction. If all the equipment is five-year property your depreciation deduction would total $25,250 computed as follows: $3,500 ($10,000 × 35%) for 1st quarter purchases, $2,500 ($10,000 × 25%) for 2nd quarter purchases, $15,000 ($100,000 × 15%) for 3rd quarter purchases and $4,250 ($85,000 × 5%) for 4th quarter purchases. If however, you had elected to expense $5,000 of the $85,000 equipment, the mid-quarter convention would not have applied and the half-year convention would have yielded a total first year depreciation deduction of $40,000 (20% of total $200,000), a $14,750 increase.

▶ **PLANNING TIP:** One way around the depreciation conventions is to make an election to expense or deduct immediately up to $500,000 worth of equipment in 2013 [Code Sec. 179]. The expensing election is available for property that is used for personal as well as business purposes if the business use predominates [Reg. § 1.179-1(d)(1)]. You may not claim an expensing deduction for (1) property used outside the United States, (2) air conditioning units, or (3) or heating units. Once you have made the election to expense part or all of the basis of business property, that basis is no longer considered in computing whether the mid-quarter convention applies. For further discussion, see ¶ 11,045.

Tax-Free Transfers

A special rule applies if you place property in service and later in the same year you transfer the property to a related party in a tax-free transfer [¶ 11,035]. For purposes of determining whether your transferee meets the 40 percent threshold, the date of the transfer between you two is the date the transferee is deemed to place the property into service. However, if the transferee is subject to the mid-quarter convention, the allowable depreciation is governed by the date the property was originally placed in service by you.[69]

Example 11-17: The sole owner of a calendar-year corporation puts property into service on February 1 and then transfers it to the corporation on November 1. For purposes of determining whether or not the corporation is subject to the mid-quarter convention, the property is considered placed in service on November 1. But if the corporation must use the mid-quarter convention, allowable depreciation is computed from the midpoint of the first quarter.

Optional Tables

The IRS has issued four tables that may be used to compute depreciation for property subject to the mid-quarter convention.[70] The tables, one for each quarter during the year property is placed in service, are reproduced starting in this section.

---

[69] LTR 8948015 (Aug. 31, 1989).

[70] Treas. Dept., IRS Publication 946, "How to Depreciate Property" (2013 Ed.), Appendix A, pp. 71-73.

Table 4. 3-, 5-, 7-, 10-, 15-, and 20-year Property—Half-year Convention; Property Placed in Service in the 1st Quarter

If the Recovery Year Is:	*and the Recovery Period Is:* 3-year	5-year	7-year	10-year	15-year	20-year
	the Depreciation Rate Is:					
1	58.33	35.00	25.00	17.50	8.75	6.563
2	27.78	26.00	21.43	16.50	9.13	7.000
3	12.35	15.60	15.31	13.20	8.21	6.482
4	1.54	11.01	10.93	10.56	7.39	5.996
5		11.01	8.75	8.45	6.65	5.546
6		1.38	8.74	6.76	5.99	5.130
7			8.75	6.55	5.90	4.746
8			1.09	6.55	5.91	4.459
9				6.56	5.90	4.459
10				6.55	5.91	4.459
11				0.82	5.90	4.459
12					5.91	4.460
13					5.90	4.459
14					5.91	4.460
15					5.90	4.459
16					0.74	4.460
17						4.459
18						4.460
19						4.459
20						4.460
21						0.565

3-, 5-, 7-, 10-, 15-, and 20-year Property—Mid-quarter Convention; Property Placed in Service in the 2nd Quarter

If the Recovery Year Is:	*and the Recovery Period Is:* 3-year	5-year	7-year	10-year	15-year	20-year
	the Depreciation Rate Is:					
1	41.67	25.00	17.85	12.50	6.25	4.688
2	38.89	30.00	23.47	17.50	9.38	7.148
3	14.14	18.00	16.76	14.00	8.44	6.612
4	5.30	11.37	11.97	11.20	7.59	6.116
5		11.37	8.87	8.96	6.83	5.658
6		4.26	8.87	7.17	6.15	5.233
7			8.87	6.55	5.91	4.841
8			3.34	6.55	5.90	4.478
9				6.56	5.91	4.463
10				6.55	5.90	4.463
11				2.46	5.91	4.463

If the Recovery Year Is:	*3-year*	*5-year*	*7-year*	*10-year*	*15-year*	*20-year*
	and the Recovery Period Is:					
	the Depreciation Rate Is:					
12					5.90	4.463
13					5.91	4.463
14					5.90	4.463
15					5.91	4.462
16					2.21	4.463
17						4.462
18						4.463
19						4.462
20						4.463
21						1.673

3-, 5-, 7-, 10-, 15-, and 20-year Property—Mid-quarter Convention; Property Placed in Service in the 3rd Quarter

If the Recovery Year Is:	*3-year*	*5-year*	*7-year*	*10-year*	*15-year*	*20-year*
	and the Recovery Period Is:					
	the Depreciation Rate Is:					
1	25.00	15.00	10.71	7.50	3.75	2.813
2	50.00	34.00	25.51	18.50	9.63	7.289
3	16.67	20.40	18.22	14.80	8.66	6.742
4	8.33	12.24	13.02	11.84	7.80	6.237
5		11.30	9.30	9.47	7.02	5.769
6		7.06	8.85	7.58	6.31	5.336
7			8.86	6.55	5.90	4.936
8			5.53	6.55	5.90	4.566
9				6.56	5.91	4.460
10				6.55	5.90	4.460
11				4.10	5.91	4.460
12					5.90	4.460
13					5.91	4.461
14					5.90	4.460
15					5.91	4.461
16					3.69	4.460
17						4.461
18						4.460
19						4.461
20						4.460
21						2.788

3-, 5-, 7-, 10-, 15-, and 20-year Property—Mid-quarter Convention; Property Placed in Service in the 4th Quarter

If the Recovery Year Is:	*and the Recovery Period Is:*					
	3-year	*5-year*	*7-year*	*10-year*	15-year	*20-year*
	the Depreciation Rate Is:					
1	8.33	5.00	3.57	2.50	1.25	0.938
2	61.11	38.00	27.55	19.50	9.88	7.430
3	20.37	22.80	19.68	15.60	8.89	6.872
4	10.19	13.68	14.06	12.48	8.00	6.357
5		10.94	10.04	9.98	7.20	5.880
6		9.58	8.73	7.99	6.48	5.439
7			8.73	6.55	5.90	5.031
8			7.64	6.55	5.90	4.654
9				6.56	5.90	4.458
10				6.55	5.91	4.458
11				5.74	5.90	4.458
12					5.91	4.458
13					5.90	4.458
14					5.91	4.458
15					5.90	4.458
16					5.17	4.458
17						4.458
18						4.459
19						4.458
20						4.459
21						3.901

.08 Listed Property

To deduct an expense for "listed property," higher level of substantiation is required than for other types of property. No deduction (or credit) is allowed for listed property unless the taxpayer can substantiate each expenditure or use by adequate records or sufficient evidence corroborating the taxpayer's own statement [Code Sec. 274(d)(4); Temp. Reg. § 1.274-5T(a)(4) and (c)].

Listed property includes the following:

- Passenger automobiles;
- Other forms of transportation if the property's nature lends itself to personal use;
- Entertainment, recreational and amusement property;
- Computers and peripheral equipment;
- Cellular telephones and similar telecommunications equipment (only prior to January 1, 2010); and
- Any other property specified by regulation [Code Sec. 280F(d)(4)(A)].

> ▶ **PRACTICE POINTER:** Since the cost of cell phones and other similar telecommunications equipment are no longer characterized as listed property beginning in 2010, they can be deducted or depreciated like other business property, and are no longer subject to the strict substantiation requirements of Code Sec. 274(d).

The following elements of each expenditure or use for listed property must be substantiated:

- The amount of each separate expenditure;
- The amount of each business/investment use based on the appropriate measure (i.e., mileage for vehicles, time for other listed property) and the total use of the listed property for the tax year;
- The date of the expenditure or use; and
- The business purpose of the expenditure or use [Code Sec. 274(d); Temp. Reg. § 1.274-5T(b)(6)].

To establish these elements and satisfy the adequate records requirement, a taxpayer must maintain a summary of expenses (such as an account book, diary, log, statement of expense, trip sheets, or similar record) and documentary evidence (such as receipts or paid bills) [Temp. Reg. § 1.274-5T(c)(2)]. Taxpayers who cannot substantiate an element by adequate records may substantiate expenses or use by their own statement plus corroborative evidence to establish each element [Temp. Reg. § 1.274-5T(c)(3)].

An employer must substantiate its business and investment use of listed property by showing that, all or a portion of the use of the listed property is by employees in the employer's trade or business. If any employee used the property for personal purposes, the employer must show that it included an appropriate amount in the employee's gross income [Temp. Reg. § 1.274-5T(e)(2)(i)(A)].

To substantiate the business or investment use of listed property provided to an employee, the employer may rely on records unless the employer knows or has reason to know that this evidence is not accurate. The employer must retain a copy of these records, if available. Alternatively, an employer may rely on a statement submitted by the employee that provides sufficient information to allow the employer to determine the business or investment use of the property, unless the employer knows or has reason to know that the statement is not based on either adequate records or the employee's own corroborated statement. [Temp. Reg. § 1.274-5T(e)(2)(ii)].

50-Percent Business Test

If listed property is used more than 50 percent for business in the tax year that it is placed in service, depreciation may be computed using the regular MACRS depreciation, bonus depreciation or the Code Sec. 179 expensing deduction.

If listed property is not used more than 50 percent for business in the tax year that it is placed in service, depreciation must be computed using the straight-line method under the MACRS alternative depreciation system (ADS) and no first-year bonus depreciation deduction or Code Sec. 179 expense allowance may be claimed [Code Sec. 280F(b)(1), (b)(3) and (d)(1); Reg. § 1.280F-6(d)].

For purposes of the 50-percent test, qualified business use is any use of the property in a trade or business, *except*:

- The leasing of the property to someone who has a 5 percent or more ownership in the business;
- The use of the property as compensation for services unless the amount of the compensation is reported on the appropriate information return (and, where required, income tax is withheld on the compensation);
- The use of the property as compensation to someone who has a 5 percent or more ownership interest in the business—even when the compensation is properly reported on an information return; and
- The use of property for investment purposes.

Example 11-18: Mr. Johnson is a 50 percent owner of XYZ, Inc. XYZ provides Johnson with a home computer. Johnson uses the computer 45 percent of the time in XYZ's business, 30 percent of the time for personal investing, and 25 percent for entertainment purposes. As required, XYZ reports the value of Johnson's 55 percent nonbusiness use on his Form W and withholds income tax on it. Result: Only 45 percent of the computer's use is considered a qualified business use. So XYZ must use straight-line depreciation under ADS to compute its deductions.

Employee-Owned Listed Property

If you own listed property for use in your employer's business, you may claim depreciation on the property only if your use is (1) for the convenience of your employer and (2) required as a condition of employment [Code Sec. 280F(d)(3)]. Your use of the property is regarded as for your employer's convenience only if your use is for a substantial business reason of your employer. Your use is considered a condition of employment only if it is required for you to properly perform your duties.

Example 11-19: Mr. Nelson is an inspector for a construction company with many construction sites in the local area. Nelson is required to travel to the various construction sites on a regular basis. The company does not furnish Nelson an automobile and does not explicitly require him to use one. However, the company reimburses him for his expenses in traveling to the various sites. Result: Nelson's use of the car is for the convenience of his employer and is required as a condition of his employment. So he may claim depreciation on the car to the extent of the business use.

Example 11-20: Ms. Bronson is a sales manager for a manufacturing company. She frequently takes work home at night. She buys a home computer to help her track sales, do departmental budgets, write reports and so forth. Result: Bronson does not meet the convenience-of-employer or the condition-of-employment requirements. So she may not claim depreciation on her computer.

▶ **OBSERVATION:** The IRS has ruled that no depreciation is allowed for a computer unless there is a clear showing that the employee cannot properly perform the duties of employment without it.[71] However, the Tax Court has taken a more liberal position. The court allowed a couple without access to a computer at work to write off their home computer because it "substantially aided" them in the performance of their job.[72]

Recapture

If the listed property satisfies the more-than-50-percent business use requirement in the tax year it is placed in service but fails to meet that test in a later tax year, previous depreciation deductions (including bonus depreciation and any amount expensed under Code Sec. 179) claimed in tax years before business dropped are subject to recapture. The recapture amount is the difference between the depreciation (including any bonus allowance and Code Sec. 179 allowance) claimed prior to the recapture year and the amount of depreciation that could have been claimed under ADS (without claiming any Code Sec. 179 allowance or bonus depreciation). Beginning in the recapture year and throughout the remaining ADS recovery period, depreciation must be computed using ADS [Code Sec. 280F(b)(2); Code Sec. 168(k)(2)(D)(i)(II); Temp. Reg. § 1.280F-3T(c) and (d)].

.09 Dispositions

A *disposition* is the permanent withdrawal of property from use in your trade or business. A disposition may be made by sale, exchange, retirement, abandonment, or destruction. If you dispose of property before you have fully recovered your cost, you are entitled to a depreciation deduction in the year of disposition. Your deduction is determined as if you disposed of the property in the middle of the year or the middle of the quarter, depending on the convention that was used when the property was originally placed in service. However, you cannot claim any depreciation deduction for property you place in service and dispose of in the same year [Reg. § 1.168(d)-1].

If you transfer property to a related party in a tax-free transfer [¶ 11,035], the normal rule for dispositions does not apply. Instead, you compute your depreciation deduction as if you retained the property for the entire year. Then the full year's deduction is allocated between you and your related-party transferee, according to which portion of the year each of you held the property.[73]

Mass Asset or General Asset Accounts

Beginning with depreciable assets placed in service in tax years ending after October 10, 1994, you may elect to place assets subject to MACRS in one or more general asset accounts [Code Sec. 168(i)(4)]. You claim one deduction for the mass asset account, computed on the combined adjusted bases of the individual properties. Taxpayers owning a lot of depreciable property can group almost any type of property into one or more classes. They can treat each class of property as a single asset. All property in a class must be like-kind. A class may contain only property that (1) uses the same depreciation method, recovery period and convention; (2) is placed in service in the same year; and (3) is in the same asset class [Reg. § 1.168(i)-1].

---

[71] Rev. Rul. 86-129, 1986 CB 48; LTR 8725067 (Mar. 25, 1987).

[72] *T.C. Cadwallader*, 57 TCM 1030, Dec. 45,856(M), TC Memo. 1989-356, *aff'd*, CA-7, 90-2 USTC ¶ 50,597, 919 F2d 1273.

[73] LTR 8948015 (Aug. 31, 1989).

Disposition of item from mass asset account. An asset in a general asset account is disposed of when ownership of the asset is transferred or when the asset is permanently withdrawn from use either in the taxpayer's trade or business or in the production of income. A disposition includes the sale, exchange, retirement, physical abandonment, or destruction of an asset. A disposition also occurs when an asset is transferred to a supplies, scrap, or similar account [Reg. § 1.168(i)-1(e)(1)]. No loss is realized upon the disposition of an asset from the general asset account because immediately before a disposition of any asset in a general asset account, the asset is treated as having an adjusted basis of zero [Reg. § 1.168(i)-1(e)(2)(i)]. Any amount realized on a disposition will be taxed as ordinary income to the extent the sum of the unadjusted depreciable basis of the general asset account and any expensed cost for assets in the account exceeds any amounts previously recognized as ordinary income upon the disposition of other assets in the account. The adjusted depreciable basis and the depreciation reserve of the general asset account are not affected as a result of a disposition of an asset from the general asset account [Reg. § 1.168(i)-1(e)(2)(iii)].

Example 11-21: ABC Corp. maintains one general asset account for ten machines. The machines cost a total of $10,000 and were placed in service in June. Of the ten machines, one machine costs $8,200 and nine machines cost a total of $1,800. Assume this general asset account has a depreciation method of 200 percent declining balance, a recovery period of 5 years, and a half-year convention. As of January 1, the following year, the depreciation reserve of the account is $2,000 [($10,000 – $0) × 40 percent / 2]. On February 8, ABC sells the machine that costs $8,200 to an unrelated party for $9,000. The machine has an adjusted basis of zero. On its tax return for that year, ABC reports $9,000 as ordinary income because such amount does not exceed the unadjusted depreciable basis of the general asset account ($10,000), plus any expensed cost for assets in the account ($0), less amounts previously recognized as ordinary income ($0). The unadjusted depreciable basis and depreciation reserve of the account are not affected by the disposition of the machine. Thus, the depreciation allowance for the account is $3,200 (($10,000 – $2,000) × 40 percent) [Reg. § 1.168(i)-1(e)(2)(v), Ex. 1].

¶11,045 CODE SEC. 179 EXPENSING DEDUCTION

Instead of depreciating tangible personal property under MACRS, certain taxpayers (not estates, trusts, or certain noncorporate lessors) may elect to deduct all or part of the cost of qualifying property purchased for use in a trade or business in the year the property was placed in service [Code Sec. 179(a)]. This type of deduction is called the Section 179 expensing deduction and may be claimed in lieu of any other type of cost recovery. The expensing election is available for property used for personal as well as business purposes provided the business use predominates [Reg. § 1.179-1(d)(1)].

The Code Sec. 179 dollar limitation in 2013 is $500,000 and the investment limitation is $2 million [Code Sec. 179(b)(1)]. For tax years beginning after 2013, the dollar limit is $25,000 and the investment limitation is $200,000 unless otherwise extended by Congress [Code Sec. 172(b)(2)].

When the taxpayer is a component member of a controlled group, Code Sec. 179(d)(6)(A) only allows one election for all the component members of the controlled group. However in Information Letter 2013-0016, the IRS concluded that S corporations that are members of a controlled group are not treated as a single taxpayer subject to the rule that limits the controlled group's maximum annual Code Sec. 179 expense deduction. Therefore these S corporations are treated as separate entities for purposes of the expensing deduction and each S corporation can make a separate Code Sec. 179 election up to the maximum election amount.

Amounts ineligible for expensing as a result of these limitations cannot be carried forward and expensed in a later year. Instead, the excess cost can only be recovered through depreciation deductions.

.01 Placed in Service Requirement

The Code Sec. 179 election must be made on the tax return for the year in which the property is "placed in service" [Code Sec. 179(c)(1)(B)].[74] Placed in service is defined to mean "the time that property is first placed by the taxpayer in a condition or state of readiness and availability for a specifically assigned function, whether for use in a trade or business, for the production of income, in a tax-exempt activity, or in a personal activity" [Reg. § 1.179-4(e)]. If the property is used partially for business, a deduction under Code Sec. 179 is allowed only if the business use is more than 50 percent of the property's use [Reg. § 1.179-1(d)].

Idle Asset Rule

Depreciation deductions may be available under the "idle asset" rule in situations where an asset, while not in actual use, was nevertheless devoted to the business of the taxpayer and was ready for use should the occasion arise as discussed in *Piggly Wiggly Southern, Inc.*[75] In *C.R. Douglas*,[76] the owner of an S corporation and her husband were not entitled to a flow-through deduction under Code Sec. 179 for expenses of an aircraft owned by the S corporation because the aircraft was never used in the conduct of the business. The aircraft could not be depreciated pursuant to the "idle asset" rule because it was never available for its alleged business function.

.02 Increased Dollar Limitation for Enterprise Zone Business

An enterprise zone business (as defined in Code Sec. 1397C) which conducts trade or business activities within an empowerment zone (as defined in Code Sec. 1391(b)(2)) may increase the annual dollar limitation ($500,000 for tax years beginning in 2013) by the lesser of $35,000 or the cost of Code Sec. 179 property that is qualified zone property (as defined in Code Secs. 1397D, 1397A). However, in applying the investment limitation ($2 million for tax years beginning in 2013), only one-half of the cost of qualified zone property is taken into account (the full cost of Code Sec. 179 property that is not qualified zone property is counted toward the investment limitation) [Code

---

[74] *S.H. Patton*, 116 TC 206, Dec. 54,307 (2001); *J. Rosser*, 99 TCM 1035, Dec. 58,107(M), TC Memo. 2010-6; *C.M. Willock*, 99 TCM 1314, Dec. 58,183(M), TC Memo. 2010-75, *aff'd in part, vac'd in part, rem'd in part*, CA-4, 2011-1 USTC ¶ 50,369.

[75] *Piggly Wiggly Southern, Inc.*, 84 TC 739, Dec. 42,039 (1985), *aff'd*, CA-11, 86-2 USTC ¶ 9789, 803 F2d 1572.

[76] *C.R. Douglas*, 102 TCM 238, Dec. 58,748(M), TC Memo. 2011-214.

Sec. 1397A(a)(2)]. The $35,000 increase is subject to recapture if the qualified zone property ceases to be used in the empowerment zone [Code Sec. 1397A(b)].

Farm businesses in an empowerment zone do not qualify as enterprise zone businesses and are ineligible for this increased Code Sec. 179 annual dollar limitation if the aggregate unadjusted bases (or, if greater, the fair market value) of the assets owned by the taxpayer which are used in the farm business and the aggregate value of assets leased by the taxpayer which are used in the farm business exceed $500,000 [Code Sec. 1397C(d)(5)].

Empowerment zone designations are scheduled to expire on December 31, 2013 [Code Sec. 1391(d)(1)(A)(i)].

.03 Annual Dollar Limit

If only one asset is placed in service during the year and its cost is less than the maximum permitted dollar limit, the Code Sec. 179 deduction is limited to that cost. The total cost that can be deducted in each year is limited to the taxable income from the active conduct of any trade or business during the tax year. Expensing deductions that are disallowed because of the taxable income limit are carried over to succeeding tax years. You use carryover deductions on a first-in-first-out basis—that is, carryovers from earlier years are used first [Reg. § 1.179-3(a)]. Employees as well as small business owners are eligible to take advantage of the Section 179 expensing deduction. Employees must be able to show that their purchase is for the convenience of their employer or as a condition of employment.

If your combined cost of items placed in service during 2013 exceeds $2 million, you can write off each item's nonexpensed cost through MACRS. The amount you expense of each item must be subtracted from the item's basis. This reduced basis is the amount you use to compute your MACRS deduction. Therefore, electing the expense deduction reduces your MACRS deduction.

> ▶ **OBSERVATION:** The expensing deduction can be a way to avoid the effect of the mid-quarter convention [¶11,040]. Reason: Property expensed is not included in determining whether the mid-quarter convention applies [Reg. § 1.168(d)-1(b)(4)].

> **Example 11-22:** XYZ, Inc., a calendar-year taxpayer, puts two items of personal property into service, each costing $20,000. One is put into service in February and the other in November. If XYZ expenses the February item, it will get a $20,000 expensing deduction, but its depreciation deduction is subject to the mid-quarter rules. Its deduction for the November item will be only 12.5 percent of a full year's deduction (one-half of a quarter). On the other hand, if it expenses the November item, it will still get a $20,000 expensing deduction but the mid-quarter rules will not apply. So it gets a half-year's depreciation on the February item.

Expensing Cap for SUVs

A taxpayer's maximum Code Sec. 179 expensing deduction for SUVs is capped at $25,000 regardless of the year [Code Sec. 179(b)(5)]. The limitation applies to SUVs that weigh 14,000 pounds or less (in place of the present law 6,000 pound rating). For this purpose, an *SUV* is defined to exclude any vehicle that:

- Is designed to seat more than nine individuals rearward of the driver's seat;
- Is equipped with an open cargo area, or a covered box not readily accessible from the passenger compartment, of at least six feet in interior length; or
- Has an integral enclosure, fully enclosing the driver compartment and load carrying device, does not have seating rearward of the driver's seat, and has no body section protruding more than 30 inches ahead of the leading edge of the windshield [Code Sec. 179(b)(5)(B)(ii)].

Example 11-23: During 2013, a calendar year taxpayer acquires and places in service an SUV that costs $70,000. The SUV is used 100 percent in the taxpayer's business. The taxpayer may expense $25,000 under Code Sec. 179. The remaining adjusted basis of $45,000 is eligible for an additional depreciation deduction of $4,500 under the general depreciation rules (automobiles are five-year recovery property). The remaining $40,500 of cost ($70,000 original cost less $29,500 deductible currently) would be recovered in 2013 and subsequent years pursuant to the general depreciation rules.

Proration Not Required

The expense deduction under Code Sec. 179 is determined without any proration based on the period of time the business equipment has been in service during the tax year or the length of the tax year in which the property is placed in service [Reg. § 1.179-1(c)(1)]. Thus, the expensing deduction is available regardless when in the year the equipment is purchased and the expensing deduction is not prorated to reflect the portion of the year that the taxpayer owned the business property. This means that you can purchase business equipment at year-end, and expense the cost as if you owned it for the entire year.

.04 Investment Limit

If the combined cost of personal property placed in service during the year exceeds $500,000 in 2013, then the $2 million investment limitation is reduced dollar-for-dollar by the excess over $500,000 in 2013. Married couples (whether filing jointly or separately) are subject to the same dollar limitations as single taxpayers. The same is true for a group of controlled corporations.

Investment Limit Applied to Partnerships and S Corporations

For a partnership or S corporation, the taxable income limitation applies at both the entity level and at the shareholder or partner level [Code Sec. 179(d)(8)]. This limit means that the partnership or S corporation determines the amount of its Code Sec. 179 deduction and then allocates the deduction among its partners or shareholders based on their interest in the entity. Pursuant to Reg. § 1.179-2(b)(3)(iv), a partner or S corporation shareholder that is a calendar-year taxpayer is subject to (a) the dollar limitation for Code Sec. 179 property placed in service by the partner or S corporation shareholder during that year and (b) its allocable share of the Code Sec. 179 deduction from any partnership or S corporation with a tax year ending that year.[77]

Each partner or shareholder then adds the amount allocated to him or her from the partner or S corporation on Schedule K-1 to his or her other nonpartnership Code Sec. 179 expenses and applies the maximum dollar limit to this total. To ease recordkeeping and reporting burdens, when determining whether a partner has exceeded the annual investment limit, the partner does not count any of the Code Sec. 179 property placed in service by the partnership.

A partnership (or S corporation) may not allocate its Code Sec. 179 expense deduction for depreciable property to a partner (or an S corporation shareholder) if the partnership or S corporation has no taxable income. Partnerships and S corporations may carry forward the disallowed portion (as a result of the taxable income limitation) at the entity level. Partners may not claim a Code Sec. 179 expensing deduction in a year when their partnership reported no business income.[78] Reg. § 1.179-2(c)(2) provides that the partnership may not allocate to its partners as a Code Sec. 179 expense deduction for any tax year more than the partnership's taxable income limitation for that tax year, and a partner may not deduct as a Code Sec. 179 expense deduction for any tax year more than the partner's taxable income limitation for that tax year.

> ▶ **PLANNING TIPS:** Consider your business income for the year and your ability to benefit from the expensing deduction before purchasing the business property and placing it in service in the year you have a business loss. In order to claim an expensing deduction for property, you must place the property in service during the year you want to claim the deduction. Thus, if you want to buy business property this year but will not have sufficient business income to support the expensing deduction, wait until next year to place the property in service if you expect to have more profit in the following tax year. An alternative would be to make the election in a loss year in order to preserve your right to it but to carry the deduction forward to future tax years.

.05 Taxable Income Limit

Your expensing deduction cannot exceed the taxable income you and your spouse (if filing a joint return) derive from the active conduct of any trade or business during the year. Note that you can combine your income from all sources in meeting the "taxable income" threshold including the following: (1) Code Sec. 1231 gains (or losses); (2) interest from working capital of your trade or business; (3) wages, salaries, tips, or other pay earned as an employee. Taxable income is figured without regard to: (1) the Code Sec. 179 expense deduction; (2) the self-employment tax deduction; and (3) any net operating loss carryback or carryforward.

> **NOTE:** If you are an employee, you are considered to be engaged in the active conduct of the trade or business of your employment. So wages or other compensation you receive as an employee count as your business income for purposes of the Code Sec. 179 deduction [Reg. § 1.179(c)(6)(iv)]. Any cost that is

[77] Rev. Proc. 2008-54, 2008-2 CB 722.

[78] *D.L. Hayden*, CA-7, 2000-1 USTC ¶ 50,219, 204 F3d 772.

not deductible in one tax year because of this limit can be carried over to the next tax year [Reg. § 1.179-3].

▶ **PLANNING TIP:** Your ability to combine incomes from other actively conducted businesses makes the expensing election available to you even if the cost of your business equipment exceeds the income generated by the business in the start-up years provided you have income from other sources in those years. You can even count the salary you earn as an employee as well as the salary of your spouse if you file a joint return in computing the amount of your "taxable income" for Code Sec. 179 purposes [Reg. § 1.179-2(c)(6)(iv) and (7)].

Example 11-24: You open a new sideline business as a sole proprietorship and spend $20,000 to purchase the necessary equipment for the start-up year. Your new business only earns $10,000 in its start-up year. Your spouse works full-time and you continued to work full-time while starting your new business. Your joint taxable income for the year was $100,000. That year, you can claim an expensing deduction in the amount of $20,000. If you had opened your new business as a corporation rather than a sole proprietorship your expensing deduction would have been limited to $10,000, which was the amount of your taxable income from the business for the year.

.06 Property Eligible for Expensing Deduction

Property (new or used) is eligible for the Code Sec. 179 expensing election if it is:

1. Tangible Code Sec. 1245 property as defined in Code Sec. 1245(a) (3),
2. Depreciable under Code Sec. 168 (i.e., depreciable under MACRS), and
3. Acquired by purchase for use in the active conduct of a trade or business [Code Sec. 179(d) (1); Reg. § 1.179-4].

Qualified Real Property

The Code Sec. 179 expensing allowance for qualified real property is available for eligible property placed in service in 2012 and 2013 [Code Sec. 179(f) (1)]. Any amount disallowed by reason of the taxable income limitation may not be carried forward to a tax year that begins after 2013 and such amount is recovered through depreciation deductions as if no Code Sec. 179 election had been made [Code Sec. 179(f) (4) (A)]. If the disallowed amount is carried over from a tax year other than the taxpayer's last tax year beginning in 2013, the amount is treated as attributable to property placed in service on the first day of the taxpayer's last tax year beginning in 2013. For the last tax year of the taxpayer beginning in 2013, the amount determined under the business income limitation of Code Sec. 179(b) (3) (A) for the tax year is determined without regard to the carryover limitation rules of Code Sec. 179(f) (4) and Code Sec. 179(f) (4) (C)].

Code Sec. 1245 Property

Code Sec. 1245 property includes the following broad classifications of depreciable property:

1. Personal property;
2. Other tangible property (not including most buildings and their structural components) that:
   a. Is used as an integral part of manufacturing, production, or extraction, or of furnishing transportation, communications, electricity, gas, water, or sewage disposal services;
   b. Is a research facility used in connection with any of the activities listed in (a), above; or
   c. Is a facility used in connection with any of the activities listed in (a) for the bulk storage of fungible commodities;
3. That part of any real property that has an adjusted basis reflecting amortization deductions;
4. Single-purpose agricultural or horticultural structures; and
5. Storage facilities (other than buildings and their structural components) that are used in connection with the distribution of petroleum or primary products of petroleum.
6. Any railroad grading or tunnel bore.

Land and Code Sec. 1250 land improvements, such as buildings and other permanent structures and their components are real property and do not qualify for expensing under Code Sec. 179. Code Sec. 1250 land improvements, for example, include swimming pools, paved parking lots, wharves, docks, bridges, and fences. However, certain land improvements are Code Sec. 1245 property and thus qualify for Code Sec. 179 expensing. Specifically, Code Sec. 1245 land improvements are land improvements that qualify as other tangible property because they are used as an integral part of manufacturing, production, or extraction, or of furnishing transportation, communications, electricity, gas, water, or sewage disposal services.

Property contained in or attached to a building that is not a structural component, such as refrigerators, grocery store counters, office equipment, printing presses, testing equipment, and signs can qualify for expensing under Code Sec. 179.

Trade or Business Use Requirement

To qualify for Code Sec. 179 expensing, property must be used more than 50 percent in the active conduct of the taxpayer's trade or business [Reg. § 1.179-2(c)(6)]. If a property is used for the production of income (i.e. investment), the property does not qualify for the expensing allowance.

Qualifying property typically includes office equipment, bookcases, file cabinets, furniture, display cases, and mobile trailers. The Tax Court has approved an employee's Code Sec. 179 deductions for a computer, printer, and camera purchased for use in the taxpayer's work as a telemarketing sales manager for the business telephone directory.[79] The expensing deduction is available for property that is used for personal as well as business purposes if the business use predominates (more than 50 percent) [Reg.

---

[79] *S.A. Mulne*, 72 TCM 111, Dec. 51,447(M), TC Memo. 1996-320.

§ 1.179-1(d)(1)]. The definition of property eligible for immediate expensing also includes horses.

Off-the-Shelf Computer Software

Off-the-shelf computer software qualifies as Code Sec. 179 property if the software is placed in service by the taxpayer in a tax year before 2014 and is acquired by purchase for use in the active conduct of the taxpayer's trade or business [Code Sec. 179(d)(1)(A); Reg. § 1.179-4]. Off-the-shelf computer software is defined as software that is: (1) readily available for purchase by the general public, (2) subject to a nonexclusive license, and (3) that has not been substantially modified. Computer software does not include any database or similar item unless it is in the public domain and is incidental to the operation of otherwise qualifying computer software [Code Secs. 179(d)(1)(A)(ii), 197(e)(3)(A)(i)].

Qualified Liquid Fuel Refineries

Taxpayers may make an irrevocable election to expense 50 percent of the cost of a qualified refinery property [Code Sec. 179C(a)]. The expensing deduction is allowed for the tax year in which the qualified refinery property is placed in service. The remaining 50 percent of the cost is recovered under either Code Sec. 168 or Code Sec. 179B (the election for small business refiners to expense certain qualified capital costs). An election for a particular tax year is made on the taxpayer's return for that year. Once made, the election may be revoked only with IRS consent [Code Sec. 179C(b)].

Qualified refinery property eligible for expensing includes any portion of a qualified refinery: (1) the original use of which commences with the taxpayer; (2) which is placed in service by the taxpayer after August 8, 2005, and before January 1, 2014; (3) which meets certain production capacity requirements (in the case of an expansion of an existing refinery); (4) which meets all applicable environmental laws in effect on the date such portion was placed in service; (5) no written binding contract for the construction of which was in effect on or before June 14, 2005; and (6) the construction of which is subject to a written binding construction contract entered into before January 1, 2010, which is placed in service before January 1, 2010, or, in the case of self-constructed property, the construction of which began after June 14, 2005 and before January 1, 2010 [Code Sec. 179C(c)(1)].

A "qualified refinery" means any refinery located in the United States that is designed to serve the primary purpose of processing liquid fuel from crude oil or qualified fuels [Code Sec. 179C(d)]. Qualified fuels include oil produced from shale and tar sands; gas produced from geopressured brine, Devonian shale, coal seams, or a tight formation or biomass; and synthetic fuels produced from coal. The definition of a "qualified refinery" also includes a refinery located in the United States that is designed to serve the primary purpose of processing liquid fuel from crude oil or qualified fuels (as defined in Code Sec. 45K(c)), or directly from shale or tar sands [Code Sec. 179C(d)].

.07 Property Not Eligible for Expensing Deduction

The following types of property are ineligible for the Section 179 expensing deduction and therefore must be depreciated under the general depreciation rules [Code Secs. 179(d)(1) and 50(b)]:

- Property used 50 percent or less of the time in a trade or business;
- Property used predominately outside the United States [Code Sec. 50(b)(1)];
- Property used in connection with furnishing lodging, except the following [Code Sec. 50(b)(2)];
   a. Nonlodging commercial facilities that are available to those who are not using the lodging facilities on the same basis as they are available to those using the lodging facilities [Code Sec. 50(b)(2)(A)];
   b. Property used by a hotel or motel in connection with the trade or business of furnishing lodging where the predominant portion of the accommodation is used by transients [Code Sec. 50(b)(2)(B)];
   c. The portion of the basis of a certified historic structure that is for qualified rehabilitation expenditures [Code Sec. 50(b)(2)(C)];
   d. Any energy property that includes either: (a) equipment that uses solar energy to generate electricity, to heat or cool a structure, to provide hot water for use in a structure, or to provide solar process hear, or (b) equipment used to produce, distribute, or use energy derived from a geothermal deposit, up to (but not including) the electrical transmission stage [Code Sec. 50(b)(2)(D)]. Property used by tax-exempt organizations;
- Property used by foreign persons or entities;
- Portable air conditioning or portable heating units [Code Sec. 179(d)(1)];
- Property you hold only for the production of income, such as investment property, plus rental property (provided renting property is not your trade or business), and property that produces royalties;
- Real property, including buildings and their structural components;
- Property used by tax-exempt organizations that is not predominantly used in connection with an unrelated business income activity [Code Sec. 179(f)(1); Code Sec. 50(b)(4)];
- Property used by governmental units;
- Certain property noncorporate lessors lease to others unless you manufactured the property or the term of the lease is less than 50 percent of the property's class life and for the first 12 months after the property is transferred to the lessee, the sum of the deductions related to the property that are allowed to you solely under Code Sec. 162 (except rents and reimbursed amounts) is more than 15 percent of the rental income from the property;
- If the property was acquired from a related person (e.g., your parents or children or a corporation in which you own more than 50 percent of the stock);
- If the property was acquired by one member of a controlled group from another member of the same group; and
- If the property's basis is determined in whole or in part by its adjusted basis in the hands of the person from whom it was acquired (gift) or under stepped-up basis rules for property acquired from a decedent [Reg. § 1.179-4(c)(1)(iv)].

.08 Basis Limitation on Expensing Deduction

In general, the amount that is eligible for the expensing deduction is the taxpayer's basis in the property. Basis for expensing purposes does not include any basis that is determined by reference to the basis of other property. This could occur if a taxpayer purchased a new piece of equipment and traded in old equipment. The taxpayer's basis in the new equipment would include the adjusted basis of the equipment traded in for the new equipment. The taxpayer would only be able to expense under Code Sec. 179 the amount he or she paid for new equipment.

> **Example 11-25:** Husband and wife purchase a new piece of equipment that cost $5,000. They trade in their old equipment that cost $2,000. Even though their basis in the new equipment is $7,000, they can only claim a Code Sec. 179 deduction on the $5,000 amount they paid.

If taxpayers acquire property in a nontaxable like-kind exchange, the adjusted basis of the old asset is excluded in computing the expense deduction for the new asset.

When taxpayers sell or otherwise dispose of Code Sec. 179 property they must increase the basis of the property by any unused carryover of disallowed Code Sec. 179 deduction.

.09 Recapture

If taxpayers dispose of expensed property before the end of the MACRS recovery period for the property, they must recapture the tax benefit received from the expensing deduction. [Code Sec. 179(d)(10); Reg. § 1.179-3(f)(2)]. The same recapture rule applies to any qualified enterprise zone property that ceases to be used in an empowerment zone by an enterprise zone business [Code Sec. 1397A(b)]. Taxpayers must include in income the difference between: (1) the expensing deduction (and depreciation deductions, if any) claimed before the year of disposition; and (2) the deductions that would have been allowed under regular MACRS without expensing.

Recapture also applies where there is no disposition, but business use of the property falls below 50 percent of total use. For example, if the taxpayer expenses an item and later converts it to personal use, he or she would be subject to recapture. (Note: There are different recapture rules for listed property [¶ 11,040].)

.10 How to Make the Election

Taxpayers should make their Code Sec. 179 election on Form 4562, *Depreciation and Amortization.*

As a general rule, an election must be made on the taxpayer's first income tax return for the tax year to which the election applies (whether or not the return is timely) or on an amended return filed within the time prescribed by law (including extensions) for filing a return for that year, and an election, once made, may not be revoked without the IRS' consent. However, for tax years beginning before 2014, a taxpayer can make or revoke an election to claim a Code Sec. 179 expense deduction on an amended return without first obtaining consent of the IRS.

The election is made for a prior tax year by filing an amended federal tax return for the tax year to which the election applies. A separate election must be made for each tax year in which a Code Sec. 179 expense deduction is claimed [Reg. § 1.179-5(a)]. The election must specify the items of Code Sec. 179 property and the portion of the cost of each item to be expensed. The amended return must also include an adjustment to taxable income to account for the Code Sec. 179 election and any collateral adjustments to taxable income or tax liability, such as to account for depreciation on the property for which the Code Sec. 179 election was made. Adjustments must also be made on returns for succeeding tax years, if they are affected by the election [Reg. § 1.179-5(c)(2)(i)]. The taxpayer must maintain records which identify each piece of Code Sec. 179 property and reflect how and from whom the property was acquired and when the property was placed in service.

If a taxpayer elected to expense only a portion of the cost basis of an item of Code Sec. 179 property for a tax year before 2014, the taxpayer can file an amended return for that tax year and increase the portion to be expensed without first obtaining the consent of the IRS. Similarly, if the taxpayer did not make an election to expense the cost basis of an item of Code Sec. 179 property, the taxpayer can file an amended return for that tax year and elect to expense any portion of the cost basis of the item without first obtaining the consent of the IRS. An increase in the amount expensed is not treated as a revocation of a prior Code Sec. 179 election for that year [Reg. § 1.179-5(c)(2)(ii)].

.11 Revoking the Election

For tax years after 2002 and before 2014, a taxpayer who wishes to revoke a Code Sec. 179 election can revoke the entire election, revoke the election of a specific item of property, or revoke a selected dollar amount with respect to a specific item of property [Reg. § 1.179-5(c)(3)(i)]. The election can be revoked without first obtaining consent of the IRS by filing an amended federal tax return for the tax year to which the revocation applies. The amended return must include an adjustment to taxable income for the revocation of the election and any collateral adjustments to taxable income or tax liability, such as to account for depreciation on the property for which the election was revoked. Adjustments must also be made on returns for succeeding tax years, if they are affected by the revocation. Once an election has been revoked, it cannot be reversed; the revocation is irrevocable [Reg. § 1.179-5(c)(3)(ii)].

Example 11-26: Taxpayer owns and operates a jewelry store. She purchases and places in service two items of Code Sec. 179 property—a cash register costing $4,000 (5-year MACRS property) and office furniture costing $10,000 (7-year MACRS property). On her timely filed federal tax return, she elected to expense under Section 179 the full cost of the cash register and, with respect to the office furniture, claimed the depreciation allowable. In November of that year, she realizes that it would have been more advantageous to make an election under Sec. 179 to expense the full cost of the office furniture rather than the cash register. She may file an amended federal tax return revoking the expensing election for the cash register, claiming the depreciation for the cash register, and making an election to expense under Sec. 179 the cost of the office furniture. The amended return must include an adjustment for the depreciation previously claimed for the office furniture, an adjustment for the depreciation allowable for the cash register, and any other collateral adjustments to taxable income or to the tax liability. In addition, once Taxpayer revokes the election for the entire cost basis of the cash register, Taxpayer can no longer expense under Sec. 179 any portion of the cost of the cash register [Reg. § 1.179-5(c)(4), Ex. 1].

In some cases, the taxpayer can file an amended return to increase the amount expensed under Code Sec. 179. If the taxpayer elected to expense only a portion of the cost basis of an item of Code Sec. 179 property, the taxpayer can file an amended return for that tax year and increase the portion to be expensed without first obtaining IRS consent. Similarly, if the taxpayer did not make an election to expense the cost basis of an item of Code Sec. 179 property, the taxpayer can file an amended return for that tax year and elect to expense any portion of the cost basis of the item without first obtaining IRS consent. An increase in the amount expensed is not treated as a revocation of a prior Code Sec. 179 election for that year.

.12 Advantages of Expensing Deduction

By taking advantage of the expensing deduction under Code Sec. 179, the small business owner will accomplish the following two goals:

- The taxpayer will lower the cost of purchasing property for your trade or business by recovering the cost of the asset immediately rather than spreading out the depreciation deductions over several years; and
- The taxpayer will avoid the complex record keeping that is required when you depreciate property. Sec. 179 enables you to simply write off immediately (up to the statutory limits) the cost of business property in the year purchased. Compare the difference if you decide to depreciate the asset instead. Since business property usually falls into the 5- or 7-year depreciation category, it could take you up to 7 years to benefit fully from the tax deductions.

Example 11-27: Keith Miller is a self-employed accountant. He purchased and put into service $300,000 in office equipment and furniture. By electing under Code Sec. 179 to take the maximum deduction, he would be able to deduct the entire cost of the new equipment and furniture.

If you have a start-up business with no income you may still take advantage of the expensing deduction if you or your spouse have income that year from other sources.

¶11,050 MACRS AND REAL ESTATE

Real estate is divided into two classes for figuring MACRS depreciation: residential rental real estate and nonresidential real estate [Code Sec. 168(b), (c)]. A building is considered residential rental property only if 80 percent or more of the gross rents come from dwelling units. A dwelling unit is a house or apartment used to provide living accommodations. It does not include a unit of a hotel, motel, or any other establishment in which more than half of the units are used on a transient basis.

If you own a building and use one of the units as a personal residence, you include that unit's rental value in determining if the 80 percent test is met.

Example 11-28: Ms. McDonald owns a six-unit building, five residential apartments and one professional office. She lives in one unit and rents out the other four apartments and the office. Gross annual rent from the office: $15,000. Gross rent from each of the five apartments: $12,000, total $60,000. Result: Assuming the rental value of McDonald's apartment is also $12,000, her building is considered a residential rental property—even though less than 80 percent of her actual rents come from the apartments. When you figure in the rental value of her apartment, exactly 80 percent ($60,000/$75,000) comes from residential rents.

.01 How to Figure the Depreciation Deduction

For real estate subject to MACRS, the recovery period for residential rental property is 27.5 years. For nonresidential property, the recovery period is 39 years if the property was placed in service on or after May 13, 1993 [Code Sec. 168(c)]. For nonresidential property placed in service after December 31, 1986, and before May 13, 1993, the recovery period is 31.5 years. The 31.5-year recovery period also applies to property placed in service as late as December 31, 1993, if:

- A taxpayer entered into a binding contract to buy or build the property before May 13, 1993 (or acquired the contract from someone who entered into it before May 13, 1993), and
- Construction started before May 13, 1993.

There is no accelerated depreciation for MACRS real estate. You must use straight-line depreciation [Code Sec. 168(b)(3)].

▶ **OBSERVATION:** Anything with an ADR class life [¶11,040] of less than 27.5 years is not considered real estate. Because land improvements—for example, parking lots, sidewalks, roads, and fences—have a 20-year ADR life,[80] you can depreciate them more rapidly than real estate. They qualify as 15-year property and you can write them off using the 150 percent declining balance method of depreciation.

The applicable depreciation convention for real estate is the mid-month convention. (Unlike personal property, there is no special rule for substantial fourth-quarter purchases of real estate.) Any real property—residential or nonresidential—that you place in service during a year is depreciable from the midpoint of the month it is placed in service. (The mid-month convention also applies in the year of disposition.) So, unlike personal property with its half-year convention, the size of your first-year deduction depends on when you place the property in service.

Example 11-29: Mr. Green buys an office building for $240,000, $40,000 of which is allocable to the land. He places the building in service on October 8. His depreciation deduction for a full year would be $200,000 divided by the 39-year recovery period, or $5,128. Since he is considered to have placed the building in service in mid-October, he is entitled to 2½ months of depreciation for the year. So his deduction is $1,068 (5/24 × $5,128).

---

[80] Rev. Proc. 88-22, 1988-1 CB 785.

Example 11-30: Same facts as in Example 11-29, except that Green puts the property into service on April 10. Now he is entitled to $8^1/_2$ months of depreciation that year. So his deduction is $3,632 (17/24 × $5,128).

Because the mid-month convention applies, you do not have to make any adjustment in your real estate depreciation for short tax years.

.02 Optional Tables

Instead of computing depreciation as just described, you may use optional tables issued by the IRS. These tables can be found in IRS Publication 946, *How to Depreciate Property.*[81]

There are separate tables for residential rental and nonresidential properties. Each table lists the percentage depreciation to be applied to the unadjusted basis of a property in each tax year and varies according to which month the property was first placed in service.

.03 Alternative Depreciation System (ADS)

In lieu of regular MACRS depreciation, you may elect to use the ADS to depreciate real estate. You can make this election on a property-by-property basis. For example, if you put two apartment buildings into service in one year, you can use regular MACRS on one and elect ADS on the other. You must make the election to use ADS in the year you place the property in service. Once you make the election, it is irrevocable.

Under ADS, you write off the cost of your property using the straight-line method, the mid-month convention and a 40-year recovery period. The same recovery period is used for both residential and nonresidential properties. ADS is also used in computing the alternative minimum tax [Ch. 16].

.04 Additions or Improvements

You treat an addition or improvement to a building as a separate property under MACRS. You do not simply add it to the depreciable basis of the building. Instead, you must depreciate the addition or improvement separately, using straight-line depreciation, the mid-month convention and appropriate recovery period (e.g., 27.5 years for an improvement to a residential rental property). Depreciation begins on the later of (1) the date on which you place the addition or improvement in service or (2) the date on which you place the building in service [Code Sec. 168(i)(6)].

If you are leasing property and make an improvement to it, you must use the normal MACRS recovery period for the improvement—regardless of the length of the lease. For example, if you lease land for 20 years, and erect a nonresidential building on it, you must use a 39-year recovery period (31.5 years if the building is placed in service after December 31, 1986 and before May 13, 1993) to figure your depreciation deductions.

In *Amerisouth XXXII,*[82] the Tax Court concluded that an apartment complex's structural components were depreciable as residential real property over 27.5 years. The taxpayer's argument that the apartment complex was a collection of over 1,000 components

---

[81] Rev. Proc. 89-15, 1989-1 CB 816; Treas. Dept., IRS Publication 946, *How to Depreciate Property* (2013 Ed.).

[82] *Amerisouth XXXII,* 103 TCM 1324, Dec. 58,975(M), TC Memo. 2012-67.

depreciable as personal property over periods ranging from five to 15 years was rejected. The taxpayer conducted a cost-segregation study that separated the components at issue into 12 categories. To the extent the taxpayer owned the utility lines, they were structural components depreciable as residential real property. Similarly, the components in the special HVAC, special plumbing, special electric, finish carpentry, millwork, interior windows and mirrors and special painting categories generally were structural components because they were permanent and related to the operation or maintenance of an apartment building. However, the clothes-dryer vents had no connection to the apartments' general ventilation system and, therefore, were personal property, as were the dedicated gas lines in the common laundry rooms. Moreover, electrical outlets specifically for use by refrigerators, stoves, washers and dryers were also depreciable as personal property, as were cable, telephone and data outlets, because they were used with specific pieces of equipment.

OTHER DEPRECIATION SYSTEMS

¶11,055 ACCELERATED COST RECOVERY SYSTEM

The Accelerated Cost Recovery System (ACRS) applies to depreciable property placed in service after 1980 and before 1987. ACRS has been replaced by MACRS [¶11,030], but it continues to govern current deductions for property you originally placed in service in those years.

In many ways, ACRS is similar to MACRS. They both allow accelerated depreciation of property over a fixed period specified by law. But in several key respects, ACRS differs from MACRS:

- ACRS has no 7- or 20-year property classes;
- Cars and trucks are in the 3-year class rather than the 5-year class;
- The recovery period for real estate is much shorter under ACRS than MACRS;
- Instead of MACRS-prescribed depreciation methods (with depreciation tables optional), ACRS mandates the use of tables;
- ACRS does not permit a depreciation deduction in the year personal property is disposed of; and
- ACRS has no special depreciation rule that applies when a large amount of property is placed in service in the last quarter of the year.

.01 Recovery Period for Personal Property

The cost of equipment, machinery and other personal property you placed in service under ACRS is generally written off over 3-, 5-, 10- or 15-year periods. The precise period depends on what ACRS class your property falls in [former Code Sec. 168(c); note that all ACRS references to the Internal Revenue Code are to the Code as it existed prior to the Tax Reform Act of 1986].

3-year property includes cars, light-duty trucks, property used in research and experimentation, and all other property with an ADR midpoint life [¶11,040] of four years or less.

5-year property covers all depreciable personal property not included in any other class, such as most kinds of production machinery, office furniture and equipment, and heavy-duty trucks.

10-year property includes railroad tank cars, mobile and prefab homes, certain coal burning equipment, public utility property with an ADR midpoint life of 18 to 25 years and real estate with an ADR midpoint life of 12.5 years or less (e.g., theme park structures).

15-year property covers public utility property with an ADR midpoint life of more than 25 years.

.02 Depreciation Methods for Personal Property

You find your ACRS deduction for each year of the recovery period by multiplying the unadjusted basis of the property (less any expensing deduction claimed) by a percentage prescribed by law. The applicable percentage depends on the property's class and the number of years since you placed the property in service [former Code Sec. 168(b)(1)]. The prescribed percentages are reproduced in Table 5.

Table 5. ACRS Depreciation of Personal Property

If the recovery year is:	*The applicable percentage for the class of property is:*			
	3-year	*5-year*	*10-year*	*15-year public utility*
1	25	15	8	5
2	38	22	14	10
3	37	21	12	9
4		21	10	8
5		21	10	7
6			10	7
7			9	6
8			9	6
9			9	6
10			9	6
11				6
12				6
13				6
14				6
15				6

Example 11-31: Mr. Baker bought a mobile home for $47,000 that he rented out. The mobile home is 10-year property under ACRS. In the eighth depreciation year for the item, Mr. Baker can claim a depreciation deduction of $4,230 for the mobile home (9 percent of $47,000).

NOTE: The depreciation percentages for each year are based on a 150 percent declining balance method of depreciation in the early years of the recovery period and a switch to straight line in the later years [¶11,040]. They are figured under a half-year depreciation convention for the year the property was placed in service [¶ 11,040]. So, as with MACRS, your first-year deduction under ACRS was the same no matter when property is placed in service during a year.

If you dispose of ACRS property before the end of its last depreciation year, you cannot claim a deduction for the year of disposition [former Code Sec. 168(d)(2)].

Alternate Depreciation Method

ACRS provides a straight-line depreciation method [¶ 11,040]in lieu of the specified depreciation percentages. ACRS also allows alternate recovery periods [former Code Sec. 168(b)(3)] as listed in Table 6.

Table 6. Alternate ACRS Depreciation

Type of Property	Recovery Periods Available
3-year property	3, 5, or 12 years
5-year property	5, 12, or 25 years
10 year property	10, 25, or 35 years
15-year public utility property	15, 35, or 45 years

The straight-line method and alternate recovery periods had to be elected in the year you originally placed the property into service (i.e., before 1987). If you elected the alternate method, you use the half-year convention in both the year the property was placed in service and in the year following the end of the recovery period. Like regular ACRS, no deduction is allowed in the year you dispose of the property. And you cannot revoke your election without IRS consent.

.03 ACRS and Real Estate

You generally depreciate all real estate, both residential and nonresidential, in the same way under ACRS (unlike MACRS where residential and nonresidential properties have different recovery periods). Like ACRS personal property, you find your percentage depreciation rate for each year from a table prescribed by law [former Code Sec. 168(b)(2)]. The percentages are based on a 175 percent declining balance method switching to straight line [¶ 11,040]. However, because of statutory changes made in the recovery period and depreciation convention during the years ACRS was in effect, there are four different tables. The one you use depends on when your property was placed in service:

- For real estate placed in service after 1980 and before March 16, 1984, the table percentages are based on a 15-year recovery period. And any property placed in service during a year is depreciated from the first day of the month you place it into service;
- For real estate placed in service after March 15, 1984, and before June 23, 1984, the recovery period is 18 years. But property continues to be depreciable from the first day of the month it is placed in service;
- For real estate placed in service after June 22, 1984, and before May 9, 1985, the recovery period is 18 years, but a mid-month convention applies. Property placed in service during any month is depreciable from the midpoint of that month; and
- For real estate placed in service after May 8, 1985, and before 1987, the recovery period is 19 years with a mid- month depreciation convention.

The ACRS real estate tables are reproduced in Table 7.

Table 7. ACRS Real Estate Depreciation

Table I 15-year Real Property (other than low-income housing) Placed in Service After 1980 and Before March 16, 1984

Year	Month Placed in Service 1	2	3	4	5	6	7	8	9	10	11	12
1	12%	11%	10%	9%	8%	7%	6%	5%	4%	3%	2%	1%
2	10%	10%	11%	11%	11%	11%	11%	11%	11%	11%	11%	12%
3	9%	9%	9%	9%	10%	10%	10%	10%	10%	10%	10%	10%
4	8%	8%	8%	8%	8%	8%	9%	9%	9%	9%	9%	9%
5	7%	7%	7%	7%	7%	7%	8%	8%	8%	8%	8%	8%
6	6%	6%	6%	6%	7%	7%	7%	7%	7%	7%	7%	7%
7	6%	6%	6%	6%	6%	6%	6%	6%	6%	6%	6%	6%
8	6%	6%	6%	6%	6%	6%	5%	6%	6%	6%	6%	6%
9	6%	6%	6%	5%	5%	6%	5%	5%	5%	6%	6%	6%
10	5%	6%	5%	6%	5%	5%	5%	5%	5%	5%	6%	5%
11	5%	5%	5%	5%	5%	5%	5%	5%	5%	5%	5%	5%
12	5%	5%	5%	5%	5%	5%	5%	5%	5%	5%	5%	5%
13	5%	5%	5%	5%	5%	5%	5%	5%	5%	5%	5%	5%
14	5%	5%	5%	5%	5%	5%	5%	5%	5%	5%	5%	5%
15	5%	5%	5%	5%	5%	5%	5%	5%	5%	5%	5%	5%
16	—	—	1%	1%	2%	2%	3%	3%	4%	4%	4%	5%

Table II 18-year Real Property (placed in service after March 15, 1984 and before June 23, 1984)

Year	Month Placed in Service 1	2	3	4	5	6	7	8	9	10-11	12
1	10%	9%	8%	7%	6%	6%	5%	4%	3%	2%	1%
2	9%	9%	9%	9%	9%	9%	9%	9%	9%	10%	10%
3	8%	8%	8%	8%	8%	8%	8%	8%	9%	9%	9%
4	7%	7%	7%	7%	7%	7%	8%	8%	8%	8%	8%
5	6%	7%	7%	7%	7%	7%	7%	7%	7%	7%	7%
6	6%	6%	6%	6%	6%	6%	6%	6%	6%	6%	6%
7	5%	5%	5%	5%	6%	6%	6%	6%	6%	6%	6%
8-12	5%	5%	5%	5%	5%	5%	5%	5%	5%	5%	5%
13	4%	4%	4%	5%	5%	4%	4%	5%	4%	5%	5%
14-18	4%	4%	4%	4%	4%	4%	4%	4%	4%	4%	4%
19	—	—	1%	1%	1%	2%	2%	2%	3%	3%	4%

Table III

19-year Real Property
(placed in service after May 8, 1985 and before 1987)
(19-Year 175% Declining Balance)
(Assuming Mid-Month Convention)
Month Placed in Service

Year	1	2	3	4	5	6	7	8	9	10	11	12
1	8.8%	8.1%	7.3%	6.5%	5.8%	5.0%	4.2%	3.5%	2.7%	1.9%	1.1%	0.4%
2	8.4%	8.5%	8.5%	8.6%	8.7%	8.8%	8.8%	8.9%	9.0%	9.0%	9.1%	9.2%
3	7.6%	7.7%	7.7%	7.8%	7.9%	7.9%	8.0%	8.1%	8.1%	8.2%	8.3%	8.3%
4	6.9%	7.0%	7.0%	7.1%	7.1%	7.2%	7.3%	7.3%	7.4%	7.4%	7.5%	7.6%
5	6.3%	6.3%	6.4%	6.4%	6.5%	6.5%	6.6%	6.6%	6.7%	6.8%	6.8%	6.9%
6	5.7%	5.7%	5.8%	5.9%	5.9%	5.9%	6.0%	6.0%	6.1%	6.1%	6.2%	6.2%
7	5.2%	5.2%	5.3%	5.3%	5.3%	5.4%	5.4%	5.5%	5.5%	5.6%	5.6%	5.6%
8	4.7%	4.7%	4.8%	4.8%	4.8%	4.9%	4.9%	5.0%	5.0%	5.1%	5.1%	5.1%
9	4.2%	4.3%	4.3%	4.4%	4.4%	4.5%	4.5%	4.5%	4.5%	4.6%	4.6%	4.7%
10-19	4.2%	4.2%	4.2%	4.2%	4.2%	4.2%	4.2%	4.2%	4.2%	4.2%	4.2%	4.2%
20	0.2%	0.5%	0.9%	1.2%	1.6%	1.9%	2.3%	2.6%	3.0%	3.3%	3.7%	4.0%

Alternate Depreciation Method

Straight-line depreciation could have been elected for ACRS real estate in the year a property was placed in service. For 15-year property, ACRS allows alternate recovery periods of either 15, 35 or 45 years. For 18-year property, the recovery periods are 18, 35 or 45 years. And for 19-year real estate, the periods are 19, 35 or 45 years.

Improvements to ACRS Real Estate

If you make an improvement or addition to property being depreciated under ACRS, you cannot write off the improvement or addition under ACRS. As long as the improvement or addition was placed in service after 1986, you must depreciate it using a longer recovery period and the straight-line method under MACRS [¶11,050].

¶11,060 USEFUL LIFE DEPRECIATION SYSTEM

You could write off depreciable personal and real property placed in service before 1981 under the useful life (or facts and circumstances) system. You generally recover the cost of the property over the estimated useful life of the property, using a reasonable depreciation method [Reg. §1.167(a)-1]. However, for property placed in service after 1970, you were allowed to elect the Asset Depreciation Range [¶11,040] [Reg. §1.167(a)-11(a)].

.01 Useful Life

The useful life of a property is an estimate of how long you can expect to use it in your trade or business. It is not how long the property will last, but how long it will continue to be useful to you, taking into account the frequency of use, your repair policy, and the conditions in the area surrounding the property.

Suppose you placed property into service before 1981 and the facts on which you based your estimated useful life have now changed significantly. You may revise your estimate if (1) there is a clear and convincing basis for your change and (2) the change in the estimate is significant [Reg. § 1.167(a)-1(b)].

.02 Depreciation Methods

Straight-line and declining balance methods of depreciation [¶ 11,040] are permitted under the useful life system. However, you may use 200 percent declining balance only for property that was new when you placed it in service and had a useful life of three years or more. Depreciable real property is generally limited to 125 percent declining balance (for residential rental property) or straight line (for other real estate).

If you want to change the depreciation method you have been using, you generally must file Form 3115 with the Internal Revenue Service. You must file the form in the first 180 days of the tax year the change is to take effect.

> ▶ **OBSERVATION:** If you have been depreciating property under the declining balance method, you may now want to switch to the straight-line method. The declining balance method will leave you with a portion of your cost unrecovered at the end of the property's useful life; the straight-line method won't. Note: You can make a switch from the declining balance method to the straight-line method without filing Form 3115.

.03 Salvage Value

The salvage value is the secondhand value of property at the expected time of disposition [¶ 11,001]. The total amount that can be written off under the useful life system is ordinarily the adjusted basis of the property less the property's salvage value. Once determined, salvage value doesn't change due to price fluctuations. However, it may be changed if you revise a property's useful life [discussed above)]. You may ignore salvage value to the extent of 10 percent of the cost of the property. Note: Salvage value is ignored completely under ACRS and MACRS.

¶ 11,065 DEPRECIATION METHODS NOT BASED ON YEARS

You must make an election to determine your depreciation according to a method that is not based on a prescribed period of years. If you would otherwise be subject to the AMT, you will like one of these methods because no AMT adjustment will be needed if your depreciation is not expressed in terms of a number of years [Code Sec. 168(f)(1)].

.01 Unit-of-Production Method

Under the unit-of-production method, your depreciation deduction is based on the estimated number of units that depreciable property will produce before it wears out [Reg. § 1.167(b)-0(b)].

Example 11-32: A machine costs $10,000. You estimate that the machine will produce 20,000 units before it is no longer useful. If it produces 2,500 units, your depreciation deduction is $1,250 ($10,000 × 2,500/20,000).

The unit-of-production method is especially suitable for figuring depreciation of equipment used in mining, oil wells and timber working.

.02 Operating-Day Method

The operating-day method allows you to figure depreciation based on the number of days of life the equipment is expected to have.

Example 11-33: You buy a machine for $15,000. The life of the machine is estimated to be 1,000 days. If you use it on 200 days during the year, your deduction is $3,000 ($15,000 × 200/1,000).

This method may be used on rotary drilling equipment and other machinery where the major depreciation factor is the wear and tear from use.[83]

.03 Income Forecast Method

The income forecast method is specifically limited to recover the costs of assets such as film, video tape, sound recordings, copyrights, books, and patents [Code Sec. 167(g)(6)].

The income forecast method of depreciation permits you to recover the depreciable basis of property over the anticipated income to be earned by the property. The income forecast method is typically used to depreciate show business assets in an effort to prevent a distortion of income caused by the uneven flow of income produced by those assets. It can lead to bigger write-offs earlier in the life of the asset because it allows a company to write off the cost of assets as the income it produces accrues.

Example 11-34: Video Game, Inc. manufacturers video games. They have found that 25 percent of the income attributable to a video game is earned during the first year that the video game is released. According to the income forecast method, Video Game, Inc. can write off 25 percent of the costs associated with manufacturing video games during the first year, provided the salvage value is minimal.

The income forecast method cannot be used to calculate the depreciation of consumer durables subject to rent-to-own contracts placed in service after August 5, 1997.[84] Instead, qualified rent-to-own property is subject to depreciation under MACRS and is treated as three-year property. The income forecast method cannot be used to depreciate amortizable Section 197 intangibles [Code Sec. 167(g)(6)].

---

83 Rev. Rul. 56-652, 1956-2 CB 125.

84 *ABC Rentals of San Antonio, Inc.*, CA-10, 96-2 USTC ¶50,208, 97 F3d 392, *vacated, on reh'g*, CA-10, 98-1 USTC ¶50,340, 142 F3d 1200, *on remand*, 77 TCM 1229, Dec. 53,217(M), TC Memo. 1999-14 and 79 TCM 1484, Dec. 53,749(M), TC Memo. 2000-47; *see also* Rev. Rul. 95-52, 1995-2 CB 27.

Computation of Depreciation Using the Income Forecast Method

Code Sec. 167(g) provides that depreciation deductions are figured by multiplying the cost basis of the property (but only amounts satisfying the Section 461(h) economic performance standard) by a fraction, the numerator of which is the year's income generated by the property, and the denominator of which is all income earned before the close of the 10th year following the year in which the property was placed in service. The depreciation deduction for the 10th tax year after the placed-in-service tax year equals the taxpayer's entire remaining basis in the property [Code Sec. 167(g)(1)(C)].

Participations and Residuals Included in Basis

A taxpayer may include participations and residuals in the adjusted basis of a property in the tax year that it is placed in service, but only to the extent that the participations and residuals relate to income estimated to be earned in connection with the property before the close of the tenth tax year after the tax year the property was placed in service [Code Sec. 167(g)(7)(A)].

As an alternative to including such participations and residuals in the adjusted basis of the property and recovering their cost over a 10-year period, a taxpayer may exclude the participations and residuals from the adjusted basis of the property and deduct them in full in the year that they are actually paid [Code Sec. 167(g)(7)(D)(i)]. The Conference Committee Report (H.R. Conf. Rep. No. 108-755) states that the decision to currently deduct these expenses may be made on a property-by-property basis but must be applied consistently with respect to a given property thereafter.

Participations and residuals are defined as costs the amount of which by contract varies with the amount of income earned in connection with the property [Code Sec. 167(g)(7)(B)].

Income from the property defined. The term "income from the property," for purposes of computing depreciation under the income forecast method, is defined as the taxpayer's gross income from the property [Code Sec. 167(g)(5)(E)].

How proposed regulations change computation of depreciation. In proposed regulations the IRS has revised how depreciation is computed under the income forecast method. Prop. Reg. § 1.167(n)-4(a) provides that a taxpayer's depreciation allowance for income forecast property is generally an amount that bears the same relationship to the depreciable basis of the property that the "current year income" for that year bears to the "forecasted total income" for the property.

Revised computation method. The proposed regulations introduce a revised computation to be used by taxpayers when conditions necessitate using a revised forecasted total income that differs from the forecasted total income used in computing depreciation allowances in previous years [Prop. Reg. § 1.167(n)-4(b)(1)]. Thus, for example, a taxpayer using the income forecast method for a motion picture would increase the forecast of total income to be earned from the motion picture if it becomes apparent that the motion picture is more popular than originally expected. After that realization, the taxpayer should use the revised computation to compute the allowance for income forecast depreciation for the motion picture. Under the revised computation, the unrecovered depreciable basis of the income forecast property is multiplied by a fraction—the numerator is current year income and the denominator is obtained by subtracting from revised forecasted total income the amounts of current year income from prior tax years.

When revised computation is required. The revised computation must be used if *forecasted total income* in the prior tax year is either:

- Less than 90 percent of "revised forecasted total income" for the year; or
- Greater than 110 percent of "revised forecasted total income" for the year [Prop Reg. § 1.167(n)-4(b)(2)].

Additional catch-up allowance. Several special rules exist for computing allowances for depreciation under the income forecast method. A special rule applies for certain basis redeterminations whereby an additional "catch up" allowance for depreciation is allowed in the year that basis is redetermined [Prop. Reg. § 1.167(n)-4(c)(1)]. Under this special rule, the additional depreciation allowance is an amount equal to the cumulative allowances for depreciation that would have been permitted in previous years had the basis redetermination amount been included in basis in the year the property was placed in service. It is intended that this additional allowance will make up for the potential back-loading of depreciation deductions that may otherwise occur if the additional amount were taken into account over the remaining income from the property and diminish the amount of look-back interest that may otherwise accrue. For example, contingent amounts are payments made to an author when actual book sales exceed a certain level. The contingent payments are not added to basis of the assets until the tax year in which all events occur which firmly establish the amount of the payments. These contingent basis amounts would be treated as basis redetermination amounts and would increase the basis of income forecast property in the year paid or incurred. Prop. Reg. § 1.167(n)-4(c)(1) provides for an additional catch-up allowance for depreciation in the year that basis is redetermined. The additional depreciation allowance would be equal to the cumulative allowances for depreciation that would have been recovered through depreciation allowances in prior years if the basis redetermination amount had been included in depreciable basis in the tax year that the book was originally placed in service.

Example 11-35: David, an accrual basis movie producer, enters into a contract with Eve, an author, under which David will make a film based on Eve's book. Eve performs no services for David to use the book as a basis for David's film. David pays Eve a fixed dollar amount upon entry into the agreement and promises to pay Eve a contingent payment of five percent of David's income from the film, beginning after the film has earned $100,000 (net of distribution costs). David estimates that forecasted total income from the film will be $200,000. The film earns $65,000 of current year income in year one, $30,000 in year two, and $25,000 in year three. David takes allowances for depreciation in year one ($65,000 divided by $200,000, multiplied by the basis of the film) and year two ($30,000 divided by $200,000, multiplied by the basis of the film). In year three, David's liability to Eve becomes fixed and David pays Eve $1,000. The $1,000 incurred by David is a basis redetermination amount that increases the basis of the film for purposes of computing David's depreciation allowance for the film for year three. In addition to the year three allowance based on current year income ($25,000 divided by $200,000 multiplied by the basis of the film, which includes for year three the $1,000 basis redetermination amount), David is entitled to an additional allowance for depreciation for year three under Prop. Reg. § 1.167(n)-4 (c)(1). This additional allowance is $475, the sum of the allowance of $325 that would have been allowed in year one ($65,000 divided by $200,000, multiplied by the $1,000 payment to Eve) and the allowance of $150 that would have been allowed in year two ($30,000 ÷ $200,000 × $1,000) if the $1,000 had been included in basis in the year that the film was placed in service.

Final year depreciation. A taxpayer may deduct as a depreciation allowance the remaining depreciable basis of income forecast property depreciated under the income forecast method in the earlier of:

- The year in which the taxpayer reasonably believes that the asset will produce no current income and no income in any subsequent tax year up to and including the 10th tax year after the property is placed in service; or
- The 10th year following the year the asset is placed in service [Code Sec. 167(g)(1)(C); Prop. Reg. § 1.167(n)-4(d)(1)].

Use of the income forecast method is elected on a property-by-property basis. Once elected, the income forecast method is a method of accounting that may not be changed without IRS consent. Modifications to forecasted total income to take into account information that becomes available after the property is placed in service in accordance with these proposed regulations is not a change in a method of accounting requiring IRS consent.

Computation of income. Prop. Reg. § 1.167(n)-3(a) provides that *current year income* is the income from an income forecast property for the current year (less the distribution costs of the income forecast property for such year), determined in accordance with the taxpayer's method of accounting. All income earned in connection with the income forecast property is included in current year income. In the case of a film, television show, or similar property, such income includes, but is not limited to:

- Income from foreign and domestic theatrical, television, and other releases and syndications;
- Income from releases, sales, rentals, and syndications of video tape, DVD, and other media; and
- Incidental income associated with the property, such as income from the financial exploitation of characters, designs, titles, scripts, and scores, but only to the extent that such incidental income is earned in connection with the ultimate use of such items by, or the ultimate sale of merchandise to, persons who are not related to the taxpayer.

***Forecasted total income* defined.** Taxpayers are required at the end of the tax year in which income forecast property is placed in service to make an accurate projection of all anticipated income to be earned from the income forecast property based on the conditions known to exist at that time. This estimate is referred to as *forecasted total income,* the sum of current year income for the year that income forecast property is placed in service, plus all income from the income forecast property that the taxpayer reasonably believes will be includible in current year income in subsequent tax years (as adjusted for distribution costs) up to and including the 10th tax year after the year in which the income forecast property is placed in service. Forecasted total income is based on the conditions known to exist at the end of the tax year for which the income forecast property is placed in service [Prop. Reg. § 1.167(n)-3(b)].

Revised forecasted total income. Taxpayers must evaluate the accuracy of their forecasts annually. In order to perform these evaluations of forecasted total income, taxpayers must compute *revised forecasted total income.* If information is discovered in a tax year following the year in which income forecast property is placed in service indicating that forecasted total income is inaccurate, a taxpayer must compute revised forecasted total income for the tax year. Revised forecasted total income is based on the conditions known to exist at the end of the tax year for which the revised forecast is being made.

Revised forecasted total income is defined as the sum of current year income for the current tax year and all prior tax years, plus all income from the income forecast property that the taxpayer reasonably believes will be includible in current year income in tax years after the current tax year up to and including the 10th tax year after the year in which the income forecast property is placed in service [Prop. Reg. § 1.167(n)-3(c)]. Taxpayers must use the revised computation if forecasted total income in the immediately preceding tax year falls outside a range bounded on the low end by 90 percent of revised forecasted total income for the current tax year, and on the upper end by 110 percent of revised forecasted total income for the current tax year. (In the situation where revised forecasted total income was used to compute income forecast depreciation in the immediately preceding tax year, this comparison is made by comparing the revised forecasted total income for the current tax year to revised forecasted total income for the immediately preceding tax year.) Taxpayers may elect to alter their computations of income forecast depreciation (using the revised computation detailed below) when revised forecasted total income differs from forecasted total income.

Syndication income from television series. Pursuant to Code Sec. 167(g)(5)(B), income from the syndication of a television series need not be included in the income forecast computation prior to the fourth tax year beginning after the date the first episode of the series is placed in service, unless an "arrangement relating to syndication" in the future exists. In such a case, syndication income is included in the income forecast computation at the time the arrangement relating to future syndication is made. This special rule also applies for purposes of applying the look-back method.

An *arrangement relating to syndication* of a series of television shows means any arrangement other than the first run exhibition agreement. For example, an arrangement for exhibition of a television series by individual television stations is an arrangement for syndication if it results in an exhibition of one or more episodes of the series beginning after one or more episodes of the series have been exhibited on a television network. A first-run exhibition agreement is an agreement under which any episode (including a pilot episode) of a television series is first placed in service within a particular market [Prop. Reg. § 1.167(n)-3(d)(2)].

Disposition of the property. Special rules apply if income forecast property is disposed of prior to the end of the 10th tax year after the year the property is placed in service. In such a case, Code Sec. 167(g)(5)(E) requires that for purposes of applying the look-back method, income from the disposition of the property is to be taken into account. Failure to apply a similar rule for purposes of computing income forecast depreciation in the year of disposition may permit a depreciation differential that would not be corrected through the operation of the look-back method (because the differential would arise in a year for which the period of time to which look-back interest would apply would be zero). Accordingly, the proposed regulations require taxpayers to take income from the disposition of income forecast property into account in the year of disposition in computing revised forecasted total income both for purposes of computing its income forecast depreciation and for purposes of applying the look-back method [Prop. Reg. § 1.167(n)-d(1)].

Example 11-36: ABCo places in service income forecast property with a depreciable basis of $100, and estimates that forecasted total income from the property will be $200. In tax year one, current year income is $80. The depreciation allowance for year one is $40, computed by multiplying the depreciable basis of the property of $100 by the fraction obtained by dividing current year income of $80 by forecasted total income of $200.

Example 11-37: Assume the same facts as in example above. In year two, the taxpayer's current year income is $40. In addition, the taxpayer computes revised forecasted total income to be $176. The taxpayer is required to compute its depreciation allowance for this property using the revised computation because forecasted total income in year one of $200 is greater than 110 percent of revised forecasted total income in year two (110 percent of $176 = $193.6). The depreciation allowance for tax year two computed under the revised computation is $25, computed by multiplying the unrecovered depreciable basis of $60 by the fraction obtained by dividing current year income of $40 by $96 (revised forecasted total income of $176 less current year income from prior tax years of $80).

Example 11-38: Assume the same facts as in example above. Because the taxpayer used the revised computation in year two, the revised computation applies in year three. In year three, the taxpayer's current year income is $32. The depreciation allowance for year three computed under the revised computation is $20, computed by multiplying the unrecovered depreciable basis of $60 by the fraction obtained by dividing current year income of $32 by $96 (revised forecasted total income of $176 less current year income from tax years prior to the change in estimate tax year of $80) [Prop. Reg. § 1.167(n)-4.]

Look-back calculation required. If you claimed depreciation deductions under the income forecast method in prior years you must adjust taxable income for the third and tenth tax year following the year the property was placed in service by the difference between the depreciation calculated using actual income amounts and estimated income amounts. You either pay or receive interest on the calculated underpayment or overpayment, respectively, of tax for each of the prior tax years. You must pay interest to the extent that depreciation, calculated using estimated rather than actual income from the property, was too rapid. You will receive interest if depreciation was too slow. The look-back method does not apply if:

- The property had a cost basis of $100,000 or less [Code Sec. 167(g)(3)], or
- Actual income earned in connection with the property for the period before the close of the recomputation years is within 10 percent of the estimated income used to compute the original deductions [Code Sec. 167(g)(4)].

In order to apply the look-back method, prior year allowances for depreciation for income forecast property are recomputed using revised forecasted total income for the recomputation year in lieu of forecasted total income (or, if appropriate, revised forecasted income) from the property that was used in the computation of depreciation under the income forecast method in the prior year. If a taxpayer sells or otherwise disposes of income forecast property, the amount realized upon the disposition of the property is included in determining revised forecasted total income from the property in the year of disposition. These recomputed depreciation allowances are then used to determine either a hypothetical overpayment of tax or a hypothetical underpayment of tax.

Generally, taxpayers must determine the hypothetical overpayment or underpayment of tax arising from the change in depreciation allowances by recomputing their tax liability. Thus, a taxpayer's tax liability for each prior year is recomputed by substituting the recomputed depreciation allowances for the depreciation allowances originally claimed. The recomputed tax liability is then compared to the taxpayer's actual liability. For purposes of this comparison, the taxpayer must determine the actual tax liability for each prior year based on the information available on the later of:

- The due date of the return, including extensions;
- The date of an amended return;
- The date a return is adjusted by examination; or
- The date of any previous application of the look-back requirement for the income forecast property.

The result of this comparison is a hypothetical overpayment or underpayment of tax for each prior year in which allowances for depreciation were claimed for income forecast property subject to the look-back method.

Pass-through entities that are not closely held pass-through entities must use a simplified method to compute their hypothetical overpayment or underpayment for each prior year in which allowances for depreciation were claimed for income forecast property subject to the look-back method.

Regardless of the method used, the resulting hypothetical overpayments or underpayments are then used to compute interest that is to be charged or credited on each of these amounts. Interest is generally computed from the due date of the return (not including extensions) for the years in which changes in depreciation allowances occur to the due date of the recomputation year (not including extensions). Special rules are provided for taxpayers who do not use the simplified method where changes in depreciation allowances affect tax liability in years other than the year in which the changes in depreciation allowances occur. Interest is computed using the overpayment rate under Code Sec. 6621. The amounts resulting from these computations are netted to arrive at look-back interest due to the taxpayer or payable to the government for the recomputation year. For purposes of computing taxable income, look-back interest is treated as interest on an overpayment or underpayment of tax. Under Code Sec. 167(g)(5)(D), look-back interest required to be paid is treated as a tax liability for penalty purposes.

12

Business Deductions

BUSINESS EXPENSES IN GENERAL

What is a deductible expense? . . . . ¶ 12,001
Expenses incurred in trade, business, or profession . . . . ¶ 12,005
Tax treatment of capital expenditures . . . . ¶ 12,010
Distinguishing repairs from capitalized expenses . . . . ¶ 12,011
Environmental clean-up costs . . . . ¶ 12,012
Expenses for tax-exempt income . . ¶ 12,015
Enhanced charitable deductions . . ¶ 12,020
Expenses for political purpose . . . . ¶ 12,025
Illegal business or payment . . . . . . ¶ 12,030
Lobbying expenses . . . . ¶ 12,035
Business start-up expenses . . . . . . ¶ 12,040

COMPENSATION FOR SERVICES

Deduction for compensation . . . . . ¶ 12,045
Reasonableness of compensation . . . . ¶ 12,050
Payment for services . . . . ¶ 12,055
Commissions . . . . ¶ 12,060
Bonuses and other additional compensation . . . . ¶ 12,065
Severance pay . . . . ¶ 12,070
Fees to attorneys, accountants, and other professionals . . . . ¶ 12,075
Golden parachute payments . . . . . ¶ 12,080
Compensation cap for publicly held corporations . . . . ¶ 12,085
Executive compensation limits for financial institutions participating in TARP . . . . ¶ 12,086
Health insurance provider $500,000 deduction limit . . . . ¶ 12,087

RENT, ADVERTISING, INSURANCE

Rent . . . . ¶ 12,095
Advertising expenses . . . . ¶ 12,100
Insurance premiums . . . . ¶ 12,105
Interest expenses . . . . ¶ 12,110

MISCELLANEOUS TRADE OR BUSINESS EXPENSES

Expenses of self-employeds . . . . . ¶ 12,115
Expenses incurred in trade or business by employee . . . . ¶ 12,120
Home office deduction . . . . ¶ 12,125
Education expenses . . . . ¶ 12,130
Uniforms and work clothes . . . . . . ¶ 12,135

SPECIAL DEDUCTION PROBLEMS

Research and experimental expenditures . . . . ¶ 12,145
Deduction for domestic production activities . . . . ¶ 12,150

Energy-efficient commercial building deduction . . . . ¶12,151
Film and television production costs . . . . ¶12,152

DEPLETION DEDUCTION

What is depletion? . . . . ¶12,155
Who is entitled to the deduction for depletion? . . . . ¶12,160
Figuring the depletion deduction . . . . ¶12,165
Cost depletion . . . . ¶12,170
Percentage depletion . . . . ¶12,175
Treatment of bonuses and royalties . . . . ¶12,180

SPECIAL DEPLETION PROBLEMS

Depletion of timber . . . . ¶12,185
Books of account . . . . ¶12,190

MINING EXPENSES

Mine exploration expenditures . . ¶12,195
Mining development expenditures . . . . ¶12,200

FARMERS' EXPENSES

Expenses of farmers . . . . ¶12,205
Soil and water conservation expenditures . . . . ¶12,210
Amortization of reforestation expenditures . . . . ¶12,215

COMMUNITY RENEWAL PROVISIONS

Incentives to stimulate growth in renewal communities . . . . ¶12,220

BUSINESS EXPENSES IN GENERAL

A broad variety of costs qualify as deductible business expenses. Some of these are discussed in other chapters: For example, retirement plan contributions are covered in Chapter 3, fringe benefits provided by employer to employees in Chapter 4, travel and entertainment in Chapter 10 and depreciation in Chapter 11. This chapter brings together a diverse group of deductible expenses incurred in business by companies, self-employeds, and employees alike. The write-offs range from compensation, insurance, home offices and education to depletion and farming expenses.

¶12,001 WHAT IS A DEDUCTIBLE EXPENSE?

When taxpayers purchase property that is used in their trade or business, the expense can be either deducted currently as an ordinary and necessary business expense, or capitalized and recovered through depreciation or amortization deductions over a period of time as prescribed by statute [Code Secs. 167, 168]. A taxpayer who meets certain conditions as discussed in ¶11,045 can also elect under Code Sec. 179 to expense immediately the cost of acquiring tangible personal property that is used in the active conduct of a trade or business. Taxpayers will generally prefer to deduct their expenses as ordinary and necessary business expenses under Code Sec. 162.

In order for an expenditure to be deductible, it must be (1) ordinary and necessary; (2) paid or incurred during the tax year; and (3) related to carrying on a trade or business [Code Sec. 162; Reg. §1.162-1].

.01 Ordinary and Necessary

An *ordinary* expense is one that is commonly incurred in your trade or business. It may vary, depending on the time, place and circumstances under which it is incurred.[1] A *necessary* expense need not be "essential." It may be necessary if it is "appropriate and helpful" to your business or occupation.[2]

Among items included as business expenses are: management expenses; commissions; labor; supplies; incidental repairs; operating expenses of automobiles used in the trade or business; traveling expenses incurred while away from home in the pursuit of a trade or business; advertising and other selling expenses; insurance premiums against fire, storm, theft, accident, or other similar business losses; rents paid for use of business property; and expenses incurred to protect advantageous business agreements.[3] [Reg. § 1.162-1(a)].

.02 How Expenses Are Treated on the Return

Business expenses are generally deducted from your adjusted gross income [Code Sec. 62(a)(1)]. If you are the sole owner of an unincorporated business, you must report business income and expenses on Schedule C (Form 1040). Partnerships are required to file Form 1065 and a Schedule K listing the total of the partners' share of income, deductions, credits, etc. Each partner's distributive share of specially allocated items is shown on the appropriate line of his Schedule K-1.

For further discussion of employee business expenses, see ¶ 12,120.

.03 Which Deductions Will the IRS Challenge

Based on a study conducted by the General Accounting Office ("GAO"), the business deductions most likely to be vigorously contested by the IRS involve the following:

1. **Inadequate documentation of expenses**. When the IRS raises this issue, they are claiming that you failed to provide documentation or evidence of a claimed business expense or did not have adequate documentation necessary to deduct a claimed expense. In the absence of supporting evidence critical to support the business deduction, the IRS will argue that the expense has been distorted for tax purposes. For example, in *Interex, Inc.*[4] the Court of Appeals for the First Circuit denied a corporation's deduction for legal and accounting services after its president and sole shareholder could not explain how the corporation's tax and legal advisor calculated the amount of the deduction. The taxpayer could not describe the nature of the legal and accounting services provided to the corporation. The court concluded that the absence of key details about the expenses proved that they were distorted.
2. **Deduction of unreasonable compensation.** The IRS is likely to claim in these cases that the closely held corporations deducted more than was reasonable for an officer's salary or for rent on rental property owned by a corporate officer. The

---

[1] *T.H. Welch*, SCt, 3 USTC ¶ 1164, 290 US 111, 54 SCt 8; *Dunn & McCarthy, Inc.*, CA-2, 43-2 USTC ¶ 9688, 139 F2d 242; *Kentucky Util. Co.*, CA-6, 68-1 USTC ¶ 9361, 394 F2d 631.

[2] *S.B. Heininger*, SCt, 44-1 USTC ¶ 9109, 320 US 467, 64 SCt 249.

[3] *T.J. Enterprises, Inc.*, 101 TC 581, Dec. 49,473 (1993).

[4] *Interex, Inc.*, CA-1, 2003-1 USTC ¶ 50,272, 321 F3d 55.

disallowed deductions will be labeled as disguised dividends to the individuals receiving the salary or rent and will thus be taxable as income [¶12,050].

3. **No trade or business existed**. The IRS will disallow the deductions taxpayers claim from a for-profit trade or business because the IRS finds that the taxpayers are not engaged in a profit-making activity. These will be "hobby loss" cases where the taxpayer deducted expenses for an activity that the IRS characterizes as recreational in nature rather than constituting a trade or business [Ch. 23].
4. **Personal expenses not deductible.** In these cases the taxpayers will claim deductions for business-related expenses that the IRS will claim were actually personal in nature. Personal expenses such as nonbusness related life insurance premiums and rent on an apartment used solely as a personal residence are not deductible.
5. **Inadequate substantiation of expenses.** The IRS will argue expenses for meals, entertainment, travel, and automobiles have not been substantiated adequately. Not only must a taxpayer show that such an expense is ordinary and necessary to the taxpayer's business, but also that the expense is directly related to or associated with the business. Automobile and travel expenses are the most commonly disallowed expenses for inadequate substantiation.

¶12,005 EXPENSES INCURRED IN TRADE, BUSINESS, OR PROFESSION

.01 General Rule

Expenses paid or incurred by an individual to purchase property used in the taxpayer's trade, business or profession are gathered on Schedule C and deducted from the entrepreneur's adjusted gross income [Code Sec. 62(a)(1); Temp. Reg. § 1.62-1T(c)(1)]. They are not limited to actual out-of-pocket "expenses," but may also include losses, bad debts, depreciation, etc. [¶12,115]. To be deductible as ordinary and necessary expenses of a trade, business or profession, the expenses must be:

- *Directly* connected with the taxpayer's trade, business or profession [Code Sec. 162(a); Reg. § 1.162-1]; and
- *Reasonable* in amount.[5]

.02 Examples of Deductible Expenses

Dissolution and Liquidation Expenses

Dissolution and liquidation expenses of a corporation are deductible as ordinary and necessary business expenses in the year dissolution occurs.[6]

Expenses for Handicapped

Costs up to $15,000 to make any facility or vehicle used in a trade or business more accessible and usable to the handicapped or elderly are currently deductible [Code Sec. 190]. See also Ch. 14 for availability of tax credit.

---

[5] *Lincoln Elec. Co.*, CA-6, 49-2 USTC ¶9388, 176 F2d 815, *cert. denied,* 338 US 949, 70 SCt 488.

[6] *Idaho Power Co.*, SCt, 74-2 USTC ¶9521, 418 US 1, 94 SCt 2757.

Banks Can Deduct Currently Loan Origination Costs

In *PNC Bancorp*,[7] the Court of Appeals for the Third Circuit held that a bank could deduct currently the internal and external costs that they incur in connection with the issuance of loans to their customers because expenses were a routine part of the banks' daily business, and the services procured with these outlays were integral to the basic execution of the banking business for decades.

Merger Investigation Costs

In *Wells Fargo & Co.*,[8] the Eighth Circuit held that a bank could currently deduct its officers' salaries and its investigatory and due diligence legal fees incurred in connection with its acquisition by a consolidated group. However, expenses incurred after the determined "final decision" date were incurred to facilitate consummation of the acquisition, and therefore, required capitalization.

Merger Termination Fee

In *Santa Fe Pacific Gold Co.*,[9] the Tax Court concluded that a merger termination fee paid to clear the way for a merger with another suitor was a currently deductible expense under Code Sec. 162.

Costs of Meeting ISO 9000 International Quality Standards

Costs incurred to obtain, maintain, and renew ISO 9000 certification of international standards for quality management systems are generally deductible as ordinary and necessary business expenses even though the businesses derive some long-term benefits from the certification.[10]

Deduction Allowed for Removal of Depreciable Asset

Costs incurred to retire and remove an old depreciable asset deductible even though the expenses were incurred in connection with the installation of a replacement asset.[11]

Legal and Litigation-Related Expenses: Corporations: Takeover Expenses

In *Staley Manufacturing Co.*,[12] most of the investment banker fees incurred by a corporation in defending against a series of unsolicited but eventually successful takeover bids were deductible as ordinary and necessary business expenses. However, to the extent that the bankers' evaluation of the corporation's stock helped to facilitate the merger, fees relating to facilitative work were capital expenditures. In Letter Ruling 200911002, the IRS ruled that a corporation could deduct payments it made to settle a securities class action lawsuit, including legal fees and other administrative fees attributable to the lawsuit and its settlement. It was irrelevant that some of the settled claims had some connection to a stock offering.

---

[7] *PNC Bancorp*, CA-3, 2000-1 USTC ¶50,483, 212 F3d 822.

[8] *Wells Fargo & Co.*, CA-8, 2000-2 USTC ¶50,697, 224 F3d 874.

[9] *Santa Fe Pacific Gold Co.*, 132 TC No. 12 (2009).

[10] Rev. Rul. 2000-4, 2000-1 CB 331.

[11] Rev. Rul. 2000-7, 2000-1 CB 712.

[12] *Staley Mfg. Co.*, CA-7, 97-2 USTC ¶50,521, 119 F3d 482.

Bank FDIC Fees

In *Metrocorp Inc.*,[13] entrance and exit fees paid to the FDIC by the taxpayer on its acquisition of a failed savings and loan association in a conversion transaction did not provide significant future benefits and were therefore currently deductible as ordinary and necessary business expenses.

License and Insurance Expenses

Expenses incurred by trucking company for license premiums, permits, fees and insurance were deductible even though these expenses partially benefited the following tax year.[14]

Stock Redemption Settlement Payment

Settlement payment made to former CEO to terminate an employment agreement including amounts paid to redeem company stock.[15]

¶12,010 TAX TREATMENT OF CAPITAL EXPENDITURES

.01 What Is a Capitalized Expense

A capital expenditure is an outlay to acquire property or make a permanent improvement that extends beyond the tax year. Code Sec. 263(a) provides that no immediate deduction is allowed for: (1) any amount paid for new buildings or for permanent improvements or betterments made to increase the value of any property or estate; or (2) any amount paid in restoring property or in addition to depreciation which represents an allowance for exhaustion. Capitalized expenses are written off by means of a series of amortization, depreciation, or depletion deductions over a number of years.

In addition, amounts paid to acquire, produce, or improve real or tangible personal property must be capitalized [Reg. § 1.263(a)-1(a)]. Note that the capitalization rules do not change the tax treatment of any amount that is specifically addressed in another provision of the Internal Revenue Code such as: (1) Code Sec. 263A which requires taxpayers to capitalize the direct and allocable indirect costs to property produced by the taxpayer and property acquired for resale; and (2) Code Sec. 195 which requires taxpayers to capitalize certain costs as start-up expenditures. For further discussion of Code Sec. 263A, see ¶17,045 and for further discussion of Code Sec. 195, see ¶12,040.

Reg. § 1.263(a)-1(d) provides the following examples of capital expenditures:

1. An amount paid to acquire or produce a unit of real or personal tangible property [Reg. § 1.263(a)-2];
2. An amount paid to improve a unit of real or personal tangible property [Reg. § 1.263(a)-3];

[13] *Metrocorp, Inc.*, 116 TC 211, Dec. 54,308 (2001).

[14] *U.S. Freightways Corp.*, CA-7, 2001-2 USTC ¶50,731, 270 F3d 1137.

[15] *Chief Industries, Inc.*, 87 TCM 1002, Dec. 55,554(M), TC Memo. 2004-45.

3. An amount paid to acquire or create intangibles [Reg. § 1.263(a)-3];
4. An amount paid or incurred to facilitate an acquisition of a trade or business, a change in capital structure of a business entity, and certain other transactions [Reg. § 1.263(a)-5];
5. An amount paid to acquire or create interests in land, such as easements, life estates, mineral interests, timber rights, zoning variances, or other interests in land;
6. An amount assessed and paid under an agreement between bondholders or shareholders of a corporation to be used in a reorganization of the corporation or voluntary contributions by shareholders to the capital of the corporation for any corporate purpose [Code Sec. 118; Reg. § 1.118-1]; and
7. An amount paid by a holding company to carry out a guaranty of dividends at a specified rate on the stock of a subsidiary corporation for the purpose of securing new capital for the subsidiary and increasing the value of its stockholdings in the subsidiary. This amount must be added to the cost of the stock in the subsidiary.

.02 Tax Treatment of Success-Based Fees

Reg. § 1.263(a)-5(a) provides that a taxpayer must capitalize an amount paid to facilitate a business acquisition or reorganization transaction. Such costs include those incurred in the process of investigating or otherwise pursuing the transaction.

An amount that is contingent on the successful closing of a transaction described in Reg. § 1.263(a)-5(a) as a "success-based fee" is presumed to facilitate the transaction. A taxpayer may rebut the presumption that the expense must be capitalized by maintaining sufficient documentation to establish that a portion of the fee is allocable to activities that do not facilitate the transaction.

The treatment of success-based fees has generated considerable controversy between taxpayers and the IRS. Disputes have arisen regarding the type and extent of documentation required to establish that a portion of a success-based fee is allocable to activities that do not facilitate a business acquisition or reorganization transaction. In Rev. Proc. 2011-29,[16] the IRS provides a safe harbor election for allocating a success-based fee between activities that facilitate a covered transaction and activities that do not. Rev. Proc. 2011-29 applies to a taxpayer that:

1. Pays or incurs a success-based fee for services performed in the process of investigating or otherwise pursuing a transaction described in Reg. § 1.263(a)-5(e)(3); and
2. Makes the safe harbor election.

The IRS will not challenge a taxpayer's allocation of a success-based fee between activities that facilitate a transaction described in Reg. § 1.263(a)-5(e)(3) and activities that do not facilitate the transaction if the taxpayer:

1. Treats 70 percent of the amount of the success-based fee as an amount that does not facilitate the transaction;
2. Capitalizes the remaining 30 percent as an amount that does facilitate the transaction; and

[16] Rev. Proc. 2011-29, IRB 2011-18, 746.

3. Attaches a statement to its original federal income tax return for the tax year the success-based fee is paid or incurred, stating that the taxpayer is electing the safe harbor, identifying the transaction, and stating the success-based fee amounts that are deducted and capitalized.

An election under Rev. Proc. 2011-29 applies only to the transaction for which the election is made and, once made, is irrevocable. Moreover, the election applies with respect to all success-based fees paid or incurred by the taxpayer in the transaction for which the election is made.

.03 Types of Expenses That Are Capitalized

Takeover Expenses

The U.S. Supreme Court held in the seminal case, *Indopco, Inc.*,[17] that financial and legal expenses to facilitate a corporation's own friendly takeover must be capitalized rather than deducted currently because the takeover benefits the corporation generally and the benefits extend beyond the tax year in which the costs were incurred [¶12,075].

Legal Fees Incurred to Defend Against Lawsuit That Arose with Respect to an Acquisition or a Liability Assumed in an Acquisition

Legal fees incurred to defend against an antitrust suit that arose with respect to an acquisition or a liability assumed in an acquisition must be capitalized.[18]

Salaries in Connection with an Acquisition

In *D.J. Lychuk*,[19] an S corporation had to capitalize salaries and benefits paid in connection with the acquisition of automobile financing installment contracts.

Mutual Fund Start-Up Costs and Loan Origination Costs

Mutual fund start-up costs must be capitalized because the business benefits from the mutual fund profits far beyond the year in which the fund was started up.[20]

Payments to Eliminate Competition

If the restraint is for a definite term, the cost may be written off over that time period. However, if the restriction is permanent or indefinite, no deduction is allowed. If an agreement not to compete is part of indivisible contract for sale of all assets of a business, no deduction is allowed.[21]

Intangibles

The cost of acquiring business goodwill, trademarks, patents and other intangibles may be amortized over 15 years [Code Sec. 197; See Ch. 11]. The economic benefit from below-market financing can be an amortizable intangible asset if the taxpayer can establish a fair market value and limited useful life.[22]

---

[17] *Indopco*, SCt, 92-1 USTC ¶50,113, 503 US 79, 112 SCt 1039; *F.W. Woodward*, SCt, 70-1 USTC ¶9348, 397 US 572.

[18] *American Stores Co.*, 114 TC 458, Dec. 53,901 (2000); *Illinois Tool Works, Inc.*, CA-7, 2004-1 USTC ¶50,130, 355 F3d 997.

[19] *D.J. Lychuk*, 116 TC 374, Dec. 54,353 (2001).

[20] *FMR Corp.*, 110 TC 402, Dec. 52,745 (1998).

[21] *B.T. Babbitt, Inc.*, 32 BTA 693, Dec. 8976, *acq.* 1935-2 CB 2; *Toledo Blade Co.*, 11 TC 1079, Dec. 16,736 (1948), *aff'd*, CA-6, 50-1 USTC ¶9234, 180 F2d 357, *cert. denied*, 340 US 811, 71 SCt 38.

[22] *Federal Home Loan Mortgage Corp.*, 121 TC 279, Dec. 55,333 (2003).

Payments for Customer Lists and Brokerage Accounts

Customer lists are written off over 15 years because they are Section 197 assets.

Asbestos Removal Expenses

The cost of removing asbestos insulation from equipment and buildings[23] must be capitalized. But in *Cinergy Corp*,[24] the Court of Federal Claims held that a taxpayer may deduct the cost of removing and encapsulating deteriorating asbestos that it had installed in an office building because the work wasn't done to refurbish the building or prepare it for a new use and the cost represented only a small fraction of the building's value.

▶ **PRACTICE TIPS:** The court in Norwest[25] held that asbestos removal costs must be capitalized when performed in conjunction with an overall plan of building rehabilitation. This does not necessarily mean that all asbestos removal costs must be capitalized if they are performed independent of other remodeling projects. All asbestos removal work should therefore be performed, where possible, independent of other renovation projects. This separation will improve your chance to deduct your asbestos removal costs. You should separate the asbestos removal project from the overall building renovation by taking the following steps:

1. Renovate the building and remove the asbestos at different times, preferably in different tax years.
2. Have different contractors renovate the building and remove the asbestos.
3. Pay for the building renovation and asbestos removal with separate checks.
4. Make sure that the asbestos removal and building renovation are not part of one big full-blown general plan of rehabilitation.

Greenmail Paid to Corporate Raider

"Greenmail," which is an amount paid to eliminate a corporate raider's threat to a target company must be amortized over the life of the stock purchase agreement if the premiums are really paid to purchase stock.[26]

Costs Incurred to Change Manufacturing Process

Costs incurred by a company to initially adopt a manufacturing process must be capitalized because the new plan provide significant long-term benefits lasting substantially beyond the end of the tax year.[27]

.04 Exceptions to *INDOPCO*

In the following situations the IRS has allowed an immediate deduction of specific expenses, even though the outlays produced some future benefit:

---

[23] LTR 9240004 (June 29, 1992).

[24] *Cinergy Corp.*, FedCl, 2003-1 USTC ¶ 50,302, 55 FedCl 489.

[25] *Norwest Corp.*, 108 TC 265, Dec. 52,008 (1997).

[26] *Wrangler Apparel Corp.*, DC-NC, 96-2 USTC ¶ 50,634, 931 FSupp 420.

[27] LTR 9544001 (July 21, 1995).

- Advertising expenses,[28] including graphic design costs for product packaging;[29]
- Marketing and advertising costs incurred before regulatory approval of a product for sale;[30]
- Incidental building repairs that don't appreciably prolong useful life;[31]
- Severance pay;[32]
- Costs of opening new retail stores;[33] and
- Employer's training costs related to an existing line of business.[34] This means that amounts paid or incurred for training, including the costs of trainers and routine updates of training materials, are deductible as business expenses even though they may have some future benefit. Training costs must be capitalized only where the training is intended to obtain future benefits significantly beyond those traditionally associated with training provided in the ordinary course of business. For example, the cost of training employees of an electric utility to operate a new nuclear plant would be capitalized because these expenses are akin to start-up costs of a new business.

▶ **PRACTICE TIP:** If you want your *INDOPCO*-type business expenses to be deductible, adopt the following strategies:

1. Never link your business expense to anything that is called "new" or "innovative." In fact, avoid using these buzz words at all costs. They will trigger the attention of the IRS. If you use these words the IRS will think that your everyday business expenses have long-term benefits and should thus be capitalized. For example, expenses incurred to train employees to operate new equipment should be in an "existing line of business."
2. Clearly identify the importance of the immediate or short-term benefits that will result from your expenditure of funds. In doing so you hopefully will de-emphasize any attendant long-term benefits. For example, expenses incurred to train employees should be incurred to improve performance in the regular conduct of your business.
3. Focus on the recurring nature of the expenses to show that they must be spent frequently and are therefore not one-time expenses with long-term lasting effects.
4. Argue that any long-term benefits are merely an incidental, unintended and unanticipated by-product.
5. If applicable, call the expenditure a repair intended to fix something that's wrong or broken. Avoid the terms overhaul, renovation, improvement, remodeling, refurbishment, betterment, or advancement. These make the expense look like a capital expense. Maintain a periodic maintenance program for your business so expenditures can be consistently lumped into the immediately deductible improvement category of expenses.

---

[28] Rev. Rul. 92-80, 1992-2 CB 57.

[29] *RJR Nabisco, Inc.*, 76 TCM 71, Dec. 52,786(M), TC Memo. 1998-252.

[30] FSA 199939035 (Aug. 9, 1999).

[31] Rev. Rul. 94-12, 1994-1 CB 36.

[32] Rev. Rul. 94-77, 1994-2 CB 19.

[33] LTR 9645002 (June 21, 1996).

[34] Rev. Rul. 96-62, 1996-2 CB 9.

6. Rather than lumping a group of expenses into one big pot, divide them up into separate individual expenses that look more like business expenses that are incurred each year.

.05 Capitalization Requirements for Intangibles

A taxpayer must capitalize the following amounts paid with respect to intangibles:

1. Amounts paid to create or enhance a separate and distinct intangible asset that is capable of being sold or transferred apart from a trade or business;
2. Amounts paid to acquire any intangible from another party in a purchase or similar transaction;
3. Amounts paid to create an intangible relating to financial interests, prepaid expenses, memberships and privileges, rights obtained from a government agency, contract rights, contract terminations, benefits arising from the provision, production, or improvement of real property, and amounts spent to defend or perfect title to intangible property); or
4. Amounts paid to facilitate an acquisition or creation of an intangible described above in (1)-(3) [Reg. § 1.263(a)-4(b)(1)]. In determining whether an amount is paid to facilitate a transaction, the fact that the amount would or would not have been paid but for the transaction is relevant but is not determinative. An amount paid to determine the value or price of an intangible is an amount paid in the process of investigating or otherwise pursuing the transaction [Reg. § 1.263(a)-4(e)].

Amounts Paid to Create or Enhance a Separate and Distinct Intangible Asset

A taxpayer must capitalize an amount paid to create or enhance a separate and distinct intangible asset [Reg. § 1.263(a)-4(b)(1)(iii)]. A separate and distinct intangible asset is a property interest of ascertainable and measurable value in money's worth that is subject to protection under state, federal, or foreign law and the possession and control of which is intrinsically capable of being sold, transferred or pledged separate and apart from a trade or business. A fund or similar account is treated as a separate and distinct intangible asset of the taxpayer if amounts in the fund may revert to the taxpayer. Amounts paid to create or terminate contract rights do not create a separate and distinct intangible asset. Furthermore, an amount paid to create a package design, computer software, or an income stream from the performance of services under a contract is not treated as an amount that creates a separate and distinct intangible asset [Reg. § 1.263(a)-4(b)(3)].

.06 Election to Capitalize Rights and Benefits Not Exceeding 12 Months

A taxpayer is not required to capitalize amounts paid to create any right or benefit that does not last longer than the earlier of: (1) 12 months beyond the date the taxpayer realizes the right or benefit; or (2) the end of the next tax year after payment is made [Reg. § 1.263(a)-4(f)(1)]. For contract terminations, the duration of the benefit is the unexpired term of the agreement. If the original agreement contains a provision that allows termination after a certain notice period, an amount paid to shorten the notice period creates a benefit for the time the notice was shortened. However, there are exceptions to this 12-month rule for amounts paid to create or facilitate the creation of a: (1) financial interest, such as an ownership interest, a debt interest, or a financial instrument; (2) Section 197 intangible, such as goodwill, patent, copyrights, trademarks, and permits; and (3) intangible of indefinite duration, such as a license granted by the government that allows the taxpayer to operate a business [Reg. § 1.263(a)-4(f)]. A taxpayer may elect not to apply the 12-month rule to categories of similar transactions. A taxpayer makes the election by treating the amounts as capital expenditures in its timely filed original federal income tax return (including extensions) for the tax year during which the amounts are paid. In the case of an affiliated group of corporations filing a consolidated return, the election is made separately with respect to each member of the group and not with respect to the group as a whole. In the case of an S corporation or partnership, the election is made by the S corporation or by the partnership and not by the shareholders or partners [Reg. § 1.263(a)-4(f)(7)].

.07 *De Minimis* Rule

Under the *de minimis* rule in Reg. § 1.263(a)-4(d)(6)(v), a taxpayer is not required to capitalize amounts paid to another party to create, originate, enter into, renew or renegotiate an agreement providing the taxpayer the right to use or be compensated for the use of tangible or intangible property if the aggregate of all amounts paid with respect to the agreement does not exceed $5,000. If the aggregate of all amounts paid with respect to that agreement exceeds $5,000, then all amounts must be capitalized. An amount paid in the form of property is valued at its fair market value at the time of the payment. A taxpayer that reasonably expects to create, originate, enter into, renew or renegotiate at least 25 similar agreements during the tax year may establish a pool of agreements for purposes of determining the amounts paid with respect to the agreements in the pool. Under this pooling method, the amount paid with respect to each agreement included in the pool is equal to the average amount paid with respect to all agreements included in the pool. A taxpayer computes the average amount paid with respect to all agreements included in the pool by dividing the sum of all amounts paid with respect to all agreements included in the pool by the number of agreements included in the pool.

¶12,011 DISTINGUISHING REPAIRS FROM CAPITALIZED EXPENSES

.01 General Rule for Capital Expenditures

Code Sec. 262 requires the capitalization of amounts paid to acquire, produce, or improve tangible property whereas Code Sec. 162 allows the deduction of all ordinary and necessary business expenses, including the costs of certain supplies, repairs, and maintenance. It is often very difficult for taxpayers to distinguish business expenses which are deductible under Code Sec. 162 in the year incurred from capitalized expenses which are deductible over a period of time by means of annual depreciation deduction under Code Sec. 262. The distinction between capitalized improvements and deductible repairs is not always clear. But here is a useful general guide:

> A repair is expenditure for the purpose of keeping the property in an ordinarily efficient operating condition. It does not add to the value of property, nor does it appreciably prolong its life. It merely keeps the property in an operating condition over its probable useful life for the uses for which it was acquired. Expenditures for repair purposes are distinguishable from those for replacements, alterations, improvements or additions that prolong the life of the property, increase its value, or make it adaptable to a different use. . . . [O]ne is a deductible maintenance charge, while the others are additions to capital investment that should be capitalized over time.[35]

The IRS has released final regulations that provide a general framework for distinguishing capital expenditures from deductible supply, repair and maintenance costs. The regulations provide rules for the following:

- Materials and supplies [Reg. § 1.162-3];
- Repairs and maintenance [Reg. § 1.162-4];
- Capital expenditures [Reg. § 1.263-1];
- Amounts paid for acquisition/ production of tangible property [Reg. § 1.263(a)-2)]; or
- Amounts paid for the improvement of tangible property [Reg. § 1.263(1)-3].

.02 Costs of Materials and Supplies

The cost of nonincidental materials and supplies are generally deducted in the tax year first used or consumed [Reg. § 1.162-3(a)(1)]. The terms "materials and supplies" are defined in Reg. § 1.162-3(c)(1) as tangible property used or consumed in the taxpayer's business operations that is not inventory and that:

- Is a component that is acquired to maintain, repair, or improve a unit of tangible property owned, leased, or serviced by the taxpayer, but is not acquired as part of any single unit of tangible property;
- Consists of fuel, lubricants, water, and similar items that are reasonably expected to be consumed in 12 months or less, beginning when used in a taxpayer's operations;
- Is a unit of property that has an economic useful life of 12 months or less, beginning when the property is used or consumed in the taxpayer's operations;
- A unit of property with an acquisition or production cost less than $200; or
- Is identified by the IRS in published guidance as materials and supplies.

Optional Election to Capitalize Rotable and Temporary Spare Parts

Rotable and temporary spare parts are materials and supplies that are deducted in the year used or consumed unless the taxpayer elects an optional method of accounting for the parts [Reg. § 1.162-3(a)(2)]. A rotable spare part is defined in Reg. § 1.162-3(c)(2) as a material or supply which is installed on a unit of property, removed from the property, repaired or improved, and either reinstalled on the same or other property or stored for later installation. Temporary spare parts are components used temporarily until a new or repaired part can be installed and then are

---

[35] *Illinois Merchants Trust Co., Ex.*, 4 BTA 103, Dec. 1452, *acq.* 1926-2 CB 2.

removed and stored for later installation. Standby emergency spare parts are parts acquired for a particular machine and set aside to avoid substantial operational time loss. Standby spare parts are usually expensive, and they are not subject to periodic replacement, acquired in quantity, repaired or reused.

Only amounts paid for rotable, temporary or standby emergency spare parts qualify for an optional election to capitalize and depreciate as a separate asset [Reg. § 1.162-3(d)(1)]. The election would apply to amounts paid to acquire or produce any rotable, temporary or standby emergency spare part. Any property for which this election is made shall not be treated as a material or a supply. This limitation is necessary so different recovery periods could not apply to a capitalized material or supply and the property it improves or repairs [Reg. § 1.162-3(d)(1)]. The term produce means construct, build, install, manufacture, develop, create, raise, or grow [Reg. § 1.63-(c)(6)].

How to Make Optional Election

The taxpayer makes this optional election to capitalize the amounts paid to acquire or produce a rotable, temporary, or standby emergency spare part in the year that amounts are paid by beginning to recover the costs when the asset is placed in service. The election must be made on a timely filed original federal tax return (including extensions) for the tax year the asset is placed in service. A taxpayer may revoke the election by filing a request for a private letter ruling and obtaining the IRS consent. The IRS will grant the request if the taxpayer acted reasonably and in good faith and the revocation will not prejudice IRS interests. The election may not be made or revoked by filing an application for change in accounting method or, before obtaining IRS consent to make a late election or to revoke the election, by filing an amended federal tax return [Reg. § 1.162-3(d)(3)].

.03 Election to Capitalize Repair and Maintenance Costs

A taxpayer may make an annual election to opt out of expensing repair and maintenance costs if the taxpayer treats the costs as capital expenditures on its books and records. A taxpayer must elect to capitalize these expenses on its return. An electing taxpayer must also depreciate the expenditures. treat amounts paid for repair and maintenance to tangible property as amounts paid to improve that property and as an asset subject to the allowance for depreciation if the taxpayer incurs these amounts in carrying on the taxpayer's trade or business and if the taxpayer treats these amounts as capital expenditures on its books and records regularly used in computing income.

The election applies to all amounts paid for repair and maintenance to tangible property that the taxpayer treats as capital expenditures on its books and records for the tax year [Reg. § 1.263(a)-3(n)(1)]. The taxpayer must begin to depreciate the cost of the improvements amount when they are placed in service [Reg. § 1.263(a)-3(n)(2)]. In the case of a partnership or S corporation, the election is made by the partnership or S corporation and not by the partner or shareholder.

The election is made by attaching a statement to the taxpayer's timely filed original tax return (including extensions) for the tax year in which the repair and maintenance expenditures are paid. The statement must be titled "Section 1.263(a)-3(n) Election" and must include the taxpayer's name, address, taxpayer identification number, and a statement that the taxpayer is making the election to capitalize repair and maintenance costs under Reg. § 1.263(a)-3(n). The election may not be made by filing an application for a change in method of accounting or, unless permission to file a late election is first obtained, on an amended return.

.04 *De Minimis* Safe Harbor Expensing Rule

A *de minimis* expensing safe harbor is available under Reg. § 1.263(a)-1(f). This safe harbor will enable taxpayers to deduct certain amounts paid or incurred to acquire or produce a unit of tangible property. If the taxpayer has (1) an Applicable Financial Statement (AFS), (2) written accounting procedures for expensing amounts paid or incurred for such property under certain dollar amounts, and (3) treats such amounts as expenses on its AFS in accordance with its written accounting procedures, the taxpayer may deduct up to $5,000 per invoice. In order for taxpayer to take advantage of the $5,000 *de minimis* safe harbor, they must have written book policies in place at the start of the tax year that specify a per-item dollar amount (up to $5,000) that may be expensed for financial accounting purposes [Reg. § 1.263(a)-1(f)(1)(i)]. The taxpayer's AFS could be one of the following in descending priority: (i) A financial statement required to be filed with the Securities and Exchange Commission (SEC) (the 10-K or the Annual Statement to Shareholders); (ii) A certified audited financial statement that is accompanied by the report of an independent certified public accountant (or in the case of a foreign entity, by the report of a similarly qualified independent professional) that is used for credit purposes; reporting to shareholders, partners, or similar persons; or any other substantial nontax purpose; or a financial statement (other than a tax return) required to be provided to the federal or a state government or any federal or state agency (other than the SEC or IRS) [Reg. § 1.263(a)-1(f)(4)].

For smaller businesses, Reg. § 1.263(a)-1(f)(1)(ii) provides a safe harbor for taxpayers without an AFS and the per-item or invoice threshold amount in that situation is $500.

Election Procedures

The *de minimis* safe harbor must be elected annually by including a statement with the taxpayer's tax return for the year elected. The irrevocable election applies to all qualifying expenses, including materials and supplies that satisfy the requirements for qualification. An election to use the safe harbor may not be made through the filing of an application for change in accounting method. A late election may be made on an amended return only with IRS consent [Reg. § 1.263(a)-1(f)(5)].

> **Example 12-1:** Taxpayer provides consulting services to its customers. In Year 1, N pays amounts to purchase 50 laptop computers and 50 office chairs to be used by its employees. Each laptop computer costs $400, and has an economic useful life of more than 12 months. Each office chair costs $100. Taxpayer has an applicable financial statement and a written accounting policy at the beginning of the year to expense amounts paid for units of property costing $500 or less. N treats amounts paid for property costing $500 or less as an expense on its applicable financial statement in Year 1. If taxpayer properly elects to apply the *de minimis* safe harbor under Reg. § 1.263(a)-1(f) to amounts paid in Year 1, then taxpayer must apply the de minimis safe harbor to amounts paid for the computers and the office chairs and may deduct the amounts paid for the computers and the office chairs in the tax year paid [Reg. § 1.162-3(h), Ex. 14].

Taxpayers Without Applicable Financial Statements

A safe harbor is also available for taxpayers without an AFS. The per-item or invoice threshold amount in that case is $500. The IRS argued that it was justified in imposing that lower threshold since there would be less assurance that the accounting procedures clearly reflect income. The $500 limit (like the $5,000 ceiling for taxpayers with applicable financial statements) is all or nothing; if the cost of an invoice or item exceeds the applicable limit, then no portion of the cost is deductible under the safe harbor [Reg. § 1.263-1(f)(1)(ii)].

Special Rules for Determining Invoice Price

An anti-abuse rule in Reg. § 1.263-1(f)(6) prohibits taxpayers from "manipulating a transaction" to avoid the $5,000 or $500 per item limit. The rule specifically prohibits "componentization" of an item of property. For example, a taxpayer who purchases a truck cannot split the cost of the truck into three components (such as the engine, cab and chassis) on three invoices in order to avoid the dollar limit. A taxpayer must include all additional costs, such as delivery fees, installation services, and similar costs that are included on the same invoice as the invoice for the cost of the property. If these additional costs are not included on the same invoice as the property the taxpayer may, but is not required to, include the additional costs in the item of property.

.05 Safe Harbor for Routine Maintenance on Property

Under a routine maintenance safe harbor, an amount paid is deductible if it is for recurring activities that a taxpayer expects to perform to keep a unit of property in its ordinarily efficient operating condition [Reg. § 1.263(a)-3(i)]. The activities are routine only if, at the time the unit of property is placed in service, the taxpayer reasonably expects to perform the activities more than once during the class life of the unit of property.

Routine maintenance activities for buildings includes, for example, the inspection, cleaning, and testing of the building structure or each building system, and the replacement of damaged or worn parts with comparable and commercially available replacement parts. Routine maintenance may be performed any time during the useful life of the building structure or building systems. However, the activities are routine only if the taxpayer reasonably expects to perform the activities more than once during the 10-year period beginning at the time the building is placed in service by the taxpayer. Factors to be considered in determining whether maintenance is routine include the recurring nature of the activity, industry practice, manufacturers' recommendations, and the taxpayer's experience with similar or identical property [Reg. § 1.263(a)-3)(i)(1)(i)]. The routine maintenance safe harbor does not apply to amounts paid for repairs, for maintenance, and for improvements to network assets such as railroad track, oil and gas pipelines, water and sewage pipelines, power transmission and distribution lines, and telephone and cable lines.

The safe harbor includes amounts paid for property with an economic useful life of 12 months or less if the taxpayer's accounting procedures in place at the beginning of the tax year provide for the current deduction of such amounts. The cost of each item of short-lived property that is deductible under this *de minimis* rule may not exceed

$5,000 ($500 for taxpayers without an applicable financial statement). The taxpayer's accounting procedures do not need to put a dollar cap on the cost of an item of short-lived property that it expenses under its accounting procedures. For example, if the taxpayer's accounting procedures expense all assets with a useful life of 12 months or less, the *de minimis* safe harbor applies to all such amounts unless the property costs more than $5,000 per invoice/item (or more than $500 if the taxpayer does not have an applicable financial statement). An electing taxpayer must apply the *de minimis* safe harbor to all amounts, including eligible materials and supplies.

Routine maintenance for property other than buildings is the recurring activities that a taxpayer expects to perform as a result of the taxpayer's use of the unit of property to keep the unit of property in its ordinarily efficient operating condition. Routine maintenance activities include, for example, the inspection, cleaning, and testing of the unit of property, and the replacement of damaged or worn parts of the unit of property with comparable and commercially available replacement parts. Routine maintenance may be performed any time during the useful life of the unit of property. However, the activities are routine only if, at the time the unit of property is placed in service by the taxpayer, the taxpayer reasonably expects to perform the activities more than once during the class life of the unit of property. A taxpayer's expectation will not be deemed unreasonable merely because the taxpayer does not actually perform the maintenance a second time during the class life of the unit of property, provided that the taxpayer can otherwise substantiate that its expectation was reasonable at the time the property was placed in service. Factors to be considered in determining whether maintenance is routine and whether the taxpayer's expectation is reasonable include the recurring nature of the activity, industry practice, manufacturers' recommendations, and the taxpayer's experience with similar or identical property. With respect to a taxpayer that is a lessor of a unit of property, the taxpayer's use of the unit of property includes the lessee's use of the unit of property [Reg. § 1.263(a)-3(i)(1)(ii)].

Routine maintenance does not include the following: (i) amounts paid for a betterment to a unit of property; (ii) amounts paid for the replacement of a component of a unit of property for which the taxpayer has properly deducted a loss for that component; (iii) amounts paid for the replacement of a component of a unit of property for which the taxpayer has properly taken into account the adjusted basis of the component in realizing gain or loss resulting from the sale or exchange of the component; (iv) amounts paid for the restoration of damage to a unit of property for which the taxpayer is required to take a basis adjustment as a result of a casualty loss or relating to a casualty event; (v) amounts paid to return a unit of property to its ordinarily efficient operating condition, if the property has deteriorated to a state of disrepair and is no longer functional for its intended use; (vi) amounts paid to adapt a unit of property to a new or different use; (vii) amounts paid for repairs, maintenance, or improvement of network assets; or (viii) amounts paid for repairs, maintenance, or improvement of rotable and temporary spare parts to which the taxpayer applies the optional method of accounting for rotable and temporary spare parts under Reg. § 1.162-3(e) [Reg. § 1.263(a)-3(i)(3)].

.06 Amounts Paid to Improve Tangible Property

Amounts paid to improve a unit of tangible property must be capitalized [Reg. § 1.263(a)-3(a)]. A unit of property is improved if amounts are paid for activities performed by the taxpayer resulting in:

- A betterment to the unit of property;
- A restoration of the unit of property; or
- Adaptation of the unit of property to a new or different use [Reg. § 1.263(a)-3(d)].

A unit of property for this purpose consists of a group of functionally interdependent components, such as the parts of a machine, with the machine being treated as a unit of property [Reg. § 1.263(a)-3(e)(1)]. In the case of a building, the building (including its structural components) is a unit of property [Reg. § 1.263(a)-3(e)(2)]. However, certain major systems of the building, such as heating, air conditioning, and ventilation (HVAC), plumbing, and electrical, are treated as separate units of property for purposes of determining whether there has been a capitalizable betterment, restoration, or adaption to the system [Reg. § 1.263(a)-3(e)(2)(ii)].

Removal Costs

The cost of removing a depreciable asset or a component of a depreciable asset is not capitalized as an improvement if the taxpayer realizes gain or loss on the removed asset or component. If a taxpayer disposes of a component of a unit of property and the disposal is not a disposition on which gain or loss is realized, then the taxpayer deducts the costs of removing the component if the removal costs directly benefit or are incurred by reason of a repair to the unit of property. Otherwise the removal costs are capitalized as part of the improvement costs to the unit of property [Reg. § 1.263-3(g)(2)].

.07 Safe Harbor for Small Taxpayers with Buildings

An annual safe harbor election is also available for buildings owned or leased by a taxpayer with an unadjusted basis (i.e., generally cost) no greater than $1 million [Reg. § 1.263(a)-3(h)(4)].

The taxpayer must have average annual gross receipts of $10 million or less during the three preceding tax years. Gross receipts are specially defined and include income from sales (unreduced by cost of goods), services, and investments [Reg. § 1.263(a)-3(h)(3)(i)].

In the case of a lessee, the unadjusted basis of the building is equal to the total amount of (undiscounted) rent paid or expected to be paid over the entire lease term, including expected renewal periods.

Under the new exception, the small taxpayer is not required to capitalize improvements if the total amount paid for repairs, maintenance, improvements and similar activities during the year that are performed on the building does not exceed the lesser of $10,000 or two percent of the unadjusted basis of the building. Amounts deducted under the *de minimis* rule or the new safe harbor for routine maintenance are counted toward the $10,000 limit. No amount is deductible under the safe harbor for buildings if this limit (or the $1 million adjusted basis limit) is exceeded. The safe harbor is applied separately to each building owned or leased by the taxpayer [Reg. § 1.263(a)-3(h)(1)].

Eligible property includes a building (including structural components and building systems) owned or leased by a qualifying taxpayer and also portions of buildings that are owned or leased and considered separate units of property under the regulations, such as an individual condominium or cooperative unit or office space. The safe harbor does not apply to costs paid with respect to exterior land improvements that are separate units of property.

The irrevocable election is made annually on a timely filed (including extensions) original income tax return. In the case of a partnership or S corporation that owns or leases a building, the partnership or S corporation makes the election. The election may not be made by filing an application for a change in accounting method or on an amended return unless permission to file a late election on an amended return is first obtained [Reg. § 1.263(a)-3(h)(6)].

.08 Capitalization of Betterments

A taxpayer must capitalize as an improvement an amount paid for a betterment to a unit of property [Reg. § 1.263(a)-3(j)(1)]. An amount is paid for a betterment to a unit of property only if it: (i) ameliorates a material condition or defect that either existed prior to the taxpayer's acquisition of the unit of property or arose during the production of the unit of property, whether or not the taxpayer was aware of the condition or defect at the time of acquisition or production; (ii) is for a material addition, including a physical enlargement, expansion, extension, or addition of a major component (as defined in paragraph (k)(6) of this section) to the unit of property or a material increase in the capacity, including additional cubic or linear space, of the unit of property; or (iii) is reasonably expected to materially increase the productivity, efficiency, strength, quality, or output of the unit of property [Reg. § 1.263(a)-3(j)(1)(i)-(iii)].

Application of Betterment Rules to Buildings

An amount is paid to improve a building if it is paid for a betterment to a building, condominium, cooperative, leased building or leased portion of building. For example, an amount is paid to improve a building if it is paid for an increase in the efficiency of the building structure or any one of its building systems (for example, the HVAC system) [Reg. § 1.263(a)-3(j)(2)(ii)].

.09 Capitalization of Restorations

A taxpayer must capitalize as an improvement an amount paid to restore a unit of property, including an amount paid to make good the exhaustion for which an allowance is or has been made [Reg. § 1.263(a)-3(k)(1)]. An amount restores a unit of property only if it: (i) is for the replacement of a component of a unit of property for which the taxpayer has properly deducted a loss for that component, other than a casualty loss; (ii) is for the replacement of a component of a unit of property for which the taxpayer has properly taken into account the adjusted basis of the component in realizing gain or loss resulting from the sale or exchange of the component; (iii) is for the restoration of damage to a unit of property for which the taxpayer is required to take a basis adjustment as a result of a casualty loss; (iv) returns the unit of property to its ordinarily efficient operating condition if the property has deteriorated to a state of disrepair and is no longer functional for its intended use; (v) results in the rebuilding of the unit of property to a like-new condition after the end of its class life; or (vi) is for the replacement of a part or a combination of parts that comprise a major component or a substantial structural part of a unit of property [Reg. § 1.263(a)-3(k)(1)(i)-(vi)].

Application of Restorations to Buildings

An amount is paid to improve a building if it is paid to restore a building, condominium, cooperative, leased building or portion of building [Reg. § 1.263(a)-3(k)(2)]. For example, an amount is paid to improve a building if it is paid for the replacement of a part or combination of parts that comprise a major component or substantial structural part of the building structure or any one of its building systems (for example, the HVAC system).

Restoration of Damage from Casualty

The amount paid for restoration of damage to the unit of property that must be capitalized is limited to the excess of (1) the taxpayer's basis adjustments resulting from the casualty event, over (2) the amount paid for restoration of damage to the unit of property that are otherwise considered capitalizable restorations. Casualty-related expenditures in excess of this limitation may be deducted as repair expenses if they so qualify [Reg. § 1.263(a)-3(k)(4)].

> **Example 12-2:** A storm damages a building with an adjusted basis of $500,000. The cost of restoring the building is $750,000, consisting of a roof replacement ($350,000) and clean-up/repair costs ($400,000). A $500,000 casualty loss is claimed. The cost of the roof must be capitalized as an improvement because it is a major component and substantial structural part of the building. The remaining $400,000 clean/up repair costs must be capitalized to the extent of the $150,000 excess of the building's adjusted basis ($500,000) over the capitalized cost of the roof ($350,000). The remaining $250,000 of repair/clean-up costs ($400,000 – $150,000) may be currently deducted [Reg. § 1.263(a)-3(k)(7), Ex. 5(ii)].

Rebuilt Like New

A capitalizable restoration includes rebuilding a unit of property to a like-new condition after the end of its class life. A property is rebuilt to a like-new condition if it is brought to the status of new, rebuilt, remanufactured, or similar status under the terms of any federal regulatory guideline or the manufacturer's original specifications. A comprehensive maintenance program, conducted according to the manufacturer's original specifications, even though substantial, does not return a unit of property to like-new condition [Reg. § 1.263(a)-3(k)(5)].

¶12,012 ENVIRONMENTAL CLEAN-UP COSTS

.01 Distinguishing Deducted and Capitalized Environmental Expenses

Expenses incurred by a business in removing and disposing of environmental waste generally are deductible expenses under Code Sec. 162, but the expenses must be capitalized under Code Sec. 263 to the extent they relate to pollution that occurred before the business bought the property. In addition, a company must capitalize the cost of cleaning toxic chemicals stored on the land because the company will receive long-term benefits from the clean-up efforts.

In *United Dairy Farmers, Inc.*,[36] the court held that a corporation which bought contaminated land had to capitalize the expenses incurred for environmental remediation, and the costs incurred for engineering and new site feasibility studies. However, in Rev. Rul. 94-38,[37] the IRS held that a corporation that discharged hazardous waste as part of its manufacturing process was allowed a current business expense deduction for ongoing soil remediation and groundwater treatment costs incurred to clean up the land and treat groundwater, because they did not produce permanent improvements or otherwise provide significant future benefits. Those expenditures did not increase the value of the property after they were made in comparison to its value before it was contaminated and thus were not capital expenditures. However, taxpayers were required to capitalize the cost of groundwater treatment facilities that had a useful life substantially beyond the tax year. Moreover, because the construction of these facilities constituted production within the uniform capitalization rules, direct costs and a portion of indirect costs were required to be capitalized. For further discussion of the uniform capitalization rules, see ¶ 17,045.

In Rev. Rul. 98-25,[38] the IRS concluded that costs incurred by a manufacturer to replace underground storage tanks (USTs) containing waste by-products (including the costs of removing, cleaning, and disposing of the old USTs and of acquiring, installing, filling, and monitoring of the new USTs) were deductible as ordinary and necessary business expenses. Since the new USTs were merely filled with waste, sealed, and buried indefinitely, they had no remaining useful life or salvage value for the manufacturer and, thus, did not have to be capitalized. The IRS distinguished the USTs from the groundwater treatment facilities in Rev. Rul. 94-38, which had useful lives that extended beyond a single tax year.

In Rev. Rul. 2004-18,[39] the IRS clarified Rev. Rul. 94-38 and Rev. Rul. 98-25 to provide that costs incurred to clean up land that a taxpayer contaminated with hazardous waste by the operation of the taxpayer's manufacturing plant must be included in inventory costs. Rev. Rul. 2005-42[40] elaborated further by providing that environmental remediation costs are properly allocable to inventory without regard to whether those costs are incurred before, during, or after production in compliance with Reg. § 1.263A-1(c)(2).

In Rev. Rul. 2004-17,[41] the IRS ruled that amounts paid by a manufacturer to clean up environmental contamination that occurred in prior years do not qualify for relief under the claim of right rules in Code Sec. 1341 because the manufacturer wasn't repaying an amount that was previously included in gross income. Therefore, the taxpayer could not deduct the clean-up costs. Instead, these expenses had to be included in inventory costs.

---

[36] *United Dairy Farmers, Inc.*, CA-6, 2001-2 USTC ¶ 50,680, 267 F3d 510.

[37] Rev. Rul. 94-38, 1994-1 CB 35, as clarified by Rev. Rul. 2004-18, 2004-1 CB 509.

[38] Rev. Rul. 98-25, 1998-1 CB 998, clarified by Rev. Rul. 2004-18, 2004-1 CB 509.

[39] Rev. Rul. 2004-18, 2004-1 CB 509.

[40] Rev. Rul. 2005-42, 2005-2 CB 67.

[41] Rev. Rul. 2004-17, 2004-1 CB 516. *See also* *Alcoa, Inc.*, CA-3, 2007-2 USTC ¶ 50,824, 509 F3d 173.

In *Kerr-McGee Corp.*,[42] the Court of Federal Claims held that the taxpayer must not only show that remediation costs were undertaken to return the property to its pre-contamination condition pursuant to federal or state statutory mandate but the taxpayer must also show that the expenses were not incurred to improve the property's value or change its use.

.02 Specified Liability Loss Treatment for Environmental Waste Disposal Expenses

The expenses incurred by taxpayers to clean up heavily polluted sites may be eligible for specified liability loss (SLL) under Code Sec. 172(f)(1)(B)(i)(iv). For further discussion of SLLs, see ¶ 13,110.02. SLLs may be carried back ten years under Code Sec. 172(f)(6). Expenses for remediation of environmental contamination qualify as SLLs if they are deductible expenses incurred in satisfaction of a liability under federal or state law requiring the remediation of environmental contamination [Code Sec. 172(f)(1)]. Additionally, the act or failure to act giving rise to the liability must occur at least three years before the beginning of the tax year; and the taxpayer must have used the accrual method throughout the period(s) during which the act or failure to act giving rise to the liability occurred [Code Sec. 172(f)(1)(B)(ii)].

¶12,015 EXPENSES FOR TAX-EXEMPT INCOME

Business expenses allocable to tax-exempt income are not deductible [Code Sec. 265(a)(1)]. In addition, no deduction is allowed for interest on a loan to buy or carry tax-exempt securities [Ch. 9]. Thus, if one-eighth of a service fee for investment management were attributable to tax-exempt interest, one-eighth of the income generated by that income would be disallowed.[43]

An unrecognized involuntary conversion gain [Ch. 7] is not tax-exempt income for this purpose.[44] Likewise, tax-free parsonage or off-base military housing allowances do not cause the disallowance of deductions for home mortgage interest and property taxes.

¶12,020 ENHANCED CHARITABLE DEDUCTIONS

A donor's deduction for the contribution of "ordinary income property" is usually limited to the donor's basis in the contributed property [Code Sec. 170(e)(1)]. "Ordinary income property" is appreciated property which, if sold at its fair market value on the date of contribution, would give rise to ordinary income or short-term capital gain. "Ordinary income property" includes:

1. Inventory and stock in trade, Code Sec. 306 (stock acquired in a nontaxable transaction, which produces ordinary income if sold), stock of a collapsible corpora-

---

[42] *Kerr-McGee Corp.*, FedCl, 2007-2 USTC ¶50,556, 77 FedCl 309.

[43] *C.K. Herbst*, 2 TCM 361, Dec. 13,337(M) (1943).

[44] *Cotton States Fertilizer Co.*, 28 TC 1169, Dec. 22,570 (1957), *acq.* 1958-1 CB 4.

tion to the extent it would produce ordinary income under Code Sec. 341 if sold, stock in certain foreign corporations to the extent it would produce ordinary income if sold, works of art created by the donor, manuscripts prepared by the donor, and letters and memoranda;

2. Capital assets (including stock) held for less than the required holding period for long-term capital gain treatment at the time contributed; and
3. Depreciable, tangible real or personal property and mining property used in a taxpayer's trade or business, to the extent of any gain that would have been treated as ordinary income because of depreciation had the property been sold at its fair market value at the date of contribution [Reg. § 1.170A-4(b)(1)].

There are some exceptions to this rule. One exception to this general rule enables corporate donors to deduct basis plus one-half of the unrealized appreciation for property that is contributed for use in the care of the ill, needy, or infants [Code Sec. 170(e)(3)].

C corporations may claim an enhanced deduction for contributions of inventory to charitable organizations that are: (1) used in a manner consistent with the charity's tax-exempt purpose solely for the care of the ill, needy, or infants; (2) not transferred in exchange for money, other property or services; and (3) substantiated by a written statement that their use will be consistent with such requirements. Donated property that meets these requirements is deductible at an amount that is the lesser of: (1) the basis of the property plus one half of the excess of fair market value over the basis; or (2) twice the basis [Code Sec. 170(e)(3)].

.01 Contributions of Scientific Property Used for Research

Another exception to the general rule enables a corporate donor to deduct basis plus one-half of the unrealized appreciation in ordinary income property that is contributed to a college, university, or scientific tax-exempt organization for use in research [Code Sec. 170(e)(4)]. For both exceptions, however, the donor's deduction cannot exceed two times the donor's basis in the contributed property.

The augmented deduction for the contribution of research property is available to corporations other than an S corporation, a personal holding company, or a service organization [Code Sec. 170(e)(4)(D)]. The contributed property must be scientific equipment or apparatus that is contributed to a qualified donee: a college, university, or tax-exempt scientific research organization [Code Sec. 41(e)(6)]. The deduction for contributions to a private foundation is limited to the donor's basis.

In order to qualify for the larger deduction, the following requirements must be met [Code Sec. 170(e)(4)(B)(i)-(vii)]:

1. The contributed property must be constructed by the taxpayer;
2. The contribution must be made within two years of construction;
3. The original use of the property must be by the donee;
4. Substantially all the use of the property by the donee (i.e., at least 80 percent) must be for research or experimentation in physical or biological sciences;
5. The donee may not transfer the property in exchange for money, other property, or services; *and*

6. The taxpayer must receive a written statement from the donee stating that requirements (4) and (5) will be met.

In addition to property constructed by the donor corporation, property that has been assembled by the donor corporation is also eligible for the enhanced deduction for contributions of scientific property for research [Code Sec.170(e)(4)(B)]. According to the Joint Committee on Taxation, Technical Explanation of the Tax Relief and Health Care Act of 2006 (P.L. 109-432) (JCX-50-06), there is no intention that old or used components assembled by the donor corporation into scientific property will qualify for the enhanced deduction.

.02 Charitable Contributions of Food Inventory

Corporate or noncorporate taxpayers can claim an enhanced deduction for donations of food inventory from any trade or business if the food is contributed before January 1, 2014 [Code Sec. 170(e)(3)(C)(iv)]. The deduction may be claimed by any trade or business of a corporate or noncorporate taxpayer including an S corporation and sole proprietorship.

Donated food inventories must consist of "apparently wholesome food" which is defined as food intended for human consumption that meets all quality and labeling standards imposed by federal, state, and local laws and regulations even though the food may not be readily marketable due to appearance, age, freshness, grade, size, surplus, or other conditions [Code Sec. 170(e)(3)(C)(i)(II)].

The amount of the enhanced deduction for donated food inventory equals the lesser of (1) the donated item's basis plus one-half of the item's appreciation, or (2) two times the donated item's basis. For a taxpayer other than a C corporation, the total deduction for donations of food inventory during the tax year is limited to a maximum of 10 percent of the taxpayer's net income from all sole proprietorships, S corporations, or partnerships (or other non-C corporation) from which the contributions are made.

¶12,025 EXPENSES FOR POLITICAL PURPOSE

Generally, no business deduction is allowed for direct or indirect payments for political purposes. Indirect contributions include: (1) admission to a dinner or program where the proceeds of the affair would benefit a political party or candidate; (2) admission to an inaugural ball, parade, concert, or similar event that is identified with a candidate or party; and (3) advertising in a publication (including a convention program) where the proceeds benefit a party or candidate [Code Sec. 276(a)].

¶12,030 ILLEGAL BUSINESS OR PAYMENT

Operating expenses of an illegal (under state law) or questionable business are deductible.[45] But expenses of an inherently illegal nature, such as bribery and protection

[45] *N. Sullivan*, SCt, 58-1 USTC ¶9368, 356 US 27, 78 SCt 512.

payments, are not deductible[46] [Code Sec. 162(c), (f), (g); Reg. §§1.162-18, -21]. No deductions or credits are allowed for amounts paid for illegal trafficking in drugs listed in the Controlled Dangerous Substances Act or the law of the state where the activity is conducted [Code Sec. 280E]. However, the general disallowance of deductions doesn't affect the deduction from gross receipts for cost of goods sold. A deduction for payments to foreign government employees is disallowed only if it violates the Foreign Corrupt Practices Act [Code Sec. 162(c)(1)]. Formerly, the deduction would be disallowed if it would be illegal under any U.S. law. The Sixth Circuit has allowed a deduction for legal kickback payments that meet the "ordinary and necessary" business expense test.[47]

.01 Fines Not Deductible

Treble damages paid by a taxpayer when he breaches a contract will not be deductible because the damages constitute a nondeductible fine designed to punish.[48] Code Sec. 162(f) "bars the deduction of fines and penalties imposed to sanction or punish conduct which a well-defined government policy seeks to proscribe."

.02 Restitution Payment to Bank Not Deductible

Restitution payments made by the chief executive officer (CEO) of a bank who illegally purchased bank stock were capital expenditures rather than ordinary and necessary business expenses.[49] Since the CEO's violation arose from the purchase of stock, which is a capital asset, and since the restitution payment enabled him to retain the stock, the payment was characterized as a capital expenditure.

.03 Reimbursement of Embezzled Funds Deductible

An S corporation was allowed to deduct as an ordinary and necessary business expense amounts paid to reimburse its client for money that was embezzled from the client by the S corporation's employee.[50]

¶12,035 LOBBYING EXPENSES

The cost of lobbying is generally deductible if it is an ordinary and necessary business expense. No deduction is allowed for the expense of influencing federal or state legislation or the actions of high-level federal officials of the executive branch [Code Sec. 162(e)(1)]. This covers not only the cost of a hired lobbyist but also amounts paid for the preparation, planning and coordinating of lobbying activities. The disallowance rule does not apply to lobbying connected with country, city, and other local legislation. And it does not cover communications with government officials compelled by sub-

[46] *G.A. Comeaux*, 10 TC 201, Dec. 16,238 (1948), *acq.* 1948-1 CB 1, *aff'd*, CA-10, 49-2 USTC ¶9358, 176 F2d 394. *Excelsior Baking Co.*, DC-MN, 49-1 USTC ¶9132, 82 FSupp 423.

[47] *Raymond Bertolini Trucking Co.*, CA-6, 84-2 USTC ¶9591, 736 F2d 1120.

[48] *J.W. Hawronsky*, 105 TC 94, Dec. 50,814 (1995).

[49] *L.A. Mitchell*, 67 TCM 3015, Dec. 49,869(M), TC Memo. 1994-237, *aff'd*, CA-6, 96-1 USTC ¶50,042, 73 F3d 628.

[50] *P.D. Musgrave*, 73 TCM 1721, Dec. 51,821(M), TC Memo. 1997-19.

poena or federal or state law. Taxpayers may allocate their costs between legislative branch lobbying and executive branch lobbying in determining the nondeductible amount by consistently using any reasonable method of allocating costs to lobbying activities [Reg. § § 1.162-28(a)(1), 1.162-29(c)(2)].

A business cannot indirectly take a deduction for contributions to noncharitable tax-exempt organizations, such as trade associations, to the extent they are allocable to nondeductible lobbying activities. These tax-exempt organizations generally must give dues payers an estimate of the portion of the dues allocable to these activities. This is called the *notice requirement.* As an added precaution against unwarranted deductions, the law provides that a noncharitable tax-exempt organization must report on its annual return its total nondeductible lobbying expenditures and the amount of its dues that are allocable to those expenditures. This is called the "reporting requirement."

Certain tax-exempt organizations may qualify for exemption from the reporting requirements of Code Sec. 6033(e) if substantially all of the dues paid to the organization are nondeductible. A social welfare organization, agricultural and horticultural organization, or business league will not be required to report lobbying expenditures to members if:

- More than 90 percent of all annual dues are received from persons, families, or entities who each pay annual dues of $155 in 2013 or less [Code Sec. 512(d)(1)]; or

- More than 90 percent of all annual dues are received from Code Sec. 501(c)(3) organizations, state and local governments whose income is exempt from tax, or from the exempt organizations that are automatically excepted from the reporting rules.

There is a special exception to the disallowance rule for small amounts of "in-house expenditures." If a taxpayer's in-house expenditures (not including allocable overhead) do not exceed $2,000 during a year, they are deductible (assuming they are not connected with a political campaign or grass-roots lobbying) [Code Sec. 162(e)(5)(B)]. For deduction purposes, in-house expenditures include materials and labor other than (1) payments to a professional lobbyist and (2) dues and similar payments. And they include overhead costs. So, for example, if a taxpayer's in-house expenditures are $1,800 and allocable overhead costs are $1,000, then $2,800 is deductible.

.01 Lobbying Expenditures of Exempt Organizations

The disallowance rule applies to dues or similar payments made to tax-exempt organizations to the extent the funds are used for lobbying activities [Code Sec. 162(e)(3)] [Ch. 23]. So, for example, if a tax-exempt organization uses 25 percent of its dues to lobby for federal or state legislation, 25 percent of each member's dues are not deductible. The organization will generally provide members with annual statements reporting what portion of dues payments are nondeductible. For further discussion see Ch. 23.

¶12,040 BUSINESS START-UP EXPENSES

.01 Deduction of Start-Up and Organizational Expenditures and 15-Year Amortization for Excess

All taxpayers including single-member LLCs, corporations, sole proprietors and partnerships can elect to deduct up to $5,000 of start-up expenditures in the tax year in which their trade or business begins [Code Sec. 195(b)]. The $5,000 amount must be reduced (but not below zero) by the amount by which the start-up expenditures exceed $50,000. The remainder of any start-up expenditures—those that are not deductible in the year in which the trade or business begins—must be ratably amortized over the 180-month period (15 years) beginning with the month in which the active trade or business begins [Code Sec. 195(b)(1)(B); Reg. § 1.195-1(a)].

Taxpayers Eligible for Code Sec. 195 Deduction

In general, the Code Sec. 195 deduction may be claimed by a taxpayer who incurs start-up expenditures and enters into a trade or business. In the case of start-up expenditures incurred by a corporate taxpayer (including a subchapter S corporation), the amortization deduction must be claimed on the income tax return for that corporation and is not deductible as a special item by any shareholder. In the case of a sole proprietor, the amortization deduction may be claimed as a deduction for the trade or business with respect to which the start-up expenditures were paid or incurred. In the case of start-up expenditures incurred by a partnership, the amortization deduction may be taken into account in computing the taxable income of the partnership. In the case of qualifying investigatory expenses incurred in connection with the acquisition of a partnership interest, the amortization deduction should be claimed by the partner who incurred such expenses.

Corporations may elect to deduct up to $5,000 (but not below zero) of organizational expenditures for the tax year in which the corporation begins business [Code Sec. 248(a)]. For further discussion, see ¶ 20,045.

For further discussion of deduction by partnerships of expenditures incurred to organize a partnership, see ¶ 24,020.

.02 Expenses Eligible for Section 195 Deduction

Business start-up expenditures are expenses incurred after that taxpayer makes the decision to establish a particular business and prior to the time the business actually begins operating. An enterprise ceases to incur start-up expenses when it becomes an active trade or business.[51] Start-up expenses deductible under Code Sec. 195 include amounts paid or incurred in connection with the following activities:

- Investigating the possibility of creating or acquiring an active trade or business including preopening costs, which are amounts spent for any activity engaged in for profit and for the production of income. These activities must be engaged in before

[51] *F. Lee Bailey*, 103 TCM 1499, Dec. 59,011(M), TC Memo. 2012-96.

the day on which the active trade or business begins, in anticipation of the activity becoming an active trade or business.

- Creating an active trade or business.
- Any activity engaged in for profit and for the production of income before the day on which the active trade or business begins, in anticipation of such activity becoming an active trade or business [Code Sec. 195(c)(1)(A)].

In addition, the expenditure must be one that would be allowable as a deduction if it were paid or incurred in connection with the expansion of an existing trade or business in the same field you have entered [Code Sec. 195(c)(1)].

When to Deduct

Start-up expenses are not deductible until the business actually begins to operate as a trade or business. If a taxpayer acquires a preexisting trade or business, operations begin on the date of acquisition and start-up expenses may be deductible on that date. Operations do not begin for a newly formed business until the business first performs the activities for which it was created [Code Sec. 195(b)(1), (c)(2)(B)]. If a taxpayer incurs start-up expenses but decides not to go into business, the taxpayer may not deduct the start-up expenses.

Timing of Investigatory Expenses Crucial for Deduction

The IRS has also ruled that expenditures a corporation incurred in conducting a preliminary due diligence investigation before deciding to submit a letter of intent qualified as start-up expenditures under Code Sec. 195.[52] However, the expenses incurred after the decision to submit the letter of intent, which included legal and accounting firm fees, were neither deductible nor amortizable start-up expenditures under Code Sec. 195. Rather, they were part of the cost of acquiring the target business.

Distinguish Acquisition Costs from Section 195 Expenses

Start-up expenses do not include amounts paid or incurred as part of the acquisition cost of a trade or business. The IRS has concluded that expenses incurred in connection with investigating the acquisition of a bank after the taxpayer had engaged in a general search or preliminary investigation did not constitute start-up costs that were eligible for amortization under Code Sec. 195.[53] Instead, the IRS ruled that the expenditures were nondeductible, capital expenditure incurred in connection with the acquisition of the bank.

> **NOTE:** The purchase of common stock is the acquisition of an investment interest and is therefore not considered an Code Sec. 195 amortizable start-up cost. Note that the costs incurred in investigating the purchase of common stock could be eligible for amortization under Code Sec. 195 if the acquisition of the common stock is actually the acquisition of the assets of the business. A buyer would be acquiring the assets of a business if the acquired corporation becomes a member of an affiliated group that includes that buyer and a consolidated income tax return is filed for that group.

---

[52] LTR 199901004 (Sept. 28, 1998).

[53] LTR 9825005 (Mar. 9, 1998).

In Rev. Rul. 99-23,[54] the IRS approved as Code Sec. 195 expenses any expenditure incurred in the course of a general search for, or investigation of, an active trade or business in order to determine whether to enter a new business and which new business to enter (other than costs incurred to acquire capital assets that are used in the search or investigation). However, expenditures incurred in the attempt to acquire a specific business do not qualify as start-up expenditures because they are acquisition costs that must be capitalized under Code Sec. 263. The nature of the cost must be analyzed to determine whether it is an investigatory cost incurred to facilitate the "whether" and "which" decision, or an acquisition cost incurred to facilitate consummation of the purchase of a business.

For example, the IRS concluded in Rev. Rul. 99-23 that costs incurred to conduct industry research and to evaluate publicly available financial information are investigatory costs eligible for amortization as start-up expenditures under Code Sec. 195. However, the costs relating to the appraisals of assets and an in-depth review of books and records to establish the purchase price are capital acquisition costs. Similarly, the IRS concluded that costs incurred to evaluate potential businesses should be classified as investigatory costs eligible for amortization as start-up expenditures under Code Sec. 195. However, the costs incurred to draft regulatory approval documents prior to the time the decision was made to acquire the business are not start-up expenditures under Code Sec. 195.

The IRS also concluded that cost of "preliminary due diligence" services provided prior to the time the taxpayer decided to buy the business (including the costs of conducting research on the industry and in reviewing financial projections) are typical of the costs incurred during an investigation to determine whether to acquire a new business and which new business to acquire. Thus, these costs are investigatory costs that are eligible for amortization as start-up expenditures under Code Sec. 195. The costs related to "due diligence" services provided after that time, however, relate to the attempt to acquire the business and must be capitalized under Code Sec. 263 as acquisition costs. Thus, the "due diligence" costs incurred to review internal documents, books and records, and to draft the acquisition agreements are not eligible for amortization under Code Sec. 195.

.03 Examples of Start-Up Expenses

Start-up expenses could include advertising costs, salaries and wages paid to employees who are being trained and their instructors, travel expenses incurred in lining up prospective distributors, suppliers, or customers, and salaries and fees paid or incurred for executives, consultants, and similar professional services. Eligible expenses also include investigatory costs incurred in reviewing a prospective business prior to reaching a final decision to acquire or enter that business. These could include expenses incurred to analyze potential markets, products, labor supply, transportation facilities, etc.

.04 Deemed Election

A taxpayer is deemed to have made an election under Code Sec. 195(b) to amortize start-up expenditures for the tax year in which the active trade or business to which

[54] Rev. Rul. 99-23, 1999-1 CB 998, as corrected by Announcement 99-89, IRB 1999-36, 408.

the expenditures relate begins. Thus, the taxpayer does not need to formally elect to deduct start-up expenses.

A taxpayer may choose to forgo the deemed election by affirmatively electing to capitalize its start-up expenditures on a timely filed federal income tax return (including extensions). The election either to amortize start-up expenditures or to capitalize start-up expenditures is irrevocable and applies to all start-up expenditures that are related to the active trade or business. A change in the characterization of an item as a start-up expenditure is a change in method of accounting. A change in the determination of the tax year in which the active trade or business begins also is treated as a change in method of accounting if the taxpayer amortized start-up expenditures for two or more tax years [Reg. § 1.195-1(b)].

Example 12-3: Corporation X incurs $3,000 of start-up expenditures that relate to an active trade or business that begins on July 1, 2013. Corporation X is deemed to have elected to amortize start-up expenditures under Code Sec. 195(b) in 2013. Therefore, Corporation X may deduct the entire amount of the start-up expenditures in 2013 [Reg. § 1.195-1(c), Ex. 1].

Example 12-4: The facts are the same as in the example above except that Corporation X incurs start-up expenditures of $41,000. Corporation X is deemed to have elected to amortize start-up expenditures in 2013. Therefore, Corporation X may deduct $5,000 and the portion of the remaining $36,000 that is allocable to July through December ($36,000/180 × 6 = $1,200) in 2013, the tax year in which the active trade or business begins. Corporation X may amortize the remaining $34,800 ($36,000 – $1,200 = $34,800) ratably over the remaining 174 months [Reg. § 1.195-1(c), Ex. 2].

COMPENSATION FOR SERVICES

Compensation paid for personal services is a deductible business expense if: (1) ordinary and necessary; (2) reasonable; (3) for personal services actually rendered in connection with a trade or business, or related to "nonbusiness" activities; and (4) actually paid or incurred during the tax year. The name by which the compensation is designated, the basis on which it is determined and the form in which it is paid are immaterial.

¶12,045 DEDUCTION FOR COMPENSATION

Taxpayers may claim a deduction for ordinary and necessary business expenses, including "a reasonable allowance for salaries or other compensation for personal services actually rendered" [Code Sec. 162(a)(1); Reg. § 1.162-7; see ¶ 12,050]. Courts often determine the deductibility of compensation by applying the following two-prong test: (1) is the amount of compensation reasonable, and (2) is the payment purely for services rendered [Reg. § 1.162-7(a)]. Wages paid *solely* for services that are personal to the employer (for example, to domestics) are not deductible [Code Sec. 262(a); Reg.

§ 1.262-1(b)(3)]. For a discussion of when (timing issues) taxpayers can claim deductions for compensation, see Ch. 18.

.01 Child Employed by Parent

Wages (except the cost of meals and lodging) paid to a minor child for services actually rendered as a bona fide employee in the taxpayer's business are deductible even if the child uses the wages for part of his own support.[55]

¶12,050 REASONABLENESS OF COMPENSATION

The reasonableness of compensation paid to employees can be determined by examining the following five factors considered by the Ninth Circuit in the seminal case, *Elliotts, Inc.*:[56]

1. The employee's role in the company or the overall significance of the employee to the company; relevant considerations include the position held by the employee, hours worked, and duties performed,[57] as well as the general importance of the employee to the success of the company;
2. A comparison of the employee's salary with salaries paid by similar companies for similar services;
3. The character and condition of the company (which takes into account the company's size and complexity);
4. Conflicts of interest, i.e., does a relationship exist between the taxpaying company and its employee that might permit the company to disguise nondeductible corporate distributions of income as salary expenditures; and
5. Internal consistency in a company's treatment of payments to employees. An additional factor is whether an independent investor would be willing to compensate the employee as the taxpayer compensated the employee.

In *Metro Leasing & Dev. Corp.*,[58] the Ninth Circuit noted that "the perspective of an independent investor is but one of many factors that are to be considered when assessing the reasonableness of an executive officer's compensation." See ¶ 12,050.04 for further discussion of the independent investor test.

The reasonableness of compensation is a question of fact to be determined on the basis of all the facts and circumstances. Employers may deduct compensation paid to employees provided the compensation is reasonable. In deciding whether the compensation is reasonable the following factors must be weighed: (a) the employee's qualifications; (b) the nature, extent, and scope of the employee's work; (c) the size and complexity of the business; (d) a comparison of salaries paid with sales and net income;

---

[55] Rev. Rul. 72-23, 1972-1 CB 43; Rev. Rul. 73-393, 1973-2 CB 33; *W.E. Eller*, 77 TC 934, Dec. 38,391 (1981).

[56] *Elliotts, Inc.*, CA-9, 83-2 USTC ¶9610, 716 F2d 1241; *Aries Communications Inc.*, 105 TCM 1585, Dec. 59,504(M), TC Memo. 2013-97.

[57] *American Foundry*, CA-9, 76-1 USTC ¶9401, 536 F2d 289.

[58] *Metro Leasing & Dev. Corp*, CA-9, 2004-2 USTC ¶50,308, 376 F3d 1015.

(e) the prevailing general economic conditions; (f) comparison of salaries with distributions to shareholders; (g) the prevailing rates of compensation for comparable positions in comparable concerns; (h) amount of salary paid to employee in previous years; (i) the salary policy of the corporation as to all employees; and (j) whether the employee and employer dealt at arm's length.

.01 Compensation or Dividend

In profitable years, corporations may prefer to distribute profits in the form of deductible compensation rather than as nondeductible dividends. The IRS does not approve of this means of distributing earnings and profits and will attempt to recast the so-called "salary" as nondeductible dividends. As a result, they often audit this issue because they are trying to prevent the distribution of corporate profits disguised as deductible salaries and bonuses to controlling shareholders/employees.

In *O.S.C. & Associates Inc.*,[59] the Court of Appeals for the Ninth Circuit held that a corporation may not deduct a large portion of the incentive payments made to employee-shareholders because the payments looked more like a stock distribution based on ownership interests than compensation for services rendered. The following factors were considered in determining whether the employee/shareholder's compensation was really disguised dividends:

- Whether the bonuses were in exact proportion to the officers' stockholdings;
- Whether the payments were made in lump sum rather than as the services were rendered;
- Whether there was a complete absence of formal dividend distributions by an expanding corporation;
- Whether the system of bonuses was completely unstructured having no relation to services rendered;
- Whether the company's consistently negligible taxable income indicated that the bonus system was based on funds available rather than on services rendered;
- Whether bonus payments were made only to the four officer-stockholders and to no other employees.

CEO's $17.5 Million Bonus Deduction Sanctioned

In *Menard, Inc.*[60] the Court of Appeals for the Seventh Circuit concluded that a $17.5 million bonus paid to a company's CEO was deductible as reasonable compensation and was not a disguised dividend. The court found that the bonus paid was not excessive because the executive performed services that were delegated to staff in other comparable companies. He received a large bonus because it compensated him for his added assumption of risk and the additional responsibilities he assumed on behalf of the company. The court approved his large bonus because the taxpayer micromanaged his

---

[59] *O.S.C. & Associates Inc.*, 73 TCM 3231, Dec. 52,127(M), TC Memo. 1997-300, *aff'd*, CA-9, 99-2 USTC ¶50,765, 187 F3d 1116, *cert. denied*, SCt, 120 SCt 1831. *See also, Labelgraphics, Inc.*, CA-9, 2000-2 USTC ¶50,648, 221 F3d 1091; *Haffner's Service Stations, Inc.*, 83 TCM 1211, Dec. 54,644(M), TC Memo 2002-38, *aff'd*, CA-1, 2003-1 ¶50,333, 326 F3d 1.

[60] *Menard, Inc.*, CA-7, 2009-1 USTC ¶50,270, 560 F3d 620.

business, the board of directors was dependent on him, and the amount of work he performed was normally handled by two or more directors in other companies.

In *Multi-Pak Corp.*,[61] the Tax Court concluded that a corporation could deduct all of the compensation paid to its CEO and sole shareholder as reasonable compensation because: (1) the CEO made every important decision for the taxpayer's operations; (2) as a result of the CEO's decisions and leadership, the company was one of the more successful of its kind; (3) the company treated the CEO pay in a consistent manner.

.02 Catch-Up Pay Justified in Profitable Years

The courts have approved the deduction of an exorbitant amount of compensation paid to an employee in the corporation's profitable years after years of undercompensation in the leaner years.[62] As a result, businesses that underpay employees/shareholders in the start-up years can catch up in later years when the business becomes more profitable and still deduct the compensation. A corporation will not lose its deduction for reasonable compensation paid an employee simply because it started out business life as sole proprietorship which was later absorbed by a corporation.

The court will uphold catch-up pay in profitable years if the compensation was reasonable and was directly attributable to the executive's hard work, talent, and considerable experience. The court will also look at the company's prior years of grossly undercompensating. A corporation can claim deductions for catch-up compensation allocable to services performed in prior years when the business operated as a sole proprietorship if (1) the predecessor entity was completely absorbed by the new corporation; (2) the employee was undercompensated in those years; and (3) the successor corporation benefited from those undercompensated services.[63]

There is no precise rule to determine the exact amount of compensation that is considered reasonable. It is an amount that would ordinarily be paid for like services by like enterprises under like circumstances [Reg. § 1.162-7(b) (3)]. The facts in each case control. For example, a company is justified in paying more to an owner-employee who is instrumental in boosting company profits than to an owner-employee who has little impact on profits.[64] The Tax Court has upheld a family business's deduction of 70 percent of the bonus paid to its president, even though she was essentially a self-made entrepreneur.[65] The court considered her low compensation in previous years before she had turned the business around. The large bonus was justified not only by her substantial efforts but also by the fact that she had been undercompensated in previous years before the business became successful.

---

[61] *Multi-Pak Corp.*, 99 TCM 1567, Dec. 58,253(M), TC Memo. 2010-39.

[62] *Alpha Medical Inc.*, CA-6, 99-1 USTC ¶ 50,461, 172 F3d 942; *Comtec Systems, Inc.*, 69 TCM 1581, Dec. 50,405(M), TC Memo. 1995-4, *motion denied*, 70 TCM 52, Dec. 50,747(M), TC Memo. 1995-310.

[63] *J. Radtke*, CA-7, 90-1 USTC ¶ 50,113, 895 F2d 1196.

[64] *Hendricks Furniture, Inc.*, 55 TCM 497, Dec. 44,666(M), TC Memo. 1988-133.

[65] *Max Burton Enterprises*, 74 TCM 652, Dec. 52,254(M), TC Memo. 1997-421.

.03 Compensation Paid by Closely-Held Corporations to Shareholder-Employees

A corporation can deduct from its taxable income a "reasonable allowance for salaries or other compensation for personal services actually rendered" [Code Sec. 162(a)(1); Reg. §§ 1.162-7, 1.162-9]. Dividends, however, are not deductible because they are not an expense, but a distribution to shareholders. Therefore, there is an incentive for owners to characterize/disguise dividends as salary in order to deduct the distributions as a business expense. Because of the potential for avoiding taxation in this manner, Reg. § 1.162-7(b)(1) provides that "special scrutiny should be given to compensation paid by a corporation whose stock is closely held." The requirement that compensation be in a reasonable amount and for services actually rendered ensures that a corporation may not improperly lessen its tax burden by characterizing earnings distributions as salary.

The IRS is very sensitive to the possibility that some of the dollars paid as deductible compensation are really nondeductible dividend distributions and have been improperly deducted as compensation. The IRS therefore has a general policy of disallowing compensation paid by closely-held corporations to shareholder-employees when those shareholder-employees have not received dividend distributions. As a result this issue is one of the most frequently litigated tax questions today. The courts have struggled to come up with a fair test for deciding when compensation will be deemed reasonable and a recent case lists the factors should be considered in determining how much compensation paid to shareholder/employees is reasonable.

The courts and the IRS will consider the following factors established in *Owensby & Kritikos, Inc.*,[66] in determining whether compensation paid to shareholder/employees is reasonable:

- The employee's qualifications;
- The nature, extent, and scope of the employee's work;
- The size and complexities of the employer's business;
- A comparison of salaries paid with the employer's gross and net income;
- The prevailing general economic conditions;
- A comparison of salaries with distributions to officers and retained earnings;
- The prevailing rates of compensation for comparable positions in comparable concerns;
- The salary policy of the employer as to all employees;
- The amount of compensation paid to the employee in previous years;
- The employer's financial condition;
- Whether the employer and employee dealt at arm's length;
- Whether the employee guaranteed the employer's debt;

---

[66] *Owensby & Kritikos, Inc.*, CA-5, 87-2 USTC ¶9390, 819 F2d 1315; *See also Pepsi-Cola Bottling Co.*, CA-10, 76-1 USTC ¶9107, 528 F2d 176; *Eberl's Claim Service, Inc.*, CA-10, 2001-1 USTC ¶50,396, 249 F3d 994; *Leonard Pipeline Contractors, Ltd.*, CA-9, 98-1 USTC ¶50,356, 142 F3d 1133, *on remand*, 76 TCM 376, Dec. 52,856(M), TC Memo. 1998-315, *aff'd without op.*, CA-9, 2000-1 USTC ¶50,208, 210 F3d 384; *Pulsar Components Int'l*, 71 TCM 2436, Dec. 51,236(M), TC Memo. 1996-129.

• Whether the employer offered a pension plan or profit-sharing plan to its employees; and

• Whether the employee was reimbursed by the employer for business expenses.

In *Brewer Quality Homes, Inc.*,[67] the court concluded that the taxpayer was not permitted to deduct the entire amount of compensation paid by a mobile home retailing business to its founder, principal officer and 50 percent shareholder because the amount of compensation was unreasonable under a nine-factor test. The court concluded that the excess monies paid the executive were in fact disguised dividends.

▶ **PRACTICE POINTER:** To avoid the audit that resulted in years of litigation for the taxpayer in *Brewer Quality Homes*, closely held businesses should be sure to follow a consistent policy of dividend distributions to shareholders and officers. This practice will ensure that substantial bonuses declared at year-end when the earnings of a business are known will not be characterized as disguised dividends by the IRS. In profitable years, corporations may prefer to distribute profits in the form of deductible compensation rather than as nondeductible dividends. The IRS does not approve of this means of distributing earnings and profits and will attempt to recast the so-called salary as nondeductible disguised dividends that are taxed once at the corporate level and again at the shareholder level. The IRS therefore has a general policy of disallowing compensation paid by closely held corporations to shareholder-employees when those shareholder-employees have not received dividend distributions. As a result, this issue is one of the most frequently litigated tax questions today.

.04 Independent Investor Test

One method used to analyze the reasonableness of shareholder/employee compensation is the independent investor test[68] which asks "whether an inactive, independent investor would be willing to compensate the employee as he was compensated."[69] According to this test, the compensation package should be viewed from the perspective of a hypothetical independent investor. This means that, after considering the dividend and return on equity enjoyed by a disinterested stockholder, you must ask whether a stockholder would sanction the compensation paid to the employee.

▶ **PRACTICE TIP:** The bottom line is that a closely held business can pay a shareholder/employee enormous salaries and still deduct the compensation if they can prove that the salary was actually earned by the employees and that the business was a success as a result of the efforts of the employee. The investor's perspective on compensation paid to CEOs cannot be overlooked when companies decide whether salaries and dividends paid to executives are reasonable

[67] *Brewer Quality Homes, Inc.*, 86 TCM 29, Dec. 55,219(M), TC Memo. 2003-200, *aff'd in unpublished per curiam opinion*, CA-5, 2005-1 USTC ¶50,114.

[68] *Dexsil Corp.*, CA-2, 98-1 USTC ¶50,471, 147 F3d 96, *on remand*, 77 TCM 1973, Dec. 53,372(M), TC Memo. 1999-155; *Rapco, Inc.*, 69 TCM 2238, Dec. 50,544(M), TC Memo. 1995-128, *aff'd*, CA-2, 96-1 USTC ¶50,297, 85 F3d 950; *Exacto Spring Corp.*, CA-7, 99-2 USTC ¶50,964, 196 F3d 833; *Wechsler & Co.*, 92 TCM 138, Dec. 56,594(M), TC Memo. 2006-173.

[69] *Elliotts, Inc.*, CA-9, 83-2 USTC ¶9610, 716 F2d 1241; *Damron Auto Parts, Inc.*, 82 TCM 344, Dec. 54,430(M), TC Memo. 2001-197; *Trucks, Inc.*, DC-Neb., 84-1 USTC ¶9418; *Shaffstall Corp.*, DC-Ind., 86-2 USTC ¶9566; *Alpha Medical Inc.*, CA-9, 99-1 USTC ¶50,461, 172 F3d 942; *Rapco Inc.*, CA-2, 96-1 USTC ¶50,297.

and in turn deductible. This means that in good times, when investors enjoy a healthy stream of profits, they would supposedly be more likely to sanction generous compensation packages paid to those in charge of generating the profits. If, however, the tables are turned and the investment fails to deliver the promised rewards, the hypothetical investor will look askance at executives who are going home with all the profits and leaving the investor empty-handed.

The following factors should be considered when you use the independent investor test to determine whether compensation payments to shareholder/employees are reasonable:

- The investor's anticipated rate of return on his or her investment; and
- The investor's actual return on his or her investment after executive compensation has been taken into account.[70]

¶12,055 PAYMENT FOR SERVICES

In addition to being reasonable, the compensation, to be deductible, must be paid purely for services. If the purported compensation is actually a payment for the transfer of property by the employee, then it is a nondeductible capital expenditure. A payment may be a dividend if it is excessive and bears a close relationship to the employee's stockholdings [Reg. § § 1.162-7, -8].

¶12,060 COMMISSIONS

All amounts paid for services including commissions are deductible, the same as ordinary salaries [Reg. § 1.162-1(a)].

.01 Advances to Salespersons

These amounts, originally intended as loans, but later considered paid by the employer, are compensation to the salespersons and deductible by the employer in the year charged off.[71]

.02 Buying and Selling Commissions

Commissions paid in buying and selling property, such as securities and real estate, are generally not deductible by the investor, trader, or dealer. These are either added to the property's cost or offset the selling price, and thereby determine the gain or loss on the property's later sale. However, a dealer in securities may deduct commissions as an ordinary and necessary business expense [Reg. § 1.263(a)-2(e)]. Selling commissions deducted for estate tax purposes can *not* be offset against the selling price [Code Sec. 642(g)].

---

[70] *Mulcahy, Pauritsch, Salvador & Co., Ltd.*, CA-7, 2012-1 USTC ¶ 50,349, 680 F3d 867.

[71] Rev. Rul. 69-465, 1969-2 CB 27.

¶12,065 BONUSES AND OTHER ADDITIONAL COMPENSATION

Compensation paid to employees in addition to their regular salary or wage is deductible by the employer only if the total compensation package is reasonable. Any excess (unreasonable) amount is not deductible [Reg. § 1.162-9]. For fringe benefits, see Chapter 4.

.01 Wages During Military Reserve Leaves

Amounts paid by employers to employees while they are on leave to attend National Guard or Army and Navy Reserve training are additional compensation and are deductible [Code Sec. 162(a)].

.02 Employee Benefits

Amounts paid for dismissal wages, unemployment benefits and guaranteed annual wages are deductible.

Payments to an employee because of injuries (even if paid in a lump sum) are deductible to the extent not compensated for by insurance or otherwise [Reg. § 1.162-10].

Amounts paid under sickness, accident, hospitalization (including reimbursement of Medicare premiums to active or retired employees and contributions to welfare fund for these premiums[72]), recreational, welfare or similar benefit plans are also deductible. If, however, these amounts may be used to provide benefits under a deferred compensation pension, or profit-sharing plan, they are deductible under the rules covering such plans [Reg. § 1.162-10].

Contributions to retirement plans may be deductible. The tax rules are covered in Chapter 3.

.03 Employer's Deduction for Restricted Property Transferred to Employee

An employer who gives restricted property as compensation to his employee may claim a deduction equal to the amount included in the employee's gross income.

Code Sec. 83(h) entitles an employer to claim a deduction for property transferred in connection with performance of services if the person performing the services also actually includes the property in income [Reg. § 1.83-6(a)(1); See Ch. 2].

A corporation transferring stock to its employees as compensation will not be entitled to a compensation deduction if the employees fail to include the value of the stock in their gross income.[73]

Deduction from Nonqualified Stock Option Election by Target's Officers

The IRS concluded, when dealing with nonqualified stock options modified to facilitate a merger, that the deduction resulting from the Code Sec. 83(b) election by

---

[72] Rev. Rul. 67-315, 1967-2 CB 85.

[73] *Venture Funding, Ltd.*, Dec. 52,637, 110 TC 236, Dec. 52,637, *aff'd in unpublished per curiam opinion*, CA-6, 99-2 USTC ¶50,972, 198 F3d 248, *cert. denied*, 530 US 1205.

the target's officers to pay tax in the year the option was exercised, could only be claimed by the acquiror, not the target.[74]

▶ **PRACTICE POINTERS:** To ensure that employers will be able to successfully claim deductions for stock transferred to employees to compensate for services performed:

Employers should send employees who receive property in exchange for services Forms W-2 or Forms 1099-MISC indicating receipt of the property. This will eliminate the need for employers to police their employees tax return to see if they reported the receipt of property on their tax returns as required in Code Sec. 83;

Payroll taxes should be deducted and withheld from payments made to employees in exchange for services; and

Be consistent in your treatment of tax items. It would be grossly inconsistent to omit reporting receipt of the stock as income, to fail to send employees the requisite information forms and then to claim a tax deduction for the value of the stock. This will send up a flare to the IRS.

¶12,070 SEVERANCE PAY

Severance payments made by companies to its employees are deductible as ordinary and necessary business expenses.[75] Even though severance payments made by a taxpayer to its employees in connection with a business downsizing may produce some future benefits, such as reducing operating costs and increasing operating efficiencies (and thus look like expenses that should be capitalized) severance payments principally relate to previously rendered services of those employees. Therefore, such severance payments are deductible as Code Sec. 162 ordinary and necessary business expenses. Severance pay is also subject to FICA withholding.[76]

¶12,075 FEES TO ATTORNEYS, ACCOUNTANTS, AND OTHER PROFESSIONALS

Fees paid to attorneys and other professionals are deductible if incurred in one of the following situations [Code Sec. 212(3); Reg. §§1.162-1, 1.212-1]:

- In a transaction directly connected with, or closely resulting from a trade, business or profession;
- In producing or collecting income, or managing, conserving or maintaining property held for the production of income; or
- In the determining, collecting or refunding of any tax.

---

[74] FSA 200206003 (Oct. 22, 2001).

[75] Rev. Rul. 94-77, 1994-2 CB 19.

[76] *K.H. Donnel*, FedCl, 2001-2 USTC ¶50,664, 50 FedCl 375, but see *In re Quality Stores, Inc.*, DC-MI, 2010-1 USTC ¶50,250, *aff'd*, CA-6, 2012-2 USTC ¶50,551, *cert. granted* Oct. 2, 2013.

The deduction of legal fees depends on the origin and character of the claim for which the expenses were incurred and whether the claims bears a sufficient nexus to the taxpayer's business or to the income produced.[77] In essence, when determining whether a particular legal expense is deductible, taxpayers should look to the event that prompted the taxpayer to seek legal services. The expenses will be deductible as business expenses only if the origin of the claim is rooted in the taxpayer's trade, business, or profession. For example, a clinical professor of medicine could not deduct legal expenses incurred in connection with a state audit of her university as ordinary and necessary business expenses on Schedule C. Instead, the costs were characterized as unreimbursed employee business expenses that could be claimed only as miscellaneous itemized deductions on Schedule A. Although the taxpayer maintained a business that was separate from her employment at the university, the origin and character of the claim with respect to which the expenses were incurred did not bear a sufficient nexus to that business. The fact that the legal services might have resulted in damage control necessary to fend off negative publicity and salvage her outside business relationships was irrelevant because the state audit, which had nothing to do with her business, was the precipitating event.[78]

The U.S. Supreme Court has held that legal fees paid in defending a criminal action are deductible if they are an ordinary and necessary business expense, even if the defense is unsuccessful.[79] A disallowance of the deduction must be supported by some governmental statement of a national or state public policy considered to be frustrated.

.01 Deductible

Fees for defense of malpractice suit, disbarment proceedings, conspiracy and fraud charges, mail fraud proceedings,[80] suit against a director of a corporation, expense of defending against a court martial;[81] attorney's fees in connection with additional income tax on taxpayer's (or transferor's) business,[82] or in suit to recover income tax deficiencies assessed on property held for production of income,[83] or in will contest resulting in increase of taxpayer's share of trust income;[84] legal and accounting fees in contesting income tax deficiency and fraud penalties and effecting compromise settlement;[85] tax or investment counseling fees paid by a corporation for the benefit of its executives;[86] legal fees in suit for negligent destruction of rental property;[87] malpractice insurance premiums paid by nonpracticing retiring attorney;[88] litigation

[77] *D. Gilmore*, SCt, 63-1 USTC ¶9285, 372 US 39, 83 SCt 623; *J.A. Cavanaugh*, 104 TCM 610, Dec. 59,264(M), TC Memo. 2012-324.

[78] *E.T. Test*, CA-9, 2002-2 USTC ¶50,692, *cert. denied*.

[79] *W.F. Tellier*, SCt, 66-1 USTC ¶9319, 383 US 687, 86 SCt 1118.

[80] *S.B. Heininger*, SCt, 44-1 USTC ¶9109, 320 US 467, 64 SCt 249; *J. DiFronzo*, 75 TCM 1693, Dec. 52,545(M), TC Memo. 1998-41.

[81] *L.C. Howard*, CA-9, 53-1 USTC ¶9213, 202 F2d 28.

[82] *B.P. O'Neal*, 18 BTA 1036, Dec. 5795, *acq.* 1930-2 CB 45; *J.C. Kelley*, 38 BTA 1292, Dec. 10,520, *acq.* 1939-1 CB 19.

[83] *H.E. Cammack*, 5 TC 467, Dec. 14,680 (1945), *acq.* 1945-1 CB 2.

[84] *S.E. Tyler*, 6 TC 135, Dec. 14,948 (1946), *acq.* 1946-1 CB 4.

[85] *Greene Motor Co.*, 5 TC 314, Dec. 14,623 (1945), *acq.* 1945-1 CB 3.

[86] Rev. Rul. 73-13, 1973-1 CB 42.

[87] *T. Pate*, CA-10, 58-1 USTC ¶9482, 254 F2d 480.

[88] *M.A. Steger*, 113 TC 227, Dec. 53,570 (1999).

expenses paid in connection with filing suit against a securities firm whose unwise investment practices resulted in loss of the employer's retirement funds.[89]

.02 Nondeductible

Fees in suing for slander[90], or libel[91] (unless livelihood threatened);[92] fees to recover nontaxable damages for personal injuries suffered on business trip;[93] defense of contested election by public officer;[94] defense of title to property;[95] legal advice as to selection of securities for gift; preparation of a will; obtaining or defending a suit for divorce or separate maintenance,[96] even if expenses are to conserve income-producing property;[97] (but fees are deductible if incurred for the production or collection of alimony or separate maintenance payments that are includible in gross income [Reg. § 1.262-1]); defense of assault or bribery charges (neither business connected).[98]

.03 Capital Expenditures

Occasionally, an attorney's fee may be a capital expenditure. Examples are fees paid to secure a long-term lease of real estate;[99] fees for reducing an assessment for a local benefit;[100] and fees for tax advice on changing corporate capital structure (merger, stock split and proposed redemption).[101] In addition, legal fees paid to defend a sole shareholder from charges of criminal tax evasion will not be deductible if they are really a constructive dividend to the shareholder.[102]

.04 Cost of Corporate Takeover Attempt

Takeover costs paid to the acquiring company (greenmail, cost of repurchasing stock, etc.) are treated as capital costs and must be written off over a period of years. And the U.S. Supreme Court has said that financial and legal expenses a company incurred to facilitate its own takeover are capital expenses because they created significant benefits that lasted well beyond the tax year in which the takeover occurred[103] [¶ 12,010].

In *Staley Manufacturing, Co.*,[104] the court held that the investment banking fees paid by a corporation in an unsuccessful attempt to block a hostile takeover bid were currently deductible as ordinary and necessary business expenses because the corporation did not obtain a long-term benefit from making the expenditures. Only the following expenses had to be capitalized:

---

[89] *Sklar, Greenstein & Scheer, P.C.*, 113 TC 135, Dec. 53,505 (1999).

[90] *E.E. Lloyd*, 22 BTA 674, Dec. 6779, *aff'd*, CA-7, 3 USTC ¶ 873, 55 F2d 842.

[91] *R.E. Kleinschmidt*, 12 TC 921, Dec. 16,998 (1949).

[92] *P. Draper*, 26 TC 201, Dec. 21,701 (1956), *acq.* 1956-2 CB 5.

[93] *J.D. Murphy*, 48 TC 569, Dec. 28,541 (1967).

[94] Rev. Rul. 1, 1953-1 CB 36.

[95] *S.W.C. Lumpkin*, CA-4, 44-1 USTC ¶ 9200, 140 F2d 927, *cert. denied*, 322 US 755, 64 SCt 1266; *J.C. Coughlin*, 3 TC 420, Dec. 13,791 (1944).

[96] *F.G. Robins*, 8 BTA 523, Dec. 2889.

[97] *D. Gilmore*, SCt, 63-1 USTC ¶ 9285, 372 US 39, 83 SCt 623; *T. Patrick*, SCt, 63-1 USTC ¶ 9286, 372 US 53, 83 SCt 618; *E.T. Test*, CA-9, 2002-2 USTC ¶ 50,692, *cert. denied*, 1538 US 961.

[98] *B.S. Nadiak*, CA-2, 66-1 USTC ¶ 9262, 356 F2d 911; *M. Margoles*, 27 TCM 319, Dec. 28,905(M), TC Memo. 1968-58.

[99] *W.P. Davidson*, 27 BTA 158, Dec. 7827, *nonacq.* 1933-1 CB 16.

[100] Rev. Rul. 70-62, 1970-1 CB 30.

[101] Rev. Rul. 67-125, 1967-1 CB 31.

[102] *L.C. Hood*, Dec. 54,020 115 TC 172, Dec. 54,020 (2000).

[103] *Indopco, Inc.*, SCt, 92-1 USTC ¶ 50,113, 503 US 79, 112 SCt 1039.

[104] *A.E. Staley Mfg. Co.*, CA-7, 97-2 USTC ¶ 50,521, 119 F3d 482.

- Expenses incurred to evaluate the company stock in order to facilitate the eventual merger;
- Fees paid to defend against an unwanted acquisition;
- Fees paid to maintain and protect long-range business plans; and
- Fees paid to establish corporate policy.

A company can amortize over the life the loan the amount of costs and fees paid to attorneys and investment bankers in order to obtain financing for corporate takeovers, mergers, and leverage buyouts.[105]

The Tax Court concluded that a bank had to capitalize rather than deduct currently the costs incurred by the bank in evaluating whether or not to go forward with a proposed merger. These expenses included amounts paid to a law firm for preacquisition investigations and due-diligence reviews and the salaries paid to the acquired bank's officers who worked on the nuts and bolts of the proposed acquisition.[106] The pre-merger investigatory costs, in accordance with *INDOPCO* had to be capitalized because they were connected to a transaction that was expected to produce a significant long-term benefit to the taxpayer.

¶12,080 GOLDEN PARACHUTE PAYMENTS

Golden parachute agreements are contracts that corporations enter into with their key personnel in which the corporation agrees to pay the employee amounts in excess of their usual compensation if control or ownership of the corporation changes. Concerned that golden parachutes triggered by changes in control provide corporate funds to subsidize officers or other highly compensated individuals, Congress enacted the Code Sec. 280G golden parachute rules. These rules basically impose a nondeductible 20 percent excise tax under Code Sec. 4999 on the recipient of an excess parachute payment.

Payments made under golden parachute agreements are designated *parachute payments* that are defined in Code Sec. 280G(b)(2)(A) as any payment in the nature of compensation to (or for the benefit of) a *disqualified individual* (such as a top officer or highly compensated individual) if:

- Payment is contingent on a change in the ownership of a corporation, the effective control of a corporation, or the ownership of a substantial portion of the assets of a corporation (a change in ownership or control); and
- The aggregate present value of the payments in the nature of compensation which are contingent on such change equals or exceeds an amount equal to three times the base amount. [Code Sec. 280G(b)(2)(A); Reg. § 1.280G-1, Q&A-2]. The base amount is the individual's annualized includible compensation for the base period

[105] *Fort Howard Corp.*, Dec. ¶ 51,610, 107 TC 187, Dec. 51,610 (1996).

[106] *Norwest Corp.*, 112 TC 89, Dec. 53,277 (1999), *aff'd in part and rev'd in part*, CA-8, 2000-2 USTC ¶ 50,697, 224 F3d 874.

(i.e., the most recent five tax years ending before the date on which the change in ownership or control occurs) [Code Sec. 280G(b)(3)(A), (d)(2)].

For discussion of the modification of the golden parachute rules for financial institutions that sell troubled assets to the Treasury through the Troubled Asset Relief Program (TARP), see ¶ 12,086.

.01 Tax Consequences of Parachute Payments

Code Sec. 280G denies a deduction to a corporation for any *excess parachute payment*, which is an amount equal to the excess of any parachute payment over the portion of the disqualified individual's base amount that is allocated to such payment[107] [Code Sec. 280G(b)(1)].

The employee/executive receiving the payments must pay a nondeductible excise tax (in addition to income taxes) equal to 20 percent of the amount of the excess parachute payment [Code Sec. 4999].

The excess amount is also subject to social security and Medicare taxes without any offset for the 20 percent excise tax.

.02 *Parachute Payment* Defined

Code Sec. 280G(b)(2)(A) defines a *parachute payment* as any payment in the "nature of compensation" to (or for the benefit of) a disqualified individual (such as a top officer or highly compensated individual) if:

- Payment is contingent on a change in the ownership or effective control of the corporation, or in the ownership of a substantial portion of the assets of the corporation (a change in ownership or control); and
- The aggregate present value of the payments in the nature of compensation which are contingent on such change equals or exceeds an amount equal to three times a "base amount" [Code Sec. 280G(b)(2)(A); Reg. § 1.280G-1, Q&A-2].

.03 Change in Ownership or Control

Reg. § 1.280G-1, Q/A-27(a), provides that a change in the ownership of a corporation occurs on the date that any one person, or more than one person acting as a group, acquires ownership of stock of the corporation that, together with stock held by such person or group, possesses more than 50 percent of the total fair market value or total voting power of the stock of such corporation. Reg. § 1.280G-1, Q/A-27(b) provides that persons will not be considered to be acting as a group merely because they happen to purchase or own stock of the same corporation at the same time, or as a result of the same public offering. However, persons will be considered to be acting as a group if they are owners of a corporation that enters into a merger, consolidation, purchase, or acquisition of stock or similar business transaction with the corporation.

Reg. § 1.280G-1,Q/A-27(c), also provides that stock underlying a vested option is considered owned by an individual who holds the vested option (and the stock underlying an unvested option is not considered owned by an individual who holds

---

107 *Square D Co.*, Dec. 55,308, 121 TC 168, Dec. 55,308 (2003), *aff'd*, CA-7, 2006-1 USTC ¶ 50,162, 438 F3d 739.

the unvested option). If the option is exercisable for stock that is not substantially vested, the stock underlying the option is not treated as owned by the individual who holds the option.

Reg. § 1.280G-1, Q/A-29, provides that a change in the ownership of a substantial portion of a corporation's assets occurs on the date that any one person, or more than one person acting as a group, acquires (or has acquired during the 12-month period ending on the date of the most recent acquisition by such person or persons) assets from the corporation that have a total gross fair market value equal to or more than one-third of the total gross fair market value of all of the assets of the corporation immediately prior to such acquisition or acquisitions.

Transfers from Corporation to Joint Venture with Shared Ownership

In *Yocum*,[108] the court concluded that Code Sec. 280G applies to any payment contingent on a "change . . . in the ownership of a substantial portion of the assets of the corporation." The court emphasized that this language is not limited to transfers to wholly unrelated parties and contains no exception for transfers of property from one corporation to another entity, even if both entities have some overlapping ownership. Therefore the court concluded that a transfer of assets from a corporation to a joint venture in which it was a copartner was a change in the ownership of a substantial portion of the assets of the corporation under the Code Sec.280G golden parachute rules. Thus the transfer triggered an excise tax under Code Sec. 4999 on a significant portion of the value of a corporate officer's stock that became vested as a result of the transfer under the terms of a restricted stock agreement.

Restricted Stock Treated as Outstanding

In Rev. Rul. 2005-39,[109] the IRS concluded that unvested shares of restricted stock, for which an Code Sec. 83(b) election is made, are treated as outstanding stock for purposes of determining:

- Whether a corporation has experienced a change in ownership or control under Code Sec. 280G(b)(2)(A)(i); and
- The amount of stock held by a shareholder for purposes of testing whether the shareholder is a disqualified individual under Reg. § 1.280G-1, Q/A-17.

The IRS reached this conclusion because generally, stock—including restricted stock—that is transferred to an employee in connection with the performance of services is treated as substantially vested when the employee makes an election under Code Sec. 83(b), and the employee is considered the owner of the stock.

.04 How to Avoid Golden Parachute Limitations

In order to circumvent the golden parachute limitations, taxpayers often attempt to creatively structure their agreements as something other than a golden parachute agreement. With this in mind, taxpayers try to make the payments resemble payments that are exempted from the parachute limitations. The following payments are exempt from the parachute rules:

---

108 *R.H. Yocum*, FedCl, 2005-2 USTC ¶ 50,470, 66 FedCl 579.

109 Rev. Rul. 2005-39, 2005-2 CB 1.

- Payments with respect to a small business corporation;
- Payments with respect to a corporation no stock in which is readily tradable on an established securities market if certain shareholder approval requirements are satisfied;
- Payments to or from a qualified plan;
- Certain payments made by a tax-exempt Code Sec. 501(c)(3) corporation undergoing a change in ownership or control but only if such organization is subject to an express statutory prohibition against inurement of net earnings to the benefit of any private shareholder or individual;
- Certain payments of reasonable compensation for services to be rendered on or after the change in ownership or control [Reg. § 1.280G, Q&A 5];
- Termination payments triggered by an employer's reorganization where the payments can be allocated to a noncompete covenant.[110]

Contrast these payments with payments that replace compensation that would have been earned by an executive if he had continued to perform services for the remainder of his employment contract. Taxpayers involved in ownership shifts who resort to such techniques must prove the reasonableness of any payments received in connection with the change in corporate ownership or control. Parties to a severance agreement should thus be prepared (1) to prove that the payments they received were not triggered by a change in business ownership, (2) to describe in great detail what services were performed in exchange for payments received, and (3) to justify payments received by reference to comparable rates within the industry or historical rates of compensation for that individual.[111]

Example 12-5: A small business corporation operates two businesses. The corporation sells the assets of one of its businesses, and these assets represent a substantial portion of the assets of the corporation. Because of the sale, the corporation terminates its employment relationship with persons employed in that business. Several of these employees are highly-compensated individuals to whom the owners of the corporation make severance payments in excess of three times each employee's base amount. Since the corporation is a small business corporation immediately before the change in ownership or control, the payments are not parachute payments [Reg. § 1.280G-1, Q&A-6, Ex.1].

Example 12-6: Assume the same facts as in Example 12-5, except that the corporation is not a small business corporation. If no stock in the corporation is readily tradable on an established securities market (or otherwise) immediately before the change in ownership or control and the shareholder approval requirements are met, the payments are not parachute payments [Reg. § 1.280G-1, Q&A-6, Ex. 2].

---

[110] LTR 200110025 (Dec. 8, 2000).

[111] *J.N. Balch*, Dec. 48,976, 100 TC 331, Dec. 48,976 (1993), *aff'd sub nom, R.G. Cline*, CA-7, 94-2 USTC ¶ 50,468, 34 F3d 480.

Example 12-7: Stock of Corporation S is wholly owned by Corporation P, stock of which is readily tradable on an established securities market. The Corporation S stock equals or exceeds one-third of the total gross fair market value of Corporation P, and thus, represents a substantial portion of the assets of Corporation P. Corporation S makes severance payments to several of its highly-compensated individuals that are parachute payments under Code Sec. 280G. Because stock in Corporation P is readily tradable on an established securities market, the payments are not exempt from the definition of parachute payments [Reg. § 1.280G-1, Q&A-6, Ex. 3].

.05 *Disqualified Individual* Defined

A *disqualified individual* under Code Sec. 280G(c) includes an employee or independent contractor of the corporation who is with respect to the corporation a shareholder, officer, or a highly compensated individual. An individual will be treated as an employee-shareholder if at any time he owns more than 1 percent of the fair market value of the outstanding shares of all classes of the corporation's stock. Even if a person owns less than 1 percent, he or she may still be deemed a disqualified individual if he or she is an officer or highly-compensated

An individual will be treated as highly compensated if he or she is a member of the group consisting of the lesser of the highest paid 250 employees or the highest paid 1 percent of employees.

.06 Types of Parachute Payments

Parachute payments are defined as a "payment in the nature of compensation." This means that parachute payments may take the form of cash, the right to receive cash, a transfer of property, pensions, insurance or annuity proceeds, as well as other payments (such as fringe payments) that arise out of the employment relationship. In addition, both nonstatutory and statutory stock options will be treated as property transferred, for parachute purposes, not later than the time at which the options become substantially vested, whether or not they have a readily ascertainable fair market value.

.07 Valuation of Compensatory Stock Options

In Rev. Proc. 2003-68,[112] the IRS has provided rules for valuing compensatory stock options for purposes of the golden parachute rules. According to Rev. Proc. 2003-68, a taxpayer may value a stock option, without regard to whether the option is on publicly or nonpublicly traded stock, using any valuation method that is consistent with generally accepted accounting principles and which takes into account the factors provided in Reg. § 1.280G-1, Q&A 13. Important factors include the following:

- The spread, which is the difference between the option's exercise price and the value of the option property at the time of vesting;
- The volatility of the underlying stock, which is the probability of the property increasing or decreasing in value; and
- The *option term,* which is how long the holder has to exercise the option.

[112] Rev. Proc. 2003-68, 2003-2 CB 398.

Recalculation

The value of an option may be recalculated during the 18-month period beginning on the date of the change in ownership or control [Reg. § 1.280G-1, Q/A-33]. Recalculation is permitted if, during the redetermination period, either of the following occurs: (1) there is a change in the term of the option due to a termination of employment, or (2) there is a change in the volatility of the stock. For purposes of redetermining the value of the option, an employer is permitted to use a method other than the method used in making the initial determination, provided that both methods are permitted under Rev. Proc. 2003-68. If the value of an option is recalculated under this revenue procedure, parachute payments and excess parachute payments must be recalculated using the redetermined valuation. However, the base amount does not have to be re-apportioned; instead, the base amount allocated to the parachute payment is permitted to remain the same, with any adjustment to the excise tax made with respect to the option. This adjustment may be claimed only by filing an amended return for the tax year that includes the payment date.

Valuation Safe Harbor

- The safe harbor valuation method is based on the *Black-Scholes* model and takes into account, as of the valuation date, the following factors:
- The volatility of the underlying stock;
- The exercise price of the option;
- The value of the stock at the time of the valuation (the *spot price*); and
- The term of the option on the valuation date.

The safe harbor value of the option equals (1) the number of shares covered by the options multiplied by (2) the spot price of the stock, then multiplied by (3) a valuation factor. To determine the valuation factor, the taxpayer must determine the volatility, spread, and option term factors, as described below.

Volatility

The taxpayer must determine whether the volatility of the underlying stock is low, medium, or high. If the valuation is based on a substituted option, volatility is determined based on the stock under the substituted option. For this purpose, a low volatility stock has an annual standard deviation of 30 percent or less. A medium volatility stock has an annual standard deviation greater than 30 percent but less than 70 percent. A high volatility stock has an annual standard deviation of 70 percent or greater. If the stock is publicly traded on an established securities market, the expected volatility of the underlying stock used for purposes of volatility must be the volatility for the most recent year disclosed in the most recent financial statements of the corporation. If the stock is not publicly traded, the volatility is assumed to be the same as the volatility for a comparable corporation that is publicly traded.

¶12,085 COMPENSATION CAP FOR PUBLICLY HELD CORPORATIONS

A publicly held corporation's deduction for compensation paid to a "covered employee" during the tax year is limited to $1 million [Code Sec. 162(m)(1)].

.01 Covered Employee Defined

A "covered employee" is defined in Code Sec. 162(m)(3) as any employee if as of the close of the tax year, (1) the employee is the chief executive officer (CEO) or is an individual acting in such capacity, or (2) the employee's total compensation for the year must be reported to shareholders because the employee is among the four highest compensated officers (other than the CEO). Reg. § 1.162-27(c)(2)(ii) generally provides that named executive officers subject to disclosure are: (i) the principal executive officer (PEO), principal financial officer (PFO) or someone acting in a similar capacity regardless of compensation level; (ii) the three most highly compensated executive officers other than the PEO and the PFO who were serving as executive officers; and (iii) up to two additional individuals for whom disclosure would have been provided but for the fact that the individual was not serving as an executive officer at the end of the tax year.[113] The time for determining whether an employee is a covered employee by virtue of being highly compensated is made as of the close of the tax year.[114] The $1 million compensation deduction limit paid to covered employees of a publicly held corporation doesn't apply to a foreign corporation.[115]

Coordination with Disallowed Golden Parachute Payments

The $1 million threshold is reduced (but not below zero) by excess golden parachute payments that are not deductible under the golden parachute provisions of Code Sec. 280G [¶ 12,080] [Code Sec. 162(m)(4)(F); Reg. § 1.162-27(g)].

> **Example 12-8:** The CEO of ABCo is paid $1,500,000 in compensation for the tax year. Of this amount, $600,000 is an excess parachute payment. Because the excess parachute payment reduces the $1 million deduction limitation to $400,000, ABCo can deduct $400,000, because $500,000 of the compensation is nondeductible.

.02 Publicly Held Corporation Defined

A publicly held corporation is defined as any corporation issuing any class of securities required to be registered under section 12 of the Securities Exchange Act of 1934, i.e., a corporation the securities of which are listed on a national securities exchange or that has $5 million or more of assets and 500 or more shareholders [Code Sec. 162(m)(2); Reg. § 1.162-27(c)(1)(i)]. Whether a corporation is publicly held is determined on the last day of the corporation's tax year. Accordingly, a publicly held corporation that becomes private during its tax year is not subject to Code Sec. 162(m) [Reg. § 1.162-27(c)(1)(i)]. A publicly held corporation includes all corporations in the affiliated

---

[113] Notice 2007-49, 2007-1 CB 1429.

[114] LTR 201321017 (Feb. 20, 2013).

[115] LTR 200916012 (Dec. 23, 2008).

group of the publicly held corporation whether or not a consolidated return is filed. A publicly held subsidiary is subject to separate SEC reporting requirements and so is excluded from the affiliated group of its parent. Separate treatment of publicly held subsidiaries is effective as of the first regularly scheduled shareholder meeting of the publicly held subsidiary that occurs more than 12 months after December 2, 1994 [Reg. § 1.162-27(j) (2) (ii)].

.03 Compensation Defined

Compensation for purposes of the Code Sec. 162(m) (3) deduction limitation includes all amounts paid during the tax year whether paid in cash, stock, options, the corporation's stock, or other property, if the compensation would otherwise be deductible as remuneration for services performed by a covered employee [Code Sec. 162(m) (4) (E); Reg. § 1.162-27(c) (3)].

Compensation does not include:

1. Compensation in the form of payments from qualified retirement plans or nontaxable fringe benefits [Reg. § 1.162-27(c) (3)],
2. Remuneration that is not treated as wages for purposes of the Federal Insurance Contributions Act (FICA) [Code Sec. 3121(a) (5) (A) through Code Sec. 3121(a) (5) (D)],
3. Any benefit that is reasonably anticipated to be excludable from gross income under the Code.

For discussion of withholding rules imposed on $1 million-plus supplemental wages, see ¶ 14,225 and ¶ 15,015.

.04 Exemptions from $1 Million Cap

The following types of compensation are specifically excluded from the $1 million limit:

- Commissions generated solely on account of income generated by the employee's efforts [Reg. § 1.162-27(d)];
- "Performance-based" compensation paid to covered employees will not be subject to the $1 million deduction limit if:
  - — It is payable solely on account of the attainment of one or more preestablished, objective performance goals but only if (i) the performance goals are determined by a compensation committee of the board of directors of the taxpayer which is comprised solely of two or more outside directors, (ii) the material terms under which the remuneration is to be paid, including the performance goals, are disclosed to shareholders and approved by a majority of the vote in a separate shareholder vote before payment of such remuneration, and (iii) before any payment of such remuneration, the compensation committee certifies that the performance goals and other material terms were in fact satisfied [Code Sec. 162(m) (4) (C); Reg. § 1.162-27(e) (2)]. In Rev. Rul. 2008-13,[116] the IRS concluded that compensation paid to an executive is not qualified performance-based com-

[116] Rev. Rul. 2008-13, IRB 2008-10, 518. *See also* LTR 200804004 (Sept. 21, 2007).

pensation-based compensation for purposes of Code Sec. 162(m), even if the compensation is paid upon the attainment of the performance goal, if the plan agreement or contract provides for payment of compensation to an executive upon the attainment of a performance goal or for (1) termination without "cause" or for "good reason" or (2) voluntary retirement. This ruling expands the scope of Letter Ruling 200804004 where the IRS determined that incentive awards paid to a corporate executive did not qualify as performance-based compensation under Code Sec. 162(m) because the awards would be paid even if the performance goals were not attained if the executive terminated his or her employment for good reason or the company terminated the employment arrangement without cause.

— Stock options and stock appreciation rights are deemed to satisfy the performance goal requirement if: (1) the grant or award is made by the compensation committee; (2) the plan under which the option or right is granted states the maximum number of shares with respect to which options or rights may be granted during a specified period to any employee; and (3) under the terms of the option or right, the amount of compensation the employee can receive is based solely on an increase in the value of the stock after the date of the grant or award [Prop. Reg. § 1.162-27(e)(2)(vi)].

— In Rev. Rul. 2012-19,[117] the IRS concluded that dividends paid on restricted stock and dividend equivalents paid on restricted stock units (RSU) must satisfy the performance-based compensation rules of Code Sec. 162(m) separately from the stock and the RSUs. Thus, even if the rights to the stock and RSUs are performance-based, the dividends and equivalents are not automatically performance-based.

— The goals are established in writing by a committee of two or more "outside directors" during the first 90 days (or first 25 percent) of a "performance period" relating to the employee's performance of service when the outcome of the performance is still substantially uncertain. A corporate director qualifies as an "outside director" and is, thus, eligible to grant awards and make other determinations under performance-based compensation plans if he is not a current employee, a former employee receiving compensation (other than under a tax-qualified pension plan) or a current or former officer [Reg. § 1.162-27(e)(3)]. However, a director is not disqualified solely because he or she is a former officer of a corporation that previously was a member of the employer's affiliated group, but is no longer affiliated because it has been spun off or liquidated. In Rev. Rul. 2008-32,[118] the IRS concluded that a member of a publicly held corporation's board of directors, who had been an interim CEO of the company, did not qualify as an "outside director." Therefore, he could not set performance based compensation goals to allow the corporation to avoid the Code Sec. 162(m)(1) $1 million compensation deduction limit on compensation paid to its executives. An outside director is one who doesn't receive remuneration in any capacity other than as a director [Reg. § 1.162-27(e)(3)(i)(D)]. Remuneration for this purpose includes

[117] Rev. Rul. 2012-19, IRB 2012-28, 16.

[118] Rev. Rul. 2008-32, IRB 2008-27, 6.

any payment in exchange for goods or services. Remuneration is received by a director in each of the following circumstances: (1) remuneration is paid, directly or indirectly, to the director personally or to an entity in which the director has a beneficial ownership interest of greater than 50 percent; (2) remuneration, other than *de minimis* remuneration, was paid by the publicly held corporation in its preceding tax year to an entity in which the director has a beneficial ownership interest of at least five percent but not more than 50 percent; and (3) remuneration, other than *de minimis* remuneration, was paid by the publicly held corporation in its preceding tax year to an entity by which the director is employed or self-employed, other than as a director. Remuneration that was paid by the publicly held corporation in its preceding tax year to an entity is *de minimis* if payments to the entity did not exceed five percent of the gross revenue of the entity for its tax year ending with or within that preceding tax year of the publicly held corporation. However, remuneration in excess of $60,000 is not *de minimis*. Under Reg. § 1.162-27(e)(3)(iv), remuneration is not for personal services unless two requirements are satisfied. First, the remuneration must be paid to an entity for legal, accounting, investment banking, and management consulting services performed for the corporation. Second, the director must perform significant services (whether or not as an employee) for the corporation, division, or similar organization (within the entity) that actually provides the personal services to the publicly held corporation, or more than 50 percent of the entity's gross revenues for the entity's preceding tax year are derived from the personal-service-providing-organization;

— The material terms of the performance goals are disclosed to and approved by a majority of the shareholders in a separate shareholder vote before payment is made;

— The compensation committee certifies in writing that the performance goals were met before any payment is made; and

— The compensation committee has discretion only to reduce, but not to increase, the amount of compensation payable under the performance formula.

- Payments to a qualified retirement plan (including salary reduction payments under a 401(k) plan);
- Benefits and other amounts excluded from an employee's gross income (e.g., tuition reimbursements under an educational assistance plan); and
- Compensation paid under a written contract that was binding on February 17, 1993, and at all times thereafter, unless after February 17, 1993, there has been a material modification of the terms of the contract or it has been renewed [Reg. § 1.162-27(h)].
- Compensation paid under an agreement that existed prior to the corporation becoming publicly held and disclosed in the initial public offering (IPO) is not subject to the $1 million ceiling for 3 years after becoming public. The $1 million deduction limit does not apply to any compensation plan that existed before the corporation became publicly held to the extent that the plan was disclosed in the prospectus accompanying the IPO [Reg. § 1.162-27(f)(1)]. In addition, the $1 million deduction limit does not apply to a privately held corporation that went public without an IPO.

Example 12-9: Prior to the start of a fiscal year, Corporation S establishes a bonus plan under which Alice Able, the chief executive officer, will receive a cash bonus of $500,000, if year-end corporate sales increase by at least 5 percent. The compensation committee retains the right, if the performance goal is met, to reduce the bonus payment to Alice if, in its judgment, other subjective factors warrant a reduction. The bonus will be deductible.

Example 12-10: Bob Best is the general counsel of Corporation R, which is engaged in patent litigation with Corporation S. Representatives of Corporation S have informally indicated to Corporation R a willingness to settle the litigation for $50,000. Subsequently, the compensation committee of Corporation R agrees to pay Bob a bonus if Bob obtains a formal settlement for at least $50,000. The bonus to Bob is not deductible because the performance goal was not established at a time when the outcome was substantially uncertain.

¶12,086 EXECUTIVE COMPENSATION LIMITS FOR FINANCIAL INSTITUTIONS PARTICIPATING IN TARP

Under the Troubled Asset Relief Program (TARP), the federal government is authorized to purchase troubled assets from financial institutions, either through a public auction or directly from the institution. During the period in which financial assistance under TARP remains outstanding, each TARP recipient will be subject to the $500,000 deduction limit for compensation paid to "covered executives" under Code Sec. 162(m)(5). There is no threshold amount of assistance an entity must receive to be classified as a TARP recipient for these purposes.

.01 Covered Executives

"Covered executives" include the chief executive officer (CEO) and the chief financial officer (CFO) of an applicable employer (or an individual acting in that capacity), at any time during a portion of the tax year that includes the TARP authorities period. It also includes any employee who is one of the three highest compensated officers of the employer for the year (other than the CEO and CFO).

¶12,087 HEALTH INSURANCE PROVIDER $500,000 DEDUCTION LIMIT

.01 General Rule

Code Sec. 162(m)(6) imposes a $500,000 deduction limitation rule on the aggregate amount of "applicable individual remuneration" and "deferred deduction remuneration" paid by a covered health insurance provider to an "applicable individual" for services performed by the applicable individual. The deduction limit will apply whether the remuneration is paid during the tax year in which the services are performed or in a later tax year. For example, if an applicable individual has $500,000 or more of applicable individual remuneration attributable to services provided in a disqualified tax year, the amount that exceeds $500,000 is not deductible in any tax year. The deferred deduction remuneration attributable to that tax year would not be deductible in any tax year either. However, if an applicable individual has less than $500,0000 in applicable individual remuneration for a disqualified tax year, and has deferred deduction remuneration attributable to the same disqualified tax year that when combined with the applicable individual remuneration for the year exceeds $500,000, all of the applicable individual remuneration is deductible in that disqualified tax year. In such a case, the amount of deferred deduction remuneration deductible in future tax years is limited to the excess of $500,000 over the amount of the applicable individual remuneration for that tax year [Prop. Reg. § 1.162-31(e)(1)].

.02 Applicable Individuals

The $500,000 deduction limit applies only for remuneration earned by an applicable individual. Applicable individuals include officers, directors, and employees of a covered health insurance provider, and can include independent contractors [Code Sec. 162(m)(6)(F)].

.03 Applicable Individual Remuneration

"Applicable individual remuneration" is the aggregate amount of remuneration that would otherwise be deductible for services performed by an applicable individual. If the remuneration is deductible in the current tax year, it does not matter whether the services were performed in the current tax year or another tax year. Applicable individual remuneration includes commission based pay, performance-based compensation, and remuneration payable under an existing binding contract [Code Sec. 162(m)(6)(D); Prop. Reg. § 1.162-31(b)(10)].

Applicable individual remuneration for a disqualified tax year (i.e., a year in which the employer is a covered health insurance provider as defined in Prop. Reg. § 1.162-31(b)(6)), may include remuneration for services performed in a year before the year in which the deduction for the remuneration is allowable. For example, a discretionary bonus granted and paid to an applicable individual in a disqualified tax year in recognition of services performed in prior tax years is applicable individual remuneration for that disqualified tax year. In addition, a grant of restricted stock in a disqualified tax year with respect to which an applicable individual makes an election under Code Sec. 83(b) is applicable individual remuneration for the disqualified tax year of the covered health insurance provider in which the grant of the restricted stock is made [Prop. Reg. § 1.162-31(b)(10)]. Applicable individual remuneration does not include any deferred deduction remuneration with respect to services performed during any tax year [Prop. Reg. § 1.162-31(b)(10)].

.04 Deferred Deduction Remuneration

Deferred deduction remuneration is remuneration that would be applicable individual remuneration for services performed during the tax year except that the deduction is allowable (without regard to this limitation) in a subsequent year.

.05 Order of Application and Calculation of Deduction Limits

The deduction limit of $500,000 is applied first to applicable individual remuneration attributable to a disqualified tax year, and is reduced (but not below zero) by the amount of the applicable individual remuneration against which it is applied. If the applicable individual also has deferred deduction remuneration attributable to that disqualified tax year that becomes otherwise deductible in a subsequent tax year, the deduction limit (as reduced) is applied to that amount of deferred deduction remuneration in the first tax year in which it becomes otherwise deductible. The deduction limit is then further reduced (but not below zero) by the amount of the deferred deduction remuneration against which it is applied. If the applicable individual has an additional amount of deferred deduction remuneration attributable to services performed in the original disqualified tax year that becomes otherwise deductible in a subsequent tax year, the deduction limitation, as further reduced, is applied to that amount of deferred deduction remuneration in the tax year in which it is otherwise deductible. This process continues for future tax years in which deferred deduction remuneration attributable to services performed by the applicable individual in the original disqualified tax year is otherwise deductible. No deduction is allowed in any tax year for any applicable individual remuneration or deferred deduction remuneration attributable to services performed in a disqualified tax year to the extent that it exceeds the deduction limitation for that disqualified tax year at the time the deduction limitation is applied to the remuneration [Prop. Reg. § 1.162-31(e)(2)(i)].

.06 Application to Payments

A payment of deferred deduction remuneration may include remuneration attributable to services performed in earlier tax years of a covered health insurance provider. In that case, a separate deduction limitation applies to each portion of the payment that is attributed to services performed in a different disqualified tax year. Any portion of a payment that is attributed to a disqualified tax year is deductible only to the extent that it does not exceed the deduction limit that applies for that disqualified tax year, as reduced by the amount of applicable individual remuneration and deferred deduction remuneration attributable to services performed in that year that were deductible in an earlier tax year. Amounts attributable to services performed by an applicable individual must be attributed to services performed by the applicable individual in the earliest year to which the amount can be attributed under the tax year attribution rules [Prop. Reg. § 1.162-31(e)(2)(ii)].

RENT, ADVERTISING, INSURANCE

¶12,095 RENT

Tenants can deduct rent for property they use to the extent it is used in their trade, business or profession [Code Secs. 162(a)(3), 212]. Payments for leasing machinery and equipment can also be deducted.

.01 Advance Rental

A cash method taxpayer generally may not deduct prepaid rent in the year paid because it is not an ordinary and necessary business expense for that year. Prepaid rental payments are in part a consideration for the use of rented premises for years subsequent to the tax year in which they are paid. Therefore the entire amount cannot properly be considered an ordinary and necessary expense of carrying on the business during the tax year, and only the part properly attributable to the process of earning income during the tax years may be deducted from gross income for those years. The taxpayer must deduct prepaid rent ratably over the years in which the taxpayer uses the property. In *Baton Coal Co.*,[119] the Tax Court held that rental payments must be apportioned as an expense over the life of the lease. Thus, only the portion allocation to a particular year can be deducted in that year.

> **Example 12-11:** Company ABCo enters into a 10-year lease under which it is required to pay rent of $2,000 a year. During the first year, it pays not only the $2,000 allocable to that year but the entire $20,000 rent for the 10-year period. It may deduct only $2,000 during the first year. The remaining $18,000 must be deducted ratably, $2,000 a year, over the remaining 9 years.

However, in *Zaninovich*,[120] the Court of Appeals for the Ninth Circuit indicated that an advance rental prepayment limited to one year of a 20-year lease was deductible in full in the year of payment and did not have to be prorated. Thus, a calendar-year taxpayer who made a lease prepayment covering a one-year period from December through November in December of the current year was entitled to deduct the entire amount in the year of payment.

Some courts have applied a 3-prong test for allowing a current deduction for advance rental payments:[121] (1) actual payment of the item; (2) a substantial business reason for making the payment; and (3) the item's prepayment cannot cause a material distortion in the taxpayer's taxable income.

.02 Lease Cancellation Payments

Amounts paid by a landlord for canceling a lease are capital expenditures recoverable through deductions spread over the unexpired term of the lease.[122] If the sum is paid by the tenant for canceling his lease, the total cost of canceling the lease and any unamortized improvements to the leasehold are deductible in the year of cancellation.[123]

.03 Payments Under Lease

Payments for using machinery and equipment under lease agreements are deductible as rent if there is compelling evidence of a true rental and not a sale. Otherwise, the

---

[119] *Baton Coal Co.*, 19 BTA 169, Dec. 5882, *aff'd*, CA-3, 2 USTC ¶788, 51 F2d 469, *cert. denied*, 284 US 674, 52 SCt 129.

[120] *M.J. Zaninovich*, CA-9, 80-1 USTC ¶9342, 616 F2d 429.

[121] *J.J. Grynberg*, Dec. 41,439, 83 TC 255, Dec. 41,439 (1984).

[122] *H.B. Miller*, Dec. 3464, 10 BTA 383.

[123] *A.J. Cassatt*, CA-3, 43-2 USTC ¶9579, 137 F2d 745.

payments (except for interest and other charges) are part of the purchase price and are not deductible (but you are allowed depreciation on the property).

In *Yearout Mechanical & Engineering, Inc.*[124] the Tax Court concluded that a mechanical contractor could deduct amounts paid for renting equipment from its controlling shareholders. The rental agreements entered into with the shareholders were hybrid arrangements that contained features of both long-term leases and short-term rental agreements. There was a valid business reason for the arrangement. The taxpayer's management determined that incurring additional long-term debt or comparable commitments under a long-term lease was imprudent given the untested line of business. Additionally, short-term rentals were infeasible, given an increase in the construction business and a demand for construction equipment that exceeded supply on the third-party rental market. The payments made under the hybrid arrangements were reasonable and not more than the taxpayer would have been required to pay as a result of an arm's-length bargain.

Lease Agreement Treated as Purchase or Sale

To determine if your payments are rent, you must first establish that your agreement is a lease rather than a conditional sales contract. If you acquire title to or equity in the property, the agreement should be treated as a conditional sales contract. Any one or more of the following conditions indicate that the so-called lease is really a purchase or sale:

- Portions of periodic payments apply specifically to an equity to be acquired by the lessee;
- Lessee will acquire title on payment of a stated amount of "rent" that must be paid in any event;
- Total amount that the lessee must pay for a relatively short period of use is very large compared with the amount needed to get transfer of title;
- Periodic payments materially exceed current fair rental value;
- Property may be bought under an option at a price that is (a) nominal in relation to value of property at the time option may be exercised, or (b) relatively small compared with total required payments;
- Part of the "rent" is specifically designated interest or is easily recognizable as the equivalent of interest; and
- Total rental payments plus option price approximate price at which property could have been bought plus interest and carrying charges.

Transfer of Title Not Essential

The fact that the agreement does not provide for the transfer of title or specifically precludes transfer of title does not prevent the contract from being a sale of an equitable interest in the property. Thus, the agreement is a sale if (1) total rents over a relatively short period approximate the price at which the property could have been bought plus interest and carrying charges and (2) the lessee may continue to use the property over

[124] *Yearout Mechanical & Engineering, Inc.*, 36 TCM 158, Dec. 57,540(M), TC Memo 2008-217.

its entire useful life for relatively nominal or token payments, even if there is no provision for the passage of title.[125]

.04 Leveraged Lease Transactions

In Rev. Proc. 2001-28,[126] the IRS provides guidelines it will use for advance ruling purposes in determining whether certain transactions purporting to be leases of property are, in fact, leases for federal income tax purposes. Why is this important? Different tax consequences result from whether a transaction is characterized as a lease. They will be treated as either financing arrangements or as sales of the subject property depending on the characterization. Rev. Proc. 2001-28 applies to *leveraged leases,* which involve three parties: a lessor, a lessee and a lender to the lessor. In general, these leases are net leases, the lease term covers a substantial part of the useful life of the leased property, and the lessee's payments to the lessor are sufficient to discharge the lessor's payments to the lender.

The IRS will consider the lessor in a leveraged lease transaction to be the owner of the property and the transaction a valid lease if all the guidelines described below are met:

- *Minimum unconditional "at risk" investment.* The lessor must have made a minimum unconditional "at risk" investment in the property which should be equal to at least 20 percent of the cost of the property.
- *Lease term and renewal options.* The lease term must include all renewal or extension periods except renewals or extensions at the option of the lessee at fair rental value at the time of such renewal or extension.
- *Purchase and sale rights.* No lessee may have a contractual right to purchase the property from the lessor at a price less than its fair market value at the time the right is exercised.
- *Investment by lessee.* Rules must be specified concerning the permitted investment in the property by the lessee, including the specifications regarding severable and nonseverable improvements to the property.
- *No Lessee loans or guarantees.* No member of the lessee group may loan funds to the lessor to acquire the property.
- *Profit motive required.* The lessor must represent and demonstrate that it expects to receive a profit from the transaction beyond the value of the tax deductions, allowances, credits, and other tax attributes arising from the transaction. In meeting this rule, overall profit and positive cash flow requirements must be met.

The actual requirements for the ruling request are set forth in Rev. Proc. 2001-29.[127]

.05 Leased Acquisition Costs

A proportionate part of sums paid to acquire a lease for business reasons, can be deducted each year of the lease [Reg. § 1.162-11(a)]. Lease-acquisition costs may be amortized over the lease term [Code Sec. 178(a); Reg. §§ 1.178-1, -3]. However, any lease renewals (including renewal options and any other period for which you reasonably expect the lease to be renewed) must be included in figuring the amortization

---

[125] Rev. Rul. 55-540, 1955-2 CB 39.

[126] Rev. Proc. 2001-28, 2001-1 CB 1156.

[127] Rev. Proc. 2001-29, 2001-1 CB 1160.

period, but only if less than 75 percent of the lease-acquisition cost is for the lease's remaining term (excluding any renewal period remaining on the lease acquisition date).

A district court in *ABC Beverage Corp.*,[128] allowed a taxpayer that exercised an option to purchase property it had been leasing to deduct a portion of the amount tendered in the transaction as a lease termination payment. The deductible portion of the purchase price was attributable to buying out the lease that called for excessive rent.

¶12,100 ADVERTISING EXPENSES

Advertising expenditures (except indirect political contributions [¶ 12,025]) are deductible as business expenses, if they are ordinary and necessary and bear a reasonable relation to the business activities of the taxpayer. The cost of goodwill advertising that keeps the advertiser's name before the public is deductible. But the cost of advertising intended to promote or defeat legislation is not deductible. Advertising that encourages charitable contributions or the buying of U.S. savings bonds qualifies as a deductible expense [Reg. § 1.162-20(a)(2)].

.01 Deductible

Examples of deductible expenses include: expenses of car dealer for sponsoring sports car racing;[129] of slaughterhouse for sponsoring race car displaying company name;[130] of auto agency outfitting and supporting local youth baseball team;[131] of professional sports club for financing construction of local hall of fame;[132] of slot machine leasing company for furnishing pencils, balloons, calendars, etc. to clubs and lodges that leased machines from company.[133]

.02 Nondeductible

Examples of nondeductible expenses include: lock and safe business for maintaining parade horses that did not link company name with show entries;[134] of tax expert for maintaining yacht that flew pennant bearing numerals "1040";[135] of realtor for maintaining Moorish "castle" as residence;[136] of restaurant intending to promote or defeat legislation, political parties or candidates.[137]

> **NOTE:** The IRS has said that, except in very unusual circumstances, advertising costs are currently deductible and don't have to be capitalized.[138] Advertising costs must be capitalized only where the advertising is specifically directed toward obtaining future benefits significantly beyond those traditionally associ-

---

[128] *ABC Beverage Corp.*, DC-MI, 2008-2 USTC ¶ 50,533, 577 FSupp2d 935.

[129] *Lang Chevrolet Co.*, 26 TCM 1054, Dec. 28,648(M), TC Memo. 1967-212.

[130] *D.O. Hestnes*, 47 TCM 528, Dec. 40,650(M), TC Memo. 1983-727, *cert. denied*, 106 SCt 234.

[131] *J. Dahl*, 24 BTA 1167, Dec. 7337, *acq.* 1932-1 CB 3.

[132] Rev. Rul. 66-277, 1966-2 CB 42.

[133] *Ohio Novelty Co.*, 6 TCM 1128, Dec. 16,096(M) (1947).

[134] *L.W. Rolland*, 18 TCM 702, Dec. 23,725(M), TC Memo. 1959-161, *aff'd*, CA-5, 61-1 USTC ¶ 9190, 285 F2d 760.

[135] *R.L. Henry*, 36 TC 879, Dec. 24,994 (1961).

[136] *D.B. Kenerly*, 47 TCM 1244, Dec. 41,048(M), TC Memo. 1984-117.

[137] *Pickrick Inc.*, DC-GA, 65-2 USTC ¶ 9543.

[138] Rev. Rul. 92-80, 1992-2 CB 57.

ated with normal product advertising or with institutional or good will advertising (e.g., ad costs to allay public opposition to granting of a nuclear power plant license).

¶12,105 INSURANCE PREMIUMS

.01 Life Insurance Premiums

Premiums are not deductible if paid by the person insured [Code Sec. 262(a); Reg. § 1.262-1(b)(1)]. Such premiums are personal rather than business or "nonbusiness" expenses. For example, premiums you pay on an ordinary life policy you take out on your life (with your spouse or other dependents as beneficiaries) are not deductible.

A company may not deduct premiums paid on any life insurance policy, or endowment or annuity contract covering the life of any of its officers or employees if the company is directly or indirectly a beneficiary under the policy or contract [Code Sec. 264(a); Reg. § 1.264-1(a)]. This means that premiums paid by an employer on the life of any employee are not deductible while the employer is a beneficiary, even if only to the extent of the cash surrender value.[139]

A partner in a partnership who takes out an insurance policy on his or her own life and names his or her partners as beneficiaries to induce them to retain their investments in the partnership, will be considered a beneficiary and the insurance premiums will not be deductible.

The deduction prohibition described above does not apply to the following [Code Sec. 264(b)]:

- Any annuity contract described in Code Sec. 72(s)(5). This includes certain qualified pension plans, certain retirement annuities, individual retirement annuities, and qualified funding assets; and
- Any annuity contract to which Code Sec. 72(u) applies. This includes annuity contract held by other than natural persons.

However, premiums a company pays on the life of an officer or employee *are* deductible if the company is neither directly nor indirectly a beneficiary *and* the premium is an ordinary and necessary business expense [Code Sec. 162(a)]

Group Insurance Premiums

Premiums paid by an employer on group-permanent and group-term life insurance are deductible [Ch. 4]. For taxability to the employee, see Ch. 2.

Loan Insurance

If you insure your own life or the life of another person with a financial interest in your business to get a loan for business purposes (policy in favor of lender), you may not deduct the premiums [Code Sec. 264(a)(1)]. The proceeds would be used to liquidate the debt, so you are indirectly a beneficiary.[140]

---

[139] Rev. Rul. 66-203, 1966-2 CB 104.

[140] Rev. Rul. 68-5, 1968-1 CB 99.

Certain Partnership Insurance

A partner cannot deduct premiums on insurance on his own life, irrevocably naming his co-partners as sole beneficiaries to induce them to stay in the business. (In accomplishing his purpose, jeopardy to a taxpayer's interest in the partnership is removed and his interest in the business is favorably affected.[141]) [Reg. § 1.264-1(b)].

Split-Dollar Life Insurance Plan

Split-dollar life insurance plans are a popular nonqualified employee benefit that calls for a sharing of premium costs, cash values, and death benefits. The insured, who is usually the employee signs a contractual agreement with his or her employer, whereby the employer agrees to pay all or a portion of the employee's life insurance premiums and the employee pays the balance, if any. For discussion of tax treatment of split-dollar arrangements see Ch. 2.

.02 Premiums on Insurance Other Than Life—Fire, Burglary, and Others

Premiums on fire,[142] burglary, storm, theft, and accident insurance covering property used in a trade, business or profession, or in connection with the production of income or the management, conservation or maintenance of property held for the production of income, are deductible [Code Secs. 162(a), 212; Reg. § § 1.162-1, 1.212-1]. The Tax Court held that premiums paid after a business use ends and the property is offered for sale must be capitalized.[143] Insurance on property used for personal purposes, for example, fire insurance on your home, is a nondeductible personal expense [Code Sec. 262(a); Reg. § 1.262-1]. Premiums paid to insure against your sudden dismissal from employment for reasons other than your own actions or disability are deductible.[144]

Employers' Liability Insurance and Other Business Types

Premiums on other insurance such as public liability, worker's compensation, credit, fidelity, indemnity bonds, use and occupancy, and the like are deductible, if incurred in (1) carrying on a trade, business or profession, (2) the production or collection of income, or (3) the management, conservation or maintenance of property held for the production of income. Some premiums may have to be capitalized [Ch. 12]. Insurance premiums paid by a coal mine for black lung liability insurance coverage were capital expenditures that could not be currently deducted because the coal mine received benefits beyond the current tax year in which the expenditures were made.[145] Premiums on overhead insurance that reimburses the taxpayer for business overhead expenses incurred during prolonged periods of disability are deductible, if the policy expressly states that it is overhead insurance.[146]

Health, Accident, and Disability Insurance

If an employer buys group hospitalization and surgical insurance for employees and their families, the premiums paid are deductible as ordinary and necessary business expenses. The purchase must be in consideration of services rendered.

---

141 Rev. Rul. 73, 1953-1 CB 63.

142 *J.L. Bell*, 13 TC 344, Dec. 17,192 (1949), *acq.* 1949-2 CB 1.

143 *M.R. Lenington*, 25 TCM 1350, Dec. 28,201(M), TC Memo. 1966-264.

144 LTR 8321074 (Feb. 22, 1983).

145 *Black Hills Corp.*, CA-8, 96-1 USTC ¶ 50,036, 73 F3d 799.

146 Rev. Rul. 55-264, 1955-1 CB 11.

Employers who provide group health plans will be penalized if their plan does not provide continuation coverage (see below) to employees and their beneficiaries.

▶ **OBSERVATION:** An employer's highly compensated employees cannot exclude from their gross income contributions made by the employer to a group health plan unless all of the employer's group health plans provide continuation coverage.

To meet the continuation coverage requirement, a plan must provide employees and their qualified beneficiaries the choice of continuing to be covered by the employer's group health plan if they experience a "qualifying event." A qualifying event is a covered employee's death, termination, divorce, and eligibility to receive Medicare benefits. A qualifying event can also involve the end of coverage eligibility for a dependent child under the plan guidelines or a bankruptcy proceeding involving the employer [Code Sec. 4980B(f)(2)(B)(v)].

If any of the qualifying events occur, the plan must provide an election period of at least 60 days to covered employees, their spouses, and their dependent children during which they may choose to continue coverage under the plan [Code Sec. 4980B(f)(5)].

If an employer's group health plan fails to make continuation coverage available to qualified beneficiaries, the employer will be subject to an excise tax. In general, the tax is $100 per day during the noncompliance period for each failure. For certain combined groups of beneficiaries, $200 per day is the maximum tax that can be imposed [Code Sec. 4980B(c)(3)].

NOTE: Any governmental or church plan is excluded from the tax. What's more, the tax doesn't apply to a group health plan that fails to meet the continuing coverage requirements, if the qualifying event occurred in a calendar year right after a calendar year during which the employer usually had fewer than 20 employees on a typical business day [Code Sec. 401(d), (e), 4980B(d)].

.03 Health Insurance Payments of Self-Employeds and S Corp Shareholders

Self-employed taxpayers are entitled to claim a deduction for all or a portion of the amount they pay for health insurance for themselves, their spouse, and dependents [Code Sec. 162(l); Ch. 9]. The deduction for health insurance expenses of self-employed individuals is 100 percent beginning in 2003 and thereafter [Code Sec. 162(1)(1)(A)]. The deduction may also be claimed by individuals as well as S corporation shareholders who own more than 2 percent of the stock or voting power, general partners, and limited partners receiving guaranteed payments. This is a deduction from your adjusted gross income—rather than an itemized medical expense deduction. Any premiums that cannot be deducted as an adjustment to income be deducted as part of their medical expenses on Schedule A, Form 1040 to the extent total medical expenses exceed 10 percent of adjusted gross income [Code Sec. 213(a); ¶9100]. The expenses that are deductible for adjusted gross income are not taken into account in figuring if the threshold for the itemized medical expense deduction is met.

Example 12-12: Susan Walters is a self-employed attorney. She earns an annual salary of $200,000. She spent $3,000 on medical insurance for herself. She may deduct $3,000.

The deduction for health insurance expenses of self-employed individuals cannot be claimed in any month in which he or she is also eligible to participate in a subsidized health plan maintained by his or her employer or the employer of his or her spouse. The amount of your deduction will be limited to your earned income derived from the trade or business for which the insurance plan was established. If you were also eligible to participate in any subsidized health plan maintained by your employer or your spouse's employer for any month or part of month in the year, amounts paid for health insurance coverage for that month cannot be used to figure the deduction. For example, if you were eligible to participate in a subsidized health plan maintained by your spouse's employer from September 30 through December 31, you cannot use amounts paid for health insurance coverage for September through December to figure your deduction.

¶12,110 INTEREST EXPENSES

In a closely held corporation, a shareholder or group of shareholders may loan money to the corporation at fair market interest rates. The corporation must pay interest to the shareholders on the amount borrowed. The interest received by the shareholder is taxed as ordinary income. If advances from shareholders to a corporation are characterized as loans, the corporation can deduct interest it pays on the loans if : (1) the debtor is legally liable for the debt, (2) both parties intend for the debt to be repaid, and (3) a true debtor-creditor relationship exists [Code Sec. 163(a)]. If, however, the advances are characterized as equity, payments on the advances are constructive dividends and are not deductible. For further discussion of constructive dividends, see ¶ 2085. Certain interest must be capitalized as discussed further in ¶ 12,110.03 and Chapter 17.

.01 Determining Whether an Advance Is Debt or Equity

The following 11 nonexclusive factors which were applied by the court in *Roth Steel Tube Co.*[147] should be considered when deciding whether an advance made to a company by a shareholder is debt or equity:

1. The names given the instruments, if any, evidencing the debt.
2. The presence or absence of a fixed maturity date and schedule of payments.
3. The presence or absence of a fixed rate of interest and interest payments.
4. The source of repayments.
5. The adequacy or inadequacy of capitalization.
6. The identity of interest between the creditor and the stockholder.
7. The security, if any, for the advances.

---

[147] *Roth Steel Tube Co.*, CA-6, 86-2 USTC ¶9676, 800 F2d 625, *cert. denied*, 107 SCt 1888.

8. The corporation's ability to obtain financing from an outside lending institution.
9. The extent to which the advances were subordinated to the claims of outside creditors.
10. The extent to which the advances were used to acquire capital assets.
11. The presence or absence of a sinking fund to provide repayments.

No single factor is controlling; the weight to be afforded a given factor depends on the facts and circumstances of the case.

In *Indmar Products Co.*,[148] the Sixth Circuit reversed the Tax Court to hold that advances made by the taxpayer's majority stockholders were loans rather than equity contributions because the advances exhibited clear, objective indicia of *bona fide* debt. Therefore the taxpayer could claim a deduction under Code Sec. 163(a) for the interest payments. The appellate court found that the following Roth Steel factors indicated that the advances were loans: (1) the fixed rate of interest and the regular interest payments indicate that the advances were *bona fide* debt; (2) the history of executed notes indicated that loans existed; (3) the advances are documented by demand notes with a fixed rate of interest and regular interest payments; (4) the taxpayer repaid a significant portion of the unpaid advances by taking on additional debt thus indicating that the presence of a loan; (5) the advances were used for working capital which supports a finding of debt.

.02 Interest on Corporate-Owned Life Insurance (COLI) Policies

Corporations often set up a corporate owned life insurance (COLI) program and purchase life insurance on the lives of its employees whereby the company will receive most if not all of the proceeds when the employee dies. The company borrows against the value of the life insurance policies at an interest rate just above the rate at which inside buildup is credited under the policy, and the company then deducts the interest it pays on these loans. However, no deduction is available for interest paid to any life insurance, annuity, or endowment contract that covers any individual, unless that individual is a key person [Code Sec. 264(a)(4)].

If the policy or contract covers a key person, you can deduct the interest to the following extent:

- The aggregate debt is not more than $50,000 for that key person [Code Sec. 264(e)(1)], and
- The interest paid or accrued for any month is not more than the Moody's Corporate Bond Yield Average-Monthly Average Corporates for that month [Code Sec. 264(e)(2)(B)].

A ***key person*** is an officer or 20 percent owner. However, the number of individuals you can treat as key persons is limited to the greater of (1) five individuals, or (2) the lesser of 5 percent of the total officers and employees of the company or 20 individuals [Code Sec. 264(e)(3)].

---

148 *Indmar Products Co.*, CA-6, 2006-1 USTC ¶50,270, 444 F3d 771, *rev'g*, 89 TCM 795, Dec. 55,936(M), TC Memo. 2005-32.

In the case of a taxpayer other than a natural person, no deduction is allowed for the portion of the taxpayer's interest expense allocable to the unborrowed policy cash surrender value [Code Sec. 264(f)]. An exception exists for a policy owned by an entity engaged in business covering one specified individual who is an employee, officer, or director of the business at the time first covered [Code Sec. 264(f)(4)(A)]. This means that unless one of the exceptions described below applies, you will lose an allocable portion of any interest deduction if you own a life insurance policy, or an annuity or endowment contract with "inside buildup." This occurs where the policy's or contract's cash surrender value exceeds the amount of any loans taken out with respect to the policy or contract.

You will qualify for any exception to this rule if the policy or contract is owned by an entity engaged in a trade or business if that policy or contract covers only one individual and that individual is, when first covered by the policy or contract, one of the following:

- A 20 percent owner of the entity [Code Sec. 264(f)(4)(A)(i)]; or
- An individual other than a 20 percent owner who is an officer, director, or employee of the trade or business [Code Sec. 264(f)(4)(A)(ii)].

A policy or contract covering a 20 percent owner of an entity will not be treated as failing to meet either of these requirements because the policy or contract covers the joint lives of the 20 percent owner and the owner's spouse [Code Sec. 264(f)(4)(A)].

COLI Attacked as Sham

In *American Electric Power Co.*[149] the Court of Appeals for the Sixth Circuit concluded that a taxpayer's COLI program was an economic sham and denied interest deductions on policy loans. The taxpayer purchased life insurance policies on the lives of over 20,000 of its employees, named itself as the beneficiary on all policies and deducted policy loan interest. The court concluded that the COLI plan was an economic sham because the transaction had no practicable economic effects other than the creation of income tax losses. The court noted that the taxpayer did nothing more than "show a deductible expense on paper, without actually suffering any of the ordinary economic consequences of paying the money," because circular netting transactions obviated the obligation to ever actually repay the underlying policy loans. The court did not go so far as to reject the use of all COLI plans but warned taxpayers that the favorable life insurance tax rules cannot be abused by taxpayers who want to create bogus tax deductions, as was done in this case.

The deduction of interest on COLI plans will only be respected by the courts if the plans have real economic consequences. This conclusion mirrors those reached by the Court of Appeals for the Third and Eleventh Circuits who both found that that similar COLI plans were economic shams. In *In re CM Holdings*,[150] the court concluded that the transaction as a whole lacked economic substance, and thus was an economic sham. In

---

[149] *American Electric Power Co.*, CA-6, 2003-1 USTC ¶50,416, 326 F3d 737, *cert. denied*, 540 US 1104, 124 SCt 1043.

[150] *In re CM Holdings*, CA-3, 2002-2 USTC ¶50,596, 301 F3d 96; *Dow Chemical Co.*, CA-6, 2006-1 USTC ¶50,126, 435 F3d 594.

Winn-Dixie Stores, Inc.,[151] the court concluded that the broad-based COLI program lacked sufficient economic substance to be respected for tax purposes.

.03 Capitalization of Interest Expense

Under the uniform capitalization rules, interest paid or incurred during the production period of certain types of property must be capitalized [Code Sec. 263A(f)(1)]. [See Ch. 17]. Property subject to the interest capitalization rules is referred to as "designated property" which is defined as:

1. All real property produced by a taxpayer; and
2. Tangible personal property (other than inventory or property held primarily for sale to customers in the ordinary course of a trade or business) with a class life of 20 years or more under the modified accelerated cost recovery depreciation system (MACRS) (long-life property);
3. Tangible personal property produced by a taxpayer if it either has a class life of 20 years or more, an estimated production period of more than 1 year and total estimated production costs of more than $1 million; or
4. Tangible personal property with an estimated production period of more than 2 years [Code Sec. 263A(f)(1)(B); Code Sec. 163A(f)(4)(A); Reg. § 1.263A-8(b)].

MISCELLANEOUS TRADE OR BUSINESS EXPENSES

¶12,115 EXPENSES OF SELF-EMPLOYEDS

Certain types of business expenses are generally associated with self-employed business and professional people. They are claimed on Schedule C of Form 1040. The IRS has said that so-called statutory employees—a hybrid group of workers that includes outside salespeople, truck drivers, insurance salespeople, etc.—are not employees for income tax purposes. They are treated as self-employed taxpayers and deduct their business expenses on Schedule C.[152] If self-employeds have expenses below $5,000, don't show a loss and meet other tests, they can use Schedule C-EZ.

.01 Self-Employment Taxes

When computing adjusted gross income, a self-employed individual may deduct one-half of the self-employment tax that he or she paid that year [Code Sec. 164(f)]. The 0.9 percent Additional Medicare tax imposed on self-employment income beginning in 2013 is not included in this deduction. For further discussion of the Additional Medicare tax, see ¶ 15,050.

[151] *Winn-Dixie Stores, Inc.*, CA-11, 2001-2 USTC ¶50,495, 254 F3d 1313, *cert. denied*, 535 US 986; *Dow Chemical Co.*, CA-6, 2006-1 USTC ¶50,126, 435 F3d 594.

[152] Rev. Rul. 90-93, 1990-2 CB 33.

.02 Fees for Right to Practice

The following items are *not* deductible: bar examination fees and other expenses incurred in securing admission to the bar; similar fees and expenses incurred by physicians, dentists, accountants and others for securing the right to practice their professions [Reg. § 1.212-1(f)]; fees paid to hospital to practice as staff member (capital expenditure).[153]

.03 Travel Expenses of Self-Employed

If a taxpayer legitimately maintains a home office which is his or her principal place of business, he or she is entitled to a special perk. [See Ch. 12 for more on home office deduction]. The daily transportation expenses incurred when traveling between an office in a home, which now becomes one of your work locations and other work locations regardless of whether the location is regular or temporary, or is within or outside of their metropolitan area is deductible.[154] The daily transportation expenses incurred in going between the home office and other work locations must be incurred in the same trade or business.[155]

> **Example 12-13:** Bob is an architect who uses the basement in his home as his principal place of business. When he is working he drives from his home to client's homes, job sites, the interior designer's office, and various showrooms and fabricators. His transportation costs for all these trips are deductible because he is traveling from one work site (his home) to another work location.

> **Example 12-14:** George is a self-employed tree cutter who works in national forests all over the country. The Tax Court has held that he was entitled to deduct all vehicle expenses that he incurred traveling between his home and his multiple job sites and between the job sites themselves.[156]

For further discussion of deduction of travel expenses, see Ch. 10.

¶12,120 EXPENSES INCURRED IN TRADE OR BUSINESS BY EMPLOYEE

.01 Employee Business Expenses In General

Employees can deduct the same types of expenses as self-employeds. Employee business expenses are claimed on Form 2106. Any expense incurred by an employee is not deductible unless it is required by the employment agreement[157] or is incident to performing his duties.[158]

---

[153] *G.L. Heigerick*, Dec. 27,846, 45 TC 475 (1966).

[154] Rev. Rul. 99-7, 1999-1 CB 361.

[155] *E.R. Curphey*, 73 TC 766, Dec. 36,753 (1980).

[156] *C.W. Walker*, Dec. 49,460, 101 TC 537.

[157] *F.M. Magill*, 4 BTA 272, Dec. 1501.

[158] *G. Tyler*, 13 TC 186, Dec. 17,127 (1949), *acq.* 1949-2 CB 3.

The following expenses are deductible:

- Employment agency fees and other expenses in seeking employment in the same trade or business even if employment is not secured, but not if employment is sought in new trade or business;[159]
- Cost of medical examination required as condition of employment;[160] and
- Cost of meals eaten by state troopers, while on duty, at a public restaurant adjacent to the highway they were patrolling.[161]

.02 Reimbursed Expenses

The fact that employees have been reimbursed for certain expenses does not, of itself, convert an item to deductible status. The expense must be justified by the Code. For example, a reimbursement could be a disguised form of compensation.

Generally, reimbursements or other expense allowances made under an *accountable plan*—one in which the employee substantiates the expenses and must return excess allowances to the employer—need not be reported on the employee's tax return. And the employee does not have to claim an offsetting deduction for his or her expenses [Ch. 20]. However, reimbursements or allowances not from an accountable plan must be reported on the employee's return. The employee can then deduct his business expenses—but only as a miscellaneous itemized deduction. And miscellaneous expenses are deductible only to the extent their total exceeds 2 percent of the employee's adjusted gross income [¶ 9140]. Net result: If the employee's miscellaneous expenses don't reach the 2 percent mark, he or she has no deduction to offset the taxable reimbursement.

Reimbursement Must Be Claimed

Employees may not claim a deduction for amounts which their employer would have reimbursed if the employees had made a claim for the expense.[162]

Reporting Requirements

The employee's method of reporting business expenses on the return depends on whether or not an accounting is made to the employer. Form 2106 is used to report an employee's business deductions on the return. No accounting, reporting, or recordkeeping is required for incidental expenses [Reg. §§ 1.162-17, 1.274-5].

Per Diem Arrangements

An employer can provide its employees with per diem travel allowances for away-from-home travel at a fixed per diem rate [Ch. 10]. If the allowance does not exceed the government-approved maximum which is released annually, the expenses are considered accounted for provided the employee is required to (1) keep a record of time, place, and his expenses' business purpose and (2) give the same information to the

---

[159] *L.F. Cremona*, 58 TC 219, Dec. 31,369 (1972), *acq.* 1975-2 CB 1; Rev. Rul. 75-120, 1975-1 CB 55; Rev. Rul. 77-16, 1977-1 CB 37.

[160] Rev. Rul. 58-382, 1958-2 CB 59.

[161] *K.W. Christey*, CA-8, 88-1 USTC ¶9205, 841 F2d 809, *cert. denied*, 489 US 1016.

[162] *H.E. Podems*, 24 TC 21, Dec. 20,955 (1955); *N.E. Kennelly*, 56 TC 936, Dec. 30,911 (1971), *aff'd*, CA-2, 72-1 USTC ¶9348, 456 F2d 1335.

employer. The employee does not have to keep track of actual expenses for travel, lodging, or meals.

If an employee receives a per diem allowance in excess of the approved rate, only the excess is taxable. In other words, the expenses are deemed to be substantiated to the extent of the maximum rate. If an employee receives a total per diem amount before the trip and it exceeds the approved rate, the employer does not have to require the employee to return the excess. The plan is still treated as accountable as long as the employee is required to return any portion allocable to days not actually traveled.

Example 12-15: The Orwell Welding Company provides its manager, David Dean, with a per diem travel allowance of $120 per day for five days. Assume the applicable government-approved maximum rate is $100 per day. As long as Dean meets the above per diem requirements, only the excess ($20 per day) will be taxable to him as compensation and thus subject to payroll and income taxes.

Example 12-16: Dean is given a per diem allowance equal to the government rate: $100 per day. His away-from-home meetings were productive and he wraps up his business in only four days (though provided with a five-day allowance). As long as Orwell Welding Co. required him to return the amount attributable to the day he was not traveling, only that amount (if not returned) will be taxable to him as compensation.

Employee expense arrangements, for tax purposes, are divided into two categories: *accountable plans* and *nonaccountable plans.* An allowance paid under an accountable plan is generally tax-free to the employee. It is not subject to payroll taxes, nor is it reported on the employee's tax return. The employee only reports the employer payment as income if expenses exceed the allowance and the employee wants to deduct the difference. In contrast, payments under a nonaccountable plan are considered taxable wages. The employer must withhold on the payments and report them on the employee's Form W-2 [Ch. 10].

Any expenses incurred by the employee in excess of amounts reimbursed are deductible by the employee, but only to the extent that, when combined with other miscellaneous expenses, they exceed 2 percent of the taxpayer's adjusted gross income.

Proving expenses. Employees who receive payments under an accountable plan ordinarily will not be called on to prove their expenses unless [Reg. §§1.162-17(d)(1), 1.274-5(b)(4)]:

- They claim a deduction for an excess of expenses over reimbursements; or
- They are related to the employer [Ch. 13]; or
- It is determined that the employer's accounting procedures for reporting and substantiating employees' expenses were not adequate.

What is "adequate accounting?" To "adequately account" to an employer, the employee must submit a record describing the business nature and the amount of each expense. For travel, entertainment and gift costs, the employee must substantiate the amount, date, place (or description of the item, for gifts), business purpose and business relationship of the expenditure that has been recorded at or near the time of the expenditure. There must also be supporting documentary evidence. Only this kind of proof will qualify as *adequate accounting,* except when records were destroyed or if it is impossible to get the evidence [Ch. 10] [Reg. §§1.162-17(b)(4), 1.274-5(c)(2)].

Jury Duty Pay

If employees serving on a jury must give their employer all or part of their jury duty pay in return for receiving their regular pay during the jury service period, the jury duty pay turned over to the employer is deducted from the employee's adjusted gross income [Code Sec. 62(a)(13)].

.03 Expenses of School Teachers

Prior to January 1, 2014, teachers of kindergarten through grade 12 who worked at least 900 hours during a school year could claim an above-the-line deduction for up to $250 annually of expenses paid or incurred for books, supplies (other than nonathletic supplies for courses of instruction in health or physical education), computer equipment (including related software and services) and other equipment, and supplementary materials used by the eligible educator in the classroom [Code Sec. 62(a)(2)(D)].

¶12,125 HOME OFFICE DEDUCTION

Code Sec. 280A(c)(1) permits a taxpayer to deduct home office expenses if part of the taxpayer's home is used regularly and exclusively:

1. As the taxpayer's principal place of business for any trade or business,[163]
2. As a place to meet with the taxpayer's patients, clients, or customers in the normal course of the taxpayer's trade or business, or
3. In the case of a separate structure such as a studio or garage that is not attached to the dwelling unit, in connection with the taxpayer's trade or business.

Taxpayers may also deduct the following:

- Expenses that are allocable to space within the home used on a regular basis for the storage of inventory or product samples held for use in the taxpayer's trade or business of selling products at retail or wholesale, if the dwelling unit is the sole fixed location of the trade or business [Code Sec. 280A(c)(2)];
- Expenses that are attributable to the rental of the entire home or just a portion of it [Code Sec. 280A(c)(3)]; and
- Expenses that are allocable to the portion of the home used on a regular basis in the taxpayer's trade or business of providing day care for children, for individuals who have attained age 65, or for individuals who are physically or mentally incapable of caring for themselves [Code Sec. 280A(c)(4)].

---

[163] In *K. Dunford,* 106 TCM 130, Dec. 59,609(M), TC Memo. 2013-189, the Tax Court denied the taxpayer's home office deduction for failure to prove that there was an identifiable portion of their motor home used exclusively for business purposes. The court found it implausible that the taxpayers used an unenclosed countertop in a cramped motor home exclusively as their home office.

To qualify under the exclusive use test, a taxpayer must use a specific part of his or her home only for his or her business. A taxpayer does not satisfy the exclusive use test if he or she uses the part of the home both for business and for personal purposes unless, for example, the taxpayer uses part of the home as a daycare facility. A taxpayer who is an employee may deduct expenses attributable to a business use of a residence only if that use is for the convenience of the taxpayer's employer.

Taxpayers may only deduct home office expenses up to the amount of gross income derived from use of the home office as reduced by (1) the deductions allocable to the use; and (2) the allowable trade or business expenses that are not allocable to the use of the dwelling unit for the tax year (for example, advertising, wages, and supplies) [Code Sec. 280A(c)(5)].

For discussion of the tax impact of selling a home after using a portion of it as your home office, see ¶ 7020.

.01 What Qualifies as Your Home

To be eligible to claim the home office deduction, the taxpayer must live in a *dwelling unit,* which includes a house, apartment, condominium, mobile home, boat, or similar property that provides basic living accommodations such as sleeping space, toilet, and cooking facilities. All other structures next to or near the dwelling unit, such as a separate garage or shed in your back yard, would also qualify. Hotels, motels, or inns do not qualify.

> **Example 12-17:** A florist, who operates a flower shop in town, grows roses for the shop in a greenhouse behind her house. Since she uses the greenhouse exclusively and regularly in her business, it qualifies as a separate structure and she can deduct related expenses.

.02 Trade or Business Use Required

You must be using your home in connection with a "trade or business" to claim a deduction for its business use. Using your home to pursue or manage a hobby or to engage in a money-making activity that is not a trade or business will not qualify. For further discussion of hobby losses, see ¶ 13,085.

> **Example 12-18:** A real estate developer manages his personal investment portfolio from an office in his basement. In his office, he reads financial newspapers, reports, and periodicals, clips bond coupons, and makes investment decisions for his personal account over the phone. He does not make investments for others as a broker or dealer. He is denied a deduction for the business use of his home because he is not in the trade or business of investing.

.03 Exclusive Use of Home Office Required

This is an all-or-nothing test. "Exclusive use" means *only* for business. If you or any members of your family use your home office for *any* personal purposes, you fail the exclusive use test. Even occasional personal use is enough to disqualify your home office. You must dedicate a room or some portion of your home to your home office and use it for nothing else in order to qualify for a home office deduction. In *Anderson*,[164] the Tax Court held that taxpayers who lived in a bed and breakfast they owned and operated couldn't deduct expenses relating to those parts of the inn used for both business and personal purposes.

Example 12-19: A self-employed tailor uses his dining room as both his sewing center and for occasional family meals. He will fail the exclusive use test. To qualify the dining room for the deduction, he should remove the dining-related objects and move in his sewing machine, etc.

Example 12-20: A self-employed piano teacher claimed a home office deduction for her piano studio as well as for the rooms adjacent to her piano studio where piano students and their parents waited for piano lessons to either begin or end. She also used the adjacent rooms for personal purposes. Since the rooms other than the actual piano studio were not used exclusively for teaching, her deduction for those other rooms was denied.[165]

Exclusive Use When Two Businesses Are Involved

If you use your home office for more than one business, a home office deduction will be allowed only if each and every business satisfies all the home office tests discussed above. Even if only one of your two businesses fails one part of the test, you lose your entire home office deduction, even for the one business that otherwise met all the requirements.

Example 12-21: Alfred Hamacher was employed as an administrator at an acting school and was an independent actor. He used a home office for his two businesses: his acting career and his job as acting school administrator. Because the acting school provided him with a suitable office, the court found that the use of a home office for his administrator job was for his own personal convenience, comfort, and economy rather than for the convenience of his employer as required by law. Alfred's home office deductions were denied completely even for the otherwise qualifying use. If Alfred had used his home office only for activities relating to his acting career, his home office deductions probably would have been allowed.[166]

Using Home as Storage Unit for Taxpayer's Inventory

If a taxpayer is in the trade or business of selling products at retail or wholesale and his home is the sole fixed location of the trade or business, he can claim deductions for space in his home that is used regularly for storing inventory or product samples (or both) [Code Sec. 280A(c)(2)]. To claim the deduction, the inventory or product samples must be stored in a separately identifiable space suitable for storage [Prop. Reg. § 1.280A-2(e)].

---

[164] *C.E. Anderson*, 91 TCM 791, Dec. 56,439(M), TC Memo. 2006-33.

[165] *H.J. Langer*, CA-8, 93-1 USTC ¶50,191, 989 F2d 294; *J.A. Walz*, TC Summary Opinion 2005-1.

[166] *A.W. Hamacher*, 94 TC 348, Dec. 46,444 (1990).

Example 12-22: An attorney who worked both in private practice and in government service stored his law library and files in one room of his house rather than rent warehouse space. He was denied a storage space deduction because he was not in the trade or business of selling products at wholesale or retail.[167]

Example 12-23: An orthodontist who used the attic and basement of his house to store inactive dental records, was denied a storage space deduction for these areas because he was not in trade or business of selling products at wholesale or retail.[168]

.04 Principal Place of Business

A home office can qualify as your principal place of business if:

- You use it exclusively[169] and regularly to conduct administrative or management activities of a trade or business; and
- There is no other fixed location where you conduct these substantial administrative or management activities of your trade or business [Code Sec. 280A(c) (1)].

Some of the activities that the IRS considers to be administrative or managerial in nature include billing customers, clients or patients, keeping books and records, setting up appointments and forwarding orders or writing reports.

The bottom line is that you will still qualify for the home office deduction even if the essence of your business is performed outside of the home. This means that many businesspeople and professionals who administer their business from a home office location, but sell or provide goods or services outside of the home office can shelter some of their income from tax by claiming a home office deduction. Their ability to claim the home office deduction will not be affected by the fact that they conduct substantial nonadministrative or nonmanagement business activities at a fixed location of the business outside the home (such as meeting with customers, clients or patients at a fixed location of the business away from home).

The business use must be more than occasional or incidental.[170] In order to sustain a home office deduction, the taxpayer must be able to prove that his or her home office was regularly used as a place for meeting clients in the normal course of business. The Congressional committee reports provide that "[e]xpenses attributable to *incidental* or *occasional* trade or business use of an exclusive portion of a dwelling unit would not be deductible [as a home office deduction] even if that portion of the dwelling unit is used for no other purpose." S. Rept. No. 94-938, 94th Cong., 2d Sess. 148-149 (1976); see H. Rept. No. 94-658, 94th Cong., 1st Sess. 161 (1975). (Emphasis added.)

---

[167] *J.O. Druker*, CA-2, 83-1 USTC ¶9116, 697 F2d 46, *cert. denied*,461 US 957.

[168] *L.E. Pearson*, 43 TCM 1508, Dec. 39,055(M), TC Memo. 1982-295.

[169] *B.A. Ong*, 103 TCM 1624, Dec. 59,030(M), TC Memo. 2012-114.

[170] *D.T. Robinson*, CA-3, 2012-2 USTC ¶50,455; *E.G. Jackson*, 76 TC 696, Dec. 37,875 (1981).

Who Will Benefit

The broad definition of *principal place of business* is beneficial to self-employed taxpayers and independent contractors who maintain an office at home to perform paper work but provide their professional services outside the home. It means that people like interior designers, consultants, repair technicians, electricians, plumbers, independent sales representatives, painters, artists, dancers, and actors who maintain a home office for billing, ordering and scheduling purposes but provide their services in locations outside of their homes will finally be able to claim a home office deduction. It will also help any independent contractors such as physicians who work in hospitals and clinics outside their homes but maintain the home office for administrative and managerial purposes.

The home office deduction will not be denied even if:

- Administrative or management activities in connection with your business are performed by others outside your home;
- You carry out administration or management activities at sites that are not fixed locations of the business, such as hotels, cars, or project sites;
- If you conduct some minimal administration or managerial activities at a fixed location of the business outside your home provided the administrative or managerial activities are not substantial and consist basically of doing a little bit of paperwork; and
- You have suitable space to conduct administrative or management activities outside your home, but choose to use your home office for those activities.

Example 12-24: Dr. Sams, a self-employed anesthesiologist, sees patients at several local hospitals where he is not provided any office space. The doctor maintains an office at home where he performs routine administrative and management activities including reviewing patient charts, bookkeeping, correspondence, calling doctors, patients and insurance companies, and keeping current with continuing medical education requirements. Prior to the change in the law, the U.S. Supreme Court concluded in *Soliman*,[171] that his principal place of business was not his home office, because he performed the "essence of the professional service" at the hospitals. Because he failed to meet with patients at home, his home office deduction was denied. Effective on January 1, 1999 as a result of a change in the law, he can claim a home office deduction for the portion of his home that he used exclusively and regularly to conduct the administrative or management activities associated with his profession. The fact that he did a little paperwork at the hospitals will not affect his deduction.

Example 12-25: Katia Popov is a violinist who performs with orchestras and contracts with various studios to record music for the movie industry. She worked for 24 contractors in numerous locations with no office or practice room. Popov lived with her husband in an apartment. The apartment's living

---

[171] *N.E. Soliman*, SCt, 93-1 USTC ¶ 50,014, 506 US 168, 113 SCt 701.

room served as Popov's home office. The room was sparsely furnished and used exclusively for an office and she spent hours each day practicing in that room. The Ninth Circuit concluded that she was entitled to a home office deduction for her practice space in her living room because it was used exclusively as her principal place of business.[172]

.05 How Employees Can Claim the Home Office Deduction

Employees will only be able to claim a home office deduction if they can prove that they are using the home office for the convenience of the employer, not the employee. The question whether an employee chose not to use suitable space made available by the employer for administrative activities is relevant to deciding whether or not the employee is using his or her home office for the convenience of the employer rather than primarily for the convenience of the employee.

.06 Travel Between Home Office and Other Work Sites

Once taxpayers have established a part of their home as a home office they can begin to deduct the daily transportation expenses incurred when traveling between an office in their home to another work location of that business, regardless of whether the location is regular or temporary, or is within or outside of the metropolitan area. The daily transportation expenses incurred in going between the home office and other work locations must be incurred in the same trade or business.[173]

Example 12-26: Betty is an interior designer who uses the basement in her home as her principal place of business. When she is working she drives from her home to client's homes, job sites, the architect's office, design centers, furniture showrooms, carpet wholesalers, upholsterers, and drapery fabricators. Her mileage for all these trips is deductible as business mileage because she is traveling from one work site (her home) to another.

.07 Form 8829

Self-employed taxpayers who file Schedule C (Form 1040) must figure the business use of their home on Form 8829, *Expenses for Business Use of Your Home*. Unfortunately, taxpayers may find that jumping through all the hoops in order to claim a home office deduction may not result in much tax savings. Homeowners will find that they are already deducting in full their real estate taxes and mortgage interest. In addition they are already deducting their casualty losses to the extent they exceed $100 plus 10 percent of adjusted gross income. What are left are utilities, rent, insurance, security system, maintenance, and depreciation. These normally nondeductible expenses will be deductible if taxpayers have a qualifying home office but the deduction will be limited by the percentage of the home that is used for the home office.

The first step in deducting these expenses is figuring out what percentage of the home is used for business purposes so expenses can be allocated to business use.

[172] *K.V. Popov*, CA-9, 2001-1 USTC ¶50,353, 246 F3d 1190.

[173] *E.R. Curphey*, 73 TC 766, Dec. 36,753 (1980); Rev. Rul. 99-7, 1999-1 CB 361.

Figuring the Percentage of Residential Space Used for Business

There are two methods to use in establishing the business percentage of a home.

Method one. Measure the total square footage of the home and then measure the square footage of the home office. Divide the size of the office by the total size of the home and multiply by 100.

> **Example 12-27:** Larry runs a newsletter business out of the basement in his home. He uses the basement exclusively and regularly for his business and it is his principal place of work. Larry's entire home including the basement measures 4,000 square feet. The basement alone measures 800 square feet. He can deduct 20 percent (800 divided by 4000 × 100 = 20 percent) of his home office-related expenses.

Method two. If all the rooms in the house are about the same size, an alternate way of computing the percentage of the home that is used for business is to divide the number of room(s) used for business purposes by the total number of rooms in the house.

> **Example 12-28:** Robert lives a seven-room home and he uses one room in his house exclusively and regularly for his insurance business. He can determine the business usage of his house by dividing one room by seven rooms which yields 14.3 percent business usage.

The business part of the expenses is figured by applying the percentage to the total of each expense.[174]

Deductible Expenses

The deduction for the home's business use (other than for expenses deductible in any event, like mortgage interest) is limited to gross income reduced by *all* deductible expenses, including business expenses not related to the use of the home itself. To compute how much can be deducted, divide all expenses into three categories: (1) the unrelated expenses, (2) direct expenses, and (3) indirect expenses.

Unrelated expenses do not benefit the home office. They benefit only the personal living space in the home. These include repairs to personal areas of the home, lawn care, building a swimming pool, landscaping, and painting a room not used for business. These unrelated expenses that benefit only the part of a home used for personal purposes *cannot* be deducted.

Direct expenses are directly related to the business use of a portion of the home. They are fully deductible and include painting or repairing the specific room used for the home office.

Indirect expenses are incurred to operate and maintain the entire home and would be incurred whether or not a business is operated out of the home. They benefit both the business and personal parts of the home. Only the percentage of indirect expenses

---

[174] Treas. Dept., IRS Publication 587, "Business Use of Your Home" (2013 Ed.), p. 6.

allocated to the business use of the home will be deductible. Examples of indirect expenses include the following:

Real estate taxes and home mortgage interest. If you own your home you can already deduct your real estate taxes and mortgage interest. If you maintain a home office, however, you will be deducting the portion of your real estate taxes and mortgage interest that is allocated to business use of your home on Schedule C (as figured on Form 8829) with the balance deducted on Schedule A as an itemized deduction.

Rent. If you rent rather than own your home, you can deduct the portion of your rent allocable to the business use of your home. Renters cannot typically deduct real estate taxes and mortgage interest. If they qualify for the home office deduction, however, they will be able to deduct their rent plus utilities. Their rent usually includes a pass through of the owner's real estate taxes, mortgage interest, and depreciation. Renters will therefore find that a home office deduction can generate a big tax savings.

Casualty losses. Whether or not you can deduct casualty losses that damaged or destroyed your home depends on whether the damage occurred to the portion of your home used for business or for personal purposes. If the loss occurs on property you use solely for business purposes, such as a home office, the entire loss is deductible. If the loss occurs on property you used for both personal and business use, the business percentage of the loss is fully deductible. If the loss occurs on property used only for personal purposes, the loss may be deducted if:

- You itemize deductions;
- Your casualty loss is not covered by insurance;
- Each loss suffered exceeds $100 [Code Sec. 165(h)];
- The total of all casualties suffered during the year exceeds 10 percent of your adjusted gross income after subtracting $100 from each loss suffered [Code Sec. 165(h)(2)(A)]; and
- The casualty losses results from one of the following events: a fire, a storm, a shipwreck, a theft, or similar casualties provided they were sudden (not gradual or progressive), unexpected (not anticipated), and unusual (not occurring commonly).

Utilities and services. You can deduct the portion of your utilities and services that is allocable to the business use of your home. The deductible expenses include expenses for electricity, gas, trash removal, water, and cleaning services.

If you have only one telephone, only optional phone services used exclusively for your business, such as call waiting, call forwarding, speed or three-way calling, extra directory listings, or phone equipment rentals are deductible. You can deduct the *second* phone line if it is maintained solely for your business. No deduction is allowed for any charges associated with maintaining the *first* phone line into your home since this is considered a nondeductible personal living expense.

Homeowners insurance. You can deduct the percentage of your homeowners insurance that relates *only* to the business use of your home.

Repairs. You can deduct the costs of repairs and labor that relate to the business use of your home. For example, if you repair your furnace or leaking roof, the repairs benefit the entire home. If you use 25 percent of your home for business, 25 percent of the total roof repair bill would be deductible.

Security systems. You can deduct the business percentage of the expenses you incur to maintain and monitor a security system installed to protect the doors and windows in your home. You can also claim a depreciation deduction for the percentage of the cost of installing the security system that relates to the business use of the home.

Depreciation. You can claim depreciation on the cost of business property that you buy for use in your home office. Typically, your purchases will qualify as business property depreciable under MACRS as either 5-year or 7-year property. Five-year property includes computers and peripheral equipment, typewriters, calculators, adding machines and copies. Seven-year property includes office furniture and equipment such as desks, files, and safes. The portion of your house's cost allocated to the home office may be depreciated over 39 years. For depreciation purposes, the basis of the house is the lower of the fair market value of the house at the time you started to use a part of it for business, or its adjusted basis, exclusive of the land. Only that part of the cost basis allocated to your office is depreciable.

Election to Expense Costs Immediately

You may also elect to recover the cost of office furniture and equipment in the year of purchase with a deduction under Code Sec. 179 provided the business property is placed in service during that year. This deduction would be in lieu of recovering the cost over time through depreciation deductions. For further discussion, see ¶ 11,045.

> ▶ **OBSERVATION:** Deductions for the business use of your home will not create a business loss or increase a net loss from your business.[175]

Carryforward Allowed

A carryforward is allowed for any home office deduction that is disallowed by the gross income limit. Deductions carried over continue to be allowable only up to the income from the business from which the expenses arose, whether or not the dwelling unit is used as a residence during the tax year [Code Sec. 280A(c)(5)].

Example 12-29: Baker operates a retail sales business from his home. His use meets the requirements for deducting expenses for the home's business use. He uses 20% of the home for business. His gross income, expenses for the business, and computing expenses for the business use of the home are as follows:

Gross income from business use of home	$12,000	
Total expenses:		
(1) Business percentage (20%) of mortgage interest and real estate taxes	$2,000	
(2) Expenses for business in home not allocable to the home itself (cost of goods sold, telephone, supplies, labor, etc.)		9,000

[175] *M.H. Visin*, 86 TCM 279, Dec. 55,269(M), TC Memo. 2003-246, *aff'd in unpublished opinion*, 2005-1 USTC ¶ 50,199, *cert. denied*.

(3) Other expenses attributable to home's business use:		
(a) Maintenance, insurance, utilities (20%)	800	
(b) Depreciation (20%)	1,600	
Gross income limitation:		
Total of (1) and (2) (allowable in full)		11,000
Limit on further deductions		$ 1,000
Subtract expenses in (3)(a)		$ 800
Limit on further deductions		$ 200
Depreciation ((3)(b))		$ 1,600
Depreciation allowable		$ 200
Carryover expenses to following year (subject to income limit in that year)		$ 1,400

NOTES: Tenants who meet the office-at-home rules can deduct an allocable portion of their rent payments (instead of depreciation, taxes and the like). Employees cannot claim landlord-type deductions (e.g., depreciation) on account of renting a home-office to their employer [Code Sec. 280A(c)(6)].

.08 New Simplified Method Available for Home Office Deductions

In Rev. Proc. 2013-13,[176] the IRS provided a new simplified, optional method for taxpayers who want to claim a home office deduction. This safe harbor method is an alternative for qualifying taxpayers and does not replace the existing method of calculating home office expenses on Form 8829, *Expenses for Business Use of Your Home*. Under the safe harbor method, a taxpayer determines the amount of deductible expenses for a qualified business use of the home by multiplying the allowable square footage by the prescribed rate. The new optional deduction is limited to $1,500 per year based on $5 per square foot for up to 300 square feet. The safe harbor method is unavailable to an employee with a home office if the employee receives advances, allowances, or reimbursements for expenses related to the qualified business use of the employee's home under a reimbursement or other expense allowance arrangement.

Homeowners using the new safe harbor will not be able to depreciate the portion of their home used in a trade or business. However, they will be able to claim allowable mortgage interest, real estate taxes, and casualty losses on the home as itemized deductions on Schedule A of Form 1040. The new option is available beginning with the 2013 return that most taxpayers will file in 2014; it is not available for 2012 returns. Taxpayers using the simplified option will not file Form 8829 but will be filing a new simplified form.

Election Procedures

A taxpayer may elect from year to year whether to use the safe harbor method or to calculate and substantiate actual expenses. A taxpayer elects the safe harbor method by using the method to compute the deduction for the home office on his or her

[176] Rev. Proc. 2013-13, IRB 2013-6, 478.

timely filed, original federal income tax return for the tax year. Once made, an election for the tax year is irrevocable. A change from using the safe harbor method in one year to actual expenses in a succeeding tax year, or vice-versa, is not a change in method of accounting and does not require IRS consent.

Deduction Otherwise Allowable

A taxpayer electing the safe harbor method generally cannot deduct any actual expenses related to the home office for that year with the following exceptions:

- A taxpayer who elects the safe harbor method may also claim deductions in that year for qualified residence interest, property taxes, and casualty losses on Form 1040, Schedule A. They cannot however, deduct any portion of these expenses from the gross income derived from the home office, either for purposes of determining the net income derived from the business or for purposes of determining the gross income limitation. However, taxpayers with a home office who also have a rental use of the same home must allocate a portion of the expenses to the rental use of the home.
- A taxpayer who elects the safe harbor method may deduct trade or business expenses unrelated to the home office for that tax year (for example, expenses for advertising, wages, and supplies).

Depreciation in Year Safe Harbor Elected

A taxpayer electing the safe harbor method for a tax year cannot deduct any depreciation (including any additional first-year depreciation) or Code Sec. 179 expense for the part of the home that is used for the home office for that tax year. The depreciation deduction allowable for that portion of the home for that tax year is deemed to be zero.

Depreciation in Year Other Than Safe Harbor Year

If a taxpayer uses the safe harbor method for a tax year and then decides to go back to the regular method of substantiating actual expenses for purposes of claiming the home office deduction for any subsequent tax year, the taxpayer must calculate the depreciation deduction allowable in the subsequent year for the portion of the home that is used as a home office by using the appropriate optional depreciation table applicable for the property, regardless of whether the taxpayer used an optional depreciation table for the property in its placed-in-service year. The optional depreciation tables for MACRS property are provided in the annual IRS Publication 946, *How To Depreciate Property*. The appropriate optional depreciation table is based on the depreciation system, depreciation method, recovery period, and convention applicable to the Code Sec. 1250 property in its placed-in-service year.

.09 Day Care Providers May Claim Home Office Deduction

Taxpayers who use a space in their home on a regular basis for providing day care may be able to deduct the business expenses for that part of their home even if they also use the same space for nonbusiness purposes. To qualify for this exception they must meet both of the following requirements:

- They must be in the trade or business of providing day care for children, persons age 65 or older, or persons who are physically or mentally unable to care for themselves.

- They must have applied for, been granted, or be exempt from having a license, certification, registration, or approval as a day care center or as a family or group daycare home under state law.

Taxpayers will not satisfy these requirements if their application, license or other authorization has been rejected or revoked [Code Sec. 280A(c)(4)(B)].

Computing Amount of Deduction

When home-office deductions are claimed for day care provided in portions of the home that are also put to nonbusiness use, two allocations are necessary. However, the IRS has said that you are not required to keep detailed records of the number of hours a given room is used for day care. A room that is available for day care use throughout the business day and is regularly used as part of the day care routine can be treated as used for day care during all business operation hours. The deduction is figured as follows [Code Sec. 280A(c)(4)]:[177]

1. Multiply the annual home expenses (mortgage interest, taxes, utilities, etc.) by a fraction-the square footage of the home available for day care divided by the home's total square footage.
2. Next, multiply the amount in (1) above by a second fraction-the total hours during the year the day care business is operated (including preparation and cleanup time) divided by the total number of hours in the year (8,760).

Example 12-30: Joan Brown, a licensed day care provider, uses her home 250 days a year for day care. She spends 11 hours daily on this plus another hour each day for preparation and cleanup [3,000 hours (12 hours × 250 days per year)]. The Browns' home has a total of 1,600 square feet with personal living area totaling 400 square feet. The Browns' total annual home expenses come to $10,000 this year. Joan Brown figures her deduction for day services as follows:

1. $10,000 home expenses × 1,200/1,600 = $7,500
2. $7,500 × 3,000 hours/8,760 hours = $2,568.49

NOTE: Form 8829 has special lines for day care providers to calculate the area of the home that is used for day care, as well as the percentage of hours devoted to day care. If, in Example 12-30 above, Joan Brown's day care business was in operation for only part of the year, the 8,760 hour figure would have to be adjusted to take into account only the total number of hours in that part of the year.

Actual Meal Costs

Day care providers can either deduct 100 percent of the actual cost of food consumed by their day care recipients or deduct the optional standard meal and snack rates shown in Table 1 below.

Optional Standard Meal and Snack Rates

Family day care providers can deduct standard meal and snack rates for food served in their day care home to eligible children instead of maintaining detailed records and receipts of food purchased for use in their day care business.[178]

---

[177] Rev. Rul. 92-3, 1992-1 CB 141.

[178] Rev. Proc. 2003-22, 2003-1 CB 577.

For these purposes:

1. A family day care provider is a person engaged in the business of providing family day care.
2. Family day care is childcare provided to eligible children in the home of the family day care provider. The care must be nonmedical, not involve a transfer of legal custody, and generally last less then 24 hours each day.
3. Eligible children are minor children receiving family day care in the home of the family day care provider.

Day care providers can compute the deductible cost of each meal and snack actually purchased and served to an eligible child during the time period they provided family day care using the standard meal and snack rates shown in the following table that illustrates the rates for meals and snacks in effect from July 1, 2013 through June 30, 2014.[179]

Table 1 - CHILD AND ADULT CARE FOOD PROGRAM (CACFP)
[Per Meal Rates in Whole or Fractions of U.S. Dollars Effective from July 1, 2013–June 30, 2014]

Day Care Homes	Breakfast		Lunch and Supper		Snack	
	TIER I		TIER I		TIER I	
CONTIGUOUS STATES	$1.28		$2.40		$0.71	
ALASKA	2.04		3.89		1.16	
HAWAII	1.49		2.81		0.83	

.10 Home Office Deduction Flow Chart

To determine at a glance if you are eligible for a home office deduction, consult the following chart:[180]

[179] Federal Register Doc. 2013-17997, Vol. 78, No. 144, July 26, 2013.

[180] Treas. Dept., IRS Publication 587, "Business Use of Your Home, (Including Use by Day-Care Providers)" (2013 Ed.), p. 4.

Figure A. **Can You Deduct Business Use of the Home Expenses?** Do not use this chart if you use your home for the storage of inventory or product samples, or to operate a daycare facility. See *Exceptions to Exclusive Use,* earlier, and *Daycare Facility,* later.

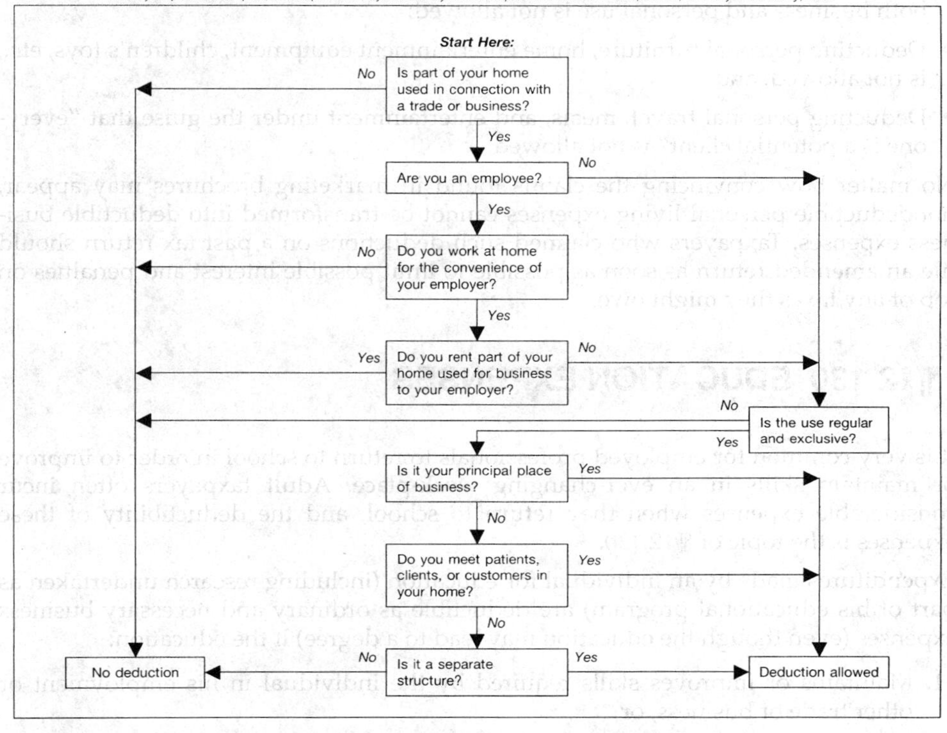

.11 Bogus Home-Based Business Schemes May Trigger Audit

The IRS has warned taxpayers about the establishment of bogus home-based businesses as a tax avoidance device designed to convert personal expenses into deductible business expenses.[181] The IRS listed the following examples of personal expenses that are not deductible but are commonly claimed as business expenses in home-based business tax avoidance schemes:

- Deducting all or most of the cost and operation of a personal residence. For example, placing a calendar, desk, filing cabinet, telephone, or other business-related item in each room does not increase the amount that can be deducted;
- Deducting a portion of the house payment is not allowed if the business is not legitimate;
- Paying young children a salary for services, such as Xeroxing, answering telephones, washing cars, and then deducting these costs as business expenses is not allowed;
- Deducting education expenses from the salary wrongfully paid to children as employees also is not allowed;

[181] Rev. Rul. 2004-32, 2004-1 CB 621; IRS News Release IR-2002-13.

- Deducting excessive car and truck expenses when the vehicle has been used for both business and personal use is not allowed;
- Deducting personal furniture, home entertainment equipment, children's toys, etc., is not allowed; and
- Deducting personal travel, meals, and entertainment under the guise that "everyone is a potential client" is not allowed.

No matter how convincing the claims found in marketing brochures may appear, nondeductible personal living expenses cannot be transformed into deductible business expenses. Taxpayers who claimed such deductions on a past tax return should file an amended return as soon as possible to limit possible interest and penalties on top of any taxes they might owe.

¶12,130 EDUCATION EXPENSES

It is very common for employed professionals to return to school in order to improve or maintain skills in an ever-changing work-place. Adult taxpayers often incur considerable expenses when they return to school, and the deductibility of these expenses is the topic of ¶12,130.

Expenditures made by an individual for education (including research undertaken as part of his educational program) are deductible as ordinary and necessary business expenses (even though the education may lead to a degree) if the education:

1. Maintains or improves skills required by the individual in his employment or other trade or business, or
2. Meets the express requirements of the individual's employer, or the requirements of applicable law or regulations, imposed as a condition to the retention by the individual of an established employment relationship, status, or rate of compensation [Reg. § 1.162-5(a)].

In order for an employee to claim a deduction under Code Sec. 162 for educational expenses, the taxpayer must have established a trade or business before pursuing the new degree.[182] The amount of time necessary for a taxpayer to establish a trade or business as an employee is subjective and no set standards have been established. Working as a graduate teaching assistance does not qualify as an established trade or business because the employment is only temporary.[183] A taxpayer can take a temporary leave of absence of "one year or less"[184] from his or her employment in order to pursue an advanced degree and still be able to deduct education expenses. For example, in *M.O. Furner*,[185] the Court of Appeals for the Seventh Circuit held that a junior high social studies teacher, who took a year off from teaching in order to pursue a full time graduate course in history, was permitted to deduct the cost of attending graduate school as an education expense, even though she accepted a different position upon graduation.

---

[182] *D.J. Primuth*, 54 TC 374, Dec. 29,985 (1970).

[183] *A.M. Jungreis*, 55 TC 581, Dec. 30,600 (1970).

[184] Rev. Rul. 68-591, 1968-2 CB 73.

[185] *M.O. Furner*, CA-7, 68-1 USTC ¶9234, 393 F2d 292.

Example 12-31: An attorney in the tax department of a law firm wants to improve her tax skills and attends a masters program in taxation. Even though this program leads to the taxpayer obtaining a masters of laws in taxation (LL.M. in taxation), the costs associated with obtaining the degree are deductible.[186]

Example 12-32: The taxpayer is a schoolteacher. The state school board requires that all teachers in that state be periodically certified. As part of the certification renewal process, teacher must either present evidence of college credits in professional or academic subjects earned during the life of the certificate or pass an examination on five books selected by the state's department of education. The taxpayer decides to take college courses to satisfy her employer's employment requirements. She may deduct the costs she incurs in taking such courses.[187]

Example 12-33: The taxpayer, who had two years' experience as an Army administrator and planner, took two years off to attend Harvard Business School to obtain an MBA. After receiving his degree, he returned to a similar line of work to that which he had prior to getting his MBA degree. He will be able to deduct his tuition expenses because he had sufficient time to establish himself as a business manager before taking two years off to pursue the MBA which equipped him to be a better manager than he had been prior to earning the advance degree.[188]

Example 12-34: A salesman in a dental laboratory that manufactured a protective mouth guard needed by athletes could deduct expenses incurred to obtain an MBA after the taxpayer's employer told him that pursuing the MBA would speed his advancement within the company and enhance his business skills. The company, however, did not require the taxpayer to obtain the MBA. The Tax Court concluded that MBA courses provided the taxpayer with a general background to perform tasks and activities that he had performed previously for his employer. The court found that the MBA qualified the taxpayer to perform the same general duties he performed before enrolling in the program. Thus, the taxpayer's MBA did not meet a minimum education requirement of

---

[186] LTR 9112003 (Dec. 18, 1990). But see *P.R. Wassenaar*, 72 TC 1195, Dec. 36,359 (1979), where the Tax Court held that a student who had a clerkship in the summer before he graduated from law school and was also pursuing a LL.M in taxation had not established a trade or business before pursuing the advanced degree and could therefore not deduct the expenses. Similarly, in *P. Weyts*, 85 TCM 999, Dec. 55,076(M), TC Memo 2003-68, an individual could not deduct the costs of obtaining an LLM, a JD or an MBA as trade or business expenses because he had not established himself in his trade or business. Although the taxpayer worked as a summer associate for two firms while a member of the state bar, he failed to establish that his compensation and assignments were similar to other full-time associates. Moreover, the record established that the taxpayer enrolled in each degree program immediately after completion of the preceding one. As such, he had an "uninterrupted continuity in his legal education" and was not entitled to the claimed deductions.

[187] *N.P. Hill*, CA-4, 50-1 USTC ¶9310, 181 F2d 906.

[188] *S.G. Sherman*, 36 TCM 1191, Dec. 34,621(M), TC Memo. 1977-301.

his employer. Nor did the MBA qualify him to perform a new trade or business. Therefore the taxpayer could deduct the amount of substantiated MBA tuition expenses.[189]

However, even if any of the above requirements are met, expenses are **not** deductible if the education either:

- Meets minimum educational requirements of the taxpayer's current employment or trade or business; or
- Qualifies the taxpayer for a new trade or business [Reg. § 1.162-5(b)].[190]

Example 12-35: The taxpayer is an attorney licensed to practice in Ohio. She takes a review course to prepare for the Kentucky bar exam. This expenditure is not deductible. Passing the bar is the minimum educational requirement for the practice of law in each individual state.

Example 12-36: The taxpayer is an instructor at a university. She wants to become a full-time facility member and must obtain a graduate degree in order to be promoted. The costs of obtaining that graduate degree are not deductible because obtaining this degree is required to meet the minimum standard to become a full-time faculty member [Reg. § 1.162-5(b)(2)(iii)].[191]

Example 12-37: The taxpayer is an engineer who decides to become a lawyer. The tuition costs the engineer incurs in obtaining a law degree are nondeductible because they qualify the engineer for a new trade or business [Reg. § 1.162-5(b)(3)].

Example 12-38: The taxpayer, who was an Army officer involved in troop training, decided to attend Harvard Business School to obtain an MBA. The taxpayer will not be able to deduct the costs associated with obtaining the degree because the taxpayer's education qualified him for a new trade or business. The taxpayer's position in the Army was far different from the job he took as a business consultant after obtaining his MBA.[192]

---

[189] *D.R. Allemeier*, 90 TCM 197, Dec. 56,131(M), TC Memo. 2005-207. But see *R.T. Smith*, 41 T.C.M. 1186, Dec. 37,792(M), TC Memo 1981-149, where the cost of obtaining an MBA was disallowed because the taxpayer's position as a quality-control foreman required him to have only a basic understanding of business and the MBA was at a "level and of a nature not proximately related to the skills required of him in his employment."

[190] *L.A. Singleton-Clark*, T.C. Summary Opinion 2009-182 (nurse could deduct costs of obtaining MBA/HCM because she was already performing the functions for which the degree qualified her and the degree did not qualify her for a new trade or business); *C.N. Ortega*, T.C. Summary Opinion 2009-120 (education expenses not deductible because qualifies taxpayer for new business or trade).

[191] *A. Mitrevics*, 22 TCM 271, Dec. 25,992(M), TC Memo. 1963-67.

[192] *J.S. Schneider*, 47 TCM 675, Dec. 40,682(M), TC Memo. 1983-753.

.01 Maintaining or Improving Skills

Deductible educational costs to maintain or improve skills include those refresher courses or courses dealing with current developments as well as academic and vocational courses [Reg. § 1.162-5(c)].

.02 Requirements of Employer

If, after meeting the minimum educational requirements for the job, you must obtain additional education to keep your present job status or pay rate, those expenses are deductible. Education that also allows advancement in the employer firm will not necessarily be disallowed under the "requirements of employer" criterion. The deduction is allowed if education resulting in advancement is required for you to be kept as an employee at your present level [Reg. § 1.162-5(c)].

> ▶ **IMPORTANT:** The fact that you hold a job is not absolute proof that you have met the minimum requirements of that trade or business. The cost of subsequent education may still be nondeductible even though it is required by your employer.

Example 12-39: Allison Parke, who has completed two years of a normal three-year law school course leading to a law degree, is hired by a law firm to do legal research and perform other functions on a full-time basis. As a condition to continued employment, Ms. Parke is required to obtain the degree and pass the state bar exam. Parke completes her law school education by attending night school and she takes a bar review course in order to prepare for the state bar exam. The law courses and bar review course constitute education required to meet the minimum educational requirements for qualification in Parke's trade or business and thus, the expenditures for such courses are not deductible [Reg. § 1.162-5(b)(2)].

.03 Other Deductible Expenses

The following table illustrates when education expenses are deductible:[193]

---

[193] Treas. Dept., IRS Publication 17, "Your Federal Income Tax" (2013 Ed.), p. 194.

Table 2. Are Work-Related Education Expenses Deductible?

Start Here

Is the education required by your employer or the law to keep your present salary, status, or job?

Yes → Does the requirement serve a bona fide business requirement of your employer?

No → Does the education maintain or improve skills needed in your present work?

(Does the requirement serve a bona fide business requirement of your employer?) No → Does the education maintain or improve skills needed in your present work?

(Does the requirement serve a bona fide business requirement of your employer?) Yes → Is the education needed to meet the minimum educational requirements of your present trade or business?

(Does the education maintain or improve skills needed in your present work?) Yes → Is the education needed to meet the minimum educational requirements of your present trade or business?

(Does the education maintain or improve skills needed in your present work?) No → Your education is **not** qualifying work-related education.

(Is the education needed to meet the minimum educational requirements of your present trade or business?) Yes → Your education is **not** qualifying work-related education.

(Is the education needed to meet the minimum educational requirements of your present trade or business?) No → Is the education part of a program of study that will qualify you for a new trade or business?

(Is the education part of a program of study that will qualify you for a new trade or business?) Yes → Your education is **not** qualifying work-related education.

(Is the education part of a program of study that will qualify you for a new trade or business?) No → Your education is qualifying work-related education.

Which Educational Expenses Are Deductible?

Deductible education expenses include amounts spent for tuition, books, supplies, typing, lab fees, and similar items as well as certain travel and transportation costs.[194] No deduction is allowed for travel expenses that would be deductible only on the grounds that the travel itself constitutes education. However, this prohibition does not apply to travel that is a necessary adjunct to an educational activity that would give rise to a business deduction.

Travel and Transportation Expenses

The school where you take job-related classes is considered to be a work location and thus subject to the general work-related travel rules [Ch. 10]. And that means you can deduct the costs of the one-way trips from work to class. Whether you can deduct the costs incurred to travel between your home and class, however, depends on whether the school is a "temporary work location."[195]

For travel within your city or locality, the school is considered "temporary" if you attend the classes on a short-term basis (generally a matter of days or weeks). So any course of study that lasts beyond one semester is probably "regular" (as opposed to temporary) and therefore nondeductible.

---

[194] *M.L. McCulloch*, 55 TCM 259, Dec. 44,609(M), TC Memo. 1988-84.

[195] *H.S. Case*, 50 TCM 1291, Dec. 42,438(M), TC Memo. 1985-530.

For travel outside your city or locality, the school is considered temporary (and thus deductible) if the education lasts less than one year.[196]

> ▶ **OBSERVATION:** If your main office is in your home, the expenses incurred between your home office and school are considered to be expenses incurred to go between two work locations. Therefore, they are deductible.

The cost of travel for personal reasons is not deductible [Reg. § 1.162-5(d)].

Teachers' Education Expenses

The education expenses of teachers are often deductible. The minimum educational requirements for a position in an educational institution are the minimum level of education (in college hours or degree) normally required when persons are first employed. If there is no minimum level, a teacher is considered to meet the minimum educational requirements (as to the deductibility of expenses) when he or she becomes a faculty member. All teaching and related duties are considered to be the same general type of work. Thus, education expenses incurred by a classroom teacher for a change from elementary to secondary school, or from one subject to another or from teacher to principal would be deductible. Expenses incurred to qualify for a permanent certificate to teach in another state would also be deductible [Reg. § 1.162-5(b)(2), (3)]. A teacher has been allowed an education expense deduction for full-time graduate study, even though not actively employed at the time. The IRS limits this to a suspension of a year or less to qualify for the deduction.

> **Example 12-40:** Joe Frank, who holds a bachelor's degree, is employed by UPI University as an instructor in economics. He enrolls in graduate courses as a candidate for a graduate degree. Joe may become a permanent faculty member only if he obtains a graduate degree. He may continue as an instructor only so long as he shows satisfactory progress toward obtaining his degree. The costs of the graduate courses are not deductible, since they constitute education required to meet the minimum educational requirements for qualification in Joe's trade or business.

Travel as a Form of Education

The general rule is that no deduction may be claimed by any taxpayer (teachers, professors, and others) for travel expenses incurred as a form of education [Code Sec. 274(m)(2)]. For example, a high school French teacher cannot deduct expenses associated with traveling to France just so the teacher can be exposed to the French language. Similarly, an architect cannot deduct expenses associated with traveling to Italy to view and study the architecture. However, in *Jorgensen*,[197] the Tax Court allowed a teacher to deduct all travel and tuition expenses for university courses in Greece and Asia because the courses maintained or improved skills required in the teacher's employment as a high school English teacher. The court approved the deduction because: (1) the educational activities involved more than just travel to an interesting

---

[196] Rev. Rul. 99-7, 1999-1 CB 361.

[197] *A. Jorgensen*, 79 TCM 1926, Dec. 53,855(M), TC Memo. 2000-138; but see *T.W. Keller*, 71 TCM 3228, Dec. 51,427(M), TC Memo. 1996-300 (no deduction allowed because university did not require professor to travel abroad as a condition of sabbatical).

locale; (2) there were regularly scheduled lectures as well as a structured syllabus, extensive reading assignments; (3) the course work qualified for academic credit; and (4) the instructors satisfied American teaching standards.

A teacher's traveling expenses (including travel while on sabbatical leave) may be deductible if the teacher can prove that the period of travel was an ordinary and necessary business expense under Reg. § 1.162-5(a). A period of travel will only qualify if the majority of the activities performed during such period directly maintain or improve skills required by the employer or trade or business. The approval of a travel program by an employer or the fact that travel is accepted by an employer in the fulfillment of its requirements for retention of rate of compensation, status, or employment does not prove that the required relationship exists between the travel involved and the duties of the individual in his particular position [Reg. § 1.162-5(d)].

▶ **PRACTICE POINTER FOR TEACHERS:** There are situations where a teacher's traveling expenses may be deductible if he or she can prove that the travel was an ordinary and necessary business expense under Reg. § 1.162-5(a). For example, a teacher may deduct all travel and tuition costs for overseas courses if the courses maintain or improve skills required in the teacher's employment. The following factors will help the teacher support the conclusion that the travel was primarily for business purposes: (1) the teacher engaged in educational activities that amounted to much more than simply travel to an interesting destination; (2) the teacher attended regular scheduled lectures; (3) the coursework included structured syllabi; (4) the coursework included extensive reading assignments; (5) the course work qualifies for academic credit; and (6) the instructors abroad satisfy American teaching standards.

NOTE: Employees may only deduct the cost of courses in foreign countries as a business expense subject to the 2 percent floor on miscellaneous deductions [Ch. 9].

For discussion of employer-provided educational assistance plans, see Ch. 4. For discussion of deduction by teacher of amounts spent from their own money to purchase books and supplies, see ¶ 12,120.

Educational Travel Mixed With Pleasure

If a taxpayer travels away from home primarily for educational enrichment, his or her expenditures for travel, meals, and lodging while away from home are deductible. However, if the taxpayer also engages in some personal activity such as sightseeing, social visiting, entertaining, or other recreation, the portion of the expenses attributable to such personal activity constitutes nondeductible personal or living expenses and is not allowable as a deduction. If the taxpayer's travel away from home is primarily personal, the expenditures for travel, meals, and lodging (other than meals and lodging during the time spent in participating in deductible educational pursuits) are not deductible. Whether a particular trip is primarily personal or primarily to obtain education and therefore deductible depends upon all the facts and circumstances of each case. An important factor to consider in making the determination is the relative amount of time devoted to personal activity as compared with the time devoted to educational pursuits [Reg. § 1.162-5(e)(1)].

Example 12-41: A self-employed tax attorney takes a one-week course in new developments in taxation that is offered in New York City. Her primary purpose in going to New York is to take the course, but she also takes a side trip to Atlantic City for one day, takes a sightseeing trip while in New York, and entertains some personal friends. Her transportation expenses to New York and return to home are deductible but her transportation expenses to Atlantic City are not deductible. Her expenses for meals and lodging while away from home will be allocated between educational pursuits and personal activities. Those expenses which are entirely personal, such as sightseeing and entertaining friends, are not deductible [Reg. § 1.162-5(e)(2), Ex. 1].

¶12,135 UNIFORMS AND WORK CLOTHES

You can deduct as an ordinary and necessary business expense the cost and upkeep of work clothes that you must wear as a condition of your employment provided the clothing is not suitable for everyday wear. The clothing must be specifically required by your employer in order for the clothing to be deductible. For example, uniforms worn by delivery workers, firefighters, health care workers, nurses, police officers, letter carriers, professional athletes, and transportation workers (air, rail, bus, etc) will qualify for the deduction. All clothing, special shoes, hats, and coats will qualify for the deduction. This includes protective clothing required for work, including safety shoes or boots, safety glasses, hard hats, and work gloves. The following workers should be able to deduct their special safety garments: carpenters, cement workers, chemical workers, electricians, fishing boat crew members, machinists, oil field workers, pipe fitters, steamfitters, and truck drivers.

Musicians and entertainers can deduct the cost of theatrical clothing and accessories if they are not suitable for everyday wear. The courts, however, have denied a deduction for the purchase and maintenance of specially purchased clothing, make-up and hair-styling worn by well-known rock stars and performers because the clothing is "adaptable for general and personal wear" and the rock stars failed to show that the particular clothes would not have been purchased but for the employment.[198]

If you purchase clothing that displays your employer's logo those purchases will qualify for the deduction.[199] Generally, armed forces uniforms may not be deducted by those on active duty. However, if you are an armed forces reservist, you can deduct the unreimbursed cost of your uniform if military regulations restrict you from wearing it except while on duty as a reservist. You can only deduct, however, the excess of these costs over a uniform gratuity received for uniforms required for training and drills. If local military regulations forbid you from wearing fatigue uniforms when you are off

---

[198] *D.V. Teschner*, 74 TCM 1108, Dec. 52,339(M), TC Memo. 1997-498.

[199] *L.K. Williams*, 62 TCM 110, Dec. 47,464(M), TC Memo. 1991-317, *aff'd in an unpublished opinion*, 996 F2d 1230.

duty, you can deduct the amount by which the cost of buying and keeping up these uniforms is more than the uniform allowance you receive.

Students at armed forces academy cannot deduct the cost of their uniforms if they replace regular clothing. However, the cost of insignia, shoulder boards, and related items will be deductible. You can, however, deduct the cost of your uniforms if you are a civilian faculty or staff member of a military school.

SPECIAL DEDUCTION PROBLEMS

¶12,145 RESEARCH AND EXPERIMENTAL EXPENDITURES

A taxpayer may use one of three alternative methods to account for research and experimental expenditures incurred in connection with his or her trade or business:

1. Currently deduct the expenditures in the year in which they are paid or incurred [Code Sec. 174(a)];
2. Treat the expenditures as deferred expenses, amortizable over a period of at least 60 months beginning in the month that benefits are first realized from the expenditures [Code Sec. 174(b) Reg. § 1.174-1]; or
3. Amortize the expenditures over 10 years beginning in the tax year in which they are paid or incurred [Code Sec. 59(e)].

A taxpayer that fails to account for its research and experimental expenditures using one of these three methods is generally required to capitalize the expenditures.

.01 Definition of Research and Experimental Expenditures

The term *research or experimental expenditures,* as used in Code Sec. 174, means expenditures incurred in connection with the taxpayer's trade or business which represent research and development costs in the experimental or laboratory sense. The term generally includes all costs incident to the development or improvement of a product. The term includes the costs of obtaining a patent, such as attorneys' fees expended in making and perfecting a patent application. Expenditures represent research and development costs in the experimental or laboratory sense if they are for activities intended to discover information that would eliminate uncertainty concerning the development or improvement of a product. Uncertainty exists if the information available to the taxpayer does not establish the capability or method for developing or improving the product or the appropriate design of the product. Whether expenditures qualify as research or experimental expenditures depends on the nature of the activity to which the expenditures relate, not the nature of the product or improvement being developed or the level of technological advancement the product or improvement represents [Reg. § 1.174-2(a)(1)].

In Prop. Reg. § 1.174-2(a)(1), the definition of "research or experimental expenditures" is liberalized to provide that the ultimate success, failure, sale, or use of the product is not relevant to determining eligibility to claim deductions under Code Sec. 174. Costs may be eligible for deduction under Code Sec. 174 if paid or incurred after production begins but before uncertainty concerning the development or improvement of the product is eliminated.

The term *product* includes any pilot model, process, formula, invention, technique, patent, or similar property, and includes products to be used by the taxpayer in its trade or business as well as products to be held for sale, lease, or license [Reg. § 1.174-2(a)(3)]. The term *pilot model* means any representation or model of a product that is produced to evaluate and resolve uncertainty concerning the product during the development or improvement of the product. The term includes a fully-functional representation or model of the product or a component of the product [Prop. Reg. § 1.174-2(a)(4)].

A Code Sec. 174 deduction is only available for research or experimental expenditures to the extent that the amount of the expenditure is reasonable under the circumstances. In general, the amount of an expenditure for research or experimental activities is reasonable if the amount would ordinarily be paid for like activities by like enterprises under like circumstances. Amounts supposedly paid for research that are not reasonable under the circumstances may be characterized as disguised dividends, gifts, loans, or similar payments. This reasonableness requirement does not apply to the reasonableness of the type or nature of the activities themselves [Reg. § 1.174-2(a)(9)].

Costs that are eligible for the Code Sec. 174 deduction include not only costs paid or incurred by the taxpayer for research or experimentation undertaken directly by him but also to expenditures paid or incurred for research or experimentation carried on in his behalf by another person or organization (such as a research institute, foundation, engineering company, or similar contractor). However, any expenditures for research or experimentation carried on in the taxpayer's behalf by another person are not eligible Code Sec. 174 expenditures to the extent that they represent expenditures for the acquisition or improvement of land or depreciable property, used in connection with the research or experimentation, to which the taxpayer acquires rights of ownership [Reg. § 1.174-2(a)(10)].

> **Example 12-42:** Z is a wine producer who is researching and developing a new wine production process that involves the use of a different method of crushing the grapes. In order to test the effectiveness of the new grape crushing methods, Z incurs $2,000 in labor and materials to conduct the test on this part of the new manufacturing process. The $2,000 of the costs represents research and development costs in the experimental or laboratory sense. Therefore, the $2,000 incurred qualifies as research or experimental expenditures under Code Sec. 174 because it is a cost incident to the development or improvement of a component of a process [Prop. Reg. § 1.174-2(a)(11), Ex. 9].

The following expenditures do not qualify as research or experimental expenditures: (1) quality control testing other than testing to determine if the design of the product is appropriate; (2) efficiency surveys; (3) management studies; (4) consumer surveys; (5) advertising or promotions; (6) the acquisition of another's patent, model, production or process; or (7) research in connection with literary, historical, or similar projects [Reg. § 1.174-2(a)(6)].

.02 Realistic Prospect Test

To qualify as deductible research expenditures, the taxpayer must show a realistic prospect of using the technology to engage in a trade or business, not just as an investor. In addition, the expenses cannot be related to the taxpayer's personal use.[200] Code Sec. 174(a)(1) does not require that the taxpayer actually be engaged in a trade or business at the time of the expenditure in order to qualify for the deduction.[201] However, the expenditures must still be incurred "in connection" with the taxpayer's trade or business. Specifically, there must be a "realistic prospect" at the time of the expenditure that the taxpayer will enter a trade or business involving the technology being developed.[202]

Several factors are relevant in determining if a taxpayer is just a passive investor or has a realistic prospect of, at some time, engaging in a trade or business connected with the research and development expenditures as follows:

- The parties' intent;
- The financial resources of the taxpayer to market a developed product;
- Marketing and promotional materials indicating plans to market the product;
- The taxpayer's exercise of control over the person or entity doing the research;
- The taxpayer's business activity during the years at issue; and
- The taxpayer's and others' experience who are involved in the research.[203]

.03 Current Expense Method

Under the current expense method, a taxpayer may treat qualifying research and experimental expenditures that are incurred in connection with a trade or business as currently deductible in the year in which they are paid or incurred regardless of how they are recorded on the books[204] [Code Sec. 174(a); Reg. § 1.174-3(a)]. If the current expense method is adopted, the method applies to all research and experimental expenditures paid or incurred in the year of adoption and all subsequent years, unless a different method is authorized by the IRS. In no event will the taxpayer be permitted to adopt one method for part of the expenditures relative to a particular project and adopt for the same year a different method of treating the balance of the expenditures relating to the same project [Code Sec. 174(a)(3); Reg. § 1.174-3(a)].

Adoption Without Consent

IRS consent is not required if the taxpayer adopts the current expense method for the first year in which he or she pays or incurs research or experimental expenditures. The taxpayer may do so by claiming a deduction for his research or experimental expendi-

---

[200] *M. Mayrath*, CA-5, 66-1 USTC ¶9250, 357 F2d 209.

[201] *E.A. Snow*, SCt, 74-1 USTC ¶9432, 416 US 500, 94 SCt 1876; *R.F. Cleveland*, CA-4, 62-1 USTC ¶9142, 297 F2d 169.

[202] *L.H. Diamond*, CA-4, 91-1 USTC ¶50,186, 930 F2d 372; *LDL Research & Dev. II, Ltd.*, CA-10, 97-2 USTC ¶50,643, 124 F3d 1338; *S.D. Kantor*, CA-9, 93-2 USTC ¶50,433, 998 F2d 1514.

[203] *N. Lewin*, CA-4, 2003-1 USTC ¶50,330, 335 F3d 345; *R.E. Kantor*, CA-9, 93-2 USTC ¶50,433, 998 F2d 1514; *W.L. Zink*, CA-5, 91-1 USTC ¶50,219, 929 F2d 1015; *Scoggins*, CA-9, 95-1 USTC ¶50,061, 46 F3d 950; LTR 200145011 (Aug. 3, 2001).

[204] Rev. Rul. 58-78, 1958-1 CB 148; LTR 9524008 (Mar. 15, 1995).

tures. If the taxpayer fails to adopt the method for the first year in which he incurs such expenditures, he cannot do so in subsequent years without IRS consent [Reg. § 1.174-3(b)(1)].

Change of Method

You must file the application for change by the end of the first tax year to which the change applies. You must attach a copy of the letter of permission to the return for the first tax year to which the change applies [Reg. § 1.174-3(b)(3)].

.04 Treatment as Deferred Expenses

If you defer your research and experimental expenditures and charge them to a capital account, you must deduct them ratably over a period of 60 months or more [Code Sec. 174(b)]. You start with the month you first benefit from the expenditures. If there are two or more projects, you may select different deferral periods for each. If, however, the property resulting from such expenditures has a determinable useful life, such capitalized expenditures are recoverable by way of depreciation or depletion. Also, if the expenditures that you elected to defer result in the development of depreciable property, you must recover the unrecovered costs from the time the asset first becomes depreciable by way of depreciation. Rapid write-offs, to the extent they exceed the amount allowable had the research and experimental expenditures been capitalized and deducted ratably over 10 years, are considered adjustments for determining the alternative minimum tax of noncorporate taxpayers [Ch. 16] [Code Sec. 56(b)(2)].

Election of Method

You must make the election no later than the time for filing the return for the tax year (including extensions) the expenditures are paid or incurred. You make the election by a signed statement attached to the return [Reg. § 1.174-4(b)(1)]. The election cannot be made simply by claiming the deduction on the return.[205] The election does not apply to an expenditure paid or incurred before the year of election [Code Sec. 174(b); Reg. § 1.174-4].

Change of Method

Once adopted, this method must be followed unless the IRS consents to a change. You must file the application by the end of the first tax year for which the change applies. You must attach a copy of the permission to the return for the first tax year to which the change applies [Reg. § 1.174-4(b)(2)].

.05 Exceptions

Generally, the option to defer the expenses or deduct them in the year paid or incurred does not apply to: (1) expenditures for land or depreciable or depletable property, even if it is to be used in research or experimentation (but depreciation and depletion on such property are considered research and experimental expenditures); or (2) exploration expenditures incurred for minerals, oil or gas [Code Sec. 174(c), (d); Reg. § 1.174-2(b), (c)]. However, research and experimental expenditures, themselves, are deductible in the year paid or incurred even if they result (as a product of the research and experimentation) in depreciable property to be used in your trade or business. If

[205] Rev. Rul. 76-324, 1976-2 CB 77.

the expenditures are for the construction or manufacture of depreciable property by another, they are deductible only if incurred at your order or risk.

.06 Adjustment of Basis

Expenses deferred (discussed above) are included in figuring the adjusted basis of the property for which they are paid or incurred. The adjusted basis, however, must be reduced by the deferred expenses allowed as deductions to the extent there is a tax benefit (but not less than the amount allowable for the tax year and prior years) [Code Sec. 1016(a)(1), (14); Reg. § 1.1016-5(j)].

.07 Computer Software Costs

Costs incurred to develop computer software for the developer's own use or for sale or lease to others may be treated as current expenses under rules applicable to research and experimental expenditures under Code Sec. 174(a).[206] Developers may currently deduct such costs or treat the costs as capital expenditures amortizable over 60 months from completion of development under Code Sec. 174(b) or over 36 months under the rules applicable to the depreciation of computer software under Code Sec. 167(f)(1). In addition, the IRS will not question the tax treatment of software costs that are included in the capitalized and depreciable cost of hardware. Finally, software leasing or licensing costs may be deducted as rental payments under Reg. § 1.162-11.

Computer Software Defined

Computer software is any program or routine (any sequence of machine-readable code) that is designed to cause a computer to perform a desired function or set of functions and the documentation required to describe and maintain that program or routine. It includes all forms and media in which the software is contained, whether written, magnetic, or otherwise. Computer programs of all classes, for example, operating systems, executive systems, monitors, compilers and translators, assembly routines, and utility programs as well as application programs, are included. Computer software also includes any incidental and ancillary rights that are necessary to effect the acquisition of the title to, the ownership of, or the right to use the computer software.

Computer software does not include any data or information base described in Reg. § 1.197-2(b)(4) (for example, data files, customer lists, or client files) unless the data base or item is in the public domain and is incidental to a computer program. Nor does it include any cost of procedures that are external to the computer's operation.

Tax treatment. The tax treatment of computer software costs will be determined depending on whether the costs were incurred:

- To develop computer software for the developer's own use or for sale or lease to others;
- To acquire computer software; or
- In connection with leased or licensed software as discussed further below.

[206] Rev. Proc. 2000-50, 2002-2 CB 601, as modified by Rev. Proc. 2007-16, IRB 2007-4, 358 (regarding change in accounting method).

Costs of developing computer software. The IRS will not question the tax treatment of costs connected with developing computer software (whether or not the particular software is patented or copyrighted) if all costs properly attributed to the development of the software are either:

- Consistently treated as current expenses that are deducted in full in accordance with the rules similar to those applicable under Code Sec. 174(a) to research and experimental expenditures; or
- Consistently treated as capital expenditures that are amortized ratably over a period of 60 months from the date of completion of the development as provided by Code Sec. 174(b), or over 36 months from the date the software is placed in service as provided in Code Sec. 167(f)(1).

Cost of acquired computer software. The IRS will not question treatment of:

- Costs that are included, without being separately stated, in the cost of the computer hardware if the costs are consistently treated as a part of the cost of the hardware that is capitalized and depreciated; or
- Costs that are separately stated if the costs are consistently treated as capital expenditures for an intangible asset the cost of which is to be recovered by amortization deductions ratably over a period of 36 months beginning with the month the software is placed in service as provided under the rules applicable to the depreciation of computer software under Code Sec. 167(f)(1).

Leased or licensed computer software. Where you lease or license computer software for use in your trade or business, the IRS will not question a deduction properly allowable under Reg. § 1.162-11 as a rental expense. This means that the cost of licensing software for business use for a specific period of time may be deducted over that term in the same manner that a business tenant may under Reg. § 1.162-11 deduct the cost of acquiring a leasehold over the lease term.

However, an amount described in Reg. § 1.162-11 is not currently deductible if, without regard to that regulation, the amount is properly chargeable to capital account [Reg. § 1.197-2(a)(3)].

Change in accounting method. Any change in your treatment of software costs is a change in accounting method, subject to automatic change provisions. A change in useful life is also considered a change in method of accounting.[207] This means that any taxpayer wanting to change his or her method of accounting must follow IRS automatic change in method of accounting provisions. To change your accounting method, you must file Form 3115, *Application for Change in Accounting Method.*

---

[207] Rev. Proc. 2007-16, IRB 2007-4, 358.

¶12,150 DEDUCTION FOR DOMESTIC PRODUCTION ACTIVITIES

.01 Deduction for U.S. Manufacturers

Code Sec. 199 provides that C corporations, S corporations, partnerships, sole proprietorships, cooperatives, and estates and trusts may claim a manufacturing deduction equal to up to 9 percent of the lesser of the taxpayer's *qualified production activities income* (QPAI) or taxable income (determined without regard to the deduction for income attributable to domestic production activities) for the year.
Qualified production activities include:

- Manufacturing, production, growth or extraction in the United States of certain tangible personal property, computer software, films and videotapes, sound recordings (such as discs, tapes, or other phonorecordings), electricity, natural gas, or potable water;
- Construction performed in the United States; and
- Engineering or architectural services performed in the United States for construction projects in the United States [Code Sec. 199(c)(4)(a)].

Eligible taxpayers may claim a manufacturing deduction equal to the phased-in percentage of the lesser of taxable income (or an individual's adjusted gross income) or qualified production activities income. In applying these rules, only items that are attributable to the actual conduct of a trade or business are taken into account [Code Sec. 199(d)(5)].

Special Rule for Puerto Rico

For purposes of the domestic production activities deduction, the term "United States" only includes the 50 States and the District of Columbia, as well as U.S. territorial waters. It does not include U.S. possessions or territories. However, if a taxpayer has gross receipts from sources within the Commonwealth of Puerto Rico, then Puerto Rico will be considered part of the United States if all of those receipts are subject to the U.S. federal income tax [Code Sec. 199(d)(8)]. Thus, if a taxpayer has gross receipts from qualified production activities within Puerto Rico and those receipts are subject to U.S. income tax, then such receipts will be considered domestic production gross receipts. Moreover, wages paid by the taxpayer to a bona fide resident of Puerto Rico for services performed in Puerto Rico will be considered "wages" for purposes of calculating the 50-percent W-2 wage limitation. The special rule that permits Puerto Rico to be deemed part of the United States for purposes of the domestic production activities deduction under Code Sec. 199 applies to the first eight tax years beginning after December 31, 2005, and before January 1, 2014 [Code Sec. 199(d)(8)(C)]. Thus, prior to January 1, 2014, a taxpayer with gross receipts from qualified production activities within Puerto Rico, which are subject to U.S. federal income taxes, may treat those receipts as domestic production gross receipts.

Deduction Amount

The Code Sec. 199 domestic production activities deduction is equal to nine percent of the lesser of:

- The qualified production activities income of the taxpayer for the year; or
- The taxpayer's taxable income (determined without regard to this provision) for the year [Code Sec. 199(a)(2)].

If the taxpayer is an individual, these calculations use adjusted gross income, rather than taxable income [Code Sec. 199(d)(2)].

Taxpayers may claim a domestic production activities deduction on Form 8903, *Domestic Production Activities Deduction.*

W-2 Wage Limitation

The amount of the manufacturing deduction cannot exceed 50 percent of the W-2 wages paid by the taxpayer as an employer during the tax year [Code Sec. 199(b)(1)]. W-2 wages must relate to the taxpayer's domestic production gross receipts (DPGR) [Code Sec. 199(b)(2)(B); Reg. § 1.199-2]. Thus, to determine W-2 wages taxpayers must determine their total W-2 wages, and then determine the portion that is properly allocable to DPGR. In the case of pass-through entities such as partnerships and corporations, each partner or shareholder shall be treated as having W-2 wages for the year in an amount equal to such person's allocable share of the W-2 wages of the partnership or S corporation for the year [Code Sec. 199(d)(1)(A)(iii)]. A taxpayer's W-2 wages must be paid by the taxpayer with respect to employment of employees by the taxpayer during the year. W-2 wages are the sum of wages plus the total amount of elective deferrals, compensation deferred and the amount of designated Roth contributions [Code Sec. 199(b)(2)(A)]. The Emergency Economic Stabilization Act of 2008 modified the W-2 wage limitation by defining the term W-2 wages for qualified films to include any compensation for services performed in the United States by actors, production personnel, directors, and producers [Code Sec. 199(b)(2)].

In Rev. Proc. 2006-47,[208] the IRS provides methods for calculating W-2 wages for purposes of the Code Sec. 199 manufacturing deduction. Rev. Proc. 2006-47 specified the mandatory use of one of three methods for calculating the W-2 wages:

- Unmodified box method—total wages in either Box 1 or Box 5 (Medicare wages) of all Forms W-2 filed with SSA by the taxpayer;
- Modified Box 1 method—total entries in Box 1 of Forms W-2 filed with respect to employees of the taxpayer minus certain nonwage amounts in Box 1; and
- Tracking wages method—total wages subject to federal income tax withholding that are paid to employees of the taxpayer minus supplemental unemployment compensation benefits plus elective deferrals reported in Box 12 under Code Secs. 401(k), 403(b), and 457 plans.

---

[208] Rev. Proc. 2006-47, 2006-2 CB 869.

Affiliated Groups

In the case of corporate taxpayers that are members of certain affiliated groups, the manufacturing deduction is determined by treating all members of such groups as a single taxpayer and the deduction is allocated among such members in proportion to each member's respective amount (if any) of qualified production activities income [Code Sec. 199(d)(4)(A)]. An expanded affiliated group is an affiliated group as defined for purposes of consolidated returns, except that the stock ownership threshold is reduced to 50 percent from 80 percent, and insurance companies and corporations that elect to use a possessions tax credit are not excluded [Code Sec. 199(d)(4)(B)]. Except as provided in regulations, the qualified production activities deduction is allocated among the members of the group in proportion to the member's respective amount (if any) of qualified production activities income [Code Sec. 199(d)(4)(C)].

.02 *Qualified Production Activities Income* (QPAI) Defined

In general, QPAI is equal to the taxpayer's domestic production gross receipts, reduced by the sum of the following:

- The costs of goods sold that are allocable to such receipts;
- Other deductions, expenses, or losses that are directly allocable to such receipts; and
- A ratable share of other deductions, expenses, and losses that are not directly allocable to such receipts or another class of income [Code Sec. 199(c)(1)].

For purposes of determining cost of goods sold, any item or service brought into the United States is treated as acquired by purchase, and its cost is not less than its value immediately after it entered the United States [Code Sec. 199(c)(3)(A)]. Except as provided otherwise by the Treasury, the value of property is its customs value [H.R. Conf. Rep. No. 108-755]. Similar rules apply in determining the adjusted basis of leased or rented property where the lease or rental gives rise to domestic production gross receipts [Code Sec. 199(c)(3)(A)]. These rules also apply if the item or service was imported into the United States without an arm's-length transfer price [H.R. Conf. Rep. No. 108-755]. However, if the taxpayer had exported the property for further manufacture, the increase in cost or adjusted basis cannot exceed the difference between the property's value when it was exported, and its value when it was brought back into the United States [Code Sec. 199(c)(3)(B)].

.03 Domestic Production Gross Receipts (DPGR)

Domestic production gross receipts (DPGR) are defined as a taxpayer's gross receipts that are derived from one or more of the following:

- Any lease, rental, license, sale, exchange or other disposition of qualifying production property (QPP) that was manufactured, produced, grown, or extracted (MPGE) by the taxpayer in whole or in significant part within the Unites States[209] [Code Sec. 199(c)(4)(A)(i)(I); Reg. § 1.199-3(a)(1)]. The term MPGE includes "manufacturing, producing, growing, extracting, installing, developing, improving, and creating QPP; making QPP out of scrap, salvage, or junk material as well as from new or raw

[209] *J.T. Longino*, 105 TCM 1491, Dec. 59,487(M), TC Memo. 2013-80.

material by processing, manipulating, refining, or changing the form of an article, or by combining or assembling two or more articles" [Reg. § 1.199-3(e)(1)]. In Field Attorney Advice 20133302F,[210] the IRS concluded that a pharmacy care provider's photo processing activities by which it produced photo products from raw materials such as paper, ink, chemicals and blank computer disks constituted MPGE under Reg. § 1.199-3(e)(1). However, the process of affixing a customer's intangible files to a CD or DVD not manufactured by the taxpayer was not considered a MPGE activity.

When the taxpayer contracts with an unrelated third party for the manufacturing of its products, the taxpayer must have the "benefits and burdens of ownership of the QPP under federal income tax principles during the period the MPGE activity occurs" [Reg. § 1.199-3(e)(1)]. In *ADVO, Inc.*,[211] a corporation engaged in direct mail advertising, was denied a domestic production activities deduction for the cost of its direct advertising materials. The gross receipts attributable to the taxpayer's printed direct mail advertising and distribution products did not qualify as QPP because the taxpayer contracted its actual printing out to third-party printers. The taxpayer did not manufacture the advertising packages, but only produced intangible property used by printers to produce tangible personal property in the form of the packages. The taxpayer did not have the benefits and burdens of ownership of the QPP as defined in Reg. § 1.199-3(e)(1) during the period of manufacturing.

Qualifying production property generally includes any tangible personal property, computer software, or sound recordings [Code Sec. 199(c)(5)]. Excluded from the definition of tangible property is land, real property, computer software, sound recordings, qualified films, and electricity, natural gas, or potable water [Reg. § 1.199-3(j)(2)]. Gross receipts derived from customer and technical support, telephone and other telecommunication services, online services (such as Internet access services, online banking services, providing access to online electronic books, newspapers, and journals), and other similar services do not constitute gross receipts derived from a lease, rental, license, sale, exchange, or other disposition of computer software [Reg. § 1.199-3(i)(6)(ii)]. Code Sec. 199(c)(4)(C) provides a special rule for government contracts. Property will be treated "as disposed of" if it is produced under a contract with the federal government and title was transferred to the government before production of the property is complete. This government contracts exception eliminated the requirement that DPGR must be attributable to the "dispostion" of QPP for purposes of the Code Sec. 199 deduction. Therefore, the IRS concluded in Technical Advice Memorandum 201314043,[212] that a taxpayer could claim the deduction for amounts received under a government contract, even though it did not deliver the QPP that was the subject of the contract to its government customer.

---

[210] Field Attorney Advice (FAA) 20133302F (Aug. 19, 2013).

[211] *ADVO, Inc.*, 141 TC No. 9, Dec. 59,670 (2013).

[212] TAM 201314043 (Nov. 28, 2012).

The regulations provide the following two safe harbor exceptions for computer software:

— Gross receipts derived from providing computer software for customer use online will be treated as DPGR if (1) the taxpayer sells the software both online and affixed to a tangible medium (e.g., a CD) or via in Internet download, (2) the software has only minor or immaterial differences from the online software and (3) the software has been manufactured, produced, grown or extracted by the taxpayer in whole or in significant part in the U.S. [Reg. § 1.199-3(i)(6)(iii)(A)].

— Gross receipts derived from providing computer software that has been manufactured, produced, grown or extracted by the taxpayer in whole or in significant part in the U.S. for customer use online will be treated as DPGR if another person sells substantially identical software to its customers affixed to a tangible medium or via an Internet download [Reg. § 1.199-3(i)(6)(iii)(B)]. Substantially identical software is defined as (1) having the same functional result as the online software (from the customer's perspective) and (2) having a significant overlap of features or purposes with the online software [Reg. § 1.199-3(i)(6)(iv)(A)].

- Any lease, rental, license, sale, exchange or other disposition of any qualified film produced by the taxpayer in the United States [Code Sec. 199(c)(4)(A)(i)(II); Reg. § 1.199-3(a)(1)(ii)]. A qualified film for purposes of the Code Sec. 199 deduction includes any copyrights, trademarks, and other intangibles with respect to a qualified film produced by the taxpayer [Code Sec. 199(c)(6)]. The Code Sec. 199 deduction for qualified films is not affected by the methods and means of distributing the film. For example, the distribution of a qualified film via the Internet (whether the film is viewed online or downloaded or whether or not there is a fee charged) is now considered to be a disposition of the film for purposes of determining domestic production gross receipts. Reg. § 1.199-3(k)(1) provides that the term qualified film means any motion picture film or video tape, or live or delayed television programming (film), if no less than 50 percent of the total compensation relating to the production of such film is compensation for services performed in the United States by actors, production personnel, directors, and producers [Reg. § 1.199-3(k)(1)]. Under this safe harbor, the taxpayer's direct labor and overhead costs to produce the film in the United States must account for 20 percent or more of the film's total costs. The not-less-than-50-percent-of-the-total-compensation requirement is calculated using a fraction. The numerator is the compensation for services performed in the United States and the denominator is the total compensation for services regardless of where the production activities are performed [Reg. § 1.199-3(k)(5)].

  The term *actors* includes players, newscasters, or any other persons who are compensated for their performance or appearance in a film. The term *production personnel* includes writers, choreographers, and composers who are compensated for providing services during the production of a film, as well as casting agents, camera operators, set designers, lighting technicians, make-up artists, and other persons who are compensated for providing services that are directly related to the production of the film. The definition of a qualified film generally does not include tangible personal property embodying the qualified film, such as DVDs or videocassettes [Reg. § 1.199-3(k)(1)].

Example 12-43: X creates a television program in the United States that includes scenes from films licensed by X from unrelated persons Y and Z. Assume that Y and Z produced the films licensed by X. The not-less-than-50-percent-of-the-total-compensation requirement is determined by reference to all compensation for services paid in the production of the television program, including the films licensed by X from Y and Z, and is calculated using a fraction. The numerator of the fraction is the compensation for services performed in the United States and the denominator is the total compensation for services regardless of where the production activities are performed. However, for purposes of calculating the denominator, in determining the total compensation paid by Y and Z, X need only include the total compensation paid by Y and Z to actors, production personnel, directors, and producers for the production of the scenes used by X in creating its television program [Reg. § 1.199-3(k)(10), Ex. 6].

- Any lease, rental, license, sale, exchange or other disposition of electricity, natural gas, or potable water produced by the taxpayer within the United States [Code Sec. 199(c)(4)(A)(i)(III); Reg. § 1.199-3(a)(1)(iii)].
- Construction performed in the United States [Code Sec. 199(c)(4)(A)(ii)]. This includes activities that are directly related to the erection or substantial renovation of residential and commercial buildings and infrastructure. The Conference Report provides that substantial renovation includes structural improvements, but not mere cosmetic changes, such as painting (H.R. Conf. Rep. No. 108-755).
- Engineering or architectural services performed in the United States for construction in the United States [Code Sec. 199(c)(4)(A)(iii); Reg. § 1.199-3(a)(3)]. In *Gibson & Associates*,[213] the Tax Court concluded that an engineering and heavy highway construction company's receipts from several bridge and highway projects arose from the construction of real property and, thus, qualified as domestic production gross receipts. The court found that the taxpayer erected real property when it added additional lanes, driveways, ramps, traffic rails, bridge decks, and retaining walls to existing roads. The taxpayer's work was not routine maintenance, and the rehabilitation of one or more components of real property was not just a repair. The taxpayer's renovation of major components often extended the useful life of the structures as a whole on account of the intricate interaction of all of the components and, thus, resulted in a more permanent increment in the longevity, utility, and worth of the structure as a whole that, in turn, increased the useful life of the overall structure.
- Income derived from the lease, rental, license, sale, exchange, or other disposition of computer software include advertising income and product-placement income which is compensation for placing or integrating advertising or a product into the computer software [Reg. § 1.199-3(i)(5)(ii)(B)]. An exception is made for income derived from customer and technical support, telephone and other telecommunication services, online services such as Internet access services, online banking services, and providing access to online electronic books, newspapers, and journals [Reg. § 1.199-3(i)(6)(ii)]. However, under the "third-party comparable exception" in Reg. § 1.199-3(i)(6)(iii), gross receipts from direct use of computer software qualify as DPGR if another person derives gross receipts from the disposition of substantially

---

[213] *Gibson & Associates,* 136 TC No. 10, Dec. 58,552 (2011).

identical software to its customers, by a tangible medium (such as a disk or DVD) or download from the Internet. In CCA 201226025, IRS Chief Counsel rejected the application of this exception to a seller of online software. Therefore the IRS denied the Code Sec. 199 deduction for income from the software. However, if the taxpayer could show that an individual component of its software had a substantially identical offline counterpart, gross receipts attributable to that component should qualify as DPGR and be eligible for the Code Sec. 199 deduction.

- Gross receipts include gross receipts derived from the sale, exchange, or other disposition of agricultural products only if (1) the taxpayer performs storage, handling, or other processing activities (other than transportation activities) with respect to the products, and (2) the products are consumed in connection with, or incorporated into, the manufacturing, production, growth, or extraction of qualifying production property, by the taxpayer or by some other party [H.R. Conf. Rep. No. 108-755].

In Rev. Rul. 2011-24,[214] the IRS analyzed several situations where a telecommunications company provided services to a customer to determine whether the provider received domestic production gross receipts (DPGRs) from its customers. The court concluded that gross receipts derived from the performance of services generally do not qualify as DPGRs. In situations where the provider's gross receipts were derived from the performance of telecommunications services without the lease or rental of equipment, the provider's receipts do not constitute DPGRs. In situations where the provider rented or leased equipment that was located on the customer's premises, along with providing services, the provider's gross receipts were derived from a combination of the performance of telecommunications services and the rental of the customer premises equipment, with the latter receipts qualified as DPGR. Receipts derived from the performance of telecommunications services, on the other hand, did not constitute DPGRs.

.04 Exclusions from DPGRs

Domestic production gross receipts do not include gross receipts derived from the following:

- **Sale of food and beverages.** Domestic production gross receipts do not include gross receipts derived from the sale of food and beverages prepared by the taxpayer at a retail establishment [Code Sec. 199(c)(4)(B)(i)]. Note that food processing generally is a qualified production activity, but the sale of food and beverages prepared by the taxpayer at a retail establishment is not. For instance, the Conference Report provides that operations at a meat packing plant give rise to qualified domestic production gross receipts, but a chef's creation of a venison sausage for his or her restaurant does not [H.R. Conf. Rep. No. 108-755]. However, a single taxpayer may operate food processing facilities, as well as retail facilities that sell the produced goods and other foods and beverages.

Example 12-44: Red Hot Mama, Inc., makes and sells fruit and vegetable salsas of all varieties. The company buys the fruits and vegetables used in their salsas. They prepare and package the various salsas at their food processing facility and then sell the packaged salsas to retailers. Red Hot Mama also operates retail

[214] Rev. Rul. 2011-24, IRB 2011-41, 485.

facilities that sell the salsas along with other snack foods and freshly made fruit and vegetables smoothies prepared from the salsas at the retail establishment. The gross receipts from Red Hot Mama's retail operations are qualified domestic production gross receipts to the extent they represent receipts from the sale of their salsas, but are nonqualified to the extent they represent receipts from the sale of the freshly made smoothies prepared at the retail establishment. However, Red Hot Mama may allocate part of the beverage receipts to qualified receipts to the extent of the value of the ingredients used to make the beverages. Red Hot Mama's sale of salsas to unrelated retailers provides a value for the ingredients it uses to make the smoothies for retail sale (H.R. Conf. Rep. No. 108-755).

- **Transmission or distribution of electricity, natural gas, or potable water.** Domestic production gross receipts do not include gross receipts derived from the transmission or distribution of electricity, natural gas, or potable water [Code Sec. 199(c)(4)(B)(ii)].[215] Note that DPGRs include gross receipts from the production in the United States of electricity, gas, and potable water, but exclude gross receipts from the transmission of these items. Thus, gross receipts from the production of electricity are DPGR, whether the producing facility is part of a regulated utility or is an independent power facility. However, if the taxpayer is an integrated producer that generates electricity and delivers it to end users, its DPGR does not include gross receipts that are properly attributable to the transmission of the electricity from the generating facility to the final customers or to a point of local distribution [H.R. Conf. Rep. No. 108-755].

Example 12-45: A owns a wind turbine that generates electricity. B owns a local distribution network. C owns a high-voltage transmission line. A sells its turbine-produced electricity to B, which uses its distribution network to sell the electricity to its customers. A contracts with C to transmit the electricity to B. A's receipts from the sale of the electricity to B are DPGR. C's gross receipts from transporting the electricity and B's receipts from distributing the electricity to its customers, are not DPGR. If A makes direct sales of electricity to customers in B's service area and B receives remuneration for the distribution of electricity, B's receipts are not DPGR. If A, B, and C are related taxpayers, they must allocate their gross receipts among their production, distribution and transmission activities [H.R. Conf. Rep. No. 108-755].

- **Receipts derived from related parties.** DPGRs do not include gross receipts derived from property leased, licensed, or rented by the taxpayer for use by any related person [Code Sec. 199(c)(7)(A)] Persons are related in this situation if they are members of a controlled group of corporations or an affiliated service group, or are other entities under common control [Code Sec. 199(c)(7)(B)].

[215] CCA 201208029 (Dec. 1, 2011) (a natural gas exploration and production company's gross receipts derived from the sale of leasehold rights under a oil, gas and mineral exploration lease were not DPGR).

.05 Qualified Production Activities Income of Pass-Through Entities (Other Than Cooperatives)

The manufacturing deduction is available to pass-through entities, including S corporations, partnerships, estates, and trusts (but not agricultural or horticultural cooperatives, as discussed further below). The deduction is applied at the partner or shareholder level of a pass-through entity. All items applicable to the deduction are passed through to the partner or shareholder. Partnerships and S corporations may calculate a partner's or shareholder's share of qualified production activities income (QPAI) and W-2 wages at the entity level in order to calculate the domestic production activities deduction.[216]

.06 Qualified Production Activities Income of Agricultural and Horticultural Cooperatives

Member-owned agricultural and horticultural cooperatives may also claim a deduction equal to qualified production activities income derived from agricultural or horticultural products that are manufactured, produced, grown, or extracted by cooperatives, or that are marketed through cooperatives, as it provides for qualified production activities income of other taxpayers. In Letter Ruling 20112012,[217] the IRS concluded that for purposes of computing a grain farmers' cooperative's Code Sec. 199 domestic production activities deduction, the cooperative's qualified production activities income and taxable income were to be computed without regard to any deduction for grain payments to members or patrons.

In addition, the amount of any patronage dividends or per-unit retained allocations paid to a member of an agricultural or horticultural cooperative that is allocable to the portion of qualified production activities income of the cooperative is deductible from the gross income of the member. In order to qualify, such amount must be designated by the organization as allocable to the deductible portion of qualified production activities income in a written notice mailed to its patrons. The cooperative cannot claim a dividends-paid deduction for such amounts.

.07 Alternative Minimum Tax (AMT)

The manufacturer's deduction is allowed for purposes of computing alternative minimum taxable income (AMTI) (including adjusted current earnings). When you compute AMTI, the deduction is determined by reference to the lesser of the qualified production activities income (as determined for the regular tax) or the AMTI (in the case of an individual, adjusted gross income as determined for the regular tax) without regard to this deduction. For individual taxpayers, the calculation of the deduction is the same for both income tax and AMT liability. For other taxpayers, however, the deduction for AMT purposes is calculated as the applicable percentage of the lesser of (1) the taxpayer's qualified production activities income (determined without regard to available tax credits), or (2) the taxpayer's alternative minimum taxable income (determined without regard to this deduction) [Code Sec. 199(d)(6)].

---

216 Rev. Proc. 2007-34, 2007-1 CB 1345.

217 LTR 20112012 (Mar. 23, 2011).

¶12,151 ENERGY-EFFICIENT COMMERCIAL BUILDING DEDUCTION

A taxpayer may claim a deduction under Code Sec. 179D(a) for part or all of the cost of energy efficient commercial building property that the taxpayer places in service prior to January 1, 2014. Typically this deduction will be claimed by the private owner or tenant of a commercial building, a government owner of a commercial building, or the architect or engineer of a government-owned commercial building. Owners of buildings and tenants/lessees would be able to reduce their basis in the building by the amount of the deduction.

.01 Definition of Energy Efficient Commercial Building Property

"Energy efficient commercial building property" is defined in Code Sec. 179D(c)(1) as depreciable property that satisfies each of the following conditions:

1. The property is installed on or in any building that is located in the United States;
2. The property is installed as part of the interior lighting systems; the heating, cooling, ventilation, and hot water systems; or the building envelope; and
3. It is certified that the interior lighting systems, heating, cooling, ventilation, and hot water systems, and the building envelope that have been incorporated into the building, or that the taxpayer plans to incorporate into the building subsequent to the installation of such property, will reduce the total annual energy and power costs with respect to the combined usage of the building's heating, cooling, ventilation, hot water, and interior lighting systems by 50 percent or more.

.02 Maximum Amount of the Deduction

The maximum amount of the deduction may not exceed the excess (if any) of (i) the product of $1.80 and the square footage of the building, over (ii) the aggregate amount of the Code Sec. 179D deductions allowed with respect to the building for all prior tax years [Code Sec. 179D(b)].

In the event that the installation of energy efficient commercial building property does not achieve the 50-percent reduction in total annual energy and power costs required by Code Sec. 179D(c)(1)(D), a partial deduction is available in Code Sec. 179D(d)(1) in an amount not to exceed the product of $0.60 and the square footage of the building, for each system that satisfies the requirements of Code Sec. 179D(d)(1) (the permanent rule). While the taxpayer may claim a partial Code Sec. 179D deduction for each system, the taxpayer may not claim partial deductions that in total exceed the overall limitation of (i) the product of $1.80 and the square footage of the building, over (ii) the aggregate amount of the Code Sec. 179D deductions allowed with respect to the building for all prior tax years.

An interim lighting rule allows for an alternate method of calculating a partial deduction for interior lighting systems. This rule provides a partial deduction for part or all of the cost of certain energy efficient commercial building property installed as part of a lighting system that reduces the lighting power density of the building by more than 25 percent (50 percent in the case of a warehouse) [Code Sec. 179D(f)].

Under the permanent rule, property that would be energy efficient commercial building property but for the failure to achieve the target 50-percent reduction in energy and power costs required under Code Sec. 179D(c)(1)(D) is partially qualifying commercial building property if it is installed as part of a system that satisfies the applicable energy savings percentage.

.03 Energy Savings Percentages Required

In Notice 2012-26,[218] the IRS revises Notice 2008-40[219] and Notice 2006-52[220] to provide that property installed as part of the interior lighting system is partially qualifying property under the permanent rule if the installation of such property will reduce the total annual energy and power costs with respect to the combined usage of the building's heating, cooling, ventilation, hot water systems by 15 percent or more. The total annual energy and power costs with respect to interior lighting systems must be reduced by 25 percent or more. The total annual energy and power costs with respect to the building envelope must be reduced by 10 percent or more.

The following table summarizes the energy savings percentages permitted under Notice 2006-52, Notice 2008-40 and Notice 2012-26.

Summary of Energy Savings Percentages Provided by IRS Guidance

	Energy Savings Percentages permitted under Notice 2006-52	Energy Savings Percentages permitted under Notice 2008-40	Energy Savings Percentages permitted under Notice 2012-26
Interior Lighting Systems	16 2/3	20	25
Heating, Cooling, Ventilation, and Hot Water Systems	16 2/3	20	15
Building Envelope	16 2/3	10	10
Effective for property placed in service	January 1, 2006 - December 31, 2008	January 1, 2006 - December 31, 2013	Effective date of Notice 2012-26 - December 31, 2013; if Code Sec. 179D is extended beyond December 31, 2013, also effective (except as otherwise provided in an amendment of Code Sec. 179D or the guidance thereunder) during the period of the extension

.04 Limitation on Deduction for Partially Qualifying Property

A taxpayer who owns, or is a lessee of, a commercial building and installs partially qualifying energy efficient commercial building property may claim a partial deduction for each qualifying system. However, because the deduction for each such system is

---

[218] Notice 2012-26, IRB 2012-17, 847.

[219] Notice 2008-40, 2008-1 CB 725.

[220] Notice 2006-52, 2006-1 CB 1175.

limited to $0.60 per square foot, the sum of all partial deductions claimed cannot exceed the excess (if any) of (i) the product of $1.80 and the square footage of the building, over (ii) the aggregate amount of the Code Sec. 179D deductions allowed with respect to the building for all prior tax years.

.05 Certification Process for Energy-Efficient Commercial Property Deduction

Before a taxpayer may claim the Code Sec. 179D deduction with respect to property installed on or in a commercial building, the taxpayer must obtain a certification with respect to the property. The certification must be provided by a qualified individual and satisfy the requirements of Code Sec. 179D (c) (1). A taxpayer is not required to attach the certification to the return on which the deduction is taken. Taxpayers must maintain such books and records as are sufficient to establish the entitlement to, and amount of, any deduction claimed by the taxpayer [Reg. § 1.6001-1 (a)]. Accordingly, a taxpayer claiming a deduction under Code Sec. 179D should retain the certification as part of the taxpayer's records. A certification will be treated as satisfying the requirements of Code Sec. 179D (c) (1) if the certification contains all of the following:[221]

1. The name, address, and telephone number of the qualified individual.
2. The address of the building to which the certification applies.
3. A statement providing that the changes being incorporated into the building will reduce the total annual energy and power costs.

¶12,152 FILM AND TELEVISION PRODUCTION COSTS

To encourage domestic film production, Code Sec. 181 allows the owner of a qualified film or television production to elect to deduct production costs in the year that they are incurred instead of capitalizing the costs and recovering them through depreciation deductions. The owner of the production makes the election and claims the deduction. The election is usually made in the first year that production costs are paid or incurred. The production costs are then deducted each year that the costs are paid or incurred.

The Code Sec. 181 expensing incentive differs depending on when film or television production commenced:

- To qualify for the election on productions that commence after October 22, 2004 and before January 1, 2008, the aggregate production cost may not exceed $15 million and 75 percent of the compensation paid with respect to the production must be for services performed in the U.S.
- To qualify for the election on productions that commence after December 31, 2007, the first $15 million of an otherwise qualified film or television production may be treated as an expense in cases where the aggregate cost of production exceeds the dollar limitation.

---

[221] Notice 2006-52, 2006-1 CB 1175, as clarified and amplified by Notice 2008-40, 2008-1 CB 725, as modified by Notice 2012-26, IRB 2012-13, 576.

The $15 million amounts are increased to $20 million in both cases for productions in low income communities or distressed areas or isolated areas of distress). The deduction is recaptured if the production ceases to be a qualifying production either before or after it is placed in service. The deduction is also treated as a depreciation deduction for purposes of the Code Sec. 1245 recapture rules [Code Sec. 1245(a)(2)(C)].

.01 75-Percent Compensation Test

A production is not a qualified production unless at least 75 percent of the total "compensation" paid with respect to the production is "qualified compensation" paid for services performed in the United States. A service is performed in the United States if the principal photography to which the service relates occurs within the United States and the person performing the service is physically present in the United States. Special rules apply to fully and partially animated productions [Reg. § 1.181-3(d)]. U.S. possessions and territories are not included in the definition of the United States [Reg. § 1.181-3(f)(3)].

The term compensation means payments made by an owner of the production for services performed in the United States by actors, directors, producers, and production personnel who are being compensated for providing services directly related to production. Payees include writers, choreographers, and composers providing services during production, casting agents, camera operators, set designers, lighting technicians, and make-up artists [Code Sec. 181(d)(3)(A); Reg. §§ 1.263A-(e)(2)(i)(B), 1.181-3(c)].

.02 Production Costs

"Production costs" are eligible for expensing. In addition, the $15 or $20 million production cost limit is determined by reference to "production costs." A production cost is defined as any cost of the type subject to capitalization under the uniform capitalization rules of Code Sec. 263A but for the fact that amounts expensed under this provision are exempted from all capitalization requirements [Reg. § 1.181-1(a)(3)].

Production costs include:

- Participations and residuals compensation paid for services,
- Compensation paid for property rights,
- Noncompensation costs, and
- Costs related to obtaining financing for the production, including premiums for a completion bond.

Production costs do not include:

- Costs paid or incurred to distribute or exploit a production, including advertising and print costs and
- Costs to prepare a new release or new broadcast of an existing film or video, such as a DVD release or re-broadcast.

No Double Deduction

Production costs deducted under Code Sec. 181 may not be depreciated, amortized, or otherwise deducted under any other provision of the Code. In addition, if the owner deducted any production cost in a prior tax year under a provision other than Code Sec.

181, the owner may not make an election under Code Sec. 181 in a subsequent tax year [Code Sec. 181(b); Reg. § 181-1(c)(1)].

.03 Recapture of Expensed Film and Television Production Costs

Any production costs previously deducted under Code Sec. 181 are recaptured as ordinary income in the tax year the election is voluntarily revoked or the production fails to satisfy the requirements of Code Sec. 181. In the latter instance, the Code Sec. 181 deduction is recaptured in the first tax year that [Reg. § 1.181-4(a)(1)]:

- Production costs exceed the applicable $15 or $20 million limit,
- The taxpayer expects that production costs will exceed the applicable $15 or $20 million limit,
- The production is no longer set for production,
- The owner no longer expects that the production will be set for production, or
- The owner no longer expects that the production will be a "qualified" film or television production.

For a production that has been placed in service, the recapture amount is the difference between the aggregate amount claimed under Code Sec. 181 in prior tax years and the depreciation that would otherwise have been claimed during those same tax years. If the production has not been placed in service, the entire amount previously claimed in prior tax years under Code Sec. 181 is recaptured [Reg. § 1.181-4(a)(3)].

The Code Sec. 181 deduction is also treated as a depreciation deduction for recapture purposes. Thus, upon the disposition of a production, the Code Sec. 181 deduction is subject to recapture as ordinary income to the extent of any gain [Code Sec. 1245(a)(2)(C); Reg. § 1.181-4(b)].

.04 Making and Revoking Election

The election must be made by the due date (including extensions) for filing the taxpayer's return for the year in which costs of the film or television production are first paid or incurred [Code Sec. 181(c)(1); Reg. § 1.181-2(b)(1)]. A six-month extension from the due date of the return (excluding extensions) is available if the taxpayer filed a timely original return for the year the election should have been made [Reg. § 301.9100-2]. In *L. Storey*,[222] the IRS argued that the taxpayer had failed to make the Code Sec. 181 election for the first tax year in which production costs were first paid or incurred. The court disagreed and found that the language in the Temp. Reg. § 1.181-2T(e)(1) is permissive and not mandatory. The court agreed with the taxpayer that she could not have made the election earlier because the temporary regulations under Code Sec. 181 disallowed the election until the first year in which the taxpayer reasonably expected the film would be set for production. The court pointed to Reg. § 1.181-2T(a)(3), which describes a taxpayer timely making an election later than the year that production costs are first incurred because he or she previously did not satisfy the reasonable expectations requirements. The court further found that the taxpayer's elections were imperfect. However, they were adequate under the doctrine of substan-

---

[222] *L. Storey*, 103 TCM 1631, Dec. 59,031(M), TC Memo. 2012-115.

tial compliance and production costs were deductible as expenses in the year in which the costs were incurred rather than having to be capitalized and depreciated.

Reasonable Expectation Requirement

The election cannot be made in the tax year that production costs are first paid or incurred unless the owner reasonably expects, based on all available facts and circumstances, that the production will be set for production and when completed will be a qualified film or television production. In addition, the owner must reasonably expect that the $15 or $20 million production cost limit will never be exceeded [Reg. § 1.181-2(b)(1)(iii)]. If an election is delayed because of the preceding reasonable expectation requirement, production costs paid or incurred in prior tax years may be deducted in the tax year the election is allowed (i.e., in the tax year that the reasonable expectation requirement is satisfied) [Reg. § 1.181-2(b)(2)].

There is no particular form for claiming the deduction. Instead, an election statement with specified information is attached to the return for the tax year of the election [Reg. § 1.181-2(c)(2)(i)]. An information statement is also required in any subsequent year in which production expenditures are deducted [Reg. § 1.181-2(c)(2)(ii)].

Once the election is made, it may not be revoked without IRS consent [Code Sec. 181(c)(2)]. However, the IRS will grant its consent if the owner attaches a revocation statement to its return and recaptures the expensed amount [Reg. § 1.181-2(d)].

DEPLETION DEDUCTION

¶12,155 WHAT IS DEPLETION?

Minerals, oil and gas, other natural deposits (including soil in place[223]), and timber are known as wasting assets. The gradual reduction of the original amount by removal for use is known as *depletion.* The theory is that the annual deduction for depletion and depreciation, in the aggregate, will return the cost or other basis of the property plus later allowable capital additions [Reg. § § 1.611-1, -5].

Property means each separate interest you own in each mineral deposit in each separate tract or parcel of land. It includes working or operating interests, royalties, overriding royalties, production payments, and net profits interests. Contiguous areas acquired at the same time from the same owner constitute a single separate tract or parcel of land. Areas included in separate conveyances or grants from separate owners are separate tracts or parcels, even if the areas are contiguous [Code Sec. 614(a); Reg. § 1.614-1(a)(1)].

---

[223] Rev. Rul. 79-411, 1979-2 CB 246.

¶12,160 WHO IS ENTITLED TO THE DEDUCTION FOR DEPLETION?

.01 Owner of an Economic Interest

To qualify for depletion deductions, you must own an *economic interest* in the property. This means you have an interest in the mineral deposit or timber and must look solely to income from production for a return of your capital [Reg. § 1.611-1(b)(1)].

The U.S. Supreme Court has ruled that contract coal miners have no economic interest in the coal they mine.[224]

Example 12-46: An adjacent upland owner who provides the only available drilling site for oil from submerged coastal lands is entitled to depletion on the share of net profits received from the producer for use of the lands.[225]

Example 12-47: A processor under contracts with oil producers to extract casinghead gasoline from natural gas they deliver to it is not entitled to depletion, since it has no capital investment in the mineral deposit being depleted.[226]

For an individual taxpayer, the deduction is subtracted from gross income to arrive at adjusted gross income.

.02 Lessor and Lessee

No specific rule can be laid down for making the apportionment, and each case must be decided on its own merits.

If the value of any leased mineral or timber property must be ascertained to figure the basis for depletion, the value of the interests of the lessor and lessee may be found separately. If they are figured as of the same date, they may not exceed the value of the property as a whole on that date [Reg. § 1.611-1(c)].

Minimum Royalties

If lessees agree that they will pay a minimum royalty to be applied against the price or royalty per unit, lessors take depletion even if the minerals covered by that royalty are not extracted. The depletion is computed as if the minerals had been removed. No further deduction is allowed, of course, when actual removal takes place [Reg. § 1.612-3(b)(1)]. If all the minerals are not extracted and the lease is ended, lessors must adjust their capital account by restoring the depletion deductions taken in prior years for the minerals paid for in advance, but not extracted. The same amount must be reported as income [Reg. § 1.612-3(b)(2)].[227]

---

224 *Paragon Jewel Coal Co.*, SCt, 65-1 USTC ¶9379, 380 US 624, 85 SCt 1207.

225 *Southwest Exploration Co.*, SCt, 56-1 USTC ¶9304, 350 US 308, 76 SCt 395.

226 *Bankline Oil Co.*, SCt, 38-1 USTC ¶9154, 303 US 362, 58 SCt 616.

227 *F.L. Engle*, SCt, 84-1 USTC ¶9134, 464 US 206, 104 SCt 597.

Overriding Royalties

Lessees who transfer their interest in the property, but retain their royalty interests, share an equitable portion of the depletion allowance with the lessor. It is immaterial whether the transfer is by assignment or by a sublease, since an economic interest in the property has been retained.

Delay Rentals

Amounts paid for the privilege of deferring development are ordinary income to the lessor and not subject to depletion [Reg. § 1.612-3(c)(1)].

Shut-in Royalties

Shut-in royalties are treated the same as delay rentals.[228]

.03 Life Tenant and Remainderman

The life tenant gets depletion until his death. Then the remainderman gets it [Reg. § 1.611-1(c)(3)].

.04 Sale of Entire Economic Interest

If you lease or transfer property subject to depletion but retain an economic interest in that property, you are entitled to the deduction.

¶12,165 FIGURING THE DEPLETION DEDUCTION

There are two methods for calculating depletion: cost depletion and percentage depletion. Under the cost depletion method, each year's deduction is a portion of your depletable basis in the property. With percentage depletion, deductions are a specified percentage of your income from the property [Code Sec. 613(b); Reg. § 1.613-2(a)]. The percentage is specified for each natural resource.

Depletion is generally claimed on Schedule E of Form 1040. However, depletion on an operating oil and gas interest is claimed on Schedule C.

¶12,170 COST DEPLETION

This method, also known as ***valuation depletion,*** applies to all types of property subject to depletion. Under it, the basis is the same as that for figuring gain on the sale of the property, and may be more or less than cost. The basis is divided by the estimated number of units (tons of ore, barrels of oil, thousands of cubic feet of natural gas, feet of timber) in the ground to arrive at the depletion unit. The deduction for a tax year is the depletion unit multiplied by the number of units sold within the year.

---

[228] *F.I. Johnson*, CA-5, 61-1 USTC ¶9307, 287 F2d 544.

.01 How to Figure Cost Depletion

The basis for depletion under the cost method is the adjusted basis for determining gain on a sale [Code Sec. 612; Reg. § 1.612-1(a)]. If you can use percentage depletion, you should still figure out what your deduction would be under the cost depletion method. That way, if the cost depletion deduction turns out to be larger, you can claim it.

Depletion under the cost method is figured as follows [Reg. § 1.611-2(a)(1)]:

(Adjusted basis/Total remaining mineral units) × Number of units sold

▶ **OBSERVATION:** It is the number of units sold (not the number produced) that determines the allowance.

Example 12-48: On January 1, the Russell Co. owned property subject to depletion, with a basis in its hands of $1,000,000. The recoverable reserves (the total remaining mineral units) were estimated at 100,000 units. The unit cost was $10, and if 5,000 units were sold during the year, the depletion deduction would be $50,000 (assuming no capital additions).

Important exceptions to the cost method are considered in ¶ 12,175, ¶ 12,180, ¶ 12,185.

.02 Determining Adjusted Basis

In general, the property's adjusted basis, for cost depletion purposes, is figured by following the same rules as apply when determining gain from the sale of the property [see Ch. 6] [Code Sec. 612]. The exceptions to this rule are explained below.

.03 Charges to Capital Account

In figuring the adjusted basis, certain additions must be made to capital account. In the case of mines and oil and gas properties, capital expenditures allocable to the mine or well itself are recoverable through depletion; capital expenditures allocable to plant or equipment are recoverable through depreciation.

Capital Additions to Mines

Expenditures for plant and equipment (except maintenance and repairs) are ordinarily recoverable through depreciation. But in certain cases, expenditures for equipment necessary to maintain normal output are chargeable to expense (deductible) [Reg. § 1.612-2]. For operating oil and gas properties, depreciation is allowed on machinery, tools, pipes, and similar items, and also on installation costs if they are not deducted as intangible drilling expenses [Reg. § 1.611-5(b)(4)].

Intangible Drilling Costs

An operator can either charge intangible drilling and development costs to capital, recovering them through depletion or depreciation (depending on the nature of the expenditure), or deduct the costs as expenses. A binding election must be made on the return for the first tax year the costs are sustained. If the costs are not deducted on this return, you are considered to have elected to capitalize them [Code Sec. 263(c); Reg. § 1.612-4]. There are exceptions to the general rule denying current deductions for capital expenditures. Examples are intangible drilling and development costs for oil and gas wells, and geothermal wells, and the like [Code Sec. 263(c)]. Cash basis taxpayers can only deduct their intangible drilling and development costs in the year in which the payment is required under a drilling contract, not in a prior year.[229]

If the operator has elected to capitalize intangible drilling and development costs, an additional option is available. This option permits a deduction as an ordinary loss of the intangible drilling and development costs incurred in drilling a nonproductive well.

Intangible drilling and development costs of oil and gas wells must be capitalized and amortized ratably over 60 months for computing a corporation's earnings and profits starting with the month production begins [Code Sec. 312(n)(2)(A)].

Intangible drilling and development costs include the cost to operators of any drilling or development work (excluding amounts payable only out of production or the gross proceeds of production, and amounts properly allocable to cost of depreciable property) done for them by contractors under any form of contract, including turnkey contracts [Reg. § 1.612-4(a)].

Intangible drilling costs incurred in drilling a well in consideration of an assignment of an interest in a lease are capital expenditures, and may not be deducted as business expenses.[230] However, intangible drilling and development expenses incurred in acquiring an operating or working interest may be treated as deductible expenses [Reg. § 1.612-4(a)].

The deductions for depletion that reduced the adjusted basis of the property are recaptured if the property is disposed of. The amounts previously deducted are treated as ordinary income to the extent they exceed the amounts that would have been deducted had the costs been capitalized. The recapture rules are similar to those involving Sec. 1245 property [Ch. 8] [Code Sec. 1254(b)(1)].

Reduction of benefits. Every corporation that is an integrated oil company must reduce its deduction for intangible drilling costs to 70 percent of what it could otherwise deduct. The remaining 30 percent must be deducted ratably over a 60-month period starting with the month the costs are paid or incurred [Code Sec. 291(b)].

.04 Incorrect Estimate of Remaining Units

If it is discovered that the remaining units have been incorrectly estimated, the annual depletion allowance for the tax year and later years will be based on the revised estimate [Code Sec. 611(a); Reg. § 1.611-2(c)(2)].

Example 12-49: The United Coal Co. bought mineral property for $3,000,000 when the recoverable reserves (remaining units) were estimated at 300,000 units. United did not use percentage depletion. 40,000 units were extracted during the year but only 25,000 were sold. The depletion deduction is $250,000 (($3,000,000/300,000) × 25,000).

---

[229] *F.F. Hardesty*, CA-5, 42-1 USTC ¶ 9449, 127 F2d 843; *Rowan Drilling Co.*, CA-5, 42-2 USTC ¶ 9628, 130 F2d 62; *H. Hunt*, CA-5, 43-1 USTC ¶ 9440, 135 F2d 697.

[230] Rev. Rul. 71-579, 1971-2 CB 225.

Example 12-50: In Example 12-49, suppose one year later it is discovered that the property actually contains 500,000 units. Assuming that no capital additions are to be made, the adjusted basis would be $2,750,000 ($3,000,000 – $250,000 depletion taken in the prior year), and if 30,000 units were sold the following year the depletion deduction would be $165,000 (($2,750,000/500,000) × 30,000). Note that the revision in the remaining units does not affect the basis for depletion. It would have been $2,750,000 (assuming no capital additions) if the revised estimate of the remaining units had not been made.

.05 Elective Safe Harbor for Oil and Gas Recoverable Reserves

The IRS has provided taxpayers with domestic oil and gas producing properties with an elected safe harbor in determining the recoverable reserves for cost depletion purposes.[231] If the election is made, a taxpayer's estimate of the total recoverable reserves from each domestic oil and gas producing property will be treated as being equal to 105 percent of the property's proved reserves as defined in 17 CFR § 210.4-10(a) of Regulation S-X, for purposes of computing cost depletion. An electing taxpayer must attach a statement to a timely filed income tax return for the first tax year for which the safe harbor is elected and the election cannot be revoked for that tax year. The election applies to all of the taxpayer's domestic oil and gas producing properties and will be effective for the tax year in which it is made and all subsequent tax years until revoked.

¶12,175 PERCENTAGE DEPLETION

Percentage depletion is an alternate method of computing depletion. Under this method, a specified percentage of the *gross income from the property* is taken as a depletion deduction. The percentage depletion may not exceed 50 percent (100 percent for oil and gas properties of the "taxable income from the property" (figured without depletion allowance). But see the following allowance discussion [Code Sec. 613(a); Reg. § 1.613-1(a)]. The percentage method applies to geothermal wells and deposits, certain oil and gas wells, coal mines, metal mines, and certain other deposits, but not to timber. For those properties to which the percentage method applies, the deduction should be figured under both the cost method and the percentage method, and the larger deduction taken [Code Sec. 613(a); Reg. § 1.613-1]. Also, the basis of the property must be reduced by the larger allowance [Reg. § 1.1016-3(b)(1)].

.01 Oil, Gas, and Geothermal Wells

Percentage depletion is permitted only for: (1) certain domestic gas wells and (2) oil and gas wells of small independent producers and royalty owners. In general, the percentage depletion rate for oil and gas is 15 percent of the gross income from the property [Code Sec. 613(e)(1)(B)].

Applicable Percentages for Depletion of Marginal Oil and Gas Properties

Each year, the IRS updates the applicable percentage under Code Sec. 613A to be used in determining percentage depletion for marginal properties. Code Sec. 613A(c)(6)(C)

[231] Rev. Proc. 2004-19, 2004-1 CB 563.

defines the term "applicable percentage" for purposes of determining percentage depletion for oil and gas produced from marginal properties. The applicable percentage is the percentage (not greater than 25 percent) equal to the sum of 15 percent, plus one percentage point for each whole dollar by which $20 exceeds the reference price (determined under Code Sec. 45K(d) (2) (C)) for crude oil for the calendar year preceding the calendar year in which the tax year begins. The reference price determined under Code Sec. 45K(d) (2) (C) for 2012 is $94.53.[232]

Domestic Gas Production

Geothermal wells, which consist of natural heat stored in rocks or aqueous liquid or vapor, are eligible for percentage depletion. The well must be located in the U.S. or its possessions [Code Sec. 613(e) (1)].

Grandfather Rule

Producers of gas sold under a *fixed contract* regarding any geothermal deposit in the U.S. or its possessions that is determined to be a gas well can take a depletion allowance equal to 22 percent of the gross income from the property's domestic production. A *fixed contract* is a contract under which the price cannot be adjusted to reflect any increase in seller's tax resulting from the repeal of percentage depletion [Code Sec. 613A(b) (1)].

Independent Producers and Royalty Owners

The test to qualify for percentage depletion is based on *average daily production* for the tax year from domestic oil and gas wells. This is the result of dividing aggregate production by the number of days in the tax year. The amount of your average daily production to which depletion applies is the amount of average daily production that doesn't exceed 1,000 barrels or 6 million cubic feet of natural gas. For production that includes both oil and gas, the exemption is allocated between the two [Code Sec. 613A(c) (1)].

The Independent producer's exemption is not available to: (1) any producer who owns or controls a retail outlet for the sale of oil or gas or petroleum products; (2) any producer who engages (directly or through a related person) in refining more than 50,000 barrels on any day during the tax year. A *retailer* is a taxpayer with gross receipts of over $5 million for the tax year from the sale of these products [Code Sec. 613A(c) (2) (B)].

***Related Person* Defined**

A person is a related person with respect to a taxpayer if a significant ownership interest in either the taxpayer or the person is held by the other, or if a third person has a significant ownership interest in both the taxpayer and the person. The term "significant ownership interest" means:

- With respect to any corporation, 5 percent or more in value of the outstanding stock of such corporation,
- With respect to a partnership, 5 percent or more interest in the profits or capital or such partnership, and

---

232 Notice 2013-53, IRB 2013-36.

- With respect to any estate or trust, 5 percent or more of the beneficial interests in such estate or trust.

For purposes of determining significant ownership interest, an interest owned by or for a corporation, partnership, trust, or estate shall be considered as owned directly both by itself and proportionately by its shareholders, partners, or beneficiaries, as the case may be [Code Sec. 613A(d)(3)].

Gross Income from the Property

Gross income from the property generally is the amount for which you sell the oil or gas in the immediate vicinity of the well. If the oil or gas is processed or transported or both, gross income is figured using the average market or field price before processing or transportation [Reg. § 1.613-3].

In figuring gross income for percentage depletion, a lessee must exclude from actual gross income the amount of rents and royalties paid to the lessor [Code Sec. 613(a); Reg. § 1.613-2(c)(5)]. If royalties in the form of bonus payments have been paid in any year, lessees must exclude from gross income the part of the payments that are allocable to the products sold during the tax year.[233] Percentage depletion is not allowed for lease bonuses or advance royalties for oil, gas or geothermal properties—regardless of the actual production of the property [Code Secs. 613(e)(3), 613A(d)(5)].

Taxable income from the property is *gross income from the property,* less the allowable deductions directly related to the mineral property on which depletion is claimed. Deductions not directly related to the property are fairly allocated [Reg. § 1.613-5(a)]. The charitable contribution deduction is not subtracted.[234] This applies to qualifying gas well production.

.03 Other Depletable Mineral Interests

The percentage of gross income depletion for mines, wells and other natural deposits ranges from 22% (e.g., sulfur and uranium) to 5% (e.g., gravel, peat[235] and clay) depending on whether the location is within or outside the U.S. [Code Sec. 613(b); Reg. § 1.613-2(a)(2)].

An amount equal to any rents and royalties paid or incurred for the property must be excluded in determining gross income [Code Sec. 613(a); Reg. § 1.613-2(c)(5)].

Gross Income from the Property

Gross income from the property in connection with percentage depletion for mines means gross income from mining. Mining includes more than merely the extraction of ores or minerals from the ground. Mining also includes (1) the treatment processes considered as mining to the extent they are applied by the mine owner or operator to the mineral or the ore and (2) the transportation of ores or minerals from the point of extraction to the plants or mills where the ordinary treatment processes are applied, but not in excess of 50 miles (unless the IRS rules otherwise) [Code Sec. 613(c)(1), (2); Reg. § 1.613-4(h)]. Any process that is not necessary to bring the minerals to shipping form is not part of

---

[233] *Canadian River Gas Co.,* CA-2, 45-2 USTC ¶ 9450, 151 F2d 954, *cert. denied,* 327 US 793, 66 SCt 818.

[234] Rev. Rul. 60-74, 1960-1 CB 253.

[235] Rev. Rul. 57-336, 1957-2 CB 325.

the treatment process.[236] The U.S. Supreme Court holds that a lessee of mining property must deduct ad valorem and royalty taxes it paid before figuring gross income from property for percentage depletion purposes.[237]

> **NOTE:** Percentage depletion is to be based on the constructive income from the raw product if marketable in that form (whether or not marketable at a profit), and not on the value of the finished product.[238]
>
> The percentage depletion on oil shale is figured on its value after the extraction and retorting of the shale oil, but before hydrogenating and refining [Code Sec. 613(c)(4)(H)].
>
> Cash or trade discounts actually allowed by a taxpayer must be subtracted from the sales price in determining gross income from the property [Reg. § 1.613-4(e)(1)].
>
> **NOTE:** The *extraction of ores or minerals from the ground* includes the extraction by mine owners or operators of ores or minerals from the waste or residue of their prior mining such as a tailing dump or a culm bank. This does not apply to a buyer of the waste or residue or a buyer of the rights to extract ores or minerals from the waste or residue [Code Sec. 613(c); Reg. § 1.613-4(i)].
>
> The depletion deduction may be figured (without regard to any election) either on the percentage basis or on the general rule basis, whichever gives the greater deduction [Code Sec. 613(a); Reg. § 1.613-1(a)].

Business Interruption Insurance

Proceeds from a policy insuring against loss of mining profits are not taken into account in figuring percentage depletion, since they are not considered gross income from mining.[239]

Taxable Income from the Property

Such income generally has the same meaning as for oil, gas, and geothermal wells, above. However, the deduction for mining expenses is reduced by gain on sale of depreciable property that is taxed as ordinary income, and which is allocable to the property [Ch. 8]. Records must be kept in determining the gain on the property [Code Sec. 613(a); Reg. § 1.613-5(b)(5)].

Reduction of Benefits

The amount allowable as a deduction for coal and iron ore percentage depletion by corporations is reduced by 20% of the amount of the excess of the deduction over the property's adjusted basis [Code Sec. 291].

.04 Percentage Depletion Allowed Through No Cost Basis

It is possible and not unusual for a taxpayer to recover tax-free, through percentage depletion, an amount greater than the property's cost. It follows that you may recover a larger amount tax-free through depletion than you could through a sale or other

---

[236] Rev. Rul. 62-5, 1962-1 CB 88; Rev. Rul. 64-49, 1964-1 CB 218.

[237] *U.S. Steel Corp.*, DC-NY, 67-1 USTC ¶ 9459, 270 FSupp 253, *aff'd*, CA-2, 71-2 USTC ¶ 9505, 445 F2d 520, *cert. denied*, 405 US 917, 92 SCt 940.

[238] *Cannelton Sewer Pipe Co.*, SCt, 60-2 USTC ¶ 9553, 364 US 76, 80 SCt 1581.

[239] *C. Guthrie*, CA-6, 63-2 USTC ¶ 9722, 323 F2d 142.

disposition of the property. These inequalities are ignored. The law allows the deduction although the cost has been recovered.[240]

¶12,180 TREATMENT OF BONUSES AND ROYALTIES

If a lessor receives a bonus in addition to royalties, a cost depletion deduction for the bonus is figured as follows [Reg. § 1.612-3(a)]:

$$\frac{\text{Basis} \times \text{Bonus}}{\text{Bonus} + \text{Estimated Royalties}} = \text{Depletion Deduction}$$

The depletion allowance figured above is deducted from the lessor's basis for depletion; the remainder of the basis is recoverable through depletion deductions as the royalties are received later.

Example 12-51: Assume that the lessor's basis for depletion is $2,000,000, that he receives a bonus of $1,000,000, and that he is to receive a royalty of one-fourth of the minerals produced by the lessee, it being estimated that the royalty payments will amount to $3,000,000. The depletion deduction on account of the receipt of the bonus would be $500,000, figured as follows:

$2,000,000 × $1,000,000 ÷ ($1,000,000 + $3,000,000) = $500,000.

SPECIAL DEPLETION PROBLEMS

¶12,185 DEPLETION OF TIMBER

This depletion is based on the adjusted basis for figuring gain on a sale. It does not include any part of the land's cost. Depletion occurs when the timber is cut and is figured by the cost method only.

.01 Figuring the Deduction

The deduction each year is the number of timber units cut multiplied by the depletion unit. The unit is figured as follows [Code Sec. 611; Reg. § 1.611-3(b)(2)]:

$$\frac{C + P + A}{U + (\text{or} -)\ YX + (\text{or} -)} = \text{Depletion unit}$$

C equals the adjusted basis of the timber on hand at the beginning of the year.

P equals the cost of any timber purchased during the year.

A equals capital additions during the year other than purchases.

---

[240] *Elliott Petroleum Corp.*, CA-9, 36-1 USTC ¶9184, 82 F2d 193; *Louisiana Iron & Supply Co.*, 44 BTA 1244, Dec. 12,040, *acq.* 1941-2 CB 8.

U equals the number of units of timber on hand at the beginning of the year.

X equals the number of units to be added or deducted in order to adjust the total remaining units (U) to conform to the actual quantity of units remaining.

Y equals the number of units acquired during the year.

The loss to be deducted for forest fire is found the same way. If timber contains turpentine, that portion of the total cost or other basis reasonably allocable to turpentine may be amortized or recovered through depletion deductions on any reasonable basis over the period of actual turpentining.[241]

NOTE: A map and statement (Form T) giving the data required by the regulations must be attached to the return if depletion of timber is claimed [Reg. § 1.611-3(h)].

.02 When to Claim Depletion

Claim your depletion allowance as a deduction in the year of sale or other disposition of the products cut from the timber, unless you choose to treat the cutting of timber as a sale or exchange. Include allowable depletion for timber products not sold during the tax year the timber is cut as a cost item in the closing inventory of timber products for the year. The inventory is your basis for determining gain or loss in the tax year you sell the timber products.

¶12,190 BOOKS OF ACCOUNT

Separate accounts should be kept in which there should be recorded the basis of the property, any allowable capital additions, and all other adjustments. The annual depletion deduction should be credited to the mineral property accounts or to the depletion reserve accounts [Reg. § 1.611-2(b)]. It is not necessary to adopt any particular method of bookkeeping, but records must be accurate.

As to timber, there are special requirements for the books of account [Reg. § 1.611-3(c)(1)], and, as a general rule, separate accounts must be kept for each "block" of timber [Reg. § 1.611-3(d)(1)].

MINING EXPENSES

¶12,195 MINE EXPLORATION EXPENDITURES

Exploration expenditures are those expenses incurred in ascertaining the existence, extent, quality, or quantity of a new mineral deposit. You may elect to deduct domestic exploration expenditures incurred in hard mineral operations [Code Sec. 617(a)(1); Reg. § 1.617-1(a)]. Expenses to discover oil and gas deposits, called geological and geophysical expenses, must be capitalized.

---

241 Rev. Rul. 90-61, 1990-2 CB 39.

Expenditures for capital equipment or improvements used in exploration are not exploration expenditures if the cost is recoverable through depreciation. However, the depreciation is an exploration expenditure [Reg. § 1.617-1(b)(2)].

You may elect an unlimited deduction of exploration expenditures paid during the tax year as to any domestic mineral deposit (other than oil and gas) subject to the depletion allowance [Reg. §§ 1.617-1(a), -2(b)(1)]. If this election is made, the capitalized exploration costs must therefore be deductible only on abandoning the exploration project or the property.

Mining exploration costs are an adjustment in figuring the alternative minimum tax [Ch. 26] [Code Sec. 56(a)(2)]. The costs that are deducted for regular tax purposes must be recovered through 10-year straight line amortization for the alternative minimum tax.

> **Example 12-52:** Blake incurred a one-time mining exploration expense of $1,000. He gets a deduction for that amount on his return. For alternative minimum tax purposes, he must spread $1,000 over a 10-year period starting with the year the expenditure was incurred.

.01 Recapture

Once the property reaches the development stage, all previously deducted exploration expenditures must be recaptured. You have two choices about the recapture: (1) You can elect, as to all mines reaching the production stage during the tax year (on which deductions have been allowed), to include in gross income an amount equal to the adjusted exploration expenditures. Or, (2) If you do not so elect, you cannot take otherwise deductible depletion allowances until the sum of the allowances not taken equals the adjusted exploration expenditures. Adjusted exploration expenditures are those which produced a tax benefit. Therefore, depletion allowances not taken reduce total adjusted exploration expenditures. You must make this election annually [Code Sec. 617(b)(2); Reg. § 1.617-3(b)].

Recapture also applies to sales and assignments, causing ordinary gain to the extent of the deducted exploration expenditures. Transferees in tax-free exchanges will eventually have to recapture the deductions [Reg. § 1.617-4(a)(2)]. Partnerships are subject to special rules [Code Sec. 617(g)].

The above rules do not apply to expenditures: (1) to acquire or improve depreciable property (although depreciation on such property qualifies as an expenditure); (2) that are deductible without regard to these provisions; (3) that are part of the acquisition cost [Code Secs. 616, 617; Reg. § 1.616-1(b)].

The adjusted basis of the mine or of the deposit is not reduced by depletion disallowed when the unlimited exploration expenditure is elected [Code Sec. 617(e)(1)].

.02 Reduction of Benefits

For corporations, 30 percent of domestic mining exploration costs must be amortized ratably over a 60-month period. The remaining 70 percent, together with similar costs of noncorporate taxpayers, is eligible for expensing [Code Sec. 291(b)].

Any deductible exploration expense is a deduction for adjusted gross income on your tax return.

¶12,200 MINING DEVELOPMENT EXPENDITURES

Expenses for the development of a mine or natural deposit (other than an oil or gas well) that contains commercially marketable quantities of the ore or mineral are deductible as follows:

- The expenses can be deducted in the year paid or incurred [Code Sec. 616(a); Reg. § 1.616-1(a)]; or
- You may elect to deduct the expenses proportionately as the ore or mineral benefited by them is sold (deferred expense). While the mine or deposit is in the development stage, this election is limited to the development expenses in excess of the net receipts from production within the tax year. (Expenditures not in excess of such receipts are deductible in full.) This election is not binding on future years. It may be made on the return or by a statement filed with the timely filed return (including extensions) for the tax year to which the election applies [Code Sec. 616(b); Reg. § 1.616-2(a)].

For purposes of calculating alternative minimum taxable income the expenses are amortized over 10 years [Code Sec. 56(a)(2)]

Example 12-53: Mine A was in the development stage throughout the year. If the development expenses incurred during the year are $5,000, the whole amount is either deductible that year, or, at your election, deferred to be deducted ratably as the ore or mineral is sold.

Example 12-54: Mine C was in the development stage from January to August. From August to December of that year, it was in the productive stage. Development expenses from January to August amounted to $5,000 and from August to December, $1,000. If the net receipts from the sale of minerals produced that year are $3,000, you have an option to:

- Deduct $6,000 that year, or
- Deduct $3,000 that year and defer $3,000 to be deducted ratably as the ore or mineral is sold. (The $3,000 represents your $5,000 pre-production development expenses not in excess of the $3,000 net receipts. The $3,000 to be deferred represents the $1,000 development expenses incurred in the productive stage plus the $2,000, which is the excess of your $5,000 of pre-production development expenses over the $3,000 of net receipts.)

The above rules do not apply to expenditures: (1) to acquire or improve depreciable property (although depreciation on such property qualifies as an expenditure); (2) that are deductible without regard to these provisions; (3) that are part of the acquisition cost [Code Secs. 616, 617; Reg. § 1.616-1(b)].

Mining development costs are an adjustment in figuring the alternative minimum tax [Ch. 16] [Code Sec. 56(a)(2)]. The costs that are deducted for regular tax purposes must be recovered through 10-year straight line amortization for the alternative minimum tax.

.01 Reduction of Benefits

For corporations, 30 percent of domestic mining exploration costs must be amortized ratably over a 60-month period. The remaining 70 percent, together with similar costs of noncorporate taxpayers, is eligible for expensing [Code Sec. 291(b)(1)].

.02 Adjusted Basis of Mine or Deposit

Deferred development expenses are included in figuring the adjusted basis when the mine or deposit is sold. The adjusted basis is reduced by the deferred deductions to the extent they reduced tax liability (but not less than the amount allowable). These expenses are not factors in figuring the adjusted basis for depletion purposes [Code Sec. 616(c); Reg. § 1.1016-5(f)].

FARMERS' EXPENSES

¶12,205 EXPENSES OF FARMERS

The expenses of preparing, developing, and operating a farm are either ordinary and necessary current business expenses or capital expenditures. A farmer's income and expenses are reported on Schedule F of Form 1040, 1041, or 1065. Special rules limit the deductions available to farm syndicates. See the discussion of farming syndicates below. Losses of farmers are discussed in Ch. 13.

.01 Business Expenses

During the productive period of the farm, the ordinary and necessary current expenses of farming are deductible [Reg. § 1.162-12(a)].

Examples of Deductible Expenses

The following are deductible business expenses for farmers:[242]

- Rations bought and furnished to sharecroppers;
- Feed purchased (grain, hay, silage, mill feeds, concentrates and other roughages, and cost of grinding, mixing, and processing feed) [but see the discussion of farming syndicates below];
- Machine hire (payments for use of threshing, combining, silo filling, baling, ginning, and other machines);
- Seeds and plants bought (but see the discussion of farming syndicates below);
- Supplies purchased (spray material, poisons, disinfectants, cans, barrels, baskets, egg cases, bags, etc.);

[242] Treas. Dept., IRS Publication 225, "Farmer's Tax Guide" (2013 Ed.), pp. 20-25.

- Repairs and maintenance of farm machines and equipment;
- Breeding fees;
- Fertilizers and lime (cost of commercial fertilizers, lime and manure purchased during the year, the benefit of which is of short duration) [see also election];
- Veterinary and medicine for livestock;
- Storage and warehousing expense;
- Insurance on farm property, except farmer's dwelling (buildings, improvements, equipment, crops and livestock);
- Water rent (farm share of expense); and
- Blacksmith and harness repair.

Examples of Nondeductible Expenses

The following are examples of expenses the farmer may not deduct:

- Loss of growing plants, produce, and crops;
- Repayment of loans;
- Estate, inheritance, legacy, succession, and gift taxes;
- Loss of livestock;
- Losses from sales or exchanges between related persons;
- Cost of raising unharvested crops;
- Cost of unharvested crops bought with land;
- Club dues and membership fees with the exception of boards of trade, business leagues, chambers of commerce, civic or public service organizations, professional associations, trade associations, and real estate boards;
- Fines and penalties.
- Value of products raised by farmer and used for board of hired help;
- Expense of raising products consumed by farmer and his or her family;
- Cost of producing or acquiring donated products[243] [see Ch. 12];
- Value of labor of farmer, his wife, or minor children (but reasonable wages paid to child for service on farm are deductible);
- Cotton acreage allotments;[244] and
- Expenses of planting and developing citrus groves (see below).

During the development of the farm, a farmer may elect to capitalize ordinary and necessary expenses incidental to current operation instead of deducting them [Reg. § 1.162-12(a)].

Citrus and almond grove expenses. In general, the costs of planting, cultivating, maintaining, and developing citrus and almond groves must be capitalized if they have a pre-production period of more than two years. However, an election can be made to deduct all these pre-productive costs [Code Sec. 263A(d)(3)(C)]. The election does not

---

243 Rev. Rul. 75-11, 1975-1 CB 27.

244 Rev. Rul. 66-58, 1966-1 CB 186.

apply under certain circumstances. For example, it does not apply to the cost of planting, cultivating, maintaining, or developing any citrus or almond grove incurred before the end of the fourth tax year after the trees were planted [Code Sec. 263A(d)(3)(C)]. The costs of replanting a grove lost by disease, freeze or other casualty generally are deducted currently [Code Sec. 263A(d)(2)(A)].

Election to deduct fertilizer and lime expenditures. You may elect to treat as a deductible expense expenditures for fertilizer, lime, ground limestone, marl, or other materials used to enrich, neutralize, or condition your farm land, or for the application of these materials. You make the election by taking the deduction on a timely filed return for the year. It may not be revoked without consent of the IRS [Code Sec. 180(c); Reg. §§1.180-1, -2].

.02 Capital Expenditures

Expenditures during the preparatory period, when the property is made ready for development, are not deductible as business expenses. They are capital expenditures [Ch. 11; ¶12,110] [Reg. §1.162-12(a)], except for fertilizer and lime expenditures (above) the farmer elects to deduct.

The cost of farm machinery, equipment, and buildings (other than dwellings) whether incurred in the preparatory period or another period is not deductible as an expense, but is a capital expenditure, and deduction is allowed for depreciation. Likewise, amounts spent to buy work, breeding or dairy animals are regarded as investments of capital, and depreciation is allowed, unless the animals are included in inventory [Reg. §1.162-12(a)].

.03 Farming for Pleasure

If you operate a farm for recreation or pleasure and not on a commercial basis, and farm expenses exceed farm receipts, you need not include in income the receipts from the sale of farm products. The expenses will be treated as personal expenses; that is, not deductible [Reg. §1.162-12(b)(1)]. Farm expenses in excess of receipts are deductible only if the farming is engaged in for profit [Ch. 13].

.04 Prepaid Expenses

Cash basis taxpayers with excess prepaid farm supplies for the tax year are not allowed a deduction for the excess prepaid farm supplies earlier than the time when they actually use or consume those items. A taxpayer has excess prepaid farm supplies to the extent that the amount of the taxpayer's prepaid farm supplies for the tax year exceeds 50 percent of the taxpayer's deductible farming expenses (other than prepaid farm supplies) for the tax year. Qualified farm-related taxpayers are excepted from this requirement. A taxpayer is a qualified farm-related taxpayer if (1) the taxpayer's principal residence is on a farm, the taxpayer's principal occupation is farming, or the taxpayer is a member of the family of a person whose principal residence is on a farm or whose principal occupation is farming; (2) the aggregate prepaid farm supplies for the three tax years preceding the tax year are less than 50 percent of the aggregate deductible farming expenses (other than prepaid farm supplies) for those three tax years or the taxpayer has excess prepaid farm supplies for the tax year by reason of any change in business operation directly attributable to extraordinary circumstances [Code Sec. 464(f)].

¶12,210 SOIL AND WATER CONSERVATION EXPENDITURES

Farmers may deduct in the tax year paid or incurred expenses for soil and water conservation and the prevention of erosion of land used in farming [Code Sec. 175(a); Reg. § 1.175-1]. Endangered species recovery expenditures are included along with soil and water conservation expenditures and land erosion prevention expenditures as a type of expenditure that may be currently deducted by a farmer under Code Sec. 175. The deduction cannot be more than 25 percent of the farmer's gross income from farming during the tax year (see .01 below). The expenditure must be made to further the business of farming and, if not deducted, must be capitalized [Reg. §§ 1.175-1, -2(a)]. Examples of deductible expenditures include the treatment and moving of earth. However, farmers may not deduct expenditures to buy, construct, install, or improve depreciable structures or facilities.

The deduction applies to land used by the farmer or the farmer's tenants for the production of crops, fruits or other agricultural products or for the sustenance of livestock [Code Sec. 175(c)(2)]. It does not apply when you rent farm land at a fixed rental (unless you materially help manage or operate the farm), engage in forestry or timber growing, or run a farm as a hobby [Reg. § 1.175-3]. If the expenditures are made for newly acquired farm land, the deduction applies if the land is put to the same type of farming use as that immediately preceding its acquisition. However, if land will be put to a different use (i.e., pasture or timber land cultivated for crops), the expenditures are preparatory expenses and must be capitalized [Reg. § 1.175-4(a)(2)].

> **NOTE:** Expenditures that can be deducted currently are limited to amounts incurred that are consistent with a conservation plan approved by the Department of Agriculture's Soil Conservation Service [Code Sec. 175(c)(3)(A)(i)].

.01 Deductible Expenditures

Expenditures for treating and moving earth (including—but not limited to—leveling, conditioning, grading, terracing, contour furrowing, and restoring soil fertility); eradication of brush; planting of windbreaks; construction, control and protection of diversion channels, drainage ditches, irrigation ditches, earthen dams, watercourses, outlets and ponds [Code Sec. 175(c)(1); Reg. § 1.175-2(a)(1)].

.02 Nondeductible Expenditures

Expenditures to buy, construct, install, or improve depreciable structures, appliances, or facilities, or any amount deductible under other provisions. Expenditures for depreciable property include cost of materials, supplies, wages, fuel, hauling and dirt moving for structures such as tanks, reservoirs, pipes, conduits, canals, dams, wells or pumps made of masonry concrete, tile, metal or wood [Code Sec. 175(c)(1); Reg. § 1.175-2(b)]. For deductibility of assessments for depreciable property, see .03 below.

.03 Limitations

Regulations have established the following limitations for deductions:

- The amount deductible for the tax year cannot exceed 25 percent of gross income from farming during the tax year. *Gross income from farming* means gross income from all of your farms. It does not, however, include gains from sale of assets such as farm machinery or gains from the disposition of land [Reg. § 1.175-5(a)]; and
- Expenditures over the amount allowable for any tax year can be carried over to the following tax year and considered the first expenditure in that year. However, the total deduction for each succeeding year (carryover plus actual expenditures made during the tax year) is still limited to 25 percent of gross income from farming during the tax year.

Example 12-55: Mr. McDonald had $12,000 gross income from farming this year. His soil and water conservation expenditures were $3,500. McDonald can deduct $3,000 (.25 × $12,000) this year. The balance, $500, can be carried over to next year and considered the first such expenditure in that year.

Example 12-56: Assume that McDonald had $10,000 gross income from farming this year, and that his soil and water conservation expenditures were $2,100. He can deduct $2,500 this year, and his carryover to next year would be $100, figured as shown below:

Carryover from last year	$500
Expenditures this year	2,100
Total	$2,600
Deduction (limited to .25 × $10,000)	2,500
Carryover to next year	$100

Amounts deducted either in the year paid or incurred or a carryover year are considered in figuring a net operating loss [Ch. 13] [Reg. § 1.175-5(a)(3)].

.04 Election to Expense or Capitalize

The method (deduction or capitalization) can be adopted without consent for the first tax year the expenditures are paid or incurred. For adoption at any other time, IRS consent is required. Once adopted, the method applies to all soil and water conservation expenditures for the tax year and later tax years, and must be followed consistently, unless the IRS consents to a change. However, you may request authorization to capitalize (or, if the election to deduct is not made, to deduct) soil and water conservation expenditures for a special project or a single farm.

The request for adoption (or a change) must be filed not later than the time required for filing the return [Code Sec. 175(d)(2); Reg. § 1.175-6(d)].

▶ **OBSERVATION:** You should distinguish between (1) soil and water conservation expenditures and (2) expenses for maintenance and repair of structures built for soil and water conservation purposes or to prevent erosion. Expenses for maintenance and repair are deductible when paid or incurred without limit. They cannot be carried over and deducted in a succeeding year.[245]

.05 Assessments

Assessments levied by a soil or water conservation or drainage district in order to defray expenditures made by such district may also be deductible. A deduction is allowed for so much of the assessment, not otherwise allowable as a deduction, as is paid or incurred to satisfy expenses which could have been deducted by the taxpayer as soil or water conservation expenses, or endangered species recovery expenditure if he had paid or incurred them [Code Sec. 175(c)(1); Reg. § 1.175-2(c)].

The amount of the district's assessment that may be deducted by any one farmer cannot exceed 10 percent of the total amount of the assessment attributable to the acquisition of depreciable assets [Code Sec. 175(c)(1)]. Thus, if an assessment by a district against its members in the total amount of $1 million includes $100,000 attributable to the acquisition of depreciable property, no one member may deduct a total of more than $10,000. To the extent that the assessment against a member exceeds the 10-percent limit, the excess is a capital expenditure which must be added to the basis of the farm property involved. If an assessment which exceeds the 10-percent limit is payable in installments, each installment is to be divided between a deductible portion and a capitalized portion.

Generally, if the amount of the assessment paid (attributable to the acquisition of depreciable property by the district) exceeds 10 percent of the total amount which has or will be assessed against the farmer as his share of the cost to the district in acquiring the property, only 10 percent of the assessment is deductible in the year when paid by the farmer, and the remaining 90 percent is deductible ratably over the following nine tax years. However, if the amount which otherwise would be spread over the nine-year period amounts to $500 or less, the full assessment is allowed as a deduction in the year of payment [Code Sec. 175(f)].

¶12,215 AMORTIZATION OF REFORESTATION EXPENDITURES

Up to $10,000 ($5,000 for married taxpayers filing separately) of qualified reforestation expenses for each qualified timber property may be currently deducted in the tax year paid or incurred [Code Sec. 194(b)]. All qualified reforestation expenditures in excess of the annual limitation may be capitalized and amortized over 84 months if the taxpayer so elects [Code Sec. 194(a)].

Qualified reforestation expenditures are direct costs that are incurred in connection with forestation or reforestation by planting or seeding, including the cost of (1) site preparation, (2) seeds or seedlings, and (3) labor and tools [Code Sec. 194(c)(3)(A); Reg. § 1.194-3(c)]. The expenditures must relate to a site located in the United States that will contain trees in significant commercial quantities and that is held by the taxpayer for growing and ultimately cutting trees for sale or use in the commercial

245 Treas. Dept., IRS Publication 225, "Farmer's Tax Guide" (2013 Ed.), pp. 28-31.

production of timber products. The site must be at least one acre which is planted with tree seedlings in the manner normally used in forestation or reforestation [Code Sec. 194(c)(1); Reg. § 1.194-3(a)]. Amounts deducted as amortization are subject to recapture under Sec. 1245 if the property is sold prematurely [Ch. 8].

COMMUNITY RENEWAL PROVISIONS

¶12,220 INCENTIVES TO STIMULATE GROWTH IN RENEWAL COMMUNITIES

The following tax incentives exist to stimulate investment and job creation in the renewal communities:

.01 Types of Incentives for Renewal Communities

Capital Gain

A zero-percent capital gains rate applies to qualified capital gain from the sale of qualified renewal community assets held for more than five years. The tax-free capital gain treatment applies to qualified community assets, which include: (1) qualified community stock, (2) qualified community partnership interests, and (3) qualified community business property [Code Sec. 1400F(b)(1)]. Qualified capital gain is defined as any gain recognized on the sale of a capital asset or property used in the trade or business under Code Sec. 1231(b) (for example, depreciable property and real property used in the business and not held for sale to customers) [Code Sec. 1400F(c)(1)]. Qualified gain does not include gain attributable to periods before January 1, 2002, or after December 31, 2014 [Code Sec. 1400F(c)(2)].

The following types of capital gains generated from a renewal community business will not be eligible for the exclusion: gain attributable to real property or an intangible asset that is not an integral part of a renewal community business [Code Sec. 1400B(e)(4)]; gain that would be treated as ordinary income under the Code Sec. 1245 or Code Sec. 1250 depreciation recapture provisions, if Code Sec. 1250 applied to all depreciation rather than the additional depreciation [Code Sec. 1400B(e)(3); Code Sec. 1400F(c)(3)]; gain that is attributable directly or indirectly, in whole or in part, to a transaction with a related party [Code Sec. 1400B(e)(5)].

Renewal Community Employment Credit

For further discussion, see Ch. 14.

Commercial Revitalization Deduction for Renewal Communities

A *commercial revitalization deduction* allows taxpayers who construct or rehabilitate nonresidential buildings in renewal communities to deduct either: (a) 50 percent of qualifying expenses for the tax year in which a qualified building is placed in service, or (b) all of the qualifying expenses ratably over a 10-year period beginning with the month in which the building is placed in service [Code Sec. 1400I(a)];

Increased Expensing Under Code Sec. 179 for Renewal property

For further discussion, see Ch. 11.

Work Opportunity Credit for Youth in Renewal Communities

For further discussion, see Ch. 14.

Commercial Revitalization Expenditure Amounts

This covers an election to recover the cost of building.

In Rev. Proc. 2003-38,[246] the IRS explains how a taxpayer may elect under Code Sec. 1400I(a) to recover the cost of the building using a more accelerated method than is otherwise allowable under the Code Sec. 168 depreciation provisions. The IRS also released guidance that sets forth the time and manner for states to make allocations under Code Sec. 1400I, of commercial revitalization expenditure amounts to a new or substantially rehabilitated building that is placed in service in a renewal community.

In Rev. Proc. 2006-16,[247] the IRS explains how a commercial revitalization agency may retroactively allocate commercial revitalization expenditure amounts for buildings located in the expanded area of a renewal community pursuant to Code Sec. 1400E(g). The IRS also explains how a taxpayer may make a commercial revitalization deduction election under Code Sec. 1400l(a) for these buildings and may deduct the increased expensing amount under Code Sec. 1400J for Code Sec. 179 property that is placed in service in the expanded area of a renewal community pursuant to Code Sec. 1400E(g).

.02 Empowerment Zones

To stimulate investment in empowerment zones, taxpayers doing business in these areas will be entitled to the following tax incentives:

- Employers doing business in any of the designated empowerment zones will be entitled to an empowerment zone employment credit equal to 20 percent of the first $15,000 of qualified wages paid to full-time or part-time employees [Code Sec. 1396] (for detailed discussion, see Ch. 14).
- Depreciable business property placed in service in the empowerment zone is eligible for increased Code Sec. 179 expensing deduction [Code Sec. 1397A]. For detailed discussion, see Ch. 11.
- A taxpayer can elect to roll over, or defer the recognition of, capital gain realized from the sale or exchange of any qualified empowerment zone asset purchased after December 21, 2000, and held for more than one year where the taxpayer uses the proceeds to purchase other qualifying empowerment zone assets in the same zone within 60 days of the sale of the original empowerment zone asset [Code Sec. 1397B]. The recognition of the rollover gain is deferred until the sale of the replacement asset by reducing the basis of the replacement asset by the amount of the realized gain which is not recognized [Code Sec. 1397B(b)(4)]. See ¶8105.
- Qualified businesses operating in enterprise communities and empowerment zones are eligible to finance property with tax-exempt private activity bonds [Code Sec. 1394]. Qualified enterprise zone facility bonds issued to finance property in an enterprise community may be issued only while the enterprise community designation is in effect and are fully subject to the state private activity bond volume limitations.

---

[246] Rev. Proc. 2003-38, 2003-1 CB 1017, as modified by Rev. Proc. 2006-16, 2006-1 CB 539.

[247] Rev. Proc. 2006-16, 2006-1 CB 539.

Losses and Bad Debts

13

LOSSES IN GENERAL

Deductible losses . . . . ¶ 13,001
Amount deductible . . . . ¶ 13,005

LOSSES IN BUSINESS OR PROFIT TRANSACTIONS

Loss incurred in trade or business . . . . ¶ 13,010
Transaction entered into for profit . . . . ¶ 13,015

CASUALTY AND THEFT LOSSES

Casualty losses . . . . ¶ 13,020
Theft losses . . . . ¶ 13,025
Special tax return rules for casualties and thefts . . . . ¶ 13,030
Worthless stock . . . . ¶ 13,040
Demolition of buildings . . . . ¶ 13,045
Abandonment losses . . . . ¶ 13,050
Losses of farmers . . . . ¶ 13,055
Loss distinguished from capital expenditure . . . . ¶ 13,060

DISALLOWED LOSSES

Wash sales . . . . ¶ 13,065
Sham sales . . . . ¶ 13,070
Sales to related taxpayers . . . . ¶ 13,075
Gambling losses . . . . ¶ 13,080
Hobby losses and expenses . . . . . . ¶ 13,085
Passive losses . . . . ¶ 13,090
At-risk rules . . . . ¶ 13,100
Losses from vacation homes . . . . . ¶ 13,105

NET OPERATING LOSS DEDUCTION

What is a net operating loss (NOL) . . . . ¶ 13,110
Determining net operating loss . . ¶ 13,115
Carryover of unused portion of net operating loss . . . . ¶ 13,120

BAD DEBT DEDUCTIONS

Overview of bad debts . . . . ¶ 13,125
Amount deductible . . . . ¶ 13,130
Business bad debts . . . . ¶ 13,135
Nonbusiness bad debts . . . . ¶ 13,140
Advances to relatives . . . . ¶ 13,145
Advances to corporations by stockholders . . . . ¶ 13,150
Deposits in closed banks . . . . ¶ 13,155
Worthless bonds . . . . ¶ 13,160
Bad debt and loss distinguished . . . ¶ 13,165
Recovery of bad debts . . . . ¶ 13,170
Loss on sale of pledged property other than on purchase money mortgage . . . . ¶ 13,175

LOSSES IN GENERAL

Taxpayers can deduct losses and bad debts in appropriate circumstances. The specific deduction rules depend on such factors as whether the loss or bad debt arose in connection with the taxpayer's business investments or is personal. The rules are explained in this chapter. Capital losses of individuals are discussed in Chapter 8; for corporate capital losses, see Ch. 20.

¶13,001 DEDUCTIBLE LOSSES

.01 Harvesting Paper Losses

An investor who has seen the value of his or her stocks invested in mutual funds held outside of tax-sheltered retirement accounts decline, may be able to turn this paper loss into a tax advantage by selling the stocks that have declined in value in order to recognize the loss and generate tax savings. This is known as "harvesting" paper losses. Taxpayers should get out their calculator and see if the following strategies will work for them. Consider selling the losers now in order to lock in a valuable capital loss this year. Sell enough of the losers to cover any capital gains plus $3,000 of ordinary income. Taxpayers will be able to use up to $3,000 of their capital losses to offset $3,000 of ordinary income generated from wages, and interest each year.

Example 13-1: You have $50,000 of capital gain from the sale of XYZCo stock that you sold earlier this year. In addition, your ABCo stock has plummeted in value. You should sell enough of your shares in ABCo stock to generate a capital loss sufficient to shelter your $50,000 capital gain plus an extra $3,000 capital loss to shelter your salary, bonus and interest income. Any extra capital loss can be carried over indefinitely to future tax years until the earlier of your death or when the losses are used up.

Before harvesting paper losses from stock that has declined in value, figure out the current tax benefit of recognizing the loss. When searching for capital assets to sell off, avoid antiques and other collectibles that are taxed at the maximum long-term tax rate of 28 percent.

.02 What Losses Are Deductible

In one sense, taxpayers suffer a loss each time their wealth decreases in value. But they may claim no write-off unless certain requirements are met. For example, if a stock is worth less than its purchase price, the investor may not claim a deduction until the shares are sold.

For individuals, only the following losses are eligible for a deduction [Code Sec. 165(c); Reg. § 1.165-1(e)]:

- Losses incurred in a trade or business.
- Losses incurred in a transaction entered into for profit.
- Losses from fires, storms, shipwreck, other casualty or theft, whether or not connected with a trade or business or incurred in a transaction entered into for profit.

Example 13-2: Mr. Edwin is a self-employed real estate agent. During the year, he sold his auto at a loss and bought a new one. To the extent Edwin's auto is used for business, he is entitled to deduct the loss. But to the extent Edwin uses the auto for personal travel, he gets no deduction.

A corporation is not subject to these limitations, so all its losses generally are deductible. Consequently, a corporate taxpayer does not need a business or profit connection to write off a loss. In fact, a corporation may be able to deduct a loss when it disposes of nonbusiness property used by stockholders for personal purposes.

Of course, the corporate deduction can be limited by other tax rules, such as the prohibition for write-offs on entertainment facilities [Ch. 10].

A related deduction is allowed for bad debts [¶ 13,125]. If someone owes you money and does not pay, you may be entitled to a deduction [Code Sec. 166; Reg. § 1.166-1].

Example 13-3: Mr. Edwin, a real estate agent, lends $5,000 to a client for the purpose of using the proceeds as the downpayment on a house Edwin wants to sell. When the debt comes due several years later, the client has no property and is unable to pay. Edwin can deduct $5,000 as a business bad debt in the year the debt is due.

NOTE: It is possible for a deduction to be allowed under the loss rules as well as the bad debt rules. In this situation, a taxpayer must treat the deduction as a bad debt and not as a loss.[1]

A taxpayer may deduct voluntary as well as involuntary losses. For example, losses from the voluntary sale of business property are deductible. Also, taxpayers can deduct an involuntary loss, such as from theft or a casualty.

To be deductible, losses must be due to closed and completed transactions, fixed by identifiable events. In addition, losses must be real losses that are actually sustained during the tax year for which claimed [Reg. § 1.165-1(b)].

Special rules apply to certain losses, such as loss on the sale of income-producing property that was formerly used as a residence, loss from worthless stock, loss from voluntary removal of buildings, loss due to obsolescence of nondepreciable property, and losses of farmers [¶ 13,040-¶ 13,055].

Some losses are specifically disallowed, such as loss on "wash sales," loss on sales to certain related taxpayers, losses from passive activities in excess of passive income, gambling losses in excess of winnings, losses from the rental of a vacation home that is also used as a personal residence and hobby losses [¶ 13,065 et seq.].

Taxpayers may be able to offset business, casualty, and theft losses of the current year against income from past and future years. This is the "net operating loss" deduction [¶ 13,110 et seq.].

Taxpayers can generally deduct losses from passive activities (i.e., activities they do not materially participate in) and vacation home rentals only to the extent of their passive income. But they can carry over losses that are disallowed in the year incurred and deduct them against passive and vacation home income in future years. Additionally, they can deduct these losses against salary, interest, dividend, and other income once the passive activity is disposed of.

¶13,005 AMOUNT DEDUCTIBLE

In general, the amount of the loss deduction is figured the same way as a loss on a sale [Code Sec. 165(b)]. It is the difference between the amount realized and the adjusted basis of the property [Ch. 6]. In any event, the amount of the loss cannot be more than the adjusted basis of the property [Reg. § 1.165-1(c)]. Insurance, salvage value and other recoveries reduce the deductible loss [Code Sec. 165(a); Reg. § 1.165-1(c)].

Example 13-4: Ms. Juliet owns a ski shop. She purchased 10 pairs of skis at a total cost to her of $2,000. She hoped to sell the skis for $4,000, but market conditions forced her to sell them at a bargain price of only $1,000. Her amount realized (selling price) is $1,000, while her adjusted basis (what she paid) is $2,000. Her deductible loss is the difference between the two, or $1,000.

NOTE: Taxpayers do not necessarily have a deductible loss when they sell property for less than they intended or for less than its market value. To have a loss, they must sell for less than their basis.

There are special rules that apply to personal casualty and theft losses and losses of business property by casualty and theft [¶ 13,030].

LOSSES IN BUSINESS OR PROFIT TRANSACTIONS

¶13,010 LOSS INCURRED IN TRADE OR BUSINESS

A trade or business is a regular occupation or calling carried on for a living or for profit. An individual may claim a deduction under Code Sec. 165(c) for losses incurred in a trade or business. The loss does not have to be incurred in a principal trade or business if the taxpayer is engaged in several occupations. An isolated activity or transaction generally is not a trade or business.

Example 13-5: Mr. Smith bought a new refrigerator for his home and sold it at a loss after deciding it was not big enough for his needs. He is not entitled to a deduction. Mr. Jones is a butcher who bought a refrigerator for his store and sold it at a loss because it did not fit his requirements. He has a deductible loss.

Taxpayer cannot claim a loss deduction on the sale of business or investment property (e.g., a business car) to the extent the property is used for personal reasons. And they cannot deduct a loss on the sale of an entertainment facility, even if they used it exclusively for business entertainment purposes [Ch. 10].

.01 Anticipated Profits or Wages

A taxpayer cannot claim a deduction for loss of anticipated profits or wages because the lost profits or wages are not taxed to the taxpayer in the first place.

Example 13-6: As a result of personal injuries, Ms. Green lost anticipated income from writing. Green cannot claim a deduction for expected income not yet earned.[1]

.02 Legal Damages

A taxpayer can deduct damages paid under a judgment to settle a suit or claim arising out of trade or business, or transaction entered into for profit. However, the taxpayer cannot deduct damages for personal losses.

Payment by a corporate president and director to settle suit for mismanagement is deductible.[2] Damages paid for the fraudulent claim of fire loss are not deductible when it frustrates public policy.[3]

.03 Fines Not Deductible

Treble (triple) damages are not deductible because they constitute a nondeductible fine [Code Sec. 162(f)].[4] The Internal Revenue Code "bars the deduction of fines and penalties imposed to sanction or punish conduct which a well-defined government policy seeks to proscribe." Treble damages are penalties that serve a deterrent and a retribution function similar to a criminal fine and thus are not deductible.

▶ **OBSERVATION:** Business expense deductions are not disallowed for being in violation of public policy, unless the type of expense is specifically disallowed by a provision of the tax law (e.g., bribing government officials) [Code Secs. 162(c), (f), (g)]. On the other hand, loss deductions can be denied on the ground of frustrating public policy.[5]

.04 Repayment of Embezzled Funds

An embezzler who includes embezzled income on his or her tax return is entitled to a deduction for reimbursing the victims in the year in which restitution is made. But the amount of the deduction cannot exceed the amount embezzled. The deduction is not based on the value of any assets which the embezzler may have purchased with the embezzled funds.[6] Payments to a bank as restitution for a relative's embezzlement, though, are nondeductible gifts.[7]

.05 How Involuntary Conversions Are Treated on Return

Taxpayers can deduct losses from their trade or business from gross income to arrive at adjusted gross income. This type of deduction *(deductions from adjusted gross income)* should be distinguished from personal casualty losses, which are claimed as itemized deductions [Ch. 1]. Taxpayers should report a sale, exchange, or involuntary conversion of property used in their trade or business on Form 4797, *Sale of Business*

---

1 *J. Greenway*, 40 TCM 24, Dec. 36,860(M), TC Memo. 1980-97.

2 *Great Island Holding Corp.*, 5 TC 150, Dec. 14,582 (1945), *acq.* 1945 CB 3.

3 *C. O'Brien*, CA-9, 63-2 USTC ¶9668, 321 F2d 227, *aff'g*, 36 TC 957, Dec. 25,010 (1961) on other grounds.

4 *J.W. Hawronsky*, 105 TC 94, Dec. 50,814 (1995).

5 Rev. Rul. 82-74, 1982-1 CB 110; Rev. Rul. 77-126, 1977-1 CB 47.

6 *D.E. Greenman*, DC-FL, 92-1 USTC ¶50,272, 711 FSupp 1556, *aff'd without op.*, 914 F2d 268.

7 *P.E.L. Lingham*, 36 TCM 649, Dec. 34,417(M), TC Memo. 1977-152.

Property. However, involuntary conversions of property due to casualty or theft are reported on Form 4684, *Casualties and Theft.*

¶13,015 TRANSACTION ENTERED INTO FOR PROFIT

Individual taxpayers can deduct a loss incurred in any transaction entered into for profit, even though not connected with a trade or business [Code Sec. 165(c)(2); Reg. § 1.165-1(e)]. Profit is used in its ordinary and usual sense. It has been defined as the gain on invested capital or the receipt of money in excess of the amount spent. It must be of a tangible or pecuniary nature and capable of measurement.

Example 13-7: You cannot deduct a payment you make on a promise to a relative to repay him for any loss sustained on securities he bought. This is not a transaction entered into for profit. However, the loss on sale of a residence you converted to rental use is a transaction entered into for profit and is deductible.[8] Penalties for a premature withdrawal of funds from a time savings account, including amounts that exceed interest accrued or already paid on the account, are allowable loss deduction[9] [Ch. 9].

.01 Sale of Gift and Inherited Property

A sale of property acquired by gift or inheritance may be a transaction for profit that gives rise to a deductible loss. It depends on how the taxpayer uses the property. Ordinary investment property is treated as held for profit unless the taxpayer's conduct shows contrary intent.

Example 13-8: The loss was allowed where a taxpayer inherited a private residence and planned to rent or sell it from time of acquisition. A joint owner was also allowed to deduct the loss on the sale of personal residence when there was an intention to sell it after it was inherited from the co-owner.[10] A loss on the sale of an inherited necklace was deductible when the taxpayer had no intention of using the necklace, but always intended to dispose of it at the best possible price. A loss deduction was allowed on the sale of an inherited yacht never used for personal purposes, when there was no intent to use it for such purposes.

.02 Sale of Stock

Under ordinary conditions, the purchase of stock shows an intention to receive profits, and a loss on its sale is allowed. But the loss may not be deductible if you have a nonprofit motive when the stock is acquired.[11]

---

[8] *Heiner v. Tindle*, SCt, 1 USTC ¶ 299, 276 US 582, 48 SCt 326.

[9] Rev. Rul. 82-27, 1982-1 CB 32.

[10] *P. Miller Est.*, 26 TCM 229, Dec. 28,367(M), TC Memo. 1967-44.

[11] *E.T. Weir*, CA-3, 40-1 USTC ¶ 9200, 109 F2d 996, *cert. denied*, 310 US 637, 60 SCt 1080; *R.D. Dresser*, CtCls, 3 USTC ¶ 866, 55 F2d 499, 74 CtCls 55, *cert. denied*, 287 US 635, 53 SCt 85.

Example 13-9: Loss on sale of stock in country club is not deductible when you buy the stock to become a member. Nor can you deduct the loss on the sale of stock you knew to be worthless when you bought it [¶ 13,040].

.03 How Losses from Transactions Entered into for Profit Are Treated on Return

Deductible losses in any transaction entered into for profit, even though not for your trade or business, are deductions *from* adjusted gross income if (1) you held the property for the production of rents or royalties, or (2) the loss is from the sale or exchange of capital assets (deduction is subject to capital loss limitation), or (3) the loss is due to securities becoming worthless (subject to capital loss limitation). You report a loss on the sale or exchange of property held for the production of rents or royalties on Form 4797 [Ch. 8]. You report a loss on the sale or exchange of capital assets and a loss on securities that become worthless on Schedule D of Form 1040.

CASUALTY AND THEFT LOSSES

¶13,020 CASUALTY LOSSES

Individual taxpayers can deduct losses from fire, storm, shipwreck, or other casualty, even though not incurred in a trade or business or in a transaction entered into for profit [Code Sec. 165(c)(3); Reg. § 1.165-7]. A "casualty" is an event due to some sudden, unexpected, or unusual cause. Generally, this means an accident or some sudden invasion by a hostile agency. It need not be due to natural causes. The progressive deterioration of your property through a steadily operating cause is not a casualty; nor is it a casualty when you lose an article through your own negligence or carelessness. A casualty loss may arise from the demolition or evacuation of a taxpayer's home in a disaster area.

.01 IRS Provides Relief for Homeowners with Corrosive Drywall

In Rev. Proc. 2010-36,[12] the IRS has provided relief to homeowners who have suffered property losses due to the effects of certain imported drywall installed in homes between 2001 and 2009. The ruling allows affected taxpayers to treat damages from corrosive drywall as a casualty loss and provides a "safe harbor" formula for determining the amount of the loss.

The IRS provides the following relief:

- Individuals who pay to repair damage to their personal residences or household appliances resulting from corrosive drywall may treat the amount paid as a casualty loss in the year of payment.
- Taxpayers who have already filed their income tax return for the year of payment generally have three years to file an amended return and claim the deduction. The amount of a loss that may be claimed depends on whether the taxpayer has a

[12] Rev. Proc. 2010-36, IRB 2010-42, 439.

pending claim for reimbursement (or intends to pursue reimbursement) of the loss through property insurance, litigation or otherwise.

- In cases where a taxpayer does not have a pending claim for reimbursement, the taxpayer may claim as a loss all unreimbursed amounts paid during the tax year to repair damage to the taxpayer's personal residence and household appliances resulting from corrosive drywall.
- If a taxpayer does have a pending claim (or intends to pursue reimbursement), a taxpayer may claim a loss for 75 percent of the unreimbursed amount paid during the tax year to repair damage to the taxpayer's personal residence and household appliances that resulted from corrosive drywall.

A taxpayer who has been fully reimbursed before filing a return for the year the loss was sustained may not claim a loss. A taxpayer who has a pending claim for reimbursement (or intends to pursue reimbursement) may have income or an additional deduction in subsequent tax years depending on the actual amount of reimbursement received.

.02 Deduction Limited to Property Losses on Owner's Property

Code Sec. 165(a) and (c)(3) allows an individual taxpayer to deduct "losses of property not connected with a trade or business or a transaction entered into for profit, if such losses arise from fire, storm, shipwreck, or other casualty." Generally, only the owner of the property damaged by a casualty is entitled to a deduction for a casualty loss sustained to that property.

Casualty Loss in Leasehold/Coop Ownership Situations

Where a taxpayer has a leasehold interest in property that is damaged by a casualty, the taxpayer is entitled to deduct a casualty loss sustained to that leasehold interest. In *C.A. Alphonso*,[13] the Court of Appeals for the Second Circuit reversed the Tax Court to hold that a stockholder in a residential co-op had a sufficient property interest under state law to claim a casualty loss deduction for her share of an assessment to fix damage to a retaining wall that collapsed and caused considerable damages on the co-op's premises. After reviewing the terms of the taxpayer's lease, the court found that she had a shared right with all other building residents to use the co-op's grounds and that under state law, her right to use the grounds, shared with other co-op residents and their respective guests was a property interest in the grounds. Therefore the taxpayer held a property interest in the co-op grounds that were sufficient to sustain a casualty loss deduction.

Actual Physical Damage Required

The IRS and most courts have determined that a casualty loss is allowed only for the actual physical damage resulting from the casualty.[14]

---

[13] *C.A. Alphonso*, CA-2, 2013-1 USTC ¶50,179, *rev'g*, 136 TC 247, Dec. 58,574 (2011).

[14] *A.E. West*, CA-3, 58-2 USTC ¶9906, 259 F2d 704; *C.A. Peterson*, 30 TC 660, Dec. 23,044 (1958); Rev. Rul. 70-16, 1970-1 CB 36.

Example 13-10: Mr. Smith's cottage on the shore escaped damage when a hurricane demolished neighboring cottages. But the value was reduced because the area might suffer again from hurricanes. No loss is allowed for the reduction in value.

However, one court has allowed a deduction for loss in value of property resulting from a casualty even though there was no physical damage to the property. Diminution of property value resulted from a landslide which cut off street access to the taxpayer's property.[15]

Example 13-11: Ms. Muller's home built on a bluff was partially isolated when the bluff suddenly slid and the home's value declined because of poor access to it. The loss in value was allowed even though the home itself was not physically damaged.

The courts have not recognized "buyer resistance" as a basis for a casualty loss.[16] A casualty loss was denied to a couple who claimed that the O.J. Simpson murders and the ensuing media frenzy caused the value of their home to plummet as a result of buyer resistance after the double murders and the subsequent public focus on O.J. Simpson whose home was in close proximity to theirs.[17] Because the taxpayers failed to allege any physical damage to their property as a result of their proximity to O.J. Simpson's house, they failed to establish their entitlement to a casualty loss deduction under the law. The reduction in the value of their home could not be construed as catastrophic in nature.

.03 Deductible Whether Business or Personal

Taxpayers can deduct casualty losses from business, personal or investment property. However, the type of property determines the amount of the deduction [Code Sec. 165(c); Reg. § 1.165-7].

▶ **OBSERVATION:** Taxpayers can deduct a loss from the destruction of a personal-use property only if the loss is from a casualty. However, they can deduct a loss from the destruction of business or investment property, even though it fails to qualify as a casualty [¶ 13,010; ¶ 13,015]. For example, a condemnation loss of business or investment property is deductible; a condemnation loss of personal-use property, such as a residence, is not.

Deductible Casualty Losses

Examples of deductible losses include:

- Automobile damages to a car caused by faulty driving (but not a willful act or willful negligence); damages to a car from faulty driving by operator of another auto [Reg. § 1.165-7(a)(3)];
- Drought damages if unusual in area (not from normal dry spell); foundation of residence weakened by subsoil shrinkage due to unusually severe drought;[18]

---

[15] *W.K. Stowers*, DC-MS, 59-1 USTC ¶ 9186, 169 FSupp 246.

[16] *C.W.P. Kamanski*, CA-9, 73-1 USTC ¶ 9371, 477 F2d 452.

[17] *M.N. Caan*, DC-CA, 99-1 USTC ¶ 50,349.

[18] Rev. Rul. 54-85, 1954-1 CB 58.

- Sonic boom damage caused by airplane breaking the sound barrier;[19]
- Vandalism damage;[20]
- Damage to exterior house paint from sudden and severe smog containing high chemical fume concentration;[21]
- Attorney's fees and court costs paid from award in suit to recover casualty losses, if court finds a deductible casualty;[22] and
- Losses from deposits or accounts in certain insolvent financial institutions [Code Sec. 165(l)].

Nondeductible Casualty Losses

Following are example of disallowed casualty losses:

- Damages paid to another to cover personal injury by a car (unless used for business purposes);[23]
- Moth damage to fur coat;[24]
- Loss of livestock from disease (does not meet the suddenness test);[25]
- Tree and shrub damage on residential property caused by disease or insects (but damage by freeze and mass attack by southern pine beetles is deductible);[26]
- Loss of purse, package or other article left on a bus or train; loss of valuable ring that slipped from finger;
- Termite damage (unless it meets suddenness test);[27]
- Loss on sale of residence due to condemnation of property as part of a site for flood prevention construction;[28] and
- Man's payment to his mistress to keep her from revealing their extramarital affair and the fact that she was pregnant was not deductible as a casualty loss.[29]

.04 Amount Deductible as Personal Casualty Loss

Limitations Imposed on Casualty Losses

The amount of a taxpayer's personal casualty loss deduction is the lesser of: (1) *the sustained loss*—that is, the property's value just before the casualty less its value immediately afterward—or (2) *the adjusted basis of the property* for figuring loss on a sale [Code Sec. 165(h); Reg. § 1.165-7(b)]. This amount eligible for a deduction is reduced by:

- Insurance;
- Amounts received from an employer or disaster relief agencies to restore the property;

---

[19] Rev. Rul. 60-329, 1960-2 CB 67.

[20] *B.E. Davis*, 34 TC 586, Dec. 24,246 (1960), *acq.* 1963-2 CB 4.

[21] Rev. Rul. 71-560, 1971-2 CB 126.

[22] *I.J. Hayutin*, 31 TCM 509, Dec. 31,419(M), TC Memo. 1972-127, *aff'd*, CA-10, 75-1 USTC ¶ 9108, 508 F2d 462.

[23] *F. Anderson*, CA-10, 36-1 USTC ¶ 9085, 81 F2d 457.

[24] Rev. Rul. 55-327, 1955-1 CB 25.

[25] Rev. Rul. 61-216, 1961-2 CB 134.

[26] *R.J. Lloyd*, DC-WA, 61-2 USTC ¶ 9674; *Nelson*, TC Memo. 1968-35.

[27] Rev. Rul. 63-232, 1963-2 CB 97.

[28] Rev. Rul. 70-16, 1970-1 CB 36.

[29] *R.C.Y. Ing*, CA-9, 96-1 USTC ¶ 50,100, 73 F3d 369.

- Other compensation for lost property;
- $100.
- After these reductions are made for each casualty, the remaining loss amounts are added up for the year. Write off this aggregate figure to the extent it exceeds 10 percent of adjusted gross income.

For losses sustained on personal-use property, claim a deduction only to the extent damages are not covered by insurance and only if taxpayers file a timely insurance claim with respect to the loss [Code Sec. 165(h)(5)(E)]. In other words, taxpayers cannot deduct a loss covered by insurance if they choose not to make a claim. In *M.D. Ambrose,*[30] the Court of Federal Claims found that a taxpayer's failure to provide timely proof of their loss to their insurance provider did not preclude them from deducting the loss under Code Sec. 165(h)(5)(E). According to the court, the plain language of the statute merely requires a basic demand for compensation in order for the taxpayer to qualify to deduct the loss.

> ▶ **OBSERVATION:** The above limitation does not apply to a casualty loss of business or investment property. In some instances, they can come out ahead by forgoing an insurance claim—if their premium payments will increase—and claiming the tax deduction in its place.

A taxpayer's deductible loss is not reduced by food, medical supplies and other forms of subsistence received that are not replacements of lost property. Nor is a loss reduced by unrestricted cash gifts.

If the insurance proceeds received exceed the taxpayer's loss and the taxpayer replaces the property, the taxpayer has taxable income only to the extent that his or her amount realized exceeds the replacement cost.

If the taxpayer sustains more than one loss from a single event, only one $100 reduction is made. If spouses file jointly, they are treated as one taxpayer. Separate losses sustained by the same act, therefore, bring only one reduction [Reg. § 1.165-7(b)(4)].

How to Prove a Loss in Value

Taxpayers should use competent appraisals to prove the difference between the value of the property immediately before and immediately after the casualty. The reasonable cost of repairs necessary to restore damaged property to its condition immediately before the casualty may be acceptable evidence of the loss of value. However, loss is measured by the difference in value, not the amount of repair bills. Repairs must be limited to damage sustained [Reg. § 1.165-7(a)(2)].

A loss involving both realty and improvements (buildings, ornamental trees, and shrubbery) is treated as a single loss that is measured by the actual decrease in the entire property's value [Reg. § 1.165-7(b)]. The cost of clearing property of debris is part of the loss deduction. However, when more than one item of personal property is involved, the decrease in fair market value or adjusted basis is figured separately for each item and then combined to find the deduction.

Sentimental values are not considered in determining loss on the destruction, damage, or theft of family portraits, heirlooms, or keepsakes.

---

30 *M.D. Ambrose*, CA-FC, 2012-2 USTC ¶ 50,518.

Exclusion of Insurance Proceeds

Taxpayers may receive insurance proceeds for expenses incurred while their principal residence is not usable because of fire, storm, or other casualty. To the extent the insurance compensates them for extraordinary living expenses, the proceeds are income tax-free. (Extraordinary expenses are defined as the actual expenses incurred to live away from a residence less the normal expenses that would have been incurred had the taxpayer been able to stay there). The IRS has said that the excludable amount of insurance payments does not have to be measured on a year-by-year basis. The exclusion should instead be calculated at the end of the "loss period" when the homeowner reoccupies the home.[31]

Taxpayers may be able to defer gain on insurance proceeds received to compensate for the destruction of or damage to their home. They generally defer the gain by purchasing a new home or rebuilding the old one within two years [Code Sec. 1033].

Special Relief Available in Federally Declared Disaster Area

Taxpayers in federally declared disaster areas (see ¶5100.10 for list of these areas) are entitled to take advantage of the following special tax relief:

- The 10 percent of AGI limitation applicable to personal casualty loss deductions is waived for personal casualty losses that are "net disaster losses" [Code Sec. 165(h)(3)(A)]. A "net disaster loss" means the excess of the personal casualty losses attributable to a federally declared disaster over personal casualty gains [Code Sec. 165(h)(3)(B)]. The $100 per-casualty floor applies in all years after December 31, 2009 [Code Sec. 165(h)(1)]. The amount of the standard deduction claimed by a taxpayer is increased by the amount of his or her disaster loss deduction [Code Sec. 63(c)(1)(D)]. Unlike the basic standard deduction, for purposes of calculating AMT income, the portion of the standard deduction amount attributable to the disaster loss deduction is allowed as a deduction [Code Sec. 56(b)(1)(E)].
- The two-year time period within which taxpayers must purchase appropriate replacement property and thereby defer gain is extended to *four* years in federally declared disaster areas [Code Sec. 1033(h)(1)(B)].
- Insurance proceeds for unscheduled personal property including miscellaneous items not specifically listed or insured under the insurance policy, that were part of the home's contents are automatically received tax-free no matter what the taxpayer does with the money [Code Sec. 1033(h)(1)(A)(i)]. There is no need for taxpayers to calculate whether the insurance recovery represents gain.
- Other insurance proceeds for the home and its contents can be lumped together and treated as a *common pool of funds* for purposes of the replacement break. Thus, if taxpayers buy a replacement home (or replacement personal property), they can elect to recognize gain only to the extent the insurance proceeds for all of these items exceed replacement costs [Code Sec. 1033(h)(1)(A)(ii)]. They do not have to calculate gain on individual items. They can therefore defer paying tax on insurance proceeds only to the extent that they spend an amount equal to their common pool of funds, which are the insurance proceeds received for the residence plus the separately scheduled contents. For further discussion, see Ch. 7.

---

[31] Rev. Rul. 93-43, 1993-2 CB 69.

- Losses occurring in a federally declared disaster area may be deducted on the tax return for the tax year immediately preceding the tax year in which the disaster occurred. See ¶5100.10 for a list of areas designated as disaster areas. The election to deduct a disaster loss for the preceding year must be made by filing a return, an amended return on Form 1040X, or a claim for a refund on or before the later of: (1) the due date of the taxpayer's return (determined without regard to any extensions) for the tax year in which the disaster actually occurred, or (2) the due date of the taxpayer's income tax return (determined with regard to extensions of time to file the return) for the tax year immediately preceding the tax year in which the disaster actually occurred. The loss is measured as of the date of the disaster. Otherwise, you deduct the loss in the year sustained [Code Sec. 165(i); Reg. § 1.165-11]. If you need a copy of last year's tax return in order to make the disaster election, complete Form 4506, *Request for Copy of Tax Form,* and send it to the IRS Service Center where the return was originally filed. Individuals in areas designated as federal disaster areas need not pay a fee to obtain a copy of an old tax return, provided they write "Disaster" along the top margin of Form 4506.

Insurance proceeds received when government authority forces evacuation of the taxpayer's residence because of a fire, storm, or other casualty are also tax-free. However, taxpayers do owe tax on payments received for the loss of rental income or damage to the property. The tax-free break also does not apply to the extent the residence is used for business purposes [Code Sec. 123; Reg. § 1.123-1].

.05 Figuring Business Casualty Loss

The amount of a taxpayer's business casualty loss depends on whether the property is completely destroyed or only partially destroyed. If the property is entirely destroyed, the taxpayer's loss is the amount of his or her adjusted basis for determining loss on a sale [Ch. 6] less any insurance, salvage value or other recovery [Code Sec. 165(b); Reg. § 1.165-7(b)(1)].

> **Example 13-12:** Mr. Flynn's insured shop was demolished by hurricane. Flynn originally purchased the shop for $100,000 but had taken $15,000 worth of depreciation write-offs. Thus, his adjusted basis was $85,000. Flynn received $80,000 from his insurance company. Thus, his deduction is $5,000 ($85,000 – $80,000), the difference between the adjusted basis and the insurance recovery.

If only part of the property is destroyed, the taxpayer's loss is measured by the decrease in the property's fair market value, up to the taxpayer's adjusted basis in the property. The taxpayer can generally use the cost of reasonable repairs to determine how much the property has declined in value [Reg. § 1.165-7(a)(2)(ii)].

Allocation of Loss

A loss incurred in a trade or business or in any transaction entered into for profit is determined by reference to the "single, identifiable property" damaged or destroyed. Thus, for example, in determining the fair market value of the property before and after the casualty in a case where damage by casualty has occurred to a building and ornamental or fruit trees used in a trade or business, the decrease in value is measured by taking the building and trees into account separately, and not together as an integral part of the realty, and separate losses are determined for the building and trees [Reg. § 1.165-7(b)(2)(i)].

In Technical Advice Memorandum 200902011[32] the IRS described the factors that should be examined to arrive at a reasonable unit of property for purposes of calculating a casualty loss deduction. The IRS determined that each damaged line, circuit and substation of the electric utility taxpayer was a single, identifiable property that could be considered a reasonable unit of property for purposes of the casualty loss deduction because each performs a discrete, identifiable function.

.06 When to Deduct a Casualty Loss

The time to deduct a casualty loss is the tax year in which the taxpayer actually sustains the loss [Reg. § 1.167-7(a)(1)].

If the taxpayer does not collect insurance or other reimbursement in the loss year, but there is a reasonable prospect of recovery by insurance or reimbursement, the loss is not sustained until it can be determined with reasonable certainty whether the reimbursement will be received. If a portion of the loss is not covered by insurance or reimbursement, the loss on that portion is sustained in the year the casualty occurs.

Example 13-13: Ms. Smith's business property with a $10,000 basis, insured for $8,000, was destroyed last year. Smith expected the $8,000 insurance claim to be paid in full last year when she had a $2,000 loss. Because she recovered only $7,500 the following year with no chance of getting the full $8,000, she may claim a $500 loss for that year.

If the taxpayer deducts a loss in one year and is compensated for it in a subsequent year, the taxpayer does not recompute tax for the earlier year. Instead, the amount received for the loss is taxed as income in the year received, but only to the extent taxable income was actually reduced by a deduction in the earlier year [Reg. § 1.165-1(d)(2)].

Example 13-14: Last year, Mr. Parker had an adjusted gross income (AGI) of $60,000 and suffered a $10,000 personal casualty loss. The insurance company refused to pay his claim, so Parker is entitled to a deduction. After subtracting $100 and 10 percent of Parker's AGI (the limitations for personal losses), only $3,900 is actually deductible. The insurance company finally investigated Parker's claim the following year and paid him the full $10,000. Result: Because Parker only received s a loss deduction of $3,900 last year, he will treat only $3,900 of the proceeds as income the following year.

.07 Carrybacks and Carryovers

When an individual taxpayer's deductible casualty losses exceed taxable income for the tax year, the excess is considered a net operating loss. As such, the taxpayer may carry back the loss to offset income of prior years and carry forward the loss to offset income of future years under the net operating loss provisions [Code Sec. 172(d)(4)(C)]. All

[32] TAM 200902011. *See also* TAM 201014052.

deductible casualty losses qualify even though the property involved is personal, and you are not in business [Reg. § 1.172-3(a)(3)(iii)]. See ¶ 13,110 et seq.

¶13,025 THEFT LOSSES

Losses from theft, larceny, robbery, or embezzlement are deductible if proven [Code Sec. 165(c)(3); Reg. § 1.165-8]. The cost of recovering stolen property is deductible as a theft loss. In determining whether a theft loss under Code Sec. 165(c)(3) has occurred, courts often examine state law in the jurisdiction where the loss was sustained, but in *R.F. Goeller*,[33] the U.S. Court of Federal Claims concluded that state criminal law statutes were irrelevant in determining whether the taxpayers had suffered a theft loss under Code Sec. 165 when a real estate investment became worthless. Instead, the court looked at the plain, ordinary, contemporary, common meaning of the term "theft loss." In the interest of uniform administration of the federal revenue statues, it made more sense to require courts to adopt a relatively uniform federal definition of a term, rather than requiring an investigation of different state criminal law each time a theft loss deduction is claimed.

.01 Amount Deductible

Theft losses are generally treated as casualty losses for tax purposes. For personal property, each theft loss is deductible only to the extent it exceeds $100. No deduction is allowed if total casualty losses (including thefts) for the year are 10 percent or less of adjusted gross income [Code Sec. 165(h)(2)]. In applying the casualty loss rules to thefts, your fair market value of the property immediately after a theft is considered to be zero [Reg. § 1.165-8(c)]. The taxpayer's loss must be reduced by (1) amounts received from an insurance company, or the value of any claim against the company; and (2) surety or fidelity bond proceeds, or amount of claim against the bonding company. Taxpayers cannot take a theft deduction for unreported income that has been embezzled from them. They may deduct, as a theft loss, amounts loaned to a corporation as a result of the corporation's fraudulent financial reports before it became bankrupt.

If their property is protected by insurance, they cannot deduct a personal theft loss unless they file a timely claim.

.02 When to Deduct Theft Loss

Taxpayers can generally deduct casualty losses in the year that the theft loss was "sustained." However, for embezzlements and other thefts, the taxpayer may not find out about the loss until it's too late to amend a return for the year the loss was sustained. So that the deduction is not lost, a special rule applies: Theft losses are

---

[33] *R.F. Goeller*, FedCl, 2013-1 USTC ¶ 50,238; *Ramsay Scarlett & Co.*, 61 TC 795, Dec. 32,507 (1974), *aff'd*, CA-4, 75-2 USTC ¶ 9634, 521 F2d 786. *See J.M. Urtis*, 105 TCM 1428, Dec. 59,470(M), TC Memo. 2013-66 (theft loss deduction allowed for home repair fraud).

considered "sustained" and deductible in the year in which the loss is discovered [Code Sec. 165(e); Reg. § 1.165-8(a)(2)].[34]

.03 Theft Loss Denied When Reasonable Prospect of Recovery Exists

A theft loss deduction will not be allowed in situations where the victim has a *reasonable prospect of recovery*. According to this rule, even after they discover a theft loss, if a claim for reimbursement exists during that year and there is a "reasonable prospect of recovery," then the theft loss will be deductible only when it can be ascertained with reasonable certainty that they will not be reimbursed for the loss [Reg. § 1.165-1(d)(2)(i)].[35]

This means that a taxpayer, hoping to claim a theft loss, must prove with reasonable certainty that, as of the end of the tax year, his or her loss would never be recovered. The taxpayer must prove that he or she has exhausted reasonable prospects of recovery and that it is reasonably certain that he or she will never get the money back. For example, an investor may not claim a theft loss deduction for securities losses attributable to unauthorized trades because the investor had litigation pending to recover some of his or her losses.[36] As a result, there was a reasonable prospect that the investor would recover some of the stolen money by year-end.

.04 Theft Loss Unavailable for Declining Stock Prices

Losses arising on account of a decline in the value of stock owned by the taxpayer, where the decline is due to a fluctuation in the market price of the stock or to other similar causes, generally are not deductible under Code Sec. 165(a) as a theft loss. A mere shrinkage in the value of stock owned by the taxpayer, even though extensive, doesn't give rise to a loss deduction if the stock has any recognizable value on the date claimed as the date of the loss [Reg. § 1.165-4(a)].

A deduction may be claimed, however: (1) if the stock is worthless and has no recognizable value [see ¶ 13,040]; or (2) when the loss is actually sustained as a result of a sale or exchange (i.e., sale to a third party). Losses from a sale or exchange of stock held for investment are capital losses and may be deducted subject to capital loss limits under Code Sec. 1211 and Code Sec. 1212 [Code Sec. 165(f); see Ch. 8 for further discussion]. Under Code Sec. 1211(b), individual taxpayers can recognize capital losses only to the extent of capital gains plus $3,000. Code Sec. 1212(b) allows noncorporate taxpayers to carry forward unrecognized capital losses, treated as either short-term or long-term capital losses, to subsequent tax years, but it does not allow them to carry back unrecognized capital losses to prior tax years. The distinction between a capital loss and a theft loss is significant because a capital loss is deductible only against capital gains and no more than $3,000 of ordinary income in each year (with the unused deduction being carried forward to later tax years), whereas a theft loss is immediately deductible in full against all taxable income.

---

[34] *M.L. Alison*, SCt, 52-2 USTC ¶ 9571, 344 US 167, 73 SCt 191; *Gwinn Bros. & Co.*, 7 TC 320, Dec. 15,250 (1946), *acq.* 1946-2 CB 2.

[35] *D.S. Alioto*, CA-6, 2012-2 USTC ¶ 50,659, 699 F3d 948.

[36] *H.L. Jeppsen*, CA-10, 97-2 USTC ¶ 50,878, 128 F3d 1410, *cert. denied*, 524 US 916.

In *D.R. Schroerlucke*,[37] the court denied a former WorldCom employee's theft loss claim based on the collapse of WorldCom because the stock's decline in value was not due to a theft as defined by state law. According to the court nothing was taken or appropriated and there was no theft by deception, theft by conversion, or theft of services. Although the stock later declined in value, the court found no evidence to show that the corporation's executives had any specific intent to take or appropriate the stock by devaluation or by any other means as required to prove theft under state law.

.05 Theft Loss Treatment for Ponzi Scheme Victims

The IRS provided tax relief to victims of Ponzi-type fraudulent investment schemes (without specific mention of Bernard Madoff) in the form of:

1. Rev. Rul. 2009-9,[38] which clarifies the income tax law governing the treatment of losses from Ponzi-type investment schemes and addresses seven specific tax issues that victims of Madoff-type schemes may confront; and
2. Rev. Proc. 2009-20,[39] which provides a safe harbor for determining the proper time and amount of loss that may be claimed by affected taxpayers.
3. Form 4684, *Casualties and Thefts*, now includes a section for claiming a deduction for theft losses resulting from an investment in a Ponzi-type scheme.

Rev. Rul. 2009-9 uses an example involving an investor who is a victim of a Ponzi scheme to determine the nature of the loss, limitations on the loss, the year the loss is deductible, the amount deductible as a theft loss, the amount of the net operating loss carryback, whether the theft loss qualifies for claim of right benefits, and whether the mitigation provisions apply.

Safe Harbor in Rev. Proc. 2009-20

In Rev. Proc. 2009-20, the IRS provided an optional safe harbor for qualified investors that experienced losses in investment arrangements that were discovered to be criminally fraudulent. The safe harbor allows them to treat their losses from Ponzi schemes as theft losses in the year of discovery when certain conditions are met. In Rev. Proc. 2011-58,[40] the IRS modified the Ponzi scheme safe harbor found in Rev. Proc. 2009-20 so it will be easier for investors to claim a theft loss deduction under Code Sec. 165 for losses suffered when the lead figure in the Ponzi scheme has died.

The existing safe harbor in Rev. Proc. 2009-20 required that the lead figure in the scheme be under criminal indictment or the subject of a criminal complaint that has not been withdrawn. The loss could be deducted as a theft loss in the year of discovery which was defined as the tax year of the investor in which the indictment, information, or complaint was filed. The amount of the deduction is calculated by multiplying the amount of the qualified investment by 95 percent, for a qualified investor that does not pursue any potential third-party recovery; or 75 percent, for a qualified investor that is pursuing or intends to pursue any potential third-party recovery; and subtracting from this product the sum of any actual recovery and any potential insurance/SIPC recovery. The amount of the deduction is not further reduced by potential direct recovery or

---

[37] *D.R. Schroerlucke*, FedCl, 2011-2 USTC ¶50,642, 100 FedCl 584.

[38] Rev. Rul. 2009-9, 2009-1 CB 735.

[39] Rev. Proc. 2009-20, 2009-1 CB 749.

[40] Rev. Proc. 2011-58, IRB 2011-50.

potential third-party recovery. In Rev. Proc. 2011-58, the IRS broadened the definition of an investment loss: (1) to include schemes in which a civil complaint is brought against the lead figure by a state or federal authority that has not been withdrawn; (2) to make an exception for the nonwithdrawal requirement for indictments or complaints withdrawn due to the lead figure's death. These changes are retroactively applicable to losses for which the discovery year is a tax year beginning after December 31, 2007.

These changes were necessary because since Rev. Proc. 2009-20 was released, the deaths of some lead figures in Ponzi schemes made it impossible to charge them with criminal theft. Qualified investors in these cases were therefore unable to satisfy the definition of a qualified loss in Rev. Proc. 2009-20 and were therefore precluded from using the optional safe harbor. Rev. Proc. 2011-58 remedies this situation by retroactively expanding the definition of qualified loss. Rev. Proc. 2011-58 also clarifies that the terms "indictment," "information," and "criminal complaint" in Rev. Proc. 2009-20 have meanings similar to the use of those terms in the Federal Rules of Criminal Procedure.

Lack of Direct Investment with Perpetrator Does Not Preclude Theft Loss

In Chief Counsel Advice 201213022, the IRS concluded that losses suffered by Ponzi scheme victims who invested through the fund managers, rather than directly with perpetrators of the Ponzi scheme can still be deducted as theft losses under Code Sec. 165. The IRS found that there was privity between the taxpayers and the perpetrator because the perpetrator intended to misappropriate their money.

¶13,030 SPECIAL TAX RETURN RULES FOR CASUALTIES AND THEFTS

Generally, the way you report casualties (including thefts) depends on whether you have a net gain or loss from casualties and whether you held the property for personal purposes or for business or investment purposes.

You may have a gain from a casualty when an insurance recovery or other reimbursement exceeds your loss.

.01 Personal Casualty and Theft Losses

If you had only one loss, and no gains, during the year and the loss was on a single item, you can report the loss on Schedule A, Form 1040. If there was more than one casualty or theft, or if more than one item was involved, you use Form 4684, *Casualties and Thefts,* to figure the loss. The final amount gets transferred to Schedule A.

Allocation of Loss

You must allocate losses on property used for both business and pleasure before deducting them. Your business losses are wholly deductible for adjusted gross income, but your personal losses are deductible only above $100 per loss and 10 percent of adjusted gross income on all of your combined casualty and theft losses for the year.

> **Example 13-15:** Ms. Syms had an adjusted gross income of $50,000. Her car, which she used 75 percent of the time for business and 25 percent for pleasure, was totally destroyed in an accident. After receiving an insurance settlement,

Syms still had a remaining theft loss of $1,200. Syms can deduct $900 on her return. There is a $900 business casualty loss (75 percent × $1,200), but no personal casualty loss, because the loss didn't exceed the threshold limit ($100 and 10 percent of adjusted gross income).

.02 Gains and Losses from Casualties or Thefts

When you have both gains and losses from casualties or thefts, a special computation is made on Form 4684, *Casualties and Thefts.*

Special Netting of Personal Casualty and Theft Gains and Losses

You must net gains and losses from personal casualties or thefts. If your recognized gains exceed your recognized losses from these transactions, then you treat all of these gains and losses as capital gains and losses. In this case, your losses will not be subject to the 10 percent of adjusted gross income floor. However, you must apply the $100 floor before the netting computation is made. If your recognized losses exceed recognized gains, your losses are fully deductible to the extent of your gains. Losses in excess of gains are subject to the 10 percent of adjusted gross income floor [Code Sec. 165(h)(2); 1231(a)].

Example 13-16: Mr. Smith has an adjusted gross income of $100,000 (exclusive of any personal casualty losses). During the year, Smith had a $50,000 gain from an insurance recovery for the destruction by fire of his personal residence. He also had a $40,000 casualty loss after applying the $100 floor. Smith treats all his casualties as capital gains and losses. He can disregard the 10 percent adjusted gross income rule.

Example 13-17: Assume the same facts as in Example 13-16 except that Smith's casualty losses for the year are $70,100 (not $40,000). The first $50,000 of losses will be allowed as a deduction in full against Smith's gain. Of the remaining $20,000 (after subtracting the $100 floor), $10,000 is deductible—$20,000 less the 10 percent-of-AGI floor.

Section 1231 Property and Separate Netting of Gains and Losses

You do not net casualty gains and losses on property used in business with personal casualties. Instead, you net business casualties with gains or losses from "Section 1231 property" (i.e., property used in your trade or business, or held for the production of rents or royalties and held for more than one year) [Ch. 8]. If your gain on the casualty is subject to depreciation recapture, you do not include the recaptured gain in the netting computation. You then net the gains not subject to recapture and the losses separately from other gains and losses from Section 1231 assets. If the result is a net gain, you net the gain again with the gains and losses from other Section 1231 assets. If this also results in a net gain, you treat the casualty gains and losses as capital gains and losses (if the requisite holding period has been satisfied except to the extent the recapture rules apply); if it results in a net loss, you treat the casualty gains and losses as ordinary gains and losses [Ch. 8].

If the result of the separate netting of the business casualty gains and losses is a net loss, you keep the casualty or theft gains and losses separate from any gains and losses from other Section 1231 assets. You treat the losses as fully deductible ordinary losses, and the gains as ordinary gains.

¶13,040 WORTHLESS STOCK

If any security that is a capital asset becomes worthless during the tax year, the loss is treated as a capital loss on the last day of the tax year [Code Sec. 165(g)(1)]. An exception from this capital loss treatment applies for certain worthless securities in a domestic corporation affiliated with the taxpayer [Code Sec. 165(g)(3)]. Proposed regulations provide that the abandonment of a security establishes the worthlessness of the security to the taxpayer. In order to abandon a security, a taxpayer must permanently surrender and relinquish all rights in the security and receive no consideration in exchange. Whether a transaction is properly characterized as an abandonment or other type of transaction would be determined based on all the facts and circumstances [Prop. Reg. § 1.165-5(i)].

.01 Definition of *Security*

For these purposes *security* means the following:

- Share of stock in a corporation;
- Right to subscribe to, or to receive, a share of stock in a corporation; or
- A bond, debenture, note, or certificate, or other evidence of indebtedness to pay a fixed or determinable sum of money, which has been issued with interest coupons or in registered form by a domestic or foreign corporation or by any government or political subdivision [Code Sec. 165(g)(2); Reg. § 1.165-5(a)].

.02 Stock Must be Totally Worthless

In order to claim a capital loss for a worthless security, the law requires that the taxpayer show that the security became wholly or totally worthless during the year [Reg. § 1.165-4]. To abandon a security, a taxpayer must permanently surrender and relinquish all rights in the security and receive no consideration in exchange for the security. All the facts and circumstances must be examined to determine whether the transaction is an abandonment rather than a sale, exchange, contribution to capital, dividend, or gift [Reg. § 1.165-5(i)].

No deduction will allowed for partial worthlessness or for mere decline in value. Failure to prove that the stock became wholly worthless at the close of the year in question will result in the denial of your claim for a capital loss. No deduction will be allowed solely on account of a decline in the value of stock owned by a taxpayer when the decline is due to a fluctuation in the market price of the stock. A mere shrinkage in the value of stock owned by a taxpayer, even though extensive, does not give rise to a deduction under section 165(a) if the stock has any recognizable value on the date claimed as the date of loss [Reg. § 1.165-4(a)].[41] Worthlessness is generally shown by a relevant identifiable event which clearly evidences destruction of both the potential and liquidating values of a stock. If you owe money on the purchase price of the stock, you may not claim a deduction until the loan is paid off. You may establish the loss by a bona fide sale before the stock becomes entirely worthless.

Even if a stock meets the definition of a *security* for purposes of the special worthless security loss deduction provision, ascertaining when a security becomes worthless causes serious problems for the investor. Ordinarily, the loss of value may be established only by some *fixed and identifiable event,* such as bankruptcy, cessation from doing business, liquidation, or the appointment of a receiver. In exceptional cases in which the liabilities of the corporation are greatly in excess of assets and there is no reasonable expectation or hope that a continuation of the business will result in profit to the shareholders, no identifiable event is necessary to establish worthlessness. Generally, however, as long as there is a "reasonable hope and expectation that assets will exceed the liabilities of the corporation in the future," the corporation's stock is not worthless. Thus, if a shareholder may receive new shares in a reorganized, bankrupt corporation or a liquidating dividend, the stock generally is not worthless. The taxpayer must show worthlessness by the lack of a liquidating value and by identifiable events that indicate the lack of a reasonable expectation that the shares may become valuable in the future.

A taxpayer who waits until the occurrence of an identifiable event may find that the loss is disallowed because he is unable to show that the stock had any value in a prior year. If the taxpayer does not claim the loss in the earliest year possible, he faces the risk that the statute of limitations may run.

> ▶ **PLANNING TIP:** To ensure that the statute of limitations does not run on your worthless stock, you should claim a loss for the earliest year when it may possibly be allowed and to renew the claim in subsequent years if there is any reasonable chance of its being applicable to the income for those years.[42] The Code recognizes the difficulty of ascertaining the proper year of worthlessness by allowing a seven-year, instead of the usual three-year, statute of limitation for claiming a loss deduction [Code Sec. 6511(d)]. This means that you have seven years from the due date of your tax return to amend it in order to deduct a worthless security loss. In any event, it is advisable to take the deduction for the earliest year in which the security appears to be worthless. The safest course, notwithstanding the liberal seven-year rule, is for the taxpayer to give him- or herself the benefit of the doubt.

In the alternative, investors should consider selling the nearly-worthless security, even for a nominal amount, before it becomes definitely worthless. This will do two things: (1) establish the date of the loss and (2) avoid questions regarding the financial state of the corporation.

---

[41] *P.B. Osborne*, 70 TCM 243, Dec. 50,794(M), TC Memo. 1995-353, *aff'd*, CA-6, 97-2 USTC ¶ 50,524.

[42] *M.K. Young*, CA-2, 41-2 USTC ¶ 9744, 123 F2d 597.

.03 Character of Loss

The deductibility of losses associated with buying and selling securities depends on whether you are classified as a securities dealer/trader or merely a securities investor. The losses of a securities investor who only invests for personal use are deductible as capital losses because the securities are capital assets [Code Sec. 165(g); Reg. § 1.165-5(d)]. The losses of a securities dealer/trader (defined below) are fully deductible as ordinary losses.

A noncorporate taxpayer may deduct capital losses only to the extent of his or her capital gain with any excess capital loss deductible against $3,000 of ordinary income [Code Sec. 1211(b)]. Capital losses not used to reduce capital gains or ordinary income in the tax year in which they are sustained are carried forward to the next tax year [Code Sec. 1212(b)]. The carryover of losses goes on indefinitely until you use up the losses or die.

Capital assets are property owned whether or not it is connected with a trade or business. An exception is provided for stock held primarily for sale to customers in the ordinary course of a trade or business [Code Sec. 1221(a)(1)]. Other exceptions include inventory, real estate, depreciable property used in a trade or business, certain copyrights, and literary, musical, or artistic compositions.

.04 Who Qualifies as a Securities Dealer/Trader

A dealer/trader in securities is one who has an established place of business and who regularly engages in the purchase and resale of securities to customers [Reg. § 1.471-5]. The securities transactions must be substantial, frequent, regular, and continuous and the taxpayer must earn his or her livelihood primarily from the sale of securities [Reg. § 1.212-1(g)]. It is critical for the taxpayer to have customers, an established place of business and a dealer's license or certifications from the securities industry.[43] An investor who merely manages investments for his own personal account is not in the trade or business of investing. Therefore that investor's losses will only be deductible as capital losses. In determining whether a dealer or investor exists, courts will consider the following factors:

- Investment intent;
- The nature of the income derived from the activity; and
- The frequency, extent and regularity of securities transactions.[44]

To be classified as a securities dealer the following must be true:

- Trading activity must be substantial, frequent, regular and continuous enough to constitute a trade or business (sporadic trading does not constitute a trade or business); and
- The taxpayer must seek to catch the swings in the daily market movements, and to profit from these short-term changes, rather than to profit from the long-term holding of investments. Courts look at whether your securities income is princi-

[43] *S. Marrin*, 73 TCM 1748, Dec. 51,826(M), TC Memo. 1997-24, *aff'd*, CA-2, 98-2 USTC ¶ 50,490, 147 F3d 147.

[44] *H.C. Van der Lee*, CA-2, 2012-2 USTC ¶ 50,638, 501 Fed Appx 30, *aff'g*, 102 TCM 329, Dec. 58,772(M), TC Memo. 2011-234; *H.H. Hart*, 73 TCM 1684, Dec. 51,812(M), TC Memo. 1997-11, *aff'd in unpublished memo*, 98-1 USTC ¶ 50,163, 135 F3d 764, *cert. denied*, 525 US 846.

pally derived from frequent and substantial sales of securities rather than from dividends, interest, or long-term appreciation.

A trader buys and sells securities with reasonable frequency in an effort to catch the swings in the daily market movements and thus profit on a short-term basis. On the other hand, an investor purchases securities to be held for capital appreciation and income, usually without regard to short-term developments that would influence the price of the securities on the daily market.[45]

To qualify as a securities dealer and to have losses be fully deductible, the taxpayer must have customers, an inventory of securities and sales must be substantial, frequent, and regular. If trading activities do not rise to this level, the taxpayer will be classified as a mere investor for his or her own account and losses will be subject to the capital loss limitations. In addition, the taxpayer will not be entitled to deduct all of the ordinary and necessary expenses of carrying on that investment activity under Code Sec. 162. Under Code Sec. 212, however, investment expenses will be deductible as a miscellaneous itemized deduction to the extent that total miscellaneous itemized deductions exceed two percent of adjusted gross income [Ch. 9].

.05 Worthless Security Deduction Following Entity Reclassification

When an election is made to change the classification of an entity from a corporation to a disregarded entity, the shareholder of that entity is allowed a worthless security deduction if the fair market value of the entity's assets, including intangible assets such as goodwill and going concern value, does not exceed the entity's liabilities.[46]

Reg. § 301.7701-3(g)(1)(iii) provides that an eligible entity classified as an association that elects to be classified as a disregarded entity is deemed to distribute all of its assets and liabilities to its single owner in liquidation of the association. Reg. § 1.332-2(b) provides that a parent corporation that completely liquidates its 80-percent-or-more-owned subsidiary may claim a worthless stock loss only if the parent receives nothing for its stock because the entity's liabilities exceed FMV (under water). A shareholder therefore receives no payment for its stock in a liquidation if, at the time of the liquidation, the FMV of the corporation's assets is less than its liabilities. Thus, the worthless stock deduction may be claimed in situations where the FMV of the reclassified entity's assets are less than the entity's liabilities so that the parent receives no payment on the deemed liquidation of the entity. In determining the FMV of a corporation's assets, all of its assets, including tangible and intangible assets (such as goodwill and going concern value) and assets that may not appear on the corporation's balance sheet, must be taken into account.

¶13,045 DEMOLITION OF BUILDINGS

Generally, taxpayers must add losses incurred in connection with the demolition of buildings to their basis in the land upon which the demolished building was located [Code Sec. 280B]. This means the taxpayer may claim no deduction until the taxpayer disposes of the land.

---

45 *C.H. Liang*, 23 TC 1040, Dec. 20,917 (1955), *acq.* 1955-1 CB 4.

46 Rev. Rul. 2003-125, 2003-2 CB 1243.

.01 Demolition of Home in a Disaster Area

A taxpayer can claim a casualty loss deduction when he or she is forced to abandon or demolish a residence because of a disaster if (1) the residence is located in a federally declared disaster area, (2) demolition or evacuation is ordered by the state or local government within 120 days of the federal determination, and (3) the residence has been rendered unsafe because of the disaster [Code Sec. 165(k)].

¶13,050 ABANDONMENT LOSSES

A loss incurred in a business or in a transaction entered into for profit that arises from the sudden termination of usefulness in that business or transaction of any nondepreciable property can be deducted if the business or transaction is discontinued or the property is permanently discarded from use in that business or transaction. The tax year in which the loss is actually sustained is not necessarily the tax year in which there is an overt act of abandonment or loss of title to the property [Reg. § 1.165-2(a)].

When depreciable property is abandoned, the difference between the taxpayer's adjusted basis in the property and any salvage value may be recognized as a loss [Reg. § 1.167(a)-8].

.01 Act of Abandonment Required

The intention to abandon standing alone is not sufficient to establish a recognition event; instead, there must be an affirmative act of abandonment of an asset, or placing the asset in a supplies or scrap account. You must be able to show permanent withdrawal from business use such as the sale, exchange, or actual abandonment of the asset [Reg. § 1.167(a)-8(a)].[47] The IRS concluded in Field Attorney Advice 20133101F[48] that a taxpayer was not entitled to claim an abandonment loss deduction for costs incurred in an attempted stock offering because the planned stock offering was merely postponed rather than abandoned or terminated as required under Code Sec. 165(a) in order to claim an abandonment loss.

Intangible assets such as leases may be the subject of an abandonment loss. An abandonment loss does not result simply from cessation of use, or mere diminution in a property's value because diminution in value fails to satisfy the requirement that a loss be "evidenced by closed and completed transactions, fixed by identifiable events." Losses from sales or exchanges, or from casualties, are not eligible abandonment losses. In addition, you may not claim an abandonment loss for stock in trade or property held in inventory that has declined in value [Reg. § 1.165-2].

.02 Abandonment Loss Claimed in Year Loss Sustained

A taxpayer may claim the abandonment loss deduction in the year the loss is actually sustained. This is not necessarily the tax year when the act of abandonment or the loss of title to the property occurs [Reg. § 1.165-2].

---

[47] FSA 200141026.

[48] Field Attorney Advice 20133101F (Aug. 7, 2013).

Example 13-18: Amounts spent in drilling test holes to find water for a business are capital expenditures. However, if sufficient water is not found and the project is abandoned, the entire cost is deductible as a loss.[49]

A loss deduction is available for goodwill allocable to the abandoned part of a business.[50]

.03 Distinguish Abandonment Losses from Predevelopment Capital Expenditures

Expenses incurred by a real estate developer in connection with the acquisition of real estate can only be deducted as an abandonment loss if the acquisition was actually abandoned.[51] If the expenditures are merely part of an integrated plan that was not implemented the loss will be denied. Distinguish abandonment losses from predevelopment costs incurred in the process of acquiring a capital asset which must be capitalized.

¶13,055 LOSSES OF FARMERS

Losses incurred in the operation of a farm as a business are deductible in the same manner as losses from any other trade or business, including carryover and carryback of the net operating loss [Reg. § 1.165-6; Code Sec. 172].[52] Thus, if a farmer operates a farm in addition to being engaged in another trade or business, and sustains a loss from the farm operation, the amount of loss sustained may be deducted from gross income received from all sources, provided that the farm is not operated for recreation or pleasure. Farming losses may, however, be subject to the "at-risk" limitation set forth in Code Sec. 465. See ¶ 13,100 for further discussion of the at-risk limitation. In addition, passive investors in farming syndicates may be limited by the passive loss rules as set forth in Code Sec. 469 and as discussed further in ¶ 13,090.

.01 Deterioration of Crops in Storage

A farmer cannot claim a deduction for deterioration or shrinkage in weight or decrease in value of farm products held for favorable markets. However, the shrinkage can be reflected in inventory for farmers who use an inventory method of accounting [Reg. § 1.165-6(b)].

.02 Destruction of Prospective Crops

A taxpayer cannot deduct a loss due to destruction by frost, storm, flood, or fire. This is a loss of anticipated profits [Reg. § 1.165-6(c)]. See ¶ 13,010.

.03 Livestock or Produce

Casualty or theft losses of livestock or produce bought for sale are deductible if the taxpayer reports income on the cash method. If the taxpayer reports income on an

---

[49] Rev. Rul. 61-206, 1961-2 CB 57.

[50] *C.M. Strauss*, DC-LA, 62-1 USTC ¶ 9131, 199 FSupp 845.

[51] *FRGC Investment, LLC*, 84 TCM 508, Dec. 54,926(M), TC Memo. 2002-276.

[52] Treas. Dept., IRS Publication 225, "Farmers' Tax Guide" (2012 Ed.), p. 26.

accrual method, the taxpayer should claim casualty and theft losses on property bought for sale by omitting the item from the closing inventory for the year of the loss. A separate deduction may not be claimed.

If the taxpayer raises and sells livestock, plants, produce, and crops the taxpayer cannot deduct a loss for the value of losses suffered, except as a loss reflected in inventory. A loss not reflected in inventory that results from the death of any purchased livestock may be deducted like any other business casualty loss if it is not compensated for by insurance or otherwise. This applies when death is the result of disease, exposure, injury or an order of state or federal authorities. The taxpayer's deductible amount is his or her actual purchase price less any depreciation allowable. The cost of any feed, pasture or care that has been deducted as an expense of operating cannot be included as part of the cost of the stock to determine the loss [Reg. § 1.165-6(d)].

> **NOTE:** If a state or the federal government pays for livestock killed or other property destroyed for which a loss was claimed in a prior year, you must include the amount received as income in the year the payment is made.

.04 Loss Reflected in Inventory

If the taxpayer's gross income is determined by the use of inventories, they cannot take a deduction separately for livestock or products lost during the year, whether bought for resale or produced on the farm. These losses will be reflected in inventory by reducing the livestock or products on hand at the close of the year. This reduces gross income from the business by the amount of the loss [Reg. § 1.165-6(f)(2)].

.05 Operating a Farm and Another Business

If the taxpayers own and operate a farm and also have another trade, business or calling, they can deduct farm operation losses from gross income received from other sources (1) only if they engaged in the farming for profit [¶ 13,085] and (2) only to the extent allowed by the passive loss rules under Code Sec. 465 if they do not materially participate in the farming activity [¶ 13,090].

.06 How Farm Operating Losses Are Treated on Return

A taxpayer may claim farm operating losses as deductions from adjusted gross income if they operate the farm as a business or hold the property for the production of rents or royalties. If they operate the farm themselves, they should report an operating loss on Schedule F of Form 1040. If they rent farm land out for a flat fee, they should report any loss from the rental activity on Schedule E of Form 1040. If rental income is based on farm production or crop shares, taxpayers should report any rental activity loss on both Schedule E and Form 4835.

.07 NOLs of Farmers

The carryback period for a farming loss is five years [Code Sec. 172(b)(1)(G)]. The carryforward period for losses is 20 years. A farming loss is defined as the lesser of: (1) the amount of a taxpayer's net operating loss for the tax year if only income and deductions attributable to the taxpayer's farming business were taken into account; or (2) the amount of the net operating loss for the tax year [Code Sec. 172(i)].

.08 Application of Uniform Capitalization Rules to Farmers

The uniform capitalization (UNICAP) rules of Code Sec. 263A apply to plants and animals produced by certain partnerships, corporations, and tax shelters required to use the accrual method of accounting regardless of the length of the preproductive period of the plant or animal. For further discussion of the UNICAP rules see ¶17,045. For other taxpayers engaged in a farming business, the uniform capitalization rules do not apply to the cost of producing plants with a preproductive period of two years or less or to the costs of producing animals regardless of the length of their preproductive period [Code Sec. 263A(d)]. The uniform capitalization rules do not apply to:

1. Certain costs to replace destroyed or damaged plants or
2. Eligible farmers who make an election not to have the uniform capitalization rules apply to their farming businesses.

Farming business is defined in Code Sec. 263A(e)(4) as the trade or business of farming and includes the operation of a nursery or sod farm, and the raising or harvesting of trees bearing fruit, nuts, or other crops, or ornamental trees other than evergreen trees that are more than six years old when severed. Reg. § 1.263A-4(a)(4) defines a farming business as a trade or business involving the cultivation of land or the raising or harvesting of any agricultural or horticultural commodity. Examples include the trade or business of operating a nursery or sod farm; the raising or harvesting of trees bearing fruit, nuts, or other crops; the raising of ornamental trees (other than evergreen trees that are more than six years old at the time they are severed from their roots); and the raising, shearing, feeding, caring for, training, and management of animals. The term *harvesting* does not include contract harvesting of an agricultural or horticultural commodity grown or raised by another.

Similarly, merely buying and reselling plants or animals grown or raised entirely by another is not raising an agricultural or horticultural commodity [Reg. § 1.263A-4(a)(4)]. A taxpayer is engaged in raising a plant or animal, rather than the mere resale of a plant or animal, if the plant or animal is held for further cultivation and development prior to sale. In determining whether a plant or animal is held for further cultivation and development prior to sale, consideration will be given to all of the facts and circumstances, including: the value added by the taxpayer to the plant or animal through agricultural or horticultural processes; the length of time between the taxpayer's acquisition of the plant or animal and the time that the taxpayer makes the plant or animal available for sale; and, in the case of a plant, whether the plant is kept in the container in which it was purchased, replanted in the ground, or replanted in a series of larger containers as it is grown to a larger size.

.09 Limitation on Farming Losses

The amount of net farm losses that taxpayers, other than C corporations, who receive Commodity Credit Corporation loans or certain other farm subsidies may claim is limited to the greater of $300,000 ($150,000 for a married taxpayer filing separately) or the taxpayer's net farm income for the prior five tax years [Code Sec. 461(j)(4)(B)(i)]. The loss that is limited is referred to as the "excess farm loss" [Code Sec. 461(j)(4)(A)].

In the case of a partnership or S corporation, the limit is applied at the partner or shareholder level, so that partners and shareholders take into account their proportionate distributive shares of farm income, gain, loss, and deduction allocated to them by the partnership or S corporation. The partner or shareholder also takes into account applicable subsidies received by a partnership or S corporation during the tax year, regardless of whether the subsidies are treated as income for federal tax purposes [Code Sec. 461(j)(5)(B)].

A loss that is disallowed in one tax year by this provision is carried forward indefinitely to the next tax year and treated as a deduction attributable to a farming business of the taxpayer in that tax year [Code Sec. 461(j)(2)].

¶13,060 LOSS DISTINGUISHED FROM CAPITAL EXPENDITURE

Some items that seem like losses are really nondeductible contributions of capital.

.01 Contributions to Corporation or Partnership

A stockholder may not claim a loss deduction for voluntary capital contributions to a corporation. These are treated as capital expenditures that increase the stock's basis. Taxpayers may realize a loss if they are forced to make advances to the corporation from which they can expect no return.[53] Advances by partners to partnerships are generally treated the same as advances by stockholders to corporations [Ch. 20].

.02 Surrender of Stock to Corporation

Taxpayers may make a capital contribution by surrendering part of their stock to a corporation. Generally, the cost of the surrendered stock increases the retained stock's basis, so no "loss" deduction is available.

DISALLOWED LOSSES

¶13,065 WASH SALES

The wash-sale provisions were designed to prevent investors holding stock that has depreciated in value from realizing a loss for tax purposes by selling it, while at the same time maintaining the investment by repurchasing the same or substantially identical stock. A wash sale occurs when taxpayers buy substantially identical stock or securities within 30 days before or after the sale of such securities. They cannot currently deduct losses on wash sales. Instead, they add the disallowed loss to their basis in the newly acquired securities, which increases loss or reduces gain when they eventually sell the stock [Code Sec. 1091; Reg. §§1.1091-1, -2]. Thus, while taxpayers cannot prematurely claim losses, they can receive an investment return that is partially or wholly tax-free. Options to purchase or sell securities are securities in their own right and are subject to the wash sale rules.

NOTE: Taxpayers must clearly identify wash sale transactions on Schedule D [Instructions for Schedule D].

---

[53] *G.A.E. Kohler Est.*, 37 BTA 1019, Dec. 10,052, *acq.* 1938-2 CB 18.

Example 13-19:

	Item	*Date of Purchase*	*Cost*	*Date of Sale*	*Selling Price*	*Indicated Loss*
(A)	100 shares of X stock	1-5-13	$10,000	2-19-13	$8,500	$1,500
(B)	100 shares of X stock	2-9-13	$9,000			

The indicated loss of $1,500 on the sale of the 100 shares in lot A is disallowed because within 30 days before the sale, identical stock (lot B) was bought. The basis of stock in lot B becomes $10,500 ($9,000 + $1,500). The result would be the same if identical securities were bought within 30 days after the sale.

The taxpayer's loss on the sale of securities will also be disallowed if the taxpayer's spouse, controlled company, or another related taxpayer buys replacement securities within the prohibited time period.

The wash sale provisions do not apply to sales of stock or securities that result in a profit. Nor do they apply to commodity futures contracts since these are not considered stock or securities. Shares acquired within the 61-day period need not be in the same quantity as the shares sold for the wash sale provisions to apply. But you can deduct a loss to the extent the number of shares sold exceed the number purchased.

For discussion of the application of the wash sale rules to mutual funds, see ¶ 6090.

.01 Short Sales

Rules similar to the general wash sale rules apply to losses realized on the closing of a short sale of stock or securities if you either sell or sell short substantially identical stock or securities. The 30-day period is measured from the date of the closing [Code Sec. 1091(e)].

.02 The Holding Period

For securities bought in connection with a wash sale includes the period for which you held the original securities [Code Sec. 1223(4); Reg. § 1.1223-1].

Example 13-20:

	Item	*Date of Purchase*	*Cost*	*Date of Sale*	*Selling Price*	*Indicated Loss*
(C)	100 shares of X stock	3-3-13	$5,000	8-29-13	$4,500	$500
(D)	100 shares of X stock	9-2-13	$4,600	5-1-14	$4,500	

The indicated loss of $500 on the sale of 100 shares in lot C is disallowed because within 30 days after the sale, identical stock or securities (lot D) were bought. The basis of the securities in lot D becomes $5,100 ($4,600 plus $500). The recognized loss on the sale of lot D is $600 ($5,100 – $4,500). The period held is counted as follows: From March 3, 2013 to August 29, 2013 and September 2, 2013 to May 1, 2014. Thus, the securities in lot D were held more than one year, and the loss is treated as long-term capital loss. Note: The original securities (lot C) were not held from August 29, 2013 to September 2, 2013, so that period cannot be included in the holding period.

.03 Substantially Identical Stock or Securities

The wash sale provisions apply only when you purchase securities that are substantially identical to those sold. The securities must be the same in all important particulars. Any significant difference in the securities purchased and those sold, such as bonds with different interest rates or stock in different corporations, renders the wash sale rules inapplicable.

.04 Dealers

The wash sale rules do not apply if you are a dealer in stock or securities and the loss is sustained in a transaction made in the ordinary course of your business [Code Sec. 1091(a)].

¶13,070 SHAM SALES

Although you can sell property for the sole purpose of writing off a loss, you get a deduction only if the sale is bona fide. A sham transaction made only for the record will not suffice. For example, if there is a repurchase agreement, the sale is termed a sham and your loss deduction disallowed. The IRS considers the following circumstances in determining whether there is a repurchase agreement: (a) the relationship, business association, or friendship between you and purchaser; or (b) actual repurchase of the property.[54] What's more, a loss on a real sale to a related taxpayer may be disallowed [¶13,075].

¶13,075 SALES TO RELATED TAXPAYERS

No loss deduction is allowed when you sell property to certain related taxpayers. If the related taxpayer later sells the property, his gain is reduced by the amount of your disallowed loss. Once the Code Sec. 267's related-party provisions apply to a particular year, their application does not change even if there is a subsequent change in the debtor-creditor relationship. In *Ronald Morgan Cadillac, Inc.*[55] an accrual basis corporation was denied an interest deductions and a related carryback of losses on a note held by a related cash basis taxpayer, despite the sale of that note to an unrelated party. The original holder of the note was a related party to the taxpayer. Once the note and the accrued and unpaid interest were sold to an unrelated party, the taxpayer attempted to deduct interest payments and carry back the resulting losses to satisfy tax liabilities in a previous year. The limitation on interest deductions, however, applied to that tax year and continued to apply to all holders of the note in that year until the interest was actually paid.

---

[54] *S.M. Shoenberg*, CA-8, 35-1 USTC ¶9333, 77 F2d 446, *cert. denied*, 296 US 586, 56 SCt 101.

[55] *Ronald Morgan Cadillac, Inc.*, CA-9, 2004-2 USTC ¶50,394, *cert. denied*, 4/18/05.

.01 Family Losses

No deduction is allowed for a sale or exchange made, directly or indirectly, between:

- Husband and wife;
- Brothers and/or sisters (whole or half-blood); or
- Ancestors and lineal descendants [Code Sec. 267(b), (c); Reg. § 1.267(b)-1].

The loss is disallowed even if the sale is made indirectly. The sale of stock on a stock exchange by one family member followed the same day by the purchase of the same number of shares of the same stock at similar prices by another family member is considered an indirect sale between members of the family.

A forced sale is treated the same as a voluntary sale. For example, a loss sustained by a mortgagor on foreclosure sale to a family member as mortgagee is not deductible.

The no-deduction rule does not apply to any transfer incident to a divorce [Code Sec. 267(g)].

.02 Sales Between Corporation and Shareholders

No deduction is allowed if a sale is made, directly or indirectly, between a shareholder and a corporation if the shareholder owns more than 50 percent in value of the outstanding stock of the corporation, directly or indirectly [Code Sec. 267(b)(2); Reg. § 1.267(c)-1].

.03 Sales Between Taxpayer and Exempt Organization

No deduction is allowed if you sell property to a tax-exempt organization controlled by you or your family [Code Sec. 267(b)(9); Reg. § 1.267(b)-1].

.04 Sales Between Executor and Estate Beneficiary

Except for transactions in satisfaction of a pecuniary bequest, no deduction is allowed if an executor of an estate sells property to a beneficiary of such estate [Code Sec. 267(b)(13)]. Reason: An estate and a beneficiary of an estate are treated as related persons for purposes of:

- The disallowance of a loss on the sale of an asset to a related person [Code Sec. 267(b)]; and
- The disallowance of capital gain treatment on the sale of depreciable property to a related person [Code Sec. 1239].

.05 Constructive Ownership of Stock

In applying the above rules, you are considered to own not only the stock registered in your name, but stock you constructively own under rules explained below [Code Sec. 267(c); Reg. § 1.267(c)-1].

Stock Ownership Rule

Stock owned, directly or indirectly, by or for a corporation, partnership, estate or trust, is considered as being owned proportionately by or for its shareholders, partners, or beneficiaries.

> **Example 13-21:** Mr. Albert owns 60 percent of Corp. P's stock, and Corp. P owns all the stock of Corp. Q. Albert is the constructive owner of 60 percent of

Corp. Q's stock. Since Albert owns more than 50 percent in value of the stock of Corp. Q, a loss on the sale of property to the corporation would be disallowed. Furthermore, a loss on property sold by the corporation to Albert would also be disallowed.

Example 13-22: Mr. Crowley and Mr. Dillon are members of the C&D Partnership that owns 4,000 of the 5,000 shares of Corp. U. Crowley's proportionate interest in the partnership is 60 percent. In addition, Crowley personally owns 500 shares of stock of Corp. U. Dillon, a 40 percent partner, does not personally own any shares of Corp. U. Crowley is the constructive owner of 2,400 shares of U stock (60 percent of 4,000) and the actual owner of 500 shares. Since Crowley is the owner of more than 50 percent in value of the outstanding stock of Corp. U, a loss would be disallowed on any sale of property between the partnership and Crowley.

Partnership Rule

An individual who actually or constructively (other than under the family attribution rule) stock in a corporation is considered as owning the stock owned, directly or indirectly, by or for a partner.

Example 13-23: Same facts as in Example 13-22. Under rule (1) above, Mr. Dillon is treated as the owner of 40 percent of the shares owned by C&D Partnership—or 1,600 shares. And since he is the constructive owner of these shares, he is also treated as owning the 2,900 shares actually and constructively owned by Crowley. Since this makes Dillon a more-than-50 percent owner of U, any loss on a sale of property between Dillon and U is not deductible.

Family Rule

A taxpayer is treated as owning the stock owned, directly or indirectly, by a member of his or her family (spouse; brothers and sisters, whether by the whole or half-blood; ancestors, and lineal descendants) [Code Sec. 267(c)(4)].

Example 13-24: Mr. Easton owns 30 percent, his wife 10 percent, and his wife's brother (Easton's brother-in-law) 20 percent of the stock of Corporation V. Easton is the constructive owner of 10 percent of V stock and the actual owner of 30 percent (40 percent in all). Since Easton is the owner of less than 50 percent in value of the outstanding stock of Corporation V, a loss would be allowed on a sale of property between them. Mrs. Easton is the constructive owner of 50 percent of V stock (the 30 percent owned by Mr. Easton plus the 20 percent owned by her brother) and the actual owner of 10 percent (60 percent in all). Since Mrs. Easton is the owner of more than 50 percent in value of the outstanding stock of Corporation V, a loss would be disallowed on a sale of property between them.

.06 Recognized Gain on Resale

If your loss on a sale to a related taxpayer is disallowed and the related taxpayer later sells the property at a gain, a special rule limits the income tax consequences. The related taxpayer pays tax on the gain from the sale of the property only to the extent that it exceeds your disallowed loss [Code Sec. 267(d); Reg. § 1.267(d)-1].

Example 13-25: Mr. Clark bought stock for $7,500 and sold the stock to his wife, Martha, for $5,000. The $2,500 loss is disallowed. Martha sells the stock for $8,000. Her recognized gain is $500, figured as follows:

Martha's selling price	$8,000
Her basis	5,000
Gain	$3,000
Disallowed loss	2,500
Excess of gain over disallowed loss (gain taxed)	$ 500

There is a similar result when losses are disallowed under the wash sale provisions [¶ 13,065].

Divisible Property

Suppose you sell property at a loss to a related taxpayer and the relative later sells a part. A proportionate part of your disallowed loss is allocated to the partial sale and reduces the relative's taxable gain.

Example 13-26: Mrs. Harry sold class A stock which had cost her $1,100 and common stock which had cost her $2,000 to her spouse for a lump sum of $1,500. The loss of $1,600 ($3,100 less $1,500) was disallowed. When the spouse bought the shares, the value of class A stock was $900 and the value of the common stock was $600. The spouse later sold the class A stock for $2,500. His gain is $1,400, determined as follows:

Selling price by spouse of class A stock		$2,500
Less: Basis allocated to class A stock ($900/$1,500 × $1,500)		900
Gain		$1,600
Less: Disallowed loss sustained by Harry on class A stock sale:		
Basis of class A stock to Harry	$1,100	
Amount realized by Harry on class A stock ($900/$1,500 × $1,500)	900	
Disallowed loss to Harry on class A stock sale		200
Taxable gain on sale of class A stock by spouse		$1,400

Exchange or Gift of Property by Buyer

Suppose your relative exchanges the property for other property in a nontaxable exchange, and then sells the other property. The gain on the sale of the other property is reduced by your disallowed loss, just as though the property sold were the original property bought from you. But only the person who bought the original property gets the benefit of the rule. Thus, if your relative gives the property to another person, the other person would have to pay the full tax if he sold the property at a gain.

¶13,080 GAMBLING LOSSES

.01 Tax Treatment of Gambling Losses

The Internal Revenue Code treats gambling losses in one of two ways depending on whether the gambler is characterized as a casual or professional gambler. Taxpayers who are engaged in the trade or business of gambling are characterized as professional gamblers and may deduct both their gambling losses plus all wagering costs and all gambling related nonwagering business expenses, such as transportation, meals and entertainment, admission, subscription and data fees against their gambling winnings above the line as a trade or business expense in arriving at adjusted gross income [Code Sec. 62(a)(1)].

In contrast, taxpayers who are not in the trade or business of gambling are typically called recreational or casual gamblers and may deduct their gambling losses less favorably below the line as an itemized deduction in arriving at taxable income [Code Sec. 63(a)].[56] If, however, a taxpayer claims the standard deduction rather than itemizing deductions, the taxpayer will be unable to net the gambling winnings against gambling losses, except to the extent they occur as part of a single transaction.[57]

Irrespective of whether the taxpayer is a professional or a casual gambler, "losses from wagering transactions shall be allowed only to the extent of the gains from such transactions" [Code Sec. 165(d); Reg. § 1.165-10].

.02 Gambling Winnings Defined

Gambling winnings are defined in Code Sec. 3402 (q)(4)(A) as proceeds from a wager that is determined by reducing the amount received by the amount of the wager. This means basically that every gambling transaction in a casino including every pull of the lever or push of a button on a slot machine could result in gambling winnings. It is up to the taxpayer to prove gambling losses and taxable income.

.03 Gambling Defined as Trade or Business

In *Groetzinger*,[58] the United Stated Supreme Court addressed the issue of whether a taxpayer's gambling activity was a trade or business. The Court concluded that Groetzinger was engaged in the trade or business of gambling because he devoted 60 to 80 hours each week for 48 weeks to parimutuel wagering, primarily on greyhound races. In addition, the taxpayer gambled at racetracks 6 days a week and spent a substantial amount of time studying racing forms, programs, and other materials. Even though the taxpayer received income from other sources during the year, the taxpayer had no

[56] *R.L. Hill*, 63 TCM 2323, Dec. 48,059(M), TC Memo. 1992-140; *R.V. Johnston*, 25 TC 106, Dec. 21,295 (1955); *R. Cromley*, 96 TCM 42, Dec. 57,497(M), TC Memo. 2000-176; *H.H. Heidelberg*, 36 TCM 566, Dec. 34,392(M), TC Memo. 1977-133.

[57] *G.D. Shollenberger*, 98 TCM 667, Dec. 58,044(M), TC Memo. 2009-306.

[58] *R.P. Groetzinger*, SCt, 87-1 USTC ¶9191, 480 US 23, 107 SCt 980.

other profession or type of employment during the 48 weeks he devoted to gambling. The Supreme Court stated that in order for a taxpayer to be engaged in a trade or business, "the taxpayer must be involved in the activity with continuity and regularity and * * * the taxpayer's primary purpose for engaging in the activity must be for income or profit. A sporadic activity, a hobby, or an amusement diversion does not qualify." The Supreme Court concluded that "if one's gambling activity is pursued full time, in good faith, and with regularity, to the production of income for a livelihood, and is not a mere hobby, it is a trade or business." In Reg. § 1.183-2(b), the IRS provides a nonexclusive list of nine factors that should be considered when determining a taxpayer's profit motive as follows:

1. *Manner in which the taxpayer carries on activity.* If the taxpayer conducts the gambling activities in a businesslike manner, such as maintaining complete books and records, a profit motive is likely to exist.
2. *Expertise of taxpayer/consultants.* Extensive study and consultation with experts indicates profit motive.
3. *Time and effort expended in carrying on the activity.* Devotion of time and effort to conducting gambling activities indicates profit motive.
4. *Expectation that assets may increase in value.* May apply to gambling activities because asset involved in gambling usually is cash.
5. *Success of the taxpayer in carrying on other activities.* Taxpayer's success in other nongambling business activities may indicate a profit motive.
6. *Taxpayer's history of income/losses realized in activity.* History of substantial gambling losses may indicate that taxpayer does not conduct the gambling activities for profit.
7. *Amount of occasional profits from activity.* Occasional gambling gains may indicate a profit objective.
8. *Taxpayer's financial status.* If taxpayer does not have substantial income from nongambling activities, it may indicate that taxpayer engages in gambling for profit.
9. *Personal pleasure or recreation.* Since gambling at a casino is commonly understood to be a pleasant amusement, a taxpayer has to show that there is no pleasure in gambling such as the absence of friends or family members when gambling.

.04 Professional Gamblers

In the following cases, the Tax Court held that the taxpayers were professional gamblers and were therefore entitled to report gambling winnings and losses on Schedule C, *Profit or Loss from Business* and deduct both wagering costs and gambling related nonwagering business expenses from gambling winnings:

In *R.A. Mayo,*[59] the Tax Court held that the taxpayer was a professional gambler who engaged in gambling on horse races. The court distinguished the nongambling business expenses from gambling expenses and held that the deduction of wagering losses was limited under Code Sec. 165(d) to the amount of wagering gains. Therefore the

[59] *R.A. Mayo,* 136 TC 81, Dec. 58,524 (2011); AOD-2011-06, IRB 2012-3.

taxpayer could fully deduct nongambling business expenses to offset other ordinary incomes or carry over the net gambling loss to other tax years. Note that the IRS Chief Counsel has issued an action on decision recommending acquiescence to the Tax Court's decision in *R.A. Mayo.*

In *J.F. Chow,*[60] the Tax Court held that a retired physician was a professional gambler and could deduct her gambling loss on Schedule C because she engaged in gambling activities with continuity and regularity. The court reached this result even though she had no business plan, did not seek or follow expert advice, and did not adhere to her alleged pattern of strategic times to gamble because she had disposed of a substantial amount of property for gambling purposes, and this disposition could severely reduce their future income. This fact proved to the court that the gambling activity was much more than a hobby.

In *T.M. Le,*[61] the Tax Court concluded that the taxpayers who believed in feng shui were professional gamblers. They used feng shui to determine their "lucky days" to gamble. During every weekend and off days, the taxpayers traveled 130 miles each way to casinos and gambled for long hours. The court found that even though they gambled primarily on weekends, the number of hours devoted to gambling activities was similar to the number they worked for their jobs during the weekdays. Moreover, the court stated that investment decisions in a stock or a business based on feng shui or some other cultural judgment would not by itself be "irrational" and the fact that the approach was unsuccessful did not make it irrational. Instead, the court believed that the taxpayers used their best judgment and successfully tested their business approach.

In *L.M. Myers,*[62] the Tax Court found that a taxpayer who spent 25-35 hours per week working at the trucking business and about 40 hours per week on the gambling activity was a professional gambler because she approached the activity in a businesslike manner, relied upon the expertise of her own observations and those of casino employees, spent a considerable amount of time playing slot machines, showed that she had business acumen in her operation of a trucking company, made an occasional profit from the activity and admitted that she viewed the activity as work, deriving no personal pleasure from the gambling.

In *J. Castagnetta,*[63] the Tax Court concluded that a taxpayer who was part-time truck driver who also spent 40 hours per week on handicapping and betting on horse races was a professional gambler because he gambled in a businesslike manner, he carried on the activity in accordance with practices learned from extensive study and consultation with experts, and he used much of his personal time and effort to carry on the activity. He maintained numerous statistics for each horse race and used this information for handicapping horse races. He also reviewed videotapes of the horse races for further study, used a computer to maintain his gambling activity, read numerous books on gambling and handicapping horse races, and regularly sought advice from and provided advice to other gamblers.

---

[60] *J.F. Chow,* 99 TCM 1193, Dec. 58,155(M), TC Memo. 2010-48, *aff'd,* CA-9, 2012-2 USTC ¶50,585, *cert. denied,* 133 SCt 1304 (02/19/2013).

[61] *T.M. Le,* TC Summary Op. 2010-94 (July 19, 2010).

[62] *L.M. Myers,* TC Summary Op. 2007-194 (Nov. 19, 2007).

[63] *J. Castagnetta,* TC Summary Op. 2006-24 (Feb. 13, 2006).

.05 Casual Gamblers

In the following cases, the Tax Court concluded that the taxpayers were casual gamblers:

In *S.B. Whitten*,[64] the Tax Court concluded that a contestant who appeared on TV's Wheel of Fortune was not a professional gambler because he was not in the trade or business of either gambling or appearing as a contestant on a television game show. Therefore, his expenses including the cost of meals, transportation and lodging for the contestant and his family were deductible only as a miscellaneous itemized deduction subject to the 2 percent floor.

In *R.L. Moore*,[65] the Tax Court concluded that an individual who worked 40 hours a week as a traveling x-ray technician and gambled at slot machines in casinos when he was off work was not a professional gambler because he did not engage in his gambling activities in a businesslike manner nor did he attempt to increase his profitability in this venture. He failed to maintain records of his gambling transactions and never consulted with gambling experts. His income was derived primarily from his work as an x-ray technician and he enjoyed gambling in his free time.

In *D.J. Hastings*,[66] the Tax Court concluded that an accounting and consulting business owner who gambled primarily on weekends and holidays for at least eight hours at a time was not in the trade or business of gambling because she failed to show a profit motive. The taxpayer did not carry on her gambling activities in a businesslike manner. The taxpayer failed to maintain records of her gambling transactions despite her professional background as an accountant. Moreover, her occasional and weekend gambling activity did not indicate a profit objective.

In *M.N. Merkin*,[67] the Tax Court concluded that a psychiatrist's activity of playing video poker did not rise to the level of a trade or business activity because he failed to prove that his primary objective for gambling was to earn income or make a profit. Moreover, he did not carry on his gambling activity in a businesslike manner as evidenced by his failure to maintain any receipts, books, or records and his sole reliance on the casinos to track all of his playing time, betting history, wins, and losses. Even though he read video poker magazines and kept abreast of the machines and their respective payout histories at the casino, he did not use this knowledge to adjust his gambling strategies.

In *Calvoa*,[68] the Tax Court held that the owner of a textile corporation was not in the trade or business of gambling and therefore could not deduct his gambling losses as a business expense on Schedule C. The substantial time that the taxpayer invested in preparing for his gambling trips and developing a strategy for playing slot machines failed to rise to the level of a trade or business because the taxpayer failed to provide daily contemporaneous records of his gambling activities. Additionally, the taxpayer's

---

[64] *S.B. Whitten*, 70 TCM 1064, Dec. 50,963(M), TC Memo. 1995-508.

[65] *R.L. Moore*, 102 TCM 74, Dec. 58,707(M), TC Memo. 2011-173.

[66] *D.J. Hastings*, 97 TCM 1355, Dec. 57,774(M), TC Memo. 2009-69.

[67] *M.N. Merkin*, 95 TCM 1576, Dec. 57,459(M), TC Memo. 2008-146.

[68] *J. Calvoa*, 93 TCM 988, Dec. 56,862(M), TC Memo. 2007-57.

livelihood did not depend on playing the slot machines. His primary income came from his salary from an unrelated business where he was president and 100-percent owner.

In *M. Ferguson*,[69] the Tax Court concluded that a building operator engineer who spent more than 1,000 hours of his free time during the year at issue playing video poker was not a professional gambler because his gambling activities did not have the requisite profit motive to support a conclusion that he was engaged in the trade or business of gambling. He did not carry on his poker activity in a businesslike manner in that he did not maintain adequate books or records, but relied on casino records to track his wins and losses. In addition, he did not seek additional assistance with or adjust his strategy, even though he never had a winning year.

.06 Practice Pointers for Characterization as Professional Gambler

Classification of a gambler as either a professional or casual gambler can have significant tax differences. Taxpayers who want to establish themselves as professional gamblers should take note of the following guidelines:

1. Professional gamblers should conduct their business in a professional businesslike manner. Separate books and bank accounts should be maintained for all gambling activities. They should maintain a daily log of gambling wins and losses, execute a written business plan, and document their successful business strategies.
2. Professional gamblers should be able to prove their extensive study of written materials in the field of gambling and engage in regular consultation with gambling experts.
3. Professional gamblers should be able to exhibit actual or honest profit motive.
4. Professional gamblers should be able to show that their livelihood depends on gambling.

¶13,085 HOBBY LOSSES AND EXPENSES

The IRS and the courts are often suspicious of taxpayers claiming business deductions in connection with activities that look more like hobbies than businesses. For that reason, activities such as ownership of a sailboat or yacht are subject to strict scrutiny. The IRS fears that taxpayers are actually deducting personal living expenses associated with a hobby rather than deducting ordinary and necessary business expenses as required by law. As a result, the law requires taxpayers writing off expenses incurred in operating and maintaining any hobby to prove that they were operating a business activity and that they had a profit motive.

Deductions for an activity not carried on for profit (e.g., hobbies such as stamp collecting) are treated as miscellaneous itemized deductions, which means that they are deductible only to the extent that they exceed 2 percent of adjusted gross income. However, hobby expenses that are attributable to rental or royalty income (e.g., renting out a yacht) generally are deductible up to the amount of hobby income—these

[69] *M. Ferguson*, TC Summary Op. 2007-30 (Feb. 28, 2007).

expenses are not subject to the 2 percent floor [Code Secs. 62, 67; Temp. Reg. § § 1.62-1T, 1.67-1T].

> **NOTE:** The hobby loss rules also apply to an S corporation [Chapter 21] engaged in activity not carried on for profit.

The hobby loss rules also apply to an S corporation [Chapter 21] engaged in activity not carried on for profit. Taxpayers are not subject to the hobby loss rules if they can show that the activity was engaged in with an actual and honest intent to make a profit [Code Sec.183; Reg. § § 1.183-1–1.83-4]. Whether the requisite profit objective exists is determined by looking at all the surrounding facts and circumstances [Reg. § 1.183-2(b)]. In determining whether such objective exists, it may be sufficient that there is a small chance of making a large profit [Reg. § 1.183-2(a)]. Greater weight is given to objective facts than to taxpayer's mere statement of intent. There is a rebuttable presumption that your activity is engaged in for a profit, thus enabling you to deduct your losses, if you can show that profit resulted from the activity in three out of five consecutive years [Code Sec. 183(d); Reg. § 1.183-1(a)].

.01 Aggregating Activities to Circumvent Hobby Loss Limitations

In order to avoid the Code Sec. 183 hobby loss limitations, taxpayers often try to aggregate activities that would separately be considered hobbies with other similar activities to create one profitable activity not subject to the hobby loss limits. The IRS regulations sanction these combinations if the certain requirements are satisfied.

Reg. § 1.183-1(d)(1) provides that if the taxpayer is engaged in several undertakings, they can be combined to constitute one activity. The following factors must be considered when deciding whether a taxpayer can aggregate activities for purposes of the hobby loss limitations. The three primary factors to consider are:

1. The degree of organizational and economic interrelationship of various undertakings;
2. The business purpose which is (or might be) served by carrying on the various undertakings separately or together in a trade or business or in an investment setting; and
3. The similarity of various undertakings.

Generally, the IRS will accept the taxpayer's characterization of several undertakings either as a single activity or as separate activities. However, the taxpayer's characterization will not be accepted when it appears it is artificial and cannot be reasonably supported under the facts and circumstances of the case.

For example, Reg. § 1.183-1(d)(1) provides that where land is held primarily with the intent to profit from increase in its value, and the taxpayer also engages in farming on that land, the farming and the holding of the land will only be considered a single activity if the farming activity reduces the net cost of carrying the land for its appreciation in value. Thus, farming and holding of the land will be considered a single activity only if the income derived from farming exceeds the deductions attributable to the farming activity.

In *Keanini*,[70] the Tax Court held that a taxpayers' dog breeding and grooming operation could be aggregated and considered a single activity for purposes of the

[70] *S. Keanini*, 94 TC 41, Dec. 46,354 (1990).

Code Sec. 183(a) hobby loss rules. Similarly, in *Engdalh*,[71] the court held that the holding of land and the breeding, raising, and selling of horses on that land constituted a single activity because the primary purpose of purchasing the land was the breeding, raising, and selling of the horses. In *Estate of E. Brockenbrough*,[72] the court concluded that the taxpayers' operation of a farm that simultaneously involved horse breeding and rodeos was a single, for-profit activity. The two activities were complementary in nature and shared a close organizational and economic relationship.

But in *Estate of R.E. Stangeland*,[73] the court concluded that a consulting business could not be aggregated with several businesses involving retail stores, restaurants, retail developments and a small airplane rental operation because the businesses had separate management and locations and functioned as separate units.

.02 Horse Breeding and Showing

In the case of horse racing, breeding and showing, taxpayers only have to show a profit in two out of seven consecutive years ending with the current year in order to claim deductions in connection with horse activity [Code Sec. 183 (d); Reg. § 1.183-1(c)(1)]. In *Routon*,[74] taxpayers were entitled to claim deductions in connection with their Arabian horse-breeding and training activity because they engaged in the activity with the intent of realizing a profit. Although the activity produced losses, it was operated in a businesslike manner, and the taxpayers maintained adequate books and records, consulted with Arabian horse industry experts, invested half of their annual income in the undertaking, devoted substantial time to the activity, and did not ride the horses for pleasure. Moreover, the taxpayer created two other successful business ventures with respect to which he had limited expertise at the outset, and the record established that he intended for the horse-breeding activity to generate a profit.

In *Topping*,[75] the Tax Court concluded that a taxpayer's equestrian activities were an integral part of her equestrian-based interior design business and were therefore conducted for profit as a single activity. The taxpayer was successful in this case because she proved that she generated prospective clients for her interior design business as a result of her exposure and reputation as an equestrian rider, as well as her popularity in a local equestrian club. She showed that virtually all of her clients were equestrian-related contacts who depended on her knowledge and expertise of horses in designing horse barns and interiors of recreational homes related to equestrian activities. Since the taxpayer's current and potential clientele were very wealthy individuals, the court found that her exposure and reputation as a professional equestrian rider materially benefited her design activities.

---

[71] *T.N. Engdahl*, 72 TC 659, Dec. 36,167 (1979) (Acq.).

[72] *Estate of E. Brockenbrough*, 76 TCM 1063, Dec. 53,006(M), TC Memo. 1998-454.

[73] *Estate of R.E. Stangeland*, 100 TCM 156, Dec. 58,308(M), TC Memo. 2010-185.

[74] *R.A. Routon*, 83 TCM 1062, Dec. 54,609(M), TC Memo. 2002-7. *See also M.T. Helmick*, Dec. 57,947(M), TC Memo. 2009-220; *R.S. Miller*, 96 TCM 211, Dec. 57,548(M), TC Memo. 2008-224; *M.E. Blackwell*, 102 TCM 137, Dec. 58,722(M), TC Memo. 2011-188.

[75] *T.L. Topping*, 93 TCM 1120, Dec. 56,903(M), TC Memo. 2007-92.

In most horse breeding cases, however, the taxpayers typically fail to prove that they engaged in horse-related activities for the purpose of making a profit, so expenses incurred are deductible only to the extent of income generated by the activity.[76]

.03 Election Available to Postpone Profit Determination

If your activity did not make a profit in the early years you can make an election to extend the time frame for determining whether or not your business has been profitable. You may elect to delay a determination regarding whether the presumption applies until the close of the fourth (or sixth, in the case of horse racing, breeding or showing) tax year after the tax year in which the taxpayer first engages in the activity. You can make the Code Sec. 183(e) election to suspend the presumption until the close of the fourth (or sixth, in the case of horse racing, breeding or showing) tax year from the time the activity is started by filing Form 5213, *Election to Postpone Determination As To Whether the Presumption Applies That an Activity is Engaged in for Profit,* with the IRS no later than three years after the due date of your return (determined without extensions) for the first tax year in which you engaged in the activity [Code Sec. 183(e)]. If you have received written notice from the IRS proposing to disallow deductions attributable to the activity, you must file Form 5213 within 60 days of receiving the notice. By making the election, you automatically extend the statute of limitations for a deficiency during any year in the suspension period to at least two years after the return's due date for the last year in the five (or seven) year period.

.04 How to Prove an Activity Is Engaged in For Profit

To guide you in proving that an activity is engaged in for profit, the IRS has provided a list of factors that should be taken into account as follows [Reg. § 1.183-2(b)]:

- Conduct your activity in a businesslike manner. This means that you should keep detailed and accurate records of all income generated, expenses, activities, maintenance, repairs, etc.;[77] In order to prove a profit motive, taxpayers need to have a business plan including a budget and separate bank account. It behooves taxpayers trying to prove a profit motive to keep accurate records of all business activity including records of income and expenses. In addition, it is a good idea for

[76] *See L.L. Foster*, 104 TCM 90, Dec. 59,131(M), TC Memo. 2012-207; *J.M. Chandler*, CA-9, 2012-2 USTC ¶50,584; *T.L. Phemister*, 63 TCM 2759, Dec. 48,153(M), TC Memo. 1992-221; *J. Freed*, 88 TCM 288, Dec. 55,755(M), TC Memo. 2004-215; *M.G. Bunney*, 86 TCM 233, Dec. 55,256(M), TC Memo. 2003-233; *E. Giles*, 89 TCM 770, Dec. 55,932(M), TC Memo. 2005-28; *R.E. Corrigan*, 89 TCM 1313, Dec. 56,034(M), TC Memo. 2005-119; *R.E. Cramer*, 80 TCM 114, Dec. 53,971(M), TC Memo. 2000-229; *L.J. Novak*, 80 TCM 128, Dec. 53,976(M), TC Memo. 2000-234; *R.J. McKeever*, 80 TCM 358, Dec. 54,040(M), TC Memo. 2000-288; *C.A. McGee*, 80 TCM 438, Dec. 54,067(M), TC Memo. 2000-308; *R.L. Beck*, 82 TCM 347, Dec. 54,431(M), TC Memo. 2001-198; *J.E. Hastings*, 84 TCM 663, Dec. 54,968(M), TC Memo. 2002-310; *T.T. Kuberski*, 84 TCM 178, Dec. 54,840(M), TC Memo. 2002-200.

[77] *W.L. Wilmot*, 102 TCM 599, Dec. 58,839(M), TC Memo. 2011-293 (photography activity not engaged in for profit); *W. Hellings*, 67 TCM 1988, Dec. 49,626(M), TC Memo. 1994-24 (charter boat deductible); *D.E. Wesley*, 93 TCM 1062, Dec. 56,885(M), TC Memo. 2007-78 (professional musician could not deduct cost of recording equipment because activity not conducted in businesslike manner). *See R.J. Zenzen*, 102 TCM 58, Dec. 58,701(M), TC Memo. 2011-167 (taxpayer's drag racing activity not engaged in for profit).

taxpayers to obtain expert advice from a professional in the field on how to operate the business for a profit;[78]

- Be able to show your wide expertise or the expertise of your advisors in the activities;
- Be able to show the substantial time and effort that you spent in conducting your activity;[79]
- Be able to show that you expected the asset to appreciate in value;
- Be able to show your successes in carrying on other ventures in your life;
- Be able to explain that your losses were attributable to circumstances beyond your control such as drought, disease, fire, theft, weather damages, or depressed market conditions or that they occurred during the initial or start-up stage of the activity. Be able to show some years when the business was profitable;
- Be able to show the amount of occasional profits, if any, which you earned;[80]
- Be able to show you were not rich and that you needed the activity in question to be profitable to support your family and children;
- Avoid indicating that you, your family, and your friends derived any personal pleasure or recreational benefits from the activity. In *Brown*,[81] the Tax Court concluded that the taxpayer operated his gold mining activity for profit and therefore could deduct expenses in excess of income from the activity. One of the factors that influenced the court's decision was the fact that the taxpayer sacrificed his entire weekends to travel alone to the mine and even faced risks of injury while visiting the site; and
- Be able to show that you entered into the activity with a profit motive—not just to claim tax deductions for what otherwise would be a nondeductible personal expense. For example, in *M.P. Remler*,[82] married taxpayers were not entitled to deduct expenses attributable to their autistic child's education because the special education activity was not a *bona fide* business activity engaged in for profit. The couple satisfied only one of the nine factors that are evaluated in determining whether an activity is entered into for profit. Moreover, the couple's reimbursement under the Individuals with Disabilities in Education Act (IDEA) did not establish that they engaged in the special education of their son with the primary intent of making a profit. In *R.L. Rowden*,[83] a taxpayer could not deduct expenses associated with ownership and maintenance of an airplane because none of the activities related to the airplane was a trade or business. The court concluded that the taxpayer's primary purpose for engaging in the activities was not income or profit. His recordkeeping was disorganized and unreliable, he did not have an expectation that assets used in the activity would appreciate, he did not have had a good-faith expectation of realizing a profit on his operation, he introduced no

[78] *A. Zarins*, 81 TCM 1375, Dec. 54,282(M), TC Memo. 2001-68, *aff'd in unpublished order*, 2002-1 USTC ¶50,471.

[79] *R.D. Bagley*, DC-CA, 2013-2 USTC ¶50,462.

[80] *D.W. Wolf*, 67 TCM 2327, Dec. 49,705(M), TC Memo. 1994-93, *aff'd in unpublished per curiam opinion*, CA-4, 96-1 USTC ¶50,039 (yacht not deductible).

[81] *Brown*, TC Summary Op. 2001-184.

[82] *M.P. Remler*, 90 TCM 502, Dec. 56,196(M), TC Memo. 2005-265, *aff'd in unpublished opinion*, CA-9, 2007-2 USTC ¶50,813.

[83] *R.L. Rowden*, 97 TCM 1159, Dec. 57,744(M), TC Memo. 2009-41.

evidence regarding the financial performance of his aircraft maintenance activity for previous years or evidence regarding occasional profits, and the individual's full-time job allowed the individual to conduct the aircraft maintenance activity at a loss.

- Avoid discussing with the IRS agent or in a courtroom how valuable the tax deductions were to you on your tax return.[84]

It is possible for a taxpayer to prove that a sailboat racing activity was engaged in with an actual and honest intent to make a profit if the taxpayer can show that the activity was conducted in a businesslike manner and that any losses suffered were attributable to unforeseen and/or circumstances beyond the taxpayer's control.[85]

¶13,090 PASSIVE LOSSES

Special rules govern loss deductions from "passive" activities. These so-called passive loss rules were designed primarily to prevent taxpayers from using inflated losses generated by tax shelters to offset ordinary income from salaries, wages, dividends, and interest [Ch. 24]. Under the passive loss provisions [Code Sec. 469; Reg. § 1.469-1], taxpayers can generally deduct a loss from a passive activity only to the extent of income from other passive activities. The loss cannot be deducted against active income (e.g., salary or self-employment earnings) or portfolio income (e.g., your investment income from dividends or interest). Disallowed passive activity losses are suspended until the taxpayer either has offsetting passive income or disposes of his or her entire interest in the passive activity in a taxable transaction.

Code Sec. 469(c)(1) provides that the term "passive activity" means any activity (1) which involves the conduct of any trade or business, and (2) in which the taxpayer does not materially participate. Rental activities are also considered to be passive activities under Code Sec. 469(c)(2). However, a real estate professional can deduct rental losses against nonrental income if he or she materially participates in the rental activity as discussed later in this chapter.

Losses from a working interest in an oil or gas property are not subject to the passive activity limitations, as long as the taxpayer holds the interest either directly or through an entity that doesn't limit the taxpayer's liability (e.g., a general partnership) [Code Sec. 469(c)(3)(A); Reg. § 1.469-1(e)(4)]. The credit attributable to a working interest in an oil and gas property may be claimed to the extent of the taxpayer's regular tax liability allocable to the activity's net income.

.01 How the Passive Loss Rule Works

For purposes of the passive activity loss rule, all of the taxpayer's taxable income is divided into three parts:

---

[84] *K.F. Mattfeld*, 63 TCM 2991, Dec. 48,210(M), TC Memo. 1992-273, *aff'd in unpublished opinion*, 15 F3d 1087 (sailboat not deductible).

[85] *R. Schwartz*, 85 TCM 1058, Dec. 55,094(M), TC Memo. 2003-86, and 88 TCM 167, Dec. 55,730(M), TC Memo. 2004-193 (supplemental opinion).

- Regular income from wages and salary or professional fees;
- Portfolio (or investment) income is gross income (other than income derived in the ordinary course of a trade or business) that is attributable to (1) interest; annuities; royalties; dividends on C corporation stock; income (including dividends) from a real estate investment trust, regulated investment company, real estate mortgage investment conduit, common trust fund, controlled foreign corporation, qualified electing fund, or cooperative; (2) dividends on S corporation stock; (3) the disposition of property that produces income of a type described in (1); and (4) the disposition of property held for investment [Temp. Reg. § 1.469-2T(c)(3)(i)]. Temp. Reg. § 1.469-2T(c)(3)(ii) identifies several sources of income that are not considered portfolio income. This income includes "income from investments made in the ordinary course of a trade or business of furnishing insurance or annuity contracts or reinsuring risks underwritten by insurance companies." The phrase "made in the ordinary course of a trade or business" contemplates (1) that the investment occur at a time when the taxpayer is conducting a trade or business or reinsuring risks, and (2) that the investment be an ordinary and necessary part of the business of reinsuring risks;[86] and
- Passive income, such as is generated by most tax shelters and other types of passive investments.

As a general rule, there will be no traffic across these three parts. Thus, regular income will be offset by deductions permitted by the Code, (*e.g.*, home mortgage interest and state and local property taxes). The passive loss rules provide that passive losses may only be used to offset income earned from that (or another) passive activity, not to offset regular or investment income. In sum, salary and portfolio income are separated from passive activity losses and credits. The passive loss limitation ensures that salary and portfolio income cannot be offset by tax losses from passive activities until the amount of such losses is determined on a fully taxable disposition. However, a taxpayer's passive losses can shelter his passive income.

More specifically, deductions from passive trade or business activities to the extent that they exceed the income from all passive activities (except portfolio income) generally may not be deducted against compensation for services or portfolio income (interest, dividends, or gain from the sale of property held for investment). Portfolio income, which includes interest, annuities, and dividends, as well as gain from the disposition of bonds, stocks, annuities, or other property held for investment, is not treated as income from a passive activity [Code Sec. 469(e)(1)(A)].

> **Example 13-27:** The taxpayer invests in three risky partnerships which promise huge long-term financial rewards and abundant tax deductions. Partnership 1 invests in harnessing solar energy to generate electricity. Partnership 2 invests in oil and gas wells, and Partnership 3 invests in an independent filmmakers. Partnership 1 generated a profit and your share in the profit was $2,000. That same year, Partnership 2 and 3 each generated losses of $100,000. The taxpayer's income is $600,000 without regard to these investments. If the passive loss rules did not apply, taxable income for the year would be $402,000 [$600,000 – $200,000 ($100,000 × 2) + $2,000].

---

[86] *H.V. More*, 115 TC 125, Dec. 54,002 (2000).

If the passive loss rules are applied to the same facts, the taxpayer cannot deduct the $200,000 passive losses in excess of $2,000 passive gain and taxable income for the year would be $600,000 [$600,000 + $2,000 – $2,000].

.02 Taxpayers Affected

The passive loss rules generally apply to individuals, estates, trusts, closely held C corporations to a limited extent as discussed below, and personal service corporations [Code Sec. 469(a)(2)]. Even though the passive loss rules do not apply to grantor trusts, partnerships, and S corporations directly, they do apply to owners of such entities.

Special Rule for Closely Held Corporations

Closely held corporations are subject to the passive activity limitations. A corporation is a "closely held corporation" if it satisfies the following requirements [Code Sec. 469(j)(1); Temp. Reg. § 1.469-1T(g)(2)(ii)]:

- It is a C corporation;
- At any time during the last half of the tax year more than 50 percent in value of the corporation's outstanding stock is owned, directly or indirectly, by five or fewer individuals; and
- It is not a personal service corporation.

Special passive loss rules exist for closely held corporations [Code Sec. 469(e)(2)]. A closely held corporation can offset net active income with its passive activity loss. It can also offset the tax attributable to its net active income with its passive activity credits. However, a closely held corporation cannot offset its portfolio income with its passive activity loss. Net active income is defined as the corporation's taxable income figured without any income or loss from a passive activity or any portfolio income or loss.

> **Example 13-28:** A closely held C corporation has $400,000 of passive losses from a rental activity, $500,000 of active business income and $100,000 of portfolio income. The passive losses reduce the active business income to $100,000, but may not be applied against the portfolio income.

Personal Service Corporation Defined

The passive activity loss rules apply to personal service corporations in an attempt to prevent investors from sheltering personal service income simply by incorporating as a personal service corporation and then using that entity to purchase passive activity investments and deduct passive losses. A taxpayer is a *personal service corporation* if all of the following requirements are met [Code Sec. 469(j)(2); Temp. Reg. § 1.469-1T(g)(2)(i)]:

- The taxpayer is a C corporation (not an S corporation);
- The principal activity of the taxpayer during the "testing period" (defined below) for the tax year is the performance of personal services;
- During the testing period such services are substantially performed by employee-owners. This requirement is met if more than 20 percent of the corporation's compensation cost for its activities of performing personal services during the testing period is for personal services performed by employee-owners.

- Employee-owners own more than 10 percent of the fair market value stock of the outstanding stock in the taxpayer on the last day of the testing period. Ownership is determined under the attribution rules of Code Sec. 318, with the following modification: a shareholder will be considered as owning the same proportion of the stock owned, directly or indirectly, by or for the corporation as the shareholder owns in the corporation.

A person is generally considered an employee-owner of a personal service corporation if both the following apply [Reg. § 1.441-3(g)]:

1. He or she is an employee of the corporation on any day of the testing period. Any shareholder who performs personal services for, or on behalf of, the corporation will be treated as an employee even if the legal form of that person's relationship to the corporation is such that the person would be considered an independent contractor for other purposes.
2. The person owns *any* outstanding stock of the corporation on any day of the testing period.

Personal services are those in the fields of health (including veterinary services), law, engineering, architecture, accounting, actuarial science, performing arts, and consulting.

Definition of *Testing Period*

Generally, the *testing period* for a particular tax year is the preceding tax year [Reg. § 1.441-3(c)(2)]. However, in the case of a new corporation, the testing period is the period beginning on the first day of the tax year and ending on the earlier of:

- The last day of the tax year, or
- The last day of the calendar year in which the tax year begins.

Special Rules Regarding Publicly Traded Partnerships

The passive activity loss rules apply to a taxpayer's income or loss from a passive activity held through a publicly traded partnership (PTP) which is defined as a partnership whose interests are traded on an established securities market or are readily tradable on a secondary market [Code Sec. 469(k)(2)]. Taxpayers can offset losses from passive activities of a PTP only against income or gain from passive activities of the same PTP. Similarly, they can offset credits from passive activities of a PTP only against the tax on the net passive income from the same PTP.

.03 Passive Activity Defined

A *passive activity* is one of the following:

- The conduct of any trade or business activity in which taxpayers do not "materially participate" during the tax year [Code Sec. 469(c)(1)(B)]; or
- Any rental activity regardless whether or not they materially participate in the activity [Code Sec. 469(c)(2)]. There are special rules for real estate rental activities and real estate professionals which are discussed in detail later.

Activities That Are Not Considered Passive Activities

The following activities are not passive activities and are therefore not subject to the passive activity loss limitation (but they may be subject to the at-risk rules, discussed later):

- Trade or business activities in which you materially participated for the tax year;
- A working interest in an oil or gas well which you hold directly or through an entity that does not limit your liability (such as a general partner interest in a partnership). It does not matter whether you materially participated in the activity for the tax year [Code Sec. 469(c)(3)(A); Temp. Reg. § 1.469-1T(e)(4)(i)]. However, if, but for this rule, your interest in an oil or gas well would be an interest in a passive activity and you have a net loss from the well for the tax year, your disqualified deductions from the well for the year will be treated as passive activity deductions for the year and a ratable portion of your gross income from the well will be treated as passive activity gross income for the year [Temp Reg. § 1.469-1T(e)(4)(ii)];

  Disqualified deductions. A taxpayer's "disqualified deductions" from an oil or gas well for a tax year are the taxpayer's deductions attributable to the well and allocable to the tax year and with respect to which economic performance occurs at a time during which the taxpayer's only interest in the working interest is held through an entity that limits the taxpayer's liability with respect to the drilling or operation of the well [Temp. Reg. § 1.469-1T(e)(4)(ii)(C)(2)].
- The rental of a dwelling unit that was also used for personal purposes during the year for more than the greater of 14 days or 10 percent of the number of days during the year that the home was rented at a fair rental;
- An activity of trading personal property for the account of those who own interests in the activity. [Temp Reg. § 1.469-1T(e)(6)]; and
- Rental real estate activities in which the taxpayer materially participated as a real estate professional, as discussed later.

.04 Material Participation

The definition of *material participation* is important because the taxpayer will not have their losses limited by the passive loss rules if he or she can prove material participation in an activity [Code Sec. 469(h)]. An individual materially participates in an activity if, based on all of the facts and circumstances, the individual participates in the activity on a "regular, continuous, and substantial basis"[87] during the year (facts and circumstances test) [Temp. Reg. § 1.469-5T(a)(1)], or the individual participates in the activity for more than 500 hours during the year (500-hour test) [Temp. Reg. § 1.469-5T(a)(1)]. A taxpayer will be found to materially participate in an activity if the taxpayer satisfies the following seven tests:

1. Prove participation in the activity for more than 500 hours during the tax year [Temp. Reg. § 1.469-5T(a)(1)]. For purposes of this test, any "participation" is

[87] *P.D. Montgomery*, 105 TCM 1865, Dec. 59,566(M), TC Memo. 2013-151 (satisfied "regular, continuous and substantial" test); *A. Iverson*, 103 TCM 1128, Dec. 58,921(M), TC Memo. 2012-19 (failed to satisfy test).

counted unless the work is not of a type that is customarily done by an owner of such an activity and one of the principal purposes for the performance of such work is to avoid the passive loss rules, or if the work is done in the taxpayer's capacity as an investor. Work performed as an investor includes the following:

a. Studying and reviewing financial statements or reports on operations of the activity
b. Preparing or compiling summaries or analyses of the finances or operations of the activity for your own use
c. Monitoring the finances or operations of the activity in a nonmanagerial capacity [Temp. Reg. § 1.469-5T(f) (2) (ii)].

Temp. Reg. § 1.469-5T(f) (4) provides that the extent of an individual's participation in an activity may be established by any reasonable means. Contemporaneous daily time reports, logs, or similar documents are not required if the extent of such participation may be established by other reasonable means. Reasonable means may include the "identification of services performed over a period of time and the approximate number of hours spent performing such services during such period, based on appointment books, calendars, or narrative summaries."

The Tax Court has held that while the regulations permit some flexibility, they do not allow a post event "ballpark guesstimate" of time committed to participation in a rental activity or the unverified undocumented testimony of taxpayers.[88] For purposes of these requirements, work in an activity is treated as "participation" only if the taxpayer owns an interest in the activity (directly or indirectly) at the time the work is done. This means that work of a nonowner employee is generally not treated as participation. In addition, any participation by a spouse in the activity is treated as participation by the taxpayer, even if a joint return is not filed.

> ▶ **PLANNING TIP:** If the taxpayer is going to be involved in an activity for at least one day a week for a 52-week year, the taxpayer should make certain that each day consists of 10 hours, so that he or she would participate for 520 hours for the 52-week year. In contrast, if the taxpayer worked only 7 hours per day once a week for the 52-week year, participation would total only 364 hours, which is below the 500-hour threshold.

2. Prove that participation constitutes substantially all of the participation in the activity of all individuals for the tax year, including participation of individuals who did not own any interest in the activity [Temp. Reg. § 1.469-5T(a)(2)].
3. Prove that the taxpayer participated in the activity for more than 100 hours during the tax year and participated in the activity at least as much as any other individual (including individuals who did not own any interest in the activity) for the year [Temp. Reg. § 1.469-5T(a)(3)].
4. The activity is a significant participation activity and participation in all such activities exceeds 500 hours. A significant participation activity is one in which

[88] *R. Vandergrift*, 103 TCM 1092, Dec. 58,916(M), TC Memo. 2012-14; *J.F. Moss*, 135 TC 365, Dec. 58,336; *A.H. Jafarpour*, 103 TCM 1880, Dec. 59,087(M), TC Memo. 2012-165; *P.T.W. Lum*, 103 TCM 1557, Dec. 59,019(M), TC Memo. 2012-103; *B. Bartlett*, 106 TCM 102, Dec. 59,602(M), TC Memo. 2013-182.

the taxpayers participate more than 100 hours during the tax year but do not materially participate under any of the other six tests [Temp. Reg. § 1.469-5T(a)(4)].

5. Prove that the taxpayer materially participates in the activity for any five of the preceding ten tax years [Temp. Reg. § 1.469-5T(a)(5)].
6. The activity is a personal service activity in which the taxpayer materially participated for any three (whether or not consecutive) preceding tax years [Temp. Reg. § 1.469-5T(a)(6)]. An activity is a personal service activity if it involves the performance of personal services in the fields of health (including veterinary services), law, engineering, architecture, accounting, actuarial science, performing arts, consulting, or any other trade or business in which capital is not a material income-producing factor.
7. The taxpayer must satisfy a facts and circumstances test proving that the taxpayer participated on a "regular, continuous, and substantial" basis [Temp. Reg. § 1.469-5T(a)(7)]. A taxpayer will not be considered to have materially participated in an activity under this final test if he or she participated in the activity for 100 hours or less during the year.

Material Participation by a Trust

Neither the Code nor the regulations explain how one determines whether a trust materially participates in a business for purposes of the passive activity rules in Code Sec. 469(h). The only guidance is in the legislative history which indicates that a trust materially participates in an activity if a "fiduciary, in his capacity as such, is so participating." The only court opinion addressing how a trust establishes material participation for purposes of Code Sec. 469 is *Mattie K. Carter Trust*,[89] where the district court held that in determining material participation for trusts, the activities of the trust's fiduciaries, employees, and agents should be considered to determine whether the trust's participation is "regular, continuous, and substantial." The Court rejected the government's position that the determination should be made solely by referring to the activities of the trustee, finding this approach arbitrary and creating unnecessary statutory ambiguity.

In direct opposition to the decision in *Mattie K. Carter*, the IRS took the view in Technical Advice Memorandum 201317010,[90] that the only way for a trust to establish material participation for purposes of Code Sec. 469(h) is for the fiduciaries, in their capacities as fiduciaries, to be involved in the operations of the relevant activities on a "regular, continuous, and substantial basis." The only relevant activities are those of the fiduciaries. Based on the facts in that technical advice memorandum, the IRS concluded that the two trusts did not materially participate in the activities of two S corporations because the IRS declined to attribute the activities of the owners to the trusts. The IRS only viewed the activities of the fiduciaries' as relevant for purposes of establishing whether the trusts materially participated.

---

[89] S. Rep't No. 99-313, 99th Cong., 2d Sess. at 735 (1985); *Mattie K. Carter Trust*, DC-TX, 2003-1 USTC ¶ 50,418, 256 FSupp2d 536.

[90] TAM 201317010 (Jan. 18, 2013). *See also* TAM 200733023 (Aug. 17, 2007) (trust materially participated only if its fiduciaries so participate); LTR 201029014 (April 7, 2010) (trust could materially participate if the trustee met the standard in Code Sec. 469(h)(1)).

In order for a trust to establish material participation, the following guidelines should be followed:

1. The trust must establish who is acting as a fiduciary on the trust's behalf. The individuals could include agents, employees or advisors.
2. The trust must establish which fiduciary's hours will count in determining material participation.
3. The trust must determine what hours will qualify as participation for purposes of proving material participation.

The issue of material participation by trusts and estates is also important in order to avoid exposure to the 3.8 percent net investment income tax which is imposed on estates and trusts on their undistributed net investment income which includes income from any passive activities [Code Sec. 1411(a)(2)]. To avoid exposure to the NIIT, the estate or trust could establish material participation in the operation of the trade or business which had generated net investment income because the NIIT is not imposed on the income from the operation of an active trade or business [Prop. Reg. § 1.1411-4(a)]. See ¶ 15,170 for detailed discussion of the net investment income tax.

Retiree Allowed to Claim Farming Losses Based on Deceased Husband's Participation

In Technical Advice Memorandum 200911009 the IRS allowed a decedent's surviving spouse to satisfy the material participation requirements for claiming losses related to farming activity (ordinarily passive activity losses) based on her deceased husband's material participation in farming before his retirement. Before his death, the taxpayer's husband conducted the farming activity of raising cattle through an LLC owned by a trust. An exception under Code Sec. 2032A(b)(5)(C) authorizes the IRS to use "any application" of the rule to allow surviving spouses to meet the material participation requirement if already met by the decedent. The IRS interpreted the statute to allow a retired taxpayer to use the accumulated time of material participation by a deceased spouse prior to retirement to fulfill the requirements for claiming the farming losses. As long as the decedent had materially participated in five of the eight years before retirement and the taxpayer was retired at the time of his death, she would be treated as materially participating in the farming activity under Code Sec. 469(h)(3).

Limited Partners and Material Participation

Limited partners are treated differently, however, because the Code presumes that limited partners do not materially participate in their limited partnerships. Under Code Sec. 469(h)(2), a limited partner's interest in a limited partnership isn't treated as an interest in which the taxpayer materially participates, except to the extent provided in the regulations. Thus, Code 469(h)(2) treats losses from an "interest in a limited partnership as a limited partner" as presumptively passive.

Prop. Reg. § 1.469-5(e)(2) permits an individual taxpayer to establish material participation in a limited partnership but limits the individual taxpayer to only three of the seven regulatory tests (listed above) that ordinarily are available to prove the point. Prop. Reg. § 1.469-5(e)(3)(i) provides that an interest in an entity will be treated as an interest in a limited partnership as a limited partner if:

1. The entity in which such interest is held is classified as a partnership for federal income tax purposes under § 301.7701-3; and
2. The holder of such interest does not have **rights to manage the entity** (emphasis added) at all times during the entity's tax year under the law of the jurisdiction in which the entity was organized and under the governing agreement [Prop. Reg. 1.469-5(e)(3)(i)].

Note that these proposed regulations ease definition of a limited partnership interest because they eliminate the temporary regulations' reliance on limited liability for purposes of determining whether an interest is an interest in a limited partnership as a limited partner under Code Sec. 469(h)(2). Instead, the proposed regulations adopt an approach that relies on the individual partner's right to participate in the management of the entity. The proposed regulations focus on the individual partner's right to participate in the management of the entity when distinguishing limited partners from general partners for purposes of applying the Code Sec. 469 PAL limitations. This new focus will make it easier for individuals holding partnership interests to satisfy the material participation test because fewer partnership interests will be presumed to be limited partners for PAL purposes as they were under the temporary regulations.

Judicial Interpretations

A number of courts have addressed whether the holder of a limited liability company (LLC) should be treated as holding an interest in a limited partnership as a limited partner for purposes of applying the Code Sec. 469 material participation tests that limit the ability of the taxpayer to deduct losses. After suffering five defeats on this issue, the IRS has recently acquiesced in one case. For example, in *S.A.Gregg,*[91] an Oregon district court concluded that, in the absence of regulations to the contrary, LLC members would not be considered limited partners under the limited partner presumption found in Code Sec. 469(h)(2). In *Garnett,*[92] the Tax Court applied the general partner exception to hold that owners of interests in LLCs and LLPs are general partners, and not limited partners, for purposes of determining whether they materially participated in the LLC or LLP under the temporary Code Sec. 469 material participation regulations. In *Thompson,*[93] the Court of Federal Claims held that since an LLC member was not a limited partner under State law, the Code Sec. 469(h)(2) did not apply to limit the ability of the LLC member to deduct passive losses. Most recently, the Tax Court in *Newell,*[94] concluded that Code Sec. 469(h)(2) did not apply to the managing member of an LLC and that the member fell within the general partner exception in Temp. Reg. § 1.469-5T(e)(3)(ii). On April 5, 2010, the IRS issued an Action on Decision acquiescing in the result only in *Thompson*. This means that the IRS accepts the court's holding in the case and will follow it in disposing of cases with similar controlling facts. However, acquiescence in result only indicates that the IRS either disagrees with or has concern with some or all of the court's reasoning.

---

[91] *S.A. Gregg,* DC Ore., 2001-1 USTC ¶ 50,169, 186 FSupp2d 1123.

[92] *P.D.Garnett,* 132 TC 368, Dec. 57,875 (2009).

[93] *J.R. Thompson,* FedCl, 2009-2 USTC ¶ 50,501, *acq. in result only,* AOD 2010-02, 2010-14 IRB 515.

[94] *L.E. Newell,* 99 TCM 1107, Dec. 58,127(M), TC Memo. 2010-23; *S.K. Hegarty,* TC Summary Op. 2009-153.

> ▶ **PLANNING POINTER:** *Garnett* and *Thompson* offer LLC and LLP members greater tax planning opportunities than are available to limited partners for establishing that they have materially participated in the business of the LLC or LLP. As a result of the pro-taxpayer decisions in *Garnett* and *Thompson*, entrepreneurs can now begin offsetting their losses generated by their businesses from salary or investment income. For example, assume that the taxpayer is a successful dermatologist and a limited partner in a money-losing laser-treatment center. Assume further that the taxpayer's wife is the owner of a profitable beauty salon and spa and a limited partner in a money-losing health food store. Under *Garnett* and *Thompson*, losses from the two money-losing investments could offset the salary and investments earned by two taxpayers in the other two profitable businesses.

The presumption that a limited partnership interest is passive applies even if the partner owns the limited partnership interest indirectly through a tiered-entity arrangement (*e.g.*, owning a general partnership interest or stock in an S corporation, which in turn owns a limited partnership in another entity). Thus, the income or loss attributable to a limited partner will generally be passive.

Ways Around the Limited Partner Bias

There are two ways in which to circumvent the limited partner bias. First, a partner can prove that the limited partnership interest constituted material participation in an activity if the partner can show that he or she:

- Participated in the activity for more than 500 hours,
- Materially participated in the activity for any five tax years during the preceding 10 tax years, or
- Materially participated for any three preceding tax years in a personal service activity.

Second, a partner will not be treated as a limited partner if the partner was a general partner in the partnership at all times during the partnership's tax year ending with or within the partner's tax year. This is called the general partner exception.

.05 Rental Activities

All rental activities (except those in which the taxpayer materially participated as a real estate professional under Code Sec. 469(c)(7)) will be treated as passive [Code Sec. 469(c)(2)]. An investment activity will be treated as a rental activity for purposes of the passive loss limitation if:

- Tangible property (real or personal) is used by customers or held for use by customers, and
- The gross income received or expected to be received is principally for the use of that property, whether or not the use is under a lease, a service contract or any other type of arrangement.

Exceptions

The taxpayer's activity will not be considered a rental activity for purposes of the passive loss rules in the following situations:

- *Short-term rentals.* An activity involving the use of tangible property is not a rental activity if, on average, the period for which each customer uses the property is seven days or less [Temp. Reg. § 1.469-1T(e)(3)(ii)(A)]. This exception excludes short-term property rentals, such as automobiles, video cassettes, tuxedos, and tools. This exception also applies to short-term rentals of real property, including hotels and parking lots.

- *Significant personal services.* If the average term of the rental of tangible property is greater than seven days but less than 30 days, the activity will not be considered a rental activity if significant personal services are provided [Temp. Reg. § 1.469-1T(e)(3)(ii)(B)]. Only personal services performed by individuals are considered to be "significant personal services" for purposes of this exception [Temp. Reg. § 1.469-1T(e)(3)(iv)]. In addition, in determining significant personal services, certain "excluded services" are not taken into account. These excluded services include services necessary to permit the lawful use of the property, construction services or those which extend the useful life of the property, and those services which are customarily provided in long-term rentals of high-grade commercial and residential property, such as janitorial services.

- *Extraordinary personal services.* Even if property is used for more than 30 days, an activity will not be considered a rental activity if *extraordinary personal services* are provided in connection with the activity [Temp. Reg. § 1.469-1T(e)(3)(ii)(C)]. Extraordinary personal services are provided only if the services are performed by individuals and the customers' use of the property is incidental to receipt of the services. For example, the use by patients of a hospital's boarding facilities is incidental to the receipt of personal services from the hospital's staff. On the other hand, the long-term use of a photocopier would not qualify for this exception, even if frequent maintenance and service is required.

In *F.A. Assaf,*[95] the passive activity loss rules did not preclude a married couple from deducting leasing activity losses incurred by their limited liability company (LLC). The LLC, which owned the real property, also provided substantial support services to its attorney tenants, including answering phones, taking messages, clerking services, and other secretarial services. Thus, the payments made to the LLC were principally for the services provided, not for the space leased and, therefore, the taxpayers qualified for the extraordinary personal services exception to the passive activity rules. In addition, the wife spent a substantial amount of time on the leasing activities and legal support services and, therefore, materially participated in the LLC's activities. Therefore, because the LLC's activities were nonpassive, its losses could be netted against other income.

In Rev. Rul. 2005-64,[96] the IRS explains the circumstances under which losses incurred by a taxpayer who provides air transportation activity through a pass-through entity are passive losses under Code Sec. 469. The IRS concludes that an S corporation's lease of an aircraft for another's use, supplying neither pilot nor crew, is a rental activity and, therefore, a passive activity. Thus, losses incurred by the individual through the S corporation are subject to the passive loss limitations.

---

[95] *F.A. Assaf,* 89 TCM 694, Dec. 55,915(M), TC Memo. 2005-14.

[96] Rev. Rul. 2005-64, 2005-2 CB 600.

However, if the S corporation provides a pilot and crew to operate and maintain the aircraft, and food and fuel for travel, then the S corporation has provided "extraordinary personal services" in connection with the use of the aircraft and the aircraft rental is incidental to the customers' receipt of services [Temp. Reg. § 1.469-1T(e)(3)(ii)(C)]. An activity involving the use of tangible property is not a rental activity if extraordinary personal services are provided by the owner of the property in connection with making the property available for use by customers. Even though providing air transportation services is not a rental activity, it may still be a passive activity if the individual/sole owner of the S corporation fails to materially participate in the activity. If the owner does materially participate, the provision of air transportation services is not a passive activity and losses are not subject to the passive loss limitations.

- *Rentals incidental to nonrental activities.* The rental of property is treated as incidental to a nonrental activity only if: (i) the principal purpose for holding the property is investment and gross rental income is less than 2 percent of the lesser of the basis or fair market value of the property, (ii) the principal purpose for holding the property is use in a trade or business, the property was so used during at least two of the last five tax years, and the gross rental income is less than 2 percent of the lesser of the basis or fair market value of the property, (iii) the property is held primarily for sale to customers in the ordinary course of a trade or business, and the rental income is recognized in the year of sale, or (iv) the property is tax-exempt lodging [Temp. Reg. § § 1.469-1T(e)(3)(ii)(D) and (e)(3)(vi)].
- *Nonexclusive use.* Making property available for use is not a rental activity if the property is available during business hours for nonexclusive use by various customers [Temp. Reg. § 1.469-1T(e)(3)(ii)(E)]. This exception would apply, for example, to a golf course which sells annual memberships but which is also open on a daily basis to the public.
- *Property made available for use in nonrental activity.* If the taxpayer owns an interest in a partnership, S corporation, or joint venture which is conducting a nonrental activity, it does not constitute a rental activity when the taxpayer provides property for use in the activity in the taxpayer's capacity as an owner [Temp. Reg. § § 1.469-1T(e)(3)(ii)(F) and (e)(3)(vii)].

Self-Rental Recharacterization Rule

Code Sec. 469(c)(2) provides that income received by a taxpayer from rental activity is generally deemed passive regardless of the level of the taxpayer's participation unless the "self-rental rule" under Reg. § 1.469-2(f)(6) applies.

Reg. § 1.469-2(f)(6) provides that income from rental realty is not passive activity income if the property is rented for use in a trade or business activity in which the taxpayer materially participates for the tax year. According to this so-called "self-rental rule," when a taxpayer rents property to his own business, the rental income (which normally would be passive income) is not characterized as passive activity income. Thus, affected taxpayers are unable to use passive activity losses from their rental properties to offset rental income earned from their wholly owned businesses. They cannot artificially create passive activity income from another activity in order to absorb passive losses.

For example, in *G. Beecher*,[97] a married couple was precluded from applying losses from their various rental properties to offset rental income derived from leases of their property as office space to their wholly owned lessee corporations. The court recharacterized the couple's rental income as nonpassive income under the self-rental rule of Reg. § 1.469-2(f)(6) because the couple materially participated in the business activities of the lessee corporations.

In *Carlos*,[98] a couple who owned and rented two commercial real estate properties to two separate, wholly owned businesses in which they materially participated could not treat their combined net income from the two properties as nonpassive self-rental income. Instead, the income from the income-generating rental property was treated as a self-rental and, thus, excluded from passive activity loss computations under Reg. § 1.469-2(f)(6), whereas the loss generated by the second property was treated as a separate passive loss. Similarly, in *T.P. Krukowski*,[99] rents received by the sole shareholder of two C corporations from his lease of an office building to one of the corporations, a law firm in which he was a partner, were recharacterized as nonpassive income that could not be used to offset his losses on the lease of another building to the other corporation.

In *J. Veriha*,[100] the taxpayer could not offset one company's losses from truck rentals against another wholly owned company's income from truck rentals. The court found that the losses from one rental business were passive because they were from a rental activity , but the income from the other rental business was nonpassive, based on the material participation self-rental rule under Reg. § 1.469-2(f)(6). The taxpayer owned and materially participated in a trucking business, and controlled two companies from which the trucking business leased its tractors and trailers. He classified income from one leasing company and a net loss from the other as passive. The court disagreed and found that income from an "item of property" rented to, and for use in, a nonpassive activity in which the taxpayer materially participates should be treated as nonpassive.

In *F.J. Dirico*,[101] the Tax Court held that the passive activity loss self-rental rule didn't apply to telecommunication tower and land rental income derived by a taxpayer from his wholly owned S corporation. The taxpayer's wholly-owned S corp leased access to the towers to unrelated third parties in what was a rental activity rather than a trade or business. Therefore, the taxpayer's income from those leases constituted passive activity income (or loss). The court found that application of the self-rental rule to the taxpayer's tower and land rentals to the S corporation would depend on the existence of two conditions: (1) the S corporation must have used the properties in a trade or business activity (which, for purposes of the passive loss rules is an activity other than a rental activity), and (2) the taxpayer must have materially participated in that trade or business activity. The court found that the S corporation's leasing of towers and land to unrelated third parties was a rental activity

---

[97] *G. Beecher*, CA-9, 2007-1 USTC ¶ 50,379, 481 F3d 717. *See also L.A. Samarasinghe*, 103 TCM 1152, Dec. 58,925(M), TC Memo. 2012-23.

[98] *T.R. Carlos*, 123 TC 275, Dec. 55,748 (2004).

[99] *T.P. Krukowski*, 114 TC 366, Dec. 53,888 (2000), *aff'd*, CA-7, 2002-1 USTC ¶ 50,219, 279 F3d 547; *C.F. Sidell*, 78 TCM 423, Dec. 53,537(M), TC Memo. 1999-301, *aff'd*, CA-1, 2000-2 USTC ¶ 50,751, 225 F3d 103; *S.C. Shaw*, 83 TCM 1194, Dec. 54,640(M), TC Memo. 2002-35; *A.R. Fransen*, DC-LA, 98-2 USTC ¶ 50,776, *aff'd*, CA-5, 99-2 USTC ¶ 50,882, 191 F3d 599.

[100] *J. Veriha*, 139 TC No. 3, Dec. 59,122 (2012).

[101] *F.J. Dirico*, 139 TC 396, Dec. 59,253 (2012).

because the services provided by the S corporation were the types of services provided by any lessor or landlord. The S corporation did not use the properties in a trade or business and the court therefore concluded that the self-rental rule did not apply to the rental income received by the taxpayer.

.06 Code Sec. 469 Groupings

The definition of *activity* is important for purposes of the passive loss rules because passive losses generated by an activity will be deductible only against passive income generated by the same activity. For grouping purposes, trade or business activities are defined as activities that:

- Involve the conduct of a trade or business;
- Are conducted in anticipation of the commencement of a trade or business; or
- Involve deductible research or experimental expenditures.

It may be advantageous to consider grouping trade or business activities and rental activities for purpose of applying the passive activity loss and credit limitation rules of Section 469 [Reg. § 1.469-4]. Reg. § 1.469-4(c) permits a taxpayer to group trades or businesses together to satisfy the material participation standards [¶ 13,090.04] and avoid characterization as a passive activity. Under Reg. § 1.469-4(c)(1), trade or business activities or rental activities may be treated as a single activity if the activities constitute an appropriate economic unit for the measurement of gain or loss for purposes of the PAL rules.

Reason: Grouping can be beneficial because once two activities have been grouped into one larger activity, taxpayers only need to show materially participation in the activity as a whole. On the other hand, if the two activities are separate, taxpayers are required to show material participation in each activity which can be more difficult. In addition, if the activities are grouped together for tax purposes, taxpayers will be in a better position to use up any suspended passive losses because they have disposed of the activity.

The greatest opportunity for circumvention of the passive activity loss rules lies in the combination of rental activities (always passive and often producing losses) with trade or business activities (often active and producing income). As a result, taxpayers will only be able to group activities together if those activities form an *appropriate economic unit* for measuring gain or loss under the passive activity rules [Reg. § 1.469-4(c)(1)]. In determining whether activities constitute an appropriate economic unit and therefore may be treated as a single activity, consider the following factors:

- Similarities and differences in types of trades or business;
- The extent of common control;
- The extent of common ownership;
- Geographical location; and
- Interdependencies between activities such as whether the activities purchase or sell goods among themselves, involve products or services that are normally provided together, have the same customers, have the same employees, or use a single set of books and records to account for the activities [Reg. § 1.469-4(c)(2)].

Example 13-29: Taxpayers own a bakery and a movie theater at a shopping mall in Baltimore and a bakery and movie theater in Philadelphia. Depending on all the relevant facts and circumstances, there may be more than one reasonable method for grouping the activities. For example, taxpayers may be able to group the movie theaters and the bakeries into: (1) one activity, (2) a movie theater and a bakery activity, (3) a Baltimore activity and a Philadelphia activity, or (4) four separate activities [Reg. § 1.469-4(c)(3), Example 1].

Grouping Rental and Nonrental Activities

In general, taxpayers cannot group a rental activity with a trade or business activity. Reason: Most rental activities are considered to be passive and trade or business activities are considered to be passive only if taxpayers do not materially participate. However, the activities can be grouped together if the activities form an appropriate economic unit and:

- The rental activity is insubstantial in relation to the trade or business activity or visa versa, or
- Each owner of the trade or business activity has the same proportionate ownership interest in the rental activity [Reg. § 1.469-4(d)(i)]. A husband and wife who file a joint return are treated as one taxpayer.

In *L. Candelaria*,[102] a district court concluded that a lessor company and a related lessee partnership could be grouped as a single economic unit because the company's rental activity was insubstantial in relation to the partnership's business activity for purposes of Reg. § 1.469-4(d). Its rental activity was conducted solely for the partnership's benefit and it existed only to enhance the partnership's business activities. The partnership provided services to the community at large and its business activity was not dependent on the company's rental activity. In addition, the company's activity was insubstantial in comparison to that of the partnership under the 80/20 rule because its gross and net incomes were less than 20 percent of the combined totals of the two businesses. Therefore, the company's losses qualified for an exception to the passive loss rules and could be treated as deductible nonpassive losses.

Grouping Real Property Rentals and Personal Property Rentals

Generally, an activity involving the rental of real property and an activity involving the rental of personal property cannot be treated as a single activity and grouped together for tax purposes. However, personal property provided in connection with the real property may be treated as a single activity [Reg. § 1.469-4(d)(2)].

No Grouping Allowed: Limited Partners and Limited Entrepreneurs

Limited partners and limited entrepreneurs may not group the following activities with any other activity in another type of business [Reg. § 1.469-4(d)(3)]:

- Holding, producing, or distributing motion pictures films or video tapes;
- Farming;

[102] *L. Candelaria*, DC-TX, 2007-2 USTC ¶ 50,758, 518 FSupp2d 852.

- Leasing personal property;
- Exploring for, or exploiting, oil and gas resources; or
- Exploring for, or exploiting geothermal deposits.

If the taxpayer owns an interest as a limited partner or a limited entrepreneur in an activity described in the list above, the taxpayer may group that activity with another activity in the same type of business if the grouping forms an appropriate economic unit as discussed earlier.

A limited entrepreneur is a person who has an interest in a business organization other than as a limited partner and does not activity participate in the management of the business organization. This includes owners of interests in limited liability companies.

> **Example 13-30:** Farmer owns and operates a farm. Farmer is also a member of a limited liability company that conducts a cattle-feeding business. Farmer does not actively participate in the management of the LLC. In addition, Farmer is a limited partner in an oil and gas production limited partnership. Because Farmer does not actively participate in the management of the cattle LLC, Farmer is a limited entrepreneur in cattle LLC. Farmer's cattle-feeding business may not be grouped with any other activity that does not involve farming. Moreover, Farmer's farm may not be grouped with the cattle-feeding activity unless the grouping constitutes an appropriate economic unit for the measurement of gain or loss for purposes of the passive loss rules.

Activities Conducted Through Another Entity

A personal service corporation, closely held corporation subject to the passive loss rules, partnership, or S corporation must group its activities using the rules discussed in this section. Once the entity groups its activities, partners or shareholders of the entity may group those activities with each other, with activities conducted directly by the partner or shareholder, and with activities conducted through other Code Sec. 469 entities. A shareholder or partner may not treat activities grouped together by an Code Sec. 469 entity as separate activities [Reg. § 1.469-4(d)(5)].

Personal Service and Closely Held Corporations

Taxpayers may group an activity conducted through a personal service or closely held corporation with their other activities only to determine whether they materially or significantly participated in those other activities.

No Grouping of PTPs

Taxpayers may not group activities conducted through a publicly traded partnership (PTP) with any other activity, including an activity conducted through another PTP.

No Regrouping Allowed

Once taxpayers have grouped their activities together or have decided to keep them separate, they may not regroup them in future years unless the original grouping was clearly inappropriate or became inappropriate due to a material change in facts and circumstances. This means that once activities have been grouped together or kept separate, taxpayers must be consistent in the treatment of these activities in subsequent tax years [Reg. § 1.469-4(e)(1), (2)].

IRS May Regroup

The IRS has the authority under the regulations to regroup a taxpayer's activities if any of the activities resulting from the taxpayer's groupings are not an appropriate economic unit and a principal purpose of the taxpayer's grouping is to circumvent the passive loss rules [Reg. § 1.469-4(f)(1)].

Example 13-31: Five doctors operate five separate medical practices. Each of the doctors has tax shelter or real estate investments that generate passive losses. All five doctors form a partnership to buy and operate X-ray equipment. They receive limited partnership interests and do not materially participate in the X-ray business. Accordingly, they treat the X-ray business as a passive activity and the income it generates as passive income. On their tax returns, the doctors treat the partnership's services as a separate activity from their medical practices and offset the passive income generated by the X-ray partnership against the passive losses generated by their tax shelters and other real estate investments. According to the IRS, the medical practice and the X-ray business constitute an appropriate economic unit. The X-ray business cannot be treated as a separate activity. Moreover, the IRS would view the circumvention of the passive loss rules as the principal reason for treating the medical practices and the X-ray services as separate activities. The medical practices and the X-ray partnership should be treated as a single activity. The passive income thus generated by the X-ray business could *not* be used to offset their passive losses from tax shelters and real estate investments. Unless those activities also generated passive income, the passive losses could not be deducted at this time. The IRS also has the authority to assert the accuracy-related penalty against the doctors in this situation according to Code Sec. 6662 [Reg. § 1.469-4(f)(2), example.

Regs Provide "Fresh Start" Opportunity for Regrouping Activities to Avoid 3.8 percent Net Investment Income Tax

The net investment income surtax under Code Sec. 1411 imposes 3.8 percent surtax on the net investment income of certain individuals as well as of estates and trusts. [For detailed discussion of this tax, see ¶ 15,170.] Because the 3.8 percent surtax applies to income from a passive investment activity, but not from income generated by an activity in which the taxpayer is a material participant, taxpayers who invest in passive investments may want to increase their participation in the activity to qualify as a material participant in the activity and avoid paying the 3.8 percent net investment income tax. As explained in Temp. Reg. § 1.469-5T(a), a taxpayer can establish material participation by satisfying any one of seven tests, including: participation in the activity for more than 500 hours during the tax year; and participation in the activity for more than 100 hours during the tax year, where the individual's participation in the activity for the tax year isn't less than the participation in the activity of any other individual (including individuals who aren't owners of interests in the activity) for the year.

In order to satisfy these tests and qualify as a material participant, taxpayers who own more than one passive investment should consider grouping or regrouping their activities. Under proposed reliance regulations, taxpayers subject to the 3.8 percent net investment income surtax under Code Sec. 1411 may do a one-time regrouping under Prop. Reg. § 1.469-11(b)(3)(iv). The proposed regulations provide that taxpayers may regroup their activities in 2013 or 2014 if the taxpayer meets the applicable income threshold and has net investment income. A taxpayer may only regroup activities once pursuant to Prop. Reg. § 1.469-11(b)(3)(iv)(A).

IRS Notice Required

Taxpayers are required to report their groupings and regroupings of activities to the IRS.[103] A taxpayer must file a written statement with its original income tax return for the first tax year in which two or more trade or business activities or rental activities are originally grouped or regrouped as a single activity. If a taxpayer adds a new trade or business activity or a rental activity to an existing grouping for a tax year, the taxpayer must file a written statement with the taxpayer's original income tax return for that year. This statement must identify the names, addresses, and employer identification numbers for the trade or business activities or rental activities that are being grouped as a single activity. In addition, any statement reporting a new grouping of two or more trade or business activities or rental activities as a single activity must contain a declaration that the grouped activities constitute an appropriate economic unit for the measurement of gain or loss for purposes of the PAL rules. Taxpayers must report to the IRS, as part of their annual income tax return, their groupings and regroupings of activities and the addition of specific activities within their existing groupings of activities.

The statement reporting a regrouping must contain an explanation of why the taxpayer's original grouping was determined to be clearly inappropriate or the nature of the material change in the facts and circumstances that makes the original grouping was clearly inappropriate.

Special rules for groupings by partnerships and S corporations. Partnerships and S corporations must comply with the disclosure instructions for grouping activities provided for on Form 1065, *U.S. Return of Partnership Income* and Form 1120S, *U.S. Income Tax Return for an S Corporation*, respectively. Generally, compliance with the applicable form requires disclosing the entity's groupings to the partner or shareholder by separately stating the amounts of income and loss for each grouping conducted by the entity on attachments to the entity's annual Schedule K-1. The partner or shareholder is not required to make a separate disclosure of the groupings disclosed by the entity unless the partner or shareholder: (1) groups together any of the activities that the entity does not group together, (2) groups the entity's activities with activities conducted directly by the partner or shareholder, or (3) groups the entity's activities with activities conducted through other Code Sec. 469 entities. A shareholder or partner may not treat activities grouped together by a Code Sec. 469 entity as separate activities.

Reporting of pre-existing groupings required only upon change. A taxpayer is not required to file a written statement reporting the grouping of the trade or business activities and rental activities that have been made prior to January 25, 2010 (pre-existing groupings) until the taxpayer makes a change to the grouping.

Effect of failure to report. If a taxpayer is engaged in two or more trade or business activities or rental activities and fails to report whether the activities have been grouped

[103] Rev. Proc. 2010-13, IRB 2010-4, 329.

as a single activity, then each trade or business activity or rental activity will be treated as a separate activity for purposes of applying the PAL and credit limitation rules of Code Sec. 469. A timely disclosure shall be deemed made by a taxpayer who has filed all affected income tax returns consistent with the claimed grouping of activities and makes the required disclosure on the income tax return for the year in which the failure to disclose is first discovered by the taxpayer. If the failure to disclose is first discovered by the IRS, however, the taxpayer must also have reasonable cause for not making the disclosures. Although this default rule will generally result in unreported activities being treated as separate activities, the IRS may still regroup a taxpayer's activities to prevent tax avoidance.

▶ **PLANNING TIPS FOR GROUPING ACTIVITIES:** The facts and circumstances test now used to define *activity* afford taxpayers a degree of latitude in making the proper groupings of business and rental activities to produce the least amount of passive loss. The following guidelines should be considered in grouping activities:

- Characterize loss-generating activities as active and income-generating activities as passive where the activities reasonably can be considered an "appropriate economic unit."
- Divide each rental property in which the taxpayer owns an interest into a separate activity so that suspended losses related to the property can be claimed when the taxpayer disposes of the rental property.
- Rental activities producing losses should be combined with a trade or business activity in which you materially participated so that the losses can offset active income.
- Rental properties that are passive by definition and cannot be aggregated with an active trade or business should be grouped into units that are likely to be disposed of at the same time, because any loss on disposition is subject to limitation if it is not a disposal of the entire, or at least a substantial portion of the activity.

.07 Real Estate Professionals

A real estate professional will be able to treat rental real estate activities as nonpassive under Code Sec. 469(c)(7), and therefore, will be eligible to deduct losses from rental real estate activities against wages, salary, or professional fees if the following requirements are satisfied:

- More than half of the personal services performed during the tax year are performed in real property trades or businesses [Code Sec. 469(c)(7)(B)(i)]. For purposes of this rule *real property trade or business* is defined as "any real property development, redevelopment, construction, reconstruction, acquisition, conversion, rental, operation, management, leasing, or brokerage trade or business." This list omits real estate lending, financing, or consulting;
- The real estate professional materially participates in real property trades or businesses during the tax year. Whether the taxpayer "materially participates" in rental real estate activities is determined as if each of the taxpayer's interests in rental real estate is a separate activity-unless an election is made to treat all interests in rental real estate as one activity as provided in Code Sec. 469(c)(7)(A).

A taxpayer who fails to formally elect to aggregate real estate rental activities cannot treat them as one activity for purposes of the qualifying real estate professional rules.[104] A qualifying real estate professional who wants to make the aggregation election must file an election statement with his original income tax return for the tax year for which it is made [Reg. § 1.469-9(g)(3). According to Rev. Proc. 2011-34,[105] real estate professionals can obtain relief if they have failed to timely file the election under Reg. § 1.469-9(g)(1) which allows taxpayers to make late elections to treat all interests in rental real estate as a single rental real estate activity for purposes of the passive loss rules. In order to be eligible for an extension of time to make the election, a taxpayer must provide a sworn statement representing that all necessary steps were taken except for the timely filing of the election, and that the taxpayer had reasonable cause for the failure to make a timely election. Any taxpayer receiving relief under Rev. Proc. 2011-34 will be treated as having made a timely election to treat all interests in rental real estate as a single rental real estate activity as of the tax year for which the late election was requested.

A taxpayer can demonstrate *material participation* under seven different tests. The most common method is for a taxpayer to prove based on contemporaneous documents (not "ballpark guesstimates")[106] that he participated in an activity for more than 500 hours during the tax year; and that

- The taxpayer performs *more than* 750 hours of services during the tax year in real property trades or businesses in which he or she materially participates [Code Sec. 469(c)(7)(B)(ii)]. The taxpayer has the burden of proof on this issue. The taxpayer cannot be vague, unsupported or contradictory.[107] In the case of a joint return, these requirements are satisfied only if either spouse *separately* satisfies the more than 750 hours requirement [Code Sec. 469(c)(7)(B)]. The participation of both spouses cannot be combined to determine whether either spouse materially participates in an activity.[108]

In *J. F. Moss*,[109] the Tax Court concluded that an individual who owned four real estate rental properties could not count the hours that he considered himself "on call" to perform services on the properties toward the 750-hour threshold required to be considered a real estate professional for purposes of the passive activity loss rules. The taxpayer was required to actually "perform" the services that are counted toward the 750-hour threshold.

Thus, material participation alone is insufficient to qualify for relief under Code Sec. 469(c)(7). The taxpayer must also work more than 750 hours in real property trades or businesses. A closely held C corporation is eligible to deduct losses from real estate activities if more than 50 percent of the gross receipts of the corporation were derived from real property trades or businesses in which the corporation materially participated [Code Sec. 469(c)(7)(D)(i)]. The 750-hour test does not apply to closely held C corporations.

---

104 *K. Jahina*, TC Summary Op. 2002-150.

105 Rev. Proc. 2011-34, IRB 2011-24, 875.

106 *G. Merino*, 106 TCM 36, Dec. 59,586(M), TC Memo. 2013-167.

107 *W. Harnett*, CA-11, 2012-2 USTC ¶ 50,665, 496 Fed Appx 963, *aff'g*, 102 TCM 148, Dec. 58,725(M), TC Memo. 2011-191 (2011).

108 *D. DeGuzman*, DC-NJ, 2001-2 USTC ¶ 50,560, 147 FSupp2d 274.

109 *J.F. Moss*, 135 TC 365, Dec. 58,336 (2010).

Personal services, performed by an employee will not be treated as performed in real property trades or businesses, unless the employee is a 5 percent owner (under Code Sec. 416(i)(1)(B)) in the employer. For example, only a real estate agent, working as an independent contractor rather than as an employee (unless he owns 5 percent or more of the real estate agency), will qualify as performing services in real property trades or businesses. One way around the 5 percent owner rule is to grant stock options to the employee at an exercise price exceeding current fair market value (making it unlikely that the employee will exercise the option in the future) so that the employee is a 5 percent owner. Any person with an option to acquire stock is deemed to own such stock [Code Sec. 318(a)(4)].

In *Z. Lapid*,[110] the real estate activities of married taxpayers, which included both a trade or business and rental activity, generated only nondeductible passive losses. The trade or business involved owning four hotel condominiums that served as units in hotels whose day-to-day operations were managed by hotel management companies. Because the taxpayers failed to establish material participation, their activity with the units was passive. Hours that the wife spent studying and tracking their investments were deemed *investment activity* and, therefore, did not count toward material participation.

Limited Partners and Material Participation

A limited partner generally cannot be deemed to materially participate in a limited partnership activity unless one of the following applies:

- The limited partner participates in the activity for more than 500 hours;
- The limited partner materially participated in the activity for any five tax years during the ten tax years that immediately precede the tax year;
- The activity is a personal source activity and the limited partner materially participated in the activity for any three tax years preceding the tax year. These restrictions on the ability of a limited partner to materially participate apply to the limited partner's share of any income, loss, deduction, or credit from an activity attributable to a limited partner interest.

$25,000 Offset for Real Estate Activities

If either spouse actively participate in a rental real estate activity, they can use annually up to $25,000 of loss from the activity to offset their nonpassive income from sources such as wages and dividends [Code Sec. 469(i)(1)]. Similarly, they can offset credits from the rental real estate activity against the tax on up to $25,000 of nonpassive income after taking into account any losses allowed under this exception. In order to qualify for the $25,000 offset, the taxpayer must be an individual (or the taxpayer's estate for the tax years ending less than two years after the date of the taxpayer's death), and the taxpayer must actively participate in the rental real estate activity. The $25,000 amount is an aggregate for both losses and tax credits. Low-income housing and rehabilitation investment tax credits can be used as part of the

---

[110] *Z. Lapid*, 88 TCM 313, Dec. 55,764(M), TC Memo. 2004-222. *See also A. H. Jafarpour*, 103 TCM 1880, Dec. 59,087(M), TC Memo. 2012-165; *S.R. Wilson*, 103 TCM 1553, Dec. 48,031(M), TC Memo. 2012-101; *N.T. Uyemura*, 103 TCM 1555, Dec. 59,018(M), TC Memo. 2012-102; *P.T. Lum*, 103 TCM 1557, Dec. 59,019(M), TC Memo. 2012-103.

overall $25,000 whether or not the individual actively participates in the rental real estate activity to which the credit relates.

If taxpayers are married, filing a separate return, and live apart from their spouse for the entire tax year, their offset amount cannot exceed $12,500 [Code Sec. 469(i)(5)(A)]. However, if they live with their spouse at any time during the year and are filing a separate return, they cannot take advantage of this special offset to reduce their nonpassive income or tax on nonpassive income.

10 Percent Ownership Interest Required

Taxpayers do not actively participate in a rental real estate activity unless their interest in the activity (including a spouse's interest) was at least 10 percent by value of all interests in the activity throughout the year. For purposes of determining the 10 percent ownership requirement, separate buildings are treated as separate rental real estate activities if the degree of integration of the business and other relevant factors do not mandate treating them as parts of a larger activity such as a chain of similar stores [Code Sec. 469(i)(6)].

What Is Active Participation?

For purposes of special $25,000 offset available to real estate professionals, note that active participation is not the same as material participation. The active participation standard is considerably less demanding than the material participation standard. For example, the active participation standard can be satisfied without regular, continuous, and substantial involvement in operations, so long as you participate in the making management decisions or arranging for others to provide services (such as repairs), in a significant and *bona fide* sense. Management decisions that are relevant in this context include approving new tenants, deciding on rental terms, approving capital or repair expenditures, and other similar decisions. Services provided by an agent are not attributed to the principal, and a mere formal and nominal participation in management, in the absence of a genuine exercise of independent discretion and judgment, will be insufficient to meet the active participation standard.

> **Example 13-32:** Taxpayer owns and rents out an apartment that formerly was his primary residence, or that he used as a part-time vacation home. He will be treated as actively participating even if he hires a rental agent and others to provide services, such as repairs, so long as he participates in the decision-making process and exercise independent discretion and judgment in the management of the apartment.

A limited partner, to the extent of his limited partnership interest, is not treated as meeting the active participation standard [Code Sec. 469(i)(6)(C)]. In addition, a lessor under a net lease is unlikely to have the degree of involvement which active participation entails.

In the following example, a taxpayer who purchases an undivided interest in a shopping mall does not actively participate in the investment and will be unable to benefit from the $25,000 offset rule.

Example 13-33: A taxpayer purchases an interest from a promoter, based on a prospectus describing the investment opportunity and stressing the tax benefits of the $25,000 rule. Since one of your principal interests in the investment is to shelter income, the taxpayer relies on a professional management company which also holds an interest in the shopping mall to make all significant management decisions. In order to create an evidentiary record purporting to show active participation, the management company sends out letters detailing operating expenses, changes in tenants and new lease terms. The management company also informs about market trends, and requests approval of decisions to seek certain types of retailers as tenants. The taxpayer ratifies these decisions without independently exercising judgment. The taxpayer has not actively participated in this activity.

The $25,000 allowance is applied by first netting income and loss from all of the taxpayer's rental real estate activities in which he actively participates. If there is a net loss for the year from such activities, net passive income (if any) from other activities is then applied against it, in determining the amount eligible for the $25,000 allowance.

Example 13-34: Taxpayer has $25,000 of losses from a rental real estate activity in which he actively participates. If he also actively participates in another rental real estate activity, from which he has $25,000 of gain, resulting in no net loss from rental real estate activities in which he actively participates, then no amount is allowed under the $25,000 allowance for the year whether or not he has net losses from other passive activities for the year.

A single $25,000 loss limit is allowed in the aggregate as opposed to allowing a $25,000 loss for each activity. This $25,000 allowance must be allocated if there is more than one property involved and losses exceed $25,000. First, losses are treated as allowed before credits. Second, the allocation over all loss properties is done on a *pro rata* basis with respect to the losses (or credits) from each activity [Code Sec. 469(i)(3)(D)].

Example 13-35: Taxpayer qualifies for the full $25,000 offset. He has $10,000 of losses from activity No. 1 and $40,000 from activity No. 2. Under the *pro rata* allocation rule, $5,000 of loss is treated as allowed from activity No. 1 and $20,000 is treated as allowed from activity No. 2.

.08 Income Limitations

The $25,000 maximum offset amount ($12,500 for married individuals filing separate returns and living apart at all times during the year) is reduced, but not below zero, by 50 percent of the amount by which adjusted gross income exceeds $100,000 ($50,000 if married filing separately). If modified adjusted gross income is $150,000 or more ($75,000 or more if married filing separately), generally this special offset cannot be used [Code Sec. 469(i)(3)(A)].

To determine modified adjusted gross income for these purposes start with adjusted gross income and exclude the following [Code Sec. 469(i)(3)(F)]:

- Taxable social security and tier 1 railroad retirement benefits;
- Deductible contributions to individual retirement accounts (IRA) and Code Sec. 501(c)(18) pension plans;
- Interest from qualified U.S. savings bonds used to pay qualified higher education expenses;
- Amounts received from an employer's adoption assistance program;
- Any passive activity loss, or any rental real estate loss allowed because you materially participated in the rental activity as a real estate professional;
- Any overall loss from a publicly traded partnership;
- The deduction allowed for interest on student loans;
- The deduction allowed for tuition and related expenses; or
- The deduction allowed for income from domestic production activities.

The phaseout rule does not apply, or applies separately, in the case of the rehabilitation credit [Code Sec. 469(i)(3)(B)], the commercial revitalization deduction [Code Sec. 469(i)(3)(C)], and the low-income housing credit [Code Sec. 469(i)(3)(D)]. For the rehabilitation credit, the phaseout range for the $25,000 passive loss deduction is between $200,000 and $250,000 of adjusted gross income (phaseout is 50 percent of the adjusted gross income in excess of $200,000). The phaseout rules do not apply to any portion of the passive activity loss or credit for the tax year that is attributable to the low-income housing credit or the revitalization deduction.

Order of Phaseout of $25,000 Amount

The phaseout of the $25,000 amount should be applied in the following order:

- To the portion of the passive activity loss to which the exception for the commercial revitalization deduction does not apply;
- To the portion of such loss to which the exception for the commercial revitalization deduction applies;
- To the portion of the passive activity credit to which the special phaseout rule for the rehabilitation credit or the exception for the low-income housing credit does not apply;
- To the portion of such credit to which the special phaseout rule for the rehabilitation credit applies; and
- To the portion of such credit to which the exception for the low-income housing credit applies [Code Sec. 469(i)(3)(E)].

Carryover of $25,000 Offset

When losses from rental activities are not currently allowed because they exceed the $25,000 allowance, they are carried forward and may be deductible under the $25,000 rule in a subsequent year, assuming that the owner actively participates in the activity in the subsequent year. However, a change in the nature of your involvement with the activity does not trigger the allowance of deductions carried over from prior years. Thus, if the taxpayer begins to participate actively in an activity in which he or she did not so participate in prior years, the rule allowing up to $25,000 of losses from rental activities against nonpassive income does not apply to losses from the activity carried over from such prior years.

> **Example 13-36:** A landlord does not actively participate in the rental of his investment condominium and suffers $10,000 in loss all of which is carried over to the following tax year. In the following tax year, he actively participates in the activity and breaks even for the year (no income or loss). He may not deduct the $10,000 in losses carried over from the prior year under the $25,000 offset rule.

> **Example 13-37:** Same as above except the landlord actively participates in both tax years, and the loss from the prior year was $35,000 so that $10,000 carried over to the following year. In this case the carried over loss would be deductible under the $25,000 offset rule.

.09 Passive Losses Suspended and Carried Forward

The passive activity loss rules allow taxpayers to deduct passive activity losses only from passive activity income. Any disallowed losses and credits for the tax year are suspended and carried forward (but not back) indefinitely and are allowed in subsequent years against passive activity income [Code Sec. 469(b)]. Any passive loss or credit carried forward is allowed only to the extent that there is net passive income in a subsequent year or the activity is disposed of to a nonrelative in a taxable transaction.

An allocation of the suspended losses is required if taxpayers own interests in more than one passive activity and at least one of them generates net passive income. In this situation, carry forward only the net loss from all activities and use the following allocation formula to determine how much of the net loss from all activities is assigned to each of the activities that generated the loss [Temp. Reg. § 1.469-1T(f) (2)]:

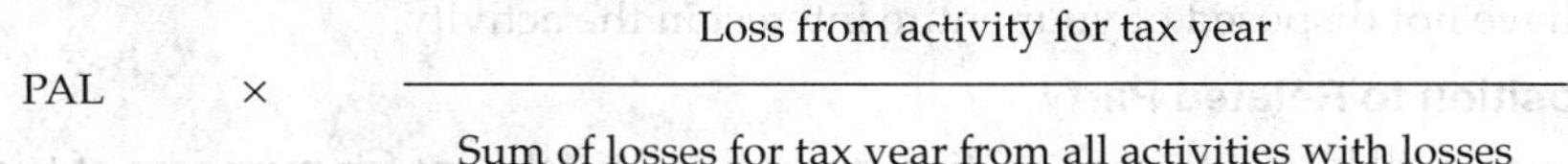

$$\text{PAL} \times \frac{\text{Loss from activity for tax year}}{\text{Sum of losses for tax year from all activities with losses}}$$

In other words, the amount of the suspended losses from each passive activity is determined on a *pro rata* basis. With respect to each activity, the portion of the loss that is suspended and carried forward is determined by the ratio of net losses from that activity to the total net losses from all passive activities for the year. In general, passive activity losses are used to offset passive activity income before the application of any other losses from nonpassive activities or net operating losses.

.10 Dispositions of Passive Activities

When a taxpayer has a passive activity loss that cannot be used because the taxpayer does not have sufficient passive activity income, the disallowed passive activity loss is suspended and either:

- Carried forward to reduce passive activity income generated in future years as discussed above; or

- Deducted in full or in part when the taxpayer disposes of his or her entire interest in the passive activity to an unrelated party in a fully taxable transaction [Code Sec. 469(g)(1)(A)].

  ▶ **PLANNING POINTER:** Code Sec. 469(g)(1)(A) provides that taxpayers who dispose of their entire interest in a passive activity or a former passive activity in a taxable disposition may deduct all suspended losses first against that year's passive income and then against any nonpassive activity income.

Mark-to-Market Election Does Not Trigger Deduction of Suspended Losses

A noncorporate taxpayer may elect to treat a capital asset or property used in the taxpayer's trade or business on a certain day as having been sold on the same day for an amount equal to its fair market value and as having been reacquired for an amount equal to its fair market value on the same date (this election was designed to permit taxpayers to take advantage of the reduced capital gains rate for qualified 5-year gain). This mark-to-market election is not a disposition for purposes of Code Sec. 469(g)(1)(A). Therefore, the gain included in gross income as a result of the mark-to-market election may be passive activity gross income that can be offset by passive activity deductions, but the election does not affect the determination of passive activity losses that are disallowed under Code Sec. 469.[111]

Partial Dispositions

If taxpayers dispose of substantially all of an activity, they may treat the interest disposed of as a separate activity, provided they can establish with reasonable certainty: (1) the amount of prior year deductions and credits disallowed under the passive activity rules that is allocable to the substantial part of the disposed activity [Reg. §1.468-1(f)(4)], and (2) the amount of gross income and any other deductions and credits for the current year that is allocable to the part of the disposed activity [Reg. §1.469-4(g)(2)].

How can this partial disposition rule be helpful? This rule will allow taxpayers to claim suspended passive losses when the passive activity is disposed of even though they have not disposed of your entire interest in the activity.

Disposition to Related Party

Taxpayers will be not treated as disposing of an investment for purposes of triggering suspended losses, if they dispose of the investment in an otherwise fully taxable transaction to a related party [Code Sec. 469(g)(1)(B). The term *related party* includes members of your family including brothers, sisters, spouse, ancestors and lineal descendants and other persons bearing a relationship to the taxpayer described in Code Secs. 267(b) and 707(b)(1) [Code Sec. 469(g)(1)(B)]. In the event of a related party transaction, the suspended losses are not triggered but rather remain suspended until the investment is sold to an unrelated party. The suspended losses may be offset by income from other passive activities.

Capital Loss Rule

To the extent that any loss recognized on a fully taxable disposition of a taxpayer's entire interest in a passive activity is a loss from the sale or exchange of a capital asset, such loss is limited to the amount of gains from the sale or exchange of capital

[111] Notice 2002-29, 2002-1 CB 797.

assets for that year plus, for individuals, $3,000. The limitation on the deductibility of capital losses is applied before the determination of the amount of losses allowable on the disposition under the passive loss rule.

Example 13-38: Taxpayer has a capital loss of $10,000 on the disposition of a passive activity. The taxpayer is allowed to deduct $5,000 of previously suspended ordinary losses as a result of the disposition. $5,000 of ordinary losses is allowed. Assuming the taxpayer has no other capital gains or losses for the year, the capital loss deduction against ordinary income is limited to $3,000. The balance of the capital loss from the disposition is carried forward and allowed in accordance with the provisions determining the deductibility of capital losses.

Disposition of Entire Interest by Installment Sale

An installment sale of a taxpayer's interest in an activity in a fully taxable transaction triggers the allowance of the suspended losses. The losses are allowed pro rata in each year you receive payment on the installment obligation. The losses are allowed in the ratio of the gain recognized in each year to the gross profit you realized (or will realize) on the sale when payment is completed.

Disposition by Gift

If a taxpayer disposes of any passive activity by gift the suspended passive activity losses are not allowed as a deduction in any tax year. Instead, the basis of the transferred interest is increased by the amount of the unused suspended passive activity losses.

Dispositions by Death

In the case of a transfer of a passive activity interest because the owner of the interest has died, the suspended passive activity losses are allowed as a deduction against the taxpayer's income in the year of death, but only to the extent that such passive activity losses exceed the amount by which the basis of the interest in the passive activity in the hands of the transferee is increased under the rules for determining the basis of property acquired from a decedent [Code Sec. 469(g)(2)].

Example 13-39: If the basis of an interest in a passive activity in the hands of a transferee is increased by $6,000 and unused passive activity losses of $8,000 were allocable to the interest at the date of death, then the decedent's deduction for the tax year would be limited to $2,000 ($8,000 – $6,000).

Suspended PALS Deductible After Switch to S Corp

In *St. Charles Investment Co.*[112] the Court of Appeals for the Tenth Circuit reversed the Tax Court to hold that an S corporation could deduct the suspended passive activity losses incurred when it was a C corporation. As a result of this taxpayer victory, S corporations with suspended PALs from years as a C corporation will be able to deduct

[112] *St. Charles Inv. Co.*, CA-10, 2000-2 USTC ¶50,840, 232 F3d 773, *rev'g*, 110 TC 46, Dec. 52,548 (1978).

those losses in full after conversion to S corporation status regardless of their entity status at the time of the deduction.

.11 IRS Audit Guidelines

Taxpayers who are claiming any passive activity losses on their income tax returns, should be aware of the comprehensive 200-page IRS audit manual that was designed to alert revenue agents and tax auditors to potential audit issues involving passive activity losses. The guide not only identifies the audit issues but outlines the approach to be taken on those issues. It is a virtual bible for those who claim passive activity losses. The manual provides that a return reflecting or suggesting any of the following red flags should be considered for a passive income audit:

- Large income items reflected on Form 8582, *Passive Activity Loss Limitations*;
- Overall net loss from a disposition listed on Form 8582;
- Like-kind exchange and losses listed on Schedule E;
- Partial sale of interests with losses claimed;
- Multiple properties and sales with short holding periods;
- Net income on rentals with little or no depreciation, involving land, or relating to self-rented property;
- Rental real estate losses in excess of $25,000 where no Form 8582 is attached;
- Schedule C, entitled "Real Estate Management";
- Forms 8582 with large flow-through losses in Part I for Rental Real Estate with active participation;
- Rentals on Schedule E where there are few expenses, thus suggesting possible net leases;
- Returns with large losses in the block for nonpassive losses on Schedule E, Part II, particularly if the first two digits of the employee identification number (EIN) are from out-of-state; and
- Schedule C or F with losses and an out-of-state EIN, particularly if wages, labor or management fees, are a line item deduction.

The IRS manual identified the following issues as ones that require a second look by agents and examiners:

- Returns with Schedule K-1 that reflect low ownership percentage, out-of-state addresses, or limited partners;
- Returns where an activity involves renting or leasing equipment and a loss is claimed. Be sure that self-employment tax is paid if the activity involves equipment leasing and income is generated;
- The offsetting of "self-charged" management fees passed through from real estate partnerships, S corporations, and joint ventures against nonpassive income derived by the S corporation from those fees;[113]

[113] *D.H. Hillman*, 114 TC 103, Dec. 53,768 (2000), *rev'd*, CA-4, 2001-1 USTC ¶50,354, 250 F3d 228, *supplemental opinion*, 118 TC 323, Dec. 54,711 (2002).

- Taxpayers recharacterizing interest income as passive income. Review the computation supporting the recharacterization.

.12 Passive Activity Credits

Certain tax credits that arise in connection with a passive activity are generally treated in the same manner as passive deductions. That is, these tax credits may be used to offset the tax that is attributable to passive income but not the tax that is attributable to nonpassive income (income tax attributable to salary and dividend income.) The amount of tax attributable to net passive income is the difference between the tax that you would have to pay on all income, and the tax that you would have to pay on taxable income other than net passive income. Under both computations, the tax effect of credits is disregarded.

In general, unused credits arising from passive activities, like unused passive losses, are suspended and carried forward indefinitely. However, unlike losses, suspended credits are not specifically allowed when you dispose of the passive activity. Instead, the suspended credits are aggregated with credits relating to the taxpayer's nonpassive activities for purposes of determining whether all such credits are allowable in light of other limitations applicable to the use of credits (for example, the general business credit percentage of tax liability limitation and the provision that credits cannot be used to reduce regular tax liability to less than tentative minimum tax liability). In addition, the treatment of such credits is determined in all respects by the general rules applicable to such credits, including carryover periods. However, credits that are subject to special limitations continue to be subject to such limitations when they cease to be limited by the passive activity rules.

¶13,100 AT-RISK RULES

Like the passive loss rules [¶ 13,090], the *at-risk rules* were designed to limit tax shelter losses. The at-risk rules provide that an individual or closely held corporate taxpayer who is engaged in an activity may only deduct a loss generated by an activity (including interest expense) to the extent that the taxpayer is at-risk for the activity at the close of the tax year [Code Sec. 465]. A taxpayer is considered at risk in an activity to the extent of: (1) cash and the adjusted basis of property contributed by him to the activity; plus (2) any amounts borrowed for use in the activity if he is personally liable for repayment or if property other than property used in the activity is pledged as security. The amount that you have at risk in an activity is the amount that you could actually lose as a result of the investment. A taxpayer is at risk for money borrowed for use in the activity to the extent that the taxpayer is liable personally for repayment or to the extent the taxpayer has pledged property as security. Under Code Sec. 465(b)(3), at risk amounts do not include money borrowed from related parties (recourse or nonrecourse), or from any person who has an interest in the activity, which could include having a capital interest or an interest in the net profits of the activity.

.01 Reason for At-Risk Rule

Like the passive loss rules, Congress created the at-risk rules to limit tax shelter investors from offsetting wages and dividends with losses generated from activities financed by nonrecourse loans where investors were not personally liable for the amount invested in circular investment schemes.

.02 Definition of Loss

For purposes of the at-risk rule, the term *loss* means the excess of the deductions allocable to the specific activity for the year, without regard to the at-risk limitation, over the income received or accrued by the investor during the same year from the same activity [Code Sec. 465(d)].

.03 Carryover of Loss

Any loss disallowed because it exceeds the amount at-risk in one year is suspended and may be deducted in the succeeding tax years, subject to the at-risk limits in each of those years [Code Sec. 465(a)(2)]. There is no limit to the number of years to which a taxpayer may carry over a loss disallowed as a result of the at-risk rules [Reg. § 1.465-2(b)]. The amount of loss which is deductible in a particular year reduces the amount at risk (but not below zero) for that activity for subsequent tax years. Thus, if a loss exceeds the at-risk amount, it will not be allowed in the next year unless the at-risk amount is also increased by investing more money in the activity. The amount of loss which is allowed for a tax year cannot reduce the amount at risk below zero [Reg. § 1.465-3(a)].

> **Example 13-40:** The amount at risk in an activity is $100 and if $120 is distributed to the taxpayer from the activity or if a $120 recourse loan is converted to nonrecourse, the amount at risk is reduced to negative $20. In order for the taxpayer to restore the amount they have at risk in the activity to zero, the amount at risk must be increased by $20. Thus, in such a case, if in the succeeding tax year, they incur a loss of $40, the amount at risk must increased by $60 ($40 + $20) in order for the full $40 to be allowed under Code Sec. 465.

.04 What to File

Taxpayers should Form 6198, *At-Risk Limitations,* to compute the amount of loss that they can deduct from an activity covered by the at-risk rules. The form must be filed with their return if: (1) they have a loss from any part of an activity that is covered by the at-risk rules, and (2) they are not at risk for some of their investment in the activity.

.05 Interplay with Passive Activity Rules

Taxpayers should apply the at-risk rules before applying the passive activity rules discussed above. This means the maximum possible passive loss deduction is the amount that taxpayers have at-risk in the investment, regardless of how much passive income they have from other activities. On the other hand, the at-risk amounts are reduced by losses allowed by the at-risk rules, even though they are not deductible under the passive loss rules.

> **Example 13-41:** This year taxpayer invests $5,000 in a limited partnership. The partnership borrows $45,000 and invests the $50,000 total in a farming operation. Due to the high degree of leverage, the partnership generates $7,500 worth of tax losses. Since taxpayer has only $5,000 at risk in the investment, his loss

deduction cannot exceed that amount. Taxpayer's deduction is further reduced by the passive loss rules. If taxpayer has only $500 of passive income, he can deduct only $500 of the loss.

.06 Who Is Affected

The at-risk rules apply to the investments and trade or business activities of all individuals and to certain closely held corporations other than S corporations [Code Sec. 465(a)(1)]. For purposes of the at-risk rules, a corporation is a closely held corporation if at any time during the last half of the tax year, more than 50 percent in value of its outstanding stock is owned directly or indirectly by or for five or fewer individuals. When determining whether 50 percent in value of the stock is owned by five or fewer individuals, apply the following rules (discussed in Code Sec. 544):

- Stock owned directly or indirectly by or for a corporation, partnership, estate, or trust is considered owned proportionately by its shareholders, partners, or beneficiaries;
- An individual is considered to own the stock owned directly or indirectly by or for his or her family. Family includes only brothers and sisters (including half brothers and sisters), a spouse, ancestors, and lineal descendants; and
- If a person holds an option to buy stock, he or she is considered to be the owner of that stock.

.07 What Activities Are Covered

The at-risk rules apply to each activity engaged in by a taxpayer in carrying on a trade or business or for the production of income. Some of the specific types of activities subject to these rules are [Code Sec. 465(c)]:

- Farming;
- Exploring for, or exploiting, oil and gas;
- Holding, producing, or distributing motion picture films or videotapes;
- Equipment leasing including personal property and certain other tangible property that is depreciable or amortizable. Equipment leasing does not include leases of master sound recordings and similar contractual arrangements for tangible or intangible assets associated with literary, artistic, or musical properties, such as books, lithographs of artwork, or musical tapes. The equipment leasing exclusion is not available for leasing activities related to other at-risk activities, such as motion picture films, and video tapes, farming, oil and gas properties, and geothermal deposits. Equipment leasing by closely held corporations is not subject to the at-risk rules;
- Exploring for, or exploiting, geothermal deposits (for wells started after September 1978);
- Real estate activities acquired after 1986 including personal property and services that are incidental to making real property available as living accommodations. For example, making personal property, such as furniture, and services available when renting a hotel or motel room or a furnished apartment is considered incidental to making real property available as living accommodations.

.08 Aggregation Rules

The aggregation rules allow taxpayers to treat certain at-risk activities that are a trade or business and that need be treated as separate activities as a single activity if the following requirements are satisfied:

1. The taxpayer actively participates in the management of the trade or business. This means the taxpayer makes decisions involving the operation or management of the activity, performing services for the activity, and hiring and discharging employees; or
2. The trade or business is carried on by a partnership or S corporation and 65 percent or more of its losses for the tax year are allocable to persons who actively participate in the management of the trade or business [Code Sec. 465(c) (3) (B)].

Factors that indicate active participation include:

- Participating in decisions involving performing services for the trade or business;
- Actually performing services for the trade or business; and
- Hiring and discharging employees (this must include employees other than the manager).[114]

These aggregation rules also apply to the following five activities, which ordinarily are treated as separate activities [Code Sec. 465(c) (2) (A), (C)]:

- Each film or videotape;
- Each leased piece of Code Sec. 1245 property;
- Each farm;
- Each oil and gas property; and
- Each geothermal property.

Aggregation by Partners and S Corporation Shareholders

Partners and S corporation shareholders may aggregate the following activities engaged in by their partnership or S corporation:

- Films and videotapes;
- Farms;
- Oil and gas properties; and
- Geothermal properties [Temp. Reg. § 1.465-1T(a)].

Example 13-42: A partnership or S corporation is engaged in the activity of exploring for, or exploiting, oil and gas resources with respect to 10 oil and gas properties. The partner or S corporation shareholder may aggregate those properties and treat the aggregated oil and gas activities as a single activity. If that partnership or S corporation also is engaged in the activity of farming with respect to two farms, the partner or shareholder may aggregate the farms and

[114] Joint Committee on Taxation, General Explanation of the Revenue Act of 1978 (JCS-1-79), p. 131 (March 12, 1979).

treat the aggregated farming activities as a single separate activity. The partner or shareholder may not aggregate the farming activity with the oil and gas activity [Temp. Reg. § 1.465-1T(a)].

Single year aggregation. Partners and S corporation shareholders must, however, treat all leasing of Code Sec. 1245 property that is placed in service in any tax year of the partnership or S corporation as one activity [[Code Sec. 465(c) (2) (B) (i)].

.09 Amounts Considered at Risk

You are considered to be at risk for an activity to the extent of the following:

- The amount of money and the adjusted basis of other property you have contributed to the activity, and
- Amounts borrowed for use in the activity if you are personally liable for repayment or you pledge property (other than property used in the activity) as security for the loan [Code Sec. 465(b) (1)].

Keep in mind that loans will only qualify as amounts at risk if you are personally liable for repayment or if you have pledged property as security for the borrowed amount [Code Sec. 465(b) (2)]. The amount considered at risk is the net fair market value of your interest in the pledged property. The net fair market value of property is its fair market value (determined on the date the property is pledged) less any prior (or superior) claims to which it is subject. However, no property will be taken into account as security if it is directly or indirectly financed by debt that is secured by property you contributed to the activity.

At-Risk Amount Limited if Lender Has Interest in Activity or Is Related Party

Under the at-risk rules, borrowings (recourse or nonrecourse) from a related person or from any person who has an interest in the activity are not treated as at-risk amounts [Code Sec. 465(b) (3)]. This prohibited-interest borrowing rule applies to the so-called catch-all group of activities that are subject to the at-risk rules as well as to the original list of enumerated activities (e.g., motion pictures, farming, equipment leasing) [Reg. § 1.465-8(a) (1)]. These catch-all activities would include activities engaged in by the taxpayer, either in carrying on a trade or business, or in the production of income and would include for example, holding real estate [Code Sec. 465(c) (3)]. See ¶ 13,140 for list of catch-all activities.

Disqualifying Interest in Activity Defined

Amounts borrowed with respect to an activity will not increase the borrower's amount at risk in the activity if the lender has an interest in the activity other than that of a creditor or is related to a person (other than the borrower) who has an interest in the activity other than that of a creditor. This *disqualifying interest* rule applies even if the borrower is personally liable for the repayment of the loan or the loan is secured by property not used in the activity [Reg. § 1.465-8(a) (1)]. For purposes of determining a corporation's amount at risk, an interest in the corporation as a shareholder is not a disqualifying interest in any activity of the corporation. Thus, amounts borrowed by a corporation from a shareholder may increase the corporation's amount at risk. In addition, for purposes of determining a taxpayer's amount at risk in an activity of holding real property, financing that is secured by real property used in the activity and is qualified nonrecourse financing is not a disqualifying interest in any activity [Reg. § 1.465-8(a)(2)].

Loans for which the borrower is personally liable for repayment. If a borrower is personally liable for the repayment of a loan for use in an activity, a person shall have a disqualifying interest in the activity other than that of a creditor only if the person has either a capital interest in the activity or an interest in the net profits of the activity. A *capital interest* in an activity means an interest in the assets of the activity that is distributable to the owner of the capital interest upon the liquidation. The partners of a partnership and the shareholders of an S corporation are considered to have capital interests in the activities conducted by the partnership or S corporation. It is not necessary for a person to have any incidents of ownership in the activity in order to have an interest in the net profits of the activity. For example, an employee or independent contractor any part of whose compensation is determined with reference to the net profits of the activity will be considered to have an interest in the net profits of the activity [Reg. § 1.465-8(b)(1)].

Example 13-43: A, the owner of a herd of cattle sells the herd to partnership BCD. BCD pays A $10,000 in cash and executes a note for $30,000 payable to A. Each of the three partners, B, C, and D, assumes personal liability for repayment of the amount owed A. In addition, BCD enters into an agreement with A under which A is to take care of the cattle for BCD in return for compensation equal to 6 percent of BCD's net profits from the activity. Because A has an interest in the net profits of BCD's farming activity, A is considered to have an interest in the activity other than that of a creditor. Accordingly, amounts payable to A for use in that activity do not increase the partners' amount at risk even though the partners assume personal liability for repayment.

Example 13-44: Assume the same facts as in Example 13-43 except that instead of receiving compensation equal to 6 percent of BCD's net profits from the activity, A instead receives compensation equal to 1 percent of the gross receipts from the activity. A does not have a capital interest in BCD. A's interest in the gross receipts is not considered an interest in the net profits. Because B, C, and D assumed personal liability for the amounts payable to A, and A has neither a capital interest nor an interest in the net profits of the activity, A is not considered to have an interest in the activity other than that of a creditor with respect to the $30,000 loan. Accordingly, B, C, and D are at risk for their share of the loan if the other provisions of section 465 are met.

Example 13-45: Assume the same facts as in Example 13-43 except that instead of receiving compensation equal to 6 percent of BCD's net profits from the activity, A instead receives compensation equal to 6 percent of the net profits from the activity or $15,000, whichever is greater. A is considered to have an interest in the net profits from the activity and accordingly will be treated as a person with an interest in the activity other than that of a creditor [Reg. § 1.465-8(b)(4)].

Nonrecourse loans secured by assets with a readily ascertainable fair market value. In the case of a nonrecourse loan for use in an activity where the loan is secured by property which has a readily ascertainable fair market value, a person shall be considered a person with a qualifying interest in the activity other than that of a creditor only if the person has either a capital interest in the activity or an interest in the net profits of the activity [Reg. § 1.465-8(c)].

Example 13-46: X is an investor in an activity described in section 465(c)(1). In order to raise money for the investment, X borrows money from A, the promoter (the person who brought X together with other taxpayers for the purpose of investing in the activity). The loan is secured by stock unrelated to the activity that is listed on a national securities exchange. X's stock has a readily ascertainable fair market value. A does not have a capital interest in the activity or an interest in its net profits. Accordingly, with respect to the loan secured by X's stock, A does not have an interest in the activity other than that of a creditor.

Nonrecourse loans secured by assets without a readily ascertainable fair market value. In the case of a nonrecourse loan for use in an activity where the loan is secured by property that does not have a readily ascertainable fair market value, a person shall have a disqualifying interest in the activity if the person stands to receive financial gain (other than interest) from the activity or from the sale of interests in the activity. Persons who stand to receive financial gain from the activity include persons who receive compensation for services rendered in connection with the organization or operation of the activity or for the sale of interests in the activity. Such a person will generally include the promoter of the activity who organizes the activity or solicits potential investors in the activity. [Reg. § 1.465-8(d) (1)].

Example 13-47: A is a motion picture promoter and he organizes the activity and solicits potential investors. For these services A is paid a flat fee of $130x. This fee is paid out of the amounts contributed by the investors to the activity. X, one of the investors in the activity, borrows money from A for use in the activity. X is not personally liable for repayment to A of the amount borrowed. As security for the loan, X pledges an asset that does not have a readily ascertainable fair market value. A is considered a person with an interest in the activity other than that of a creditor with respect to this loan because the asset pledged as security does not have a readily ascertainable fair market value, X is not personally liable for repayment of the loan, and A received financial gain from the activity. Accordingly, X's amount at risk in the activity is not increased despite the fact that property was pledged as security [Reg. § 1.465-8(d)(2)].

Related Person Defined

For these purposes, *related persons* include the following Code Sec. 465(b) (3) (C)]:

- Members of the family, but only brothers and sisters (both whole and half blood) spouse, ancestors (parents, grandparents, etc.), and lineal descendants (children, grandchildren, etc.);

- Two corporations that are members of the same controlled group of corporations determined by applying a 10 percent ownership test;
- The fiduciaries of two different trusts, or the fiduciary and beneficiary of two different trusts, if the same person is the grantor of both trusts;
- Certain educational or charitable organizations and a person who directly or indirectly controls one of these organizations;
- A corporation and an individual who owns directly or indirectly more than 10 percent of the value of the outstanding stock of the corporation;
- A trust fiduciary and a corporation of which more than 10 percent in value of the outstanding stock is owned directly or indirectly by or for the trust or by or for the grantor of the trust;
- The grantor and fiduciary or the fiduciary and beneficiary of any trust;
- A corporation and a partnership if the same persons own over 10 percent in value of the outstanding stock of the corporation and more than 10 percent of the capital interest or the profits interest in the partnership;
- Two S corporations if the same persons own more than 10 percent in value of the outstanding stock of each corporation;
- An S corporation and a regular corporation if the same persons own more than 10 percent in value of the outstanding stock of each corporation;
- A partnership and a person who owns directly or indirectly more than 10 percent of the capital or profits of the partnership;
- Two partnerships if the same persons directly or indirectly own more than 10 percent of the capital or profits of each;
- Two persons who are engaged in business under common control; and
- An executor of an estate and a beneficiary of that estate.

.10 Amounts Not Considered at Risk

You are not at risk for amounts protected against loss through the following financing arrangements:

- Nonrecourse financing (as discussed below and subject to the exception for *qualified nonrecourse financing*);
- Guarantees;
- Stop-loss agreements; or
- Other similar loss limiting arrangements [Code Sec. 465(b)(4)].

For example, you will not be considered to be at risk for the equity capital you have invested in an activity if you are protected against economic loss by an agreement or arrangement for compensation or reimbursement. The IRS and the courts will look through artfully structured transactions to determine whether investors, particularly limited partners, have any realistic possibility of suffering an economic loss. If they determine that the investor will be immunized from suffering an economic loss as a result of a web of guarantees, then he or she will not be at-risk for tax purposes.[115]

.11 Nonrecourse Financing

Nonrecourse financing is financing for which the taxpayer is not personally liable in the event of a default. Financing is nonrecourse if the debt holder's only remedy in the event of a failure is to take the property securing the loan (through foreclosure or voluntary transfer) and to sell it. For example, if you borrow money to contribute to an investment and the lender's only recourse is your interest in the activity or to the property used in the activity, the loan will be termed a nonrecourse loan. You are not at risk with respect to amounts protected against loss through nonrecourse financing unless you can establish that you have *qualified nonrecourse financing* [Code Sec. 465(b)(5)].

.12 Qualified Nonrecourse Financing Exception

Taxpayers are at risk with respect to their share of any qualified nonrecourse financing secured by real property used in the activity of holding real property [Code Sec. 465(b)(6)(A)]. Qualified nonrecourse financing is defined as any financing for which no one is personally liable for repayment and that is:

- Borrowed in connection with the activity of holding real property which includes the holding of personal property and providing services incidental to making real property available as living accommodations [Code Sec. 465(b)(6)(E)(i)]. In determining whether qualified nonrecourse financing is secured only by real property used in that activity, disregard property that is incidental to the activity of holding real property. In addition, disregard other property if the total gross fair market value of that property is less than 10 percent of the total gross fair market value of all the property securing the financing;
- Nonconvertible from a debt obligation to an ownership interest, [Code Sec. 465(b)(6)(B); Reg. § 1.465-27(b)]; and
- Loaned or guaranteed by any federal, state, or local government, or borrowed from a *qualified person:* someone who actively and regularly engages in the business of lending money [Code Sec. 465(b)(6)(D)(i); Code Sec. 49(a)(1)(D)(iv)]. The following people are not qualified persons: (a) a related person unless the financing is commercially reasonable and on the same terms as loans involving unrelated persons; (b) a person who acquired the property from a related person; or (c) a person who receives a fee due to investment in the real property or a person related to that person.

Application of Qualified Nonrecourse Financing Exception to Partnerships

For partnerships, the qualified nonrecourse financing test is made at both the partner and partnership level. The amount of qualified nonrecourse financing for which the partners are treated at risk cannot exceed the total amount of qualified nonrecourse financing at the partnership level [Reg. § 1.465-27(b)(4)]. A partner's share of any

[115] *R.L. Whitmire,* 109 TC 266, Dec. 52,327 (1997), *aff'd,* CA-9, 99-1 USTC ¶ 50,563, 178 F3d 1050; *D.H. Hillman,* 114 TC 103, Dec. 53,768 (2000), *rev'd,* CA-4, 2001-1 USTC ¶ 50,354, 250 F3d 228, *supplemental opinion,* 118 TC 323, Dec. 54,711 (2002).

qualified nonrecourse financing is determined on the basis of the partner's share of liabilities of the partnership incurred in connection with that financing [Code Sec. 465(b)(6)(C)].

.13 Recapture

Losses you previously deducted must be recaptured when your at-risk amounts fall below zero. This can happen if you receive a distribution, your nonrecourse debt increases or you receive a loan guarantee. When your loss is recaptured, you have taxable income to the extent your at-risk basis is reduced below zero [Code Sec. 465(e)].

> **Example 13-48:** You invest $50,000 in a business venture subject to the at-risk rules. You are not personally liable for any of the debts of the business, so your at-risk amount is your original investment of $50,000. Over the course of several years, you deduct losses of $25,000. You subsequently borrow $35,000 in nonrecourse debt from the local bank. The debt is secured by business property. You must recapture $10,000 of the loss deductions, since your at-risk amount ($50,000 less $25,000 less $35,000) is reduced below zero.

The amount you recapture in any year is limited to the excess of losses you previously claimed over amounts you previously recaptured [Code Sec. 469(b)(6)]. This means that in the above example you would not have to recapture more than $15,000 in future years unless you claim additional loss deductions.

Finally, you may deduct recaptured income in a subsequent year to the extent your at risk amount increases above zero. So, for example, if you were to make an additional contribution to the business of $10,000 or more, you would be allowed to deduct the recaptured $10,000.

¶13,105 LOSSES FROM VACATION HOMES

The tax consequences of owning a vacation home will depend on whether your vacation home, which includes your house, apartment, condominium, house trailer, or boat, is classified for tax purposes as a residence, a rental property, or a hybrid of both. This classification depends on the amount of time that you or your family personally use the home compared to the number of days it is rented to outsiders at a fair rent. If you rent out your vacation home and also use it yourself, losses attributable to rental-type expenses (such as depreciation and maintenance) will not be allowed in full because they must be divided between your rental use and personal use. Deductible expenses unrelated to the rental (such as property taxes and mortgage interest), however, are still deductible in full against your other income [Code Sec. 280A(b)].

.01 Vacation Home as Residence

Your vacation home qualifies as a residence if you use the property during the year for personal purposes for the greater of:

- 14 days, or
- 10 percent of the days the property is rented out [Code Sec. 280A(d)(1)]. If your personal use falls below these strict levels, then any loss is fully deductible (subject to the passive loss rules [¶ 13,090]and the hobby loss rules [¶ 13,085]).

The easiest scenario tax-wise occurs when you simply use your vacation home as a second home and do not rent it out. In this situation, the following expenses are deductible:

- Mortgage interest (up to $1 million of acquisition indebtedness and up to $100,000 of home equity debt on a loan taken out for purposes other than to buy, build, or substantially improve the home). Before buying your second vacation home with a mortgage, keep in mind that you may only claim mortgage interest deductions with respect to one vacation home.
- Real estate taxes; and
- Casualty losses provided they are reduced by $100 per occurrence and to the extent that such losses for the year exceed 10 percent of your adjusted gross income.

.02 Tax-Free Rent-14-Day Limit

If you rented out your vacation home to others for less than 15 days during the year, all the rental income you receive for those 14 days will be tax-free [Code Sec. 280A(g)]. You do not even have to report the rental income on your tax return. This can be a great windfall if you are lucky enough to own a second home in an area adjacent to a special sporting event such as the Olympics or a major golf tournament for which people will pay thousands to rent your place for a limited two-week period.

For example, if you can rent out your beach house for only 14 days the entire year and charge rent of $5,000 a week, you will receive $10,000 tax-free per year. But keep in mind that you can only rent the place out for a maximum of 14 days per year for the income to be tax-free. You would be wise to take advantage of this tax break before it is repealed. In addition to receiving 14 days worth of tax-free income, you will still be entitled to deduct on Schedule A your real estate tax payments and your mortgage interest payments because your vacation home still qualifies as a qualified personal residence for purposes of the mortgage interest deduction [Code Sec. 163(h)(4)(A)]. You will not, however, be able to deduct any other expenses you incurred in connection with renting the property.

.03 Personal Use Ceiling

Code Sec. 280A limits an owner's deductions with respect to use of a vacation home, including a condominium, if the owner's personal use of the unit exceeds the greater of 14 days or 10 percent of the number of days during the year for which the unit is rented at a fair rental. This is called the personal use ceiling. In essence the law classifies the dwelling as a residence if the owner's personal use exceeds the personal use ceilings. Once the property is characterized as a "residence," the owner may only claim deductions up to amount of income received from the property.

In one case, a couple who personally used their vacation condominium for 27 days out of the year had not exceeded the personal use ceiling, so they were entitled to deduct all their condo-related expenses. The court did not look at how many days the condo was actually rented which was only 200 days (the taxpayers had exceeded 10 percent of 200) but at the number of days that the condo was available for rent which was 365 days of the year according to the lease agreement.[116]

In computing personal use of a vacation home, you must count one personal day for every day or part of a day that the home is used by you or your family members for personal purposes. Any day that the home is rented out to anyone at a fair market rental—including family members—for use as their principal residence is not counted as a personal use day by you [Code Sec. 280A(d)(3)(A)]. On the other hand, any day that the home is rented for less than a fair market rental is counted as a personal day. Any day that you spend doing repair or maintenance work isn't counted as a personal use day. Any day that you let someone use the home in exchange for some other dwelling will be considered a personal use day.

Example 13-49: Sally uses her beach house for 30 days during the year and rents it at a fair rental for 200 days. She uses her house as a residence during the year because her 30 personal use days exceed 10 percent of the 200 days that the unit was rented.

Example 13-50: Bill donates a week in his mountain retreat to a charity auction. This week will count towards Bill's personal use of the home for purposes of determining his right to deduct expenses.

A special rule applies if the owner rents the principal residence (or holds it out for rental) at a fair market rental for a consecutive period of 12 months or more. The owner's use of the property as a principal residence for a part of any tax year during which the rental period extends is not treated as personal use. The rental period may be less than 12 months if the property is sold or exchanged at the end of the period [Code Sec. 280A(d)(4)]. This rule is helpful if the owner moves to a new residence before selling the old one. The owner may be able to claim full tax savings from renting out the old home while seeking a buyer—even though the owner lived in the home for more than 14 days during the year.

.04 Hybrid Use

If owners rent their vacation home for more than 14 days a year and also use it personally more than 14 days a year or 10 percent of the days that the home was rented at a fair rental, the vacation home will be classified as a hybrid or mixed-use property and all income must be reported on Schedule E and all expenses must be divided or allocated between the days the home is rented and the days the owner personally used the home [Code Sec. 280A(e)].

Example 13-51: Mom uses her beach house for 30 days during the year and rents it at a fair rental for 200 days. She has a hybrid or mixed use and must report all income and divide expenses between rental use and personal use and report them on Schedule E (Form 1040) because her 30 personal use days

[116] *M. Razavi*, CA-6, 96-1 USTC ¶50,060, 74 F3d 125.

exceed the greater of 14 days or 10 percent of the 200 days that the unit was rented.

Example 13-52: You own a condominium in a resort area. You rent it out at a fair rental price for a total of 170 days during the year. For 12 of these days, the tenant was not able to use the apartment and allowed you to use it even though you did not refund any of the rent. Your family actually used the apartment for 10 of those days. Therefore, the apartment is treated as having been rented for 160 (170 – 10) days. Your family also used the apartment for 7 other days during the year. You used the apartment as a home because you used it for personal purposes for 17 days. That is more than the greater of 14 days or 10 percent of the total days it was rented. You must report all income and divide expenses between rental use and personal use and report them on Schedule E.

When you have a hybrid or mixed-use property you must divide your expenses into three groups and then deduct them on Schedule E to the extent of rental income as follows [Prop. Reg. § 1.280A-3(d)(3)]:

- Mortgage interest, property taxes, or casualty losses allocable to the rental period.
- Operating expenses (maintenance, repairs, utilities) relating to the rental period.
- Depreciation only to the extent the rental income exceeds the deductions in the previous items.

You deduct interest and taxes attributable to your personal use period on Schedule A. Operating expenses and depreciation attributable to the personal use period are not deductible.

Expenses that cannot be claimed this year because of the income limitation rule, can be carried forward and used in a future year when there is sufficient rental income to cover it.

You must allocate the three categories of deductions between rental use and personal use. This allocation is based on the ratio of the number of days the unit was used for rental purposes divided by the total number of days that the unit was used for any purpose other than for repairs or maintenance. The resulting allocation of expenses to rental use is deductible only to extent of gross rental income. "Gross rental income" is defined as gross receipts from renting the unit minus expenses incurred to attract tenants such as realtors' fees and advertising expenses. You cannot use rental losses to offset nonrental income.

Example 13-53: You rent your ski lodge in Aspen for a three month period from December, January, and February, (90 days) use it yourself 2 weeks in December and have a week vacant. The lodge was used for rental for 83 days (90 days minus 7 vacant days). You add in the two weeks you used it and find that the total use of the place was 97 days. You can allocate 83/97ths of the expenses to the rental.

Example 13-54: Mr. and Mrs. Smith own a second home that they rented out during the year for 100 days and occupied themselves for 25 days. During the year, they spent $5,200 for interest and taxes, $4,000 maintaining the property, and they have $2,000 in depreciation. Their gross rental income is $6,300. Under the allocation formula, 80 percent of their expenses are attributable to the rental period (100 days out of 125 days)—$4,160 of the interest and taxes, $3,200 of the maintenance and $1,600 of the depreciation. The Smiths can deduct the $4,160 interest and taxes in full. They can deduct $2,140 of their maintenance expenses ($6,300 less $4,160). The remaining maintenance expenses, as well as the depreciation, are not deductible. The Smiths can also deduct the $1,040 of interest and taxes allocable to the personal use period.

▶ **OBSERVATION:** The result in the example is based on the IRS position for allocating interest and taxes on a rental vacation home. The Tax Court and the Ninth and Tenth Circuit Courts have adopted a different position.[117] These courts maintain that the proper allocation of interest and taxes to the rental period should be: the number of rental days to the number of days in the whole year. Under this approach, you could be entitled to deduct more of your operating expenses and depreciation.

For example, with this more liberal rule, the Smiths in the above example would allocate only $1,425 of their interest and taxes to the rental of the second home. That means that the Smiths can deduct the entire $4,800 because their rental income in excess of the interest and tax deduction is $4,875 ($6,300 less $1,425). Result: The Tax Court formula gives the Smiths $2,660 more in deductions than using the IRS formula.

.05 Vacation Home as Rental Property

Your vacation home will be treated like a pure rental property if your personal use of the property doesn't exceed the greater of 14-days or 10 percent of the days the property is rented out during the year at a fair rental. You report rental income and deductions on Schedule E (Form 1040). Your deductions related to renting the vacation home will be limited by the passive activity loss rules found in Code Sec. 469. Use Form 8582, *Passive Activity Loss Limitations,* to determine the amount of the deductible loss reported on Schedule D. [See ¶ 13,090]

Passive Loss Rule Limitation

The passive loss rules provide that the income and deductions resulting from renting your vacation home will automatically be passive in nature unless you qualify for the active participation exception discussed further below. The passive loss limitations require you to deduct losses from passive activities such as rental activities, only against income from such passive activities. This means that your operating expenses, such as utilities, maintenance, insurance, advertising, commissions, as well as depreciation, property taxes, and mortgage interest can be deducted only to offset your passive rental income. You cannot use the deductions to offset your active income from wages or income from your trade or business. Unused passive losses

[117] *D.D. Bolton,* 77 TC 104, Dec. 38,075 (1981), *aff'd,* CA-9, 82-2 USTC ¶ 9699, 694 F2d 556; *E.G. McKinney,* 41 TCM 1272, Dec. 37,832(M), TC Memo. 1981-181, *aff'd,* CA-10, 83-2 USTC ¶ 9655, 732 F2d 414.

can, however, be carried forward to offset your gain when you eventually sell the property.

Active Participation Exception

Up to $25,000 of your deductions related to the vacation property can be applied against your income from other sources if:

- Your adjusted gross income is less than $150,000 (the deduction is reduced once your adjusted gross income is over $100,000 and is completely phased out once your income hits $150,000) [Code Sec. 469(i)(3)(A)];
- You and your spouse had at least a 10 percent interest in the activity during the tax year; and
- You actively participated in the management of the property. Any excess rental loss exceeding $25,000 can be carried forward and applied against ordinary income in later years [Code Sec. 469(c)(7)].

What Is Active Participation?

You will *actively participate* in the management of the property if you approve new tenants, decide on rental terms, approve capital or repair expenditures and make other similar decisions. Keep in mind that the Tax Court has held that you will be unable to benefit from the $25,000 allowance if a management or rental agent handles all aspects of renting the vacation unit and maintaining it.[118]

Keep in mind that in order to prove active participation with respect to maintaining your vacation property you do not need to show regular, continuous and substantial involvement in the operation of the activity as would be required under Code Sec. 469(c)(7) the "material participation" exception for real estate professionals.

In *C.M. Akers*,[119] the Tax Court concluded that the owner of a cabin available for rent was not entitled to deduct expenses that exceeded the income from the property because the house was characterized as a residence rather than a rental property for purposes of Code Sec. 280A. In the eyes of the court, the taxpayer failed to prove that personal use of the cabin did not exceed the greater of 14 days or 10 percent of the days it was rented at fair rental. Since the cabin was rented for less than 15 days, no income from the rental was included in his return, and he was not allowed to deduct any expenses related to the rental of the cabin.

The court also concluded that, the individual's rental of the cabin was not a "rental activity" under Code Sec. 469(j)(8), since the average period of customer use was three days and he was therefore not allowed a $25,000 offset for losses against passive income [Temp. Reg. § 1.469-1T(e)(3)(i) and (ii)(A)].

.06 Planning Strategies for Vacation Home Owners

Negotiate mortgage on vacation home without points. Negotiate the loan on your vacation without points because points paid to secure a loan for a vacation home are not deductible in full in the first year as they are for a primary residence. Instead, they must be amortized over the life of the loan.

---

[118] *J.R. Madler*, 75 TCM 2025, Dec. 52,629(M), TC Memo. 1998-112.

[119] *C.M. Akers*, 99 TCM 1354, Dec. 58,193(M), TC Memo. 2010-85.

If you want your vacation home to qualify as a rental property rather than a residence, be certain that your personal use of the property never exceeds the greater of 14 days or 10 percent of the total rental time. Be creative with your use of personal use days. Because use of the dwelling unit for repairs or maintenance will be disregarded in calculating the number of days for which the unit is used for personal purposes, coordinate any family vacation with the upkeep of the rental unit. A personal use day by one's family members will not be considered a personal use day of the home if the owner spends time cleaning, repairing, or maintaining the home. A vacation home is not treated as rented at fair rental for any day on which it was used for personal purposes. You will be charged an entire day of personal use even if you use the property for only part of the day. Days spent repairing or maintaining the home will be disregarded in calculating the number of personal use days if your principal purpose for using the home was to perform repair or maintenance work, even if family members also used it for recreational purposes on that day.

Example 13-55: Dad spends three hours on Saturday and three hours on Sunday painting the beach house. The rest of the days are spent relaxing with the family. These days do not count as personal use days because Dad spent time cleaning on those days.

A vacation home will be considered to have been used by its owner for personal purposes if for any part of a day the home is used:

- For personal purposes by the taxpayer, any other person who owns an interest in the home, or the relatives (spouses, brothers, sisters, parents) of either;
- By any individual who uses the home under a reciprocal or exchange arrangement, whether or not rent is charged; and
- By any individual who uses the home and does not pay a fair rental.

Example 13-56: You rent your beach house to Emily, who in turn rents her house at a ski resort to you. You each pay a fair rental price. You are treated as using your house for personal purposes on the days that Emily uses it because your house is used by Emily under an arrangement that allows you to use her house.

Example 13-57: You and your sister are co-owners of an apartment at a ski resort. You rent the unit out to vacationers whenever possible. The unit is not used as a main house by anyone. Your sister uses the unit for two weeks every year. Because your sister has an interest in the unit, both of you are considered to have used the unit for personal purposes during those two weeks.

You use a dwelling unit for personal purposes if:

- You donate the use of the unit to a charitable organization;
- The organization sells the use of the unit at a fund-raising event; and
- The purchaser uses the unit.

Example 13-58: Dad donates a week in his mountain retreat to a charity auction. The charity auctions the use of the unit to the highest bidder who actually uses the unit for a week. This week will count towards Dad's personal use of the home.

Sale of Vacation Home

The sale of your vacation home will only qualify for the $250,000 home sale exclusion ($500,000 on a joint return) if you convert your vacation home to your primary residence and live in the home as your principal residence for two out of five years before the date you sell it. For further discussion of the home sale exclusion, see ¶ 7001 [Code Sec. 121(a)]. This exclusion is allowed once every two years when you sell or exchange the home. For further discussion of the Housing Assistance Tax Act of 2008, which provided that gain from sale of principal residence which is allocated to nonqualified use is not excluded from income, see ¶ 7001.

Reporting requirements. If you are eligible to take advantage of the exclusion and your sale proceeds do not exceed $250,000 or $500,000 on a joint return, you do not need to even report the sale on your tax return. Use Schedule D (Form 1040), *Capital Gains and Losses* to report any profit that exceeds the exclusion amount. Keep in mind that you cannot deduct a loss from the sale of your main home.

Treatment of sale proceeds depends on use of vacation home. If you have not converted your vacation home to your main home, then treatment of the gain or loss depends on whether the home was classified as rental property or as a second residence. If the vacation home was classified as a second residence because it was used the greater or 14 days or 10 percent of the rental period, then the gain on the sale will be treated as capital gain taxed at a maximum tax rate of 15 percent. If the vacation home qualifies as rental property because the personal use did not exceed the greater of 14 days or 10 percent of the rental period, the gain will be also be treated as a capital gain and any loss will be deductible as a capital loss. If you sell land on which you had hoped to build a vacation home, you may not exclude any of the gain on the sale because the land does not qualify as your main home under the law.

Home office in vacation home. If you used part of your vacation home as a home office, you probably claimed depreciation deductions for the business use of the home. These depreciation deductions reduced your home's basis. If you now sell your home, you may not exclude the portion of your gain attributable to allowed or allowable post-May 6, 1997 depreciation deductions [Code Sec. 121(d)(6)]. Instead, you must now pay depreciation recapture tax at a 25 percent rate because it constitutes unrecaptured Section 1250 gain under the law [Ch. 12].

NET OPERATING LOSS DEDUCTION

¶13,110 WHAT IS A NET OPERATING LOSS (NOL)

.01 Net Operating Losses of Individuals

If a taxpayer has a net operating loss (NOL), the losses of a bad year can be used to offset the profits of a good year [Code Sec. 172; Reg. §§1.172-1-1.172.8]. Thus, taxpayers may use a NOL to reduce taxable income in other years. Here's how: In general, taxpayers can carry the NOL back for two years and deduct it from income earned in earlier years, and carry it forward for 20 years and deduct it from income in those later years. If taxpayers carry back a NOL, they must refigure tax for the carryback year. For further discussion of NOLs of corporations, see ¶20,115–¶20,140.

.02 Refund Claims

If it turns out that the individual taxpayer, estate, or trust owes less tax for that year, they can get a quick refund by filing Form 1045, *Application for Tentative Refund.* Form 1045, however, may be used only if filed within one year after the close of the NOL year (but not before Form 1040 or Form 1041 for the NOL year is filed). Form 1045 is processed within the later of 90 days after being filed or 90 days after the last day of the month that includes the due date (including extensions) for filing Form 1040 or Form 1041 for the loss year [Code Sec. 6411(b)].

As an alternative to Form 1045, an individual may file Form 1040X for each carryback year to claim a refund. Form 1040X must generally be filed within three years after the due date of the return for the NOL year. Estates and trusts file an amended Form 1041, *U.S. Income Tax Return for Estates and Trusts.* (There is no Form 1041X; use Form 1041 as issued for the carryback year and check the amended return box.) If an amended return is filed, the taxpayer must still attach the NOL computations using the Form 1045 computation schedules. The IRS generally processes an amended return within six months after filing. Note: Taxpayers have the option of disregarding the carryback period and simply carry the NOL forward—if that's to their tax advantage. There are special rules that restrict deductible operating loss. Thus, in computing the NOL and the carrybacks and carryovers, taxpayers may have to adjust (modify) deductions and income for the years involved.

> **NOTE:** The loss must be from the operation of a trade, business, or profession, or from casualty or theft. A loss due to confiscation of a business by a foreign government can also qualify for the net operating loss.[120]

.03 Computing Net Operating Loss of Individuals

The net operating loss (NOL) of an individual or other noncorporate taxpayer is computed in the same manner as taxable income or loss, except that the following adjustments must be made [Code Sec. 172(d); Reg. §1.172-3]:

---

[120] *L. Alvary,* CA-2, 62-1 USTC ¶9493, 302 F2d 790.

1. *Exemptions.* An individual may not take any personal and dependency exemptions into account, and a trust or estate may not claim the Code Sec. 642(b) personal exemption deduction.
2. *Net operating loss deduction.* No deduction may be taken for a net operating loss carryback or carryover from another tax year.
3. *Nonbusiness deductions.* Nonbusiness deductions are deductible only to the extent of nonbusiness income including nonbusiness capital gains in excess of nonbusiness capital losses [Code Sec. 172(d)(4); Reg. § 1.172-3(a)(3)].
4. *Nonbusiness capital losses.* Nonbusiness capital losses may be deducted only to the extent of nonbusiness capital gains. Any excess cannot be deducted [Code Sec. 172(d)(2) and (4)(A)].
5. *Nonbusiness capital gains.* Nonbusiness capital gains are first offset against nonbusiness capital losses. Any net nonbusiness capital gain is then used to reduce the excess of the ordinary nonbusiness deductions over ordinary nonbusiness gross income. Any remaining nonbusiness capital gain offsets business capital loss. A taxpayer's capital gains are determined without regard to the 50-percent exclusion for gain from qualified small business stock provided in Code Sec. 1202 (i.e., this deduction is not allowed in computing the NOL) [Code Sec. 172(d)(2)(B)].
6. *Business capital losses.* Business capital losses may be deducted up to the sum of (1) business capital gains and (2) the amount arrived at by subtracting from nonbusiness capital gain any nonbusiness capital losses, personal exemptions, and nonbusiness deductions. Any excess cannot be deducted in determining the net operating loss [Code Sec. 172(d)(2); Reg. § 1.172-3(2)(i); Reg. § 1.172-3(c)].
7. *Manufacturing deduction.* The Code Sec. 199 deduction for domestic production activities is not allowed in computing the NOL [Code Sec. 172(d)(7)].

As a result of these modifications, the amount of loss that may be carried back or forward as a net operating loss deduction is reduced.

Example 13-59: Brian Bond had a business capital loss of $7,000. In addition, he had ordinary nonbusiness income of $6,000, ordinary nonbusiness deductions of $7,000, nonbusiness capital gains of $10,000, and nonbusiness capital losses of $5,000.

These are offset against each other as follows:

Nonbusiness capital gain		$10,000	
Nonbusiness capital loss		($5,000)	
Remaining nonbusiness capital gain		$5,000	
Nonbusiness deductions	($7,000)		
Nonbusiness income	$6,000		
Excess deductions		($1,000)	
Remaining nonbusiness capital gain			$4,000
Offset against business capital loss			($7,000)
Remaining business capital loss			($3,000)

The $3,000 remaining business loss may not be claimed in computing the NOL.

.04 Years to Which NOL May Be Carried Back

Under Code Sec. 172(b) (1), an NOL is generally carried back two years and forward 20 years. There are special rules for NOLs for specified losses, resulting in NOLs that may be carried back more than two years. The general rule under Code Sec. 172(b) (2) is that an NOL is used in the following order until exhausted:

- Carried back to the second preceding tax year;
- Carried back to the first preceding tax year; and
- Carried forward to the following 20 tax years.

The taxpayer has the option to make an election provided in Code Sec. 172(b) (3) to waive the entire carryback period. This election must be made by the due date (including extensions of time) for filing the taxpayer's return and will be irrevocable.

Consult Table 1 to determine the appropriate NOL carryback and carryover period.

Table 1. NOL Carryforward and Carryback

	General Carryback	General Carryforward
NOLs arising in tax years beginning before 8/6/97 (and certain casualty, theft, and disaster-related losses)	3 years	15 years
Beginning after 8/5/97 and ending on or before 12/31/00	2 years	20 years
Ending after 12/31/00 and before 1/1/03	5 years	20 years
Ending on or after 1/1/03	2 years	20 years

▶ **PLANNING POINTER:** Failure to follow IRS procedure will preclude use of longer NOL carryback. In *Tualatin Valley Builders Supply, Inc.*,[121] the Court of Appeals for the Ninth Circuit concluded that a taxpayer could not use the special 5-year carryback period because the taxpayer failed to follow IRS procedures for choosing that carryback period.

.05 Exceptions to Regular Carryback/Carryforward Rule

The following NOL carrybacks are *not* subject to the regular two-year carryback and 20-year carryforward limits:

- Eligible small businesses (ESBs) can elect to carry back 2008 and 2009 NOLs for three, four or five years, instead of the normal two years [Code Sec. 172(b)(1)(H)]. An ESB is a trade or business that meets a $15 million gross receipts test for the tax year in which the loss arose [Code Sec. 172(b)(1)(H)(iv)]. The $15 million gross receipts test is satisfied if the average annual gross receipts for the business for the three-taxable-year period ending with a tax year does not exceed $15 million [Code Sec. 172(b)(1)(H)(iv)]. The carryforward period for NOLs remains at 20 years whether or not the taxpayer elects to use an extended carryback period [Code Sec. 172(b)(1)(A)(ii)]. ESBs that qualify for the extended carryback period for 2008 and

[121] *Tualatin Valley Builders Supply, Inc.*, CA-9, 2008-1 USTC ¶ 50,280, 522 F3d 937.

2009 NOLs must make an affirmative election to use the longer carryback period by taking the steps outlined in Rev. Proc. 2009-26.[122]

- *Real estate investment trusts (REITs).* An NOL sustained by a REIT may be carried forward to the 20 years following the loss year. However, no loss carryback is available [Code Sec. 172(b)(1)(B); Reg. § 1.172-10].
- *Specified liability losses.* Special carryback periods apply in the case of specified liability losses. A specified liability loss (SLL) is a separate NOL that can be carried back 10 years from the tax year of the loss [Code Sec. 172(b)(1)(C)]. SLLs include (1) amounts attributable to product liability or expenses incurred in investigating, opposing, or settling claims against the taxpayer on account of product liability; and (2) expenses paid to satisfy a liability under a federal or state law requiring the reclamation of land, decommissioning of a nuclear power plant, dismantling a drilling platform, remediation of environmental contamination or a payment under any workers compensation act [Code Sec. 172(f)]. In Letter Ruling 201006028, the IRS determined that a homebuilder's liabilities arising from its breach of warranties provided to new homebuyers did not qualify as product liabilities under Code Sec. 172(f)(4) and therefore the NOLs attributable to deduction for repairing the homes were not SLLs subject to the special 10-year carryback under Code Sec. 172(b)(1)(C). An election to apply the general rules must be made on or before the due date of the taxpayer's return, including any filing extensions, for the tax year of the NOL. Once made, the election is irrevocable for that tax year [Code Sec. 172(f)(6); Reg. § 1.172-13(c)]. For purposes of the 10-year carryback of product liability losses, the U.S. Supreme Court ruled in *United Dominion Industries, Inc.*,[123] that the amount of an affiliated group's product liability loss (PLL) is to be calculated on a consolidated, single-entity basis, not by determining PLLs separately for each company.
- *Three-year carryback for NOLs attributable to casualty losses and federally declared disasters for individuals, farmers, and small businesses.* Although the general carryback period for an NOL is two years, the portion of an NOL that is an "eligible loss" is carried back three years. An eligible loss is defined as:

  1. The portion of an individual's NOL attributable to casualty and theft losses and
  2. The portion of an NOL attributable to a federally declared disaster in the case of a taxpayer engaged in the trade or business of farming or a taxpayer that is a small business [Code Sec. 172(b)(1)(F)].

  In this situation, a small business means any trade or business (including one conducted in or through a corporation, partnership, or sole proprietorship) with average gross receipts of less than $5 million in gross receipts for a three-year period [Code Secs. 448(c), 172(b)(1)(F)(iii)]. Losses attributable to a federally declared disaster that occurs after 2007 and before January 1, 2010 (whether or not the taxpayer is a farmer) are now treated as a qualified disaster loss eligible for a five-year carryback.

---

[122] Rev. Proc. 2009-26, IRB 2009-19, 935.

[123] *United Dominion Industries, Inc*, SCt, 2001-1 USTC ¶ 50,430, 532 US 822, 121 SCt 1934; *Intermet Corp.*, 117 TC 133, Dec. 54,503 (2001), *nonacq.* IRB 2003-18.

- *Five-year carryback for farming losses.* The carryback period for a farming loss is five years, effective for net operating losses for tax years beginning after December 31, 1997 [Code Sec. 172(b)(1)(G)]. The carryforward period remains at 20 years. A farming loss is defined as the lesser of:

  1. The amount of a taxpayer's NOL for the year if only income and deductions attributable to the taxpayer's farming business were taken into account; or

  2. The amount of the NOL for the year [Code Sec. 172(i)].

  The term "farming business" is defined in Code Sec. 263A(e)(4) as the trade or business of farming and includes the operation of a nursery or sod farm, and the raising or harvesting of trees bearing fruit, nuts, or other crops, or ornamental trees other than evergreen trees which are more than six years old when severed.

- *Five-year carryback for qualified disaster losses.* Qualified disaster losses that arise in tax years beginning after December 31, 2007 and before January 1, 2010, in connection with federally declared disasters declared after that date are eligible for a five-year carryback [Code Sec. 172(b)(1)(J)]. "Qualified disaster losses" are the lesser of: (1) the sum of Code Sec. 165 losses occurring within a disaster area and attributable to a federally declared disaster, plus the deduction for qualified disaster expenses allowable for the year under Code Sec. 198A; or (2) the NOL for that year [Code Sec. 172(j)(1)]. A qualified disaster loss may not include any amounts with respect to any property used in connection with any private or commercial golf course, country club, massage parlor, hot tub facility, suntan facility, or any store selling alcoholic beverages for consumption off premises; or any gambling or animal racing property [Code Sec. 172(j)(4)].

  Alternative tax. A taxpayer electing the five-year carryback will not be subject to the general rule limiting a taxpayer's NOL deduction to 90 percent of alternative minimum taxable income (AMTI) [Code Sec. 56(d)(3)]. Instead, the taxpayer may offset up to 100 percent of AMTI with such NOL carryback.

- *Five-year carryback for Gulf Opportunity Zone losses.* A five-year net operating loss carryback period is provided for "qualified Gulf Opportunity Zone losses" (GO-Zone losses) that arise in tax years ending on or after August 28, 2005 [Code Sec. 1400N(k)].

- *Five-year carryback for timber losses in Gulf Opportunity Zone, Rita GO Zone, and Wilma GO Zone.* A taxpayer with qualified timber property located in the Gulf Opportunity Zone, Rita GO Zone, or Wilma GO Zone may carryback NOLs attributable to pre-January 1, 2007, income and losses with respect to such property for five years, effective for losses that arise in tax years ending on or after August 28, 2005 [Code Sec. 1400N(i)].

Election to Forego Carryback

You can elect to waive the entire NOL carryback period [Code Sec. 172(b)(3)]. Instead, you may use it only in the carryover period. To make this choice, you must attach a statement to your tax return for the NOL year. The statement must show that you elect to forgo the carryback and that it is being made under Sec. 172(b)(3) [Code Sec. 172(b)(3)]. The election must be made by the due date of the return (including extensions). Once you make the election for any NOL year, it is irrevocable.

.03 Who Is Entitled to NOL Relief?

All taxpayers are entitled to the net operating loss deduction. It can be claimed even if you are not in business during the carryback or carryover year [Code Sec. 172; Reg. § 1.172-1]. Although corporations are also allowed to write off NOLs, a special tax rule has been designed to prevent profitable corporations from acquiring unprofitable corporations merely to take advantage of their loss write-offs [Ch. 20].

In LTR 200927031, the IRS ruled that a social club may carry forward its NOLs incurred in years in which it was a tax-exempt entity to years when it is a taxable entity.

¶13,115 DETERMINING NET OPERATING LOSS

A net operating loss is computed the same way as taxable income. Deductions are made from gross income and if the deductions are more than gross income, you have a net operating loss. However, special rules limit what you can deduct in computing a net operating loss. In general, the rules do not allow you to deduct net capital losses or nonbusiness losses in computing the net operating loss.

.01 Business and Nonbusiness

It is necessary first to separate business from nonbusiness items of income and expense.

Business Income

Business income is not only income from your trade or business; salary or wages you earn as an employee are also considered business income. Also, gain from the sale or exchange of depreciable property or real estate you use in your business is included in business income.

Business Deductions

Aside from deductions from your trade or business, personal casualty and theft losses are also business deductions. So are moving expenses and employee business expenses such as travel, transportation, union dues and work clothes required for work. Individual stockholder losses from S corporations are also business deductions.

Nonbusiness Income

Nonbusiness income is income that is not from your trade or business. Examples are dividends, annuities, income from an endowment, interest on investments, and income from S corporations.

Nonbusiness Deductions

Nonbusiness deductions are those not from your trade or business, or are not related to employment. These include medical expenses, alimony, charitable contributions, and contributions to a personal retirement plan. If you do not itemize deductions, nonbusiness deductions include the standard deduction.

.02 Adjustments in Figuring NOL

If your deductions exceed your income so that your tax return shows a loss for the year, certain adjustments have to be made in the loss figure shown on the return. The resulting amount is your net operating loss.

The following items reduce the amount of your loss [Code Sec. 172(d); Reg. § 1.172-3]:

- Net operating loss from any other year;
- Deduction for personal exemptions [Ch. 1];
- Nonbusiness capital losses are deductible only up to nonbusiness capital gains. Any excess cannot be deducted;
- Nonbusiness deductions may be subtracted only from nonbusiness income, including any nonbusiness capital gains that remain after deducting nonbusiness capital losses. Any excess of nonbusiness deductions over nonbusiness income cannot be deducted;
- Business capital losses may be deducted only up to the total business capital gains plus any nonbusiness capital gains that remain after deducting nonbusiness capital losses and other nonbusiness deductions. A net capital loss cannot be deducted; and
- Contributions for a self-employed person to a self-employment retirement plan [Ch. 3].

Example 13-60: The following example illustrates how net operating loss is computed. Mr. Miller owns a small store and he has the following income and deductions:

Income:	
Salary earned as part-time salesman	$26,225
Interest on savings	425
Net long-term capital gain on sale of real estate in business	2,050
Total income	$28,700
Deductions:	
Net loss from small business (sales of $67,000 minus expenses of $100,000)	$33,000
Net short-term capital loss on sale of stock	900
Net loss from rental property	50
Personal exemption	3,200
Small business investment company stock loss	300
Loss on small business stock	620
Total deductions	$38,070

Miller's deductions exceed his income by $9,370 ($38,070-$28,700). However, to compute Miller's net operating loss, certain of his deductions must be modified. He cannot deduct the following:

Nonbusiness net short-term capital loss	$ 900
Personal exemption	3,650
Total adjustments to net loss	$5,450

When these items are eliminated, total deductions are $32,650 ($38,070 - $5,450). Total deductions then exceed income by $3,920 ($32,650 – $28,700). This is Miller's NOL.

.03 Capital Loss Carryover

Because of the distinction between business and nonbusiness capital gains and losses, you must find how much of any capital loss carryover is a business capital loss and how much is a nonbusiness capital loss [Reg. § 1.172-3(b)].

¶13,120 CARRYOVER OF UNUSED PORTION OF NET OPERATING LOSS

For NOLs arising in tax years prior to August 6, 1997, net operating losses (as adjusted above) were used first to reduce income of the third preceding year. If any loss remained, it was carried to the second preceding year, then to the first preceding year, and then it was carried forward to future years, as described in ¶ 13,110. However, taxpayers must make adjustments to their taxable income for each year to which the loss is applied [Code Sec. 172(b)(2); Reg. § 1.172-4(b)].

NOLs arising in tax years after August 5, 1997, generally can only be carried back two years. [See ¶ 13,110].

Important: Taxpayers can elect to waive the carryback and have the NOL apply against only future operating income [Code Sec. 172(b)(3)]. If taxpayers make this election, it must apply for both regular tax and alternative minimum tax purposes.[124]

.01 Determining the Carryover

After determining the year to which taxpayers will initially carry an NOL, they will need to calculate how much of it they can carry back or forward to that year.

If the net operating loss is less than the taxable income of the first year to which it is carried, simply subtract the loss from the taxable income in that year.

Example 13-61: Mr. Miller suffers a $12,000 net operating loss (as adjusted) that he carries back one year. When he filed his return for that year, his taxable income was $30,000. Miller offsets the $30,000 of income by the full $12,000 loss, so his taxable income now drops to $18,000. Miller files an amended return and claims a refund.

---

[124] *R. Plumb*, 97 TC 632, Dec. 47,802 (1991); *M.S. Nemitz*, 130 TC No. 9, Dec. 57,438 (2008).

If the NOL is more than taxable income of the first year to which it is carried, taxpayers must adjust that year's taxable income to see how much of the loss will be used up then and how much will be carried over to the following year [Reg. § 1.172-5]. These are the key adjustments you must make:

1. Capital losses are only deductible to the extent of your capital gains. A net capital loss is not allowed;
2. Deduct any prior net operating loss carrybacks or carryovers. The earliest losses are deducted first;
3. Recompute deductions that are dependent on adjusted gross or taxable income. This applies, for example, to medical expenses (deductible only to the extent they exceed 7 1/2 percent of adjusted gross income) and to charitable contributions (generally deductible to the extent they don't exceed 50 percent of adjusted gross income). Special rule: For charitable contributions only, add back any carrybacks or carryovers deducted in the previous step; and
4. Taxpayers may not claim any personal or dependency deductions.

Example 13-62: Mr. Smith suffers a $30,000 NOL (as adjusted) that he carries back two years. His tax return, as a single taxpayer with no dependents, looked like this:

Salary	$30,000
Taxable interest and dividends	5,000
Total	$35,000
Less: Net capital loss	(1,000)
Adjusted gross income (AGI)	$34,000
Less: Itemized deductions:	
$20,000 charitable gift—deduction limited to 50% of AGI	17,000
$3,000 medical expenses—only amount above 7 1/2% of AGI deductible	450
Taxes, mortgage interest, etc.	3,450
Personal exemption in 2010	3,650
Taxable income	$9,450

Because the $30,000 NOL carried back exceeds the taxable income for that year, it is necessary to adjust Smith's taxable income as follows:

Salary	$30,000
Taxable interest and dividends	5,000
Net capital loss not allowed	0
Modified adjusted gross income	$35,000
Less: Itemized deductions:	
Recomputed charitable gift	17,500
Recomputed medical expenses	375
Taxes, mortgage interest, etc.	3,450
Personal exemption not allowed	0
Modified taxable income	$13,675

The adjustments give Smith a higher taxable income. His operating loss offsets 100 percent of this income, so Smith is entitled to a refund of any tax paid for that year. The remainder of the loss is carried forward to be used against later years' income as needed. Note: If Smith's following-year taxable income is insufficient to absorb 100 percent of the remaining loss, it will be necessary to adjust that year's income in the same manner.

BAD DEBT DEDUCTIONS

¶13,125 OVERVIEW OF BAD DEBTS

The general rule is that a deduction is allowed for "any debt which becomes worthless within the tax year." [Code Sec. 166; Reg. § 1.166-1]. The fact that the debtor is a family member or other related interest does not preclude deduction of a bad debt if the debt was bona fide and worthlessness has been established. A bona fide debt is a debt that arises from "a debtor-creditor relationship based upon a valid and enforceable obligation to pay a fixed or determinable sum of money" [Reg. § 1.166-1(c)].[125] A gift or contribution to capital will not be considered "debt" for purposes of claiming a bad debt deduction under Code Sec. 166 and it is important for taxpayers to distinguish these two types of transactions if the taxpayer wants to claim a bad debt deduction. See ¶ 13,145 and ¶ 13,150. Whether a purported loan is a bona fide debt for tax purposes is determined from the facts and circumstances of each case. Transactions between family members are subject to added scrutiny to determine the true character of a purported loan.[126] The presumption that transactions between family members are gifts may be rebutted by an affirmative showing that a real expectation of repayment and intent to enforce the collection of the indebtedness existed.

Note that a worthless security or worthless corporate bond may not be deducted as a bad debt [Code Secs. 165(g)(2)(C), 166(e)]. See ¶ 13,160. Creditors can deduct the loss resulting from the worthlessness or inability to collect these bad debts, provided the debts had a value when acquired or created.[127]

Business creditors are treated differently from nonbusiness creditors for tax purposes, however, because business creditors can claim bad debt deductions even when the debts are not totally worthless. Nonbusiness bad debts are deductible by taxpayers (other than corporations) only as short-term capital losses, are subject to the limitations on deductions for capital losses, and are reported on Schedule D (Form 1040) [Code

[125] *J.H. Kean*, 91 TC 575, Dec. 45,046 (1988); *J. Shaw*, 106 TCM 54, Dec. 59,589(M), TC Memo. 2013-170.

[126] *J.J. Caligiuri*, CA-8, 77-1 USTC ¶9225, 549 F2d 1155, *aff'g*, 34 TCM 1386, Dec. 33,480(M), TC Memo. 1975-319; *C. Perry*, 92 TC 470, Dec. 45,533 (1989), *aff'd*, CA-5, *in an unpublished opinion*, 912 F2d 1466 (1990), *cert. denied*, 111 SCt 1418.

[127] *A.J. Eckert*, SCt, 2 USTC ¶714, 283 US 140, 51 SCt 373; *M.E. John*, 88 TCM 437, Dec. 55,800(M), TC Memo. 2004-257.

Sec. 166(d)]. A business bad debt occurs when (1) the debt generating the loss was created or acquired in the course of the taxpayer's trade or business (such as a trade receivable); or (2) the worthless debt is incurred in the trade or business of the taxpayer [Code Sec. 166(d)(2); Reg. § 1.166-5(b)].

A business bad debt is deductible by both corporate and noncorporate taxpayers to the full extent of its worthlessness, without limitation. Thus, corporate bad debts—whether business or nonbusiness—are fully deductible in the year they become worthless [Code Sec. 166(a)]. An S corporation may not claim a bad debt deduction for a partially worthless nonbusiness bad debt.[128]

.01 Worthlessness Defined

Whether a debt is worthless depends on the facts and circumstances of each situation, including the value of any collateral securing the debt and the financial condition of the debtor [Reg. § 1.166-2(a)]. The taxpayer has the burden of proving that his or her debt is worthless and failure to do so will result in denial of the bad debt deduction.[129] The taxpayer should be able to show an identifiable event that renders the debt worthless and uncollectible.[130] Legal action is not necessary to prove that the debt is worthless if the surrounding circumstances indicate that the debt is worthless and uncollectible and that legal action to enforce payment would in all probability not result in the satisfaction of execution on a judgment [Reg. § 1.166-2(b)]. Bankruptcy is generally considered an indication of the worthlessness of at least a part of an unsecured and unpreferred debt [Reg. § 1.166-2(c)]. The bad debt deduction is limited to the difference between the claim and the amount received on distribution of the bankrupt's assets [Reg. § 1.166-1(d)(2)]. The word "worthless" is defined as destitute of worth, having no value, valueless, or useless.

.02 When Debtor Contributes to Worthlessness

It is well settled that certain actions by a lender preclude a bad debt deduction. A taxpayer cannot deduct a worthless debt where its actions, standing alone, made the debt uncollectible.[131] For example, a lender can't voluntarily release a solvent debtor and then claim a deduction for a worthless debt.[132] However, the Tax Court has refused to adopt an absolute rule that a taxpayer may never deduct a debt as worthless if the taxpayer contributed to the worthlessness. For example, in *ABC Beverage Corp.*,[133] the Tax Court held that a lender wasn't barred from claiming a bad debt deduction just because the lender's legitimate business decisions contributed to the worthlessness of the debt. The court considered the following factors in determining the appropriateness of allowing a business deduction based on a partially worthless debt where the debtor contributed to the worthlessness:

- The sound business judgment of the corporate officers,
- The value of the collateral securing the debt,

---

[128] Rev. Rul. 93-36, 1993-1 CB 187.

[129] *J. Shaw*, 106 TCM 54, Dec. 59,589(M), TC Memo. 2013-170; *M.A. Bishop*, 105 TCM 1597, Dec. 59,505(M), TC Memo. 2013-98.

[130] *M.E. John*, 88 TCM 437, Dec. 55,800(M), TC Memo. 2004-257.

[131] *Pepsi Americas, Inc.*, FedCl, 2002-1 USTC ¶50,326, 52 FedCl 41.

[132] *Roth Steel Tube Co.*, 68 TC 213, Dec. 34,416 (1977), *aff'd*, CA-6, 80-1 USTC ¶9410, 620 F2d 1176.

[133] *ABC Beverage Corp.*, 92 TCM 268, Dec. 56,620(M), TC Memo. 2006-195.

- Whether the debtor is a going concern with the potential to earn a future profit, and
- Whether the identifiable events occurred to render the debt worthless during the year in which the taxpayer claimed the deduction.

.03 Where to Deduct Bad Debt

If the bad debt was created, acquired, or incurred in a taxpayer's trade or business, it should be reported on Schedule C, Form 1040 (Schedule F, Form 1040, if farming is involved). However, if a business bad debt is incurred by an individual in a trade or business as an employee, it is reported as a miscellaneous itemized deduction for unreimbursed employee business expenses on Schedule A of Form 1040. If a debt is a nonbusiness bad debt, i.e., it is not created, acquired, or incurred in the taxpayer's trade or business, it is treated as a short-term capital loss and should be reported on Schedule D, Form 1040 [Code Sec. 166(d)]. When you deduct specific bad debts, you must attach an explanatory statement to your return. According to IRS Pub. 17, *Your Federal Income Tax,* your statement must show: (1) the nature of the debt (including the amount); (2) the name of the debtor and any business or family relationship to the taxpayer; (3) the date the debt became due; (4) the efforts made to collect the debt; and (5) the reason for determining the debt to be worthless.

.04 Existence of Bona Fide Debt

In order for a bad debt to be deductible, there must be a valid, bona fide enforceable debt. There must also be a debtor-creditor relationship which exists when one person, by contract or law, is obliged to pay another an amount of money, certain or uncertain, either currently or at some future date. There is no debt, however, if the obligation to repay is subject to a contingency and that contingency has not occurred [Reg. § 1.166-1(c)].

The courts have identified and considered the following factors to use in determining whether bona fide debt exists: (1) the names given to the certificates evidencing the indebtedness; (2) the presence or absence of a fixed maturity date; (3) the source of payments; (4) the right to enforce payment of principal and interest; (5) participation in management flowing as a result; (6) the status of the contribution in relation to regular corporate creditors; (7) the intent of the parties; (8) "thin" or inadequate capitalization; (9) identity of interest between creditor and stockholder; (10) source of interest payments; (11) the ability of the corporation to obtain loans from outside lending institutions; (12) the extent to which the advance was used to acquire capital assets; and (13) the failure of the debtor to repay on the due date or to seek a postponement.[134]

¶13,130 AMOUNT DEDUCTIBLE

The amount deductible is the taxpayer's adjusted basis in the debt for determining loss from a sale or exchange [Code Sec. 166(b); Reg. § 1.166-1(d)]. This may or may not be

[134] *J.M. Herrera*, 104 TCM 540, Dec. 59,246(M), TC Memo. 2012-308, *aff'd*, CA-5, 2013-2 USTC ¶ 50,586.

the same as the face amount of the debt. See Ch. 6. No deduction is allowed when the taxpayer's basis cannot be proven.[135]

Example 13-63: Mr. Ames buys a $1,000 note for $700. His basis in the note is $700, and that is the amount deductible if the debt becomes worthless.

¶13,135 BUSINESS BAD DEBTS

A bad debt is considered a business bad debt only if it was created or acquired in the course of a taxpayer's trade or business or the debt became worthless in the course of a taxpayer's trade or business [Reg. § 1.166-5(b)(2)]. The taxpayer's motivation for making the debt must be primary and dominant to his or her trade or business; significant motivation is not sufficient.[136]

Taxpayers can deduct business bad debts in full to the extent they become partially or completely worthless during the tax year [Code Sec. 166]. Whether a debt is worthless depends on the facts and circumstances of each situation, including the value of any collateral and the financial condition of the debtor [Reg. § 1.166-2(a)]. See ¶ 13,125.

For discussion on how qualifying professionals can write off billings that become uncollectible see ¶ 18,175.

.01 Tax Treatment of Business Bad Debt and Nonbusiness Bad Debt

The tax treatment of worthless debt instruments or loans turns on whether the worthless loan is a business bad debt or a nonbusiness bad debt. From a tax perspective, treatment as a business bad debt is preferable because a business bad debt is fully deductible under Code Sec. 166(a) whereas a nonbusiness bad debt is deductible only as a short-term capital loss under Code Sec. 166(d). Code Sec. 166(d)(1) provides that nonbusiness bad debts may be treated as short-term capital losses subject to the $3,000-per-year loss limitation for capital losses. Code Sec. 166(d)(2) defines a nonbusiness bad debt as a debt other than (1) a debt created or acquired in connection with the taxpayer's trade or business, or (2) the loss from worthlessness that is incurred in the taxpayer's trade or business.

Taxpayers are subject to limits on deduction of their capital losses. For noncorporate taxpayers, both net long-term capital losses and short-term capital losses may be used to offset any capital gains (without regard to holding periods), and the excess may be deducted to the extent that it does not exceed the lesser of (1) $3,000 ($1,500 for married individuals filing separate returns), or (2) the excess of the capital losses over the capital gains [Code Sec. 1211(b)]. This means that individual taxpayers can always use capital losses to shelter capital gains. However, if the taxpayer's capital losses for a year exceed his capital gains, the excess is deductible only up to a maximum of $3,000.

For corporations, losses from the sale or exchange of capital assets may only be used to offset capital gains [Code Sec. 1211(a)]. Noncorporate taxpayers who have more capital

---

[135] *R.K. Skinner v. Eaton*, 34 F2d 576, *aff'd*, CA-2, 44 F2d 1020.

[136] *E. Generes*, SCt, 72-1 USTC ¶ 9259, 405 US 93.

losses than can be used in a tax year may be allowed to carry over the excess capital losses and apply them to capital gains and a portion of their ordinary income for an unlimited number of tax years [Code Sec. 1212]. Corporate taxpayers may only carry over unused capital losses for the five years following the capital loss year, but are allowed to carry back unused capital losses to the three years preceding the capital loss year.

> **Example 13-64:** James had $30,000 of ordinary income, a net short-term capital loss of $500, and a net long-term capital loss of $300. His total capital loss deduction is $800.

.02 Investment Activities as a Nonbusiness

When a taxpayer invests his or her own money and manages his or her own investments, these activities do not amount to a trade or business.[137] Investors who invest their own funds in public or privately held companies earn investment returns; they are investing, not conducting a trade or business, even when they make their entire living by investing. "No matter how extensive his activities may be, an investor is never considered to be engaged in a trade or business with respect to his investment activities."[138] When loans are made by a shareholder-employee predominately to protect his or her investment in a company rather than his salary as an employee, the loans will be treated as nonbusiness bad debts.[139]

A common factor used by the courts to distinguish mere investing from conducting a trade or business is whether the investor receives compensation rather than just investment return. In other words if the taxpayer receives not just a return on his investment but compensation attributable to those services, then the investment activity is more likely to rise to the level of a trade or business.[140]

In *T.A. Dagres*,[141] the Tax Court concluded that a venture capital fund manager was allowed a business bad debt deduction under Code Sec. 166(a) for a loan he made to a deadbeat business associate who promised to provide leads on investment opportunities. The court concluded that the taxpayer made the loans only to protect what he considered a valuable source of leads on promising companies in which he could invest the money of the fund and earn substantial income. Since that motive was enhancing the future investment opportunities of his trade or business, the court concluded that he provided the requisite business nexus for claiming a bad debt deduction. Thus, the taxpayer was in the business of managing investments and the loan was proximately related to that business and could be written off as a business bad debt.

---

[137] *A.J. Whipple*, SCt, 63-1 USTC ¶9466, 373 US 193, at 200, 202, 83 SCt 1168.

[138] *M. King*, 89 TC 445, at 459, Dec. 44,174 (1987), citing *E. Higgins*, SCt, 41-1 USTC ¶9233, 312 US 212, at 216, 218, 61 SCt 475.

[139] *H.R. Haury*, 104 TCM 121, Dec. 59,139(M), TC Memo. 2012-215.

[140] *T.A. Dagres*, 136 TC 263, Dec. 58,581 (2011).

[141] *Id.*

¶13,140 NONBUSINESS BAD DEBTS

Nonbusiness bad debts are debts that are not related to the taxpayer's trade or business when they are created, acquired, or become worthless. A debt that arose in the taxpayer's trade or business, becomes a nonbusiness debt in the hands of a donee, executor, or transferee who was not in the trade or business when the debt arose. No deduction is allowed for a partially worthless nonbusiness bad debt [Code Sec. 166(d); Reg. § 1.166-5].

NOTE: Debts owed to corporations are business debts by definition.

Example 13-65: During the year, Mr. Lane, a sole proprietor, made the following loans:

To	Amount	Type	Unrecoverable
Sister	$2,000	Nonbusiness	$1,000
Mother	$1,000	Nonbusiness	$1,000
Customer 1	$3,000	Business	$1,000
Customer 2	$5,000	Business	$2,000

Mr. Lane can deduct $4,000 for bad debts that year: $1,000 that his mother owes him, $1,000 of the $3,000 that Customer 1 owes him and $2,000 of the $5,000 that Customer 2 owes him. Mr. Lane gets no deduction for the $1,000 that his sister owes him because partially worthless nonbusiness bad debts are not deductible.

▶ **IMPORTANT:** When a noncustodial parent doesn't pay court-ordered child support, the custodial parent has no choice but to pay the children's bills out of his or her own pocket. The IRS has said the custodial parent in such a situation cannot take a nonbusiness bad debt deduction for the unpaid support. Reason: The custodial parent has no basis in the debt; the debt is the obligation of the noncustodial parent.[142]

.01 Loans by Officers or Employees

Uncollectible loans made by corporate officers or employees are generally nonbusiness bad debts. The business of the corporation is not the business of its employees or officers. However, a loan may be a business debt if it was required as a condition of your employment, not just to protect your investment in the company. In one case, the Tax Court allowed a corporate president to take a business bad debt deduction for a loss on a business-related guarantee of the corporation debt. The court said his primary motivation was to protect his job.[143]

.02 Loans by a Stockholder to a Corporation

Shareholders who lend money to their corporations will only be able to deduct *bona fide* debts that become worthless during the year under Code Sec. 166(a)(1) if the debts arise from debtor-creditor relationships based upon valid and enforceable

---

[142] Rev. Rul. 93-27, 1993-1 CB 32.

[143] *I. Rosati*, 29 TCM 1661, Dec. 30,473(M), TC Memo. 1970-343.

obligations to pay fixed or determinable amounts of money [Reg. § 1.166-1(c)]. A contribution to capital does not qualify as *bona fide* debt for purposes of Code Sec. 166. The ultimate question is "whether the investment, analyzed in terms of its economic reality, constitutes risk capital entirely subject to the fortunes of the corporate venture or represents a strict debtor-creditor relationship."[144] The names given to documents evidencing the indebtedness, the presence or absence of a fixed maturity date, the source of repayments, the right to enforce repayment of the advance, the intent of the parties, the failure of the corporation to repay on the due date, and other factors are considered to determine whether a payment is a contribution to capital or *bona fide* debt.[145] No one factor is controlling, and the determination of whether there is a loan or a contribution to capital is a question of fact which must be decided on the basis of all the relevant facts and circumstances.

In *Bowers*,[146] the Court of Appeals for the Fourth Circuit held that a loan made personally by a corporate employee to a significant customer of the corporation was made predominantly to maintain the enhanced level of the employee's income resulting from his handling of the customer's transactions. Therefore, when the debt from the customer to the employee became worthless, it was deductible as a business bad debt.

The test for deciding whether a transaction is proximately related to trade or business was established by the U.S. Supreme Court in *E. Generes*[147] in which the Court held that, where the taxpayer is both an employee and shareholder, the taxpayer's "dominant motivation" underlying the transaction(s) at issue determines whether the transaction(s) is proximately related to the taxpayer's trade or business. In the event a taxpayer's dominant motivation is business-related, the taxpayer may deduct. Oppositely, if the taxpayer's dominant motivation is investment-related, the taxpayer may not deduct. Thus, whether a bad debt may be properly characterized as deductible depends on the intent of the taxpayer.

In determining whether the advances to the corporation gave rise to a bona fide debt as opposed to an equity investment, some courts have relied on the following factors cited in *A.R. Lantz Co.*:[148]

1. Labels on the documents evidencing the (supposed) indebtedness,
2. Presence or absence of a maturity date,
3. Source of payment,
4. Right of the (supposed) lender to enforce payment,
5. Lender's right to participate in management,
6. Lender's right to collect compared to the regular corporate creditors,

---

144 *Calumet Industries*,95 TC 257, Dec. 46,872 (1990); *Fin Hay Realty Co.*, CA-3, 68-2 USTC ¶ 9438, 398 F2d 694; *D. Bynum, Jr.*, 95 TCM 1060, Dec. 57,315(M), TC Memo. 2008-14.

145 *Texas Farm Bureau*, CA-5, 84-1 USTC ¶ 9247, 725 F2d 307; *Am. Offshore*, 97 TC 579, Dec. 47,750 (1991).

146 *J.N. Bowers*, CA-4, 83-2 USTC ¶ 9569, 716 F2d 1047; *H. Litwin* DC-KS, 91-1 USTC ¶ 50,229, *aff'd*, CA-10, 93-1 USTC ¶ 50,041, 983 F2d 997.

147 *E. Generes*, SCt, 72-1 USTC ¶ 9259, 405 US 93, 92 SCt 827.

148 *A.R. Lantz*, CA-9, 70-1 USTC ¶ 9308, 424 F2d 1330.

7. Parties' intent,
8. Adequacy of the (supposed) borrower's capitalization,
9. Whether stockholders' advances to the corporation are in the same proportion as their equity ownership in the corporation,
10. Payment of interest out of only "dividend money," and
11. Borrower's ability to obtain loans from outside lenders.

In *J.C. Ramig*,[149] corporate shareholder and employee were not entitled to bad-debt deductions for amounts advanced to, and paid on or behalf of the corporation because they represented equity investments, rather than loans. The court reasoned that: (1) the company could not obtain loans from outside lenders and it was therefore not likely it could have repaid the advances from its own earnings; (2) the parties did not provide for interest or a repayment date; (3) there was no evidence the company had repaid similar charges in the past; and (4) the taxpayer failed to show that his payments for equipment rentals were made as a guarantor for the corporation.

.03 Nonbusiness Bad Debt Deductible as Short-Term Capital Loss

You treat a nonbusiness bad debt as a short-term capital loss in the year of worthlessness. (Because debts owed to corporations are always business debts, this restriction does not apply to them.)

> **Example 13-66:** Ms. Zale had a nonbusiness bad debt of $3,200 owed to her which became worthless this year. The debt of $3,200 is considered a short-term capital loss. If Zale had no other capital gains and losses this year, the debt is deductible only to the extent of $3,000, and the balance ($200) is carried over to the following year.

¶13,145 ADVANCES TO RELATIVES

If you lend money to relatives and they fail to pay you back, your ability to deduct the loss depends on how the advance to the relative is characterized for tax purposes. First, you must establish whether the advance to the relative was a gift or a loan. If the advance that will never be repaid turns out to be characterized as a gift, you will be unable to claim a deduction because no debtor-creditor relationship was created when you gave your relative the money.

The next step is to determine whether the advance was a business or nonbusiness bad debt. If the intra-family advance that subsequently became worthless qualifies as a business bad debt it will be deductible under Code Sec. 166(a) as it becomes wholly or partially worthless to the full extent of its worthlessness. On the other hand, if the intra-family advance qualifies as a nonbusiness bad debt, it will only be deductible when it becomes wholly worthless and then only as a short-term capital loss regardless of the time it has been outstanding [Code Sec. 166(d)(1)(B)]. A short-term capital loss is

[149] *J.C. Ramig*, CA-9, 2012-2 USTC ¶50,639.

deducted on Schedule D and offsets dollar-for-dollar your short-term capital gain. Any excess can be used to offset long-term capital gains dollar-for-dollar. When short-term capital losses exceed capital gain, the excess can offset up to $3,000 of ordinary income in the year the loss occurs. You can carry forward any unused balance of the short-term capital loss [Code Secs. 1211, 1212, 1222].

You can claim a bad debt as a short-term capital loss if you satisfy the following requirements:

- You must be able to prove that the debt arose from a valid debtor/creditor relationship based on a valid and enforceable obligation to pay a fixed or determinable sum of money [Reg. § 1.166-1(c)]. You must be able to show that the obligation to repay was not contingent and was made with a reasonable expectation, belief, and intention that the advance would be repaid.
- The debt must be completely worthless and you must have no reasonable expectation of future payment.[150] Your deduction will be denied if even a modest fraction of the debt can be recovered [Reg. § 1.166-5(a)(2)]. The law is strict on this point because the government is afraid that everyone will try to deduct all loans/gifts made to family members and friends as nonbusiness bad debts. For this reason, in order to successfully claim a short-term capital loss for advances to deadbeat relatives, you must prove that the debt is totally worthless in the year that you claim the loss.

When you are claiming a short-term capital loss, attach a statement to your Schedule D explaining the following:

- Why you are claiming the deduction;
- Why you lent the money;
- The name of the debtor;
- What actions you took to recover the money;
- Why the debt is worthless this year; and
- When the debt was due.

To be sure that your intra-family loan will be deductible as a loss in the event that the relative defaults, pay attention to the following:

1. Check Applicable Federal Rates to determine the minimum rate required by the IRS.
2. Set terms including amount, interest rate, payment schedule, and length of loan. Don't agree in advance to forgive any part of the loan.
3. Retain a lawyer to draw up a formal note establishing the terms of the loan.
4. If a house is purchased with the loan, draw up a mortgage and get title insurance.
5. Record the loan at the appropriate county office.

---

[150] *M.A. Buchanan*, CA-7, 96-2 USTC ¶50,334, 87 F3d 197, *cert. denied*, 519 US 950, 117 SCt 363.

¶13,150 ADVANCES TO CORPORATIONS BY STOCKHOLDERS

These advances may be loans or capital contributions (additional investment). If the advance is in fact a loan, it is subject to the rules governing bad debts.

In *Cerand & Co.*,[151] the Tax Court looked at the following factors to conclude that advances made by a taxpayer to related corporations were capital contributions rather than loans:

- There was no certificate memorializing the debt or fixed maturity date or repayment schedule;
- Repayments were sporadic, not uniform in amount and depended on financial success and the resulting ability to pay; and
- Based on the corporation's thin capitalization and no business history, third-party lenders would not have made similar loans on similar terms.

As a result of the court's characterization of the advances as capital contributions rather than loans, when the borrower went out of business, the taxpayer could only claim the losses as capital losses.

¶13,155 DEPOSITS IN CLOSED BANKS

Code Sec. 165(l) provides that a taxpayer may elect to treat certain losses in an insolvent financial institution as a casualty or theft loss if the taxpayer can prove that the loss resulted from the bankruptcy or insolvency of the institution and if the taxpayer is a qualified individual. A *qualified individual* is any individual except anyone who is an officer of the qualified financial institution, who owns at least one percent in value of the outstanding stock of the institution, and certain relatives and persons related to such persons [Code Sec. 165(l)(2)].

In one case, the CEO of a failed S & L was denied a deduction for his lost personal deposits in the S & L because the taxpayer was an officer of the S & L in the years he claimed the losses and was not a qualified individual entitled to an ordinary loss deduction under Code Sec. 165(l).[152] The taxpayer could not deduct the deposits as bad debts under Code Sec. 166 because he failed to prove that the deposits became wholly worthless during the years in issue. The taxpayers also tried to deduct the debts as ordinary and necessary business expenses under Code Sec. 162. The Tax Court rejected this attempt with the explanation that Code Sec. 162 does not apply to debts.

However, deposits not made in the course of your business are subject to the usual rule for nonbusiness bad debts and are treated as short-term capital losses [Code Sec. 166(d)(1); Reg. §1.166-5]. Your total net capital losses (for the current year and any carryovers) can offset up to $3,000 of your salary, dividends, and other income for the

---

[151] *Cerand & Co.*, 82 TCM 755, Dec. 54,514(M), TC Memo. 2001-271.

[152] *C.L. Fincher*, 105 TC 126, Dec. 50,859 (1995).

year. Your deduction is reduced to the extent you are compensated by deposit insurance. Your deposit is simply treated as a loan to the bank.

.01 Election to Treat as an Ordinary Loss

You also may elect to deduct a deposit the bank will not repay as an ordinary loss incurred in a transaction entered into for profit [Code Sec. 165(l)]. A special rule allows you to get a full deduction up to a maximum amount of $20,000 per year ($10,000 for married taxpayers filing separately) [Code Sec. 165(l)(5)(B)(ii)].

However, you may not make this election if any part of the deposit is insured under federal law. Additionally, you must reduce the $20,000 ceiling by the amount of insurance proceeds you reasonably expect to receive under state law.

> **NOTE:** If you own one percent or more of the financial institution or are an officer, you cannot elect to treat your deposit as an ordinary loss or a casualty loss. You also cannot make an election if you are related to an owner or officer.

¶13,160 WORTHLESS BONDS

The bad debt rules do not apply to bonds issued by corporations or governments [Code Secs. 165(g)(2)(C), 166(e)]. This is true whether the holder of the bond is a corporate or noncorporate taxpayer. However, as with any worthless security, you may be entitled to a capital loss deduction.

.01 Exception

Worthless securities held by a bank or trust company are treated as bad debts [Code Sec. 582]. And there is a conclusive presumption of complete or partial worthlessness when a bank or trust company must charge off a debt in whole or in part in obedience to specific orders of the banking authorities.

¶13,165 BAD DEBT AND LOSS DISTINGUISHED

The difference between a bad debt and loss may be important for two reasons: (1) you cannot take a deduction for property that declines in value (e.g., stock certificates) without a sale or exchange, but you may be able to deduct partially worthless business bad debts; and (2) ordinarily, the statute of limitations for you to file a refund claim for a loss deduction is three years after you filed the return. The statute of limitations is seven years for a bad debt.

.01 Voluntary Cancellation or Forgiveness

These voluntary cancellations of a debt do not give rise to deductible losses. However, you may be able to take a bad debt deduction if the debt is actually worthless. That deduction may be allowed because the debt is worthless, not because it is forgiven. For example, you can deduct the difference between a note's face value and the amount received in compromise if your debtor has no assets out of which the entire amount can be collected by suit. In some cases, even though the debt was not worthless when you forgave it, you can take a loss deduction when there is some payment in exchange for the forgiveness.

Deductible as a Loss

The debt cancellation is a loss when made in exchange for a security interest (or lien) for other debts previously unsecured.[153]

A loss resulting from a dispute over the correctness of book charges and credits in connection with business transactions in a compromised account is deductible in the year in which settled by compromise or otherwise.[154]

Loss under composition agreement is deductible in the year the agreement was made.[155]

Capital Transactions Not Deductible

If a shareholder gratuitously forgives a debt owed to him by the corporation, the transaction amounts to a contribution to the capital of the corporation [Reg. § 1.61-12]. No loss deduction is allowed.

.02 Endorsers and Guarantors

If you incur a loss from a loan guaranty, you receive the same treatment as if you had made the loan directly. Thus, you can generally deduct the loss in full if the guaranty is connected with your trade or business. If you entered into a guaranty for profit, the loss is a short-term capital loss. If you operate on the cash basis of accounting, you get no bad debt deduction until you pay the note.

> **Example 13-67:** Francis endorses John's note. John defaults and Francis has to pay. Ordinarily, John owes Francis the amount paid. If this debt is worthless, Francis may take a deduction.

The deduction may be disallowed if the endorser cannot prove he intended to collect the debt.

> **Example 13-68:** Father endorsed his son's note, without investigating the son's financial prospects. Father made no effort to collect from the son when he had to pay the son's debt. The bad debt deduction is denied on the ground that the transaction was in effect a gift to the son.

¶13,170 RECOVERY OF BAD DEBTS

In the year you recover part or all of a bad debt previously deducted, you must include the recovery in your income to the extent that it reduced your tax in an earlier year. A recovery is a return of an amount you deducted or took a credit for in an earlier year.

---

[153] *First National Bank of Durant, Okla.*, 6 BTA 545, Dec. 2259, *acq.* 1927-2 CB 2.

[154] *Kansas City Pump Co.*, 6 BTA 938, Dec. 2373.

[155] *Pacific Novelty Co.*, 5 BTA 1017, Dec. 2047, *acq.* 1927-1 CB 5.

Generally, you must include part or all of the recovered amounts in income in the year you receive the recovery.

> **Example 13-69:** Mr. Stone's tax return showed a short-term capital loss deduction of $300 when his debtor failed to pay a $300 debt. The following year, the debtor paid Stone the $300. Stone includes the $300 in gross income that year. He does not make the adjustment by filing an amended return the previous year.

.01 Tax Benefit Rule

This rule comes into play if you deducted a bad debt from your gross income and later collect all or part of the debt. Your recovery is included in your income only to the extent that the deduction reduced your tax (by any amount) in an earlier year. The recovery amount is excludable from income if the deduction reduced your taxable income but did not reduce your tax liability [Ch. 2].

¶13,175 LOSS ON SALE OF PLEDGED PROPERTY OTHER THAN ON PURCHASE MONEY MORTGAGE

If a mortgagor makes a voluntary conveyance of property to the mortgagee, the property's fair market value is considered as payment of the unpaid balance of the obligation. If the fair market value of the property is less than the amount owed, the difference, if uncollectible, is a bad debt deductible by the mortgagee. If there is a foreclosure and someone other than the mortgagee bids on the property for less than the obligation, the mortgagee has a bad debt deduction for the difference between the obligation and the amount received. If the mortgagee bids on the property, the deduction is the difference between the obligation and the bid price [Reg. § 1.166-6]. For repossessions of installment sale property, see Chapter 19.

14 Tax Credits—Estimated Tax for Individuals

PERSONAL TAX CREDITS

Child and dependent care credit . . ¶ 14,001

Earned income credit . . . . ¶ 14,005

Credit for the elderly and permanently disabled . . . . ¶ 14,010

Adoption expenses credit . . . . . . ¶ 14,015

Child tax credit . . . . ¶ 14,020

Hope Scholarship Credit/ American Opportunity Tax Credit . . . . ¶ 14,025

Lifetime Learning Credit . . . . ¶ 14,030

Health Coverage Tax Credit . . . . . ¶ 14,035

Residential energy property credit . . . . ¶ 14,040

Residential alternative energy expenditures credit . . . . ¶ 14,045

First-time homebuyer credit . . . . ¶ 14,047

GENERAL BUSINESS CREDIT

Figuring the general business credit . . . . ¶ 14,050

Investment credit . . . . ¶ 14,055

Low-income housing credit . . . . . ¶ 14,060

Work opportunity tax credit . . . . . ¶ 14,065

Orphan drug credit . . . . ¶ 14,075

Research tax credit . . . . ¶ 14,080

Enhanced oil recovery credit . . . . ¶ 14,085

Disabled access credit . . . . ¶ 14,090

Renewable electricity production credit . . . . ¶ 14,095

Clean renewable energy bond credit . . . . ¶ 14,096

Empowerment zone and renewal community employment credit . . . . ¶ 14,100

Indian employment credit . . . . . . ¶ 14,105

Employer social security credit on tips (FICA tip credit) . . . . ¶ 14,110

Credit for small business pension plan start-up expenses . . . . . . ¶ 14,115

Small employer health insurance tax credit . . . . ¶ 14,120

Code Sec. 36B premium assistance tax credit . . . . ¶ 14,121

Credit for employers providing child care assistance for employees . . . . ¶ 14,125

Employer wage credit for activated military reservists . . . . ¶ 14,126

Railroad track maintenance credit . . . . ¶ 14,127

Mine rescue team training tax credit . . . . ¶ 14,128

Retirement savings contribution credit . . . . ¶ 14,130

New markets tax credit . . . . ¶ 14,135

Homebuilder's credit for new energy-efficient homes . . . . ¶ 14,140

Manufacturer's credit for energy-efficient appliances . . . . ¶ 14,145

Advanced nuclear facility business tax credit . . . . ¶ 14,150

Credit for installation of alternative fueling stations . . . . ¶ 14,155
Worker retention credit . . . . ¶ 14,156
Election to claim accelerated AMT and research credits in lieu of bonus depreciation . . . . . . ¶ 14,157
Carbon dioxide capture credit . . . . ¶ 14,158
Credits for certain uses of gasoline and special fuels . . . . ¶ 14,165
Fuel production credits . . . . ¶ 14,170
Agricultural chemicals security tax credit . . . . ¶ 14,171
Credit for interest paid on mortgage credit certificates . . . . ¶ 14,175
Plug-in electric drive motor vehicle credit . . . . ¶ 14,180
Credit for holders of qualified zone academy bonds . . . . ¶ 14,185
Alternative motor vehicle credit . . ¶ 14,195

PAYMENT OF ESTIMATED TAX BY INDIVIDUALS

What is estimated tax? . . . . ¶ 14,200
Who must make estimated tax payments . . . . ¶ 14,205
When to pay estimated tax . . . . . . ¶ 14,210
How to figure estimated tax . . . . . ¶ 14,215
Penalty for underpaying estimated tax . . . . ¶ 14,220

BACKUP WITHHOLDING

Backup withholding on interest, dividends, and certain other payments . . . . ¶ 14,225

PERSONAL TAX CREDITS

¶14,001 CHILD AND DEPENDENT CARE CREDIT

The child and dependent care tax credit is a nonrefundable credit available to offset a percentage of employment-related expenses incurred for household services and for the care of a qualifying individual incurred so the taxpayer can be gainfully employed. The expenses must be for periods during which the taxpayer is gainfully employed or is in active search of gainful employment [Code Sec. 21(a); Reg. § 1.21-1(a)].

.01 Who May Claim the Credit?

A taxpayer may claim the dependent care credit if the taxpayer incurred expenses to care for a qualifying individual while the taxpayer is at work or looking for work. A qualifying individual is defined as:

- A qualifying child (as defined for purposes of the dependency exemption [Ch. 1]) who has not attained age 13; A qualifying child is the taxpayer's child or a descendant of the taxpayer's child (i.e., grandchild); or the taxpayer's sibling (including half-brothers and half-sisters) or step-sibling or a descendant of the taxpayer's sibling or step-sibling who have not attained the age of 13 [Code Sec. 21(b)(1)(A)]. The child must be a U.S. citizen during the relevant years.[1]

---

[1] *L.M. Carlebach,* 139 TC No. 1, Dec. 59,127 (2012).

- An individual who lives with the taxpayer for more than one-half of the tax year, is incapable of self care, and is the taxpayer's dependent or if the individual would qualify as the taxpayer's dependent but for one or more of the following reasons: (1) the taxpayer or spouse was claimed as a dependent on another person's return (and thus was not eligible to claim dependency exemptions), or (2) the individual receiving care could not be claimed as a dependent because he or she was married and filed a joint return, or (3) the individual receiving care could not be claimed as a dependent because his or her gross income equaled or exceeded the exemption amount ($3,900 in 2013) [Code Sec. 21(b)(1)(B)]. A taxpayer's dependent is someone who is a qualifying child or a qualifying relative. A qualifying relative is (1) a person who has the same principal abode as the taxpayer and is a member of the taxpayer's household, or who is a relative such as a parent, step-parent, sibling, step-sibling, aunt, uncle, in-law, child, or grandchild, (2) for whom the taxpayer provides over one-half of the person's support for the year, (3) who is not a qualifying child of another taxpayer, and (4) whose gross income is less than the exemption amount [Code Sec. 152(d)].

- The taxpayer's spouse, if the spouse is physically or mentally incapable of caring for himself or herself and has the same principal place of abode as the taxpayer for more than half of the tax year [Code Sec. 21(b)(1)(C)]. An individual is physically or mentally incapable of self-care if, as a result of a physical or mental defect, the individual is incapable of caring for his or her hygiene or nutritional needs, or requires full-time attention of another person for his or her own safety or the safety of others. The inability of an individual to engage in any substantial gainful activity or to perform the normal household functions of a homemaker or care for minor children because of a physical or mental condition does not of itself establish that the individual is physically or mentally incapable of self-care [Reg. § 1.21-1(b)(4)].

To be a qualifying individual for purposes of the dependent care credit, a physically or mentally disabled dependent or spouse must have the same principal place of abode as the taxpayer for more than one-half of the year [Code Sec. 21(b)(1)]. An individual will not be treated as having the same principal place of abode as the taxpayer if, at any time during the tax year, the relationship between the individual and the taxpayer is in violation of local law [Code Sec. 21(e)(1)].

.02 Employment-Related Expenses Defined

Expenses are employment-related expenses only if they enable the taxpayer to be gainfully employed. The nature of the taxpayer's work is somewhat irrelevant. It can be as an independent contractor, an employee, part-time or full-time. Employment may consist of services performed within or outside the taxpayer's home and include self-employment. The expenses must be for the care of a qualifying individual or for household services performed during periods when the taxpayer is gainfully employed or is in active search of gainful employment. Work as a volunteer or for a nominal consideration is not considered gainful employment in this situation [Reg. § 1.21-1(c)(1)]. If expenses are paid for a period of time and the taxpayer is gainfully employed or in active search of gainful employment during only part of that time, the expenses must be allocated on a daily basis [Reg. § 1.21-1(c)(2)].

Short, Temporary Absence Exception

A taxpayer who is gainfully employed is not required to allocate expenses during a short, temporary absence from work, such as for vacation or minor illness, provided that the care-giving arrangement requires the taxpayer to pay for care during the absence. An absence of two consecutive calendar weeks is a short, temporary absence. Whether an absence longer than two consecutive calendar weeks is a short, temporary absence is determined based on all the facts and circumstances [Reg. § 1.21-1(c)(2)(ii)].

Part-Time Employment

A taxpayer who is employed part-time generally must allocate expenses for dependent care between days worked and days not worked. However, if a taxpayer employed part-time is required to pay for dependent care on a periodic basis (such as weekly or monthly) that includes both days worked and days not worked, the taxpayer is not required to allocate the expenses. A day on which the taxpayer works at least one hour is a day of work [Reg. § 1.21-1(c)(2)(iii)].

Care for Child Outside Home

Expenses for child care services outside the taxpayer's home qualify for the credit if the expenses are incurred to care for a dependent under the age of 13. If the child turns 13 in mid-year, the taxpayer can only claim the credit for expenses incurred prior to the child's 13th birthday [Code Sec. 21(b)(1)(A)].

Care for Parent Outside Home

A taxpayer can also claim a credit for expenses for the out-of-home care of a dependent, other than a qualifying child (such as a parent), if (1) the dependent also spends at least 8 hours a day in the taxpayer's household, and (2) the care is provided in a qualified dependent care center [Code Sec. 21(b)(2)(B); Reg. § 1.21-1(e)(2)]. The term *dependent care center* means any facility that provides full-time or part-time care for more than six individuals (other than individuals who reside at the facility) on a regular basis during the year, and receives a fee, payment, or grant for providing services for the individuals (regardless of whether the facility is operated for profit) [Code Sec. 21(b)(2)(D); Reg. § 1.21-3(e)(2)(ii)].

The social security and federal unemployment tax paid on household and dependent care wages are considered to be part of the total amount paid for household and dependent care.

Educational Programs

Expenses for a child in a nursery school or a pre-school program for children below the level of kindergarten are for the care of a qualifying individual and may be considered employment-related expenses. In addition, expenses for before- or after-school care of a child in kindergarten or a higher grade may qualify. But the expenses associated with education beginning at the kindergarten level, however, are not considered expenses incurred for the care of a qualifying individual [Reg. § 1.21-1(d)(5)].

Summer School, Day Camp

The costs of summer school and tutoring programs are not qualifying employment-related expenses because they are educational in nature. Expenses for overnight camps are not employment-related expenses [Code Sec. 21(b)(2); Reg. § 1.21-1(d)(6)]. However, the cost of a day camp or similar program may be for the care of a qualifying individual and an employment-related expense, even if the day camp specializes in a particular activity.

Household Services

Expenses for household services may be employment-related expenses if the services are ordinary and usual services performed in the taxpayer's home and are necessary for the maintenance of the household and attributable to the care of the qualifying individual. Services of a housekeeper are household services if the services are provided, at least in part, to the qualifying individual. Services performed by chauffeurs, bartenders, or gardeners are not considered household services [Code Sec. 21(b)(2)(A); Reg. § 1.21-1(d)(3)]. If an expense is partly for household services or for the care of a qualifying individual and partly for other goods or services, a reasonable allocation must be made. Only so much of the expense that is allocable to the household services or care of a qualifying individual is an employment-related expense. An allocation must be made if a housekeeper or other domestic employee performs household duties and cares for the qualifying children of the taxpayer and also performs other services for the taxpayer. No allocation is required, however, if the expense for the other purpose is minimal or insignificant or if an expense is partly attributable to the care of a qualifying individual and partly to household services.

Manner of Providing Care

The manner of providing care need not be the least expensive alternative available to the taxpayer. The cost of a paid caregiver may be an expense for the care of a qualifying individual even if another caregiver is available at no cost [Reg. § 1.21-1(d)(4)].

Indirect Expenses

Expenses that relate to, but are not directly for the care of a qualifying individual, such as application fees, agency fees, and deposits, may be for the care of a qualifying individual and may be employment-related expenses if the taxpayer is required to pay the expenses to obtain the related care. However, forfeited deposits and other payments are not for the care of a qualifying individual if care is not provided [Reg. § 1.21-1(d)(11)].

.03 Amount of Credit

Taxpayers with adjusted gross income of $15,000 or less are allowed a credit equal to 35 percent of employment-related expenses. The credit is reduced by one percentage point for each $2,000 of adjusted gross income, or fraction thereof, above $15,000 through $43,000. Taxpayers with adjusted gross income over $43,000 are allowed a credit equal to 20 percent of employment-related expenses. The maximum amount of employment-related expenses to which the credit may be applied is $3,000 if there is one qualifying individual or $6,000 if there are two or more qualifying individuals [Code Sec. 21(c)]. For married taxpayers, the expenses taken into account in calculating the credit may not exceed the earned income of the spouse who earns the lesser amount [Code Sec. 21(d)(1)]. Thus, a married person with a nonworking spouse cannot claim the credit, unless the nonworking spouse is incapable of self-care or is a full-time student. If the nonworking spouse is incapable of self-care or is a student, that person is deemed to have earned income of $250 for each month of disability or school attendance if there is one qualifying child or dependent, or $500 if there are two or more children or dependents [Code Sec. 21(d)(2)]. Table 1 outlines the maximum credits available to taxpayers as follows:

Table 1. Maximum Dependent Care Credit

Maximum Credits

Adjusted Gross Income	Applicable Percentage	One Qualifying Individual	Two or More Qualifying Individuals
$15,000 or less	35%	$1,050	$2,100
$15,001—17,000	34%	1,020	2,040
$17,001—19,000	33%	990	1,980
$19,001—21,000	32%	960	1,920
$21,001—23,000	31%	930	1,860
$23,001—25,000	30%	900	1,800
$25,001—27,000	29%	870	1,740
$27,001—29,000	28%	840	1,680
$29,001—31,000	27%	810	1,620
$31,001—33,000	26%	780	1,560
$33,001—35,000	25%	750	1,500
$35,001—37,000	24%	720	1,440
$37,001—39,000	23%	690	1,380
$39,001—41,000	22%	660	1,320
$41,001—43,000	21%	630	1,260
$43,001 and over	20%	600	1,200

Deemed Earned Income

The amount of your work-related expenses during the tax year may not exceed your earned income for the year. If you are married, the expenses may not exceed the lower-paid spouse's earnings for the year. This means that a married taxpayer with a nonworking spouse may not be able to claim the dependent care credit unless the nonworking spouse is incapable of taking care of himself or is a full-time student. If the nonworking spouse is incapable of self-care or is a full-time student and therefore has no earned income, Code Sec. 21(d)(2) provides the dollar limit on deemed earned income of a taxpayer's spouse who is either a full-time student, or physically or mentally incapable of caring for himself is $250 a month if there is one dependent and $500 a month if there are two or more dependents.

Example 14-1: The taxpayer works full-time outside of her home. She has an infant and a three-year-old child. Her husband is attending medical school and has no other earned income. The taxpayer has adjusted gross income of $14,000 for the year and pays $6,000 a year for a live-in nanny. Under Code Sec. 21(d)(2) her husband's deemed income is $500 a month for the 12 months. The couple's credit would be $2,100 (35% × $6,000) for the year. The 35 percent credit rate is available because the wife's adjusted gross income is less then $15,000. If her adjusted gross income had been over $43,000, the percentage would have been reduced to 20 percent of the work-related expenses and the credit would be $1,200.

There is an overall limit on the child care credit and the credit for the elderly and permanently disabled [¶ 14,010]. These combined credits are allowed to the extent they do not exceed your tax liability.

.04 Payments to Relatives

The credit is available for child care payments you make to a relative, provided you are not eligible to claim a dependency exemption for the relative. If the relative is your child (as defined in Code Sec. 152(f)(1) [See Ch. 1]), the child must be at least 19 years of age. [Code Sec. 21(e)(6); Reg. §1.21-4(a)].

.05 Filing Requirements

In order to claim the credit for child and dependent care expenses, a taxpayer must file Form 1040 or Form 1040-A or Form 1040NR. The credit cannot be claimed on Form 1040EZ or on Form 1040NR-EZ. A taxpayer must complete Form 2441, *Child and Dependent Care Expenses*, and attach it to Form 1040, Form 1040A, or Form 1040NR.

.06 Provider Identification Test

A taxpayer must identify all persons or organizations that provide care for his or her child or dependent. Use Part I for Form 2441 to show the information. To identify the care provider, the taxpayer must give the provider's name, address, and taxpayer identification number. If the care provider is an individual, the taxpayer identification number or his social security number or individual taxpayer identification number must be provided. If the care provider is an organization, then the employer identification number (EIN) is required. If the taxpayer is unable to furnish this information, the taxpayer must be able to show that due diligence was used in trying to furnish the necessary information. Even though the taxpayer is unable to provide the information required, he or she may still claim the credit if the taxpayer can show to the IRS that he or she exercised due diligence in attempting to provide the required information [Code Sec. 21(e)(9)].

.07 Filing Status

In order to claim the credit for child and dependent care expenses, the taxpayer's filing status must be single, head of household, qualifying widow(er) with dependent child, or married filing jointly [Code Sec. 21(e)(4)]. If a taxpayer is married at the close of the tax year, a joint return must be filed in order for the dependent care credit to be claimed [Code Sec. 21(e)(2); Reg. §1.21-3(a)]. If either spouse dies during the tax year and it is possible to file a joint return for the survivor and the deceased spouse, the credit is allowed only if a joint return is made. If the surviving spouse remarries before the end of the tax year in which his spouse died, the credit is allowed on the decedent's separate return [Reg. §1.21-3(c)].

.08 Divorced and Separated Taxpayers

A special rule applies to a divorced or legally separated taxpayer, a taxpayer separated under a written separation agreement, or a taxpayer who lives apart from his spouse for the last six months of the tax year [Code Sec. 21(e)(5)]. The custodial parent is entitled to a dependent care credit for any child who: (1) is under age 13, or is physically or mentally incapable of self-care, (2) receives over half of his or her support during the calendar year from one or both parents, and (3) is in the custody of one or both parents for more than one-half of the calendar year [Reg. § 1.21-1(b)(5)].

The custodial parent is the parent having custody for the greater portion of the calendar year [Code Sec. 152(e)(4)]. The custodial parent is entitled to the credit even though the noncustodial parent can claim the child as a dependent. The noncustodial parent will be able to claim the child's exemption because the custodial parent released his or her right to the exemption by signing Form 8332, *Release/Revocation of Claim to Exemption for Child by Custodial Parent*, or a similar statement.

An individual who is legally separated under a decree of divorce or of separate maintenance is not considered to be married for purposes of the child and dependent care credit [Code Sec. 21(e)(3); Reg. § 1.21-3(b)]. In addition, a married person who lives apart from his spouse for the last six months of the tax year, files a separate return, maintains a household which is for more than half the year the principal place of abode of a qualifying dependent, and furnishes over half the cost of maintaining the household for the year is not considered married when computing the credit [Code Sec. 21(e)(4); Reg. § 1.21-3(b)].

> ▶ **TAX TIP:** If your employer has a plan that lets you put pre-tax dollars in a child care reimbursement account, you need to choose between participating in that plan and claiming the credit. The employer's plan has these advantages: (1) The plan dollar limits are higher; (2) the employer's plan exclusion gives a tax benefit at your highest tax rate, while the child care credit for you will probably be limited to 20 percent (if your adjusted gross income exceeds $43,000); and (3) payments under an employer's plan are exempt from social security and Medicare taxes.

Taxpayers may claim the full benefit of certain nonrefundable personal credits, which include the child and dependent care credit, to offset their regular tax as opposed to only the amount by which the regular tax exceeds the alternative tentative minimum tax [Ch. 16].

¶14,005 EARNED INCOME CREDIT

The *earned income credit* (EIC) is a refundable tax credit for eligible low-income workers [Code Sec. 32(a)]. As a result, if the EIC exceeds the worker's tax liability, he or she can get a check from the IRS for the excess. The credit is based on earned income, which includes wages, salaries, and other employee compensation, plus earnings from self-employment. The amount of the credit is determined by multiplying an individual's earned income by a credit percentage, subject to a possible phaseout. Different credit percentages and phaseout percentages are provided for low-income workers who have no qualifying children, one qualifying child, and more than one qualifying child. The worker claims the credit by filing Schedule EIC of Form 1040 or 1040A. If you do not have a qualifying child, you can use Form 1040EZ to claim the credit. A low-income employee with one or more children can cash in on an advance credit before he or she files a tax return. The employee simply gives his or her employer a completed Form W-5, and the employer then includes part of the credit in each of the employee's paychecks.

.01 Qualifying Children

Tests of Qualifying Child Status

Relationship test. A qualifying child for purposes of the EIC must be (1) a son, daughter, or stepchild of the taxpayer or a descendent of a son, daughter, or stepchild of the taxpayer or (2) a brother, sister, stepbrother, or stepsister of the taxpayer or a descendent of a brother, sister, stepbrother, or stepsister of the taxpayer [Code Sec. 32(c)(3)(A)]. A child who is legally adopted by a taxpayer or placed with the taxpayer for legal adoption by the taxpayer is treated as a taxpayer's own child by blood [Code Sec. 152(f)(1)(B)]). A brother or sister includes a brother or sister by the half-blood [Code Sec. 152(f)(4)]. A foster child is treated as a child of a taxpayer. A foster child is an individual placed with the taxpayer by an authorized placement agency or by judgment, decree, or court [Code Sec. 152(f)(1)(C)].

Age test. The child must not have reached age 19 (age 24 if the child is a student) before the close of the calendar year in which the tax year of the taxpayer begins [Code Sec. 152(c)(3)(A)]. The age requirement does not apply to a child who at any time during the calendar year is permanently and totally disabled as defined in Code Sec. 22(e)(3) [Code Sec. 152(c)(3)(B)].

Married children. A child (including a foster child) who is married at the close of the taxpayer's tax year is not a qualifying child unless the taxpayer can claim a dependency exemption for the child (or is unable to claim a dependency exemption) solely because the taxpayer signed a waiver that allows his or her spouse to claim the dependency exemption as a noncustodial parent under the special rule described in Code Sec. 152(e) for divorced or separated parents [Code Sec. 32(c)(3)(B)].

Principal place of abode and residency test. The child (including a foster child) must have the same principal place of abode as the taxpayer for more than one-half of the tax year [Code Sec. 152(c)(1)(B)]. This test must be satisfied even if the special rule applicable to divorced parents as described in Code Sec. 152(e) allows the taxpayer, who is a divorced or separated noncustodial parent, to claim a dependency exemption [Code Sec. 32(c)(3)(A)]. The principal place of abode must be in the United States [Code Sec. 32(c)(3)(C)]. Note that for purposes of claiming a dependency exemption it is not necessary for a child to have a principal place of abode in the United States.

Temporary absences due to special circumstances, including absences due to illness, education, business, vacation, or military service, are disregarded.

In determining whether a child's principal place of abode is in the United States, for any period during which a member of the armed forces is stationed outside the United States on extended active duty, the member is considered to be maintaining a principal place of abode in the United States. Thus, a child living with a member of the armed forces for more than one-half of the tax year would satisfy the U.S. residency test [Code Sec. 32(c)(4)]. Extended active duty means any period of active duty for a period in excess of 90 days or for an indefinite period [Code Sec. 32(c)(4)].

Support test does not apply. A taxpayer is not required to provide more than one-half of the support of an individual in order for a child to be a qualifying child.

Married taxpayers filing separately. If the parents of a qualifying child file separate returns, the child is treated as the qualifying child of the parent with whom the child resided the longest period of time during the tax year. If the child resides with both parents an equal amount of time, the child is the qualifying child of the parent with the highest adjusted gross income [Code Sec. 32(c)(1)(c)].

Tie-breaker rule. According to the tie-breaker rule, if two or more taxpayers are otherwise entitled to treat an individual as a qualifying child and they both want to treat the child as a qualifying child on their return, then the individual shall be treated as the qualifying child of the taxpayer who (a) is a parent of the individual, or (b) has the highest adjusted gross income for the year [Code Sec. 32(c)(1)(C)(i)]. If the parents do not file a joint return together, the child will be treated as the qualifying child of (a) the parent with whom the child resided for the longest period of time during the tax year, or (b) if the child resides with both parents for the same amount of time during such tax year, the parent with the highest adjusted gross income [Code Sec. 32(c)(1)(C)(ii)].

Identification requirement. The taxpayer must include the name, age, and TIN (i.e., social security number) of the child on the tax return. The omission of the correct TIN required under Code Sec. 32(c)(3)(D) is treated as a mathematical or clerical error under Code Sec. 6213(g)(2)(F) and any additional tax resulting from the disallowance of the credit is summarily assessed. The identification requirements are prerequisites to claiming the EIC, and are not merely a part of the definitions of eligible individuals and qualifying children.

.02 Earned Income Defined

The definition of *earned income* includes wages, salaries, tips, self-employment income, strike benefits, long-term disability benefits received before retirement, tip income, and income received as a statutory employee and any other employee compensation if includible in income for the tax year.

Members of the military may make an election to treat combat zone compensation that is otherwise excluded from gross income under Code Sec. 112 as earned income for purposes of the earned income credit [Code Sec. 32(c)(2)(B)(vi)].

.03 Investment Income Defined

You cannot claim the EIC if your investment income is more than $3,300 in 2013 [Code Sec. 32(i)]. *Investment income* includes taxable interest and dividends, tax-exempt interest, capital gain net income, the excess of aggregate passive income over passive losses, and net income from rents and royalties not derived in the ordinary course of business. The IRS has announced that low-income taxpayers who realize gain from the sale of business assets need not count such gain as investment income that might disqualify them from entitlement to the EIC. Gain that is treated as long-term capital gain does not constitute disqualified income for purposes of the EIC. However, that gain is includible in a taxpayer's total income figure.[2]

.04 Computing the Credit

In 2013, the amounts listed in the following chart are used to determine the earned income tax credit under Code Sec. 32(b). The "earned income amount" is the amount

[2] Rev. Rul. 98-56, 1998-2 CB 667.

of earned income at or above which the maximum amount of the earned income credit is allowed. The "threshold phaseout amount" is the amount of adjusted gross income (or, if greater, earned income) above which the maximum amount of the credit begins to phase out. The "completed phaseout amount" is the amount of adjusted gross income (or, if greater, earned income) at or above which no credit is allowed. The threshold phaseout amounts and the completed phaseout amounts shown in the table below for married taxpayers filing a joint return include the increase provided in Code Sec. 32(b)(3)(B)(i), as adjusted for inflation in 2013.

Table 2. Earned Income Tax Credit—2013

	Number of Qualifying Children			
Item	*One*	*Two*	*Three or More*	*None*
Earned Income Amount	$9,560	$13,430	$13,430	$6,370
Maximum Amount of Credit	$3,250	$5,372	$6,044	$487
Threshold Phaseout Amount (Single, Surviving Spouse, or Head of Household)	$17,530	$17,530	$17,530	$7,970
Completed Phaseout Amount (Single, Surviving Spouse, or Head of Household)	$37,870	$43,038	$46,227	$14,340
Threshold Phaseout Amount (Married Filing Jointly)	$22,870	$22,870	$22,870	$13,310
Completed Phaseout Amount (Married Filing Jointly)	$43,210	$48,378	$51,567	$19,680

Earned Income Tax Credit—2014

	Number of Qualifying Children			
Item	*One*	*Two*	*Three or More*	*None*
Earned Income Amount	$9,720	$13,650	$13,650	$6,480
Maximum Amount of Credit	$3,305	$5,460	$6,143	$496
Threshold Phaseout Amount (Single, Surviving Spouse, or Head of Household)	$17,830	$17,830	$17,830	$8,110
Completed Phaseout Amount (Single, Surviving Spouse, or Head of Household)	$38,511	$43,756	$46,997	$14,590
Threshold Phaseout Amount (Married Filing Jointly)	$23,260	$23,260	$23,260	$13,540
Completed Phaseout Amount (Married Filing Jointly)	$43,941	$49,186	$52,427	$20,020

Certain Nonresident Aliens Ineligible for Credit

A nonresident alien cannot claim the earned income credit unless he or she is married to a U.S. citizen or resident and both spouses choose to be treated as residents for the entire year.

Military Personnel

If you are in the U.S. military on extended active duty outside the United States, you are considered to live in the United States during that duty period, and you may be able to claim the EIC as long as you meet the other rules.

If you and someone else both take care of a qualifying child, then only the one with the higher adjusted gross income may be eligible to claim the credit for that child. If you are the eligible party but you cannot claim the credit (say, because your earned income is too high), then no one can claim the credit for the child.

.05 Sanctions for Failing to Follow EIC Rules

The following sanctions will be imposed for abusing the rules and regulations that apply to the EIC [Code Sec. 32(k)]:

- If you are caught fraudulently claiming the EIC, you will be ineligible to claim the EIC for the next ten years;
- If you erroneously claim the EIC due to reckless or intentional disregard of rules or regulations, you will be ineligible to claim the EIC for the next two years;
- If you are denied the EIC because you made a false claim, you may claim the EIC in later years only if you recertify yourself. This means that you must demonstrate your current eligibility under standards and reporting requirements that will be set forth in regulations to be issued by Treasury; and
- Paid return preparers are required to fulfill certain due diligence requirements on returns they prepare where they claim the EIC. The penalty for failure to meet these requirements is increased from $100 to $500 for each failure to satisfy the due diligence requirements for all returns required to be filed after December 31, 2011 [Code Sec. 6695(g)]. This penalty is in addition to any other penalty imposed under the law.

.06 How to Avoid the Due Diligence Penalty

When paid preparers of federal income tax returns or claims for refund file returns claiming the EIC, the paid tax return preparers are required to file a due diligence checklist on Form 8867, *Paid Preparer's Earned Income Credit Checklist*, with the return claiming the credit.

The IRS imposes a $100 penalty on tax return preparers for each failure to comply with due diligence requirements in determining a taxpayer's eligibility to claim the earned income credit [Code Sec. 6695(g)]. In addition, the return preparer must retain a copy of Form 8867 for three years from the later of the due date of the return (determined without regard to any extension of time for filing), or the date the return or claim for refund was filed [Reg. § 1.6695-2(b)(4)]. Reg. § 1.6695-2(a) subjects all paid return preparers, whether an individual or firm, who determine eligibility for the EIC and who fail to satisfy the due diligence requirements, to the due diligence penalty. Reg. § 1.6695-2(c)(1) provides further that before imposing the penalty on a firm based on an employee's failure to comply with the due diligence requirements, the IRS must establish that a member of its principal management participated in or knew of the failure. A firm would be subject to the penalty if it failed to establish reasonable and appropriate procedures to ensure compliance with the due diligence requirements. A penalty will be imposed if the firm established procedures to ensure compliance but disregarded those procedures through willfulness, recklessness, or gross indifference [Reg. § 1.6695-2(c)(2)].

Isolated Infringements Ignored

The IRS will not apply the EIC due diligence penalty for a particular return or claim for refund if the preparer can satisfy the IRS that, based on all the facts and circumstances:

1. The preparer's normal office procedures was reasonably designed and routinely followed to ensure compliance with the due diligence requirements; and
2. Failure to meet the requirements on one the return or claim for refund was isolated and inadvertent [Reg. § 1.6695-2(c)].

.07 Taxpayer Identification Number (TIN) Required

No EIC is allowed to a taxpayer who fails to provide his or her TIN (Social Security number) or the TIN of his or her spouse (if married) on the tax return for the year for which the credit is claimed [Code Sec. 32(c)(1)(F)]. In addition, no EIC will be allowed to a taxpayer who has one or more qualifying children if none of the qualifying children are properly identified by name, age, and TIN on the tax return for the year for which the credit is claimed [Code Sec. 32(c)(1)(G)].

¶14,010 CREDIT FOR THE ELDERLY AND PERMANENTLY DISABLED

Taxpayers may qualify for this special credit if they are a U.S. citizen or resident and are:

- Age 65 or older by the end of the tax year; or
- Under age 65 at the tax year's end and
  a. Are retired on permanent and total disability
  b. Did not reach mandatory retirement age before the current year and
  c. Received taxable disability benefits in the current year [Code Sec. 22(b)].

The credit is equal to 15 percent of eligible income. The maximum credit for a married couple when both are older than age 65 is $1,125 [Code Sec. 22(a)].

.01 Figuring the Credit

To figure the credit, you must first determine your base amount. Then you subtract from your base amount: (1) any nontaxable social security or other nontaxable pension and disability benefits, and (2) part of your AGI, depending on the level of your income.

The base amounts are listed in the table below:

Table 3. Base Amounts for the Credit for the Elderly and Permanently Disabled

	If your filing status is:	*Your base amount is:*
1.	Single, a head of household, or a surviving spouse, and 65 or older	$5,000
	Under 65 and retired on permanent and total disability	5,000
2.	Married filing jointly and Both you and your spouse are 65 or older	7,500
	Both you and your spouse are under 65 and one of you retired on permanent and total disability	5,000
	Both you and your spouse are under 65 and both of you retired on permanent and total disability	7,500
	One of you is 65 or older, and the other is under 65 and retired on permanent and total disability	7,500
	One of you is 65 or older, and the other is under 65 and not retired on permanent and total disability	5,000
3.	Married filing separately and did not live with your spouse at any time during the year and 65 or older	3,750
	Younger than 65 and retired on permanent and total disability	3,750

The base amount for taxpayers under 65 is limited to the amount received as disability income. On joint returns, if one spouse is over 65, but both are qualified individuals, the initial amount is increased to a maximum of $5,000 plus the amount received as disability income by the younger spouse.

Base Amount Reductions

Your credit base must be reduced by nontaxable social security, railroad retirement benefits, or other exempt pension benefits you receive. The base amount is also reduced by one-half of the amount of your adjusted gross income above the following income levels: $7,500 for single persons; $10,000 for married persons filing jointly; or $5,000 for married persons filing separately [Code Sec. 22(c), (d)].

> **NOTE:** *Nontaxable social security* includes disability benefits, any amounts that are withheld to pay premiums on supplementary Medicare insurance, and any reduction because of receiving a benefit under workers' compensation.

.02 Credit for Husband and Wife

Generally, the credit is available to married couples who file a joint return. The credit is figured on your combined income, and the credit base is reduced by the total exempt pension income above the permitted level. Certain married taxpayers living apart can qualify for the credit [Code Sec. 22(e)(1)].

.03 What Is Permanent and Total Disability?

A person is considered to be permanently and totally disabled if he or she is unable to engage in any substantial gainful activity because of a physical or mental impairment which can be expected to result in death or which has lasted or can be expected to last for a continuous period of not less than 12 months [Code Sec. 22(e)(3)]. A physician must certify that the condition has lasted or can be expect to last continuously for 12 months or more, or that the condition will probably result in death.

A *substantial gainful activity* is performing significant duties over a reasonable period of time while working for pay or profit. This means that you will only be entitled to the credit if you can show the following:

- You have *not* worked full-time or part-time at your employer's convenience;
- You have *not* been paid at least the minimum wage, and
- You have *not* performed substantial productive work activities.

You will not lose your credit if the work you perform is undertaken to take care of yourself or your home, to work on hobbies, to engage in institutional therapy or training, or to attend school, clubs, social programs, and similar activities. Performing these activities, may, however, indicate that you are capable of engaging in substantial gainful activity and result in a denial of the credit. See Example 14-5 below.

Just because an individual has not worked for some time, is not, by itself, conclusive evidence that he or she cannot engage in substantial gainful activity. The IRS could look at prior work experience in an effort to deny the credit.

Examples 14-3 and 14-4 illustrate situations where the taxpayers are considered engaged in a substantial gainful activity and are unable to claim the credit.

> **Example 14-2:** Barbara, a former school teacher, retired because of her disability. She is 58 years old and now works full-time as a babysitter for a salary. She is not entitled to the credit even though she retired on a disability because she is still able to perform the duties of her new job in a full-time competitive work situation. It doesn't matter that the nature of her new work differs from the nature of her original employment.

> **Example 14-3:** Barry, a former stockbroker, retired because of his terminal illness. He was 61 years old and now drives a truck for a charitable organization. He is not paid for this work and is responsible for setting his own hours. The number of hours that he works each week ranges from 10 hours to 40 hours. Barry is not entitled to the credit because his ability to drive the truck each week indicates that he is able to engage in substantial gainful activity. It doesn't matter that he is not paid for this work.

The following Example 14-5 illustrates how a person must prove that he is engaged in neither a substantial nor a gainful activity in order to qualify for the credit.

> **Example 14-4:** Wally retired because of his disability. He is 63 years old. He took a job on a trial basis in order to see if he was up to performing the work. The trial period lasted for 6 months and Wally was paid the minimum wage. Since Wally was disabled, he was assigned only light duties of a nonproductive nature. For purposes of claiming the credit, Wally was not engaged in a substantial activity because his duties were nonproductive. In an attempt to deny Wally's credit, however, the IRS will look to Wally's receipt of the minimum wage as evidence that he was engaged in a gainful activity. In the absence of more facts to establish that he was unable to engage in both a substantial and gainful activity, the credit will be denied.

Physician's Statement

A taxpayer younger than age 65 must have his or her physician complete a statement certifying that he or she is permanently and totally disabled. This statement should be attached to your tax return and a copy should be kept for your records. No statement is required if a physician's statement was filed in prior years and the statement provided that due to continued disabled condition, the taxpayer was unable to engage in any substantial gainful activity during the tax year.

¶14,015 ADOPTION EXPENSES CREDIT

Law in 2013. The following two tax breaks are available to individuals who pay or incur expenses to adopt a child in 2013:

1. Employees who incur adoption-related expenses may be able to exclude from income a certain annually adjusted portion of their expenses if their employer has an adoption assistance program in place and either pays or reimburses the employees qualified adoption expenses [Code Sec. 137]. See ¶ 4115.
2. The adoptive parent may also be able to claim a refundable adoption tax credit for qualified adoption expenses associated with adopting a child under age 18 or a special needs child of any age.

.01 Dollar Limitations

In 2013, a credit in the amount of $12,970 will be allowed for an adoption of any child with or without special needs [Code Sec. 23(a)(3)].

Why Did the Code Sections Change?

The Patient Protection and Affordable Care Act of 2010 and the Tax Relief Act of 2010 temporarily designated Code Sec. 23 as Code Sec. 36C for 2010 and 2011. As designated, Code Sec. 36C provided a temporary refundable adoption credit, and an increase in the maximum adoption credit to $13,170, in 2010 and 2011. In 2012 and thereafter these temporary changes no longer apply and in 2012 and thereafter, the credit is redesignated as Code Sec. 23 and is no longer refundable.

Beginning January 1, 2012, all nonrefundable personal tax credits are allowed to the full extent of the taxpayer's regular tax and AMT liability [Code Sec. 26(a)]. Thus, the adoption credit may be claimed against both regular tax liability (reduced by any foreign tax credit claimed) and AMT liability. The adoption credit can be carried forward for up to five years if the credit exceeds the taxpayer's regular tax and AMT reduced by the sum of the other nonrefundable credits (except the adoption credit, residential energy-efficient property credit, and the first-time homebuyer credit for the District of Columbia [Code Sec. 23(c)].

.02 Income Phaseout Rules

The available adoption credit begins to phase out for taxpayers with modified adjusted gross income (MAGI) in 2013 in excess of $194,580 and is completely phased out for taxpayers with MAGI of $234,580 or more [Code Sec. 23(b)(2)(A)].

For further discussion of the employer-provided adoption assistance program, see ¶4115.

.03 Qualified Expenses

Qualified expenses are defined as the reasonable and necessary adoption fees, court costs, attorney fees, and other expenses directly related to adopting an eligible child. Taxpayers are also entitled to claim the adoption credit for expenses paid or incurred for an unsuccessful domestic adoption (not unsuccessful foreign adoption) [Code Sec. 36C].

.04 Computation of MAGI for Adoption Credit Purposes

MAGI for the year in which the adoption credit may be claimed is computed by taking adjusted gross income and reducing the income by the following exclusions:

- Foreign earned income exclusion or the foreign housing exclusion or deduction under Code Sec. 911;
- Exclusion for income from Guam, American Samoa, and the Northern Mariana Islands under Code Sec. 931; and
- Exclusion of income from Puerto Rico under Code Sec. 933 [Code Sec. 23(b)(2)(B)].

To determine the amount by which the credit must be reduced by taxpayers over the income threshold, the otherwise excludable amount is multiplied by a fraction with a numerator that is the amount by which the taxpayers income exceeds $189,710 in 2012 and a denominator that is $40,000 [Code Sec. 23(b)(2)].

> ▶ **PRACTICE POINTER:** Note that MAGI as computed differently for purposes of the adoption tax credit and the exclusion for employer-provided adoption benefits.

.05 Adoption Credit Not Refundable

In 2012 and thereafter, the adoption credit is redesignated as Code Sec. 23 and is no longer refundable.

.06 Eligible Child

An eligible child is defined for purposes of both the adoption expense exclusion and the adoption credit (see ¶14,015) as:

- Any child under age 18. If the child turned 18 during the year, the child is an eligible child for the part of the year he or she was under age 18.
- An eligible child who is physically or mentally incapable of caring for himself or herself [Code Sec. 23(d)(2)(B)].

The child may not be the child of the taxpayer's spouse (i.e., a stepchild) [Code Sec. 23(d)(1)(C)].

.07 Special Needs Adoptions

In 2013, the credit in the amount of $12,970 is allowed for the adoption of a child with special needs [Code Sec. 23(a)(3)].

A child is a child with special needs if:

1. The child is a citizen or resident of the United States or its possessions at the time the adoption process begins;
2. A state (including the District of Columbia) has determined that the child cannot or should not be returned to his or her parents home;
3. The state has determined that the child will not be adopted unless assistance is provided to the adoptive parents. Factors used by states to make this determination include: (a) a childs ethnic background and age, (b) the childs membership in a minority or sibling group, and (c) whether the child has a medical condition, or a physical, mental, or emotional handicap [Code Sec. 23(d)(3)].

.08 Adopted Child Needs Identification Number

The adopted child must have some official form of identification in order for the adoptive parents to claim tax benefits with respect to the adoption of that child on their tax return [Code Sec. 23(f)(2)]. Any of the following will suffice:

- A social security number (SSN). If the child needs a SSN, apply on Form SS-5;
- An individual taxpayer identification number (ITIN) if the child is a resident or nonresident alien and not eligible for an SSN. If the child needs an ITIN, apply on Form W-7; or
- An adoption taxpayer identification number (ATIN), which is a temporary TIN for children who are placed for adoption and a SSN is unavailable or cannot be secured. File Form W-7A with the IRS to obtain an ATIN. In order for the ATIN to be assigned, the child must be placed for adoption by an authorized placement agency that includes (in addition to governmental and private placement organizations) biological parents and other persons authorized by state law to place children for legal adoption. In addition, parents in the process of a domestic U.S. adoption are advised to write "U.S. adoption pending" in the exemption section of their tax return in place of the child's social security number and attach a copy of documentation from the adoption agency or other authority to show that the child was placed in the home for legal adoption.

.09 Qualified Adoption Expenses

Qualified adoption expenses include reasonable and necessary adoption fees, court costs, attorney fees, travel expenses (including meals and lodging) while away from home, and adoption expenses directly related to the adoption of a child [Code Secs. 23(d)(1), 137(d)]. All reasonable and necessary expenses required by a state as a condition of adoption are qualified adoption expenses including the cost of construction, renovations, alterations, or purchases specifically required by the state to meet the needs of the adopted child.

Qualified adoption expenses do *not* include the following:

- Expenses incurred in violation of state or federal law or in carrying out any surrogate parenting arrangement,
- Expenses incurred in connection with the adoption by an individual of a child who is the child of such individual's spouse, and
- Expenses which are reimbursed under an employer program or otherwise [Code Sec. 23(d)(1)(D)].

.10 When To Claim Adoption Credit

The following tables explain when to take the credit:

Adopting a child who is a U.S. citizen or resident.

IF taxpayer pays qualifying expenses in ...	THEN take the credit in ...
Any year before the year the adoption is final.	The year after the year of the payment.
The year the adoption is final.	The year the adoption is final.
Any year after the year the adoption is final.	The year of the payment.

Adopting a foreign child.

IF taxpayer pays qualifying expenses in ...	THEN take the credit in ...
Any year before the year the adoption is final.	The year the adoption is final.
The year the adoption is final.	The year the adoption is final.
Any year after the year the adoption is final.	The year of the payment.

Finality Safe Harbor for Children Receiving IR2, IR3, or IR4 Visa

In Rev. Proc. 2005-31,[3] the IRS provides that it will not challenge a taxpayers treatment of the adoption of a child who receives an IR2, IR3, or IR4 visa as final in:

- The tax year in which the competent authority enters a decree of adoption; or
- The tax year in which a home state court enters a decree of re-adoption or the home state otherwise recognizes the decree of the foreign country, if that year is one of the next two tax years after the year in which the competent authority enters the decree.

IR2 visa. An IR2 visa is a visa issued to a foreign-born child who is not an orphan, who was adopted in the foreign-sending country while under the age of 16 years, and who has been in the legal custody of, and has resided with the adoptive parent for at least two years.

IR3 visa. An IR3 visa is a visa issued to an orphan after a full and final adoption of the orphan has occurred in the foreign country. An IR3 visa is issued if (1) the competent authority of the foreign country severs the parental rights of the biological or any previous adoptive parents and establishes a parent-child relationship between the orphan and the adoptive parent or parents, and (2) the adoptive parent or parents see the orphan before or during the adoption proceeding.

IR4 visa. An IR4 visa is a visa issued to an orphan if (1) a simple adoption occurs in the foreign country, or (2) the competent authority of the foreign-sending country grants legal guardianship or custody either to the prospective adoptive parent or parents or to an individual or agency acting on behalf of the prospective adoptive parent or parents.

In Rev. Proc. 2005-31,[4] the IRS provides guidance to taxpayers on the finality of foreign adoptions but does not apply to adoptions governed by the Hague Convention on Protection of Children and Co-operation in Respect of Intercountry Adoption (Convention) which became effective in the United States on April 1, 2008. Rev. Proc. 2005-31 provides taxpayers with safe harbors for claiming the adoption credit and

---

[3] Rev. Proc. 2005-31, 2005-1 CB 1374.

[4] Rev. Proc. 2005-31, 2005-1 CB 1374.

exclusion for Convention adoptions, and guidance on filing amended returns to claim the credit or exclusion for Convention adoptions that became final in 2008 or 2009. Rev. Proc. 2005-31 continues to apply to foreign adoptions not governed by the Convention (non-Convention adoptions).

In Rev. Proc. 2010-31,[5] the IRS provided safe harbors for determining the finality of a foreign adoption governed by the Hague Convention on Protection of Children effective in the United States on April 1, 2008. In addition, guidance is provided to taxpayers on filing amended returns to claim the adoption credit or exclusion for Convention adoptions that became final in 2008 and 2009.

.11 Substantiation Requirements

In addition to filling out Form 8839, *Qualified Adoption Expenses*, eligible taxpayers must include with their tax returns the adoption-related documents listed below in order to substantiate an adoption or attempted adoption. The document(s) should be attached to the taxpayer's income tax return for the year that the credit is claimed.

Substantiation Requirements for Finalized Domestic and Foreign Adoptions

1. For a domestic or foreign adoption finalized in the United States, an adoption order or decree establishing that the taxpayer's adoption of the eligible child has been finalized and the date finalized.
2. For a foreign adoption governed by the Hague Convention and finalized in another country:
    a. Hague Adoption Certificate (Immigrating Child),
    b. An IH-3 visa, or
    c. A foreign adoption decree, translated into English.
3. For a foreign adoption from a country that is not party to the Hague Convention:
    a. A foreign adoption decree, translated into English, or
    b. An IR-2 or IR-3 visa.

Substantiation Requirements for Domestic Adoptions That Are Not Final

1. An adoption taxpayer identification number, obtained by the taxpayer for the child, included on the taxpayer's income tax return (instead of attaching a document),
2. A home study completed by an authorized placement agency,
3. A placement agreement with an authorized placement agency,
4. A document signed by a hospital official authorizing the release of a newborn child from the hospital to the taxpayer for legal adoption,
5. A court document ordering or approving the placement of a child with the taxpayer for legal adoption, or
6. An original affidavit or notarized statement signed under penalties of perjury from an adoption attorney, government official, or other person, stating that the signor:

[5] Rev. Proc. 2010-31, IRB 2010-40.

a. Placed or is placing a child with the taxpayer for legal adoption, or

b. Is facilitating the adoption process for the taxpayer in an official capacity, summarizing the facilitation.

Substantiation Requirements for Special Needs Adoptions

In addition to a copy of the adoption order or decree, a taxpayer claiming the credit for a special needs child must attach a copy of the state determination of special needs to the taxpayer's income tax return for the year that the taxpayer claims the credit. The special needs determination must include information establishing that the state has made a determination of special needs for the eligible child.

.12 How to Claim Adoption Credit

Use Form 8839, *Qualified Adoption Expenses,* to claim an adoption credit or an adoption expense exclusion (see ¶4115). The adoption credit and income exclusion for employer-provided adoption benefits cannot be claimed on Form 1040A. They may only be claimed on Form 1040 or Form 1040NR. Taxpayers may claim the credit or exclusion if their filing status is single, head of household, qualifying widow(er), or married filing jointly. If, however, the adoptive parents are legally separated under a decree of divorce or separate maintenance agreement, or if they lived apart for the last six months of the tax year, they may claim the credit or exclusion on a separate return, provided the parents home is the childs home for more than half the year and the parent pays more than half the cost of keeping up the home for the year.

.13 Double Dipping Prohibited

Although an adopting parent may claim both a credit and an exclusion in connection with the adoption of an eligible child, both may not be claimed for the same adoption-related expenses [Code Sec. 36C(b)(3)].

¶14,020 CHILD TAX CREDIT

The child tax credit is $1,000 per qualifying child beginning January 1, 2013 [Code Sec. 24(a)].

.01 Tax Liability Limitation

Beginning January 2012, all nonrefundable personal tax credits are allowed to the full extent of the taxpayer's regular tax and AMT liability [Code Sec. 26(a)]. Thus, the credit may be claimed against both regular tax liability (reduced by any foreign tax credit claimed) and AMT liability.

.02 Income Limitations

The credit will begin to phase out when modified adjusted gross income reaches the amounts shown in Table 4 [Code Sec. 24(b)(2)].

Table 4. Phaseout Amounts for Child Tax Credits

Filing Status	Phaseout Begins
Single	$ 75,000
Joint	$110,000
Married Filing Separately	$ 55,000

NOTE: These figures are not indexed for inflation.

The credit is reduced by $50 for each $1,000 of modified adjusted gross income over the threshold.

Modified gross income for purposes of the child tax credit is your adjusted gross income but without applying the following exclusions:

- Code Sec. 911 (foreign earned income exclusion or the foreign housing exclusion);
- Code Sec. 931 (exclusion for income from Guam, American Samoa and the Northern Mariana Islands); and
- Code Sec. 933 (exclusion of income from Puerto Rico) [Code Sec. 24(b)(1)].

.03 Qualifying Child Defined

Multipurpose Definition

A uniform definition of *qualifying child* applies for purposes of the child tax credit and the dependency exemption under Code Sec. 152(c) with the additional requirement that the child be under 17 years of age and be a United States national, citizen or resident [Code Sec. 24(c)]. A qualifying child for purposes of the child tax credit must also be the taxpayer's dependent [Code Sec. 24(a)]. See Ch. 1 for discussion of the dependency exemption.

Tests of Qualifying Child

To be a taxpayer's qualifying child, a person must satisfy the following tests.

Relationship. A qualifying child for purposes of the child care credit includes the taxpayer's children and their descendants, as well as the taxpayer's siblings (including half-siblings and step-siblings) and their descendants [Code Sec. 152(c)(1)(A)]. A taxpayer's child may also be the taxpayer's stepchild; a child legally adopted by the taxpayer or lawfully placed with the taxpayer for legal adoption by the taxpayer; or a foster child who has been placed with the taxpayer by an authorized placement agency or by a judgment, decree or other order of any court of competent jurisdiction [Code Sec. 152(f)]. A qualifying child must be a United States national, citizen, or resident [Code Secs. 24(c)(2) and 152(b)(3)]. In situations of divorce and multiple support agreements, the relationship between the child and the taxpayer is significant because the child tax credit attaches to the dependent exemption, i.e., only the taxpayer entitled to the dependent exemption is entitled to the child tax credit if the child is a qualifying child.

Residence. A qualifying child must share the same principal place of abode as the taxpayer for more than one-half of the tax year [Code Sec. 152(c)(1)(B)].

Support. A qualifying child must not provide more than one-half of his or her own support for the calendar year in which the taxpayer's tax year begins [Code Sec. 152(c)(1)(C); Code Sec. 24(c)(1)].

Age. The child must be less than 17 years of age, determined as of the close of the calendar year [Code Sec. 24(c)(1)]. When credit is claimed, the name and taxpayer identification number for each qualifying child must be included on the return.

.04 Refundable Portion of Child Tax Credit

The child tax credit is refundable for all taxpayers beginning January 1, 2013 to the extent of 15 percent of the amount by which the taxpayer's earned income for the year exceeds a threshold amount. The reduced earned income threshold amount of $3,000 for the credit applies through December 31, 2017 [Code Sec. 24(d)(4)]. Therefore, for tax years beginning before 2018, the child tax credit may be refundable to the extent of 15 percent of the taxpayer's earned income in excess of $3,000. Taxpayers with three or more children must calculate the refundable portion of the credit using the excess of their Social Security taxes over the earned income credit, instead of the 15-percent amount, if it results in a greater refundable credit [Code Sec. 24(d)(1)].

For purposes of determining the eligibility of any individual for benefits or assistance (or the amount or extent of benefits or assistance) under any federal program or any state or local program financed in whole or in part with federal funds, any payment made to a taxpayer as a refundable child tax credit in 2013 will not be taken into account as income, nor taken into account as resources, for a period of 12 months from receipt by the taxpayer [Code Sec. 6409].

The Court of Appeals for the Tenth Circuit has found that the nonrefundable portion of the child tax credit is not exempt from the bankruptcy estate. The refundable portion of the credit was exempt from the bankruptcy estate under state law.[6]

.05 Stacking Rules

If a taxpayer has several credit carryovers in a year, special stacking rules tell you the order in which credits are used to reduce tax liability. Here's the order in which the credit carryovers are generally applied:

- Nonrefundable personal credits;
- Other credits;
- Business credits;
- Investment tax credit; and
- Refundable credits, which are not limited by the alternative minimum tax, are then applied first to reduce the taxpayer's tax liability for the year. Any remaining credit in excess of the tax liability for the year is refunded to the taxpayer.

¶14,025 HOPE SCHOLARSHIP CREDIT/AMERICAN OPPORTUNITY TAX CREDIT

.01 American Opportunity Tax Credit

From January 1, 2013 through December 31, 2017, the American Opportunity tax credit is worth up to $2,500 per eligible student. The credit is computed by taking an

[6] *In re Borgman*, CA-10, 2012-2 USTC ¶50,637, 698 F3d 1255.

amount equal to 100 percent of qualified tuition and related expenses not in excess of $2,000 plus 25 percent of those expenses in excess of $2,000, but not in excess of $4,000 [Code Sec. 25A(i)(1)]. This elective credit is claimed on Form 8863, *Educational Credits (American Opportunity and Lifetime Learning Credits)*. If a parent claims a child as a dependent, then only that parent may claim the credit for the child. The credit cannot be claimed by both the parent and the student. The credit is a "per student" credit which means that the credit may be claimed for each eligible student in a family However, for each eligible student, the credit may be claimed for no more than four tax years [Code Sec. 25A(i)(2); Reg. § 1.25A-3(b), (c)].

Example 14-5: Parent pays qualified tuition and related expenses for Dependent Son to attend University. Parent claims Dependent Son as a dependent on his federal income tax return. Parent is allowed an education tax credit on his return. Dependent Son may not also claim an education tax credit on his own tax return [Reg. § 1.25A-1(f)(2), Ex. 1].

.02 Refundability

Forty percent of a taxpayer's otherwise allowable American Opportunity credit is refundable in tax years 2013 through 2017. This means that taxpayers who have a zero tax bill can obtain up to a $1,000 tax refund from the IRS for each eligible student. However, if the taxpayer claiming the credit is a child who has unearned income subject to the "kiddie tax" under Code Sec. 1(g), none of the credit is refundable [Code Sec. 25A(i) (6)]. The refundable portion of the credit is generally available to bona fide residents of U.S. possessions, but cannot be claimed by those residents in the U.S. A bona fide resident of a possession with a mirror code tax system (Commonwealth of the Northern Mariana Islands, Guam, and the Virgin Islands) may claim the refundable portion of the credit in the possession in which the individual is a resident.

The nonrefundable portion of the American Opportunity credit can be offset against the excess of the sum of the regular tax plus AMT liabilities over the sum of the other nonrefundable credits allowable (other than the American Opportunity, adoption, residential energy-efficient property credit, and the plug-in electric vehicle credits) and the foreign tax credit [Code Sec. 25A(i) (5)].

.03 Income Phaseout Ranges

In 2013, the modified AGI (MAGI) phaseout limits for taxpayers claiming the American Opportunity Tax Credit are between $80,000 and $90,000 for single filers ($160,000 and $180,000 for joint filers). The modified credit is ratably reduced by the amount bearing the same ratio to the credit as the excess of the taxpayer's MAGI over $80,000 bears to $10,000. These amounts double to $160,000 and $20,000 for joint filers [Code Sec. 25A(i) (4)]. MAGI is the taxpayer's AGI with any amounts excluded under the provisions for foreign or U.S. possessions earned income and foreign housing expenses. The credit may not be claimed by married taxpayers who file separate returns [Code Sec. 25A(g)].

Example 14-6: In 2013, Olivia was a full-time student at a university with tuition and related expenses of $10,000. Her unmarried father paid her tuition and wants to claim the American Opportunity Tax Credit on her behalf. The father's MAGI was $82,000. The ratio of the excess of his MAGI over $80,000, $2,000, to $10,000 is 1/5 (($82,000 – $80,000)/$10,000). The $2,500 credit claimed by the father is reduced by 1/5, so he can only claim a $2,000 credit ($2,500 – (1/5 × $2,500)).

.04 Qualified Tuition and Related Expenses

Qualified tuition and related expenses include the tuition and fees and course materials required for the enrollment or attendance of the taxpayer, the taxpayer's spouse or any of the taxpayer's dependents for courses of instruction at eligible educational institutions which include undergraduate, graduate level and professional degree programs [Code Sec. 25A(i)(3)]. Typically, a fee would be treated as a qualified tuition and related expense if it must be paid to the eligible educational institution by students as a condition of their enrollment or attendance. Fees for books, supplies, and equipment used in a course of study as well as nonacademic fees would be included in the definition only if they must be paid to the eligible educational institution for the enrollment or attendance of the student [Reg. § 1.25A-2(d)(2)]. If the student can purchase the books, supplies and equipment anywhere (not just in the university bookstore) the cost does not constitute a related expense.

Example 14-7: Bob is a photography major at his state university. He is required to purchase a specific camera for his classes. Even though the camera is available in the school bookstore, he may purchase the camera anywhere he chooses. The cost of the camera is not a qualified expense because Bob was not required to purchase it from the university bookstore.

Qualified tuition and related expenses do not include the costs of room and board, insurance, medical expenses (including student health fees), transportation, student activity fees, and similar personal, living, or family expenses, regardless of whether the fee must be paid as a condition of the student's enrollment or attendance of the student at the institution [Reg. § 1.25A-2(d)(3)]. If a student is required to pay a fee (such as a comprehensive fee or a bundled fee) to an eligible educational institution that combines charges for qualified tuition and related expenses with charges for personal expenses, the portion of the fee that is allocable to personal expenses is not included in qualified tuition and related expenses. The determination of what portion of the fee relates to qualified tuition and related expenses and what portion relates to personal expenses must be made by the institution using a reasonable method of allocation [Reg. § 1.25A-2(d)(4)].

No credit is available for expenses relating to any course of instruction or other education that involves sports, games, hobbies, or any noncredit course unless the course or other education is part of the student's degree program [Code Sec. 25A(f)(1)(B); Reg. § 1.25A-2(d)(5)].

.05 No Double Dipping

You cannot use the AOTC to shelter from tax amounts that are already excludable from gross income under other provisions in the Internal Revenue Code. This means that you cannot claim a credit for tax-free scholarships (Code Sec. 117), tax-free employer assistance (Code Sec. 127) or educational expenses already deducted as a business expense under Code Sec. 162.

If you pay qualified tuition and fees on behalf of a student in 2013, you have the option of electing either the AOTC, the Lifetime Learning Credit [¶ 14,030], or the exclusion from gross income for distributions from a Coverdell education savings account [Ch. 3]. You cannot claim more than one of these education benefits. If, however, you have more than one qualifying student, you may claim the AOTC for each eligible student's qualified tuition and related expenses and a Lifetime Learning Credit for one or more other students' qualified tuition and related expenses.

.06 Election

You make an election to claim the AOTC by attaching Form 8863, *Education Credits (American Opportunity, HOPE and Lifetime Learning Credits,* to the tax return for the tax year in which the credit is claimed [Reg. § 1.25A-1(d)]. In addition, you may elect to claim the AOTC on an amended, as well as an original, tax return.[7] The amended return must be filed before the expiration of the limitations period for filing a credit or refund claim for the tax year in which the education credit was claimed. You are not allowed to claim a carryforward of an unused education credit or excess qualified expenses. In addition, an education credit in excess of your tax liability for the tax year cannot be refunded.

.07 Reporting Requirements Imposed on Schools

Educational institutions that receive payments of tuition and related expenses are required under Code Sec. 6050S to file information returns on Form 1098-T, "Tuition Statement," for each individual who is or has been enrolled for any academic period and for whom reportable transactions are made during the calendar year. In addition, any person engaged in a trade or business of making payments under an insurance arrangement as reimbursements or refunds of tuition and related expenses would have to file a Form 1098-T with the IRS for each individual for whom it makes reimbursement or refunds [Reg. § 1.6050S-1(a)]. In addition, the schools are required to provide this same material to each student or individual who is included on the information return. Educational institutions must file Form 1098-T with the IRS by February 28 of the year following the year the payment was received. If taxpayers elect to file these forms electronically, the deadline is extended until April 1. Educational institutions that file Form 1098-T must provide the same information to students and individuals named on the form by January 31. No penalties will be imposed for failure to file correct information returns or correct statements if a good faith effort was made to comply with the reporting requirements.[8]

---

[7] Notice 99-32, 1999-1 CB 1185.

[8] Notice 2000-62, 2002-2 CB 587.

¶14,030 LIFETIME LEARNING CREDIT

.01 Amount of Credit for Other Taxpayers

A taxpayer who does not meet the requirements for claiming the American Opportunity Tax Credit (AOTC), i.e., one that takes less than a half-time academic course load, one who is not a candidate for a degree, certificate, or other postsecondary credential program, one who has completed two years of postsecondary education, or one who has been convicted of a Federal or State felony regarding a controlled substance before the end of the year in which the academic period ends, may claim the Lifetime Learning Credit.

The Lifetime Learning Credit equals 20 percent of up to $10,000 of qualified tuition and related expenses paid to an eligible educational institution during the year for education furnished to the taxpayer, the taxpayer's spouse, and any claimed dependent during any academic period beginning during the year [Code Sec. 25A(c); Reg. § 1.25A-4(a)]. Therefore, the maximum credit that may be claimed in 2013 is $2,000. There is no limit to the number of years the lifetime learning credit can be claimed for each eligible student [Reg. § 1.25A-4(b)]. However, a taxpayer cannot claim both the AOTC and Lifetime Learning Credit for the same student in one year, but if a parent has two qualifying students, the parent can claim the AOTC for one student and the LLC for the other student.

The student must be enrolled at an eligible educational institution but, unlike the AOTC, the student need not be enrolled on at least a half-time basis. Instead, the student is eligible for the Lifetime Learning Credit if he or she is taking a few or even just one undergraduate or graduate-level class to acquire or improve job skills (assuming that the other requirements for the credit are satisfied). Another difference between the AOTC and the Lifetime Learning credit, is that the Lifetime Learning credit is not limited to expenses for the first two years of post-secondary education. This means that you may claim the credit for graduate-level degree costs.

.02 Qualified Tuition and Related Expenses

The term *qualified tuition and related expenses* is defined as the tuition and fees required for the enrollment or attendance of a student for courses of instruction at an eligible educational institution. Typically, a fee would be treated as a qualified tuition and related expense if it must be paid to the eligible educational institution by students as a condition of their enrollment or attendance. Fees for books, supplies, and equipment used in a course of study as well as nonacademic fees (fees that are not used directly for, or allocated to, an academic course of study) would be included in the definition only if they must be paid to the eligible educational institution for the enrollment or attendance of the student [Reg. § 1.25A-2(d)(2)]. If the student can purchase the books, supplies and equipment anywhere (not just in the university bookstore) the cost does not constitute a related expense.

Example 14-8: Bob is a photography major at his state university. He is required to purchase a specific camera for his classes. Even though the camera is available in the school bookstore, he may purchase the camera anywhere he chooses. The cost of the camera is not a qualified expense because Bob was not required to purchase it from the university bookstore.

Qualified tuition and related expenses do not include the costs of room and board, insurance, medical expenses (such as student health fees), transportation, student activity fees, and similar personal, living, or family expenses, whether or not paid to the eligible educational institution [Reg. § 1.25A-2(d)(3)].

Qualified tuition and related expenses do not include expenses relating to any course of instruction or other education that involves sports, games, hobbies, or any noncredit course unless the course or other education is part of the student's degree program, or in the case of the Lifetime Learning Credit, the student takes the course to acquire or improve job skills [Code Sec. 25A(f)(1)(B); Reg. § 1.25A-2(d)(5)].

Example 14-9: Taxpayer A, a professional photographer, enrolls in an advanced photography course at a local community college. Although the course is not part of a degree program, Taxpayer A enrolls in the course to improve her job skills. The course fee paid by Taxpayer A is a qualified tuition and related expense for purposes of the Lifetime Learning Credit [Reg. § 1.25A-4(b)(2), Ex. 1].

Example 14-10: Taxpayer B, a stockbroker, plans to travel abroad on a photo-safari for his next vacation. In preparation for the trip, Taxpayer B enrolls in a noncredit photography class at a local community college. Because Taxpayer B is not taking the photography course as part of a degree program or to acquire or improve his job skills, amounts paid by Taxpayer B for the course are not qualified tuition and related expenses for purposes of the Lifetime Learning Credit [Reg. § 1.25A-4(b)(2), Ex. 2].

.03 Election

You make an election to claim the Lifetime Learning Credit by attaching Form 8863, *Education Credits (American Opportunity and Lifetime Learning Credits)*, to the return for the tax year in which the credit is claimed [Reg. § 1.25A-1(d)]. In addition, you may elect to claim the Lifetime Learning credit on an amended, as well as an original, tax return. The amended return must be filed before the expiration of the limitations period for filing a credit or refund claim for the tax year in which the education credit was claimed. You are not allowed to claim a carryforward of an unused education credit or excess qualified expenses. In addition, an education credit in excess of your tax liability for the tax year cannot be refunded.

.04 Income Phaseout

In 2013, the phaseout range for the Lifetime Learning Credit is between $53,000 and $63,000 for single taxpayers and between $107,000 and $127,000 for joint filers [Code Sec. 25A(d)(2)].

.05 Reporting Requirements Imposed on Schools

Educational institutions that receive payments of tuition and related expenses are required under Code Sec. 6050S to file information returns on Form 1098-T, *Tuition Statement*. In addition, the schools are required to provide this same material to each student or individual who is included on the information return.

¶14,035 HEALTH COVERAGE TAX CREDIT

The health coverage tax credit (HCTC) is a refundable tax credit equal to 72.5 percent of the amount paid during eligible coverage months for qualifying health insurance coverage for the taxpayer and any qualifying family member after February 12, 2011 [Code Sec. 35(a)]. The HCTC is scheduled to terminate on December 31, 2013. The HCTC is claimed by filing Form 8885, *Health Coverage Tax Credit*. There are no dollar limits on the amount of HCTC that may be claimed annually, and the credit doesn't phase out at higher levels of adjusted gross income.

.01 Eligible Individuals Defined

The basic categories of individuals who are eligible to claim the HCTC include:

- Trade adjustment assistance (TAA) recipients;
- Alternative TAA recipients; and
- Required individuals (age 55 or over as of the first day of the month) during any month that a pension benefit is paid by the Pension Board Guaranty Corporation (PBGC) [Code Sec. 35(c)].

.02 Eligible Coverage Month Defined

An *eligible coverage month* occurs when, on the first day of the month during the taxpayer's tax year, the taxpayer: (1) is an eligible individual, (2) is covered by a qualified health insurance plan on which the taxpayer paid the premiums, (3) has no other specified coverage, and (4) is not imprisoned by any federal, state or local authority [Code Sec. 35(b)].

.03 Qualified Health Insurance Costs Defined

The following ten categories of health insurance will be considered qualified coverage for purposes of the HCTC [Code Sec. 35(e)(1)]:

- COBRA coverage (a plan providing COBRA coverage to an eligible individual or a qualifying family member cannot reject payment from the HCTC advance payment program because it does not come directly from a COBRA qualified beneficiary. A plan that terminates an individual's COBRA coverage requirements for this reason faces Code Sec. 4980 excise taxes which are generally, $100 per day per beneficiary for period of noncompliance;[9]
- State-based continuation coverage under a state law that requires such coverage;
- A qualified state high risk pool;

---

[9] Notice 2005-50, 2005-2 CB 14.

- Health insurance programs offered to state employees;
- Health insurance programs comparable to state employees' health plan;
- An arrangement entered into by the state and a group health plan, an issuer of health insurance coverage, an administrator, or an employer;
- A state arrangement with a private sector health care coverage purchasing pool;
- A state-operated health plan that does not receive any federal financial assistance;
- A group health plan available through the employer of an eligible spouse; or
- An individual health insurance policy not defined above, which was in effect for the entire 30-day period prior to the date that the individual separated from employment that qualifies the individual as a TAA or PBGC recipient [Code Sec. 35(e)].

.04 *Other Specified Coverage* Defined

A taxpayer will have *other specified coverage* if he or she has:

- Any insurance that is considered to be for medical care under a health plan maintained by the employer of the taxpayer or the taxpayer's spouse and at least 50 percent of the cost is paid or incurred by the employer;
- Any insurance coverage under a cafeteria plan in which the premiums are paid or incurred by the employer in lieu of a right to receive cash benefits or other qualified benefits under a cafeteria plan;
- Participation in Medicare, Medicaid, or State Child Health Insurance Programs; and
- Participation in a health benefits plan for federal employees and military personnel [Code Sec. 35(f)].

An individual who is entitled to or receives benefits from the Veterans Administration is not treated as having other specified coverage which would disqualify him from claiming the HCTC.[10] When determining whether an employer pays or incurs at least 50 percent of the cost of coverage consider (1) the basis for determining the dollar amount of the cost; (2) the effect of cafeteria plan contributions under Code Sec. 125; and (3) the category of coverage. If the proportion of the cost of coverage paid or incurred by an employer varies with the category of coverage, the amount paid or incurred by the employer for each category is determined on an aggregate basis. Thus, for example, in a plan that makes coverage available in self-only and family categories, the portion of the cost of family coverage paid or incurred by the employer is determined by dividing the total cost of such coverage by the total amount the employer pays or incurs for such coverage.

¶14,040 RESIDENTIAL ENERGY PROPERTY CREDIT

Individuals who own a dwelling unit in the United States and use it as their principal residence are eligible for a nonrefundable personal credit for qualified energy efficiency improvements (building envelope components such as energy-efficient doors and win-

[10] Notice 2005-50, 2005-2 CB 14.

dows) and residential energy property expenditures (such as energy-efficient heat pumps, furnaces, central air conditioners and water heaters) [Code Sec. 25C(a)(2)]. The energy improvements must be installed in or on the dwelling unit and originally placed in service by the individual after December 31, 2011 and before January 1, 2014 [Code Sec. 25C(g)(2)].

.01 Credit Amount

The credit amount equals 10 percent of the amount paid or incurred for qualified energy efficiency improvements, not including installation costs, plus the amount paid or incurred, including labor costs, for residential energy property expenditures. Certain dollar limits apply, including a $200 limit for windows, $50 for an advanced main air circulating fan; $150 for any qualified natural gas, propane, or oil furnace or hot water boiler; and $300 for any item of energy-efficient building property meeting minimum energy standards (electric heat pump water heater, electric heat pump, geothermal heat pump, central air conditioner, and natural gas, propane, or oil water heater). The aggregate amount of the credit allowed for a taxpayer cannot exceed $500 reduced by the credit amounts allowed [Code Sec. 25C(b)].

¶14,045 RESIDENTIAL ALTERNATIVE ENERGY EXPENDITURES CREDIT

In 2008 through 2016, the residential energy-efficient property credit applies to expenditures incurred by homeowners who install the following energy-efficient property in their homes:

1. 30 percent of the qualified *solar electric property* expenditures made by the taxpayer during the year,
2. 30 percent of the qualified *solar water heating* property expenditures made by the taxpayer during the year,
3. 30 percent of the qualified *fuel cell property* expenditures made by the taxpayer during the year,
4. 30 percent of the qualified *small wind energy property* expenditures made by the taxpayer during the year, and
5. 30 percent of the qualified *geothermal heat pump property* expenditures made by the taxpayer during the year [Code Sec. 25D(a)].

In Notice 2009-41,[11] the IRS issued interim guidance, pending the issuance of regulations, relating to the credit for residential energy-efficient property under Code Sec. 25D. The notice provides procedures that manufacturers may follow to certify that property satisfies certain conditions of Code Sec. 25D as well as guidance regarding the conditions under which taxpayers seeking to claim the credit may rely on a manufacturer's certification.

[11] Notice 2009-41, IRB 2009-19, 933.

.01 Credit Limits

Beginning in 2009, the annual credit maximums for qualified solar electric property expenditures, solar hot water heaters, wind turbines, and geothermal heat pumps were eliminated [Code Sec. 25D(b)(1)]. The maximum annual credit for each half kilowatt of electric capacity from fuel cell plants remains at $500.

.02 Eligible Categories of Alternative Energy Property

Solar Electric Property

The term "qualified solar electric property expenditure" means an expenditure for property which uses solar energy to generate electricity for use in a dwelling unit located in the United States and used as a residence by the taxpayer [Code Sec. 25D(d)(2)]. For tax years 2009 through 2016, 30 percent of qualified solar electric property expenditures made during a tax year qualify for the residential alternative energy credit. There is no annual maximum credit amount applicable to expenditures made in 2009 through 2016 for qualified solar electric property.

Solar Water Heating Property

The term "qualified solar water heating property expenditure" means an expenditure for property to heat water for use in a dwelling unit located in the United States and used as a residence by the taxpayer if at least half of the energy used is derived from the sun [Code Sec. 25D(d)(1)].

Qualified Fuel Cell Property Expenditure

The term "qualified fuel cell property expenditure" means an expenditure for qualified fuel cell property (as defined in Code Sec. 48(c)(1)) installed on or in connection with a dwelling unit located in the United States and used as a principal residence by the taxpayer [Code Sec. 25D(d)(3)]. In the case of joint occupancy of a dwelling unit with regard to which qualified fuel cell property is installed, the maximum annual amount of fuel cell expenditures by all occupants cannot exceed $1,667 for each half kilowatt of capacity of the qualified fuel cell property [Code Sec. 25D(e)(4)]. This is the equivalent of the annual credit maximum of $500 for each half kilowatt of electric capacity from fuel cell plants.

Qualified Small Wind Energy Property

An expenditure for property that uses a wind turbine to generate electricity for use in connection with a dwelling unit located in the United States and used as a residence by the taxpayer is a qualified small wind energy property expenditure [Code Sec. 25D(d)(4)]. Thirty percent of such expenditures made in a tax year qualify for the residential alternative energy credit for property placed in service during tax years 2008 through 2016 [Code Sec.25D(a)(4)].

Qualified Geothermal Heat Pump Property

Equipment that uses the ground or ground water as a thermal energy source to heat a U.S. residential dwelling unit, or as a thermal energy sink to cool the unit, and meets the Energy Star program requirements in effect at the time the expenditure is made, is qualified geothermal heat pump property [Code Sec. 25D(d)(5)(B)]. An expenditure for qualified geothermal heat pump property installed on or in connection with a dwelling unit located in the United States and used as a residence by the taxpayer is a qualified geothermal heat pump property expenditure [Code Sec. 25D(d)(5)(A)]. Thirty percent of such expenditures made in a tax year qualify for the residential alternative energy credit for property placed in service during tax years 2008 through 2016 [Code Sec. 25D(a)(5)].

.03 Offset of Credit Against AMT

After 2008, the residential alternative energy credit can be offset against the excess of both regular tax and AMT liabilities over the sum of the credits for dependent care, the elderly and disabled, adoption, child tax, home mortgage interest, education expenses, saver's, and nonbusiness energy property [Code Sec. 25D(c)(1)].

.04 Carryforward

If the energy credit exceeds the excess of both regular tax and AMT liabilities over the sum of the personal credits, the excess can be carried to the next tax year and added to any residential energy credit for that tax year [Code Sec. 25D(c)(2)(B)].

¶14,047 FIRST-TIME HOMEBUYER CREDIT

No Credit May Be Claimed in 2012. Note that this credit terminated for purchases made after May 1, 2010 except for:

- Purchases made through September 30, 2010, if the taxpayer entered into a written binding contract before May 1, 2010 to close on the purchase of a principal residence before July 1, 2010 [Code Sec. 36(h)(2)].
- Taxpayers who served on qualified official extended duty service outside the United States for at least 90 days after December 31, 2008 and before May 1, 2010. For these taxpayers (and their spouses), the credit applies to homes purchased before May 1, 2011; and to homes purchased before July 1, 2011 if the taxpayer enters into a written binding contract before May 1, 2011, to close on the purchase before July 1, 2011 [Code Sec. 36(h)(3)].

The first-time homebuyer was able to claim a refundable tax credit pursuant to Code Sec. 36 equal to the lesser of:

- $8,000 ($4,000 if the taxpayer is married filing separately), or
- 10 percent of the purchase price of the principal residence purchased in the United States;
- Long-time homebuyers qualified for a reduced credit of $6,500 ($3,250 if married filing a separate return) [Code Sec. 36(b)(1)(D)].

No credit was allowed for the purchase of any residence if the purchase price exceeded $800,000.

The deadline for closing home purchases in order to qualify for the first-time homebuyer credit was extended from June 30, 2010, to September 30, 2010. This deadline applies to any eligible homebuyer who entered into a binding purchase contract prior to May 1, 2010.

For property purchased after August 4, 1997, and before January 1, 2012, a first-time homebuyer of a principal residence in the District of Columbia is entitled to a tax credit of up to $5,000 of the purchase price of the residence through the end of 2011 [Code Sec. 1400C(i)].

Special filing and documentation requirements apply to taxpayers claiming the homebuyer credit.

.01 How to Claim the Credit

To avoid refund delays, those who entered into a purchase contract before May 1, 2010, but closed after that date, should attach to their return a copy of the pages from the signed contract showing all parties' names and signatures if required by local law, the property address, the purchase price, and the date of the contract.

Besides filling out Form 5405, *First-Time Homebuyer Credit and Repayment of the Credit*, all eligible homebuyers must also include with their return one of the following documents:

- A copy of the settlement statement showing all parties' names and signatures if required by local law, property address, sales price, and date of purchase. Normally, this is the properly executed Form HUD-1, *Settlement Statement*.
- For mobile home purchasers who are unable to get a settlement statement, a copy of the executed retail sales contract showing all parties' names and signatures, property address, purchase price, and date of purchase.
- For a newly constructed home where a settlement statement is not available, a copy of the certificate of occupancy showing the owner's name, property address, and date of the certificate.

Besides providing a tax benefit to first-time homebuyers and purchasers who haven't owned homes in recent years, the law allows a long-time resident of the same main home to claim the credit if they purchase a new principal residence. To qualify, eligible taxpayers must show that they lived in their old homes for a five-consecutive-year period during the eight-year period ending on the purchase date of the new home. Homebuyers claiming this credit can avoid refund delays by attaching documentation covering the five-consecutive-year period:

- Form 1098, Mortgage Interest Statement, or substitute mortgage interest statements,
- Property tax records, or
- Homeowner's insurance records.

.02 Principal Residence Defined

A taxpayer's principal residence is defined as the one the taxpayer lives in most of the time and can be a house, houseboat, house trailer, cooperative apartment, condominium, or other type of residence. Vacation homes and rental property do not qualify for this credit. In *R. Grosso*,[12] a district court concluded that a married couple was not entitled to a first-time homebuyer tax credit for a townhouse that they purchased for

[12] *R. Grosso*, DC-Pa., 2011-2 USTC ¶ 50,744.

their son since the townhouse was not their principal residence and they had no intention of using it as such.

The definition of purchase excludes property acquired from a person related to the person acquiring the property or the spouse of the person acquiring the property, if married. A related person includes a spouse, parent, grandparent, child, or grandchild [Code Sec. 36(c)(2)].

First-Time Homebuyer Credit Only Available to Individuals

In *J. Trugman*,[13] the Tax Court concluded that a couple was not entitled to claim the first-time homebuyer credit because their principal residence was purchased through the couple's S corporation. Even though they were the sole shareholders of the S corporation, the purchase of the home by the S corporation did not qualify them as purchasers of the home because Code Sec. 36 provides that only an individual can claim the credit.

.03 Income Thresholds

After November 6, 2009, the full credit is available to individual taxpayers with modified adjusted gross income (MAGI) between $125,000 and $145,000 and between $225,000 and $245,000 for joint filers in the year of purchase. Those with higher incomes do not qualify.

For homes purchased prior to November 7, 2009, the credit is phased out for individual taxpayers with MAGI between $75,000 and $95,000 and between $150,000 and $170,000 for joint filers in the year of purchase. Those with higher incomes do not qualify.

.04 Eligibility

Two types of individuals are eligible to claim the first-time homebuyer credit:

- First-time homebuyers—An individual (and, if married, the individual's spouse) who has not had a present ownership interest in a principal residence during the three-year period ending on the date of the home purchase can qualify for a credit of up to $8,000. The maximum credit is reduced to $7,500 for purchases made before 2009 [Code Sec. 36(c)(1)].
- Long-time residents of the same principal residence—An individual can qualify for a maximum credit of $6,500 if the home is purchased after November 6, 2009, and the individual (and spouse, if married) owned and used the same residence as a principal residence for a consecutive five-year period during the eight-year period ending on the date of the purchase [Code Sec. 36(c)(6)].

The following taxpayers are ineligible for the credit: (1) a nonresident alien [Code Sec. 36(d)(1)]; (2) A taxpayer who acquires the home from a related person. For homes purchased after November 6, 2009, this restriction also applies to homes purchased from a person related to the taxpayer's spouse [Code Sec. 36(d)(2)]; (3) A taxpayer who can be claimed as another taxpayer's dependent [Code Sec. 36(d)(3)]; (4) A taxpayer under the age of 18 on the date of purchase for a home purchased after November 6,

[13] *J. Trugman*, 138 TC 390, Dec. 59,065 (2012). *See also Rospond*, TC Summary Op. 2012-47 (LLC cannot claim credit). *Runyan*, TC Summary Op. 2012-42 (trust beneficiary cannot claim credit).

2009; (5) A married taxpayer whose spouse has attained the age of 18 on the date of the purchase is treated as having also attained the age of 18 [Code Sec. 36(b)(4)].

In *R.D. Packard,*[14] the Tax Court concluded that a couple was entitled to claim the first-time homebuyer credit on their joint return even though the husband and wife each qualified under a different criteria for qualifying under Code Sec. 36(c).

.05 Extension of Credit if on Official Extended Duty Outside United States

In the case of any individual (and, if married, the individual's spouse) who serves on qualified official extended duty service outside of the United States for at least 90 days during the period beginning after December 31, 2008, and ending before May 1, 2010, the expiration date of the first-time homebuyer credit is extended for one year, through May 1, 2011 (July 1, 2011, in the case of an individual who enters into a written binding contract before May 1, 2011, to close on the purchase of a principal residence before July 1, 2011).

.06 Application of First-Time Homebuyer Credit to Unmarried Taxpayers

The first-time homebuyer credit is also available to co-owners who could include same-sex couples and family members or other non-married individuals who buy a home together. In Notice 2009-12,[15] the IRS provides that if two or more unmarried individuals buy a principal residence, they can allocate the first-time homebuyer credit between the individual owners using any reasonable method that does not allocate any portion of the credit to a taxpayer not eligible to claim that portion. The total amount allocated cannot exceed the smaller of $8,000 or 10 percent of the purchase price.

A reasonable method is any method that does not allocate all or a part of the credit to a co-owner who is not eligible to claim that part of the credit. A reasonable method includes allocating the credit between taxpayers who are eligible to claim the credit based on (1) the taxpayers' contributions towards the purchase price of a residence as tenants in common or joint tenants, or (2) the taxpayers' ownership interests in a residence as tenants in common.

Example 14-11: A and B, who are not married, purchased their first principal residence as tenants in common on June 29, 2009. They do not have MAGI in excess of the MAGI threshold. A contributes $45,000 and B contributes $15,000 towards the $60,000 purchase price of a residence. Each owns a one-half interest in the residence as tenants in common. The allowable credit is limited to 10 percent of the purchase price, or $6,000. A and B may allocate the allowable $6,000 credit three-fourths to A and one-fourth to B based on their contributions toward the purchase price of the residence, one-half to each based on their ownership interests in the residence, or using any other reasonable method (for example, the entire credit to A or B).

---

[14] *R.D. Packard,* 139 TC 390, Dec. 59,244 (2012).

[15] Notice 2009-12, IRB 2009-6, 446.

.07 Credit Repayment Requirements

2008 Purchases

The purchase of a qualified home acquired after April 8, 2008, and before January 1, 2009, triggers repayment of the first-time homebuyer credit as an additional tax on the taxpayer's return payable in annual installments over 15 years. A sale or change in use of a home purchased after April 8, 2009, and before January 1, 2009, within that 15 year period triggers immediate repayment of the credit. The maximum credit for 2008 is 10 percent (up to $7,500) of the purchase price.

2009 and Early 2010 Purchases

For homes purchased after 2008, the first-time homebuyer credit does not have to be repaid unless the taxpayer sells the home or ceases to use it as a principal residence within 36 months after purchasing it. In either case, the credit is recaptured only to the extent there is gain on the sale, determined using an adjusted basis that is reduced by the amount of the credit previously taken. The maximum credit for 2009 and early 2010 is 10 percent (up to $8,000) for first-time buyers. The credit expired in 2010 for most taxpayers. However, individuals on official extended active duty outside the United States for more than 90 days have additional time. They must have entered into a binding contract of purchase before May 1, 2011, and closed the contract before July 1, 2011.

IRS Notices

The IRS is mailing Notice CPO3a, *Repaying Your First-Time Homebuyer Credit*, to taxpayers who purchased a qualified home in 2008 and who begin repaying the credit with their 2010 returns. The IRS will send these annual reminders to taxpayers until the credit is repaid. The IRS also will mail courtesy notices to taxpayers who purchased homes in 2009 and early 2010 reminding them of the repayment rule if they sell the home or if there is a change in use. Notice CPO3b, will be sent to taxpayers for the three years after they receive the credit. In addition, the IRS will mail Notice CPO3c when it learns through information matching that a taxpayer's home, for which the credit has been claimed, is no longer his or her principal residence.

GENERAL BUSINESS CREDIT

The general business credit is a limited nonrefundable credit against income tax that is claimed after all other nonrefundable credits except the credit for prior year minimum tax. The general business credit for a tax year is the sum of:

1. The business credit carryforwards to such year,
2. The amount of the current year business credit, and
3. The business credit carrybacks to such year [Code Sec. 38(a)].

¶14,050 FIGURING THE GENERAL BUSINESS CREDIT

.01 General Rules for Computing Credits

The general business credit is a limited nonrefundable credit against income tax that is claimed after all other nonrefundable credits except the credit for prior year minimum tax [Code Sec. 53]. The credit is the sum of (1) the business credit carryforwards to such year, (2) the amount of the current year business credit, and (3) the business credit carrybacks to such year [Code Sec. 38(a)]. If the sum of any business credit carryforwards for the tax year plus the amount of the current year business credit for the tax year is greater than the tax liability limitation for the tax year, the excess, to the extent attributable to the current year business credit, may be carried back one tax year and forward 20 tax years [Code Sec. 39(a)(1)]. The total carryover period is, therefore, 21 years (i.e., the sum of the one-year carryback period and the twenty year carryforward period). An unused credit is carried back to the earliest of the 21-year period (i.e., the carryback year) and then carried forward to each of the other 20 years in the carryforward period [Code Sec. 39(a)(2)]. Compute the general business credit using this five-step process:

1. Separately figure each of the individual credits that make up the business credit.
2. Combine the credits *other than the empowerment zone employment credit* into a single, general business credit (including any carrybacks and carryovers from other tax years).
3. Apply the combined credit dollar-for-dollar against your net income tax liability, as adjusted, for the year. For purposes of the combined credit, net income tax liability must be reduced by the greater of
   a. Tentative minimum tax liability, if any [Chapter 16], or
   b. 25 percent of net regular tax liability above $25,000 ($12,500 if file a separate return, unless spouse is not entitled to any business credit) [Code Sec. 38(c)(1)].
4. Separately apply the empowerment zone employment credit against net income tax liability, as adjusted. Net income tax liability must be reduced by the greater of
   a. 75 percent of tentative minimum tax, or
   b. 25 percent of regular tax liability above $25,000 ($12,500), after subtracting out the combined credit (other than the empowerment zone employment credit or the New York Liberty Zone business employee credit or the specified credits) [Code Sec. 38(c)(2)]. Net effect: Unlike the combined credit, use the empowerment zone employment credit against up to 25 percent of alternative minimum tax (AMT) liability [Ch. 16].
5. Carry the unused credits back to the first tax year before the year the credit arises and carry any unused credit forward to each of the 20 years after the credit arises until the credit is all used up [Code Sec. 39(a)].

NOTE: When the general business credit is carried back and then forward, the individual credits are deemed to be used up in the order listed in Code Sec. 38(b) [Code Sec. 38(d)(1)].

¶14,055 INVESTMENT CREDIT

The investment credit consists of the sum of [Code Sec. 46]:

- The rehabilitation credit [Code Sec. 47];
- The energy credit [Code Sec. 48(a)];
- The advanced coal project credit [Code Sec. 48A];
- The gasification project credit [Code Sec. 48B];
- The qualifying advanced energy project credit [Code Sec. 48(C)]; and
- The therapeutic discovery project credit for tax years beginning in 2010 and 2011 [Code Sec. 48D].

The investment credit, which will consist of the sum of all five, is claimed as part of the general business credit [Code Sec. 38]. You claim the investment credit on Form 3468, *Investment Credit*. You may not claim the investment credit for property used predominantly outside the United States [Code Sec. 50(b)(1)(A)]. In addition, property used for lodging or by tax-exempt organizations, governmental units or foreign persons or entities is ineligible for the investment credit [Code Sec. 50(b)(2) and (3)].

.01 Investment Credit Recapture

If property on which you took an investment credit is disposed of prematurely, or ceases to qualify as investment credit property, you must recapture part or all of the investment credit [Code Sec. 50(a)(1)]. Recapture means that you must add back to the tax due in the year of disposition a certain amount of the credit previously claimed. The recaptured amount is the difference between the credit taken (including carrybacks and carryforwards) and the credit allowed for actual use [Code Sec. 50(a)]. The recaptured amount decreases ratably over time. If the property was disposed of within one year after being placed in service, all of the credit is recaptured. If the property was disposed of in later years, the amount of the credit recaptured is as shown in Table 5[Code Sec. 50(a)(1)(B)].

Table 5. Rates of Investment Credit Recaptured

If disposed of:	The recapture percentage:
After 1 year	80%
After 2 years	60%
After 3 years	40%
After 4 years	20%
After 5 years	None

▶ **TAX RETURN TIP:** Investment credit recapture is computed on Form 4255, *Recapture of Investment Credit.*

.02 Rehabilitation Credit

The credit for rehabilitation expenditures is provided to encourage restoration of existing certified historical structures instead of construction of a new building. The rehabilitation credit is one of the components of the investment credit [Code Sec. 46]. Generally, a two-tier rehabilitation credit applies for qualified rehabilitation expenditures:

- 20 percent for rehabilitation of certified historic structures; and
- 10 percent for rehabilitation of buildings (other than certified historic structures) originally placed in service before 1936 [Code Sec. 47(a), (c)(1)(B)].

The 20 percent historic rehabilitation credit is available for both residential and nonresidential buildings. However, the 10 percent credit is limited to nonresidential property [Code Sec. 47(a)]. The rehabilitation credit may be claimed on Form 3468, *Investment Credit.*

Qualified rehabilitation expenditures do not include the costs of acquiring the property or enlarging a building. In order to qualify for the credit, a building must be substantially rehabilitated. A rehabilitation is substantial if expenditures during the 24-month period selected by you and ending with or within the tax year exceed the greater of (1) $5,000, or (2) the adjusted basis of the building as of the first day of the 24-month period. However, a 60-month period may be used if the rehabilitation is reasonably expected to be carried out in phases which are set out in architectural plans and specifications completed before the rehabilitation began [Code Sec. 47(c)].

In addition, property other than a certified historic structure must satisfy the following structural requirements:

- 50 percent or more of the existing external walls must be retained in place as external walls;
- 75 percent or more of the existing external walls must be retained in place as internal or external walls; and
- 75 percent or more of the building's existing internal structural framework must be retained in place [Code Sec. 47(c)]. This means that completely gutted buildings cannot qualify for the rehabilitation credit.

Definition of Certified Historic Structure

A *certified historic structure* is any building which is listed in the National Register, or is located in a registered historic district, and is certified by the Secretary of the Interior to the Secretary of the Treasury as being of historic significance to the district.

> **NOTE:** If you rehabilitate an historic structure and then donate a scenic easement in the building to charity, you cannot double dip and claim the rehabilitation credit for rehabilitating the portion of the building that you gave away and for which you claimed a charitable deduction. Your rehabilitation expenses must be reduced by the charitable donation.[16]

---

16 *Rome I, Ltd.*, 96 TC 697, Dec. 47,324 (1991).

.03 Business Energy Credit

The Emergency Economic Stabilization Act of 2008 (EESA) extended the energy credit through December 31, 2016 [Code Sec. 48(a)(2)(A)(i)(II), (3)(A)(ii), (c)(1)(D), (2)(D)]. In addition, EESA made the energy credit 100 percent allowable against the alternative minimum tax [Code Sec. 38(c)(4)(B)(v)]. Thus, the energy credit can offset 100 percent of the alternative minimum tax.

Investment Credit Election

A taxpayer may make an irrevocable election to treat certain qualified property that is part of a qualified investment credit facility placed in service in 2009 through 2013 as energy property eligible for a 30-percent investment credit under [Code Sec. 48(a)(5)]. If the election is made, no production credit will be allowed under Code Sec. 45 for any tax year with respect to any qualified investment credit facility [Code Sec. 48(a)(5)(B)].

For purposes of the credit, qualified investment credit facilities are facilities otherwise eligible for the Code Sec. 45 production tax credit with respect to which no credit under Code Sec. 45 has been allowed. Qualified facilities include those producing electricity using wind, closed-loop biomass, open-loop biomass, geothermal energy, landfill gas, municipal solid waste (trash), hydropower, or marine and hydrokinetic renewable energy. In order to qualify for the election, wind facilities must be placed in service in 2009 through 2012. All other facilities must be placed in service in 2009 through 2013 in order to qualify [Code Sec. 48(a)(5)(C)].

Qualified property is property that is (1) tangible personal property or (2) other tangible property (not including a building or its structural components), but only if such property is used as an integral part of the qualified investment credit facility and with respect to which depreciation (or amortization in lieu of depreciation) is allowable [Code Sec. 48(a)(5)(D)].

In Notice 2009-52,[17] the IRS provided the requirements for electing the energy investment tax credit in lieu of the production tax credit for property that is an integral part of a renewable electric energy facility. The election is irrevocable and must be made on Form 3468, *Investment Credit*, with a timely filed return (including extensions) filed for the year the property is placed in service. Taxpayers must make a separate election for each qualified facility. A statement with detailed technical information about the facility and the property, signed under penalty of perjury by the taxpayer or someone authorized to bind the taxpayer, must be attached to Form 3468.

Property Eligible for 10 Percent Nonrefundable Energy Credit

- A nonrefundable 10 percent energy credit is available for stationery microturbine property and other energy property placed in service during the tax year.
- A nonrefundable 10 percent energy credit is available for combined heat and power systems (CHPS) which is property: (1) that uses the same energy source for the simultaneous or sequential generation of electrical power, mechanical shaft power, or both, in combination with the generation of steam or other forms of useful thermal energy (including heating and cooling applications); (2) that pro-

[17] Notice 2009-52, IRB 2009-25, 1094.

duces at least 20 percent of its total useful energy in the form of thermal energy that is not used to produce electrical or mechanical power (or a combination thereof), and produces at least 20 percent of its total useful energy in the form of electrical or mechanical power (or a combination thereof); and (3) the energy efficiency percentage of which exceeds 60 percent [Code Sec. 48(c)(3)(A)]. CHPS property does not include property used to transport the energy source to the generating facility or to distribute energy produced by the facility [Code Sec. 48(c)(3)(C)(iii)].

- A nonrefundable 10 percent energy credit is available for geothermal heat pump systems which include any equipment that uses the ground or ground water as a thermal energy source to heat a structure [Code Sec. 48(a)(3)(A)(vii)].

Property Eligible for 30 Percent Nonrefundable Energy Credit

A 30 percent nonrefundable energy credit is available for:

1. Qualified fuel cell property with a credit cap of $1,500 per half kilowatt of capacity [Code Sec. 48(c)(1)(B)].
2. Equipment that uses solar energy to generate electricity to heat or cool a structure (including provide hot water) or provide solar process heat,
3. Equipment that illuminates the inside of a structure using fiber-optic distributed sunlight (Code Sec. 48(a)), and
4. Qualified small wind energy property expenses [Code Sec. 48(a)(2)(A)(i)(IV), (3)(A)(vi)]. Qualified small wind energy property is property that uses a qualifying small wind turbine (one with a nameplate capacity of not more than 100 kilowatts) to generate electricity [Code Sec. 48(c)(4)]. The $4,000 credit cap applicable to qualified small wind energy property has been eliminated for periods after 2008, thus allowing an uncapped 30 percent credit to be claimed for such property [Code Sec. 48(c)(4)].

.04 Advanced Coal Project Credit

The advanced coal project investment credit under Code Sec. 48A is available only to taxpayers who apply for and receive certification that their project satisfies the relevant requirements. The IRS and Energy Department have jointly established programs to evaluate applications for such certifications using a competitive bidding process. This investment tax credit is available for power generation projects that use integrated gasification combined cycle (IGCC) or other advanced coal-based electricity generating technologies.

Advanced Project Credit Amount

The credit amount is:

1. 30 percent of the qualified investment for the tax year for IGCC projects, and
2. 15 percent of the qualified investment for projects using other advanced coal-based generation technologies [Code Sec. 48A(a)(3)].

Taxpayers seeking subsidies for their advanced coal projects under the program will file applications for certification. Up to $2.55 billion in credits will be allocated to taxpayers whose applications for certification are approved [Code Sec. 48A(d)(3)(A)]. The IRS is authorized to allocate an additional $1.25 billion for advanced coal-based generation technology projects [Code Sec. 48A(d)(3)(B)(iii)].

Certification Requirements

A project is a qualifying advanced coal project that obtains certification if the IRS determines that:

1. The project uses an advanced coal-based generation technology to power a new electric generation unit or to refit or repower an existing electric generation unit (including an existing natural gas-fired combined cycle unit);
2. The fuel input for the project, when completed, will be at least 75-percent coal;
3. The electric generation unit or units at the project site will have a total nameplate generating capacity of at least 400 megawatts;
4. A majority of the output of the project is reasonably expected to be acquired or utilized;
5. The applicant/taxpayer provides evidence of ownership or control of a site of sufficient size to allow the proposed project to be constructed and to operate on a long term basis; and
6. The project will be located in the United States [Code Sec. 48A(e)(1)].

In addition, the project must include equipment that separates and sequesters at least 65 percent of the projects' total carbon dioxide emissions [Code Sec. 48A(d)(2)(A)(ii)]. This percentage increases to 70 percent if the credits are later reallocated by the IRS [Code Sec. 48A(e)(1)(G)].

The IRS will give high priority to (1) projects that include greenhouse gas capture capability, (2) projects that increase by-product utilization, (3) projects that demonstrate the greatest separation and sequestration percentage of total carbon dioxide emissions, and (4) applicants who have research partnerships with an eligible educational institution are also to receive high priority [Code Sec. 48A(e)(3)].

The IRS is required to recapture the benefit of any allocated credit if the project fails to attain or maintain the carbon dioxide separation and sequestration requirements [Code Sec. 48A(i)]. In addition, the IRS is required to disclose which projects receive credit allocations, including the taxpayer's identity and credit amount [Code Sec. 48A(d)(5)].

.05 Gasification Project Credit

The gasification project credit under Code Sec. 48B is available only to taxpayers who have applied for and received certification that their project satisfies the relevant criteria. The IRS and Energy Department jointly established programs to evaluate applications for these certifications using a competitive bidding process. The total amount of qualifying gasification credit that can be allocated under the program cannot exceed $350 million [Code Sec. 48B(d)(1)]. The IRS is authorized to allocate an additional $250 million in qualifying gasification project credits for projects that include equipment that separates and sequesters at least 75 percent of the project's total carbon dioxide emissions [Code Sec. 48B(d)(1)]. The IRS is required to recapture the benefit of any allocated credit if the project fails to attain or maintain the 75-percent separation and sequestration requirements [Code Sec. 48B(f)].

In general, the qualifying gasification project credit for any tax year is equal to 30 percent of the qualified investment for the tax year [Code Sec. 48B(a)]. The qualified investment for any tax year is the basis of eligible property placed in service by the taxpayer during the tax year that is part of the qualifying gasification project. Eligible property is limited to property for which depreciation or amortization is available and (1) the construction, reconstruction, or erection which is completed by the taxpayer, or (2) which is acquired by the taxpayer, if the original use of the property commences with the taxpayer [Code Sec. 48B(b)(1)].

The basis of property, for purposes of calculating the qualified investment, is reduced to the extent the property was financed by tax-exempt private activity bonds or subsidized energy financing Code Sec. 48B(b)(2).

A qualifying gasification project is a project that:

1. Employs gasification technology,
2. Will be carried out by an eligible entity, and
3. Any portion of the qualified investment of which is certified under the qualifying gasification program as eligible for a credit under Code Sec. 48B.

The qualified investment in a particular project cannot exceed $650 million [Code Sec. 48B(c)(1)]. Since the credit is equal to 30 percent of the qualified investment, the maximum credit for any single project is $195 million.

.06 Credit for Investment in Advanced Energy Facilities

The IRS and the U.S. Department of Energy have established Phase II of the tax credit program under Code Sec. 48C for qualifying investments in advanced energy property projects.[18] Under Phase II, the qualifying Code Sec. 48C advanced energy project tax credit for a tax year is an amount equal to 30 percent of the qualified investment, up to $100 million for that tax year. The qualified investment for any tax year is the basis of eligible property that is placed in service by the taxpayer during that year.

A qualifying advanced energy project is a project that meets the following requirements: (1) the project re-equips, expands, or establishes a manufacturing facility for the production of "specified advanced energy property" or property that, after further manufacture, will become specified advanced energy property; (2) the IRS has certified that part or all of the qualified investment in the project is eligible for a credit under Code Sec. 48C; and (3) the project does not produce any property which is used in the refining or blending of any transportation fuel (other than renewable fuels).

Specified advanced energy property means any of the following: (1) property designed for use in the production of energy from the sun, wind, geothermal deposits or other renewable resources; (2) fuel cells, microturbines, or an energy storage system for use with electric or hybrid-electric motor vehicles; (3) electric grids to support the transmission of intermittent sources of renewable energy, including property for the storage of such energy; (4) property designed to capture and sequester carbon dioxide and sequester carbon dioxide emissions; (5) property designed to refine or blend renewable fuels (but not fossil fuels) or to produce energy conservation technologies (including energy-conserving lighting technologies and smart grid technologies); (6) new plug-in electric drive motor vehicles, qualified plug-in electric vehicles, or components that are designed specifically for use with

[18] Notice 2013-12, IRB 2013-10, 543.

such vehicles, including electric motors, generators, and power control units; or (7) other property designed to reduce greenhouse gas emissions.

Eligible property is any property (other than a building or its structural components) that meets the following requirements: (1) the property is necessary for the production of specified advanced energy property; (2) the property is (a) tangible personal property, or (b) other tangible property (not including a building or its structural components) that is used as an integral part of the qualifying advanced energy project; and (3) depreciation (or amortization in lieu of depreciation) is allowable with respect to the property.

.07 Therapeutic Discovery Tax Credit

A 50-percent nonrefundable investment tax credit is available to companies with 250 or fewer employees that make qualified investments in qualifying therapeutic discovery projects [Code Sec. 48D].

Qualifying Therapeutic Discovery Project Program

In Notice 2010-45,[19] the IRS established the Qualifying Therapeutic Discovery Project Program and outlined the procedures that an eligible taxpayer should follow to apply for certification from the IRS that a qualified investment in a qualifying therapeutic discovery project is eligible for the credit.

Qualifying Therapeutic Discovery Project Defined

A "qualifying therapeutic discovery project" is defined in Code Sec. 48D(c) as a project which is designed:

1. To treat or prevent diseases or conditions by conducting pre-clinical activities, clinical trials, and clinical studies, or carrying out research protocols, for the purpose of securing approval of a product from the FDA,
2. To diagnose diseases or conditions or to determine molecular factors related to diseases or conditions by developing molecular diagnostics to guide therapeutic decisions, or
3. To develop a product, process, or technology to further the delivery or administration of therapeutics.

Eligible Taxpayer

The credit is available only to companies having 250 or fewer employees [Code Sec. 48D(c)(2)]. For purposes of this definition, all persons treated as a single employer under Code Sec. 52(a) (controlled group of corporations) or Code Sec. 52(b) (partnerships, proprietorships that are under common control) or under Code Sec. 414(m) (affiliated service groups) or Code Sec. 414(o) (separate organizations, employee leasing arrangements) are treated as a single employer [Code Sec. 48D(c)(2)]. For these purposes, the term "employee" includes both full-time and part-time employees but does not include leased employees.

Qualified Investment

The qualified investment for any year is the aggregate amount of the costs paid or incurred in such year for expenses necessary for and directly related to the conduct of

[19] Notice 2010-45, IRB 2010-23, 734.

a qualifying therapeutic discovery project. Code Sec. 48D(b)(3) provides that the qualified investment for any year with respect to any qualifying therapeutic discovery project does not include any cost for:

1. Remuneration paid to "covered employees" which is defined as the chief executive officer or the four highest paid officers in the company,
2. Interest expenses,
3. Facility maintenance expenses which are costs paid or incurred to maintain a facility, including mortgage or rent payments, insurance payments, utility and maintenance costs, and the costs of employing maintenance personnel [Code Sec. 48D(c)(3)],
4. Any service costs, or
5. Any other expense appropriate to carry out the purposes of the qualifying therapeutic discovery credit.

Selection Criteria

Companies must apply to the IRS to obtain certification for qualifying investments. Code Sec. 48(d)(3) provides that in determining qualifying projects, the IRS will consider only those projects that show reasonable potential to:

1. Result in new therapies to treat areas of unmet medical need or to prevent, detect, or treat chronic or acute disease and conditions,
2. Reduce long-term health care costs in the United States, or
3. Significantly advance the goal of curing cancer within a 30-year period.

In addition, Code Sec. 48D(d)(3)(B) provides that the IRS will take into consideration the projects which have the greatest potential to: (1) create and sustain (directly or indirectly) high quality, high paying jobs in the United States, and (2) advance the United States' competitiveness in the fields of life, biological, and medical sciences.

Part of Investment Credit

The Therapeutic Discovery Credit is part of the investment credit and the basis of any property that is part of a qualifying therapeutic discovery project and subject to an allowance for depreciation is included in the credit base for purposes of applying the investment credit at-risk limitation rules [Code Secs. 46(6) and 49(a)(1)(C)(vi)]. If a credit is allocated under the qualifying therapeutic discovery project program for an expenditure for property subject to an allowance for depreciation, the basis of that property is reduced by the amount of the credit [Code Sec. 48D(e)(1)].

No Double Benefits

The Therapeutic Discovery Credit will not be allowed for any investment for which bonus depreciation is allowed. Furthermore, any expense taken into account under the program for the year also may not qualify for the research credit or the orphan drug credit. If a credit is allowed for an expenditure related to property subject to depreciation, the basis of the property is reduced by the amount of the credit [Code Sec. 48D(e)(1)]. Additionally, expenditures taken into account in determining the credit are nondeductible to the extent of the credit claimed that is attributable to such expenditures.

Recapture

If an investment ceases to be a qualified investment, the IRS will provide for the recapture of the appropriate percentage of the grant amount as determined by the IRS.

Application Process

Eligible applicants should apply for certification for tax credits available under the Qualifying Therapeutic Discovery Project Program by filing Form 8942, *Application for Certification of Qualified Investments Eligible for Credits and Grants Under the Qualifying Therapeutic Discovery Project Program.* A separate application for certification must be submitted for each project for which an eligible taxpayer is seeking certification of a qualified investment.

The taxpayer must inform the IRS if the plans for a qualifying therapeutic discovery project change in any significant respect from the information set forth in the application for certification at any time prior to the date of certification. A significant change is any change, including any change that would affect the continuing accuracy of a statement made in the application, that a reasonable person would conclude might have influenced evaluation of the application.

¶14,060 LOW-INCOME HOUSING CREDIT

.01 General Rules for Claiming Credit

The owner of a qualified low-income housing project that is constructed, rehabilitated, or acquired may claim the low-income housing credit in each of 10 tax years in an amount equal to the applicable credit percentage appropriate to the type of project, multiplied by the qualified basis allocable to the low-income units in each qualified low-income building. The applicable percentage is generally based on the month the building is placed in service or, at the election of the taxpayer, the month in which the taxpayer and housing credit agency agree to the amount of housing credit allocated to the building [Code Secs. 42(a) and (b)(2)(A)]. The IRS prescribes credit percentages which yield, over the 10-year credit period, a credit having a present value equal to 70 percent of the qualified basis of a new building that is not federally subsidized, 30 percent of the qualified basis of a new building that is federally subsidized, and 30 percent of the qualified basis of an existing building [Code Secs. 42(a) and (b)].

.02 State Agency Credit Ceiling

Generally, the amount of the low-income housing credit for any tax year for any building may not exceed the housing credit allocated to that building, although the allocation limitation does not apply to buildings financed with certain tax-exempt obligations [Code Sec. 42(h)(1)(A) and (h)(4)]. The allocation is made by a state housing credit agency, which is limited in the dollar amount of housing credit allocations it may make in a year. The allocation must generally be made not later than the close of the calendar year in which the building is placed in service, unless the allocation is subject to one of the exceptions discussed in Code Sec. 42(h)(1)(B). The housing credit agency must allocate credits under a qualified allocation plan which sets selection criteria and provides a procedure for monitoring compliance with credit requirements and reporting noncompliance to the IRS [Code Sec. 42(m)(1)].

A state's housing credit allotment for each year must be apportioned among the state and local housing credit agencies within the state. A housing agency may allocate credits only to buildings located within the jurisdiction of the governmental unit of which the agency is a part. Allocations may be received from different agencies with overlapping jurisdictions and can be made for whole projects, as well as separately for individual buildings. At least 10 percent of the state's credit allocation must be set aside for projects in which tax-exempt charitable and social welfare organizations materially participate [Code Sec. 42(h)(5)(B)].

The housing credit allocations of any state for any calendar year are limited by the state credit ceiling, which is the sum of:

1. The unused carryforward component, which is the unused state housing credit ceiling for the preceding calendar year;
2. The population component, which is the greater of: (a) $2,590,000, or (b) the state population multiplied by $2.25 in 2013 [Code Sec. 42(h)(3)(C)(ii)];[20]
3. The returned credit component, which is the amount of housing credit ceiling returned in the calendar year; and
4. The national pool component, which is the amount of unused credit carryover assigned to the state [Code Sec. 42(h)(3)(C)].

.03 Definitions

A *qualified low-income housing project* is one that meets minimum set-aside requirements. This means that:

- 20 percent or more of the combined residential rental units in the project are occupied by those with incomes of 50 percent or less of area median income (as adjusted for family size); or
- 40 percent or more of the combined residential rental units are occupied by those with incomes of 60 percent or less of area median income (as adjusted for family size) [Code Sec. 42(g)].

Eligible residential units must be used by the general public, and all of the units in a project must be used on a nontransient basis. Generally, a unit is nontransient if the initial lease term is six months or greater. Additionally, no hospital, nursing home, sanitarium, lifecare facility, retirement home, or trailer park can be a qualified low-income project. However, the portion of the building used to provide supportive services for the homeless does qualify.

A housing unit generally is eligible for the low-income housing credit if occupied entirely by the tenants who are married full-time students filing joint returns or single parents. [Code Sec. 42(i)(3)(D)(i)]. The low-income housing credit is available for units occupied entirely by married full-time students filing a joint income tax return or single parents who are full-time students, provided that neither the students nor their children can be claimed as a dependent on someone else's return [Code Sec. 42(i)(3)(D)(ii)].

[20] Rev. Proc. 2012-41 IRB 2012-45, 539.

The *qualified basis* of a low-income housing building is the lesser of (1) or (2) [Code Sec. 42(c)(1)]:

$$\text{(1) Eligible basis} \times \frac{\text{Low-income housing units in building}}{\text{All units in building}}$$

$$\text{(2) Eligible basis} \times \frac{\text{Total floor space in low-income housing units}}{\text{Total floor space of all units}}$$

Eligible basis is the new building's adjusted basis but not the land's cost. Eligible basis for an existing building is your acquisition cost plus any capital improvements you made by the end of the first tax year of the credit period [Code Sec. 42(d)].

A resident manager's unit is included in figuring the building's eligible basis under Code Sec. 42(d) but excluded from the fraction under Code Sec. 42(c).[21]

Your depreciable basis for the project is not reduced by the low-income housing credit.

To encourage the construction of low-income housing in certain high-cost areas, the eligible basis of a new building or the eligible basis of an existing building undergoing substantial rehabilitation can be 130 percent of the basis claimed for depreciation. This exception, however, does not apply to federally subsidized buildings other than HUD Community Development Block Grants.

The eligible basis used to compute the low-income housing tax credit of a new low-income building is the adjusted basis of the building as of the close of the first tax year of the credit period [Code Sec. 42(d)(1)]. In an effort to prevent double dipping that would occur, for example, if the owner of a building received both the low-income housing credit and a federal-interest subsidy or federal grant with respect to the building, the law provides that the eligible basis will be reduced if a federal grant is made with respect to the same building. The eligible basis of the building for the tax year and all succeeding tax years will be reduced to the extent of the federal grant [Code Sec. 42(d)(5)]. An exception to this basis reduction rule exists, however, for certain rental assistance programs under Code Sec. 42(g)((2)(B)(i). Certain types of federal rental assistance payments do not result in a reduction in the eligible basis of a low-income housing building [Reg. § 1.42-16].

.04 Compliance Issues

Substantial Rehabilitation Expenditures

The rehabilitation expenditures paid or incurred during any 24-month period must be at least equal to the greater of:

1. 20 percent of the adjusted basis of the rehabilitated building as of the first day of the 24-month period; or
2. $6,400 (in 2013) per low-income housing unit in the rehabilitated building, determined by dividing the qualified basis attributable to the rehabilitation

[21] Rev. Rul. 92-61, 1992-2 CB 7.

expenditures by the number of low-income units in the building [Code Sec. 42(e)(3)(A)(ii)].

New student exception to low-income housing rules. A unit providing student housing will qualify as a low-income unit if the unit is occupied by an individual who is (1) a student who has previously been under the care and placement of a state agency responsible for administering a foster care program, specifically, a plan under part B or part E of title IV of the Social Security Act or (2) enrolled in a job training program receiving assistance or (3) entirely by full-time students who are single parents [Code Sec. 42(i)(3)(D)].

General public use requirement clarified. The general public use requirement that must be met in order to claim the low-income housing credit is clarified to allow rental of units to certain favored groups without losing eligibility for the low-income housing credit [Code Sec. 42(g)(9)]. Specifically, low-income housing projects will not fail to meet the general public use requirement due to occupancy restrictions or preferences in favor of tenants:

- With special needs,
- Who are members of a specified group under a federal program or state program or policy that supports housing for such specified group, or
- Who are involved in artistic or literary activities.

.05 Recapture of Credit on Disposition of Qualified Building

The requirement to post a bond upon disposition of an interest in a qualified low-income building to avoid the recapture of previously claimed low-income housing credit amounts has been repealed for interests in buildings disposed of after July 30, 2008. The recapture of credit amounts from previous years upon disposition of an interest in a building will not occur if it is reasonable to expect the building to continue to operate as a qualified low-income building for the remainder of the compliance period.

However, if a building (or interest therein) is disposed of during the compliance period and there is any reduction of the qualified basis of the building which results in an increase of the amount that would be recaptured in the year of disposition or any subsequent year, then the period for assessment of any deficiency related to the increase in tax will be three years. The three-year statute of limitations begins on the date the taxpayer notifies the IRS of the reduction of the basis. The assessment may be made within the three-year period notwithstanding any other provision that would prevent the assessment [Code Sec. 42(j)(6)].

▶ **TAX RETURN TIP:** The low-income housing credit is claimed by the building owner on Form 8586, *Low-Income Housing Credit.* The authorized housing credit agency will send the building owner an allocation of credit on Form 8609, *Low-Income Housing Credit Allocation and Certification.* The building owner must complete this schedule each year of the 15-year compliance period, regardless of whether he or she claimed a credit for the tax year. The building owner should use Form 8611, *Recapture of Low-Income Housing Credit*, to calculate the recapture portion of a low-income housing credit taken in a previous year and later disallowed.

NOTE: If you are a recipient of a credit from a flow-through entity (partnership, S corporation, estate or trust), use Form 8586 to claim the credit. The flow-through entity completes an additional Form 8586 and attaches that form and Form 8609 to its return.

¶14,065 WORK OPPORTUNITY TAX CREDIT

The Work Opportunity Tax Credit (WOTC) provides employers with an incentive to hire persons from targeted groups having a particularly high unemployment rate or other special employment needs [Code Sec. 51]. The credit is computed by taking a percentage of the qualified wages paid during an employee's first year of employment, based on the number of hours worked. Because the WOTC will terminate with respect to wages paid to persons who begin work for the employer before January 1, 2014, employers thinking of hiring WOTC-eligible individuals and taking advantage of this valuable tax credit, should begin the hiring and complicated certification process well before December 31, 2013 [Code Sec. 51(c)(4)(B)].

.01 General Rules for Claiming WOTC

For targeted individuals hired on or before December 31, 2013, employers generally may claim a WOTC equal to 40 percent of the first $6,000 of qualified wages paid per employee (for a maximum WOTC of $2,400) during an employee's first year of employment provided the employee performs at least 400 hours of service [Code Sec. 51(a)]. The following exceptions to these rules are listed below:

- For qualified summer youth employees, only $3,000 of wages are taken into consideration when computing the amount of the WOTC [Code Sec. 51(d)(7)];
- The credit is 25 percent for employees who have completed at least 120 hours, but less than 400 hours of service for the employer [Code Sec. 51(i)(3)];
- The amount of first-year wages taken into account in computing the WOTC for qualified veterans can be as high as $12,000, $14,000, or $24,000 for qualified veterans, if certain requirements discussed below are satisfied [Code Sec. 51(b)(3)]; and
- For long-term family aid recipients, the maximum credit is $9,000 (up to $10,000 first-year wages × .4) and up to $10,000 of second-year wages × .5) [Code Sec. 51(e)].

.02 Groups Eligible to Claim WOTC

The work opportunity tax credit provides an elective credit to employers that hire individuals from the following targeted groups [Code Sec. 51]:

- Qualified IV-A recipient—An individual who is a member of a family receiving assistance under a state plan approved under part A of title IV of the Social Security Act relating to Temporary Assistance for Needy Families (TANF). The assistance must be received for any 9 months during the 18-month period ending on the hiring date.

- Qualified veterans who are members of families receiving food stamps for at least a 3-month period during the 12-month period ending on the hiring date, who have service-connected disabilities, or who are unemployed;
- Qualified ex-felons hired no more than one year after the later of their conviction or release from prison [Code Sec. 51(d)(4)];
- Designated community resident who is at least age 18 but not yet age 40 on the hiring date and lives within an empowerment zone, enterprise community, renewal community, or rural renewal county;
- Vocational rehabilitation referrals certified to have physical or mental disabilities that result in a substantial handicap to employment;
- Summer youth employee who performs services for the employer between May 1 and September 15 and is at least 16 years of age but not yet 18 on the hiring date, has never worked for the employer before and lives in empowerment zone, enterprise community, or renewal community [Code Sec. 51(d)(7)];
- Recipient of supplemental nutrition assistance program (SNAP) benefits (food stamps) who is at least age 18 but not yet age 40 on the hiring date and is a member of a family that has received SNAP benefits for the 6-month period ending on the hiring date or is no longer eligible for food stamps but the family received food stamps for at least 3 months of the 5-month period ending on the hiring date;
- Recipient of Supplemental Security Income (SSI) for any month ending during the 60-day period ending on the hiring date; and
- Recipient of long-term family assistance who is an individual who is a member of a family that (1) has received TANF payments for at least 18 consecutive months ending on the hiring date, or (2) receives TANF payments for any 18 months (whether or not consecutive) beginning after August 5, 1997, and the earliest 18-month period beginning after August 5, 1997, ended during the past 2 years, or (3) stopped being eligible for TANF payments because federal or state law limits the maximum period such assistance is payable and the individual is hired not more than 2 years after such eligibility ended [Code Sec. 51(d)(10)].

The work opportunity credit is part of the general business credit and may be carried back and forward accordingly [Code Sec. 38(b)(2)]. The credit is computed on Form 5884, *Work Opportunity Credit*. The taxpayer may elect not to have the credit apply for any tax year [Code Sec. 51(j)(1)].

The amount of wages that an employer may take into account in computing the amount of the WOTC differs for the various categories of qualified veterans, as follows:

1. Veteran is member of family receiving assistance under food stamp program for at least three months, all or part of which is during the 12-month period ending on the hiring date [Code Sec. 51(d)(3)(A)(i)]. The maximum WOTC for hiring qualified veterans in this category is $2,400 (.4 × $6,000 maximum qualifying first-year wages).
2. Veteran has a service-connected disability and has a hiring date that isn't more than one year after having been discharged or released from active duty in the

U.S. Armed Forces [Code Sec. 51(d)(3)(A)(i)(I)]. The maximum WOTC for hiring these veterans is $4,800 (.4 × $12,000 maximum qualifying first-year wages).

3. Veteran has a service-connected disability and has aggregate periods of unemployment during the one-year period ending on the hiring date of six months or more [Code Sec. 51(d)(3)(A)(i)(II)]. The maximum WOTC for hiring these veterans is $9,600 (.4 × $24,000 maximum qualifying first-year wages).
4. Veteran has aggregate periods of unemployment during the one-year period ending on the hiring date which equal or exceed four weeks (but less than six months) [Code Sec. 51(d)(3)(A)(iii]. The maximum WOTC for hiring these veterans is $2,400 (.4 × $6,000).
5. The individual has aggregate periods of unemployment during the one-year period ending on the hiring date of six months or more [Code Sec. 51(d)(3)(A)(iv)]. The maximum WOTC for hiring these veterans is $5,600 (.4 × $14,000 maximum qualifying first-year wages).

.03 Tax-Exempt Employers Hiring Veterans

Tax-exempt organizations generally cannot claim the WOTC [Code Sec. 52(c)]. However, effective for individuals hired after November 21, 2011, a tax-exempt organization may claim a credit against its Federal Insurance Contribution Act (FICA) tax obligation for hiring WOTC-eligible qualified veterans [Code Sec. 3111(e)(1)].

The WOTC is allowed against the social security tax that the tax-exempt employer would otherwise have to pay on the wages of all its employees during the "applicable employment period" which is the one-year period beginning with the day the veteran begins work for the tax-exempt organization [Code Secs. 52(c)(2) and 3111(e)]. Any credit that exceeds the employer social security tax for the period the credit is claimed may be carried forward and will be included in the qualified tax-exempt organization's cumulative calculation on Form 5884-C filed for a subsequent tax period.

The credit for hiring qualified veterans, which can't exceed the OASDI tax otherwise payable for employment of all the tax-exempt employees during the "applicable employment period," is calculated as it normally would be under Code Sec. 51, but with the following modifications:

- The general credit percentage of qualifying first-year wages is 26 percent (instead of 40 percent).
- The credit percentage of qualifying wages is 16.25 percent (instead of 25 percent) for a qualified veteran who has completed at least 120, but less than 400, hours of service for the employer.
- The tax-exempt employer may only take into account wages paid to a qualified veteran for services in furtherance of the activities related to the purposes or function constituting the basis of the organization's exemption under Code Sec. 501 [Code Sec. 3111(e)(2) and (3)].

Tax-exempt organizations that are entitled to claim the WOTC must file Form 5884-C, *Work Opportunity Credit for Qualified Tax-Exempt Organizations Hiring Qualified Veterans* to calculate the cumulative credit for all qualified veterans. Form 5884-C, which is filed separately and should not be attached to any other return, should be filed after the tax-exempt files its employment tax return for the tax period for which the credit is claimed. This form can be filed immediately after the qualified tax-exempt organization files its employment tax return and it must be filed within 2 years from the date the tax reported on the employment tax return was paid, or 3 years from the date the employment tax return was filed, whichever is later.

The qualified tax-exempt organization using Form 5884-C must calculate the cumulative credit to which the qualified tax-exempt organization is entitled for all qualified veterans hired on or after November 22, 2011. The qualified tax-exempt organization must reduce the cumulative credit by any credits claimed on any Forms 5884-C filed for prior tax periods. The amount refunded will be limited to the amount of employer social security tax reported on the employment tax return filed by the qualified tax-exempt organization for the employment tax period for which the credit is claimed. Any excess credit (i.e., any credit that exceeds the employer social security tax for the period the credit is claimed) may be carried forward and will be included in the qualified tax-exempt organization's cumulative calculation on Form 5884-C filed for a subsequent tax period to the extent provided in the instructions to Form 5884-C.

.04 Certification of Targeted Group Membership Required

An employer will only be able to claim the WOTC if on or before the day the individual begins work, the employer has obtained certification from a designated local agency (DLA) stating that the individual is a member of a targeted group; or (2) on or before the day the individual is offered employment, the employer has completed a pre-screening notice on Form 8850, *Pre-Screening Notice and Certification Request for the Work Opportunity Credit*, and no later than 28 days after the individual begins work the employer submits the signed notice to the DLA [Code Sec. 51(d)(13)(A)].

A veteran will be treated as certified by the DLA as having aggregate periods of unemployment meeting the requirements of Code Sec. 51(d)(3)(A)(ii)(II) or Code Sec. 51(d)(3)(A)(iv), if he or she is certified by the local agency as being in receipt of unemployment compensation under state or federal law for not less than six months during the one-year period ending on the hiring date [Code Sec. 51(d)(13)(D)(i)(I)]. A veteran will be treated as certified by the DLA as having aggregate periods of unemployment meeting the requirements of Code Sec. 51(d)(3)(A)(iii), if he or she is certified by the local agency as being in receipt of unemployment compensation under state or federal law for not less than four weeks (but less than six months) during the one-year period ending on the hiring date [Code Sec. 51(d)(13)(D)(i)(II)].

¶14,075 ORPHAN DRUG CREDIT

.01 Orphan Drug Credit

Taxpayers may be able to elect the nonrefundable orphan drug credit for 50 percent of qualified clinical drug testing expenses paid or incurred for the clinical testing of low or unprofitable drugs used in certain rare diseases or conditions through December 31, 2013 [Code Sec. 45C]. These drugs are commonly called orphan drugs. The orphan drug credit is a component of the general business credit, which means that for credits arising in post-1997 years) an unused credit may be carried back to the first tax year before the year the credit arose and then any unused credit is carried forward to each of the 20 years after the credit arises until you have used it up [¶ 14,050].

Clinical testing means any human clinical testing that:

- Is carried out under an exemption for a drug being tested for a rare disease;
- Occurs after the date such drug is designated as a drug for a rare disease, but before the date on which an application for such drug is approved; and
- Is conducted by or on behalf of the taxpayer who applied for the drug to be tested [Code Sec. 43C(b)(2)].

Expenses eligible for the orphan drug credit are defined in part by reference to the Code Sec. 41 definition of expenses qualifying the research tax credit [¶ 14,080].

¶14,080 RESEARCH TAX CREDIT

Most taxpayers including individuals, estates, trusts, organizations, or corporations carrying on a trade or business may claim a nonrefundable research tax credit for research expenses paid or incurred before January 1, 2014 [Code Sec. 41(h)(1)(B)]. The research and experimentation (R&E) credit was designed to provide tax incentives for incremental increases in research and development spending. The credit was intended to "stimulate a higher rate of capital formation and to increase productivity" and "to encourage business firms to perform the research necessary to increase the innovative qualities and efficiency of the U.S. economy."[22] This means that the taxpayer must increase research spending over a specified base amount in order to qualify for the research tax credit.

The research credit consists of three separately calculated component credits. These component credits are: (1) the incremental research credit [Code Sec. 41(a)(1)], (2) the credit for basic research payments to universities and other qualified organizations (available only to C corporations) [Code Sec. 41(a)(2)], and (3) the credit for energy research consortium payments [Code Sec. 41(a)(3)].

The research credit is a component credit of the general business credit under Code Sec. 38 and is nonrefundable. Therefore, the research credit is subject to the general business credit tax liability limitation of Code Sec. 38 and to the general business credit carryback and carryforward rules of Code Sec. 39.

.01 Credit Amount

The research expense credit is claimed on Form 6765, *Credit for Increasing Research Activities*, as one of the components of the general business credit.

The research credit is the sum of: (1) 20 percent of the excess of qualified research expenses for the current tax year over a base period amount, (2) 20 percent of the basic research payments made to a qualified organization, and (3) 20 percent of the amounts paid or incurred by a taxpayer in carrying on any trade or business to an energy research consortium for qualified energy research [Code Sec. 41(a)]. Special

---

[22] S. Rept. No. 97-144 (1981), 1981-2 CB 412; H.R. Rept. No. 97-201 (1981), 1981-2 CB 352.

base period adjustments are required where there is an acquisition or disposition of the major portion of a business that paid or incurred research expenses.

Base Amount

For purposes of calculating the Code 41(a)(1) incremental research credit, the base period amount is the product of the taxpayer's fixed-base percentage and average annual gross receipts for the four tax years preceding the credit period [Code Sec. 41(c)]. The base amount may not be less than 50 percent of the qualified research expenses for the credit year. In the case of a new taxpayer with no prior tax years, the average annual gross receipts for the four tax years preceding the credit year is zero. If, with respect to any credit year, the taxpayer has been in existence for one, two, or three previous tax years, then the average annual gross receipts of the taxpayer for the four tax years preceding the credit year is the average annual gross receipts for the number of tax years preceding the credit year [Reg. § 1.41-3(a)]. The fixed-base percentage (aggregate qualified research expenses compared to aggregate gross receipts for 1984 through 1988 tax years) may not exceed 16 percent [Code Sec. 41(c)].

Gross Receipts Defined

The term "gross receipts" is broadly defined in Reg. § 1.41-31(c)(1) to include the total amount, as determined under the taxpayer's method of accounting, derived by the taxpayer from all its activities and from all sources. Excluded are: (1) returns or allowances; (2) receipts from the sale or exchange of capital assets; (3) repayments of loans or similar instruments; (4) receipts from a sale or exchange not in the ordinary course of business; (5) amounts received with respect to sales tax or other similar state and local taxes if, under the applicable state or local law, the tax is legally imposed on the purchaser of the good or service, and the taxpayer merely collects and remits the tax to the taxing authority; and (6) amounts received by a taxpayer in a tax year that precedes the first tax year in which the taxpayer derives more than $25,000 in gross receipts other than investment income [Reg. § 1.41-3(c)(2)]. A taxpayer's gross receipts for any tax year are reduced by sales returns and allowances that are made during the tax year [Code Sec. 41(c)(7)]. Gross receipts of a foreign corporation include only gross receipts that are effectively connected with the conduct of a trade or business within the United States, the Commonwealth of Puerto Rico, or other possessions of the United States [Reg. § 1.41-3(c)(3)].

In *Union Carbide Corp.*,[23] the Court of Appeals for the Second Circuit affirmed the Tax Court (and the Supreme Court declined to review the case) to conclude that a consolidated group was not entitled to additional research credits for supplies used to conduct research on products that were in the process of being manufactured for sale and were, in fact sold, because the expenditures were not qualified research expenses. The supplies, which would have been used during the manufacturing regardless of any research performed, did not qualify as an amount paid or incurred for supplies used in the conduct of qualified research under Code Sec. 41(b)(2)(A)(ii)]. Indirect research costs, such as amounts incurred during the production process upon which the qualified research was conducted, and not during the conduct of the qualified research itself, were excluded under Reg. § 1.41-2(b)(2). The court found that the taxpayer's projects did not fulfill the "process of experimentation test" required to

---

[23] *Union Carbide Corp.*, 97 TCM 1209, Dec. 57,753(M), TC Memo. 2009-50, *aff'd*, CA-2, 2012-2 USTC ¶ 50,553, 697 F3d 104, *cert. denied*, 133 SCt 1626 (03/18/2013).

show that it was qualified research because the taxpayer did not perform any post-testing analysis or comparisons of the data collected.

In *Hewlett-Packard Co.*,[24] the Tax Court concluded that a corporate taxpayer had to include nonsales income, including dividends, interest, rent, and other income in its average annual gross receipts for purposes of calculating the base amount used for determining the amount of the research tax credit. The fact that Code Sec. 41(c)(6), as in effect during the tax years at issue (1999-2001), required that gross receipts for these purposes be "reduced by returns and allowances made during the taxable year" did not limit the meaning of "gross receipts" to sales or service income generated in the ordinary course of business. The court reasoned that gross receipts are generally not limited to sales receipts in the tax code and that corporate research budgets are generally based on a business's expected income stream regardless of the source. Moreover, a narrower definition would allow taxpayers to manipulate the base amount over time by characterizing the same types of income as derived from the ordinary course of business in some years but not others.

In *Deere & Co.*,[25] a U.S. corporation with foreign subsidiaries was required to include the annual gross receipts of its foreign subsidiaries in the calculation of its average annual gross receipts for the four tax years prior to the tax year for which it claimed the credit for increasing research activities. *Deere* established that a taxpayer is required to include in its gross receipts the sales the taxpayer made to third parties in foreign countries through its foreign branches. Code Sec. 41(c)(6) provides that in the case of a foreign corporation, there shall be taken into account only gross receipts which are effectively connected with a trade or business within the United States, the Commonwealth of Puerto Rico, or any possession of the United States.

But in *Procter & Gamble Co.*,[26] a federal district court concluded that a consumer products company could exclude receipts from intercompany sales to its foreign subsidiaries when determining gross receipts for the purposes of calculating its research tax credit. The court found that the company's research tax credit computation was proper because purely intercompany transactions are properly disregarded under Code Sec. 41(f). Code Sec. 41(f)(1)(A) and Reg. § 1.41-6(i) do not distinguish between calculations of research expenses and gross receipts; rather, the "single taxpayer" provisions are applicable to the entire credit calculation, not simply to the determination of research expenses. There was no basis for distinguishing between intercompany transactions with foreign subsidiaries and those with domestic subsidiaries. The exclusion of intercompany transactions in general was warranted because intercompany sales do not represent sales to the company's customers. The court found that including international intercompany transfers in the gross receipts calculation would result in the multiple counting of transactions which are merely administrative or legal in nature.

---

[24] *Hewlett-Packard Co.*, 139 TC 255, Dec. 59,200 (2012).

[25] *Deere & Co.*, Dec. 57,969, 133 TC 246 (2009); *Union Carbide Corp.*, 97 TCM 1209, Dec. 57,753, TC Memo. 2009-50.

[26] *Procter & Gamble Co.*, DC-OH, 2010-2 USTC ¶ 50,554, 733 FSupp2d 857.

Energy Research Consortium

An energy research consortium is an organization:

- That is a tax-exempt organization and operated primarily to conduct energy research or is organized and operated primarily to conduct energy research in the public interest;
- That is not a private foundation;
- To which at least five unrelated persons paid or incurred amounts to such organization during the calendar year for energy research; and
- To which no single person paid or incurred during the calendar year more than 50 percent of the total amounts received by such organization for energy research during such calendar year [Code Sec. 41(f)(6)].

.02 What Expenses Qualify for the Research Credit?

An expense will qualify for the research credit if it satisfies the following three requirements found in Code Sec. 41(d)(1):

1. The expenses must qualify as a research and experimental expenditures under Code Sec. 174 [Code Sec. 41(d)(1)(A); Reg. § 1.174-2; Ch. 12]. Therefore, an expenditure must be a Code Sec. 174 expense to constitute "qualified research" under Code Sec. 41.[27] Code Sec. 174 does not define the phrase "research and experimental expenditures," but provides that Code Sec. 174 does not apply to expenditures for "the acquisition or improvement of property to be used in connection with the research or experimentation and of a character which is subject to the allowance" for depreciation. [Reg. § 1.174-2(b)(2)]. In *TG Missouri Corp.*,[28] the Tax Court held that costs incurred by a manufacturer of molded products to which the taxpayer added design and engineering modifications before selling them to customers were properly included as qualified research expenses when calculating its research credit. The cost of the production molds sold to customers could be treated as the cost of supplies for purposes of the research credit because the production molds were not assets of a character subject to the allowance for depreciation under Code Secs. 41(b)(2)(C) and 174(c). Based on the statutory language, the phrase "property of a character subject to the depreciation allowance" meant property that is depreciable in the hands of the taxpayer, and was not a reference to just the character of the property itself. *Research and experimental expenditures* are defined in Code Sec. 174 and Reg. § 1.174-2 as expenditures incurred in connection with the taxpayer's trade or business which represents research and development costs in the experimental or laboratory sense. The term generally includes all such costs incident to the development or improvement of a product or the costs of obtaining a patent, such as attorneys' fees expended in making and perfecting a patent application. Expenditures for activities intended to discover information that would eliminate uncertainty concerning the development or improvement of a product would also qualify. In this situation, the term *product* includes any pilot model, process, formula, invention, technique, patent, or similar property, and includes products to be used by the taxpayer in its trade or business as well as products to be held for sale, lease, or license. The term *research or experimental expenditures* does not include expenditures for

---

[27] *Norwest Corp.*, 110 TC 454, Dec. 52,758 (1998).

[28] *TG Missouri Corp.*, Dec. 57,991, 133 TC 278 (2009).

a. The ordinary testing or inspection of materials or products for quality control (quality control testing)
b. Efficiency surveys
c. Management studies
d. Consumer surveys
e. Advertising or promotions
f. The acquisition of another's patent, model, production, or process or
g. Research in connection with literary, historical, or similar projects.

2. According to the "discovery test," expenses must be undertaken to discover information which is technological in nature and which when applied will be useful in the development of a new or improved business component of the taxpayer [Code Sec. 41(d)(1)(B)]; and
3. According to the "process of experimentation test," substantially all of the research activities must constitute elements of a process of experimentation related to a new or improved function, performance, or reliability or quality of a business component. Research relating to style, taste, cosmetic, or seasonal design factors will not qualify [Code Sec. 41(d)(1)(C)].

Process of Experimentation Test

A *process of experimentation* is a process designed to evaluate one or more alternatives to achieve a result where the capability or the method of achieving that result, or the appropriate design of that result, is uncertain at the beginning of the research activities. The taxpayer's activities must be directed at resolving uncertainty regarding the development or improvement of a business component. The process must fundamentally rely on the principles of the physical or biological sciences, engineering, or computer science. A taxpayer is required to identify the uncertainty regarding the development or improvement of a business component that is the object of the taxpayer's research activities. A taxpayer is also required to identify one or more alternatives intended to eliminate that uncertainty. Additionally, a taxpayer is required to identify and to conduct a process of evaluating the alternatives [Reg. § 1.41-4(a)(5)]. Such a process may involve, for example, modeling, simulation, or a systematic trial and error methodology. A process of experimentation must be an evaluative process and generally should be capable of evaluating more than one alternative [Reg. § 1.41-4(a)(5)].

A federal district court in *Trinity Industries, Inc.*[29] concluded that a shipbuilder qualified for the research and experimentation credit for all costs associated with developing two prototype ships. As long as a taxpayer could prove that at least 80 percent of research activities were elements of a "process of experimentation," all associated expenses could qualify for the credit.

Substantially all requirement. Substantially all of the research activities must constitute elements of a process of experimentation for a qualified purpose [Code Sec. 41(d)(1)(C)]. The substantially all requirement is satisfied only if 80 percent or more of the research activities, measured on a cost or other consistently applied reasonable

[29] *Trinity Industries, Inc.*, DC Tex., 2010-1 USTC ¶ 50,219.

basis, constitute elements of a process of experimentation for a qualified purpose. This requirement is applied separately to each business component [Reg. § 1.41-4(a)(6)]. The requirement is satisfied if 20 percent or less of a taxpayer's research activities do not constitute elements of a process of experimentation for a qualified purpose, so long as these remaining activities are considered expenses under Code Sec. 174 and are not ineligible activities under Code Sec. 41(d)(4) [Reg. § 1.41-4(a)(6), (a)(8), Ex. (4)].

Shrinking-back rule. If all of the requirements for qualified research (as defined in Code Sec. 41(d)) are not met with respect to a business component (e.g., product) the test is then applied at the next most significant subset of elements of the business component. This shrinking back of the product is continued until either a subset of elements of the component that satisfies the requirement is reached or the most basic element of the component is reached and that element also fails to satisfy the test. This rule is not intended to exclude qualified research expenses from the credit. It is intended to ensure that expenses attributable to qualified research activities are eligible for the credit [Reg. § 1.41-4(b)(2)].

> **Example 14-12:** Joe Long develops a new truck carburetor and also modifies the truck engine so that it is compatible with the new carburetor. If the modifications to the engine as a whole (including the development of the new carburetor) do not satisfy the requirements for qualified research, those requirements are applied to the next most significant subset of elements of the engine. If the next most significant subset is the carburetor, then the tests for qualified research are applied at that level [Reg. § 1.41-4(b)(3)].

Qualified research expenses that are eligible for the research tax credit consist of:

- Wages for employees involved in the research activity;
- Cost of supplies used in research;
- Time-sharing costs for computer use in the conduct of research; and
- 65 percent of the costs of contracting with another party to conduct research on the taxpayer's behalf (contract research expenses) [Code Sec. 41(b)].

100 percent of contract research expenses paid to an eligible small business, institution of higher education, or federal laboratory for qualified research that is energy research qualify as qualified research expenses. In the case of amounts paid to a qualified research consortium, 75 percent (rather than 65 percent as in (4) above) of amounts paid for qualified research on behalf of the taxpayer and one or more unrelated taxpayers is treated as qualified research expenses eligible for the research credit.

.03 Ineligible Activities

The following items are ineligible for the Section 174 election and may not be taken into account for purposes of the credit:

- Research done outside the United States, the Commonwealth of Puerto Rico, or any possession of the United States [Reg. § 1.41-4(c)(7)].
- Research in the social sciences, arts, or humanities [Reg. § 1.41-4(c)(8)].

- Ordinary testing or inspection of materials or products for quality control [Reg. § 1.174-2(a)(1)].
- Market and consumer research [Reg. § 1.174-2(a)(1)].
- Advertising or promotion expenses [Reg. § 1.174-2(a)(1)].
- Management studies and efficiency surveys [Reg. § 1.41-4(c)(6)].
- Research to find and evaluate mineral deposits, including gas and oil [Code Sec. 174(d)].
- Acquisition or improvement of land or of certain depreciable or depletable property used in research [Code Sec. 174(c)].
- Acquisition of another person's patent, model, production, or process [Reg. § 1.174-2(a)(1)].
- Research funded by another person, or any governmental entity, by means of a grant or contract [Code Sec. 41(d)(4); Reg. § 1.41-4(c)(9)].
- Research conducted after commercial production [Code Sec. 41(d)(4)(A); Reg. § 1.41-4(c)(2)].
- Research for the adaptation of existing business components [Code Sec. 41(d)(4)(B); Reg. § 1.41-4(c)(3)].
- Research for the duplication of an existing business component [Code Sec. 41(d)(4)(C); Reg. § 1.41-4(c)(4)].
- Research costs incurred in developing computer software primarily for the taxpayer's own internal use is eligible for the credit only if the software is used in
  a. Qualified research undertaken by the taxpayer
  b. A production process that meets the requirements for the credit. Any other research activities for internal-use software are not eligible for the credit [Code Sec. 41(d)(4)(E)].

.04 Commercial Computer Software

Taxpayers who have sought a research tax credit for the development of computer software have been uniformly unsuccessful as illustrated in the cases below. In *Tax & Accounting Software Corporation.*,[30] the Court of Appeals for the Tenth Circuit held that research costs incurred in developing tax preparation and accounting software for sale to accountants were ineligible for a research credit because they failed to satisfy the process of experimentation requirements under Code Sec. 41. The court concluded that to qualify for the credit, taxpayers must show that they were uncertain that the end result of the process of experimentation was technically feasible at the time the research commenced. Because the taxpayer in this case conceded that its programmers did not question the technical feasibility of the products under development, the taxpayers failed to satisfy the process of experimentation requirement.

---

[30] *Tax & Accounting Software Corp.*, CA-10, 2002-2 USTC ¶ 50,623, 301 F3d 1254, *cert. denied*, 539 US 903.

Similarly, in *Eustace*,[31] the sole shareholders of an insurance software development company were denied their research tax credits because the company's process in enhancing its software failed to satisfy either the discovery or the process of experimentation tests of Code Sec. 41(d)(1). Despite the taxpayers' assertion that the statutory standard for research and development merely required a process of trial and error, it was determined that the research failed to produce an innovation in underlying principle, and was not designed to dispel uncertainty about the technological possibility of developing similar software.

In *Wicor, Inc.*,[32] a gas utility corporation was not entitled to a research credit because its development of a computerized integrated customer information system did not constitute qualified research. There was no evidence to show that the project exceeded what was already known in the field of computer science. Moreover, the means for achieving the final result were not certain at the onset, and it did not result in any new discoveries in the field of computer science.

In *United Stationers, Inc.*,[33] an office products wholesaler was denied a research tax credit for expenses incurred in modifying purchased computer software to improve its recordkeeping, marketing, and inventory control. The corporation merely applied and built upon pre-existing information and did not discover any technological information or expand existing computer science principles. Further, the projects did not involve experimentation because there was no uncertainty with respect to their designs or development. In any event, the projects constituted internal use software and were specifically excluded from the credit since they were not innovative and did not involve a significant economic risk.

In *Norwest Corp.*,[34] the Tax Court held that a bank holding company's internal use software projects did not meet the standards for qualified research since they involved basic and routine principles of software development that did not result in new knowledge about computer science and there was no significant technical risk.

> ▶ **TAX PLANNING TIP:** Even if your research expense fails to qualify for the research tax credit, it may qualify for expensing [Ch. 11] or 60-month amortization [Ch. 12] [Code Sec. 174].

.05 Substantiation of Eligible Expenses

A taxpayer must retain records in sufficiently usable form and detail to substantiate the credit. To facilitate compliance and administration, the IRS and taxpayers may agree to guidelines for the keeping of specific records for purposes of substantiating the credit [Reg. § 1.41-4(d)].

In *B. Shami*,[35] the Tax Court concluded that wages paid by an S corporation to its shareholders and executives were not qualified expenses for purposes of the research credit because the individuals failed to substantiate that they conducted research or

---

[31] *N.E. Eustace*, CA-7, 2003-1 USTC ¶ 50,133, 312 F3d 905, *cert. denied*, 123 S.Ct. 2247.

[32] *Wicor, Inc.*, DC-WI, 2000-2 USTC ¶ 50,833, 116 FSupp2d 1028, *aff'd*, CA-7, 2001-2 USTC ¶ 50,576, 263 F3d 659.

[33] *United Stationers Inc.*, CA-7, 99-1 USTC ¶ 50,136, 163 F3d 440, *cert. denied*, 527 US 1023.

[34] *Norwest Corp.*, 110 TC 454, Dec. 52,758 (1998).

[35] *B. Shami*, 103 TCM 1415, Dec. 58,989(M), TC Memo. 2012-78.

engaged in the direct supervision of research activities that constituted qualified research as required by Reg. § 1.41-4(d). Moreover, they failed to substantiate their claimed wage allocations because they failed to provide any documentation that established how much time they spent performing research and development services during the tax years at issue and the testimony they offered was self-serving and unreliable. Further, there was insufficient evidence to estimate the appropriate allocation of wages between qualified and nonqualified services.

.06 Allocation of Research Credit in Controlled Groups

The IRS explained in Notice 2013-20,[36] that for tax years beginning after December 31, 2011, controlled groups must allocate the group credit to each member of the controlled group in proportion to each member's contribution of qualified research expenses, basic research payments, and amounts paid or incurred to energy research consortiums (QREs) to the controlled group's total QREs for the tax year. Such allocation methodology must also be applied to determine the portion of a group credit that is allocated to, and within, a consolidated group that is a member of a controlled group under Reg. § 1.41-6(d)(1) and (3). For example, X, a controlled group consisting of 3 members, B, C, and D, has a $100 credit for the taxable year. X's total QREs for the taxable year is $1000. B paid $200 of the QREs, C paid $300 of the QREs, and D paid $500 of the QREs during the taxable year. Based on the proportion of each member's contribution of QREs to the controlled group's total QREs for the taxable year, B is allocated a $20 credit.

¶14,085 ENHANCED OIL RECOVERY CREDIT

A credit is available for costs related to enhanced oil recovery (EOR) projects, also called tertiary recovery projects [Code Sec. 43]. The credit is equal to up to 15 percent of qualified enhanced oil recovery costs attributable to qualified domestic EOR projects [Code Sec. 43(a); Reg. § 1.43-1(a)].

The enhanced oil recovery credit is part of the general business credit [¶ 14,050]. Thus, the same limitations and carryover rules of that credit apply to the enhanced oil recovery credit.

Suppose property qualifies as an integral part of more than one qualified enhanced oil recovery project. Then you can include that project's cost in the credit base only once.

.01 Enhanced Oil Recovery Costs

These include costs paid or incurred on a qualified enhanced oil recovery project located in the U.S. and involving one or more tertiary recovery methods. The credit can be as much as 15 percent of the following types of costs [Code Sec. 43(c)]:

- Depreciable or amortizable tangible property that is an integral part of the project;
- Intangible drilling and development costs [Ch. 12];

  NOTE: For an integrated oil company, the credit base includes the intangible drilling costs that taxpayers must capitalize under Code Sec. 291(b)(1).

[36] Notice 2013-20, IRB 2013-15, 902.

- Costs of tertiary injectants for which an amortization deduction can be claimed; and
- Any amount that is paid or incurred to construct a gas treatment plant for certain specified purposes in Alaska.

.02 At-Risk Limit

Enhanced oil recovery project costs eligible for the credit are limited to the amount for which you are at-risk in the project [Code Sec. 43(c)(3)]. This means that any item's credit base will be reduced to the extent that it was financed with nonqualified nonrecourse financing.

.03 Phaseout of Credit

The enhanced oil recovery credit under Code Sec. 43 for any tax year is reduced if the "reference price," determined under Code Sec.45K(d)(2)(C), for the previous year is greater than $28 multiplied by that year's inflation adjustment factor. The credit is phased out in any tax year in which the reference price for the preceding calendar year exceeds $28 (as adjusted) by at least $6. The inflation adjustment factor for 2013 is 1.5968. Because the reference price, as determined under Code Sec. 45K(d)(2)(C), for 2012 ($94.53) exceeds $28 multiplied by the inflation adjustment factor for 2012 ($44.71) by $49.82, the enhanced oil recovery credit for qualified costs paid or incurred in 2013 is phased out completely. The GNP implicit price deflator to be used for calendar year 2012 is 115.387.[37]

¶14,090 DISABLED ACCESS CREDIT

Costs that an eligible small business incurs to remove architectural and transportation barriers to the handicapped and elderly can result in tax benefits. The business can elect to take a deduction of up to $15,000 each year for eligible access expenditures [Code Sec. 190; Ch. 12]. In lieu of this deduction, eligible small businesses may be able to claim the disabled access credit for similar expenses. The disabled access credit was designed to reduce the cost of complying with the Americans with Disabilities Act of 1990 (ADA). This law requires businesses to make accommodations for disabled workers and customers. The nonrefundable credit is equal to 50 percent of the amount of the eligible expenses that exceed $250, but not more than $10,250 [Code Sec. 44(a)]. Thus, the maximum credit allowable is $5,000 [50 percent of $10,000 ($10,250 less $250)].

The credit is claimed on Form 8826, *Disabled Access Credit*, which should be attached to the taxpayer's tax return. In order to claim the credit, the small business must have the duty to comply with the ADA. In *Arevalo*,[38] the Court of Appeals affirmed the Tax Court to conclude that an individual was not entitled to claim the disabled access tax credit because the taxpayer did not have the obligation to comply with the ADA. The small business, not the taxpayer, had the duty to comply with the ADA because the business was responsible for all business decisions.

---

[37] Notice 2013-50, IRB 2013-32, 134.

[38] *E.R. Arevalo*, CA-5, 2007-1 USTC ¶50,166, 469 F3d 436; *J.M. Sita*, CA-7, 2009-1 USTC ¶50,275; *O.D. Snyder*, 97 TCM 1504, Dec. 48,039(M), TC Memo. 57,812; *M.P. Loveland*, 97 TCM 1509, Dec. 48,040(M), TC Memo. 57,813(M).

.01 Eligible Small Business

An eligible small business is one (1) whose gross receipts for the prior tax year did not exceed $1 million or (2) who employed no more than 30 full-time employees during the preceding tax year. (Full-time employees work at least 30 hours a week for at least 20 weeks during the year.) [Code Sec. 44(b)].

.02 Eligible Public Accommodations Access Expenses

Eligible access expenditures means amounts paid or incurred by an eligible small business to enable it to comply with applicable requirements of the Americans With Disabilities Act of 1990 [Code Sec. 44(c)(1)]. Qualified expenses include amounts the taxpayer pays or incurs:

- To remove architectural, communication, physical or transportation barriers that keep the handicapped from gaining access to the premises;
- To provide qualified interpreters or other effective methods of making aurally delivered materials available to the hearing-impaired;
- To provide qualified readers, taped texts and other effective methods of making visually delivered materials available to the visually impaired;
- To acquire or modify equipment or devices for the disabled; and
- To provide other similar services, modifications, materials or equipment [Code Sec. 44(c)(2)].

.03 Credit Denied for Equipment Purchased in Normal Course of Business

Code Sec. 44(c)(2)(D) provides that the disabled access credit will be available for expenditures made to acquire or modify equipment for individuals with disabilities. You must distinguish equipment purchased to comply with the needs of the disabled and equipment purchased that is generally useful to all patients and merely the disabled in a general sense without addressing their specific needs. For example, the IRS held that a dentist could not claim a disabled access credit for x-ray machines used for all his patients, including those in wheelchairs.[39] Similarly in Fan,[40] the Tax Court held that a dentist's purchase of a video camera system for use in his practice was not an eligible access expenditure for purposes of the disabled access credit because the new system had a general applicability and usefulness to all his patients and failed to permit patients to be treated who were previously excluded. Similarly, an optometrist's purchase of a field analyzer, which plots the visual field of a patient, and a hand-held topographer, which makes a map of the eye and screens for irregularities, did not qualify as eligible access expenditures. As a result, his claimed disabled access credit was disallowed. The taxpayer acquired the equipment in the normal course of his business rather than to comply with applicable requirements of the Americans with Disabilities Act of 1990 (ADA).[41]

---

[39] FSA 200024048 (Mar. 21, 2000).

[40] *S.T. Fan*, 117 TC 32, Dec. 54,419 (2001).

[41] *L.D. Svoboda*, 91 TCM 643, Dec. 56,402(M), TC Memo. 2006-1; *D. Taye-Channell*, 91 TCM 662, Dec. 56,411(M), TC Memo. 2006-8; *R.E. Galyen*, 91 TCM 762, Dec. 56,436(M), TC Memo. 2006-30.

But in *Hubbard*,[42] the Tax Court held that the cost of special equipment purchased for use in an optometric practice qualified for the disabled access tax credit because the equipment was purchased expressly for the purpose of enabling the taxpayer to treat disabled patients.

Expenses for Improving Web Access Ineligible for Credit

The IRS has concluded that specially developed software expense incurred by a business to improve web-access for the disabled are not eligible for the disabled access credit because the web-based business failed to satisfy a physical presence requirement.[43]

The improved web access failed to qualify because a nexus failed to exist between the software expenses incurred to improve access to the business website and the actual physical premises as required by the ADA.

.04 Special Rules

In determining the credit and if the limitations are met, all members of a corporation's controlled group are treated as one person. For a partnership, the $10,250 annual limit applies at both the partnership and partner levels. A similar rule applies for an S corporation [Code Sec. 44(d)(3)].

You cannot get a double benefit for expenses you incur to remove barriers to the handicapped. So expenses you claim for the credit cannot also be claimed for the up-to-$15,000 deduction [Ch. 12].

> ▶ **OBSERVATION:** The deduction is available to all businesses-not just small businesses as with the credit. You should figure the credit before taking the deduction. Reason: The credit reduces your tax liability dollar-for-dollar, while the deduction only reduces your income subject to tax. But expenditures in excess of the credit qualify for the deduction.

The amount of the credit is not included in the adjusted basis of any property with respect to which a credit is determined [Code Sec. 44(d)(7)].

The disabled access credit is part of the general business credit [¶ 14,050]. Thus, the same limitations and carryover rules apply. The portion of the unused business credit for any tax year that is due to the disabled access credit cannot be carried back to any tax year ending before November 5, 1990.

¶ 14,095 RENEWABLE ELECTRICITY PRODUCTION CREDIT

A nonrefundable credit is available under Code Sec. 45 for the domestic production of electricity from qualified energy resources produced at a qualifying facility during a 5- or 10-year period that generally begins on the date that the taxpayer places the facility in service [Code Sec. 45(a)]. The electricity must be sold by the taxpayer to an unrelated person during the tax year [Code Sec. 45(a)(2)(B)].

---

[42] *D.B. Hubbard*, 86 TCM 276, Dec. 55,268(M), TC Memo. 2003-245.

[43] Chief Counsel Advice 200411042 (Feb. 6, 2004).

A taxpayer may make the election to treat Code Sec. 45 qualified facilities as energy property eligible for the 30-percent investment credit under Code Sec. 48(a)(5) if the facility is placed in service after 2008 and the construction of the facility begins before January 1, 2014. In Notice 2013-60,[44] the IRS provided guidance and a safe harbor to determine when construction had begun on a "qualified facility" for purposes of the renewable electricity production tax credit or the energy investment tax credit. For further discussion of investment tax credit, see ¶ 14,055. In order to make the election to treat qualified facilities as energy property, qualified property must also be acquired or constructed, reconstructed, or erected by the taxpayer and the original use of the property must commence with the taxpayer [Code Sec. 48(a)(5)(D)].

.01 Qualified Facilities

Qualified energy resources and facilities include the following [Code Sec. 45(d)]:

1. A wind facility (i.e., a facility using wind to produce electricity) which is owned by the taxpayer. The credit for a wind facility may be claimed if construction of the facility begins before January 1, 2014 [Code Sec. 45(d)(1)];
2. A closed-loop biomass facility is a facility that uses any organic material from a plant which is planted exclusively for the purpose of being used at a qualifying facility to produce electricity. The credit for a closed-loop biomass facility may be claimed if construction of the facility begins before January 1, 2014. These facilities no longer are required to be placed in service before that date in order to qualify for the credit [Code Sec. 45(d)(2)];
3. An open-loop biomass facility that uses agricultural livestock waste nutrients (e.g., poultry waste) to produce electricity. The facility must be rated at not less than 150 kilowatts. If the owner of the facility is not the producer of the electricity, the lessee or operator of the facility claims the credit. The credit for an open-loop biomass facility may be claimed if construction of the facility begins before January 1, 2014. These facilities no longer are required to be placed in service before that date in order to qualify for the credit [Code Sec. 45(d)(3)];
4. A geothermal or solar energy facility (i.e., a facility using geothermal or solar energy to produce electricity) owned by the taxpayer. The credit for a geothermal facility may be claimed if construction of the facility begins before January 1, 2014. These facilities no longer are required to be placed in service before that date in order to qualify for the credit [Code Sec. 45(d)(4)];
5. A landfill gas facility (i.e., a facility producing electricity from gas derived from the biodegradation of municipal solid waste) owned by the taxpayer. The credit for a landfill gas facility may be claimed if construction of the facility begins before January 1, 2014. These facilities no longer are required to be placed in service before that date in order to qualify for the credit [Code Sec. 45(d)(6)];
6. A trash combustion facility (i.e., a facility which burns municipal solid waste to produce electricity) owned by the taxpayer. The credit for a trash facility may be claimed if construction of the facility begins before January 1, 2014. These facilities no longer are required to be placed in service before that date in order to qualify for the credit [Code Sec. 45(d)(7)]. The definition of municipal solid waste

[44] Notice 2013-60, IRB 2013-42, clarifying Notice 2013-29, IRB 2013-20, 1085.

has been modified to exclude paper that is commonly recycled and that has been segregated from other solid waste [Code Sec. 45(c)(6)];

7. A qualifying hydropower facility. The credit for a qualified hydropower facility may be claimed if construction of the facility begins before January 1, 2014. These facilities no longer are required to be placed in service before that date in order to qualify for the credit [Code Sec. 45(d)(9)]. In the case of a hydropower facility, an efficiency improvement or addition to capacity required for the facility to be qualified will be treated as placed in service before January 1, 2014, if the construction or the improvement or addition begins before that date [Code Sec. 45(d)(9)(C)];

8. An Indian coal production facility. The credit may be claimed for sales of Indian coal produced at an Indian coal production facility during the eight-year period beginning on January 1, 2006 and ending on December 31, 2013 [Code Sec. 45(e)(10)]. Indian coal is defined as coal produced from reserves that on June 14, 2005, were owned by a federally recognized tribe of Indians or were held in trust by the United States for a tribe or its members [Code Sec. 45(c)(9)]. The credit is subject to reduction for grants, tax-exempt, bonds, subsidized energy financing, and other credits allowed to property that is part of the project. Only U.S. production may be taken into account [Code Sec. 45(e)(10)(C)]; and

9. Marine and hydrokinetic renewable energy facilities if owned by the taxpayer. The credit for a marine and hydrokinetic renewable energy facility may be claimed if construction of the facility begins before January 1, 2014 [Code Sec. 45(d)(11)]. These facilities no longer are required to be placed in service before that date in order to qualify for the credit. The facility must produce electric power from marine and hydrokinetic renewable energy and have a nameplate capacity rating of at least 150 kilowatts [Code Sec. 45(d)(11)]. Marine and hydrokinetic renewable energy is energy derived from (1) waves, tides, and currents in oceans, estuaries, and tidal areas; (2) free flowing water in rivers, lakes, and streams; (3) free flowing water in an irrigation system, canal, or other man-made channel, including projects that utilize nonmechanical structures to accelerate the flow of water for electric power production purposes; or (4) differentials in ocean temperature (ocean thermal energy conversion). The term does not include energy derived from any source that uses a dam, diversionary structure (except for irrigation systems, canals, and other man-made channels), or impoundment for electric power production [Code Sec. 45(c)(1)].

.02 Credit Amount

The inflation adjustment factor to be used in computing the renewable electricity production credit for calendar year 2013 is 1.5063 for qualified energy resources and refined coal, and 1.1538 for Indian coal. The reference price is 4.53 cents per kilowatt hour for facilities producing electricity from wind. The reference price for fuel used as feedstock for refined coal production is $58.23 per ton. The amount of the credit is 2.3 cents per kilowatt hour on sales of electricity produced from wind energy, closed-loop biomass, geothermal energy and solar energy, and 1.1 cents per kilowatt hour on sales of electricity produced from open-loop biomass, small irrigation power facilities, landfill gas facilities, trash combustion facilities, qualified hydropower facilities, and marine and hydrokinetic energy facilities. The credit for refined coal production is $6.590 per ton. The credit for Indian coal production is $2.308 per ton. The renewable electricity production credit is not subject to a phaseout in 2013.[45]

The credit is computed on Form 8835, *Renewable Electricity, Refined Coal, and Indian Coal Production Credit,* and is part of the general business credit, subject to applicable limitations, as well as applicable carryback and carryforward rules [¶ 14,050].

.03 Credit Availability

The Clean Coal Credit is available regardless of whether the taxpayer owns the refined coal production facility in which the coal is produced. The taxpayer may lease or operate a facility owned by another person and still claim the credit for the refined coal the taxpayer produces at the facility. In order to qualify for the credit, at least 80 percent of the total value of the facility must have been improved or added after October 22, 2004, in order for the taxpayer to qualify for the credit.[46]

¶14,096 CLEAN RENEWABLE ENERGY BOND CREDIT

.01 Clean Renewable Energy Bonds

Clean renewable energy bonds (CREBs) may be issued from 2006 through 2009 to finance capital expenditures by tax-exempt electricity producers to increase their capacity to produce electricity from clean renewable sources [Code Sec. 54]. The bonds may be issued by governmental bodies, cooperative electricity companies, or cooperative lenders owned by cooperative electricity companies. A taxpayer holding a CREB may claim a nonrefundable credit equal to the interest that the bond would otherwise pay [Code Sec. 54(a)]. The credit is not available for any bond issued after December 31, 2009 [Code Sec. 54(m)].

.02 New Clean Renewable Energy Bonds

New clean renewable energy bonds (New CREBs) may be issued by qualified issuers to finance qualified renewable energy facilities [Code Sec. 54C]. The provisions regarding new clean renewable energy bonds apply to obligations issued after October 3, 2008. Qualified renewable energy facilities are facilities that: (1) qualify for the tax credit under Code Sec. 45 (other than Indian coal and refined coal production facilities), without regard to the placed-in-service date requirements of that section; and (2) are owned by a public power provider, governmental body, or cooperative electric company.

The term "qualified issuers" includes: (1) public power providers; (2) a governmental body; (3) cooperative electric companies; (4) a not-for-profit electric utility that has received a loan or guarantee under the Rural Electrification Act; and (5) clean renewable energy bond lenders. The term "public power provider" means a State utility with a service obligation. A "governmental body" means any State or Indian tribal government, or any political subdivision thereof. The term "cooperative electric company" means a mutual or cooperative electric company. A clean renewable energy bond lender means a cooperative that is owned by, or has outstanding loans to, 100 or more cooperative electric companies.

---

[45] Notice 2013-33, IRB 2013-22.

[46] Notice 2010-54, IRB 2010-40, 403.

¶14,100 EMPOWERMENT ZONE AND RENEWAL COMMUNITY EMPLOYMENT CREDIT

.01 General Rules for Claiming the Credit

Special tax incentives exist for any employer engaged in a trade or business located in an empowerment zone [Code Sec. 1396(a)] or a renewal community zone [Code Sec. 1400H]. The IRS announced in IR-2013-78[47] that all empowerment zone designations in effect on December 31, 2009, remain in effect through December 31, 2013.

These zones are basically poor urban or rural areas designated as such by the federal government. [Code Sec. 1391(b)(2)]. For example, the overall poverty rate must be 20 percent or higher and the area must exhibit a condition of pervasive poverty, unemployment, and general economic distress [Code Sec. 1392].

Through the end of 2013, employers doing business in certain empowerment zones are entitled to a tax credit for qualified wages paid to employees who work and live in the zones [Code Sec. 1391(d)(1)(A)(i)]. The empowerment zone employment credit is equal to 20 percent of the first $15,000 of qualified wages paid to full-time or part-time employees [Code Sec. 1396(b) and (c)]. The employee must live in the empowerment zone and must perform substantially all of his work in the zone in the employer's trade or business [Code Sec. 1396(d)].

D.C. Zone Employment Credit

Employers in the D.C. Zone may claim a 20-percent credit against income tax for qualified wages paid to eligible employees in empowerment zones under Code Sec. 1396 through the end of 2011 (not extended) [Code Sec. 1400(f)].

The same type of employment credit is extended to employers doing business in renewal communities, with the difference that the renewal community credit is equal to 15 percent of the first $10,000 of qualified wages, as opposed to 20 percent of the first $15,000 for empowerment zones. In order to be entitled to the credit, qualified full-time or part-time wages must be paid to employees who work and live in the renewal communities [Code Sec. 1400H(b)]. Other than the amount of the credit, the renewal communities are treated as empowerment zones for purposes of the employment credit [Code Sec. 1400H(a)].

These credits are claimed on Form 8844, *Empowerment Zone and Renewal Community Employment Credit*, and, although part of the general business credit, they are not a part of the general business credit limitation computation. The credit amounts are calculated separately, as are the yearly limitations on the amount of each credit that may be claimed against a taxpayer's tax liability.

¶14,105 INDIAN EMPLOYMENT CREDIT

Prior to January 1, 2014, employers of enrolled members of an Indian tribe (or spouses of enrolled members) can claim a credit for wages and health insurance

[47] IR-2013-78, Sept. 27, 2013; Notice 2013-38, IRB 2013-25, 1251.

provided to an Indian who works on an Indian reservation. The credit is available to the extent the business paid more for wages or health insurance during the current tax year than it paid in 1993 [Code Sec. 45A(a)]. Employers should use Form 8845, *Indian Employment Credit*, to compute the credit. Form 8845 should be attached to the employer's tax return.

¶14,110 EMPLOYER SOCIAL SECURITY CREDIT ON TIPS (FICA TIP CREDIT)

A nonrefundable income tax credit is available to employers operating food and beverage establishments for a portion of employer social security taxes paid or incurred on employee cash tips [Code Sec. 45B(a)]. Employee tip income is treated as employer-provided wages for purposes of Federal Insurance Contributions Act (FICA) taxes (Social Security and Medicare) [Code Sec. 3121(q)]. Therefore, tip income is subject to both the employee and employer portions of the FICA taxes, up to the FICA taxable wage base.

Thus, food and beverage establishments can claim an income tax credit equal to the employer's share of FICA taxes (7.65 percent) paid on tip income that exceeds the amount of tips treated as wages for minimum wage purposes [Code Sec. 45B].

The credit applies to tips received from customers in connection with the delivery or serving of food or beverages, regardless of whether the food or beverages are for consumption on the premises of the establishment [Code Sec. 45B(b)(2)]. Employers cannot deduct any FICA tax that is claimed as a credit. But an employer can elect in any year not to have FICA tax eligible for the credit treated as a credit. The credit is available whether or not the employee reported the tips on which the employer-FICA taxes were paid.

.01 Minimum Wage Level Frozen for Purposes of FICA Tip Credit

Employers operating food and beverage establishments may continue to compute the amount of the FICA tip credit based on the federal minimum wage in effect on January 1, 2007 ($5.15 per hour) even though the Fair Minimum Wage Act of 2007 increased the minimum wage from $5.15 per hour to $7.25 per hour over a two-year period [Code Sec. 45B(b)(1)(B)]. Since the tip credit only applies to tips in excess of those treated as wages for purposes of satisfying the federal minimum wage provision, any increase in the minimum wage amount would create a reduction in the tip credit. By freezing the minimum wage amount used to calculate the credit ($5.15 per hour), the change allows businesses to continue to claim the full tip credit despite any increase in the federal minimum wage. Use Form 8846, *Credit for Employer Social Security and Medicare Taxes Paid on Certain Employee Tips*, to compute the credit.

In Rev. Rul. 2003-64,[48] the IRS ruled that a tax-exempt social club that operated a country club could claim the social security tax credit under Code Sec. 45B for the portion of employer FICA taxes paid with respect to employee tips received from both members and nonmembers when it computed its unrelated business income tax (UBIT). The club, which had a clubhouse where food and beverages were served to

48 Rev. Rul. 2003-64, 2003-1 CB 1036.

members and their nonmember guests, had paid FICA taxes on all tips earned by its employees and the tips were received in connection with the club's food and beverage service. Therefore, the club could calculate the credit on the basis of all tips received by its employees, not just the tips received from nonmembers.

¶14,115 CREDIT FOR SMALL BUSINESS PENSION PLAN START-UP EXPENSES

.01 Credit Basics

A nonrefundable income tax credit is available for a small business that adopts a new qualified defined benefit or defined contribution plan (including a 401(k) plan), a SIMPLE plan or a SEP [Code Sec. 45E]. The credit equals 50 percent of the start-up costs incurred to create or maintain a new employee retirement plan [Code Sec. 45E(a)]. The credit is limited to $500 in any tax year and it may be claimed for qualified expenses incurred in each of the three years beginning with the tax year in which the plan becomes effective [Code Sec. 45E(b)]. Expenses offset by the credit may not be claimed as a deduction for the year.

.02 Who May Claim

The credit may be claimed by an employer who did not employ more than 100 employees with compensation in excess of $5,000 in the preceding year [Code Sec. 45E(c)(1)]. The credit is available for costs paid or incurred in tax years beginning after December 31, 2001, with respect to qualified employer plans that are first effective after that date. An employer must not have established or maintained a qualified employer plan during the three-tax-year period immediately preceding the first tax year in which the new plan is effective [Code Sec. 45E(c)(2)]. The new plan can be disqualified for the credit if the prior qualified employer plan received contributions or accrued benefits for substantially the same employees as the new plan will cover.

The aggregation rules apply in determining the number of an employer's employees [Code Sec. 45E(e)(1)]. Under the aggregation rules, all members of a controlled group of corporations are considered one employer. All trades or businesses under common control are treated as a single employer. All employees of the members of an affiliated service group are treated as employed by a single employer. In addition, all eligible employer plans are treated as one eligible employer plan [Code Sec. 45E(e)(1)]. The employer and any predecessor must not have been a member of a controlled group in which a member established or maintained a qualified retirement plan (that received contributions or accrued benefits for the same employees covered by the new plan) during the three-tax-year test period. The credit is allowed as part of the general business credit for the tax year in which the plan becomes effective [Code Sec. 38(b)(14)].

.03 Eligible Plan

An eligible employer plan includes a new qualified defined benefit plan, defined contribution plan (including a 401(k) plan), savings incentive match plan for employees (SIMPLE) plan, or simplified employee pension (SEP) plan [Code Secs. 45E(d)(2),

4972(d)]. The plan must cover at least one employee who is not a highly compensated employee [Code Sec. 45E(d)(1)(B)].

.04 Qualified Start-Up Costs

Qualified start-up costs are any ordinary and necessary expenses incurred to establish or administer an eligible plan or to educate employees about retirement planning [Code Sec. 45E(d)(1)(A)]. The credit is limited to 50 percent of the qualified start-up costs, not to exceed $500, incurred in the first year the new plan is effective and in each of the two years following [Code Sec. 45E(b)]. In addition, the amount of qualified costs and allowable credit are determined by applying the aggregation rules [Code Sec. 45E(e)(1)]. Therefore, an employer's qualified costs include the costs incurred for all eligible employer plans within the employer's control group and the credit is attributable to the employers within the group.

¶14,120 SMALL EMPLOYER HEALTH INSURANCE TAX CREDIT

.01 Credit Basics

Under Code 45R, an "eligible small employer" may claim the 35-percent small business health care credit (25 percent in the case of a tax-exempt eligible small employer) for nonelective contributions (i.e., premiums) paid to purchase health insurance for employees if the employer maintains a "qualifying arrangement" for the premiums paid for health coverage in tax years 2010 through 2013 [Code Sec. 45R; Prop. Reg. § § 1.45R-1, -2, -3, -4, and -5].[49]

Beginning in 2014, an eligible small employer must participate in an insurance Small Business Health Options Program (SHOP) Exchange (now called SHOP MARKETPLACE) in order to claim the small business health care credit and the credit percentage increases to 50 percent (35 percent in the case of an eligible tax-exempt employer). However, the credit may only be claimed for two consecutive tax years beginning after 2013. Thus, an eligible small employer at most may claim a credit in six tax years (2010 – 2013 + two consecutive tax years that begin after 2013).

Note that only the portion of the premiums paid (or considered paid) by the employer for its employees' coverage under a qualifying arrangement is taken into account in computing the credit. Amounts paid by an employee are not counted [Prop. Reg. § 1.45R-3(g)(1)]. For example, if an employer pays 80 percent of the premiums for employees' coverage, with employees paying the other 20 percent pursuant to a salary reduction arrangement under a cafeteria plan, only the 80 percent premium amount paid by the employer counts in calculating the credit.

Component of General Business Credit

The small employer health insurance credit is a component of the general business credit [Code Sec. 38(b)(36); Prop. Reg. § 1.45R-5(a)]. The general business credit may

[49] Notice 2010-44, IRB 2010-22, 717, as amplified by Notice 2010-82, IRB 2010-51 (effective for tax years 2011, 2012 and 2013).

be carried back one year and forward 20 years. For a tax-exempt employer, the credit is a refundable credit, so that even if the employer has no taxable income, the employer may receive a refund (so long as it does not exceed the employer's income tax withholding and Medicare tax liability).

Credit Allowed in Full Against Alternative Minimum Tax

The small employer health insurance credit may be claimed in full against both regular and alternative minimum tax (AMT) liabilities [Code Sec. 38(c)(4)(B)(vi); Prop. Reg. § 1.45R-5(b)]. This rule is effective for credits in tax years beginning after December 31, 2009, and to carrybacks of such credits.

.02 Eligible Small Employer Defined

An eligible small employer (must be determined each year): (1) has 25 or fewer full-time equivalent employees (FTEs) employed during its tax year; (2) the average annual wages of the FTEs is not greater than $50,000 in 2010 through 2013; and (3) the employer has a qualifying arrangement in effect [Code Sec. 45R(d)(1)]. Because the limitation on the number of employees is based on FTEs, an employer with 25 or more employees could qualify for the credit if some of its employees work part-time. For example, an employer with 46 half-time employees (meaning each employee is paid wages for 1,040 hours) has 23 FTEs and therefore may qualify for the credit. In determining the number of FTEs and the average annual wages paid to these employees, an employee is taken into account even if the employee is not enrolled in the health insurance plan.

An employer that otherwise meets the requirements for the credit does not fail to be an eligible small employer merely because the employees of the employer are not performing services in a trade or business. For example, a household employer that otherwise satisfies the requirements of Code Sec. 45R is eligible for the credit [Prop. Reg. § 1.45R-2(a)]. An employer located outside of the U.S. (including a U.S. Territory) must have income effectively connected with the conduct of a trade or business in the U.S. to qualify as an eligible small employer [Prop. Reg. § 1.45R-2(a)].

The number of FTEs during a tax year is equal to the total number of hours of service for which employees were paid wages by the employer divided by 2,080. The result, if not a whole number, is rounded to the next lowest whole number [Code Sec. 45R(d)(2)(A)]. However, if, after dividing the total hours of service by 2,080 [the number of hours in a 52-week work year assuming a 40-hour work week (52 × 40 = 2,080)] the resulting number is less than one, the employer rounds up to one FTE [Prop. Reg. § 1.45R-1(a)(9); Prop. Reg. 1.45R-2(e). In making this computation, only the first 2,080 hours of service per employee are taken into account. Hours in excess of this amount are not counted [Code Sec. 45R(d)(2)(B)]. An employee's hours in excess of this amount (i.e., overtime hours) are not taken into account in determining the number of FTEs. An employee's hours of service for a year include [Prop. Reg. § 1.45R-2(d)(1)]:

1. Each hour for which an employee is paid, or entitled to payment, for performing duties for the employer during the employer's tax year (rule 1); and
2. Each hour for which an employee is paid, or entitled to payment, by the employer on account of a period of time during which no duties are performed due to vacation, holiday, illness, incapacity (including disability), layoff, jury duty, military duty or leave of absence (i.e., paid leave) (rule 2).

No more than 160 hours of service are required to be counted for an employee on account of any single continuous period during which the employee performs no duties.

The IRS allows any one of the following three methods for determining the actual number of hours an employer's employees has worked during the employer's tax year [Prop. Reg. § 1.45R-2(d)(2)]:

1. Actual hours of service from records of hours worked and hours for which payment is made or due for vacation, holiday, illness, incapacity, etc., as described in rule 1 and rule 2 above;
2. Days-worked equivalency whereby an employee is credited with 8 hours of service for each day for which the employee would be required to be credited with at least one hour of service under rule (1) or rule (2) above; or
3. Weeks-worked equivalency whereby the employee is credited with 40 hours of service for each week for which the employee would be required to be credited with at least one hour of service under rule (1) or rule (2) above.

Employers may apply different methods for different classifications of employees, if the classifications are reasonable and consistently applied. For example, an employer may use the actual hours worked method for all hourly employees and the weeks-worked equivalency method for all salaried employees. In addition, employers may change the method for calculating employees' hours of service for each tax year [Prop. Reg. § 1.45R-2(d)(2)].

.03 Qualifying Arrangement Defined

The employer must make nonelective contributions through a qualifying "arrangement." The arrangement must require an employer to make a nonelective contribution on behalf of each employee who enrolls in a qualified health plan offered to employees by the employer in an amount equal to a uniform percentage, but not less than 50 percent, of the premium cost of the qualified health plan (the "uniformity" requirement) [Code Sec. 45R(d)(4); Prop. Reg. §§ 1.45R-1(a)(15), 1.45R-2(a)]. An employer contribution is considered a nonelective contribution so long as it is *not* made through a salary reduction arrangement [Code Sec. 45R(e)(3); Prop. Reg. § 1.45R-1(a)(12)]. For tax years beginning after 2013, the arrangement must offer the insurance through a SHOP exchange. For earlier tax years, the arrangement may, but is not required to, offer the insurance through a SHOP exchange [Code Sec. 45R(d)(4)].

.04 Employee Defined

An employee is defined as an individual who is an employee of the eligible small employer under the common law [Prop. Reg. § 1.45R-1(a)(5)(i); Reg. § 31.3121(d)-1(c)]. The following individuals are not considered employees [Code Sec. 45R(e)(1); Prop. Reg. § 1.45R-1(a)(5)(iii) and (v)]: (1) any self-employed persons, independent contractors, partners or sole proprietors; (2) shareholders owning more than two percent of an S corporation; (3) owners of more than 5-percent of other businesses; or (4) any family member of these owners or partners. A family member is defined as a child (or descendant of a child); a sibling or step-sibling; a parent (or ancestor of a parent); a step-parent; a niece or nephew; an aunt or uncle; or a son-in-law, daughter-in-law, father-in-law, mother-in-law, brother-in-law or sister-in-law; (5) any other member of the household of these owners and partners who qualifies as a dependent [Reg. § 1.45R-1(a)(8)].

Special Rule for Seasonal Employees

Seasonal workers who work for 120 or fewer days during the tax year are not considered employees when determining FTEs and average annual wages [Code Sec. 45R(d)(5)(A); Reg. § 1.45R-1(a)(5)(iv)]. Premiums paid on behalf of seasonal employees may be taken into account in determining the credit even if their hours of service and wages are not taken into account because they do not work more than 120 days. The 120-day test is applied by taking into account any day of work regardless of the number of hours worked on that day. A seasonal worker is defined as a worker who performs labor or services on a seasonal basis and retail workers employed exclusively during holiday seasons [Code Sec. 45R(d)(5)(B); Prop. Reg. § 1.45R-1(a)(15)].

The following spouses are not considered employees by operation of ownership attribution rules: (1) the employee-spouse of a shareholder owning more than two percent of the stock of an S corporation; (2) the employee-spouse of an owner of more than five percent of a business; (3) the employee-spouse of a partner owning more than a five percent interest in a partnership; and (4) the employee-spouse of a sole proprietor [Reg. § 1.45R-1(a)(5)(iii)].

Leased employees are considered employees [Code Sec. 45R(e)(1)]. However, premiums for health insurance coverage paid by a leasing organization for a leased employee are not taken into account by the service recipient in computing the service recipient's small employer health insurance credit.

Ministers

Whether a minister is an employee or self-employed for purposes of the credit is determined under the common law test for determining worker status. If, under the common law test, a minister is self-employed, the minister is not taken into account in determining an employer's FTEs and premiums paid because a self-employed individual is excluded from the term "employee" for purposes of the credit. If, under the common law test, the minister is an employee, the minister is taken into account in determining an employer's FTEs and premiums paid by the employer for the minister's health insurance coverage can be taken into account in computing the credit. A tax-exempt employer's credit cannot exceed the total of the tax-exempt eligible small employer's income tax and Medicare tax withholding and its Medicare tax liability for the year. Because compensation of a minister performing services in the exercise of his or her ministry is not subject to Social Security or Medicare tax under FICA, a minister has no wages for purposes of computing an employer's average annual wages [Prop. Reg. § 1.45R-1(a)(5)(vi)].

Wages Defined

Wages for purposes of the provision are defined by reference to Code Sec. 3121(a), relating to the definition of wages for Federal Insurance Contributions Act (FICA) purposes but without regard to the wage base limitation [Code Sec. 45R(e)(4); Prop. Reg. § 1.45R-1(a)(22)].

.05 How to Claim Credit

The credit is computed on Form 8941, *Credit for Small Employer Health Insurance Premiums*, and is generally claimed on Form 3800, *General Business Credit*. A tax-exempt employer claims the credit by filing a Form 990-T, *Exempt Organization Business Income Tax Return* with an attached Form 8941 showing the calculation of the claimed credit [Prop. Reg. § 1.45R-5(a)]. The small employer health insurance credit is subject to reduction (but not below zero) if the employer has more than 10 full-time employees or the average annual wages of FTE's exceeds $25,000 in 2013 (as adjusted for inflation beginning in 2014). The small employer health insurance credit is reduced by the sum of: (1) The product of: (a) the credit amount, and (b) the number of the employer's FTE's for the tax year in excess of 10, divided by 15; and (2) The product of: (a) the credit amount, and (b) the employer's average annual wages in excess of the applicable dollar amount for the tax year ($25,000 in tax years beginning in 2010-2013), divided by the applicable dollar amount [Code Sec. 45R(c)].

Example 14:13: For the 2013 tax year, a qualified employer has 12 FTEs and average annual wages of $30,000. The employer pays $96,000 in health care premiums for those employees, which does not exceed the average premium for the small group market in the employer's state, and otherwise meets the requirements for the credit. The credit is calculated as follows: (1) Initial amount of credit determined before any reduction: (35% × $96,000) = $33,600; (2) Credit reduction for FTEs in excess of 10: ($33,600 × 2/15) = $4,480; (3) Credit reduction for average annual wages in excess of $25,000: ($33,600 × $5,000/$25,000) = $6,720; (4) Total credit reduction: ($4,480 + $6,720) = $11,200; (5) Total 2013 tax credit: ($33,600 – $11,200) = $22,400.

Example 14:14: Assume the same facts except that the tax year is 2014. The reduction is computed identically (without regard to the inflation adjustment to the $25,000 dollar amount) except that the credit rate is 50 percent. (1) Initial amount of credit determined before any reduction: (50% × $96,000) = $48,000; (2) Credit reduction for FTEs in excess of 10: ($48,000 × 2/15) = $6,400; (3) Credit reduction for average annual wages in excess of $25,000: ($48,000 × $5,000/$25,000) = $9,600; (4) Total credit reduction: ($6,400 + $9,600) = $16,000; (5) Total 2014 tax credit: ($48,000 – $16,000) = $32,000 [Prop. Reg. § 1.45R-3(c)(3)].

¶14,121 CODE SEC. 36B PREMIUM ASSISTANCE TAX CREDIT

The Code Sec. 36B premium assistance tax credit is a refundable credit which is available beginning January 1, 2014. This credit was designed to make health insurance affordable to individuals and families with modest incomes (i.e., between 100 percent and 400 percent of the federal poverty level, or FPL) who are not eligible for other health insurance coverage, such as Medicare, Medicaid or affordable employer sponsored health insurance plans. Individuals and small businesses that are eligible to claim the credit will be able to purchase private health insurance through competitive marketplaces called Exchanges or Health Insurance Marketplaces.

Open enrollment to purchase health insurance for 2014 through the Marketplace began October 1, 2013, and continues through March 31, 2014 [Q&A No. 2]. If an individual enrolls in an employer-sponsored plan, he isn't eligible for the Code Sec. 36B premium tax credit, even if the plan is unaffordable or fails to provide minimum value [Q&A No. 10].

The amount of the Code Sec. 36B premium tax credit that may be claimed by the taxpayer is based on a sliding scale. Those who have a lower income receive a larger credit to help cover the cost of their insurance and those with a higher income will receive a lower credit. If the amount of the credit is more than the amount of an individual's tax liability, he will receive the difference as a refund. If an individual owes no tax, he can get the full amount of the credit as a refund [Q&A No. 13].

.01 Eligibility

Individuals are eligible for the Code Sec. 36B premium tax credit if they satisfy the following requirements:

1. Enroll one or more family members in a "qualified health plan" which is purchased through the Marketplace;
2. Have "household income" between 100 percent and 400 percent of the federal poverty line (FPL) for the taxpayer's family size [Code Sec. 36B(c)(1)(A); Reg. § 1.36B-2(b)(1)];
3. Aren't able to get "affordable coverage" through an eligible employer plan that provides "minimum value";
4. Aren't eligible for other "minimal essential coverage" under a government-sponsored program, such as Medicaid, Medicare, Children's Health Insurance Program (CHIP) or the Department of Defense's health care program, TRICARE;
5. File a joint return, if married; and
6. Aren't claimed as a dependent by another person [Q&A No. 5].

.02 Qualified Health Plan

A qualified health plan is defined a health plan that is certified as eligible to be offered via an Exchange. However, a catastrophic plan is not a qualified health plan for purposes of the premium assistance credit [Code Sec. 36B(c)(3)(A); Reg. § 1.36B-1(c)].

.03 Household Income

Household income is defined in Reg. § 1.36B-1(e) as an individual's modified adjusted gross income plus that of every other individual in his family for whom he can properly claim a personal exemption deduction and who is required to file a federal income tax return [Code Sec. 36B(d)(2)]. Modified adjusted gross income is the adjusted gross income on his federal income tax return plus any excluded foreign income, nontaxable Social Security benefits (including tier 1 railroad retirement benefits), and tax-exempt interest received or accrued during the tax year. It doesn't include Supplemental Security Income (SSI) [Reg. § 1.36B-1(e)(2); Q&A No. 7].

To be eligible for the premium tax credit, individuals and families must have annual household income between 100 percent and 400 percent of the federal poverty line [Code Sec. 36(c)(1)(A)]. In Q&A No. 6, the IRS explains that eligibility for a certain year is based on the most recently published set of poverty guidelines at the time of the first day of the annual open enrollment period. Thus, the tax credit for 2014 will be based on the 2013 guidelines (which for residents of the 48 contiguous states or Washington, D.C.) are:

- $11,490 (100 percent) up to $45,960 (400 percent) for one individual.
- $15,510 (100 percent) up to $62,040 (400 percent) for a family of two.
- $23,550 (100 percent) up to $94,200 (400 percent) for a family of four.

.04 Affordable Coverage

An employer-sponsored plan will be considered "affordable" for an employee and related individuals if the portion of the annual premium an individual must pay for self-only coverage does not exceed the required contribution percentage (9.5 percent for tax years beginning before January 1, 2015) of the taxpayer's household income [Code Sec. 36B(b)(3)(A)(i)]. The affordability test applies only to the portion of the annual premiums for self-only coverage and doesn't include any additional cost for family coverage. If the employer offers multiple health coverage options, the affordability test applies to the lowest-cost option available to the individual that also satisfies the minimum value requirement. If the employer offers any wellness programs, the affordability test is based on the premium the individual would pay if he received the maximum discount for any tobacco cessation programs, and did not receive any other discounts based on wellness programs [Q&A No. 8].

.05 Minimum Value

An employer-sponsored plan provides "minimum value" if the plan covers at least 60 percent of the expected total allowed costs of benefits provided to an employee [Code Sec. 36B(c)(2)(C)(ii); Prop. Reg. § 1.36B-6(a)]. Regulations issued by the Secretary of Health and Human Services apply in determining the percentage of "the total allowed costs of benefits" provided under a group health plan or health insurance coverage that are covered by that plan or coverage [Reg. § 1.36B-2(c)(3)(vi)]. The plan is responsible for determining whether it provides minimum value. In most cases, the plan may use the IRS provided calculator for this purpose. In Notice 2012-31,[50] the IRS described several methods for determining minimum value.

Under the proposed regulations, an eligible employer sponsored plan's minimum value percentage is determined by dividing: (1) the plan's anticipated covered medical spending for benefits provided under a particular essential health benefits (EHB) benchmark plan for the minimum value standard population based on the plan's cost sharing provision by (2) the total anticipated allowed charges for EHB coverage provided to the MV standard population [Prop. Reg. § 1.36B-6(c)].

The MV standard population for this purposes is a standard population developed and described through summary statistics by the Department of Health and Human Services. The MV standard population is based on the population covered by a typical self-insured group health plan [Prop. Reg. § 1.36B-6(b)]. The proposed regulations provide the following four methods for determining MV [Prop. Reg. § 1.36B-1(d)]:

---

[50] Notice 2012-31, IRB 2012-20, 906.

1. An MV calculator provided on the IRS website or the Health and Human Services website. As explained below, certain adjustments to the calculator result are permitted;
2. Any safe harbor method authorized by the IRS and HHS;
3. Actuarial certification, if the employer's plan has nonstandard features that are incompatible with the calculator and may materially affect the MV percentage; and
4. For plans in the small group market, conformance with the requirements for a level of bronze, silver, gold, or platinum coverage.

The MV percentage computed by the IRS MV calculator may be adjusted to the extent of the value of any benefit included in any EHB benchmark that is outside the parameters of the MV calculator. The adjustment must be made based on an actuarial analysis that complies with the rules for actuarial certification (item (3) above) [Prop. Reg. § 1.36B-6(e)].

Adjustments for Wellness

In determining a plan's MV percentage, nondiscriminatory wellness program incentives that affect deductibles, copayments, and other cost-sharing are treated as earned only if the incentive relates to tobacco use [Prop. Reg. § 1.36B-6(c)(2)].

Adjustments for Health Savings Accounts

Employer contributions during a plan year to health savings accounts offered with the employer plan are taken into account in determining the plan's share of costs and, therefore, are counted toward and increase the plan's MV percentage [Prop. Reg. § 1.36B-6(c)(3)]. The amount taken into accounting in determining the MV percentage is the amount of expected spending for health care costs in the benefit year [Prop. Reg. § 1.36B-6(c)(5)].

Adjustments for Health Reimbursement Arrangements

New amounts made available for the current plan year under a health reimbursement arrangement that is integrated with an employer plan are also taken into account toward the plan's MV percentage if the amounts may only be used to reduce cost-sharing for the covered medical expenses and may not be used to pay insurance premiums [Prop. Reg. § 1.36B-6(c)(4)]. The amount taken into accounting in determining the MV percentage is the amount of expected spending for health care costs in the benefit year [Prop. Reg. § 1.36B-6(c)(5)].

.06 Minimal Essential Coverage

The Code Sec. 36B premium assistance credit cannot be claimed for any month during the tax year with respect to an applicable taxpayer or family member who is eligible for "minimum essential coverage" through an employer plan that is "affordable" and provides "minimum value." Minimum essential coverage includes employer-sponsored health coverage that is affordable and provides minimum value as well as certain government programs that sponsor health plan coverage such as Medicare and Medicaid. An applicable taxpayer (or member of the applicable taxpayer's family) who chooses to enroll in an employer-sponsored plan that is not affordable or does not provide minimum value is not eligible for a premium assistance tax credit during the months of enrollment (i.e., the credit will be determined without regard to enrolled family members) [Reg. § 1.36B-2(c)(3)(vii)(A)].

Under Code Sec. 5000A(f)(1)(E), the Secretary of Health and Human Services, in coordination with the Secretary of the Treasury, may designate health benefits coverage not specified in Code Sec. 5000A as providing minimum essential coverage. In Notice 2013-41,[51] the IRS provided guidance on whether or when, for purposes of the Code Sec. 36B premium tax credit, an individual is eligible for minimum essential coverage under certain government-sponsored health programs or other coverage designated as minimum essential coverage.

.07 Reconciling Premium Tax Credit with Advance Credit Payments

Taxpayers can choose to have the credit paid in advance to their insurance company to lower the amount paid for monthly premiums, or they can claim all of the credit when they file their tax return for the year. If they choose to have the credit paid in advance, they must reconcile the amount paid in advance with the actual credit computed when they file their tax return. Individuals can choose to have the credit paid in advance to their insurance company to lower what they pay for their monthly premiums, and then reconcile the amount paid in advance with the actual credit computed when they file their tax return. A taxpayer who receives excess advance payments must treat the excess amount as additional tax under Code Sec. 36B(f)(2). Taxpayers whose credit amount exceeds the amount of advance payments for the tax year may receive the excess as an income tax refund. Taxpayers who do not seek advance credit payments also may claim the premium tax credit on the income tax return [Code Sec. 36B(f)(1); Reg. § 1.36B-4(a)(1)].

.08 Information Reporting by Exchanges/Marketplace

An Exchange/Marketplace makes an advance determination of credit eligibility for individuals enrolling in coverage through the Exchange/Marketplace and seeking financial assistance. Using information available at the time of enrollment, the Exchange/Marketplaces determines (1) whether the individual meets the income and other requirements for advance credit payments, and (2) the amount of the advance payments. Advance credit payments are made monthly to the issuer of the qualified health plan in which the individual enrolls. The Exchange/Marketplace will send an individual an information statement showing the amount of his premiums and advance credit payments by January 31 of the year following the year of coverage. For example, an individual will receive the 2014 information statement by January 31, 2015, and can use this information to compute his premium tax credit on his 2014 tax return and to reconcile the advance credit payments made on his behalf with the amount of the actual premium tax credit [Q&A No. 12].

Code Sec. 36B(f)(3) directs Exchanges/Marketplaces to report to the IRS on or before January 31 of the year following the calendar year of coverage and to taxpayers the following information for each qualified health plan in which an individual or a member of the individual's family enrolls: (1) the name, address, and taxpayer identification number (TIN), or date of birth if a TIN is not available, of an individual enrolling, or

[51] Notice 2013-41, IRB 2013-29, 60.

enrolling a family member, in coverage and approved for advance credit payments (taxpayer), and the name and TIN of the individual's spouse, if applicable; (2) the name, address, and TIN, or date of birth if a TIN is not available, of an adult enrolling in coverage or enrolling one or more members of a family in coverage and either not requesting or not approved for advance credit payments (responsible adult); (3) the name and TIN, or date of birth if a TIN is not available, and dates of coverage for each individual covered under the plan; (4) the monthly premium for the applicable benchmark plan used to compute advance credit payments; (5) for a responsible adult, the premium for the applicable benchmark plan that would apply to the individuals enrolled in a qualified health plan; (6) the monthly premium for the plan or plans in which a taxpayer, responsible adult, or family member enrolls, without reduction for advance credit payments, including the amount of premiums for a stand-alone dental plan allocated to pediatric dental benefits; (7) the amount of the advance credit payments made on a taxpayer's behalf each month; (8) the name of the qualified health plan issuer and the issuer's employer identification number (EIN); (9) the qualified health plan policy number; (10) the Exchange's unique identifier; and (11) any other information specified by forms or instructions or in published guidance [Prop. Reg. § 1.36B-5(b)(1)].

¶14,125 CREDIT FOR EMPLOYERS PROVIDING CHILD CARE ASSISTANCE FOR EMPLOYEES

.01 Amount of Credit

Employers may claim a tax credit for providing child care assistance to employees in all tax years after December 31, 2012 [Code Sec. 45F]. The tax credit is equal to 25 percent of qualified expenses for employee child care and 10 percent of qualified expenses for child care resource and referral services [Code Sec. 45F(a)]. The maximum total credit that may be claimed by a taxpayer cannot exceed $150,000 per tax year [Code Sec. 45F(b)]. Form 8882, *Credit for Employer-Provided Child Care Facilities and Services,* should be used to calculate and claim the credit.

Any deductions an employer may be entitled to for these expenses are reduced by the amount of these credits. If the credits are taken for expenses of acquiring, constructing, rehabilitating, or expanding a facility, the employer's basis in the facility is reduced by the amount of the credits.

.02 Eligible Expenses

Credit-eligible expenses include costs paid or incurred [Code Sec. 45F(c)]:

- To acquire, construct, rehabilitate or expand property that is to be used as part of the employer's child care facility;
- In operation of the employer child care facility, including the costs of training and certain employee compensation; or
- Under a contract with a child care facility to provide child care services to employees of the taxpayer.

.03 Child Care Facilities

A qualified child care facility is a facility the "principal use" of which is to provide child care assistance and that also meets the requirements of all applicable laws and regulations of the state and local government in which it is located, including the licensing requirements applicable to a child care facility [Code Sec. 45FR(c)(2)]. The principal use requirement is waived if the facility is located in the principal residence of the operator of the facility [Code Sec. 45F(c)(2)(A)].

A facility will not be treated as a qualified child care facility for purposes of the taxpayer claiming the employer-provided child care credit, unless:

1. Enrollment is open to the taxpayer's employees during the tax year,
2. In the event that the facility is the taxpayer's principal trade or business, at least 30 percent of the enrollees at the facility are the dependents of the taxpayer's employees, and
3. Use of the child care facility cannot discriminate in favor of highly-compensated employees [Code Sec. 45F(c)(2)(B)].

.04 Qualified Child Care Resources and Referrals Expenditures

Qualified child care resource and referral expenses are amounts paid or incurred under a contract to provide child care resource and referral services to the employees of the taxpayer. Expenditures for these services cannot discriminate in favor of highly compensated employees of the employer.

.05 Recapture

Credits claimed in connection with a facility are subject to recapture for the first ten years after the facility is placed in service. The amount of recapture is reduced over the ten-year recapture period. Recapture takes effect if the taxpayer either ceases operation of the care facility or transfers its interest in the facility without securing an agreement to assume recapture liability for the transferee.

¶14,126 EMPLOYER WAGE CREDIT FOR ACTIVATED MILITARY RESERVISTS

Eligible small businesses may be able to qualify for a 20-percent tax credit for differential wage payments made to qualified employees called up for active military duty before January 1, 2014 [Code Sec. 45P(f)]. The payments are made to compensate members of the National Guard or Reserves who are called up to active military duty and whose higher-paying civilian jobs are temporarily suspended while they receive the lower military pay. The Code Sec. 45P credit is claimed by a civilian employer who voluntarily provides military differential pay in an amount equal to the difference between the civilian pay and military pay.

.01 Qualified Payments

Qualified payments (1) must be made by a small business employer to a qualified employee for any period during which the employee is performing service in the uniformed services while on active duty for a period of more than 30 days, (2) must represent all or a portion of the wages that the employee would have received from the employer for performing services for the employer, and (3) must not exceed $20,000 per year [Code Sec. 45P(b)(1)].

.02 Eligible Small Business Employer

An eligible small business employer must employ, on average, fewer than 50 employees on business days during the tax year, and provide eligible differential wage payments to every qualified employee under a written plan [Code Sec. 45P(b)(3)]. A qualified employee must be employed by the small business employer during the 91-day period immediately preceding the period for which the for differential wage payment is made [Code Sec. 45P(b)(2)].[52]

The credit reduces the employer's compensation deduction and any other credits otherwise allowable with respect to compensation paid [Code Secs. 45P(c), 280C(a)]. The differential wages credit is part of the Code Sec. 38 general business credit.

¶14,127 RAILROAD TRACK MAINTENANCE CREDIT

The railroad track maintenance credit, which is part of the general business credit applies to qualifying expenditures paid or incurred before January 1, 2014. The credit assists small and mid-sized railroads in upgrading their tracks and related infrastructure, and in maintaining those railroads as a viable alternative to shipping freight via over-the-road trucking. The credit is equal to 50 percent of any qualified railroad track maintenance expenditures paid or incurred by an eligible taxpayer during the tax year [Code Sec. 45G(a)].

.01 Eligible Taxpayers

Eligible taxpayers include any Class II or Class III railroad, and any person who transports property using the rail facilities of a Class II or Class III railroad or who furnishes railroad-related property or services to such a railroad, but only regarding miles of track assigned to that person by the railroad [Code Sec. 45G(c)]. Railroads are classified as Class II or Class III by the Surface Transportation Board of the Department of Transportation [Code Sec. 45G(e)(1)].

.02 Qualified Railroad Track Maintenance Expenditures

Qualified railroad track maintenance expenditures include gross expenditures (whether or not otherwise chargeable to capital account) for maintaining railroad track (including roadbed, bridges, and related track structures) owned or leased as of January 1, 2005, by a Class II or Class III railroad. Qualified expenditures are determined regardless of any consideration for such expenditures (e.g., discounted shipping rates, the increment in a markup of track materials prices, debt forgiveness) given to a track assignee by the Class II or Class III railroad that made the track assignment [Code Sec. 45G(d)]. The taxpayer's basis in the track is reduced by the allowable credit [Code Sec. 45G(e)(3)].

[52] Notice 2010-15, IRB 2010-6, 390.

.03 Limitations

The credit is limited to $3,500 multiplied by the sum of (1) the number of miles of railroad track owned or leased by an eligible taxpayer as of the close of its tax year, and (2) the number of miles of track assigned to the eligible taxpayer by a Class II or Class III railroad that owns or leases the track at the close of the tax year. Each mile of track may be taken into account only once, either by the owner or the assignee. The assignment of a mile of track by a Class II or Class III railroad can only be made once in a tax year, and is treated as made at the close of the assignment tax year. The railroad cannot take the credit for any assigned mile, and the assignment must be taken into account for the assignee's tax year that includes the effective date of the assignment [Code Sec. 45G(b)].

¶14,128 MINE RESCUE TEAM TRAINING TAX CREDIT

The mine rescue training team credit, which was available through December 31, 2013, may be claimed by eligible employers for mine rescue team training expenses [Code Sec. 45N(e)].

.01 Credit Amount

The credit amount is equal to the lesser of:

- 20 percent of the training program costs paid or incurred during the tax year for each qualified mine rescue team employee, including wages paid while attending the training program; or
- $10,000 [Code Sec. 45N(a)].

.02 Eligible Employer

An eligible employer is any taxpayer that employs individuals as miners in underground mines located in the United States [Code Sec. 45N(c)]. A qualified mine rescue team employee is a full-time employee who is a miner eligible for more than six months of the tax year to serve as a mine rescue team member because he or she has either:

- Completed, at minimum, an initial 20-hour instruction course as approved by the Mine Safety and Health Administration's Office of Educational Policy and Development; or
- Received at least 40 hours of refresher training [Code Sec. 45N(b)].

.03 Wages

Wages are defined as all compensation including noncash benefits under Code Sec. 3306(b), but without regard to any dollar limitation [Code Sec. 45N(d)]. The credit amount is determined on Form 8923, *Mine Rescue Team Training Credit,* and claimed as part of and subject to the limitations of the general business credit.

¶14,130 RETIREMENT SAVINGS CONTRIBUTION CREDIT

A nonrefundable tax credit is available for contributions made by eligible taxpayers to a retirement plans such as a 401(k) plan, 403(b) annuity, Code Sec. 457 plan of a state or local government, SIMPLE plan, or SEP, as well as for traditional or Roth IRA contributions. To be eligible for the credit, taxpayers must at least 18 years old and cannot be claimed as a dependent on another taxpayer's return [Code Sec. 25B(c)(1)]. Students who are enrolled for 12 hours or more in any five months of the years are considered to be full-time students and are not eligible for the credit.

The maximum annual contribution eligible for the credit is $2,000 and the maximum credit is $1,000 per eligible individual [Code Sec. 45N(a)]. In 2013 the maximum retirement savings contribution credit rate is 50 percent, which is completely phased out when adjusted gross income exceeds $59,000 (joint filers), $44,250 (head of household), and $29,500 (single and married filing separately) as illustrated in the following table [Code Sec. 25B(b)]:[53]

Table 6. Retirement Saver's Credit—2013

Adjusted Gross Income

Joint return		*Head of a household*		*All other cases*		*Applicable percentage*
Over	*Not over*	*Over*	*Not over*	*Over*	*Not over*	
$0	$35,500	$0	$26,625	$0	$17,750	50
35,500	38,500	26,625	28,875	17,750	19,250	20
38,500	59,000	28,875	44,250	19,250	29,500	10
59,000	—	44,250	—	29,500	—	0

The credit may be claimed in addition to any deduction or exclusion that otherwise applies to the contribution. However, the amount of any eligible contribution is reduced by any distributions from a qualified retirement plan or IRA in the year for which the credit is claimed or the two tax years preceding the year the credit is claimed. The amount of an otherwise eligible contribution is also reduced by distributions received after the close of the tax year in which the credit is claimed and before the due date for the return for the year of the credit. Form 8880, *Credit for Qualified Retirement Savings Contribution*, is used to calculate the amount of the credit, which is then reported on Form 1040.

[53] IRS New Release IR-2012-77, October 18, 2012.

¶14,135 NEW MARKETS TAX CREDIT

.01 General Rules for Claiming the Credit

Through December 31, 2013, taxpayers can claim a new markets tax credit on a credit allowance date in an amount equal to the applicable percentage of the taxpayer's qualified equity investment in a qualified community development entity (CDE) [Code Sec. 45D(a)]. The new markets tax credit was created to provide a tax incentive to taxpayers making investments in low-income communities. The credit allowance date for any qualified equity investment is the date on which the investment is initially made and each of the six anniversary dates thereafter. The applicable percentage is five percent for the first three credit allowance dates and six percent for the remaining credit allowance dates.

¶14,140 HOMEBUILDER'S CREDIT FOR NEW ENERGY-EFFICIENT HOMES

An eligible contractor can claim a tax credit of either $1,000 or $2,000 for building a qualified new energy-efficient home that a person acquires from a contractor after December 31, 2005, and prior to January 1, 2014, for use as a residence [Code Sec. 45L(a) and (g)]. An *eligible contractor* is a person who constructs a new energy-efficient home, or a manufacturer that produces a qualified new energy-efficient manufactured home [Code Sec. 45L(b)(1)].

.01 Qualified New Energy-Efficient Home

In order to be considered a qualified new energy-efficient home, the dwelling must be located in the United States, must meet specified energy saving requirements, must be purchased or be acquired by a person from the eligible contractor before January 12, 2014, for use as a residence. In addition, a qualified new energy-efficient home must receive a written certification that describes its energy-saving features including the energy-efficient building envelope components used in its construction and the energy-efficient heating or cooling equipment that has been installed [Code Sec. 45L(c) and (d)].

.02 Credit Amount

The applicable amount of the credit depends on the energy savings realized by the home. The maximum credit is $2,000 for homes and manufactured homes that meet rigorous energy-saving requirements; alternatively, manufactured homes that meet a less demanding test may qualify for a $1,000 credit. The taxpayer's basis in the property is reduced by the amount of any new energy-efficient home credit allowed with respect to that property [Code Sec. 45L(e)].

¶14,145 MANUFACTURER'S CREDIT FOR ENERGY-EFFICIENT APPLIANCES

A credit may be claimed for the manufacture of energy-efficient appliances such as dishwashers, clothes washers, and refrigerators manufactured in calendar years 2012 or 2013. The credit is a part of the general business credit and will be used to determine a taxpayer's current year business credit [Code Sec. 38(b)(24)]. The credit is claimed only by the manufacturers of energy-efficient appliances. Consumers may not claim the credit.

The total amount of credit available is equal to the sum of the credit amount separately calculated for each type of qualified energy-efficient appliance produced by the taxpayer during the year. The credit amount for each type of qualified appliance is determined by multiplying the eligible production for that type of appliance by the type's applicable amount [Code Sec. 45M(a)(2)]. There are three types of qualified energy-efficient appliances for purposes of this new credit, as follows:

.01 Appliances Eligible for Credit

Dishwashers

Dishwashers manufactured in 2011, 2012 or 2013 may be eligible for a $50 or $75 credit as follows:

- $50 for dishwashers manufactured in calendar year 2011, 2012 or 2013 that use no more than 295 kilowatt hours of electricity per year and 4.25 gallons of water per normal dishwasher cycle (4.75 gallons of water for dishwashers designed for greater than 12 place settings) [Code Sec. 45M(b)(1)(D)].
- $75 for dishwashers manufactured in calendar year 2011, 2012 or 2013 that use no more than 280 kilowatt hours of electricity per year and 4.0 gallons of water per normal dishwasher cycle (4.5 gallons of water for dishwashers designed for greater than 12 place settings) [Code Sec. 45M(b)(1)(E)].

Clothes Washers

Clothes washers manufactured in 2011, 2012 or 2013 may be eligible for a $225 credit as follows:

- $225 for top-loading clothes washers manufactured in calendar year 2011, 2012 or 2013 that meet or exceed a 2.4 modified energy factor and do not exceed a 4.2 water consumption factor [Code Sec. 45M(b)(2)(F)(i)].
- $225 for front-loading clothes washers manufactured in calendar year 2011, 2012 or 2013 that meet or exceed a 2.8 modified energy factor and do not exceed a 3.5 water consumption factor [Code Sec. 45M(b)(2)(F)(ii)].

Refrigerators

Refrigerators manufactured in 2011, 2012 or 2013 may be eligible for a $150 or $200 credit as follows:

- $150 for refrigerators manufactured in calendar year 2011, 2012 or 2013 that consume at least 30 percent less energy than the 2001 energy conservation standards [Code Sec. 45M(b)(3)(E)].
- $200 for refrigerators manufactured in calendar year 2011, 2012 or 2013 that consume at least 35 percent less energy than the 2001 energy conservation standards [Code Sec. 45M(b)(3)(F)].

.02 Eligible Production

The eligible production amount for a particular type of energy-efficient appliance is determined by subtracting the average number of qualified appliances described above that the taxpayer produced during the base period from the number of appliances of the same type that the taxpayer produced during the applicable calendar year. Only qualified appliances produced in the United States apply [Code Sec. 45M(c)(2)].

.03 Credit Amount Limitations

The aggregate credit allowed will be limited to $25 million, reduced by the amount of the credit allowed to the taxpayer or any predecessor of the taxpayer for all prior tax years beginning after December 31, 2010 [Code Sec. 45M(e)(1)]. Credits for the most energy-efficient refrigerators and clothes washers will not count against the $25 million limit [Code Sec. 45M(e)(2)].

¶14,150 ADVANCED NUCLEAR FACILITY BUSINESS TAX CREDIT

A business tax credit may be claimed for energy production from advanced nuclear power facilities [Code Secs. 38(b)(21) and 45J]. The credit is equal to 1.8 cents times the number of kilowatt hours of electricity that are: (1) produced by the taxpayer at an advanced nuclear power facility during the eight-year period beginning on the date the facility was originally placed in service; and (2) sold by the taxpayer to an unrelated person during the tax year.

It may only be claimed during the eight-year period beginning on the date the facility was originally placed in service. A qualifying advanced nuclear power facility is any advanced nuclear facility that (1) is owned by the taxpayer, (2) uses nuclear energy to produce electricity, and (3) was placed in service after August 8, 2005, and before January 1, 2021.

Any nuclear facility with a reactor design (or a substantially similar design of comparable capacity) approved before 1994 by the Nuclear Regulatory Commission is not a qualifying advanced nuclear power facility. The facility must be located in the United States or a U.S. possession [Code Sec. 45J(e) applying Code Sec. 45(e)(1)].

The amount of the business tax credit that is allowed per tax year, per facility, is limited to the ratio of the national megawatt capacity limitation of the facility to the total megawatt nameplate capacity of the facility under a national limitation [Code Sec. 45J(b)(1)]. The amount of the credit allowable any year will not exceed an amount that bears the same ratio to $125 million as the national megawatt capacity limitation allocated to the facility bears to 1,000 [Code Sec. 45J(c)(1)].

¶14,155 CREDIT FOR INSTALLATION OF ALTERNATIVE FUELING STATIONS

A credit may be claimed for the installation of alternative fueling stations used in a trade or business, or installed at the taxpayer's residence before January 1, 2014 (January 1, 2015, in the case of property relating to hydrogen) [Code Sec. 30C(g)]. A taxpayer has the option not to claim this credit [Code Sec. 30C(e)(4)]. The tax basis of any property for which the credit is claimed will be reduced by the portion of the property's cost that is taken into account in computing the credit [Code Sec. 30C(e)(1)].[54]

.01 Interaction with Expensing Election Under Code Sec. 179

No alternative fuel vehicle refueling property credit will be allowed with respect to the portion of the cost of any property taken into account under the Code Sec. 179 election to expense certain depreciable business assets.

.02 Maximum Credit Allowed

A taxpayer is allowed a tax credit of up to 30 percent of the cost of "qualified alternative fuel vehicle refueling property," that is placed in service during the year [Code Sec. 30C(a)]. In addition to the 30-percent limit, there is an annual cap on the credit's dollar amount. For commercial retail taxpayers for whom the property would be subject to a depreciation deduction, the maximum yearly credit is $30,000. However, taxpayers who install qualified vehicle refueling property at their principal residence are limited to a $1,000 annual credit [Code Sec. 30C(b)]. A taxpayer may carry forward unused credits for 20 years.

The credit is claimed on Form 8911, *Alternative Fuel Vehicle Refueling Property Credit.*

.03 Qualified Alternative Fuel Vehicle Refueling Property Defined

To qualify for the credit, the property (may not include a building or its structural components) must satisfy the following requirements:

- Be of a character that would be subject to the depreciation deduction;
- Be property originally used by the taxpayer;
- Be at the site at which the vehicle is refueled (if the property is for the storage or dispensing of alternative fuels into the fuel tank of a vehicle propelled by the fuel); or
- Be located at the point where the vehicles are recharged (if the property is for recharging electrically-propelled vehicles) [Code Sec. 30C(c)(1)].

These rules also apply to refueling property installed at a residence, except that the property does not have to qualify for the depreciation deduction [Code Sec. 30C(c)(2)]. In order to qualify for the credit, the fuels to be stored or dispensed must be:

---

[54] Notice 2007-43, 2007-1 CB 1318.

- At least 85 percent in volume consist of one or more of the following: ethanol, natural gas, compressed natural gas, liquefied natural gas, liquefied petroleum gas, or hydrogen [Code Sec. 30C(c)(1)(A)];
- Electricity (if the property is for recharging electrically-propelled vehicles) [Code Sec. 30C(c)(2)(C)]; or
- Any mixture of biodiesel and diesel fuel (determined without regard to any use of kerosene) containing at least 20 percent of biodiesel [Code Sec. 30C(c)(1)(B)].

No alternative fuel vehicle refueling property credit is allowed for property that is used predominately outside the United States [Code Sec. 30C(e)(3)].

¶14,156 WORKER RETENTION CREDIT

.01 Credit Basics

If a qualified individual begins work for a qualified employer after February 3, 2010, and before January 1, 2011, the employer is exempt from paying its share of the individual's old-age, survivors, and disability insurance (OASDI) taxes or Railroad Retirement Tax Act (RRTA) Tier 1 taxes from March 19, 2010, through December 31, 2010 [Code Secs. 3111(d) and 3221(c)]. The employer can claim a credit of up to $1,000 for retaining the newly hired worker for at least 52 consecutive weeks. The credit is claimed on Form 5884-B, *New Hire Retention Credit*, which requires employers to enter the worker's Social Security number, the date the worker began employment, the worker's wages during the first 26 weeks of consecutive employment, and the worker's wages during the second 26 weeks of consecutive employment.

.02 Credit Amount

For each retained worker, a qualified employer's general business credit is increased by the lesser of:

- $1,000, or
- 6.2 percent of the retained worker's wages during a 52-week consecutive period [Act Sec.102(a) of P.L. 111-147].

The credit applies for the first tax year in which the retained worker satisfies the 52-week test [Act Sec. 102(a)(2) of P.L. 111-147]. It cannot be carried back to any tax year beginning before March 18, 2010 [Act Sec. 102(c) of P.L. 111-147].

.03 Qualified Employees

The retention credit applies to a retained worker who is also a qualified individual for purposes of the payroll tax holiday [Act Sec. 102(b) of P.L. 111-147]. Qualified individuals are individuals who:

1. Begin employment with qualified employers after February 3, 2010, and before January 1, 2011;
2. Certify, by signed affidavits under penalties of perjury, that they were not employed for more than 40 hours during the 60-day period ending on the date their employment with the qualified employer begins;

3. Are not hired to replace another employee of the qualified employer, unless the other employee voluntarily quit or was fired with cause; and
4. Are not related to the employer in a way that would make them ineligible for the work opportunity credit [Code Secs. 3111(d)(3) and 3221(c)(3)].

Generally, a qualified employer is any employer other than the United States, any state, any local government, or any instrumentality of the preceding. However, a qualified employer includes any public higher education institution [Code Secs. 3111(d)(2) and 3221(c)(2)].

A retained worker is a qualified individual:

1. Who is employed by the taxpayer on any date during the tax year,
2. Who is employed by the taxpayer for a period of not less than 52 consecutive weeks, and
3. Whose wages for the employment during the last 26 weeks of the 52-week period are equal to at least 80 percent of the wages for the first 26 weeks.

The credit applies when a qualified employer hires an otherwise qualified individual to replace an individual whose employment was terminated for cause or due to other facts and circumstances. For example, an employer that reopens a factory that was closed due to lack of demand may rehire qualified individuals who had worked for the employer but were terminated when the factory was closed. In contrast, an employer that terminates the employment of an individual not for cause, but in order to take advantage of these hiring incentives, is not eligible for the payroll tax holiday or the retention credit [Joint Committee on Taxation, Technical Explanation of the Hiring Incentives to Restore Employment Act (JCX-4-10)].

Employees can use Form W-11, *Hiring Incentives to Restore Employment (HIRE) Act Employee Affidavit*, to certify that they have not been employed for more than 40 hours during the 60 days before their hiring date.[55]

¶14,157 ELECTION TO CLAIM ACCELERATED AMT AND RESEARCH CREDITS IN LIEU OF BONUS DEPRECIATION

The Code 168(k)(4) election allows corporations to increase their Code Sec. 38(c) business credit limit and Code Sec. 53(c) AMT credit limit in lieu of claiming the 50 percent bonus depreciation deduction for certain property.

In Rev. Proc. 2009-33,[56] the IRS provides guidance to corporations regarding:

1. The property eligible for the election provided by Code Sec. 168(k)(4)(H),
2. The time and manner for making the elections, and

[55] IRS News Release, IR-2010-33, March 18, 2010.

[56] Rev. Proc. 2009-33, IRB 2009-29,150.

3. The computation of the amount by which the business credit limitation and AMT credit limitation may be increased if the new elections are made.

.01 Election to Accelerate AMT Credit in Lieu of Bonus Depreciation Provided for Round 3 Extension Property

A corporation may elect to forgo bonus depreciation on "round 3 extension property" and claim unused AMT credits from tax years beginning before January 1, 2006 [Code Sec. 168(k)(4)(J)]. Round 3 extension property is defined as property which is eligible qualified property solely by reason of the one-year extension of the bonus depreciation allowance to property acquired after December 31, 2007, and placed in service in 2013, and, in the case of longer-period production property and certain noncommercial aircraft, property placed in service in 2014 [Code Sec. 168(k)(4)(J)(iv)]. Bonus depreciation is discussed further at ¶ 11,001.

.02 Amount of Credit

The business credit and AMT credit limits are increased by the Code Sec. 168(k)(4) election by the "bonus depreciation amount" which is equal to 20 percent of the difference between first-year depreciation on eligible property, computed with bonus depreciation, and first-year depreciation computed without bonus depreciation [Code Sec. 168(k)(4)(C)(i)]. The maximum credit is limited to the lesser of $30 million or six percent of the increased credits. The bonus depreciation amounts and maximum credits are determined separately for property that is and is not "extension" property. However, the bonus depreciation amount for any year must not exceed the maximum increase amount reduced by the sum of the bonus depreciation amounts determined for all prior tax years [Code Sec. 168(k)(4)(C)(ii)].

.03 Eligible and Extension Property Defined

Eligible Qualified Property

Eligible qualified property is property that is (1) acquired after March 31, 2008 and before January 1, 2014, (2) placed in service before January 1, 2014 (or before January 1, 2015, for longer-period production property and certain noncommercial aircraft), and (3) eligible for the bonus depreciation deduction. No binding written purchase contract may be in effect before April 1, 2008 [Code Sec. 168(k)(2)(A) and (4)(D)].

Eligible Qualified Property with Longer Production Period

In the case of eligible qualified property with a longer production period that is entitled to an extended December 31, 2014, placed-in-service deadline, only the portion of the property's basis that is attributable to manufacture, construction, or production (1) after March 31, 2008, and before January 1, 2010, and (2) after December 31, 2010, and before January 1, 2014 is taken into account under the progress expenditures rule in computing the credit [Code Sec. 168(k)(4)(D)(iii)].

.04 Election Rules

If a corporation previously made an election to forgo bonus depreciation then that election will apply to round 3 extension property unless the corporation makes an election not to forgo bonus depreciation on round 3 extension property [Code Sec. 168(k)(4)(J)(ii)]. A previous election to forgo bonus depreciation includes an election to forgo bonus depreciation for the corporation's first tax year beginning after March 31, 2008, an election to forgo bonus depreciation with respect to extension property, and an election to forgo bonus depreciation on round 2 extension property.

If the election to forgo bonus depreciation applies to round 3 extension property, the bonus depreciation amount, maximum amount, and maximum increase amount are computed separately for eligible qualified property which is round 3 extension property. These computations are not combined with any amounts computed for eligible qualified property which is not round 3 extension property and which is subject to a prior election [Code Sec. 168(k)(4)(J)(ii)(II)].

Election Rules for Corporations with No Previous Election to Forgo Bonus Depreciation

If a corporation did not previously make an election to forgo bonus depreciation, the corporation may make an election to forgo bonus depreciation in its first tax year ending after December 31, 2012, and each subsequent tax year. However, if the election is made, it only applies to round 3 extension property [Code Sec. 168(k)(4)(J)(iii)].

.05 Time and Manner for Making Election

A corporation must make this election by the due date (including extensions) of the taxpayer's federal income tax return. If the taxpayer has missed this deadline, a late election may be made. A C corporation makes the Code Sec. 168(k)(4) extension property election by:

1. Claiming the refundable credit on the appropriate line of the Form 1120, *U.S. Corporation Income Tax Return*;
2. Filing, with the Form 1120, the Form 3800, *General Business Credit*, or Form 8827, *Credit for Prior Year Minimum Tax—Corporations*, or both, as applicable;
3. Filing, with the Form 1120, the Form 4562, *Depreciation and Amortization (Including Information on Listed Property)*, indicating that the taxpayer used the straight line method and did not claim the bonus first year depreciation deduction for all extension property; and
4. Providing written notification to any partnership in which the taxpayer is a partner that the taxpayer is making the extension property election. This notification must be made on or before the due date (including extensions) of the taxpayer's federal income tax return. If the taxpayer makes a late extension property election, the notification to the partnership must be made no later than the date the taxpayer files its federal income tax return containing the late election.
5. If a corporation previously made an election under Code Sec. 168(k)(4)(A) to forgo bonus depreciation for its first tax year beginning after March 31, 2008, or made an election to forgo bonus depreciation with respect to extension property under Code Sec. 168(k)(4)(H)(ii) for its first tax year ending after December 31, 2008, the election to forgo bonus depreciation will apply to round 2 extension property, unless the corporation makes an election not to forgo bonus depreciation on round 2 extension property [Code Sec. 168(k)(4)(I)(ii)].
6. If a corporation did not previously make an election under Code Sec. 168(k)(4)(A) to forgo bonus depreciation in its first tax year beginning after March 31, 2008, and

did not make an election to forgo bonus depreciation with respect to extension property under Code Sec. 168(k)(4)(H)(ii) for its first tax year ending after December 31, 2008, the corporation may make an election to forgo bonus depreciation in its first tax year ending after December 31, 2010, and each subsequent tax year. However, if the election is made, it only applies to round 2 extension property [Code Sec. 168(k)(4)(I)(iii)].

An S corporation makes the Code Sec. 168(k)(4) extension property election by:

1. Making appropriate adjustments to the appropriate line of the Form 1120S, *U.S. Income Tax Return for an S Corporation*;
2. Attaching to the Form 1120S a statement indicating that the taxpayer is making the extension property election and a statement showing the computation of the increases to the business credit and AMT credit limitations;
3. Filing, with the Form 1120S, the Form 4562 indicating that the taxpayer used the straight line method and did not claim the bonus first year depreciation deduction for all extension property; and
4. Providing written notification to any partnership in which the taxpayer is a partner that the taxpayer is making the extension property election. This notification must be made on or before the due date (including extensions) of the taxpayer's federal income tax return for its first tax year ending after December 31, 2008. If the taxpayer makes a late extension property election, the notification to the partnership must be made no later than the date the taxpayer files its federal income tax return containing the late election.

Members of a controlled group of corporations are treated as one taxpayer for purposes of the Code Sec. 168(k)(4) election. Therefore, if any member of a controlled group makes the election not to apply Code Sec. 168(k)(4) to extension property, the election is binding on all other members of the controlled group. If all members of a controlled group are members of an affiliated group of corporations that file a consolidated return, the common parent of the consolidated group makes the election not to apply Code Sec. 168(k)(4) to extension property on behalf of all members of the consolidated group.

A corporation that did not make the Code Sec. 168(k)(4) election may make the Code Sec. 168(k)(4) extension property election by attaching a statement to its return. If the election is made, the election applies to all extension property placed in service by the taxpayer.

¶14,158 CARBON DIOXIDE CAPTURE CREDIT

The carbon dioxide capture credit is a general business credit that provides incentives to taxpayers that capture carbon dioxide at certain industrial facilities and either permanently dispose of the gas in a geologic formation or use it in certain enhanced oil or natural gas recovery efforts [Code Sec. 45Q].

The credit applies to carbon dioxide captured at industrial facilities located in the United States or its possessions that (1) are owned by the taxpayer, (2) have carbon capture equipment installed, and (3) capture at least 500,000 metric tons of carbon dioxide during the tax year [Code Sec. 45Q(c) and (d)(1)].

In Notice 2009-83,[57] the IRS provided that a taxpayer must satisfy the following three requirements to be eligible to claim the Code Sec. 45Q credit:

- Own an industrial facility where carbon capture equipment is placed in service,
- Capture no less than 500,000 metric tons of qualified carbon dioxide during the tax year at the industrial facility, and
- "Physically or contractually ensure" that the qualified carbon dioxide is securely stored in a "geological formation."

Carbon dioxide capture credits are claimed by the person who captures and physically or contractually ensures the disposal of qualified carbon dioxide in secure geological storage or its use as a tertiary injectant in a qualified enhanced oil or natural gas recovery project (EOR project) [Code Sec. 45Q(d)(5)]. In addition, the person claiming the credit must own an industrial facility at which carbon capture equipment is placed in service and such equipment must capture at least 500,000 metric tons of qualified carbon dioxide during the tax year at the facility [Code Sec. 45Q(c)]. In addition, the carbon dioxide used as a tertiary injectant must be disposed of in secure geological storage [Code Sec. 45Q(a)].

The credit is generally claimed by the owner of an industrial facility where the carbon dioxide is captured if the owner physically or contractually ensures its disposal in secure geological storage [Code Sec. 45Q(d)(5)].

.01 Credit Amounts

The carbon dioxide capture credit for 2013 is (1) $21.25 per metric ton of qualified carbon dioxide (CO2) that is captured by the taxpayer at a qualified facility, disposed of in secure geological storage, and not used by the taxpayer as a tertiary injectant in a qualified enhanced oil or natural gas recovery project; and (2) $10.63 per metric ton of qualified CO2 that is captured by the taxpayer at a qualified facility, used as a tertiary injectant in a qualified enhanced oil or natural gas recovery project, and disposed of by the taxpayer in secure geological storage [Code Sec. 45Q(a)].[58]

¶14,165 CREDITS FOR CERTAIN USES OF GASOLINE AND SPECIAL FUELS

Generally, individuals, estates, trusts, or corporations can claim a credit for the federal excise taxes paid for the nonhighway use of gasoline and special fuels. These include gasoline or special fuels used in farming and special fuels used in local transit systems and for aviation or commercial fishing purposes. Quarterly refund payments are allowed for claims of at least $1,000 [Code Secs. 34, 6420, 6421, 6424, 6427]. Examples of

---

[57] Notice 2009-83, IRB 2009-44, as modified by Notice 2011-25, IRB 2011-14.

[58] Notice 2013-34, IRB 2013-23, 1198.

nonhighway use include operating a power lawn mower, stationary engines, or engines for use in construction, mining, or timbering projects.

Any individual, estate, trust, or corporation claiming the credit must file and attach Form 4136, *Credit for Federal Tax Paid on Fuels,* to the income tax return.

Instead of waiting to claim an annual credit on Form 4136, taxpayers may be able to file:

- Form 8849, *Claim for Refund of Excise Taxes,* to claim a periodic refund; or
- Form 720, *Quarterly Federal Excise Tax Return,* to claim a credit against fuel tax liability.

But taxpayers cannot claim on Form 4136 any amounts that were claimed on Form 8849 or Form 720.

¶14,170 FUEL PRODUCTION CREDITS

.01 Credit for Producing Fuel from Nonconventional Sources

The nonconventional fuel production credit is an income tax credit allowed for the domestic production of oil, gas, and synthetic fuels derived from nonconventional sources that are sold to nonrelated persons. This credit is included in the computation of the general business credit (see Code Sec. 38(b)(22)) and is subject to the limitations applicable to the general business credit. Any unused credit may be carried back one year and carried forward 20 years [Code Sec. 39].

The credit can be claimed for coke or coke gas (1) produced in facilities that were placed in service before January 1, 1993, or after June 30, 1998, and before January 1, 2010, and (2) sold during the period beginning on the later of January 1, 2006, or the date the facility is placed in service, and ending on the date that is four years after the date such period began [Code Sec. 45K(g)(1)]. A coke and coke gas facility, for purposes of the nonconventional source fuel credit, does not include facilities that produce petroleum-based coke or coke gas [Code Sec. 45K(g)(1)].

Qualified fuels that are eligible for the credit include (1) oil produced from shale and tar sands, (2) gas produced from geopressured brine, Devonian shale, coal seams, or a tight formation, (3) gas produced from biomass, and (4) liquid, gaseous, or solid synthetic fuels produced from coal (including lignite), including such fuels when used as feedstocks [Code Sec. 45K(c)(1)].

Amount of Credit

The IRS has published the nonconventional source fuel credit, inflation adjustment factor and reference price for calendar year 2012, which is used to determine the tax credit allowable under Code Sec. 45K. For calendar year 2012, the credit is available only for fuel produced from coke or coke gas (other than from petroleum-based products) and is not subject to phase-out. The reference price that is used to determine the allowable tax credit for coke or coke gas for calendar year 2012 is $94.53 and the inflation adjustment factor is 1.1922. Accordingly, the nonconventional source fuel credit is $3.58 per barrel-of-oil equivalent ($3.00 × 1.1922).[59]

.02 Alcohol Fuels Credit

The alcohol fuels credit is composed of four separate credits:

- The alcohol mixture credit,
- The alcohol credit,
- The small ethanol producer credit [Code Sec. 40], and
- The second generation biofuel producer credit [Code Sec. 40(a)].

The first three credit components will terminate for sales or uses that occur: (1) for any period after December 31, 2011 *or* (2) for any period before January 1, 2012 when the rates of tax under Code Sec. 4081(a)(2)(A) on gasoline, diesel fuel, and kerosene are 4.3 cents per gallon [Code Sec. 40(e)(1)].

The second generation biofuel producer credit component of the alcohol fuels credit applies to qualified biofuel production after December 31, 2008 and before January 1, 2014 [Code Sec. 40(b)(6)(H), (e)(3)].

.03 Cellulosic Biofuels Producer Credit (Now Called the "Second Generation Biofuel Producer Credit)"

The $1.01 per gallon nonrefundable income tax credit for the production of qualified cellulosic biofuel has been (1) renamed the "second generation biofuel producer credit," (2) has been expanded to include fuel derived from various algae, and (3) will expire after December 31, 2013 [Code Sec. 40(b)(6)(J)]. The term "qualified second generation biofuel" means any second generation biofuel which is produced by the taxpayer and sold to another person (1) for use in the production of a qualified second generation biofuel mixture in a trade or business (other than casual off-farm production), (2) for use as a fuel in a trade or business, or (3) who sells the second generation biofuel at retail to another person and places such second generation biofuel in the fuel tank of such other person [Code Sec. 40(b)(6)(C)].

If second generation biofuel is derived from algae and sold for refining into a fuel which meets the Environmental Protection Agency (EPA) requirements and the refined fuel is not excluded as either black liquor or crude tall oil, it is treated as the sale of a qualified second generation biofuel under Code Sec. 40(b)(6)(C)(i). In addition, the fuel will be treated as meeting the EPA requirements in the hands of the seller, and will not be excluded as either black liquor or crude tall oil in the hands of the seller [Code Sec. 40(b)(6)(G)].

The cellulosic biofuel producer credit which is a component of the Code Sec. 40 alcohol fuels credit is generally subject to the carryforward rules of the general business credit but Code Sec. 40(e)(2) limits the carryover of any unused alcohol fuels credit to a fixed period after the termination date of the credit. Thus, upon termination of the cellulosic biofuel producer credit, the carryover period of any unclaimed credit amount will be limited to the three subsequent tax years.

---

[59] Notice 2013-25, IRB 2013-17.

Taxpayer Option Not to Elect Alcohol Fuels Credit

Taxpayers also have the option of electing to not claim the alcohol fuels credit [Code Sec. 40(f)]. The election or revocation must be made before the expiration of the three-year period beginning on the due date of the return for such tax year (determined without regard to extensions).

.04 Biodiesel Fuels Credit

The nonrefundable biodiesel fuels income tax credit consists of the sum of the following three credits: the biodiesel mixture credit [Code Sec. 40A(b)(1)], the biodiesel credit [Code Sec. 40A(b)(2)], and the small agri-biodiesel producers credit [Code Sec. 40A(b)(4)]. The biodiesel fuels credit is treated as a general business credit and applies to fuel produced, and sold or used before January 1, 2014 [Code Sec. 40A(g)].

¶14,171 AGRICULTURAL CHEMICALS SECURITY TAX CREDIT

.01 Who May Claim Credit

Effective for expenses paid or incurred after May 22, 2008, and before December 31, 2012, a 30-percent credit is available for qualified chemical security expenditures incurred by an eligible agricultural business. The credit is limited to $100,000 per facility. This amount is reduced by the aggregate amount of the chemical security tax credits allowed for the facility in the prior five years [Code Sec. 45O(b)]. In addition, each taxpayer's annual credit is limited to $2 million [Code Sec. 45O(c)]. The term "taxpayer" includes controlled groups [Code Sec. 45O(g)]. The taxpayer's deductible expenses are reduced by the amount of the credit claimed [Code Sec. 280C(f)]. The credit is a component of the general business credit and is claimed on Form 8931, *Agricultural Chemicals Security Credit* [Code Sec. 45O(a)].

.02 Key Definitions

"Qualified chemical security expenditures" are defined as amounts paid for:

- Employee security training and background checks;
- Limitation and prevention of access to controls of specified agricultural chemicals stored at a facility;
- Tagging, locking tank valves, and chemical additives to prevent the theft of specified agricultural chemicals or to render such chemicals unfit for illegal use;
- Protection of the perimeter of specified agricultural chemicals;
- Installation of security lighting, cameras, recording equipment, and intrusion detection sensors;
- Implementation of measures to increase computer or computer network security;
- Conducting security vulnerability assessments;
- Implementing a site security plan; and
- Other measures provided for by regulation.

Amounts listed above are only eligible to the extent they are incurred by an eligible agricultural business for protecting specified agricultural chemicals [Code Sec. 45O(d)]. "Eligible agricultural businesses" are businesses that: (1) sell agricultural products, including specified agricultural chemicals, at retail predominantly to farmers and ranchers; or (2) manufacture, formulate, distribute, or aerially apply specified agricultural chemicals [Code Sec. 45O(e)].

"Specified agricultural chemicals" means: (1) fertilizer commonly used in agricultural operations, and (2) any pesticide including all active and inert ingredients which are used on crops grown for food, feed, or fiber [Code Sec. 45O(f)].

¶14,175 CREDIT FOR INTEREST PAID ON MORTGAGE CREDIT CERTIFICATES

States and localities can issue mortgage credit certificates (MCC) to qualified first-time homebuyers.[60] These are certificates issued under a qualified mortgage certificate program by the state or political subdivision with authority to issue qualified mortgage bonds to provide financing on a taxpayer's residence. Qualified homebuyers will receive a MCC indicating the portion of the principal debt that qualifies for the credit and the credit percentage rate.

.01 Who May Claim Credit

First-time homebuyers may claim a tax credit for a portion of the mortgage interest paid during the year in which the qualified residence is used as a principal residence [Code Sec. 25].

.02 Amount of Credit

The amount of the MCC is equal to the certificate credit rate (which must be not less than 10 percent or more than 50 percent of the rate specified by the issuer on the MCC) times the mortgage interest paid or accrued by the taxpayer during the tax year on the remaining principal of the certified indebtedness amount [Code Sec. 25(a)(1) and (d)(1); Temp. Reg. § 1.25-2T(b)]. If the certificate credit rate exceeds 20 percent, the maximum credit is limited to $2,000. For a residence owned by two or more persons, the $2,000 limit is prorated among such persons according to their respective interests in the residence [Code Sec. 25(a)(2); Temp. Reg. § 1.25-2T(d)]. Therefore, only individuals who purchase lower-priced residences may benefit from a credit rate in excess of 20 percent. The taxpayer's deduction for interest on the qualifying mortgage is reduced by the amount of the credit [Code Sec. 163(g); Temp. Reg. § 1.163-6T. See Ch. 9].

> **Example 14-15:** Mr. Smith received a mortgage credit certificate specifying a 50 percent credit rate. For the tax year, he pays mortgage interest of $5,000. Of this amount, he is entitled to the maximum mortgage credit of $2,500 plus an interest deduction for the remaining $2,500.

---

[60] Rev. Proc. 2013-27, IRB 2013-24, 1243.

.03 Tax Liability Limitation

The credit for interest paid on MCCs may not exceed the excess (if any) of the regular tax over the tentative minimum tax for the tax year, reduced by the sum of the nonrefundable personal credits other than the adoption credit, the child credit, the saver's credit, the residential alternative energy credit, the first-time homebuyers credit for the District of Columbia, and this credit for interest paid on MCCs [Code Sec. 25(e)(1)(C)(ii)].

A three-year carryforward is provided for any unused credit for interest paid on MCCs. Any credit that is unused after three years is lost [Code Sec. 25(e)(1); Temp. Reg. §1.25-2T(d)(2)]. If unused credits from two prior tax years are carried forward to a subsequent tax year, the unused credit from the earlier of the two prior years must be taken into account before the unused credit from the later of those two years [Temp. Reg. §1.25-2T(d)(2)(ii)].

.04 Reporting Requirements

The credit for interest on mortgage credit certificates is computed on Form 8396, *Mortgage Credit Interest.* Any carryforward to the succeeding tax year is computed in Part II of Form 8396. The deduction for home mortgage interest on Schedule A of Form 1040 must be reduced by the amount shown on line 3 of Form 8396. MCC recipients must file a statement with the lender, under penalties of perjury, establishing their eligibility for a MCC. Persons who make a material misstatement due to negligence are subject to a $1,000 penalty. A $10,000 penalty applies if such material misstatement is due to fraud. Lenders that make certified loans under MCC programs are also required to file reports on Form 8329, *Lender's Information Return for Mortgage Credit Certificates (MCCs)*. Each failure to file a report is subject to a $200 penalty unless it can be shown that the failure was due to reasonable cause and not to willful neglect [Code Sec. 6709]. States or political subdivisions that have or create programs under which MCCs may be issued should use Form 8330, *Issuer's Quarterly Information Return for Mortgage Credit Certificates (MCCs),* for each issue of MCCs. The form is filed on a quarterly basis beginning with the quarter in which the election to issue MCCs is made.

¶14,180 PLUG-IN ELECTRIC DRIVE MOTOR VEHICLE CREDIT

A credit is available for qualified plug-in electric drive motor vehicles placed in service by the taxpayer equal to the sum of:

a. A base amount of $2,500, and
b. $417 for a vehicle drawing propulsion energy from a battery with at least 5 kilowatt hours of capacity plus $417 for each additional kilowatt hour of capacity in excess of 5 kilowatt hours, up to a maximum aggregate of $5,000 based on kilowatt hour capacity [Code Sec. 30D(b)(3)]. Therefore the total credit allowed for a vehicle is limited to $7,500.

The credit may be claimed on Form 8834, *Qualified Plug-in Electric and Electric Vehicle Credit.*

.01 Credit Amount

The minimum credit amount is $2,500 if the vehicle battery has 4 but less than 5 kilowatt hours of capacity. The credit maximum is $7,500 consisting of the $2,500 base amount plus the $5,000 maximum predicated on battery kilowatt hour capacity. The plug-in electric drive motor vehicle credit is a permanent credit and applies to taxpayers who acquire vehicles after December 31, 2009.

Taxpayers can elect to not have the new qualified plug-in electric drive motor vehicle credit apply to their vehicle [Code Sec. 30D(f)(6)].

.02 Qualified Plug-in Electric Drive Motor Vehicle

A vehicle manufacturer must comply with a 17-item checklist and submit this certification to the IRS in order to certify that the vehicle is eligible for the Code Sec. 30D plug-in vehicle credit.[61] A purchaser of a motor vehicle may rely on the manufacturer's certification concerning the vehicle and the amount of the credit allowable with respect to the vehicle. The purchaser may claim a credit in the certified amount with respect to the vehicle if the following requirements are satisfied:

1. The vehicle is placed in service by the taxpayer after December 31, 2009, and is acquired by the taxpayer after December 31, 2009;
2. The original use of the vehicle commences with the taxpayer;
3. The vehicle is acquired for use or lease by the taxpayer, and not for resale; and
4. The vehicle is used predominantly in the United States.

In addition the vehicle must:

a. Have a gross vehicle weight rating of less than 14,000 pounds,
b. Be a self-propelled vehicle designed for transporting persons or property on a street or highway, and
c. Be propelled to a significant extent by an electric motor drawing electricity from a battery having a capacity of at least 4 kilowatt hours that can be recharged from an external source [Code Sec. 30D(d)(1)].

Furthermore, the vehicle must be in compliance with the applicable provisions of the Clean Air Act for the vehicle's particular make and model year [Code Sec. 30D(f)(7)]. A motor vehicle is defined as any vehicle manufactured primarily for use on public streets, roads, and highways that has at least 4 wheels [Code Sec. 30D(d)(2)].

.03 Phaseout of Credit

When 200,000 new qualified plug-in electric drive motor vehicles have been sold for use in the United States after December 31, 2009 by a manufacturer, the phaseout will be triggered as to that manufacturer's vehicles. The phaseout period begins with the second calendar quarter following the calendar quarter that includes the date the 200,000th unit is sold [Code Sec. 30D(e)(2)]. For the first two quarters of the phaseout period, the credit is cut to 50 percent of the otherwise allowable full credit amount. The

[61] Notice 2009-89, IRB 2009-48, as modified by Notice 2012-54, IRB 2012-52, 773.

credit is cut to 25 percent for the third and fourth quarters of the phaseout period. Thereafter, there is no credit allowed.

.04 Disqualified Property

No new qualified plug-in electric drive motor vehicle credit is allowed for property used predominately outside of the United States except for aircraft, rolling stock, and motor vehicles of U.S. persons that are operated to and from the U.S. [Code Sec. 30D (f) (4)]. In addition the amount of any deduction or other credit allowable for a new qualified plug-in electric drive motor vehicle must be reduced by the amount of the new qualified plug-in electric drive motor vehicle credit allowed under Code Sec. 30D. [Code Sec. 30D (f) (2)].

.05 Business or Personal Use

If the plug-in electric drive motor vehicle is used in a trade or business and, is therefore, subject to depreciation, the credit allowed for the business use portion is treated as part of the general business credit and that portion is not allowed to calculate the new qualified plug-in electric drive vehicle credit [Code Secs. 30D (c) (1) and 38 (b) (35)]. If the plug-in electric drive motor vehicle is considered personal property, the credit will be treated as if it is part of the nonrefundable personal credits [Code Sec. 30D (c) (2) (A)]. This treatment allows the credit to be claimed against a taxpayer's regular tax and alternative minimum tax (AMT) liabilities in years that Code Sec. 26 (a) (2) applies. In years when Code Sec. 26 (a) (2) does not apply (after 2009), the plug-in credit must be offset against the excess of the taxpayer's regular tax plus AMT liabilities over the sum of the nonrefundable personal credits allowable (except this credit, the adoption credit, the residential alternative energy property credit) and the foreign tax credit [Code Sec. 30D (c) (2) (B)].

.06 Property Used by Tax-exempt Entity

If the plug-in electric drive motor vehicle will be used by a tax-exempt organization, governmental unit or foreign person or entity and is not subject to a lease, the seller of the vehicle can claim the credit provided the seller clearly discloses in writing to the entity the amount of any credit allowable with respect to the vehicle [Code Sec. 30D (f) (3)].

.07 Plug-In Electric Vehicle Credit Extended for 2-Wheeled Vehicles and 3-Wheeled Electric Vehicles

The plug-in electric drive motor vehicle credit is available for 2- and 3-wheeled plug-in electric vehicles acquired during 2012 or 2013 [Code Sec. 30D (g)].The credit is equal to the applicable amount with respect to each new qualified 2- or 3-wheeled plug-in electric drive vehicle. The applicable amount is equal to the lesser of:

1. 10 percent of the cost of the qualified 2- or 3-wheeled plug-in electric drive vehicle; or
2. $2,500 [Code Sec. 30D (g) (2)].

In order for a vehicle to qualify as a 2- or 3-wheeled plug-in electric drive vehicle, the vehicle must have 2 or 3 wheels, be made by a manufacturer, and be acquired for use or lease by the taxpayer and not resale. The original use of the vehicle must begin with the taxpayer. In addition, the vehicle must:

1. Have a gross vehicle weight rating of less than 14,000 pounds;
2. Be primarily manufactured for use on public streets, roads, and highways;
3. Be able to achieve a speed of at least 45 miles an hour;
4. Be propelled to a significant extent by an electric motor drawing electricity from a battery having a capacity of at least 2.5 kilowatt hours that can be recharged from an external source; and
5. Be acquired after December 31, 2011, and before January 1, 2014 [Code Sec. 30D(g)(3)].

The amount of any deduction or other credit allowable for a new vehicle must be reduced by the amount of any new qualified vehicle credit allowed under Code Sec. 30D [Code Sec. 30D(f)(2)]. Moreover, the vehicle must be in compliance with (1) the applicable provisions of the Clean Air Act for the vehicle's particular make and model year (or applicable air quality State law provisions where a Clean Air Act waiver is in effect), and (2) the vehicle safety provisions of 49 U.S.C. 30101-30169 [Code Sec. 30D(f)(7)].

¶14,185 CREDIT FOR HOLDERS OF QUALIFIED ZONE ACADEMY BONDS

A tax credit is available for financial institutions such as banks, insurance companies, and corporations actively engaged in the business of lending money, if they hold *qualified zone academy bonds* (QZABs) [Code Sec. 1397E(a)]. A QZAB is a bond issued by a state or local government to finance certain eligible public school purposes. The financial institutions are entitled to a nonrefundable tax credit in an amount equal to a credit rate (set by the Treasury Department) multiplied by the face amount of the bond. The credit rate applies to all QZABs purchased in each month. The credit is claimed on Form 8912, *Credit to Holders of Tax Credit Bonds*. The provisions of Code Sec. 1397E terminated in the fall of 2008 and are only applicable to bonds issued on or before October 3, 2008. However, state and local governments may continue to issue qualified zone academy bonds after October 3, 2008 under Code Sec. 54E.

.01 General Rules for Claiming the Credit

A taxpayer holding a QZAB will be entitled to a credit for each year that it holds the bond. The amount of the credit is includible in gross income, but the credit may be claimed against regular income tax and AMT liability.

The credit rate for a qualified zone academy bond will be the rate published daily by the Bureau of Public Debt on its Internet site for state and local government bonds at http://www.publicdebt.treas.gov. The qualified zone academy bond credit rate shall be applied to a qualified zone academy bond on the first day on which there is a binding contract in writing for the sale or exchange of the bond. The credit rate will be determined by the Department of the Treasury based on its estimate of the yield on outstanding AA rated corporate bonds of a similar maturity for the business day immediately prior to the date on which there is a binding contract in writing for the sale or exchange of the bond.

A qualified zone academy bond (QZAB) is a bond issued as part of an issue if: (1) 100 percent of the available project proceeds of the issue are to be used for a qualified purpose with respect to a qualified zone academy established by an eligible local education agency; (2) the bond is issued by the state or a local government and the academy is located within its jurisdiction; and (3) the issuer designates the bond as a QZAB, certifies that it has written assurances of the required private contributions with respect to the academy, and certifies that it has the written approval of the eligible local education agency for the bond issuance [Code Sec. 54E(a)].

A qualified purpose, with respect to any particular qualified academy includes: (1) rehabilitating or repairing the public school facility in which the academy is established; (2) providing equipment for use at the academy; (3) developing course materials for use in the academy; and (4) training teachers and other school personnel in the academy [Code Sec. 54E(d)(3)].

A qualified zone academy is a public school (or academic program within a public school) established by and operated under the supervision of an eligible local education agency (generally, the local public school board) to provide education or training below the post-secondary level if: (1) the school or program is designed in cooperation with business to enhance the academic curriculum, increase graduation and employment rates, and better prepare students for the rigors of college and the increasingly complex workforce; (2) students in the school or program will be subject to the same academic standards and assessments as other students educated by the local education agency; (3) the comprehensive education plan of the school or program is approved by the local education agency; and (4) the public school is located in an empowerment zone or enterprise community; or (b) there is a reasonable expectation, at the date of issuance of the bonds, that at least 35 percent of the students in the school or program will be eligible for free or reduced-cost school lunches under the National School Lunch Act [Code Sec. 54E(d)(1)].

The local education agency that established the academy must have written commitments from private entities to make qualified contributions having a present value, as of the date the bonds are issued, of not less than 10 percent of the proceeds of the issue [Code Sec. 54E(b)]. Qualified contributions include: (1) equipment for use in the academy, including state-of-the-art technology and vocational equipment; (2) technical assistance in developing curriculum or training teachers in order to promote appropriate market-driven technology in the classroom; (3) services of employees as volunteer mentors; (4) internships, field trips, or other educational opportunities outside the academy for students; or (5) any other property or service specified by the local education agency [Code Sec. 54E(d)(4)].

.02 National QZAB Limits

Code Sec. 54E(c) establishes a national QZAB limit for each year. The authority of state and local governments to issue QZABs has been extended through 2013. Therefore, state and local governments are authorized to issue up to $400 million[62] of QZABs in 2013 and these funds can be used to finance renovations, equipment purchases, developing course material, and training teachers and personnel at a qualified zone academy [Code Sec. 54E(c)(1)].

¶14,195 ALTERNATIVE MOTOR VEHICLE CREDIT

.01 General Rules for Claiming the Credit

A number of tax credits collectively titled the Alternative Motor Vehicle Credit may be claimed by taxpayers who purchase a new qualifying vehicle. If a qualifying vehicle is leased to a consumer, the leasing company may claim the credit. These credits are designed to encourage the development, manufacture, and use of alternative fuel motor vehicles [Code Sec. 30B]. This credit is equal to the sum of the following five separate credit components:

- The qualified fuel cell motor vehicle credit for the purchase of a new qualified fuel cell motor vehicle placed in service before January 1, 2015 [Code Sec. 30B(b)],
- The advanced lean burn technology motor vehicle credit for the purchase of a new advanced lean burn technology motor vehicle placed in service before January 1, 2011 [Code Sec. 30B(c)],
- The qualified hybrid motor vehicle credit for the purchase of a new qualified hybrid motor vehicle placed in service before January 1, 2011 [Code Sec. 30B(d)],
- The qualified alternative fuel motor vehicle credit for the purchase of a qualified alternative fuel motor vehicle placed in service before January 1, 2011 [Code Sec. 30B(e)], and
- The plug-in conversion credit for the conversion of a motor vehicle to a qualified plug-in electric drive motor vehicle before January 1, 2012 [Code Sec. 30B(a)(5)].

Common Requirements for all Components of Alternative Motor Vehicle Credit

There are distinct requirements for each of the first four components of the Alternative Motor Vehicle Credit (not plug-in conversion credit). The following three requirements, however, are common to each of the credits:

1. The original use of the vehicle must commence with the taxpayer,
2. The vehicle must be acquired for use or lease by the taxpayer and not for resale, and
3. The vehicle must be made by a manufacturer.

The credit is claimed on Form 8910, *Alternative Motor Vehicle Credit.*

As of June 30, 2010, the following passenger automobiles and pick-up trucks with a gross vehicle weight rating of 8,500 pounds or less qualify for the hybrid motor vehicle credit if purchased before the January 1, 2011, credit termination date [Code Sec.

[62] Notice 2013-3, IRB 2013-7.

30B(d)(2)(A) and (k)(2)]. The original use of the vehicle must begin with the taxpayer claiming the credit (i.e., the vehicle must be new when purchased).

The full credit amount listed below may only be claimed up to the end of the first calendar quarter after the calendar quarter in which the manufacturer records its sale of 60,000 hybrid or advance lean burn technology vehicle to a retail dealer. For the second and third calendar quarters after the quarter in which the 60,000th vehicle is sold, taxpayers may claim 50 percent of the credit. For the fourth and fifth calendar quarters, taxpayers may claim 25 percent of the credit. No credit is allowed for later quarters.

Hybrid or lean technology Toyota vehicles (including Lexus vehicles manufactured by Toyota) purchased before October 1, 2006, qualify for 100 percent of the credit. Taxpayers buying qualifying Toyota vehicles from October 1, 2006, through March 31, 2007, may claim 50 percent of the otherwise allowable credit. Vehicles purchased from April 1, 2007, through September 30, 2007, are eligible for 25 percent of the credit. The credit is not allowed for vehicles purchased after September 30, 2007.

50 percent of the otherwise allowable credit may be claimed for Honda vehicles purchased from January 1, 2008, through June 30, 2008, and 25 percent for vehicles purchased from July 1, 2008, through December 31, 2008. No credit will be allowed for purchases after December 31, 2008.

50 percent of the otherwise allowable credit may be claimed for Ford and Mercury vehicles purchased from April 1, 2009, through September 30, 2009, and 25 percent for vehicles purchased from October 1, 2009, through March 31, 2010.

The following list of vehicles qualify for the hybrid motor vehicle credit if the vehicle was placed in service before January 1, 2011:[63]

2011 Model Year Hybrid Vehicles (as of December 30, 2010)

Model Year	Make	Model	Credit Amount
2011	BMW	Active Hybrid 750i	$900
		Active Hybrid Li	$900
		Active Hybrid X6	$1,550
2011	Cadillac	Escalade Hybrid (2WD & 4WD)	$2,200
2011	Chevrolet	Tahoe Hybrid C1500 2WD	$2,200
		Tahoe Hybrid K1500 4WD	$2,200
		Silverado Hybrid C15 2WD	$2,200
		Silverado Hybrid K15 4WD	$2,200
2011	GMC	Sierra Hybrid C15 2WD	$2,200
		Sierra Hybrid K15 4WD	$2,200

[63] Notice 2009-37, IRB 2009-18, 898.

Model Year	Make	Model	Credit Amount
		Yukon Hybrid C1500 2WD	$2,200
		Yukon Hybrid K1500 4WD	$2,200
		Yukon Denali Hybrid K1500 4WD	$2,200
2011	Mercedes Benz	ML450 Hybrid	$2,200
2011	Nissan	Altima Hybrid	$2,350
2011	Porsche	Cayenne S Hybrid	$1,800

2010 Model Year Hybrid Vehicles (as of 01-04-10)

Model Year	Make	Model	Credit Amount	NOTE:
2010	BMW	ActiveHybrid X6	$1,550	
2010	Cadillac	Escalade Hybrid (2WD & 4WD)	$2,200	
2010	Chevrolet	Malibu Hybrid	$1,550	
		Silverado Hybrid C15 2WD	$2,200	
		Silverado Hybrid K15 4WD	$2,200	
		Tahoe Hybrid C1500 2WD	$2,200	
		Tahoe Hybrid K1500 4WD	$2,200	
2010	Ford	Escape Hybrid 4x2	$3,000	If purchased before 04-01-09: Full Credit Amount
			$1,500	If purchased on 04-01-09 and on or before 09-30-09 Credit is 50% ($1500)
			$750	If purchased on 10-01-09 and on or before 03-31-10 Credit is 25% ($750)
		Escape Hybrid 4x4	$2,600	If purchased before 04-01-09: Full Credit Amount

Model Year	Make	Model	Credit Amount	NOTE:
			$1,300	If purchased on 04-01-09 and on or before 09-30-09 Credit is 50% ($1,300)
			$650	If purchased on 10-01-09 and on or before 03-31-10 Credit is 25% ($650)
		Fusion Hybrid	$3,400	If purchased before 04-01-09: Full Credit Amount
			$1,700	If purchased on 04-01-09 and on or before 09-30-09 Credit is 50% ($1,700)
			$850	If purchased on 10-01-09 and on or before 03-31-10 Credit is 25% ($850)
2010	GMC	Sierra Hybrid C15 2WD	$2,200	
		Sierra Hybrid K15 4WD	$2,200	
		Yukon Hybrid C1500 2WD	$2,200	
		Yukon Hybrid K1500 4WD	$2,200	
		Yukon Denali Hybrid C1500 2WD	$2,200	
		Yukon Denali Hybrid K1500 4WD	$2,200	
2010	Mercury	Mariner Hybrid 4x2	$3,000	If purchased before 04-01-09: Full Credit Amount
			$1,500	If purchased on 04-01-09 and on or before 09-30-09 Credit is 50% ($1500)
			$750	If purchased on 10-01-09 and on or before 03-31-10 Credit is 25% ($750)
		Mariner Hybrid 4x4	$2,600	If purchased before 04-01-09: Full Credit Amount

Model Year	Make	Model	Credit Amount	NOTE:
			$1,300	If purchased on 04-01-09 and on or before 09-30-09 Credit is 50% ($1,300)
			$650	If purchased on 10-01-09 and on or before 03-31-10 Credit is 25% ($650)
		Milan Hybrid	$3,400	If purchased before 04-01-09: Full Credit Amount
			$1,700	If purchased on 04-01-09 and on or before 09-30-09 Credit is 50% ($1,700)
			$850	If purchased on 10-01-09 and on or before 03-31-10 Credit is 25% ($850)
2010	Mercedes-Benz	S 400 Hybrid	$1,150	
		ML 450 Hybrid	$2,200	
2010	Nissan	Altima Hybrid	$2,350	

2009 Model Year Hybrid Vehicles (as of 03-19-2009)

Make	Model	Credit Amount
Cadillac	Escalade Hybrid 2WD	$2,200
Cadillac	Escalade Hybrid All Wheel Drive	$1,800
Chevrolet	Tahoe Hybrid C1500 2WD	$2,200
Chevrolet	Tahoe Hybrid K1500 4WD	$2,200
Chevrolet	Silverado Hybrid C15 2WD	$2,200
Chevrolet	Silverado Hybrid K15 4WD	$2,200
Chevrolet	Malibu Hybrid	$1,550
Chrysler	Aspen Hybrid	$2,200
Dodge	Durango Hybrid	$2,200
Ford	Escape Hybrid 2WD	$3,000
Ford	Escape Hybrid 4WD	$1,950
GMC	Sierra Hybrid C15 2WD	$2,200

Make	Model	Credit Amount
GMC	Sierra Hybrid K15 4WD	$2,200
GMC	Yukon Hybrid C1500 2WD	$2,200
GMC	Yukon Hybrid K1500 4WD	$2,200
Mazda	Tribute Hybrid 2WD	$3,000
Mazda	Tribute Hybrid 4WD	$1,950
Mercury	Mariner Hybrid 2WD	$3,000
Mercury	Mariner Hybrid 4WD	$1,950
Nissan	Atima Hybrid	$2,350
Saturn	Aura Hybrid	$1,550
Saturn	Vue Hybrid	$1,550

2008

Make	Model	Credit Amount
Ford	Escape Hybrid 2WD	$3,000
Ford	Escape Hybrid 4WD	$2,220
Mercury	Mariner Hybrid 2 WD	$3,000
Mercury	Mariner Hybrid 4WD	$2,200

2007

Make	Model	Credit Amount
Chevrolet	Silverado 2WD Hybrid Pickup Truck	$ 250
Chevrolet	Silverado 4WD Hybrid Pickup Truck	$ 650
Ford	Escape Hybrid 2WD	$2,600
Ford	Escape Hybrid 4WD	$1,950
GMC	Sierra 2WD Hybrid Pickup Truck	$ 250
GMC	Sierra 4WD Hybrid Pickup Truck	$ 650
Honda	Accord AT	$1,300
Honda	Accord Navi	$1,300
Honda	Civic CVT	$2,100

Make	Model	Credit Amount	
Lexus*	GS450h	**Purchase Date**	
		1-1-06 / 9-30-06	$1,550
		10-1-06 / 3-31-07	$ 775
		4-1-07 / 9-30-07	$ 387.50
		10-1-07	$ 0
Lexus*	RX 400h 4WD	**Purchase Date**	
		1-1-06 / 9-30-06	$2,200
		10-1-06 / 3-31-07	$1,100
		4-1-07 / 9-30-07	$ 550
		10-1-07	$ 0
Lexus*	RX 400h 2WD	**Purchase Date**	
		1-1-06 / 9-30-06	$2,200
		10-1-06 / 3-31-07	$1,100
		4-1-07 / 9-30-07	$ 550
		10-1-07	$ 0
Mercury	Mariner Hybrid 4WD	$1,950	
Saturn	Vue Green Line	$ 650	
Toyota*	Camry Hybrid	**Purchase Date**	
		1-1-06 / 9-30-06	$2,600
		10-1-06 / 3-31-07	$1,300
		4-1-07 / 9-30-07	$ 650
		10-1-07	$ 0
Toyota*	Prius	**Purchase Date**	
		1-1-06 / 9-30-06	$3,150
		10-1-06 / 3-31-07	$1,575
		4-1-07 /9-30-07	$ 787.50
		10-1-07	$ 0
Toyota*	Highlander Hybrid 2WD	**Purchase Date**	
		1-1-06 / 9-30-06	$2,600

Make	Model	Credit Amount	
		10-1-06 / 3-31-07	$1,300
		4-1-07 / 9-30-07	$ 650
		10-1-07	$ 0
Toyota*	Highlander Hybrid 4WD	**Purchase Date**	

2006

Make	Model	Credit Amount	
Chevrolet	Silverado 2WD Hybrid Pickup Truck	$ 250	
Chevrolet	Silverado 4WD Hybrid Pickup Truck	$ 650	
Ford	Escape Hybrid 2WD Front Wheel Drive	$2,600	
Ford	Escape Hybrid 4WD	$1,950	
GMC	Sierra 2WD Hybrid Pickup Truck	$ 250	
GMC	Sierra 4WD Hybrid Pickup Truck	$ 650	
Honda	Accord Hybrid AT w/updated calibration*	$1,300 $ 650 - Vehicles without updated calibration	
Honda	Accord Hybrid Navi AT w/updated calibration*	$1,300 $ 650 - Vehicles without updated calibration	
Honda	Civic Hybrid CVT	$2,100	
Honda	Insight CVT	$1,450	
Lexus*	RX400h 2WD	**Purchase Date**	
		1-1-06 / 9-30-06	$2,200
		10-1-06 / 3-31-07	$1,100
		4-1-07 / 9-30-07	$ 550
		10-1-07	$ 0
Lexus*	RX400h 4WD	**Purchase Date**	
		1-1-06 / 9-30-06	$2,200
		10-1-06 / 3-31-07	$1,100
		4-1-07 / 9-30-07	$ 550

Make	Model	Credit Amount	
		10-1-07	$ 0
Mercury	Mariner 4WD Hybrid	$1,950	
Toyota*	Highlander 2 WD Hybrid	**Purchase Date**	
		1-1-06 / 9-30-06	$2,600
		10-1-06 / 3-31-07	$1,300
		4-1-07 / 9-30-07	$ 650
		10-1-07	$ 0
Toyota*	Highlander 4WD Hybrid	**Purchase Date**	
		1-1-06 / 9-30-06	$2,600
		10-1-06 / 3-31-07	$1,300
		4-1-07 / 9-30-07	$ 650
		10-1-07	$ 0
Toyota*	Prius	**Purchase Date**	
		1-1-06 / 9-30-06	$3,150
		10-1-06 / 3-31-07	$1,575
		4-1-07 / 9-30-07	$ 787.50
		10-1-07	$ 0

2005

Make	Model	Credit Amount	
Ford	Escape HEV 2WD	$2,600	
Ford	Escape HEV 4WD	$1,950	
Honda	Accord Hybrid AT	$ 650	
Honda	Accord Hybrid Navi AT	$ 650	
Honda	Civic Hybrid CVT	$1,700	
Honda	Civic Hyrid MT	$1,700	
Honda	Insight CVT	$1,450	
Toyota*	Prius	**Purchase Date**	
		1-1-06 / 9-30-06	$3,150

Make	Model	Credit Amount	
		10-1-06 / 3-31-07	$1,575
		4-1-07 / 9-30-07	$ 787.50
		10-1-07	$ 0

No credit is available for:

- Purchases of Toyota and Lexus hybrid vehicles after September 30, 2007;
- Purchases of Honda hybrid vehicles on or after January 1, 2009; and
- Purchases of Ford or Mercury hybrid vehicles on or after April 1, 2010.

Coordination with Other Credits

Taxpayers with qualified motor vehicles that are used in a trade or business and subject to depreciation will claim the alternative motor vehicle credit as a part of and subject to the rules of the general business credit. Thus, any unused credit in a tax year will be eligible to be carried back three years and forward 20 years [Code Secs. 30B(g)(1) and 38(b)(25)].

Tax-Exempt Entities

Generally, the buyer of a qualified vehicle would claim the credit. However, the seller (but not the lessor) of a qualified vehicle to a tax-exempt entity, a governmental unit or a foreign entity may claim the credit, if the seller gives written notice of intent to claim the credit and the credit's amount to the buyer [Code Sec. 30B(h)(6)].

Motor Vehicle Defined

Motor vehicle means any vehicle that is manufactured primarily for use on public streets, roads and highways, and which has at least four wheels [Code Secs. 30(c)(2) and 30B(h)(1)].

.02 Fuel Cell Motor Vehicle Credit

The first component of the alternative motor vehicle credit is the qualified fuel cell motor vehicle credit for qualifying vehicles placed in service during 2006 through 2014 [Code Sec. 30B(b)]. To be eligible as a qualifying fuel cell motor vehicle, the motor vehicle must meet the several criteria discussed below in addition to the three requirements common to all qualifying alternative vehicles as discussed in ¶ 14,195.

In the case of passenger automobiles or light trucks, two additional criteria must be met. The vehicle must be certified as meeting or exceeding the Bin 5, Tier II emission standard established in the regulations under the Clean Air Act for that make and model year vehicle [Code Sec. 30B(b)(3)(B)]. For states, such as California, that have passed equivalent qualifying emission standards, the vehicle is required to also be certified for those standards for that particular make and model year [Code Sec. 30B(h)(10)(A)]. In addition, the vehicle must be propelled by power derived from one or more cells which convert chemical energy directly into electricity by combining oxygen with hydrogen fuel [Code Sec. 30B(b)(3)(A)].

Credit Amount

The amount of credit attributable to the placing in service of a qualified fuel cell motor vehicle during the tax year is determined using the Table 7[Code Sec. 30B(b) (1)].

Table 7. Fuel Cell Motor Credit Amounts

If vehicle gross vehicle weight rating of:	New qualified fuel cell motor vehicle credit is:
Not more than 8,500 lbs	$8,000
(if placed in service after December 31, 2009	$4,000
More than 8,500 lbs but not more than 14,000 lbs	$10,000
More than 14,000 lbs but not more than 26,000 lbs	$20,000
More than 26,000 lbs	$40,000

Qualified fuel cell vehicles that meet the definition of either a passenger automobile or light truck and meet certain standards for increased fuel efficiency will be able to increase their credit amount based on the increase in fuel efficiency over the 2002 city fuel economy standards [Code Sec. 30B(b) (2) (A)]. The additional amount is determined using Table 8.

Table 8. Additional Fuel Efficiency Credit Amounts

In the case of a vehicle which achieves a fuel economy (expressed as a percentage of the 2002 model year city fuel economy) of:	The additional credit amount is:
At least 150 percent but less than 175 percent	$1,000
At least 175 percent but less than 200 percent	$1,500
At least 200 percent but less than 225 percent	$2,000
At least 225 percent but less than 250 percent	$2,500
At least 250 percent but less than 275 percent	$3,000
At least 275 percent but less than 300 percent	$3,500
At least 300 percent	$4,000

The 2002 model year city fuel economy for such vehicles is determined using Table 9 [Code Sec. 30B(b) (2) (B)].

Table 9. 2002 Model Year City Fuel Economy by Weight Class

Passenger Automobile If vehicle inertia weight class is:	2002 model year city fuel economy is:
1,500 or 1,750 lbs	45.2 mpg
2,000 lbs	39.6 mpg
2,250 lbs	35.2 mpg
2,500 lbs	31.7 mpg
2,750 lbs	28.8 mpg
3,000 lbs	26.4 mpg
3,500 lbs	22.6 mpg
4,000 lbs	19.8 mpg
4,500 lbs	17.6 mpg

Passenger Automobile If vehicle inertia weight class is:	2002 model year city fuel economy is:
5,000 lbs	15.9 mpg
5,500 lbs	14.4 mpg
6,000 lbs	13.2 mpg
6,500 lbs	12.2 mpg
7,000 to 8,500 lbs	11.3 mpg

Light Trucks If vehicle inertia weight class is:	2002 model year city fuel economy is:
1,500 or 1,750 lbs	39.4 mpg
2,000 lbs	35.2 mpg
2,250 lbs	31.8 mpg
2,500 lbs	29.0 mpg
2,750 lbs	26.8 mpg
3,000 lbs	24.9 mpg
3,500 lbs	21.8 mpg
4,000 lbs	19.4 mpg
4,500 lbs	17.6 mpg
5,000 lbs	16.1 mpg
5,500 lbs	14.8 mpg
6,000 lbs	13.7 mpg
6,500 lbs	12.8 mpg
7,000 to 8,500 lbs	12.1 mpg

.03 Advanced Lean Burn Technology Motor Vehicle Credit

The second component of the alternative motor vehicle credit is the advanced lean burn technology motor vehicle credit for qualifying vehicles placed in service during 2006 through 2010 [Code Sec. 30B(c)]. To be eligible as a qualified advanced lean burn technology motor vehicle, the motor vehicle must meet several criteria in addition to the three requirements common to all qualifying alternative vehicles as discussed in ¶ 14,195.

An advanced lean burn technology motor vehicle must be a passenger automobile or light truck with an internal combustion engine that is (1) designed to operate primarily using more air than is necessary for complete combustion of the fuel, (2) incorporates direct injection, and (3) achieves at least 125 percent of the 2002 model year city fuel economy [Code Sec. 30B(c)(3)(A)]. Vehicles from model year 2004 and later must also receive a certificate that the vehicle meets or exceeds the Bin 5, Tier II emission standard established under the Clean Air Act for that make and model year, if the gross vehicle weight rating is 6,000 pounds or less. Vehicles with a gross vehicle weight rating of more than 6,000 pounds but not more than 8,500 pounds must be certified to meet or exceed the Bin 8, Tier II emission standard established under the Clean Air Act [Code Sec. 30B(c)(3)(A)(iv)].

Credit Amount

The credit amount attributable to the placing in service of a new qualified advanced lean burn technology motor vehicle during the tax year is determined by using Table 10 [Code Sec. 30B(c)(2)(A)].

Table 10. Credit Amounts for Advanced Learn Burn Technology Motor Vehicles

In the case of a vehicle which achieves a fuel economy (expressed as a percentage of the 2002 model year city fuel economy) of:	The credit amount is:
At least 125 percent but less than 150 percent	$400
At least 150 percent but less than 175 percent	$800
At least 175 percent but less than 200 percent	$1,200
At least 200 percent but less than 225 percent	$1,600
At least 225 percent but less than 250 percent	$2,000
At least 250 percent	$2,400

Conservation Credit

The credit amount for new advanced lean burn technology motor vehicles may be increased by a conservation credit [Code Sec. 30B(c)(2)(B)]. The conservation credit is determined by first calculating the lifetime fuel savings. The lifetime fuel savings is equal to the excess, if any, of:

1. 120,000 divided by the 2002 model year city fuel economy for the vehicle inertia weight class, over
2. 120,000 divided by the city fuel economy for the vehicle [Code Sec. 30B(c)(4)].

The conservation credit is based on the lifetime fuel savings expressed in gallons of gasoline from the table below:

Table 11. Additional Conservation Credit Measured by Lifetime Fuel Savings

In the case of a vehicle which achieves a lifetime fuel savings (expressed in gallons of gasoline) of:	The conservation credit amount is:
At least 1,200 but less than 1,800	$250
At least 1,800 but less than 2,400	$500
At least 2,400 but less than 3,000	$750
At least 3,000	$1,000

The following new vehicles qualify for the advance lean burn technology credit if purchased before the January 1, 2011, termination date [Code Sec. 30B(k)(2)]. Volkswagen vehicles (including Audi) are subject to a credit phaseout if purchased after June 30, 2010.

2010 Model Year New Advanced Lean Burn Technology Motor Vehicle Credit Amounts

- 2010 Audi A3 2.0L TDI Automatic
  - — If purchased before 7-01-10—$1,300
  - — If purchased on or after 7-01-10 and on or before 12-31-10—$650

- 2010 Audi Q7 3.0L TDI
  - — If purchased before 7-01-10—$1,150
  - — If purchased on or after 7-01-10 and on or before 12-31-10—$575
- 2010 BMW 335d Sedan—$900
- 2010 BMW X5 xDrive35d—$1,800
- 2010 BMW ActiveHybrid x6—$1,550
- 2010 Mercedes GL 350 BlueTEC—$1,800
- 2010 Mercedes ML 350 BlueTEC—$900
- 2010 Mercedes R 350 BlueTEC—$1,550
- 2010 Volkswagen Golf 2.0L TDI Automatic
  - — If purchased before 7-1-2010—$1,700
  - — If purchased on or after 7-01-10 and on or before 12-31-10—$850
- 2010 Volkswagen Golf 2.0L TDI Manual
  - — If purchased before 7-1-2010—$1,300
  - — If purchased on or after 7-01-10 and on or before 12-31-10—$650
- 2010 Volkswagen Jetta 2.0L TDI Sedan
  - — If purchased before 7-1-2010—$1,300
  - — If purchased on or after 7-01-10 and on or before 12-31-10—$650
- 2010 Volkswagen Jetta 2.0L Sportwagen
  - — If purchased before 7-1-2010—$1,300
  - — If purchased on or after 7-01-10 and on or before 12-31-10—$650
- 2010 Volkswagen Touareg 3.0L TDI
  - — If purchased before 7-1-2010—$1,150
  - — If purchased on or after 7-01-10 and on or before 12-31-10—$575

2009 Model Year New Advanced Lean Burn Technology Motor Vehicle Credit Amounts

- 2009 Audi Q7 3.0L TDI
  - — If purchased before 7-1-2010—$1,150
  - — If purchased on or after 7-01-10 and on or before 12-31-10—$575
- 2009 BMW 335d Sedan—$900
- 2009 BMW X5 xDrive35d—$1,800
- 2009 Mercedes GL 320 BlueTEC—$1,800
- 2009 Mercedes ML 320 BlueTEC—$900
- 2009 Mercedes R 320 BlueTEC—$1,550
- 2009 Volkswagen Jetta 2.0L TDI Sedan
  - — If purchased before 7-1-2010—$1,300
  - — If purchased on or after 7-01-10 and on or before 12-31-10—$650

- 2009 Volkswagen Jetta 2.0L TDI Sportswagen
  - — If purchased before 7-1-2010—$1,300
  - — If purchased on or after 7-01-10 and on or before 12-31-10—$650
- 2009 Volkswagen Touareg 3.0L TDI
  - — If purchased before 7-1-2010—$1,150
  - — If purchased on or after 7-01-10 and on or before 12-31-10—$575

.04 Hybrid Motor Vehicle Credit

The third component of the alternative motor vehicle credit is the hybrid motor vehicle credit for qualifying vehicles placed in service after December 31, 2005, and before January 1, 2011 [Code Sec. 30B(d)]. The qualified hybrid motor vehicle credit for passenger automobiles or light trucks with a gross vehicle weight rating (GVWR) of no more than 8,500 pounds terminates for vehicles purchased after December 31, 2010 [Code Sec. 30B(k)(2)]. The qualified hybrid motor vehicle credit for all other vehicles terminates for those vehicles purchased after December 31, 2009 [Code Sec. 30B(k)(3)]. To be eligible as a qualified hybrid motor vehicle, the vehicle must meet several criteria discussed below in addition to the three requirements common to all qualifying alternative vehicles as discussed in ¶ 14,195.

The hybrid motor vehicle must draw propulsion energy from onboard sources of stored energy that are both an internal combustion or heat engine using consumable fuel, and a rechargeable energy storage system [Code Sec. 30B(d)(3)(A)]. Passenger automobiles or light trucks must receive a certificate of conformity under the Clean Air Act, and meet or exceed the equivalent qualifying California low emission vehicle standard under § 243(e)(2) of the Clean Air Act for that make and model year.

In addition, if the vehicle has a gross weight rating of 6,000 pounds or less, it must meet or exceed the Bin 5, Tier II emission standard established in the regulations under the Clean Air Act for that make and model year. Vehicles with a gross weight rating of more than 6,000 pounds but not more than 8,500 pounds must meet or exceed the Bin 8, Tier II emission standard.

Finally, the vehicle must have a maximum available power of at least:

- 4 percent, in the case of a passenger automobile or light truck with a gross vehicle weight rating of not more than 8,500 pounds;
- 10 percent, in the case of a vehicle which has a gross vehicle weight rating of more than 8,500 pounds but not more than 14,000 pounds; or
- 15 percent, in the case of a vehicle which has a gross vehicle weight rating in excess of 14,000 pounds [Code Sec. 30B(d)(3)(A)(i), (ii), and (iii)].

Vehicles from model years 2004 through 2007, other than passenger automobiles or light trucks with a gross weight rating of not more than 8,500 pounds with an internal combustion or heat engine, must receive a certificate of conformity under the Clean Air Act as meeting the emission standard established in the regulations for either a diesel heavy duty engine or an ottocycle heavy duty engine [Code Sec. 30B(d)(3)(A)(iv)].

The term qualified hybrid motor vehicle shall not include any vehicle which is not a passenger automobile or light truck if the vehicle has a gross vehicle weight rating of less than 8,500 pounds [Code Sec. 30B(d)(3)(A)].

Credit Amount

The credit amount attributable to the placing in service of a qualified hybrid motor vehicle during the tax year, in the case of passenger automobiles or light trucks with a gross vehicle weight rating of not more than 8,500 pounds, is determined by referring to credit amounts determined under Code Sec. 30B(c)(2)(A), the advanced lean burn technology motor vehicle credit, as represented by Table 12 [Code Sec. 30B(d)(2)(A)(i)].

Table 12. Hybrid Motor Vehicle Credit

In the case of a vehicle which achieves a fuel economy (expressed as a percentage of the 2002 model year city fuel economy) of:	The credit amount is:
At least 125 percent but less than 150 percent	$400
At least 150 percent but less than 175 percent	$800
At least 175 percent but less than 200 percent	$1,200
At least 200 percent but less than 225 percent	$1,600
At least 225 percent but less than 250 percent	$2,000
At least 250 percent	$2,400

The credit amount for qualified hybrid motor vehicles that are passenger automobiles or light trucks with a GVWR of no more than 8,500 pounds may be increased by a conservation credit [Code Sec. 30B(d)(2)(A)(ii)].The conservation credit for qualified hybrid motor vehicles is determined in the same manner as the conservation credit for advanced lean burn technology motor vehicles by first calculating the lifetime fuel savings. The lifetime fuel savings is equal to the excess, if any, of:

1. 120,000 divided by the 2002 model year city fuel economy for the vehicle inertia weight class, over
2. 120,000 divided by the city fuel economy for the vehicle [Code Sec. 30B(c)(4)].

The conservation credit is based on the lifetime fuel savings expressed in gallons of gasoline from the lifetime fuel savings table below:

Table 13. Additional Conservation Credit for Hybrid Motor Vehicles

In the case of a vehicle which achieves a lifetime fuel savings (expressed in gallons of gasoline) of:	The conservation credit amount is:
At least 1,200 but less than 1,800	$250
At least 1,800 but less than 2,400	$500
At least 2,400 but less than 3,000	$750

If the qualified hybrid motor vehicle is not a passenger automobile or light truck with a gross vehicle weight rating under 8,500 pounds, the credit amount is equal to an applicable percentage times the qualified incremental hybrid cost of the vehicle as certified by the manufacturer [Code Sec. 30B(d)(2)(B)]. The applicable percentages are as follows:

- 20 percent, if the vehicle achieves an increase in city fuel economy relative to a comparable vehicle of at least 30 percent but less than 40 percent;
- 30 percent, if the vehicle achieves an increase in city fuel economy relative to a comparable vehicle of at least 40 percent but less than 50 percent; and
- 40 percent, if the vehicle achieves an increase in city fuel economy relative to a comparable vehicle of at least 50 percent [Code Sec. 30B(d)(2)(B)(ii)].

The qualified incremental hybrid cost is equal to the amount of the excess of the manufacturer's suggested retail price (MSRP) for the hybrid vehicle over the MSRP of a comparable vehicle. The incremental hybrid cost cannot exceed:

- $7,500, if the hybrid vehicle has a gross vehicle weight rating of not more than 14,000 pounds;
- $15,000, if the hybrid vehicle has a gross vehicle weight rating of more than 14,000 pounds but not more than 26,000 pounds; or
- $30,000, if the hybrid vehicle has a gross vehicle weight rating of more than 26,000 pounds [Code Sec. 30B(d)(2)(B)(iii)].

.05 Alternative Fuel Motor Vehicle Credit

The fourth component of the alternative motor vehicle credit is the alternative fuel motor vehicle credit for qualifying vehicles placed in service during 2006 through 2010 [Code Secs. 30B(e) and (k)(4)]. To be eligible as an alternative motor vehicle, the vehicle must meet several criteria in addition to the three requirements common to all alternative vehicles as discussed in ¶ 14,195 [Code Sec. 30B(e)(4)(A)]. The alternative fuel motor vehicle must only be capable of operating using an alternative fuel which include compressed natural gas, liquefied natural gas, liquefied petroleum gas, hydrogen, and any liquid at least 85 percent of the volume of which consists of methanol [Code Sec. 30B(e)(4)(A)(i)].

Credit Amount

The amount of credit attributable to the placing in service of a qualified alternative fuel motor vehicle is equal to the applicable percentage times the incremental cost of the vehicle [Code Sec. 30B(e)(1)]. The applicable percentage is: 50 percent, plus 30 percent, if the vehicle:

- Has received a certificate of conformity under the Clean Air Act and meets or exceeds the most stringent standard available for certification under the Clean Air Act for that make and model year vehicle (other than a zero emission standard); or
- Has received an order certifying the vehicle as meeting the same requirements as vehicles which may be sold or leased in California and meets or exceeds the most stringent standard available for certification under the state laws of California for that make or model year vehicle (other than a zero emission standard). For a qualified alternative fuel motor vehicle with a gross vehicle weight rating of more than 14,000 pounds, the most stringent standard available shall be the standard available for certification on August 8, 2005 [Code Sec. 30B(e)(2)].

Incremental Cost

Incremental cost for any qualified alternative fuel motor vehicle is equal to the excess of the manufacturer's suggested retail price (MSRP) for the vehicle over the MSRP for a gasoline or diesel fuel motor vehicle of the same model, to the extent that amount does not exceed:

- $5,000, if the vehicle has a gross vehicle weight rating of not more than 8,500 pounds;
- $10,000, if the vehicle has a gross vehicle weight rating of more than 8,500 pounds but not more than 14,000 pounds;
- $25,000, if the vehicle has a gross vehicle weight rating of more than 14,000 pounds but not more than 26,000 pounds; and
- $40,000, if the vehicle has a gross vehicle weight rating of more than 26,000 pounds [Code Sec. 30B(e)(3)].

Mixed-Fuel Vehicles Credit

The qualified alternative fuels motor vehicle credit may be claimed in a reduced amount for vehicles that use a mixture of alternative fuel and petroleum-based fuels [Code Sec. 30B(e)(5)]. A qualifying mixed-fuel vehicle is one that:

- Has a gross vehicle weight rating of more than 14,000 pounds;
- Is certified by the manufacturer as being able to perform efficiently in normal operation on a combination of an alternative fuel and a petroleum-based fuel;
- Either: has received a certificate of conformity under the Clean Air Act or has received an order certifying the vehicle as meeting the same requirements as vehicles which may be sold or leased in California.

The vehicle must meet or exceed the low emission vehicle standard for that make and model year vehicle, and satisfy the following requirements: (1) the original use of the vehicle must commence with the taxpayer (2) the vehicle must be acquired for the use or lease of the taxpayer and not for resale, and (3) the vehicle must be made by a manufacturer [Code Sec. 30B(e)(5)(B)].

Credit amount. The credit amount for mixed-fuel vehicles is expressed as a percentage of the new qualified alternative fuel motor vehicle credit. If a mixed fuel vehicle uses a 75/25-percent mixture (at least 75-percent alternative fuel and at most 25-percent petroleum based fuel), it is eligible for 70 percent of the credit. If it uses a 90/10-percent mixture (at least 90-percent alternative fuel and at most 10-percent petroleum-based fuel), it is eligible for 90 percent of the qualified alternative fuels motor vehicle credit [Code Sec. 30B(e)(5)(A)].

.06 Plug-in Electric Drive Motor Vehicle Conversion Credit

The fifth and final component of the alternative motor vehicle credit is the plug-in conversion credit [Code Sec. 30B(i)]. The credit is available with respect to any motor vehicle placed in service after February 17, 2009 which is converted to a qualified plug-in electric drive motor vehicle [Code Sec. 30B(a)(5)]. This credit is not applicable to any conversions made after December 31, 2011 [Code Sec. 30B(i)(4)]. Qualification is determined without regard to whether the vehicle was made by a manufacturer or whether the original use commenced with the taxpayer who is seeking the credit [Code Sec. 30B(i)(2)].

The plug-in conversion credit is equal to 10 percent of the cost of converting the vehicle, up to $40,000, for a maximum credit of $4,000. The plug-in conversion credit is treated as part of the alternative motor vehicle credit and may be claimed even if another alternative motor vehicle credit under Code Sec. 30B(a)(1) through Code Sec. 30B(a)(4) was claimed for the same motor vehicle in any preceding tax year [Code Sec. 30B(a)(5)].

In 2011, for purposes of the plug-in conversion credit, a qualified plug-in electric drive motor vehicle is a motor vehicle that:

a. Is propelled significantly by an electric motor drawing electricity from a battery with a capacity of at least 4 kilowatt hours,

b. Uses an external source of electricity to recharge such battery,

c. Has a gross vehicle weight rating of less than 14,000 pounds,

d. Is treated as a motor vehicle under title II of the Clean Air Act (a self-propelled vehicle designed for transporting persons or property on a street or highway), and

e. Is acquired for use or lease by the taxpayer and not for resale [Code Sec. 30B(i)(2)].

There is no recapture of the alternative motor vehicle credit if the property ceases to be eligible due to conversion to a qualified plug-in electric drive motor vehicle [Code Sec. 30B(h)(8)].

PAYMENT OF ESTIMATED TAX BY INDIVIDUALS

¶14,200 WHAT IS ESTIMATED TAX?

.01 Types and Amounts of Income Requiring Estimated Payments

The federal income tax system is often referred to as a "pay-as-you-go tax." This means that the IRS wants you to pay the tax as soon as taxable income is received. The IRS does not want to wait until April 15 (or later if you file for extensions) to receive the taxes the Service is owed. Estimated tax is the method used to prepay tax on income that is not subject to withholding. [For discussion of withholding, see Ch. 15].

.02 Payment Procedures

If you must make estimated tax payments, use Form 1040-ES payment vouchers. Each payment voucher has a date when the voucher is due for the calendar year. Except for the first-time filers, each voucher is preprinted by the IRS with your name, address, and social security number. When payment is due, you send the appropriate voucher and payment to the IRS Center listed in the instructions to the form.

¶14,205 WHO MUST MAKE ESTIMATED TAX PAYMENTS

Estimated income tax payments are used to provide for current payment of income taxes not collected through withholding. Estimated tax is the amount of income tax (including alternative minimum tax that the taxpayer anticipates owing, plus any self-employment tax, less any credits [Code Sec. 6654(g)].

.01 Situations Requiring Estimated Tax Payments

Individuals who have income that is not subject to withholding must pay estimated tax. Typically estimated tax is owed on the following types of income: income from self-employment, bonuses, commissions, interest, dividends, rents, royalties, alimony, and gains from the sale of assets, prizes, lottery winnings, and awards or any other type of payment where the payor has not withheld income tax at the source. Estimated tax is used to pay income tax as well as self-employment and alternative minimum tax.

Employers of domestic workers who fail to satisfy their obligations for FICA and FUTA withholding, through regular estimated tax payments or increased tax withholding from their own wages, may be subject to estimated tax penalties.

Consult the following chart to determine whether a taxpayer has to pay estimated tax.[64]

.02 Exceptions

There are two exceptions to the imposition of a penalty on underpayment of estimated taxes. An individual is not required to make quarterly payments if estimated tax liability (after amounts withheld and credit) for the current year is less than $1,000 [Code Sec. 6654(e)(1)]. In addition, no payments are required if a U.S. citizen or resident alien did not have any tax liability for the preceding tax year and that year was a full tax year [Code Sec. 6654(e)(2)]. Under circumstances of hardship or following an individual's retirement or disability, the penalty for failure to pay estimated tax may be waived [Code Sec. 6654(e)].

Criminal Penalty

If an addition to tax is assessed under Code Sec. 6654 for underpayment of estimated tax, the taxpayer may be liable for a criminal penalty under Code Sec. 7203 if the failure to pay the estimated tax was willful.

[64] Treas. Dept., IRS Publication 505, "Tax Withholding and Estimated Tax" (2013 Ed.), p. 24.

Figure 2-A. **Do You Have To Pay Estimated Tax?**

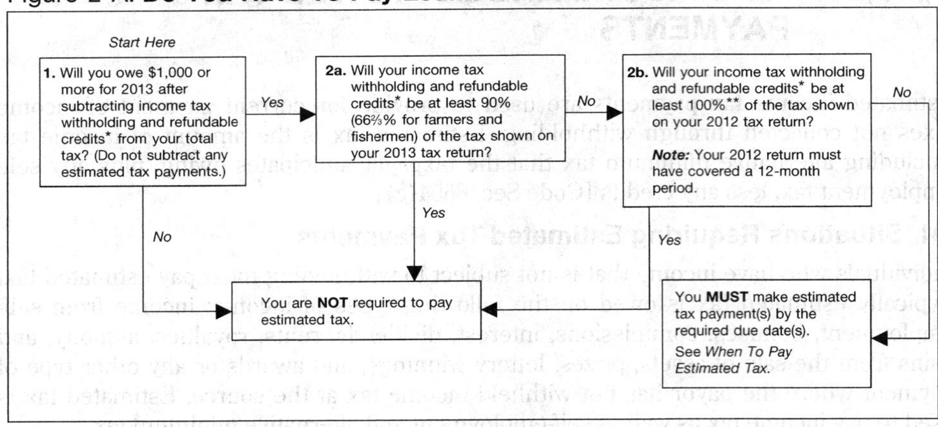

* Use the refundable credits shown on the 2013 Estimated Tax Worksheet, line 13b.

** 110% if less than two-thirds of your gross income for 2012 and 2013 is from farming or fishing and your 2012 adjusted gross income was more than $150,000 ($75,000 if your filing status for 2013 is married filing a separate return).

Example 14-16: In April 2014, Ms. Richards completes her income tax return for tax year 2013. She properly computes her tax liability to be $12,000 on an income of $72,000. Since her withholding this year was only $9,000, she still owes $3,000. Her tax liability last year was only $8,000, so Richards pays no penalty this year. Reason: Her withholding this year was more than 100 percent of the tax she paid last year. The $9,000 withholding amount she paid is treated as estimated tax payments made in four equal installments on the due date for each quarterly payment.

Example 14-17: In 2013, Richards expects to owe taxes of $15,000 on an adjusted gross income of $100,000. Halfway through the year, only $5,000 had been withheld from her pay, and she has made no estimated tax payments. At this rate, she will have to pay an underpayment penalty. Suppose, however, Richards increases her wage withholding so that by the end of the year, $15,000 has been withheld from her pay. Her withholding for the year equals 100 percent of her tax liability for the year. Withholding is treated as having been made in equal installments throughout the year. Thus, there is no penalty.

.03 Year-End Tax Planning To Avoid Penalty

If, toward the end of the year, you have underpaid estimated tax, you can increase the amount of wage withholding by claiming fewer allowances. If you already claim no allowances, you can request your employer to withhold an additional amount. The result: You can avoid the penalty for an underpayment that occurred earlier in the year.

¶14,210 WHEN TO PAY ESTIMATED TAX

A calendar-year taxpayer's first estimated tax payment (either in full or in an installment) is due for a current tax year when the calendar-year taxpayer files his or her income tax return for the prior year. Payment is sent with a payment-voucher included in the Form 1040-ES, *Estimated Tax for Individuals*. Payment due dates that apply for calendar-year taxpayers are detailed below. However, special payment due dates apply for farmers and fishermen and for fiscal year taxpayers.

.01 Estimated Tax Payment

You pay estimated tax in quarterly installments by filing the appropriate Form 1040-ES payment voucher with the IRS Service Center listed in the instructions to the form. The payment dates are as shown in Table 14 [Code Sec.6654(c)].

Table 14. Estimated Tax Payment Due Dates

Required installments	Required payment due dates
Jan. 1–March 31	April 15
April 1–May 31	June 15
June 1–Aug. 31	September 15
Sept. 1–Dec. 31	January 15 next year

If you must pay by April 15, you may pay the entire year's estimated tax then or pay 25 percent on each of these dates: April 15, June 15, Sept. 15 and the following Jan. 15. Your installment payments may be lowered if income is annualized, or if you base installment payments on the amount of your last year's tax [Code Sec. 6654(d)].

Keep in mind that if the payment due date falls on Saturday, Sunday, or legal holiday, the next business day is the due date of the estimated tax payment.

You may apply a credit for overpayment of your previous year's income tax against your current year's first installment or equally divide the credit among all the installments. You must elect to apply the overpayment against a later installment. You make the election by attaching a statement to the return showing the overpayment and indicating which installment it should be applied against. Also, you may elect to credit the overpayment to an estimated tax payment arising after the overpayment arose but before the election is made.[65]

> **Example 14-18:** Mr. Roberts makes an estimated tax payment of $10,000 for the year and receives an extension to file his return until August 15. When the return is filed on August 15, it shows a tax liability of only $8,000. Roberts may elect to credit the $2,000 overpayment to the April 15 estimated tax payment.

Return as Last Installment

Calendar-year taxpayers who first come within the estimated tax requirements after September 1, 2013, should make an estimated tax installment payment by January 15, 2014.

---

[65] Rev. Rul. 99-40, 1999-2 CB 441.

How to amend. You may use the Amended Estimated Tax Schedule on page 2 of Form 1040-ES instructions to figure if your estimated tax needs to be increased or decreased. You may pay the estimated tax, or the rest of the tax in equal installments on the remaining payment dates. If you make the amendment after September 15 of the tax year, your payment must be made by January 15 of the next year.

Example 14-19: Mr. Jones figures a 2014 estimated tax of $800 when he files his 2013 income tax return on April 15. Later, on September 15, 2013, he discovers that his estimated tax should be reduced by $150. The amount payable on January 15, 2013, will be $50, computed as follows:

1.	Amended estimated tax	$650
2.	Less estimated tax payments:	
	April 15, June 15, and September 15, at $200 each	600
3.	Unpaid balance	$ 50
4.	Amount to be paid on January 15, 2012	$ 50

How to Submit Estimated Tax Payments

There are three ways to make estimated tax payments:

1. Credit an overpayment on your tax return to next year's estimated tax;
2. Send in your payment with a payment-voucher from Form 1040-ES; or
3. Pay electronically using the Electronic Federal Tax Payment System (EFTPS).

.02 Special Terms for Certain Types of Taxpayers

Farmers and Fishermen

A special estimated tax rule is provided for farmers and fishermen in Code Sec. 6654(i)].[66] A taxpayer qualifies as a farmer or fisherman for the current tax year if at least two-thirds of the taxpayer's total gross income was from farming or fishing in either the prior or current tax year [Code Sec. 6654(i)(2)]. Under Code Sec. 6654(i)(1)(A), only one installment payment must be made farmers or fishermen. Under Code Sec. 6654(i)(1)(B), the installment is due on January 15 of the following tax year and qualifying farmers and fishermen who choose not to make the required estimated tax installment payment are not subject to an estimated tax addition to tax if they file their returns and pay the full amount of tax due by March 1 of the following tax year [Code Sec. 6654(i)(1)(D)].

Fiscal Year Taxpayers

Fiscal year taxpayers whose tax year does not start on January 1 substitute corresponding months in their fiscal year instead of those indicated for paying the installments by calendar year taxpayers.[67] If you are a fiscal year taxpayer your payment dates are:

- The 15th day of the 4th month of your fiscal year;
- The 15th day of the 6th month of your fiscal year;

[66] Notice 2013-5, IRB 2013-9, 529.

[67] Rev. Rul. 99-40, 1999-2 CB 441.

- The 15th day of the 9th month of your fiscal year; and
- The 15th day of the 1st month after the end of your fiscal year.

Thus, for a fiscal year starting July 1, the payment due dates are October 15, December 15, March 15th and July 15. The last payment need not be made if you file your income tax return by the last day of the first month after the end of your fiscal year and pay all the tax you owe with your return.

Example 14-20: Ms. Holt's fiscal year begins October 1. Her quarterly installment payment of estimated tax is due January 15, March 15, June 15, and October 15 of the following year.

Nonresident Aliens

An alien who must pay estimated tax uses Form 1040-ES (NR), U.S. Estimated Tax for Nonresident Alien Individuals.

¶14,215 HOW TO FIGURE ESTIMATED TAX

.01 General Calculation

In figuring your estimated tax payments, you must estimate your tax for the year and reduce it by estimated withholding and other credits against your tax. You should consider all available facts that will affect your income, deductions, and credits during the year. In estimating your tax before reducing it for estimated withholding and other credits, you may be able to use last year's tax (including self-employment and alternative minimum taxes), or annualize income. For the lowest amount of estimated taxes that must be paid to avoid penalties, see ¶14,220.

▶ **OBSERVATION:** You must be careful to make adjustments both for changes in your own situation and changes in the tax law. For example, changes in your personal life such as having a baby or buying a home will require you to adjust your withholding.

A worksheet is provided on Form 1040-ES for you to compute your estimated tax liability. Although you do not file the worksheet with the payment voucher, it is almost a necessity to figure your estimated tax.

.02 Figuring Your Adjusted Gross Income

- Compute your expected AGI for the year, which is your expected total income less your expected adjustments to income.
- Include in your total income everything you expect to receive during the year, even if it is subject to withholding. However, you can exclude income that is tax-exempt, like interest from municipals.
- Reduce your total income by adjustments you expect to take on your income tax return. These may include deductions for IRA or Keogh contributions. If you expect to have self-employment income, figure your self-employment tax first and then subtract half of it as an adjustment [Ch. 12].

¶14,220 PENALTY FOR UNDERPAYING ESTIMATED TAX

.01 General Penalty Terms

If estimated income taxes are underpaid by an individual, a penalty is imposed equal to the interest that would accrue on the underpayment for the period of the underpayment.

The penalty for not paying enough estimated tax is interest charged at the current underpayment rate. The penalty is based on the federal short-term interest rate plus three percentage points [Code Sec. 6621]. Because this rate is adjusted every calendar quarter, you calculate the penalty separately for each estimated tax installment. Normally, you would have to compound interest daily, but this would render the calculations extremely complex. A special exception allows you to ignore the compound interest requirement for the estimated tax penalty [Code Sec. 6622]. In addition to the interest charge, willful failure to pay estimated taxes is a misdemeanor punishable by the fine of $25,000 ($100,000 for corporations) or jail for not more than one year, or both. The penalty is not deductible and can be avoided if the amount of each required installment is 25 percent of your required annual payment.

The IRS has ruled that an individual who makes required annual estimated tax payments properly based on a late-filed return for a previous year won't have to pay an estimated tax underpayment penalty.[68]

The penalty can be avoided if the amount of each *required installment* is 25 percent of the *required annual payment*. For most taxpayers, the required annual payment is the lesser of:

- 90 percent of the tax shown on the current year's return (or if no return was filed, 90 percent of the tax for the year); or
- 100 percent of the tax shown on the preceding tax year's return (if the tax year consisted of 12 months and a return was filed for that year) [Code Sec. 6654(d)].

If your tax liability less withholding is under $1000, the penalty does not apply. Also you don't have a penalty for a current year's underpayment if you had no tax liability in the prior year and you were a U.S. citizen or resident for the entire year. The prior tax year must have been a 12-month period [Code Sec. 6654(e)].

Example 14-21: Adam, who is single and 24 years old, was unemployed for most of last year. He earned $3,100 in wages before he was laid off, and he received $3,000 in unemployment compensation. He had no other income. He did not have to pay income tax because his gross income was less than the filing requirement for a single person under age 65. He filed a return only to have his withheld income tax refunded to him. The following year he began a home improvement business. He made no estimated tax payments that year. Even though he did owe tax that year, Adam does not owe an underpayment penalty because he had no tax liability for the prior year.

[68] Rev. Rul. 2003-23, 2003-1 CB 511.

The year's withholdings are equally divided among the installment periods, unless you prove a different allocation, or unless more than one tax year begins in a calendar year [Code Sec. 6654(g)]. This allows you to adjust your withholding to avoid a penalty.

Example 14-22: Last year Smith paid income tax of $3,000. This year, his tax liability is $6,000. He paid no estimated tax to cover this year's tax bill and plans to pay the tax when he files the return on April 15. Smith's underpayment penalty for each required installment is computed on 25 percent of the lesser of: 10 percent of the tax shown on this year's return (90 percent × $6,000) or 100 percent of last year's tax bill ($3,000). Thus, the underpayment penalty is figured on $750 (25 percent of $3,000) for each required installment. A separate computation of any penalty must be made for each installment due date. This is because the interest rate that determines the penalty fluctuates quarterly.

.02 Estimated Tax Penalty Safe Harbor

An individual is generally subject to the penalty on the difference between the tax payments (including withholding) made by the installment due date and the lesser of the following:

1. The installment amount due based on 90 percent of the tax shown on the current tax year's return (if no return is filed for the tax year, 90 percent of the actual tax liability for the year),
2. For a taxpayer with adjusted gross income of $150,000 ($75,000 for married taxpayer filing separately) or less, the installment amount due based on 100 percent of the tax shown on the return for the preceding tax year, if such year was a full tax year,
3. For a taxpayer with adjusted gross income of more than $150,000 in the *preceding* year, the installment amount due based on 110 percent of the tax shown on the return for the preceding tax year, if such year was a full tax year,
4. The installment amount based on 90 percent of the tax as computed by placing the taxpayer's taxable income for the months of the tax year prior to the due date on an annualized basis [Code Sec. 6654(d)].

Example 14-23: Taxpayer filed a 2012 income tax return, for a full tax year, showing a tax of $10,000 on adjusted gross income exceeding $150,000. Taxpayer figures that in 2013 his income will remain the same, but his tax will increase to $16,000. He also estimates that the total amount of income tax that will be withheld from his 2013 income will be $12,000. Since his estimated tax will be at least $1,000, he should compare the amount of tax to be withheld in 2013, $12,000, with the lesser of (1) 90 percent of the tax to be shown on his 2013 return or (2) 110 percent of the tax shown on his 2011 return. Taxpayer will not meet the 90-percent test because $14,400 (90 percent of $16,000) is more than the $12,000 expected to be withheld during 2013. However, he will meet the 110-percent test because the $12,000 tax expected to be withheld in 2013 is more than 110 percent of his $10,000 tax on last year's return. As a result, Taxpayer need not make estimated tax payments for 2013.

Example 14-24: If, in Example 14-23 above, Taxpayer estimates that only $9,000 would be withheld for 2013, his estimated tax for 2013 would be $7,000 ($16,000 minus $9,000). He should make estimated tax payments for 2013 because his estimated tax will be at least $1,000 and the amount to be withheld, $9,000, is less than 110 percent of the tax shown on his 2012 return and less than 90 percent of the $16,000 tax expected to be shown on his 2013 return. For 2013, Taxpayer must make estimated tax payments totaling $2,000 to bring his total payment for 2013 up to the $11,000 required under the prior-year's-tax test. Payments of $500 should be made by each installment due date for 2013.

Taxpayers who discover that they are falling short of the estimated tax safe harbors can avoid the penalty by: (1) completing a new Form W-4 requesting that the employer increase tax withholding during the remainder of the year or (2) making larger estimated tax payments.

.03 Married Taxpayers Filing Separate Returns

For purposes of claiming the credit for estimated tax paid, if a married couple makes separate estimated tax payments and files separate returns, each may take a credit only for his or her own payments. If they make joint estimated tax payments, but subsequently file separate returns, they must decide how to divide the payments between them. One may claim all of the estimated tax paid and the other none, or they may divide it in any other way on which they agree. If they cannot agree, they must then divide the payments in proportion to each spouse's individual tax as shown on their separate returns.

.04 Estimated Tax Installments Based on Annualized Income

If your income fluctuates unevenly throughout the year, a special rule allows you to make payments of less than 25 percent of your estimated tax liability in those periods when your income is at a peak. The rule is called the annualized income method of computing estimated tax. Use of the annualized income installment method, provided on a worksheet contained in the instructions to Form 2210, *Underpayment of Estimated Tax by Individuals, Estates and Trusts*, may reduce or eliminate the penalty that would otherwise be due. The total amount of installments for the year should equal 90 percent of your estimated tax liability (66⅔ percent for farmers and fishermen). However, your payments can be weighted toward the end of the year. The computations include self-employment and alternative minimum taxes, in addition to regular income tax.

Your first step is to annualize income up to the month each installment is due. To annualize income, you multiply your taxable income to the end of the period covered by the installment (figured without deducting personal exemptions) by 12, divide by the number of months from the beginning of the tax year to the end of the installment period, and subtract personal exemptions to which you are entitled on the installment due date. The payment on the due date for the current year's first installment must equal or exceed 22.5 percent of the tax figured on the annualized income. For succeeding installments, payments must be at least 45 percent, 67.5 percent, and 90 percent of the annualized tax [Code Sec. 6654(d)].

Example 14-25: Mr. Jones is married and files a joint tax return. He claims three exemptions and has no alternative minimum tax liability. He chooses to annualize income to pay estimated tax.

1.	Wages received during Jan.-Mar.		$ 5,000
2.	Actual adjusted gross income		$ 5,000
3.	Annualized adjusted gross income [$5,000 × 4]		$20,000
4.	Less: Itemized deductions [$2,000 × 4 = $8,000]		
	Exemptions [3 × $3,200]	9,600	17,600
5.	Annualized taxable income		$ 2,400
6.	Tax at 10 percent		$ 240

If Jones' withholding through March and estimated tax payment for the 1st installment period are at least $54 (22.5 percent of $240), he does not owe a penalty for that period.

Alternative Minimum Taxable Income; Self-Employment Income

To annualize for the alternative minimum tax, you add the annualized preferences to the annualized adjusted gross income. You add or subtract annualized adjustments. Then you deduct your allowable annualized alternative minimum tax itemized deductions and your exemption to arrive at your annualized alternative minimum taxable income. Self-employment income is annualized for the period covered by the installment in the same way as taxable income and alternative minimum taxable income.

Lower Required Installments

If you figure your estimated tax by annualizing income, each installment payment may be the lesser of: the required installment (90 percent × current year's estimated tax divided by 4) or the annualized income installment. If the annualized income installment for the payment period is less than the required installment, you only need to pay the annualized income installment [Code Sec. 6654(d)(2)].

Recapture. If you pay the annualized income installment, you must add your savings for that payment period (the difference between the amount you pay and the required installment) to the required installment for the next payment period. If you also pay only the annualized income installment for the later payment period, you must add your savings for that later period (the difference between the required installment for that payment period (as increased) and the annualized income installment for that period) to the required installment for the next payment period [Code Sec. 6654(d)].

Example 14-26: Mr. Lee estimates that his taxable income for next year will be from wages subject to withholding and a gain on a sale of a parcel of land that he expects to sell in August. He estimates the tax to be $8,000; His tax bill last year was $7,400. Based on these estimates, the required annual payment for next year's tax bill is $7,200. This is the lesser of: $7,200 ($8,000 × 90 percent) or $7,400 (last year's tax bill). The required installment for each pay period is $1,800 ($7,200 × 25 percent). He also estimates withheld taxes of $4,000 ($1,000 allocated to each payment period due date). For payment periods, he figures the tax on the annualized income for the 1st and 2nd periods will be $6,000; 3rd, $9,000 and 4th, $8,000. Lee's payments for the year will total $7,200 [$1,350 + $1,350 + $2,700 + $1,800] computed as follows:

Required annual payment:	
Lesser of: $7,200 ($8,000 × 90%) or $7,400 (last year's tax bill)	$7,200
Required installment for each pay period:	
($7,200 × 25%)	$1,800
1st payment period:	
Annualized income installment:	
($6,000 × 22.5%)	$1,350
Withholding for 1st period	1,000
Payment required	$ 350
2nd payment period:	
Required installment:	
($1,800 + $450, difference between $1,800 and $1,350 installment payment for 1st period)	$2,250
Annualized income installment:($6,000 × 45% = $2,700 – $1,350, tax paid, 1st period)	$1,350
Less:Withheld tax, 2nd period	1,000
Payment required	$ 350
3rd payment period:	
Required installment:	
($1,800 + $900, difference between $2,250 and $1,350 installment payment for 2nd period)	$2,700
Annualized income installment:	
($9,000 × 67.5% = $6,075 less $2,700 installment payments for 1st and 2nd periods)	$3,375
This is more than the required installment (as increased) Less:Withheld tax, 3rd period	1,000
Payment required	$1,700
4th payment period:	
Required installment (no increase) ($7,200 × 25%)	$1,800
Annualized income installment [$7,200 ($8,000 × 90%) less $5,400, (prior payments)]	$1,800
Less:Withheld tax, 4th period	1,000
Payment required	$ 800

▶ **OBSERVATION:** Annualization usually necessitates an amendment of prior tax computations for the year. It is most useful when the larger part of a taxpayer's income is received in the latter part of the year.

▶ **TAX RETURN TIP:** You must make computations relating to the penalty on Form 2210. You should attach it to the return for any underpayment and a reliance on an exception. However, you need not file this form if your withholding plus estimated tax payments equal or exceed 100 percent (or 110 percent) of your preceding year's tax (assuming you can use that safe harbor) or if you owed no tax for the preceding year. IRS computers are programmed to compute the amounts due.

▶ **OBSERVATION:** To calculate the amount of estimated tax due, you use either the appropriate tax table or tax rate schedule, whichever is most advantageous.[69]

.05 How the Penalty Is Applied

You figure the current underpayment penalty [Ch. 27] separately for each installment. The penalty is applied to the difference between the amount you actually paid (including withheld taxes) and the amount that you should have paid if the estimated tax were the lesser of: 90 percent (66²/3 percent for farmers and fishermen) of the amount shown on the final return, or 100 percent (or 110 percent) of the tax shown on your preceding tax year's return (assuming you can use that safe harbor) [Code Sec. 6654(b), (d)]. The charge runs from date of the installment until you pay the amount or until the filing date of the tax return, whichever is earlier.

Underpayment

This is the excess of your required installment (or, if it is lower, your annualized income installment) for a payment period over the portion of the amount you paid by the due date that is not applied to an underpayment for an earlier payment period.

How underpayments are applied. You figure the period of underpayment by applying estimated tax payments to any underpayments on earlier installments in the order in which such installments were required to be paid.

Figuring the penalty. The penalty for the first period of underpayment is figured on the total underpayment for the payment period. Later periods of underpayment for that payment period is from the day after an applied payment to the date of the next applied payment or April 15 of the following year, whichever is earlier. The penalty for each of the later periods of underpayment will be figured on the balance of the underpayment for the payment period as of the beginning of each later period of underpayment.

To figure your penalty for a payment period with more than one period of underpayment, figure a penalty amount separately for each of the periods of underpayment using the number of days in each period of underpayment, the correct underpayment balance, and the appropriate penalty rates [Ch. 27].

Overpayment

If you overpay an installment, you carry the overpayment to the next period and add it to your withholding and estimated tax payment for that later period.

---

69 Rev. Proc. 83-79, 1983-2 CB 597.

In addition to the interest charge, willful failure to pay estimated taxes is a misdemeanor punishable by a fine of $25,000 ($100,000 for corporations), or jail for not more than one year, or both [Code Sec. 7203].

.06 Waiver of Penalty

A limited waiver of the penalty applies if the IRS determines that the underpayment is due to casualty, disaster, or other unusual circumstance and if denying the waiver would be against equity and good conscience. The IRS can also waive the penalty for reasonable cause during the first two years after you reach age 62 or become disabled [Code Sec. 6654(e)(3)].

BACKUP WITHHOLDING

The main purpose of backup withholding on interest, dividends, and certain other payments is to make sure that you report all taxable income on your tax returns.

¶14,225 BACKUP WITHHOLDING ON INTEREST, DIVIDENDS, AND CERTAIN OTHER PAYMENTS

Payers of interest, dividends, and other specified payments for which information reporting is required (reportable payments) must apply backup withholding to those payments if the payee does not furnish a correct taxpayer identification number. Backup withholding also applies if the IRS notifies a payer to begin withholding because a payee underreported reportable payments or if a payee fails to certify that he or she is not subject to backup withholding after the IRS notifies the payer of underreporting. Withholding requirements apply to other types of payments, including gambling winnings, pension, and retirement distributions, and distributions of Indian gaming profits. In addition, taxpayers can enter into voluntary agreements to have withholding apply to some payments, including social security and unemployment benefits, payments from employers that are not treated as wages, eligible rollover distributions, and some types of government payments. A payee can use Form W-9 to certify that taxpayer identification number be provided, that payee is not subject to withholding for notified payee underreporting, or that payee is exempt from backup withholding. A payee subject to backup withholding for underreporting can seek IRS determination to stop backup withholding.

.01 Backup Withholding Requirements

Banks, businesses and other payors of dividends, interest, and certain other *reportable payments* must pay backup withholding at a rate of 28 percent (fourth lowest tax rate in effect in 2013) [Code Sec. 3406(a)(1)].[70]

Backup withholding is made by deducting and withholding income tax from payments made to payees in the following four situations:

---

[70] Announcement 2003-45, 2003-2 CB 73.

- *A Trigger*—The payee failed to furnish the payor a TIN (Taxpayer Identification Number) [Code Sec. 3406(a)(1)(A); Ch. 26];
- *B Trigger*—The IRS notified the payee that the TIN furnished to them by the payor was incorrect [Code Sec. 3406(a)(1)(B)];
- *C Trigger*—The IRS notified the payor to start backup withhold on interest or dividends because the payee did not report or underreported interest or dividends on his or her tax return (but only after at least 4 notices are given over a 120-day period, see below) [Code Sec. 3406(a)(1)(C); Code Sec. 3406(c)(1)(B)]; and
- *D Trigger*—The payor failed to certify that the payee was exempt from backup withholding [Code Sec. 3406(a)(1)(D)].

Banks or other businesses that pay taxpayers interest and dividends give recipients Form W-9 so they can report and certify TINs or to enable eligible payees to claim an exemption from withholding [Code Sec. 3406(a), (b)]. TINs must be provided under penalties of perjury only for payments of interest, dividends, patronage dividends and payments subject to broker reporting [Code Sec. 3406(e)(1)].

C Trigger—Withholding After Notification of Underreporting from IRS

The C trigger listed above requires a payor to withhold on reportable interest or dividend payments if the payee has failed to report and pay tax on interest and dividends and the IRS or a broker has notified the payor of this fact. If a payor receives notice from a broker, the payor is required only to withhold on accounts identified by the broker [Reg. § 31.3406(c)-1(c)(3)(i)(B)].

After receipt of the notice from the IRS concerning payee underreporting, the payor must exercise reasonable care to identify all existing accounts of the payee so that withholding commences on these accounts. The payor is permitted to search any computer or other recordkeeping system for the region, division or branch that serves the geographic area where the payee's mailing address is located and that is established or maintained to reflect reportable interest payments [Reg. § 31.3406(c)-1(c)(3)(ii)]. New accounts are typically not subject to backup withholding if the payee provides the payor with a Form W-9 (or an acceptable substitute) stating that the payee is not subject to withholding. An exception to this rule exists if the payor knows or has reason to know that the payee statement on the form is untrue [Reg. § 31.3406(c)-1(c)(3)(iii)].

Notice to Payees

The payor is required to notify the payee that withholding due to underreporting has started. The payor must send the notice within 15 days after the date that the payor makes the first payment subject to withholding [Reg. § 31.3406(c)-1(d)]. The IRS has set forth specific rules concerning the form, content, and manner of delivery of a notice that a payor must send to a payee or broker.[71] If the IRS notifies the payor of an incorrect TIN, the payor must promptly, within the 30 days before withholding, notify the payee. The payor must also notify the IRS if a new TIN is furnished by the payee [Code Sec. 3406 (c)(4), (d)(2), (e)(2), (h)(8), (9)]. The payor should then begin withholding with payments made after the thirtieth day after the date notification is received from the IRS.

---

[71] Rev. Proc. 93-37, 1993-2 CB 477.

The withholding will remain in effect until January 1 of the following year if, before the preceding December 2, the IRS notified the payor and the payee that the backup withholding was no longer required. The IRS must provide these notices to all payees by October 15 [Code Sec. 3406(c)(3)(C)].

.02 When Does Backup Withholding Begin?

Payors can begin backup withholding usually within 30 days after they are notified by the IRS. However, in most cases of underreporting of interest and dividends, it cannot begin until the IRS sends at least four notices to you over a 120-day period. Also, special rules apply for the period for starting and stopping withholding. For example, a payor may elect to begin or stop withholding on shorter notice than 30 days if the IRS determined actual underreporting of any reportable interest and dividends. A 60-day exemption applies if you sign a certification that you are awaiting a TIN [Code Sec. 3406(c)(1)-(5), (e)(5)].

.03 Payments Subject to Backup Withholding

Backup withholding applies to most types of payments that are reported on Form 1099s. These include:

- Interest payments reported on Form 1099-INT [Code Sec. 3406(b)(1)(A)];
- Dividends reported on Form 1099-DIV [Code Sec. 3406(b)(1)(A)];
- Patronage dividends (but only if at least one half of the payment is in money) reported on Form 1099-PATR [Code Sec. 3406(b)(2)(A)(iii)];
- Rents, profits, or other gains reported on Form 1099-MISC;
- Royalty payments reported on Form 1099-MISC;
- Commissions, fees, or other payments for work performed by an independent contractor, reported on Form 1099-MISC;
- Payments by brokers reported on Form 1099-B; and
- Payments by fishing boat operators, but only the part that is in money and that represents a share of the proceeds of the catch, reported on Form 1099-MISC) [Code Sec. 3406(b)(3)(D)].
- Payments that must be reported on an information return under Code Sec. 6041, relating to payments of $600 or more made in the course of business to another person [Code Sec. 3406(b)(3)(A)];
- Payments of remuneration for services of a kind that are required to be reported on an information return (Form 1099-MISC) under Code Sec. 6041A(a) [Code Sec. 3406(b)(3)(B)];
- Gross proceeds on transactions required to be reported by a broker or barter exchange on an information return (Form 1099-B) under Code Sec. 6045 [Code Sec. 3406(b)(3)(C)];
- Payments of royalties aggregating $10 or more in a calendar year to be reported pursuant to Code Sec. 6050N [Code Sec. 3406(b)(3)(E)]; and
- Payments made after December 31, 2011, in settlement of payment card transactions [Code Sec. 3406(b)(3)(F)].

.04 Payees and Payments Exempt From Backup Withholding

The following payees are exempt from backup withholding [Code Sec. 3406(g)(1)]:

- A tax-exempt organization, an individual retirement plan, or a custodial account established under Code Sec. 403(b)(7);
- The United States or any of its agencies or instrumentalities;
- A state, the District of Columbia, a possession of the United States, or any of their subdivisions or instrumentalities;
- A foreign government, or any of its political subdivisions, agencies or instrumentalities; [Code Secs. 3406 (g)(1)(A), 6049(b)(4)]
- An international organization or any of its agencies or instrumentalities.
- *Payees awaiting TINs.* Payees awaiting receipt of their TIN will be exempt from backup withholding for a period of up to 60 days [Reg. § 31.3406(g)-3(a)(1]. Once the payee has received the TIN, the taxpayer will be required to furnish it to all payors in a timely manner, or backup withholding will commence;
- *Beneficiaries of estates and trusts.* A beneficiary of a trust or estate is only subject to backup withholding if the trust or estate is a payor of a reportable payment. This means that backup withholding applies only to payments that must be reported on an information return. [For further discussion of information returns, see Ch. 26]; and
- *Foreign persons.* Payments of interest made to foreign persons are generally not subject to information reporting and therefore these payees are not subject to backup withholding [Reg. § 1.1441-1(b)(1)].

The following payments are exempt from backup withholding:

- Interest, dividend and broker or barter payments of not more than $10 [Reg. § 31.3406(b)(4)-1];
- Taxable dividends pursuant to Code Sec. 302 [Reg. § 31.3406(b)(2)-4(b)(1)];
- Amounts relating to the disposition of certain stock pursuant to Code Sec. 306 [Reg. § 31.3406(b)(2)-4(b)(1)];
- Additional consideration paid in connection with certain reorganizations pursuant to Code Sec. 356 [Reg. § 31.3406(b)(2)-4(b)(1)];
- Certain distributions ordered by the Securities and Exchange Commission because of Code Sec. 1081(e)(2) [Reg. § 31.3406(b)(2)-4(b)(1)];
- Exempt-interest dividends paid by a regulated investment company, as defined in Code Sec. 852(b)(5)(A) [Reg. § 31.3406(b)(2)-4(b)(2)];
- Net commissions paid to an unincorporated special insurance agent [Reg. § 31.3406(b)(3)-1(b)(2)];
- Distributions from an IRA annuity [Reg. § 31.3406(g)-2(c)(2)];
- Distributions from an owner-employer plan [Reg. § 31.3406(g)-2(c)(3)];
- Distributions from a pension, annuity, profit-sharing, stock bonus plan, or other plan deferring the receipt of compensation [Reg. § 31.3406(g)-2(c)(1)];
- Certain surrenders of a life insurance contract [Reg. § 33.3406(g)-2(c)(4)]; and

- Foreign source interest payments made on deposits outside the U.S. by foreign branches of U.S. banks to U.S. persons [Reg. § 1.1441-1(b)(4)].

.05 Penalties

Civil and criminal penalties are imposed for giving false information to avoid backup withholding. The civil penalty is $500. The criminal penalty is a $1,000 maximum fine plus imprisonment for up to one year [Code Sec. 7205(b)].

.06 Relief in Cases of Undue Hardship

The IRS has the authority to stop, or not start, backup withholding for notified payee underreporting where withholding would cause undue hardship to the payee and it is unlikely that such underreporting will occur again [Code Sec. 3406(c)(3)]. The following factors determine whether withholding will cause undue hardship under Reg. § 31.3406(c)-(1)(g)(6):

- Whether the backup withholding, when combined with other withholding and estimated tax payments, would result in significant overwithholding;
- Whether the payee's health, including his ability to pay foreseeable medical expenses as a result of the withholding, would be affected;
- Whether the payee relies upon the interest and dividend income to meet his necessary living expenses;
- Whether the payee's income is fixed or limited;
- Whether the payee can liquidate other assets, such as stocks and bonds, to meet his living expenses and the resulting consequences;
- Whether the payee had reported and timely paid his most recent year's tax liability (including interest and dividend income); and
- Whether the payee has filed a bankruptcy petition.

Innocent Spouse Relief

The backup withholding provisions will apply to both husband and wife if underreporting is found on a joint return. Both spouses will be subject to backup withholding on accounts in their individual names as well as on joint accounts [Reg. § 31.3406(c)-1(h)]. A spouse who files a joint return on which underreported interest is determined may protect his or her accounts from backup withholding by establishing that: (1) he or she is an innocent spouse, or (2) there is a bona fide dispute as to whether he or she is an innocent spouse. [Reg. § 31.3406(c)-1(h)(2)(i)]. For further discussion of innocent spouse relief, see ¶ 26,006.

Income Tax Withholding, Employment and Net Investment Income Tax

FEDERAL INCOME TAX WITHHOLDING

Purpose of withholding . . . . ¶ 15,001
Who must withhold? . . . . ¶ 15,005
Who is subject to withholding? . . ¶ 15,010
Wages subject to withholding . . . . ¶ 15,015
How to figure withholding . . . . . . ¶ 15,020
Withholding allowances . . . . ¶ 15,025
Withholding allowance certificate, Form W-4 . . . . ¶ 15,030
Withholding tax on pensions, annuities, and other deferred income . . . . ¶ 15,040
Income tax withholding and nonresident aliens . . . . ¶ 15,045

SOCIAL SECURITY (FICA) TAXES

Tax on wages . . . . ¶ 15,050
Covered employment . . . . ¶ 15,055
Exempt employment . . . . ¶ 15,060
Partially covered employment . . . ¶ 15,065
Employer-employee relationship . . . . ¶ 15,070
Wages subject to FICA . . . . ¶ 15,075
Payments not taxed as wages . . . . ¶ 15,080
Federal Self-Employment Contributions Act (SECA) taxes . . . . . . ¶ 15,085
What is self-employment? . . . . ¶ 15,090
Self-employment income . . . . ¶ 15,095
Special rules for certain forms of self-employment income . . . . ¶ 15,105

FEDERAL AND STATE UNEMPLOYMENT TAXES

Tax on employers under the Federal Unemployment Tax Act (FUTA) . . . . ¶ 15,110
FUTA tax credits . . . . ¶ 15,115
Returns and payment of tax . . . . . ¶ 15,120
Employer's records . . . . ¶ 15,125

PAYROLL TAX RETURNS, DEPOSITS, RECORDS, AND REFUNDS

General obligations . . . . ¶ 15,130

WITHHELD INCOME TAX REPORTING REQUIREMENTS

How employer reports and pays tax . . . . ¶ 15,135
Statement to employees, Form W-2 . . . . ¶ 15,140
Withholding adjustments . . . . ¶ 15,145
Record retention . . . . ¶ 15,150
Refunds and credits . . . . ¶ 15,155
Penalties . . . . ¶ 15,160

EMPLOYMENT TAX REFUNDS AND ADJUSTMENTS

How to make adjustments . . . . ¶ 15,165

NET INVESTMENT INCOME TAX

Overview of Net Investment Income Tax . . . . ¶ 15,170

Employers are subject to a complex array of payroll taxes and withholding requirements. These provisions grow more numerous each year, as the federal and state governments place increasing emphasis on the taxation of employee benefits to raise revenues. Payroll taxes are also becoming more expensive to employers, as the social security taxable wage base escalates, and new penalties for filing errors and nonpayment of tax proliferate. This chapter explains the employer's duties in regard to withholding of federal income tax, collection and payment of social security taxes, and federal and state unemployment tax payments. There are strong similarities among these various taxes as to their definitions of employee and wages, but separate treatments of each have been provided due to numerous exceptions and special rules. Recordkeeping requirements, payroll tax deposit and return procedures, and practical suggestions for keeping the employment tax bill to a minimum are also included.

FEDERAL INCOME TAX WITHHOLDING

¶ 15,001 PURPOSE OF WITHHOLDING

Employers are required to withhold federal income taxes from their employees' wages in amounts determined by each employee's withholding allowance certificate and government withholding tax tables [Code Sec. 3402(a)]. Neither employer nor employee can claim an income tax deduction for amounts of federal income tax withheld. However, the withheld tax is credited against the total tax due. The withheld sums must be paid to the IRS on a quarterly basis. An employer who fails to pay taxes withheld from its employees' wages is liable for the unpaid taxes. Liability for unpaid taxes extends to any "responsible person" required to collect, truthfully account for, and pay over any withheld tax. A taxpayer who willfully fails to do so will be liable for a penalty equal to the total amount of the tax evaded, or not collected, or not accounted for and paid over [Code Sec. 6672(a)]. A "'person' . . . includes an officer or employee of a corporation . . . who . . . is under a duty to perform the act in respect of which the violation occurs." Code Sec. 6671(b). Thus, an employee may be liable under Code Sec. 6672(a) if he (1) is a person who is "required to collect, truthfully account for, [or] pay over" the taxes (a responsible person), and (2) willfully fails to do so. See ¶ 15,160 for further discussion.

¶ 15,005 WHO MUST WITHHOLD?

Employers who pay wages to employees must withhold income tax from the wages paid, in an amount determined according to the formula or tables at ¶ 15,020.

.01 Employers

Employers required to withhold income tax from wages paid to employees include individuals, partnerships, estates, trusts, trustees in bankruptcy,[1] corporations, and unincorporated organizations. Churches, colleges and organizations that are themselves exempt from income tax must withhold from employees, as must the governments of the United States, Puerto Rico, the District of Columbia, states, cities, school districts and other political subdivisions, instrumentalities, and agencies [Code Sec. 3401(d); Reg. § 31.3401(d)-1].

The employer's representatives, for the most part, handle the mechanical details of withholding. When a corporate employer has branch offices, the branch manager or other representative may actually perform the duties of the employer. A payroll processing firm may be engaged to deduct taxes and prepare paychecks, but the legal responsibility for withholding and paying tax still rests with the employer [Reg. § 31.3403-1].

.02 Persons Controlling Wage Payments

Persons other than the actual employer may be required or permitted to withhold tax.

- If the person for whom an individual performs services does not have control of the wage payments, then the person having control must withhold [Code Sec. 3401(d)(1); Reg. § 31.3401(d)-1(f)]. Most often, bonding companies or sureties are not liable for the withholding taxes of the insured contractor. For example, a bonding company furnished funds with which to meet a contractor's payroll by giving the bank on each payday a draft to cover the payroll. The bonding company was held not liable for the withholding tax;[2]
- One who pays wages for a nonresident alien individual, foreign partnership, or foreign corporation not engaged in a trade or business within the U.S., is considered an employer even though the services are not performed for him [Code Sec. 3401(d)(2); Reg. § 31.3401(d)-1(e)]. See also ¶ 15,045;
- Fiduciaries, agents, and others who have control over or who pay employees' wages may perform the employer's duties when authorized by the IRS [Code Sec. 3504; Reg. § 31.3504-1(a)]; and
- Lenders, sureties, or other persons who pay wages directly to employees of another are liable to the U.S. for withholding taxes related to these wages plus interest. In addition, any creditor who lends money knowing that the loan will be used to meet payroll is subject to a limited liability [Code Sec. 3505(b)].[3]

Employee leasing companies will be considered employers for payroll tax purposes and will be responsible to withhold tax on employee income and to collect and remit payroll taxes to the U.S.[4]

Regulations clarify the tax liability of lenders, sureties, and other third parties that lend funds for wages of employees either directly or through the account of the

---

[1] *W. Otte*, SCt, 74-2 USTC ¶ 9822, 419 US 43, 95 SCt 247.

[2] *Firemen's Fund Indemnity Co.*, CA-9, 54-1 USTC ¶ 49,026, 210 F2d 472.

[3] Rev. Proc. 78-13, 1978-1 CB 591, as corrected by Announcement 78-136, IRB 1978-38, 16.

[4] *Total Employment Company, Inc.*, DC-FL, 2004-1 USTC ¶ 50,177, 305 BR 333.

employer [Reg. § 31.3505-1]. Code Sec. 3505(b) states that the third party providing funds for an employee's wages is liable to pay the withholding tax, along with interest that is not paid by the employer. The lender's liability for the withholding taxes is limited to an amount equal to 25 percent of the amount of wages supplied for the employer's account. The regulations state that the third party will be liable to pay the interest in addition to the withholding tax, but only to an overall maximum of 25 percent of the amount of the funds supplied by the lender. The regulations conform to judicial interpretation[5] and clarify that interest will continue to be computed in addition to any withholding tax liability, but only to an overall maximum of 25 percent of the amount of the funds supplied by the lender. The period of limitations for collection of the withholding taxes and interest is ten years [Code Sec. 6502(a); Reg. § 31.3505-1(d)(1)].

¶15,010 WHO IS SUBJECT TO WITHHOLDING?

Employers must withhold employees' income tax only if the legal relationship of employer-employee exists for the services for which the compensation is paid [¶ 15,070]. It is not necessary that the services be continuing at the time that the wages are paid [Reg. § 31.3401(d)-1(b)]. Thus, for example, employers who pay wages to former employees on January 16, for services the latter performed during the week of January 5-9, when the employer-employee relationship existed, must withhold the tax when the wages are paid.

.01 Who Are Employees?

An employer-employee relationship exists if the person for whom services are performed has the right to control and direct the individual who performs the services [¶ 15,070]. This control must extend not only to the result to be accomplished by the work, but also to the details and means by which that result is accomplished. Employers do not have to actually direct or control the way the services are performed; it is enough if they have the right to do so.

The IRS has drawn a distinction between skilled professionals and other workers. Professionals can be deemed subject to a company's control even when they rely on their own expertise and knowledge to get the job done. In a private ruling, the IRS categorized a professional as an employee simply because the company had general control over the way the professional performed his job.[6]

Types of Employees

Managers, officers, directors. No distinction is made for withholding purposes between classes or grades of employees. However, a corporate officer is an employee, but a director of a corporation in his or her capacity as such is not. Withholding, therefore, is required on officers' salaries, but not on directors' fees [Reg. § 31.3401(c)-1(f)].

---

[5] *Metro Constr. Co.*, CA-9, 79-2 USTC ¶ 9530, 602 F2d 879; *Intercontinental Ind., Inc.*, CA-6, 81-1 USTC ¶ 9129, 635 F2d 1215; *Hannan Co.*, 639 F2d 284.

[6] LTR 9201001 (Sept. 24, 1991).

Minors, students. Minors are treated the same as other employees. For example, tax is withheld from the wages of students working during vacation, even if they will not earn enough to pay income tax (unless they file proper certificates (Form W-4) to claim exempt status [¶ 15,025]); see ¶ 15,060 for newspaper carriers under 18.

Partners. If an employer-employee relationship in fact exists, it does not matter that the employee is called a partner [Reg. § 31.3401(c)-1(e)].

Substitutes who are properly working in place of regular employees are considered employees for purposes of withholding.[7]

Unlawful business. An individual performing services in an illegal activity for wages may nonetheless be an employee.[8]

.02 Self-Employed Persons

Individuals who are in fact partners, independent contractors, or sole proprietors of a business are not subject to withholding on their drawings or earnings in such capacities.

Examples of self-employed persons include:

> auctioneers, contractors, subcontractors, dentists, doctors, freelance professional models,[9] lawyers, off-duty police officers performing security work outside the scope of their employment,[10] public stenographers, veterinarians, and others who follow an independent trade, business, or profession, in which they offer their services to the public [Reg. § 31.3401(c)-1(c)].

Direct sellers and real estate agents are classified as self-employeds if:

- Substantially all of their income for services as real estate agents or direct sellers are directly related to sales or other output;
- Their services are performed under a written contract that calls for them not to be treated as employees for tax purposes [Code Sec. 3508].

So-called statutory employees (a hybrid between employees and independent contractors) are treated like employees for FICA taxes. But the IRS has said that statutory employees, which include such workers as truck drivers, newspaper distributors and carriers, insurance salespeople, and outside salespeople, are not employees for income tax purposes and are not subject to income tax withholding [¶ 15,060, ¶ 15,070].[11]

A special formula is provided to compute an employer's liability for failure to withhold income taxes or the employee's share of FICA taxes in certain situations involving worker reclassification by the IRS [Code Sec. 3509].

> ▶ **TAX ALERT:** An employer will not be held liable for employment taxes (FICA, FUTA, or income tax withholding) if there is a reasonable basis for treating an individual as self-employed. To get this special break, the employer must file all required federal returns, including information returns, on a basis consistent

[7] Rev. Rul. 70-438, 1970-2 CB 231.

[8] Rev. Rul. 60-77, 1960-1 CB 386.

[9] Rev. Rul. 71-144, 1971-1 CB 285. But see Rev. Rul. 74-332, 1974-2 CB 327 (where models supervised by agency).

[10] *C. Specks*, 104 TCM 746, Dec. 59,283(M), TC Memo. 2012-343.

[11] Rev. Rul. 90-93, 1990-2 CB 33.

with treatment of the worker as self-employed. The employer (or the employer's predecessor) must not have treated any worker in a substantially similar position as an employee. However, this relief is not available for any arrangement employers may have for services provided to them by certain technical personnel, such as engineers, computer programmers, and systems analysts. In these cases, the employment relationship between the business and the technical service specialist will be determined under the common law rules[12] [¶ 15,070].

A reasonable basis for treating an individual as an independent contractor can be established through one or more of the following tests: judicial precedent; published IRS rulings; technical advice from the IRS with respect to the particular employer, or a letter ruling to the employer; a past IRS audit, if there was no assessment pertaining to the employer's treatment of individuals in the same position as the worker whose status is in question; a long-standing, recognized practice in the industry in which the worker is engaged.[13]

The surest way to avoid misclassifying an employee is to request an IRS ruling as to whether your worker is an employee or an independent contractor by submitting Form SS-8, available at any IRS district office. Meanwhile, note that withholding of income or social security tax from an individual's wages, or the filing of an employment tax return with respect to those wages, is considered treatment of the individual as an employee.

¶15,015 WAGES SUBJECT TO WITHHOLDING

Only those payments that are wages for income tax purposes are subject to withholding.

.01 What Are Wages?

Wages are pay to employees for services [Code Sec. 3401(a)]. A payment can be wages whether it is called a salary, fee, bonus, signing bonus, overtime pay, award, commission, vacation pay, severance pay, royalty, payments for accumulated leave or even retirement pay. Wages can be paid in property, such as stocks, bonds, or other property transferred in exchange for the employee's services. The property's fair market value when it is transferred is the amount of the wages [Reg. § 31.3401(a)-1(a)(4)]. Early termination payments to departing employees will also be considered wages subject to FICA tax.

▶ **PRACTICE POINTER:** For payroll tax purposes, wages include all remuneration for employment regardless of the form of the payment. Even sign-on bonuses, early termination settlements, noncompete amounts, and royalties paid under an employment contract—no matter how worded—will be considered wages subject to FICA, FUTA, and income tax withholding. For example, a shareholder of a closely held corporation can not circumvent federal employment taxes by disguising wages as royalties or rent.[14]

---

[12] Treas. Dept., IRS Publication 15-A, "Employer's Supplemental Tax Guide" (2013 Ed.), pp. 7-9.

[13] Rev. Proc. 85-18, 1985-1 CB 518.

[14] *Charlotte's Office Boutique, Inc.*, 121 TC 89, Dec. 55,254 (2003), *supplemental decision*, 87 TCM 998, Dec. 55,551(M), TC Memo. 2004-43, *aff'd*, CA-9, 2005-2 USTC ¶ 50,593, 425 F3d 1203 (wages

The same kind of payment may be wages subject to withholding under some conditions but not under other conditions, or only a portion of a payment may be subject to withholding as wages. Also, some payments for employment may be excluded from wages [Reg. § 31.3401(a)-2]. Withholding is based upon wages actually or constructively paid, regardless of when wages were earned [Reg. § 31.3402(a)-1].

Wages Subject to Withholding

Overtime pay; dismissal pay [Reg. § 31.3401(a)-1(b)(4)]; certain reimbursed employment agency fees;[15] social security tax or state unemployment tax, paid by the employer on behalf of an employee (without deduction from the employee's pay) [Reg. § 31.3401(a)-1(b)(6)]; severance pay;[16] payments equivalent to difference between employee's normal wages and amounts received from the state while serving in the National Guard;[17] guaranteed annual wage payments;[18] financial counseling fees paid by a corporation for the benefit of its executives.[19]

Items Not Subject to Withholding

Occasional supper money given for overtime work [Reg. § 1.132-6(d)(2)]; qualified tuition reductions for undergraduate studies given by an educational organization to its employees [Code Sec. 117(d), 3401(a)(19)]; compensation paid to former employees in the Armed Forces or National Guard;[20] facilities or privileges of small value furnished to employees generally, to promote health, goodwill or efficiency, such as entertainment, medical services and courtesy discounts on purchases [Reg. § 31.3401(a)-1(b)(10)]; merchandise of nominal value [Reg. § 1.132-6(e)]; scholarship and fellowship grants [Code Sec. 117(b)]; union strike benefits;[21] reimbursement for uniforms if the payments are properly identified when made, the expenses are substantiated and unsubstantiated reimbursements are returned [Reg. § 31.3401(a)-1(b)(2)]; medical care reimbursements made under self-insured medical reimbursement plan [Ch. 5] [Code Sec. 3401(a)(20)].

Employers that transfer property to employees in connection with the performance of services need not deduct and withhold income tax to qualify for a compensation deduction [Reg. § 1.83-6(a)]. Under the rule, the employer will be allowed a deduction for the amount included in the gross income of the employee. If the employer timely complies with the Form W-2 or 1099 reporting requirements regarding the amount includible in the employee's income, the employee will be deemed to have included the amount in gross income.

Statutory or qualified stock options: withholding not required. For qualified stock options, the definition of wages for FICA tax purposes excludes remuneration on account of a transfer of a share of stock pursuant to an exercise of an ISO or ESPP

(Footnote Continued)

cannot be disguised as royalties or rents); Rev. Rul. 2004-109, 2004-2 CB 958 (bonuses for signing or ratifying a contract are wages); Rev. Rul. 2004-110, 2004-2 CB 960 (amounts paid to cancel employment contract are wages).

[15] Rev. Rul. 73-351, 1973-2 CB 323.

[16] *K.H. Donnel*, FedCl, 2001-2 USTC ¶ 50,664, 50 FedCl 375.

[17] Rev. Rul. 68-238, 1968-1 CB 420.

[18] Rev. Rul. 61-68, 1961-1 CB 429.

[19] Rev. Rul. 73-13, 1973-1 CB 42.

[20] Rev. Rul. 69-136, 1969-1 CB 252.

[21] *A. Kaiser*, SCt, 60-2 USTC ¶ 9517, 363 US 299, 80 SCt 1204; Rev. Rul. 61-136, 1961-2 CB 20; Rev. Rul. 68-424, 1968-2 CB 419; Rev. Rul. 75-475, 1975-2 CB 406.

option, or on account of a disposition of stock acquired through such an exercise [Code Sec. 3121(a)]. Similar changes were made with respect to Railroad Retirement Act and FUTA taxes [Code Secs. 3231(e), 3306(b)]. Gains resulting from a disqualifying disposition of stock acquired through exercise of a qualified stock option or reportable under the 85/100-percent ESPP option rule are subject to income tax at ordinary rates. However, the employer is not required to withhold income tax in the event of a disqualifying disposition of stock [Code Sec. 421(b)]. Furthermore, withholding is not required with respect to amounts taxable under the 85/100-percent rule [Code Sec. 423(c)]. See discussion at Ch. 2. The IRS has taken the position that compensation may have to be reported on Form W-2 whether or not income tax is withheld, and has specifically stated that income realized from a disqualifying disposition of statutory stock (whether through an ESPP or ISO) must be reported as compensation on Form W-2 [Reg. § 1.6041-2(a)(1); Notice 2002-47].[22]

Payments Subject to Withholding Under Special Rules

Back pay and back overtime pay. Back pay and back overtime pay are subject to withholding even if paid as a result of a settlement or court judgement.[23] In *Cleveland Indians Baseball Co.,*[24] the United States Supreme Court held that a professional baseball club that remitted FICA and FUTA taxes with respect to the portion of a fund created in settlement of an employment dispute that was allocable to back pay owed to certain players was not entitled to a refund of those taxes. The back pay was subject to FICA and FUTA withholding in the tax years in which the amounts were paid to the players, rather than in the years to which the payments were related.

Board and lodging. The value of meals or lodging furnished to an employee is not subject to withholding if the employee can exclude the value of the meals or lodging from income [Reg. § 31.3401(a)-1(b)(9)]. The value is excludable if (1) meals or lodging are furnished on the employer's business premises (generally the employee's place of employment); (2) they are furnished for the employer's convenience; and (3) for lodging (but not meals), the employee must accept the lodging as a condition of employment [Code Sec. 119].

Cafeteria plans. Under a cafeteria plan [Ch. 4], employer contributions are excluded from the wages of an employee and not subject to withholding to the extent that qualified benefits are elected by the employee [Code Sec. 125; Prop. Reg. § 1.125-1].

Cash-or-deferred (Sec. 401(k)) plan contributions. Amounts that an employee elects to have the employer defer from salary into a trust under a profit-sharing or stock bonus plan on the employee's behalf are not includible in an employee's gross income. Such deferrals are thus not subject to withholding [Reg. § 31.3401(a)(12)-1]. (See ¶ 15,040 for withholding on distributions of such deferred income.) But amounts that an employee elects to receive as cash under such a plan are wages subject to withholding.

Commissions. Commissions generally are wages subject to withholding. But if a retail commission salesperson, usually paid in cash, receives a noncash payment (such as a sales prize), it is not subject to withholding if the prize's fair market value is included as other compensation reported on the Form W-2 [¶ 15,140] [Code Sec.

---

[22] Notice 2002-47, 2002-2 CB 97.

[23] Rev. Rul. 72-268, 1972-1 CB 313; Rev. Rul. 80-364, 1980-2 CB 294.

[24] *Cleveland Indians Baseball Co.,* SCt, 2001-1 USTC ¶ 50,341, 532 US 200, 121 SCt 1433; see also Rev. Rul. 55-203, 1955-1 CB 114.

3402(j); Reg. § 31.3402(j)-1].[25] An insurance salesperson is not a retail commission salesperson for this purpose.[26]

Decedent's payments. Payments after an employee's death representing unpaid compensation for services rendered by a deceased employee are not subject to withholding.[27]

Dependent care assistance payments. Such payments are not subject to withholding as long as it's reasonable to believe that the employee would be able to exclude these payments [Ch. 4][Code Sec. 3401(a)(18)]. An employee can exclude an amount equal to the smaller of (1) his or her earned income or (2) $5,000 ($2,500 if married filing separately) [Code Sec. 129(a)(2)].

Educational expenses. Job-related educational expense payments are not subject to withholding if the education maintains or improves skills required by the individual's employment or other trade or business, or is a condition of employment. However, if the education is required to meet the minimum educational requirements for the job, or the education will qualify the individual for a new trade or business, then the educational payments are subject to withholding [Ch. 12] [Reg. § 1.162-5].[28] The employee must substantiate his or her educational expenses to the person providing the payment, and return any unspent amounts.[29]

Fishing wages. A commercial fisherman's services as a crew member of a specified boat for one tax year did not constitute service excepted from employment under Code Sec. 3401(a)(17), and, thus, was subject to withholding. The taxpayer received payments to fund health insurance premiums, which constituted compensation for services rendered on the boat that did not represent a share of the boat's catch of fish, did not depend on the amount of the boat's catch and were not paid solely for additional duties for which additional cash remuneration is traditional in the industry.[30] The Tax Court held that a member of a fishing boat crew was self-employed because he was compensated solely from the proceeds of the sale of the boat's catch, even though operating expenses were subtracted from the proceeds before the crew's compensation was determined.[31]

Gambling winnings. Withholding is imposed on winnings of more than $5,000 from sweepstakes, wagering pools, and lotteries. Withholding is generally imposed on other types of gambling winnings (including pari-mutual pools with respect to horse races, dog races, and jai alai) only if the winnings exceed $5,000 and are at least 300 times the wager. In Rev. Proc. 2007-57,[32] the IRS informed poker tournament sponsors, including casinos that poker winnings are subject to withholding if the proceeds are more than $5,000 from a wager placed in any sweepstakes, wagering pool, or lottery [Code Sec. 3402(q)]. The term "wagering pool" includes "all pari-mutuel betting pools, including on- and off-track racing pools, and similar types of betting pools." The withholding rate is equal to the third lowest rate applicable to single

[25] Rev. Rul. 57-18, 1957-1 CB 354; Rev. Rul. 68-216, 1968-1 CB 413.

[26] Rev. Rul. 57-551, 1957-2 CB 707.

[27] Rev. Rul. 86-109, 1986-2 CB 196.

[28] Rev. Rul. 78-184, 1978-1 CB 304.

[29] Conference Report on H.R. 1720 [Family Support Act of 1988].

[30] Rev. Rul. 77-102, 1977-1 CB 299.

[31] *J.E. Anderson*, 123 TC 219, Dec. 55,721 (2004), *aff'd in unpublished, per curiam, opinion*, CA-1, 2005-2 USTC ¶ 50,455.

[32] Rev. Proc. 2007-57, 2007-2 CB 547.

filers which currently is 25 percent. In addition, the payor of gambling winnings from these activities must report winnings of more than $600 by filing Form W-2G, *Certain Gambling Winnings*, with the IRS on or before February 28 (March 31 if filed electronically) of the year following the year in which the winnings are paid. Backup withholding is required if the winner of reportable amounts does not furnish his TIN to the payor. No withholding is required on winnings from bingo, keno, or slot machines. However, for winnings of $1,200 or more from a bingo game or slot machine and for winnings of $1,500 or more from a keno game, the payor must file Form W-2G [Code Secs. 3402(q), 6041; Reg. § 1.6041-1]. Withholding is imposed on proceeds from wagering transactions other than bingo, keno or slot machines at the rate stated above if such proceeds exceed $5,000, regardless of the odds of the wager.

Golden parachute contracts. Payments under golden parachute contracts, like any termination pay, are subject to withholding.[33]

Insurance and annuity premiums. Payments to employees to buy individual hospitalization coverage that are includable in employees' income are subject to withholding.[34] But if the payments are actually reimbursements of premiums actually paid by employees to insurers, the payments are excludable from income.[35] Group-term life insurance premiums are not subject to withholding, even though premiums for coverage in excess of $50,000 are income taxable to employees [Code Sec. 79(a)(1), 3401(a)(14)]. Premiums paid by an exempt organization [Ch. 23] to buy an employee annuity are exempt from withholding.[36]

IRA contributions paid by employer. Amounts paid for individuals to retirement arrangements are not wages subject to withholding as long as it is reasonable to believe that the employees will be entitled to deductions for such payments [Ch. 3] [Code Sec. 3401(a)(12); Reg. § 31.3401(a)(12)-1(d)].

Loans, interest-free and below-market. The amount treated as additional compensation to the employee [Ch. 2] is not subject to income tax withholding. But the amount deemed additional compensation must be reported on Form W-2 as other compensation.

Moving expenses are not subject to withholding if, when paid, it is reasonable to believe that the employee can deduct them. Reimbursements or allowances in excess of moving expenses are subject to withholding [Ch. 9] [Code Sec. 3401(a)(15); Reg. § 31.3401(a)(15)-1].

Pensions and retirement pay distributions are subject to withholding unless the recipient elects exemption from withholding on Form W-4P. For withholding procedures, see ¶ 15,040.

Qualified or nonqualified stock options. When employees exercise their rights in nonqualified stock options, the excess of the stock's fair market value over the option price is wages subject to withholding.[37] Withholding also applies to amounts paid to employees to cancel these options.[38] Statutory stock options will not trigger payroll tax withholding. See discussion below under Statutory stock options.

---

[33] Treas. Dept., IRS Publication 15-A, "Employer's Supplemental Tax Guide" (2013 Ed.), p. 13.

[34] Rev. Rul. 85-44, 1985-1 CB 22.

[35] Rev. Rul. 61-146, 1961-2 CB 25.

[36] *Canisius College*, CA-2, 86-2 USTC ¶ 9700, 799 F2d 18, *cert. denied*, 481 US 1014.

[37] Rev. Rul. 67-257, 1967-2 CB 359.

[38] Rev. Rul. 67-366, 1967-2 CB 165.

Retirement plan payments by employer. Payments to or from a trust or annuity plan (including a Sec. 403(b) annuity purchased by a public school or tax-exempt organization), made to or for employees and their beneficiaries, are not subject to withholding unless payments are compensation for services [Reg. § 31.3401(a)(12)-1].

Supplemental unemployment compensation benefits (SUBs). Under Code Sec. 3402(o)(2), the term supplemental unemployment compensation benefits (SUBs) is defined as "amounts which are paid to an employee, pursuant to a plan to which the employer is a party, because of an employee's involuntary separation from employment (whether or not such separation is temporary), resulting directly from a reduction in force, the discontinuance of a plan or operation or other similar conditions." Code Sec. 3402(o) provides that any supplemental unemployment compensation benefit paid to an individual should be treated "as if it were payment of wages" by the employer for income tax withholding purposes. Therefore, the benefit is subject to income tax withholding.

In *In re Quality Stores, Inc.*,[39] this language was interpreted by the bankruptcy, district, and appellate courts to mean that SUB payments are *not* wages and, therefore, while subject to income tax withholding, are not subject to FICA withholding. However, the Court of Appeals for the Federal Circuit, in *CSX Corp.*[40] reached the opposite conclusion. The Supreme Court has granted the government's Petition for a Writ of Certiorari in *In re Quality Stores, Inc.* and that case will be decided by the high court in the 2013-2014 term. The government argues that in construing Code Sec. 3402(o), the Sixth Circuit court failed to recognize that Code Sec. 3402(o) is expressly limited to income tax rather than FICA withholding. The government argued that this was a key factor in the Federal Circuit's *CSX Corp.* decision treating SUB payments as wages subject to FICA.

Traveling expenses. Traveling expenses, and other bona fide, ordinary and necessary expenses incurred, or reasonably expected to be incurred, in an employer's business and specifically advanced or reimbursed to employees, are not wages if the employees (within a reasonable period of time) substantiate their expenses to the person providing the advance or reimbursement, and return any unspent amounts. Wages and expense money need not be paid separately, but if one payment includes both items, each should be shown on the pay stub separately [Reg. § 31.3401(a)-4(a)].

Wages as community property. Total wages paid to the husband are wages subject to withholding. The wife's share of the tax withheld may be credited against her tax if she files separately.[41]

Consult the chart for special rules that apply to services and payments.[42]

---

[39] *In re Quality Stores, Inc.*, CA-6, 2012-2 USTC ¶ 50,551, *reh'g denied*, 2013-1 USTC ¶ 50,150, *cert. granted* Oct. 2, 2013.

[40] *CSX Corp.*, CA-Fed, 2008-1 USTC ¶ 50,218, 518 F3d 1328.

[41] *D.W. Smith*, 9 TCM 933, Dec. 17,921(M) (1950).

[42] Treas. Dept., IRS Publication 15, "(Circular E), Employer's Tax Guide (For use in 2013)," pp. 37-41.

15. Special Rules for Various Types of Services and Payments

Section references are to the Internal Revenue Code unless otherwise noted.

Special Classes of Employment and Special Types of Payments	Treatment Under Employment Taxes		
	Income Tax Withholding	**Social Security and Medicare (including Additional Medicare Tax when wages are paid in excess of $200,000)**	**FUTA**
Aliens, nonresident.	See Publication 515, Withholding of Tax on Nonresident Aliens and Foreign Entities, and Publication 519, U.S. Tax Guide for Aliens.		
Aliens, resident:			
1. Service performed in the U.S.	Same as U.S. citizen.	Same as U.S. citizen. (Exempt if any part of service as crew member of foreign vessel or aircraft is performed outside U.S.)	Same as U.S. citizen.
2. Service performed outside U.S.	Withhold	Taxable if (1) working for an American employer or (2) an American employer by agreement covers U.S. citizens and residents employed by its foreign affiliates.	Exempt unless on or in connection with an American vessel or aircraft and either performed under contract made in U.S., or alien is employed on such vessel or aircraft when it touches U.S. port.
Cafeteria plan benefits under section 125.	If employee chooses cash, subject to all employment taxes. If employee chooses another benefit, the treatment is the same as if the benefit was provided outside the plan. See Publication 15-B for more information.		
Deceased worker:			
1. Wages paid to beneficiary or estate in same calendar year as worker's death. See the Instructions for Forms W-2 and W-3 for details.	Exempt	Taxable	Taxable
2. Wages paid to beneficiary or estate after calendar year of worker's death.	Exempt	Exempt	Exempt
Dependent care assistance programs.	Exempt to the extent it is reasonable to believe amounts are excludable from gross income under section 129.		
Disabled worker's wages paid after year in which worker became entitled to disability insurance benefits under the Social Security Act.	Withhold	Exempt, if worker did not perform any service for employer during period for which payment is made.	Taxable
Employee business expense reimbursement:			
1. Accountable plan.			
a. Amounts not exceeding specified government rate for per diem or standard mileage.	Exempt	Exempt	Exempt
b. Amounts in excess of specified government rate for per diem or standard mileage.	Withhold	Taxable	Taxable
2. Nonaccountable plan. See section 5 for details.	Withhold	Taxable	Taxable
Family employees:			
1. Child employed by parent (or partnership in which each partner is a parent of the child).	Withhold	Exempt until age 18; age 21 for domestic service.	Exempt until age 21
2. Parent employed by child.	Withhold	Taxable if in course of the son's or daughter's business. For domestic services, see section 3.	Exempt
3. Spouse employed by spouse. See section 3 for more information.	Withhold	Taxable if in course of spouse's business.	Exempt
Fishing and related activities.	See Publication 334, Tax Guide for Small Business.		
Foreign governments and international organizations.	Exempt	Exempt	Exempt

Publication 15 (2013) Page 37

Special Classes of Employment and Special Types of Payments	Treatment Under Employment Taxes		
	Income Tax Withholding	Social Security and Medicare (including Additional Medicare Tax when wages are paid in excess of $200,000)	FUTA
Foreign service by U.S. citizens:			
1. As U.S. government employees.	Withhold	Same as within U.S.	Exempt
2. For foreign affiliates of American employers and other private employers.	Exempt if at time of payment (1) it is reasonable to believe employee is entitled to exclusion from income under section 911 or (2) the employer is required by law of the foreign country to withhold income tax on such payment.	Exempt unless (1) an American employer by agreement covers U.S. citizens employed by its foreign affiliates or (2) U.S. citizen works for American employer.	Exempt unless (1) on American vessel or aircraft and work is performed under contract made in U.S. or worker is employed on vessel when it touches U.S. port or (2) U.S. citizen works for American employer (except in a contiguous country with which the U.S. has an agreement for unemployment compensation) or in the U.S. Virgin Islands.
Fringe benefits.	Taxable on excess of fair market value of the benefit over the sum of an amount paid for it by the employee and any amount excludable by law. However, special valuation rules may apply. Benefits provided under cafeteria plans may qualify for exclusion from wages for social security, Medicare, and FUTA taxes. See Publication 15-B for details.		
Government employment: State/local governments and political subdivisions, employees of:			
1. Salaries and wages (includes payments to most elected and appointed officials.) See chapter 3 of Publication 963, Federal-State Reference Guide.	Withhold	Generally, taxable for (1) services performed by employees who are either (a) covered under a section 218 agreement or (b) not covered under a section 218 agreement and not a member of a public retirement system (mandatory social security and Medicare coverage), and (2) (for Medicare tax only) for services performed by employees hired or rehired after 3/31/86 who are not covered under a section 218 agreement or the mandatory social security provisions, unless specifically excluded by law. See Publication 963.	Exempt
2. Election workers. Election individuals are workers who are employed to perform services for state or local governments at election booths in connection with national, state, or local elections. **Note.** File Form W-2 for payments of $600 or more even if no social security, or Medicare taxes were withheld.	Exempt	Taxable if paid $1,600 or more in 2013 (lesser amount if specified by a section 218 social security agreement). See Revenue Ruling 2000-6.	Exempt
3. Emergency workers. Emergency workers who were hired on a temporary basis in response to a specific unforeseen emergency and are not intended to become permanent employees.	Withhold	Exempt if serving on a temporary basis in case of fire, storm, snow, earthquake, flood, or similar emergency.	Exempt
U.S. federal government employees.	Withhold	Taxable for Medicare. Taxable for social security unless hired before 1984. See section 3121(b)(5).	Exempt

Special Classes of Employment and Special Types of Payments	Treatment Under Employment Taxes		
	Income Tax Withholding	Social Security and Medicare (including Additional Medicare Tax when wages are paid in excess of $200,000)	FUTA
Homeworkers (industrial, cottage industry):			
1. Common law employees.	Withhold	Taxable	Taxable
2. Statutory employees. See section 2 for details.	Exempt	Taxable if paid $100 or more in cash in a year.	Exempt
Hospital employees:			
1. Interns	Withhold	Taxable	Exempt
2. Patients	Withhold	Taxable (Exempt for state or local government hospitals.)	Exempt
Household employees:			
1. Domestic service in private homes. Farmers, see Publication 51 (Circular A).	Exempt (withhold if both employer and employee agree).	Taxable if paid $1,800 or more in cash in 2013. Exempt if performed by an individual under age 18 during any portion of the calendar year and is not the principal occupation of the employee.	Taxable if employer paid total cash wages of $1,000 or more in any quarter in the current or preceding calendar year.
2. Domestic service in college clubs, fraternities, and sororities.	Exempt (withhold if both employer and employee agree).	Exempt if paid to regular student; also exempt if employee is paid less than $100 in a year by an income-tax-exempt employer.	Taxable if employer paid total cash wages of $1,000 or more in any quarter in the current or preceding calendar year.
Insurance for employees:			
1. Accident and health insurance premiums under a plan or system for employees and their dependents generally or for a class or classes of employees and their dependents.	Exempt (except 2% shareholder-employees of S corporations).	Exempt	Exempt
2. Group-term life insurance costs. See Publication 15-B for details	Exempt	Exempt, except for the cost of group-term life insurance includible in the employee's gross income. Special rules apply for former employees.	Exempt
Insurance agents or solicitors:			
1. Full-time life insurance salesperson.	Withhold only if employee under common law. See section 2.	Taxable	Taxable if (1) employee under common law and (2) not paid solely by commissions.
2. Other salesperson of life, casualty, etc., insurance.	Withhold only if employee under common law.	Taxable only if employee under common law.	Taxable if (1) employee under common law and (2) not paid solely by commissions.
Interest on loans with below-market interest rates (foregone interest and deemed original issue discount).	See Publication 15-A.		
Leave-sharing plans: Amounts paid to an employee under a leave-sharing plan.	Withhold	Taxable	Taxable
Newspaper carriers and vendors: Newspaper carriers under age 18; newspaper and magazine vendors buying at fixed prices and retaining receipts from sales to customers. See Publication 15-A for information on statutory nonemployee status.	Exempt (withhold if both employer and employee voluntarily agree).	Exempt	Exempt

Special Classes of Employment and Special Types of Payments	Treatment Under Employment Taxes		
	Income Tax Withholding	Social Security and Medicare (including Additional Medicare Tax when wages are paid in excess of $200,000)	FUTA
Noncash payments:			
1. For household work, agricultural labor, and service not in the course of the employer's trade or business.	Exempt (withhold if both employer and employee voluntarily agree).	Exempt	Exempt
2. To certain retail commission salespersons ordinarily paid solely on a cash commission basis.	Optional with employer, except to the extent employee's supplemental wages during the year exceed $1 million.	Taxable	Taxable
Nonprofit organizations.	See Publication 15-A.		
Officers or shareholders of an S Corporation. Distributions and other payments by an S corporation to a corporate officer or shareholder must be treated as wages to the extent the amounts are reasonable compensation for services to the corporation by an employee. See the Instructions for Form 1120S.	Withhold	Taxable	Taxable
Partners: Payments to general or limited partners of a partnership. See Publication 541, Partnerships, for partner reporting rules.	Exempt	Exempt	Exempt
Railroads: Payments subject to the Railroad Retirement Act. See Publication 915, Social Security and Equivalent Railroad Retirement Benefits, for more details.	Withhold	Exempt	Exempt
Religious exemptions.	See Publication 15-A and Publication 517, Social Security and Other Information for Members of the Clergy and Religious Workers.		
Retirement and pension plans:			
1. Employer contributions to a qualified plan.	Exempt	Exempt	Exempt
2. Elective employee contributions and deferrals to a plan containing a qualified cash or deferred compensation arrangement (for example, 401(k)).	Generally exempt, but see section 402(g) for limitation.	Taxable	Taxable
3. Employer contributions to individual retirement accounts under simplified employee pension plan (SEP).	Generally exempt, but seesection 402(g) for salary reduction SEP limitation.	Exempt, except for amounts contributed under a salary reduction SEP agreement.	
4. Employer contributions to section 403(b) annuities.	Generally exempt, but see section 402(g) for limitation.	Taxable if paid through a salary reduction agreement (written or otherwise).	
5. Employee salary reduction contributions to a SIMPLE retirement account.	Exempt	Taxable	Taxable
6. Distributions from qualified retirement and pension plans and section 403(b) annuities. See Publication 15-A for information on pensions, annuities, and employer contributions to nonqualified deferred compensation arrangements.	Withhold, but recipient may elect exemption on Form W-4P in certain cases; mandatory 20% withholding applies to an eligible rollover distribution that is not a direct rollover; exempt for direct rollover. See Publication 15-A.	Exempt	Exempt
Salespersons:			
1. Common law employees.	Withhold	Taxable	Taxable
2. Statutory employees.	Exempt	Taxable	Taxable, except for full-time life insurance sales agents.
3. Statutory nonemployees (qualified real estate agents, direct sellers, and certain companion sitters). See Publication 15-A for details.	Exempt	Exempt	Exempt
Scholarships and fellowship grants (includible in income under section 117(c)):	Withhold	Taxability depends on the nature of the employment and the status of the organization. See *Students, scholars, trainees, teachers, etc.* on the next page.	
Severance or dismissal pay.	Withhold	Taxable	Taxable

Special Classes of Employment and Special Types of Payments	Treatment Under Employment Taxes		
	Income Tax Withholding	Social Security and Medicare (including Additional Medicare Tax when wages are paid in excess of $200,000)	FUTA
Service not in the course of the employer's trade or business (other than on a farm operated for profit or for household employment in private homes).	Withhold only if employee earns $50 or more in cash in a quarter and works on 24 or more different days in that quarter or in the preceding quarter.	Taxable if employee receives $100 or more in cash in a calendar year.	Taxable only if employee earns $50 or more in cash in a quarter and works on 24 or more different days in that quarter or in the preceding quarter.
Sick pay. See Publication 15-A for more information.	Withhold	Exempt after end of 6 calendar months after the calendar month employee last worked for employer.	
Students, scholars, trainees, teachers, etc.:			
1. Student enrolled and regularly attending classes, performing services for:			
a. Private school, college, or university.	Withhold	Exempt	Exempt
b. Auxiliary nonprofit organization operated for and controlled by school, college, or university.	Withhold	Exempt unless services are covered by a section 218 (Social Security Act) agreement.	Exempt
c. Public school, college, or university.	Withhold	Exempt unless services are covered by a section 218 (Social Security Act) agreement.	Exempt
2. Full-time student performing service for academic credit, combining instruction with work experience as an integral part of the program.	Withhold	Taxable	Exempt unless program was established for or on behalf of an employer or group of employers.
3. Student nurse performing part-time services for nominal earnings at hospital as incidental part of training.	Withhold	Exempt	Exempt
4. Student employed by organized camps.	Withhold	Taxable	Exempt
5. Student, scholar, trainee, teacher, etc., as nonimmigrant alien under section 101(a)(15)(F), (J), (M), or (Q) of Immigration and Nationality Act (that is, aliens holding F-1, J-1, M-1, or Q-1 visas).	Withhold unless excepted by regulations.	Exempt if service is performed for purpose specified in section 101(a)(15)(F), (J), (M), or (Q) of Immigration and Nationality Act. However, these taxes may apply if the employee becomes a resident alien. See the special residency tests for exempt individuals in chapter 1 of Publication 519.	
Supplemental unemployment compensation plan benefits.	Withhold	Exempt under certain conditions. See Publication 15-A.	
Tips:			
1. If $20 or more in a month.	Withhold	Taxable	Taxable for all tips reported in writing to employer.
2. If less than $20 in a month. See section 6 for more information.	Exempt	Exempt	Exempt
Worker's compensation.	Exempt	Exempt	Exempt

.02 Supplemental Wages in Excess of $1 Million

If the sum of a supplemental wage payment and all other supplemental wage payments paid by an employer (including amounts paid by to an employee during the calendar year) exceeds $1 million, the withholding rate on the supplemental wages in excess of $1 million are equal to the maximum rate of tax in effect for that year [Reg. § 31.3402(g)-1(a)(2)]. Thus, the mandatory flat rate for supplemental wages in excess of $1 million is 39.6 percent in 2013. A supplemental wage payment may be in the form of a holiday bonus, a commission, dismissal pay, a back pay award, overtime pay or vacation pay.

Supplemental Wages Defined

In addition to regular wage payments, an employee may receive supplemental wages which could include commissions, bonuses, nonqualified deferred compensation includible in income, and back pay. Whether wages are classified as regular wages or supplemental wages may have significance in determining the amount of income tax required to be withheld because special withholding rules apply when employees receive supplemental wages. The issue for employers is when they must withhold income tax from these supplemental wages and how much must be withheld.

In Rev. Rul. 2008-29,[43] the IRS provides guidance on how an employer determines the amount of income required to be withheld for tax purposes on the following payments of supplemental wages: (1) commissions paid at fixed intervals with no regular wages paid to the employee, (2) commissions paid at fixed intervals in addition to regular wages paid at different intervals, (3) draws paid in connection with commissions, (4) commissions paid to the employee only when the accumulated commission credit of the employee reaches a specific numerical threshold, (5) a signing bonus paid prior to the commencement of employment, (6) severance pay paid after the termination of employment, (7) lump sum payments of accumulated annual leave, (8) annual payments of vacation and sick leave, and (9) sick pay paid at a different rate than regular pay.

Withholding Methods for Supplemental Wages

The regulations provide guidance on the following withholding methods:

1. *Aggregate procedure*. Under the aggregate procedure method, the employer can determine the amount of withholding on supplemental wages of $1 million or less by aggregating the amount of supplemental wages with the regular wages paid for the current payroll period or for the most recent payroll period of the year of the payments, and treating the aggregate as if it were a single wage payment for the regular payroll period [Reg. § 31.3402(g)-1(a)(6)].
2. *Optional flat rate withholding*. If supplemental wages are $1 million or less, the employer has the option to disregard the amount of regular wages paid to an employee as well as the withholding allowances claimed by an employee on Form W-4, *Employee's Withholding Allowance Certificate*, and use a flat withholding rate of 28 percent [Reg. § 31.3402(g)-1(a)(7)]. In order for employers to use optional flat rate withholding, an employer must have withheld income tax from

[43] Rev. Rul. 2008-29, IRB 2008-24, 1149.

regular wages, and the supplemental wages must be separately paid or stated on the employer's records.

3. *Mandatory flat rate withholding.* If the supplemental wages exceed $1 million, the employer must withhold income tax at the maximum income tax rate, currently 39.6 percent in 2013 [Reg. § 31.3402(g)-1(a)(2)].

Special Rules

Supplemental wages paid by other businesses under common control should be taken into account in determining whether the employer has paid $1 million of supplemental wages to an employee in the calendar year [Reg. § 31.3402(g)-1(a)(3)(i)]. In addition, payments by third-party agents of the employer must be taken into account to determine whether mandatory flat rate withholding applies [Reg. § 31.3402(g)-1(a)(3)(ii)]. A *de minimis* rule allows agents to disregard payments by the employer (and vice versa) if the agent or employer's payments do not exceed $100,000 [Reg. § 31.3402(g)-1(a)(iv)].

.03 Fringe Benefits and Withholding

The fair market value of noncash fringe benefits is treated as wages subject to withholding. However, amounts paid specifically either as advances or reimbursements for traveling or other bona fide ordinary and necessary expenses incurred or reasonably expected to be incurred in the business of the employer are not wages and are not subject to withholding or FICA [Reg. § 31.3401(a)-1(b)(2); Reg. § 31.3121(a)-1(h)]. In *HB&R, Inc.,*[44] the Eighth Circuit held that a company need not withhold income taxes or pay FICA on the roundtrip airfare provided to employees whose regular routine involved working for three weeks in remote areas and then spending three weeks at home. The airfare was deemed an ordinary and necessary business expense of the employer and therefore exempt from payroll taxes.

When to Withhold

You can treat taxable fringe benefits as paid on an annual, semiannual, quarterly, or pay-period basis, and withhold accordingly. You may also change your withholding basis as often as you wish in the course of a year, as long as taxable benefits are treated as paid no later than December 31. The value of a single fringe benefit may be apportioned over several pay periods, even if the benefit is actually received all at once. The same withholding basis does not have to be used for all employees. No formal election of basis is required; nor do you have to notify the government of its choice of basis.

Special Accounting Rule

The value of taxable fringe benefits that are *actually provided* during the last two months of the calendar year may be treated as paid during the subsequent calendar year. Withholding on these benefits is therefore deferred into the next year. No formal election of this special rule is required (other than informing employees), and you can choose to use it for some benefits while disregarding it for others. Exceptions: This rule cannot be applied to the value of benefits received by the employee

---

[44] *HB&R, Inc.*, CA-8, 2000-2 USTC ¶ 50,795, 229 F3d 688; *M. Jordan*, CA-8, 2007-2 USTC ¶ 50,603, 490 F3d 677.

during the first ten months of the calendar year, even if those benefits are not treated as paid until December 31.

You must notify employees if you plan to use this special accounting rule. Notification must be made between the time of the employee's last paycheck of the calendar year, and the time the employee receives Form W-2 (generally, January 31 of the following calendar year [¶15,140]). Employees must, in turn, use this rule for all purposes (e.g., for taking deductions related to the fringe benefit) and for the same period.

Optional Withholding on a Company Vehicle

The value of an employee's personal use of a company car is includible in gross income, unless it can be specifically excluded as a *working condition fringe* or as a *de minimis fringe benefit*. The value of the personal use is generally its fair market value. But optional valuation rules are provided: the auto lease valuation rule; the vehicle cents-per-mile rule; and the commuting-use-only rule [Ch. 4]. [Reg. §1.61-21(c)(2)(iii)].

You may choose whether to withhold income tax on the value of an employee's personal use of a company car. If you elect not to withhold, you must notify the employee of this election and must include the fair market value of the personal use on Form W-2. Withholding of social security tax is mandatory, however [¶15,075]. When withholding income tax and social security tax, you may treat the value of the personal use as paid on a pay period, quarterly, semiannual, or annual basis.

.04 Tips Subject to Withholding

All cash tips received by an employee are wages for FICA tax purposes and must be reported to the employer unless the cash tips received during a single calendar month total less than $20. Cash tips include tips received from customers, charged tips distributed to the employee by his or her employer, and tips received from other employees under any tip-sharing arrangement. Thus, both directly and indirectly tipped employees must report tips received to their employer. Noncash tips (such as tickets or gift certificates) from customers are not wages for FICA tax purposes and are not reported to the employer. All cash tips and noncash tips are includable in an employee's gross income and subject to federal income taxes [Code Sec. 3121(q)]. The employee must give the employer a written statement of cash tips by the 10th day of the month after the month in which the tips are received [Code Sec. 6053(a); Reg. §31.6053-1(a)]. The statement can be filed in a paper statement or may be filed electronically. The employer should withhold the employee share of FICA taxes on the reported tips from the wages of the employee (other than tips) or from other funds made available by the employee for this purpose. The employer pays both employer and employee shares of FICA taxes in the same manner as the taxes on the employee's nontip wages and includes the reported tips on the employee's Form W-2, *Wage and Tax Statement*.

If an employee fails to report tips to his or her employer, the employee is liable for the employee share of FICA taxes on those unreported tips. The employee is liable for the employee share of FICA taxes on the unreported tips. The employee pays his or her share of FICA taxes by completing Form 4137, *Social Security and Medicare Tax on Unreported Tip Income*, and filing it with Form 1040 for the year in which the tips are actually received by the employee. If an employee fails to report tips to his or her employer, the employer is not liable for the employer share of FICA taxes on the unreported tips until notice and demand for the taxes is made to the employer by the IRS. The employer is not liable to withhold and pay the employee share of FICA taxes on the unreported tips. Notice and demand is made by the IRS when it advises the employer in writing of the amount of tips received by an employee who failed to report or underreported tips to the employer.

How to Distinguish Tips and Service Charges

The IRS released Rev. Rul. 2012-18[45] in order to help taxpayers distinguish tips which are subject to special FICA tax rules from service charges which must be treated as wages. Taxpayers have until on or after January 1, 2014 to comply with the treatment of service charges under Rev. Rul. 2012-18 where the IRS defined service charges as mandatory add-on fees to food and beverage bills that are distributed to wait staff by the employer. The IRS advised taxpayers to rely on the following four criteria when determining whether a payment is a tip or a service charge: (1) payment of a tip must be made free from compulsion; (2) the customer must have the unrestricted right to determine the amount of the tip; (3) the tip should not be the subject of negotiation or dictated by employer policy; and (4) generally, the customer has the right to determine who receives the tip. The IRS used the following examples to explain the difference.

Example 15-1: A restaurant's menu specifies that an 18% charge will be added to all bills for parties of 6 or more customers. The customer's bill for food and beverages for her party of 8 includes an amount on the "tip line" equal to 18% of the price for food and beverages and the total includes this amount. The customer did not have the unrestricted right to determine the amount of the payment because it was dictated by employer policy. The customer did not make the payment free from compulsion. The 18% charge is not a tip. The amount included on the tip line is a service charge dictated by the restaurant.

Example 15-2: A restaurant includes sample calculations of tip amounts beneath the signature line on its charge receipts for food and beverages provided to customers. The actual tip line is left blank. The customer's charge receipt shows sample tip calculations of 15%, 18% and 20% of the price of food and beverages. The customer inserts the amount calculated at 15% on the tip line and adds this amount to the price of food and beverages to compute the total. The amount the customer entered on the tip line is a tip.

Aggregate Estimation Method Approved

In *Fior D'Italia*,[46] the Supreme Court sanctioned the IRS method of calculating the FICA taxes that a restaurant owes on tips that its employees may have received but did not report. According to the high court, when employees are suspected of failing to report all of their cash tips, the IRS may go the employer and collect the employer's share of

---

[45] Rev. Rul. 2012-18, as amplified by Announcement 2012-25, IRB 2012-26, June 20, 2012 and Announcement 2012-50, IRB 2012-52, Dec. 13, 2012.

[46] *Fior D'Italia, Inc.*, 2002-1 USTC ¶50,459, 536 US 238, 122 SCt 2117.

the FICA tax based on the aggregate estimate of all the tips that the restaurant's customers paid its employees. To make this calculation, the IRS examines the restaurant's credit card slips for the year in question and then calculates total tips by multiplying the tip rates by the restaurant's receipts.

NOTE: Employers also owe FICA tax on tip income they allocate to employees on Form W-2, but only after the government issues a notice and demand for the tax. (See ¶ 15,015 for allocation procedures and income tax withholding requirements. Returns and payment procedures are covered at ¶ 15,170.) Employees must pay a penalty of 50 percent of the social security tax due on any tips they willfully fail to report to their employers as required [Code Sec. 6652(b); Reg. § 31.6652(c)-1].

Tip Reporting by Large Food and Beverage Establishments

Large food and beverage establishments must use Form 8027, *Employer's Annual Information Return of Tip Income and Allocated Tips* to make annual reports to the IRS on receipts from food or beverage operations and tips reported by employees. All employees receiving $20 or more a month in tips must report 100 percent of their tips to their employer. Form 8027 need not be filed for: (1) any fast food operation; (2) any food or beverage operation operated for less than one month in the calendar year; (3) any food or beverage operation where tipping is not customary (such as in a cafeteria-style operation [Reg. § 31.6053(j)(18)]; or where (4) at least 95 percent of total sales (other than carryout) had a service charge of 10 percent or more.

Large food and beverage establishments are those that provide food or beverages for which tipping is customary, and which normally employ 10 or more employees on a business day. For the 10-employee test, those who have a stock value interest of 50 percent or more in their corporate businesses are not counted as employees [Code Sec. 6053(c)(4); Reg. § 31.6053-3(j)(7)]. Food and beverage operations at different locations are treated as separate operations for reporting purposes. This is true even though the same operations are conducted in a single building but in different locations. Fast-food and cafeteria-style operations that are conducted without table service or customary tipping are excepted from filing Form 8027 [Reg. §§ 31.6053-3(h), (j)(17) and (18)].

Employers should consult Rev. Proc. 2012-37[47] for guidance on preparing and electronically filing Form 8027.

Voluntary Tip Reporting Compliance Agreements

The IRS has developed a Tip Rate Determination/Education Program (TRD/EP) in order to enhance tax compliance among tipped employees. The program offers employers the opportunity to voluntarily enter into one of two types of agreements: a Tip Reporting Alternative Commitment (TRAC) agreement or a Tip Rate Determination Agreement (TRDA). Both are available for industries in which tipping is customary. The IRS has extended the TRD/EP indefinitely, due to the significant increase in tip reporting through the voluntary compliance program.[48] All employers with establishments where tipping is customary and underreporting has occurred are

---

[47] Rev. Proc. 2012-37, IRB 2012-41, 449.

[48] IRS News Release, IR-2004-117, Sept. 16, 2004.

eligible to apply to apply for either TRDA or TRAC by submitting an application letter to the employer's area IRS chief, Examination/Compliance Division, Attn: Tip Coordinator.

A TRAC agreement obligates a business to educate its employees on their tip-reporting obligations and to institute formal employee tip-reporting procedures. In return, the IRS agrees to base the business's liability for social security and Medicare taxes for an employee solely on reported tips and any unreported tips discovered during an IRS audit of the employee. A TRDA requires that at least 75 percent of an employer's tipped employees voluntarily enter into a Tipped Employee Participation Agreement. Tip rates for all job classifications are then determined using historical data. If participating employees fail to report tips at or above these rates, the employer will provide the IRS with information (name, social security number, wages, hours, and sales) on the nonconforming employees. Employers are also required to furnish similar information on employees choosing not to participate in the program.

While employers are liable for FICA taxes on previously unreported tips for a six-month validation period, participation assures the employer that prior periods will not be examined during the period that the TRDA is in effect. In addition, the IRS will not initiate any tip examinations of the employer during the life of the TRDA. The employer is thus immune from potentially costly and time-consuming tip-reporting audits conducted at the employer's level. On April 29, 2013, the IRS announced that it is considering updating TRDAs and TRACs in order to improve employee tip reporting compliance and use technological advancements to decrease taxpayer and administrative burdens.[49]

¶15,020 HOW TO FIGURE WITHHOLDING

Withholding from gross wages may be figured ordinarily by either the wage-bracket withholding tables or the percentage method. Graduated rates apply in figuring withholding. Each method is arranged by payroll periods and divided into two separate schedules for married (including surviving spouse) and single (including head of household) taxpayers. You can use the percentage method for some employees while using the wage-bracket table for others. And you can change from one method to another without IRS approval. Generally, you must use the percentage method for quarterly, semiannual, or annual payroll periods, unless you use an authorized alternative method (see below).The amount you withhold under either method depends on the schedule you use (as to the payroll period and the employee's marital status), the number of withholding allowances claimed by the employee on the withholding allowance certificate [¶15,025] and the amount of the employee's earnings.

You may use alternative methods of withholding that result in substantially the same amount of tax withheld as the percentage or wage-bracket methods.

---

[49] Announcement 2013-29, IRB 2013-18, 1024; Announcement 2013-33, IRB 2013-20, 1098.

.01 Percentage Method

The amount to be withheld using the percentage method is determined as follows [Code Sec. 3402(a), (b); Reg. § 31.3402(b)-1]:

1. Multiply one withholding allowance shown in the table below by the number of allowances claimed by the employee [¶ 15,025]. Note: This table is found on page 42 in IRS Publication 15, *(Circular E), Employer's Tax Guide for Use in 2013.*
2. Subtract that amount from the employee's wage to find net wages used to figure withholding.
3. Apply the proper rate found in IRS Publication 15.

Table 1. Percentage Method—2013 Amount for One Withholding Allowance

Payroll Period	One Withholding Allowance	Payroll Period	One Withholding Allowance
Weekly	$ 75.00	Semiannually	$1,950.00
Biweekly	$150.00	Annually	$3,900.00
Semimonthly	$162.50	Daily or miscellaneous (each day of the payroll period) . .	$ 15.00
Monthly	$325.00		
Quarterly	$975.00		

Example 15-3: During 2013, an unmarried employee is paid $600 weekly. This employee has in effect a Form W-4 claiming two withholding allowances. Using the Percentage Method, tax in the amount of $52.60 should be withheld from the taxpayer's wages computed as follows:

1. Total wage payment	$600.00
2. One allowance	$ 75.00
3. Allowances claimed on Form W-4	2
4. Multiply line 2 by line 3	$150.00
5. Amount subject to withholding (subtract line 4 from line 1)	$450.00
6. Tax to be withheld on $450.00 from Table for Percentage Method of Withholding (Table 1—Weekly Payroll Period)—single taxpayer	$52.60

.02 Wage-Bracket Withholding Method

Under this method, the amount to be withheld is found directly from the wage-bracket tables which can be found in IRS Publication 15, *(Circular E), Employers Tax Guide (For use in 2013)* on pages 44-65. They are set up by payroll period (weekly, biweekly, semimonthly, monthly, and daily or miscellaneous), with separate tables for married and single taxpayers. The employer uses the bracket in which the wage payment fits and withholds the amount found in the column for the number of withholding allowances claimed [¶ 15,025] [Code Sec. 3402(c); Reg. § 31.3402(c)-1].

When wages are in excess of the last wage bracket in the table, you should refer to the percentage method withholding table indicated.

.03 Alternative Methods

In addition to the percentage and wage-bracket methods, several alternative methods of computing withholding are available. In Publication 15-A, the IRS provides the following alternative methods: (1) formula tables for percentage method withholding (for automated payroll systems), (2) wage bracket percentage method tables (for automated payroll systems), and (3) combined income, social security, and Medicare tax withholding tables. Some of the alternative methods explained in Publication 15-A, *Employer's Supplemental Tax Guide (Supplement to Circular E, Employer's Tax Guide, Publication 15)* are annualized wages, average estimated wages, cumulative wages, and part-year employment.

.04 When No Payroll Period Is Specified

If employers pay wages without regard to any payroll period, or if they pay wages for a period not otherwise provided for by the percentage method schedule or wage-bracket tables, they can find the amount withheld by using the table for a daily or miscellaneous payroll period of the same length, or if the percentage method is used, by applying the amount of the withholding exemption for such period [Code Secs. 3402(b)(1), (2), 3402(c)(2), (3)].

Short Period

Employers may use the weekly payroll period table to determine the amount to be withheld when the period covered by the payments is less than one week [Code Secs. 3402(b)(3), 3402(c)(4)].

Figuring Withholding by Annualizing Wages

Employers can figure withholding by annualizing wages and finding the amount as follows:

1. Multiply wages for the payroll period by the number of these periods in the calendar year;
2. Determine the amount to be withheld from step (1) on an annual basis; then
3. Divide the result by the number of payroll periods[50] [Reg. § 31.3402(h)(2)-1].

.05 Part-Year Employment Method of Withholding

Employers can figure withholding by the part-year employment method if the employee requests it. This request must state under penalty of perjury:

- The last day of employment (if any) by any employer before the current term of continuous employment, if the employee was previously employed during the year in which the current term of employment began;
- That the employee will work no more than 245 days during the current year; and
- That the employee will use the calendar-year accounting period.

[50] Rev. Rul. 66-328, 1966-2 CB 454.

Employers figure withholding in the following order [Reg. § 31.3402(h)(4)-1(c)]:

1. Add the wages for the current payroll period to the total wages paid to the employee for all prior periods included in the current term of continuous employment;
2. Divide total wages computed in (1) above by the total payroll periods to which that amount relates, plus an equal number of payroll periods in the employee's continuous unemployment just before the current term of continuous unemployment. Omit from the term of continuous unemployment any days before the start of the calendar year;
3. Determine the total tax that would have been withheld if average wages (computed in (2) above) had been paid for the number of payroll periods determined in (2) above (including the equivalent number of payroll periods);
4. Find the excess, if any, of the tax computed in (3) above over the total tax already withheld for all payroll periods during the current term of continuous employment.

.06 Vacation Pay

Withholding on vacation allowances is the same as for regular wage payments made for the vacation period. If employees get extra pay for working during their vacation, it is treated as a supplemental payment (discussed above) [Reg. § 31.3402(g)-1(c)].

.07 Sick Pay

Payments by employers under sick-pay plans are considered wages subject to income tax withholding [Reg. § 31.3401(a)-1(b)(8)]. Payments by a third party, such as an insurance company or trust, are not subject to withholding, unless the payee so requests on Form W-4S or similar statement. A request for withholding, or change or cancellation of withholding, applies to payments made eight days after the request, and even earlier if the payer agrees [Code Sec. 3402(o)(5); Reg. § 31.3402(o)-3(i)].

> **NOTE:** A third-party that is paid an insurance premium and not reimbursed on a cost-plus-fee basis is treated as an employer rather than as an agent. That means the third party is liable for both the employee's and employer's share of social security and Medicare taxes with respect to sick pay, unless the liability is transferred to the employer.[51]

.08 Wages Paid on Behalf of Two or More Employers

If an agent, fiduciary, or other person pays the wages of an employee of two or more employers, withholding is figured on the total amount [Reg. § 31.3402(g)-3].

.09 Withholding on Average Estimated Wages

Withholding on average estimated wages can be made, with necessary adjustments for any quarter, without IRS approval. You can also use an estimate in figuring tips an employee will report in a given quarter. You determine the amount to be withheld and then deduct it from each regular wage payment. You can make adjustments during the quarter and within 30 days thereafter to reflect tips actually reported by the employee [Code Sec. 3402(h)(1); Reg. § 31.3402(h)(1)-1(b)].

---

[51] Notice 91-26, 1991-2 CB 619; as corrected by Notice 91-26A, 1991-2 CB 629.

.10 Voluntary Withholding

If employees find that withholding will not cover their tax liability, they can claim fewer allowances on the withholding allowance certificate (W-4) than they would normally be entitled to given their marital status, number of dependents, etc. [¶15,025]. For example, a married person can request withholding at the higher single rate in order to have more income tax withheld from wages. In addition, employees may request (by filing a new Form W-4) that you increase their withholding by a specific dollar amount. In turn, you must honor such requests automatically, and give effect to revised Forms W-4 in the first payroll period that ends on or after the thirtieth day after the employer receives the new W-4 [¶15,030]. Increased amounts that you are requested to withhold are then considered tax required to be deducted and withheld [Code Sec. 3402(i)(2); Reg. §31.3402(i)-1(a)].

.11 When Allowances for Claimed Exemptions Offset Regular Wages

If the amount of regular wages due an employee for two or more consecutive payroll periods of one week or more is less than the amount claimed as exempt from tax given the employee's withholding allowances, you may elect a special method to find the tax to be withheld on supplemental wages received for those payroll periods:

1. Average the total regular and supplemental payments over the payroll periods;
2. Figure the tax to be withheld on the average amount for each payroll period; then
3. Subtract the tax withheld on the regular wages from the tax to be withheld on the average wages. The remainder is the tax you withhold on the supplemental payments [Reg. §31.3402(g)-1(b)].

.12 Withholding on Nonwage Payments

A voluntary agreement between an employer and an employee can cover payments for an employee's service not within the term wages (for example, domestic and farm workers' wages [¶15,015]). The agreement is effective for a period the employer and employee mutually agree on, but either one can end it by giving notice to the other. No special form is prescribed for the employee's request. However, Form W-4 must be attached to the request. Certain payments such as noncash pay for services not in the course of an employer's business, certain moving expense reimbursements and employer-paid group-term life insurance premiums may not be withheld on under a voluntary agreement [Code Sec. 3402(p); Reg. §§31.3401(a)-3, 31.3402(p)-1]. For withholding on pension and annuity payments, see ¶15,040; for withholding on supplemental unemployment compensation, see ¶15,015.

¶15,025 WITHHOLDING ALLOWANCES

Employees can claim on their withholding allowance certificate (Form W-4) one withholding allowance for each exemption they report on their income tax return [Ch. 1]. They may also claim a special withholding allowance [discussed below]and additional withholding allowances for items described below. Spouses who are each employed must allocate their total allowances between their allowance certificates. An allocation also must be made if one spouse, or one single person, holds more than one job at the same time [Code Sec. 3402(f), 3402(m); Reg. §§31.3402(f)(1)-1, 31.3402(f)(2)-1, 31.3402(m)-1].

.01 Exemption from Withholding

An employee who had no tax liability last year and anticipates none this year may complete a withholding allowance certificate, Form W-4, claiming that he or she is exempt from withholding. An employee cannot withhold income tax from an employee who has filed such a properly executed Form W-4 [Code Sec. 3402(n); Reg. §31.3402(n)-1]. Forms W-4 on which employees claim exemption from withholding expire on the 15th day of the second month following the end of the tax year. Therefore, employees must file a new Form W-4 by each February 15 if they wish to continue to claim exempt status [Reg. §31.3402(f)(4)-2(c)]. Exemption from income tax withholding does not affect the employee's liability for social security taxes.

Consult the following chart to determine if you are eligible to claim an exemption from withholding on Form W-4:[52]

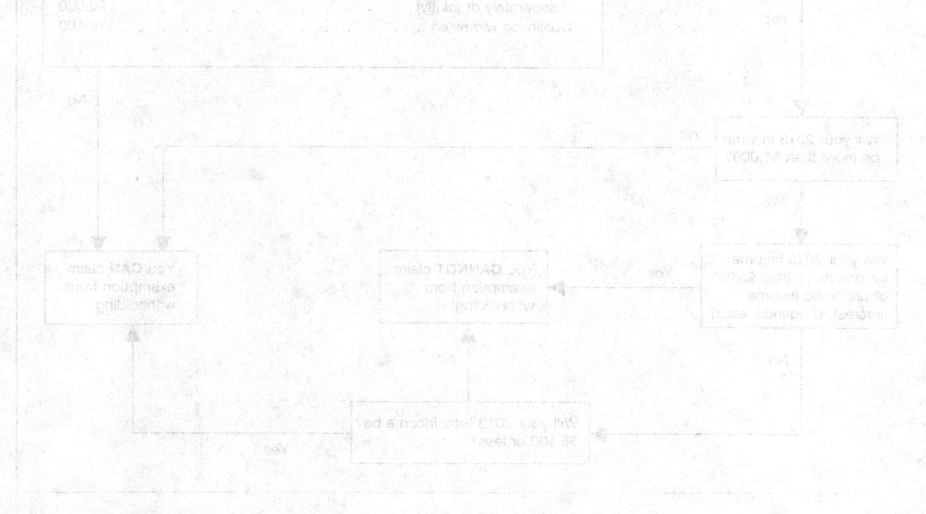

52 Treas. Dept., IRS Publication 505, "Tax Withholding Estimated Tax" (For use in 2013), p 12.

Figure 1-A. **Exemption From Withholding on Form W-4**

Note. Do not use this chart if you are 65 or older or blind, or if you will itemize your deductions, claim exemptions for dependents, or claim tax credits. Instead, see the discussions in this chapter under *Exemption From Withholding.*

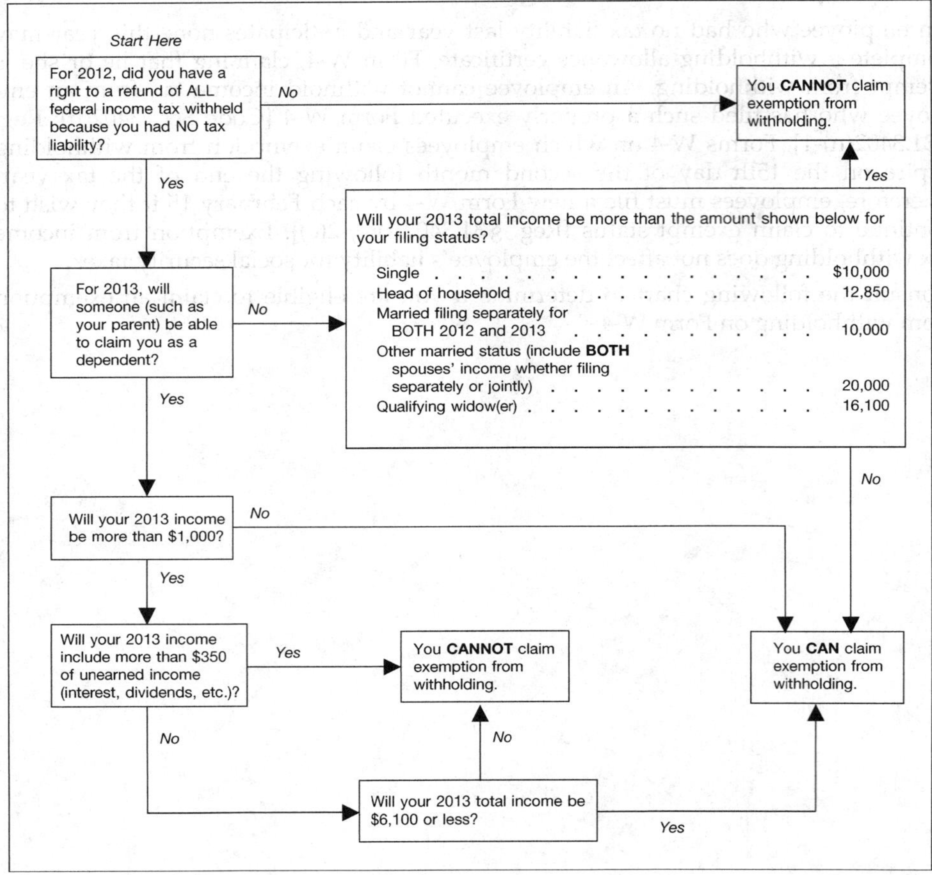

.02 Additional Withholding Allowances

Employees with substantial adjustments to income, deductions, credits and nonwage income can avoid overwithholding by claiming additional withholding allowances on Form W-4. Besides itemized deductions, employees can count deductible adjustments to income that include alimony, deductible retirement contributions (IRA and Keogh plans), net losses from business and net operating loss carryovers. Allowances remain in effect until the employee files a new Form W-4 [Code Sec. 3402(m); Reg. § 31.3402(m)]. Form W-4 includes worksheets to help you figure your withholding allowances. Be sure to adjust withholding for the new child tax credit and higher education credit.

Because tax credits directly lower your tax, you need to figure withholding allowances for tax credits separately from allowances based on deductions. The Personal Allowances Worksheet on Form W-4 allows you to take an additional allowance if you have child or dependent care expenses for which you plan to claim a credit. If you do not meet this expense threshold, or plan to claim other tax credits (see below) not taken into account on Form W-4, you can use one of the following alternate methods of figuring withholding allowances.

Alternative Withholding Allowance Methods

The IRS sanctions two alternative methods of calculating withholding allowances.

- Allowances may be determined without using the worksheets provided on Form W-4. The calculation must be based on current withholding schedules, tax rate schedules, and the Form 1040ES (Estimated Tax for Individuals) worksheet, and it must be more accurate than the Form W-4 method; or
- An employee may use an alternative method that takes into account tax credits that are not mentioned on Form W-4.

This alternative method may also be used if the employee is entitled to claim more than one allowance for child and dependent care expenses.

The *deduction equivalent* of the tax credits must first be determined. This is done by multiplying the total estimated amount of the credits by the applicable factor, which can be found in Table 1-3 on page 10 of IRS Publication 505, *Tax Withholding and Estimated Tax*. The factors as they are applied for tax year 2013 are shown in Table 2.

Table 2. Deductions and Adjustments Worksheet (Form W-4)

Table 1-3. Deductions and Adjustments Worksheet (Form W-4)—Line 5

a. Married Filing Jointly or Qualifying Widow(er)

If combined income from all sources is:	Multiply credits by:
$0 – 42,000	10.0
$42,001 – 96,000	6.7
$96,001 – 175,000	4.0
$175,001 – 260,000	3.6
$260,001 – 430,000	3.0
$430,001 – 480,000	2.8
$480,001 and over	2.5

b. Single

If combined income from all sources is:	Multiply credits by:
$0 – 19,000	10.0
$19,001 – 46,000	6.7
$46,001 – 100,000	4.0
$100,001 – 200,000	3.6
$200,001 – 430,000	3.0
$430,001 and over	2.5

c. Head of Household

If combined income from all sources is:	Multiply credits by:
$0 – 30,000	10.0
$30,001 – 65,000	6.7
$65,001 – 145,000	4.0
$145,001 – 230,000	3.6
$230,001 – 430,000	3.0
$430,001 – 460,000	2.8
$460,001 and over	2.5

d. Married Filing Separately

If combined income from all sources is:	Multiply credits by:
$0 – 21,000	10.0
$21,001 – 48,000	6.7
$48,001 – 87,500	4.0
$87,501 – 130,000	3.6
$130,001 – 215,000	3.0
$215,001 – 240,000	2.8
$240,001 and over	2.5

The result is included in the amount entered on line 5 of the "Deductions and Adjustments Worksheet" on Form W-4. An employee may use the worksheet for this purpose, even if it would not otherwise be used.

Married persons figure their withholding allowances on the basis of their combined wages and allowable items (see above). However, this does not apply if they filed separate returns for the prior year and expect to file separately for the current year. An employee with two employers can divide the total number of allowances to which he or she is entitled among his or her jobs, but the employee can claim each particular withholding allowance with only one employer at a time [Code Sec. 3402(m); Reg. §31.3402(m)-1].

¶15,030 WITHHOLDING ALLOWANCE CERTIFICATE, FORM W-4

Every employee must furnish his or her employer with a signed withholding exemption certificate (Form W-4) on or before starting employment [Code Sec. 3402(f)(2)(A)]. It is used to:

- Claim the total number of withholding allowances;
- Ask the employer to withhold an additional amount from gross pay; or
- Claim exemption from withholding [¶15,025].

Employees who don't file a W-4 are subject to withholding as if they had claimed zero allowances [Reg. §31.3402(f)(2)-1(a)]. Furthermore, these employees are treated as single persons until they file a Form W-4 that indicates married status [Code Sec. 3402(l)]. Penalties are imposed for false or fraudulent statements, for failing to supply a certificate, or for misstating withholding allowances [¶15,160]. The certificate is invalid for any altering or unauthorized additions to the Form W-4 [Reg. §31.3402(f)(2)-1(e)].

An employee can claim a special withholding allowance for himself or herself, and additional allowances for certain dependents and other factors. Claims for withholding allowances remain in effect until the employee files a new certificate because of a change in circumstances [discussed below].

.01 Employer's Responsibility Regarding Questionable W-4s

An employer is not required to determine whether employees have claimed more than the number of allowances to which they are entitled [Reg. §31.3401(e)-1(b)].

.02 New Employees

Employers must verify that each new employee is legally eligible to work in the United States. This will include completing the Immigration and Naturalization Service (INS) Form I-9, *Employer Eligibility Verification Form.*

These employees must furnish a Form W-4 with their identification numbers [¶15,165] to their employers on or before the date employment starts. Employers are required to request a W-4 from each new employee, and must give immediate effect to each form submitted [Code Sec. 3402(f); Reg. §31.3402(f)(1)-1(a)].

Example 15-4: Kane starts work on Feb. 4, and gives his employer a Form W-4 that claims three allowances. The next pay period ends on Feb. 15. In figuring the withholding from Kane's salary on that date and thereafter, these three allowances will be used.

.03 Filing an Amended W-4 on Change in Status

An employee may file a new withholding allowance certificate at any time if the number of allowances he or she is eligible to claim increases (for example, due to the birth of a child).

An employee *must* file a new certificate within ten days if the number of allowances he or she can claim decreases due to a change in circumstances [Reg. § 31.3402(f)(2)-1(b)]. Here are some examples of cases where withholding allowances decrease:

- An employee becomes legally separated or divorced, or the spouse claims his or her own allowance on a separate certificate;

  NOTE: The *death* of a spouse (or other dependent) doesn't affect withholding until the next year, but requires filing of a new certificate by December 1 (if possible) of the year in which the death occurred. If the employee qualifies as a surviving spouse with a dependent child, the status of married individual may be claimed for the following two years [Code Sec. 2(a)].

- The support of a dependent for whom the employee claimed a withholding allowance is taken over by someone else, so that the employee no longer expects to furnish more than half the dependent's support for the year;
- An employee has been claiming additional withholding allowances for estimated itemized deductions, while his or her spouse was not employed. When the spouse begins employment, a smaller number of additional withholding allowances may be authorized; and

When to Give Effect to Revised Forms W-4

You may give effect to a new certificate filed by an employee with respect to the next wage payment made on or after the date the revised certificate is furnished. You must give effect to revised W-4s no later than the start of the first payroll period ending on or after the 30th day after the date that you receive the revised W-4 [Code Sec. 3402(f)(3)].

Example 15-5: Johnson is paid semimonthly on the 1st and 15th of each month. She files a revised Form W-4 with her employer on January 2. Her new withholding amount must be reflected in her February 1 paycheck.

Anticipated Changes in Circumstances

An employee may not file a Form W-4 that claims married status unless the employee is actually married at the time the certificate is filed. When employees anticipate a decrease in the number of withholding allowances they can claim, owing to a change of circumstance that will take effect in the next calendar year (see the note regarding death of a spouse, above), the employees should file a revised W-4 on or before

December 1 (if possible). In these latter cases the employer should not give effect to the revised W-4 until the next calendar year [Reg. § 31.3402(f)(2)-1(c)].

.04 How Much to Withhold to Avoid the Penalty

To determine how much to withhold, complete all applicable Form W-4 worksheets. This basically means that you have to compute your entire tax return in advance without the benefit of the actual IRS forms or computer programs to run the numbers for you. To help you compute your current withholding amount, take a look at IRS Publication 505, *Tax Withholding and Estimated Tax.* Also look at Publication 919, *How Do I Adjust My Withholding?* because it has the current tax rate schedules and tables.

.05 Tax Law Changes May Affect Withholding

When figuring your estimated tax or how much income tax you want withheld from wages do not overlook legislative changes which become effective this year. These include the inflation-adjusted credits and deductions which could reduce your overall tax bill and decrease the amount of tax that should be withheld.

¶15,040 WITHHOLDING TAX ON PENSIONS, ANNUITIES, AND OTHER DEFERRED INCOME

The withholding procedures used for pension, annuity and deferred income payments parallels those used for wage withholding. But different rates and rules apply depending on the type of payment. Payors of pensions, annuities, and other deferred income must withhold income tax from all designated distributions made by them, unless the recipient claims exemption from withholding on Form W-4P.

A designated distribution is any distribution or payment from an employer-deferred compensation plan (that is, a qualified employer plan or other deferred-compensation plans); any type of IRA; or a commercial annuity (annuity, endowment, or life insurance contract issued by an insurance company [Ch. 3]) [Code Sec. 3405(e)(1); Temp. Reg. § 35.3405-1T Q&A-2].

.01 The Withholding Rate

The rate withheld depends on whether the distribution is periodic or nonperiodic. In either case, however, the amount withheld can never exceed the amount of money plus the fair market value of other property (other than securities of the employer corporation) received in a distribution. For this reason, a payor will not have to liquidate employer securities qualifying for special deferral of net unrealized appreciation, merely to satisfy withholding rules. If a payor has more than one program under which designated distributions can be paid, then each program must be treated separately. Also, the value of a noncash distribution is determined as of the last valuation date before the distribution [Code Sec. 3405(e)(8); Temp. Reg. § 35.3405-1T Q&A-8].

.02 Periodic Payments

Income tax is withheld as it is on wages, but it is calculated separately at the graduated rates set forth in the appropriate withholding table. The amount withheld is based on prescribed payment periods designated in the annuity or pension contract and the information on the Withholding Certificate for Pension or Annuity Payments (Form W-4P). If a W-4P is not filed and an election to avoid withholding is not made, tax is withheld as if the recipient were married and claimed three withholding allowances [Code Sec. 3405(a)(4)]. A payee is treated as married with three allowances even if the payor knows the payee is single [Temp. Reg. § 35.3405-1T, B-4].

Payees who elect that no tax be withheld make this election on Form W-4P. Such an election must be given effect under the rules that apply to Forms W-4 [¶ 15,030] [Code Sec. 3405(a)(3)]. And the election remains in effect until revoked by the payee. If the recipient doesn' t furnish his taxpayer identification number (TIN) to the payor or if the IRS has notified the payor that the TIN is incorrect, an election is not effective [Code Sec. 3405(e)(12)]. The payor must give notice of the right to make this election no earlier than six months before and no later than the first payment date. Follow-up notices of a payee's right to make, renew, or revoke any election must be given at least once each year. Furthermore, payees who had benefits suspended due to reemployment must again be notified when benefits are reinstated [Temp. Reg. §§ 35.3405-1T, D-1].

.03 Nonperiodic Distributions

The amount withheld from nonperiodic distributions, depends on whether or not you choose to have the distributions transferred directly into an eligible plan (such as another qualified retirement plan or an IRA). There is no withholding on a direct transfer. But if the transfer is not direct, there is a mandatory withholding of 20 percent of the amount transferred. This 20 percent must be withheld even though you may have made a tax-free rollover. (Of course, you get back any excess withholding when you file your tax return for the year.)

> ▶ **IRS GUIDANCE:** The IRS has issued regulations in the form of a series of questions and answers to guide employers and plan administrators in complying with the withholding rules. Here's a rundown of the some of the regulation's key questions and answers [Reg. § 31.3405(c)-1T, Q&A-1(c)(2)].

How does a plan go about making a direct rollover? The distributing plan must pay the amount of the distribution directly to the new plan selected by the employee. Any "reasonable" means of payment is acceptable. For example, the distributing plan can make a wire transfer or can mail a check to the rollover plan. The check or wire transfer must be payable to the trustee of the plan or, if there is no trustee, to the custodian or issuer of the contract under the plan.

Can an employee direct the plan to roll over only part of his or her distribution? Yes. An employee can choose to receive payment of part of a distribution and ask the plan to make a direct rollover of the remainder. However, where an employee wants to divide a distribution, the plan can require the direct rollover to be at least $500. If the total distribution is less than $500, the plan does not have to permit the employee to divide the distribution.

What if the employee's distribution is very small, say, $100 or $200? A plan can limit direct rollovers to total distributions of $200 or more. A plan can, however, permit direct rollovers regardless of the amount of the distribution, or it can set the minimum below $200.

If a plan has to make direct rollovers to other plans, does that mean it also has to accept rollovers? No. A plan can refuse to accept rollover contributions. Or a plan can limit the types of plans from which it will accept rollovers or the types of rollover contributions it will accept (for example, cash or cash equivalents).

Suppose an employee is to receive a series of distributions that are eligible to be rolled over, for example, period payments over less than 10 years. Does the plan have to get new directions for each payment? No. The plan can treat the employee's election to make or not to make a direct rollover as applying to all payments in a series, provided the employee is on notice that his or her election will not apply to future payments. The employee must, however, be able to change the election for future payments at any time.

Can the employee elect not to have tax withheld from a distribution that is not directly rolled over? No. If a distribution is eligible to roll over, the only way the employee can avoid having tax withheld is to elect a direct rollover.

If a distribution consists of property other than cash, how does the plan withhold? As a general rule, if a distribution consists solely of property or does not include enough cash to satisfy the 20 percent withholding obligation, the plan must either sell the property or receive cash from the employee to pay the withholding. However, employer securities do not have to be sold to satisfy the withholding obligation.

What is undue hardship? It generally means more than just inconvenience or increased costs. The plan administrator should be prepared to show problems in developing forms, mailing notices, processing responses, updating computer systems or training personnel.

Avoiding Withholding for Nonperiodic Distributions

If a retirement plan pays out a benefit in the form of employee securities, the net unrealized appreciation on the employer securities may be excluded from the employee's gross income. The IRS has said that to the extent net unrealized appreciation is excludable from gross income, the appreciation is not subject to withholding [Temp. Reg. § 31.3405(c)-1T, Q&A-1(c)(2), Temp. Reg. § 35.3405-1T].

Distributions Delivered Outside the United States and Its Possessions

Pension benefits and other similar payments delivered outside the United States and its possessions are subject to withholding. However, if the payee certifies to the payor that he or she isn't a U.S. citizen or resident alien or an expatriate for tax avoidance purposes, then the recipient may elect no withholding [Code Sec. 3405(e)(13)].

.04 Payor's Liability for Withholding

The payor of a designated distribution is generally liable for the payment of the tax required to be withheld. However, in some cases, such as qualified plans [Ch. 3], the plan administrator must withhold, and is liable for, payment of the tax. The plan administrator can, instead, direct the payor to withhold if the payor is furnished with the required information. The rules relating to wage withholding and deposits apply to tax withheld on designated distributions.

Form 945 is used by payors to remit withheld taxes once a year [Code Sec. 3405(d); Temp. Reg. § 35.3405-1T]. Also, payees must furnish their correct TINs for an election out of withholding to be valid [Code Sec. 3405(e)(12)].

¶15,045 INCOME TAX WITHHOLDING AND NONRESIDENT ALIENS

The taxation of income earned by non-U.S. citizens depends on whether the individual is classified as a resident alien or a nonresident alien. Resident aliens are taxed on their worldwide income, as are U.S. citizens. A nonresident alien is generally subject to tax on U.S.-source income and on foreign-source gross income effectively connected with a U.S. trade or business. Generally, U.S.-source income received by a nonresident non-U.S. citizen that is not "effectively connected with a U.S. trade or business" is subject to a flat 30 percent withholding tax (or lower tax rate provided by treaty) [Code Secs. 1441, 1442; Reg. § 1.1441-1(b)]. U.S. source net income that is effectively connected to a trade or business is subject to tax in the same manner as income earned by U.S. citizens [Code Sec. 871(a) and (b)]. The 30 percent (or lower treaty rate) tax is imposed on payments of U.S.-source interest that is not effectively connected with a U.S. trade or business. See also Ch. 28.

.01 Who Must Withhold?

Usually, an agent that makes income payments is responsible for withholding on payments received by nonresident aliens. Agents include U.S. citizens, resident or resident alien fiduciaries, resident partnerships, and U.S. and foreign corporations [Code Secs. 1441(a), 1442(a); Reg. § 1.1441-1].

A corporation that pays dividends may assume that shareholders are U.S. citizens or residents if their addresses are in the U.S., if the corporation does not know their status. If the address is a foreign one, or changed from a foreign one to one in the U.S., tax must be withheld, unless a written statement asserting U.S. citizenship is furnished by the individual [Reg. § 1.1441-1(b)(3)].

> **NOTE:** Special rules apply to partnerships (both foreign and domestic). Partnerships with income effectively connected with the conduct of a trade or business in the United States must pay a withholding tax equal to the applicable percentage of the effectively connected taxable income that is allocable to its foreign partners. The applicable percentage is 35 percent for both noncorporate and corporate partners [Code Sec. 1446].

.02 Payments Subject to Withholding

Withholding may be required on fixed or determinable periodic income. This includes dividends, interest (other than original issue discount), rents, royalties, premiums, annuities, remuneration, emoluments, and other income of this type. Withholding also is required on gain from the disposal of timber, coal, or iron ore that is treated as gain from a sale or exchange of the timber, coal, or iron ore, original issue discount that accrued but was not included in income before an original issue discount was sold or a payment made on the obligation, and gains from the sale or exchange of patents, copyrights, secret processes and formulas, goodwill, trademarks, trade brands, franchises, and like property to the extent that such gains are from payments that are contingent on the productivity, use, or disposition of the property sold or exchanged [Code Sec. 1441(b); Reg. § 1.1441-2].

Income Effectively Connected with U.S. Trade or Business

Withholding on payments (except wages) is generally not required if: (a) income is effectively connected with the nonresident aliens' U.S. trade or business and is includible in their gross income, and (b) they file a withholding exemption statement (Form 4224) with the withholding agent [Code Sec. 1441(c); Reg. § 1.1441-4]. However, effectively connected income earned by foreign persons through U.S. partnerships may be subject to withholding [as discussed above]. See Ch. 28.

Withholding Rates

When withholding is required, the rate is generally 30 percent of the income items, unless a lower treaty rate applies. The withholding rates on wages paid to nonresident aliens for services in the U.S. are the same as for foreign taxpayers. Foreign students and exchange visitors are subject to a 14 percent withholding rate on the taxable portion of their scholarships or grants [Code Secs. 1441(b); 1442; Reg. §§ 1.1441-1, 1.1441-2, 1.1441-4(b)(1)].

.03 Who Is Subject to Withholding?

Withholding on *noneffectively connected* income applies to nonresident alien individuals (including alien residents of Puerto Rico), foreign partnerships, and foreign corporations. Foreign students and exchange visitors are subject to the same withholding rates as other nonresident aliens except for the taxable portion of their scholarships or grants [Ch. 5] [Code Sec. 1441; Reg. §§ 1.1441-1, 1.1441-2]. Note that effectively connected income earned by foreign partners in U.S. partnership may be subject to withholding [discussed above]. See Ch. 28.

.04 Tax Treaties on Withholding Rates

Lower withholding rates are provided in a number of tax conventions with foreign countries. To obtain the lesser treaty rate or exemption, the recipient must file Form 1001 with the withholding agent. The reduced rate for dividends applies when the payor's records show the stockholder's address is in the foreign country concerned.[53]

.05 Withholding on Sales of U.S. Real Property by Foreign Persons

This withholding serves to collect tax that may be owed by the foreign person. A buyer or other transferee who acquires a U.S. real property interest from a foreign person must deduct and withhold the lesser of 10 percent of the amount realized by the transferor (foreign person), or the transferor's maximum tax liability (the maximum amount that the IRS determines the transferor could owe on its gain on the sale, plus the transferor's unsatisfied prior withholding tax liability as to that interest) [Code Sec. 1445(a); Reg. § 1.1445-1].

Buyers use Form 8288, *U.S. Withholding Tax Return for Dispositions by Foreign Persons of U.S. Real Property Interests* to report and pay withheld tax. Foreign transferors use Form 8288-A, *Statement of Withholding on Dispositions by Foreign Persons of U.S. Real Property Interests* to report transactions.

Special rules apply to distributions by corporations and for partnerships, trusts and estates [Code Sec. 1445(e); Reg. § 1.1445-5c(1)(i)]. If a domestic partnership, domestic trust, or domestic estate disposes of a United States real property interest, the

[53] Rev. Rul. 66-55, 1966-1 CB 360.

partnership, trustee, or executor must withhold a tax equal to 35 percent (or, to the extent provided in regulations, 15 percent) of the gain realized to the extent that the gain is allocable to a foreign person who is a partner or beneficiary of the partnership, trust, or estate or is allocable to a portion of the trust treated as owned by a foreign person under the grantor trust rules. This rule involving withholding by partnerships, estates, and trusts only comes into play when distributions from the sale of U.S. real property are made to a foreign person who is a partner or beneficiary. If the partner or beneficiary is not a foreign person, no income tax is required to be withheld from the distribution. The IRS has not exercised its regulatory authority to reduce the withholding rate to 15 percent.

.06 Withholding Rules for Nonresident Alien Employees

In general, an employer must withhold federal social security and Medicare taxes tax at the 30 percent rate on compensation paid to a nonresident alien individual for labor or personal services performed in the United States, unless that pay is specifically exempted from withholding or subject to graduated withholding [Code Sec. 3402(a)(1). This rule applies regardless of the employer's place of residence, the place where the contract for service was made, or the place of payment.[54]

Illegal Aliens

Foreign workers who are illegal aliens are subject to U.S. taxes in spite of their illegal status. U.S. employers or payers who hire illegal aliens may be subject to various fines, penalties, and sanctions imposed by U.S. Immigration and Customs Enforcement. If employers or payers choose to hire illegal aliens, the payments made to those aliens are subject to the same tax withholding and reporting obligations that apply to other classes of aliens. Illegal aliens who are nonresident aliens and who receive income from performing independent personal services are subject to 30 percent withholding unless exempt under some provision of law or a tax treaty. Illegal aliens who are resident aliens and who receive income from performing dependent personal services are subject to the same reporting and withholding obligations that apply to U.S. citizens who receive the same kind of income.

Nonresident alien individuals should use Form 8233, *Exemption From Withholding on Compensation for Independent (and Certain Dependent) Personal Services of a Nonresident Alien Individual* to claim a tax treaty exemption from withholding on some or all compensation paid for the following: self-employment (called independent personal services in tax treaties); dependent personal services; personal services income; noncompensatory scholarship or fellowship income from the same withholding agent.

30 Percent Withholding Rate

Employers must withhold at the statutory rate of 30 percent on all payments unless the alien enters into a withholding agreement or receives a final payment exemption. The amount of pay subject to 30 percent withholding may be reduced by the personal exemption amount ($3,900 for 2013) if the alien gives the employer a properly completed Form 8233. A nonresident alien is allowed only one personal exemption.

---

[54] Treas. Dept., IRS Publication 515, "Withholding of Tax on Nonresident Aliens and Foreign Entities" (2013 Ed).

However, individuals who are residents of Canada, Mexico, or South Korea, or are U.S. nationals generally are entitled to the same exemptions as U.S. citizens. Students and business apprentices may claim an additional exemption for their spouse if a joint return is not filed, and if the spouse has no gross income for the year and is not the dependent of another taxpayer. They also may claim additional exemptions for children who reside with them in the United States at any time during the year, but only if the dependents are U.S. citizens or nationals or residents of the United States, Canada, or Mexico. They may not claim exemptions for dependents who are admitted to the United States on "F2," "J2," or "M2" visas unless such dependents have become resident aliens.

Each allowable exemption must be prorated according to the number of days during the tax year during which the alien performs services in the United States. Multiply the number of these days by $10.68 (the daily exemption amount for 2013) to figure the prorated amount. A U.S. national is an individual who owes his sole allegiance to the United States, but who is not a U.S. citizen. Such an individual is usually a citizen of American Samoa or a Northern Mariana Islander who chose to become a U.S. national.[55]

Withholding agreements. Pay for personal services of a nonresident alien who is engaged during the tax year in the conduct of a U.S. trade or business may be wholly or partially exempted from withholding at the statutory rate if an agreement has been reached between the IRS and the alien as to the amount of withholding required. This agreement will be effective for payments covered by the agreement that are made after the agreement is executed by all parties. The alien must agree to timely file an income tax return for the current tax year.

Final payment exemption. The final payment of compensation for independent personal services may be wholly or partially exempt from withholding at the statutory rate. This exemption applies to the last payment of compensation, other than wages, for personal services rendered in the United States that the alien expects to receive from any withholding agent during the tax year. To obtain the final payment exemption, the alien, or the alien's agent, must file the forms and provide the information required by the IRS. This information includes, but is not limited to, the following items:

- A statement by each withholding agent from whom amounts of gross income effectively connected with the conduct of a U.S. trade or business have been received by the alien during the tax year. It must show the amount of income paid and the amount of tax withheld. The withholding agent must sign the statement and include a declaration that it is made under penalties of perjury.
- A statement by the withholding agent from whom the final payment of compensation for personal services will be received showing the amount of final payment and the amount that would be withheld if a final payment exemption is not granted. The withholding agent must sign the statement and include a declaration that it is made under penalties of perjury.

---

[55] *Id.*

- A statement by the alien that he or she does not intend to receive any other amounts of gross income effectively connected with the conduct of a U.S. trade or business during the current tax year.
- The amount of tax that has been withheld (or paid) under any other provision of the Code or regulations for any income effectively connected with the conduct of a U.S. trade or business during the current tax year.
- The amount of any outstanding tax liabilities, including any interest and penalties, from the current tax year or prior tax periods.
- The provision of any income tax treaty under which a partial or complete exemption from withholding may be claimed, the country of the alien's residence, and a statement of sufficient facts to justify an exemption under that treaty.

The alien must give a statement, signed and verified by a declaration that it is made under the penalties of perjury, that all the information provided is true, and that to his or her knowledge no relevant information has been omitted.

If satisfied with the information provided, the IRS will determine the amount of the alien's tentative income tax for the tax year on gross income effectively connected with the conduct of a U.S. trade or business. Ordinary and necessary business expenses may be taken into account if proved to the satisfaction of the Commissioner or his delegate. The IRS will provide the alien with a letter stating the amount of the final payment of compensation for personal services that is exempt from withholding, and the amount that would otherwise be withheld that may be paid to the alien due to the exemption. The amount of pay exempt from withholding cannot be more than $5,000. The alien must attach a copy of the letter to his or her income tax return for the tax year for which the exemption is effective.

Tax treaties. Under some tax treaties, pay for independent personal services performed in the United States is treated as business income and taxed according to the treaty provisions for business profits. Under other tax treaties, pay for independent personal services performed in the United States is exempt from U.S. income tax only if the independent nonresident alien contractor performs the services during a period of temporary presence in the United States (usually not more than 183 days) and is a resident of the treaty country. Independent nonresident alien contractors use Form 8233 to claim an exemption from withholding under a tax treaty.

Wages Paid to Employees—Graduated Withholding

Salaries, wages, bonuses, or any other pay for personal services paid to nonresident alien employees are subject to graduated withholding in the same way as for U.S. citizens and residents if the wages are effectively connected with the conduct of a U.S. trade or business. Any wages paid to a nonresident alien for personal services performed as an employee for an employer are generally not subject to the 30 percent withholding if the wages are subject to graduated withholding. The 30 percent withholding does not apply to pay for personal services performed as an employee for an employer if it is effectively connected with the conduct of a U.S. trade or business and is specifically exempted from the definition of wages. The amount of wages subject to graduated withholding may be reduced by the personal exemption amount ($3,900 for 2013).

Special rule for certain agricultural workers. The 30 percent withholding does not apply to pay for personal services performed by a foreign agricultural worker in the

United States on an H2A visa. However, if the total wages are $600 or more and the worker does not give the employer a TIN, the employer may need to backup withhold.

Pay that is not wages. Employment for which the pay is not considered wages (for graduated income tax withholding) includes, but is not limited to, the following items:[56]

- Agricultural labor if the total cash wages paid to an individual worker during the year is less than $150 and the total paid to all workers during the year is less than $2,500. But even if the total amount paid to all workers is $2,500 or more, wages of less than $150 per year paid to a worker are not subject to income tax withholding if certain conditions are met.
- Services of a household nature performed in or about the private home of an employer, or in or about the clubrooms or house of a local college club, fraternity, or sorority. A local college club, fraternity, or sorority does not include an alumni club or chapter and may not be operated primarily as a business enterprise. Examples of these services include those performed as a cook, janitor, house-keeper, governess, gardener, or houseparent.
- Certain services performed outside the course of the employer's trade or business for which cash payment is less than $50 for the calendar quarter.
- Services performed as an employee of a foreign government, without regard to citizenship, residence, or where services are performed. These include services performed by ambassadors, other diplomatic and consular officers and employees, and nondiplomatic representatives. They do not include services for a U.S. or Puerto Rican corporation owned by a foreign government.
- Services performed within or outside the United States by an employee or officer (regardless of citizenship or residence) of an international organization designated under the International Organizations Immunities Act.
- Services performed by a duly ordained, commissioned, or licensed minister of a church, but only if performed in the exercise of the ministry and not as an employee of the United States, a U.S. possession, or a foreign government, or any of their political subdivisions. These also include services performed by a member of a religious order in carrying out duties required by that order.
- Tips paid to an employee if they are paid in any medium other than cash or, if in cash, they amount to less than $20 in any calendar month in the course of employment.
- Compensation paid to a nonresident alien (other than a resident of Puerto Rico) for services performed outside the United States is not considered wages and is not subject to withholding.

Special instructions for Form W-4. A nonresident alien subject to wage withholding must give the employer a completed Form W4 to enable the employer to figure how much income tax to withhold. Note that a nonresident alien cannot claim exemption from withholding on Form W4. Use Form 8233 to claim a tax treaty exemption from

---

[56] *Id.*

withholding. In completing Form W4, nonresident aliens should use the following instructions instead of the instructions on Form W4:

- Check "Single" on line 3 (regardless of actual marital status);
- Claim only one withholding allowance on line 5, unless a resident of Canada, Mexico, or South Korea, or a U.S. national; and
- Write "Nonresident Alien" or "NRA" above the dotted line on line 6.

Nonresident alien employees are not required to request an additional withholding amount, but they can choose to have an additional amount withheld on line 6.

Students and business apprentices from India. Students and business apprentices who are eligible for the benefits of Article 21(2) of the United States India income tax treaty can claim additional withholding allowances on line 5 for their spouses. In addition, they can claim an additional withholding allowance for each dependent who has become a resident alien.

Reporting requirements for wages and withheld taxes paid to nonresident aliens. The employer must report the amount of wages and deposits of withheld income and social security and Medicare taxes by filing Form 941.

Form W-2. The employer also must report on Form W-2 the wages subject to NRA withholding and the withheld taxes. You must give copies of this form to the employee. If the employee submits Form 8233 to claim exemption from withholding under a tax treaty, the wages are reported on Form 1042-S and not in box 1 of Form W-2. Wages exempt under a tax treaty may still be reported in the state and local wages boxes of Form W-2 if such wages are subject to state and local taxation. For more information, see the instructions for these forms.

Social security and Medicare tax. The employer generally must also withhold FICA and file Form 941, Employer's Quarterly Federal Tax Return. In certain cases, wages paid to students and railroad and agricultural workers are exempt from FICA. Wages paid to nonresident alien students, teachers, researchers, trainees, and other nonresident aliens in "F1," "J1," M1," or "Q" nonimmigrant status are not subject to FICA. See Publication 15, *Employer's Tax Guide*, for the rules on withholding.

Beginning in 2013, the withholding rates for social security and Medicare have increased. Also, in addition to withholding Medicare tax at 1.45 percent, you must withhold a 0.9 percent Additional Medicare Tax from wages you pay in excess of $200,000 in a calendar year. See ¶ 15,050.03 for further discussion.

Federal unemployment tax (FUTA). The employer must pay FUTA and file Form 940, *Employer's Annual Federal Unemployment (FUTA) Tax Return*. Only the employer pays this tax; it is not deducted from the employee's wages. In certain cases, wages paid to students and railroad and agricultural workers are exempt from FUTA tax. For more information, see the instructions for these forms. Wages paid to nonresident alien students, teachers, researchers, trainees, and other nonresident aliens in "F1," "J1," "M1," or "Q" nonimmigrant status are not subject to FUTA tax.

Pay for dependent personal services. Dependent personal services are personal services performed in the United States by a nonresident alien individual as an employee rather than as an independent contractor. Pay for dependent personal services is subject to nonresident alien withholding and reporting as follows:

Graduated rates. Ordinarily, employers must withhold on wages for dependent personal services using graduated rates. The nonresident alien must complete Form W4 and report wages and income tax withheld on Form W-2. However, employers do not have to withhold if any of the following four exceptions applies.

- **Exception 1**. Compensation paid for labor or personal services performed in the United States is deemed not to be income from sources within the United States and is exempt from U.S. income tax if:

  — The labor or services are performed by a nonresident alien temporarily present in the United States for a period or periods not exceeding a total of 90 days during the tax year;

  — The total pay does not exceed $3,000; and

  — The pay is for labor or services performed as an employee of, or under a contract with: (a) a nonresident alien individual, foreign partnership, or foreign corporation that is not engaged in a trade or business in the United States, or (b) a U.S. citizen or resident alien individual, a domestic partnership, or a domestic corporation, if the labor or services are performed for an office or place of business maintained in a foreign country or in a possession of the United States by this individual, partnership, or corporation.

  If the total pay is more than $3,000, the entire amount is income from sources in the United States and is subject to U.S. tax. Also, compensation paid for labor or services performed in the United States by a nonresident alien in connection with the individual's temporary presence in the United States as a regular member of the crew of a foreign vessel engaged in transportation between the United States and a foreign country or a U.S. possession is not income from sources within the United States.

- **Exception 2**. Compensation paid by a foreign employer to a nonresident alien for the period the alien is temporarily present in the United States on an "F," "J," or "Q" visa is exempt from U.S. income tax. For this purpose, a foreign employer means:

  — A nonresident alien individual, foreign partnership, or foreign corporation, or

  — An office or place of business maintained in a foreign country or in a U.S. possession by a domestic corporation, a domestic partnership, or an individual U.S. citizen or resident.

  Employers can exempt the payment from withholding if they can reliably associate the payment with a Form W-8BEN containing the taxpayer identification number of the payee.

- **Exception 3**. Compensation paid to certain residents of Canada or Mexico who enter or leave the United States at frequent intervals is not subject to withholding. These aliens must either:

  — Perform duties in transportation services (such as a railroad, bus, truck, ferry, steamboat, aircraft, or other type) between the United States and Canada or Mexico; or

  — Perform duties connected with an international project, relating to the construction, maintenance, or operation of a waterway, viaduct, dam, or bridge crossed by, or crossing, the boundary between the United States and Canada or the boundary between the United States and Mexico.

To qualify for the exemption from withholding during a tax year, a Canadian or Mexican resident must give the employer a statement with the employee's name, address, and identification number, and certifying that the resident: (a) is not a U.S. citizen or resident; (b) is a resident of Canada or Mexico, whichever applies; and (c) expects to perform the described duties during the tax year in question.

The statement can be in any form, but it must be dated and signed by the employee and must include a written declaration that it is made under penalties of perjury.

Canadian and Mexican residents employed entirely within the United States. Neither the transportation service exception nor the international projects exception applies to the pay of a resident of Canada or Mexico who is employed entirely within the United States and who commutes from a home in Canada or Mexico to work in the United States. If an individual works at a fixed point or points in the United States (such as a factory, store, office, or designated area or areas), the wages for services performed as an employee for an employer are subject to graduated withholding.

- **Exception 4**. Compensation paid for services performed in Puerto Rico by a nonresident alien who is a resident of Puerto Rico for an employer (other than the United States or one of its agencies) is not subject to withholding. Compensation paid for either of the following types of services is not subject to withholding if the alien does not expect to be a resident of Puerto Rico during the entire tax year:
  - — Services performed outside the United States but not in Puerto Rico by a nonresident alien who is a resident of Puerto Rico for an employer other than the United States or one of its agencies; or
  - — Services performed outside the United States by a nonresident alien who is a resident of Puerto Rico, as an employee of the United States or any of its agencies.

To qualify for the exemption from withholding for any tax year, the employee must give the employer a statement showing the employee's name and address and certifying that the employee: (a) is not a citizen or resident of the United States, and (b) is a resident of Puerto Rico who does not expect to be a resident for that entire tax year. The statement must be signed and dated by the employee and contain a written declaration that it is made under penalties of perjury.

Tax treaties. Pay for dependent personal services under some tax treaties is exempt from U.S. income tax only if both the employer and the employee are treaty country residents and the nonresident alien employee performs the services while temporarily living in the United States (usually for not more than 183 days). Other treaties provide for exemption from U.S. tax on pay for dependent personal services if the employer is any foreign resident and the employee is a treaty country resident and the nonresident alien employee performs the services while temporarily in the United States.

Pay for teaching. This category is given a separate income code number because some tax treaties provide at least partial exemption from withholding and from U.S. tax. Pay for teaching means payments to a nonresident alien professor, teacher, or researcher by a U.S. university or other accredited educational institution for teaching or research work at the institution. Graduated withholding of income tax usually applies to all wages, salaries, and other pay for teaching and research paid by a U.S. educational institution during the period the nonresident alien is teaching or performing research at the institution. A nonresident alien temporarily in the United States on an "F1," "J1," "M1," or "Q1" visa is not subject to social security and Medicare taxes on pay for services performed to carry out the purpose for which the alien was admitted to the United States. Social security and Medicare taxes should not be withheld or paid on this amount. If an alien is considered a resident alien, that pay is subject to social security and Medicare taxes even though the alien is a nonimmigrant. This rule also applies to FUTA (unemployment) taxes paid by the employer. Teachers, researchers, and other employees temporarily present in the United States on other nonimmigrant visas or in refugee immigration status are fully liable for social security and Medicare taxes unless an exemption applies from one of the totalization agreements in force between the United States and several other nations.

Under most tax treaties, pay for teaching or research is exempt from U.S. income tax and from withholding for a specified period of time when paid to a professor, teacher, or researcher who was a resident of the treaty country immediately prior to entry into the United States and who is not a citizen of the United States. The U.S. educational institution paying the compensation must report the amount of compensation paid each year which is exempt from tax under a tax treaty on Form 1042-S. The employer should also report the compensation in the state and local wages boxes of Form W-2 if the wages are subject to state and local taxes, or in the social security and Medicare wages boxes of Form W-2 if the wages are subject to social security and Medicare taxes.

Pay during studying and training. This category refers to pay (as contrasted with remittances, allowances, or other forms of scholarships or fellowship grants for personal services performed while a nonresident alien is temporarily in the United States as a student, trainee, or apprentice, or while acquiring technical, professional, or business experience. Wages, salaries, or other compensation paid to a nonresident alien student, trainee, or apprentice for labor or personal services performed in the United States are subject to graduated withholding.

SOCIAL SECURITY (FICA) TAXES

¶15,050 TAX ON WAGES

Two parallel federal tax systems exist to fund retirement and disability benefits for most workers:

- The Federal Insurance Contributions Act (FICA or social security tax) [Code Secs. 3101-3128]; and
- The Railroad Retirement Tax Act (RRTA) [Code Secs. 3201-3241].

.01 FICA

FICA imposes two taxes on most employers and employees:

- Old-age, survivors, and disability insurance (OASDI) taxes to fund social security benefits [Code Sec. 3111(a)], and
- Hospital insurance (HI) taxes commonly known as Medicare provides funding for hospital and hospital service insurance for those 65 years of age or older [Code Sec. 3111(b)].

For 2013, the FICA tax rate for employers and employees is 7.65 percent each—6.2 percent for OASDI up to the wage base and 1.45 percent for HI. For 2013, an employee pays:

1. 6.2 percent Social Security tax on the first $113,700 of wages (maximum tax is $7,049.40 [6.20 percent of $113,700], plus
2. 1.45 percent Medicare tax on the first $200,000 of wages ($250,000 for joint returns; $125,000 for married taxpayers filing a separate return), plus
3. 2.35 percent Medicare tax (regular 1.45 percent Medicare tax + 0.9 percent additional Medicare tax) on all wages in excess of $200,000 ($250,000 for joint returns; $125,000 for married taxpayers filing a separate return) [Code Sec. 3101(b)(2)].

.02 Medicare Taxes Imposed on Wages and Investments

New Medicare Taxes in 2013

The 2010 Patient Protection and Affordable Care Act (PPACA) increased Medicare tax for most taxpayers effective in 2013 as follows:

- A 0.9 percent Additional Medicare Tax will be imposed on taxpayers (other than corporations, estate, or trusts) receiving wages with respect to employment in excess of $200,000 ($250,000 in the case of joint filers and surviving spouses, and $125,000 in the case of a married taxpayer filing separately) [Code Sec. 3101(b)(2)]. The threshold amounts are not indexed for inflation;
- A 0.9 percent Additional Medicare Tax will be imposed on an individual's net earnings from self-employment in excess of these threshold amounts [Code Sec. 1401(b)(2)];
- Higher-income taxpayers with investment income will be subject to a new 3.8 percent unearned net investment income tax (NIIT) on their net investment income (NII). The unearned income Medicare tax is imposed on the lesser of (a) net investment income, (2) the excess of modified gross income over the above threshold amounts [Code Sec. 1411(a)]. For further discussion, see ¶15,170.

.03 Additional Medicare Tax

Beginning in 2013, a 0.9 percent Additonal Medicare Tax will be imposed on the employee portion for individuals who have wages in excess of $200,000 ($250,000 in the case of married taxpayer's filing jointly, $125,000 in the case of a married taxpayer filing separately). The additional tax on wages increases the employee portion of Medicare tax to 2.35 percent (1.45 percent + 0.9 percent) for taxpayers with earned income in excess of the threshold amount. Note that the additional tax on wages is imposed only on employees. Although employers are not subject to the matching excise tax, they do have a withholding obligation and are liable for the tax if they fail to withhold the required tax from employees. Employers are required to withhold the additional 0.9 percent Medicare tax on wages in excess of $200,000.

Beginning in 2013, a 0.9 percent Additional Medicare Tax is imposed on self-employment income in excess of $200,000 ($250,000 in the case of married taxpayer's filing jointly, $125,000 in the case of a married taxpayer filing separately). The net effect of the additional tax on net earnings from self-employment is to increase the Medicare tax to 3.8 percent (2.9 percent + 0.9 percent) for taxpayers with earned income in excess of the threshold amount.

.04 RRTA

The RRTA replaces the social security system for railroad workers. RRTA taxes are divided into two tiers. The first tier is based on combined railroad retirement and social security credits, using social security benefit formulas. The second tier is based on railroad service only and is comparable to the pensions paid over and above social security benefits in other heavy industries. The employer's Tier 1 tax on compensation paid to employees is equal to the amount the employer would pay under FICA (that is, 7.65 percent of the employee's covered compensation) [Code Sec. 3221(a)].

Railroad Worker Defined

An RRTA employer is a railroad carrier or any company that (1) is directly or indirectly owned or controlled by or under common control with a railroad carrier, and (2) operates any equipment or facility or performs any service (except trucking service, casual service, and the casual operation of equipment or facilities) in connection with the transportation of passengers or property by railroad, or the receipt, delivery, elevation, transfer in transit, refrigeration or icing, storage, or handling of property transported by railroad. Employers do not include street, interurban, or electric railways that are not operated as part of a general steam-railroad system of transportation; or companies engaged in mining coal, supplying coal to an employer if delivery is not beyond the mine tipple, and operating equipment or facilities in these activities [Code Sec. 3231(a); Reg. § 31.3231(a)-1]. Employees under RRTA include any individual who is in the service of one or more employers, including as an officer of an employer [Code Sec. 3231(b); Reg. § 31.3231(b)-1].

Taxable Wages

Taxable wages under FICA, and taxable compensation under RRTA, comprise all current compensation paid to an employee by the employer for covered employment, including tips and gratuities; commissions that are part of compensation; bonuses; gifts from employers to employees; most awards and prizes; reimbursements of employee business expenses under nonaccountable plans; standby pay; back pay awards; dismissal pay; supplemental unemployment benefits; employee FICA taxes paid by the employer; dividends recharacterized as compensation; and the cash value of all remuneration paid in any medium other than cash. See ¶ 15,075 for further discussion of the definition of wages.

Taxable wages do not include some employee achievement awards, reimbursements of employee business expenses under accountable plans, reimbursements of moving expenses that the employer reasonably believes are deductible by the employee, scholarships and fellowships, most employer contributions to health savings accounts (HSAs) and Archer medical savings accounts (MSAs), and dividends paid to an employee stock option plan (ESOP) [Code Secs. 3401(a), 3121(a), 3231(e) and 3306(b)]. See ¶ 15,060 for further discussion of exempt employment.

.05 Multiple Employers

If an employee works for more than one employer in a calendar year, each employer withholds the employee's FICA tax and pays the employer's share of tax as if it were the only employer during the year. (For the exception for successor employers, see below.) A refund or credit is allowed to employees for any excess social security tax the employees may pay [Code Sec. 6413(c)(1)].

> **Example 15-6:** Mr. Hunter left his job at First National Bank on June 30, 2013, at which time he had earned $113,700 in wages. He earned another $113,700 during the second half of the year in his new job at Community Savings and Loan, giving him an annual wage of $227,400. Hunter can get a refund for the OASDI tax he paid on the last $113,700 of wages he earned at Community Savings; that is the amount by which his wages for the year exceeded the $113,700 taxable wage base.

> **NOTE:** The credit for excess payment by employees is limited to the OASDI tax since there no longer is wage base for the Medicare tax.

.06 Successor Employer

In figuring the wage limitation, a successor employer who takes over a business can count the wages paid by the predecessor employer to the workers who continue in the employ of the successor employer [Code Sec. 3121(a)(1)].

Employers must withhold employees' tax through deductions from each salary or wage payment [Code Sec. 3102; Reg. § 31.3102-1]. Employers of agricultural workers and domestics may use their own judgment in deciding whether to withhold the tax from each payment or wait until the tests for coverage have been met [¶ 15,060]. The tax collected must be deposited with an authorized bank or Federal Reserve Bank. If employers deduct less than the correct amount of tax from employees, the employers become liable for the full amount [Code Sec. 3102(c)(4); Reg. § 31.3102-1(c)]. But they are not liable for non-payment of the employee's share of tax on tips if employee funds are not sufficient to permit deduction of the employee tax by the 10th day of the month after the tips are paid [¶ 15,015].

Social security tax is imposed regardless of an employee's age. Employees are subject to the tax on all covered earnings even if they are minors (unless they are employed by a parent [¶ 15,060]), have reached the retirement age or are already collecting social security benefits.

.07 Application for EIN

Within seven days after the first payment of wages, employers must apply for an employer identification number (EIN) by filing Form SS-4. Employers hiring household domestics may be assigned a number without their having to file an application [Reg. § 31.6011(b)-1(a)(2)].

A self-employed person engaged in a trade or business who does not already have an EIN should file Form SS-4 with the IRS [Reg. § 301.6109-1(d)].

Employees who have no social security (ID) numbers must apply for one on Form SS-5 within seven days after they are hired. They must file earlier if they leave the job before the seventh day [Reg. § 31.6011(b)-2].

Duties of Employer and Employee

Employers must include their assigned EIN on all records, correspondence, claims or other returns required under the law and regulations. They should have only one EIN [Reg. § 31.6011(b)-1(d)]. If they acquired the business of another employer, the newly combined business cannot use the number assigned to the other employer.

Employees must notify their employers of their ID numbers as soon as they are hired. If they have no ID numbers, they must show their employers (1) a receipt from the Social Security Administration indicating that an application has been filed, or (2) an application (or statement containing similar information) on Form SS-5, or a duplicate of the form the employees have filed or intend to file with the Administration [Reg. § § 31.6011(b)-2, 301.6109-1].

The name and ID number of each employee must be entered on the records, returns, and claims of employers. If employees fail to advise employers of their ID numbers, employers must request the numbers. If employees do not have social security numbers, employers must advise them of the requirement. If employees then fail or refuse to file an application, employers must state that fact by affidavit when they file their returns. If employees do not have ID numbers or receipts when employers file their returns on Form 941, employers should attach the employees' Forms SS-5 or statements. Employers should keep copies of these forms or statements [Reg. § § 31.6011(b)-2, 301.6109-1].

.08 Record Maintenance

Employer's Responsibilities

Employers must keep accurate records of all remuneration paid employees, whether in cash or a medium other than cash. While no particular form is prescribed, the system of accounting must show that the employer's tax liability was correctly figured and taxes paid.

The records for *each* employee must show the following:

- The name, address, occupation, and social security (ID) number;
- The total amount (including any deductions) and date of each wage, annuity, or pension payment, and the period and character of the services covered by the payment (including the period for which the employee was paid while absent due to sickness or injury and the amount and weekly rate of such payments);
- The amount of pay and reported cash tips subject to the tax;
- The fair market value of in-kind wages paid; and
- The amount of employees' tax withheld or collected and the date collected, if different from the date of the payment [Reg. § 31.6001-5(a)].

If the dollar amounts in (2) and (3) above are not the same, the reason for the difference should be made a part of the record.

The employer also must keep copies of all returns, schedules, and other statements. The records must be kept for a period of four years after the date the tax became due or was paid, whichever is later [¶ 15,150] [Reg. § § 31.6001-1(b), (e)].

Statements to Employees

As explained at ¶15,140, every employer who withholds taxes must furnish the employee an Annual Wage and Tax Statement (Form W-2) by January 31 of the next year (or within 30 days after the last payment of wages is made, if the employee leaves during the year and requests a statement at that time). [Reg. §31.6051-1(d)(1)]. It must show total wages subject to social security and the total social security tax withheld. If only social security has been withheld (as for domestics), the employer should check the statutory employee checkbox in Box 15 of the W-2. The employer uses Copy A of the W-2 as an information return.

Employee's Responsibilities

Employees generally need not keep records. However, it is advisable that they maintain permanent records of the name and address of each employer, their period of employment, the taxable wages, the tax withheld and the receipts furnished by each employer. Because they must report monthly tips of $20 or more to their employers, employees also should keep records of tip income.

Self-Employed Person's Responsibilities

Self-employed individuals are not required to keep any specific records. However, like employees, they should keep their own records to establish eligibility for benefits. Also, the self-employment income statement is included on their income tax return. Because the IRS has three years to review the return (longer in some cases), records should be held for at least that long.

¶15,055 COVERED EMPLOYMENT

Employers and employees are liable for the social security tax only on the wages paid and received in covered employment [Code Sec. 3121(b)]. An employer under FICA is the person for whom an individual performs any service as an employee [Code Sec. 3401(d)].

.01 Employment Within the United States

Generally, any service performed in the U.S. by employees for their employers, regardless of the citizenship or residence of either, is considered covered employment [Code Sec. 3121(b)]. For this purpose, the U.S. includes the U.S. Virgin Islands, Puerto Rico, Guam, and American Samoa [Code Sec. 3121(e)(2)]. All employment within the U.S. is covered, except for certain exempt occupations [¶15,060].

.02 Employment Outside the United States

Employment outside the United States is covered *if* the service is rendered by a U.S. citizen for an American employer [Code Sec. 3121(b), (h)]. But services that would be exempt if performed in the U.S. remain exempt.

A U.S. citizen working outside the U.S. for a foreign affiliate of a U.S. firm may be covered at the option of the U.S. firm, if the latter owns not less than 10 percent of the foreign affiliate's voting stock. The U.S. firm must agree with the Secretary of the Treasury to pay the social security tax and cover all the U.S. citizens employed by the affiliate. Employers must file Form 2032, *Contract Coverage Under Title II of the Social Security Act*, for such workers to be covered [Code Sec. 3121(l)(1)].

> **NOTE:** If the foreign subsidiary holds over 50 percent of the voting stock of another foreign company, the U.S. citizens employed by the latter also may be covered.

Social security taxes can also be imposed on covered employment if an international agreement provides for coverage under the U.S. system.

.03 Maritime and Aircraft Personnel

On American Craft

Work outside the U.S. is covered if the contract of hire was made in the U.S., or if while the employee is working on the craft, it touches at a port in the U.S., Puerto Rico, the U.S. Virgin Islands, Guam, or American Samoa.

On Foreign Craft

Work on a foreign vessel is covered if performed by U.S. citizens for a U.S. employer. But work on a foreign vessel within the U.S. is exempt if (1) it is performed by an alien or for a foreign employer, and (2) the individual is employed on and in connection with such vessel when it is outside the U.S. [Code Sec. 3121(b)(4)].

.04 Agricultural Labor

There is a two-part test for coverage of farm employment. Cash wages paid to farm workers are subject to social security and Medicare taxes if the employer meets one of the following tests:

- The employer pays cash and noncash wages of $2,500 or more to all employees for agricultural labor during the year.
- The employer pays the employee $150 or more in cash wages in a calendar year [Code Sec. 3121(a)(8); Reg. § 31.3121(a)(8)-1]. For further discussion see ¶ 15,060.

.05 Family Employment

Children Who Work for Their Parents

Individuals age 18 or older who are employed by a parent in the parent's trade or business are subject to FICA tax.

Spouses Who Work for Their Spouse

Wages earned by an individual in the employ of a spouse in the spouse's trade or business are subject to FICA.

¶ 15,060 EXEMPT EMPLOYMENT

Employers and employees are liable for the social security tax only on the wages paid and received in covered employment [Code Sec. 3121(b)]. Coverage depends on factors such as the nature of the work performed, the amount of pay, the nature of the employer, and whether the employees are covered by some other federal retirement system.

Covered employment includes most forms of employment, except for:

- Americans who work outside the United States for non-American employers [Code Sec. 3121(b)];
- Foreign temporary agricultural workers [Code Sec. 3121(b)(1)];
- Domestic service performed in a local college club, or local chapter of a college fraternity or sorority, by a student who is enrolled and is regularly attending classes at a school, college, or university [Code Sec. 3121(b)(2)];
- Service not in the course of the employer's trade or business, or domestic service in a private home of the employer, performed by an individual under the age of 21 in the employ of his father or mother, or performed by an individual in the employ of his spouse or son or daughter [Code Sec. 3121(b)(3)(B)];
- Compensation for certain services performed by a child under age 18 in the employ of his or her father or mother [Code Sec. 3121(b)(3)(A)];
- Particular types of federal workers and office-holders [Code Sec. 3121(b)(5) and (6)];
- Most state and city workers who are not covered by retirement systems [Code Sec. 3121(b)(7)];
- Some religious workers [Code Sec. 3121(b)(8)];
- Certain students who work for schools and hospitals [Code Sec. 3121(b)(10) and (13)];
- Workers for foreign governments and international organizations [Code Sec. 3121(b)(11) and (15)];
- Sharecroppers [Code Sec. 3121(b)(16)];
- Domestic services performed by persons under the age of 18 [Code Sec. 3121(b)(21)]; and
- Fishing boat crew members who are compensated only by a portion of the catch [Code Sec. 3121(b)(20)].

  NOTE: Service performed on a fishing boat will not be considered employment where the following requirements exist: (1) the individual receives no more than $100 per trip which is contingent on a minimum catch and is paid solely for additional duties (such as mate, engineers, or cook) for which additional cash remuneration is traditional in the industry; (2) the individual receives a share of the boat's catch of fish or a share of the proceeds from the sale of such catch, and (3) the amount of the individual's share depends on the amount of the boat's catch of fish, and (4) the operating crew of the boat is normally made up of fewer than 10 individuals [Code Sec. 3121(b)(20); Reg. § 31.3121(b)(20)-1].

FICA taxes apply only to compensation above certain thresholds for:

- Childcare;
- Domestic services and casual labor [Code Sec. 3121(a)(7)];
- Agricultural labor [Code Sec. 3121(a)(8)];
- Home workers [Code Sec. 3121(a)(10)]; and
- Workers for tax-exempt organizations [Code Sec. 3121(a)(16)].

Reported cash tips of less than $20 per month are also exempt from FICA [Code Sec. 3121(a)(12)(B)].

.01 Agricultural Labor

Wages from farm labor are subject to FICA if the employer pays more than $2,500 to all employees for agricultural labor during the year in cash and noncash wages, or if a worker is paid more than $150 in cash by that one employer during the year. Only cash wages paid to farm workers are subject to social security and Medicare taxes. Cash wages include checks, money order, and any other kind of money or cash. It does not include food, lodging, clothing, transportation, passes and other goods and services.[57]

Exception

An employee's wages will not count toward the $2,500 test if the employee is a seasonal worker who is employed as a hand harvest laborer and is paid on a piece rate basis in an operation that has been, and is customarily and generally recognized as having been, paid on a piece rate basis in the region of employment, commutes daily from his or her permanent residence to the farm on which he or she is so employed, and has been employed in agriculture fewer than 13 weeks during the preceding calendar year. [Code Sec. 3121(a)(8)]

Sometimes farm workers are supplied to a farmer by a crew leader. If a crew leader pays the crew members for their work, and the crew leader is not designated as the farmer's employee in writing, the workers are considered employees of the crew leader [Code Sec. 3121(o); Reg. § 31.3121(o)-1]. Farmers are covered as self-employed persons [¶ 15,095]. Agricultural workers from any foreign country, lawfully admitted on a temporary basis, are not covered [Code Sec. 3121(b)(1); Reg. § 31.3121(b)(1)-1].

.02 Household Employees (Nanny Tax)

If a taxpayer has a household employee including a nanny or housekeeper working in his or her home in 2013 the taxpayer needs to pay state and federal employment tax if the nanny receives $1,800 or more in cash wages annually, regardless of the number of days the person works [Code Sec. 3121(a)(7)(A), (B); Reg. § 31.3121(a)(7)-1(a)(2)]. The employer does not have to withhold federal income tax from the household employee's wages unless the employee requests withholding and the employer agrees.

Although persons performing domestic services in a private home may be in covered employment, they are not subject to FICA unless and until they have sufficient wages to meet the above test. In figuring the employer's and the domestic's social security tax, the cash wages may, at the employer's option, be rounded to the nearest dollar [Code Sec. 3121(i)(1); Reg. § 31.3121(i)-1].

Domestic service is defined as services of a household nature performed by an employee in or about the private home of his or her employer. Such service includes those performed by cooks, waiters, butlers, housekeepers, governesses, maids, valets, nannies, baby sitters, janitors, laundresses, caretakers, handymen, gardeners, and chauffeurs of automobiles for family use. Services not of a household nature, such as services performed as a private secretary, tutor, or librarian, are not included in

---

[57] Treas. Dept., IRS Publication 51, "(Circular A), Agricultural Employer's Tax Guide For Use in 2013," p. 10.

domestic service even though such services may be performed in the employer's private home [Reg. § 31.3121(a)(7)-1(a)(2)].

Household workers under the age of 18 are exempt from social security taxation and coverage unless their principal occupation is household employment. As a result, you will have no paper work to complete or taxes to pay for your part-time babysitters or other household workers under age 18 even if you pay them over $1,800 for the year. There is an exception, however, for domestic workers who are under age 18 and who work full-time as a domestic. For example, if your cleaning lady is 16 years old and dropped out of school to be a domestic, she would still be covered by the social security system and you would have to pay social security tax on her behalf if you pay her more than $1,800 per year.

Domestic service performed in a local college club or local chapter of a college fraternity or sorority is covered unless it is performed by students enrolled and regularly attending classes at a school, college or university [Code Sec. 3121(b)(2); Reg. § 31.3121(b)(2)-1].

For 2013, the FICA tax rate for employers and employees is 7.65 percent each—6.2 percent for OASDI up to the wage base, and 1.45 percent for HI (maximum). For 2013, an employee pays:

1. 6.2 percent Social Security tax on the first $113,700 of wages (maximum tax is $7,049.40 [6.20 percent of $113,700], plus
2. 1.45 percent Medicare tax on the first $200,000 of wages ($250,000 for joint returns; $125,000 for married taxpayers filing a separate return), plus
3. 2.35 percent Medicare tax (regular 1.45 percent Medicare tax + 0.9 percent additional Medicare tax) on all wages in excess of $200,000 ($250,000 for joint returns; $125,000 for married taxpayers filing a separate return) [Code Sec. 3101(b)(2)]. For further discussion of the Additional Medicare Tax, see ¶ 15,050.

For 2014, the FICA tax rate for employees and employers is 7.65 percent each—6.2 percent for OASDI up to the wage base, and 1.45 percent for HI (no maximum). For 2014, an employee pays:

1. 6.2 percent Social Security tax on the first $117,000 of wages maximum tax is $7,254 [6.20 percent of $117,000], plus
2. 1.45 percent Medicare tax on the first $200,000 of wages ($250,000 for joint returns; $125,000 for married taxpayers filing a separate return), plus
3. 2.35 percent Medicare tax (regular 1.45 percent Medicare tax + 0.9 percent additional Medicare tax) on all wages in excess of $200,000 ($250,000 for joint returns; $125,000 for married taxpayers filing a separate return) [Code Sec. 3101(b)(2)]. For further discussion of the additional Medicare tax, see ¶ 15,050.

Schedule H

The employer must report and pay social security and Medicare taxes (FICA) and federal unemployment taxes (FUTA) for any domestic help on his or her 1040 personal income tax return. The employer must complete Schedule H, file it with the federal income tax return, and pay household employment taxes, if the answer is yes to any of the following questions:

1. Did you pay cash wages of $1,800 or more in 2013 to any one household employee? (Do not count wages you paid to your spouse, your child under age 21, your parent, or any employee under age 18)
2. Did you withhold federal income tax during 2013 for any household employee?
3. Did you pay total cash wages of $1,000 or more in any calendar quarter of 2012 or 2013 to household employees? **Caution:** The $1,800 per year test applies only to questions 1 and 2. The $1,000 per quarter test applies here in question 3.

Cash Wages

Cash wages include wages paid with checks, money orders, etc. Cash wages do not include the value of food, lodging provided at the taxpayer's home for the taxpayer's convenience and as a condition of employment, clothing, and other noncash items given to a household employee. However, cash given to an employee in place of these items is included in cash wages. If the employer reimburses the amount the employee pays to commute to the employer's home by public transit such as bus or train, these reimbursements are not wages.

Do not include the value of parking provided to employees at or near the employer's home or near a location from which the employee commutes to the employer's house. See ¶ 4100 for further discussion of transportation fringe benefits.

Employers only have to pay social security tax on domestic help if the workers qualify as employees rather than independent contractors. If someone is an independent contractor, the employer will not owe social security taxes on those wages. That responsibility lies with the independent contractor. The employer is required to send the worker an annual 1099 Form, totaling their earnings for the year. The form is due by January 31 of the year following the year they worked.

In general, a domestic will be an employee if the employer set the hours, provides materials and supplies, and give detailed instruction on how the job should be completed. An independent contractor, on the other hand, sets his or her own hours, uses his or her own equipment, and works for a variety of clients.

Example 15-7: You hire Alice to clean your house and to care for your children. Alice follows your specific instructions about housework and child care duties. You provide the household equipment and supplies that Alice needs to do her work. Alice is your household employee and since you pay her $200 a week, you must pay household employment taxes and file Schedule H.

Example 15-8: You hire James to care for your lawn. James runs a lawn service and offers his services to the general public. He provides his own tools and supplies in addition to hiring and paying his own workers. James is an independent contractor rather than your household employee and you need not pay federal employment taxes nor file Schedule H on his behalf.

Wages Not Counted

When deciding whether an employer is subject to the federal employment taxes, do not count wages paid to the following individuals even if they were paid more than $1,800 during 2013:

- A spouse;
- A child who is under age 21;
- A parent unless both of the following conditions apply:
  a. A parent cares for a child who lives with them and the child is under age 18 or has a physical or mental condition that requires the personal care of an adult for at least 4 continuous weeks in a calendar quarter.
  b. Taxpayer is divorced and has not remarried, or is a widow or widower, or is living with a spouse whose physical or mental condition prevents him or her from caring for your child at least 4 continuous weeks in a calendar quarter.
- An employee under age 18 at any time during the year unless providing household services is the employee's principal occupation. If the household employee is also a student under age 18, providing household services will not be considered the employee's principal occupation [Code Sec. 3121(b)(21)].

Example 15-9: Taxpayer hires Maria who is 17 years old as a full-time nanny. She would be covered by the Social Security system and taxpayer would have to pay Social Security tax on her behalf if the taxpayer pays her more than $1,800 per year.

Example 15-10: Taxpayer hires Anna who is 17 years old as a weekend and evening babysitter. Anna is a full-time student during the day. Taxpayer need not pay household employment taxes for Anna even if he pays her more than $1,800 per year because Anna is a student and providing household services is not considered to be her principal occupation.

.03 Casual Labor

Occasional, incidental, or irregular services not in the course of the employer's trade or business are excluded from covered employment unless the employee receives $100 or more in cash for any calendar year [Code Secs. 3121(a)(7)(A), (C); Reg. §§31.3121(a)(7)-1(b), (c)]. Services performed for a corporation are not excluded from covered employment under this exception [Reg. §31.3121(a)(7)-1(a)(1)].

.04 Certain Family Employment

Services performed by a child under age 18 in the employ of a parent are exempt. Domestic service in a private home and service not in the course of an employer's trade or business are exempt when performed by a child under 21 in the employ of a parent or by an individual in the employ of a spouse, son, or daughter. However, domestic service by a parent in the home of a son or daughter is generally covered if the son or daughter (1) is widowed, divorced and has not remarried, or has a spouse living in the home who has a mental or physical condition that results in the spouse being incapable of caring for the employer's child for at least four continuous weeks in the calendar quarter in which the services are rendered; and (2) the employer's child or stepchild is under 18 or has a mental or physical condition that requires the personal care and supervision by an adult for at least four continuous weeks in the quarter in which service is performed [Code Sec. 3121(b)(3)(B); Reg. §31.3121(b)(3)-1].

Services performed by any family member for another family member's corporation are not exempt for social security purposes.

.05 Clergy

Duly ordained, commissioned, or licensed ministers of a church performing duties in the exercise of their ministry and members of religious orders performing duties required by their order are not in covered employment [Code Sec. 3121(b)(8)(A); Reg. §31.3121(b)(8)-1]. However, social security coverage can be elected by members of a religious order subject to vows of poverty, or any autonomous subdivision of such order, by filing Form SS-16, *Certificate of Election of Coverage.* The election of coverage must be irrevocable and applicable to all current and future members of the order. Services by members of the religious order which has elected coverage are deemed to have been performed by such members as employees of the order or subdivision [Code Sec. 3121(r); Reg. §31.3121(r)-1].

Ministers and members of a religious order who are not under a vow of poverty are generally considered self-employed. However, they may elect out of social security coverage by filing an application for exemption from self-employment tax [¶15,090]. The application is made on Form 4361, *Application for Exemption From Self-Employment Tax for Use by Ministers, Members of Religious Orders and Christian Science Practitioners,* and must be accompanied by a statement that the applicant opposes coverage on conscientious or religious grounds.

Service in the employ of a church or church-controlled tax-exempt organization is generally covered. However, a one-time election to exclude such services from coverage may be made by the organization [(j) below].

.06 Students FICA Exemption

Code Secs. 3101 and 3111 impose social security and Medicare taxes (FICA taxes) on employees and employers equal to a percentage of the wages received by an employee. The Code Sec. 3121(b)(10) "student FICA exemption" exempts employers from withholding and paying FICA tax on services performed "if the services are performed by a student who is enrolled and regularly attending classes" at the school, college, or university. The IRS has construed the student exception to exempt from taxation students who work for their schools "as an incident to and for the purpose of pursuing a course of study." Taxpayers qualifying for the student FICA exception are not required to pay FICA taxes on their wages.

An institution is a school, college, or university only if its primary function is formal instruction, it has a regular faculty and curriculum, and it has a regularly enrolled student body (i.e., the primary function test) [Reg. §31.3121(b)(10)-2(c)]. An employee is a student only if the services he provides are incidental to the course of study, and if the educational aspect of the relationship predominates over the service aspect. Moreover, an employee whose normal work schedule is 40 hours or more per week is considered a full-time employee and therefore services performed by that individual aren't incidental to the course of study (full-time employee rule) [Reg. §31.3121(b)-(10)-2(d)].

Supreme Court Resolves Medical Student FICA Dispute in Favor of IRS

In *Mayo Foundation for Medical Education and Research,*[58] the Supreme Court unanimously upheld the validity of Reg. § 31.3121(b)(10)-2(d)(3)(iii), which provides that all persons who work more than 40 hours per week for an employer should be treated as employees. Therefore the IRS can now classify medical residents who work from 50 to 80 hours per week, as employees subject to FICA taxes, rather than as students exempt from FICA.

In reaching its unanimous decision, the Supreme Court looked at the language of Reg. § 31.3121(b)(10)-2(d)(3)(iii) which limits the FICA student exception to students who work only part-time or less than 40 hours a week. The court therefore focused on the number of hours an individual works in contrast to the number of hours spent in school. In the view of the court, employees who are working more than 40 hours a week are considered full-time employees and have filled the conventional measure of available time with work rather than study. Therefore, the Court concluded that the medical residents did not fall within the scope of the student FICA exception because they worked more than 40 hours per week; therefore, they were full-time employees and their compensation for health care and patient services was subject to FICA taxes. The Court reasoned that they are the kind of workers that Congress intended to both contribute to and benefit from the Social Security system.

The IRS released Rev. Proc. 2005-11[59], as well as final regulations on the exception from employment taxes for services provided by students who are also enrolled and attending classes at a "school, college, or university" (SCU) [Code Sec. 3121(b)(10); Reg. § 31.3121(b)(10)-2]. Rev. Proc. 2005-11 provides standards for determining whether or not services performed by a student while employed by a public or private nonprofit SCU qualify for the student FICA exception safe harbor. The rules provide that an institution of higher learning will only qualify for the student FICA student exception if its primary function is conducting educational activities. The rules also narrow the class of students eligible for the FICA student exception by making it unavailable to career employees who work more than 40 hours a week and who are eligible to participate in benefits offered by their employers.

The regulations provide standards for determining whether an employer qualifies as a SCU and whether an employee is a student for purposes of the student FICA exception. The regulations also provide that full-time employees are not students for purposes of the exception, and outline relevant factors to be taken into account in determining if the exception applies to the services provided by other employees.

Safe Harbor

In order to qualify for the safe harbor available in Rev. Proc. 2005-11, the following requirements must be satisfied:

- The employer must qualify as *institution of higher education,* which means any public or private nonprofit SCU that meets the requirements set forth in Department of

[58] *Mayo Foundation for Medical Education & Research,* SCt, 2011-1 USTC ¶ 50,143, 131 SCt 704, *aff'g,* CA-8, 2009-1 USTC ¶ 50,432.

[59] Rev. Proc. 2005-11, 2005-1 CB 307.

Education regulations [Reg. § 31.3121(b)(10)-2(c)]. An organization is a SCU if (a) its primary function is the presentation of formal instruction; (b) it normally maintains a regular faculty and curriculum, and (3) it normally has a regularly enrolled body of students in attendance at the place where its educational activities are regularly carried on.

- The employee must qualify as a *student,* which means that the employee's services for the SCU must be "incident to and for the purpose of pursuing a course of study" at the SCU [Reg. § 31.3121(b)(10)-2(d)(3)(i)].

Half-time undergraduate students or *half-time graduate or professional students* are eligible for the student FICA exception if they perform services for an institution of higher education where they are enrolled. The term *half-time graduate or professional student* means an enrolled graduate or professional student who is carrying at least a half-time academic workload at an SCU.

Safe harbor unavailable for certain employees. The safe harbor will be unavailable to the following employees:

- A full-time employee (working 40 or more hours per week) because the services performed by a full-time employee are not incident to and for the purpose of pursuing a course of study [Reg. § 31.3121(b)(10)-2(d)(3)(iii)].
- The services of a professional employee because such services cannot generally be considered to be incident to and for the purpose of pursuing a course of study. A professional employee is defined in as an employee whose work: (a) requires knowledge of an advanced type in a field of science or learning, (b) requires the consistent exercise of discretion and judgment, and (c) is predominantly intellectual and varied in character (as opposed to routine mental, manual, mechanical, or physical work) and is of such character that the output produced or the result accomplished cannot be standardized in relation to a given period of time [Reg. § 31.3121(b)(10)-2(d)(3)(v)(B)(1)].
- An employee who receives or is eligible to receive employment benefits because such services cannot generally be considered to be incident to and for the purpose of pursuing a course of study. An employee's services are not eligible for the safe harbor if the individual is eligible: (a) for vacation, sick leave, or paid holiday benefits; (b) to participate in any qualified retirement plan that is established or maintained by the institution, or would be eligible to participate if age and service requirements were met; (c) to receive an allocation of employer contributions or would be eligible to receive such allocations if age and service requirements were met, or if contributions were made by the employee; (d) to receive an annual deferral by nonelective employer contributions under an eligible deferred compensation plan or would be eligible for such annual deferrals if plan requirements were met, or if contributions were made by the employee to a salary reduction plan; (e) for reduced tuition because of the individual's employment relationship with the institution; or (f) to receive one or more of the following employment benefits: life insurance, qualified educational assistance, dependent care assistance programs, and adoption assistance because of the individual's employment relationship with the institution.

.07 Newspaper Carriers and News Vendors

Qualifying newspaper distributors and carriers are direct sellers taxed as independent contractors rather than employees [Code Sec. 3508(b)(2)(A)(iii)]. A person engaged in the trade or business of the delivery or distribution of newspapers or shopping news (including any services that are directly related to such trade or business, such as solicitation of customers or collection of receipts) qualifies as a direct seller, provided:

- Substantially all the remuneration for the performance of the services is directly related to sale or other output rather than to the number of hours worked, and
- The services performed by the person are performed pursuant to a written contract between such person and the service recipient, and
- The contract provides that the person will not be treated as an employee for Federal tax purposes.

The law applies to newspaper distributors and carriers whether or not they hire others to assist in the delivery of newspapers. The law also applies to newspaper distributors and carriers operating under either a buy-sell distribution system (where the newspaper distributor or carriers purchase the newspapers from the publisher) or an agency distribution system.

Service performed by workers under age 18 of age in the assembly and house-to-house delivery or distribution of newspapers are not considered employees [Code Sec. 3121(14)(A)]. News vendors, regardless of age, who sell papers or magazines to the ultimate consumer at a fixed price, and whose compensation is the excess of such price over what they pay for the papers or magazines, are not considered employees. This is true even if the news vendor is guaranteed a minimum amount for such service, or is credited with any unsold papers or magazines that are returned [Code Sec. 3121(b)(14); Reg. §31.3121(b)(14)-1].

.08 Railroad Workers

These workers are covered by their own federal retirement system, so they are excluded from FICA coverage [Code Sec. 3121(b)(9); Reg. §31.3121(b)(9)-1].

.09 Communist Organizations

Service in the employ of any organization is exempt if performed in a year during any part of which the organization is required to register as a Communist organization under the Internal Security Act of 1950 [Code Sec. 3121(b)(17); Reg. §31.3121(b)(17)-1].

.10 Nonprofit Organizations

Service in the employ of a nonprofit organization is generally not exempt, except in the case of certain members of the clergy and certain students working in a school or college are exempt [discussed above]. However, no social security tax is imposed on wages paid to employees of nonprofit organizations exempt from federal income tax under Sec. 501(a) or under Sec. 521 (generally religious, charitable, etc. organizations and farmers' cooperatives), if the employee earns less than $100 during the year [Code Sec. 3121(a)(16)]. This limited exemption does not apply to employees of stock bonus, pension, or profit-sharing trusts.

NOTE: Employees of nonprofit organizations who are covered on a mandatory basis by the Federal Employees' Retirement System are treated as federal employees under the social security system. They are covered employees only if hired after 1983.

Election of Church Exemption

A church or a qualified church-related organization may make a one-time election to exclude, for FICA tax purposes, services performed in the employ of the church or organization. If the election is filed, their employees are subject to self-employment tax [¶ 15,085, ¶ 15,090] [Code Sec. 3121(w)(2)].

.11 Government Employees

The Social Security system now covers most federal employees except those specifically exempted. State and local government employees must be covered unless they are covered by a retirement system (see below).

Federal Employees

The following employees are *not* exempt from FICA coverage [Code Sec. 3121(b)(5), (6)]:

- All federal civilian employees hired after 1983 are covered, including those previously employed, if the period of separation lasted at least 365 days. Only continuous noncovered federal employment since 1983 is a basis for exclusion from FICA coverage, for services performed after 1983. If the break in domestic federal service was due to service in an international organization or temporary military duty, and the person is exercising reemployment rights, the employee is not automatically covered;
- Legislative branch employees are covered unless they were covered by the Civil Service Retirement System on December 31, 1983 (subject to special rules) [Code Sec. 3121(b)(5)(G)];
- All members of the U.S. armed forces, whether on active duty or inactive duty training, and all Peace Corps members are directly covered [Code Sec. 3121(m), (p)]; and
- The president, vice-president, and members of Congress; all sitting federal judges, including retired judges reassigned to active duty; and all executive level and senior executive service appointees are covered.

NOTE: Employees (including members of Congress) who choose to participate in the Federal Employees' Retirement System are still in covered employment and must pay social security tax [Code Sec. 3121(b)(5)].

Exempt federal employees. As explained above, service for the federal government or its instrumentalities is exempt if performed by an individual continuously employed since 1983. Also exempt is service by an individual who receives an annuity under the federal civil service retirement system; service by an inmate in a penal institution; service by a student nurse in a federal hospital; and temporary service during disasters [Code Sec. 3121(b)(5), (6)].

Employees of State and Local Governments

Employees of any state, its political subdivisions, or any instrumentality wholly owned by one or more state or political subdivisions are covered by social security, unless they are covered by a retirement system related to their government employment. Certain classes of state and local government employees are exempt [Code Sec. 3121(b)(7)(F); Reg. §31.3121(b)(7)-2].

Employees who are presently covered by a retirement system related to their government employment, and who are therefore not covered by social security, may be brought into the social security system through agreements with the Secretary of Health and Human Services. The employees must vote in favor of social security coverage by secret ballot. If a majority of the members eligible to vote, vote in favor of coverage, all are covered [Social Security Act Sec. 218(d)(3)]. State and local governments cannot terminate so-called Section 218 social security coverage. State and local governments that had elected coverage and then withdrawn (as they were allowed to do before 1984) can voluntarily rejoin, assuming their employees did not automatically become subject to social security coverage as of July 2, 1991. However, state and local governments that elect to rejoin the system are then precluded from terminating coverage.

Special rules apply to employees of publicly owned and operated transportation systems [Code Sec. 3121(j); Reg. §31.3121(j)-1].

Employees of Foreign Governments

Foreign government employees are exempt [Code Sec. 3121(b)(11)]. Services performed for an instrumentality wholly owned by a foreign government may be exempt if the foreign government gives a similar exemption to employees of the U.S. government or its instrumentalities [Code Sec. 3121(b)(12)]. Services performed for an international organization, such as the United Nations, are not covered employment [Code Sec. 3121(b)(15); Reg. §§31.3121(b)(11), (12), (15)-1]. In addition, wages are exempt to the extent they are subject to similar social security taxes or contributions of a foreign country under an international agreement [Code Secs. 3101(c), 3111(c)].

> **NOTE:** U.S. citizens employed in the U.S., Puerto Rico, Guam, American Samoa and the U.S. Virgin Islands by foreign governments or their instrumentalities, or by international organizations, can be covered as self-employed individuals [¶15,095].

¶15,065 PARTIALLY COVERED EMPLOYMENT

Suppose an employee performs both exempt and covered service for the same employer. If half or more of the employee's time during any pay period is devoted to FICA-exempt employment, then all the employment during that pay period is considered exempt. If less than half of the employee's time during the pay period is devoted to FICA-exempt employment, all the employment is considered covered employment. *Pay period* means the period (not more than 31 consecutive days) wages are ordinarily paid to employees by the employer [Code Sec. 3121(c); Reg. §31.3121(c)-1].

Suppose part of the services rendered by an individual for one person during a pay period is performed as an employee and part is performed not as an employee (e.g., as an independent contractor). In such a case, only the services performed as an employee should be subjected to this test. Services performed in another capacity are excluded from FICA tax (but see ¶15,085-¶15,090 for coverage of self-employed persons).

NOTE: Domestic service or agricultural labor is FICA-covered employment even if certain pay is not considered wages. Therefore, the above test does not apply if an employee works part-time as a servant in the employer's home (or as a hired hand on his farm) and part time at the employer's place of business. If the pay for domestic or agricultural services meets the earnings test for those services [¶15,022, ¶15,060], all of the employee's wages are FICA-taxable.[60]

¶15,070 EMPLOYER-EMPLOYEE RELATIONSHIP

Creation of the employer-employee relationship affords the employee some valuable benefits but also imposes a number of expensive obligations on the employer as follows:

- The employer must withhold federal income taxes on the employee's compensation;
- The employer must collect and pay social security and Medicare taxes on the worker's compensation under the Federal Insurance Contribution Act (FICA) [¶15,022];
- The employer must pay unemployment taxes on the employee's wages under the Federal Unemployment Tax Act (FUTA);
- The employer must comply with workplace safety laws and federal and state labor laws including worker's compensation laws; and
- The employer may have to provide fringe benefits for employees, such as making contributions to a pension or retirement plans and providing health and life insurance, vacation pay, and paid sick leave for the employee. In addition, employers with 50 or more employees must grant employees the right to take up to 12 weeks of unpaid leave with the right to reinstatement under the Family and Medical Leave Act.

Plainly, business owners will bolster their profit margins if they classify a worker as an independent contractor rather than an employee. Independent contractor status relieves them from having to satisfy many onerous and expensive obligations. Most workers, on the other hand, prefer being classified as employees because their employer will then provide benefits such as paid vacations, health, and life insurance and make tax-free contributions to retirement savings plans.

.01 Independent Contractor Status—Pros and Cons

If a worker is classified as an independent contractor, he or she must pay his or her own self-employment tax (SECA), which is the combined FICA taxes that would be shared by an employee and employer. This amounts to a total of 15.3 percent on the first $113,700 of income in 2013. This figure will be even more for higher income earners because there is no longer an income cap on the Medicare portion (2.90 percent) of the tax. See ¶15,085.

---

[60] Rev. Rul. 55-386, 1955-1 CB 120.

Despite the drawback of being subject to SECA tax, independent contractor status offers the following advantages to workers:

- Independent contractors do not have to pay federal unemployment tax (FUTA);
- Trade or business expenses that otherwise would not be deductible (or only partially deductible) for employees become fully deductible on the Schedule C of an independent contractor. The expenses of an employee, on the other hand, are deductible only to the extent they exceed 2 percent of the taxpayer's adjusted gross income. In addition, they are subject to the income limitations imposed on itemized deductions; and
- Independent contractors can establish their own retirement plans and deduct contributions to the plan, offering them greater flexibility than may be available with the employer's plan.

▶ **TAX TIP:** A ruling as to whether a person is an employee or self-employed may be obtained from the IRS by submitting Form SS-8 [¶ 15,010].

.02 Who Is an Employee?

For some workers it is easy to determine what category they fall into. The IRS regulations specifically provide that in many situations "physicians, lawyers, dentists, veterinarians, contractors, subcontractors, public stenographers, auctioneers" are independent contractors. These are people who follow an independent trade, business, or profession in which they offer their services to the general public.

Generally, the common law tests for the employer-employee relationship are used [Code Sec. 3121(d)(2)]. Under these tests the employer-employee relationship exists when the person for whom services are performed has the right to control and direct the person who performs the services, not only as to the result of the work, but also as to the details and means to accomplish it [Reg. § 31.3121(d)-1(c)]. (But see ¶ 15,010 for different standard applied when workers are professionals.)

In addition to this primary test of control, the IRS applies a 20-factor test[61] to determine whether an employer-employee relationship exists.

Unfortunately, the 20-factor test will not resolve all classification dilemmas easily because it fails to prioritize the 20 factors. As a result you never know which factor or group of factors is viewed by the IRS as dispositive. The IRS may reach a different classification than you do simply because they afford more weight to one or more of the 20 factors.

If you seek certainty regarding your work status you can obtain a private letter ruling, but be aware that this route can be expensive and time-consuming.

▶ **TAX TIP:** In addition, you can consult IRS Form SS-8, *Determination of Employee Work Status for Purposes of Federal Employment Taxes and Income Tax Withholding,* which lists 19 really important questions and more than 100 not-so-important questions to help you determine the nature of a work relationship.

The following list summarizes the 20-factor test:

1. *Instructions:* Employees are usually instructed when, where, and how work is to be performed.

---

[61] Rev. Rul. 87-41, 1987-1 CB 296.

2. *Training:* Employees are usually trained because the employer wants the services performed in a particular manner.
3. *Integration:* Employees are usually subject to control by the employer when the success or continuation of a business depends upon the performance of those services.
4. *Services rendered personally:* Employees will perform the services themselves but the employer will control the methods and results of the job.
5. *Hiring, supervising, and paying assistants:* Employees will be hired, supervised, and paid by their employer. These activities generally show control over the employee.
6. *Continuing Relationship:* Employees will have a continuing relationship with their employer.
7. *Set hours of work:* Employees will have their hours set by the employer.
8. *Full-time required:* Employees will usually be required to work full-time on their employer's business and will be restricted from doing other work.
9. *Doing work on employer's premises:* Employees will usually perform the work on their employer's premises.
10. *Order or sequence set:* Employees will usually be required to perform the services in the order set by the employer, rather than being free to follow their own pattern of work.
11. *Oral or written reports:* Employees will be required to submit oral or written reports accounting for their actions.
12. *Method of payment:* Employees will usually be paid by the hour, week, or month.
13. *Paying business or traveling expenses:* Employees' business or travel expenses will usually be paid by their employer.
14. *Furnishing tools and materials:* Employees will usually be furnished the necessary tools and materials by their employer.
15. *Significant investment:* Independent contractors will usually make a significant investment in facilities used in performing services for another.
16. *Working for more than one firm at a time:* Independent contractors usually work for more than one firm at a time.
17. *Making services available to the general public:* Independent contractors usually make their services readily available to the general public.
18. *Possibility of discharge:* Employees can usually be discharged by their employers.
19. *Right to terminate:* Employees have the right to end their relationship with an employer at any time without incurring liability.
20. *Realization of profit or loss:* Independent contractors can realize a profit or suffer a loss as a result of their services.

Courts will examine each set of facts to determine who controls the workers. In a nutshell, if the person hiring the workers sets all the rules, the workers are usually employees. If the workers call the shots, then the workers are independent contractors. In a regulation, the IRS reduces the 20-factor test to its essence which is whether the business owner controls the worker and the manner in which he or she works, if yes, then the worker is an employee. Reg. § 31.3121(d)-1(c)(2) provides the following description of the employment relationship:

> Generally [the employer/employee] relationship exists when the person for whom services are performed has the right to control and direct the individual who performs the services, not only as to the result to be accomplished by the work but also as to the details and means by which that result is accomplished.
>
> In addition, the regulation stresses the importance of the employer's right to discharge the employee, and the employer's furnishing of a place of work and tools for work.

Example 15-11: Ann Decker is an attorney who worked as an assistant for Mary Brant, another attorney. Ann is required to comply with Mary's instructions about when, where and how her work should be performed. Either Ann or Mary could terminate the work relationship on two weeks notice. Ann performed services full time at Mary's office and was paid an hourly wage. In addition, Mary furnished the necessary supplies and reimbursed Ann with the necessary supplies and reimbursed her work-related travel expenses. The IRS concluded that Ann was an employee for income tax purposes.[62]

▶ **TECHNICAL SERVICE WORKERS:** A special safe-harbor that granted independent contractor status to so-called technical service workers, engineers, designers, computer programmers, drafters, and other similarly skilled workers has been closed off. As a result, the status of these workers must be determined under the common law tests above. In light of recent IRS crackdowns on employers who misclassify employees, it is prudent to first determine whether a technical service worker is an employee, and then to determine whether the worker is employed by a service broker or provider, or by the client firm or end-user of the service. To do so, apply the common law test of who controls the method and result of the work. If the worker appears to be under the control of another party, the other factors mentioned above can help you determine whether it is your firm that exerts this control, or whether a technical service firm is actually the employer. Calling a worker a freelancer will not make them an independent contractor in the eyes of the IRS if they were really employees and are therefore entitled to participate in the company's 401(k) and stock purchase plans.

.03 Special Cases

The following workers are considered statutory employees (even though they may not be employees under the common law tests) if they perform services for pay in the prescribed circumstances [Code Sec. 3121(d)(3); Reg. § 31.3121(d)-1]:

---

[62] LTR 9534002 (May 16, 1995). See also *Donald G. Cave A. Professional Law Corp.*, 101 TCM 1224, Dec. 58,558 (M), TC Memo. 2011-48, *aff'd*, CA-5, 2012-1 USTC ¶ 50,258, where the Court of Appeals for the Fifth Circuit affirmed the Tax Court and concluded that all attorneys of the law firm were common law employees based on the degree of control exercised by the firm over their work, the firm's provision of facilities for their use, and the permanence of the relationship of the lawyers with the law firm.

- Corporate officers [Reg. § 1.3121(d)-1(b)];
- Agents or commissioned drivers who deliver produce, meat products, bakery products, beverages (other than milk) or laundry or dry-cleaning services for a boss;
- Full-time life insurance salespersons;
- Individuals who work at home under the direction of the party that provides the supplies and the materials for the work; and
- Certain traveling salespersons.

Also, some independent contractors are treated as statutory nonemployees, such as real estate agents and direct sellers (see below).

Full-time traveling or city salespersons (other than agent-drivers or commission-drivers, mentioned below) are employees, if they solicit orders for one principal from wholesalers, retailers, contractors, hotels, restaurants and the like, for merchandise for resale or business supplies [Code Sec. 3121(d)(3)(D)]. Their entire or principal business activity must be soliciting for one principal. Multiple-line salespersons generally are not employees under this rule. If salespersons solicit orders merely for one principal, they will not be excluded solely because of sideline sales activities on behalf of one or more persons. In this case, the salespersons are employees only of those for whom they primarily solicit orders; they are not employees of the other persons [Reg. § 31.3121(d)-1(d)(3)].

Agent-drivers or commission drivers are employees if they distribute meat, vegetable, fruit, bakery, or beverage (except milk) products, or handle laundry or dry cleaning services for their principal[63] [Code Sec. 3121(d)(3)(A); Reg. § 31.3121(d)-1(d)(1)]. This group includes those who operate their own trucks or trucks owned by their employer; those who serve customers designated by the company as well as those solicited on their own; and those whose pay is based on commissions or the difference between the price they charge their customers and the price they pay to the company for the products or services [Reg. § 31.3121(d)-1(d)(3)(i)].

Full-time life insurance salespersons are employees [Code Sec. 3121(d)(3)(B)]. To determine their status, the common law test is first applied. If the conditions of this test are met, they are employees regardless of other tests. If they are not employees under the common law test, they are nonetheless covered if their entire or principal business activity is devoted to soliciting life insurance or annuity contracts primarily for one company.[64]

Insurance company's outside sales agents are independent contractors. An insurance company's outside sales agent was held an independent contractor because the company did not significantly control the manner in which he sold insurance because: (1) the company did not provide specific instructions or training for selling insurance; (2) the company paid for certain limited expenses while the agent covered the reminder, including rent, employee salaries and the cost of equipment for an outside office; (3) the agent was free to hire his own assistants; (4) the agent did not

[63] Rev. Rul. 73-260, 1973-1 CB 412.

[64] Rev. Rul. 54-309, 1954-2 CB 261; Rev. Rul. 59-103, 1959-1 CB 259.

work on the insurance company's premises; (5) the agent's pay was determined entirely on a commission basis; (6) the agent set his own hours and was not required to report to the company on a regular basis.

Homeworkers are employees (and their wages are subject to FICA taxes) if they meet either the common law tests or the following tests: (1) They do work under terms furnished by the person for whom the services are performed on materials furnished by and required to be returned to that person, and (2) they are paid at least $100 in cash in any calendar year [Code Sec. 3121(a)(10), 3121(d)(3)(C)]. The pay is based on wages paid in the year rather than on pay earned during the year. To qualify as a homeworker, an individual must personally perform substantially all the services involved. Individuals who work at home are not employees if they have a substantial investment in the facilities used in connection with their job (other than facilities for transportation), or if the services are in the nature of a single transaction, and not part of a continuing relationship with the employer.[65]

Real estate agents and direct sellers are classified as independent contractors if they meet two tests: (1) substantially all of their income for services as real estate agents or direct sellers must be directly related to sales or other output; (2) their services are performed under a written contract that provides they will not be treated as employees for federal tax purposes [Code Sec. 3508]. Direct sellers include individuals engaged in the trade or business of selling consumer products on a commission basis (as opposed to a fixed, hourly rate), but does not include sales people working in a permanent retail establishment [Code Sec. 3508(b)(2)(A)(ii)]. For example, a door-to-door salesman would be an independent contractor.

Corporate officers who perform no services or only minor ones, and who are not entitled to receive (directly or indirectly) any pay are not employees but any fees they earn may be subject to self-employment tax [¶15,085] [Code Sec. 3121(d)(1); Reg. §31.3121(d)-1(b)].

Corporate directors may be employees if they act as officers or perform services for the corporation other than taking part in meetings of the board of directors.[66] Your company should distinguish any fees paid to an individual for services as a director from any remuneration for services as an officer or employee, in order to keep the fees free of FICA tax to the company.

Bank directors serving on bank committees are presumed not to be employees if the committee (1) consists exclusively of directors or (2) consists primarily of directors and the committee operates like a committee that includes only directors. But the bank must treat committee members who are not directors as employees and pay the tax on their pay unless the bank gets a contrary ruling from the IRS.[67]

Partners

Bona fide members of a partnership are employers, not employees, so remuneration received by a partner from the partnership is not wages from FICA-covered employment. But a partner who conducts the business of the partnership may be subject to

[65] *A. Ware*, DC-MI, 94-1 USTC ¶50,126, 850 FSupp 602, *aff'd*, CA-6, 95-2 USTC ¶50,553, 67 F3d 574.

[66] *Veterinary Surgical Consultants, P.C.*, 117 TC 141, Dec. 54,527 (2001), *aff'd in unpublished opinion*, CA-3, 2003-1 USTC ¶50,141, *cert denied*, 123 SCt 2621; Rev. Rul. 57-246, 1957-1 CB 338.

[67] Rev. Rul. 68-597, 1968-2 CB 463.

the self-employment tax[68] [¶ 15,085]. The Fifth Circuit Court of Appeals has held that a partner can be an employee of his partnership. In ruling that a partner can exclude from gross income the meals and lodging furnished him for the convenience of the partnership, the court said it is "possible for a partner to stand in any one of a number of relationships with his partnership, including those of creditor-debtor, vendor-vendee, and employee-employer."[69]

Newspaper Distributors and Carriers Treated as Direct Sellers

Qualifying newspaper distributors and carriers are classified as direct sellers and are thus taxed as independent contractors rather than employees [Code Sec. 3508(b)(2)(A)(iii)]. A person engaged in the trade or business of the delivery or distribution of newspapers or shopping news (including any services that are directly related to such trade or business, such as solicitation of customers or collection of receipts) qualifies as a direct seller, provided:

- Substantially all the remuneration for the performance of the services is directly related to sale or other output rather than to the number of hours worked, and
- The services performed by the person are performed pursuant to a written contract between such person and the service recipient, and
- The contract provides that the person will not be treated as an employee for federal tax purposes.

The classification as direct seller applies to newspaper distributors and carriers whether or not they hire others to assist in the delivery of newspapers. The classification also applies to newspaper distributors and carriers operating under either a buy-sell distribution system (where the newspaper distributor or carriers purchase the newspapers from the publisher) or an agency distribution system.

Note that this clarification of newspaper distributors and carriers as direct sellers only addresses the worker classification issue for income and employment taxes only. It has no impact whatsoever on the interpretation or applicability of Federal, State, or local labor laws.

Guidance for Limo Drivers

The IRS has provided guidance for its examiners to follow in determining whether limo drivers are employees or independent contractors.[70] The IRS divides the limousine industry into the three following categories:

- Pure dispatch services;
- Pure transportation services, which own cars and employ drivers; and
- Mixed service providers, which are typical in this industry and present all the classification problems.

The following two factors are critical when classifying limo drivers: (1) significant investment in equipment, and (2) realization of profit or loss. The IRS says that the absence of either of these factors indicates that a driver is an employee, and no further analysis is necessary. If both factors are present, further analysis is required.

---

68 Rev. Rul. 69-184, 1969-1 CB 256.

69 *A.L. Armstrong*, CA-5, 68-1 USTC ¶9355, 394 F2d 661.

70 Employment Tax Procedures: Classification of Workers Within the Limousine Industry, 3/13/97.

For these purposes, a limo driver has made a significant investment and is therefore an independent contractor if he or she owns or leases his or her own vehicle. The examiners are advised to closely examine whether a purported ownership, loan, or lease is bona fide for tax purposes.

Manicurists Employees

Manicurists working at a nail salon were employees of the salon operator because the salon owner provided most of the supplies, controlled the cash, issued paychecks, and had the right to fire the manicurists at any time. In addition, insurance, telephone, advertising, utilities, and similar expenses were paid by the salon operator.[71]

Carpet and Tile Installers Independent Contractors

Carpet[72] and tile[73] installers were independent contractors because the hirer maintained control over its carpet installers only to the extent that they needed a ready, able, work force that could successfully complete installation jobs when needed. The installers retained their independence with respect to the sequence, manner, and skill with which jobs were completed. Installers bore the risk of profit or loss on their jobs, controlled their own work force, owned and used their own tools and supplies.

Bakery Workers

Bakery workers were common law employees after looking at the following factors and concluding that they did not set their hours, were assigned production levels, and could not leave until those quotas were met, and were paid a fixed wage based on amount produced:

- Degree of control;
- Investment in facilities;
- Opportunity for profit or loss;
- Right to discharge;
- Integral part of the business;
- Permanency of the relationship; and
- Relationship the parties thought they created.[74]

.04 Relief for Worker Misclassification

If an employer classifies an employee as an independent contractor and there is no reasonable basis for doing so, the employer may be held liable for employment taxes for that worker.

Relief Provisions

If an employer has a reasonable basis for not treating a worker as an employee, the employer may be relieved from having to pay employment taxes for that worker. To obtain relief, the employer must file all required federal information returns on a basis consistent with the employer's treatment of the worker. The employer (or the

---

[71] *LA Nails Inc.*, DC-MD, 98-1 USTC ¶50,438.

[72] *Consolidated Flooring Services*, FedCl, 97-2 USTC ¶50,680, 38 FedCl 450, later proceeding, FedCl, 99-1 USTC ¶50,434, 42 FedCl 878, later proceeding, FedCl, 2000-2 USTC ¶50,553.

[73] *U.V. Jones*, 94 TCM 230, Dec. 57,071(M), TC Memo. 2007-249.

[74] *Ewens & Miller, Inc.*, 117 TC 263, Dec. 54,561 (2001).

employer's predecessor) must not have treated any worker holding a substantially similar position as an employee for any periods beginning after 1977.

Misclassified Workers Can File Form 8919

Workers who have been misclassified as independent contractors by their employers must use Form 8919, *Uncollected Social Security and Medicare Taxes on Wages,* to calculate and report their share of uncollected Social Security and Medicare taxes. The form should be attached to the taxpayer's Form 1040. Form 8919 requires the employee to indicate why he or she is filing the form. Misclassified workers should no longer use Form 4137, *Social Security and Medicare Tax on Unreported Tip Income.* This form should only be used by employees who receive tips.

In addition to completing Form 8919, workers must satisfy one of several criteria demonstrating that they were an employee, such as showing that they were a Code Sec. 530 designated employee, showing that they received correspondence from the IRS stating that they were an employee, or showing that they filed a Form SS-8, *Determination of Worker Status for Purposes of Federal Employment Taxes and Income Tax Withholding.*

Code Sec. 3509 Relief

When an employer treats services performed by an employee as though they were performed by a nonemployee and fails to withhold the required income or social security taxes, Code Sec. 3509 provides that the employer's liability for the unpaid amounts is determined as a fraction of the employee's wages that are subject to income tax withholding and as a fraction of the employee social security taxes required to be withheld. The applicable amounts are 1.5 percent of wages (increased to three percent where no information returns (Forms 1099) are filed) for income tax purposes and 20 percent of the employee's portion of the social security taxes that must be withheld (increased to 40 percent where no information returns are filed). The employer's portion of the social security taxes must be paid in full. Note that Code Sec. 3509 cannot be used to determine an employer's liability for any period within the current calendar year. If the employer fails to withhold due to an employee misclassification and the misclassification is recognized before the due date of the quarterly employment tax return for the last calendar quarter of a year, the employer should make up the amounts during the current year.

Form 4670 Relief

If the employer does not qualify for the reduced rates under Code Sec. 3509, the employer may still find relief from employment tax liability by providing evidence that the employee reported the income on his or her federal income tax return and paid the federal income tax due. To qualify for this relief, the employee must sign Form 4669, *Statement of Payments Received,* and state that the income was reported and the taxes attributable to the income were paid. In addition, the employer must complete and sign Form 4670, *Request of Relief from Payment of Income Tax Withholding,* and submit this form along with Form 4669 to the IRS. This relief does not, however, relieve employers of any penalties or additions to tax for failure to withhold the employment tax.

Section 530 Safe Harbor

Businesses that misclassify workers as independent contractors instead of as employees may escape liability for past and future employment taxes (FICA, FUTA, and federal income tax withholdings) by showing that they qualify for relief under Section 530 of the Revenue Act of 1978 ("Section 530"). Section 530 relief will prevent the IRS from classifying the worker as an employee. An employer will be entitled to Section 530 relief even though it failed to timely file some information returns dealing with workers it treated as independent contractors.[75] In an audit the IRS has an obligation to inform employers of their right to seek Section 530 relief. This is particularly helpful to small businesses that might not otherwise be aware of this available relief. Note that Section 530 relief is available only to employers and that employees cannot claim relief under its provisions.[76]

An employer who misclassified workers as independent contractors instead of as employees, may escape liability for all employment taxes, if they satisfy the following three requirements that are found in Section 530 of the Revenue Act of 1978 ("Section 530").[77]

1. The employer must have had a reasonable basis for not treating the workers as employees. An employer will be treated as having a reasonable basis if the treatment of the worker was in reasonable reliance on any of the following sources:
   - Judicial precedent, published rulings, or technical advice relating to the taxpayer.
   - A past IRS audit in which there was no employment tax assessment attributable to the treatment of the individuals holding positions substantially similar.
   - A long standing recognized practice of a significant segment of the industry in which the individual was engaged.
2. The employer (and any predecessor business) must have treated the workers and any similar workers as independent contractors for all applicable periods beginning after December 31, 1977.
3. The employer must have filed Form 1099 MISC, *Miscellaneous Income,* for each worker, if that form was required.

The business will be relieved from all federal employment tax liability as well as any related interest or penalties if the employer satisfies the Section 530 requirements.

No 530 Relief for Technical Service Workers

Section 530 relief is unable in a situation where a worker provides technical services for a client pursuant to an arrangement between the business and the client. Technical services employees include engineers, designers, drafters, computer programmers, systems analysts or other similarly skilled workers engaged in a similar line of work. Thus, the wages of technical service personnel who provide services in third-party situations are subject to FICA and FUTA taxes with respect to remuneration paid and

---

[75] *Medical Emergency Care Associates,* 120 TC 436, Dec. 55,154 (2003).

[76] *A.H. Ahmed,* CA-8, 98-2 USTC ¶50,570, 147 F3d 791.

[77] *Peno Trucking Inc.,* CA-6, 2008-2 USTC ¶50,580; *R. Porter,* DC-IA, 2008-2 USTC ¶50,479, 569 FSupp 2d 862.

services performed after 1986. The withdrawal of protection from employment tax liability on remuneration paid to technical service personnel under Section 530 applies only with respect to "three-party" situations where specified services are provided for a client of a technical services firm under an agreement between the firm and the client.

Industry Practice Safe Harbor

When applying the industry practice safe harbor, the IRS will gather sufficient information and will then consider whether a reasonably prudent business under similar circumstances would have relied on the evidence of industry practice to treat its workers as independent contractors. The extent of the business's knowledge of industry practice, whether obtained through personal experience, a survey, or through an advisor is relevant. In addition, the reasonableness or unreasonableness of the reliance may turn on the source of the information from which the business derived knowledge of the industry practice.

The IRS and the courts have been liberal when interpreting the industry practice safe harbor. A practice will qualify as an industry practice even if less than one quarter of the taxpayer's competitors follow similar practices. Moreover, a new industry can initiate its own industry practice and qualify for relief under the industry practice safe harbor. For example, a company can rely on a self-conducted industry survey to conclude that its workers are independent contractors thus entitling them to employment tax relief under the industry practice safe harbor of Section 530.[78]

In order to determine industry practice:

- Examine business records, such as corporate minutes or unanimous consents in lieu of directors' meetings, to determine whether any written record exists that shows the reason for treatment of workers as independent contractors.
- Interview the workers themselves to determine what reasons were given to them by the business when establishing their status as independent contractors.
- Interview key workers in the business. In some cases, it may be disclosed, or other objective evidence may show, that some reason other than industry practice drove the company's decision to treat its workers as independent contractors.

After they have gathered sufficient information, the IRS agents should consider whether a reasonably prudent business under similar circumstances would have relied on the evidence of industry practice to treat its workers as independent contractors. The extent of the business's knowledge of industry practice, whether obtained through personal experience, a survey, or through an advisor is relevant. In addition, the reasonableness or unreasonableness of the reliance may turn on the source of the information from which the business derived knowledge of the industry practice.

The IRS and the courts have been very liberal when interpreting the industry practice safe harbor. A practice will qualify as an industry practice even if less than one quarter of the taxpayer's competitors follow similar practices. In addition, a practice may qualify for relief under the safe harbor even though it was implemented after the enactment of Section 530. A new industry can begin its own industry practice and

[78] *General Investment Corp.*, CA-9, 87-2 USTC ¶9453, 823 F2d 337; *Options for Senior America Corp.*, DC-MD, 98-2 USTC ¶50,620, 11 FSupp2d 666.

qualify for relief under the industry practice safe harbor. A recent example of a court's liberal view of the industry practice safe harbor was in a case where the court held that a company could rely on a self-conducted industry survey to conclude that its workers were independent contractors thus entitling them to employment tax relief under Section 530.[79]

Section 530 Relief Applies on Entity-by-Entity Basis, Not Consolidated Basis

The IRS held that if parent and subsidiaries file a consolidated corporate return, Section 530 relief applies on an entity-by-entity basis for determining the substantive consistency test, rather than on a consolidated basis. The fact that one of the subsidiary corporations served as paying agent doesn't matter.[80]

Tax Court Jurisdiction Expanded

The Tax Court has the jurisdiction to review IRS determinations that: (1) service providers are employees or independent contractors for employment tax and income tax withholding purposes, or (2) the organization for which services are performed is not entitled to relief from employment taxes under Section 530; and (3) concern the proper amount of employment tax that is due under the above determinations [Code Sec. 7436(a)]. In order to petition the Tax Court to review your employment tax dispute, you must first receive from the IRS by certified or registered mail a "Notice of Determination Concerning Worker Classification Under Section 7436." You must then file your petition for review with the Tax Court before the 91st day after the IRS mails you the Notice of Determination. The Tax Court's jurisdiction to review Code Sec. 7436 employment tax issues includes the determination of the proper amount of employment tax [Code Sec. 7436(a)].

The IRS has released Notice 2002-5[81] regarding Tax Court jurisdiction in employment status proceedings. Information is provided regarding when and how the IRS will issue a Notice of Determination of Worker Classification and how taxpayers petition for Tax Court review of the determinations under Code Sec. 7436.

Interest Accrual May Be Stopped During Tax Court Review

Taxpayers involved in worker classification disputes may make a remittance to stop the accrual of interest yet still receive a notice of determination and retain the right to petition the Tax Court for review of the worker classification issue [Reg. § 31.6205-1(a)(6)(ii)]. Keep in mind that the deposit stops the running of interest only on the amount that is actually remitted and does not earn interest while in the hands of the IRS.

The benefits of having the worker classification dispute heard in the Tax Court are numerous. First, the Tax Court is an economical forum because the person for whom the services are performed need not pay a dime of the taxes up front while the case is pending before the Tax Court.

Second, the Tax Court will listen to both sides of the story and determine the facts on their own rather than relying on an administrative record to determine the facts of the case.

---

[79] *Options for Senior America Corp.*, DC-MD, 98-2 USTC ¶ 50,620, 11 FSupp2d 666.

[80] LTR 200129008 (Dec. 15, 2000).

[81] Notice 2002-5, 2002-1 CB 320.

Third, the party that wins is entitled to claim costs and fees from the opposing party [Code Sec. 7436(d)(2)].

Finally, the Tax Court is a pro-taxpayer forum rather than a rubber stamp for the IRS.

Voluntary Worker Classification Settlement Program

In 2011, the IRS has launched a new Voluntary Classification Settlement Program (VCSP) that will enable qualifying employers to resolve past worker classification controversies by voluntarily reclassifying their workers as employees for federal employment tax purposes.[82] The program is available to businesses, tax-exempt organizations, and government entities that are currently treating their workers (or a class or group of workers) as independent contractors or other nonemployees and want to prospectively treat the workers as employees. Employers eligible to participate in the program may voluntarily reclassify their workers as employees for future tax periods with limited federal employment tax liability for the past nonemployee treatment. To participate in the program, the taxpayer must meet certain eligibility requirements, apply to participate in VCSP, and enter into a closing agreement with the IRS.

To be eligible for the program an applicant must:

- Consistently have treated the workers (or a class or group or workers) in the past as independent contractors or other nonemployees and want to prospectively treat the workers as employees,
- Have filed all required Forms 1099 for the workers for the previous three years,
- Not currently be under audit by the IRS, and
- Not currently be under audit by the Department of Labor or a state agency concerning the classification of these workers. A taxpayer that was previously audited by IRS or DOL concerning the classification of the workers will only be eligible if the taxpayer has complied with the results of that audit.

However, once a taxpayer chooses to reclassify certain of its workers as employees, all workers in the same class must be treated as employees for employment tax purposes.

Employers interested in participating in VCSP must submit an application using Form 8952, *Application for Voluntary Classification Settlement Program*, at least 60 days before they want to begin treating the workers as employees. They must also submit a valid Power of Attorney on Form 2848. Once submitted, the IRS will review the application and verify the taxpayer's eligibility. Employers accepted into the program will enter into a closing agreement with the IRS to finalize the terms of the VCSP and will simultaneously make full and complete payment of any amount due under the closing agreement. An employer accepted into the VCSP will agree to prospectively treat the class of workers as employees for future tax periods and in exchange:

1. Pay 10 percent of the employment tax liability that may have been due on compensation paid to the workers for the most recent tax year, determined under the reduced rates of Code Sec. 3509, which alleviates the tax discrepancies that arise when a worker who has been treated as an independent contractor is reclassified as an employee.

---

[82] Anouncement 2011-64, IRB 2011-41, 503.

2. Will not be liable for any interest and penalties on the liability;
3. Will not be subject to an employment tax audit for the worker classification of the workers for prior years; and
4. Agree for the first three years under the program, to be subject to a special six-year statute of limitations, rather than the usual three years that generally applies to payroll taxes.

In Announcement 2012-45,[83] the IRS modified the VCSP to: (1) permit a taxpayer under IRS audit, other than an employment tax audit, to be eligible to participate in the VCSP; (2) clarify the current eligibility requirement that a taxpayer that is a member of an affiliated group is not eligible to participate in the VCSP if any member of the affiliated group is under employment tax audit; (3) clarify that a taxpayer is not eligible to participate in the VCSP if the taxpayer is contesting in court the classification of the class or classes of workers from a previous audit by the IRS or the Department of Labor; and (4) eliminate the requirement that a taxpayer agree to extend the period of limitations on assessment of employment taxes as part of the VCSP closing agreement with the IRS.

In Announcement 2012-46,[84] the IRS announced that it was changing the eligibility requirements to allow more employers, particularly larger ones, to apply for the VCSP. Under the program as expanded, employers under IRS audit (other than an employment tax audit) can qualify for the VCSP. Also, employers allowed into the program will no longer be subject to a special six-year statute of limitations, instead of the usual three-year limitation period that normally applies to payroll taxes. Until June 30, 2013, the IRS waived the eligibility requirement that an employer must file Forms 1099 with respect to workers they are seeking to reclassify for the past three years.

In IRS News Release IR-2013-23,[85] the IRS announced that a modified VCSP was temporarily available to taxpayers who would otherwise be eligible for the current VCSP but have not filed all required Forms 1099 for the previous three years for the workers who need to be reclassified. Eligible taxpayers that took advantage of this limited, temporary eligibility expansion agreed to prospectively treat workers as employees and received partial relief from federal employment taxes. This temporary expansion was available through June 30, 2013.

¶15,075 WAGES SUBJECT TO FICA

Wages subject to social security tax include wage amounts within the annual wage base [¶15,050], whether paid in cash, benefits, or any other form, to employees for services in covered employment [Code Sec. 3121(a)]. *Wages* are defined as "all remuneration for employment" arising out of an employment relationship unless specially exempted [Reg. §31.3121(a)-1]. (See ¶15,080 for payments not taxed as wages.) This means that taxable wages include the following: salaries, fees, Christmas gifts and bonuses,[86] bonuses paid in installments to retired employees for past

[83] Anouncement 2012-45, IRB 2012-51, 724.

[84] Anouncement 2012-46, IRB 2012-51, 725.

[85] IRS News Release IR-2013-23, Feb. 27, 2013.

[86] Rev. Rul. 71-53, 1971-1 CB 279; Rev. Rul. 70-471, 1970-2 CB 199.

services,[87] employee stock bonuses,[88] severance pay,[89] sales contest prize awards (cash or cash value paid to salesperson directly or to salesperson's spouse),[90] sales commissions (but not if paid to former customers),[91] payments made to tenured teachers or other employees to force them to resign,[92] or to benefits paid under reduction-in-force program,[93] payments made to employees as consideration for cancellation of an employment contract and relinquishment of contract rights,[94] and age discrimination settlement payments because they represent lost wages.[95] But note that if no employment relationship exists, wages for withholding purposes do not exist. This means that damages received by an unsuccessful job applicant who charged the company with age discrimination will not be considered wages and will therefore not be subject to withholding because the job applicant was not an employee at the time he received the damages.[96]

The basis of the wage is immaterial. For example, wages are taxable whether paid on an hourly, daily, weekly, monthly, or annual basis, or on a piece-work or a percentage-of-the-profits basis [Reg. § 31.3121(a)-1(c), (d)].

The amount of wages paid in a form other than money is the fair market value of what is received at the time of receipt [Reg. § 31.3121(a)-1(e)]. If wages are paid in a foreign currency, the official rate of exchange when the payment is made is used to determine the value of the payment in U.S. currency for purposes of the tax and the limitation on taxable wages.

.01 Fringe Benefits

Fringes are subject to FICA tax unless specifically excluded from the definition of wages [¶ 15,080] [Code Sec. 3121(a)]. The taxable value of a noncash fringe benefit is the excess of the fringe benefit's fair market value over any amount paid for it by the employee. The fair market value is the amount an individual would have to pay for the benefit in an arm's length transaction [Reg. § 1.61-21(b)(2)].

Employers may elect not to withhold income tax on an employee's personal use of a company car [¶ 15,015], but they must nonetheless withhold and pay social security tax on the value of that use.

> **NOTE:** If an employer elects to treat an employee's company car use as 100 percent personal in nature, the employer and employee will each owe FICA tax on what may in fact be an exaggerated amount of personal use. For this reason, the all-use-as-personal-use valuation of company car use works best for employees whose regular wages exceed the social security wage base (OASDI, $110,100 in 2012).

---

[87] Rev. Rul. 57-92, 1957-1 CB 306.

[88] *Indianapolis Glove Co.*, CA-7, 38-2 USTC ¶ 9505, 96 F2d 816.

[89] *K.H. Donnel*, FedCl, 2001-2 USTC ¶ 50,664, 50 FedCl 375.

[90] Rev. Rul. 68-216, 1968-1 CB 413.

[91] Rev. Rul. 69-452, 1969-2 CB 181.

[92] *P.F. Klender*, DC-MI, CA-6, 2006-1 USTC 50,347, 450 F3d 185; *Univ. of Pittsburgh*, CA-3, 2007-2 USTC ¶ 50,789, 507 F3d 165; *D.F. Appoloni*, CA-6, 2006-1 USTC ¶ 50,347, 450 F3d 185, *cert. denied* 1/16/07, but see *N.D. State Univ.*, CA-8, 2001-2 USTC ¶ 50,485, 255 F3d 599; *nonacq.* IRB 2001-53 (re-released 1/24/2007), AOD 2007-001.

[93] *CSX Corp.*, FedCl, 2008-1 USTC ¶ 50,218, 518 F3d 1328.

[94] Rev. Rul. 2004-110, 2004-2 CB 950. But see *N.D. State Univ.*, CA-8, 2001-2 USTC ¶ 50,485, 255 F3d 599; *nonacq.* IRB 2001-53 (re-released 1/24/2007), AOD 2007-001.

[95] *C. Gerstenbluth*, CA-2, 2013-2 USTC ¶ 50,494, *aff'g*, DC-NY, 2012-2 USTC ¶ 50,612.

[96] *R. Newhouse*, CA-8, 98-2 USTC ¶ 50,768, 157 F3d 582.

.02 Employer Payment of Employee's Share of Tax

If an employer pays an employee's share of social security tax or any state unemployment insurance tax, without deducting the tax from the employee's wages, the amount of the tax payment itself becomes income subject to income tax withholding [¶ 15,015] and social security tax. Exception: Employer payments of domestics' or agricultural employees' tax [Code Sec. 3121(a)(6)].

.03 Tips

Employers owe and must withhold social security tax on all tips (cash or charge) of $20 or more in a calendar month if employees make written reports of tips to employers [Code Sec. 3102(c)]. For further discussion see ¶ 15,015.

.04 Agent-Drivers' and Commission Drivers' Wages

Agent-drivers or commission drivers who are employees [¶ 15,070] may submit a statement of their gross receipts, expenses (other than transportation), and their truck's fair rental value to their employers. The difference between their gross receipts and the total of their expenses and the truck's rental value is wages. If no statement is furnished, the difference between the price paid to the principal for the products or services they distribute and the suggested selling price to the customers is wages.[97]

.05 Sick Pay

Sick pay payments made by an employer or a third party (such as an insurance company) are taxable if they are not made under a plan established by the employer and if they are paid before the expiration of six calendar months following the last calendar month the employee worked for the employer [Code Sec. 3121(a)(4); Reg. § 31.3121(a)(14)-1]. Any payment attributable to an employee's contribution is not taxable under these rules.

> **NOTE:** A third-party payer acting as the employer's agent will be liable for withholding and depositing only the employee's share of the tax on covered payments, if it promptly notifies the employer of the sick pay payments it has made.[98] If such a third-party payer does not notify the employer within the time required for the deposit of FICA tax on the payments, the third-party payer becomes liable for the employer's share of FICA as well. In addition, the third-party payer must give each recipient employee a Form W-2 by January 31 that shows any federal income tax withheld, the amount of the sick pay the employee must include in income, the amount not includible in income due to the employee's contributions to the sick pay plan, the amount of sick pay subject to FICA, and the amount of FICA tax withheld on the payments. On the other hand, a third-party payer that is paid an insurance premium and not reimbursed on a cost-plus-fee basis is treated as an employer rather than as an agent. That means the third party is liable for both shares of social security and Medicare taxes, unless the liability is transferred to the employer.[99]

See ¶ 15,080 for instances where sick pay is not subject to FICA.

---

[97] Rev. Rul. 73-260, 1973-1 CB 412.

[98] P.L. 97-123, Sec. 3[d].

[99] Notice 91-26, 1991-2 CB 619; as corrected by Notice 91-26A, 1991-2 CB 629.

.06 Deferred Compensation Plans

Taxable wages include employer contributions, made at an employee's election, to a qualified retirement plan, tax-sheltered annuity, or cash-or-deferred (Sec. 401(k)) plan [Code Secs. 3121(a)(5), 3121(v)]. In regard to cash-or-deferred plans, amounts that an employee elects to have his employer defer from salary into a trust under a profit-sharing or stock bonus plan are taxable, regardless of whether the cash-or-deferred arrangement is part of a cafeteria plan [Ch. 4]. Any cash the employee elects to receive under a cash-or-deferred arrangement is also taxable. Amounts deferred under eligible state and local deferred compensation plans [Code Sec. 457] and state pick-up plans [Code Sec. 414(h)(2)]are also taxable [Code Sec. 3121(v)(1)(B)].

Inclusion of Nonqualified Deferred Compensation

Code Sec. 409A provides that all amounts deferred for all tax years under a nonqualified deferred compensation plan that does not comply with requirements relating to distributions, acceleration of benefits, and elections are currently includible in gross income to the extent not subject to a substantial risk of forfeiture and not previously included in gross income. If a taxpayer fails to include these amounts, in addition to current income inclusion, interest at the underpayment rate plus one percentage point is imposed on the underpayments that would have occurred if the compensation had been includible in income when first deferred, or if later, when not subject to a substantial risk of forfeiture. The amount required to be included in income is also subject to a 20-percent additional tax. For further discussion, see ¶3170 and ¶15,115.

.07 Insurance Payments

Employer-provided group-term life insurance premiums are subject to FICA to the extent the coverage is includible in gross income (i.e., exceeds $50,000) [Code Sec. 3121(a)(2)(C)]. Generally, however, payments under a plan established by an employer to provide for employees or their dependents on account of death, or medical or hospital expenses due to sickness or disability, are not taxable [See ¶15,080].

> **NOTE:** Suppose employers continue to provide taxable group-term life insurance coverage to someone who has left their employment. The former employee is responsible for paying his or her portion of the FICA taxes. The Form W-2 must separately show the portion of the wages that consists of the payment for taxable group-term life insurance and the FICA tax owed by the former employee [Code Secs. 3102(d), 3202].

¶15,080 PAYMENTS NOT TAXED AS WAGES

The law specifically exempts certain forms of compensation from social security tax.

> ▶ **OBSERVATION:** Employers can realize payroll savings by making sure they are not collecting and paying tax on payments that are not wages for FICA tax purposes. They can substitute FICA tax-free forms of compensation for regular cash wages whenever practical.

.01 Employee Achievement Awards

Awards are excluded as wages for social security tax if it is reasonable to believe that an employee will be able to exclude them from income [Ch. 4] [Code Sec. 3121(a)(20)].

.02 Payments in Kind; Meals and Lodging

Pay in any medium other than cash is not taxable, if paid for (1) domestic service in private home, (2) farm labor, or (3) service not in the course of the employer's trade or business. *Pay in any medium other than cash* includes lodging, food, clothing, car tokens, transportation passes or tickets, and other goods or commodities [Code Secs. 3121(a)(7)(A), 3121(a)(8)(A); Reg. §§31.3121(a)(7)-1, 31.3121(a)(8)-1]. If the noncash remuneration is *not* paid for services indicated in (1), (2) and (3) above, it is included in wages according to the following guidelines:

> Items furnished to employees are not taxable wages if the items are of small value compared to total pay and are furnished for employees' health, contentment, goodwill, or efficiency. But items furnished to employees are taxable wages if their value is an appreciable part of the pay. Thus, board and lodging furnished to employees on vessels or in isolated localities, living quarters furnished to apartment house superintendents, and meals furnished to restaurant employees are taxable wages. Payments made directly to an employee's landlord by the employer are considered cash and are therefore also taxable wages.[100]

The value of meals or lodging furnished by an employer is not subject to FICA tax if at the time the meals or lodging is furnished it is reasonable to believe the employee will be able to exclude the items from income [Code Sec. 3121(a)(19)]. Generally, such items are excludable if (1) they are furnished on the employer's business premises; (2) they are furnished for the employer's convenience; and (3) for lodging, the employee must accept the lodging as a condition of employment [Ch. 4] [Code Sec. 119].

.03 Employee Business Expenses

Advances, allowances or reimbursements for travel and other ordinary and necessary expenses incurred (or reasonably expected to be incurred) by an employee in the course of the employer's business are not wages. The employee must substantiate his or her expenses to the employer within a reasonable amount of time and return any unspent amounts [Ch.10] [Reg. §§1.62-2, 31.3121(a)-3]. Wages and expense money need not be paid separately, but if one payment includes both items, each should be separately identified on the pay stub.

.04 Sick Pay

Payments to or on behalf of an employee on account of sickness, accident, disability, or medical or hospitalization expenses are not taxable wages, *if* they are made after the expiration of six calendar months following the last month the employee worked for the employer. This rule applies even if the payments are not made under a plan. For payments made under a plan, see ¶15,075 [Code Sec. 3121(a)(4); Reg. §31.3121(a)(4)-1].

---

[100] Rev. Rul. 54-384, 1954-2 CB 366.

.05 Payments Under Employee Benefit, Trust, or Annuity Plans

Generally, payments made under a plan established by the employer on account of sickness, accident disability, medical or hospital expenses due to sickness or disability, or death, are not taxable wages (but see the discussion of sick pay above and ¶15,075). Likewise, payments under a plan that are made upon or after the termination of employment because of death, age-related retirement, or retirement for disability are not taxable. These exclusions from FICA taxable wages apply also to payments made on account of the employee's dependents [Code Secs. 3121(a)(2), 3121(a)(13); Reg. §§31.3121(a)(2)-1, 31.3121(a)(13)-1]. Important exception: employer-provided group-term life insurance coverage in excess of $50,000 [¶15,075]. Benefits provided employees under a cafeteria plan are excluded from wages [Ch. 4] [Code Sec. 3121(a)(5)(G)], except group-term life insurance premiums for coverage in excess of $50,000, and amounts deferred or cash received under a cash-or-deferred plan [Ch. 3, Ch. 4; ¶15,075]. Payments made on account of sickness or disability under a statute in the nature of a workers' compensation act are excluded from wages for FICA purposes [Prop Reg. §31.3121(a)(2)-1(d)(1)].

Social security law also excludes the following:

- Any payment made to, or on behalf of an employee or beneficiary

  a. From or to a trust described in Code Sec. 401(a) that is exempt from tax under Code Sec. 501(a) at the time of the payment, unless the payment is made to an employee of the trust as remuneration for services rendered as the employee and not as a beneficiary of the trust

  b. Under or to an annuity plan which, at the time of the payment, is a plan described in Code Sec. 403(a)

  c. Under or to an annuity contract under Code Sec. 403(b) other than a payment for the purchase of the contract by reason of a salary reduction agreement (whether evidenced by a written instrument or otherwise) [Code Secs. 3121(a)(5)(A), (B), (D)].

- Any payment under or to an exempt governmental deferred compensation plan [Code Sec. 3121(a)(5)(E)]; and

- Any payment to supplement pension benefits under a plan or trust to take into account some or all of the increase in the cost of living since retirement, but only if the supplemental payments are under a plan which is treated as a welfare benefit plan under ERISA [Code Sec. 3121(a)(5)(F)].

  ▶ **IMPORTANT:** A payment that would have been made regardless of retirement, death, or retirement for disability is not excluded from FICA tax [Code Sec. 3121(a)(13)].

  NOTE: Employer contributions to IRAs under a simplified employee pension plan (SEP) are not subject to FICA tax.

- Any elective deferrals permitted under a SEP, although excludable from income, are includable in the definition of wages for FICA (and FUTA) purposes [Code Sec. 3121(a)(5)(C)].

.06 Other Types of Payments

The following payments are not considered wages for social security purposes:

- Employer payments of domestic or agricultural employees' social security or state unemployment insurance taxes;
- Payments to employees (other than sick or vacation pay) after they reach retirement age if they do not work for the employer during the period for which the payment is made [Code Sec. 3121(a); Reg. §§31.3121(a)(6)-1, 31.3121(a)(9)-1, 31.3121(a)(11)-1];
- Tuition payments, if for courses related to the employer's business [Ch. 4] [Code Sec. 3121(a)(20)];
- Payments under a dependent care assistance program, if believed to be excludable from gross income when paid [Ch. 4] [Code Sec. 3121(a)(18)];
- Moving expenses if when paid the employee is likely to be able to take a deduction for income tax purposes [Ch. 9];
- Employment agency fees paid directly to the agency;
- Occasional supper money furnished because of overtime work;
- Early retirement incentive payments to college or university professors in exchange for relinquishing tenure rights are not treated as FICA wages but surrender of contractual property rights;
- Differential wages paid to employees who leave their job to go on active military duty;[101]
- Severance payments made by a bankrupt retailer to its employees pursuant to pre- and post-bankruptcy petition severance programs were not wages for FICA purposes because the payments fell within the Code Sec. 3402(o)(2) exception to wages for supplemental unemployment compensation benefits.[102]

  ▶ **OBSERVATION:** Businesses that are run through two or more related corporations that share common employees may be able to designate one of the companies as a common paymaster for both. Only the common paymaster is considered the employer for social security tax purposes, so the most tax a business will owe on a shared employee's wages is the single-employer maximum tax.

¶15,085 FEDERAL SELF-EMPLOYMENT CONTRIBUTIONS ACT (SECA) TAXES

.01 Amount of Tax

A tax is imposed on self-employment income of self-employed individuals each year. The tax rate consists of a component for old-age, survivors, and disability insurance (OASDI) and a component for hospital insurance (HI). Generally, no tax is payable when net earnings from self-employment are less than $400. The self-employment tax rates and the maximum earnings base subject to tax are as follows:

---

[101] Rev. Rul. 2009-11, IRB 2009-18, 896.

[102] *In re Quality Stores, Inc.*, DC-MI, 2010-1 USTC ¶50,250, *aff'd*, CA-6, 2012-2 USTC ¶50,551, *cert. granted* Oct. 2, 2013.

Calendar Year	Maximum Earnings Base	Tax Rate
2013	$113,700	12.40% (OASDI)
	No limit	2.90% (HI)

An additional Medicare tax of 0.9 percent is imposed on self-employment income if self-employment income exceeds $200,000 ($250,000 in the case of a joint return, $125,000 in the case of married filing separately). Thus, a single taxpayer will pay a 2.9 percent tax on self-employment income of up to $200,000 and a 3.8 percent tax on self-employed income in excess of $200,000 [Code Sec. 1401(b)(2)]. For further discussion of the additional Medicare tax, see ¶ 15,050.

.02 Computing Self-Employment Tax Liability

A deduction in figuring a taxpayer's net earnings from self-employment is available for purposes of computing the self-employment tax [Code Sec. 1402(a)(12)]. A self-employed individual may also deduct one-half of the self-employment tax for the year in arriving at adjusted gross income [Code Sec. 164(f)]. The 0.9 percent Medicare tax is not taken into account for purposes of either deduction. If a self-employed individual also has wages subject to social security taxes, the wages are deducted from the maximum earnings base subject to the self-employment tax.

For self-employed workers, the FICA tax is 15.3 percent—12.4 percent for OASDI and 2.9 percent for HI. The 0.9 percent additional Medicare tax similarly applies to self-employment income in excess of $200,000 ($250,000 of combined self-employment income on a joint return, $125,000 for married taxpayers filing a separate return). [Code Sec. 1401(b)(2)]. In effect, this makes the Medicare tax rate 3.8 percent for self-employment income in excess of these amounts. For further discussion of the additional Medicare tax, see ¶ 15,050.

.03 Fiscal Years

A taxpayer need not prorate the tax or earnings base for a fiscal year that overlaps the date of a rate or earnings base change. For example, if a self-employed individual has a fiscal year beginning October 1, 2013, the 2013 earnings base ($113,700) and the 2013 tax rate (15.3 percent) apply to his fiscal tax year. If a partner's tax year is different from the tax year of the partnership, the partner's tax year governs in determining the applicable self-employment rate [Code Sec. 1402(a); Reg. § 1.1402(a)-2(e)].

¶ 15,090 WHAT IS SELF-EMPLOYMENT?

Generally, only individuals who carry on a trade or business as proprietors or partners, or who render services as independent contractors, are self-employed and have self-employment income. The term trade or business does not include all business endeavors. Persons paid for making occasional speeches are not engaged in a trade or business but may be so considered if they seek speaking engagements for which they receive lecture fees or other compensation, and if they fill such engagements with reasonable regularity.[103] Illegal activities may be a trade or business.[104]

---

[103] Rev. Rul. 55-431, 1955-2 CB 312, amplified by, Rev. Rul. 77-356, 1977-2 CB 317.

[104] Rev. Rul. 60-77, 1960-1 CB 386.

.01 Clergy

Duly ordained, commissioned, or licensed ministers of churches, Christian Science practitioners and members of religious orders (except those who have taken a vow of poverty) are considered self-employed as to services that they perform. They are subject to self-employment tax, unless they get an exemption on conscientious or religious grounds. An application to be exempt from self-employment tax under Code Sec. 1402(e)(1) must be filed by the due date of the return for the second tax year ending after their net earnings from these services are at least $400. The application must include a statement that the applicant opposes acceptance of public insurance benefits on conscientious or religious grounds. Individuals already covered cannot apply for an exemption. An exemption is irrevocable once granted. Coverage generally starts with the first tax year the individual has net earnings of $400 or more (any part of which is from services as a minister, member, or practitioner) and for all succeeding tax years [Code Sec. 1402(e)(4); Reg. §§1.1402(c)-3(e)(2), 1.1402(c)-5, 1.1402(e)-2A, 4A].

.02 Excluded Services

Persons are *not* self-employed if they engage in any of the following:

- Services performed in public office [Reg. §1.1402(c)-2(a)(1)]. However, state and local government officials paid on a fee basis are covered, unless their state covers them as employees [Code Sec. 1402(c)(1); Reg. §1.1402(c)-2, 1.1402(c)-3(f)];
- Services performed as a railroad worker [Reg. §1.1402(c)-4]. (These workers have their own retirement system);
- Services performed by a member of a religious order who has taken a vow of poverty [Code Sec. 1402(c); Reg. §1.1402(c)-5];
- Services by a member of a religious sect, if the sect: (1) provides for dependent members; (2) is opposed to all life, health and accident insurance; and (3) has been in existence continuously since December 31, 1950. A member of such a sect must apply for an exemption on Form 4029, *Application for Exemption From Social Security and Medicare Taxes and Waiver of Benefits*. This is filed by the return's due date for the first tax year that includes self-employment income. If none is filed by that date, the member has until three months to comply after receiving notice from the IRS that a timely application was not filed [Code Sec. 1402(g); Reg. §1.1402(h)-1];
- Services as a newspaper carrier under the age of 18 [Reg. §1.1402(c)-3(b)]; and
- Pay for services as an employee is not pay from self-employment, except for certain news vendors 18 years of age or over [¶15,060]. In this connection, terms such as employee and wages have the meanings explained in ¶15,070 and ¶15,075. Also, certain fishing crewmen [¶15,015] are treated as self-employed [Code Sec. 1402(c)(2)(F)].

.03 Tax Advantages of Self-Employed Status

Independent contractor status has some tax advantages, as follow:

- The independent contractor does not pay federal unemployment taxes (FUTA);
- Trade or business expenses that otherwise would not be deductible (or only partially deductible) for employees become fully deductible on the Schedule C of an independent contractor. The expenses of an employee, on the other hand, are

deductible only to the extent they exceed 2 percent of the taxpayer's AGI. They are subject to the overall limitations on itemized deductions contained in Code Sec. 68; and

- Independent contractors are entitled to establish their own retirement plans and deduct contributions to the plan, lending greater flexibility than may be available from the employer's plan.

¶15,095 SELF-EMPLOYMENT INCOME

.01 Net Earnings

Self-employment income, or net earnings from self-employment, is income a taxpayer earns from a trade or business as a sole proprietor or partner, less deductions attributable to the trade or business [Code Sec. 1402]. Income that is excluded from gross income for income tax purposes is generally excluded from self-employment income. However, no deduction is allowed for net operating losses, personal and dependent exemptions, earnings deposited by a commercial fisherman into a capital construction fund, and the qualified production activities deduction.

A self-employed individual may deduct 100 percent of premiums for medical care insurance for themselves, their spouses, their dependents, and their child under age 27. The deduction is taken from gross income in arriving at adjusted gross income [Code Sec. 162(l)(1)].

.02 Optional Methods of Computing Net Earnings

Taxpayers who had a loss or a small amount of income from self-employment may find it beneficial to file Schedule SE and use either optional method in Part II of Schedule SE.[105] The optional method may increase the amount of self employment tax paid but may afford the taxpayers the following benefits:

- The optional method may give the taxpayer credit toward social security coverage.
- The optional method may qualify the taxpayer to claim the earned income credit or give the taxpayer a larger credit.
- Using the optional method may qualify the taxpayer to claim the additional child tax credit or give the taxpayer a larger credit.
- The optional methods may help the taxpayer qualify for the child and dependent care credit.
- The optional method of computing net earnings from self-employment may be used to figure self-employed health insurance deduction.

Farm Optional Method

Taxpayers may use this method to compute their net earnings from farm self-employment if their gross farm income was $6,960 or less or their net farm profits were less than $5,024. Under this method, taxpayers report two-thirds of gross farm

[105] Treas. Dept. 2013 Instructions for Schedule SE (Form 1040), p. SE-6.

income—up to $4,640 as net earnings. This method can increase or decrease net earnings from farm self-employment even if the farming business had a loss.

Nonfarm Optional Method

Taxpayers may use this method to compute their net earnings from farm self-employment if their net nonfarm profits were less than $5,024 and also less than 72.189 percent of gross nonfarm income. To use this method, the taxpayer must also be regularly self-employed. This requirement is satisfied if actual net earnings from self-employment were $400 or more in two of the three years preceding the year the nonfarm optional method is used. The net earnings of $400 or more could be from either farm or nonfarm earnings or both. The net earnings include the taxpayer's distributive share of partnership income or loss subject to self employment tax. Use of the nonfarm optional method from nonfarm self-employment is limited to 5 years but the 5 years do not have to consecutive.

Under this method, taxpayers should report as net earnings two-thirds of their gross nonfarm income, up to $5,024 or 72.189 percent of gross nonfarm income. But the taxpayer cannot report less than his or her actual net earnings from nonfarm self-employment.

Using Both Optional Methods

If the taxpayer uses both methods, the taxpayer can report less than his or her actual net earnings from farm and nonfarm self-employment, but cannot report less than actual earnings from non-farm self-employment. If the taxpayer uses both methods to compute net earnings, he or she cannot report more than $4,640 of net earnings from self-employment.

.03 Income Earned Abroad

Foreign earned income (but not the housing amount) that qualifies for exclusion from income tax under Code Sec. 901(a)(1) [Ch. 28] is nonetheless included as net earnings from self-employment [Code Sec. 1402(a)(11)]. This inclusion applies to residents of Puerto Rico, the U.S. Virgin Islands, Guam, or American Samoa. They must treat self-employment income the same as U.S. residents, except that a Puerto Rican resident must include income from Puerto Rican sources in gross income as well [Code Secs. 1402(a)(6), 7651; Reg. §§1.1402(a)-2, -9, -12].

.04 Partners' Income

Partners' earnings from self-employment include their distributive share of the partnership net income, whether or not distributed. Guaranteed payments and other items that must be accounted for separately[106] [Ch. 24] also are included in the self-employment income computation. However, if the true nature of the relationship between the partner and the partnership is that of employee-employer, the partner's distributive share may be subject to FICA instead [¶15,070].

If the individual and the partnership are on different tax years, the same rules apply to the partner's distributive share as apply for income tax [Ch. 24] [Reg. §1.1402(a)-2(e)].

---

[106] Rev. Rul. 65-272, 1965-2 CB 217.

Suppose a partner dies before the end of the partnership's tax year. Then his self-employment net earnings should include his distributive share of the partnership's ordinary income or loss for the partnership tax year, except his share attributable to any interest in the partnership after he died. For this purpose, the partnership's ordinary income or loss is treated as if it were realized or sustained ratably over the partnership tax year. Although the partner's *distributive share* includes the share that goes to his estate or any person succeeding to his rights because of his death, it does not include any share from a partnership interest not held at death [Code Sec. 1402(f); Reg. § 1.1402(f)-1(a)(3)].

Generally, retirement payments received by retired partners are net earnings from self-employment, except for certain periodic payments made by a partnership on account of retirement under a written plan [Code Sec. 1402(a)(10); Reg. § 1.1402(a)-17].

.05 S Corporations and Payroll Taxes

When income is passed through to an individual from an S corporation, it is not treated as self-employment income that is subject to self-employment tax under Code Sec. 1402.[107] However, a shareholder who is an officer of the S corporation and who performs services for the S corporation is considered an employee and reasonable compensation for these services is subject to FICA, FUTA, and income tax withholding.[108] For further discussion of this issue which has spawned much litigation, see ¶21,051.

.06 Income From Other Sources

Directors' Fees

Directors are in a trade or business when not employees. Therefore, their fees and other pay for services as such, including attendance at meetings and serving on standing committees, are earnings from self-employment.[109] Fees paid to a director who also serves as an employee of the same corporation constitute self-employment earnings only if they are paid separately from earnings, or designated as separate earnings when paid with earnings from employment.

> **NOTE:** Directors' fees are treated as self-employment income in the year they are paid [Code Sec. 1402(a)].

Fiduciaries' Fees

Fees received by fiduciaries not in a trade or business are not self-employment income. Usually only professional fiduciaries are considered to be engaged in a trade or business, and the fees received by them are self-employment income. However, even if individuals are not considered professional fiduciaries, they may be subject to the self-employment tax, if they carry on an active trade or business in the administration of an estate.

---

107 Rev. Rul. 59-221, 1959-1 CB 225.

108 *Joseph M. Grey Public Accountant P.C.*, 119 TC 121, Dec. 54,871, *aff'd in unpublished opinion*, CA-3, 2004-1 USTC ¶50,214; LTR 9530005 (Apr. 26, 1993).

109 Rev. Rul. 57-246, 1957-1 CB 388; Rev. Rul. 68-595, 1968-2 CB 378.

Research Funds

Persons who receive research grants to do independent research work are independent contractors. They must include the funds in their self-employment income.

International organizations. U.S. citizens employed in the U.S. by a foreign government, its instrumentalities or by an international organization are considered self-employed individuals [Code Sec. 1402(c)(2); Reg. § 1.1402(c)-3]. If employed by an international organization, they are considered self-employed even though they are also covered by the Civil Service Retirement Act.[110]

Trust income. When beneficiaries have the sole right to operate trust property for their joint profit, their distributive shares of the profits may be self-employment income from a joint venture or partnership.[111]

¶15,105 SPECIAL RULES FOR CERTAIN FORMS OF SELF-EMPLOYMENT INCOME

Not all self-employment income is considered net earnings. The rules are described here [Code Sec. 1402(a); Reg. § 1.1402(a)].

.01 Dividends

Dividends are included only by dealers in stock or securities, and then only if received in the course of their business as dealers. The Tax Court held in *Rudman*,[112] that a commodities dealer's trades through another broker were subject to self-employment tax.

.02 Interest

Business loan interest is included, even if the lender is not in the business of making loans. For instance, interest received by merchants on their accounts or notes receivable is included. Interest on nonbusiness loans is excluded. Interest on corporate and government securities is included only by a dealer in securities.

.03 Rentals

Real Estate Rentals

Rentals from real estate and personal property leased with it, including rentals in crop shares, generally are excluded from self-employment income [Code Sec. 1402(a)(1); Reg. § 1.1402(a)-4(a)]. Rentals from real estate less any related deductions are included only by real estate dealers, and then only if they are received in the course of their business as dealers. Owners of boarding houses, apartment houses, tourist homes, or motels (where services also are rendered to the occupants), are subject to self-employment taxes. Services are considered rendered if they are primarily for the occupants' convenience. Supplying maid service, for example, constitutes such services, but furnishing heat and light or collecting trash does not. Payments to supervising beneficiaries of trust property and their distributive share of profits from rentals of office space are considered rental income and are excluded when comput-

---

110 Rev. Rul. 66-69, 1966-1 CB 204.

111 Rev. Rul. 64-220, 1964-2 CB 335.

112 *K.M. Rudman*, 118 TC 354, Dec. 54,726 (2002).

ing net earnings from self-employment. They do not render services to the occupants.[113]

Farmland Rental Payments

However, under the so-called farm rental exception of Code Sec. 1402(a)(1), the rentals derived by the owner or tenant of land are not excluded from the computation of net earnings from self-employment if the following two conditions exist:

- The owner or tenant *materially participates* in the production of the agricultural or horticultural commodity grown on the land; and

- The income is derived under an arrangement, between the owner or tenant and another individual, which provides that the other individual will produce agricultural or horticultural commodities on such land, and that there will be material participation by the owner or tenant in the production or the management of the production of such agricultural or horticultural commodities.

Reg. § 1.1402(a)-4(b)(2) provides that farm rental income will be included for self-employment tax purposes, when the income is subject to a sharecropping or other rental agreement wherein material participation by the owner or tenant is required in the production or management of the agricultural commodities. The contractual arrangement may be either oral or written, but it must impose the requirement to produce one or more agricultural goods on the land of the owner or tenant [Reg. § 1.1402(a)-4(b)(3)]. Moreover, the scope of the arrangement must require that the owner or tenant materially participate in either the production or management of the commodities. The term production includes planting, cultivating, and harvesting crops, and the furnishing of machinery, implements, seed, and livestock [Reg. § 1.1402-4(b)(3)(ii)]. *Management of production* refers to managerial decision making in the production of the commodities such as: when to plant, cultivate, dust, spray, or harvest the crop; making inspections and advising; decisions on types of crops, rotation plans, and the types of equipment to be furnished [Reg. § 1.1402(a)-4(b)(3)].

According to IRS Publication No. 225, *Farmer's Tax Guide*, a taxpayer is considered to participate materially if he or she has an arrangement with a tenant for the taxpayer's participation and the taxpayer meets one of the following tests:

- The taxpayer does any three of the following: (a) pays, using cash or credit, at least half the direct costs of producing the crop or livestock, (b) furnishes at least half the tools, equipment, and livestock used in the production activities, (c) advises or consults with the tenant, and (d) inspects the production activities periodically;

- The taxpayer regularly and frequently makes or takes an important role in management decisions substantially contributing to, or affecting the success of, the enterprise;

- The taxpayer works 100 hours or more spread over a period of five weeks or more in activities connected with agricultural production; or

---

[113] Rev. Rul. 64-220, 1964-2 CB 335.

- The taxpayer does things that considered in their totality, show he or she is materially and significantly involved in the production of the farm commodities.[114]

A great deal of confusion exists in the interpretation of Code Sec. 1402(a)(1) as it relates to the imposition of self-employment tax on farm rent. Recently, the Tax Court has decided conversely on two self-employment tax cases related to farmland rents.[115] In *Bot*,[116] the Court of Appeals for the Eighth Circuit affirmed the Tax Court to hold that retired farmers who had a crop-sharing arrangement with their sons were liable for self-employment tax on value-added payments received from an agricultural co-op where they were still active members. However, in other related cases, the Eighth Circuit has held that the farm rental payments were not subject to self-employment tax. The IRS has announced that it will not follow any Eighth Circuit cases holding that farm rental payments weren't subject to self-employment tax.[117]

According to the IRS, if under the overall scheme of farming operations it was understood that the farmer materially participated, then the income received from the lessee is subject to self-employment tax regardless of whether material participation was explicitly called for under the written or oral lease.

.04 Conservation Reserve Program Payments

The Conservation Reserve Program (CRP) is a U.S. Department of Agriculture (USDA) voluntary conservation reserve program that offers annual "rental" payments to owners and operators for converting highly erodible cropland normally devoted to the production of an agricultural commodity to less intensive use. Under the CRP, a participating owner who enrolls land in the program doesn't relinquish control of the land to the USDA, and the USDA doesn't engage in any activities with respect to the land that constitute "use" of the land by the USDA. Taxpayers participating in the CRP maintain control over and free access to their premises. Although the CRP restricts the taxpayer's use of the property—i.e., the taxpayers cannot plant certain crops and engage in certain activities with respect to the enrolled property, which the taxpayer agrees to in exchange for consideration—the Government doesn't take possession of the property or acquire the right to use the property for its own purposes.

In *R.J. Morehouse*,[118] the Tax Court concluded that a taxpayer who received payments under CRP was liable for self-employment tax under Code Sec. 1401. The court found that the CRP payments were includible in the taxpayer's self-employment income because he was engaged in a trade or business during the years in issue and there was a nexus between his trade or business and the CRP payments he received. The Court further held that CRP payments weren't "rentals from real estate" under Code Sec. 1402(a)(1). The Tax Court agreed with and adopted the analysis of the Sixth

---

[114] Treas. Dept., IRS Publication 225, "Farmer's Tax Guide For Use in Preparing 2013 Returns," p. 74.

[115] *G.E. Johnson*, 87 TCM 1057, Dec. 55,566(M), TC Memo. 2004-56 (farmland rent not included in net earnings subject to self-employment tax since the rent was not measured by the taxpayers' participation in farming activities); *J.J. Solvie*, 87 TCM 1049, Dec. 55,565(M), TC Memo. 2004-55 (rent received for a hog barn was subject to self-employment tax since the rent was not paid at fair market value but rather it was tied to the taxpayer's farming success).

[116] *R.J. Bot*, 118 TC 138, Dec. 54,653 (2002), *aff'd*, CA-8, 2004-1 USTC ¶50,112, 353 F3d 595.

[117] AOD 2003-003.

[118] *R.J. Morehouse*, 140 TC No. 16, Dec. 59,568 (2013).

Circuit in *F.J. Wuebker*[119] on whether CRP payments were excluded from the calculation of net earnings from self-employment as "rentals from real estate" under Code Sec. 1402(a)(1). In *Wuebker*, the Court of Appeals for the Sixth Circuit reversed the Tax Court to hold that payments received by a farmer for participating in the CRP were income from farming and subject to self-employment tax under Code Sec. 1401. Although the payments were described as rentals, they weren't paid for use of the land and didn't fall within the self-employment-income exception for real estate rentals. Following the *Wuebker* decision, the IRS issued Notice 2006-108,[120] where the Service held that CRP rental payments were not payments for the right to use or occupy real property. The CRP rental payments were made in exchange for conducting activities that meet the commitments of a CRP contract and are therefore rentals from real estate.

.05 Profit or Loss from Business or Profession

Income and deductions reported in Schedule C of Form 1040 are included; but not if related to services not considered as being self-employment [¶15,090]. No net operating loss is allowable.

> ▶ **OBSERVATION:** Although the mere receipt of royalties probably is not a trade or business, royalties from a trade or business of writing books that generate royalties will be considered self-employment income.[121]

.06 Gain or Loss From Disposing of Property

Such gain or loss is excluded if it is from (1) the sale or exchange of capital assets; (2) the cutting of timber or disposal of timber, coal, or iron ore [Ch. 8]; (3) the sale, exchange, or involuntary conversion of property other than inventory or property held for sale to customers.

.07 Income of the Clergy

Retirement benefits received from a church plan by a minister after he or she retires and the rental value or allowance of a parsonage, including utilities, furnished to a minister after retirement are no longer considered earnings from self-employment that are subject to self-employment taxes [Code Sec. 1402(a)(8)]. The self-employment income of members of the clergy of any religious order includes amounts received for the performance of services and duties [Code Sec. 1402(c)(4)].

FEDERAL AND STATE UNEMPLOYMENT TAXES

¶15,110 TAX ON EMPLOYERS UNDER THE FEDERAL UNEMPLOYMENT TAX ACT (FUTA)

The Federal Unemployment Tax Act (FUTA) imposes a tax on employers who employed one or more persons in covered employment on at least one day in each of 20 weeks during the current or preceding calendar year or who paid wages (in

[119] *F.J. Wuebker*, 110 TC 431, Dec. 52,748 (1998), *rev'd*, CA-6, 2000-1 USTC ¶50,254, 205 F3d 897.

[120] Notice 2006-108, IRB 2006-51, 1118.

[121] Rev. Rul. 55-385, 1955-1 CB 100.

covered employment) of at least $1,500 ($20,000 for agricultural labor or $1,000 for household employees) in a calendar quarter in the current or preceding calendar year [Code Sec. 3306(a)]. The tax is based on the first $7,000 of certain wages paid during the calendar year to each employee.

.01 FUTA Tax Rate

Employers pay FUTA tax at a rate of 6.0 percent on the first $7,000 of covered wages paid to each employee during a calendar year, regardless of when those wages were earned. The minimum threshold for FUTA deposits is $500.

.02 Covered Employment

Wages include all pay for employment except for the wages explained below [Code Sec. 3306(b)]. Payments made in a medium other than cash are measured by their cash value. Certain benefits may be included as taxable wages. Tips reported to the employer are considered wages [Code Sec. 3306(s)]. Sick pay is also considered wages under FUTA, whether paid by the employer or by a third-party payer, when payments are made within 6 months after the last month the recipient was employed [Reg. § 31.3306(b)(4)-1].

The following payments are not considered to be wages and thus are not subject to FUTA withholding:

- Payments over $7,000 by one employer during a calendar year [Code Sec. 3306(b)(1)]. (Certain successor employers may count wages paid by the predecessor employer as paid by themselves [Reg. § 31.3306(b)(1)-1(b)]);
- Payments to or on behalf of employees or their dependents under a plan or system providing benefits for (a) sickness or accident disability, (b) medical or hospitalization expenses in connection with sickness or accident disability, or (c) death [Code Sec. 3306(b)(2)]. Thus employer-provided group-term life insurance is not wages under FUTA. But a payment that would have been made regardless of retirement, death, or disability is not excluded from FUTA [Code Sec. 3306(b)(10)];
- Payments, not intended as wages, made from a trust exempt from tax under Sec. 501(a), or payments under or to a qualified annuity plan, or payments under a cafeteria plan. Payments under a simplified employee pension plan (SEP) are also excluded, but elective deferrals under the SEP (though excludable from income for income tax purposes) are includible for employment tax purposes [Code Sec. 3306(b)(5)];
- Payments of a domestic or agricultural employee's social security tax or any tax imposed under a state unemployment compensation law [Code Sec. 3306(b)(6)];

  NOTE: In the case of domestic service in a private home, local college club, or local chapter of a college fraternity or sorority, the term "employer" means any person who paid wages in cash of $1,000 or more during the current or preceding calendar year for such services [Code Sec. 3306(a)(3)]. For agricultural workers, the employer's agricultural payroll must be $20,000 or more during any calendar quarter in the current or preceding calendar year; or ten workers or more must be employed during some portion of a day (whether or not at the same time) during any 20 different weeks in the current or preceding year [Code Sec. 3306(a)(2)].

- Pay, other than in cash, for services not in the course of the employer's trade or business [Code Sec. 3306(b)(7)];
- Nonlump-sum payment of supplemental unemployment benefits (SUB);[122]
- Tips, unless they are reported by the employee to the employer. For example, tips reported in writing and taken into account under the state minimum wage law are wages[123] under FUTA [Code Sec. 3306(s)];
- Payments to or on behalf of employees for moving expenses if it is reasonable to believe that employees will be allowed deductions for such payments [Ch. 9] [Code Sec. 3306(b)(9)].
- Remuneration, other than in cash, for agricultural labor [Code Sec. 3306(b)(11)];
- Payments to aliens admitted to the United States to perform agricultural labor pursuant to sections 214(c) and 101(a)(15)(H) of the Immigration and Nationality Act [Code Sec. 3306(c)(1)(B)];
- Any payment or benefit furnished to employees for dependent care assistance programs, if it is reasonable to believe that they will be allowed to exclude such payments or benefits from income [Ch. 4] [Code Sec. 3306(b)(13)];
- Fringe benefits provided to or on behalf of employees [Ch. 4] if it is reasonable to believe that they will be allowed to exclude the benefits from income [Code Sec. 3306(b)(16)]; and
- Employee achievement awards if it is reasonable to believe that these benefits are excludable from the employee's income [Ch. 4] [Code Sec. 3306(b)(16)].

In general, compensation is treated as wages for purposes of FUTA when it is actually or constructively received by the employee. Normally, wages are defined as all remuneration for employment. When dealing with nonqualified deferred compensation, however, the issues become murky. Under Code Sec. 3306(r)(2), any amount deferred under a nonqualified deferred compensation plan is included in the employee's FUTA wages at the later of: (1) when the services are performed, or (2) when there is no substantial risk of forfeiture of the employee's right to the deferred amount.

An amount deferred under a nonqualified deferred compensation plan will not be subject to a *substantial risk of forfeiture* and, thus will be included in the employee's wage base, when the employee can take the money out of the account with no strings attached. In other words the money is his without the need to prove that he is performing substantial services for the employer. See Ch. 3 and ¶ 15,075.

¶15,115 FUTA TAX CREDITS

.01 Amount of FUTA Tax Credit

The amount of FUTA tax paid by an employer may be offset by credits of up to 5.4 percent (known as the "normal credit" and "additional credit") against their FUTA tax liability for amounts paid to a state unemployment compensation fund by January 31 of the subsequent year. The net FUTA tax rate for most employers is 0.6

[122] Rev. Rul. 90-72, 1990-2 CB 211.

[123] Rev. Rul. 78-335, 1978-2 CB 254.

percent (i.e., 6.0 percent – 5.4 percent).[124] States experiencing financial difficulties can borrow funds from the federal government to pay unemployment benefits. However, if a state defaults on its repayment of the loan, the normal credit available is reduced. This effectively increases the employer's FUTA tax rate by 0.3 percent beginning with the second consecutive January 1 in which the loan isn't repaid, then an additional 0.3 percent annually thereafter [Code Sec. 3302(c)]. Thus, the net FUTA tax rate paid by an employer in a state that has had an unpaid loan with the federal government for two consecutive years will be 0.3 percent higher than the net 0.6 percent rate used by employers in states without past due loans. The net FUTA tax rate continues to rise 0.3 percent for each additional year that the loans remain unpaid.

Code Sec. 3302(g) provides that a state with an outstanding loan may repay any advances using its unemployment trust fund account in lieu of having the credit reduction rules apply to its employers.

Possible Credit Reduction States for 2013

The following states and the Virgin Islands will be credit reduction states in 2013, unless they repay their outstanding federal employment loans by November 10, 2013, because, according to the Department of Labor, they have had an outstanding federal unemployment compensation loan for at least two years: Arizona, Arkansas, California, Connecticut, Delaware, Georgia, Indiana, Kentucky, Missouri, Nevada, New Jersey, New York, North Carolina, Ohio, Rhode Island, South Carolina, the Virgin Islands, and Wisconsin.

0.6 Percent Credit Reduction

Employers in Arizona and Delaware face a possible 0.6 percent credit reduction on their 2013 FUTA tax return (maximum $42 increase per employee) because of their state's failure to repay its outstanding federal loans for three consecutive years.

0.9 Percent Credit Reduction

Employers in Arkansas, California, Connecticut, Georgia, Kentucky, Missouri, Nevada, New Jersey, New York, North Carolina, Ohio, Rhode Island, the Virgin Islands, and Wisconsin face a possible 0.9 percent credit reduction on their 2013 FUTA tax return (maximum $63 increase per employee) because of their state's failure to repay its outstanding federal loans for four consecutive years.

1.2 Percent Credit Reduction

Employers in Indiana and South Carolina face a possible 1.2 percent credit reduction on their 2013 FUTA tax returns (maximum $84 increase per employee) because of their state's failure to repay its outstanding federal loans for five consecutive years.

.02 State Payments Made After FUTA Due Date

Taxpayers who fail to pay state taxes by January 31 (or an extended due date of the federal return) will be limited to a credit of only 90 percent of the normal 90 percent tax credit; that is, 4.86 percent of taxable wages. This reduction does not apply to a bankruptcy trustee if the payment is late without fault of the trustee and due to the bankruptcy case [Code Secs. 3302(a)(3), (5)]. However, the state tax must be paid and

[124] Treas. Dept. IRS Publication 15 *(Circular E), Employer's Tax Guide For Use in 2013*, p. 29.

any credit or refund claim must be filed within three years after the federal return was filed, or two years after payment of the federal tax [Code Sec. 6511(a); see ¶15,205].

Refunds

Refunds will be granted to employers who pay their federal tax without taking credit for state taxes paid, if the state taxes were paid after the due date for filing the federal return but within two years after payment of the federal tax.

¶15,120 RETURNS AND PAYMENT OF TAX

Employers generally must deposit FUTA taxes on a quarterly basis. However, under Reg. § 31.6302(c)-(3), employers whose accumulated FUTA taxes (i.e., FUTA taxes for the current quarter plus undeposited FUTA taxes for prior quarters) do not exceed $500 are not subject to the deposit requirements until the quarter in which accumulated FUTA taxes exceed $500. For the last calendar quarter, the employer must compute the balance of tax due for the entire year.

Use Form 940, *Employer's Annual Federal Unemployment (FUTA) Tax Return,* to report annual FUTA taxes. The form must be filed by January 31 of the year following the calendar year to which the tax relates, but employers who make timely quarterly deposits of tax are allowed an additional ten days to file the return [Reg. § 31.6071(a)-1]. Taxpayers must deposit FUTA tax electronically using EFTPS.

.01 Filing Extension

The time for filing the return may be extended for not over six months on application to the IRS [Code Sec. 6081(a); Reg. § 1.6081-1(a)] with a statement of the reasons for the delay. If it is shown that undue hardship would result, the time for paying the tax may be extended for not over six months [Code Sec. 6161(a)(1)].

.02 Amended Return

An employer amending a previously filed return must complete a new Form 940, using the amounts that should have been used on the original return. The return should be signed with a statement attached explaining why an amended return is being filed. The employer should be certain to use a Form 940 for the year it is amending and write "AMENDED RETURN" at the top of the form and file it at the same location as the original return was filed.

.03 Refunds and Adjustments

Taxes, including interest, penalties and additions, that have been erroneously, illegally or wrongfully collected may be credited or refunded to the taxpayer [Code Sec. 6402(a)]. The claim for refund should be filed with the IRS. It must be filed within three years after filing the return or two years after paying the tax, whichever period expires later [Code Sec. 6511(a)].

.04 Additional Penalties

Additions and penalties for failure to file returns, failure to pay taxes when due, false returns, and the like, are similar to those shown in ¶15,160.

¶15,125 EMPLOYER'S RECORDS

Every employer must keep permanent records showing the following information:

- Total wages paid during calendar year with distinct label of taxable and nontaxable pay;
- The amount of contributions paid into each state unemployment fund, for services subject to the state tax, showing separately (a) payments made and not deducted from the employees' pay, and (b) payments made and deducted (or to be deducted) from the employees' pay; and
- The information required to be shown on the return and the extent of the tax liability.

Employers who consider that they are not subject to tax should keep records showing the number of individuals employed on each day [Reg. §31.6001-1(d)].

The records must be accessible for inspection and the records for a given year must be preserved for four years from the date the tax for that year becomes due or is paid, whichever is later [Reg. §31.6001-1(e)(2)].

PAYROLL TAX RETURNS, DEPOSITS, RECORDS, AND REFUNDS

¶15,130 GENERAL OBLIGATIONS

An employer who must withhold income taxes from wages or who is liable for paying and collecting social security taxes must make a quarterly return on Form 941, *Employer's Quarterly Federal Tax Return.* Form 944, *Employer's Annual Federal Tax Return,* was designed to reduce burden on small employers by permitting eligible small employers to file one employment tax return to report their social security, Medicare, and withheld federal income taxes (referred to herein as their "employment tax liability") for an entire taxable year instead of four employment tax returns (one for each quarter). Eligible employers are those with employment tax liability of $1,000 or less.

.01 Optional Filing of Form 944

Employers that otherwise would be required to file Form 944 can notify the IRS if they want to elect to file Form 941, *Employer's Quarterly Federal Tax Return,* instead of Form 944 annually.

When to File Form 944

File Form 944 by January 31, after the end of the calendar year. File Form 944 only once for each calendar year. If Form 944 is filed electronically, do not file a paper Form 944.

Who Must File Form 944

The employer must Form 944 if the IRS has notified the employer that he must file Form 944 instead of Form 941 to report any of the following amounts:

- Wages paid by the employer.
- Tips the employees have received.
- Federal income tax that the employer has withheld.
- Both the employer's and the employee's share of social security and Medicare taxes.
- Current year's adjustments to social security and Medicare taxes for fractions of cents, sick pay, tips, and group-term life insurance.
- Credit for COBRA premium assistance payments.

Who Cannot File Form 944

The following employers cannot file Form 944:

1. Employers who are not notified. If the IRS does not notify the employer to file Form 944, the employer should not file Form 944;
2. Household employees. If the employer employs only household employees, do not file Form 944;
3. Agricultural employers. If the employer employs only agricultural employees, the employer should not file Form 944.

.02 Form 940

Employers required to pay federal unemployment (FUTA) taxes must file an annual return on Form 940, *Employer's Annual Federal Unemployment (FUTA) Tax Return*. The deadline for filing these returns may be extended if timely deposits have been made during the period. When to deposit the withheld taxes depends on the total amount withheld. Civil and criminal penalties may be imposed for failure to withhold taxes, pay over withheld taxes, or file returns.

.03 Form 945 Used for Nonpayroll Withheld Taxes

Use Form 945, *Annual Return of Withheld Federal Income Tax,* to report withheld federal income tax from nonpayroll payments which include:

- Military retirement,
- Gambling winnings,
- Indian gaming profits,
- Voluntary withholding on certain government payments, and
- Backup withholding.

Report all federal income tax withholding from nonpayroll payments or distributions on one Form 945. Do not file more than one Form 945 for any calendar year.

Do not report on Form 945 federal income tax withheld on distributions to participants from nonqualified pension plans (including nongovernmental Code Sec. 457(b) plans) and some other deferred compensation arrangements that are wages and are reported on Form W-2.

WITHHELD INCOME TAX REPORTING REQUIREMENTS

¶15,135 HOW EMPLOYER REPORTS AND PAYS TAX

Withheld income taxes (as well as employer-employee social security taxes) must be paid into a Federal Reserve bank or other authorized depositary electronically with a few exceptions. The exceptions apply primarily to businesses with $2,500 or less in quarterly tax liabilities that pay when filing their returns.

Penalties may be imposed if deposits are paid to an IRS Center. The date of receipt is stamped by the authorized bank to help determine the timeliness of the deposit [Reg. § 31.6302-(h)(5)]. A deposit mailed on or before the second day before the due date is timely even though it may be received after the due date; the date of the postmark is considered the date of the deposit [Code Sec. 7502(e); Reg. § 301.7502-1(a)]. But this timely mailing rule does not apply to deposits of $20,000 or more, if the deposit is made by an employer who deposits any tax more than once a month [(a) below]. Deposits of $20,000 or more that are not paid into an authorized bank by the due date will be considered late, regardless of when mailed [Code Sec. 7502(e)(3)].

.01 When Deposits Are Made

The IRS provides specific rules for the payment of employment taxes. There are two general classes of employers: monthly depositors and semi-weekly depositors. An employer's status as a monthly or semi-weekly depositor depends on the employer's prior deposit history rather than on current deposit liabilities. Under a so-called look-back rule, an employer looks back to the amount of its payroll tax accumulated during a prior 12-month base period to determine its current deposit schedule. This base period ends with the preceding June 30. The base period for the 2013 deposit schedule is July 1, 2012 through June 30, 2013. This enables employers to determine their status several months prior to the beginning of each year.

> ▶ **IRS NOTIFICATION:** The IRS will tell employers by November of each year which schedule they are to follow for the coming year. So employers need not even figure out which method to use on their own.

New Employers

New employers are considered to have a zero amount of accumulated taxes for any calendar quarter in which the employer did not exist [Reg. § 31.6302-1(b)(4)].

Adjustments. When determining the tax liability for a base period quarter, employers look at the tax liability shown on the original return. Any adjustments for the quarter made on a supplemental return are not taken into account. However, adjustments made on a Form 941-X, *Adjusted Employer's Quarterly Federal Tax or Claim for Refund*, that is attached to a Form 941 for a later period are taken into account in determining the tax liability for that later period [Reg. § 31.6302-1(b)(5)].

Threshold for Deposits Increases for Small Businesses

Employers generally deposit FUTA taxes on a quarterly basis. If the accumulated FUTA taxes do not exceed $500 the employers are not subject to the deposit requirements until the quarter in which the accumulated FUTA taxes exceed $500 [Reg. § 31.6302(c)-3(a)(2)]. If FUTA tax liability for a calendar year exceeds deposits for the year, the employer may pay the balance with the annual return if it does not exceed $100. Otherwise, the balance must be deposited with an authorized financial institution [Reg. § 31.6302(c)-3].

Semiweekly Depositors

Employers that accumulate over $50,000 in withheld taxes in any base period year make deposits as shown in Table 3 [Reg. § 31.6302-1(b)(3), (c)(2)].

Table 3. Deposit Schedule for Semiweekly Withholding Deposits

Payment Dates	Deposit Dates
Wednesday, Thursday, and/or Friday	On or before the following Wednesday
Saturday, Sunday, Monday, and/or Tuesday	On or before the following Friday

Deposits are required only on banking days. If a deposit is due on a non-banking day, it can be made on the next banking day. Semi-weekly depositors are always guaranteed at least three banking days before they have to make a deposit, assuming that the required deposit was not $100,000 or more (which would subject them to the next-day deposit rule).

Example 15-12: Baker Corp. is subject to the semi-weekly rule because it had more than $50,000 of employment taxes that had to be deposited during the base period. Baker's employees are paid every Monday. On the Monday, January 1, Baker accumulated $10,000 in employment taxes. Baker has a deposit obligation of $10,000 that must be satisfied on or before the following Friday, January 5.

Example 15-13: Assume the same facts as in Example 15-12, except that Baker has two pay dates, Monday and Friday. On the Friday, January 5, Baker accumulated $8,000 in taxes on wages paid. Friday, January 5, falls within a different semi-weekly period than the first Monday, January 1. Thus, Baker has two separate deposit obligations: $10,000 that must be satisfied by Friday, January 5, and $8,000 that must be satisfied by the following Thursday, January 11.

Special end-of-quarter procedure: Suppose a required semi-weekly deposit includes taxes for two different quarters. Then a special deposit procedure is provided. The employer has to use separate deposit coupons to remit the payroll taxes for each quarter, even though both deposits were due the same day [Reg. § 31.6302-1(c) (2) (i)].

Example 15-14: Eden Corp. has two weekly paydays, Wednesday and Friday and the company pays some employees on Wednesday, March 21. Other employees are paid on Friday, March 23. Payroll taxes for both paydays are due on Wednesday, March 28. However, the taxes for the Wednesday payday are first quarter taxes, while the taxes for the Friday payday are second quarter taxes. Result: Eden must use separate deposit coupons to remit the taxes.

Next-Day Deposit Rule

Suppose accumulated taxes reach $100,000. Then employers would have to make a deposit by the next banking day. The next-day rule applies even if the employer is normally a monthly or semiweekly depositor. To determine if the $100,000 threshold is met [Reg. § 31.6302-1(c)(3)]:

- A monthly depositor considers only those employment taxes accumulated in the calendar month in which the day occurs; and
- A semiweekly depositor takes into account only those employment taxes accumulated in the Wednesday-Friday or Saturday-Tuesday semi-weekly periods in which the day occurs.

NOTE: A monthly depositor immediately becomes a semi-weekly depositor if it becomes subject to the next-day rule. It retains this status for at least the remainder of the current year and the following year.

Example 15-15: On Monday, January 1, Fairwood Corp. accumulated $110,000 in employment taxes as to wages paid on that date. Fairwood has a $110,000 deposit obligation that must be satisfied by the next banking day, regardless of its deposit status. If it was not subject to the semiweekly rule on January 1, Fairwood becomes subject to this rule as of the following January 5.

Example 15-16: Graham Co. is subject to the semiweekly rule. On Monday, January 1, it accumulated $110,000 in employment taxes. Graham has a $110,000 deposit obligation that must be satisfied by the next banking day, Tuesday, January 2. On this day, Graham accumulated an additional $30,000 in employment taxes. Although it had a prior $110,000 deposit obligation incurred earlier in the semiweekly period, Graham has an additional and separate deposit obligation of $30,000 that must be satisfied.

Makeup Date

The makeup date for a monthly depositor is the return due date for the period in which the shortfall occurred. For semiweekly or next-day depositors, shortfalls must be deposited by the first Wednesday or Friday (whichever is earlier) falling on or after the 15th day of the month following the month in which the deposit is required [Reg. § 31.6302-1(f)(3)].

▶ **PENALTY ABATEMENT:** In addition to the safe harbor, penalties are abated if an employer shows that the failure to deposit the full amount of employment taxes was due to a reasonable cause (as provided in Code Sec. 6656(a)).

.02 When to File the Quarterly Return

The quarterly return and any undeposited payments that may be remitted with it are due by the last day of the month following the period covered by the return. However, if timely deposits in full have been made for all three months of a quarter, the employer is allowed 10 additional days for filing [Reg. § 31.6071(a)-1]. Form 942 is used for withholding on wages of domestics (unless the employer has elected to use

Form 941), and Form 943 is used for agricultural workers' pay [Reg. § 31.6011(a)-4(a)]. Table 4 summarizes the due dates.

Table 4. Due Dates for FUTA Payments

Quarters	Quarter Ending	Due Date	Due Date if timely deposits have been made
Jan.-Feb.-Mar.	March 31	April 30	May 10
Apr.-May-June	June 30	July 31	Aug. 10
July-Aug.-Sept.	Sept. 30	Oct. 31	Nov. 10
Oct.-Nov.-Dec.	Dec. 31	Jan. 31	Feb. 10

Amounts deposited with banks are credited against the taxes shown on the quarterly return [Code Sec. 6302(c); Reg. § 31.6302-1].

Final Return

The last Form 941 filed by an employer who goes out of business or ceases to pay wages must be marked final return. The return must be accompanied by a statement showing the date of the last payment of wages and indicating where and by whom required records will be kept. The same procedure must be followed when a business is sold or otherwise transferred to another employer; in such cases the accompanying statement must also include the name and address of the purchaser and the date of the sale [Reg. § 31.6011(a)-6]. In the event of a sale or transfer, both the predecessor and successor employers should file a Form 941 for the quarter in which the sale or transfer took place. However, if both employers agree, the successor can furnish the W-2 forms to employees who continue to work for the successor employer. When filing Forms 941 and W-3, *Transmittal of Income and Tax Statements,* successor and predecessor must each include the other's name, address, and identification number. Predecessor employers file Forms W-2 for employees who were employed only by them, and must keep their Forms W-4 on file. The transferred employees must provide the successor with new Forms W-4 as the successor now becomes responsible for deducting and withholding tax from wages paid to the transferred employees. [¶ 15,030].

Seasonal employers and those who only temporarily stop paying wages are relieved from filing Form 941 for quarters when they regularly have no tax liability because they have paid no wages. To alert the IRS that you will not have to file a return for one or more quarters during the year, you should check the seasonal employer box on the 941.

.03 Employers Who Fail to Collect or Pay Tax

Any employer that has failed to collect, account for and pay over employees' FICA tax or income tax withheld from wages, or has failed to make deposits, payments or tax returns may be required in the future to deposit the taxes by the close of the second banking day after collection in a special trust account for the U.S. government [Code Sec. 7512(a); Reg. § 301.7512-1(b)]. In addition, monthly returns (Form 941-M) and monthly payments of tax may be required. Severe penalties are levied for failure to make deposits and payments [¶ 15,160] [Reg. §§ 31.6011(a)-5(a), 31.6071(a)-1, 31.6151-1(a)].

▶ **TAX TIP:** No matter how secure a future source of funding appears, an employer should never hold back payroll tax payments as a bridge loan to tide the company over. Persons who have discretion over the disbursing of company funds and who knowingly allow payroll taxes to go unpaid will be held personally liable for 100 percent of the unpaid tax [See ¶15,160; Code Sec. 6672(a); Reg. § 301.6672-1].

The courts and the IRS view payroll taxes as trust funds that do not belong to the taxpayer, but which are being held in trust for the government. A high standard exists for a taxpayer to establish reasonable cause for failure to pay and file returns for withheld employment taxes. In *Diamond Plating Co.,*[125] a manufacturing company's financial hardship and the alleged misfeasance of its treasurer did not excuse its failure to timely file employment tax returns and deposit employment taxes.

.04 No Extensions of Time to File

The IRS does not grant extensions of time to file Form 941 [Reg. § 31.6081(a)-1(a)]. Also, there are no extensions granted for paying the tax [Reg. § 31.6161(a)(1)-1]. But when the due date of a deposit falls on a Saturday, Sunday or legal holiday, the next business day is the due date [Code Sec. 7503; Reg. § 301.7503-1].

.05 Returns and Payment of Tax Withheld on Payments to Nonresident Aliens or Foreign Entities

Tax withheld on payments to nonresident alien individuals, foreign partnerships, or foreign corporations must be reported by the withholding agent on Form 1042. An information return (Form 1042S) must also be submitted. These are filed with the Director, Internal Revenue Service Center, Philadelphia, Pennsylvania [Code Sec. 1461; Reg. § 1.1461-3].

The withholding agent deposits withheld taxes into an authorized bank using a Federal Tax Deposit Coupon Form, under rules similar to those governing deposits of withheld income and employment taxes described above [Reg. §§ 1.1461-3, 1.1461-4, Reg. § 31.6302-1(h)].

A nonresident alien, foreign partnership, or corporation must file a Form 4224 to get an exemption from withholding on effectively connected income.

A resident alien may claim an exemption from U.S. withholding tax by filing Form 1078 (Certificate of Residence) or similar statement with the withholding agent [Reg. § 1.1441-5].

.06 Employers Going Out of Business

Employers going out of business are required to furnish wage statements both to employees and to the Social Security Administration (SSA) on termination of an employer's operations [Reg. §§ 31.6051-1(d)(1)(ii); 31.6071(a)-1(a)(3)(ii)]. This requirement affects employers and their employees in the year the employer ceases to pay wages. The employer is required to file a final Form 941, *Employer's Quarterly Federal Tax Return,* to file Forms W-2, *Wage and Tax Statement,* and W-3, *Transmittal of Wage and Tax Statements,* with SSA and to furnish Form W-2 [¶15,140] to the employees at the same time the employer is required to file the final Form 941. However, if the

---

[125] *Diamond Plating Co.,* CA-7, 2005-1 USTC ¶50,107, 390 F3d 1035.

final return is a monthly return, the employer must furnish the required statement on or before the last day of the month in which the final return is required to be filed. In no event may the employer furnish the required statement later than January 31 of the year after the calendar year to which it relates. These requirements do not apply to employers with respect to their domestic employees.

¶15,140 STATEMENT TO EMPLOYEES, FORM W-2

An employer must give each employee three copies (copies B, C, and 2) of the *Wage and Tax Statement*, Form W-2 (or Form 1099-R for withholding on annuity, pension, or other deferred payments) by January 31 of the year succeeding each calendar year. Employees who separate from service during the calendar year may be given a W-2 at any time after termination of employment, but no later than January 31 of the succeeding year. However, if a terminated employee requests that a W-2 be furnished earlier, you must provide the W-2 on or before the later of the 30th day after the day of the request, or the 30th day after the day on which the last payment of wages is made [Reg. § 31.6051-1(d)(1)]. Forms W-2 must be given, even though no income tax or social security tax was withheld, if wages equal or exceed the amount of one withholding exemption. A W-2 must also be given to an employee who filed a proper certificate claiming that he is exempt from income tax withholding [¶ 15,025] [Code Sec. 6051; Reg. § 31.6051-1]. Employees covered by certain deferred compensation plans [Ch. 3] also get a W-2. Penalties are imposed for fraudulent W-2s and failure to furnish W-2s [¶ 15,160].

.01 What to Include on Form W-2

Form W-2 must show the total wages paid (including noncash payments and reported tips), the total amount of elective deferrals from wages, the amounts deducted during the preceding year for income and social security taxes, any advance payments of the earned income credit [¶ 15,035], and any amounts furnished to the employee under a dependent care assistance plan [Ch. 4] [Code Sec. 6051(a)(9)]. It must include the employer's name, address, and identification number (EIN) and the employee (TIN) [Code Sec. 6051(a); Reg. § § 31.6051-1(a), 31.6109-1].

.02 Special Reporting Rules

Sick pay from an insurance company or other third-party payor that must be shown on Form W-2. Box 2 should include the amount of income tax withheld from the sick pay by the third party payor. Box 1 should include the amount of sick pay the employee must include in income. Box 4 should include employee social security tax withheld by the third party payor, while Box 3 should include the amount of the sick pay subject to social security tax. Report in Box 13 any amount of sick pay not includible in income because the employee contributed to the sick pay plan, and label it with the code for nontaxable sick pay.

Third-party payors who withhold on these payments must furnish employers with W-2s no later than January 15 of the year following that in which payments were made. Employers, in turn, must furnish similar W-2s to employees no later than January 31 of that year unless binding agreements between employers and payors designate the payors as employers' agents for furnishing W-2s [Code Sec. 6051(f); Reg. § 31.6051-3].

Dependent Care Assistance Payments

The total amount paid or incurred under a dependent care assistance plan should be reported in Box 10 of the W-2. This amount must also be included in income taxable and social security taxable wages (Boxes 1 and 3, respectively) to the extent they exceed the limit on excludable payments [¶ 15,015]. They should be included in the year the dependent care is provided, even if you pay for the care in a later year.

Deferred Compensation

Qualified plan contributions. Employers who make contributions to (that is, allow employees to defer compensation into) a Sec. 401(k) cash-or-deferred arrangement, a Sec. 403(b) salary reduction agreement to purchase an annuity contract, a Sec. 408(k)(6) salary reduction simplified employee pension, a Sec. 457 deferred compensation plan for state and local government employees or a Sec. 501(c)(18)(D) tax-exempt organization plan must enter the total elective deferral (including any excess) in Box 13 with the appropriate code. These employers must also check the deferred compensation checkbox in Box 15, as well as the pension plan checkbox (except for contributions to a nonqualified pension or Sec. 457 plan).

Nonqualified plan distributions. Employers must report the total amount of distributions to an employee from a nonqualified deferred compensation plan or a Sec. 457 plan in Box 11. This amount should also be included as income in Box 1.

Group-Term Life Insurance

Employers who provide employees with more than $50,000 of group-term life insurance must include the cost of coverage over $50,000 as income in Box 1 and social security wages in Box 3. This excess coverage must also be reported in Box 13 and labeled with the correct code. The cost of the excess coverage is computed from a government table [Ch. 4] [Reg. § 1.79-3].

Employee Business Expenses

Advances or reimbursements to employees made under an accountable plan are generally excluded from gross income and social security tax and need not be reported on the W-2. However, if an employee receives a per diem or mileage allowance, the employer must include in income (Box 1) and social security wages (Box 3) any amounts received in excess of the government-specified rates [Ch. 10]. Such excess amounts should also be reported in Box 13 and labeled with the appropriate code.

Tip Income

Box 1 of Form W-2 (Wages, tips, other compensation) should include the amount of tips reported by the employee to the employer. The amount of reported tips should also be shown in Box 7 (social security tips), even if the employer did not have sufficient employee funds from which to collect the FICA tax. On the other hand, Box 8 is reserved for the amount of tip income allocated to the employee by a large food or beverage establishment [¶ 15,015]. Allocated tips are not included in Box 1 nor in Box 7.

Armed Forces Pay

A statement must be furnished covering pay for service in the armed forces if any tax is withheld or if any taxable compensation was paid [Ch. 2]. It must show the total taxable compensation paid and the tax withheld [Code Sec. 6051(b); Reg. §31.6051-1(a)(2)].

Health Insurance Coverage

Code Sec. 6051(a)(14) provides that an employer must disclose on each employee's Form W-2 the value of the employee's health insurance coverage sponsored by the employer.

If an employee enrolls in employer-sponsored health insurance coverage under multiple plans, the employer must disclose the aggregate value of all such health coverage (excluding the value of a health flexible spending arrangement). To determine the value of employer-sponsored health insurance coverage, the employer calculates the applicable premiums for the tax year for the employee under the rules for COBRA continuation coverage under Code Sec. 4980B(f)(4), including the special rule for self-insured plans. The value that the employer is required to report is the portion of the aggregate premium. If the plan provides for the same COBRA continuation coverage premium for both individual coverage and family coverage, the plan would be required to calculate separate individual and family premiums.

.03 When the Business Is Sold or Transferred

If another employer acquires or succeeds to a going concern, and the services of the predecessor employer's employees are continued, the successor employer may agree to assume responsibility for furnishing Forms W-2 to those continuing employees. In such a case, all wages paid by both employers (including *other compensation* paid or the uncollected employee tax on tips) are included in the W-2 given to the employees by the successor employer.[126] No IRS consent is required.

.04 Extension of Time

Employers who show good cause may be granted an extension of time not exceeding 30 days for furnishing employees' copies or filing Form W-2 with the IRS. The application must be filed by when the Form W-2 would normally be given to employees or filed with the IRS, respectively. It must be in writing, signed by the employer or his agent, and must state detailed reasons for the request [Reg. §§31.6051-1(d)(2), 31.6081(a)-1(a)(3)].

.05 Filing Requirements

Employees must attach the tax return copy of each W-2 they receive to their final income tax return for the year. If employees get an additional Form W-2 after filing their returns, they must file an amended return with the new Form W-2 attached. An employer may replace lost or destroyed copies with a new copy marked "Reissued Statement," but a reissued W-2 should not be sent to the Social Security Administration.[127]

---

[126] Rev. Proc. 2004-53, 2004-2 CB 320.

[127] Notice 90-66, 1990-2 CB 350, as corrected by Announcement 90-136, IRB 1990-50, 19.

Correcting Form W-2

Corrections are made on Form W-2c, *Statement of Income and Tax Amounts*, for errors made in previously filed Forms W-2 and W-3. Form W-3c should be used to transmit the corrections made for Form W-2c. Form W-2c (without transmittal Form W-3c) may also be used to correct errors in employees' names or social security numbers as well as to make corrections for one employee's W-2. Forms W-2c not delivered to employees must be kept by employers.

> ▶ **OBSERVATION:** Employers who correct a W-2 before transmittal should give the corrected copy to the employee. Employers indicate the correction by marking the "void" box on the original Form W-2, Copy A.

Employers must make a reasonable effort to deliver the Form W-2 or Form W-2c to an employee. Mailing it to the last known address is enough. If it cannot be delivered, it should be kept as part of the employer's records for four years.

Where to File

Employers must file Copy A of Forms W-2, *Wage and Tax Statement*, with Form W-3, *Transmittal of Income and Tax Statements*. Payers of wages should file Forms W-2 with one Form W-3. These forms must be filed with the Social Security Administration (SSA) as indicated in W-3 instructions by the last day of February after the calendar year to which the statements apply [Reg. § 31.6071(a)-1(a)(3)].

Corrected Statements

Form W-2c, *Corrected Income and Tax Statement*, is used by an employer (or other payer) to correct errors in previously filed Forms W-2. Copy A of Form W-2c should be filed with the SSA. Form W-2c may be submitted alone (without a W-3c) to correct only an employee's name and/or TIN or to make corrections for only one employee.

Form W-3c, *Transmittal of Corrected Income and Tax Statements*, is used to accompany copies of Form W-2c. A separate Form W-3c must be used for each type of W-2. Form W-3c alone (without accompanying Forms W-2c) may be used to correct an EIN or establishment number. The original copy of Form W-3c indicates the proper SSA office at which to file it.

¶15,145 WITHHOLDING ADJUSTMENTS

Errors made by employers in withholding or paying the tax for any quarter may be adjusted without interest, in a later quarter of the same year [Code Sec. 6205(a)(1)]. The method of making the adjustment depends on when the error was discovered.

.01 Errors Found Before Quarterly Return Filed

Suppose too little tax was withheld from employees. Then the correct amount should be shown in the return and the undercollection deducted from the next wage payment. If too much was withheld, a receipt should be obtained from the employees showing date and amount of repayment to them. If repayment to the employees is not made before Form 941 is filed, the amount collected must be included on the return and the adjustment is made on the return for a following quarter [Reg. §§ 31.6205-1(c), 31.6413(a)-1].

.02 Errors Found After Quarterly Return Filed

Suppose the employer collects and pays more than the correct amount of the employee's tax (unless the employee requested extra income tax withholding [¶15,025]). Then the employer may adjust the overcollection by repaying or reimbursing the employee for the amount of the overcollections in any quarter of the same calendar year. The employer may also reimburse the employee by applying the overcollection against taxes to be withheld in any later quarter of the same calendar year [Reg. § 31.6413(a)-1(b)(2)(ii)]. If the overcollection is repaid, a written receipt with the amount and date should be obtained and kept as part of the employer's records. The necessary adjustment is made by a deduction on the return for any later quarter of the same calendar year [Reg. § 31.6413(a)-2(b)].

The employer may report an underpayment on the return for any later quarter of the same calendar year or file a supplemental return for the period when the wages were paid. An underpayment reported by the due date of the return for the period in which the error was found is considered an adjustment. If the error is not reported as an adjustment, the underpayment should be reported on the return for the next period in the calendar year or immediately on a supplemental return [Reg. § 31.6205-1(c)(2)].

Employers may reimburse themselves for an undercollection of tax by deductions from the employee's pay on or before the last day of the calendar year. The employer and employee can settle the item between themselves within the year, if the deduction is not made [Reg. § 31.6205-1(c)(4)].

> **NOTE:** Employers should attach a statement to Form 941 explaining (a) what the error was; (b) ending date of each quarter in which the error was made; (c) the amount of the error for each quarter; (d) the quarter in which the error was found; and (e) how the matter was settled with the employee.[128]

.03 Adjusting Tax Reported on Tips

If employers do not have enough wages or funds available from which to collect the correct amount of the employee's social security tax on tips, they should deduct the uncollected tax as an adjustment on Form 941.[129]

¶15,150 RECORD RETENTION

All required records must be retained until the later of four years after the tax is paid or four years after the due date of the tax. Records relating to a claim for a refund, credit, or abatement should be held until four years after the claim is filed [Reg. § 31.6001-1(e)(2)].

.01 Employers' Records

Employers must show the persons employed during the year; their taxpayer identification numbers (TINs); addresses; wages and reported tips subject to withholding; amounts and dates of payments and deductions; and the periods of employment to

---

[128] Instructions for Form 941.

[129] Instructions for Form 941.

which they apply [Reg. § 31.6001-5]. Withholding allowance certificates and employees' notices of changes in withholding status should also be kept.

.02 Employees

Employees usually don't have to keep records (except for claims' purposes), but they should retain the duplicate copy of the Form W-2 [Reg. § 31.6001-1(d)].

¶15,155 REFUNDS AND CREDITS

If employers pay the IRS more than the amount withheld from their employees, they can get a refund or credit [Code Sec. 6402(a), 6414; Reg. § 301.6402-1]. The credit for an overpayment that was not withheld from the employee may be taken as a deduction on a return of tax withheld on Form 941. A statement explaining the deduction must be attached to the return [Reg. § 31.6414-1].

.01 Employee Refunds and Credits

The amounts withheld during the year from employees are credited against their tax liability for the year. If the amount withheld exceeds the tax due, the excess will be refunded on timely application [Code Secs. 6401(b), 6402(a); Reg. § 301.6402-1]. Fiscal year taxpayers must claim credit for the entire tax withheld during the calendar year that ends in the fiscal year for which the return is filed.

.02 Nonresident Aliens

Withholding agents [¶15,045] who pay more than the correct amount withheld from a nonresident alien may file a claim for credit for the overpayment on the appropriate form or may claim a credit for the overpayment on Form 1042. Withholding agents cannot claim credit for the overpayment on Form 1042, if they already filed a claim for credit or refund on the appropriate form or a claim for refund on Form 1042 [Reg. §§ 301.6402-2, 1.6414-1].

¶15,160 PENALTIES

Employers may be liable for penalties and interest for not collecting tax, not filing a return, not depositing taxes, nonpayment of tax, fraudulent withholding statements or for failing to supply correct information returns. They may also be subject to criminal penalties. Employees may be subject to civil and/or criminal penalties for filing fraudulent withholding allowance certificates and failing to supply a correct TIN.

> ▶**PRACTICE WARNING:** Taxpayers should not rely on a third party to fulfill their obligation to collect and pay employment taxes to the government. The Court of Appeals for the Third Circuit held that a business was liable for overdue employment taxes even though it paid the taxes in full to its payroll firm, which then embezzled some of the funds. The court emphasized that it is well established that a taxpayer's reliance on a third party to fulfill its tax

obligations will not release the taxpayer from its obligation to collect and pay employment taxes to the government.[130]

The following is an overview of penalties that may be imposed in regard to employment taxes. See Ch. 27 for a more detailed treatment of tax penalties.

.01 Employer Penalties

Employers who fail to report and pay employment taxes may be liable for penalties for failure-to-deposit and failure-to-pay as well as underpayment interest. In addition, regardless of the form of business, any person who is responsible for collecting, accounting for, or paying overwithheld taxes (called *trust fund taxes* because they are held in trust for the government) and willfully fails to do so will be liable for the trust fund recovery penalty, or the 100-percent penalty in an amount equal to 100 percent of the unremitted trust fund taxes [Code Sec. 6672].

For purposes of the trust fund taxes, the term *person* includes an officer or employee of a corporation, LLC, or a member or employee of a partnership, who is under a duty to collect the taxes [Code Sec. 6671(b)]. A responsible person is willful if he had knowledge of the tax delinquency and knowingly failed to rectify it when there were available funds to pay the tax bill. The responsible party need not exhibit an intent to defraud the IRS or some other evil motive; all that is necessary to demonstrate willfulness is the existence of an intentional act to pay other creditors before the federal government. While willfulness may not be established by proof of mere negligence, willful conduct also includes a reckless disregard for obvious or known risks. A person may not immunize himself from the consequences of his actions by wearing blinders which will shut out all knowledge of the liability for and the nonpayment of his withholding taxes. A person is liable under the reckless disregard standard if he (1) clearly ought to have known (2) there was a grave risk that withholding taxes were not being paid and if (3) he did not know, he was in a position to find out about the failure to pay.

Failure to Withhold and Pay Over Tax

Employers required to withhold tax are liable for paying this tax, whether or not it is collected from the employee [Code Sec. 3403; Reg. § 31.3403-1], unless the employee files a return and pays the underwithheld tax. Employers do not owe interest on the tax if they show to the IRS that timely supplementary returns covering the underwithheld tax were filed[131] [¶ 15,145]. However, an employee's payment of underwithheld taxes does not necessarily relieve an employer of any penalties or additions to tax for failure to withhold or pay over tax [Code Sec. 3402(d); Reg. § 31.3402(d)-1]. Persons responsible for withholding and paying over tax (whether or not officers of the corporation) may be held personally liable if they willfully fail to pay the tax.[132] Discharges in personal bankruptcy will not shield them from liability for the tax.[133] Severe health problems are not a shield from liability.[134]

---

[130] *Pediatric Affiliates*, CA-3, 2007-1 USTC ¶ 50,477, 230 Fed Appx 167, *aff'g*, DC-NJ, 2006-1 USTC ¶ 50,201.

[131] Rev. Rul. 86-10, 1986-1 CB 358.

[132] *R.L. Gephart*, CA-6, 87-1 USTC ¶ 9319, 818 F2d 469; *In re Nutt*, DC-FL, 2003-1 USTC ¶ 50,395, *aff'g*, 2002-2 USTC ¶ 50,753.

[133] *O.J. Sotelo*, SCt, 78-1 USTC ¶ 9446, 436 US 268, 98 SCt 1795, *reh'g denied*, 438 US 907.

[134] *D.S. Savage*, DC-CA, 2006-1 USTC ¶ 50,202.

Who Is a Responsible Person?

Before the 100 percent trust fund penalty may be assessed against an individual, that person must be characterized as a person who was responsible to withhold and pay over payroll taxes, and one who willfully failed to do so. There is no single factor that determines whether an individual is a responsible person. Numerous courts addressing this issue have concluded that indicia of responsibility include whether the individual:

- Is an officer or member of the board of directors;
- Owns shares or possesses an entrepreneurial stake in the company;
- Is active in the management of day-to-day affairs of the company;
- Has the ability to hire and fire employees;
- Makes decisions regarding which, when, and in what order outstanding debts or taxes will be paid;
- Exercises control over daily bank accounts and disbursement records, and
- Has check-signing authority.

The courts have generally found that a *responsible person* is one who has ultimate authority over expenditure of funds in the organization. It is not necessary for the officer himself to write the checks, so long as the individual has significant authority and control over the corporation's finances. Responsibility hinges on status, duty, and authority, not knowledge. Delegation of that authority, however, to another will not relieve a taxpayer of responsibility for payment of federal withholding taxes.[135] The authority to sign checks is only one of several factors that need to be considered in determining whether an individual has significant authority and control over the day to day financial operations of a corporation to render him or her a responsible person. It is not necessary for the officer or director to write the checks, so long as the individual has significant authority and control over the corporation's finances.[136]

> **Example 15-17:** The taxpayer was chairman of the board and had the overall financial responsibilities at the company including signing payroll tax returns. When his business experienced cash flow problems, he failed to collect and send his employees' payroll taxes to the IRS. He met with an IRS agent who agreed to a payment plan, which he failed to pay. The taxpayer was forced to shut down production and file for bankruptcy. The IRS assessed a 100-percent penalty against the taxpayer for failure to collect and pay over payroll taxes because he was the responsible person within the organization. The court agreed and concluded that he knowingly and voluntarily paid other creditors and business expenses while the payroll tax liabilities were accruing. Thus, he

---

[135] *In re Battles*, BC-DC-AL, 2000-2 USTC ¶50,734.

[136] *C.B. Erwin*, DC-NC, 2013-1 USTC ¶50,181; *J.M. Horovitz*, DC-PA, 2008-1 USTC ¶50,186, 543 FSupp2 441; *J.C. Tornes*, DC-OH, 2008-2 USTC ¶50,431; *R.C. Savona*, DC-CA, 2008-1 USTC ¶50,342; *S.K. Verret*, CA-5, 2009-1 USTC ¶50,248, 312 Fed Appx 615; *D.R. Ferguson*, CA-8, 2007-1 USTC 70,265, 484 F3d 1068; *S. Lindsey*, CA-10, 2002-2 USTC ¶50,698, 48 Fed Appx 302; *Davis*, DC-LA, 2009-1 USTC ¶50,375. *Jefferson*, CA-7, 2008-2 USTC ¶50,587, 546 F3d 477.

willfully failed to collect and pay over the payroll taxes and was subject to the 100-percent responsible person penalty.[137]

The IRS had aggressively pursued collection of the responsible person penalty. In *Lubetzky*,[138] the Court of Appeals for the First Circuit held a corporate treasurer liable for six quarters of his employer's withholding taxes despite his superiors' orders to pay other creditors before paying the IRS. The court noted that although the primary liability for failing to pay withholding tax is the employer's responsibility, a penalty for such a failure equal to the unpaid tax can be collected from any person (including a bookkeeper) who is required but willfully fails to pay over the withheld taxes.

Note that a contrary result was reached in *Vinick*,[139] where the First Circuit previously held that a corporate officer, who was also a certified public accountant and treasurer of the company, lacked the requisite control over the corporation's finances for the period in question to render him a responsible person even though he had check-writing authority because he had no involvement in the day-to-day operations of the company. The IRS has announced its nonacquiescence to this result.

The court in *Lubetzky* has made it clear that taxpayers who are in charge of their corporation's day-to-day finances will have a difficult time avoiding the responsible person penalty. Even though the taxpayer's superiors told him not to pay the IRS before paying creditors so the company could remain afloat, the taxpayer was penalized for not paying withholding taxes.

Check Writer Not Responsible Person

In *J. Tarpoff*,[140] an unusual taxpayer victory, a district court held that the head buyer of a packaging facility was not liable for the trust fund recovery penalty because he was not the responsible person. The court found that he did not have sufficient control of the company's finances to allocate funds to pay other creditors in preference to paying the IRS. The individual was not an officer, member, manager, owner or shareholder of the company and never attended a board of directors' meeting. He did not have supervisory authority over accounting, finance or payroll and he did not have the authority to determine who to pay or the priority of payments.

In *R.D. Bunch*,[141] a district court concluded that the chairman of the board of a nonprofit corporation was a responsible person for payment of withholding taxes. As a board member, the individual had full control over the corporate affairs, received monthly financial reports and exerted significant control over the financial affairs of the corporation by providing the corporation with operating funds. The individual's claim that he played a nominal role and that he lacked actual knowledge of the corporation's affairs could not absolve him of his responsibility to pay the withholding taxes. The corpora-

---

[137] *E.Ghandour*, CA-FC, 97-2 USTC ¶50,926, 132 F3d 52.

[138] *I. Lubetzky*, CA-1, 2005-1 USTC ¶50,207; *J. Doulgeris*, DC-FL, 2009-2 USTC ¶50,544. See also *T.L. Jenkins*, CA-FC, 2012-1 USTC ¶50,630.

[139] *A.W. Vinick*, CA-1, 2000-1 USTC ¶50,263, 205 F3d 1, *nonacq.* See also *C.B. Erwin*, CA-4, 2010-1 USTC ¶50,354, 591 F3d 313; *R.A. Smith*, CA-10, 2009-1 USTC ¶50,263, 555 F3d 1158; *J.D. Salzillo*, CA-FC, 2005-1 USTC ¶50,324, 66 FedCl 23 (chief financial officer of bankrupt company not responsible person, despite having check-signing authority, because the company's president maintained absolute control of all finances).

[140] *J. Tarpoff*, DC-IL, 2012-1 USTC ¶50,201.

[141] *R.D. Bunch*, DC-Tenn., 2012-1 USTC ¶50,246.

tion had sufficient funds to pay the withholding taxes but it repaid the individual's loans instead. Moreover, the individual knew that the withholding taxes were not being paid as of the fourth quarter of the first tax year at issue. However, the corporation continued to pay other creditors, to meet payroll, and to repay the individual's loans. The individual failed to support his allegations that the funds the corporation received were encumbered and, therefore, could not be used to pay the unpaid trust fund taxes.

The court also found that Bunch, as responsible person, had knowledge of the taxes owed and failed to pay them when there were available funds to pay the government. Throughout the entire period of time at issue, Perceptions had access to sufficient funds from which the delinquent taxes could have been paid. In fact, the amounts paid to Bunch personally in repayment of his loans to the corporation were more than sufficient to meet the company's withholding tax liability. The court found that even if Bunch did not have actual knowledge of the tax delinquency, his conduct in this case clearly constitutes the requisite recklessness to meet the willfulness element. Bunch clearly should have known of the clear risk that withholding taxes were not being paid, if, from nothing more, the fact that he was required to loan money to Perceptions near the middle of each month for it to meet its financial obligations. He was thus fully aware of the corporation's financial difficulties and he had complete access to the corporation's books of accounts and the monthly financial reports to the board of directors. Even if those reports were not forthcoming, he clearly had the authority to ask for those reports at any time. Bunch could not avoid liability by "wearing blinders" to avoid obtaining actual knowledge of the tax delinquency.

Procedures for Appealing Trust Fund Penalty Assessments

Taxpayers may appeal a proposed trust fund penalty assessment and request an Appeals conference if they observe the following procedures:

- If the proposed penalty assessment for any tax period is $25,000 or less, a taxpayer may appeal the proposed assessment by submitting two copies of a small case appeal request. The taxpayer must identify the issues he or she is contesting and explain the basis of his or her disagreement. The IRS emphasized that the taxpayer should describe whether he or she had the duty and authority to collect and pay over trust fund taxes; and
- A taxpayer may appeal a proposed penalty assessment of more than $25,000 by submitting a formal protest. The formal protest must identify the issues, describe the taxpayer's authority, and cite any law or other authority on which the taxpayer relies.[142]

A stay against collection of the 100-percent penalty is available if: (1) a bond is posted; (2) payment is made to start a refund suit; and (3) a refund claim is filed and court proceedings are brought within 30 days after denial of such claim [Code Sec. 6672(b); Reg. § 301.6672-1].

Failure to File Return or Pay Tax

Unless due to reasonable cause and not to willful neglect, the penalty for failure to file a return is 5 percent of the unpaid tax for a month or fraction of a month, with an extra 5

---

[142] Rev. Proc. 2005-34, 2005-1 CB 1233.

percent for each additional month or fraction. The maximum penalty is 25 percent. If the failure to file is fraudulent, the penalty is increased to 15 percent with a maximum of 75 percent. For failure to file within 60 days of the due date, the minimum penalty is the lesser of $135 or 100 percent of the amount of tax required to be shown on the return. The penalty for failure to pay tax (unless the failure is due to reasonable cause and not willful neglect) is 0.5 percent of the unpaid tax shown on the return less credits and less any part of the tax paid on or before the beginning of each month; the maximum penalty is 25 percent. If for the same month an employer is penalized for both failure to pay and failure to file, that month's penalty for not filing may be reduced by 0.5 percent [Code Sec. 6651(a)].

Willful failure to file a return, supply required information, keep required records, or pay a tax is a misdemeanor punishable by a fine of not more than $25,000 ($100,000 for corporations) and/or one year imprisonment [Code Sec. 7203]. Anyone who willfully attempts to evade any tax is guilty of a felony punishable by a fine of not more than $100,000 ($500,000 for corporations) and/or imprisonment for not more than five years [Code Sec. 7201].

Failure-to-Deposit Penalty

Unless the failure is due to reasonable cause and not willful neglect, failure to make timely deposits of withheld taxes in an authorized government depositary is subject to a penalty equal to the applicable percentage of the amount of the underpayment [Code Sec. 6656]. The applicable percentage is: 2 percent if the failure is for not more than 5 days; 5 percent if more than 5 days but not more than 15 days; 10 percent if more than 15 days; 15 percent is the deposit is not paid by the earlier of the 10th day after receiving a delinquency notice or the date the IRS sends a notice and demand for immediate payment [Ch. 27] [Code Sec. 6656(b)].

A deposit will be applied to the most recent period or periods within the specified tax period to which the deposit relates, unless the person making the deposit designates a different period to which the deposit should be applied [Code Sec. 6656(e)(1)].

The IRS will apply federal tax deposits to the most recently ended deposit period to which the deposit relates and will apply any excess to deposit periods ending on or after the date of the deposit in period-ending-date order. The application of deposits to the most recently ended deposit period will, in some cases, prevent the cascading of penalties where a depositor either fails to make deposits or makes late deposits. When a depositor receives a penalty notice, he or she may, within 90 days of the date of the penalty notice, contact the IRS and designate the deposit period to which the deposits are to be applied.[143]

Safe Harbor

The IRS will consider a depositor to have satisfied its deposit obligations even if there is a shortfall in the amount of taxes required to be deposited for a deposit period [Reg. § 31.6302-1(f)]. A shortfall will be treated as a liability for a deposit period (the make-up period) ending immediately before the shortfall make-up date and after the end of any other deposit period ending before the shortfall make-up date. Thus, if a shortfall make-

[143] Rev. Proc. 2001-58, 2001-2 CB 579.

up date falls on the same date a deposit is due for another deposit period, the IRS will apply a deposit made on the shortfall make-up date to the shortfall liability first. Any excess will then be applied to deposit periods other than the make-up period beginning with the most recently ended of such other periods. If a deposit is made before the shortfall make-up date but after the end of a deposit period for which the deposit obligation has not been satisfied, the IRS will apply the deposit to the liability for that deposit period first before applying any excess to the shortfall.

A depositor that has accumulated $100,000 or more of employment taxes must deposit those taxes by the close of the next banking day [Reg. § 31.6302-1(c)(3)]. The deposit is treated as a liability for a deposit period ending on the day in which the deposit accumulates in excess of $100,000 in employment taxes.

Failure to File Correct Information Returns

Employers who (1) fail to file an information return (for example, a Form W-2) by the due date, (2) fail to include all the information required to be shown on the return, or (3) include incorrect information on the return are subject to a penalty, the amount of which depends on when, if at all, a correct information return is filed [Code Sec. 6721(a)(2)].

Code Sec. 6721 sets forth a three-tier penalty structure depending on when taxpayers supply the missing information as follows:

1. If any of the reporting failures are corrected within 30 days after the return's filing date, the amount of the penalty is $15 per return, with a yearly maximum of $75,000. The maximum annual amount applicable to small businesses with respect to a correction made within 30 days is $25,000. For nearly all information returns, these penalty rates apply if returns or corrected returns are filed by March 30 (March 31 in leap years) because most information returns must be filed by February 28 (February 29 in leap years) [Code Sec. 6721(b)(1); Reg. § 301.6721-1(b)(1)].
2. If the failure is corrected within a period that runs from 31 days after the due date up to August 1 of the calendar year in which the return was required to be filed, the amount of the penalty is $30 per return, with a maximum yearly amount of $150,000, with a maximum annual amount of $50,000 for small businesses [Code Sec. 6721(b)(2); Reg. § 301.6721-1(b)(2)].
3. If the failure is corrected after August 1, the penalty is $50 per return, with a maximum yearly amount of $250,000. The maximum annual amount applicable to small businesses for a correction made after August 1 is $100,000 [Code Sec. 6721(a)(1); Reg. § 301.6721-1(a)(1)].

If a failure to file a correct information return is due to intentional disregard of the filing requirements, the penalty is the greater of $100 per failure or 10 percent of the aggregate amount required to be reported on the return. The $250,000 maximum does not apply in such cases; nor do the small business or *de minimis* exceptions [Ch. 27] [Code Sec. 6721(e)].

Failure to Furnish Wage and Tax Statement

An employer who fails to furnish an employee with a correct payee statement (e.g., the Annual Wage and Tax Statement or W-2) by the due date, or who fails to include all of the information required to be shown on the statement, is subject to a penalty of $50 for each failure (maximum penalty $100,000 per year) [Code Sec. 6722(a); Reg. § 301.6722-1(a)]. There is no de minimis exception, no break for small businesses, and no exception for corrected omissions and inaccuracies [Ch. 27].

If the failure is due to intentional disregard, the penalty is increased to $100 per statement or, if greater, 10 percent of the amount required to be shown on the statement. There is no $100,000 maximum in such cases [Code Sec. 6722].

Fraudulent Withholding Statement or Failure to Furnish Statement

An employer that willfully furnishes a false or fraudulent wage and tax statement or that willfully fails to furnish such a statement is subject to a penalty of $50 per fraudulent or unfurnished statement [Code Sec. 6674]. In addition, that employer is also subject to a fine of not more than $1,000 and/or imprisonment for not more than one year [Code Sec. 7204].

.02 Employee Penalties

A $500 civil penalty is imposed for claiming more withholding allowances [¶ 15,025] on Form W-4 than there is a reasonable basis for claiming, if such a claim results in reduced withholding. A reasonable basis for a claim exists if the number of allowances is computed in accordance with Form W-4 instructions. Thus, the penalty applies to statements relating to withholding exemptions, estimated itemized deductions, absence of tax liability, and other false statements made to reduce withholding. However, the penalty does not apply if withholding is not reduced as a result of the statements, or if the tax liability is paid by withholding and estimated taxes [Code Sec. 6682(b); Reg. § 301.6682-1(a)].

A criminal penalty is imposed if false or fraudulent information is willfully given on the withholding allowance certificate or if there is an intentional failure to give information that would result in increased withholding. The employee is subject to a fine of up to $1,000 or imprisonment for not over one year, or both [Code Sec. 7205(a)].

> **NOTE:** The criminal penalty above is in addition to any other penalty. Thus, for example, the criminal penalty for willful evasion [Code Sec. 7201] is not barred if prosecution for a false certificate is also possible [Code Sec. 7205(a)].

EMPLOYMENT TAX REFUNDS AND ADJUSTMENTS

¶ 15,165 HOW TO MAKE ADJUSTMENTS

Refunds and adjustments are allowed for underpayments and overpayments of employment tax by both employers and employees. If employers do not collect enough tax from employees, or withhold too much, the mistake generally should be reflected on the next return. An error in the employee's tax generally will be matched by an error in the employer's share.

The limitation period on both assessments and refunds is the same as for income taxes [¶ 15,155]. In general, a social security tax refund can be claimed within three years after the filing of the return or within two years from the payment of the tax, whichever is later. Interest is allowed on the overpayment.

.01 Adjusted Employer's Quarterly Federal Tax Return or Claim for Refund

Employers must use Form 941-X, *Adjusted Employer's Quarterly Federal Tax Return or Claim for Refund,* to adjust errors discovered on previously filed Forms 941 and 941-SS. You are required to file Form 941-X separately from Form 941 or Form 941-SS.

.02 Adjusted Employer's Annual Federal Tax Return for Agricultural Employees or Claim for Refund

Employers must use Form 943-X, *Adjusted Employer's Annual Federal Tax Return for Agricultural Employees or Claim for Refund,* to adjust errors discovered on previously filed Form 943. File Form 943-X separately from Form 943.

.03 Adjusted Employer's Annual Federal Tax Return or Claim for Refund

Employers must use Form 944-X, *Adjusted Employer's Annual Federal Tax Return or Claim for Refund,* to adjust errors discovered on previously filed Forms 944 and 944-SS. You are required to file Form 944-X separately from Form 944 or Form 944-SS.

.04 Adjusted Annual Return of Withheld Federal Income Tax or Claim for Refund

Employers must use Form 945-X, *Adjusted Annual Return of Withheld Federal Income Tax or Claim for Refund,* to adjust errors discovered on previously filed Form 945. File Form 945-X separately from Form 945.

NET INVESTMENT INCOME TAX

¶15,170 OVERVIEW OF NET INVESTMENT INCOME TAX

Beginning in 2013, a 3.8 percent net investment income tax (NIIT) is imposed on the lesser of: (1) an individual's net investment income (NII) for the tax year, or (2) any excess of modified adjusted gross income (AGI) for the tax year over a threshold amount [Code Sec. 1411(a)(1)]. The NIIT is also imposed on the undistributed net investment income of an estate or trust with AGI in excess of the dollar amount at which the highest tax bracket for an estate or trust begins ($11,950 in 2013 and increasing to $12,150 in 2014). Unfortunately, the 3.8 percent surtax may not be deducted anywhere on the federal income tax return. Taxpayers (including individuals and estate and trusts) subject to the NIIT should use Form 8960, *Net Investment Income Tax—Individuals, Estate and Trusts,* to compute the 3.8 percent tax. Individuals should report the tax on Form 1040 and estates and trusts should report it on Form 1041.

.01 Taxpayers Subject to NIIT

The 3.8 percent NIIT is imposed on the NII of the following taxpayers:

- Individuals who are citizens or residents of the United States [Prop. Reg. § 1.1411-2(a)];
- Estates and most trusts (see exceptions below) are subject to the 3.8 percent net investment income tax on the lesser of: (1) their undistributed NII, or (2) any excess of their AGI over the dollar amount at which the highest tax bracket for estates and trusts begins ($11,950 for 2013 and increasing to $12,150 in 2014) [Code Sec. 1411(a)(2)]. Undistributed NII is defined in Prop. Reg. § 1.1411-3(e)(2) as an estate's or trust's NII determined just as it would be for an individual and then reduced by distributions of net investment income to beneficiaries and charitable deductions;
- A bankruptcy estate of a debtor who is treated as an individual for purposes of the NIIT. Therefore the bankruptcy estate is subject to the same lower $125,000 threshold amount as a married taxpayer filing a separate return [Prop. Reg. § 1.1411-2(a)(2)(iii)].

Taxpayers Subject to Special NIIT Rules

- **Nonresident aliens are not subject to NIIT**. Special rules apply to nonresident aliens (NRAs) in Prop. Reg. § 1.1411-2(a). If a nonresident alien individual is married to a U.S. citizen or resident, the spouses are treated as married filing separately for purposes of Code Sec. 1411 and the U.S. citizen or resident is subject to the married filing separately threshold for purposes of computing the NIIT while the nonresident alien spouse is not subject to the tax [Prop. Reg. § 1.1411-2(a)(2)]. If a married couple with one spouse who is a nonresident alien elects to treat the nonresident alien as a resident of the U.S. under Code Sec. 6013(g), they may make a similar election for purposes of the NIIT by following Prop. Reg. § 1.1411-2(a)(2)(i)(B)(2). The effect of this election is that the spouses will include their combined income in the net investment income tax calculation and apply the $250,000 threshold for taxpayers filing a joint return.
- **Trusts not subject to NIIT** [Code Sec. 1411(e)(1); Prop. Reg. § 1.1411-3(b)]:
  - — Trusts that are exempt from income taxes (e.g., charitable trusts and qualified retirement plan trusts exempt from tax under Code Sec. 501, and charitable remainder trusts exempt from tax under Code Sec. 664;
  - — A trust in which all of the unexpired interests are organized and operated exclusively for religious, charitable, scientific, literary, or educational purposes, or to foster national or international amateur sports competition (but only if no part of its activities involve the provision of athletic facilities or equipment), or for the prevention of cruelty to children or animals as described in Code Sec. 170(c)(2)(B);
  - — Trusts that are classified as "grantor trusts" under Code Secs. 671-679. A grantor trust is treated as owned by the grantor for income tax purposes and all items of trust income, loss, credit and deduction are reported by the grantor on the grantor's tax return. As a result of achieving grantor trust status, the trust entity has no income to which the NIIT would apply; and
  - — Trusts that are not classified as "trusts" for federal income tax purposes such as real estate investment trusts (REITs) and common trust funds) [Code Sec. 1411(e)(2)].

- Electing small business trusts (ESBTs), which are treated as two separate trusts when a portion of the ESBT's holdings is S corporation stock, are subject to special computational rules. ESBTs are treated as two separate trusts for computational purposes, but are consolidated when determining the AGI threshold [Prop. Reg. § 1.1411-3(c)(1)];
- Charitable remainder trusts are also subject to special computational rules. Although, the trust itself isn't subject to the net investment income tax, the annuity and unitrust distributions may constitute net investment income to the noncharitable recipient [Prop. Reg. § 1.1411-3(c)(2)];
- Foreign estates and trusts are generally not subject to the net investment income tax if they have little or no connection to the United States. However, to the extent the income is earned or accumulated for the benefit of, or distributed to, U.S. persons, the net investment income of a foreign estate or foreign trust will be subject to the tax [Prop. Reg. § 1.1411-3(c)(3)].

.02 Computation of Tax

Individual taxpayers compute their exposure to the NIIT (also called the "unearned income Medicare contribution tax") by taking 3.8 percent of the lesser of: (1) the individual's net investment income (NII) for the year, or (2) the excess (if any) of the individual's MAGI over an unindexed threshold amount [Code Sec. 1411(a)(1)]. Individuals will owe NIIT if they have NII and also have MAGI over the following thresholds which are not indexed for inflation: [Code Sec. 1411(b)].

Filing Status	Threshold Amount
Married filing jointly	$250,000
Married filing separately	$125,000
Single	$200,000
Head of household (with qualifying person)	$200,000
Qualifying widow(er) with dependent child	$250,000

Example 15-18: In 2013, an unmarried U.S. citizen, has MAGI of $190,000, which includes $50,000 of NII. She has a zero exposure to the 3.8 percent surtax on unearned income because the threshold amount for a single individual is $200,000. If in 2014, she has MAGI of $220,000, which includes $50,000 of NII, she has a NIIT of $760 (3.8 percent multiplied by $20,000) [Prop. Reg. § 1.1411-2(b)(2)].

Example 15-19: Married taxpayers, who file a joint return, collectively earn $270,000 in wages and have $80,000 of NII in 2013. Their MAGI is $350,000. They must pay a 3.8 percent NIIT on the lesser of their: (1) $80,000 of NII, or (2) $100,000 ($350,000 – $250,000) MAGI in excess of the $250,000 threshold for married taxpayers filing jointly. They must pay NIIT in the amount of $3,040 (.038 × $80,000) in 2013.

Example 15-20: In 2013, a single taxpayer receives no wages or self-employment income. He does, however, earn $3.2 million in NII from a stock and bond portfolio that is not part of a qualified employee benefit plan. She will incur a 3.8 percent NIIT on the lesser of her: (1) $3.2 million NII, or (2) $3 million ($3,200,000 – $200,000) MAGI in excess of the $200,000 threshold amount for a single taxpayer. Thus, she must pay $114,000 (.038 × 3,000,000) in NIIT 2013.

The net investment income tax is subject to the estimated tax provisions. Therefore, individuals, estates, and trusts that are subject to the tax should adjust their income tax withholding or estimated payments to account for the tax increase in order to avoid underpayment penalties.

.03 MAGI Defined

MAGI is defined for purposes of the NIIT as AGI plus any amount excluded as foreign earned income under Code Sec. 911(a)(1), less properly allocated deductions [Code Sec. 1411(d)].

.04 Net Investment Income Defined

Determining what income constitutes NII subject to the net investment income tax is key to finding ways to minimize exposure to the 3.8 percent surtax on unearned income. If taxpayers can reduce their NII, they will be able to reduce exposure to the tax.

Code Sec. 1411(c) defines net investment income tax as the sum of the following three categories of income under Code Sec. 1411(c) reduced by certain expenses properly allocable to that income [Prop. Reg. § 1.1411-4(a)(1)]:

1. Category I: Gross income from interest, dividends, annuities royalties, and rents other than such income derived in the ordinary course of a trade or business not described in Category II [Code Sec. 1411(c)(1)(A)((i)]. Gross income from royalties includes amounts received from mineral, oil, and gas royalties and amounts received for the privilege of using patents, copyrights, secret processes and formulas, goodwill, trademarks, trade-brands and franchises.

2. Category II: Other gross income derived from a trade or business that either (1) trades financial instruments or commodities, or (2) is considered a "passive activity." The term "financial instruments" is defined in Prop. Reg. § 1.1411-5(c)(1) as stocks and other equity interests, evidences of indebtedness, options, forward or futures contracts, notional principal contracts, any other derivatives, or any short positions or partial units in any of these items. The term "passive activity" is defined in general in Code Sec. 469 as one in which the taxpayer does not materially participate on a regular, continuous and substantial basis. Rental activity of real estate or equipment is deemed to be passive unless the equipment rentals last seven days or less [Temp. Reg. § 1.469-1T(e)(3)(A)]. In addition, the rental activity of a real estate professional (i.e., someone for whom more than half of their personal services performed in trades or businesses are performed in real property trades or businesses in which the taxpayer materially participates, and who performs more than 750 hours of service during the tax year in that real property trade) is not treated as a passive activity under Code Sec. 469(c)(7).

3. Category III: Net gain, if taken into account in computing taxable income, attributable to the disposition of property held in a passive activity trade or business, or the business of trading in financial instruments or commodities [Code Sec. 1411(c)(1)(A)(iii)].

The proposed reliance regulations are effective January 1, 2014, but may be relied on prior to that date until final regulations are issued.

Examples of properly allocable deductions include early-withdrawal penalties, investment interest expense, investment advisory and brokerage fees, expenses directly related to rental and royalty income, and state and local income taxes allocable to items included in investment income [Prop. Reg. § 1.1411-4(f)(3)(i)].

Examples of income taken into account in computing NII include: gains from the sale of stocks, bonds, and mutual funds; capital gain distributions from mutual funds; gain from the sale of investment real estate (including gain from the sale of a second home that is not a principal residence); gains from the sale of interests in partnerships and S corporations (to the extent taxpayer was a passive owner) [Code Sec. 1411(c)]. The 3.8 percent surtax applies to a trade or business only if it is a Code Sec. 469 passive activity of the taxpayer or a trade or business involved in trading Code Sec. 475(e)(2) financial instruments or commodities [Code Sec. 1411(c)(2)].

CFCs and PFICs. Dividends and gains from the stock of a controlled foreign corporation (CFC) and passive foreign investment company (PFIC) are included in computing NII. The rules apply to an individual, estate or trust that is a U.S. shareholder of a CFC, or that is a U.S. person that directly or indirectly owns an interest in a qualified electing fund (which involves an election made with respect to a PFIC) [Prop. Reg. § 1.1411-10].

Treatment of child's investment income from Form 8814. The amount of a child's interest, dividends and capital gains that parents include on their Form 1040 for kiddie tax purposes from Form 8814, *Parent's Election to Report Child's Interest and Dividends* is included in calculating the parent's NII. However, the calculation of the parent's net investment income does not include (a) amounts excluded from Form 1040 due to the threshold amounts on Form 8814, and (b) amounts attributable to Alaska Permanent Fund Dividends.

Income exclusions. Income excluded from the computation of NII and therefore not be subject to the 3.8 percent surtax are: wages, unemployment compensation; operating income from a nonpassive business, Social Security benefits, veterans benefits, tax-exempt bond interest, gain on the sale of a principal residence excludable under Code Sec. 121, alimony, tax exempt interest (e.g., earned on state or local obligations); self-employment income, Alaska permanent fund dividends; gain on tax-free exchanges of insurance policies under Code Sec. 1035, gain excluded on like-kind exchanges under Code Sec. 1031, gain excluded on the sale of qualified small business stock under Code Sec. 1202, and distributions from the following tax-favored retirement plans: Code Sec. 401(a) (qualified pension, profit-sharing and stock bonus plans): Code Sec. 403(a) (qualified annuity plans), Code Sec. 403(b) (plans for employees of public schools and tax-exempt organizations); Code Sec. 408 (traditional IRAs); Code Sec. 408A (Roth IRAs); and Code Sec. 457(b) (deferred compensation plans of state and local governments and tax-exempt organizations).

Trade or business exclusion. Also excluded from NII is income from trades or businesses conducted by a sole proprietor, partnership, or S corporation (but investment income, gain, or loss on working capital isn't treated as derived from a trade or business and thus is subject to the NIIT [Code Sec. 1411(c)(3)].Gain or loss from a disposition of an interest in a partnership or S corporation is taken into account by the partner or shareholder as NII only to the extent of the net gain or loss that the transferor would take into account if the entity had sold all its property for fair market value immediately before the disposition [Code Sec. 1411(c)(4)].

Home sale gain. The net investment income tax will not apply to any amount of gain realized from sale of a principal residence if the gain is already excluded from gross income under Code Sec. 121 which exempts from gross income the first $250,000 ($500,000 in the case of a married couple) of gain recognized on the sale of a principal residence. However, gain attributable to depreciation adjustments (which cannot be excluded from income under Code Sec. 121(d)(6)) is included in NII. Moreover, gains from the sales of second homes are subject to NIIT if the taxpayer has MAGI exceeding the applicable threshold.

Alternative Minimum Tax 16

INDIVIDUALS		CORPORATIONS	
Alternative minimum tax for individuals	¶16,001	Alternative minimum tax for corporations	¶16,025
Tax adjustments	¶16,005	Adjusted current earnings	¶16,030
Tax preferences	¶16,010	Preferences	¶16,035
AMT exemptions	¶16,015	Exemption and tax rate	¶16,040
Alternative minimum tax credit	¶16,020	Credits	¶16,045

INDIVIDUALS

¶16,001 ALTERNATIVE MINIMUM TAX FOR INDIVIDUALS

The Internal Revenue Code provides special income tax breaks for certain kinds of income and expenses. Using these breaks may reduce your regular income tax but subject you to the alternative minimum tax (AMT) in its place.

The alternative minimum tax (AMT) is an alternative taxing system imposed under Code Sec. 55. Individuals must use Form 6251, *Alternative Minimum Tax—Individuals,* to compute their AMT liability, while corporations must use Form 4626, *Alternative Minimum Tax—Corporations.* Estates and trusts use Schedule I of Form 1041, *U.S. Income Tax Return for Estates and Trusts.*

The AMT was originally directed at wealthy taxpayers who offset taxable income through the clever use of deductions, exemptions and credits that receive preferential treatment under the tax laws. The AMT was created to make sure that these resourceful taxpayers, who legitimately arrange their affairs to minimize their tax liability, pay their fair share of tax. As a result, the AMT includes in its taxable base many of the items that the regular tax system allows you to exclude.

So-called adjustments and preference items that provide you with favorable treatment under the regular income tax rules are eliminated under the alternative minimum tax rules. This broadened tax base (in excess of an exemption amount as discussed in ¶16,015) is subject to AMT rates that are lower than the top regular income tax rates. Generally, all taxpayers subject to regular income tax are subject to the AMT, although small corporations are exempt. A taxpayer's AMT for the tax year is the excess of the tentative minimum tax over the taxpayer's regular tax liability. AMT must be paid in addition to the regular tax liability [Code Sec. 55(a)]. For example, if a taxpayer's tentative minimum tax for a tax year is $100,000 while his regular tax is $75,000, he must pay an AMT of $25,000 in addition to the $75,000 regular tax for the total tax of $100,000.

The AMT is perceived as a concern to high-income taxpayers only. But that's not necessarily the case.[1] Those who are not wealthy may be required to pay the AMT. Reason: AMT income is increased by some of the most common tax breaks—state and local income and property taxes, interest on home equity loans, personal and dependency exemptions, and employee business expenses. Thus, for example, taxpayers who live and work in high-tax states and cities may have unexpected AMT liabilities. An alarming number of unintended taxpayers have felt the pinch of the AMT because the numbers involved in the AMT computation were not indexed for inflation.

.01 AMT Tax Rates

The AMT tax is imposed against individuals (including nonresident aliens), estates, trusts, and corporations (including foreign corporations engaged in a U.S. trade or business). A two-tiered, graduated rate schedule is applicable to noncorporate taxpayers. In 2013, the lower tier consists of a 26 percent tax rate which applies to income up to the following amounts:

Married Individuals Filing Separate Returns	$ 89,750
Joint Returns, Unmarried Individuals (other than surviving spouses), and Estates and Trusts [Code Sec. 55(b)(1)].	$179,500

In 2013, the upper tier 28 percent tax rate applies to excess taxable income above the amounts listed above.

.02 Treatment of Capital Gains for AMT Purposes

A taxpayer is required under Code Sec. 55(b)(3) to reduce alternative minimum taxable income (AMTI) by the applicable exemption amount [¶16,015] and by the amount of the long-term capital gain subject to the 25 percent, 20 percent, 15 percent, or 5 percent capital gains rates. A tentative minimum tax is computed on the AMTI as reduced by the exemption amount and long-term capital gain. The tentative minimum tax is then increased by the amount of tax paid on the long-term capital gain for regular tax purposes. The taxpayer's minimum tax liability is the difference between regular tax liability and the tentative minimum tax liability as increased by the regular tax paid on the long-term gain.

Under the formula for computing the AMT for capital gains, an individual's tentative minimum tax may not exceed the total of:

1. The tentative minimum tax computed without regard to Code Sec. 55(b)(3) on the individual's "taxable excess" (i.e., alternative minimum taxable income in excess of the applicable exemption amount), reduced by the *lesser* of (a) net capital gain or (b) the total of adjusted net capital gain and unrecaptured Code Sec. 1250 gain; plus

---

[1] *S.W. Katz*, 87 TCM 1222, Dec. 55,612(M), TC Memo. 2004-97; *N.E. Holly*, 75 TCM 1752, Dec. 52,564(M), TC Memo. 1998-55, *appeal dismissed*, CA-4, 99-1 USTC ¶50,151.

2. Zero percent of so much of the adjusted net capital gain (or, if less, taxable excess) that does not exceed the amount on which tax is computed under Code Sec. 1(h)(1)(B); plus
3. 15 percent of the taxpayer's adjusted net capital gain (or, if less, taxable income) in excess of the amount of tax determined under Step (2), above or, in tax years beginning after December 31, 2012, if less, the excess of (a) the amount of taxable income that would (without regard to the capital gains rules) be taxed at a rate below 39.6 percent, over (b) taxable income reduced by adjusted net capital gain; plus
4. In tax years beginning after December 31, 2012, 20 percent of the taxpayer's adjusted net capital gain (or, if less, taxable income) in excess of the amount of tax determined under Steps (2) and (3), above; plus
5. 25 percent of the amount of taxable income in excess of the total of the amounts determined under steps (1), (2), and (3), above [Code Sec. 55(b)(3)].

For the purposes of the preceding formula, the term "net capital gain" is defined as the excess of net long-term capital gain for the tax year over net short-term capital loss for the tax year [Code Sec. 1222(11)]. The term "adjusted net capital gain" is defined in Code Sec. 1(h)(3) as net capital gain reduced (but not below zero) by the sum of unrecaptured Code Sec. 1250 gain (as defined in Code Sec. 1(h)(7)) and 28 percent rate gain (as defined in Code Sec. 1(h)(4)), plus qualified dividend income [Code Sec. 1(h)(11)].

Dividends Taxed as Capital Gains for Regular Tax and AMT Purposes

Dividends received by individual shareholders are taxed as net capital gain [Code Sec. 55(b)(3)(C)]. See ¶8001. This means that dividends will be taxed at rates of 0 percent, 15 percent and 20 percent for both regular tax and AMT purposes. Dividends are included in calculating taxable income for regular tax purposes and AMTI for AMT purposes.[2]

.03 Computation of the Alternative Minimum Tax

The AMT is a separately computed tax that is paid only if your tax bill computed under the AMT system exceeds your tax bill computed under the regular way. If the AMT applies to you, you are taxed on a much larger income base, which is why you will have a bigger tax bill when the AMT is triggered.

To determine whether you are subject to the AMT, first you must figure your Federal income tax under the regular rules. Then you recompute your tax under the AMT rules. If you owe more under the AMT system than you owed under the regular tax system, you must pay the higher AMT bill.

To calculate your AMT exposure, you first start with your adjusted gross income from Form 1040 (before personal exemptions) and add back the necessary adjustments, which are the deductions and tax preference items that are allowed under the regular tax rules but are disallowed or limited when computing AMT.

You can calculate your AMT liability as follows [Code Sec. 55]:

1. Start with taxable income from Form 1040.
2. Add or subtract certain adjustments [Code Secs. 55(b)(2)(A), 56 and 58; see ¶16,005].

---

[2] *T. Weiss*, 129 TC 175, Dec. 57,206 (2007).

3. Add all tax preference items [Code Secs. 55(b)(2)(B), 57; see ¶16,010].
4. The sum is the alternative minimum taxable income (AMTI) which is often characterized as the heart of the AMT [Code Sec. 55(b)(2)].
5. Subtract the applicable exemption amount, if any [¶16,015]. This equals the alternative minimum tax base (AMTB).
6. Multiply AMTB by the alternative minimum tax rates (26 percent of the first $175,000 of AMTB plus 28 percent of the excess of AMTB over $175,000). This will result in the tentative minimum tax. If this figure exceeds your regular tax bill, you owe AMT.
7. Subtract the regular tax liability.
8. This is the AMT that must be paid in addition to the regular tax. The result of this computation is that the taxpayer pays the higher of the tentative minimum tax or the tax liability on taxable income computed on Form 1040 without consideration of the AMT.

.04 Adjustments and Tax Preferences

When taxpayers compute AMT liability, the critical component is determining alternative minimum tax income (AMTI), which is the figure through which selected tax deductions and exemptions are reclaimed. The adjustments and tax preference items that individuals must take into account when computing AMTI are:

1. Accelerated depreciation on property placed in service after 1986 [Code Sec. 56(a)(1)]. Accelerated depreciation on pre-1987 real property over straight-line depreciation [Code Sec. 57(a)(6)]. Depreciation on property placed in service after 1986 and before January 1, 1999, is computed by using the generally longer class lives prescribed by the alternative depreciation system of Code Sec. 168(g) and either (a) the straight-line method in the case of property subject to the straight-line method under the regular tax or (b) the 150-percent declining balance method in the case of other property. Depreciation on property placed in service after December 31, 1998, is computed by using the regular tax recovery periods and the AMT methods described in the previous sentence. Depreciation on property acquired after September 10, 2001, and before January 1, 2005 (January 1, 2006, for certain property), which is allowed an additional allowance under Code Sec. 168(k) for the regular tax, is computed without regard to any AMT adjustments [Code Sec. 56(a)(1)].
2. Mining exploration and development costs are capitalized and amortized over a 10-year period [Code Sec. 56(a)(2)].
3. Taxable income from a long-term contract (other than a home construction contract) is computed using the percentage of completion method of accounting [Code Sec. 56(a)(3)].
4. Amortization of pre-1987 and post-1986 pollution control facilities [Code Secs. 56(a)(5), 57(a)(6)]. The amortization deduction allowed for pollution control facilities placed in service before January 1, 1999 (generally determined using 60-month amortization for a portion of the cost of the facility under the regular tax), is calculated under the alternative depreciation system (generally, using

longer class lives and the straight-line method). The amortization deduction allowed for pollution control facilities placed in service after December 31, 1998, is calculated using the regular tax recovery periods and the straight-line method.

5. Certain itemized deductions are not allowed [Code Sec. 56(b)(1)(A)(i)].
6. Deductions for State, local, and foreign real property taxes; State and local personal property taxes; State, local, and foreign income, war profits, and excess profits taxes; and State and local sales taxes are not allowed [Code Sec. 56(b)(1)(A)(ii)].
7. Medical expenses are allowed only to the extent they exceed 10 percent of the taxpayer's adjusted gross income [Code Sec. 56(b)(1)(B)].
8. The standard deduction and personal exemptions are not allowed [Code Sec. 56(b)(1)(E)].
9. The amount allowable as a deduction for circulation expenditures are capitalized and amortized over a three-year period [Code Sec. 56(b)(2)].
10. The amount allowable as a deduction for research and experimentation expenditures from passive activities are capitalized and amortized over a 10-year period [Code Sec. 56(b)(2)].
11. The regular tax rules relating to incentive stock options do not apply [Code Sec. 56(b)(3)].
12. The excess of the deduction for percentage depletion over the adjusted basis of each mineral property (other than oil and gas properties) at the end of the tax year is not allowed [Code Sec. 57(a)(1)].
13. The amount by which excess intangible drilling costs (i.e., expenses in excess of the amount that would have been allowable if amortized over a 10-year period) exceed 65 percent of the net income from oil, gas, and geothermal properties is not allowed. This preference applies to independent producers only to the extent it reduces the producer's AMTI (determined without regard to this preference and the net operating loss deduction) by more than 40 percent) [Code Sec. 57(a)(2)].
14. Tax-exempt interest income on private activity bonds (other than qualified 501(c)(3) bonds issued after August 7, 1986, and certain housing bonds issued after July 30, 2008) is included in AMTI [Code Sec. 57(a)(5)].
15. Use of the installment method of accounting by dealers in personal property [Code Sec. 57(a)(6)].
16. Passive farm and passive business activity losses [Code Sec. 58].
17. Certain net operating loss deductions [Code Sec. 56(a)(4), (d)].
18. A nonresident alien's net gain from the disposition of U.S. real property interests [Code Sec. 897(a)(2)].
19. Gains on the sale of certain small business stock [Code Sec. 57(a)(7)]. Seven percent of any gain realized on the sale of qualified small business stock and excluded from gross income under Code Sec. 1202 is generally treated as a tax preference item. Since the exclusion generally equals 50 percent of the realized gain, only 3.5 percent of the gain recognized is treated as a tax preference item.

However, for stock acquired after September 27, 2010, and before January 1, 2014, the excluded gain is not a tax preference item [Code Sec. 1202(a)(4)]. See ¶ 8105.

.05 Tax Planning to Avoid the AMT

Advance planning to reduce or eliminate AMT positive adjustments may help to reduce or eliminate the effect of the AMT. To best determine the strategy that will reduce your exposure to the AMT, you should estimate your taxable income and alternative minimum taxable income (AMTI) for this year and next year and calculate your expected tax bill for both years. Use Form 1040 and the accompanying schedules to estimate your income tax bill. Use Form 6251, *Alternative Minimum Tax-Individuals,* to estimate your AMTI and to calculate your exposure to the AMT. Remember, of course, that legitimate tax planning based on bona fide transactions is always acceptable to the IRS, but that sham transactions designed solely for tax savings purposes will be recharacterized by the IRS to reflect economic reality.

In a tax year when AMT liability is inevitable, you may want to consider accelerating the receipt of ordinary income and postponing deductions until the following year. Assuming that you will be in a greater than 26 or 28 percent tax bracket in the following year, ordinary income would be shifted in the AMT year to a lower 26 or 28 percent tax bracket. This will result in a significant tax savings. You may also want to consider such strategies as electing out of the installment sale method in order to accelerate the recognition of income.

You should also consider deferring deductible expenses out of the AMT year so they will be deductible in a later year when income will be taxed at rates exceeding 26 or 28 percent. This strategy makes sense because a deduction may be worth 39.6 percent for a taxpayer in the highest tax bracket and will be worth only 26 or 28 percent in the year the taxpayer is subject to the AMT.

In addition, deferring deductions away from an AMT year makes sense because the benefits of some regular tax deductions, such as state and local income taxes and real estate taxes, are lost completely in the AMT year. The payment of these items should be postponed to a subsequent, non-AMT year. Examples of deferral-type preferences that should be shifted to a non-AMT year are prepaid real estate taxes, medical expenses, miscellaneous itemized deductions, such as professional fees, and state and local tax payments. If preferences are deferred or accelerated from one tax year to another, the marginal rates in those two years will generally determine whether it is beneficial to defer or accelerate the preferences. Taxes will be saved if the shifting of preferences increases income in the year with the lower marginal rate and decreases it in the higher marginal rate year.

A common positive adjustment under the AMT arises when executives exercise their incentive stock options. To avoid the impact of the AMT when taxpayers exercise incentive stock options, the taxpayers should consider spreading the exercise of incentive stock options over multiple years to offset the large adjustment that would arise if all options were exercised in one year. See ¶ 16,005.

Another AMT-minimization strategy involves accelerated depreciation. Because any excess depreciation over straight-line depreciation taken on property must be added back when computing alternative minimum taxable income, taxpayers should choose straight-line depreciation over the accelerated depreciation method.

Optional 10-Year Write-Off of Certain Tax Preferences

Another strategy is to make an election under Code Sec. 59(e) to claim a longer write-off of certain expenses in order to avoid an AMT preference. With this election, taxpayers have the option of avoiding deductions for certain expenditures classified as tax preference items if, instead of claiming the deductions entirely in one tax year, they elect to claim the deductions ratably over a 3-, 5-, or 10-year period [Code Sec. 59(e)]. A three-year period is allowed only for circulation expenditures under Code Sec. 173, whereas a five-year period is allowed for intangible drilling and development expenditures incurred or paid in tax years beginning after 1989 [Code Sec. 263(c)]. Expenditures that qualify for a 10-year period are research and experimental expenditures [Code Sec. 174(a)], intangible drilling and development expenditures [Code Sec. 263(c)] paid or incurred in tax years beginning before 1990, mine development expenditures [Code Sec. 616(a)], and mining exploration expenditures [Code Sec. 617(a)].

Election periods begin with the tax year in which an expenditure is made. However, the write-off period for intangible drilling and development costs (IDC) begins in the month the IDC are paid or incurred [Code Sec. 59(e)(1)]. The election can be made with respect to any portion of any qualified expenditure [Code Sec. 59(e)(4)(A)]. The amount amortized is determined without regard to Code Sec. 291, which otherwise requires a 20 percent reduction of certain corporate preference items for regular tax purposes [Code Sec. 59(e)(2)].

How to make the election. The election must be made by attaching a statement to the income tax return (or amended return) for the tax year in which the qualified expenditure is made and the amortization begins. The statement must be filed no later than the date prescribed by law for filing the original return (including any extensions) for that tax year [Reg. § 1.59-1(b)(1)]. The statement must include:

- The taxpayer's name, address, and taxpayer identification number; and
- The type and specific amount of qualified expenditures identified in Code Sec. 59(e)(2) that the taxpayer is electing to deduct ratably over the applicable period of time [Reg. § 1.59-1(b)(1)].

Taxpayers making the election are not required to specify the type and amount of qualified expenditures for each activity or project, or to provide a description of each activity or project to which the expenditures relate. However, taxpayers must maintain books and records sufficient to support their allocation of Code Sec. 59(e) expenditures to reduce the gain otherwise recognized on the disposition of a property, project, or activity, as is required by Code Sec. 1016(a)(20)]. The election may be made for any portion of any qualified expenditure paid or incurred during the tax year. However, the election must be made for a specific dollar amount subject to election under Code Sec. 59(e), and cannot be made by reference to a formula [Code Sec. 59(e)(2)].

Revocation and modification of election. IRS consent is required to revoke an election [Code Sec. 59(e)(4)(B); Reg. § 1.59-1(c)]. The amount subject to the election may not be modified on an amended return filed after the due date of the original return.[3] IRS consent to a revocation will be granted only in rare and unusual circumstances. The request for revocation must contain all of the information necessary to demonstrate such rare and unusual circumstances, sufficient to justify the revocation. The application for consent to revoke the election must be made in the form of a letter ruling request, and must be submitted prior to the end of the tax year the applicable amortization period ends. If granted, the revocation will be effective in the earliest tax year for which the period of limitations has not expired. The remaining unamortized costs are deductible in the tax year the revocation is effective [Reg. § 1.59-1(c)].

In conclusion, in planning for minimization of a taxpayer's AMT exposure, taxpayers should strive to:

- Minimize the impact of the AMT;
- Take advantage of the AMT exemption;
- Analyze projected income and deductions in the current and subsequent tax years and strive to avoid various adjustments and preferences that subject the taxpayers to the AMT;
- Accelerate income in a year that taxpayers are subject to AMT and postpone deductions; and
- Minimize the impact of AMT preferences that do not result in an AMT credit.

¶16,005 TAX ADJUSTMENTS

To the extent that you defer tax from one year to another, you experience a financial benefit—the use of money over time. Many tax breaks, like accelerated depreciation, provide you with this kind of deferral. For the AMT, you must adjust your income to eliminate some or all of the deferral benefit.

In the early years, your adjustment is added to your AMT income (AMTI) [Code Sec. 55(b)(2)(A)]. But, in the later years (when you pay the deferral back for regular tax purposes), your adjustment reduces your AMTI and actually provides you with an AMT savings at that time. This type of adjustment acts as an *averaging device* and prevents you from being taxed twice on the same income: once for regular tax purposes and again for the alternative minimum tax.

The exemption amount may substitute for regular tax deductions that are added back as AMT adjustments. For example, your personal and dependency exemptions are not allowed for AMT purposes. So you must add them back to your taxable income to calculate your AMT liability. In their place, you are entitled to a specific AMT exemption if your AMT income does not exceed certain levels [¶ 16,015].

The tax law specifies which items are to be treated as adjustments and which ones are to be treated as preferences. The tax treatment of AMT adjustments differs from preferences. Adjustments involve substitution of AMT treatment of an item for the regular tax treatment. A preference involves the addition of the difference between

[3] LTR 9607001 (Oct 31, 1995); LTR 9848003 (July 29, 1998).

the AMT treatment and the regular tax treatment. The following are the adjustments used to compute AMTI [Code Sec. 56, 58].

.01 Itemized Deductions

In general, an individual or other noncorporate taxpayer may deduct most itemized deductions when computing AMTI, subject to some exceptions. The itemized deduction for medical expenses is deductible against AMTI only to the extent medical expenses exceed 10 percent of regular tax adjusted gross income. The requirement that high-income taxpayers reduce their itemized deductions under Code 68 [see ¶9,001] does not apply for AMT purposes [Code Sec. 56(b)(1)(F)]. Any reduction for regular tax purposes is reflected as a negative adjustment on line 6 of Part I of Form 6251, *Alternative Minimum Tax—Individuals,* in computing AMTI.

In addition, individuals may not claim an itemized deduction for the taxes described in Code Sec. 164(a)(1), (2) or (3) when computing AMTI Code Sec. 56(b)(1)(A)(ii). Therefore, the following taxes are added back when computing AMTI:

- State and local, and foreign, real property taxes[4] [Code Sec. 164(a)(1)];
- State and local personal property taxes [Code Sec. 164(a)(2)];
- State and local, and foreign, income, war profits, and excess profits taxes [Code Sec. 164(a)(3)];
- State and local general sales taxes [Code Sec. 164(b)(5)(A)].

If a taxpayer elects to claim a deduction under Code Sec. 164(b)(5)(A) for general sales taxes in 2013 [see discussion in ¶9030], this amount must be added back to AMTI just like the deduction for state and local income taxes must be added back if that deduction is taken. Taxpayers in states with no state-wide income tax (Alaska, Florida, Nevada, South Dakota, Texas, Washington, and Wyoming) who elect to deduct the general sales taxes paid may now become subject to the AMT. Note that Delaware, Hawaii (an excise tax treated as sales tax), Montana, New Hampshire and Oregon have no general sales tax and Alaska only has some *local* general sales tax, therefore, no tables appear in the IRS instructions for Form 1040, Schedule A, for these states.

> ▶ **PRACTICE POINTER:** Taxpayers are advised to compare whether claiming the state and local income tax or the general sales tax will result in the lowest possible tax liability. If the taxpayer lives in a state with no income tax, the taxpayer should determine whether claiming the deduction for general sales taxes paid will result in exposure to the AMT. The net result may be that, although a taxpayer's regular tax liability may be lowered, if the taxpayer must pay the AMT, he or she may lose most or all of the advantage of taking the sales tax deduction. Taxpayers in states with a state income tax that is less than or equal to the general sales tax rate (Alaska (some local sales taxes), Arizona, Connecticut, Florida, Illinois, Indiana, Maryland, Michigan, Mississippi, Nevada, Pennsylvania, South Dakota, Tennessee, Texas, Washington and Wyoming) will need to compare the amount of income tax paid to the amount of sales tax paid to determine the greatest deduction, especially if the taxpayer purchased a

---

[4] *L. Ostrow*, CA-2, 2006-1 USTC ¶50,116, 430 F3d 581 (no deduction allowed when computing AMTI for co-op's real estate taxes [Code Sec. 164(a)]).

big-ticket item during the year. In those states where the income tax rate is greater than the general sales tax rate, the choice would appear to be clear, unless the taxpayer has purchased an automobile, boat or other specified item that may generate a sales tax bill in excess of the income tax bill.

.02 Standard Deduction

The standard deduction is not allowed in computing AMTI [Code Sec. 56(b)(1)(E)]. However, for tax years beginning after December 31, 2007, there is an allowance for the portion of the standard deduction attributable to the disaster loss deduction [Code Secs. 63(c)(1)(D), 56(b)(1)(E)]. For purchases on or after February 17, 2009, there is a similar allowance for the motor vehicle sales tax deduction [Code Sec. 63(c)(1)(E)]. Therefore, individuals who claim the standard deduction for regular tax purposes enter the standard deduction as a positive adjustment on Form 6251, *Alternative Minimum Tax—Individuals.*

.03 Personal and Dependency Exemptions

Personal and dependency exemptions may not be claimed for AMT purposes [Code Sec. 56(b)(1)(E)]. This adjustment is not separately listed on Form 6251, *Alternative Minimum Tax—Individuals.* It is, however, taken into account in Part I of the Form 6251, line 1 where taxpayers provide their regular taxable income *before exemptions* in computing alternative minimum taxable income (AMTI).

.04 Miscellaneous Itemized Deductions

Taxpayers may not deduct amounts deducted as miscellaneous itemized deductions on Schedule A when they compute the AMT [Code Sec. 56(b)(1)(A)(i)]. Therefore miscellaneous deductions must be added back when computing AMTI and are reflected as a positive adjustment on Form 6251, *Alternative Minimum Tax—Individuals.* Miscellaneous itemized deductions are defined as all itemized deductions other than certain specified itemized deductions which are listed in Code Sec. 67(b). The specified itemized deductions which are not miscellaneous itemized deductions and therefore need not be added back when a taxpayer is computing AMTI are:

1. The deduction for interest under Code Sec. 163;
2. The deduction for taxes allowed under Code Sec. 164;
3. Casualty, theft, and wagering loss deductions allowed under Code Sec. 165(c)(3) and (d);
4. Charitable contribution deductions allowed under Code Sec. 170 and Code Sec. 642(c);
5. Medical expense deductions allowed under Code Sec. 213;
6. Any deduction for impairment-related work expenses;
7. The deduction for a share of estate tax allowed under Code Sec. 671(c) to a person including income in respect of a decedent in gross income;
8. Any deduction allowable in connection with personal property used in a short sale;
9. The deduction described in Code Sec. 1341 allowed to a taxpayer who establishes after the close of a tax year in which an amount is included in income that the taxpayer did not have an unrestricted right to the income;

10. The deduction allowed under Code Sec. 72(b)(3) when annuity payments cease before a taxpayer's investment is recovered;
11. The deduction allowed under Code Sec. 171 for amortizable bond premium; and
12. The deduction allowed under Code Sec. 216 for shareholders of a cooperative housing corporation.

Unreimbursed employee business expenses are claimed as miscellaneous itemized deductions on Schedule A and therefore can subject a taxpayer to AMT liability.

.05 Medical and Dental Expenses

Medical and dental expenses are claimed as an itemized deduction for regular tax purposes to the extent they exceed 10 percent of an individual's adjusted gross income in tax years beginning after December 31, 2012 [Code Sec. 213(a)]. There is a transition rule for older individuals. For minimum tax purposes, the deduction remains limited to medical expenses in excess of 10 percent of adjusted gross income [Code Sec. 56(b)(1)(B)]. The difference, if any, between the allowable regular tax and the AMT medical expense deduction is reflected as a positive adjustment on Form 6251, *Alternative Minimum Tax—Individuals*.

.06 Home Mortgage Deduction

Interest on a home mortgage which is deductible for regular tax purposes may not be deducted for AMT purposes if the mortgage was taken out:

1. After June 30, 1982, and used for a purpose other than to buy, build, or substantially improve a taxpayer's principal residence or a "qualified dwelling" that is used by the taxpayer for personal purposes for the greater of—
   a. 14 days, or
   b. 10 percent of the days during the year that it is rented at fair market value [Code Sec. 56(e)(1)], or
2. Before July 1, 1982, and is secured by property that, at the time the mortgage was taken out, was not the taxpayer's principal residence or a qualified dwelling used by the taxpayer or a member of the taxpayer's family [Code Sec. 56(e)(3)].

A "qualified dwelling" is any house, apartment, condominium, or (if not used on a transient basis) mobile home. The term includes any structures or other property appurtenant to these types of dwellings [Code Sec. 56(e)(2)].

An individual who refinanced a mortgage after June 30, 1982, for an amount in excess of the original mortgage may not deduct the interest related to the excess when computing AMTI. Interest on refinancing indebtedness up to the amount of the original mortgage remaining at the time of the refinancing is deductible for AMT purposes if the interest on the original mortgage was deductible for AMT purposes [Code Sec. 56(e)(1)]. The portion of any home mortgage interest which is deducted on Schedule A but which is not allowed for AMT purposes is reflected as a positive adjustment on Form 6251, *Alternative Minimum Tax—Individuals*.

In Rev. Rul. 2005-11,[5] the IRS concluded that interest paid on a home mortgage that was refinanced more than once is deductible as qualified housing interest for AMT

---

[5] Rev. Rul. 2005-11, 2005-1 CB 816.

purposes if the mortgage that was refinanced was qualified housing interest and the amount of the mortgage indebtedness is not increased. The instructions to Form 6251, *Alternative Minimum Tax—Individuals,* allow an AMT deduction for interest paid on mortgages refinanced more than once and include a worksheet to help taxpayers determine the correct home mortgage interest adjustment. As clarified by Rev. Rul. 2005-11, a taxpayer should include in the worksheet calculation qualified housing interest on a mortgage that previously was refinanced.

Example 16-1: The taxpayer borrowed $100,000 to purchase a principal residence. The outstanding principal balance on the mortgage was $90,000, and the taxpayer refinanced the $90,000 balance. The refinanced amount equaled the amount of the outstanding principal, so the interest paid or accrued on the mortgage is deductible as qualified housing interest for AMT purposes because the interest is qualified housing interest and the amount of the loan is not increased.

Six years later, the outstanding principal balance on the mortgage was $80,000. The taxpayer refinanced the $80,000 balance of the mortgage and borrowed an additional $30,000. The taxpayer did not use the $30,000 to acquire, construct, or substantially improve a principal residence. When the taxpayer refinanced the mortgage, the interest on the mortgage was qualified housing interest to the extent of the outstanding principal balance of the original mortgage. Therefore, for AMT purposes, the taxpayer may deduct only the interest paid or incurred on $80,000 and not the interest attributable to the additional $30,000 that was borrowed.

.07 Investment Interest Expense Deduction

For regular tax purposes, investment interest expense is deductible to the extent of total investment income under Code Sec. 163(d). See ¶ 9020. To determine the amount of investment interest deductible for AMT purposes, a taxpayer is required to refigure investment income, gains, and expenses taking into account all AMT adjustments and preferences that apply [Code Sec. 56(b)(1)(C)(v)]. These refigured amounts are the items listed in Part II of Form 4952, *Investment Interest Expense Deduction*, for determining net investment income.The difference between the regular and AMT investment interest deduction is entered as a positive adjustment on Form 6251 if the regular deduction is greater. If the regular deduction is less, the adjustment is entered as a negative amount.

.08 Depreciation Deductions

Depreciation claimed as a deduction for regular tax purposes is an item of tax adjustment to the extent that it exceeds the depreciation allowable for AMT purposes. This means that the ability of taxpayers to claim depreciation deductions is severely limited for purposes of the AMTI computation.

Depreciation That Must Be Refigured for AMT Purposes

For purposes of the AMTI computation, you must refigure depreciation, including depreciation allocable to costs for:

- Property placed in service after December 31, 1998, that is depreciated for the regular tax using the 200-percent declining balance method (generally 3-, 5-, 7-, and 10-year property under the modified accelerated cost recovery system (MACRS));
- Tangible property placed in service after 1986 and before 1999 that was depreciated using a faster method than the alternative depreciation system. If the transitional election was made, this rule applies to property placed in service after July 31, 1986; and
- Section 1250 property placed in service after 1998 that is not depreciated for the regular tax using the straight line method.

Depreciation That Is Not Refigured for AMT Purposes

You need not refigure depreciation for the AMT for:

- Residential rental property placed in service after December 31, 1998;
- Nonresidential real property with a class life of 27.5 years or more placed in service after 1998 that is depreciated for the regular tax using the straight line method;
- Other Section 1250 property placed in service after 1998 that is depreciated for the regular tax using the straight-line method;
- Property other than Section 1250 property, placed in service after 1998 that is depreciated for the regular tax using the 150-percent declining balance method or the straight-line method;
- Property for which you elected to use the alternative depreciation system for the regular tax;
- Property that is qualified property eligible for the special depreciation allowance. The special allowance is deductible for the AMT and there is also no adjustment required for any depreciation figured on the remaining basis of the qualified property;
- Motion picture films, videotapes, or sound recordings;
- Property depreciated under the unit-of-production method or any other method not expressed in a term of years; and
- Qualified Indian reservation property [Code Sec. 56(a) (1) (A) (ii)].

How Depreciation Is Refigured for AMT Purposes

If the property was placed in service before 1999, refigure depreciation for the AMT using the alternative depreciation system (ADS) of Code Sec. 168(f), with the same convention used for the regular tax. If the property was placed in service after 1998 and the property was depreciated for the regular tax using the 200-percent declining balance method, for AMT purposes, use the 150-percent declining balance method. You should switch to the straight line method the first tax year it gives a larger deduction, and use the same convention and recovery period used for the regular tax [Code Sec. 168(c); Code Sec. 56(a) (1) (A) (ii)].

Bonus Depreciation

If bonus depreciation is claimed on MACRS property acquired after December 31, 2007, then regular tax depreciation and AMT depreciation is computed in the same manner.

In addition, the bonus depreciation allowance is also claimed in full for AMT purposes. For further discussion of bonus depreciation, see ¶ 11,001.01.

.09 Gain or Loss from Sale of Business Property

If you claimed a gain or loss from the sale or exchange of post-1986 depreciable property, or claimed a casualty gain or loss to business or income-producing property, you will have to refigure it for AMT purposes because basis adjustments required for AMT purposes will affect gain or loss. For AMT purposes, you must adjust the basis of property to take into account depreciation claimed.

.10 Incentive Stock Options

An incentive stock option (ISO) is an option granted by a corporation to its key executives to purchase stock of the corporation at a certain price. Companies often include ISOs in a key executive pay package as a way to attract and retain valued employees. Upon the exercise of the IOS, the executive receives stock in the corporation. No income is recognized when stock is received upon exercise of an ISO [Code Sec. 421(a)(1)].

The impact of AMT exposure when ISOs are exercised should not be overlooked. The employee "exercises" a stock option when he or she accepts the offer to sell the stock subject to the option. A promise to pay the option price is not an exercise of the option unless the employee is personally liable to sell at that time. ISOs defer tax until the shares of option stock are sold, and turn what would otherwise be compensation (ordinary income) into long-term capital gains, which is eligible for favorable tax treatment. If a taxpayer (including a trust) holds onto ISOs for at least two years after receipt, the difference between pre-set "the exercise price" and the stock selling price is taxed as capital gain [Code Sec. 422(a)(1)]. This amount, which is called the "bargain element," is considered an adjustment for alternative minimum tax purposes [Code Sec. 56(b)(3)]. No taxable income is recognized when an ISO is granted or exercised [Code Secs. 421(a), 422(a); see also Ch. 2]. However, the difference between the fair market value of the stock and the exercise price is an item of AMT tax preference and can trigger a significant AMT liability in the year of exercise if a large amount of appreciated stock is involved [Code Sec. 56(b)(3)]. The taxpayer must generally report the excess, if any, of:

1. The fair market value of the stock acquired through exercise of the option (determined without regard to any lapse restriction) when its rights in the acquired stock first become transferable or when these rights are no longer subject to a substantial risk of forfeiture, over
2. The amount paid for the stock, including any amount paid for the option used to acquire the stock.

If you acquired stock by exercising an ISO and disposed of that stock in the same year, the tax treatment under the regular tax and the AMT is the same, and no adjustment is required. Be sure to increase the AMT basis of any stock acquired through the exercise of an ISO by the amount of the adjustment.

The Tax Court has held that the difference between the adjusted AMT base and the regular tax basis of stock received through the exercise of an ISO is not a tax adjustment taken into account in the calculation of an alternative tax NOL (ATNOL) deduction in the year the stock is sold. Furthermore, it held that the sale of stock received through the exercise of ISOs was a sale of a capital asset and thus did not create an ATNOL.[6]

For AMT purposes, Code Sec. 83 applies to determine the compensation income (if any) attributable to ISOs. Property is not taxable under Code Sec. 83 until it is either transferable or no longer subject to a substantial risk of forfeiture. Therefore, a taxpayer who exercises an ISO that is substantially vested must include in AMT income (AMTI), the excess of the fair market value of the stock acquired through exercise of the option (determined without regard to any lapse restriction) when rights in the acquired stock first become transferable or when these rights are no longer subject to a substantial risk of forfeiture, over the amount paid for the stock, including any amount paid for the ISO used to acquire the stock [Code Sec. 56(b)(3)]. Thus, the more rapidly the underlying stock appreciates, the greater the risk the employee will owe ATM on the exercise of the option. This is because AMTI includes the difference between the fair market value of the stock on the date the ISO is exercised and the price paid for the stock (the "ISO spread") [Code Sec. 56(b)(3)]. However, keep in mind that the AMT only applies if it is higher than the taxpayer's regular income tax [Code Sec. 55(a)].

If the stock is not substantially vested in the year of exercise, income is includible under the Section 83 rules for AMT purposes when the stock becomes substantially vested. Property is substantially nonvested when it is both subject to a substantial risk of forfeiture and is nontransferable [Reg. § 1.83-3(c)]. Under Prop. Reg. § 1.83-3(c)(1), a substantial risk of forfeiture exists only where rights in transferred property are "conditioned, directly or indirectly, upon the future performance (or refraining from performance) of substantial services by any person, or upon the occurrence of a condition related to a purpose of the transfer if the possibility or forfeiture, is substantial." Property is not transferred subject to a substantial risk of forfeiture if the employer is required to pay the fair market value of a portion of such property to the employee when the property is returned. The risk that the value of property will decline during a certain period of time does not constitute a substantial risk of forfeiture. A nonlapse restriction, standing by itself, will not result in a substantial risk of forfeiture. In general, restrictions on the transfer of property, whether contractual or by operation of law, will not result in a substantial risk of forfeiture. Therefore, transfer restrictions that will not result in a substantial risk of forfeiture include, but are not limited to, restrictions that if violated, whether by transfer or attempted transfer of the property, would result in the forfeiture of some or all of the property, or liability by the employee for any damages, penalties, fees or other amount.

Example 16-2: On January 3, 2013, YCo grants to Quinn, an officer of YCo, a nonstatutory option to purchase YCo common stock. Although the option is immediately exercisable, it has no readily ascertainable fair market value when it is granted. Under the option, Quinn has the right to purchase 100 shares of YCo common stock for $10 per share, which is the fair market value of a share on the date of grant of the option. On May 1, 2013, YCo sells its common stock

---

[6] *E. Marcus*, 129 TC 24, Dec. 57,053 (2007).

in an initial public offering (IPO). Pursuant to an underwriting agreement entered into in connection with the IPO, Quinn agrees not to sell, otherwise dispose of, or hedge any YCo common stock from May 1 through November 1 of 2013 ("the lock-up period"). Quinn exercises the option and YCo shares are transferred to Quinn on August 15, 2013, during the lock-up period. The underwriting agreement does not impose a substantial risk of forfeiture on the shares because the provisions of the agreement do not condition Quinn's rights in the shares upon anyone's future performance (or refraining from performance) of substantial services or on the occurrence of a condition related to the purpose of the transfer of shares to Quinn. Accordingly, neither Code Sec. 83(c)(3) nor the imposition of the lock-up period by the underwriting agreement preclude taxation under Code Sec. 83 when the shares resulting from exercise of the option are transferred to Quinn [Prop. Reg. § 1.83-3(c)(4), Ex. 6].

In a pair of technical advice memorandums, the IRS concluded that notwithstanding stock transfer restrictions, compensation attributable to the exercise of ISOs is included in income when the shares purchased with the ISOs are transferred.[7]

You must then increase your AMT basis of any stock acquired through the exercise of an ISO by the amount of the adjustment. If you acquired stock by exercising an ISO and you disposed of that stock in the same year, the tax treatment under the regular tax and the AMT is the same (no adjustment is required).

▶ **PRACTICE POINTER:** It is important for you to retain adequate records for both the AMT and regular tax so that you can figure your adjusted gain or loss in the year that you sell the stock because your AMT basis in stock acquired through an ISO is likely to differ from your regular tax basis.

Example 16-3: Mr. Kelly exercises an incentive stock option for 100 shares of his employer's stock. The exercise price is $25 per share, and the fair market value is $75. The adjustment in the year of exercise is $50 per share for a total of $5,000. This amount must be added to his income for AMT purposes even though exercising the option is not a taxable event for regular tax purposes. Kelly's basis for regular tax purposes is $25 per share and for AMT purposes is $75. When Kelly sells the stock several years later, he pays regular tax on the options but reduces his income in that year for AMT purposes—since the stock was previously subject to the AMT.

Section 83(b) Election

Stock received pursuant to the exercise of an ISO may in some cases be nontransferable and subject to a substantial risk of forfeiture. In this situation, no AMT adjustment is immediately required. As noted above, the AMT adjustment is made when the rights in the stock first become transferable or are no longer subject to a substantial risk of forfeiture. However, a taxpayer may instead choose to take the AMT adjustment into account in the tax year of exercise by making a Section 83(b) election for AMT purposes. Although a Section 83(b) election may not be made with respect to stock

[7] TAM 200338010 (May 22, 2003); TAM 200338011 (May 22, 2003).

received as the result of the exercise of an ISO for regular tax purposes (see Code Sec. 83(e)(1)), this prohibition does not apply for AMT purposes. The rationale is apparently based on Code Sec. 56(b)(3), which provides that the ISO rules do not apply for purposes of the AMT. A Section 83(b) AMT election (like a regular Section tax 83(b) election) must be made within 30 days after the stock is transferred to the taxpayer.[8]

If the election is made, the excess of the stock's fair market value when the option is exercised (determined without regard to any lapse restriction) over the exercise price (including any amount paid for the option) is included in AMTI (i.e., as an adjustment on Form 6251). The employer should also be entitled to an AMT deduction equal to the amount included in the employee's AMTI [Code Sec. 83(h)]. When the stock is sold, AMT gain (the difference between the selling price and fair market value at time of exercise) would be long-term capital gain (assuming the requisite holding period is satisfied). For regular tax purposes, the gain is equal to the difference between the selling price and the exercise price (including any amount paid for the option). The difference between the regular tax gain and AMT gain is reported as a negative adjustment on Form 6251.

In *A.J. Kadillak*,[9] an individual who made a valid Code Sec. 83(b) election following the exercise of ISOs was required to recognize the excess of the vested and nonvested stock's fair market value over the exercise price for purposes of AMTI. The capital loss limitations of Code Secs 1211 and 1212 applied for purposes of determining AMTI. Therefore, although the nonvested stock was forfeited in the year after the exercise of the option, the taxpayer was not entitled to carry back his AMT capital losses or AMT net operating losses to reduce his AMTI for the prior year.

AMT capital loss cannot be carried back. In *Merlo*,[10] an individual exercised incentive stock options and realized a capital loss for AMT purposes when the taxpayer's acquired stock became worthless. The court held that the taxpayer who paid AMT on the exercise of the incentive stock options was subject to the same capital loss limitations for regular tax and AMT purposes and could not carry back a capital loss in figuring the AMT. The taxpayer therefore had to apply the regular tax capital loss limitations when calculating his alternative minimum taxable income (AMTI). Since the net regular capital loss was excluded in computing the net operating loss (NOL) deduction and since the ATNOL was the same as the regular NOL with certain adjustments to taxable income under the AMT provisions, the taxpayer's AMT capital loss could not be used to create an ATNOL that could be carried back to the prior tax year.

.11 Passive Activity Gains and Losses

Passive activity gains and losses must be refigured for AMT purposes by taking into account all adjustments, preferences, and any suspended losses that apply to that

[8] Treas. Dept., IRS Form 6251, *Alternative Minimum Tax—Individuals* (for 2013 returns), Instructions, p. 2.

[9] *A.J. Kadillak*, 127 TC 184, Dec. 56,670 (2006), *aff'd*, CA-9, 2008-2 USTC ¶50,462, 534 F3d 1197.

[10] *R.J. Merlo*, 126 TC 205, Dec. 56,494 (2006), *aff'd*, CA-5, 2007-2 USTC ¶50,554, 492 F3d 618; *P. Norman*, DC-CA, 2006-2 USTC ¶50,429, *aff'd*, CA-9, 2008-2 USTC ¶50,467; *M. Spitz*, 92 TCM 121, Dec. 56,589(M), TC Memo. 2006-168; *J.N. Palahnck*, 127 TC 118, Dec. 56,644 (2006), *aff'd per curiam*, CA-2, 2008-2 USTC ¶50,577, 544 F3d 471.

activity. For example, your deductions for post-1986 depreciation and tax-exempt interest would not be allowed and would reduce the amount of your passive activity loss, thus increasing taxable income.

Example 16-4: A partner in a partnership receives a Schedule K-1 (Form 1065) from the partnership that shows the following:

- A passive activity loss of $10,000;
- A depreciation adjustment of $1,000 on post-1986 property; and
- An adjustment of $1,000 for adjusted gain or loss.

Because the adjustments are not allowed for the AMT, the partner must first reduce the passive activity loss by those amounts. The result is a passive activity loss for the AMT of $8,000. This amount would be used to refigure the allowable passive activity loss for the AMT.

.12 Publicly Traded Partnership (PTP)

If you had losses from a PTP, you will have to refigure the loss using any AMT adjustments and preferences and any AMT prior year disallowed loss.

.13 Tax Shelter Passive Farm Activities

Losses from any tax shelter farm activity that consists of a farming syndicate, as defined in Code Sec. 464(c), and are disallowed when computing AMTI [Code Sec. 58(a)(2)(A)]. A loss that is disallowed under the tax shelter farm activity rule may be carried forward for AMT purposes [Code Sec. 58(a)(1)(B)]. More specifically, deductions in excess of the gross income allocable to each passive farm activity are disallowed. Each farm is treated as a separate activity. Income from one passive farm activity cannot be netted against another passive farm activity loss. Thus, each activity is treated as a separate basket for purposes of the farm activity loss rule.

In applying the limitations on losses from passive activities or tax shelter farming activities, the amount of losses subject to limitation under Code Sec. 58 is reduced by the amount (if any) of the taxpayer's insolvency at the close of the tax year. Pursuant to Code Sec. 108(d)(3), "insolvency" is the excess of liabilities over the fair market value of the taxpayer's assets.

Since Code Sec. 58(a)(1) denies a deduction for farm loss from any tax shelter farm activity in the computation of your AMTI, you must refigure any gain or loss from a tax shelter passive farm activity taking into account all AMT adjustments and preferences and any AMT prior year disallowed losses. If the amount is a gain, include it on the AMT Form 8582. If the amount is a loss, instead of including it on the form, carry the loss forward to use against gains or losses from tax shelter passive farm activities next year.

A *tax shelter farm activity* is either: "any farming syndicate" as defined as a partnership or any other enterprise other than a corporation which is not an S corporation engaged in the trade or business of farming, if:

1. A partnership or any other enterprise other than a corporation which is not an S corporation engaged in the trade or business of farming is a farming syndicate if:

(a) at any time interests in such partnership or enterprise have been offered for sale in any offering required to be registered with any Federal or State agency having authority to regulate the offering of securities for sale; or more than 35 percent of the losses during any period are allocable to limited partners or limited entrepreneurs.

2. A taxpayer, when computing his or her alternative minimum taxable income, is fully allowed the losses attributable to the farming activity in the tax year when the taxpayer disposes of his entire interest in the tax shelter farm activity. Thus, a taxpayer could time the sale of his or her interest to occur within a tax year in which other tax preferences would give rise to a significant AMT liability, which would then be sheltered by the farming activity loss.

.14 Alternative Minimum Tax Net Operating Loss Deduction

Corporate and noncorporate taxpayers must adjust the net operating loss (NOL) deduction when computing AMTI [Code Sec. 56(a)(4)]. The NOL for AMT purposes is figured the same way as it is for regular tax purposes with certain modifications [Code Sec. 56(d)(1)]. First, the loss cannot offset more than 90 percent (increased to 100 percent for NOLs from 2001 and 2002) of AMTI (loss may not be carried back, only carried forward)[11] determined without regard to this deduction. Second, the operating loss is subject to the AMT adjustments and preferences, but preferences are taken into account only to the extent they increased the NOL for regular tax purposes [Code Sec. 56(d)(1)(A), (B)]. Consider the bargain element of incentive stock options, which is treated as a preference items for AMT purposes. In computing AMTI for the year in which an option is exercised, a taxpayer must include the difference between the stock's fair market value at the time of the exercise and its actual price, a difference that is not included in regular tax computations. This difference must be added back to the regular income base used to calculate the taxpayer's alternative tax NOL deduction.

> **Example 16-5:** You have gross income of $20,000 and deductions of $35,000, of which $10,000 are due to AMT adjustments and preference items. Your NOL for regular tax purposes is $15,000. However, the AMT net operating loss for the year is limited to $5,000 [$20,000 – ($35,000 – $10,000)]. You can carry the $5,000 loss forward or back to reduce income that is subject to AMT in those years.

> **Example 16-6:** You have an income of $100,000 and losses totaling $150,000, of which $40,000 are tax preference items. While the NOL for regular taxation is $50,000, AMTI may not be reduced by the tax preference items. Thus, your income may be reduced by only a loss of $110,000, leaving an alternative tax NOL of $10,000.

.15 Circulation Expenses

Noncorporate taxpayers who deduct circulation expenditures (i.e., the costs of establishing, maintaining, or increasing the circulation of a newspaper, magazine, or other

[11] *Metro One Telecommunications, Inc.*, CA-9, 2013-1 USTC ¶50,107, 704 F3d 1057.

periodical) from regular taxable income by expensing them must compute AMTI as if the expenditures were capitalized and ratably amortized over a three-year period [Code Sec. 56(b)(2)]. If the expenditures create a tax loss for the taxpayer, all unrecovered expenditures may be claimed against AMTI. Recomputed deductions must also be reflected in the amount of gain or loss included in AMTI. If property for which deductions have been recomputed is sold, the adjusted basis of the property must be based on adjusted circulation deductions rather than the deductions used to calculate regular taxable income.

.16 Research and Experimentation Costs

If noncorporate taxpayers have deducted research and experimental costs from regular taxable income by expensing them, they must recompute these deductions when computing their AMTI by capitalizing the costs and ratably amortizing them over a 10-year period. No AMT adjustment is required if the taxpayer has materially participated in the activity that produced the expenses [Code Sec. 56(b)(2)(D)].

.17 Mining Exploration and Development Costs

Taxpayers may be able to fully deduct mining exploration and development costs incurred during the year for regular tax purposes; however, deductions for mining exploration and development costs are not allowed for AMT purposes. Instead, taxpayers must ratably amortize costs incurred after 1986 over a 10-year period [Code Sec. 56(a)(2)(A). However, if taxpayers abandon the mine as worthless, an immediate write-off is allowed for both the regular tax and the AMT [Code Sec. 56(a)(2)(B)].

> ▶ **PRACTICE POINTER:** There is no AMT adjustment for mining exploration and development costs if taxpayers elect to deduct them ratably over 10 years for regular tax purposes as provided in Code Sec. 59(e).

.18 Long-Term Contracts

Special accounting methods are used for reporting income from long-term contracts.[12] A *long-term contract* is a building, installation, construction, or manufacturing contract that is not completed in the tax year in which it is entered into [Code Sec. 460(f)(1); Reg. § 1.460-1(a)(1)]. See Ch. 19. A manufacturing contract is a long-term contract only if it involves manufacturing a unique item not usually found in the manufacturer's finished goods inventory, or the item takes more than 12 months to complete [Code Sec. 460(f)(2); Reg. § 1.460-1(b)(1)].

> ▶ **OBSERVATION:** A contract that meets the definition is considered a long-term contract even though you expected it to be completed within the tax year.

Percentage of Completion Method

Generally, for regular tax purposes you must determine taxable income on long-term contracts entered into after July 10, 1989, by using the percentage of completion method [Code Secs. 56(a)(3), 460(a)]. The percentage of completion method need not be used for home construction contracts or any other construction contract entered into by a taxpayer who estimates that the contract will be completed within two years and whose average annual gross receipts for the three tax years preceding the tax year in which the contract is entered into do not exceed $10,000,000. Nor must it be

---

[12] Rev. Rul. 92-28, 1992-1 CB 153.

used for a portion of qualified ship contracts and residential construction contracts. [Code Sec. 460(e)]. Under the percentage of completion method, the amount of income generated by the contract is taxed to you based on the percentage of work you complete each year.

When figuring your AMTI, you must use the percentage-of-completion method [Code Sec. 460(b)] to determine your income from any long-term contract other than a home construction contract [Code Sec. 56(a)(3)]. The percentage of the contract completed is determined by using the simplified procedures for allocation of costs prescribed by Code Sec. 460(b)(3).

Exception for Home Construction Contracts

The percentage of completion method is not required for to any home construction contract [Code Sec. 460(e)(1)].

.19 Pollution Control Facilities

For regular tax purposes, taxpayers may be able to write off the cost of a pollution control facility (e.g., septic tax) over a 60-month amortization period [Code Sec. 169]. For property placed in service after 1986 and before 1999, the deduction for AMT purposes is determined under the alternative depreciation system [Code Sec. 56(a)(5)]. For property placed in service after 1998, figure the AMT depreciation for pollution control facilities under Code Sec. 168 using the straight-line method.

.20 Domestic Production Activities Deduction

The domestic production activities deduction is allowed for both individuals and corporations against the AMT. For individuals, the calculation of the deduction is the same for both regular income tax and AMT liability. For other taxpayers, however, the deduction for AMT purposes is calculated as a stated percentage (nine percent in 2010 and thereafter) of the lesser of (1) the taxpayer's qualified production activities income (determined without regard to available AMT adjustments) or (2) the taxpayer's alternative minimum taxable income (determined without regard to this deduction) [Code Sec. 199(a)].

.21 Unlawful Discrimination Damages

Gross income generally does not include the amount of any damages received by individuals (other than punitive damages) due to personal physical injuries, including death [Code Sec. 104(a)(2)]. Other damages are usually included in gross income. Expenses, such as costs and fees that are incurred in recovering damages are treated as miscellaneous itemized deductions, which are not taken into account in computing the AMT. However, an above-the-line deduction is allowed for fees and costs paid in connection with certain civil rights claims, most notably a claim of unlawful discrimination. The amount so excluded from gross income is limited to the amount of the judgment or settlement that was includible in the taxpayer's gross income. Because this amount is allowed as an above-the-line deduction, it is not taken into account in computing the AMT.

.22 Income Averaging for Farmers and Fishermen

Individuals engaged in the farming or fishing business may elect to average their income over three years in order to reduce their regular tax liability. This reduction in the regular tax could lead to a higher AMT, which is computed without income averaging. Thus, solely for purposes of computing the AMT, the regular income tax liability of a farmer or fisherman is computed without income averaging. Consequently, the AMT will be reduced by nonapplication of the income averaging rules when computing AMT [Code Sec. 55(c)(2)].

.23 Alcohol Fuels Credit Adjustment

AMTI does not include the alcohol fuels credit included in a taxpayer's gross income under Code Sec. 87 [Code Sec. 56(a)(7)].

¶16,010 TAX PREFERENCES

Taxpayers subject to the AMT, must add so-called tax preference items to taxable income when computing AMTI for AMT purposes [Code Sec. 55(b)(2)(B)]. Preferences can take the form of deductions, lower tax rates, or exclusions that generated tax savings under regular tax purposes. Generally, only the amount of the benefit received less the benefit otherwise allowed is counted as a tax preference item. Code Sec. 57 defines these tax preference items. The major tax preferences include the following items.

.01 Depletion

Taxpayers must refigure depletion deductions for purposes of the AMTI computation. This means that they must use only income and deductions allowed for the AMT when refiguring the limit based on taxable income from the property under Code Sec. 613(a) and the limit based on taxable income, with certain adjustments, under Code Sec. 613A(d)(1). In addition, depletion deductions for mines, wells, and other natural deposits under Code Sec. 611 are limited to the property's adjusted basis at the end of the year, as refigured for the AMT, unless the taxpayer is an independent producer or royalty owner claiming percentage depletion for oil and gas wells under Code Sec. 613A(c). This limit must be figured separately for each property. When refiguring the property's adjusted basis, take into account any AMT adjustments made this year or in previous years that affect basis (other than current year depletion).

The excess of the deduction for depletion under Code Sec. 611 over the adjusted basis of the depletion property at the end of the tax year (determined without regard to the depletion deduction for the tax year) is a tax preference item and must be added back to regular income when computing AMTI, unless the deduction for depletion was computed in accordance with Code Sec. 613A(c) [Code Sec. 57(a)(1)].

Example 16-7: Taxpayers claimed a deduction for percentage depletion of $50 with respect to property having a basis of $10 (disregarding the percentage depletion deduction). When computing your AMTI they would have a tax preference item in the amount of $40.

.02 Intangible Drilling Costs

If taxpayers claimed deductions for intangible drilling costs (IDCs) of oil, gas, or geothermal wells, they will have to refigure IDCs for purposes of the AMT. When computing AMTI, add back the amount by which the "excess intangible drilling costs" exceed 65 percent of "net income from the oil, gas, or geothermal properties." Be sure to figure the preference for all oil and gas properties separately from the preference for all geothermal properties.

> **Example 16-8:** Taxpayers have $100 of net oil and gas income (and a $65 net income offset) and $80 of excess intangible drilling costs. They would add back a tax preference in the amount of $15.

The term *net income from oil, gas, and geothermal properties* is determined without regard to deductions for excess intangible drilling costs [Code Sec. 57(a)(2)(C)]. The amount of *excess intangible drilling cost* is the amount of the excess, if any, of the taxpayer's regular tax deduction for such costs (deductible under Code Sec. 263(c) or 291(b) over the amount that would have been allowable if the taxpayer had amortized the cost over 10 years on a straight-line method [Code Sec. 57(a)(2)(B)].

Steps in Figuring Excess IDCs

Figure excess IDCs as follows:

1. Determine the amount of IDCs allowed for the regular tax under Code Sec. 263(c) or Code Sec. 291(b), but do not include any Code Sec. 263(c) deduction for nonproductive wells; and
2. Subtract the amount that would have been allowed if IDCs had been amortized over a 120-month period starting with the month that production from the well begins.

Net income is determined by taking the gross income that received or accrued during the tax year from all oil, gas, and geothermal wells and reducing the gross income by the deductions allocable to these properties (reduced by the excess IDCs). When refiguring net income, use only income and deductions allowed for the AMT.

> ▶ **PRACTICE POINTER:** There is no AMT adjustment for intangible drilling costs if you elect to deduct them ratably over 60 months as provided in Code Sec. 59(e).

Exception for Independent Oil Producers

Note that independent oil and gas producers (not integrated oil companies as defined in Code Sec. 291(b)(4)), do not have to compute preference items for excess percentage depletion deductions because the preference for IDCs from oil and gas wells does not apply to them [Code Sec. 57(a)(2)(E)]. However, this benefit is limited. The reduction in alternative minimum taxable income by reason of this rule may not exceed 40 percent of the alternative minimum taxable income for the year determined without regard to this exception or the alternative tax net operating loss deduction.

.03 Tax-Exempt Interest from Private Activity Bonds

When computing AMTI, add back tax-exempt interest on specified private activity bonds which means any private bond issued after August 7, 1986 where the interest is tax exempt [Code Sec. 57(a)(5)(C)].

Certain Housing Bonds Get More Favorable AMT Treatment

The following types of tax-exempt housing bonds, if issued after July 30, 2008, are not treated as private activity bonds for AMT purposes. Thus interest generated by these housing bonds will not be subject to AMT and will *not* be an AMT tax preference item that need be added to the taxpayer's regular taxable income base in computing the taxpayer's alternative minimum taxable income (AMTI):

- An exempt facility bond if it is part of an issue, 95 percent or more of the net proceeds of which are to be used to provide qualified residential rental projects;
- A qualified mortgage bond; and
- A qualified veterans' mortgage bond [Code Sec. 57(a)(5)(C)(iii)].

Mutual Fund Tax-Exempt Dividends

Tax-exempt dividends paid by a regulated investment company (RIC), which is commonly known as a mutual fund, are treated as interest on specified private activity bonds to the extent the dividends are attributable to interest on the bonds received by the company, minus an allocable share of the expenses paid or incurred by the company in earning the interest.

Child's Tax-Exempt Interest from Private Activity Bonds

If your child is subject to the "kiddie tax," and you have made the election to report your child's interest and dividend on your tax return by filing Form 8814, *Parent's Election to Report Child's Interest and Dividends,* any tax-exempt interest your child receives from specified private activity bonds will be considered a preference item for purposes of the AMT and must added back when computing AMTI.

.04 Accelerated Depreciation of Property Acquired Before 1987

If you acquired real property before 1987, the difference between the depreciation that would have been allowable if the straight line method had been used and the accelerated depreciation that you claimed for regular tax purposes is considered a tax preference item [Code Sec. 57(a)(6)]. As a result, when computing AMTI, you must use the straight-line method to figure depreciation on real property if for regular tax purposes you had used accelerated depreciation using pre-1987 rules. This means that you must use a recovery period of 19 years for 19-year real property and 15 years for low-income housing. For leased personal property other than recovery property, add back the amount by which your regular tax depreciation using the pre-1987 rules exceeds the depreciation allowable using the straight-line method.

For leased 10-year recovery property and leased 15-year public utility property, add back the amount by which your regular tax depreciation exceeds the depreciation allowable using the straight line method with a half-year convention, no salvage value, and a recovery period of 15 years (22 years for 15-year public utility property) [Code Sec. 57(a)(6)].

.05 Exclusion for Gains on Sale of Small Business Stock

If certain conditions are met, noncorporate investors may exclude some or all of the gain realized on the sale or exchange of small business stock held for more than five years. The percentage exclusion for qualified small business stock sold by an individual is 50 percent for stock acquired before February 18, 2009, 75 percent for stock acquired after February 17, 2009 and before September 28, 2010, and 100 percent for stock acquired after September 27, 2010 and before January 1, 2014 [Code Sec. 1202(a)]. For further discussion of the exclusion of gain realized on sale of qualified small business stock, see ¶ 8105.

Generally, a percentage of the excluded gain is classified as a tax preference item when computing an investor's alternative minimum taxable income (AMTI) to determine liability for AMT. The applicable percentages are as follows:

- For tax years ending before May 7, 1997, 50 percent of the excluded gain was treated as a tax preference item;
- For tax years ending after May 6, 1997, on sales or exchanges before May 6, 2003, 42 percent of the amount excluded was treated as a tax preference item. However, this amount was reduced to 28 percent if stock qualified under a five-year holding period for capital assets; and
- For sales or exchanges on or after May 6, 2003, only seven percent of the 50-percent exclusion is treated as a tax preference item when computing AMTI [Code Sec. 57(a)(7)]. However, none of the excluded gain is a tax preference item for stock acquired after September 27, 2010, and before January 1, 2014 [Code Sec. 1202(a)(4)].

Since seven percent of the exclusion is treated as a preference for AMT purposes under Code Sec. 57(a)(7), only 3.5 percent (50% × 7%) of the investor's total realized gain for the sale or exchange of small business stock will be used in the computation of AMTI. The AMTI rules that applied to five-year property have also been eliminated because the special capital gains tax rates that pertained to five-year property were eliminated.

¶16,015 AMT EXEMPTIONS

In 2013, the AMT exemption amounts under Code Sec. 55(d)(1) are:

Joint Returns or Surviving Spouses	$80,800
Unmarried Individuals (other than Surviving Spouses)	$51,900
Married Individuals Filing Separate Returns	$40,400
Estates and Trusts	$23,100

There is a $40,000 exemption amount for corporations and a $22,500 exemption amount for estates or trusts [Code Sec. 55(d)(1)(D), (d)(2)].

.01 AMT Exemption Phaseout

The AMT exemption amount for an individual, estate, or trust is reduced in 2013 by 25 percent for each $1 of AMTI in excess of:

- $153,900 for married individuals filing a joint return and surviving spouses,
- $115,400 for unmarried individuals,
- $76,950 for married taxpayers filing a separate return, and
- $76,950 for estates or trusts [Code Sec. 55(d)(3)].

In 2013, the AMT exemption amounts are completely phased out when AMTI reaches $477,100 for married taxpayers filing joint returns and surviving spouses, $323,000 for unmarried taxpayers, and $238,550 for married taxpayers filing a separate return, and $169,350 for estates or trusts.

▶ **TAX RETURN TIP:** Individuals compute their AMT liability on Form 6251. It is attached to Form 1040 and filed at the same time and place that Form 1040 is filed.

.02 Kiddie Tax AMT Exemption Amount

A child who is subject to the kiddie tax will be subject to the AMT. The child will compute a tentative minimum tax in much the same way as an individual taxpayer. However, the AMT exemption for the child will be limited to (1) the sum of the child's earned income for the year plus $7,150 in 2013, or (2) $33,750 [Code Sec. 59(j)(1)]. The child's exemption amount and their ultimate AMT liability is not dependent upon the computation of the parent's alternative minimum taxable income or AMT exemption amount.

¶16,020 ALTERNATIVE MINIMUM TAX CREDIT

.01 Who May Claim the AMT Credit

If an individual is subject to AMT in any year, the amount of tax exceeding the taxpayer's regular tax liability is allowed as a credit (the "AMT credit") in any subsequent tax year to the extent the taxpayer's regular tax liability exceeds his or her tentative minimum tax liability that year [Code Sec. 53]. For individuals, the AMT credit is allowed only to the extent that the taxpayer's AMT liability results from adjustments that are timing in nature. The individual AMT adjustments relating to itemized deductions and personal exemptions are not timing in nature, and no minimum tax credit is allowed with respect to these items.

Any unused credit may be carried forward indefinitely as a credit against regular tax liability. However, it is limited to the extent that the regular tax liability reduced by other nonrefundable credits exceeds the tentative minimum tax for the tax year. The credit may not be used to offset any future AMT liability.

.02 Nonrefundable Personal Credits

For tax years beginning after December 31, 2011, all nonrefundable personal tax credits are allowed to the full extent of the taxpayer's regular tax and AMT liability. For this purpose, the regular tax liability is first reduced by the amount of any applicable foreign tax credit [Code Sec. 26(a)(2)].

There are no nonrefundable personal credits excluded from the application of the general tax liability rule after 2011. Thus, there is no longer any need for a separate tax liability limitation rule as part of any nonrefundable credit provision. As a result, the tax liability rules have been stricken for the adoption credit, the child tax credit, the American Opportunity credit, the saver's credit, the residential energy efficient property credit, the plug-in electric vehicle credit, the alternative motor vehicle credit, and the new qualified plug-in electric vehicle credit Code Secs. 30(c)(2), 30B(g)(2) and 30D(c)(2)]. Therefore beginning in 2013, these credits can be offset against regular tax and AMT liabilities, after reduction for any foreign tax credit, just as all other nonrefundable personal credits.

.03 Reason for AMT Credit

Without the AMT tax credit for deferral preferences, you could end up paying a double tax—AMT in the year that an adjustment or preference provides you with a regular tax benefit and again in the regular tax system in the year the deferral ends. To mitigate this problem, you can claim a minimum tax credit against your regular income tax for AMT paid in 1987 or later [Code Sec. 53]. The credit is a function of your AMT liability for the year. Essentially, you subtract that portion of your AMT that is attributable to exclusion items (i.e., those tax breaks that permanently avoid regular income tax). The remainder is available as a credit against your *regular* tax liability for a subsequent year. For example, assume you must include the bargain element on the exercise of an incentive stock option in AMTI but you will not realize the income for regular tax purposes until you sell the stock. If the AMT exceeds the regular tax liability as a result of this deferral preference, you will be entitled to an AMT credit in future years to offset any regular tax liability resulting in that year.

Exclusion preferences that result from the permanent exclusion of income from regular taxable income are ineligible for the credit because exclusion preferences result in a permanent reduction of the regular tax whereas deferral preferences create the potential for double taxation when they affect the timing of income recognition under the regular tax. Exclusion preferences, on the other hand, never reverse and, therefore, cannot cause double taxation. In order to determine the amount of AMT attributable to deferral preferences, the AMT actually paid for the year is reduced by the amount of AMT that would have been paid if only exclusion preferences existed. The balance is the amount of AMT attributable to deferral preferences.

.04 AMT Credit Relief for Individuals with Long-Term Unused Credits

If an individual has a long-term unused minimum tax credit for any tax year beginning before January 1, 2013, the minimum tax credit allowable for that year will not be less than the "AMT refundable credit amount" regardless of the minimum tax credit otherwise allowed to the taxpayer [Code Sec. 53(e)(1)]. Any additional amount of credit is refundable [Code Sec. 53(e)(4)].

The "AMT refundable credit amount" is defined as the amount equal to the greater of: (1) 50 percent of the long-term unused minimum tax credit, or (2) the amount (if any) of the AMT refundable credit amount determined for the taxpayer's previous year [Code Sec. 53(e)(2)].

Before January 1, 2008, any underpayment of outstanding tax which is attributable to the application of Code Sec. 56(b)(3) (and any outstanding interest or penalty associated with such underpayment) is abated. No credit shall be allowed with respect to any abated amount [Code Sec. 53(f)(1)].

Individuals and fiduciaries must calculate the credit on Form 8801, *Credit for Prior Year Minimum Tax—Individuals, Estates, and Trusts.* Form 8827, *Credit for Prior Year Minimum Tax—Corporations,* is used by corporations to figure any minimum tax credit for alternative minimum tax incurred in prior years and any minimum tax credit carryforward that may be used in future years. Estates and trusts must use Schedule I of Form 1041, *U.S. Income Tax Return for Estates and Trusts.*

.05 Carryforward Permitted

The AMT credit can be carried forward indefinitely, but it cannot be carried back. The credit only offsets the excess of the regular tax over the AMT and thus, the AMT credit cannot offset the AMT itself in future years.

.06 AMT Foreign Tax Credit

Taxpayers may use 100 percent of the AMT foreign tax credit when computing AMT liability. See Ch. 28.

CORPORATIONS

¶16,025 ALTERNATIVE MINIMUM TAX FOR CORPORATIONS

Corporations are separate taxable entities and are subject to the AMT. If a corporation has a net capital gain for any tax year, the corporation will pay an alternative tax if it is less than the tax computed in the regular manner. Under the alternative tax, the portion of the corporation's taxable income that is net capital gain is subject to a maximum tax rate of 35 percent. The alternative tax rate is applied to the lesser of a corporation's net capital gain or its taxable income [Code Sec. 1202(a)(2)]. Because the top corporate tax rate is currently 35 percent, this method of application has no immediate impact on corporations.

If the alternative tax applies, it is computed as follows:

1. Subtract the net capital gains (net long-term capital gain over the net short-term capital loss) from the corporation's net taxable income.
2. Compute a partial tax on the remaining taxable income using the corporate graduated tax rates.
3. Add to the partial tax computed above 35 percent of the net capital gains (or, if less, 35 percent of the corporation's taxable income).

The resulting amount is used if it is less than the tax computed under the regular corporate tax rates [Code Sec. 1201(a)].

To calculate a corporation's AMT, use the format outlined for individuals as modified below. The adjustments pertaining only to individuals (e.g., personal and dependency exemptions, home equity indebtedness, and medical expenses) do not apply. Instead, corporations are subject to several special adjustments.

> ▶ **TAX RETURN TIP:** A corporation's AMT liability should be reported in Form 4626, *Alternative Minimum Tax—Corporations*, unless the corporation qualifies as a small business as discussed below.

.01 No AMT for Small Businesses

Corporations that satisfy the definition of *small corporations* are exempt from the corporate AMT [Code Sec. 55(e)]. Some businesses that fit into the definition of small corporation will therefore be able to avoid an added level of complexity that vexes taxpayers subject to the AMT. Moreover, the companies will also avoid the compliance costs associated with being subjected to the dreaded AMT.

.02 Treatment as a Small Corporation

A qualifying small corporation will be exempt from the AMT if it satisfies the gross receipts test. Therefore, a corporation's AMT bill will be zero for any tax year that the corporation has average annual gross receipts of $5 million or less for its first three tax years beginning after December 31, 1993. For subsequent tax years, the corporation will be exempt from the AMT if its average annual gross receipts for all three-tax-year periods endings before the tax year does not exceed $7,500,000 [Code Sec. 55(e)(1)]. However, this amount is reduced to $5,000,000 for the first three-year-period following 1993 (or portion of that period, if the corporation has not been in existence for that long) that is taken into account for this purpose. Once a corporation qualifies as a small corporation, it will continue to be exempt from the AMT for as long as its average annual gross receipts for the prior three-year period does not exceed $7,500,000. If the corporation was in existence for less than three years at the time it seeks to qualify for the exemption, then the gross receipts test is applied based on the period during which it has existed.

A new corporation is treated as having a tentative minimum tax of zero and thus is not subject to the AMT for the first tax year that the corporation is in existence (regardless of its gross receipts for the year). The allowable credit against the regular tax for prior year minimum tax liability of a small corporation is limited to the amount by which the corporation's regular tax liability (reduced by other credits) exceeds 25 percent of the excess (if any) of the corporation's regular tax (reduced by other credits) over $25,000. If a corporation ceases to be a small corporation, it cannot qualify as such for any subsequent tax year and the AMT will apply only prospectively. In applying the small corporation exemption, any reference to the corporation includes its predecessors.

> **Example 16-9:** XYZ corporation came into existence in 2011 and is neither aggregated with a related, existing corporation nor treated as having a predecessor corporation. It will qualify as a small corporation for its first year of existence, 2011, regardless of its gross receipts for that year. In order to qualify as a small corporation for 2011, XYZ's gross receipts for 2011 must be $5 million or less. If XYZ qualifies for 2011, it will also qualify for 2013 if its average gross receipts for the two-tax-year period including 2011 and 2012 is $7.5 million or less. If XYZ does not qualify for 2012, it cannot qualify for 2013 or any subsequent year. If XYZ qualifies for 2013, it will qualify for 2014 if its average gross receipts for the three-tax-year period including 2011, 2012 and 2013 is $7.5 million or less.

.03 Definition of *Gross Receipts*

Temp. Reg. § 1.448-1T(f)(2)(iv) defines *gross receipts* as total sales (net of returns and allowances) and all amounts received for services, plus any income from investments (e.g., interest, dividends, rents, royalties, and annuities) and from incidental or outside sources. It also includes original issue discount and tax-exempt income. Gross receipts are reduced by the taxpayer's adjusted basis in capital assets and Code Sec. 1231 assets sold. Gross receipts do not include the repayment of loans or sales tax collected from the consumer.

How to Satisfy the Gross Receipts Test

For purposes of applying the gross receipts test to determine eligibility for the AMT exemption for small corporations, the following rules apply [Code Sec. 55(e)(1)(D)]:

- Aggregate gross receipts of related entities and predecessor corporations. Entities are related if they are treated as members of the same controlled group of corporations or are members of an affiliated service group;
- Annualize gross receipts for any tax year of less than 12 months. If you only have gross receipts for a six-month tax year, you must double gross receipts for purposes of the gross receipts test;
- Reduce gross receipts by the amount of returns and allowances; and
- If the corporation has not been in existence for an entire three-year period, the gross receipts test should be applied for the years it was in existence.

.04 How to Avoid Aggregation

Requiring corporations to include the gross receipts of any related or predecessor corporation can tip small corporations over the $7.5 million gross receipts mark and thus result in corporations failing to qualify for exemption from the AMT. Keep in mind that entities are related if they are treated as a single employer under the rules of Code Sec. 52(a) or Code Sec. 52(b) (commonly controlled businesses) or Code Sec. 414(m) or Code Sec. 414(o) (affiliated service group). In addition, under Code Sec. 1563(a), controlled groups are affiliated companies in either a parent-subsidiary relation [Code Sec. 1563(a)(1)], with the parent owning more than 50 percent of the subsidiary's vote and value), or a brother-sister corporation relation [Code Sec. 1563(a)(2)]. In order to avoid jeopardizing qualifying for the exemption under the gross receipts, practitioners and small business owners should be careful to plan around the brother-sister rules in order to avoid the impact of the aggregation rules.

Small corporations that would otherwise qualify for the AMT exemption should try and avoid using multiple entities that would not have to be aggregated under the gross receipts test. They should deliberately arrange multiple corporations so that the interests would not have to be aggregated. Take for example the rules regarding brother-sister groups. These rules require five or fewer shareholders (including individuals, estates, or trusts) to own:

- At least 80 percent of the combined voting power of all classes of voting stock or at least 80 percent of the value of all classes of stock of each corporation; and
- More than 50 percent of the voting power of all classes of stock entitled to vote or more than 50 percent of the total value of all classes of stock of each corporation, taking into account the stock ownership of each person only to the extent it is identical with respect to each corporation.

Example 16-10: Alan and Bob are individual shareholders who are equal shareholders in two separate corporations which each have gross receipts of less than $5 million. They each want their corporations to qualify for the AMT exemption. As a result, they each own no more than 25 percent of each other's corporations so they will deliberately fail the aggregation requirement under the gross receipts test.

.05 Consequences to a Small Corporation of Losing Exemption

When a corporation fails the gross receipts test because gross receipts exceed $5 million and the corporation fails to qualify for the AMT exemption, the only good news is that the corporation's AMT liability will be calculated only on a prospective basis. This fresh start approach means that only transactions entered into after the corporation has lost its exempt status will be subject to the AMT [Code Sec. 55(e) (2)].

Example 16-11: A corporation is exempt from the AMT from 2010 through the year 2012. In 2013, the corporation's gross receipts exceed $7.5 million and the corporation is subject to the AMT. The fresh start date is January 1, 2013. Beginning on that date, the corporation will have to consider the impact of the AMT on the activities engaged in by the corporation.

After a corporation has lost small corporation status, the corporation must determine AMT liability by making certain modifications for transactions and investments that arose on or after the change date [Code Sec. 55(e) (2)]. The change date is the first day of the first tax year for which the corporation ceases to be a small corporation [Code Sec. 55(e) (4)]. After the change date, the corporation should become more aware of the following seven tax consequences [Code Sec. 55(e) (2) (A) through (G)]:

- The depreciation and pollution control adjustments will apply to property placed in service after the change date;
- The mining exploration and development cost adjustments will apply to costs paid or incurred on or after the change date;
- The long-term contract adjustements applies only to contracts entered into on or after the change date;
- The AMT net operation loss applies as if the change date were substituted for January 1, 1987 each place it appears and the day before the change date were substituted for December 31, 1986 each place it appears;
- The limitation on the allowance of negative adjustments based on prior adjusted current earnings (ACE) when determining the corporate ACE adjustment applies only to prior tax years beginning on or after the change date;
- There is not depreciation ACE adjustment; and
- The ACE earnings and profits adjustment and ACE depletion adjustment apply as if the day before the change date were substituted for December 1, 1989.

Exceptions

The seven modifications to the computation of AMT listed above do not apply to any item acquired in certain corporation acquisitions (e.g., an Code Sec. 381 transaction), or to any substituted or carry-over basis property if the property was subject to the modifications while held by the transferor. This is property where the basis of the property in the hands of the corporation is determined by reference to the basis of the property in the hands of the transferor [Code Sec. 55(e)(3)].

¶16,030 ADJUSTED CURRENT EARNINGS

The adjustments described here apply exclusively to corporations.

Corporations add 75 percent of the difference between their *adjusted current earnings (ACE)* (a figure similar to a corporation's earnings and profits used with respect to dividends) and their alternative minimum taxable income (determined without regard to the adjustment required for adjusted current earnings or the alternative tax net operating loss deduction) [Code Sec. 56(g); Reg. § 1.56(g)-1]. If their alternative minimum taxable income (as adjusted) exceeds their adjusted current earnings, 75 percent of the excess is subtracted from their alternative minimum taxable income.

.01 Depreciation

For property placed in service beginning in 1994, corporations use the same depreciation write-offs for ACE that they use in calculating pre-adjustment AMTI [Code Sec. 56(g)(4)(A)(i)]. The alternative depreciation system is used for property placed in service after 1989 and before 1994. This generally includes using the straight line method over a recovery period [Ch. 11]. For depreciation on property placed in service before 1990 to which the MACRS applies, the property's adjusted basis (as determined for purposes of computing alternative minimum taxable income as of the close of the last tax year beginning before 1990) is recovered on a straight line basis over the remaining recovery period using the alternative depreciation system [Code Sec. 56(g)(4)(A)(i)].

Example 16-12: Acme Corp. acquires three depreciable assets. It would depreciate them as follows for ACE purposes if the assets were placed in service after 1989 and before 1994.

Asset	*AMT Depreciation*	*ACE Depreciation*	*Difference*
Truck	$35,000	$20,000	$15,000
Forklift	20,000	10,000	10,000
Computer	15,000	10,000	5,000
ACE depreciation adjustment			$30,000

Its AMT is $4,500 more than it otherwise would be by virtue of the ACE adjustment. Reason: Acme has $600,000 of preadjustment AMTI. Assuming the depreciation adjustment is the only factor in computing ACE, Acme's ACE is $630,000 (preadjustment AMTI plus the $30,000 ACE depreciation adjustment). Acme treats 75 percent of the difference between preadjustment AMTI and ACE ($630,000 – $600,000 = $30,000 × 75 percent = $22,500) as an add-back to be included in Acme's AMTI subject to tax. Thus, Acme's AMT is $4,500 higher (20 percent AMT tax rate times $22,500) by virtue of the ACE adjustment. If Acme had placed the three assets in service after 1993, its AMTI would be reduced by

$22,500 for an AMT savings of $4,500. Reason: Acme could use the same depreciation method for ACE that it uses for preadjustment AMTI.

For property placed in service after 1998, the AMT depreciation adjustment uses the 150 percent declining balance method over the property's shorter regular MACRS recovery period. Prior to 1999, it was based on using the 150 percent declining balance method over the property's class life.

.02 Intangible Drilling Costs

Intangible drilling costs paid or incurred in tax years starting after 1989 are capitalized and amortized over a 60-month period starting with the month the costs were paid or incurred if the taxpayer is an integrated oil company [Code Sec. 56(g) (4) (D) (i)].

.03 Depletion

Depletion is computed using the cost method for property placed in service after 1989 [Code Sec. 56(g) (4) (F)]. For any tax year beginning after 1992, this adjustment is not required by independent oil and gas producers and royalty owners.

Assume part of a taxpayer's alternative tax energy preference deduction is due to depletion or intangible drilling costs. The taxpayer must then reduce basis for computing depletion or intangible drilling costs in subsequent years [Reg. § 1.56(g)-1(s)].

.04 Installment Sales

For installment sales, adjusted current earnings are computed as if the corporation did not use the installment method. However, if the special rule for nondealers applies [Ch. 19], the installment method can be used with respect to the gain for which interest is paid [Code Sec. 56(g) (4) (D) (iv)].

.05 Miscellaneous Adjustments

More information: Refunds of federal income taxes are not included in adjusted current earnings [Reg. § 1.56(g)-1(c) (4) (ii)]. What's more, there is no ACE adjustment when a corporation distributes appreciated property to shareholders if a shareholder assumes a liability in connection with a distribution of property or if a nonshareholder makes a contribution to capital that is excluded from the corporation's income. Any inside buildup from life insurance contracts (minus the portion of premium attributable to insurance coverage) has to be included in ACE.

In the case of any amount (with limited exceptions, such as for cancellation of debt income) excluded from gross income for purposes of computing alternative minimum taxable income but taken into account in determining earnings and profits, that amount is included in income as if it were includible in gross income for purposes of computing alternative minimum taxable income, but is reduced by any deduction that would have been allowable in computing alternative minimum taxable income if that amount were includible in gross income [Code Sec. 56(g) (4) (B)]. No deduction is allowed for any item that is not deductible for purposes of computing earnings and profits [Code Sec. 56(g) (4) (C)].

> ▶ **OBSERVATION:** The ACE adjustment is not required for an S corporation, regulated investment company, real estate investment trust (REIT) or real estate mortgage investment conduit (REMIC) [Code Sec. 56(g)(6)].

.06 Nonstatutory Stock Option Exercise

The IRS has ruled that the compensation deduction that a company is entitled to on exercise of nonstatutory stock options is also allowed for purposes of computing adjusted current earnings for AMT purposes.[13] When a corporation transfers stock on exercise of a nonstatutory compensatory stock option, and the option did not have a readily ascertainable fair market value at grant, the option grantee has compensation income for the difference between the exercise price and the option stock's fair market value at exercise. The corporation gets an equal compensation deduction at that time under Code Sec. 83(h) and Code Sec. 162. In this situation, the IRS says that the corporation's earnings and profits are reduced by the amount of the compensation deduction. As a result, the deduction also is allowed in computing the AMT ACE adjustment.

¶16,035 PREFERENCES

When computing AMT, corporations add tax preference items back to taxable income in the same manner as do individuals [¶16,010]. The following tax preferences and adjustments of a corporate taxpayer are subject to the minimum tax:

1. Accelerated depreciation on property placed in service after 1986 [Code Sec. 56(a)(1)];
2. Accelerated depreciation on pre-1987 real property over straight-line depreciation [Code Sec. 57(a)(6)];
3. Accelerated depreciation on leased personal property (personal holding companies only) [Code Sec. 57(a)(6)];
4. The excess of expensed mining exploration and development costs over 10-year amortization [Code Sec. 56(a)(2)];
5. Any method of reporting income from long-term contracts other than the percentage-of-completion method [Code Sec. 56(a)(3)];
6. Amortization of pre-1987 and post-1986 pollution control facilities [Code Secs. 56(a)(5), 57(a)(6)];
7. Use of the installment method of accounting for dealer sales [Code Sec. 56(a)(6)];
8. 75 percent of the amount by which a corporation's adjusted current earnings exceed its alternative minimum taxable income [Code Sec. 56(c)(1), (g)];
9. Capital construction funds of shipping companies [Code Sec. 56(c)(2)];
10. The special deduction allowed under Code Sec. 833 to Blue Cross/Blue Shield and other tax-exempt insurance providers [Code Sec. 56(c)(3)];
11. Certain depletion deductions [Code Sec. 57(a)(1)];
12. Reserves for losses on bad debts of financial institutions [Code Sec. 57(a)(4)];
13. Intangible drilling costs [Code Sec. 57(a)(2)];
14. Tax-exempt interest on certain private activity bonds [Code Sec. 57(a)(5)]; and
15. Certain net operating loss deductions [Code Sec. 56(a)(4), (d)].

13 Rev. Rul. 2001-1, 2001-1 CB 726.

¶16,040 EXEMPTION AND TAX RATE

Corporations can deduct a $40,000 exemption amount from AMT income. The exemption is phased out in the same manner as for individuals. For every dollar of corporate AMT income above $150,000 (not adjusted for inflation), 25 percent of the exemption is phased out. The exemption is eliminated when AMT income reaches $310,000 [Code Sec. 55(d)(2), (3)(C)].

¶16,045 CREDITS

In computing the adjusted net minimum tax for corporations, the amount of net minimum tax is not reduced by the amount of the net minimum tax for exclusion preferences and adjustments. Rather, the entire amount of their net minimum tax is available for a minimum tax credit carryforward. The adjusted net minimum tax is increased by the disallowed portions of the nonconventional fuels credit and the electric vehicle credit, as in the case of noncorporate taxpayers [Code Sec. 53(d)(1)(B)(iv)].

Corporations use Form 8827, *Credit for Prior Year Minimum Tax—Corporation,* to figure the minimum tax credit, if any, for AMT incurred in prior tax years and to figure any minimum tax credit carryforward.

.01 Accelerating Certain AMT Credits

Corporations or consolidated groups with AMT credits from pre-2007 tax years may continue to accelerate the use of these credits instead of claiming the Code Sec. 168(k) additional bonus depreciation for eligible property. To accelerate the use of these credits, an election must be made under Code Sec. 168(k)(4). Companies that would not benefit from claiming bonus depreciation will find this provision helpful. For further discussion, see ¶14,157.

Inventory

INVENTORIES IN GENERAL

Need for inventory . . . . ¶ 17,001
Income from business . . . . ¶ 17,005
Goods included in inventory . . . . ¶ 17,010

PRICING INVENTORIES: IDENTIFICATION

First-in, first-out method . . . . ¶ 17,015
Last-in, first-out method . . . . ¶ 17,020

PRICING INVENTORIES: VALUATION

Valuing inventories . . . . ¶ 17,025
Costing inventory under LIFO . . . ¶ 17,030
Goods unsellable at normal prices . . . . ¶ 17,035
Book inventories . . . . ¶ 17,040
Uniform capitalization rules (UNICAP) . . . . ¶ 17,045
Methods of valuation in special industries . . . . ¶ 17,050
Methods disapproved . . . . ¶ 17,055
Basis . . . . ¶ 17,060

FARM INVENTORY AND ACCOUNTING

Income from farming . . . . ¶ 17,065
Inventories of farmers and livestock raisers . . . . ¶ 17,070

INVENTORIES IN GENERAL

Inventory consists of goods purchased or manufactured for resale and supplies used in the production of goods or the provision of services. Inventory accounting is necessary to properly match costs with revenues.[1]

The taxpayer's inventory should include all finished or partly finished goods and, in the case of raw materials and supplies, only those which have been acquired for sale or which will physically become a part of merchandise intended for sale. This includes containers, such as kegs, bottles, and cases, whether returnable or not, if title thereto will pass to the purchaser of the product to be sold in the container. Merchandise should be included in the inventory only if the taxpayer has title to the item. Accordingly, the seller should include in his inventory goods under contract for sale but not yet segregated and applied to the contract and goods out upon consignment, but should exclude from inventory goods sold (including containers) if title has passed to the purchaser [Reg. § 1.471-1].

[1] Statement 1 and 2 of Accounting Research Bulletin (ARB) No. 43 (330-10-10-1).

¶17,001 NEED FOR INVENTORY

Code Sec. 471 provides that whenever the use of inventories is necessary to clearly determine the income of the taxpayer, inventories must be maintained by the taxpayer. Reg. § 1.471-1 generally requires a taxpayer to account for inventories when the production, purchase, or sale of merchandise is an income-producing factor in the taxpayer's business.

An inventory is a list of goods on hand held for sale. In every business in which the production, purchase or sale of merchandise is an income-producing factor, you must determine an inventory of unsold goods on hand at the beginning and end of each year in order to clearly reflect income [Code Sec. 471; Reg. § § 1.446-1(a)(4)(i), 1.471-1]. This is necessary because (1) some of the merchandise produced or bought during the year may not be sold during the year or (2) the merchandise sold during the year may include all that was produced or bought during the year, plus some that was produced or bought in a prior year. In some businesses, the use of inventories is not a practical method of figuring income and is not permitted. For example, real estate dealers may not use an inventory method.

Taxpayers who maintain inventory must use accrual accounting for purchases and sales [Ch. 18] [Reg. § 1.446-1(c)(2)(i)].[2]

> ▶ **OBSERVATION:** When organizing a new business and adopting an accounting method, you should consider using an accrual method, even though inventories are not required at the start. In the event that later developments make inventories necessary, there would be no need for you to apply for permission to change accounting methods.

There are four main issues related to the subject of inventory: (1) the extent to which inventory must be used in figuring gross profit [¶17,005], (2) determining what goods must be included [¶17,010], (3) identifying the goods remaining in inventory [¶17,015, ¶17,020], and (4) determining inventory value [¶17,025-¶17,060].

¶17,005 INCOME FROM BUSINESS

The first step in determining a business' net income (or loss) is to figure its gross profit (or loss). Inventories are an important element in calculating the gross profit of many businesses.

Current rules require that costs you incur in producing real or tangible personal property or costs incurred in acquiring property for resale be capitalized. The so-called uniform capitalization rules are covered in ¶17,045.

.01 Gross Profit

Gross profit from a business means the total receipts (less returns and allowances) minus the cost of goods sold. To figure the cost of goods sold, add the costs of inventory at the start of the tax year, merchandise and materials bought or produced

---

[2] Rev. Rul. 69-536, 1969-2 CB 109, as amplified by Rev. Rul. 86-149, 1986-2 CB 67.

during the year and all other costs related to obtaining or producing the merchandise (including all costs that must be capitalized under the uniform capitalization rules). Then you subtract inventory at the close of the tax year from this total. The result is the net cost of goods sold.

The usual items included in the cost of goods sold are direct and indirect labor, materials and supplies consumed, freight-in and a proportion of overhead expenses. The Ninth Circuit[3] and the IRS agree[4] that price rebates or price adjustments can be included in the cost of goods sold, even though they are illegal under state law and are clearly precluded as a business expense deduction. For accounting purposes, you reflect unreimbursed casualty and theft losses of inventory during the year through the increase in the cost of goods sold by properly reporting opening and closing inventories. However, such losses sustained by manufacturers and producers could be excluded from inventory under the uniform capitalization rules [Reg. § 1.263A-1(e)(3)(iii)(D)].

Example 17-1: A business shows receipts of $30,000 ($31,500 gross sales less $1,500 returns and allowances); inventory of goods at the start of the year, $3,700; inventory of goods at the end of the year, $3,000; and merchandise bought during the year for sale, $15,000. Costs incurred during year in connection with the purchase and production of goods for sale are labor, $7,500; material and supplies, $600; and other costs, $200. The gross profit is $6,000. In addition to the amount spent during the year [the excess of receipts ($30,000) over disbursements ($23,300)], the cost of goods that were sold out of the inventory on hand at the beginning of the year must be reflected. The calculation is as follows:

1. Total receipts from business, $31,500, less returns and allowances, $1,500		$30,000
COST OF GOODS SOLD		
2. Inventory at beginning of year	$ 3,700	
3. Merchandise bought for sale	15,000	
4. Labor	7,500	
5. Material and supplies	600	
6. Other costs	200	
7. Total (lines 2 to 6)	$27,000	
8. Less inventory at end of year	3,000	
9. Net cost of goods sold (line 7 minus line 8)		$24,000
10. Gross profit from business		$ 6,000

NOTE: Depreciation and cost depletion may be considered in determining the gross profit of a mining, manufacturing, or merchandising business. When depreciation and cost depletion are included in the cost of goods produced,

[3] *Sobel Wholesale Liquors*, CA-9, 80-2 USTC ¶ 9690, 630 F2d 670, *acq.* 1982-2 CB 2.

[4] Rev. Rul. 82-149, 1982-2 CB 56.

these items should be reported in the same amounts as in your financial report [Reg. § 1.471-11(c)(3)].

▶ **TAX RETURN TIP:** Sole proprietors should compute cost of goods sold in Part II of the Schedule C, Form 1040. Gross profit is figured in Part I of Schedule C. Regular corporations figure cost of goods sold on Schedule A of Form 1120, partnerships on Schedule A of Form 1065.

.02 Donated Items

A deduction may be claimed for inventory—whether manufactured by the taxpayer or acquired for resale—that's donated to a charity. As a general rule, the amount of the deduction is cost or other basis in the property (just as if it had been sold) [Code Sec. 170(e)(1)].

If a taxpayer makes a contribution of property that would have generated ordinary income (or short-term capital gain), the taxpayer's charitable contribution deduction is generally limited to the property's adjusted basis [Code Sec. 170(e)(1)(A)].

How the donation is handled on the return depends on whether the items were manufactured or acquired in the same year they were given away or were in opening inventory at the beginning of the year [Reg. § 1.170A-1(c)(4)].

> **Example 17-2:** A calendar year accrual-basis taxpayer contributed to a church property from inventory having a fair market value of $600. The closing inventory at the end of the prior year included $400 of costs attributable to the acquisition of such property, and in the prior year the taxpayer deducted $50 of administrative and other expenses attributable to such property. Under Code Sec. 170(e)(1)(A) and Reg. § 1.170A-4(A), the amount of the charitable contribution allowed is $400 ($600 -[$600 - $400]). The cost of goods sold to be used in determining gross income may not include the $400 which was included in opening inventory for that year [Reg. § 1.170A-1(c)(4), ex. 1].

Property Not Included in Opening Inventory

Taxpayers may not claim a charitable contribution deduction for property donated in the same year it is acquired or manufactured. The cost or other basis of this property is treated as part of the cost of goods sold in the contribution year [Ch. 9; Ch. 12].

Property Included in Opening Inventory

Taxpayers should claim a charitable deduction for cost or other basis in the donated property. They may also reduce cost of goods sold by the same amount. Non-inventoried overhead costs remain deductible the same way as if the goods had not been donated.

There are special rules for donations of inventory that are used for the care of the ill, needy or infants [Ch. 20] [Code Sec. 170(e)(3)(A)(i); Reg. § 1.170A-4A].

.03 Goods Withdrawn for Personal Use

If taxpayers withdraw goods from inventory for personal use and pay for them with their own funds, the cost of those goods is excluded from the total amount of merchandise bought for sale. It is as if they bought them directly from the wholesaler, rather than taking them from business inventory. If they do not pay for the withdrawn goods, they must make adjustments to avoid understating net profit from the business. Without the adjustments, the cost of goods withdrawn for personal use would be charged against the total sales of the business. How to adjust: Credit the purchases account with the merchandise withdrawn for personal use and charge the proprietors' drawing accounts with the cost of the withdrawn merchandise. A separate account should be kept of all goods withdrawn for personal or family use.

¶17,010 GOODS INCLUDED IN INVENTORY

The IRS may require a taxpayer to use an inventory method of accounting if: (1) the taxpayer produced, purchased, or sold merchandise and (2) the taxpayer's production, purchase, or sale of that merchandise was an income-producing factor. Your inventory includes all finished or partly finished goods. Raw materials and supplies (including containers) are included only if they have been acquired for sale, or will physically become a part of merchandise intended for sale. Merchandise is included only if you have title. Goods you buy (including containers) that are currently in transit are included in your inventory if you have title, even if you do not have physical possession yet. But goods (including containers) out on consignment are included in the seller's inventory [Reg. § 1.471-1]. Your inventory at the start of the tax year should be identical with your preceding year's closing inventory. You may not take depreciation on inventories and stock in trade.

▶ **OBSERVATION:** Determining who has title to inventory may be significant for businesses that value inventory at the lower of cost or market. That's because buyers can't get the tax benefit of price declines until they have title to the goods.

.01 Items Excluded from Inventory

Among the items not included in inventory are capital assets, investments, equipment and similar assets, cash, notes and accounts receivables.

In *Osteopathic Medical Oncology & Hematology, PC*,[5] the Tax Court held that chemotherapy drugs administered by employees of a medical corporation as an indispensable part of its services were not "merchandise" and need not be inventoried under Reg. § 1.471-1. Therefore, the taxpayer properly used the cash method to expense their cost. The IRS has acquiesced in the result of the case and agrees that, under similar circumstances, prescription drugs or similar items administered by healthcare providers are not merchandise within the meaning of Reg. § 1.471-1.

Similarly, in *RACMP Enterprises, Inc.*,[6] the Tax Court held that a concrete contractor was not required to use the accrual method because the materials that were used in providing its services were not merchandise held for sale and so they did not have to be inventoried. However, prior cases and ruling have held the following to be inventoriable merchandise of service businesses: eyeglass frames sold by an optometrist; artificial limbs and orthopedic braces sold by a taxpayer engaged in the business of fitting disabled persons with these devices; caskets sold at cost by an undertaker as

---

[5] *Osteopathic Medical Oncology & Hematology, PC*, 113 TC 376, Dec. 53,629 (1999) (*Acq. in result*, 2001 CB xvi).

[6] *RACMP Enterprises*, 114 TC 211, Dec. 53,825 (2000).

a part of overall funeral services; metals sold in connection with electroplating services; and the cost of the paper and ink used in the production of newspapers.

.02 Sales-Based Vendor Allowances

Buyers of consumer goods often receive discounts if they purchase a certain quantity or volume of goods. A vendor may also offer a discount in order to increase sales of end-of-season merchandise or of merchandise with an approaching expiration date. Reg. § 1.471-3(b) treats trade or other discounts as a reduction in the purchase of the inventory to which they relate, rather than as gross income.

Prop. Reg. § 1.471-3(e) provides that the amount of a sales-based vendor allowance (an allowance, discount, or price rebate a taxpayer earns by selling specific merchandise) is a reduction in the cost of the merchandise sold or deemed to be sold under the inventory cost flow assumption (such as first-in, first-out; last-in, first-out; or a specific goods method) that the taxpayer uses to identify the costs in ending inventory. This amount decreases cost of goods sold and does not reduce the inventory cost or value of goods on hand at the end of the tax year.

In CCA 200945034, the IRS concluded that returned/defective merchandise vendor allowances should be treated as a discount that reduces the cost of inventory under Reg. § 1.471-3(b), even though the allowances were provided in lieu of actual merchandise returns and were characterized as compensation for defective goods. The allowances were akin to a trade discount because they did not depend on proof of actual defects or upon return or disposition of defective merchandise. The allowances were not part of total sales because in negotiating the allowances, the vendors and the taxpayer reached an agreed-upon net selling price for all merchandise. The IRS also concluded that the allowances should reduce the cost of all merchandise purchased from the vendor, not just the merchandise found to be defective, because the allowances were not tied to specific items of defective inventory, but instead related to all purchased merchandise items.

PRICING INVENTORIES: IDENTIFICATION

¶17,015 FIRST-IN, FIRST-OUT METHOD

The *first-in, first-out (FIFO) method* is a way to identify goods in closing inventory. Under this method, the goods first bought are considered those first sold. You can value FIFO inventories at cost or at *lower of cost or market* [¶ 17,025]. The "cost" of the inventory on hand at the end of the year is the cost of the goods last bought. But if the quantity of ending inventory is greater than the amount bought at the last price, the excess is inventoried at the next to the last price, and so on. FIFO may be used if you buy the same type of merchandise at different prices during the year and it is so intermingled that you cannot identify it with specific invoices [Reg. § 1.471-2(d)].

> **Example 17-3:** Assume that the inventory at the end of the year shows 275,000 units of a certain article on hand and the last three invoices for that article are June 29, 100,000 at $1.00; September 30, 80,000 at $1.10; December 10, 125,000 at $0.95. If the goods cannot be identified with specific invoices and FIFO is used,

the inventory would show 125,000 at $0.95, 80,000 at $1.10 and the remainder (70,000) at $1.00. Total inventory: $276,750.

Example 17-4: Assume the same facts as in Example 17-3, except that market value at year end is $1.00 per unit. If the taxpayer uses lower of cost or market to value inventory, the cost of the ending FIFO inventory would be $268,750 (125,000 at $0.95 plus 150,000 at $1.00).

¶17,020 LAST-IN, FIRST-OUT METHOD

When prices are rapidly rising, the election of the *last-in, first-out (LIFO) inventory method* will result in a higher cost of goods sold and a lower taxable gain when the goods are sold. With IRS approval, any taxpayer who must maintain inventory records can use the last-in, first-out (LIFO) method provided it accurately reflects income [Code Sec. 472; Reg. §§1.472-1, 1.472-3]. The goods most recently bought or produced are treated as the first goods sold so that the goods you have on hand at the close of the year are treated as those you bought or produced earliest.

You must value LIFO inventories at cost. If you adopt the LIFO method and the closing inventory of the preceding year is not at cost, you may have to make an adjustment to restate opening inventory. Adjustments are required to write down from actual cost "subnormal goods" to reverse writedowns of normal goods that are recorded at market value.[7] But you can spread the income attributable to the preceding year's writedown adjustments over three years, starting with the LIFO election year [Code Sec. 472(d)].

.01 Differences Between Inventory Treatment Using LIFO Versus FIFO

Under LIFO, you treat the inventory at the end of the year as being composed of the earliest acquired goods. Under FIFO, you treat inventory at the end of the year as composed of the latest acquired goods [¶17,015].

Example 17-5: Assuming the same facts in each case, closing inventory is figured under (1) FIFO and (2) LIFO as follows:

	(1) First-in, first-out	*(2) Last-in, first-out*
Sales 5,000 units@ $4.00	$20,000	$20,000
Cost of sales:		
Opening inventory (2,000 units@ $1.00)	2,000	$ 2000
Purchases (5,000 units@ $3.00)	15,000	15,000
Total	$17,000	$17,000

[7] Rev. Proc. 76-6, 1976-1 CB 545; Rev. Rul. 76-282, 1976-2 CB 137.

Less: Closing inventory:				
(FIFO) 2,000 units@ $3.00	6,000	11,000		
(LIFO) 2,000 units@ $1.00			2,000	15,000
Gross profit on sales		$ 9,000		$ 5,000

Example 17-6: Assume that there are 150 units in inventory at the end of the year and purchases during the period are:

1st purchase 100 units @ $1.00	$100
2nd purchase 200 units @ $1.10	$220
3rd purchase 250 units @ $1.20	$300
4th purchase 100 units @ $1.25	$125

For the first-in, first-out method., the goods on hand are considered to have been acquired by the most recent purchases; therefore the inventory is composed of:

From 4th purchase: 100 units @ $1.25	$125
From 3rd purchase: 50 units @ $1.20	60
Cost of inventory	$185

For the last-in, first-out method, the sales are assumed to consist of the last goods purchased, and the inventory at the end of the period is assumed to consist of any opening inventory and the earliest purchases. Therefore the inventory is composed of:

From the 1st purchase: 100 units @ $1.00	$100
From the 2nd purchase: 50 units @ $1.10	55
Cost of inventory	$155

Using the LIFO method may be desirable in a period of rising prices. It produces a smaller profit than the FIFO method by eliminating from income the effect of an increase in the market value of the inventory. Businesses most likely to benefit by the LIFO method are those in which:

- The value of the inventory is large compared with other assets and sales;
- Production covers a long period; and
- The price of goods included in inventory is subject to wide fluctuations.

But in a period of declining prices, the reverse is true, since LIFO users will be unable to offset a decline in the market value of their inventory against their income.

.02 Application for, and Use of, LIFO

Elect application of the LIFO inventory method by submitting Form 970, *Application to Use LIFO Inventory Method,* or a statement acceptable to the IRS, to the return for the first tax year you use the method [Reg. § 1.472-3]. If this method is used for the first time in valuing closing inventories, file Form 970 (or an acceptable alternative attachment) with the return. Once adopted, the taxpayer must continue to use the LIFO method unless the IRS requires a change to another method, or authorizes a change that is requested by filing Form 3115 [Ch. 18] [Reg. § 1.472-5].

Elect LIFO for the entire inventory or just for specified items (such as raw materials). In the LIFO application, specify which part of the inventory will be affected by election of the LIFO method. The IRS, however, can require use of the LIFO method for other items in the taxpayer's inventory if it finds this is necessary for a clear reflection of income. It may also require use of LIFO for similar goods of any other trades or businesses [Reg. § 1.472-2(i)]. With a new taxable entity (e.g., a corporation), approval to use LIFO is required even if the new business is formed from companies that had permission to use LIFO and the transaction was tax free.

Taxpayers cannot change to *dollar value LIFO* [¶ 17,030] from another LIFO method without IRS consent. Special adjustments are required when a change is allowed or when a change in the content of pools is allowed or required [Reg. § § 1.472-8(f) (1),(2)].

LIFO Conformity

The IRS will invalidate a LIFO election if during the election year you use FIFO or any other valuation method for your financial reports [Code Sec. 472(c); Reg. § 1.472-2(e)].[8] This rule is applicable to "financially related corporations" (specially defined for these purposes) as if they were single businesses [Code Sec. 472(g)(1)]. LIFO taxpayers may use other inventory methods in financial and credit statements to explain or supplement the primary presentation of income in those statements [Reg. § 1.472-2(e)(i)(v)]. Also, the IRS has held that the LIFO conformity requirement doesn't apply to financial forecasts.[9] You may use the dollar-value method of pricing inventory [Ch 17,030] for income tax purposes while continuing to use the specific goods method for purposes of financial reporting, without violating the "LIFO conformity" rule. Both are LIFO methods [Code Secs. 472(c), (e); Reg. § 1.472-2(e)(8)].[10]

PRICING INVENTORIES: VALUATION

¶17,025 VALUING INVENTORIES

The two most popular ways to value inventories are:

- Cost; and
- Cost or market, whichever is lower [Reg. § 1.471-2(c)].

The method you use to value inventories must conform to the best accounting practice in your trade or business, clearly reflect your income and be consistent from year to year [Reg. § 1.471-2(b)].

A new business entity may adopt either method. Once a method is adopted, the taxpayer may not change it without IRS permission. The adopted method must be used

[8] Rev. Rul. 75-49, 1975-1 CB 151.

[9] Rev. Rul. 88-84, 1988-2 CB 124.

[10] Rev. Rul. 85-129, 1985-2 CB 158.

for the entire inventory. Exceptions exist for (1) goods inventoried by the last-in, first-out method [¶ 17,020], and (2) animals inventoried by the unit-livestock-price [¶ 17,070] method [Reg. § 1.471-2(d)]. Consistency is important in valuing inventory from year to year.

.01 Single Method for More Than One Trade or Business

If you have more than one trade or business, the IRS may require you to use the same valuation method for similar goods in different trades or businesses, if necessary to clearly reflect income [Reg. § 1.471-2(d)].

.02 Change of Inventory Valuation Method

To change your method of inventory valuation, file Form 3115 to request the IRS's permission within the tax year for which the change is to be effective [Reg. § 1.446-1(e)(3)]. The IRS will not permit the change if tax reduction is the principal reason for the request.

.03 Inventories at Cost

The cost of merchandise bought during the year is the invoice price minus trade or other discounts, plus freight and other charges paid to obtain the goods [Reg. § 1.471-3]. To this net invoice price should be added transportation or other necessary charges incurred in acquiring possession of the goods. In the case of merchandise produced by the taxpayer, cost is defined as (1) the cost of raw materials and supplies entering into or consumed in connection with the product, (2) expenditures for direct labor, and (3) indirect production costs incident to, and necessary for, the production of the particular article, including in such indirect production costs an appropriate portion of management expenses, but not including any cost of selling or return on capital, whether by way of interest or profit [Reg. § 1.471-3(b)].

The cost of goods on hand at the beginning of the tax year or other accounting period is the amount at which they were included in the closing inventory of the preceding period unless the taxpayer has changed his method of accounting for inventories to conform with the uniform capitalization rules of Code Sec. 263A [See ¶ 17,045 for further discussion of these rules].

Any goods in an inventory that are unsellable at normal prices or in the normal way because of damage, imperfections, shop wear, changes of style, odd or broken lots, or other similar causes, including second-hand goods taken in exchange, should be valued, if such goods consist of raw materials held for use or consumption, upon a reasonable basis taking into consideration the usability and condition of the goods, but in no case shall such value be less than the scrap value [Reg. § 1.471-2(c)].

Cash Discounts

Cash discounts are reductions in the invoice cost attributable to prompt payment. Vendors offer a reduction in purchase price if payment is made within a specified period. Cash discounts that approximate a fair interest rate may be treated in either of two ways, but you must be consistent. You may either:

- *Deduct cash discounts from purchases.* If you adopt this method, cash discounts will reduce the cost of goods sold. The invoice price after the cash discount is the price at which the goods in the inventory are valued.
- *Credit cash discounts to a discount account.* If you adopt this method, the credit balance in this account at the end of the tax year is included in income. The cost of goods sold is not reduced by cash discounts taken.[11]

If the second method is used, the IRS says that you may not deduct the average amount of cash discount received from the invoice price of the merchandise on hand at the close of the tax year[12] [Reg. § 1.471-3(b)]. In contrast to the IRS, which only permits the actual discount to be taken into account, the courts have taken a more lenient approach.[13]

Merchandise Manufactured by Taxpayer

Generally, the cost of goods manufactured is determined under the uniform capitalization rules. An exception to the uniform capitalization rules applies to personal property purchased for resale by a taxpayer that has had average annual gross receipts of $10,000,000 or less for the preceding three tax years. Such taxpayers will determine the cost of goods purchased according to their inventory price less trade or other discounts plus freight-in (freight, delivery, and other necessary costs of acquiring possession). In situations where the uniform capitalization rules do not apply, the cost of goods manufactured is the total of: (1) the cost of the raw materials and supplies consumed in the process, (2) the expenditures for direct labor, including overtime costs,[14] and (3) indirect production costs, including a reasonable proportion of management expenses, but excluding all selling expenses [Reg. § 1.471-3(c)].

> **NOTE:** Loss on the sale of supplier's stock you buy to get merchandise for use in your business is part of your inventory cost, not a capital loss.[15] But you must prove that you bought the stock to get merchandise.[16]

Inventory Capitalization Rules

In general, taxpayers must determine the cost of goods manufactured under the uniform capitalization rules. As a result, taxpayers must now capitalize into the cost of products certain other indirect costs that were previously classified as period costs and, so, were deductible at the end of the accounting period in which they were incurred. As a result, they are included in the cost of inventory and deducted as the inventory is sold. This often means costs are deductible later than under the old rules. The capitalization rules [¶ 17,045] apply both to merchandise bought for resale and to goods manufactured by a taxpayer for resale. Under the uniform capitalization rules, depreciation on manufacturing equipment or plant is required to be included in the cost of manufacturing the goods. Other expenditures that are part of the cost of goods manufactured include: (1) Cost of containers and packages that are an integral part of

---

[11] Rev. Rul. 73-65, 1973-1 CB 216.

[12] Rev. Rul. 69-619, 1969-2 CB 111.

[13] *Leedom & Worrall Co.*, 10 BTA 825, Dec. 3563; *J.M. Radford Grocery Co.*, 19 BTA 1023, Dec. 6066 (1930) *(Nonacq.)*.

[14] Rev. Rul. 69-373, 1969-2 CB 110.

[15] *Western Wine & Liquor Co.*, 18 TC 1090, Dec. 19,207 (1952), *appeal dismissed*, 205 F2d 420 *(Acq.)*; *Clark*, 19 TC 48, Dec. 19,247 (1952) *(Acq.)*.

[16] *McGhee Upholstery Co.*, 12 TCM 1455, Dec. 20,060(M) (1953).

the product manufactured, and (2) Overhead expenses, including rent, heat, light, power, insurance, taxes, maintenance, labor, and supervision [Reg. § 1.263A-1(e)(3)]. Reimbursements of federal excise taxes where the merchandise to which the reimbursements relate is included in ending inventory is treated as a reduction of cost. Cost does not include illegal bribes and kickbacks, fines and penalties, or treble damage payments under antitrust laws.

.04 Inventories at Lower of Cost or Market

For normal goods in inventory, market means the aggregate of the current bid prices prevailing at the date of the inventory of the basic elements of cost reflected in inventories of goods purchased and on hand, goods in process of manufacture, and finished manufactured goods on hand [Reg. § 1.471-4(a)]. The basic elements of cost include direct materials, direct labor, and indirect costs required to be included in inventories by the taxpayer.

If the company is actually selling items at less than the original or replacement costs, then it can write down the items to the actual selling prices. But you cannot use this selling price exception unless you can show an item-by-item breakdown of costs and sales prices-even if your company is conforming to the best accounting practices of the industry.[17] The rules for determining market value apply to goods bought and on hand, as well as to the basic elements of cost (materials, labor and overhead) for items in the process of being manufactured or finished and on hand. It does not apply to goods on hand or in process for delivery on a contract at fixed prices, if the contract legally cannot be canceled. These goods must be inventoried at cost [Reg. § 1.471-4].

▶ **OBSERVATION:** The lower of cost or market method is a conservative accounting method for balance sheet and credit qualifications, but not necessarily so for income tax purposes. Any income reductions for the year in which inventory is reduced to market are offset by a comparable decrease in the cost of goods sold in the next year. Before adopting this method, your business should consider the risk of falling into a higher tax bracket that might increase its total tax liability over a two-year period.

On the date the inventory is being valued, you compare the market value of each article with its cost. The lower figure is taken as the inventory value [Reg. § 1.471-4(c)]. For this comparison, the cost of goods in the closing inventory that were also on hand at the beginning of the year is their opening inventory price.[18]

Example 17-7: At the close of the year, a taxpayer had on hand:

	Cost	Market
Bricks	$2,000	$2,400
Coal	2,000	1,700

The bricks would be inventoried at $2,000; the coal at $1,700.

Example 17-8: 100 tons of the commodity were bought at $74 a pound on August 15 and on October 1 another 50 tons were bought at $64 a pound.

---

[17] *Tog Shop, Inc.*, DC-GA, 89-2 USTC ¶ 9554, 721 FSupp 300.

[18] Rev. Rul. 70-19, 1970-1 CB 123.

The entire 150 tons were on hand at the close of the year. The market value at the close of the year was $72 a pound. If cost or market, whichever is lower is used, the 100 tons would be inventoried at market or $72 a pound; the 50 tons would be inventoried at cost, or $64 a pound.

.05 Shrinkage Estimates for Inventory

If a physical inventory is taken at year end, the amount of shrinkage for the year is known. If a physical inventory is not taken at year end, shrinkage through year end will be based on an estimate or not taken into account until the following year.

The courts have approved use of the shrinkage accrual method for adjusting inventory. In one case, the court approved a supermarket and drug store operator that did not physically count inventory at year-end, but used *cycle counting*, which means that they conducted physical inventory counts on a rotating basis throughout the year.[19] In cycle counting, the excess of book inventory records over inventory amounts determined by physically counting the inventory is treated as shrinkage (e.g., bookkeeping errors, breakage, theft). The court approved the taxpayer's computation of the annual shrinkage rate as a percentage of gross sales, taking into consideration facts such as merchandising techniques, store size, and regional differences. This shrinkage rate was used to reduce inventories and increase costs of goods sold.

In another case where a discount retailer also used the shrinkage accrual method, the Tax Court concluded that the taxpayer's method of determining estimated shrinkage clearly reflected income and conformed to widely accepted industry practice.[20] In a third case involving a national department store, the appellate court held that the method the national department store chain used to maintain book inventories that estimated inventory shrinkage at year-end based on a percentage of sales clearly reflected income.[21]

A business may determine its year-end closing inventory by taking a reasonable deduction for shrinkage (e.g. inventory loss due to undetected theft, breakage, bookkeeping errors) [Code Sec. 471(b)]. As a result of this provision, businesses are saved from the burden of actually having to take a year-end inventory in order to determine if any inventory shrinkage has occurred.

The deduction for the estimated inventory shrinkage may be claimed only if the business:

1. Normally takes a physical count of its inventories at each business location on a regular and consistent basis; and
2. Makes proper adjustments to its inventories and to its estimating methods to the extent its estimates are more or less than the actual shrinkage [Code Sec. 471(b)].

Example 17-9: ABCorp manufactured and sold paper clips. On January 2, ABCorp took an inventory of its paper clips. No other inventories were taken

[19] *Kroger Co.*, 73 TCM 1637, Dec. 51,803(M), TC Memo. 1997-2.

[20] *Wal-Mart Stores, Inc.*, CA-8, 98-2 USTC ¶50,645, 153 F3d 650.

[21] *Dayton Hudson Corp.*, CA-8, 98-2 USTC ¶50,644, 153 F3d 660.

that year. When ABCorp filed its tax return for the year, the corporation claimed a deduction for inventory shrinkage. ABCorp failed to qualify for the inventory shrinkage deduction because it did not take inventories on a regular and consistent basis as required in Code Sec. 471(b)(1).

Example 17-10: Same facts as in Example 17-9 except that ABCorp took an inventory every three months with the last inventory taking place on October 2. When ABCorp filed its tax return for the year, the corporation claimed a deduction for inventory shrinkage. ABCorp will qualify for the inventory shrinkage deduction in this example because it did take inventories on a regular and consistent basis as required in Code Sec. 471(b)(1).

The IRS has provided guidance on: (1) how to change accounting methods for estimating inventory shrinkage; and (2) the workings of the retail safe harbor method which may be used by taxpayers to estimate inventory shrinkage.[22] The retail safe harbor method was established for taxpayers who are primarily engaged in the resale of personal property to the general public to use where physical inventories are normally taken at each location at least annually. The IRS establishes procedures to follow if a retailer wants to change to the retail safe harbor method of accounting (or to some other method where the taxpayer's present method does not estimate inventory shrinkage). If these procedures are followed the change will be automatic.

The retail safe harbor method uses a historical ratio of shrinkage to sales to estimate the inventory shrinkage that occurred between the date of the last physical inventory and the end of the tax year. This historical ratio is based on the actual shrinkage established by all physical inventories taken during the most recent three tax years and the sales for related periods. The most recent three tax years include the tax year for which the shrinkage estimate is to be made and the two prior tax years.

Taxpayers using the last-in first-out (LIFO) inventory method must allocate shrinkage among their various LIFO inventory pools in a reasonable and consistent manner.

You will need to request IRS consent to change to a method of accounting for estimating inventory shrinkage in computing ending inventory using: (1) The retail safe harbor method regardless of whether your present method of accounting estimates inventory shrinkage; or (2) A method other than the retail safe harbor method, provided your present method does not estimate inventory shrinkage and your new method of accounting (that estimates inventory shrinkage) clearly reflects income. Follow the IRS procedures in requesting this change.[23]

.06 Rolling-Average Method

The IRS traditionally has viewed rolling-average inventory valuation as a method of accounting that does not clearly reflect income, especially when inventory is held for several years or costs fluctuate substantially, but in Rev. Proc. 2008-43,[24] the IRS announced that the rolling-average method of valuing inventories for financial accounting purposes clearly reflected income for federal income tax purposes provided a

[22] Rev. Proc. 98-29, 1998-1 CB 857.

[23] Rev. Proc. 98-29, 1998-1 CB 857.

[24] Rev. Proc. 2008-43, 2008-2 CB 186.

taxpayer meets one of the two newly created safe harbors. The IRS also provided procedures by which a taxpayer may obtain automatic consent to change to a rolling-average method.

Rolling-Average Method Safe Harbors

A taxpayer's use of the rolling-average method for financial accounting purposes to value inventories for federal income tax purposes will be deemed to clearly reflect income if:

1. The taxpayer recomputes the rolling average cost of an inventory item on one of the following bases: (a) each time the taxpayer purchases or produces an additional unit or units of that item; or (b) on a regular basis but no less frequently than once per month; and
2. The taxpayer satisfies one of the following conditions:
   a. The variance percentage, as determined under section 4.02 of this revenue procedure, does not exceed one percent; or
   b. The entire inventory of a taxpayer's trade or business turns at least four times per year, as determined under section 4.03 of this revenue procedure.

Determination of variance percentage. The variance percentage is determined by:

1. Subtracting the cost of the ending inventory of the trade or business computed using the taxpayer's rolling-average method from the cost of the ending inventory of the trade or business computed using either the FIFO method or the specific identification method to determine the variance; and then
2. Dividing the variance by the aggregate rolling-average cost of the inventory.

Determination of inventory turns. The number of times that the entire inventory of a taxpayer's trade or business turns during a tax year is equal to the cost of goods sold divided by average inventory (average of beginning and ending inventory). A taxpayer that uses a LIFO cost-flow assumption for tax purposes must calculate inventory turns using rolling-average cost and a FIFO cost-flow assumption.

Procedures for Changing Methods of Accounting

Taxpayers are granted IRS consent to change to a rolling-average method of accounting.

¶17,030 COSTING INVENTORY UNDER LIFO

Value the opening inventory for the first tax year that LIFO is used at the actual cost of the goods on hand. The unit cost for an item is the average of the cost of all items, as if they were all bought at the same time at the same price [Reg. § 1.472-2(c)]. If this unit cost is $5 and the inventory remained constant at 1,000 units, the LIFO inventory value would always be $5,000 because these first units would always be considered to remain in stock.

If the closing inventory is larger than the opening inventory, the cost of the increase, or increment, generally is determined from purchases or manufacturing costs during the year in one of three ways: cost of earliest units, cost of latest units or average cost. The IRS may accept another method that correctly reflects income [Reg. § 1.472-2(d)].

Example 17-11: Bell Co. adopted the LIFO method. The opening inventory was 10 units at $10 a unit. During the year, Bell Co. bought 10 units: 1 in January at $11, 2 in April at $12, 3 in July at $13, and 4 in October at $14. The closing inventory had 15 units. Depending on the method used for valuing inventory increases, the closing inventory will be:

	(a) Most recent purchases			(b) In order of acquisition			(c) At an annual average	
10 @	$10	$100	10 @	$10	$100	10 @	$10	$100
4 @	$14 (October)	$56	1 @	$11 (January)	$11	5 @	$13 (130/10)	$65
1 @	$13 (July)	$13	2 @	$12 (April)	$24			
			2 @	$13 (July)	$26			
Totals:								
15		$169	15		$161	15		$165

Example 17-12: Bell Co.'s closing inventory for the following year is 13 units. This is a decrease of 2 units from the opening inventory from Example 17-11. The value of the reduced inventory must be determined from the 15 units in opening inventory in the order of acquisition and by the method used to value inventory increases. The closing inventory value depends on the method used to value the increases. If the increase for the preceding tax year was taken:

	(a) By reference to most recent purchases			(b) In order of acquisition			(c) On average basis	
10 @	$10	$100	10 @	$10	$100	10 @	$10	$100
1 @	$13	$13	1 @	$11	$11	3 @	$13	$39
2 @	$14	$28	2 @	$12	$24			
Totals								
13		$141	13		$135	13		$139

.01 Manufacturers and Raw Materials

Manufacturers, who have elected the LIFO inventory method for raw materials under Code Sec. 472(a), are required to: (1) elect that method for a *good* or *goods,* which may include one or more raw material goods that will become part of the merchandise intended for sale, and (2) make the LIFO election for the entire good or goods (not for only a part of the good or goods) [Reg. § 1.472-1(c)]. This means that a taxpayer who was in a business involving rebuilding and selling used automobile engines to auto repair shops could use FIFO to value used engines blocks that were one of the raw materials of the remanufactured engines and can elect to use LIFO for specified goods subject to inventory. The use of LIFO, however, had to be limited to one or more of the raw materials in a class of goods that constitute tangible, movable objects rather than labor and overhead.[25] This means that LIFO could be adopted for just the raw materials that go into the finished products, or it may be used for everything that goes into the finished products, but it is not available for any other combination. You may figure the cost of finished goods and goods in process any way that clearly reflects income; but you may need to make adjustments for raw materials integrated in the goods [Reg. § 1.472-1(c)].

Example 17-13: Opening inventory consists only of 20 units of raw material at 6¢ a unit. Raw material bought during the year cost 10¢ a unit. Closing inventory has 12 units of raw material and 12 units of finished goods. Processing cost is 4¢ a unit, overhead 1¢ a unit. The closing inventory value is figured:

Raw materials	Raw material	Finished goods
12 at 6¢	72¢	
8 at 6¢		$ .48
4 at 10¢		.40
Processing cost (4¢ × 12)		.48
Overhead (1¢ × 12)		.12
	72¢	$1.48

Dollar-Value Costing

This method of costing LIFO inventories uses dollar values rather than physical quantities of goods. The inventory is viewed in terms of pools, not individual items. Pools may be classified by broad product categories, by departments, or by any other logical grouping. The *dollar-value LIFO* method requires you to match dollar values in the closing and opening inventories at base year (your first LIFO year) prices. You then make adjustments to reflect increases or decreases in current prices.

The *base year cost* is established for the entire inventory in the *pool* at the beginning of the first tax year the method is adopted. This pool remains the same for all later years unless the IRS approves a change as a change of accounting method [Ch. 18]. The base-year cost is the total cost of all items in the pool [Reg. § 1.472-8(a)].

You generally must establish the closing inventory value for the pool by the *"double extension" method.* However, the District Director may accept a link chain method if the double extension method is impractical. In addition, closing inventory value for the pool can be established by an inventory price index method, explained below. If this method is used, you do not have to show that the double extension is impractical. You must attach a detailed explanation of the link method, or inventory price index method, or any other index method to the return for the first year that dollar value is adopted [Reg. § 1.472-8(e) (1), (2) and (3)].

The Double Extension Method

The *double extension method* is basically a way to state, in dollar amounts, the value of the increase or decrease in closing inventory in relation to the base year cost [Reg.

[25] *Consolidated Mfg., Inc.*, CA-10, 2001-1 USTC ¶ 50,400, 249 F3d 1231.

§ 1.472-8(e)(2)]. The base year unit cost of a new item entering the pool is its price or production cost; but the IRS may accept a reconstructed base year unit cost if necessary.

To apply the method, you find the cost of the closing inventory at the unit cost for the base year and the unit cost for the current year, then divide the total current cost by the total cost at base year unit cost to get a ratio that is applied to increases in inventory for the year. The current year cost may be consistently determined by one of the methods described above for valuing inventory increases or decreases (e.g., cost of earliest units, latest units or average cost).

There is an inventory increase for the year when the total dollar value of the closing inventory at base year unit costs exceeds the base year cost. You convert the inventory increase to current dollar value by applying the ratio, or percentage, derived from the comparative base year and current year costs. This figure is the LIFO value of the increase. You record and account for each year's increase as a separate unit.

There is an inventory decrease when the closing inventory for a year is less than the opening inventory with both computed at base year unit costs. Decreases or liquidations of inventory must be absorbed first by the latest previous increase and then successively by the next earlier increases until the decrease is fully absorbed. The ratio established for a particular year's increase is also used when that increase is liquidated. Base year inventory is reduced only when the total of all decreases is more than the total of all increases.

Example 17-14: Electing the dollar value LIFO method for the base year. Bay Co. properly establishes a pool for items A, B, and C. The inventory on January 1 is: A-1,000 units at a cost of $5 a unit; B-2,000 units at $4; C-500 units at $2; for a total base year cost of $14,000. The total current year cost of the December 31st closing inventory, determined from items last bought during the year, is $24,250. This includes: A-3,000 units at a unit cost of $6; B-1,000 units at $5; C-500 units at $2.50. At the base year unit costs (A-$5, B-$4, C-$2) the closing inventory cost is $20,000. The closing inventory value is $21,275 computed as follows:

1. Closing inventory at base year cost	$20,000
Base year inventory cost	$14,000
Increase in inventory*	$ 6,000

2. $24,250 (inventory at current year unit cost)/$20,000 (inventory at base year unit cost) = 121.25% (ratio of current cost to base year cost)

* If cost of the closing inventory at base year unit costs were equal to or less than base year inventory cost, that would be the closing inventory value.

	Closing inventory base year cost	Ratio of current year cost to base year cost	Closing inventory value
Base cost	$14,000	100%	$14,000
Increase	6,000	121.25%	7,275
Total	$20,000		$21,275

Example 17-15: On December 31, of the second year, Bay Co. of Example 17-14 has a current year cost of $27,000 and a cost of $18,000 at base year unit costs for its closing inventory. The base year cost of the opening inventory was $20,000 so the $2,000 reduction in inventory reduces the $6,000 increase. The closing inventory value for the second year is $18,850 computed as follows:

	Closing inventory base year cost	Ratio of current year cost to base year cost	Closing inventory value
Base cost	$14,000	100%	$14,000
Increase	4,000	121.25%	4,850
Total	$18,000		$18,850

Manufacturers' and Processors' Pools

Manufacturers' and processors' pools include the entire inventory of a natural business unit. This may be an entire business or a separate division of a business. The circumstances surrounding the operation of an organization determine whether it has one or more natural business units. You can establish separate pools for substantially similar inventory items that are not part of a natural business pool. Goods bought from others for wholesaling or retailing must be pooled as they are for merchandisers [Reg. § 1.472-8(b)].[26] The Tax Court has held that inventory items purchased as part of a bargain purchase of a business constituted different items than subsequently produced and otherwise identical inventory.[27]

Merchandisers' Pools

Merchandisers' pools must be established by major lines, types, or classes of goods, according to customary business classification. One example is a department of a department store [Reg. § 1.472-8(c)].

Inventory Price Index Method (IPIC)

If this method of accounting is elected, use government-issued consumer or producer price indexes to compute the LIFO value of a dollar-value inventory pool. Once adopted, it applies to all inventory items reported using the LIFO method. Most taxpayers can establish dollar-value LIFO pools under special rules and may elect to compute an inventory price index for valuing the pools by reference to the stated price change percentages contained in consumer or producer price indexes that are published by the federal government [Reg. § 1.472-8(e)(3)]. Use of the inventory price computation method allows taxpayers to use price indexes prepared by the United States Bureau of Labor Statistics (BLS) instead of computing it on their own. The inventory price index method is preferred by taxpayers because the IRS will accept it as an accurate and reliable manner of computing an index [Code Sec. 472(f); Reg. § 1.472-8(e)(3)(i)].

The appropriate inventory price indexes are used to value pools by referring to 80 percent (100 percent for eligible small businesses, defined the same way as for the adoption of simplified dollar-value LIFO (discussed below) of the price changes found in

[26] Rev. Rul. 82-192, 1982-2 CB 102.

[27] *Hamilton Industries, Inc.*, 97 TC 120, Dec. 47,501 (1991). *But see* TAM 9328002 (Mar. 5, 1993) (separate LIFO pools must be maintained for goods acquired in bargain purchase).

the selected indexes. After an index election is made, you can withdraw it only with IRS consent [Code Sec. 472(f); Reg. § 1.472-8(e)(3)]. In order to adopt the IPIC method of accounting, Form 970 must be filed and contain a list of:

- Dollar-value pools, including a description of the items in each pool;
- The United States Bureau of Labor Statistics (BLS) table selected for each pool;
- The representative month, if applicable;
- The BLS categories to which items in a pool will be assigned;
- The method of assigning items to categories; and
- The method of computing the IPI (that is, the double-extension or link-chain IPIC method) [Reg. § 1.472-8(e)(3)(iv)(A)].

.02 Simplified Dollar-Value LIFO

There is a *simplified dollar-value LIFO election* for businesses with average annual gross receipts for the preceding three-year period of $5 million or less [Code Sec. 474]. It is designed to allow small businesses to use LIFO without undue complexities or excessive compliance costs.

This simplified LIFO method calls for inventory pools grouped by Bureau of Labor Statistics (BLS) Producer and Consumer general price index categories. Annual cost changes are indexed by reference to BLS monthly published indexes. Cumulative indexes, developed by the link-chain method, are also used.

Businesses that previously elected the single pool method can continue using it under prior law rules or can revoke it without IRS consent. But you cannot use the new simplified method and the old single pool method at the same time.

Inventory values using simplified dollar-value LIFO generally follow the usual rules found in the regulations for regular dollar-value LIFO inventories [Reg. § 1.472-8]. However, the main differences are:

- The way in which inventory items are pooled;
- Use of published indexes to find an annual index component for each pool; and
- The technique used to compute the cumulative index for a pool for any given year.

Establishing Inventory Pools

Retailers using the retail method group their pools by the 11 general categories in the BLS consumer price index for all urban consumers. All other taxpayers use the 15 general two-digit categories in the monthly BLS producers' prices and price indexes for commodity groupings and individual items. You measure the annual change in costs for each general category pool as a whole by the percentage change for the year in the published index for that category. Present dollar inventory values are discounted back to equivalent values in the base year through the link-chain approach (a current cumulative index is constructed from year-by-year index components), rather than by the double-extension method (comparing the dollar amount of inventory items measured in present year prices against the dollar amount of the same inventory items in base year prices).

Selecting an Index

You select a month of the year whose index you will use to measure annual changes in your pool. You must use the same month in later years unless the IRS consents to a change. Originally released BLS index figures are used, unless corrected figures are published before you file your return-the index figure that's actually used for the year must be adhered to next year (any over- or undervaluation will adjust itself automatically at the end of next year).

Rules Applying to Year of Change

The first year that the simplified dollar-value LIFO method is used is the base year. Converting to this method may involve adjustments, but doesn't require IRS consent. On a change from FIFO, you assign inventory items to the new pools, combine their values, and the total is your base year layer. As with other LIFO methods, a change from a method that allows inventories to be stated at less than cost (e.g., FIFO) requires you to restore any previous writedowns from cost to income. (The base year dollar values will include these amounts.) Conversion from another LIFO method is done similarly, but preexisting LIFO layers must be preserved and prior year layers restated in base year dollars by comparing the prices paid to the item's present value.

.03 Qualified Liquidations of LIFO Inventories

Generally, inventory replacement adjustments are allowed for liquidations caused by an embargo, international boycott, Energy Department regulations or requests, or a major foreign trade interruption. The Treasury Secretary acknowledges this by publishing a notice in the Federal Register that replacement of any class of goods is difficult or impossible [Code Sec. 473(d)(3)].

Basis

Goods that replace LIFO qualified liquidated inventory are taken into the purchases account and reflected in closing inventory at the inventory cost basis of the goods replaced. However, the cost of replacement goods is determined in the order of acquisition (latest units) when the closing inventory is larger than the opening inventory and the liquidated inventory has not been completely replaced before the replacement year ends.

A replacement period is limited to three years after the liquidation year. It may be shorter if the IRS so specifies.

Adjustments

If you replace liquidated goods, in part or in full, and reflect them in the closing inventory, you can increase or decrease income for the liquidating year by the difference between the cost of the replaced goods and the LIFO basis of the liquidated inventory. [Code Sec. 473(b)].

.04 Vehicle Pool Method

In Rev. Proc. 2008-23,[28] the IRS provides an alternative dollar-value LIFO pooling method, the Vehicle-Pool Method, for retail dealers and wholesale distributors (collec-

---

[28] Rev. Proc. 2008-23, IRB 2008-12, 664.

tively, "resellers") of cars and light-duty trucks. This revenue procedure also provides the exclusive procedures for obtaining automatic consent to change to the Vehicle-Pool Method.

Under the Vehicle-Pool Method, a reseller with new vehicles (i.e., new cars, new light-duty trucks, and new crossover vehicles, including SUVs, vans, minivans, and other similar vehicles) may establish a New Vehicle pool for all new vehicles. In addition, under this method, a reseller with used vehicles (i.e., used cars, used light-duty trucks, and used crossover vehicles, including SUVs, vans, minivans, and other similar vehicles) may establish a Used Vehicle pool for all used vehicles. No pool established under this revenue procedure may include a vehicle with a gross vehicle weight that exceeds 14,000 pounds. A reseller is granted IRS consent to change to the Vehicle-Pool Method.

¶17,035 GOODS UNSELLABLE AT NORMAL PRICES

Goods in inventory that cannot be sold at normal prices or used in the normal way should be valued at *bona fide selling prices* less the direct cost of disposition. However, in no case should taxpayers write down goods below scrap value. This applies whether the inventory is taken at cost or at cost or market. *Bona fide selling price* is the actual offering price of the goods during a period ending not later than 30 days after the inventory date. Goods may be unsellable at normal prices because of imperfection, shop wear, change of style, odd lots, or other causes, including second-hand goods taken in exchange [Reg. § 1.471-2(c)].

The Supreme Court has ruled that manufacturers cannot write down their excess inventory to scrap value until it is actually scrapped, sold, or offered for sale at a lower price.[29] They must value their excess inventory at replacement cost (if lower than actual cost), or must alter their accounting methods to do so. In making the adjustments, the IRS approves in advance this change in accounting method [Ch. 18].[30] Procedures to follow have been set forth by the IRS.[31]

¶17,040 BOOK INVENTORIES

The IRS allows taxpayers to use book or perpetual inventories [Reg. § 1.471-2]. The purpose of a book inventory is to show the goods on hand as of any given date. It must show proper credit for goods you sell or use during the year, as well as charges for goods you buy or produce. Additions and subtractions to the book inventory are made on the basis of the actual cost of goods bought or produced. Taxpayers must verify the balances shown by the book inventories by taking physical inventories at reasonable intervals and making adjustments to conform with them. If they use the lower of cost or market method, closing inventory of each tax year should be adjusted for each article, as shown in ¶ 17,025 [Reg. § 1.471-4].

---

[29] *Thor Power Tool Co.*, SCt, 79-1 USTC ¶9139, 439 US 522, 99 SCt 773; Rev. Rul. 83-59, 1983-1 CB 103.

[30] Rev. Rul. 80-60, 1980-1 CB 97.

[31] Rev. Proc. 80-5, 1980-1 CB 582.

¶17,045 UNIFORM CAPITALIZATION RULES (UNICAP)

Under the uniform capitalization (UNICAP) rules manufacturers and certain retailers and wholesalers must capitalize direct costs and an allocable portion of most indirect costs that benefit or are incurred because of production, development or resale activities [Code Sec. 263A(a)]. Capitalized costs are generally treated in one of two ways. Costs allocable to goods included in inventory become part of the inventory's value. You will then recover your costs when you sell or otherwise dispose of the inventory. Other capitalized costs are included in the basis of property you produce, rather than being claimed as a current deduction. You will recover these costs annually through depreciation or amortization deductions [Reg. § 1.263A-1(c) (3)].

.01 Who Is Subject to the UNICAP Rules?

Taxpayers are subject to the UNICAP rules if they: (1) produce real or tangible personal property for use in business, or (2) produce real or tangible personal property for sale to customers, or (3) acquire property for resale [Reg. § 1.263A-1(a) (3) (i)]. However, this rule does not apply to taxpayers who acquire personal property for resale if their annual gross receipts do not exceed $10 million for the three previous years [Code Sec. 263A(b) (2) (B); Reg. § 1.263A-1(b)].

.02 When Do You Produce Property?

Taxpayers produce property if they construct, build, install, manufacture, develop, improve, create, raise, or grow the property [Reg. § 1.263A-2(a) (1) (ii)]. Producers must capitalize direct and indirect costs without regard to whether those costs are incurred before, during, or after the production period [Reg. § 1.263A-2(a) (3)]. Reg. § 1.263A-2(a) (3) (ii) specifically requires real estate developers to capitalize property taxes "if, at the time the taxes are incurred, it is reasonably likely that the property will be subsequently developed."[32]

> **NOTE:** The Tax Court held in *Von-Lusk*[33] that a real estate developer organized to manage, hold, and develop land had to capitalize preliminary land development costs including property taxes and payments made to independent contractors such as lobbyists, engineers and lobbyists. The expenses were incurred in meeting with government officials, obtaining building permits and zoning variances, negotiating permit fees, performing engineering and feasibility studies, drafting architectural plans and in paying a mortgage company to review and direct independent contractors' work. The Tax Court concluded that the payments were the first purposeful steps of land development, and were costs allocable to property "produced" by the partnership. The fact that the property wasn't developed or physically changed in anyway was irrelevant to the court because the steps taken were ancillary to constructing the buildings. In addition, the fact that local regulations may prevent the planned development from ever taking place didn't mean payments weren't development costs. Instead, the expenditures were allocable to property "produced" by the taxpayer and the

---

[32] *J.J Reichel*, 112 TC 14, Dec. 53,205 (1999).

[33] *Von-Lusk*, 104 TC 207, Dec. 50,466 (1995); *Louisiana Land & Exploration Co.*, CA-5, 47-1 USTC ¶9266, 161 F2d 842.

taxpayer had to capitalize the direct and indirect costs (such as property taxes) of the property [Reg. § 1.263A-2(a)(3)(ii)].

Property produced under a contract is treated as produced by the taxpayer to the extent that the taxpayer makes payments or otherwise incurs costs in connection with the property [Reg. § 1.263A-2(a)(1)(ii)(B)]. Tangible personal property includes intellectual or creative property such as films, sound records, video tapes, books, artwork, photographs, or similar property containing words, ideas, concepts, images or sounds [Reg. § 1.263A-2(a)(2)]. The IRS has concluded that the cost of a "demo" tape produced by an unknown songwriter seeking to find a record company to sell his music must be capitalized under the UNICAP rules because the sound recording was tangible personal property.[34] It failed to fit into the qualified creative expense exception to the UNICAP rules [Code Sec. 263A(h)(1)]. See ¶ 17,045.09 for further discussion. Since the demo tape was similar to a video tape and motion picture film, the cost of producing the sound recording was not a qualified creative expense. Similarly, the IRS has concluded that a taxpayer who produced, published, and distributed books must keep inventories and is subject to the UNICAP rules. Accordingly, it must capitalize its direct costs and all indirect costs that were properly allocable to tangible personal property that it produced.[35]

Tangible personal property does not include stocks, securities, debt instruments, mortgages or loans [Reg. § 1.263A-2(a)(2)(B)(2)]. In *Suzy's Zoo*,[36] the Court of Appeals for the Ninth Circuit affirmed the Tax Court to hold that a small greeting card company that contracts with third parties to manufacture its products was a "producer" and therefore subject to the uniform capitalization rules under Code Sec. 263A. The Court found that the company failed to qualify under either the *routine producer order* or the *small reseller* exception because it was a "producer" that actually produced its paper products under Code Sec. 263A.

▶ **OBSERVATION:** The capitalization rules require the deduction of certain costs later than would otherwise occur. For instance, retirement plan contributions are usually deducted when made. But, contributions for a worker who manufactures inventory are capitalized as part of the cost of the inventory and, therefore, not deductible until the products are sold.

The capitalization rules are not intended to affect inventories valued on a basis other than cost. Thus, the rules do not affect inventories valued at market using the lower of cost or market method. However, the rules do apply to the valuation of inventories at cost using the lower of cost or market rule [Reg. § 1.263A-1(a)(3)(iv)].

.03 Accounting Method Changes

You may need to change your accounting method to properly value your inventories in compliance with the UNICAP rules. The IRS has provided guidance for changing methods of accounting for costs subject to the UNICAP rules.[37] You will be deemed to have obtained the consent of the IRS to change your method of accounting if you comply with the IRS guidelines. You will have to file Form 3115 (*Application for*

[34] LTR 9643003 (July 10, 1996).

[35] Chief Counsel Advice 200727014 (July 19, 2007).

[36] *Suzy's Zoo*, 114 TC 1, Dec. 53,701 (2001), *aff'd*, CA-9, 2001-2 USTC ¶ 50,766, 273 F3d 875.

[37] Rev. Proc 2008-52, IRB 2008-36, 587, as amplified, clarified, and modified by Rev. Proc. 2009-39, IRB 2009-38, 371.

Change in Accounting Method) with your original or amended tax return as well as send a copy to the IRS National Office in D.C.

In Rev. Proc. 2006-11,[38] the IRS outlines the alternative routes a taxpayer may take to change its method of accounting to comply with simplified service cost and production capitalization rules.

In Rev. Proc. 2006-12,[39] the IRS outlines how to obtain automatic consent to capitalize costs of intangibles allowed under Reg. §§1.263(a)-4, 1.263(a)-5, and 1.167(a).

Advance Consent

Reg. §§1.263A-2 require costs to be capitalized under the simplified service cost method and the simplified production method. They clarify what property qualifies as a self-constructed asset produced on a routine and repetitive basis, under either the simplified service cost method or the simplified production method. A change in either a taxpayer's treatment of mixed service costs, to comply with either of these methods is a change of accounting method. In the past, the IRS granted automatic consent for both those changes of accounting method. The IRS will allow taxpayers to request advance consent for their accounting method rather than wait and determine whether the automatic-consent rules apply.

How To Apply for Advance Consent

Taxpayers interested in obtaining advance consent from the IRS should take the following steps:

- A taxpayer must submit a Form 3115 the date that is 30 days after the end of the taxpayer's year for which the change is requested;
- Any Code Sec. 481(a) adjustment must be made over a two-year period. Code Sec. 481 adjustments are necessary to prevent items from being omitted or duplicated upon the change of accounting method;
- A taxpayer may request advance consent even if its case is being audited, before IRS Appeals, or in litigation;

  NOTE: Small resellers can change their method of accounting for costs. A small reseller must obtain consent to change its method of accounting for costs that are subject to the UNICAP rules.[40] If the small reseller complies with all IRS provisions, it will be deemed to have obtained the consent of the IRS to change its method of accounting. A small reseller is any taxpayer that acquires real or personal property and whose average annual gross receipts for the three immediately preceding tax years does not exceed $10 million. The procedure applies to a small reseller of personal property changing from a permissible UNICAP method to a permissible non-UNICAP inventory capitalization method and a formerly small reseller changing from a permissible non-UNICAP inventory capitalization method to a permissible UNICAP method in the first tax year that it does not qualify as a small reseller. To qualify for the automatic consent, the small reseller must complete Form 3115, *Change in Method of Accounting*, and

[38] Rev. Proc. 2006-11, 2006-1 CB 309.

[39] Rev. Proc. 2006-12, 2006-1 CB 310, as modified by Rev. Proc. 2006-37, 2006-2 CB 499.

[40] Rev. Proc 2008-52, IRB 2008-36, 587, as amplified, clarified, and modified by Rev. Proc. 2009-39, IRB 2009-38, 371; and Rev. Proc. 2011-17, IRB 2011-5, 441; and Rev. Proc. 2010-44, IRB 2010-49, 811.

attach it to its return. In addition, an Code Sec. 481(a) adjustment must be made in order to complete the change in accounting method.

.04 Property Excluded from Capitalization Rules

The uniform capitalization rules do not apply to the following types of property [Code Sec. 263A(b)(2)(B), (c); Reg. § 1.263A-1(b)]:

- Property used for personal or nonbusiness purposes [Code Sec. 263A(c)(1)];
- Property produced under a long-term contract [Code Sec. 263A(c)(4)]; and
- Personal property bought for resale if average annual gross receipts for the three preceding years are $10 million or less [Code Sec. 263A(b)(2)(B); Reg. § 263A-1(b)].

  NOTE: To make this determination, include in the calculation the average annual gross receipts from all businesses, not just those generated from the resale of personal property.[41]
- Property produced for use if substantial construction occurred before March 1, 1986;
- Timber and ornamental trees [Code Sec. 263A(c)(5)];
- Costs allocable to "cushion gas" and emergency gas [Reg. § 1.263A-1(b)(8)];
- Certain intangible drilling and development costs incurred for oil, gas, or geothermal wells, and mineral property [Reg. § 1.263A-1(b)(7)];
- The costs of certain producers using a simplified production method are not subject to UNICAP if their total indirect costs are $200,000 or less, as discussed further below [Reg. § 1.263A-2(b)(3)(iv)(A)];
- A small reseller may disregard de minimis production activities [Reg. § 1.263A-3(a)(2)(ii)]. A reseller's production activities are de minimis if gross receipts from the sale of the produced property and labor costs of the production activities are less than 10 percent of total gross receipts and labor costs, respectively, for the entire trade or business [Reg. § 1.263A-3(a)(2)(iii)(A)(ii)];
- Costs incurred in certain farming businesses [Reg. § 1.263A-1(b)(3)];
- Qualified creative expenses paid or incurred by certain free-lance authors, photographers, and artists [Reg. § 1.263A-1(b)(5)];
- Certain not-for-profit activities [Reg. § 1.263A-1(b)(6)];
- Certain property that is substantially constructed [Reg. § 1.263A-1(b)(10)];
- Certain property provided incident to the provision of services by the taxpayer if the property provided to the client is *de minimis* in amount and not inventory in the hands of the service provider [Reg. § 1.263A-1(b)(11)];
- Certain producers with total indirect costs of $200,000 or less [Reg. § 1.263A-1(b)(12)]; and
- The origination of loans is not considered the acquisition of intangible property for resale [Reg. § 1.263A-1(b)(13)].

---

[41] Rev. Proc. 2008-52, IRB 2008-36, 587, as amplified, clarified, and modified by Rev. Proc. 2009-39, IRB 2009-38, 371; and Rev. Proc. 2011-17, IRB 2011-5, 441; and Rev. Proc. 2010-44, IRB 2010-49, 811.

.05 Costs Subject to UNICAP Rules

Taxpayers subject to the UNICAP rules must capitalize all direct and certain indirect costs properly allocable to property produced or property acquired for resale. The four categories of costs that must be allocated are as follows [Reg. § 1.263A-1(g)]:

- *Direct material costs*-Producers must capitalize direct material costs [Reg. § 1.263A-1(e)(2)(i)(A)];
- *Direct labor costs*-Producers must capitalize direct labor costs [Reg. § 1.263A-1(e)(2)(i)(B)];
- *Indirect costs*-Producers and resellers must capitalize indirect costs [Reg. § 1.263A-1(e)(3)]; and
- *Service costs*-Producers and resellers must capitalize service costs that are a type of indirect cost [Reg. § 1.263A-1(e)(4)].

Resellers must capitalize the acquisition costs of property acquired for resale [Reg. § 1.263A-1(e)(2)(i)].

.06 Cost Allocation Methods

There are various detailed or specific (facts-and-circumstances) cost allocation methods that you may use to allocate direct and indirect costs (including service costs) to property produced and property acquired for resale. In addition, in lieu of a facts-and-circumstances allocation method, you may use one of the simplified methods (as discussed further below) to allocate direct and indirect costs [Reg. § 1.263A-1(f)(1)].

Specific Identification Method

This method traces costs to a cost objective, such as a function, department, activity, or product, on the basis of a cause and effect or other reasonable relationship between the costs and the cost objective [Reg. § 1.263A-1(f)(2)].

Burden Rate

A burden rate allocates an appropriate amount of indirect costs to production or resale activities using predetermined rates that approximate the actual amount of indirect costs incurred. Burden rates (such as ratios based on direct costs or hours) must be developed in accordance with acceptable accounting principles and applied in a reasonable manner. You may allocate different indirect costs on the basis of different burden rates. Thus, for example, you may use one burden rate for allocating the cost of rent and another burden rate for allocating the cost of utilities [Reg. § 1.263A-1(f)(3)].

Standard Cost Method

This standard cost method allocates an appropriate amount of direct and indirect costs to property produced through the use of preestablished standard allowances, without reference to costs actually incurred [Reg. § 1.263A-1(f)(3)(ii)].

Reasonable Allocation Method

Use any other reasonable allocation method to allocate direct and indirect costs provided: (1) the total costs actually capitalized under the method do not differ significantly from the costs that would be capitalized using one of the other methods specifically mentioned by the IRS above; (2) the method is applied consistently; and

(3) the allocation method is not being used to circumvent the UNICAP rules [Reg. § 1.263A-1(f)(4)].

.07 Definition of Costs and How to Allocate Them

How costs are classified determines how the costs will be allocated, as described here.

Direct Material Costs

Direct material costs include the costs of the materials that become an integral part of specific property produced and those materials that are consumed in the ordinary course of production and that can be identified or associated with particular units or groups of units of property produced [Reg. § 1.263A-1(e)(2)(i)(A)].

How to allocate direct material costs. Direct material costs must be allocated to the property produced or acquired to resell using your method of accounting for materials such as specific identification, FIFO, LIFO, or any other reasonable allocation method [Reg. § 1.263A-1(g)(1)].

Direct Labor Costs

Direct labor costs include the costs of labor that can be identified or associated with particular units or groups of units of specific property produced. For this purpose, labor encompasses full-time and part-time employees, as well as contract employees and independent contractors. Direct labor costs include all elements of compensation other than employee benefit costs. Elements of direct labor costs include basic compensation, overtime pay, vacation pay, holiday pay, sick leave pay, shift differential, payroll taxes, and payments to a supplemental unemployment benefit plan [Reg. § 1.263A-1(e)(2)(i)(B)].

How to allocate direct labor costs. Direct labor costs are generally allocated to property produced or acquired to resell using a specific identification method, standard cost method, or any other reasonable allocation method. All elements of compensation, other than basic compensation, may be grouped together and then allocated in proportion to the charge for basic compensation. You will not be treated as using an erroneous method of accounting if direct labor costs are treated as indirect costs under your allocation method, provided such costs are capitalized as required under the UNICAP rules [Reg. § 1.263A-1(g)(2)].

Indirect Costs

Indirect costs include all costs other than direct material costs and direct labor or acquisition costs. You must capitalize all indirect costs allocable to property produced or acquired for resale when the costs directly benefit or are incurred because of production or resale activities. Indirect costs may be allocable to both production and resale activities, as well as to other activities that are not subject to the UNICAP rules. If you are subject to the UNICAP rules, you must make a reasonable allocation of indirect costs among production, resale, and other activities [Reg. § 1.263A-1(e)(3)].

How to allocate indirect costs. Indirect costs are generally allocated to departments or activities for resale using either a specific identification method, a standard cost method, a burden rate method, or any other reasonable allocation method [Reg. § 1.263A-1(g)(3)].

Examples of indirect costs. Indirect costs that must be capitalized to the extent they are properly allocable to property produced or acquired for resale include the following:

- Indirect labor costs [Reg. § 1.263A-1(e)(3)(ii)(A)];
- Officers' compensation [Reg. § 1.263A-1(e)(3)(ii)(B)];
- Pension and other related costs [Reg. § 1.263A-1(e)(3)(ii)(C)];
- Employee benefit expenses [Reg. § 1.263A-1(e)(3)(ii)(D)];
- Indirect material costs [Reg. § 1.263A-1(e)(3)(ii)(E)];
- Purchasing costs [Reg. § 1.263A-1(e)(3)(ii)(F)];
- Handling costs such as attaching wheels and handlebars to a bicycle acquired for resale [Reg. § 1.263A-1(e)(3)(ii)(G)];
- Storage costs [Reg. § 1.263A-1(e)(3)(ii)(H)];
- Cost recovery such as depreciation and amortization [Reg. § 1.263A-1(e)(3)(ii)(I)];
- Depletion [Reg. § 1.263A-1(e)(3)(ii)(J)];
- Rent, including the cost of renting equipment, facilities or land [Reg. § 1.263A-1(e)(3)(ii)(K)];
- Taxes attributable to labor, materials, supplies, equipment, land, or facilities used in production or resale activities [Reg. § 1.263A-1(e)(3)(ii)(L)];
- Insurance, including the cost of insurance on plant or facility, machinery, equipment, materials, property produced or property acquired for resale [Reg. § 1.263A-1(e)(3)(ii)(M)];
- Utilities, including the cost of electricity, gas and water [Reg. § 1.263A-1(e)(3)(ii)(N)];
- Repairs and maintenance of equipment or facilities [Reg. § 1.263A-1(e)(3)(ii)(O)]. In Rev. Rul. 2005-42,[42] the IRS concluded that like repair costs, environmental remediation costs incurred by a taxpayer to clean up land and to treat groundwater that the taxpayer contaminated with hazardous waste from its production activities are costs that directly benefit or are incurred by reason of the performance of the production activities even if the condition that necessitated the remediation arose during prior taxable periods [Reg. § 1.263A-2(a)(3)(i)]. As with repair costs, environmental remediation costs are properly allocable to inventory without regard to whether those costs are incurred before, during, or after production. [Reg. § 1.263A-1(c)(2)] Likewise, remediation costs are allocable under Reg. § 1.263A-1(c)(1) to the property produced during the tax year in which the costs are incurred;
- Engineering and design costs such as expenses incurred prior to the beginning of production [Reg. § 1.263A-1(e)(3)(ii)(P)];
- Spoilage, including the cost of rework labor, scrap, and spoilage [Reg. § 1.263A-1(e)(3)(ii)(Q)];
- Tools and equipment [Reg. § 1.263A-1(e)(3)(ii)(R)];
- Quality control and inspection [Reg. § 1.263A-1(e)(3)(ii)(S)];

[42] Rev. Rul. 2005-42, 2005-2 CB 67.

- Bidding costs incurred in the solicitation of contracts [Reg. § 1.263A-1(e)(3)(ii)(T)];
- Licensing and franchise costs [Reg. § 1.263A-1(e)(3)(ii)(U)];
- Interest incurred during the production period [Reg. § 1.263A-1(e)(3)(ii)(V)]. Although interest is generally deductible under Code Sec. 63, interest costs which are paid or incurred during the production period and, which are allocable to real or tangible personal property produced by the taxpayer (either for his own use or to sell) that has a long useful life, such as real property or property with a class life of 20 years of more, must be capitalized under Code Sec. 263A(f). Real property includes the structural components of buildings and inherently permanent structures. Capitalized interest is treated as cost of the property produced and is recovered upon sale or other disposition; and
- Capitalizable service costs [Reg. § 1.263A-1(e)(3)(ii)(W)].

Indirect costs excluded from capitalization. The following indirect costs need not be capitalized and thus may be deducted currently:

- Royalties paid for licensed trademark;

  In *Robinson Knife Manufacturing Co.*,[43] the United States Court of Appeals for the Second Circuit reversed the Tax Court to hold that a manufacturing company selling kitchen tools labeled with trademarks licensed from third parties was entitled to deduct royalty payments to those third parties as ordinary and necessary business expenses under Code Sec. 162. The IRS had argued and the Tax Court found that under Code Sec. 263A, the royalties must be capitalized and made part of Robinson's inventory costs. The appellate court disagreed and concluded that the company's royalty payments (1) were calculated as a percentage of sales revenue from inventory and (2) were incurred only upon the sale of that inventory; therefore, the payments were not "properly allocable to property produced" under Reg. § 1.263A-1(e)(3)(i) and, therefore, should be deducted currently rather than capitalized.

  IRS Nonacquiescence. The IRS did not acquiesce to the Second Circuit's decision in *Robinson Knife Manufacturing Co.* This means that the IRS will not follow the Second Circuit's holding in cases involving the same legal issues unless the case is appealable to the Second Circuit. The IRS disagreed with the Second Circuit's analysis and believes that the company incurred the royalty expenses ''by reason of'' its production activities. Therefore, in their view, the royalty payments were production costs within the meaning of Reg. § 1.263A-1(e)(3)(i) that must be capitalized.

  Issuance of Proposed Regs. In response to *Robinson Knife,* the IRS issued proposed regulations clarifying that sales-based royalties are productions costs required to be capitalized under Code Sec. 263A and allocated to inventory sold during the tax year [Prop. Reg. § 1.263A-1(c)(5)]. According to the IRS, the Second Circuit "misconstrued the nature of costs required to be capitalized."

- Selling and distribution costs such as marketing, selling, advertising, and distribution costs [Reg. § 1.263A-1(e)(3)(iii)(A)];

[43] *Robinson Knife Manufacturing, Co.*, 97 TCM 1037, Dec. 57,710(M), TC Memo. 2009-9, *rev'd*, CA-2, 2010-1 USTC ¶ 50,300, 600 F3d 121 (AOD-2011-1, Feb. 9, 2011) (Non-Acq. Announcement, Feb. 2, 2011).

- Research and experimental expenditures [Reg. § 1.263A-1(e)(3)(iii)(B)];
- Code Sec. 179 costs (the election to expense certain depreciable business assets) [Reg. § 1.263A-1(e)(3)(iii)(C)], [Ch. 11];
- Code Sec. 165 losses [Reg. § 1.263A-1(e)(3)(iii)(D)], [Ch. 13];
- Cost recovery allowances on temporarily idle equipment and facilities [Reg. § 1.263A-1(e)(3)(iii)(E)];
- Taxes assessed on the basis of income including only state, local, foreign income and franchise taxes [Reg. § 1.263A-1(e)(3)(iii)(F)];
- Strike expenses associated with hiring employees to replace striking personnel (but not the wages of replacement personnel), costs of security, and legal fees associated with settling strikes [Reg. § 1.263A-1(e)(3)(iii)(G)];
- Warranty and product liability costs incurred in fulfilling product warranty obligations for products that have been sold and costs incurred for product liability insurance [Reg. § 1.263A-1(e)(3)(iii)(H)];
- Storage costs relating to inventory incurred by a taxpayer at an on-site storage facility that is physically attached to and integrally part of a retail sale facility [Reg. § 1.263A-1(e)(3)(iii)(I)];[44]
- Unsuccessful bidding expenses incurred in the solicitation of contracts not awarded to the taxpayer [Reg. § 1.263A-1(e)(3)(iii)(J)]; and
- Deductible service costs that do not directly benefit or are not incurred because of production or resale activities. Examples are costs incurred in conjunction with overall management, policy guidance, general financial planning, personnel policy, quality control policy, and marketing [Reg. § 1.263A-1(e)(3)(iii)(K); Reg. § 1.263A-1(e)(4)(ii)(B)].

Service Costs

Service costs that must be capitalized are indirect costs such as general and administrative costs that may be identified specifically with or directly benefit a service department or function [Reg. § 1.263A-1(e)(4)(i)(A)]. Service departments are administrative, service, or support departments including the personnel, purchasing operations, materials handling, accounting, data processing, security and legal services departments [Reg. § 1.263A-1(e)(4)(iii)].

How to allocate service costs. Service costs are a type of indirect costs that may be allocated using a specific identification method, a standard cost method, a burden rate method, or any other reasonable allocation method. Generally, if you use a specific identification method or another reasonable allocation method, you must

[44] To qualify for this exception, the on-site storage costs must relate to property sold by a taxpayer "exclusively" to retail customers. In *Load, Inc.*, CA-9, 2009-1 USTC ¶ 50,194, 554 F3d 785, expenses that a taxpayer incurred to place manufactured homes on sales lots were not deductible as ordinary and necessary business expenses; instead, they had to be capitalized as inventory costs. While expenses may be excluded from inventory if incurred at an on-site storage facility, this exception only applies if the taxpayer's expenses relate to property sold "exclusively" to retail customers. In this case, the taxpayer's expenses were incurred to place manufactured homes on the lots to assist local independent salespersons in selling the homes; thus, although the taxpayer participated in the sale of the home from the lots to retail customers, it did not sell the homes exclusively to customers.

allocate service costs to particular departments or activities based on a factor or relationship that reasonably relates the service costs to the benefits received from the service departments or activities. For example, a reasonable factor for allocating legal services to particular departments or activities is the number of hours of legal services attributable to each department or activity.

Mixed Service Costs

Mixed service costs are service costs that are partially allocable to production or resale activities (capitalized) and partially allocable to non-production or non-resale activities (deductible). For example, a personnel department may incur costs to recruit factory workers (allocable to production activities) and it may incur costs to develop wage, salary, and benefit policies (allocable to non-production activities) [Reg. § 1.263A-1(e)(4)(ii)(C)]. You must allocate mixed service costs, under either a direct reallocation method (discussed below), a step-allocation method (discussed below), or any other reasonable allocation method [Reg. § 1.263A-1(g)(4)(i)].

The IRS's Large and Mid-Size Business Division has issued a directive to the field warning that retailers have improperly treated their merchandising departments as mixed service costs departments under the UNICAP rules.[45] The IRS takes the position that a retailer's merchandising or purchasing department is not a service department under the UNICAP rules and so the costs incurred by the department are not mixed service costs. The IRS concluded that before a cost can be a mixed service cost, it must be a service cost. A service cost is an indirect cost that can be identified specifically with a service department or function or that directly benefits or is incurred by reason of a service department or function [Reg. § 1.263A-1(e)(4)(i)(A)].

***De minimis* rule for mixed service costs.** If 90 percent or more of a mixed service department's costs are deductible service costs, you may elect not to allocate any portion of the service department's costs to property produced or acquired for resale. For example, if 90 percent of the costs of your industrial relations department benefit your overall policy-making activities, you are not required to allocate any portion of these costs to a production activity. Under this election, however, if 90 percent or more of a mixed service department's costs are capitalizable service costs, you must allocate 100 percent of the department's costs to the production or resale activity benefited. For example, if 90 percent of the costs of your accounting department benefit your manufacturing activity, you must allocate 100 percent of the costs of the accounting department to the manufacturing activity [Reg. § 1.263A-1(g)(4)(ii)].

Methods for allocating mixed service costs. There are two methods of allocating mixed service costs:

- The direct reallocation method; and
- The step allocation method [Reg. § 1.263A-1(g)(4)(iii)].

Under the *direct reallocation method,* the total costs (direct and indirect) of all mixed service departments are allocated only to departments engaged in production or resale activities and then from those departments to particular activities. This direct reallocation method ignores benefits provided by one mixed service department to other mixed service departments, and also excludes other mixed service departments

---

[45] Industry Director Directive #2 on Mixed Service Costs.

from the base used to make the allocation. An example of the direct reallocation method is as follows [Reg. §1.263A-1(g)(4)(iii)(C)]:

Example 17-16: (i) ABC, Inc. has the following five departments: the Assembling Department, the Painting Department, and the Finishing Department (production departments), and the Personnel Department and the Data Processing Department (mixed service departments). ABC allocated the Personnel Department's costs on the basis of total payroll costs and the Data Processing Department's costs on the basis of data processing hours.

(ii) Under a direct reallocation method, allocates the Personnel Department's costs directly to its Assembling, Painting, and Finishing Department, and not to its Data Processing department.

Department	Total Dept. Costs	Amount of Payroll Costs	Allocation Ratio	Amount Allocated
Personnel	$ 500,000	$ 50,000	—	($500,000)
Data Proc'g	250,000	15,000	—	
Assembling	250,000	15,000	15,000/285,000	26,315
Painting	1,000,000	90,000	90,000/285,000	157,895
Finishing	2,000,000	180,000	180,000/285,000	315,790
	$4,000,000	$350,000		

(iii) After ABC allocates the Personnel Department's costs, ABC then allocates the costs of its Data Processing Department in the same manner.

Department	Total Dept. Cost After Initial Allocation	Total Data Proc. Hours	Allocation Ratio	Amount Allocated	Total Dept. Cost After Final Allocation
Personnel	$ 0	2,000	—	—	$ 0
Data Proc'g	250,000	—	—	($250,000)	
Assembling	276,315	2,000	2,000/10,000	50,000	326,315
Painting	1,157,895	0	0/10,000	0	1,157,895
Finishing	2,315,730	8,000	8,000/10,000	20,000	2,515,790
	$4,000,000	12,000			$4,000,000

Under a *step allocation,* a sequence of allocations will be made. First, the total costs of the mixed service departments that benefit the greatest number of other departments are allocated to (1) other mixed service departments, (2) departments that incur only deductible service costs, and (3) departments that exclusively engage in production or resale activities. You continue to allocate mixed service costs in this manner until all mixed service costs are allocated to departments that exclusively engage in production or resale activities. Thus a step allocation method recognizes the benefits provided by one mixed service department to another mixed service department and also includes mixed services that have not yet been allocated in the base used to make the allocation. An example of the step-allocation is as follows [Reg. § 1.263A-1 (g) (4) (iii) (C)]:

Example 17-17: (i) Taxpayer DEF, Inc. has the following five departments: the Manufacturing Department (a production department), the Marketing Department and the Finance Department (departments that incur only deductible service costs), the Personnel Department and the Data Processing Department (mixed service departments). DEF uses a step allocation method and allocates the Personnel Department's costs on the basis of total payroll costs and the Data Processing Department's costs on the basis of data processing hours. DEF's Personnel Department benefits all four of DEF's other departments, whereas its Data Processing Department benefits only three departments. Because DEF's Personnel Department benefits the greatest number of other departments, DEF first allocates its Personnel Department costs to its Manufacturing, Marketing, Finance and Data Processing departments, as follows:

Department	Total Dept. Costs	Amount of Payroll Costs	Allocation Ratio	Amount Allocated
Personnel	$ 500,000	$ 50,000	—	($500,000)
Data Proc'g	250,000	15,000	15,000/300,000	25,000
Finance	250,000	15,000	15,000/300,000	25,000
Marketing	1,000,000	90,000	90,000/300,000	150,000
Manufac'g	2,000,000	180,000	180,000/300,000	300,000
	$4,000,000	$350,000		

(ii) Under a step allocation method, the denominator of DEF's allocation ratio includes the payroll costs of its Manufacturing, Marketing, Finance, and Data Processing departments.

(iii) Next, DEF allocates the costs of its Data Processing Department on the basis of data processing hours. Because the costs incurred by DEF's Personnel Department have already been allocated, no allocation is made to the Personnel Department.

Department	Total Dept. Cost After Initial Allocation	Total Data Proc. Hours	Allocation Ratio	Amount Allocated	Total Dept. Cost After Final Allocation
Personnel	$ 0	2,000	—	—	$ 0
Data Proc'g	275,000	—	—	($275,000)	0
Finance	275,000	2,000	2,000/10,000	55,000	330,000
Marketing	1,150,000	0	0/10,000	0	1,150,000
Manufac'g	2,300,000	8,000	8,000/10,000	220,000	2,520,000
	$4,000,000	12,000			$4,000,000

(iv) Under the second step of DEF's step allocation method, the denominator of DEF's allocation ratio includes the data processing hours of its Manufacturing, Marketing, and Finance Departments, but does not include the data processing hours of its Personnel Department (the other mixed service department) because the costs of that department have previously been allocated.

.08 Elective Simplified Methods-In General

Taxpayers who manufacture or resell personal property cannot deduct the direct cost and some portions of the indirect cost of producing their inventory as an immediately deductible business expense. Instead, they must capitalize the cost under the uniform capitalization rules and allocate it to the value of their inventory. Different methods are available to allocate these costs under Code Sec. 263A based on the special characteristics of each taxpayer's business. To streamline the process, the IRS has developed simplified methods of allocating the costs.

The simplified production method under Reg. § 1.263A-2(b) determines aggregate amounts of costs which are allocable to produced "eligible property." The simplified service cost method under Reg. § 1.263A-1(h) allows taxpayers to determine capitalizable mixed service costs incurred during the tax year with respect to "eligible property." These simplified methods of cost allocation apply to self-constructed assets produced by the taxpayer on a routine and repetitive basis in the ordinary course of the taxpayer's production activities. Property eligible for these methods includes self-constructed tangible personal property that is considered produced on a routine and repetitive basis in the ordinary course of a taxpayer's trade or business. Property produced on a routine and repetitive basis means units of tangible personal property that are mass-produced. Mass-produced property occurs when numerous substantially identical assets are manufactured within a tax year using standardized designs and assembly-line techniques. Further, the applicable recovery period for the assets must not be longer than three years or the property must be a material or supply that will be used or consumed within the three years of production [Reg. § 1.263A-1(h)(2)(i)(D)].

Because the simplified methods are less accurate and precise than the facts and circumstances method, property that is mass-produced or property with a high turnover are better suited for these methods. A change in the treatment of a taxpayer's mixed service costs to comply with these rules is considered a change of accounting method for which a Code Sec. 481 adjustment is required [Reg. § 1.263A-1(k)]. The IRS will consent to the change, provided certain administrative procedures are followed.

Taxpayers may elect to use simplified methods for determining what costs must be included in inventory. Basically, these methods start out with inventory calculated without regard to the capitalization rules. Add to this the additional costs that must be inventoried under the capitalization rules. Simplified procedures are available both for producers and retailers/wholesalers. Make the election on a timely filed return for the first tax year to which the inventory capitalization rules apply. Changes to or from these simplified methods in later tax years require IRS consent.

Simplified Production Method

Producers, regardless of their levels of gross receipts may elect to use the simplified production method to determine the additional Code Sec. 263A costs properly allocable to ending inventories of property produced and other "eligible property" on hand at the end of the tax year [Reg. § 1.263A-2(b)]. This method was designed to reduce the administrative burdens of complying with the Code Sec. 263A capitalization rules in situations where mass production of assets occurs on a repetitive and routine basis, with a typically high turnover rate for the produced assets. The simplified production method is inappropriate for use in accounting for casual or occasional production of property.

The amount of additional Code Sec. 263A costs that is allocable to eligible property remaining on hand at the close of the tax year under the simplified production method is computed by multiplying the Code Sec. 471 costs on hand at the end of the year by an absorption ratio [Reg. § 1.263A-2(b)(3)(i)(A)]. The absorption ratio generally is equal to the additional Code Sec. 263A costs incurred during the year divided by the Code Sec. 471 costs incurred during the year [Reg. § 1.263A-2(b)(3)(ii)(A)].

Additional Code Sec. 263A costs are the costs, other than interest, that were not capitalized under the taxpayer's method of accounting immediately prior to the effective date of Code Sec. 263A but that are required to be capitalized under Code Sec. 263A [Reg. § 1.263A-1(d)(3)]. Code Sec. 471 costs generally are the costs, other than interest, that the taxpayer capitalized under its method of accounting immediately prior to the effective date of Code Sec. 263A [Reg. § 1.263A-1(d)(2)].

Eligible property. A taxpayer who elects to use the simplified production method generally must use the method for all production activities associated with the following categories of eligible property [Reg. § 1.263A-2(b)(2)(i)]:

1. *Inventory property.* Stock in trade or other property properly includible in the inventory of the taxpayer [Reg. § 1.263A-2(b)(2)(i)(A)].
2. *Non-inventory property held for sale.* Non-inventory property held by a taxpayer primarily for sale to customers in the ordinary course of the taxpayer's trade or business [Reg. § 1.263A-2(b)(2)(i)(B)].
3. *Certain self-constructed assets.* Self-constructed assets substantially identical in nature to, and produced in the same manner as, inventory property produced by the taxpayer or other property produced by the taxpayer and held primarily for sale to customers in the ordinary course of the taxpayer's trade or business [Reg. § 1.263A-2(b)(2)(i)(C)].
4. *Self-constructed assets produced on a repetitive basis.* Self-constructed assets produced by the taxpayer on a routine and repetitive basis in the ordinary course of the taxpayer's trade or business [Reg. § 1.263A-2(b)(2)(i)(D)].

IRS defines "eligible property." In Rev. Rul. 2005-53,[46] the IRS clarified the types of property that qualify as "eligible property" and the application of the term "routine and repetitive" for purposes of the simplified service cost and simplified production methods (simplified methods) of accounting for capital costs under Code Sec. 263A. For purposes of the simplified methods, "eligible property" is produced on a "routine and repetitive" basis in the ordinary course of a trade or business if the assets are either mass-produced (numerous identical goods that are manufactured using standardized designs and assembly line techniques) or have a high degree of turnover.

Example 17-18: U, a manufacturer of office equipment, produces numerous identical copiers during the year using assembly line techniques. U leases the copiers and does not hold them for sale. U is producing copiers on a routine

[46] Rev. Rul. 2005-53, 2005-2 CB 425.

and repetitive basis for purposes of the simplified methods because the copiers are mass-produced.

Example 17-19: X, an electric utility, regularly purchases identical meters and installs them on its customers' properties. The meters measure the amount of electric current used by X 's customers. X does not manufacture meters. X is not producing meters on a routine and repetitive basis for purposes of the simplified methods because the meters are neither mass-produced by X nor have a high degree of turnover. Mass production does not include installation of meters and meters do not have a short useful life.

Example 17-20: Z, a company that owns and operates a national chain of restaurants, continually constructs new restaurants each year. Z generally uses a standardized design when constructing new restaurants. However, local zoning laws and the physical characteristics of the specific construction site require Z to modify the design for each new restaurant. Z is not producing restaurants on a routine and repetitive basis for purposes of the simplified methods because the restaurants neither are mass-produced nor have a high degree of turnover.

NOTE: *Small producer exception.* A producer that uses the simplified production method and, during its tax year, incurs total indirect costs of $200,000 or less may treat the addition Code Sec. 263A costs allocable to eligible property remaining on hand at the close of the tax year as zero. In computing the $200,000 threshold, any nonproduction costs not required to be capitalized, such as selling and distribution costs may be excluded [Reg. § 1.263A-2(b)(3)(iv)].

Simplified Resale Method

The simplified resale method provides a simplified method for determining the additional costs properly allocable to property acquired for resale and other "eligible property" on hand at the end of the tax year. Generally, the simplified resale method is only available to a trade or business exclusively engaged in resale activities. However, certain resellers with property produced as a result of *de minimis* production activities or property produced under contract may elect the simplified resale method [Reg. § 1.263A-3(d)(2)]. Eligible property includes any real or personal property such as stock in trade that is acquired for resale. If you are engaged in both production and resale activities in the same business, you may use the simplified production method but not the simplified resale method [Reg. § 1.263A-3(a)(4)].

Under the simplified resale method, the additional capitalized costs allocable to eligible property remaining on hand at the close of the tax year are computed by taking the "combined absorption ratio" and multiplying it by the Code Sec. 471 costs remaining on hand at year end (Code Sec. 471 assets defined above) [Reg. § 1.263A-3(d)(3)]. The resulting product is the additional costs that are added to your ending Code Sec. 471 costs to determine capitalized costs. The *combined absorption ratio* is the sum of the storage and handling costs absorption ratio and the purchasing costs absorption ratio defined below. The storage and handling costs absorption ratio is determined by taking the *current year's storage and handling costs* (total storage costs plus the handling costs incurred during the year relating to the property acquired for resale and other eligible property) and dividing them by the beginning inventory plus the current year's purchases [Reg. § 1.263A-3(d)(3)(i)(D)]. The purchasing costs absorption ratio is determined by dividing the current year's purchasing costs (the total purchasing costs incurred during the year that relate to the property acquired for resale) and dividing it by the current year's purchases.

Historic Absorption Ratio

The *historic absorption ratio election* is available to producers and resellers using either the simplified production or the simplified resale method, but not a facts-and-circumstances allocation method. When the historic absorption ratio method is elected, taxpayers are relieved from the time-consuming and expensive requirement of determining an absorption ratio annually (ratio of additional Code Sec. 263A costs to Code Sec. 471 costs). Instead, the historic method applies the ratio for a three-year test period immediately preceding the first year for which the election is effective [Reg. § 1.263A-2(b)(4)(i)]. The absorption ratio is computed by taking the total Code Sec. 263A costs incurred during the three-year "test period" divided by the Code Sec. 471 costs incurred during the test period [Reg. § 1.263A-2(b)(4)(ii)]. You will use this same historic ratio for five years without determining actual addition Code Sec. 263A costs. In the sixth year following the three-year test period, you will again compute your actual additional Code Sec. 263A costs and a new absorption ratio. If the actual absorption ratio for this recomputation year differs from the historic absorption ratio by no more than one half of one percentage point, you can continue to use the previously computed historic ratio for the recomputation year and the following five tax years. If the sixth year ratio is not within 0.5 percent, you must use an actual absorption ratio for the next three years-years six, seven, and eight-called the updated test period. At the end of this three year period, a new historic absorption ratio based on the prior three-year-period is applied for the next five years (years 9-13) [Reg. § 1.263A-2(b)(4)(C)(2)].

You elect the historic absorption ratio method by attaching a statement to your tax return for the tax year in which the election is made showing the actual absorption ratios determined under the simplified production method during its first test period. This statement must disclose the historic absorption ratio to be used during your qualifying period. A similar statement must be attached to the return for the first tax year within any subsequent qualifying period [Reg. § 1.263A-2(b)(4)(C)(2)(iv)]. Rev. Proc. 95-25[47] provides the exclusive procedure for a taxpayer on a simplified production or simplified resale method of account for fewer than three tax years to obtain consent to make a historic absorption ratio election. This procedure is applicable only for a taxpayer's first, second, or third tax year.

Simplified Service Cost Method

Producers and resellers are eligible to use the simplified service cost method whether or not the simplified resale method is elected [Reg. § 1.263A-1(h)]. Under this method, the amount of capitalized mixed service costs is determined by multiplying total mixed service costs by an allocation ratio [Reg. § 1.263A-1(h)(3)(i)]. Producers may use either a labor-based allocation ratio or a production cost allocation ratio [Reg.

---

[47] Rev. Proc. 95-25, 1995-1 CB 701.

§ 1.263A-1(h)(3)(ii)]. To determine the labor-based allocation ratio, producers take the Code Sec. 263A labor costs and divide them by the total labor costs.

Code Sec. 263A labor costs are the total labor costs (excluding labor costs included in mixed service costs) allocable to property produced and acquired for resale and subject to the UNICAP rules. Total labor costs are the sum of labor costs (excluding labor costs included in mixed service costs) incurred in all parts of your trade or business during the year [Reg. § 1.263A-3(d)(3)(i)(F)].

Producers may elect to apply a production cost allocation ratio which is determined by taking the Code Sec. 263A production costs and dividing them by the total costs incurred during the year [Reg. § 1.263A-1(h)(5)(ii)]. *Code Sec. 263A production costs* are the total costs (excluding mixed service costs and interest) incurred in your trade or business during the tax year that are allocable to produced property under Code Sec. 263A. Total costs are all direct and indirect costs (excluding mixed service costs and interest) incurred in your trade or business during the year that are allocable to produced property as well as all other costs of your trade or business.

.09 Exclusions from Uniform Capitalization Rules

Freelance Authors, Photographers and Artists—The Qualified Creative Expense Exception

Freelance authors, photographers, and artists are exempt from the UNICAP rules if their expenses qualify under the qualified expense exception [Code Sec. 263A(h)(1)]. Thus, the qualified creative expenses incurred by free-lance authors, photographers, and artists in the trade or business (rather than as an employee) of being a writer, photographer, or artist can be deducted currently. To qualify, the expense must not be related to printing, photographic plates, motion pictures films, videotapes, or similar items. A freelance writer, photographer, or artist is a self-employed individual whose personal efforts create (or may reasonably be expected to create) a literary manuscript, musical composition, dance score, photograph, negative, picture, painting, sculpture, statue, etching, drawing, cartoon, graphic design, or original print edition [Code Sec. 263A(h)(3)]. These taxpayers may therefore deduct the costs of producing their original works in the year in which the expense is incurred. To determine whether an expense is paid or incurred in the business of being an artist, you must consider whether the item created is original or unique. In addition, aesthetic value is afforded greater value than utilitarian use [Code Sec. 263A(h)(3)(C)(ii)]. For example, expenses paid in making jewelry, silverware, pottery, furniture, and other household items generally are not considered to be paid or incurred in the business of being an artist.

Personal Service Corporations

The UNICAP exemption for writers, photographers, and artists also applies to the expenses of a personal service corporation which directly relates to the activities of the qualified employee-owner [Code Sec. 263A(h)(3)(D)]. A qualified employee-owner is an individual who is a writer, photographer, or artist who owns (including ownership by members of his or her family) substantially all of the stock of the corporation. Thus, corporations owned by authors, photographers, or artists may currently deduct the costs of producing original works provided the principal activity of the corporation is performing personal services directly related to the artistic activities.

Photographers and Filmmakers

A current deduction is not available to expenses related to "printing, photographic plates, motion picture films, videotapes or similar items." [Code Sec. 263A(h)(2)].

.10 Farming

Special rules apply to costs incurred in a farming business [see ¶ 17,070].

.11 Interest Capitalization Rules

Interest you incur in producing property must be capitalized as an indirect cost of production under the UNICAP rules [Code Sec. 263A(f)]. The interest capitalization rules do not apply unless the property is produced for use in a trade or business or for an activity engaged in for profit [Reg. § 1.263A-8(b)(4)]. The *avoided cost method* is used to determine the amount of capitalized interest. This method requires the capitalization of interest to the extent that it would not have been incurred during the production period if you had used the money spent on production expenditures to pay down outstanding indebtedness. You will recover the capitalized interest through depreciation deductions or through cost of sales. If a property consists of a depreciable component and a nondepreciable component, such as a building and the lot on which it is located, any interest that must be capitalized with respect to the property must be added to the basis of the depreciable component [Reg. § 1.263A-8(a)(2)].

Designated Property

Only designated property is subject to the interest capitalization rules. *Designated property* includes:

- All real property (land, buildings, and permanent structures) produced by you; and
- Tangible personal property produced by or for you if it either has a class life of 20 years or more, an estimated production period of more than one year and total estimated production costs of more than $1 million, or an estimated production period of more than two years [Code Sec. 263A(f)(1)(B); Reg. § 1.263A-8(b)].

Property with a production period of 90 days or less and total production expenditures that do not exceed $1 million divided by the number of days in the production period will not be considered designated property [Reg. § 1.263A-8(b)(4)]. The production period of a property, generally, begins on the date production begins and ends on the date the property is ready to be placed in service or is ready to be held for sale [Code Sec. 263A(f)(4)(B)].

In the case of real property, designated property may be divided into units that could consist of individual apartments, condominiums, offices, or spaces in a shopping mall if the units are expected to be separately placed in service or sold [Reg. § 1.263A-10(b)(2)].

The amount of interest that must be capitalized under the avoided cost method is determined separately for each unit of designated property produced by or for you.

Traced Debt

Indebtedness directly allocable to production expenditures is considered *traced debt.* Interest on traced debt is capitalized first and is referred to as the "traced debt amount" [Reg. § 1.263A-9(b)]. If the production expenditures exceed the amount of traced debt, interest on other debt (nontraced debt) is capitalized to the extent this interest could have been reduced if production expenditures had not been incurred. This second category of capitalized interest is referred to as the *excess expenditure amount* [Reg. § 1.263A-9(c)]. A traced debt amount and excess expenditure amount are calculated for each tax year, or shorter computation period, during which production of the unit takes place. You may elect an annual computation period that corresponds to your tax year or divide the tax year into two or more computation periods of equal length.

Safe Harbor Leases

The uniform capitalization rules for interest require the capitalization of interest paid or incurred during the production of property with both a long production period and a long useful life. Interest directly attributable to expenditures with respect to this property is considered traced debt and must be capitalized first. Interest on any other debt that the taxpayer incurred during the production of designated property must also be capitalized to the extent that the debt could have been avoided if there were no production expenditures. Eligible debt refers to the calculation of the amount of interest that is required to be capitalized as related either to direct or indirect debt. Reg. § 1.263A-9 provides that eligible debt does not include a purchase money obligation given to a lessee by the lessor in a safe harbor leasing transaction. Therefore, capitalization of interest on the obligation is not required. Safe harbor leases allowed property owners to transfer depreciation and investment tax credits to another party in return for cash and an interest-bearing note. The interest would be deducted by the lessor and included in income by the lessee. Even though the safe harbor leasing rules no longer exist, formerly qualifying transactions are still respected as leases.

Accounting Method Changes

If you need to change your method accounting to comply with the interest capitalization rules, you must follow the conditions prescribed by the IRS. You will be deemed to have obtained the consent of the IRS to change your method of accounting if you comply with all IRS provisions, which include requiring you to file Form 3115 with your original or amended return as well as send a copy to the IRS National Office in D.C.

¶17,050 METHODS OF VALUATION IN SPECIAL INDUSTRIES

.01 Dealers in Securities

A *dealer in securities* is one who regularly: (1) buys securities for resale to customers, or (2) offers to enter into, assume, offset, assign, or otherwise end positions in securities with customers in the ordinary course of a trade or business [Code Sec. 475(c)(1)].

The following general rules apply to certain securities held by a dealer [Code Sec. 475(a)]:

- Any security that is inventory in the dealer's hands must be included in inventory at its fair market value;
- Any security that is not inventory in the dealer's hands and held at year's end is considered as sold by the dealer at its fair market value on the year's last business day. The dealer must take into account any gain or loss in figuring income for that tax year; and
- Gain or loss in the securities' later sale is adjusted to reflect gain or loss already taken into account under the mark-to-market rule [Code Sec. 475(a)]. See Ch. 8 for further discussion of the mark-to-market rule.

Example 17-21: On May 15, Steven Shearer, a securities dealer, buys Ace Corp. stock, held for sale to customers, for $400. On December 31, the Ace stock has a fair market value of $800. Shearer must recognize a $400 gain for the year. On June 15, of the following year, Shearer sells the stock for $600. He adjusts the amount of gain recognized to take into account the gain recognized on December 31 of the previous year ($400).

Result: Shearer has a $200 loss [$800 ($400 stock basis + $400 gain recognized) less $600 amount realized.

A dealer in securities generally treats any gain or loss taken into account under the above rules as ordinary income or loss. However, these rules don't apply during the period when the security is (1) a hedge with respect to a security, position, right to income, or a liability that is not subject to the mark-to-market rules, (2) held by the taxpayer other than in its capacity as a dealer in securities, or (3) improperly or untimely identified by the taxpayer [Code Sec. 475(d)(3)]. A *security* is:

- Any share of corporate stock;
- Any partnership or beneficial ownership interest in a widely held or publicly traded partnership or trust;
- Any note, bond, debenture, or other evidence of indebtedness;
- Any interest rate, currency or equity notional principal contract;
- Any evidence of an interest in, or a derivative financial instrument in, any of the foregoing securities, or any currency, including any option, forward contract, short position, or any similar instrument in those securities or currency; and
- Any position that is not one of the foregoing securities that is clearly identified in the dealer's records as a hedge before the close of the day on which it is acquired or entered into or at any other times.

The mark-to-market rules do not apply to:

- Securities held for investment;
- Any debt instrument acquired (including originated) by a dealer in the ordinary course of a trade or business (provided it is not held for sale); and
- Any security that is a hedge as to a position, right to income, or a liability that is not a security in the taxpayer's hands [Code Sec. 475(b)].

NOTE: These exceptions generally do not apply unless the security or debt instrument is identified in the dealer's records as qualifying before the end of the day on which it is acquired, originated or entered into [Code Sec. 475(b)(2)].

The uniform capitalization rules, the rules requiring the capitalizing of certain interest and carry charges as to straddles or the wash sale rules do not apply to any security to which the mark-to-market rules apply. However, any loss recognized under mark-to-market is subject to the straddle rules [Ch. 8; Ch. 13] [Code Sec. 475(d)(1)]. Taxpayers who must change their accounting method to meet the current rules are treated as having initiated the change with IRS consent. Any adjustment is taken into account ratably over five tax years.

.02 Farmers and Livestock Raisers

[See ¶ 17,070].

.03 Manufacturers

Comprehensive capitalization rules apply to the manufacture of inventory goods [¶ 17,045].

.04 Miners and Like Producers-Allocation of Costs

This method may be used when two or more products of a different selling value are produced by a uniform process [Reg. § 1.471-7].

Example 17-22: When coal is used to produce gas, a by-product (coke) may result. The production cost may be allocated to the gas and to the coke in proportion to their respective selling values.

.05 Retail Merchants

The methods that department stores and large retailers most commonly use to value their inventory is the conventional retail inventory method. A taxpayer may use the retail inventory method to value ending inventory for a department, a class of goods, or a stock-keeping unit. A taxpayer maintaining more than one department or dealing in classes of goods with different percentages of gross profit must compute cost complements separately for each department or class of goods [Prop. Reg. § 1.471-8(d)].

The retail inventory method of accounting uses a formula to convert the retail selling price of ending inventory to an approximation of cost (retail cost method) or an approximation of lower of cost or market (retail LCM method). A taxpayer may use the retail inventory method instead of valuing inventory at cost under Reg. § 1.471-3 or lower of cost or market under Reg. § 1.471-4 [Prop. Reg. § 1.471-8(a)].

A taxpayer computes the value of ending inventory under the retail inventory method by multiplying a cost complement by the retail selling prices of the goods on hand at the end of the taxable year [Prop. Reg. § 1.471-8(b) (1)]. The cost complement is a ratio computed as follows:

- The numerator is the value of beginning inventory plus the cost of goods purchased during the taxable year. A taxpayer may not reduce the numerator of the cost complement by the amount of an allowance, discount, or price rebate a taxpayer earns by selling specific merchandise [Prop. Reg. § 1.471-8(b) (2) (ii)]. A retail LCM method taxpayer may not reduce the numerator of the cost complement for an allowance, discount, or price rebate that is related to or intended to compensate for a permanent markdown of retail selling prices [Prop. Reg. § 1.471-8(b) (2) (iii)]. Thus, in the case of markdown allowances and margin protection payments, the value of ending inventory as computed under the retail LCM method is reduced solely as a result of the reduction in retail selling price, avoiding an unwarranted additional reduction in inventory value for a single markdown allowance and more reasonably approximating LCM.

- The denominator is the retail selling prices of beginning inventory plus the retail selling prices of goods purchased during the year (that is, the bona fide retail selling prices of the items at the time acquired), adjusted for all permanent markups and markdowns, including markup and markdown cancellations and corrections. The denominator is not adjusted for temporary markups or markdowns [Prop. Reg. § 1.471-8(b) (2)]. Finally, the proposed regulations clarify that, under the retail inventory method, taxpayers do not adjust the cost complement or ending retail selling prices for temporary markdowns and markups.

The cost complement is then multiplied by the retail selling price of ending inventory to determine the ending inventory value [Prop. Reg. § 1.471-8(b) (2) (i)].

For inventory valuation purposes, Reg. § 1.471-3(a) generally provides that the cost of purchases during the year generally includes invoice price less trade or other discounts. A sales-based allowance is based on a retailer's sales volume (sales-based allowance). A volume-based allowance is based on the quantity of merchandise a retailer purchases. A markdown allowance or margin protection payment may relate to a retailer's reduction in retail selling price. Under Prop. Reg. § 1.471-3(e), the amount of an allowance, discount, or price rebate a taxpayer earns by selling specific merchandise (a sales-based vendor allowance) is a reduction in the cost of the merchandise sold and does not reduce the inventory cost or value of goods on hand at the end of the tax year.

¶17,055 METHODS DISAPPROVED

The following methods of taking or valuing inventory are specifically disapproved [Reg. § 1.471-2(f)]:

- Deducting from the inventory a reserve for price changes, or an estimated depreciation in its value;
- Taking work in process, or other parts of the inventory, at a nominal price or at less than its proper value;
- Omitting portions of the stock on hand;
- Using a constant price or nominal value for so-called normal quantity of materials or goods in stock;
- Including stock in transit, either shipped to or from the taxpayer, when the title is not vested in the taxpayer;

- Using the direct cost method by allocating only the variable indirect production costs to the costs of goods produced while treating fixed costs as currently deductible period costs.
- Using the *prime cost method* by treating all indirect production costs as currently deductible period costs; and
- Writing down inventory based solely on sales activity rather than true market value.[48]

¶17,060 BASIS

If property should have been included in inventory, its basis is the last inventory value [Code Sec. 1013; Reg. § 1.1013-1].

FARM INVENTORY AND ACCOUNTING

¶17,065 INCOME FROM FARMING

.01 Accounting Methods of Farmers

Farmers have the option of choosing an accounting method for their farm business when they file their first income tax return that includes a Schedule F. However, farmers cannot use the crop method for any tax return, including the first tax return, unless the farmer receives approval from the IRS. Generally, farmers may use any of the following accounting methods:

- Cash method—Under the cash method, all items of income that the farmer actually or constructively receives during the year are included in gross income. If property or services are received, the farmer must include their fair market value in income. Expenses are deducted in the tax year in which the expenses are actually paid.
- Accrual method—Under the accrual method, the farmer includes an amount in income in the tax year in which all events that fix the farmer's right to receive the income have occurred and the farmer can determine the amount with reasonable accuracy. Expenses are deducted when: (1) the all-events test has been met which will occur when all events have occurred that fix the fact of liability and the liability can be determined with reasonable accuracy; and (2) economic performance has occurred.
- Special methods of accounting for certain items of income and expenses.
- Combination (hybrid) method using elements of two or more of the above.

A farmer that operates two or more separate and distinct businesses can use a different accounting method for each business. No business is considered to be separate and distinct unless a different set of books and records is maintained for each business.

---

48 Rev. Rul. 77-364, 1977-2 CB 183.

Change in Accounting Method

Once a farmer has set up an accounting method, the farmer must receive IRS approval before changing to another method [Reg. § 1.471-6(a)]. A change in accounting method includes a change in:

- The overall method, such as from cash to an accrual method, and
- The farmer's treatment of any material item, such as a change in the farmer's method of valuing inventory (for example, a change from the farm-price method to the unit-livestock-price method). To obtain approval, the farmer must file Form 3115 and may also be required to pay a fee.

When Accrual Method Mandated

Although most farmers use the cash method of accounting because it is much easier to keep cash method records, the following farmers must use the accrual method of accounting:

1. A corporation (other than a family corporation) that had gross receipts of more than $1 million for any tax year beginning after 1975 [Code Sec. 447(a)].
2. A family corporation that had gross receipts of more than $25,000,000 for any tax year beginning after 1985 [Code Sec. 447(d)(2)].
3. A partnership with a corporation as a partner.
4. A tax shelter.

Note that items 1, 2, and 3 above do not apply to an S corporation or a business operating a nursery or sod farm, or the raising or harvesting of trees (other than fruit and nut trees).

Family Corporation Defined

A family corporation is generally a corporation that meets one of the following ownership requirements [Code Sec. 447(d)]:

- Members of the same family own at least 50 percent of the total combined voting power of all classes of stock entitled to vote and at least 50 percent of the total shares of all other classes of stock of the corporation.
- Members of two families have owned, directly or indirectly, since October 4, 1976, at least 65 percent of the total combined voting power of all classes of voting stock and at least 65 percent of the total shares of all other classes of the corporation's stock.
- Members of three families have owned, directly or indirectly, since October 4, 1976, at least 50 percent of the total combined voting power of all classes of voting stock and at least 50 percent of the total shares of all other classes of the corporation's stock.

Tax Shelter Defined

A tax shelter is a partnership, noncorporate enterprise, or S corporation that meets either of the following tests:

1. Its principal purpose is the avoidance or evasion of federal income tax.
2. It is a farming syndicate, which is an entity that meets either of the following tests:

- Interests in the activity have been offered for sale in an offering required to be registered with a federal or state agency with the authority to regulate the offering of securities for sale.
- More than 35 percent of the losses during the tax years are allocable to limited partners or limited entrepreneurs. A limited partner is defined as one whose personal liability for partnership debts is limited to the money or other property the partner contributed or is required to contribute to the partnership. A limited entrepreneur is one who has an interest in an enterprise other than as a limited partner and does not actively participate in the management of the enterprise.

Deferral of Crop Insurance Proceeds

A cash-basis farmer who receives insurance proceeds as a result of destruction of, or damage to, crops may make an election to include those proceeds in income in the year following the year of damage or destruction if the income from the crops would normally have been reported in the following year [Code Sec. 451(d); Reg. § 1.451-6]. Federal payments received as a result of (a) destruction or damage to crops caused by drought, flood, or any other natural disaster or (b) the inability to plant crops because of such a natural disaster are treated as insurance proceeds received as a result of destruction of, or damage to, crops for this purpose [Code Sec. 451(e); Reg. § 1.451-7]. If, however, a cash-basis farmer receives the proceeds in the year following the casualty year, he merely includes them in income in that year without making the election [Reg. § 1.451-6(a)].

Crop Method

You may use the crop basis method to figure the income from crops that take more than one year to grow and sell. This is a special variation of the accrual basis, and the entire cost of producing the crop must be deducted in the year you realize the gross income from the crop [Reg. § 1.61-4(c)]. You must file an application to use this method within 180 days after the start of the tax year to be covered by the return [Ch. 18].

.02 Income Averaging for Farmers and Commercial Fishermen

Individuals engaged in a fishing or commercial fishing business can elect to average all or part of their "farm income" over a three-year period [Code Sec. 1301(a); Reg. § 1.1301-1(a)]. The purpose of the three-year averaging option is to enable a farmer or fisherman to equalize the wide differences in their tax liabilities that may occur each year as a result of uncontrollable factors such as weather, natural and man-made disasters, and the overall farm or fishing economy. Farmers and commercial fishermen making this election should complete Schedule J (Form 1040), *Income Averaging for Farmers and Fishermen,* to compute their tax and attach it to their Form 1040. An electing eligible individual taxpayer must do the following:

1. Designate all or part of his or her taxable income for the year from the business of farming as "elected farm or commercial fishing income" (including gain from the sale of property, except land, regularly used in the taxpayer's farming business for a substantial period);
2. Allocate one-third of the "elected farm or commercial fishing income" to each of the prior three tax years; and

3. Determine current year tax liability by determining the sum of:
   a. Current year tax liability without the elected farm income allocated to the three prior tax years; plus
   b. The increase in the tax liability for each of the three prior tax years by taking into account the allocable share of the elected farm income for those years [Code Sec. 1301; Reg. § 1.1301-1(a)].

Fishing Business Defined

The availability of income averaging for fishermen applies to individuals engaged in a fishing business, not recreational fishermen [Code Sec. 1301(a)]. A fishing business is defined as the conduct of commercial fishing where the harvested fish enter commerce or are intended to enter commerce through sale, barter or trade [Code Sec. 1301(b)(4)]. Fishing means the catching, taking, or harvesting of fish; the attempted catching, taking, or harvesting of fish; any activities that reasonably can be expected to result in the catching, taking, or harvesting of fish; or any operations at sea in support of or in preparation for the catching, taking, or harvesting of fish. Fishing does not include any scientific research activity conducted by a scientific research vessel. Fish means finfish, mollusks, crustaceans, and all other forms of marine animal and plant life, other than marine mammals and birds. Catching, taking, or harvesting includes activities that result in the killing of fish or the bringing of live fish on board a vessel [Reg. § 1.1301-1(b)(1)(i)].

An individual engaged in a farming or fishing business includes a sole proprietor of a farming or fishing business, a partner in a partnership engaged in a farming or fishing business, and a shareholder of an S corporation engaged in a farming or fishing business, but not a C corporation shareholder, or employee or a trust or estate [Code Sec. 1301(b)(2); Reg. § 1.1301-1(b)(1)(iii)].

Identification of Items Attributable to Farming or Fishing Business

Farm and fishing income includes items of income, deduction, gain, and loss attributable to an individual's farming or fishing business. Farm and fishing losses include any net operating loss carryover or carryback or net capital loss carryover to an election year. Income, gain, or loss from the sale of development rights, grazing rights, and other similar rights is not treated as attributable to a farming business. In general, farm and fishing income does not include compensation received as an employee. However, a shareholder of an S corporation engaged in a farming or fishing business may treat compensation received from the corporation as farm or fishing income if the compensation is paid by the corporation in the conduct of the farming or fishing business. If a crewmember on a vessel engaged in commercial fishing is compensated by a share of the boat's catch of fish or a share of the proceeds from the sale of the catch, the crewmember is treated as engaged in a fishing business and the compensation is treated for such purposes as income from a fishing business [Reg. § 1.1301-1(e)(1)(i)].

Determination of Amount That May Be Elected Farm Income

The maximum amount of income that an individual may elect to average (electible farm income) is the sum of any farm and fishing income and gains, minus any farm and fishing deductions or losses (including loss carryovers and carrybacks) that are allowed as a deduction in computing the individual's taxable income [Reg. § 1.1301-1(e)(2)(i)(A)]. Individuals conducting both a farming business and a fishing business must calculate electible farm income by combining income, gains, deductions, and losses derived from the farming business and the fishing business [Reg. § 1.1301-1(e)(2)(i)(B)]. Electible farm income may not exceed taxable income, and electible farm income from net capital gain attributable to a farming or fishing business may not exceed total net capital gain. Subject to these limitations, an individual who has both ordinary income and net capital gain from a farming or fishing business may elect to average any combination of the ordinary income and net capital gain [Reg. § 1.1301-1(e)(2)(i)(D)].

Alternative Minimum Tax (AMT)

Both a farmer and a fisherman may choose to use the income averaging rules to reduce their regular tax liability. Since the amount of a taxpayer's AMT is equal to the excess of the taxpayer's tentative minimum tax over his or her regular tax, such a reduction in the taxpayer's regular tax could end up leading to a higher AMT liability. Thus, solely for purposes of computing any AMT liability, the regular tax is determined without regard to averaging of farm and fishing income [Code Sec. 55(c)(2)]. Consequently, the AMT, that is, the excess of that taxpayer's tentative minimum tax over the regular tax, will be smaller by not applying the income averaging rules when computing AMT.

¶17,070 INVENTORIES OF FARMERS AND LIVESTOCK RAISERS

.01 Accounting for Inventory

Farmers who are required to keep an inventory must keep a complete record of their inventory that shows the actual count of the inventory as well as all factors that enter into its valuation, including quality and weight, if applicable. Generally, a farmer who produces, purchases, or sells merchandise must keep an inventory and use the accrual method for purchases and sales of merchandise. An exception is available for "qualifying taxpayers" or "qualifying small business taxpayers."

Exceptions

If the taxpayer is a qualifying taxpayer or a qualifying small business taxpayer that has an eligible business, the taxpayer may use the cash method of accounting, even if the farmer produces, purchases, or sells merchandise. A qualifying taxpayer can also choose not to keep an inventory, even if the taxpayer does not change to the cash method.

A qualifying taxpayer is defined as a taxpayer that has average annual gross receipts of $1 million or less for the three-year tax period ending with that prior tax year. Note that a tax shelter cannot be a qualifying taxpayer.

A qualifying small business taxpayer is defined as a taxpayer that: (1) for each prior tax year has average annual gross receipts of $10 million or less for the three-tax-year period ending with that prior tax year; and (2) whose principal business activity is not an ineligible activity.[49] Note that the qualifying small business exception does not apply to a farming business. However, if the taxpayer is a qualifying small business taxpayer engaged in a farming business, this exception may apply to the taxpayer's nonfarming businesses.

What Is Included in Inventory

The following items must be included in the farmer's inventory:

1. *Hatchery business.* Taxpayers in the hatchery business and on the accrual method of accounting must include in inventory eggs in the process of incubation.
2. *Products held for sale.* All harvested and purchased farm products held for sale or for feed or seed, such as grain, hay, cotton, etc., must be included in inventory.
3. *Supplies.* Supplies acquired for sale or that become a physical part of items held for sale must be included in inventory.
4. *Livestock.* Livestock held primarily for sale must be included in inventory. Livestock held for draft, breeding, or dairy products can either be depreciated or included in inventory.
5. *Growing crops.* Generally growing crops need not be included inventory. However, if the crop has a preproductive period of more than two years, the costs associated with the crop must be capitalized or included in inventory.
6. *Items held for sale.* Inventory should include all items held for sale, or for use as feed, seed, etc., whether raised or purchased, that are unsold at the end of the year.

.02 Inventory Valuation Methods

Farmers who must value inventories to determine taxable income may do so on the basis of cost, or cost or market, whichever is lower. However, a simpler method for farmers is the "farm-price method." In addition, farmers raising livestock may value their inventories of animals according to either the "farm-price method" or the "unit-livestock-price method."

For inventory capitalization rules that apply to farmers and ranchers, see the discussion of capitalizing farming costs below.

.03 Farm-Price Method

Under this method, you value inventories at market price less the direct cost of disposition. Market price is the current price at the nearest market in the quantities you usually sell. Cost of disposition includes broker's commissions, freight, hauling to market, and other marketing costs. If you use this method, it must be applied to the entire inventory except livestock inventory that you elect to value under the unit-livestock-price method. If you used a different method to value inventories in prior years and switch to the farm-price method, you must get IRS permission for the change [Reg. § 1.446-1(e), 1.471-6(d)].

---

[49] Rev. Proc. 2002-28, 2002-1 CB 815, as modified by Rev. Proc. 2011-14, IRB 2011-4.

.04 Unit-Livestock-Price Method

This method takes into consideration, the difficulty of establishing the exact cost of producing and raising each animal. Under this method, you group or classify animals that you raise by class. Animals within a class are then valued at a standard unit price [Reg. § 1.471-6(e)]. The IRS must approve the method you use to classify animals.[50] To find the unit cost for each classification, you must take into account the age and kind of animals included within a class. This is so that normal costs incurred in producing the animals will be reflected. You must annually reevaluate your unit livestock prices and adjust the prices upward or downward to reflect increases or decreases in the costs of raising livestock. IRS approval is not required for these adjustments. Any other changes in unit prices or classifications do require IRS approval.

Example 17-23: If it costs $15 to produce a calf and $7.50 each year to raise a calf to maturity, the classification and unit prices would be as follows: calves, $15; yearlings, $22.50; two-year-olds, $30; mature animals, $37.50.

If you are using the farm-price method and want to switch to the unit-livestock-price method, you must get IRS approval[51] for the change. However, if you have filed returns on the basis of inventories at cost, or cost or market, whichever is lower, you may adopt the unit-livestock-price method without formal application [Reg. § 1.471-6(h)].

.05 Livestock Included in Inventory

Accrual basis farmers must include in inventory all livestock raised or purchased for sale. But you may treat livestock acquired for draft, breeding, or dairy purposes as depreciable capital assets, or include them in inventory. Although you may use either method, whatever you choose must be applied consistently from year to year.

For preproductive period costs, see the discussion of capitalizing farming costs below. If you use the unit-livestock method, it applies to all livestock raised, whether for sale or for breeding, draft or dairy purposes.[52] Livestock that you purchase must be included in inventory at cost. However, farmers still have the option to either inventory or capitalize livestock purchased for breeding, draft, or dairy purposes [Reg. § 1.471-6(g)]. Once you elect a method, it can be changed only with IRS consent [Ch. 18].[53]

In figuring gain or loss from livestock in inventory, the inventory value takes the place of the original cost, if any.[54]

.06 Capitalizing Farming Costs Under UNICAP Rules

Taxpayers must capitalize the cost of producing all plants and animals except the costs of producing plants with pre-productive periods of less than two years or the costs of replanting and developing plants lost or damaged by a casualty. In addition, soil and water conservation expenditures described in Code Sec. 175 and fertilizer described in Code Sec. 180 incurred during the pre-productive period must be capitalized under

---

[50] Treas. Dept., IRS Publication 225, "Farmer's Tax Guide" (2013 Ed.), p. 7.

[51] Treas. Dept., IRS Publication 225, "Farmer's Tax Guide" (2013 Ed.), p. 7.

[52] *J. Catto*, SCt, 66-1 USTC ¶9376, 384 US 102, 86 SCt 1311.

[53] Rev. Rul. 60-60, 1960-1 CB 190.

[54] Rev. Rul. 60-60, 1960-1 CB 190.

Code Sec. 263A. However, these expenditures are not subject to capitalization under the UNICAP rules except to the extent that they must be capitalized as pre-productive period costs [Reg. § 1.263A-4(b)(1)].

A taxpayer that grows a plant which will have more than one crop or yield is engaged in the production of two types of property, the plant and the crop or yield of the plants. That means that, for example, the orange farmer would be engaged in the production of the orange and the orange tree. The regulations clarify the proper tax treatment of field costs including the costs of irrigating and fertilizing, that are incurred after a crop or yield is harvested but before the crop or yield is disposed of, which do not benefit and are unrelated to the crop or yield that has been harvested. These costs do not have to be capitalized to the harvested crop or yield because they relate to the plant or a future crop or yield rather than to the harvested crop or yield.

Reg. § 1.263A-4(b)(2) also provides that the following factors are relevant in determining whether the crop or yield is produced in sufficient quantities to be harvested and marketed in the ordinary course: (1) whether a harvested crop or yield is more than de minimis, although less than expected at the maximum bearing stage, based on a comparison of the quantities per acre harvested in the year in question to the quantities per acre expected to be harvested when the plant reaches full maturity; and (2) whether the sales proceeds exceed the costs of harvest and make a reasonable contribution to an allocable share of farm expenses.

.07 Farming UNICAP Exceptions

Under Code Sec. 263A(d)(3), farmers who are not required under Code Sec. 447 to use an accrual method of accounting and who are not prohibited from using the cash method by Code Sec. 448(a)(3) (qualified taxpayers) are eligible for two exceptions to the UNICAP requirements as follows:

- They do not have to capitalize costs of producing plants with a pre-productive period of two years or less, or animals, in a farming business [Code Sec. 263A(d)(1)]; and
- They may elect out of the UNICAP requirements for the costs of producing plants in a farming business [Code Sec. 263A(d)(3)].

Reg. § 1.263A-4(a)(4)(i) provides that those engaged in contract harvesting, reselling plants or animals that are not self-produced, and processing that is not incident to growing or harvesting agricultural or horticultural commodities are not producing property in a farming business. However, the final regulations clarify that a taxpayer is engaged in the production of property in a farming business, rather than the mere resale of plants or animals, if the plant or animal is held for further cultivation or development before its sale. A list of factors is provided in the Reg. § 1.263A-4(a)(4)(i) to assist you in determining whether a plant or animal is held for further cultivation or development prior to sale or merely held for resale.

.08 More Than Two-Year Preproductive Period

Qualified taxpayers must capitalize only the costs of producing plants that have a pre-productive period of more than two years. For a plant grown in commercial quantities in the United States, this determination is based on the nationwide weighted average preproductive period of the plant. In Notice 2013-18,[55] the IRS has provided the following list of commercially grown plants with nationwide weighted average preproductive periods in excess of two years: almonds, apples, apricots, avocados, blueberries, cherries, chestnuts, coffee beans, currants, dates, figs, grapefruit, grapes, guavas, kiwifruit, kumquats, lemons, limes, macadamia nuts, mangoes, nectarines, olives, oranges, peaches, pears, pecans, persimmons, pistachio nuts, plums, pomegranates, prunes, tangelos, tangerines, tangors, and walnuts.

▶ **PRACTICE POINTER:** Notice 2013-18 provides certainty to farmers who grow crops that appear on the list. They now know that they will have to elect out of UNICAP if they want to currently deduct their preproductive development costs.

.09 Election Not to Capitalize Costs

A qualified taxpayer may elect to deduct, rather than capitalize preproductive costs, automatically on its original federal income tax return for the tax year in which the taxpayer would otherwise be required to capitalize costs under Code Sec. 263A. This is accomplished by not applying the UNICAP rules and by applying the special rules specified in Reg. § 1.263A-4(d)(4), such as required use of the alternative depreciation system. If this automatic election isn't made in that year, the taxpayer may make the election by filing Form 3115, *Application for Change in Accounting Method,* using the appropriate procedures for filing that form [Reg. § 1.263A-4(d)(3)].

---

[55] Notice 2013-18, IRB 2013-14, 742; Rev. Proc. 2013-20, IRB 2013-14.

18 Accounting

ACCOUNTING METHODS

Methods of accounting . . . . ¶ 18,001

Cash receipts and disbursements method . . . . ¶ 18,005

Constructive receipt—cash basis . . ¶ 18,010

Income paid to third parties—assignments . . . . ¶ 18,015

Constructive payment—cash basis . . . . ¶ 18,020

Accrual basis . . . . ¶ 18,025

Accounting methods must clearly reflect income . . . . ¶ 18,030

Records . . . . ¶ 18,035

Reconstruction of income . . . . . . ¶ 18,040

Change in accounting method . . . ¶ 18,045

Adjustments required by change in accounting method . . . . ¶ 18,050

ACCOUNTING PERIODS

Accounting periods . . . . ¶ 18,055

Change in accounting period . . . . ¶ 18,060

How to request a change in accounting period . . . . ¶ 18,065

Returns for periods of fewer than 12 months . . . . ¶ 18,070

Special rule for tax year election by partnerships, S corporations, electing S corporations, and personal service corporations . . . . . . ¶ 18,075

WHEN TO REPORT INCOME

Period in which items of gross income reported . . . . ¶ 18,080

Compensation for services . . . . . . ¶ 18,085

Dividends . . . . ¶ 18,090

Interest and discounts . . . . ¶ 18,095

Discount and interest on U.S. savings bonds . . . . ¶ 18,100

Rent and deferred rent transactions . . . . ¶ 18,105

Income from sale of property or stock . . . . ¶ 18,110

Prepaid income . . . . ¶ 18,115

Disputed income . . . . ¶ 18,120

Repaid income . . . . ¶ 18,125

WHEN TO CLAIM DEDUCTIONS

When deductions may be claimed . . . . ¶ 18,130

Deductions limited to amount at risk . . . . ¶ 18,135

Passive activities loss limitations . . . . ¶ 18,140

Vacation or incentive bonuses . . . . ¶ 18,145

Advertising expenses . . . . ¶ 18,150

Interest . . . . ¶ 18,155

Taxes . . . . ¶ 18,160

Medical expenses . . . . ¶ 18,165

Contributions . . . . ¶ 18,170
Bad debts and losses . . . . ¶ 18,175
Reserves for expenses and losses . . . . ¶ 18,180
Deductions for farmers prepaying 50 percent or more of farming expenses . . . . ¶ 18,185
Depreciable property . . . . ¶ 18,190

ACCOUNTING METHODS

An accounting method is a set of rules used to determine when and how you report your income and expenses. The regular method of accounting you use to keep your books is generally used in computing your income for tax purposes. The method used must clearly reflect taxable income.

¶18,001 METHODS OF ACCOUNTING

A taxpayer's methods of accounting determine the time for reporting income and expenses. No one method of accounting is appropriate for all taxpayers. Therefore, the tax law requires each taxpayer to adopt the forms and methods of accounting suitable for his or her purpose [Code Sec. 446(a); Reg. § 1.446-1(a)(2)]. The two principal methods of accounting are:

- The cash receipts and disbursements, or *cash basis,* method of accounting [¶ 18,005]; and
- The *accrual basis* method of accounting [¶ 18,025].

If you are a cash-basis taxpayer, you generally take income into account when you receive it and deduct expenses when you pay them. On the other hand, if you are an accrual-basis taxpayer, you take income into account when you earn it and deduct expenses when you incur them. Other methods of accounting used include the installment sales method of accounting [¶ 19,001], long-term contracts method [¶ 19,075], and farmers' crop basis [¶ 17,065]. Hybrid methods may also be used [(a) below].

C corporations, partnerships that have a C corporation as a partner, tax shelters, and tax-exempt trusts with unrelated business income generally cannot use the cash method (or a hybrid method reporting partly on a cash method). However, the cash method continues to be available to: businesses (but not tax shelters) with average annual gross receipts (less returns and allowances) of $5 million or less for the preceding three years (or the shorter period they conducted business); employee-owned service businesses in the field of health, law, accounting, engineering, architecture, actuarial science, performing arts or consulting (qualified personal service corporations); and farming and timber businesses [Code Sec. 448(b)].

.01 Hybrid Accounting Method

You can use a combination of accounting methods if it clearly reflects income and you use it consistently. If you use the accrual basis for purchases and sales, you can use the cash basis for all other income and expense items. You cannot, however, combine cash basis for income with accruals of expenses [Code Sec. 446(c); Reg. § 1.446-1(c)(1)(iv)].

The IRS has said that you are not required to have strict book-tax accounting conformity. You can use different accounting methods, provided you maintain workpapers that document all adjustments between book and taxable income. The IRS approved a company's use of the cash method of accounting for income taxes, even though the company maintained accrual books.[1]

.02 More Than One Trade or Business

If you are engaged in two or more separate and distinct businesses, you may use a different method for each. That means, however, you must keep separate books and records [Code Sec. 446(d); Reg. § 1.446-1(d)].

.03 Income Solely From Wages

If your income is derived solely from wages, you are not required to keep formal books. Your accounting method may be established from your tax returns, copies of them, or other records [Reg. § 1.446-1(b)(2)].

.04 Safe Harbor Methods of Accounting

Safe Harbor for Purchasers of Previously Leased Vehicles

The IRS has created a safe harbor method of accounting for capital cost reduction (CCR) payments by those taxpayers in the business of purchasing motor vehicles subject to lease from dealers.[2] The safe harbor method of accounting excludes the capital cost reduction payments from both the purchaser's gross income and its basis in the vehicle. Taxpayers have automatic consent to a change to this method without filing Form 3115, *Application to Change a Method of Accounting.* A CCR payment is defined as any payment made by an individual leasing a motor vehicle at the beginning of the lease that reduces the total amount paid during the lease term. A CCR payment may be:

- A cash down payment;
- The trade-in value of the individual's used vehicle;
- A rebate or incentive supplied by the manufacturer;
- Credits earned under a credit card reward program; or
- The first or last monthly rental payment.

Excluded from the definition of CCR payment are refundable security deposits; extended service plan fees; sales, leases, excise, use, or *ad valorem* taxes paid in advance or collected by the dealer; or administrative fees made in connection with a motor vehicle lease.

Safe Harbor for Truck Tires

The IRS has provided a safe harbor method of accounting for the cost of original and replacement tires for most trucks used in business activities in Rev. Proc. 2002-27.[3] The new method is called the *original tire capitalization method* and it requires truck purchasers to capitalize the cost of the original tires and depreciate them using the same depreciation method, recovery period and convention that apply to the truck,

---

[1] LTR 9103001 (June 19, 1990); AOD No. 1991-07.

[2] Rev. Proc. 2002-36, 2002-1 CB 993.

[3] Rev. Proc. 2002-27, 2002-1 CB 802.

and allows the truck purchaser to deduct the cost of replacement tires as an expense in the tax year in which they are installed on the vehicle. In order to use this method, the taxpayer must use it for all original and replacement tires on its qualifying vehicles.

> **Example 18-1:** A taxpayer puts a light truck in service in 2009. He replaces the tires during 2011 and again during 2013. He would depreciate the original tires as part of the truck over the truck's five year MACRS recovery period (even though they are replaced in 2012), and expense the cost of the replacement tires in 2011 and 2013.

A taxpayer who wants to change to the original tire capitalization method must follow the IRS procedure established to make an automatic change in accounting method with one modification. Include the statement: Automatic Change Filed Under Rev. Proc. 2002-27, on the appropriate line on Form 3115 requesting the change. The automatic accounting method will be unavailable to taxpayers who have a tire-cost issue under consideration in examination, before appeals, or before a federal court, or pending in examination. In Chief Counsel Advice 200252091, the IRS said that a taxpayer who has not elected the original tire capitalization method can currently deduct the cost of retread tires as a repair if the retread is consumable in less than one year.

Safe Harbor for Auto Part Remanufacturers and Resellers

In Rev. Proc. 2003-20,[4] the IRS provided a safe harbor method of accounting that remanufacturers and resellers of rebuilt automotive parts can use to value their inventory of rebuildable cores. Taxpayers using the lower of cost or market inventory method can value their inventory of cores by reference to prices in an established core supplier market. This method is called the core alternative valuation method. To change to this method, a taxpayer must file Form 3115.

Safe Harbor for Heavy Equipment Industries

In Rev Proc. 2006-14,[5] the IRS provided a safe harbor accounting method for heavy equipment dealers. The safe harbor allows them to approximate the cost of their heavy equipment parts inventory using a replacement cost method. A taxpayer is a "heavy equipment dealer" only if the taxpayer sells new heavy equipment under an agreement with one or more heavy equipment manufacturers or distributors and earns a majority of its revenue from the sale, or sale and lease, of new heavy equipment.

Replacement cost method. Under the replacement cost method, a taxpayer must determine the cost of the heavy equipment parts in its inventory by reference to the replacement cost of the heavy equipment parts using a standard price list which states the price at which the equipment can be purchased on the date of the inventory. If the price is unavailable on the current price list, then taxpayers should use the price at which the equipment was last offered for purchase. The price list must be a standard price list that is widely used and recognized by the heavy equipment industry. It must be used for business purposes by the heavy equipment dealer industry and the taxpayer

---

[4] Rev. Proc. 2003-20, 2003-1 CB 445.

[5] Rev. Proc. 2006-14, 2006-1 CB 350.

must use it in the ordinary course of business to purchase heavy equipment. In addition, taxpayers must satisfy book conformity and recordkeeping requirements.

Audit protection. For taxpayers currently using the replacement cost valuation method, the IRS is offering audit protection without filing Form 3115. Additionally, the taxpayer's use of the replacement cost accounting method will not be raised as an issue in a tax year that ends before April 30, 2005. Moreover, if the replacement cost method is currently an issue, it will no longer be pursued by the IRS.

Taxpayers wishing to switch to the replacement cost method should file Form 3115.

Safe Harbor for Depreciation of Rotable Spare Parts

In Rev. Proc. 2007-48,[6] the IRS provided a safe harbor method of accounting to treat rotable spare parts as depreciable assets, rather than as inventory, effective for tax years ending on or after December 31, 2006. Taxpayers can obtain automatic consent to adopt the new safe harbor if they account for their rotable spare parts in accordance with specific provisions in Rev. Proc. 2007-48. Changing treatment of rotable spare parts is a change in method of accounting subject to the rules of Code Sec. 446 and Code Sec. 481. If a taxpayer is not eligible for an automatic change to the safe harbor method of accounting, the taxpayer may request to change its method of accounting for treating rotable spare parts by filing Form 3115.

A taxpayer relying on the safe harbor method of accounting for rotable spare parts must:

1. Capitalize the cost of the rotable spare parts under Code Sec. 263 and depreciate these parts under Code Sec. 168,
2. Establish one or more pools for the rotable spare parts,
3. Identify the disposed rotable spare parts, and
4. Determine the depreciable basis of the rotable spare parts for depreciation purposes.

If taxpayers follow the safe harbor provided in Rev. Proc. 2007-48, the IRS will not challenge the taxpayer's treatment of the pools of rotable spare parts as depreciable assets.

Safe Harbors for Motor Vehicle Dealerships

In Rev. Proc. 2010-44,[7] the IRS provided two safe harbor accounting methods for motor vehicle dealerships: the retail sales facility safe harbor method; and the reseller without production activities safe harbor method. The IRS also provided procedures for obtaining automatic consent to change to the safe harbor methods. Under the retail sales facility safe harbor method, a dealership is not required to capitalize certain handling and storage costs incurred at its retail sales facility. Under the reseller without production activities safe harbor method, the cost of certain handling activities performed on vehicles, other than the cost of vehicle parts, is not required to be capitalized to the extent incurred at the dealership's retail sales facility. Any motor vehicle dealership may use either or both of the safe harbor methods.

---

[6] Rev. Proc. 2007-48, 2007-2 CB 110.

[7] Rev. Proc. 2010-44, IRB 2010-49, 811.

Safe Harbors for Telecom Network Asset Costs

The IRS has issued three revenue procedures that provide safe harbors for the accounting treatment of network assets owned by wireless and wireline telecommunications carriers. The guidance also allows eligible companies to obtain automatic IRS consent to change to the permitted methods of accounting.

In Rev. Proc. 2011-22,[8] the IRS provides a safe harbor method for determining the depreciation period for certain tangible assets used by wireless telecommunications carriers. Rev. Proc. 2011-22 applies to depreciable assets used primarily to provide wireless telecom or broadband services by mobile phones. It is limited to mobile telephone switching offices (MTSOs) and cell sites. The guidance lists the typical equipment used at MTSOs and cell sites, including antenna towers.

In Rev. Proc. 2011-27,[9] the IRS provides two safe harbor methods for determining the amount of wireline telecom network asset repair and replacement costs that should be capitalized and deducted. Rev. Proc. 2011-27 applies to all real and personal property used by a wireline carrier to provide wireline telecommunication or broadband services.

In Rev. Proc. 2011-28,[10] the IRS provides two similar safe harbors for capitalizing/deducting wireless telecom carrier network costs. Rev. Proc. 2011-28 applies to all real and personal property used by a wireless carrier to provide wireless telecommunication or broadband services.

¶18,005 CASH RECEIPTS AND DISBURSEMENTS METHOD

The cash receipts and disbursements method of accounting (the cash method) is the method most commonly used by individuals. Under this method, income is generally recognized in the year of actual or constructive receipt and expenses are deductible in the year of actual payment [Reg. § 1.446-1(c)(1)(i)]. Income is recognized when actually or constructively received in the form of cash, a cash equivalent, or other property with an ascertainable value. Property may be a cash equivalent if it can be valued with reasonable certainty and is received without any substantial restrictions on its use or disposition. Cash equivalents include checks, notes, credits, letters of credit, forgiveness of debt, assumptions of liabilities, and any other property with an ascertainable value [Code Sec. 451].

A cash basis taxpayer generally accounts for deductions in the year in which the taxpayer makes actual payment in cash or in property that is a cash equivalent [Reg. § 1.461-1(a)(1)]. Payments in the form of refundable deposits or notes are not currently deductible.

.01 Who May Use

The cash method is limited to S corporations, sole proprietorships, and partnerships that have no C corporation partners. Qualified personal service corporations may also

[8] Rev. Proc. 2011-22, IRB 2011-18, 737.

[9] Rev. Proc. 2011-27, IRB 2011-18, 740.

[10] Rev. Proc. 2011-28, IRB 2011-18, 743.

use the cash method if they are substantially involved in performing services in the fields of health, law, accounting, performing arts, etc. Also, all of their stock must be substantially owned (at least 95 percent in value) by employees performing services in these fields, their estates, or anyone acquiring an ownership interest by reason of that person's death within the past 24 months [Code Sec. 448(a); Temp. Reg. § 1.448-1T(a)].

.02 Qualifying Small Businesses May Use Cash Method

Small business taxpayers with gross receipts of $10 million or less may use the cash method for their eligible trades or businesses.[11] Qualifying taxpayers will not be required to maintain inventories under Code Sec. 471 to use accrual accounting or to capitalize various indirect costs under Code Sec. 263A. The main advantage of the cash method is the ability to defer income until payment is actually or constructively received instead of having to take income into account when the customer is billed. The cash method of accounting provides for a more accurate matching of tax accounting practices and the actual receipt of income and therefore promotes tax deferral. Deductions for inventory items or material items used in a business, however, will have to be deferred until the later of payment or use of the item.

Who Will Benefit?

Service businesses that also sell related products, such as a plumber who also sells plumbing supplies will benefit from using the cash method of accounting. The cash method will generally be unavailable to manufacturers, wholesalers, retailers, miners, certain publishers, and sound recorders unless they are principally a service business or perform certain kinds of custom manufacturing.

What Taxpayers Qualify for Small Business Exclusion?

A qualifying small business for these purposes is one that (1) has average annual gross receipts of $10 million or less, and (2) is not prohibited from using the cash method under Code Sec. 448. For example, corporations, and partnerships with corporate partners, generally must use an accrual method if their gross receipts are more than $5 million.

A qualifying small business may use the cash method for all of its trades or businesses if the taxpayer satisfies any one of the following three tests and did not previously change (and was not previously required to have changed) from the cash method to an accrual method for any trade or business as a result of becoming ineligible to use the cash method.

1. The taxpayer reasonably determines that is principal business activity is described in a North American Industry Classification System (NAICS) code (published by the Department of Commerce; information regarding the codes can be found at www.census.gov) other than one of the following ineligible codes:

   - Mining activities (North American Industry Classification System (NAICS) codes 211 and 212);
   - Manufacturing (NAICS codes 31-33);

[11] Rev. Proc. 2002-28, 2002-1 CB 815, as modified by Rev. Proc. 2011-14, IRB 2011-4.

- Wholesale trade (NAICS code 42);
- Retail trade (NAICS codes 44 and 45); and
- Information industries (NAICS codes 5111 and 5122).

2. Notwithstanding that the taxpayer's principal business activity is described in one of the ineligible NAICS codes, the taxpayer reasonably determines that its principal business activity is the provision of services (including the provision of property incidental to those services).
3. Notwithstanding that the taxpayer's principal business activity is described in one of the ineligible NAICS codes, the taxpayer reasonably determines that its principal business activity is the fabrication or modification of tangible personal property upon demand in accordance with customer design or specifications.

Provision of Services Essential

A qualifying small business taxpayer may use the cash method for all of its trades or businesses if its principal business activity is the provision of services, including the provision of property incident to those services. For example, a publisher whose principal business activity is the sale of advertising space in its publications is eligible to use the cash method even though the taxpayer's principal business activity would otherwise be ineligible.

A qualifying small business taxpayer may use the cash method for all of its trades or businesses if its principal business activity is the fabrication or modification of tangible personal property upon demand in accordance with customer design or specifications. This test will not be met if the customer merely chooses among preselected options, such as size, color, or materials, offered by the taxpayer or if the taxpayer must make only minor modifications to its basic design to meet the customer's specifications.

> **Example 18-2:** Susan is a sofa manufacturer that only produces sofas upon receipt of a customer order. Customers are allowed to pick among 150 different fabrics offered by Susan or to provide their own fabric, which Susan will use to finish the customer's sofa. Susan's principal business activity is ineligible for the cash method under the NAICS code 33 because Susan does not provide sofas incident to the performance of services. Instead, Susan performs certain services (upholstering) incident to the sale of sofas. Susan also does not fabricate or modify tangible personal property because customers merely choose among preselected options and Susan only makes minor modifications to the basic design of its sofa. Susan may not use the cash method under this revenue procedure.

Gross Receipts Requirement

A taxpayer has average annual gross receipts of $10 million or less if the taxpayer's average annual gross receipts for the three-year period ending with the prior tax year does not exceed $10 million.

Gross receipts is defined in a manner that is consistent with Temp. Reg. 1.448-1T(f)(2)(iv). Gross receipts for a tax year equal all receipts derived from all of a taxpayer's trades or businesses that must be recognized under the method of accounting actually used by the taxpayer for that tax year for federal income tax purposes [Temp. Reg. § 1.448-1T(f) (2) (iv)]. For example, gross receipts include total sales (net of returns and allowances) and all amounts received from services, interest, dividends, and rents. However, gross receipts do not include taxes collected by the taxpayer and remitted to the state or local taxing authority. If the taxpayer has been in existence for less than the three-taxable-year period, the taxpayer must determine its average annual gross receipts for the number of years (including short tax years) that the taxpayer has been in existence. In the case of a short tax year, a taxpayer's gross receipts must be annualized by multiplying the gross receipts for the short tax year by 12 and then dividing the result by the number of months in the short tax year [Code Sec. 448(c) (3) (B) and Temp. Reg. § 1.448-1T(f) (2) (iii)].

Example 18-3: Albert is a plumbing contractor who installs plumbing fixtures in customers' homes and businesses. Albert also has a store that sells plumbing equipment to homeowners and other plumbers who visit the store. Albert derives 60 percent of his total receipts from plumbing installation (including amounts charged for parts and fixtures used in installation) and 40 percent of total receipts from the sale of plumbing equipment through its store. Albert determines that his principal business activity is plumbing installation, which is included in the construction activities described in NAICS code 23. Albert may use the cash method for both business activities.

Automatic Accounting Method Change

A qualifying small business taxpayer that wants to use the cash method for an eligible trade or business must follow the automatic change in accounting method provisions established by the IRS[12] with certain modifications. If the taxpayer is under examination, before an appeals office, or before a federal court regarding any income tax issue, the taxpayer must provide a copy of the Form 3115, *Application for Change in Accounting Method,* to the examining agent, appeals officer, or counsel for the government at the same time that it files the copy of the Form 3115 with the National Office. The Form 3115 must contain the name and telephone number of the examining agent, appeals officer, or counsel for the government. Taxpayers filing Form 3115 for a change in method of accounting under this revenue procedure should write "Filed under Rev. Proc. 2003-20" at the top of their Form 3115.

Taxpayers that do not want to account for inventories under Code Sec. 471 must make any necessary change from the taxpayer's current method of accounting for inventoriable items to treat them as nonincidental materials and supplies under Reg. § 1.162-3. Taxpayers may file a single Form 3115 for both changes. The Section 481(a) adjustment must take into account both increases and decreases in the applicable account balances such as accounts receivable, accounts payable, and inventory.

---

[12] Rev. Proc. 2003-20, 2003-1 CB 445.

¶18,010 CONSTRUCTIVE RECEIPT—CASH BASIS

Constructive receipt occurs when an item is credited to the taxpayer's account, set apart for the taxpayer, or otherwise made available so the taxpayer may draw upon it at any time. However, income is not constructively received if the taxpayer's control of its receipt is subject to substantial limitations or restrictions. Thus, if a corporation credits its employees with bonus stock, but the stock is not available to such employees until some future date, the mere crediting on the books of the corporation does not constitute receipt [Reg. § 1.451-2].

.01 Examples of Constructive Receipt

- Interest on savings bank deposits is fully taxable when credited, without reduction for any forfeiture on a premature withdrawal.[13]
- Interest coupons are reported for the year the coupons matured, unless there are no funds available for payment [Reg. § 1.451-2(b)].
- Brokerage account profits not withdrawn are taxable in the year earned, even if the account may be wiped out by losses in later years.[14]
- Checks issued in one year and received in another are constructively received in the year of issuance, if they were available to you in the earlier year[15] or you agreed to accept payment in that year.[16] When compensation for services is due and payable, you cannot defer recognition of the income by requesting the employer, customer, or client to delay payment or to place the funds in an escrow or other account to be paid out at a later time.[17]
- A bonus for majority stockholder is constructively received in the year authorized, even though not paid until the next year. This assumes that the corporation had enough funds and the shareholder could sign the check to pay out the bonus.[18]

.02 Special Rules

Acceptance

A taxpayer is not legally obligated to accept income to be taxed under the constructive receipt doctrine. If the money is subject to the taxpayer's control, it is constructively received whether actually accepted or not. The taxpayer cannot shift income to another year by refusing to accept what has been properly tendered under a prior agreement.[19] For example, a retiree verbally refused to accept a pension and kept uncashed checks received under the pension plan. The court concluded that the checks were income constructively received.[20] But there was no constructive receipt when an employee

---

[13] Rev. Rul. 75-21, 1975-1 CB 367.

[14] *W.S. Webb*, CA-2, 3 USTC ¶1196, 67 F2d 859.

[15] *H.B McEuen*, CA-5, 52-1 USTC ¶9281, 196 F2d 127.

[16] Rev. Rul. 68-126, 1968-1 CB 194.

[17] Rev. Rul. 70-435, 1970-2 CB 100.

[18] *F.F. Haack*, 41 TCM 708, Dec. 37,616(M), TC Memo. 1981-13.

[19] *H.B Hurd*, 12 BTA 368, Dec. 4045.

[20] *W.A. Hedrick*, CA-2, 46-1 USTC ¶9214, 154 F2d 90, *cert. denied*, 329 US 719, 67 SCt 53.

refused to accept salary voted but not credited, and the corporation used the money for charitable purposes the employee suggested.[21]

Salary

A taxpayer may constructively receive compensation if the money is credited to the taxpayer, and the taxpayer may withdraw it at anytime.[22] There needn't be a book entry setting the money apart, if it is otherwise made available.[23] However, whether or not there is constructive receipt depends on the facts in each case. If there are no funds to make the payment (e.g., the employer is insolvent), there is no constructive receipt.[24]

Amounts taken out of a taxpayer's wages by his or her employer to pay insurance, buy savings bonds, pay union dues, or pay income taxes, are constructively received by the taxpayer and must be included in his or her gross income for that year. If the employer uses wages to pay his or her debts, or if wages are attached, they are also constructively received by the taxpayer.

Controlling Shareholders

Shareholdersdid not constructively receive bonuses in the year authorized by the corporation due to substantial restrictions on their payment.

Deferred Execution of Notes

An agreement to execute promissory notes in a later year is a cash equivalent.[25]

Dividends

For constructive receipt of dividends, see ¶ 18,090.

For a discussion of endowment and life insurance proceeds, see Ch. 5.

¶18,015 INCOME PAID TO THIRD PARTIES—ASSIGNMENTS

A taxpayer may agree that income he or she is entitled to receive be paid to a third party. This raises the question of who pays the tax on the income—the one making the agreement or the person to whom it is paid.

.01 Assignment of Income from Property

If a taxpayer owns an interest in property and agrees that the income from the property will be paid to a third party—without there being any transfer of title to the property producing the income. The income remains taxable to the property owner; it is not taxable to the third party. It doesn't matter whether the income is to be earned in the future or has already been earned.[26] But if the taxpayer made a legal transfer of a

[21] *A.P. Giannini*, CA-9, 42-2 USTC ¶9595, 129 F2d 638.

[22] *W. Burns*, CA-5, 1929 CCH D-9144, 31 F2d 399, *cert. denied*, 280 US 564.

[23] *J.J. Cooney*, 18 TC 883, Dec. 19,154.

[24] *Northern Trust Co.*, 8 BTA 685, Dec. 2922, *acq.* 1928-1 CB 23.

[25] *R.M. Evans*, 55 TCM 902, Dec. 44,797(M), TC Memo. 1988-228.

[26] *G.A. Eubank*, SCt, 40-2 USTC ¶9788, 311 US 122, 61 SCt 149; *P.R.G. Horst*, SCt, 40-2 USTC ¶9787, 311 US 112, 61 SCt 144.

property interest to a third party, he or she is taxed on the income arising under the agreement.[27]

.02 Assignment of Earnings

A taxpayer is taxed on a payment earned for personal services, even if he or she assigns it to another. The result is the same whether the assignment is for income to be earned,[28] or income already earned for past services.

Examples of Assigned Income

Taxable to assignor. Assignment of earned commissions to third party by insurance agent;[29] assignment of cash dividends on stock (ownership of stock is retained by assignor);[30] assignment of rent[31] or lease[32] (real property owned by assignor); assignment by a beneficiary of trust income for a short period (one year);[33] assignment of dividends after declaration date and before payment date by a life income beneficiary of a trust;[34] share of partnership income assigned;[35] assignment by husband to wife of patent license contracts between him and a corporation, if he, as majority stockholder, had power to cancel the contract;[36] Medicare fees assigned by physicians to exempt organizations, though deductible as charitable contributions.[37]

Taxable to assignee. Transfer of stock to a son and subsequent dividends on the stock, even when the father retained possession of stock certificate;[38] assignment by life beneficiary of trust of part of the trust income for rest of his life.[39]

¶18,020 CONSTRUCTIVE PAYMENT—CASH BASIS

Generally, as a cash-basis taxpayer, you cannot deduct expenses before you make actual payment. However, you can deduct expenses that are treated as an offset against amounts owed to you in the year of the offset.[40] In such cases, the obligation for the deducted expense is fully discharged by the offset. For example, interest charged by a broker on debt owed by you on the usual type of margin account is constructively paid when the broker makes collections for your account.[41]

---

[27] *B.M. Holmes Est.*, 1 TC 508, Dec. 12,942 (1943); *J.S. Austin*, CA-6, 47-1 USTC ¶9247, 161 F2d 666, *cert. denied*, 332 US 767.

[28] *G.C. Earl*, SCt, 2 USTC ¶4961, 281 US 111, 50 SCt 241.

[29] *G.A. Eubank*, SCt, 40-2 USTC ¶9788, 311 US 122, 61 SCt 149.

[30] *A.H. Van Brunt*, 11 BTA 406, Dec. 3778.

[31] *Bing*, CA-2, 26 F2d 1017.

[32] *G.R. Shafto*, CA-4, 57-2 USTC ¶9859, 246 F2d 338.

[33] *S.H. Schaffner*, SCt, 41-1 USTC ¶9355, 312 US 579, 61 SCt 759.

[34] Rev. Rul. 74-562, 1974-2 CB 28.

[35] *O.M. Mitchel*, CA-2, 1 USTC ¶193, 15 F2d 287, *cert. denied*, 273 US 759.

[36] *J. Sunnen*, SCt, 48-1 USTC ¶9230, 333 US 591, 68 SCt 715.

[37] Rev. Rul. 70-161, 1970-1 CB 15.

[38] *A.W.E. Capel*, 7 BTA 1076, Dec. 2711, *acq.* 1928-1 CB 6.

[39] *E.T. Blair*, SCt, 37-1 USTC ¶9083, 300 US 5, 57 SCt 330.

[40] *R.C. Reynolds*, 44 BTA 342, Dec. 11,796.

[41] Rev. Rul. 70-221, 1970-1 CB 33.

¶18,025 ACCRUAL BASIS

Under an accrual method of accounting, income is includible in gross income when all the events have occurred that fix the right to receive the income and the amount can be determined with reasonable accuracy [Reg. § 1.451-1(a)]. All the events that fix the right to receive income generally occur when (1) the required performance takes place, (2) payment is due to the taxpayer, or (3) payment is received by the taxpayer, whichever happens earliest. Similarly, expenses are deducted by accrual basis taxpayers when they are incurred, regardless of whether the expenses are paid at that time [¶ 18,080; ¶ 18,130].

Example 18-4: On September 1, 2012, a paving contractor laid a sidewalk for Mason City. Payment was not received until 2013. If the contractor reports on the accrual basis, the income is included in his 2012 return (when earned). If he reports on the cash basis, the payment is included in his 2013 return (when received).

Example 18-5: On November 1, 2012, Walker bought a machine and gave his one-year 9 percent note for $500. On November 1, 2013, he paid the note and interest ($545). If he reports on the accrual basis, $7.50 interest is deductible in 2012, and $37.50 is deductible in 2013 (over the period the liability is actually incurred). If he reports on the cash basis, the $45 is deductible in 2013 (when paid).

.01 Farming

A corporation engaged in the trade or business of farming (other than an S corporation) generally must use the accrual method if it has gross receipts in excess of $1 million. Exception: Incorporated family farms need not use the accrual method unless they have gross receipts exceeding $25 million. A family farming corporation is one where 50 percent or more of the total combined voting power of all classes of stock entitled to vote and at least 50 percent of all other classes of stock of the corporation is owned by members of the same family [Code Sec. 447].

¶18,030 ACCOUNTING METHODS MUST CLEARLY REFLECT INCOME

No matter which accounting method you use, it must clearly reflect your income [Code Sec. 446(b); Reg. § 1.446-1(a)(2)]. It is important that you treat items of income and expense consistently from year to year. So, even if you use the cash basis to keep your accounts and make your return, unusual cases may arise when a payment you make during the year is not currently deductible.

Here are some examples of such unusual cases:

- *Commissions, fees, and printing costs* paid in one year by a taxpayer in securing a loan for 10 or 15 years, covered by a mortgage on property to be leased, are not deductible in full in the year of payment, but should be spread over the period of the loan, even if taxpayer's return is made on the cash basis.[42]
- *Insurance premiums* that are business or investor's expenses paid in advance for more than one year by cash basis taxpayer are deductible ratably over the period to which they relate (IRS and Court of Appeals for the 1st Circuit).[43] But the Court of Appeals for the 8th Circuit holds that these premiums may be deducted in the year paid.[44]
- *A subsidiary corporation* that sold goods produced by the parent company acquired title before selling to customers. So the IRS required it to maintain inventories and recomputed its income on the accrual basis.[45]
- *Advance season ticket sales* for a baseball team's future games were deferred to the year that the games were played in order to more clearly match income with expenses in *Tampa Bay Devil Rays, Ltd.*[46]

.01 Rounding Off to Whole Dollars

You may round off amounts on internal transactions to the nearest dollar if a penny elimination account is maintained and you follow the procedure with reasonable consistency.

¶18,035 RECORDS

The accounting records you keep must be sufficient to enable you to determine your actual income. These records generally take the form of your regular books of account and supporting documentation. They should reflect the following essential information [Reg. § 1.446-1(a)(4)]:

- If the production, purchase, or sale of merchandise is an income-producing factor, you must take inventories into account at the beginning and end of the year [Ch. 17];
- You must properly classify expenditures during the year as capital or expense; and
- If you are recovering the cost of an asset through depreciation, amortization or depletion, any expenditure (other than ordinary repairs) made to restore the property or prolong its useful life must be added to the property account or charged against the appropriate reserve. The expenditures are not deductible expenses [Chs. 11, 12].

---

[42] *J.S. Lovejoy*, 18 BTA 1179, Dec. 5830.

[43] Rev. Rul. 70-413, 1970-2 CB 103; *Boylston Market Ass'n*, CA-1, 42-2 USTC ¶9820, 131 F2d 966.

[44] *Waldheim Realty & Inv. Co.*, CA-8, 57-2 USTC ¶9717, 245 F2d 823.

[45] *Thomas Nelson, Inc.*, DC-TN, 88-1 USTC ¶9339, 694 FSupp 428, *amended*, 734 FSupp 810.

[46] *Tampa Bay Devil Rays, LTC.*, 84 TCM 394, Dec. 54,893(M), TC Memo. 2002-248; *Artnell Co*, CA-7, 68-2 USTC ¶9593, 400 F2d 981, *on remand*, 29 TCM 403, Dec. 30,055(M), TC Memo. 1970-85.

¶18,040 RECONSTRUCTION OF INCOME

If you have no regular method of accounting or your records are incomplete, inaccurate, lost, or destroyed, the IRS may reconstruct your income by whatever method seems appropriate [Code Sec. 446(b); Reg. § 1.446-1(b)(1)].

.01 Net Worth Method

The IRS first establishes your *net worth* (difference between the assets and the liabilities) at the start of the tax year. Any increase in your net worth during the tax year is added to your nondeductible expenses. This amount is compared with the amount reported on your return. If the reported amount is smaller than the income as reconstructed, and the additional funds did not come from a nontaxable source (such as gift or inheritance),[47] they are unreported income on which you owe an additional tax. The courts have approved using the net worth method in reconstructing income from gambling, a tavern-restaurant, slot machines, a general store, used car business, and black market operations, among others. The net worth method also has been upheld by the Supreme Court as a basis for conviction for tax evasion.[48]

.02 Percentage Method

The IRS reconstructs your income by determining your total sales or receipts and applying to this amount an average percentage of gross profit.[49] It also can reconstruct taxable income by applying to your gross income an average percentage of taxable income to gross income.[50] The percentage used is taken either from returns you filed in previous years or from figures reflecting percentages of taxpayers in similar trades or businesses.[51] However, the experience of other taxpayers cannot be used if your business conditions are unlike those of the businesses used for comparison.[52]

.03 Bank Deposit Method

The IRS includes in your income the total amounts you deposited in the tax year, after eliminating:

- Duplications (such as transfers of funds between banks);
- Amounts identified as not being income receipts; and
- Total receipts you reported as income.

Unexplained bank deposits are presumed to be income; the burden of proving otherwise is on you.[53]

---

47 *B. Goodman*, 20 TCM 997, Dec. 24,934(M), TC Memo. 1961-201.

48 *M.L. Holland*, SCt, 54-2 USTC ¶9714, 348 US 121, 75 SCt 127; *D. Freidberg*, SCt, 54-2 USTC ¶9713, 348 US 142, 75 SCt 138; *D. Smith*, SCt, 54-2 USTC ¶9715, 348 US 147, 75 SCt 194; *E.B. Calderon*, SCt, 54-2 USTC ¶9712, 348 US 160, 75 SCt 186.

49 *B. Fairman*, 8 TCM 30, Dec. 16,785(M).

50 *M. & B. Rubin, Inc.*, 10 BTA 866, Dec. 3570.

51 *F.G. Bishoff*, CA-3, 1 USTC ¶310, 27 F2d 91.

52 *W. Stratman*, 8 TCM 560, Dec. 17,032(M).

53 *R.L. Hague Est.*, CA-2, 43-1 USTC ¶9258, 132 F2d 775, *cert. denied*, 318 US 787, 63 SCt 983.

.04 Excess Cash Expenditure Method

With this method, the IRS reconstructs income by comparing the amount you spent with the amount the return shows was available to you as income. Income has been reconstructed from amounts spent for machinery, equipment, real estate, and living expenses, and from amounts spent for medical and entertainment expenses.

¶18,045 CHANGE IN ACCOUNTING METHOD

The IRS has the power to require a taxpayer to change accounting methods when the IRS thinks that the taxpayer is using a method that does not clearly reflect income. Even though the IRS may require a taxpayer to change its accounting method from one that does not clearly reflect income to one that more clearly reflects income, the IRS does not have the discretion to require a change from a method of accounting that clearly reflects income to a method that, the IRS's view, more clearly reflects income.[54]

IRS examiners are required to resolve any timing issue as an accounting method change and to make the change in the earliest tax year under examination with an Code Sec. 481(a) adjustment as discussed further below. Generally, you must obtain the IRS's consent before changing your method of accounting. Consent is required even if the new method is proper or permitted under the Code or Regulations [Code Sec. 446(e); Reg. §1.446-1(e)(2)].

.01 What Is a Change in Method?

A change in the method of accounting includes a change in the overall plan of accounting for gross income or deductions or a change in the treatment of any material item used in such overall plan. Although a method of accounting may exist without the necessity of a pattern of consistent treatment of an item, in most instances a method of accounting is not established for an item without such consistent treatment. A material item is any item that involves the proper time for the inclusion of the item in income or the taking of a deduction. In determining whether a taxpayer's accounting practice for an item involves timing, generally the relevant question is whether the practice permanently changes the amount of the taxpayer's lifetime income. If the practice does not permanently affect the taxpayer's lifetime income, but does or could change the tax year in which income is reported, it involves timing and is therefore a method of accounting. Changes in method of accounting include the following:

- Change from the cash receipts and disbursement method to an accrual method, or vice versa;[55]
- Change involving the method or basis used in the valuation of inventories;
- Change from the cash or accrual method to a long-term contract method, or vice versa;
- Certain changes in computing depreciation or amortization (as discussed in detail below);

---

[54] Rev. Proc. 99-28, 1999-2 CB 109.

[55] Rev. Proc. 72-52, 1972-2 CB 833.

- Change involving the adoption, use or discontinuance of any other specialized method of computing taxable income, such as the crop method; and
- Situations in which consent is required prior to adoption of the new accounting method [Reg. § 1.446-1(e)(2)(ii)(a)].
- The IRS's denial of a deduction under the related party rules of Code Sec. 267 is a change of accounting method.[56]

The following changes are *not* considered changes in method of accounting:

- Correction of mathematical or posting errors, or errors in the computation of tax liability (such as errors in computation of the foreign tax credit, net operating loss, percentage depletion, or investment credit);
- Adjustment of any item of income or deduction that does not involve the proper time for the inclusion of the item of income or the taking of a deduction. For example, corrections of items that are deducted as interest or salary, but that are in fact payments of dividends, and of items that are deducted as business expenses, but which are in fact personal expenses, are not changes in method of accounting;
- Addition to bad debt reserve (although such adjustment may involve the question of the proper time for the taking of a deduction, such items are traditionally corrected by adjustment in the current and future years); and
- A change in treatment resulting from a change in underlying facts [Reg. § 1.446-1(e)(2)(ii)(b)].
- Removing the Code Sec. 163(j) interest deduction limit is not a change in accounting method.[57]

Changes in Depreciation or Amortization That Are a Change in Method of Accounting

The following changes in depreciation or amortization are considered changes in accounting method [Reg. §§ 1.167(e)-1(a)(1), 1.446-1(e)(2)(ii)(d)(2)].

- A change in the treatment of an asset from nondepreciable or nonamortizable to depreciable or amortizable, or vice versa;
- A correction to require depreciation or amortization in lieu of a deduction for the cost of depreciable or amortizable assets that had been consistently treated as an expense in the year of purchase, or vice versa;
- A change in the depreciation or amortization method, period of recovery, or convention of a depreciable or amortizable asset;
- A change from not claiming to claiming the additional first year depreciation deduction and the resulting change to the amount otherwise allowable as a depreciation deduction for the remaining adjusted depreciable basis of, qualified property, 50-percent bonus depreciation property, or qualified New York Liberty Zone property, provided the taxpayer did not make the election out of the additional first year

[56] *R.J. Bosamia*, CA-5, 2011-2 USTC ¶ 50,688, 661 F3d 250.

[57] CCA 201202021 (Jan. 16, 2012).

depreciation deduction (or did not make a deemed election out of the additional first year depreciation deduction);

- A change from claiming the 30-percent additional first year depreciation deduction to claiming the 50-percent additional first year depreciation deduction or vice versa. This paragraph does not apply if a taxpayer is making a late election or revoking a timely valid election;
- A change from claiming to not claiming the additional first year depreciation deduction for an asset that is not qualified property, 50-percent bonus depreciation property, or qualified New York Liberty Zone property, and the resulting change to the amount otherwise allowable as a depreciation deduction for the property's depreciable basis;
- A change in salvage value to zero for a depreciable or amortizable asset for which the salvage value is expressly treated as zero by Code Sec. 168(b)(4);
- A change in the accounting for depreciable or amortizable assets from a single asset account to a multiple asset account (pooling), or vice versa, or from one type of multiple asset account (pooling) to a different type of multiple asset account (pooling); and
- A change in the method of identifying which mass assets accounted for in multiple asset accounts or pools have been disposed [Reg. § 1.446-1(e)(2)(ii)(d)(2)].

Changes in Depreciation or Amortization That Are Not a Change in Accounting Method

The following changes in depreciation or amortization are *not* considered changes in accounting method:

- An adjustment in the useful life of a depreciable or amortizable asset;
- A change in computing depreciation or amortization allowances in the same year that use of an asset changes in the taxpayer's hands;
- The making of a late depreciation or amortization election or the revocation of a timely valid depreciation or amortization election;
- A change in salvage value of a depreciable or amortizable asset; and
- Any change in the placed-in-service date of a depreciable or amortizable asset [Reg. § 1.446-1(e)(2)(ii)(d)(3)].

The IRS has released an automatic consent procedure that allows taxpayers to change their method of accounting for certain depreciable or amortizable property after its disposition.[58] The guidance applies to taxpayers changing from an impermissible method of accounting for depreciation of property that has been disposed of by the taxpayer during the year of change, and for which the taxpayer did not take into account any depreciation allowance, or took into account some depreciation but less than that allowable in the year of change or any prior tax year. The change does not apply to certain property held by tax-exempt organizations, a property for which a taxpayer is revoking a timely valid depreciation election or making a late depreciation election, a

---

[58] Rev. Proc. 2007-16, IRB 2007-4, 358.

property for which the taxpayer deducted the cost or other basis of the property as an expense, and any property disposed of by a taxpayer in a nonrecognition transaction.

.02 IRS Consent Required

You make an application to change an overall method of accounting or the accounting treatment of any item by filing Form 3115, *Application for Change in Accounting Method*, with the IRS within the year of change [Reg. § 1.446-1(e)(3)(i)]. Consent is required for accounting method changes unless the IRS has provided an automatic accounting method change procedure.[59] Part I of Form 3115 requests specific information for automatic change requests; Part II requests information for all change requests. Ordinarily, a taxpayer must file a separate Form 3115 for each change in accounting method. The IRS provided an exception to this rule in Rev. Proc. 2012-19[60] and Rev. Proc. 2012-20[61] which allow taxpayers to request multiple changes on a single Form 3115. Rev. Proc. 2012-19 addresses accounting method changes to the treatment of repairs versus capital expenses. Rev. Proc. 2012-20 addresses accounting method changes under the depreciation rules and the treatment of general asset accounts.

If you wait to file the Form 3115 after the close of the tax year in which you want to make the change, extensions will be granted only in unusual and compelling circumstances. If you need to file for an extension, the IRS recommends that you make your request as early as possible, so the IRS will have enough time to respond before the tax return for the year of change is due.

If you have been under examination by the IRS for at least 12 consecutive months as of the first day of a tax year, you may only file your Form 3115 during the first 90 days of that tax year. However, this 90-day window is not available if your method of accounting is an issue that the examining agent is considering. In that situation, you must supply a copy of the Form 3115 to the examining agent.

Form 3115 must be filed:

- Any time during the first 180 days of the tax year, if the taxpayer is not under examination; or
- Any time during the 120-day period following the end of the examination for taxpayers under examination, even though a subsequent examination may have already commenced.

There is an exception to the 120-day rule for taxpayers who have been notified by the IRS that the accounting method change is an *issue under consideration* in a subsequent audit. In these situations, you must provide a copy of Form 3115 to the appeals officer or the government's counsel in a court case.

The IRS will take several factors into consideration before deciding whether to grant your request to change accounting methods. The IRS will consider whether the change will create or shift profits or losses between the trades or businesses and whether the proposed method will clearly reflect income. If you request a change in accounting method for one business, you must identify all other businesses by name and the

---

[59] For automatic change requests procedures, see Rev. Proc. 2011-14, IRB 2011-4, 330, as modified and clarified in various specific situations.

[60] Rev. Proc. 2012-19, IRB 2012-14, 689.

[61] Rev. Proc. 2012-20, IRB 2012-14, 700.

method of accounting used by each for the particular item that is the subject to the requested accounting method change.

If you have kept separate books and records and have used different accounting methods for separate businesses, you must file a Form 3115 and pay a user fee for each business if you want to change the accounting method of each business.

.03 Automatic Consent Procedures

You can obtain automatic consent to accounting method changes by completing Form 3115 and attaching it to your timely filed (including extensions) original tax return for the year of change. A copy of the form must be filed with the IRS National Office. No user fee is imposed for requesting automatic consent. Rev. Proc. 2011-14[62] describes the procedures taxpayers may use to obtain automatic consent for a change in method of accounting for more than 30 areas.

¶18,050 ADJUSTMENTS REQUIRED BY CHANGE IN ACCOUNTING METHOD

In conjunction with an accounting method change, a Section 481(a) adjustment is often required to prevent amounts from being duplicated or omitted [Code Sec. 481(a); Reg. § 1.481-1].[63]

The number of tax years over which a Section 481 adjustment should be taken into account may differ from four years to one year. In certain cases, the difference creates a disincentive for certain taxpayers to change their method of accounting in the required tax year. Taxpayers may change their method of accounting to take any Section 481 adjustments resulting from the change into account over either a four year period for a net positive adjustment and for a one year period for a net negative adjustment.[64] Taxpayers may elect to use a one-year adjustment period in lieu of the four-year period for positive adjustments if the net adjustment for the change is less than $25,000. Taxpayers may rely on these administrative procedures by filing a Form 3115, *Application for Change of Accounting Method.*

When a Section 481 adjustment is made, the income of the transition year may consist of two elements:

- Taxable income figured under the new method; and
- Adjustments between the old and the new method.

> **Example 18-6:** Mr. Green, changing from the cash to the accrual basis, has taxable income of $20,000 figured on the accrual basis. His books at the start of the year show: Accounts receivable, $30,000; accounts payable, $14,000; inven-

[62] Rev. Proc. 2011-14, IRB 2011-4, 330, as modified and clarified in various specific situations.

[63] *Color Arts, Inc.*, 85 TCM 1104, Dec. 55,103(M), TC Memo. 2003-95.

[64] Rev. Proc. 2011-14, IRB 2011-4, 330, as modified and clarified in various specific situations.

tory, $5,000. taxable income after adjustments for items that are treated differently under the old and new methods is $41,000:

1. Taxable income figured on accrual basis		$20,000
2. Adjustments:		
(a) Add: (1) Items not previously reported as income:		
Accounts receivable Jan. 1	$30,000	
(2) Items previously deducted:		
Inventory Jan. 1	$5,000	
Total to be added		35,000
Total		$55,000
(b) Subtract items not previously deducted:		
Accounts payable Jan. 1		14,000
3. Taxable income after adjustments		$41,000

If the net amount of your adjustments is an increase in taxable income of not more than $3,000 (or is any decrease), you make the entire amount of the adjustment in the year of change [Code Sec. 481]. But if the increase in income exceeds $3,000, you may make the adjustment by:

- A three-year allocation method;
- An allocation under the new method of accounting; or
- Any other method agreed on between you and the IRS [Code Sec. 481(b), (c); Reg. § 1.481-2(a), (b)].

NOTE: You generally make the election of a relief method in a statement filed with the IRS when permission to change the accounting method is requested [¶ 18,045].

.01 Three-Year Allocation Method

The tax is reduced to the amount that you would have paid if you had received one-third of the increase in your income in the year of the change and one-third in each of the two preceding years. To qualify for this method, you must have used the old method of accounting for the two years preceding the change-over year [Code Sec. 481(b)(1); Reg. § 1.481-2(a), (d)].

Example 18-7: Assume the same facts as in Example 18-6, and that Green used the cash method in the two prior tax years. Since the adjustments increase taxable income by $21,000 ($41,000 adjusted taxable income less $20,000 taxable income before adjustments), Green may allocate the additional income as follows: $7,000 to each of the two previous tax years and $7,000 to the current tax year.

Allocation Under New Method of Accounting

If you can establish your taxable income under the new method for any number of years consecutively preceding the change-over year, the tax is reduced to the amount that you would have paid if (1) you figured the tax for those preceding years under the new method, and (2) you allocated the then remaining adjustments to the change-over year [Code Sec. 481(b)(2); Reg. § 1.481-2(b), (d)].

> **Example 18-8:** Assume the same facts as in Example 18-6, and that Green recomputed the tax for two prior tax years on the accrual basis. On this basis, the taxable income for the tax year two years ago was increased by $6,000 and for the tax year one year ago by $7,000. Thus, $13,000 of the $21,000 adjustments were allocated to those years. The balance, $8,000, is taken into account in figuring the tax for the current year (the change-over year).

Finally, special rules apply to carrybacks and carryovers of net operating losses and capital losses [Code Sec. 481(b)(3)(A); Reg. § 1.481-2(c)(2)].[65]

ACCOUNTING PERIODS

¶18,055 ACCOUNTING PERIODS

.01 General Rules

Taxable income is figured on the basis of the taxpayer's annual accounting period. This may be either the calendar year or a fiscal year [Code Sec. 441(b)(1)]. A *fiscal year* means (1) an accounting period of 12 months ending on the last day of any month other than December, or (2) an annual accounting period varying from 52 to 53 weeks, subject to the rules below.

Some general rules follow:

- If you do not keep books, you must use a calendar year [Code Sec. 441(b)(2)];
- You may not prepare your return based on an accounting period that ends on a date other than the last day of a calendar month. If you do make such a choice, you must compute net income on a calendar year basis.[66] Exception: Electing a 52-53 week period, described below;
- A newly organized corporation may file its return on a fiscal-year basis without applying to the IRS for permission. To qualify, the fiscal-year basis must be definitely established and the books kept on a fiscal-year basis before the close of the first fiscal year;
- A sole proprietor must report business and personal income on the basis of the same tax year. For example, you may not operate your business on a fiscal-year basis, and file your individual return on a calendar year basis;[67] and
- Special rules, covered in ¶ 18,075 limit the selection of a fiscal year of a Partnership, S corporation, electing S corporation, and personal service corporation. Briefly, these

---

[65] Rev. Rul. 64-245, 1964-2 CB 130.

[66] Rev. Rul. 85-22, 1985-1 CB 154.

[67] Rev. Rul. 57-389, 1957-2 CB 298.

entities must choose a tax year that conforms with the tax years of its partners, shareholders, or owner-employees. See ¶ 18,075 for a more detailed discussion.

.02 52-53 Week Fiscal Year

A 52-53 week fiscal year is an accounting period that varies from 52 to 53 weeks and always ends on the same day of the week. If you regularly keep your books on the basis of this type of year, you may also use it to figure your taxable income [Code Sec. 441(f)(1)]. There are two kinds of 52-53 week fiscal years:

- Your accounting period may end on the same day of the week that occurs for the last time in a particular calendar month. The year may end as many as six days before the end of the month; or
- The year may end on the same day of the week that falls nearest to the end of a particular calendar month. In that case, the year may end as many as three days before or after the end of the month.If you do not keep books regularly on the basis of a 52-53 week year, you may elect this period if, at the time of election, you conform your books to this basis. After that, you must continue to keep your books and report income on this basis [¶ 18,060–¶ 18,070].

Effective Dates

The due dates of returns and effective dates of tax law changes are often based on the beginning or ending of tax years. In such cases, the following rules apply:

- A 52-53 week year is considered to begin on the first day of the calendar month nearest to the first day of the 52-53 week year; and
- It is considered to end or close on the last day of the calendar month ending nearest to the last day of the 52-53 week year [Code Sec. 441(f)(2)(A)].

Example 18-9: Assume that a new tax rate applies to tax years beginning after December 31. A 52-53 week year starting on any day within the period December 26 to January 4, is treated as starting on January 1.

Example 18-10: Assume that a return is due by the 15th of the 3rd month following the close of the fiscal year. A 52-53 week year ending on June 1 is considered as ending on May 31. The return, therefore, must be filed by Aug. 15.

Election

If you are a new taxpayer, you do not need permission to use a 52-53 week fiscal year. If you are switching to this type of fiscal year, you make the election by attaching a statement to the return for the first period for which the election is made. It should show:

- The calendar month with reference to which the new 52-53 week year ends;
- The day of the week on which the tax year will always end; and
- Whether it will end on

  a. The date the day occurs for the last time in the calendar month, or

  b. The date it occurs nearest to the end of the calendar month.

The Commissioner's prior approval is not needed as long as the 52-53 week year being elected ends on a day that refers to the same month in which the taxpayer's prior year ended. In other cases, see the general rules outlined in ¶ 18,055 above, or the special rules for partners and partnerships in Chapter 24. Also see ¶ 18,070 for rules regarding short tax years resulting from changes to or from 52-53 week years.

¶18,060 CHANGE IN ACCOUNTING PERIOD

You may want to change from a calendar year to a fiscal year, from a fiscal year to a calendar year, or from one fiscal year to another fiscal year. This is called a change in accounting period. You must file a fractional-year return for the part of the year between the close of the old period and the start of the new. This period is called the *short tax year* [¶ 18,070][Code Sec. 443(a)].

Special rules apply to short tax periods resulting from a change to or from a 52-53 week accounting period. In the year that the 52-53 week period is adopted, periods of more than 358 days and periods of less than 7 days are not treated as short periods. You treat the former as full years; you add the latter to the following tax year [Code Sec. 441(f)(2)(B)].

> **Example 18-11:** Assume that a corporation is on a calendar-year basis for 2013. It elects to report income for 2014 on the basis of a 52-53 week period, ending on the Tuesday nearest to the end of December. The first tax period following the change will consist of the period from January 5, 2014, through December 31, 2014, plus the short period of 4 days, January 1 through January 4, 2014. No fractional return is required for the short period since it is less than 7 days.

> **Example 18-12:** Assume the same facts as in Example 18-11, except that the corporation was on a fiscal year ending November 30. The first full tax year will consist of the period from January 5, 2014, through December 31, 2014. A fractional year return will be required for the short tax year beginning December 1, 2013, and ending January 4, 2014, since this period consists of more than 6 but less than 359 days.

In Rev. Proc. 2003-62,[68] the IRS provides rules for individuals filing on a fiscal year basis to obtain automatic approval to change to a calendar year. The procedures don't apply if the individual has an interest in a passthrough entity. Certain interests in passthrough entities will be disregarded. A disregarded passthrough entity is one that generates income exceeding the lesser of $500,000 or five percent of the individual's gross income. In addition, Rev. Proc, 2003-62 limits carryback of net operating losses over $50,000. The procedures extend the deadline for filing Form 1128 to the deadline for filing the individual's tax return (including extensions) for the first year the change is effective.

---

[68] Rev. Proc. 2003-62, 2003-2 CB 299.

¶18,065 HOW TO REQUEST A CHANGE IN ACCOUNTING PERIOD

Generally, a change in accounting period must be approved by the IRS [Code Sec. 442; Reg. § 1.442-1(a)]. The taxpayer applies for the change on Form 1128, *Application to Adopt, Change, or Retain a Tax Year,* by the 15th day of the second calendar month after the short period ends. For example, to change to a calendar year, file by the 15th day of February of the next year. If there is a substantial business reason for the change, it will usually be approved (e.g., to change to a year that coincides with your natural business cycle).[69] The taxpayer and the IRS must agree to the terms, conditions and adjustments required [Reg. § 1.442-1(b)].

A change ordinarily will not be approved if it substantially reduces tax liability. This could be the case if the change shifted income or deductions to another year or another taxpayer (e.g., a short tax year has a substantial net operating loss). However, even in these cases, approval may be obtained if the taxpayer can establish a business purpose for the requested change and agrees to certain adjustments to eliminate the distortions in taxable income [Reg. § 1.442-1(b)(2)].

.01 Taxpayers Not Required to File Form 1128

Certain taxpayers are not required to file a Form 1128 in order to obtain IRS approval to change their accounting period. Instead, they simply notify the IRS of the change by filing a statement with the IRS District Director in the district where their return is filed. Usually the statement accompanies the short-period return required as a result of the change [Reg. § 1.442-1(b)(2)]. The statement indicates the authority for the change (usually a regulation or revenue ruling) and provides any other information that is necessary to show that the taxpayer is eligible to make the change. The following taxpayers need not file Form 1128 to change their existing tax year:

Corporations

Rev. Proc. 2006-45[70] sets forth the exclusive procedures for certain corporations to obtain automatic approval to change their annual accounting period under Code Sec. 442 and Reg. § 1.442-1(b). Corporations complying with Rev. Proc. 2006-45 will be deemed to have established a business purpose and obtained the approval of the IRS to change their accounting period.

Partnerships, S corporations, Electing S corporations, Personal Service Corporations, Trusts

Rev. Proc. 2006-46[71] provides the exclusive procedures for partnerships, S corporations, electing S corporations, personal service corporations, and trusts to obtain automatic approval to adopt, change, or retain their annual accounting period under Code Sec. 442

[69] Rev. Proc. 2011-14, IRB 2011-4, 330, as modified and clarified in various specific situations.

[70] Rev. Proc. 2006-45, 2006-2 CB 851 (as modified and clarified by Rev. Proc. 2007-64, IRB 2007-42 for corporation leaving a consolidated group).

[71] Rev. Proc. 2006-46, 2006-2 CB 859.

and Reg. § 1.442-1(b). Partnerships, S corporations, electing S corporations, personal service corporations, and trusts complying with Rev. Proc. 2006-46 will be deemed to have established a business purpose and obtained IRS approval to adopt, change, or retain their annual accounting period.

Individuals

A newly married individual changing to the tax year of his or her spouse so they can file a joint return [Reg. § 1.442-1(d)]need not file Form 1128. The newly married husband or wife adopting the annual accounting period of the other spouse must file a Federal income tax return for the short period required by that change on or before the 15th day of the 4th month following the close of the short period. If the due date for any such short-period return occurs before the date of marriage, the first tax year of the other spouse ending after the date of marriage cannot be adopted. The short-period return must contain a statement at the top of page one of the return that it is filed under the authority of Reg. § 1.422-1(d).

> **Example 18-13:** *H* and *W* marry on September 25, 2013. *H* is on a fiscal year ending June 30, and *W* is on a calendar year. *H* wishes to change to a calendar year in order to file joint returns with *W*. *W*'s first tax year after marriage ends on December 31, 2013. *H* may not change to a calendar year for 2013 since, under Reg. § 1.422-1(d), he would have had to file a return for the short period from July 1 to December 31, 2012, by April 15, 2013. Since the date of marriage occurred subsequent to this due date, the return could not be filed. Therefore, *H* cannot change to a calendar year for 2013. However, *H* may change to a calendar year for 2014 by filing a return by April 15, 2014, for the short period from July 1 to December 31, 2013. If *H* files such a return, *H* and *W* may file a joint return for calendar year 2014 (which is *W*'s second tax year ending after the date of marriage) [Reg. § 1.422-1(d), Ex.].

Tax-Exempt Organizations

An exempt organization that has not changed its tax year within 10 calendar years and meets the other requirements of Rev. Proc. 85-58 need not file Form 1128.[72]

If you regularly keep books on the calendar or fiscal year, but erroneously file returns on a different basis, you do not need permission to file returns for later years based on the way the books are kept.

¶18,070 RETURNS FOR PERIODS OF FEWER THAN 12 MONTHS

Most income tax returns cover an accounting period of 12 months. However, shorter periods may be used when you (a) file your first or final return, and (b) change an accounting period.

[72] Rev. Proc. 85-58, 1985-2 CB 740.

.01 First or Final Returns

Short-period returns are required of new taxpayers filing their first returns and of taxpayers ending their existence. This applies to all kinds of taxpayers, such as corporations, partnerships, estates, trusts, and decedents. These returns are prepared and filed, and the taxes paid, as if they were returns for a 12-month period ending on the last day of the short period. The income of the short period is not annualized, nor are personal exemptions or tax credits prorated. A decedent's return, however, may be filed and the tax paid as if he had lived to the end of his last tax year [Code Sec. 443; Reg. § 1.443-1(a)(2)].

.02 Change of Accounting Period

You may have to file a return for fewer than 12 months when you change accounting periods. Unlike first or final short period returns, you must place these returns on an annual basis [Code Sec. 443(b)]. This is done as follows [Code Sec. 443; Reg. § 1.443-1(b)(1)]:

1. Multiply the short period modified taxable income (i.e., gross income minus deductions allowed for the short period) by 12;
2. Divide the result by the number of months in the short period;
3. Figure the tax on the result on an annual basis, using the tax rate schedules;
4. Divide the result by 12; and
5. Multiply the result by the number of months in the short period.

Example 18-14: JPS Corporation had net income before tax of $20,000 for the four-month short period ending April 30. Annualized taxable income is $60,000 ($20,000 × 12/4). The tax on this amount is $10,000. To annualize the tax, multiply it by 4/12. Result: $3,333.

Individual Taxpayers

If you file a short-period return due to a change in accounting period, you have to follow three additional special rules:

- You cannot use the tax tables to compute your tax liability [Code Sec. 3(b)(1)]. You must use the tax rate schedules [Ch. 1];
- You must use your actual amount of itemized deductions to compute short period taxable income. You cannot use the standard deduction [Reg. § 1.443-1(b)(1)(iv)]; and
- Your deduction for personal exemptions is prorated. This is done by apportioning them in the ratio that the number of months in the short tax year bears to 12 [Code Sec. 443(c); Reg. § 1.443-1(b)(1)].

Example 18-15: Mr. Roberts is married with one child. He and his wife file a joint return. They decide to change from a fiscal year ending March 31 to a calendar year. Gross income for the short period April 1-December 31, is $43,000. Itemized deductions for the short period total $8,700. His three exemptions for the year come to $8,100. The tax for the short period is computed as follows:

Gross income for short period		$43,000
Less: Deductions	$8,700	
9/12 of exemptions	6,075	14,775
		28,225
		× 12/9
Annualized taxable income		$37,633
Tax on annualized taxable income		$ 5,645
Tax for 9-month period (9/12 of tax on annualized taxable income)		$ 4,234

Net Operating Loss

In computing taxable income for a short year, you apply a net operating loss deduction against the actual income for the short period before placing the income on an annual basis.[73]

Alternative Minimum Tax

Your alternative minimum taxable income for the short period is placed on an annual basis by multiplying it by 12 and dividing the result by the number of months in the short period. Your alternative minimum tax is computed on that annualized income. Then the tax is reduced by using the ratio that the number of months in the short year bears to 12 [Code Sec. 443(d)]. For detailed discussion of the alternative minimum tax, see Chapter 16.

Credits

If any credit against your tax depends upon the amount of any item of income or deduction, the credit must be computed upon the annualized value of the item and then applied against your tax figured on an annual basis. If the credit limitation is based on taxable income, you must annualize your income [Reg. § 1.443-1(b)(1)].

Example 18-16: Suppose that in Example 18-15 above, Mr. Roberts and his wife qualify to take the tax credit for child care expenses. Suppose also that their actual child care expenses exceed the $3,000 limitation when there is one qualifying child. Since their annualized short period gross income is $57,333 ($43,000 × 12/9), the applicable percentage is 20 percent and the amount of the credit on an annualized basis is $600. Subtracting this from the annualized tax of $5,645 gives you an annualized tax after credits of $5,045. Result: Tax after credits for the 9-month period is $3,784 ($5,045 × 9/12).

52-53 Week Year

In annualizing your income for short tax years resulting from a change to or from a 52-53 week accounting period [¶ 18,055], your computation is made on a daily basis [Code Sec. 441(f)(2)(B)].

[73] Rev. Rul. 65-163, 1965-1 CB 205.

Refund for relief. To prevent hardship, you can apply for a refund if the tax figured under the annualized method is greater than the tax figured on actual income for the 12-month period starting with the first day of the short period. This would occur, for instance, if the short period covered your peak business season.

Your eligibility for this relief is determined by establishing the actual taxable income for the 12 months *beginning* with the first day of the short period. The tax on your actual taxable income for the 12-month period is then multiplied by a fraction (the numerator being your actual taxable income for the short period and the denominator being your taxable income for the 12-month period). Your tax for the short period computed under this method cannot be less than your tax on the unannualized income for the short period (with some modifications) [Code Sec. 443(b)(2); Reg. § 1.443-1(b)(2)].

Noncorporate taxpayers who are not in existence at the end of the 12-month period may figure their tax based on the 12 months ending with the last day of the short period. The same rule applies to a corporation that has disposed of substantially all of its assets before the end of the 12-month period [Code Sec. 443(b)(2)(B); Reg. § 1.443-1(b)(2)].

Example 18-17: GVW Inc. had income for a 4-month short period beginning September 1, of $41,000, and for a 12-month period ending the following August 31, of $85,000. Its tax without placing the income on an annual basis would be $6,150. Its tax computed under the exception is:

Taxable income for 12-month period	$85,000
Tax on income for 12-month period	$17,150
Tax for short period: $17,500 × 41,000/$85,000	$ 8,272

The corporation's tax for the 4-month short period is $8,272 (the greater of the two alternative calculations). If the exception is not elected, the tax is $10,023 (4/12 of the $30,070 tax on $123,000 annualized income).

How to apply for relief. To use the relief method, you must first file a return and pay the tax under the general method. Then, you apply to the IRS to use the optional method. The application is made in the form of a claim for credit or refund which shows how the taxable income and tax for the 12-month period were computed. The deadline for applying is the due date (including extensions) of your return for the first tax year which ends at least one year after the first day of the short period [Code Sec. 443(b)(2)(A); Reg. § 1.443-1(b)(2)(v)(a)].

¶18,075 SPECIAL RULE FOR TAX YEAR ELECTION BY PARTNERSHIPS, S CORPORATIONS, ELECTING S CORPORATIONS, AND PERSONAL SERVICE CORPORATIONS

Partnerships, S corporations, and personal service corporations (PSCs) are required to conform their tax years to that of their owners (i.e., normally a calendar year). However, an exception to this general rule is provided for businesses that satisfactorily demonstrate that there is a business purpose for having a different fiscal business year.

Partnerships, S corporations, electing S corporations (corporations electing to be S corporations), and PSCs generally must follow certain procedures to obtain automatic approval to adopt, change, or retain their annual accounting periods. In general, these entities must choose a tax year that conforms with the tax years of its partners, shareholders, or owner-employees. Rev. Proc. 2006-46[74] sets forth the exclusive procedures that these entities must follow in order to obtain automatic approval to adopt, change, or retain their annual accounting periods. Rev. Proc. 2002-39[75] provides the procedures that taxpayers must follow to establish a business purpose and request the approval of the IRS to adopt, change, or retain a taxpayer's annual accounting period. The rules established in this notice apply to taxpayers outside the scope of the rules allowing for automatic approval to adopt, change or retain an annual accounting period.

.01 Minimum Distributions Required by PSCs

If your PSC elects a fiscal year, it must make *minimum distributions* to the employee-owners before the end of the calendar year. If the PSC doesn't meet this requirement for an election year, its deductions for payments to owner-employees is limited [Code Sec. 280H(a); Temp. Reg. § 1.280H-1T(b)].

Essentially, the minimum distribution requirement is a mechanical test designed to minimize the benefits of tax deferral created by the fiscal-year election. Under the test, amounts paid to you and other owner-employees in the deferral period (the number of months between the end of the fiscal year and December 31) must equal or exceed the lesser of amounts determined under the preceding year test or three-year average test [Code Sec. 280H(c); Temp. Reg. § 1.280H-1T(c)].

For the preceding year test, amounts paid to the owner-employees in the preceding year and includible in their gross income are divided by the number of months in the year and then multiplied by the number of months in the deferral period. Note: For purposes of this calculation, you don't include payments which represent gain from the sale or exchange of property between you and other owner-employees and your PSC or dividends paid by the corporation.

---

74 Rev. Proc. 2006-46, 2006-2 CB 859.

75 Rev. Proc. 2002-39, 2002-1 CB 1046, as modified by Rev. Proc. 2003-34, 2003-1 CB 856.

> **Example 18-18:** A PSC paid $120,000 to its owner-employees during the year ended October 31, 2013 (a full 12-month year). To apply the preceding-year test for the year ended October 31, 2014, the testing amount is $20,000 ($120,000 ÷ 12 months = $10,000; $10,000 × 2 months) [Code Sec. 280H(f); Temp. Reg. § 1.280H-1T(c)(2)].

In the three-year average test, amounts paid (as defined above) to you and other owner-employees for the immediately prior three years are divided by the PSC's *adjusted taxable income* for the same period to give you the *applicable percentage.* Adjusted taxable income is the sum of your PSC's taxable income plus amounts included in the owner-employees' gross incomes (excluding gains on sales and dividends.) The applicable percentage is then multiplied by your PSC's adjusted taxable income for the deferral period of the year being tested.

Tax Pointer

Your PSC is deemed to have satisfied both the three-year average test and the preceding year test for the first year it is in existence.

Even if your PSC fails to satisfy the minimum distribution requirements, it can still deduct what is called the ***maximum deductible amount.***

.02 Maximum Deductible Amount

If your PSC doesn't meet the minimum distribution requirement for any applicable election year, the amount of applicable payments it can deduct for that year is limited to a maximum deductible amount. That amount is the sum of (1) the applicable amounts paid in the deferral period plus (2) the applicable amounts paid in the deferral period divided by the number of months in the deferral period multiplied by the number of months in the nondeferral period. The ***nondeferral period*** is the portion of the applicable election year that comes after the deferral period [Temp. Reg. § 1.280H-1T(d)].

> **Example 18-19:** XYZ Personal Service Corporation elects to retain a fiscal tax year that ends on January 31. XYZ, which has three owner-employees, does not meet the minimum distribution requirements for the year. XYZ paid the three owner-employees $143,000 in compensation for the year. Result: XYZ's maximum deductible amount for the year is $156,000—$143,000 (applicable payments during the deferral period) plus $13,000 ($143,000 divided by 11 months in the deferral period multiplied by one month in the nondeferral period).

Carryover of Disallowed Amounts

Payments to owner-employees that can't be deducted aren't lost. They're carried over and treated as paid or incurred in the next tax year. And there's no time limit on how long they can be carried forward [Code Sec. 280H(b)].

WHEN TO REPORT INCOME

The question often is not *whether* you include an item in income but *when* you should include it. The rules generally have evolved from IRS rulings and court decisions.

¶18,080 PERIOD IN WHICH ITEMS OF GROSS INCOME REPORTED

.01 Cash Basis

Cash basis taxpayers report all income subject to tax actually or constructively received, in cash or its equivalent, during the year [Code Sec. 451; Reg. § 1.451-1]; for constructive receipt, see ¶ 18,010.

Checks

Checks are income in the year you receive them, even though you cash them in a later year.[76] This is so, even if you receive the check too late to cash it in the year of receipt.[77] However, if you do not cash the check until the next year at the request of the drawer, you include the check in your income in the year you cash it.[78] For dividend checks, see ¶ 18,090.

.02 Accrual Basis

If you are on the accrual basis, you include in gross income all income subject to tax that accrues during the year. You accrue income when all the events have occurred that fix your right to receive it, the amount can be reasonably estimated and your right to receive it is not subject to substantial restrictions (the *all events test*). The right to receive income becomes fixed at the earliest of (a) required performance; (b) the date payment becomes due; or (c) the date payment is made. When you make a reasonable estimate, you include in income any difference between the estimated and exact amount in the year the exact amount is determined [Reg. § 1.451-1]. You do not have to accrue income if the right to receive it depends on some future occurrence.[79]

Uncollectible Amounts

You are not required to accrue income for an amount that probably you will never receive. The courts generally do not require the accrual of payments of interest, rents, or royalties if the payments are uncollectible when they are due. If an obligation is not collectible when the right to receive it arises, nothing accrues.[80]

In Rev. Rul. 2003-10,[81] the IRS addressed the tax year in which an accrual method vendor would accrue income when the vendor's customer disputes its liability to the vendor in the following three situations:

- If a taxpayer using an accrual method of accounting overbills a customer due to a clerical mistake in an invoice and the customer discovers the error and, in the

[76] *H.A. Fromson*, Fed Cl, 94-2 USTC ¶ 50,425, 32 FedCl 1; *J.M. Butler*, 19 BTA 718, Dec. 6003, *acq.* 1931-2 CB 11; *U.A. Lavery*, CA-7, 46-2 USTC ¶ 9406, 158 F2d 859.

[77] *C.F. Kahler*, 18 TC 31, Dec. 18,884.

[78] *L.M. Fischer*, 14 TC 792, Dec. 17,636 (1950), *acq.* 1950-2 CB 2; *A.V. Johnston*, 23 TCM 2003, Dec 27,083(M), TC Memo. 1964-323.

[79] *American Central Utilities Co.*, 36 BTA 688, Dec. 9782, *acq.* 1938-1 CB 2; *Cuba RR Co.*, 9 TC 211, Dec. 15,970 (1947), *acq.* 1947-2 CB 2; FSA 20124103F (Aug. 22, 2012).

[80] *M.E. Schlude*, SCt, 63-1 USTC ¶ 9284, 372 US 128, 83 SCt 601.

[81] Rev. Rul. 2003-10, 2003-1 CB 288.

following tax year, disputes its liability for the overbilled amount, then the taxpayer accrues gross income in the tax year of sale for the correct amount;

- A vendor would not accrue gross income in the tax year of sale if, during the tax year of sale, the customer disputes its liability to the taxpayer because the taxpayer shipped the incorrect goods; and
- If a vendor ships excess quantities of goods and the customer agrees to pay for the excess quantities of goods, gross income would be accrued in the tax year of the sale.

Nonaccrual Experience (NAE) Accounting Method

Qualifying professionals who have billings to be written off as uncollectible may use any nonaccrual-experience (NAE) method of accounting that clearly reflects the taxpayer's actual experience or any one of the five safe harbor NAE methods listed below to write off their bad debts. The NAE method is available only to a taxpayer using an accrual method of accounting that either provides services in a field described in Code Sec. 448(d)(2)(A) (health, law, engineering, architecture, accounting, actuarial science, performing arts, or consulting), or that meets the $5 million annual gross receipts test of Code Sec. 448(c). The taxpayer may not charge interest or penalties for failure to timely pay the amount charged for the performance of services.

A taxpayer who is qualified to use an NAE method of accounting is not required to accrue any portion of amounts billed for the performance of services that, on the basis of the taxpayer's experience, and to the extent determined under the computation or formula used by the taxpayer and allowed under Reg. § 1.448-2 will not be collected. A taxpayer is qualified to use an NAE method of accounting if the taxpayer uses an accrual method of accounting with respect to amounts to be received for the performance of services by the taxpayer and either: (1) provides services in the health, law, engineering, architecture, accounting, actuarial science, performing arts, or consulting fields, or (2) has average annual gross receipts that do not exceed $5 million [Code Sec. 448(d)(5)]. In addition, the professional must charge no interest or penalties for failure to timely pay the amount charged.

> **NOTE:** A corporation or partnership meets the $5,000,000 gross receipts test of Code Sec. 448(d)(5) if the average annual gross receipts of the entity for the 3-taxable-year period ending with such prior tax year does not exceed $5,000,000.

In Rev. Proc. 2006-56,[82] the IRS provides procedures to enable the taxpayer to request IRS consent to make certain changes to, from, or within a NAE method of accounting and to adopt certain NAE methods. In Rev. Proc. 2011-46,[83] the IRS provided a book safe harbor method of accounting for taxpayers using the nonaccrual-experience (NAE) method of accounting under Code Sec. 448(d)(5) and Reg. § 1.448-2. To be eligible, taxpayers must also use an accrual method and must either: (1) provide services in fields described in Code Sec. 448(d)(2)(A) or (2) meet the $5 million annual gross receipts test of Code Sec. 448(c).

---

[82] Rev. Proc. 2006-56, 2006-2 CB 1169, as modified by Rev. Proc. 2011-14, IRB 2011-4, as modified and amplified by Rev. Proc. 2011-46, IRB 2011-42.

[83] Rev. Proc. 2011-46, IRB 2011-42, 518.

Safe harbors—In general. A taxpayer that satisfies one of the safe harbor NAE method identified in Reg. § 1.448-2 is not required to accrue any portion of amounts to be received from the performance of services that, on the basis of the taxpayer's experience, and to the extent determined under the computation or formula used by the taxpayer and allowed under the safe harbors in Reg. § 1.448-2, will not be collected. Taxpayers may use a NAE method of accounting to determine the amount they can write off. Reg. § 1.448-2 provides the following five safe harbors:

Safe harbor 1: Revenue-based moving average method. A taxpayer may use a NAE method under which the taxpayer determines the uncollectible amount by multiplying its accounts receivable balance at the end of the current tax year by a percentage (revenue-based moving average percentage). The revenue-based moving average percentage is computed by dividing the total bad debts sustained, adjusted by recoveries received, throughout the applicable period by the total revenue, resulting in accounts receivable earned throughout the applicable period. See paragraph (g) Example 4 of this section for an example of this method [Reg. § 1.448-2(f)(1)].

Safe harbor 2: Actual experience method.

1. *Option A: Single determination date.* A taxpayer may use a NAE method under which the taxpayer determines the uncollectible amount by multiplying its accounts receivable balance at the end of the current tax year by a percentage (moving average NAE percentage) and then increasing the resulting amount by 5 percent. The taxpayer's moving average NAE percentage is computed by dividing the total bad debts sustained, adjusted by recoveries that are allocable to the bad debts, by the determination date of the current tax year related to the taxpayer's accounts receivable balance at the beginning of each tax year during the applicable period by the sum of the accounts receivable at the beginning of the each tax year during the applicable period
2. *Option B: Multiple determination dates.* Alternatively, in computing its bad debts related to the taxpayer's accounts receivable balance at the beginning of each tax year during the applicable period, a taxpayer may use the original determination date for each tax year during the applicable period. That is, the taxpayer may use bad debts sustained, adjusted by recoveries received that are allocable to the bad debts, by the determination date of each tax year during the applicable period rather than the determination date of the current tax year [Reg. § 1.448-2(f)(2)].

Safe harbor 3: Modified Black Motor method. A taxpayer may use a NAE method under which the taxpayer determines the uncollectible amount by multiplying its accounts receivable balance at the end of the current tax year by a percentage (modified Black Motor moving average percentage based on valuation formula addressed in *Black Motor Co.*,[84] and then reducing the resulting amount by the bad debts written off during the current tax year relating to accounts receivable generated during the current tax year. The modified Black Motor moving average percentage is computed by dividing the total bad debts sustained, adjusted by recoveries received, during the applicable period by the sum of accounts receivable at the end of each tax year during the applicable period [Reg. § 1.448-2(f)(3)].

---

[84] 41 BTA 300, Dec. 10,996 (1940), *aff'd*, CA-6, 42-1 USTC ¶ 9265, 125 F2d 977.

Safe harbor 4: Modified moving average method. A taxpayer may use a NAE method under which the taxpayer determines the uncollectible amount by multiplying its accounts receivable balance at the end of the current tax year by a percentage (modified moving average percentage). The modified moving average percentage is computed by dividing the total bad debts sustained, adjusted by recoveries received, during the applicable period other than bad debts that were written off in the same tax year the related accounts receivable were generated by the sum of accounts receivable at the beginning of each tax year during the applicable period [Reg. § 1.448-2(f)(4)].

Safe harbor 5: Alternative NAE method. A taxpayer may use an alternative NAE method that clearly reflects the taxpayer's actual NAE, provided the taxpayer's alternative NAE method meets the self-test requirements described below [Reg. § 1.448-2(f)(5)].

Self-test requirement. Alternatively, taxpayers may use a method that reflects their actual experience. However, taxpayers must demonstrate how they determine actual experience and must self-test to determine whether their method meets the actual experience standard. Self-testing must be performed in the first year that the taxpayer uses an NAE method. If the taxpayer's actual experience is less than the amount written-off under the taxpayer's NAE method, the IRS will allow the taxpayer to apply the NAE method. If the taxpayer's experience exceeds the NAE write-off, the taxpayer cannot use its NAE method for that year and must change to another method [Reg. § 1.448-2(e)].

Taxpayers not using a safe harbor must continue to self-test every three years. If the write-off under the NAE method is less than 110 percent of the actual uncollectible amount, the IRS will accept the taxpayer's NAE method. A company that acquires a major portion of another company may include data from the predecessor company. A company that disposes of a major portion of a trade or business may not use data from the business it disposed of.

State and Local Tax Refunds

In Rev. Rul. 2003-3,[85] the IRS ruled that a state or local income or franchise tax refund is includible in the income of a taxpayer using the accrual method of accounting when the taxpayer receives payment or notice that the refund claim has been approved, whichever is earlier. Any change in the timing of a taxpayer's inclusion in income of state or local income taxes or franchise tax refunds to conform with this ruling constitutes a change in method of accounting. Therefore, a taxpayer that wants to accrue state or local income or franchise tax refunds in the year payment or notification of approval of the refund claim is received must file Form 3115.

Prepaid Income

Prepaid income generally is reported in the year received. You cannot prorate it over the period in which you are to perform the services.[86] The IRS permits a one-year deferral in the recognition of certain prepaid income where payments are received in

---

[85] Rev. Rul. 2003-3, 2003-1 CB 252.

[86] *Doyle, Dane, Bernbach, Inc.*, 79 TC 101, Dec. 39,199 (1982) (*Nonacq.* 1988-1 CB 1) (*Withholding of Nonacq and Acq.*, IRB 2003-2).

one year for services to be rendered in the next succeeding year.[87] However, there are some exceptions [¶18,085].

Stock Brokerage Commissions

Under the all-events test, an accrual method stock brokerage firm must accrue commission income on the trade date, rather than the settlement date, which occurs several days later.[88] On the *trade date* a stock broker will execute a customer's order to buy or sell securities. The securities are not actually transferred that day and payment is not due until the settlement date, which is within three business days according to SEC requirements. Between the trade and settlement dates, the broker performs certain functions to record, confirm, and book the customer's trade. A security is not credited to the customer's account until the actual settlement date.

According to the all-events test, it is the fixed right to receive the income that is controlling and not whether any money has changed hands [Reg. § 1.446-1(c)(1)(ii)]. The execution of an order on behalf of a customer is the essential service that a stock brokerage performs and is the time when the discount broker's right to receive the commission and the customer's obligation to pay the commission arose. All events performed by the brokerage after the trade date are of a ministerial and mechanical nature and exist merely to confirm the trade that was executed.

¶18,085 COMPENSATION FOR SERVICES

.01 Cash Basis

If you are on the cash basis, you include compensation in income for the year you actually or constructively receive it [Reg. § 1.451-1(a); ¶18,010].[89] Generally, it is immaterial that your employer, using the accrual basis, deducted the compensation in the previous year. Part of your pay deferred under an employment contract is not income in the year earned until you actually receive payment or it is made available to you later. At the same time, your employer can deduct deferred compensation payments only in the year they are actually paid or transferred unless an exception (inventory, depreciable property) to that rule applies [Reg. § 1.461-1(a)(1)].[90] Special rules apply to a salaried partner [Ch. 24]. Money placed in an educational benefit trust set up by a corporation for the education of employees' children is deferred compensation taxable to the employees and deductible by the corporation when paid out of the trust.[91]

Advances to Salespersons

If a salesperson is under an employment contract that provides that advances are a debt owed to the employer, the advances are not taxable upon receipt. However, if the advances were originally intended as loans but are later charged off, they are additional compensation to the salesperson and are deductible by the employer in the

---

[87] Rev. Proc. 2011-14, IRB 2011-4, 330, as modified and clarified in various specific situations; Rev. Proc. 2011-18, IRB 2011-5, 443.

[88] *Charles Schwab Corp.*, CA-9, 99-1 USTC ¶50,109, 161 F3d 1231, *cert. denied*, 120 SCt 67; Rev. Rul. 74-372, 1974-2 CB 147.

[89] *C.F. Zittel*, 12 BTA 675, Dec. 4102; *W.B. Massey*, CA-5, 44-2 USTC ¶9384, 143 F2d 429.

[90] Rev. Rul. 69-650, 1969-2 CB 106.

[91] Rev. Rul. 75-448, 1975-2 CB 55; *R.T. Armantrout*, CA-7, 78-1 USTC ¶9232, 570 F2d 210.

year charged off.[92] If the contract guarantees a certain monthly sum, advances up to the guarantee are income upon receipt.[93]

.02 Accrual Basis

Under an accrual method of accounting, income is includible in gross income when all the events have occurred that fix the right to receive the income and the amount can be determined with reasonable accuracy (the all-events test) [Code Sec. 461(h)(4)]. All the events that fix the right to receive income generally occur when (1) the required performance takes place, (2) payment is due to the taxpayer, or (3) payment is received by the taxpayer, whichever happens earliest [Reg. § 1.451-1]. In *Trinity Industries, Inc.*,[94] the Tax Court held that an accrual basis taxpayer had to accrue income once the all-events test was satisfied, even if payment was postponed until a later year. Thus the taxpayer had to accrue the full contract price of goods in the year of delivery. Accrual was not postponed by the purchasers' assertion of rights to withhold deferred payments under the common law claim of offset.

.03 Restricted Property

If property you receive for performing services is subject to a substantial risk of forfeiture, you do not generally include the property's value in income until the time when the restrictions lapse as discussed in Ch. 2 [Code Sec. 83].

.04 Advance Payments for Goods and Services

Generally, advance payments (e.g., paying two years of rent up-front when the lease is signed) are income in the year received for both cash and accrual basis taxpayers (provided there are no restrictions on the use of the funds) [Reg. § 1.451-5]. A payment for extended warranty coverage will be classified as an advance payment includable in income in the year of receipt.[95]

An accrual method taxpayer in certain specified and limited circumstances may defer the inclusion in gross income of payments received (or amounts due and payable) in one tax year for services to be performed by the end of the next succeeding tax year.[96] A payment is an advance payment if: (1) including the payment in gross income for the tax year of receipt is a permissible accounting method for federal income tax purposes, (2) the payment is recognized by the taxpayer (in whole or in part) in revenues in its applicable financial statement for a subsequent tax year, and (3) the payment is for certain specified activities, including the performance of services or the use of intellectual property.

In general, advance payments are not taxable until the taxpayer has *complete dominion and control* over the income (e.g., no possibility of having to refund the money). For example, refundable security deposits paid to a utility, such as a phone company or an electric company, as a guarantee that future bills will be paid are not taxable to the

---

[92] *C.E. Shockey*, 6 TCM 1092, Dec. 16,075(M); Rev. Rul. 69-465, 1969-2 CB 27.

[93] *K. Drummond*, 43 BTA 529, Dec. 11,649.

[94] *Trinity Industries, Inc.*, 132 TC No. 2, Dec. 57,718 (2009).

[95] LTR 9424075 (Jan. 26, 1994).

[96] Rev. Proc. 2004-34, 2004-1 CB 991, as modified and clarified by Rev. Proc. 2011-18, IRB 2011-5, 443; Rev. Proc. 2011-14, IRB 2011-4, 330, as modified and clarified in various specific situations.

company until the deposits are actually used to pay the bills.[97] Until the deposit is applied to pay a customer's bill, the utility is obligated to return the deposit and so lacks dominion and control over it.[98]

Accrual-basis taxpayers and those using a long-term contract method of accounting, though, have a choice of when to include certain advance payments. The choice extends to advance payments for (1) the sale or disposition in a future year of goods primarily held for sale to customers, or (2) building, installing, constructing or manufacturing items that won't be completed until a later tax year [Reg. § 1.451-5].

The advance payments may generally be included in income either: (1) when you receive them, or (2) when includible under your normal method of accounting. This method of accounting is either the method used for tax purposes or for financial reporting, whichever would result in the payments being included in income earlier. *Exception:* For long-term contracts, you use the accounting method you use for tax purposes. The method used for your financial reports is disregarded.

Example 18-20: HF Inc., a manufacturer of household furniture, is an accrual basis taxpayer. In December HF receives an $8,000 advance payment on a $20,000 order. The furniture is shipped in that month but not delivered and accepted by the customer until January of the following year. HF may include the $8,000 advance payment in the taxable income of either year.

A payment is an advance payment eligible for deferral if the payment is for one of the following purposes: (1) services; (2) goods; (3) use (including by license or lease) of intellectual property; (4) limited occupancy or use of property if ancillary to the provision of services (for example, advance payments for the use of rooms or other quarters in a hotel, booth space at a trade show, campsite space at a mobile home park, and recreational or banquet facilities, or other uses of property, so long as the use is ancillary to the provision of services to the property user); (5) sale, lease, or license of computer software; (6) guaranty or warranty contracts ancillary to the above items; (7) subscriptions; (8) memberships in most organizations; or (9) any combination of the above items.

Excluded from the definition of *advance payments* are the following types of income items:

- Rent;
- Insurance premiums;
- Debt instruments, deposits, letters of credit, notional principal contracts, options, forward contracts, futures contracts, foreign currency contracts, credit card agreements, financial derivatives, including prepayments of interest;
- Service warranty contract payments;
- Warranty and guaranty contracts where a third party is the primary obligor;

[97] *Indianapolis Power & Light Co.*, SCt, 90-1 USTC ¶ 50,007, 493 US 203, 110 SCt 589.

[98] *Oak Industries*, 96 TC 559, Dec. 47,262 (1991); *American Telephone & Telegraph Co.*, 55 TCM 16, Dec. 44,549(M), TC Memo. 1988-35.

- Payments subject to the foreign withholding rules in Code Secs. 871(a), 881, 1441, or 1442; and
- Property transferred in connection with the performance of services to which Code Sec. 83 applies.

.05 Up-Front Cash for Advance Trade Discount

Up-front cash advances received by a wholesaler from a retailer in exchange for an advance trade discount do not constitute gross income in the year of receipt if, like security deposits, they are subject to repayment if the taxpayer fails to satisfy the volume commitment. Even though the taxpayer may have had complete dominion over the money received, the advances are not an accession to wealth since the taxpayer may have to return the money. The tax treatment of cash advance trade discounts is comparable to the tax treatment of customer security deposits in *Indianapolis Power & Light Co.*, where the Supreme Court held that customer security deposits were not income to the utility because the utility was obligated to repay the money when the taxpayer terminated utility service. In *Westpac Pacific Food*,[99] the Court of Appeals for the Ninth Circuit reversed the Tax Court to conclude that up-front cash advances received by a wholesaler from a retailer in exchange for an advance trade discount did not constitute gross income in the year of receipt.

The IRS has announced that it will follow the Ninth Circuit decision in *Westpac Pacific Food* with respect to taxpayers that adopt the advance trade discount method of accounting.[100] Thus, accrual method taxpayers may treat advance trade discounts as reductions in the cost of goods sold, rather than as income when received.

.06 Deferring Income on Prepaid Gift Cards

The sale of gift cards and gift certificates is widespread in the retail industry. Typically, a retailer sells a gift certificate or gift card to a buyer who then gives the card to a donee who redeems the card at the retailer who then provides goods or services to the holder. For income tax purposes, payment for a gift certificate or gift card was viewed as payment for goods or services to be provided in the future. If a customer uses a gift card to purchase merchandise or services from a participating merchant, the participating merchant is obligated to accept the gift card as payment for its goods or services and the gift card entity is obligated to reimburse the participating merchant for the sales price of the goods or services purchased with the gift card. Under the terms of a typical gift card service agreement, the entity selling the gift card entity is primarily liable to the customer for the value of the gift card until the card expires or is redeemed.

The Supreme Court established in *M.E. Schlude*,[101] that amounts received by an accrual method taxpayer for goods or services to be provided in the future (advance payments) must be included in gross income in the tax year of receipt. There are however, two exceptions to this general rule in Reg. § 1.451-5 and Rev. Proc. 2004-34.[102] Reg. § 1.451-5

---

[99] *Westpac Pacific Foods*, CA-9, 2006-2 USTC ¶ 50,369, 451 F3d 970.

[100] Rev. Proc. 2007-53, 2007-2 CB 233.

[101] *M.E. Schlude*, SCt, 63-1 USTC ¶ 9284, 372 US 128, 83 SCt 601.

[102] Rev. Proc. 2004-34, 2004-1 CB 991, as modified and clarified by Rev. Proc. 2011-18, IRB 2011-5, 44; Rev. Proc. 2011-14, IRB 2011-4, 330, as modified and clarified in various specific situations.

generally allows accrual method taxpayers a limited deferral for advance payments received for the sale of goods. The taxpayer may defer recognition of this income until the payments are recognized in revenues under the taxpayer's method of accounting. However, Reg. § 1.451-5(c) provides that a taxpayer generally may not defer advance payments for inventoriable goods beyond the end of the second tax year following the year the taxpayer receives substantial advance payments.

Rev. Proc. 2004-34 provides a "deferral method" of accounting that allows an accrual method taxpayer receiving advance payments for goods or services to defer recognizing income to the extent the taxpayer defers recognizing the payments as revenues in its "applicable financial statement." If the taxpayer does not include advance payments as revenues in its applicable financial statement in the year of receipt, the taxpayer must include the advance payments in gross income in the next succeeding taxable year. Therefore, under Rev. Proc. 2004-34, the retailer could defer recognizing the advance payment from the sale of the gift card. Today, however, gift cards are commonly sold by one retailer and redeemed either by that retailer or by others (related or unrelated to the selling entity) under a gift card service agreement.

In Rev. Proc 2011-18,[103] the IRS provided that a taxpayer that sells gift cards redeemable through other entities should be treated the same as a taxpayer that sells gift cards that only it redeems. Therefore in Rev. Proc 2011-18 the IRS modified the definition of advance payments in Rev. Proc. 2004-34 to allow deferral of advance payments received under "eligible gift cards" redeemable through another entity that may or may not be related to the taxpayer. An eligible gift card sale was defined as the sale of a gift card (or gift certificate) if:

1. The taxpayer was primarily liable to the customer (or holder of the gift card) for the value of the card until redemption or expiration, and
2. The gift card was redeemable by the taxpayer or by any other entity that is legally obligated to the taxpayer to accept the gift card from a customer as payment for goods or services.

Example 18-21: W is an S corp. that operates an affiliated restaurant corporation and manages other affiliated restaurants. W administers a gift card program for participating restaurants that operate under different trade names. Under the gift card program, W and each of the restaurants sell gift cards, which are issued with W's brand name and are redeemable at all participating restaurants. The restaurants sell the gift cards to customers and remit the proceeds to W. W is liable to the customer for the value of the gift card until redemption, and the restaurants are obligated under an agreement with W to accept the gift card as payment for food, beverages, taxes, and gratuities. When a customer uses a gift card to make a purchase at one of the restaurants, W is obligated to reimburse that restaurant for the amount of the purchase, up to the total gift card value. In W's applicable financial statement, W recognizes revenue from the sale of a gift card when a gift card is redeemed at a restaurant. W tracks

[103] Rev. Proc. 2011-18, IRB 2011-5, 443, modified and clarified by Rev. Proc 2013-29, IRB 2013-33, 141.

sales and redemptions of gift cards electronically and is able to determine the extent to which advance payments are recognized in revenues in its applicable financial statement for the taxable year of receipt. The payments received by W from the sale of gift cards are advance payments because they are payments for eligible gift card sales and W is therefore eligible to use the deferral method.

If a gift card is redeemable by an entity whose financial results are not included in the taxpayer's applicable financial statement, a payment will be treated as recognized by the taxpayer in income to the extent the gift card is redeemed by the entity during the year. For a taxpayer without an applicable financial statement, if a gift card is redeemable by an entity, including an entity whose financial results are not included in the taxpayer's financial statement, a payment will be treated as earned by the taxpayer to the extent the gift card is redeemed by the entity during the year.

Some taxpayers were unable to take advantage of the deferral method of accounting sanctioned in Rev. Rul. 2004-34 (as modified by Rev. Proc. 2011-18) solely because the taxpayer never recognized eligible gift card sales in revenues in its applicable financial statement payments or, for taxpayers without an applicable financial statement, the payment was never earned by the taxpayer because the payment was earned by the unrelated redeeming entity. To remedy this unintended consequence, the IRS provided in Rev. Proc. 2013-29[104] that for purposes of Rev Proc 2004-34, if a gift card is redeemable by an entity whose financial results are not included in the taxpayer's applicable financial statement, a payment will be treated as recognized by the taxpayer in revenues in its applicable financial statement to the extent the gift card is redeemed by the entity during the year. And, for a taxpayer without an applicable financial statement, if a gift card is redeemable by an entity whose financial results are not included in the taxpayer's financial statement, a payment will be treated as earned by the taxpayer to the extent the gift card is redeemed by the entity during the year.

Example 18-22: On November 1, 2013, *A*, in the business of giving dancing lessons, receives an advance payment for a one-year contract commencing on that date and providing for up to 48 individual, one-hour lessons. *A* provides eight lessons in 2013 and another 35 lessons in 2014. In its applicable financial statement, *A* recognizes 1/6 of the payment in revenues for 2013, and 5/6 of the payment in revenues for 2014. *A* uses the Deferral Method. For federal income tax purposes, *A* must include 1/6 of the payment in gross income for 2013, and the remaining 5/6 of the payment in gross income for 2014.

.07 Special Exception for Inventoriable Goods

A special rule applies if the taxpayer receives an advance payment for the sale of inventoriable goods (including a gift certificate) that cannot be satisfied with identifiable goods and the taxpayer (1) has received *substantial advance payments,* and (2) has on hand (or available through normal source of supply) enough substantially similar goods to satisfy the agreement in the year the payments are received. If these conditions are met, all advance payments received by the end of the second tax year after the one in

104 Rev. Proc. 2013-29, IRB 2013-33, 141.

which the substantial payments were received must be included in income (if not previously included) [Reg. § 1.451-5(c)(1)(i)]. Advance payments received under an agreement are "substantial" if total payments received under the agreement since inception equal or exceed the total costs and expenditures reasonably estimated as includible in inventory for that agreement [Reg. § 1.451-5(c)(3)]. If advance payments are included in income in the second tax year under this exception, the taxpayer must deduct as part of his cost of goods sold and eliminate from inventory the costs and expenditures included in inventory at the end of that year for those goods (or substantially similar goods) on hand. If no such goods are on hand by the last day of that second year, the taxpayer must deduct the estimated cost of goods necessary to satisfy the agreement. These estimated costs may not be deducted in another year. However, any variances between the estimated costs and the actual costs determined later must be taken into account as an adjustment to the cost of goods sold in the year the taxpayer completes his obligations under the agreement. Any advance payments received after that second year are fully taxable in the year received.

¶18,090 DIVIDENDS

Dividends are subject to tax if they are unqualifiedly subject to the shareholder's demand [Reg. § 1.301-1(b)]. This applies to both cash and accrual basis taxpayers.

> **Example 18-23:** A dividend is fully and unqualifiedly available to Turner in the year the dividend is declared. He can obtain it merely for the asking. Although Turner does not actually receive the dividend until the following year, it is taxable in the year it is declared.

> **Example 18-24:** Mr. Benton, a stockbroker, buys stock for Mr. Mason in Benton's name. Benton is Mason's duly appointed agent. Benton receives a dividend for Mason on December 14, 2013, but transmits it to Mason by check on January 2, 2014. It is taxable to Mason in 2013.

.01 Dividend Checks Mailed on Last Day of Tax Year

If a dividend is declared payable on December 31, but the corporation follows the practice of mailing the dividend checks so that they will not be received until January, you do not have constructive receipt in December, and the dividend is January income [Reg. § 1.451-2(b)], even if you are on the accrual basis.[105] For treatment of other checks received by the cash basis taxpayer, see ¶ 18,080.

.02 Income from Building and Loan Associations

An amount credited to the shareholders of a building and loan association is constructively received in the year of credit, if it passes without restriction to the shareholder.

---

[105] *Tar Prods. Corp.*, CA-3, 42-2 USTC ¶ 9662, 130 F2d 866; *American Light & Traction Co.*, CA-7, 46-2 USTC ¶ 9312, 156 F2d 398.

But if the amount accumulated is not available to you until maturity, the total amount credited is income to you in the year of maturity [Reg. § 1.451-2(b)].

.03 Patronage Dividends and Per-Unit Retains

Patronage dividends and per-unit retains are generally taxable in the year received, whether you are on the cash or accrual basis [Code Sec. 1385(a); Reg. § 1.1385-1(a)]. See Ch. 23 for patrons' income from cooperatives.

¶18,095 INTEREST AND DISCOUNTS

.01 Interest

If you are on the cash basis, interest is generally taxable when you actually or constructively [¶ 18,010] receive it. Accrual method taxpayers report interest for the year in which it accrues, unless received earlier [¶ 18,115]. And you may not report interest income net of interest expense on funds borrowed to make the investment.[106]

.02 Discount Instruments

Even as a cash-basis taxpayer, you may owe tax on bonds, notes and other instruments acquired for less than their face value. The rules for original issue discount and market discount are explained at Ch. 2.

.03 Certificates of Deposit

An increase in value of nonnegotiable and growth savings certificates issued by banks is included in a cash-basis taxpayer's gross income in the year the increase occurs, since you can redeem the certificate in that year.[107] Interest earned by a cash-basis taxpayer on a one-year or shorter certificate that is not credited or made available for withdrawal is not includible in your gross income until maturity.

¶18,100 DISCOUNT AND INTEREST ON U.S. SAVINGS BONDS

.01 U.S. Savings Bonds Issued at a Discount

Series EE bonds are the only U.S. savings bonds currently issued at a discount. You pay less than the face amount for the bonds. The face amount is payable to you at maturity. The difference between the purchase price and the redemption value is taxable interest. The amount that accrues in any tax year is measured by the actual increase in the redemption price occurring in that year[108] [See ¶ 2070].

On May 1, 2005, interest rates became fixed for the life of the new Series EE bonds. Thus, starting May 1, 2005, investors who buy a new Series EE U.S. savings bond will receive for the life of the bond whatever interest rate is in effect at the time of purchase. Prior to the change, interest rates on series EE bonds changed every six months.

---

[106] *M.P. Murphy*, 92 TC 12, Dec. 45,411 (1989).

[107] Rev. Rul. 66-45, 1966-1 CB 95.

[108] U.S. Savings Bonds, Series E and EE, Redemption Value Tables.

▶ **OBSERVATION:** Series EE bonds were first offered in 1980. Before then, Series E bonds were issued and many are still outstanding ,although they have fully matured.

Cash Basis

If you own either Series E or EE bonds you may:

- Defer reporting the interest until the earlier of the year you cash in the bonds or the year in which they finally mature (method 1); or
- Choose to report the increase in redemption value as interest each year (method 2).

If you want to change your method of reporting the interest from method 1 to method 2, you may do so with IRS permission. However, in the year of change, you must report all interest accrued to date and not previously reported for the bonds. There is a way to get automatic IRS approval of the change. However, it may be used no more often than once every five years. You attach a completed Form 3115 to your return for the year you are switching methods. You must also attach a statement saying that you agree to report all untaxed interest when the bonds are redeemed, mature or are disposed of, whichever is earlier.

NOTE: If you plan to redeem Series EE bonds in the same year that you will pay for higher educational expenses, you should use method 1. See below.

If a taxpayer dies owning savings bonds, the entire increment that had not been taxed is reported as income in respect of a decedent [Ch. 25] not includible in the recipient's income until actually or constructively received. However, the decedent's personal representative may elect to include it in the decedent's final return.[109] An election cannot be made in an amended return filed after the due date of the original return or in an original return not timely filed.[110]

Accrual Basis

If you are an accrual taxpayer, you must report interest on U.S. savings bonds each year as the interest accrues. You cannot defer reporting interest until the bonds are cashed or mature.

Series E or EE Bonds Held Beyond Maturity

Let's say that you are a cash-basis taxpayer who holds Series E or EE bonds after maturity. If you have elected to report the taxable increment on the accrual basis, you must continue to do so, unless you get permission to change. On the other hand, if you have elected to report on redemption or maturity, you report the entire increment in the year of *final* redemption or *extended* maturity.

.02 U.S. Savings Bonds Issued on a Current Income Basis

Unlike EE bonds, HH bonds are current-income securities. Taxpayers pay face value for the bonds and receive interest payments by direct deposit to their checking or savings account every six months until maturity or redemption. HH bonds are often used to supplement retirement income.

Unlike Series EE bonds issued on a discount basis, U.S. savings bonds are issued at par with interest payable semiannually by Treasury check. The interest is taxable (1)

---

[109] Rev. Rul. 68-145, 1968-1 CB 203.

[110] Rev. Rul. 55-655, 1955-2 CB 253.

when received, for those on the cash basis, or (2) when accrued, for those on the accrual basis. The interest accrues when it becomes payable. Owners of matured Series H or HH bonds may continue to hold the bonds at interest after maturity. Interest for the extended period should be reported when received or accrued.

.03 Education Savings Bonds

Taxpayers may be able to exclude from income all or part of the interest received on redeeming qualified U.S. Savings Bonds if they pay qualified higher educational expenses during the year. See ¶ 2070.

¶ 18,105 RENT AND DEFERRED RENT TRANSACTIONS

.01 Rent in General

Generally, advance rents, royalties, and bonuses received upon execution of a lease are includible in gross income in the year received [Reg. § 1.61-8(b); Code Sec. 467]. This rule applies to both cash-and accrual-method taxpayers, even though payments are returnable if the terms of the lease are unfulfilled.[111] Security deposits may or may not be includible in the lessor's income depending on the rights and obligations assumed by the lessee when the deposits are made. If the deposits are made to ensure the lessee's performance of the lease terms and conditions and are returnable to the lessee upon termination of the lease, the amounts are not rental income to the lessor.[112] Advance rentals must be included in income for the year of receipt regardless of the period covered or the method of accounting employed by the taxpayer [Reg. § 1.61-8(b)].

Lease Cancellation

An amount received by a lessor from a lessee for cancelling a lease constitutes gross income for the year in which it is received, since it is essentially a substitute for rental payments [Reg. § 1.61-8(b)].

.02 Deferred Payments for Use of Property or Services

Rental and interest income attributable to a *deferred rental agreement* must be reported and deducted as if both parties were on the accrual method of accounting [Code Sec. 467]. Generally, a deferred rental payment agreement *(Section 467 rental agreement)* is any agreement for the use of tangible property involving over $250,000 in rental payments, under which (1) at least one payment is made after the calendar year of the paid usage, or (2) there are rent increases over the term of the agreement. The accrual method that the lessor and lessee must use factors an interest element into the deferred payments. Thus, the lessor reports as income and the lessee deducts an amount equal to the sum of: (1) the *accrued rent* for the year, and (2) interest on the amounts taken into account for prior years which remain unpaid.

---

[111] Rev. Rul. 57-537, 1957-2, CB 52.

[112] *In re Point Lorne Development Corp.* DC-CA, 71-1 USTC ¶ 9250.

Accrued rent for the year is calculated by adding rents allocated according to the rental agreement to the present value of rents to be paid after the close of the period. Interest is calculated at 110 percent of the Applicable Federal Rate (AFR), compounded semiannually, in effect when the agreement is entered into with respect to debt instruments having a maturity equal to the term of the agreement. There are special rules for agreements that don't allocate rents and for tax avoidance transactions.

Tax Avoidance

If you receive rent under a deferred payment agreement that is deemed to have a tax avoidance purpose, you must refigure your rental income to recognize a level amount of rent each year—the constant rental amount.

For agreements that are considered tax avoidance transactions, your accrued rental income for the year is the "constant rental amount." This is the amount which, if received at the close of each lease period (i.e., the 12-month period starting on the first day the agreement applies), would result in an aggregate present value equal to the present value of the aggregate payments required under the agreement. Present value is calculated at 110 percent of the AFR, compounded semiannually.

What is a tax avoidance transaction? Agreements that meet certain conditions are presumed to be *tax avoidance transactions.* The test applies to *disqualified leasebacks* or *long-term agreements.* These are deferred payment rental agreements under which the term of the agreement exceeds 75 percent of the property's recovery period *and* a principal purpose for the increasing (i.e., stepped) rents is tax avoidance. The test also applies to agreements that don't provide how rents are to be allocated [Code Sec. 467(b)].

Determining if a principal purpose of a deferred payment rental agreement is tax avoidance boils down to a question of the facts and circumstances of the particular situation.

A tax avoidance purpose might be presumed if, under the lease, the lessee had an option to renew at a rental amount significantly less than the rental amounts payable during the later years of the lease.

Safe harbors. There are certain safe harbor situations where a tax avoidance purpose will be presumed not to exist. These primarily apply to stepped rental agreements. The protected circumstances include:

- Rent increases based on price index changes;
- Rents figured based on a percentage-of-receipts formula;
- Reasonable rent holidays, such as for a short period of time after the inception of a lease; and
- Changes in rent related to changes in amounts paid to unrelated third parties (e.g., insurance, maintenance, or real estate taxes).

Recapture

Lessors who pass the tax-avoidance test are subject to a special recapture provision on the leased property's disposition. Any gain realized is ordinary income to the extent rent accruals that would have been taken into account had the rent leveling provision applied exceed actual accruals to the transfer date [Code Sec. 467(c)].

Example 18-25: Mr. Smith has a $25,000 gain on the sale of an office building. Accrued rents were $2,000 at the date of sale, but would have been $3,000 if the rent leveling provisions had applied. Result: $1,000 of the gain is ordinary income.

¶18,110 INCOME FROM SALE OF PROPERTY OR STOCK

.01 Sale of Property

You report gain from the sale of property in the year there is a *closed transaction.* For a *cash basis* taxpayer, that is usually when you receive the purchase price. An *accrual basis* taxpayer realizes gain when a sale is completed (see below), and you have an unqualified right to receive payment. This usually occurs when the buyer becomes unconditionally liable to pay the purchase price.[113]

When a Sale Is Completed

A sale of real property generally occurs at the earlier of the time (1) title is conveyed by a deed, or (2) possession and the burdens and benefits of ownership are, from a practical standpoint, transferred to the buyer. The transfer of possession and of the burdens and benefits of ownership need not be complete. When the *bundle of rights* or attributes of ownership acquired by the buyer outweigh those retained by the seller, the sale is completed.[114] Sales of personal property are governed by the same rules. But most sales of personal property will occur when title passes. For tax purposes, the local law of sales determines when title passes.

Contingent Payments

If all or part of the consideration for the sale of property is an agreement to make future payments of a contingent character, the transaction is not closed for tax purposes. No part of the contingent payments is income until you have recovered your capital. After that, the payments are taxed as capital gain, if the asset was a capital asset.[115]

Example 18-26: Ms. Jones sold property to a corporation for a percentage of its profits for five years. Since the payments were contingent on earnings, they were not income until received, and then only to the extent they represented gain over the basis of the property.[116]

The tax rules for deferred payment sales are discussed at Ch. 19.

.02 Sale of Stock Through a Broker

The question of when a sale of stock becomes a closed transaction arises if you make a sale at the end of one tax year but do not receive delivery of the certificates until the

[113] *North Texas Lumber*, SCt, 2 USTC ¶484, 281 US 11, 50 SCt 184.

[114] *2 Lexington Ave. Corp.*, 26 TC 816, Dec. 21,847 (1956) *(Acq.).*

[115] *E.A. Logan*, SCt, 2 USTC ¶736, 283 US 404, 51 SCt 550.

[116] *D.D. Yerger*, DC-PA, 44-1 USTC ¶9282, 55 FSupp 521.

next year. Both cash and accrual basis taxpayers recognize gain or loss from sales of securities made on an established market on the trade date [Code Sec. 453(k)(2)]. Sales of publicly traded property such as stocks and bonds do not qualify for the installment method where payment is received in the following year [Ch. 19] [Code Sec. 453(k)(2)(A)].

.03 Payments or Property in Escrow

Suppose part or all of the property's purchase price is placed in escrow by the buyer. Then you (the seller) should not include the amount placed in escrow in your gross sales until you actually or constructively receive it, whether you are on the cash or accrual basis. However, on performing the terms of the contract and escrow agreement, you realize taxable income, even though you may not accept the money until the following year.

¶18,115 PREPAID INCOME

Generally, prepaid income is taxable in the year of receipt, whether the taxpayer is on the cash or accrual basis. However, there are exceptions for accrual basis taxpayers receiving prepaid subscription income, certain prepaid membership dues, and advance payments.

.01 Prepaid Subscriptions

Publishers on an accrual basis may elect to report prepaid subscriptions over the subscription period instead of reporting it all in the year received [Code Sec. 455(a); Reg. § 1.455-1]. But, if the taxpayer's liability ends or the taxpayer goes out of existence, the taxpayer must report any unreported amount in that year [Code Sec. 455(b); Reg. § 1.455-4]. The election generally applies to all prepaid subscriptions of the trade or business for which it is made. However, income that will be earned within 12 months of receipt may either be included in the election or reported in the year received [Code Sec. 455(c); Reg. § 1.455-6(c)].

How to Elect Reporting Throughout Subscription Period

A taxpayer can make the election without IRS consent for the first tax year in which he or she receives subscription income [Code Sec. 455(c); Reg. § 1.455-6(a)]. The taxpayer makes the election by attaching a statement to a timely filed return indicating the amount of prepaid subscription income, the period over which the taxpayer's liability extends, and the method of allocating income to each period [Reg. § 1.455-6(a)]. Consent is required at any other time. The taxpayer must file the application with the IRS, within 90 days (plus allowable 90-day extension)[117] after the start of the first year to which the election is to apply [Reg. § 1.455-6(b)]. The election is effective for the year of election and all later years. The taxpayer can revoke the election only with IRS consent [Code Sec. 455(c); Reg. § 1.455-2(c)].

---

[117] Rev. Proc. 94-32, 1994-1 CB 627.

.02 Prepaid Membership Dues

Certain membership organizations without capital stock, operating on the accrual basis, may elect to spread dues covering 36 months or less over the membership period. For example, this would apply to automobile clubs like the AAA [Code Sec. 456; Reg. § 1.456-1].

¶18,120 DISPUTED INCOME

A dispute regarding the taxpayer's right to receive an amount that the taxpayer claims is due postpones the time for taxing the claim. Amounts recovered as a result of the dispute usually are taxable: (1) under the accrual method when the dispute is terminated by a settlement, a final judgment by the highest court, or a final judgment of a lower court if no appeal is taken and the time for appeal expires;[118] and (2) under the cash method, when the taxpayer receives the amounts.[119] However, taxability is not postponed beyond the time when you receive disputed amounts under a claim of right and without restriction as to their disposition, even if the receipt takes place during a dispute.[120] (Income impounded, withheld or escrowed during a dispute as to your right to receive it is not taxable until the funds are released to you or the dispute is terminated.)[121]

An offer to compromise a claim for a lesser amount does not create taxable income,[122] but an unconditional concession as to part of the claim fixes the time for accrual of the conceded amount. (See ¶ 18,080 for income not expected to be collected.)

¶18,125 REPAID INCOME

.01 Cash Basis

If you receive income under a claim of right, it is income in the year you receive it. To be taxable under the claim of right doctrine, you must receive the income without restriction as to its disposition. You must include the income even though your right to retain it is disputed and all or part of it may have to be repaid in a later year because the right to its use proves not to have been unrestricted. However, you can deduct the repayment in the later year,[123] even if the government received no tax benefit in the year the income was reported because you had a net loss.[124] The Supreme Court has held

---

[118] *H. Liebes & Co.*, CA-9, 37-2 USTC ¶9361, 90 F2d 932.

[119] *Sanford & Brooks Co.*, SCt, 2 USTC ¶636, 282 US 359, 51 SCt 150; *W. Koelle*, 7 BTA 917, Dec. 2676, *acq.* 1928-1 CB 18.

[120] *North American Oil Consolidated*, 286 US 417, 53 SCt 613.

[121] *North American Oil Consolidated*, 286 US 417, 53 SCt 613.

[122] *Triboro Coach Corp.*, 29 TC 1274, Dec. 22,911, *acq.* 1960-2 CB 7.

[123] *Universal Oil Products Co.*, CA-7, 50-1 USTC ¶9260, 181 F2d 451, *cert. denied*, 340 US 850, 71 SCt 78.

[124] *M.P. O'Meara*, 8 TC 622, Dec. 15,683 (1947), *acq.* 1947-2 CB 3.

that the deduction taken for repayment must be reduced by any depletion taken on income received under a claim of right.[125]

Example 18-27: Mr. Toby is a cash basis taxpayer who was involved in a lawsuit with the Bex Corporation, arising from a contract dispute. The court settled the dispute in his favor, awarding him $2,000. Although Bex said it would appeal the judgment, it was ordered by the court to pay immediately without restriction. Bex did appeal the decision and the appellate court reversed the lower court's decision the following year. Toby was forced to repay the $2,000. Toby must include the $2,000 in his income in the year of receipt and he may deduct the $2,000 repayment the following year.

▶ **SPECIAL RELIEF:** A number of factors may prevent you from receiving enough benefit from the deduction to offset the tax you paid when you received the income. For instance, you may be in a lower tax bracket. If the repayment exceeds $3,000, a relief provision applies. The inequity is corrected by reducing your tax for the year of repayment. In essence, the reduction is equal to the amount of tax you previously had to pay on the income you are now repaying. If the reduction exceeds the tax for the current year, the excess is refunded or credited as an overpayment [Code Sec. 1341; Reg. § 1.1341-1]. If you are a cash-basis taxpayer who reported the income on the constructive receipt basis, but have never actually received it, you are considered to have made the repayment in the year you were required to relinquish your right to receive the income.

Exceptions to Relief Provisions

The above provisions do not apply to: (1) bad debts [Ch. 13], (2) legal expenses incurred in contesting repayment of the income previously included, or (3) sales of inventory [Code Sec. 1341(b)(2); Reg. § § 1.1341-1(f),(g),(h)].

.02 Accrual Basis

Similar rules apply if you are an accrual-basis taxpayer and you receive income under a claim of right. The year in which the income first accrues is considered the year in which you receive the income. You are entitled to a deduction in the year the obligation to repay accrues.

WHEN TO CLAIM DEDUCTIONS

It is critical that you claim deductions in the proper year. You may lose entirely a deduction claimed in the wrong year.

---

[125] *Skelly Oil Co.*, SCt, 69-1 USTC ¶ 9343, 394 US 678, 89 SCt 1379; *Cities Service Oil Co.*, CtCls, 72-2 USTC ¶ 9560, 462 F2d 1134, 199 CtCls 89, *cert. denied*, 409 US 1063, 93 SCt 558.

¶18,130 WHEN DEDUCTIONS MAY BE CLAIMED

.01 Cash-Basis Taxpayers

Cash-basis taxpayers must claim deductions in the year you make payment in cash or its equivalent [Code Secs. 461, 7701(a)(25); Reg. § 1.461-1(a)(1)]. But a note is not the equivalent of cash. So, if you give your note in payment, you cannot claim the deduction until you pay the note, even if it is secured by collateral.[126] However, you can deduct a payment with money borrowed from another party when paid; not later, when you repay the loan.[127]

.02 Accrual-Basis Taxpayers

An accrual method taxpayer generally may deduct a liability in the tax year in which (1) all events occur that determine the fact of liability, (2) the amount of the liability can be determined with reasonable accuracy and (3) economic performance has occurred (the "all events test") [Code Sec. 461(h); Reg. § 1.461-1(a)(2)]. (But see below for a discussion of the recurring items exception.)

If you have actually incurred a liability, and if there is uncertainty only as to the exact amount and date it must be discharged, you may set up a reasonable estimate as an accrual. You take any difference in the estimate and the exact amount into account in the year of exact determination [Reg. § 1.461-1(a)(2)]. But if an actual liability is not incurred until the happening of some contingency, you do not accrue any amount until the contingency occurs.[128] Similarly, taxpayers cannot claim a deduction for anticipated warranty expenses which were required by state law but had not yet been incurred by the taxpayer.[129]

Code Sec. 461(h) places accrual method taxpayers on the cash method for tort liabilities. The deductions that a major car manufacturer could claim with respect to its tort settlement obligations were limited to the cost of annuities that it purchased to fund the settlement payments.[130] The manufacturer's deduction of the full amount of its liability in one year caused a distortion of income, since actual payments to the tort claimants would be extended over many years. Only the amounts paid for the annuities were deductible each year. To offset the disallowance of the future payments, the manufacturer could exclude its annuity income, which corresponded exactly to the anticipated future payments.

Establishing the Fact of Liability

In order to prove that a taxpayer has satisfied the all events test, the taxpayer must show that all the events have occurred that establish the fact of liability. This is the first prong of the all events test and the test is satisfied when (1) the event fixing the

[126] *F.D. Quinn*, CA-5, 40-1 USTC ¶ 9403, 111 F2d 372.

[127] *T.A. Granger*, CA-4, *aff'g an unpublished opinion*, March 6, 1980, 37 TCM 1849-20, Dec. 35,550(M), TC Memo. 1978-474; *J.H. Crain*, CA-8, 35-1 USTC ¶ 9217, 75 F2d 962.

[128] *Blaine, Mackay, Lee Co.*, CA-3, 44-1 USTC ¶ 9230, 141 F2d 201.

[129] *Chrysler Corp.*, CA-6, 2006-1 USTC ¶ 50,155, 436 F3d 644.

[130] *Ford Motor Co.*, CA-6, 95-2 USTC ¶ 50,643, 71 F3d 209.

liability, whether that be the required performance or other event occurs, or (2) payment is unconditionally due.[131]

In Rev. Rul. 2011-29,[132] the IRS concluded that an employer using an accrual method of accounting may claim a deduction in the current year for a fixed amount of bonuses payable to a group of employees even though the employer did not know the identity of the employees who will receive a bonus or the amount of any particular bonus until after the end of the tax year. According to the court, the taxpayer's obligation to pay the bonuses was fixed at the end of the year in which the services were provided because (1) the taxpayer was obligated to pay the bonuses; and (2) any bonus allocable to an employee who was not employed on the date when the bonuses were paid was reallocated to other eligible employees.

The court cited *United States v. Hughes Properties, Inc.*,[133] to support the proposition that the all-events test will be satisfied even though the identity of the ultimate recipients and the amount, if any, each employee will receive could not be determined prior to the end of the tax year. In that case, the Supreme Court allowed a casino operator to deduct amounts guaranteed for payment of progressive slot machine jackpots that had not yet been won by casino patrons. The Court reasoned that the taxpayer had a fixed obligation to pay the guaranteed amounts, and that the identification of the eventual recipients of the progressive jackpots was inconsequential. The Court noted that "[t]he obligation is there, and whether it turns out that the winner is one patron or another makes no conceivable difference as to basic liability."

Economic Performance

Generally, you cannot deduct business expenses until economic performance occurs (usually when you provide the underlying services or property). However, the following exceptions apply:

- *3½ month rule exception.* Under the 3½ month exception to the general rule of economic performance, a taxpayer is allowed to treat services or property as provided to it as the taxpayer makes payment to the person providing the services or property, if the taxpayer can reasonably expect the person to provide the services or property within 3½ months after the date of payment [Reg. § 1.461-4(d)(6)(ii)]. The IRS has privately ruled that a taxpayer engaged in direct mail advertising could deduct prepaid year-end postage costs reasonably expected to be used within 3½ months.[134]
- *Recurring item exception.* Under the Code Sec. 461(h)(3) recurring item exception to the general rule of economic performance, a liability is treated as incurred for a tax year if:
  1. At the end of that tax year, all events have occurred that establish the fact of the liability and the amount can be determined with reasonable accuracy;
  2. Economic performance occurs on or before the earlier of (a) the date the taxpayer files a timely (including extensions) return for that tax year; or (b) the 15th day of the 9th calendar month after the close of that tax year (i.e., 8½ months);

[131] Rev. Rul. 2007-3, 2007-1 CB 350; LTR 201246029 (July 31, 2012).

[132] Rev. Rul. 2011-29, IRB 2011-49.

[133] *Hughes Properties, Inc.*, 86-1 USTC ¶9440, 476 US 593 (1986).

[134] LTR 200709003 (Sept. 18, 2006).

3. The liability is recurring in nature; and
4. Either (a) the amount of the liability is "not material"; or (b) accrual of the liability results in a "better matching" of the liability with the income to which it relates than would result from accruing the liability for the tax year in which economic performance occurs [Code Sec. 461(h)(3)(A); Reg. § 1.461-5(b)(1)].

In determining whether a liability is material, consideration is given to the amount of the liability in absolute terms and in relation to the amount of other items of income and expense attributable to the same activity [Reg. § 1.461-5(b)(4)(i)]. A liability is "material" if it is material for financial statement purposes under generally accepted accounting principles [Section 1.461-5(b)(4)(ii)]. A liability that is immaterial for financial statement purposes under generally accepted accounting principles may be material for purposes of the materiality requirement of the recurring item exception [Reg. § 1.461-5(b)(4)(iii)].

In determining whether the matching requirement of the recurring item exception is satisfied, generally accepted accounting principles are an important factor, but are not dispositive [Reg. § 1.461-5(b)(5)(i)].

In Rev. Rul. 2012-1,[135] the IRS clarified the "not material" and "better matching" requirements under the recurring item exception in the context of a one-year lease liability and a one-year service contract liability. For service contract type liabilities, the recurring item exception applies differently depending on whether the contract is for the provision of services as distinguished from insurance or warranty-type contracts. For liabilities arising out of the provision of services to the taxpayer, the ruling clarifies that the taxpayer must satisfy either the "not material" or "better matching" requirement. For liabilities arising out of the provision of insurance, warranty or similar service contract liabilities, the better matching requirement is deemed to be met.

In Rev. Proc. 2008-25,[136] the IRS provided a safe harbor accounting method for accrual method taxpayers that incur FICA tax and FUTA tax (i.e., payroll tax) liabilities for bonuses and vacation pay, as well as other compensation. Under the safe harbor, a taxpayer is treated as satisfying the requirements for the recurring item exception in Reg. § 1.461-5(b)(1)(i) for its payroll tax liability in the same tax year in which all events have occurred that establish the fact of the compensation liability and the amount of the compensation liability can be determined with reasonable accuracy. Procedures are provided for taxpayers to obtain automatic consent to change to this accounting method.

In Rev. Rul. 2007-3,[137] the IRS concluded that a liability for services or insurance is not fixed by the mere execution of a contract for the future provision of services or insurance. Instead, the liability is fixed and can therefore be deducted only when payment for the services or insurance was due and paid, not in the year the contract was executed. The mere execution of the contract in the year prior to the payment did not establish the taxpayer's liability. A taxpayer who wants to change its treatment of liabilities for services or insurance to comply with this ruling must obtain the consent

135 Rev. Rul. 2012-1 IRB 2012-2, 255.

136 Rev. Proc. 2008-25, IRB 2008-13, 686.

137 Rev. Rul 2007-3, 2007-1 CB 350.

of the IRS under Code Sec. 446(e) by following the procedures in Rev. Proc. 2011-14.[138]

The following chart gives the general rules for when economic performance occurs with respect to various expenses for accrual-method taxpayers.

Type of Liability	When Incurred	Regulation
Awards, prizes and jackpots paid by taxpayer	Payment	1.461-4(g)(4)
Barter transactions	Include lesser of costs incurred or property/services received	1.461-4(d)(4)(ii)
Breach of contract	Payment	1.461-4(g)(2)
Capital expenditures	Include in basis when goods delivered or $3^1/_2$ month rule	1.461-4(d)(6)(ii)
Employee benefits	When otherwise deductible under Code Secs. 404, 404A, or 419	1.461-4(g)(4)
Escrow accounts—funds paid through third parties	When transferred to person to whom liability is owed	1.461-(g)(1)(i)
Installment contracts	As each installment is performed or delivered	1.461-4(d)(6)(iv)
Insurance, warranty, and service contract liabilities	Payment	1.461-4(g)(5)
Interest	As economically accrued	1.461-4(e)
Liabilities arising out of a violation of law	Payment	1.461-4(g)(2)
Licensing fees	Payment	1.461-4(g)(6)
Long term contracts—percentage completion method	Earlier of payment or time property/service is provided	1.461-4(d)(2)(ii)
Property provided to the taxpayer by another person	Taxpayer receives property or pays within $3^1/_2$ months of receipt	1.461-4(d)(2)(i)
Property or services to be provided by the taxpayer	As taxpayer incurs related costs	1.461-4(d)(4); 1.461-4(g)(4)
Real estate developers—estimated cost of future improvements	Request consent to add costs to basis	Rev. Proc. 92-29
Real estate taxes	Payment or as accrued	1.461-4(g)(4)
Rebates and refunds	Payment	1.461-4(g)(3)

[138] Rev. Proc. 2011-14, IRB 2011-4, 330, as modified and amplified by Rev. Rul. 2012-1 IRB 2012-2, 255.

Type of Liability	When Incurred	Regulation
Recurring costs	Include if payment or delivery occurs sooner of $8^1/2$ months from year close or time return is due	1.461-5(b)
Services provided to the taxpayer by another person	When services performed or $3^1/2$ month rule	1.461-4(d)(2)
Taxes other than creditable foreign taxes or real estate taxes	Payment	1.461-4(g)(6)
Tort and workers compensation claims	Payment	1.461-4(g)(2)
Use of property provided of use	Ratable over period	1.461-4(d)(3)(i)

There are seven types of expenses that can be deducted only when paid: workers' compensation act or tort liabilities; breach of contract liabilities; rebates and refunds; awards, prizes and jackpots; liabilities for insurance, warranty and service contracts; and taxes (other than creditable foreign taxes) [Reg. § 1.461-4(g)]. Important: Although these liabilities are designated as payment-only liabilities, you may still be able to accelerate your deductions by taking advantage of the recurring item rule (as discussed above).

.03 Contested Liabilities

A taxpayer may claim a deduction for a contested liability prior to resolution of the contest if the following requirements are met:

- The taxpayer contests an asserted liability;
- The taxpayer transfers money or other property to provide for the satisfaction of the asserted liability and relinquishes all control over the money or other property transferred;
- The contest with respect to the asserted liability exists after the time of the transfer; and
- But for the fact that the asserted liability is contested, a deduction would be allowed for the tax year of the transfer under the economic performance test [Code Sec. 461(f); Reg. § 1.461-2(a)].

This special rule does not apply with respect to a deduction for income, war profits, and excess profits taxes imposed by the authority of any foreign country or possession of the United States, including a tax paid in lieu of a tax on income, war profits, and excess profits otherwise generally imposed by any foreign country or possession of the United States [Code Sec. 461(f); Reg. § 1.461-2(a)(2)].

If any portion of the contested amount that is deducted under this special rule for the tax year of transfer is subsequently refunded when the contest is settled, that portion is includible in gross income for the tax year of receipt or for an earlier year if the refund was properly accruable for that earlier year. However, this provision does not apply to items the recovery of which are excluded from income under the tax benefit rule [Reg. § 1.461-2(a)(3)].

Example 18-28: ABCo, an accrual-basis taxpayer, contests $200 of a $1,000 asserted real property tax liability in 2007 but pays the entire liability to the taxing authority. The contest is settled in 2012, and ABCo receives a refund of $50. It deducts $1,000 for the tax year 2007 and includes $50 in gross income for the tax year 2012 (assuming the tax benefit regulations do not apply to that amount) [Reg. § 1.461-2(a)(4), Ex. 2].

Example 18-29: In June 2011, BoCo pays, under protest, the amount of $5,268 in satisfaction of its liability for property taxes. In July 2011, the corporation contests the tax liability in a court action. The court action is terminated in August of 2013 with a final determination that the corporation was liable for only $4,576 in taxes. The full amount of the protested payment ($5,268) is deducted on the corporation's 2011 return. However, the $692 overpayment is income on the corporation's 2013 return, unless the 2011 deduction of the overpayment did not result in an income tax benefit in 2011 within the meaning of Code Sec. 111 (the tax benefit rule).

Contest **Defined**

A *contest* is a bona fide dispute regarding the proper evaluation of the law or of the facts necessary to determine the existence or correctness of the amount of an asserted liability. It is not necessary to institute legal proceedings to establish the existence of a contest—an affirmative act denying the validity or accuracy (or both) of the asserted liability that is made to the person asserting such liability is sufficient to be considered a contest. An example of such an act would be the inclusion of a written protest with the payment of the asserted liability [Reg. § 1.461-2(b)(2)].

Transfers to Provide for Satisfaction of Asserted Liability

A taxpayer may provide for the satisfaction of an asserted liability by transferring money or other property beyond the taxpayer's control to any of the following [Reg. § 1.461-2(c)(1)]:

- The person asserting the liability;
- An escrowee or trustee pursuant to a written agreement among the taxpayer, the escrowee or trustee, and the person asserting the liability that the money or other property be delivered in accordance with the settlement of the contest;
- An escrowee or trustee pursuant to an order of the United States, any state or political subdivision, any federal or state agency or instrumentality, or a court that the money or other property be delivered in accordance with the settlement of the contest;
- A court with jurisdiction over the contest; or
- A qualified settlement fund [Reg. § 1.468B-1(b)].

For the money or other property to be transferred beyond the taxpayer's control, the taxpayer must relinquish all authority over the money or other property [Reg. § 1.461-2(c)(1)(ii)]. The following are not transfers to provide for the satisfaction of an asserted liability [Reg. §§ 1.461-2(c)(1)(iii), 1.461-2(g)(2)]: (1) purchasing a bond to guarantee payment of the asserted liability; (2) an entry on the taxpayer's books of account; (3) a transfer to an account that is within the control of the taxpayer; (4) a transfer of any indebtedness of the taxpayer or of any promise by the taxpayer to provide services or property in the future; and (5) a transfer to a person (other than the person asserting the liability) of any stock of the taxpayer or of any stock or indebtedness of a person related to the taxpayer.

> **Example 18-30:** GBCo contests a liability asserted by a contractor for services rendered. To provide for the contingency that it may have to pay the liability, the company establishes a separate bank account in its name and transfers an amount equal to the amount of the liability from its general account. The transfer does not qualify as a transfer to provide for the satisfaction of an asserted liability because the company has not transferred the money beyond its control [Reg. § 1.461-2(c)(2), Ex. 1].

In *Goodrich Corp.*,[139] a corporation was not entitled to claim a deduction for its transfer of notes to a trust to satisfy its subsidiary's contested IRS tax liabilities because there was no written agreement between the trust, the taxpayer and the IRS as required by Reg. § 1.461-2(c) (1) (ii).

Contest must exist after time of transfer. A contest with respect to an asserted liability exists after the time of transfer only if the contest is pursued after the transfer. Thus, the contest must be neither settled nor abandoned at the time of the transfer. A contest may be settled by a decision, judgment, decree, or other order of any court of competent jurisdiction that has become final or by written or oral agreement between the parties [Reg. § 1.461-2(d)].

Deduction otherwise allowed. A contested liability may be deducted only if the deduction is otherwise allowable [Code Sec. 461(f) (4)]. The existence of the dispute must be the sole factor preventing a deduction for the tax year of the transfer or for an earlier tax year for which the amount would be accruable by an accrual basis taxpayer. Neither Code Sec. Sec. 461(f) nor the regulations may be construed to give rise to a deduction because both sections relate only to the timing of otherwise allowable deductions [Reg. § 1.461-2(e) (1)].

> **Example 18-31:** Mary, an accrual-basis individual taxpayer, makes a gift to a friend. She pays the entire amount of gift tax assessed against her but contests the tax. Gift taxes are not deductible. The requirements for deducting a contested liability are not satisfied because the deduction would not be allowed for the tax year of transfer even if she had not contested the gift tax liability [Reg. § 1.461-2(e)(3), Ex. 1].

The question of whether the deduction is otherwise allowable is determined after application of the economic performance rules [Code Sec. 461(f); Reg. § 1.461-2(e) (2)]. Economic performance occurs for liabilities requiring payment to another person arising out of any workers compensation act or any tort, or any other designated liability [Reg. § 1.461-4(g)], as payments are made to the person to which the liability is owed.

---

[139] *Goodrich Corp.*, WDNC, 2012-1 USTC ¶ 50,159, 406 FSupp2d 445.

Except as provided for designated settlement funds, economic performance does not occur when a taxpayer transfers money or other property to a trust, an escrow account, or a court to provide for the satisfaction of an asserted workers compensation, tort, or other designated liability that the taxpayer is contesting unless the trust, escrow account, or court is the person to which the liability is owed or the taxpayer's payment to the trust, escrow account, or court discharges the taxpayer's liability to the claimant. Rather, economic performance occurs in the tax year the taxpayer transfers money or other property to the person that is asserting the workers compensation, tort, or other designated liability that the taxpayer is contesting or in the tax year that payment is made from a trust, an escrow account, or a court registry funded by the taxpayer to the person to which the liability is owed.

Example 18-32: Eve is a defendant in a class action suit for tort liabilities. In 2011, Eve establishes a trust for the purpose of satisfying the asserted liability and transfers $10,000,000 to the trust. The trust does not satisfy the designated settlement requirements. In 2013, the trustee pays $10,000,000 to the plaintiffs in settlement of the litigation. Economic performance with respect to Eve's liability to the plaintiffs occurs in 2013 and she may deduct the $10,000,000 payment to the plaintiffs that year.

Contested Liability Trusts Used as Tax Shelters

The IRS has issued a notice warning that certain transactions that use contested liability trusts improperly to attempt to accelerate deductions for contested liabilities under Code Sec. 461(f) are *listed transactions* for purposes of the tax shelter registration and notification rules discussed in Ch. 26.[140]

If a taxpayer claimed accelerated deductions in conjunction with an abusive contested liability trust, the IRS has announced that the taxpayer has claimed an improper method of accounting and must change to a permissible accounting method by filing amended returns for all open years and eliminating the improper deductions. If the limitations period has expired on the first year in which the impermissible method was used, the entire amount of the Section 481(a) adjustment must be included in the first open year.[141]

.04 Overlapping Items

Although you cannot use the expenses, liabilities, or deficit of one year to reduce your income of a later year, regulations recognize that in a business of any magnitude there are certain overlapping items [Reg. § 1.461-1(a)(3)].

▶ **OBSERVATION:** The important thing is that you follow a consistent policy, making sure your income of any year is not distorted.

---

[140] Notice 2003-77, 2003-2 CB 1182.

[141] Rev. Proc. 2004-31, 2004-1 CB 986.

.05 Method of Payment

Suppose that you are a cash-basis taxpayer and that you pay by check. Then you can deduct the payment when you deliver the check, if you pay it on presentation.[142] You cannot deduct checks that you postdated to another tax year before the date shown.[143]

▶ **OBSERVATION:** The same reasoning should apply to other itemized deductions as well.

You can take an immediate deduction for charitable contributions or medical expenses charged on a credit card.[144]

Example 18-33: Mr. Smith contributes to a college fund. He sends the college a check in late December. The check is dated December 31. The college does not deposit or cash the check until January of the following year. The contribution is considered made in the year the check was dated and Smith takes the deduction that year [Reg. § 1.170A-1(b)].

For accrual-basis taxpayers, the payment method usually does not affect the time for deducting the expenses. The IRS has concluded that an accrual method manufacturer could claim a deduction for cooperative advertising services in the year the services were performed even though the required claim form was not submitted until the following year.[145] According to the IRS under the *all events test,* the taxpayer's liability to pay the retailer was incurred in Year 1, the year in which the services are performed, provided the manufacturer was able to reasonably estimate this liability. The IRS viewed the submission of the claim and proofs of performance by the retailer as a mere technicality and not a requirement for deductibility. The event establishing the taxpayer's obligation to pay the rebate was the performance of the services. After the services were performed, the requirement that a claim or documentation be submitted to obtain payment was merely the mechanism for requesting payment. As a result, the IRS viewed the form submission requirements as merely ministerial in nature. Since the activity that triggered the rebate occurred in Year 1, the IRS allowed the deduction in Year 1, provided the amount of the rebate could be determined with reasonable accuracy.

▶ **PRACTICE TIP:** Accrual basis taxpayers who can prove that the claim form is a mere technicality will be able to deduct the payment in the year the services are rendered rather than having to wait until the actual claim form is filed.

.06 Prepaid Expenses

Expenses such as rent, interest and insurance premiums are, generally, not deductible in full if they cover more than one tax year [Ch. 12, ¶ 18,155]. You must prorate the deduction over the total time period for which you made the payment.

Example 18-34: Mr. Wallace, a cash-basis taxpayer on the calendar year, owns a small store. On July 1, 2013, he pays an insurance premium of $3,000 for a policy that is effective July 1, 2013, for a three-year period ending June 30, 2016. He may deduct $500 in 2013, $1,000 in 2014 and 2015, and $500 in 2016.

---

[142] *M.J. Spiegel Est.,* 12 TC 524, Dec. 16,898 (1949) *(Nonacq. Withdrawn).*

[143] *B. Griffin,* 49 TC 253, Dec. 28,706 (1967).

[144] Rev. Rul. 78-38, 1978-1 CB 67.

[145] Rev. Rul. 98-39, 1998-2 CB 198.

Example 18-35: Mr. Thomas owns a small store and is a calendar-year, cash-basis taxpayer. On July 1, 2013, he pays $1,000 for an insurance policy that runs through June 30, 2014. He may deduct the $500 in 2013 and $500 in 2014.

Cash-Basis Tax Shelter's Prepaid Expenses

Tax shelters generally cannot use the cash method. To the extent that the cash method can still be used, a tax shelter cannot deduct prepaid expenses before *economic performance* occurs (described above for accrual-basis taxpayers) [Code Sec. 461(i)]. For this rule, the recurring item exception to the economic performance requirement does not apply. A *tax shelter* is:

- A partnership or other enterprise (except a C corporation) in which interests were offered for sale in an offering that must be registered with a federal or state agency;
- A partnership or enterprise if over 35 percent of the losses are allocable to limited partners; or
- Any partnership, entity, plan or arrangement whose principal purpose is tax avoidance or evasion as defined in Code Sec. 6662(d)(2)(C).

Example 18-36: XYZ oil and gas shelter management fees are treated as incurred when the management services are rendered. The cost of prepaid supplies is treated as incurred when the supplies are used. Research and development costs are deductible as the contract research occurs. Prepaid drilling costs, even under a noncancellable turnkey contract, would be deductible only as the drilling occurs.

A special exception is made for oil and gas shelters if economic performance occurs before the close of the 90th day after year end. The maximum deduction allowed under this exception is limited to the cash investment in the tax shelter.

¶18,135 DEDUCTIONS LIMITED TO AMOUNT AT RISK

The *at-risk rules* generally prevent you from claiming tax shelter deductions in excess of your financial commitment in the activity. For detailed discussion of the at-risk rules, see ¶ 13,100.

¶18,140 PASSIVE ACTIVITIES LOSS LIMITATIONS

Basically, this tax shelter limitation prevents you from using a loss from a *passive activity* (for example, limited partners' interests in a business) to shelter *active income* (for example, salary) or *portfolio income* (for example, dividends, interest, and capital gains). You are allowed to write off a tax shelter loss only against your other tax shelter income. For a detailed discussion of passive loss rules, see ¶ 13,090 and ¶ 24,020 [Code Sec. 469].

¶18,145 VACATION OR INCENTIVE BONUSES

Special rules govern the time for deducting vacation or incentive pay and bonuses.

.01 Vacation or Incentive Pay

An employer's deduction for vacation or incentive pay in a particular year is limited to: (1) amounts that are *actually received* (as defined below) by the employee during that year, and (2) if vested as of the last day of that year, received by employees within two and one-half months after the end of that year [Code Sec. 404(a)(11)]. The employer's deduction may not be based solely on the funding or vesting of vacation or severance pay, even if that funding or vesting results in the inclusion of the vacation or severance pay in the taxable income of the employee on or before 2½ months after the end of the tax year. What matters for deduction purposes is whether or not the employee actually received the money. Any other vacation pay earned in the employer's tax year is deductible when paid (and not when it is first includible in the employee's income by virtue of its being substantially vested) [Code Sec. 404(a)(5)]. See Ch. 3 for further discussion of deferred compensation.

The term *actually received* is defined as:

- Not intended to include letters of credit, promissory notes or other evidences of indebtedness, whether or not the evidence is guaranteed by any other instrument or by any third party;
- Not including a promise to provide services or property in the future, whether or not evidenced by a written agreement; or
- Not including an amount transferred as a loan, refundable deposit, contingent payment, or amount set aside in a trust.

The IRS provides that an employer changing its method of accounting to comply with Code Sec. 404(a)(11), will be treated as making a change initiated by the taxpayer with the consent of the IRS. Employers need not make a formal request. In addition, the change must be made with an Code Sec. 481 adjustment that will be taken into account ratably over a three-tax-year period beginning with the first taxable ending after July 22, 1998. See Ch. 3 for further discussion.

.02 Accrual of Bonuses

If the exact amount of a bonus cannot be determined and paid until the year following the year of accrual, the bonus may be deducted by the accrual-basis taxpayer in the year of accrual if:

- The total bonuses are determinable through a formula in effect before the end of the year;
- Before the end of the year the employer obligates itself to make payment by notifying each employee (individually, or in a group) either orally or in writing of the percentage of the total bonus payment to be awarded to him or her; and
- Payment is made as soon after the close of the year as is administratively feasible.[146]

For the time for deducting contributions to tax-qualified retirement plans, see Ch. 3.

[146] *Truck and Equipment Corp.*, 98 TC 141, Dec. 47,984 (1992).

¶18,150 ADVERTISING EXPENSES

If you use the cash basis, you deduct these expenses in the year you pay them. If you use the accrual basis, you deduct them in the year they accrue. Although the benefits of advertising may continue for several years, you need not capitalize the cost and write it off over the later years.[147] The IRS has specifically stated that advertising costs are deductible even though advertising has some future benefit.[148] The Supreme Court's decision in *Indopco*[149] [Ch. 12] does not affect the treatment of advertising costs as business expense which are generally deductible under Section 162.[150] The Tax Court concluded that graphic design costs for cigarette packages were deductible advertising expenses even though they may produce future patronage or goodwill and look like capital expenses that have a long-term benefit to the taxpayer and should therefore be capitalized over the economic lives of the cigarettes to which they attach.[151] The court held that advertising costs are generally deductible even though the advertising may have some future effect on future patronage or goodwill. The Tax Court concluded that the long-term benefits associated with product packaging design are benefits traditionally associated with business advertising and did not justify capitalization of the expenses. For discussion of deduction of advertising expenses, see Ch. 12.

¶18,155 INTEREST

If you are on the cash basis, you ordinarily deduct interest when you actually pay it,[152] unless you prepay the interest [discussed below]. If you are an accrual-basis taxpayer, you deduct interest as it accrues; interest accrues ratably over the period.[153]

> **NOTE:** You treat interest on debt you use to finance the production of inventory as part of the cost of that inventory—and deduct the interest as the items are sold.

Your interest deductions for any year generally cannot exceed the amount of interest economically accrued.[154] This means that you must generally allocate payments on indebtedness to principal to the extent they exceed interest accrued at the stated or effective rate.

---

[147] *E.H. Sheldon & Co.*, CA-6, 54-2 USTC ¶9526, 214 F2d 655.

[148] Rev. Rul. 92-80, 1992-2 CB 57; Rev. Rul. 94-12, 1994-1 CB 36.

[149] *Indopco*, SCt, 92-1 USTC ¶50,113, 503 US 79, 112 SCt 1039.

[150] Rev. Rul. 92-80, 1992-2 CB 57.

[151] *RJR Nabisco, Inc.*, 76 TCM 71, Dec. 52,786(M), TC Memo. 1998-252 *(Nonacq.)*.

[152] *Mass. Mutual Life Ins. Co.*, SCt, 3 USTC ¶1045, 288 US 269, 53 SCt 337.

[153] *Handlery Hotels, Inc.*, CA-9, 82-1 USTC ¶9106, 663 F2d 892.

[154] Rev. Rul. 83-84, 1983-1 CB 97.

Exception: You can use the *Rule of 78* to figure deductible interest on short-term (five years or less) consumer loans that meet specific criteria (e.g., level installment payments).[155] Under this rule, interest for any given year is the total interest payable over the term of the loan multiplied by a fraction. The fraction is the years remaining on the loan at the beginning of the year divided by the sum of the years of the loan period. This method results in larger deductions in the early years than the economic accrual method.

.01 Prepaid Interest

If you are a cash-basis taxpayer and pay interest in advance, you must allocate the interest deduction over the period of the loan. Generally, points that you pay on a mortgage used to buy or improve your principal residence can be fully deducted in the year of payment. The payment must be an established business practice in the area and must not exceed amounts generally charged for such home loans [Code Sec. 461(g)(2)]. And while you must pay the points directly, the IRS has said you satisfy this requirement if you pay over at closing an amount equal to or greater than the points (say, as a down payment or escrow deposit).[156]

Exclusions

Individuals cannot deduct points that are allocable to mortgage amounts in excess of $1 and must deduct points paid for a second home, vacation home, investment property, or trade or business property or to refinance a loan used to purchase or improve a principal residence over the term of the loan.[157]

.02 Insurance Policy Loan

Interest on a life insurance policy loan, which by the terms of the contract is added to the principal of the loan if not paid when due, cannot be deducted as *interest paid* by a cash basis taxpayer.[158]

.03 Discount on a Note

In general, you can deduct interest on an original issue discount instrument as it accrues—whether the issuer is a cash or accrual taxpayer. For discount instruments issued after July 1, 1982, you calculate the interest using the economic accrual (i.e., not straight line) method [Ch. 2] [Code Sec. 163(e)].

> **Example 18-37:** Ms. Coe, on the cash basis, receives $1,000 cash for a note in the amount of $1,387.05 (12 percent interest), payable in five equal annual installments. (The note has an original issue discount of $387.05.) Of the $277.41 first payment, $120 (12 percent of $1,000) is deductible as interest.

However, there are exceptions for: (1) instruments issued by natural persons before March 2, 1984; and (2) loans between natural persons that are not made in the course of the lender's business, are not in excess of $10,000 when combined with prior loans and do not have tax avoidance as one of their principal purposes. If these exceptions are

---

155 Rev. Proc. 2009-39, IRB 2009-38, 371.

156 Rev. Proc. 94-27, 1994-1 CB 613.

157 Rev. Rul. 87-22, 1987-1 CB 146; *P.G. Cao*, CA-9, 96-1 USTC ¶50,167, 78 F3d 594.

158 *N.C. Prime*, 39 BTA 487, Dec. 10,605; *H.P. Keith*, CA-2, 44-1 USTC ¶9138, 139 F2d 596.

met, you can deduct the interest when it would normally be deductible under your usual method of accounting (e.g., when paid by a cash basis taxpayer) [Code Sec. 1272(a)(2)(E)].

High-Yield Discount Instruments

Special rules apply to certain high yield corporate discount obligations. The tax law recharacterizes part of the discount as a dividend, which is not deductible [Ch. 20].

.04 Allocating Interest Expense Among Expenditures

You can fully deduct interest payments on some loans (for example, business interest). Other interest payments (such as consumer or investment interest) are nondeductible or deductible within limitations. To determine how much of your interest you can deduct, you must allocate it among the various categories of interest. The IRS has developed a set of complex rules to allocate interest expenses [Temp. Reg. § 1.163-8T].

The allocation rules apply to the following types of interest:

- Passive activity interest—either currently deductible or placed in a suspense account and carried over to a future year [Ch. 13].
- Investment interest—generally deductible to the extent of net investment income [Ch. 9].
- Trade or business interest—fully deductible.
- Personal interest—nondeductible since 1991 [Ch. 9].
- Residence interest—generally deductible if debt is used to acquire or substantially improve residence; $100,000 limit on debt secured by a residence but used for other purposes [Ch. 9].

Payments to Third Parties

Special rules apply if the loan proceeds are not paid directly to the borrower. If the lender gives the loan proceeds to a third party (e.g., a property seller), that disbursement is an expenditure from the loan proceeds. If cash isn't given (e.g., a loan assumption or seller financing), the debt is treated as if you made an expenditure from the proceeds for the purpose for which the debt was incurred [Temp. Reg. § 1.163-8T(c)(3)].

Repayment of Principal

If the loan proceeds are allocated to more than one expense when repayment of principal occurs, the principal payment is allocated in the following order [Temp. Reg. § 1.163-8T(d)]:

1. Personal expenses;
2. Investment expenses and passive activity expenses (other than (3) below);
3. Rental real estate passive activity expenses where you actively participate in the activity;
4. Expenses allocable to activities where you were formerly a passive investor, but now are a material participant; then
5. Trade or business expenses.

If loan proceeds are allocated to two or more expenses within one of the five classes above, you treat expenses in the order the amounts were allocated (e.g., by the dates that checks were drawn on the account). You can treat allocations occurring on the same day as occurring in any order you choose.

▶ **OBSERVATION:** If you want to avoid the allocation rules, do not mix together borrowed and nonborrowed funds in the same account. That way you can use only the nonborrowed funds for personal expenditures. What's more, you'll have good documentation of how you used borrowed funds. You can also achieve this goal by maintaining separate accounts for separate classes of expenditures or financing only one expenditure per loan.

Another good move is to deposit the proceeds of loans with different interest rates into different accounts. This will make it easy for you to use the loans with the higher interest rates for expenditures that are subject to the least limitations on deductibility.

Finally, to simplify things, use the proceeds from the sale of an asset that was purchased with borrowed funds (that have not been fully repaid yet) to acquire a similar type of asset. For example, if you sell stock bought with borrowed funds, use the proceeds to buy other investments, or leave the cash in a savings account. This way, you'll avoid having to reallocate loan proceeds when an asset is sold (or otherwise disposed of).

NOTE: Sometimes, you may have to make a trade-off between what approach is easiest vs. which one will save you the most tax dollars. From the standpoint of simplicity, segregated accounts and loans make the most sense. From the standpoint of tax savings, however, it may pay to deliberately trigger the allocation rules in some cases. Bottom line: You have to decide on a case-by-case basis whether the potential tax savings are significant enough to warrant the extra work involved in applying the allocation rules.

Passthrough Entities

Special rules govern the allocation of debt where you use the proceeds for contributions to or purchases of interests in passthrough entities (i.e., partnerships and S corporations). Generally, you allocate the proceeds and associated interest expense among all the entity's assets using any *reasonable method.*

Special rules also come into play to allocate debt incurred by a passthrough entity that is used for distributions to the owners. Under the general rule, the allocation is made in accordance with the owner's use of the proceeds.[159]

¶18,160 TAXES

.01 Cash-Basis Taxpayers

You may deduct as taxes only the amount you actually pay during the year.[160]

---

[159] Notice 89-35, 1989-1 CB 675; Notice 88-37, 1988-1 CB 522.

[160] *B.I. Powell*, 26 BTA 509, Dec. 7651 *(Acq.)*.

.02 Accrual-Basis Taxpayers

An accrual basis taxpayer deducts taxes as they accrue. A tax accrues when all the events have occurred that fix the amount of the tax and determine the taxpayer's liability to pay it.[161] See ¶ 18,130 for discussion of all events test. A tax that is imposed retroactively cannot accrue before enactment of the law imposing it.[162] The economic performance rules may apply; see ¶ 18,130. For contested taxes, see ¶ 18,130.

Foreign Tax Credit

A foreign tax that is claimed as a credit accrues for the year to which it relates, even if contested and not paid until a later year. However, you may claim a credit for that year only for the amount of tax actually paid. An additional credit is allowed when the contested liability is finally determined.[163]

State Income Taxes

State income taxes generally accrue in the year in which you earn the income (on which the state tax is paid).[164] But an increase in state taxes accrues when the amount is finally determined by litigation or default, or you acknowledge liability.

Franchise Taxes

Several states impose corporate franchise taxes based on income which accrue when all the events have occurred that fix the liability.

Property Taxes

As a general rule, economic performance occurs as the tax is paid to the governmental authority that imposed the tax. [Reg. § 1.461-4(g)(6)].

Election to ratably accrue real property taxes. You may elect to accrue and deduct taxes ratably over the period imposed. You may make the election for each separate trade or business (or for "nonbusiness" activities if accounted for separately). It can be adopted *without consent* for the first year you incur real property taxes, if you make the election by the return due date for the tax year (including extensions). For adoption at any other time, you must make a written request to the IRS not later than 90 days (180 days with extension)[165] after the start of the tax year to which the election applies (but see note below) [Reg. § 1.461-1(c)].

> **NOTE:** The IRS eased this special election rule. Taxpayers can automatically make (or revoke) the special election to ratably accrue real property taxes. The consent of the IRS is not required.[166]

Payroll Taxes

An accrual basis employer can deduct its payroll tax liability in the year the all events test and recurring item exception are met, even though the compensation to which it relates is deferred compensation deductible under Code Sec. 404 in the following

---

[161] *General Dynamics Corp.*, SCt, 87-1 USTC ¶ 9280, 481 US 239, 107 SCt 1732.

[162] *Union Bleachery*, CA-4, 38-2 USTC ¶ 9361, 97 F2d 226.

[163] Rev. Rul. 58-55, 1958-1 CB 266, as amplified by Rev. Rul. 84-125, 1984-2 CB 125.

[164] Rev. Rul. 72-490, 1972-2 CB 100.

[165] Rev. Proc. 94-32, 1994-1 CB 627.

[166] Rev. Proc. 92-28, 1992-1 CB 745, as amplified by Rev. Proc 94-32, 1994-1 CB 627.

year.[167] See ¶18,130 for further discussion of the all events test and the recurring item exception.

¶18,165 MEDICAL EXPENSES

The medical expense deduction [Ch. 9] is claimed for amounts actually paid during the tax year. However, you may deduct medical expenses you pay by bank credit cards in the year charged [Ch. 18].[168] In general, you cannot claim a deduction for accruals or prepaid expenses. But you can deduct prepaid expenses that are part of nursing home or continuing care facility entrance fees.[169]

¶18,170 CONTRIBUTIONS

Generally, you can deduct charitable contributions in the year paid. Pledge or accrual is not sufficient to substantiate a deduction[170] [Ch. 9]. However, you deduct a charitable contribution made through a bank credit card in the year the charge is made, regardless of when you repay the bank [¶18,130].[171] Another special rule allows accrual-basis corporations to deduct contributions authorized by their boards of directors before the contributions are actually paid [Ch. 20]. You deduct contributions of property in the year the gift is completed.

.01 Contribution of Stock Certificate

You make a deductible contribution of a properly endorsed stock certificate when you unconditionally deliver the certificate to the donee or the donee's agent. If you deliver the certificate to the donor's agent or to the issuing corporation for transfer, you make the contribution when stock is transferred on the corporate books [Reg. § 1.170A-1(b)].

¶18,175 BAD DEBTS AND LOSSES

.01 Bad Debts

You can deduct these debts in the year they become worthless. Except for corporations, nonbusiness bad debts must be completely worthless to be written off. But you can deduct partially worthless business debts [Ch. 13].

.02 How Professionals Can Write Off Bad Debts

Qualifying professionals who have billings to be written off as uncollectible may use any nonaccrual-experience (NAE) method of accounting that clearly reflects the taxpayer's actual experience or any one of the five safe harbor NAE methods discussed in ¶18,080.02.

---

[167] Rev. Rul. 2007-12, 2007-1 CB 685.

[168] Rev. Rul. 78-39, 1978-1 CB 73.

[169] Rev. Rul. 93-72, 1993-2 CB 77.

[170] Rev. Rul. 78-38, 1978-1 CB 67.

[171] Rev. Rul. 78-38, 1978-1 CB 67.

.03 Losses

You can generally deduct these amounts in the year sustained. They must be evidenced by closed and completed transactions fixed by identifiable events [Ch. 13].

Sales of Property and Stock

You can generally deduct losses from sales of property or stock in the year there is a *closed transaction* [¶ 18,110].

Mortgage Foreclosure

Generally, loss to the mortgagor resulting from a foreclosure is sustained when the period of redemption expires.[172] However, circumstances may warrant deduction in the year of the foreclosure sale as where taxpayers, though financially able, refused to pay the taxes because of the low value of the property.[173] In effect, they have abandoned the property. If they litigate the validity of the foreclosure sale, no loss occurs until the litigation is finally settled.[174] Also, if they make a bona fide claim that the sale is invalid, the time for deduction may be postponed until that claim is settled, although there is no formal court action.[175]

Casualty Losses

You can deduct casualty losses whether they relate to business, nonbusiness or investment property. The type of property determines the amount of your deduction. The time to deduct a casualty loss usually is the tax year in which you actually sustain the loss. A deduction is allowed for the previous year if the loss was attributable to a disaster occurring in an area qualifying for federal disaster relief [Ch. 13].

¶18,180 RESERVES FOR EXPENSES AND LOSSES

A reserve is an amount set aside out of current income for meeting expenditures to be made in a later tax year. Taxpayers (other than financial institutions) cannot deduct reserves for bad debts [Ch. 13].

.01 Cash Basis

Under the cash basis, you may take deductions only in the year of payment. So you cannot take deductions for additions to a reserve.

.02 Accrual Basis

If your books are kept on the accrual basis, you make take a deduction if there is a present liability to support the deduction. The cases are in conflict as to whether you can deduct reasonably accurate estimates of expenses before the year in which the services actually are rendered and your liability to make actual payments arises. Some circuit courts have allowed the deduction for the year in which the income for

---

[172] *Derby Realty Corp.*, 35 BTA 335, Dec. 9563, *appeal dismissed*, CA-6, 92 F2d 999.

[173] *K.T. Peterman*, CA-9, 41-1 USTC ¶9387, 118 F2d 973; *J. Abelson*, 44 BTA 98, Dec. 11,761 *(Nonacq.)*.

[174] *W.Z. Morton*, CA-4, 39-2 USTC ¶9554, 104 F2d 534.

[175] *Burke, Ltd.*, 3 TC 1031, Dec. 13,997 (1944) *(Acq.)*.

the services was taxable, or in which the obligation to perform them arose.[176] The Tax Court disagrees.[177] See ¶ 18,130 for the rule when an actual liability has been incurred, but the amount is uncertain.

Examples of reserves held not deductible include:

- Anticipated loss on contract to buy merchandise;[178]
- Reserve for self-insurance;[179] and
- Anticipated refunds for future years' insurance policy cancellations.[180]

¶ 18,185 DEDUCTIONS FOR FARMERS PREPAYING 50 PERCENT OR MORE OF FARMING EXPENSES

.01 Purpose for Rule

To prevent abuse of mismatched income and deductions by taxpayers who are not active, full-time farmers, Code Sec. 464 limits the amount that cash-basis taxpayers can deduct in the year of payment for prepaid farm supplies and certain poultry-related expenses.

.02 How Deduction is Limited

To the extent that prepaid farm expenses exceed 50 percent of total deductible farming expenses (excluding prepaid supplies) for the tax year, the amount over 50 percent may be deducted only in the year the supplies are actually used or consumed. This limitation applies only if the taxpayer has had excess farming expenses for three consecutive tax years [Code Sec. 464(f)(3)].

.03 *Farming* Defined

For Code Sec. 464 purposes, *farming* means the cultivation of land or the raising or harvesting of any agricultural or horticultural commodity including the raising, shearing, feeding, caring for, training, and management of animals. Only trees bearing fruit or nuts are treated as agricultural commodities. Accordingly, a farmer raising livestock, fish, poultry, bees, dogs, flowers, and/or vegetables is engaged in farming [Code Sec. 464(e)(1)].

.04 *Prepaid Farm Supplies* Defined

The limitation on the deduction of excess prepaid farm supplies applies to a variety of items commonly purchased by farmers. Prepaid farm supplies include poultry, feed, seed, fertilizer, and other supplies used in raising or producing farm assets, the costs of which are allowed as deductions for a subsequent years under the year-of-deduction rules [Code Sec. 464(a), (b), (f)(4)].

---

[176] *P. Harrold*, CA-4, 52-1 USTC ¶ 9107, 192 F2d 1002; *E.W. Schuessler*, CA-5, 56-1 USTC 9368, 230 F2d 722.

[177] *Natl. Bread Wrapping Machine Co.*, 30 TC 550, Dec. 23,027 (1958).

[178] *Adams-Roth Baking Co.*, 8 BTA 458, Dec. 2865.

[179] Rev. Rul. 69-512, 1969-2 CB 24.

[180] *A.M. Brown*, SCt, 4 USTC ¶ 1223, 291 US 193, 54 SCt 356.

.05 Year of Deduction Rule

Farmers may only deduct expenses related to feed, seed, fertilizer, and other similar farm supplies in the tax years the supplies are actually used or consumed [Code Sec. 464(a)].

.06 Poultry Expenses

The cost of poultry (including egg-laying hens and baby chicks) purchased for use in a trade or business must be capitalized and deducted ratably over the lesser of 12 months or their useful life in the trade or business [Code Sec. 464(b)(1)]. The cost of poultry purchased for sale must be deducted for the tax year in which the poultry is sold or otherwise disposed of [Code Sec. 464(b)(2)].

Example 18-38: Farmer spends $1,000 on feed for his pigs on September 1, 2013. The animals consume $400 worth of the feed before January 1, 2014. The remaining $600 of feed is consumed in 2014. Under the year-of-deduction rules, $400 is allowed as a deduction in 2013, and $600 is allowed in 2014. The $400 paid for feed consumed in 2013 is not subject to the prepaid farm supplies limitation since that portion of the total feed expense was deductible in the year of payment. However, the $600 paid for feed consumed in 2014 is a prepaid farm expense because, under the year-of-deduction rules, the expense is allowed in a year after the year of payment.

.07 *Excess Prepaid Farm Supplies* Defined

Only a taxpayer's excess prepaid farm supplies are subject to the limitation and are not currently deductible. Excess prepaid farm supplies are defined as prepaid farm supplies for the tax year to the extent that the amount of those supplies exceeds 50 percent of the deductible farming expenses for the tax year (other than prepaid farming supplies) [Code Sec. 464(f)(4)(A)]. Deductible farming expenses include the operating expenses of the farm such as ordinary and necessary farming expenses under Code Sec. 162, interest and taxes paid, depreciation allowances on farm equipment and other deductible expenses [Code Sec. 464(f)(4)(C)].

Under the prepaid farm supplies limitation, cash-basis taxpayers may deduct the cost of excess prepaid farm supplies only in the year the supplies are actually used or consumed unless the taxpayer is a qualified farm-related taxpayer who may deduct the entire cost of prepaid farm supplies, regardless of when the supplies are used or consumed. Excess prepaid farm supplies are prepaid farm supplies to the extent that the amount of such supplies exceeds 50 percent of deductible farming expenses (other than prepaid supplies) for the year [Code Sec. 464(f)].

.08 Taxpayers Subject to Limitation

Cash basis taxpayers with excess farm supplies can be subject to the limitation on excess deductions unless they are qualified farm-related taxpayers. Specifically, the deduction limitation for prepaid farm supplies applies to a taxpayer for any tax year in which the taxpayer [Code Sec. 464(f)(3)]:

1. Does not use the accrual method of accounting;
2. Has excess prepaid farming supplies; and
3. Is not a "qualified farm-related taxpayer" [Code Sec. 464(f)(2)].

.09 *Qualified Farm-Related Taxpayer* Defined

A *qualified farm-related taxpayer* is any taxpayer:

1. Whose principal residence (see ¶ 7005 for definition) is on a farm;
2. Who has the principal occupation of farming; or
3. Who is a member of the family of a taxpayer described in (i) or (ii), above [Code Sec. 464(f)(3)]. A taxpayer's family is determined with reference to his or her grandparent and includes the spouses of such related persons [Code Sec. 464(f)(3)(B)(iii); Code Sec. 464(c)(2)(E)].

The Eleventh Circuit has held that a corporation, not just an individual, may have a "principal occupation of farming," and therefore qualify as a farm-related taxpayer under [Code Sec. 464].[181] But the same court also concluded that a medical doctor who owned a cattle feeding business was a limited entrepreneur who did not actively participate in the cattle feeding business and, therefore, was entitled to deduct only the cost of feed purchased that was actually consumed by the cattle during the year. The operation or management of the feedlot, where the cattle were fed and fattened, was conducted by the feedlot manager, whom the doctor had no right to supervise or fire. The decisions made by the doctor were limited to those that an investor makes.[182] Additionally, a *qualified farm-related taxpayer* must meet either one of the following tests:

1. The aggregate prepaid farm supplies for the three tax years preceding the year at issue are less than 50 percent of the total deductible prepaid farming supplies (other than prepaid farm supplies) for those three years [Code Sec. 464(f)(3)(A)(i)]; or
2. The taxpayer has excess prepaid farm supplies for the year because of a change in business operations directly attributable to extraordinary circumstances. A taxpayer has excess prepaid farm supplies to the extent that prepaid farm supplies are greater than 50 percent of deductible farming expenses (other than prepaid supplies) for the year. Extraordinary circumstances include fire, storm, other casualty, disease or drought, and government crop diversion programs [Code Sec. 464(f)(3)(A)(ii)].

Because the expenses for three consecutive years are examined, most active farmers easily qualify as qualified farm-related taxpayers and, therefore, will be able to deduct prepaid expenses without limitation (unless they make substantial prepayments every year).

.10 Impact on Deductible Amounts

If the taxpayer is subject to the prepaid expense limitation and has excess prepaid farm supplies, the excess portion of the those supply expenses is deducted in later years under the year-of-deduction rules In other words, excess prepaid feed, seed, fertilizer, and similar expenses are deducted in the year they are used or consumed; the excess cost of poultry used in a trade or business is capitalized and deducted ratable over the

---

[181] *Golden Rod Farms, Inc.*, CA-11, 97-2 USTC ¶ 50,507, 115 F3d 897.

[182] *G.L. Wallace Est.*, CA-11, 92-2 USTC ¶ 50,387, 965 F2d 1038.

lesser of 12 months or their useful life; and the cost of poultry purchased for sale is deducted in the year of disposition. The deduction of the portion of prepaid farm supplies that is not "excess" is not subject to the limitation, and non-excess expenses are generally deductible in the year of payment.

¶18,190 DEPRECIABLE PROPERTY

Even as a cash-basis taxpayer, you generally cannot currently deduct the full payment for business and investment assets that you will use for longer than one year. Instead, you recover your basis in these assets over a period of time through depreciation and amortization deductions [Chs. 11 and 12].

.01 Intangible Property

Intangibles can be defined as assets that you cannot see or touch. If you acquire a business and part of the purchase price included intangibles such as goodwill, trademark and trade names, you can amortize the cost of these intangibles, which are called *Section 197 intangibles* over 15 years [Code Sec. 197]. To qualify for the 15-year amortization, you must hold the intangibles in connection with your trade or business or in an activity engaged in for the production of income. Your basis in the intangible will be written off ratably over the same 15-year period, starting with the month the intangible is acquired, regardless of its actual useful life. No other depreciation, amortization, or business expense deduction may be claimed on the intangible that is amortized under this provision. For further discussion, see ¶ 11,005.

Installment and Deferred Payment Sales

INSTALLMENT SALES IN GENERAL

Installment method of reporting in general . . . . ¶ 19,001
Taxpayers eligible to use the installment method . . . . ¶ 19,005
One-payment rule . . . . ¶ 19,010

HOW TO REPORT SALES UNDER THE INSTALLMENT METHOD

Figuring installment sale income in general . . . . ¶ 19,015
Computation of gain in installment sale . . . . ¶ 19,020
Installment sales with a contingent sales price . . . . ¶ 19,025
Depreciation recapture . . . . ¶ 19,030
Interest charge on tax deferral . . . . ¶ 19,035
Pledges of installment obligations . . . . ¶ 19,040
Related party sales . . . . ¶ 19,045
Disposition of installment obligations . . . . ¶ 19,050

DEFERRED PAYMENT SALES

Deferred payment sales not on the installment plan . . . . ¶ 19,055

REPOSSESSIONS

Repossession of personal property . . . . ¶ 19,060
Real property repossessed by seller . . . . ¶ 19,065

SPECIAL SALES PROBLEMS

Sale of real property in lots . . . . . ¶ 19,070
Long-term contracts . . . . ¶ 19,075

INSTALLMENT SALES IN GENERAL

The installment method permits a taxpayer to include in gross income all or a portion of the realized gain in an installment sale of property in the tax year or years in which one or more installment payments are received, rather than in the tax year in which the installment sale itself takes place [Code Sec. 453(a)]. A sale at a loss does not qualify for the installment method of reporting. Code Sec. 453 applies to taxpayers with qualifying installment sales of real and noninventoriable personal property, including intangible property and noninventory farm property. In order to qualify as an installment sale, at least one payment for the property must be received in a tax year after the disposition takes place. For qualifying taxpayers, the installment method of reporting is an excellent way to lock in gains while deferring the recognition of income.

¶19,001 INSTALLMENT METHOD OF REPORTING IN GENERAL

An *installment sale* is a sale of property where one or more payments are received after the close of the tax year in which the sale took place. This method basically allows the taxpayer to spread the tax consequences of a sale over a number of years. The installment method cannot be used for (1) the sale of personal property by a person who normally sells property of the same type on the installment plan, (2) the sale of real property held for sale to customers in the ordinary course of business, or (3) any disposition of personal property under a revolving credit plan [Code Secs. 453(l) and 453(k)(1)]. The installment method can, however, be used for sales of personal or real property by investors and others who are *not* in the business of selling that type of property. For example, if a taxpayer sells a pleasure boat and receives payments over a three-year period, the taxpayer may report gain using the installment method. However, if the taxpayer is in the business of selling boats and makes a sale with a three-year payment period, the taxpayer is considered a *dealer* and must report all the gain in the year of sale, regardless of when payments are received [Code Sec. 453]. (Installment reporting cannot be used by dealers for sales after 1987.) The installment method of reporting does not change the character of any gain as ordinary income or capital gain.

Although dealers are generally prohibited from reporting sales on the installment method, an exception is made for dispositions of certain timeshares and qualified unimproved residential lots, if interest is paid on the deferred tax. For residential lots, the seller must not be required to make improvements [Code Sec. 453(l)(2)]. In addition, gain on property used or produced in the trade or business of farming may be reported using the installment method, even if the sale would otherwise be considered a dealer sale [Code Sec. 453(l)(2).

.01 Authorization of Partial Payment Installment Agreements

The IRS is authorized to enter into partial installment agreements with taxpayers. These agreements provide for only partial payment of the taxpayer's liability over the life of the agreement. The IRS must review partial payment installment agreements at least every two years. The primary purpose of this review is to determine whether the financial condition of the taxpayer has significantly changed so as to warrant an increase in the value of the payments being made.

.02 When to Forego the Installment Method

Even though the installment method of reporting may result in a tax savings to the seller because it defers the reporting of some of the income from the sale of property, it does not make sense to use the installment sale method of reporting in every qualifying transaction. Keep in mind that usage of the method is mandatory unless the taxpayer elects out of reporting an installment sale on the installment method [Code Sec. 453(d); Temp. Reg. § 15A.453-1T(d)(1)] and pays the tax owed in full in the year the property is sold even if the taxpayer may not be paid all of the selling price in that year [Temp. Reg. § 15A.453-1T(d)(2)].

The election out of the installment method must be made on or before the due date of the return (including extensions) for the tax year of sale. To make the election out, do not report your sale on Form 6252. Instead report the entire gain on Schedule D, Form 1040 or Form 4797, *Sales of Business Property*, whichever applies to your situation.

You may qualify for an automatic extension of six months from the due date of the return, excluding extensions, to make this election [Reg. §§301.9100-2(b) and (d)].

Ask yourself the following questions to determine whether you should elect out of the installment reporting method or avoid structuring your sale of property as an installment sale:

- *Will you be in a higher tax bracket in future years?* If yes, elect out. You should project as much as possible what your income and expense picture will be in the years of the anticipated reporting of income from the installment sale. If you expect a large amount of future income, adding more to it in the form of installment sale reporting (especially if the installment sale will generate substantial ordinary income or yield short term gain taxed as ordinary income) will only result in a bigger tax bill in the later years.
- *Do you have capital losses this year?* If yes, elect out. If you have capital losses this year, electing out of the installment method may increase your current capital gains this year which in turn will allow you to deduct more current capital losses this year. By electing out, the gain on the sale will be taxed in the year of the sale and the capital losses can offset your capital gains.
- *Would you have to pay interest on the deferral?* If yes, elect out. The benefits of tax deferral inherent in the installment method of reporting are negated in certain situations. For example, if the sale involves a nondealer disposition of non-farm or non-personal-use property, and the sale price is more than $150,000, and the aggregate face amount of all similar installment obligations that arose during the year that are outstanding at the close of the year exceed $5 million, the seller must pay interest on the deferred tax attributable to the installment obligation [Code Sec. 453A(b)(2); see ¶19,035 for further discussion]. If you would have to pay interest on the deferral, the installment method of reporting becomes less attractive and you should elect out.
- *Do you need the cash now?* If yes, don't enter into an installment sale. For example, if you had a large mortgage on the property that you sold, you may need the cash to pay off that mortgage. Receiving the payments over time may help your tax situation but may leave you unable to pay off the debts you owe on the property you sold.
- *Do you have suspended passive activity losses?* If yes, elect out. If the property sold was a passive activity with suspended passive activity losses (PALS) because the activity failed to produce sufficient income to offset the losses, reporting the income on the installment sale method may limit your ability to deduct those losses now. If you report the income from the sale of the passive activity on the installment method, the suspended PALS cannot be deducted in full in the year of sale. You must spread out the deduction of your passive losses over the years of income reporting. On the other hand, by electing out of the installment method, you can deduct in full all the suspended losses in the year you report all the gains from the sale.
- *Do you have to report depreciation recapture?* If yes, elect out. If the property you sold on the installment method was depreciated, the depreciation would be recaptured

and taxed as ordinary income in the year of sale under Code Sec. 1245 or Code Sec. 1250. This rule applies even if no payments are received in the year of the sale.

.03 Electing Out of the Installment Method

If an installment sale has occurred, it must be reported on the installment method, unless you elect out. You must make the election out on or before the due date of the return (including extensions) for the tax year of the disposition [Code Sec. 453(d)(2)]. After you have elected out, do not report your sale on Form 6252. Instead report the entire gain on Schedule D (Form 1040) or Form 4797, *Sales of Business Property*, whichever applies to your situation. Once you elect out, you generally cannot revoke the election. Your only hope at this point is to beg the IRS to revoke your election out and allow you to report on the installment method.

When IRS Permits Late Election Out

The IRS may permit a late election to be made only in rare circumstances where good cause is shown for not making a timely election out [Temp. Reg. § 15A.453-1(d)(3)(ii)]. To be granted the ability to make a late election out of the installment method of reporting, you must request it from the IRS and indicate the grounds on which it should be granted. One of the only reasons that the IRS will accept for failing to make a timely election out is an honest taxpayer mistake. For example, if you instructed your paid tax return preparer to elect out of installment method of reporting, but the preparer forgot to do so, the IRS may allow you a second chance to file an amended return and make your election out.

The IRS does *not* consider the following reasons to be good cause for failing to make a timely election out of using the installment method:

- Subsequent change in circumstances or law;
- Subsequent change of taxpayer's mind; or
- Desire to simplify your income tax reporting.[1]

For example, a recharacterization of a transaction as a sale in a tax year subsequent to the tax year in which the transaction occurred will not justify a late election. This means that you cannot initially report a transaction as a lease and then decide that you would be better off reporting it as an installment sale. You will be unable to make the switch at this point.

Revocation of Election Out

In general, an election out of the installment method of reporting is irrevocable and the election may only be revoked with the consent of the IRS [Code Sec. 453(d)(3)].[2] You will not be allowed to revoke the election if either of the following situations applies:

- One of the purposes is to avoid federal income tax; or
- The tax year in which any payment was received has closed [Temp. Reg. § 15A.453-1(d)(4)].

---

[1] Rev. Rul. 90-46, 1990-1 CB 107.

[2] LTR 9233044 (May 21, 1992); LTR 8938067 (June 29, 1989); LTR 8830030 (Apr. 29, 1988).

Revocation of an election is not permitted where you simply have a change of mind, whether due to changed circumstances, subsequent events, or occurrences beyond your control.

The IRS may, however, permit the revocation of your election out, if the election was the result of an inadvertent error, clerical mistake or lack of communication between you and your return preparer.[3] For example, if you intended to use the installment method but did not due to a failure in communications between you and your return preparer, clerical error, inadvertence, or similar mistake, a revocation may be granted.

Automatic Six-month Extension

If you timely filed your tax return and failed to make the election out, you may still make the election by filing an amended return within 6 months of the due date of your return (excluding extensions). Write "Filed pursuant to section 301.9100-2" at the top of the amended return and file it at the same place you filed your original return.

¶19,005 TAXPAYERS ELIGIBLE TO USE THE INSTALLMENT METHOD

Under current law, you can use the installment method for reporting income from dispositions of:

- Personal property, if you do not regularly sell or otherwise dispose of property on the installment plan (that is, a nondealer sale of personal property);

  NOTE: Income from the sale of a partnership interest including income from the sales of real estate by the partnership[4] generally qualifies for installment reporting. However, you may not use installment reporting to the extent the income is attributable to inventory [Ch. 24].[5]

- Real property not held by you for sale to customers in the ordinary course of a trade or business, such as property you use in a trade or business or hold for the production of income;
- Certain timeshares and residential lots by dealers who elect to pay interest on the tax deferred because of using the installment method; and
- Property you use or produce in the business of farming [Code Sec. 453(l)(2)(A)].

.01 Sales Ineligible for Installment Method of Reporting

The installment method of reporting is unavailable for the following transactions:

- To report gains from sales of inventory of personal property [Code Sec. 453(b)(2)(B)];

---

[3] LTR 9225012 (Mar. 16, 1992).

[4] *R.W. Parker*, 104 TCM 823, Dec. 59,299(M), TC Memo. 2012-357.

[5] Rev. Rul. 89-108, 1989-2 CB 100.

- Sales of real estate or personal property by dealers or other persons who regularly sell such property under an installment plan in the ordinary course of business [Code Sec. 453(b)(2)(A)]. This rule is designed to limit the use of the installment method by taxpayers to defer payment from sales of real estate held as a capital asset or as a Section 1231 asset. In *Tietig*,[6] the court held that a real estate developer was not entitled to report the sale of residential lots using the installment method. The installment method was unavailable because the dealer failed to show that he sold residential lots to an individual;
- For sales under revolving credit plans [Code Sec. 453(k)];
- For sales of publicly traded stock, securities or other publicly traded property; This prohibition does not does not apply to unregistered restricted stock sold in a private placement;
- Sales that result in a loss;
- Sales of depreciable property to a related party (e.g., a more than 50 percent controlled corporation), unless it can be shown that tax avoidance was not one of the principal purposes of the transaction [Code Sec. 453(g)];

  ▶ **PLANNING TIP:** You may use the installment reporting on the sale of nondepreciable property to a related person, but if the related person disposes of the property within two years of the original sale, the amount realized on the second sale is treated as a payment received by the original seller [Code Sec. 453(e)].

- Sale of a partnership interest for the portion of the proceeds that are attributable to the partnership's unrealized receivables.[7]

If a transaction fails to qualify for installment treatment, you must report the gains or losses from the sale on your tax return in the year of the sale.

¶19,010 ONE-PAYMENT RULE

You are only required to receive one installment payment to qualify for use of the installment sale method [Code Sec. 453(b)(1); Temp. Reg. § 15A.453-1(b)(1)]. This means that installment sale reporting is available to a seller who receives just one lump-sum payment in a tax year subsequent to the year of sale.

Example 19-1: Property is sold in December for $50,000. Assume alternatively:

1. The down payment is $5,000. The balance under the contract is payable in $5,000 installments over nine years, beginning the following year; or
2. Again the down payment is $5,000. The $45,000 balance of the purchase price is due the following year; or
3. The property is sold with no down payment. The full purchase price of $50,000 is paid the following year.

Each of these transactions is an installment sale because each one involves a payment occurring after the year of sale.

---

[6] *E.C. Tietig*, CA-11, 2003-1 USTC ¶ 50,205.

[7] *L.M. Mingo*, 105 TCM 1857, Dec. 59,564(M), TC Memo. 2013-149.

.01 Bond or Other Debt Received as Payment

Any bond or other evidence of debt received from the buyer that has interest coupons attached or that can be readily traded on an established securities market is treated as a payment in the year received. There no longer is a requirement that the bond or other evidence of indebtedness be issued by a corporation or government or political subdivision of a government.

HOW TO REPORT SALES UNDER THE INSTALLMENT METHOD

¶19,015 FIGURING INSTALLMENT SALE INCOME IN GENERAL

You must use the installment sale method of reporting your installment sales unless you elect out [Code Sec. 453(d); Temp. Reg. § 15A.453-1T(a); see ¶ 19,001 for discussion of electing out]. Use Form 6252 to report a sale of property as an installment sale in the year it takes place and to report payments received in later years. Be sure to attach the completed form to your federal income tax return.

The installment method permits you to spread the gross profit generated from the sale of property over the entire period during which payments are received. Each payment is considered to contain a pro rata recovery of both costs and profits. A *gross profit ratio* is applied to each installment payment when it is received and that portion of each payment representing the element of gain is included in the seller's gross income for that tax year [Code Sec. 453(c)].

In general, the installment method requires you to break down the payments you receive each year from an installment sale into three parts:

- Interest;
- Return of investment (basis) in the property sold; and
- Profit.

If interest is included in a payment, you must report separately all the interest as ordinary income on your tax return. Interest is generally not included in a down payment. However, you may have to treat a part of each later payment as interest, even if it is not called interest in your agreement with the buyer.

The rest of each installment payment is treated as if it were made up of two parts. One part is a return of your investment (basis) in the property you sold. The other part is your gain from the sale. If you took depreciation deductions on the asset, part of your gain may be recaptured as ordinary income.

Income that arises from the installment sale method is reported, for tax purposes, when the income is actually received. To determine what part of the installment payment is gain, multiply each payment received by the gross profit percentage which is the anticipated total gross profit divided by the total contract price. The result is subject to tax, while the rest is return of basis. The following example illustrates how installment sale reporting may save you taxes:

Example 19-2: Taxpayer owns 100 shares of the Widget Corporation, a privately held corporation, with a basis of $100 per share—a total of $10,000. He sells the shares in Year 1 for a total price of $50,000. He has gain of $40,000. However, he will receive payment as follows: $10,000 down and the balance in four equal, annual installments of $10,000, plus interest. Therefore, the gross profit is $40,000. Under installment reporting, the proportion of the gross profit ($40,000) to the contract price ($50,000) yields an 80 percent gross profit ratio. With respect to each payment, including the down payment, 20 percent will be a tax-free return of capital and 80 percent will be a realized and recognized gain.

Under the installment sale method, the gain is characterized by the original transaction and depends on the nature of the asset and the period for which the asset was held. If shares are a capital asset and the applicable long-term holding period requirement is met, the gain will be characterized as long-term capital gain; however, capital losses can be used to offset the capital gain. The interest received in addition to the principal is ordinary income.

¶19,020 COMPUTATION OF GAIN IN INSTALLMENT SALE

A taxpayer recognizes income on the payments received in a year from an installment sale in the proportion that the gross profit bears to the contract price [Code Sec. 453(c)]. The key terms are defined here.

.01 Gross Profit

Gross profit is the selling price minus the adjusted basis of the property sold. Commissions and other selling expenses are added to the seller's basis in order to determine the proportion of the payments that constitute gross profit from the disposition [Temp. Reg. § 15A-453-1(b)(2)(v)].

.02 Selling Price

The *selling price* is the gross sales price of the property to the buyer without reduction for any existing mortgage or other lien on the property, whether assumed or taken subject to the buyer. The selling price includes the cash and notes (at face value) received from the buyer. Selling expenses do not reduce the sales prices. The selling price does not include interest, whether stated or unstated [Temp. Reg. § 15A.453-1(b)(2)(ii)].

.03 Contract Price

The *contract price* is the total of all principal payments you are to receive on the installment sale minus that portion of any qualifying indebtedness that is assumed or taken subject to by the buyer. However, the amount of qualifying indebtedness that is taken into account for this purpose is limited to the seller's adjusted basis in the property [Temp. Reg. § 15A.453-1(b)(2)(iii)]. Qualifying indebtedness includes:

- Any mortgage or other the indebtedness that encumbers the property; and
- Any indebtedness not secured by the property but incurred or assumed by the purchaser incident to his acquisition, holding, or operation of the property in the ordinary course of business or investment.

Qualifying indebtedness excludes liabilities incident to the disposition of the property (*e.g.*, legal fees relating to the taxpayer's sale of the property) or an obligation functionally unrelated to the acquisition, holding or operating of the property.

Example 19-3: Seller has basis in property of $100,000 and sells property for $240,000. Buyer assumes Seller's $160,000 mortgage and makes a cash payment of $80,000. Seller incurs $24,000 of expenses in connection with the sale. The amount of the first-year payment equals $116,000, determined as follows:

Seller's basis	$100,000
plus selling costs	24,000
Seller's adjusted basis	124,000
Mortgage assumed by Buyer	$160,000
Less Seller's adjusted basis	124,000
	$ 36,000
Plus cash payment	$ 80,000
Payment in Year of Sale	$116,000

.04 Payments Received in Installment Sale

Sellers apply their *gross profit ratio* to *payments received* during the year under the installment obligation. In this context, payments received include amounts actually or constructively received under an installment obligation [Temp. Reg. § 15A.453-1(b)(3)(i)]as discussed here.

Cash

Payments may be cash or other property, including foreign currency, marketable securities, and evidences of indebtedness that are payable on demand or readily tradable [Code Sec. 453(f)(4); Temp. Reg. § 1.453A-1(b)(3)(i)]. *Readily tradable* in this context refers to an obligation that is: (a) in registered form, (b) issued with interest coupons attached, or (c) is issued in any other form designed to render it readily tradable in an established securities market [Temp. Reg. § 15A.453-1(e)(4)(iv)].

An obligation is in *registered form* if (1) it is registered as to principal, income, or both, and (2) its transfer must be effected by surrendering the instrument to the issuer, and having the issuer re-issue the instrument or issue a new instrument. [Temp. Reg. § 15A.453-1(e)(1)(i)].

Exclusion of Debt

Evidence of the buyer's indebtedness is generally excluded from the term *payment* (whether or not payment of such indebtedness is guaranteed by another person) [Code Sec. 453(f)(3)]. An exception is provided for bonds or other evidences of indebtedness of the buyer (notes) that are payable on demand or readily tradable [Code Sec. 453(f)(4)(A); Temp. Reg. § 15A.453-1(e)(1)(i)(A)]. A bond or other evidence of indebtedness is readily tradable if it was issued with interest coupons attached or in registered form or in any form designed to render such bond or other evidence of indebtedness readily tradable in an established securities market [Code Sec. 453(f)(5); Temp. Reg. § 15A.453A-1(e)(1)(i)].

Secured Liability

Payments received include evidence of a liability that is secured directly or indirectly by cash or a cash equivalent, such as a bank certificate or treasury note [Temp. Reg. § 15A.453-1(b)(3)(i)].

.05 Like-Kind Exchanges

The value of like-kind property is not included in the total contract price or considered as a payment received in the year of sale. Specifically, the contract price is reduced by the value of property received to the extent that it qualifies for nonrecognition of gain under Code Sec. 1031. The gross profit is reduced by the amount of gain not recognized [Code Sec. 453(f)(6)]. For further discussion of like-kind exchanges, see ¶ 6050.

> **Example 19-4:** Seller sells property with a basis of $100,000 for $250,000. As consideration, Buyer gives Seller like-kind property worth $50,000 in addition to Buyer's installment obligation of $200,000. Buyer will make a $25,000 payment in the year of the sale; the remaining $175,000 will be paid in the following year. The contract price is $200,000; the gross profit equals $100,000. The gross profit percentage equals 50 percent ($100,000/$200,000). Seller realizes and recognizes $12,500 (50 percent of $25,000) in the year of the sale and $87,500 (50 percent of $175,000) in the following year.

.06 Payments With Wrap-Around Mortgage

One method of purchasing mortgaged property involves the use of a wrap-around note. A *wrap-around* refers to the purchaser's installment obligation to pay the seller an amount sufficient to cover an existing mortgage liability. Ordinarily, the seller will use payments received on the installment obligation to service the wrapped indebtedness. Pursuant to Temp. Reg. § 15A.453-1(b)(3)(ii), the buyer of property with an existing mortgage is treated as having assumed the wrapped mortgage, even though title to the property has not passed in the year of sale and the seller remains liable for payments on the wrapped indebtedness.

In the hands of the seller, the wrap-around installment obligation will have a basis equal to the seller's basis in the property which was the subject of the installment sale, increased by the amount of gain recognized in the year of sale, and decreased by the amount of cash and the fair market value of other nonqualifying property received in the year of sale.

The amount of any indebtedness assumed or taken subject to by the buyer (other than wrapped indebtedness) is to be treated as cash received by the seller in the year of sale. Therefore, the gross profit ratio with respect to the wrap-around installment obligation is a fraction, the numerator of which is the face value of the obligation less the taxpayer's basis in the obligation and the denominator of which is the face value of the obligation [Temp. Reg. § 15A.453-1(b)(3)(ii)].

Example 19-5: Investor sells property to Buyer. The property is encumbered by a first mortgage with a principal amount of $500,000 and a second mortgage with a principal amount of $400,000, for a selling price of $2 million. Investor's basis in the property is $700,000. According to the agreement between the parties, passage of title is deferred and Buyer does not assume and purportedly does not take subject to either mortgage in the year of sale. Buyer pays investor $200,000 in cash and issues a wrap-around mortgage note with a principal amount of $1.8 million bearing adequate interest. Buyer is deemed to have acquired property subject to the first and second mortgages (wrapped indebtedness) totaling $900,000. The contract price is $1.3 million (selling price of $2 million less $700,000 mortgages within the seller's basis assumed or taken subject to). Gross profit is also $1.3 million (selling price of $2 million less $700,000 basis). Accordingly in the year of sale, the gross profit ratio is 1 ($1.3 million/$1.3 million). Payment in the year of sale is $400,000 ($200,000 cash received plus $200,000 mortgage in excess of basis ($900,000 − $700,000)). Therefore investor recognizes $400,000 gain in the year of sale ($400,000 × 1). In the hands of investor, the wrap-around installment obligation has a basis of $900,000, equal to investor's basis in the property ($700,000) increased by the gain recognized by investor in the year of sale ($400,000) reduced by the cash received by investor in the year of sale ($200,000). Investor's gross profit with respect to the note is $900,000 ($1.8 million face amount less $900,000 basis in the note) and investor's contract price with respect to the note is its face amount of $1.8 million. Therefore, the gross profit ratio with respect to the note is 1/2 ($900,000/$1.8 million) [Temp. Reg. § 15A.453-1T(b)(3), Example 5].

¶19,025 INSTALLMENT SALES WITH A CONTINGENT SALES PRICE

The formula for reporting gain on the installment method presumes that there is an easily determinable amount realized and gross profit, but sometimes the gross profit or the contract price is not determinable because the selling price is contingent. You may still use the installment method of reporting for contingent payment sales unless you elect to use another method [Temp. Reg. § 15A.453-1(c)(1)].

Contingent payment sales are transactions in which the aggregate sales price cannot be determined by the end of the tax year of sale. They do not include transactions involving an equity element, *e.g.*, a retained interest in the property sold, an interest in a joint venture or partnership, an equity interest in a corporation [Temp. Reg. § 15A.453-1(c)(1)]. Unless the taxpayer elects to report the gain resulting from such a sale in the year of sale, it is reported on the installment method. The Temporary Regulations prescribe rules for allocating your basis (including selling expenses except for selling expenses of dealers in real estate) to payments received and to be received in transactions where the gross profit or the total contract price (or both) cannot be readily ascertained. The rules are designed to distinguish contingent payment sales in the following situations:

- A maximum selling price is determinable;
- No maximum selling price is determinable but the term over which payments are to be received is determinable; and
- No maximum selling price or term of payments is determinable.

In addition, the regulations specify situations where an alternate allocation of cost recovery called the *income forecast computation* may be permissible [Temp Reg. § 15A.453-1(c)(1)].

.01 Maximum Stated Selling Price

If the sales price is contingent but a maximum price is stated in the contract, the seller determines a maximum selling price by assuming that all of the contingencies contemplated by the agreement are met. A contingent payment sale will be treated as having a stated maximum selling price if under the terms of the agreement the maximum amount of sale proceeds that will be received can be determined as of the end of the tax year in which the sale takes place. The maximum selling price will be the highest price that can be received, assuming that all contingencies operate in the seller's favor [Temp. Reg. § 15A.453-1(c)(2)(i)(A)]. In other words, the gross profit ratio applied to each payment will be computed by assuming that any unresolved contingencies are fulfilled so as to require the payment of the maximum amount. When the maximum selling price is reduced, the seller recomputes the gross profit ratio.

> **Example 19-6:** Investor sells stock in Widget Corporation, a privately held corporation, for a down payment of $100,000 plus five percent of the net profits of Widget Corporation for the next nine years. The contract provides for a maximum amount payable of $1,000,000. Investor's basis in the stock is $100,000. The selling price and the contract price both equal $1,000,000. The gross profit is $900,000. Thus, the gross profit ratio is 90 percent—$900,000 (gross profit) divided by $1,000,000 (contract price). Thus, $90,000 of the first payment is realized as gain; $10,000 is a tax-free recovery of capital.

.02 Fixed Term of Years

If the installment obligation is payable over a fixed term of years but no maximum selling price is stated, the seller basis (inclusive or selling price) will be allocated to the tax years in which payment may be received under the agreement in equal annual increments. But if in any tax year no payment is received or the payment is less than the basis allocated to that year, no loss is allowed, unless the year is the final payment year [Temp. Reg. § 15A.453-1(c)(3)(i)]. Gain is recognized to the extent that payments received exceed the *pro rata* portion of the seller's adjusted basis for the property [Temp. Reg. § 15A.453-1(c)(3)(i)]. These rules are called the ratable basis recovery rules. In short, these rules provide that, in the case of an installment sale in which the maximum selling price cannot be determined, but the period over which payments are to be received is fixed, the taxpayer's basis shall be allocated equally over the tax years in which payments may be received under the installment sale agreement.

Depending upon the particular terms of an otherwise valid installment sale, the ratable basis recovery rules may have the effect of accelerating the recognition of income on a contingent installment transaction while deferring the recognition of losses [See Temp. Reg. § 15A.453-1(c)(7)]. A taxpayer may use an alternative method of basis recovery where the regulations would substantially and inappropriately defer basis recovery. In Letter Ruling 200415006, the IRS approved use of an alternate method of basis recovery on a contingent payment installment plan where the alternative method would result in basis recovery more than twice as fast as under the normal basis recovery rules. Note that a taxpayer must receive a ruling from the IRS before using an alternative method of basis recovery. The ruling request must be filed before the due date (including extensions) of the return for the tax year in which the first payment is received.

Courts Strike Down Tax Shelters Abusing Ratable Basis Recovery Rules

In *Boca Investerings Partnership*,[8] tax shelter partnership was created by a U.S. corporation and a foreign corporation that was not subject to U.S. tax. The partnership relied on a series of investment transactions that involved use of contingent installment sale transactions where the gain was recovered on a ratable basis. The transactions were designed to exploit the terms of the ratable basis recovery rules found in Temp. Reg. § 15A.453-1(c)(3)(I). That regulation supplies a general rule of *ratable basis recovery* for situations where a seller at least knows the maximum period over which the purchase price will be paid. The partnership formed between the domestic entities and the foreign entities in *Boca Investerings* took advantage of this regulation by first buying, then immediately selling a debt instrument on an installment basis in an effort to create losses that could be used to shelter capital gains. The court concluded that the only logical explanation for the partnership's formation was the exploitation of Temp. Reg. § 15A.453-1T(c)(3)(I) and the creation of a paper tax loss to absorb its enormous capital gains. The court concluded that the absence of a non-tax business purpose was fatal to the recognition of the entity for tax purposes.

In Saba Partnership,[9] a case involving facts similar to those in *Boca Investerings*, the partnerships involved in the transactions also relied on the ratable basis recovery rules found in Temp. Reg. § 15A.453-1T(c) to allocate their gains to a nontaxable foreign entity, and their losses to the taxpayer, who attempted to deduct them as capital losses. The court found that the partnerships engaged in financial transactions with the sole purpose of exploiting the ratable basis recovery rules and were not organized or operated for a nontax, business purpose. According to the court, the taxpayer that formed the partnerships failed to show that they engaged in even a minimal amount of

---

[8] *Boca Investerings Partnership*, CA-DC, 2003-1 USTC ¶ 50,181, 314 F3d 625, *cert. denied*, 124 SCt 180.

[9] *Saba Partnership*, 78 TCM 684, Dec. 53,604(M), TC Memo. 1999-359, *vacated and remanded*, CA-DC, 2002-1 USTC ¶ 50,145, 273 F3d 1135, *supplemental opinion*, 85 TCM 817, Dec. 55,035(M), TC Memo. 2003-31.

business activity as required under the standard articulated in *Moline Properties, Inc.*[10] As a result, they were also disregarded for federal income tax purposes.

If in any year the seller receives no payment or the amount of the payment received is less than the adjusted basis for the property allocated to that tax year, the seller does not recognize a loss unless the tax year is the final payment year or the agreement has become worthless. Rather, the excess of the basis for the property allocated to that year over the payment received in the tax year is added to the succeeding year's basis. Any basis that remains at the end of the installment payment period is treated as a loss in the final year of payment (or earlier, if the obligation becomes worthless).

.03 Neither Maximum Selling Price Nor Fixed Term

Sales in which there is no stated maximum price and no specified number of years are rare. If the transaction qualifies as an installment sale, the adjusted basis of the property is recovered in equal annual installments over a 15-year period commencing with the date of the sale. No immediate loss is allowed if payments received in one year are less than the basis allocated to that year. However, the excess of the basis not recovered in one year over the payment received in such year is spread over the remaining balance of the 15-year period. Even after the expiration of the 15-year period, the unrecovered remaining basis is not allowed as a loss but is carried forward until the basis is recovered or the agreement is determined to be worthless. In a situation where property is disposed of on the installment method without reference to a maximum sales price or time limit, an issue exists as to whether or not the property was sold in the first place. The transaction may be treated as a lease or as a licensing agreement; therefore, the threshold issue is whether or not the seller made a transfer of substantial rights [Temp. Reg. § 15A.453-1T(c)(3)].

.04 Income Forecast Method for Basis Recovery

When either depreciable or depletable property is sold where payments are based on estimated receipts or units produced by or from the property, the taxpayer's basis may be recovered by use of an income forecast method. Thus, where the property sold is a mineral property or a motion picture, the taxpayer may be able to use the income forecast method [Temp. Reg. § 15A.453-1(c)(6)]. Under the income forecast method, the taxpayer's cost in any one tax year is recovered by prorating the basis in the following manner:

$$\text{Basis} \times \frac{\text{Payment received (net of interest)}}{\text{Estimated total payments}}$$

.05 Foreign Currency or Fungible Goods

Installment sales that specify that payment is to be made in foreign currency or identified fungible goods are contingent payment sales, because the value of the payment varies in relation to the U.S. dollar. In such cases, basis is recovered according

[10] *Moline Properties, Inc.*, SCt, 43-1 USTC ¶9464, 319 US 436, 63 SCt 1132.

to the ratio that the number of units paid during the year bears to the total number of units payable [Temp. Reg. § 15A.453-1 (c) (5)].

.06 Special Rule to Avoid Substantial Distortion

The basis recovery rules for contingent payment sales reported on the installment method may defer or accelerate recovery of the taxpayer's basis. Where this distortion occurs, Temp. Reg. § 15A.453-1 (c) (7) allows the taxpayer to use an alternative method if it can be established (prior to the due date of the return including extensions) that the prescribed method would substantially and inappropriately defer recovery of basis. In order to be successful with the use of this alternative method, the taxpayer must show that:

- The alternative method is a reasonable method of ratably recovering basis; and
- Under the method, the taxpayer will likely recover basis twice as fast as if the prescribed rate had been used. In meeting these criteria, the taxpayer may rely upon current or recent data (*e.g.*, sales, profit, or other factual data that is subject to verification). Future projections may be allowable where a specific event has already occurred (*e.g.*, corporate stock has been sold for future payments contingent on profits and an inadequately insured major plant facility of the corporation has been destroyed).

Although a taxpayer may be successful in recovering basis at a faster rate than the general rules allow, the IRS may be successful in certain situations in slowing the rate of recovery. Where the prescribed method inordinately accelerates a write-off, the IRS may require an alternate method of basis recovery unless the taxpayer is able to demonstrate either that the method used is a reasonable one or, would not result in recovery at twice the rate of the one proposed by the IRS. Again, the taxpayer may rely upon contemporaneous or immediate past data to support his or her position.

¶19,030 DEPRECIATION RECAPTURE

If a taxpayer reports the gain on the sale of depreciable property, all the depreciation (cost recovery) deductions recaptured as ordinary income are taxable under Code Secs 1245 and 1250 in the year of the disposition, regardless of the term over which the payments are to be made [See Ch. 8 for definitions of Code Secs 1245 and 1250 property, respectively]. For purposes of determining the recapture of depreciation, payments under the contract are treated as received in the year of disposition. The amount recaptured that is included in income increases the adjusted basis of the property disposed of for purposes of determining the gross profit ratio on the balance of the gain (if any) to be reported.

Example 19-7: J sells depreciated real estate to B for $2,000,000 to be paid in installments over a five-year period. The property has an adjusted basis of $800,000. Of the $1,200,000 gain, assume that $300,000 is recaptured as ordinary income under Code Sec. 1250. J includes the $300,000 recaptured as ordinary income in the year of the disposition. In determining the gross profit ratio for purposes of the installment sale method, the adjusted basis of the property equals $1,100,000 [$800,000 (adjusted basis) plus $300,000 (amount recaptured)]. The gross profit rate equals 45 percent—selling price ($2,000,000) less adjusted basis ($1,100,000) divided by $2,000,000 (total contract price).

.01 How to Handle 25 Percent Gain on Installment Sales of Depreciable Property

The IRS has provided guidance on how individual taxpayers should treat an installment sale of depreciable real property when the gain to be reported includes both 25 percent-rate gain (unrecaptured Code Sec. 1250 gain) and 15 percent-rate gain (adjusted net capital gain taxed at a maximum rate of 15 percent). This problem will arise when you have the following scenario:

- You are using the installment method to report the sale of a capital asset such as investment property you have held for more than one year and the gain portion of each payment received is taxed at a maximum rate of 15 percent, and
- You are selling depreciable property acquired after 1986 and part of that gain representing depreciation recapture is taxed at a maximum rate of 25 percent.

The IRS provides that if the capital gain from an installment sale consists of both 25 percent-rate gain and 15 percent-rate gain, as in the example above, the 25 percent-rate gain is taken into account as payments are received before any 15 percent-rate gain is included [Reg. § 1.453-12(a)]. If the taxpayer is otherwise in a 15 percent tax bracket, the 25 percent-rate gain is taxed at a 15 percent rate, and the 15 percent-rate gain is taxed at a 10 percent rate.

Example 19-8: You sell an office building for $800,000 and make a gain of $400,000, of which $200,000 is taxed at a maximum rate of 25 percent and the other $200,000 is taxed at a maximum rate of 15 percent. The buyer makes four equal annual installment payment of $200,000. Half of each payment is taxable gain. Reg. § 1.453-12 provides that the gain portion of the first two payments is taxed at a maximum rate of 25 percent ($100,000 gain part of each $200,000 installment × 2), and the gain part of the second two payments is taxed at a maximum rate of 15 percent.

▶ **PLANNING POINTER:** As a result of the front-loading rule found in Reg. § 1.453-12, when you sell depreciable real estate on the installment method, the earlier payments that you receive will be taxed at a higher rate than the later payments.

.02 Installment Method and Section 1231 Property

Under Code Sec. 1231(c), net Code Sec. 1231 gain that would otherwise be taxed as long-term capital gain, is taxed as ordinary income to the extent of a taxpayer's non-recaptured net Code Sec. 1231 losses for the preceding five years. Code Sec. 1231 gain from an installment sale that is recharacterized as ordinary gain under Code Sec. 1231(c) is deemed to consist first of 25 percent rate gain and then of 15 percent rate gain. Installment gain characterized as ordinary gain under Code Sec. 1231(a) because there is a net loss under Code Sec. 1231 for a tax year, is treated as consisting of 25 percent gain first, before 15 percent gain for purposes of determining how much 25 percent gain remains to be taken into account in later years [Reg. § 1.453-12(d)].

¶19,035 INTEREST CHARGE ON TAX DEFERRAL

Nondealer sellers who enter into installment sales of their real or personal property may have to pay interest charges on their deferred tax liability if both of the following requirements are satisfied:

- The sales price of the property is greater than $150,000 [Code Sec. 453A(b)(1)];
- The installment obligation is outstanding as of the close of the tax year; and
- The face amount of all of nondealer installment obligations held by the taxpayer that arose during such year and that are outstanding at the close of such year exceeds $5 million [Code Sec. 453A(b)].

In determining whether the nondealer seller has exceeded the $5 million threshold for any tax year, the face amount of installment obligations arising during the year and outstanding as of the close of the year are reduced by the amount treated as a payment on such obligations for such tax year under the pledge rules discussed below. In addition, partnerships and S corporations should apply the $5 million threshold at the partner or shareholder level.

.01 Treatment of Interest

Any interest paid on a deferred installment sale tax liability will be treated as interest and taken into account in computing the amount of any deduction allowable to the taxpayer for interest paid or accrued during the tax year [Code Sec. 453A(c)]. The interest will be deductible by individuals if it is trade or business or investment expense interest but not if it is nondeductible personal interest.

.02 Sales Exempt from Nondealer Rule

The following installment sales are exempt from the special nondealer rule which charges taxpayers interest on deferred tax liabilities:

- Dispositions of property used in the business of farming [Code Sec. 453A(b)(3)(B)];
- Dispositions of personal use property which is defined as property that is substantially used outside of the taxpayer's trade or business or investment activity [Code Sec. 453A(b)(3)(A)]; and
- Dispositions of timeshares or residential lots [Code Sec. 453A(b)(4)].

.03 How to Calculate Interest on Deferred Tax Liability

Under Code Sec. 453A(c)(2), the interest equals the product of the applicable percentage of the deferred tax liability with respect to the obligation multiplied by the underpayment rate in effect under Code Sec. 6621(a)(2) for the month with or within which the tax year ends.

In order to calculate the amount of interest owed by the nondealer seller on the deferred tax liability, follow the following five steps:

1. Subtract $5 million from the total face value of installment notes from all sales made during the year that are subject to the interest and outstanding as of the

close of the tax year. Notes that are fully paid within the year of the sale are excluded from the total.

2. Divide the difference (the result in Step (1)) by the total face value of the obligations outstanding as of the close of the tax year. Exclude notes that are fully paid by year-end. This result equals the *applicable percentage* that is calculated in the year of the sale.
3. For each year that a note subject to the rule remains outstanding, multiply the gains still postponed under the installment method at year-end by the maximum tax rate. This is the deferred tax liability.
4. Multiply the deferred tax liability (the result in Step (3)) by the applicable percentage found in Step (2).
5. Multiply the result in Step (4) by the underpayment rate (that is the interest rate charged on late payments of tax) in effect for the month with or within which the taxpayer's tax year ends. This calculation gives the interest payable for the year on the tax still deferred under the installment method.

In Chief Counsel Advice 201021020, the IRS concluded that the computation of the Code Sec. 453A interest payment isn't affected by the fact that the installment sale occurred on the last day of the taxpayer's short tax year and that the interest isn't computed by applying a weighted average. The IRS also explained that the Code Sec. 453A interest is deductible for the year that the required addition to tax is imposed.

.04 Trap for Unwary

The nondealer interest rules present a trap for the unwary because a whole year's interest charge is imposed on nondealer installment obligations regardless of when the sale took place. The interest is calculated with respect to nondealer real property installment obligations outstanding at the end of a tax year so that an entire year's interest is payable even if the sale took place on December 31 and the proceeds of the installment note are collected on January 1 of the following year.

> ▶ **TAX PLANNING TIP:** You should therefore consider staggering sales of property subject to the interest rule over several years to avoid meeting the $5 million threshold. For example, assume you are a calendar-year taxpayer who wants to sell two properties, each for $4 million. If you sell them during the same year, interest will be triggered. However, if you make one sale in December and the other in January, thus straddling two years for tax purposes, the interest rule won't apply because the sales that arose during each year don't exceed $5 million, even though the sales price of each sale exceeds $150,000.

¶19,040 PLEDGES OF INSTALLMENT OBLIGATIONS

The pledge rule provides that if a seller pledges an installment obligation to secure a loan, the net proceeds, (the gross loan proceeds less the direct expenses of obtaining the loan), of the secured loan will be treated as a payment received on such installment obligation on the later of:

- The date that the indebtedness is secured; or
- The date that the net proceeds are received by the seller [Code Sec. 453A(d)(1)].

As a result, the pledge will trigger taxable gain for the seller who pledges the installment note.

The amount treated as a payment received in this situation will not exceed the excess of the total contract price over any payments received under the contract before the secured loan was incurred [Code Sec. 453A(d)(2)]. The total amount of gain that can be recognized on an obligation as a result of secured loans and the receipt of payments cannot exceed the total gain from the installment sale. Actual payments received on the installment obligation subsequent to the receipt of the loan proceeds are not taken into account until such subsequent payments exceed the loan proceeds that were treated as payments.

> **Example 19-9:** Seller disposes of property for an installment note. The disposition is properly reported using the installment method. Seller only recognizes gain as the deferred payments are received. If Seller pledges the installment note as security for a loan, Seller would be required to treat the proceeds of the loan as payment on the installment note to the extent that he or she had the right to satisfy all or a portion of the indebtedness with the installment obligation.

In addition, any arrangement that gives the taxpayer the right to satisfy an obligation with an installment note will be treated the same as a direct pledge of the installment note. As a result, that taxpayer must treat the loan proceeds as an installment payment and must recognize the loan proceed amount as gain [Code Sec. 453A(d)(4)].

The pledge rule does not apply to the following types of installment dispositions:

- Installment method sales made by a dealer in timeshares and residential lots where the taxpayer elects to pay interest under Code Sec. 453(l)(3);
- Sales of personal use property;
- Sales of property used or produced in the trade or business of farming; or
- Dispositions where the sales price does not exceed $150,000 [Code Sec. 453A(b)(1)].

¶19,045 RELATED PARTY SALES

Two special rules limit the use of installment reporting between related persons. First, the sale must be tested against Rule One. If Rule One does not apply, the sale must be tested against Rule Two. A *related person* for purposes of both rules includes spouses, children, grandchildren, parent, grandparent, sibling, controlled corporation, partnership, trust, or estate.

.01 Related Sale Rule One

If a taxpayer sells depreciable property to a related person (i.e., a controlled entity), as defined in Code Sec. 1239(b), except that the term also includes two or more partnership having a relationship to each other described in Code Sec. 707(b)(1)(B), the taxpayer cannot report the sale using the installment method. Instead, all payments to be received are considered received in the year of sale. Payments to be received include the total of all noncontingent payments and the fair market value of any contingent payments. When payments are contingent but the fair market value may not be reasonably ascertained, the basis will be recovered ratably by the seller and conformity with regard to the recognition of income and the treatment of basis between the buyer and the seller will be required.

Exceptions

If no significant tax deferral benefit will be derived from the sale and if it can be shown to the satisfaction of the IRS that avoidance of federal income tax was not one of the principal purposes of the sale, Related Sale Rule One will not apply and installment reporting may be used for sales of depreciable property to related persons.

.02 Related Sale Rule Two

If a seller makes an installment sale of property to a related person who resells the property before the installment payments are made in full, the seller must treat the amount realized by the related party has having been received at the time of the second disposition [Code Sec. 453(e)(1)]. The resale of property by a related party must be made within two years of the original disposition in order to trigger the resale rule [Code Sec. 453(e)(2)(A)]. The two-year period is tolled (suspended) if the buyer's risk of loss is *substantially lessened* by a put (an option to sell) on the property, by another person's holding a call (an option to buy) on the property, or by a short sale or other transaction lessening the risk of loss [Code Sec. 453(e)(2)(B)].

Exceptions

If the taxpayer can show, to the satisfaction of the IRS that neither the first disposition to the related person nor the second disposition had as one of its principal purposes the avoidance of federal income tax, Related Sale Rule Two does not apply and installment reporting may be used for related party resales. This exception is intended to apply to involuntary dispositions, such as foreclosures, or to subsequent installment sales with terms that are equivalent to or longer than those of the first sale. In addition, Related Sale Rule Two does not apply to an involuntary conversion if the initial sale occurred before the threat or imminence of conversion (destruction, theft, seizure, or condemnation) or if the second disposition occurred after the death of the installment seller or buyer [Code Sec. 453(e)(6)].

.03 Computation of Gain

The gain that must be reported by the seller when the related party resells the property is based on the gross profit ratio on the original installment sale.

Fair Market Value When the Disposition Is Not a Sale or Exchange

If the related purchaser disposes of the property in a transaction that is not a sale or exchange, the amount realized by the initial seller is the fair market value of the transferred property [Code Sec. 453(e)(4)].

Limitation on Amount Treated as Received

When a member of a family group makes an installment sale of property to a related person (first disposition) and the related party sells the property fewer than two years before the first disposition and before the installment payments are made in full (second disposition), the person who made the first disposition must treat the amount realized on the second disposition as received by the person making the first disposition. The amount treated as received by the initial seller in any one tax year is limited to the difference between [Code Sec. 453(e)(3)]:

- The lesser of the total amount realized from the second disposition of the property before the close of the tax year or the total contract price for the first disposition; and
- The sum of: (a) the total amount of payments received with respect to the first disposition before the close of such tax year and (b) the total amount treated as received with respect to the first disposition for prior years under the resale rule. Subsequent payments received by the initial seller from the related party may be recovered without tax consequences until they equal the amount realized upon the disposition that resulted in acceleration of the installment gain.

.04 Related Persons

Related person includes the following relationships:

- Members of an immediate family including children, grandchildren, and parents;

  NOTE: Transactions between a husband and wife or a former husband wife if incident to a divorce are not subject to the related party rule since there's no taxable gain. A transfer is incident to a divorce if it occurs within one year after the date on which the marriage ends or is related to the end of the marriage.

- A partnership in which the person is a partner;
- A trust in which the person is a beneficiary or which the person is treated as owning under the grantor trust rules;
- A corporation and a shareholder if the shareholder owns directly or indirectly more than 50 percent of the value of that corporation's outstanding stock. [Code Sec. 267(b)(2)];
- Two corporations that are members of the same controlled group. [Code Sec. 267(b)(3)];
- A fiduciary of a trust and a corporation, if more than 50 percent of the outstanding stock's value is owned directly or indirectly by or for the trust or by or for the trust's grantor;
- Any trust's grantor and fiduciary, and any trust's fiduciary and beneficiary;
- The fiduciaries of two different trusts, and the fiduciaries and beneficiaries of two different trusts, if you are both trusts' grantor;
- A fiduciary of a trust and a corporation if the trust or grantor owns more than 50 percent in value of the corporation;
- Certain educational and charitable organizations, and you or the members of your family if you directly or indirectly control the organization;
- Two S corporations if one person owns more than 50 percent in value of the outstanding stock of each corporation. [Code Sec. 267(b)(11)];
- An S corporation and a C corporation if one person owns more than 50 percent in value of each corporation's outstanding stock. [Code Sec. 267(b)(12)];
- An executor and a beneficiary of the estate; and

- A corporation and a partnership if one person owns more than 50 percent in value of the corporation's outstanding stock and more than 50 percent of the capital interest, or profits interest in the partnership.

.05 Exceptions

There are a number of exceptions to the resale rule:

- It does not apply to a sale or exchange of stock to the issuing corporation;
- It does not apply to an involuntary conversion if the initial sale occurred before the threat or imminence of conversion;
- It does not apply to a second disposition after the death of the installment seller or buyer; and
- It does not apply to any transaction that does not have the avoidance of tax as one of its principal purposes. This exception is intended to apply to involuntary dispositions, such as foreclosures, or to subsequent installment sales with terms that are equivalent to or longer than those of the first sale [Code Sec. 453(e)(6)].

¶19,050 DISPOSITION OF INSTALLMENT OBLIGATIONS

If you dispose of your installment obligation from an installment sale, the entire amount of the gain or loss from that disposition is recognized in the year of disposition. A disposition generally includes a sale, exchange, cancellation, bequest, gift,[11] distribution, or transmission of an installment obligation which includes the buyer's note, deed of trust, or other evidence that the buyer will make future payments to you. Increasing the interest rate on an installment obligation and substituting a new obligor is not a disposition of the obligation.[12] There is also no disposition for assigning an installment obligation as collateral for a loan. But if installment obligations are transferred to a financial institution at a discount, or at face value less certain charges, and substantial incidents of ownership are relinquished, then there is a disposition.[13] The IRS has concluded in Letter Ruling 201144005[14] that modification of a stock purchase agreement and promissory note would not constitute a disposition of an installment obligation under Code Sec. 453B. Therefore the seller did not need to recognize gain or loss at that time.

When you are using the installment and you dispose of the installment obligation, you generally have a gain or loss to report. It is considered gain or loss on the sale of the property for which you received the installment obligation. If the original installment sale produced ordinary income, the disposition of the obligation will likewise result in ordinary income or loss. If the original sale resulted in a capital gain, the disposition of the obligation will result in a capital gain or loss.

When the installment obligation is sold or exchanged, the gain or loss is the difference between your basis in the obligation and the amount realized [Code Sec. 453B(a)]. If you dispose of the obligation in any other way, for example, when you

[11] Rev. Rul. 72-264, 1972-1 CB 131.

[12] Rev. Rul. 82-122, 1982-1 CB 80.

[13] Rev. Rul. 65-185, 1965-2 CB 153.

[14] LTR 201144005 (Aug. 2, 2011).

give the installment obligation to someone else or cancel the buyer's debt to you, the gain or loss is the difference between your basis in the obligation and its fair market value at the time of the disposition.

The basis of an installment obligation is the difference between the face value of the obligation over an amount equal to the income that would be returnable if the obligation were satisfied in full.

Example 19-10: Mr. Bottoms sold unimproved land for $20,000. He bought the property two years ago at a cost of $12,000. In the year of sale Bottoms received $5,000 in cash and the buyer's notes for $15,000, payable in later years. Two years after the installment, before the buyer made any further payments, Bottoms sold the notes for $15,000. Bottoms' basis in the notes sold is $9,000, figured as follows:

Selling price of property (also contract price)	$20,000
Cost of property	12,000
Total profit	$ 8,000
Percentage of profit (proportion of each payment reportable as income, $8,000/$20,000)	40%
Unpaid balance of notes	$15,000
Amount of income reportable if the notes were paid in full (40% of $15,000)	6,000
Basis of notes sold (excess of unpaid balance of notes over amount of income reportable if the notes were paid in full)	$9,000

Bottoms has to include $6,000 in his gross income (the difference between the amount realized from the sale of the installment obligation, $15,000, and his basis in that obligation, $9,000).

Example 19-11: In 2009, Mr. Hobson sold for $100,000 (exclusive of 9 percent interest) real property that he had purchased in 1998 and which had an adjusted basis of $60,000. Payment was to be made as follows: cash for $30,000; installment obligation for $70,000, payable by the buyer in semiannual installments of $10,000 each, the first to be paid on April 1, 2010. The profit was $40,000, which will be accounted for as the $100,000 due on the contract is paid. Accordingly, 40 percent of each payment is profit.

	Face value	*Recognized gain (40%)*	*Return of capital or basis (60%)*
2009 payments	$ 30,000	$12,000	$18,000
2010 payments	$ 20,000	$ 8,000	$12,000
2011 payments	$ 20,000	$ 8,000	$12,000
2012 payments	$ 20,000	$ 8,000	$12,000
2013 payments	$ 10,000	$ 4,000	$ 6,000
Total	$100,000	$40,000	$60,000

Assume that before any payment is made, Hobson assigned the installment obligation (face value $50,000) for $35,000. If the obligation were satisfied in full, $50,000 would be received. Of that amount 40 percent is income ($50,000 × 40% = $20,000). The basis of the installment obligation is the difference between the face amount of the obligation ($50,000) and the amount of income that would be returnable if the installment obligation were satisfied in full ($20,000): $50,000 – $20,000 = $30,000. The recognized gain is $5,000 ($35,000 – $30,000).

.01 Acquisition from Decedent

Installment obligations that the decedent would have reported on the installment basis if the decedent had lived are taxed to the successor as *income in respect of decedent (IRD)*. This means that unreported income attributable to an installment obligation held by a person at death is treated as IRD and the estate or beneficiary must include that unreported gain in income as payments are received [Code Sec. 691(a)(4); Reg. § 1.691(a)-5]. If an installment obligation is sold or given away by the estate or beneficiary or is canceled, IRD is recognized by the transferor to the extent the fair market value of the installment obligation or the amount received upon sale, whichever is greater, exceeds the decedent's remaining basis. The estate also recognizes IRD if the decedent's will forgives the obligation or the obligation is transferred to the obligor [Code Sec. 691(a)(2) and Code Sec. 691(a)(5)].

.02 Tax-Free Transfers of Installment Obligations

In some cases, installment obligations may be transferred without tax being imposed on disposition. These include: transfers to a controlled corporation in exchange for stock [Ch. 6]; contributions to a partnership in exchange for partnership interest; distributions by a partnership to a partner; certain exchanges of property for stock or securities involving corporate reorganizations [Ch 22]; certain liquidations of subsidiaries [Ch. 22] [Code Sec. 453B(d)].

.03 Transfers Between Spouses or Incident to Divorce

No gain or loss is recognized for any transfers of installment obligations from an individual to a spouse, or to a former spouse, if made incident to a divorce.[15] The transferee receives the same tax treatment that would have applied to the transferor [Ch. 6] [Code Sec. 453B(g)]. These transfers are treated as nontaxable gifts.

> **NOTE:** The transferor must recognize gain on the transfer of installment obligations to a trust.

.04 Change in Form of Collateral Securing Installment Obligation

The mere substitution of collateral securing an installment obligation is not a disposition of the obligation,[16] but when the security for the note changes to cash and marketable securities, the holder will be deemed to have received payment in full, according to the IRS[17] [Reg. § 15a. 453-1(b)(3)(i)].

---

15 *A.S. Yankwich*, 83 TCM 1208, Dec. 54,643(M), TC Memo 2002-37.

16 Rev. Rul. 55-5, 1955-1 CB 331.

17 LTR 9238005 (June 8, 1992).

DEFERRED PAYMENT SALES

¶19,055 DEFERRED PAYMENT SALES NOT ON THE INSTALLMENT PLAN

A deferred payment sale is an installment sale where you do not report the gain on the installment method. Instead, you report the entire amount of gain in the year of the sale even if the installment obligations are payable over several years.

NOTE: The installment method is not available for dealer dispositions of property [¶19,005].

.01 Gain or Loss in Year of Sale

In general, if you are a cash-method seller, you must report the fair market value of the buyer's obligations (in addition to the cash and value of property you receive for the sale) as the amount realized on the sale in the year of their receipt. If you are an accrual seller, you generally report the face amount of the buyer's obligations (in addition to the property's value and the amount of cash that you receive) for the year of sale.

If, at the time of the sale, you reported a fair market value of less than face value the amount reported becomes your basis in the obligation; and a proportionate part of each payment collected later represents income. If the obligation has an indeterminable fair market value, subsequent payments are exempt until your basis in the obligation is recovered (see below). The distinction between collections on obligations with a discounted value and those with no determinate value is important, because the former results in ordinary income, while the latter may qualify for capital gain treatment. Only in unusual circumstances will obligations be considered to have no fair market value [Reg. § 1.453-6].

.02 Collections on Discounted Notes

If an obligation's fair market value is less than face value, the fair market value (1) is included in the amount realized to compute gain or loss at the time of sale, and (2) determines the creditor's basis in the obligation for computing future gain. In later years, part of each payment received is regarded as a return of capital, and the remainder is taxable income. The portion that is exempt as a return of capital bears the same ratio to each payment received as the fair market value of the obligation at the time of the sale bore to its face value.[18] If the issuer of the obligation is an individual, the taxable portion of each payment is ordinary income. If the issuer of the obligation is a corporation, the gain is capital gain only if the collection qualifies as a bond retirement.

Example 19-12: Ms. Brown sold realty, which had an adjusted basis of $60,000, for $100,000, payable as follows: cash, $35,000; first mortgage assumed, $20,000; second mortgage for $45,000 payable by the buyer in 5 annual installments of $9,000 each (exclusive of 9 percent stated interest), the first to be paid the

[18] *A.B. Culbertson*, 14 TC 1421, Dec. 17,725 (1950) (*Acq.* 1950-2 CB 1).

following year. The fair market value of the second mortgage note was 66²/₃ percent of face value, or $30,000. The $40,000 realized gain is reported under the deferred payment method as follows:

Proceeds realized:		
Cash		$35,000
First mortgage (assumed by purchaser; therefore valued at par)		20,000
Second mortgage	$45,000	
Discount on second mortgage (33¹/₃%)	15,000	30,000
		$85,000
Adjusted basis		60,000
Realized gain		$25,000

The balance of the realized gain ($15,000) will be reported as the 5 annual installments are paid:

	Year 1	*Year 2*	*Year 3*	*Year 4*	*Year 5*
Collected	$9,000	$9,000	$9,000	$9,000	$9,000
Less 66²/₃% already reported	6,000	6,000	6,000	6,000	6,000
Realized (ordinary) gain to be reported	$3,000	$3,000	$3,000	$3,000	$3,000

.03 Indeterminate Market Value

If the fair market value of an obligation cannot be determined, you are entitled to a return of capital before reporting any profits [Reg. § 1.453-6(a)(2)]. The basis of the property sold, reduced by any cash, or other property having a fair market value that you receive on the sale, becomes your basis in the obligation with an indeterminate market value for computing gain or loss on collection. If the property sold was a capital asset, collection may result in capital gain [Reg. § 1.453-6]. Contingent rights to future payments have been held to have an indeterminate fair market value.[19]

Example 19-13: Assume the same facts as in Example 19-12, except that the second mortgage notes had an indeterminate fair market value. The order of the payment is:

Cash	$ 35,000
First mortgage (assumed by purchaser and therefore valued at par)	20,000
First annual installment	9,000
Second annual installment	9,000
Third annual installment	9,000
Fourth annual installment	9,000
Fifth annual installment	9,000
Total	$100,000

[19] *E.A. Logan*, SCt, 2 USTC ¶736, 283 US 404, 51 SCt 550 (1931).

The adjusted basis is $60,000. The cash ($35,000), first mortgage ($20,000) and $5,000 of the first annual installment (total $60,000) are a return of capital. $4,000 of the first annual installment and all of the subsequent installments are recognized gain when received. If all the installments are paid when due, Brown will report realized gain as follows: return for Year 1, $4,000; Year 2, $9,000; Year 3, $9,000; Year 4, $9,000; Year 5, $9,000 (total $40,000).

REPOSSESSIONS

¶19,060 REPOSSESSION OF PERSONAL PROPERTY

Your gain or loss on the repossession of personal property in a deferred payment sale *not* on the installment plan [¶ 19,055] is the difference between the fair market value of the property on the date of repossession and the basis of the defaulted obligation adjusted, for other amounts realized or costs incurred in the repossession. However, you report the entire taxable gain or deductible loss in the year of sale. Therefore, the basis of the obligation to be used is its face value or fair market value, whichever was used in computing gain or loss for the year of sale. Nature of the gain or loss depends on the obligation, rather than the original sale. If the obligation is discharged by repossession of the property, any gain will be ordinary income. If the repossession results in a loss that is a nonbusiness bad debt, it will be reported as a short-term capital loss. If the loss is a business bad debt, it will be so reported.

¶19,065 REAL PROPERTY REPOSSESSED BY SELLER

No loss is recognized and no bad debt deduction is allowed when you repossess real property to satisfy a purchase obligation. You recognize gain on repossession only to the extent of the cash (or other property) you received, less the gain on the original sale you already included in income. The amount of your taxable gain, however, is limited to the gain on the original sale less repossession costs and gain previously reported as income [Reg. § 1.1038-1]. The nonrecognition of gain rules do not apply when real property is reconveyed to the estate of a deceased seller.[20]

If you reported the original sale on the installment basis, the repossession gain retains the same character as the gain on the original sale. If the sale was by a dealer, the gain is ordinary income; otherwise, it is either capital gain or Sec. 1231 gain [Code Sec. 1038; Reg. § 1.1038-1]. Your holding period includes the period you held the property before its original sale, but excludes the period starting with the day after date of the original

[20] Rev. Rul. 69-83, 1969-1 CB 202.

sale and ending with date you reacquired the property [Reg. § 1.1038-1(g)]. If the original sale was not an installment sale, and the title passed to the buyer, repossession gain from a voluntary reconveyance generally is ordinary income.

Example 19-14: Mr. Brown sold a building in Year 1 for $60,000, $10,000 cash and a $50,000 mortgage, payable $10,000 annually starting in Year 2. His adjusted basis was $48,000. Brown elected to report the income from the sale on the installment basis. His gain was $12,000, or 20 percent of the selling price, and he reported a $2,000 gain in Years 2, 3 , 4, and 5. The buyer defaulted in year 6 and Brown repossessed the property at a cost of $500. Brown's gain on repossession is $32,000 ($40,000 cash received minus $8,000 already reported as income), but his recognized gain is limited to $3,500 ($12,000 gain on the original sale minus $500 repossession costs and $8,000 already reported as income).

If any part of the debt obligation remains unsatisfied, its basis becomes zero. Hence, any later recovery is income. The basis of the repossessed property is the adjusted basis of the obligations (including the basis of unsatisfied obligations) plus (1) any repossession gain and (2) repossession costs. Adjusted basis of the obligations is the excess of the face amount of the obligations over the gain that would be reported if the obligations were satisfied in full [Code Sec. 1038; Reg. § 1.1038-1(g)].

Example 19-15: The basis of the repossessed property in Example 19-14 is $20,000, determined as follows:

Obligations (face amount)	$20,000
Less 20% unreported profits	4,000
Adjusted basis of obligations	$16,000
Repossession gain	3,500
Repossession costs	500
Basis of repossessed property	$20,000

If you took a bad debt deduction for the partial or complete worthlessness of the obligations before the repossession and the repossession satisfies the debt, you must add back to income the deduction if a tax benefit resulted from it. Basis is increased accordingly [Code Sec. 1038(d); Reg. § 1.1038-1(f)].

.01 Repossession of Seller's Residence

If the repossessed property was your principal residence, and gain was either excluded or not recognized on the original sale, special rules may apply. If you do not resell the property within a year after repossession, the rules above apply. If you do resell within a year, in effect the repossession is disregarded, and the resale is considered a sale of the property occurring on the original sales date; the price deemed received is the resale price, including mortgages plus the cash or other property retained from the original sale. Using this selling price, the amount of your gain that is exempt or not recognized is recomputed [Ch. 7]. If the recomputation shows the taxable gain is more or less than that reported in the year of the original sale, you make an adjustment by taking the difference into account in the return for the year of resale [Reg. § 1.1038-2].

SPECIAL SALES PROBLEMS

¶19,070 SALE OF REAL PROPERTY IN LOTS

A real estate development company will often acquire a tract of land and divide it into parcels or lots for easier sales. Ordinarily this requires an outlay for development such as surveying, installation of sewers, paving, and the like. These costs must be recorded on company books and equitably apportioned to the separate lots.

The sale of each lot is treated as a separate transaction and gain or loss must be figured separately on each lot. Thus, gain or loss on every lot sold must be determined and not deferred until the entire tract has been disposed of [Reg. § 1.61-6(a)].

▶ **OBSERVATION:** If you sell your entire property, you may defer your gain or loss until later years, for example, under the nonrecognition rules of like-kind exchanges [Ch. 6].

The allocation of costs is problematic in making the computation. Foot frontage, release prices, tentative sales prices, and assessed valuation have all been used. The tentative sales price method is shown in Example 19-16.

Example 19-16: The cost of the land, including the improvements, was $25,000 and the development company expects to sell the lots for $100,000. The cost of any one lot is 25 percent of the sale price at which it was offered for sale to the public on the day the tract was first opened.

		Tentative sales price		*Estimated cost price*	
Lot No.	*No. of lots*	*Each Lot*		*Total Lots*	
1-10	10	$5,500	$55,000	$1,375	$13,750
11-20	10	3,000	30,000	750	7,500
21-25	5	2,000	10,000	500	2,500
26-30	5	1,000	5,000	250	1,250

¶19,075 LONG-TERM CONTRACTS

Special accounting methods are used for reporting income from long-term contracts.[21] Generally, contracts for the manufacture, building, installation, or construction of property, if not completed within the tax year they are entered into are characterized as long-term contracts [Code Sec. 460(f); Reg. § 1.460-1(b)(1)]. A manufacturing contract, however, is not a long-term contract unless it requires the manufacture of a unique item or an item normally requiring more than 12 months to complete.

[21] Rev. Rul. 92-28, 1992-1 CB 153.

Code Sec. 460 generally requires that long-term contracts be accounted for under the percentage-of-completion method (PCM) and that taxpayers make a look-back computation of interest to compensate the government (or the taxpayer) for any underestimation (or overestimation) of income from the contract.

A contract is considered completed under the long-term contract rules on the earlier of: (1) when the contract's subject matter is used by the customer for its intended purpose and at least 95 percent of the total allocable contract costs have been incurred by the taxpayer, or (2) when there is final completion and acceptance [Reg. § 1.460-1(c)(3)].

Home construction contracts and other real property construction contracts that satisfy a two-year test and a $10 million gross receipts test don't have to use the percentage-of-completion method and instead can use the completed contract method [Reg. § 1.460-1(a)(2)]. For further discussion, see ¶ 19,075.02.

Contracts for the production or installation of real property or improvements to real property (construction contract) are considered to be long-term contracts as long as they are not completed within the tax year in which they are executed. In determining whether a contract is completed within the tax year in which it is entered into, all contract costs incurred and activities performed by the taxpayer, by any parties related to the taxpayer, and by the customer must be taken into account [Reg. § 1.460-1(c)(1)]. In determining whether a contract is a long-term contract, it is irrelevant whether title in the property manufactured or constructed under the contract is delivered to the customer [Reg. § 1.460-1(b)(2)].

Contracts characterized as *for the sale of property* may still qualify as long-term contracts, if manufacture, building, installation or construction of the property was necessary in order for the taxpayer's contractual obligations to be fulfilled and if such manufacture, building, installation or construction was not completed at the time that the contract was executed [Reg. § 1.460-1(b)(2)(i)].

In order for manufacturing contracts to qualify as long-term contracts, the contract must not be completed within the tax year in which it is executed, and the contract must involve the manufacture of either: (1) a unique item of a type that is not normally included in the finished goods inventory of the taxpayer; or (2) an item that normally requires more than 12 calendar months to complete [Code Sec. 460(f)(2); Reg. § 1.460-2(a)].

Unique defined. Unique in this context means designed for the needs of a specific customer. To determine whether an item is designed for the needs of a specific customer, a taxpayer must consider the extent to which research, development, design, engineering, retooling, and similar activities (customizing activities) are required to manufacture the item and whether the item could be sold to other customers with little or no modification. A contract may require the taxpayer to manufacture more than one unit of a unique item. If a contract requires a taxpayer to manufacture more than one unit of the same item, the taxpayer must determine whether that item is unique by considering the customizing activities that would be needed to produce only the first unit. For this purpose, a taxpayer must consider the activities performed on its behalf by a subcontractor.

.01 Safe Harbors

An item is not unique if it satisfies one or more of the following safe harbors. If an item does not satisfy one or more safe harbors, the determination of uniqueness will depend on the facts and circumstances. The safe harbors are:

- *Short production period.* An item is not unique if it normally requires 90 days or less to complete. In the case of a contract for multiple units of an item, the item is not unique only if it normally requires 90 days or less to complete each unit of the item in the contract;
- *Customized item.* An item is not unique if the total allocable contract costs attributable to customizing activities that are incident to or necessary for the manufacture of the item do not exceed 10 percent of the estimated total allocable contract costs allocable to the item. In the case of a contract for multiple units of an item, this comparison must be performed on the first unit of the item and the total allocable contract costs attributable to customizing activities that are incident to or necessary for the manufacture of the first unit of the item must be allocated to that first unit; and
- *Inventoried item.* A unique item ceases to be unique no later than when the taxpayer normally includes similar items in its finished goods inventory [Reg. § 1.460-2].

  ▶ **OBSERVATION:** A contract that meets the definition is considered a long-term contract even though you expected that it would be completed within the tax year.

Generally, you must determine taxable income on long-term contracts by using the percentage of completion method based on a cost-to-cost comparison [Code Sec. 460(a)]. The income from exempt construction contracts may be determined using the completed-contract method, the exempt-contract percentage-of-completion method or any other permissible method [Code Sec. 460(e)].

.02 Percentage of Completion Method (PCM)

Code Sec. 460 allows the receipt of taxable income from a long-term contract to be deferred under the percentage-of completion method. This accounting method is frequently used in connection with long-term construction projects, because it is difficult to determine the net profitability of a construction project because of fluctuating and unforeseen expenses.

The term "long-term contract" is defined as "any contract for the manufacture, building, installation, or construction of property if such contract is not completed within the tax year in which the contract is entered into" [Code Sec. 460(f)(1)]. The Regulations also clarify that "[a] contract is for the manufacture, building, installation, or construction of property if the manufacture, building, installation, or construction of property *is necessary* for the taxpayer's contractual obligations to be fulfilled and if the manufacture, building, installation, or construction of that property has not been completed when the parties enter into the contract" [Reg. § 1.460-1(b)(2)(i) (emphasis added)].

Most long-term contracts must be accounted for under the percentage of completion method of accounting [Code Sec. 460(a)]. Although the percentage of completion method generally requires taxpayers to recognize income and costs from a long-term contract as the contract is being completed, taxpayers may elect to postpone such recognition until the first tax year in which at least 10 percent of the contract costs have been incurred as of the end of that year [Code Sec. 460(b)(5)]. In applying the percentage of completion method to long-term contracts, incorrect cost or income estimates will generally give rise to interest liability or income upon completion of the contract.

In *Koch Industries, Inc.*,[22] the Court of Appeals for the Tenth Circuit reversed a federal district court to conclude that a corporation was not entitled to use the percentage-of-completion accounting method to defer the receipt of income received for warranting that highways would meet certain performance standards over a specified period of time. The court found that the warranty agreements did not require the taxpayer to perform "manufacture, building, installation, or construction" to fulfill its contractual obligations as required under Reg. § 1.460-1(b)(2)(i). Rather, the warranties included detailed performance standards which the taxpayer's pavement and structures were required to meet. Although it was virtually certain that some work would be performed at some point during the warranty period, the taxpayer had no obligation to perform any work on the highway unless and until the highway and/or structures failed to meet the performance standards included in the warranty agreements.

According to the Regulations, this type of contingent activity is "a nonlong term contract activity that is never incident to or necessary for the manufacture or construction of property under a long-term contract." [Reg. § 1. 460-1(d)(2)]. Thus, the court concluded that the income received by the taxpayer in consideration of these agreements was ineligible for the percentage-of-completion method of accounting because it is derived from non-long-term contract activity.

Exceptions

Home construction contracts and other real property construction contracts that satisfy a two-year test and a $10 million gross receipts test don't have to use the percentage-of-completion method and instead can use the completed contract method [Reg. §§ 1.460-1(a)(2), 1.460-3(b)(1)]. Under the completed contract method, a taxpayer doesn't report income until a contract is complete, even though payments are received in years before completion [Reg. § 1.460-4(d)]. The $10 million gross receipts test is satisfied if a taxpayer's (or predecessor's) average annual gross receipts for the three tax years preceding the contracting year do not exceed $10 million.

A home construction contract is a construction contract where 80 percent or more of the estimated total contract costs are reasonably expected to be attributable to the building, construction, reconstruction, or rehabilitation of dwelling units contained in buildings containing four or fewer dwelling units and to improvements to real property directly related to the dwelling units [Code Sec. 460(e)(6)(A)]. The proposed regulations expand the scope of the home construction contract exemption by providing that a contract for the construction of common improvements is considered a contract for the construction of improvements to real property directly related to the dwelling unit(s) and located on the site of such dwelling unit(s), even if the contract is not for the construction of any dwelling unit. Therefore, under the proposed

---

[22] *Koch Industries, Inc.*, DC-KS, 2008-2 USTC ¶ 50,465, 564 FSupp2d 1276, *rev'd*, CA-10, 2010-1 USTC ¶ 50,362.

regulations, a land developer that is selling individual lots (and its contractors and subcontractors) may have long-term construction contracts that qualify for the home construction contract exemption.

Note that each townhouse or row house is a separate building. The proposed regulations expand what is considered a townhouse or rowhouse, for purposes of the home construction contract exemption, to include an individual condominium unit. This will have the effect of allowing each condominium unit to be treated as a separate building for purposes of determining whether the underlying contract qualifies as a home construction contract. The IRS has ruled that land sale contracts aren't home construction contracts eligible for the completed contract method where the land developer isn't performing the construction contract activities with respect to the dwelling units.[23]

A taxpayer that uses the percentage of completion method (PCM) or the exempt contract percentage-of-completion method (or elects the 10-percent method or special alternative minimum taxable income (AMTI) method, or that adopts or elects a cost allocation accounting method or changes to another method with the IRS's consent) must apply the method consistently for all similarly classified contracts until the taxpayer obtains consent under Code Sec. 446 to change to another accounting method [Prop. Reg. § 1.460-5(g)]. A taxpayer-initiated accounting method change is allowed only on a cut-off basis so a Code Sec. 481(a) adjustment is not permitted or required.

The cut-off method would be continued only for taxpayer-initiated changes from:

- A permissible PCM method to another permissible PCM method for long-term contracts for which PCM is required; and
- A cost allocation method that complies with the Reg. § 1.460-5 rules to another complying cost allocation method.

Amounts reported as Code Sec. 481(a) adjustments would generally be taken into account in the tax year they are reported. A look-back computation would not be required upon contract completion simply because the taxpayer has changed its accounting method, but would be required if actual costs or the contract price differ from the estimated amounts notwithstanding that an accounting method change occurred. Taxpayers may not change or otherwise use a method of accounting in reliance on the proposed regulations until they are finalized [Prop. Reg. § 1.460-4(g)].

IRS Targets Improper Use of Contract Method of Accounting

The IRS's Large and Mid-size Business Division (LMSB) has issued a directive to auditors in the field warning that there is a growing trend within the construction industry in which taxpayers are using the completed contract method in situations where it doesn't apply or improperly deferring completion under this accounting method. The completed contract method of accounting is generally the preferred tax method used in the construction industry since it allows the taxpayer to defer the recognition of income and expenses until the contract is complete. In the directive, the IRS takes the position that when each home is sold, the contract is considered complete and income should be recognized. The abuse targeted by the IRS involves large master planned communities that take many years to complete. Taxpayers are

[23] LTR 200552012 (Sept. 27, 2005).

deferring income from the sale of the homes many years into the future (5, 10, 15 years or more). Therefore, the subsequent sale of one of these homes could be a taxable transaction long before the builder recognized income from the initial sale of the home. The IRS notes that this is an obvious abuse of the tax law. Therefore, the IRS has labeled this issue a mandatory audit issue to ensure consistent treatment and to prevent widespread abuse.[24]

.03 Look-back Method

For the look-back method, the recognition of income and expense must be postponed until the end of the first tax year in which you have incurred at least 10 percent of the actual total contract cost. Therefore, income and expense will be allocated to a different tax year if the first tax year that the 10 percent threshold is exceeded based on actual costs differs from the first tax year theat the 10 percent threshold is exceeded based on estimated costs [Code Sec. 460(b)(5)].

When a long-term contract is completed, you must "look back" and calculate taxes that would have been payable each year if actual total costs had been known [Code Secs. 460(b)(3)-(5); Reg. § 1.460-6]. You must pay interest on taxes that would have been due if actual total costs were known. Conversely, the IRS must pay you interest if taxes were overpaid for any year. The look-back method must be applied to the portion of any contract reported on the percentage of completion method. Form 8697 is used to compute the interest under the look-back method.

The first step of the look-back method is to reapply the percentage of completion method using actual contract price and costs rather than estimated contract price and costs. The second step requires you to recompute tax liability for each year of the contract using gross income as reallocated under the look-back method. If there is any difference between the recomputed tax liability and the tax liability as previously determined for a year, such difference is treated as a hypothetical underpayment or overpayment of tax to which you must apply a rate of interest equal to the overpayment rate, compounded daily. You will receive or pay interest if the net amount of interest applicable to hypothetical overpayments exceeds or is less than the amount of interest applicable to hypothetical underpayments.

The look-back method does not apply to: (a) any home construction contract; or (b) any other construction contract entered into by a taxpayer who:

- Estimates the contract will be completed within two years from the date the contract begins; and
- Has average annual gross receipts for the three tax years preceding the tax year in which the contract is entered into that do not exceed $10 million.

Also, the method does not apply to any contract completed within two years of the contract start date if the contract's gross price (as of contract completion) does not exceed the lesser of: (a) $1 million, or (b) 1 percent of the taxpayer's average annual gross receipts for the three tax years before the contract completion's tax year [Code Secs. 460(b)(3)(B), (e)].

[24] IRS Large and Mid Size Business Industry Directive on Super Completed Contract Method (April 5, 2007).

Example 19-17: Arco Corp., a calendar-year taxpayer, entered into a long-term contract that would be completed in two years. In the year the contract was entered into, the gross income reported on that contract by its using the percentage of completion method was $50,000. When the contract was completed, the profit that should have been reported in the year the contract was entered into was $90,000. Assume a 7 percent interest rate applied and that Arco is in the 35 percent tax bracket. For the contract year, Arco's tax underpayment was $14,000 [$40,000 ($90,000 – $50,000) × 35 percent]. Thus, Arco must pay $980 in interest on its tax underpayment for the contract year.

Election Not to Apply the Look-Back Method in *De Minimis* Cases

Manufacturers and construction contractors whose long-term contracts otherwise are subject to the look-back method, may elect not to apply the look-back method with respect to a long-term contract in *de minimis* cases. A *de minimis case* is a situation in which, for each prior contract year, there is only a 10 percent difference between the cumulative taxable income (or loss) under the contract using estimated contract price and costs and the cumulative taxable income (or loss) using actual contract price and costs [Code Sec. 460(b)(6); Reg. § 1.460-6(j)].

Thus, after making the election, when a long-term contract is completed, a taxpayer would be required to apply the first step of the look-back method (the reallocation of gross income using actual, rather than estimated, contract price and costs), but is not required to apply the additional steps of the look-back method if the application of the first step resulted in *de minimis* changes to the amount of income previously taken into account for each prior contract year.

Taxpayer should make the election not to apply the look-back method to long-term contracts in *de minimis* cases by attaching a statement to their timely filed federal income tax return (including extensions) for the tax year the election is effective or to an amended return for that year. This statement must have the legend "NOTIFICATION OF ELECTION UNDER SECTION 460(b)(6)"; provide the taxpayer's name and identifying number and the effective date of the election; and identify the trades or businesses that involve long-term contracts [Reg. § 1.460-6(j)].

The election applies to all long-term contracts completed during the tax year for which the election is made and to all long-term contract completed during subsequent tax years, unless the election is revoked with IRS consent [Code Sec. 460(b)(6)(D)].

An election not to apply the look-back method automatically revokes an election under Reg. § 1.460-6(e) to use the delay reapplication method [Reg. § 1.460-6(j)].

Example 19-18: Bruce Glasser enters into a three-year contract, and he has completed the work under the terms of the contract, he finds that the annual net income under the contract using the actual contract price and costs is $200,000, $300,000 and $500,000 respectively for years 1, 2, and 3 under the percentage of completion method. If Glasser makes the proper election, he need not apply the look-back method if he reported net income under the contract of between $180,000 and $220,000 as of the end of year 1, and between $270,000 and $330,000 as of the end of year 2.

Election Not to Reapply the Look-Back Method

A taxpayer also has the option of electing not to reapply the look-back method with respect to a contract, if, as of the close of any tax year after the contract is completed, the cumulative taxable income or loss under the contract is within 10 percent of the cumulative look-back income or loss as of the close of the most recent year in which the look-back method was applied (or would have applied but for the application of the *de minimis* exception described above). In applying this rule, amounts that are taken into account after completion of the contract are not discounted.

Thus, an electing taxpayer need not apply or reapply the look-back method if amounts that are taken into account after the completion of the contract are ***de minimis***.

The election applies to all long-term contracts completed during the tax year for which the election is made and to all long-term contracts completed during subsequent tax years, unless the election is revoked with IRS consent.

> **Example 19-19:** Tom Hall enters into a three-year contract and reports taxable income of $12,250, $15,000, and $12,750, respectively, for Years 1 through 3 of the contract. Upon completion of the contract, cumulative look-back income is $40,000 and 10 percent of this amount is $4,000. After the completion of the contract, Hall incurs additional costs of $2,500 in each of the next three succeeding years of the contract. Hall may elect not to reapply the look-back method for Year 4 because the cumulative amount of contract taxable income ($40,000 – $2,500 = $37,500) is within 10 percent of contract look-back income as of the completion of the contract ($40,000). Finally, Hall does not reapply the look-back method for Year 6 because the cumulative amount of contract taxable income ($32,500) is within 10 percent of contract look-back income as of the last application of the look-back method ($35,000).

In addition, when you apply the look-back method, only one rate of interest applies for each accrual period. An accrual period begins the day after the return due date (without extensions) for the tax year and ends on the return due date for the following tax year. The applicable rate of interest is the overpayment rate in effect for the calendar quarter in which the accrual period begins [Code Secs. 6621, 460(b)(2)(C)].

.04 Midcontract Change in Taxpayers Under Long-term Contract

The tax treatment following a midcontract change in taxpayers of a contract accounted for under a long-term contract method depends on whether the change is a ***constructive completion transaction*** or a ***step-in-the-shoes transaction.***

The step-in-the-shoes rules apply to the following transactions [Reg. § 1.460-4(k)(3)]:

1. Transfers to which Code Sec. 361 applies if the transfer is in connection with a tax-free reorganization described in Code Sec. 368(a)(1)(A), (C) or (F);
2. Transfers to which Code Sec. 361 applies if the transfer is in connection with a reorganization described in Code Sec. 368(a)(1)(D) or (G), provided the requirements of Code Sec. 354(b)(1)(A) and (B) are met;
3. Distributions to which Code Sec. 332 applies, provided the contract is transferred to an 80-percent distributee;

4. Transfers described in Code Sec. 351;
5. Transfers to which Code Sec. 361 applies if the transfer is in connection with a reorganization described in Code Sec. 368(a)(1)(D) with respect to which the requirements of Code Sec. 355 (or so much of Code Sec. 356 as relates to Code Sec. 355) are met;
6. Transfers (e.g., sales) of S corporation stock;
7. Conversion to or from an S corporation;
8. Members joining or leaving a consolidated group;
9. Contributions to which Code Sec. 721(a) applies;
10. A transfer of partnership interests; and
11. Distributions to which Code Sec. 731 applies (other than the distribution of the contract).

Constructive Completion Rules

The constructive completion rules apply to all other transactions [Reg. § 1.460-4(k)(2)]. In the constructive completion transaction, the old taxpayer is treated as completing the contract and the new taxpayer is treated as entering into a new contract on the transaction date. However, allocable contract costs do not include any consideration paid, or costs incurred, as a result of the transaction that are allocable to the contract.

In the case of a step-in-the-shoes transaction, the former taxpayer's obligation to account for the contract terminates on the date of the transaction and is assumed by the new taxpayer. The new taxpayer must assume the former taxpayer's methods of accounting for the contract, with both the contract price and allocable contract costs based on amounts taken into account by both parties [Reg. §§ 1.460-4(k)(3)(ii) and (iii)]. However, in the case of a tax avoidance transaction, the IRS may allocate income with respect to a transferred long-term contract between the previous and new taxpayers.

The amount of gain realized on a transfer of a contract is relevant, for example, in determining the amount of gain recognized with respect to the contract in a Section 351 transaction in which the former taxpayer receives from the new taxpayer money or property other than stock of the transferee [Reg. § 1.460-4(k)(3)(ii)(B)].

For constructive completion transactions, the look-back method is applied by the old taxpayer with respect to pretransaction years upon the transaction date and, if applicable, by the new taxpayer with respect to posttransaction years upon contract completion. For step-in-the-shoes transactions, the look-back method is applied only by the new taxpayer upon contract completion. The new taxpayer must account for pre- and posttransaction years, with special rules governing the calculation of look-back interest in the case of pre-transaction years. The former taxpayer in such cases must provide certain information to the new taxpayer in order to enable the new taxpayer to make the necessary look-back calculations.

Corporations— Tax Rates, Income, Deductions, Gains, and Losses

TAXING THE CORPORATION

What is a corporation? .... ¶20,001

How corporations are taxed ..... ¶20,005

Rate of tax .... ¶20,010

CORPORATE INCOME

Income of a corporation .... ¶20,015

Capital contributions .... ¶20,020

Property distributions received from other corporations .... ¶20,025

Other corporate income .... ¶20,030

Schedule M-3 (Form 1120) requiring corporations to reveal more aggressive transactions .... ¶20,035

CORPORATE DEDUCTIONS

Deductions of corporations in general .... ¶20,040

Special deductions for corporations .... ¶20,045

Dividends received from domestic corporations .... ¶20,050

Dividends received from foreign corporations .... ¶20,055

Dividends on certain public utility preferred stock .... ¶20,060

Limitations on dividends-received deductions .... ¶20,065

Charitable contributions .... ¶20,070

CAPITAL GAINS AND LOSSES OF CORPORATIONS

Capital gains and losses in general .... ¶20,075

Gain on disposition of depreciable property .... ¶20,080

PURCHASES, SALES AND DISTRIBUTIONS OF CORPORATE SECURITIES AND PROPERTIES

Corporation dealing in its own stock .... ¶20,085

Corporation dealing in its own obligations .... ¶20,090

Income from discharge of indebtedness .... ¶20,095

Effect of property distributions on corporation .... ¶20,100

Effects of distributions on corporation's earnings and profits .. ¶20,105

Allocating purchase price in asset sales .... ¶20,110

NET OPERATING LOSSES OF CORPORATIONS

What is a net operating loss? ..... ¶20,115

Net operating losses in general .. ¶20,120

Years to which a net operating loss may be carried .... ¶20,125

Figuring the net operating loss . . ¶20,130
Net operating loss carryover disallowed for substantial change of ownership . . . . ¶20,140

ACCUMULATED EARNINGS TAX

The accumulated earnings tax in general . . . . ¶20,145
Income subject to the tax . . . . ¶20,150
Avoiding the accumulated earnings tax . . . . ¶20,155

AFFILIATED AND RELATED CORPORATIONS

Affiliated corporations—consolidated returns . . . . ¶20,160
Controlled corporations—multiple tax limitations . . . . ¶20,165
Disallowance of benefits of graduated corporate rates and accumulated earnings credit . . . . . ¶20,170
Allocation among related corporations . . . . ¶20,175

TAXING THE CORPORATION

¶20,001 WHAT IS A CORPORATION?

A corporation is a taxable entity, separate and distinct from its owners or shareholders. Generally, if an organization is incorporated under state laws, it will be taxed as a corporation. However, for federal income tax purposes, a corporation need not be "incorporated." An association, joint-stock company, insurance company, or a trust or partnership that operates as an association or corporation may be treated as a corporation for federal income tax purposes even though it is not technically a "corporation" [Code Sec. 7701(a)(3); Reg. § 301.7701-2]. The following businesses will be taxed as corporations:

- A business formed under a federal or state law that refers to it as a corporation, body corporate, or body politic;
- A business formed under a state law that refers to it as a joint-stock company or joint-stock association;
- An insurance company;
- Certain banks;
- A business wholly owned by a state or local government;
- A business specifically required to be taxed as a corporation by the Internal Revenue Code (for example, certain publicly traded partnerships);
- Certain foreign businesses; and
- Any other business that elects to be taxed as a corporation by filing Form 8832.

.01 Classification of Business Entities Organized in Multiple Jurisdictions

Several jurisdictions have enacted provisions that enable a business entity to be treated as created or organized under the laws of more than one jurisdiction at the same time: a dual-chartered entity. The IRS takes the position that an entity organized in more than one jurisdiction is treated as a corporation for tax purposes if it takes a corporate form in any of those jurisdictions [Reg. § 301.7701-2(b)(9)]. Furthermore, a business entity organized both in the U.S. and in a foreign entity is treated a domestic entity for tax purposes [Reg. § 301.7701-5(a)].

.02 Check-the-Box for Entity Classification

Most unincorporated businesses (except a publicly traded partnerships) can simply check a box on Form 8832, *Entity Classification Election,* indicating whether they want to be taxed as a corporation or a partnership [Reg. §§ 1.761-1, 301.7701-1, 1.7701-2, 1.7701-3, 1.7701-4 and 1.7701-6]. The "check-the-box" regulations provide a simplified elective procedure for entities to be classified for federal tax purposes as partnerships, even if they have corporate characteristics [Reg. §§ 301.7701-1 through 301.7701-3]. Domestic and foreign business entities are no longer forced to figure out where they stand under the complex four-factor test that existed under the old Kintner regulations [See Ch. 30]. All revenue rulings and procedures that applied the archaic rules under the Kintner regulations are obsolete to the extent that they use the prior classification regulations to differentiate between partnerships and corporations.

The final check-the-box regulations make life simpler for limited liability companies (LLCs) that want to be taxed as partnerships. LLCs combine the limited liability benefit of corporations with the major tax benefit of doing business as a partnership—avoiding tax at the entity level and the ability to pass through taxable income, losses and credits to the partner level [¶ 24,001, ¶ 30,080].

The check-the-box regulations were created because the historical distinctions between corporations and partnerships were eroded by a rash of state statutes that afforded partnership tax status to unincorporated entities that looked much like corporations. For example, even though limited liability is an attribute normally associated with corporations, some state partnership statutes provide that no partner is liable for all of the debts of the partnership. As a result, taxpayers can achieve partnership tax status for businesses that, in all meaningful aspects, are virtually indistinguishable from a corporation.

For detailed discussion of the check-the-box regulations, see ¶ 30,080.

¶20,005 HOW CORPORATIONS ARE TAXED

.01 The Basic Framework

Corporations are subject to double taxation. The first level of tax must be paid by the corporation on its earnings. The second level of tax is due when the earnings are distributed to shareholders as dividends. Each shareholder must pay taxes separately on his or her share of the dividends [Code Secs. 11, 301(c)]. To make matters worse, the corporate is denied a deduction for distribution of dividends.

Most ordinary business corporations are subject to tax on a graduated tax rate structure. A penalty surtax, the accumulated earnings tax, may be imposed when a corporation retains earnings beyond the reasonable needs of the business [¶ 20,145 et seq.]. The corporation also may have to pay an alternative minimum tax [¶ 16,025–¶ 16,045].

.02 Corporate Estimated Tax

A corporation must make four estimated tax payments throughout the year if it expects its tax to be $500 or more. Generally, each payment must be at least 25 percent of the required annual payment. The required annual payment is 100 percent of the tax shown on the return for the current tax year. Corporations with assets of $1 billion or more must also pay 100 percent of the amount due. However, certain small corporations may base the required annual payment on 100 percent of the tax shown on the return for the preceding tax year if this amount is less. Corporations may elect to use an annualized income installment or an adjusted seasonal installment if the installment is less than the amount computed under the general rules [Code Sec. 6655]. If a corporation fails to pay a correct installment of estimated tax by the due date, it is generally subject to an underpayment penalty [Code Sec. 6655]. The installments generally can be based on a pro rata portion of the corporation's estimated annual tax liability. Alternatively, the quarterly installments can be based on the corporation's annualized taxable income or the corporation's adjusted seasonal taxable income.

When Installment Payments are Due

For calendar-year corporations, the due dates for estimated tax payments are:

Required Installment	*Due Date*
1st	April 15
2nd	June 15
3rd	September 15
4th	December 15

The estimated tax installments of corporations using fiscal years are due on the 15th day of the fourth, sixth, ninth, and twelfth months of the tax year [Code Sec. 6655(i)]. If any due date falls on a weekend or legal holiday, the next regular workday is substituted.

.03 Corporate Tax Returns

Unless exempt from taxation, all domestic corporations including corporations in bankruptcy must file an income tax return on Form 1120 each year, whether or not they have income. An S corporation [Ch. 21] uses Form 1120S. Corporations with tax preferences use Form 4626, *Alternative Minimum Tax—Corporations*, to determine alternative minimum tax liability [Ch. 16]. Consolidated returns are discussed in ¶20,160. Also see Ch. 26 for additional filing requirements for corporations. The due date for the corporate return is March 15 for calendar year corporations and the 15th day of the third month following the close of the fiscal year for corporations on the fiscal-year basis.

Uncertain Tax Position Schedule

Corporations must report uncertain tax positions on Form 1120, Schedule UTP, *Uncertain Tax Position Statement* with Form 1120 if the corporation has total assets that equal or exceed $50 million [Reg. § 1.6012-2(a)(4)].

Although the requirement to file Schedule UTP will ultimately apply to corporations with at least $10 million in assets, the requirement will be phased-in over a five-year period. The asset threshold is expected to reach $10 million in 2014, but is only $50 million in 2013.

Schedule UTP requires a "concise description" of each UTP for which a corporation or related entity has recorded a reserve in an audited financial statement, or for which no reserve has been recorded because of expected litigation. A related party is any entity that has a relationship to the corporation described in the rules for transactions between related parties [Code Sec. 267(b)].

A "concise description" must provide the relevant facts affecting the tax treatment of the position, and information that will apprise the IRS of the identity of the tax position and the nature of the issue. The description should not exceed a few sentences and should not assess the hazards of litigation. The IRS will view a description as inadequate if it merely indicated that an issue was unsettled, but did not describe the issue or any of the facts.

If a reserve is not recorded based on expectation to litigate, the UTP must be reported if the tax position is one which the corporation or related party determines that the probability of settling with the IRS is less than 50 percent and, under applicable accounting standards, no reserve was recorded in the audited financial statements because the corporation intends to litigate and it has determined that it is more likely than not to prevail on the merits in the litigation.

The initial reporting of a reserve will trigger reporting of the tax position taken on the return, but subsequent reserve increases or decreases related to the tax position will not require reporting.

The taxpayer must rank by size the reported tax positions (including transfer pricing and other valuation positions). The size of the tax position is based on the amount of the U.S. federal income tax reserve (including interest and penalties separately identified in the books and records as associated with the particular position) recorded for that position. The taxpayer must also designate the tax positions for which the reserve exceeds 10 percent of the aggregate amount of the reserves for all tax positions reported on the schedule. If a reserve is recorded for multiple tax positions, then a reasonable allocation of that reserve among the tax positions to which it relates must be made in determining the size of each tax position.

.04 Special Treatment Corporations

Certain corporations are taxed in different ways, at different rates or with additional deductions. These include:

- S corporations [Ch. 21];
- Personal holding companies [Ch. 23];
- Regulated investment companies (RICs) [Ch. 23];
- Real estate investment trusts (REITs) [Ch. 23];
- Real estate mortgage investment conduits [Ch. 23];
- Private foundations [Ch. 23];
- Exempt organizations with unrelated business income [Ch. 23];
- Farmers' cooperatives [Ch. 23]; and
- Foreign corporations [Ch. 28].

.05 Transfers to Controlled Corporations—Section 351 Exchanges

Code Sec. 351 provides that taxpayers (individuals or groups) will not recognize gain if they transfer property (or money and property) to a corporation (being formed or already formed) in exchange for stock of that corporation if they "control" the corporation after the exchange [exception: nonqualified preferred stock is not treated as stock transferred for property] [Code Sec. 351(g)(2); see ¶22,055.03 for further discussion]. The requisite control exists if the shareholders own 80 percent of the corporation's voting stock and 80 percent of each class of non-voting stock after the exchange. Any property other than stock of the corporation will be considered boot and will be subject to tax. In addition, the Code Sec. 351 exchange must have economic substance and service a legitimate business purpose.

In *Shell Petroleum, Inc.*,[1] a federal district court found that an oil producing taxpayer was entitled to a federal income tax refund of nearly $19 million, plus interest based on the carryback of consolidated net capital losses. The court found that the taxpayer's restructuring transaction qualified for nonrecognition of gain or loss under Code Sec. 351(a) and that its business purpose withstood the IRS's sham transaction argument. The taxpayer engaged in a restructuring transaction in which exploration and production assets (producing and non-producing properties) were transferred to a newly formed subsidiary in exchange for shares of auction-preferred stock sold to unrelated investors. The court found the transaction to have economic substance in that it served a legitimate business purpose by increasing cash flow and preserving long-term properties even though the transaction was structured to maximize tax benefits.

The tax-free treatment will not apply in the following situations:

- The corporation is an investment company such as a regulated investment company, a real estate investment trust or a corporation with substantial investment property [Code Sec. 351(e); Reg. § 1.351-1(c)(1)];
- Property is transferred in a bankruptcy or similar proceeding in exchange for stock used to pay creditors; and
- The stock is received in exchange for the corporation's debt (other than a security) or for interest on the corporation's debt (including a security) that accrued while the debt was held.

Tax Filing Reminder

Both the corporation and any person involved in a nontaxable exchange of property for stock must attach to their income tax returns a complete statement of all facts pertinent to the exchange as discussed in Reg. § 1.351-3.

Control

To be in control of a corporation, the investor or group of investors must own, immediately after the exchange, at least 80 percent of the total combined voting power of all classes of stock entitled to vote and at least 80 percent of the outstanding shares of each class of nonvoting stock outstanding [Code Sec. 368(c); Reg. § 1.351-1(a)].

---

[1] *Shell Petroleum, Inc.*, DC-TX, 2008-2 USTC ¶50,422.

Example 20-1: Mr. Hunter owned 2,000 of the 3,000 shares of voting common stock of Homer Corporation, and 85 of the 100 shares of nonvoting preferred stock. Hunter transfers property to the corporation, in return for which the corporation gives him 7,000 shares of newly issued common stock. No gain is recognized because Hunter is now in control of the corporation. He owns 90 percent of the voting stock (9,000 of 10,000) and 85 percent of the other class of stock (85 of 100 shares).

Example 20-2: When starting up a corporation, Mr. Whitman contributed a building worth $200,000 (his basis in it is $50,000) in exchange for 200 shares of stock, and Mr. Bloom contributed equipment worth $100,000 in exchange for 100 shares. The corporation issued no other stock at that time. No gain or loss is recognized on the transaction since Whitman and Bloom are controlling shareholders after the exchange.

The nonrecognition provision applies only to *contributed property*. It does not apply to services rendered or to be rendered to the corporation. Note that the value of stock received for services is income to the recipient. The nonrecognition provisions do not apply to unsecured debts and claims against the corporation for accrued but unpaid interest on a debt [Code Sec. 351(d)]. The term *property* for purposes of the nonrecognition provisions does not include property of a relatively small value when compared to the value of stock and securities already owned or to be received for services by the transferor if the main purpose of the transfer is to qualify for nonrecognition of gain. Property transferred will not be considered to be of relatively small value if its fair market value is at least 10 percent of the fair market value of the stock and securities already owned or to be received for services by the transferor.

Example 20-3: Mr. Smith contributed property worth $4,000 and services worth $6,000 in exchange for 10 shares of stock with a fair market value of $10,000. If he is a controlling shareholder, Smith would owe tax on the $6,000 of stock received in exchange for services, but not on the stock he received in exchange for the property.

Successive Transfers Permissible

In Rev. Rul. 2003-51,[2] the IRS concluded that a transfer of assets to a domestic corporation in exchange for an amount of stock in the corporation, which constituted control, satisfied the control requirement of Code Sec. 351 even though, pursuant to a binding agreement entered into by the transferor with a third party prior to the exchange, the transferor transferred the stock of the corporation to another corporation simultaneously with the transfer of assets by the third party to the second corporation, and immediately thereafter, the transferor and the third party were in control of the second corporation. Even though the first transfer was followed by a transfer of the stock received, treatment of the first transfer as a transfer described in Code Sec. 351 was not inconsistent with the purposes of that provision. The transfers qualified as

[2] Rev. Rul. 2003-51, 2003-1 CB 938.

successive transfers. Accordingly, the second transfer did not cause the first transfer to fail to satisfy the control requirement of Code Sec. 351.

Nonqualified Preferred Stock

Nonqualified preferred stock is treated as property other than stock for purposes of Code Sec. 351. Generally, it is preferred stock if it possesses any of the following features:

- The holder has the right to require the issuer or a related person to redeem or buy the stock;
- The issuer or a related person is required to redeem or buy the stock;
- The issuer or a related person has the right to redeem or buy the stock and, on the issue date, it is more likely than not that the right will be exercised; or
- The dividend rate on the stock varies with reference to interest rates, commodity prices, or similar indices [Code Sec. 351(g)(2)].

Illusory participation rights. In order for stock to be treated as participating in corporate growth to any significant extent (and, thus, avoid being classified as preferred stock for purposes of Code Sec. 351), there must be a real and meaningful likelihood that the shareholder will actually participate in the earnings and growth of the corporation [Code Sec. 351(g)(3)(A)]. This clarification was added to thwart possible attempts by some taxpayers to avoid characterization of an instrument as nonqualified preferred stock by including illusory participation rights or including terms that the taxpayers could argue create an unlimited dividend.

Example 20-4: ABCo has two classes of stock: Class A Common and Class A Preferred. The preferred stock has preferential rights on liquidation and is entitled to the same dividends as may be declared on the common stock. If ABCo pays no dividends to holders of the common and preferred stock, Class A Preferred will be classified as nonqualified preferred stock.

Example 20-5: The preferred stock of BabCO entitles shareholders to a dividend equal to the greater of 7 percent or the dividends that common stock shareholders receive. If the common stock shareholders are not expected to receive dividends greater than 7 percent, BabCo's preferred stock will be classified as nonqualified preferred stock.

Disproportionate Exchanges

When more than one person transfers property to the corporation in exchange for corporate stock, the stock they receive need not be in the same proportion as the property they contribute. However, the transaction will be recharacterized, according to its true nature, as though (1) the exchanges had been proportionate and (2) the shareholder who received stock of lesser value than the property transferred made a gift or paid compensation or extinguished a debt to the shareholder who received the larger amount [Reg. § 1.351-1(b)].

Example 20-6: Mr. Alexander and Mr. Benton organize a corporation with 1,000 shares of common stock. Alexander transfers property worth $10,000 in exchange for 200 shares of stock while Benton transfers property worth $10,000 to the corporation in exchange for 800 shares of stock. No gain or loss is recognized. However, Alexander is deemed to have transferred 300 shares (worth $6,000) to Benton. If Benton had worked for Alexander, the disproportionate exchange would be taxed as compensation. If, say, Benton were Alexander's son and the deemed transfer was gratuitous, it would be treated as a gift.

.06 Assumption of Liabilities in Section 351 Exchanges

The Code Sec. 351 exchange of property for stock in a controlled corporation will still be tax-free even if the corporation assumes a liability of the transferor [Code Sec. 357(a); see Ch. 22]. The term *liability* includes any fixed or contingent obligation to make payment [Code Sec. 358(h)(3)]. A recourse liability is treated as assumed if the transferor has agreed to and is expected to satisfy the liability, whether or not the transferor has been relieved of the liability [Code Sec. 357(d)(1)(A)]. For further discussion, see Ch. 22. If the assumption of liabilities has no real business purpose or if the main purpose in the exchange is tax avoidance, the assumption of the total liability is treated as a cash payment by the corporation to the transferor [Code Sec. 357(b)(1)]. In addition, if the total liabilities assumed exceeds the total of the adjusted basis of the property transferred, then the excess will be treated as a gain from the sale of the property (capital or not as the case may be) [Code Sec. 357(c)(1); Reg. §§1.357-1, -2]. Reason: Code Sec. 357(c) provides that contributing property with liabilities in excess of basis can trigger immediate recognition of gain in the amount of the excess. The Code treats discharging a liability the same as receiving money because the taxpayer improves his economic position when he exchanges property that is encumbered by debt. If the liabilities assumed give rise to a deduction when paid, such as trade account payable or interest, they will not be treated as liabilities for purposes of Code Sec. 357(c)(1), and no gain will be recognized [Code Sec. 357(c)(3)]. The taxpayer's basis in the stock of the controlled corporation is not reduced by the assumption of such liabilities. In Rev. Rul. 95-74,[3] the IRS concluded that the assumption of certain contingent liabilities for soil and groundwater remediation would not result in gain because the assumed liabilities would give rise to a later deduction.

Contingent Liabilities

In *Coltec Industries, Inc.*,[4] the transfer of a note in exchange for assumption of contingent asbestos liabilities had no meaningful purpose and so was ignored for tax purposes under the economic substance doctrine.

In *Black & Decker Corp.*,[5] the court concluded that a contingent liability that was transferred fell within the Code Sec. 357(c)(3) exception to the excess basis rule for liability the payment of which would give rise to a deduction. Therefore, the liabilities

[3] Rev. Rul. 95-74, 1995-2 CB 36.

[4] *Coltec Industries, Inc.*, CA-FC, 2006-2 USTC ¶50,389, 454 F3d 1340.

[5] *Black & Decker Corp.*, CA-4, 2006-1 USTC ¶50,142, 436 F3d 431, *aff'g in part, rev'g in part and rem'g* DC decisions; *cert. denied* 2/20/07, *rev'g and rem'g*, DC-MD, 2004-2 USTC ¶50,390.

transferred did not reduce stock basis. Note: This case was decided prior to the enactment of Code Sec. 358(h), which would have required the taxpayer to reduce its basis by the amount of the transferred liabilities.

Nonrecourse liabilities are treated as assumed by the transferee of the property to which the nonrecourse liability is subject [Code Sec. 357(d)(1)(B)]. The amount of the nonrecourse liability is reduced by the lesser of (1) the amount of liability which an owner of other assets has not transferred and has agreed with the transferee to, and is expected to, satisfy, or (2) the fair market value of such other assets [Code Sec. 357(d)(2)(B)].

Example 20-7: Mr. Baker transfers property with a $5,000 adjusted basis to his controlled corporation in exchange for stock worth $6,000. The corporation agrees to assume a $3,000 liability on the property and gives Baker $1,000 of cash. Thus, Baker received consideration worth $10,000. His realized gain is $4,000. But his recognized gain is $1,000 (cash received). If the exchange is tax-motivated, though, Baker's recognized gain is $4,000 (cash plus liability assumed). All or part of a recourse liability is deemed to be assumed if the transferee has agreed to, and is expected to, satisfy the liability whether or not the transferor is relieved of the liability [Code Sec. 357(d)(1)(A)]. This determination is made based on the facts and circumstances [Code Sec. 357(d)(1)(A)].

Example 20-8: Donald Peracchi contributed to a controlled corporation land with liabilities in excess of his basis in the property. In an effort to avoid a tax problem under Code Sec. 357(c), Peracchi also executed a promissory note, promising to pay the corporation over a million over a term of ten years at 11 percent interest. The court concluded that he had a basis of over a million dollars in the note, which was its face value. Since, the aggregate liabilities of the property contributed to the corporation do not exceed its basis, Peracchi did not recognize any gain under Code Sec. 357(c). The court found that the transfer of Peracchi's note to the controlled corporation had substantial economic effect because of the possibility that the business might go into bankruptcy and have to be enforced.[6]

The taxpayer recognizes gain to the extent that the liabilities assumed exceed the total of the adjusted basis of the property transferred to the controlled corporation [Code Sec. 357(c)]. The assumption of liabilities by the controlled corporation generally reduces the taxpayer's basis in the stock of the controlled corporation. If the corporation assumes a liability of the transferor, the person who transferred the property is considered to have received taxable gain up to the fair market value of the liability that was assumed. Thus, he subtracts the liability in figuring his basis [Code Sec. 358(d)(1); Reg. § 1.358-3]. Transfers of liabilities that would be deductible by the shareholder when paid (e.g., accounts payable) or of certain liquidating payments to a retiring partner [Ch. 24] are not counted as liabilities [Code Secs. 357(c)(3), 358(d)(2)]. If Code Sec. 357(c) gain is realized when a nonrecourse liability is assumed by the transferee

[6] *D.J. Peracchi*, CA-9, 98-1 USTC ¶ 50,374, 143 F3d 487.

corporation and all of the property to which the debt is subject is not transferred by the transferor, then the basis step-up is limited to the amount of gain that would have been recognized if only a pro rata portion of the liability were assumed [Code Sec. 362(d)(2)].

Basis Determination

The corporation's basis in the property acquired from a controlling shareholder is the shareholder's basis in the property, increased by any gain recognized by the shareholder on the exchange [Code Sec. 362(a)].

The shareholder's basis in the stock received is the same as the basis of the property exchanged, increased by any gain recognized on the transaction, and decreased by the fair market value of any other property or money received in the exchange and any loss recognized on the exchange [Code Sec. 358(a); Reg. § 1.358-1].

> **Example 20-9:** Mr. Trent transfers property to Sutton Corp. in exchange for its controlling stock worth $150,000. Trent's adjusted basis in the property was $100,000. His basis in the Sutton Corp. stock is $100,000.

> **Example 20-10:** Same facts as Example 20-9, except that Sutton gives Trent $5,000 in addition to the stock. Trent has a recognized gain of $5,000 (since the money is not covered by the nonrecognition provision). His basis in the stock is still $100,000 ($100,000 basis in stock less $5,000 cash received plus $5,000 recognized gain).

> **Example 20-11:** Mr. Smith transferred property with an adjusted basis of $500,000 and subject to a mortgage of $100,000 to a controlled corporation in a nontaxable exchange. He received stock worth $550,000. His basis for the stock is $400,000 (the $500,000 adjusted basis of the property transferred less the $100,000 mortgage).

Code Sec. 358(h) provides that the basis of stock received in a tax-free transfer to a controlled corporation is reduced (but not below the stock's fair market value) by the amount of any liability that: (1) is assumed in exchange for the stock, and (2) did not otherwise reduce the transferor's basis in the stock because of the assumption. The amount of liability is determined as of the date of the exchange. The purpose of this provision is to limit taxpayers from accelerating or duplicating losses through the assumption of liabilities. Except as provided by the IRS, this rule does not apply if, as part of the exchange, the trade or business associated with the liability is also transferred to the corporation.

> **Example 20-12:** Ann Marlboro transfers assets with an adjusted basis and fair market value of $100 to her wholly-owned corporation and the corporation assumes $40 of liability (the payment of which would give rise to a deduction). Thus, the value of the stock received by Ann is $60. The basis of Ann's stock is $60. No basis reduction is required because of the assumption of the liability because payment of the liability would give rise to a deduction.

Filing Requirement

Both the shareholder and controlled corporation taking part in the exchange must file a statement describing the pertinent facts with their income tax returns for the year of the exchange [Reg. § 1.351-3].

¶20,010 RATE OF TAX

.01 Current Corporate Tax Rates

Corporations are subject to tax on their taxable income as shown in the following Table 1 [Code Secs. 11, 1201].

Table 1. Corporate Tax Rates

If taxable income is: Over	But not over	Tax is	Of the amount over
$ 0	$ 50,000	15%	$ 0
50,000	75,000	$7,500 + 25%	50,000
75,000	100,000	13,750 + 34%	75,000
100,000	335,000	22,250 + 39%	100,000
335,000	10,000,000	113,900 + 34%	335,000
10,000,000	15,000,000	3,400,000 + 35%	10,000,000
15,000,000	18,333,333	5,150,000 + 38%	15,000,000
18,333,333		35%	

.02 Personal Service Corporations Taxed at Flat 35 Percent Rate

Personal service corporations (PSCs) are denied the benefits of the graduated corporate rate structure outlined above. Instead they are taxed at a flat 35 percent income tax rate [Code Sec. 11(b)(2)]. A *personal service corporation* is any corporation in which:

- Substantially all of the corporation's activities involve the performance of services in the fields of health, law, engineering, architecture, accounting, actuarial science, performing arts, or consulting [Code Sec. 448(d)(2)(A); Temp. Reg. § 1.448-1T(e)(4)(i) (the function test)]; and
- At least 95 percent of the corporation's stock is owned directly or indirectly by: (a) employees performing services, (b) retired employees who had performed the personal services, (c) any estate of the employee or retiree described in (a) or (b) above, or (d) any person who acquired the stock of the corporation as a result of the death of an employee or retiree (but only for the 2-year period beginning on the date of the employee's or retiree's death [Code Sec. 448(d)(2)(B); Temp. Reg. § 1.448-1T(e)(5)(i) (the ownership test)[7]].

The IRS has the authority to reallocate a PSC's income deductions and other tax allowances if two requirements are met:

[7] Treasury shares should be disregarded in applying the ownership test under the PSC rules. *Robertson Strong & Apgar Architects, PC*, TC Summary Opinion 2007-48.

- Substantially all of the corporation's services are performed for or on behalf of a single other corporation, partnership or entity; and
- The principal purpose for forming or using the PSC is the avoidance of federal income tax by reducing the income of any employee-owner or by securing for such person the benefit of a tax allowance that would not otherwise be available [Code Sec. 269A(a); Reg. § 1.269A-1(a)]. See Ch. 18, Ch. 30.

Example 20-13: The Tax Court concluded in *Alron Engineering & Testing Corporation*,[8] that a corporation engaged in geotechnical testing and engineering services was not a PSC after concluding that geotechnical testing was not within the field of engineering because it did not require the same education, training, and mastery as engineering. There were no standard minimum requirements to provide geotechnical testing services under state law, and technicians were not bound by state or board licensing or review. Although geotechnical testing data could be used in the corporation's engineering analysis, the data could be used for other purposes and by other parties as well. Thus the two lines of services could function mutually exclusively. Thus the court concluded that since geotechnical testing was not in the field of engineering, 95 percent of the corporation's time was not devoted or incident to the field of engineering.

Example 20-14: The Tax Court concluded in *Lykins*,,[9] that a corporation providing investment and accounting services was not a PSC because less than 95 percent of the time of the corporation's employees was spent on the accounting services. Thus substantially all of the corporation's activities were not performed in a qualifying field under Code Sec. 448(d)(2), and the function test of the PSC definition was not met.

In *Rainbow Tax Services, Inc.*,[10] the Tax Court concluded that a bookkeeping and tax return preparation business was engaged in providing accounting services and therefore qualified as a PSC even though the accounting services performed by the taxpayer did not require a CPA license. The court noted that the tax return preparation activities performed by the taxpayer required extracting information relating to financial transactions, analyzing that information, and then summarizing and reporting that information on a tax return. The court concluded that these activities clearly qualified as services in the field of accounting. [Temp. Reg. § 1.448-1T(e)(5)(vii), Ex. 1(i)].

In *W.W. Eure, M.D., Inc.*,[11] the Tax Court concluded that a professional medical corporation, incorporated under state law, that operated as a radiation oncology treatment facility was a PSC because 95 percent or more of its employees' time was spent providing healthcare directly to patients or performing incidental services.

---

[8] *Alron Eng'g & Testing Corp.*, 80 TCM 603, Dec. 54,102(M), TC Memo. 2000-335.

[9] *Ron Lykins, Inc.*, 91 TCM 804, Dec. 56,441(M), TC Memo. 2006-35.

[10] *Rainbow Tax Services*, 128 TC 42, Dec. 56,860(M) (2007).

[11] *W.W. Eure, M.D., Inc.*, 93 TCM 1237, Dec. 56,938(M), TC Memo. 2007-124.

In *Calpo Hom & Dong Architects, Inc.*,[12] the Tax Court concluded that a corporation that provided architectural services was a PSC because the corporation met the ownership test since it was 100 percent owned by licensed architects. The corporation also met the function test because 95 percent of its time was devoted to the performance of services in the field of architecture.

In *Grutman-Mazler Engineering Inc.*,[13] an engineering company was a qualified personal service corporation subject to a flat 35-percent income tax rate because it satisfied both the function and ownership. The function test was satisfied because 95 percent or more of its employees' time was spent providing engineering services, as defined by state law, or services incidental to engineering services. The ownership test was met because all of the company's stock was held by employees performing services in connection with a qualifying field, in this case, engineering, which included surveying and mapping.

In *Kraatz & Craig Surveying, Inc.*,[14] the Tax Court concluded that a land surveying corporation was performing services in the field of engineering and was thus a PSC. The court found that both legislative history and the dictionary supported the inclusion of surveying and mapping in the definition of engineering in Temporary Reg. § 1.448-1T(e)(4).

.03 Corporations and Alternative Minimum Tax

Corporations are separate taxable entities and are subject to an alternative minimum tax (AMT). To calculate a corporation's AMT, use the format outlined in ¶ 16,025. The adjustments pertaining only to individuals (e.g., personal and dependency exemptions, home equity indebtedness, and medical expenses) do not apply. Instead, corporations are subject to several special adjustments.

> ▶ **TAX RETURN TIP:** Taxpayers should report a corporation's AMT liability (unless it qualifies for the small corporation exception discussed below) on Form 4626.

.04 Small Corporations Exempt from AMT

Small business corporations are exempt from the corporate AMT [Code Sec. 55(e)]. Some businesses that fit into the definition of small corporation will therefore be able to avoid an added level of complexity that vexes taxpayers subject to the AMT. Moreover, the companies will also avoid the compliance costs associated with being subjected to the dreaded AMT.

A corporation will qualify as a *small corporation* and be exempt from the AMT if it satisfies a so-called *gross receipts test*. According to this test, the corporation's AMT bill will be zero for a tax year if that year is the corporation's first tax year in existence (regardless of its gross receipts for the year) or:

- That tax year is one of the corporation's first three tax years and its average annual gross receipts for those years does not exceed $5,000,000; or

---

[12] *Calpo, Hom & Dong Architects, Inc.*, 93 TCM 1306, Dec. 56,956(M), TC Memo. 2007-140. *See also Robertson Strong & Apgar Architects, PC*, TC Summary Opinion 2007-48.

[13] *Grutman-Mazler Engineering, Inc.*, 95 TCM 1551, Dec. 57,450(M), TC Memo. 2008-140.

[14] *Kraatz & Craig Surveying, Inc.*, 134 TC 167, Dec. 58,178 (2010).

- Its average annual gross receipts for all three-tax-year periods beginning after 1993 and ending before that tax year does not exceed $7.5 million [Code Sec. 55(e)(1)].

For detailed discussion, see ¶ 16,025.

CORPORATE INCOME

¶ 20,015 INCOME OF A CORPORATION

Generally, gross income of a domestic corporation includes the same items and is figured in the same way as gross income of an individual. A *domestic corporation* is one that is created or organized in the United States or under the laws of the United States or of any other state or territory [Code Sec. 7701(a)(4)]. A *foreign corporation* is one that is not domestic [Code Sec. 7701(a)(5)].

.01 Taxable Income

Corporate taxable income is gross income less the deductions allowed to corporations [¶ 20,040]. There is no intermediary step of calculating an adjusted gross income. The following are the major sources of corporate income:

- Gross profit from sales [Ch. 17];
- Dividends [Ch. 2];
- Interest [Ch. 2];
- Rents and royalties [Ch. 2]; and
- Gains and losses [¶ 20,075, ¶ 20,080, ¶ 20,110-¶ 20,140].

These additional factors must be considered in determining corporate income:

- Receipts that are contributions to capital [¶ 20,020];
- Property distributions received by corporations [¶ 20,025];
- Rentals paid to shareholders of a lessor corporation [¶ 20,030]; and
- Income from a sinking fund [¶ 20,030].

¶ 20,020 CAPITAL CONTRIBUTIONS

A contribution of money or property to the capital of a corporation will be excluded from the corporation's gross income, regardless of whether it was made by a shareholder or by nonshareholder outsiders. The exclusion is not available unless the motivation behind a contribution was a capital improvement made to strengthen the capital structure of the corporation. If a contributor to the capital of a corporation receives goods or services in return, the contributions may not be excluded from the corporation's income [Code Sec. 118(a)].

.01 Contributions by Shareholders

If a corporation requires additional capital for conducting its business, and obtains these funds through voluntary pro rata payments from shareholders, the amounts received are not income [Reg. § 1.118-1]. They are capital contributions and are added to the stock's cost. The corporation's basis in property acquired as a contribution to capital is generally the same as the shareholder's basis, see Ch. 6. One court held that a shareholder can create basis in his C corporation by contributing a unsecured negotiable promissory note to the business.[15] The court examined the note closely and found that it was an ordinary, negotiable, recourse obligation which must be treated as genuine debt for tax purposes because:

- The taxpayer was creditworthy and was likely to have the funds to pay the promissory note if necessary;
- The value of the note was its face value since it had a fixed term and a market rate of interest commensurate with the taxpayer's creditworthiness. In addition, nothing in the record suggested that the corporation couldn't borrow against the note to raise cash; and
- The note was fully transferable and enforceable by third parties, such as hostile creditors of the corporation. By increasing his personal exposure to the creditors of the company, the taxpayer increased his economic investment in the corporation, and a corresponding increase in basis was therefore justified.

.02 Contributions by Nonshareholders

Any contributions made by nonshareholders are also not considered income to the corporation. The following special rules govern these contributions:

Property Other Than Money

When a nonshareholder contributes property other than money (for example, land contributed by a governmental unit to induce the corporation to locate its business in a particular community), the corporation's basis in the property is zero [Code Sec. 362(c)(1)].

Property Acquired with Money Contributions

If a nonshareholder makes a capital contribution of money, the corporation's basis in any property bought with the money during the 12 months after the contribution is reduced by the contribution. Any money not used during that period reduces the corporation's basis in other property held at the end of the 12-month period in the following order:

1. Depreciable property;
2. Property subject to amortization;
3. Property subject to depletion (except percentage depletion);
4. Other property.

The corporation's basis in property for each category must be reduced to zero before going to the next category. The basis of property in each category is reduced in proportion to the relative bases of the properties, but a different adjustment may be made if the IRS consents. Request for the change should be filed with the return for the tax year the property was transferred to the corporation [Code Sec. 362(c)(2); Reg. § 1.362-2(c)].

---

[15] *D.J. Peracchi*, CA-9, 98-1 USTC ¶50,374, 143 F3d 487, *rev'g and rem'g* TC.

Example 20-15: On February 14, the local development council gives $25,000 to XYZ Corporation to induce it to keep its office in town. XYZ's total basis in depreciable property is $500,000. If, one year later, XYZ has not yet purchased any property with the money, it must reduce its total basis in the depreciable property by $25,000.

Contribution to Water and Sewerage Utilities in Aid of Construction

Code Sec. 118(c) provides special rules for water and sewage disposal utilities. A regulated public utility that provides water or sewerage disposal services is allowed to treat any amount of money or property received from any person as a tax-free contribution to capital if such amount: (1) was a contribution in aid of construction (which does not include a connection fee), and (2) was not included in the taxpayer's rate base for rate-making purposes.

¶20,025 PROPERTY DISTRIBUTIONS RECEIVED FROM OTHER CORPORATIONS

If the company owns stock in another corporation, the company takes into income the fair market value of in-kind property distributions. However, that amount is reduced (but not below zero) by: (1) any liability of the distributing corporation assumed by the company in connection with the distribution, and (2) any liability to which the property is subject immediately before and after the distribution [Code Sec. 301(b); Reg. § 1.301-1(g)].

The company's basis in the property it receives in the distribution is the property's fair market value [Code Sec. 301(d)].

¶20,030 OTHER CORPORATE INCOME

Two common types of income also taxable to a company are corporate rental income paid to shareholders and income from a sinking fund.

.01 Corporate Rental Income Paid Directly to Shareholders

If the company leases property to others, the rent is taxable to it, even though the rent is paid directly to its shareholders and bondholders.[16] This applies even if the lease is in perpetuity and without a condition defeating its force or operation.[17]

Example 20-16: Acme Construction Co. leased property to Baker Construction Co., the annual rental being $500,000. Instead of paying $500,000 to Acme, Baker paid $200,000 to Acme's shareholders and $300,000 to its bondholders. The transaction is treated as if the following had been done: (1) Baker paid the

---

[16] *Rensselaer & Saratoga R.R. Co.*, CA-2, 1 USTC ¶15, 249 Fed. 726, *cert. denied*, 246 US 671, 38 SCt 424.

[17] *Joliet & C.R.. Co.*, SCt, 42-1 USTC ¶9222, 315 US 44, 62 SCt 442.

$500,000 rent to Acme (which must include it in income), and (2) Acme then paid a dividend of $200,000 to its shareholders and $300,000 to its bondholders.

The rent is constructively received by the lessor corporation. Its shareholders may be held liable as transferees for the corporation's tax on the rental income[18] [Ch. 27].

.02 Income from a Sinking Fund

If the company issues bonds, it may establish a sinking fund to pay the debt. Usually, the corporation must make payments at stated intervals to a trustee appointed for this purpose. Property in the fund is a corporate asset and the company reports any income or gain from it [Reg. § 1.61-13(b)].

Example 20-17: Widget Co. issues $500,000 of ten-year bonds to purchase some new equipment. Each year, Widget deposits $40,000 in a sinking fund to accumulate cash to pay off the bonds when they mature. Income earned on money in the sinking fund must be included in Widget's gross income.

¶20,035 SCHEDULE M-3 (FORM 1120) REQUIRING CORPORATIONS TO REVEAL MORE AGGRESSIVE TRANSACTIONS

A corporation with total assets (non-consolidated or consolidated for all corporations included within a tax consolidation group) of $10 million or more on the last day of the tax year must complete Schedule M-3 (Form 1120), *Net Income (Loss) Reconciliation for Corporations With Total Assets of $10 Million or More.* Corporations and partnerships with less than $10 million in total assets not otherwise required to file Schedule M-3 are currently permitted to voluntarily file Schedule M-3. These taxpayers may continue to voluntarily file Schedule M-3 and may elect to file Schedule M-3 Parts I, II, and III or to file Schedule M-3 Part I and to file Schedule M-1 in place of Schedule M-3 Parts II and III. These corporations and partnerships will not be required to file Form 1120 Schedule B, Form 1065 Schedule C, or Form 8916-A.

Corporations must use Schedule M-3 to reconcile income and deductions from their financial statement and tax return. The form is designed to improve the transparency of corporate transactions, identify taxpayers who may have engaged in aggressive transactions, and target high-risk taxpayers for audit.

.01 Who Must Complete Schedule M-3

Any domestic corporation (including a U.S. consolidated tax group consisting of a U.S. parent corporation and additional includible corporations listed on Form 851, *Affiliations Schedule*) required to file Form 1120, *U.S. Corporation Income Tax Return,* that reports

---

[18] *Western Union Tel. Co.,* CA-2, 44-1 USTC ¶9254, 141 F2d 774, *cert. denied,* 322 US 751, 64 SCt 1262.

on Schedule L of Form 1120 total consolidated assets at the end of the corporation's tax year that equal or exceed $10 million must complete and file Schedule M-3.

If the parent corporation of a U.S. consolidated tax group files Form 1120 and files Schedule M-3, all members of the group must file Schedule M-3. However, if the parent corporation of a U.S. consolidated tax group files Form 1120 and any member of the group files Form 1120-PC, *U.S. Property and Casualty Insurance Company Income Tax Return*, or Form 1120-L, *U.S. Life Insurance Company Income Tax Return*, that member must either:

- Fully complete Schedule M-3 as if the member filed Form 1120; or
- Complete Schedule M-3 by including the sum of all differences between the member's income statement net income (or loss) and taxable income (differences) (regardless of whether the difference would otherwise be reported elsewhere on Part II or on Part III) on Part II, line 26, Other income (loss) items with differences, and separately state and adequately disclose each difference in a supporting schedule.

.02 Who Is Not Required to File Schedule M-3?

Schedule M-3 is not required for any taxpayers other than those identified above. Thus, taxpayers required to file the following forms need not file Schedule M-3:

- Form 1065, *U.S. Return of Partnership Income*;
- Form 1120-REIT, *U.S. Income Tax Return for Real Estate Investment Trusts*;
- Form 1120-F, *U.S. Income Tax Return of a Foreign Corporation*;
- Form 1120-H, *U.S. Income Tax Return for Homeowners Associations*; and
- Form 1120-SF, *U.S. Income Tax Return for Settlement Funds.*

In addition, Schedule M-3 is not required for any member of a U.S. consolidated tax group if the parent corporation of the group files Form 1120-PC or Form 1120-L.

.03 Change in Schedule M-3 Requirements for Corporations and Partnerships with $10 Million to $50 Million in Total Assets Effective for Tax Years Ending December 31, 2014 and Later

The IRS has announced that effective for tax years ending December 31, 2014 and later, corporations and partnerships with at least $10 million but less than $50 million in total assets at year end will be permitted to file Schedule M-1 in place of Schedule M-3, Parts II and III. Schedule M-3, Part I, lines 1-12 will continue to be required for these taxpayers. Those taxpayers electing to file Schedule M-1 must report book income on Schedule M-1, line 1, equal to the book income amount reported on Schedule M-3, Part I, line 11. Corporations and partnerships with $10 million to $50 million in total assets may voluntarily file Schedule M-3 Parts II and III rather than Schedule M-1. This change applies to corporations and partnerships filing Forms 1120, 1120-C, 1120-F, 1120S, 1065 and 1065B. Corporations and partnerships filing Forms 1120, 1120-C, 1120-F, 1120S, 1065 and 1065B with $10 million to $50 million in total assets will not be required to file Form 1120 Schedule B, Form 1065 Schedule C or Form 8916-A.

CORPORATE DEDUCTIONS

¶20,040 DEDUCTIONS OF CORPORATIONS IN GENERAL

Corporations are generally entitled to claim the same deductions as an individual taxpayer [Code Secs. 161-196]. Corporations, may not, however, claim the standard deduction, any personal exemptions, or deductions medical expenses or alimony payments [Code Secs. 211-223]. In addition, corporations can offset capital losses only against capital gains [Code Sec. 1211]. The following are the more common deductions available to corporations:

- Salaries and wages [¶ 12,045];
- Rent [¶ 12,090];
- Repairs [¶ 12,095];
- Bad debts [¶ 13,125];
- Interest [¶ 9005];
- Taxes [¶ 9030];
- Charitable contributions [¶ 20,070];
- Casualty losses [¶ 13,020];
- Depreciation [¶ 11,001];
- Amortizable bond premium [¶ 9155];
- Depletion [¶ 12,155];
- Advertising [¶ 12,100; ¶ 18,150];
- Contributions to pension and profit-sharing plans [¶ 3001]; and
- Net operating loss deduction [¶ 20,135].

The cost of most lobbying [¶ 12,035] and club dues [¶ 10,045] is no longer deductible. Publicly held corporations cannot deduct more than $1 million of compensation paid to key executives [¶ 12,085]and only 50 percent of the cost of business meals and entertainment is deductible [¶ 10,040].

> ▶ **OBSERVATION:** Because there is no provision for adjusted gross income for a corporation, there is no distinction between deductions for adjusted gross income and itemized deductions.

.01 Disallowed Deductions

Deductions, credits and other allowances may be disallowed if the principal purpose for organizing a corporation[19] or acquiring control or property of a corporation is to secure tax benefits which the taxpayer would not otherwise be able to claim. The disallowance will apply if:

---

[19] *Made Rite Inv. Co.*, CA-9, 66-1 USTC ¶ 9284, 357 F2d 647, *aff'g* TC *per curiam.*

- A person or persons obtains control of the corporation, or
- The corporation obtains property (with a carryover or transferred basis) from another corporation not then controlled by the former or its stockholders; and
- The principal purpose for the acquisition is evading or avoiding taxes through the benefits of a deduction, credit or allowance that would not otherwise be available[20] [Code Sec. 269(a); Reg. § § 1.269-1–1.269-6].

In the context of Code Sec. 269, "principal purpose" means that the evasion or avoidance purpose must be more important than any other purpose. In considering what is the principal purpose, all tax avoidance purposes must be aggregated and compared with the aggregate business purposes for the acquisition. To prevail, the taxpayers need to prove only that the avoidance or evasion of tax was not the principal purpose for the acquisition. The relevant purpose is the purpose which existed at the time of the acquisition; however, facts occurring before and after the acquisition may be considered to the extent they tend to support or negate the proscribed purpose.[21]

Control means ownership of stock with at least 50 percent of the total combined voting power of all classes of stock entitled to vote; or at least 50 percent of total value of shares of all classes of stock [Code Sec. 269(a); Reg. § 1.269-1(c)].

Person includes an individual, trust, estate, partnership, association, company, or corporation [Reg. § 1.269-1(d)].

The IRS, however, may allow a part of the otherwise disallowed deduction or credit if the partial allowance does not result in the tax evasion or avoidance for which the acquisition was made. The IRS may also allocate gross income deductions, credits, or allowances, between or among the corporations or properties if, again, it determines the allocation will not result in the avoidance or evasion of federal income tax [Code Sec. 269(c); Reg. § 1.269-4].

See also ¶ 20,140 for limitation of net operating loss carryover when one corporation acquires another; and Ch. 22 for treatment of various carryovers when one corporation acquires another in a reorganization.

¶20,045 SPECIAL DEDUCTIONS FOR CORPORATIONS

In addition to the general business deductions, a corporation may claim deductions for [Code Secs. 241-249; Reg. § 1.241-1]:

- Organizational expenditures [Code Sec. 248];
- Dividends received from other domestic corporations [¶ 20,150] [Code Sec. 243; Reg. § 1.243-1]; and
- Dividends received from foreign corporations [¶ 20,055] [Code Sec. 245; Reg. § 1.243-2].

---

[20] *Capri, Inc.*, 65 TC 162, Dec. 33,477 (1975); *Plains Petroleum Co.*, 78 TCM 130, Dec. 53,467(M), TC Memo. 1999-241.

[21] *K.L. Love*, 103 TCM 1887, Dec. 59,088(M), TC Memo. 2012-166.

▶ **OBSERVATION:** Except for a deduction for dividends paid on certain preferred stock of public utilities [¶20,060], and the deduction for organizational expenditures, the special deductions differ from general deductions in that the special deductions are for amounts *received* rather than *paid.*

.01 Organizational Expenditures

Corporations (including S corporations) can elect to currently deduct up to $5,000 of their organizational expenditures for the tax year in which they begin business [Code Sec. 248(a)(1)]. The $5,000 limit is reduced (but not below zero) by the amount by which the organizational expenditures exceed $50,000 [Code Sec. 248(a)(2)]. Expenditures not currently deducted are deducted ratably over the 180-month period beginning with the month in which the corporation begins business [Code Sec. 248(a)(2); Reg. § 1.248-1(a)]. The election applies only to expenditures incurred before the end of the tax year that the corporation begins business, regardless of whether it is on the cash or accrual basis, or whether the expenditures are paid in the tax year they were incurred [Code Sec. 248(a); Reg. § 1.248-1(a)].

To be deductible, the organizational expenditure must be: (1) incident to the corporation's creation; (2) chargeable to capital account; and (3) of a character that would be amortizable over the corporation's life [Code Sec. 248(b); Reg. § 1.248-1(b)(1)]. This includes: fees paid for legal services in drafting the corporate charter, bylaws, minutes of organizational meetings, and terms of original stock certificates; fees paid for accounting services; expenses of temporary directors, and of organizational meetings of directors or stockholders; and fees paid to the state of incorporation [Reg. § 1.248-1(b)(2)].

The following expenditures are not organizational expenditures for purposes of Code Sec. 248:

- Expenditures connected with issuing or selling shares of stock or other securities, such as commissions, professional fees, and printing costs. This is so even where the particular issue of stock to which the expenditures relate is for a fixed term of years.
- Expenditures connected with the transfer of assets to a corporation.
- Expenditures connected with the reorganization of a corporation, unless directly incident to the creation of a corporation [Reg. § 1.248-1(b)(3)].

Deemed Election

A corporation is deemed to have made an election to deduct such expenditures for the tax year in which the corporation begins business. Thus, the corporation does not need to formally elect to deduct start-up expenses. A corporation may elect to forego the deemed election for these expenditures by affirmatively electing to capitalize its organizational expenses on a timely filed federal income tax return (including extensions) for the tax year in which the corporation begins business. The election either to amortize organizational expenditures or to capitalize such expenditures is irrevocable and applies to all organizational expenditures of the corporation [Reg. § 1.248-1(c)].

Example 20-18: Corporation X incurs $3,000 of organizational expenditures and begins business on July 1, 2013. Corporation X is deemed to have elected to amortize organizational expenditures under Code Sec. 248(a) in 2013. Therefore,

Corporation X may deduct the entire amount of the organizational expenditures in 2013, the tax year in which Corporation X begins business [Reg. § 1.248-1(e), Ex. 1].

Example 20-19: The facts are the same as in the example above, except that Corporation X incurs organizational expenditures of $41,000. Corporation X is deemed to have elected to amortize organizational expenditures under Code Sec. 248(a) in 2013. Therefore, Corporation X may deduct $5,000 and the portion of the remaining $36,000 that is allocable to July through December 2013 ($36,000/180 × 6 = $1,200) in 2013, the tax year in which Corporation X begins business. Corporation X may amortize the remaining $34,800 ($36,000 - $1,200 = $34,800) ratably over the remaining 174 months [Reg. § 1.248-1(e), Ex. 2].

.02 Business Start-Up Costs

All taxpayers, including corporations, single-member LLCs, sole proprietors, and partnerships, can elect to deduct up to $5,000 of their start-up expenditures for the tax year in which their active trade or business begins [Code Sec. 195(b)(1)(A)]. The $5,000 limit is reduced by the amount by which the start-up expenditures exceed $50,000 [Code Sec. 195(b)(1)(A)]. Remaining start-up expenditures can be deducted ratably over the 180-month period beginning with the month in which the active trade or business begins [Code Sec. 195(b)(1)(B)]. See ¶ 12,040 for detailed discussion.

.03 When Business Commences

A corporation may claim a deduction under Code Sec. 248 for organizational expenses over a period beginning with the month in which the corporation begins business. The words "begins business," however, do not have the same meaning as "in existence." Mere organizational activities, such as the obtaining of the corporate charter, are not alone sufficient to show the beginning of business. If the activities of the corporation have advanced to the extent necessary to establish the nature of its business operations, however, it will be deemed to have begun business. For example, the acquisition of operating assets which are necessary to the type of business contemplated may constitute the beginning of business [Reg. § 1.248-1(d)].

The IRS has adopted a three-prong test for determining when a company starts business. A company first functions as a going concern when: (1) it acquires the assets needed to conduct business; (2) the assets are put to productive use; and (3) the business is producing income.[22] See also Ch. 12.

¶20,050 DIVIDENDS RECEIVED FROM DOMESTIC CORPORATIONS

Dividends are taxed twice: (1) as the distributing corporation's income, and (2) as income to the recipient. Dividends are taxed *three times* if paid to a corporation and then

---

[22] Rev. Rul. 99-23, 1999-1 CB 998, as corrected by Ann. 99-89, IRB 1999-36, 408.

distributed to shareholders. For example, if Acme Corporation receives a dividend from Beta Corporation and then distributes the dividend income to its individual stockholders, Beta's earnings would be taxed twice at the corporate level and once at the individual stockholder's level. The dividends-received deduction minimizes this tax impact by taxing only a small portion of dividend income received by corporations. The size of the dividends-received deduction depends on the relationship of the shareholder and distributing corporations:

.01 70 Percent Dividend Deduction

If the company owns less than 20 percent of the issuing corporation's stock (by vote and value), the company may deduct 70 percent of the dividends it receives or accrues from that corporation [Code Sec. 243(a)(1)].

.02 80 Percent Dividend Deduction

If the company owns over 20 percent or more of the issuing corporation, the company may deduct 80 percent of the dividends received [Code Sec. 243(c)(1)].

.03 100 Percent Dividend Deduction

Members of an affiliated group of corporations (described next) may deduct 100 percent of dividends received from another member. Also, corporations may deduct 100 percent of dividends received from small investment companies. The 80 percent (70 percent if less than 20 percent owned) of taxable income limitation does not apply to this deduction [Code Sec. 246(b); Reg. § 1.246-2].

.04 Dividends Received from Affiliated Group Member

Corporations can fully deduct certain qualifying dividends: ones received by the corporation that is a member of the same affiliated group of corporations as the corporation distributing the dividends [¶ 20,160]. For this purpose, affiliated groups may include insurance companies. Special rules apply to affiliated groups that include insurance companies. *Qualifying dividends* are dividends either: (a) paid out of post-1963 earnings and profits, or (b) paid by a corporation electing the Puerto Rico and possessions tax credit [Ch. 28] [Code Sec. 243(a)(3), (b)(1)].

.05 Holding Period Requirements

To qualify for the dividends-received deduction, the following must be met:

- The company must own the stock on the dividend record date[23] (the day that a stock must be held if the stockholder is to receive a dividend); and
- The company must have held the stock for a minimum period of time. This means at least 46 days during the 91-day period beginning 45 days before the taxpayer becomes entitled to the dividend (the ex-dividend date) [Code Sec. 246(c)(1)(A)].

For a preferred stock, the holding period must be met during the 181-day period that begins 90 days before the date on which the stock becomes ex-dividend [Code Sec. 246(c)(2)].

---

[23] *J.L. O'Brien Co.*, CA-3, 62-1 USTC ¶ 9393, 301 F2d 813, *cert. denied*, SCt, 371 US 820, 83 SCt 37.

The company cannot count the days it held the original stock if the company's risk of loss is diminished [Code Sec. 246(c)(4)]. The corporation's minimum holding period does not include any period during which the company's risk of loss with respect to the stock is diminished because the company:

- Has an option to sell, is under a contractual obligation to sell or has made (and not closed) a short sale of substantially identical stock or securities, or
- Is the grantor of an option to buy substantially identical stock or securities, or
- Has reduced the risk by virtue of holding one or more other positions (including a futures or forward contract or an option) with respect to substantially similar or related property [Code Sec. 246(c)(4)]. The company will reduce the risk of loss if changes in the fair market values of the stock and the positions held are reasonably expected to vary inversely [Reg. § 1.246-5(b)(2)].

Property is considered substantially similar or related to the stock investment if the fair market values of the stock and the other property primarily reflect the performance of a single firm or enterprise, the same industry or industries, the same economic factor or factors (such as interest rates, commodity prices or foreign-currency exchange rates), and changes in the fair market value of the stock are reasonably expected to approximate changes in the fair market value of the other property [Reg. §1.246-5(b)(1)]. A corporation may be treated as having diminished its risk of loss on a stock investment if it acquires an offsetting position in substantially similar stock of another company. But the fact that two corporations are in the same industry does not automatically make their stocks substantially similar.

When Is the Dividends-Received Deduction Unavailable?

A corporate shareholder does not qualify for a dividends-received deduction on the following types of dividends received:

- If the corporation held the common stock less than 46 days during the 91-day period beginning 45 days before the stock becomes ex-dividend with respect to the dividend [Code Sec. 246(c)(1)(A)];
- If the corporation held the preferred stock less than 91 days during the 181-day period beginning 91 days before the stock becomes ex-dividend with respect to the dividend if the dividends received on it are for a period or periods totaling more than 356 days [Code Sec. 246(c)(2)];
- If the dividend was received from a real estate investment trust;
- The dividend was received from a corporation exempt from tax under Code Sec. 501 as a charitable organization or Code Sec. 521 as a farmers' cooperative association either for the tax year of the distribution or the preceding tax year [Code Sec. 246(a)(1)]; and
- If the corporation is under an obligation (pursuant to a short sale or otherwise) to make related payments for positions in substantially similar or related property. This usually covers payments by the corporation equivalent to dividends declared on stock "borrowed" to cover a short sale; but it is not restricted to that situation [Code Sec. 246(c)(1)(B)].

¶20,055 DIVIDENDS RECEIVED FROM FOREIGN CORPORATIONS

The dividends-received deduction can apply, in a modified form, to distributions received by a domestic corporation from foreign corporations (other than a passive foreign investment company) if certain ownership requirements are met. If the company owns at least 10 percent of the foreign corporation from which it receives dividends, the company can claim a 70 percent (80 percent in the case of a 20 percent or more owned corporation) deduction of the U.S.-source portion of dividends received from the foreign corporation [Code Sec. 245(a)]. The allowable deduction is based on the proportion of the foreign corporation's post-1986 earnings that have been subject to U.S. corporate income tax and that have not been distributed [Code Sec. 245(a)(3)]. Amounts of Subpart F income previously taxed that are distributed to U.S. shareholders reduce earnings and profits in arriving at the proportion.

.01 Wholly Owned Foreign Corporations

If all of the income of a foreign corporation is effectively connected with a U.S. business [Ch. 28] for a tax year, the foreign corporation is taxed at U.S. rates. A domestic corporation that owns all the stock of such a foreign corporation for the entire year may deduct 100 percent of the dividends paid out of these earnings and profits, if it also owns all of the stock for its entire tax year when the dividends are received [Code Sec. 245(b)(1)].

> **NOTE:** Dividends from a foreign corporation paid out of earnings and profits accumulated by a domestic corporation when it was subject to U.S. income tax are treated as dividends from a taxable domestic corporation [Code Sec. 243(e); Reg. §§1.243-3(a)(1), 1.245-1(a)(2)].

¶20,060 DIVIDENDS ON CERTAIN PUBLIC UTILITY PREFERRED STOCK

Corporations are allowed a deduction for a portion of the dividends that they receive on certain preferred stock issued by a public utility. The amount of the deduction is computed as follows [Code Sec. 244(a)]:

1. Determine the amount received as dividends on preferred stock issued before October 1, 1942 by a public utility.
2. Multiply the amount determined in (1) by 40 percent (which is the fraction whose numerator is 14 percent and whose denominator is 35 percent).
3. Multiply the difference between the amount determined in (1) and the amount determined in (2) by 70 percent (100 percent with respect to qualifying dividends (i.e., dividends distributed by one member of an affiliated group to another member of that same group).

Public utilities are allowed a deduction for a portion of the dividends that they pay on preferred stock issued before October 1, 1942. The amount of a public utility's deduction is computed as follows [Code Sec. 247(a)]:

1. Determine the amount that is the lesser of the amount of dividends paid during the tax year on its preferred stock or its taxable income for the tax year (computed without the deduction allowed for dividends paid).
2. Multiply the amount determined in (1) by 40 percent (which is the fraction whose numerator is 14 percent and whose denominator is 35 percent).

The amount of dividends paid does not include any amount distributed with respect to dividends unpaid and accumulated in any tax year ending before October 1, 1942. Amounts distributed with respect to dividends unpaid and accumulated for a prior tax year are deemed distributed with respect to the earliest year or years for which there are dividends unpaid and accumulated.

¶20,065 LIMITATIONS ON DIVIDENDS-RECEIVED DEDUCTIONS

The dividends-received deductions are subject to certain limitations.

.01 Limitation Based on Taxable Income

The total amount the company can deduct for domestic dividends eligible for the 70-percent deduction, [¶20,050], dividends received from certain public utilities [¶20,060], and dividends received from foreign corporations [¶20,055] is limited with respect to dividends received from 20-percent-owned corporations to 80 percent of the company's modified taxable income and is limited with respect to dividends received from other corporations to 70 percent of the company's modified taxable income [Code Sec. 246(b)(1)]. Modified taxable income is taxable income computed without regard to the following deductions:

- Net operating loss,
- Deduction for income from domestic production activities,
- Dividends eligible for the 70-percent deduction,
- Dividends paid or received on certain public utility preferred stock, and
- Dividends received from certain foreign corporations.

The capital loss carryback to the tax year and the basis adjustment for extraordinary dividends [discussed below] are also disregarded [Code Sec. 246(b)(1)].

> **NOTE:** This limitation does not apply if the company has an NOL for the year [¶20,120]. In determining whether a corporation has an NOL for a tax year, the deductions allowed for dividends received are computed without regard to this limitation. [Code Sec. 246(b)(2); Reg. § 1.246-2].

Example 20-20: Rex Corporation owns 25 percent of the voting stock of Domestic Corporation. Rex receives $80,000 in business income and $100,000 in dividends from Domestic. Its deductions for the current tax year are $100,000 in business expenses and a $10,000 net operating loss deduction. The dividends-received deduction is limited to $64,000 (instead of $80,000), computed as follows:

1. Gross income		$180,000
2. Business deductions		100,000
3. Taxable income before net operating loss deduction and dividends-received deduction		$ 80,000
4. Div. rec. ded. (80% × $80,000)	$64,000	
5. Net operating loss deduction	10,000	74,000
6. Taxable income		$ 6,000

If the corporation's business deductions totaled $100,001 so that item 3 is $79,999, the taxable income limitation would not apply. In this case, after deducting the 80 percent of the dividends received ($80,000), item 6 would be a net operating loss of $1; so the dividends-received deduction would not be limited to 80 percent of taxable income.

.02 Limitation for Debt Financed Portfolio Stock

If the company borrows money to buy stock, the interest on the debt is usually deductible. The combination of interest deductions and the dividends-received deductions can effectively shelter the company's earnings. To reduce this tax benefit, the deduction for dividends received on debt financed portfolio stock is limited [Code Sec. 246A(a)]. The amount of the deduction depends on how much of the stock is debt financed. The limitation does not apply to the 100 percent dividends-received deduction for dividends between members of the same affiliated group and dividends received by small business investment companies [Code Sec. 246A(b)]. Special rules apply to stock of banks or bank holding companies [Code Sec. 246A(c)(3)(A)].

Portfolio Stock

Portfolio stock includes all stock of a corporation, unless, as of the beginning of the ex-dividend date: (1) the company owns at least 50 percent of the total voting power of the other corporation's stock and at least 50 percent of the total value of the stock, or (2) the company owns at least 20 percent of the total voting power and 20 percent of the total value of the stock and five or fewer corporate shareholders own stock possessing at least 50 percent of the total voting power of the corporation and having a value equal to at least 50 percent of the total value of the corporation's stock [Code Sec. 246A(c)(2)]. Portfolio stock is *debt financed* if there is any indebtedness (including purchase money indebtedness) directly attributable to the company's investment in it [Code Sec. 246A(c)(1), (d)(3)(A)].

NOTE: Proceeds from a short sale are treated as indebtedness for the period beginning on the date the proceeds are received and ending on the date the sale is closed [Code Sec. 246A(d)(3)(B)].

The Reduced Deduction

The reduced deduction is figured as follows [Code Sec. 246A(a)]:

1. Find the *average indebtedness percentage* by dividing the average amount of portfolio indebtedness on the stock during the base period (see below) by the average amount of the adjusted basis of the stock during the base period.
2. Subtract the average indebtedness percentage from 100 percent, and multiply this percentage to the amount of the dividend received.
3. Multiply this figure by 70 percent (80 percent for a 20-percent-owned corporation as defined in Code Sec. 243(c)(2)).

The Base Period

The *base period* is the shorter of:

- The period beginning on the ex-dividend date for the dividend prior to the present one and ending on the day before the ex-dividend date for the present dividend; or
- The one-year period ending on the day before the ex-dividend date for the dividend involved [Code Sec. 246A(d)(4)].

If the stock is not held through the entire base period, only that portion of the period that the stock is held is considered in determining the average indebtedness percentage [Code Sec. 246A(d)(2)].

Any reduction in the dividends-received deduction required by the above rules may not be greater than the interest deduction allocable to such dividend (including any deductible short sale expense) [Code Sec. 246A(e)]. Where the borrower and the dividend recipient are different taxpayers, the regulations may disallow the interest deduction of the borrower or provide other treatment instead of reducing the dividends-received deduction [Code Sec. 246A(f)].

> **Example 20-21:** Jay Corp. pays a dividend of $1 per share per quarter. The ex-dividend dates are January 16, April 16, July 16, and October 16. On January 17, Kay Corp. buys 1,000 shares of Jay Corp. for $100,000. Kay holds 22 percent of Jay Corp. stock. Kay Corp. borrows $60,000 of the purchase price at an interest rate of 10 percent per year. Assume that the stock is portfolio stock. On April 16, when the entire debt is still outstanding, Kay Corp. received dividends on the stock totaling $1,000. If the stock purchase had not been financed, Kay Corp. would be entitled to a dividends-received deduction of 80 percent of $1,000, or $800. The average indebtedness percentage is 60 percent ($60,000 ÷ $100,000). Therefore, only 40 percent (100 percent less 60 percent) of the dividend received, or $400, is eligible for the dividends-received deduction. The deduction is 80 percent of $400, or $320.

The dividends-received deduction for debt financed portfolio stock is limited in instances where dividends are received from certain foreign corporations engaged in business in the U.S. [Code Secs. 246A(a), 245(a)]. In figuring the deduction, start off with the ***unfinanced*** portion of the portfolio stock owned by the domestic company. Then, multiply this by the appropriate portion of the foreign corporation's effectively connected income (70 percent or 80 percent, depending on whether the company owns 20 percent of the foreign corporation).

Example 20-22: 70 percent of Domestico's portfolio stock of Foreignco is debt financed, and 60 percent of Foreignco's gross income is effectively connected with the conduct of a U.S. business. Domestico owns 20 percent of Foreignco. Thus, it gets an 80 percent dividends-received deduction. And Domestico may deduct only 14.4 percent (30 percent unfinanced portion × 80 percent dividends-received deduction × 60 percent effectively connected income) of any dividends received from the foreign corporation.

.03 Gain Must Be Recognized for Certain Extraordinary Dividends

When you make the basis reduction because of an extraordinary dividend, the untaxed portion of the dividend cannot reduce basis below zero. Gain must be recognized in the tax year in which the extraordinary dividend is received to the extent that the untaxed portion exceeds basis [Code Sec. 1059(a)(2)]. This means that immediate gain recognition is required, as opposed to the former rule that allowed gain to be deferred until the tax year in which the stock was sold or otherwise disposed of by the corporate shareholder. This gain is treated as gain from the sale or exchange of the stock

Example 20-23: ABCo owns 83 percent of BBBCo and ABCo has basis of $150,000 in that stock. This year, ABCo receives a $170,000 distribution from BBBCo in a non-pro rata distribution considered to be an extraordinary dividend. Since ABCo owns more than 80 percent of BBBCo, the entire $170,000 is untaxed and ABCo must reduce its basis in BBBCo stock by the amount of the untaxed extraordinary dividend. This year, ABCo must recognize gain of $20,000, the amount by which the untaxed distribution ($170,000) exceeds basis ($150,000).

Extraordinary Dividend Defined

A dividend is extraordinary if its amount is equal to or greater than 10 percent of the stock's adjusted basis (5 percent for preferred dividends) [Code Sec. 1059(c)(1), (2)]. However, the company has the option of determining the status of a distribution as an extraordinary dividend by reference to the share's fair market value on the day before the ex-dividend date in lieu of its adjusted basis. To use this option, the company must prove the fair market value to the IRS [Code Sec. 1059(c)(4)].[24] Special rules apply for dividends paid before the declaration date and dividends on certain qualifying stock.

The definition of an *extraordinary dividend* covers certain distributions in partial liquidation and non-pro rate redemptions of stock. Untaxed dividends result because a corporate shareholder can generally deduct at least 70 percent of dividends received from another corporation (the deduction increases to an 80 percent deduction, if at least 20 percent of the distributing corporation is owned by the corporate shareholders, and to a 100 percent deduction, if at least 80 percent of the distributing corporation is owned by the corporate shareholders). If a dividend is in the form of property, its amount is the fair market value, reduced (but not below zero) by any liability assumed by the company and any liability to which the property is subject to immediately before and after the distribution [Code Sec. 1059(d)(2)].

---

[24] Rev. Proc. 87-33, 1987-2 CB 402.

All dividends received with respect to the same stock that have ex-dividend dates within an 85-day period are treated as one dividend. All dividends received with respect to the same stock whose ex-dividend dates are within a 365-day period are extraordinary dividends if their aggregate amount is greater than 20 percent of the stock's adjusted basis [Code Sec. 1059(c)(3)].

Example 20-24: C Corp. purchased 100 shares of common stock of D Corp., a nonaffiliated domestic corporation on January 10. The adjusted basis of the stock to C Corp. is $1,000 ($10 per share). Assume that the purchase of the stock was not financed. D Corp. declares a dividend of $1.50 per share and the ex-dividend date is September 13. The dividend of $150 is paid to C Corp. on September 27. C Corp. sells the D Corp. stock on December 31. Of the $150, 70 percent or $105 is eligible for the dividends-received deduction. Because the amount of the dividend exceeds 10 percent of the stock's adjusted basis (10 percent × $1,000 = $100), and the stock was not held for more than two years before the ex-dividend date, the stock's basis is reduced by the untaxed portion of the dividend ($105). The adjusted basis of the stock is $895 ($1,000 – $105). This increases the amount of the gain or decreases the amount of the loss on the subsequent sale.

The definition of *extraordinary dividend* includes a redemption which is treated as a dividend as a result of the option attribution rules. As a result of this expansion, companies can no longer try to avoid tax on distributions by using the option attribution rules to characterize a redemption as a dividend. Where redemption is treated as an extraordinary dividend, the basis reduction applies without regard to holding period, and only the basis in the stock actually redeemed is taken into account [Code Sec. 1059(e)(1)(A)].

Special Extraordinary Dividend Rule

If an individual receives, with respect to any share of stock, qualified dividend income (i.e., a dividend taxed as long-tern net capital gain) from one or more dividends that are extraordinary dividends, then any loss on the sale of the stock to the extent of the extraordinary dividends will be treated as long-term capital loss [Code Sec. 1(h)(11)(D)(ii)]. In other words, if, with respect to any share of stock, an individual receives an extraordinary dividend that's eligible for treatment as qualified dividend income, any loss on the sale of the stock must be treated as a long-term capital loss to the extent of the dividend. The holding period of the stock on which the extraordinary dividend is paid is not taken into account in determining whether an individual is subject to the extraordinary dividend rule or whether the loss on the stock (to the extent of the extraordinary dividends) is long-term capital loss.

Example 20-25: You purchase and sell 100 shares of ABCo at a $10,000 loss and also receive a $10,000 extraordinary dividend from the company during the year. You then incur $10,000 in net long-term capital gain and $10,000 in short-term capital gain in other unrelated transactions. You must use your $10,000 ABCo loss to offset the net long-term capital gain, leaving $10,000 of short-term capital gain to be taxed at ordinary income tax rates. Without the extraordinary dividend rule, you could characterize the loss as short-term and use it to offset the short-term capital gain, allowing your net $10,000 gain to be taxed at preferable long-term capital gain rates.

¶20,070 CHARITABLE CONTRIBUTIONS

In general, a corporation may deduct the same types of charitable contributions that are deductible by individuals [Ch. 9]. However, there are some additional restrictions on the corporate deduction. Donations made to fraternal societies and those made to trusts, community chests, funds or foundations for use outside the U.S. or its possessions are not deductible by the corporation [Code Sec. 170(c)(2), (4); Reg. § 1.170A-11(a)]. Likewise, a corporation may not deduct amounts paid to its tax-exempt parent corporation as charitable contributions. These payments are treated as dividends.[25] The same rules apply to a corporation as apply to individual taxpayers for contributions of income and remainder interests in trust and the contribution of the right to use property [Ch. 9] [Code Sec. 170(f)(2); Reg. § 1.170A-6].

The deduction for donated property is generally determined by its fair market value at the time of the contribution. However, there are important exceptions. For example, the value of the contribution must be reduced by the amount of gain which would not be long-term capital gain if the property were sold at its fair market value. Thus, the donor of appreciated ordinary income property or other property that does not meet the long-term capital gain holding period [Ch. 8] may deduct only the basis in the property rather than its full fair market value [Ch. 9] [Code Sec. 170(e)(1)(A)].

> **Example 20-26:** This year, Acme Inc. makes a charitable contribution of computer equipment that it had purchased a few years ago. The fair market value of the equipment at the time of the contribution is $5,000, but Acme had depreciated the equipment for tax purposes down to $3,000. Because $2,000 would have been recognized as ordinary income (under the depreciation recapture rules) if Acme were to sell it at its fair market value, the amount of the contribution must be reduced by $2,000. Acme may deduct only $3,000.

A special rule applies when inventory property held primarily for sale to customers, or real or depreciable property used in a trade or business is given by a corporation (other than an S corporation) to a public charity or private operating foundation. This rule permits a deduction equal to the sum of the corporation's basis in the property plus up to one-half of the amount that would not be long-term capital gain if the corporation sold the property at its fair market value. However, the corporation cannot take a deduction exceeding twice the basis of the property. No deduction is allowed for any part of the unrealized appreciation that would be ordinary income resulting from recapture of certain items if the corporation sold the property [Code Sec. 170(e)(3)(C); Reg. § 1.170A-4A].

---

[25] *Crosby Valve & Gage Co.*, CA-1, 67-2 USTC ¶9529, 380 F2d 146, *cert. denied*, SCt, 389 US 976, 88 SCt 477.

To qualify, the charity must:

- Use the property in a way related to its exempt purpose and solely for the care of the ill, the needy or infants;
- Not exchange the property for money, other property, or services; and
- Give the corporation a statement representing compliance with the other two conditions.

Additionally, the property, if subject to the Food, Drug, and Cosmetic Act, must satisfy all Act requirements on the date of the transfer and for 180 days before that date. This special rule also applies to contributions of certain newly manufactured research equipment to a qualified tax-exempt research organization for research or experimentation, including research training, made by a corporation other than an S corporation, personal holding company, or personal service corporation [Code Sec. 170(e)(3), (4); Reg. § 1.170A-4A(a)].

Example 20-27: The Roper Sled Company made a qualified contribution of children's sleds to St. Mark's Church this year. The property's fair market value at the date of the contribution is $1,000, and the basis of the property is $600. The amount of gain that would not have been long-term capital gain if the property had been sold is $400 ($1,000 – $600). The deductible contribution is the $600 basis plus one-half of the $400—or $800.

Example 20-28: Same facts as in Example above, except that the Roper Sled Company has a $200 basis in the property. The amount of gain which would not have been long-term capital gain if the property had been sold is now $800 ($1,000 – $200). The basis plus one-half of this amount is $600. Since the deductible contribution cannot exceed twice Roper's basis in the property, the deduction is limited to $400.

.01 Time for Deduction

If the corporation is on the cash-basis method, it can deduct contributions only in the year paid [Reg. § 1.170A-1]. However, if it's an accrual-basis corporation, it can elect to deduct contributions authorized by its board of directors during the tax year, if they are paid within 2½ months after the tax year ends [Reg. § 1.170A-11(b)]. The corporation makes the election by reporting the contribution on the return, and attaching a declaration that the resolution authorizing the contribution was adopted by the board of directors during the tax year. This must be verified by a statement signed by an officer authorized to sign the return that it is made under the penalties of perjury. A copy of the resolution authorizing the contribution also must be attached to the corporation's return [Reg. § 1.170A-11(b)(2)].

.02 Amount Deductible

In general, the total deductions under Code Sec. 170(a) for any tax year is limited to 10 percent of the corporation's taxable income [Code Sec. 170(b)(2)(A)]. For this purpose, taxable income must be computed without regard to certain deductions and losses, namely: (1) the deduction for charitable contributions, (2) the deductions for certain dividends received and for dividends paid on certain preferred stock of public utilities, (3) any net operating loss carryback, (4) the deduction for income attributable to domestic production activities, and (5) any capital loss carryback [Code Sec. 170(b)(2)(C)]. For charitable contributions of inventory or property, the deduction is typically limited to the corporation's basis in the property up to 10 percent of the corporation's taxable income [Code Sec. 170(e)].

The corporation must reduce its deduction for the donation of appreciated property to its basis if the contribution is: (1) made to or for the use of private nonoperating foundations; (2) for a contribution of tangible personal property that is used by the charity in a way unrelated to its exempt purpose; or (3) of any patent, copyright (other than a copyright not qualifying as a capital asset), trademark, trade name, trade secret, know-how, software (other than software that is readily available for purchase by the general public, subject to a nonexclusive license, and not substantially modified), or similar property or applications or registrations of such property [Code Sec. 170(e)(1)(B); Reg. § 1.170A-4(b)(3)].

Example 20-29: Glass Co. gave $5,000 to a domestic community chest. Its taxable income plus special deductions (but not deducting contributions) was $45,000. It had no capital loss during the tax year. The charitable contribution deduction is $4,500 (10 percent of $45,000). The $500 that is not deductible currently is carried forward, subject to the rules discussed below.

Alternative Minimum Tax

For contributions of tangible personal property, such as artwork and collectibles, and contributions of other property the difference between the fair market value of donated appreciated property and the adjusted basis of that property is not treated as a tax preference item for AMT purposes [Ch. 16].

.03 Carryover

The corporation can carry over contributions in excess of the 10 percent limit to the five succeeding tax years. However, the total of contributions actually made during the later year plus the carryover are subject to the 10 percent limit [Code Sec. 170(d)(2); Reg. § 1.170A-11(c)]. Also, the corporation must reduce a carryover to the extent that the excess contribution carried over reduces taxable income and increases a net operating loss carryover.

Example 20-30: Assume that in 2013, Glass Co. in Example 20-29 had a taxable income (figured without contributions, special deductions, net operating loss carryback and capital loss carryback) of $50,000, and that it gave $4,800 to the American Red Cross. The deduction would be figured as follows:

Contributions actually made in 2013	$ 4,800
Carryover from 2012	500
Total	$ 5,300
Amount deductible in 2013 (10% × $50,000)	5,000
Excess (available for carryover to 2014)	$ 300

▶ **OBSERVATION:** In calculating its charitable contribution, the corporation must first deduct its current year's contribution, and then deduct its carryover from the prior years (beginning with the most recent years). As a result, it is possible that an amount will be carried over for more than five years, after which it will be lost.

CAPITAL GAINS AND LOSSES OF CORPORATIONS

¶20,075 CAPITAL GAINS AND LOSSES IN GENERAL

Overall, capital gains and losses of corporations and individuals arise in the same way—from the sale or exchange of a capital asset [Ch. 8]. Occasionally, some capital gain transactions may be given ordinary income treatment, like disposing of property for which accelerated depreciation deductions were claimed [Ch. 8] or the sale or exchange of depreciable property between an individual and his or her controlled corporation [Ch. 8].

A corporation, like an individual, balances net long-term capital gain or loss against net short-term capital gain or loss to arrive at the year's net capital gain [Ch. 8]. However, there are two key differences in the rules that apply to corporations:

- Corporations can only deduct capital losses to the extent of capital gains. Anything in excess of capital gain cannot be deducted that year. [Code Sec. 1211(a); Reg. § 1.1211-1(a)(1)]; and
- There are special carryback and carryforward of net capital loss rules for corporations described here.

.01 Where to Report Capital Gains and Losses

A corporation reports its capital gains and losses on Schedule D of Form 1120, or Form 1120S if it elects S corporation treatment.

Generally, a corporation must pay an alternative minimum tax [Ch. 16] equal to 20 percent of the excess of its tentative minimum tax over its regular income tax liability [Code Sec. 55(b)(1)(B)]. Capital gains are fully included in a corporation's alternative minimum taxable income.

.02 Carrybacks and Carryovers of Net Capital Losses

Although a corporation cannot claim a deduction in the current year for a net capital loss, it can carry the loss back to each of the three years before the loss year. If the carrybacks do not absorb the entire loss, the rest can be carried over to each of the five years after the loss year. A net capital loss is first carried back to the earliest tax year to which it is allowed. If the corporation has two or more carryovers to the same year, it first uses the loss occurring on an earlier date to reduce the net capital gains and then the next carryover is applied [Code Sec. 1212(a); Reg. § 1.1212-1]. A capital loss carryback may not increase or create the corporation's net operating loss [¶ 20,130] [Code Sec. 1212(a)(1)(A)(ii)] for the tax year in which the carryback is applied. Furthermore, regardless of origin, all carrybacks and carryovers are treated as short-term capital losses for carryback and carryover purposes.

Example 20-31: In Year 4, Widget Corp. has a net capital loss of $40,000. Its net capital gains in Years 1, 2 and 3 were $23,000, $12,000, and $6,000, respectively. The first year to which Widget can carry back its Year 4 net capital loss is Year 1. The $23,000 net capital gain for that year is completely used up by the $40,000. The excess ($17,000) is carried to Year 2 where it entirely offsets the $12,000 net capital gain for that year. The $5,000 remaining net capital loss is deducted in Year 3 from the $6,000 net capital gain for that year, reducing it to $1,000. The net capital loss has been completely used up, so there is no capital loss carryover for other tax years.

Example 20-32: Baker Corp. has a net capital loss of $32,000 in Year 4. Its net capital gains in Years 1, 2 and 3 were $102,000, $15,000, and $10,000, respectively. It also had a net operating loss of $100,000 in Year 1. Baker cannot carry back its net capital loss to Year 1 because that would increase its net operating loss for that year. It can carry back $15,000 of its net capital loss to Year 2. For Year 3, Baker can carry back $10,000 of the net capital loss to offset the $10,000 net capital gain of Year 3. The balance of the net capital loss ($7,000) will be available as a loss carryover for tax years 5-9.

Foreign expropriation capital losses cannot be included in a capital loss carryback [Code Sec. 1212(a)(1)(A)(i)]; a special ten-year carryforward is allowed instead. Regulated investment companies are allowed an eight-year carryover, but no carryback [Code Sec. 1212(a)(1)(C)(i)]. A tentative carryback adjustment [Ch. 27]is available, enabling corporations to obtain a speedy refund or credit for an overpayment resulting from a carryback.

Capital loss carryovers may be lost upon a substantial change of ownership [¶ 20,140].

.03 Special Rules on Carrybacks

Net capital losses cannot be carried back to any tax year in which the corporation is [Code Sec. 1212(a)(3)]:

- A regulated investment company as defined in Code Sec. 851 [Ch. 23];
- A real estate investment trust as defined in Code Sec. 856 [Ch. 23]; or

¶20,080 GAIN ON DISPOSITION OF DEPRECIABLE PROPERTY

All or part of the gain the corporation has from disposing of Sec. 1245 or 1250 property (that is, depreciable property with a fair market value in excess of its adjusted basis) may be ordinary income [Ch. 8]. The deductions for mining exploration expenses [Ch. 12] and certain farm expenses may be recaptured under similar rules.

If the corporation distributes Sec. 1245 or Sec. 1250 property to a shareholder, it measures its ordinary income from the distribution as if the property had been sold at fair market value at the time of distribution [Code Secs. 1245(a), 1250(a); Reg. §§1.1245-1(c), 1.1250-1(a)(4)]. This applies to dividend distributions, liquidations and stock redemptions that otherwise would be tax-free [Code Secs. 1245(d), 1250(h); Reg. §§1.1245-6(b), 1.1250-1(c)(2)]. However, the amount of ordinary gain from the disposition is limited to the corporation's recognized gain when the distributee or transferee takes the corporation's basis for the property as its own basis in:

- Liquidation of a controlled subsidiary [Ch. 22];
- Transfer to a controlled subsidiary [Ch. 6]; or
- Exchange for stock or securities in a reorganization [Ch. 22].

This limit applies to exempt farmers' cooperatives [Ch. 23]but not other tax-exempt organizations [Code Secs. 1245(b)(3), 1250(d)(3); Reg. §§1.1245-4(c)(2), 1.1250-3(c)(1)].

.01 Additional Recapture on Disposition of Sec. 1250 Property

Additional complexity is added to the recapture rules of the Code Sec. 1250 by Code Sec. 291. This provision requires that 20 percent of the excess of the amount that would be treated as ordinary income, if the property were Code Sec. 1245 property, over the amount recaptured as ordinary income under Code Sec. 1250, also be recaptured as ordinary income.

Example 20-33: Boxcar, Inc. sells Code Sec. 1250 property at a gain of $100,000. Assume that, under Code Sec. 1250, $20,000 of such gain is recapturable as ordinary income. Assume further that, if the property were Code Sec. 1245 property, $50,000 of the gain would be recaptured as ordinary income under Code Sec. 1245. Under these assumptions, the corporation would recapture $20,000 of the gain as ordinary income and $6,000 (20 percent of $30,000 ($50,000 Code Sec. 1245 recapture less $20,000 Code Sec. 1250 recapture) of the gain as ordinary income under Code Sec. 291.

PURCHASES, SALES AND DISTRIBUTIONS OF CORPORATE SECURITIES AND PROPERTIES

¶20,085 CORPORATION DEALING IN ITS OWN STOCK

The corporation recognizes no gain or loss when it disposes of its own stock, including treasury stock, in exchange for money, other property, or as payment for services [Code Sec. 1032(a); Reg. §1.1032-1(a)]. Nor does the corporation recognize gain or loss on the lapse or acquisition of an option on its stock. However, the corporation does recognize gain or loss when it transfers restricted property to an employee. Its recognized gain or loss is the amount it claimed as a deduction [Ch. 22] [Reg. §1.83-6(b)].

The corporation may recognize gain or loss if it receives its own stock in the exchange, unless the corporation acquires its own stock in exchange for other shares of its own stock (including treasury stock) [Reg. §1.1032-1(b)].

Example 20-34: Able Co. owns real estate worth $3,000, but having an adjusted basis of $2,500, which it exchanges for shares of its own stock having a fair market value of $3,000. The $500 gain is taxable.

¶20,090 CORPORATION DEALING IN ITS OWN OBLIGATIONS

The corporation may issue its own obligations (bonds, debentures, notes or other debt-bearing instruments) in three ways:

- At face value (price printed on the obligation);
- At a premium (price more than face amount); or
- At a discount (price less than face amount).

Special rules apply to convertible bonds that are repurchased at a premium and to obligations that are part of investment units which include options [Reg. §§1.61-12(c)(4), 1.163-4(a)(2)].

.01 Obligations Issued at Face Value

The corporation does not realize gain or loss when it issues its obligations at face value [Reg. §1.61-12(c)(1)]. If it repurchases them for more than the issue price, the excess of the issue price plus any amount of original issue discount deducted prior to repurchase or minus any amount of premium returned as income prior to repurchase can be deducted as an interest expense [Reg. §1.163-4(c)]. If the corporation repurchases them for less than the adjusted issue price, the difference is discharge of indebtness income[26] [Reg. §1.61-12(c)(3)].

Example 20-35: Last year, Burke Corp. issued 500 bonds with a face value of $1,000 each, receiving $500,000 for them. If it repurchases 100 bonds this year for $95,000, it has income of $5,000 ($100,000 – $95,000); if it repurchases the 100 bonds for $103,000, it can deduct $3,000 ($103,000 – $100,000).

.02 Obligations Issued at a Premium

When the corporation issues obligations at a premium, the premium is income and should be prorated or amortized over the life of the obligations [Reg. §1.61-12(c)(2)]. If the corporation repurchases the obligations for a price in excess of their adjusted issue price, the excess (repurchase premium) can be deducted as interest for the tax year that the repurchase occurs. However, if the issue price of the obligation was determined under Code Sec. 1273(b)(4) or 1274, any repurchase premium is not deductible in the year of the repurchase but instead must be amortized over the term of the debt instrument in the same manner as original issue discount. If an issuer repurchases a debt instrument for an amount less than its adjusted issue price, the excess of the

[26] *Kirby Lumber Co.*, SCt, 2 USTC ¶814, 284 US 1, 52 SCt 4.

adjusted issue price over the repurchase price is discharge of indebtedness income [Reg. § 1.61-12(c) (3)].

Example 20-36: Hale Co. issues $100,000 of its 20-year bonds for $110,000. After five years (Hale has reported $2,500 as income), the bonds are repurchased for $115,000. Since the repurchase price ($115,000) exceeds the adjusted issue price ($110,000 – $2,500 = $107,500) Hale gets a $7,500 deduction on account of the repurchase.

Example 20-37: Assume the same facts as in Example above, except that the bonds were repurchased for $95,000. The adjusted issue price less the repurchase price is $12,500. Hale will recognize that excess as income in the year of repurchase.

.03 Obligations Issued at a Discount

If the corporation issues the obligations at a discount, it can deduct the net amount of the discount, which should be prorated or amortized over the life of the obligations [Reg. § 1.163-4(a)]. If the obligations are bought back by the corporation before maturity, at a price in excess of the issue price plus any amount of original issue discount deducted prior to repurchase or minus any amount of premium returned as income prior to repurchase, the excess of the repurchase price over the issue price adjusted for amortized premium or deducted discount is deductible as interest for the tax year [Reg. § 1.163-4(c)]. If an issuer repurchases a debt instrument for an amount less than its adjusted issue price, the excess of the adjusted issue price over the repurchase price is discharge of indebtedness income [Reg. § 1.61-12(c) (3)].

Example 20-38: If Judd Co. issues $100,000 of its 20-year bonds for $90,000, a portion of the discount will be deducted each year as interest. After two years, Judd repurchases the bonds. If it pays more than the adjusted issue price, the difference is a deductible expense; if it pays less, Judd has taxable income on the repurchases.

.04 Treatment of Unamortized Balance Upon Refinancing

If the corporation refinances or refunds obligations before maturity, the corporation amortizes the unamortized premium or discount on the old bonds over the life of the new bonds.[27] In certain liquidations and reorganizations, a successor corporation may continue to amortize bond discount or premium on bonds taken over from the predecessor corporation.

---

[27] *Virginia Electric & Power Co.*, DC-VA, 43-2 USTC ¶ 9613, 52 FSupp 835.

.05 Portion of C Corporation's Deduction Disallowed If High-Yield Discount Obligation

Special rules apply to certain high-yield discount obligations that are defined as debt instruments (e.g., bonds, debentures, notes, and certificates) that have the following attributes [Code Sec. 163(i)(l)]:

- *Five-year maturity.* The instrument's maturity date is more than five years from the date of issue;
- *AFR plus five.* The instrument's yield to maturity equals or exceeds the sum of the applicable federal rate (AFR) for the month in which it is issued and five percentage points. The IRS may by regulation permit the use of a rate that is higher than the federal rate if the taxpayer establishes that the higher rate is based on the same principles as the AFR and that it is appropriate for the term of the instrument;
- *Significant OID.* The instrument has significant original issue discount. An instrument has significant OID if

  a. The aggregate amount that would be included in gross income with respect to the instrument for periods before the close of any accrual period defined in Code Sec. 1272(a)(5), that ends more than five years after the date of issue; exceeds

  b. The sum of the aggregate amount of interest to be paid under the instrument before the close of such accrual period and the instrument's issue price (defined in Code Secs. 1273(b) and 1274(a)) multiplied by its yield to maturity [Code Sec. 163(i)(2)].

In determining whether a debt instrument is an applicable high yield debt instrument, the following special rules apply: (1) any payment under the instrument is assumed to be made on the last day permitted under the instrument, and (2) any payment to be made in the form of another obligation of the issuer or a related person is assumed to be made when the obligation is required to be paid in cash or in property other than such obligation. For purposes of determining whether a debt instrument's term is greater than five years or whether it has significant OID, this payment assumption rule applies to payment in stock as well as payment in other forms of obligation. Payment in stock is not taken into account, however, for purposes of determining the instrument's yield to maturity [Code Sec. 163(i)(3)].

C corporations may not deduct the disqualified portion of original issue discount (OID) on an applicable high yield discount obligation issued after July 10, 1989. Further, the remainder of the OID on such instruments may not be claimed as a deduction until paid [Code Sec. 163(e)(5)].

The disqualified portion of the original issue discount on any applicable high yield discount obligation is the lesser of the amount of that original issue discount or the portion of the total return on that obligation which bears the same ratio to the total return as the disqualified yield on the obligation bears to the yield to maturity on the obligation [Code Sec. 165(e)(5)(C)]. "Disqualified yield" means the excess of the yield to maturity on the obligation over the sum of the applicable federal rate in effect for the calendar month in which the obligation was issued plus six percentage points. The "total return" is the amount that would have been original issue discount on the obligation if interest based on a fixed rate and payable unconditionally at fixed periodic intervals of one year or less were included in the stated redemption price at maturity.

The dividend equivalent portion of any amount includible in gross income of a corporation in respect of an applicable high yield discount obligation is treated as a dividend received by the corporation from the corporation issuing the obligation [Code Sec. 163(e)(5)(B)]. The dividend equivalent portion is the portion of the amount includible in income that is attributable to the disqualified portion of the original issue discount on the obligation and would have been treated as a dividend if it had been a distribution made by the issuing corporation with respect to its stock.

> **Example 20-39:** Grand Corp. issues a bond with an issue price of $1,000 and yield of 20 percent to maturity in 10 years. All interest is payable at maturity. Assume the AFR is 9 percent. Thus, the bond is subject to the high-yield discount obligation rules.
>
> The return on the instrument in the first year is $200 ($1,000 × 20%). The adjusted price is $1,200 at the end of the year ($1,000 plus $200). The disqualified yield is 5 percent. That is the 20 percent yield to maturity less the sum of the 9 percent AFR plus six percentage points. This disqualified yield is 25 percent (5/20 of the yield to maturity). The amount of the disqualified portion in the first year is $50 (25% × $200). The return on the instrument at the end of the second year is $240 ($1,200 times 20%), and the disqualified portion is $60 (25% × $240).

> **Example 20-40:** Assume the same facts as in Example 20-37. If Grand distributes $120 in cash to bondholders at the end of the second year, $30 ($120 ×25%) is considered payment from the disqualified portion. The other $90 is a deductible interest payment.

¶20,095 INCOME FROM DISCHARGE OF INDEBTEDNESS

Generally, corporations must treat debt forgiveness as income. However, there are special rules for bankrupt and insolvent debtors [Ch. 2] [Code Sec. 108(a)(1)].

¶20,100 EFFECT OF PROPERTY DISTRIBUTIONS ON CORPORATION

Generally, a corporation recognizes no gain or loss for distributing property (including its stock or stock rights) to its shareholders [Code Sec. 311(a)]. A corporation does, however, have taxable gain on property that it distributes to the extent the property's fair market value exceeds its basis. The gain is determined as if the corporation sold the property at fair market value [Code Sec. 311(b)].

NOTE: The IRS is authorized but has not to date issued regulations that prevent partnership or trust interest distributions from being used to circumvent the above rules. The amount of gain recognized on a nonliquidating distribution of a partnership or trust interest would be computed without regard to any loss from property that was contributed to the partnership or trust for the principal purpose of recognizing such loss on the distribution [Code Sec. 311(b)(3)].

.01 Depreciable Property

If a corporation makes a dividend distribution of property subject to recapture under Code Secs. 1245, 1250, 1252, or 1254, it must recognize ordinary income on the disposition, which will be measured as if the corporation sold the property for fair market value [¶20,080] [Code Sec. 1245(a), (d), 1250(a), (h); Reg. §§1.1245-1 et seq., 1.1250-1 et seq.].

.02 Property Distributed at Bargain Price to Shareholder

If a corporation transfers property in a sale or exchange to another shareholder at a bargain price, the corporation is deemed to have made a distribution. How much of the distribution is taxable as a dividend depends upon the corporation's current and accumulated earnings and profits (E&P) at the time of the distribution [Ch. 2]. The general rules for determining whether a distribution is considered a taxable dividend are as follows:

- A distribution is a taxable dividend to the extent of the corporation's E&P;
- Distributions in excess of E&P represent a return of capital and reduce the basis of the shareholder's stock; and
- Any excess, after basis has been recovered, is treated as capital gain.

If the amount paid for the property by the shareholder is less than the property's adjusted basis, the amount of distribution is the excess of the fair market value over the purchase price.

Example 20-41: Batson Corp. sold property to shareholder Richard Grayson for $2,000. The property's fair market value is $10,000. The amount of the distribution to Grayson is $8,000.

¶20,105 EFFECTS OF DISTRIBUTIONS ON CORPORATION'S EARNINGS AND PROFITS

A corporation's earnings and profits (E&P) must be adjusted when it distributes property to its shareholders.

.01 General Rule

If the distribution is in the form of money, the E&P are decreased by the amount of money distributed. Upon the distribution of a corporation's obligations, the E&P are decreased by the principal amount of the obligations (issue price for original issue discount obligations) [Code Sec. 312(a)(1), (2)]. For distributions of other property,

E&P are generally decreased by a corporation's adjusted basis in the distributed property [Code Sec. 312(a)(3); Reg. § 1.312-1(a)-(c)].

Example 20-42: Maple Co. distributes $5,000 to a shareholder. Before the distribution, Maple's earnings and profits are $7,500. The distribution decreases its earnings by $5,000, leaving a balance of $2,500 in the earnings and profits account.

Example 20-43: Deluxe Corporation, with E&P of $500,000, distributes property with an adjusted basis of $150,000 and a fair market value of $100,000 to its shareholders. The distribution decreases its E&P by $150,000 (adjusted basis), leaving a balance of $350,000 in the E&P account.

.02 Distributing Appreciated Property

A corporation's distribution of appreciated property increases its E&P by the excess of the property's fair market value over the property's adjusted basis [Code Sec. 312(b)]. The distribution then results in a decrease to E&P using fair market value instead of adjusted basis to measure the decrease. The net effect is that the E&P are decreased by the property's basis.

Example 20-44: Acme Corporation with E&P of $500,000 distributes real property with an adjusted basis of $100,000 and fair market value of $150,000 to its shareholders. The distribution increases Acme's E&P by $50,000 ($150,000 fair market value less $100,000 adjusted basis), and then decreases it by $150,000 (the property's fair market value), leaving a balance of $400,000 in the E&P account.

.03 Adjustments for Liabilities

The adjustments just described must be reduced by any liability on the property distributed, and the amount of any liability of the corporation assumed by a shareholder in connection with the distribution [Code Sec. 312(c); Reg. §§ 1.312-3, 1.312-4].

Example 20-45: Engel Co. distributed to its sole shareholder, John Kane, as a dividend in kind, a vacant lot. On that date, the lot had a fair market value of $50,000 and was subject to a mortgage of $10,000. The adjusted basis of the lot was $31,000. The earnings and profits were $10,000. The dividend received by Kane is $30,000 ($50,000, the fair market value – $20,000 mortgage). The earnings and profits of Engel after this transaction is $20,000 + $19,000 – $30,000 = $9,000.

.04 Distributions Not Taxed to Distributee

If a corporation makes partially or wholly tax-free distributions to its shareholders, it must file Form 5452 by February 28 of the following year. These distributions are considered wholly or partially nontaxable only because the corporation's earnings and profits are less than the distributions. If the corporation does not furnish the required information, the IRS may assume it has redetermined its distributions to be fully taxable as dividends.

.05 Allocation of Earnings

When a corporation distributes the stock of a corporation it controls [Ch. 22], part of the earnings and profits of the corporation must be allocated to the controlled corporation [Code Sec. 312(h)(1); Reg. § 1.312-10]. This allocation of earnings and profits between distributing and controlled corporations must be made in most tax-free distributions, exchanges, or transfers of property [Reg. § 1.312-11]. A similar allocation is also required in a Type C or Type D tax-free reorganization [Code Sec. 312(h)(2)].

.06 Discharge of Indebtedness

The amount of any debt discharge (including amounts excluded from gross income) increases corporate earnings and profits. However, any debt discharge amount that is used to reduce bases of corporate depreciable property under Sec. 1017 does not increase its earnings and profits [Code Sec. 312(l)(1)].

¶20,110 ALLOCATING PURCHASE PRICE IN ASSET SALES

Generally, in an applicable asset acquisition both the buyer and the seller must use the residual allocation method to allocate the purchase price received for determining the buyer's basis or the seller's gain or loss [Code Sec. 1060]. Briefly, under the residual allocation method, the goodwill and going concern value is the excess of the business's purchase price over the aggregate fair market values of the tangible assets and the identifiable intangible assets other than goodwill and going concern value. The method used here is the same as the one for allocating purchase price to assets following a stock purchase [Reg. § 1.338-6]. The price of the assets acquired must be reduced by cash and cash-like items; the balance is allocated first to certain tangible assets, followed by certain intangibles (neither allocation can be more than the assets' fair market values). The remaining cost must then be allocated to goodwill and going concern value.

Both the buyer and seller in an applicable asset acquisition are bound for tax purposes by the terms of their written agreements as to the allocation of any consideration or the value of any of the assets. However, their agreement is not binding if the IRS determines that the allocation (or value) is not appropriate.

.01 Applicable Asset Acquisition

An applicable asset acquisition is any transfer of assets constituting a business in which the seller's basis is determined wholly by reference to the consideration (usually the purchase price) paid for the assets [Code Sec. 1060(c)]. For this rule, a group of assets will constitute a business if their character is such that goodwill or going concern value could under any circumstances attach to the assets. For example, a group of assets that would constitute an active trade or business within the meaning of Code Sec. 355 (involving the distribution of a controlled corporation's stock) will in all events be considered a business. In addition, businesses that are not active businesses under Code Sec. 355 will also be subject to this rule.

NOTE: The mandatory allocation rule covers both direct and indirect transfers of a business. Taxpayers must apply the special allocation rules to a sale of a business by an individual or a partnership, or a sale of a partnership interest in which the basis of the purchasing partner's proportionate share of the partnership's assets is adjusted to reflect the purchase price.

.02 Information Required

The seller and buyer must file information returns on Form 8594, *Asset Acquisition Statement,* disclosing amounts allocated to goodwill or going concern value, and to any other categories of assets or specific assets [Code Sec. 1060(b); Reg. § 1.1060-1(e)(1)].

Additional Reporting Requirement

If a taxpayer owns more than 10 percent of a business, the taxpayer must furnish any information required by the IRS if an interest in the business is transferred or if the taxpayer enters into an employment contract, covenant not to compete, royalty or lease agreement, or other agreement with the buyer. The buyer also must furnish any information that the IRS may require.

The seller and the purchaser in an asset acquisition each must report information concerning the amount of consideration in the transaction and its allocation among the assets transferred. The seller and purchaser also must report information concerning subsequent adjustments to consideration [Reg. § 1.1060-1(e)(1)]. The seller and the purchaser must each file asset acquisition statements on Form 8594, *Asset Acquisition Statement,* with their income tax returns for the tax year that includes the purchase date.

If the amount of consideration allocated to any asset by the seller or the purchaser is increased (or decreased) after the tax year that includes the purchase date, the seller or purchaser making the increase (or decrease) must file a supplemental asset acquisition statement on Form 8594 with the income tax return for the tax year in which the increase is properly taken into account [Reg. § 1.1060-1(e)(2)].

NET OPERATING LOSSES OF CORPORATIONS

¶20,115 WHAT IS A NET OPERATING LOSS?

The amount of a loss from a business activity that can be carried over to other years is known as a net operating loss (NOL). The NOL is the amount of business deductions in excess of business gross income plus or minus certain adjustments. Note that nonbusiness casualty and theft losses are treated as business losses for NOL purposes.

An NOL sustained in one year may be used to reduce the taxable income for another year. It may be carried back to earlier years and yield tax refunds. If not exhausted in earlier years (or if the taxpayer elects not to used the carryback), it may be carried forward to later years and reduce the tax for those years.

For a discussion of NOLs of individuals, see ¶ 13,110– ¶ 13,120.

¶20,120 NET OPERATING LOSSES IN GENERAL

If a corporation's allowable deductions exceed its annual gross income, as modified, the corporation can carry the resulting net operating loss back or forward and deduct the loss in other tax years to reduce income in those years. The aggregate of the carrybacks and carryovers to a year is the net operating loss deduction [Code Sec. 172(a); Reg. § 1.172-1(a)].

.01 Who May Claim Net Operating Loss Deduction

All corporations are entitled to the net operating loss deduction in computing their income tax, except:

- Life insurance companies
- Mutual insurance companies other than marine mutual insurance companies;
- Regulated investment companies [Code Sec. 852(b)(2)(B)];
- S corporations. S corporation losses are passed through to their shareholders [Code Sec. 1366(a)];
- Partnerships. Partnership losses are passed through to their parents who deduct partnership losses [Code Sec. 703(a)(2)(D)].

The general rules governing a net operating loss are similar to those for individuals [Ch. 13]; but the adjustments for figuring net operating losses and net operating loss carryovers differ.

.02 Refund Claim

Taxpayers can obtain refunds by filing an application for a tentative carryback adjustment. A net operating loss, business credit carryback or a capital loss carryback may give rise to a tentative carryback adjustment for a prior tax year. The application generally must be filed on or after the date the return is filed for the tax years in which the losses or credits arose. It also must be filed within 12 months of the end of the tax year in which the losses or credits arose. Corporations file Form 1139, *Corporation Application for Tentative Refund.* The IRS has 90 days to make any refund or credit. However, it must issue any refunds within 45 days to avoid paying interest.

Form 1139 must be filed within one year after the close of the NOL year (but not before the return for the NOL year is filed). In lieu of Form 1139, the corporation may file a separate Form 1120X for each carryback year. The form must be filed within three years after the due date of the return for the NOL year.

¶20,125 YEARS TO WHICH A NET OPERATING LOSS MAY BE CARRIED

In the case of a net operating loss that arises in a tax year beginning after August 5, 1997, the NOL is normally carried back two years. Any loss remaining after the two-year carryback period is then carried forward 20 years, starting with the year after the loss year and then to each succeeding year for 19 more years or until the loss is completely used up. Any portion of a net operating loss remaining after the 20-year carryover period is nondeductible [Code Sec. 172(b)(1)(A)]. A taxpayer may make an irrevocable election to waive the two-year carryback period [Code Sec. 172(b)(3)].

.01 Five-Year Carryback for 2008 and 2009 NOLs

An eligible small business (ESB) may elect to carry back 2008 and 2009 NOLS for three, four, or five years, instead of the normal two years [Code Sec. 172(b)(1)(H)]. An ESB is a trade or business that meets a $15 million gross receipts test for the tax year in which the loss arose [Code Sec. 172(b)(1)(H)(iv)]. The $15 million gross receipts test is satisfied if the average annual gross receipts for the business for the three-year period ending with a tax year does not exceed $15 million [Code Sec. 172(b)(1)(H)(iv)]. The carryforward period for NOLs remains at 20 years whether or not the taxpayer elects to use an extended carryback period [Code Sec.172(b)(1)(A)(ii)]. ESBs that qualify for the extended carryback period for 2008 and 2009 NOLs must make an affirmative election to use the longer carryback period by taking the steps outlined in Rev. Proc. 2009-26.[28]

.02 Three-Year Carryback for Certain Nols Attributable to Casualty Losses and Federally Declared Disasters for Individuals, Farmers, and Small Businesses

Although the general carryback period for an NOL is two years, the portion of an NOL that is an "eligible loss" is carried back three years. An eligible loss is defined as (1) the portion of an individual's NOL attributable to casualty and theft losses and (2) the portion of an NOL attributable to a federally declared disaster in the case of a taxpayer engaged in the trade or business of farming or a taxpayer that is a small business [Code Sec. 172(b)(1)(F)]. Losses attributable to a federally declared disaster that occurs after 2007 and before January 1, 2010 (whether or not the taxpayer is a farmer) are now treated as a qualified disaster loss eligible for a five-year carryback.

.03 Five-Year Carryback for Farming Losses

The carryback period for a farming loss is five years, effective for NOLs beginning after December 31, 1997 [Code Sec. 172(b)(1)(G)]. The carryforward period remains at 20 years. A farming loss is defined as the lesser of:

1. The amount of a taxpayer's net operating loss for the tax year if only income and deductions attributable to the taxpayer's farming business were taken into account, or

2. The amount of the net operating loss for the year [Code Sec. 172(i)].

The term "farming business" is defined in Code Sec. 263A(e)(4) as the trade or business of farming and includes the operation of a nursery or sod farm, and the raising or harvesting of trees bearing fruit, nuts, or other crops, or ornamental trees other than evergreen trees which are more than six years old when severed.

---

[28] Rev. Proc. 2009-26, IRB 2009-19, 935.

.04 Five-Year Carryback for Qualified Disaster Losses

Qualified disaster losses that arise in tax years beginning after December 31, 2007, in connection with federally declared disasters declared after that date are eligible for a five-year carryback [Code Sec. 172(b)(1)(J)].

.05 Five-Year Carryback for Gulf Opportunity Zone Losses

A five-year net operating loss carryback period is provided for "qualified Gulf Opportunity Zone losses" (GO-Zone losses) that arise in tax years ending on or after August 28, 2005 [Code Sec. 1400N(k)].

.06 Five-Year Carryback for Timber Losses in Gulf Opportunity Zone, Rita GO Zone, and Wilma GO Zone

A taxpayer with qualified timber property located in the Gulf Opportunity Zone, Rita GO Zone, or Wilma GO Zone may carryback NOLs attributable pre-January 1, 2007, income and losses with respect to such property for five years, effective for losses that arise in tax years ending on or after August 28, 2005 [Code Sec. 1400N(i)].

.07 Five-Year Carryback for Certain Electric Utilities

Electric utilities may elect, in a tax year that ends after December 31, 2005, and before January 1, 2009, a five-year NOL carryback period for NOLs generated in tax years ending in 2003, 2004, and 2005. The five-year carryback period, however, only applies to an amount of the NOL loss equal to the taxpayer's investment in certain electric transmission property or pollution control equipment expenditures in the tax year that precedes the election year [Code Sec. 172(b)(1)].

.08 10-Year Carryback for Specified Liability Losses

The portion of an NOL attributable to the sum of certain product liability claims and statutory and tort liability losses is referred to as a specified liability loss [Code Sec. 172(f)]. The carryback period for a specified liability loss is 10 years [Code Sec. 172(b)(1)(C)].

¶20,130 FIGURING THE NET OPERATING LOSS

The net operating loss of a corporation is the excess of the deductions over gross income, with some adjustments [Code Sec. 172(a), (b), (c)]. Because of the required adjustments, the net operating loss is not necessarily the same as the loss shown on Form 1120. The adjustments are:

1. A dividends received deduction is allowed in full if claiming the deduction results in a loss [Code Sec. 172(d)(5)]. A corporation owning less than 20 percent of the distributing corporation may deduct 70 percent of the dividends received or accrued. The deduction is increased to 80 percent for a corporation owning at least 20 percent of the distributing corporation.

Example 20-46: A corporation has $300,000 of income from manufacturing, $400,000 of expenses, and $100,000 of dividend income. It has a net operating loss computed as follows:

Income from manufacturing	$300,000	
Dividend income	100,000	400,000
Expenses	$400,000	
Tentative taxable income		$0
Minus 70% dividends received deduction		$70,000
Net operating loss		($70,000)

If, however, the full dividends received deduction does not result in a loss, the deduction will be subject to an additional limitation on taxable income.

2. A deduction for dividends paid on certain preferred stock of public utilities is allowed in full without regard to the percentage limitations imposed by Code Sec. 247 [Code Sec. 172(d)(5)].
3. The dividends-received deduction allowed under Code Sec. 244 for certain preferred stock of public utilities is allowed in full, without regard to the limitation of such deduction to the taxpayer's taxable income, if claiming the deduction results in a loss [Code Sec. 172(d)(5)].
4. A net operating loss deduction resulting from losses suffered in other years cannot be used to increase the loss of the tax year since this would result in a longer carryback or carryover period than is allowable under the Code [Code Sec. 172(d)(1); Reg. § 1.172-2(a)(1)(i)].
5. The manufacturer's deduction allowed under Code Sec. 199 for domestic production activities is not allowed [Code Sec. 172(D)(7)].

A corporation is not required to make an adjustment for capital gains and losses [Code Sec. 172(d)(2)].

¶20,140 NET OPERATING LOSS CARRYOVER DISALLOWED FOR SUBSTANTIAL CHANGE OF OWNERSHIP

After a substantial ownership change, such as when one corporation purchases another, an acquiring corporation can only deduct the net operating losses of the acquired corporation up to the amount of the Sec. 382 limitation [Code Sec. 382(a)]. In order for a corporation to deduct even this amount, a business continuity test must be satisfied. The purpose of this provision is to prevent the trafficking of losses when an ownership change occurs. The legislative history explains that the Code Sec. 382 limitation is necessary following a change in ownership because new shareholders otherwise would have an opportunity to contribute income-producing assets (or divert income opportunities) to the corporation, thus inappropriately accelerating the use of net operating loss carryovers. The Code Sec. 382 limitation is intended to prevent a corporation from obtaining greater loss utilization than it could have achieved absent a change in ownership.[29]

Code Sec. 382 imposes limitations on the use of pre-change tax losses of purchased loss corporations [Code Sec. 382(a)]. Loss corporation means a corporation entitled to use a net operating loss carryover or having a net operating loss for the tax year in which the ownership change occurs [Code Sec. 382(k)(1)]. An old loss corporation means any corporation with respect to which there was an ownership change and which before the ownership change had a net operating loss [Code Sec. 382(k)(2)].

.01 Substantial Ownership Change

The crucial event that triggers the application of the Sec. 382 limitation is an "ownership change". There is an "ownership change" if, immediately after any owner shift involving a five-percent shareholder or any "equity structure shift" the percentage of stock of the loss corporation that is owned by one or more 5-percent shareholders has increased by more than 50 percentage points over the lowest percentage of stock of the loss corporation owned by such shareholders at any time during the testing period (generally a three-year period) [Code Sec. 382(g); Temp. Reg. § 1.382-2T(a)(1)]. There is an owner shift involving a 5-percent shareholder if there is any change in the respective ownership of stock of a corporation and such change affects the percentage of stock of such corporation owned by any person who is a 5-percent shareholder before or after the change [Code Sec. 382(g)(2)].

There is an "equity structure shift" when there is a reorganization (not including an "F" reorganization and not including a "D" or "G" reorganization unless the corporation to which the assets are transferred acquires substantially all of the transferor's assets and the stock, securities), and other properties received by the transferor, as well as the other properties of the transferor, are distributed pursuant to a plan of reorganization [Code Sec. 382(g)(3)].

NOTE: A triggering ownership change can take place even if no single shareholder acquires 5 percent of the corporation's stock. A group of persons who have a formal or informal understanding among themselves to make a coordinated acquisition of stock is treated as a single entity for purposes of applying the ownership change rules [Reg. § 1.382-3]. Also, if a 50 percent stockholder claims a worthless stock deduction during the three-year testing period after an ownership change, the shareholder is treated as having acquired such stock on the first day of the first succeeding tax year and will not be treated as having owned such stock during any prior period [Code Sec. 382(g)(4)(D)].

.02 Small Shareholders

The term "5 percent shareholder" is important for purposes of determining whether an ownership change has occurred. As discussed above, an ownership change is defined as a change in the percentage of ownership of the loss corporation's stock owned by the "5 percent shareholders" of more than 50 percentage points (by value) over a 3-year period [Code Sec. 382(g); Temp. Reg. § 1.382-2T(a)(1)]. A "5 percent shareholder" is defined as:

---

[29] S. Rep. No. 99-313 at 232 (1986).

- Any person holding 5 percent or more of the corporation's stock, directly or indirectly, during the testing period;
- A "public group" consisting of individual shareholders who each own less than 5 percent of a loss corporation ("small shareholders") and are aggregated and treated as a single 5 percent shareholder;
- A "5 percent entity" (i.e., the public group of a partnership, corporation, estate, or trust that directly or indirectly owns 5 percent or more of the loss corporation, and the owners of which are not 5 percent shareholders); and
- A public group of the loss corporation, a first-tier entity or a higher-tier entity identified as a 5 percent shareholder under Reg. § 1.382-2T(j)'s segregation rules (under which the public shareholders of a loss corporation may be separated into two or more groups, each of which is treated as a 5% shareholder, as a result of certain transactions).

In Notice 2010-49,[30] the IRS addressed stock ownership changes involving small shareholders and described two general approaches for tracking ownership changes: the ownership tracking approach and the purposive approach. Under the ownership tracking approach, all changes in ownership are tracked without regard to the particular circumstances, resulting in the segregation of small shareholders into a new public group that is treated as a five-percent shareholder. In contrast, the "purposive" approach focuses more sharply on the circumstances in which abuses are likely to arise. Under this approach, it is unnecessary to track acquisitions of stock by small shareholders because they generally cannot acquire loss corporation stock and cannot take advantage of the existing net operating losses. In Prop. Reg. § 1.382-3 the IRS expands the "purposive" approach thus reducing the need to track changes of stock ownership for corporation that have net operating losses. Although small shareholders are generally aggregated and treated as one 5 percent shareholder, this aggregation rule is applied separately to small shareholders of parties to certain Code Sec. 368 reorganizations. The proposed regulations would make the segregation rules inoperative to transfers of loss corporation stock to small shareholders by 5 percent entities or individuals who are 5 percent shareholders. In these cases, the stock transferred would be treated as being acquired proportionately by the public groups existing at the time of the transfer. This rule would also apply to transfers of ownership interests in 5 percent entities to public owners and to 5 percent owners who are not 5 percent shareholders [Prop. Reg. § 1.382-3(j)(13)].

.03 Continuity of Business

As a general rule, if the new loss corporation does not continue the business enterprise of the old loss corporation at all times during the two-year period beginning on the change date, the Code Sec. 382 limitation for any post-change year will be zero, which means that the new loss corporation's NOL carryovers are *completely* disallowed [Code Sec. 382(c)].

.04 Section 382 Limitation

This Code Sec. 382 limitation is an amount equal to the loss corporation's value immediately before the ownership change, multiplied by the highest of the adjusted

[30] Notice 2010-49, IRB 2010-27, 10.

federal long-term rates in effect for any month in the three-calendar-month period ending with the calendar month in which the change date occurs [Ch. 22] [Code Sec. 382(b)(1)]. Similar limitations are applied to excess credits and net capital losses [Ch. 22] [Code Sec. 383].

.05 Limitation Not Triggered by Ownership Changes Pursuant to Certain Restructuring Plans

The Code Sec. 382(a) limitation will not apply in the case of an ownership change occurring pursuant to a restructuring plan of a taxpayer that is (1) required under a loan agreement or a commitment for a line of credit entered into with the Department of the Treasury under the Emergency Economic Stabilization Act of 2008, and (2) intended to result in a rationalization of the costs, capitalization, and capacity with respect to the manufacturing workforce of, and suppliers to, the taxpayer and its subsidiaries [Code Sec. 382(n)(1)]. This exception will not apply in the case of any subsequent ownership change unless the subsequent ownership change also meets the requirements of the exception [Code Sec. 382(n)(2)].

An ownership change that would be otherwise excepted from the application of the Code Sec. 382(a) limitation will instead remain subject to the limitation if, immediately after such ownership change, any person (other than a voluntary employees' beneficiary association described in Code Sec. 501(c)(9)) owns stock of the new loss corporation possessing 50 percent or more of the total combined voting power of all classes of stock entitled to vote, or of the total value of the stock of such a corporation. In determining the stock ownership, related persons will be treated as a single person.

ACCUMULATED EARNINGS TAX

¶20,145 THE ACCUMULATED EARNINGS TAX IN GENERAL

A corporation's earnings are subject to a double tax—one at the corporate level as the income is earned, and another at the shareholder level when the earnings are distributed as dividends. See ¶20,005. Shareholders may be tempted to avoid the second tax by accumulating the earnings at the corporate level. To prevent this tax avoidance technique, the accumulated earnings tax is imposed on a corporation at a rate of 20 percent beginning in 2013 (increased from 15 percent in tax years 2003 through 2012) on the accumulated taxable income of a corporation if the corporation accumulates earnings beyond its reasonable business needs. This tax is imposed in addition to the regular corporate income tax [Code Secs. 531, 532(a)]. The tax (payable in addition to the regular tax payable by a corporation) is imposed on accumulated taxable income exceeding the $250,000 minimum accumulated earnings credit ($150,000 for personal service corporations engaged in the fields of health, law, engineering, architecture, accounting, actuarial science, performing arts, or consulting) [Code Sec. 535(c)(2)].

A corporation's directors are responsible for determining how much dividends should be paid to avoid liability for accumulated earnings tax. Under certain conditions, they may be personally liable for allowing a corporation to be subject to the tax. If there is evidence of negligence in permitting the accumulation and consequent underpayment of tax, an additional penalty tax can be imposed.[31]

.01 Corporations Liable for Tax

Every taxable corporation (other than domestic or foreign personal holding companies, or passive foreign investment companies, and exempt corporations) is subject to the accumulated earnings tax if it is formed or used to avoid the income tax that would otherwise be paid by shareholders [Code Sec. 532(a), (b); Reg. § 1.532-1(a)(1)]. Publicly held corporations are subject to accumulated earnings tax.[32] The tax is imposed without regard to the number of the corporation's shareholders [Code Sec. 532(c)].

> **NOTE:** S corporations are not subject to this tax since all of their earnings generally are passed through and taxed to the shareholders rather than the corporation [Ch. 21].

Tax avoidance need not be the accumulation's sole or dominant purpose for the tax to apply. Liability is incurred whenever one of the purposes for accumulation is avoiding the shareholders' income taxes.[33] The fact that the corporation's earnings have accumulated beyond the reasonable needs of the business does show a purpose to avoid shareholders' income taxes, unless the corporation proves the contrary by a preponderance of evidence [Code Sec. 533(a); Reg. § 1.533-1(a)(1)].

Reasonable Needs of the Business

The most important question is whether or not the earnings have been allowed to accumulate beyond the reasonable needs of the business, present or reasonably anticipated. Some of the reasons which may justify an accumulation of earnings are: a corporation's plans for bona fide business expansion;[34] plans for plant replacement; plans to acquire a business enterprise by purchasing its stock or assets; the need to establish a sinking fund to retire bona fide business indebtedness; or to provide working capital or inventory for the business [Reg. § 1.537-2(b)]. The plans must be "specific, definite and feasible" [Reg. § 1.537-1(b)]. To prove that a specific, definite, and feasible plan for the use of the accumulated funds exist, the taxpayer should have appropriate documentation indicating that the accumulation is for reasonable business purposes.[35]

In *Haffner's Service Stations Inc.*,[36] the court required a clearly substantiated plan for the use of the accumulated funds in order to avoid being subject to the accumulated earnings tax. Examples of specific plans for use of the accumulated earnings would include the need to redeem either shares which are part of a stockholder's gross estate or stock held by a private foundation that constitutes business holdings [Ch. 23] [Code Sec. 537(a); Reg. § 1.537-1(c), (d)]. In addition, earnings may be accumu-

---

[31] Rev. Rul. 75-330, 1975-2 CB 496.

[32] *American Metal Products Corp.*, CA-8, 61-1 USTC ¶ 9332, 287 F2d 860, *aff'g*, 34 TC 89, Dec. 24,142 (1960).

[33] *Donruss Co.*, SCt, 69-1 USTC ¶ 9167, 393 US 297, 89 SCt 501.

[34] *Otto Candies, LLC*, DC-LA, 2003-1 USTC ¶ 50,516, 288 FSupp2d 730; *Tri-City Advertising, Inc.*, 54 TCM 1537, Dec. 44,524(M), TC Memo. 1988-19.

[35] *Northwestern Ind. Tele. Co.*, CA-7, 97-2 USTC ¶ 50,859, 127 F3d 643, *aff'g* TC; *cert. denied*, 525 US 810, 119 SCt 41.

[36] *Haffner's Service Stations, Inc.*, CA-1, 2003-1 ¶ 50,333, 326 F3d 1.

lated to pay reasonably anticipated product liability losses [Code Sec. 537(b)(4); Reg. § 1.537-1(a), (f)].

> **NOTE:** Listed and readily marketable securities purchased out of earnings and profits must be valued at net liquidation value, not cost, in determining whether earnings were unreasonably accumulated.[37]

Unreasonable Accumulations

Accumulations for the following objectives indicate they may be beyond reasonable business needs: loans to shareholders; expending corporate funds for stockholders' personal benefit; loans having no reasonable relation to conduct of the business; loans to another corporation controlled by common stockholders and whose business is not that of the taxpayer corporation; investments not related to the corporation's business; or retention of earnings to provide against unrealistic hazards [Reg. § 1.537-2(c)].

.02 Burden of Proof

Once the IRS has determined that a corporation has accumulated earnings to avoid stockholders' income taxes, the corporation has the burden of proving the contrary [Code Sec. 533(a); Reg. § 1.533-1(a), (b)]. However, special rules apply to proceedings in the Tax Court, and the government has the burden of proof if [Code Sec. 534(a); Reg. § § 1.534-1 through 1.534-4]:

- Before the notice of deficiency for accumulated earnings tax was mailed, the government failed to notify the corporation by certified or registered mail that the proposed deficiency includes an accumulated earnings tax; or
- Within 60 days after mailing the notification mentioned above, the corporation submits a statement of the grounds (and facts sufficient to show the basis of the grounds) on which it relies to establish that the accumulation was not beyond the reasonable needs of its business. An additional 30 days may be granted for good cause.

¶20,150 INCOME SUBJECT TO THE TAX

The accumulated earnings tax is imposed on *accumulated taxable income, not* on surplus earnings above reasonable accumulation for the present year [Code Sec. 531]. Accumulated taxable income is adjusted taxable income [discussed below]minus the sum of: (1) the dividends-paid deduction [discussed below]and (2) the accumulated earnings credit [discussed below] [Code Sec. 535(a); Reg. § 1.535-2].

.01 Adjusted Taxable Income

Adjusted taxable income is taxable income with the following adjustments [Code Sec. 535(b); Reg. § 1.535-2]:

1. Add back the net operating loss deduction;
2. Add back the capital loss carryback or carryover (unless the corporation is a mere holding or investment company);

---

[37] *Ivan Allen Co.*, SCt, 75-2 USTC ¶ 9557, 422 US 617, 95 SCt 2501.

3. Add back the deduction for dividends received;
4. Either:
   a. Add the excess of the charitable contributions deduction allowed over the amount actually paid during the year; or
   b. Subtract the excess of charitable contributions actually paid during the year over the contributions deduction allowed;

   ▶ **OBSERVATION:** The net effect is that you deduct the full amount of the charitable contributions in the year they are actually paid.
5. Subtract federal income tax (contested income tax deficiency not deductible);[38]
6. Subtract taxes included in the foreign tax credit;
7. Subtract the disallowed net capital loss, reduced by the amount of any nonrecaptured capital gains deductions (unless the corporation is a mere holding or investment company). This insures that the same net capital gain is not used to reduce the net capital loss deduction more than once. The reduction is limited to the amount of the corporation's accumulated earnings and profits as of the close of the preceding tax year.
8. Subtract the net capital gain (computed without regard to carrybacks or carryovers), less the tax attributable to it. This figure is further reduced by net capital losses from prior years. Net capital loss carryforwards are treated as short-term capital losses. In the case of a foreign corporation, only gains and losses that are effectively connected with the conduct of a trade or business within the United States (and not exempt from tax under treaty) may be taken into account.

Special rules apply to figure the adjusted taxable income of holding and investment companies. The deduction for net capital loss and capital loss carryovers are not allowed. A net short-term capital gain deduction is allowed to the extent that it does not exceed capital loss carryovers to such year. The accumulated earnings and profits cannot be less than they would have been had these provisions applied to all tax years beginning after July 18, 1984 [Code Sec. 535(b)(8)].

.02 Dividends-Paid Deduction

From adjusted taxable income, subtract (1) dividends paid during the tax year (excluding dividends paid during first 2½ months of tax year if these were deducted for previous year); (2) dividends paid within 2½ months after close of tax year; and (3) consent dividends [Ch. 2].

The rules for the dividends-paid deduction of personal holding companies [Ch. 23] also apply here, except that no dividend carryover is allowed for purposes of the accumulated earnings tax, and the deduction for dividends paid after the close of the tax year is mandatory and unlimited.

No dividends-paid deduction is allowed for the accumulated earnings tax for any stock redemption by a mere holding or investment company that is not a regulated investment company [Code Sec. 562(b)]. Under prior law, dividend treatment could

[38] *Metro Leasing & Dev. Corp.*, CA-9, 2004-2 USTC ¶50,308, 376 F3d 1015, *aff'g*, 119 TC 8, Dec. 54,809 (2002).

be avoided through using stock redemptions, by means of which the shareholder would get capital gains treatment and the investment company would be free from the accumulated earnings tax.

.03 Accumulated Earnings Credit

From adjusted taxable income, also subtract the accumulated earnings credit. The credit is designed so that the accumulated earnings tax applies only to the amount unreasonably accumulated. The tax is not imposed unless accumulated earnings exceed $250,000 ($150,000 for certain personal service corporations) [Code Sec. 535(c)(2); Reg. § 1.535-3].

The accumulated earnings credit allowed is the *greater* of:

- Earnings and profits of the tax year retained for the reasonable needs of the business minus net capital gains (reduced by the tax on such gains); or
- $250,000 ($150,000 for a corporation the principal function of which is the performance of services in the field of health, law, engineering, architecture, accounting, actuarial science, performing arts, or consulting) *minus* the excess of accumulated earnings and profits at the end of preceding tax year reduced by dividends paid during the first 2 1/2 months of the tax year.

For a mere holding or investment company, the accumulated savings credit is the difference (if any) between $250,000 and the corporation's accumulated earnings and profits (reduced by dividends paid during the first 2 1/2 months of the year) as of the close of the preceding tax year.

> **Example 20-47:** Calendar year XYZ Corp had accumulated earnings and profits of $120,000 at the end of 2012. On March 1, 2013, it distributed $50,000 as taxable dividends. In 2012, XYZ's capital gain, minus the tax attributable to such gain, was $10,000. It had no capital loss. XYZ retained $30,000 for the reasonable needs of the business. Using the first formula, the credit would be $20,000 ($30,000 – $10,000). Using the second formula, the credit would be $180,000 ($250,000 – $70,000 ($120,000 – $50,000)). XYZ has an accumulated earnings credit of $180,000 under the second formula.

¶20,155 AVOIDING THE ACCUMULATED EARNINGS TAX

A corporation can avoid owing the tax by increasing its dividends-paid deduction to the point where the sum of the deduction and the accumulated earnings credit equals its adjusted taxable income. If the corporation is unwilling (or unable) to pay a dividend, it may increase its dividends-paid deduction by making a *consent dividend.* Consent dividends are phantom distributions that are treated as having been made to the stockholders on the last day of the corporation's tax year and immediately reinvested in the corporation as paid-in capital [Code Secs. 561(a)(2), 565; Reg. § 1.561-1(a)]. Interest is imposed on underpayments of the accumulated earnings tax from the due date of the tax return with respect to which that tax is imposed.

AFFILIATED AND RELATED CORPORATIONS

¶20,160 AFFILIATED CORPORATIONS—CONSOLIDATED RETURNS

An affiliated group of corporations may elect to be taxed as a single unit and thus eliminate intercompany gains and losses. This permits the affiliated group to file a consolidated return, rather than separate returns. Taxpayers often try to qualify their subsidiary corporations as members of a consolidated group because of the many advantages that exist in filing consolidated return as listed below. The privilege of filing a consolidated return is extended to all the corporations that have been members of the affiliated group at any time during the tax year provided they file consent before the last day for filing the return. The filing of a consolidated return by all of the affiliated corporations is considered such consent [Code Secs. 1501, 1502; Reg. § 1.1502-75(b)].

A group that filed (or was required to file) a consolidated return for the immediately preceding year must file a consolidated return for the current tax year unless an election to discontinue is made [Reg. § 1.1502-75(a)(2)]. A group is considered as remaining in existence for a tax year as long as the common parent remains the common parent and at least one subsidiary that was affiliated with it at the end of the prior year remains affiliated with it [Reg. § 1.1502-75(d)]. An affiliated group of corporations that did not file a consolidated return for the immediately preceding tax year may file a consolidated return instead of separate returns for the tax year, provided each member of the group during any part of the tax year consents no later than the due date (including extensions) for filing the common parent's return for the tax year [Reg. § 1.1502-75(a)(1)]. To consent, each subsidiary executes Form 1122, *Authorization and Consent of Subsidiary Corporation to Be Included in a Consolidated Income Tax Return,* which is attached to the consolidated return made on Form 1120 for the group by the common parent [Reg. § 1.1502-75(h)(2)]. If a member of the group fails to file Form 1122, the IRS has the discretion to determine that such member has joined in the making of the consolidated return. If the IRS makes this determination, the member is treated as if it had filed a Form 1122 for the year [Reg. § 1.1502-75(b)(2)]. Consents are required only for the first consolidated return year. The common parent must prepare Form 851 (Affiliations Schedule), which is also attached to Form 1120 [Reg. § 1502-75(h)).

In *Falconwood Corp,*[39] an affiliated group that survived the downstream merger of its former common parent into a subsidiary could use a postmerger loss to offset the group's prior year income. The step transaction doctrine was not applicable because the restructuring had an independent business purpose and, therefore, the taxpayer was bound to follow the consolidated return regulations.

---

[39] *Falconwood Corp.*, CA-FC, 2005-2 USTC ¶ 50,597, 422 F3d 1339, *rev'g and rem'g*, FedCl, 2004-1 USTC ¶ 50,242.

.01 What Is an Affiliated Group?

Generally, an affiliated group is one or more chains of corporations connected through stock ownership with a common parent corporation which is an includible corporation provided the following two requirements be met:

- The common parent must directly own stock possessing at least 80 percent of the total voting power of at least one of the other includible corporations and having a value equal to at least 80 percent of the total value of stock of the corporation; and
- Stock meeting the 80 percent test in each includible corporation other than the common parent must be owned directly by one or more of the other includible corporations [Code Sec. 1504(a)].

Most corporations will be considered "includible" corporation and can be part of the affiliated group for consolidated return purposes with the following exceptions [Code Sec. 1504(b), (c), (e)]:

- Corporations exempt from tax, other than a title-holding company described in Sec. 501(c)(2) and the exempt organizations deriving income from it [Ch. 23] [Code Sec. 1504(e)];
- Insurance companies subject to tax under Code Sec. 801;
- Foreign corporations;
- Corporations electing the possession tax credit [Ch. 28];
- Regulated investment companies [Ch. 23];
- Real estate investment trusts [Ch. 23];
- A DISC as defined in Code Sec. 992(a)(1); and
- An S corporation.

The term *stock* for purposes of determining whether there is an affiliated group does not generally include certain preferred stock [Code Sec. 1504(a); Reg. § 1. 1502-1(g)(2)(i)]. Excluded stock is stock with each of the following characteristics: (1) it is not entitled to vote, (2) it is limited and preferred as to dividends, (3) it does not significantly participate in corporate growth, (4) it has redemption and liquidation rights that do not exceed the issue price of such stock, except for a reasonable redemption or liquidation premium, and (5) it is not convertible into another class of stock [Code Sec. 1504(a)(4)].

.02 Importance of Voting Stock

Most litigation in this area involves determining whether the stock to be counted in determining affiliated group status is *voting stock.* The most important feature in determining whether stock is voting stock is the ability to elect the board of directors and thereby have a say in the control of the business.[40] The Tax Court has refused to apply this so-called mechanical test and instead examined all the facts surrounding the management of the company and the voting rights of the various classes of its stock, its board and the members of the board.[41] As a result, in determining whether the 80

[40] Rev. Rul. 69-126, 1969-1 CB 218.

[41] *Alumax*, CA-11, 99-1 USTC ¶ 50,210, 165 F3d 822.

percent voting power requirement under Code Sec. 1504(a) is satisfied, so a subsidiary can be included in a consolidated group, the court also considered the rights given to a special class of nonvoting stock and concluded they were equivalent to voting stock. As a result the nonvoting stock was considered voting stock for purposes of determining whether the corporations could be consolidated.

▶ **PRACTICE WARNING:** Now that the mechanical test can no longer be relied on to determine whether stock should be counted in determining affiliated group status, be sure to consider the voting rights of all classes of stock. You may find that the minority nonvoting stock holders actually have so much control over the management of the corporation that the 80 percent voting power requirement is not satisfied.

.03 Changing the Election

Once a group files a consolidated return, it must continue to do so as long as it exists, unless the IRS consents to a discontinuance. A group generally continues to exist as long as the common parent and at least one subsidiary remain.

.04 Considerations in Filing Consolidated Return

Whether a consolidated return is advantageous depends on the facts in each case. To enable you to assess better the advisability of electing a consolidated return, Table 2 lists the most common advantages and disadvantages in filing consolidated returns.

Table 2. Advantages and Disadvantages of Filing Consolidated Returns

Advantages	Disadvantages
1. Current offset of each member's ordinary losses against other members' profits in many instances; similarly as to treatment for capital gains and losses. Carryback and carry forward of losses may be greater against a bigger consolidated income.	1. Locked-in effect of filing consolidated return (can be painful). IRS permission is required to discontinue consolidated return filing, and must be for good cause.
2. Deferral of income on intercompany transactions.	2. Deferral of loss on intercompany transaction.
3. Intercompany dividends are 100 percent tax-free.	3. Recordkeeping complications from deferred intercompany transactions.
4. Centralization of tax structure.	4. Possible loss of all or portion of foreign tax and investment credits.
5. Group use of foreign taxes paid by a member in excess of its limitations on foreign tax credits; similar group use of business credits.	5. Necessity to make adjustments in opening and closing inventories for intercompany profits.
6. Use by other members of excess of the following attributes over limitations: (a) charitable contributions and (b) soil and water conservation of tax structure.	6. Subsidiary's tax year must conform to parent's; may result in short year and possible reduction in loss carry-over.
7. Ability to establish joint profit-sharing or stock bonus plans [Ch. 3].	7. Many unique minority shareholder problems and possible derivative actions.
8. The LIFO conformity requirement applies to affiliated corporations [Ch. 17] [Code Sec. 472(g)(2)].	

The Supreme Court concluded in *United Dominion Industries, Inc.*,[42] that product liability expenses of individual members of an affiliated group of five corporations could be counted toward the consolidated net operating loss being carried back on the group's consolidated tax return. This decision is good news to affiliated groups where some of the members have incurred large product liability losses even though the corporations were individually solvent. This decision aggregates the product liability losses so they can be carried back on the group's consolidated return.

.05 Intercompany Transactions

The consolidated return regulations generally treat intercompany transactions on a" single entity basis". The single entity approach for intercompany transactions is an integral part of the overall tax treatment of affiliated groups filing consolidated returns under Code Sec. 1502. Treating intercompany transactions on a single entity basis is required to clearly reflect consolidated taxable income ("CTI") and consolidated tax liability ("CTL"). However, in certain circumstances, the IRS may exercise discretion and grant consent, under Reg. § 1.1502-13(e)(3), to a consolidated group to treat some or all intercompany transactions (other than intercompany transactions with respect to stock or obligations of members of a consolidated group) on a separate entity basis (that is, without the application of Reg. § 1.1502-13). Consent under Reg. § 1.1502-13(e)(3) may require changes in the methods of accounting for intercompany transactions of members of a consolidated group. In Rev. Proc. 2009-31,[43] the IRS provides rules detailing the procedures for consolidated groups to elect under Reg. § 1.1502-13(e)(3) to account for intercompany transactions on a separate entity basis. These requests must be submitted as a private letter ruling request and apply to all members of the consolidated group. The election may generally be revoked without IRS consent, or automatic revocation may occur. In addition, the IRS can revoke or modify the election if the circumstances under which the ruling was granted change substantially and it is determined that single-entity reporting is necessary in order to clearly reflect income and tax liability. The IRS sets forth the time and manner in which requests for consent must be filed and provides a checklist to facilitate the filing and handling of requests under Reg. § 1.1502-13(e)(3) by specifying the information that should be included so that applications will be as complete as possible when originally filed.

.06 Consolidated Returns Barred After Termination

Once a corporation terminates its membership in a consolidated group, it generally thereafter cannot be included in any consolidated return filed by the same group before the 61st month starting after the first tax year in which the corporation stopped being a member.[44] The IRS will allow certain taxpayers to receive an automatic waiver of the 60-month waiting period for reconsolidating returns. To get an automatic waiver, the deconsolidated corporation must be included in the affiliated group's timely filed consolidated return for the tax year that includes the date it most

[42] *United Dominion Industries*, SCt, 2001 USTC ¶ 50,430, 532 US 822, 121 SCt 1934, *rev'g and rem'g*, CA-4, 2000-1 USTC ¶ 50,310, 208 F3d 452. *See subsequent case at United Dominion Industries*, CA-4, 2001-2 USTC ¶ 50,571, 259 F3d 193.

[43] Rev. Proc. 2009-31, IRB 2009-27, 107.

[44] Rev. Proc. 2002-32, 2002-1 CB 959, as modified by Rev. Proc. 2006-21, IRB 2006-24, 1050, to improve electronic filing of returns and to reduce reporting requirements.

recently became an affiliated group member. In addition, a statement containing the following information must be attached to the return:

- Name, address, and employer identification number of the relevant corporations;
- Information regarding the taxable income of the relevant corporations; and
- Analysis pertaining to the effect of the disaffiliation and subsequent consolidation.

When the waiver is granted, it is binding on the consolidated group filing the consolidated return and there can be no revocation by the consolidated group. The waiver is binding as of the date the deconsolidated corporation most recently became a current group member-unless permission is given for the whole group to stop filing a consolidated return.

¶20,165 CONTROLLED CORPORATIONS—MULTIPLE TAX LIMITATIONS

Members of a controlled group of corporations are treated as a single corporation for applying the graduated tax rate brackets below the top 35 percent bracket. The rate structure is apportioned equally among them or shared as they elect (see the description of the election below). Members of a controlled group are treated as one corporation for purposes of the additional 5 percent surtax tax on corporations with incomes over $100,000 but less than $335,000 and the 3 percent surtax on corporations with taxable income in excess of $15,000,000 [¶20,010]. This additional tax is divided among the members in the same manner as they share in the group's single taxable income amount in each bracket [Code Sec. 1561(a)]. For purposes of allocating the maximum amount in each tax bracket among members of a controlled group, the taxable income of a controlled group is taken into account and any increase in the tax attributable to the additional tax on taxable income over $100,000 equal to the lesser of 5 percent or $11,750 is also divided among the component members in the same manner as the maximum amount in each rate bracket is apportioned among members of the controlled group.

.01 Accumulated Earnings Credit

Members of a controlled group of corporations are limited to one accumulated earnings credit totaling $250,000 ($150,000 for certain personal service corporations) which must be divided *equally* among the component members [¶20,150] [Code Sec. 1561(a)(2)].

.02 Alternative Minimum Tax

The AMT exemption available to corporations in the amount of $40,000 is divided equally among the members of a controlled group, unless all of the members consent to an apportionment plan providing for an unequal allocation of the exemption [Ch. 16] [Code Secs. 55(d)(2), 1561(a)(3)]. You must file the consent of an apportionment plan with the District Director or the Service Center where the component member files its return [Reg. § 1.58-1(c)(3)(ii)].

.03 Controlled Groups

Controlled groups fall into four main categories [Code Sec. 1563(a); Reg. § 1.1563-1(a)(1)(i)]:

- Parent corporations and their 80 percent subsidiaries (basically the same as the parent-subsidiary group that is eligible to file a consolidated return [¶ 20,160]).
- Brother-sister corporations. These are two or more corporations at least 50 percent owned by five or fewer individuals, estates or trusts. The stock ownership of each person is taken into account only to the extent that such stock ownership is identical with respect to each corporation.
- Combined groups, see Reg § 1.1563-1(a)(4); or
- Life insurance controlled groups. See Reg. § 1.1563-1(a)(5).

Special attribution rules apply to determine stock ownership [Code Sec. 1563(d), (e); Reg. § § 1.1563-2(b)(1), 1.1563-3(b)(1)]. For example, a person is considered to own the stock of a corporation if he or she (1) owns an option to buy the stock, (2) is a 5 percent or more owner of a partnership or corporation which owns such stock, or (3) has children or grandchildren under 21 years of age who own such stock.

Excluded Corporations

Some corporations are not counted as members of a group, even if they are controlled. A corporation that is a member of a controlled group of corporations on December 31 of any tax year will be treated as an excluded member of the group for the tax year including that December 31 if the corporation: (1) is a tax-exempt corporation that has no unrelated business income; (2) it is a foreign corporation that does not have income effectively connected with a U.S. business [Ch. 28]; (3) it is an S Corporation; (4) it is an insurance company (other than an insurance company that is a member of a controlled group of insurance companies); or (5) it is a franchised corporation (the stock is sold to the corporate employees, and the corporation sells or distributes products of another group member) [Code Sec. 1563(b)(2); Reg. § 1.1563-1(b)(2)(ii)].

.04 Election

The election to apportion the graduated tax rate amounts is made with respect to members' tax years including the same December 31. All corporations that were members of the group on that day must consent to an apportionment plan if the amounts are not divided equally [Code Sec. 1561(a)].

¶20,170 DISALLOWANCE OF BENEFITS OF GRADUATED CORPORATE RATES AND ACCUMULATED EARNINGS CREDIT

If the corporation, or five or fewer individuals in control of a corporation, transfer property (other than money), directly or indirectly, to a newly created corporation or a corporation not actively engaged in business at the time it was acquired and after the transfer the transferor or transferors are in control of the transferee corporation, the controlled corporation can lose its benefits of graduated corporate rates and the accumulated earnings credit [¶20,150]. The tax breaks are lost unless it is proven that getting graduated rates and the credit was not a major purpose of the transfer. However, the IRS can allow the benefits and credit in part or allocate it among the corporations [Code Sec. 1551(a); Reg. § 1.1551-1(a)].

.01 Control

A corporation controls another a corporation if it owns at least 80 percent of the voting power or value of all classes of stock [Code Sec. 1551(b); Reg. § 1.1551-1(e)(1)(i)].

A group of five or fewer individuals controls corporations if (1) they own at least 80 percent of the voting power or value of the stock of each corporation, and (2) they own more than 50 percent of the total combined voting power of all classes of stock entitled to vote or more than 50 percent of the total value of shares of all classes of stock of each corporation, taking into account only each one's least percentage of ownership in each corporation [Code Sec. 1551(b)(2)].

In either case, the constructive ownership rules at Ch. 13 apply.

Example 20-48: Alice owns 50 percent of the voting stock of Alpha Corporation and 30 percent of the voting stock of Beta Corporation. Betty, on the other hand, owns 30 percent of the voting stock of Alpha Corporation and 50 percent of the voting stock of Beta Corporation. As a result, they together own at least 80 percent of the voting stock of both corporations, and taking into account each one's least percentage ownership with respect to each corporation, they own more than 50 percent of the voting stock of each corporation.

Individual	Alpha Corporation	Beta Corporation	Least % Ownership
Alice	50	30	30
Betty	30	50	30
Total	80	80	60

¶20,175 ALLOCATION AMONG RELATED CORPORATIONS

The IRS can distribute, apportion, or allocate gross income, deductions, credits or allowances among organizations, trades or businesses owned or controlled by the same interests if it determines that it is necessary to prevent tax evasion or to clearly reflect the taxpayer's income [Code Sec. 482; Reg. § 1.482-1(a)(2)].[45]

Example 20-49: A subsidiary corporation rented a building it owned to the parent corporation. The parties arbitrarily adjusted the rental each year to result in the lowest possible combined tax. In such case, the accounts will be adjusted to show fair rental value.

[45] Rev. Proc. 99-32, 1999-2 CB 296.

The IRS will also impute the following: interest on interest-free or low-interest intercompany loans or advances; payment for certain services rendered by one related corporation for another and for the use or occupation of tangible or intangible property of one related corporation by another; and profit to the seller of tangible property to a related party [Reg. § 1.482-2(a)(ii)]. Income or deductions so allocated may later actually be transferred between the involved corporations without further tax consequences.[46]

[46] Rev. Proc. 99-32, 1999-2 CB 296.

S Corporations 21

ELECTING S CORPORATION STATUS

Becoming an S corporation . . . . . . ¶21,001
Advantages of operating as an S corporation . . . . ¶21,002
Drawbacks of an S corporation election . . . . ¶21,003
Comparison of S corporations, C corporations, and partnerships . . . . ¶21,005
Electing S corporation taxation . . ¶21,010
Requirements for taxation as S corporation . . . . ¶21,011
Eligible S corporation shareholders . . . . ¶21,012
100 shareholder limit . . . . ¶21,013
Trusts eligible to be S corporation shareholders . . . . ¶21,014
One class of stock requirement . . . ¶21,015
S corporation's tax year . . . . ¶21,016
Effect of S election on corporation . . . . ¶21,020
Terminating the S election . . . . ¶21,025

OPERATING AS AN S CORPORATION

Tax on S corporation income . . . . . ¶21,030
Treatment of certain gains . . . . ¶21,035
Pass-throughs to shareholders . . . . ¶21,040
Treatment of losses and deductions . . . . ¶21,045
Treatment of distributions . . . . ¶21,050
S corporations and payroll taxes . . ¶21,051
Adjustments to basis of stock . . . . ¶21,055

ELECTING S CORPORATION STATUS

S corporations are hybrid business entities. They combine the flexibility of a partnership with the advantages of operating in the corporate format. However, unlike regular corporations, S corporations are generally not treated as taxable entities for federal income tax purposes. Instead, once an S corporation election has been made, the corporation's income passes through to the S corporation shareholders. These shareholders then pay tax on S corporation income whether or not distributed. This pass-through-of-income principle parallels the tax treatment afforded entities taxed as partnerships.

¶21,001 BECOMING AN S CORPORATION

If a domestic corporation satisfies certain requirements, it may be exempt from federal income tax if an election is made by the shareholders to be treated for tax purposes as an S corporation. After a timely election is made, the electing corporation will be taxed like a partnership but also will be able to enjoy all the advantages of operating in the corporate form for all other purposes. The advantages and the drawbacks are discussed in ¶21,002 and ¶21,003. Briefly, a corporation is eligible to become an S corporation if:

- The corporation satisfied the requirements of S corporation status [¶21,011];
- All shareholders must consent to S corporation status [¶21,010];
- The corporation files Form 2553, *Election by a Small Business Corporation*, to indicate it selects S corporation status by certified mail (return receipt requested), registered mail, or a preapproved private delivery service, as listed in ¶26,065; and
- The corporation uses an appropriate tax year [¶21,016].

The burden of proof is on the taxpayer to file an S corporation election. For example, in *Higbee*,[1] the shareholders asserted that they had mailed Form 2553, but had no proof. The court held the S corporation election to be invalid. The IRS will be more lenient if the issue arises before audit, rather than in the courts as discussed in ¶21,010.

¶21,002 ADVANTAGES OF OPERATING AS AN S CORPORATION

The following is a brief summary of the main advantages of electing to be taxed as an S corporation:

- *Avoidance of double taxation.* S corporation earnings are generally taxed only once, at the shareholder level.

  ▶ **OBSERVATION:** This method of taxation is particularly beneficial when the individual tax rates are lower than the tax rate of the corporation.
- *Shareholders get an immediate deduction for losses.* Like partnerships, S corporation losses are passed through to shareholders and can offset income from other sources.

  ▶ **OBSERVATION:** These losses may be deducted subject to passive activity loss rules [Ch. 13] affecting some shareholders and the restriction that losses claimed do not exceed basis in S corporation stock and loans to the corporation.

  NOTE: If a shareholder does not have sufficient adjusted basis in stock or debt pass-through losses can be carried forward to succeeding tax years when the shareholder's basis is increased.

---

[1] *M. Higbee*, TC Summary Op. 2002-128.

- *No accumulated earnings tax penalty.* S corporation income can be accumulated without restriction and paid out later to shareholders tax-free to the extent of stock and debt basis. Tax is owed, however, when the income is earned.

- No personal holding company (PHC) tax.

  ▶ **OBSERVATION:** If the S corporation has carryover regular corporation earnings and profits, it is subject to passive income rules that restrict passive earnings in a way similar to the personal holding company tax [¶23,020].

  NOTE: Regular corporations must pay the PHC tax if they have a certain dollar amount of passive income and a restricted number of shareholders. S corporations that have no carryover regular corporation earnings and profits can have the benefits of unlimited amounts of passive income and can avoid the PHC tax. This break makes the initial election of S status particularly attractive for the holding of passive investments.

- *Family income splitting.* S corporations can be used to transfer business profits to children in lower tax brackets subject to the kiddie tax as discussed in ¶2170. See also ¶21,070.

  NOTE: Although this type of arrangement is permitted, the S corporation must pay a reasonable salary to S corporation officers or the IRS will adjust the distribution of corporate income to reflect the real contributions to the operation of the business.

- Tax-exempt interest pass-through.

  ▶ **OBSERVATION:** The tax-exempt income retains its character in shareholder's hands. Regular corporation tax-exempt interest distributed to the shareholders as dividends is subject to tax. Partnerships also can pass-through tax-exempt income.

- *Charitable contributions.* Although regular corporations are subject to a 10 percent of taxable income limit on charitable contribution deductions [¶20,070], shareholders can deduct their share of S corporation's contributions subject to the more liberal limits applicable to individuals [¶9075].

- *Earnings may be distributed free of FICA, FUTA, and Employment Taxes.* Distributions from an S corporation are free from FICA, FUTA, and other employment taxes such as State Unemployment Insurance. The problem is that some S corporations have abused this exemption and have paid their S corporation shareholders dividend distributions rather than wages which would be subject to FICA, FUTA, and the other employment taxes. Although dividends received by S corporation shareholders are taxable for federal income tax purposes, S corporations can avoid all employment taxes by making distributions instead of compensating wages to their shareholder-employees. The bad news is that the IRS has targeted the issue of S corporations paying distributions instead of wages. The IRS challenges the cases on two grounds: (1) for companies that pay some but "unreasonably low" salaries, the IRS will seek to increase the amount of salaries paid; and (2) for companies that pay no salaries at all but make distributions, the IRS will try to recharacterize the distributions as wages subject to employment tax. In *J. Radtke*,[2] the court concluded that S corporations are required to pay reasonable salaries to S corporation shareholders. For further discussion, see ¶21,051.

- *Protection from creditors.* An S corporation provides its shareholders with protection from corporation debts and against the corporation's creditors.
- *No recharacterization of pass-through items.* S corporations pass through certain items of income, expense to shareholders without recharacterization [Code Sec. 1366(a)(1)(A)].

.01 Gifts of S Corporation Stock

Shareholders can make gifts of stock yearly to their children. Because differences in voting rights are allowed in an S corporation, shareholders can retain control of the corporation by holding voting stock while giving gifts of nonvoting stock to children. If shareholders keep these stock gifts within the limits of the gift tax exclusion [Ch. 29], no gift tax will result. The limitation on valuation freezes, though, could reduce the estate tax savings [Ch. 29].

¶21,003 DRAWBACKS OF AN S CORPORATION ELECTION

Here are some drawbacks that should be considered when making an S election:

- Only one class of stock is allowed. For further discussion, see ¶21,015.

  ▶ **OBSERVATION:** Even though S corporations can issue voting and nonvoting stock, the fact that all the stock must be common restricts the ability to include investors with different interests. C corporations can issue preferred, common, and convertible stock without restriction. Partnership agreements may provide for an unlimited variety of interests.

An IRS ruling showed that an S corporation owner could, with care, impose restrictions and conditions on the shares transferred to other family members. This ruling concluded that imposing transfer restrictions and forced redemption conditions on some shares under the terms of a sole S shareholder's will, would not create a second class of stock.[3]

- *Passive income restrictions.* If the S corporation has accumulated C corporation earnings and profits, it could lose that S election if it violates the passive income test [Ch. 21].

  ▶ **OBSERVATION:** Even if the election is not lost, the S corporation will have to pay a corporate tax in any year in which passive income exceeds the prescribed limits.

- Fringe benefit restrictions.

---

[2] *J. Radtke*, CA-7, 90-1 USTC ¶50,113, 895 F2d 1196, *aff'g*, DC-WI, 89-2 USTC ¶9466, 712 F. Supp. 143. See also *Nu-Look Design, Inc.*, CA-3, 2004-1 USTC ¶50,138, 356 F3d 290, *cert. denied*, 125 SCt 60; *Yeagle Drywall Co.*, 82 TCM 814, Dec. 54,528(M), TC Memo. 2001-284, *aff'd in unpublished opinion*, CA-3, 2003-1 USTC ¶50,141, *cert. denied*, 123 SCt 2623.

[3] LTR 9022024 (Feb. 28, 1990).

NOTE: In Notice 2008-1,[4] the IRS concluded that a two-percent shareholder-employee may deduct amounts paid for insurance if the insurance plan was established by the S corporation. A plan is considered to be established by the S corporation if the S corporation makes the premium payments in the current year or the two-percent shareholder makes the premium payments and is, then, reimbursed by the S corporation. Payments, whether made directly by the S corporation or reimbursed by the S corporation, must be included in the shareholder's wages and reported on the shareholder's Form W-2, *Wage and Tax Statement*.

One of the major disadvantages of an S election is that if a shareholder owns more than 2 percent of the corporation's stock, he is not eligible for tax-sheltered fringe benefits he could have enjoyed if his corporation had been a C corporation. However, S corporations can offer their other employees the same tax-qualified retirement plans available to employees of C corporations. Some restrictions, though, apply to retirement plan loans [Ch. 3].

Fringe benefits subject to the 2 percent shareholder rule include:

- The cost of group term life insurance coverage up to $50,000 [Code Sec. 79];
- Amounts received from accident and health plans [Code Sec. 105];
- Contributions by an employer to accident and health plans [Code Sec. 106];
- Meals and lodging furnished for the convenience of the employer [Code Sec. 119];
- Employee achievement awards [Code Sec. 74(c)];
- Cafeteria plans [Code Sec. 125];
- Qualified transportation fringe benefits [Code Sec. 132(f)];
- Adoption assistance programs [Code Sec. 137(c)(2)];
- Contributions by the corporation to health savings accounts [Code Sec. 223]; and
- Qualified moving expenses reimbursements [Code Sec. 132(g)].

Some fringe benefits are not subject to the 2 percent shareholder rules. Therefore the corporation can deduct the cost of these fringe benefits up to the limits specified by the statutory limits regardless of the percentage of stock that the recipient shareholder owns. Moreover, they are excluded from the employee's income. The following fringe benefits qualify for full deductions:

- Pension and profit-sharing plans [Code Sec. 401(c)(1)];
- Compensation for injury or sickness [Code Sec. 104(a)(3)];
- Educational assistance programs [Code Sec. 127];
- Dependent care assistance [Code Sec. 129];
- No-additional-cost services, qualified employee discounts, working condition fringes, *de minimis* fringes, qualified retirement planning services and on-premises athletic facilities [Code Sec. 132].

The IRS has said that health and accident insurance premiums paid by S corporations for more-than-2 percent shareholder-employees must be treated as compensation for income tax purposes. (They are not, however, treated as compensation for FICA tax

[4] Notice 2008-1, 2008-1 CB 251.

purposes.) Result: The company payments are deductible by the corporation on Form 1120S, are subject to income tax withholding and must be reported on the shareholder-employee's Form W-2.[5]

- Tax years. An S corporation generally must operate on a calendar year basis unless it can establish a valid business purpose for a different tax year. An S corporation can elect to use a tax year other than a required year if certain procedures are followed [¶21,016].

  ▶ **OBSERVATION:** Under those procedures, an S corporation must make payments that are intended to represent the value of the tax deferral obtained by its shareholders through using a tax year different from the required tax year.

- Less favorable deductions.

  ▶ **OBSERVATION:** C corporate deductions may be more favorable than individual tax deductions. Your S corporation is not eligible for these special corporate deductions. One of the most significant is the dividends received deduction [¶20,050].

- Carryovers from regular corporation years.

  ▶ **OBSERVATION:** A C corporation with net operating loss and other such tax attributes could lose these tax benefits if it makes an S election. Carryovers between a C and an S corporation are not allowed. Also, when making the switch, S corporation years count in computing the maximum carryover period. If the S election is in effect for the entire carryover period, the C corporation carryover will be permanently lost [¶21,045].

- Shareholder redemption followed by spin-off may be taxable. For example, an S corporation's distribution of the stock of a subsidiary immediately after acquiring 100 percent control of it via redemption of its other 50 percent shareholder's stock was held not to qualify for nonrecognition as a tax-free spin-off under Code Sec. 355.[6]

¶21,005 COMPARISON OF S CORPORATIONS, C CORPORATIONS, AND PARTNERSHIPS

Table 1 summarizes the differences between partnerships, regular (i.e., C) corporations, and S corporations.

---

[5] Announcement 92-16, IRB 1992-5, 53, clarifying Rev. Rul. 91-26, 1991-1 CB 184.

[6] *D.P. McLaulin Jr.*, CA-11, 2002-1 USTC ¶50,156, 276 F3d 1269, *aff'g*, 115 TC 255, Dec. 54,047 (2000).

Table 1. Comparison of Entity Features

Points to Consider	S Corporations	C Corporations	Partnerships
Ownership limitations	100 shareholder limit and qualification requirements to be shareholders [¶21,010].	No limit on number or class of shareholders.	No limit on number or class of partners.
Liability exposure	Except in rare circumstances, shareholders are only liable for capital contributions.	Except in rare circumstances, shareholders are only liable for capital contributions.	General partners are personally, jointly, and severally liable for partnership obligations. Limited partner liable for capital contributions only.
Tax year	S corporation generally must use a calendar year unless business purpose shown for a fiscal year. S corporations can elect to use a tax year other than a required year if they follow specific procedures. Electing S corporations must make payments to the federal government that are intended to represent the value of the tax deferral obtained by the shareholders through the use of a tax year different from the required tax year [¶21,010].	Calendar or fiscal year permitted. Tax year does not have to match shareholders' tax years.	Must generally use same tax year as majority-interest partners (principal partners if majority partners don't have same tax year, or year resulting in least income deferral if principal partners don't have same tax year) unless business purpose show n for a different tax year. Partnerships can elect to use a tax year other than a required year if they follow specific procedures [Ch. 18; Ch. 24]. Electing partnerships must make payments (required payments) to the federal government that are in tended to represent the value of the tax deferral obtained by the partners through the use of a tax year different from the required tax year.
Federal tax return	Form 1120S, information return.	Form 1120, corporate income tax return [Ch. 20].	Form 1065, information return.

Points to Consider	S Corporations	C Corporations	Partnerships
Alternative minimum tax	Applies only at shareholder level. No ACE adjustment [Ch. 16].	Applies at corporate level. ACE adjustment [Ch. 16].	Applies only at partner level. No ACE adjustment [Ch. 16; Ch. 24].
Liquidation of business	No tax at corporate level (except for built-in gains) [¶21,035].	Double tax on corporate and shareholder levels [Ch. 22].	No tax at partnership level [Ch. 24].
Treatment of income and losses	Corporate income determined at entity level and passed through to each shareholder and taxed at shareholders' rates. Some S corps. pay tax on built-in gains and excess net passive income. Income and loss items that affect a shar eholder's tax liability are separately stated—e.g., charitable contributions and depletion [¶21,040].	All corporate income taxed at corporate level and again taxed at shareholder level when distributed as dividends. Some C corporations taxed as personal holding companies and can be taxed on excess accumulated income [Ch. 20; Ch. 23].	Same as S corp. except no tax on built-in gains or tax on passive income [Ch. 24].
Net operating losses	Losses pass through to shareholders and are deductible to the extent of their stock and debt basis. Losses may be carried back or forward [¶21,045].	Deductible only by the corporation in a year which it has offsetting income. Losses may be carried back or forward [Ch. 20].	Same pass-through rules as S corp.
Tax-exempt income	Tax-exempt income of corporation retains its character when passed through to the shareholders. It increases shareholders' stock bases [¶21,040].	Tax-exempt income increases corporate earnings and profits and is not taxed at corporate level. If distributed to shareholders as dividends, it is subject to tax.	Same pass-through rule as S corp.
Capital gains	Capital and Code Sec. 1231 gains pass through to shareholders and retain their character at shareholder level [¶21,035; ¶21,040].	Capital and Sec. 1231 gains taxed at corporate rate [Ch. 20].	Same rule as S corp. except no tax at partnership level on capital gains [Ch. 24].

Points to Consider	S Corporations	C Corporations	Partnerships
Capital losses	Capital losses pass through to shareholders and retain their character at the shareholder level. Losses offset capital gains and then up to $3,000 of ordinary income. May be carried forward indefinitely [¶21,035; ¶21,040].	Capital losses deducted at corporate level only to the extent of capital gains. Losses may be carried back 3 years or forward 5 years [Ch. 10].	Same rule as S corp. [Ch. 24].
Accumulated earnings	All income is passed through and taxed at shareholder level. S corps. with carryover C corp. earnings and profits are subject to corporate tax on excess passive income and distributions of accumulated earnings and profits taxed as dividend income [Ch. 21].	Corps. may accumulate income for reasonable business needs. Up to $150,000 for personal service corporations and $250,000 for other C corps. may be accumulated without question. Unreasonable accumulations subject to tax [Ch. 20].	All income taxed to partners whether distributed or not [Ch. 24].
Distributions and income allocations	Distributions are taxed to the extent they exceed a shareholder's basis in stock and debts. Corporation recognizes gain on distribution of appreciated property. Income may only be allocated in proportion to shareholdings [¶21,050].	Distributions taxed as ordinary income and allocated on basis of shareholders. C corp. will generally recognize gain on sale or distribution of appreciated property [Ch. 20].	Distributions taxed to the extent they exceed partner's basis in partnership interest and partnership debt. Distributive income shares may be allocated by agreement of the partners. Partnership does not recognize gain on distribution of appreciated property [Ch. 14].
Fringe benefits	Owner of more than 2 percent of S corp. shares cannot receive tax-free certain fringe benefits including, employer-provided health care, meals and lodging, and life insurance [¶21,002].	Shareholder- employees may receive tax-qualified fringe benefits without restriction [Ch. 4].	All partners not eligible for tax-free fringes.

Points to Consider	S Corporations	C Corporations	Partnerships
Retirement plans	Generally the same rules and limitations apply to S corps. as to C corps. with respect to qualified plans. S corps. do, however, have restrictive fringe benefit rules. Benefits only available to shareholders owning 2 percent or less of S stock.	C corp. can provide a broad variety of defined benefit and defined contribution plans, including those involving the corporation's own stock [Ch. 3].	Partners must establish own retirement plans.
Investment interest deduction	Shareholder deducts his share of the S corp.'s investment interest to the extent of his net investment income limitation [Ch. 9].	No limitation.	Partner may deduct his share of partnership's interest up to the extent of his net investment income limitation.
Dividends received	Taxed only to extent they exceed shareholder's basis in stock and debt.	C corp. can deduct 70 percent (80 percent if dividends received from 20 percent-or- more owned corp.) of dividends received from domestic corporations [Ch. 20].	Same rule as S corp.
FICA taxes	Tax payable by the corporation and the employees [Ch. 15].	Tax paid by the corporation.	Self-employment tax applies to salary and drawings.

¶21,010 ELECTING S CORPORATION TAXATION

An important benefit of establishing Subchapter S status is the ability to pass the S corporation's profits and losses through to the shareholders who then report them on their individual income tax returns, thus avoiding double taxation of corporate earnings. As the Supreme Court stated in *Gitlitz*[7] "[s]ubchapter S allows shareholders of qualified corporations to elect a 'pass-through' taxation system under which income is subjected to only one level of taxation." In order to take advantage of this benefit, a corporation must be a qualified corporation whose shareholders elect such treatment. An election may be made only with the consent of all of the shareholders of the corporation at the time of the election [Reg. § 1.1362-1]. Certain eligible entities that timely file S corporation elections will be deemed to have elected to be classified as associations taxable as corporations.

[7] *Gitlitz*, 2001-1 USTC ¶50,147, 531 US 206, 209 (2001).

.01 S Corporation Election Procedures

Small business corporations do not automatically receive S corporation tax status. In order for the favorable subchapter S tax rules to apply, a qualifying corporation must elect S corporation status and all shareholders at the time of the election must consent to the election and timely file Form 2553, *Election by a Small Business Corporation* [Code Sec. 1362(a)]. A qualifying small corporation may make an election to be treated as an S corporation (1) at any time during the preceding tax year, or (2) at any time during the tax year and on or before the 15th day of the third month of the tax year by filing Form 2553, *Election by a Small Business Corporation* [Code Sec. 1362(b)(1); Reg. § 1.1362-6(a)(2)]. This election should be sent by certified mail (return receipt requested), registered mail, or a preapproved private delivery service (e.g., Federal Express, Airborne Express, DDHL, or United Parcel Service).

In *Fankhouser*,[8] the Tax Court denied S status to a taxpayer because the IRS had no record of receiving Form 2553. The taxpayer had not sent it registered or certified mail and the taxpayer had no mailing record. If the taxpayer had mailed the form either registered or certified mail, the election would have been protected under Code Sec. 7502(c) even if the IRS never received the form [Ch. 26]. However, in Letter Ruling 200211023,[9] the IRS granted S status from the date of incorporation, even though it had no record of receiving Form 2553 and there was no proof the taxpayer mailed it.

Under Code Sec. 1362(b)(3), if an S corporation election is made after the 15th day of the 3rd month of the tax year and on or before the 15th day of the 3rd month of the following tax year, then the S corporation election is treated as made for the following tax year. If the election is late or if no election is made but the IRS finds there was reasonable cause for the failure to make a timely election, the IRS may still treat the election as on-time [Code Sec. 1362(b)]. Extensions of time to file an S corporation election are not granted ahead of time; however, the IRS may treat late-filed subchapter S elections as timely if there is a reasonable cause for the late filing [Code Sec. 1362(b)(5)].

Code Sec. 1361(b)(1)(B) limits the permitted shareholders of an S corporation to domestic individuals, estates, certain trusts, and certain exempt organizations. Code Sec. 1361(d)(1)(A) provides that a QSST is a permitted S corporation shareholder if the beneficiary of the QSST makes an election by signing and filing an election statement with the IRS. Reg. § 1.1361-1(j)(6)(iii) provides that the QSST election must be made within the 16-day-and-2-month period beginning on the day that the S corporation stock is transferred to the trust. Code Sec. 1361(c)(2)(A)(v) provides that an ESBT is a permitted S corporation shareholder if the trustee of the trust makes an election by signing and filing an election statement with the IRS. The election must be filed within the same time requirements as prescribed for filing a QSST election [Reg. § 1.1361-1(m)(2)(iii)].

Under Code Sec. 1361, an S corporation may elect to treat certain wholly owned subsidiaries as QSubs by filing Form 8869, *Qualified Subchapter S Subsidiary Election* with the IRS. The election may be filed at any time during the tax year [Reg.

---

[8] *E. Fankhauser*, 76 TCM 437, Dec. 52,872(M), TC Memo. 1998-328; *R.E. Dansby*, 97 TCM 1358, Dec. 57,775(M), TC Memo. 2009-70.

[9] LTR 200211023 (Dec. 14, 2001).

§ 1.1361-3(a)(3)]. The effective date of the election is the date specified on the form (provided the date specified is not earlier than two months and 15 days before the date of the filing and the date specified is not more than 12 months after the date of the filing), or on the date the election form is filed if no date is specified [Reg. § 1.1361-3(a)(4)]. If an election form specifies an effective date more than two months and 15 days prior to the date on which the election form is filed, it will be effective two months and 15 days prior to the date it is filed. If an election form specifies an effective date more than 12 months after the date on which the election is filed, it will be effective 12 months after the date it is filed.

NOTE: For election purposes, *month* means a period starting on the same day of any calendar month on which the corporation's tax year began, and ending with the close of the day before the corresponding day of the next calendar month. If there is no such corresponding day, the month ends with the close of the last day of the succeeding calendar month. Also, for the election, the new corporation's tax year begins on the date that it has shareholders, acquires assets or begins doing business, whichever is the first to occur [Reg. § 1.1362-6(a)(2)(ii)(C)].

Example 21-1: Ace Corp., a calendar year small business corporation, began its first tax year on January 7. To be an S corporation starting with its first tax year, Ace must make the election before March 22 of that same year. An election made earlier than January 7 of that year, would not be valid.

Example 21-2: Assume the same facts as Example 21-1, except that Ace begins its first tax year on November 8. To be an S corporation starting with its first tax year, Ace must make the election during the period that begins November 8, and ends before January 23 of the following year.

.02 S Corporation Shareholder Consent Required

The S corporation election is only valid if all S corporation shareholders at the time of the election consent to the election [Code Sec. 1362(a)(2)].[10] If the election is to be retroactive to the beginning of the year, all shareholders who owned stock that year (prior to the election) must sign the form [Code Sec. 1362(b)(2)(B); Reg. § 1.1362-6(b)(3)].

Example 21-3: On January 1, Baker Corp., operating on a calendar year, had 15 shareholders. On January 31 of that same year, two of Baker's shareholders, Richard Able and Bob Davis, sold their shares to Ben Proctor, Alex Reese, and Tom Tucker. On March 1 of that year, Baker Corp. filed its election to be an S corporation for that tax year. For the election to be effective, all those who owned shares from January 1 through March 1 of that year must consent to the election (including Able and Davis).

▶ **IMPORTANT:** Even if your corporation makes a timely election after the start of a tax year and on or before the 15th day of the third month, the election won't

---

[10] *Cabintaxi Corp.*, CA-7, 95-2 USTC ¶50,445, 63 F3d 614.

be effective until the following year if, at all times during the pre-election period, your corporation was not fully eligible to make the election or *any* stockholder during that period did not consent [Code Sec. 1362(b)(2); Reg. § 1.1362-6(a)(2)(ii)(B)].

Once a valid election is made, new shareholders need not consent to that election [Reg. § 1.1362-6(a)(2)(i)]. A shareholder's consent must be in the form of a written statement that sets forth the name, address, and taxpayer identification number of the shareholder, the number of shares of stock owned by the shareholder, the date (or dates) on which the stock was acquired, the date on which the shareholder's tax year ends, the name of the S corporation, the corporation's taxpayer identification number, and the election to which the shareholder consents. The statement must be signed by the shareholder under penalties of perjury. The consent statement should be attached to the corporation's election statement [Reg. § 1.1362-6(b)].

If an S corporation election is invalid because shareholder consents were omitted, Reg. § 1.1362-6(b)(3)(iii) provides that the S corporation can request an extension of time to furnish the consents. No user fee is required.

.03 Relief for Late S Corporation Elections

Taxpayers who want their business to be taxed as an S corporation for 2013 must file an S election on Form 2553, any time during 2013 or before March 15, 2014. If the election is filed after this date, the S election will not be effective until the following year. Failure to file could mean double taxation of earnings. Taxpayers who miss the deadline should not despair. In Rev Proc 2013-30,[11] the IRS simplified and consolidated the provisions for requesting relief for late S corporation elections under Code Sec. 1362, late QSST elections, late ESBT elections, late QSub elections, and late corporate classification elections. This procedure now represents the exclusive method by which taxpayers may apply for relief for these late elections. If these automatic relief provisions do not apply, the corporation may seek relief by filing a private letter ruling request with the IRS (in which case a user fee will apply). If no relief is sought from an untimely election, an S corporation election that is faulty only because it is filed after the due date will be treated as made for the following tax year [Code Sec. 1362(b)(3)]. The IRS ordinarily will not issue rulings or determination letters if the IRS has already provided an automatic approval or administrative procedure for an S corporation to obtain relief for late S corporation, QSST, QSub or ESBT elections.

How to Make Election

A taxpayer may request relief for a late S corporation election by completing the proper election form, attaching the required supporting documents, and filing it with the IRS by: (1) attaching the election form to the S corporation's current year Form 1120S within three years and 75 days after the date the election is intended to be effective; (2) attaching the election form to one of the S corporation's late-filed prior year Forms 1120S; (3) filing the election form independent of Form 1120S within three years and 75 days after the date the election is intended to be effective.

---

[11] Rev. Proc. 2013-30, IRB 2013-36, 173.

Other Requirements for Election

The requesting taxpayer must also include a statement that describes: (1) its reasonable cause for the failure to make a timely S corporation election or that the failure to make a timely election was inadvertent, and (2) the diligent actions that were made to correct the mistake upon its discovery. The election form must indicate at the top that it is filed "pursuant to Rev Proc 2013-30." Supporting statements including a "Reasonable Cause/Inadvertence Statement" must be signed under penalty of perjury. When the IRS receives the completed request for relief, IRS will determine whether the requirements for granting additional time to file the election under Subchapter S have been satisfied and will notify the requesting taxpayer of its determination.

.04 Reasonable Cause for Late or Inadvertent Defective Election

The S corporation must show reasonable cause for the late election. In most private letter rulings on relief from late elections, taxpayers were granted inadvertent termination relief under Code Sec. 1362(b)(5) if the taxpayer could establish reasonable cause for the failure to make a timely election and could show that granting the relief would not prejudice government interests and a proper election was filed within 20 days of the ruling. The IRS has been liberal in granting relief for late or inadvertent S corporation elections.[12]

The IRS has the authority to give taxpayers a break where the S corporation election was ineffective because it failed to meet statutory requirements, or where the election was inadvertently terminated as a result of some mistake made by one of the shareholders. The IRS can waive the effect of an inadvertent defective S election if the IRS finds that:

- The election was not effective because of a failure to qualify as a small business corporation or to obtain the required shareholder consents;
- The circumstances resulting in such ineffective election were inadvertent; and
- Within a reasonable period of time after discovering the circumstances causing the invalidity, the corporation takes steps to correct the ineffective election, specifically, the corporation becomes a small business corporation or acquires the requisite shareholder consents [Code Sec. 1362(f)].

.05 Late Elections in Community Property States

When stock of the corporation is owned by husband and wife as community property (or the income from the stock is community property), each person having a community property interest in the stock or its income must consent to the S election in order for it to be valid [Reg. § 1.1362-6(b)(2)(i)].

In Rev. Proc. 2004-35,[13] the IRS provided automatic relief for late filing of shareholder consent for spouses of S corporation shareholders in community property states [Arizona, California, Idaho, Louisiana, Nevada, New Mexico, Texas, Washington, and Wisconsin]. This relief provision is effective for all relief applications, including those

---

[12] LTR 201227004 (July 6, 2012); LTR 201222034 (May 18, 2012); LTR 201216030 (April 20, 2012); LTR 201127008 (July 8, 2011); LTR 201119009 (May 13, 2011); LTR 201104014 (Jan. 28, 2011); LTR 201049023 (Dec. 10, 2010); LTR 200919021 (Jan. 30, 2009); LTR 9837012 (May 28, 1997); LTR 9735008 (May 23, 1997); LTR 9735020 (May 30, 1997); LTR 9735019 (May 30, 1997); LTR 9735026 (May 30, 1997), but see LTR 201123013 (June 10, 2011) (no reasonable cause established).

[13] Rev. Proc. 2004-35, 2004-1 CB 1029.

already under consideration by the IRS, provided the taxpayers satisfy all eligibility and procedural requirements. If denied relief under this revenue procedure, a corporation may request relief under Reg. § 1.1362-6(b)(3)(iii) or request inadvertent invalid election relief by requesting a letter ruling. Automatic relief is available if the following conditions are met:

- The S corporation election is invalid solely because the Form 2553, *Election by a Small Business Corporation*, failed to include the signature of a community property spouse who was a shareholder solely pursuant to state community property law; and
- Both spouses have reported all items of income, gain, loss, deduction, or credit consistent with the S corporation election on all affected federal income tax returns.

A shareholder that satisfies the requirements of Rev. Proc. 2004-35 will be deemed to have (1) reasonable cause for the failure to consent to the S corporation elections, (2) made the request for the extension of time to file a consent within a reasonable time under the circumstances, and (3) satisfied the requirement that the interests of the government will not be jeopardized by treating the election as valid. Accordingly, the shareholder will automatically be granted relief to file the late shareholder consent.

.06 S Election Doubles as Deemed Check-the-Box Corporation Election

An eligible entity that wants to be classified as an S corporation may elect to be classified as an association under Reg. § 301.7701-3(c)(1)(i) by filing Form 8832, *Entity Classification Election*, and electing to be an S corporation under Code Sec. 1362(a) by filing Form 2553. If an eligible entity fails to file a timely Form 2553, Rev. Proc. 2013-30[14] provides a simplified method for requesting relief. The method provided is in lieu of the letter ruling process ordinarily used to obtain relief for late elections. Accordingly, user fees do not apply. For further discussion see ¶ 21,010.03.

¶21,011 REQUIREMENTS FOR TAXATION AS S CORPORATION

To qualify for taxation as an S corporation, the corporation must satisfy the following requirements set forth in Code Sec. 1361(b)(1):

- Be a domestic corporation. See ¶ 21,011.
- Have no more than 100 shareholders. See ¶ 21,013.
- Have only eligible shareholders which include individuals, decedent's estates, certain prescribed trusts, but no nonresident aliens. See ¶ 21,012.
- Have only one class of stock. See ¶ 21,015.

.01 Domestic Corporation

The corporation must be a domestic corporation organized in the United States (including any territory) which is not an ineligible corporation [Code Sec. 1361(b)(1)].

[14] Rev. Proc. 2013-30, IRB 2013-36, 173.

.02 Ineligible Corporations

An *ineligible corporation* is defined as:

- A financial institution that uses the reserve method of accounting for bad debts described in Code Sec. 585;
- An insurance company (other than certain stock casualty insurance companies);
- A corporation electing the Puerto Rico and possessions tax credit under Code Sec. 936; or
- A DISC or former DISC [Code Sec. 1361(b)(2)].

.03 S Corporation Must File Return

Every small business corporation which has made an S corporation election must file a tax return for each tax year on Form 1120-S, *U.S. Income Tax Return for an S Corporation* even though the entity itself is not subject to tax [Code Sec. 6037(a)]. The return must report income and allowable deductions as well as the names and addresses of all shareholders, the number of shares owned by each shareholder at all times during the year, the amount of money and other property distributed by the corporation to them and their pro-rata share of corporation items [Reg. § 1.6037-1]. Each S corporation required to file a return must furnish each person who is a shareholder a copy of the information shown on the Form 1120-S [Code Sec. 6037(b)]. S corporations must also deliver a copy of each shareholder's Schedule K-1 to them on or before the filing due date of the return.

.04 Penalty for Failure to File S Corporation Return

S corporations that fail to file Form 1120S each year as required under Code Sec. 6037 are subject to an entity level penalty. The penalty is assessed each month (or portion thereof) that the failure continues, for a maximum of twelve months [Code Sec. 6699(a)]. The base penalty is $195 per shareholder for each month, or fraction of a month, during which the failure continues, up to a maximum of twelve months [Code Sec. 6699(b)]. An S corporation can avoid the penalty if it shows reasonable cause for failing to meet its filing obligation [Code Sec. 6699(c)]. If the S corporation files a return with incomplete return information, but submits the missing information within 30 days of the IRS's request that it do so, or within 30 days following a second notice requesting the missing information, the penalty may be abated.[15]

¶21,012 ELIGIBLE S CORPORATION SHAREHOLDERS

.01 Shareholder Eligibility

Code Sec. 1361(b) restricts S shareholder eligibility to U.S. citizens, resident individuals, estates, certain trusts described in Code Sec. 1361(c)(2), and certain tax-exempt organizations described in Code Sec. 1361(c)(6). For further discussion of the trusts that are eligible to own S corporation stock, see ¶21,014. Tax exempt organizations described in Code Secs. 401(a), 501(c)(3), and 501(a) (so-called qualified tax exempt shareholders) can be shareholders in an S corporation and will count as one share-

[15] IRM 20.1.2.10.3 (09-04-2009).

holder for purposes of determining the number of shareholders in an S corporation [Code Sec. 1361(b)(1)(B), (c)(6)].

The acquisition of S stock by an ineligible shareholder will result in the inadvertent termination of the S election. A partnership is an ineligible S corporation shareholder but a partnership may hold S corporation stock as a nominee for an individual, trust or estate that is eligible to be an S corporation shareholder [Reg. § 1.1361-1(e)(1)]. In addition, an entity classified as an association that is taxable as a corporation under Reg. § 301.7701-2 may elect to be treated as an S corporation if it otherwise qualifies to be an S corporation [Reg. § 1.1361-1(c)].

Individual Retirement Accounts

Individual retirement accounts (IRAs) (including Roth IRAs) are not otherwise eligible S corporation shareholders [Reg. § 1.1361-1(h)(1)(vii)]. In Rev. Rul. 92-73,[16] the IRS provides that traditional IRAs are ineligible S corporation shareholders because the beneficiaries of a traditional IRA is not taxed currently on S corporation's income whereas the beneficiaries of the permissible S corporation shareholder trusts listed in Code Sec. 1361(c)(2)(A) are taxed currently on the trust's share of such income. In *Taproot Administrative Services, Inc.*,[17] the Court of Appeals for the Ninth Circuit affirmed the Tax Court to conclude that a Roth IRA was an ineligible S corporation shareholder.

Nonresident Aliens

A nonresident alien is an ineligible shareholder [Code Sec. 1361(b)(1)(C)]. A nonresident alien is defined as an individual who is neither a citizen of the United States nor a resident in the United States for at least one-half of the year [Code Sec. 7701(b)(1)(B)]. For purposes of this rule, a dual resident alien who claims special tax benefits under an international treaty is considered a nonresident alien.

A U.S. shareholder whose nonresident alien spouse has a current ownership interest in his stock under local law (such as a community property interest under foreign law) is ineligible to be an S corporation shareholder [Reg. § 1.1361-1(g)].

.02 Qualified Subchapter S Subsidiaries (QSubs)

Code Sec. 1361 allows S corporations to have wholly owned qualified Subchapter S subsidiaries (QSubs) and not run afoul of the S corporation qualification rules. This means that an S corporation can drop or divide up separate divisions of its business into 100 percent owned subsidiaries and not jeopardize its S election. To qualify for this treatment, the parent S corporation must:

- Elect to treat a wholly owned subsidiary as a qualified subchapter S subsidiary (QSub); and
- Own 100 percent of the stock of the subsidiary, which must be a domestic corporation that would be an eligible to be an S corporation (as discussed above) if the stock were owned by the shareholders of the parent [Code Sec. 1361(b)(3); Reg. § 1.1361-2(a)].

---

[16] Rev. Rul. 92-73, 1992-2 CB 224.

[17] *Taproot Administrative Services, Inc.*, 133 TC 202, Dec. 57,950 (2009), *aff'd*, CA-9, 2012-1 USTC ¶ 50,256, 679 F3d 1109.

After the QSub election is made, except as discussed below, the QSub is not treated as a separate corporation; the QSub election results in a deemed liquidation of the subsidiary into the parent. Following the deemed liquidation, all the subsidiary's assets, liabilities and items of income, deductions, and credits are treated as those of the parent S corporation [Code Sec. 1361(b)(3)(A); Reg. § 1.1361-4(a)(1)]. In essence, the stock of the QSub is disregarded for federal tax purposes, except for purposes of meeting the 100 percent stock ownership requirement [Reg. § 1.1361-4(a)(4)]. QSubs which generally are disregarded as entities separate from their owners for federal tax purposes will be treated as separate entities for federal employment tax and related reporting requirement purposes [Reg. § 1.1361-4(a)(7)].

Because the liquidation is a deemed liquidation, there is no need to file Form 966, *Corporate Dissolution or Liquidation*. However, a final return for the subsidiary may have to be filed if it was a separate corporation prior to the date of the deemed liquidation. No final return is required if this election is being made pursuant to a reorganization under Code Sec. 368(a)(1)(F) and Rev. Rul. 2008-18.[18]

If the QSub ceases to qualify as such because the parent revokes the election or because the QSub ceases to qualify, another QSub election for the subsidiary may not be made for five years without the consent of the IRS.

It is possible to set up multiple tiering of QSub subsidiaries and not run afoul of the rules. For example, you could own 100 percent of the stock of Corp. A, which in turn owns 100 percent of Corp. B, which owns 100 percent of Corp. C. If you have made an S election for A and a QSub election for B, Corp. A may elect to treat Corp. C as a QSub [Reg. § 1.1361-2(b)]. If, however, there is a break in the chain of elections, the lower-tier subsidiaries will be disqualified from treatment as QSubs [Reg. § 1.1361-2(c), Ex. 4].

.03 Mechanics of QSub Election

An S corporation will make a QSub election for an eligible subsidiary by filing Form 8869, *Qualified Subchapter S Subsidiary Election*, with the IRS. The parent S corporation can make the QSub election at any time during the tax year. However, the effective date of the election depends upon when it is filed. The effective date of the QSub election is the date that Form 8869 is filed unless the election form specifies a different date [Reg. § 1.1361-3(a)(3)].

A QSub election form may specify an effective date that is up to two months and 15 days prior to the date on which the QSub election is filed or up to 12 months after the election is filed. The QSub election does not have to be made within the first two months and 15 days of the tax year. Instead, it can be made up to one year in advance [Reg. § 1.1361-3(a)(3)]. Extensions may be available [Reg. § 1.1361-3(a)(5)]. File Form 8869 with the IRS Service Center where the subsidiary filed its most recent return. However, if the parent S corporation forms a subsidiary and makes a valid election effective upon formation, submit Form 8869 to the service center where the parent S corporation filed its most recent return. The IRS will notify the corporation whether or not the QSub election is accepted. The corporation should generally receive a determination within 60 days after it has filed Form 8869. If the IRS questions whether Form 8869 was filed, an acceptable proof of filing is:

[18] Rev. Rul. 2008-18, IRB 2008-13, 674.

- A certified or registered mail receipt (timely post-marked) from the U.S. Postal Service, or its equivalent from a designated private delivery service;
- A Form 8869 with an accepted stamp;
- A Form 8869 with a stamped IRS received date; or
- An IRS letter stating that Form 8869 has been accepted.

For discussion of relief from late elections, see ¶21,010.

The QSub election form must be signed by the president, treasurer, assistant treasurer, chief accounting officer or any other corporation officer authorized to sign the S corporation's return [Reg. §1.1361-3(a)(1)].

.04 Effects of QSub Election

The QSub election will have the following effects:

- When an S corporation makes a valid QSub election for a subsidiary, the subsidiary is deemed (in a legal fiction) to have liquidated into the parent S corporation immediately before the election is effective. The stock of the subsidiary is cancelled (or redeemed) and, in exchange, the assets of the subsidiary are transferred to the parent corporation. This liquidation is generally treated as a tax-free transaction under Code Sec. 332, which provides that the parent recognizes no gain or loss as a result of the liquidation. Similarly, Code Sec. 337 provides that the subsidiary recognizes no gain or loss on the transaction.
- The tax treatment of the liquidation, alone or in the context of any larger transaction, generally is determined under all relevant Code provisions and general tax law principles, including the step transaction doctrine [Reg. §1.1361-4(a)(2)]. The step transaction doctrine looks at a transaction in its entity rather than at its component steps individually. For example, if James sells property to Bill who in turn sells it to George, the step transaction doctrine looks at the transaction as a sale from James to George. The step transaction doctrine will ignore intermediate steps if they lack economic substance and are only used to accomplish indirectly what cannot be accomplished directly.
- Corporations may move freely between QSub and S corporation status, provided there is no intervening period for which the corporation is treated as a C corporation [Reg. §1.1361-5(d)].
- The QSub status of a corporation continues until it terminates. If a QSub election terminates, the corporation is treated as a new corporation acquiring all of its assets (and assuming all of its liabilities) from the S corporation in exchange for stock of the new corporation immediately before the termination [Code Sec. 1361(b)(3)(C)]. The tax treatment of the termination is determined under the Code and general tax law principles, including the step transaction doctrine [Reg. §1.1361-5(b)]. The tax treatment of QSubs is changed when the sale of QSub stock terminates the QSub election. The stock sale is treated as a sale of an undivided interest in the assets and liabilities of the QSub that is equal to the percentage of the stock sold, followed immediately by the deemed creation of the new corporation in a transaction that can qualify for tax free treatment under Code Sec. 351 [Code Sec. 1361(b)(3)(C)(ii)].
- A nondebtor parent corporation's revocation of its S corporation status and the resulting termination of its debtor subsidiary's status as a QSub is not an unlawful

post-petition transfer of estate property. The debtor's QSub status is controlled solely by its parent. Since the debtor does not have the right to control its QSub status, the debtor's bankruptcy estate does not have that right either. Therefore, the bankruptcy estate has no standing to challenge the revocation of the debtor's QSub status. Moreover, the debtor does not have a property interest in its QSub status because a tax classification over which the debtor has no control is not a legal or equitable property interest for bankruptcy purposes.[19]

- An election by an S corporation to treat a subsidiary as a QSub does not produce an item of income, so no basis adjustment will be allowed by the S corporation shareholders in their stock in the QSub. Making the QSub election is considered a deemed liquidation that qualified for tax-free treatment under Code Sec. 332. Therefore, no gain or loss will be recognized from such a liquidation and no item of income be created.[20]

.05 Revoking QSub Status

Reg. § 1.1361-3(b) provides procedures for revoking QSub status. The parent must file a statement including the parent's and QSub's names, addresses and employer identification numbers with the service center where the S corporation's most recent tax return was properly filed. If the parent does not specify the date for revocation of QSub status, it will be the date the statement is filed. If the parent specifies a date, it cannot be more than two months and 15 days before (or more than 12 months after) the date the revocation statement is filed.

If a QSub election is revoked, such status cannot be reelected for five years without IRS consent. However, under Reg. § 1.1361-5(d)(1), if a QSub election is revoked or otherwise terminated, but the corporation was never a C corporation after the revocation, an S election within 5 years is permissible without IRS consent.[21]

.06 Relief from Inadvertently Invalid QSub Election

The IRS has the authority to grant relief to inadvertent invalid qualified subchapter S subsidiary elections and terminations in the same manner that it does for inadvertent S corporation elections and terminations [Code Sec. 1362(f)]. See ¶ 21,010 for further discussion.

¶21,013 100 SHAREHOLDER LIMIT

.01 Maximum of 100 Shareholders

An S corporation can have no more than 100 shareholders [Code Sec. 1361(b)(1)(A)]. For purposes of counting the number of shareholders to determine whether the 100-shareholder limit is exceeded, all family members can elect to be treated as one shareholder [Code Sec. 1361(c)(1)(B)]. The term *members of the family* is defined as the common ancestor, the lineal descendants of the common ancestor, and the spouses (or former spouses) of the lineal descendants or common ancestor. The common

---

[19] *In re: The Majestic Star Casino, LLC*, CA-3, 2013-1 USTC ¶ 50,338, 716 F3d 736.

[20] *R Ball for R Ball III by Appt.*, 105 TCM 1257, Dec. 59,440(M), TC Memo. 2013-39.

[21] LTR 9823016 (Mar. 4, 1998).

ancestor cannot be more than six generations removed from the youngest generation of shareholders at the time the S election is made. A spouse (or former spouse) will be treated as being of the same generation as the individual to whom he or she is (or was) married [Code Sec. 1361(c)(1)(B)(i)].

The applicable date for determining if a common ancestor is more than six generations removed from the youngest generation of shareholders is the latest of: (1) the date the S corporation election under Code Sec. 1362(a) is made, (2) the earliest date that a family member first holds stock in the corporation, or (3) October 22, 2004. Reg. § 1.1361-1(e)(3)(i) provides further that any legally adopted child of an individual, any child who is lawfully placed with an individual for legal adoption by that individual, and any eligible foster child of an individual will be treated as a child of the individual by blood.

.02 Nominees

Stock that is held by a nominee, guardian, custodian, or other agent is counted as owned by the beneficial owner and not by the nominee shareholder. Thus, a custodian who holds stock in an S corporation on behalf of three beneficial owners is not counted as a shareholder of the corporation; however, the three beneficial owners are counted. A partnership may hold S corporation stock as a nominee for a person who will be treated as the shareholder. However, if the partnership is the beneficial owner of the stock, then the partnership is the shareholder, and the corporation will not qualify as a small business corporation [Reg. § 1.1361-1(e)(1)].

.03 Minors

Under the rule discussed above for stock held by nominees, a minor is considered to be the shareholder even though the stock is held in the name of a guardian or custodian. If two or more minors own stock held in the name of a guardian or custodian, each minor is considered to be a separate shareholder. Where stock has been transferred to a minor under a state Uniform Transfers to Minors Act, the stock is considered to be owned by an individual (the minor) and not by the trust even though a form of fiduciary relationship is created by gifts under such an act [Reg. § 1.1361-1(e)(1)].

For purposes of the election, the estate or trust of a deceased member of the family will be considered to be a member of the family during the period in which the estate or a trust holds stock in the S corporation. Additionally, for purposes of the election, the members of the family will include:

1. Each potential current beneficiary of an electing small business trust who is a member of the family;
2. The income beneficiary of a qualified subchapter S trust (QSST) who makes the QSST election, if that income beneficiary is a member of the family;
3. Each beneficiary of a trust who is a member of the family, if the trust was created primarily to exercise the voting power of stock transferred to it;
4. The member of the family for whose benefit a trust described in Code Sec. 1361(c)(2)(A)(vi) was created;
5. The deemed owner of a trust treated as wholly owned under the grantor trust rules if that deemed owner is a member of the family; and

6. The owner of an entity disregarded as an entity separate from its owner under Reg. § 301.7701-3 if that owner is a member of the family [Reg. § 1.1361-1(e)(3)(ii)].

Two Elections Made by One Family

If a corporation has two or more elections in effect and the members of one family for which the election has been made (the inclusive family) include all the members of another family for which the election was also made (the subsumed family), then the members of the inclusive family will be counted as one shareholder as long as the inclusive family's election is in effect, and the members of the subsumed family will not be counted as a separate and additional shareholder.

Effective Date

The election will be effective as of the first day of the corporation's tax year designated by the shareholder making the election. Any election will remain in effect until terminated.

> ▶ **PLANNING POINTER:** The increase in the number of permitted shareholders to 100 and the treatment of a family group as one shareholder was designed by lawmakers to enable extended families to continue their S corporations without the need to resort to partnerships when families grow and the number of shareholders increases. The election to treat members of a family as a single S corporation shareholder will allow multi-generational family-owned businesses to take advantage of S corporation status despite growth in family size.

Prior to the time when the 100-shareholder limit became law, taxpayers circumvented the old no-more-than 35 shareholders requirement by relying on Rev. Rul. 94-43,[22] which authorized the formation of multiple family-owned S corporations or partnerships each consisting of fewer than the requisite number of shareholders.

¶21,014 TRUSTS ELIGIBLE TO BE S CORPORATION SHAREHOLDERS

Certain trusts are allowed to own S corporation stock. However, trusts must comply with strict rules to continue to be eligible S corporation shareholders. As a result, an S corporation and its tax advisors must constantly monitor its trust shareholders' elections, trust agreements, and their subsequent modifications, to make certain that they comply with S corporation eligibility rules.

The following six types of trusts are eligible to be S corporation shareholders:

- A grantor trust or a trust that distributes all its income to its sole beneficiary who is treated as the trust owner [Code Sec. 1361(c)(2)(A)(i)];
- A voting trust [Code Sec. 1361(c)(2)(A)(iv)];
- A testamentary trust, which is a trust to which S stock is transferred under a will, but only for two years starting with the day of the transfer [Code Sec. 1361(c)(2)(A)(iii); Reg. § 1.1361-1(h)(1)(iv)];
- A qualified Subchapter S trust (QSST) [Reg. § 1.1361-1(j)];

[22] Rev. Rul. 94-43, 1994-2 CB 198.

- An electing small business trust (ESBT) [Code Sec. 1361(c)(2)(A)(v); Reg. § 1.1361-1(c), (h), (j)]; or
- A qualified subpart E trust that continues in existence after the death of the deemed owner is a permitted shareholder, but only for the 2-year period beginning on the day of the deemed owner's death [Code Sec. 1361(c)(2)(A)(ii); Reg. § 1.1361-1(h)(3)(ii)]. Qualified subpart E trusts include both grantor trusts and trusts in which a person other than the grantor is treated as the owner under Code Sec. 678.

.01 Grantor Trusts

A grantor trust may be an S corporation shareholder if the following requirements are satisfied:

- The grantor is an individual;
- The grantor is not a nonresident alien;
- The grantor is treated as owning all of the trust [Code Sec. 1361(c)(2)(A)(i) and Code Secs. 671–677]; and
- The grantor consents to the S election only for the period that it is to be a shareholder of the S corporation [Reg. § 1.1362-6(b)(2); Reg. § 1.1361-1(h)(1)(i)].

For further discussion and characteristics of grantor trusts, see ¶ 25,115.

.02 Voting Trusts

The following requirements must be satisfied in order for a voting trust to qualify as an S corporation shareholder:

- The trust must be in writing;
- The trust must give right-to-vote stock to one or more trustees;
- All distributions must be for the benefit of the beneficial owners;
- The title and possession of the S corporation stock must vest in the beneficiaries at the end of the trust; and
- The trust must terminate on or before a specific time period or event under its terms, or by state law [Reg. § 1.1361-1(h)(1)(v)].

.03 Testamentary Trusts

A testamentary trust is created in an individual's will to prevent a beneficiary from owning S corporation stock until the time that the decedent designates in his or her will. Typically a parent establishes a testamentary trust for S corporation stock that he or she does not wish a young or irresponsible child to inherit prior to the time when the child can manage the stock responsibly. These trusts are also used in the second marriage situation in conjunction with the qualified terminable interest property (QTIP) trusts. For further discussion, see ¶ 29,120.

A testamentary trust must satisfy the following requirements:

- S corporation stock must be transferred to the trust pursuant to the terms of a will;
- S corporation stock must be transferred only for the two-year period beginning on the day the stock is transferred to the trust; or

- S corporation stock must be transferred pursuant to the terms of an electing trust as defined in Reg. § 1.645-1(b)(2) during the election period as defined in Reg. § 1.645-1(b)(6), or deemed to be distributed at the close of the last day of the election period, but in each case only for the two-year period [Reg. § 1.1361-1(h)(1)(iv)].

.04 Trusts Owned by a Beneficiary (Code Sec. 678 Trusts)

A Code Sec. 678 trust allows the donor to exercise gift-giving flexibility so that the donee (beneficial owner) can decide whether or not to elect S corporation status.

A trust owned by a beneficiary (a person other than a grantor) is allowed to be a shareholder of an S corporation, provided the beneficiary is:

- An individual; and
- Not a nonresident alien [Code Sec. 1361(c)(2)(A)(i); Code Sec. 678].

.05 Qualified Subchapter S Trusts (QSSTs)

A QSST is a trust that:

1. Distributes (or is required to distribute) currently all its income to one individual who is a U.S. citizen or resident;
2. Includes only one income beneficiary during the life of the current income beneficiary;
3. Owns stock in one or more S corporations;
4. Distributes any portion of the trust corpus only to the current income beneficiary during the beneficiary's lifetime, including the time at which the trust terminates; and
5. Terminates the income interest of the current income beneficiary upon the death of the beneficiary or the termination of the trust, whichever occurs first [Code Sec. 1361(d)].

A QSST is eligible to hold S stock if the current income beneficiary makes an election to treat the trust as an S shareholder [Reg. § 1.1361-3(a)]. If a husband and wife filing jointly who are both U.S. citizens or residents are designated beneficiaries of a trust, they are treated as a single beneficiary for purposes of meeting the QSST requirement [Reg. § 1.1361-1(j)(2)(i)]. If any QSST distribution satisfied the grantor's legal obligation to support the income beneficiary, the trust ceases to be a QSST as of the date of the distribution [Reg. § 1.1361-1(j)(ii)(B)]. The reason for this is that the grantor would then be treated either as the trust's owner under the grantor trust rules or as a trust beneficiary. If a QSST sells its S stock, the QSST election is terminated with respect to the stock sold, and gain or loss on the sale is that of the trust as a separate taxpayer and not that of the income beneficiary [Reg. § 1.1361-1(j)(8)].

Disposition of S Corporation Stock by QSST and Application of Passive Activity Losses and At-Risk Amounts

The disposition of S corporation stock by a trust electing QSST status is treated as a disposition of the stock by the QSST beneficiary for purposes of applying the Code Sec. 465 at-risk limitations and the Code Sec. 469 passive activity loss rules [Reg. § 1.1361-1(j)(8)]. Therefore, the beneficiary of a QSST is generally allowed to deduct suspended losses under the at-risk and passive loss rules when the trust disposes of the S corporation stock [Code Sec. 1361(d)(1)]. This change is made only with respect to the Code Sec. 465 and Code Sec. 469 limitations. Thus, upon the disposition of subchapter S stock, the QSST election terminates as to the stock sold and any gain or loss recognized on the sale will continue to be that of the trust, not the income beneficiary.

QSST and ESBT Conversions

A trust may convert from a QSST to an ESBT by signing the appropriate election and filing it with the service center where the S corporation files its income tax return [Reg. § 1.1361-1(j)(12)(ii)]. The election must state at the top of the document "ATTENTION ENTITY CONTROL—CONVERSION OF A QSST TO AN ESBT PURSUANT TO SECTION 1.1361-1(j)." A separate election must be made with respect to the stock of each S corporation held by the trust.

A trust is eligible to convert from a QSST to an ESBT if it meets the following requirements:

- The trust meets all of the requirements to be either an ESBT or a QSST as the case may be.
- The trustee and the current income beneficiary of the trust make the appropriate election with respect to the stock of each S corporation held by the trust.
- The trust has not converted from an ESBT to a QSST or visa versa within the 36 month period preceding the effective date of the new election.
- The date on which the new election is to be effective can not be more than 15 days and 2 months after the date on which the election is filed and can not be more than 12 months after the date on which the election is filed. If an election specifies an effective date more than 15 days and 2 months prior to the date on which the election is filed, it will be effective 15 days and 2 months prior to the date on which it is filed. If an election specifies an effective date more than 12 months after the date on which the election is filed, it will be effective 12 months after the date it is filed [Reg. § 1.1361-1(j)(12)].

.06 Electing Small Business Trust (ESBT)

An electing small business trust (ESBT) may be a shareholder of an S corporation [Code Sec. 1361(c)(2)(A)(v)]. An ESBT is subject to income tax at the highest individual income tax rate (currently 35 percent) on the portion of the trust which consists of stock in one or more S corporations ("S portion") [Code Sec. 641(c)]. The income from the S portion of an ESBT is not included in the beneficiaries' income. The only items of income, loss, or deduction taken into account in computing the taxable income of the S portion of an ESBT are: (1) the items of income, loss, or deduction allocated to it as an S corporation shareholder under the rules of subchapter S, (2) gain or loss from the sale of the S corporation stock, and (3) to the extent provided in regulations, any state or local income taxes and administrative expenses of the ESBT properly allocable to the S corporation stock. An ESBT can deduct interest on debt incurred to acquire S corporation stock when computing the taxable income of the S portion of the ESBT [Code Sec. 641(c)(2)(C)].

An ESBT must meet the following requirements:

- An ESBT may only have the following types of beneficiaries: individuals, estates, charitable organizations, or a state or local government that holds a contingent interest in the trust and is not a potential contingent beneficiary (PCB) [Code Sec. 1361(e)(1)(A)(i)]. PCBs of an ESBT are counted as shareholders of the S corporation for purposes of determining whether the corporation qualifies for the S corporation election. Powers of appointment, to the extent they are not exercised, are disregarded in determining the PCBs of an ESBT. Thus, a PCB does not include anyone by virtue of a power of appointment that remained unexercised during the relevant period [Code Sec. 1361(e)(2)]. If PCBs of an ESBT disqualify a corporation in which the ESBT holds stock from S corporation status, the ESBT can remedy the situation by disposing of the offending shares within one year [Code Sec. 1361(e)(2)];

- Special rules apply for a power of appointment that can be exercised in favor of an exempt organization that is an eligible S corporation shareholder under Code Sec. 1361(c)(6). The definition of a power of appointment for purposes of the PCB rules is based on the definitions provided in Code Secs. 2041 and 2514 and the accompanying regulations [Code Sec. 1361(e)(2); Reg. § 1.1361-1(m)(vi)(A)].
- All members of a class of unnamed charities permitted to receive distributions under a discretionary distribution power held by a fiduciary that is not a power of appointment will be considered collectively to be a single PCB for purposes of determining the number of permissible shareholders unless the power is actually exercised. In that case, each charity that actually receives distributions would also be a PCB. The ESBT election requirements require a trust containing such a power to indicate its present in the election statement. This PCB definition applies only to powers to distribute to one or more members of a class of unnamed charities which is unlimited in number. It doesn't apply to a power to make distributions to or among particular named charities [Reg. § 1.1361-1(m)(4)(vi)].
- No interest in the trust may be acquired by purchase which means any acquisition of property with a cost basis determined under Code Sec. 1012 [Code Sec. 1361 (e)(1)(A)(ii)]. Thus, interests in qualifying trusts must be acquired by gift, bequest or other non-purchase acquisition; and
- The trustees must elect to be treated as an ESBT by filing a statement with the IRS. The statement must be filed with the same service center where the ESBT files its Form 1041. If the trust satisfies the ESBT requirements, the trust will be treated as an ESBT as of the date of the election [Code Sec. 1361(e)].

  ▶ **PLANNING TIP:** As a result of the addition of ESBTs to the list of eligible S corporation shareholders, S corporations are now able to take advantage of two common estate planning trusts, the spray trust and the accumulation trust. These trusts may now be funded with S corporation stock.

The trustee of an ESBT must file an election generally within 2 months and 16 days from the day that stock is transferred to the trust. The trustee must file a statement that:

- Contains the name, address, and taxpayer identification number of all potential current beneficiaries, the trust, and the corporation;
- Identifies the election as an election made under Code Sec. 1361(e)(3);
- Specifies the date on which the election is to become effective (not earlier than 15 days and two months before the date on which the election is filed);

- Specifies the date or dates on which the stock of the corporation was transferred to the trust;
- Provides all information and representations necessary to show that all potential current beneficiaries meet the shareholder requirements of Code Sec. 1361(b)(1); and
- States that the trust qualifies as an ESBT. In the case of newly electing S corporations, the trustee may attach the ESBT election to the Form 2553, *Election by a Small Business Corporation.* For purposes of the ESBT's consent to the S corporation election, only the trustee need consent to the S corporation election.

A charitable remainder annuity trust and a charitable remainder unitrust cannot be electing small business trusts [Code Sec. 1361(e)(1)(B)(iii)].

¶21,015 ONE CLASS OF STOCK REQUIREMENT

Code Sec. 1361(b)(1)(D) prohibits an S corporation from having more than one *class* of stock. If an S corporation issues a second class of stock, it ceases to fit the definition of a small business corporation, and its S corporation status is automatically terminated [Code Sec. 1362(d)(2)(A)]. A corporation is treated as having only one class of stock if all the corporation's outstanding shares confer identical rights to distribution and liquidation proceeds rather than different voting rights. Stock may have differences in voting rights and still be considered one class of stock.

.01 Identical Rights to Distribution and Liquidation Proceeds

Reg. § 1.1361-1(l)(2) provides that the determination of whether all outstanding shares of stock confer identical rights to distribution and liquidation proceeds is made based on the corporate charter, articles of incorporation, bylaws, applicable state law and binding agreements relating to distribution and liquidation proceeds. Although a corporation is not treated as having more than one class of stock so long as the governing provisions provide for identical distribution and liquidation rights, any distributions (including actual, constructive, or deemed distributions) that differ in timing or amount are to be given appropriate tax effect in accordance with the facts and circumstances.

.02 Buy-Sell and Redemption Agreements

Bona fide agreements to redeem or buy stock at the time of death, divorce, disability, or termination of employment are disregarded for the one-class-of-stock rules. Also disregarded are buy-sell agreements among shareholders, redemption agreements, and agreements restricting the transferability of stock unless: (1) an agreement's principal purpose is to circumvent the one-class-of-stock rules, and (2) the agreement establishes a purchase price that, at the time of the agreement, is significantly above or below the stock's fair market value [Reg. § 1.1361-1(l)(2)(iii)]. The IRS has concluded that an S corporation's redemption of a portion of its nonvoting stock did not create a second class of stock and therefore did not terminate the corporation's subchapter S election.[23]

[23] LTR 201207002 (Oct. 18, 2011).

.03 Second Class of Stock

Reg. § 1.1361-1(l)(4)(i) provides that "[i]nstruments, obligations, or arrangements are not treated as a second class of stock unless (1) the instrument "constitutes equity or otherwise results in the holder being treated as the owner of stock under general principles of Federal tax law"; and (2) a "principal purpose" of issuing the instrument is "to circumvent the rights to distribution or liquidation proceeds conferred by the outstanding shares of stock" [Reg. § 1.1361-1(l)(4)(ii)]. A "call option, warrant, or similar instrument" is treated as a second class of stock if: (1) "taking into account all the facts and circumstances," the warrant "is substantially certain to be exercised"; and (2) the warrant "has a strike price substantially below the fair market value of the underlying stock on the date that the [warrant] is issued" [Reg. § 1.1361-1(l)(4)(iii)(A)].[24]

Safe Harbors for Call Options

A safe harbor is available for call options which will not be treated as a second class of stock if: (1) "it is issued to a person that is actively and regularly engaged in the business of lending and issued in connection with a commercially reasonable loan to the corporation"; or (2) A call option that is issued to an individual who is either an employee or an independent contractor in connection with the performance of services for the corporation or a related corporation is not treated as a second class of stock if the call option is nontransferable within the meaning of Reg. § 1.83-3(d); and the call option does not have a readily ascertainable fair market value at the time the option is issued [Reg. § 1.1361-1(l)(4)(iii)(B)]. A call option is not treated as a second class of stock if, on the date the call option is issued, transferred or materially modified, the strike price of the call option is at least 90 percent of the fair market value of the underlying stock on that date. A good faith determination of fair market value by the corporation will be respected unless it can be shown that the value was substantially in error and the determination of the value was not performed with reasonable diligence to obtain a fair value. Failure of an option to meet this safe harbor will not necessarily result in the option being treated as a second class of stock [Reg. § 1.1361-1(l)(4)(iii)(C)].[25]

.04 Treatment of Straight Debt

An instrument or obligation that is straight debt is generally not treated as a second class of stock [Reg. § 1.1361-1(l)(5)(i)]. *Straight debt* means any written unconditional promise to pay a fixed amount on demand or on a specified date if: (1) the interest rate and interest payment dates are not contingent on profits, the borrower's discretion, or similar factors; (2) the debt cannot be converted directly or indirectly into stock; and (3) the creditor is an individual (other than a nonresident alien), an estate, trust eligible to hold stock in an S corporation, or a person actively and regularly engaged in the business of lending money [Code Sec. 1361(e)(5); Reg. § 1.1361-1(l)(5)].

.05 Inactive Shareholders

Individuals may wish to invest in an S corporation without being actively involved in its day-to-day operations. Others may want to invest in an S corporation without becoming involved in its day-to-day management but may want to have something

---

[24] *Santa Clara Valley Housing Group, Inc.*, DC-CA, 2012-1 USTC ¶ 50,169.

[25] LTR 201043015 (Oct. 29, 2010); LTR 201104008 (Jan. 28, 2011).

to say about certain major corporate decisions such as a merger, liquidation, or sale of a substantial corporate asset.

▶ **WHAT TO DO:** The corporation can issue common stock with full voting rights to those shareholders who will actively manage the business, common stock whose voting rights are limited to certain key issues to those shareholders who are not interested in actively managing the business but do want to be heard on certain major issues, and nonvoting stock to those shareholders who prefer to be pure investors.

▶ **CAUTION:** In general, losses from a passive activity (an interest in an active business in which taxpayer doesn't materially participate) are currently deductible only against income from passive activities [Ch. 13].

.06 Weighted Voting Rights

When an S corporation is organized, some shareholders may contribute capital in the form of money or assets; others may contribute services. In such cases, the shareholders contributing services frequently want to make sure that they control the corporation, even though the number of shares they hold wouldn't automatically guarantee it. It also sometimes happens that, in forming an S corporation, minority shareholders, looking to protect their investment, will want to put one or more of their members on the board of directors, or in some other way be able to exercise some influence, even though the number of shares they own ordinarily does not guarantee them this power.

A solution is to issue common stock to the various shareholders with voting rights specifically geared to guaranteeing them control, the right to elect directors, the right to veto certain actions taken by a majority of the board of directors, or the right to do whatever they happen to be interested in doing.

¶21,016 S CORPORATION'S TAX YEAR

An S corporation, regardless of when it became an S corporation, may use either a calendar tax year or any other tax year for which it establishes a business purpose—or makes a Code Sec. 444 election to qualify for using some other 52-53 week fiscal year [Ch. 18] [Code Sec. 1378; Reg. § 1.1378-1(a)].

Note that deferral of income to shareholders will not be treated as a valid *business purpose*. [Code Sec. 1378(b)]. Once an accounting period has been selected, the taxpayer is generally precluded from making a change unless the IRS sanctions the change. Typically, the IRS will require proof that there is a substantial business purpose for making the change. However, in certain situations as discussed further below, automatic approval of a change in accounting periods may be available. The IRS has waived a number of limitations that made it hard for corporations to automatically change annual accounting periods.

The IRS has issued Rev. Proc. 2006-46,[26] which provides the exclusive procedures for an S corporation to obtain automatic approval to adopt, change, or retain its annual accounting period under Code Sec. 442. An S corporation that complies with Rev.

[26] Rev. Proc. 2006-46, 2006-2 CB 859.

Proc. 2006-46 will be deemed to have a business purpose and will obtain the approval of the IRS to adopt, change, or retain its annual accounting period. The IRS may deny an adoption, change, or retention of an annual accounting period under this guidance only if the required forms are not timely filed or if the taxpayer fails to meet the scope or any term and condition.

.01 Changes Requiring IRS Approval

The following changes are not automatic and thus may not be implemented by a taxpayer without the approval of the IRS:

- A change from the cash to the accrual method or vice versa (unless the change is an authorized automatic change);
- A change in the method of valuing inventory; and
- A change in the method of calculating depreciation (except for certain very limited changes).

.02 Electing a Tax Year Different from the Required Tax Year

An S corporation can elect to use a tax year that is different from the required tax year (generally, the calendar year). Certain restrictions apply to this so-called Sec. 444 election. However, if your S corporation establishes a business purpose for its tax year, it is not required to make a Sec. 444 election to use such a year [Code Sec. 444; Temp. Reg. § 1.444-1T].

An S corporation is eligible to make and continue a Sec. 444 election if all the following three conditions are met [Code Sec. 444; Temp. Reg. § 1.444-2T].

Not a Member of a Tiered Structure

The S corporation is not a member of a tiered structure other than a tiered structure that consists only of partnerships or S corporations (or both) all of which have the same tax year. An S corporation is considered a member of a tiered structure if the S corporation directly owns any portion of a deferral entity, or a deferral entity directly owns any portion of the S corporation [Temp. Reg. § 1.444-2T]. For purposes of Temp. Reg. § 1.444-2T, solely with respect to an S corporation shareholder, the term *deferral entity* does not include the following entities: (a) a trust that is treated as an electing small business trust (ESBT) under Code Sec. 1361(e) or (b) a trust described in Code Sec. 401(a) or Code Sec. 501(c)(3) that is exempt from tax under Code Sec. 501(a). [Reg. § 1.444-4(a), (b).] An S corporation with either such trusts as a shareholder may make an election under Code Sec. 444.

> **NOTE:** This means the S corporation can own no ownership interest in an entity that defers income tax payment, nor can this entity own an ownership interest in the S corporation.
>
> ▶ **OBSERVATION:** This condition prevents shareholders from multiplying the benefits of the three-month deferral period by passing income through various organizations. An exception permits electing a fiscal year if all the members of a tiered structure have the same tax year [Code Sec. 444(d)(3); Temp. Reg. § 1.444-2T(e)].

No Previous Fiscal Year Elected

The S corporation must not have previously elected a fiscal year.

Deferral Period Requirements Satisfied

The S corporation elects a year that meets the deferral period requirements. The deferral period is the number of months between the start of the tax year elected and the end of the first required tax year ending within the elected year. For example, if a tax year beginning October 1, 2013, and ending September 30, 2014, is elected and a calendar year is required, the deferral period of the elected tax year is three months (October 1, 2013 to December 31, 2013) [Temp. Reg. § 1.444-1T].

S corporations can make an election to change a tax year only if the deferral period is the shorter of: (1) three months, or (2) the deferral period of the tax year being changed. If the current tax year is the required tax year, the deferral period is zero. So no change is allowed.

> **Example 21-4:** Acme Corp., an S corporation, uses a calendar tax year, which is also its required tax year. Because Acme's deferral period is zero, it is not able to make a Sec. 444 election.

> **Example 21-5:** Beta Corp., a newly formed S corporation, began operations on December 1. Beta's shareholders use a calendar year for their individual returns. Beta wants to make a Sec. 444 election to adopt a September 30 tax year. Its deferral period for the tax year beginning December 1, is three months (September 30 to December 31).

Making the Election

An S corporation makes a Sec. 444 election by filing Form 8716, *Election to Have a Tax Year Other Than a Required Tax Year.* This form must be filed by the earlier of: (1) the 15th day of the fifth month after the month that includes the first day of the tax year for which the election will first be effective, or (2) the due date (without regard to extensions) of the income tax return resulting from the Sec. 444 election. Also, your S corporation must attach a copy of the form to the Form 1120S for the first tax year for which the election is made [Temp. Reg. § 1.444-3T].

> **Example 21-6:** Echo Corp., an S corporation, began operations on September 10 and is qualified to make a Sec. 444 election to use a tax year ending September 30. Echo must file Form 8716 by December 16, which is the due date of its tax return for the period September 10 to September 30.

> **Example 21-7:** Assume the same facts as in Example 21-6, except that Echo began operations on October 20. It must file Form 8716 by March 15 of the following year, the 15th day of the 5th month after October 20—when the election will first be effective.

Required Payment

If an S corporation makes an election to have a tax year other than the required tax year, the entity must make a required payment for any tax year that the Sec. 444

election is in effect and the required payment amount exceeds $500 [Code Sec. 7519; Reg. § 1.7519-1].

▶ **OBSERVATION:** This required payment represents the tax deferral that you and the other owners would otherwise receive as a result of adopting a fiscal year.

The required payment for any year that a Sec. 444 election is in effect (i.e., the applicable election year) equals the excess of: 36 percent multiplied by the S corporation's net base year income over the net required payment balance.

The *net required payment balance* is the total amount of required payments reduced by refunds for all prior election years. The applicable percentage for an S corporation is 100 percent, unless more than 50 percent of your S corporation's net income for the short tax year that otherwise would have resulted is allocable to shareholders that would not have been eligible to include this short tax year income over a four-year period.

The *base year* is the preceding tax year. For example, if you are computing required payments for the April 1, 2013, to March 31, 2014, tax year, the base year is the tax year starting April 1, 2012, and ending March 31, 2013 [Reg. § 1.7519-1(b)(3)].

Net income is the combination of your corporation's items of income and expenses (other than credits and tax-exempt income).

If the S corporation was a C corporation for its base year, the C corporation's taxable income is treated as the S corporation's net income for the base year.

If an applicable election year is your S corporation's first tax year of existence, your new corporation does not have a base year. Therefore, the required payment is zero.

The S corporation's *net base year income* equals the sum of the deferral ratio (number of months in deferral period over number of months in tax year) multiplied by your S corporation's net income for the prior tax year, plus the excess of the deferral ratio multiplied by the total amount of applicable payments the S corporation made during the prior tax year over the total amount of the applicable payments your S corporation made during the deferral period of that prior year [Reg. § 1.7519-1(b)(5)].

Applicable payments. These are amounts paid by the S corporation that are includible in a shareholder's gross income. For example, this would include an officer's compensation, wages, or rental costs paid to any shareholder. Dividends that your S corporation pays and gain on the sale of property between a shareholder and the corporation are not included [Code Sec. 7519(d)(3)].

NOTE: If the S corporation was a C corporation for its base year, the corporation will be treated as an S corporation for the base year for the applicable payments.

Example 21-8: Lane Corp. is an S corporation with a Section 444 fiscal year ending on September 30. Lane's taxable income for the tax year starting October 1, 2012, is $300,000. This is the base year for fiscal 2013. During fiscal year 2013, Lane pays its sole shareholder, Mr. Barton, a monthly salary of $20,000. Lane also pays Barton a $30,000 bonus on September 15, 2013. Thus, Lane's applicable payments for fiscal 2013 are $270,000, of which $60,000 are applicable payments deductible during the deferral period of the base year (October 1 through December 31, 2012. Lane has a net required payment balance of zero because its required payments for prior years are completely offset by refunds in those years. Based on these facts, Lane's required payment for 2013 is $29,700, determined as follows [Code Sec. 7519(b)(2), (1)]:

Net income	$300,000		
Multiplied by deferral ratio	3/12	$75,000	
Plus: Applicable payments	$270,000		
Multiplied by deferral ratio	3/12	$67,500	
Less aggregate amount of applicable payments deductible during deferral period of base year	60,000	7,500	
Net base year income			$82,500
Required payment (36 percent of $82,500)			$29,700

Handling the required payment. The S corporation reports the required payment on Form 8752, *Required Payment or Refund Under Section 7519.* If the payment is more than $500, it is paid when Form 8752 is filed. The S corporation can also make this payment with federal tax deposit coupons. No payment is required if the required payment is $500 or less. However, Form 8752 must still be filed.

The S corporation must file Form 8752 and make the required payment (or report the zero amount) by May 15 of the calendar year following the calendar year in which the applicable election year begins. For example, if an S corporation's applicable election year begins July 1, 2013, Form 8752 must be filed by May 15, 2014 [Reg. § 1.7519-2(a)(4)(ii)].

Terminating the Election

The election to use a tax year different from the regular tax year remains in effect until it is terminated. This happens when your S corporation:

- Changes to the required tax year;
- Liquidates;
- Willfully fails to comply with the required payments or distributions; or
- Becomes a member of a tiered structure.

If the election is terminated, another Sec. 444 election cannot be made for any tax year.

.03 Natural Business Year

A *natural business year* is an accounting period that has a substantial business purpose for its existence. In determining if a substantial business purpose for a requested tax year exists, both tax as well as nontax factors must be considered. A nontax factor is the annual cycle of business activity. However, significant weight is given to tax factors. A prime consideration is whether the change would create a substantial distortion of income. Any deferral of income to shareholders is not a business purpose.

The natural business year is determined by a 25 percent test. This test is designed for businesses with a busy season. The natural business year ends with that season. To figure this test:

1. Compute gross receipts from sales and services for the most recent 12-month period that ends with the last month of the requested fiscal year. Divide the gross receipts of the last two months of this 12-month period by this 12-month figure.
2. Make the same computation for the two 12-month periods just before the 12-month period used above.
3. Compare the results. If each of the three results equals or exceeds 25 percent, the fiscal year is the natural business year.

If the S corporation qualifies for more than one natural business year, the year producing the highest average of the three percentages is the natural business year.

Example 21-9: Ace Corp., an S corporation, wants to use a May 31 tax year. Ace's gross receipts for April and May total $100,000. Receipts for the year ending May 31 come to $300,000. Assume Ace has similar revenue patterns for the prior two years. The May 31 tax year qualifies as a natural business year because 33 percent of gross receipts are earned in the last two months of that year.

¶21,020 EFFECT OF S ELECTION ON CORPORATION

S corporations compute their taxable income in the same manner individuals calculate their taxable income. Determination of the tax liability of an S corporation shareholder requires accounting of the shareholder's pro rata share of the corporation's items of income, losses, deductions, and credits. Each of these items passes through to S shareholders and is then subject to individual limits on deductibility. For example, the IRS concluded in Rev. Rul. 2000-43[27] that S corporations are precluded from treating charitable contributions as made in prior years because S corporations compute their tax liability in the same manner as individuals and the election is unavailable to individuals. The fact that accrual-basis corporations are permitted to make this election under Code Sec. 170(a)(2) did not persuade the IRS to decide in favor of the S corporation.

For each tax year the S election remains in effect, your corporation is, with certain exceptions, exempted from all federal income taxes. The following exceptions apply:

- Capital gains tax [¶ 21,035];
- Tax on built-in gains [¶ 21,035];
- Tax on recomputing a prior-year investment credit [¶ 21,030];
- LIFO recapture tax [¶ 21,030]; and
- Tax on excess net passive income [¶ 21,030].

▶ **OBSERVATION:** When your corporation elects S status, only so-called built-in gains (gain allocable to the period before the S election took effect) are subject to

[27] Rev. Rul. 2000-43, 2000-2 CB 333.

corporate taxation. These gains can be taxed if sales are made within ten years after the S election.

¶21,025 TERMINATING THE S ELECTION

The S election is terminated in *any* of the following circumstances [Code Sec. 1362(d); Reg. § 1.1362-2]:

- The election is revoked.
- The business ceases to qualify as an S corporation. S corporation status can be terminated at any time if the business ceases to qualify as an S corporation [Code Sec. 1362(d)(2)]. The following events will result in termination:
  - — Having more than 100 shareholders;
  - — Transferring stock in the S corporation to an ineligible shareholder, such as a corporation, partnership, an ineligible trust or a nonresident alien;
  - — Creating a class of stock other than the voting and nonvoting common stock allowed; and
  - — Acquiring a subsidiary, other than a QSub.
- The passive investment income restrictions on corporations with earnings and profits are violated.

S corporation status will terminate if both of the following conditions occur for three consecutive tax years [Code Sec. 1362(d)(3); Reg. § 1.1362-2(a)]:

- The S corporation has accumulated earnings and profits (from years as a C corporation); and
- Passive investment income for each year is more than 25 percent of gross receipts.

Passive investment income generally means gross receipts derived from royalties, rents, dividends, interest, annuities, and sales or exchanges of stock or securities (gross receipts from such sales or exchanges being taken into account for purposes of this paragraph only to the extent of gains therefrom) [Code Sec. 1362(d)(3)(C)]. However, the term *passive investment income* does not include dividends from the stock held by an S corporation in certain C corporations provided such dividends are attributable to the earnings and profits of a C corporation derived from the active conduct of a business [Code Sec. 1362(d)(3)(E)]. Gross receipts from dispositions of capital assets (other than stock and securities) will be taken into account only to the extent of the capital gain net income therefrom [Code Sec. 1362(d)(3)].

This termination is effective as of the first day of the tax year starting after the third consecutive tax year with excess passive investment income.

> ▶ **OBSERVATION:** If your corporation elected S status from its inception, it may have unlimited amounts of passive investment income. It will have no earnings from a non-S corporation status.

See ¶ 21,030 for discussion of passive income tax.

In the event of an inadvertent termination of S corporation status or an inadvertent defective S election, the IRS can waive the termination or the effect of an invalid election. For further discussion, see ¶21,010.

.01 Intentional Disqualification

An S corporation can intentionally disqualify itself by deliberately failing to meet the general requirements for S status. Thus, for example, issuance of a second class of stock or issuing stock to a nonqualifying trust would result in termination of the S election.[28] An intentional termination can only be effective as of the date it occurs; it is not retroactive.

If a corporation's status as an S corporation is terminated, the corporation generally must wait five tax years before it can again become an S corporation, unless the IRS consents to an earlier election [Code Sec. 1362(g)].

.02 Revoking S Corporation Status

A change in ownership does not of itself revoke an S election. There's no requirement that the new shareholder affirm the S corporation treatment. Instead, S corporation status can only be revoked if shareholders who collectively own more than 50 percent of the outstanding shares consent to the revocation. The consenting shareholders must own their stock in the S corporation at the beginning of the day the revocation is filed. The revocation is effective for the whole year if made on or before the 15th day of the third month of the year. The revocation may specify an effective date on or after the actual revocation date, even if this results in a split tax year [Code Sec. 1362(d)(1)].

.03 Treatment of S Termination Year

If the corporation terminates its S election during a tax year, two short tax years result. The first, an S corporation short tax year, ends on the day before the termination is effective. The second, a C corporation short tax year, starts on the day the termination is effective and ends on the day the tax year would have ended had no termination occurred [Code Sec. 1362(e)(1)].

Example 21-10: S Corp. has 100 shareholders. On June 4, S Corp. acquires a 1001sth shareholder. S Corp.'s election terminates as of June 4, and two short tax years result. Its S corporation short tax year starts January 1 and ends on June 3, the date before the termination. Its C corporation tax year begins on June 4, the day of the termination and ends on December 31.

.04 Computation of Income in S Termination Year

Generally, shareholders compute items of corporate income, loss, deductions, and credits for the full tax year without closing the corporation's books on the termination date (but see "Exception," below). They allocate these items between the two short tax years on a daily basis. The shareholders report the amounts allocated to the S corporation short tax year under the general S corporation rules. The corporation uses the

[28] *T.J. Henry Assoc., Inc.*, 80 TC 886, Dec. 40,110 (1983), *acq.* 1984-2 CB 1; LTR 9607003 (Nov. 3, 1995).

amounts allocated to the C corporation short tax year to compute its tax for that period. This tax must be determined on an annualized basis. This pro rata allocation formula does not apply to an S corporation year in which there is a sale or exchange of 50 percent or more of the corporation's stock [Code Sec. 1362(e)(1), (2), (5), (6)].

The two short tax years are counted as only one year when figuring net operating loss or other carryovers [¶21,045]. Also, the due date for both returns (without extensions) is the same date as the return for the short C corporation year [Code Sec. 1362(e)(6)].

Exception

The corporation can elect to compute income, loss, deductions and credits for both short period returns under the normal tax accounting rules *only* if all persons who were shareholders at any time during the S corporation termination year and all persons owning stock on the first day of the short C corporation year consent to the election. Under this election, items of income, etc., would be attributed to the two short tax years according to when they were actually realized or incurred [Code Sec. 1362(e)(3); Reg. § 1.1362-3(b)].

.05 No Termination of S Status in ESOP Rollover to IRA

In Rev. Proc. 2004-14,[29] the IRS paved the way for rollovers of S corporation stock from employee stock ownership plans (ESOPs) to taxpayer's individual retirement accounts (IRAs). For further discussion of ESOPs, see ¶3160. The IRS concluded that in a direct rollover from the ESOP to the IRA, the S corporation's election will not be terminated. In order for the rollover to not impact on the S corporation's election the following three requirements must be satisfied: First, the terms of the ESOP must require that the S corporation repurchase its stock immediately upon the ESOP's distribution to the IRA. Second, pursuant to the terms of the ESOP, (1) the S corporation must actually repurchase its stock contemporaneously with, and effective on the same day as, the distribution, or (2) the ESOP is permitted to assume the rights and obligations of the S corporation to repurchase the stock immediately upon the distribution to an IRA and the ESOP actually repurchases the stock contemporaneously with, and effective on the same day as, the distribution. Third, no income, loss, deduction, or credit attributable to the distributed S corporation stock under Code Sec. 1366 can be allocated to the participant's IRA.

.06 No Termination of S Status by Chapter 11 Bankruptcy Petition

In *A. Mourad*,[30] the court held that the filing of a voluntary petition under Chapter 11 of the Bankruptcy Code did not cause the termination of a corporation's status as an S corporation. As a result, the corporation's sole shareholder had to include the entity's post-petition income on his individual return.

---

[29] Rev. Proc. 2004-14, 2004-1 CB 489.

[30] *A. Mourad*, CA-1, 2004-2 USTC ¶50,419, 387 F3d 27, *aff'g*, 121 TC 1, Dec. 55,211 (2003).

OPERATING AS AN S CORPORATION

¶21,030 TAX ON S CORPORATION INCOME

For each year an election is in effect, the S corporation is usually exempt from all federal income taxes [Code Sec. 1363(a)]. However, see ¶ 21,035 for a possible exception for certain gains. Also, see below for possible tax on excess passive investment income.

A shareholder of an S corporation is taxed on his or her pro-rata share of the corporation's income, loss, deduction, or credit [Code Sec. 1366(a)(1); Reg. § 1.1366-1]. This allocation on a per-share, per-day basis means that income is allocated to the shareholder according to the number of shares held *and* the number of days they were held [discussed below]. Items of income, loss, deduction, and credit are separately allocated to each shareholder whenever separate treatment could affect tax liability. These items are reported on the shareholder's personal tax return subject to applicable rules and limitations. The balance of the corporation's income or loss is aggregated and passed through to the shareholders as *nonseparately computed income or loss.* This income is reported on Schedule E, Form 1040, and is incorporated as income or loss in the computation of each shareholder's taxable income. Finally, each shareholder's pro rata share of corporate items of tax preference income is used to compute personal alternative minimum tax liability [Code Sec. 1366].

> **NOTE:** If any shareholder terminates the shareholder's interest in the corporation, all affected shareholders and the corporation can agree to make an allocation as if the tax year consisted of two tax years, the first of which ended on the date of the termination. An affected shareholder means any shareholder whose interest is terminated and all shareholders to whom such shareholder transferred shares during the year [Code Sec. 1377(a)(2)]. If the terminating shareholder transferred shares to the corporation, all persons who were shareholders during the year are affected shareholders.

Shareholders who will have to pay tax on their pro rata share of S corporate income include owners or *beneficial shareholders* who are defined as taxpayers whose position of leadership, control and risk of loss in the S corporation, as well as compensation is consistent with being an owner, rather than a mere employee of the S corporation.[31] In this situation, courts will ignore the fact that the beneficial shareholder never actually paid for the S corporation shares.

.01 How to Compute S Corporation Taxable Income

S corporations are required to compute their taxable income so the income can be passed through to shareholders based on their pro rata share. When computing taxable income, S corporations are required to separate all items of income, loss, and deductions into one of two groups. All items of income, loss and deduction that are not separately stated must be combined to compute the nonseparately computed income or loss of the S corporation under Code Sec. 1366(a)(1)(B); Reg.

---

[31] *S.D. Pahl,* CA-9, 98-2 USTC ¶ 50,602, 150 F3d 1124, *aff'g,* 71 TCM 2744, Dec. 51,287(M), TC Memo. 1996-176.

§ 1.1366-1(a)(3)]. The group consists of the separately stated income and deductions which include any income (including tax-exempt income), loss, or deduction that may have to be separately reported by the individual shareholders [Code Sec. 1363(b)]. Typically separately stated items include rents, royalties, interest, dividends, and capital gains or losses realized by the corporation. The character of any item of income, loss, deduction, or credit is determined as if that item were realized directly from the source from which realized by the S corporation, or incurred in the same manner as incurred by the corporation.

> **Example 21-11:** An S corporation has capital gain on the sale or exchange of a capital asset. A shareholder's pro rata share of the gain will also be characterized as a capital gain regardless of whether the shareholder is otherwise a dealer in that type of property.

Corporate profit and loss will be reallocated among family members in certain circumstances. This situation could arise when an individual, who is a member of the family of one or more shareholders of an S corporation, provides services for the S corporation, or furnishes capital to the corporation without being paid for these efforts. All the facts and circumstances are considered in determining a reasonable allowance for services rendered for, or capital furnished to the S corporation. The amount that would ordinarily be paid to obtain comparable services or capital from neither a person who is a family member nor shareholder is one factor to be considered [Code Sec. 1366(e)]. Similar rules apply to services rendered, or capital furnished, to an S corporation by a pass-through entity in which a member of a shareholder's family holds an interest [Reg. § 1.1366-3(a)]. If the pass-through entity does not receive reasonable compensation for the services rendered or capital furnished, the IRS may prescribe adjustments to the pass-through entity and the corporation as necessary to reflect the value of the services rendered or the capital furnished.

> **Example 21-12:** The stock of an S corporation is owned 50 percent by Dad and 50 percent by Son. For the tax year, the corporation has items of taxable income equal to $70,000. Compensation of $10,000 is paid by the corporation to Dad for services rendered during the tax year, and no compensation is paid to Son, who rendered no services. Based on all the facts and circumstances, reasonable compensation for the services rendered by Dad would be $30,000. The IRS has the discretion to allocate up to an additional $20,000 of the $70,000 of the corporation's taxable income to Dad for services rendered.

Generally, S corporations compute taxable income the same as a partnership. However, S corporations can deduct organizational expenditures much like a corporation can deduct these expenses under Code Sec. 248 [Code Sec. 1363(b)(3)]. See ¶ 20,045 for discussion of organizational expenditures. In addition, the deductions allowable to individuals are generally allowed to S corporations, with the following exceptions which may not be deducted by the S corporation [Code Sec. 1363(b)]:

- Personal exemptions;
- Foreign taxes;
- Charitable contributions;
- Expenses for the production of income (other than in a trade or business);
- Medical expenses;
- Alimony;
- Taxes, interest, and business depreciation by a cooperative housing corporation tenant-stockholder;
- Moving expenses;
- Payments to an IRA;
- Deduction for contributions to an Archer MSA or health savings account;
- Interest on education loans;
- Deduction for tuition and fees;
- Oil and gas depletion; and
- Net operating loss deduction [¶ 21,045].

NOTE: Foreign taxes, charitable contributions, and depletion deductions are passed through to shareholders to be used in computing your individual tax liability. Also, the corporate dividends-received deduction [Ch. 20]is not allowed.

Most elections affecting the computation of items derived from S corporations must be made by the corporation. However, certain elections must be made separately by each shareholder, including those relating to: (1) mining exploration expenses, and (2) foreign taxes [Code Sec. 1363(c)].

An S corporation's recovery of interest expense must be reported by its shareholders, according to the Tax Court,[32] even though the interest had been deducted prior to the corporation's election when the company was a C corporation. The tax benefit rule [Ch. 2]was applied at the entity level; and, accordingly, the recovery passed through to the S shareholders to the extent that the prior C corporation benefited from the interest deduction.

.02 Estimated Taxes

Although S corporations generally are not subject to tax on taxable income, there are limited exceptions. When an exception applies, S corporations must make estimated tax payments [Ch. 26] [Code Sec. 6655].

S corporations are required to make estimated tax payments for tax liability attributable to the following three items:

- Built-in gains tax that is imposed on S corporations that dispose of assets that appreciated in value during the years when the corporation was a C corporation [Code Secs. 1374, 6655(g)(4); See ¶ 21,035];
- The receipt of passive investment income in excess of 25 percent of total annual gross receipts if your corporation has earnings and profits from a year in which it was not an S corporation (discussed below) [Code Sec. 1375]; and

[32] *T.A. Frederick*, 101 TC 35, Dec. 49,165 (1993).

- The recapture of investment tax credits claimed during a tax year in which the corporation was not an S corporation (discussed below) [Code Sec. 1371(d)(2)].

The required annual estimated tax payment is the lesser of: (1) 100 percent of the tax shown on the return for the tax year or (2) 100 percent of the tax liability incurred by virtue of the built-in gains tax and tax due because of investment credit recapture, plus 100 percent of the tax due on the passive investment income reported by the S corporation in the preceding year.

.03 Tax on Passive Income

S corporations may be subject to tax if it has: (1) C corporation earnings and profits left over at the close of a tax year, *and* (2) more than 25 percent of its gross receipts is passive investment income [Code Sec. 1375(a)]. Passive investment income generally means gross receipts from interest, dividends, rents, royalties, and annuities [Code Sec. 1362(d)(3)(C)]. However, dividends received by an S corporation from a C corporation subsidiary are not treated as passive investment income to the extent the dividends are attributable to the earnings and profits of the C corporation derived from the active conduct of a business [Code Sec. 1362(d)(3)(E)].

If the corporation has excess net passive income for the year, it must pay a tax on this amount or its taxable income (determined without regard to any dividends-received deductions or net operating loss deduction), if lower, at the maximum corporate tax rate for the year [Ch. 20] [Code Sec. 1375(a)]. The IRS can waive this tax if (1) the S corporation had previously determined in good faith that it had no C corporation earnings and profits and (2) the S corporation distributed these earnings and profits within a reasonable time after they were discovered [Code Sec. 1375(d)].

Net Passive Income

Net passive income is the corporation's passive investment income reduced by allowable deductions directly connected with producing it (other than deductions for net operating loss, dividends received, and amortization of organizational expenditures) [Code Sec. 1375(b)(2)].

Excess Net Passive Income

Excess net passive income is the corporation's net passive income for the year multiplied by the following fraction [Code Sec. 1375(b)(1)]:

$$\frac{\text{Passive investment income for year - 25 percent of gross receipts for year}}{\text{Passive investment income for year}}$$

> **Example 21-13:** S Corp. has $120,000 in gross receipts; $60,000 taxable income; $50,000 in passive investment income and $10,000 in expenses directly attributable to passive investment income. Its net passive income is $40,000 ($50,000 passive investment income minus $10,000 expenses). The amount by which passive investment income for the year exceeds 25 percent of gross receipts is $20,000 [$50,000 passive investment income minus $30,000 (25 percent of $120,000 gross receipts)].
>
> The corporation's excess net passive income is $16,000 [$40,000 net passive income times 2/5 ($20,000 of passive income in excess of 25 percent of gross receipts divided by $50,000 passive income)]. This is less than the corporation's

taxable income. The corporation's tax on excess net passive income therefore is $5,600 (35 percent of $16,000).

Limitations and Special Rules

Excess net passive income cannot exceed the corporation's taxable income (computed without any deductions for net operating loss, dividends received from certain corporations, or amortization of organizational expenditures). Also, only the credit for certain uses of gasoline and special fuels is allowed against the passive income tax [Code Sec. 1375(c)]. However, when determining the amount of passive investment income, do not take into account any recognized built-in gain or loss of the S corporation for any tax year in the recognition period [Code Sec. 1375(b)(4)].

> **NOTE:** The rule under Sec. 1375(b)(4) applies generally for tax years starting after 1986, but only for returns filed under an S election made after 1986. *Recognition period* is the 10-year period starting with the first day of the tax year for which the corporation was an S corporation.

Pass-Through Reduction

If the S corporation is liable for a passive investment income tax, each item of passive investment income is reduced by its portion of the tax to determine the amount of its corporate pass-through to shareholders [Code Sec. 1366(f)(3)].

.04 Tax on Recomputing a Prior-Year Investment Credit

This tax might apply if the corporation claimed the investment credit on a prior year's corporate income tax return before it became an S corporation. If the S corporation makes an early disposition of the property, the S corporation is liable for paying the tax. However, S corporation shareholders might be subject to the recapture if their stock interest in the S corporation is reduced by more than one-third [Reg. § 1.47-4(a)(2)].

> ▶ **OBSERVATION:** Electing to be treated as an S corporation in itself is not treated as a disposition. Therefore, an S election does not automatically trigger recapture of a credit taken before the election was effective [Code Sec. 1371(d)].

> ▶ **TAX TIP:** Recapture occurs only if shareholder's stock interest is reduced below two-thirds of what it was when the property giving rise to the credit was placed in service by the corporation. Thus, if business considerations permit, they can avoid recapture by selling down no lower than the two-thirds mark until after the recapture period for the property has elapsed (in general, five years from when the property was placed in service).

.05 Recapture of LIFO Benefits on Converting to S Corporation

If a LIFO-method C corporation elects to become an S corporation, it will have to recapture the benefits of using the LIFO method in the year it converts to S status. Consequently, the corporation will have to include a LIFO recapture amount in its gross income for its last year as a C corporation. This amount is the excess of the inventory's value using FIFO over its LIFO value at the end of the last C corporation year. The resulting increase in tax is paid over a four-year period. If your corporation was a member of an affiliated group in its last C corporation year, your converting corporation is not treated as a member of the group as to the amount included in income under the recapture rules, except to the extent provided by regulations [Code

Sec. 1363(d)]. In *Coggin Automotive Corp.*,[33] the Court of Appeals for the Eleventh Circuit reversed the Tax Court to hold that a holding company for subsidiary automobile dealerships was not required to recapture a share of the subsidiaries' LIFO inventory reserve when it converted to an S corporation [Code Sec. 1363(d)].

¶21,035 TREATMENT OF CERTAIN GAINS

A corporate-level tax (called the built-in gains tax) is imposed at the highest marginal rate applicable to corporations on an S corporation's "net recognized built-in gain" which is the gain that arose prior to the conversion of the C corporation to an S corporation. The built-in gains tax is designed to prevent corporations that had unrecognized gain on assets during C years from avoiding corporate-level tax on the gain by converting to S status and then distributing the assets. An S corporation may be liable for tax on its built-in gains if:

1. It was a C corporation prior to making its S corporation election;
2. The S corporation election was made after 1986;
3. It has a net recognized built-in gain within the recognition period; and
4. The net recognized built-in gain for the tax year does not exceed the net unrealized built-in gain minus the net recognized built-in gain for prior years in the recognition period, to the extent that such gains were subject to tax [Code Sec. 1374(c)].

The tax on built-in gains also applies if an S corporation sells, during the recognition period, assets that were acquired in a carryover basis transaction (e.g., a tax-free reorganization) in which the S corporation's basis in the assets is determined by reference to the C corporation's basis in the assets. In the case of built-in gain attributable to an asset received by an S corporation from a C corporation in a carryover basis transaction, the recognition period rules are applied by substituting the date such asset was acquired by the S corporation in lieu of the beginning of the first tax year for which the corporation was an S corporation [Code Sec. 1374(d)(8)].

.01 Recognition Period

Any unrecognized gain must be recognized by the S corporation during the "recognition period." For tax years beginning in 2011, 2012 and 2013, the "recognition period" is the five-year period beginning with the first day of the first tax year for which the corporation was an S corporation [Code Sec. 1374(d)(7)(C)]. For example, if the first day of the recognition period is July 12, 2010, the last day of the recognition period will be July 11, 2015.

The five-year period refers to five calendar years from the first day of the first tax year for which the corporation was an S corporation. The reduction in the recognition period applies separately with respect to any asset acquired in a carryover basis transaction pursuant to Code Sec. 1374(d)(8).

[33] *Coggin Automotive Corp.*, CA-11, 2002-1 USTC ¶50,448, 292 F3d 1326, *rev'g*, 115 TC 349, Dec. 54,087 (2000).

Example 21-14: C corporation elected S corporation status for its tax year beginning on January 1, 2007. C corporation will be able to sell appreciated assets it held on January 1, 2007, during 2013 without being subject to tax under Code Sec. 1374.

The purpose of the Section 1374 tax is to make sure that one or more of the following types of gain does not escape tax in connection with the transition from C status to S status:

- Gain and income that must be taxed to prevent abusive use of the S election;
- Gain and income that would have been subject to corporate income tax if the S election had not been made; and
- Gain and income that would have been taxed if the corporation had liquidated on the effective date of the S election.

Note that an S corporation's income from timber, coal, and iron ore that is afforded capital gains tax rate benefits by Code Sec. 631 is not subject to the Code Sec. 1374 built-in gains tax because the income involves the receipt of normal operating business income in the nature of rent or royalties.[34]

.02 General Features of Gain Recognition

Recognized Built-in Losses

These are the opposite of a recognized built-in gain. They are losses recognized when any asset is disposed of during the recognition period to the extent that your S corporation establishes that [Code Sec. 1374(d)(4)]:

- The asset was held by your S corporation at the start of the first tax year as an S corporation; and
- The loss is *not* more than
    a. The asset's adjusted basis at the start of the first year your S election was in effect, minus
    b. The asset's fair market value at the start of that year.

▶ **OBSERVATION:** The presumptions are different for built-in gains and losses. If a disposition during the recognition period results in a gain, your S corporation treats the full gain as a taxable built-in gain unless you can show that an exception applies. On the other hand, if there is a loss, it is presumed not to be a tax-favored built-in loss, unless you can prove otherwise.

Installment Method

If an S corporation sells an asset within the recognition period and reports the sale under the installment method of Code Sec. 453, the payments received, whether within the recognition period or not, are subject to the built-in gains tax to the extent they are built-in gains [Code Sec. 1374(d)(7)(E)].

---

[34] Rev. Rul. 2001-50, 2001-2 CB 343.

Inventory Valuation

The value of an S corporation's inventory generally is determined by reference to a sale of the entire business of the S corporation to a buyer that expects to continue to operate that business [Reg. § 1.1374-7(a)].

Partnership Items

Unless the small interest exception applies, an S corporation that owns a partnership interest at the beginning of the recognition period or transfers property to a partnership in a transaction to which Code Sec. 1374(d)(6) applies (because the adjusted basis of an asset is determined in whole or in part by reference to the adjusted basis of another asset held by the S corporation as of the beginning of the recognition period) must treat its distributive share of partnership items as if they originated with the S corporation. It does so as follows [Reg. § 1.1374-4(i)(1)]:

Step 1: Apply the rules of Code Sec. 1374(d) to the S corporation's distributive share of partnership items of income, gain, loss, or deduction included in income or allowed as a deduction to determine the extent to which it would have been treated as recognized built-in gain or loss if the partnership items had originated in and been taken into account directly by the S corporation.

Step 2: Determine the S corporation's net recognized built-in gain without the partnership items.

Step 3: Determine the S corporation's net recognized built-in gain with the partnership items.

Step 4: If the amount computed under Step 3 exceeds the amount computed under Step 2, the excess is the S corporation's partnership recognized built-in gain, and the S corporation's net recognized built-in gain is the sum of the amount computed under Step 2 plus the partnership recognized built-in gain. If the amount computed under Step 2 exceeds the amount computed under Step 3, the excess is the S corporation's partnership recognized built-in gain, and the S corporation's net recognized built-in gain is the remainder of the amount computed under Step 2 after subtracting the partnership recognized built-in gain.

These look-through rules do not apply if the fair market value of the partnership interest as of the beginning of the recognition period is less than $100,000 and the partnership interest represents less than 10 percent of the partnership's profits and capital at all times during the tax year and prior tax years in the recognition period [Reg. § 1.1374-4(i)(5)]. This exception does not apply if a corporation forms or avails of a partnership with a principal purpose of avoiding the tax on recognized built-in gains [Reg. § 1.1374-4(i)(5)].

Net Recognized Built-in Gain

Generally, for any tax year in the recognition period, this is the lesser of [Code Sec. 1374(d)(2); Reg. § 1.1374-2(a)]:

- The S corporation's taxable income determined by using all rules applying to C corporations and considering only its recognized built-in gain, recognized built-in loss, and recognized built-in gain carryover (pre-limitation amount);

- The S corporation's taxable income determined by using all rules that apply to C corporations (other than the dividends-received deduction and net operating loss deduction) (taxable income limitation); or
- The amount by which the S corporation's net unrealized built-in gain exceeds its net recognized built-in gain for all prior tax year (net unrealized built-in gain limitation).

If an S corporation's pre-limitation amount for any tax year exceeds its taxable income limitation, the amount by which its pre-limitation amount exceeds its taxable income limitation is a recognized built-in gain carryover included in its pre-limitation amount for the succeeding tax year [Reg. § 1.1374-2(c)].

▶ **OBSERVATION:** The carryover reduces the opportunity to save taxes by recognizing the built-in gain in the year your corporation would otherwise have a loss. The current year's loss does not permanently offset the corporate tax on built-in gain.

Net Operating Loss Carryforwards

Any net operating loss carryforward from a pre-S corporation tax year is allowed as a deduction against the net recognized built-in gain of your S corporation for the tax year. To determine the loss that can be carried to later tax years, the net recognized built-in gain is treated as taxable income. The same rule applies for a capital loss carryforward from a pre-C corporation tax year [Code Sec. 1374(b)(2)].

Property Acquired in Tax-Free Exchange

If any asset's adjusted basis is determined (fully or partly) by the adjusted basis of another asset held by your S corporation at the start of the first tax year for which it was an S corporation [Code Sec. 1374(d)(6)]:

- The asset is treated as held by your S corporation at the start of that first tax year, and
- Recognized built-in gain or loss is found by the fair market value and adjusted basis of the other asset at the start of that first tax year.

▶ **OBSERVATION:** This rule prevents the use of tax-free exchanges as a device for circumventing the "property owned at time of S election" requirement.

.03 Transfers of Assets from C Corporation to S Corporation—Tax on Built-in Gains

Generally, if an S corporation acquires an asset, and its basis in the asset is fully or partly determined by a C corporation's basis in the asset, then a tax is imposed on any net recognized built-in gain from the asset for any tax year beginning in the recognition period. However, when figuring the tax, the day on which the assets were acquired by the S corporation is substituted for the beginning of the first tax year that the corporation was an S corporation [Code Sec. 1374(d)(8)].

A separate determination of built-in gains tax must be made for the assets acquired in each different transfer from a C corporation to an S corporation and for the assets held by the corporation when it became an S corporation. Thus, an S corporation's Code Sec. 1374 attributes when it became an S corporation may only be used to reduce the built-in gains tax imposed on dispositions of assets that the S corporation held at that time. Similarly, an S corporation's Code Sec. 1374 attributes acquired in a transfer from a C corporation may only be used to reduce built-in gains tax imposed on dispositions of assets that the S corporation acquired in the same transaction [Reg. § 1.1374-8(b)]. Code Sec. 1374 attributes are the loss carryforwards allowed under Code Sec. 1374(b)(2) as a deduction against net recognized built-in gain and the credit and credit carryforwards allowed under Code Sec. 1374(b)(3) as a credit against the built-in gains tax [Reg. § 1.1374-1(c)].

¶21,040 PASS-THROUGHS TO SHAREHOLDERS

The character of a corporate item that is not claimed by the corporation but passed through to and reported by a shareholder is determined at the corporate level [Code Sec. 1366(b); Reg. § 1.1366-1(b)(1)].

S corporation shareholders report their pro rata share of each item of income, loss, deduction, or credit that is separately stated and a pro rata share of nonseparately stated income or loss on their individual tax returns [Code Sec. 1366(a); Reg. § 1.1366-1(a)(2)].

When it is necessary to determine the amount or character of the gross income of a shareholder, the shareholder's gross income includes the shareholder's pro rata share of the gross income of the S corporation. This is the amount of gross income of the corporation used to derive the shareholder's pro rata share of S corporation taxable income or loss [Code Sec. 1366(c); Reg. § 1.1366-1(c)].

> ▶ **OBSERVATION:** An S corporation shareholder's share of the corporation's taxable income is not self-employment income, even though it is included in gross income.

Note the treatment of the following items [Code Sec. 1366(a)]:

- *Capital gains and losses.* Gains and losses from sales or exchanges of capital assets by S corporation pass directly through to shareholders as capital gains and losses.
- *Charitable contributions.* If an S corporation contributes money or other property to a charity, the S corporation is not the taxpayer who claims the charitable deduction. Instead, the charitable deductions are passed through as separate items to each shareholder who takes into account his or her pro rata share of the contribution in determining his or her income tax liability. The charitable deduction is reported on each S corporation shareholder's Form 1120S, Schedules K and K-1 [Code Sec. 1366(a)(1)(A)]. For charitable contributions made in tax years beginning before January 1, 2014, the shareholder's basis in the stock of an S corporation making a charitable contribution of property is reduced by the shareholder's pro rata share of the adjusted basis of the contributed property [Code Sec. 1367(a)(2)].
- *Tax-exempt interest.* This passes through to shareholders, retaining its character as tax-exempt interest. It increases their basis in their S corporation's stock.

  NOTE: A later distribution of the tax-exempt interest to shareholders will not be taxable. It will merely reduce the shareholder's basis S corporation's stock.
- *Depreciation.* This is not a pass-through item. It is computed and deducted by the S corporation on its tax return in figuring taxable income or loss that is passed through to shareholders.

NOTE: The S corporation, not its shareholders, elects what method to use for computing depreciation deductions. Also, the S corporation makes the election to write off expenditures in the year of purchase, by claiming an expensing deduction [Ch. 11]. The dollar cap on expensing applies both to your S corporation and to each shareholder. The S corporation allocates the deduction among shareholders, who then take the deduction subject to the dollar limitation.

.01 Computation of Shareholder's Pro-Rata Share

A shareholder's pro-rata share of S corporation's nonseparately computed income and separately computed items depends on their percentage of stock ownership on each day of the corporation's tax year. Their pro rata share is the sum of the portions of such items that are attributable on a pro rata basis to the shares held on each day of the tax year. For this purpose, the daily portion of each item is the corporation's total amount of each item divided by the number of days in the tax year [Code Sec. 1377(a)].

Example 21-15: Electing Corp., a calendar year taxpayer, has $36,500 nonseparately computed income. The daily portion of this income is $100 ($36,500 ÷ 365). If Mr. Baker is a 50 percent shareholder for each day of the year, he must include $50 per day (or $18,250 for the year) on his tax return. If Baker had sold his stock on June 3, he would report $7,650 ($50 per day for 153 days, January 1 through June 2).

▶ **IMPORTANT:** The character of any separately computed items (e.g., capital gain, tax-exempt income, deduction or loss) realized by your corporation is passed through to you and its other shareholders. Also, your gross income includes your pro rata share of your corporation's gross income [Code Sec. 1366(b), (c)].

.02 Worthless Stock

If a taxpayer's S corporation's stock becomes worthless, the other shareholders are entitled to a capital loss deduction for whatever basis the original shareholder had for the stock. However, before computing the worthless stock deduction, the S corporation's nonseparately computed income or loss (as well as its separately computed items) for that year must be taken into account, and any required adjustments to the stock's basis must be made [Code Secs. 165(g), 1377].

¶21,045 TREATMENT OF LOSSES AND DEDUCTIONS

All losses and deductions of the S corporation (including net operating losses, depreciation and capital losses) are passed through to (and are deductible by) the S corporation shareholders. In fact, one of the more common reasons that S corporate status is chosen is the ability to flow through entity-level losses to shareholders. However, before the losses are passed through to a shareholder, the shareholder must cross several hurdles. A shareholder can deduct his pro-rata share of S corporation losses only to the extent of the total of his basis in (a) the S corporation stock, and (b) the adjusted basis of any indebtedness of the S corporation to the shareholder (basis of indebtedness) [Code Sec. 1366(d)(1)(A)].

The easiest way for a shareholder to increase basis in S corporation stock to enable the shareholder to absorb a loss pass-through is for the shareholder to make a contribution to capital. The problem here is that, if there is more than one shareholder, a contribution to capital by one shareholder becomes part of every shareholder's interest in the corporation. As a result, S corporation shareholders frequently resort to making direct loans to the corporation to increase the company's indebtedness to them. This technique seems simple, but the manner in which it is handled can make a big difference. If an S corporation repays a debt owed to a shareholder after his basis was reduced by losses and deductions passes through to him, the shareholder realizes income to the extent of the amount repaid over the reduced basis of the debt.[35]

.01 Suspended Losses

If a shareholder does not have sufficient adjusted basis in stock or debt, passthrough losses are *suspended* and carried forward to succeeding tax years when that shareholder's basis is increased [Code Sec. 1366(d)(2); Reg. § 1.1366-2].[36]

Transfers to Spouse or Incident to Divorce

If a shareholder's stock in an S corporation is transferred to a spouse, or to a former spouse incident to a divorce, any suspended loss or deduction with respect to that stock is treated as incurred by the corporation with respect to the transferee in the subsequent tax year [Code Sec. 1366(d)(2)(B)]. The amount of any loss or deduction with respect to the stock transferred shall be determined by prorating any losses or deductions disallowed for the year of the transfer between the transferor and the spouse or former spouse based on the stock ownership at the beginning of the following tax year. If a transferor claims a deduction for losses in the tax year of transfer, then if the transferor's pro rata share of the losses and deductions in the year of transfer exceeds the transferor's basis in stock and the indebtedness of the corporation to the transferor, then the limitation must be allocated among the transferor spouse's pro rata share of each loss or deduction, including disallowed losses and deductions carried over from the prior year [Reg. § 1.1366-2(a)(5)(ii)].

.02 How to Increase Stock Basis

An S corporation shareholder's ability to deduct his or her pro rata share of the corporation's losses is limited by (1) the shareholder's adjusted basis in the S corporation; plus (2) the shareholder's basis in indebtedness which is the shareholder's basis in loans made to the corporation [Code Sec. 1366(d)(1)(A), (B)]. A shareholder can deduct his pro-rata share of S corporation losses only to the extent to the total of his basis in (1) the S corporation stock, and (2) debt owed him by the S corporation.

Any genuine indebtedness of the shareholder to the corporation increases the shareholder's basis. Thus, when a shareholder loans money to the corporation, the shareholder's basis in the corporation increases and so does the amount of loss that is deductible. The shareholder can increase his or her basis in indebtedness by contributing additional capital to the corporation, or by the corporation generating and passing through to the shareholder income (both taxable income and tax-exempt

[35] *J.M. Smith*, CA-9, 70-1 USTC ¶ 9327, 424 F2d 219.

[36] *R. Broz*, CA-6, 2013-2 USTC ¶ 50,488, *aff'g*, 137 TC 46, 58, 750 (2011).

income) under Code Sec. 1367(a)(1)]. The Code does not define basis of indebtedness, but several court cases require an investment in the S corporation that constitutes "an actual economic outlay" by the shareholder to create basis of indebtedness. In *J. Maguire*,[37] the Tax Court held that a distribution of one S corporation's accounts receivable to its shareholders, followed by their contribution of the receivables to a related S corporation, increased the shareholders' basis in the second S corporation's stock and allowed them to deduct its losses. The court found that the contribution of their accounts receivable satisfied the "economic outlay" requirement for a contribution of capital because each of the couples was materially poorer after the contribution was made. The courts have required that an S corporation shareholder have the equivalent of an *economic outlay* or assumption of risk to generate sufficient Code Sec. 1367 basis for purposes of loss deductions.[38] Typically, litigation results when S corporation shareholders try to obtain basis of indebtedness by borrowing from a related entity and then engage in a back-to-back loan transaction which involves lending the proceeds to the S corporation. The issue is whether the back-to-back loan gives rise to an actual economic outlay especially when a shareholder has been made "poorer in a material sense" as a result of the loan. Reg. § 1.1366-2(a)(1) provides that a shareholder's aggregate amount of losses and deductions taken into account for any tax year of the S corporation cannot exceed that shareholder's adjusted basis in stock in the corporation and adjusted basis of any indebtedness of the corporation to that shareholder.

Bona Fide Loan Required

In order to increase a shareholder's basis of indebtedness, a loan must represent bona fide indebtedness of the S corporation that runs directly to the shareholder [Prop. Reg. § 1.1366-1(a)(2)]. A shareholder acting as guarantor of S corporation indebtedness does not create or increase basis of indebtedness simply by becoming a guarantor. Because the proposed regulations require that loan transactions represent bona fide indebtedness of the S corporation to the shareholder in order to increase basis of indebtedness, an S corporation shareholder need not otherwise satisfy the "actual economic outlay" doctrine for purposes of Code Sec. 1366(d)(1)(B).

Shareholder Guarantees

It is well established that shareholder guarantees of S corporation debt do not create debt between the S corporation and the shareholder and therefore do not increase a shareholder's basis of indebtedness. Where an S corporation shareholder acts merely as a guarantor of a loan made by another party directly to the S corporation, or acts in a capacity similar to a guarantor, the courts have held that the shareholder adjusts basis of indebtedness only to the extent the shareholder actually performs under the guarantee.[39] The proposed regulations provide that an S corporation shareholder who merely acts as a guarantor or in a similar capacity has not created basis of indebted-

---

[37] *J. Maguire*, 103 TCM 1853, Dec. 59,082(M), TC Memo. 2012-160.

[38] *L. Bergman*, CA-8, 99-1 USTC ¶ 50,475, 174 F3d 928.

[39] *P.D. Montgomery*, 105 TCM 1865, Dec. 59,566(M), TC Memo. 2013-151; *M.G. Underwood*, 63 TC 468, Dec. 33,016, *aff'd*, CA-5, 76-2 USTC ¶ 9557, 535 F2d 309; *W.H. Perry*, 47 TC 159, Dec. 28,180, *aff'd*, 68-1 USTC ¶ 9297, 392 F2d 458.

ness unless the shareholder actually makes a payment, and then only to the extent of such payment [Prop. Reg. § 1.1366-2(a)(2)(ii)].

> **Example 21-16:** A is a shareholder of S, an S corporation. In 2013, S received a loan from Bank. Bank required A's guarantee as a condition of making the loan to S. Beginning in 2014, S could no longer make payments on the loan and A made payments directly to Bank from A's personal funds until the loan obligation was satisfied. For each payment A made on the note, A obtains basis of indebtedness. Thus, A's basis of indebtedness is increased during 2014 to the extent of A's payments to Bank pursuant to the guarantee agreement [Prop. Reg. § 1.1366-2(a)(iii), Ex. 2].

Incorporated Pocketbook

The "incorporated pocketbook" theory has been relied on by some taxpayer to claim an increase in basis of indebtedness in circumstances that involve a loan directly to the S corporation from an entity related to the S corporation shareholder. In these transactions, an S corporation shareholder claims that a transfer from the related entity directly to the shareholder's S corporation was made on the shareholder's behalf and is, in substance, a loan from the related entity to the shareholder, followed by a loan from the shareholder to the S corporation. A limited number of court decisions have allowed shareholders to increase basis of indebtedness as a result of incorporated pocketbook transactions.[40] An incorporated pocketbook transaction increases basis of indebtedness only where the transaction creates a bona fide creditor-debtor relationship between the shareholder and the borrowing S corporation.

In *I. Nathel*,[41] the Court of Appeals for the Second Circuit affirmed the Tax Court to conclude that the shareholders' capital contributions to S corporations did not constitute income to the entities and did not restore or increase their tax basis in their loans to the S corporations.

S corporation shareholders should exercise extreme caution when planning a loan transaction with an S corporation. A carelessly crafted loan could result in the shareholder recognizing ordinary income when the S corporation repays the loan. If an S corporation repays a debt owed to a shareholder after his basis was reduced by losses and deductions passed through to him, the shareholder realizes income to the extent of the amount repaid over the reduced basis of the debt.[42]

In *D.G. Oren*,[43] a series of bogus circular shareholder loans to S corporations that were controlled by the same individual didn't increase basis because the loans weren't made on an at-risk basis. An *actual economic outlay* of money that would leave the shareholder *poorer in a material sense* is required to increase basis.

---

[40] *C.E. Yates*, 82 TCM 805, Dec. 54,523(M), TC Memo. 2001-280; *D.J. Culnen*, 79 TCM 1933, Dec. 53,856(M), TC Memo. 2000-139.

[41] *I. Nathel*, CA-2, 2010-1 USTC ¶ 50,443, 615 F3d 83, *aff'g*, 131 TC 262, Dec. 57,617 (2008).

[42] *J.M. Smith*, CA-9, 70-1 USTC ¶ 9327, 424 F2d 219.

[43] *D.G. Oren*, CA-8, 2004-1 USTC ¶ 50,165, 357 F3d 854. See also *M.S. Kerzner*, 97 TCM 1375, Dec. 57,783(M), TC Memo. 2009-76; *M.G. Underwood*, CA-5, 76-2 USTC ¶ 9557, 535 F2d 309; *S.P. Ruckriegel*, 91 TCM 1035, Dec. 56,485(M), TC Memo. 2006-78.

In order for loans to the S corporation to increase the shareholder's basis, the loans must have some substance or utility beyond the creation of tax deductions. Only where the shareholder provides his own money (or money he is directly liable for) to the S corporation, will basis increase. Therefore, only a shareholder who borrows money in an arm's length transaction and then loans the funds to the S corporation will be entitled to a basis increase.

In addition, the at-risk rules in Code Sec. 465 must be satisfied. The at-risk rules provide that a taxpayer engaged in an activity may deduct any loss (including interest expense) from the activity only to the extent that the taxpayer is at risk for the activity at the close of the tax year [Code Sec. 465; See Ch. 13].

The economic reality of the situation must be examined to determine whether there was a realistic chance that the taxpayer might lose the money loaned to the S corporations, or, rather, whether the funds were protected from loss. The "theoretical possibility that the taxpayer will suffer economic loss" is insufficient to satisfy the at-risk requirements. A loan to an S corporation does not create basis when the shareholder is protected from personal loss by the circular nature of the loan transactions.

> ▶ **PRACTICE POINTER:** In order for loans to increase an S corporation shareholder's basis in the S corporation enabling him to deduct losses, there must be an actual economic outlay of money by the taxpayer that would leave him poorer in a material sense. The loans must have substance or utility beyond the creation of tax deductions. Basis will only be increased if there is an actual economic outlay that made the S shareholder materially poorer. S shareholder basis is not increased by mere loan guarantees[44] or by capital contributions by another entity in which the shareholder is an owner. Similarly, a corporate shareholder's guarantee of a third party loan to the S corporation is not handled like a debt from that S corporation to the corporate shareholder unless the shareholder pays either all or part of the corporate debt. In addition, S shareholders can not increase their tax bases in the corporation for corporate debt when the debt did not run directly to them.[45] In order for basis to be increased, the S corporation shareholders either have to show for example that they in fact made corporate contributions of real property by putting a mortgage on individually owned real estate on behalf of the corporation or that they created a debt that was from the S corporation to themselves. Only when the shareholder provides his own money (or money he is directly liable for) will basis increase. Observance of all formalities when the legal obligation was created will not overcome the fact that the loans are not actual economic outlays and are not negotiated at arm's length. Remember that the IRS places intense scrutiny on loans to S corporations where the funds originate from a related party lender.

.03 Loan Guarantees Do Not Increase S Corporation Basis

No form of indirect borrowing, including shareholder guaranties of S corporation debt, will increase the shareholder's basis in the S corporation under Code Sec.

---

[44] *G. Luiz*, 87 TCM 838, Dec. 55,523(M), TC Memo. 2004-21.

[45] *A.Bean Est.*, CA-8, 2001-2 USTC ¶50,669, 268 F3d 553.

1366(b)(1)(B) until and unless the shareholder pays the obligation.[46] The mere guarantee of a loan only creates a contingent debt; however, it does not create a corporate indebtedness or generate basis sufficient to support loss deductions. In *Grojean*,[47] the Seventh Circuit held that an S shareholder's participation interest in a loan made by a bank to his S corporation, was, in effect, a guaranty. As a result, the shareholder got no basis from the transaction that would have permitted him to deduct losses passed through from the company. Take this typical situation:

> **Example 21-17:** *Year 1:* Sole shareholder's stock basis is $10,000. S Corporation gets a $7,500 bank loan, payable in two years, to meet operating expenses. Shareholder is the guarantor. The corporation's operating losses for the year are $10,000. Result: Shareholder can deduct the full $10,000 loss pass-through, but her stock basis is now zero ($10,000 – $10,000). *Year 2:* S Corporation has a $5,000 operating loss. *Result:* None of the loss is currently deductible by the shareholder. She has a zero basis in the stock and no indebtedness basis because the loan guarantee is treated as a contingent debt. She must carry over the loss until her stock and/or debt basis increases enough to absorb it.

Similarly, the Tax Court in *R. Weisberg*,[48] held that the taxpayer's loan guarantee of the corporation's line of credit did not, by itself, increase his basis in the S corporation.

In *Maloof*,[49] the Court of Appeals for the Sixth Circuit affirmed the Tax Court to conclude that an S corporation shareholder could not increase his basis in his S corporation stock or debt to reflect the amount that he was a co-obligor and guarantor on bank loans made to the S corporation. Therefore, he had insufficient basis to deduct pass-through losses on his personal returns because the taxpayer's status as a co-obligor on the loan established just the possibility, not the reality, of an economic outlay for the corporation. The taxpayer's guarantee and his pledge of his assets to the bank, without more, did not establish an economic outlay or otherwise establish "indebtedness of the S corporation to the shareholder."

Instead of guaranteeing the loan, the shareholder can personally borrow the money from a bank and lend it to the corporation. The shareholder is still liable, but now he or she has generated a basis for deducting the entire loss pass-through in Year 2. A possible disadvantage of this technique is that the loan now appears as a direct liability on the shareholder's personal financial statement.

The guarantee result may have seemed obvious because the shareholder, at the outset, was not out of pocket. Here are some other situations in which shareholders, in effect, committed their own money but still failed to generate basis.

---

[46] *B.L. Spencer*, 110 TC 62, Dec. 52,554 (1998), *aff'd without published opinion*, CA-11, 99-2 USTC ¶50,830, 194 F3d 1324.

[47] *T.F. Grojean*, CA-7, 2001-1 USTC ¶50,355, 248 F3d 572, *aff'g*, 78 TCM 1249, Dec. 53,679(M), TC Memo. 1999-425.

[48] *R. Weisberg*, 99 TCM 1223, Dec. 58,162(M), TC Memo. 2010-55.

[49] *W.H. Maloof*, CA-6, 2006-2 USTC ¶50,443, 456 F3d 645, *aff'g*, 89 TCM 1022, Dec. 55,985(M), TC Memo. 2005-75; *D.L. Russell*, CA-8, 2010-2 USTC ¶50,585, 619 F3d 908, *aff'g*, 96 TCM 302, Dec. 57,574(M), TC Memo. 2008-246.

Example 21-18: S Corporation and Partnership were owned by the same parties. Partnership lent large sums to the corporation. Result: Although the stockholders of S Corporation and the owners of Partnership were the same, the debt to Partnership was not an indebtedness to the individual partners.[50]

Example 21-19: The principal shareholder of S Corporation was also the trustee and remainderman of a trust that held a substantial note of the corporation. He claimed that the corporation was indebted to him because of his interest in the trust. Result: The debt of the corporation ran to the trust and not to the shareholder and it did not increase his basis for loss-pass-through purposes.[51]

Example 21-20: Mrs. Prashker was the sole beneficiary of her husband's estate. She established an S corporation with her son; each owned 50 percent of the stock and each had a $5,000 stock basis. Mrs. Prashker had the company borrow from her husband's estate. At year-end, the company had a $90,000 net operating loss. Mrs. Prashker claimed her 50 percent share as a loss pass-through and deducted the amount on her return. She reasoned that, as sole beneficiary of her husband's estate, she actually made the loans. Result: Only $5,000 is currently deductible. Mrs. Prashker had no debt basis with the company. The estate, not Mrs. Prashker, was the company's creditor. The loan came directly from the estate, so her current deduction was limited to her $5,000 stock basis.[52]

How to Save the Deduction

Mrs. Prashker, from the example above, could have deducted the loss in full by lending to the company herself with funds borrowed from the estate. Unfortunately, she chose a different form and was stuck with the consequences. As with the partnership and trust situations, the loan cannot be indirect. It must be made directly by the shareholder.

Example 21-21: Two S Corporations had identical owners with virtually the same holdings. When one of the companies operated at a loss, the other company advanced loans to it. Result: The shareholders' debt basis in the faltering company were not increased by the sums the other corporation advanced, and this was true even though the other company was owned by the same people.[53]

The shareholders should make direct loans to the faltering S corporations. These loans would increase their basis in the S corporation and thus increase their ability to deduct losses and other deductions.

.04 COD Income Does Not Increase Insolvent S Corporation's Stock Basis

Typically, a shareholder in an S corporation experiencing financial difficulties is unable to deduct losses because the losses generated by the financially troubled S corporation

[50] *E.J. Frankel*, 61 TC 343, Dec. 32,250 (1973), *aff'd without op.*, CA-3, 506 F2d 1051.

[51] *J.Y. Robertson*, DC-NV, 73-2 USTC ¶9645.

[52] *R.M. Prashker*, 59 TC 172, Dec. 31,583 (1972).

[53] *R.J. Lee*, 35 TCM 1157, Dec. 33,988(M), TC Memo. 1976-265.

in previous years have already soaked up the shareholder's basis in the S corporation stock. As a result, the S shareholder's unused losses become suspended. When the S corporation files for bankruptcy protection under the Federal Bankruptcy Code, creditors forgive the S corporation's debt obligations. The cancellation of indebtedness income is not taxed because Code Sec. 108 provides that cancellation of debt in a bankruptcy does not result in gross income to the extent the taxpayer is insolvent [Code Sec. 108; Ch. 2]. Even though the cancellation of debt is not included in income, S shareholders have increased their basis in S corporation stock to reflect the COD income (in the same manner as tax-exempt income) so they would have sufficient basis to deduct the suspended losses. This tactic spawned years of litigation in most of the Courts of Appeals around the country and was even addressed by the U.S. Supreme Court where the taxpayers were victorious. But that victory was short-lived as a result of the legislation in 2002 which amended the law as discussed further below.

Code Sec. 108(d)(7)(A) was amended to provide that income from the discharge of indebtedness of an S corporation that is excluded from the S corporation's income is applied at the corporate level and is not taken into account as an item of income by any shareholder and thus does not increase the basis of any shareholder's stock in the corporation. Under Code Sec. 1366(d), an S corporation shareholder cannot take into account flow-through losses and deductions of the corporation that are in excess of the shareholder's basis in the stock and debt of the S corporation. In years when the Code Sec. 108 relief applies, any such loss or deduction thus denied is treated as an NOL of the S corporation (deemed NOL) under Code Sec. 108(d)(7)(B). Code Sec. 108(d)(7)(A) closes the tax loophole created by the Supreme Court in *Gitlitz*,[54] where the high court held that insolvent S shareholders could use the S corporation's cancellation of indebtedness income to increase their stock bases thus enabling them to deduct their suspended losses. This decision was criticized by the IRS because it amounted to a windfall for investors in insolvent S corporations because they were able to increase their stock basis by the amount of the cancellation of indebtedness income which is excluded from tax by the statutory exclusion found in Code Sec. 108. This basis increase enabled them to deduct previously unused or suspended losses. This scenario, as sanctioned by the Supreme Court, permitted double dipping by taxpayers who invested in insolvent S corporations. As stated in the lone dissent to the Supreme Court opinion, this scheme creates a significant tax loophole which will "grant a solvent shareholder of an insolvent S corporation a tax benefit in the form of permission to take an otherwise unavailable deduction, thereby sheltering other, unrelated income from tax."

The IRS has issued final regulations providing guidance on the reduction of an S corporation's tax attributes when the corporation excludes COD income under Code Sec. 108.

Under the final rules, any disallowed losses or deductions, including those of a shareholder who had transferred all stock during the year, are included in an S corporation's deemed NOL. If the deemed NOL exceeds the discharged COD income, the excess

---

[54] *D.A. Gitlitz*, SCt, 2001-1 USTC ¶50,147, 531 US 206, 121 SCt 701 (2001).

deemed NOL is allocated to the shareholders as disallowed losses and deductions that can subsequently be taken into account by the shareholders.

The first tax attribute to be reduced is the taxpayer's NOL [Reg. § 1.108-7(a)(1)]. Normally, the NOLs of an S corporation are passed through to shareholders, but the reduction of attributes due to COD apply at the S corporation level under Code Sec. 108(d)(7)(A). The aggregated NOLs of shareholder that are disallowed (deemed NOL) for the year of the COD are aggregated, and that deemed NOL is what is reduced [Reg. § 1.108-7(d)(1)]. If the aggregate deemed NOL exceeds the discharge of indebtedness income, the remaining deemed NOL is allocated to the shareholders. The amount that is allocated to each shareholder is the shareholder's "excess amount," which is the excess of the shareholder's disallowed losses over the amount of discharge of indebtedness income each shareholder would have realized if the exclusion had not applied [Reg. § 1.108-7(d)(2)].

In determining the character of each shareholder's allocated excess amount, the reduced NOLs are treated as if the ordinary losses are first reduced, then any losses attributable to business property and finally any capital losses [Reg. § 1.108-7(d)(3)].

.05 When Losses Are Claimed

The S corporation shareholder claims the deduction for the tax year when the S corporation's tax year ends (the deduction is allowed for the final tax year if the shareholder dies before the end of the corporation's tax year). The shareholder's pro rata share of the loss is computed on a daily basis. For example, if the shareholder disposes of shares in the middle of the year, the shareholder would be entitled to share about one half of the corporation's operating loss for the year.

Example 21-22: Electing corporation ABC, a calendar year taxpayer, has a net operating loss of $73,000 during the current tax year. Blake, one of ten equal shareholders, has an adjusted basis of $6,000 for his shares of ABC stock. He sells the shares on June 22. Blake's pro rata share of the corporation's net operating loss to be deducted on his return is $3,440 (172 days/365 days × $7,300). Note that the stock is considered held by the buyer on the day of sale.

NOTE: Amounts for which shareholders are at risk to third parties do not increase the basis of S corporation stock to allow shareholders to deduct additional operating losses.[55]

The S corporation cannot apply a loss carryback or carryover from a nonelecting year against its income of an electing year. The carryback or carryover is not terminated by the election, but every year in which the election applies is counted in figuring the years of the carryback or carryover [Code Sec. 1371(b)].

NOTE: The prohibition against carryovers between C corporation and S corporation years is not limited to net operating losses. It also extends to carryovers of any tax attribute, such as a business credit carryover.

---

[55] *L.R. Uri*, CA-10, 91-2 USTC ¶ 50,556, 949 F2d 371; *J.L. Thomas*, CA-11, 2003-1 USTC ¶ 50,460, *aff'g*, 83 TCM 1576, Dec. 54,729(M), TC Memo. 2002-108; *E.T. Sleiman*, CA-11, 99-2 USTC ¶ 50,828, 187 F3d 1352.

Special Rule for Posttermination Transition Period (PTTP)

When an S corporation's status as an S corporation terminates, shareholders are allowed a period of time after the termination—the *posttermination transition period (PTTP)*—to take advantage for the last time of some of the benefits of the now-terminated S corporation status. At this time shareholders may claim losses and deductions previously suspended due to lack of stock or debt basis up to the amount of the stock basis as of the last day of the PTTP [Code Sec. 1366(d)]. In addition, shareholders may receive cash distributions from the corporation during the PTTP that are treated as returns of capital to the extent of any balance in the S corporation's accumulated adjustments account ((AAA) as discussed in ¶21,050) [Code Sec. 1371(e)]. Losses in excess of basis that remain disallowed at the end of the last S corporation tax year are treated as incurred by the shareholder on the last day of the PTTP. However, such losses cannot exceed the shareholder's adjusted basis in the stock on the last day of such period.

A PTTP begins on the day after the last day of the last S corporation tax year and ends on the later of:

- One year after the effective date of termination, or the due date of the last S corporation tax return (including extensions), if later; or
- The end of the 120-day period beginning on the day of the determination pursuant to an audit of the taxpayer that follows the termination of the S corporation's election and that adjusts an item of income, loss or deduction during the so-called S period (as defined in Code Sec. 1368(e)(2)) [Code Secs. 1366(d)(3); 1377(b)(1)].

The 120-day PTTP following a posttermination audit determination does not apply for purposes of allowing suspended losses to be deducted [Code Sec. 1377(b)(3)(A)]. The suspended losses are not necessarily lost forever, however, because any amount of increased income determined in the audit can be offset with the suspended losses. Tax-free distributions of money by the corporation during the 120-day period are allowed only to the extent of any increase in the AAA by reason of adjustment from the audit [Code Sec. 1377(b)(3)(B)]. Therefore, an S corporation that had failed to distribute the entire amount in its AAA during the one-year PTTP following the loss of S corporation status can no longer argue that it could distribute that amount, in addition to the amount determined in the audit, during the 120-day period following the audit. Special rule for post-termination transition period.

Any cash distribution made during the PTTP reduces the shareholder's stock basis to the extent that the distribution does not exceed the AAA. But if all shareholders consent, the S corporation may elect to treat cash distributions during this period as dividends thus enabling the corporation to avoid the accumulated earnings and personal holding company taxes [Code Secs. 1371(e), 1377(b)].

.06 Disallowing Passive Losses

There are limits on the amount of losses and credits a shareholder can claim if the shareholder does not participate in the running of the business (i.e., passive activity) [Ch. 13]. These limits are considered after the at-risk limits have been considered [Ch. 13]. *Important:* If an S corporation shareholder is actively engaged in operating the corporation's business, that shareholder is not subject to these limitations.

S corporation losses passed through to inactive shareholders cannot be used against salary and other compensation income, dividends, and interest. However, if the shareholder has income from other passive activities, losses from the S corporation can be applied against that income, even if the activities are unrelated to and different from the activities conducted by the S corporation.

You are allowed a deduction for any passive activity loss or the deduction equivalent of the passive activity credit for any tax year from rental real estate activities in which there is active participation. The amount allowed under this rule cannot be more than $25,000 ($12,500 for married persons filing separately). This amount is reduced by 50 percent of the amount by which your adjusted gross income exceeds $100,000 ($50,000 for married persons filing separately).

> ▶ **TAX BREAK:** The regulations provide a break for S corporation shareholders who make loans to, or receive them from their corporations. Under the regulations, if you lend money to your S corporation and do not materially participate in the business, your corporation's interest payments on the loan are treated as passive income to you. Result: You can offset the tax on this interest income by claiming a full deduction for your corporation's passed-through interest expense (which is considered passive) [Reg. § 1.469-7].

¶21,050 TREATMENT OF DISTRIBUTIONS

Under the Subchapter S rules, there can be no current earnings and profits (E&P) because the items of corporate income and deductions pass-through to the shareholders. Distributions are not taxable as dividends unless deemed made out of accumulated E&P [discussed below]. The rules for treatment of distributions are summarized below.

.01 Distributions When No E&P

If the S corporation has no earnings and profits, the distributions are tax free to the extent of the shareholder's adjusted stock basis. The shareholder must recognize capital gain to the extent the distribution exceeds the adjusted basis of his or her stock. The gain will be long term or short term, depending on the holding period of the shareholder's stock [Code Sec. 1368(b)].[56]

> **Example 21-23:** New calendar year S corporation has no income or loss for the year, and there are no accumulated E&P. It pays out $20,000 in cash to the sole shareholder whose stock basis is $15,000. The $20,000 distribution reduces the stock basis to zero, and the excess $5,000 is capital gain.

Appreciated Value Property

If the S corporation distributes appreciated value property to the shareholder, it is treated as if the property had been sold to the shareholder at fair market value. This will generally result in capital (or Sec. 1231) gain at the corporate level, which will retain its

[56] *J.A. D'Errico*, 103 TCM 1802, Dec. 59,071(M), TC Memo. 2012-149.

character when passed through to the shareholder. This rule does not apply to any distribution to the extent it consists of property permitted by Sections 354, 355, or 356 to be received without recognition of gain.

Example 21-24: S corporation distributes to its sole shareholder investment realty (basis, $20,000; value, $45,000) that it has held for several years. S Corp. has a $25,000 long-term capital gain, which will pass through as such to its shareholders.

.02 Distributions of Accumulated E&P

Accumulated E&P can result only from:

- Prior C corporation years;
- Undistributed taxable income from pre-1983 S corporation years; or
- Corporate acquisitions resulting in a carryover of E&P.

Any corporation that was an S corporation prior to 1983, but was not an S corporation for its first tax year beginning after December 31, 1996, may reduce its accumulated E&P as of the beginning of the first tax year beginning after May 25, 2007, by the amount of any E&P accumulated during the corporation's pre-1983 S corporation years.

When an S corporation has accumulated E&P, a distribution is treated as if made in the following order [Code Sec. 1368(c); Reg. § 1.1368-1(d)(1)]:

1. Out of the shareholder's pro-rata share of the corporation's accumulated adjustments account (defined below). This portion will be tax-free to the extent of the shareholder's stock basis, and the excess over basis will be capital gain. If the distribution is in excess of the amount in the accumulated adjustments account, then;
2. Out of the shareholder's pro rata share of accumulated E&P. This portion is taxed as a dividend. If the distribution also exceeds the amount of E&P, then;
3. It will reduce the shareholder's remaining stock basis (if any); and
4. The balance will be capital gain.

Example 21-25: Calendar-year S corporation distributes $50,000 cash. It has $10,000 accumulated E&P and no accumulated adjustments account. The sole shareholder's stock basis is $25,000. The distribution is treated as a $10,000 dividend from E&P plus $15,000 capital gain (excess of remaining $40,000 over the $25,000 stock basis).

Accumulated Adjustments Account (AAA)

The AAA is an account of the S corporation and is not apportioned among shareholders [Reg. § 1.1368-2(a)]. An S corporation's AAA generally consists of the corporation's net income that has already been taxed to the shareholders but has not yet been distributed. The account permits the S corporation to make tax-free distributions to shareholders to the extent of the amount in the account. Only S corporations with earnings and profits must maintain an AAA to determine the tax effect of distributions during years as an S corporation as well as during the post-termination transition period (PTTP) as defined by Code Sec. 1377(b)(1) and as discussed in ¶ 21,045. An S corporation without earnings and profits does not need to maintain the AAA in order to determine the tax effect of distributions. It still is advisable, however, to maintain an AAA even when not required. Form 1120S requests that the AAA be computed and disclosed on Schedule M-2. The AAA must be calculated in the event of a reorganization under Code Sec. 381(a). The regulations describe how the AAA is increased and decreased. [Reg. § 1.1368-2(a)(2), (3)]. On the first day of the first year for which a corporation has an S election in effect, the AAA is zero. The AAA is increased and decreased by S corporation items except for:

- Federal income taxes attributable to any year in which the corporation was a C corporation;
- Tax-exempt income expenses, and
- Net negative adjustments (i.e., excess of losses and deductions over income) [Reg. § 1.1368-2(a)(3)(i)(C); Code Sec. 1368(e)].

Basically the AAA is the amount which an S corporation can distribute tax-free to its shareholders before any amount is considered a distribution of accumulated E&P. It is equal to the accumulated S corporation income plus and minus adjustments shareholders were required to make to stock basis.

If the amount of the account falls below zero because of losses for any tax year, it must be offset by future income before the account can have a positive balance. After taking income and loss for the year into account, the amount in the accumulated adjustment account must be applied on a pro rata basis among all of the distributions made during the year, unless the regulations provide otherwise. For example, if the account balance at the end of the year, before distributions, is $1,000, and your corporation distributes $2,000 during the year, half of each distribution will be treated as from the accumulated adjustments account and will not be taxed [Code Sec. 1368(e)(1)].

> **NOTE:** An S corporation can elect to avoid the accumulated adjustments account treatment of distributions as tax-free reductions of stock basis. Instead, distributions will be treated as taxable dividends from any accumulated E&P from years as a C corporation. Shareholders receiving distributions during the year must consent. This election allows the S corporation to distribute E&P to avoid the tax on net passive income (¶ 21,030) [Code Sec. 1368(e)(3)].

In determining the tax treatment of distributions made by an S corporation which has accumulated E&P, the amount in the AAA is computed without regard to any negative adjustments for the year. Thus, net negative adjustments (i.e., the excess of losses and deductions over income) are disregarded [Code Sec. 1368(e)(1)(C)].

The IRS has concluded that an S corporation must reduce its AAA by the amount of a stock redemption that was characterized as a distribution under Code Sec. 301.[57] In the ruling, an S corporation redeemed, at fair market value, a portion of its stock that was owned by one of its two shareholders. The redemption was not a sale or exchange and the corporation did not make any other distributions during the tax year. At the end of the year, the shareholder's adjusted basis in the stock and the

[57] Rev. Rul. 95-14, 1995-1 CB 169.

corporation's AAA exceeded the amount of the distribution. The IRS concluded that the full amount of the redemption should be treated as a distribution that reduces the S corporation's AAA pursuant to Reg. § 1.1368-2(a)(3)(iii). The special redemption rule described in Code Sec. 1368(e)(1)(B) did not apply because the redemption was not treated as an exchange. Because the entire amount of the distribution was not included in the shareholder's income, the S corporation's AAA must be reduced by the full amount of the distribution.

¶21,051 S CORPORATIONS AND PAYROLL TAXES

When an employee-shareholder who is also an officer of the S corporation performs services for the S corporation, reasonable compensation received by the employee-shareholder for these services is subject to FICA, FUTA, and income tax withholding. Therefore, S corporation shareholders are incentivized to reduce compensation and increase dividend income because doing so will reduce exposure to payroll taxes. But S corporation employers "cannot avoid Federal employment taxes by characterizing payments to its sole employee, officer, and shareholder as dividends, rather than wages, where such payments represent remuneration for services rendered." Notwithstanding the manner in which an employer characterizes payments made to an employee, the critical fact is whether a payment is actually received as remuneration for employment [Reg. § 31.3121(a)-1(c)]. An officer who performs more than minor services for a corporation and who receives remuneration in any form for those services is considered an employee and his or her wages are subject to the employer's payment of federal employment taxes [Code Sec. 3121(d)(1); Reg. § 31.3121(d)-1(b)].[58]

.01 Recharacterization of S Corporation Distributions as Wages

S corporations often try to avoid paying payroll taxes by recharacterizing salary paid to shareholder-employees as distributions of corporate profits paid out as dividend distributions which are not subject to payroll taxes rather than as wages which are subject to payroll taxes. Therefore, the IRS and the courts are forced to recompute reasonable compensation for the shareholder-employee and recast the distributions made to them as wages.[59] The salary arrangements between closely held corporations and their shareholders have always warranted close scrutiny and this situation involving S corporations is no exception. The IRS closely scrutinizes S corporation distributions because they fear that service professionals may try to minimize payroll taxes by routing what would otherwise be self-employment income through an S corporation and then paying themselves a nominal salary. Since the amount of compensation that an S corporation pays its employee-shareholder is within the employee-shareholder's discretion, the S corporation shareholder has an incentive to claim less than a reasonable salary and characterize the payments as dividends that are not subject to employment taxes. To the extent that distributions are treated as wages, they will be subject to withholding for FICA and FUTA. Key factors used by

---

[58] *Glass Blocks Unlimited*, 106 TCM 96, Dec. 59,600(M), TC Memo. 2013-180.

[59] Rev. Rul. 74-44, 1974-1 CB 287; *J.Radtke*, DC Wis., 89-2 USTC ¶ 9466, 712 F. Supp. 143, *aff'd per curiam*, CA-7, 90-1 USTC ¶ 50,113, 895 F2d 1196.

the courts in determining whether distributions are to be treated as wages instead of dividends include:

- The extent to which the distributee controls the S corporation (when the distributee, for example, is the only director of the S corporation, that fact may be evidence that distributions are wages);
- Whether the corporation has other employees (the fact that the distributee is the only employee may be taken as evidence that distributions are wages); and
- Whether the distributee performs significant uncompensated services for the corporation.[60]

The IRS first challenged attempts by S corporation shareholder-employees to minimize compensation in favor of distributions in Rev. Rul. 74-44.[61] In that ruling an S corporation paid dividends rather than compensation to two employee-shareholders who provided services to the corporation. The IRS concluded that the dividends received by the S corporation's two sole employee-shareholders were actually wages for which the corporation had to pay FICA, FUTA and income tax withholding.

Fifteen years later, in *J. Radtke*,[62] the IRS continued to challenge the perceived payroll tax abuse and in that case the court found that funds designated as dividends were actually compensation for which an S corporation owed employment taxes. Radtke, an attorney, had created an S corporation to provide legal services. Radtke was the firm's sole director, shareholder, and full-time employee, but he took no salary, receiving instead an amount in dividend payments from the corporation. Since Radtke received the funds as dividends, rather than as wages, the corporation did not pay employment taxes on them. The IRS recharacterized the funds as wages and assessed FICA and other employment taxes on them, along with penalties and interest. The court agreed with the IRS and found that the funds were not dividends but were wages subject to payroll tax.

Similarly, in *D.E. Watson*,[63] the Court of Appeals for the Eighth Circuit affirmed the district court to conclude that an S corporation shareholder-employee's salary was unreasonably low, and the IRS was allowed to reclassify the dividends as salary subject to employment taxes. David Watson was a CPA who was the sole shareholder and employee of an S corporation which was a shareholder in a successful accounting firm. Watson typically worked long hours providing tax services to the firm's clients. His salary for the years in issue was miniscule in comparison to his very large dividend distributions. The IRS found that Watson's compensation was unreasonably low based on the significant services he provided. The courts cited Watson's 20 years of experience, his advanced degree, and the hours per week he spent as one of the primary earners at the well-established accounting firm. The courts concluded that a reasonable person in Watson's position at such a profitable firm would be expected to earn at least four times what Watson earned. The courts therefore reclassified part of

---

[60] *J. Radtke*, DC Wis., 89-2 USTC ¶9466, 712 F. Supp. 143, *aff'd per curiam*, CA-7, 90-1 USTC ¶50,113, 895 F2d 1196. See also *Spicer Accounting, Inc.*, CA-9, 91-1 USTC ¶50,103, 918 F2d 90.

[61] Rev. Rul. 74-44, 1974-1 CB 287.

[62] *J. Radtke*, DC Wis., 89-2 USTC ¶9466, 712 F. Supp. 143, *aff'd per curiam*, CA-7, 90-1 USTC ¶50,113, 895 F2d 1196. See also *Spicer Accounting, Inc.*, CA-9, 91-1 USTC ¶50,103, 918 F2d 90.

[63] *D.E. Watson*, DC-IA, 2011-1 USTC ¶50,443, *aff'd*, CA-8, 2012-1 USTC ¶50,203.

Watson's distributions as compensation and held the S corporation liable for the payroll taxes on the reclassified amount.

.02 IRS Guidelines

In IRS Fact Sheet 2008-25,[64] the IRS has provided reminders regarding the taxation of compensation paid to S corporation officers/shareholders. The IRS warns S corporations not to attempt to avoid paying payroll taxes by having their officers treat their compensation as cash distributions, payments of personal expenses, or/and loans rather than as wages. Fact Sheet 2008-25 lists the following factors that have been considered by the courts in determining reasonable compensation:

- Training and experience;
- Duties and responsibilities;
- Time and effort devoted to the business;
- Dividend history;
- Payments to nonshareholder employees;
- Timing and manner of paying bonuses to key people;
- What comparable businesses pay for similar services;
- Compensation agreements; and
- The use of a formula to determine compensation.

¶21,055 ADJUSTMENTS TO BASIS OF STOCK

.01 Adjustments under Code Sec. 1367

The S corporation will issue a shareholder a Schedule K-1 that reflects the S corporation's income, loss and deductions that are allocated to the shareholder for the year. The K-1 does not state the taxable amount of the distribution. The taxable amount of distribution is contingent on the shareholder's stock basis. It is the shareholder's sole responsibility to track his or her stock and debt basis.

In computing stock basis, the shareholder starts with the initial capital contribution to the S corporation under Code Sec. 351 or the initial cost of the stock purchased. [See ¶20,005 for discussion of Code Sec. 351]. Stock can also be acquired by gift or inheritance. If acquired by gift, the shareholder's basis is equal to the donor's basis in the property immediately prior to the gift [Code Sec. 1015]. If the stock is acquired by inheritance, Code Sec. 1014 provides that the shareholder's basis is equal to the fair market value at the decedent's date of death. That amount is then increased and/or decreased based on the flow-through amounts from the S corporation. An income item will increase stock basis while a loss, deduction or distribution will decrease stock basis.

A shareholder's stock basis is increased by each shareholder's share of the following:

1. Separately stated income items of the corporation that are passed through to shareholders, such as capital gains Code Sec. 1231 gains, tax-exempt income;

[64] IRS Fact Sheet, FS-2008-25 (Nov. 20, 2008).

2. Nonseparately stated items of income, such as S corporation ordinary income; and
3. Excess of the deductions for depletion over the basis of the property subject to depletion [Code Sec. 1367(a)(1)(C)].

A stockholder's stock basis is decreased by his share of:

1. Distributions that are not includible in the shareholder's income. This would include distributions of items that have already been taxed to the shareholder
2. Separately stated loss and deduction items of the corporation that are passed through to shareholders, such as capital losses, tax-exempt expenses;
3. Nonseparately computed loss of the corporation;
4. Corporate expenses not deductible in computing taxable income and not properly chargeable to the capital account, such as fines and penalties; and
5. The amount of the shareholder's deduction for depletion of oil and gas wells [Code Sec. 1367(a)(2)(E)].

In *M.S. Barnes*,[65] the court held that under Code Sec. 1367(a)(2), an S corporation shareholder's basis reduced by the suspended losses in the first-year basis was adequate to absorb the losses even though this meant that the losses would not be deductible that year.

The amount of losses and deductions that a shareholder takes into account for any tax year may not exceed the sum of the shareholder's adjusted bases in the stock of the S corporation and any indebtedness of the S corporation to the shareholder [Code Sec. 1366(d); Reg. § 1.1366-2(a)(1)]. A shareholder cannot deduct losses in excess of basis in S corporation stock and debt [Code Sec. 1366(d)(1)]. If a shareholder does not have sufficient basis in stock and debt to take a loss from S corporation activities, the shareholder can carry the loss forward indefinitely during the S corporation's life [Code Sec. 1366(d)(2)].

Basis includes the shareholder's investment in the stock of the corporation and loans made to the S corporation by the shareholder. Basis does not normally include amounts borrowed by the S corporation from outside sources, such as banks unless the S shareholder is the true borrower of the funds from the bank and then invests the money in or loans it to the S corporation. In this situation, the taxpayer's basis in the S corporation would be increased and would be sufficient to sustain the losses.[66]

▶ **PRACTICE POINTER:** If a shareholder in an S corporation needs to get cash into a business, the shareholder should borrow the money from the bank individually and then loan it to the business. The following formalities should be observed:

- Make sure the bank or lending institution gives the money directly to the shareholder, rather than to the S corporation;
- Be sure the name of the S corporation appears nowhere on the loan documents as a party to the transaction;

---

[65] *M.S. Barnes*, CA-DC, 2013-1 USTC ¶ 50,267, *aff'g*, 103 TCM 1424, Dec. 58,991(M), TC Memo. 2012-80.

[66] *D.E. Bolding*, CA-5, 97-2 USTC ¶ 50,554, 117 F3d 270, *rev'g*, 70 TCM 110, Dec. 50,763(M), TC Memo. 1995-326.

- Be sure that once the shareholder has the money, he or she then loans it to the S corporation with the corporation issuing a note to the shareholder for the amount of the loan; and

- Any loan repayments to the bank should come directly from the shareholder, rather than from the S corporation.

If the shareholder's basis in the stock is reduced to zero, any excess loss reduces basis (but not below zero) in any indebtedness the S corporation owes to the shareholder. The shareholder cannot currently deduct excess loss remaining after reducing both stock and debt to zero. The shareholder carries it over to later years and uses it as soon as bases in stock and debt have been increased to cover it [Code Sec. 1367(b)(2)(A)].

A shareholder in an S corporation is required to adjust the basis of his or her stock for items of income and loss for any tax year before adjusting the basis for distributions [Code Sec. 1367(a); Reg. § 1.1367-1]. For any distribution made during a tax year, the adjusted basis of the stock is determined with regard to the adjustments required to the basis of a shareholder's stock in an S corporation for the tax year. This means that the adjustments for distributions made by the S corporation during the tax year are taken into account before applying the loss limitation for the year.

.02 Ordering Rules

The order in which stock basis is increased or decreased is important. Since both the taxability of a distribution and the deductibility of a loss are dependant on stock basis, there is an ordering rule in computing stock basis. Stock basis is adjusted annually, as of the last day of the S corporation year, in the following order: (1) increased for income items and excess depletion; (2) decreased for distributions; (3) decreased for non-deductible, non-capital expenses and depletion; and (4) decreased for items of loss and deduction [Reg. § 1.1367-1(f)].

However, an elective ordering rule is available in Reg. § 1.1367-1(g) which provides that a shareholder makes the election by attaching a statement to the shareholder's timely filed original or amended return electing the alternative ordering rules and stating that the shareholder agrees to carryover any noncapital, nondeductible expenses to the succeeding tax year. Once a shareholder makes an election, the shareholder must continue to use the alternative ordering rules in future tax years unless the shareholder receives the permission of the Commissioner to change back.

.03 Restoration Rules

Income items in subsequent tax years must be used to restore basis in debt before the shareholder's basis in stock can be increased above zero. The restored basis cannot exceed the taxpayer's original basis in the debt [Reg. § 1.1367-2(c)]. If a debt has been repaid, the basis in that debt (including open account debt) must be restored before restoring basis in any remaining debts [Reg. § 1.1367-2(c)(2)]. The purpose of restoring this basis first is to offset any gain that would otherwise be realized as a result of the repayment. Restorations to bases in multiple debts owed to a single shareholder should be made in proportion to the amount by which the basis of each debt has been reduced.

.04 Open Account Debt

IRS Limits Open Account Debt of S Corporations

In *Brooks*,[67] a shareholder made a series of open account advances to his S corporation and received repayments of the advances during the same year. (To fund the activities of their businesses, S corporation shareholders make informal loans to the S corporations that do not involve formal contracts for repayment. This type of debt is referred to as "open account debt.") Because the multiple advances by the taxpayers and repayments by the corporation constituted open account indebtedness, they were treated as a single indebtedness rather than separate indebtedness; therefore, the basis of the indebtedness was properly computed by netting, at the close of the year, the advances and repayments of open account debt during the year. As a result, by restoring the basis in their debts, the advances that the taxpayers made to the S corporation shielded them from the realization of gain on debt repayments.

In response to *Brooks*, the IRS issued final regulations that define open account debt as shareholder advances not evidenced by separate written instruments and repayments on the advances, the aggregate outstanding principal of which does not exceed $25,000 at the close of the relevant tax year. The rules treat advances and repayments on open account debt as a single indebtedness. The aggregate amount applies separately to each shareholder so a corporation with ten shareholders could have $250,000 of outstanding open account debt at the end of a given year. If a shareholder lends money to the S corporation beyond the $25,000 limit, that excess is treated as standard debt evidenced by a written instrument in the following year [Reg. § 1.1367-2(a)(2)].

.05 Separate Basis Rule

The regulations adopt a per-share, per-day approach to stock basis. Each share of stock has a separate basis that is based on its original cost. The basis is increased or decreased by its proportionate share of S corporation pass-through items and distributions. S corporation adjustments are allocated to the basis of each share of stock per share, per day [Code Sec. 1377(a)(1); Reg. § 1.1367-1(c)(3)].

.06 Spillover Rule

The regulations also adopt a spillover rule dealing with the situation where the amount attributable to a share exceeds its basis. In this instance, the excess is applied to reduce (but not below zero) the remaining bases of all other shares of stock in the corporation owned by the shareholder in proportion to the remaining basis of each of those shares. [Reg. § 1.1367-1(c)(3)]. Thus, a shareholder's loss will not be limited even if the loss attributable to a share exceeds its basis as long as the shareholder owns other stock in the corporation with additional basis. This occurs when the shareholder has acquired stock in the corporation in more than one transaction at varying prices. The allocation of loss to the remaining stock is in proportion to the basis remaining after the initial allocation to each of these shares.

---

[67] *F.G. Brooks*, 90 TCM 172, Dec. 56,127(M), TC Memo. 2005-204.

.07 When Adjustments to Basis Are Made

The stock basis adjustments are determined at the end of the corporation's tax year and are generally effective as of that date [Reg. § 1.1367-1(d)(1)]. When a shareholder disposes of stock during the tax year, shareholder adjustments are deemed made immediately prior to the disposition and are allocated per share, per day in accordance with Code Sec. 1377(a). Instead of making a per share, per-day allocation based on the corporation's taxable income for the entire year, all affected shareholders and the corporation can consent to treat make an allocation as if the tax year consisted of two tax years, the first of which ended on the date that the shareholder disposed of the stock. This rule applies only to the affected shareholders. The term *affected shareholder* means any shareholder whose interest is terminated and all shareholders to whom such shareholder transferred shares during the year.

.08 Debt Basis Adjustments

When an S shareholder lends money to the corporation, the shareholder has a basis in the debt equal to the face amount of the loan. (An S shareholder's basis is not increased by third-party loans made to the S corporation-even if the S shareholder personally guarantees the loans.[68]) If the pro rata share of corporate losses exceeds a shareholder's stock basis, these losses can be deducted up to the shareholder's basis in corporate debt owed to the shareholder. [Code Sec. 1366(d)]. The losses will reduce the shareholder's basis in the debt (but not below zero) [Code Sec. 1367(a)(2)].

.09 Distributions During Loss Years

Basis adjustments for distributions made by an S corporation during the tax year are taken into account before applying the loss limitation for the year. Thus, distributions reduce the adjusted basis for determining the allowable loss for the year, but that loss does not reduce the adjusted basis for purposes of determining the tax status of the distributions.

> **NOTE:** This provision allows broader tax-free treatment of a distribution during loss years. Shareholders of an S corporation are no longer limited to tax-free treatment of a distribution only to the extent of adjusted stock basis.

.10 Adjustments to Basis of Inherited S Corporation Stock

Any person who acquires stock in an S corporation by reason of a bequest, devise or inheritance from an individual must treat as income in respect of a decedent (IRD) the pro rata share of any item of income of the corporation that would have been IRD if the income had been acquired directly from the decedent [Code Sec. 1367(b)(4)(A)]. A deduction under Code Sec. 691(c) is allowed for the estate tax attributable to an item of IRD. The stepped-up basis of the stock acquired from a decedent is reduced by the extent to which the value of the stock is attributable to items consisting of IRD [Code Sec. 1367(b)(4)(B); Reg § 1.1367-1(j)].

---

[68] *J.H. Harris*, CA-5, 90-2 USTC ¶ 50,341, 902 F2d 439.

.11 Basis Adjustment to Stock of S Corporation Making Charitable Contributions

If an S corporation contributes money or other property to a charity, each shareholder takes into account the shareholder's pro rata share of the contribution in determining its own income tax liability [Code Sec. 1366(a)(1)(A)]. The shareholder's basis in the stock of the S corporation is reduced by the amount of the charitable contribution that flows through to the shareholder [Code Sec. 1367(a)(2)(B)].

In Rev. Rul. 2008-16,[69] the IRS provided that the amount of the charitable contribution deduction a shareholder is entitled to claim may not exceed the sum of (1) the shareholder's pro rata share of the fair market value of the contributed property over the property's adjusted tax basis, and (2) the amount of the Code Sec. 1366(d) loss limitation that is allocable to the property's adjusted basis under Reg. § 1.1366-2(a)(4). Pursuant to Code Sec. 1367(a)(2)(B), the shareholder's basis in the corporate stock was reduced to zero to reflect the reduction in basis attributable to the capital loss and the reduction in basis attributable to the charitable contribution deduction. Pursuant to Code Sec. 1366(d)(2), the disallowed portion of the charitable contribution and the capital loss is treated as incurred by the corporation in the following tax year with respect to the shareholder.

---

[69] Rev. Rul. 2008-16, IRB 2008-11, 585.

Corporations—Reorganizations—Stock Redemptions

REORGANIZATIONS

General rules ¶ 22,001
Party to a reorganization ¶ 22,005
Key requirements ¶ 22,010

TYPES OF REORGANIZATIONS

Statutory merger or consolidation (Type A) ¶ 22,015
Acquiring another corporation's stock (Type B) ¶ 22,020
Acquiring another corporation's property (Type C) ¶ 22,025
Transfer of assets to another corporation (Type D) ¶ 22,030
Change in capital structure (Type E) ¶ 22,035
Change in identity, form or place of organization (Type F) ¶ 22,040
Insolvency reorganization (Type G) ¶ 22,045
Reorganizations involving foreign corporations ¶ 22,046
Reorganization chart ¶ 22,050

GAIN OR LOSS

Recognition of gain or loss ¶ 22,055
Synopsis of exchanges ¶ 22,060
Treatment of boot ¶ 22,065
Gain taxed as dividend ¶ 22,070
Limitations on deduction of duplicate built-in losses ¶ 22,071
Limitations on loss importation ¶ 22,072

BASIS

Basis to distributee-stockholder ¶ 22,075
Basis to corporation ¶ 22,080
Liabilities assumed ¶ 22,085

DIVISIVE REORGANIZATIONS

General rules ¶ 22,090
Requirements of a divisive reorganization ¶ 22,095
Tax consequences of a divisive reorganization ¶ 22,100
Divisive reorganizations involving large shareholders ¶ 22,105
Shareholders who receive boot ¶ 22,110
Basis ¶ 22,115

LIQUIDATIONS

Liquidations in general ¶ 22,120
Gain or loss on property distributions in liquidation ¶ 22,125
Nontaxable liquidation of subsidiary ¶ 22,130

CARRYOVERS

Carryovers to successor corporation ¶ 22,135
Checklist of carryover items ¶ 22,140
Special limit on net operating loss carryover ¶ 22,145
Limits on carryovers of unused credits and capital losses ¶ 22,150

STOCK REDEMPTIONS

Stock redemptions in general . . . . ¶22,155
Redemption through use of a related corporation . . . . ¶22,160
Stock redeemed to pay death taxes . . . . ¶22,165
Section 306 stock . . . . ¶22,170
Constructive ownership of stock . . ¶22,175

REORGANIZATIONS

When a corporation engages in a tax-free reorganization, it can acquire another corporation, modify its capital structure or dispose of an unwanted business without triggering a taxable gain or deductible loss at the corporate or shareholder level.

¶22,001 GENERAL RULES

A *reorganization* is a readjustment of corporate structure or ownership. It may occur when a corporation (new or existing) acquires stock or property of one or more corporations, or when an existing corporation changes its capital structure, name or form, or place of organization. Thus, for example, it may cover the merger or consolidation of a company with another; an acquisition of a subsidiary by an exchange of stock; an acquisition by a company of the assets of another in exchange for stock; a division of one company into two or more companies; or a merger of a parent company with one of its subsidiaries or a subsidiary with a parent. Additionally, a corporation can use a so-called divisive reorganization [¶22,090 et seq.] to divide its existing businesses among two or more corporate shells and then transfer some or all of those businesses to its shareholders.

There are seven types of reorganizations [Code Sec. 368(a)(1)]:

- Statutory merger or consolidation under local law (Type A) [¶22,015; ¶22,050];
- Acquiring another corporation's (target's) stock solely by exchanging stock for stock, resulting in 80 percent control of the target corporation (Type B) [¶22,020; ¶22,050];
- Acquiring at least 80 percent of a target corporation's assets by a parent corporation solely by exchanging stock for assets. Generally, the target corporation must be liquidated by distributing its shares in the parent corporation to its own shareholders (Type C) [¶22,025; ¶22,050];
- Transfer of all or part of the transferor corporation's assets to another corporation in exchange for stock in the transferee corporation that represents at least 80 percent control. Following the exchange, the stock of the transferee corporation must be distributed by the transferor corporation (Type D) [¶22,030; ¶22,050];
- Recapitalization of the capital structure within the framework of an existing corporation (Type E) [¶22,035; ¶22,050];
- Change in identity, form or place of organization of *one* corporation (Type F) [¶22,040; ¶22,050]; and
- Insolvency or bankruptcy reorganization (Type G) [¶22,045; ¶22,050].

.01 Tax Consequences of Reorganization

Once a transaction qualifies as a reorganization (as discussed below), these results follow:

- The corporation recognizes no gain or loss on the exchange, nor do the shareholders [¶22,055]. However, the corporation must recognize gain to the extent it receives cash or other taxable boot that it does not distribute to its shareholders. On the other hand, the shareholders recognize gain if the corporation distributes the boot [¶22,065];
- The basis in stock or securities surrendered carries over to and must be allocated among the stock or securities received from the corporation [¶22,075]. The same basis rule for stock or securities generally applies to the corporation. But if the corporation receives property in a tax-free reorganization, it gets the transferor's basis in that property [¶22,080]; and
- The tax attributes (loss carryovers, earnings and profits, accounting methods and the like) of the corporation whose assets are acquired are usually "inherited" by the acquiring corporation [¶22,135; ¶22,140].

.02 Reporting of Taxable Mergers and Acquisitions

Code Sec. 6043A provides that the acquiring corporation (or a stock transfer agent who records transfers of stock in the transaction) must file an information return if gain or loss is recognized by shareholders because of a second corporation's acquisition of the stock or assets of the first corporation. The information return must contain the following:

- A description of the transaction;
- The name and address of each shareholder of the acquired corporation that recognizes gain as a result of the transaction (or would recognize gain, if there was a built-in gain on the shareholder's shares);
- The amount of money and the value of stock or other consideration paid to each shareholder; and
- Such other information as future regulations may require [Code Sec. 6043A(a)].

In addition, every person required to complete a return must furnish to each shareholder, whose name must be set forth in the return, a written statement showing:

- The name, address, and phone number of the information contact of the person required to make such return;
- The information required to be shown on that return; and
- Any other information required by the IRS [Code Sec. 6043A(d)].

This written statement must be furnished to the shareholder on or before January 31 of the year following the calendar year during which the transaction occurred. The penalties for failure to comply with information reporting requirements are extended to failures to comply with Code Sec. 6043A. Code Sec. 6043A supplements the information reporting provisions of Code Secs. 6043(c) and 6045.

.03 Information Reporting

Code Sec. 6043(a)(1) provides that within 30 days after the adoption of any resolution or plan for the dissolution of a corporation or the liquidation of any amount of capital stock, the corporation must file a return setting forth the terms of the resolution or plan on Form 966 [Reg. § 1.6043-1]. The return must include the following information: (1) the name and address of the corporation; (2) the place and date of incorporation; (3) the day of the adoption of the resolution or plan and the date of any amendments or supplements; and (4) the IRS district in which the last income tax return of the corporation was filed and the tax year it covered [Reg. § 1.6043-1(b)(1)].

Information returns are required from parties involved in changes of control or substantial capital restructuring of domestic corporations [Code Sec. 6043(c); Reg. § 1.6043-4]. These rules are designed to identify corporate inversion transactions in which corporations reincorporate offshore in order to avoid U.S. tax. Only large, corporate transactions involving distributions or acquisitions of stock with a value of $100 million or more are currently reportable [Code Sec. 6043(c); Reg. § 1.6043-4(c)(1)]. Also reportable are substantial changes in a corporation's capital structure where the amount of cash and the fair market value of property provided to the corporation's shareholders is $100 million or more [Reg. § 1.6043-4(d)(1)].

Reporting Requirements

An acquisition of control or a substantial change in the capital structure of the corporation is reported to the IRS on Form 8806, *Information Return for Acquisition of Control or Substantial Change in Capital Structure*. The form must be filed before the 46th day after the acquisition of control or substantial change in the corporation's capital structure. However, in no case may the form be filed after January 5 of the year following the year in which the acquisition or change took place [Reg. § 1.6043-4(a)(3)]. In addition, a corporation required to file Form 8806 must file information returns with respect to each shareholder who receives cash, stock or other property as a result of the acquisition or restructuring [Reg. § 1.6043-4(b)(1)].

Returns with respect to shareholders are filed on Form 1096, *Annual Summary and Transmittal of U.S. Information Returns* and Form 1099-CAP, *Changes in Corporate Control and Capital Structure*. These forms must be filed by February 28 (March 31, if filed electronically) of the year following the year in which the acquisition or restructuring occurred. Form 1099-CAP must be furnished to each shareholder with respect to whom it is filed. Some shareholders are considered exempt from the filing requirement (''exempt recipients''). These types of shareholders are described below.

Information Reportable on Form 8806

Information to be reported on Form 8806 filed with the timely filed return includes:

1. The name, address and taxpayer identification number (TIN) of the reporting corporation;
2. The name, address and TIN of a common parent of the affiliated group to which the reporting corporation belonged, if any, immediately prior to the change;
3. The name, address and TIN of the acquiring corporation, if any, and a statement regarding whether the acquiring corporation was newly formed prior to the time the transaction takes place;

4. A description of the transaction or series of transactions that gave rise to the acquisition of control or the substantial change in the capital structure;
5. The date or dates of the transactions disclosed in item (5) above; and
6. A description of, and a statement of the fair market value of, any stock and other property provided to the reporting corporation's shareholders in exchange for their stock [Reg. § 1.6043-4(a)(1)].

Consent Election

Reporting corporations may elect on Form 8806 to consent to the IRS's publication of information necessary for brokers to file information returns with respect to their customers. The only information published will be the name and address of the corporation, the date of the transaction(s), a description of the shares affected by the transaction(s) and the amount of cash and fair market value of any property provided to each class of shareholders in exchange for a share.

Successor Entities

If a substantial change in the capital structure occurs through a corporation's transfer of all or substantially all of its assets to another entity, the transferor corporation is required to file all reports regarding these transactions. If the transferor corporation does not file the reports, the transferee is required to file the reports. If neither the transferor nor the transferee files the reports, they are jointly and severally liable for any penalties imposed due to the failure to report [Reg. § 1.6043-4(e)].

Reportable Acquisitions of Control

An acquisition of control occurs when a corporation acquires control of a target corporation for the first time in a stock acquisition valued at $100 million or more. The transaction is reportable if it produces distributions of stock or other property to the target's shareholders and the acquiring corporation or any of its shareholders is required to recognize gain under Code Sec. 367(a) [Reg. § 1.6043-4(c)(1)]. A reportable acquisition can occur in a single transaction or in a series of transactions.

Shareholder Relieved of a Liability

Relief from a liability is considered to be property. A shareholder receives property when a liability of the shareholder is assumed and the shareholder realizes an amount from the sale or exchange of stock as the result of a transaction that qualifies as an acquisition of control or substantial change in capital structure [Reg. § 1.6043-4(f)].

Control Defined

A shareholder corporation has control if it owns, directly or indirectly, stock that represents at least 50 percent of the total combined voting power of all stock entitled to vote, or at least 50 percent of the total value of shares of all classes of stock [Code Sec. 304(c)(1); Reg. § 1.6043-4(c)(2)].

Reportable Changes in Corporate Capital Structure

A *substantial change* in the capital structure of a corporation is reportable. A substantial change occurs when a corporation, in a transaction or a series of transactions:

1. Merges, consolidates, or otherwise combines with another corporation or transfers all or substantially all of it assets to at least one other corporation;

2. Transfers all or part of its assets to another corporation in a Title 11 or similar case and, pursuant to the plan, distributes stock or securities of that corporation; or
3. Changes its identity, form or place of organization; and
4. Is required (or any of its shareholders are required) to recognize gain under Code Sec. 367(a).

To be reportable, the value of cash and other property provided to shareholders in a transaction that qualifies as a substantial change must be at least $100 million [Reg. § 1.6-43-4(d)].

Exempt Recipients Defined

Corporations are not required to file Form 1099-CAP with regard to certain shareholders that are not clearing organizations. These shareholders are called *exempt recipients* and are described in Reg. § 1.6043-4(b)(5) as:

1. A shareholder who receives stock in an exchange that is not subject to gain recognition under Code Sec. 367(a);
2. A shareholder for which the corporation reasonably determines that the amount of cash and the fair market value of the stock and property received is not greater than $1,000;
3. A shareholder that provides a properly completed exemption certificate (see Reg. § 31.3406(h)(3)) to the corporation is: (a) a corporation (not S corporations) or a partnership; (b) an organization that is exempt from tax; (c) an individual retirement plan; (d) the U.S. government or any of its wholly owned agencies and instrumentalities; (e) a state, the District of Columbia, a possession of the United States, or any of their political subdivisions, wholly owned agencies and instrumentalities, or any pool or partnership composed exclusively of those entities; (f) a foreign government, a political subdivision of a foreign government or any wholly owned agency or instrumentality of a foreign government or political subdivision of a foreign government; (g) an international organization or any of its wholly owned agencies or instrumentalities; (h) a foreign central bank of issue; (i) a dealer in securities, commodities, or notional principal contracts that is registered under federal or state law or under the laws of a foreign country; (j) a real estate investment trust; (k) an entity registered under the Investment Company Act of 1940; (l) a common trust fund; or (m) a financial institution such as a bank, mutual savings bank, savings and loan association, building and loan association, cooperative bank, homestead association, credit union, industrial loan association, or bank or a similar organization;
4. A shareholder for which, prior to the transaction, the corporation has documentation on which it may rely allowing it to treat payments to that shareholder as made to a foreign beneficial owner or as made to a foreign payee or presumed to be made to a foreign payee; and
5. A shareholder that receives stock, cash or other property in an acquisition of control or substantial change in capital structure and the corporation, as of January 31 of the following year, does not know or have reason to know that such stock, cash, or property had been received.

Penalties for Failure To Report Corporate Acquisition or Substantial Change in Capital Structure Transactions

Failure to file the Form 8806, Form 1096, or Form 1099-CAP with regard to a change of control or substantial change in capital structure will result in penalties under Code Sec. 6652(l). The penalties for failure to file are $500 per day for each day the failure to file continues, up to a $100,000 cap for any given return. Criminal penalties under Code Sec. 7203, Code Sec. 7206, and Code Sec. 7207 may also apply [Reg. § 1.6043-4(g)].

Under Code Sec. 6045, brokers (including stock transfer agents) are required to prepare information returns and to provide corresponding payee statements regarding sales made on behalf of their customers, subject to the penalty provisions of Code Secs. 6721-6724.

¶22,005 PARTY TO A REORGANIZATION

To benefit from a tax-free reorganization, the taxpayer must be either a *party to the reorganization* or the holder of stock or securities in such a party [Code Secs. 354, 361; Reg. § 1.361-1]. Specifically, a party is: (1) a corporation resulting from a reorganization, and (2) both corporations in a reorganization resulting from the acquisition by one corporation of the stock or properties of the other [Code Sec. 368(b); Reg. § 1.368-2(f)].

> **Example 22-1:** Corporations X and Y are both parties if Corp. X is merged into Corp. Y; if Corporations X and Y are consolidated into Corp. Z, all three are parties (Type A reorganizations). Also, both are parties if Corp. X transfers substantially all of its assets to Corp. Y in exchange for voting stock (Type C) [Reg. § 1.368-2(f)].

Furthermore, if a corporation controls an acquiring corporation, it is a party to a reorganization if its stock or securities were used to acquire stock or assets of a third corporation [Code Sec. 368(b)(2); Reg. § 1.368-2(f)]. An acquiring corporation remains a party even if it transfers all or part of the stock or assets acquired to a controlled subsidiary [Code Sec. 368(a)(2)(C); Reg. § 1.368-2(f)].

A corporation is a party to a reorganization if it issues new stock certificates after a change of name (Type F reorganization), in exchange for its shareholder's stock. The same is true if a corporation issues preferred stock in exchange for its shareholders' common, as part of a recapitalization (Type E).[1]

.01 Definition of Securities

The term *securities* includes bonds and debenture notes. It typically does not include short-term purchase money notes;[2] but long-term notes may be considered securities[3] [Reg. § 1.368-1]. Securities also include rights to acquire stock issued by a corporation

[1] Rev. Rul. 72-206, 1972-1 CB 104.

[2] *Pinellas Ice & Cold Storage Co.*, SCt, 3 USTC ¶ 1023, 287 US 462, 53 SCt 257.

[3] *D.H. Burnham*, CA-7, 36-2 USTC ¶ 9544, 86 F2d 776, *cert. denied*, 300 US 683, 57 SCt 753.

that is a party to a reorganization [Reg. § 1.354-1(e)]. A debt instrument with a term of two years issued by an acquiring corporation in exchange for a security of the target corporation in an "A" reorganization is a security within the meaning of Code Sec. 354. A debt instrument with a term of five years or less is not generally a security. However, where the debt instrument is: (1) issued pursuant to a reorganization in exchange for securities in the target corporation, and (2) generally has the same terms (including maturity date) as the securities of the target corporation, the debt instrument issued by the acquiring corporation is a continuation of the holder's interest in the target corporation in substantially the same form (i.e., a security).

IRS Approves Tax-free Exchange of Short-term Notes in Statutory Merger

In Rev. Rul. 2004-78,[4] the IRS concluded that the acquiring corporation's two-year notes issued in exchange for the target corporation's notes were securities qualifying for nonrecognition treatment under Code Sec. 354. The IRS reached this result even though an instrument with a term of fewer than five years generally is not a security because the acquiring corporation's notes were issued in the reorganization in exchange for the target's securities and bear the same terms (other than interest rate) as target's securities, represent a continuation of the security's holders' investment in target in substantially the same form. Thus, the IRS concluded that the acquiring corporation's short-term notes exchanged for target's securities were securities under Code Sec. 354.

¶22,010 KEY REQUIREMENTS

A transaction can qualify as a tax-free reorganization only if the following four requirements are satisfied [Code Sec. 368; Reg. §§ 1.368-1, -2]:

.01 Plan of Reorganization

The reorganization must be done according to a plan of reorganization adopted in advance by each corporation concerned. The exchange of stock, securities, or property is not tax-free unless undertaken pursuant to the terms of this plan of reorganization.

.02 Business Purpose

The reorganization must be required by business needs and must serve a valid business purpose. It cannot be done solely as a device to avoid taxes or be merely a transfer of assets by one corporation to another under a plan having no relation to either corporation's business. In other words, if the transaction doesn't make sense apart from the tax considerations, it's likely there is no business purpose.

> **NOTE:** Although an intention to avoid tax liability will not of itself make a transaction ineffective, a plan that complies literally with the statute will not accomplish the nonrecognition of gain, if it has no other business or corporate purpose.[5]

---

[4] Rev. Rul. 2004-78, 2004-2 CB 108.

[5] *E.F. Gregory*, SCt, 35-1 USTC ¶9043, 293 US 465, 55 SCt 266; *M.S. Wilson*, CA-9, 66-1 USTC ¶9103, 353 F2d 184.

.03 Continuity of Business Enterprise (COBE)

The acquiring corporation *must*: (1) continue the target corporation's historic business (business continuity); or (2) use a significant portion of the target corporation's assets in a continuing business (asset continuity) [Reg. § 1.368-1(d)(1)]. Reg. § 1.368-1(b) provides that the continuity of business enterprise requirement is not required for a transaction to qualify as a reorganization under Code Sec. 368(a)(1)(E) (E reorganization) or under Code Sec. 368(a)(1)(F) (F reorganization).

> **Example 22-2:** If Target Corp. transfers its assets to Buyer Corp., an acquiring corporation, in exchange for stock of Buyer Corp., but Buyer Corp., pursuant to the plan of reorganization transfers the assets of Target Corp. to a third unrelated company, the continuity of business enterprise requirement would not be satisfied.

If the acquired corporation has more than one line of business, continuity of business enterprise requires only that the acquiring corporation continue a significant line of business [Reg. § 1.368-1 (d) (2) (ii)]. Also, the continuity of business enterprise requirement is satisfied if the acquiring corporation uses a significant portion of the acquired corporation's historic business assets in a business [Code Sec. 368; Reg. § 1.368-1 (d) (3)].

For example, in *Honbarrier*,[6], the Tax Court held that a statutory merger into an active trucking company of a trucking company that had sold its operating assets and invested the proceeds in tax-exempt bonds was not a tax-free A reorganization because the acquiring corporation didn' t continue the business enterprise of the acquired corporation. Rather, the acquiring corporation distributed the bulk of the assets of the acquired corporation to its shareholders.

A corporation's historic business assets are the assets used in its business historically over the long term. Business assets may include stock and securities and intangible operating assets such as good will, patents, and trademarks, whether or not they have a tax basis. In general, the determination of the portion of a corporation's assets considered significant is based on the relative importance of the assets to the operation of the business. However, all other facts and circumstances, such as the net fair market value of those assets, will be considered [Reg. § 1.368-1 (d) (3) (iii)].

> **Example 22-3:** T conducts three lines of business: manufacture of synthetic resins, manufacture of chemicals for the textile industry, and distribution of chemicals. The three lines of business are approximately equal in value. T sells the synthetic resin and chemical distribution businesses to a third party for cash and marketable securities. Six months later, T transfers all of its assets to P for P's voting stock. P continues the chemical manufacturing business without interruption. The continuity of business enterprise requirement is met. Continuity of business enterprise requires only that P continue one of T's three significant lines of business [Reg. § 1.368-1(d)(5), Ex. (1)].

---

[6] *A.L. Honbarrier*, 115 TC 300, Dec. 54,070 (2000).

Example 22-4: T manufactures boy's and men's trousers. As a part of a plan of reorganization, T sells all of its assets to a third party for cash and purchases a highly diversified portfolio of stocks and bonds on January 1, 1998. As part of the plan, T operates an investment business thereafter until June 1, 2000. On that date, the plan or reorganization culminates in a transfer by T of all its assets to P, a regulated investment company, solely in exchange for P's voting stock. The continuity of business enterprise requirement is not met. T's investment activity is not its historic business, and the stocks and bonds are not T's historic business assets.

The acquiring corporation will be treated as holding all of the businesses and assets of all of the members of the qualified group, which is one or more chains of corporations connected through stock ownership with the acquiring corporation, but only if the acquiring corporation owns directly controlling stock in at least one other corporation, and controlling stock in each of the corporations (except the acquiring corporation) is owned directly by one of the other corporations [Reg. § 1.368-1(d)(4(i), (ii)]. Each partnership of a partnership will be treated as owning the target business assets used in a business of the partnership in accordance with that partner's interest in the partnership [Reg. § 1.368-1(d)(4)(3)(A)]. The acquiring corporation will be treated as conducting a business of a partnership if members of the qualified group, in the aggregate, own an interest in the partnership representing a significant interest in that partnership business, or one or more members of the qualified group have active and substantial management functions as a partner with respect to that partnership business [Reg. § 1.368-1(d)(4)(iii)(B)].

COBE Safe Harbor for Tax-Free Reorganizations

A safe harbor is provided in Reg. § 1.368-2(k)(1) for certain transfers of assets or stock to qualify as tax-free reorganizations under Code Sec. 368(a). The safe harbor allows the transaction to satisfy the continuity of business enterprise (COBE) requirement. The safe harbor in Reg. § 1.368-2(k)(1) permits subsequent transfers of stock or assets that are characterized as either (1) a distribution to shareholders or as (2) an "other transfer." A distribution to shareholders cannot be an "other transfer."

Safe harbor treatment will be denied if there is a transfer to the former shareholders of the acquired corporation of "consideration" for their ownership interest in the acquired or surviving corporation. The safe harbor also will not apply to a transfer to the issuing (acquiring) corporation or a related person, by former shareholders of the acquiring corporation or surviving corporation of consideration initially received in the potential reorganization. However, the safe harbor continues to apply to certain other transfers, such as certain pro-rata dividend distributions by the acquiring corporation following the reorganization.

Furthermore, the restriction does not apply to transfers to a shareholder that is also the acquiring corporation. Thus, the safe harbor protects certain "upstream" mergers followed by a transfer of acquired assets.

The safe harbor for other transfers does not apply if the acquired corporation, the acquiring corporation, or the surviving corporation terminates its corporate existence in connection with the transfer of stock or assets [Reg. § 1.368-2(k)(2)].

Implication

Reg. § 1.368-2(k) makes it easier for business entities to engage in tax-free business reorganizations. For example, a transaction otherwise qualifying as a tax-free reorganization will not be disqualified because part or all of the acquired assets or stock are transferred to a corporation controlled by the acquiring corporation. This means that an otherwise tax-free reorganization will still be viable where the transfers in substance constitute only a readjustment of continuing interests in the reorganized business in modified corporate form.

.04 Continuity of Interest (COI)

There must be a continuity of interest (COI) (except in a Type E or F reorganization [¶ 22,030]) on the part of the owners of the corporation before and after the reorganization [Reg. § 1.368-1(b)]. Continuity of interest is not required for a transaction to qualify as a reorganization under Code Sec. 368(a)(1)(E) (E reorganization) or under Code Sec. 368(a)(1)(F) (F reorganization) [Reg. § 1.368-1(b)].

The purpose of the COI requirement is to prevent transactions that resemble sales from qualifying for nonrecognition of gain or loss available to corporate reorganizations [Reg. § 1.368-1(e)(1)]. COI requires that, in substance, a substantial part of the value of the proprietary interests in the target corporation be preserved in the reorganization. A proprietary interest in the target corporation is preserved if, in a potential reorganization, it is exchanged for a proprietary interest in the issuing corporation, it is exchanged by the acquiring corporation for a direct interest in the target corporation enterprise, or it otherwise continues as a proprietary interest in the target corporation. This means that the original shareholders must have an equity or ownership interest in the reorganized corporation or corporations as opposed to a mere creditor interest [Reg. § 1.368-1(e)(1)(i)].

The COI requirement is satisfied if a substantial part of the value of the proprietary interest in the target corporation (T) is preserved in the reorganization. A proprietary interest in T will be preserved if, in a potential reorganization, it:

- Is exchanged for a proprietary interest in the acquiring corporation (A),
- It is exchanged by A for a direct interest in the T enterprise, or
- It otherwise continues as a proprietary interest in T [Reg. § 1.368-1(e)(1)(i)].

The regulations do not define *substantial.* The IRS has ruled that 50 percent consideration is substantial.[7] However, the Supreme Court has ruled that stocks of 45 percent[8] and 36 percent[9] were substantial enough to satisfy the continuity of stock interest requirement.

Measuring Continuity of Interest Under the Signing Date Rule

Under the signing date rule, when determining if the continuity of interest requirement is satisfied under a contract for the reorganization that provides for fixed consideration, the consideration to be exchanged for the proprietary interests in the target corporation

[7] Rev. Rul. 66-224, 1966-2 CB 114.

[8] *J.J. Watts*, SCt, 36-1 USTC ¶ 9016, 296 US 387, 56 SCt 275.

[9] *J.A. Nelson Co.*, SCt, 36-1 USTC ¶ 9019, 296 US 374, 56 SCt 273.

is valued on the last business day before the first date such contract is a binding contract (the pre-signing date). If a portion of the consideration provided in a contract for a reorganization in which there is fixed consideration consists of other property such as boot which is identified by value, then this specified value for the boot is used to determine if continuity of interest is satisfied. If the contract doesn't provide for fixed consideration, the signing date rule does not apply [Reg. § 1.368-1(e) (2) (i)].

A contract provides for fixed consideration so as to qualify for the signing date rule if the contract provides the number of shares of each class of issuing corporation stock, the amount of money, and the other property (identified either by value or by specific description), if any, to be exchanged for all the proprietary interests in the target corporation, or to be exchanged for each proprietary interest in the target corporation. A shareholder's election to receive a number of shares of stock of the issuing corporation, money, or other property (or some combination of stock of the issuing corporation, money, or other property) in exchange for all of the shareholder's proprietary interests in the target corporation, or each of the shareholder's proprietary interests in the target corporation, will not prevent a contract from being fixed consideration [Reg. § 1.368-1(e) (2) (iii) (A)].

Binding Contract

A contract is binding if it is enforceable under applicable law against the parties to the instrument. The presence of a condition outside the control of the parties (including, for example, regulatory agency approval) will not prevent an instrument from being a binding contract. Moreover, the fact that insubstantial terms remain to be negotiated by the parties to the contract, or that customary conditions remain to be satisfied, will not prevent an instrument from being a binding contract [Reg. § 1.368-1(e) (2) (ii) (A)].

Contract Modifications

If a term of a binding contract that address the amount or type of the consideration the target shareholders will receive in a potential reorganization is modified before the closing date of the potential reorganization, the date of the modification shall be treated as the first date there is a binding contract [Reg. § 1.368-1(e) (2) (ii) (B) (1)].

A modification of a term that relates to the amount or type of consideration the target shareholders will receive in a transaction that would have resulted in the preservation of a substantial part of the value of the target corporation shareholders' proprietary interests in the target corporation if there had been no modification will not be treated as a modification if:

- The modification has the sole effect of providing for the issuance of additional shares of issuing corporation stock to the target corporation shareholders;
- The modification has the sole effect of decreasing the amount of money or other property to be delivered to the target corporation shareholders; or
- The modification has the effect of decreasing the amount of money or other property to be delivered to the target corporation shareholders and providing for the issuance of additional shares of issuing corporation stock to the target corporation shareholders [Reg. § 1.368-1(e) (2) (ii) (B) (2)].

A modification of a term that relates to the amount or type of consideration the target shareholders will receive in a transaction that would not have resulted in the preservation of a substantial part of the value of the target corporation shareholders' proprietary interests in the target corporation if there had been no modification will not be treated as a modification if:

- The modification has the sole effect of providing for the issuance of fewer shares of issuing corporation stock to the target corporation shareholders;
- The modification has the sole effect of increasing the amount of money or other property to be delivered to the target corporation shareholders; or
- The modification has the effect of increasing the amount of money or other property to be delivered to the target corporation shareholders and providing for the issuance of fewer shares of issuing corporation stock to the target corporation shareholders [Reg. § 1.368-1(e)(2)(ii)(B)(3)].

Related Person Rule

A proprietary interest in the target is not preserved if, in connection with a potential reorganization, a person related to acquiring corporation acquires, with consideration other than a proprietary interest in the acquiring corporation, stock of the target corporation or stock of the acquiring corporation furnished in exchange for a proprietary interest in the target in the potential reorganization. A proprietary interest in the target will be preserved to the extent those persons who were the direct or indirect owners of the target prior to the potential reorganization maintain a direct or indirect proprietary interest in the acquiring corporation [Reg. § 1.368-1(e)(3)].

Related Person Defined

Two corporations are *related persons* if either the corporations are members of the same affiliated group or a purchase of the stock of one corporation by another corporation would be treated as a distribution in redemption of the stock of the first corporation under Code Sec. 304(a)(2) [Reg. § 1.368-1(e)(4)(i)(A)]. Related persons do not include individual or noncorporate shareholders [Reg. § 1.368-1(e)(4)].

Impact of Subsequent Stock Sale

T shareholders are permitted to sell A stock received in a reorganization to third parties without causing the reorganization to fail to satisfy the continuity of interest requirements. Even though some courts have held otherwise, the final regulations focus the continuity of interest requirement generally on exchanges between target shareholders and the acquiring corporation. According to this approach, sales of acquiring corporation stock by former target shareholders generally are disregarded [Reg. § 1.368-1(e)(1)(i)].

> **Example 22-5:** X owns all of the stock of T. T merges into P. In the merger, X receives P stock having a fair market value of $50,000 and cash of $50,000. Immediately after the merger, and pursuant to a preexisting binding contract, X sells all of the P stock to B. The sale to B is disregarded because B is not a person related (as defined below) to P within the meaning of Reg. § 1.368-1(e)(3). Thus, the transaction satisfied the continuity of interest requirement because 50

percent of X's T stock was exchanged for P stock, preserving a substantial part of the value of the proprietary interest in T [Reg. § 1.368-1(e)(6), Ex. 1].

The IRS has found that the continuity of interest requirement was satisfied when a publicly traded acquiring corporation reacquires its shares in the open market through a broker, even if the shares are acquired from former target corporation shareholders.[10]

TYPES OF REORGANIZATIONS

¶22,015 STATUTORY MERGER OR CONSOLIDATION (TYPE A)

.01 General Process

To qualify as a Type A reorganization, the transaction must be a merger or consolidation made in accordance with state law. In a merger, one corporation acquires another corporation. The acquired company is dissolved and its assets and liabilities are taken over by the acquiring company. In a consolidation, two or more corporations combine to form a new corporation. Both of the original corporations are dissolved and the one newly-created entity survives[11] [Code Sec. 368(a) (1) (A); Reg. § 1.368-2(b) (ii)].

> **NOTE:** The tax law does not specify the type of consideration that may be given in a merger or consolidation. But securities or other property (as opposed to stock) cannot be all, or even too high a proportion, of the consideration given to the stockholders. Receipt of too much consideration other than stock has been held to break the continuity of interest [¶22,010] with the result that the reorganization was denied tax-free treatment.[12] For transfer of acquired assets to controlled subsidiary, see ¶22,025.

A *statutory merger* or *consolidation* is defined in Reg. § 1.368-2(b)(ii) as a transaction effected pursuant to the statutes necessary to effect the merger or consolidation, in which transaction, as a result of the operation of such statute or statutes, the following events occur simultaneously at the effective time of the transaction:

1. All of the assets (other than those distributed in the transaction) and liabilities (except to the extent such liabilities are satisfied or discharged in the transaction or are nonrecourse liabilities to which assets distributed in the transaction are subject) of each member of one or more combining units (each a transferor unit) become the assets and liabilities of one or more members of one other combining unit (the transferee unit); and
2. The combining entity of each transferor unit ceases its separate legal existence for all purposes; provided, however, that this requirement will be satisfied even if, under applicable law, after the effective time of the transaction, the combining entity of the transferor unit (or its officers, directors, or agents) may act or be acted against, or a member of the transferee unit (or its officers, directors, or

---

[10] Rev. Rul. 99-58, 1999-2 CB 701.

[11] Rev. Rul. 2000-5, 2001-1 CB 436.

[12] *Southwest Natural Gas Co.*, CA-5, 51-1 USTC ¶9340, 189 F2d 332, *cert. denied*, 342 US 860, 72 SCt 88.

agents) may act or be acted against in the name of the combining entity of the transferor unit, provided that such actions relate to assets or obligations of the combining entity of the transferor unit that arose, or relate to activities engaged in by such entity, prior to the effective time of the transaction.

.02 Examples of Mergers and Consolidations

The following examples from Reg. § 1.368-2(b)(ii) help define what transactions will qualify as statutory mergers or consolidations. In each example, except as otherwise provided, each of R, V, Y, and Z is a C corporation. X is a domestic limited liability company. Except as otherwise provided, X is wholly owned by Y and is disregarded as an entity separate from Y for Federal income tax purposes.

Example 22-6: Divisive transaction pursuant to a merger statute. Z transfers some of its assets and liabilities to Y, retains the remainder of its assets and liabilities, and remains in existence for tax purposes following the transaction. The transaction does not qualify as a statutory merger or consolidation because all of the assets and liabilities of Z do not become the assets and liabilities of Y. In addition, the separate legal existence of Z does not cease for all purposes.

Example 22-7: Merger of a target corporation into a disregarded entity in exchange for stock of the owner. Z merges into X and all of the assets and liabilities of Z become the assets and liabilities of X and Z's separate legal existence ceases for all purposes. In the merger, the Z shareholders exchange their stock of Z for stock of Y. The transaction qualifies as a statutory merger or consolidation because all of the assets and liabilities of Z become the assets and liabilities of one or more members of the transferee unit that is comprised of Y, the combining entity of the transferee unit, and X, a disregarded entity the assets of which Y is treated as owning for tax purposes, and Z ceases its separate legal existence for all purposes.

Example 22-8: Merger of a target S corporation that owns a QSub into a disregarded entity. The facts are the same as in Example 22-7, except that Z is an S corporation and owns all of the stock of U, a QSub. The deemed formation by Z of U is disregarded for tax purposes. The transaction is treated as a transfer of the assets of U to X, followed by X's transfer of these assets to U in exchange for stock of U. See Reg. § 1.1361-5(b)(3), Ex. 9. The transaction qualifies as a statutory merger or consolidation because all of the assets and liabilities of Z and U, the sole members of the transferor unit, become the assets and liabilities of one or more members of the transferee unit that is comprised of Y, the combining entity of the transferee unit, and X, a disregarded entity the assets of which Y is treated as owning for tax purposes, and Z ceases its separate legal existence for all purposes. Moreover, the deemed transfer of the assets of U in exchange for U stock does not cause the transaction to fail to qualify as a statutory merger or consolidation. See Code Sec. 368(a)(2)(C).

Example 22-9: Triangular merger of a target corporation into a disregarded entity. The facts are the same as in Example 22-8, except that V owns 100 percent of the outstanding stock of Y and, in the merger of Z into X, the Z shareholders exchange their stock of Z for stock of V. In the transaction, Z transfers substantially all of its properties to X. The transaction is not prevented from qualifying as a statutory merger or consolidation, provided the transaction satisfies the requirements of the forward triangular merger as provided in Code Sec. 368(a)(2)(D).

▶ **PRACTICE POINTER:** In a forward triangular merger, a controlled corporation (i.e., a subsidiary) uses its parent's stock to acquire substantially all of the property of another corporation that merges into the subsidiary. Two restrictions: (1) no subsidiary stock can be used and (2) the exchange would have qualified as a Type A reorganization had the merger been into the parent (¶22,030) [Code Sec. 368(a)(2)(D)].

Because the assets of X are treated for tax purposes as the assets of Y, Y will be treated as acquiring substantially all of the properties of Z in the merger for purposes of determining whether the merger satisfies the requirements of Code Sec. 368(a)(2)(D). As a result, the Z shareholders that receive stock of V will be treated as receiving stock of a corporation that is in control of Y, the combining entity of the transferee unit that is the acquiring corporation. Thus, the merger will satisfy the requirements of Code Sec. 368(a)(2)(D) and thus qualify as a tax-free forward triangular merger.

Example 22-10: Merger of a target corporation into a disregarded entity owned by a partnership. The facts are the same as in Example 22-9, except that Y is organized as a partnership for tax purposes. All of the assets and liabilities of Z, the combining entity and sole member of the transferor unit, do not become the assets and liabilities of one or more members of a transferee unit because neither X nor Y qualifies as a combining entity. Thus, the transaction cannot qualify as a statutory merger or consolidation.

Example 22-11: Merger of a disregarded entity into a corporation. X merges into Z and the following events occur simultaneously: all of the assets and liabilities of X (but not the assets and liabilities of Y other than those of X) become the assets and liabilities of Z and X's separate legal existence ceases for all purposes. The transaction does not qualify as a statutory merger or consolidation because all of the assets and liabilities of a transferor unit do not become the assets and liabilities of one or more members of the transferee unit and X does not qualify as a combining entity.

Example 22-12: Merger of a corporation into a disregarded entity in exchange for interests in the disregarded entity. Z merges into X and the following events occur simultaneously: all of the assets and liabilities of Z become the assets and liabilities of X and Z's separate legal existence ceases for all purposes. In the merger of Z into X, the Z shareholders exchange their stock of Z for interests in X so that, immediately after the merger, X is not disregarded as an entity separate from Y for tax purposes. Following the merger, X is classified as a partnership for tax purposes. The transaction does not qualify as a statutory merger or consolidation because immediately after the merger X is not disregarded as an entity separate from Y and, consequently, all of the assets and liabilities of Z, the combining entity of the transferor unit, do not become the assets and liabilities of one or more members of a transferee unit.

Example 22-13: Merger transaction preceded by distribution. Z operates two unrelated businesses, Business P and Business Q, each of which represents 50 percent of the value of the assets of Z. Y desires to acquire and continue operating Business P, but does not want to acquire Business Q. Pursuant to a single plan, Z sells Business Q for cash to parties unrelated to Z and Y in a taxable transaction, and then distributes the proceeds of the sale pro rata to its shareholders. Then, Z merges into Y and all of the assets and liabilities of Z related to Business P become the assets and liabilities of Y and Z's separate legal existence ceases for all purposes. In the merger, the Z shareholders exchange their Z stock for Y stock. The transaction qualifies as a statutory merger or consolidation because all of the assets and liabilities of Z, the combining entity and sole member of the transferor unit, become the assets and liabilities of Y, the combining entity and sole member of the transferee unit, and Z ceases its separate legal existence for all purposes.

Example 22-14: State law conversion of target corporation into a limited liability company. Y acquires the stock of V from the V shareholders in exchange for consideration that consists of 50 percent voting stock of Y and 50 percent cash. Immediately after the stock acquisition, V files the necessary documents to convert from a corporation to a limited liability company. Y's acquisition of the stock of V and the conversion of V to a limited liability company are steps in a single integrated acquisition by Y of the assets of V. The acquisition by Y of the assets of V does not qualify as a statutory merger or consolidation because V, the combining entity of the transferor unit, does not cease its separate legal existence. Although V is an entity disregarded from its owner for Federal income tax purposes, it continues to exist as a juridical entity after the conversion.

Example 22-15: Dissolution of target corporation. Y acquires the stock of Z from the Z shareholders in exchange for consideration that consists of 50 percent voting stock of Y and 50 percent cash. Immediately after the stock acquisition, Z files a certificate of dissolution and commences winding up its activities. Under state dissolution law, ownership and title to Z's assets does not automatically vest in Y upon dissolution. Instead, Z transfers assets to its creditors in satisfaction of its liabilities and transfers its remaining assets to Y in the liquidation stage of the dissolution. Y's acquisition of the stock of Z and the dissolution of Z are steps in a single integrated acquisition by Y of the assets of Z. The acquisition by Y of the assets of Z does not qualify as a statutory merger or consolidation because Y does not acquire all of the assets of Z as a result of Z filing the certificate of dissolution or simultaneously with Z ceasing its separate legal existence. Instead, Y acquires the assets of Z by reason of Z's transfer of its assets to Y.

Example 22-16: Merger of corporate partner into a partnership. Y owns an interest in X, an entity classified as a partnership for tax purposes, that represents a 60 percent capital and profits interest in X. Z owns an interest in X that represents a 40 percent capital and profits interest. Z merges into X. Pursuant to such law, the following events occur simultaneously at the effective time of the transaction: all of the assets and liabilities of Z become the assets and liabilities of X and Z ceases its separate legal existence for all purposes. In the merger, the Z shareholders exchange their stock of Z for stock of Y. As a result of the merger, X becomes an entity that is disregarded as an entity separate from Y for tax purposes. The transaction qualifies as a statutory merger or consolidation because all of the assets and liabilities of Z, the combining entity and sole member of the transferor unit, become the assets and liabilities of one or more members of the transferee unit that is comprised of Y, the combining entity of the transferee unit, and X, a disregarded entity the assets of which Y is treated as owning for tax purposes immediately after the transaction, and Z ceases its separate legal existence for all purposes.

Example 22-17: State law consolidation. Z and V consolidate and the following events occur simultaneously: all of the assets and liabilities of Z and V become the assets and liabilities of Y, an entity that is created in the transaction, and the existence of Z and V continues in Y. In the consolidation, the Z shareholders and the V shareholders exchange their stock of Z and V, respectively, for stock of Y. With respect to each of Z and V, the transaction qualifies as the statutory merger or consolidation all of the assets and liabilities of Z and V, respectively, each of which is the combining entity of a transferor unit, become the assets and liabilities of Y, the combining entity and sole member of the transferee unit, and Z and V each ceases its separate legal existence for all purposes.

Example 22-18: Transaction effected pursuant to foreign statutes. Z and Y, which are foreign corporations, combine, and all of the assets and liabilities of Z become the assets and liabilities of Y, and Z's separate legal existence ceases for all purposes. The transaction qualifies as a statutory merger or consolidation because the transaction is effected pursuant to statutes of the foreign country and all of the assets and liabilities of Z, the combining entity of the transferor unit, become the assets and liabilities of Y, the combining entity and sole member of the transferee unit, and Z ceases its separate legal existence for all purposes.

Example 22-19: Foreign law amalgamation using parent stock. Z and V, which are foreign corporations, amalgamate and all the assets and liabilities of Z and V become the assets and liabilities of R, an entity that is created in the transaction and that is wholly owned by Y immediately after the transaction, and Z's and V's separate legal existences cease for all purposes. In the transaction, the Z and V shareholders exchange their Z and V stock, respectively, for stock of Y. With respect to each of Z and V, the transaction qualifies as the statutory merger or consolidation of each of Z and V into R, a corporation controlled by Y because the transaction is effected pursuant to foreign law and the following events occur simultaneously at the effective time of the transaction: all of the assets and liabilities of Z and V, respectively, each of which is the combining entity of a transferor unit, become the assets and liabilities of R, the combining entity and sole member of the transferee unit, with regard to each of the above transfers, and Z and V each ceases its separate legal existence for all purposes. Because Y is in control of R immediately after the transaction, the Z shareholders and the V shareholders will be treated as receiving stock of a corporation that is in control of R, the combining entity of the transferee unit that is the acquiring corporation for purposes of Code Sec. 368(a)(2)(D).

.03 Reverse Triangular or Subsidiary Merger

In a reverse triangular merger, a parent first drops voting stock down to a subsidiary which may be newly created for this purpose. The subsidiary then merges into the target corporation, with target shareholders receiving stock of the parent in exchange for their target stock. The target corporation survives the transaction. The reverse triangular merger qualifies for tax-free treatment if: (1) after the transaction, the target corporation holds substantially all of the properties it held before the merger, and (2) the target shareholders exchanged stock constituting control (80 percent) of the target for the parent stock they received [Code Sec. 368(a)(2)(E); Reg. § 1.368-2]. In Rev. Rul. 2001-26,[13] the IRS ruled that a series of steps constituted a single integrated transaction that qualified as a reverse triangular merger since the series of integrated transactions satisfied the control-of-voting-stock requirement found in Code Sec. 368(a)(2)(E).

Example 22-20: T is a corporation all of the stock of which is owned by individual A. T has 150x dollars worth of assets and 50x dollars of liabilities. P is a corporation that is unrelated to A and T. The value of P's assets, net of liabilities, is 410x dollars. P forms corporation X, a wholly owned subsidiary, for the sole purpose of acquiring all of the stock of T by causing X to merge into T in a statutory merger (the "Acquisition Merger"). In the Acquisition Merger, P acquires all of the stock of T, and A exchanges the T stock for 10x dollars in cash and P voting stock worth 90x dollars. Following the Acquisition Merger and as part of an integrated plan that included the Acquisition Merger, T completely liquidates into P (the "Liquidation"). In the Liquidation, T transfers all of its assets to P and P assumes all of T's liabilities. The Liquidation is not accomplished through a statutory merger. After the Liquidation, P continues to conduct the business previously conducted by T. In Rev. Rul. 2008-25,[14] the IRS concluded that the merger of a controlling corporation's newly-formed subsidiary into a target corporation, followed by the target's liquidation, did not constitute a reverse subsidiary reorganization. Instead, the transaction was a qualified purchase by the controlling corporation of the target's stock followed by a Code Sec. 332 liquidation. Applying the step transaction doctrine, the IRS

---

[13] Rev. Rul. 2001-26, 2001-1 CB 1297.

[14] Rev. Rul. 2008-25, 2008-21 IRB 986.

concluded that the liquidation of the target into the controlling corporation meant that the target did not hold substantially all of its properties and the properties of the merged subsidiary, as required in a Code Sec. 368(a)(2)(E) reverse subsidiary merger.

Merged Survivors Granted New Flexibility in IRS Rulings

In Rev. Rul. 2001-24,[15] the IRS agreed that a corporate reorganization would still qualify as a tax-free reorganization under Code Sec. 368(a) if, after completing a forward triangular merger, the parent corporation went one step further and transferred its surviving subsidiary to another 100 percent owned subsidiary. Because historic continuity was preserved, and noting that such a transfer would be permitted in the case of a reverse triangular merger, the IRS agreed that the transaction continued to satisfy Code Sec. 368(a)(1)(A) and Code Sec. 368(a)(2)(D).

In Rev. Rul. 2001-25,[16] the IRS held that a reorganization qualified as a tax-free reverse triangular merger despite the fact that the surviving corporation sold half of its assets to an unrelated party immediately after the merger as part of the merger plan.

In Rev. Rul. 2002-46,[17] the IRS held that the merger of an acquiring corporation's newly formed subsidiary into a target corporation followed by the target's merger into the acquiring corporation is treated as a single statutory merger of the target into the acquiring corporation that qualifies as a reorganization under Code Sec. 368(a)(1)(A).

¶22,020 ACQUIRING ANOTHER CORPORATION'S STOCK (TYPE B)

.01 Basic Rule

If acquiring corporation exchanges any of its voting stock (or any of the voting stock of a corporation that controls it) for stock of another target corporation, a tax-free reorganization results. However, acquiring corporation must control target right after the exchange [Code Sec. 368(a)(1)(B); Reg. §1.368-2(c)].[18] However, a small amount of cash merely to round off fractional shares[19] or a nonassignable contingent contract right to receive additional voting stock[20] does not disqualify the reorganization. Nor does the exchange of debentures, in addition to the exchange of securities destroy the tax-free character of the reorganization, if the debentures are not additional consideration for the acquired stock.[21] If the exchange of debentures occurs in the course of a reorganization it will qualify for tax-free treatment. But convertible rights to purchase additional shares of stock do disqualify the reorganization.[22]

---

[15] Rev. Rul. 2001-24, 2001-1 CB 1290.

[16] Rev, Rul. 2001-25, 2001-1 CB 1291.

[17] Rev. Rul. 2001-46, 2001-2 CB 321.

[18] *G.D. Turnbow*, SCt, 62-1 USTC ¶9104, 368 US 337, 82 SCt 353; Rev. Rul. 70-65, 1970-1 CB 77.

[19] *R.M. Mills*, CA-5, 64-1 USTC ¶9474, 331 F2d 321; Rev. Rul. 66-365, 1966-2 CB 116, amplified by, Rev. Rul. 81-81 1981-1 CB 122.

[20] Rev. Rul. 66-112, 1966-1 CB 68.

[21] Rev. Rul. 98-10, 1998-1 CB 643.

[22] Rev. Rul. 70-108, 1970-1 CB 78.

Control means ownership of at least 80 percent of the voting stock and at least 80 percent of all other classes of stock [Code Sec. 368(c)(1); Reg. § 1.368-2].

Example 22-21: If Bigco exchanges 15 percent of its voting stock for at least 80 percent of the voting stock and at least 80 percent of the shares of all other classes of stock of Smallco, there is a reorganization with Bigco and Smallco as parties. If, however, Bigco also gave nonvoting stock or bonds besides voting stock, no reorganization occurs.

It does not matter whether acquiring corporation had control before the acquisition [Code Sec. 368(a)(1)(B); Reg. § 1.368-2(c)]. Thus, the stock acquired need not represent 80 percent control, if there is control after the transaction. This is commonly known as a *creeping acquisition* and is allowed for Type B reorganizations.

Example 22-22: Co. P bought 30 percent of the common stock of Co. S (with only one class of stock outstanding) for cash in Year 1. In Year 10, Co. P offers to exchange its own voting stock for all of the stock of Co. S within six months from the date of the offer. Within the six-month period, Co. P acquires an additional 60 percent of Co. S stock for its own voting stock. Co. P now owns 90 percent of the stock of Co. S and reorganization has occurred. If Corporation P had acquired 80 percent of Corporation S's stock for cash in Year 10, it could likewise acquire some or all of the remainder of such stock solely in exchange for its own voting stock and still have a reorganization.

In Rev. Proc. 2011-35,[23] the IRS provided a procedure that a corporation (Acquiring) may use to establish its basis in stock of another corporation (Target) when it acquires the Target stock in a transferred basis transaction, including B reorganizations, transfers to a controlled corporation, and certain triangular reorganizations. A survey of shareholders may be undertaken to determine the actual basis shares surrendered. When a full survey is not feasible, statistical sampling may be used. Instead of survey or sampling, approved estimation techniques may be used. The first estimation technique uses data from the master security-holder files. In general, this estimation technique uses the market price on the date of issuance. The second estimation technique uses either the target security position reports or SEC Form 13F filings. This estimation technique specifies the gathering of data for modeling share basis.

¶22,025 ACQUIRING ANOTHER CORPORATION'S PROPERTY (TYPE C)

A Type C reorganization can be described as the acquisition by one corporation of substantially all of the properties of a target corporation in exchange solely for voting stock of the acquiring corporation (or solely for voting stock of its parent) [Code Sec.

[23] Rev. Proc. 2011-35, IRB 2011-35, 890.

368(a)(1)(C); Reg. § 1.368-2(d)]. It may add a small amount of cash merely to round off fractional shares [see below].[24]

Example 22-23: If P Co. exchanges 15 percent of its voting stock for substantially all the properties of S Co., there is a tax-free "C" reorganization, with P Co. and S Co. as parties.

There also is a reorganization if a subsidiary acquires substantially all of the property of another corporation solely in exchange for the voting stock of the subsidiary's parent corporation [Code Sec. 368(a)(1)(C); Reg. § 1.368-2(d)].

Example 22-24: P Co. owns all the stock of S Co. All the assets of W Co. are transferred to S Co. in exchange for voting stock of P Co. This transaction is a tax-free Type C reorganization, with S, P, and W as parties [Reg. § 1.368-2(f)].

Generally, if acquiring corporation exchanges property pursuant to a plan of reorganization for stock and securities in target corporation, it doesn't recognize gain or loss. However, gain is recognized to the extent the corporation whose assets are acquired receives property other than stock and securities and does not distribute the property. For this purpose, transfers of property to creditors to satisfy the corporation's indebtedness in connection with the reorganization are treated as distributions under the plan [Code Sec. 361].

.01 Exception for Distribution of Appreciated Property

The distributing corporation recognizes gain (but not loss) on the distribution of appreciated property as if such property were sold to the receiving corporation at fair market value [Code Sec. 361(c)].

No gain is recognized to the distributing corporation, however, when ***qualified property*** is distributed. Qualified property is stock, stock rights, or an obligation of (1) the distributing corporation or (2) another party to the reorganization that the distributing corporation received in the exchange [Code Sec. 361(c)(2)(B)].

.02 Relaxation of Solely for Voting Stock Requirement

The rule that the acquiring corporation must give only voting stock is relaxed to this extent: If an acquiring corporation gets at least 80 percent of the fair market value of all the target corporation's property in exchange for the acquiring corporation's voting stock, it can add cash and other types of consideration such as money or other property without disqualifying the tax-free "C" reorganization [Code Sec. 368(a)(2)(B); Reg. § 1.368-2(d)]. This is called the *boot relaxation rule.*

Example 22-25: Co. P acquires Co. S's assets worth $100,000 for $92,000 of P's voting stock plus $8,000 cash. This qualifies as a tax-free Type C reorganization, even though part of the assets of Co. S is acquired for cash in addition to P's voting stock.

---

[24] Rev. Rul. 66-365, 1966-2 CB 116, amplified by Rev. Rul. 81-81, 1981-1 CB 122.

If the acquiring corporation already owns a portion of the target company's stock, will the solely for voting stock of the acquiring corporation still be satisfied? Reg. § 1.368-2(d)(4)(i) answers this question and provides that prior ownership of a portion of a target corporation's stock by an acquiring corporation generally will not prevent the solely for voting stock requirement from being satisfied, provided the following do not exceed 20 percent of the fair market value of all of the target's properties: (1) money or property (other than voting stock) distributed to the target's shareholders (other than the acquiring corporation), and (2) the assumed liabilities of the target. The regulations reverse the long held doctrine established by the IRS in Rev. Rul. 54-396 and as approved by the courts in the well-known case, *Bausch & Lomb Optical Co.*[25] which established that the acquisition of assets of a partially controlled subsidiary does not qualify as a tax-free reorganization under Code Sec. 368(a)(1)(C). The regulation would therefore eliminate a technical requirement that has always bogged down tax-free reorganizations. As a result it will now be easier for corporations to qualify for the tax-free benefits associated with reorganizations that are blessed in Code Sec. 368.

Example 22-26: Corporation P holds 60 percent of the Corporation T stock that P purchased several years also in an unrelated transaction. T has 100 shares of stock outstanding. The other 40 percent of the T stock is owned by Corporation X, an unrelated corporation. T has properties with a fair market value of $110 and liabilities of $10. T transfers all of its properties to P. In exchange, P assumes the $10 of liabilities and transfers to T $30 of P voting stock and $10 of cash. T distributes the P voting stock and $10 of cash to X and liquidates. The transaction satisfies the solely-for-voting stock requirement because the sum of $10 of cash paid to X and the assumption by P of $10 of liabilities does not exceed 20 percent of the value of the properties of T [Reg. § 1.368-2(d)(4)(ii) Ex. 1].

Assumed Liabilities

An exchange is still considered solely for voting stock if, besides giving voting stock, the acquiring corporation assumes a liability of the transferor corporation [Code Sec. 368(a)(1)(C); Reg. § 1.368-2(d)(3)].

Example 22-27: If Co. P acquires substantially all of the properties of Co. S solely for voting stock and the assumption of a mortgage on the property, the transaction will ordinarily qualify as a tax-free reorganization (but see Note 1 below).

If, however, acquiring corporation gives cash or other property, the total of their value and the value of the assumed liabilities cannot exceed 20 percent of the fair market value of the property acquired. Otherwise there is no reorganization [Code Sec. 368(a)(2)(B); Reg. § 1.368-2(d)].

---

25 *Bausch & Lomb Optical Co.*, CA-2 59-1 USTC ¶9468, 267 F2d 75, *cert. denied*, SCt, 361 US 835, 80 SCt 88.

Example 22-28: Bigco is to acquire the assets of Smallco, worth $100,000. Smallco has liabilities of $50,000, which Bigco is to assume. Bigco can give only voting stock as consideration because the liabilities alone are over 20 percent of the fair market value of the property.

NOTE 1: If the assumed liabilities are too high a proportion of the consideration given for the property, the reorganization may be denied tax-free treatment because of lack of continuity of interest[26] [¶ 22,010] [Reg. § 1.368-2(d)(1)].

NOTE 2: Even when insufficient to disqualify the tax-free reorganization, other consideration received usually is treated as boot [¶ 22,055]. In a Type C reorganization, however, other consideration in the form of nonvoting shares and securities of a party to the reorganization comprising 20 percent or less of the value of the acquired property is not regarded as boot [Reg. § 1.361-1].

.03 Amount of Property Acquired

The term *substantially all* of the properties is a relative term. The IRS considers substantially all to be at least 90 percent of the fair market value of the net assets and at least 70 percent of the fair market value of the gross assets of the transferring corporation.[27] This test affords the acquired corporation the opportunity to use some assets to distribute dividends or pay debts before the acquisition. Ultimately, it depends on the facts of any given situation.[28] Thus, 70 percent of the assets was held to be substantially all, when the value of the retained assets approximately equaled the liabilities and consisted of cash, accounts receivable and 3 percent of the inventory.[29] But 81 percent of the assets was held not to be substantially all when most of the retained assets were operating assets, not retained to liquidate liabilities.[30] On the other hand, 86 percent and 90 percent have been held to be substantially all.[31]

In determining the percentage of property transferred, value rather than cost is used.[32] The term *properties* does not include retained surplus cash which might have been paid out as a dividend before the transfer.[33]

.04 Transfer of Acquired Assets to Controlled Subsidiary

The acquiring corporation may transfer the acquired assets to a controlled subsidiary in exchange for voting stock held by the subsidiary. This exchange is normally tax-free to both and will not disqualify the tax-free status of the reorganization [Code Sec. 368(a)(2)(C)]. This is true even if acquiring corporation transfers assets to its subsidiary.[34]

NOTE 3: A transaction that qualifies as both a Type C and a Type D reorganization [¶ 22,030] is treated as Type D [Code Sec. 368(a)(2)(A)].

---

[26] *Civic Center Finance Co.*, CA-7, 49-2 USTC ¶ 9443, 177 F2d 706.

[27] Rev. Proc. 83-81, 1983-2 CB 598; Rev. Proc. 89-50, 1989-2 CB 631.

[28] *Daily Telegram Co.*, 34 BTA 101, Dec. 9263; *M. Smith*, 34 BTA 702, Dec. 9434, *acq.* 1957-2 CB 6 (test is relative); *Peabody Hotel*, 7 TC 600, Dec. 15,335 (1946), acq., 1946-2 CB 4 (no percentage determinative).

[29] Rev. Rul. 57-518, 1957-2 CB 253.

[30] *Nat. Bk. of Commerce of Norfolk*, DC-VA, 58-1 USTC ¶ 9278, 158 FSupp 887.

[31] *Schuh Trading Co.*, CA-7, 38-1 USTC ¶ 9171, 95 F2d 404.

[32] *American Foundation Co.*, CA-9, 41-2 USTC ¶ 9613, 120 F2d 807.

[33] *D. Gross*, CA-5, 37-1 USTC ¶ 9159, 88 F2d 567.

[34] Rev. Rul. 64-73, 1964-1 CB 142.

¶22,030 TRANSFER OF ASSETS TO ANOTHER CORPORATION (TYPE D)

.01 General Process

A Type D reorganization is a transfer by a corporation of some or all of its assets to a second corporation and the transfer will qualify as a tax-free reorganization under Code Sec. 368(a)(1)(D) if:

- Immediately after the transfer the transferor, or one or more of its shareholders (including persons who were shareholders immediately before the transfer), or any combination of these, are in control of the corporation to which the assets are transferred (the transferee), but only if, in pursuance of the plan; and
- Stock or securities of the transferee are distributed in a transaction that qualifies under Code Secs. 354, 355, or 356. Code Sec. 361(a) provides that "[n]o gain or loss shall be recognized to a corporation if such corporation is a party to a reorganization and exchanges property, in pursuance of the plan of reorganization, solely for stock or securities in another corporation a party to the reorganization."

Type D reorganizations can either be classified as a divisive D reorganization or a nondivisive D reorganization.

In a divisive D reorganization, a corporation transfers part of its assets to a controlled corporation and then distributes stock of the controlled corporation to shareholders in a transaction that effectively divides the existing corporation into two surviving or successor corporations. Depending on which shareholders of the dividing corporation receive which interest in each of the two survivors, the transaction can be termed a spin-off, split-off, or split-up. For further discussion of divisive reorganizations, see ¶22,090. A nondivisive D reorganization is a transaction that results in a nondivisive restructuring of an existing corporation group.

.02 *Control* Defined

Code Sec. 368(a)(1)(D) requires that a transfer by a corporation of some or all of its assets to a second corporation will be a tax-free reorganization, if immediately after the transfer the transferor, one or more of its shareholders, or any combination thereof, controls the transferee corporation. *Control* in this context means ownership of at least 50 percent of the voting stock or 50 percent of the value of all classes of stock [Code Sec. 368(a)(2)(H)]. For this purpose, the constructive ownership rules of Code Sec. 318(a), with some modification, will be applied to determine control [Code Sec. 304(c)(3)]. When a corporation contributes assets to a controlled corporation and then distributes the stock of the controlled corporation in a divisive transaction under Code Sec. 355, the fact that the shareholders of the distributing corporation dispose of part or all of the distributed stock, and the fact that the corporation whose stock was distributed issues additional stock, will not be taken into account in determining whether the "control immediately after" requirement has been satisfied.

> **NOTE:** The rules are designed to allow liquidation-reincorporation transactions that effect a bailout of earnings and profits and a step-up in basis at the cost of a capital gain tax to be treated as D reorganizations.

The stock owned by the shareholders need not be in the same proportion as it was before the transfer. However, disproportionate stock ownership may create taxable compensation or gifts from one shareholder to another [Ch. 6].

.03 Distribution Requirement

The stock and securities received by the transferor from the transferee corporation must be distributed to the transferor's shareholders in one of the following ways [Code Sec. 368(a)(1)(D)]:

- Under the plan of reorganization and together with substantially all of the corporation's remaining properties, which usually results in complete liquidation of the target corporation [Code Sec. 354(b); Reg. § 1.354-1(a)]; or
- In a divisive reorganization [¶ 22,090-¶ 22,095]. Distributions may be made if the corporation transferred only part of its assets.

Historically, the IRS and the courts have not required the actual issuance and distribution of stock and/or securities if the same person(s) owns all the stock of the transferor and transferee.

Meaningless Gesture Doctrine

Notwithstanding the requirement in Code Sec. 368(a)(1)(D) that "stock or securities of the corporation to which the assets are transferred are distributed in a transaction which qualifies under Code Sec. 355, or 356," the IRS and the courts have not required the actual issuance and distribution of stock and/or securities of the transferee corporation in circumstances where the same person or persons own all stock of the transferor corporation and the transferee corporation.[35] The IRS and the courts have viewed an issuance of stock by the transferee corporation in these situations to be a "meaningless gesture" not mandated by Code Secs. 368(a)(1)(D) and 354(b).

Reg. § 1.368-2(l)(2) provides that a Code Sec. 368(a)(1)(D) transaction will be treated as satisfying the requirements of Code Sec. 368(a)(1)(D) and Code Sec. 354(b)(1)(B) even if there is no actual issuance of stock and/or securities of the transferee corporation if the same person or persons own, directly or indirectly, all of the stock of the transferor and transferee corporations in identical proportions. In cases where no consideration is received or the value of the consideration received in the transaction is less than the fair market value of the transferor corporation's assets, the transferee corporation will be treated as issuing stock with a value equal to the excess of the fair market value of the transferor corporation's assets over the value of the consideration actually received in the transaction.

Issuance of Nominal Shares of Stock

Reg. § 1.368-2(l)(2) provides further that in cases where the value of the consideration received in the transaction is equal to the fair market value of the transferor corporation's assets, the transferee corporation will be deemed to issue a nominal share of stock to the transferor corporation in addition to the actual consideration exchanged for the transferor corporation's assets. The nominal share of stock in the transferee

---

35 *Armour, Inc.*, 43 TC 295, Dec. 27,071 (1964); *R.C. Wilson*, 46 TC 334, Dec. 27,987 (1966); Rev. Rul. 70-240, 1970-1 CB 81.

corporation will then be deemed distributed by the transferor corporation to the shareholders of the transferor corporation, as part of the exchange for the stock of such shareholders. Where appropriate, the nominal share will be further transferred through chains of ownership to the extent necessary to reflect the actual ownership of the transferor and transferee corporations. Similar treatment will apply where the transferee corporation is treated as issuing stock with a value equal to the excess of the fair market value of the transferor corporation's assets over the value of the consideration actually received in the transaction.

Example 22-29: A owns all the stock of T and S. The T stock has a fair market value of $100x. T sells all of its assets to S in exchange for $100x of cash and immediately liquidates. Because there is complete shareholder identity and proportionality of ownership in T and S, the requirements of Code Secs. 368(a)(1)(D) and 354(b)(1)(B) are treated as satisfied notwithstanding the fact that no S stock is issued. S will be deemed to issue a nominal share of S stock to T in addition to the $100x of cash actually exchanged for the T assets, and T will be deemed to distribute all such consideration to A. The transaction qualifies as a tax-free Code Sec. 368(a)(1)(D) reorganization [Reg. § 1.368-2(l)(3), Ex. 1].

IRS Permits Transfer of Target Assets into Subsidiary Following Type D Reorganization

In Rev. Rul. 2002-85,[36] the IRS held that an acquiring corporation's transfer of a target corporation's assets to a subsidiary controlled by the acquiring corporation pursuant to a plan of reorganization will not prevent a transaction that otherwise qualifies as a Type D reorganization from so qualifying. The ruling notes that neither Code Sec. Sec. 368(a)(2)(C) nor Code Sec. 368(a)(2)(A) indicates that an acquiring corporation's transfer of assets to a controlled subsidiary necessarily prevents the transaction from qualifying as a reorganization. In support of this conclusion, Reg. § 1.367(a)-3(d) was amended to provide specifically that a D reorganization followed by the transfer of all or a portion of a target corporation's assets to a controlled subsidiary pursuant to a plan of reorganization constitutes an indirect transfer of stock or securities for purposes of Reg. § 1.367(a)-3.

¶22,035 CHANGE IN CAPITAL STRUCTURE (TYPE E)

A recapitalization is an arrangement by which the stock and bonds of a corporation are readjusted as to amount, income, or priority, or an agreement of all stockholders and creditors to increase or decrease the capitalization or debts of the corporation, or both [Code Sec. 368(a)(1)(E); Reg. § 1.368-2(e)]. Cash payments received to round off fractional shares resulting from the recapitalization do not disqualify the reorganization.[37] The following illustrates recapitalization transactions:

---

[36] Rev. Rul. 2002-85, 2002-2 CB 986.

[37] Rev. Rul. 69-34, 1969-1 CB 105; Rev. Rul. 81-81, 1981-1 CB 122.

- The corporation has $200,000 par value of bonds outstanding. Instead of paying them off in cash, it discharges the obligation by issuing preferred shares, or new bonds,[38] to the bondholders;
- 25 percent of the corporation's preferred stock is exchanged for no par value common stock;
- The corporation issues preferred stock, previously authorized but unissued, for outstanding common stock;
- An exchange of outstanding preferred stock (with certain priorities as to the amount and time of payment of dividends and the distribution of the corporate assets upon liquidation) for a new issue of common stock having no such rights; and
- Outstanding preferred stock with dividends in arrears is exchanged for a similar amount of preferred stock plus stock (preferred or common) for the dividends in arrears.

The continuity of interest and continuity of business enterprise as discussed in ¶ 22,010 are not required for a recapitalization to qualify as a tax-free reorganization under Code Sec. 368(a)(1)(E) [Reg. § 1.368-1(b)].

¶22,040 CHANGE IN IDENTITY, FORM OR PLACE OF ORGANIZATION (TYPE F)

A Type F reorganization is defined in the Code as "a mere change in identity, form or place of organization of one corporation" [Sec. 368(a)(1)(F)]. Reg. § 1.368-1(b) provides that the continuity of interest and continuity of business enterprise requirements as discussed in ¶ 22,010 are not required for a transaction to qualify as a reorganization under Code Sec. 368(a)(1)(F) (F reorganization).

.01 Overlap

A Type F reorganization may also constitute a Type A, C, or D reorganization. In the event of such an overlap, the IRS has held that the transaction is treated as a Type F,[39] which is more liberal for purposes of closing the tax year and carrying back a net operating loss [¶ 22,135].

In Field Service Advice 200237017, a corporation's conversion to a limited partnership that elected to be taxed as a corporation under the check-the-box regulations was treated as a tax-free F reorganization.[40]

---

[38] *S. Neustadt Trust*, 43 BTA 848, Dec. 11,696, *aff'd*, CA-2, 42-2 USTC ¶ 9751, 131 F2d 528.

[39] Rev. Rul. 57-276, 1957-1 CB 126.

[40] See also LTR 201239003 (June 27, 2012).

¶22,045 INSOLVENCY REORGANIZATION (TYPE G)

.01 General Rules

A Type G reorganization covers transfers of assets in Bankruptcy Code cases and receiverships, foreclosures, and similar cases under federal or state law [Code Sec. 368(a)(1)(G), (3)].

To qualify as a Type G reorganization, there must be a transfer pursuant to a court-approved reorganization plan of substantially all the debtor corporation's assets to an acquiring corporation. In determining whether substantially all of the assets were transferred, the debtor corporation's need to pay creditors or to sell assets or divisions to raise cash must be taken into account. In addition, stock or securities of the acquiring corporation must be distributed in a transaction that qualifies under Code Sec. 354, 355 or 356 [¶ 22,055–¶ 22,070 and ¶ 22,090–¶ 22,115]. To satisfy this distribution requirement, some of the debtor corporation's security holders must receive stock or securities [Code Sec. 368].[41]

> **Example 22-30:** Debtor Corp. transfers all its assets to Acquiring Corp. in exchange for Acquiring stock. The stock is distributed to Debtor Corp.'s security holders and trade creditors in exchange for their claims against the corporation. Debtor Corp's shareholders get nothing for their stock.

The rules applying to Type G reorganizations are more flexible than those for other reorganizations. For example, Type G reorganizations do not have to comply with state merger laws (as do Type A). There is no requirement that former shareholders of the debtor corporation control the acquiring corporation after the exchange (as in Type D). There are no restrictions on the kind of consideration that may be issued (such as the *solely for voting* stock rule of Types B and C).

Continuity of Interest

All owners of the corporation must maintain a substantial proprietary interest in the reorganized business enterprise [¶ 22,010]. In determining whether continuity exists, the most senior class of creditors who receive stock for their claims along with all equal and junior classes (and any shareholders who receive consideration for their stock) should be treated as owners of the debtor corporation.[42] The IRS has stated that for transfers by financial institutions, the "continuity of business enterprise" requirement is satisfied if (1) the acquiring corporation assumes all of the deposits of the debtor corporation, and (2) the acquiring corporation continues to hold at least one-half of the fair market value of the assets, including mortgages and other loans, held by the debtor corporation at the time of reorganization. Assets disposed of in the ordinary course of business by the acquiring corporation will not be taken into account for this purpose.[43]

---

[41] Committee Report, P.L. 96-589.

[42] Committee Report, P.L. 96-589.

[43] Rev. Proc. 83-81, 1983-2 CB 598, Rev. Proc. 89-50, 1989-2 CB 631.

Triangular Reorganization

A triangular reorganization, in which a corporation acquires a debtor corporation using stock of its parent corporation rather than its own stock is allowed. Reverse triangular mergers are also allowed if: (1) no former shareholder of the surviving corporation receives any consideration for his or her stock, and (2) the former creditors of the surviving corporation exchange their claims for voting stock of the controlling corporation equal to at least 80 percent of the value of the debt of the surviving corporation[44] [Code Sec. 368(a)(3)(E)]. Furthermore, a corporation that acquires substantially all of the assets of a debtor corporation may transfer the assets to a controlled subsidiary.

Overlap

A Type G reorganization may also qualify as a liquidation under Code Sec. 332 [¶22,130], an incorporation under Code Sec. 351, [See Ch. 6] or some other type of Code Sec. 368 reorganization. If so, it will nevertheless be treated as a Type G reorganization. Conversely, a transaction in a bankruptcy or similar case that does not qualify as a Type G reorganization may still qualify as another type of Code Sec. 368 reorganization.

¶22,046 REORGANIZATIONS INVOLVING FOREIGN CORPORATIONS

In general, Code Sec. 367(a) provides that foreign corporations are not considered corporations for purposes of applying the corporate organization, reorganization, and liquidation rules, and determining the extent to which gain is recognized on the transfer of property by a U.S. person to a foreign corporation. Thus, transfers of property to foreign corporations that would otherwise be tax-free are treated as taxable exchanges. This rule is intended to prevent U.S. persons from deferring or escaping taxes on income by using tax-free transfers to shift appreciated assets overseas or repatriate foreign-generated earnings.

.01 Transactions Affected

The following groups of transactions are affected by these rules: (1) transfers of property from the United States (outbound transfers), and (2) other transfers (this group includes transfers into the United States (inbound transfers) and those which are exclusively foreign (foreign-to-foreign transfers)). The rules governing the transactions in the first group are generally aimed to prevent the removal of appreciated assets from a U.S. tax jurisdiction prior to their disposition. Outbound transfers of property are generally governed by Code Sec. 367(a). Transactions in the second group include those where the statutory purpose in most cases is to prevent repatriation of foreign-generated earnings. These transactions are generally governed by Code Sec. 367(b).

---

[44] Rev. Rul. 84-104, 1984-2 CB 94.

The general rule of Code Sec. 367(a) applies to the following five types of exchanges:

1. A complete liquidation of a subsidiary under Code Sec. 332;
2. A transfer to a corporation controlled by the transferor under Code Sec. 351;
3. Exchanges of stock and securities in certain reorganizations under Code Sec. 354;
4. Receipt of additional consideration in an exchange under Code Sec. 356; and
5. Nonrecognition of gain or loss in a reorganization under Code Sec. 361.

Exceptions to Reach of Code Sec. 367

Code Sec. 367(a) does not apply to the following types of transactions:

1. Transfers of property to be used in an active trade or business outside of the United States. However, certain categories of tainted assets and certain transfers of foreign branches that operated at a loss are ineligible for the trade or business exception [Code Sec. 367(a)(3); Reg. §1.367(a)-2 and Reg. §1.367-6].
2. Transfers of stock or securities may also qualify as exceptions if certain conditions are met [Reg. §1.367(a)-3]. Some exceptions require the filing of a gain recognition agreement (GRA) under which the U.S. transferor agrees to include in income the gain realized but not recognized on the initial transfer if certain triggering events occur before the close the fifth tax year following the year of the transfer. See detailed discussion below.
3. Outbound transfers of stock or securities by U.S. persons if certain conditions are satisfied.
4. Transfers of the stock or securities of a domestic corporation in a Code Sec. 355 distribution to a foreign person.

.02 Distributions Involving Foreign Corporations or Foreign Shareholders

The treatment of a distribution varies depending upon whether the corporation or shareholder is domestic or foreign. A distribution from a foreign corporation to a shareholder that is a U.S. person resulting in a dividend under Code Secs. 301(c)(1) and 316, or gain from the sale or exchange of property under Code Sec. 301(c)(3), generally is subject to U.S. income tax, with potential offset by foreign tax credits. A distribution from a domestic corporation to a shareholder that is not a U.S. person resulting in a dividend is generally taxable under Code Sec. 871 or 881 at a rate of 30 percent, subject to reduction under an applicable treaty, and the domestic corporation is responsible for withholding tax under Code Sec. 1441 or 1442. To the extent such a distribution results in gain from the sale or exchange of property to the foreign shareholder under Code Sec. 301(c)(3), such amounts are subject to U.S. income tax under Code Sec. 897(a) if the distributing corporation had been a U.S. real property holding corporation (as defined in Code Sec. 897(c)(2)) within the past five years. In such a case, the gain is subject to U.S. income tax as income effectively connected with the conduct of a trade or business within the United States.

.03 IRS Attempts to Eliminate Triangular B Reorganizations Involving Foreign Corporations—Killer B Transactions

The IRS has issued final regulations under Code Sec. 367(b) to curb abusive triangular reorganizations involving foreign corporations which are commonly referred to as "Killer B" transactions. The purpose of the regulations is to prevent the use of tax-free triangular reorganizations with a foreign corporation to avoid the taxable repatriation of a foreign subsidiary's payments to a domestic parent. The rules treat the transfer of property from the foreign subsidiary to the parent as a taxable dividend under Code Sec. 301. The regulations also impose 30-percent withholding under Code Sec. 367(a) on a deemed transfer of appreciated property from the parent to the foreign subsidiary.

The regulations apply to cross-border triangular reorganizations, including "Killer B" transactions (stock for stock), "C" reorganizations (stock for assets), reverse triangular reorganizations, and forward triangular mergers. The IRS was concerned that the reorganizations could be used to make tax-free distributions from the foreign subsidiary to the parent and tax-free contributions from a U.S. subsidiary to the foreign parent. If both corporations were foreign, no income was taxable under Subpart F.

Triangular Reorganizations

In a tax-free B reorganization, the acquiring corporation acquires the stock of a target corporation solely in exchange for the acquirer's voting stock. At the end of the transaction, the acquirer must control the target, by owning 80 percent of its voting stock. In a triangular B reorganization, the acquirer (a subsidiary corporation) uses the voting stock of its parent to acquire the target's stock. The transaction can involve a forward merger of the target into the subsidiary, or a reverse merger of the subsidiary into the target, with the target as the surviving corporation.

Deemed Repatriation

The regulations target situations in which a parent or subsidiary (or both) is foreign and the subsidiary transfers property to the parent in exchange for parent stock used to acquire the target's stock or assets. Taxpayers have claimed that the transfer of property is tax-free. The IRS, however, has viewed this tax-free treatment as an abusive device to repatriate earnings from a foreign subsidiary to the parent. Reg. § 1.367-10(c)(1) therefore deems the transfer to be a taxable dividend distribution under Code Sec. 301 from the foreign subsidiary to the parent, in the amount of money plus the fair market value of other property transferred from the sub to the parent. In treating the deemed distribution as a separate transaction occurring before the reorganization, the parent is not treated as receiving property from the subsidiary in exchange for the parent's stock in a qualifying triangular B reorganization [Reg. § 1.367(b)-10(c)(1)].

.04 Gain Recognition Agreements (GRAs)

In the case of an outbound transfer of domestic or foreign stock or securities, every U.S. transferor that is a five-percent shareholder in the transferee corporation immediately after the transfer must enter into a five-year gain recognition agreement (GRA) with respect to the transferred stock or securities to avoid gain recognition under Code Sec. 367(a) [Reg. § § 1.367-3(b), 1.367(a)-3(c), (d).

Content of the GRA

The GRA must provide the following information:

1. A statement that the document constitutes an agreement by the U.S. transferor to recognize gain.
2. A description of the transferred stock or securities.

3. A statement that the U.S. transferor agrees to comply with all the conditions and requirements including the requirement to recognize gain under the gain recognition agreement, extend the statute of limitations on assessments of tax, and file the requisite certification described below.
4. A statement that arrangements have been made to ensure that the U.S. transferor is informed of any events that affect the gain recognition agreement, including triggering events or other gain recognition events.
5. In the case of a new gain recognition agreement:
   a. A description of the event (such as the triggering event) and the applicable exception, if any, that gave rise to the new gain recognition agreement (such as a triggering event exception), including the date of the event and the name, address, and taxpayer identification number (if any) of each person that is party to the event.
   b. A description of the class, amount, and characteristics of the stock, securities, or partnership interest received in the transaction; and
   c. A calculation of the amount of the gain remains subject to the new gain recognition agreement.
6. A statement whether the U.S. transferor elects to include in income any gain recognized in the tax year during which a gain recognition occurs.
7. A statement whether a gain recognition event has occurred during the tax year of the initial transfer.
8. A statement describing any disposition of assets of the transferred corporation during such tax year other than in the ordinary course of business [Reg. § 1.367(a)-8(c)(2)].

Filing Requirements for GRA

A GRA entered into with respect to an initial transfer must be included with the timely-filed return of the U. S. transferor for the tax year during which the initial transfer occurs [Reg. § 1.367(a)-8(d)(1)]. The GRA must be signed under penalties of perjury by an agent of the U.S. transferor that is authorized to sign under a general or specific power of attorney [Reg. § 1.367(a)-8(e)(1)].

Annual Certification Requirement

The U.S. transferor must include with its timely-filed return for each of the five full tax years following the year of the initial transfer a certification that includes the following information [Reg. § 1.367(a)-8(g)]:

1. A statement of whether a gain recognition has occurred and if one has occurred, the certification must state:
   a. The amount of gain subject to the GRA.
   b. The amount of gain recognized under the GRA.
   c. A calculation of the reduction to the amount of gain subject to the GRA.

2. A complete description of any event occurring during the year that has terminated or reduced the amount of amount subject to the GRA, including a calculation of any reduction to the amount of gain subject to the GRA.
3. A statement describing any disposition of assets of the transferred corporation during the tax year not in the ordinary course of business.

Triggering Events

If one of the following triggering events occurs during the GRA term, the U.S. transferor must recognize gain and pay applicable interest with respect to any additional tax due under the GRA [Reg. § 1.367(a)-8(j)]:

1. Disposition of transferred stock or securities.
2. Disposition of substantially all of the assets of the transferred corporation unless one of the following exceptions apply:
   a. Dispositions of property described in Code Sec. 1221(a)(1) occurring in the ordinary course of business;
   b. An exchange of stock or securities described in Code Sec. 354 that is pursuant to an asset reorganization; and
   c. An exchange of stock by a corporate distributee pursuant to a complete liquidation.
3. Disposition of certain partnership interests.
4. Disposition of stock of the transferee foreign corporation.
5. Deconsolidation—A U.S. transferor that is a member of a consolidated group ceases to be a member of the consolidated group, other than by reason of an acquisition of the assets of the U.S. transferor, or by reason of the U.S. transferor joining another consolidated group as part of the same transaction.
6. Consolidation—A U.S. transferor becomes a member of a consolidated group, including a U.S. transferor that is a member of a consolidated group and that becomes a member of another consolidated group.
7. A U.S. transferor that is an individual dies, or a U.S. transferor that is a trust or estate ceases to exist.
8. The U.S. transferor fails to comply in any material respect with any requirement of this section or with the terms of the gain recognition agreement, including failure to file an annual certification.
9. GRA filed in connection with indirect stock transfers and certain triangular asset reorganizations.

¶22,050 REORGANIZATION CHART

The chart below summarizes the effects that the seven types of reorganizations have on the parties to the reorganizations.

REORGANIZATION CHART

Type of Reorg.	Parties Before Reorganization	Parties After Reorganization
A	Y merger (Y into X) X	X
A	X consolidation (X + Y) Y	W (new corp.)
B	X gives only its voting stock (all or part) for 80% control of stock of Y	X (parent) Y (subsidiary)
B	W owns 80% control of X which gives only W's voting stock (all or part) for 80% control of stock of Y	W owns 80% control of X which owns 80% control of stock of Y
C	X gives only its voting stock (all or part) for substantially all the property of Y	X owns former assets of Y X's voting stock is only asset
C	W owns 80% control of X which gives only W's voting stock (all or part) for substantially jall the property of Y	W owns 80% control of X which owns the former assets of Y W's voting stock is only asset
D	(1) X transfers all or part of its assets to Y in exchange for 50% stock control of Y	
D	(2) X distributes all of its Y stock to its (X's) stockholders	X Y controlled by X's stockholders
E*	X has a capital and debt structure before recapitalization of:	X has a capital and debt structure after recapitalization of:
E*	common stock only — issues preferred stock in exchange for 50% of the common stock	common and preferred stock
E*	common stock and bonds — issues preferred stock to pay off bonds	common and preferred stock
E*	class A common and preferred class B common stock — 50% of preferred is surrendered in exchange for class B common	class A common, class B common, and preferred stock
E*	class A common and class B common stock — all of class B may be exchanged for class A or for (new) preferred	class A common and preferred stock
F*	Y changes its name to X and substitutes stock for stock	X
F*	X N.Y. Corp. reincorporates in New Jersey	X N.J. Corp.
F*	X charter revoked or expired (reincorporates)	X
G	X (debtor) (1) transfers assets pursuant to court-approved bankruptcy plan to Y for Y stock, then (2) distributes Y stock to security holders and creditors (X stock worthless) Y	X (survivor) controlled by Y

* In Types E and F, only a few of the possible examples are given.

GAIN OR LOSS

¶22,055 RECOGNITION OF GAIN OR LOSS

Subject to certain conditions, gain or loss on exchanges in reorganizations is not recognized either to shareholders or to the corporate parties to the reorganization.

.01 Holders of Stocks and Securities

No gain or loss is recognized if stock or securities in a corporation that is a party to a reorganization [¶ 22,005] are exchanged solely for stock (except nonqualified preferred stock (NQPS) or securities in that corporation or in another corporation that is a party to the reorganization [Code Sec. 354(a); Reg. § 1.354-1]. The term *securities* includes stock warrants and rights issued by a party to the reorganization to acquire its stock [Reg. § 1.354-1(e)].

Stock rights do not include (1) rights exercisable against anyone other than the stock issuer, or (2) rights that relate to property other than stock of the rights' issuer. A stock or debt conversion privilege generally is not considered to be a separate property right received as part of a reorganization. Stock rights are treated has having no principal amount so that a taxpayer would not have to recognize any gain under Code Sec. 356 on the receipt of a stock right [Reg. § 1.356-3(b)]. This would generally be the case regardless of whether the taxpayer surrenders stock, stock rights, or debt securities as part of the reorganization. However, gain or loss must be recognized if the new property differs materially in kind or extent from the old property unless the difference is incident to readjustments of corporate structures that are required by business exigencies and that affect only a readjustment of continuing interest in properties under modified corporate forms [Reg. § 1.368-1(b)]. A significant modification of a debt instrument includes certain modifications to its interest rate and may result in an exchange of the original debt instrument for a modified instrument that differs materially either in kind or in extent [Reg. § 1.1001-3(b)].

IRS Approves Tax-Free Exchange of Short-Term Notes in Statutory Merger

In Rev. Rul. 2004-78,[45] the IRS concluded that the acquiring corporation's two-year notes issued in exchange for the target corporation's notes were securities qualifying for nonrecognition treatment under Code Sec. 354. The IRS reached this result even though an instrument with a term of fewer than five years generally is not a security[46] because the acquiring corporation's notes were issued in the reorganization in exchange for the target's securities and bore the same terms (other than interest rate) as the target's securities, represent a continuation of the security's holders' investment in target in substantially the same form. Thus, the IRS concluded that the acquiring corporation's short-term notes exchanged for target's securities were securities under Code Sec. 354.

> **NOTE:** This type of exchange is not made in divisive [¶ 22,090] or insolvency [¶ 22,045] reorganizations [Code Sec. 354(b)(1)]. If the reorganization qualifies as divisive, nontaxable exchanges may still be made under Code Sec. 355 [¶ 22,090]. See also ¶ 22,030.

.02 Boot

If the principal amount of the securities received is greater than the principal amount of the securities given up, treat the fair market value of the excess as boot. If no

---

[45] Rev. Rul. 2004-78, 2004-2 CB 108.

[46] *Pinellas Ice & Cold Storage Co.*, SCt, 3 USTC ¶ 1023, 287 US 462, 53 SCt 257; *Neville Coke & Chemical Co.*, CA-3, 45-1 USTC ¶ 9233, 148 F2d 599, *cert. denied*, SCt, 326 US 726, 66 SCt 32.

securities are surrendered, the fair market value of the securities received is treated as taxable boot [¶ 22,065]. Also, interest income is recognized to the extent the new stock, securities or other property received is attributable to accrued but unpaid interest on the securities on or after the beginning of the holding period [Code Secs. 354(a)(2), 356(d)(2)(B); Reg. § § 1.354-1(b), 1.356-3].

Example 22-31: In a tax-free recapitalization [¶ 22,035], Jones surrenders a bond in the principal amount of $1,000 in exchange for bonds in the principal amount of $1,500 with fair market value of $1,575. The fair market value of the excess principal amount is $525 ($1,575 × $500/$1,500). It is treated as boot to Jones.

NOTE: If an exchange consists of the surrender of stock for securities, no securities are given up and no stock received, the transaction resembles a redemption of the stock. In such case, the fair market value of the securities (boot) may be taxed as capital gain if the redemption is found to be disproportionate [¶ 22,155].

.03 Nonqualified Preferred Stock

Nonqualified preferred stock (NQPS) will be treated as boot for purposes of Code Secs. 351, 354, 355, 356, and 368 [Code Secs. 351(g), 354(a)(2)(C)]. For further discussion, see ¶ 22,110.02.

.04 Corporation Exchanging Property for Stock or Securities

In this type of reorganization, the transferor corporation gives up property and receives back any combination of stock, securities, or property from a transferee corporation. The transferor corporation can receive back stock, securities, or *property* without recognizing gain provided certain conditions are met [Code Sec. 361(a); Reg. § 1.361-1].

Although gain or loss generally won't be recognized to a corporation that exchanges property pursuant to a plan of reorganization for stock or securities in another corporation, the transferor corporation recognizes gain to the extent it receives property other than the stock or securities and doesn't distribute that property pursuant to the plan of reorganization [Code Sec. 361(a), (b)].

Transfers of property to creditors to satisfy the corporation's indebtedness in connection with the reorganization are treated as distributions under the plan.

Example 22-32: Corporation A transfers appreciated property to Corporation B in exchange for cash as part of a reorganization. A uses the cash to pay its creditors. A is not required to recognize gain on account of the cash received.

Generally, a distributing corporation in a reorganization recognizes gain, but not loss, on the distribution of appreciated property to its shareholders [Code Sec. 361(c)]. The corporation is treated as having sold the property to the shareholders at fair market value. There is an exception, however, which states that no gain is recognized on the distribution of the following two types of qualified property:

- Stock (or rights to acquire stock) in, or the obligation of, the distributing corporation; and

- Stock (or rights to acquire stock) in, or the obligation of, another corporation that is a party to the reorganization. These securities must have been received by the distributing corporation in the exchange.

The transfer of qualified property by the transferor corporation to its creditors in satisfaction of indebtedness is treated as a distribution pursuant to the plan of reorganization. Therefore, if the transferor corporation, as party to the reorganization, pays off its creditors with stock or debt of another corporation that is party to the reorganization, the corporation does not recognize any gain from the payments.

Suppose the acquiring corporation assumes the liability of the target corporation. For purposes of determining gain, the property's fair market value is treated as not less than the amount of the liability. The assumption of the liability generally is not treated as the receipt of other property or money [Code Sec. 357(a)]. See ¶ 22,085.

.05 Corporation Exchanging Its Own Stock or Securities for Property

If the transferor corporation gives up its own stock or securities and receives property, it also recognizes no gain or loss [Ch. 20]. If the corporation also gives up property, however, it recognizes gain or loss on this other property [Ch. 6].

¶22,060 SYNOPSIS OF EXCHANGES

Table 1 shows under what Code Section participants in exchanges made under a plan of reorganization as defined in ¶ 22,015-¶ 22,045 derive their nonrecognition of gain or loss.

Table 1. Securities Exchanged by Corporations

Exchanger		*Section*
1.	Corporation, a party to a reorganization, giving stock and securities of its own issue.	§ 1032
2.	Corporation, a party to a reorganization, giving property.	§ 361
3.	A holder, giving stock or securities as a party to a reorganization [but see ¶ 22,055].	§ 354

▶ **OBSERVATION:** A corporation giving stock or securities as a party to a reorganization may be a party giving property under Code Sec. 361 or a holder under Code Sec. 354.

¶22,065 TREATMENT OF BOOT

.01 General Rules

When boot is received by a shareholder in a corporate reorganization to which Code Secs. 354 and 356 apply, any gain realized on the exchange must be recognized to the extent of the boot received [Code Sec. 356(a)(1); Reg. § 1.356-1(a)]. In no event may the receipt of other property or money result in a deductible loss if the exchange or distribution does not result in a recognized loss [Code Secs. 356(c), 361(b)(2); Reg. §§1.356-1(a), 1.361-1].

Example 22-33: Corporation J transferred part of its assets to Corporation K for 80 percent of the voting stock and 80 percent of all other classes of stock of Corporation K, plus $50,000 in cash. This cash is boot to J, unless distributed to its shareholders.

Example 22-34: Pursuant to a plan of reorganization, Anderson exchanged 100 shares of stock of Co. X (cost to him, $5,000) for 200 shares of Co. Y into which Co. X is merging. In addition, Anderson received $200 in cash. The Y Co. shares had a fair market value of $5,500. The gain to Anderson is $700, but that gain is recognized only to the extent of $200. The basis of the Y shares becomes $5,000 [¶22,075]. If the Y stock had a fair market value of only $4,000, the loss of $800 would not be recognized and the basis of the Y shares would be $4,800. If all of Anderson's X stock did not have the same basis, the realized gain or loss would be computed separately for each basis.[47]

NOTE: For recognition of gain or loss to the giver of boot, see ¶22,055.

In Rev. Rul. 93-61, the IRS ruled that, in an acquisitive reorganization, the determination of whether boot is treated as a dividend distribution under Code Sec. 356(a)(2) (and taxed at ordinary income rates) is made by comparing the interest that the shareholder actually received in the acquiring corporation with the interest the shareholder would have received in the acquiring corporation if only stock had been received.[48] This ruling, following a Supreme Court case on point,[49] can be helpful to shareholders in a company being acquired in a cash and stock deal if dividends once again are taxed as ordinary income instead of the preferential rate for long-term capital gains. Moreover, the acquiring corporation, unwilling to issue stock when purchasing another corporation because of a reluctance to dilute corporate control, will be able to use cash to make the acquisition work for both parties.

In Rev. Rul. 93-62, the IRS also ruled that the gain recognized on the receipt of cash in an exchange of stock otherwise qualifying under Code Sec. 355 (divisive reorganization, see ¶22,095) is not treated as a dividend distribution under Code Sec. 356(a)(2).[50] Whether the payment of boot is treated as a dividend distribution is determined before the exchange. That determination is made by treating the recipient shareholder as if the shareholder had retained the distributing corporation stock exchanged for the controlled corporation stock and received the boot in exchange for distribution corporation stock equal in value to the boot.

Exchange for Sec. 306 Stock

If a corporation receives boot in exchange for Sec. 306 stock, an amount equal to the sum of the money and the fair market value of the other boot is treated as a dividend to the extent that the corporation had earnings and profits when it distributed the

---

[47] Rev. Rul. 68-23, 1968-1 CB 144.

[48] Rev. Rul. 93-61, 1993-2 CB 118.

[49] *D.E. Clark*, SCt, 89-1 USTC ¶9230, 489 US 726, 109 SCt 1455.

[50] Rev. Rul. 93-62, 1993-2 CB 118.

Sec. 306 stock. *Sec. 306 stock* refers to certain preferred stock issued as a stock dividend [¶22,170] [Code Sec. 356(e)]. This is true whether the shareholder realizes a gain or loss.

For treatment of bonds and preferred stock as boot, see ¶22,055.

How Boot Is Allocated When Shareholder Disposes of Multiple Assets

Reg. §1.356-1(b) provides that when computing the gain recognized when boot is received in exchange for a particular share of stock or security surrendered, the terms of the exchange should control provided that such terms are economically reasonable. To the extent the terms of the exchange do not specify the other property or money that is received in exchange for a particular share of stock or security surrendered, a pro rata portion of the other property and money received shall be treated as received in exchange for each share of stock and security surrendered, based on the fair market value of such surrendered share of stock or security.

Example 22-35: In an exchange to which Code Sec. 356 applies and to which Code Sec. 354 would apply but for the receipt of property not permitted to be received without the recognition of gain or loss, A (either an individual or a corporation), received the following in exchange for a share of stock having an adjusted basis to A of $85 [Reg. §1.356-1(d), Ex. 1]:

One share of stock worth	$100
Cash	25
Other property (basis $25) fair market value	50
Total fair market value of consideration received	$175
Adjusted basis of stock surrendered in exchange	$85
Total gain	90
Gain to be recognized, limited to cash and other property received	$75
A's pro rata share of earnings and profits accumulated after February 28, 1913 (taxable dividend)	$30
Remainder to be treated as a gain from the exchange of property	45

¶22,070 GAIN TAXED AS DIVIDEND

If money or other property that shareholders receive from a corporation in connection with an exchange of stock or securities has the effect of a dividend, the gain recognized may be taxed as a dividend. This rule is subject to the attribution (constructive ownership) rules explained at ¶ 22,175. The stockholders should treat their proportionate share of the earnings and profits as a dividend [Ch. 2]. Any remainder is a capital gain[51] [Code Sec. 356(a)(2); Reg. § 1.356-1].

Example 22-36: The X Co. has capital of $100,000 and earnings and profits of $50,000. In the current year the X Co. transferred all of its assets to the Y Co. in exchange for all of the stock of the Y Co. and the payment of $50,000 in cash to the stockholders of the X Co. This is a reorganization, and X and Y are parties to the reorganization. Astor, who owns 100 of the 1,000 shares of stock in the X Co. for which he paid $10,000, receives 100 shares of Y stock worth $10,000 and $5,000 in cash. The $5,000 of cash is a dividend. Suppose that instead of receiving $5,000 in cash, Astor received $7,500 in cash. Then $5,000 of that $7,500 would be taxable as a dividend, the remainder ($2,500) as capital gain.

¶22,071 LIMITATIONS ON DEDUCTION OF DUPLICATE BUILT-IN LOSSES

Code Sec. 362(e)(2) was enacted by Congress to prevent the duplication of net built-in losses in certain corporate nonrecognition transfers and applies to corporate acquisitions of property with net built-in loss in transactions described in Code 362(a) (transactions to which Code Sec. 351 applies and acquisitions of property as paid-in surplus or contributions to capital), but only if the transaction is not one in which there is an importation of built-in loss as described in Code Sec. 362(e)(1) [Reg. § 1.362-4(a)]. For further discussion of the anti-loss provisions in Code Sec. 362(e)(1), see ¶ 22,072. When a transaction is subject to Code Sec. 362(e)(2), the acquiring corporation's basis in loss property is reduced by the property's allocable portion of the transferor's net built-in loss [Code Sec. 362(e)(2)(B)]. However, under Code Sec. 362(e)(2)(C), the parties to the transaction can make an irrevocable election to apply the reduction to the transferor's basis in the stock received in the exchange instead of to the transferee's basis in the property received in the exchange. In Notice 2005-70,[52] the IRS provided guidance on making a Code Sec. 362(e)(2)(C) election. Under Notice 2005-70, an election would be considered effective once a certification was included by the transferor or, if the transferor is a controlled foreign corporation (CFC), by all of its controlling U.S. shareholders on a timely filed federal income tax return for the year of the transaction. Notice 2005-70 expressly permitted taxpayers to make a protective election that would have no effect on a transaction that is ultimately not subject to Code Sec. 362(e)(2) and also allowed other statements to be treated as effective elections if sufficient information was provided to the IRS with respect to the transfer and parties.

Example 22-37: A, an individual, owns Asset 1 (basis $90, value $60) and Asset 2 (basis $110, value $120). In a transaction to which Code Sec. 351 applies, A transfers Asset 1 and Asset 2 to X, a domestic corporation, in exchange for a single outstanding share of X stock representing all the outstanding X stock

---

[51] *E.T. Bedford Est.*, SCt, 45-1 USTC ¶ 9311, 325 US 283, 65 SCt 1157.

[52] Notice 2005-70, 2005-2 CB 694.

immediately after the transaction. A's transfer of Asset 1 and Asset 2 is a Code Sec. 362(a) transaction. For purposes of Code Sec. 362(e)(2), X's aggregate basis in those assets would be $200 ($90 + $110), which would exceed the aggregate value of the assets $180 ($60 + $120) immediately after the transaction. Accordingly, the transfer is a loss duplication transaction and A has a net built-in loss of $20 ($200 - $180). Asset 1 is loss duplication property since X's basis in Asset 1 would be $90, which would exceed Asset 1's $60 value immediately after the transaction. X's basis in Asset 2 would be $110, which would not exceed Asset 2's $120 value immediately after the transaction, so Asset 2 is not loss duplication property. X's basis in Asset 1 is $70, computed as its $90 basis under Code Sec. 362(a) reduced by A's $20 net built-in loss. X has a transferred basis of $110 in Asset 2. Under Code Sec. 358(a), A has an exchanged basis of $200 in the X stock it receives in the transaction [Reg. § 1.362-4(h), Ex. 1(i)].

.01 Basis Determinations

Whenever a person (Transferor) transfers property to a corporation (Acquiring) in a "loss duplication transaction," Acquiring's basis in each "loss duplication property" (as determined without regard to Code Sec. 362(e)(2)) is reduced by the property's allocable portion of "Transferor's net built-in loss" [Reg. § 1.362-4(b)]. This general operative rule is intended to make it easier to determine what transactions are subject to Code Sec. 362(e)(2) and how they should be treated. A "loss duplication transaction" is defined as any Code Sec. 362(a) transfer in which Acquiring's aggregate basis in the property transferred by Transferor would exceed the aggregate value of such property immediately after the transaction. The term "loss duplication property" is defined as individual property transferred in the loss duplication transaction that Acquiring would take with a basis that would exceed value immediately after the transfer. A "Transferor's net built-in loss" is defined as the excess of Acquiring's aggregate basis in property received from Transferor over the aggregate value of such property immediately after the transaction. For these purposes, Acquiring's basis in property is determined immediately after the transfer, disregarding Code Sec. 362(e)(2) but taking into account all other applicable rules [Reg. § 1.362-4(b)]. If more than one Transferor transfers property to a corporation in a Code Sec. 362(a) transaction, whether and the extent to which Code Sec. 362(e)(2) and the regs apply is determined separately for each Transferor [Reg. § 1.362-4(b)]. This is referred to as the "transferor-by-transferor" approach. In addition, a transfer can be subject to both Code Sec. 362(e)(1) and Code Sec. 362(e)(2), and that in such cases, priority is given to Code Sec. 362(e)(1).

.02 Exceptions

Exceptions to the reach of the Code Sec. 362(e)(2) anti-loss duplication rules exist for transactions in which the duplicated loss is eliminated and for transactions wholly outside the U.S. tax system. Reg. § 1.362-4(c)(1) provides that the anti-loss duplication rule does not apply to the first type of transactions to the extent that the Transferor distributes the Acquiring stock received in the transaction without recognizing gain or loss and upon completion of the transaction, no person holds Acquiring stock or any other asset with a basis determined by referring to the Transferor's basis in the distributed Acquiring stock. Reg. § 1.362-4(c)(2) provides further that transactions outside the U.S. tax system qualify for the exception if (i) the transaction is between persons not connected to the United States (that is, neither the Transferor nor the Acquiring is a U.S. person, a person otherwise required to file a U.S. tax return for the year of the transaction, a CFC or a CFP on the date of the transaction); (ii) the transaction does not become relevant for federal tax purposes within two years of the transfer (i.e., the transfer occurs more than two years prior to the date when either the Transferor or the Acquiring becomes a person required to file a U.S. return, a CFC or a CFP, or a person acquires the loss duplication property or stock received in a loss duplication transaction in a transferred basis transaction, as described in Reg. § 1.362-4(d)(3)(ii)(E) through Reg. § 1.362-4(d)(3)(ii)(G); and (iii) the transaction is not undertaken pursuant to a plan to reduce or avoid federal taxes [Reg. § 1.362-4(c)(2)]. For purposes of the administrative relief granted for transactions outside the United States, CFPs are treated in the same manner as CFCs. The reason that CFCs are ineligible for relief is that a CFC could not reasonably expect a transfer to have no relevance for federal income tax purposes, and so the administrative relief is not warranted. The same is true with respect to CFPs.

.03 Code Sec. 362(e)(2)(C) Election

The Code Sec. 362(e)(2)(C) election can be made protectively, but once made, the election is irrevocable. The Code Sec. 362(e)(2)(C) election will be effective only if two conditions are met: (i) a written, binding agreement to make a Code Sec. 362(e)(2)(C) election must be executed by the Transferor and the Acquiring before a statement under Code Sec. 362(e)(2)(C) (a "Code Sec. 362(e)(2)(C) statement") is filed; and (ii) a Code Sec. 362(e)(2)(C) statement must be filed in accordance with the regulations [Reg. § 1.362-4(d)(1)]. The effect of the Code Sec. 362(e)(2)(C) election is that an amount equal to the portion of the Transferor's net built-in loss that would otherwise be applied to reduce asset basis is allocated among the Acquiring shares received or deemed received in the exchange (in proportion to the value of such shares) and applied to reduce the Transferor's basis in each such share. In such a case, the Acquiring's basis in the loss duplication property received from the Transferor in the transaction is not determined under Code Sec. 362(e)(2) [Reg. § 1.362-4(d)(2)].

.04 Code Sec. 362(e)(2)(C) Statement

The transferor and the transferee must execute a written, binding agreement (called a "Code Sec. 362(e)(2)(C) statement") and it must be in effect prior to the time that the election is filed. The Code Sec. 362(e)(2)(C) statement must provide detailed filing guidance depending on the identities and filing duties of the parties involved [Reg. § 1.362-4(d)]. The "Code Sec. 362(e)(2)(C) statement" must be titled as such, identify the Transferor and the Acquiring by name and TIN (if any), state that the Transferor and the Acquiring have entered into a written, binding agreement to make the election, and state the date of the transaction to which the election applies [Reg. § 1.362-4(d)(3)(i)]. A Code Sec. 362(e)(2)(C) statement is not required and may not be filed by a U.S. person that is not otherwise required to file a U.S. return. The term "U.S. return" is defined as a return of income that must be filed under Code Sec. 6012 or an information return under Code Sec. 6031that the taxpayer is unconditionally required to file [Reg. § 1.362-4(g)(6)]. The statement is filed by the Transferor, if the Transferor is otherwise required to file a U.S. return for the year of the transaction. If the Transferor is a CFC or CFP at the time of the transaction and is not otherwise required to file a U.S.

return, the statement is treated as filed by all of the Transferor's controlling U.S. shareholders or reporting U.S. partners, respectively. If the Transferor is not otherwise required to file a U.S. return and is not a CFC or CFP, then the statement is filed by the Acquiring, if the Acquiring is otherwise required to file a U.S. return in the year of the transaction, or by all of the Acquiring's controlling U.S. shareholders, if the Acquiring is a CFC at the time of the transaction and is not otherwise required to file a U.S. return. The statement must be filed with a timely filed original U.S. tax return for the year of the transfer [Reg. § 1.362-4(d)(e)(ii)(A) through Reg. § 1.362-4(d)(3)(ii)(D)].

A "controlled foreign corporation (CFC)" is defined as any corporation under Code Sec. 957 or 953(c) [Reg. § 1.362-4(g)(7)]. A "controlling U.S. shareholder" is defined as any person treated as such under Reg. § 1.964-1(c)(5) because such person owns either a direct interest in the CFC or an interest treated as owned by reason of an interest in a partnership, estate, trust, or corporation [Reg. § 1.362-4(g)(8)]. A "controlled foreign partnership (CFP)" is defined as any partnership treated as such for purposes of Code Sec. 6038 [Reg. § 1.362-4(g)(9)]. A "reporting U.S. partner" is defined as any partner of a CFP that is required to file an information return with respect to the CFP under Code Sec. 6038 [Reg. § 1.362-4(g)(10)]. For purposes of determining the person that must file a Code Sec. 362(e)(2)(C) statement, CFPs are treated in the same manner as CFCs. Although a CFP may not be required to file a U.S. return, the reporting U.S. partners of a CFP have a relationship to the CFP, and a filing obligation with respect to the CFP's activities, that is materially the same as that of the controlling U.S. shareholders of a CFC. Thus, the reporting U.S. partners of a CFP have the same reporting requirements under the final regulations as the controlling U.S. shareholders of a CFC.

If neither the Transferor nor the Acquiring is a person required to file a U.S. tax return, a CFC or a CFP at the time of the transaction but at some time later either the Transferor or the Acquiring becomes a person required to file a U.S. return, a CFC or a CFP, a Code Sec. 362(e)(2)(C) statement must be filed with the original U.S. return for the tax year in which such event occurs [Reg. § 1.362-4(d)(3)(ii)(E), (e)(ii)(F)].

.05 Transfers by Partnerships/ S Corporations

If a partnership or S corporation transfers property in a loss duplication transaction with respect to which a Code Sec. 362(e)(2)(C) election is made, any reduction to the basis in the Acquiring stock received by the partnership or S corporation in exchange for the loss duplication property is treated as an expenditure of the partnership or expense of the S corporation [Reg. § 1.362-4(e)]. However, if a person transfers property to an S corporation in a loss duplication transaction, any resulting reduction under Code Sec. 362(e)(2) and the regs to the S corporation's basis in the property received is not treated as an expense of the S corporation [Reg. § 1.362-4(f)].

¶22,072 LIMITATIONS ON LOSS IMPORTATION

The anti-loss importation limitations apply in both Code Sec. 334(b)(1)(B) and Code Sec. 362(e)(1). Code Sec. 334(b)(1)(B) applies to corporate acquisitions of loss property in liquidations described in Code Sec. 332 (complete liquidation of subsidiary). Code Sec. 362(e)(1) applies to corporate acquisitions of loss property in transactions described in Code Sec. 362(a) (transactions to which Code Sec. 351 applies and acquisitions of property as paid-in surplus or contributions to capital, each a Code Sec. 362(a) transaction) and in transactions described in Code Sec. 362(b) (reorganizations). The application and effect of the anti-loss importation provisions are materially identical, and so the proposed regulations use the same nomenclature and operating rules for both anti-loss importation provisions.

The anti-loss importation provisions apply when a corporation acquires property that is described in Code Sec. 362(e)(1)(B) in a transaction described in Code Sec. 332, 362(a), or 362(b), and, under the generally applicable basis rules (other than the anti-loss duplication rule in Code Sec. 362(e)(2)), the acquiring corporation (Acquiring) would take the property with an aggregate basis in excess of "value" (generally equal to fair market value). When an anti-loss importation rule applies, Acquiring's basis in each such property is equal to the property's value. To the extent Acquiring receives property in the transaction that is not subject to the anti-loss importation rules, Acquiring's basis in the property is determined under generally applicable basis rules, including Code Sec. 362(e)(2). The determination of whether a Code Sec. 362 transaction is a loss importation transaction is made by reference to the net amount of built-in gain and built-in loss in all importation property acquired from all transferors in the transaction. This approach, differs from the transferor-by-transferor approach of Code Sec. 362(e)(2), which expressly focuses on the net built-in loss transferred by a particular transferor in a Code Sec. 362(a) transaction [Prop. Reg. § 1.362-3(c)(3)].

.01 Importation Property

Property will be considered Code Sec. 362(e)(1)(B) importation property if the following two conditions are satisfied: (1) any gain or loss recognized on a disposition of the property would not be subject to federal income tax in the hands of the transferor immediately before the transfer [Code Sec. 362(e)(1)(B)(i)]; (2) any gain or loss recognized on a disposition of the property would be subject to federal income tax in the hands of the transferee immediately after the transfer [Code Sec. 362(e)(1)(B)(ii)]. A hypothetical sale analysis is used in Prop. Reg. § 1.362-3(c)(2) to identify importation property. Under this approach, the actual tax treatment of any gain or loss that would be recognized on a sale of the property, first by the transferor immediately before and then by Acquiring immediately after the transfer, would determine whether an individual property is importation property. Property would be importation property only if two conditions were satisfied; (1) if any gain or loss that would be recognized on a hypothetical sale of the property by the transferor immediately before the transfer would not be subject to federal income tax in the hands of the transferor, the first condition would be satisfied; (2) if any gain or loss that would be recognized on a hypothetical sale of the property by Acquiring immediately after the transfer would be subject to federal income tax in the hands of Acquiring, the second condition would be satisfied [Prop. Reg. § 1.362-3(c)(2)]. In general, the determination would be made by reference to the tax treatment of the hypothetical seller of the transferred or acquired property, that is, whether the hypothetical seller would take the gain or loss into account in determining its federal income tax liability [Prop. Reg. § 1.362-3(d)]. If a hypothetical seller is a partnership, an S corporation, or a grantor trust, the gain or loss by the partners', shareholders', or owners' gain or loss is used to identify importation property [Prop. Reg. § 1.362-3(d)(2)].

If any gain or loss realized on a hypothetical sale would be includible in income by more than one person, the property is treated as tentatively divided into separate portions in proportion to the allocation of gain or loss to each person [Prop. Reg. § 1.362-3(e)].

.02 Loss Importation Transaction

Once the importation property has been identified, Acquiring determines the aggregate basis that it would have in all importation property acquired in the transaction (including the tentatively divided portions of transferred property), without regard to the anti-loss importation provisions or Code Sec. 362(e)(2). If the aggregate basis of the importation property exceeds such property's aggregate value, the transaction would be a loss importation transaction and subject to the anti-loss importation provisions. If the aggregate basis of importation property does not exceed such property's value, the anti-loss importation provisions would have no further application [Prop. Reg. § 1.362-3(c)(3)]. If a transaction is a loss importation transaction, Acquiring's basis in each importation property received (including the tentatively divided portions of property determined to be importation property) would be an amount equal to value and this rule would apply to all importation property, regardless of whether the property's value is greater or less than its basis prior to the loss importation transaction [Prop. Reg. § 1.362-3(b)(1)]. Any property that was treated as tentatively divided for purposes of applying these provisions would cease to be treated as divided and would be treated as one undivided property (reconstituted property) with a basis equal to the sum of the bases of the portions determined under the anti-importation provision and the bases of all other portions determined under generally applicable provisions.

Filing Requirements

To facilitate the administration of both the anti-loss importation provisions and the anti-duplication provisions in Code Sec. 362(e)(2), Prop. Reg. § 1.332-6 and Prop. Reg. § 1.368-3 requires taxpayers to identify the basis and value of affected property.

BASIS

¶22,075 BASIS TO DISTRIBUTEE-STOCKHOLDER

The basis of property received in an exchange to which Code Sec. 351, 354, 355, 356, or 361 applies is the same as that of the property exchanged. This basis is decreased by:

- The fair market value of any other property (except money) received by the taxpayer;
- The amount of any money received by the taxpayer; and
- The amount of loss to the taxpayer which was recognized on such exchange; If a net built-in loss is imported into the United States in a tax-free transfer by persons not subject to U.S. tax, the corporate transferee's basis in the property transferred by such persons is its fair market value [Code Sec. 362(e)(1).

The basis is increased by:

- The amount which was treated as a dividend, and
- The amount of gain to the taxpayer which was recognized on such exchange (not including any portion of such gain which was treated as a dividend) [Code Sec. 358(a)(1); Reg. § 1.358-1(a)]. The basis of any other property received is its fair market value on the date of exchange [Code Sec. 358(a)(2); Reg. § 1.358-1].

Example 22-38: Pursuant to a plan of reorganization, Mr. Albert exchanged 100 shares of stock of the X Co. he had bought for $10,000 for 200 shares of Y Co. stock having a fair market value of $11,000. No gain is recognized on the exchange. The cost basis of the Y shares to Albert is $10,000.

Example 22-39: Mr. Vickers surrenders stock that has a basis of $1,000 in his hands in a tax-free recapitalization. He receives in exchange stock that has a value of $500 and a bond with a value of $750. The bond is boot [¶ 22,055]. Actual gain on the deal is $250. Any part treated as a dividend is taxed as such; the remainder, if any, is taxed as a capital gain. The basis of the new stock is $500 determined as follows: $1,000 (basis of old stock) minus $750 (value of the other property), plus $250 (gain taxed), or $500. The basis of the bond is $750.

.01 Allocation of Basis

If several kinds of stock or securities are received in an exchange or distribution, basis must be allocated among the properties received in proportion to their relative fair market values [Code Sec. 358(b)(1); Reg. § 1.358-2]. If, as the result of an exchange or distribution under Code Sec. 354, 355 or 356, a shareholder who owned stock of only one class before the transaction owns stock of two or more classes after the transaction, then the basis of all the stock held before the transaction must be allocated among the stock of all classes (whether or not received in the transaction) held immediately after the transaction in proportion to the fair market values of the stock of each class [Reg. § 1.358-2(a)(2)]. If a security holder who owned only one class of securities before the transaction, owns securities or stock of more than one class, or owns both stock and securities, then the basis of all the securities held before the transaction must be allocated among all the stock and securities (whether or not received in the transaction) held immediately after the transaction in proportion to the fair market values of the stock of each class and the securities of each class.

Example 22-40: In a tax-free reorganization, Mr. Albert exchanged 100 shares of X Co. stock for 50 shares of Y Co. common stock (value $15,000) and 50 shares of Y Co. preferred stock (value $10,000). Albert's 100 shares of X Co. stock had a cost basis to him of $10,000. The total value of the Y Co. stock received is $25,000, of which $15,000, or three-fifths, is represented by the common stock and $10,000, or two-fifths, is represented by the preferred stock. The combined bases of the two classes of Y Co. stock ($10,000) are apportioned according to their respective values. The basis of the Y common stock is 3/5 of $10,000.

.02 Tracing of Basis

When all of a shareholder's stock in a target corporation is transferred in a reorganization in exchange for stock of the acquiring or issuing corporation, it may be difficult to identify physically which share of stock of the target was surrendered for which share of the acquiring or issuing corporation. Questions have arisen over whether a shareholder that sells or transfers stock received in an exchange or distribution to which Code Sec. 354, 355, or 356 applies, can identify that share as being traceable to a particular lot of exchanged shares. The courts have been in conflict. To resolve the issue, the IRS has released regulations that allow shareholders to identify the shares of the acquiring corporation sold or transferred by reference to the shares surrendered in the exchange. The regulations generally provide that the basis of each share of stock or security received in an exchange to which Code Sec. 354, 355, or 356 applies will be the same as the basis of the share(s) of stock or security(s) exchanged [Reg. § 1.358-2(a)(2)(i)].

If more than one share of stock is received in exchange for only one share of stock, the basis of the surrendered stock is allocated to the stock received in proportion to its fair market values. In the case where one share of stock is received in exchange for more than one share of stock, the basis of the surrendered stock must be allocated to the received stock in a manner that most accurately reflects that a share of stock is received in exchange for shares of stock acquired on the same date and at the same price. If such an allocation is not possible, then the basis must be allocated in a manner that minimizes the disparity in the holding periods of the surrendered stock whose basis is allocated to any particular share of stock received [Reg. § 1.358-2(a)(2)(i)].

Example 22-41: S, an individual, owns 20 shares of Corporation X stock with a basis of $4 each. In a merger of X into Corporation Y, S receives 2 shares of Y stock in exchange for each share of his X stock. Thus, S ends up with 40 shares of Y stock after the transaction. S recognizes no gain or loss on the exchange, and will hold the 40 shares of Y stock with a basis of $2 each.

A special rule applies if stock of more than one class are received in exchange for stock, or if boot is received. In such a case, the basis will be determined under the terms of the exchange if such terms specify which shares are received in exchange for a particular class of stock, and such terms are economically reasonable. To the extent the terms of the exchange do not provide that, a pro rata portion of the shares of stock of each class received and a pro rata portion of the boot received will be treated as received in exchange for each share of stock surrendered, based on the fair market value of the surrendered stock [Reg. § 1.358-2(a)(2)(ii)].

Example 22-42: S, an individual, owns 10 shares of Class A stock of Corporation X with a basis of $3 each, 10 shares of Class A stock of X with a basis of $9 each, and 10 shares of Class B stock of X with a basis of $3 each. In a recapitalization, S surrenders all of his shares of Class A stock in exchange for 20 shares of new Class C stock and 20 shares of new Class D stock. S recognizes no gain or loss on the exchange. On the date of the exchange, each share of Class A stock is worth $6, each share of Class C stock is worth $2, and each share of Class D stock is worth $4. The terms of the exchange do not specify that shares of Class C or Class D stock are received in exchange for particular shares of Class A stock. Under Reg. § 1.358-2(a)(2)(ii), a pro rata portion of the shares of Class C and Class D stock received will be treated as received in exchange for each share of Class A stock based on the fair market value of the surrendered shares of Class A stock. Therefore, S is treated as receiving one share of Class C stock and one share of Class D stock in exchange for each share of Class A stock. Under Reg. § 1.358-2(a)(2), S has 10 shares of Class C stock, each of which has a basis of $1, and 10 shares of Class C stock, each of which has a basis of $3. In addition, S has 10 shares of Class D stock, each of which has a basis of $2, and 10 shares of Class D stock, each of which has a basis of $6. S's basis in each share of Class B stock remains $3 [see Reg. § 1.358-2(c), Ex. 3].

A special situation arises in the case of a Code Sec. 354 or 356 exchange in which the shareholder receives no property, with a fair market value less than that of the stock surrendered in the transaction. For example, such a situation may arise in a reorganization involving commonly controlled corporations where the issuance of stock would constitute a meaningless gesture. First, the shareholder or security holder is treated as receiving the stock, securities, or boot actually received in the transaction and an amount of stock of the issuing corporation (i.e., the acquiring corporation or its parent) that has a value equal to the excess of the value of the surrendered stock or securities over the value of the stock, securities, and boot actually received in the transaction. If the shareholder owns only one class of stock of the issuing corporation, the stock deemed received by the shareholder will be stock of that same class. If the shareholder owns multiple classes of stock, the stock deemed received will be stock of each such class owned by the shareholder immediately prior to the transaction, in proportion to the value of the stock of each class.

Then, the stock or securities of the issuing corporation held by the shareholder or security holder are treated as recapitalized. In the recapitalization, the shareholder or security holder is treated as surrendering all of its stock and securities in the issuing corporation in exchange for the stock and securities of the issuing corporation that the shareholder or security holder actually holds immediately after the transaction. The stock treated as surrendered in the recapitalization includes the stock or securities held immediately prior to the transaction, the stock or securities actually received, and the stock deemed received in the transaction. The basis of each share of stock and security deemed received or actually received in the exchange is determined under the general tracing rules of the regulations [Reg. § 1.358-2(a)(2)(iii)].

Example 22-43: S, an individual, holds all 100 outstanding shares of Corporation X stock with a basis of $1 each and all 100 outstanding shares of Corporation Y stock with a basis of $2 each. Y acquires the assets of X in a "D" reorganization, in which S surrenders his X stock but does not receive any additional Y stock. Immediately before the reorganization, the fair market value of each share of X and Y stock is $1. S recognizes no gain or loss in the transaction. S is deemed to have received shares of Y stock with an aggregate fair market value of $100 in exchange for his X stock. Given the number of outstanding shares of Y stock and their value immediately before the reorganization, S is deemed to have received 100 shares of Y stock in the reorganization. Under Reg. § 1.358-2(a)(2)(i), each of those shares has a basis of $1. The Y stock is then deemed to be recapitalized. In the recapitalization, S is treated as receiving 100 shares of Y stock in exchange for the Y stock that he held immediately prior to the reorganization and the Y stock that he is deemed to have received in the reorganization. Under Reg. § 1.358-2(a)(2)(i), immediately after the reorganization, S holds 50 shares of Y stock with a basis of $2 and 50 shares of Y stock with a basis of $4 [Reg. § 1.358-2(c), Ex. 10].

Code Sec. 355 Distributions

In the case of a Code Sec. 355 distribution, the basis of the stock with respect to which the distribution is made is allocated between such stock and the stock received in proportion to their fair market values. If one share of stock is received with respect to more than one shares of stock, then the basis of each share of stock of the distributing corporation must be allocated to the stock received in a manner that reflects to the greatest extent possible that a share of stock received is received with respect to shares of stock acquired on the same date and at the same price. If such an allocation is not possible, the basis of each share of stock of the distributing corporation must be allocated to the shares of stock received in a manner that minimizes the disparity in the holding periods of the stock with respect to which such shares of stock are received [Reg. § 1.358-2 (a) (2) (iv)].

Example 22-44: S, an individual, acquired 5 shares of Corporation X stock on Date 1 for $4 each and 5 shares of X stock on Date 2 for $8 each. X owns all of the outstanding stock of Corporation Y. The fair market value of the X stock is $1800. The fair market value of the Y stock is $900. In a Code Sec. 355 distribution, X distributes all of the Y stock pro rata to its shareholders. No stock of X is surrendered in the distribution. S receives 2 shares of Y stock with respect to each share of X stock. S recognizes no gain or loss on the receipt of the Y stock. Because S receives 2 shares of Y stock with respect to each share of X stock, the basis of each share of X stock is allocated between such share of X stock and two shares of Y stock in proportion to their fair market values. Therefore, each of the 5 shares of X stock acquired on Date 1 will have a basis of $2 and each of the 10 shares of Y stock received with respect to those shares will have a basis of $1. In addition, each of the 5 shares of X stock acquired on Date 2 will have a basis of $4 and each of the 10 shares of Y stock received with respect to those shares will have a basis of $2 [Reg. § 1.358-2(c), Ex. 12].

A special rule applies if stock of more than one class are received in distribution for or if boot is received. In such a case, the basis will be determined under the terms of the distribution if such terms specify which shares are received with respect to a particular share of stock or class of stock , and the terms are economically reasonable. To the extent the distribution terms do not provide that, a pro rata portion of the shares of stock of each class received and a pro rata portion of the boot received will be treated as received with respect to each share of stock of the distributing corporation, based on their fair market values [Reg. § 1.358-2 (a) (2) (v)].

Stock Acquired at Different Times and Prices

If a shareholder receives stock in exchange for, or with respect to, stock acquired on different dates and at different prices, then the received stock are divided into segments based on the relative fair market values of the exchanged stock or securities, or the stock with respect to which the distribution is made [Reg. § 1.358-2(a)(2)(vi)].

If the shareholder cannot identify the shares of stock that are received in exchange for, or with respect to, particular shares of stock, then the shareholder may designate which shares of stock are received in exchange for, or with respect to, a particular share of stock. The designation must be consistent with the terms of the exchange or distribution. The designation must be made on or before the first date on which the basis of the stock received is relevant. Such a relevant date may be, for example, the date on which the stock is sold or otherwise transferred. The designation is binding for purposes of determining the tax consequences of a subsequent sale or exchange of such stock. In the case where the shareholder holder cannot establish, and fails to designate, the particular shares of stock received, then the shareholder is treated as selling or transferring a share of stock received in exchange for, or with respect to, the share of stock that was purchased or acquired at the earliest date [Reg. § 1.358-2(a)(2)(vii)].

Example 22-45: S, an individual, acquired 20 shares of Corporation X stock on Date 1 for $3 each and 10 shares of X stock on Date 2 for $6 each. In a merger of X into Corporation Y, S receives 2 shares of Y stock in exchange for each share of X stock, or 60 shares of Y stock total. S recognizes no gain or loss on the exchange. S is not able to identify which shares of Y stock are received in exchange for each share of X stock. Under Reg. § 1.358-2(a)(2)(i), S has 40 shares of Y stock with a basis of $1.50 each, which are treated as having been acquired on Date 1. S also holds 20 shares of Y stock with a basis of $3 each, which are treated as having been acquired on Date 2. Under Reg. § 1.358-2(a)(2)(vii), on or before the date on which the basis of a share of Y stock received becomes relevant, S may designate which of the shares of Y stock have a basis of $1.50 and which have a basis of $3 [Reg. § 1.358-2(c), Ex. 1].

For basis in divisive reorganizations, see ¶ 22,115.

¶22,080 BASIS TO CORPORATION

The basis of property acquired by a corporation in connection with a tax-free reorganization is the same as it would be in the transferor's hands, increased by any gain recognized to the transferor on the transfer [Code Sec. 362(b); Reg. § 1.362-1].

Example 22-46: X Corporation owns property with a basis of $10,000 and a fair market value of $20,000. X Corporation transfers the property to Y Corporation for all of Y's stock, and distributes the Y stock to the X Corporation shareholders. This is a reorganization, and the exchange is nontaxable. Y Corporation's basis in the property received from X Corporation is $10,000.

If a corporation acquires stocks or securities in a corporation that is a party to the reorganization, the corporation's basis in the stock or securities is the same as the basis of the property it exchanged, with the same basis adjustments discussed in ¶ 22,075 [Code Sec. 358(a)(1); Reg. § 1.358-1]. However, the stock or securities a corporation acquires retain the basis they had in the hands of the transferor if the corporation exchanges its stock or securities (or its parent's stock or securities) as all or part of the consideration for the transfer [Code Sec. 362(b); Reg. § 1.362-1].

¶22,085 LIABILITIES ASSUMED

.01 Basic Rule

Acquisitive Reorganization

If the acquiring corporation acquires property encumbered with a liability and assumes the liability, the exchange will still be tax-free, unless the purpose was to avoid taxes or the assumption had no business purpose [Code Sec. 357(a)(2), (b); Reg. § 1.357-1]. Only liabilities specifically treated as assumed under Code Sec. 357(c) will result in a basis step-up for the transferee corporation. A recourse liability (or portion thereof) is treated as assumed only if the transferee has agreed to and is expected to satisfy the liability whether or not the transferor has been relieved of the liability [Code Sec. 357(d)(1)]. In a situation where more than one person agrees to satisfy a liability, only one would be expected to satisfy the liability. A nonrecourse liability is treated as having been assumed by the transferee of any asset that is subject to the liability unless the owner of other assets subject to the same nonrecourse liability agrees with the transferee to satisfy the liability (up to the fair market value of the other assets) [Code Sec. 357(d)(2)]. See Ch. 6 and Ch. 10.

However, the acquiring corporation's assumption of liability decreases the basis to the transferor of the property he receives in the exchange [Code Sec. 358(d); Reg. § 1.358-3]. But see an exception discussed below.

> **Example 22-47:** Corporation X transfers its property with a basis of $100,000 to Corporation Y in return for voting stock of Y and the assumption of a $25,000 mortgage on the property. No gain or loss is recognized to either corporation. X's basis for the stock received is $75,000.

IRC Rules for Assumed Liability

Code Sec. 301(b)(2) has historically provided that the amount of a corporate distribution must be reduced if the transferee assumes a liability of the corporation or receives property subject to a liability. It has not, however, provided specific rules for determining the amount of liabilities assumed. The IRS has made it clear in Reg. § 1.301-1(g) that the amount of liabilities assumed in connection with a distribution under Code Sec. 301 should be determined in accordance with the rules of Code Sec. 357(d). Code Sec. 357(d) prescribes the following rules:

- A recourse liability is treated as assumed if, based on all facts and circumstances, the transferee has agreed to, and is expected to, satisfy the liability. The transferor need not be relieved of the liability.
- A nonrecourse liability is treated as assumed by the transferee of any asset subject to the liability, except that the liability treated as assumed is reduced by the lesser of (1) the liability that the owner of other assets not transferred to the transferee that are also subject to the liability is expected to satisfy, or (2) the fair market value of those other assets subject to the liability.

.02 Assumption of Liabilities in Excess of Basis (Transfers to Controlled Corporation)

Gain is recognized by the corporate transferor to the extent that liabilities assumed by the transferee in a transfer to a controlled corporation under Code Sec. 351 or in a Code Sec. 368(a)(1)(D) divisive reorganization involving Code Sec. 355 distribution exceed the total of the adjusted basis, in the hands of the transferor, of the properties transferred [Code Sec. 357(c)]. Acquisitive "D" reorganizations that occur on or after October 22, 2004, are excluded from the application of Code Sec. 357(c). Acquisitive "D" reorganizations are excepted from this gain recognition rule because, unlike the divisive "D" reorganizations, the former result in a complete liquidation of the corporate transferor. Since the transferor's liabilities are limited to its assets, which are transferred to the subsidiary corporation in the transaction, and the transferor ceases to exist, the assumption of liabilities may not enrich the transferor in any way. The rule conforms the treatment of acquisitive "D" reorganizations to that of other acquisitive reorganizations.

In *Seggerman Farms, Inc.*,[53] family members who transferred farm equipment and property to their wholly owned corporation had to recognize gain on the transfers under Code Sec. 357 to the extent that the amount of liabilities assumed, plus the amount of liabilities to which the property was subject, exceeded the total of the adjusted basis of the transferred assets.

No Gain from Excess Liabilities in Acquisitive Reorganizations

In Rev. Rul. 2007-8,[54] the IRS ruled that taxpayers will not recognize gain on a transfer of excess liabilities in connection with a transfer of property for stock that qualifies as an "A," "C," acquisitive "D," or acquisitive "G" reorganization and that is also subject to Code Sec. 351. For further discussion of Code Sec. 351, see ¶ 6075.

Rev. Rul. 2007-42 sets forth two situations in which the transferor corporation ceases to exist and cannot be enriched as the result of the assumption of its liabilities. Thus the ruling concludes in both situations that taxpayers will not be required to recognize gain on the transfers in excess of liabilities pursuant to Code Sec. 357(c)(1).

In situation 1, individual A owns all the stock of corporations X and Y. Y acquires all the assets of X in exchange for Y stock and the assumption of X's liabilities. X liquidated and distributed the Y stock to A. The sum of the liabilities exceeded X's basis in the assets

---

[53] *Seggerman Farms, Inc.*, CA-7, 2002-2 USTC ¶ 50,728, 308 F3d 803.

[54] Rev. Rul. 2007-8, 2007-1 CB 469.

transferred to Y. The transaction qualified as a "D" reorganization and a nontaxable exchange under Code Sec. 351 (transfer of property for stock).

In situation 2, individual A owns X, and B, an unrelated individual, owns Y. The exchange of stock for assets by X and Y are similar to situation 1. In addition, B transfers property to Y so that the Y stock held by X and Y after the transaction amounts to "control" under Code Sec. 368(c). The transfer by X of all its assets and liabilities to Y for stock, followed by the liquidation of X, is a "C" reorganization. X's and B's transfers of property to Y are nontaxable under Code Sec. 351.

Basis of Property Encumbered by Liabilities

The basis of property encumbered by a liability can never exceed the fair market value of the transferred property. This is especially important in situations where one or more assets secure a single liability and the assets are transferred to different subsidiaries. Each subsidiary is not allowed to count the liability in determining the basis of the asset. The transferee's basis can not be increased under Code Sec. 362(a) (in a Code Sec. 351 transfer to a controlled corporation) or under Code Sec. 362(b) (in a reorganization) above the property's fair market value by gain recognized by the transferor as a result of the assumption of a liability. This rule applies to liabilities related to property transferred in Code Sec. 351 exchanges, the determination of permissible consideration in a C reorganization, the treatment of transfers by corporate parties to a reorganization, transfers by certain trust funds to a regulated investment company (RIC) and property subject to a transferor's liability in a Code Sec. 1031 exchange.

> **NOTE:** In determining the amount of liabilities assumed, the liability is excluded for a cash basis transferor to the extent that its payment by the transferor would have resulted in a deduction or would have constituted payments to partners under Code Sec. 736(a). However, the liability will be included to the extent that the obligation resulted in the creation of, or an increase in, the basis of any property. Also, the excluded liabilities cannot reduce the transferor's basis in stock received [Code Sec. 357(c)(3)].

.03 Prevention of Duplication/Acceleration of Loss through Liability Assumption

In an acquisitive reorganization under Code Sec. 368(a)(1)(D), the transferor must generally transfer substantially all its assets to the acquiring corporation and then go out of existence. Assumption of its liabilities by the acquiring corporation thus does not enrich the transferor corporation, which ceases to exist and whose liability was limited to its assets in any event, by corporate form. This welcome change conforms the treatment of acquisitive reorganizations under Code Sec. 368(a)(1)(D) to that of other acquisitive reorganizations.

Change of Control Following Transfer

No gain or loss is recognized when a taxpayer transfers property to a corporation in exchange for stock and immediately after the exchange that taxpayer controls the corporation. However, the taxpayer will recognize gain to the extent the taxpayer receives money or other property (boot) as part of the exchange [Code Sec. 351]. The assumption of liabilities by the controlled corporation generally is not treated as boot, except that the taxpayer recognizes gain to the extent that the liabilities assumed exceed the total of the adjusted basis of the property transferred to the controlled corporation [Code Sec. 357(c)]. The assumption of liabilities by the controlled corporation generally reduces the taxpayer's basis in the stock of the controlled corporation. The taxpayer's basis in the stock of the controlled corporation is the same as the basis of the property contributed to the controlled corporation, increased by the amount of any gain recognized on the exchange, and reduced by the amount of any money or property received, and by the amount of any loss recognized by the transferor [Code Sec. 358].

The assumption of such liabilities that would give rise to a deduction is not treated as money received by the taxpayer in determining whether the taxpayer has gain on the exchange. Similarly, the taxpayer's basis in the stock of the controlled corporation is not reduced by the assumption of such liabilities.

.04 Basis of Property in Exchange Involving Assumption of Liabilities

Code Sec. 358(h) provides that the basis of stock received in a tax-free transfer to a controlled corporation is reduced (but not below the stock's fair market value) by the amount of any liability which (1) is assumed by another person as part of the exchange, and (2) did not otherwise reduce the transferor's basis in the stock because of the assumption. The amount of the liability is determined as of the date of the exchange. The purpose of this change is to limit taxpayers from accelerating or duplicating losses through assumptions of liabilities. Code Sec. 358(h)(1)(A) provides that the basis reduction rule of Code Sec. 358(h) only applies to the amount of any liability that is assumed by *another person* (i.e., a party other than the person transferring the property in exchange for stock) [Code Sec. 358(h)(1)(A)]. Without this clarification, an assumption of liabilities by the party transferring the property to the corporation in exchange for its stock would permit such transferor to reduce the basis of the stock received in the exchange by the amount of the liability.

Except as provided by the IRS, this rule doesn't apply if, as part of the exchange, the trade or business associated with the liability is also transferred to the corporation.

> **Example 22-48:** Ann Marlboro transfers assets with an adjusted basis and fair market value of $100 to her wholly-owned corporation and the corporation assumes $40 of liability (the payment of which would give rise to a deduction). Thus, the value of the stock received by Ann is $60. Code Sec. 358(h) requires that the basis of Ann's stock be reduced to $60 (a reduction equal to the amount of the liability). No basis reduction is required if the transferred assets consist of the trade or business, or substantially all the assets, with which the liability is associated.

The term *liability* in this context includes any fixed or contingent obligation to make payment [Code Sec. 358(h)(3)]. A recourse liability is treated as assumed if the transferor has agreed to, and is expected to satisfy, the liability, whether or not the transferor has been relieved of the liability [Code Sec. 357(d)(1)(A)].

.05 Assumption of Environmental Liabilities Does Not Reduce Basis

The IRS concluded in Rev. Rul. 95-74[55] that contingent environmental liabilities that have not been deducted or capitalized and are assumed by a newly formed subsidiary in

[55] Rev. Rul. 95-74, 1995-2 CB 36.

a Section 351 exchange are not liabilities for purposes of Sections 357(c)(1) and 358(d). Therefore, the contingent environmental liabilities assumed by a subsidiary should not reduce the parent company's basis in the subsidiary's stock and the parent should not be required to recognize a gain because of the transfer of contingent liabilities to the subsidiary.

DIVISIVE REORGANIZATIONS

¶22,090 GENERAL RULES

For various reasons, a corporation may want to dispose of one or more of its business interests. It can accomplish this result by selling off the underlying assets and distributing the proceeds to the shareholders. But this triggers a two-level tax. First, the corporation must recognize gain on the sale of any appreciated assets. Second, the shareholders have taxable income or gain on the distribution (depending on whether the payout is classified as a dividend or a return of shareholder's investment in the company).

A corporation can avoid one or both of these tax consequences by engaging in a so-called divisive reorganization [See ¶ 22,030]. The corporation divides what was formerly held in one corporate shell into two or more corporate shells. Then it distributes the stock in the new corporation (or corporations) to shareholders, who may give up some or all of their stock in the original corporation.

> ▶ **TAX-FAVORED RESULT:** Neither the corporation nor its shareholders generally owe tax with this scheme unless the shareholders end up with cash, property, or other taxable boot in addition to tax-free stock.

.01 Types of Divisive Reorganizations

There are three types of divisive reorganizations under Code Sec. 355—split-ups, split-offs, and spin-offs. Each type of division divides the corporate entity into two or more corporations, with the stock of the new corporation in the hands of some or all of the original shareholders. The purpose of the divisive reorganization rules found in Code Sec. 355 is to permit tax-free restructuring of several businesses among existing shareholders. Distinguish this from a pre-arranged plan designed to avoid corporate-level gain in transactions that resemble sales.

Split-Ups

With a tax-free *split-up,* the parent corporation distributes all of its assets to two or more controlled corporations (which may or may not be newly formed). Then it distributes the stock of the controlled corporations to shareholders, who give up stock in the parent.

> **Example 22-49:** Central Corporation creates Able and Baker Corporations. Central then transfers its manufacturing business to Able in exchange for all of Able's stock. Central also transfers its remaining repair business to Baker in exchange for all of Baker's stock. Finally, Central distributes the Able and Baker

stock to its own shareholders, who give up their stock in Central. Result: The transaction qualifies as a tax-free split-up.

Split-Offs

In a *split-off,* the parent corporation keeps some of its assets and transfers the balance to one or more controlled corporations. Then the corporation transfers the stock of the controlled corporations to some or all of its shareholders, who give up some or all of their stock in the parent. With a split-off, the parent corporation remains in business, but in a trimmed-down form.

Example 22-50: Same as Example 22-49, except that Central creates only Able Corporation. Central keeps its manufacturing business and transfers the repair business to Able. Then Central distributes the Able stock to its shareholders, who give up 50 percent of their stock in Central. Result: The transaction now is a tax-free split-off.

Spin-Offs

In a *spin-off,* a corporation distributes to its shareholders stock that it owns in a controlled corporation. Its shareholders do not surrender any stock in the parent corporation.

Example 22-51: Same as Example 22-50, except that Central's shareholders get Able stock without giving up any of their Central stock.

Type D Reorganization-Style Spin-Off Does Not Qualify for Tax Deferral

In *South Tulsa Pathology Laboratory Inc.*,[56] the Tax Court held that the transfer of stock of a controlled corporation to its shareholders (spin-off) followed by the immediate sale of the spun-off company to a third party failed to qualify as a tax-free D reorganization under Code Sec. 368(a)(1)(D) because the transaction was a device to distribute earnings and profits lacking in sufficient business purpose. The taxpayer failed to satisfy the Code Sec. 355 requirements as discussed below.

.02 How to Satisfy the Section 355 Requirements

In order for a divisive D reorganization to qualify as a tax-free reorganization, the following four requirements of Code Sec. 355 must be satisfied:

- Solely stock in the controlled corporation must be distributed to shareholders;
- The distribution cannot be used principally as a device to distribute earnings and profits of the distributing corporation or the controlled corporation. A transaction is a device to distribute earnings and profits if there is a: (a) pro rata distribution among the shareholders of the distributing corporation, (b) subsequent sale or exchange of stock of the distributing or the controlled corporation after a distribution, (c) sale or exchange negotiated or agreed upon before the distribution [Reg. § 1.355-2(d)(2)];

---

[56] *South Tulsa Pathology Laboratory Inc.*, 118 TC 84, Dec. 54,633 (2002).

- The active business requirement of Code Sec. 355(b) must be satisfied; and
- All of the controlled corporation's stock held by the distributing corporation, or an amount constituting control, must be distributed.

In addition to these statutory requirements, the distribution must have an independent corporate business purpose and there must be continuity of proprietary interest after the distribution [Reg. § 1.355-2(b) and (c)].

.03 Safe Harbors Under Reg. § 1.355-2(d)(5)

A taxpayer may be able to prove that the spin-off was not a device for the distribution of earnings and profits by qualifying for the safe harbors available under Reg. § 1.355-2(d)(5)(ii) that require proof of the following:

- Accumulated or current earnings and profits for the tax year of the distribution, and
- The presence of a valid corporate business purpose, which is as a "real and substantial non-Federal tax purpose germane to the business of the distributing corporation, the controlled corporation, or the affiliated group * * * to which the distributing corporation belongs" [Reg. § 1.355-2(b)(4), (d)(3)(ii)].

.04 Section 355(e) Enacted to Prevent Sales Disguised as Tax-free Reorganizations

Prior to the addition of Code Sec. 355(e) to the Code in 1997, corporations often used divisive reorganizations as a tax-free means of disposing of businesses with appreciated assets. Such deals were commonly known as *Morris Trust transactions* after the case that first sanctioned these deals. In a number of highly publicized transactions, which caught the attention of lawmakers, overly creative taxpayers disguised a sale as a tax-free divisive reorganization by abusing Code Sec. 355. For example, a corporation would distribute the stock of one of its subsidiaries that had appreciated assets to its shareholders in a so-called tax-fee spin-off under Code Sec. 355 and, pursuant to a prearranged plan, an unrelated corporation would acquire the distributed subsidiary. In this transaction, the distributing corporation would pay no tax on what amounted to the sale of appreciated assets hidden in the subsidiary that it spun off tax-free. Lawmakers reacted to this abuse by enacting Code Sec. 355(e), which was called the anti-Morris Trust provision. Code Sec. 355(e) was intended to eliminate tax-free spin-offs that look more like a sale than a reorganization because taxpayers had pre-arranged plans designed to avoid corporate-level tax. Code Sec. 355(e) imposes a corporate-level tax on the distributing corporation if there is an otherwise tax-free distribution that is part of a plan or series of related transactions in which one or more persons acquire, directly or indirectly, at least a 50 percent interest in either the distributing corporation or any controlled corporation. If that occurs, the distributing corporation is taxed on the amount by which the distributed stock's fair market value exceeds it basis.

.05 The Anti-*Morris Trust* Provisions

Code Sec. 355(e) requires a distributing corporation to recognize gain on the distribution of a controlled corporation if, pursuant to a "plan or series of related transactions," one or more persons acquires directly or indirectly more than 50 percent by vote or value of the stock of either the distributing or controlled corporation. Code Sec. 355(e) also creates a rebuttable presumption that any acquisition occurring two years before or after a Code Sec. 355 distribution is part of such a plan "unless it is established that the distribution and the acquisition are not pursuant to a plan or series of related transactions" [Code Sec. 355(e)(2)(B).

For purposes of determining whether one or more persons has acquired a 50 percent interest, the Section 318(a)(2) attribution rules generally apply and the aggregation rules of Code Sec. 355(d)(7)(A) apply so that all related persons are treated as one person [Code Sec. 355(e)(4)(C)]. In addition, if a successor corporation in an A, C, or D reorganization acquires the assets of the distributing or any controlled corporation, the shareholders (immediately before the acquisition) of the successor corporation are treated as if they acquired stock in the corporation whose assets were acquired [Code Sec. 355(e)(3)(B)].[57]

.06 What Is a Plan or Series of Related Transactions?

Whether two transactions are part of the same "plan or series of related transactions" is determined by a subjective test that depends ultimately on the intentions and expectations of the parties. Whether a distribution and an acquisition are part of a plan is determined based on all the facts and circumstances [Reg. § 1.355-7(b)(1)]. The regulations set forth a number of nonexclusive factors that tend to show the presence or absence of a plan [Reg. § 1.355-7(b)(3)]. The weight to be given each of the facts and circumstances depends on the particular case, and the existence of a plan is not determined merely by comparing the number of plan and nonplan factors [Reg. § 1.355-7(b)(1)].

The following facts and circumstances show that a distribution and an acquisition are part of a plan:

- In the case of an acquisition (other than involving a public offering) after a distribution, at some time during the two-year period ending on the date of the distribution, there was an agreement, understanding, arrangement, or substantial negotiations regarding the acquisition or a similar acquisition. The weight to be accorded this fact depends on the nature, extent, and timing of the agreement, understanding, arrangement, or substantial negotiations. The existence of an agreement, understanding, or arrangement at the time of the distribution is given substantial weight;
- In the case of an acquisition involving a public offering after a distribution, at some time during the two-year period ending on the date of the distribution, there were discussions by Distributing or Controlled with an investment banker regarding the acquisition or a similar acquisition. The weight to be accorded this fact depends on the nature, extent, and timing of the discussions;
- In the case of an acquisition (other than involving a public offering) before a distribution, at some time during the two-year period ending on the date of the acquisition, there were discussions by Distributing or Controlled with the acquirer regarding a distribution. The weight to be accorded this fact depends on the nature, extent, and timing of the discussions. In addition, in the case of an acquisition (other than involving a public offering) before a distribution, the acquirer intends to cause a

[57] Rev. Rul. 98-27 1998-1 CB 1159.

distribution and, immediately after the acquisition, can meaningfully participate in the decision regarding whether to make a distribution;

- In the case of an acquisition involving a public offering before a distribution, at some time during the two-year period ending on the date of the acquisition, there were discussions by Distributing or Controlled with an investment banker regarding a distribution. The weight to be accorded this fact depends on the nature, extent, and timing of the discussions; and
- In the case of an acquisition either before or after a distribution, the distribution was motivated by a business purpose to facilitate the acquisition or a similar acquisition [Reg. § 1.355-7(B)(3)].

.07 Safe Harbors—In General

The IRS has announced that it will no longer issue private letter rulings on whether a transaction qualifies for nonrecognition treatment under Code Sec. 355.[58] To afford taxpayers some measure of security before moving forward, the regulations list nine detailed safe harbor transactions. If the taxpayer's acquisition and distribution fall within one of the safe harbors, then they are not treated as part of a plan, and the distributing corporation need not apply the facts and circumstances test.

Safe Harbor I

A distribution and an acquisition occurring after the distribution will not be considered part of a plan if:

- The distribution was motivated in whole or substantial part by a corporate business purpose other than a business purpose to facilitate an acquisition of the acquired corporation; and
- The acquisition occurred more than six months after the distribution and there was no agreement, understanding, arrangement, or substantial negotiations concerning the acquisition or a similar acquisition during the period that begins one year before the distribution and ends six months thereafter [Reg. § 1.355-7(d)(1)].

Safe Harbor II

A distribution and an acquisition occurring after the distribution will not be considered part of a plan if:

- The distribution was not motivated by a business purpose to facilitate the acquisition or a similar acquisition; and
- The acquisition occurred more than six months after the distribution and there was no agreement, understanding, arrangement, or substantial negotiations concerning the acquisition or a similar acquisition during the period that begins one year before the distribution and ends six months thereafter; and
- No more than 25 percent of the stock of the acquired corporation (Distributing or Controlled) was either acquired or the subject of an agreement, understanding, arrangement, or substantial negotiations during the period that begins one year before the distribution and ends six months thereafter [Reg. § 1.355-7(d)(2)].

---

[58] Rev. Proc. 2013-32, IRB 2013-28, 55.

Safe Harbor III

If an acquisition occurs after a distribution, there was no agreement, understanding, or arrangement concerning the acquisition or a similar acquisition at the time of the distribution, and there was no agreement, understanding, arrangement, or substantial negotiations concerning the acquisition or a similar acquisition within one year after the distribution, the acquisition and the distribution will not be considered part of a plan [Reg. § 1.355-7(d)(3)].

Safe Harbor IV

A distribution and an acquisition (other than involving a public offering) occurring before the distribution will not be considered part of a plan if the acquisition occurs before the date of the first disclosure event regarding the distribution. This rule will not apply to:

- A stock acquisition if the acquirer or a coordinating group of which the acquirer is a member is a controlling shareholder or a 10-percent shareholder of the acquired corporation (Distributing or Controlled) at any time during the period beginning immediately after the acquisition and ending on the date of the distribution; and
- An acquisition that occurs in connection with a transaction in which the aggregate acquisitions are of stock possessing 20 percent or more of the total voting power of the stock of the acquired corporation (Distributing or Controlled) or stock having a value of 20 percent or more of the total value of the stock of the acquired corporation (Distributing or Controlled) [Reg. § 1.355-7(d)(4)].

Safe Harbor V

A distribution that is pro rata among the Distributing shareholders and an acquisition (other than involving a public offering) of Distributing stock occurring before the distribution will not be considered part of a plan if the acquisition occurs after the date of a public announcement regarding the distribution; and there were no discussions by Distributing or Controlled with the acquirer regarding a distribution on or before the date of the first public announcement regarding the distribution. This rule does not apply to:

- A stock acquisition if the acquirer or a coordinating group of which the acquirer is a member is a controlling shareholder or a 10-percent shareholder of Distributing at any time during the period beginning immediately after the acquisition and ending on the date of the distribution; and
- An acquisition that occurs in connection with a transaction in which the aggregate acquisitions are of stock possessing 20 percent or more of the total voting power of the stock of Distributing or stock having a value of 20 percent or more of the total value of the stock of Distributing [Reg. § 1.355-7(d)(5)].

IRS approves spin-off despite simultaneous merger. In Rev. Rul. 2005-65,[59] the distribution of the stock of a pharmaceuticals corporation's wholly owned subsidiary following a merger with another pharmaceuticals corporation was not part of a plan of reorganization that would cause the recognition of gain under Code Sec. 355(e). The

---

[59] Rev. Rul. 2005-65, 2005-2 CB 684.

distribution, which was publicly announced prior to any consideration of a merger, was substantially motivated both before and after the merger by the intent to alleviate capital allocation problems between the pharmaceuticals corporation and its subsidiary and, thus, had a business purpose unrelated to the subsequent acquisition. Furthermore, the distribution would have occurred at approximately the same time and in a similar form even if the acquisition had not occurred.

Safe Harbor VI

A distribution and an acquisition involving a public offering occurring before the distribution will not be considered part of a plan if the acquisition occurs before the date of the first disclosure event regarding the distribution in the case of an acquisition of stock that is not listed on an established market immediately after the acquisition, or before the date of the first public announcement regarding the distribution in the case of an acquisition of stock that is listed on an established market immediately after the acquisition [Reg. § 1.355-7(d)(6)].

Safe Harbor VII

An acquisition (other than involving a public offering) of Distributing or Controlled stock that is listed on an established market is not part of a plan if, immediately before or immediately after the transfer, none of the transferor, the transferee, and any coordinating group of which either the transferor or the transferee is a member is:

- The acquired corporation (Distributing or Controlled);
- A corporation that the acquired corporation (Distributing or Controlled) controls;
- A member of a controlled group of corporations of which the acquired corporation (Distributing or Controlled) is a member;
- A controlling shareholder of the acquired corporation (Distributing or Controlled); or
- A 10-percent shareholder of the acquired corporation (Distributing or Controlled).

This rule does not apply to a transfer of stock by or to a person if

- The corporation the stock of which is being transferred knows, or has reason to know, that the person or a coordinating group of which such person is a member intends to become a controlling shareholder or a ten percent shareholder of the acquired corporation (Distributing or Controlled) at any time after the acquisition and before the date that is two years after the distribution; and
- If a transfer of stock results immediately, or upon a subsequent event or the passage of time, in an indirect acquisition of voting power by a person other than the transferee, paragraph (d)(7)(i) of this section does not prevent an acquisition of stock by such other person from being treated as part of a plan [Reg. § 1.355-7(d)(7)].

Safe Harbor VIII

If, in a transaction to which Code Secs. 83 or 421(a) or (b) applies, stock of Distributing or Controlled is acquired by a person in connection with such person's performance of services as an employee, director, or independent contractor for Distributing, Controlled, a related person, a corporation the assets of which Distributing, Controlled, or a related person acquires in a reorganization, or a corporation that acquires the assets of Distributing or Controlled in such a reorganization (and the stock acquired is not excessive by reference to the services performed), the acquisition and the distribution will not be considered part of a plan. This rule does not apply to a stock acquisition if the acquirer or a coordinating group of which the acquirer is a member is a controlling shareholder or a 10-percent shareholder of the acquired corporation (Distributing or Controlled) immediately after the acquisition [Reg. § 1.355-7(d)(8)].

Safe Harbor IX

If stock of Distributing or Controlled is acquired by a retirement plan of Distributing or Controlled (or a retirement plan of any other person that is treated as the same employer as Distributing or Controlled), the acquisition and the distribution will not be considered part of a plan. This rule does not apply to the extent that the stock acquired pursuant to acquisitions by all of the qualified plans during the four-year period beginning two years before the distribution, in the aggregate, represents more than ten percent of the total combined voting power of all classes of stock entitled to vote, or more than ten percent of the total value of shares of all classes of stock, of the acquired corporation (Distributing or Controlled) [Reg. § 1.355-7(d)(9)].

Example 22-52: Distributing (D) owns all of the stock of Controlled (C) and distributes the stock of C in a distribution to which section Code Sec. 355 applies. D is in business 1 and is relatively small in its industry and wants to combine with X, a larger corporation also engaged in business 1. C is in business 2. X and D begin negotiating for X to acquire D, but X does not want to acquire C. To facilitate the acquisition of D by X, D agrees to distribute all the stock of C pro rata before the acquisition. Prior to the distribution, D and X enter into a contract for D to merge into X subject to several conditions. One month after D and X enter into the contract, D distributes C and, on the day after the distribution, D merges into X. As a result of the merger, D's former shareholders own less than 50 percent of the stock of X. The issue is whether the distribution of C and the merger of D into X are part of a plan. No safe harbor applies to this acquisition. To determine whether the distribution of C and the merger of D into X are part of a plan, D must consider all the facts and circumstances. The following tends to show that the distribution of C and the merger of D into X are part of a plan: X and D had an agreement regarding the acquisition during the two-year period ending on the date of the distribution and the distribution was motivated by a business purpose to facilitate the merger. Because the merger was agreed to at the time of the distribution, the distribution of C and the merger of D into X are part of a plan [Reg. § 1.355-7(j), Ex.1].

Acquisitions Unaffected by Anti-*Morris Trust* Provisions

The following acquisitions are not affected by the anti-*Morris Trust* provisions and will thus still qualify as tax-free divisive reorganizations [Code Sec. 355(e)(3)(A)]:

- The acquisition of stock in the controlled corporation by the distributing corporation;
- The acquisition by a person of stock in a controlled corporation by reason of holding stock in the distributing corporation;

- The acquisition by a person of stock in any successor corporation of the distribution corporation or controlled corporation by reason of holding stock in such distributing or controlled corporation; and
- The acquisition of stock in the distributing corporation or any controlled corporation to the extent that the percentage of stock owned directly or indirectly in such corporation by each person owning stock in such corporation immediately before the acquisition does not decrease. This exception is not applicable if the stock held before the acquisition was acquired pursuant to a plan, or series of related transactions, to acquire a 50 percent or greater interest in the distributing or controlled corporation, as discussed further above [Code Sec. 355(e)(3)(A)(iv)].

These exceptions do not apply if the stock held before the acquisition was acquired pursuant to a plan, or series of related transactions, to acquire a 50 percent or greater interest in the distributing corporation or any controlled corporation. [Code Sec. 355(e)(3)(A)].

Information to Be Filed

When a corporation distributes stock or securities of a controlled corporation, it must attach a statement to its tax return for the year of the distribution. The statement must demonstrate that the distribution complies with the tax rules governing divisive reorganizations [¶ 22,095].

When shareholders receive a distribution, they must attach a statement to their return that lists the stock or securities that were surrendered (if any), the stock or securities that they received and the names and addresses of all the involved corporations [Reg. § 1.355-5].

¶22,095 REQUIREMENTS OF A DIVISIVE REORGANIZATION

Code Sec. 355(a) provides that a corporation may distribute stock and securities in a controlled corporation to its shareholders in a tax-free spin-off if:

- Each of the distributing corporation and controlled corporation is engaged, immediately after the distribution, in the active conduct of a trade or business,
- Each trade or business has been actively conducted throughout the five-year period ending on the date of the distribution, and
- Neither trade nor business has been acquired in a transaction in which gain or loss was recognized within the five-year period [Code Sec. 355(b)(1)(A), (2)(B), and (C)]. A corporation can make a tax-free distribution of stock (or securities) in another corporation only if it satisfies the following six requirements:

.01 Business Purpose

The corporation must have a bona fide business purpose both for dividing its assets between two or more corporations and for distributing stock or securities to its shareholders [Reg. § 1.355-2(b)]. The business purpose is not satisfied if the parent company's goals could have been achieved through a nontaxable transaction that (1) would not have required the distribution of a controlled corporation's stock, and (2) was neither impractical nor unduly expensive. A business purpose for the spin-off can include: increasing stock values;[60] improving the subsidiary's image in the marketplace,[61] splitting off the stock of some shareholders engaged in serious disputes that adversely affect operations, a reduction of state and/or local taxes (but not federal taxes); compliance with an antitrust divestiture order; splitting off a particular business to the shareholder most able to run it; and enabling a key employee to buy stock of a subsidiary without also buying stock of the parent (if state law prevents the subsidiary from issuing stock directly to the employee) [Reg. § 1.355-2(b)(3)].

In Rev. Rul. 2003-55,[62] the IRS ruled that the distribution of stock in an Section 355 transaction will still satisfy the business purpose requirement even if the original business purpose motivating the distribution can't be achieved because of an unexpected change in circumstances after the distribution that was brought about by deteriorating market conditions that soured a planned initial public offering.

In Rev. Rul. 2003-52,[63] the IRS ruled that the distribution of a controlled farming corporation's stock to split up its two businesses among different family members satisfied the business purpose requirement even though it was motivated in part by the shareholders' personal considerations. These included furthering the personal estate planning needs of the parties and promoting family harmony and prosperity.

If the corporation has a business purpose for dividing its assets but not for distributing stock of the controlled corporation, it does not satisfy the business purpose requirement.

> **Example 22-53:** Candy Corporation makes candy and toys. Its management wants to protect the candy business from the risks of the toy business by spinning off the toy business to shareholders. Under the tax rules, however, Candy does not have a business purpose for the spin-off. The reason: Candy can accomplish its full objective by putting the toy business in a subsidiary corporation. So there is no business purpose for making a distribution of stock to Candy's shareholders.

> **NOTE:** A shareholder purpose for effecting a reorganization (e.g., estate planning) is not a bona fide business purpose because it is not a corporate purpose.

.02 Active Business Requirement

In order for a corporation distribution to qualify for nonrecognition treatment under Code Sec. 355 immediately after the distribution, both the distributing corporation and the controlled corporation must be engaged in the active conduct of a trade or business.

A corporation is treated as engaged in the active conduct of a trade or business if it meets the following four tests under Code Sec. 355(b)(2):

---

[60] Rev. Rul. 2004-23, 2004-1 CB 585.

[61] Rev. Rul. 2003-110, 2003-2 CB 1083.

[62] Rev. Rul. 2003-55, 2003-1 CB 961.

[63] Rev. Rul. 2003-52, 2003-1 CB 960.

1. The corporation is engaged in the active conduct of a trade or business.
2. The trade or business was actively conducted for the five-year period ending on the date of the distribution.
3. The trade or business was not acquired in a taxable transaction during the five-year period ending on the date of the distribution.
4. Neither the distributee corporation nor the distributing corporation acquired control, directly or indirectly, over the controlled (distributed) corporation conducting the trade or business in a taxable transaction within five years before the distribution.

Each of these four tests is discussed below.

1. The corporation is engaged in the active conduct of a trade or business [Code Sec. 355(b)(2)(A)].

   Special rules for determining active conduct in the case of affiliated groups. In order to determine if a corporation meets this test, all members of the corporation's separate affiliated group (SAG) are treated as one corporation [Code Sec. 355(b)(3)(A)]. For this purpose, an SAG with respect to any corporation means the affiliated group which would be determined under Code Sec. 1504(a) if such corporation were the common parent and Code Sec. 1504(b) did not apply [Code Sec. 355(b)(3)(B)].

   If a corporation became a member of a SAG as a result of one or more transactions in which gain or loss was recognized, any trade or business conducted by the corporation at the time the corporation became such a member will be treated as acquired in a transaction in which gain or loss was recognized in whole or in part [Code Sec. 355(b)(3)(C)]. This type of acquisition is, therefore, subject to Code Sec. 355(b)(2)(C) and may qualify as an expansion of an existing trade or business conducted by either the distributing corporation or the controlled corporation.

   The above active business test rules apply to distributions occurring after May 17, 2006. However, they do not apply to any distribution in a transaction that is (i) made pursuant to an agreement that was binding on May 17, 2006, and at all times thereafter, (ii) described in a ruling request submitted to the IRS on or before such a date, or (iii) described on or before such a date in a public announcement or in a filing with the Securities and Exchange Commission. The distributing corporation may irrevocably elect out of the application of this transition rule.

   Active Conduct of Trade or Business Immediately After Distribution. Code Sec. 355(b)(1) provides that Code Sec. 355(a) only applies to transactions in which both the distributing and the controlled corporation are engaged in the active conduct of a trade or business immediately after the distribution. In pursuit of this objective, both the parent corporation and each controlled corporation must perform active and substantial management and operational functions for the purpose of earning income or profit. [Reg. § 1.355-3(b)(2)]. Activities performed by a corporation include activities performed by employees of an affiliate and in certain cases by shareholders of a closely held corporation, if such activities are performed for the corporation. For example, activities performed by a corporation include activities performed for the corporation by its sole shareholder. However, the activities of employees of affiliates (or, in certain cases, shareholders) are only taken into account during the period such corporations are affiliates (or persons are shareholders) of the corporation [Reg. § 1.355-3(b)(2)(iii)].

In Rev. Rul. 2007-42,[64] the IRS concluded that a distributing corporation was engaged in the active conduct of a trade or business for purposes of Code Sec. 355(b) where the corporation owned a "significant interest" in a limited liability company (LLC) classified as a partnership for federal tax purposes and the LLC performed the activities required for an active trade or business under Reg. § 1.355-3(b)(2). For further discussion of LLCs, see Chapter 30.

Treatment of a separate affiliated group. Solely for purposes of determining whether a corporation is engaged in the active conduct of a trade or business, all members of a corporation's SAG will be treated as one corporation. Therefore, transfers of assets (or activities) that are owned (or performed) by the SAG immediately before and immediately after the transfer are disregarded and are not acquisitions [Prop. Reg. § 1.355-3(b)(1)(ii)].

Subsidiary SAG members are treated like divisions of the distributing or controlled corporation, as the case may be, and the controlled corporation may be a member of the distributing corporation's SAG during the pre-distribution period. Prop. Reg. § 1.355-3(b)(1)(ii) also provides that a stock acquisition that results in a corporation becoming a subsidiary SAG member is treated as an asset acquisition, thereby substantially reducing the applicability of Code Sec. 355(b)(2)(D). Notwithstanding this rule, however, purchases of stock of the controlled corporation during the pre-distribution period may be subject to Code Sec. 355(a)(3)(B).

Prop. Reg. § 1.355-3(b)(2)(v) provides that, for purposes of Code Sec. 355(b), a corporation can be attributed the trade or business assets and activities of a partnership. In particular, the proposed rules allow a partner to be attributed the partnership's trade or business assets and activities if the partner owns a significant interest in the partnership. Thus, the proposed regulations yield results similar to the rules regarding the satisfaction of the continuity of business enterprise requirement.

Transition Relief for Corporate Divisions Affected by Change to Active Business Rule. In Notice 2007-60,[65] the IRS provided transition relief regarding the application of Code Secs. 355(b)(2)(C) and (D) to certain trade or business acquisitions between members of affiliated groups under Reg. § 1.355-3(b)(4)(iii) to reflect the enactment of Code Sec. 355(b)(3). The IRS will not challenge the distributing corporation's acquisition, or the acquisition by its separate affiliated group (SAG), of additional stock of the controlled corporation as a violation of Code Sec. 355(b)(2)(C) with respect to the controlled corporation, provided the transaction satisfies the requirements of Code Sec. 355(b)(2)(D), as in effect before the enactment of Code Sec. 355(b)(3). The relief applies to distributions effected on or before the date the proposed regulations that modify the active trade or business rules to reflect the enactment of Code Sec. 355(b)(3) are published as temporary or final regulations.

2. **Five-Year Pre-Distribution Active Conduct of Trade or Business.** Both the retained and distributed business must have been actively conducted throughout the five-year pre-distribution period [Code Sec. 355(b)(2)(B)]. In Rev. Rul.

[64] Rev. Rul. 2007-42, 2007-2 CB 44.

[65] Notice 2007-60, 2007-2 CB 466.

2002-49,[66] the IRS held that the five-year active trade or business was satisfied when, during the five-year period before a spin-off, a corporation holding a membership interest in a member-managed LLC, purchased the remaining interests in the LLC, contributed a portion of the LLC's business to a newly formed controlled corporate subsidiary and then distributed its stock in the controlled subsidiary to the corporate parent's shareholders.

Impact of Business Changes on Five-Year Active Trade or Business. Changes in a trade or business, product line or product capacity during the five-year period prior to a spin-off will be disregarded provided the changes do not constitute the acquisition of a new or different business [Code Sec. 355(b)(2)(B); Reg. § 1.355-3(b)(3)(ii)]. For example, the addition of new product lines, the dropping of old products, changes in production capacity will be disregarded in determining whether an active trade or business has been conducted by a corporation throughout the five-year period preceding a spin-off. Moreover, if a business purchased, created, or otherwise acquired another trade or business in the same line of business, then the acquisition of that other business is ordinarily treated as an expansion of the original business, unless that purchase, creation, or other acquisition constitutes the acquisition of a new or different business. In Example (7) of Reg. § 1.355-3(c), corporation X had owned and operated a department store in the downtown area of the City of G for six years before acquiring a parcel of land in a suburban area of G and constructing a new department store. Three years after the construction, X transferred the suburban store and related business assets to new subsidiary Y and distributed the Y stock to X's shareholders. Citing Reg. § 1.355-3(b)(3)(i) and (ii), the example concludes that the spin-off was tax-free.

In Example (8) of Reg. § 1.355-3(c), corporation X had owned and operated hardware stores in several states for four years before purchasing the assets of a hardware store in State M where X had not previously conducted business. Two years after the purchase, X transferred the State M store and related business assets to new subsidiary Y and distributed the Y stock to X's shareholders. Citing Reg. § 1.355-3(b)(3)(i) and (ii), the example concludes that X and Y both satisfy the requirements of Code Sec. 355(b).

Distinguish expansions of existing businesses from acquisitions of new ones. In Rev. Rul. 2003-18,[67] the IRS concluded that the acquisition of an automobile franchise by a automobile dealer engaged in the sale and service of a different brand of automobile was an expansion of the existing business rather than an acquisition of a new one. The IRS explained that the brands were similar, the business activities were the same for the two brands, and the operation of the acquired franchise required the experience that the corporation had developed while operating the original business. Thus, the IRS concluded that each of the dealerships was engaged in the active conduct of a five-year active trade or business immediately after the distribution and the spin-off was tax-free.

Similarly, in Rev. Rul. 2003-38,[68] the IRS concluded that taxpayers who operated a retail shoe shore in shopping malls and other locations and then expanded to sell

[66] Rev. Rul. 2002-49, 2002-2, CB 288.

[67] Rev. Rul. 2003-18, 2003-1 CB 467.

[68] Rev. Rul. 2003-38, 2003-1 CB 811.

shoes on the Internet, merely expanded their existing business rather than acquire a new or different business under Reg. § 1.355-3(b)(3)(ii). As a result, the spin-off was tax-free. The IRS concluded that the creation of the Internet web site by a shoe retailer to sell shoes on-line did not constitute the acquisition of a new or different business under Reg. § 1.355-3(b)(3)(ii). Instead, it was an expansion of the existing retail shoe store business. Therefore, the taxpayers were engaged in the active conduct of a five-year active trade or business immediately after the distribution and the spin-off was tax-free.

▶ **PLANNING POINTER:** When a taxpayer's business has expanded and undergone a character change, it is often difficult to determine whether the taxpayer has actively conducted a trade a business throughout the five-year period prior to a spin-off for purposes of Code Sec. 355. A distribution of stock following the spin-off will only be tax-free if the taxpayer can prove that this requirement was satisfied. Based on the IRS conclusions in Rev. Rul. 2003-18 and Rev. Rul. 2003-38, a business expansion will not constitute a change significant enough to violate the five-year active business requirement if: (i) the product sold in the new business is similar to the product sold by the old business, (ii) the business activities associated with the operation of the old business are the same as the business activities associated with the operation of the new business, and (iii) the operation of the new business requires use of the experience and know-how that the taxpayer developed in the operation of the original business. Taxpayers engaged in the active conduct of a trade or business may separate, or spin off, a subsidiary into a separate company and make tax-free distributions of stock in the new company to the parent company and shareholders by following these guidelines.

3. **Trade or Business Not Acquired in Taxable Transaction During Five-Year Predistribution Period.** The distributed business must not have been acquired during a five-year period ending on the date of the distribution in a transaction that triggered gain or loss recognition [Code Sec. 355(b)(2)(C), (D); Reg. § 1.355-3(b)(4), (5)].

Example 22-54: Since 1984, Corporation A has operated seven retail clothing establishments: six in State X and one in State Y. It has been unable to find reliable suppliers for its State Y store, so it transfers that store to controlled Corporation B. Then it distributes the Corporation B stock to a Mr. Z, a shareholder from State Y, in exchange for his stock in Corporation A. After the distribution to Mr. Z, both Corporation A and B operate active businesses that have been in existence for more than five years. So the split-off of Corporation B qualifies as a tax-free divisive reorganization.

In *McLaulin*,[69] the Court of Appeals for the 11th Circuit held that a parent corporation's distribution of its subsidiary stock to shareholders was a taxable transaction because the parent had acquired control of the subsidiary shortly before the distribution.

---

69 *D.P. McLaulin Jr.*, CA-11, 2002-1 USTC ¶ 50,156, 276 F3d 1269.

The contemporaneous redemption and distribution failed to satisfy the active trade or business requirement because control of the subsidiary was acquired by the parent within five years of a transaction in which gain was recognized by the 50 percent shareholder, thus violating the conditions of Code Sec. 355(b)(2)(D)(ii).

4. **Neither Distributee Corporation Nor Distributing Corporation Acquired Control Over Controlled (Distributed) Corporation Conducting Trade Or Business In Taxable Transaction Within Five Years Before Distribution.** Code Sec. 355(b)(2)(D) requires that neither the distributee corporation nor the distributing corporation acquire control, directly or indirectly, over the controlled (distributed) corporation conducting the trade or business in a taxable transaction within five years before the distribution. The purpose of this provision is to prevent creative taxpayers from arranging their affairs in order to avoid dividends that would be otherwise be distributed and taxed. By taking advantage of Code Sec. 355(a) these taxpayer might try and avoid taxation of these dividends by using the tax-free distribution rules of Code Sec. 355.

.03 Not a Device for Distributing Earnings and Profits

The distribution to the shareholders must not be principally a device to pay out corporate earnings and profits. If, for example, a distribution looks like a dividend, it will be taxed as a dividend—even if it follows the other tax law requirements for divisive reorganizations [Code Sec. 355(a)(1)(B); Reg. § 1.355-2(d)(2)]. See also ¶ 22,030.

Reg. § 1.355-2(d)(2) provides that the presence of any of the following factors will be evidence of device:

1. **Pro rata distribution.** A distribution that is pro rata or substantially pro rata among the shareholders of the distributing corporation presents the greatest potential for the avoidance of the dividend provisions of the Code and, in contrast to other types of distributions, is more likely to be used principally as a device. Accordingly, the fact that a distribution is pro rata or substantially pro rata is evidence of device [Reg. § 1.355-2(d)(2)(i)].
2. **Subsequent sale or exchange of stock.** A sale or exchange of stock of the distributing or the controlled corporation after the distribution is evidence of device. Generally, the greater the percentage of the stock sold or exchanged after the distribution, the stronger the evidence of device. In addition, the shorter the period of time between the distribution and the sale or exchange, the stronger the evidence of device [Reg. § 1.355-2(d)(2)(ii)].

.04 Distribution of Stock or Securities

The parent corporation must distribute (1) stock of the controlled corporation (or corporations) to the stockholders, or (2) securities of the controlled corporation to its security holders [Code Sec. 355(a)(1)(A)].

The distribution must consist of all the stock or securities of the controlled corporation that the parent corporation held immediately before the distribution, or an amount to constitute control [Code Sec. 355(a)(1)(D); Reg. § 1.355-2].

.05 Control

The distributing corporation must distribute an amount of stock in the controlled corporation constituting control [Code Sec. 355(a)(1)(D)(ii)]. Control means the ownership of stock with at least 80 percent of the total voting power and at least 80 percent of the total number of shares of all other classes of stock of the corporation [Code Sec. 368(c)]. The principles of the step-transaction doctrine will no longer be applied to determine whether a distributed corporation was a controlled corporation immediately before the distribution solely because of any post-distribution acquisition or restructuring of the distributed corporation, whether prearranged or not.[70]

.06 Continuity of Interest

There must be continuity of interest by those who owned the business prior to the spin-off in order for the nonrecognition treatment provided in Code Sec. 355 to apply [Reg. § 1.355-2(c)].

In order to satisfy the continuity of interest requirement, one or more persons who, directly or indirectly, were the owners of the enterprise before the distribution or exchange are required to own, in the aggregate, an amount of stock establishing a continuity of interest in each of the modified corporate forms in which the enterprise is conducted after the separation [Reg. § 1.355-2(c)(1)].

> **Example 22-55:** For more than five years, corporation X has been engaged directly in one business, and indirectly in a different business through its wholly owned subsidiary, S. The businesses are equal in value. At all times, the outstanding stock of X has been owned equally by unrelated individuals A and B. For valid business reasons, A and B cause X to distribute all of the stock of S to B in exchange for all of B's stock in X. After the transaction, A owns all the stock of X and B owns all the stock of S. The continuity of interest requirement is met because one or more persons who were the owners of X prior to the distribution (A and B) own, in the aggregate, an amount of stock establishing a continuity of interest in each of X and S after the distribution [Reg. 1.355-2(c)(2), Ex.1].

.07 Distributions Involving Disqualified Investment Corporations

Code Sec. 355(g) provides that certain distributions involving disqualified investment corporations are excluded from the application of Code Sec. 355. This exception applies to distributions in which:

1. Either the distributing corporation or the controlled corporation is a disqualified investment corporation immediately after the transaction in which the distribution occurs, and
2. Any person, who did not hold a 50-percent or greater interest in such a disqualified investment corporation immediately before the transaction, holds such an interest immediately after the transaction [Code Sec. 355(g)(1)].

In this situation, a transaction also means a series of transactions [Code Sec. 355(g)(4)].

[70] Rev. Rul. 98-27, 1998-1 CB 1159.

Disqualified Investment Corporation

A disqualified investment corporation is defined as any distributing or controlled corporation having investment assets with a fair market value that is two-thirds or more of the fair market value of all its assets. For distributions occurring during such one-year period, the fair market value of the investment assets is increased to three-quarters or more of the fair market value of all of the corporation's assets [Code Sec. 355(g) (2) (A)].

Investment Assets

Investment assets include cash, corporate stock or securities, partnership interests, debt instruments, options, forward contracts, futures contracts, notional principal contracts, derivatives, foreign currency, or any similar asset [Code Sec. 355(g) (2) (B) (i)].

An exception applies for assets used in certain financial trades or businesses if substantially all of the income of the business is derived from persons who are not related to the person conducting the business. To qualify for the exception, the assets must be held for use in the active and regular conduct of:

1. A lending or finance business within the meaning of Code Sec. 954(h) (4),
2. A banking business conducted through a bank, a domestic building and loan association, or any similar institution that may be specified by the IRS, or
3. An insurance business which is licensed, authorized, or regulated by an applicable insurance regulatory body [Code Sec. 355(g) (2) (B) (ii)].

Another exception applies to any security held by a dealer in securities that is subject to the mark-to-market accounting method under Code Sec. 475(a) [Code Sec. 355(g) (2) (B) (iii)].

In addition, stock or securities in a 20-percent controlled entity (with respect to the distributing or controlled corporation) are not considered investment assets. This exception also applies to debt instruments, options, derivatives, forward or futures contracts, or notional principal contracts issued by such a controlled entity. A look-through rule applies to treat the distributing or controlled corporation as owning its ratable share of assets of any 20-percent controlled entity. For the purpose of this exception, a 20-percent controlled entity means a corporation in which the distributing or controlled corporation owns (directly or indirectly) stock, except that "20 percent" is substituted for "80 percent" and any preferred stock is not taken into account [Code Sec. 355(g) (2) (B) (iv)].

A partnership interest or a debt instrument or other evidence of indebtedness issued by a partnership is also not treated as an investment asset in certain cases. This exception applies if one or more of the partnership's trades or businesses is taken into account (or would be taken into account if the five-year business history requirement of Code Sec. 355(b) (2) (B) is disregarded) by the distributing or controlled corporation in order to determine if the distribution satisfies the active business requirement of Code Sec. 355(b). For this purpose, the distributing or controlled corporation is treated as owning its ratable share of the assets of the partnership [Code Sec. 355(g) (2) (B) (v)].

50-Percent or Greater Interest

To determine if any person holds a 50-percent or greater interest in a disqualified investment corporation immediately after the distribution, the "vote or value" test of Code Sec. 355(d)(4) is used. For this purpose, the attribution rules of Code Sec. 318 apply [Code Sec. 355(g)(3)]. This means that where a person holds 50 percent of the voting power (but not the value) of the distributing corporation prior to the transaction and 50 percent of the value of either the distributing or controlled corporation immediately after the transaction, the disqualified investment corporation rules apply.

¶22,100 TAX CONSEQUENCES OF A DIVISIVE REORGANIZATION

Once the above requirements are satisfied, a distribution of stock or securities generally will not trigger gain or loss recognition to shareholders or security holders [Code Sec. 355(a)]. It makes no difference whether the distribution is pro rata, stock is surrendered, or if there is a plan of reorganization.

Equally important, the distribution will not trigger gain or loss at the corporate level [Code Sec. 355(c) if the distribution is not made under a plan of reorganization; Code Sec. 361(c) if it is made under such a plan].

Note, however, that the distributing corporation must recognize gain (but not loss) if the distribution to the other shareholders includes anything other than stock or securities in the controlled corporation. This means that the corporation must recognize gain if it distributes cash or appreciated property (boot) to its shareholders [Code Sec. 355(c)]. The rule dovetails with the well-established concept that a distribution of boot is taxable to shareholders [¶ 22,110].

.01 Tax Treatment of Lapse of Stock Restrictions in Connection with Spin-Off

In Rev. Rul. 2002-1,[71] the IRS concluded that neither parent corporation nor its spun-off subsidiary would recognize gain or loss on the lapse of stock restrictions on compensatory stock or the exercise of nonqualified stock options to acquire the stock of both companies. In addition, each company is entitled to deduct amounts includible in its respective employees' income as a result of the lapse of restrictions on either company's stock and the exercise of options to acquire either company's stock.

.02 Treatment of Transfers to Creditors in Divisive Reorganizations

The amount of money plus the fair market value of other property that a distributing corporation in the context of a reorganization under Code Sec. 368(a)(1)(D) and Code Sec. 355 can distribute to its creditors without gain recognition under Code Sec. 361(b)(3) is limited to the aggregate basis of the assets contributed to the controlled corporation.

---

[71] Rev. Rul. 2002-1, 2002-1 CB 268.

¶22,105 DIVISIVE REORGANIZATIONS INVOLVING LARGE SHAREHOLDERS

Under the current tax rules, the parent corporation may have to recognize gain (but not loss) when it distributes to its shareholders stock or securities of one or more controlled corporations.

The gain recognition rule applies when the parent corporation makes a *disqualified distribution*. This is defined as a distribution of *disqualified stock* to a shareholder, if, immediately after the distribution, the shareholder owns a 50-percent or greater interest (by vote or value) in either the parent corporation or a distributed controlled corporation [Code Sec. 355(d)(2)].

Disqualified stock is any stock in the parent corporation or any controlled corporation that is acquired by purchase within five years before the distribution [Code Sec. 355(d)(3); Reg. § 1.355-6(b)(2)]]. It also can include stock in a controlled corporation that is received in the distribution.

The term *purchase* is broadly defined for purposes of this rule. It includes not only stock that is bought [Code Sec. 355(d)(5)(A); Reg. § 1.355-6(d)(1)]], but also stock received in exchange for transferring cash, marketable stock or securities or debt to a corporation controlled by the shareholder [Code Sec. 355(d)(5)(B)]. Additionally, a purchase includes stock acquired in a carryover basis transaction, including a gift, tax-free reorganization, liquidation, or contribution to a partnership or corporation, if the person or entity that surrendered that stock acquired it by purchase [Code Sec. 355(d)(5)(C)].

▶ **PLANNING POINTER:** The current crackdown on divisive reorganizations effectively extends the *"General Utilities"* repeal one step further [¶ 22,125]. It prevents taxpayers from buying an interest in a corporation (directly or indirectly) and then having the corporation distribute appreciated stock or securities to them without paying a corporate-level tax.

Example 22-56: Baker Corporation is 100 percent owned by Able Corporation. Mr. Klein buys 50 percent of Able's outstanding shares, principally because he is interested in Baker. Shortly thereafter, Able splits off its Baker stock to Klein and four other Able shareholders. Klein gets 30 percent of Baker's stock in exchange for giving up a portion of his Able stock. Result: Able must recognize gain on the Baker stock it distributes to Klein. The reason: Because Klein acquired 50 percent of Able within the prohibited five-year time period, the Baker stock split off to him is a disqualified distribution.

NOTE: Despite gain recognition at the corporate level, there are no tax consequences to shareholders. So Klein owes no tax in connection with the Able stock he gives up or the Baker stock he receives.

.01 Broad Application

Tough antiabuse rules prevent corporations from circumventing the corporate gain recognition rule by dividing stock ownership among various individuals or entities. These rules apply in the following situations:

- *Related taxpayers.* Corporations cannot avoid recognizing gain by splitting up stock ownership among related taxpayers or unrelated taxpayers who are acting in concert. Their stock holdings will be aggregated, and they will be treated as a single taxpayer. For example, if a husband and wife each buy 25 percent of a corporation, they will be treated as one taxpayer who buys 50 percent;
- *Owners of stock or securities.* Any owner of an entity (a corporation, partnership, estate, or trust) is treated as owning a proportionate amount of all the stock or securities held by that entity. For example, if a taxpayer buys 40 percent of Smallco's stock and the 50 percent-owned partnership buys another 40 percent, the taxpayer is treated as owning 60 percent of Smallco—the 40 percent owned outright plus half the 40 percent owned by the partnership. Note: There is a modest escape hatch for owners of corporations. The rule applies only if the taxpayers own 10 percent or more of the corporate stock; and
- *Deemed purchases.* Taxpayers cannot avoid the five-year holding period by purchasing an interest in an entity that has held stock of a distributing or controlled corporation long enough to satisfy the holding period. Based on the preceding paragraph, the taxpayer will be treated as purchasing a proportionate amount of the distributing or controlled corporation's stock or securities on the date that the taxpayer purchased an interest in the entity or the date the entity purchased the stock or securities, whichever is later.

¶22,110 SHAREHOLDERS WHO RECEIVE BOOT

In a divisive reorganization, the stock or security holder may receive cash or other property (boot) in addition to stock or securities of a controlled corporation. Generally, the stock or security holder must recognize gain (but not loss) on the boot received. However, if the distribution has the effect of a dividend, it will be taxed as ordinary income [Code Sec. 356(a); Reg. § 1.356-1].

.01 Taxable Distributions

In addition to cash or property, the following distributions are taxable as boot:

- Distributed stock or securities of anything other than a controlled corporation;
- The principal amount of securities of a controlled corporation that exceeds the principal amount of securities surrendered [Code Sec. 355(a)(3)(A)];
- Stock of a controlled corporation that the parent corporation acquired within five years of the distribution, but only if the acquisition triggered gain or loss recognition [Code Sec. 355(a)(3)(B)];
- Any debt or obligation of the controlled corporation that is not a security; and
- Stock rights or warrants. Stock rights and warrants will be treated the same as stock in a tax-free corporate division [Reg. § 1.355-1(c)]. This is good news because stock rights and warrants are commonplace in the capital structures of corporations and are often transferred in corporate divisions. Stock rights do not include:

a. Rights exercisable against anyone other than the stock issuer, and
b. Rights that relate to property other than stock of the rights' issuer. A stock or debt conversion privilege generally is not considered to be a separate property right received as part of a reorganization.

The regulations also provide that stock rights are treated as having no principal amount so that a taxpayer would not have to recognize any gain under Code Sec. 356 on the receipt of a stock right [Reg. § 1.356-3(b)]. This would generally be the case regardless of whether the taxpayer surrenders stock, stock rights, or debt securities as part of the reorganization.

.02 Nonqualified Preferred Stock

Nonqualified preferred stock (NQPS) will be treated as boot for the purposes of Code Secs. 351, 354, 355, 356, and 368 [Code Secs. 351(g), 354(a)(2)(C)]. Thus, when a shareholder receives NQPS in a divisive reorganization, gain (but not loss) is recognized up to fair market value of the nonqualified preferred stock [Code Sec. 355(a)(3)]. Preferred stock is NQPS if it meets any one of the four following conditions [Code Sec. 351(g)(2)(A)]:

- The holder of the stock has the right to require the issuer or a related person to redeem or purchase the stock;
- The issuer or a related person is required to redeem or purchase the stock;
- The issuer or a related person has the right to redeem or purchase the stock and, as of the issue date, it is more likely than not that such right will be exercised; or
- The dividend rate on the stock varies in whole or in part (directly or indirectly) with reference to interest rates, commodity prices, or other similar indices.

The first three conditions listed above apply only in the case of rights that are exercisable or obligations that are to be performed within 20 years of the stock's issuance and are not subject to contingencies that as of the issue date make remote the likelihood of redemption or purchase [Code Sec. 351(g)(2)(B)]. In addition, such rights and obligations are not taken into account in certain circumstances involving nonpublic companies or stock issued in the compensatory context [Code Sec. 351(g)(3)].

Treatment of Preferred Stock

Code Sec. 351(g)(3)(A) provides that the term *preferred stock* means stock which is limited and preferred as to dividends and does not participate in corporate growth to any significant extent. Stock will not be treated as participating in corporate growth to any significant extent unless there is a real and meaningful likelihood of the shareholder actually participating in the earnings and growth of the corporation.

Stock described under Code Sec. 351(g)(2) will be NQPS regardless of when it was issued [Reg. § 1.356-7(a)]. Preferred stock will not be NQPS if it is received in exchange for (or in a distribution with respect to) preferred stock that is not NQPS solely because of the 20-year restrictions, and the stock received is substantially identical to the surrendered stock [Reg. § 1.356-7(b)]. When preferred stock is received in an exchange for stock that was compensation stock, the compensation stock will not be treated as NQPS, if the compensation stock was actually received for services and represented reasonable compensation for the services at the time of the transfer. This rule would apply whether the surrendered stock is common or preferred [Reg. § 1.356-7(c)].

Active Participation Requirement

In order for stock to be treated as participating in corporate growth to any significant extent (and, thus, avoid being classified as preferred stock) there must be a "real and meaningful likelihood" that the shareholder will actually participate in the earnings and growth of the corporation [Code Sec. 351(g)(3)(A)]. This clarification exists to thwart possible attempts by some taxpayers to avoid characterization of an instrument as nonqualified preferred stock by including illusory participation rights or including terms that the taxpayers could argue create an unlimited dividend.

Example 22-57: ABCo has two classes of stock: Class A Common and Class A Preferred. The preferred stock has preferential rights on liquidation and is entitled to the same dividends as may be declared on the common stock. If ABCo pays no dividends to holders of the common and preferred stock, Class A Preferred will be classified as nonqualified preferred stock.

Example 22-58: The preferred stock of BabCO entitles shareholders to a dividend equal to the greater of 7 percent or the dividends that common stock shareholders receive. If the common stock shareholders are not expected to receive dividends greater than 7 percent, BabCo's preferred stock will be classified as nonqualified preferred stock.

Giving or Receiving Other Consideration

If the security holder gives other property in the exchange besides stock or securities in a corporation which is a party to the reorganization, the security holder must recognize gain or loss on the property when the value received is more or less than its adjusted basis [Ch. 16] [Reg. § 1.358-1(a)]. If the security holder receives consideration other than the stock or securities in a corporation that is a party to the reorganization, it may be treated as boot [¶ 22,065] [Code Sec. 356(a) (1); Reg. § 1.356-1(a)].

NOTE: The term *securities* includes rights issued by a party to the reorganization to acquire its stock [Reg. § 1.354-1(e)].

¶22,115 BASIS

In a divisive reorganization, the distributee's old adjusted basis carries over and is allocated among: (1) any shares retained in the distributing corporation, and (2) any shares received in the controlled corporation (or corporations). The allocation is based on the fair market values of the retained and distributed stock (and any stock surrendered) [Code Sec. 358(c); Reg. § 1.358-2(a)(2)].

Example 22-59: Mr. Jobe owns 100 shares in Corporation X, which has a basis to him of $10,000 and a market value of $15,000. In a tax-free spin-off, he receives 100 shares of stock in Corporation Y, which has a fair market value of $5,000. After the spin-off, the basis of his X and Y stock is determined as follows:

Market value of X stock		$15,000
Market value of Y stock		5,000
Total value		$20,000
Basis of X stock after spin-of	$15,000/$20,000 × $10,000 =	$ 7,500
Basis of Y stock after spin-off	$5,000/$20,000 × $10,000 =	$ 2,500
Total basis		$10,000

Example 22-60: Ms. Frederick owns 200 shares of Corporation X stock that cost her $14,000 and has a fair market value of $40,000. In a tax-free split-off, she gives up half her X stock and receives 50 shares of preferred (value $10,000) and 50 shares of common (value $5,000) in controlled Corporation Y. Her $14,000 basis in the X stock is allocated among the three stocks she holds after the distribution as follows:

Market value of retained X stock		$20,000
Market value of Y stock—preferred		10,000
Market value of Y stock—common		5,000
Total value		$35,000
Basis of retained X stock	$20,000/$35,000 × $14,000 =	$ 8,000
Basis of Y stock—preferred	$10,000/$35,000 × $14,000 =	$ 4,000
Basis of Y stock—common	$5,000/$35,000 × $14,000 =	$ 2,000
Total basis		$14,000

If shareholders also receive taxable boot, the basis of the retained and distributed stock may have to be adjusted to reflect that boot. Once distributed, the boot has a basis equal to its fair market value.

.01 Basis to Distributing Corporation

If the parent corporation transfers property to a controlled corporation as a precursor to a divisive reorganization, the controlled corporation has the same basis in that property as the parent. But the basis is increased by any gain recognized on the transfer [Code Sec. 362(b)].

LIQUIDATIONS

¶22,120 LIQUIDATIONS IN GENERAL

A corporation is considered in liquidation when it ceases to be a going concern and its activities consist merely of winding up its affairs, paying its debts and distributing any remaining assets to shareholders. The legal dissolution of the corporation is not required. Distributions in complete or partial liquidations are treated as a full or part payment in exchange for its stock. Therefore, *liquidation* means terminating the corporate enterprise. Generally, a reorganization means a continuation of the same enterprise in a modified corporate form.

In liquidation, a corporation may either dispose of its property for cash and distribute the cash, or distribute its property to the shareholders in exchange for its capital stock. A sale or exchange of the capital stock by its shareholders will usually result in capital gain or loss to them. The following items are involved in the subject of liquidations:

- Gain or loss on property distributions in liquidation [¶ 22,125];
- Liquidation of a subsidiary [¶ 22,130];
- Basis of property received in liquidation [¶ 22,130]; and
- Liquidating distributions [Ch. 2].

¶22,125 GAIN OR LOSS ON PROPERTY DISTRIBUTIONS IN LIQUIDATION

Generally, a corporation recognizes gain or loss on a distribution of its property in complete liquidation, as if the corporation had sold the property to the distributee-shareholders at its fair market value [Code Sec. 336].

If the distributed property is subject to a liability and the shareholders assume a liability connected with the distribution, and the amount of the liability exceeds the fair market value, the property value is deemed to be not less than the amount of the liability. Thus, in this case, the corporation generally recognizes gain to the extent the liability exceeds its basis [Code Sec. 336(b)].

There is, however, an exception to the general recognition rule [discussed below]. The distribution to a parent corporation by an 80-percent-owned liquidating subsidiary is not subject to current recognition of gain [Code Sec. 337]. Within 30 days after adopting a liquidation plan, the liquidating corporation must file Form 966 with the IRS [Code Sec. 6043; Reg. § 1.6043-1].

.01 Background and Purpose

As a general rule, corporate earnings from sales of appreciated property are taxed twice—first to the corporation when the sale occurs, and again to the shareholders when the net proceeds are distributed as dividends. Under prior law, an important exception (commonly known as the *General Utilities* doctrine which grew out of a Supreme Court case, *General Utilities & Operating Co.*,[72] permitting tax-free liquidations to avoid multiple taxation of the same gain) permitted corporations to escape tax at the corporate level by distributing appreciated property to its shareholders and on certain liquidating sales of property. Broadly speaking, the *General Utilities* doctrine has been repealed. Thus, gain or loss is recognized by a corporation on a liquidating sale of its assets or on a distribution of its property in complete liquidation.

[72] *General Utilities & Operating Co.*, 36-1 USTC ¶ 9012, 296 US 200 (1935).

.02 The Code Sec. 336(e) Election—Certain Stock Sales and Distributions May Be Treated as Asset Transfers

Code Sec. 336(e) was enacted as part of the repeal of the *General Utilities* doctrine in 1986 to authorize the IRS to issue regulations that would allow taxpayers to elect to treat the sale, exchange, or distribution of at least 80 percent (by vote and value) of a corporation's stock (a qualified stock disposition or QSD) as a deemed disposition of the corporation's underlying assets. Code Sec. 336(e) provides relief from potential multiple taxation of the same economic gain, which can result by taxing a transfer of appreciated corporate stock without providing a corresponding step-up in the basis of the corporation's assets. The IRS issued final Code Sec. 336(e) regulations in 2013 and they are applicable to a QSD (80 percent of the stock) that occurs on or after May 15, 2013. The Code Sec. 336(e) is similar to the election under Code Sec. 338(h)(10) (which provides that a selling consolidated group can elect to recognize gain or loss on the deemed sale of a target's assets) for purchases of stock of a target corporation except to the extent inconsistent with Code Sec. 336(e) [Reg. § 1.336-1(a)].

A Code 336(e) election is available if a domestic corporation (seller) or S corporation shareholders dispose of stock of another corporation (target) in a qualified stock disposition. Once made, the Code Sec. 336(e) election is irrevocable [Reg. § 1.336-2(a)]. A qualified stock disposition is defined as any transaction or series of transactions in which stock of a domestic corporation meeting the requirements of Code Sec. 1504(a)(2) is sold, exchanged or distributed, or any combination thereof, by another domestic corporation or by S corporation shareholders in a disposition during the 12-month disposition period [Reg. § 1.336-1(b)(6)]. The 12-month disposition period is the 12-month period beginning with the date of the first sale, exchange or distribution of stock included in the qualified stock disposition [Reg. § 1.336-1(b)(7)]. A disposition date is, with respect to any corporation, the first day on which there is a qualified stock disposition with respect to the stock of that corporation [Reg. § 1.336-1(b)(8)].

A disposition is any sale, exchange, or distribution of stock, but only if (i) the basis of the stock in the hands of the purchaser is not determined in whole or in part by reference to the adjusted basis of the stock in the hands of the person from whom the stock is acquired or under Code Sec. 1014(a); (ii) the stock is not sold, exchanged, or distributed in a transaction to which Code Sec. 351, 354, 355, or 356 applies and is not sold, exchanged, or distributed in any transaction described in regulations in which the transferor does not recognize the entire amount of the gain or loss realized in the transaction; however, an exception applies to a distribution of stock to an unrelated person in which the full amount of stock gain would be recognized under Code Sec. 355(d)(2) or (e)(2); and (iii) the stock is not sold, exchanged, or distributed to a related person (relationship is determined generally by applying the attribution rules of Code Sec. 318(a), other than Code Sec. 318(a)(4) [Reg. § 1.336-1(b)(5), (12)].

A seller is a domestic corporation that makes a qualified stock disposition and includes a transferor and distributor of target stock [Reg. § 1.336-1(b)(1)]. All members of a seller's consolidated group are treated as a single seller, regardless of which member or members actually dispose of any stock. Any dispositions of stock made by members of the same consolidated group are treated as made by one corporation, and any stock owned by members of the same consolidated group and not disposed of is treated as stock retained by the seller [Reg. § 1.336-2(g) (2)]. Thus, a Code Sec. 336(e) election is available to a seller that directly owns stock of a target meeting the requirements of Code Sec. 1504(a) (2) and to sellers that are members of a consolidated group for the tax year including the disposition date and that, in the aggregate, own stock of the target meeting the requirements of Code Sec. 1504(a) (2). Only an amount of stock meeting the requirements of Code Sec. 1504(a) (2) needs to be disposed of, which means that not every share of stock owned by the seller needs to be disposed of. Thus, the seller or a member of the seller's consolidated group can retain a portion of the target stock.

A purchaser is any person or persons who acquire or receive stock of a target in a qualified stock disposition. This includes both a transferee and distributee of target stock [Reg. § 1.336-1(b) (2)]. Thus, a Code Sec. 336(e) election is available for sales, exchanges or distributions of target stock to both corporate and noncorporate purchasers. However, the target stock may not be sold, exchanged or distributed to a related person [Reg. § 1.336-1(b) (5) (i) (C)]. A target is any domestic corporation the stock of which is sold, exchanged, or distributed in a qualified stock disposition. An S corporation target is a target that is an S corporation immediately before the disposition date [Reg. § 1.336-1(b) (3)].

The final regulations provide two different models for the deemed transactions treated as occurring if a Code Sec. 336(e) election is made. The first model, also called the basic model, generally follows the same structure used for the deemed transactions resulting from the making of a Code Sec. 338(h) (10) election and is applicable to all qualified stock dispositions (including those consisting of taxable distributions of target stock) other than distributions described in Code Sec. 355(d) (2) or (e) (2). The second model, also called the sale-to-self model, applies to Code Sec. 355(d) (2) or (e) (2) distributions. Under the basic model, if a Code Sec. 336(e) election is made for a qualified stock disposition not described in Code Sec. 355(d) (2) or (e) (2), the seller or S corporation shareholders are not treated as having sold, exchanged, or distributed the stock disposed of in the qualified stock disposition. Instead, the "old" target is treated as selling its assets to an unrelated person in a single transaction at the close of the disposition date, but before the deemed liquidation described below (deemed asset disposition). The assets are deemed sold in exchange for the aggregate deemed asset disposition price (ADADP) determined under Reg. § 1.336-3. ADADP is allocated among the assets in the same manner as the aggregate deemed sale price (ADSP) is allocated under Reg. § 1,338-6 and Reg. 1.338-7 in order to determine the amount realized from each of the assets sold. The old target realizes the tax consequences from the deemed asset disposition before the close of the disposition date while it is owned by the seller or the S corporation shareholders. If the old target is an S corporation target, its S election continues in effect through the close of the disposition date [Reg. § 1.336-2(b) (1) (i) (A)].

The old target recognizes all of the gain realized on the deemed asset disposition. It also generally recognizes losses realized on the deemed asset disposition. However, the final regulations disallow a portion of the old target's net loss (that is, losses realized in excess of target's realized gains) recognized on the deemed asset disposition that is attributable to a distribution of target stock during the 12-month disposition period, whether or not the stock is distributed as part of the qualified stock disposition (disallowed loss rule) [Reg. § 1.336-2(b)(1)(i)(B)]. Thus, to the extent the disallowed loss rule of the final regulations applies, losses are allowed up to the amount of gains and any excess losses are permanently disallowed.

The total disallowed loss is determined by multiplying the net loss realized on the deemed asset disposition by the disallowed loss fraction. The numerator of the disallowed loss fraction is the value of the target stock, determined on the disposition date, distributed by the seller during the 12-month disposition period, whether or not the stock is distributed as part of the qualified stock disposition. The denominator of the disallowed loss fraction is the sum of the value of the target stock, determined on the disposition date, disposed of by a sale or exchange in the qualified stock disposition during the 12-month disposition period and the value of the target stock, determined on the disposition date, distributed by the seller during the 12-month disposition period, whether or not a part of the qualified stock disposition.

The amount of the disallowed loss allocated to each asset disposed of in the deemed asset disposition is determined by multiplying the total amount of the disallowed loss by the loss allocation fraction. The numerator of the loss allocation fraction is the amount of loss realized with respect to the asset and the denominator of the loss allocation fraction is the sum of the amount of losses realized with respect to each loss asset disposed of in the deemed asset disposition. To the extent the old target's losses from the deemed asset disposition are not disallowed under this rule, such losses may be disallowed under other provisions of the Code or general principles of tax law, in the same manner as if such assets were actually sold to an unrelated person [Reg. § 1.336-2(b)(1)(i)(B)(2)(iii)].

In the case of tiered targets, if an asset of the target is the stock of a subsidiary for which a Code Sec. 336(e) election is made, any gain or loss realized on the deemed sale of the stock of the subsidiary is disregarded in determining the amount of the disallowed loss. For purposes of determining the amount of disallowed loss on the deemed asset disposition by a subsidiary of target for which an election is made, the amount of the subsidiary stock deemed sold in the deemed asset disposition of the target's assets multiplied by the disallowed loss fraction with respect to the corporation that is deemed to have disposed of stock of the subsidiary is considered to have been distributed. In determining the disallowed loss fraction with respect to the deemed asset disposition of any subsidiary of the target, any sale, exchange, or distribution of its stock that was made after the disposition date is disregarded if such stock was included in the deemed asset disposition of the corporation deemed to have disposed of the subsidiary stock [Reg. § 1.336-2(b)(1)(i)(B)(2)(iv)].

The "new" target is treated as acquiring all of its assets from an unrelated person in a single transaction at the close of the disposition date, but before the deemed liquidation described below (deemed asset purchase). The assets are deemed purchased for an amount equal to the adjusted grossed-up basis (AGUB) determined under Reg. § 1.336-4. The new target allocates the consideration deemed paid in the transaction in the same manner as it would under Reg. § 1.338-6 and Reg. § 1.338-7 in order to determine the basis in each of the purchased assets. The new target remains liable for the tax liabilities of the old target, including the tax liability for the deemed disposition tax consequences [Reg. § 1.336-2(b)(1)(ii)].

The old target and the seller (or the S corporation shareholders) are treated as if, before the close of the disposition date, after the deemed asset disposition, and while the target is owned by the seller or the S corporation shareholders, the old target transferred all of the consideration deemed received from the new target in the deemed asset disposition to the seller or the S corporation shareholders, any S corporation election for the old target terminated, and the old target ceased to exist (deemed liquidation). The transfer from the old target to the seller or the S corporation shareholders is characterized for federal income tax purposes in the same manner as if the parties had actually engaged in the transactions deemed to occur under these regulations and taking into account other transactions that actually occurred or are deemed to occur. In most cases, the transfer will be treated as a distribution in complete liquidation to which Code Sec. 331 or 332 and Code Sec. 336 or 337 apply. However, the transfer may also be treated, for example, as a distribution in pursuance of a plan of reorganization, or a distribution in complete cancellation or redemption of all of its stock [Reg. § 1.336-2(b) (1) (iii)].

In the case of a distribution of target stock in a qualified stock disposition, the seller (the distributor) is deemed to purchase from an unrelated person, on the disposition date, immediately after the deemed liquidation of the old target, the amount of stock distributed in the qualified stock disposition (new target stock) and to have distributed such new target stock to its shareholders. The seller recognizes no gain or loss on the distribution of such stock [Reg. § 1.336-2(b) (1) (iv)]. If the seller or an S corporation shareholder retains any target stock after the disposition date, the seller or the S corporation shareholder is treated as purchasing the retained stock from an unrelated person (also referred to as new target stock for purposes of the regulations) on the day after the disposition date for its fair market value. The holding period for the retained stock starts on the day after the disposition date [Reg. § 1.336-2(b) (1) (v)].

Under the sale-to-self model, if a Code Sec. 336(e) election is made with respect to a qualified stock disposition resulting, in whole or in part, from a disposition described in Code Sec. 355(d) (2) or (e) (2), the old target is treated as selling its assets to an unrelated person in a single transaction at the close of the disposition date in exchange for the ADADP which is allocated among the assets in the same manner as ADSP is allocated under Reg.§ 1.338-6 and Reg. § 1.338-7 in order to determine the amount realized from each of the sold assets. The old target realizes the tax consequences from the deemed asset disposition before the close of the disposition date while it is owned by the seller. Under this model, the old target is not deemed to liquidate after the deemed asset disposition [Reg. § 1.336-2(b) (2) (i) (A)].

The old target recognizes all of the gain realized on the deemed asset disposition. Losses realized on the deemed asset disposition are generally recognized by the old target. However, a portion of the old target's net loss (that is, losses realized in excess of target's realized gains) recognized on the deemed asset disposition that is attributable to a distribution of target stock during the 12-month disposition period is disallowed under the disallowed loss rule. As discussed above, the total disallowed loss is determined by multiplying the net loss realized on the deemed asset disposition by the disallowed loss fraction, and the amount of the disallowed loss allocated to each asset disposed of in the deemed asset disposition is determined by multiplying the total amount of the disallowed loss by the loss allocation fraction [Reg. § 1.336-2(b) (2) (i) (B)].

Immediately after the deemed asset disposition, the old target is treated as acquiring all of its assets from an unrelated person in a single, separate transaction at the close of the disposition date (but before the deemed distribution described below) in exchange for an amount equal to the AGUB. The old target allocates the consideration deemed paid in the transaction in the same manner as the new target would under Reg. § 1.338-6 and Reg. § 1.338-7 in order to determine the basis in each of the purchased assets [Reg. § 1.336-2(b)(2)(ii)].

In the case of parent-subsidiary chains of corporations making Code Sec. 336(e) elections, the deemed asset disposition of a higher-tier subsidiary is considered to precede the deemed asset disposition of a lower-tier subsidiary, and the old target's deemed purchase of all its assets is considered to precede the deemed asset disposition of a lower-tier subsidiary [Reg. § 1.336-2(b)(2)(C)]. Immediately after the old target's deemed purchase of its assets, the seller is treated as distributing the stock of the old target actually distributed to its shareholders in the qualified stock disposition. No gain or loss is recognized by the seller on the distribution. Additionally, if stock of the target is sold, exchanged, or distributed outside of the Code Sec. 355 transaction but still as part of a qualified stock disposition described, in whole or in part, in Code Sec. 355(d)(2) or (e)(2), no gain or loss is recognized by the seller on such sale, exchange, or distribution [Reg. § 1.336-2(b)(2)(iii)(B)].

If the seller retains any target stock after the disposition date, the seller is treated as having disposed of the retained old target stock, on the disposition date, in a transaction in which no gain or loss is recognized, and then, on the day after the disposition date, purchasing the stock so retained from an unrelated person for its fair market value. The holding period for the retained stock starts on the day after the disposition date [Reg. § 1.336-2(b)(2)(iv)].

The Code Sec. 336(e) election does not generally affect the federal income tax consequences to the purchaser with respect to the acquisition of the target stock. However, the tax consequences of the deemed asset disposition and liquidation of the target may affect the purchaser's consequences. For example, if the seller distributes the stock of the target to its shareholders in a qualified stock disposition for which a Code Sec. 336(e) election is made, any increase in the seller's earnings and profits as a result of the old target's deemed asset disposition and liquidation into the seller may increase the amount of a distribution to the shareholders constituting a dividend [Reg. § 1.336-2(c)]. A minority shareholder of the target recognizes gain or loss (as permitted under the general principles of tax law) on its sale, exchange, or distribution of the target stock. A minority shareholder who retains its target stock does not recognize gain or loss with respect to its shares of the target stock. The minority shareholder's basis and holding period for that target stock are not affected by the Code Sec. 336(e) election. Notwithstanding this treatment of the minority shareholder, if a Code Sec. 336(e) election is made, the target will still be treated as disposing of its assets in the deemed asset disposition [Reg. § 1.336-2(d)].

In order to make a Code Sec. 336(e) election, the seller(s), or in the case of an S corporation target, all of the S corporation shareholders, and the target must enter into a written, binding agreement to make the election and a Code Sec. 336(e) election statement must be attached to the relevant return [Reg. § 1.336-2(h)]. If the seller(s) and the target are members of a consolidated group, the election statement is filed on a timely filed consolidated return and the common parent of the consolidated group must provide a copy of the Code Sec. 336(e) election statement to the target on or before the due date (including extensions) of the consolidated group's consolidated federal income tax return. If the target is an S corporation, the election statement is filed on the S corporation's timely filed return. If the seller and the target are members of an affiliated group but do not join in the filing of a consolidated return, the election statement is filed with both the seller's and the target's timely filed returns [Reg. § 1.336-2(h)].

The old target and the new target should file Form 8883, *Asset Allocation Statement Under Section 338*, to report the results of the deemed asset disposition, making appropriate adjustments as necessary to account for a Code Sec. 336(e) election. The final regulations permit taxpayers to make a protective Code Sec. 336(e) election if they are unsure as to whether a transaction constitutes a qualified stock disposition. If such an election is made, it will not have any effect if the transaction does not constitute a qualified stock disposition, but it will otherwise be binding and irrevocable [Reg. § 1.336-2(j)].

.03 Nonrecognition on Distributions in Complete Liquidations

Liquidating transfers within an affiliated group are a nonrecognition event. The basis in the hands of the corporation receiving the property is generally the same as it was in the hands of the transferor corporation (carryover basis). However, if gain or loss is recognized by the liquidating corporation with respect to such property, the basis of the property is the fair market value at the time of the distribution [Code Sec. 334(b)(1)]. For liquidations in which an 80 percent corporate shareholder receives property with a carryover basis, nonrecognition of gain or loss applies for any property actually distributed to the controlling corporate shareholder. Gain, but not loss, is recognized to a minority shareholder that receives property in such a liquidation. Nonrecognition is generally denied under the 80 percent corporate shareholder exception when the shareholder is a tax-exempt corporation or a foreign corporation [¶ 22,130] [Code Secs. 337, 367].

A corporation that transfers all or substantially all of its assets to a tax-exempt entity would recognize gain or loss as if the transferred assets were sold at their fair market values [Reg. § 1.337(d)-4(a)(1)]. However, no gain or loss would be recognized on transferred assets that are used by the exempt entity in an activity subject to the unrelated business income tax. In that case, gain would be recognized when the exempt entity sold the assets or stopped using them in an unrelated trade or business [Reg. § 1.337(d)-4(b)(1)].

.04 Consequences of Property Transfer to RICs and REITs

It is well established that C corporations must recognize gain when they distribute appreciated property in connection with a complete liquidation [Code Secs. 336, 337]. In order to circumvent this rule when distributing appreciated property, C corporations have converted to pass-through entities entity as S corporations [see Ch. 21], RICs [see ¶ 23,075] or REITs [see ¶ 23,095] which are not taxed at the corporate level. In order to prevent this tax-avoidance scheme, Reg. § 1.337(d)-7(a) and Reg. § 1,337(d)-7(b)(1) generally provide that if property of a C corporation becomes the property of a RIC or

REIT by the qualification of that C corporation as a RIC or REIT or by the transfer of assets of that C corporation to a RIC or REIT (a conversion transaction), then the RIC or REIT will be subject to tax on the net built-in gain in the converted property under the rules of Code Sec. 1374 (called the "general rule"). This general rule, however, does not apply if the C corporation transferor makes a "deemed sale election" provided for under Reg. § 1.337(d)-7(c) to recognize gain and loss as if it sold the converted property to an unrelated person at fair market value [Reg. § 1.337(d)-7(a)(1)].

The general rule will not apply: (1) to the extent that the conversion transaction qualifies for nonrecognition treatment as a like-kind exchange under Code Sec. 1031 or as an involuntary conversions under Code Sec. 1033 (the exchange exception); (2) to a conversion transaction when the C corporation that owned the converted property is a tax-exempt entity *to the extent* that gain would not be subject to tax if a deemed sale election were made [Reg. § 1.337(d)-7(d)]. Thus, the tax-exempt exception applies to the extent the deemed sale gain with respect to the converted property would be exempt from tax under Code Sec. 501(a) because that portion of the gain would not be subject to tax under any code provision had a deemed sale election been made. This is the case even though the tax-exempt exception does not apply to the extent the deemed sale gain with respect to the converted property would be subject to tax under Code Sec. 511.

Example 22-61: X is a REIT, Y is a C corporation, and X and Y are not related. X owned a building that it leased for commercial use (Property A). Y owned a building leased for commercial use (Property B). On January 1, Year 3, Y transferred Property B to X in exchange for Property A in a nonrecognition transaction under Code Sec. 1031(a). Immediately before the exchange, Properties A and B each had a value of $100, X had an adjusted basis of $60 in Property A, Y had an adjusted basis of $70 in Property B. The transfer of property (Property B) by Y (a C corporation) to X (a REIT) is a conversion transaction that qualifies as a nonrecognition transaction under Code Sec. 1031(a) as to Y; thus, Y does not recognize any of its $30 gain [Reg. § 1.337(d)-7(d)(3)(ii), Ex. 1].

.05 Limitations on the Recognition of Losses

1. A liquidating corporation cannot recognize loss for any distribution of property to a related person (under Code Sec. 267), unless the property is distributed to all shareholders on a pro rata basis *and* the property was not acquired by the liquidating corporation in a Sec. 351 transaction or as a contribution to capital during the five years preceding the distribution [Code Sec. 336(d)]. The corporation can, however, recognize losses in the case of a distribution in a *complete* liquidation [Code Sec. 267(a)(1)].
2. If property is contributed to the corporation in advance of its liquidation primarily to recognize a loss on the property's sale or distribution and eliminate or limit corporate level gain, the basis (for loss) of any property acquired by the corporation in a Sec. 351 transaction or as a capital contribution is reduced (not below zero) by the excess of the property's basis on the contribution date over its fair market value on that date. It is presumed (except as provided in regulations) that any Sec. 351

transaction or capital contribution within a two-year period of the adoption of the plan of complete liquidation has such a principal purpose. It is also presumed that acquisitions after the adoption of the plan have such a principal purpose [Code Sec. 336(d)].

.06 Nonliquidating Distributions of Appreciated Property

The distributing corporation must generally recognize gain if appreciated property (other than an obligation of the corporation) is distributed to its shareholders outside of complete liquidation [Code Sec. 311(b)].

.07 Conversion from C Corporation to S Corporation

The S corporation must recognize gain on a sale or distribution of appreciated property to its shareholders to the extent the appreciation occurred (a) when the corporation was a C corporation and (b) within ten years after the S election was made. However, once the S corporation waits out the 10-year period, no corporate-level tax is imposed on a sale or distribution of the property [Ch. 21] [Code Sec. 1374].

The liquidation of a C corporation into an S corporation is governed by the generally applicable subchapter C rules, including the provisions of Code Secs. 332 and 337 allowing the tax-free liquidation of a corporation into its parent corporation [¶ 22,130]. Following a tax-free liquidation, the built-in gains of the liquidating corporation may later be subject to tax under Code Sec. 1374 on a subsequent disposition [Ch. 21]. An S corporation will also be eligible to make a Code Sec. 338 election resulting in the immediate recognition of all the acquired C corporation's gains and losses (and the resulting imposition of a tax) [Ch. 21].

¶22,130 NONTAXABLE LIQUIDATION OF SUBSIDIARY

A parent corporation recognizes no gain or loss if it receives property (including money) in a complete liquidation of a subsidiary (except as described below for the stock purchase election) provided the parent corporation owns 80 percent of the value and voting power of the subsidiary [Code Sec. 332(b)]. In addition, the following requirements must be met [Code Sec. 332(b); Reg. § § 1.332-2 through 1.332-4]:

- The parent corporation must be the owner of stock in the liquidating corporation meeting the requirements of Code Sec. 1504(a)(2) applicable in determining whether that corporation qualifies as a member of an affiliated group [Ch. 20] [Code Sec. 332(b)]. Such ownership must exist on the date the liquidation plan is adopted and continue until property is received in liquidation; and
- The subsidiary's distribution is in complete cancellation or redemption of all of the subsidiary's stock; and
- The distribution of all of the subsidiary's property is made to the parent corporation in the same tax year, unless there is a series of distributions. In that case, the transfer must be made within three years from the close of the tax year in which the first distribution is made [Code Sec. 332(b)(2), (3); Reg. § 1.332-3, -4].

NOTE: For a liquidation of a subsidiary involving a foreign corporation, see Code Sec. 367, which provides that a liquidation into a foreign parent is taxed to the liquidating corporation, except to the extent provided in Reg. § 1.367(e)(2).

▶ **OBSERVATION:** The gain or loss of minority shareholders is determined without regard to Code Sec. 332 because it does not apply to that part of distributions in liquidation received by minority shareholders [Reg. § 1.332-5]. Additionally, liquidations into a tax-exempt parent (as long as the exempt parent does not use the property in an unrelated trade or business) or a foreign corporation do not qualify for this nonrecognition rule [Code Sec. 336(d)(3)].

Gain is recognized on a distribution to a corporation that does not qualify as an 80 percent owner without applying a consolidated return regulation [Reg. § 1.1502-34], which aggregates the stock of affiliated group members for determining if the 80 percent ownership is met. [Code Sec. 355(b)(2)(D)].

.01 Basis of Property Received

Generally, the parent corporation's basis for the property received is the same as the subsidiary's basis [Code Sec. 334(b)(1); Reg. § 1.334-1]. If, however, gain or loss is recognized by the liquidating corporation, the parent corporation's basis for the property received is the fair market value at the time of the distribution [Code Sec. 334(b)(1)].

.02 Election to Treat Stock Purchase as Asset Acquisitions

Code Sec. 338 attempts to treat as equals for tax purposes the purchase of an 80 percent or more interest in the stock of the target corporation with a purchase of the target's assets. In general, the goals are to: (1) ensure that the target and its shareholders bear the same tax burden on a sale of the target's stock that they would have incurred on a sale of its assets followed by a complete liquidation; (2) provide the buyer with a cost basis in the assets of the target; and (3) terminate the tax attributes of the target and start afresh, without regard to whether or not the target is actually liquidated.

To achieve these objectives, Code Sec. 338 generally permits an acquiring corporation that purchases an 80-percent or greater interest in another corporation during a period of no more than 12 months, to make an election to treat the stock purchase as a purchase of all of the target's assets for their fair market value in a single transaction [Code Sec. 338(a)]. As a result of this election, the old target's tax attributes are eliminated. Benefit: the basis of the assets will be stepped up to the purchase price of the stock thus increasing depreciation deductions. To make the election under Code Sec. 338, file Form 8023, *Elections Under Section 338 for Corporations Making Qualified Stock Purchases.* Once made, the election is irrevocable [Code Sec. 338(g)(3)]. In addition to Form 8023, a Form 8883, *Asset Allocation Statement Under Section 338* describing the details of the deal must be filed.

Generally, to set up a purchase of stock to obtain assets, the acquiring corporation must: (1) make a qualifying purchase of the stock of the target corporation and (2) not later than the 15th day of the ninth month following the month of the acquisition date make the appropriate election. A qualifying purchase is a purchase of stock meeting the requirements of Code Sec. 1504(a)(2) applicable in determining whether that corporation qualifies as a member of an affiliated group [Ch. 20], during a 12-month acquisition period [Code Sec. 338(d)(3)].

Once the Code Sec. 338 election is made, the following tax consequences result:

- The target (old target) is treated as if it sold all of its assets at the close of the acquisition date at fair market value in a single transaction and the target must recognize gain or loss on the hypothetical asset sale, after which it returns as a new corporation with a cost basis in its assets and none of its former tax attributes [Code Sec. 338(b)].
- The target corporation is treated as a new corporation which purchased all of the assets as of the beginning of day after the acquisition date [Code Sec. 338(a)(2)].

Type of Code Sec. 338 Elections

An election to treat a qualified stock purchase as an asset purchase is either an express election under Code Sec. 338(g) or deemed election under Code Sec. 338(e).

If the acquiring corporation makes a Code Sec. 338(g) express election, old target's gain or loss from the deemed asset sale is included in old target's final return unless it is a member of a consolidated group or is an S corporation.

Under Code Sec. 338(h)(10), if there is a qualified stock purchase of a target that is a member of a consolidated group, the acquiring corporation and selling consolidated group can jointly elect to have the selling consolidated group recognize (and report) gain or loss as though the target sold all of its assets in a single taxable transaction while still a member of the selling group, and then liquidated.

No gain or loss is recognized by the target corporation as a result of an election by the acquiring corporation. However, the election will trigger any depreciation or investment credit recapture by the target corporation and will terminate its tax attributes, such as net operating loss carryovers. Normally, recapture items will be associated with the final return of the target corporation for the tax year ending on the date of acquisition. However, if for some reason recapture income is included in the income of the new corporation that is included in the consolidated return filed with the acquiring corporation, it must be separately accounted for and may not be absorbed by losses or deductions of other members of the group.

> **NOTE:** The depreciable assets of a target corporation qualify as ACRS or MACRS recovery property. Moreover, the acquiring corporation is not bound by the target corporation's ACRS or MACRS recovery period and method.

***Purchase* Defined**

An Code Sec. 338 election may be made only for a transaction that qualifies as a *purchase* within the meaning of Code Sec. 338(h)(3), which provides that stock will not be considered to be purchased if it is acquired:

- In a carryover basis transaction;
- From a decedent;
- In an exchange to which Code Secs. 351, 354, 355 or 356 apply;
- In a transaction in which the transferor does not recognize the entire amount of the gain or loss; or
- From a related person such as a family member, partnership, estate or trust whose stock is attributed (options don't count) to the acquiring corporation under Code Sec. 318(a) [Code Sec. 338(h)(3)(A); Reg. § 1.338-2(b)(2)].

Stock acquired from a related corporation (including stock acquired in a carryover basis transaction following a qualified stock purchase and election with respect to the transferor) will satisfy the purchase requirement if at least 50 percent in value of the related corporation's stock was purchased [Code Sec. 338(h)(3)(C)]. The relationship will be tested immediately after the transaction [Reg. § 1.338-3(b)(3)(ii)].

The acquiring corporation is not treated as having purchased stock in a third corporation that it constructively owns as a result of purchasing the stock in another (the second) corporation. Instead, if a qualified stock purchase and election are made with respect to the second corporation, the deemed purchase of the third corporation's stock will, if it satisfies the 80 percent ownership requirement, be treated as a qualified stock purchase permitting an election by the second corporation (as discussed further below) [Code Sec. 338(h)(3)(B)].

> **Example 22-62:** XYZ Corp. acquires 80 percent of the stock of Target Corp. which owns 80 percent of ABC Corp. stock. XYZ Corp. can't elect to treat ABC Corp. as a target because it is treated as owning only 64 percent (80 percent of 80 percent) of its stock. However, when the Sec. 338 election is made, Target Corp. is treated as having sold all of its assets, and as a new corporation that purchased the assets, including 80 percent of the stock of, ABC Corp. Target Corp. can elect to have its deemed purchase of ABC Corp.'s stock treated as an asset acquisition.

Qualifying for Code Sec. 338 Election

To make a Code Sec. 338(h)(10) election the following conditions must exist [Reg. § 1.338(h)(10)-1(d)]:

- P must make a qualified stock purchase of T stock from either a selling consolidated group, a selling affiliate or from S corporation shareholders. Acquisition of corporate stock could be from a bankrupt parent corporation,[73] or a foreign subsidiary.[74] A purchase of a share of stock in target occurs so long as more than a nominal amount is paid for the shares. Stock in a target affiliate acquired by new target in the deemed asset sale of target's own assets would be considered purchased if under the general principles of tax law, new target is considered to own stock of the target affiliate meeting the requirements of Code Sec. 1504(a)(2), notwithstanding the fact that no purchase price may be allocated to target's stock in the target affiliate [Reg. § 1.338-3(b)(2)];
- A Code Sec. 338(h)(10) election is made jointly by P and T shareholders on Form 8023. The instructions on the form provide more guidance on making the election. The Code Sec. 338(h)(10) election must be made not later than the 15th day of the ninth month beginning after the month in which the acquisition date occurs [Code Sec. 338(g)(1)]. The acquisition date is the day within the 12-month acquisition period on which the 80 percent purchase requirement is satisfied [Code Sec. 338(h)(2)]. Rev. Proc. 2003-33,[75] provides that corporate taxpayers have an automatic

---

[73] *Ralphs Grocery Co.*, 101 TCM 1087, Dec. 58,529(M), TC Memo. 2011-25.

[74] LTR 201220020 (Feb. 17, 2012).

[75] Rev. Proc. 2003-33, 2003-1 CB 803.

12-month extension of time to make an election under Code Sec. 338 on Form 8023. To benefit from the automatic extension taxpayers must file Form 8023 no later than 12 months after the discovery of the failure to file the election. A single statement, filed under penalties of perjury by all required filers, must be attached to the Form 8023;

- The Code Sec. 338(h)(10) election is irrevocable [Code Sec. 338(g)(3)];
- A combined deemed sale return must be filed for all targets from a single selling consolidated group; and
- Gains and losses recognized on the deemed sale of assets by targets included in the combined return are treated as the gains and losses of a single target.

Consequences of Code Sec. 338(h)(10) Election

If a Code Sec. 338(h)(10) election is made, the following consequences will result.

- **The transaction will be treated as a taxable sale of all old T's assets.** Old T will recognize gain or loss as if, while old T was a member of the consolidated group, it sold all of its assets in a single transaction as of the close of the acquisition date (but before the deemed liquidation). Old T's gain or loss on each assets and the computation of the deemed selling price is determined under Reg. § 1.338(h)(10)-1(f).
- **Deemed liquidation for old target.** Old T is treated as if, whereas T is a member of the selling consolidated group, it distributed all of its assets in complete liquidation. This deemed liquidation is considered to take place as of the close of the acquisition date but after the deemed sale of its assets.
- **Basis of T stock not acquired.** The basis of T stock retained by the selling consolidated group is its fair market value.
- **Nonrecognition treatment for target stock.** No gain or loss is recognized on the sale or exchange by the S group (or the selling affiliate or an S corporation shareholder) to P of stock of T included in the QSP. This gain is ignored. If T is an S corporation immediately before T's acquisition date, the sale or exchange of old T stock to P on the acquisition date does not result in termination of the S election.

Example 22-63: S1 owns all of the T stock and T owns all of the stock of T1 and T2. S1 is the common parent of a consolidated group that includes T, T1, and T2. P makes a qualified stock purchase of all of the T stock from S1. A Code Sec. 338(h)(10) election is made for T and for the deemed purchase of T1. An election is not made for T2. S1 does not recognize gain or loss on the sale of the T stock and T does not recognize gain of loss on the sale of the T1 stock because T and T1 are Code Sec. 338(h)(10) targets. Thus, gain or loss realized on the sale of T or T1 stock is not taken into account in earnings and profits. However, because the election was not made for T2, T must recognize any gain or loss realized on the deemed sale of the T2 stock.

Example 22-64: The results would be the same if S1, T, T1, and T2 are not members of any consolidated group, because S1 and T are selling affiliates [Reg. § 1.338(h)(10)-1(e), Ex. 1].

- **Availability of Code Sec. 338(h)(10) election in certain multi-step transactions.** Notwithstanding anything to the contrary in Reg. § 1.338-3(c)(1)(i), a Code Sec. 338(h)(10) election may be made for T where P's acquisition of T stock, viewed independently, constitutes a qualified stock purchase and, after the stock acquisition, T merges or liquidates into P (or another member of the affiliated group that includes P), whether or not, under relevant provisions of law, including the step transaction doctrine, the acquisition of the T stock and the merger or liquidation of T qualify as a tax-free reorganization. If a Code Sec. 338(h)(10) election is made in a case where the acquisition of T stock followed by a merger or liquidation of T into P qualifies as a tax-free reorganization, P's acquisition of T stock is treated as a qualified stock purchase and is not treated as part of a reorganization [Reg. § 1.338(h)(10)-1(c)(2)].
- **Estimated tax.** If a transaction eligible for the election under Code Sec. 338(h)(10) occurs, estimated tax would be determined based on the stock sale, unless and until the parties agree to make a Code Sec. 338(h)(10) election, on which estimated tax consequences would be based on the deemed asset sale [Code Sec. 338(h)(13)].

CARRYOVERS

¶22,135 CARRYOVERS TO SUCCESSOR CORPORATION

When the assets of a corporation are acquired by a corporation in a tax-free liquidation or reorganization, the successor corporation may, under conditions described below, carry over certain tax benefits, privileges, elective rights, and obligations [¶ 22,140] of the predecessor corporation [Code Sec. 381(a)(c); Reg. § 1.381(a)-1].

.01 When a Carryover Is Allowed

The carryover provisions apply to the following.

Liquidation of a Subsidiary

When the controlling parent corporation takes over the property of a subsidiary in a complete liquidation of the subsidiary [see ¶ 22,130][Code Sec. 381(a)(1); Reg. § 1.381(a)-1(b)(1)].

Reorganizations

When the successor corporation acquires assets of another corporation in the following types of reorganization:

- A statutory merger or consolidation (Type A) [¶ 22,015];
- An acquisition by the corporation of properties of another corporation for stock (Type C) [¶ 22,025];
- A transfer of assets for controlling stock, if there is a single transferee corporation and the transferor distributes all of the stock, securities and properties it receives as well as its other properties under a plan of reorganization (certain Type D) [¶ 22,030];

- A mere change in identity, form, or place of organization of one corporation (Type F) [¶ 22,040]; and
- An insolvency reorganization, if there is a single transferee corporation and the transferor distributes all of the stock, securities and properties it receives as well as its other properties under a plan of reorganization (certain Type G; ¶ 22,045) [Code Sec. 381(a)(2); Reg. § 1.381(a)-1(b)(1)].

NOTE: The carryover provisions do not apply to partial liquidations, divisive reorganizations, or reorganizations not listed above [Reg. § 1.381(a)-1(b)(3)]. A Type B reorganization [¶ 22,020] is not included since only the stock is acquired and the controlled corporation remains in existence. However, if it is liquidated, there will be a Type C reorganization. Type E is not included because only a single corporation is involved in a recapitalization [¶ 22,035].

.02 Importance of Dates for Carryover Benefits

The successor corporation takes over the carryovers as of the close of the day of distribution (for a liquidated subsidiary) or the day of transfer (for a reorganization) [Code Sec. 381(a)].

NOTE: The following rules apply to liquidations and reorganizations entitled to carryover benefits (but not Type F reorganizations) [Code Sec. 381(b); Reg. §§ 1.381(b)-1, 1.381(c)(1)-1]:

The tax year of the predecessor corporation ends on the date the assets are transferred from the predecessor to the successor corporation. Amounts retained to pay taxes, director fees and dissolution expenses do not affect this date.[76] The predecessor should file a return for the tax year ending with that date. If the predecessor remains in existence, it should also file a return for the tax year beginning on the day following the date of transfer and ending with the date its year would have ended had there been no transfer.

Generally, the date of transfer is the day the transfer is completed. However, if specified statements are filed, it may be the day when substantially all the property has been transferred and the predecessor has ceased all operations except liquidating activities. The latter date also applies if completion of the transfer is unreasonably postponed [Reg. § 1.381(b)-1(b)].

.03 Net Operating Loss or Net Capital Loss Carryback

The successor corporation is not entitled to carry back to a tax year of a predecessor a net capital loss or a net operating loss incurred in a tax year ending after the date of transfer [Code Sec. 381(b)(3)]. However, in a Type F reorganization [¶ 22,040], the successor corporation's loss can be carried back against the predecessor's pre-merger profits.

NOTE: The Second Circuit held that a triangular merger of a 62 percent controlled subsidiary into a 100 percent controlled shell was a Type F reorganization, even though the subsidiary's minority shareholders had to exchange their stock for the controlled shell's parent's stock.[77]

---

[76] Rev. Rul. 70-27, 1970-1 CB 83.

[77] *Aetna Casualty & Surety Co.*, CA-2, 77-1 USTC ¶ 9120, 568 F2d 811, *reh'g denied*, CA-2, 77-1 USTC ¶ 9261, 568 F2d 823.

Example 22-65: On December 31, 2013, Corporations X and Y transfer all their property to Z in a consolidation. If Z has a net operating loss or net capital loss in 2014, it cannot be carried back to a tax year of X or Y.

Example 22-66: On December 31, 2013, Corporation X merges into Corporation Y in a statutory merger, with Y's charter continuing after the merger. If Y has a net operating loss or a net capital loss in 2014, the loss cannot be carried back to a tax year of X, but is a carryback to a tax year of Y.

Example 22-67: X reorganizes by changing its name to Y. Y may carry back a net operating or net capital loss to a tax year of X before the reorganization.

¶22,140 CHECKLIST OF CARRYOVER ITEMS

The following items may be carried over subject to the conditions described:

- *Net operating loss.* The successor corporation may carry over net operating losses of the predecessor, subject to the special limitations shown at ¶22,145. However, the carryover to the first tax year ending after the date of transfer is limited to a fraction of the successor corporation's taxable income for that year (figured without regard to any net operating loss deduction). The fraction is the number of days in the tax year after the transfer over the total number of days in the tax year [Code Sec. 381(c)(1)(B); Reg. §1.381(c)(1)-1(d)]. Any deferred minimum tax liability attributable to the carryover is also acquired [Reg. §1.381(c)(1)-1(a)(3)];
- *Earnings and profits.* Earnings and profits of the predecessor become those of the successor corporation. But an earnings and profits deficit of either corporation may be applied only against the successor corporation's earnings and profits accumulated after the assets' date of transfer. The earnings and profits of the successor corporation's first tax year that may be reduced by the predecessor's deficit is in the same ratio to the total of the successor corporation's undistributed earnings for the year as the number of days of the year after the transfer bears to the total days in the year [Code Sec. 381(c)(2); Reg. §1.381(c)(2)-1(a)];
- *Capital loss carryover.* The successor corporation is entitled to use the unexhausted portion of the predecessor's capital loss carryover. The first year in which the loss may be deducted is the first tax year of the successor corporation ending after the date of transfer of assets. The amount that can be used in the first year, however, is limited to a fraction of the successor corporation's capital gain net income for that year. The fraction is the number of days in the tax year after the transfer over the total number of days in the tax year [Code Sec. 381(c)(3); Reg. §1.381(c)(3)-1];
- *Method of accounting.* When the acquiring corporation continues to operate a trade or business of the parties as a separate and distinct trade or business after the date of distribution or transfer, the acquiring corporation must use a carryover accounting method for each continuing trade or business. The carryover method requirement applies to the overall method of accounting (for example, an accrual method of

accounting) and any special method of accounting (for example, the percentage of completion method of accounting) used by each trade or business after the date of distribution or transfer. The acquiring corporation need not secure the Commissioner's consent to continue a carryover method [Reg. §§1.381(c)(4)-1(a)(2), 1.381(c)(5)-1(a)(2)].

- *Inventories.* The successor corporation values inventories received from the predecessor on the same basis as the predecessor. However, if the carryover of the method of taking inventory results in the corporation having more than one method of taking inventory, the successor corporation may adopt a particular method or combination of methods of taking inventory [Code Sec. 381(c)(5); Reg. §1.381(c)(5)-1];
- *Depreciation.* The successor corporation figures depreciation on acquired assets the same way the predecessor did. But total depreciation on a particular asset may not exceed the predecessor's adjusted basis. A change of method may be made with IRS consent [Ch. 11] [Code Sec. 381(c)(6); Reg. §1.381(c)(6)-1];
- The successor corporation can use the ADR system on property acquired from a predecessor only if the predecessor elected it for the property [Ch. 11] [Reg. §1.167(a)-11(e)(3)];
- *Installment sales method.* If the successor corporation acquires installment obligations which the predecessor reported on the installment basis, the corporation also reports the income on the installment basis [Code Sec. 381(c)(8); Reg. §1.381(c)(8)-1];
- *Amortization of bond discount or premium.* If the successor corporation assumes liability for bonds of the predecessor issued at a discount or premium, the corporation is treated as the predecessor in determining the amortization deductible or includible in income [Code Sec. 381(c)(9); Reg. §1.381(c)(9)-1];
- *Exploration and development expenditures.* The successor corporation can deduct certain mining development expenditures [Ch. 12] when the predecessor has previously so elected [Code Sec. 381(c)(10); Reg. §1.381(c)(10)-1];
- *Contributions to employee benefit trusts or plans.* The successor corporation is considered to be the predecessor in determining deductions for contributions of an employer to qualified employees' trusts or annuity plans [Code Sec. 381(c)(11); Reg. §1.381(c)(11)-1]. See Ch. 3;
- *Recovery of tax benefit items.* If the successor corporation is entitled to the recovery of amounts previously deducted or credited by the predecessor, the corporation must include in its income the amounts that would have been a tax benefit to the predecessor on the recovery [Code Sec. 381(c)(12)];
- *Involuntary conversions.* The successor corporation is treated as the predecessor when there is an involuntary conversion [Ch. 7] [Code Sec. 381(c)(13); Reg. §1.381(c)(13)-1];
- *Dividend carryover to personal holding company.* If the successor corporation is a personal holding company, it may include a dividend carryover of its predecessor in figuring the dividends-paid deduction [Ch. 23] to the same extent as the predecessor [Code Sec. 381(c)(14); Reg. §1.381(c)(14)-1];

- *Obligations of predecessor.* The successor corporation may deduct amounts that arise out of an obligation of the predecessor if:
  a. The obligation is assumed by the corporation,
  b. The obligation gives rise to a liability after the date of transfer,
  c. The liability, if paid or accrued by the predecessor after that date, would have been deductible by it. The obligation was not reflected in the consideration transferred by the corporation for the property [Code Sec. 381(c)(16); Reg. § 1.381(c)(16)-1];
- *Deficiency dividend of personal holding company.* If the successor corporation pays a personal holding company deficiency dividend of its predecessor, it is entitled to the deficiency dividend deduction [Ch. 13] [Code Sec. 381(c)(17); Reg. § 1.381(c)(17)];
- *Percentage depletion on ore extraction from prior mining residue.* The successor corporation can claim percentage depletion on prior mining residue acquired from the predecessor [Code Sec. 381(c)(18); Reg. § 1.381(c)(18)-1];
- *Charitable contributions over prior years' limitation.* If the predecessor corporation has a charitable contribution carryover on the date of the transfer, the successor corporation can use the carryover (within the limit [Ch. 20]) only in tax years beginning after that date that are not more than five tax years after the year the excess contribution was made [Code Sec. 381(c)(19); Reg. § 1.381(c)(19)-1];
- *Life insurance companies.* A successor life insurance company may take into account, under special regulations, certain items of a predecessor life insurance company [Code Sec. 381(c)(22); Reg. §§ 1.381(c)(22)-1, (d)-1];
- *General business credit.* The successor corporation carries over items the predecessor used to account for the general business credit [Ch. 14] [Code Sec. 381(c)(24)];
- *Deficiency dividend of regulated investment company or real estate investment trust.* If the successor corporation pays a deficiency dividend of its predecessor, such predecessor is entitled to the deficiency dividend deduction [Code Sec. 381(c)(23)]. See Ch. 23;
- *Foreign tax credit.* The successor corporation may carry over any unused foreign taxes of the predecessor, but the credit is subject to a limitation that includes only post-merger foreign taxable income attributable to the same business that caused the predecessor's foreign tax liability [Ch. 28];
- *Credit for prior year minimum tax liability.* The successor corporation can take into account the items required to be taken into account for purposes of the credit for prior year minimum tax liability in respect of the distributor or transferor corporation [Code Sec. 381(c)(25)]; and
- *Enterprise zone provisions.* The successor corporation must take into account the items required to be taken into account for purposes of the enterprise zone provisions in respect of the distributor or transferor corporation [Code Sec. 381(c)(26)].

¶22,145 SPECIAL LIMIT ON NET OPERATING LOSS CARRYOVER

Under certain conditions, a limit (described below) is placed on the net operating loss (NOL) carryover that is available to the acquiring corporation in tax-free reorganizations described in Code Sec. 381(a) [¶ 22,135]. The NOL carryover after a substantial change of ownership also may be disallowed or reduced [Ch. 20]. This is to prevent profitable corporations from trafficking *loss corporations* solely to use the losses to offset the acquiring corporation's gains.

Code Sec. 382(a) limits, after a more than 50 percent change in stock ownership, the amount of prechange NOLs (or other loss attributes such as research and development credits or capital losses) that a corporation (referred to as a loss corporation) may use to offset taxable income in the tax years or periods following an ownership change. *Prechange losses* include NOL carryovers to the tax year in which the ownership change occurs and any NOL incurred during that tax year to the extent such NOL is allocable to the portion of the year ending on the date of the ownership change [Code Sec. 382(d)(1)]. An ownership change is deemed to have occurred if, on a required measurement date (a testing date), the aggregate percentage ownership interest of one or more 5-percent shareholders of the loss corporation is more than 50 percentage points greater than the lowest percentage ownership interest of such shareholder(s) during the (generally) 3-year period immediately preceding such testing date (the testing period) [Code Sec. 382(g)(1) and (2); Code Sec. 382(i)(1)(3); Reg. § 1.382-2(a)(4)].

The amount of the limitation each year is equal to the product of the fair market value of all the stock of the loss corporation immediately before the ownership change multiplied by the applicable long-term tax-exempt rate.

.01 Determining Stock Ownership for Purposes of Section 382

Code Sec. 382(l)(3)(A) provides that, with certain exceptions, the constructive ownership rules of Code Sec. 318 apply in determining stock ownership. Under the first of those exceptions, set forth in Code Sec. 382(l)(3)(A)(i), the family attribution rules of Code Sec. 318(a)(1) provide that an individual and all members of his family (spouse, children, grandchildren, and parents) are treated as one individual. Code Sec. 382(h)(6)(iv) provides further that, if an individual may be treated as a member of more than one family, such individual will be treated as a member of the family with the smallest increase in percentage ownership (to the exclusion of all other families).

In *Garber Industries Holding Co.*,[78] a stock sale between siblings who were five-percent owners of a loss corporation increased one sibling's percentage ownership of the corporation by more than 50 percentage points. Such an owner shift was a change in ownership for purposes of Code Sec. 382 that required the corporation to reduce its claimed NOL deduction for both regular and AMT purposes. The stock sale could not be disregarded by treating the siblings as one individual under the constructive

[78] *Garber Industries Holding Co.*, 124 TC 1, Dec. 55,901 (2005), *aff'd*, CA-5, 2006-1 USTC ¶ 50,109, 435 F3d 555.

ownership rules. Since the sibling shareholders were not children or grandchildren of an individual shareholder of the loss corporation, their holdings could not be aggregated for purposes of applying Code Sec. 382.

There are limitations on a corporation's NOL carryforwards following a worthless stock deduction by 50 percent shareholders. In addition, there are limitations on using preacquisition losses to offset built-in gains [Code Sec. 382(g), (h)].

The following rules apply generally to more-than-50-percent-owner shifts or equity structure changes and to reorganization plans. Briefly, after a substantial ownership change, however effected, the taxable income available for offset by pre-change NOLs is limited to a prescribed rate times the loss corporation's value immediately before the change [Code Sec. 382]. To figure the annual limitation, multiply the loss corporation's value immediately before the ownership change by the federal long-term tax-exempt rate published by the IRS. The rate used is the highest rate in effect for any month in the three-month period ending with the month in which the ownership change occurs. Built-in losses and gains are subject to special rules.

> **Example 22-68:** Rich Corp. acquires Loss Corp. for the fair market price of $100,000. Prior to the acquisition, Loss Corp. had $300,000 of NOLs, and the federal long-term rate (FLTR) was 8 percent. When multiplying the fair market value of Loss Corp. ($100,000) by the FLTR (8 percent), Rich Corp. cannot use more than $8,000 per year of Loss Corp.'s NOLs to offset its gains.

In Notice 2010-50,[79] the IRS provided guidance concerning how to measure an owner shift in a loss corporation, for purposes of applying the Code Sec. 382 limitation on the use of NOLs, when the loss corporation has more than one class of stock outstanding whose values fluctuate relative to each other. The guidance addresses two methodologies for measuring value. These include the "full value methodology," in which value of all shares is measured by "marking" the shares to value on every test date, but daily fluctuations in value between testing dates are ignored, and the "hold constant principle" (HCP) that looks to the relative value of a tested share on its acquisition date and only marks acquired shares to value. Until additional guidance is issued, the IRS will not challenge any reasonable application of either the full value methodology or the HCP provided a single methodology is applied consistently.

¶22,150 LIMITS ON CARRYOVERS OF UNUSED CREDITS AND CAPITAL LOSSES

Similar rules for disallowance or reduction of NOL carryovers for changes in ownership [Ch. 20; ¶ 22,145]also apply to carryovers of capital losses, foreign tax credits, and unused business credits [Code Sec. 383]. In addition, to carry over unused foreign tax credit, the overall limitation [Ch. 28] must also be applied.

Applicable generally to ownership changes occurring after 1986, certain excess credits are subject to special limitations [Code Sec. 383]. These limitations are similar to the

[79] Notice 2010-50, IRB 2010-27, 12.

rules on NOL carryovers (under Code Sec. 382) explained at Ch. 20. Capital loss carryforwards and the deduction equivalent of credit carryforwards are limited to an amount determined on the basis of the tax liability that is attributable to so much of the taxable income as does not exceed the Sec. 382 limitation for the tax year.

STOCK REDEMPTIONS

¶22,155 STOCK REDEMPTIONS IN GENERAL

Usually, when a corporation redeems its stock from a shareholder, the transaction is treated as if the shareholder sold its stock to the corporation. Any profit is taxed as capital gain. However, what looks like a redemption is sometimes a disguised dividend (taxable as ordinary income). It is, therefore, necessary to distinguish between a dividend and a sale or exchange. The rules of Code Sec. 302, which are called the antifraud rules, are designed to prevent a shareholder from fraudulently structuring a stock redemption as a sale, which is taxed at favorable capital gains tax rates rather than as a dividend, which is usually taxed at ordinary income rates. The first antifraud provision provides that when a corporation redeems stock, there is a presumption that a dividend has been distributed and the taxpayer is taxed at ordinary income rates to the extent of the corporation's earnings and profits [Code Sec. 316(a)]. Therefore, unless the dividend is a qualified dividend, the distribution will be taxed at the highest individual tax rates. If the corporation has no earnings and profits at the time the redemption occurs, but generates earnings by the end of the year, the redemption is nevertheless treated as a dividend [Code Sec. 316(a)(2)]. If the corporation's earnings and profits are insufficient to cover the distribution, the basis of all the shareholder's stock is reduced to zero. The remainder of the proceeds will typically be taxed as capital gain [Code Sec. 301(c)].

.01 Sale or Exchange and Dividend Distinguished

A taxpayer can prove that a distribution is a sale rather than a dividend by showing that:

- It is not essentially equivalent to a dividend under the net effects test discussed below [Code Sec. 302(b)(1)];

  NOTE: In determining whether a redemption is not equivalent to a dividend, the fact that it fails to meet the other conditions is not considered.

- It meets the *substantially disproportionate* (or 80 percent) *test* discussed below *and* leaves the shareholder with less than 50 percent of the total voting power after redemption [Code Sec. 302(b)(2)];
- The distribution is a complete termination of the shareholder's stock in the corporation [Code Sec. 302(b)(3); Reg. § 1.302-4]; or
- The distribution is a redemption of stock held by a noncorporate shareholder in partial liquidation of the distributing corporation [Code Sec. 302(b)(4)].

  NOTE: The substantially disproportionate test and the complete redemption test are safe harbors. That's because they are objective and mechanical with a higher degree of certainty than the net effects test which depends on the facts and circumstances of each case.

.02 Net Effects Test

To qualify for sale or exchange treatment, the redemption must result in a meaningful reduction of the shareholder's proportionate interest in the corporation. A redemption is essentially equivalent to a dividend, and is taxed as such, if it meets a *net effects test* [Code Sec. 302(b)(1)]. It meets the test if all the circumstances show that, as a practical matter, the shareholder's relationship to the corporation did not change.[80] If the test is met, the mere presence of a business purpose for the redemption is irrelevant and does not change the result.[81]

Ordinarily, a dividend results if there is a pro rata redemption of the only class of stock outstanding, or a redemption of one class of stock (except Sec. 306 stock [¶22,170]) when all the other classes are held in the same proportion. However, the redemption of voting preferred stock without a reduction in a shareholder's ownership of common stock may qualify as a substantially disproportionate redemption under Code Sec. 302(b)(2) if the shareholder owns no common stock either directly or constructively.[82] The IRS will sometimes apply a substance over form analysis to determine the true character of the stock acquisition transaction.[83]

The effect of the redemption on voting control, share of earnings, and share of assets is important in determining whether the redemption is "essentially equivalent to a dividend." Even a big drop in ownership interest (e.g., from 85 percent to 60 percent) does not avoid dividend treatment if the shareholder retains voting control.

.03 Substantially Disproportionate Test

A redemption is substantially disproportional and therefore will qualify as an exchange, provided the following tests are satisfied immediately after the redemption:

1. The stockholder owns less than 50 percent of the total combined voting power of all classes of stock immediately after the redemption,
2. The ratio of his holdings of voting stock immediately after the redemption to all the voting stock in the corporation at that time is less than 80 percent of the ratio which the voting stock he owned immediately before the redemption bore to the entire voting stock in the corporation at that time, and
3. The stockholder's ownership of common stock (whether voting or nonvoting) after and before redemption also meets the 80 percent test. These tests will be applied to each stockholder individually, regardless of the effect of the distribution on the other stockholders [Code Sec. 302(b)(2)(C)].

In addition, the corporation's redemption may not be pursuant to a plan which is in reality a series of redemptions which result in the aggregate in a distribution which is not substantially disproportionate. Where events are clearly part of an overall, integrated plan to reduce a shareholder's interest in a corporation, the IRS provides in Rev. Rul. 75-447[84] that the sequence of events will be disregarded and effect will only

---

[80] *E.J. Seabrook*, DC-OK, 66-1 USTC ¶9416, 253 FSupp 652.

[81] *M.P. Davis*, SCt, 70-1 USTC ¶9289, 397 US 301, 90 SCt 1041, *reh'g denied*, 397 US 1071.

[82] Rev. Rul. 81-41, 1981-1 CB 121.

[83] LTR 9342005 (July 22, 1993).

[84] Rev. Rul. 75-447, 1975-2 CB 113.

be given to the overall outcome when determining whether a distribution is substantially disproportionate in a plan calling for a stock redemption accompanied either by an issuance of new stock or by a shareholder's sale of stock.

The constructive ownership rules of Code Sec. 318 will apply when making a determination as to whether a redemption is substantially disproportionate.

Example 22-69: XYZ Corp. has one class of stock, voting common, 100 shares of which are outstanding immediately before a redemption. Smith owns 70 shares, Jones owns 25 shares and Taylor owns 5 shares. The shareholders are not related. X redeems 50 shares of Smith's stock, 6 shares of Jones' stock and 4 shares of Taylor's stock for a total of 60 shares redeemed. In order to determine whether the redemption is substantially disproportionate with respect to any of the aforementioned shareholders, the following chart may be used:

Shareholders	*Before Redemption Shares Owned*	*Total*	*%*	*After Redemption Shares Owned*	*Total*	*%*
Smith	70	100	70	20	40	50
Jones	25	100	25	19	40	47.5
Taylor	5	100	5	1	40	2.5

The redemption of Smith's is not substantially disproportionate because, although his current holdings ratio (50%) is less than 80% of his previous holdings (70% × 80% = 56%), his stock ownership after redemption is exactly 50% of all of the outstanding voting stock, but the law requires his stock ownership to be less than 50% in order for the redemption to qualify as substantially disproportionate with respect to him.

The redemption of Jones's shares is not substantially disproportionate either. Although he owns only 47.5% of all outstanding voting stock after redemption, his holdings ratio after the redemption is greater than his holdings ratio before the redemption (47.5% v. 25%).

The redemption of Taylor's shares is substantially disproportionate. His percentage of ownership in the corporation is well below 50% after the redemption (2.5%) and his holdings ratio after the redemption (2.5%) is less than 80% of his holdings ratio before the redemption (5% × 80% = 4%).

The substantially disproportionate percentage tests do not apply to nonvoting preferred stock.

.04 Complete Termination of Shareholder's Stock

A complete termination of the shareholder's stock interest in the corporation qualifies for capital gains treatment if, after the redemption, the shareholder owns no stock in the corporation, either actually or constructively. The constructive ownership rules in ¶ 22,175 apply, with one exception. The exception prevents application of the family attribution rules, if the conditions discussed below apply and if there are no prior transfers of the kind described below.

.05 Partial Liquidations

A distribution in redemption of stock held by a noncorporate shareholder is treated as a distribution in partial liquidation if it is (1) not essentially equivalent to a dividend (determined at the corporate level) and (2) under a plan that occurs within the tax year in which the plan is adopted or within the next tax year [Code Sec. 302(e)]. Another setup that qualifies is a distribution (whether or not pro rata) caused by a distributing corporation's termination of business. Other distributions may also qualify under regulations yet to be issued.

NOTE: The IRS has broad regulatory powers to stop the use of split-ups, split-offs and the like (under Code Secs. 327, 351, 355, etc.) to avoid the partial liquidation rules [Code Sec. 346(b)].

.06 Stock Ownership

In applying the above tests, take into account stock attribution rules which are explained at ¶ 22,175. They apply here except as otherwise noted below.

.07 Other Rules

A formal retirement of the redeemed stock is not required. The corporation may continue to hold it as treasury stock.

Special rules apply to redemptions from a controlled corporation; redemptions to pay death taxes; redemption of Sec. 306 stock; and liquidating dividends [Ch. 2; ¶ 22,160-¶ 22,175]. A corporation gets no deduction for any amount it pays or incurs in connection with its stock's redemption.

.08 When Constructive Ownership Rules Do Not Apply

The rules for attribution between family members do not apply if [Code Sec. 302(c)(2); Reg. § 1.302-4]:

- Immediately after the redemption, the taxpayer had no interest in the corporation other than as a creditor. The taxpayer cannot be an officer,[85] director, or employee;
- The taxpayer does not reacquire an interest (other than by bequest or inheritance) within ten years from the redemption date. If the taxpayer does acquire such an interest, he or she is assessed an additional tax, at dividend rates, for the redemption year (the statute of limitations is automatically extended); and
- The taxpayer files an agreement: (1) to notify the IRS within 30 days if such interest is acquired, and (2) to keep copies of the return and other records showing the tax that would have been payable if the redemption had been a dividend. The agreement must be filed with the return.

Example 22-70: Husband and wife each own 50 percent of the stock of a corporation. All the husband's stock is redeemed, and husband meets the above conditions. The husband is entitled to treat this as a sale of his stock, because the family constructive ownership rules do not apply. If they did apply, he would still constructively own his wife's shares, and the redemption would not be complete.

---

[85] Rev. Rul. 75-2, 1975-1 CB 99.

NOTE: Family attribution rules under Code Sec. 318(a)(1) may be waived *only* by an entity and its beneficiaries if those through whom ownership is attributed to the entity join in the waiver. The entity and the beneficiaries would be liable for any acquisitions by them within the ten-year period and the statute of limitations would be open to assess any deficiency [Code Sec. 302(c)(2)(C)].

.09 Prior Stock Transfers to Avoid Tax

The family attribution rules *do* apply under either of the following two conditions, but only if tax avoidance was a principal purpose [Code Sec. 302(c)(2)(B); Reg. § 1.302-4(g)].

- If a purchaser acquired any part of the redeemed stock, directly or indirectly, within the previous 10 years from a person whose stock would have been attributed to the purchaser at the time of redemption [Reg. § 1.302-4(g)(1); or

  Example 22-71: Solely to reduce taxes, the only shareholder of a corporation gives half of the stock to his son. Five years later, there is a complete redemption of all of the son's shares. The rules relating to constructive ownership between members of a family apply.

- If, at the time of redemption, any person owned stock that would be attributed to the distributee and such person acquired any stock in the corporation directly or indirectly from the distributee within the 10-year period ending on the date of the distribution, and such stock so acquired from the distributee is not redeemed in the same transaction [Reg. § 1.302-4(g) (2)].

  Example 22-72: If, in Example 22-71, the father's shares were redeemed and the father otherwise terminated his interest in the corporation, the redemption would be treated as a sale or exchange.

NOTE: These rules do not apply to distributions in liquidation [Reg. § 1.302-1].

In Letter Ruling 200930011[86] the IRS concluded that a redemption agreement allowing two of four family members to surrender interests in a corporation in exchange for promissory notes from the corporation resulted in gain to those individuals. A father and his three sons owned shares in a corporation, and the father and one son decided to end their participation in the corporation's business. To that end, the father gave some shares to the two sons who would retain corporate interests, and the corporation gave 15-year promissory notes to the father and the withdrawing son in exchange for redemption of their shares in the corporation. The IRS concluded that the father's gift of shares to his sons was not intended as a means of avoiding federal income tax under Code Sec. 302(c)(2)(B).

---

[86] LTR 200930011 (April 13, 2009).

¶22,160 REDEMPTION THROUGH USE OF A RELATED CORPORATION

Code Sec. 304 was enacted primarily to prevent the owner of multiple corporations from converting what would otherwise be dividend income from one corporation (the issuing corporation) to capital gain by selling its stock to another corporation that he controls. Code Sec. 304 requires certain related corporate transactions to be recast as redemptions for tax purposes, which may result in dividend income, capital gain, and/or basis recovery, depending on the particular situation.

.01 Sale to Related Corporation (Other Than a Subsidiary)

If one or more persons are in control of each of two corporation and in return for property,one of the corporations acquires stock in the other corporation from the person so in control, then such property will be treated as a distribution in redemption of the stock of the corporation acquiring such stock [Code Sec. 304(b)(2)]. The dividend amount is determined by treating the transaction as if the property were distributed by the acquiring corporation to the extent of its earnings and profits and then by the corporation whose stock is issued (the issuing corporation) to the extent of its earnings and profits [Code Sec. 304(b)(2)].

Generally, when stock from one member of an affiliated group is transferred to another member of the group (in a Sec. 304(a) transaction), proper adjustments must be made in (1) the adjusted basis of any intragroup stock and (2) the earnings and profits of any member of this group, to the extent necessary to carry out this rule's purposes. *Intragroup stock* means any stock in a member of an affiliated group held by another member of this group [Code Sec. 304(b)(4)].

The contribution-to-capital rule will not apply if the shareholder is treated as having exchanged its stock under Code Sec. 302(a) [relating to stock redemption in general (¶22,155)]. Thus, if Sec. 302(a) applies, the acquiring corporation will be treated as buying the stock, for example, for purposes of Code Sec. 338 [relating to certain stock purchases treated as asset acquisition (¶22,130)].

Effect on Basis

In a Code Sec. 304 transaction, the acquiring corporation acquires stock of the issuing corporation in return for property. The stock is acquired from one or more persons who were in control of both the acquiring and issuing corporations. The property is treated as received in redemption of acquiring corporation stock.

If the transaction is treated as a Code Sec. 301 distribution, the acquiring corporation's basis in issuing corporation stock is, generally, the transferor's basis plus any gain recognized in the transfer [Code Sec. 362]. The transferor's basis in acquiring corporation stock is the same as transferor's basis in the issuing corporation stock surrendered [Prop. Reg. § 1.304-2(a)(3)]. Any basis reduction with respect to acquiring corporation stock that is required by Code Sec. 301(c)(2) is applied to reduce the adjusted basis of each share of acquiring corporation stock directly held or deemed held by the transferor on a pro rata, share-by-share basis [Prop. Reg. § 1.304-2(a)(4)].

If the transaction is not treated as a 301 distribution, the property received by the transferor is treated as a redemption or a payment in exchange for stock. In that case, the basis and holding period of the acquiring corporation stock treated as redeemed is the same as the basis and holding period of the issuing corporation stock actually surrendered. The acquiring corporation takes a cost basis in the issuing corporation stock it acquires [Prop. Reg. § 1.304-2(a)(5)].

.02 Sale to Subsidiary

If a subsidiary, in return for property, acquires stock of its parent corporation from a shareholder of the parent corporation, the acquisition of such stock will be treated as if the parent corporation had redeemed its own stock in exchange for the property. A corporation is a parent corporation if it meets the 50 percent ownership requirements [Code Sec. 304(a)(2); Prop. Reg. § 1.304-3(a)].

.03 Control

Control means ownership of 50 percent or more of the voting power or 50 percent or more of the total value of all classes of stock.

> **NOTE:** The rules in ¶ 22,175 on constructive ownership apply in determining control, except that 5 percent is substituted for 50 percent [Code Sec. 304(c)(3)].

¶22,165 STOCK REDEEMED TO PAY DEATH TAXES

.01 Special Relief

When someone dies, it may be necessary to redeem some of the stock the decedent held in order to pay death taxes in situations where corporate stock represents a significant portion of the decedent's estate. If the redemption is treated as a dividend, the entire amount received could be taxable. However, relief is granted in Code Sec. 303 by treating the redemption as a sale—so that only the amount received in excess of the decedent's stock basis is taxable. To qualify for this tax relief, all of the following conditions must be met [Code Sec. 303; Reg. § § 1.303-1 to 1.303-3]:

- The value of the stock redeemed is included in the decedent's gross estate for estate tax purposes [described below].
- The stock is redeemed after death and within three years and 90 days after the filing of the estate tax return; or, if a petition was filed with the Tax Court, within 60 days after its decision becomes final; or, if deferred payment of estate taxes is elected, within the time permitted for the estate tax installments in a closely held business interest [Code Sec. 303(b)(1)].
- The stock is redeemed for an amount not more than the estate and inheritance taxes (including interest), plus the funeral and administration expenses allowable as deductions to the estate. There is no requirement that the proceeds be needed to pay these items or that they be used to pay them. However, any excess over the allowable amount is a dividend.

> **NOTE:** Stock that can qualify for capital gain is limited to stock redeemed from a shareholder whose interest in the estate is reduced (either directly or through a binding obligation to contribute) by the payment of death taxes and funeral and administration expenses. Special rules also limit the amount of qualifying redemption distributions made more than four years after the death.

- The value of the stock must exceed 35 percent of the value of the decedent's adjusted gross estate (gross estate less deductions for administration expenses, debts, taxes and losses). For this purpose, the stock of two or more corporations may be treated as stock of a single corporation if 20 percent or more of the stock of each *directly*[87] owned by the decedent is included in the gross estate [Code Sec. 303(b)].

Example 22-73: Adjusted gross estate of decedent who died is $1 million. The sum of death taxes and funeral and administration expenses is $275,000. Included in gross estate is stock, valued as follows:

Corporation X	$200,000
Corporation Y	400,000
Corporation Z	200,000

Stock of Corporations X and Z included in gross estate is all of their outstanding stock. If treated as stock of a single corporation, it has value of over $350,000 (35 percent of adjusted gross estate). Likewise, Corporations Y's stock has value of over $350,000. Distribution in redemption of stock X and Z, or stock Y, in amounts not totaling more than $275,000 can be considered distribution in payment for stock.

.02 Qualifying Stock

The stock need not be owned by the decedent at death, nor does it have to be redeemed from the decedent's estate, *as long as its value is includible in the decedent's gross estate.* Examples of this are stock the decedent transferred within three years of death and stock the estate distributed before the redemption. However, stock redeemed from a purchaser for value does not qualify even though it was part of the decedent's estate.

Stock received after death can qualify if its basis is determined by reference to qualified stock included in the estate. An example is a nontaxable stock dividend paid to the estate after decedent's death.

¶22,170 SECTION 306 STOCK

.01 General Rules

In order to prevent a shareholder from withdrawing earnings and profits of a corporation at capital gain tax rates rather than ordinary income tax rates, lawmakers created *Section 306 stock.* Section 306 stock refers to certain preferred stock issued as a nontaxable stock dividend or in a transaction in which no gain or loss is recognized. The Section 306 stock can also include rights and common stock that is reclassified in a recapitalization proceeding.[88] When Section 306 stock is sold by a shareholder the amount realized is treated as a distribution under Code Sec. 301. Any amount treated as ordinary income will be treated as a dividend received from the corporation eligible for the same tax rates as long-term capital gain [Code Sec. 306(a) (1) (D)].

---

[87] *O.E. Byrd Est.*, CA-5, 68-1 USTC ¶9139, 388 F2d 223.

[88] Rev. Rul. 81-91, 1981-1 CB 123.

Section 306 stock includes the following:

- Stock that is received as a nontaxable stock dividend (other than common stock received as a stock dividend on common stock) [Reg. § 1.306-3(c)];
- Stock (other than common) received in a corporate reorganization, split-off, split-up, or spin-off, to the extent that the effect was substantially the same as the receipt of a stock dividend [Reg. § 1.306-3(d)];
- Stock received in exchange for Section 306 stock [Reg. § 1.306-3(e)];
- Stock with a transferred or substituted basis, determined on the basis of Section 306 stock in the hands of any person [Reg. § 1.306-39e)]; or
- Stock (other than common) received from a controlled corporation in a tax-free exchange under Code Sec. 351, if the receipt of money in lieu of the stock would, to any extent, have been treated as a dividend, determined by applying the constructive ownership rules subject to a substitution of 5 percent for the 50 percent limitation with respect to attribution to or from corporations.

.02 Sale of Section 306 Stock

When Sec. 306 stock is sold the amount realized will be taxed as ordinary income up to the stock's ratable share of the earnings at the time of issuance. If the amount realized exceeds the stock's ratable share of the corporation's earnings and profits, the excess, to the extent of gain, is treated as capital gain. However, no loss is recognized [Code Sec. 306(a)(1); Reg. § 1.306-1].

Any amount treated as ordinary income under Code Sec. 306 will be treated as a dividend for purposes of:

- The reduced capital gains tax rates [see ¶ 8001]
- Other purposes specified by the IRS [Code Sec. 306(a)(1)(D)].

.03 Redemption of Section 306 Stock

The general dividend rules apply in determining the tax status of the proceeds [Ch. 2]. The portion that is covered by corporate earnings and profits at the time of the redemption is a dividend and is taxed as ordinary income [Code Sec. 306(a)(2); Reg. § 1.306-1].

.04 Exceptions

The rules regarding gains on Section 306 do not apply in the following situations [Code Sec. 306(b); Reg. § 1.306-2]:

- A shareholder completely terminates his or her actual and constructive interest in the corporation;
- The redemption is in complete or partial liquidation;
- The shareholder can prove that a principal purpose was not tax avoidance; and
- The transaction is one in which gain or loss is not recognized.

NOTE: Sec. 306 stock also includes any stock (other than common stock) acquired in a Sec. 351 tax-free exchange if the receipt of money (instead of the stock) would have been treated as a dividend at the time. [Code Sec. 306(c)(3)]

Sec. 351 provides for the nonrecognition of all or part of the gain or loss on certain transfers to a controlled corporation in exchange for stock.

¶22,175 CONSTRUCTIVE OWNERSHIP OF STOCK

The tax consequences of some transactions depend on how much stock is owned by the shareholder in a particular corporation. In these cases, the shareholders are deemed to own not only his or her own stock, but also stock belonging to others that is treated as the shareholder's under the attribution rules below. In applying these rules, the shareholder is considered an owner of stock whether owned directly or indirectly [Code Sec. 318; Reg. § 1.318-1 to 1.318-4].

The general attribution rules below apply to stock redemptions [¶22,155-¶22,160]; preferred stock bailouts [¶22,170]; liquidation of subsidiaries [¶22,130]; and net operating loss carryovers [Ch. 20, ¶22,145]. Special rules apply to sales between corporations and shareholders [Ch. 13]; personal holding companies [Ch. 23]; and in determining whether a corporation comes within a controlled group [Ch. 20].

.01 Family Members

A shareholder is considered the owner of the stock owned by a spouse (unless legally separated or divorced), children and adopted children, grandchildren, and parents [Code Sec. 318(a)(1); Reg. § 1.318-2]. But see ¶22,155 for exceptions.

Example 22-74: Taxpayer owns 20 of the 100 outstanding shares of stock of a corporation. Taxpayer's wife owns 20 shares of such stock. Taxpayer's son owns 20 shares. Taxpayer's grandson owns 20 shares. Taxpayer is considered to own 80 shares. Taxpayer's wife and son also are each considered to own 80 shares. But taxpayer's grandson is considered to own only 40 shares, that is, his own and his father's; he is not considered to own the stock of his grandparents.

Example 22-75: Mr. Hicks owns no stock of the Ecks Corp. His wife, however, owns 25 percent and his son owns 26 percent of the stock. Hicks is constructive owner of 51 percent of the Ecks Corp. stock.

.02 Partnerships and Estates

A partnership (or S corporation) or estate owns the stock of its partners or beneficiaries. Partners or beneficiaries own *proportionately* the stock of the partnership or estate [Code Sec. 318(a) (2), (3); Reg. § § 1.318-2, -3].

Example 22-76: Mr. Heeney has a 50 percent interest in a partnership. The partnership owns 50 of the 100 outstanding shares of stock of a corporation, the remaining 50 shares being owned by Heeney. The partnership is considered as owning 100 shares. Heeney is considered as owning 75 shares (his own 50 plus 50 percent of partnership's 50).

.03 Trusts

A trust owns the stock of its beneficiary, unless the beneficiary has only a remote, contingent interest (it is remote if its value cannot exceed 5 percent of the value of the trust property). Trust beneficiaries own the trust's stock in proportion to their interests in the trust. (These trust rules do not apply to exempt employee trusts.) [Code Sec. 318(a)(2), (3); Reg. § 1.318-2, -3.]

> **Example 22-77:** A testamentary trust owns 25 of the outstanding 100 shares of stock of a corporation. Mr. Drake, who holds a vested remainder in the trust having a value, determined actuarially, equal to 4 percent of the value of the trust property, owns the remaining 75 shares. Since Drake's interest in the trust is vested rather than contingent (whether or not remote), the trust is considered as owning 100 shares. Drake is considered as owning 76 shares (75 + 4% × 25).

Grantor-owned Trust

[Ch. 25]. There is mutual attribution between the trust and any grantor or other person treated as its owner [Code Sec. 318(a)(2), (3)].

.04 S Corporations

An S corporation is treated as a partnership for purposes of the constructive ownership rules [Code Sec. 318(a)(5)(E)].

.05 Corporations

If a shareholder owns, or is deemed to own 50 percent or more in value of a corporation's stock, the shareholder is considered an owner of any stock the corporation owns, in the ratio of the value of his or her stock to the value of all the corporation's stock. The corporation in turn owns the shareholder's stock in other corporations [Code Secs. 318(a)(2), (3); Reg. §§ 1.318-1, -2].

> **Example 22-78:** Ms. Foster and Mr. Hopkins, unrelated individuals, own 70 percent and 30 percent in value of the stock of M Corp. respectively. M Corp. owns 50 of the 100 outstanding shares of stock of O Corp., the remaining 50 shares being owned by Foster. M Corp. is considered as owning 100 shares of O Corp., and Foster is considered as owning 85 shares of O Corp. (50 + 70 percent of 50).

.06 Options

If the shareholder has options to acquire stock (or options to acquire an option), the shareholder is considered to own the stock even though the option is only exercisable after a period of time has elapsed[89] [Code Sec. 318(a)(4); Reg. § 1.318-3]. Warrants or convertible debentures are considered options if the shareholder has the right to acquire the stock at his or her election.[90]

---

89 Rev. Rul. 89-64, 1989-1 CB 91.

90 Rev. Rul. 68-601, 1968-2 CB 124, clarified, Rev. Rul. 89-64, 1989-1 CB 91.

Example 22-79: Mr. Newman and Ms. Taylor, unrelated individuals, own all of the 100 outstanding shares of stock of a corporation, each owning 50 shares. Newman has an option to acquire 25 of Taylor's shares, and has an option to acquire a further option to acquire the remaining 25 of Taylor's shares. Newman is considered as owning the entire 100 shares of stock of the corporation.

.07 Constructive Ownership as Actual Ownership

Stock constructively owned by the shareholder under the above rules is treated as actually owned (it can be reattributed from the shareholder to others).

Example 22-80: The rules provide that husband, wife, and son are each considered as owning 80 shares. If the remaining 20 shares are owned by another corporation wholly owned by husband, wife, and son then all are considered to own the stock in fact owned by that corporation.

.08 Exceptions

There are two exceptions to the above rules:

- Stock attributed to a partnership, estate, trust or corporation under the attribution to rules cannot be reattributed under the attribution from rules [Code Sec. 318(a) (5) (C); Reg. § 1.318-4]; and
- Stock attributed to an individual under the family attribution rules cannot be reattributed under those rules [Reg. § 1.318-4].

Corporations—Personal Holding Companies, Etc.—Exempt Organizations

PERSONAL HOLDING COMPANIES

Personal holding company (PHC) tax . . . . ¶ 23,001
The PHC income requirement . . . . ¶ 23,005
The stock ownership requirement . . . . ¶ 23,010
Corporations exempt from PHC tax . . . . ¶ 23,015
Income subject to PHC tax . . . . . . ¶ 23,020
Rate of tax, returns, and payment . . . . ¶ 23,025
Deficiency dividend . . . . ¶ 23,030
Consolidated returns . . . . ¶ 23,040

REGULATED INVESTMENT COMPANIES (RICs)

Tax on RICs (mutual funds) . . . . . . ¶ 23,075
Requirements to be taxed as RIC . . ¶ 23,080
Venture capital companies . . . . ¶ 23,085
Figuring the tax on RICs . . . . ¶ 23,090

REAL ESTATE INVESTMENT TRUSTS (REIT)

What is a REIT . . . . ¶ 23,095
Gross income requirement . . . . . . ¶ 23,096
Asset test . . . . ¶ 23,097
Distribution requirement . . . . ¶ 23,098
Tax-free division of REIT . . . . ¶ 23,099

REAL ESTATE MORTGAGE INVESTMENT CONDUITS (REMICs)

Real estate mortgage investment conduits (REMICs) in general . . . . ¶ 23,100

EXEMPT ORGANIZATIONS

Exempt organizations in general . . ¶ 23,105
Report requirements for exempt organizations . . . . ¶ 23,106
Lobbying activities by tax-exempt organizations . . . . ¶ 23,107
Political campaign activities by exempt organizations . . . . ¶ 23,108
Code Sec. 527 political organizations and exempt organizations . . ¶ 23,109
Types of exempt organizations . . ¶ 23,110

PRIVATE FOUNDATIONS

Private foundations defined . . . . . ¶ 23,115
Tax on investment income . . . . ¶ 23,120
Prohibited acts of private foundations . . . . ¶ 23,125
Tax on self-dealing . . . . ¶ 23,130
Tax on undistributed income . . . . . ¶ 23,135
Tax on excess business holdings . . ¶ 23,140
Tax on speculative investments . . ¶ 23,145
Tax on improper expenditures . . . . ¶ 23,150
Nonexempt trusts treated as private foundations . . . . ¶ 23,151

UNRELATED BUSINESS INCOME

Exempt organizations subject to tax on unrelated business income . . . . ¶23,160
Unrelated business defined . . . . . ¶23,165
Income from unrelated business . . ¶23,170
Unrelated debt-financed income . . ¶23,175
Unrelated business taxable income (UBTI) tax rates, returns, and payments . . . . ¶23,180

PENALTIES IMPOSED ON EXEMPT ORGANIZATIONS

Excess benefit transactions . . . . . . ¶23,185
Tax on exempt organizations involved in tax shelters . . . . ¶23,190

PERSONAL HOLDING COMPANIES

¶23,001 PERSONAL HOLDING COMPANY (PHC) TAX

The personal holding company (PHC) tax was enacted when the highest corporate tax rate was much lower than the highest personal income tax rate and taxpayers retained investments in corporations where the income would be taxed at the lower corporate rate. To eliminate this loophole, Congress enacted the PHC tax to ensure that personal holding companies are taxed at the higher, personal holding company tax rates regardless of whether or not the PHCs were formed with the intention of accumulating earnings or profits. The PHC tax is aimed at closely held corporations with income mainly from investments [Code Sec. 541]. In 2013, the PHC tax rate was increased from 15 percent to 20 percent to reflect the maximum tax rate applicable to qualified dividends for such periods. The tax is computed by multiplying undistributed PHC income by 20 percent. Qualified dividends are taxed at capital gains rates and effective January 1, 2013, a top capital gains tax rate of 20 percent (increased from 15 percent) became applicable [Code Sec. 1(h)].

.01 Alternative Minimum Tax (AMT)

Like other corporations, PHCs pay AMT on their tax preferences [Ch. 16]. You calculate a PHCs AMT in the same manner as you would calculate a C corporation's AMT with the exception of circulation expenditures described in Code Sec. 173. To the extent that circulation costs are currently deducted by the PHC for regular tax purposes, they must be amortized over three years when calculating the AMT income for a PHC [Code Sec. 56(b)(2)(C)].

.02 What Is a Personal Holding Company?

A corporation is a PHC only if: (1) at least 60 percent of its adjusted ordinary gross income is *personal holding company income* [Code Sec. 542(a)(1)] [¶23,005] *and* (2) five or fewer individuals own more than 50 percent of its stock [Code Sec. 542(a)(2)] [¶23,010]. The tests are applied each year to the situation as it exists that year.

¶23,005 THE PHC INCOME REQUIREMENT

A corporation becomes a PHC only when 60 percent or more of its adjusted ordinary gross income for the tax year is PHC income [Code Sec. 542(a)(1)]. To find adjusted ordinary gross income, first reduce gross income by capital gains and Code Sec. 1231 gains. This is ordinary gross income. Then reduce ordinary gross income by the amount of: *leasing income* (rents, etc.) your corporation receives for the use of tangible personal property it manufactures as a substantial activity during the tax year; *interest* on judgments, tax refunds, condemnation awards and U.S. obligations held for sale by a dealer; *rents* to the extent of related deductions for property taxes, interest, rent incurred and depreciation (except depreciation on tangible personal property not customarily leased to any one lessee for more than three years); *mineral, oil, and gas royalties* and income from working interests to the extent of related deductions for depletion, property and severance taxes, interest and rent incurred [Code Sec. 543(b)]. Rents and royalties not eliminated are the adjusted amounts included in personal holding company income.

.01 Personal Holding Company Income

The term "personal holding company income" means the portion of the adjusted ordinary gross income which consists of the following:

- *Dividends, interest, royalties, and annuities.* Royalties are those other than mineral, oil, gas, and copyright royalties. Computer software royalties received by certain companies that are actively engaged in the business of developing computer software are not personal holding company income under specified conditions [Code Secs. 543(d), 553(a)];
- *Rent* adjusted for the use of, or the right to use, corporate property. Adjusted rents are not personal holding company income if they are at least 50 percent of adjusted ordinary gross income and dividend distributions exceed the amount by which personal holding company income (computed with certain adjustments) exceeds 10 percent of ordinary gross income;
- *Adjusted mineral, oil and gas royalties.* Adjusted mineral, oil and gas royalties are PHC income unless:
  a. They are at least 50 percent of adjusted ordinary gross income
  b. Trade or business deductions (except compensation paid to shareholders for personal services and deductions specifically allowable under sections other than Code Sec. 162) are at least 15 percent of adjusted ordinary gross income and
  c. PHC income (computed with certain adjustments) is 10 percent or less of ordinary gross income;
- *Copyright royalties.* Copyright royalties includes compensation, however designated, for the use of, or the right to use, copyrights in works protected by U.S. copyright law. Copyright royalties (not including royalties received for the use of, or right to use, copyrights on works created in whole or in part by any shareholder) are not counted if they are at least 50 percent of ordinary gross income, personal holding company income (with certain adjustments) is not more than 10

percent of ordinary gross income, and the sum of trade or business deductions allocable to the royalties (other than deductions for compensation for personal services rendered by shareholders, deductions for royalties paid or accrued, and deductions specifically allowable under a provision other than Code Sec. 162) equals or exceeds 25 percent of the amount by which the ordinary gross income exceeds the sum of the royalties paid or accrued and depreciation and amortization deductions allowed with respect to the copyright royalties;

- *Produced film rents,* unless they constitute 50 percent or more of ordinary gross income;
- *Payments for the use of tangible corporate property by a shareholder* who owns, directly or indirectly, 25 percent or more in value of the outstanding stock at any time during the tax year. However, it applies only if the corporation has other PHC income for the tax year in excess of 10 percent of its ordinary gross income;
- *Payments under personal service contracts,* if the individual who is to perform the services is named in the contract or can be designated by someone other than the corporation, and directly or indirectly owns 25 percent or more in value of the outstanding corporate stock at any time during the tax year;[1] and
- Taxable income from estates and trusts is PHC income [Ch. 25].

¶23,010 THE STOCK OWNERSHIP REQUIREMENT

Even if a corporation meets the income test [¶23,005], it is not classified as a PHC unless more than 50 percent in value of its outstanding stock is owned, directly or indirectly, by five or fewer individuals any time during the last half of the tax year. Under this rule, certain charitable organizations and qualified employer retirement plan trust are considered individuals [Code Sec. 542(a)(2); Reg. § 1.542-3].

The following rules determine whether a corporation meets the stock ownership requirement and whether payments under personal service contracts, payments for use of property, and copyright royalties are personal holding company income [¶23,005] [Code Sec. 544; Reg. § § 1.544-1 to -7]:

1. *Stock not owned by individual.* Stock owned, directly or indirectly, by or for a corporation, partnership, estate, or trust is considered owned proportionately by its shareholders, partners, or beneficiaries [Code Sec. 544(a)(1)];
2. *Family and partnership ownership.* A taxpayer is considered to own the stock owned, directly or indirectly, by or for his or her family or partner. A taxpayer's family includes only brothers and sisters (whole or half-blood), spouse, ancestors, and lineal descendants [Code Sec. 544(a)(2)];

   NOTE: Despite these attribution rules, any particular shares of stock are counted only once in determining whether a taxpayer satisfies the 50 percent ownership requirement. In general, shares are attributed in a manner that produces the highest concentration of ownership in five or fewer individuals. Once ownership of shares is attributed to a particular shareholder, no one else (not even the direct owner) is deemed to own them for purposes of the 50 percent test.[2]

---

[1] Rev. Rul. 75-67, 1975-1 CB 169.

[2] Rev. Rul. 89-30, 1989-1 CB 274.

3. *Options.* If a taxpayer has an option to acquire stock, the taxpayer is considered the owner of the underlying stock. This applies to an option to acquire an option, and each one of a series of options. The option rule takes precedence over the family and partnership rules [Code Sec. 544(a)(3)];
4. *Constructive ownership.* Stock constructively owned by a taxpayer as a result of applying rule 1 or (3) above is treated as actually owned by the taxpayer in again applying rule 1 or in applying rule 2 so as to make another the stock's constructive owner, but stock constructively owned by an individual by reason of the family and partnership attribution rules is not treated as owned for purposes of again applying those rules to make someone else the constructive owner of such stock; the family, partnership, and option attribution rules apply for purposes of the stock ownership requirement only if the effect is to make the corporation a personal holding company and apply for purposes of determining whether income from personal service contracts, the use of property by shareholders, and copyright royalties have to be included in personal holding company income [Code Sec. 544(a)(5)]; and
5. *Convertible securities.* Outstanding securities convertible into stock (whether or not convertible during the tax year) are considered as outstanding stock, but only if including all such securities will make the corporation a PHC or will make income from personal service contracts, the use of property by shareholders, or copyright royalties personal holding company income [Code Sec. 544(b)].

¶23,015 CORPORATIONS EXEMPT FROM PHC TAX

The following entities cannot be treated as personal holding companies and are exempt from PHC tax [Code Sec. 542(c)]:

- Corporations exempt from the income tax under Subchapter F [Code Sec. 501 through Code Sec. 530]; For further discussion see ¶23,110;
- Banks, as defined in Code Sec. 581, domestic building and loan associations, life insurance companies, and surety companies;
- Certain lending or finance companies [Code Sec. 542(c)(6)];
- Foreign corporations [Code Sec. 542(c)(5)];
- A small business investment company, unless a shareholder owns a 5 percent or more interest in a concern receiving funds from the company [Code Sec. 542(c)(7)];
- A corporation under court jurisdiction in a bankruptcy or similar case, unless a major purpose of the court proceeding is to avoid PHC tax [Code Sec. 542(c)(8)];
- A real estate investment trust (REIT) [Code Sec. 856(h)(3)(B)].

¶23,020 INCOME SUBJECT TO PHC TAX

The personal holding company tax is a tax on the *undistributed personal holding company income.*

.01 Undistributed PHC Income

Undistributed PHC income is a personal holding company's taxable income for regular income tax purposes with certain adjustments minus the dividends-paid deduction (discussed below) [Code Sec. 545(b); Reg. § 1.545-1]. The personal holding company's taxable income is adjusted as follows:

- *Taxes.* A PHC can deduct federal income taxes and foreign income and profits taxes not deducted in figuring taxable income. A PHC can also deduct certain foreign taxes attributable to dividends it receives from foreign subsidiaries that are deemed to have been paid by the domestic corporations [Ch. 28]. The accumulated earnings tax and the personal holding company tax are *not* deductible [Code Sec. 545(b)(1); Reg. § 1.545-2(a)];
- *Charitable contributions.* A PHC can deduct charitable contributions with the same taxable income limitation as for an individual [Ch. 9] but without any carryover. Taxable income for purposes of the contribution limitation is figured without the charitable deduction [Ch. 20], certain expense and depreciation deductions, special deductions (other than organizational expenditures) and net operating loss or capital loss carryback to the tax year [Code Sec. 545(b)(2); Reg. § 1.545-2(b)];
- *Expenses and depreciation* allocable to the operation and maintenance of property may not exceed rent the corporation receives for the use of the property unless: (a) the rent was the highest obtainable, or if none was received, none was obtainable; (b) the property was held in the course of a business carried on in good faith for profit; and (c) it was reasonable to expect that operation of the property would result in a profit, or the property was necessary to the business [Code Sec. 545(b)(6); Reg. § 1.545-2(h)];
- *Net capital gains.* A deduction is allowed for the PHC's net capital gain, but reduced by the taxes on such net capital gain [Code Sec. 545(b)(5); Reg. § 1.545-2(e)]. The reduction is the difference between: (1) the tax on the total taxable income and (2) the tax on the taxable income, excluding the net capital gain;
- For gains and losses realized by a foreign corporation, the PHC tax is calculated by taking into account only capital gains and losses that are effectively connected with the conduct of a U.S. trade or business and are not exempt by treaty [Code Sec. 545(b)(7)];
- *Net operating loss* deduction is not allowed; but a deduction is allowed for the net operating loss of the preceding year figured without the special deductions (except organizational expenditures) [Code Sec. 545(b)(4); Reg. § 1.545-2(d)];
- *Dividends-received* deduction is not allowed [Code Sec. 545(b)(3); Reg. § 1.545-2(c)]; and
- *Income for a short period* [Ch. 18] need not be annualized [Code Sec. 546].

After these adjustments are made, the dividends-paid deduction is subtracted to find undistributed PHC income [Code Sec. 545(a); Reg. § 1.545-1].

.02 Dividends-Paid Deduction

The PHC can subtract the following: (1) dividends that it paid during the year, (2) consent dividends, (3) the dividend carryover, and (4) certain dividends that it paid after the close of the tax year. The figure arrived at is the undistributed personal holding company income, which is the basis of the tax [Code Sec. 561; Reg. § § 1.561-1, -2].

Dividends Paid During the Tax Year

Only taxable dividends can be subtracted. Thus, the PHC must pay dividends out of earnings or profits [Ch. 2] [Code Sec. 562; Reg. § 1.562-1(a)]. However, any distribution to the extent of the undistributed PHC income is considered a taxable dividend, even if it is not paid out of earnings. Such dividends also are taxable to the stockholders [Code Sec. 316(b)(2); Reg. § § 1.316-1, 1.563-3]. This prevents an inequity when undistributed PHC income exceeds earnings, as could occur when certain deductions are disallowed.

Example 23-1: XYZ, Inc., a personal holding company with no accumulated earnings, has $5,000 earnings for the tax year. However, its adjusted PHC taxable income is $15,000, due to the disallowance of $10,000 of deductions. To avoid the PHC tax, XYZ must pay out $15,000 of dividends. However, if it could only subtract dividends paid from earnings, the maximum subtracted would be $5,000, leaving an undistributed personal holding company income of $10,000 subject to PHC tax. The exception above permits the subtraction of $15,000. The $15,000 is taxable to shareholders, even though earnings and profits are just $5,000.

NOTE: The personal holding company's distribution of appreciated property results in a dividends-paid deduction equal to the adjusted basis (*not* fair market value) of the property in the hands of your company at the time of the distribution. Reg. § 1.562-1(a) is used to determine the amount of deduction.[3]

Generally, in figuring undistributed PHC income, the PHC may subtract only the part of a liquidating dividend chargeable to accumulated earnings and profits. However, distributions of undistributed PHC income in a complete liquidation (including a distribution in redemption of stock [Ch. 22]) concluded within a 24-month period may be treated as dividends [Code Secs. 316(b)(2), 562(b)]. The dividend cannot be more than the undistributed PHC income for the year of distribution. Distributions between corporate and noncorporate shareholders must be allocated, and amounts the corporation pays to noncorporate shareholders may not be subtracted unless designated as dividend distributions [Reg. § § 1.316-1(b)(2), 1.562-1(b)(2)].

If the PHC files a consolidated return with an affiliated group and must also file a separate PHC schedule, the company can subtract a dividend distribution to another group member if it would be a taxable dividend to a recipient who is not a member of an affiliated group [Code Sec. 562(d); Reg. § 1.562-3].

Dividends paid after the close of the tax year [see below], but removed from PHC income in the tax year, may not be subtracted again by the company in the year actually distributed [Code Sec. 563(b)].

---

[3] *A.S. Fulman*, SCt, 78-1 USTC ¶9247, 434 US 528, 98 SCt 841.

Dividends That Cannot Be Deducted from Undistributed PHC Income

Nontaxable dividends, including nontaxable stock dividends and nontaxable stock rights [Code Sec. 312]; preferential dividends, including a distribution that is not made to all shareholders within the same class of stock in proportion to their shareholdings, or one that violates the dividend preference of any class of stock [Code Sec. 562(c); Reg. § 1.562-2].

Consent Dividends

A PHC may claim the dividends-paid deduction without impairing its cash position by paying cash dividends that are immediately returned to the corporation in the form of a loan or capital contribution [Code Sec. 565; Reg. §§ 1.565-1 through 6]. However, if the consent of the shareholders is obtained, it is presumed that a dividend was paid and then invested in the corporation without an actual distribution. The corporation treats the consent dividend as paid-in surplus or as a contribution to capital, with a corresponding reduction in its earnings and profits. The consent dividend will be taxable to the shareholders the same as a cash dividend. Since it is theoretically reinvested by the shareholder, the shareholder's stock basis is correspondingly increased [Code Sec. 1016(a)(12); Reg. § 1.1016-5(h)].

Dividend Carryover

If dividends exceeded adjusted taxable income in each of the two prior tax years, the sum of the excess dividends for those two years may be carried over to the current tax year. If there is an excess only in the first preceding year, only that amount is carried over. If the excess is in the second preceding year, it is reduced by the excess of taxable income over the dividends paid in the first year. Any balance is then carried over to the current tax year [Code Sec. 564(b); Reg. § 1.564-1].

> **NOTE:** *Dividends* referred to above include the following: (a) dividends paid during the tax year; (b) dividends paid before the 15th day of the third month following its close; and (c) consent dividends. They do not include the dividend carryover [Code Sec. 564(b)(1)].

Dividends Paid After the Close of the Tax Year

A PHC can elect to take a deduction for dividends paid after the close of the tax year and within 2 1/2 months after its close. However, the deduction cannot exceed the following: (1) the undistributed PHC income figured without the deduction for dividends paid after the close of the year; or (2) 20 percent of the dividends paid during the year, not including consent dividends or the deduction for dividends paid after the close of the preceding year [Code Sec. 563(b); Reg. § 1.563-2].

In figuring the accumulated earnings tax [Ch. 20], the PHC can deduct without election or restriction dividends paid after the close of the tax year and within 2 1/2 months after its close [Code Sec. 563(a); Reg. § 1.563-1].

.03 Foreign Corporations

When 10 percent or less of the value of the outstanding stock of a foreign corporation subject to the tax is owned by U.S. citizens or residents, domestic corporations, partnerships, estates, or trusts during the last half of the tax year, only the same percentage of the PHC's undistributed PHC income is taxed [Code Sec. 545(a)]. The greatest percentage of ownership during the period is used.

¶23,025 RATE OF TAX, RETURNS, AND PAYMENT

The personal holding company tax rate on undistributed personal holding company income increased from 15 percent to 20 percent effective January 1, 2013. [Code Sec. 541]. A PHC files a single return for both the income tax and the personal holding company tax. A separate Schedule PH (Form 1120), *U.S. Personal Holding Company (PHC) Tax* is provided for the PHC tax. The PHC pays the tax at the same time as the income tax [Ch. 26].

¶23,030 DEFICIENCY DIVIDEND

If a corporation is subject to the PHC tax for a prior tax year, a procedure is available that allows the corporation to make a dividend distribution to its shareholders even though the distribution does not qualify for a dividends-paid deduction. This procedure relieves the corporation from paying the deficiency, or entitles it to a refund or credit if any part of the deficiency has been paid [Code Sec. 547(d)].

> ▶ **OBSERVATION:** This means that shareholders are currently taxed because of this distribution. Also, the PHC tax can be completely wiped out for the corporation.

This remedy does not extend to interest and penalties. It is not available at all if any part of the deficiency was due to fraud or willful failure to file a timely return.

In most cases, the first step toward paying a deficiency dividend is to sign an agreement with the IRS regarding the corporation's liability for the personal holding company tax. This is known as a *determination*. The determination date ordinarily is the date that the agreement is mailed to your corporation, but it is the date that the agreement is signed if a dividend is paid before the mailing date but on or after the date of signing. The term *determination* also means a decision by the Tax Court, a judgment, decree, or other court order that has become final, or a closing agreement [Ch. 27]. The corporation must pay the deficiency dividend within 90 days after the determination date. The corporation must file a claim for a deduction within 120 days after the determination date. A refund claim can be filed by your corporation within 2 years from the determination date [Code Sec. 547; Reg. § § 1.547-1 to -7].

¶23,040 CONSOLIDATED RETURNS

The PHC tax does not apply to affiliated corporations filing a consolidated return, unless 60 percent or more of the adjusted ordinary gross income of the group is PHC income. Generally, this does not apply if any member of the group (including the common parent): (1) is exempt from the PHC tax or (2) received 10 percent or more of its adjusted ordinary gross income from sources outside the affiliated group, and 80 percent or more of the income from outside sources was PHC income [Code Sec. 542(b); Reg. § 1.542-4].

If, for any of the reasons stated above, the general rule does not apply, then each corporation will be treated separately and, if it meets the personal holding tests, each will be separately subject to the PHC tax.

REGULATED INVESTMENT COMPANIES (RICs)

¶23,075 TAX ON RICs (MUTUAL FUNDS)

.01 Tax Treatment of RICs

A regulated investment company (RIC) (more commonly known as a mutual fund) is a widely held corporation or common trust fund that acts as investment agents for its shareholders, typically investing in government and corporate securities and distributing dividend and interest income earned from the investments as dividends to their shareholders. The RIC entity may avoid paying corporate tax if the RIC distributes all of its earnings and profits to its shareholders [Code Sec. 852(b)]. Unlike ordinary corporations, a RIC may claim a deduction for dividend payments against ordinary income and net capital gains. RIC taxation is available only if the entity satisfies several requirements discussed in detail below, including one that at least 90 percent of its gross income consist of interest, dividends, and certain other income types.

.02 Excise Tax Imposed on RIC Undistributed Income

An excise tax under Code Sec. 4982(a) is imposed "on every regulated investment company for each calendar year." The excise tax is equal to 4 percent of the excess, if any, of (1) the "required distribution" for the calendar year, over (2) the distributed amount for that same calendar year. The tax is payable on or before March 15 of the following calendar year. The RIC should use Form 8613, *Return of Excise Tax on Undistributed Income of Regulated Investment Company*, to report the excise tax. If a RIC has more than one mutual fund, each mutual fund should file a separate Form 8613. "Required distribution" is defined in Code Sec. 4982(b), with respect to any calendar year, as the sum of (A) 98 percent of the RIC's ordinary income for that calendar year, plus (B) 98.2 percent of the RIC's "capital gain net income for the 1-year period ending on October 31 of such calendar year." "Capital gain net income" is defined in Code Sec. 4982(e)(2)(A) as having the same meaning given to that term by Code Sec. 1222(9), "determined by treating the one-year period ending on October 31 of any calendar year as the company's taxable year." Code Sec. 1222(9) provides that "[t]he term 'capital gain net income' means the excess of the gains from sales or exchanges of capital assets over the losses from such sales or exchanges."

For discussion of RIC capital loss carryovers see ¶23,090. For discussion of the investor's tax treatment of mutual fund distributions, see Chapter 6.

Entities Exempt from Excise Tax

The following RICs are exempt from the Code Sec. 4982 excise tax: (1) A RIC that is a tax-exempt qualified pension, profit-sharing, or stock bonus plan; (2) A RIC that is a segregated asset account of a life insurance company; (3) RIC investments of less than $250,000 made in connection with the organization of a RIC; (4) entities whose ownership of an interest in the RIC would not preclude the application of look-through rules under Code Sec. 817(h)(4) related to segregated accounts of certain annuity and life insurance contracts. Specifically, these entities include qualified annuity plans, IRAs, including Roth IRAs, certain government plans, and a pension plan described in Code Sec. 501(c)(18). In addition, another RIC not subject to the excise tax may hold stock in a RIC without negating its exemption from the excise tax [Code Sec. 4982(f)].

Election to Use Tax Year

A RIC can make an irrevocable election to have its tax year applied in lieu of the one-year period ending on October 31 if its tax year ends with the month of November or December [Code Sec. 4982(e)(4)].

¶23,080 REQUIREMENTS TO BE TAXED AS RIC

To qualify for the tax benefits afforded RICs (no taxation at entity level), a corporation must meet the following requirements:

- *Registration.* The corporation must either be registered under the Investment Company Act of 1940 or be a certain type of common trust fund [Code Sec. 851(a); Reg. § 1.851-1(b)].

  NOTE: A corporation that elects to be treated as a business development company under the Investment Company Act is eligible to be a RIC [Code Sec. 851(a)(1)(B)].

- *Election.* The corporation must file an election to be taxed as a RIC with its return for the tax year. The election is binding for future years [Code Sec. 851(b)(1); Reg. § 1.851-2(a)].
- *Gross income.* At least 90 percent of the corporations gross income must be derived from:

  — Dividends,

  — Interest,

  — Payments with respect to securities loans (as defined in Code Sec. 512(a)(5)),

  — Gains from the sale or other disposition of stock or securities or foreign currencies,

  — Other income (including but not limited to gains from options, futures, or forward contracts) derived with respect to its business of investing in such stock, securities, or currencies,

  — Net income derived from an interest in a qualified publicly traded partnership,

  — At the close of each quarter of the tax year at least 50 percent of the value of its total assets is represented by cash and cash items (including receivables),

  — Government securities and securities of other regulated investment companies, and

  — Other securities limited to an amount not greater in value than five percent of the value of the total assets of the taxpayer and to not more than 10 percent of the outstanding voting securities of such issuer [Code Sec. 851(b)].

- *Diversification of assets.* At the close of each quarter of the tax year, at least 50 percent of the value of the corporation's total assets must be cash and cash items (including receivables), government securities, and securities of other RICs [Code Sec. 851(b)(3)]. Other securities may also be included, but the amount that the taxpayer owns in any one corporation cannot be: (1) greater in value than 5 percent of the value of the taxpayer's total assets and (2) more than 10 percent of the outstanding voting securities of the issuing corporation. In the case of a venture capital company, the 10 percent rule may be waived in order to permit the venture capital company to qualify as a RIC [¶23,085]. Also, at the close of each quarter, the mutual fund must not have more than 25 percent of the value of its total assets invested in the securities (other than government securities or the securities of other RICs) of any one corporation or of two or more corporations which the mutual fund controls, and which are engaged in the same, similar or related business [Code Sec. 851(b)(3); Reg. §1.851-2(c)]. At the close of each quarter of the tax year, the corporation, not more than 25 percent of the value of its total assets can be invested in the securities of one or more qualified publicly trade partnerships [Code Sec. 851(b)(3)(B)(iii)]. In Rev. Proc. 2009-42,[4] the IRS explained the conditions under which a RIC that holds a partnership interest in a Public-Private Investment Partnership (PPIP) created under the Public-Private Investment Program is treated for purposes of Code Sec. 851(b)(3) as if it directly invested in the assets held by the PPIP. Under the Program, the Treasury Department and private investors partner to form PPIPs, which acquire certain commercial and residential mortgage-backed securities.

- Special rules are applied to venture capital companies [¶23,085]. For purposes of applying the diversification requirements, a RIC's investment in refunded bonds is an investment in government securities to the extent that an acquisition of the refunded bonds would be treated as an acquisition of the government securities that were deposited in the escrow for the bonds.[5]

- *Distribution of income.* The company must distribute to shareholders dividends (not counting capital gain dividends) at least equal to the sum of: (a) 90 percent of its investment company taxable income plus (b) 90 percent of the excess of its tax-exempt interest over its disallowed tax-exempt interest deductions [Code Sec. 852(a); Reg. §1.852-1]. The dividends may be paid during the tax year, or after its close [¶23,090].

  For purposes of determining the taxable income of a RIC, Code Sec. 852(b) separates a RIC's net capital gain from its other income (identified as *investment company taxable income*). Code Sec. 852(b)(3) imposes a tax on the excess of the RIC's net capital gain over its deduction for dividends paid determined with reference to capital gains dividends only. A RIC is not allowed any deduction for expenses against its net capital gain. A RIC's investment company taxable income equals its taxable income (exclusive of net capital gain) reduced by allowable expenses and its deduction for dividends paid determined without regard to capital gains dividends and exempt-interest dividends. Thus, the basic pattern for taxing a RIC's income treats its expenses as allocable only to its investment company taxable income (exclusive of net capital gain).

---

[4] Rev. Proc. 2009-42, 2009-40 IRB 459.

[5] Rev. Rul. 2003-84, 2003-2 CB 289.

NOTE: A waiver of the RIC distribution rule may be provided when the failure to meet the rule results from prior year distributions necessary to avoid the excise tax on the undistributed income of a RIC [¶23,090] [Code Sec. 852(a)(2)(B)].

The distributions made by the RIC to shareholders will be deductible by the RIC provided the distributions are pro rata and not preferential. The RIC may not: (1) distribute dividends in any manner that prefers or favors any share of stock of a class over any other share of stock of that same class, and (2) prefer one share of stock over another class except to the extent that one class is entitled to the preference [Code Sec. 562(c)]. Distributions made to RIC shareholders may vary and yet not forfeit deductibility as dividends. Mutual fund distributions will qualify as deductible dividends under Code Sec. 562 even if variations exist in distributions made to different shareholders provided the differences exist solely as a result of the allocation and payment of fees and expenses.[6]

.01 Saving Features

Under the *de minimis* asset test failure rule, the failure is forgiven if it is cured in a timely fashion. The rule is available if a RIC fails to meet one of the asset tests in Code Sec. 851(b)(3) due to the ownership of assets the total value of which does not exceed the lesser of:

- One percent of the total value of the RIC's assets at the end of the quarter for which the assets are valued, and
- $10 million [Code Sec. 851(d)(2)(B)(i)].

Where the *de minimis* rule applies, the RIC is considered to have satisfied the asset tests if, within six months of the last day of the quarter in which the RIC identifies that it failed the asset test the RIC:

- Disposes of assets in order to meet the requirements of the asset tests, or
- The RIC otherwise meets the requirements of the asset tests [Code Sec. 851(d)(2)(B)(ii)].

A savings mechanism is also available for other (non-*de minimis*) asset test failures, provided that:

- Following the identification of the failure to satisfy the asset tests, the RIC sets forth in a schedule a description of each asset that causes the RIC to fail to satisfy the asset test [Code Sec. 851(d)(2)(A)(i)];
- The failure to meet the asset tests is due to reasonable cause and not due to willful neglect [Code Sec. 851(d)(2)(A)(ii)]; and
- Within six months of the last day of the quarter in which the RIC identifies that it failed the asset test, the RIC (a) disposes of the assets which caused the asset test failure, or (b) otherwise meets the requirements of the asset tests [Code Sec. 851(d)(2)(A)(iii)].

---

[6] Rev. Proc. 99-40, 1999-2 CB 565.

In the case of an asset test failure other than a *de minimis* failure, a tax is imposed in an amount equal to the greater of:

- $50,000, or
- The amount determined by multiplying the highest rate of tax imposed on corporations (currently 35 percent) by the net income generated during the period of asset test failure by the assets that caused the RIC to fail the asset test [Code Sec. 851(d)(2)(C)(i)].

.02 Gross Income Test Failures

An RIC that fails to meet the gross income test shall nevertheless be considered to have satisfied the test if (following the identification of the failure to meet the test for the tax year):

- The RIC set forth in a schedule, a description of each item of its gross income; and
- The failure to meet the gross income test is due to reasonable cause and is not due to willful neglect [Code Sec. 851(i)(1)].

In addition, a tax is imposed on any RIC that fails to meet the gross income test equal to the amount by which the RIC's gross income from sources which are not qualifying income exceeds one-ninth of its gross income from sources which are qualifying income [Code Sec. 851(i)(2)].

> **Example 23-2:** A RIC has $900 million of gross income from sources which are qualifying income, and $150 million of gross income from other sources. A tax of $50 million is imposed. The tax is the amount by which the $150 million gross income from sources which are not qualifying income exceeds $100 million, which is one ninth of $900 million (Joint Committee on Taxation, *Technical Explanation of H.R. 4337, the ''Regulated Investment Company Modernization Act of 2010''* (JCX-49-10)).

.03 Calculation of Investment Company Taxable Income

Taxes imposed for failure of the asset or income tests are deductible for purposes of calculating investment company taxable income of a RIC [Code Sec. 852(b)(2)(G)].

.04 Deficiency Dividend Procedure

Under Code Sec. 860, a qualified investment entity, i.e., a RIC, may avoid being disqualified as a special tax entity or being subject to tax on deficiency dividends (other than interest and penalties) if a "determination" results in an adjustment, which could preclude compliance with the normal income distribution requirements. Essentially, an amount deductible as a deficiency dividend is included in computing the deduction for dividends paid. A RIC that uses the deficiency dividends procedures is subject to interest and penalties on the amount of the adjustment, but only up to the amount of the deficiency deduction allowed. A RIC is allowed a deduction for a deficiency dividend only if, among other things, there is a determination that results in an adjustment for the year in which the deficiency dividend is paid.

In Rev. Proc. 2009-28,[7] the IRS provided procedures for which the filing by a RIC of Form 8927, *Determination Under Section 860(e)(4) by a Qualified Investment Entity*, is

[7] Rev. Proc. 2009-28, 2009-20 IRB 1011.

treated as a self-determination for purposes of the deficiency dividend procedures of Code Sec. 860.

A "determination", as defined under Code Sec. 860(e), includes: (1) a final decision of the Tax Court or any other court of competent jurisdiction, (2) a closing agreement [Code Sec. 7121], (3) a tax liability agreement signed by the IRS and the taxpayer, and (4) a statement of "self-determination," which is a statement by the taxpayer attached to its amendment or supplement to the tax return for the relevant tax year [Code Sec. 860(e)(4)].

The date of the determination controls the timeliness of certain acts that the RIC must perform. No distribution of property will be considered deficiency dividends unless the property is distributed within 90 days after the determination and unless a claim for a deficiency dividend deduction with respect to the distribution is filed pursuant to Code Sec. 860(g) [Code Sec. 860(f)(1)].

Code Sec. 860(g) provides that no deficiency dividend deduction shall be allowed unless a claim is filed within 120 days after the date of the determination. The claim must be filed on Form 976, *Claim for Deficiency Dividends Deductions by a Personal Holding Company, Regulated Investment Company, or Real Estate Investment Trust.*

Rev. Proc. 2009-28 provides that if a RIC properly completes Form 8927, and files it with the IRS, in accordance with the applicable instructions, then the form will be treated as a statement of self-determination and therefore constitute a determination for purposes of Code Sec. 860(e). The procedures apply certain principles contained within the timely-mailing-as-timely-filing rules of Code Sec. 7502. Thus, if Form 8927 is sent by U.S. mail or by proper use of a private delivery service (PDS), then the date of the determination is the postmark date determined using the principles of Reg. § 301.7502-1(c) (regarding registered and certified mail) and any applicable guidance (as enumerated in the procedures) regarding designated PDSs. If the Form 8927 is filed with the IRS by any other means, then the date of the determination is the date the form is received by the IRS.

Taxpayers are encouraged to request a return receipt or other comparable evidence of actual receipt by the IRS to establish that the Form 8927 was delivered. If the taxpayer does not have proof of actual delivery, *prima facie* evidence that the Form 8927 was delivered to the IRS is sufficient.

.05 Personal Holding Companies

A PHC without accumulated earnings and profits can elect RIC status. PHCs with accumulated earnings and profits can make distributions to qualify. However, the highest corporate tax rate is imposed on the undistributed investment company taxable income to any RIC that is a PHC [¶ 23,001 et seq.] [Code Sec. 852(b)(1)].

¶23,085 VENTURE CAPITAL COMPANIES

An investment company that furnishes capital for corporations chiefly engaged in developing new products is a *venture capital company.* In determining whether an investment company satisfies the requirement that it invest at least 50 percent of its assets in certain investments to qualify as a regulated investment company, the investment company may include in its investments the value of any securities of an issuer, whether or not the company owns more than 10 percent of the outstanding voting securities of the issuer, the basis of which, when added to the basis of the investment company for securities of such issuer previously acquired, did not exceed five percent of the value of the total assets of the company at the time of the subsequent acquisition of securities. This rule does not apply to the securities of an issuer if the company has continuously held any security of such issuer for 10 or more years preceding the quarter of the tax year. To qualify for this special rule, the investment company must have the SEC certify, not earlier than 60 days before the close of the tax year, that it is principally engaged in the furnishing of capital to other corporations, which are principally engaged in the development or exploitation of inventions, technological improvements, new processes, or products not previously generally available [Code Sec. 851(e)(1); Reg. § 1.851-6].

¶23,090 FIGURING THE TAX ON RICs

RICs are taxed on investment company taxable income at the same rates as corporations in general. See ¶ 23,010 for corporate tax rates. A RIC that is also a personal holding company is taxed at the highest corporate rate [¶ 23,080]. Investment company taxable income is taxable income with the following adjustments:

- Excess of net long-term capital gain over net short-term capital loss is excluded;
- No net operating loss deduction is allowed;
- Special deductions listed in Ch. 20 are not allowed (except organizational expenditures); and
- Dividends paid during the tax year (other than capital gain and exempt-interest dividends) can be deducted.

Adequate shareholder records need not be kept for a corporation to qualify as a RIC. However, investment company taxable income of a RIC that does not keep adequate shareholder records is taxed at the highest corporate rate (the same treatment is provided for RICs that are personal holding companies [¶ 23,080]) [Code Sec. 852(a)].

In addition, a tax is imposed on the excess of net long-term capital gain over (1) net short-term capital loss and (2) capital gain dividends paid during the tax year [Code Sec. 852; Reg. § 1.852-2, -3]. See below for treatment of undistributed long-term capital gain under certain conditions.

For any calendar year, a nondeductible excise tax applies on every RIC, equal to 4 percent of the excess, if any, of the required distribution for the calendar year over the distributed amount for the calendar year [Code Sec. 4982]. The excise tax is to be paid not later than March 15 of the succeeding calendar year. *Required distribution* for any calendar year means the sum of 98 percent of the RIC's ordinary income for the calendar year, plus 98 percent of the RIC's capital gain net income for the one-year period ending on October 31 of the calendar year. This is increased by the excess, if any, of the grossed-up required distribution for the preceding calendar year over the distributed amount for the preceding calendar year.

.01 Qualified Dividends Paid by Mutual Funds and Other RICs

A mutual fund (RIC) shareholder can include as part of qualifying dividend income any dividends designated by the mutual fund as qualifying dividends [Code Sec. 854(b)(1)(B)]. In order for the RIC to designate the amount as qualified dividend income, the entity's qualified dividend income must be less than 95 percent of its gross income. The aggregate amount designated as qualified dividends may not exceed the aggregate dividends received during the year [Code Sec. 854(b)(1)(C)]. In addition, the amount designated as qualifying dividend income may not exceed the sum of: (1) the qualified dividend income of the RIC for the tax year; and (2) the amount of any earnings and profits distributed for the tax year accumulated in a tax year in which the RIC rules did not apply [Code Sec. 854(b)(1)(C)]. In Rev. Rul. 2005-31,[8] the IRS announced that it is allowing dividend designations to total more than the dividend distributions, which, when coupled with a rule that computes qualified dividend income without reduction for expenses, results in greater tax savings for investors.

When the aggregate of qualifying dividends received by a RIC during the year are less than 95 percent of the RIC's *gross income,* the dividends paid by the RIC that are eligible for capital gains treatment are limited to the aggregate qualifying dividends received by the RIC. *Gross income* includes only the excess of net short-term capital gain from sales or dispositions of stock or securities, over net long-term capital loss from such sales or dispositions included in gross income [Code Sec. 854(b)(1)(B)(ii)].

Capital Gain Dividend

A RIC may make capital gain dividend distributions to shareholders only out of a RIC's net capital gain for the year, which is the excess of its net long-term capital gain over its net short-term capital loss [Code Sec. 852(b)(3)(C)]. A capital gain dividend must be reported to the IRS and its shareholders on Form 1099 [Code Sec. 852(b)(3)(C)]. Capital gain dividends may not be the subject of an individual's dividends exclusion or a corporation's dividends received deduction under Code Sec. 243 [Code Sec. 854(a)].

Undistributed Long-Term Capital Gain

RICs may treat undistributed long-term capital gain as if:

- It had been distributed to its shareholders;
- The capital gains tax had been paid by the shareholder (rather than the company); and
- The amount constructively distributed (less the capital gains tax) had been reinvested by the shareholder in the company.

A shareholder will: (1) include this amount in figuring long-term capital gain; (2) get a credit against tax equal to the capital gains tax paid by the company on the amount; and (3) add the amount (less the tax) to stock basis. Thus, the adjusted basis of each shareholder's shares in the RIC is increased by the difference between the amount of the includible capital gains from the dividend and the tax the shareholder is deemed to

[8] Rev. Rul. 2005-31, 2005-1 CB 1084.

have paid with respect to those shares. Thus, the adjusted basis of each shareholder's shares in the RIC is increased by the difference between the amount of the includible capital gains from the dividend and the tax the shareholder is deemed to have paid with respect to those shares. Within 30 days after the close of the tax year, the company must file Form 2438, *Undistributed Capital Gain Tax Return,* and pay the tax on the undistributed gain. A notice of the amount constructively distributed must be given to each shareholder on Form 2439 within 60 days after the end of the fund's tax year and should be attached to each taxpayer's tax return to substantiate the credit claimed [Code Sec. 852(b)(3)(D); Reg. § 1.852-4, -9(b)].

.02 Exempt-Interest Dividend

A tax-exempt dividend is any dividend (or part of it) so designated by the company in a written notice mailed to its shareholders within 60 days after the close of its tax year. A RIC must report the tax items in written statements furnished to shareholders [Code Sec. 852(b)(5)(A)(i)]. Exempt-interest dividends are allowed only if, at the close of each quarter of its tax year, at least 50 percent of the value of the company's total assets is tax-exempt obligations. An upper-tier RIC that is a qualified fund of funds may pass through exempt-interest dividends and foreign tax credits to its shareholders, without having to meet the 50-percent asset requirement [Code Sec. 852(g)]. A qualified fund of funds is a RIC if, at the close of each quarter of the tax year, at least 50 percent of the value of its total assets is represented by interests in other RICs [Code Sec. 852(g)(2)]. The amount of the dividend cannot be more than the excess of the exempt interest over the disallowed exempt-interest deductions. A shareholder treats exempt-interest dividends as interest excludable from gross income [Code Sec. 852(b)(5)]. Any loss on the sale or exchange of RIC stock held for six months or less is disallowed to the extent exempt-interest dividends are received for the stock [Code Sec. 852(b)].

.03 Foreign Tax Credit

Instead of claiming a tax credit or deduction for foreign taxes on its own return, a RIC may elect to have its shareholders claim the credit or deduction on their returns. Although the company loses the credit or deduction for the foreign taxes, it may add the amount of such taxes to its dividends-paid deduction. To qualify for the election, the company must have more than 50 percent of the value of its total assets at the close of the tax year invested in foreign securities, and must distribute at least 90 percent of its investment company taxable income. An upper-tier RIC that is a qualified fund of funds may pass through foreign tax credits, even though, at the close of the tax year, not more than 50 percent of the value of its total assets consist of stock and securities in foreign corporations [Code Sec. 852(g)(1)(B)]. A notice of the election must be sent to shareholders within 60 days after the end of the fund's tax year [Code Sec. 853; Reg. § 1.853-1-4]. A RIC must report the tax items in written statements furnished to shareholders [Code Sec. 853(c)]. For an explanation of the foreign tax credit, see Ch. 28.

.04 Shareholders' Dividends-Received Deduction

Dividends received by individuals from most sources are taxed at capital gains tax rates with certain modifications [Code Sec. 1(h)(11)]. See Ch. 2. Code Sec. 854(b)(1)(A) allows a corporate shareholder that receives a dividend from a RIC to claim a dividends received deduction with respect to the amount of the distribution designated by the RIC as a dividend. Code Sec. 854(b)(1)(B) provides that the aggregate amount that may be designated by a RIC as a dividend for purposes of the dividends received deduction may not exceed the aggregate amount of dividends received by the RIC during the tax year. The same restriction is imposed on the amount that may be designated by the RIC as a dividend for purposes of claiming the lower rates on dividends [Code Sec. 854(b)(1)(B)]. If the aggregate dividends received by a RIC during any tax year are less than 95 percent of its gross income, a corporate shareholder that receives a dividend from a RIC that has met the minimum distribution requirements of Code Sec. 852(a) may claim a dividends received deduction under Code Sec. 243 with respect to the amount of the distribution designated by the RIC as a dividend [Code Sec. 854(b)(1)(A)].

.05 Dividends Declared After Year-End (Spillover Dividends)

If dividends are declared after year-end (commonly referred to as spillover dividends) but before the filing date of the return, they may be treated as having been paid in the tax year covered by the return if the company elects. However, they must actually be paid to the shareholders not later than the date of the next regular dividend payment after the declaration and within 12 months after the close of the tax year. These dividends are treated by the shareholders as income of the tax year in which the dividends are actually distributed. Notice to shareholders must be given not later than 45 days after the close of the tax year in which the distribution is made [Code Sec. 855; Reg. § 1.855-1].

A spillover dividend must be declared before the later of:

- The 15th day of the ninth month following the closing of the tax year, or
- The extended due date for filing the corporation's return for the tax year (when such a filing extension occurs) [Code Sec. 855(a)(1)].

Under the new rules, the entire dividend must be distributed to shareholders no later than the date of the first dividend payment *of the same type of dividend* (such as ordinary income dividend or capital gain dividend) after the declaration, and during the 12 months after the tax year is closed [Code Sec. 855(a)(2)].

.06 Preference Items for Alternative Minimum Tax

The adjusted current earnings of a RIC are not treated as a tax preference subject to the minimum tax [Code Sec. 56(g)(6)].

.07 Earnings of Liquidating RICs

Any amount that a liquidating RIC may take as a deduction for dividends paid with respect to an otherwise tax-free liquidating distribution to an 80 percent corporate owner is includible in the income of the recipient corporation. The includible amount is treated as a dividend received from the RIC. The liquidating RIC may designate the amount as a dividend eligible for the 70 percent dividends-received deduction [Code Sec. 332(c)]. The liquidating corporation will not recognize gain on the liquidating distribution and the recipient corporation will hold the assets at a carryover basis, even where the amount received is treated as a dividend [Code Sec. 334(b)].

.08 RIC Capital Loss Carryover

A RIC may carry forward net capital losses indefinitely [Code Sec. 1212(a)].[9] A RIC computes net capital loss carryovers in the same manner as individuals. See ¶ 8051.

REAL ESTATE INVESTMENT TRUSTS (REIT)

¶23,095 WHAT IS A REIT

The real estate investment trust (REIT) is a tax-preferred entity that permits investors to buy shares in real estate investment property and real estate mortgages. In essence, a REIT is a mutual fund that invests exclusively in real estate. A REIT operates much the same way as a mutual fund because it is publicly traded on the stock market and is completely liquid. To qualify as a REIT, an entity must satisfy a two-part income test found in Code Sec. 856(c)(2) and Code Sec. 856(c)(3). See ¶ 23,096 for further discussion. In addition, there is an asset test imposed in Code Sec. 856(c)(4). See ¶ 23,097 for further discussion. REITS are also subject to a distribution requirement imposed in Code Sec. 857. For further discussion, see ¶ 23,098.

A REIT must receive most of its income from passive real estate related investments and not engage in any active trade or business. It is a pass-through entity that is also required to distribute income to shareholders who in turn pay tax on the income. If an electing entity meets the qualifications for REIT status, the portion of its income that is distributed to the investors each year generally is taxed to the investors without the imposition of tax at the REIT level.

A REIT must satisfy a number of tests on an annual basis relating to the following attributes of the entity: (1) organizational structure, (2) source of income, (3) nature of assets, and (4) distribution of income. These tests are intended to allow pass-through treatment only if there is a pooling of investment arrangement, if the entity's investments are basically in real estate assets, and its income is passive income from real estate investment, rather than income from the operation of a business involving real estate. In addition, substantially all of the entity's income must be passed through to its shareholders on a current basis. A REIT may elect to be taxed in a manner substantially similar to a RIC [¶ 23,090]. However, unlike a RIC, there is no pass-through of the foreign tax credit.

Capital gain or loss is realized on the sale or redemption of a REIT investment. A REIT cannot carry back a net operating loss. However, a 20-year carryover is allowed [Code Sec. 172(b)(1)(B)].

.01 Electing REIT Status

A qualifying corporation, trust or association may choose to be a REIT by making an election on Form 1120-REIT [Code Sec. 856]. The election is irrevocable [Code Sec. 856(c); Reg. § 1.856-2(b)]. When it qualifies for REIT status, a corporation, trust or association must adopt or change to a calendar-year accounting period [Code Sec. 859].

---

9 Rev. Rul. 2012-29, IRB 2012-42, 475.

An entity that has not engaged in any active business may change its annual accounting period to a calendar year without IRS approval, for electing REIT status [Code Sec. 859(b)].

Taxpayers may revoke the REIT election voluntarily, but the organization may not make a new REIT election for the four tax years after this revocation.

.02 Organization and Tax Requirements

In addition to the income and investment requirements discussed in ¶ 23,096, a REIT must [Code Sec. 856(a); Reg. § 1.856-1]:

- Be managed by one or more trustees or directors;
- Have beneficial interests represented by transferable shares or certificates;
- Be taxable as a domestic corporation (but for the REIT provisions); and
- Be beneficially owned by at least 100 persons (for at least 335 days of a tax year) and five or fewer persons may not own, either actually or constructively, more than 50 percent of the stock. A pension or profit-sharing trust is no longer counted as a single individual for purposes of this rule. Rather, beneficiaries of qualified employees' pension or profit-sharing trusts [Ch. 3] are treated as holding stock in the REIT in proportion to their actuarial interests in the trust [Code Sec. 856(h)(3)(A)(i)].

An entity that otherwise meets the applicable requirements may elect REIT status, even if it meets the PHC stock ownership test, or if it had fewer than 100 shareholders, provided that the entity was not a REIT in any prior year [Code Sec. 856(h)]. Also, to elect REIT status, the electing entity must either have been treated as a REIT for all tax years, or must have no earnings and profits accumulated for any year in which the entity was in existence and not treated as a REIT [Code Sec. 857(a)].

.03 Excise Tax Imposed on REIT Undistributed Income

An excise tax of four percent is imposed on undistributed REIT income under Code Sec. 4981. The nondeductible excise tax is computed on any excess of the "required distribution" over the "distributed amount" [Code Sec. 4982(a)]. The tax is reported on Form 8612, *Return of Excise Tax on Undistributed Income of Real Estate Investment Trusts* and is due on or before March 15 of the year following the calendar year for which it is calculated [Code Sec. 4981(d)]. If more time is needed to file the form, use Form 7004, *Application for Automatic Extension of Time To File Certain Business Income Tax, Information, and Other Returns.* Note, however, that Form 7004 does not extend the time for payment of tax. Form 8612 must be signed and dated by the president, vice president, treasurer, assistant treasurer, chief accounting officer, or by any other officer (such as tax officer) authorized to sign. Receivers, trustees, or assignees must sign and date any return that they are required to file on behalf of the REIT.

The "required distribution" for each year is, generally, the sum of (1) 85 percent of the REIT's ordinary income plus (2) 95 percent of the REIT's net capital gain income [Code Sec. 4981(b)(1)]. The computation may also include a "grossed up required distribution," which is the sum of amounts from earlier years that have not been deemed to be distributed plus current taxable income without regard to any deduction for dividends paid [Code Sec. 4981(b)(2)]. Dividends declared in October, November or December of a year and made payable to shareholders of record in such months are deemed to have been paid by the REIT and received by its shareholders on December 31 of such year, so long as the dividends are actually paid during January of the following year.[10]

.04 Prohibited Transactions Rules

A 100-percent tax is imposed on the net income (including any foreign currency gain) of a REIT from prohibited transactions [Code Sec. 857(b)(6)(A)]. A *prohibited transaction* is the sale or other disposition of property held for sale in the ordinary course of a trade or business other than foreclosure property [Code Sec. 857 (b)(6)(B)(iii)]. In determining the amount of net income derived from prohibited transactions, losses from such transactions (and deductions attributable to prohibited transactions in which a loss was incurred) may not be taken into account [Code Sec. 857(b)(6)(B)(ii)]. However, the amount of any net loss from prohibited transactions may be taken into account in computing REIT taxable income.

.05 Records and Information

The trust must keep records of all its investments. It also must keep records of the actual stock ownership in the Revenue District where it files its return. For this, the trust must ask some record shareholders to supply the names of the actual stock owners each year. Shareholders who do not give the information to the trust must attach it to their income tax return. A trust that does not keep this ownership record is subject to a penalty of $25,000 ($50,000 for intentional violations [Code Sec. 857(f)]).

.06 Preference Items for Alternative Minimum Tax

The adjusted current earnings of a REIT are not treated as a tax preference subject to the alternative minimum tax [Code Sec. 56(g)(6)].

.07 Reduction of Corporate Preference Items

Corporate shareholders of a REIT may reduce the amount of additional section 1250 ordinary income that they have to recognize by treating a capital gain dividend as paid out of that amount. Any dividend so treated is section 1250 gain for any corporate shareholder [Code Sec. 291(d)].

.08 Safe Harbor Provided for Distressed Mortgage Debt Held by REITs

In Rev. Proc. 2011-16,[11] the IRS provided a safe harbor when mortgage loans held by REITs that have experienced default or for which there is a significant risk of default have been modified in order to substantially reduce the risk of default. The safe harbor is available if both of the following conditions are satisfied:

1. The REIT or servicer of the loan (the "pre-modified loan") reasonably believes that there is a significant risk of default of the pre-modified loan on maturity of the loan or at an earlier date. One relevant factor in determining the risk of default is how far in the future the possible default may be.
2. The REIT or servicer reasonably believes that the modified loan presents a substantially reduced risk of default, as compared with the pre-modified loan.

---

[10] Conference Committee Report to the Tax Reform Act of 1996 (P.L. 99-514).

[11] Rev. Proc. 2011-16, IRB 2011-5, 440.

If these conditions are satisfied, then for purposes of ascertaining under Reg. § 1.856-5(c)(2) the "loan value of the real property" securing that loan, a REIT may treat the modification as not being a new commitment to make or purchase a loan, and the modification of the mortgage loan will not be treated as a prohibited transaction under Code Sec. 857(b)(6).

Rev. Proc. 2011-16 also provides that the IRS will not challenge a REIT's treatment of a loan as being in part a "real estate asset" for purposes of Code Sec. 856(c)(4) if the REIT treats the loan as being a real estate asset in an amount equal to the lesser of:

1. The value of the loan as determined under Reg. § 1.856-3(a), or
2. The loan value of the real property securing the loan as determined under Reg. § 1.856-5(c) and Rev. Proc. 2011-16.

¶23,096 GROSS INCOME REQUIREMENT

Code Sec. 856 sets forth a number of requirements that taxpayers must satisfy in order for an entity to qualify for tax-preferred REIT status, and the favorable tax treatment afforded earnings distributed to investors. The two-part gross income test in Code Sec. 856(c)(2) must be satisfied on an annual basis. Failure to satisfy the gross income test could subject the REIT to penalty excise tax or to REIT disqualification for the year of the failure and four succeeding tax years.

There are two categories of income that a REIT must satisfy each year under Code Sec. 856(c)(2) and (3):

- At least 95 percent of the entity's gross income must be from rents from real property; and
- At least 75 percent of the entity's gross income must be from real property sources.

Under the Code Sec. 856(c)(2) gross income test, at least 95 percent of a REIT's gross income[12] (excluding gross income from prohibited transactions) must be derived from passive-type income, such as:

- Dividends;
- Interest;
- Rents from real property;[13]
- Gain from the sale or other disposition of stock, securities, and real property;

[12] LTR 201246013 (Aug. 20, 2012) (income inclusions attributable to a REIT's stock ownership in controlled foreign corporations and passive foreign investment companies constitute qualifying income under Code Sec. 856(c)(2)).

[13] LTR 201314002 (Oct. 9, 2012). ("data center" buildings with components designed to store and protect documents and data constitute "real property"); LTR 201204006 (Oct. 24, 2011) (large, welded steel frames bolted to sign superstructures with the top sign consisting of an LED video screen constitute "real property"); LTR 201143011 (July 19, 2011) (outdoor steel billboard structures that were part of the building structures, or separately constructed structures in the case of the tower steel billboard structures constitute "real property"); LTR 201129007 (April 6, 2011) (wireless and broadcast communications towers and sites on which such towers are located (including fencing, shelters, and permanently installed backup generators) constitute "real property").

- Abatements and refunds of taxes on real property;
- Income and gain derived from foreclosure property;
- Amounts received for entering into agreements (i) to make loans secured by mortgages on real property or on interests in real property or (ii) to purchase or lease real property (including interests in real property and interests in mortgages on real property); and
- Gain from the sale or other disposition of a real estate asset which is not a prohibited transaction [Code Sec. 856(c)(2)].

Under the Code Sec. 856(c)(3) 75-percent gross income test, a REIT is required to show that at least 75 percent of its gross income, other than gross income from prohibited transactions, is derived from "real property." Qualifying types of income for this 75-percent category include:

- Rents from real property;
- Interest on obligations secured by real estate mortgages or real estate interests;
- Gain from the sale of real property;
- Dividends and other distributions from qualified REITs;
- Abatements and refunds of taxes on real property;
- Income and gain from foreclosure property;
- Amounts received or accrued as consideration for agreeing to make loans secured by real estate mortgages or real estate interests or to purchase or lease real estate;
- Gain from the sale or disposition of a real estate asset is not a prohibited transaction; and
- Qualified temporary investment income [Code Sec. 856(c)(3)].

A REIT's failure to meet the 95-percent and 75-percent gross income tests will not result in disqualification of the REIT if:

1. After the REIT identifies the failure to meet the requirements, it provides a description of each item of its gross income described in the tests in a schedule filed in accordance with IRS regulations, and
2. The failure to satisfy the tests is due to reasonable cause and not due to willful neglect [Code Sec. 856(c)(6)].

.01 Interest Rate or Hedging Agreements

Any income from a hedging transaction or any income from a transaction entered into to manage currency fluctuations will not be considered gross income for purposes of the 95-percent income test or 75-percent income test to the extent the transaction hedges any indebtedness incurred to acquire or carry real estate assets [Code Sec. 856(c)(5)(G)(i) and (ii)]. For these purposes, a hedging transaction is defined in Code Sec. 1221(b)(2)(A) as any transaction entered into by the REIT primarily to manage the risk of interest rate or price changes or currency fluctuations with respect to borrowings made or to be made, or ordinary obligations incurred by the REIT. Any hedging transaction must be clearly identified as such before the close of the day on which it was acquired, originated or entered into [Code Sec. 1221(a)(7)].

.02 Qualified Temporary Investment Income

If a REIT receives new equity capital and temporarily invests the proceeds in stock or debt instruments, then income from these investments (interest, dividends or gains from the sale of the instruments) that is received during the one-year period beginning on the date the capital is received is treated as qualifying income for purposes of the 75-percent income test [Code Sec. 856(c)(5)(D)]. New capital is any amount received by the REIT in exchange for stock or certificates of beneficial interests in the REIT or in a public offering of debt obligations of the REIT that have maturities of at least five years.

.03 Use of Foreign Currency Gains in REIT Income and Asset Tests

Passive foreign exchange gain and real estate foreign exchange gain are generally excluded from gross income for purposes of the 95-percent and 75-percent income tests, respectively, for REIT qualification effective for gains and items of income [Code Sec. 856(n)]. Thus, foreign currency gain does not hinder an entity's ability to satisfy the income tests, but it also does not assist in qualification.

Real estate foreign exchange gain is foreign currency gain attributable to:

- An item of income or gain to which the 75-percent income test applies (rents, gains from the disposition of real estate, etc.);
- The acquisition or ownership of obligations secured by mortgages on real property or on interests in real property (other than foreign currency gain attributable to an item of income or gain to which the 75-percent test applies); or
- Becoming or being the obligor under obligations secured by mortgages on real property or interests in real property (other than foreign currency gain attributable to an item of income or gain to which the 75-percent test applies) [Code Sec. 856(n)(2)(A)].

Real estate foreign exchange gain also includes foreign currency gain attributable to a qualified business unit (QBU) of the REIT under Code Sec. 987, but only if (1) the QBU meets the 75-percent income test, and (2) at least 75 percent of the QBU's assets are represented by real estate assets, cash and cash items, and government securities under Code Sec. 856(c)(4)(A) at the close of each quarter that the REIT directly or indirectly holds the QBU [Code Sec. 856(n)(2)(B)].

Passive foreign exchange gain includes:

- Real estate foreign exchange gain;
- Foreign currency gain that is attributable to an item of income or gain to which the 95-percent income test applies;
- Foreign currency gain attributable to the acquisition or ownership of obligations (other than foreign currency gain attributable to an item of income or gain to which the 95-percent test applies); or
- Foreign currency gain attributable to becoming or being the obligor under obligations (other than foreign currency gain attributable to an item of income or gain to which the 95-percent test applies) [Code Sec. 856(n)(3)(A) and (B)].

.04 Dealing or Trading in Securities

If a REIT engages in dealing in or substantial and regular trading of securities, any foreign currency gain it derives from that trading will constitute gross income that does not qualify under the 75-percent and 95-percent income tests. In other words, those gains will not be considered qualified income that can be used to satisfy the income tests. However, this treatment does not apply to income that is not gross income under the hedging rules of Code Sec. 856(c)(5)(G) [Code Sec. 856(n)(4)].

.05 "Rents from Real Property"

"Rents from real property" include: (1) rents from interests in real property; (2) charges for services customarily furnished or rendered in connection with the rental of real property, whether or not such charges are separately stated; and (3) rent attributable to personal property leased under, or in connection with, a lease of real property, but only if the rent attributable to the personal property does not exceed 15 percent of the total rent for the year attributable to both the real and personal property leased under, or in connection with, the lease [Code Sec. 856(d)(1)].[14]

The term "rents from real property" includes charges for services customarily furnished or rendered in connection with the rental of real property, whether or not the charges are separately stated. Services rendered to tenants of a particular building will be considered customary if, in the geographic market in which the building is located, tenants in buildings of a similar class are customarily provided with the service. In particular, in geographic areas where it is customary to furnish electricity or other utilities to tenants in buildings of a particular class, the submetering of those utilities to tenants in the buildings will be considered a customary service [Reg. § 1.856-4(b)(1)].

.06 Impermissible Tenant Service Income

Note that real property rentals qualify for both the 95 percent and the 75 percent tests above. This does not include *impermissible tenant service income*, which means any amount received or accrued by a REIT for services it furnishes to the tenants of its property, or for managing or operating the property [Code Sec. 856(d)(2)(C); Code Sec. 857(d)(7)(A)]. However, services rendered or management or operation provided through an independent contractor are not treated as furnished by a REIT [Code Sec. 856(d)(7)(C)(i)]. If impermissible tenant service income exceeds 1 percent of all the income from the property during the tax year, then none of the income from the property qualifies as *rents from real property* [Code Sec. 856(d)(7)(B)]. This means that even a relatively small amount of impermissible services income may disqualify a REIT's real estate rentals for purposes of the statutory qualification tests.[15]

.07 Taxable REIT Subsidiaries

Although rents generally qualify as income for both the 95-percent and 75-percent gross income tests, rents may be disqualified if the REIT provides certain services to tenants. Rents from real property do not include amounts received or accrued from a tenant in

---

[14] LTR 201317001 (Jan. 16, 2013) (amounts received by a prison owner-operator under government contracts to "house" prisoners and detainees were payments to use space within a specific building and would be treated as "rents from real property").

[15] Rev. Rul. 98-60 1998-2 CB 751.

which the REIT directly or indirectly owns at least a 10-percent interest. Amounts received from a taxable REIT subsidiary are not excluded from rents under this rule [Code Sec. 856(d)(2)(B)].

A REIT may own one or more *qualified REIT subsidiaries* and treat all of the subsidiary's' assets, liabilities and items of income, deduction and credit as its own. A qualified REIT subsidiary is defined as a corporation, if all of its stock is held by the REIT [Code Sec. 856(i)(2)]. The ability to own taxable REIT subsidiaries expands the range of activities in which a REIT and its subsidiaries can engage because income from a taxable REIT subsidiary is not treated as impermissible tenant service income [Code Sec. 856(d)(7)(C)(i)]. This means that a taxable REIT subsidiary can provide noncustomary services to a REIT's tenants or manage or operate properties for third parties without causing amounts received or accrued by the REIT, directly or indirectly, to be disqualified as rents from real property. Moreover, securities of taxable REIT subsidiaries are excepted from the 10 percent vote and value limitations on a REIT's ownership of securities of a single issuer. However, no more than 25 percent of the value of a REIT may be represented by securities of one or more taxable REIT subsidiaries [Code Sec. 856(c)(4)(B)(ii) and (iii)].

To qualify as a taxable REIT subsidiary, both the REIT subsidiary and the REIT must join in an election which can only be revoked with the consent of both parties [Code Sec. 856(l)(1)]. IRS consent is not required for either the election or the revocation. File Form 8875, *Taxable REIT Subsidiary Election*, to make the election.

The following entities will not qualify as taxable REIT subsidiaries:

- A REIT itself cannot be a taxable REIT subsidiary; and
- Corporations that directly or indirectly operate or manage lodging or health care facilities, or provide any person rights to any brand name under which such a facility is operated, also cannot be taxable REIT subsidiaries [Code Sec. 856(l)(3)].

A lodging facility is a hotel, a motel, or a property providing lodging in which more than half of the rooms or dwelling units in the property are used on a transient basis [Code Sec. 856(d)(9)]. A health care facility is a licensed facility that provides medical, nursing, or ancillary services, such as a hospital, nursing home, or home for assisted living [Code Sec. 856(e)(6)(D)(ii), (l)(4)].

A corporation cannot be treated as a taxable REIT subsidiary if it directly or indirectly provides another person with the franchising, licensing, or other rights to the brand name under which the hotel or other lodging facility or the health care facility is operated [Code Sec. 856(l)(3)(B)]. However, a corporation that provides rights to operate or manage a hotel or other lodging facility to an eligible independent contractor can still be treated as a taxable REIT subsidiary [Code Sec. 856(d)(8)(B)]. The corporation must hold the rights as a franchisee, licensee, or in a similar capacity and must own the hotel or other lodging facility or lease it from the REIT [Code Sec. 856(l)(3)]. Under this exception, a taxable REIT subsidiary, though prohibited from operating a lodging facility, may nevertheless hire an independent contractor to do so. An eligible independent contractor for these purposes is an independent contractor or a related person that is actively engaged in the trade or business of operating qualified lodging facilities for any person who is not related to the REIT or the taxable REIT subsidiary [Code Sec. 856(d)(9)(A)]. There is no similar exception that allows a taxable REIT subsidiary to hire an independent contractor to operate a health care facility.

.08 REIT Lodging Facilities Subsidiary Exception Expanded to Health Care Property

A taxable REIT subsidiary can rent a health care facility from its parent REIT and hire an independent contractor to operate such a facility. The rents paid to the parent REIT would be qualifying rental income for purposes of the 75-percent and 95-percent gross income tests [Code Sec. 856(d)(8)(B)].

A taxable REIT subsidiary is not considered to be operating or managing a qualified health care property or a qualified lodging facility other than through an independent contractor solely because:

1. The taxable REIT subsidiary directly or indirectly possessed a license, permit, or similar instrument enabling it to do so; or
2. The taxable REIT subsidiary employs individuals working at such facility or property located outside the United States, but only if an eligible independent contractor is responsible for the daily supervision and direction of such individuals on behalf of the TRS pursuant to a management agreement or similar service contract [Code Sec. 856(d)(8)(B)].

An eligible independent contractor is an independent contractor or a related person that, at the time of entering into a management agreement or other service contract with a taxable REIT subsidiary to operate a qualified lodging facility or qualified health care property, is actively engaged in the trade or business of operating qualified lodging facilities or qualified health care properties for any person who is not related to the REIT or the TRS [Code Sec. 856(d)(9)(A)]. A person will not fail to be an eligible independent contractor if:

- The taxable REIT subsidiary pays the expenses for operating the qualified health care property or qualified lodging facility under the management agreement or service contract with the contractor;
- The taxable REIT subsidiary receives the revenues from the qualified health care property or qualified lodging facility, less operating expenses and fees paid to the contractor; or
- The REIT receives income from the contractor under an existing lease of another property that was in effect as of the later of January 1, 1999, or the earliest date that a taxable REIT subsidiary of the REIT entered into a management agreement or a service contract with the contractor with respect to the qualified health care property or qualified lodging facility [Code Sec. 856(d)(9)(B)].

As with lodging facilities, the rule that a taxable REIT subsidiary cannot provide another person with the franchising, licensing, or other rights to the brand name under which the health care facility is operated does not apply if the taxable REIT subsidiary provides rights to operate or manage a health care facility to an eligible independent contractor [Code Sec. 856(l)(3)].

.09 Services Provided by REIT Subsidiary to Tenant

In LTR 200828025,[16] the IRS concluded that a REITs provision of steam and electricity to the tenants of a commercial office building was a customary service provided in commercial office buildings in the area and not considered impermissible services rendered to the tenants. Thus, under Reg. § 1.512(b)-1(c)(5), the furnishing of heat and light are not considered services rendered to the occupant and therefore would not cause amounts received from tenants for those utility services to be treated as impermissible tenant service income under Code Sec. 856(d)(2)(C) and Code Sec. 856(d)(7). Therefore, rents received by the REIT were not treated as unrelated business taxable income (UBTI).

In Rev. Rul. 2002-38,[17] the IRS indicated that a REIT's income derived from its taxable REIT subsidiary's services to its tenants didn't give rise to impermissible tenant service income and therefore didn't prevent the REIT from qualifying as a REIT under Code Sec. 856(d)(2)(C). Similarly in Rev. Rul. 2004-24,[18] amounts received by a REIT for furnishing attended or unattended parking facilities to tenants didn't give rise to impermissible tenant service income. Why? Furnishing parking facilities is a service customarily furnished or rendered in connection with the rental of real property under Code Sec. 856(d)(1)(B) and therefore did not disqualify the REIT. In Rev. Rul. 2003-86,[19] the IRS concluded that a joint venture partnership between a REIT and an independent contractor of the REIT could provide noncustomary services to tenants of the REIT without causing the rents paid by the tenants to the REIT to fail to qualify as rents from real property under Code Sec. 856(d). Why? Code Sec. 856(d)(7)(C)(i) provides that services furnished or rendered through an independent contractor from whom the REIT does not derive or receive any income, are not treated as furnished, rendered, or provided by the REIT for purposes of Code Sec. 856(d)(7)(A). Thus, services rendered by the independent contractor did not give rise to impermissible tenant service income since the REIT derived no income from the independent contractor.

> **Example 23-3:** A REIT forms a taxable REIT subsidiary to provide housekeeping services to its tenants. No service charges are separately stated from the tenant's rents. The REIT pays the subsidiary 160 percent of its direct cost to provide the services reported by the subsidiary on its return as gross income. The subsidiary rendered the services rather than the REIT because the subsidiary: (1) had employees performing all the housekeeping services; (2) paid all costs for providing the services; and (3) rented space for carrying out the services, making no other payments to the REIT. Since the subsidiary rendered the services, no impermissible tenant service income prevented the REIT from qualifying as a REIT under Code Sec. 856(d)(2)(C).

.10 Safe Harbors for Rent-Producing Real Property

Safe harbors are provided for certain sales of rent-producing real property. Under the safe harbor rule, the REIT may sell property that is a real estate asset and not be subject to the 100-percent penalty, if the following requirements are met:

[16] LTR 200828025 (April 8, 2008).

[17] Rev. Rul. 2002-38, 2002-2 CB 4.

[18] Rev. Rul. 2004-24, 2004-1 CB 550.

[19] Rev. Rul. 2003-86, 2003-2 CB 290.

1. The REIT must have held the property for at least two years [Code Sec. 857(b)(6)(C)(i)].
2. The total expenditures made by the REIT, or any of its partners, during the two years preceding the sale of the land may not exceed 30 percent of the net selling price of the property [Code Sec. 857(b)(6)(C)(ii)]. If the property was acquired through foreclosure or lease termination, the term "expenditures" includes those costs paid by, or for the account of, the mortgagor or lessee after default became imminent. The term "expenditures" does not include costs relating to foreclosure property if the property is not foreclosed upon, costs incurred in order to comply with governmental requirements, loan advances, and costs incurred to restore the property after a fire, storm, or other casualty loss [Code Sec. 857(b)(6)(E)].
3. The REIT must not sell more than seven properties (other than foreclosure properties or property covered by the Code Sec. 1033 involuntary conversion rules) during the tax year or the aggregate adjusted bases of property sold must not exceed 10 percent of the aggregate bases of all the REIT's assets at the beginning of the REIT's tax year [Code Sec. 857(b)(6)(C)(iii)]. The total adjusted basis of all the REIT's assets, including the property that has been sold, is determined using depreciation deductions that are used for purposes of computing earnings and profits. All sales resulting in a gain or loss are included. The sale of more than one parcel of property to one buyer in one transaction is considered to be one sale, and the term "sale" does not include transactions where the net selling price is less than $10,000 [Code Sec. 857(b)(6)(E)(vi)]. A third alternative is available, under which the fair market value of property (other than foreclosure or Code Sec. 1033 property) sold during the tax year must also not exceed 10 percent of the fair market value of all of the REIT's assets at the beginning of the tax year [Code Sec. 857(b)(6)(C)(iii)].
4. Land or improvements that are not acquired through foreclosure or lease termination must be held for rent for a period of not less than two years [Code Sec. 857(b)(6)(C)(iv)]. However, if developed land is held in order to derive a gain from its sale, the safe harbor rule will not apply simply because the property is rented at a rate substantially lower than that charged for comparable property.
5. If the seven sales limitation in item (3), above, is not satisfied, the safe harbor may still apply if substantially all the marketing and development expenditures with respect to the property sold were made through an independent contractor [Code Sec. 857(b)(6)(C)(v)]. The determination of whether a particular sale qualifies for the prohibited transaction safe harbor is made on a property-by-property basis.

.11 Safe Harbor Rule for Sales of Timber Property

A safe harbor provides that certain sales of REIT timber property will not be considered sales of property held for sale in the ordinary course of business. The purpose of this safe harbor is to permit a REIT that holds timberland to make sales of timber property without being considered a dealer, provided there has not been significant development of the property. Under this rule, a sale of a real estate asset by a REIT will not be a prohibited transaction under Code Sec. 857(b)(6)(D) if the following six requirements are met:

1. The asset must have been held for at least four years in connection with the trade or business of producing timber;
2. The aggregate expenditures made by the REIT (or a partner of the REIT) during the two-year period preceding the date of sale that (a) are includible in the basis of the property (other than timberland acquisition expenditures), and (b) are directly related to the operation of the property for the production of timber or for the preservation of the property for use as timberland, must not exceed 30 percent of the net selling price of the property;
3. The aggregate expenditures made by the REIT (or a partner of the REIT) during the two-year period preceding the date of sale (a) that are includible in the basis of the property and (b) that are not directly related to the operation of the property for the production of timber or the preservation of the property for use as timberland must not exceed five percent of the net selling price of the property;
4. The REIT either: (a) does not make more than seven sales of property (other than sales of foreclosure property or sales covered by the involuntary conversion rules) during the tax year; or (b) the aggregate adjusted bases (as determined for purposes of computing earnings and profits) of property sold during the year (other than sales of foreclosure property or sales covered by the involuntary conversion rules) do not exceed 10 percent of the aggregate bases (as determined for purposes of computing earnings and profits) of all assets of the REIT as of the beginning of the tax year; or (c) the fair market value of the property sold during the tax year does not exceed 10 percent of the fair market value of all of the REIT's assets at the beginning of the tax year;
5. If the requirement of 4(a), above, is not satisfied, substantially all of the marketing expenditures with respect to the property must be made by persons who are independent contractors with respect to the REIT and from whom the REIT does not derive any income; and
6. The sales price on the sale of the property cannot be based in whole or in part on income or profits of any person, including income or profits derived from the sale of such properties.

¶23,097 ASSET TEST

At the close of each quarter of the tax year [Code Sec. 856(c) (4)]:

- 75 percent or more of the value of the trust's total assets must be in real estate assets, cash and cash items[20] (including receivables), and government securities [Code Sec. 856(c) (4) (A)];
- Not more than 25 percent of the value of its total assets may be represented by securities (other than government securities);

[20] Rev. Rul. 2012-17, IRB 2012-25, 1018 (money market fund shares qualified as "cash item" for purposes of Code Sec. 856(c)(4)(A)); LTR 201310020 (Dec. 5, 2012) (boat slips at a marina leased by a REIT were "real estate assets").

- Not more than 20 percent of the value of its total assets may be represented by securities of one or more taxable REIT subsidiaries; and
- Except with respect to a taxable REIT subsidiary and government securities, the REIT may not hold the securities of a single issuer in a quantity that:
  a. Have a value greater than the value of 5 percent of the REIT's total assets,
  b. Represent more than 10 percent of the total voting power of the outstanding securities of the issuer, or
  c. Represent more than 10 percent of the total value of the outstanding securities of the issuer [Code Sec. 856(c) (4) (B)].

The following arrangements are not considered securities for purposes of the rule that a REIT cannot own more than 10 percent of the value of the outstanding securities of a single issuer:

a. Any loan to an individual or an estate;
b. Any rental agreement;
c. Any obligation to pay rents from real property;
d. Any security issued by a state or its political subdivisions, the District of Columbia, a foreign government or its political subdivisions, or the Commonwealth of Puerto Rico, but only if the determination of any payment received or accrued under such security does not depend in whole or in part on the profits of any entity not described in this category, or payments on any obligation issued by such entity;
e. Any security issued by a REIT; and
f. Any other arrangement that, as determined by the IRS, is excepted from the definition of a security [Code Sec. 856(m) (1)].

In addition, any debt issued by a partnership, and not described above, is not considered a security: (1) to the extent of the REIT's interest as a partner in the partnership and (2) if at least 75 percent of the partnership's gross income (excluding income from prohibited transactions) is derived from sources referred to in Code Sec. 856(c) (3) such as rents, dividends, interest, etc. [Code Sec. 856(m) (4)].

.01 *De Minimis* Asset Failures of 5 Percent or 10 Percent Tests

The requirements must be satisfied each quarter. A REIT will not lose its REIT status for failing to satisfy the 5 percent or 10 percent test in a quarter if the failure is due to the ownership of assets with a total value that does not exceed the lesser of: (1) one percent of the total value of the REIT's assets at the end of the quarter for which such measurement is done or (2) 10 million dollars; provided in either case that the REIT either disposes of the assets within six months after the last day of the quarter in which the REIT identifies the failure, or otherwise meets the requirements of those rules by the end of such time period [Code Sec. 856(c) (7) (B)]. It may be possible for a REIT to satisfy the requirements without a disposition, for example, by increasing its other assets in the case of the 5 percent rule, or by the issuer modifying the amount or value of its total securities outstanding in the case of the 10 percent rule.

.02 Larger Asset Test Failures (Whether of 5-Percent or 10-Percent Test, or of 75-Percent or Other Asset Test)

If a REIT fails to meet any of the asset test requirements for a particular quarter and the failure exceeds the *de minimis* threshold, the REIT will be deemed to have satisfied the requirements if:

1. Following the REIT's identification of the failure, the REIT files a schedule with a description of each asset that caused the failure;
2. The failure was due to reasonable cause and not to willful neglect;
3. The REIT disposes of the assets within six months after the last day of the quarter in which the identification occurred (or the requirements of the rules are otherwise met within such period); and
4. The REIT pays a tax on the failure. The tax that the REIT must pay on the failure is the greater of (1) $50,000, or (2) an amount determined by multiplying the highest corporate tax rate by the net income generated by the assets for the period beginning on the first date of the failure and ending on the date the REIT has disposed of the assets. Such taxes are treated as excise taxes, for which the deficiency provisions of the excise tax rules apply [Code Sec. 856(c)(7)(C)].

¶23,098 DISTRIBUTION REQUIREMENT

To qualify as a REIT, an entity generally must distribute to its shareholders during the tax year the sum of 90 percent of its ordinary taxable income (determined without the deduction for dividends paid) and 90 percent of its net income from foreclosure property, over its excess noncash income [Code Sec. 857(a)]. The IRS has the authority to waive this distribution requirement if the taxpayer's failure to satisfy its requirements results from the taxpayer having to make distributions in order to avoid imposition of certain excise taxes.

.01 Distribution of Income

"REIT taxable income" is defined as taxable income with the following adjustments [Code Sec. 357 (b)(2)]:

- Special deductions listed in Ch. 20 are not allowed (except for organizational expenses);
- Dividends paid (computed without net income from foreclosure property) can be deducted;
- Any increase in income from a change in accounting method is included;
- Net income from foreclosure property is excluded [Code Sec. 857(b)(2)];
- Any taxes paid for failing to satisfy the gross income or asset tests, any tax on redetermined rents and deductions and excess interest, and any tax paid to avoid termination of REIT status may be deducted; and
- Net income derived from prohibited transactions is excluded.

A 4 percent excise tax applies to the undistributed amount that should have been distributed [Code Sec. 4981(a)]. The dividends may be declared and paid during the tax year or after its close, generally under the same conditions as RICs [¶ 23,090] [Code Secs. 857, 858; Reg. §§ 1.857-1 through 10, 1.858-1].

.02 Distribution of Stock

In Rev. Proc. 2010-12,[21] the IRS provided guidance on stock distributions by publicly traded REITs and RICs. If a RIC or REIT makes a qualifying distribution, the IRS will treat the distribution of stock as a dividend. The amount of such stock distribution will be treated as equal to the amount of money that could have been received instead of stock. In addition, if a RIC or REIT makes a qualifying distribution and some shareholders receive a combination of stock and money that differs from the combination received by other shareholders and if the fair market value of the stock on the date of distribution differs from the amount of money that could have been received instead, those differences do not cause the distribution to be treated as a preferential dividend.

The IRS further provides that if a RIC or REIT makes a qualifying distribution and some shareholders receive a combination of stock and money that differs from the combination received by other shareholders and if the fair market value of the stock on the date of distribution differs from the amount of money that could have been received instead, those differences do not cause the distribution to be treated as a preferential dividend.

A qualifying distribution must meet all of the following requirements:

1. The distribution is made by the corporation to its shareholders with respect to its stock;
2. Stock of the corporation is publicly traded on an established securities market in the United States;
3. The distribution is declared on or before December 31, 2012, with respect to a tax year ending on or before December 31, 2011 (subject to special timing rules for certain distributions, including distributions made after the close of the tax year);
4. Pursuant to such declaration, each shareholder may elect to receive the shareholder's entire entitlement under the declaration in either money or stock of the distributing corporation of equivalent value, subject to a limitation on the amount of money to be distributed in the aggregate to all shareholders with the value of the distributed shares determined under the formula in item (5) below;
5. The calculation of the number of shares to be received by any shareholder will be determined over a period of two weeks ending as close as practicable to the payment date based upon a formula utilizing market prices that is designed to equate in value the number of shares to be received with the amount of money that could be received instead; and
6. With respect to any shareholder participating in a dividend reinvestment plan (DRIP), the DRIP applies only to the extent that, in the absence of the DRIP, the shareholder would have received the distribution in money under item (4), above.

---

[21] Rev. Proc. 2010-12, IRB 2010-3, 269.

¶23,099 TAX-FREE DIVISION OF REIT

A REIT can engage in the active conduct of a trade or business at the level required for a tax-free spin off under Code Sec. 355(d).[22] The IRS reasoned that as long as the REIT can show that its activities in connection with qualifying rents from real property rise to a level that constitutes activities and substantial management and involvement with operational functions, it can satisfy the active trade or business requirement of a tax-free division.

A REIT may avoid being disqualified as a special tax entity or being subject to tax on deficiency dividends (other than interest and penalties) if a "determination" results in an adjustment, which could preclude compliance with the normal income distribution requirements [Code Sec. 860]. Essentially, an amount deductible as a deficiency dividend is included in computing the deduction for dividends paid. A REIT that uses the deficiency dividends procedures is subject to interest and penalties on the amount of the adjustment, but only up to the amount of the deficiency deduction allowed. A REIT is allowed a deduction for a deficiency dividend only if, among other things, there is a determination that results in an adjustment for the year in which the deficiency dividend is paid.

In Rev. Proc. 2009-28,[23] the IRS provided procedures describing when the filing by a REIT of Form 8927, *Determination Under Section 860(e)(4) by a Qualified Investment Entity,* will be treated as a "self-determination" for purposes of the deficiency dividend procedures of Code Sec. 860.

A "determination," as defined under Code Sec. 860(e), includes: (1) a final decision of the Tax Court or any other court of competent jurisdiction, (2) a closing agreement [Code Sec. 7121], (3) a tax liability agreement signed by the IRS and the taxpayer, and (4) a statement of "self-determination," which is a statement by the taxpayer attached to its amendment or supplement to the tax return for the relevant tax year [Code Sec. 860(e)(4)].

The date of the determination controls the timeliness of certain acts that the REIT must perform. No distribution of property will be considered deficiency dividends unless the property is distributed within 90 days after the determination and unless a claim for a deficiency dividend deduction with respect to the distribution is filed pursuant to Code Sec. 860(g) [Code Sec. 860(f)(1)].

Code Sec. 860(g) provides that no deficiency dividend deduction shall be allowed unless a claim is filed within 120 days after the date of the determination. The claim must be filed on Form 976, *Claim for Deficiency Dividends Deductions by a Personal Holding Company, Regulated Investment Company, or Real Estate Investment Trust.*

---

[22] Rev. Rul. 2001-29, 2001-1 CB 1348.

[23] Rev. Proc. 2009-28, 2009-20 IRB 1011.

REAL ESTATE MORTGAGE INVESTMENT CONDUITS (REMICs)

¶23,100 REAL ESTATE MORTGAGE INVESTMENT CONDUITS (REMICS) IN GENERAL

.01 General Rules

A real estate mortgage investment conduit (REMIC) is an entity that is formed to hold a fixed pool of mortgages secured by interests in real property, with multiple classes of interests held by investors. REMICs are widely used securitization vehicles for mortgages and the tax rules can be found in Code Secs. 860A through 860G. For an entity to qualify as a REMIC, all of the interests in the entity must consist of one or more classes of regular interests and a single class of residual interests. In addition, those interests must all be issued on the startup day [Reg. § 1.860G-2(k)].

A regular interest is treated as debt of the REMIC [Code Sec. 860G(a)(1)]. In addition, terms of a regular interest are fixed on the startup day and must (1) unconditionally entitle the holder to receive a specified principal amount (or other similar amount), and (2) provide that interest payments at or before maturity are based on a fixed rate (or to the extent provided in regulations, at a variable rate).

An entity qualifies as a REMIC only if, among other things, as of the close of the third month beginning after the startup day and at all times thereafter, substantially all of its assets consist of qualified mortgages and permitted investments [Code Sec. 860D(a)(4)]. This asset test is satisfied if the entity owns no more than a *de minimis* amount of other assets [Reg. § 1.860D-1(b)(3)(i)]. As a safe harbor, the amount of assets other than qualified mortgages and permitted investments is *de minimis* if the aggregate of the adjusted bases of those assets is less than one percent of the aggregate of the adjusted bases of all of the entity's assets [Reg. 1.860D-1(b)(3)(ii)].

The net income of a REMIC, after accounting for the regular interests, generally is passed through to and taken into account by the holders of the residual interests. Amounts includible in income (or deductible as a loss) by holders of REMIC interests are treated as portfolio income (or loss). This income (or loss) is not taken into account in determining the loss from a passive activity [Ch. 13]. An investor can purchase either a regular or residual interest. If the distributing REIT designates a distribution as a capital gain dividend, shareholders treat it as capital gain. Under Code Sec. 857(c), the dividends received deduction is *not* available for dividends from a REIT because dividends received from a REIT are not considered dividends for purposes of the Code Sec. 243 dividends received deduction.

Regular Interest

A regular interest is treated like a bond for tax purposes, even though it may be issued in the form of stock or an interest in a partnership or trust. An investor may receive taxable interest payments and a tax-free return of principal. The investor must use the accrual method of accounting to determine the amount of interest to include in income each year. Interests purchased at a discount are subject to the original issue discount and market discount rules [Ch. 2].

If a regular interest in a REMIC is sold at a profit, some or all of the gain may be ordinary income, rather than capital gains. To calculate the ordinary income portion, the investor must first determine how much interest the instrument would have yielded during the period the investor held it using a rate equal to 110 percent of the applicable federal rate as of the beginning of the holding period. The excess of that figure over the amount that the investor actually took into income is ordinary income.

Example 23-4: Ms. Moore purchased a regular interest for $10,000. Two years later, she sold it for $10,700—a $700 profit. Moore received $1,800 of taxable income from the REMIC. However, she would have gotten $2,000 of interest if the REMIC had yielded 110 percent of the applicable federal rate. Thus, $200 ($2,000 less $1,800) of her profit is ordinary income and the other $500 is capital gains.

Residual Interest

A residual interest is, in essence, the right to what is left after the regular interest is paid. A residual interest owner gets the difference between the cash flow from the mortgage payments and the lesser amount paid out to regular interest owners. The return fluctuates, for instance, if mortgagors default on payments or pay off early. Residual interests are taxed like partnership interests. Residual interest owners take into income an allocable portion of the REMIC's income or lossregardless of whether the income has been distributed. Generally, the allocation is made quarterly, based on the number of days each investor held the residual interest. REMICs may also pass through to investors certain costs that may be deducted (subject to the 2 percent floor for deducting miscellaneous itemized deductions).

In determining the REMIC's net income, interest-type payments to regular interest holders are deductible.

Basis is increased by the amount of taxable income and reduced by deductible losses. However, investors deduct losses only to the extent of basis. Excess losses are carried over and used only to offset income from the same REMIC.

.02 Qualification as a REMIC

To qualify as a REMIC, the entity must [Code Sec. 860D(a)]:

- Elect REMIC status, which applies for the tax year and all prior tax years;
- Have only regular or residual interests;
- Have only one class of residual interests (and all distributions, if any, to these interests are pro rata);
- Have substantially all of the assets consist of qualified mortgages and permitted investments at all times after the end of the third month starting after the REMIC's start-up day;
- Use a calendar year as its tax year;

- Have reasonable arrangements designed to ensure that residual interests in it are not held by disqualified organizations; and
- Make available information necessary for applying the tax on certain transfers of residual interests.

NOTE: Although after the third month substantially all of the REMIC's assets must, at all times, consist only of qualified mortgages and permitted assets, this asset test does not apply during the REMIC's liquidation period [Code Sec. 860D(a)(2)(A)(4), F(a)(2)(A)(4), F(a)(4)(B)].

Regular Interests

These are interests that allow owners interest payments based on a fixed rate or fixed portion of the interest payments on qualified mortgages [Code Sec. 860G(a)(1)].

A regular interest in a REMIC must be issued on the start-up day with fixed terms and must be designated as a regular interest.

These interests can be issued in the form of debt, stock, partnership interests, interests in a trust, or any other form allowed by state law.

▶ **OBSERVATION:** The owner of a regular interest in a REMIC is considered to be a debt instrument for income tax purposes whether or not it is in the form of a debt instrument. Thus, the OID, market discount, and income-reporting rules that apply to bonds and other debt instruments [Ch. 2] also generally apply to a regular interest in a REMIC.

Residual Interests

A residual interest is an interest in a REMIC that is not a regular interest. It is designated as a residual interest by the REMIC [Code Sec. 860G(a)(2)].

.03 Taxation of Interest

Regular Interests

A regular interest owner must use an accrual method to determine the amount includible in gross income [Code Sec. 860B(b)]. Any gain is ordinary income to the extent of a portion of unaccrued original issue discount on the interest.

Residual Interests

If a taxpayer acquires a residual interest in a REMIC, the taxpayer is liable for tax on his or her pro rata share of the REMIC's taxable income, whether or not distributed. Code Sec. 860E(a)(6) provides rules for determining the alternative minimum taxable income of a taxpayer holding residual interests in a REMIC.

.04 Taxation of the REMIC

Generally, a REMIC is not a taxable entity. The REMIC's income generally is taken into account by owners of regular and residual interests (above). However, the REMIC is subject to tax on prohibited transactions, on certain amounts contributed to it after the start-up date, and on its net income from foreclosure property. It may be required to withhold on amounts paid to foreign holders of interests. In addition, a tax is imposed on transfers to disqualified organizations [Code Secs. 860A, 860E, 860G].

Foreclosure Property

A REMIC must pay tax each year on its net income from foreclosure property. The tax is imposed at the top marginal corporate rate (currently 35 percent). Net income from foreclosure property is computed as if the REMIC were a REIT [¶ 23,095] [Code Sec. 860G(c)].

> ▶ **OBSERVATION:** If a REMIC acquires this kind of property and receives amounts with respect to the property that would not be treated as certain types of qualifying income if received by a REIT, the REMIC is subject to tax on these amounts. For example, rents from real property and interest on obligations secured by mortgages on real property are excluded qualifying income, while gain from the sale of foreclosure property held primarily for sale to customers is taxed.

Contributions After the Start-Up Date

The REMIC must pay an annual tax equal to 100 percent of the value of contributions made to it after the start-up date. This tax does not apply to cash contributions:

- Made to facilitate a clean-up call or a qualified liquidation;
- Made during the three months after the start-up day;
- Made to a qualified reserve fund by a residual interest holder;
- In the nature of a guarantee; or
- Permitted by regulations [Code Sec. 860G(d)].

> **NOTE:** A clean-up call is the prepayment of the remaining principal balance of a class of regular interests when the administrative costs associated with servicing that class outweigh the benefits of maintaining it.

Tax on Prohibited Transactions

Because a REMIC essentially is designed to hold mortgages contributed to it when it is organized, the conditions under which it can dispose of these mortgages are limited. In addition, penalties are imposed if a REMIC holds assets other than qualified mortgages and certain permitted investments. A 100 percent tax is imposed on net income from prohibited transactions [Code Sec. 860F(a)].

.05 Modification of REMICs

A real estate mortgage investment conduit (REMIC) is an entity that is formed to hold a fixed pool of mortgages secured by interests in real property, with multiple classes of interests held by investors. REMICs are widely used securitization vehicles for mortgages and the tax rules can be found in Code Secs. 860A through 860G. For an entity to qualify as a REMIC, all of the interests in the entity must consist of one or more classes of regular interests and a single class of residual interests. In addition, those interests must all be issued on the startup day [Reg. § 1.860G-2(k)].

The legislative history of the REMIC provisions indicates that Congress intended the provisions to apply only to an entity that holds a substantially fixed pool of real estate mortgages and related assets and that "has no powers to vary the composition of its mortgage assets."[24]

General Debt Modification Rule

Reg. § 1.1001-3(c)(1)(i) defines a "modification" of a debt instrument as any alteration, including any deletion or addition, in whole or in part, of a legal right or obligation of the issuer or holder of a debt instrument, whether the alteration is evidenced by an express agreement (oral or written), conduct of the parties. Reg. § 1.1001-3(e) governs which modifications of debt instruments are "significant." Reg. § 1.1001-3(b) provides that a significant modification produces a deemed exchange of the original debt instrument for a new debt instrument.

Under Reg. § 1.860G-2(b), related rules apply to determine REMIC qualification. If there is a significant modification of an obligation that is held by a REMIC, then the modified obligation is treated as one that was newly issued in exchange for the unmodified obligation that it replaced. Thus, even if an entity initially qualifies as a REMIC, one or more significant modifications of loans held by the entity may terminate the qualification if the modifications cause less than substantially all of the entity's assets to be qualified mortgages.

Certain loan modifications, however, are not significant for purposes of Reg. § 1.860G-2(b)(1), even if the modifications are significant under the rules in Reg. § 1.1001-3. In particular, under Reg. § 1.860G-2(b)(3)(i), if a change in the terms of an obligation is "occasioned by default or a reasonably foreseeable default," the change is not a significant modification for purposes of Reg. § 1.860G-2(b)(1), regardless of the modification's status under Reg. § 1.1001-3.

In Rev. Proc. 2009-45,[25] the IRS sets forth conditions under which modifications to the terms of certain commercial mortgage loans that are at risk of default will not cause the IRS to challenge the tax status of REMICs that hold the loans or to assert that those modifications give rise to prohibited transactions.

> **Example 23-5:** S services mortgage loans that are held by R, a REMIC. Borrower B is the issuer of one of the mortgage loans held by R. B's mortgage loan is due upon maturity. The real property securing B's mortgage loan is an office building. All of B's required payments on the mortgage loan have been timely, and the loan is not scheduled to mature for another 12 months. In order to repay the loan when it matures, B will have to refinance the maturing mortgage loan into a newly issued mortgage loan. The following factors, however, indicate that refinancing options may be unavailable when the mortgage loan matures: current economic conditions in the relevant credit markets, and the current market value of the real property securing the loan. B provides a written factual representation to S showing that B will probably not be able to repay or refinance the mortgage loan at maturity. S reasonably believes that, if the loan to B is not modified, there is a significant risk of default by B upon maturity of the mortgage loan. Therefore, S and B agree to modify the mortgage loan by extending its maturity and increasing the interest rate. S reasonably believes that this modification reduces the risk of default. The modification is a

[24] S. Rep. No. 99-313 99th Cong., 2d Sess. 791-92, 1986-3 (Vol. 3) C.B. 791-92.

[25] Rev. Proc. 2009-45, 2009-40 IRB 471.

significant modification under Reg. § 1.1001-3(e). S reasonably believed that the pre-modification loan presented a significant risk of default and that the modification substantially reduced that risk. The IRS concluded that the modification fell within the safe harbor of Rev. Proc. 2009-45. Thus, the IRS will not challenge the tax status of the REMIC that holds the loans or assert that those modifications give rise to prohibited transactions.

In order for a REMIC to qualify for the safe harbor provided by Rev. Proc. 2009-45, the following conditions are satisfied:

1. The pre-modification loan must not be secured by a residence that contains fewer than five dwelling units and that is the principal residence of the issuer of the loan.
2. Either—(1) If a REMIC holds the pre-modification loan, then as of the end of the three-month period beginning on the startup day, no more than ten percent of the stated principal of the total assets of the REMIC must be represented by loans fitting the following description: At the time of contribution to the REMIC, the payments on the loan must be overdue by at least 30 days or a default on the loan was reasonably foreseeable; or (2) If an investment trust holds the pre-modification loan, then as of all dates when assets were contributed to the trust, no more than ten percent of the stated principal of all the debt instruments held by the trust may be represented by instruments with payments that were overdue by 30 days or more or for which default was reasonably foreseeable.
3. The holder or servicer reasonably must believe that there is a significant risk of default of the pre-modification loan upon maturity of the loan or at an earlier date. In a determination of the significance of the risk of a default, one relevant factor is how far in the future the possible default may be. In appropriate circumstances, a holder or servicer may reasonably believe that there is a significant risk of default even though the foreseen default is more than one year in the future.
4. The holder or servicer must reasonably believe that the modified loan presents a substantially reduced risk of default, as compared with the pre-modification loan.

If all four conditions are satisfied, the IRS will not:

- Challenge a REMICs qualifications on the grounds that the modifications are not the exceptions listed under Reg. § 1.860G-2(b)(3);
- Contend that the modifications are prohibited transactions under Code Sec. 860F(a)(2) on the ground that the modifications resulted in one or more dispositions of qualified mortgages;
- Challenge a securitization vehicle's classification as a trust under on the grounds that the modifications manifest a power to vary the investment of the certificate holders; and
- Challenge a securitization vehicle's qualification as a REMIC on the grounds that the modifications result in a deemed reissuance of the REMIC regular interests.

IRS Provides Relief to REMICs Holding Modified Mortgages Under Federal Assistance Program

In Rev. Prov. 2009-23,[26] the IRS has issued guidance describing the conditions under which it will not challenge the tax status of REITs that hold mortgage loans modified under the Home Affordable Modification Program. The IRS will not: (1) challenge a REMICs qualification on the grounds of an improper modification of a mortgage, or that they result in a deemed reissuance of the REMIC regular interests; (2) contend that the modifications are prohibited transactions under on the grounds that the modifications result in one or more dispositions of qualified mortgages; or (3) challenge a securitization vehicles trust classification under on the grounds that the modifications manifest a power to vary the investment of the certificate holders. This guidance is effective for loan modifications on or after March 4, 2009.

EXEMPT ORGANIZATIONS

¶23,105 EXEMPT ORGANIZATIONS IN GENERAL

.01 Tax Benefits

Nonprofit organizations such as charitable, religious, or educational institutions, are entitled to take advantage of the following tax benefits: (1) they are entitled to an exemption from federal income tax, (2) they are eligible to claim tax deductions for contributions, (3) they have access to tax-exempt financing through state and local governments, and (4) they generally are exempt from state and local taxes.

.02 Tax-Exempt Purposes

A charitable organization must operate primarily in pursuit of one or more tax-exempt purposes which include religious, charitable, scientific, educational, literary, testing for public safely, to foster international amateur sports competition, or for the prevention of cruelty to animals or children [Code Sec. 501(a)]. The nonprofit organization may be in the form of a trust or a corporation, but are exempt only if they apply for an exemption as one of those organizations described in Code Sec. 501(c), (d), (e) or (f) [¶ 23,110] or as an employee pension, profit-sharing or stock bonus plan qualified under Code Sec. 401(a) [Ch. 3]. Despite the exemption, an organization may still be subject to tax on unrelated business income (UBTI) [¶ 23,155 et seq.].

.03 Internet Fundraising Sanctioned

A tax-exempt organization can use an internet fundraising platform to raise money for a project without jeopardizing the organization's qualification as a tax-exempt charity under Code Sec. 501(c)(3) if the web site or e-mail solicitations complies with the following rules:[27]

---

[26] Rev. Proc. 2009-23, 2009-17 IRB 884.

[27] Information Letter #20130001, March 29, 2013.

- An organization applying for recognition of tax-exempt status under Code Sec. 501(c)(3) must describe its actual and planned fundraising activities in its application, Form 1023, *Application for Recognition of Exemption under Section 501(c)(3) of the Internal Revenue Code*. The organization must report any expenses incurred on Form 1023 and its annual information tax returns (e.g., Form 990, Form 990-EZ or Form 990-PF).
- An organization that is raising funds, and has not received recognition as exempt from tax under Code Sec. 501(c)(3), should make a clear statement in the solicitation material (whether on a website or otherwise). The statement should be conspicuous, easily recognizable, and state that the organization has not received Code Sec. 501(c)(3) recognition and, therefore, contributions may not be deductible.
- A Code Sec. 501(c)(3) organization cannot be organized or operated for the benefit of private interests, such as the creator or the creator's family. No part of a Code Sec. 501(c)(3) organization's net earnings may inure to the benefit of any private shareholder or individual. The organization should consider whether payments or benefits to fundraisers or other private parties may be excessive or may constitute impermissible direct or indirect private benefit or private inurement.
- The organization must consider any fees that a fundraiser or any other private party may charge and determine whether payment of such fees, and any other aspect of the arrangement between the organization and the private party, is reasonable and is consistent with Code Sec. 501(c)(3) status.
- An organization that provides something of value to donors in exchange for donations must consider carefully the possibility that doing so may violate the rules against private benefit or private inurement and must comply with any substantiation and disclosure requirements for quid pro quo contributions.
- The organization should consider any state laws and regulations that may apply to internet fundraising by nonprofit or tax-exempt organizations.

¶23,106 REPORTING REQUIREMENTS FOR EXEMPT ORGANIZATIONS

An exempt organization must keep books and records to show tax compliance. The organization must be able to document the sources of receipts and expenditures reported on its annual return and on any tax returns it must file. Records must support income, expenses, and credits reported on exempt organization annual returns and tax returns. For example, an organization needs to keep records of revenues derived from, and expenses attributable to, an unrelated trade or business so that it can properly prepare Form 990-T, *Unrelated Business Income Tax Return*, and calculate its unrelated business taxable income. However, even if no return is filed, records must be maintained showing activities conducted, income received and expenses incurred. Books and records must be available for IRS inspection. If the IRS examines an organization's returns, the organization must have records to explain items reported.

.01 Form 990

All tax-exempt organizations must file an annual information return on Form 990, *Return of Organization Exempt From Income Tax.* Tax-exempt organizations that do not file a required information form for three consecutive years automatically lose their federal tax-exempt status [Code Sec. 6033(j)(1)]. If an organization loses its exemption, it will have to reapply with the IRS to regain its tax-exempt status [Code Sec. 6033(j)(2)]. Any income received between the revocation date and renewed exemption may be taxable. Form 990-series returns and e-Postcards are due by the 15th day of the 5th month after an organization's tax year ends.

.02 How Tax-Exempts Can Reinstate Lost Tax-Exempt Status

For further discussion of how tax-exempt organizations who lose their tax exempt status can reinstate that status, see ¶ 26,170.

.03 Small Tax-Exempts May File e-Postcard

Small tax-exempt organizations may file the simpler Form 990-N, *Electronic Notice (e-Postcard) for Tax-Exempt Organizations Not Required to File Form 990 or 990-EZ,* rather than the standard Form 990 or Form 990-EZ if their annual gross receipts are $50,000 or less. For further discussion of which small tax-exempts may file e-postcards, see ¶ 26,170.

For further discussion of the reporting requirements imposed on tax-exempt organizations see ¶ 26,170.

Private foundations are general religious, charitable, or educational exempt organizations that are essentially private in nature [¶ 23,115]. Strict requirements and severe penalties are applied to private foundations for specified acts (or failures to act) [¶ 23,120 et seq.].

.04 Application for Exemption

Every organization claiming exemption from tax must file an application with the IRS. Special forms are provided for the following types of organizations:

- For those claiming exemption under Code Sec. 501(c)(3), Form 1023, *Application for Recognition of Exemption Under Section 501(c)(3) of the Internal Revenue Code*;
- Under Code Sec. 501(c)(2), (4) through (10), (12), (13), (15), (17) and (19), Form 1024, *Application for Exemption Under Section 501(a)*;
- Under Code Sec. 521 (farmers' cooperative associations), Form 1028, *Application for Recognition of Exemption Under Section 521 of the Internal Revenue Code*; and
- Under Code Sec. 528 (homeowners' associations), Form 1120-H, *U.S. Income Tax Return for Homeowners Associations.*

Organizations for which no special form is provided must file an application prescribed by the IRS together with any required information [Reg. § 1.501(a)-1]. A copy of the articles of incorporation and the latest financial statement must be attached to the application. Subordinate organizations under the control of a central organization can apply for exemptions on a group basis.[28]

[28] Rev. Proc. 96-40, 1996-2 CB 301.

NOTE: Every new supplemental unemployment compensation benefits trust (SUB), VEBA, or group legal services plan must timely advise the IRS of its application for tax-exempt status. Exempt SUBs or plans already in existence must also give notice, within an IRS-established time period [Code Sec. 505]. Also, benefits provided by a plan cannot discriminate in favor of highly compensated employees.

The exemption application, and supporting papers are open to public inspection. On request, the IRS must supply the basis on which an exemption is granted [Code Sec. 6104(a); Reg. § 301.6104(a)-1].

In addition to the proof of exemption, tax-exempt corporations must file annual information returns [Ch. 26]. Tax-exempt organizations must make copies of its exemption application and information returns for the previous three years available for public inspection. The tax-exempt organization must also provide copies to individuals who request them, unless it makes the documents widely available by posting them on a readily accessible World Wide Web site.

.05 Disallowed Losses

No deduction is allowed for the loss on a sale between an exempt organization and a taxpayer (or a taxpayer's family) that controls it [Ch. 13] [Code Sec. 267(a)(1), (b)(9); Reg. § 1.267(b)-1].

.06 Private Inurement Prohibition and Loss of Tax-Exemption

Code Sec. 501(c)(3) provides that no substantial part of the net earnings of a Code Sec. 501(c)(3) tax-exempt charitable organization can inure to the benefit of any private shareholder or individual. Tax-exempt status may therefore be jeopardized, for example, if insiders, such as private shareholders or individuals, improperly benefit from the organization's earnings.[29]

Supplemental unemployment benefit trusts and Code Sec. 401(a) governmental plans and church plans may lose their exempt status if they engage in *prohibited activities* [Code Sec. 503; Reg. § 1.503(a)-1]. Examples of prohibited acts are payment of unreasonable compensation or lending of money at low interest rates to persons connected with the organization [Code Sec. 503(b); Reg. § 1.503(b)-1]. An organization that loses its exempt status under Code Sec. 501(c)(3) because of excessive lobbying can never become exempt under Code Sec. 501(c)(4) as a social welfare organization [Code Sec. 504]. Those religious, charitable and educational organizations that are private foundations are subject to a number of penalty taxes for engaging in prohibited acts [¶ 23,125], but lose their exemption only for willful repeated acts or a willful and flagrant act [¶ 23,115] [Code Sec. 507(a)].

---

29 *United Cancer Council*, CA-7, 99-1 USTC ¶ 50,248, 165 F3d 1173.

¶23,107 Lobbying Activities by Tax-Exempt Organizations

Tax-exempt organizations may risk loss of their exempt status if lobbying activities constitute a substantial part of the organization's activities. To avoid losing their exempt status due to excessive lobbying, public charities (except for churches and affiliated group members) can elect to be subject to a tax equal to 25 percent of their *excess expenditures* for the tax year [Code Secs. 501(h), 504, 4911(a)(11)]. The election is made on Form 5768, *Election/Revocation of Election by an Eligible Section 501(c)(3) Organization to Make Expenditures to Influence Legislation,* and is effective for the year in which it is filed.

Excess lobbying expenditures are the greater of (1) the excess of lobbying expenditures over the lobbying nontaxable amount or (2) the excess of grass-roots expenditures over 25 percent of the lobbying nontaxable amount. Grass-roots and lobbying expenditures are both attempts to influence legislation, but grass-roots does not include communication with a government official or employee. The *lobbying nontaxable amount* is a certain percentage of the lobbying expenditures [Code Sec. 501(h)]. The Supreme Court has held that the requirement that an organization cannot engage in substantial lobbying activities to qualify for tax exemption does not violate either the First or Fifth Amendment.[30]

.01 Disclosure of Lobbying Expense by Tax-Exempt Organizations

Tax-exempt organizations, other than Code Sec. 501(c)(3) organizations (e.g., trade associations), that pay or incur nondeductible lobbying expenditures must provide an annual information return to their members estimating the portion of members' dues that was used for lobbying expenses [Code Sec. 6033(e)(1)(A)]. The members, in turn, may not deduct the portion of their dues that was used for lobbying expenses. Organizations that fail to provide such notices or that underestimate the actual amount of dues allocable to nondeductible lobbying expenditures will be subject to tax on the aggregate amount of dues allocable to the expenditures made during the tax year that was not reported on the notices [Code Sec. 6033(e)(2)].

The IRS has enumerated the specific circumstances in which certain exempt organizations will be deemed to satisfy the reporting and notice requirements of Code Sec. 6033(e)(3).[31] There are three situations when a tax-exempt organization will not have to provide the information returns:

- When the organization has only *de minimis* (i.e., not more that $2,000) in-house lobbying expenses [Code Sec. 6033(e)(1)(B)(ii)];
- When the organization elects to pay the proxy tax (see below) on its lobbying expenditures [Code Sec. 6033(e)(2)(A)]; or
- When the organization establishes that substantially all the dues up to $105 in 2012 are paid by members who are not entitled to deduct such dues when computing their taxable income [Code Sec. 6033(e)(3)].

---

[30] *Taxation with Representation of Washington,* SCt, 83-1 USTC ¶9365, 461 US 540, 103 SCt 1997.

[31] Rev. Proc. 98-19, 1998-1 CB 547.

.02 Proxy Tax

A noncharitable tax-exempt organization may choose to forgo the information return requirement if it pays a proxy tax on the total amount of its lobbying expenditures (up to the amount of dues and other similar payments received by the organization. The tax rate is equal to the highest corporate rate in effect for the tax year (i.e., currently 35 percent). If the organization chooses to pay the proxy tax, no amount of the dues paid by members will be deemed nondeductible as a result of the organization's lobbying activities.

.03 Lobbying Activities Prohibited

Taxpayers are denied a deduction for contributions to a charity that conducts lobbying activities under the following circumstances:

- The charity conducts lobbying activities of direct financial interest to the donor's trade or business; and
- A principal purpose of the contribution was to gain a deduction for a lobbying expense that would otherwise have been nondeductible [Code Sec. 170(f)(9)].

¶23,108 Political Campaign Activities by Exempt Organizations

.01 Political Campaign Activities Prohibited

The IRS imposes strict guidelines on political campaign activities used by tax-exempt organizations to educate voters in elections.[32] Tax-exempt organizations are prohibited from participating or intervening in any way in any political campaign on behalf of, or in opposition to, any candidate for public office [Code Sec. 501(h)(1)]. Tax-exempt organizations that violate this strict prohibition could face revocation of their tax-exempt status and the imposition of excise taxes on the amount of money spent on that activity. In cases of flagrant violation of the law, the IRS has specific statutory authority to make an immediate determination and assessment of tax. Also, the IRS can ask a federal district court to enjoin the organization from making further political expenditures. Moreover, contributions to organizations that lose their Code Sec. 501(c)(3) status because of political activities are not deductible by the donors for federal income tax.

All Code Sec. 501(c)(3) organizations such as charities, schools and churches are prohibited from participating in, or intervening in (including the publication or distribution of statements), any political campaign on behalf of (or in opposition to) any candidate for public office. This means, for example, that they cannot:

1. Endorse any candidate;
2. Make donations to a candidate's campaign;
3. Engage in fundraising for a candidate;
4. Distribute statements for or against a particular candidate; or

---

[32] Rev. Rul. 2007-41, 2007-1 CB 1421.

5. Engage in any activity that may be beneficial or detrimental to any candidate for public office.

Even activities that encourage people to vote for or against a particular candidate on the basis of nonpartisan criteria violate the political campaign prohibition of Code Sec. 501(c)(3). Some political campaign activities or expenditures are not prohibited under the law. Distinguishing prohibited activities from those that are permitted, requires an analysis of all the facts and circumstances in each case. For example, tax-exempt organizations may sponsor debates or forums to educate voters, but if these debates and forums show a preference for or against a particular candidate, they become a prohibited activity. Tax-exempt organizations can also engage in advocating for or against issues and to a limited extent ballot initiatives or other legislative activities.

The IRS also considers a website to be a form of communication and cannot be viewed as a means of circumventing the prohibition against participating in political campaign activities. If a tax-exempt organization posts something on its website that endorses or opposes a candidate for public office, the organization will be treated as if it had distributed printed material, oral statements or broadcasts and will be subject to the same scrutiny and sanctions from the IRS.

.02 Individual Activity by Religious Leaders

In order for religious organizations to retain their tax-exempt status, religious leaders are prohibited from making partisan comments in official organization publications or at official church functions. The IRS encourages religious leaders who speak or write in their individual capacity to clearly indicate that their comments are personal and not intended to represent the views of the organization.[33]

Example 23-6: A candidate running for the Senate publishes a full-page ad in the local newspaper listing five prominent rabbis who have personally endorsed him. In the ad, each rabbi's affiliation with his synagogue is listed. The ad states, "Titles and affiliations of each individual are provided for identification purposes only." The candidate's campaign committee pays for the ad. Since the ad was not paid for by any of the listed synagogues, was not published in an official synagogue publication, and the endorsement was made by each rabbi in a personal capacity, the ad does not constitute campaign intervention by any of the listed synagogues.

Example 23-7: A minister publishes a monthly church newsletter that is distributed to all church members. In each issue, the minister has a column titled, "My Views." The month before the election, the minister states in the "My Views" column, "It is my personal opinion that a certain presidential candidate should be elected." For that one issue, the minister pays from his personal funds the portion of the cost of the newsletter attributable to the "My Views" column. Even though he paid part of the cost of the newsletter, the newsletter is an

---

[33] Treas. Dept., IRS Publication 1828, "Tax Guide for Churches and Religious Organizations," (2012 Ed.) p. 7.

official publication of the church. Since the endorsement appeared in an official publication of the church, it constitutes campaign intervention attributed to the church.[34]

.03 Religious Organizations Inviting Candidates to Speak

Religious organizations that invite candidates to speak at their events must be ever mindful of the prohibitions against political campaign activity so they do not jeopardize their tax-exempt status. The IRS advises the religious organization that invites a candidate to speak to take the following steps:

- Provide an equal opportunity to all political candidates seeking the same office taking into consideration the nature of the event and the manner of presentation. For example, a religious organization that invites one candidate to speak at its well attended annual banquet, but invites the opposing candidate to speak at a sparsely attended general meeting, will likely be found to have violated the political campaign prohibition, even if the manner of presentation for both speakers is otherwise neutral;
- Do not indicate any support of or opposition to the candidate. The religious organization should explicitly make this disclaimer when the candidate is introduced and in all communications concerning the candidate's attendance at the religious organization; and
- The religious organization should not engage in any political fundraising.

If a religious organization invites several candidates to speak at a public forum, the forum would be a prohibited political activity if it showed a bias for or against any candidate. To avoid having the public forum be treated as a prohibited campaign activity, it should consider the following facts:

a. Whether questions for the candidate are prepared and presented by an independent nonpartisan panel;

b. Whether the topics discussed by the candidates cover a broad range of issues that the candidates would address if elected to the office sought and are of interest to the public;

c. Whether each candidate is given an equal opportunity to present his or her views on the issues discussed;

d. Whether the candidates are asked to agree or disagree with positions, agendas, platforms or statements of the organization; and

e. Whether a moderator comments on the questions or otherwise implies approval or disapproval of the candidates.

Example 23-8: A minister invited three congressional candidates for the district in which the church is located to address the congregation, one each on three successive Sundays, as part of regular worship services. Each candidate was given an equal opportunity to address and field questions on a wide variety of

---

[34] Treas. Dept., IRS Publication 1828, "Tax Guide for Churches and Religious Organizations," (2012 Ed.) p. 8.

topics from the congregation. The minister's introduction of each candidate included no comments on their qualifications or any indication of a preference for any candidate. The actions do not constitute political campaign intervention by the church.

Example 23-9: A rabbi invited a candidate for the Senate to preach to the congregation on the Saturday prior to the November election. During his remarks, the candidate stated, "I am asking not only for your votes, but for your enthusiasm and dedication, for your willingness to go the extra mile to get a very large turnout on Tuesday." The rabbi invited no other candidate to address the congregation during the Senatorial campaign. Because these activities took place during official worship services, they are attributed to the synagogue. By selectively providing synagogue facilities to allow the candidate to speak in support of his campaign, the synagogue's actions constitute political campaign intervention.[35]

If a religious organization invites a political candidate (including church or synagogue members) to speak in a noncandidate capacity, the religious organization must ensure that:

- The individual speaks only in a noncandidate capacity;
- Neither the individual nor any representative of the church or synagogue makes any mention of his or her candidacy or the election;
- No campaign activity may occur in connection with the candidate's attendance; and
- The religious organization clearly indicates the capacity in which the candidate is appearing and should not mention the individual's political candidacy or the upcoming election in the communications announcing the candidate's attendance at the event.

Voter Guides

During campaign season, religious organizations commonly distribute voter guides that are designed to educate voters on the candidates' position on various political issues. The IRS provides that these guides may be used solely to educate voters, rather than as an attempt to favor or oppose candidates for elected public office. The following aspects of voter guides should be analyzed to determine whether a church or religious organization's publication or distribution of voter guides constitutes prohibited political campaign activity:

- Whether the candidate's positions are compared to the organization's position.
- Whether the guide includes a broad range of issues that the candidates would address if elected to the office sought.
- Whether the description of issues is neutral.

---

[35] Treas. Dept., IRS Publication 1828, "Tax Guide for Churches and Religious Organizations," (2012 Ed.) p. 11.

- Whether the descriptions of candidates' positions are either:
  a. The candidate's own words in response to questions, or
  b. A neutral, unbiased and complete compilation of all candidates' positions.

Business Activity

Religious organizations must also be careful that their business activities, such as the selling or renting of mailing lists, the leasing of office space, or the acceptance of paid political advertising, do not constitute participation or intervention in a political campaign. Factors that should be considered in determining whether the religious organization has engaged in prohibited political campaign activity include whether:

- The good, service, or facility is available to the candidates on an equal basis;
- The good, service or facility is available only to candidates and not the general public; and
- The activity is an ongoing activity of the organization or whether it is conducted only for the candidate.

Rating of Candidates Prohibited

The political campaign prohibition of Code Sec. 501(c)(3) may be violated even though the tax-exempt organization had a nonpartisan motive. For example, a tax-exempt bar association's rating of candidates for elective judicial office constituted a prohibited intervention or participation in political campaigns in *Ass'n of the Bar of the City of New York*.[36] In that case, a local bar association lost its tax-exempt status because its rating of candidates for judgeships at the municipal, state and federal level constituted prohibited intervention or participation in political campaigns. The ratings were communicated to the members and the public and constituted indirect political activity, not merely the dissemination of objective data, as argued by the association. The U.S. Court of Appeals for the Second Circuit held that the "voter education activities" of the Association of the Bar of the City of New York constituted prohibited campaign activities, even though these activities were nonpartisan and in the public interest.

Sanctions for Violations

An organization engaging in prohibited political campaign activities may lose its exempt status and be subject to excise tax on the amounts spent on those activities [Code Sec. 4955]. For egregious violations, the IRS has the authority under Code Sec. 6852 to make an immediate determination and assessment of tax. The IRS could also ask a district court to enjoin the organization from making further political expenditures under Code Sec. 7409. In addition, donors who make contributions to organizations that lose their tax-exempt section 501(c)(3) status as a result of prohibited political activities would not be able to claim deductions for their contributions to these organizations.

---

[36] *Ass'n of the Bar of the City of New York*, CA-2, 88-2 USTC ¶9535, 858 F2d 876, *cert. denied*, 490 US 1030, 109 SCt 1768.

¶23,109 Code Sec. 527 Political Organizations and Exempt Organizations

.01 Disclosure Requirements

A Code Sec. 527 organization is a political organization set up to accept contributions and make expenditures for a political campaign or similar activities. Code Sec. 527 provides limited tax-exempt status to *political organizations,* including parties, committees, and associations organized and operated primarily for the purpose of directly or indirectly accepting contributions or making expenditures for an *exempt function,* which means influencing or attempting to influence the selection, nomination, election or appointment of specific types of federal or state officials. The organizations generally don't pay tax on contributions they receive but are subject to tax on their net investment income and certain other income at the highest corporate income tax rate, which now stands at 35 percent. Donors are exempt from gift tax on their contributions to these organizations.

The IRS provided guidance on the reporting and disclosure requirements for tax-exempt Code Sec. 527 political organizations in Rev. Rul. 2003-49[37] and imposed the following three reporting and disclosure requirements: (1) an initial notice of status, (2) periodic reports of contributions and expenditures, and (3) annual returns. These requirements are discussed in detail below.

Within 24 hours after the date on which the Code Sec. 527 organization is established, the Code Sec. 527 organization will have to provide notice to the IRS electronically and in writing that it is to be treated as a Code Sec. 527 organization on Form 8871, *Political Organization Notice of Section 527 Status.* On Form 8871, the political organizations must disclose their existence, purpose and staff. An organization is exempt from these disclosure requirements if:

- It reasonably anticipates that it won't have gross receipts of $25,000 or more for any tax year;
- It is subject to Code Sec. 527 solely because of Code Sec. 527(f)(1) (which provides that if a Code Sec. 501(c) tax-exempt organization) expends any amount during the tax year for an exempt function, such as influencing the nomination or election of a state or federal official, then it is taxed as if it were a political organization;
- It is a person required to report under the Federal Election Campaign as a political committee;
- The organization is a political committee of a state or local candidate; or
- The organization is a state or local committee of a political party [Code Sec. 527(e)(5)].

A newly established political organization need not file Form 8871 if it reasonably anticipates that its annual gross receipts will be less than $25,000 for its first six tax years. However, if an organization in fact, does have annual receipts of $25,000 or more

[37] Rev. Rul. 2003-49, 2003-1 CB 903.

for any tax year, it must file Form 8871 within 30 days of receiving $25,000 in a single tax year to continue to be tax-exempt.

If the organization has a material change in any of the information reported on Form 8871, it must file an amended Form 8871 within 30 days of the material change. A final Form 8871 must be filed within 30 days of a political organization's termination.

.02 Periodic Reporting Requirements

In addition to notifying the IRS of their existence and purpose, periodic reporting requirements are imposed on certain tax-exempt organizations. A tax-exempt political organization must report periodically certain contributions it receives and expenditures it makes [Code Sec. 527(j)]. The required periodic reporting form is Form 8872, *Political Organization Report of Contributions and Expenditures*. Tax-exempt political organizations that accept contributions or make expenditures for an exempt function during a calendar year must file periodic reports on Form 8872, beginning with the first month or quarter during the calendar year in which they accept contributions or make expenditures. The following tax-exempt political organizations are excepted from the periodic reporting requirements: (1) any organization excepted from the requirement to file Form 8871, and (2) any qualified state or local political organization.

A tax-exempt political organization that does not timely file Form 8872, or that fails to include the information required on the Form 8872, must pay a penalty to the IRS in an amount calculated by multiplying the amount of contributions and expenditures that are not disclosed by the highest corporate tax rate [Code Sec. 527(j)(1)].

A political organization, whether or not tax-exempt, with more than $100 of taxable income must file an annual income tax return on Form 1120-POL, *U.S. Income Tax Return for Certain Political Organizations* [Code Sec. 6012(a)(6)]. The form is due on or before the 15th day of the third month after the close of the organization's tax year [Code Sec. 6072(b)]. Forms 1120-POL are not required to be available for public inspection.

.03 Requirements for Tax-Exempt Hospital

A hospital will qualify for tax-exempt status if it is organized and operated for a charitable purpose and otherwise satisfies the requirements of Code Sec. 501(c)(3).

Code Sec. 501(r) imposes requirements in addition to, but not in lieu of, the requirements otherwise applicable to a tax-exempt organization. The requirements generally apply to any tax-exempt organization that operates at least one hospital facility. Code Sec. 501(r)(2) provides that a hospital facility generally includes: (1) an organization that operates a facility required by a state to be licensed, registered, or similarly recognized as a hospital; and (2) any other facility that the IRS determines has the provision of hospital care as its principal purpose. Code Sec. 501(r) applies to hospital organizations on a facility-by-facility basis.

The following requirements are imposed on each hospital facility [Code Sec. 501(r)(2)(B); Prop. Reg. § 1.501(r)-1(b)(15)]:

Community Health Needs Assessment

Each hospital facility is required to conduct a community health needs assessment at least once every three years and adopt an implementation strategy to meet the community needs identified through such assessment [Code Sec. 501(r)(3); Prop. Reg. § 1.501(r)-3(b)]. Each hospital facility is required to make the assessment widely available. Failure to complete a community health needs assessment in any applicable three-year period results in a penalty of up to $50,000. The community health needs assessment "may be based on current information collected by a public health agency or non-profit organizations and may be conducted together with one or more organizations, including related organizations."[38]

Financial Assistance Policy

Each hospital facility is required to adopt, implement, and widely publicize a written policy requiring the organization to provide, without discrimination, care for emergency medical conditions [Code Sec. 501(r)(4)(B); Prop. Reg. § 1.501(r)-4(b)(1)]. The financial assistance policy must indicate the eligibility criteria for financial assistance and whether such assistance includes free or discounted care. For those eligible for discounted care, the policy must indicate the basis for calculating the amounts that will be billed to such patients. The policy must also indicate how to apply for such assistance. If a hospital does not have a separate billing and collections policy, the financial assistance policy must also indicate what actions the hospital may take in the event of nonresponse or nonpayment, including collections action and reporting to credit rating agencies.

"The policy must prevent discrimination in the provision of emergency medical treatment, including denial of service, against those eligible for financial assistance under the facility's financial assistance policy or those eligible for government assistance."[39] Each hospital facility also is required to adopt and implement a policy to provide emergency medical treatment to individuals. The policy must prevent discrimination in the provision of emergency medical treatment, including denial of service, against those eligible for financial assistance under the facility's financial assistance policy or those eligible for government assistance.

Limitation on Charges

Code Sec. 501(r)(5) requires a hospital organization to limit amounts charged for emergency or other medically necessary care that is provided to individuals eligible for assistance under the organization's financial assistance policy to not more than the amounts generally billed to individuals who have insurance covering such care. In addition, a hospital facility may not use gross charges (i.e., "chargemaster" rates) when billing individuals who qualify for financial assistance.

It is intended that amounts billed to those who qualify for financial assistance may be based on either the best, or an average of the three best, negotiated commercial rates, or Medicare rates.[40]

---

[38] Joint Committee on Taxation, *Technical Explanation of the Revenue Provisions of the "Reconciliation Act of 2010," as amended, in combination with the "Patient Protection and Affordable Care Act"* (JCX-18-10), at 81, March 21, 2010.

[39] Technical Explanation at 82.

[40] Technical Explanation at 82.

Billing and Collection Requirements

Code Sec. 501(r)(6) requires a hospital organization to forego extraordinary collection actions against an individual before the organization has made reasonable efforts to determine whether the individual is eligible for assistance under the hospital organization's financial assistance policy. "Extraordinary collections include lawsuits, liens on residences, arrests, body attachments, or other similar collection processes."[41] "Reasonable efforts' includes notification by the hospital of its financial assistance policy upon admission and in written and oral communications with the patient regarding the patient's bill, including invoices and telephone calls, before collection action or reporting to credit agencies is initiated."[42]

Excise Tax for Failure To Meet Hospital Exemption Requirements

Code Sec. 4959 imposes a $50,000 excise tax on a hospital that fails to meet Code Sec. 501(r) requirements for any tax year. In addition, Code Sec. 6033(b) imposes reporting requirements on hospitals.

.04 Joint Ventures Between Tax-Exempts and For-Profits

In Rev. Rul. 98-15[43] the IRS established the framework for the creation of joint ventures between tax-exempts and for-profits by providing that a tax-exempt organization may form and participate in a partnership and meet the operational test only if:

- Participation in the partnership furthers a charitable purpose; and
- The partnership arrangement permits the exempt organization to act exclusively in furtherance of its exempt purpose and only incidentally for the benefit of the for-profit partners.

In *Redlands Surgical Services*,[44] a tax-exempt health corporation wanted to enter into a partnership with a for-profit entity in order to operate a surgical center. The Tax Court found that Redlands Surgical Services wasn't entitled to exemption because it wasn't operated exclusively for charitable purposes in view. The court supported this view by noting that Redlands Surgical Services had given effective control over its sole activity (operation of a surgical center) to its for-profit partners. Affirming the Tax Court, the Court of Appeals for the Ninth Circuit held that the nonprofit entity effectively ceded control over the operation of the joint venture to its for-profit partner and thereby conferred a private benefit that impermissibly served private interests. In doing so, the taxpayer was no longer operated exclusively for exempt purposes as required by law.

In Rev. Rul. 2004-51,[45] the IRS concluded that the tax-exempt university continued to qualify for tax exemption even after it contributed part of its assets to and conducted part of its activities through an LLC, which was 50-percent owned with a for-profit entity. The IRS reasoned that the activities conducted through the LLC constituted a trade or business that was substantially related to the exercise and performance of the university's exempt purposes and functions. Even though the LLC arranged and conducted all aspects of the teacher training seminars, the university alone approved the curriculum,

[41] Technical Explanation at 82.

[42] Technical Explanation at 82.

[43] Rev. Rul. 98-15, 1998-1 CB 718.

[44] *Redlands Surgical Services*, CA-9, 2001-1 USTC ¶50,271, 242 F3d 904.

[45] Rev. Rul. 2004-51, 2004-1 CB 974.

training materials and instructors, and determined the standards for successfully completing the seminars. Therefore, the university was not subject to the unrelated business income tax on its distributive share of the LLC's income.

▶ **PLANNING POINTER:** Even though the facts addressed in Rev. Rul. 2004-51 involve a university, the ruling paves the way for other tax-exempt organizations to engage in joint ventures with for-profit entities without risking loss of their tax-exempt tax status under Code Sec. 501(c)(3). The ruling maps out the steps that a business-minded tax-exempt organization must take before entering into a business venture with a for-profit entity.

In *St. David's Health Care System*,[46] the Court of Appeals for the Fifth Circuit concluded that a nonprofit hospital would no longer qualify for tax exemption if its activities in a joint venture furthered the private, profit-seeking interests of its for-profit partner. The court concluded that when a nonprofit in a joint venture cedes control over the partnership to its for-profit partner, it is assumed the partnership's activities substantially further the for-profit's interests. A settlement was finally reached, however, that will allow St. David's to continue operating as a tax-exempt entity even though it entered into a joint venture with a for-profit health care company.

▶ **PLANNING POINTER:** This landmark settlement paves the way not only for other tax-exempt hospitals but for other tax-exempt organizations to engage in joint ventures with for-profit entities without risking loss of their tax-exempt tax status under Code Sec. 501(c)(3). More ammunition is provided to the business-minded tax-exempt organizations by Rev. Rul. 2004-51, as discussed above, where the IRS maps out how they will analyze whether the joint venture affects the organization's tax-exempt status.

.05 Guidance to Hospitals on Physician Recruitment

The IRS has detailed the tax consequences of physician recruitment incentives provided by tax-exempt hospitals in Rev. Rul. 97-21 and in numerous private letter rulings.[47] To retain tax-exempt status, a hospital that provides recruitment incentives to nonemployee private practice physicians must provide those incentives in a manner that does not cause the hospital to be organized or operated for the benefit of private interests. A hospital will violate this test and lose its tax-exempt status if it engages in the following activities:

- Substantial activities that fail to further the hospital's exempt purposes or that do not bear a reasonable relationship to the accomplishment of those purposes;
- Activities that result in inurement of the hospital's net earnings to a private shareholder or individual. An activity may result in inurement if it is structured as a device to distribute the net earnings of the hospital;

[46] *St. David's Health Care System*, CA-5, 2003-2 USTC ¶50,713, 349 F3d 232.

[47] Rev. Rul. 97-21, 1997-1 CB 121; LTR 200307094 (Nov. 20, 2002); LTR 199949039 (Sept. 8, 1999); LTR 9726020 (Mar. 31, 1997).

- Substantial activities that cause the hospital to be operated for the benefit of a private interest rather than public interest so that it has a substantial nonexempt purpose; and
- Substantial unlawful activities through either direct or indirect means.

¶23,110 TYPES OF EXEMPT ORGANIZATIONS

.01 Exempt Organizations

The following types of organizations, with exceptions, qualify for exemption:

- *Corporations organized under an Act of Congress,* which are instrumentalities of the U.S. exempt from federal income taxes under such act [Code Sec. 501(c)(1)];
- *Corporations paying all income to exempt organizations* [Code Sec. 501(c)(2); Reg. § 1.501(c)-(2)-1];
- *Religious, charitable, educational, etc., organizations* [Code Sec. 501(c)(3); Reg. § 1.501(c)(3)-1];
- *Churches,* conventions or associations of churches [Code Sec. 501(c)(3); Reg. § 1.501(c)(3)-1];
- *Civic leagues* or organizations operated exclusively for the promotion of social welfare [Code Sec. 501(c)(4); Reg. § 1.501(c)(4)-1];
- *Labor, agricultural, or horticultural organizations* (including certain fishermen's organizations) [Code Sec. 501(c)(5), (g); Reg. § 1.501(c)(5)-1];
- *Business leagues,* chambers of commerce, real estate boards, boards of trade or professional football leagues not organized for profit whose earnings do not benefit any private shareholder or individual [Code Sec. 501(c)(6); Reg. § 1.501(c)(6)-1];
- *Clubs* organized and operated substantially for pleasure, recreation, and other nonprofitable purposes, whose net earnings do not benefit any private shareholder (but not if charter, bylaws or other written policies provide for discrimination) [Code Sec. 501(c)(7), (i); Reg. § 1.501(c)(7)-1];
- *Fraternal beneficiary societies,* orders, or associations operating under the lodge system and providing insurance benefits to their members or their dependents[48] [Code Sec. 501(c)(8); Reg. § 1.501(c)(8)-1];
- *Voluntary employees' beneficiary associations* meeting certain requirements [Code Sec. 501(c)(9); 505; Reg. § 1.501(c)(9)-1];
- *Fraternal orders* operating under the lodge system and not providing insurance benefits for members [Code Sec. 501(c)(10); Reg. § 1.501(c)(10)-1];
- *Teachers' retirement fund associations* [Code Sec. 501(c)(11)];
- *Benevolent life insurance associations,* mutual ditch or irrigation companies, mutual or cooperative telephone companies, or like organizations [Code Sec. 501(c)(12); Reg. § 1.501(c)(12)-1];

---

[48] *Grange Ins. Ass'n of California.,* CA-9, 63-1 USTC ¶9455, 317 F2d 222.

- *Cemetery companies* [Code Sec. 501(c)(13); Reg. § 1.501(c)(13)-1];
- *Credit unions* [Code Sec. 501(c)(14)(A)];
- *Credit counseling organizations* that provide educational information to the general public on budgeting, personal finance, financial literacy, saving and spending practices, and the sound use of consumer credit must be organized and operated according to special rules in order to be exempt from federal income taxation under Code Sec. 501(q). Debt management plan services provided by exempt organizations that do not meet these standards are treated as an unrelated trade or business. The standards are consistent with the requirements in IRC Chief Counsel Advice 200431023 and 200620001 for determining tax-exempt status for credit counseling organizations.

  A credit counseling services organization will only be tax-exempt if it: (1) qualifies as a charitable or educational organization, or (2) a social welfare organization, and is organized and operated according to the following requirements [Code Sec. 501(q)(1)]:

  — *Tailored credit counseling services.* The organization must provide credit counseling services tailored to consumers' specific needs and circumstances [Code Sec. 501(q)(1)(A)(i)].

  — *No loans.* The organization must make no loans to debtors (other than loans with no fees or interest), and must not negotiate loans on behalf of debtors [Code Sec. 501(q)(1)(A)(ii)].

  — *Incidental credit improvement services.* The organization can provide services that improve a consumer's credit record, history, or rating, but only if those services are incidental to providing credit counseling services. The organization cannot charge a separately-stated fee for credit record, history, or rating improvement services [Code Sec. 501(q)(1)(A)(iii)].

  — *No refusal to provide services.* The organization must not refuse to provide credit counseling services due to a consumer's inability to pay, ineligibility for debt management plan enrollment, or unwillingness to enroll in a debt management plan [Code Sec. 501(q)(1)(B)].

  — *Reasonable fee policy.* The organization must establish and implement a fee policy that: (i) requires that any fee charged to a consumer is reasonable; (ii) allows waiver of fees if the consumer is unable to pay; and (iii) except as allowed by state law, prohibits charging a fee based on a percentage of the consumer's debt, the consumer's payments to be made under a debt management plan, or the consumer's projected or actual savings resulting from debt management plan enrollment [Code Sec. 501(q)(1)(C)].

  — *Independent board members with public interest.* The organization must at all times have a board of directors or other governing body ("board") that is controlled by persons who represent the broad interests of the public (e.g., public officials, persons having special knowledge or expertise in credit or financial education, community leaders). Not more than 20 percent of the board's voting power may be vested in persons who are employed by the organization or will benefit financially, directly or indirectly, from its activities (other than through the receipt of reasonable directors' fees, or the repayment of consumer debt to creditors other than the organization or its affiliates). In addition not more than

49 percent of the board's voting power may be vested in persons employed by the organization or who will benefit financially, directly or indirectly, from its activities (other than through the receipt of reasonable directors' fees) [Code Sec. 501(q)(1)(D)].

— *Limited ownership of related service providers.* The organization must not own more than 35 percent of the total combined voting power of a corporation, the profits interest of a partnership, or the beneficial interest of an estate or trust, any of which are in the trade or business of lending money, repairing credit, or providing debt management plan services, payment processing or similar services. This does not apply if the corporation, partnership, or trust is a charitable organization [Code Sec. 501(q)(1)(E)].

— *Referral fees.* The organization must receive no amount for providing referrals to others for debt management services, and must pay no amount to others for obtaining consumer referrals [Code Sec. 501(q)(1)(F)]. For example, if an organization pays or receives a fee for using or maintaining a locator service for consumers to find a credit counseling organization, the fee is not considered a referral [Joint Committee on Taxation, Technical Explanation of the Pension Protection Act of 2006 (JCX-38-06)].

- *Banks providing reserves and deposit insurance* [Code Sec. 501(c)(14)(B), (C)];
- *Small mutual insurance companies* or associations other than life or marine with gross receipts under $150,000 [Code Sec. 501(c)(15); Reg. § 1.501(c)(15)-1]. Property and casualty insurance companies (whether stock or mutual) with net written premiums (or direct written premiums, if greater) not exceeding $350,000 are exempt from tax. Those whose premiums are between $350,000 and $1.2 million may elect to be taxed only on taxable investment income [Code Secs. 501(c)(15), 831];
- *Corporations organized by farmers' cooperatives* [Code Sec. 501(c)(16); Reg. § 1.501(c)(16)-1];
- *Qualified supplemental unemployment benefit trusts* meeting certain requirements [Code Secs. 501(c)(17), 505; Reg. § 1.501(c)(17)-1];
- *Trusts forming part of pension plans* [Reg. § 1.501(c)(18)-1];
- *Armed Forces members' organizations* [Code Sec. 501(c)(19), (23); Reg. § 1.501(c)(19)-1];
- *Qualified group legal services organizations or trusts* meeting certain requirements [Code Secs. 501(c)(20), 505; Prop. Reg. § 1.501(c)(20)-1];
- *Black Lung Act trusts* that satisfy coal mine operators' liabilities for black lung benefits and buy liability insurance [Code Sec. 501(c)(21); Reg. § 1.501(c)(21)-1];
- *Trusts created to satisfy certain withdrawal liability payments* of multiemployer pension plans [Code Sec. 501(c)(22)];
- *Title-holding companies* meeting certain requirements [Code Sec. 501(c)(25)];
- *Athletic organizations* promoting amateur sports competition [Code Sec. 501(c)(3)];
- *Religious or apostolic associations* or corporations [Code Sec. 501(d); Reg. § 1.501(d)-1];

- *Hospital service organizations* (but not a cooperative hospital laundry)[49] [Code Sec. 501(e)];
- *Cooperative service organizations of operating educational organizations* (school investment funds) [Code Sec. 501(f)];
- *Child care organizations* whose services are available to the public [Code Sec. 501(k)];
- *Farmers' cooperative* marketing and purchasing associations [Code Sec. 521; Reg. § 1.521-1];
- *Political organizations* operated primarily to influence selection, appointment, nomination or election of public office seekers. A fund of an elected official to receive contributions for newsletters can also qualify [Code Sec. 527; Reg. § 1.527-1, -7];
- *Qualified homeowners' associations* (e.g., condominium and residential real estate management associations) [Code Sec. 528; Reg. § 1.528-1 to -10];
- *Qualified state tuition programs* [Code Sec. 529; 5110];
- *Clubs.* College fraternities;[50] country clubs[51] (even though club got its principal income from a bar or restaurant, if only members or guests were served);[52] riding clubs (if admission charged outsiders for annual rodeo is merely to defray expenses).[53]
- *Religious, charitable, educational, etc., organizations.* Daughters of the American Revolution; Salvation Army; Red Cross; Navy Relief Society; U.S. Lawn Tennis Association; Woodrow Wilson Foundation; the U.S.O.; U.S. Olympic Association;
- *Business leagues, etc.* Fruit growers association organized to promote sale of apples grown in state;[54] to promote sale and use of processed agricultural product;[55]
- *Medical clinic.* An outpatient medical clinic organized and operated exclusively for charitable, scientific and educational purposes and treating indigent patients, qualified as a tax-exempt Code Sec. 501(c)(3) organization even though it was organized as a for-profit organization because it was done so only to comply with Illinois law, which restricted the medical group from organizing as a not for-profit corporation.[56] The fact that the IRS granted tax-exempt status to this medical clinic is good news to health care providers seeking to practice in states where the corporate statutes prohibit medical practices and clinics from forming as tax-exempt entities; and
- *Hospital.* A nonprofit hospital was an exempt organization even though it entered into a partnership with a for-profit health care business because contractual terms clearly protected the nonprofit, charitable pursuits of the hospital.[57] See ¶ 23,105.06.

---

[49] *HCSC-Laundry*, SCt, 81-1 USTC ¶ 9202, 450 US 1, 101 SCt 836.

[50] Rev. Rul. 69-573, 1969-2 CB 125.

[51] *Coeur d'Alene Country Club*, DC-ID, 46-1 USTC ¶ 9181, 64 FSupp 540, *appeal dismissed*, 157 F2d 330.

[52] Rev. Rul. 44, 1953-1 CB 109; Rev. Proc. 71-17, 1971-1 CB 683.

[53] *Clements Buckaroos*, 21 TCM 83, Dec. 25,336(M), TC Memo. 1962-18.

[54] *Washington State Apples, Inc.*, 46 BTA 64, Dec. 12,233, *acq.* 1942-1 CB 17.

[55] Rev. Rul. 67-252, 1967-2 CB 195.

[56] North Share Medical Specialists, S.C., DOC. 1996-31095.

[57] *St. David's Health Care System*, CA-5, 2003-2 USTC ¶ 50,713, 349 F3d 232.

.02 Examples of Nonexempt Organizations

The following are examples of organizations not considered to be exempt:

- *Clubs.* Automobile clubs;[58]
- *Farmers' cooperatives.* Advertising association;[59] scavenger service;[60] marketing building materials on cooperative basis;[61]
- *Cemeteries.* Operation of cemetery used only by organizer and descendants;[62]
- *Private organizations.* Jockey Club of New York; private hospital operated for benefit of physicians in charge;[63] and
- *Business leagues, etc.* Stock exchange; commodity exchange; nurses' association operated primarily as an employment agency for its members;[64] business league operated primarily to publish yearbook comprised largely of members' paid ads.[65]
- *Down-payment-assistance programs.* These programs are funded by home-sellers or other interested parties to provide cash assistance to homebuyers who cannot afford to make the minimum down payment or pay the closing costs required when purchasing a home.[66] Contrast this commercial activity with ones that also offer such assistance but are funded by broad-based fundraising and are operated to assist low-income families in purchasing homes or to redevelop economically depressed areas, which are tax-exempt.

.03 Feeder Organizations

An organization operated primarily to carry on a trade or business for profit cannot claim tax exemption on the ground that all its profits are payable to one or more exempt organizations [Code Sec. 502(a)]. That is, its own activities must be of an exempt nature to gain tax exemption. A feeder organization is taxable on its entire income, not just the portion it designates as its unrelated business income. *Trade or business,* for this rule, does not include the rental of realty or of personal property rented out with such realty unless it is more than incidental in amount. *Rents* are similar to those excluded for unrelated business taxable income [¶23,170]. It also does not include a business in which most of the work is performed voluntarily, nor one that sells merchandise, substantially all of which is donated (for example, a thrift shop) [Code Sec. 502(b); Reg. §1.502-1(d)]. A separate organization that pays its profits to an exempt organization is not a feeder organization subject to tax if its workers perform without pay or the merchandise that it sells is received as a gift or contribution [Code Sec. 502(b)(2), (3)].

---

58 *Calif. State Auto. Ass'n.*, CA-9, 49-2 USTC ¶9325, 175 F2d 752, *cert denied*, 338 US 905, 70 SCt 307.

59 *National Outdoor Advertising Bureau*, CA-2, 37-1 USTC ¶9289, 89 F2d 878.

60 *Sunset Scavenger Co.*, CA-9, 36-2 USTC ¶9367, 84 F2d 453.

61 Rev. Rul. 73-308, 1973-2 CB 193.

62 Rev. Rul. 65-6, 1965-1 CB 229.

63 *Sonora Community Hospital*, CA-9, 68-2 USTC ¶9528, 397 F2d 814.

64 Rev. Rul. 61-170, 1961-2 CB 112.

65 Rev. Rul. 65-14, 1965-1 CB 236.

66 Rev. Rul. 2006-27, 2006-1 CB 915; *Partners In Charity, Inc.*, 141 TC No. 2, Dec. 59,612 (2013).

PRIVATE FOUNDATIONS

¶23,115 PRIVATE FOUNDATIONS DEFINED

Private foundations enable taxpayers to achieve philanthropic, family, financial, estate planning and other tax goals without losing complete control over their assets. To achieve these objectives, however, the foundation must comply with a number of detailed rules, requirements, and prohibitions. Failure to follow these requirements will subject the foundation and its directors or trustees to substantial liability.

.01 *Private Foundations* Defined

Private foundations are best defined as what they are not. Thus, the tax law [Code Sec. 509] states that they include *all* exempt charities under Code Sec. 501(c)(3) [¶23,110] *except the following:*

- A church, school or educational organization that supports state schools, a hospital or medical research association, a governmental unit, or a charitable organization that is supported by the government or the general public [Code Secs. 170(b)(1)(A), 509(a)(1); Reg. §1.170A-9]. (A medical research organization is not a private foundation merely because it does not commit itself to spend every contribution for research within five years of receipt [Reg. §1.509(a)-2(b)]);

  NOTE: The public support tests used for public charities described above differ in many important respects from those used for the publicly supported organizations described in (2) below. For detailed descriptions of the public charities above that qualify under Code Sec. 170(b)(1)(A), see Ch. 9.

- An organization that normally receives: (a) from the general public (persons who are not disqualified [¶23,140]) and from governmental units more than one-third of its annual support in any combination of (1) gifts, grants, contributions or membership fees and (2) gross receipts from admissions, sales or services performed in a related trade or business and (b) no more than 1/3 of its annual support from the sum of (1) gross investment income and (2) the excess of unrelated business taxable income from businesses [¶23,170]over the unrelated business income tax [¶23,155] [Code Sec. 509(a)(2); Reg. §1.509(a)-3]. Contributions and payment for services are both counted as support (for example, a $10 gift plus $5 ticket payment would make up $15 public support). But payments by any person or government bureau for services rendered cannot exceed $5,000 or 1 percent of the total support, whichever is greater [Reg. §1.509(a)-3(b)]. Gross investment income includes interest, dividends, rents and royalties, but not net capital gains [Code Sec. 509(e)]. In addition to gifts and contributions, gross investment income, and gross receipts, the total support of an organization also includes net income from unrelated business activities [¶23,160] but not net capital gains [Code Sec. 509(d)];

  ▶ **OBSERVATION:** Failure to satisfy the above support test is not necessarily fatal, because the IRS may look at the experience of an organization over a four-year period to determine its "normal" sources of support [Reg. §1.509(a)-3(c)]. Special rules are provided for new organizations [Reg. §1.509(a)-3(d), (e)].

- An organization exclusively for the benefit of one or more organizations described in (1) or (2) above [Code Sec. 509(a)(3); Reg. § 1.509(a)-4]; and
- An organization operated exclusively to test for public safety [Code Sec. 509(a)(4)].

.02 Notification of Status

Because the activities of private foundations are severely restricted [¶ 23,125], both new *and* old charitable organizations are presumed to be private foundations unless they claim public charity status [Reg. § 1.508-1(b)]. Therefore, an organization that claims to be an exempt charity must notify the IRS on Form 1023, *Application for Recognition of Exemption* [Reg. § 1.508-1(a)]. It should provide information that it is not a private foundation, plus any further information necessary to establish that it qualifies as a public charity [Reg. § 1.508-1(b)(2)]. An organization that fails to give notice by 15 months from the end of the month in which it was organized will not be exempt [Code Sec. 508(a); Reg. § 1.508-1(a)]. No deductions are allowed for charitable contributions received after the loss of exemption [Code Sec. 508(d)(2); Reg. § 1.508-2].

Private foundations are subject to the public inspection requirements that currently apply to public charities and all other tax-exempt organizations that file annual information returns. This means that private foundations must comply with requests from individuals who want to see a copy of the foundation's annual information return including Form 990-PF, *Return of Private Foundation or Section 4947(a)(1) Nonexempt Charitable Trust Treated as a Private Foundation,* and Form 4720, *Return of Certain Excise Taxes Under Chapters 41 and 42 of the IRC* [Reg. § 301.6104(d)-1(b)(4)]. Each copy of a return made available to the public must include all information furnished to the IRS on the return, including all schedules, attachments and supporting documents. A copy of Form 990, for example, includes those parts of the return that show compensation paid to specific persons. In addition, a private foundation is required to:

- Make its annual information return available for public inspection at its principal office during regular business hours for 180 days after the foundation publishes notice of the availability of its return;
- Allow public inspection of the foundation's exemption application at the foundation's principal office; and
- Provide copies of the exemption application upon request [Code Sec. 6104(d)].

Unlike other tax-exempt organizations, a private foundation must disclose to the general public, the names and addresses of its contributors [Reg. § 301.6104(d)-1(b)(4)(ii)].

The following organizations need not provide notice on Form 1023: churches (including church organizations, religious schools, mission societies and youth groups); public charities whose annual gross income normally is $5,000 or less; subordinate organizations (except private foundations) covered by a group exemption letter; and certain nonexempt charitable trusts [¶ 23,195] [Code Sec. 508(c); Reg. § 1.508-1(a)(3), (b)(7)].

.03 Tax on Termination of Status

Code Sec. 507 provides that a private foundation may terminate its private foundation status by voluntarily notifying the IRS of its plan to terminate and by paying a tax equal to the lower of: (1) all of the increases in income, estate, and gift taxes that would have been imposed on the foundation and all substantial contributors if the foundation had been liable for income taxes and if its contributors had not received deductions for contributions to the foundation, or (2) the value of its net assets valued either as of the first day on which the foundation took action culminating in loss of its exempt status or as of the day on which it ceased to be a foundation, whichever is greater [Code Sec. 507(d); Reg. § 1.507-5(a)].

The termination tax may also be imposed on the private foundation if: (1) the organization notifies the IRS of its intent to terminate, or (2) IRS gives notice of the forfeiture of exempt status for willful and flagrant violations of the prohibitions on foundations [Code Sec. 507(a); Reg. § 1.507-1]. In either case, tax assessments recapture the total tax benefits (with interest) flowing from the foundation's prior exempt status [Code Sec. 507(c); Reg. § 1.507-5, -8]. The recapture tax cannot exceed the value of the foundation's net assets [Code Sec. 507(e); Reg. § 1.507-4, -7]. The IRS may abate the tax if the foundation itself goes public and so operates for at least five years or if it distributes its assets to one or more public charities that have existed continuously for at least five years [Code Sec. 507(b); Reg. § 1.507-9]. If this tax is imposed on the foundation, deductions for gifts and bequests to the foundation are not allowed.

In Rev. Rul. 2003-13,[67] the IRS explained when distribution of a private foundation's assets will, by itself, terminate the foundation. In the first situation, a private foundation distributed all of its net assets to an exempt organization that had been in existence for at least 60 months. In the second situation, the facts are the same as in the first situation except that the exempt organization has been in existence for fewer than 60 months. In the third situation, the facts are the same as in the first situation, but the exempt organization is a Section 509(a)(2) organization. In the fourth situation, the facts were the same as in the third situation but the exempt organization is a Section 509(a)(3) organization. The IRS concluded in the first situation that the distribution terminated the private foundation because the exempt organization has been in existence for at least 60 months. The outcomes are different in the three other situations. In the second situation, distribution did not terminate the private foundation because the exempt organization had not been in existence for at least 60 months. In the third and fourth situations, distribution did not terminate the private foundation because the exempt organizations were not Section 509(a)(1) organizations.

.04 Transfers of Assets Between Private Foundations

Private foundations may transfer assets to other private foundations for the following reasons:

- To reduce operating and administrative costs;
- To eliminate dissension that occurred after a personal family crisis such divorce or death;
- To allow organizers to achieve different charitable objectives; or
- To take advantage of business and tax advantages available by operating in a different business form.

---

[67] Rev. Rul. 2003-13, 2003-1 CB 305.

In Rev. Rul. 2002-28,[68] the IRS provided guidance on the filing obligations and excise tax issues that arise when a private foundation transfers all of its assets to other foundations under Code Sec. 507(b)(2). The IRS issued this formal guidance in response to the hundreds of ruling requests it had received from taxpayers seeking assurances that proposed transfers of private foundation assets to other private foundations would be tax-free. This issue is frequently audited because taxpayers often attempt to circumvent the onerous private foundation termination tax by transferring assets between private foundations. The termination tax is imposed under Code Sec. 507(c) when private foundations fail to follow the prescribed procedures for terminating their tax-favored status as private foundations.

Rev. Rul. 2002-28 analyzed the following three common types of asset transfers by a private foundations:

- A private foundation, after satisfying all its outstanding liabilities, distributes all its remaining assets in equal shares to three other private foundations, with the original foundation dissolving the following day according to state law;
- The trustees of a charitable trust that is classified as a private foundation trust decide that the trust's charitable purpose can be more effectively accomplished by operating in corporate form. Therefore they create a not-for-profit corporation to carry on the trust's charitable activities, The not-for-profit corporation is classified as a private foundation under Code Sec. 509(a). The trust then transfers all its assets to the not-for-profit corporation; and
- In order to eliminate the costs of maintaining two separate private foundations, two previously separate foundations with similar objectives transfer all their assets to a single newly formed private foundation.

The IRS reviewed the three situations and concluded that a private foundation that transfers all its assets to one or more private foundations in a transfer described in Code Sec. 507(b)(2) (where the transferee foundation is not treated as a newly created organization), is not required to notify the IRS that it plans to terminate it private foundation status. Since the private foundation did not provide notice and did not terminate, it was not subject to the Section 507(c) termination tax. If any of the foundations had provided notice and terminated they would have been subject to the termination tax. However, if the foundation gives notice of termination after it has transferred all its assets to another organization, the termination tax will be zero.

Tax Return Filing Requirements

A private foundation that has disposed of all its assets and terminates its private foundation status must file a Form 990-PF, *Return of Private Foundation or Section 4947(a)(1) Nonexempt Charitable Trust Treated as a Private Foundation*, for the tax year of the disposition and must comply with any expenditure responsibility reporting obligations on the return. A private foundation that has disposed of all its assets and does not terminate its private foundation status must file a Form 990-PF for the tax year of the disposition and must comply with any expenditure responsibility reporting obligations on the return, but does not need to file returns in the following tax

[68] Rev. Rul. 2002-28, 2002-1 CB 941, as modified and amplified by Rev. Proc. 2008-52, 2008-36 IRB 587.

years if it has no assets and does not engage in any activities. If the private foundation receives additional assets or resumes activities in later years, it must resume filing Form 990-PF for those years.

¶23,120 TAX ON INVESTMENT INCOME

Private foundations must pay a 2 percent tax on their net investment income for the tax year [Code Sec. 4940; Reg. §53.4940-1]. Investment income includes interest, dividends, rents and royalties to the extent they are not taxed as unrelated business income [¶23,155]. A private foundation's net investment income for purposes of computing tax on the foundation under Code Sec. 4940 does not include any distributions from trusts and estates. Therefore, private foundations may exclude distributions from estates and trusts when determining net investment income under Code Sec. 4940(c).[69]

Private foundations that want to exclude distributions from trusts and estates from net investment income should write "Filed pursuant to Notice 2004-35" on the front page of Form 990-PF. Private foundations seeking refund of taxes paid in the past should file amended returns and likewise indicate that they are "Filed pursuant to Notice 2004-35." Net capital gains are also subject to the investment tax. Capital losses are taken into account only as an offset to gains. This tax is reported on Form 990. Foreign private foundations pay a 4 percent tax on gross investment income from U.S. sources. This tax also applies to nonexempt private foundations, to the extent that it, plus the unrelated business income tax that would have been imposed, exceeds the foundation's regular tax.

A private foundation is not subject to the 2 percent tax if it qualifies as an exempt operating foundation. An *exempt operating foundation* is one that:

- Is an operating foundation;
- Has been publicly supported for at least ten years;
- Has a governing body that consists of individuals at least 75 percent of whom are not disqualified individuals [¶23,130]and is broadly representative of the general public; and
- Has no foundation officer who is at any time during the tax year a disqualified individual [Code Sec. 4940(d)].

The tax may be reduced from 2 percent to 1 percent in certain circumstances. To qualify for the reduced rate, the foundation's current-year distributions must exceed a minimum. Under Code Sec. 4940(e)(2), the minimum equals the average fair market value of current-year noncharitable assets, multiplied by the average payout (as a percentage of asset value) for the past five tax years, plus 1 percent of current year net investment income [Code Sec. 4940(e)(2)].

Example 23-10: Foundation ABC has a 5 percent average distribution ratio for the past five years, $1 million of current-year net investment income, and $25 million average fair market value of current-year assets. It must distribute at

[69] Notice 2004-35, 2004-1 CB 889.

least $1.26 million (($25 million x .05) + ($1 million × 0.01)) to be eligible for the 1 percent rate.

¶23,125 PROHIBITED ACTS OF PRIVATE FOUNDATIONS

Heavy excise taxes are imposed on private foundations for certain prohibited acts (or failures to act). These taxes apply as well to the foundation manager and in certain cases to substantial contributors [¶ 23,130]. Government officials may be penalized for dealings with the foundation. There is also a tax on the termination of the exempt status of the foundation [¶ 23,115]. If a violation is willful and flagrant, or if the foundation, its manager, a disqualified person [¶ 23,130] or government official is liable for excise tax for a prior violation, a penalty equal to the tax is also imposed [Code Sec. 6684; Reg. § 301.6684-1]. Since the taxes are excises, they are not deductible as taxes [Ch. 9].

Briefly, the following are penalized acts:

- Self-dealing [¶ 23,130];
- Failure to distribute income [¶ 23,135];
- Excessive holdings in a business [¶ 23,140];
- Investments which jeopardize the charitable purpose [¶ 23,145]; and
- Improper expenditures (for example, propaganda to influence legislation) [¶ 23,150].

> **NOTE:** Governing instruments of private foundations must include provisions prohibiting income accumulations and the other prohibited acts [Code Sec. 508(e)(1); Reg. § 1.508-3]. Gifts and bequests to foundations not complying are not deductible [Code Sec. 508(d)(2)(A)]. Private foundations must also file information returns [Ch. 26].

.01 Abatement of First Tier Taxes

The IRS may abate the first tier private foundation excise taxes provided for in Code Secs. 4942 through 4945 (but not penalty tax on self-dealing, [Code Sec. 4941(a)]). The foundation must establish that the violation of the foundation rules was due to reasonable cause and not willful neglect, and was corrected within an appropriate correction period [Code Sec. 4962].

¶23,130 TAX ON SELF-DEALING

.01 General Rules

Code Sec. 4941(a)(1) imposes an excise tax on each act of self-dealing between a disqualified person and a private foundation [Reg. § 53.4941(a)-1]. The term "self-dealing" includes any direct or indirect sale or exchange, or leasing, of property between a private foundation and a disqualified person [Code Sec. 4941(d)(1)(A)]. Also included is the direct or indirect transfer to, or use by or for the benefit of a disqualified person of the income or assets of a private foundation [Code Sec.

4941(d)(1)(E)]. The term "disqualified person" with respect to a private foundation includes a person who is a substantial contributor to the foundation, a foundation manager, and a member of the family of a disqualified person [Code Sec. 4946(a)(1)].

Activities Considered to Be Self-dealing

The following activities constitute acts of self-dealing:

- The sale or exchange of property between a private foundation and a disqualified person [Code Sec. 4941(d)(1)(A)];
- The transfer of property by a disqualified person to a private foundation if the foundation assumes a mortgage or similar lien that was placed on the property prior to the transfer, or takes subject to a mortgage or similar lien that a disqualified person placed on the property within the 10-year period ending on the date of transfer [Code Sec. 4941(d)(2)(A); Reg. § 53.4941(d)-2(a)(2)];
- In general, the leasing of property between a disqualified person and a private foundation [Reg. § 53.4941(d)-2(b)];
- The lending of money or other credit between a private foundation and a disqualified person [Reg. § 53.4941(d)-2(c)];
- In general, the furnishing of goods, services, or facilities between a private foundation and a disqualified person. For example, if a foundation furnishes personal living quarters to a disqualified person (other than a foundation manager or employee) without charge, such furnishing will be an act of self-dealing [Reg. § 53.4941(d)-2(d)(1)];
- The payment of compensation (or payment or reimbursement of expenses) by a private foundation to a disqualified person [Code Sec. 4941(d)(1)(D)];
- The transfer to, or use by or for the benefit of, a disqualified person of the income or assets of a private foundation. For example, the indemnification (of a lender) or guarantee (of repayment) by a private foundation with respect to a loan to a disqualified person will be treated as a use for the benefit of a disqualified person of the income or assets of the foundation [Reg. § 53.4941(d)-2(f)(1)]; and
- The indemnification by a private foundation of a foundation manager for compensatory expenses will be an act of self-dealing unless such payment when added to other compensation paid to such manager results in a total compensation package that is reasonable. A compensatory expense includes any penalty tax that is owed by the foundation manager provided the expense was not incurred by the manager in connection with a civil proceeding arising out the manager's performance of services on behalf of the foundation or any expense resulting from the manager's act or failure to act [Reg. § 53.4941(d)-2(f)(4)].

Payments Not Considered as Self-dealing

Noncompensatory indemnification of foundation managers against liability for defense in civil proceedings and the purchase of a single insurance policy to provide coverage for managers are viewed as expenses for the foundation's administration and operation rather than compensation for the manager's services and do not constitute acts of self-dealing [Reg. § 53.4941(d)-2(f)(3) and (5)].

Estate Administrative Exception

Reg. § 53.4941(d)-1(b)(3) (sometimes referred to as the "estate administration exception") provides a limited exception to the self-dealing rules to permit the orderly administration of an estate or trust, allowing flexibility to shift assets to carry out the decedent's intent under the will or trust, providing all of the conditions in the regulation are met. The term "indirect self-dealing" does not include a transaction with respect to a private foundation's interest or expectancy in property held by an estate (or revocable trust, including a trust that has become irrevocable on the grantor's death), if:

1. The trustee of a revocable trust either possesses a power of sale with respect to the property, or has the power to reallocate the property to another beneficiary;
2. The transaction is approved by the probate court having jurisdiction over the trust;
3. The transaction occurs before a revocable trust is considered subject to Code Sec. 4947;
4. The trust receives an amount that equals or exceeds the fair market value of the private foundation's interest or expectancy in the property at the time of the transaction; and
5. The transaction results in the private foundation receiving an interest or expectancy at least as liquid as the one it gave up [Reg. § 53.4941(d)-1(b)(3)].

In Letter Ruling 201016084, the IRS ruled that a proposed allocation and distribution to a surviving spouse and a private foundation of the net proceeds from the sale of a residence pursuant to the settlement of the decedent spouse's estate did not constitute an indirect act of self-dealing between the surviving spouse and the foundation under Code Sec. 4941 because the transaction qualified for the estate administration exception in Reg. § 53.4941(d)-1(b)(3).

Disqualified Persons

A disqualified person is any of the following [Code Sec. 4946(a)]:

- A substantial contributor (see below);
- The foundation manager
- The owner of more than 20 percent of the total combined voting power of a corporation, the profits interest of a partnership, or the beneficial interest of a trust or unincorporated enterprise if that corporation, partnership, trust, or unincorporated enterprise is a substantial contributor to the foundation;
    a. A member of the family of any of the above (i.e., an individuals spouse, ancestors, children, grandchildren, great grandchildren, and the spouses of children, grandchildren, and great grandchildren);
    b. A trust or estate in which any of the foregoing persons owns more than 35 percent of the beneficial interest; or
    c. A government official (e.g., an individual who holds an elective office in the executive or legislative branch of the U.S. government, an appointed office in the executive or judicial branch of the U.S. government, a position listed in Schedule C of Rule VI of the Civil Service Rules or the compensation for which is equal to or greater than the lowest rate of basic pay for the Senior Executive

Service under 5 U.S.C. Sec. 5382, or an elective or appointive public office in the executive, legislative, or judicial branch of the government of a state or U.S. possession).

Substantial Contributor

A substantial contributor is any person (including a corporation) who alone or with his spouse has contributed or bequeathed a total of more than $5,000 to a private foundation, but only if such gifts and bequests exceed 2 percent of all gifts and bequests received from all donors.[70] If a person is a substantial contributor in any year, he remains one for later years [Code Secs. 4946(a)(2), 507(d)(2); Reg. § 1.507-6].

A person's status as a substantial contributor will be terminated if (1) neither the person nor a related person made a contribution to the foundation within the last ten years; (2) at no time during the ten-year period was that person or related person a manager of the foundation; and (3) the person's aggregate contributions are insignificant when compared to the contributions to that foundation by one other person [Code Sec. 507(d)(2)(C)].

Initial Taxes

A tax is imposed on the disqualified person at 10 percent of the amount involved in the self-dealing. The foundation manager who knowingly participated is subject to a 5 percent tax ($20,000 maximum), unless the foundation managers participation was not willful and was due to reasonable cause [Code Sec. 4941(a); Reg. § 53.4941(a)-1]. The tax is reported on Form 4720 by private foundations with Form 990 (or Form 1041-A by nonexempt trusts).

Additional Taxes

The disqualified person is liable for an additional tax of 200 percent of the amount involved if the self-dealing act is not corrected within 90 days after the deficiency notice is mailed. The foundation manager is liable for 50 percent of the amount for refusal to agree to a correction. Code Sec. 4941(b), (c)(2); Reg. §§ 53.4941(b)-1, (c)-1, (e)-1(d)].

¶23,135 TAX ON UNDISTRIBUTED INCOME

A private foundation is subject to tax if it does not make qualifying distributions in an amount at least equal to its minimum investment return (with certain adjustments). The minimum investment return is five percent of the excess of the aggregate fair market value of all assets of the foundation (other than those that are used or held for use directly in carrying out the foundations exempt purpose) over the acquisition indebtedness with respect to such assets. There is an initial tax of 30 percent on the undistributed income and an additional 100 percent tax if required distributions are not made within 90 days after the deficiency notice [Code Sec. 4942].

In general, the tax does not apply if the organization was created before May 27, 1969, and is required to accumulate income. Nor does it apply to a private operating

[70] *M. Graham*, 83 TCM 1137, Dec. 54,628(M), TC Memo. 2002-24.

foundation that is, one that spends at least 85 percent of its income directly for the active conduct of its charitable purposes and meets certain other qualifying tests [Code Sec. 4942(a)(1); Reg. § 53.4942(b)].

Also, an amount a private foundation sets aside for a specific charitable project is treated as distributed income if (1) such amount is to be paid out within five years and (2) the project is one that can be better accomplished by the set-aside than by an immediate payment of funds [Code Sec. 4942(g)(2)]. Set-asides commonly arise when a foundation awards a grant for a long-term project or awards a matching grant.

¶23,140 TAX ON EXCESS BUSINESS HOLDINGS

An excise tax is imposed on a private foundation if it has excess business holdings. The initial tax is 10 percent of the value [Code Sec. 4943(a)(1)]. It is imposed on the last day of the foundation's tax year but is determined on that day when excess holdings were the largest. An additional tax of 200 percent is imposed if the excess holdings are not disposed of within a specified period [Code Sec. 4943(b)].

Excess business holdings are, with respect to the holdings of any private foundation in any business enterprise, the amount of stock or other interest in the enterprise that the foundation would have to dispose of to a person other than a disqualified person in order for the remaining holdings of the foundation in that enterprise to be permitted holdings [Code Sec. 4943(c)(1)]. Permitted holdings in an incorporated business enterprise are 20 percent of the voting stock (reduced by the percentage of voting stock owned by all disqualified persons). Permitted holdings in a partnership are 20 percent of profits interests (reduced by the percentage of profit interests owned by disqualified persons) [Code Sec. 4943(c)(2)]. There may be no permitted holdings in a sole proprietorship. Excess business holdings (as defined) may consist of stock in a corporation or a partnership interest if not related to the foundation's charitable purpose. The foundation may not hold any interest in a sole proprietorship [Code Sec. 4943; Reg. § 53.4943-3].

¶23,145 TAX ON SPECULATIVE INVESTMENTS

.01 Excise Tax Imposed

If a private foundation invests in a manner that jeopardizes the carrying out of its charitable purpose, the private foundation and the foundation manager are penalized by an excise tax [Code Sec. 4944; Reg. § 53.4944-1-6]. The initial tax on the foundation is 10 percent of the investment, imposed each year until the earliest of (1) the mailing of a deficiency notice, (2) the assessment of the tax, or (3) the removal of the investment from jeopardy. The additional tax is 25 percent of the investment if not sold within 90 days after deficiency notice. The foundation manager who knowingly participated without use of reasonable care is subject to initial and additional taxes of 5 percent each ($10,000 maximum for initial tax and $20,000 for additional tax) [Code Secs. 4944(d)(2), 4961, 4963; Reg. §§ 53.4944-1, -2, -4, -5].

.02 Program-Related Investments

A "program-related investment" (PRI) will not be classified as an investment which jeopardizes the carrying out of the exempt purposes of a private foundation and therefore will not subject the private foundation to excise tax. A PRI is an investment whose primary purpose is to accomplish a charitable, religious, scientific, or other qualified purpose (even if the purposes are carried out by noncharitable organizations) with no significant purpose either to produce income or capital appreciation or to accomplish legislative or political activity [Reg. § 53.4944-3(a)(1)].

The IRS has released proposed regulations that provide new examples illustrating investments that qualify as PRIs under the private foundation rules. The charitable activities described in the new examples are based on published guidance and on financial structures described in private letter rulings. The new examples reflect current investment practices and they illustrate that:

- An activity conducted in a foreign country furthers a charitable purpose if the same activity would further a charitable purpose if conducted in the United States;
- The charitable purposes served by a PRI are not limited to situations involving economically disadvantaged individuals and deteriorated urban areas;
- The recipients of PRIs need not be within a charitable class if they are the instruments for furthering a charitable purpose;
- A potentially high rate of return does not automatically prevent an investment from qualifying as program-related;
- PRIs can be achieved through a variety of investments, including loans to individuals, tax-exempt organizations and for-profit organizations, and equity investments in for-profit organizations;
- A credit enhancement arrangement may qualify as a PRI; and
- A private foundation's acceptance of an equity position in conjunction with making a loan does not necessarily prevent the investment from qualifying as a PRI [Prop. Reg. § 53.4944-3(b)]

¶23,150 TAX ON IMPROPER EXPENDITURES

If a private foundation makes *taxable expenditures,* the private foundation and the foundation manager are penalized by an excise tax. The initial tax on the foundation is 20 percent of the expenditure [Code Sec. 4945(a)(1)]. An additional tax of 100 percent is imposed if the foundation does not recover the expenditures, to the extent possible, within 90 days after deficiency notice [Code Sec. 4945(b)]. The initial tax on the manager who knowingly participated is 5 percent (maximum $10,000) and the additional tax is 50 percent (maximum $20,000). No tax is imposed if the manager was not willful and used reasonable care [Code Secs. 4945, 4961, 4963].

Generally, taxable expenditures are outlays designed to:

- Influence legislation through lobbying or propaganda;
- Influence election outcomes or to carry on voter registration drives;
- Fund certain discriminatory study or travel grants to individuals;

- Make grants to an organization unless the organization is described in Code Sec. 509(a) or is an exempt operating foundation or the private foundation exercises expenditure responsibility with respect to the grant; and
- Fund any purpose that would not support a charitable deduction if the foundation were taxable [Code Sec. 4945(d); Reg. § 53.4945-2-6].

> ▶ **OBSERVATION:** Grants to exempt operating foundations from other foundations are not subject to the expenditure responsibility requirements [Code Sec. 4945(d)(4)].

¶23,151 NONEXEMPT TRUSTS TREATED AS PRIVATE FOUNDATIONS

Both charitable and split-interest trusts that are not exempt from tax may be subject to some of the same requirements and restrictions that are imposed on exempt private foundations [¶23,115 et seq.] and must file an annual return on Form 5227, *Split-Interest Trust Information Return* [Code Sec. 4947; Reg. § § 53.4947-1, 53.6011-1(d)].

A 30 percent excise tax is imposed on the undistributed income of a private foundation [Code Sec. 4942(a)]. Undistributed income is defined as the amount by which the distributable amount exceeds the qualifying distributions made before such time out of the distributable amount [Code Sec. 4942(c)]. Code Sec. 4942(d) defines *distributable amount* as the minimum investment return (plus certain refunds of amounts previously taken into account as qualifying distributions) reduced by the taxes imposed on the private foundation under Code Sec. 4940. Reg. § 53.4942(a)-2(b)(2) provides that the distributable amount of a private foundation shall be increased by the income portion of distributions from trusts described in Code Sec. 4947(a)(2).

In *Ann Jackson Family Foundation*,[71] the Court of Appeals for the Ninth Circuit held that Treas. Reg. § 53.4942(a)-2(b)(2) was invalid to the extent that it required including in the private foundation's distributable amount for the year the full amount of the income portion of distributions from split-interest trusts. In light of this decision, the IRS has issued guidance in Notice 2004-36[72] to private foundations on the treatment of distributions received from a Code Sec. 4947(a)(2) split-interest trust in computing a foundation's distributable amount under Code Sec. 4942. Pending further guidance, private foundations should compute the distributable amount under Code Sec. 4942(d) without regard to Reg. § 53.4942(a)-2(b)(2).

---

[71] *Ann Jackson Family Foundation*, CA-9, 94-1 USTC ¶50,068, 15 F3d 917.

[72] Notice 2004-36, 2004-1 CB 889.

UNRELATED BUSINESS INCOME

¶23,160 EXEMPT ORGANIZATIONS SUBJECT TO TAX ON UNRELATED BUSINESS INCOME

Code Sec. 511(a) imposes a tax on the unrelated business taxable income (UBTI) of tax-exempt organizations. UBTI is income that is unrelated to the exercise or performance by such organization of its charitable, educational, or other purpose or function constituting the basis for its tax exemption [Code Sec. 511(a)]. Otherwise tax-exempt organizations are taxed on income unrelated to the purposes that entitle them to exemption [¶23,110].

The income subject to tax is from unrelated businesses or is unrelated debt-financed income [¶23,175] [Code Secs. 511-515]. UBTI is the gross income derived by any tax-exempt organization from any unrelated trade or business it conducts [Code Sec. 512(a)(1)]. The unrelated business income tax (UBIT) is imposed on UBTI in an effort to force tax-exempt organizations to focus on the achievement of their tax-exempt purpose or function rather than on becoming profitable entities. Income generated by a tax-exempt organization from a trade or business that is substantially related to its tax-exempt purpose will escape taxation. To be *substantially related*, the activity "must contribute importantly to the accomplishment of [the organization's tax-exempt] purposes" [Reg. § 1.513-1(d)(2)].

For a discussion on the unrelated income tax rates, returns and payments, see ¶23,200. The unrelated business tax can be offset by the foreign tax credit [¶28,001] [Code Sec. 515]. A charitable deduction is allowed in figuring unrelated business taxable income [¶23,170].

> ▶ **OBSERVATION:** Church books may be examined only to the extent necessary to determine any UBI tax liability, and then only if the Regional Commissioner believes it has UBI and gives advance notice. However, this restriction does not interfere with the IRS's examination of an organization's religious activities for determining its exempt qualification [Reg. § 301.7605-1(c)].

¶23,165 UNRELATED BUSINESS DEFINED

In determining whether a trade or business run by a tax-exempt organization is unrelated, it is irrelevant whether or not the organization needs the income. If the business is not substantially related to the exercise or performance of the charitable, educational, or other purpose constituting the basis for exemption under Code Sec. 501, it is an unrelated trade or business [Code Sec. 513(a)].

A tax-exempt organization will be subject to UBIT if the following three conditions exist:

- The income of the exempt organization is from a trade or business;
- The trade or business is *regularly carried on* by the tax-exempt organization rather than being from a sporadic activity; and

- The trade or business is not substantially related to the performance by the charity of its tax-exempt function. The business is substantially related only if the activity (not the proceeds from it) contributes importantly to the accomplishment of the exempt purposes of the organization [Reg. § 1.513-1].[73]

In *Ocean Pines Association, Inc.*,[74] the Court of Appeals for the Fourth Circuit affirmed the Tax Court to conclude that the income of a tax-exempt homeowners association from member fees for use of parking lots and a beach club was UBTI. According to the court, operating the parking lots and beach club did not promote "social welfare" because the facilities were not available to the general public and the fees income benefited the private interests of the association's members. Since operating the parking lots and beach club did not promote social welfare, it did not contribute to or advance the association's tax exempt purpose. Therefore, the income was not substantially related to the association's exempt purpose which was to promote the common good and welfare of the general public.

.01 Special Rule for Trusts

For an exempt employees' trust or an exempt supplemental unemployment benefit trust, the term *unrelated trade or business* means any business regularly carried on by the trust or by a partnership of which it is a member [Code Sec. 513(b); Reg. § 1.513-1]. The income from the business is taxable [Code Sec. 512; Reg. § 1.512(a)-1].

.02 Excluded from Definition of Unrelated Trade or Business

Code Sec. 513(a) states that the term "unrelated trade or business" does not include any trade or business:

1. In which substantially all the work in carrying on the trade or business is performed for the organization without compensation;
2. That is carried on by a tax-exempt organization or by a governmental college or university primarily for the convenience of its members, students, patients, officers or employees; or
3. That consists of selling merchandise, substantially all of which has been received by the organization as gifts or contributions.

In addition, unrelated trade or business does *not* include:

- Qualified public entertainment activities (e.g., fairs and expositions) conducted by exempt charitable, social welfare or agricultural organizations;
- *Qualified convention or trade show activity* regularly conducted by exempt unions or trade associations [Code Sec. 513(d); Reg. § 1.513-3]; and
- Specified services provided by one hospital to others if the services could have been provided tax free by a cooperative organization of exempt hospitals and the services meet certain other tests [Code Sec. 513(e)].

---

[73] *American Bar Endowment*, 86-1 USTC ¶ 9482, 477 US 105 (1986).

[74] *Ocean Pines Ass'n, Inc.*, CA-4, 2012-1 USTC ¶ 50,225, 672 F3d 284; *Flat Top Lake Ass'n*, CA-4, 89-1 USTC ¶ 9180.

.03 Convention and Trade Show Exception

A *convention and trade show activity* is any activity of a kind traditionally conducted at conventions, annual meetings, or trade shows. A convention and trade show activity includes, but is not limited to, any activity one of the purposes of which is to attract persons in an industry generally (without regard to membership in the sponsoring organization) as well as members of the public to the show for the purpose of: (1) displaying industry products, (2) stimulating interest in, and demand for, industry products or services, or (3) educating persons engaged in the industry in the development of new products and services or new rules and regulations affecting the industry [Code Sec. 513(d)(3)(A)].

To qualify for the trade show exclusion, the activity must meet all of the following conditions:

- It must be conducted in conjunction with an international, national, state, regional, or local convention, annual meeting, or show conducted by a qualifying organization;
- One of the purposes must be the promotion and stimulation of interest in, and demand for, the products and services of that industry in general, or which educate persons in attendance regarding new developments or products and services related to the exempt activities of the organization; and
- The show must be designed to achieve such purpose through the character of the exhibits and the extent of the industry products displayed [Code Sec. 513(d)(3)(B); Reg. § 1.513-3(c)(2)].

In Rev. Rul. 2004-112,[75] the IRS concluded that internet activities conducted by a trade association on a supplementary trade show website operated in conjunction with a trade show were not subject to UBIT. This ruling extends the current-law exception from UBIT for qualified convention and trade show activity to internet activities that are connected with a convention, annual meeting or trade show. However, activities on an internet website that were made available to the public around-the-clock, solely for a two-week period that did not overlap or coincide with any convention, meeting or trade show conducted by the association did not qualify for the trade show UBIT exception.

.04 When Is a Sale Related to the Tax-Exempt Function?

If the primary purpose behind a sale is to further the organization's exempt purpose, the sale is related and income earned from that sale will be exempt, even though the item has a utilitarian function or value. Where the purpose of the sale is solely to generate income, the income generated will be taxable. In determining the primary purpose underlying the sale, the IRS will consider the degree of connection between the item and the charity's function. The overall impression conveyed by the article is also considered. If the dominant impression one gains from viewing or using the article correlates to its original article, picture or likeness, the article sold is substantially related to the original for tax purposes. If, however, the noncharitable use or function predominates, the sale would be unrelated and the income generated from the sale would be subject to UBIT.

[75] Rev. Rul. 2004-112, 2004-2 CB 985.

Example 23-11: *Occasional food stand.* If an exempt organization operates a sandwich stand during the week of an annual county fair, it is not regularly carrying on a business and the income generated will not constitute UBIT. But if the tax-exempt operates a public parking lot one day each week, the income will be UBIT.

Example 23-12: *Experimental agricultural production facility.* Milk and cream production from an experimental dairy herd maintained by a research organization is a related business. But manufacture of ice cream and pastries is not a related business.

Example 23-13: *Training school.* A school trains children in singing and dancing for professional careers. Performances before audiences by the students contribute importantly to the school's tax-exempt purpose of training. Thus, the income from admissions to the performances is exempt.

Example 23-14: *Job center for disabled.* In Letter Ruling 9438013, the IRS ruled that income from a job center operated for the handicapped was not UBTI. An exempt organization provided residential placement for mentally and physically handicapped adults. The organization also operated a working ranch where handicapped residents provided all of the manual labor for various aspects of the ranch. The ranch provided training and education and permitted the handicapped person to assume responsibilities. The IRS ruled that the income from the food, lodging, rental and other activities will not generate UBIT because the project furthered charitable purposes and was related to the organization's exempt purpose.

Example 23-15: *Museum shops.* In Letter Ruling 9550003, the IRS ruled that income received by a tax-exempt museum from the sale of the following items was not UBTI because the products contributed to the museum's tax-exempt educational mission: books, tapes, records, films, compact disks, toys on period topics, collectibles, reproductions and adaptations of prototypes in the museum's art collections, food representative of the products carried in the time period represented in the museum and Christmas cards, ornaments and decorations that were reproductions of originals found in the museum's collection. In addition, products such as film, batteries, flashbulbs, ponchos, and umbrellas, which were sold for the convenience of visitors, enabled them to devote a greater portion of their time to viewing the museum and were thus substantially related to the museum's exempt purposes. On the other hand, products such as prepackaged foods, toiletries, tobacco products, newspapers, magazines, candy, pain relievers, golf clothing and accessories, metal polish, neckties, caps, souvenirs, mementos, shirts and books, and services such as engraving and gift wrapping, which did not relate to the museum's collections and did not contribute importantly to the accomplishment of the exempt purposes, were subject to UBIT. In addition, sales of furniture, dinnerware, silverware, pewter, stemware, rugs, and lamps that were not reproductions or adaptations were subject to UBIT because their primary purpose was to generate income, rather than to encourage personal learning experiences about the museum's collection. The IRS also concluded that the museum's extensive off-site sales activities were subject to UBIT, because the primary purpose behind these activities was a commercial one.

Example 23-16: *Insurance coverage.* In Letter Ruling 9535004, the IRS ruled that a national amateur softball organization's income from providing team liability and accident insurance coverage to its members through an unrelated, for-profit agent-broker was subject to UBIT because the activity was not substantially related to the tax-exempt purpose. Similarly, in a technical advice memorandum,[76] the IRS concluded that sales of life insurance policies by a fraternal society to member's widows were not substantially related to its exempt purpose. A federal district court concluded that a credit union's sale of credit life and disability insurance was related to its tax-exempt purposes and, therefore, did not generate UBTI.[77]

Example 23-17: *Tax-exempts income from magazine.* In *Arkansas State Police Ass'n,*[78] a tax-exempt organization that maintained tight control over a magazine that bore its name could not avoid UBIT from advertising revenues simply by funneling the magazine's operations through a publishing contract.

Example 23-18: *Travel and tours activities of tax-exempt organizations.* Travel tour programs are often offered by tax-exempt organizations, such as colleges, universities, museums, and historical societies. To determine whether the income generated by the tours is taxed as UBTI, examine the nature, scope, and motivation for the tour to determine whether there is a connection between a particular tour and the organization's exempt purpose [Reg. § 1.513-1(d)(2)]. Where the primary purpose for the tour is to further the organization's charitable, religious or educational purpose, the income earned will not be UBTI. It is only where the primary purpose for the tour is unrelated to the organization's tax-exempt purpose, that the income received will be taxed as UBTI [Reg. § 1.513-7(a)].

Example 23-19: *Receipt of real estate commissions.* In Letter Ruling 201015037, the IRS ruled that the receipt of commissions by a tax-exempt organization that directs, coordinates, and integrates health care services in connection with a real estate leasing activity was not considered UBTI because that activity was not regularly carried on by the health care services provider.

---

76 TAM 201320023 (Feb. 20, 2013).

77 *Bellco Credit Union,* DC-CO, 2010-1 USTC ¶ 50,343.

78 *Ark. St. Police Ass'n,* CA-8, 2002-1 USTC ¶ 50,269, 282 F3d 556.

▶ **PRACTICE POINTERS:** Travel and tour activities sponsored by tax-exempt organizations will be tax-free if the following guidelines are followed [Reg. § 1.513-7(a)]:

- The tours should include scheduled instruction or curriculum related to the destinations being visited.
- The travel tours should relate and contribute importantly to the accomplishment of the organization's tax-exempt purpose, rather than be designed to simply generate revenues for the tax-exempt organization.
- In order to prove that tours offered by an educational institution are substantially related to the institution's educational purpose, the tours should include a substantial amount of required study, lectures, report preparation, examination and should qualify for academic credit.
- Educational materials should be prepared by the tax-exempt organization or be provided to tour participants in connection with the tours. The materials should describe the educational opportunities on the tours and should emphasize the opportunity for members to learn more about the organization's tax-exempt purpose.
- The tours should offer scheduled instruction, organized study or group discussion in areas related to the organization's tax-exempt purpose.
- Members of the tax-exempt organization's administrative staff should accompany each tour group. In addition, the staff members should have special expertise in the area and play an educational role in the tours.
- Socializing and fostering goodwill among members should not be the primary goal of the travel tour. Rather the tour should contribute importantly to the organization's educational purposes. The tour program should not be primarily social and recreational in nature. The scheduled activities should be part of a coordinated educational program.

Trade or Business Activities

A trade or business includes any activity carried on to produce income. It makes no difference if it is not profitable; the business could still be unrelated. An activity remains a business even when carried on within a larger aggregate of similar activities that may or may not be related to the exempt purpose [Code Sec. 513(c)]. Advertising income from publications of exempt organizations in excess of expenses or any loss is unrelated (therefore, taxable), whether or not the publications are related to the exempt purpose [Reg. § 1.512(a)-1(f)]. In *National Education Association of the United States,*[79] the Tax Court found that a tax-exempt labor organization must allocate a portion of its membership dues to circulation revenue from its two magazines because their members had a legal right to receive the magazines. Therefore a portion of the membership dues had to be allocated to circulation income. The allocation generated a profit in circulation income, requiring the payment of UBIT on advertising revenue.

---

[79] *National Education Ass'n of the U.S.,* 137 TC 100, Dec. 58,769 (2011).

Income Exempt from Tax

Income from a trade or business is not subject to tax if [Code Sec. 513(a); Reg. § 1.513-1(e)]:

- Substantially all the work (generally, 85 percent or more) is performed for the organization without pay. For example, an orphanage runs a secondhand clothing store, all the work being performed by volunteers.
- As to religious, charitable or educational organizations, and state universities, it is carried on primarily for the convenience of its members, students, patients, officers, or employees. For example, a college operates a laundry for laundering dormitory linen and students' clothing.
- The business is the selling of merchandise, substantially all of which is received as gifts or contributions. For example, activities commonly known as thrift shops.

The following events will not result in unrelated taxable business income tax:

- The exchanging or renting of donor mailing lists by an exempt organization with or to other exempt organizations will constitute royalty income and will therefore be excluded from UBTI by Code Sec. 512(b)(2)];[80]
- Exempt organizations receiving income from certain unsolicited distributions of low-cost articles incidental to soliciting charitable contributions [Code Sec. 513(h)(1)(A)]. In 2013, *low-cost* means articles costing $10.20 or less;
- Qualified trade shows or conventions at which suppliers to the sponsoring organization's members sell products or services, and convention activities of charitable organizations and social welfare organizations; and
- Receiving qualified sponsorship payments [Code Sec. 513(i)].

Qualified Sponsorship Payment

Qualified sponsorship payments are those made by a person engaged in a trade or business to a tax-exempt organization where there is no arrangement or expectation of a substantial return benefitother than the use or acknowledgment of the payor's name, logo, or product lines [Code Sec. 513(i)(2)(A)]. For this purpose, use or acknowledgment does not include advertising. The use of promotional logos or slogans that are an established part of the sponsor's identity does not, by itself, constitute advertising.

***Substantial return benefit* defined.** A *substantial return benefit* is any benefit other than: (1) a use or acknowledgment of the payor's name or logo in connection with the exempt organization's activities, or (2) certain goods or services that have an insubstantial value. If a sponsor receives a substantial benefit return in exchange for its payment, its qualified sponsor payment is UBTI and subject to federal tax. Generally, benefits such as complimentary tickets, pro-am playing spots, and receptions for donors have an insubstantial value only if they have a fair market value of not more than 2 percent of the payment [Reg. § 1.513-4(c)(2)].

Exclusive sponsorships. The right to be the only sponsor of an activity, or the only sponsor from a particular trade, business, or industry generally is not a substantial

[80] *Common Cause,* 112 TC 332, Dec. 53,428 (1999); *Planned Parenthood Federation of America, Inc.,* 77 TCM 2227, Dec. 53,429(M), TC Memo. 1999-206.

return benefit. Thus, payments for exclusive sponsorship arrangements may be a qualified sponsorship payment. However, if in return for a payment, the organization agrees that products or services will not be sold or provided in connection with an organization's activities, the payor has received a substantial return benefit and the portion of the payment attributable to the exclusive provider arrangement is not a qualified sponsorship payment [Reg. § 1.513-4(c)(2)(v)].

> **Example 23-20:** ABCo, who makes ice cream, contributes $5,000 to a homeless shelter. In return for the contribution, the tax-exempt organization agrees to carry ABCo corporate logo on its monthly newsletter that it mails to contributors. The $5,000 contribution would not be subject to the UBIT because ABCo will not obtain any substantial return benefit for its contribution.

A *qualified sponsorship payment* does *not* include the following:

- Any payment if the amount of the payment is contingent upon: (a) the level of attendance at one or more events; (b) broadcast ratings; or (c) other facts indicating the degree of public exposure to one or more events [Code Sec. 513(i)(2)(B)(i)];
- Any payment that entitles the payor to an acknowledgment or advertising in regularly scheduled and printed material published by or on behalf of the tax-exempt organization. However, if the publication is related to, and primarily distributed in connection with, a specific event conducted by the tax-exempt organization, the payment may be a qualified sponsorship payment [Code Sec. 513(i)(2)(B)(ii)]; and

> **Example 23-21:** ABCo manufacturers sailboats and contributes $10,000 to Save the Bay, a tax-exempt organization. In return for the $10,000, an ad for ABCo's products will run in Save the Bay's monthly magazine. In this situation, the entire $10,000 will be subject to UBIT. If you change the facts slightly, the result is different. If, instead of the ad, ABCo would only be acknowledged in a publication distributed by the organization at its annual Save the Bay Day celebration in Annapolis, Maryland, the $10,000 would be considered a qualified sponsorship payment and would not be subject to UBIT.

- Any payment made in connection with a qualified convention or trade show activity. This generally refers to conventions or trade shows conducted by certain tax-exempt organizations that have as one of their purposes the promotion of interest in the products and services of the industry in general or the purpose to educate the attendees regarding new developments or products and services related to the exempt activities of the organization [Code Sec. 513(i)(2)((B)(ii)(II)].

Loss of tax-exempt status. An exempt organization can have its tax-exempt status revoked if it conducts an excessive amount of unrelated business. The IRS has stated that if unrelated income is less than 5 percent of gross income, the exempt organization is probably safe from having its exempt status revoked. If more than 5 percent of an exempt organization's gross income comes from unrelated sources, its exempt status still may be safe. This percentage isn't the only factor that determines if exempt status is in jeopardy. Other factors include the amount of time an exempt organization spends on its unrelated business and how much of its income is used for exempt programs.

¶23,170 INCOME FROM UNRELATED BUSINESS

Gross income from an unrelated business includes both the gross income of an unrelated business regularly carried on by the exempt organization and a percentage of unrelated debt-financed income [¶ 23,175] [Code Secs. 512(a)(1), 514(a)(1)].

.01 Foreign Corporations

UBI of a foreign organization includes income from U.S. sources that is not effectively connected with a U.S. business as well as all UBI that is effectively connected [Ch. 28] [Code Sec. 512(a)(2); Reg. § 1.512(a)-1(g)].

If the unrelated business is conducted with the exempt organization as a partner, the organization must include in its income its distributive share of the gross income of the partnership, less directly connected deductions. It must make the necessary adjustments for the exclusions and deductions below [Code Sec. 512(c)].

.02 Exclusions from Gross Income

The following types of income received by tax-exempt organizations will be tax-free and thus will not constitute UBTI [Code Sec. 512(b); Reg. § 1.512(b)-1]:

- Dividends, interest, and annuities [Code Sec. 512(b)(i)];
- Royalties [Code Sec. 512(b)(2)]. Royalty income includes income generated by the tax-exempt organization's participation in an affinity credit card program. This type of royalty income will be tax-free as long as the contracts with the tax-exempt organizations don' t require them to provide more than minimally necessary or a *de minimis* amount of services;[81]

  ▶ **PRACTICE POINTER:** Tax-exempt organizations wishing to enter into affinity credit card and similar arrangements in an effort to generate tax-free income should be sure that their contracts with the credit card or other types of companies do not require them to provide more than a *de minimis* amount of services. In addition, the tax-exempt organization should avoid providing promotional services and mailing list management outside of the contract requirements.[82] After a string of losses, the IRS has decided not to pursue cases challenging tax-exempt organizations' affinity credit card arrangements and rentals of mailing lists unless the tax-exempt organization provided more than a *de minimis* amount of services.[83]

- Rents from real or personal property are generally excluded [Code Sec. 512(b)(3)(A)]. However, rents from personal property leased with real property are taxed if they exceed 10 percent of the total rents from all property leased. In addition, all rentsfrom real as well as personal propertyare taxed if: (1) over 50 percent of the total rents determined when the lessee first places personal property

[81] *Oregon St. Univ. Alumni Ass'n.*, CA-9, 99-2 USTC ¶ 50,879, 193 F3d 1098.

[82] *Sierra Club, Inc.*, CA-9, 96-2 USTC ¶ 50,326, 86 F3d 1526, *on remand*, 77 TCM 1569, Dec. 53,299(M), TC Memo. 1999-86.

[83] IRS Memorandum Doc. 20006813 (March 7, 2000).

in service are attributable to personal property: or (2) the total rents are contingent on profits. Also, rents from debt-financed property are taxable [¶ 23,175];

- Capital gains and losses, except for the cutting of timber treated as a sale;
- Income taxed as debt-financed income (including otherwise excluded rents, dividends, interest, capital gains, annuities and royalties) [¶ 23,175];
- Income derived from research for state and local governments or the U.S., its agencies or instrumentalities;
- Income from research by a college, university, or hospital and by an organization operating primarily for fundamental research, the results of which are freely available to the general public;
- Income from limited partnership interest of certain testamentary charitable trusts;
- Dues of agricultural or horticultural organizations not to exceed $155 in 2013; and
- Income earned by tax-exempt organizations from bingo games is not taxed [Code Sec. 513(f)]. *Bingo game* means any game of bingo where, in the presence of all persons placing wagers in the game, the following events occur:
  a. Wagers are placed
  b. The winners are determined
  c. The distribution of prizes or other property is made [Code Sec. 513(f)(2)].

A nonprofit organization's instant bingo games will fail to qualify for the bingo game exception if the players do not place markers over randomly called numbers in an attempt to form a preselected pattern.[84] The players can not purchase a prepackaged card from a series of similarly situated cards. The bingo must involve the random selection of numbers by a caller and must require the players to participate in the game by covering the squares on his card that correspond to randomly drawn numbers. The winners may not be predetermined outside the presence of other players.

> ▶ **PRACTICE TIP:** If you want the income generated by your tax-exempt organization's bingo game to be tax-free, be sure that all the requirements of the Code Sec. 513(f) are met. The critical requirement is that players place markers over randomly called numbers in an attempt to form a preselected pattern. In addition, the winners must be determined in the presence of everyone playing the game.

.03 Deductions from Gross Income

To arrive at UBTI, the exempt organization may deduct from gross income the deductions directly connected with the carrying on of the trade or business, subject to the following exceptions or limitations [Reg. § 1.512(b)-1]:

- Any deductions directly connected with items excluded from income are not deducted. See the previous discussion for items of excluded income.
- The deduction for charitable contributions is allowed (whether or not directly connected with the carrying on of the business), but cannot exceed 10 percent of

[84] *Julius M. Israel Lodge of B'Nai B'rith No. 2113*, CA-5, 96-2 USTC ¶ 50,562, 98 F3d 190.

the unrelated business taxable income of an organization taxed as a corporation figured without the charitable contribution deduction. For an exempt trust's charitable deduction, see ¶ 23,190.

- The net operating loss deduction is allowed, except that any income or deduction excluded in figuring the UBI is not taken into account in determining the net operating loss or deduction for any tax year, or the amount of the net operating loss carryback or carryover.

Specific Deduction

The organization also gets a specific deduction of $1,000. For a diocese, religious order, or association of churches, each parish, individual church, or other local unit can claim a specific deduction of the lower of $1,000 or gross income from the unrelated business carried on by the local unit [Code Sec. 512(b)(12); Reg. § 1.512(b)-1(h)].

> ▶ **OBSERVATION:** A trust taxed on unrelated business taxable income receives no deduction for personal exemption [Ch. 15], but the $1,000 specific deduction is allowed.

.04 Special Rules

Special rules apply to social clubs, voluntary employee benefit associations, veterans' organizations, and controlled organizations.

Social Clubs

Social clubs generally exclude only exempt function income. Thus, clubs must pay tax on investment income but do not pay tax on dues, fees, and similar charges paid by members for club services and facilities rendered to them, their dependents or guests. In addition, they do not pay tax on investment income set aside for religious, charitable, or educational purposes. However, income from a club's unrelated business cannot be set aside and exempted from tax. If property used by the social club continuously and directly for exempt purposes (for example, a golfing area or fraternity house) is sold and replaced with other exempt-use property within one year before and three years after the sale, taxable gain is recognized only to the extent the amount realized exceeds the cost of replacement. In addition to these special exclusion rules, a social club can deduct directly connected expenses, charitable contributions within 10 percent of taxable income limitation, the net operating loss and the $1,000 specific deduction [Code Sec. 512(a)(3)].

The corporate dividends-received deduction is not considered directly connected with the production of gross income for social clubs and is not allowed as a deduction by nonexempt membership organizations. The exception also applies to membership organizations engaged primarily in gathering and distributing news to members for publication.

> ▶ **OBSERVATION:** A special rule applies to social clubs and other membership organizations to prevent them from giving up their exempt status and escaping the tax on business and investment income by using this income to serve the members at less than cost and then deducting the book loss. Nonexempt membership organizations can deduct the expenses incurred in supplying services, facilities and goods to their members only to the extent of income received

from members (including income from institutes and trade shows for the education of members) [Code Sec. 277].

Social club allowed to deduct costs of publishing magazine. The Tax Court held that a tax-exempt social club could deduct all of the costs it incurred in publishing a magazine in computing its UBTI.[85] The tax-exempt social club published a magazine, which carried paid advertisements and was distributed free of charge to both members and nonmembers of the club. For two years the club received no revenue from the magazine other than about $80,000 in advertising revenues. The club incurred $75,000 in expenses with respect to the magazine. The club deducted the expenses from the revenues to arrive at a total of $5,000 in UBTI for the two years.

The law provides that a tax will be imposed on the UBTI of tax-exempt organizations, which is generally defined as the income (not including dues and other similar fees paid by members, and certain amounts set aside for charitable purposes) derived from any unrelated trade or business that differs from the exercise or performance of the organization's exempt purpose. The organization can reduce UBTI by deducting expenses that are directly connected with the unrelated trade or business. In the case of a periodical published by an exempt organization, *UBTI* means gross income less deductions directly connected to the production of the gross income, which include both:

1. Costs directly connected with the sale and publication of advertising, and
2. Readership costs, which are costs directly connected with the production and distribution of the readership content of the periodical.

The court concluded that all expenses incurred by the ski club in producing its magazine could be deducted. The court found nothing in the legislative history to support different treatment for the deductibility of expenses incurred by social clubs and other tax-exempt organizations.

Voluntary Employee Benefit Associations (VEBAs)

Voluntary employee benefit associations are treated under the same special rules as exempt social clubs [Code Sec. 512(a)(3)]. In addition, associations can also exclude investment income set aside to provide for the payment of life, sickness, accident or other benefits [Code Sec. 512(a)(3)(B)(ii)].

> **NOTE:** Benefits provided by VEBAs to employees cannot discriminate in favor of the highly compensated. Every new VEBA must give the IRS timely notice of its application for tax-exempt status [Code Sec. 505(c)]. Exempt VEBAs already in existence must also give notice, within an IRS-established time period.

Veterans' Organizations

Veterans' organizations pay no tax on income from insurance to the extent that the income is used or set aside for insurance or charitable purposes [Code Sec. 512(a)(4); Reg. § 1.512(a)-4].

---

[85] *Chicago Metropolitan Ski Council*, 104 TC 341, Dec. 50,532 (1995).

Controlled Organizations

Among the items included in UBTI are "specified payments" that the organization receives or accrues from a controlled entity, to the extent they either reduce the controlled entity's net unrelated income or increase its net unrelated loss. Specified payments are interest, annuities, royalties, or rents, but not dividends [Code Sec. 512(b)(13)(A) and (C)]. For a controlled entity that is also tax-exempt, net unrelated income is the entity's UBTI. For a controlled entity that is taxable, net unrelated income is the portion of the entity's taxable income that would be UBTI if the entity were a tax-exempt organization with the same exempt purposes as the controlling organization. Net unrelated loss is determined under similar rules [Code Sec. 513(b)(13)(B)].

¶23,175 UNRELATED DEBT-FINANCED INCOME

A percentage of the unrelated debt-financed income of an exempt organization is taxed as unrelated business taxable income.

.01 General Rule

The income of a tax-exempt organization from debt-financed property unrelated to the exempt function is included in the computation of UBI in the same proportion that average acquisition indebtedness bears to the property's adjusted basis. Unrelated debt-financed gross income does not include income already subject to tax as UBI, but capital gains on the sale of debt-financed property are included. The same percentage of gross income is used to determine the allowable deductions. Only the percentage of deductions directly connected with the debt-financed property is allowed [Code Sec. 514(a), (b); Reg. § 1.514(a)-1, (b)-1].

> **Example 23-22:** Business or investment property is acquired by a tax-exempt organization subject to an 80 percent mortgage. Thus, 80 percent of the income and 80 percent of the deductions are taken into account. As the mortgage is paid off, the percentage taken into account diminishes.

Some exempt organizations, such as pension trusts, pension funds maintained by churches, and educational institutions [Code Sec. 514(c)(9)(C)], do not recognize UBI on income from debt-financed real property, if they satisfy six requirements [Code Sec. 514(c)(9)(B)]:

- The purchase price of the real property is a fixed amount determined as of the date of acquisition; this rule is relaxed for certain foreclosed property acquired from banks;
- The amount of the indebtedness, or the time to pay the indebtedness, is not in any way dependent on revenues, income or profits derived from the property; this requirement has also been liberalized for foreclosed property;
- The real property is not leased back to the seller (or someone related to the seller); but it can be if no more than 25 percent of the space is leased back, and the lease is on commercially reasonable terms;

- For pension trusts, the seller or lessee may not be a *disqualified person* [Code Sec. 4975(e)(2) unless no more than 25 percent of the leasable floor space is leased back to the disqualified person, and the lease is on commercially reasonable terms;
- The seller does not provide financing, unless it is on commercially reasonable terms; and
- If the real property is held by a partnership, each partner is a qualified organization, and the partnership allocations meet certain requirements [Code Sec. 514(c)(9)(B)(vi)].

.02 Debt-Financed Property

Debt-financed property is any property (for example, rental real estate, tangible personal property and corporate stock) held to produce income and that has an acquisition indebtedness [described below] at any time during the tax year (or during the 12 months preceding its disposal) [Code Sec. 514(b)(1)].[86]

Property is not included:

- If at least 85 percent of all its use is substantially related to the organization's tax-exempt purpose (if less than 85 percent of its use, to the extent of its related use) [Code Sec. 514(b)(1)(A)];
- To the extent its income is already subject to tax as income from business [¶ 23,155–¶ 23,170];
- To the extent its income is derived from research activities; and
- To the extent its use is exempt from the unrelated business tax on income from an unrelated business [¶ 23,165].

Special rules apply to related exempt organizations and to medical clinics [Code Sec. 514(b); Reg. § 1.514(b)-1].

Land Acquired for Exempt Use Within 10 Years

Subject to certain conditions, the tax does not apply to income from newly acquired land in the neighborhood of other exempt-purpose property owned by the organization if it plans to use the property within ten years of acquisition and doesn't abandon its plans. The period is 15 years for a church, and the land need not be in its neighborhood [Code Sec. 514(b)(3)(E); Reg. § 1.514(b)-1(d)].

.03 Acquisition Indebtedness

An acquisition indebtedness is the unpaid amount of any indebtedness that is:

1. Incurred in acquiring or improving the property,
2. Incurred before the acquisition or improvement, provided the indebtedness would not have been incurred but for the acquisition or improvement, or
3. Incurred after the acquisition or improvement, provided the indebtedness would not have been incurred but for the acquisition or improvement, and the incurring of

[86] *H.E. Bartels Trust*, FedCl, 2009-2 USTC ¶ 50,475.

indebtedness was reasonably foreseeable at the time of acquisition or improvement [Code Sec. 514(c)(1)].

Property Acquired Subject to a Mortgage

If the property is acquired subject to a mortgage, the amount of the mortgage is considered an acquisition indebtedness incurred in acquiring the property even though the organization did not assume or agree to pay such indebtedness. However, if mortgaged property is received by devise or bequest, the mortgage is not treated as an acquisition indebtedness for a period of 10 years from the date of acquisition. The 10-year rule is also applied to gifts if the mortgage was placed on the property more than five years before the date of the gift and the property was held by the donor for more than five years before the gift. The 10-year rule does not apply if the organization, in order to acquire the property, assumes and agrees to pay the indebtedness or makes any payment for the owner's equity in the property [Code Sec. 514(c)(2)(B)].

The extension, renewal or refinancing of an existing debt is not treated as a new debt [Code Sec. 514(c)(3)]. Nor is an FHA-insured obligation to finance low- and middle-income housing acquisition indebtedness [Code Sec. 514(c)(6)(A)(i)]. A state or local tax lien or special assessment is not a debt until the underlying tax or assessment becomes due and payable and the organization has had an opportunity to pay it [Code Sec. 514(c)(2)(C); Reg. § 1.514(c)-1].

Indebtedness incurred in performing exempt purpose

For purposes of this section, the term "acquisition indebtedness" does not include indebtedness the incurrence of which is inherent in the performance or exercise of the purpose or function constituting the basis of the organization's exemption, such as the indebtedness incurred by a credit union in accepting deposits from its members [Code Sec. 514(c)(4)].

Special rules apply to determine the basis of debt-financed property acquired in a corporate liquidation [Code Sec. 514(d); Reg. § 1.514(d)-1].

¶23,180 UNRELATED BUSINESS TAXABLE INCOME (UBTI) TAX RATES, RETURNS, AND PAYMENTS

Tax-exempt organizations are subject to tax on unrelated business taxable income which is defined as any gross income derived by a tax-exempt organization from any unrelated trade or business less the deductions connected with carrying on such trade or business [Code Sec. 512(a)(1)]. The tax is assessed on all exempt entities except federal agencies. Code Sec. 512(b)(12) provides that a $1,000 deduction is allowed in computing unrelated business taxable income. Capital gains and losses are not included in figuring unrelated business taxable income.

.01 Filing Returns and Payments

When unrelated business gross income exceeds $1,000 for the year, the exempt entity must file Form 990-T, *Exempt Organization Business Income Tax Return (and Proxy Tax Under Section 6033(e))* [Code Sec. 6033; Reg. § § 1.6012-2(e), 1.6033-2].

Certain exempt organizations must make quarterly estimated tax payments for the UBTI tax, in the same manner as regular corporate estimated income taxes [Ch. 26] [Code Sec. 6655(g)(3)].

.02 Public Inspection Rules

Code Sec. 6104(d)(1)(A)(ii) requires organizations to make available for public inspection and copying "any annual return which is filed under Code Sec. 6011 by an organization described in Code Sec. 501(c)(3) *and* which relates to any tax imposed by Code Sec. 511 (relating to imposition of tax on unrelated business income of charitable, etc., organizations)." (Emphasis added.) Code Sec. 6104(d)(1)(A)(ii) requires charities to make available for public inspection and copying only those returns and attachments to the return that are both filed under Code Sec. 6011 and that relate to the imposition of tax on unrelated business income of charitable organizations.[87]

In addition, charities must make Forms 990-T available for public inspection and copying only for the three-year period beginning on the last day prescribed for filing such return (determined with regard to any extension of time for filing).

PENALTIES IMPOSED ON EXEMPT ORGANIZATIONS

¶23,185 EXCESS BENEFIT TRANSACTIONS

.01 Intermediate Sanctions Imposed on Excess Benefit Transactions

In an attempt to curb financial abuses by tax-exempt organizations, a penalty excise tax known as intermediate sanctions will be imposed when an tax-exempt organization (Code Sec. 501(c)(3) or 501(c)(4) organization) engages in an *excess benefit transaction* under Code Sec. 4958(c)(1)(A) by directly or indirectly providing a disqualified person with an economic benefit worth more than the organization receives in return. A *disqualified person* is an person who was in a position to exercise *substantial influence* over the affairs of a tax-exempt organization at any time during the five-year period ending on the date of the excess benefit transaction [Code Sec. 4958(f)(1)(A); Reg. § 53.4958-3(a)(1)].

Tax-Exempt Revocation Standards

Reg. § 1.501(c)(3)-1(f)(2)(ii) provides that in determining whether to continue to recognize the tax-exempt status of a tax-exempt organization that engages in one or more excess benefit transactions under Code Sec. 4958(c)(1)(A), the IRS will consider the following factors:

---

[87] Notice 2008-49, IRB 2008-20, 979.

1. The size and scope of the organization's regular and ongoing activities that further exempt purposes before and after the excess benefit transaction occurred;
2. The size and scope of the excess benefit transaction in relation to the size and scope of the organization's regular and ongoing activities that further exempt purposes;
3. Whether the organization has been involved in multiple excess benefit transactions with one or more persons;
4. Whether the organization has implemented safeguards that are reasonably calculated to prevent excess benefit transactions; and
5. Whether the excess benefit transaction has been corrected or the organization has made good faith efforts to seek correction from the disqualified person(s) who benefited from the excess benefit transaction.

The regulations include an example illustrating how important the implementation of safeguards are to help preserve an entitys tax exempt status after it has engaged in an excess benefit transaction. In Reg. § 1.501(c)(3)-1(f)(2)(iv), Ex. 6, the IRS addressed a situation where a tax-exempt organization engaged in excess benefit transactions and violated the proscription against inurement under Code Sec. 501(c)(3). The tax-exempt organization did not however lose its tax-exempt status because the organization implemented safeguards directly in response to the excess benefits transactions that were calculated to prevent a repeat of the offensive behavior.

Penalties Imposed on Disqualified Persons

Penalties are imposed on disqualified persons who improperly benefit from the transactions and on organization managers who knowingly participate in the transactions. A disqualified person who benefits from an excess benefit transaction is subject to a first-tier penalty equal to 25 percent of the excess benefit [Code Sec. 4950(a)(1)]. Organization managers who knowingly, willfully and without reasonable cause participate in an excess benefit transaction are subject to a first-tier penalty tax of 10 percent of the amount of the excess benefit (up to a maximum of $20,000) [Code Sec. 4950(d)(2)]. Second-tier taxes may be imposed on a disqualified person if there is no correction of the excess benefit on or prior to the earlier of: (1) the mailing of a deficiency notice with respect to the first-tier penalty; or (2) the date of assessment. The second-tier tax is 200 percent of the amount of the excess benefit.

Safe Harbors for Organizational Managers

An organizational manager who knowingly participates in an excess benefit transaction will be subject to the 25-percent penalty tax on excess benefits received by disqualified persons as well as a 10-percent penalty tax. Two safe harbors, described here, are available to organizational managers.

Reliance on professional advice safe harbor. An organization manager's participation in a transaction will not be considered *knowing,* to the extent that, after full disclosure of the facts to an appropriate professional, the organization manager relies on a reasoned written opinion of that professional with respect to elements of the transaction within the professional's expertise. A written opinion will be considered reasoned even though it reaches an incorrect conclusion if it addresses the facts and applicable standards. However, a written opinion is not reasoned if it does nothing more than recite the facts and express a conclusion. In this situation, *appropriate professionals* are limited to:

- Legal counsel, including in-house counsel;
- Certified public accountants or accounting firms with expertise regarding the relevant tax law matters; and
- Independent valuation experts who hold themselves out to the public as appraisers or compensation consultants [Reg. § 53.4958-1(d) (4) (iii)].

Satisfaction of rebuttable presumption of reasonableness safe harbor. An organization manager's participation in a transaction is considered not knowing if the appropriate authorized body has met the requirements for the transaction to be presumed to not be an excess benefit transaction [Reg. § 53.4958-1(d) (4) (iv)]. Parties to a transaction are entitled to rely on a rebuttable presumption of reasonableness for any transaction with a disqualified person that is approved by an independent and informed board of directors or trustees (or by a committee of directors or trustees) [Reg. § 53.4958-6].

.02 What Are Excess Benefit Transactions?

Excess benefit transactions are defined in Code Sec. 4958(c) to include transactions in which a disqualified person engages in a nonfair-market-value transaction with an organization, receives unreasonable compensation, or receives payment based on the organization's income in a transaction that violates the prohibition against private inurement. Basically, an excess benefit transaction is any transaction in which an economic benefit is provided directly or indirectly to (or for the use of) any disqualified person if the value of the economic benefit provided exceeds the value of the consideration received for providing such benefit [Reg. § 53.4958-4(a)].

Three economic benefits provided to disqualified persons will not be considered excess benefits:

- Reasonable expenses for members of the governing body of an exempt organization to attend its meetings;
- An economic benefit provided to a disqualified person that the disqualified person receives solely as a member of or volunteer for the organization, if the benefit is provided to members of the public in exchange for a membership fee of $75 or less per year; and
- An economic benefit provided to a disqualified person that the disqualified person receives solely as member of a charitable class that the exempt organization intends to benefit.

> ▶ **PRACTICE TIP:** To avoid having any economic benefit provided to a disqualified individual treated by the IRS as an excess benefit, be sure to report any economic benefit as compensation on Form W-2, Form 1099 or Form 990.

This includes treating as compensation the payment of a premium for a disqualified person to cover any taxes imposed or the actual indemnification for such taxes by the exempt organization.

.03 *Disqualified Person* Defined

A *disqualified person* is defined [Code Sec. 4958(f)(1)(D)] as any individual who has been in a position to exercise substantial authority over an organization's or functionally integrated supporting organization's affairs, regardless of the individual's official title, at any time during the five-year period ending on the date of the transaction [Code Sec. 4958(f)(1)(D)]. Disqualified persons also include specified family members of an individual in a position to exercise substantial influence and 35-percent controlled entities of disqualified persons [Code Sec. 4958(f)(1); Reg. § 53.4958-3(b)(1)]. Family members include the spouse, brothers or sisters (by whole or half blood), spouses of brothers or sisters (by whole or half blood), ancestors, children, grandchildren, great grandchildren, and spouses of children, grandchildren, and great grandchildren [Code Sec. 4958(f)(1)(D); Reg. § 53.4958-3(b)(1)]. A 35-percent entity includes a corporation in which a disqualified person owns more than 35 percent of the combined voting power, a partnership in which a disqualified person owns more than 35 percent of the profits interest, or a trust or estate in which a disqualified person owns more than 35 percent of the beneficial interest [Code Sec. 4958(c)(3)(B); Reg. § 53.4958-3(b)(2)].

A person who has substantial powers, responsibilities, or interests in an organization is in a position to exercise substantial influence over the affairs of the tax-exempt organization and, therefore, is considered to be a disqualified person. This includes voting members of the governing body; presidents, chief executive officers, or chief operating officers; treasurers and chief financial officers; and persons with a material financial interest in a provider-sponsored organization [Reg. § 53.4958-3(c)].

Whether persons not included in one of the specific categories as a disqualified person is based on all relevant facts and circumstances [Reg. § 53.4958-3(a)(1); Reg. § 53.4958-3(e)]. A person may be a disqualified person with respect to transactions with more than one tax-exempt organization. In the case of multiple organizations affiliated by common control or governing documents, the determination of whether a person does or does not have substantial influence shall be made separately for each tax-exempt organization [Reg. § 53.4958-3(f)].

For supporting organizations, a disqualified person includes a substantial contributor to the organization, a family member of such substantial contributor, or 35-percent controlled entity [Code Sec. 4958(c)(3)(B)]. A "substantial contributor" is a person who has contributed or bequeathed an aggregate amount of more than $5,000 to the organization, if that amount equals more than two percent of the total contributions or bequests received by the organization for the tax year. If such a contribution or bequest is made through a trust, the term substantial contributor includes the creator of the trust [Code Sec. 4958(c)(3)(C)].

An independent contractor (such as an attorney, accountant, or investment manager or advisor) whose sole relationship to the organization is providing professional advice, but who did not have decision-making authority, generally is not a disqualified person [Reg. § 53.4958-3(e)(3)(ii)].

Two categories of persons are deemed not to have substantial influence:

- Other 501(c)(3) tax-exempt organizations; and
- Any employee who, for the period in question is not highly compensated ($115,000 in 2013) and does not fit one of the disqualified person categories in the statute or

regulations and is not a substantial contributor to the organization within the meaning of Code Sec. 507(d)(2) (contributions in excess of $5,000 that exceed 2 percent of total contributions.

If managers (officers, directors or trustees) after full disclosure of the facts to legal counsel relies on the advice of such counsel expressed in a reasoned written legal opinion that a transaction is not an excess benefit transaction under Code Sec. 4958, that manager's participation in such transactions will not be considered knowing or willful, and will ordinarily be considered due to reasonable cause, even if it is subsequently held to be an excess benefit transaction.

Compensation will be entitled to a rebuttable presumption that it is reasonable if the compensation arrangement was approved by an independent board of directors or trustees that:

- Was composed entirely of individuals unrelated to and not subject to the control of the disqualified person(s) involved in the arrangement;
- Obtained and relied upon appropriate data regarding compensation levels paid by similarly situated organizations; and
- Adequately documented the basis for its determination showing an evaluation of the individual and the basis for determining that the individual's compensation was reasonable in light of that evaluation and data [Reg. § 53.4958-6].

If the organization has annual gross receipts of less than $1 million, Reg. § 53.4958-6(c)(2)(ii) provides that the governmental body's review of compensation arrangements will be considered to have appropriate data as to comparability if it has data on compensation paid by three comparable organizations in the same or similar communities for similar services. If these three criteria are met, the subject transaction will have the benefit of a rebuttable presumption of reasonableness. This means that intermediate sanctions will not be imposed unless the IRS can rebut the presumptions by demonstrating sufficient contrary evidence to undo the independent board's determination.

Home health agencies not liable for excess benefits tax on conversion to nonexempt. In *Caracci*,[88] the Court of Appeals for the Fifth Circuit reversed the Tax Court to give a taxpayer total relief from the excess benefits tax. The taxpayer had started a home health-care agency that served the rural poor. One year later, they organized two more nonprofit home health agencies. Initially, they organized the agencies as tax-exempt entities but converted to for-profit S corporations thereafter.

Intermediate sanctions result from unauthorized personal use of church property. In five related technical advice memoranda involving a single church and different individuals related to its founder, the IRS concluded that the founder was liable for the excess benefit tax because the disqualified person used church properties for purposes that that were not substantiated to have been church business. Included in the list of activities that triggered the tax were use of church charge cards, cell phones, vehicles, and real property.[89]

---

[88] *M.T. Caracci*, CA-5, 2006-2 USTC ¶ 50,395, 456 F3d 444.

[89] LTR 200435018 (May 5, 2004); LTR 200435019 (May 5, 2004); LTR 200435020 (May 5, 2004); LTR 200435021 (May 5, 2004); LTR 200435022 (May 5, 2004).

¶23,190 TAX ON EXEMPT ORGANIZATIONS INVOLVED IN TAX SHELTERS

A tax-exempt entity that is a party to a prohibited tax shelter transaction or becomes a party to a subsequently listed transaction must pay an excise tax equal to the greater of (1) 100 percent of the entity's net income (after taking into account any tax imposed with respect to the transaction) for the year that is attributable to the transaction or (2) 75 percent of the proceeds received by the entity that are attributable to the prohibited tax shelter transaction [Code Sec. 4965(a)(1)].

Code Sec. 4965 imposes two excise taxes. First, Code Sec. 4965(a)(1) imposes an excise tax on certain tax-exempt entities that are parties to prohibited tax shelter transactions, as defined in Code Sec. 4965(e). Second, Code Sec. 4965(a)(2) imposes an excise tax on entity managers of tax-exempt entities who approve the entity as a party (or otherwise cause the entity to be a party) to a prohibited tax shelter transaction and know or have reason to know that the transaction is a prohibited tax shelter transaction. Prohibited tax shelter transactions include transactions that are identified by the IRS as potentially abusive listed tax avoidance transactions and reportable transactions that are confidential transactions or transactions with contractual protection.

.01 *Party* Defined

For purposes of Code Secs. 4965, 6033(a)(2), and 6011(g), a tax-exempt entity is a party to a transaction if it (1) facilitates the transaction by reason of its tax-exempt, tax indifferent, or tax-favored status; or (2) is identified in published guidance, by type, class, or role, as a party to a prohibited tax shelter transaction [Reg. § 53.4965-4(a)].

.02 Excise Tax Imposed on Tax-Exempt Entities

The excise tax imposed under Code Sec. 4965(a)(1) applies for the year in which the tax-exempt entity becomes a party to the prohibited tax shelter transaction and any subsequent year. The amount of tax depends on whether the tax-exempt entity knew or had reason to know that the transaction was a prohibited tax shelter transaction at the time the entity became a party to the transaction. If the tax-exempt entity did not know (and did not have reason to know) that the transaction was a prohibited tax shelter transaction at the time the entity became a party to the transaction, the tax is 35 percent in 2012 (highest corporate tax rate imposed under Code Sec. 11) multiplied by the greater of:

1. The entity's net income from the prohibited tax shelter transaction (after taking into account any other applicable taxes with respect to such transaction) for the year, or
2. 75 percent of the proceeds received by the entity for the year that are attributable to the transaction [Code Sec. 4965(b)(1)(A)].

If the tax-exempt entity knew or had reason to know that the transaction was a prohibited tax shelter transaction at the time the entity became a party to the transaction, the tax is the greater of:

1. 100 percent of the entity's net income from the transaction (after taking into account any other applicable taxes with respect to such transaction) for the year, or

2. 75 percent of the proceeds received by the entity for the year that are attributable to the transaction [Code Sec. 4965(b)(1)(B)].

Net Income and Proceeds

For purposes of Code Sec. 4965(a), the net income and proceeds attributable to the prohibited tax shelter transaction must be allocated to a particular tax year in a manner consistent with the non-plan entity's established method of accounting for federal income tax purposes. A non-plan entity that has not established a method of accounting must use the cash method to determine the amount and timing of net income and proceeds attributable to a prohibited tax shelter transaction solely for purposes of Code Sec. 4965(a). A non-plan entity that has established a method of accounting other than the cash method may nevertheless use the cash method to determine the amount of the net income and proceeds attributable to a prohibited tax shelter transaction entered into before the date of enactment of Code Sec. 4965 and allocable to pre- and post-enactment periods.

If a non-plan entity has not established a tax year for federal income tax purposes, its tax year for the purpose of determining the amount and timing of net income and proceeds attributable to a prohibited tax shelter transaction will be the annual period the entity has used in keeping its books and records.

.03 Excise Tax Imposed on Entity Managers

The manager-level excise tax under Code Sec. 4965(a)(2) will be imposed on any entity manager of a tax-exempt entity who approves the entity as a party (or otherwise causes such entity to be a party) to a prohibited tax shelter transaction and knows or has reason to know that the transaction is a prohibited tax shelter transaction. The amount of tax is $20,000 for each approval or other act causing the entity to be a party to the prohibited tax shelter transaction [Code Sec. 4965(b)(2)].

.04 *Prohibited Tax Shelter Transaction* Defined

A *prohibited tax shelter transaction* under Code Sec. 4965(e) means:

1. Listed transactions under Code Sec. 6707A(c)(2), which are transactions that are the same as, or substantially similar to, any transaction that has been specifically identified by the IRS as a tax avoidance transaction; and

2. Prohibited reportable transactions, which are: (a) confidential transactions, and (b) transactions with contractual protection [Code Sec. 4965(e)(1)].

.05 Applicable Tax-Exempt Entities

The excise tax could be imposed on any tax-exempt organizations and entities including charitable and other organizations (other than the United States), Indian tribal governments, qualified pension plans, qualified annuity plans and contracts, IRAs, and similar tax-favored savings arrangements (such as Coverdell education savings accounts, health savings accounts, and qualified tuition plans). The rules also apply to entities such as charities, churches, hospitals, museums, schools, scientific research organizations, civic and business leagues, social welfare organizations, state and local governments, labor, agricultural, or horticultural organizations, Indian tribal governments, chambers of commerce, trade associations, voluntary employees' beneficiary associations (VEBAs), and credit unions [Code Sec. 4965(c)].

.06 *Entity Manager* Defined

The term *entity manager* means the person with authority or responsibility similar to that exercised by an officer, director or trustee. In the case of plan entities, the term *entity manager* means the person who approves or otherwise causes the entity to be a party to the prohibited tax shelter transaction. An individual beneficiary (including a plan participant) or owner of a tax-favored retirement plans may be liable as an entity manager if the individual beneficiary or owner has broad investment authority under the arrangement. An entity manager who knows or has reason to know that the transaction is a prohibited tax shelter transaction must pay a tax in the amount of $20,000 for each approval [Code Sec. 4965(b)(2)]. An entity manager is an exempt organization manager, a private foundation manager, or a person with authority or responsibility similar to that exercised by an officer, director, or trustee of an organization [Code Sec. 4965(a)(2)].

Generally, the presence of certain factors may indicate that the entity manager has a responsibility to inquire further about whether a transaction is a prohibited tax shelter transaction. These factors include: whether a transaction is extraordinary for the entity; promises an exceptional return considering the amount invested; or the transaction is of significant size, either in an absolute sense or relative to the receipts of the entity.

.07 Disclosure Requirements

Every tax-exempt entity that is a party to a prohibited tax shelter transaction must provide the following information to the IRS: (a) a statement admitting that the entity is a party to the prohibited tax shelter transaction; and (b) the identity of any other party to the transaction [Code Sec. 6033(a)(2)]. Likewise, any taxable party to a prohibited tax shelter transaction must provide a statement disclosing to any other tax-exempt entity that is a party to the transaction that the transaction is a prohibited tax shelter transaction [Code Sec. 6011].

.08 Penalty for Nondisclosure

A penalty will be imposed for each failure by a tax-exempt entity to file a disclosure detailing the entity's involvement in any prohibited tax shelter transaction. The amount of the penalty is $100 for each day during which such failure continues, not to exceed $50,000 with respect to any one disclosure. The IRS has authority to make a written demand on any entity or manager subject to the penalty for nondisclosure under Code Sec. 6033(a)(2), specifying a reasonable future date when the required disclosure must be filed. Failure to comply with the IRS demand is subject to an additional penalty in the amount of $100 for each day after the expiration of the time specified in the demand during which such failure continues, not to exceed $10,000 with respect to any one disclosure [Code Sec. 6652(c)(3)(B)(ii)]. In most cases, the penalty is imposed on the tax-exempt entity. In the case of the plan entities, the penalty is imposed on the entity manager of the tax-exempt entity.

24 Partnerships

WHAT IS A PARTNERSHIP?

Tax definition . . . . ¶24,001
Check-the-box to decide entity classification . . . . ¶24,002
Partnership anti-abuse rules . . . . . ¶24,003
Publicly traded partnerships . . . . . ¶24,005
Exclusion from partnership treatment . . . . ¶24,010
Family partnerships . . . . ¶24,015

PARTNERSHIP INCOME, DEDUCTIONS, CREDITS

How a partnership reports income . . . . ¶24,020
Elections affecting computation of income . . . . ¶24,025
Book profit and taxable income distinguished . . . . ¶24,030

FIGURING A PARTNER'S TAX LIABILITY

How partners determine their tax liabilities . . . . ¶24,035
Separately stated items . . . . ¶24,040
Distribution and reconciliation schedules . . . . ¶24,045
Taking partnership income or loss into account . . . . ¶24,050
Loss is limited . . . . ¶24,055
How to determine a partner's distributive share . . . . ¶24,060
Distributive share of items due to contributed property . . . . ¶24,065

TAX YEAR OF A PARTNER AND PARTNERSHIP

Choice of tax year . . . . ¶24,070
When a partnership's tax year closes . . . . ¶24,075

TRANSACTIONS BETWEEN A PARTNERSHIP AND PARTNER OR RELATED PERSON

Partner not acting as a partner . . . . ¶24,080
Transactions between partnership and related parties . . . . ¶24,085

CONTRIBUTIONS TO A PARTNERSHIP

Tax effect of contribution . . . . ¶24,090

PARTNER'S BASIS FOR A PARTNERSHIP INTEREST

Partner's original basis and how to adjust it . . . . ¶24,095
How partnership liabilities affect basis . . . . ¶24,096

DISTRIBUTIONS TO PARTNERS

Recognition of gain or loss . . . . . . ¶24,100

Basis and holding period of property distributed . . . . ¶ 24,105

Distributions of property to transferee partners . . . . ¶ 24,110

Partnership's elective 754 adjustment to basis of undistributed property following a distribution . . . . ¶ 24,115

Distribution of unrealized receivables or inventory items . . . . . ¶ 24,120

When is a distribution a sale or exchange? . . . . ¶ 24,125

TRANSFER OF PARTNERSHIP INTEREST

Gain or loss on transfer . . . . ¶ 24,130

Basis of transferee partner . . . . ¶ 24,135

Special elective partnership basis for transferee . . . . ¶ 24,140

PAYMENTS UPON RETIREMENT OR DEATH OF PARTNER

Cross-purchase or liquidation of departing or retiring partner's interest . . . . ¶ 24,145

How installment payments are allocated . . . . ¶ 24,150

WHAT IS A PARTNERSHIP?

A partnership is not a taxable entity. It is a conduit for passing income, deductions, etc. to partners. Each year, the partnership must file a partnership return showing its total income or loss and certain separately stated items. The partners must include their distributive shares of partnership items in figuring their taxable income.

¶24,001 TAX DEFINITION

A partnership is a business entity with two or more owners [Reg. §301.7701-3(a)]. The owners could be individuals, corporations, trusts, estates or other partnerships. The hallmark of a partnership is that "the participants carry on a trade, business, financial operation, or venture and divide the profits therefrom" [Reg. §301.7701-1(a)(2)]. The term "partnership" includes a "syndicate, group, pool, joint venture, or other unincorporated organization through or by means of which any business, financial operation, or venture is carried on" [Code Sec. 761(a)]. However, a joint undertaking merely to share expenses does not create a separate entity for federal tax purposes. For example, if two or more persons jointly construct a ditch merely to drain surface water from their properties, they have not created a separate entity for federal tax purposes. Similarly, mere co-ownership of property that is maintained, kept in repair, and rented or leased does not constitute a separate entity for federal tax purposes. For example, if an individual owner, or tenants in common, of farm property lease it to a farmer for a cash rental or a share of the crops, they do not necessarily create a separate entity for federal tax purposes. [Reg. §301.7701-1(a)(2)].

In determining whether a partnership exists, the essential question is whether the parties intended to, and did in fact join together with a business purpose of sharing in the profits and losses of an undertaking or enterprise.[1] In *W.O. Culbertson*,[2] the Supreme Court stated that a partnership exists for federal tax purposes if "considering all the facts-the agreement, the conduct of the parties in execution of its provisions, their statements, the testimony of disinterested persons, the relationship of the parties, their respective abilities and capital contributions, the actual control of income and the purposes for which it is used, and any other facts throwing light on their true intent- the parties in good faith and acting with a business purpose intend to join together in the present conduct of an enterprise." In *H.M. Luna*,[3] the Tax Court provided the following eight factors to consider in determining the existence of a partnership for tax purposes:

1. The agreement of the parties and their conduct in executing its terms;
2. The contributions, if any, which each party has made to the venture;
3. The parties' control over income and capital and the right of each to make withdrawals;
4. Whether each party was a principal and co-proprietor, sharing a mutual proprietary interest in the net profits and having an obligation to share losses, or whether one party was the agent or employee of the other, receiving for his services contingent compensation in the form of a percentage of income;
5. Whether business was conducted in the joint names of the parties;
6. Whether the parties filed Federal partnership returns or otherwise represented to IRS or to persons with whom they dealt that they were joint venturers;
7. Whether separate books of account were maintained for the venture; and
8. Whether the parties exercised mutual control over and assumed mutual responsibilities for the enterprise.

A written agreement is not required to establish a partnership, but if partners want a venture to be respected as a partnership with an oral agreement, the venture must be operated as such, with separate books and records maintained and partnership tax returns filed.[4]

.01 Family Business Tax Simplification

A qualified joint venture whose only members are a husband and wife filing a joint return are treated as a partnership for federal tax purposes [Code Sec. 761(f)(1)]. A qualified joint venture is a joint venture involving the conduct of a trade or business, if: (1) the only members of the joint venture are a husband and wife, (2) both spouses

[1] *F.E. Tower*, SCt, 40-1 USTC ¶9189, 327 US 280, 66 SCt 532; *Historic Boardwalk Hall, LLC*, CA-3, 2012-2 USTC ¶50,538, 694 F3d 425, *cert denied*, May 28, 2013; *Southgate Master Fund, LLC.*, CA-5, 2011-2 USTC ¶50,648, 659 F3d 466; *J.A. Rigas*, DC-TX, 2011-1 USTC ¶50,372; *A.T. Abdolreza*, Dec. 59,588(M), TC Memo. 2013-169; Chief Counsel Advice 201323015 (Feb. 21, 2013).

[2] *W.O. Culbertson*, SCt, 49-1 USTC ¶9323, 337 US 733, 69 SCt 1210.

[3] *H.M. Luna*, 42 TC 1067, Dec. 26,967 (1964); *A.T. Azimzadeh*, Dec. 59,588(M), TC Memo. 2013-169; *R.W. Holdner*, CA-9, 2012-2 USTC ¶50,626, 483 Fed Appx 383; LTR 201323015 (June 10, 2013).

[4] *Comtek Expositions*, 85 TCM 1280, Dec. 55,147(M), TC Memo. 2003-135; *W.L. Medlin*, 86 TCM 141, Dec. 55,246(M), TC Memo. 2003-224, *aff'd*, CA-11, 2005-2 USTC ¶50,491, *cert. denied* 10/3/2005; *but see M.W. Ballantyne Est.*, CA-8, 2004-1 USTC ¶50,120, 341 F3d 802.

materially participate in the trade or business, and (3) both spouses elect to have the Code Sec. 761(f) provision apply [Code Sec. 761(f)(2)]. Material participation is determined under the passive activity limitation rules of Code Sec. 469(h), except for the rule permitting participation of the spouse of the taxpayer to be taken into account [Code Sec. 761(f)(2)(B)]. If this election is made, all items of income, gain, loss, deduction, and credit are divided between the spouses in accordance with their respective interests in the venture. Each spouse takes into account his or her respective share of these items as a sole proprietor. Thus, each spouse would account for his or her respective share on the appropriate form, such as Form 1040, Schedule C.

In a general partnership, each partner shares in the profits and liabilities of the partnership. In addition, each partner has a say in how the partnership is operated. In a limited partnership, on the other hand, the limited partners are generally liable for the partnership's liabilities only to the extent of their investment in the partnership. In exchange for this limited liability, the limited partners have no involvement in how the partnership is operated.

.02 Limited Liability Partnerships

Limited Liability Partnerships (LLP) are available in all states to enable existing professional partnerships with unlimited liability for breach of contract or negligence to be transformed into an LLP without the formality of having to liquidate and reorganize as an LLP. In order to form an LLP, the professional partnership must register with the appropriate state authority and operate as it had prior to the change in nomenclature, as well as add the term "LLP" to its partnership name in order to inform the public of the change. The LLP retains the employer identification number of its predecessor partnership. Result: members will not be subject to personal liability for breach of contract or for negligence claims resulting from their negligence or the negligence of those under their supervision.

> **NOTE:** Remember that a partner in a Professional Limited Liability Partnership (PLLP) is still liable for any personal guarantees that he/she may make on behalf of the PLLP; e.g., guaranteeing the lease on the premises operated by the firm [¶ 30,145].

> ▶ **OBSERVATION:** All jurisdictions are not alike in their treatment of the contractual obligations of their LLP; e.g., the New Jersey PLLP statute provides that all partners in a PLLP remain liable for the contractual obligations of their PLLP, such as leases or trade credit, whereas New York shields its LLP members from commercial liability.

Liability Afforded Partners in LLP

LLPs are general partnerships or limited partnerships that are created pursuant to state law. All 50 states and the District of Columbia have legislation authorizing the creation of LLPs. The liability protection afforded partners will differ from state to state.

In some states the partners in LLPs are personally liable for the commercial and other general obligations of the partnership and for the negligent actions of persons under their supervision. They are not liable, however, for negligence of their partners or of employees under another partner's supervision.

Some states offer LLP members limited protection from partnership liabilities, such as limiting the protection to malpractice claims against other partners. Other states offer full protection from liabilities, including the partnership's contractual liabilities. These are called "full shield" states.

In most states, LLP partners have the same blanket liability protection as members of an LLC. Therefore, the LLP partners are not liable for the obligations of the partnership but remain liable for their own negligent actions and the negligence of employees under their supervision. Because partners in an LLP will benefit from limited liability, many state statutes require LLPs to carry a specific amount of liability insurance.

Formation of LLP

An existing general or limited partnership generally can convert to an LLP without tax consequences by filing a registration statement. This contrasts with the formalities imposed on a taxpayer wanting to form an LLC: filing articles of organization and drafting an operating agreement.

LLPs are often formed by attorneys and accountants because these large professional partnerships have hundreds of partners scattered over the country or even on different continents and limiting liability is a big concern.

Tax Treatment of LLPs

The classification and tax treatment of LLPs is not affected by the check-the-box entity selection rules. The federal income tax status of an LLP depends on the provisions of the state law under which the partnership is formed.

¶24,002 CHECK-THE-BOX TO DECIDE ENTITY CLASSIFICATION

.01 Check-the-box Regulations

The check-the-box regulations under Reg. §301.7701-3(a) provide that a business entity that is not classified as a corporation can elect its classification for federal tax purposes. For further discussion of check-the-box regulations and limited liability companies (LLCs), see ¶30,085.

An eligible entity with at least two members can elect to be classified as either an association (and thus a corporation) or a partnership, and an eligible entity with a single owner can elect to be classified as an association or to be disregarded as an entity separate from its owner. Elections are necessary only if an eligible entity does not want its default classification or if an eligible entity chooses to change its classification.

Generally, under Reg. §301.7701-3(b)(2)(i), unless an entity elects otherwise, the entity is classified as one of the following entities:

- A partnership if it has two or more members and at least one member does not have limited liability,
- An association if all members have limited liability, or
- Disregarded as an entity separate from its owner if it has a single member that does not have limited liability.

Reg. § 301.7701-3(c)(1)(i) provides that an eligible entity may make entity classification by filing Form 8832, *Entity Classification Election.* This election will be effective on the date specified by the entity on Form 8832 or on the date filed if no such date is specified on the election form. The effective date specified on Form 8832 cannot be more than 75 days prior to the date on which the election is filed and cannot be more than 12 months after the date on which the election is filed.

If an eligible entity makes an election to change its classification, the entity cannot change its classification by election again during the 60 months succeeding the effective date of the election. An election by a newly formed eligible entity that is effective on the date of formation is not considered a change for these purposes.

An election made must be signed by: (1) each member of the electing entity who is an owner at the time the election is filed; or (2) any officer, manager, or member of the electing entity who is authorized (under local law or the entity's organizational documents) to make the election and who represents to having such authorization under penalties of perjury.

.02 IRS Clarifies Foreign Entity Check-the-Box Elections

In Rev. Proc. 2010-32,[5] the IRS provided guidance to foreign entities making check-the-box elections in situations where the entity misstates the number of owners of the foreign eligible entity on the effective date of the election. To alleviate these concerns and simplify tax administration, Rev. Proc. 2010-32 provides that if the requirements of this revenue procedure are satisfied, the IRS will treat an election under Reg. § 301.7701-3(c) to classify a foreign eligible entity as a partnership or disregarded entity, as an election that reflects the actual number of owners of the foreign entity.

Safe Harbor

Pursuant to the procedure, if a qualified entity files an otherwise valid Form 8832 to be classified as a partnership but it is later determined that the entity had a single owner as of the effective date of the election, the IRS will treat the form as an election to classify the entity as a disregarded entity. If the qualified entity elects classification as a disregarded entity, but it is later determined that the entity has two or more owners as of the effective date of the election, the IRS will treat the form as an election to classify the entity as a partnership.

In order to qualify for relief under Rev. Proc. 2010-32, the following requirements must be satisfied:

- The taxpayers must file original or amended returns consistent with the treatment of the entity as a disregarded entity or partnership.
- All required amended returns must be filed before the close of the period of limitations on assessments under Code Sec. 6501(a), and
- A corrected Form 8832 must be filed, satisfying the requirements of Reg. § 301.7701-3(c)(2)(i), and the statement "FILED PURSUANT TO REVENUE PROCEDURE 2010-32" must be included across the top of the corrected Form 8832.
- A copy of the corrected form must be attached to the amended return(s).

If a qualified entity files an otherwise valid Form 8832 electing to be classified as a disregarded entity for federal tax purposes but it is later determined that the

[5] Rev. Proc. 2010-32, 2010-36 IRB 320.

qualified entity had two or more owners for federal tax purposes as of the effective date of the election, the IRS will treat the Form 8832 as an election to classify the qualified entity as a partnership for federal tax purposes.

.03 Late Entity Classification Elections

In Rev. Proc. 2009-41,[6] the IRS extended relief with respect to a late entity classification election to both initial classification elections and changes in classification elections, and extended the time for making late entity classification elections. This guidance is the exclusive means for eligible entities to obtain relief for a late entity classification.

An entity must meet the following requirements for relief under Rev. Proc. 2009-41:

- The entity failed to obtain its requested classification as of the date of its formation or upon the entity's classification becoming relevant solely because Form 8832 was not filed timely, or
- The entity failed to obtain its requested change in classification solely because Form 8832 was not filed timely and
- The entity has not filed a federal tax or information return for the first year in which the election was intended because the due date has not passed for that year's federal tax or information return, or
- The entity filed all required federal tax returns and information returns consistent with its requested classification for all of the years the entity intended the requested election to be effective and no inconsistent tax or information returns have been filed by or with respect to the entity during any of the tax years.

Relief must be requested before three years and 75 days from the requested effective date and reasonable cause for the failure to timely make the classification election must be shown.

The IRS instructed taxpayers to write "Filed Pursuant to Rev. Proc. 2009-41" across the top of Form 8832 and attach both a declaration and the reasonable cause statement to the form. The declaration must state that the taxpayer qualifies for relief under Rev. Proc. 2009-41. Taxpayers must also explain their reason for failing to file a timely election. Applicants need not pay user fees.

.04 Effects of Changing Entity Classification

Reg. § 301.7701-3(g) describes how elective changes in an entity's classification are treated for federal tax purposes. There are four possible elective changes in classification:

1. A partnership can elect to be taxed as an association;
2. An association can elect to be taxed as a partnership;
3. An association (with a single member) can elect to be disregarded as an entity for tax purposes; and
4. A disregarded entity can elect to be taxed as an association.

[6] Rev. Proc. 2009-41, 2009-39 IRB 439.

Partnership to Association

A partnership that elects to be classified as an association is deemed to have contributed all its assets and liabilities to the association in return for stock in the association. The partnership is subsequently deemed to have liquidated by distributing the stock in the association to its partners [Reg. § 301.7701-3(g)(1)(i)].

Association to Partnership

An association that elects to be classified as a partnership is deemed to have liquidated by distributing all of its assets and liabilities to its shareholders. The shareholders are then deemed to have contributed all of the assets and liabilities to the partnership [Reg. § 301.7701-3(g)(1)(ii)].

Association to a Disregarded Entity

An eligible entity that is classified as an association and elects to be disregarded as an entity separate from its owner is deemed to have distributed all its assets and liabilities to its single owner and to subsequently have liquidated [Reg. § 301.7701-3(g)(1)(iii)].

Disregarded Entity to Association

The owner of an entity that is disregarded as an entity separate from its owner that elects to be classified as an association is deemed to have contributed all the assets and liabilities of that entity to the association in exchange for stock of the association [Reg. § 301.7701-3(g)(1)(iv)].

Adoption of Liquidation Plan by Reclassifying Entity

A plan of liquidation is deemed adopted immediately before a deemed liquidation incident to an elective change under Reg. § 301.7701-3(g), unless a formal plan of liquidation that addresses the filing of an elective change is adopted on an earlier date [Reg. § 301.7701-3(g)(2)(ii)]. This allows associations with corporate owners to avoid a conflict between entity classification rules that allow an entity to remain in existence while liquidating and the requirement under Code Sec. 332(b) that a plan of liquidation be in place in order for a corporation to avoid recognizing gain or loss on liquidating distributions from a subsidiary.

Timing of Election

Generally, an election by an entity to change its classification is treated as occurring at the start of the day for which the election is effective. Any transactions that are deemed to have occurred as the result of an elective change in an entity's classification are treated as having occurred immediately before the end of the day prior to the day the election is effective.

> **Example 24-1:** ABCo is classified as an association. ABCo elects to change its classification from an association to a partnership, effective on January 1, Year 2. ABCo is deemed to have distributed all its assets to its shareholders and liquidated, and the shareholders are deemed to have contributed the assets to the newly formed partnership, immediately before the close of December 31, Year 1. The owners of the newly formed partnership must report the transaction on December 31, Year 1. Further, December 31, Year 1, is last day of Hobson's Home Repair's tax year, as an association, and January 1, Year 2, is the first day of its tax year as a partnership.

¶24,003 Partnership Anti-Abuse Rules

In an attempt to prevent taxpayers from using partnerships to circumvent the tax laws, the IRS has issued anti-abuse regulations authorizing the IRS to recast transactions that attempt to use partnerships in a manner inconsistent with the intent of the partnership tax laws [Reg. § 1.701-2].

.01 Sham Transaction Doctrine

The anti-abuse rule described by Reg. § 1.701-2 is not the only method available to the IRS to challenge potentially abusive partnership transactions [Reg. § 1.702-2(i)]. The IRS may also rely on common law doctrine as well as nonpartnership tax provisions to recharacterize a partnership transaction or use of the partnership form which it views as abusive.

One weapon used to disregard transactions is the "sham transaction doctrine" which allows a court to disregard a transaction for tax purposes if the transaction is motivated by no business purpose other than obtaining tax benefits, and the transaction lacks economic substance because there is no reasonable expectation of profit.[7] Interest deductions, for example, may be disallowed if the indebtedness lacks substance, and exists merely in form.[8] Subjective good intentions to enter into a valid indebtedness are not generally considered.[9]

Statutory principles for disallowing transactions that lack economic substance include the passive loss rules [Code Sec. 469]and the at-risk rules [Code Sec. 465]. The transaction may also be recharacterized under accounting method principles. Code Sec. 446 requires the accounting method used by a partnership to clearly reflect the income of the partners; under Code Sec. 482, income recognized by related parties may be reallocated if necessary to clearly reflect income or prevent the evasion of taxes.

.02 Anti-Abuse Regulations

The anti-abuse rules in Reg. § 1.701-2 provide that:

- The partnership must be bona fide and each partnership transaction or series of related transactions must be entered into for a substantial business purpose;
- The form of each partnership must be respected under substance-over-form principles; and
- The tax consequences to each partner of partnership operations and of transactions among the partnership must accurately reflect the partners' economic agreement and clearly reflect the partners' income [Reg. § 1.701-2(a)].

[7] *Rice's Toyota World, Inc.*, CA-4, 85-1 USTC ¶ 9123, 752 F2d 89.

[8] *K.F. Knetsch*, SCt, 60-2 USTC ¶ 9785, 364 US 361.

[9] *G.G. Lynch*, CA-2, 60-1 USTC ¶ 9161, 273 F2d 867.

If a partnership is formed in connection with a transaction that has a principal purpose of substantially reducing the partners' aggregate federal tax liability in a manner that is inconsistent with the intent of the partnership rules in Subchapter K, the IRS can recast the transaction in order to correct the inconsistency [Reg. § 1.701-2(b)]. A transaction may be recast even though it falls within the literal words of a particular statutory or regulatory provision [Reg. § 1.701-2(b)].

In order to achieve results that are consistent with the intent of the partnership tax rules in Subchapter K, the IRS may take any of the following measures:

1. Disregard the purported partnership in whole or in part, and consider the partnership's assets and activities as owned and conducted by one or more of its purported partners [Reg. § 1.701-2(b)(1)];
2. Determine that one or more of the purported partners of the partnership should not be treated as a partner [Reg. § 1.701-2(b)(2)];
3. Adjust the method of accounting used by either the partnership or a partner in order to clearly reflect the partnership or the partner's income [Reg. § 1.701-2(b)(3)];
4. Reallocate the partnership's items of income, gain, loss, deduction, or credit [Reg. § 1.701-2(b)(4)]; or
5. Otherwise adjust the claimed tax treatment of the transaction [Reg. § 1.702-2(b)(5)].

Based on the examples provided by the IRS in the regulations, it appears that a partnership will not violate the antiabuse rules if:

- Tax benefits flow through from the partnership to the partners;
- The partnership is engaged in a bona fide business rather than an investment;
- The partnership is not formed simply as a conduit entity;
- The arrangement does not result in the pass-through of a permanent reduction in the partners' aggregate tax liability.

The antiabuse regulations also authorize the IRS to ignore the partnership entity and treat the partnership as a mere aggregate of its partners where appropriate [Reg. § 1.701-2(e)]. This abuse-of-entity provision may have an impact on some traditional uses of a partnership to:

- Invest overseas to permit the U.S. partner to calculate its foreign tax credit limitation under the look-through rules of Code Secs. 902 and 904 [Reg. § 1.701-2(f)];
- Facilitate the issuance of preferred stock while seeking to pass through an interest deduction to the partners;
- Achieve or avoid affiliated group status; or
- Avoid limitations on deductions at the corporate level (interest deductions or the dividends received deduction).

Based on examples provided in the regulations, likely candidates for added IRS scrutiny under the antiabuse rules include: (1) investment/family partnerships; (2) partnerships formed to avoid S corporation stock ownership rules; and (3) partnerships containing taxed and tax-exempt partners [Reg. § 1.701-2(d)].

.03 Economic Substance Doctrine

It is well established that taxpayers are entitled to structure their business transactions in a manner that produces the least amount of tax. However, courts have used the economic substance doctrine, a common law doctrine, to attack transactions that do not have economic substance or lack a business purpose and are designed simply to reap tax benefits outside the scope of the tax laws. To pass muster the transaction must have a reasonable possibility of showing a profit and have a business purpose for the transaction that is independent of the tax benefits. The IRS has aggressively targeted transactions that it perceives to lack economic substance. A transaction's economic substance is determined by analyzing the subjective intent of the taxpayer entering into the transaction and the objective economic substance of the transaction.

Courts have applied the economic substance doctrine to prevent taxpayers participating in transactions that are fictitious or lack economic reality and are designed simply to reap tax benefits that subvert the tax laws.[10] However, the various U.S. Courts of Appeals have differed on whether the economic substance analysis requires the application of a two-prong test, or is a facts and circumstances analysis regarding whether the transaction had a practical economic effect, taking into account both subjective and objective aspects of the transaction.

Economic Substance Doctrine Codified

The economic substance doctrine has been codified in Code Sec. 7701(o)(5)(A) which provides that the term "economic substance doctrine" means the common law doctrine under which tax benefits with respect to a transaction are not allowable if the transaction does not have economic substance or lacks a business purpose.

A transaction will only be treated as having economic substance if, apart from the federal income tax effects, it changes in a meaningful way the taxpayer's economic position, and the taxpayer has a substantial purpose for entering into the transaction or series of transactions [Code Sec. 7701(o)(1), (5)(D)].

For individual taxpayers, the codified economic substance doctrine will only apply to transactions entered into in connection with a trade or business or activity engaged in for the production of income [Code Sec. 7701(o)(5)(B)].

A state or local income tax effect that is related to a federal income tax effect is, for this purpose, treated as a federal income tax effect [Code Sec. 7701(o)(3)]; federal accounting benefit which has its origin in a reduction of federal income tax is not considered a substantial purpose for entering into a transaction [Code Sec. 7701(o)(4)].

Code Sec. 7701(o)(5)(A) eliminates the disparity among the federal circuit courts concerning application of the economic substance doctrine and clarifies that the economic substance doctrine requires an analysis of the objective effects of the transaction on the taxpayer's economic position, as well as an inquiry regarding the taxpayer's subjective motives for engaging in the transaction [Joint Committee on Taxation, *Technical Explanation of the Revenue Provisions of the "Reconciliation Act of 2010", as amended, in combination with the "Patient Protection and Affordable Care Act"* (JCX-18-10), March 21, 2010].

---

10 *Coltec Industries, Inc.*, CA-FC, 2006-2 USTC ¶50,389, 454 F3d 1340.

The profit potential of a transaction will be considered in applying the economic substance test only if the present value of the reasonably expected pre-tax profit from the transaction (taking into account fees, other transaction expenses, and, in appropriate cases as set forth in future regulations, foreign taxes) is substantial in relation to the present value of the expected net tax benefits that would be allowed if the transaction were respected [Code Sec. 7701(o)(2)(A) and (B)].

IRS Directives on Economic Substance Doctrine

On September 14, 2010, the Large and Mid-Size Business Division (now the Large Business & International Division) issued a directive requiring that the appropriate Director of Field Operations review and approve any proposal by examination to impose the codified economic substance doctrine and a related penalty in order to determine if application of the doctrine is appropriate.[11] Factors indicating that the doctrine may be appropriate include, but are not limited to, whether the transaction created no meaningful economic change on a present value basis (pre-tax), and whether the tax benefit is artificially generated by the transaction. Factors tending to show that the doctrine is not appropriate include, but are not limited to, whether the transaction was at arm's length with unrelated third parties, whether the transaction had a credible business purpose apart from federal tax benefits and whether the transaction had meaningful potential for profit apart from tax benefits.

The LB&I issued a second directive on July 15, 2011, which provides a series of inquiries that LB&I examiners and their managers must develop and analyze before seeking approval to raise the codified economic substance doctrine.[12] In addition, the July 15, 2011 LB&I Directive provides that, until further guidance is issued, the related penalty provisions are limited to the application of the economic substance doctrine and may not be imposed due to the application of any other "similar rule of law" or judicial doctrine, *e.g.*, step transaction doctrine, substance over form, or sham transaction doctrine.

Notice 2010-62

In Notice 2010-62,[13] the IRS provided interim guidance on the codification of the economic substance doctrine in Code Sec. 7701(o), which mandates the use of a conjunctive two-prong test to determine whether a transaction shall be treated as having economic substance. The first prong, found in Code Sec. 7701(o)(1)(A), requires that the transaction change in a meaningful way (apart from federal income tax effects) the taxpayer's economic position. The second prong, found in Code Sec. 7701(o)(1)(B), requires that the taxpayer have a substantial purpose (apart from federal income tax effects) for entering into the transaction.

The IRS will continue to rely on relevant case law under the common-law economic substance doctrine in applying this two-prong conjunctive test. In addition, the IRS will continue to analyze when the economic substance doctrine will apply in the same fashion as it did prior to the codification of the doctrine.

In determining whether the requirements of Code Sec. 7701(o)(1)(A) and (B) are met, the IRS will take into account the taxpayer's profit motive only if the present value of the reasonably expected pre-tax profit is substantial in relation to the present value of

---

[11] LMSB-20-0910-024.

[12] LB&I-4-0711-015.

[13] Notice 2010-62, IRB 2010-40, 411.

the expected net tax benefits that would be allowed if the transaction were respected for federal income tax purposes. In performing this calculation, the IRS will apply existing relevant case law and other published guidance.

Unless the transaction is a reportable transaction, as defined in Reg. § 1.6011-4(b), the adequate disclosure requirements of Code Sec. 6662(i) will be satisfied if a taxpayer adequately discloses on a timely filed original return (determined with regard to extensions) or a qualified amended return the relevant facts affecting the tax treatment of the transaction. The disclosure will be considered adequate only if made on a Form 8275 or 8275-R. If a transaction lacking economic substance is a reportable transaction, the adequate disclosure requirement under Code Sec. 6662(i)(2) will be satisfied only if the taxpayer meets the disclosure requirements described above and the disclosure requirements under the Code Sec. 6011 regulations. A taxpayer will not meet the disclosure requirements for a reportable transaction by only attaching Form 8275 or 8275-R to an original or qualified amended return.

In Chief Counsel Notice 2012-008, the IRS provided instructions to its personnel to ensure that the economic substance doctrine and related penalties are applied only in appropriate cases. The IRS provides that before applying the common law economic substance doctrine to a transaction, the IRS should consider all of the substantive arguments and technical analysis that are reasonably relevant to the proper tax treatment of the transaction. To ensure that the economic substance doctrines and related penalties are only raised in appropriate cases, the Chief Counsel provides that the following procedures must be followed:

1. Examination. During an examination, upon request by the IRS, Chief Counsel attorneys should provide timely assistance on economic substance. The attorneys should consider the factors outlined in the LB&I Directives and the application of appropriate case law.
2. Statutory Notices of Deficiency and Notices of Final Partnership Administrative Adjustment. Chief Counsel attorneys are required to coordinate with Division Counsel and the Office of the Associate Chief Counsel (Procedure and Administration) in order to review any proposed notice of deficiency or notice of final partnership administrative adjustment that concludes that a transaction lacks economic substance.
3. Litigation. Before raising the economic substance as a new issue in a litigation, Chief Counsel attorneys must coordinate with Division Counsel headquarters and the Office of the Associate Chief Counsel (Procedure and Administration). If the tax treatment of that transaction is the subject of one or more favorable private letter rulings or determination letters issued to the taxpayer, the appropriate course of action is to request that the Associate Chief Counsel office with jurisdiction over the transaction review and, if appropriate, revoke the applicable rulings or letters. If revocation is appropriate, attorneys should receive confirmation of the revocation before raising the economic substance doctrine as a new issue.

Pre-Codification Cases

In *Klamath Strategic Investment Fund*,[14] the Court of Appeals for the Fifth Circuit found that loan transactions made by two limited liability companies (LLCs) under a Son of BOSS tax shelter scheme lacked economic substance; therefore, they were disregarded for tax purposes. The loan agreements between a bank and the LLCS failed the economic substance test because there was no reasonable expectation that the loan transactions would produce a profit. The bank's documentation and internal communications showed that the bank did not intend the funding amount to be used as leverage for high-risk foreign currency trading; rather, the funds were to be used for relatively risk-free time deposits and to create massive tax benefits for the law partners.

In *Maguire Partners–Master Investments, LLC*,[15] the district court held that call-option spread transactions involving the simultaneous purchase of long options and a promissory note and the sale of short options that were entered into by individuals and the subsequent transfer of the transactions to their partnerships lacked economic substance. The transactions had no economic purpose except to generate inflated bases in the partnerships' assets to secure tax benefits. There was no evidence that the call-option spread was designed as a hedge generally or that it operated as a hedge.

In *New Phoenix Sunrise Corp.*,[16] the Tax Court held that a series of interconnected transactions involving a subsidiary's purchase and sale of a long and a short option in foreign currency, known as a digital option spread, the contribution of the digital option spread to a partnership, the partnership's purchase of stock and the subsequent sale of the stock at a loss lacked economic substance. The transactions were found to lack economic substance, and the entire series of transactions was a sham, because the odds of the subsidiary making a profit from the digital option spread were infinitesimally small, apart from generating significant tax losses.

¶24,005 PUBLICLY TRADED PARTNERSHIPS

.01 Definition of PTP

Publicly traded partnerships (PTP) (commonly known as *master limited partnerships*) are generally treated as corporations rather than a passthrough entity [Code Sec. 7704(a)]. However, Code Sec. 7704(c)(1) provides that Code Sec. 7704(a) does not apply to any PTP for any tax year if the partnership met the gross income requirements of Code Sec. 7704(c)(2) for the tax year and each preceding tax year beginning after December 31, 1987, during which the partnership (or any predecessor) was in existence. A partnership meets the gross income requirements for any tax year if 90 percent or more of the gross income of the partnership for the tax year consists of "qualifying income."

---

[14] *Klamath Strategic Investment Fund*, CA-5, 2009-1 USTC ¶50,395, 568 F3d 537, *on remand*, DC-TX, 2012-2 USTC ¶50,587.

[15] *Maguire Partners–Master Investments, LLC*, DC-CA, 2009-1 USTC ¶50,215, *aff'd*, CA-9, 2011-2 USTC ¶50,517.

[16] *New Phoenix Sunrise Corp.*, 132 TC 161, Dec. 57,785 (2009), *aff'd*, CA-6, 2010-2 USTC ¶50,740. *See also Nevada Partners Fund, LLC*, DC-MS, 2010-1 USTC ¶50,379, 714 FSupp2d 598, *aff'd*, CA-5, 2013-2 USTC ¶50,398.

.02 Qualifying Income Defined

"Qualifying income" is defined in Code Sec. 7704(d) as interest, dividends, real property rents, and gain from the sale or other disposition of real property (including property described in Code Sec. 1221(a)(1)). Qualifying income also includes income and gains derived from the exploration, development, mining or production, processing, refining, transportation (including pipelines transporting gas, oil or products thereof), or the marketing of any mineral or natural resource. The IRS has determined that a PTP's income from the removal, treatment, recycling, and disposal of waste products from hydraulic fracturing (fracking) is qualifying income under Code Sec. 7704(d)(1)(E).[17]

.03 COD Safe Harbor for PTPs

The IRS has provided a safe harbor under which it will not challenge a publicly traded partnership's (PTP) determination that income from the discharge of indebtedness (COD income) is qualifying income under Code Sec. 7704(d) if the COD income is attributable to debt incurred in direct connection with activities of the PTP that generate qualifying income (qualifying activities). The PTP may demonstrate that COD income is attributable to debt incurred in direct connection with the PTP's qualifying activities by any reasonable method.[18]

.04 Readily Tradable on a Securities Market

A partnership is a PTP if interests in the partnership are traded on an established securities market or are readily tradable on a "secondary market or the substantial equivalent thereof" [Code Sec. 7704(b)]. Code Sec. 7704 applies to all domestic and foreign entities treated as partnerships under Code Sec. 7701 including LLC's and other entities traded as partnerships for federal tax purposes. Interests in a partnership are readily tradable on a secondary market or the substantial equivalent of one if, taking into account all of the facts and circumstances, the partners are readily able to buy, sell, or exchange their partnership interests in a manner that is comparable, economically, to trading on an established securities market [Reg. § 1.7704-1(a)(1)]. Interests in a partnership will not be treated as readily tradable on a secondary market or the substantial equivalent of one unless:

- The partnership participates in the establishment of the market or the inclusion of its interest thereon; or
- The partnership recognizes transfers made on that market [Reg. § 1.7704-1(c)].

An established securities market in this context includes (1) A national securities exchange; (2) A national securities exchange exempt from registration because of the limited volume of transactions; (3) A foreign securities exchange that, under the law of the jurisdiction where it is organized, satisfies regulatory requirements that are analogous to the regulatory requirements under the '34 Act; (4) A regional or local exchange; (5) An interdealer quotation system that regularly disseminates firm buy or sell quotations by identified brokers or dealers by electronic means or otherwise [Reg. § 1.7704-1(b)].

Interests in a partnership that are not traded on an established securities market are readily tradable on a secondary market if, taking into account all of the facts and

---

[17] LTR 201227002 (Mar. 1, 2012).

[18] Rev. Proc 2012-28, IRB 2012-27, 4.

circumstances, the partners are readily able to buy, sell, or exchange their partnership interests in a manner that is comparable, economically, to trading on an established securities market [Reg. § 1.7704-1(c)(1)].

Reg. § 1.7704-1(c)(2) clarifies further by providing that interests in a partnership are readily tradable on a secondary market if (i) Interests in the partnership are regularly quoted by any person, such as a broker or dealer, making a market in the interests; (ii) Any person regularly makes available to the public (including customers or subscribers) bid or offer quotes with respect to interests in the partnership and stands ready to effect buy or sell transactions at the quoted prices for itself or on behalf of others; (iii) The holder of an interest in the partnership has a readily available, regular, and ongoing opportunity to sell or exchange the interest through a public means of obtaining or providing information of offers to buy, sell, or exchange the interests in the partnership; or (iv) Prospective buyers and sellers otherwise have the opportunity to buy, sell, or exchange interests in the partnership in a reasonable time frame and with the regularity and continuity.

The IRS has concluded that partnerships are not publicly trade if they use a broker-dealer's "matching" service that matches potential buyers and sellers of partnership interests in order to sell limited partnership interests. The IRS concluded that partnership interests sold through the matching service are not traded on an established securities market and are not readily tradable on a secondary market.[19]

¶24,010 EXCLUSION FROM PARTNERSHIP TREATMENT

Partnership tax treatment does not apply to unincorporated groups formed only for investment purposes (and not for the active conduct of a business) if all the other members elect to forgo such tax treatment [Code Sec. 761(a)(1); Reg. § 1.761-2(a)(2)].[20] Nor does partnership treatment apply to unincorporated groups formed only for the joint production, extraction, or use of property (but not for selling services or property produced or extracted) if all of the members so elect. However, the members must be able to compute their income independently of the computation of partnership taxable income [Code Sec. 761(a)(2); Reg. § 1.761-2(a)(3)].

To elect exclusion from partnership treatment, a partnership return must be filed on Form 1065 for the first year the exclusion was elected. The return or a separate statement must indicate that a member is electing exclusion from partnership treatment. Once the election is made, it can be changed only with IRS consent.

Under certain circumstances, a partner can elect a partial exclusion from partnership treatment. A partial exclusion requires IRS consent [Reg. § 1.761-2(c)].

---

19 LTR 201213004 (Nov. 10, 2011).

20 Rev. Rul. 65-118, 1965-1 CB 30.

Neither a complete exclusion nor a partial exclusion exempts the partners from the limitations on a partner's deductions for partnership losses or the rules regarding a partnership's required tax year.

¶24,015 FAMILY PARTNERSHIPS

A *family partnership* is a partnership whose the members are closely related by blood or marriage. Even though some family partnerships may have been created for the sole purpose of reducing the aggregate income taxes that a family unit might otherwise have to pay (by shifting some income to family members who are in lower tax brackets), the IRS recognizes the arrangement if the family members actually own their respective partnership interests. This depends on the member's intent, determined from many factors. These include the agreement, the relationship between the partner and the other parties, the partner's conduct, statements, individual abilities and capital contributions, and the control and use of income.[21]

> ▶ **OBSERVATION:** If an under-age-18 child owns his or her partnership interest, the child's partnership income may be taxed at the parent's rate, rather than at the child's lower rate [¶2170].

.01 Family Partnership Income Generated by Capital

If the partnership is one in which capital is a material income-producing factor (e.g., when substantial inventories or investments in plant or machinery are required), your family members are recognized as partners only if they acquired their capital interests in a bona fide manner and have dominion and control over their respective interests. The fact that an interest was purchased from you or another family member (or even was received from you as a gift) does not automatically taint the acquisition [Reg. § 1.704-1(e)(3)]. If a partnership interest was a gift, there are some restrictions on amounts that can be allocated to the recipient as his or her distributive share of partnership income:

- If the donor partner performs services for the partnership, an amount that represents reasonable compensation for your services must be allocated to you before the recipient's distributive share is calculated. No such allocation is required for services performed by nondonor partners; and
- The donee partner's distributive share attributable to the donated capital can't be proportionately greater than the donor's distributive share attributable to the retained capital [Reg. § 1.704-1(e)(3)].

> **NOTE:** For this provision, a partnership interest bought by one member of a family from another is treated as a gift. The term *family* here is limited to husband or wife, ancestors (for example, fathers and grandfathers) and lineal descendants (for example, sons and grandsons), and any trusts for their primary benefit [Code Sec. 704(e)(3); Reg. § 1.704-1(e)(3)(i)(a)].

---

[21] *F.E. Tower*, SCt, 46-1 USTC ¶9189, 327 US 280, 66 SCt 532; *A.L. Lusthaus*, SCt, 46-1 USTC ¶9190, 327 US 293; *W.O. Culbertson*, SCt, 49-1 USTC ¶9323, 337 US 733, 69 SCt 1210.

Example 24-2: Father sold his son a half interest in a partnership having net profits for the year of $50,000. The son performs no duties, while the father contributes services worth $10,000. $30,000 is allocated to the father ($10,000 salary plus 50 percent of the remaining $40,000). $20,000 is allocated to the son. Had the father and son both performed equal significant services, $25,000 would be allocated to each.

The IRS may also disregard the agreement and make an allocation when a donor partner indirectly creates a gift interest in the partnership [Reg. § 1.704-1(e)(3)(ii)]. Thus, if a donor partner gives property to his or her daughter who then transfers it to a partnership consisting of the partner and the daughter, the partner is considered the donor of his or her daughter's interest.

.02 Partnership Income Generated by Services

If the partnership is not one in which capital is a material income-producing factor, the IRS recognizes the family members as partners only if they contribute substantial or vital services to the partnership.

.03 Family Limited Partnerships

The family limited partnership (FLP), in which older family members are general partners and their children are limited partners in a family-owned business, has become a popular tool for shifting the wealth of the older generation to the younger generation at a reduced estate and gift tax cost. The FLP allows taxpayers to take advantage of substantial valuation discounts for lack of marketability and for holding only a minority interest in business assets. These valuation discounts will result in reduced estate taxes. In addition, the FLP may provide these benefits:

- Offer great flexibility in structuring the ownership and control of family businesses;
- Insulate family assets from the claims of creditors; and
- Provide for centralized management of family businesses.

From an income tax standpoint, FLPs avoid the compressed tax rates imposed on trusts as well as the double taxation imposed at both the corporate and shareholder levels.

How the IRS May Attack an FLP

The IRS may attack the FLP by arguing that a bona fide partnership has not been created because the parents transferring the limited partnership interest to their children effectively retained control and use of the underlying assets. As a result the IRS may set aside the FLP and tax the income earned by the FLP to the parents if the facts indicate that true ownership of the partnership was not transferred to the younger generation [Reg. § 1.704-1(e)(2)].

The IRS has become increasingly hostile to using FLPs as estate planning tools. As a result, if you are using FLPs to limit wealth transfer taxes, proceed with extreme caution. You can be sure that the IRS will take a very close look at the deal. They will want to be sure that the FLP passes muster and makes good business sense rather than being just a savvy tax-savings scheme. For further discussion of family limited partnerships, see the *Estate & Gift Tax Handbook* ¶ 261.

PARTNERSHIP INCOME, DEDUCTIONS, CREDITS

¶24,020 HOW A PARTNERSHIP REPORTS INCOME

.01 General Process

Code Sec. 701 provides that a partnership is not subject to tax. Rather, it is a conduit for passing income, deduction, and credit items through to the partners. Partners include their respective distributive shares [¶24,060] of partnership items in their personal income tax returns together with their nonpartnership income.

Information Return

A partnership files an information return on Form 1065, reporting each partner's share of income, credit, and deduction items on Schedule K-1 [¶24,045; Ch. 26]. Form 1065 and Schedule K-1 must be provided to the IRS on magnetic media, unless the partnership has 100 or fewer partners [Code Sec. 6011(e)(2)]. The partnership is subject to a monthly civil penalty ($195 times the number of its partners) for a maximum of 12 months that its return is late or incomplete without reasonable cause [Code Sec. 6698(b)]. The partnership is not liable for the penalty if its failure to file the return is due to reasonable cause.

How a Partnership Reports

First, the partnership segregates and separately states for each partner his or her distributive share of certain items [¶24,040] which have special tax significance. It then takes into account all remaining partnership items and computes its taxable income or loss, allocating to each partner his or her distributive share of that total.

Audit Tax Treatment of Partnership Items

For assessment purposes, the tax treatment of partnership income, loss, deductions and credits is determined at the partnership level [Code Sec. 6221]. Partners must report an item on their individual returns consistently with the way the item is treated on the partnership return [Code Sec. 6222(a)]. The IRS cannot adjust the treatment of an item on a tax return except through a partnership-level proceeding. Rules are provided for converting partnership items to nonpartnership items [Code Secs. 6221-6232].

The person who handles a partnership's tax matters for a specific tax year is called the tax matters partner (TMP). The TMP serves as the partnership's representative in a partnership audit, and deals with any administrative and judicial proceedings facing the partnership.

A designated TMP must be a general partner at the time of the designation, or at some time during the tax year [Code Sec. 6231(a)(7); Reg. § 301.6231(a)(7)-1(b)(1)]. If a partnership fails to designate a general partner as a TMP for a specific tax year, or if the partnership fails to designate a new TMP following the termination of a prior designation, the TMP is determined under default provisions [Reg. § 301.6231(a)(7)-1(a)].

A partnership's TMP for a partnership tax year is designated by completing the "Designation of Tax Matters Partner (TMP)" section on the bottom of page 2 of Form 1065, *U.S. Partnership Return of Income* [Reg. § 301.6231(a)(7)-1(c)]. The designation of a TMP for a partnership's tax year supersedes all prior designations when the subsequent designation is made in a certificate filed either by the current TMP, in a statement filed by general partners with a majority interest, or in a statement filed by partners with an overall majority interest [Reg. § 301.6231(a)(7)-1(h)].

.02 Partnership Tax Preferences

Partnership tax preferences are treated the same as separately stated items: the partnership does not pay any alternative minimum tax, but passes its preference items to the partners. These are included on the individual alternative minimum tax return, Form 6251 [Ch. 16][Code Secs. 55-57].

.03 Partnership's Taxable Income or Loss

Code Sec. 703(a) provides that the taxable income of a partnership is computed in the same manner as an individual's except that certain items of gain, loss, etc. must be separately stated. Moreover, the following deductions may not be claimed by a partnership [Code Sec. 703(a)(2); Reg. § 1.703-1(a)(2)]: (1) the deduction for personal exemption; (2) the standard deduction; (3) the deduction for all state and local taxes paid to foreign countries and to U.S. possessions; (4) the deduction for charitable contributions; (5) the net operating loss deduction; (6) the additional itemized deductions for individuals as follows: expenses for production of income; medical, dental, etc., expenses; expenses for care of certain dependents; alimony; and amounts representing taxes and interest paid to cooperative housing corporation; (7) the deduction for depletion on oil and gas production wells; and (8) the deduction for capital gains and the deduction for capital loss carryover.

.04 Passive Activity Losses and Credits

As a general rule, the passive loss rules provide that partners may apply losses and credits from passive activities only against income and tax from other passive activities [Code Sec. 469]. Partners cannot deduct the excess of their passive losses from an activity over income from all your passive activities against income from other sources like salaries, wages, professional fees, or income from an active business.

.05 Suspended Passive Activity Losses

These losses and credits remain suspended until: (1) the partner has passive income to offset the passive loss; or (2) the partner disposes of his or her entire interest in a passive activity in a fully taxable transaction. Suspended passive activity losses attributable to the activity and losses recognized on the disposition may be deducted from active and portfolio income. Limited partners can use suspended passive activity losses in excess of passive income in the year of disposition to offset the ordinary-income component recognized under Code Sec. 751 and other short-term and long-term gains. The passive loss rules affect individuals, estates, trusts, some closely held C corporations and personal service corporations [Code Sec. 469(a)(2)]. Even though the passive loss rules do not apply to partnerships directly, they do apply to each individual partner. See ¶ 13,090 for an in depth discussion of passive activity loss rules.

.06 Treatment of Organization and Syndication Fees

A partnership or any partner is not generally allowed a deduction for any amounts paid or incurred, directly or indirectly, to organize a partnership or to promote the sale of, or to sell, an interest in the partnership [Code Sec. 709; Reg. § 1.709-1]. However, a partnership may elect to deduct up to $5,000 of expenditures, reduced by the amount by which the expenditures exceed $50,000, with the remaining amount amortized over the 180 month (15 year) period beginning with the month in which the partnership begins business [Code Sec. 709(b)].

Beginning Business

Ordinarily, a partnership begins business when it starts the business operation for which it was organized. The mere signing of a partnership agreement alone is not sufficient to show the beginning of business. If the activities of the partnership have advanced to the extent necessary to establish the nature of its business operations, it will be deemed to have begun business. Accordingly, the acquisition of operating assets which are necessary to the type of business contemplated may constitute beginning business for these purposes. The term "operating assets," as used here, means assets that are in a state of readiness to be placed in service within a reasonable period following their acquisition [Reg. § 1.709-2(c)].

Organizational Expenses Defined

The organizational expenses are defined as expenditures which (1) are incident to the creation of the partnership; (2) are chargeable to capital account; and (3) are of a character which, if spent incident to the creation of a partnership having an ascertainable life, would be amortized over such life [Code Sec. 709(b)(3); Reg. § 1.709-2(a)].

An expenditure which fails to meet one or more of these three tests does not qualify as an organizational expense for purposes of Code Sec. 709(b). To satisfy the statutory requirements, the expense must be incurred during the period beginning at a point which is a reasonable time before the partnership begins business and ending with the date prescribed by law for filing the partnership return (determined without regard to any extensions of time) for the tax year the partnership begins business. In addition, the expenses must be for creation of the partnership and not for operation or starting the operation of the partnership trade or business [Reg. § 1.1709-2(a)].

In addition, the expense must be for an item of a nature normally expected to benefit the partnership throughout the entire life of the partnership. The following are examples of organizational expenses within the meaning of Code Sec. 709: legal fees for services incident to the organization of the partnership, such as negotiation and preparation of a partnership agreement; accounting fees for services incident to the organization of the partnership; and filing fees [Reg. § 1.709-2(a)].

The following are examples of expenses that are not organizational expenses (regardless of how the partnership characterizes them): expenses connected with acquiring assets for the partnership or transferring assets to the partnership; expenses connected with the admission or removal of partners other than at the time the partnership is first organized; expenses connected with a contract relating to the operation of the partnership trade or business (even where the contract is between the partnership and one of its members); and syndication expenses [Reg. § 1.709-2(a)].

Syndication Fees Defined

Syndication expenses are expenses connected with the issuing and marketing of interests in the partnership. Examples of syndication expenses are brokerage fees; registration fees; legal fees of the underwriter or placement agent and the issuer (the general partner or the partnership) for securities advice and for advice pertaining to the adequacy of tax disclosures in the prospectus or placement memorandum for securities law purposes; accounting fees for preparation of representations to be included in the offering materials; and printing costs of the prospectus, placement memorandum, and other selling and promotional material. These expenses must be capitalized [Reg. § 1.709-2(b)].

Liquidation of Partnership

If there is a winding up and complete liquidation of the partnership prior to the end of the amortization period, the unamortized amount of organizational expenses is a partnership deduction in its final tax year to the extent provided under Code Sec. 165 (relating to losses). However, there is no partnership deduction for capitalized syndication expenses [Reg. § 1.709-1(b)(3)].

Time and Manner of Making Election

A partnership is deemed to have made an election under Code Sec. 709(b) to amortize organizational expenses for the year in which the partnership begins business. Thus, the partnership does not need to formally elect to deduct organizational expenses. A partnership may choose to forgo the deemed election by affirmatively electing to capitalize its organizational expenses on a timely filed federal income tax return (including extensions) for the tax year in which the partnership begins business. The election either to amortize organizational expenses or to capitalize organizational expenses is irrevocable and applies to all organizational expenses of the partnership. A change in the characterization of an item as an organizational expense is a change in method of accounting to which Code Secs. 446 and 481(a) apply if the partnership treated the item consistently for two or more tax years. A change in the determination of the tax year in which the partnership begins business also is treated as a change in method of accounting if the partnership amortized organizational expenses for two or more tax years [Reg. § 1.709-1(b)(2)].

Example 24-3: Partnership X incurs $3,000 of organizational expenses after October 22, 2006, and begins business on July 1, 2013. Partnership X is deemed to have elected to amortize organizational expenses under Code Sec. 709(b) in 2013. Therefore, Partnership X may deduct the entire amount of the organizational expenses in 2013, the tax year in which Partnership X begins business [Reg. § 1.709-1(b)(4), Ex. 1].

Example 24-4: The facts are the same as in the example above except that Partnership X incurs organizational expenses of $41,000. Partnership X is deemed to have elected to amortize organizational expenses under Code Sec. 709(b) in 2013. Therefore, Partnership X may deduct $5,000 and the portion of the remaining $36,000 that is allocable to July through December of 2013 ($36,000/180 × 6 = $1,200) in 2013, the tax year in which Partnership X begins business. Partnership X may amortize the remaining $34,800 ($36,000 - $1,200 = $34,800) ratably over the remaining 174 months [Reg. § 1.709-1(b)(4), Ex. 2].

¶24,025 ELECTIONS AFFECTING COMPUTATION OF INCOME

Most elections affecting the computation of partnership income are made by the partnership and bind all the partners [Code Sec. 703(b); Reg. § 1.703-1(b)]. Elections to be made at the partnership level include those concerning the method of accounting to be used in computing partnership income, the method for computing depreciation on partnership property, the option not to use the installment sales method of reporting, the option to expense depreciable property under Code Sec. 179, the amortization of certain organization fees, and the amortization of business start-up costs. Some elections are made by individual partners rather than the partnership and a list of these elections is provided in Code Sec. 703(b). A partner may separately elect to: (1) claim an unlimited deduction on an optional basis for exploration expenses (except for oil and gas), provided that the amount deducted is recaptured once a mine reaches productions stage or is sold under Code Sec. 617 [Code Sec. 703(b)(2); ¶12,195]; (2) use his distributive share of taxes paid or accrued by the partnership to foreign countries and possessions of the United States as a credit or deduction under Code Sec. 901 [Code Sec. 703(b)(3)]; or (3) make the election to apply reductions of asset basis in connection with debt discharges excluded from income to first reduce asset basis under Code Sec. 108(b)(5), and may make separate elections with respect to qualified real property business indebtedness under Code Sec. 108(c)(3) [Code Sec. 703(b)(1)].

¶24,030 BOOK PROFIT AND TAXABLE INCOME DISTINGUISHED

A partnership's book profit should be distinguished from its taxable income. Many items enter into the determination of book profit that are not considered in figuring taxable income. For example, the items listed in ¶24,020 or items exempt from tax such as interest on municipal and state obligations do not affect partnership taxable income; yet under ordinary methods of accounting, they are taken into account in figuring book profit.

> ▶ **OBSERVATION:** When the partnership return is prepared directly from the books, it is easy for errors to occur by neglecting to exclude or include certain items. It is best first to determine the partnership's taxable income as it will appear in the partnership return by taking the regular profit and loss statement and either decreasing or increasing the book profit or loss, as required.

Example 24-5: The profit and loss statement of the Smith & Brown partnership for the tax year is as follows:

Gross receipts from sales	$316,418
Less cost of goods sold	173,618
Gross profit	$142,800

Interest received from taxable bonds and banks		1,000
Interest (tax exempt)		3,200
Short-term capital gain		1,600
Long-term capital gain		4,400
Gross profit and misc. income items		$153,000
Deduct:		
Charitable contributions	$ 3,000	
Partners' salaries ($12,500 for each partner)	25,000	
Other operating expenses	15,000	43,000
Net profit from operations and capital transactions		$110,000
Deduct interest on capital		10,000
Net profit for the year		$100,000

From this profit and loss statement, the taxable income of the Smith & Brown partnership is figured as follows:

Book profit (from profit and loss statement)		$100,000
Capital gains and losses segregated:		
Book gains on short-term transactions	$ 1,600	
Book gains on long-term transactions	4,400	
Subtract net book gain (add back net book loss) on capital asset transactions		6,000
		$94,000
Segregated income items:		
Tax-exempt interest	$ 3,200	
Subtract total segregated income items		3,200
		$90,800
Deductions not allowed:		
Charitable contributions	$ 3,000	
Add back total deductions not allowed		3,000
Partnership's taxable income		$ 93,800

The taxable income and the segregated items of the partnership would appear on the partnership return as follows:

Ordinary income	$93,800
Net gain from short-term capital asset transactions	1,600
Net gain from long-term capital asset transactions	4,400
Charitable contributions	3,000

FIGURING A PARTNER'S TAX LIABILITY

¶24,035 HOW PARTNERS DETERMINE THEIR TAX LIABILITIES

A partnership's taxable income is first computed and the character of the income determined at the partnership level. Partnership income is computed and reported on Form 1065, which is an information return used to report the income, gains, losses, deductions, and credits from the operation of a partnership. A partnership does not pay tax on its income but passes through any profits or losses to its partners. Partners must then include the partnership items on their individual income tax returns. A partnership computes taxable income in the same manner as an individual, except that certain deductions that individuals may claim may not be claimed by partnerships.

A partnership must segregate certain items of income and deductions before computing its taxable income. These items, which are outlined in Code Sec. 702 are stated separately on the Schedule K of Form 1065 according to the portion allocated to each partner. In turn, each partner is required to separately state these items on the partner's individual income tax return. [See ¶ 24,040]. Individual partners' separately stated items are allocated on Schedule K-1, which the partnership must give to each partner. Remaining income and deductions are aggregated and reported as the partnership's income or loss.

.01 Partners Must Pay Tax on Undistributed Partnership Income

A partner must pay income tax on his or her distributive share of partnership earnings in the year the partnership earns the income, regardless of whether the partner actually receives his or her distributive share. It is well settled that partners' distributions are taxed in the year the partnership receives its earnings, regardless of whether the partners actually receive their share of partnership earnings: "Few principles of partnership taxation are more firmly established than that no matter the reason for nondistribution each partner must pay taxes on his distributive share."[22] Reg. § 1.702-1 provides that a partner must separately account for his distributive share of partnership income "whether or not distributed." Consistent with this long-standing principle, courts have uniformly held that partners must currently recognize in their individual incomes their proportionate shares of partnership income, even if the partnership income was not actually distributed to them for any reason, including disputes, consensual arrangements, ignorance, concealment, or force of law.[23]

In *Burke*,[24] a partner was required to report his distributive share of partnership income on his individual income tax return even though he had not received the funds. The

[22] *J.A. Basye*, SCt, 73-1 USTC ¶ 9250, 410 US 441, 93 SCt 1080.

[23] *D.B. Heiner*, SCt, 38-2 USTC ¶ 9311, 304 US 271, 58 SCt 926; *N.S. Goldberger Est.*, CA-3, 54-1 USTC ¶ 9359, 213 F2d 78; *A.H. Earle*, CA-1, 38 F2d 965.

[24] *T.J. Burke*, CA-1, 2007-1 USTC ¶ 50,497, 485 F3d 171, *aff'g*, 90 TCM 635, Dec. 56,231(M), TC Memo. 2005-297.

court rejected the taxpayer's contention that his distributive share should not be taxed because it was placed in an escrow account pending the outcome of litigation over a dispute between the two partners. The court's conclusion was not changed by the fact that the taxpayer had no access to funds in the escrow account. Even a self-imposed restriction on the partner's access to the funds received by the partnership could not change the result.

.02 Net Operating Loss Deduction of Partner

For the purpose of determining a net operating loss deduction under Code Sec. 172, a partner must take into account his distributive share of partnership income, gain, loss, deduction, or credit. The character of any such item shall be determined as if such item were realized directly from the source from which realized by the partnership, or incurred in the same manner as incurred by the partnership. To the extent necessary to determine the allowance of the nonbusiness deductions of a partner (arising from both partnership and nonpartnership sources), the partner shall separately take into account his distributive share of the deductions of the partnership which are not attributable to a trade or business and combine such amount with his nonbusiness deductions from nonpartnership sources. The partner shall also separately take into account his distributive share of the gross income of the partnership not derived from a trade or business and combine such amount with his nonbusiness income from nonpartnership sources [Reg. § 1.702-2.]

¶24,040 SEPARATELY STATED ITEMS

A partnership segregates certain items that have special tax significance from the rest of its income, gains, losses, deductions, and credits so that each partner may take his or her distributive share of those items into account in completing an individual tax return. A partner's share of each separately stated item takes the same character it would have if the partner had realized it directly [Code Sec. 702; Reg. § 1.702-1(b)].

The regulations list specific items that must be separately stated. These include capital gains and losses, gains and losses from Sec. 1231 property, charitable contributions, dividends, foreign taxes paid by your partnership, and tax-exempt interest [Reg. § 1.702-1(a)]. However, the list in the regulations is not comprehensive. The regulations also provide that a partnership must separately state any items of income, gain, loss, deduction, or credit subject to a special allocation under the partnership agreement which differs from the allocation of partnership taxable income or loss generally [Reg. § 1.702-1(a)(8)(i)]. Under Code Sec. 911(a), if any partner is a bona fide resident of a foreign country who may exclude from his gross income the part of his distributive share which qualified as earned income as defined in Code Sec. 911(b), the earned income of the partnership for all partners must be separately stated. Similarly, all relevant items of income or deduction of the partnership must be separately stated for all partners in determining the deductibility of hobby losses.

> ▶ **OBSERVATION:** The list of items that must be separately stated changes as the tax law changes. For example, enactment of the passive loss rules dramatically increased the number of items that must be separately stated by the

partnership and separately reported by each partner. As a result, the most comprehensive listing of separately stated items is found in the partnership return schedules (Form 1065, Schedules K and K-1) for a given year [¶24,045].

Among the more significant items that must be separately stated by the partnership are ones described here.

.01 Capital Gains and Losses

A partnership reports the entire amount of its net recognized gain or loss from short-term transactions and the entire amount of its net recognized gain or loss from long-term transactions in the capital gain and loss schedule of its partnership return (Schedule D of Form 1065). Each partner must pick up his or her share of these gains and losses from the distribution schedule [¶24,045] and include them in his or her individual return *whether or not the gains and losses are distributed* [Code Sec. 702(a)(1), (2); Reg. § 1.702-1(a)(1), (2)]. Short-term or long-term treatment depends on the length of time the partnership held the asset, not the length of time the partnership interest was held.[25]

A partner's share of partnership capital loss is limited to the adjusted basis (before reduction by the current year's losses) of the partner's partnership interest at the end of the partnership year in which the loss occurred. If a partner's total losses exceed the partner's adjusted basis, the partner must allocate adjusted basis among his or her shares of partnership short-term and long-term capital losses, as well as Sec. 1231 losses and ordinary losses. Any excess can be deducted in later partnership years to the extent of the adjusted basis in those years [¶24,055] [Code Sec. 704(d)].

Example 24-6: Mr. Brenner is an equal partner in the MNO partnership. Without regard to any losses during the year, he has an adjusted basis for his partnership interest at the end of the tax year of $5,000. His current year's distributive share of MNO losses is $2,000 of short-term capital losses and $4,000 of ordinary losses. Brenner is allowed only 83.33 percent ($5,000/$6,000) of each loss, or $1,667 (83.33% × $2,000) of short-term capital loss and $3,333 (83.33% × $4,000) of ordinary loss. Brenner can carry forward $333 as a short-term capital loss and $667 as an ordinary loss.

.02 Sales, Exchanges, and Involuntary Conversions of Business Property (Sec. 1231 Assets)—Casualty and Theft Losses

A partner must take into account his or her distributive share of gains and losses from the sale, exchange, or involuntary conversion of Sec. 1231 assets [Ch. 8] and set them off against his or her individual gains and losses of the same type [Code Sec. 702(a)(3); Reg. § 1.702-1(a)(3)].

Example 24-7: A partnership equally owned by Mr. Melon and Mr. Nelson has taxable income of $40,000 and a loss of $9,000 from the sale of trucks used in the business. Melon has a Sec. 1231 gain of $5,000 from the sale of a depreciable asset used in another business he operates as a sole proprietor. He has no other income from this other business. Melon's distributable share of partnership

[25] Rev. Rul. 68-79, 1968-1 CB 310.

taxable income is $20,000 (50% of $40,000). He also has capital gain of $500 ($5,000 from the depreciable assets less $4,500, his share of the partnership Sec. 1231 loss).

Gains and losses from partnership casualties and thefts are also passed through separately to you and the other partners. You include your partnership gains and losses from casualties and thefts with the same type of casualty and theft gains and losses from other sources when determining how they should be treated [Ch. 8].

Sec. 1231 losses are limited by your adjusted basis, as discussed above.

.03 Passive Income and Deductions

In order for a partner to correctly apply the passive activity limitations, the partnership must report income or loss and credits separately for each of the following types of activities and income: trade or business activities; rental real estate activities; rental activities other than real estate; and portfolio income (income, dividends, royalties, etc.) and related deductions [Ch. 13].

When a partnership incurs an interest expense, the partner must treat the passed-through expense as a passive loss if the business is a passive activity. Under the general rule, the partner can use passive losses only to shelter passive income [¶ 24,020, Ch. 13]. However, interest income received on a loan made to the partnership is considered not to be passive income. Thus, if a taxpayer lends money to a partnership, the partner will be barred from using the interest expense paid by the partnership from sheltering the interest income received on the loan. The regulations recharacterize the interest income as passive income. *Result:* Under the regulations, the interest income is tax-free up to the partner's share of partnership interest expense [Reg. § 1.469-7].

.04 Expensing Deduction

In 2013, the maximum amount a taxpayer may expense under Code Sec. 179 is $500,000 and the investment limit is $2 million [Code Sec. 179(b)(2)(B)]. See ¶ 11,045 for further discussion. In the case of property purchased and placed in service by a partnership, the determination of whether the property is Code Sec. 179 property is made at the partnership level. The election to expense the cost of Code Sec. 179 property is made by the partnership [Reg. § 1.179-1(h), (i)].

Example 24-8: Ann owns certain residential rental property as an investment. Ann and others form ABC partnership whose function is to rent and manage such property. ABC partnership purchases and places in service office furniture costing $20,000 to be used in the active conduct of ABC's business. Although the office furniture is used with respect to an investment activity of A, the furniture is being used in the active conduct of ABC's trade or business. Therefore, because the determination of whether property is Code Sec. 179 property is made at the partnership level, the office furniture is Code Sec. 179 property and ABC may elect to expense a portion of its cost under Code Sec. 179 [Reg. § 1.179-1(h)(2)].

The expensing deduction is not claimed as a deduction by the partnership. Rather, it is separately stated and passed through to each partner and the other partners. A partner combines his or her share of the partnership's expensing deduction with his or her own such expenses (or expensing deduction from other partnerships) to determine the amount that the partner can deduct on his or her return. The partner is separately subject to the annual expensing deduction limit [Code Sec. 179(d)(8)]. See ¶ 11,045 for further discussion of expensing deduction.

Generally the basis of a partnership's Code Sec. 179 property must be reduced to reflect the amount of Code Sec. 179 expense elected by the partnership. This reduction must be made in the basis of partnership property even if the limitations of Code Sec. 179(b) and Reg. § 1.179-2 prevent a partner in a partnership from deducting all or a portion of the amount of the Code Sec. 179 expense allocated by the partnership [Reg. § 1.179-2(f)(2)].[26]

.05 Charitable Contributions

A partner deducts his or her proportionate share of partnership's contributions on his or her individual return, within the charitable contribution deduction limitations [¶ 9050] [Code Sec. 702(a)(4); Reg. § 1.702-1(a)(4)].[27]

> **Example 24-9:** Under a partnership agreement, Ms. Archer's share of partnership income or loss is 2/3. During the year, the partnership made charitable contributions of $12,000. Those contributions are not deductible by the partnership. On her personal income tax return, Archer will include $8,000 (2/3) of the partnership contributions (regardless of the income of the partnership). Suppose Archer also made a personal contribution of $2,000 to her church. Then her deduction for contributions on her individual return is $10,000, provided that amount does not exceed the limitations [¶ 9075].

.06 Investment Interest

The partnership must separately state interest paid or accrued to purchase or carry property held for investment. Each partner combines his or her share of partnership interest with his or her investment interest for purposes of applying the limitation on deductions for investment interest.

.07 Dividends Received

If a partnership has a corporate partner, a special dividends-received deduction is available to that partner for dividends received from eligible corporations by the partnership [Ch. 20]. Therefore, these dividends should be disregarded in figuring the partnership taxable income and allocated among the partners on the distribution schedule [Code Sec. 702(a)(5); Reg. § 1.702-1(a)(5)].

.08 Foreign Taxes Paid

Partners are entitled to a credit or a deduction for taxes paid by the partnership to foreign countries and U.S. possessions [Code Sec. 702(a)(6); Reg. § 1.702-1(a)(6)]. These taxes are not deductible by the partnership in figuring its taxable income. They

---

[26] Rev. Rul. 89-7, 1989-1 CB 178.

[27] The IRS booklet "Cumulative List of Organizations—Contributions to Which Are Deductible" may be obtained from the Superintendent of Documents, Government Printing Office, Wash., DC 20402.

are allocated among the partners. The election to take the foreign taxes paid by the partnership as either a credit or a deduction is made by each partner individually [¶ 24,025].

.09 Special Items

Certain items are disregarded by a partnership in computing its taxable income or loss. These are items of income, gain, loss, deductions or credits that would affect the partner's tax when combined with his or her own item of the same class. Such items are separately stated and allocated to him or her on a distribution schedule. These items include [Reg. § 1.702-1(a)(8)(i)]:

- Recovery of bad debts;
- Prior taxes and delinquency amounts [Ch. 2];
- Medical expenses [¶ 9100];
- Contributions and deductions for partners under self-employed retirement plans [Ch. 3];
- Exploration, soil and water conservation expenditures [Ch. 12];
- Gains and losses from wagering [¶ 13,080];
- Alimony [¶ 2150];
- Income, gain or loss to the partnership in a disproportionate distribution [¶ 24,125];
- Taxes and interest paid to cooperative housing corporations [Ch. 9];
- Intangible drilling and development costs [¶ 12,195]; and
- Any items subject to a special allocation under the partnership agreement that differs from the allocation of partnership taxable income or loss generally [¶ 24,060].

.10 Tax Credits

Instead of the partnership claiming available tax credits, a distributive share of each credit is passed on to each partner [Code Sec. 702(a)(7); Reg. § 1.702-1(a)(8)(ii)]. The allocation is made according to the partner's interest in the partnership's general profits, unless the partnership agreement requires a special allocation as discussed in ¶ 24,060.

Foreign Tax Credits

Partnerships must allocate foreign taxes in the same way that they allocate the income to which the taxes relate. Under Code Sec. 901(b)(5), an individual who is a partner qualifies for the foreign tax credit for his proportionate share of taxes that the partnership paid or accrued during the tax year to a foreign country or U.S possession. Under Code Sec. 706(a)(6), each partner takes into account separately his distributive share of these taxes of the partnership. Partnerships must allocate foreign tax according to the partners' interests in the partnership, in the same manner as the income to which the taxes related is allocated [Reg. § 1.704-1]. The election to claim the foreign tax credit is made by each partner. For further discussion of the foreign tax credit, see Ch. 28.

¶24,045 DISTRIBUTION AND RECONCILIATION SCHEDULES

A partner's distributive share [¶ 24,060]of separately stated items (as well as his or her distributive share of partnership income or loss) is reported on Schedule K-1, Form 1065. The capital accounts of the partners at the beginning and end of the tax year are reconciled on Schedule M, Form 1065. Schedule M-3 may be required instead of M-1. This schedule shows the relationship between the partnership's income and its capital transactions for the year. The items needed for the schedule are found in the partnership's balance sheet and distribution schedule. Each partner's capital account is reconciled on Schedule K-1, Form 1065.

¶24,050 TAKING PARTNERSHIP INCOME OR LOSS INTO ACCOUNT

After a partner picks up his or her distributive shares of separately stated items, the partner picks up his or her distributive share of partnership taxable income or loss. If the partner receives a distribution of money in excess of the adjusted basis of his or her interest in the partnership and recognizes gain under Code Sec. 731(a), for purposes of characterizing the gain under Code Sec. 469, the gain is treated as gain from the sale or exchange of a partnership interest under Temp. Reg. § 1.469-2T(e)(3)].[28]

¶24,055 LOSS IS LIMITED

If a partnership sustained a loss for the tax year, the partner's distributive share of the loss cannot exceed the adjusted basis of his or her partnership interest [Code Sec. 704(d)]. If a partner's distributive share of the loss is greater than the partner's adjusted basis of his or her partnership interest, the partners may take the excess as a deduction in later years, provided adjusted basis at that time is more than zero before the carryover loss is taken into account.

Example 24-10: Mr. Alfred and Ms. Bonnet form a partnership. They are equal partners. Alfred contributes $5,000. Bonnet contributes property worth $5,000, but with a basis to her of $1,000. The first year's operations result in a loss of $3,000. Alfred has a loss of $1,500, but Bonnet, whose loss is limited to her basis, can take only $1,000. Alfred has a basis for his partnership interest of $3,500 ($5,000 less $1,500 loss); Bonnet's basis is zero. If Bonnet later contributes $500 to the partnership, then she can take the remaining $500 loss at the end of the year she contributes.

[28] Rev. Rul. 95-5, 1995-1 CB 100.

.01 Limit Under At-Risk Rules

A partner's loss deduction generally cannot exceed the amount the partner has at risk in the activity at the end of the year [Ch. 13]. However, a partnership's nonrecourse financing (i.e., loans for which no one is personally liable) secured by real estate may increase the amount at risk if the financing is qualified nonrecourse debt for both the partner and the partnership. (This is true even for a limited partner.) Nonrecourse loans are generally qualified if made by a federal, state or local government or a lender regularly engaged in the business of lending money—but usually not a lender related to the borrower or one interested in the transaction. The amount at risk cannot be more than the total amount of the qualified nonrecourse financing at the partnership level [Code Sec. 465(b)(6)(C)].

.02 Limit Under Passive Activity Loss Rules

Losses from passive activities [Ch. 13, ¶ 24,020] may also be subject to the at-risk rules. If so, the at-risk rules are applied first to determine whether the partner is entitled to claim the loss [Temp. Reg. § 1.469-2T(d)(6)(i)]. If the loss is deductible under the at-risk rules, the passive activity rules then apply. On Form 6198, *At-Risk Limitations,* partners compute the amount at-risk and then carry the loss over to Form 8582 to determine the passive activity loss.

.03 Disallowance of Partnership Loss Duplication

The ability of partnerships to shift or duplicate losses is limited in two ways: (1) by restricting partnership allocations traceable to built-in loss property and (2) by limiting basis adjustments under Code Secs. 743 and 734 in *substantial* loss situations. There are some exceptions to these rules for investment and securitization partnerships. The following changes implement these objectives:

- *Allocations with respect to built-in loss property limited to contributing partner.* Code Sec. 704(c)(1)(C) provides that a built-in loss may be taken into account only in determining partnership items allocated to the contributing partner, and not by other partners. The basis of the contributed property in the hands of the partnership will be treated as equal to fair market value at the time of contribution for purposes of determining the amounts of items allocated to other partners. *Built-in loss* is defined as any excess of the adjusted basis of the property over its fair market value at the time of contribution [Code Sec. 704(c)(1)(C)(ii)];
- *Mandatory Code Sec. 743 adjustment to basis of partnership property following transfer of interest if substantial built-in loss exists immediately following transfer.* A partnership must adjust the basis of partnership property following a transfer of a partnership interest to reflect differences in the transferee partner's basis in its partnership interest and its proportionate share of the adjusted basis of partnership property if the partnership has a substantial built-in loss immediately after the transfer [Code Secs. 743(a) and (b)]. This adjustment is mandatory whenever a partnership interest is transferred at a time when the partnership's adjusted basis in the partnership property exceeds the property's fair market value by more than $250,000 [Code Sec. 743(d)]. An alternative basis adjustment rule is provided for electing investment partnerships, described below, and an exception is also provided for securitization partnerships in the sole business of issuing securities.

Example 24-11: ABC sells its partnership interest to XYZ for $400,000 at a time when the partnership property has an adjusted basis of $1.5 million and a fair market value of $1.2 million. The one-third share of the partnership loss allocable to ABC's interest is $100,000; however, the partnership as a whole has a $300,000 loss. Immediately following the transfer, there is a substantial built-in loss with respect to the interest because the partnership's adjusted basis in its property ($1.5 million) exceeds its fair market value ($1.2 million) by more than $250,000. The partnership will be required to make an adjustment to the adjusted basis of the partnership property with respect to XYZ. Thus, XYZ will recognize no gain or loss if the partnership immediately sells its property for fair market value.

a. The $250,000 threshold for measuring a substantial built-in loss applies regardless of the dollar value of the partnership property. There is no alternative percentage-based safe harbor in the definition of substantial built-in loss. A substantial built-in loss exists if the partnership's adjusted basis in the property exceeds its fair market value by more than $250,000 [Code Sec. 743(d)(1)].

b. *Alternative rules for electing investment partnerships.* An electing investment partnership is not treated as having a substantial built-in loss, and thus is not required to make basis adjustments to partnership property in the case of a transfer of a partnership interest [Code Sec. 743(e)(1)]. An *electing investment partnership* is defined as a partnership that (1) makes an election to have this subsection apply; (2) would be an investment company under section 3(a)(1)(A) of the Investment Company Act of 1940 but for an exemption available under Code Sec. 743; (3) has never been engaged in a trade or business; (4) holds substantially all of its assets for investment; (5) has contributed assets at least 95 percent of which consist of money; (6) allows no assets contributed to the partnership to have an adjusted basis in excess of fair market value at the time of contribution; (7) issues all partnership interests of the partnership pursuant to a private offering before the date which is 24 months after the date of the first capital contribution to the partnership; (8) has a partnership agreement that provides for substantive restrictions on each partner's ability to cause a redemption of the partner's interest; and (9) has a partnership agreement that provides for a term that is not in excess of 15 years [Code Sec. 743(e)(6)].

c. In place of the partnership level basis adjustment, the electing investment partnership members must apply a partner-level loss limitation rule which disallows the transferee partner's distributive share of losses from the sale or exchange of partnership property, except to the extent it can be established that the transferee's share of losses exceeds the loss recognized by the transferor partner (i.e., that the loss has not been duplicated by transferring the partnership interest) [Code Sec. 743(e)(2)]. The amount of the loss is reduced by the amount of any basis reduction required to be taken under Code Sec. 732(a)(2) [Code Sec. 743(e)(5)]. Under Code Sec. 732(a)(2), the basis of the property in the hands of the distributee partner cannot exceed the adjusted basis of his or her partnership interest, reduced by any money distributed in the same transaction. The disallowance applies even if the partnership is terminated under Code Sec. 708 [Code Sec. 743(e)(4)].

d. The partner-level loss limitation also restricts the ability of the transferee to transfer any losses through successive transfers of the partnership interest (except to the extent that the losses are not duplicated losses or losses offset by a prior disallowance) [Code Sec. 743(e)(2)]. Investment partnership losses disallowed under the partner-level loss limitation rule do not decrease the transferee partner's basis in its partnership interest [Code Sec. 743(e)(3)].

e. *Furnishing information to transferee partners.* An electing investment partnership is required to furnish information to any partner subject to the loss limitation rule of Code Sec. 743(e)(2) sufficient to enable the partner to compute the amount of disallowed losses [Code Sec. 6031(f)].

f. *Exception for securitization partnerships.* A securitization partnership is not treated as having a substantial basis reduction in the case of a partnership distribution, and thus is not required to make basis adjustments to partnership property [Code Sec. 734(e)]. A securitization partnership is any partnership the sole business activity of which is to issue securities that provide for a fixed principal (or similar) amount and that are primarily serviced by the cash flows of a discrete pool (either fixed or revolving) of receivables or other financial assets. These receivables or other financial asset must, by their terms, convert into cash in a finite period, but only if the sponsor of the pool reasonably believes that the receivables and other financial assets composing the pool are not acquired to be disposed of. An electing investment partnership is required to place substantive restrictions on each partner's ability to cause a redemption [Code Sec. 743(e)(6)(H)].

g. *Failure to continue to meet the definition of electing investment partnership or securitization partnership.* An electing investment partnership or securitization partnership that subsequently fails to meet the definition of an electing investment partnership or securitization partnership will be subject to the regular partnership basis adjustment rules (including mandatory basis adjustments in cases where there is a substantial built-in loss) as of the first transfer of a partnership interest that occurs after the partnership ceases to meet the applicable definition.

- *Mandatory Code Sec. 734 adjustment to basis of partnership property following distribution of property with a substantial basis reduction.* A partnership is required to make downward basis adjustments to the basis of partnership assets under Code Sec. 734 in the case of a distribution when there is a substantial basis reduction [Code Sec. 734(b) and (d)]. A *substantial basis reduction* means a downward adjustment of more than $250,000 that would be made to the basis of partnership assets if a Code Sec. 754 election were in effect. There is no percentage-of-assets alternative to the definition of a substantial basis reduction. There is an exception for securitization partnerships.

Example 24-12: ABC and DEF each contributed $2.5 million to a newly formed partnership, while GHI contributes $5 million. The partnership purchases LMN stock for $3 million and XYZ stock for $7 million. The value of each stock declines to $1 million. LMN stock is distributed to GHI in liquidation of its partnership interest. The basis of LMN stock in GHI's hands is $5 million. GHI would recognize a loss of $4 million if the LMN stock were sold for $1 million. There is a substantial basis adjustment because the $2 million increase in the adjusted basis of LMN stock is greater than $250,000. The partnership would thus be required to decrease the basis of XYZ stock (under Code Sec. 734(b)(2)) by $2 million (the amount by which the basis LMN stock was increased), leaving a basis of $5 million. If the XYZ stock were then sold by the partnership for $1 million, ABC and DEF would each recognize a loss of $2 million (rather than duplicating GHI's loss with a $6 million loss to split between them).

Electing Investment Partnerships: Reporting Requirements

Notice 2005-32[29] generally requires partners and partnerships to report their required basis adjustments as though an election under Code Sec. 754 had been made. Partnerships that are required to reduce their basis in partnership property following a transfer of a partnership interest must attach an informational statement to their annual return, as described in Reg. § 1.743-1(k)(1). The transferee must provide certain information to the partnership within 30 days of the transfer (or if the transfer occurs upon the death of a partner, within one year of the death of the deceased partner), as described in Reg. § 1.743-1(k)(2). The notice also provides rules implementing the partner-level loss disallowance rule that applies instead of the basis adjustment requirement for electing investment partnerships.

¶24,060 HOW TO DETERMINE A PARTNER'S DISTRIBUTIVE SHARE

A partner's share of income, gain, loss, deduction, or credit is determined in accordance with the partnership agreement which will include any changes agreed to by all the partners or made under the terms of the agreement [Code Sec. 704(a)]. Changes for a particular tax year are possible up to the original due date of the partnership tax return for that year [Code Sec. 761(c); Reg. § 1.761-1(c)]. Alternatively, a partner's distributive share of income, gain, loss, deduction, or credit will be determined in accordance with the partner's interest in the partnership if the partnership agreement does not provide as to the partner's distributive share of these items, or the allocation to a partner of these items under the agreement does not have substantial economic effect [Code Sec. 704(b)].

.01 Substantial Economic Effect

The allocation made by the partnership agreement is respected for tax purposes only if it has substantial economic effect [Code Sec. 704(a), Code Sec. 704(b)(2)]. As a general rule, an allocation in the partnership agreement has substantial economic effect if it meets a two-part test [Reg. § 1.704-1(b)(2)]:

---

[29] Notice 2005-32, 2005-1 CB 895.

- The allocation has an economic effect—that is, the partner who receives the allocation actually bears the economic burden or receives the economic benefit that corresponds to the allocation. This requirement is not met unless, throughout the full term of the partnership, (a) the partners' capital accounts are properly maintained, (b) liquidating distributions are made in accordance with the partners' capital account balances, and (c) any partner whose interest is liquidated is unconditionally obligated to restore a deficit capital account balance; and
- The economic effect of the allocation is substantial—that is, the allocation actually affects dollar amounts of the partners' shares of partnership income and loss, independent of tax consequences. To determine the after-tax economic benefit of detriment of an allocation to a partner, the tax consequences that result from the interaction of the allocation with such partner's tax attributes that are unrelated to the partnership are taken into account.

.02 Post-event Partnership Allocations Lack Substantial Economic Effect

Partnership allocations will lack substantial economic effect under Reg. § 1.704-1(b)(2)(iii), if partners amend their partnership agreement to create offsetting special allocations of particular items after the events giving rise to the items occurred.[30] The economic effect of an allocation is not substantial if, at the time that the allocation becomes part of the partnership agreement, the allocation fails each of these two tests:

- The after-tax consequences of at least one partner may, in present value terms, be enhanced compared to the consequences if the allocation (or allocations) were not contained in the partnership agreement; and
- There is a strong likelihood that the after-tax economic consequences of no partner will, in present value terms, be substantially diminished compared to such consequences if the allocation (or allocations) were not contained in the partnership agreement.

There are alternative tests for establishing that a partnership allocation has substantial economic effect [Reg. § 1.704-1(b)(2)(ii)(d)]. Under the alternative test, partnership allocations will have substantial economic effect if the partnership satisfies complicated optional safe harbor provisions. Generally, to satisfy the safe harbor, a partnership must maintain its book capital accounts as set forth by Reg. § 1.704-1 and make tax allocations consistent with the capital accounts.

Capital Account Maintenance Rules

Under the capital account maintenance rules of Reg. § 1.704-1(b)(2)(iv), partnership property is generally reflected on the partnership's books at historic cost, rather than at fair market value. There are, however, various situations in the regulations when partnership property is or may be reflected at fair market value. For example, a partnership may revalue its assets to their current fair market value if there is a contribution to the partnership by a new or existing partner as consideration for an interest in the partnership or a distribution from the partnership to a retiring or continuing partners as consideration for an interest in the partnership.

---

[30] Rev. Rul. 99-43, 1999-2 CB 506.

If the agreement is silent on any item or if the allocation under the agreement lacks substantial economic effect, a partner's distributive share of that item is determined by the partner's interest in the partnership (taking all facts and circumstances into account) [Code Sec. 704(b)].

Example 24-13: Mr. Able and Mr. Seeden were partners in AZ partnership. Able expected to have substantial future capital gains, while Seeden did not. Since capital losses may fully offset capital gains, but are only deductible to the extent they exceed capital gains up to $3,000, Able and Seeden amended their partnership agreement to allocate all capital losses to Able. In turn, Seeden was allocated an equivalent amount of ordinary losses. Because the purpose and effect of the new allocations were solely to reduce taxes without actually affecting shares of partnership income, it would not be recognized. The capital loss items would be allocated between the partners according to their overall share of partnership income or loss.

¶24,065 DISTRIBUTIVE SHARE OF ITEMS DUE TO CONTRIBUTED PROPERTY

When a partner contributes property to a partnership, the partnership's basis in the property generally is the same as the partner's basis in the contributed property [Code Sec. 723]. Income, gain, loss, and deductions (other than depreciation and depletion) for the contributed property are allocated among the contributing partner and the other partners, taking into consideration the difference between the property's basis and its fair market value at the time of the contribution. In this way, the partnership is not used to distort the economic realities of any gain on the sale or exchange of the property. Built-in gain (gain that is attributable to the period from the time the property was acquired to the time the property is contributed to the partnership) is specially allocated to the contributing partner [Code Sec. 704(c)].

Code Sec. 704(c) requires the difference between the fair market value and the adjusted basis of property contributed to a partnership to be allocated to the contributing partner to determine the partner's distributive share of partnership income, gain, loss, or deductions on the subsequent depreciation, depletion, or disposition of the property. The IRS requires that these allocations be made using a reasonable method consistent with the purpose of Code Sec. 704(c): preventing the shifting of tax consequences among partners with respect to precontribution gain or loss.

.01 Anti-Abuse Rule for Contributions of Property

The regulations provide a specific anti-abuse rule for contributions of property to a partnership where the property's value has appreciated or depreciated in the hands of the contributor. A method of allocation will be characterized as unreasonable if the contribution of property and the corresponding allocation of tax items are made with a view to shifting the tax consequences of built-in gain or loss among the partners in a manner that substantially reduces the present value of the partners' aggregate tax liability [Reg. § 1.704-3(a)(10)]. For tax years beginning after June 9, 2010, the tax effect of an allocation method or combination of methods on both direct and indirect partners is considered.

An "indirect partner" is defined as:

- Any direct or indirect owner of a partnership, S corporation, or controlled foreign corporation (CFC) that is a partner,
- A direct or indirect beneficiary of a trust or estate, that is a partner in the partnership, and
- Any consolidated group of which the partner in the partnership is a member [Reg. § 1.704-3(a)(10)(ii)].

TAX YEAR OF A PARTNER AND PARTNERSHIP

¶24,070 CHOICE OF TAX YEAR

.01 General Rules

A partnership and its partners each have their own tax years, which may or may not be the same. A partner is required to include in taxable income his share of any income, gain, loss, deduction, or credits of the partnership for the partnership's tax year that ends within or with his tax year [Code Sec. 706(a)].

This rule could result in a postponement of the tax on partnership income where the partnership uses a fiscal year and the partners use a calendar year.

> ▶ **OBSERVATION:** For example, if a partnership's tax year ended on January 31, a calendar-year partner's income from the partnership would be reported by the partner in his tax year ending on December 31, resulting in an 11-month deferral of income recognition.

> **Example 24-14:** Partner Ann reports income using a calendar year, while the partnership of which Ann is a member reports its income using a fiscal year ending May 31. The partnership reports its income and deductions under the cash method of accounting. During the partnership tax year ending May 31, 2013, the partnership makes guaranteed payments of $120,000 to Ann for services and for the use of capital. Of this amount, $70,000 was paid to A between June 1 and December 31, 2012, and the remaining $50,000 was paid to Ann between January 1 and May 31, 2013. The entire $120,000 paid to Ann is includible in Ann's taxable income for the calendar year 2013 (together with Ann's distributive share of partnership items set forth in Code Sec. 702 for the partnership tax year ending May 31, 2013).

To prevent partners from using the disparity between the partnership's and the partner's tax years to defer the payment of tax, the tax law restricts the partnership's right to choose a fiscal year different from the partner's tax year [Ch. 18].

Tax-Exempt Partners

In determining the tax year of a partnership, a tax-exempt partner is disregarded if it was not subject to tax on any income attributable to its investment in the partnership during the partnership's tax year immediately preceding the current year [Reg. § 1.706-1(b)(5)(i)].

Foreign Partners

A foreign partner is disregarded in determining a partnership's tax year unless the partner is allocated any gross income that is effectively connected income, and the taxation of the income is not otherwise precluded under any U.S. income tax treaty [Reg. § 1.706-1(b)(6)(i)]. The tax year of foreign partners are not disregarded in determining a partnership's tax year if no single partner (other than a disregarded foreign partner) holds a 10 percent or greater interest in the capital or profits of the partnership and if, in the aggregate, the partners that are not disregarded foreign partners do not hold a 20 percent or greater interest in the capital or profits of the partnership [Reg. § 1.706-1(b)(6)(iii)].

.02 Required Tax Year Choices for Partnerships

Unless a partnership establishes a business purpose for a different tax year, the partnership must select one of the three required tax years identified in Code Sec. 706(b)(1)(B), as described here.

Majority Interest Tax Year

The tax year of a partnership must be the *majority interest tax year* which is defined as the tax year (on a specified day) that constituted the tax year of one or more partners having an aggregate interest in profits and capital of more than 50 percent [Code Sec. 706(b)(1)(B)(i)]. This determination is made on testing days, generally the first day of the partnership's current tax year. The IRS is permitted to specify alternative testing days in order to reflect more accurately the ownership of the partnership. If a change of tax year is required under the majority interest rule, then the partnership will not be required to make another change in its tax year for either of the two tax years following the year of the change [Code Sec. 706(b)(4)(B)]. A change in ownership in the partnership may require the partnership to change to a different tax year in order to comply with Code Sec. 706(b)(1)(B).

Principal Partners' Tax Year

If there is no majority interest, the partnership must use the tax year of all its *principal partners* [Code Sec. 706(b)(1)(B)(ii)]. A principal partner is any partner having an interest in profits or capital of five percent or more [Code Sec. 706(b)(3)]. As with the majority interest tax year, a change in ownership of the partnership may result in a different required tax year under the principal partners test.

Least Aggregate Deferral Tax Year

If there is no majority interest tax year or the principal partners do not have the same tax year, the partnership generally must use a tax year that results in the least aggregate deferral of income to the partners [Code Sec. 706(b)(1)(B)(iii); Reg. § 1.706-1(b)(2)].

Example 24-15: Partnership P is on a fiscal year ending June 30. Partner A reports income on the fiscal year ending June 30 and Partner B reports income on the fiscal year ending July 31. A and B each have a 50 percent interest in partnership profits. For its tax year beginning July 1, the partnership will be required to retain its tax year since the fiscal year ending June 30 results in the least aggregate deferral of income to the partners. This determination is made as follows [Reg. § 1.706-1(b)(3)(iv), Ex. 1]:

Test 6/30	*Year End*	*Interest in Partnership Profits*	*Months of Deferral for 6/30 Year End*	*Interest x Deferral*
Partner A	6/30	.5	0	0
Partner B	7/31	.5	1	.5
Aggregate Deferral				.5

Test 7/31	*Year End*	*Interest in Partnership Profits*	*Months of Deferral for 7/31 Year End*	*Interest x Deferral*
Partner A	6/30	.5	11	5.5
Partner B	7/31	.5	0	0
Aggregate Deferral				5.5

Example 24-16: The facts are the same as in Example 24-15 except that Partner *A* reports income on the calendar year and Partner *B* reports on the fiscal year ending November 30. For the partnership's tax year beginning July 1, 1987, the partnership is required to change its tax year to a fiscal year ending November 30 because such year results in the least aggregate deferral of income to the partners. This determination is made as follows [Reg. § 1.706-1(b)(3)(iv), Ex. 2]:

Test 12/31	*Year End*	*Interest in Partnership Profits*	*Months of Deferral for 12/31 Year End*	*Interest x Deferral*
Partner A	12/31	.5	0	0
Partner B	11/30	.5	11	5.5
Aggregate Deferral				5.5

Test 11/30	*Year End*	*Interest in Partnership Profits*	*Months of Deferral for 11/30 Year End*	*Interest x Deferral*
Partner A	12/31	.5	1	.5
Partner B	11/30	.5	0	0
Aggregate Deferral				.5

A partnership may be able to use the natural business year of the partnership or other year if the partnership has a business purpose for using a different tax year [Code Sec. 706(b)(1)(C)].

A partnership may also elect to use a different tax year under Code Sec. 444. A partnership electing a tax year under Code Sec. 444 will be required to make additional payments of tax intended to compensate for any income deferrals resulting from the use of a tax year other than a required tax year.

.03 Tax Year of Newly Formed Partnerships

A newly formed partnership may adopt the following tax years without securing advance IRS approval:

- One of the required tax years (majority interest tax year, principal partners tax year, or least aggregate deferral of income as described above) [Code Sec. 706(b)(1)(B); Reg. § 1.706-1(b)(7)];
- A tax year elected under Code Sec. 444 (as discussed further below); or
- A 52-53-week tax year ending with reference to its required tax year or a tax year elected under Code Sec. 444 without the approval of the IRS.

If, however, a partnership wants to adopt any other tax year, it must establish a business purpose and obtain approval under Code Sec. 442 [Reg. § 1.441-1(c)(2)]. Any other tax year technically requires IRS permission, however, this approval may be automatically granted if the partnership adopts a natural business year. If your newly formed partnership is required to secure prior approval from the IRS for the adoption of a tax year, the partnership must file an application on Form 1128, *Application to Adopt, Change, or Retain a Tax Year*, on or before the last day of the month following the close of the tax year to be adopted. To change a tax year, the partnership must file Form 1128 with the IRS by the 15th day of the second month after the end of the short period for which a return is required because of the change [Reg. §§ 1.442-1(b)(1), 1.706-1(b)].

.04 Tax Year of Partner

A partner is not generally permitted to change to a tax year other than that of a partnership in which he is a principal partner unless he establishes a business purpose for doing so [Code Sec. 706(b)(2)]. A partner may also be eligible to obtain automatic approval to change its tax year under Rev. Proc. 2006-46.[31] Any other change requires prior IRS approval [Reg. § 1.706-1(b)(8)(i)(C)]. Partners may elect to spread their share of income ratably over four years from the partnership's short-year tax return that resulted from a change in year-end.[32]

.05 Automatic Consent Procedures to Adopt, Change, or Retain Tax Year

In Rev. Proc. 2006-46, the IRS provides the exclusive procedures for a partnership to obtain automatic approval to adopt, change, or retain its annual accounting period under Code Sec. 442 and Reg. § 1-442-1(b). Partnerships complying with Rev. Proc. 2006-46 will be deemed to have established a business purpose and obtained IRS approval to adopt, change, or retain its annual accounting period.

Natural Business Year

Automatic consent is also available if the partnership is changing to a natural business year. A tax year is considered a natural business year under this test if, for the three previous tax years, 25 percent or more of the business' gross receipts from sales and services fall within the last two months of the chosen 12-month period. A partnership that meets the gross receipts test will be granted automatic consent to change to its natural business year regardless of whether use of the natural business

[31] Rev. Proc. 2006-46, 2006-2 CB 859.

[32] Rev. Proc. 2003-79, 2003-2 CB 1036.

year results in more deferral of income than the partnership's present tax year. The taxpayer's natural business year is the year in which the highest percentage of gross receipts (larger than 25 percent) falls in the last two months of the period.

.06 Filing Requirements

A partnership that meets the requirements of the 25-percent gross receipts test and thus has automatic consent to use the natural business year, without further action, should file Form 1128, *Application to Adopt, Change or Retain a Tax Year,* by the due date (including extensions) for filing the partnership's federal income tax return for the first effective year. The partnership should include the gross receipts for the most recent 47 months (for itself or its predecessor) to show that the gross receipts test has been met. The request should be identified as an automatic approval request by labeling the form "Filed Under Rev. Proc. 2006-46." The Form 1128 should be mailed to the IRS Service Center where the taxpayer files its return (not to the national office). A copy of the Form 1128 should also be attached to the tax return filed for the first effective year.

A Form 1128 that is filed late may still be considered for processing if the partnership establishes that it acted reasonably and in good faith, and that granting an extension would not jeopardize the government's interests. Except in very unusual and compelling circumstances, an extension of time will ordinarily be denied if the application is received more than 90 days after the time required for filing Form 1128 because it will be considered to jeopardize the government's interests. If the application is received within 90 days after the time required for filing the Form 1128, relief from the late filing may be granted to the taxpayer under Reg. § 301.9100-3(b).

.07 Electing Tax Year Other Than Required Tax Year

A partnership may have a tax year other than its required tax year if it makes an election under Code Sec. 444 to use a 52-53-week tax year that ends with reference to its required tax year or a tax year elected under Code Sec. 444. A fiscal year elected under Code Sec. 444 may generally have a deferral period of no greater than three months or the deferral period of the partnership's current tax year, whichever is shorter [Code Sec. 444(b)(1)]. It is therefore easier for new partnerships to make this election. A member of a tiered structure is not eligible to elect a fiscal year under Code Sec. 444. In order to prevent abuse by an existing partnership wishing to increase the deferral period of its current tax year, a transfer of the partnership's assets to a related party (i.e., in order to create a "new" entity eligible for a maximum three-month deferral period) will be disregarded if its principal purpose was to create a greater deferral period [Temp. Reg. § 1.444-1T(b)(2)].

An Code Sec. 444 election is made by filing Form 8716, *Election to Have a Tax Year Other Than a Required Tax Year.* Code Sec. 7519 payments are required of any partnership that has elected under Code Sec. 444 to have a tax year other than a required tax year. A partnership must file Form 8752, *Required Payment or Refund Under Section 7519,* if it made a Code Sec. 444 election by filing Form 8716 and its election is in effect for the tax year. A partnership that terminates its Code Sec. 444 election or liquidates must also file Form 8752 to claim a refund of its net required payment balance [Code Sec. 7519(c)(3)]. The due date for filing Form 8752 with the required payment is the later of: (1) the 15th of the fifth month following the month that includes the first day of the tax year for which the election will first be effective; or (2) 60 days after the IRS notifies the partnership or S corporation that its request for a tax year based on business purpose has been denied [Temp. Reg. § 1.444-3T(b)].

If the partnership makes such an election, it must make a *required payment* for each year the election is in effect. The required payment represents the value of the tax deferral resulting from the use of the elected tax year. The partnership must report the required payments on Form 8752. The words "ACTIVATING BACK-UP ELECTION" should be typed or printed at the top of Form 8752.

The election remains in effect until it is terminated. The ongoing partnership can terminate its election voluntarily by changing to the required tax year. The election will be terminated by the IRS if the partnership fails to comply with the required payments. If the election is terminated, the partnership cannot make another Section 444 election for any tax year.

¶24,075 WHEN A PARTNERSHIP'S TAX YEAR CLOSES

Except in the case of a termination of a partnership or in the case of a partner whose entire interest in the partnership terminates, the tax year of a partnership shall not close as the result of the death of a partner, the entry of a new partner, the liquidation of a partner's interest in the partnership, or the sale or exchange of a partner's interest in the partnership [Code Sec. 706(c) (1)].

.01 Change of Partners

The tax year of a partnership closes or ends with respect to a partner whose entire interest in the partnership terminates, by death, liquidation, or sale or exchange [Code Sec. 706(c) (2) (A)]. As a result, the deceased partner's income will be reported on the decedent's final income tax return. Sale of less than the partner's entire interest will not result in the termination of the partner's partnership year [Code Sec. 706(c) (2) (B)]. The filing of a final return does not terminate a partnership for tax purposes if partnership agreement wind-up procedures aren't followed, even though the IRS may initially pronounce the "final" return correct. The winding up of the partnership for federal tax purposes must also comply with the winding up procedures specified in the partnership agreement.[33]

> **Example 24-17:** Ms. Allister, Mr. Biller, Mr. Calvin, and Mr. Douglas own equal shares in the ABCD partnership. For the fiscal year ending February 28, the partnership has a taxable income of $124,000. Allister, who reports on the calendar-year basis, dies July 4. Allister's final return includes the income earned by the partnership in its fiscal tax year ending February 28 and the income earned in the short period March 1 through July 4.

[33] *Harbor Cove Marina Partners Partnership*, 123 TC 64, Dec. 55,695 (2004).

A partnership's tax year does not close for a partner who makes a gift of his or her partnership interest. Income attributable to the interest up to the date of the gift is allocated to the donor.

> **Example 24-18:** Again assume the same partnership as in Example 24-17, but with Allister living. On November 30, Allister sells her entire interest. The partnership's tax year ends on November 30, as to Allister. On her return for the year which is due on April 15, Allister must include her share of partnership income for the partnership year ending October 31, and her share of partnership income for the short year, November 1, to November 30. Biller, Calvin, and Douglas are not affected by the sale and the partnership tax year does not close early for them.

.02 When a Partnership Ends

If a partnership *terminates,* its tax year closes for all partners. A partnership terminates only if (1) its operations cease, or (2) 50 percent or more of the total interest in both capital and profits is sold or exchanged within a 12-month period. There may be a "winding up period" after the partners agree to dissolve the firm [Code Sec. 708(b)(1); Reg. § 1.708-1(b)].

The gift, bequest, inheritance, or liquidation of a partnership interest is not a sale or exchange for termination purposes [Reg. § 1.708-1(b)(1)(ii)]. Thus, 50 percent or more of the partnership's assets may be distributed in liquidation of a partner's interest without terminating your partnership. But a contribution of property to a partnership, followed shortly by a distribution, may constitute a sale or exchange [Reg. § 1.731-1(c)(3)].

> ▶ **OBSERVATION:** The partnership business is not considered to end on the death of one member of a two-man partnership, if the deceased partner's estate or successor continues to share in the profits and losses of the partnership [Reg. § 1.708-1(b)].

When a partnership terminates under Code Sec. 708(b)(1)(B), the terminating partnership is treated as if that partnership first contributes all of its assets and liabilities to a new partnership in exchange for an interest in the new partnership. Following that, the terminated partnership immediately liquidates by distributing interest in the new partnership to the purchaser and the other remaining partners. Following the liquidation, the business is continued by the new partnership or it is dissolved.

The capital accounts of the partners in the old partnership will carry over intact into the new partnership [Reg. § 1.704-1(b)(2)(iv)(l)]. In addition, the deemed contribution of assets and liabilities by the old partnership to the new partnership will be disregarded in determining the capital accounts in the new partnership.

The new partnership will retain the taxpayer identification number (TIN) of the old partnership, unless it has already applied for and obtained a new TIN [Reg. § 301.6109-1(d)(2)(iii)].

The purchaser of an appreciated partnership interest will need to be sure the partnership has (or will make) an *optional adjustment to basis* election so that the purchaser can get a step-up for the purchaser's share of the basis of property inside the partnership. Under the old rules, this happened automatically because of the prior deemed distribution and contribution rules [Reg. § 1.708-1(b)(1)].

Example 24-19: Betty and Barbara each have a $100 outside basis in their equal partnership, BB. The partnership has a $200 basis in its assets. Jim purchase's Betty's interest for $400. Under the old rules, Jim and Barbara would have bases of $400 and $100, respectively, in their interests in BB and the partnership would have a $500 basis in its assets. Under the final regulations, the partners' bases in their partnership interests would be the same, but BB would have only a $200 basis in its assets unless old BB made an Code Sec. 754 election with its final return. The new partnership would have to make its own election, so that old BB's Code Sec. 754 election would not carry over to the new partnership.

.03 When Partnerships Merge and Divide

When partnerships merge or consolidate, the tax year of the new partnership is considered a continuation of the tax year of the merging partnership whose members own an interest of more than 50 percent in the capital and profits of the new partnership. The tax years of partnerships whose members own 50 percent or less interest in the new partnership are closed. If none of the members of the merging partnerships has an interest of more than 50 percent in the resulting partnership, the partnership starts with a new tax year [Code Sec. 708(b)(2); Reg. § 1.708-1(b)(2)(i)].

Example 24-20: Partnerships AB and CD merge and form partnership ABCD. Partners A and B each own 30 percent and partners C and D each own 20 percent interest in the new partnership. Because partners A and B together own an interest of more than 50 percent in the new partnership, partnership ABCD is considered a continuation of Partnership AB and takes its tax year. Partnership CD's tax year is closed on the merger.

A partnership merger or division must fall within one of two prescribed forms in order to be respected: the assets-over form merger, or the assets-up form merger. In an *assets-over merger,* the partnership that is considered terminated contributes all its assets and liabilities to the resulting partnership in exchange for an interest in the partnership; these interests are then distributed to the partners in liquidation of the terminated partnership [Reg. § 1.708-1(c)(3)(i)]. An *assets-up merger* is accomplished by distributing the assets of the terminating partnership to its partners in a liquidating distribution, following which the partners contribute the assets and liabilities to the resulting (new) partnership [Reg. § 1.708-1(c)(3)(ii)].

Divisions of partnerships take similar forms: either the severed partnership assets and liabilities are transferred in exchange for a partnership interest in the resulting entity, which is distributed to the partners (an assets-over division); or the prior partnership distributes certain assets to some or all of its partners, who then contribute the assets to a new resulting partnership (an assets-up division) [Reg. § 1.708-1(d)(3)].

In order to have a partnership division, at least two members of the prior partnership must be members of each resulting partnership that exists after the transaction. Thus, a transaction in which one of three partners separates from the business and forms a new partnership with a fourth party would not be treated as a division.

Note that mergers or divisions may not be accomplished through a bifurcation of the two forms—with some partners receiving assets and others receiving interests in the new partnership. Instead, each partner must participate in a partnership merger in the same manner. When more than two partnerships are combined, however, each combination will be viewed as a separate merger and each may be achieved using a different form (assets-over or assets-up). Divisions of a single partnership into multiple partnerships will similarly be viewed as separate transactions.

A partnership resulting from a merger of partnerships is deemed the continuation of any merging partnership whose members own more than 50 percent of the capital and profits interests [Code Sec. 708(b)(2)(A)]. Partnerships resulting from a merger or division of partnerships are considered continuations of the former partnership if the members of the resulting partnership had an interest of 50 percent or more of the prior partnership's capital and profits interests [Code Sec. 708(b)(2)(B)]. Any other resulting partnership is considered a new partnership. If the members of none of the resulting partnerships owned an interest of more than 50 percent in the capital and profits of the prior partnership, none of the resulting partnerships are considered a continuation of the prior partnership and the prior partnership is considered terminated [Reg. § 1.708-1(b)(2)(ii)].

Example 24-21: In Letter Ruling 200229031, six partnerships merged into one limited liability company (LLC) that was taxed as a partnership. The LLC is deemed to be the continuation of the partnership that contributed assets having the greatest fair market value. As such, the depreciation methods and useful lives of property from that partnership would not change. The LLC would take a carryover basis in the properties contributed by the other partnerships, and to the extent the property contributed was placed in service before 1981, their depreciation methods and useful lives would not be affected by the merger.

If more than one partnership resulting from a division is treated as continuing, the resulting partnership that is treated as the divided partnership is required to file a return for the tax year of the partnership that has been divided and to retain the employer identification number (EIN) of the former partnership. All other resulting partnerships file separate returns for the tax year beginning on the day after the date of the division. Each new entity acquires a separate new EIN [Reg. § 1.708-1(d)(2)(i)].

All resulting partnerships that are continuing are subject to preexisting elections that were made by the prior partnership. However, a post-division election made by a resulting partnership will not bind any of the other resulting partnerships [Reg. § 1.708-1(d)(2)(ii)].

Example 24-22: Mr. Marks owns 40 percent and Mr. Neale, Mr. Oliver, and Mr. Paulsen each own 20 percent interest in the capital and profits of partnership MNOP. When partnership MNOP is split into partnership MN and partnership OP, the tax year of partnership MN is considered a continuation of partnership MNOP using the same tax year since Marks and Neale together own more than

50 percent interest in partnership MNOP. Partnership OP is considered a new partnership and starts with a new tax year.

.04 Applying Economic Accrual Principles to Cash Basis Items

If a partner's interest in the partnership changes during the year, the partner's share of interest, taxes, payments for services or use of property, and other items that are accounted for under the cash method must be apportioned over each day in the period during the year in which they relate. The items are then allocated daily among the partners in proportion to their partnership interests at the end of each day to which they are assigned. For purposes of applying these rules, part of an item that relates to earlier years is assigned entirely to the first day of the tax year and any part that relates to later years is assigned entirely to the last day of the year. Required allocations to ex-partners must be capitalized [Code Sec. 706(d)].

.05 Tiered Partnerships

A partnership is a member of a tiered structure if it owns an interest in or is wholly or partly owned by an S corporation, a personal service corporation, a trust or another partnership [Ch. 18] [Temp. Reg. § 1.444-2T]. If there is a change in the interests of any partner in an "upper-tier partnership," the partner's distributive share of daily items of income and expense attributable to a lower-tier partnership must be determined under an appropriate portion test [Code Sec. 706(d)]. The formula will be based on the number of days any upper-tier partner owned lower-tier *and* upper-tier partners' respective partnership interests.

TRANSACTIONS BETWEEN A PARTNERSHIP AND PARTNER OR RELATED PERSON

¶24,080 PARTNER NOT ACTING AS A PARTNER

As a general rule, any payment made by a partnership to a partner must be classified either as a payment made to a partner acting in the capacity of a partner or as a payment made to a partner acting in the capacity of a nonpartner. If a partner engages in a transaction with the partnership other than in the capacity of a partner, the partner is not treated as a member of the partnership for that transaction [Code Sec. 707(a); Reg. § 1.707-1(a)].[34]

Such transactions include, for example, loans of money or property by the partnership to the partner or by the partner to the partnership, the sale of property by the partner to the partnership, the purchase of property by the partner from the partnership, and the rendering of services by the partnership to the partner or by the partner to the partnership. Where a partner retains the ownership of property but allows the partnership to use such separately owned property for partnership purposes (for example, to

[34] *M.G. Plotkin*, CA-11, 2012-2 USTC ¶50,688, 498 Fed Appx 954, *aff'g*, 102 TCM 450, Dec. 58,802(M), TC Memo. 2011-260 (payments made by an individual from a partnership were not partnership distributions because the individual was not a partner in the partnership).

obtain credit or to secure firm creditors by guaranty, pledge, or other agreement) the transaction is treated as one between a partnership and a partner not acting in his capacity as a partner. However, transfers of money or property by a partner to a partnership as contributions, or transfers of money or property by a partnership to a partner as distributions, are not transactions included within the provisions of Code Sec. 707(a) [Reg. § 1.707-1(a)].

Example 24-23: Ms. Perkins, an equal member of the OPQ partnership, has a basis of $1,000 for a particular asset. If she sells it to the partnership for $1,500, its fair market value, she will report a gain of $500.

Example 24-24: Assume now that Perkins in Example 24-23 pays $2,000 for partnership property that has a basis to it of $1,100. The partnership reports a gain of $900. Since the partners share equally, $300 of this gain (1/3 of $900) must be reported by Perkins on her individual return as part of her distributive share of partnership gain.

This general rule is subject to numerous exceptions, as explained below.

.01 When a Loss Is Disallowed

No deduction is allowed for losses from the sale or exchange of property (except an interest in the partnership) between (1) a partnership and a partner who owns more than a 50 percent interest in its capital or profits or (2) a partnership and another partnership, when the same persons own more than a 50 percent interest in the capital or profits of each. However, any gain realized on a later sale or exchange of the property by the purchaser is taxable only to the extent it exceeds that part of the disallowed loss allocable to the property sold [Code Secs. 267(d), 707(b)(1); Reg. § 1.707-1(b)(1)].

Example 24-25: The AFG partnership in which partner Mr. Frank owns a 60 percent interest in capital and profits transfers property at a loss of $500 to the DFH partnership, in which Frank owns a 55 percent interest in capital and profits. The AFG partnership is not allowed a deduction for the loss.

Example 24-26: The DFH partnership in Example 24-25 sells the property it got from the AFG partnership at a gain of $600. Only $100 ($600 less $500) of the gain is taxable.

Example 24-27: The DFH partnership in Example 24-25 sells the property received from the AFG partnership at a gain of $400. None of the gain is taxable.

.02 When Gain Is Ordinary Income

When property is the subject of a sale or exchange between (1) a partnership and a partner who owns over 50 percent of the capital or profits interest in the partnership or (2) two partnerships in which the same persons own more than 50 percent of the capital or profits interest, gain on the transaction is treated as ordinary income if the property is not a capital asset [Ch. 8] in the hands of the person receiving it [Code Sec. 707(b)(2); Reg. § 1.707-1(b)(2)].

Property that is not a capital asset includes trade accounts receivable, inventory, stock-in-trade, and depreciable or real property used in a trade or business.

> **Example 24-28:** Ms. Corby, who owns a 52 percent interest in the capital and profits of the CDE partnership, which sells paintings, transfers a painting from her personal collection to the partnership at a gain of $100. This amount is ordinary income to Corby.

.03 Determining Ownership of an Interest

In determining the extent of the ownership of a capital or profits interest when there is a sale or exchange between a partner and partnership, the following constructive ownership rules apply:

- An interest directly or indirectly owned by or for a corporation, partnership, estate or trust is considered to be owned proportionately by or for its shareholders, partners, or beneficiaries;
- An individual is considered to own the interest that is directly or indirectly owned by or for his or her family (including only brothers, sisters, half brothers, half sisters, spouse, ancestors, and lineal descendants); and
- If an individual is attributed with an interest under rule 1, the individual is treated as actually owning the interest for purposes of reapplying rule 1 or applying rule 2. But if the individual is attributed with an interest under rule 2, the individual is not considered to actually own the interest for purposes of attributing an interest to another person.

These rules parallel the rules for determining constructive ownership of stock [Ch. 13]. However, there is not attribution between partners [Code Sec. 707(b)(3); Reg. § 1.707-1(b)(3)].

> **Example 24-29:** If Ms. Frank, who owns only a 30 percent interest in the DFH partnership, sells property to the partnership at a $500 loss, the loss will be allowed. If, however, Mr. Howard, who also owns a 30 percent interest, were Frank's brother, the loss would not be allowed. Frank would be treated as owning more than 50 percent of the capital and profits of DFH, 30 percent directly and 30 percent by attribution from Howard.

.04 Guaranteed Payments-Salaries and Interest Paid to Partner

To the extent that payments to a partner for services or for the use of capital are determined without regard to partnership income, they are treated by the partnership in the same manner as payments made to a nonpartner [Code Sec. 707(c)]. These payments are called *guaranteed payments.*

Guaranteed payments are included as ordinary income on the partner's personal income tax return, and the partnership usually can deduct them as business expenses in computing its taxable income or loss.

Example 24-30: The BY partnership agreement provides that Mr. Bilsky, an equal partner, is to receive an annual salary of $20,000 as office manager, without regard to partnership income. After deducting the guaranteed payment, the partnership had ordinary income of $60,000. Bilsky must include $50,000 in his personal income return for that year ($20,000 guaranteed payment and $30,000 for his distributive share of partnership income). The partnership deducts the $20,000 payment as a business expense.

Guaranteed payments are not subject to withholding and are not taken into account for purposes of an employee's deferred compensation plan [Reg. § 1.707-1(c)].

To find out whether a guaranteed payment is deductible, the partnership must meet the business expense deduction tests [Ch. 12] and take into account the capital expenditure rules [Ch. 12] [Code Sec. 707(c)]. Thus, guaranteed payments to a partner for organizing your partnership or syndicating interests in the partnership are capital expenditures and not deductible [Ch. 24].

A partnership may set up a self-employed retirement plan [Ch. 3], but it gets no deduction for contributions for its partners [¶ 24,040]. When the employer of a medical partnership contributed directly to its retirement plan, the Supreme Court held that each doctor-partner had to report as income his share of the contribution. Partners may, however, claim deductions on their own returns for contributions to a self-employed retirement plan.[35]

If a partnership agreement provides that a partner who is to receive a percentage of partnership income will be paid a guaranteed minimum, the amount by which the payment exceeds his or her distributive share of partnership income constitutes a guaranteed payment.

Example 24-31: Under the HD partnership agreement, Ms. Doolittle is to receive 50 percent of the partnership income each year, but in no event will the payment be less than $10,000. One year, the partnership had taxable income of $18,000. The amount of the guaranteed payment which may be deducted by the partnership is $1,000 ($10,000 minus $9,000 distributive share).

In Rev. Rul. 2007-40,[36] the IRS concluded that a transfer of partnership property to a partner in satisfaction of a guaranteed payment constituted a taxable sale or exchange under Code Sec. 1001. The partnership received a parcel of real property and, once the property had appreciated to the point its fair market value equaled the guaranteed payment amount due to the individual partner, the partnership transferred the real property to the partner in satisfaction of the guaranteed payment. Because the transfer was a sale or exchange, it was not a distribution within the meaning of Code Sec. 731 and the nonrecognition rule of Code Sec. 731(b) did not apply. Therefore, the partnership had to recognize gain to the extent of the difference between its adjusted basis in the real property and the property's fair market value at the time it was transferred to the partner.

---

[35] *J.A. Basye*, SCt, 73-1 USTC ¶ 9250, 410 US 441, 93 SCt 1080.

[36] Rev. Rul. 2007-40, 2007-25 IRB 1426.

Fringe Benefits

A partnership has a choice when it comes to reporting the health insurance premium costs or other fringe benefits for partners. The partnership can treat the cost of the benefits as guaranteed payments for the partners' services. Result: The payments are deducted by the partnership before figuring the partners' shares of partnership income or loss. Or the partnership can treat the cost of the benefits as a reduction in distributions to the partners. Result: The benefits are not deductible by the partnership and do not affect the partners' shares of income and loss.

.05 Disguised Payments for Property or Services

A partnership must capitalize the cost of certain goods and services, such as syndication fees, purchased from its partners [¶ 24,090]. Some partnerships have attempted to avoid the capitalization rules by making allocations of income and corresponding distributions instead of direct payments to the partners. A payment that's characterized as part of the partner's distributive share of partnership income has the same effect as a partnership deduction because it reduces the income shares of the other partners.

To prevent such abuses, when a partner performs services for or transfer property to a partnership and then receives a related allocation or distribution, the transaction is treated as a payment to a nonpartner [Code Sec. 707(a)(2)(A)].

.06 Disguised Sales or Exchanges

In general, a partner recognizes no gain or loss on a contribution of money or other property to a partnership in exchange for a partnership interest [Code Sec. 721; ¶ 24,090]. Similarly, when a partnership distributions money or property to a partner, the partnership recognizes no gain or loss [Code Sec. 731(b); ¶ 24,100]. These nonrecognition rules do not apply, however, where the transaction is found to be a disguised sale of property [Code Sec. 707(a)(2)(B)]. Creative taxpayers have tried to use partnerships as a vehicle for disposing of appreciated property with no tax consequences by abusing the nonrecognition rules. For example, some partners have disguised taxable sales as tax-free contributions to the partnership followed by tax-free cash distributions. To prevent such abuses, when a contribution followed by a distribution looks like a sale or exchange, it is treated as such and the partner must recognize gain or loss on the distribution [Code Sec. 707(a)(2)(B)].

A transaction is treated as a disguised sale between a partner and a partnership when the partner contributes or transfers money or other property to a partnership and soon thereafter receives a distribution of money or other consideration from the partnership. A transaction may be deemed a sale if, based on all the facts and circumstances, the partnership's distribution of money or other consideration to the partner would not have been made but for the partner's transfer of the property [Reg. § 1.707-3(b)(1)]. Such contribution and distribution transactions that occur within two years of one another are presumed to be sales unless the facts and circumstances clearly establish otherwise (the two-year presumption rule discussed below) [Reg. § 1.707-3(c)(1)]. In all cases, however, the substance of the transaction will govern rather than its form [Reg. § 1.707-1(a)].

For example, there is no disguised sale when the transactions do not occur within two years of each other and the subsequent transfer is subject to the entrepreneurial risks of the partnership's operations [Reg. § 1.707-3(b)(1)]. In *Virginia Historic Tax Credit Fund 2001*,[37] the Court of Appeals for the 4th Circuit reversed the Tax Court and concluded that a limited partnership's exchange of state historic rehabilitation tax credits for investor contributions was a "disguised sale" for purposes of Code Sec. 707. Therefore, the limited partnership should have included the investor contributions in income for the year. The historic rehabilitation tax credits were property because they were valuable, transferrable, and embodied essential property rights. Further, the transfer of the credits for investor contributions was a sale because the exchange occurred within two years; the credits' transfer to each investor had no correlation to the investor's interest in the LP's profits; the timing and amount of the transfer were reasonably determinable; the investors had a legally enforceable right to the credits and that right was secured; and the investors had no further obligation to the partnership after the credits were transferred.

In *Canal Corp.*,[38] the Tax Court concluded that contributions of assets and liabilities by the corporation's wholly owned subsidiary to a newly formed limited liability company (LLC) (treated as a partnership for tax purposes), and the simultaneous receipt of a cash distribution, was a disguised sale under Code Sec. 707(a)(2)(B), resulting in the recognition of gain. The funds for the cash distribution originated from a bank loan, guaranteed by the subsidiary's partner in the LLC. The subsidiary agreed to indemnify the partner if the partner made payment on the guaranty. The subsidiary did not bear the economic risk of loss because the indemnity agreement lacked economic substance and was created in such a way as to limit any potential liability to the subsidiary's assets.

In *In re G-1 Holdings Inc.*,[39] the Tax Court concluded that most of an asset transfer that purported to be a tax-free capital contribution to a partnership was actually a disguised asset sale under Code Sec. 707(a)(2)(B)(iii). The limited partner transferred property to the partnership and in return received a partnership interest. As part of an integrated transaction, the limited partner then used the partnership interest to secure a nonrecourse loan in the amount of the assets' value. Thus, the loan constituted an indirect related transfer of money from the partnership to the partner. In addition, the limited partner was not subject to a substantial risk of loss because the general partner was liable for repayment of the loan. Moreover, the partnership and loan agreements contained interlocking default provisions under which the limited partner could force the partnership into liquidation if the general partner failed to pay the interest on the loan. Based on the integrated contribution and loan transactions, the principal objective of the parties was to reduce the taxes on an exchange of assets for cash.

.07 Two-Year Presumption Rule

The IRS has also established a two-year rule under which transfers between a partner and a partnership are presumed to be a sale. Under this presumption, if a partner transfers property to a partnership and the partnership transfers money or other consideration to the partner within a two-year period, then the transfers are presumed to be a sale of the property to the partnership unless the facts and circumstances clearly

---

[37] *Virginia Historic Tax Credit Fund 2001 LP*, CA-4, 2011-1 USTC ¶ 50,308, 639 F3d 129, *rev'g and rem'g*, 98 TCM 630, Dec. 58,032, TC Memo. 2009-295.

[38] *Canal Corp.*, 135 TC 199, Dec. 58,298 (2010).

[39] *In re G-1 Holdings Inc.*, DC-NJ, 2010-1 USTC ¶ 50,332.

establish otherwise. This two-year presumption applies regardless of the order of the transfers [Reg. § 1.707-3(c)]. In contrast, if the transfer of property by the partner to the partnership and the transfer of money or other consideration to the partner by the partnership take place more than two years apart, then the transfers are presumed to not constitute a sale of the property to the partnership [Reg. § 1.707-3(d)].

Notwithstanding this presumption, a transfer of money by the partnership to a partner generally is not treated as part of a sale of property by the partner to the partnership to the extent that the transfer is made to reimburse the partner for, and does not exceed the amount of, capital expenditures that:

- Are incurred during the 2-year period preceding the transfer; and
- Are incurred by the partner for property contributed to the partnership by the partner, but only to the extent the reimbursed capital expenditures don't exceed 20 percent of the fair market value of the property at the time of the contribution (preformation expenditures) [Reg. § 1.707-4(d)(2)(ii)].

In Rev. Rul. 2000-44,[40] the subsidiary incurred capital expenditures within the two-year period before the transfer of the property to the partnership and the reimbursed expenditures didn't exceed 20 percent of the fair market value of the contributed property. Thus, the reimbursement fell within the exception for reimbursement of preformation expenditures in Reg. § 1.707-4(d) and did not give rise to a disguised sale.

A partner's contribution of property to the partnership is presumed to be a taxable sale rather than a tax-free contribution if the partner receives a payment that would not have been made but for the contribution. (If the contribution and payment are not made simultaneously, the contribution is not treated as a sale if the payment is contingent on the success of the partnership.) Generally, a transaction is presumed to be a sale if payment is made within two years of the contribution. Beyond that period, the transfer is considered a bona fide contribution [Reg. § 1.707-3(c), (d)].

There are four kinds of payments that will not cause the disguised sale rules to apply: (1) reasonable guaranteed payments for capital, (2) reasonable preferred returns, (3) operating cash flow distributions, and (4) preformation expenditures [Reg. § 1.707-4].

Similarly, if a partnership sells the contributed property to a third party, the precontribution gain or loss is allocated to the contributing partner [Code Sec. 704(c)(1)(A)].

In addition, if property contributed to a partnership is distributed to another partner within seven years of the original contribution, the partner recognizes any precontribution gain or loss [Code Sec. 704(c)(1)(B)]. However, this rule doesn't apply to certain partnership transactions that have the effect of a like-kind exchange—for example, where the partnership distributes the contributed property to another partner and also distributes equivalent like-kind property to the contributing partner [Code Sec. 704(c)(1)(B)].

---

[40] Rev. Rul. 2000-44, 2000-2 CB 336.

¶24,085 TRANSACTIONS BETWEEN PARTNERSHIP AND RELATED PARTIES

When a partnership engages in a sale or exchange with a related person, losses are disallowed [Code Sec. 267(a)(1)]. When a partnership makes a payment to a related person, a deduction is allowed for that payment only when the payment is includible in the related person's income [Code Sec. 267(a)(2)].

For purposes of determining whether a loss is disallowed, the following persons are considered related: (1) a partnership and a person owning, directly or indirectly, more than 50 percent of the capital interest or profits interest in the partnership and (2) two partnerships in which the same persons own, directly or indirectly, more than 50 percent of the capital or profits interests [Code Sec. 707(b)(1)]. Also considered related are a corporation and a partnership if the same persons own more than 50 percent in value of the outstanding stock of the corporation and more than 50 percent of the capital interest or profits interest in the partnership [Code Sec. 267(b)(10)]. When the property for which a loss was disallowed subsequently is sold at a gain, gain is recognized only to the extent that it exceeds the amount of loss disallowed [Code Secs. 267(d), 707(b)].

For purposes of applying the matching rule, the following persons are considered related: (1) a partnership, (2) any person who owns (directly or indirectly) any capital or profits interest of the partnership, (3) any person who owns (directly or indirectly) any capital or profits interest of a partnership in which the partnership owns (directly or indirectly) any capital or profits interest, and (4) any person related (within the meaning of Code Sec. 267(b) or Code Sec. 707(b)(1)) to a person described in (2) or (3) [Code Sec. 267(e)(1)]. Also treated as related persons are two partnerships in which the same persons own, directly or indirectly, more than 50 percent of the capital interests or profits interest [Code Sec. 707(b)(1)]. The deduction deferred is based on the proportionate amount held in each partnership.

CONTRIBUTIONS TO A PARTNERSHIP

¶24,090 TAX EFFECT OF CONTRIBUTION

When a partnership is formed, each partner contributes money, other property, or services in return for his or her interest. A new partner may also acquire an interest by making a contribution after the partnership is formed and operating. In addition, a partner may acquire an interest in the partnership other than by making a contribution to the partnership—for example, by gift or inheritance.

.01 Nonrecognition of Gain or Loss

In general, no gain or loss is recognized to a partnership or to any partner when money, installment obligations or other property is contributed to a partnership in exchange for an interest in the partnership. This rule applies whether your partnership is newly-formed and already in existence [Code Sec. 721(a); Reg. § 1.721-1(a)]. Property in this situation includes both tangible and intangible items, such as land, cash, stock, receivables, patents, and copyrights. However, property does not include services as discussed below.

Note that losses may not be recognized when depreciated property is contributed to a partnership. The contributing partner should sell the property instead and take the loss, if possible and then contribute the sales proceeds to the partnership in exchange for an ownership interest in the partnership.

In *MAS One Limited Partnership*,[41] a partner who had guaranteed a loan on the partnership's property abandoned its partnership interest. The next day the partnership sold the property and used the proceeds to pay down the loan. As part of the loan, the guarantor partner paid the loan balance. The court ruled that a payment made by a former limited partner to satisfy a partnership's loan was income to the limited partnership, not a capital contribution.

.02 Interest Transferred as Payment for Services

If a capital interest in the partnership is received by a partner as compensation for past or future services rendered or to be rendered to the partnership, the value of the interest is a guaranteed payment and is taxed as ordinary income [¶ 24,080]. The amount of the taxable income received is the fair market value of the interest transferred as compensation. The date of valuation depends on whether the transfer was made for past services or for future services. If for past services, the valuation is made when the interest was transferred; if for future services, the valuation is made as of the time the services are rendered [Reg. § 1.721-1(b)(1), (2)]. If a person receives a profits interest for providing services to or for the benefit of a partnership in a partner capacity or in anticipation of becoming a partner, receipt of that profits interest will not be treated as a taxable event for the partner or the partnership unless the profits interest relates to a substantially certain and predictable stream of income from partnership assets, the partner disposes of the profits interest within two years of receipt, or the profits interest is a limited partnership interest in a publicly traded company.[42]

.03 Contributions of Unrealized Receivables, Inventory Items or Capital Loss Property

The character of a partnership's gain or loss on its disposition of unrealized receivables, inventory, or capital loss property is the same as if the contributing partner had disposed of them [Code Sec. 724(a)].

Unrealized Receivables

The partnership's gain or loss on contributed unrealized receivables is always ordinary [Code Sec. 724(a)].

Inventory

The partnership also has ordinary gain or loss on a taxable disposition of contributed inventory items within five years of the contribution. If the disposition occurs more than five years after the contribution, the character of the gain or loss is determined at the partnership level [Code Sec. 724(b)].

[41] *MAS One Limited Partnership*, CA-6, 2004-2 USTC ¶ 50,413, 390 F3d 427.

[42] Rev. Proc. 93-27, 1993-2 CB 343, clarified by Rev. Proc. 2001-43, 2001-2 CB 191.

Capital Loss Property

For property that was a capital asset in the partner's hands, any loss on a disposition by your partnership within five years after the contribution is a capital loss to the extent that the property's adjusted basis to the partner exceeded the property's fair market value immediately before the contribution was made [Code Sec. 724(c)].

Basis Tainting Rules

If the partnership transfers the contributed property to a transferee who takes a substituted basis (e.g., a nonrecognition transfer), the characterization rules mentioned above apply to the contributed property now in the transferee's hands [Code Sec. 724(d)(3)(A)]. Moreover, any property (except C corporation stock received in a tax-free incorporation) received by the partnership in which it takes a substituted basis also gets that treatment. Similar rules apply to a series of nonrecognition transfers.

.04 Mutual Fund Partnerships

Gain is recognized when property is contributed in exchange for a partnership interest to a partnership that would be treated as an investment company if it were incorporated. However, losses are not recognized [Code Sec. 721(b)].

The partnership is treated as an investment company if over 80 percent of the value of its assets, other than cash and nonconvertible securities, is held for investment and consists of readily marketable stocks, securities, or interests in mutual funds or real estate investment trusts [Reg. § 1.351-1(c)(1)(ii)].

> **NOTE:** This rule applies to both limited and general partnerships, regardless of whether they are publicly traded or privately formed.

PARTNER'S BASIS FOR A PARTNERSHIP INTEREST

¶24,095 PARTNER'S ORIGINAL BASIS AND HOW TO ADJUST IT

When money or property is contributed by a partner to a partnership in exchange for a partnership interest, the partner's tax basis in the partnership interest is the amount of money contributed plus the adjusted basis of the property transferred to the partnership [Code Sec. 722; Reg. § 1.722-1].

> **Example 24-32:** Mr. Sampson and Mr. Frith form a partnership. Sampson contributes $1,000 in cash and Frith contributes property worth $1,000 with an adjusted basis of $600. The basis of the property to the partnership is $600. This is also Frith's basis for his partnership interest. Sampson's basis for his partnership interest is $1,000, the amount of money he contributed.

If the property contributed to the partnership is subject to indebtedness or if the partnership assumes the partner's liabilities, the partner's basis in the partnership interest is decreased by the amount of the liabilities assumed by the other partners. The assumption of liabilities is treated as a distribution to the partner and as a cash contribution by the other partners [Reg. § 1.722-1].

If, on the other hand, a partner assumes a liability of the partnership, the assumption is treated as a contribution of money to the partnership by the partner and the partner's basis will be increased.

If a contribution to a partnership results in taxable income, that income is included in basis. For example, taxable income received because of a contribution of services in exchange for a partnership interest is included in basis [Reg. § 1.722-1]. Similarly, taxable income recognized on the contribution of property to a partnership is included in the partner's basis [Code Sec. 722].

A partner's original basis must be adjusted from time to time to prevent unintended benefits or detriments.

> ▶ **OBSERVATION:** Suppose that the value of a partners' interest increased because the partnership retained its current income. The partner is taxed on his or her share of this income even though the partnership retains it. If the partner's basis for his or her interest remained the same, a later sale of the interest would result in a second tax to the extent of any gain due to the increased value. Therefore, basis should be increased to the extent of your taxable amount.

Even if a partner cannot deduct all or part of his or her distributive shares of partnership expenses, the partner's basis in the partnership must be reduced by the full amount of your distributive shares.

The adjusted basis for a partnership interest is found under the general rule or under an alternative rule which are both discussed below.

.01 Basis Adjustment Rules

Adjustments to original basis may increase or decrease the partner's basis in a partnership interest.

Basis Increased

A partner's original basis is increased by any further contributions made to the partnership and by the partner's distributive share of:

- Partnership taxable income, capital gains and other income items separately allocated to the partners [¶ 24,040];
- Partnership tax-exempt income; and
- The excess of the depletion deduction over the basis of the depletable property [Code Sec. 705(a)(1); Reg. § 1.705-1(a)(2)].

> **Example 24-33:** Ms. Paulson's share of taxable income of the PB partnership is $2,000. She also is entitled to a $100 share of tax-exempt interest received by the partnership. The basis of Paulson's partnership interest must be increased by $2,100.

An increase in the partner's share of partnership liabilities, in any of the ways mentioned below, is considered a contribution of money by the partner to the partnership and increases the partner's basis in the partnership.

Basis Reduced

The partner's original basis is reduced (but not below zero) by cash distributions, the basis of other property distributed to the partners and by your distributive share of:

- Partnership losses (including capital losses);
- Nondeductible partnership noncapital expenditures;
- Depletion deduction for oil and gas wells [Ch. 12] [Code Secs. 705(a)(2), 733; Reg. §§1.705-1(a)(3), 1.733-1];
- Partners adjust basis to reflect the partnership's disallowed losses and unrecognized gain;[43] and
- Partners must reduce the basis in their partnership interest (but not below zero) when a partnership makes a charitable contribution of property.[44]

A decrease in a partner's share of partnership liabilities, in any of the ways mentioned below, is considered a distribution of money to the partner.

.02 Alternative Rule

In certain cases, a partner may take as his or her adjusted basis in his or her interest an amount equal to the partner's share of the partnership's adjusted basis for the property it would distribute if the partnership were terminated. The method may be used only when adjustment under the general rule is not practicable or when the IRS concludes that the result will not vary substantially from the result under the general rule. If this method is used, certain adjustments are required in figuring the partnership interest's adjusted basis. For example, adjustments might be required to reflect any significant differences due to contributions or distributions of property or transfers of partnership interests [Code Sec. 705(b); Reg. §1.705-1(b)].

Example 24-34: The ABC partnership, in which Mr. Crane, Mr. Stevens and Mr. Pound are equal partners, owns various properties with a total adjusted basis of $1,500 and has earned and retained an additional $1,500. The total adjusted basis of partnership property is thus $3,000. Each partner's share in the adjusted basis of partnership property is one-third of this amount, or $1,000. Under the alternative rule, this amount represents each partner's adjusted basis for his partnership interest.

Example 24-35: Assume that partner Crane in Example 24-34 sells his partnership interest to Mr. Dickinson for $1,250 when the partnership property (with an adjusted basis of $1,500) had appreciated in value to $3,000 and when the partnership also had $750 in cash. The total adjusted basis of all partnership property is $2,250 and the value of the property is $3,750. Dickinson's basis for his partnership interest is his cost, $1,250. However, his one-third share of the adjusted basis of partnership property is only $750. Therefore, for purposes of the alternative rule, Dickinson has an adjustment of $500 in determining the basis of his interest. This amount represents the difference between the cost of

[43] Rev. Rul. 96-10, 1996-1 CB 138.

[44] Rev. Rul. 96-11, 1996-1 CB 140.

his partnership interest and his share of partnership basis at the time of his purchase. If the partnership later earns and retains an additional $1,500, its property will have an adjusted basis of $3,750. Dickinson's adjusted basis for his interest under the alternative rule is $1,750, determined by adding $500, his basis adjustment, to $1,250 (his 1/3 share of the $3,750 adjusted basis of partnership property). If the partnership distributes $250 to each partner in a current distribution, Dickinson's adjusted basis for his interest will be $1,500 ($1,000, his 1/3 share of the remaining basis of partnership property ($3,000) plus his $500 basis adjustment). Dickinson's adjusted basis for his partnership interest, after the $500 adjustment, may be shown as follows [Reg. § 1.705-1(b), Ex.2]:

	Dickinson bought interest for $1,250	*ABC later earns and retains additional $1,500*	*ABC then distributes $250 to each partner*
1. Total adjusted basis of all ABC's property	$2,250 ($1,500 + $750)	$3,750 ($2,250 + $1,500)	$3,000 ($3,750 – $750)
2. Dickinson's share of adjusted basis of ABC property (1/3 of 1)	$ 750	$1,250	$1,000
3. Plus basis adjustment	$ 500	$ 500	$ 500
4. Dickinson's adjusted basis for his interest (2+3)	$1,250	$1,750	$1,500

¶24,096 HOW PARTNERSHIP LIABILITIES AFFECT BASIS

Code Sec. 752 specifies the adjustments that are made in a partner's basis in his or her partnership interest to reflect his or her share of the partnership's liabilities. In relevant part, Code Sec. 752 provides that: "[a]ny increase in a partner's share of the liabilities of a partnership, or any increase in a partner's individual liabilities by reason of the assumption by such partner of partnership liabilities, shall be considered as a contribution of money by such partner to the partnership" [Code Sec. 752(a)]. Accordingly, the contribution increases the partner's basis in the partnership [Code Sec. 752(a); Reg. § 1.752-1(b)]

Conversely, "[a]ny decrease in a partner's share of the liabilities of a partnership, or any decrease in a partner's individual liabilities by reason of the assumption by the partnership of such individual liabilities, shall be considered as a distribution of money to the partner by the partnership" [Code Sec. 752(b)]. Accordingly, the distribution decreases the partner's basis in the partnership (and may result in gain) [¶ 24,100] [Code Sec. 752(b)].

Liabilities are defined in Reg. § 1.752-1(a)(4)(ii) as "any fixed or contingent obligation to make payment. . . . Obligations include, but are not limited to, debt obligations, environmental obligations, tort obligations, contract obligations, pension obligations, obligations under a short sale, and obligations under derivative financial instruments such as options, forward contracts, futures contracts, and swaps."

In *Marriott International Resorts*,[45] the court concluded that an obligation to close a short sale was a Code Sec. 752 liability for which basis adjustment was required. Thus the taxpayer was required to reduce the basis of certain mortgage notes it received by the obligation to cover a short sale of U.S. Treasury securities.

Example 24-36: Mr. Vale and Mr. Brown are equal partners in the VB Partnership. This year, VB borrowed $100,000. The basis of the partnership interest of Vale and Brown is increased by $50,000 for each. Reason: Each is considered to have contributed that amount to the partnership.

Example 24-37: Assume the same facts as in Example 24-36 except that VB repays a $10,000 note. The basis of the partnership interest of Vale and Brown is decreased by $5,000 each. Reason: Each is considered to have received a distribution of that amount from the partnership.

.01 Recourse and Nonrecourse Liabilities

A partner's share of partnership liabilities depends on weather the liability is a recourse or nonrecourse liability. A liability is a recourse liability to the extent that any partner has an economic risk of loss for the liability.

A nonrecourse liability is defined as a partnership liability for which no partner (or related person) bears the economic risk of loss.

A partner's share of a recourse partnership liability equals the portion of that liability, if any, for which the partner or related person bears the economic risk of loss [Reg. § 1.752-2(a)]. The determination of the extent to which a partner bears the economic risk of loss for a partnership liability turns on whether the partner or related party can be required to make a capital contribution to the partnership, restore a deficit in his or her capital account, pay a creditor directly, or reimburse another partner for a payment by such partner to a creditor of the partnership [Reg. § 1.752-2(b) through Reg. § 1.752-2(k)].

Obligation to Make Payment if Constructive Liquidation Occurs

To determine economic risk of loss, Reg. § 1.752-2(b)(2) adopts a hypothetical worst-case scenario called a constructive liquidation which occurs when the following events all occur simultaneously:

1. All of the partnership's liabilities become payable in full;
2. With the exception of property contributed to secure a partnership liability, all of the partnership's assets, including cash, have a value of zero;
3. The partnership disposes of all of its property in a fully taxable transaction for no consideration (except relief from liabilities for which the creditor's right to repayment is limited solely to one or more assets of the partnership);
4. All items of income, gain, loss, or deduction are allocated among the partners; and
5. The partnership liquidates [Reg. § 1.752-2(b)(2)].

---

[45] *Marriott International Resorts*, CA-FC, 2009-2 USTC ¶ 50,719, 586 F3d 962.

A partner bears the economic risk of loss for a partnership liability to the extent that, if the partnership is constructively liquidated, the partner or related person would be obligated to make a payment to any person (or a contribution to the partnership) because that liability becomes due and payable and the partner or related person would not be entitled to reimbursement from another partner or person that is a related person to another partner.

Obligations Recognized

The determination of the extent to which a partner or related person has an obligation to make a payment is based on the facts and circumstances at the time of the determination. All statutory and contractual obligations relating to the partnership liability are taken into account including:

1. Contractual obligations outside the partnership agreement such as guarantees, indemnifications, reimbursement agreements, and other obligations running directly to creditors or to other partners, or to the partnership;
2. Obligations to the partnership that are imposed by the partnership agreement, including the obligation to make a capital contribution and to restore a deficit capital account upon liquidation of the partnership; and
3. Payment obligations (whether in the form of direct remittances to another partner or a contribution to the partnership) imposed by state law, including the governing state partnership statute [Reg. § 1.752-2(b)(3)].

Contingent Obligations

A contingent payment obligation is disregarded if, taking into account all the facts and circumstances, the obligation is subject to contingencies that make it unlikely that the obligation will ever be discharged. If a payment obligation would arise at a future time after the occurrence of an event that is not determinable with reasonable certainty, the obligation is ignored until the event occurs [Reg. § 1.752-2(b)(4)].

Reimbursement by Another Partner or Partnership

A partner or related person will not bear the economic risk of loss to the extent that the partner (or a related person) is entitled to receive reimbursement from another partner or related person [Reg. § 1.752-2(b)(5)].

A reimbursement is an obligation of another partner (or related person) or the partnership that effectively transfers the economic risk of loss to that other partner or the partnership. Note that a partner's state law right to subrogation with respect to a liability can be considered reimbursement and may cause the partner not to bear the economic risk of loss for the liability. Potential reimbursement from unrelated third parties (such as an insurance company) does not affect a partner's share of a recourse liability [Reg. § 1.752-2(b)(5)].

Partner Deemed to Satisfy Obligation

For purposes of determining the extent to which a partner or related person has a payment obligation and the economic risk of loss, it is assumed that all partners and related persons who have obligations to make payments actually perform those obligations, irrespective of their actual net worth, unless the facts and circumstances indicate a plan to circumvent or avoid the obligation [Reg. § 1.752-2(b)(6)].

Partner or Related Person as Lender

A partner bears the economic risk of loss for a partnership liability to the extent that the partner or a related person makes (or acquires an interest) in a nonrecourse loan to the partnership and the economic risk of loss for the liability is not borne by another partner [Reg. § 1.752-2(c)(1)]. Thus, the basis of his partnership interest is increased to the extent of the entire principal balance of the loan.

***De minimis* partner loans and guarantees.** A partner will not be considered to have the economic risk of loss for a nonrecourse loan made or guaranteed by the partner (or a related person) if: (1) the partner's interest in each item of partnership income, gain, loss, deduction, or credit for every year during the life of the partnership is 10 percent or less; and (2) the loan constitutes qualified nonrecourse financing under Code Sec. 465(b)(6) (or, in the case of a guarantee, would be qualified nonrecourse financing if the guarantor had made the loan to the partnership) [Reg. § 1.752-2(d)].

Partner Providing Property as Security for Partnership Liability

The extent to which a partner bears the economic risk of loss for a partnership liability as a result of a pledge is limited to the net fair market value of the pledged property at the time of the pledge or contribution. If a partner provides additional pledged property, the addition is treated as a new pledge and the net fair market value of the pledged property (including but not limited to the additional property) must be determined at that time. If pledged property is subject to one or more other obligations, those obligations must be taken into account in determining the net fair market value of pledged property at the time of the pledge or contribution [Reg. § 1.752-2(h)(3)].

The rule regarding partners obligated to make a payment on a liability does not apply if the partner or related person whose interest in each partnership item is 10 percent or less guarantees a loan that would otherwise be a nonrecourse loan of the partnership and would constitute qualified nonrecourse financing if the guarantor had made the loan to the partnership [Reg. § 1.752-2(d)]. The partner as lender rule does not apply if the partner or related person whose interest in each partnership item is 10 percent or less makes a loan to the partnership that constitutes qualified nonrecourse financing [Reg. § 1.752-2].

.02 Effect of Disregarded Entities on Economic Risk of Loss

Creative taxpayers have used disregarded entities to circumvent the economic risk of loss rules. The use of disregarded entities as partners creates the appearance of economic risk of loss while limiting the taxpayer's true economic exposure to loss. A disregarded business entity is an entity which is treated as separate from its owner. The IRS has released final regulations that clarify when a partner will be treated as bearing the economic risk of loss for a partnership recourse liability based on a payment obligation of a disregarded entity.

In determining the extent to which a partner bears the economic risk of loss for a partnership liability, an obligation of a disregarded business entity is taken into account only to the extent of the net value of the disregarded entity as of the date on which the partnership determines the partner's share of partnership liabilities. However, this rule will not apply to an obligation of a disregarded entity to the extent that the owners of the disregarded entity otherwise is required to make a payment with respect to such obligation of the disregarded entity [Reg. § 1.752-2(k) (1)].

Example 24-38: Alan contributes $100,000 to form a wholly owned LLC, which is treated as a disregarded entity. LLC and two unrelated parties each contribute $100,000 to form LP, a limited partnership with a calendar year as its tax year. LLC is required to make up any deficit in its capital account, but has no enforceable right to receive a contribution from Alan. The following tax year LP borrows $300,000 and purchases property for $600,000. The debt is secured by the property and is a general obligation of LP. Because LLC is a disregarded entity, Alan is treated as a partner in LP. If LP were to constructively liquidate, only LLC and not Alan, would have an obligation to make a payment on the debt. Therefore, Alan is treated as bearing the economic risk of loss only to the extent of LLC's net value, which at the end of the tax year would be zero. As a result LP's $300,000 debt would be characterized as nonrecourse [Reg. § 1.752-2(k)(6), Ex. 1.

Calculating Net Value of Disregarded Entity

The net value of a disregarded entity generally includes all assets owned by the disregarded entity that may be subject to claims of creditors, but excluding its interest in the partnership and the fair market value of property pledged to secure a partnership liability. The value is determined by subtracting all obligations, regardless of priority, that are not Reg. § 1.752-2(b) (1) payment obligations from the fair market value of the assets of the entity. The net value is not redetermined unless the obligations of the disregarded entity (that do not constitute, and are senior or of equal priority to, payment obligations of the disregarded entity) change by more than a de minimis amount; or there is more than a de minimis contribution to or distribution from the disregarded entity. Disposition of a non-de minimis asset will require an adjustment to the net value of the disregarded entity only to the extent such asset changes in value, without valuing other assets held by the disregarded entity. Changes in the owner's legally enforceable obligation to contribute to the disregarded entity are also a valuation event. However, certain transfers that remain in the entity only briefly are not valuation events [Reg. § 1.752-2(k) (2)].

Example 24-39: Assume the same facts as in the example above, but in the following year Alan contributes $250,000 to LLC that is used to purchase unimproved property. Because of the contribution, LLC's value is redetermined at the end of that tax year. At that time the value of the unimproved land has decreased to $175,000. Alan is treated as bearing the economic risk of loss for $175,000 of LP's $300,000 debt. As a result $175,000 of the debt is recharacterized as recourse, and the remaining $125,000 debt would continue to be characterized as nonrecourse [Reg. § 1.752-2(k)(6), Ex. 2].

.03 Partnership Allocations of Nonrecourse Liabilities

A nonrecourse liability is defined as a partnership liability for which no partner (or related person) bears the economic risk of loss.

Reg. § 1.752-3(a) provides that a partner's share of the nonrecourse liabilities of a partnership equals the sum of the following:

- The partner's share of partnership minimum gain;
- The amount of any taxable gain that would be allocated to the partner if the partnership disposed of (in a taxable transaction) all partnership property subject to one or more nonrecourse liabilities of the partnership in full satisfaction of the liabilities and for no other consideration; and
- The partner's share of the excess nonrecourse liabilities of the partnership as determined in accordance with the partner's share of partnership profits. The partner's interest in partnership profits is determined by taking into account all facts and circumstances relating to the economic arrangement of the partners. The partnership agreement may specify the partners' interests in partnership profits for purposes of allocating excess nonrecourse liabilities provided the interests so specified are reasonably consistent with allocations that have substantial economic effect.

For purposes of determining the amount of taxable gain, if a partnership holds multiple properties subject to a single nonrecourse liability, the partnership may allocate the liability among the multiple properties under any reasonable method [Reg. § 1.752-3(b)]. A method is not reasonable if it allocates to any item of property an amount of the liability that, when combined with any other liabilities allocated to the property, is in excess of the fair market value of the property at the time the liability is incurred. The portion of the nonrecourse liability allocated to each item of partnership property is then treated as a separate loan.

Example 24-40: The AB partnership purchases depreciable property for a $1,000 purchase money note that is a nonrecourse liability. The partnership agreement provides that all items of income, gain, loss, and deduction are allocated equally. Immediately after purchasing the depreciable property, the partners share the nonrecourse liability equally because they have equal interests in partnership profits. *A* and *B* are each treated as if they contributed $500 to the partnership to reflect each partner's increase in his or her share of partnership liabilities (from $0 to $500). The minimum gain with respect to an item of partnership property subject to a nonrecourse liability equals the amount of gain that would be recognized if the partnership disposed of the property in full satisfaction of the nonrecourse liability and for no other consideration. Therefore, if the partnership claims a depreciation deduction of $200 for the depreciable property for the year it acquires that property, partnership minimum gain for the year will increase by $200 (the excess of the $1,000 nonrecourse liability over the $800 adjusted tax basis of the property). *A* and B each have a $100 share of partnership minimum gain at the end of that year because the depreciation deduction is treated as a nonrecourse deduction. Accordingly, at the end of that year, A and B are allocated $100 each of the nonrecourse liability to match their shares of partnership minimum gain. The remaining

$800 of the nonrecourse liability will be allocated equally between *A* and *B* ($400 each) [Reg. § 1.752-3(c), Ex. 1].

.04 Preventing Duplication or Acceleration of Loss—Reg. § 1.752-7 Contingent Liabilities

In an effort to prevent a partner from transferring the tax deductions associated with contingent liabilities to the other partners in the partnership, the IRS released Reg. § 1.752-7 which provides that when a partner transfers property to a partnership subject to a Reg. § 1.752-7 liability, the liability is not treated as a liability but instead is treated as built-in loss under Code Sec. 704(c). At a later date, when the partnership satisfies all or part of a contingent liability, any resulting tax deduction or loss must be allocated to the contributing partner to the extent of the built-in loss at the date of contribution [Reg. § 1.752-7(c)(1)]. A Code Sec. 752 liability is defined as a contingent liability which, due to the uncertainty of either the amount of the debt or the likelihood of repayment, is not treated as a liability for purposes of Code Sec. 752(a) or (b).

Traditional liabilities (such as mortgages) are described in Reg. § 1.752-1. Reg. § 1.752-7 describes liabilities that have not traditionally been treated as liabilities under the partnership rules. This category includes derivatives such as options and other contingent obligations. This special category of liabilities was created because taxpayers were transferring such obligations to a partnership, thus reducing the value of their partnership interest, claiming that the obligations were not "liabilities" causing them to reduce the basis of their partnership interest, and then selling their partnership interest and claiming a loss. Under these rules, basis reduction is delayed until an event occurs that separates the partner from the liability. Triggering events include:

- A disposition or partial disposition of the partnership interest by the partner;
- A liquidation of the partner's interest in the partnership; or
- Another partner's assumption of the liability.

After a triggering event, the partnership's (or assuming partner's) deduction on the economic performance of the Reg. § 1.752-7 liability is limited. However, if the partnership (or the assuming partner) notifies the partner of the economic performance of the Reg. § 1.752-7 liability, the partner may take a loss or deduction in the amount of the prior basis reduction. These rules prevent the duplication of loss by prohibiting the partnership and any person other than the partner from whom the obligation was assumed from claiming a deduction, loss, or capital expense to the extent of the built-in loss associated with the obligation. These rules also prevent the acceleration of loss by deferring the partner's deduction or loss attributable to the obligation until the satisfaction of the Reg. § 1.752-7 liability.

The Reg. § 1.752-7 liability rules include an exception for transactions in which a partner contributes to the partnership the trade or business with which the liability is associated and the partnership continues to carry out that trade or business after the contribution. There is also a *de minimis* exception for situations in which the amount of the remaining built-in loss with respect to all Reg. § 1.752-7 liabilities assumed by the partnership (other than Reg. § 1.752-7 liabilities assumed by the partnership with an associated trade or business) in one or more Reg. § 1.752-7 liability transfers is less than the lesser of $1 million or 10 percent of the gross value of partnership assets immediately before the testing date. There is no exception for transactions in which the partner contributes substantially all of the assets associated with the liability.

DISTRIBUTIONS TO PARTNERS

¶24,100 RECOGNITION OF GAIN OR LOSS

If a partnership distributes money or property to a partner, no gain or loss is recognized to the partnership [Code Sec. 731(b)]. Gain or loss is recognized by the partner as follows:

- If the partner receives money, gain is recognized to the extent that the money exceeds the partner's basis in the partnership interest. The gain is usually capital gain. No loss is recognized unless the money is in payment of a liquidation of the partner's entire interest in the partnership [Code Sec. 731(a)];
- If the distribution consists of property other than money and it is not in liquidation of the partner's entire interest in the partnership, no gain or loss is recognized until the partner sells or disposes of the property [Code Sec. 731(b)]. But, if the property consists of unrealized receivables or inventory that has substantially appreciated in value, the distribution may be treated as a sale or exchange, and ordinary income or loss may result from the distribution [Code Sec. 751(b), ¶ 24,125];
- A contributing partner must recognize gain or loss on a distribution of contributed property to another partner that occurs within seven years of the contribution to the partnership [Code Sec. 704(c)(1)(B)]. The amount of gain or loss is equal to the amount that would have been allocated to the contributing partner if the distributed property had been sold by the partnership to the distributee partner at its fair market value at the time of the distribution. Similarly, the character of the contributing partner's gain or loss is the same as the character that would have been recognized if a sale had occurred. The recognition rules do not apply to:
    a. A distribution of property contributed to the partnership on or before October 3, 1989 [Reg. § 1.704-4(c)(1)];
    b. A deemed distribution of property in connection with a partnership termination under Code Sec. 708(b)(1)(B), or
    c. A distribution of a portion of contributed property to a noncontributing partner in a complete liquidation of the partnership under specified circumstances [Reg. § 1.704-4(c)(2)]; and
- A partner who contributes appreciated property to a partnership and receives a distribution of property, other than money, within seven years of that contribution must recognize gain in an amount equal to the lesser of: (1) the excess distribution or (2) the partner's net precontribution gain. The excess distribution is the excess, if any, of the distributed property's fair market value over the distributee partner's adjusted basis in his partnership interest [Code Sec. 737(b)(1), Reg. § 1.737-1].

¶24,105 BASIS AND HOLDING PERIOD OF PROPERTY DISTRIBUTED

Most distributions received from partnerships are tax-free to partners. Reason: If a distribution by the partnership does not represent a complete liquidation of the partner's partnership interest in the partnership, the partner takes the partnership's basis for the distributed properties. This carryover basis may not exceed the basis of the partnership interest less any money received [Code Sec. 732(a)]. If the partnership's basis in cash and property distributed exceeds the partner's basis in his or her partnership interest, the partner must allocate his basis in his partnership interest to the property received from the partnership [Code Sec. 732(c)]. The distribution reduces the partner's basis in his or her partnership interest (but not below zero) [Code Sec. 733].

Example 24-41: Ms. Armstrong, whose basis for her partnership interest is $2,500, receives a nonliquidating distribution of partnership property. If the partnership's basis for the property is $1,500, she takes that as her basis. The $1,500 reduces the basis of her partnership interest to $1,000.

Example 24-42: Armstrong has a basis of $10,000 for her partnership interest. She receives a nonliquidating distribution of $4,000 in cash and properties with a basis to the partnership of $8,000. Armstrong's basis in the distributed properties is limited to $6,000—her $10,000 basis for her partnership interest reduced by the cash distribution of $4,000. (If the partnership had made an election to adjust basis [¶24,120], it could add the $2,000 difference to the basis of its retained properties.) Armstrong's basis for her partnership interest becomes zero ($10,000 less the cash of $4,000 and her basis for the distributed property). Her basis in the distributed property is decreased to $6,000.

Partners may have a special basis adjustment for distributed property [¶ 24,140].
If the cash received exceeds the partner's basis in his or her partnership interest, Code Sec. 731(a) provides that the distribution in excess of basis is treated as a sale or exchange of the partnership interest. Because partnership interests are usually capital assets to partners under Code Sec. 741, such gain is capital gain.

Example 24-43: Anderson's basis in her partnership interest is $10,000. She receives a $12,000 cash distribution. She has owned her partnership interest for five years. Because the cash distribution exceeds her basis in her partnership interest, the excess is treated as a sale of such interest. Accordingly, she has a $2,000 long-term capital gain and her basis in her partnership interest is zero.

If the cash distributed is less than the partner's basis in his or her partnership interest, the partner will have basis remaining to allocate to the distributed property. The distributed property is classified into two groups according to Code Sec. 732(c)(1): (1) unrealized receivables and inventory, and (2) all other property. Basis allocations are made first to unrealized receivables and inventory. If basis remains, it is allocated to the other property received. See ¶ 24,120 for further discussion.

If a distribution is in complete liquidation of the partner's interest in the partnership, the partner's basis for the distributed properties is the same as the adjusted basis for the partner's partnership interest less any money received [Code Sec. 732(b); Reg. § 1.732-1(b)]. This reduced basis is allocated among the distributed properties. Unallocated basis may give rise to a capital loss.

Example 24-44: The adjusted basis of Mr. Brown's interest in the partnership is $12,000. When he retires from the partnership, he receives a liquidating distribution of $2,000 cash and $14,000 worth of real estate with an adjusted basis of $6,000 to the partnership. Brown will take $10,000 as his basis for the distributed real estate (his basis for his partnership interest, $12,000, less $2,000 cash received).

Example 24-45: Mr. Frey has $20,000 as the basis of his interest in the FGH partnership. He retires from the partnership, receiving $5,000 in cash and inventory items with a basis to the partnership of $3,000. Frey realizes a capital loss of $12,000. The basis of his interest is first reduced by the $5,000 cash. $3,000 of the remaining $15,000 basis for his interest is allocated to the inventory. The remaining $12,000 is capital loss.

.01 Holding Period

The partnership's holding period is added on or tacked onto the partner's holding period when computing the partner's holding period for distributed property. If the partner contributed the property to the partnership, the partner may also add to the beginning of the holding period the time the partner owned the property immediately before it was transferred to the partnership [Code Sec. 734(b); Reg. § 1.734-1(b)].

.02 Loss for Unallocated Basis

If the basis of the interest to be allocated on a distribution in liquidation of your entire interest is greater than the amount allocable to receivables and inventory and no other property was distributed to absorb the excess, the unallocated amount is a capital loss [Code Sec. 731(a)(2); Reg. § 1.732-1(c)(2)].

Example 24-46: Mr. Frost's interest in partnership FGH has an adjusted basis to him of $9,000. He receives as a distribution in liquidation cash of $1,000 and inventory items having a basis to the partnership of $6,000. The cash payment reduces Frost's basis to $8,000, which can be allocated only to the extent of $6,000 to the inventory items. The remaining $2,000 basis, not allocable to distributed property, is a capital loss to Frost.

.03 Special Rules

Refer to rules for specific situations that apply to certain distributions from a partnership to a partner who acquired his or her interest from another partner [¶ 24,120] and to distributions treated as sales or exchanges [¶ 24,125].

¶24,110 DISTRIBUTIONS OF PROPERTY TO TRANSFEREE PARTNERS

Distributed property may have acquired a special basis in the hands of the transferee partner. This may happen either because the partnership made an optional adjustment to the basis of its properties when he or she became a partner or because a special basis adjustment was elected for the distributed property [¶ 24,140].

The special basis adjustment may result in either an increase or a decrease in the partnership property's basis in the hands in the transferee partner and not the other partners [Code Sec. 743(b)].

When a partner receives a distribution of any property from a partnership that elected to make a special basis adjustment, the partner's basis for the distributed property is increased or decreased by the amount of the special adjustment [¶ 24,115]. A similar rule applies when the partner who made the special adjustment election receives the property [¶ 24,140] [Reg. § 1.734-2(a)].

Example 24-47: Mr. Williams acquired his interest in the ABD partnership from a previous partner. Since the partnership had made an election to adjust basis [¶ 24,115], Williams acquired a special basis for partnership property X. The adjusted basis to the partnership for this property is $1,000. Williams' special adjustment is an increase of $500. If property X is distributed to Williams, he takes $1,500 as his basis for X ($1,000 partnership basis plus $500 adjustment). If property X had been distributed to Corso, a nontransferee partner, Corso would have acquired only $1,000 as his carryover basis for X. (In such case, Williams' $500 special basis adjustment may shift over to other property. See below.)

.01 Basis Allocated to Distributed Property

Where multiple properties are distributed in a liquidating distribution or where the total carryover basis of the distributed properties exceeds the partner's basis in its partnership interest, the partner's basis in his partnership interest must be allocated among the distributed properties as provided in the following three steps:

Step One

First, to any unrealized receivables and inventory items in an amount equal to the partnership's adjusted basis in each item [Code Sec. 732(c)(1)(A)(i)]. If the partner's adjusted basis in its partnership interest (as reduced by an money distributed to the partner in the same transaction) is less than the partnership's aggregate basis in such items, the amount of the shortfall must be allocated among the distributed inventory and unrealized receivables in the following manner:

1. First, to the distributed inventory and unrealized receivables with unrealized depreciation in proportion to and to the extent of each property's unrealized depreciation, and
2. The balance, if any, to the distributed inventory and unrealized receivables in proportion to their adjusted bases (taking into account the adjustments already made).

Step Two

If any basis remains available for allocation after Step One, that basis is allocated to each distributed property (other than inventory and unrealized receivables) to the extent of each property's adjusted basis to the partnership.

Step Three

If any basis remains available for allocation after Steps One and Two, that basis is allocated first to the distributed properties (other than inventory and unrealized receivables) with unrealized appreciation in proportion to and to the extent of each property's unrealized appreciation, and the balance, if any, to the distributed properties (other than inventory and unrealized receivables) in proportion to their respective fair market values.

If the basis available for allocation after Step One is less than the amount tentatively allocated pursuant to Step Two, the amount of the shortfall must be allocated among the distributed properties (other than inventory and unrealized receivables) in the following manner: first, to the distributed properties (other than inventory and unrealized receivables) with unrealized depreciation in proportion to and to the extent of each property's unrealized depreciation, and the balance, if any, to the distributed properties (other than inventory and unrealized receivables) in proportion to their adjusted bases (taking into account the adjustments already made [Code Sec. 732(c)].

Example 24-48: A partnership with two assets, A and B, distributes them both in liquidation to a partner whose basis in its interest is $55. Neither asset consists of inventory or unrealized receivables. Asset A has a basis to the partnership of $5 and a fair market value of $40. Asset B has a basis to the partnership of $10 and a fair market value of $10. Under the Code, basis is first allocated to asset A in the amount of $5 and to asset B in the amount of $10. This is their adjusted bases to the partnership. The remaining basis adjustment is an increase totaling $40 (the partner's $55 basis minus the partnership's total basis in distributed assets of $15). Basis is first allocated to asset A in the amount of $35, which is the amount of its unrealized appreciation. There is no allocation to asset B attributable to unrealized appreciation because its fair market value equals the partnership's adjusted basis. The remaining basis adjustment of $5 is allocated according to the assets' fair market values, i.e., $4 to asset A (for a total basis of $44) and $1 to assets B for a total basis of $11 [Taxpayer Relief Act of 1997, Conference Committee Report, Act Sec. 1061].

Example 24-49: A partnership distributes both its assets, C and D, liquidation of a partners whose basis in its interest is $20. Neither asset consists of inventory or unrealized receivables. C has a basis to the partnership of $15 and a fair market value of $15, and D has a basis to the partnership of $15 and a fair market value of $5. Basis is first allocated to C and D to the extent of the partnership's basis in C and D, or $15 to each. Because the partner's basis is its interest is only $20, a downward adjustment of $10 ($30 minus $20) is required. The $10 decrease is allocated to D due to its unrealized depreciation, reducing its basis to $5. Thus, C has a $15 basis and D has a $5 basis in the hands of the distributee partner [Taxpayer Relief Act of 1997, Conference Committee Report, Act Sec. 1061].

.02 Reallocating Special Basis Adjustment

If property for which a special basis adjustment has been made is distributed to another partner, the other partner cannot take the adjustment into account. However, the original partner does not lose the benefit of the adjustment. The adjustment is reallocated to like-kind property (as defined below) retained by the partnership or applied to the basis of like-kind property distributed to the partner [Reg. § 1.704-4(d)(3)].

Like-kind Property

Like-kind property means property of the same class (stock in trade, property used in a trade or business, capital assets, and so forth) [Reg. § 1.704-4(d)(3)].

Example 24-50: Mr. Berryman is a transferee partner in the XY partnership. The partnership owns property A, a depreciable asset with a common basis to the partnership of $1,000 and a special basis adjustment to Berryman of $200. The partnership also owns property B, another depreciable asset with a common basis of $800 and a special basis adjustment to Berryman of $300. Berryman and Mr. Yudell agree that Berryman will receive a distribution of property A and Yudell will receive a distribution of property B, with all other property to remain in the partnership. As to Yudell, the basis of property B is $800, the common partnership basis. Property B will, therefore, have a basis of $800 in Yudell's hands. As to Berryman, however, the basis of property A is $1,500, the common partnership basis of $1,000 plus Berryman's special basis adjustment of $200 for property A, plus Berryman's additional special basis adjustment of $300 for property B in which he has relinquished his interest.

.03 Unused Special Basis Adjustment

Transferee partners, in liquidation of their entire partnership interest sometimes receive property for which *no* special basis adjustment has been made. The property is exchanged for an interest in property for which a special basis adjustment has been made. If the partner does not use his or her entire adjustment in determining the basis for the distributed property under the rules above, the unused amount is used by the partnership to adjust its basis for its retained property [Reg. § 1.734-2(b)(1)].

Example 24-51: On his father's death, Mr. Jones acquired by inheritance 20 percent interest in partnership ABC. Partners Ginsberg and Coleridge each have 30 percent interest. The assets of the partnership consist of $100,000 in cash and real estate worth $100,000 with a basis to the partnership of $10,000. Since the partnership elected, at the time of transfer, to adjust the basis of its property, Jones has a special basis adjustment of $45,000 for his undivided 2 interest in the real estate. The basis of Jones' partnership interest is $100,000, the basis his father had. Jones retires from the partnership and receives $100,000 in cash in exchange for his entire interest. Since Jones received no part of the real estate, his special basis adjustment of $45,000 will be allocated to the real estate, the remaining partnership property, and will increase its basis to the partnership to $55,000.

¶24,115 PARTNERSHIP'S ELECTIVE 754 ADJUSTMENT TO BASIS OF UNDISTRIBUTED PROPERTY FOLLOWING A DISTRIBUTION

.01 General Rules

Partnership distributions to a partner are generally not taxable except to the extent that the amount of any money or marketable securities distributed exceeds the partner's basis in the partnership [Code Sec. 731(a)].

Property distributed by the partnership in liquidation of a partner's interest takes a basis equal to the partner's tax basis in its partnership interest (reduced by any cash received in the liquidation) [Code Sec. 732].

Code Sec. 734(a) provides that the basis of partnership property need *not* be adjusted as the result of a distribution of property to a partner unless:

- The optional Code Sec. 754 election relating to adjustment to basis of partnership property has been made; or
- There is a substantial basis reduction which will occur if the amount of any loss recognized to the distributee partner with respect to the distribution plus, in the case of a liquidation of a partner's interest, the excess of the adjusted basis of the distributed property to the partnership immediately before the distribution over the basis of the distributed property to the distributee exceeds $250,000 [Code Sec. 734(d)(1)]. A securitization partnership is not treated as having a substantial basis reduction with respect to any distribution of property to a partner. An alternative basis adjustment rule is provided for electing investment partnerships. See ¶ 24,055 for further discussion of these exceptions.

Code Sec. 734(b)(1) provides that in order to reflect the fair market value at the time of the exchange, the partnership (with an Code Sec. 754 election in effect) increases the basis of partnership property by

- Any gain recognized by the distributee partner; and
- The excess of the adjusted basis of the distributed property to the partnership immediately before its distribution over the basis of the property to the distributee partner [Code Sec. 734(b)(1)].

Code Sec. 734(b)(2) provides that the partnership decreases the basis of partnership property by:

- Any loss recognized by the distributee partner; and
- In the case of a liquidating distribution, the excess of the basis of the property to the distributee partner over the adjusted basis of the distributed property to the partnership immediately before the distribution [Code Sec. 734(b)(2)]. Code Sec. 755(c)

provides that effective for distributions on or after October 22, 2004, when a distribution of property is made in liquidation of a partner's interest, a partnership may not decrease the basis of stock it owns in a corporate partner or other related party when it allocates basis adjustments to partnership property under Code Sec. 734. Any basis decrease that would have been allocated to a corporate partner's stock is allocated to other partnership assets. If the decrease in basis exceeds the basis of the other partnership assets, then gain is recognized by the partnership in the amount of the excess.

Code Sec. 754 Election

When a Code Sec. 754 election has been made, partners have the advantage of not being taxed on gains or losses that are already reflected in the purchase price of his or her partnership interest. A Code Sec. 754 election allows a step-up or step-down in basis under either Code Sec. 734(b) or Code Sec. 743(b) to reflect the fair market value when a partnership distributes property or transfers a partnership interest to a partner.

The partnership must file the election by the due date of the return for the year that the election is effective. The election must be in writing and (1) include the name and address of the partnership making the election, (2) be signed by any one of the partners, and (3) contain a declaration that the partnership elects, under Code Sec. 754, to apply the provisions of Code Secs. 734(b) and 743(b). There is no particular form for the election, however, the timing of the election is very important and often is the reason the election is rejected. The election must be filed no later than the due date of the partnership return, for the year in which the triggering distribution or transfer occurred [Reg. § 1.6031(a)-1(e)]. Only a partner may sign a valid Code Sec. 754 election [Reg. § 1.754-1(b)].

If a partnership fails to file the election on time, relief is available under Reg. § 301.9100-1 and -3. The IRS has approved extensions of time to make a Code Sec. 754 election. Extensions were granted where the partnership acted reasonably and in good faith and was eligible to make the election but inadvertently omitted the election when filing its return. The extension time is at the discretion of the IRS and has ranged from 60 days to 120 days.[46]

.02 Stock in a Corporate Partner or Any Person Related to Such Corporation

The partnership is prohibited from allocating any decrease in the adjusted basis of partnership property to the stock of a corporation (or any related person, as defined in Code Secs. 267(b) and 707(b)(1)) if the corporation is a partner in the partnership [Code Sec. 755(c)(1)]. A person who could be related to a corporation within the meaning of Code Sec. 267(b) would include:

- An individual and a corporation of which more than 50 percent in value of the outstanding stock is owned, directly or indirectly, by or for that individual;
- Two corporations that are members of the same controlled group;

[46] LTR 201135021 (May 17, 2011), LTR 201115002 (Jan. 3, 2011), LTR 201116010 (Dec. 23, 2010), LTR 201129024 (Apr. 12, 2011), LTR 201129030 (Apr. 12, 2011), LTR 201141001 (June 28, 2011), LTR 201122011 (Feb. 11, 2011), LTR 201114011 (Dec. 15, 2010).

- A trust fiduciary and a corporation of which more than 50 percent in value of the outstanding stock is owned, directly or indirectly, by or for the trust, or by or for the grantor of the trust;
- A corporation and a partnership if the same persons own more than 50 percent in value of the outstanding stock of the corporation and more than 50 percent of the capital or profit interest in the partnership;
- An S corporation and another S corporation if the same persons own more than 50 percent of the value in the outstanding stock of each corporation; and
- An S corporation and a regular corporation if the same persons own more than 50 percent in value of the outstanding stock of each corporation.

Additional related parties, defined in Code Sec. 707(b)(1), include:

- A partnership and a person owning, directly or indirectly, more than 50 percent of the capital interest, or the profits interest, in the partnership; or
- Two partnerships in which the same persons own, directly or indirectly, more than 50 percent of the capital interests or profits interests.

Notice 2005-32[47] generally requires partners and partnerships to report their required basis adjustments as though an election under Code Sec. 754 had been made. Partnerships that are required by the new rules to reduce their basis in partnership property following a distribution must attach to their annual return a statement setting forth the reduction and the property to which it is allocated, as described in Reg. § 1.734-1(d).

¶24,120 DISTRIBUTION OF UNREALIZED RECEIVABLES OR INVENTORY ITEMS

If a partner receives a distribution of a proportionate share of unrealized receivables or inventory, the partner is not currently taxed. When the receivables or inventory is sold or exchanged, the partner generally recognizes ordinary income or ordinary loss [Code Sec. 735(a)]. However, the partner may have capital gain or loss on the disposition of inventory items if they are sold or exchanged more than five years after the date of the distribution. The character of the gain or loss depends on the character of the items when they are sold [Code Sec. 735(a)(2); Reg. § 1.735-1(a)(2)]. Gain or loss on the sale of unrealized receivables contributed by a partner is treated as ordinary regardless of the disposition date. The partner cannot tack the partnership's holding period to his or her own holding period in determining whether inventory was held for more than five years.

> **NOTE:** Similar basis tainting rules that apply to contributed property, as explained in ¶24,090, also apply to ordinary income property distributed to you [Code Sec. 734(c)].

> **Example 24-52:** On March 10, the partnership distributes to Ms. Bowen her proportionate share of unrealized receivables. The partnership's basis in this

[47] Notice 2005-32, 2005-1 CB 895.

property, which Bowen acquired as her basis, was $1,000. If on November 10, Bowen sells these receivables for $1,500, she realizes $500 ordinary income.

Example 24-53: On February 10, the partnership distributed to Mr. Corwin his proportionate share of partnership inventory items. The partnership's basis in this property, which Corwin acquired as his basis, is $3,000. If Corwin sells the inventory items on April 10, for $4,000, he realizes ordinary income of $1,000.

Example 24-54: If Corwin, in Example 24-53 above, disposes of the distributed inventory more than five years after it was distributed to him, he will realize capital gain if the property is a capital asset in his hands.

▶ **OBSERVATION:** The distribution of unrealized receivables or inventory may give rise to ordinary income if the distribution is treated as a sale or exchange [¶24,125].

.01 Liquidating Distributions Involving Unrealized Receivables or Inventory

Payments made by the partnership to a retiring partner in exchange for the partner's interest in unrealized receivables or inventory (Section 751 property) may constitute ordinary income to the partner if the distribution is treated as a sale or exchange. For sales or exchanges (but not disproportionate distributions) of partnership interests, the requirement that the inventory be substantially appreciated in order to give rise to ordinary income treatment has been repealed. As a result, the sale of all inventory (even unappreciated) will yield ordinary income.

.02 Excluded Transactions

Two transactions are not treated as a sale or exchange for purposes of the above rule [Code Sec. 751(b)(2)]:

- A distribution of assets that you contributed to the partnership; and
- Payments that constitute a distributive share of partnership income or a guaranteed payment.

.03 Unrealized Receivables

This term means any rights (contractual or otherwise) to payment for goods delivered or to be delivered (to the extent that such payment would be treated as received for property other than a capital asset) or services rendered or to be rendered, to the extent that income arising from such rights to payment was not previously includible in income under the method of accounting employed by the partnership [Reg. § 1.751-1(c)(1)]. Such rights to payment for services must have arisen under contracts or agreements in existence at the time of sale or distribution, even though the partnership may be unable to enforce payment until a later time. For example, the term includes trade accounts receivables of a cash method taxpayer and rights to payment for goods begun but incomplete at the time of the sale or distribution [Reg. § 1.751-1(c)(1)(ii)]. The basis for such unrealized receivables shall include all costs or expenses attributable to them whether paid or accrued but not previously taken into account under the partnership method of accounting. To determine the amount of the sale price attributable to the unrealized receivables, or their value in a distribution treated as a sale or exchange, consider not only the estimated cost of completing performance of the contract, but also of the time between the sale or distribution and the time of payment.

Unrealized receivables not only include Sec. 1245 and Sec. 1250 property [Ch. 8] but also include potential Secs. 1245 and 1250 income. This means the amount which would be treated as gain under Secs. 1245(a)(1) and 1250(a) if the property were sold by the partnership at its fair market value. Any arm's-length agreement between the buyer and seller will establish fair market value.

Example 24-55: If a partnership would recognize under Sec. 1245(a)(1) gain of $600 upon a sale of an item of Sec. 1245 property and gain of $300 upon sale of its only other item of such property, the potential Sec. 1245 income of the partnership would be $900 [Reg. § 1.751-1(c)(1)(i)].

The term also includes the potential ordinary gain in the following types of property: farm land, mining property [Ch. 12]; certain oil, gas or geothermal property [Ch. 12]; stock in certain foreign corporations [Ch. 28]; and stock in a former DISC, market discount bond, or short-term obligation. The term also includes the ordinary income potential from a franchise, trademark or trade name. The gain is measured as if the partnership sold the property at fair market value at distributions [Code Sec. 751(c)(2)].

NOTE: For this rule, tiered partnerships are treated as owning a proportionate share of each other's property. So, dropping appreciated inventory and unrealized receivables into a second partnership basket will not divorce the ordinary income assets from the first partnership's interest that's being sold [Code Sec. 751(f)].

.04 What Is Inventory?

The term *inventory* is not limited to stock in trade, goods held for sale, or other items generally considered inventory. The term includes all assets of the partnership except capital assets and Sec. 1231 assets. The term also includes any other partnership property that would qualify under the above rules if held by the selling or distributee partner [Code Sec. 751(d)].

Some examples of inventory items are: accounts receivable acquired in the ordinary course of business for services or from the sale or stock in trade, unrealized receivables, and copyrights; literary, musical or artistic compositions that are not capital assets [Reg. § 1.751-1(d)(2)].

.05 What Is Substantial Appreciation?

Inventory items will be considered to have appreciated substantially in value if their fair market value is more than 120 percent of their adjusted basis to the partnership. Inventory property acquired to avoid the rules treated certain distributions as sales or exchanges is disregarded in applying the 120 percent test [Code Sec. 751(b)(3); Reg. § 1.751-1(d)(1)].

▶ **OBSERVATION:** The aggregate of all partnership inventory, specific items or groups of items, is considered in determining whether inventory has appreciated substantially in value. If the whole inventory has substantially appreciated in value, Sec. 751 applies—even if specific items distributed have not appreciated in value [Reg. § 1.751-1(d)(1)].

¶24,125 WHEN IS A DISTRIBUTION A SALE OR EXCHANGE?

A distribution is treated as a sale or exchange to the extent the distributee partner receives: (1) property other than Sec. 751 property in exchange for some or all of a partner's interest in Sec. 751 property; or (2) Sec. 751 property in exchange for some or all of the partner's interest in property other than Sec. 751 property [Code Sec. 751(b); Reg. § 1.751-1(b)].

.01 Was There an Excess Distribution?

The rules in this area do not apply to the extent that the partner receives his or her share of Sec. 751 assets or his or her share of other property.

> ▶ **OBSERVATION:** In figuring a partner's share for this purpose, the regulations require that the partner take into account any interest the partner still has in the partnership after the distribution. For example, say a partnership has Sec. 751 assets valued at $100,000. The partner has a 30 percent interest (worth $30,000), receives a distribution of $20,000 of these assets, and continues to have a 30 percent interest in the $80,000 of such assets remaining in the partnership after the distribution. Only $6,000 ($30,000 less 30 percent of $80,000) represents the partner's share of the Sec. 751 assets. The balance ($14,000) is an excess distribution [Reg. § 1.751-1(b)(1)(ii)].

.02 What Property Did the Partner Give Up?

A partner must determine what property he or she gave up for the excess distribution. The rules in this area do not apply unless the partner receives a distribution of Sec. 751 assets in exchange for an interest in other property or a distribution of other property in exchange for an interest in Sec. 751 assets.

The partner may identify the asset for which the excess distribution is made (see Example 24-56 below). Otherwise, the partner is presumed to have sold or exchanged a proportionate amount of each asset in which the partner relinquished an interest [Reg. § 1.751-1(g)].

.03 Tax Consequences of Distribution

The rules for the portion of the distribution treated as a sale or exchange are summarized in Examples 24-56 and 24-57 below. The balance of the distribution is subject to the rules for distributions in general. The exchange and distribution elements are treated separately [Reg. § 1.751-1(b)].

Tax Consequences When "Other Property" Is Distributed in Exchange for Sec. 751 Assets

The partner realizes ordinary income or loss on the sale or exchange of the Sec. 751 assets relinquished in the exchange. The partner's income or loss is the difference between (1) the partner's adjusted basis (including any special basis adjustment) for the Sec. 751 assets treated as sold or exchanged and (2) the fair market value of the other property (including money) received in exchange [Reg. § 1.751-1(b)(3)].

The partner's basis for the Sec. 751 assets treated as sold or exchanged is the basis the assets would have if the assets had been distributed just before the exchange (that is, the actual distribution) [Reg. § 1.751-1(b)(3)].

The partnership has gain or loss on the sale or exchange of the distributed property other than Sec. 751 assets. Its gain or loss is the difference between (1) its adjusted basis for the distributed property treated as sold or exchanged and (2) the fair market value of the partner's interest in the Sec. 751 assets relinquished in exchange. The character of the partnership's gain or loss depends on the kind of property it sold or exchanged [Reg. § 1.751-(b)(3)].

Example 24-56: The balance sheet of the DEF partnership is as follows:

Assets			*Capital*		
	Basis	*Market Value*		*Per Books*	*Market Value*
Cash	$ 60,000	$ 60,000	Dayton	$ 35,000	$ 60,000
Unrealized receivables	0	60,000	Edwards	35,000	60,000
			Fitter	35,000	60,000
Land & building	45,000	60,000		$105,000	$180,000
	$105,000	$180,000			

The partnership distributed to Dayton the land and building it had owned for 15 years in complete liquidation of his partnership interest. Dayton is treated as if he sold his share of the unrealized receivables for $20,000. He is taxed on $20,000 of ordinary income, as follows:

Fair market value of the assets (land & building) received in exchange for Sec. 751 property (unrealized receivables)	$20,000
Basis allocable to partner's relinquished interest in Sec. 751 property	0
Difference (treated as ordinary income)	$20,000

The following schedule may be set up to analyze the transaction:

	Dayton's interest (market value)	*Value of assets received*	*Dayton's interest (basis)*
Sec. 751 property			
Unrealized receivables	$20,000	$ 0	$ 0
Other property			
Cash	20,000	0	20,000
Land & building	20,000	60,000	15,000
	$60,000	$60,000	$35,000

Dayton's interest (at market value) in the unrealized receivables, cash, and land & building amounted to $20,000 each, for a total of $60,000. Instead of receiving his interest in each of these assets in the form of the assets themselves, at $20,000 each (total $60,000), he received his total $60,000 in land & building. Thus, $20,000 of the land & building was in exchange for his $20,000 interest in the land & building to which he was entitled; another $20,000 share of the land & building was in exchange for his $20,000 interest in the cash; the other $20,000 was in exchange for his interest in the unrealized receivables.

Tax Consequences When Sec. 751 Assets Are Distributed in Exchange for Other Property

Partners must recognize gain or loss on the sale or exchange of the other property you relinquished in the exchange. Gain or loss is the difference between (1) the partner's adjusted basis (including any special basis adjustment) for the other property treated as sold or exchanged and (2) the fair market value of the Sec. 751 assets received in exchange [Reg. § 1.751-1(b) (2)].

The partner's basis for the other property treated as sold or exchanged is the basis it would have if distributed just before the actual distribution [Reg. § 1.751-1(b) (2)].

The character of gain or loss depends on the kind of property relinquished [Reg. § 1.751-1(b) (2)].

The partnership (as constituted after the distribution) realizes ordinary income or loss on the sale or exchange of the distributed Sec. 751 assets. Its income or loss is the difference between (1) its adjusted basis for the Sec. 751 assets treated as sold or exchanged and (2) the fair market value of the partner's interest in the other property given up in exchange [Reg. § 1.751-1(b) (2)].

Example 24-57: Partner C, who has no special basis adjustment, receives a depreciated machine in liquidation of his 1/3 interest in the ABC partnership. The machine has a recomputed basis [Ch. 8] of $18,000 and the partnership books show at the time [Reg. § 1.751-1(g)]:

Assets			*Capital*		
	Adjusted Basis	*Market Value*		*Per Books*	*Market Value*
Cash	$ 3,000	$ 3,000	Liabilities . . .	$ 0	$ 0
Machine (Sec. 1245 prop.) .	9,000	15,000	Capital: A . . .	10,000	15,000
			B	10,000	15,000
Land	18,000	27,000	C	$10,000	$15,000
	$30,000	$45,000		$30,000	$45,000

The partnership has Sec. 751 property of $6,000 since the potential Sec. 1245 ordinary income for the machine is $6,000 ($15,000 fair market value less $9,000 adjusted basis). In the distribution, C got his shares of Sec. 751 property (1/3 ÷ $6,000) of $2,000 and Sec. 1231 property with a fair market value of $3,000 [1/3

× ($15,000 – $6,000)] and adjusted basis of $3,000 (1/3 × $9,000). He also received $4,000 of Sec. 1245 ordinary income property ($6,000 potential less $2,000 share above) and Sec. 1231 property with a fair market value and adjusted basis of $6,000 ($9,000 – $3,000 above). C gave up his $1,000 interest in cash and $9,000 interest in land.

Assume that the partners agree the $4,000 of Sec. 751 property (Sec. 1245 potential) in excess of C's share was in exchange for $4,000 of his land interest. C is treated as receiving 4/9 of his interest in land in a current distribution with a basis of $2,667 ($18,000/$27,000 × $4,000) and selling it to the partnership for $4,000 at a $1,333 gain. The basis of his remaining partnership interest is then $7,333 ($10,000 less $2,667 land distribution). Of the $15,000 total distribution to C, $11,000 ($2,000 ordinary income potential + $9,000 Sec. 1231 property) is not subject to the special rules of Sec. 751 (above), but is treated as a distribution. C's basis for his share of Sec. 1245 potential is zero. His basis for the remaining property is $7,333 (the basis of his partnership interest before the current distribution ($10,000) - the basis of the land treated as distributed to him ($2,667)). Thus, C's basis for the machine received from the partnership is $11,333 ($7,333 + $4,000) and his recomputed basis $13,333 ($11,333 plus $2,000 share of Sec. 1245 potential).

The partnership of A and B has an ordinary gain of $4,000 on the exchange of C's 4/9 interest in land for $4,000 of Sec. 1245 income potential (basis zero). The partnership basis for the land becomes $19,333 ($18,000 less $2,667 treated as distributed to C plus $4,000 paid for that share).

The transactions may be analyzed in the following schedule:

	C's interest (market value)	*Value of assets Received*	*C's interest (basis)*
Sec. 751 property			
Potential Sec. 1245 ordinary income for machine, $6,000 (15,000 – $9,000)	$ 2,000	$ 6,000 ($2,000+$4,000)	$ 0
Other property			
Sec. 1231 Property ($15,000 – $6,000 = $9,000)	3,000	$ 9,000 ($3,000+$6,000)	3,000
Cash	1,000	0	1,000
Land	9,000	0	6,000
Total	$15,000	$15,000	$10,000

TRANSFER OF PARTNERSHIP INTEREST

¶24,130 GAIN OR LOSS ON TRANSFER

Partners who sell or exchange their partnership interest, generally have a capital gain or loss measured by the difference between the amount realized and the adjusted basis of their partnership interest [Code Sec. 741; Reg. § 1.741-1(a)].

If the buyer assumes the partner's share of partnership liabilities, that amount is considered part of the amount realized by the partner [Reg. § 1.752-1(d)].

Example 24-58: If Mr. Abbot sells his interest in the AB partnership for $750 cash and, at the same time, the buyer assumes his $250 share of partnership liabilities, the amount realized on the transaction is $1,000. This amount is then applied against the basis of his partnership interest to determine his gain or loss.

▶ **OBSERVATION:** When a partner withdraws from a partnership, the partner may dispose of the interest by alternative methods, with different tax consequences. If the value of the partner's interest exceeds adjusted basis, and the partner would prefer capital gain (rather than ordinary income) the partner should sell or exchange his or her interest under Sec. 741. On the other hand, the taxable distributive shares of the continuing partners may be reduced, or the partnership may get a deduction, if the partner's interest is liquidated under Sec. 736 [¶ 24,145]. Thus, the tax consequences become dollars-and-cents factors in negotiating the amount to be paid by the continuing partners or by the partnership. By clearly stating intent in the agreements, partners can increase their control over the tax consequences of the transaction and reduce the chance of later litigation over such consequences.

The partnership may elect to adjust the basis of its property after a transfer to reflect your acquisition cost [¶ 24,135].

Capital gain attributable to the sale or exchange or an interest in a partnership held for more than one year is long-term capital gain. Reg. § 1.1(h)-1(a) provides that when a partnership interest is sold or exchanged, the selling partner's recognized gain or loss may consist of four components:

- Code Sec. 751(a) ordinary income;
- Collectibles gain taxed at a maximum of 28 percent;
- Unrecaptured Section 1250 gain taxed at a maximum of 25 percent; and
- Residual long-term capital gain taxed at a maximum of 15 percent.

.01 Transfer of Partnership Interest by Corporation

A corporate distribution of a partnership interest is treated somewhat like a sale—the corporation is taxed on the amount the partnership interest's fair market value exceeds its basis [Code Sec. 311(b)(1)]. Corporations have tried to offset this tax by contributing to the partnership property with a basis in excess of its fair market value before making the distribution. To prevent this abuse, regulations may provide that the contributed loss property shall not be considered when calculating the amount taxable on the distribution [Code Sec. 311(b)(3)].

.02 How Current Earnings Are Treated

A partner's distributive share of current earnings is taxed to the partner, whether or not the earnings are distributed [¶24,035; ¶24,050]. The amount so taxed increases the basis of the partner's interest in the partnership [¶24,095], so the net gain on the sale of an interest does not include the current earnings. It is only this net gain that is taxed as capital gain.

> **Example 24-59:** A partner sold his partnership interest (basis $5,000) on June 30. His share of partnership income to the date of sale was $15,000. The sale price was $20,000. The $15,000 is taxed to the partner and increases his basis for the interest to $20,000. No gain is realized on the sale since the selling price and his basis are the same.

.03 Transfers Involving Receivables or Inventory

Any recognized gain or loss due to unrealized receivables or inventory is ordinary gain or loss [¶ 24,120] [Code Sec. 751(a); Reg. § 1.751-1].

The ordinary income or loss is determined by allocating a portion of the sales proceeds and a portion of your basis to the receivables and inventory [Reg. § 1.741-1(a)].

> **Example 24-60:** C buys B's 50 percent interest in the AB partnership, which keeps its books on a cash basis. At the time, the balance sheet of the firm shows:

Assets	*Basis*	*Market Value*	*Capital*	*Basis*	*Market Value*
Cash	$ 3,000	$ 3,000	Notes payable	$ 2,000	$ 2,000
Advances for clients	10,000	10,000	Capital:		
			A	9,000	15,000
Other assets	7,000	7,000	B	9,000	15,000
Accounts receivable	0	12,000		$20,000	$32,000
	$20,000	$32,000			

The cash price C paid for his partnership interest is $15,000, representing C's share in the net assets shown above, including $6,000 for B's interest in accounts receivable. B realizes $6,000 in ordinary income, attributable to his partnership interest in unrealized receivables.

.04 Reporting Transfers

If a partner sells or exchanges all or part of his or her interest for money or other property attributable to unrealized receivables or inventory the partner must notify the partnership in writing within 30 days of the transaction or, if earlier, by January 15 of the calendar year following the calendar year of the exchange. The partner must also submit a prescribed statement with his or her income tax return for the year of sale or exchange [Reg. § 1.751-1(a)(3)]. The statement must report the amount of the partner's basis in the partnership that is attributable to unrealized receivables or inventory, as well as the portion of the amount received for the interest that is attributable to those items.

The partnership must report exchanges of partnership interests involving unrealized receivables or inventory items by filing Form 8308, *Report of a Sale or Exchange of Certain Partnership Interests,* with its partnership return for the tax year in which the exchange takes place. If a partnership isn't notified by a partner of an exchange until after it has filed its partnership return, it must file Form 8308 within 30 days of notification. The partnership must also provide a copy of Form 8308 to each transferor and transferee by the later of: January 31 of the calendar year following the year of the exchange or 30 days after it receives notice of the exchange.

.05 Not a Like-Kind Exchange

Generally, exchanges of partnership interests do not qualify for tax-free *like-kind exchange* treatment [Ch. 6][Code Sec. 1031(a)(2)(D)]. However, a like-kind exchange could in some cases be treated as a tax-free contribution to a partnership.

¶24,135 BASIS OF TRANSFEREE PARTNER

The transferee determines the original basis for his or her interest by applying the general basis rules [¶ 24,095 et seq.] [Code Sec. 742; Reg. § 1.742-1].

> ▶ **OBSERVATION:** Your *original* basis must be adjusted from time to time to prevent the unintended benefit or detriment that would otherwise result.

.01 Adjustments for Transfers

If the partnership has filed an election [¶ 24,115], it will increase or decrease the adjusted basis of its property in the amount by which the partner's basis differs from the partner's pro rata share of the partnership's adjusted basis [Code Sec. 743]. The adjustment relates only to the partner. Partners have a special basis for the adjusted properties and report it on a return for the first tax year affected [Reg. § 1.743-1]. The adjustment to the basis of the partnership's retained property is made in substantially the same manner that it is made because of a distribution [¶ 24,115]. See Example 24-61 below.

.02 How Partnership Agreements Offer Special Basis Adjustments

In some cases, the partnership agreement may provide for a special allocation of depreciation, depletion, and gain or loss on contributed property whose basis differed from its value at contribution [¶ 24,065]. A partner's share of the adjusted basis of partnership property is determined according to the rules relating to contributed property [¶ 24,065] [Code Sec. 743(b)].

.03 Effect on Depletion Allowance

If an adjustment is made to the basis of depletable property, any depletion allowance is figured separately for each partner, including the transferee partner [Code Sec. 743(b); Reg. § 1.743-1(j)(5)].

¶24,140 SPECIAL ELECTIVE PARTNERSHIP BASIS FOR TRANSFEREE

If a partner has acquired his partnership interest (1) by purchase from a former partner or another partner; or (2) from a decedent partner, he can elect to have a special basis adjustment for property other than money received in a distribution from the partnership within two years after the partnership interest was acquired. This can be done if the partnership has not made an election to have the special basis adjustment apply to its assets [¶24,135]. The partner's election will accomplish substantially the same result as if the partnership had made the election [Code Sec. 732(d)]. This special basis adjustment is the difference between the amount paid for his interest, that is, his basis for his partnership interest, and his share of the adjusted basis of the partnership assets. The special basis adjustment applies to property received in current distributions as well as to distributions in complete liquidation of the partner's interest. Reg. § 1.732-1(d)(1)(iv) provides that if the partner makes the election when a distribution of depreciable or depletable property is received, the special basis adjustment is not diminished by any depletion or depreciation on that portion of the basis of partnership property which arises from the special basis adjustment. Depletion or depreciation on that portion for the period before distribution is allowed or allowable only if the partnership made the election.

If a transferee-partner wishes to make the election, it must be made on his tax return for the year of the distribution if the distribution includes any property subject to depreciation, depletion, or amortization. If it does not include any such property, the election may be made with the return for any tax year not later than the first tax year in which the basis of the distributed property is pertinent in determining income tax.

Example 24-61: The basis to transferee partner Mr. Spire of his 25 percent interest in partnership WJKS is $17,000. When he acquired such interest by purchase, the election under Sec. 754 was not in effect. The partnership inventory had a basis to the partnership of $14,000 and a value of $16,000. Spire's purchase price reflected $500 of this difference. Thus, $4,000 of the $17,000 paid by Spire for his interest was attributable to his share of partnership inventory with a basis of $3,500. Within two years after acquiring his interest, Spire retired from the partnership and received in liquidation of his entire interest cash of $1,500, inventory with a basis to the partnership of $3,500, property X (a capital asset) with an adjusted basis to the partnership of $2,000, and property Y (a depreciable asset) with an adjusted basis to the partnership of $4,000.

The fair market value of the inventory received by Spire was 25 percent of the value of all partnership inventory and was his share of such property. It is immaterial whether the inventory Spire received was on hand when Spire acquired his interest. In accordance with Spire's election under Sec. 732(d), the amount of his share of partnership basis which is attributable to partnership inventory is increased by $500 (25 percent of the $2,000 difference between the fair market value of such property, $16,000, and its $14,000 basis to the partnership at the time Spire acquired his interest). This adjustment under Sec. 732(d) applies only for purposes of distributions to partner Spire and not for purposes of partnership depreciation, depletion, or gain or loss on disposition.

Thus, the amount to be allocated among the properties received by Spire in the liquidating distribution is $15,500 ($17,000, Spire's basis for his interest, reduced by the amount of cash received, $1,500). This amount is allocated as follows:

1. Basis of inventory items received is $4,000—$3,500 common partnership basis for such items plus the special basis adjustment of $500 which Spire would have had under Sec. 743(b).
2. Remaining basis of $11,500 ($15,500 – $4,000) is to be allocated to the remaining property distributed to Spire in proportion to their adjusted bases to the partnership and adjusting that basis by any required increase or decrease. The adjusted basis to Spire of property X is $5,111 ($2,000, the adjusted basis of property X to the partnership, plus $2,000, the amount of unrealized appreciation in property X, plus $1,111 ($4,000/$9,000 multiplied by $2,500)). The adjusted basis of property Y to Spire is $6,389 ($4,000, the adjusted basis of property Y to the partnership, plus $1,000, the amount of unrealized appreciation in property Y, plus, $1,389 ($5,000/$9,000 multiplied by $2,500)). [Reg. § 1.732-1(d)(1)(vi)].

.01 Making the Election

To elect a special basis adjustment, a partner must file an attachment with his or her tax return stating that the partner chooses to adjust the basis of property received in a distribution. The attachment must show how the special basis adjustment is computed. The election must be made with the tax return for the year of the distribution if the distribution includes any property subject to depreciation, depletion or amortization. If no such property is included in the distribution, the election need not be made until the first year in which the basis of the distributed property will affect computation of your income tax.

.02 Excluded Property

The optional method cannot be used to determine the basis for the portion of a distribution to a partner that is treated as received by the partner in a sale or exchange under Sec. 751. It does apply to the portion treated as exchanged (given up) by the partner, since such property is treated as currently distributed before the exchange [¶ 24,120]. The partner's basis for the property received is cost [Code Sec. 732(e); Reg. § 1.732-1(e)].

.03 When a Partner Must Use Special Basis

The partner must make a special basis adjustment for distributed property received, whether or not the distribution was made within two years after the partner acquired the interest, if when the partner acquired the interest:

- The fair market value of all partnership property (except money) was more than 110 percent of its adjusted basis to the partnership;
- An allocation of basis [¶24,105] on a liquidation of the partner's interest immediately after its transfer would have resulted in a shift of basis from property not subject to an allowance for depreciation, depletion or amortization to property subject to such an allowance; and
- A special partnership basis adjustment at the time of the transfer would have changed your basis for the property actually distributed [Code Sec. 732(d); Reg. § 1.732-1(d)(4)].

Example 24-62: Partnership ABK owns three parcels of land, each of which has a basis to the partnership of $5,000 and each of which is worth $55,000. It also has depreciable property with a basis and value of $150,000. Mr. Delmore purchases Mr. Koch's partnership interest for $105,000 when the election under Sec. 754 is not in effect. At this time, the value of all the partnership property is $315,000, which exceeds 110 percent of $165,000, its basis to the partnership. Four years later, the partnership dissolves and Delmore receives 1 of the 3 parcels of land which had a basis to the partnership of $5,000 and 1/3 of the depreciable property which had a basis to the partnership at that time of $45,000, 1/3 of $135,000 ($150,000 original basis less $15,000 depreciation).

Suppose Delmore's basis for his interest at the time of distribution was $100,000 and it was allocated to the properties received by him in proportion to their respective bases to the partnership. Then the basis to him for the distributed land would be $10,000 ($5,000/$50,000 × $100,000) and the basis of the depreciable property would be $90,000 ($45,000/$50,000 × $100,000). *Result:* Delmore would, in effect, apply as the basis of depreciable property a portion of the amount which he had paid for nondepreciable property.

If the partnership adjustment for transfers had been applied to the transfer of the interest, Delmore would have had a different basis for the distributed property. Therefore, Delmore *must* increase the basis of the land by a special adjustment of $50,000 ($55,000 value less $5,000 partnership basis). Hence, his basis for the land will be $55,000 ($55,000/$100,000 × $100,000) and $45,000 ($45,000/$100,000 × $100,000) for the depreciable property.

.04 How to Allocate Basis Adjustments Among Partnership Assets

Code Sec. 743(a) provides that the basis of partnership property will not be adjusted as the result of a transfer of an interest in a partnership by sale or exchange or on the death of a partner unless the election provided by Code Sec. 754 (relating to optional adjustment to basis of partnership property) is in effect with respect to such partnership or unless the partnership has a substantial built-in loss immediately after such transfer.

Code Sec. 743(b) provides for an adjustment to the basis of partnership property in the following situations:

- The transfer of an interest in a partnership by sale or exchange;
- Upon the death of a partner;
- If an election under Code Sec. 754 is in effect; or
- If the partnership has a substantial built-in loss immediately after such transfer.

The adjusted basis of the partnership property will be increased by the excess of the basis to the transferee partner of his interest in the partnership over his proportionate share of the adjusted basis of the partnership property [Code Sec. 743(b)(1)]. Alternatively, under Code Sec. 743(b)(2) the adjusted basis of the partnership property will be decreased by the excess of the transferee partner's proportionate share of the adjusted basis of the partnership property over the basis of his interest in the partnership.

The increase or decrease will constitute an adjustment to the basis of partnership property with respect to the transferee partner only. A partner's proportionate share of the adjusted basis of partnership property shall be determined in accordance with his interest in partnership capital and, in the case of property contributed to the partnership by a partner, Code Sec. 704(c) (relating to contributed property) shall apply in determining such share. In the case of an adjustment under this subsection to the basis of partnership property subject to depletion, any depletion allowable shall be determined separately for the transferee partner with respect to his interest in such property [Code Sec. 743(b)].

PAYMENTS UPON RETIREMENT OR DEATH OF PARTNER

¶24,145 CROSS-PURCHASE OR LIQUIDATION OF DEPARTING OR RETIRING PARTNER'S INTEREST

When a partner withdraws or retires from a partnership the partner can structure the departure either as a cross-purchase of the partner's interest by the remaining partners under Code Secs. 741 and 751(a), or as a liquidation of the partnership interest by the partnership under Code Sec. 736. Under Code Secs. 741 and 751(a), the sale of a partnership interest will generate capital gain or loss to the partner, except to the extent that the partner is being compensated for an interest in unrealized receivables and inventory, which produce ordinary income. Gain will result to the extent that the amount realized exceeds the adjusted basis of the partnership interest, or loss to the extent that the adjusted basis of the partnership interest exceeds the amount realized on the sale. The gain or loss will be treated as capital gain or loss unless the partnership has unrealized receivables and inventory items (collectively referred to as *Section 751 property*) [Code Sec. 741]. In this case, the partner will be treated as if the partner directly sold his or her interest in these items, resulting in ordinary income treatment. The downside to the cross-purchase is that the partnership is not entitled to a deduction for any part of the purchase price.

Payments made by a partnership in liquidation of the interest of a retired partner are governed by Code Sec. 736, which divides such payments into three categories as follows:

1. Those representing the recipient's distributive share of partnership income [Code Sec. 736(a)(1)],
2. Those deemed to be guaranteed payments [Code Sec. 736(a)(2)], and
3. Those in exchange for the partner's interest in partnership property [Code Sec. 736(b)].

If the payments are considered to represent a distributive share of partnership income or deemed to be guaranteed payments, then the amount of the payments received is taxed to the recipient as ordinary income. On the other hand, if the payments are considered to be in exchange for partnership property, then the amount received in excess of the adjusted basis of the withdrawing partner's partnership interest is taxed as capital gain.

In *D.W. Wallis,*[48] the Court of Appeals for the Eleventh Circuit affirmed the Tax Court to conclude that amounts paid to a partner in excess of his capital account for a period of time after his withdrawal from the partnership were guaranteed payments reportable as ordinary income where the payments were determined without regard to partnership income. Although the partner contended that the payments were made in exchange for his interest in the partnership and reportable as capital gain income, the payments were actually made pursuant to the partnership agreement in place of a retirement plan.

.01 Liquidation of Partnership Interest

Generally, payments made in liquidation of the partnership interest of a retiring partner or a deceased partner are treated as being made in exchange for an interest in partnership property [Code Sec. 736(b)(1); Reg. § 1.736-1(b)(1)]. However, if the retiring or deceased partner is a general partner, and capital is not a material income-producing factor for the partnership, such assets do not include unrealized receivables or goodwill (see specially treated assets below). And payments in exchange for inventory in the case of any retiring or deceased partner regardless of whether capital is an income-producing factor are treated as ordinary income [¶ 24,120].

Capital is not a material income-producing factor where substantially all the gross income of a business consists of fees, commissions, or other compensation for personal services performed by an individual. The practice of his or her profession by a doctor, dentist, lawyer, architect, or accountant will not be treated as a trade or business in which capital is a material income-producing factor even though the practitioner may have a substantial capital investment in professional equipment or in the physical plant constituting the office provided the capital investment is merely incidental to the professional practice.[49]

The remaining partners get no deduction for payments treated as distributions in exchange for assets. The payments reduce the basis for your interest and result in gain to the extent they exceed any remaining basis, or loss to the extent of any remaining basis after all payments are received. Assuming only cash is received, gain or loss is

---

[48] *D.W. Wallis,* 98 TCM 364, Dec. 57,973(M), TC Memo. 2009-243, *aff'd in an unpublished opinion, per curiam,* CA-11, 2010-2 USTC ¶ 50,766.

[49] H.R. Conf. Rep. No. 213, 103d Cong. 1st Sess. 697-98 (1993).

recognized immediately under the rules in ¶ 24,120 [Code Sec. 731(a); Reg. § 1.731-1(a)].

Example 24-63: The ABC partnership pays retired partner Mr. Celan $15,000 per year for ten years for his interest in the partnership. The basis of Celan's interest is $90,000. Of the $150,000 Celan will receive over the 10 years, $90,000 will reduce his basis and the remaining $60,000 will be capital gain.

Purchasing partners may be able to obtain amortization deductions under Code Sec. 197 for the seller's share of the partnership's good will and other intangible assets where an Code Sec. 754 election has been made. Code Sec. 197 allows the adjusted basis of any *Section 197 intangible* to be amortized ratably over a fifteen-year period beginning with the month in which the intangible was acquired [Code Sec. 197(a)]. Section 197 intangible includes goodwill, going concern value, workforce in place, business books, records, and other information bases, patents, know-how, governmental licenses and permits, covenants not to compete, and certain franchises, trademarks, and tradenames [Code Secs. 197(d)(1)(C) through (F)]. The term does not include financial interest, including interests in corporations, partnerships, trust, or estates [Code Sec. 197(e)(1)(A)]. Any amortizable Code Sec. 197 intangible is treated as property which can be depreciated under Code Sec. 167 [Code Sec. 197(f)(7)]. When a partnership owning an amortizable Code Sec. 197 intangible liquidates the interest of a partner and has a section 754 election in effect, it can generally amortize any resulting increase in the basis of Code Sec. 197 intangibles over a fifteen-year period.

▶ **PRACTICE TIP:** Partnerships holding depreciable or amortizable property, including intangible assets, that have appreciated in value should make sure that they have a Section 754 election in place so that they can amortize the increase in basis over a fifteen-year period when they liquidate the interest of a partner.

Specially Treated Assets

If the withdrawing partner is a general partner, and if capital is not a material income-producing factor of the partnership (e.g., a service-oriented partnership), payments for the following assets are not treated as payments in exchange for an interest in partnership property [Code Sec. 736(b)]:

- Amounts paid for goodwill are not treated as distributions unless the partnership agreement expressly[50] provides for reasonable payments for goodwill. If the agreement does not so provide, such amounts are other payments subject to the rules described below; and

- Amounts paid for unrealized receivables are not payments for your interest in partnership assets. They are other payments. Payments that are not made for the interest in partnership assets are either distributive shares of income or guaranteed payments, depending on whether or not they are based on income.

---

[50] *Jackson Inv. Co.*, CA-9, 65-2 USTC ¶ 9451, 346 F2d 187, *nonacq.* 1967-2 CB 4; *V.Z. Smith*, CA-10, 63-1 USTC ¶ 9211, 313 F2d 16.

Payments Based on Income

Payments measured by partnership income are distributive shares of partnership income regardless of the period over which they are paid [Code Sec. 736(a)(1); Reg. § 1.736-1(a)(3)(i)]. They are taxable to you as though you continued to be a partner and thus reduce the amount of the remaining partners' distributive shares [Reg. § 1.736-1(a)(4), (6)].

Example 24-64: Each year AB partnership pays retired partner Ms. Cummings 10 percent of partnership net income. Payments are taxed to Cummings as if she still had a 10 percent distributive share of the partnership income, loss, deductions and credits.

Payments Not Based on Income

If the payments are determined without regard to the partnership income and are not payments for an interest in partnership property [described above], they are guaranteed payments (such as salary) made to one who is not a partner. They are ordinary income to you and a deductible partnership expense [Code Sec. 736(a)(2); Reg. § 1.736-1(a)(3)(ii), -1(a)(4)].

Example 24-65: If, in Example 24-64, the payments were $100 per week rather than 10 percent of partnership net income, the payments received by Cummings are ordinary income to her and are deductible by the partnership as salary.

Income in Respect of Decedent

Amounts includible as other payments in the gross income of the successor in interest of a deceased partner are taxed to the successor the same way they would have been taxed to the decedent [Code Sec. 753; Reg. § 1.753-1(a), (d)]. Payments to the successor determined without regard to partnership income are taxed to him or her as if he or she were a partner and the payments were salary or interest on capital; that is, as ordinary income. Payments determined with reference to partnership income are taxed to the successor as if he or she were a partner receiving his or her distributive share of partnership income. The successor is allowed a deduction for any amounts that may have been included in the gross estate of the decedent [Ch. 25], but is not allowed an optional adjustment [¶ 24,140] to the basis of a deceased partner's share of receivables existing at the partner's death.[51]

.02 Reporting Gain or Loss on Installment Payments for Interest in Assets

Gain on installment payments for a partnership interest generally is not recognized until capital is recovered, unless the election below applies.

Partner's Election

If the amount paid for the interest is a fixed sum payable in installments, you may elect to report any gain or loss proportionately over the years of receipt. The gain or loss for

[51] Rev. Rul. 66-325, 1966-2 CB 249.

each year is the difference between (1) the amount treated as a distribution in that year and (2) the portion of your basis for your partnership interest attributable to such distribution [Reg. § 1.736-1(b) (6)].

Example 24-66: CBA is a personal service partnership. When partner Mr. Agee retires, the partnership's balance sheet is as follows:

Assets			*Capital*		
	Basis	*Market Value*		*Per Books*	*Market Value*
Cash	$13,000	$13,000	Liabilities . . .	$ 3,000	$ 3,000
Capital assets .	20,000	23,000	Capital		
	$33,000	$36,000	Agee	10,000	11,000
			Baker	10,000	11,000
			Colvin	10,000	11,000
				$33,000	$36,000

It is agreed that Agee's capital interest is valued at $12,000 (1/3 of $36,000) and that Agee will receive $5,000 a year for three years after his retirement. The first $5,000, however, will include Agee's share of the liabilities ($1,000) assumed by Baez and Colvin.

Tax treatment of Agee. The basis of Agee's interest is $11,000 ($10,000 investment plus $1,000, his share of liabilities). Of the $15,000 Agee is to receive, only $12,000 is in payment of his interest in partnership property. The remainder is ordinary income. Thus, Agee will have $1,000 capital gain ($12,000 minus $11,000) and $3,000 ordinary income. Agee may report the $1,000 gain at the time he receives his last payment or he may elect to allocate the gain over the 3 years. If he elects to allocate, he may report $333 capital gain and $1,000 ordinary income each year (1/3 of the total amounts of capital gain and ordinary income, respectively). The remainder of the payment is a return of capital.

Tax treatment of remaining partners. The partnership cannot deduct Agee's $1,000 capital gain since the amount represents a purchase of Agee's capital interest by the partnership. The partnership may deduct Agee's $3,000 ordinary income.

Example 24-67: Assume the same facts as in Example 24-66 except that the agreement provides for payments to Agee for three years of a percentage of annual income instead of a fixed amount. Here, Agee cannot elect to report his gain proportionately over the years. All payments received by Agee up to $12,000 are treated as payments for Agee's interest in partnership property. His gain of $1,000 is taxed only after he has received his full basis. Any payment in excess of $12,000 is treated as a distributive share of partnership income to Agee.

¶24,150 HOW INSTALLMENT PAYMENTS ARE ALLOCATED

Payments in liquidation of a partner's partnership interest may be made in installments over several years. The three methods of dividing these payments are described here.

.01 Fixed Payments

If a fixed amount (whether or not supplemented by any additional amounts) is to be received over a fixed number of years, the portion of each payment to be treated as a distribution under Code Sec. 736(b) for the tax year shall bear the same ratio to the total fixed agreed payments for such year (as distinguished from the amount actually received) as the total fixed agreed payments under Code Sec. 736(b) bear to the total fixed agreed payments under Code Secs. 736(a) and (b). The balance, if any, of such amount received in the same tax year shall be treated as a distributive share or a guaranteed payment under Code Sec. 736(a)(1) or (2). However, if the total amount received in any one year is less than the amount considered as a distribution under Code Sec. 736(b) for that year, then any unapplied portion shall be added to the portion of the payments for the following year or years which are to be treated as a distribution under Code Sec. 736(b) [Reg. § 1.736-1(b)(5)(i)].

Example 24-68: Retiring partner Mr. Smith is entitled to ten annual payments of $6,000 each for his interest in partnership property. He receives only $3,500 in Year 1. In Year 2, he receives $10,000. Of this amount, $8,500 ($6,000 plus $2,500 from Year 1) is treated as payment for his interest in assets, $1,500 as other payments under Code Sec. 736(a) [Reg. § 1.736-1(b)(5)(i)].

.02 When Amount Varies

If the retiring partner or deceased partner's successor in interest receives payments that are not fixed in amount, these payments are first treated as payments in exchange for his interest in partnership property under Code Sec. 736(b) to the extent of the value of that interest and, thereafter, all payments are treated as other payments under Code Sec. 736(a) [Reg. § 1.736-1(b)(5)(ii)].

.03 Allocation by Agreement

In lieu of the rules provided above, the allocation of each annual payment between Code Sec. 736(a) and (b) may be made in any manner to which all the remaining partners and the withdrawing partner or his successor in interest agree, provided that the total amount allocated to property under Code Sec. 736(b) does not exceed the fair market value of such property at the date of death or retirement [Reg. § 1.736-1(b)(5)(iii)].

Estates and Trusts

ESTATES AND TRUSTS IN GENERAL

How estates and trusts are taxed . . ¶25,001
Liability of fiduciaries . . . . ¶25,005
Nature of estates and trusts . . . . . . ¶25,010

WHO IS TAXABLE ON ESTATE AND TRUST INCOME

To whom estate or trust income is taxable . . . . ¶25,015
Distributable net income . . . . ¶25,020
Distributions by simple trusts . . . . ¶25,025
Distributions by estates and complex trusts . . . . ¶25,030
Beneficiary's share of each item of distributable net income . . . . ¶25,035

INCOME—CAPITAL GAINS AND LOSSES

Gross income . . . . ¶25,040
Capital gains and losses . . . . ¶25,045
Basis of property to estate or trust . . . . ¶25,050

DEDUCTIONS AND CREDITS

Deductions in general . . . . ¶25,055
Deduction for personal exemption . . . . ¶25,060
Charitable contributions . . . . ¶25,065
Depreciation or depletion . . . . ¶25,070
Net operating loss deduction . . . . ¶25,075
Expenses . . . . ¶25,080
Deduction for distributions to beneficiaries . . . . ¶25,085
Deductions in transactions between related parties . . . . ¶25,090
Credits against tax . . . . ¶25,095

RATES, RETURNS, AND PAYMENT FOR DECEDENTS, ESTATES, AND TRUSTS

Rates and returns . . . . ¶25,100
Estimated tax payment by estates and trusts . . . . ¶25,105
Tax years of estates and trusts . . . . ¶25,110

SPECIAL PROBLEMS

Grantor trust rules . . . . ¶25,115
Intentionally defective grantor trusts . . . . ¶25,116
Throwback of excess distributions by complex trusts . . . . ¶25,120
Common trust funds . . . . ¶25,125

ESTATES AND TRUSTS IN GENERAL

An estate of a deceased person, or a trust, is a separate taxable entity. The fiduciary (an executor or administrator for an estate, a trustee for a trust) must file a return and, when a tax is due, pay the tax. Generally, estates and trusts are taxed in the same manner as individuals.

¶25,001 HOW ESTATES AND TRUSTS ARE TAXED

In general, for income tax purposes, a trust is taxed as an entity separate and distinct from the grantor and the trust beneficiaries are taxed on its income just as an individual would be. The most important difference between the tax treatment of an individual and a trust is that the trust is treated as a hybrid pass-through entity. As a result, the trust is taxed on undistributed trust income (DNI) and will be able to claim a deduction when it distributes its income to its beneficiaries who are required to include these distributions in income. For further discussion of DNI, see ¶25,020.

Taxes for estates and trusts are computed by using the rate schedule specially provided for them. Special rules that affect the computing of taxable income, deductions, and credits are discussed in this chapter. These rules do not apply to certain business trusts that are more nearly associations or corporations and taxed as such. For further discussion of the taxation of estates and trusts, see *Estate & Gift Tax Handbook*, published by CCH.

Some trusts are not taxable entities. For example, a revocable trust is a separate entity for trust law purposes but is not a separate taxable entity for federal income tax purposes. A grantor of such a trust must report the trust's income and deductions on his or her individual return as if there were no trust. Trusts that do not become separate taxable entities are discussed at ¶25,115. The balance of this chapter explains the income tax on (1) trusts that are taxable entities and (2) decedents' estates. In certain cases, the trust is taxed at the grantor's rates; see ¶25,115.

.01 Allocation of Income

Generally, the income of an estate or trust is taxed either to the estate or trust through its fiduciary, or to the beneficiaries, or in part to each, depending upon the disposition of the income under the terms of the will or trust and state law. In this way, the entire taxable income of the estate or trust is taxed [¶25,015].

.02 Returns

The fiduciary of an estate (the executor or administrator, depending on whether there is a will) and the fiduciary of a trust (the trustee) must file Form 1041, *U.S. Income Tax Return for Estates and Trusts*, to report:

- The income, deductions, gains, losses, etc. of the estate or trust;
- The income that is either accumulated or held for future distribution or distributed currently to the beneficiaries;
- Any income tax liability of the estate or trust; and
- Employment taxes paid to household employees.

The filing requirements are explained in ¶25,100. The fiduciaries must also file a separate Schedule K-1 for each beneficiary. The K-1 notifies the beneficiaries of the amounts to be included on their income tax returns. For an estate, the executor or administrator, in addition to filing the estate's income tax return, generally files the decedent's final income tax return as well. The deceased person's final income tax return covers the period ending on the date of his or her death; the estate's income tax return covers the period beginning the day after death.

¶25,005 LIABILITY OF FIDUCIARIES

If you serve as a fiduciary, you assume the rights and duties of the taxpayer (the trust or estate) for income tax purposes. However, you ordinarily are not personally liable for the tax. Usually the tax is paid from the assets of the estate or trust [Code Sec. 6903; Reg. § 301.6903-1(a)]. On the other hand, if you use these assets to pay the taxpayer's debts without first satisfying the federal government's tax claim, you will be personally liable for the tax deficiency up to the amounts paid.[1]

.01 Discharge from Personal Liability

As an executor or administrator, you can apply for release from personal liability for a decedent's income and gift taxes after you have filed the returns for these taxes. You file the application at the office where the estate tax return is to be filed. If no return is required, you file the application where the decedent's last income tax return is to be filed. The IRS must notify you within nine months after receiving the application of the amount of taxes due. You are then relieved from any future deficiencies on paying the amount. You are also discharged if the IRS does not notify you within the nine-month period [Code Sec. 6905(a), (b); Reg. § 301.6905-1].

¶25,010 NATURE OF ESTATES AND TRUSTS

.01 Trust Defined

A trust is a relationship in which one person—the trustee—is the owner of the title to property, subject to an obligation to keep or use the property for the benefit of another—the beneficiary. Reg. § 301.7701-4(a) provides that the term "trust" refers to an arrangement created by a will or by an inter vivos declaration whereby trustees take title to property for the purpose of protecting or conserving it for the beneficiaries. Usually the beneficiaries of such a trust do no more than accept the benefits thereof and are not the voluntary planners or creators of the trust arrangement. However, the beneficiaries of a trust may be the persons who create it, and it will be recognized as a trust if it was created for the purpose of protecting and conserving the trust property for beneficiaries who stand in the same relation to the trust as they would if the trust had been created by others for them. Generally, an arrangement is treated as a trust if it can be shown that the purpose of the arrangement is to vest in

[1] 31 U.S.C. § 3713(b) (federal insolvency statute which gives federal liens priority over other creditors when the taxpayer is insolvent.

trustees the responsibility for the protection and conservation of property for beneficiaries who cannot share in the discharge of this responsibility. In Rev. Rul. 2013-14,[2] the IRS concluded that a Mexican Land Trust that held title to residential real property was not a trust under federal tax law. Although a Mexican bank held legal title to the property, the bank had no duties with respect to the property, and the U.S. purchaser of the property was treated as the owner of the property for tax purposes.

A trust created by an instrument other than a will is an inter vivos or living trust. This type of trust may also be called a revocable or irrevocable inter vivos trust. A trust created by will is a testamentary trust. The subject matter of the trust is often referred to as the trust res, trust principal, trust property or trust corpus. All trusts have an identifiable home base or *situs*. A trust's situs is the state whose courts have primary jurisdiction over the trust. When a trust is drafted, it is important to consider which state's law will apply and how the application of the laws in that state will affect administration of the trust. It may be necessary to move the situs of the trust in order to find laws that are the most favorable to the trust's beneficiaries. The drafter of the trust should therefore add a provision to the trust which specifically authorizes a trustee to move the situs of the trust and to change the law governing the administration of the trust.

The most common types of property making up the trust principal or trust corpus are bonds, stocks, mortgages, titles to land and bank accounts. The person who creates a trust is known as the grantor, creator, donor or settlor of the trust. As for a testamentary trust, the creator is the testator—the person who executed the will. As already indicated, once created, a trust becomes a separate taxable entity for which a return usually must be filed and taxes paid.

.02 Estate Defined

When someone dies a new legal entity comes into being to handle the business, personal and financial affairs of the decedent. The legal entity is referred to as the decedent's estate and is established under the laws of the state in which the decedent lives. The state's probate court supervises and directs the administration of the decedent's estate. An executor or personal representative administers the affairs of the estate. The named executor, if there is a will, and the administrator, if there is no will, is the fiduciary in charge of an estate. They take charge of the decedent's probate property and wind up his affairs. Probate property is defined as any property owned by the decedent at the time of death and subject to the probate process under state law. The decedent's estate, like a trust, is a separate taxable entity and the fiduciary in charge has the same tax obligations as the trustee of a trust. The decedent's estate exists until the final distribution of its assets to the heirs and other beneficiaries.

.03 Election to Treat Revocable Trust as Part of Estate

Executors have the option to make an irrevocable election to treat and tax a qualified revocable trust (QRT) as part of the deceased person's probate estate (rather than a separate trust) for federal income tax purposes [Code Sec. 645(a)]. If the election is made, an estate is able to keep the revocable trust as is, instead of having to reregister it to the estate. If an estate tax return is required, the election is effective for all tax

---

[2] Rev. Rul. 2013-14, IRB 2013-26, 1267; Rev. Rul. 92-105, 1992-2 CB 204.

years of the estate ending after the date of the decedent's death and before the date that is six months after the date of the final determination of estate tax liability [Code Sec. 645(b)(2)(B)]. However, if no estate tax return is required to be filed, the election is effective for the two years from the date of the decedent's death [Code Sec. 645(b)(2)(A)].

The election is irrevocable and must be made by both the trustee of the revocable trust and the executor of the decedent's estate by the due date for filing the estate's income tax return for its first tax year (including extensions) [Code Sec. 645(c)]. Once the deadline for the tax filing due date has passed, it is too late to make this election.

Why Election Is a Good Idea

The election to treat a QRT as part of an estate makes sense because the election will make it possible for the QRT to take advantage of income tax breaks that are only available to estates. The election is designed to ease the estate administrative burdens. If the election to treat a revocable trust as part of the estate is made, only one Form 1041 must be filed, rather than separate returns for the trust and the estate. Treating a revocable trust as part of a decedent's estate can save taxes because estates receive more favorable tax-treatment than revocable trusts receive for the following reasons:

1. Estates are allowed a charitable deduction for amounts permanently set aside for charitable purposes while post death revocable trusts are allowed a charitable deduction only for amounts paid to charities [Code Sec. 642(c)].
2. The active participation requirement imposed by the passive loss rules is waived in the case of estates (but not revocable trusts) for two years after the owner's death.
3. Estates (but not revocable trusts) can qualify for the amortization of reforestation expenditures under Code Sec. 194.
4. Trusts are required to use calendar years, but estates are not. By electing to be treated as part of the estate, a qualified revocable trust effectively can have a noncalendar or fiscal tax year during that period and engage in income deferral to postpone the payment of taxes.
5. Another reason for making the election is to avoid the generation-skipping transfer tax. While the election is in effect, the trust is not subject to the generation-skipping transfer tax.
6. The election to combine the revocable trust and the estate can simplify the winding up process traditionally associated with settling an estate. It may even eliminate the need to file a separate income tax return for the revocable trust.
7. Electing qualified revocable trusts may deduct up to $25,000 in real estate passive losses for active rental real estate activities [Code Sec. 469(i)(4)]. Trusts are typically not entitled to this deduction but qualified revocable trusts electing to be treated as part of an estate would be able to deduct active rental losses realized by the trust on the estate tax return.
8. Electing qualified revocable trusts may qualify for the $600 personal exemption deduction under Code Sec. 642(b).
9. In a situation where the revocable trust uses a pecuniary formula to fund a testamentary trust (such as a credit shelter or a marital trust), the funding of such

trust will cause either a gain or a loss if the assets have changed in value since the date of death. If the assets have declined in value, the loss that results from the funding can only be used if a Section 645 election is in place.

How to Make the Election

The election may be made whether or not an executor is appointed. If an executor is appointed, the executor and the trustee of the QRT make the election by filing Form 8855, *Election to Treat a Qualified Revocable Trust as Part of an Estate.* If an executor is not appointed, the trustee makes the election by filing Form 8855 [Reg. § 1.645-1(c)]. If an executor has been appointed, Form 8855 must be filed no later than the time for filing the Form 1041 for the first tax year of the combined electing trust and related estate. If no executor exists, Form 8855 must be filed no later than the first tax year of the electing trust regardless of income. If an extension is granted for the filing of the Form 1041 for the first tax year of the combined electing trust and related estate, Form 8855 will be timely if it is filed by the extended time for filing Form 1041 [Reg. § 1.645-1(c)].

The fiduciaries of the electing trust and the fiduciaries of the related estate each continue to have a responsibility for filing returns and paying the tax due for their respective entities even though a election to treat a QRT as part of the estate has been made. The executor must file a complete, accurate, and timely Form 1041 for the combined related estate and electing trust for each tax year during the election period. The trustee of the electing trust must timely provide the executor of the related estate with all the trust information necessary to permit the executor to file a complete, accurate, and timely Form 1041 for the combined electing trust and related estate for each tax year during the election period. The trustee and the executor must allocate the tax burden of the combined electing trust and related estate in a manner that reasonably reflects the respective tax obligations of the electing trust and related estate or gifts may result [Reg. § 1.645-1(c)].

The trustee of an electing trust for which an election will be made must obtain a taxpayer identification number (TIN) on the death of the decedent and must furnish it to the payors of the trust. The trustee must also use this TIN to file Forms 1041 as an estate during the election period. If an election will be made for a QRT, its trustee need not file a Form 1041 for the short tax year beginning with the decedent's date of death and ending Dec. 31 of that year [Reg. § 1.645-1(d)].

What Revocable Trusts Qualify for the Election

To qualify for the election, the revocable trust must be a *qualified revocable trust*. A QRT is defined as any trust, or portion of a trust, that on the date of the death of the decedent was treated as owned by the decedent because of a power held by the decedent [Code Sec. 645(b)(1)]. Retained powers could include the power to revoke the trust or the power to affect beneficial enjoyment of the income for a period commencing after the occurrence of some stated event [Code Sec. 676]. A power, exercisable by the decedent with the approval or consent of a nonadverse party does not prevent the trust from being treated as a QRT [Reg. § 1.645-1(b)(1)]. Conversely, if only the spouse, and not the decedent, holds power to revoke, the trust is not a QRT.

.04 Multiple Trusts

You can create several (multiple) trusts in one instrument and have the same trustee administer all of them. The income of each trust is taxable as income of a separate entity. Whether only one trust or more than one trust has been created depends upon your intention as determined from the trust agreement.[3] The Supreme Court has held that separate trusts are created, even if there is only one trust instrument and the trust assets are not segregated, when each beneficiary has a separate account and is granted a fixed share in the trust property.[4]

However, if tax avoidance was a principal purpose for setting up multiple trusts that have substantially the same grantor and beneficiaries, two or more trusts are treated as one and taxed accordingly. For this rule, a husband and wife are treated as one person. [Code Sec. 643(f)].

.05 Abusive Trust Schemes

Taxpayers should avoid trust arrangements that promise to reduce or eliminate federal taxes in unauthorized ways.

A legitimate trust is a form of ownership that completely separates responsibility and control of assets from all of the benefits of ownership.

> ▶ **TAX TIP:** Watch Out For the Name of the Trust: In the past, abusive trusts have had names that refer to constitutional issues, fairness, equity or patriotic themes. Sometimes they have names that resemble common business organizations or nonabusive trusts.

In the typical abusive trust arrangement, owners of the trust effectively retain control over trust assets but are promised tax benefits that are not legally available in conjunction with such control. Promoters or abusive trusts typically promise tax benefits that are unavailable under the law. The promised benefits often include the following: (1) reduction or elimination of income subject to tax; (2) deductions for personal expenses paid by the trust; (3) depreciation deductions of an owner's personal residence and furnishings; (4) a stepped-up basis for property transferred to the trust; (5) the reduction or elimination of self-employment taxes; and (6) the reduction or elimination of gift and estate taxes.

Abusive trust arrangements often use sham entities with no economic substance in order to hide the true ownership of assets and income or to disguise the economic substance of transactions that are designed to avoid federal income tax. These arrangements frequently involve more than one trust, each holding different assets of the taxpayer such as the taxpayer's business, business equipment, home or automobile, as well as interests in other trusts. Funds may flow from one trust to another trust by way of rental agreements, fees for services, purchase and sale agreements, and distributions. Some trusts purport to involve charitable purposes. In some situations, one or more foreign trusts also may be part of the arrangement. The courts will consider the following factors to determine whether a trust actually exists for tax purposes: (1) did the taxpayer's relationship to the trust property materially change after the trust was created; (2) did the trust have an independent trustee; (3) did an economic interest in the trust pass to other beneficiaries; and (4) did the taxpayer feel bound by restrictions imposed by the trust or the law of trusts. If the answer to these

---

[3] *F.W. Smith*, 25 TC 143, Dec. 21,302 (1955).

[4] *Fiduciary Trust Co.*, DC-NY, 41-1 USTC ¶9196, 36 FSupp 653; *E.P. Boyce*, CA-5, 62-1 USTC ¶9150, 296 F2d 731.

questions is no, it is likely that the trust was a sham entity devoid of economic substance. The Tax Court found this to be the case in *S.E. Vlach*,[5] where trusts established for asset protection by a doctor were found to be shams and were disregarded for tax purposes.

Red Flags

The IRS lists examples of five trust arrangements that it views as abusive. Some of the telltale characteristics of an abusive trust include the following:

1. Ownership of assets or property has not really been transferred into the trust because the original owner has retained the authority to have income earned by those assets benefit him.
2. The trustee is the promoter, or a relative or friend of the owner who simply carries out the directions of the owner whether or not permitted by the terms of the trust.
3. The trustee gives the owner: (a) checks that are pre-signed by the trustee, (b) checks that are accompanied by a rubber stamp of the trustee's signature, or (c) a credit card or a debit card so cash can readily be obtained from the trust. The assets of the trust are used for the owner's benefit.
4. The trust transforms a taxpayer's otherwise nondeductible personal, living or educational expenses into deductible items.
5. The trust seeks to avoid tax liability by ignoring either the true ownership of the assets or the true substance of the transaction.

In a nutshell, the IRS is targeting trust arrangements that ignore the true ownership of assets or the substance of the transaction. You should be suspicious of any promoter who says that you can transfer your business or home into a trust and still retain full benefit from the assets transferred into the trust while also reducing or eliminating tax. Be especially wary of anyone who says that with a trust you can now deduct your personal living expenses or claim charitable contribution deductions for payments that really benefit you and your family. The big tip off is being told by a promoter that you can set up a trust, give up no control over your assets and pay zero tax. It just does not work that way. The IRS also warns that your antennas should go up if a tax promoter suggests that you not check a proposed trust arrangement with a tax advisor, such as an attorney or accountant, or with the IRS.

If you have used one of the so-called abusive trusts in the past in order to eliminate taxes, the IRS advises you to recompute your tax liability for those years without the trusts and to file amended returns.

Dirty Dozen Tax Scams

In its list of "dirty dozen" tax scams,[6] the IRS warns taxpayers to avoid among other things, the misuse of trusts that are designed to avoid tax. According to the IRS, "[f]or years, unscrupulous promoters have urged taxpayers to transfer assets into trusts. While there are legitimate uses of trusts in tax and estate planning, some highly

---

[5] *S.E. Vlach*, 105 TCM 1690, Dec. 59,525(M), TC Memo. 2013-116; *see also L. Markosian*, Dec. 36,858, 73 TC 1235 (1980); *AMC Trust*, 90 TCM 87, Dec. 56,103(M), TC Memo. 2005-180.

[6] IRS News Release, IR-2013-33, March 27, 2013.

questionable transactions promise reduction of income subject to tax, deductions for personal expenses and reduced estate or gift taxes. Such trusts rarely deliver the tax benefits promised and are used primarily as a means of avoiding income tax liability and hiding assets from creditors, including the IRS. IRS personnel have seen an increase in the improper use of private annuity trusts and foreign trusts to shift income and deduct personal expenses. As with other arrangements, taxpayers should seek the advice of a trusted professional before entering a trust arrangement."

.06 Decanting

The term "decanting" describes the act of a trustee distributing or paying trust property directly to another trust in order to address changes in the law, reform trust terms, address trust administration problems or handle changed circumstances. Decanting enables trustees and beneficiaries to change the terms of the trusts without having to petition a court to change trust terms or rectify mistakes. A number of states have adopted decanting statutes but not all state decanting statutes are alike. Some permit decanting only if the trustee's power to invade the trust is absolute or broad rather than being limited to health, education, maintenance and support. Most expressly require that an income interest cannot be eliminated but must be preserved. Some but not all statutes provide that the decanting power cannot be used to extend the term of the trust beyond the applicable rule against perpetuities.

The act of decanting is similar to the exercise of a special power of appointment over trust property or to the discretionary distribution of property from a trust by the trustee to a beneficiary. Some states expressly state that the power to invade is a special power of appointment while other states expressly state that the power is not exercisable in favor of the trustee, the trustee's estate, the trustee's creditors, or the creditors of the trustee's estate. The restriction is necessary in order to avoid having the power to decant treated as a general power of appointment includible in the gross estate under Code Sec. 2041.

WHO IS TAXABLE ON ESTATE AND TRUST INCOME

¶25,015 TO WHOM ESTATE OR TRUST INCOME IS TAXABLE

Beneficiaries are generally taxed on distributions they receive or are entitled to receive from the estate or trust, but only to the extent of their share of its distributable net income (DNI) [¶25,020-¶25,035].

A fiduciary is taxed on the taxable income of the estate or trust. Taxable income is gross income [¶25,040] less the deductions discussed in ¶25,055 et seq.

Under certain conditions, the income of a trust is not taxed to either the beneficiaries or the fiduciary. Instead, it is taxed to the grantor or other persons having control of the trust property or income [¶25,115].

.01 Different Tax Years

Beneficiaries are taxed on the distributions for the tax year or years of the estate or trust that end within or with the beneficiary's tax year [Code Secs. 652(c), 662(c); Reg. §§1.652(c)-1, 1.662(c)-1].

Example 25-1: A beneficiary filing a return for calendar year 2013 would include distributions received from an estate having a fiscal year beginning in 2012 and ending in 2013.

NOTE: Trusts, unlike estates, may not use fiscal tax years; they are generally limited to calendar tax years [Code Sec. 645(a)].

.02 Income, Deductions, and Credits When Trust Terminates

After a trust terminates, its income, deductions and credits are attributed to the beneficiaries. However, a trust does not terminate automatically. A reasonable period is allowed for the trustee to wind up its affairs. During this period, the status of the trust income is determined under the terms of the trust instrument and state law [Reg. §1.641(b)-3].

¶25,020 DISTRIBUTABLE NET INCOME

Distributable net income (DNI) is an extremely important tax concept that is unique to the tax treatment of trusts and estates.

.01 Functions of DNI

DNI performs the following two critical functions:

- DNI measures the taxable income reportable by beneficiaries, even if the actual amount of trust or estate distributions is greater; and
- DNI limits the deductions allowed to a trust or estate for distributions made to its beneficiaries. DNI is also used to determine the character of distributions to the beneficiaries [Code Secs. 643, 652, 662; Reg. §§1.643(a)-1, 1.652(a)-2, 1.662(a)-2].

A beneficiary never reports more than his or her share of DNI. Moreover, the fiduciary's deduction for distributions cannot be more than the trust's DNI [Code Secs. 643, 651(b), 652(a), 661(a), 662(a); Reg. §§1.643(a)-0, 1.652(a)-2, 1.662(a)-2]. In addition, DNI provides the basis for allocating various classes of income among beneficiaries [Code Secs. 652(b), 662(b)].

Example 25-2: The taxpayer is the beneficiary of trust set up by his grandmother. The trust distributes $20,000 to the taxpayer in a year when DNI is computed to be $15,000. The taxpayer will report and pay taxes on only $15,000 even though he received $20,000 in cash. Similarly, the trust will only be able to deduct $15,000 as its distribution deduction even though it distributed $20,000, because the trust's deduction is limited to DNI.

.02 Income Defined for DNI Purposes

Income is defined as the amount of income of an estate or trust for the tax year determined under the terms of the governing instrument and applicable local law. However, trust provisions that depart fundamentally from traditional principles of income and principal will generally not be recognized [Reg. § 1.643(b)-1].

Thus, items such as dividends, interest, and rents are generally allocated to income, and proceeds from the sale or exchange of trust assets are generally allocated to principal. However, an allocation of amounts between income and principal pursuant to applicable local law will be respected if local law provides for a reasonable apportionment between the income and remainder beneficiaries of the total return of the trust for the year, including ordinary and tax-exempt income, capital gains, and appreciation [Reg. § 1.643(b)-1].

For example, a state statute providing that income is a unitrust amount of no less than three percent and no more than five percent of the fair market value of the trust assets, whether determined annually or averaged on a multiple year basis, is a reasonable apportionment of the total return of the trust. Similarly, a state statute that permits the trustee to make adjustments between income and principal to fulfill the trustee's duty of impartiality between the income and remainder beneficiaries is generally a reasonable apportionment of the total return of the trust [Reg. § 1.643(b)-1].

Generally, these adjustments are permitted by state statutes when the trustee invests and manages the trust assets under the state's prudent investor standard. The trust describes the amount that may or must be distributed to a beneficiary by referring to the trust's income, and the trustee, after applying the state statutory rules regarding the allocation of receipts and disbursements to income and principal, is unable to administer the trust impartially.

Allocations for apportioning the total return of a trust between income and principal will be respected regardless of whether the trust provides that the income must be distributed to one or more beneficiaries or may be accumulated in whole or in part, and regardless of which alternate permitted method is actually used, provided the trust complies with all requirements of the state statute for switching methods [Reg. § 1.643(b)-1].

A switch between methods of determining trust income authorized by state statute will not result in a taxable gift from the trust's grantor or any of the trust's beneficiaries. A switch to a method not specifically authorized by state statute, but valid under state law (including a switch via judicial decision or a binding nonjudicial settlement) may be taxable to the trust or its beneficiaries and may result in taxable gifts from the trust's grantor and beneficiaries [Reg. § 1.643(b)-1].

The IRS will respect an allocation to income of all or a part of the gains from the sale or exchange of trust assets if the allocation is made either pursuant to the terms of the governing instrument and applicable local law, or pursuant to a reasonable and impartial exercise of a discretionary power granted to the fiduciary by applicable local law or by the governing instrument, if not prohibited by applicable local law [Reg. § 1.643(b)-1].

.03 Computation of DNI

To compute DNI, start with the trust's or estate's taxable income (gross income minus deductions [¶ 25,040; ¶ 25,055 et seq.]). Then, make the following adjustments [Reg. §§ 1.643(a)-0 to 1.643(a)-7]:

1. Add back: (a) the personal exemption [¶ 25,060], (b) the distributions deduction [¶ 25,085], and (c) any net capital losses deducted by the trust or estate [Reg. § 1.643(a)-3(d)]. See ¶ 25,045.
2. Add net tax-exempt interest to taxable income as modified in number 1 above. Tax-exempt interest is reduced by: (a) any portion of the interest that is paid or set aside for charitable purposes and by (b) nondeductible expenses (such as commissions and general expenses) related to the tax-exempt interest [Ch. 12].
3. Subtract the net capital gains taxable to the trust or estate [¶ 25,045]. This includes only those gains that are allocated to corpus. Do not subtract net capital gains which are (a) paid, credited, or required to be distributed to beneficiaries or (b) paid or set aside for charitable purposes [Code Secs. 643(a)(3)]. Capital gains will be included in DNI to the extent they are, pursuant to the terms of the governing instrument and local law, or pursuant to a reasonable and impartial exercise of discretion by the fiduciary: (a) allocated to income (if income under the state statute is defined as a unitrust amount, a discretionary power to allocate gains to income must also be exercised consistently and the amount so allocated may not be greater than the excess of the unitrust amount over the amount of DNI); (b) allocated to corpus but treated consistently by the fiduciary on the trust's books, records, and tax returns as part of a distribution to a beneficiary; or (c) allocated to corpus but actually distributed to the beneficiary or utilized by the fiduciary in determining the amount that is distributed or required to be distributed to a beneficiary [Reg. § 1.643(a)-3(b)].

Example 25-3: A trust has $40,000 gross income for the year, including $9,000 capital gain which, under the trust instrument, is to be distributed one-third to the beneficiary and two-thirds to the corpus of the trust. Gross income also includes $5,000 in dividends of domestic corporations. The trust is entitled to deductions for interest, taxes, depreciation and charitable contributions amounting to $8,000. In addition to the $40,000 gross income, the trust also receives $7,000 tax-exempt interest. Distributable net income is $33,000, computed as follows:

Gross income	$40,000
Less: deductions	8,000
Taxable income as modified	$32,000
Plus: tax-exempt interest	7,000
	$39,000
Less: capital gain to be added to trust corpus (2/3)	6,000
Distributable net income	$33,000

Example 25-4: Under the terms of Trust's governing instrument, all income is to be paid to Adam for life. Trustee is given discretionary powers to invade principal for Adam's benefit and to deem discretionary distributions to be made from capital gains realized during the year. During Trust's first tax year, Trust has $5,000 of dividend income and $10,000 of capital gain from the sale of securities. Pursuant to the terms of the governing instrument and applicable local law, Trustee allocates the $10,000 capital gain to principal. During the year, Trustee distributes to Adam $5,000, representing Adam's right to trust income. In addition, Trustee distributes to Adam $12,000, pursuant to the discretionary power to distribute principal. Trustee does not exercise the discretionary power to deem the discretionary distributions of principal as being paid from capital gains realized during the year. Therefore, the capital gains realized during the year are not included in DNI and the $10,000 of capital gain is taxed to the trust. In future years, Trustee must treat all discretionary distributions as not being made from any realized capital gains [Reg. § 1.643(a)-3(e), ex. 1].

Example 25-5: The facts are the same as in Example 25-4, except that Trustee intends to follow a regular practice of treating discretionary distributions of principal as being paid first from any net capital gains realized by Trust during the year. Trustee evidences this treatment by including the $10,000 capital gain in DNI on Trust's federal income tax return so that it is taxed to Adam. This treatment of the capital gains is a reasonable exercise of Trustee's discretion. In future years Trustee must treat all discretionary distributions as being made first from any realized capital gains. [Reg. § 1.643(a)-3(e), Ex. 2].

Example 25-6: The facts are the same as in Example 25-4, except that Trustee intends to follow a regular practice of treating discretionary distributions of principal as being paid from any net capital gains realized by Trust during the year from the sale of certain specified assets or a particular class of investments. This treatment of capital gains is a reasonable exercise of Trustee's discretion. [Reg. § 1.643(a)-3(e), Ex. 3].

Example 25-7: The facts are the same as in Example 25-4, except that pursuant to the terms of the governing instrument, capital gains realized by Trust are allocated to income. Because the capital gains are allocated to income pursuant to the terms of the governing instrument, the $10,000 capital gain is included in Trust's DNI [Reg. § 1.643(a)-3(e), Ex. 4].

Example 25-8: The facts are the same as in Example 25-4, except that Trustee decides that discretionary distributions will be made only to the extent Trust has realized capital gains during the year and thus the discretionary distribution to Adam is $10,000, rather than $12,000. Because Trustee will use the amount of any realized capital gain to determine the amount of the discretionary distribution to the beneficiary, the $10,000 capital gain is included in Trust's DNI [Reg. § 1.643(a)-3(e), Ex. 5].

Example 25-9: Trust's assets consist of Blackacre and other property. Trustee is directed to hold Blackacre for ten years and then sell it and distribute all the sales proceeds to Adam. Because Trustee uses the amount of the sales proceeds that includes any realized capital gain to determine the amount required to be distributed to Adam, any capital gain realized from the sale of Blackacre is included in Trust's distributable net income for the tax year. [Reg. § 1.643(a)-3(e), Ex. 6].

Example 25-10: Under the terms of Trust's governing instrument, all income is to be paid to Adam during the Trust's term. When Adam reaches 35, Trust is to terminate and all the principal is to be distributed to Adam. Because all the assets of the trust, including all capital gains, will be actually distributed to the beneficiary at the termination of Trust, all capital gains realized in the year of termination are included in DNI [Reg. § 1.643(a)-3(e), Ex. 7].

Example 25-11: The facts are the same as Example 25-10, except Trustee is directed to pay Belinda $10,000 before distributing the remainder of Trust assets to Adam. Because the distribution to Belinda is a gift of a specific sum of money, none of Trust's DNI that includes all of the capital gains realized during the year of termination is allocated to Belinda's distribution [Reg. § 1.643(a)-3(e), Ex. 8].

Example 25-12: The facts are the same as Example 25-10, except Trustee is directed to distribute one-half of the principal to Adam when Adam reaches 35 and the balance to Adam when Adam reaches 45. Trust assets consist entirely of stock in corporation Moe with a fair market value of $1,000,000 and an adjusted basis of $300,000. When Adam reaches 35, Trustee sells one-half of the stock and distributes the sales proceeds to Adam. All the sales proceeds, including all the capital gain attributable to that sale, are actually distributed to Adam, and therefore all the capital gain is included in DNI [Reg. § 1.643(a)-3(e), Ex. 9].

Example 25-13: The facts are the same as Example 25-10, except when Adam reaches 35, Trustee sells all the stock and distributes one-half of the sales proceeds to Adam. If authorized by the governing instrument and applicable state statute, Trustee may determine to what extent the capital gain is distributed to Adam. The $500,000 distribution to Adam may be treated as including a minimum of $200,000 of capital gain (and all of the principal amount of $300,000) and a maximum of $500,000 of the capital gain (with no principal). Trustee evidences the treatment by including the appropriate amount of capital gain in DNI on Trust's federal income tax return. If Trustee is not authorized by the governing instrument and applicable state statutes to determine to what extent the capital gain is distributed to Adam, one-half of the capital gain attributable to the sale is included in DNI [Reg. § 1.643(a)-3(e), Ex. 10].

Example 25-14: The applicable state statute provides that a trustee may make an election to pay an income beneficiary an amount equal to four percent of the fair market value of the trust assets, as determined at the beginning of each tax year, in full satisfaction of that beneficiary's right to income. State statute also provides that this unitrust amount shall be considered paid first from ordinary and tax-exempt income, then from net short-term capital gain, then from net long-term capital gain, and finally from return of principal. Trust's governing instrument provides that Adam is to receive each year income as defined under state statute. Trustee makes the unitrust election under state statute. At the beginning of the tax year, Trust assets are valued at $500,000. During the year, Trust receives $5,000 of dividend income and realizes $80,000 of net long-term gain from the sale of capital assets. Trustee distributes to Adam $20,000 (4% of $500,000) in satisfaction of Adam's right to income. Net long-term capital gain in the amount of $15,000 is allocated to income pursuant to the ordering rule of the state statute and is included in DNI [Reg. § 1.643(a)-3(e), Ex. 11].

¶25,025 DISTRIBUTIONS BY SIMPLE TRUSTS

A simple trust is one which, under the trust terms, distributes only current income (it distributes no corpus), must distribute all its income and has no charitable beneficiaries [Code Sec. 651; Reg. § 1.651(a)-1]. A simple trust is primarily a conduit of income—the trust takes a deduction for the income that is required to be distributed currently, and the beneficiaries include that amount in their gross income. The terms of the trust instrument and state law determine what is income for this purpose.

.01 Income Taxable to Beneficiaries

Generally, beneficiaries must include in gross income all trust income required to be distributed to them, to the extent of the trust's DNI—regardless of whether the income is actually distributed [¶ 25,020]. For asset distributions in lieu of cash, see ¶ 25,045.

Example 25-15: Mr. Covington placed certain securities in trust for the sole benefit of his wife. The trust instrument provided that all the income be distributed to her at least once a year, that the securities themselves not be distributed to her, and that no distributions be made to anyone else. This is a simple trust. Mrs. Covington will include the trust income in her gross income each year, whether or not the fiduciary actually makes the payment to her during the tax year.[7]

If the income required to be distributed exceeds the DNI, beneficiaries are taxed only on their proportionate share of the DNI [Code Sec. 652(a); Reg. § 1.652(a)-2].

Example 25-16: A simple trust provides that Mr. Barnes is to receive 60 percent of the trust income and Ms. Cox is to receive 40 percent. The trust has the following income and disbursements during the year: $9,000 interest on corpo-

[7] Rev. Rul. 62-147, 1962-2 CB 151.

rate bonds; $4,000 capital gains allocable to corpus; $1,500 commissions, legal fees and other deductible expenses allocable to corpus; and $400 expenses allocable to income.

The trust income required to be distributed is $9,000 less $400, or $8,600. The trust's distributable net income is $9,000 (capital gains are excluded), less $1,900 (all deductible expenses), or $7,100. Although Barnes receives $5,160 ($8,600 × 60%), he will include only $4,260 ($7,100 × 60%) in income. Cox will receive $3,440 ($8,600 × 40%), but will include only $2,840 ($7,100 × 40%).

.02 Distributions of Corpus

A trust may be a simple trust one year and a complex trust another year. For example, a trust is required to distribute all of its income currently. The trustee also has a discretionary power to distribute corpus to the income beneficiary. In years when only income is distributed, the trust is a simple trust. However, if corpus is distributed, the trust becomes a complex trust for that year. When a trust ends, it is treated as a complex trust because corpus is distributed that year [Reg. § 1.651(a)-3].

¶25,030 DISTRIBUTIONS BY ESTATES AND COMPLEX TRUSTS

Complex trusts are those that are not simple trusts. They include discretionary trusts, trusts with charitable beneficiaries and trusts that accumulate income or distribute corpus. In determining inclusions for the beneficiaries and the deductions for distributions by the fiduciary, estates and complex trusts are similarly treated [Code Sec. 661-663; Reg. § 1.661(a)-1].

.01 Allocation by Tiers—Overview

For estates and complex trusts, distributions are taxed to the extent of the DNI first to the beneficiaries to whom income must be currently distributed. These are known as first-tier beneficiaries. If distributions to these beneficiaries are greater than the DNI, their shares are prorated for tax purposes. All other beneficiaries eligible to receive income are second-tier beneficiaries. They are subject to income tax on their distributions only to the extent that the DNI is greater than the amount distributed to the first-tier beneficiaries [Code Sec. 662(a)].

Example 25-17: Ms. Ames, a first-tier beneficiary, is entitled to receive $15,000 as an annual distribution from an estate, and Ms. Bates is entitled to income in the discretion of the fiduciary. (a) If the DNI is $30,000 and they each receive $15,000, each has taxable income of $15,000. (b) If the DNI is $20,000 and they both receive the same $15,000 distributions, Ames still has taxable income of $15,000 but Bates is taxed on only $5,000. The remaining $10,000 that she received is tax-free.

Distributions That Exceed Distributable Net Income

If the first-tier distributions to all beneficiaries exceed the DNI (figured without any deduction for charitable contributions), the amount to be included in each beneficiaries' gross income is figured as follows [Reg. § 1.662(a)-2(b)]:

$$\frac{\text{First tier distributions to the beneficiary}}{\text{First tier distributions to all beneficiaries}} \times \begin{array}{c}\text{Distributable net income}\\\text{(without deduction for}\\\text{charitable contributions)}\end{array} = \begin{array}{c}\text{Amount beneficiary}\\\text{includes in gross income}\end{array}$$

Example 25-18: A trust is required to distribute 50% of its current income for the tax year to Albert, the grantor's son; 25% to Bertha, the grantor's daughter; and 25% to Community Chest, a charity. The trust income is $10,000. The charitable contribution is $2,500 (25% × $10,000). The amount required to be distributed to Albert is $5,000, and the amount required to be distributed to Bertha is $2,500. Hence, the amount required to be distributed to all beneficiaries is $7,500, since the charity is not considered a beneficiary [Code Sec. 663(a)(2)]. Assume the DNI of the trust is $7,000 before the charitable deduction is taken. Albert will include $4,666.67 ($5,000/$7,500 × $7,000) in his gross income. Bertha will include $2,333.33 ($2,500/$7,500 × $7,000) in her gross income.

.02 Allocation by Tiers—Other Distributions

Beneficiaries must include in gross income all other amounts properly paid, credited, or required to be distributed to them (so-called second tier distributions) [Code Sec. 662(a)(2); Reg. § 1.662(a)-3].

▶ **OBSERVATION:** An amount is not treated as credited to you, unless it is so definitely allocated to you as to be beyond recall. Thus, "credit" for practical purposes is the equivalent of "payment." A mere entry on the books of the fiduciary will not serve as an amount credited to you, unless it cannot be changed.[8]

Example 25-19: A trust provides that each year the fiduciary must distribute $3,000 of corpus to Mr. Briant, a beneficiary. Briant will include $3,000 in his gross income to the extent of the trust's DNI.

Distributions Exceeding DNI

When the sum of the first- and second-tier distributions exceeds the DNI, the beneficiary must include in gross income only a proportionate share of the DNI (less first tier distributions). The beneficiary's share is determined as follows [Code Sec. 662(a)(2); Reg. § 1.662(a)-3]:

---

[8] *M. Stearns*, CA-2, 3 USTC ¶ 1098, 65 F2d 371, *cert. denied*, 290 US 670, 54 SCt 90.

$$\text{Distributable net income less first tier distributions} \times \frac{\text{Second tier distributions to the beneficiary}}{\text{Second tier distributions to all beneficiaries}} = \text{The beneficiary's share of distributable net income}$$

▶ **OBSERVATION:** Beneficiaries are taxed on second-tier distributions only if the first-tier distributions fail to exhaust the DNI of the estate or trust. This is so, even if the second-tier distributions are made from income. To the extent that the DNI, reduced by first-tier distributions, is less than second-tier distributions, the second-tier distributions are prorated.

Example 25-20: A trust requires the distribution of $8,000 of income to Ms. Allister annually. Any remaining income may be accumulated or distributed to Ms. Barber, Mr. Charles and Mr. Dickinson in the trustee's discretion. He may also invade corpus for the benefit of any of the four beneficiaries. During the year, the trust has $20,000 of income after deducting expenses. Distributable net income is $20,000. The trustee distributes $8,000 of income to Allister. He also distributes $4,000 each to Barber and Charles, $2,000 to Dickinson, and an additional $6,000 to Allister. The amounts taxable to each are determined as follows:

Distributable net income	$20,000
Less: first-tier distribution to Allister	8,000
Available for second-tier distributions	$12,000
Second-tier distributions:	
Allister—$6,000/$16,000 × $12,000	$4,500
Barber—$4,000/$16,000 × $12,000	$3,000
Charles—$4,000/$16,000 × $12,000	$3,000
Dickinson—$2,000/$16,000 × $12,000	$ 1,500

Allister includes $12,500 in income ($8,000 first-tier distribution plus $4,500 second-tier distribution). Barber and Charles each include $3,000 in income. Dickinson includes $1,500.

.03 Allocation by Separate Shares

The separate share rule exists in order to avoid the distortion of income that often results when a complex trust accumulates income for one beneficiary and makes taxable distributions to a different beneficiary. In determining the amount taxable to beneficiaries, allocation by tiers may work an injustice when a trust or estate is administered in substantially separate shares. To minimize this, the separate share rule provides that if a single trust or estate has more than one beneficiary, and each beneficiary has substantially separate and independent shares, the shares are treated separately for the sole purpose of determining the taxable amount [Code Sec. 663(c); Reg § 1.663(c)-1]. This treatment cannot be used to get more than one personal exemption [¶ 25,060], or to split the undistributed income of the trust into several shares which would then be taxed at lower rates.

Example 25-21: A trust with two beneficiaries has DNI of $20,000. The trustee makes a mandatory distribution of 50% of this amount, or $10,000, to beneficiary Ellen. He accumulates the other $10,000 for future distribution to beneficiary Frank. He also makes a discretionary distribution of $10,000 out of corpus to Ellen. Under the tier system, the entire DNI would be allocated to Ellen, and she would be taxed on the $20,000 received. Her tax is being measured, in part, by $10,000 of current income that can only go to Frank.

But suppose that the above trust is divided into two separate trusts, one for each beneficiary. Each trust then will have DNI of $10,000. The trustee of the trust for Ellen distributes all the income of that trust and $10,000 of the corpus to her. The trustee of the trust for Frank makes no distribution. Under these facts, Ellen would be taxed on $10,000. She actually received $20,000, but her taxable share may not exceed the DNI of the trust. The Frank trust makes no distributions, so its income of $10,000 is taxable to the trustee.

▶ **OBSERVATION:** The separate share device achieves the two-trust result in a one-trust case. The two-trust result in the above example seems more equitable since it exempts the corpus distribution and limits the tax on the beneficiaries to current income.

Separate Share Rule Applies to Estates

The separate share rule applies when the governing instrument of the estate and applicable local law create separate economic interests in one beneficiary or class of beneficiaries in such a way that their economic interests neither affect nor are affected by the economic interests of another separate beneficiary or class of beneficiaries [Code Sec. 663(c)]. The application of the separate share rule to estates is mandatory, rather than elective, where separate shares exist. It requires that the estate's income and deductions be allocated among the separate shares as if they were separate estates. According to the separate share rule, a beneficiary is taxed only on the amount of income that belongs to that beneficiary's separate share.

There are separate shares in an estate when the will and local law create separate economic interests in one beneficiary or class of beneficiaries so that the economic interests of those beneficiaries are not affected by economic interests accruing to other beneficiaries. For example, a separate share in an estate would exist where the decedent's will provides that all of the shares of a closely-held corporation go to one beneficiary and that any dividends paid to the estate by that corporation should be paid only to that beneficiary without regard to any other amounts which that beneficiary would receive under the will.

Separate Share Defined

A separate share generally is a separate economic interest in one beneficiary or class of beneficiaries of the decedent's estate. There would be separate economic interests where the economic interests of the beneficiary or class of beneficiaries neither affect nor are affected by economic interests accruing to another beneficiary or class of beneficiaries. Under this definition, a separate share generally exists only if it includes both corpus and the income attributable to that corpus and is independent from any other share [Reg. § 1.663(c)-4(a)]. This means that income earned on assets in one share (the first share) and appreciation and depreciation in the value of those assets have no effect on any other share. Similarly, the income and changes in value of any other share have no effect on the first share. Note that a gift or bequest of a specific sum of money or specific property is not a separate share [Reg. § 1.663(c)-4(a)].

.04 Special Distributions

The following items are not deductible as distributions by a trust or estate, nor are they included in gross income for the current tax year [Code Sec. 663(a)]:

1. Any gift or bequest of a specific sum of money or of specific property which, under the terms of the governing instrument, is paid in a lump sum or in not more than three installments. If, however, the instrument provides the gift or bequest is payable *only* from income (whether income for the payment year or income accumulated from a prior year), it will not be treated as a gift. Instead, it will be deductible by the trust and taxable to the beneficiary [Code Sec. 663(a)(1); Reg. § 1.663(a)-1]. For property used to satisfy a cash legacy, see ¶ 25,045.
2. Charitable distributions [Code Sec. 663(a)(2); Reg. § 1.663(a)-2]; but see ¶ 25,065.
3. Any distribution in the current tax year that was deducted by the estate or trust in a preceding tax year [Code Sec. 663(a)(3); Reg. § 1.663(a)-3].

.05 Throwback Rule

If a complex trust distributes less than its DNI, you may have to report the undistributed excess in a later year, when the trust distributes more than its DNI for that later year [¶ 25,120]. The throwback rules were eliminated for amounts distributed by a domestic trust after August 5, 1997. The throwback rules continue to apply to: (1) foreign trusts, (2) trusts that were foreign trusts but became domestic trusts, and (3) domestic trusts created before March 1, 1984, that would be treated as multiple trusts under Code Sec. 643(f) [¶ 25,011].

.06 Sixty-Five Day Rule

To avoid accumulations and the throwback rule application [¶ 25,030], this rule allows amounts paid or credited in the first 65 days of a trust tax year to be attributed to the preceding tax year [Code Sec. 663(b)(1); Reg. § 1.663(b)-1]. The 65-day rule applies only if the trustee elects it [Code Sec. 663(b)(2); Reg. §§ 1.663(b)-1, -2].

Distributions eligible for the election cannot exceed the greater of: the trust income for the tax year for which the election is made or DNI for that year. The limitation is further reduced by distributions in that year, except those amounts for which the election was claimed in a preceding tax year [Reg. § 1.663(b)-1].

The election is made on the return for the tax year in which the distribution is considered made. If no return is due, a statement of election must be filed with the IRS where the return would normally be filed. In either case, it must be made within the time for filing the return for that year (including extensions) and cannot be revoked after the return due date [Reg. § 1.663(b)-2].

Example 25-22: The Fairfield Trust, a calendar year trust, has $1,000 of income and $800 of DNI in 2013. The trust properly paid $550 to Mr. Merkle, a beneficiary, on January 10, 2013, which the trustee elected to treat as paid on December 31, 2012. The trust also properly paid $600 to him on April 25, 2013, and $450 on January 22, 2014. For 2013, the maximum amount that can be elected as properly paid or credited on the last day of 2013 is $400 ($1,000 minus $600). The $550 paid on January 10, 2013, does not reduce the maximum amount since it is treated as having been paid on December 31, 2012 [Reg. § 1.663(b)-1(a)(2), Ex.].

The administration of estates has been simplified by the extension of the 65-day rule to distribution by estates. This means an executor can elect to treat distributions paid by the estate within 65 days after the close of the estate's tax years as having been paid on the last day of the tax year [Code Sec. 663(b)].

.07 Property Distributed In Kind

In general, a property distribution by a trust or estate is taken into account for DNI purposes only to the extent of the lesser of the property's basis or its fair market value at the time of distribution. This means that the beneficiary's basis for the property will be the same as the trust's or estate's basis. However, the trust or estate may elect to treat the property distributed as a sale to you at its fair market value. If this is elected, the basis of the property in the beneficiary's hands is adjusted to reflect the gain or loss recognized by the estate or trust on the distribution [Code Sec. 643(e)].

¶25,035 BENEFICIARY'S SHARE OF EACH ITEM OF DISTRIBUTABLE NET INCOME

If DNI includes items with a special tax status, such as exempt interest, the beneficiary must determine how much of such items are included in his or her distribution. The reason for this is that such items retain their status in their hands [Code Secs. 652(b), 662(b); Reg. §§1.652(b)-1, 1.662(b)-1]. Thus, to the extent that a distribution includes exempt interest, it can be excluded from the beneficiary's return.

.01 Method of Apportionment

To determine how much of each item is included in a given distribution, apportion the net amount of each item [the gross amount of the item less the deductions allocable to it; see .03 below] among beneficiaries on a simple proportion basis, unless the governing instrument or state law requires a different allocation [Code Sec. 652(b), 662(b); Reg. §§1.652(b)-1, 1.662(b)-1]. An allocation in the trust instrument is recognized only to the extent it has an economic effect independent of its income tax consequences. Thus, if the trustee can allocate different classes of income to different beneficiaries, it is not a specific allocation by terms of the trust instrument [Reg. § 1.652(b)-2].

.02 Allocation of Deductions

As noted above, in determining the total of a particular item of DNI, the gross amount of each income item must be reduced by the deduction allocable to it. In the absence of specific instructions in the governing instrument, the deductions are allocated as follows [Reg. § 1.652(b)-3]:

1. Any deduction directly allocable to a particular class of gross income is allocated to that class.
2. If the deduction exceeds the income, the excess may be applied against any other income class the trustee chooses, with these limitations: (a) the income chosen must be included in figuring DNI, (b) a proportionate share of nonbusiness deductions must be allocated to nontaxable income and (c) excess deductions attributable to tax-exempt income may not be used as an offset against any other class of income.
3. Deductions that are not directly allocable to any particular class of income (trustee's commissions, safe deposit rentals, state income and personal property taxes, for example) are treated the same as the excess deductions; see (2) above.

Example 25-23: A trust has rents, taxable interest, dividends, and tax-exempt interest. Deductions directly attributable to the rents exceed the rental income. The excess may be allocated to the taxable interest and dividends in whatever proportions the trustee elects. However, if the excess deductions are attributable to the tax-exempt interest, they may not be allocated to the other income items.

.03 Charitable Contributions Adjustment

In determining the tax status of currently distributable income items in the beneficiary's hands, DNI is figured without regard to any part of a charitable deduction not attributable to income of the tax year. This prevents a charitable contribution from reducing the amount of current income that is otherwise taxable to the beneficiary, except to the extent the contribution is itself paid out of current income [Code Sec. 662(b); Reg. § 1.662(b)-2].

Example 25-24: A trust instrument provides that $30,000 of its income must be distributed currently to A, and the balance may either be distributed to B, distributed to a designated charity, or accumulated. Accumulated income may be distributed to B and to the charity. The trust has $40,000 of taxable interest and $10,000 of tax-exempt income, with no expenses. The trustee distributed $30,000 to A, $50,000 to charity X, and $10,000 to B.

DNI for the purpose of determining the character of the distribution to A is $30,000 (the charitable contributions deduction, for this purpose, being taken into account only to the extent of $20,000, the difference between the income of the trust for the tax year, $50,000, and the amount required to be distributed currently, $30,000).

The charitable contributions deduction taken into account, $20,000, is allocated proportionately to the items of income of the trust, $16,000 to taxable interest and $4,000 to tax-exempt income.

Under Code Sec. 662(a)(1), the amount of income required to be distributed currently to A is $30,000, which consists of the balance of these items, $24,000 of taxable interest and $6,000 of tax-exempt income. In determining the amount to be included in the gross income of B for the year, however, the entire charitable contributions deduction is taken into account, with the result that there is no DNI and therefore no amount to be included in gross income [Reg. § 1.662(b)-2, ex.1].

INCOME—CAPITAL GAINS AND LOSSES

¶25,040 GROSS INCOME

.01 Estates and Trusts

The gross income of an estate or trust is determined in the same manner as that of an individual [Reg. § 1.641(a)-2]. Thus, the taxable income of the trust or estate consists of all items of gross income received during the tax year, including the following: income required to be distributed currently to beneficiaries; income accumulated in trust for the benefit of unborn; unascertained or contingent beneficiaries; income accumulated or held for future distribution; income collected by the guardian of an infant which is to be held or distributed as the court may direct; income received by an estate of a deceased person during the period of administration or settlement of the estate; and income, which in the discretion of the fiduciary, may be distributed to the beneficiaries or accumulated [Code Sec. 641(a); Reg. § § 1.641(a)-1 through 2].

For an estate, title to personal property usually passes to the executor or administrator, but title to real property often passes to the heirs or persons named in a will at the decedent's death. Therefore, in most cases, the person who gets the real property reports the income produced by the property (such as rents), or the gain or loss from its sale [¶ 25,045]. The only complication is the proper treatment of income accrued to a decedent at the time of his or her death.

.02 Decedents

When a person dies, the executor or administrator may be required to file income tax returns for two separate and distinct taxable entities: (1) the deceased person, for the period before his or her death; and (2) the deceased person's estate.

Final Return for Decedent

If the deceased person were on the cash basis, the final return filed will include only income that he or she actually or constructively received while he was alive. A bonus received after a cash basis taxpayer's death will not be reported on his or her final return, unless it was constructively received during his or her life.[9] If he or she used the accrual method of accounting, his or her final return will include only income that accrued before his or her death. Income that accrues only because of his or her death is not included in his or her final return [Code Sec. 451(b); Reg. § 1.451-1(b)]. Deductions get similar treatment [¶ 25,055].

---

[9] *E.V. O'Daniel Est.*, 10 TC 631, Dec. 16,343 (1948), *aff'd*, CA-2, 49-1 USTC ¶ 9235, 173 F2d 966; Rev. Rul. 65-217, 1965-2 CB 214; Rev. Rul. 68-124, 1968-1 CB 44.

Income in Respect of a Decedent

Amounts that are excluded from the deceased person's final return under the above rule are taxed to the persons who receive them as a result of the decedent's death. This would include the deceased person's estate, heirs, devisees and legatees. The amounts are treated as income of the same nature and to the same extent as they would have if the deceased person had remained alive and received them [Code Sec. 691(a)]. Items apt to be included as income in respect of a decedent are interest accrued on promissory notes but not payable until after the decedent's death, deferred compensation distributions, dividends payable after death to holders of stock of record as of a date prior to death, installment obligations and commissions earned before death but not paid until later. Persons who transfer the right to receive such amounts must include in income either what they get for the right, or its fair market value, whichever is greater.

Example 25-25: Decedent kept his books on the cash basis. Shortly before his death in November, he was voted a salary payment of $10,000, to be paid in five equal annual installments beginning the following January. He could not draw any of these payments before the actual payment date. His estate collected two installments and distributed the right to the remaining three installments to the residuary legatee. The $4,000 must be included in the gross income of the estate, and the residuary legatee must include $6,000 in his income when he receives it. However, if the estate had sold the right to the three remaining installments to a person not entitled to them as a legatee, devisee or heir, or by reason of the death of the decedent, the estate would be required to include in its income the amount received or the fair market value of the right, whichever was greater.

Installment obligations. A deceased person's uncollected installment obligations, transmitted at his or her death directly to his or her estate or beneficiaries, are treated as income in respect of a decedent. The recipient reports the installment gain the same way the deceased person would have reported it [Ch. 19] [Code Sec. 691(a)(4); Reg. § 1.691(a)-5]. Any previously unreported gain from an installment sale is recognized by a deceased seller's estate if the obligation (1) passes by bequest, devise or inheritance to the obligor, or (2) is canceled by the executor [Code Sec. 691(a)(5)]. Income in respect of a deceased partner is discussed in Ch. 24.

Deductions and credits accruing after death. When not deductible on the deceased person's return, payments by an estate of the decedent's business and nonbusiness expenses, interest and taxes or foreign taxes are allowed to the estate as a deduction or credit. If the estate is not liable, the deduction or credit is allowed to the beneficiary who receives an interest in property subject to the liability and who pays off the liability [Code Sec. 691(b)(1); Reg. § 1.691(b)-1(a)].

A deduction for depletion also can be taken, but it is taken by the person who gets the income to which the depletion relates, whether or not he gets the property from which the income is derived [Code Sec. 691(b)(2); Reg. § 1.691(b)-1(b)].

Deduction for Estate Tax

Income in respect of a decedent is included in the gross estate for estate tax purposes, so it is subject to a double tax. As a relief measure, the person who reports the income can deduct the estate tax attributable to the right that he received. The income recipient can deduct a proportionate share of the federal estate tax that is attributable to the income in respect of a decedent.

In figuring the net long-term capital gains or the net capital loss, the amount of gain treated as income in respect of a decedent is reduced, but not below zero, by the amount of any deductible estate taxes attributable to a gain treated as income in respect of a decedent [Code Sec. 691(c)(4)].

Stock option. Any estate tax resulting from including an employee stock option in a decedent's estate is deductible in the year the estate or beneficiary has income resulting from disposition of stock acquired under the option [Ch. 2] [Code Sec. 421(c)(2)].

The surviving annuitant of a joint and survivor annuity gets a deduction for the proportionate estate tax each year during his life expectancy [Code Sec. 691(d); Reg. § 1.691(d)-1(a)].

¶25,045 CAPITAL GAINS AND LOSSES

The gain on the sale or exchange of a capital asset by an estate or trust must be included in its gross income. Depending on the holding period, the gain is either a short-term or long-term capital gain, and the rules prescribed for individuals apply [Ch. 8]. However, a special rule accords long-term treatment to the trust or estate even if it sells the property within one year after the deceased person's death [Code Sec. 1223(11)]. Any part of the gain that is properly paid, credited or required to be distributed during the year to the beneficiary is deductible by the fiduciary. It is taxable to the beneficiary (to the extent of the DNI), even if allocated to corpus.

.01 Capital Loss

A capital loss usually is deductible only by the estate or trust and not by the beneficiary.[10] The loss is either a short-term or long-term capital loss, and the rules for individuals apply. However, a special rule requires trusts and estates to treat losses as long-term even if the assets were sold within one year after the deceased person's death. In most states, title to real property passes directly from the deceased person to the heirs (not to the executor). In such states, gain or loss on the sale of the property is reported directly by the heir. For treatment of an unused capital loss in the trust's or estate's year of termination, see ¶ 25,055.

.02 Capital Gains Tax Rates for Estates and Trusts

Beginning in 2013, the capital gains tax rates for estates and trusts are as follows:

- A capital gains rate of 0 percent applies to the adjusted net capital gains of *estates and trusts* if the gain would otherwise be subject to the 15 percent ordinary income tax rate [Code Secs 1(h)(1)(B), 55(b)(3)(B)].

---

[10] *T.R. Beatty*, 28 BTA 1286, Dec. 8221.

- A capital gains rate of 15 percent applies to adjusted net capital gains of *estates and trusts* if the gain would otherwise be subject to the 25, 28, or 33 percent ordinary income tax rate [Code Secs 1(h)(1)(C), 55(b)(3)(C)].
- A capital gains rate of 20 percent applies to adjusted net capital gains of *estates and trusts* if the gain would otherwise be subject to the 39.6-percent ordinary income tax rate [Code Sec. 1(h)(1)(D)]. Beginning on January 1, 2013, estates and trusts are subject to a top tax rate of 39.6 percent on all taxable income in excess of the income limit of the 33-percent income tax bracket.

  See ¶ 25,100 for a discussion of income tax rates for estates and trusts beginning in 2013 and the imposition of the 3.8 percent net investment income tax on estates and trusts.

These rates apply for sales or exchanges of capital assets that are held for more than 12 months, and apply for both regular income tax and alternative minimum tax (AMT) purposes.

.03 Asset Distributions in Lieu of Cash

When a fiduciary pays a *cash* legacy by transferring an asset to the legatee, it is treated as if a sale or exchange took place between them. Gain or loss to the fiduciary is equal to the difference between the property's fair market value at its transfer and its adjusted basis in the fiduciary's hands.[11]

> **Example 25-26:** The fiduciary must pay $50,000 to the testator's child when the child becomes 25. The fiduciary is authorized to pay this amount in either cash or property worth $50,000. He elects to transfer securities worth $50,000 to satisfy the legacy. Assuming that the basis of the securities in the fiduciary's hands was $40,000, a capital gain of $10,000 is recognized. If the property transferred was not a capital asset, the $10,000 gain would be taxable as ordinary income.

The legatee is treated as the property's buyer. He or she has a basis equal to the fair market value of the property at the time of the distribution.[12]

If a trustee distributes a capital asset with the same value as a required distribution of income, it is also treated as a sale or exchange. The value is deductible by the trustee and taxable to the beneficiary to the extent of the trust's DNI.[13]

Special rules apply when the property involved is farm realty or closely held business realty [Code Sec. 1040].

.04 Distributable Net Income

In determining DNI [¶ 25,020], the fiduciary excludes gains from the sale or exchange of capital assets to the extent these gains are allocated to corpus and are not: (1) paid, credited, or required to be distributed to a beneficiary during the year, or (2) paid,

---

[11] *S.P. Suisman*, DC-CT, 36-2 USTC ¶ 9443, 15 FSupp 113, *aff'd*, CA-2, 83 F2d 1019, *cert. denied*, 299 US 573, 57 SCt 37, *reh'g denied*, 299 US 621; *W.R. Kenan Jr.*, CA-2, 40-2 USTC ¶ 9635, 114 F2d 217; Rev. Rul. 66-207, 1966-2 CB 243.

[12] *S. Ewing*, 40 BTA 912, Dec. 10,868.

[13] Rev. Rul. 67-74, 1967-1 CB 194.

permanently set aside, or to be used for a charitable purpose [Code Sec. 643(a)(3)]. Capital gains generally would be included in DNI to the extent they were, pursuant to the terms of the governing instrument or local law, or pursuant to a reasonable and consistent exercise of discretion by the fiduciary (in accordance with a power granted to the fiduciary by the governing instrument or local law): (1) allocated to income; (2) allocated to corpus but treated by the fiduciary on the trust's books, records, and tax returns as part of a distribution to a beneficiary; or (3) allocated to corpus but utilized by the fiduciary in determining the amount which is distributed or required to be distributed to a beneficiary [Reg. § 1.643(a)-3(a)]. Special rules apply to foreign trusts [¶ 25,120] [Code Sec. 643(a)(6)].

.05 Deduction for State Tax

A simple trust can deduct state income tax on capital gain retained by it in arriving at its taxable income and DNI.[14]

¶25,050 BASIS OF PROPERTY TO ESTATE OR TRUST

.01 Transfer in Trust

In the case of property transferred in trust (other than by a transfer in trust by a gift, bequest, or devise), the basis of property is the same as it would be in the hands of the grantor increased by the amount of gain or decreased by the amount of loss recognized to the grantor upon the transfer [Reg. § 1.1015-2(a)(1)].

In the case of property acquired by gift (whether by a transfer in trust or otherwise), the basis of the property for the purpose of determining gain is the same as it would be in the hands of the donor or the last preceding owner by whom it was not acquired by gift. The same rule applies in determining loss unless the basis is greater than the fair market value of the property at the time of the gift. In such case, the basis for determining loss is the fair market value at the time of the gift [Reg. § 1.1015-1(a)(1)].

Example 25-27: Ten years ago, Mr. Brown bought certain bonds for $10,000. Today, in consideration of $15,000, he transferred the bonds in trust. Brown's gain is $5,000, and the basis of the bonds to the trust is $15,000 (the basis of the bonds in the hands of Brown ($10,000) plus the gain recognized to Brown on the transfer ($5,000)).

NOTE: The basis of property acquired by gift or transfer in trust before 1921 is its fair market value on the date of gift or transfer [Code Sec. 1015(c); Reg. § 1.1015-3].

.02 Property Acquired from Decedent

Generally, the basis of property acquired from a decedent is its fair market value or its special use value on the date of death. If the executor elects to use the alternate valuation date, the basis of the property is its value on that date [Code Sec. 1014(a)(3)]. See also Ch. 6.

---

[14] Rev. Rul. 74-257, 1974-1 CB 153.

DEDUCTIONS AND CREDITS

¶25,055 DEDUCTIONS IN GENERAL

The taxable income of an estate or trust is generally computed in the same manner as an individual taxpayer [Code Sec. 641(b)]. As a result, estates and trusts ordinarily are entitled to the same deductions as individuals [Reg. § 1.641(b)-1]. Exceptions are explained below. Unlike individual taxpayers, estates or trusts may claim no standard deduction, but are entitled to a special deduction for distributions to beneficiaries [¶ 25,085].

.01 Medical and Funeral Expenses

A deceased person's medical and dental expenses paid by the estate are not deductible from the estate's taxable income [Reg. § 1.642(g)-2]. But these expenses may be deducted on the deceased person's final return, if they were not deducted in figuring the taxable estate for estate tax purposes. Funeral expenses are not deductible from the estate's taxable income in any case.[15]

Other Deductions

The deductions allowed to deceased persons depend on their accounting method. If they reported on the cash basis, the deductions would be those actually paid. If they used the accrual basis, deduction is allowed for amounts that accrue up to the date of death. Deductions cannot be taken, however, for amounts that accrued only because of their death [Code Sec. 461(b); Reg. § 1.461-1(b)]. As to deductions that accrue after their death, see ¶ 25,040.

.02 Losses

If a trust sustains a loss, the loss usually is not deductible by a beneficiary. The trust and the beneficiary are separate taxable entities, and one taxpayer cannot deduct another's losses.[16]

But when an estate or trust terminates, any unused capital loss, net operating loss carryovers, or deductions (except those for personal exemptions or charity) in excess of gross income for the last tax year can be deducted by the beneficiaries who get the estate or trust property. This is limited to (a) the remaindermen of a trust, (b) the heirs and next of kin of a person who dies without a will, and (c) the residuary legatees (including a residuary trust) of a person leaving a will [Code Sec. 642(h); Reg. § § 1.642(h)-1, -3].

.03 Trust Investment Advice Fees

Code Sec. 67(a) provides that miscellaneous itemized deductions are allowed only to the extent they exceed two percent of adjusted gross income (AGI). For purposes of this floor, the AGI of an estate or trust is computed the same way as it is for an individual, subject to certain exceptions [Code Sec. 67(e)]. One exception provides that costs paid or incurred in connection with the administration of an estate or trust

[15] Treas. Dept., IRS Publication 559, "Survivors, Executors, and Administrators For Use in Preparing 2012 Returns" (2013 Ed.), p. 19.

[16] *T.R. Beatty*, 28 BTA 1286, Dec. 8221.

that wouldn't have been incurred if the property weren't held in the estate or trust may be deducted when computing AGI [Code Sec. 67(e)(1)]. Trustees who lack expertise in money management often seek professional management advice to aid them in fulfilling their fiduciary duties and directing the investment of trust assets.

In *Michael J. Knight, Trustee of William L. Rudkin Testamentary Trust,*[17] the United States Supreme Court resolved years of litigation in a unanimous decision where the court held that fees for investment advice paid by a trust are not unique to trust administration and are therefore deductible as a miscellaneous deduction only to the extent that they exceed two percent of the trust's AGI pursuant to Code Sec. 67(a). In this important IRS victory, the high Court held that a trust's investment expenses fail to qualify for an exception to the Code Sec. 67(e)(1) floor. The Court reasoned that this exception is only available for trust-related administrative expenses that are unique to trust administration and are unlikely to be incurred by individuals. Since the Court concluded that the investment advice fees in question were not unique to the administration of a trust and are customarily incurred by individuals, they were subject to the two-percent floor for miscellaneous deductions.

> ▶ **PRACTICE POINTER:** Note that the Supreme Court decision focuses on whether or not the expenses would have been incurred by an individual. A full deduction without consideration of the two-percent floor will only be available if the taxpayer can prove that the expenses would not have been incurred by an individual.

As a result of the Supreme Court's decision in *Knight,* the IRS has withdrawn previous released proposed regulations and has released new proposed regulations that are consistent with the Supreme Court's decision.

Proposed Reg. § 1.67-4(a) states that an administration expense of an estate or a nongrantor trust is subject to the two-percent floor in Code Sec. 67(a) if the expense would be ''commonly'' or ''customarily'' incurred by a hypothetical individual owning the same property as the property owned by the estate or the nongrantor trust. The determining factor in deciding whether or not an expense is ''commonly'' or ''customarily'' incurred by a hypothetical individual owning the same property is the type of product or service that the estate or the nongrantor trust purchases, rather than the description of the cost of that product or service. In addition, expenses that do not depend on the identity of the payor (*i.e.,* whether the payor is an individual, or whether the payor is an estate or a trust) generally are expenses that are commonly or customarily incurred by an individual [Prop. Reg. § 1.67-4(b)(1)].

However, certain incremental costs of investment advice beyond the amount that normally would be charged to an individual investor would not be subject to the two-percent floor. In order to fall within the exception to the two-percent floor, the portion of the fee in excess of what is generally charged to an individual investor must be attributable to an unusual investment objective of the trust or estate or to a specialized balancing of the various parties' interests, such that a reasonable comparison with individual investors would be improper [Prop. Reg. § 1.67-4(d)].

---

[17] *Rudkin Testamentary Trust,* SCt, 2008-1 USTC ¶ 50,132, 552 US 181.

Bundled Fees

If an estate or a nongrantor trust pays a single fee, commission, or other expense (such as a fiduciary's commission, attorney's fee, or accountant's fee) for both costs that are subject to the two-percent floor and costs (in more than a *de minimis* amount) that are not, then the single fee, commission, or other expense (bundled fee) must be allocated, for purposes of computing the AGI of the trust or estate between the costs subject to the two-percent floor and those that are not. Out-of-pocket expenses billed to the trust or estate are treated as separate from the bundled fee [Prop. Reg. § 1.67-4(c)(1)].

If a bundled fee is not computed on an hourly basis, only the portion of that fee that is attributable to investment advice is subject to the two-percent floor [Prop. Reg. § 1.67-4(c)(2)].

> **Example 25-28:** A corporate trustee charges a percentage of the value of the trust income and corpus as its annual commission. In addition, the trustee bills a separate amount to the trust each year as compensation for leasing and managing the trust's rental real estate. The separate real estate management fee is subject to the two-percent floor because it is a fee commonly or customarily incurred by an individual owner of rental real estate.
>
> Taxpayers may use any reasonable method to allocate a bundled fee between costs subject to the two-percent floor and those costs that are not, including without limitation the allocation of a portion of a fiduciary commission that is a bundled fee to investment advice. However, the reasonable method standard does not apply to determine the portion of the bundled fee attributable to payments made to third parties for expenses subject to the two-percent floor or to any other separately assessed expense commonly or customarily incurred by an individual, because those payments and expenses are readily identifiable without any discretion on the part of the fiduciary or return preparer [Prop. Reg. § 1.67-4(c)(3)].

Bundled Fiduciary Fees Fully Deductible Until Regs. Finalized

In Notice 2011-37,[18] the IRS extended interim guidance allowing taxpayers to deduct the full amount of bundled fiduciary fees without regard to the application of the two-percent floor under Code Sec. 67 that would otherwise limit deduction of investment advisory fees. For tax years beginning before the date that regulations under Reg. § 1.67-4 are finalized, nongrantor trusts and estates will not be required to determine the portion of a bundled fiduciary fee that consists of costs that are fully deductible and the portion that consists of costs that are subject to the two-percent floor. Instead, taxpayers may deduct the full amount of the bundled fiduciary fee. This means that nongrantor trusts and estates do not have to "unbundle" a fiduciary fee into parts consisting of costs that are fully deductible and costs that are subject to the two-percent floor.

---

[18] Notice 2011-37, IRB 2011-20, 785.

¶25,060 DEDUCTION FOR PERSONAL EXEMPTION

Every trust or estate earning $600 or more of gross income during the tax year must file a Form 1041 [Code Sec. 6012(a)(3), (4)]. An estate or trust filing a tax return is entitled to a personal exemption similar to the one allowed individuals [Ch. 1], but the amount varies depending on the nature of the entity seeking the exemption as follows: [Code Sec. 642(b); Reg. § 1.642(b)-1].

- An estate is allowed an exemption of $600 [Code Sec. 642(b) Reg. § 1.642(b)-1(a)].
- A simple trust (a trust required to distribute all income currently [¶ 25,025]) is allowed an exemption of $300. Even though simple trusts that make distributions from principal they are called *complex trusts* for that tax year, they are still entitled to a $300 exemption that year.
- All other trusts are allowed an exemption of $100 [Code Sec. 642(b)].
- A final Form 1041 must be filed once an estate or trust is terminated. An estate is terminated at the end of the administrative proceedings and after all remaining assets have been distributed [Reg. § 1.641(b)-3(a)]. A trust is also terminated when the assets have been distributed [Reg. § 1.641(b)-3(b)]. No exemption is allowed in the year the estate or trust is terminated because the estate or trust must distribute all its income in the year of termination, and will not, therefore, have an income for the exemption to offset.
- In contrast, on a deceased person's final income tax return (Form 1040), the executor can claim a full personal exemption for the decedent [Code Sec. 151]; [Ch. 1]. The exemption is allowed for the entire year even if the decedent did not live to the end of his last tax year. No proration is required [Ch. 18].

¶25,065 CHARITABLE CONTRIBUTIONS

.01 In General

Under Code Sec. 642(c), an estate or trust may claim an unlimited charitable deduction for contributions reflecting the terms of the governing instrument. Code Sec. 642(c) specifically requires that a charitable deduction is available only if the source of the contribution is gross income, so the contribution must be traced to determine its source. If the trust's charitable contribution is made with respect to its principal (real property) not its gross income, the trust will not be allowed to claim the charitable deduction under Code Sec. 642(c) for the contribution.[19] To enable fiduciaries to act after they know the exact income for the year, they can elect to treat a current contribution as paid during the preceding tax year [Code Sec. 642(c)(1); Reg. § 1.642(c)-1]. The election must be made not later than the due date (including extensions) of the income tax return for the year after the year for which the election is made. [Reg. § 1.642(c)-1(b)(2)].

---

[19] Rev. Rul. 2003-123, 2003-2 CB 1200.

NOTE: Estates and certain inter vivos and testamentary trusts created on or before October 9, 1969, may claim a deduction from gross income for amounts which, under the terms of the will or trust, are *permanently set aside* for charitable purposes [Code Sec. 642(c)(2)]. Special rules also apply to pooled income funds [Code Sec. 642(c)(2)].

In IRS Letter Ruling 201042023,[20] the IRS concluded that a trust that donated properties to charity can claim a charitable contribution deduction under Code Sec. 642(c)(1) equal to the adjusted basis of the properties, not their higher fair market value which represented their appreciated value. The properties were purchased with trust income. The court reasoned that the trust cannot claim a charitable deduction for amounts that represent untaxed appreciation that are part of the property's fair market value. Doing so would yield a double benefit if allowed: avoiding tax on the potential gain on the appreciation and deducting not only basis but gain from gross income.

Contributions from Gross Income

Generally, only contributions of items included in gross income are deductible; tax-exempt income does not qualify.[21] Thus, no deduction will be allowed for a contribution out of the estate or trust corpus. However, a contribution from *income* allocable to corpus, such as capital gains, will qualify for the deduction, since such income is included in the gross income of the estate or trust. But no deduction is allowed to a trust for contributions allocable to its unrelated business income for the tax year [Ch. 23].

Example 25-29: A trustee, under the terms of a will, is directed to pay to a charity half of the addition to corpus each year for the duration of the trust. The only addition to the corpus for the tax year consisted of $12,000 of capital gains, and the trustee distributed $6,000 to the charity. Capital gains allocated to corpus under the terms of the will are included in trust gross income, so a charitable contribution deduction will be allowed.

Adjustment for Exempt Income

When a trust or estate has both taxable and tax-exempt income, the charitable deduction is allowed only for contributions considered as coming from gross income. Unless the governing instrument makes a different allocation, the contribution that is considered as coming from gross income bears the same proportion to the total contribution as the total gross income bears to the total income (including tax-exempt items) [Reg. § 1.642(c)-3(b)].

▶ **OBSERVATION:** To enable the estate or trust to get the full benefit of the charitable deduction, the estate's or trust's governing instrument should specifically provide that contributions be payable out of ordinary taxable income, not from tax-exempt income or long-term capital gains.

[20] LTR 201042023 (May 20, 2010).

[21] *Wellman v. Welch*, CA-1, 38-2 USTC ¶ 9508, 99 F2d 75; *M.C. Tyler Trust*, 5 TC 729, Dec. 14,747 (1945), *acq.* 1945 CB 6.

Example 25-30: A trust had $8,000 of income—consisting of $5,000 rent and $3,000 tax-exempt interest on municipal bonds. The trustee was directed to pay 25 percent of the income to charity. He made a charitable contribution of $2,000 (25 percent of $8,000). If the trust instrument is silent on the income source of the contribution, the amount considered as coming from the gross income of the trust is $1,250 ($5,000 / $8,000 × $2,000). Hence, the trust can deduct $1,250. If the trustee had been directed to pay $2,000 of the rental income to charity, he could have deducted that amount.

Similarly, when computing the amount of tax-exempt income included in distributable net income, Reg. § 1.643(a)-5(b) provides that, if the governing instrument specifically identifies the source out of which amounts are paid, permanently set aside, or to be used for such charitable purposes, the specific provisions control. In the absence of specific provisions in the governing instrument, the amount distributed is deemed to consist of the same proportion of each class of the items of income of the estate or trust as the total of each class bears to the total of all classes.

.02 Ordering Rules for Charitable Payments by Estates and Trusts

A provision in a trust, will or local law that specifically indicates the source out of which amounts are to be paid, permanently set aside, or used for a charitable purpose must have independent economic effect in addition to its income tax consequences if the allocation is to be respected for federal tax purposes [Reg. § 1.642(c)-3(b)(2)]. If the applicable provision does not have economic effect independent of income tax consequences, income distributed will consist of the same proportion of each class of the items of income as the total of each class bears to the total of all classes [Reg. § 1.643(a)-5(b)].

This rule targets charitable lead trusts which are split-interest trusts with a lead interest paid to charitable beneficiaries and a remainder interest passing to noncharitable beneficiaries. Any amounts that are not paid to charity through the annuity or unitrust payment are taxable to the charitable lead trust. The ordering rules in the charitable lead trust's governing instruments typically provide for the following ordering of classes of annuity or unitrust payment, until the class been exhausted: (1) ordinary income, (2) capital gains, (3) other income (including tax-exempt income), and (4) corpus. These ordering rules benefit the charitable lead trust because they make certain that taxable income is fully allocated before nontaxable income is allocated. They therefore minimize the amount of the trust's income that would be taxed to the trust. The IRS has consistently challenged this ordering regime because in their view it does not have economic effect.

Example 25-31: A charitable lead annuity trust has the calendar year as its tax year, and is to pay an annuity of $10,000 annually to a local charity. A provision in the trust governing instrument provides that the $10,000 annuity should be deemed to come first from ordinary income, second from short-term capital gain, third from 50 percent of the unrelated business taxable income, fourth from long-term capital gain, fifth from the balance of unrelated business taxable income, sixth from tax-exempt income, and seventh from principal. This provision in the governing instrument does not have economic effect independent of income tax consequences, because the amount to be paid to the charity is not dependent upon the type of income from which it is to be paid. Accordingly, the amount to which Code Sec. 642(c) applies is deemed to consist of the same proportion of each class of the items of income of the trust as the total of each class bears to the total of all classes [Reg. § 1.642(c)-3(b)(2), ex. 1].

Example 25-32: A trust instrument provides that 100 percent of the trust's ordinary income must be distributed currently to a local charity and that all remaining items of income must be distributed currently to a noncharitable beneficiary. This income ordering provision has economic effect independent of income tax consequences because the amount to be paid to the charitable organization each year is dependent upon the amount of ordinary income the trust earns within that taxable year. Accordingly, for purposes of Code Sec. 642(c), the full amount distributed to charity is deemed to consist of ordinary income [Reg. § 1.642(c)-3(b)(2), ex. 2].

¶25,070 DEPRECIATION OR DEPLETION

The depreciation or depletion deduction allowed to a life tenant, income beneficiary of a trust, or distributee of an estate is a deduction for purposes of determining adjusted gross income. Who gets the deduction is discussed in the following paragraphs.

NOTE: Estates and trusts cannot elect the expensing deduction [Ch. 11] [Code Sec. 179(d)(4)].

.01 Trusts

The deduction for depreciation of trust property is to be divided between the income beneficiaries and the trustee as directed in the trust instrument. If the trust instrument makes no allocation, the deduction is apportioned on the basis of the trust income (determined under the trust instrument and state law) allocable to each [Code Sec. 167(d)].

The regulations limit the allocation in the trust instrument. They provide that the share of the deduction allocated to either the trustee or a beneficiary ordinarily cannot be more than his or her pro rata share of the trust income. However, if the trust instrument or state law requires or allows the trustee to maintain a reserve for depreciation, the deduction is first allocated to the trustee for income set aside for the reserve. Any part of the deduction not used up is then divided between the beneficiaries and the trustee on the basis of the trust income (in excess of the amount set aside as a reserve) allocable to each [Reg. § § 1.167(h)-1(b), 1.642(e)-1].

Example 25-33: Mr. Hyde establishes a trust for the benefit of his son, John, and his daughter, Mary. The trust property includes an apartment house on which a depreciation allowance could be claimed. Under the terms of the trust instrument, the income of the trust is to be distributed to John and Mary in equal shares. The trust instrument also authorizes the trustee, in his discretion, to set aside income for a depreciation reserve. During the year, the trustee sets aside

$2,000 income as a reserve. Depreciation on the trust property amounts to $2,500. The trustee gets a depreciation deduction of $2,000. John and Mary each get a deduction of $250.

NOTE: If the income beneficiary is entitled to the entire income, and the instrument is silent on depreciation, the beneficiary gets the deduction. Even if the trust has no income during the year, the income beneficiary is still entitled to the deduction.[22]

.02 Estates

For an estate, the depreciation deduction is divided between the estate and the heirs, legatees and devisees on the basis of the income allocable to each [Code Sec. 167(d); Reg. § 1.167(h)-1(c)].

▶ **OBSERVATION:** If an estate or trust shares in depreciation or depletion of another trust or a partnership (or takes the deduction into account separately), the estate or trust divides the deduction among its own distributees on the same basis as it allocates its income.[23]

¶25,075 NET OPERATING LOSS DEDUCTION

Generally, estates and trusts are entitled to the net operating loss deduction. This may reduce DNI for the year to which the operating loss is carried back, so that beneficiaries may recompute their shares of the estate or trust income for the prior year.[24] However, in computing the net operating loss, the estate or trust cannot take deductions for charitable contributions or distributions to beneficiaries. A trust also must exclude income and deductions attributable to the grantor [Code Sec. 642(d); Reg. § 1.642(d)-1]. If a trust's income is allocable entirely among income beneficiaries, and the governing instrument makes no provision for depreciation, the trustee cannot take a depreciation deduction in computing the net operating loss.[25]

On termination of an estate or trust, any unused net operating loss carryovers are deductible by the beneficiaries succeeding to the estate or trust property [Code Sec. 642(h); Reg. § 1.642(h)-1].

The net operating loss deduction of a common trust fund [¶ 25,125] is allowed to the participants in the fund and not to the trust [Code Sec. 584(g); Reg. § 1.584-6].

¶25,080 EXPENSES

.01 In General

An estate or trust can deduct ordinary and necessary expenses it pays or incurs, if the expenses are:

---

[22] *S. Carol*, 30 BTA 443, Dec. 8520, *acq.* 1934-2 CB 4.

[23] Rev. Rul. 61-211, 1961-2 CB 124, as modified by, Rev. Rul. 74-71, 1974-1 CB 158.

[24] Rev. Rul. 61-20, 1961-1 CB 248.

[25] *D.B. Kearney*, DC-NY, 54-1 USTC ¶ 9113, 116 FSupp 922.

(1) trade or business expenses; (2) expenses for the production or collection of income or for managing, conserving or maintaining property held for the production of income; (3) reasonable administration expenses, including fiduciaries' fees and litigation expenses in connection with the duties of administration (except expenses allocable to the production or collection of tax-exempt income) (keep in mind that administrative expenses are deductible for income tax purposes only if they are not also claimed as deductions for estate tax purposes[26]); or (4) expenses for the determination, collection or refund of any tax [Code Secs. 162(a), 212; Reg. § 1.212-1]. Deductible expenses chargeable only to trust corpus reduce DNI and thus the amount taxable to the beneficiary. However, these expenses do not reduce the amount of income available for the income beneficiary.

A fiduciary can deduct counsel fees and other expenses of unsuccessfully contesting an income tax deficiency, or similar expenses relating to the final distribution from an expired trust.[27] Interest on overdue estate tax[28] or on legacies[29] is also deductible. But there is no deduction for interest paid by an estate on deficiencies on state inheritance taxes which are not the estate's obligation under state law.[30]

> **NOTE:** Interest paid by a trust on an unpaid balance of estate tax liability that is deferred can qualify as an administrative expense deductible by the trust.[31]

Double Deduction Not Allowed

Amounts deductible as administration expenses or losses in computing the taxable estate of a decedent are not deductible for income tax purposes unless the estate files a statement (in duplicate) to the effect that the items have not been allowed as deductions from the gross estate for estate tax purposes and that all rights to deduct them for that purpose are waived [Code Sec. 642(g); Reg. § 1.642(g)-1]. This prohibition against double deductions is also applicable to those cases where the expenses or losses are paid or incurred by trusts or other persons, instead of the estate.

The Code Sec. 642(g) double deduction prohibition rule does not apply to deductions for taxes, interest, business expenses, and other items accrued at the date of the decedent's death so that they are allowable as deductions under Code Sec. 2053(a)(3) for estate tax purposes as claims against the estate and are also allowable under Code Sec. 691(b) to the estate as deductions in respect of a decedent for income tax purposes [See Reg. § 1.642(g)-2].

¶25,085 DEDUCTION FOR DISTRIBUTIONS TO BENEFICIARIES

It is current policy to tax the income of estates and trusts only once—either to the fiduciary, or to the beneficiary, or, in part, to each. This is done by treating the estate

---

[26] Rev. Rul. 63-27, 1963-1 CB 57.

[27] *C.P. Erdman*, CA-7, 63-1 USTC ¶9391, 315 F2d 762.

[28] *W. Bingham*, SCt, 45-2 USTC ¶9327, 325 US 365, 65 SCt 1232.

[29] *B. Penrose*, DC-PA, 37-1 USTC ¶9156, 18 FSupp 413.

[30] Rev. Rul. 73-322, 1973-2 CB 44.

[31] *C.H. Ungeman*, 89 TC 1131, Dec. 44,371 (1987).

or trust as a taxable entity, and by giving it a special deduction for amounts paid or payable to the beneficiary.

.01 Simple Trusts

A simple trust gets a deduction for trust income required to be distributed currently, whether or not distributed [Code Sec. 651; Reg. § 1.651(b)-1]. For asset distributions in lieu of cash, see ¶ 25,045.

Example 25-34: The trust instrument requires all the income to be distributed currently. The trust has $10,000 income for 2013, of which $2,500 is collected in December. The trustee makes the usual quarterly payment of $2,500 to its sole beneficiary in January 2014. The trust can deduct $10,000 for 2013.

The deduction is limited to DNI [¶ 25,020]. For this purpose, DNI does not include income items (adjusted for related deductions) not included in gross income [Code Sec. 651; Reg. § 1.651(b)-1].

Example 25-35: Distributable net income is $99,000. This includes tax-exempt interest totaling $9,000. The deduction for distributions to beneficiaries cannot be more than $90,000.

.02 Estates and Complex Trusts

An estate or complex trust gets a deduction for amounts paid credited or required to be distributed to the beneficiaries. The deduction consists of the sum of (1) income required to be distributed currently (including an amount payable out of income or corpus to the extent that it is paid out of income) and (2) any other amounts paid, credited or required to be distributed for the tax year. However, the deduction cannot exceed DNI, excluding items not included in the gross income of the estate or trust [Code Sec. 661(a), (c); Reg. § § 1.661(a)-2, 1.661(c)-1]. For asset distributions in lieu of cash, see ¶ 25,045.

The amount deductible is treated as consisting of the same proportion of each class of items entering into the computation of DNI as the total of each class bears to the total DNI, unless the governing instruments or state law allocates different classes of income to different beneficiaries [Code Sec. 661(b); Reg. § 1.661(b)-1].

Example 25-36: A trust has gross income of $100,000 ($50,000 taxable income and $50,000 tax-exempt income). Its distributable net income is $98,000. It has deductions of $2,000, half of which are attributable to tax-exempt income. The deduction to the trust is limited to $49,000, since the rest of the DNI ($49,000) is deemed to be tax-exempt income.

The DNI, for purposes of computing the distributions deductions, does not include the deduction for amounts paid or permanently set aside for charity [¶ 25,065] [Code Sec. 663(a)(2)].

¶25,090 DEDUCTIONS IN TRANSACTIONS BETWEEN RELATED PARTIES

Related parties must match their deductions and income in the same year. Thus, an accrual-basis taxpayer can deduct interest, expenses, etc., paid to a related cash-basis taxpayer only when the cash-basis recipient must include a like amount in income [Code Sec. 267]. "Related parties" include, among others: (1) members of a family, (2) a grantor and his trust fiduciary, (3) fiduciaries of two trusts having the same grantor, (4) a fiduciary and a beneficiary of his trust, (5) a fiduciary and a beneficiary of another trust with the same grantor, (6) an executor of an estate and a beneficiary of the estate, and (7) a fiduciary and a corporation over 50 percent of whose stock is owned, directly or indirectly, by or for the trust or the grantor. [Code Sec. 267(b)]. See also Ch. 18 for other details.

¶25,095 CREDITS AGAINST TAX

Generally, estates and trusts are permitted the same credits that are available to individuals. For example, an estate or trust gets a credit against tax for the following:

- *Foreign taxes* not allocable to the beneficiaries [Code Sec. 642(a)].
- *Low-income housing credit* [Ch. 14] [Code Sec. 42].

RATES, RETURNS, AND PAYMENT FOR DECEDENTS, ESTATES, AND TRUSTS

¶25,100 RATES AND RETURNS

Trusts and estates of decedents are separate entities for which returns must be filed. Returns are generally filed by fiduciaries for estates or trusts, and for decedents.

.01 Tax Rates Imposed on Estates and Trusts

The following chart reflects the tax rates imposed on estates and trusts in 2013.

Estates and Trusts in 2013

If Taxable Income Is:	*The Tax Is:*
Not over $2,450	15% of the taxable income
Over $2,450 but not over $5,700	$367.50 plus 25% of the excess over $2,450
Over $5,700 but not over $8,750	$1,180 plus 28% of the excess over $5,700
Over $8,750 but not over $11,950	$2,034 plus 33% of the excess over $8,750
Over $11,950	$3,090 plus 39.6% of the excess over $11,950

.02 The 3.8 Percent Net Investment Income Tax

Beginning in 2013, estates and trusts must start paying a 3.8-percent surtax on net investment income (NII) on the lesser of (1) their "undistributed net investment income" for the year, or (2) any excess of their adjusted gross income over $11,950 in 2013 (increasing to $12,150 in 2014) which is the dollar amount at which the highest tax bracket for estates and trusts begins for the year [Code Sec. 1411(a)(2)]. The NII tax is imposed in addition to all other taxes already imposed on that income such as income tax and alternative minimum tax. Unfortunately, the 3.8 percent surtax may not be deducted anywhere on the federal income tax return. For further discussion of this tax which is also imposed on individuals, see ¶ 15,050. Taxpayers (including individuals and estate and trusts) (subject to the NIIT should use Form 8960, *Net Investment Income Tax-Individuals, Estate and Trusts*, to compute the 3.8 percent tax. Estates and trusts should report the tax on Form 1041, *U.S. Income Tax Return for Estate and Trusts*.

The following trusts are not subject to NII tax [Code Sec. 1411(e)(1); Prop. Reg. § 1.1411-3(b)]:

- Trusts that are exempt from income taxes such as charitable trusts and qualified retirement plan trusts exempt from tax under Code Sec. 501, and charitable remainder trusts exempt from tax under Code Sec. 664;
- A trust in which all of the unexpired interests are organized and operated exclusively for religious, charitable, scientific, literary, or educational purposes, or to foster national or international amateur sports competition (but only if no part of its activities involve the provision of athletic facilities or equipment), or for the prevention of cruelty to children or animals as described in Code Sec. 170(c)(2)(B);
- Trusts that are classified as "grantor trusts" under Code Secs. 671-679 [see ¶ 25.115]; a grantor trust is treated as owned by the grantor for income tax purposes and all items of trust income, loss, credit and deduction are reported by the grantor on the grantor's tax return. As a result of achieving grantor trust status, the trust entity has no income to which the NIIT would apply;
- Trusts that are not classified as "trusts" for federal income tax purposes such as real estate investment trusts (REITs) and common trust funds [Code Sec. 1411(e)(2)];
- Electing small business trusts (ESBTs), which are treated as two separate trusts when a portion of the ESBT's holdings is S corporation stock, are subject to special computational rules. ESBTs are treated as two separate trusts for computational purposes, but are consolidated when determining the AGI threshold [Prop. Reg. § 1.1411-3(c)(1)];
- Charitable remainder trusts are also subject to special computational rules. Although, the trust itself isn't subject to the NIIT, the annuity and unitrust distributions may constitute NII to the noncharitable recipient [Prop. Reg. § 1.1411-3(c)(2)]; and
- Foreign estates and trusts are generally not subject to the NIIT if they have little or no connection to the United States. However, to the extent the income is earned or accumulated for the benefit of, or distributed to, U.S. persons, the NII of a foreign estate or foreign trust will be subject to the tax [Prop. Reg. § 1.1411-3(c)(3)].

How Estates and Trust Can Minimize Exposure to 3.8 Percent NII Surtax

1. *Make Estate and Trust Distributions.* Estates and trusts can avoid exposure to the NIIT if the fiduciary (if permitted by the terms of the will or trust) makes income distributions to the beneficiaries because estates and trusts will only be subject to the surtax on "undistributed net investment income," which is defined in Prop. Reg. § 1.1411-3(e)(2) as an estate's or trust's NII determined just as it would be for an individual and then reduced by distributions of NII to beneficiaries and reduced further by any deductible charitable contributions. Distributions of income will accomplish two objectives: the beneficiaries will most likely be in a lower income tax bracket and may also have a MAGI below the threshold at which the NIIT becomes applicable.

2. *Change Estate and Trust Investments.* Estates and trusts should also consider investing in tax-exempt and tax-deferred investments in order to reduce income subject to the tax because these entities will be subject to the surtax if their AGI exceeds $11,950 in 2013 (increasing to $12,150 in 2014).

3. *Establish Material Participation by Trust.* Another tax-saving technique that estates or trusts should consider is to establish material participation by the estate or trust because NII does not include income from the operation of an active trade or business. Neither the Internal Revenue Code nor the regulations explain how to determine whether an estate or trust materially participates in a business for purposes of the passive activity loss rules in Code Sec. 469(h). The only court opinion addressing how a trust establishes material participation for purposes of Code Sec. 469 is *Mattie K. Carter Trust*,[32] where the district court held that in determining material participation for trusts, the activities of the trust's fiduciaries, employees, and agents should be considered to determine whether the trust's participation is "regular, continuous, and substantial." The court rejected the government's position that the determination should be made solely by referring to the activities of the trustee because in the court's view, this approach would create unnecessary statutory ambiguity. In direct opposition to the decision in *Mattie K. Carter*, the IRS took the view in Technical Advice Memorandum 201317010[33] that the only way for a trust to establish material participation for purposes of Code Sec. 469(h) is for the fiduciaries, in their capacities as fiduciaries, to be involved in the operations of the relevant activities on a regular, continuous, and substantial basis. Based on the facts in that technical advice memorandum, the IRS concluded that the two trusts did not materially participate in the activities of two S corporations because the IRS declined to attribute the activities of the owners to the trusts. The IRS only viewed the activities of the fiduciaries as relevant for purposes of establishing the trust's material participation. In order for a trust to establish material participation, the following guidelines should be followed: (1) The trust must establish who is acting as a fiduciary on the trust's behalf. The individuals could include agents, employees or advisors. (2) The trust must establish which fiduciary's hours will count in determining material participation. (3) The trust must

---

[32] *Mattie K. Carter Trust*, DC-TX, 2003-1 USTC ¶ 50,418, 256 FSupp 537.

[33] TAM 201317010 (Jan. 18, 2013).

determine what hours will qualify as participation for purposes of proving material participation.

4. *Use Installment Sales Method To Spread Out Taxable Gain.* One way to avoid exposure to the NIIT is to use the installment method of reporting to spread out taxable gain that would subject to the NIIT and move the gain to years where the taxpayer is not exposed to the NIIT or has lower MAGI. An installment sale is defined as a sale of property where one or more payments are received after the close of the tax year in which the sale took place For further discussion of installment sales, see Chapter 19.

.03 Decedents

If a decedent would have been required to file a return, then the executor, administrator, legal representative, or survivor must file a final return. The return is made on Form 1040, 1040EZ or 1040A. An executor or administrator may disaffirm a joint return filed by the surviving spouse.

The return covers the period from the beginning of the decedents' tax year up to and including their date of death [Code Sec. 443(a)(2); Reg. § 1.443-1(a)(2)]. For rates, see Ch. 1.

.04 Estates

A deceased person's estate income tax return is filed on Form 1041. The fiduciary must file Form 1041 if: (a) the estate's gross income is $600 or over or (b) any beneficiary is a nonresident alien [Code Sec. 6012(a)(3); Reg. § 1.6012-3(a)]. The fiduciary must file a separate Schedule K-1 (or an appropriate substitute) for each beneficiary, showing that beneficiary's share of income, deductions and credits. The fiduciary must also send a copy of Schedule K-1 to each beneficiary [Code Sec. 6034A]. The beneficiary of an estate or trust is required to file his return in a manner consistent with the information received from the estate or trust on the K-1 or any other document unless the beneficiary files a notification identifying the inconsistency [Code Sec. 6034A].

An ancillary executor or administrator must file an information return on Form 1041 for the part of the estate he or she controls [Reg. § 1.6012-3(a)(3)]. Any estate or trust fiduciary must furnish return information to the beneficiaries [Code Sec. 6034A]. Penalties are provided for failure to comply.

In his first return, the fiduciary chooses the accounting period for the estate. This may be either a calendar year or *any* fiscal year which he or she selects. Estate gross income is figured from the day following the deceased person's death [Reg. § 1.443-1]. Thus, a return may have to be filed for the short period from that date to the start of the estate's regular tax year.

> ▶ **OBSERVATION:** Although the current law drastically restricts a *trust's* ability to defer income taxation through the selection of trusts' tax years, the treatment of an *estate's* tax year is not affected [¶ 25,110].

.05 Trusts

A trust's income tax return is filed on Form 1041. The trustee must file Form 1041 if: (a) the trust has any taxable income for the tax year, or (b) its gross income is $600 or over (regardless of taxable income), or (c) any beneficiary is a nonresident alien [Code

Sec. 6012(a)(4); Reg. § 1.6012-3(a)]. The trustee must also file Form 1041-A if the trust claims charitable or other deductions for amounts paid or permanently set aside for a charity [Code Sec. 6034(a); Reg. § 1.6034-1(a)]. But this return is not required if the trust must distribute all of its net income to its beneficiaries [Code Sec. 6034(b); Reg. § 1.6034-1(b)(1)]. The trustee must file a Schedule K-1 for each beneficiary. Any estate or trust fiduciary must furnish return information to the beneficiaries [Code Sec. 6034A]. Noncompliance may be subject to $50 penalty.

Form 1041A Penalties

Penalties are imposed for failure to file or failure to provide required information on Form 1041A, *U.S. Information Return Trust Accumulation of Charitable Amounts*. Penalties are $20 per day, up to $10,000 for any one return. In the case of an organization having gross receipts exceeding $1,000,000 for any year, penalties are $100 per day up to a maximum of $50,000 [Code Sec. 6652(c)(1)]. For split-interest trusts with gross income in excess of $250,000, the penalty is $100 per day, up to a maximum of $50,000. An additional penalty may be assessed against the person required to file the return if that person knowingly fails to file the return [Code Sec. 6652(c)(2)(C)].

Confidentiality of Noncharitable Beneficiaries

Information regarding beneficiaries of split-interest trusts, other than charitable organizations, no longer must be made available to the public [Code Sec. 6104(b)].

Will or Trust Deed and Fiduciary's Statement

If requested by the IRS, the fiduciary must file a copy of the will or the trust instrument, together with his or her statement as to which provisions of the will or trust instrument determine the amount taxable to each taxpayer involved [Reg. § 1.6012-3(a)(2)].

.06 Alternative Minimum Tax

Estates and trusts must pay the alternative minimum tax (AMT) to the extent it exceeds the regular tax liability [Ch. 16]. The tax is computed under the same general rules that apply to individual taxpayers. The estate or trust applies the alternative minimum tax rates to the excess of the alternative minimum taxable income over an exemption amount. The exemption amount for estates and trusts is $22,500 [Code Sec. 55(d)(1)(D)] [Ch. 16].

The exemption is phased out at 25 cents on the dollar for alternative minimum taxable income over $75,000. The estate or trust then pays a tax of 26 percent on the first $175,000 of the taxable excess and 28 percent on each dollar above $175,000. In addition to the deductions applicable to individuals, trusts and estates are allowed additional deductions for charitable gifts, distributions and administrative costs [Code Secs. 56(a)(1); 59(c)]. Items of tax preference are allocated between the trust or estate and the beneficiaries [Reg. § 1.58-3(a)(1)].

.07 Consistency Requirement

Beneficiaries of an estate or trust must file their returns in a manner consistent with the manner reported on the trust or estate's return or must file a notice of inconsistent treatment with the IRS that identifies the inconsistent items [Code Sec. 6034A]. A beneficiary who fails to file a return in accordance with the information received from the estate or trust can generally elect to be treated as having complied with the consistency requirement. If a beneficiary fails to comply with these consistency requirements, any adjustment needed to make the treatment of items by the beneficiary consistent with the treatment of the items on the trust or estate's return is treated as a mathematical or clerical error subject to summary assessment procedures. The negligence penalty may also apply.

¶25,105 ESTIMATED TAX PAYMENT BY ESTATES AND TRUSTS

Estates and trusts must make quarterly estimated tax payments in the same manner as individuals. For individual estimated tax payments see ¶ 14,200-¶ 14,220. Estates or trusts with a short tax year must pay installments of tax on or before the 15th day of the fourth, sixth and ninth months of the tax year and the 15th day of the first month of the following tax year. The amount of each installment in a short tax year is determined by dividing the required annual payment by the number of payments required for that year. Estates and trusts generally have 45 days (rather than the 15 days allowed individuals) to compute the payments under the estimated tax annualization rules. The payment due dates are unchanged [Code Sec. 6654(l)]. First-time filers must file Form 1041-ES which includes vouchers to be included with quarterly payments.

¶25,110 TAX YEARS OF ESTATES AND TRUSTS

.01 Estate's Tax Year

Estates have flexibility in choosing their tax year. The estate's income must be reported annually on either a calendar or fiscal year basis. A fiscal year is a 12-month period ending on the last day of any month other than December [Code Sec. 441(e)]. A fiscal year election is made on Form SS-4, at the time that the estate files for its tax identification number. The first fiscal year cannot exceed 12 months, and it generally is prudent to elect the month prior to the date of death as the fiscal year-end. For example, if the decedent died on May 10, a fiscal year ending in April should be elected, making the first year May 10, 2013, to April 30, 2014.

The personal representative chooses the estate's accounting period when the first Form 1041 is filed for the estate. The estate's first tax year can be any period that ends on the last day of a month and does not exceed 12 months. The first tax year must be adopted by the due date (not including extensions) for filing the first return. After the personal representative has chosen the tax year, it cannot be changed without permission from the IRS. In addition, on the first income tax return, the personal representative chooses either the cash or accrual accounting method that will be used to report the estate's income. After an accounting method has been chosen, it cannot be changed without the consent of the IRS. An application for change is filed on IRS Form 1128.

▶ **PLANNING TIP:** The ability of an estate to adopt a fiscal year as its tax year provides a valuable income deferral opportunity. Using a fiscal year will enable a beneficiary to defer reporting taxable income from estate distributions because estate income distributed or distributable to a beneficiary is taxable to the beneficiary for the tax year in which the tax year of the estate ends [Code Sec. 662(c); Reg. § 1.662(c)-1].

Example 25-37: Alice is the beneficiary of an estate that has a tax year beginning June 1, 2013, and ending May 31, 2014. Alice is a calendar basis taxpayer. On June 1, 2013, Alice receives a distribution from the estate. She does not have to report any income resulting from this distribution until April 15, 2015, which is the due date of her 2014 individual federal income tax return.

.02 Trust's Tax Year

Trusts, unlike estates, have no flexibility in choosing their tax year. Trusts are not permitted to use fiscal tax years. They must adopt the calendar year as their tax year [Code Sec. 645(a)]. A trust beneficiary is taxed on the distributions for the tax year or years of the estate or trust that end within or with his or her tax year [Code Secs. 652(c), 662(c); Reg. §§ 1.652(c)-1, 1.662(c)-1]. However, tax-exempt and charitable trusts may use a fiscal year [Code Sec. 645].

SPECIAL PROBLEMS

¶25,115 GRANTOR TRUST RULES

.01 What Is a Grantor

A "grantor" is defined to include any person who either creates a trust, or directly or indirectly makes a gratuitous transfer of property to a trust. If a person creates or funds a trust on behalf of another person, both persons are treated as grantors of the trust [Reg. § 1.671-2(e)(1)]. A gratuitous transfer is any transfer other than a transfer made in return for fair market value. This is a determination made regardless of whether the transfer will be treated as a gift for federal gift tax purposes [Reg. § 1.671-2(e)(2)(i)].

Example 25-38: Mom creates and funds a trust for the benefit of her children. Her brother subsequently makes a gratuitous transfer to the trust. Both Mom and her brother are grantors of the trust [Reg. § 1.671-2(e)(6), Ex. 1].

If a partnership or corporation makes a gratuitous transfer to a trust, the partners or shareholders will be treated as the grantors, unless the transfer is made for a business purpose [Reg. § 1.671-2(e)(4)]. The gratuitous transfer will be treated as a distribution by the partnership or corporation to the partner or shareholders, followed by a transfer by the partners or shareholders to the trust. The partner or shareholder (not the partnership or corporation) will be treated as the trust's grantor [Reg. § 1.671-2(e)(4)].

.02 What Is a Grantor Trust

A grantor trust is a trust, whether revocable or irrevocable, in which an individual has sufficient specifically enumerated rights and/or interests in or over the trust to be considered the owner of the trust for income tax purposes.

.03 Overview of Grantor Trust Rules

In a grantor trust, all or part of the income of a trust will be taxed to the person who set up the trust or the "grantor" rather than to the trust and its beneficiaries. The grantor trust rules are found in Code Sec. 671 through Code Sec. 679. These rules were designed to make it impossible for the grantor to escape tax on the income from property transferred into a trust where the grantor retains sufficient control over the property to still be considered the owner.

In general, the grantor trust rules provide that a grantor will be treated as the owner of a trust and thus will be taxed on its income where he or she retains substantial dominion and control over the trust. A grantor of a grantor trust must report the trust's income, deductions, and credits on his or her individual income tax return as if there were no trust because a grantor type trust is not recognized as a separate taxable entity for income tax purposes. When the grantor is taxed on the income of the trust, he or she is allowed to claim the deductions, credits, and exclusions (including home sale exclusions under Code Sec. 121)[34] related to that income [Code Sec. 671; Reg. § 1.671-3(a)]. The tax year and method of accounting used by the trust are disregarded. The grantor determines the gross income from the trust properties as if the trust had not been created.[35]

The retention or possession of specifically enumerated rights and/or interests in or over the trust gives the grantor dominion and control over the trust property and/or the trust income. Code Sec. 671 provides that when the grantor or another person is treated as the owner of a portion of a trust, the grantor must report the trust's income, deductions, gain, loss and/or credits on his or her individual tax return as if there were no trust because a grantor trust is not recognized as a separate taxable entity for income tax purposes. The grantor therefore computes taxable income and credits by taking into account the trust items of income, deductions, and credits which are attributable to that portion of the trust.

If the grantor retains one or more of these specifically enumerated rights and interests that are found in Code Sec. 673 through Code Sec. 678, the trust will be classified as a "grantor trust" and the grantor or some other person with grantor-like powers will be treated as the trust's owner and taxed on its income [Reg. § 1.671-1(a)]:

- If the grantor has retained a reversionary interest in either the corpus or income of the trust [Code Sec. 673(a)];
- If the grantor or a nonadverse party has the power to control beneficial enjoyment of the corpus or the income from the trust [Code Sec. 674(a)];
- If certain administrative powers over the trust exist under which the grantor can or does benefit [Code Sec. 675];
- If the grantor or a nonadverse party has the power to revoke the trust or return the trust principal to the grantor [Code Sec. 676];
- If the grantor or a nonadverse party had the power to distribute income to or for the benefit of the grantor or the grantor's spouse [Code Sec. 677]; and

---

[34] LTR 200018021 (Jan. 21, 2000).

[35] Rev. Rul. 57-390, 1957-2 CB 326.

- If a person other than the grantor has the sole power to vest income or principal in himself or herself so he or she is treated in the same manner as a grantor of the trust [Code Sec. 678(a)].

.04 Tax Consequences of Grantor Trusts

When items of income, deduction or credit are attributed to a grantor trust, they are treated as if they had been received or paid directly to the grantor and the character of the item is treated as if it had been received or paid directly by the grantor. The existence of the trust does not change or "filter" the character of the item. This means that capital gain items will pass through the trust to the grantor as capital gain items.

The grantor is taxable on the income of a trust when, without the consent of an adverse party, the income is, or may be, paid or accumulated for the grantor's benefit, or used to pay your life insurance premiums (except on policies irrevocably payable to charity). In addition, the grantor is taxable on the income from property transferred in trust for the benefit of his spouse. In transfers for the benefit of himself or his spouse, the grantor is treated as the owner of the property transferred [Reg. § 1.677(a)-1]. Trust income used to support a child or other beneficiary whom the grantor is legally obligated to support generally is taxable to the grantor (for example, when it is used to pay his son's college tuition)[36] [Code Sec. 677; Reg. §§ 1.677(a)-1, 1.677(b)-1]. For an alimony or support trust, the wife is taxed on the payments (including any tax preference items) except to the extent the payments are for the support of minor children [Code Sec. 682; Reg. §§ 1.682(a)-1, 1.682(b)-1, 1.682(c)-1]. Some courts hold that tax-exempt income received by an alimony trust is not taxed when it is distributed to the wife,[37] but the IRS disagrees with this result[38] as do other counts.[39]

A person other than the grantor may be taxed on the trust income if he or she has a power to acquire the corpus or income of the trust. Thus, a person who has exclusive power to vest the corpus or income of a trust in himself, or who has released such power but retained controls similar to those outlined above, is taxed on the trust income [Code Sec. 678; Reg. § 1.678(a)-1], subject to these modifications:

1. If the grantor of the trust, is taxed as the owner, the other person will not be taxed under the above rule;
2. If the other person can merely use trust income to support a dependent, he or she will be taxed only to the extent it is so used [Reg. § 1.678(c)-1];
3. If the other person renounces the power within a reasonable time after learning of it, he or she will not be taxed on the trust income [Reg. § 1.678(d)-1].

Sales Between Grantor Trust and Grantor

Because a grantor trust is taxed for income tax purposes as if the grantor owns the trust assets directly, the deemed owner and the trust are treated as one and the same person. Thus, transactions between the trust and the deemed owner are ignored. In Rev. Rul.

---

[36] *G.B. Morrill*, DC-ME, 64-1 USTC ¶ 9463, 228 FSupp 734.

[37] *M.C. Ellis*, CA-6, 69-2 USTC ¶ 9665, 416 F2d 894; *A.Q. Stewart*, 9 TC 195, Dec. 15,967, *nonacq.* 1965-2 CB 7.

[38] Rev. Rul. 65-283, 1965-2 CB 25.

[39] *P.R. Kitch*, CA-10, 97-1 USTC ¶ 50,124, 103 F3d 104.

85-13,[40] the IRS sanctioned this concept and held that an apparent sale between a grantor trust and its grantor would not be regarded as a sale for income tax purposes. Therefore the grantor recognized no gain or loss on the transaction because the grantor and the trust were considered one and the same person for income tax purposes. Consider the tax-saving opportunities presently by Rev. Rul. 85-13. If the grantor sells appreciated assets to the trust, the grantor recognizes no gain under Code Sec. 1001 because the sale is ignored for income tax purposes. The opportunity to sell assets to an IDGT without recognizing gain has spawned many estate planning strategies.

.05 Income Tax Rules vs. Estate Planning Rules

The income tax rules regarding grantor trusts that result in the income of the trust being taxed to the grantor are very different from the estate tax rules which determine whether the assets in the grantor trust will be included in the grantor's estate for estate tax purposes. For estate tax purposes the trust and the deemed owner are separate persons, and under certain circumstances, the trust is not included in the deemed owner's gross estate for estate tax purposes at the death of the deemed owner. In order for the principal of the trust to be included in a grantor's estate, the decedent must have transferred property to the trust and retained an interest in the transferred property. Some of the statutorily enumerated retained interests that will result inclusion in the decedent's estate include:

- The right to possess or enjoy the transferred property,
- The right to income from the property,
- The right to designate the persons who will possess the trust property or income from it,
- Retention of certain voting rights over the stock of a controlled corporation,
- A transfer that takes effect at death where the decedent retains a reversion in the transferred property, or

Where the enumerated retained powers listed above also cause a trust to be classified as a grantor trust, income from the grantor trust will be taxed to the grantor and the trust will also be included in the decedent's estate for estate tax purposes. But there are instances where powers retained by the grantor will result in grantor trust classification but will not result in inclusion in a decedent's estate for estate tax purposes. The most popular so-called split-personality power used for this purpose is the retained administrative power over a trust found in Code Sec. 675. This power allows the grantor to exercise administrative control over the trust for the benefit of the grantor rather than the trust beneficiaries [Reg. § 1.675-1(a)]. The Code Sec. 675 retained administrative powers over a trust will result in the trust being classified as a grantor trust but will *not* result in inclusion of the trust principal in the decedent's estate for estate tax purposes.

.06 When Trust Treated as Grantor Trust

A trust will be treated as a grantor trust and the grantor taxed as the owner of the trust in the following situations:

---

[40] Rev. Rul. 85-13, 1985-1 CB 184.

- *Reversionary interest.* A trust is treated as a grantor trust when the grantor has a reversionary interest whose value at the time of the transfer of the property into the trust amounts to more than five percent of the value of the transferred property [Code Sec. 673(a)]. If the grantor's spouse retains a reversionary interest, the grantor is deemed to retain a reversionary interest as well. This rule applies if the spouse is living with the grantor at the time the interest is created. It also holds true if the individual became the grantor's spouse after the interest was created—but only for the period after the individual became a spouse. The grantor is treated as holding any power or interest held by the grantor's spouse, not only for reversionary interests but generally for all the interests retained by a grantor that would make the grantor subject to tax [Code Sec. 672(e)]. The possibility that an interest may return to the grantor or his spouse solely by inheritance under the intestacy laws is, however, not considered a reversionary interest and the grantor-trust rules will not apply. Neither does a reversionary interest exist if all that the grantor or spouse retains is an interest that can become effective only after the death, before the age of 21, of a minor beneficiary who is a lineal descendant of the grantor and holds all of the present interest of any portion of the trust.
- *Power to dispose of corpus or income.* The grantor is taxable on the trust income if he or a nonadverse party, or both, have the power to dispose of the corpus or income without the consent of any adverse party [Code Sec. 674(a); Reg. § 1.674(a)-1]. A beneficiary is ordinarily an adverse party [Reg. § 1.672(a)-1(b)]. A nonadverse party has either no beneficial interest, or one that is not substantial, or one that would not be adversely affected by the exercise of his power with regard to the trust [Code Sec. 672(b); Reg. § 1.672(b)-1]. An adverse party is any person having a substantial beneficial interest in the trust that would be adversely affected by the exercise or nonexercise of the power such as a general power of appointment over the trust property that he or she possesses respecting the trust. A nonadverse party is any other person [Code Sec. 672(a), (b); Reg. § 1.672(a)-1]. If the grantor of a trust reserves the power to take back title to the trust funds for himself, he is considered the owner of the trust, whether or not he actually exercises that power [Code Sec. 676(a)]. The grantor is taxed if he can exercise the power alone, if it can be exercised only by a nonadverse party, or if it can be exercised by both the grantor and a nonadverse party together [Code Sec. 676(a); Reg. § 1.676(a)-1]. The grantor is not taxed if the power can be exercised only by or with consent of an adverse party [Code Secs. 672(a), 676(a); Reg. § 1.676(a)-1].
- *Administrative control.* The grantor is taxable on the trust income when administrative control of the trust may be exercised primarily for his or her benefit instead of the benefit of the beneficiaries [Code Sec. 675; Reg. § 1.675-1]. The following situations illustrate this type of administrative control:
    - Power in the grantor or a nonadverse party, or both, without the approval of any adverse party, to deal with the trust property or income for less than an adequate consideration.
    - Power in the grantor or a nonadverse party, or both, that enables the grantor (or grantor's spouse) to borrow the corpus or income without adequate interest or

security, except when a trustee (other than the grantor) is authorized to make loans to *any* persons without regard to interest or security.

- When the grantor has borrowed the corpus or income and has not repaid the loan before the start of the tax year, unless the loan was made for adequate interest and security by a trustee (other than the grantor or a related or subordinate trustee subservient to the grantor).
- General powers of administration exercisable by anyone in a nonfiduciary capacity so as to benefit the grantor individually rather than the beneficiaries.

Example 25-39: Sally lives in an assisted living facility. Prior to living there, she lived in a private residence for 18 years. Sally's mother had established a trust which holds fee simple title to the residence which is the only asset in the trust. Sally is the income beneficiary of the trust and does not have the power to vest the trust corpus or income from the trust in any person. When Sally dies, the residence goes to her children who are over the age of 21. The house has never generated any income for Sally and the trustees sell it at a gain. The gain realized from the sale of the home by the trustee is not eligible for exclusion under Code Sec. 121 because Sally was not considered the owner of the trust as required under Code Sec. 121. Code Sec. 678(a) provides that a person other than the grantor will be treated as the owner of a trust if the person has power exercisable solely by himself to vest the corpus or the income from the trust in himself. Based on the trust language, Sally never had the power to vest trust corpus or income from the trust in herself and therefore could not be treated as the owner of the trust for federal income tax purposes. She was therefore ineligible to claim an exclusion for the gain realized by the trust when the trustee sold the home.

In Private Letter Ruling 201310002,[41] the IRS concluded that a trust was not a grantor trust because the administrative power that was retained by the grantor under Code Sec. 675 would only become effective after the trust return was filed and was therefore dismissed as one that would trigger grantor trust status.

.07 Reporting Requirements

Generally, the trustee must file a return on Form 1041 if the trust has gross income exceeding $600, or has taxable income, or has a beneficiary who is a resident alien [Code Sec. 6012(a)(4); Reg. § 1.6012-3(a)(1)]. Any income, deductions and credits attributable to the grantor are omitted from the return itself, and reported on a separate statement attached to it [Reg. § 1.671-4(a)]. However, if the grantor is also the trustee (or co-trustee) of a trust, and if all trust assets are treated as owned by the grantor for the tax year, then Form 1041 should not be filed. Instead, all items of income, deduction and credit are reported on the grantor's Form 1040. This rule also applies to a husband and wife who file jointly if: (1) they are the sole grantors, (2) one or both are trustees or co-trustees and (3) one or both are treated as the owner of the trust assets [Reg. § 1.671-4(b)].

---

[41] LTR 201310002 (Nov. 7, 2012).

¶25,116 INTENTIONALLY DEFECTIVE GRANTOR TRUSTS

.01 What Is an Intentionally Defective Grantor Trust (IDGT)

A popular income and estate tax planning technique involves creating a trust that deliberately triggers the grantor trust rules set forth in Code Secs 671-679. These trusts that are designed to qualify as grantor trusts are often called intentionally defective grantor trusts (IDGT). The so-called "defect" that is used to result in the grantor being treated as the owner of the trust must be carefully selected so it will not also result in the trust being included in the grantor's taxable estate. Therefore the IDGT should be irrevocable and the grantor should retain no Code Sec. 2036 or Code Sec. 2038 powers that would result in inclusion for estate tax purposes. The best "defect" is one that can easily be removed and the grantor status of the trust terminated without any tax consequences.

If the trust is drafted properly, the income and gains of the trust will be taxable to the grantor, but the assets transferred to the trust by the grantor will be excluded from the grantor's gross estate upon death. An IDGT is created when the grantor irrevocably transfers property to a trust so that the grantor is denied the actual use and enjoyment of the assets contributed to the trust and is not a trust beneficiary. The property is therefore removed from the grantor's taxable estate because the grantor has irrevocably parted with use and enjoyment of the contributed assets. The grantor must, however, reserve at least one of several powers found in Code Secs. 671 through 677 that for income tax purposes will result in the trust and all of its property still being treated as the grantor's property for income tax purposes without incurring gift tax as an additional transfer to the trust. A power often used to achieve this dual purpose is the Code Sec. 675 retained administrative power.

.02 Tax Planning Benefits Offered by IDITs

The IDGT offers the following tax planning benefits:

1. The IDGT requires creation of an irrevocable trust that intentionally violates one or more of the grantor trust rules set forth in Code Secs 671-679 so the grantor is treated as the owner of the trust and therefore taxed on the income generated by the trust at individual tax rates rather than the trust tax rates. This is an important distinction and typically will save the grantor income tax because of the compression of the tax rate brackets for trusts and estates vis-à-vis the rates for individual taxpayers. See ¶ 25,100. In 2013, trusts and estates will reach the top income tax rate of 39.6 percent when they have taxable income over $11,950 (increasing to $12,150 in 2014). In addition, in 2013 the new 3.8 percent net investment income tax will also kick in for trusts with modified adjusted gross income (MAGI) over $11,950 (increasing to $12,150 in 2014) resulting in top trust income tax rate of 43.4. 2013. In contrast, married taxpayers will not reach the 39.6 percent tax rate until they have taxable income over $450,000 in 2013. The new 3.8 percent Medicare tax on net investment income will kick in for single individuals with MAGI over

$200,000, married individuals filing jointly with MAGI over $250,000, and married individuals filing separately with MAGI over $125,000.

2. The IDGT can be used to freeze the value of the property transferred by the grantor into the trust as of the date of the transfer. This will result in removing all future appreciation from the grantor to the trust beneficiaries.
3. If assets transferred into the IDGT include closely-held business interests, partnership interests or LLC interests, the transfers may be eligible for valuation discounts for lack of control or lack of marketability.
4. The grantor can make installment sales to the IDGT. This popular wealth transfer planning technique works because of the IRS's holding in Rev. Rul. 85-13, which provides that transactions between the grantor and the grantor trust will not be a taxable event because the grantor and the trust are considered one and the same person for income tax purposes. The IRS further blessed the transaction in Rev. Rul. 2004-64,[42] which provides that the grantor's payment of income taxes attributable to the trust will not constitute a gift for federal gift tax purposes because the grantor is discharging his own legal obligation. In the typical installment sale to a IDGT, the grantor creates an irrevocable grantor trust for the benefit of descendants. The grantor makes a gift to the trust of so-called "seed" money that should be equal to at least 10 percent of the value of the assets to be sold to the trust. This seed gift will use up a portion of the grantor's lifetime gift tax exemption. The grantor then sells assets to the trust that are expected to outperform the interest rate on the note. Ideally, the assets sold to the trust would generate income (to make the interest payments) and would also qualify for valuation discounts for lack of control and lack of marketability. For example, nonvoting interests in an LLC or a Subchapter S corporation are often good assets to sell to a grantor trust. A grantor trust is also an eligible Subchapter S stockholder.

.03 Proposals to Change Taxation of Grantor Trusts

In the Obama Administration's Fiscal 2014 budget proposals and in the Treasury Department's "Greenbook," which are formally known as the "General Explanations of the Administration's Fiscal Year 2014 Revenue Proposals" (Department of the Treasury, April 2013), the Obama administration explains proposals to close the gap between the income and transfer tax rules applicable to grantor trusts. The administration explains that the lack of coordination between the two sets of rules creates tax planning opportunities to structure transactions between the deemed owner and the trust that can result in the transfer of significant wealth without gift or estate tax consequences. To eliminate this gap between the two sets of rules and the perceived tax abuse, the Obama administration makes the following proposals:

> *If a person who is a deemed owner under the grantor trust rules of all or a portion of a trust engages in a transaction with that trust that* ***constitutes a sale, exchange, or comparable transaction that is disregarded for income tax purposes by reason of the person's treatment as a deemed owner of the trust*** *(emphasis added), then the portion of the trust attributable*

---

[42] Rev. Rul. 2004-64, 2004-2 CB 7.

to the property received by the trust in that transaction (including all retained income therefrom, appreciation thereon, and reinvestments thereof, net of the amount of the consideration received by the person in that transaction)

(1) will be subject to estate tax as part of the gross estate of the deemed owner,

(2) will be subject to gift tax at any time during the deemed owner's life when his or her treatment as a deemed owner of the trust is terminated, and

(3) will be treated as a gift by the deemed owner to the extent any distribution is made to another person (except in discharge of the deemed owner's obligation to the distributee) during the life of the deemed owner.

The proposal would reduce the amount subject to transfer tax by any portion of that amount that was treated as a prior taxable gift by the deemed owner. The transfer tax imposed by this proposal would be payable from the trust.

The proposal would not change the treatment of any trust that is already includable in the grantor's gross estate under existing provisions of the Internal Revenue Code, including without limitation the following: grantor retained income trusts; grantor retained annuity trusts; personal residence trusts; and qualified personal residence trusts. Similarly, it would not apply to any trust having the exclusive purpose of paying deferred compensation under a nonqualified deferred compensation plan if the assets of such trust are available to satisfy claims of general creditors of the grantor. [Possibly a reference to a "rabbi trust"]. It also would not apply to any trust that is a grantor trust solely by reason of Code Sec. 677(a)(3) [a reference to life insurance trusts]. The proposal would be effective with regard to trusts that engage in a described transaction on or after the date of enactment. Regulatory authority would be granted, including the ability to create exceptions to this provision.

Consequences of the Obama Administration's Proposal

If enacted as proposed, this change would be the death knell to installment sales to IDGTs because the new law would eliminate all estate tax savings associated with this technique. If the assets that are sold have appreciated in value, that appreciation would be subject to estate tax no matter how long the grantor has lived and whether or not the note is paid off. Even attempts to thwart this result by terminating grantor trust status or making distributions from the trust during the grantor's life would be subject to gift tax. The only hope for planners lies in the proposal's last line which grants the IRS regulatory authority to "create exceptions to this provision" and the planning opportunities that lie therein.

Significantly, the President's fiscal year 2014 proposal specifically excludes from its scope the following trusts:

- Grantor retained income trusts (GRITs);
- Grantor retained annuity trusts (GRATs);
- Personal residence trusts;
- Qualified personal residence trusts (QPRTs);

- Trusts having the exclusive purpose of paying deferred compensation under a nonqualified deferred compensation plan if the assets of such trust are available to satisfy claims of general creditors of the grantor. This is a reference to "rabbi trusts"; and
- Any trust that is a grantor trust solely by reason of Code Sec. 677(a)(3). This exception refers to the application of income from the grantor trust to pay life insurance premiums. Therefore, certain irrevocable life insurance trusts would not be subject to estate tax inclusion merely because they are grantor trusts, if the income from the trust is used to pay premiums on policies of insurance on the life of the grantor or the grantor's spouse.

▶ **PLANNING POINTERS:** Taxpayers who are considering estate planning transactions that involve leveraged transfers to grantor trusts should proceed as soon as possible because it may be impossible to do so in the years ahead if the legislation proposed by the Obama Administration regarding grantor trusts is enacted. The proposal provides that transfers to grantor trusts that occur prior to enactment of the proposed legislation would be unaffected by the new legislation. The need to act is therefore now.

¶25,120 THROWBACK OF EXCESS DISTRIBUTIONS BY COMPLEX TRUSTS

▶ **IMPORTANT:** The throwback rules were eliminated for amounts distributed by a domestic trust after August 5, 1997. Thus, distributions from these trusts are computed without regard to any undistributed income [Code Sec. 665(c)(1)]. The throwback rules continue to apply under Code Sec. 665(c)(2), however, to: (1) foreign trusts, (2) trusts that were foreign trusts but became domestic trusts, and (3) domestic trusts created before March 1, 1984, that would be treated as multiple trusts under Code Sec. 643(f) [¶25,010]. The reason for the change is simple. The benefits of income shifting that were achieved by shifting income producing assets to trusts were eroded by the compressed income tax brackets that now apply to trusts [¶25,100]. The throwback rules were created to limit the benefit that would otherwise occur from using the lower rates applicable to one or more trusts. Since the original purpose of the throwback rules no longer exists, they were generally eliminated for domestic trusts. They still apply, however, to multiply trusts and to foreign trusts.

For trusts subject to the throwback rules, these rules ordinarily apply only to complex trusts [Reg. § 1.665(a)-0A]. But a simple trust that makes an accumulation distribution allocable to an earlier year is treated as a complex trust for that year for throwback purposes [Reg. § 1.665-1A(b)].

The throwback rule prevents tax avoidance that could occur if a trust in a lower tax bracket accumulated and paid tax on its income rather than distributing the income to a beneficiary in a higher tax bracket. When the income was distributed at a later date, little or no additional tax would be paid by the beneficiary because distributions in excess of distributable net income in the year of distribution are tax-exempt to the beneficiary [¶25,020]. Thus, trust income could be split between the trust and the beneficiary in a way that avoids the high tax to the beneficiary in a year his other income puts him in a substantially higher tax bracket than the trust. This tax avoidance device may be compounded when multiple accumulation trusts—each in a low tax bracket—are used. To forestall this, *the throwback rule taxes the beneficiaries as if the amounts had been distributed each year instead of accumulated.* In other words, the rule "throws back" the accumulated income to the years in which it was accumulated.

For detailed discussion of the throwback rules, see Estate & Gift Tax Handbook, ¶922 and ¶1041.

¶25,125 COMMON TRUST FUNDS

.01 In General

A common trust fund consists of money held by a bank, in a single federally regulated account, for investment by the bank in its capacity as a fiduciary for a number of beneficiaries. The fund is exempt from tax [Code Sec. 584(b); Reg. §1.584-1]. Each participant in the fund, however, is taxed on his or her share of the fund's income, whether distributed or not [Reg. §1.584-2]. Consequently, the bank must file an information return for the fund [Code Sec. 6032; Reg. §1.6032-1]. The fund computes its taxable income in the same manner as an individual, except that capital gains and losses are segregated, and the fund cannot deduct charitable contributions or net operating loss [Code Sec. 584(d); Reg. §§1.584-3, 1.584-6]. The partnership return Form 1065 may be used [Reg. §1.6032-1].

When participants in a common trust fund compute taxable income, they take into account the proportionate share of the capital gains or losses, and the taxable income or net loss of the fund. Excludable interest is allocated to the participants, as is the fund's net operating loss [Code Sec. 584(c); Reg. §1.584-2]. Participants must also account for their pro rata share of the fund's items of tax preference subject to the alternative minimum tax [Ch. 16] [Reg. §1.584-5].

Tax Treatment of Qualified Dividends

Qualified dividend income received by noncorporate shareholders is taxed as capital gain at a maximum 20 percent tax rate in 2013. See ¶2080 and ¶8001 for further discussion. Each common trust fund participant's proportionate share of the amount treated as qualified dividends received by the fund is treated as qualified dividend income and is therefore taxed at a maximum 20 percent rate [Code Sec. 584(c)].

Withdrawal of Participating Interest

No gain or loss is realized by the fund on the admission or withdrawal of participants. But the withdrawal of a participating interest by participants is treated as a sale or exchange of their interest resulting in a recognized gain or loss to them [Code Sec. 584(e)]. A transfer into a new trust is not a withdrawal of a participating interest.[43]

---

[43] *N. Wiggin* DC-MA, 59-1 USTC ¶9309; Rev. Rul. 60-256, 1960-2 CB 193.

Tax-Free Transfers to Regulated Investment Companies

A common trust fund can transfer substantially all of its assets to one or more regulated investment companies (RICs) without gain or loss being recognized by the fund or its participants. The fund must transfer its assets to the RICs solely in exchange for shares of the RICs and the fund must distribute the RIC shares to the fund's participants in exchange for the participants' interests in the fund. The basis of any RIC shares received by a fund participant are an allocable portion of the participant's basis in the interests exchanged [Code Sec. 584(h)].

26 Returns and Payment of Tax

INDIVIDUAL TAX RETURNS

Who must file? . . . . ¶ 26,001
Joint returns . . . . ¶ 26,005
Innocent spouse relief . . . . ¶ 26,006
Returns of minors . . . . ¶ 26,010
Return by agent . . . . ¶ 26,015
Return by fiduciary . . . . ¶ 26,020
Electronic filing of tax returns by individuals . . . . ¶ 26,025

CORPORATION TAX RETURNS

Corporation income tax returns . . ¶ 26,030
Return for short tax year . . . . ¶ 26,040

TAXPAYER IDENTIFICATION NUMBERS (TINS) AND PREPARER IDENTIFICATION NUMBERS (PTINS)

Purpose of the number . . . . ¶ 26,045
What is the identifying number? . . ¶ 26,050
Payments to others . . . . ¶ 26,055
How to get a number . . . . ¶ 26,060
Tax return preparer indentification numbers . . . . ¶ 26,061

TIME AND PLACE FOR FILING TAX RETURNS

When returns must be filed . . . . . ¶ 26,065
Extension of time to file returns . . ¶ 26,070
Where to file returns . . . . ¶ 26,075
Use of amended returns . . . . ¶ 26,080
Substitute tax forms . . . . ¶ 26,085

SUPPORTING INFORMATION

Additional information that must be filed with the return . . . . . ¶ 26,090
How long to retain your tax records . . . . ¶ 26,095

PAYMENT OF TAX

When individual tax must be paid . . . . ¶ 26,100
When corporate tax must be paid . . . . ¶ 26,105
When estates and trusts pay tax . . ¶ 26,110
Exempt organizations . . . . ¶ 26,115
Extension of time to pay tax . . . . . ¶ 26,120
Payment procedures . . . . ¶ 26,125
Electronic Federal Tax Payment System (EFTPS) . . . . ¶ 26,130

INFORMATION RETURNS

Information returns in general . . . . ¶ 26,135
Return for business payments . . . . ¶ 26,140
Returns for interest paid . . . . ¶ 26,145
Returns for dividends paid . . . . . . ¶ 26,150
Reporting requirements imposed on corporations when employees exercise stock options . . . . ¶ 26,155

Group-term life insurance premiums . . . . ¶26,160
Certain liquidations or terminations . . . . ¶26,165
Information returns for tax-exempt organizations and trusts . . . . ¶26,170
Partnership, fiduciary, S corporation, and limited liability company returns . . . . ¶26,180
Returns for foreign items and foreign organizations . . . . ¶26,185

TAX-SHELTERS

Obligations imposed on tax shelter participants . . . . ¶26,210

INDIVIDUAL TAX RETURNS

This section deals with those individuals who must file income tax returns. These include returns of minors as well as those filed by an agent or fiduciary. A key question for married couples is whether they can, or should, file joint or separate returns.

¶26,001 WHO MUST FILE?

Whether you must file an income tax return generally depends on your gross income, age and filing status [Ch. 1]. Categories of filers include the following:

- Individuals [Ch. 1];
- Minors [¶26,010];
- Self-employed persons [Ch. 1];
- Executors, administrators, or legal representatives [¶26,020];
- U.S. citizens living abroad [Ch. 28];
- Residents of Puerto Rico [Ch. 28]; and
- Aliens [Ch. 28].

.01 Who Should File?

Even if you are not required to file under the dollar limits listed in Ch. 1, you should file to get a refund if income tax was withheld from your pay. Examples are students working part-time during the school year or during the summer and other part-time wage earners. Also, file if you can take the earned income credit [Ch. 14].

.02 Signing the Return

An agent may be appointed to prepare and sign a return on behalf of another taxpayer provided the return is accompanied by a power of attorney (or copy of one) authorizing the attorney to represent the taxpayer in making, executing, or filing the return [Reg. §1.6012-1(a)(5)]. The taxpayer or an authorized agent must sign the Federal income tax return in order for it to be a valid return [¶26,015] [Code Sec. 6061; Reg. §1.6061-1].

Any taxpayer who prepares the return as a fiduciary, parent or guardian, or executor or administrator, must sign the return. A husband and wife must each sign a joint return (or a fiduciary may sign for either one[1]). A return with no signature or incompletely signed may be considered *no return* and subject to penalties.[2]

If you file a tax return on behalf of your child or a child for whom you are a guardian, you should sign the child's name where indicated, adding: "By [your signature], Parent [or Guardian]for minor child."

.03 Signature by Tax Return Preparer

A tax return preparer must sign the return or claim for refund after it is completed and before it is presented to the taxpayer (or nontaxable entity) for signature. If the preparer is unavailable for signature, another preparer should review the entire preparation of the return or claim for refund, and then sign the return or claim for refund. If more than one income tax return preparer is involved in the preparation of the return or claim for refund, the individual preparer who has the primary responsibility as between or among the preparers for the overall substantive accuracy of the preparation of such return or claim for refund is considered the income tax return preparer for purposes of this paragraph [Reg. § 1.6695-1(b)].

Example 26-1: A taxpayer employs *X* to prepare his estate tax return, and claims for refund of taxes. *X* assigns *Y* to prepare *T*'s return. *Y* obtains the information necessary for completing the return and forwards the information to *C*, a computer tax service which performs the mathematical computations and prints the return by means of computers. *C* then sends the completed return to *Y* who reviews the accuracy of the return. *Y* is the individual preparer who is primarily responsible for the overall accuracy of *T*'s return. *Y* must sign the return as preparer [Reg. § 1.6695-1(b)(4), Ex. 1].

Example 26-2: *X* partnership is a national accounting firm which prepares returns. *A* and *B*, employees of *X*, are involved in preparing the tax return of *T* Corporation. After they complete the return, *C*, a supervisory employee of *X*, reviews the return. The mathematical computations and carried-forward amounts are proved by *D*, an employee of *X*'s comparing and proving department. The policies and practices of *X* require that *P*, a partner, finally review the return. The scope of *P*'s review includes reviewing the information provided by applying to this information his knowledge of *T*'s affairs, observing that *X*'s policies and practices have been followed, and making the final determination with respect to the proper application of the tax laws to determine *T*'s tax liability. *P* may or may not exercise these responsibilities, or may exercise them to a greater or lesser extent, depending on the degree of complexity of the return, his confidence in *C* (or *A* and *B*), and other factors. *P* is the individual preparer who is primarily responsible for the overall accuracy of *T*'s return. *P* must sign the return as preparer [Reg. § 1.6695-1(b)(4), Ex. 2].

---

[1] Rev. Rul. 67-191, 1967-1 CB 318.

[2] *J.U. Reaves*, CA-5, 61-2 USTC ¶ 9703, 295 F2d 336; *N.T. Olpin*, CA-10, 2001-2 USTC ¶ 50,730, 270 F3d 1297.

Example 26-3: *C* Corp. maintains an office in Seattle, Washington, to prepare partnership returns. *C* makes arrangements with individuals (but provides no working facilities) in several states to collect information from partners of a partnership and to determine their tax liabilities. *E*, an individual, who has such an arrangement in Los Angeles with *C*, collects information from *T*, a general partner, and completes a worksheet kit supplied by *C* which is stamped with *E*'s name and an identification number assigned to *E* by *C*. In this process, *E* classifies this information in appropriate income and deduction categories for the tax determination. The completed worksheet kit signed by *E* is then mailed to *C*. *D*, an employee in *C*'s office, reviews the worksheet kit. *D* does not review the information obtained from *T* for its validity or accuracy. *D* may, but did not, make the final determination with respect to the proper application of tax laws to the information. The data from the worksheet is entered into a computer and the return form is completed. The return is prepared for submission to *T* with filing instructions. *E* is the individual preparer primarily responsible for the overall accuracy of *T*'s return. *E* must sign the return as preparer [Reg. § 1.6695-1(b)(4), Ex. 3].

Example 26-4: *X* employs *A*, *B*, and *C* to prepare gift tax returns for taxpayers. After *A* and *B* have collected the information from the taxpayer, the return form is completed by computer service. On the day the returns prepared by *A* and *B* are ready for their signatures, *A* is away from the city for one week on another assignment and *B* is on detail to another office for the day. *C* may sign the returns prepared by *A*, provided that *C* reviews the information obtained by *A* relative to the taxpayer, and *C* reviews the preparation of each return prepared by *A*. *C* may not sign the returns prepared by *B* because *B* is available [Reg. § 1.6695-1(b)(4), Ex. 4].

.04 Faxed Copy of Signature Okay if Authenticated

The IRS has agreed to accept a faxed copy of a manual signature provided the faxed signature is properly authenticated.[3] Here's what would have to occur in order for the faxed signature to be accepted by the IRS. The Service Center would contact the taxpayer by telephone, verify the taxpayer's identification, and offer to transmit a "jurat notice" to the taxpayer by fax. If the taxpayer agrees to sign the return by fax, the IRS would exchange fax telephone numbers with the taxpayer and advise him that his faxed signature will be treated as an original signature and become part of the taxpayer's return.

.05 Electronically Signed Tax Returns

The IRS requires all taxpayers who file their tax returns electronically (e-file) to use electronic signatures. The IRS has eliminated the paper signature document for e-filed returns. To electronically sign a return, taxpayers must create a personal identification number (PIN). Each married taxpayer filing a joint return must create and use his own

[3] Service Center Advice 200137053, August 14, 2001.

individual PIN. There are two ways to create an IRS e-signature PIN: (1) self-select PIN method; or (2) the practitioner PIN method.

Self-select PIN Method

Taxpayers who are preparing their own returns using software must use the self-select PIN method which allows taxpayers to select five numbers (except all zeros) to enter as their electronic PIN signature. As part of the verification process, taxpayers must also provide either their AGI listed on last year's tax return or their PIN used to e-file their return last year. In addition, taxpayers must include their date of birth.

Practitioner PIN Method

Taxpayers who use a volunteer or paid tax preparer may use either the practitioner PIN method or the self-select PIN method. The practitioner PIN method allows taxpayers to authorize their tax preparer to enter or generate a five-digit PIN on their behalf. The taxpayer must sign Form 8879, *IRS e-file Signature Authorization,* which is retained by the practitioner but not mailed to the IRS. Some tax preparers may use an electronic signature pad for Form 8879 this year. Taxpayers who are age 16 and younger must use the practitioner PIN method.

IRS-issued Electronic Filing PIN

If taxpayers are using the self-select PIN method and they cannot remember their adjusted gross income from last year or their PIN from last year, the IRS will issue a temporary Electronic Filing PIN (EFP.) The taxpayer's identity still must be verified. Most tax software will contain a link to the EFP tool or it can be found on the IRS website. The EFP will generate a five-digit number that can be substituted for the PIN. The taxpayer can then return to the self-select PIN method, use the temporary EFP in place of the PIN requirement, and complete the signature process.

Signing Joint Return When Spouse Unavailable

If a taxpayer's spouse is serving in a combat zone and the taxpayer does not have power of attorney, the taxpayer can still create a self-select PIN for a spouse and e-file the return. After e-filing the return, the taxpayers should submit a signed statement explaining the situation along with Form 8453, *U.S. Individual Income Tax Transmittal for an IRS e-file Return.* If the taxpayer has a power of attorney for a military spouse or anyone who must file a tax return, the taxpayer can use the self-selection PIN method to sign their return. The taxpayer must also attach the power of attorney to Form 8453 and mail both to the IRS.

¶26,005 JOINT RETURNS

If two married taxpayers elect to file a joint return, it is much the same as if they combined their income, deductions and exemptions and each reported half on a separate return. (Two married taxpayers may file a joint return even though one spouse has no income or deductions.) To determine when taxpayers are considered married, see Ch. 1.

.01 Liability for Tax

When spouses sign and file a joint tax return, each one is fully responsible for any tax deficiency that might subsequently result from that filing including interest or penalties even if only one spouse earned all the income. The legal term for this is *joint and several liability* [Code Sec. 6013(d)(3); Reg. § 1.6013-4(b)]. However, one spouse may be relieved of liability for tax (including interest, penalties and deficiency) if he or she qualifies for innocent spouse relief as discussed in ¶ 26,006.

.02 Change in Election to File Jointly or Not

If spouses choose to file separate returns, they can later change this election and file jointly. When they do, the joint return replacing the separate returns must be filed within three years after the due date for the original returns [Code Sec. 6013(b); Reg. § 1.6013-2]. However, if a joint return has been filed, the spouses cannot elect to file "late" separate returns after the original due date [Reg. § 1.6013-1(a)].

.03 Joint Return on Death of Spouse

If a spouse dies during the tax year, the surviving spouse may file a joint return with the deceased spouse unless the surviving spouse remarries before the end of the year. In that case, the surviving spouse can file a joint return with his or her new spouse [Code Sec. 6013(a)(2); Reg. § 1.6013-1(d)(1), (2)]. Usually, the return is made by the executor or administrator. However, the surviving spouse can file a joint return if no executor or administrator is appointed before the due date for filing the return [Code Sec. 6013(a)(3); Reg. § 1.6013-1(d)(3)].

Also, an executor or administrator later appointed can disaffirm a joint return filed by you. The disaffirmance is made on a separate return for your deceased spouse within one year after the due date of your return [Code Sec. 6013(a)(3); Reg. § 1.6013-1(d)(5)].

If an executor or administrator has been appointed, both the executor and the surviving spouse must sign a joint return. If there has been no appointment, write in the signature area "Filing as surviving spouse," and show the date of death in the name and address space.

.04 When Separate Returns May Be Better

It's usually wiser to file jointly. But not always. Taxpayers should consider filing separate returns in the following situations: (1) If either spouse has substantially larger miscellaneous itemized expenses, medical expenses or casualty losses than the other, separate returns may save tax because of the percentage rule [Ch. 9, Ch. 13](for example, medical expenses can only be deducted if they exceed 10 percent of your adjusted gross income (AGI). If one spouse's AGI is lower as a result of filing separately, each spouse may be able to deduct more of his or her medical expenses and reduce his or her tax bill); (2) if each spouse can obtain a larger benefit from a net operating loss deduction by applying it to a separate income. Separate filing also may be wise if one spouse is facing the alternative minimum tax [Ch. 16]. Other situations exist where filing separately may be an advantage. So, if both spouses have income, figure the tax both ways to make sure.

¶26,006 INNOCENT SPOUSE RELIEF

When spouses sign a joint tax return, each spouse is fully responsible for any tax bill that might result from that filing including interest or penalties even if only one spouse earned all the income.[4]

The legal term for this result is joint and several liability [Code Sec. 6013(d)(3)]. Joint and several liability applies to all joint returns filed, even under circumstances such as: (1) divorce, (2) a divorce decree stating that one former spouse will accept responsibility for any tax liability on returns filed while married, (3) an underpayment that is the sole responsibility of the other spouse, or (4) where one spouse earns all of the income. This means that both spouses are responsible for the total tax bill even if all the income is earned by only one spouse. The harshness of this rule is mitigated by innocent spouse relief which is an escape hatch for a qualifying spouse [Code Sec. 6015].

The three following relief measures are available to a spouse seeking innocent spouse relief:

1. **Innocent spouse relief**. Code Sec. 6015(b) allows a taxpayer to elect relief from understatements of tax attributable to erroneous items of the other spouse if the taxpayer had no reason to know of the understatement and, taking into account all the facts and circumstances, it is inequitable to hold the taxpayer liable; or
2. **Separate liability relief**. Code Sec. 6015(c) allows a taxpayer who is divorced or legally separated from, or no longer living with, the spouse or former spouse with whom the joint return was filed to elect to allocate a deficiency (or a portion of a deficiency) to the other spouse, as if the spouses had filed separate tax returns; or
3. **Equitable relief**. Code Sec. 6015(f) provides that a taxpayer may request, under "procedures prescribed by the Secretary," relief from a tax understatement or underpayment when the taxpayer does not qualify for relief under the other two subsections and it would be inequitable to hold the taxpayer liable considering all the facts and circumstances.

.01 Innocent Spouse Relief Election

Code Sec. 6015(b) provides that a spouse may make an election for innocent spouse relief [Reg. § 1.6015-2(a)]. To qualify for this relief the spouse must prove that:

1. A joint return was filed for the tax year;
2. On the return there is an "understatement of tax" attributable to "erroneous items" of one individual filing the joint return. An *erroneous item* is any income, deduction, credit, or basis if it is omitted or incorrectly reported on the joint return.
3. In signing the return the requesting spouse did not know and had no "reason to know" of the item giving rise to the understatement. Courts have found that taxpayers have a reason-to-know test in two situations: First, a spouse may have reason to know of an understatement reflected on the tax filings. Second, even if a

[4] *M.B. Butler*, 114 TC 276, Dec. 53,869 (2000).

spouse is not aware of sufficient facts to give her reason to know of the substantial understatement, the spouse nevertheless may know enough facts to put him or her on notice that an understatement exists. Notice is provided if the spouse knows sufficient facts such that a reasonably prudent taxpayer in the same position would be led to question the legitimacy of the deduction. In this situation, a duty of inquiry arises, which, if not satisfied by the spouse, may result in constructive knowledge of the understatement being imputed to the spouse. The following four factors should be considered in reaching that result: (1) the spouse's education, (2) the spouse's involvement in the family's financial affairs, (3) the presence of unusual or lavish expenditures beyond the family's norm, and (4) the other spouse's evasiveness or deceitfulness concerning the family's finances.[5]

In *W.L. Greer*,[6] the Court of Appeals for the Sixth Circuit followed five other courts of appeals to deny innocent spouse relief under Code Sec. 6015(b) under the "knowledge of the transaction" test. In the court's view, the spouse more than likely had reason to know of the understatement because she had knowledge of the underlying transaction giving rise to the claimed tax benefits.

All of the facts and circumstances must be considered in determining whether the requesting innocent spouse had reasons to know of an erroneous item including the nature of the item and the amount of the item relative to other items; the couple's financial situation; the innocent spouse's business experience; the extent of the innocent spouse's participation in the activity that resulted in the erroneous item; whether the innocent spouse failed to inquire at or before the time the return was signed about items on the return or omitted from the return that a reasonable person would question; and whether the erroneous item represented a departure from a recurring pattern reflected in prior years' returns [Reg. § 1.6015-2].

4. It would be "inequitable" to hold the spouse liable for the deficiency attributable to the understatement [Reg. § 1.6015-2(a)]. All of the facts and circumstances must be considered in determining whether it is inequitable to hold a requesting spouse jointly and severally liable for an understatement. One relevant factor is whether the requesting spouse significantly benefited, directly or indirectly, from the understatement. A significant benefit is any benefit in excess of normal support. Evidence of direct or indirect benefit may consist of transfers of property or rights to property, including transfers received several years after the year of the understatement. For example, if an innocent spouse receives property (including life insurance proceeds) from the nonrequesting spouse that is traceable to items omitted from gross income that are attributable to the nonrequesting spouse, the innocent spouse will be considered to have received significant benefit from those items. [Reg. § 1.6015-2(d)]. In *P.E. Campbell*,[7] a spouse who had limited involvement in the family's finances was entitled to innocent spouse relief because she did not have reason to know that, at the time of signing the joint

---

[5] *P.A. Price*, CA-9, 89-2 USTC ¶ 9598, 887 F2d 959.

[6] *W.L. Greer*, CA-6, 2010-1 USTC ¶ 50,228, *aff'd*, 97 TCM 1075, Dec. 57,722(M), TC Memo. 2009-20.

[7] *P.E. Campbell*, 91 TCM 735, Dec. 56,430(M), TC Memo. 2006-24.

return, there was an understatement of tax on the return attributable to her husband's participation in a sham straddle transaction. Furthermore, it was not equitable to hold her liable for the tax deficiency because she did not benefit from the transaction and, given her assets and limited number of years remaining in the work force, imposing the tax liability on her would result in a severe economic hardship.

5. The innocent spouse applies for relief within two years after the IRS has begun its first collection activities against the requesting spouse [Code Sec. 6015(b)(1)(E)]. In *N.W. McGee*,[8] the Tax Court held that the two-year statute of limitations on requesting innocent spouse relief did not apply when the IRS failed to provide the spouse with adequate notice of the right to claim such relief. Reg. § 1.6015-5(b)(2)(i) provides that collection-related activities include: (1) notice of intent to levy and the taxpayer's right to a collection due process hearing; (2) offsetting a refund from another tax year; or (3) filing a suit or claim that puts the requesting spouse on notice that the IRS intends to collect the tax from property belonging to that spouse. For example, garnishment of wages or a notice of intent to levy against the property of the electing spouse would constitute collection activity against the electing spouse but mailing the notice of deficiency and demand for payment to the last known address of the electing spouse, addressed to both spouses, would not constitute sufficient notice. A taxpayer's overpayment and the IRS use of that overpayment as a credit to other tax amounted to a collection activity for purposes of innocent spouse relief and the taxpayer's bid for innocent spouse relief was denied.[9]

Reason to Know Defined

All of the facts and circumstances to be considered in determining whether the requesting innocent spouse had reasons to know of an erroneous item include the nature of the item and the amount of the item relative to other items; the couple's financial situation; the innocent spouse's educational background and business experience; the extent of the innocent spouse's participation in the activity that resulted in the erroneous item; whether the innocent spouse failed to inquire at or before the time the return was signed about items on the return or omitted from the return that a reasonable person would question; and whether the erroneous item represented a departure from a recurring pattern reflected in prior years' returns (e.g., omitted income from an investment regularly reported on prior years' returns) [Reg. § 1.6015-2(c)].

Inequitable Defined

All of the facts and circumstances must be considered in determining whether it is inequitable to hold a requesting spouse jointly and severally liable for an understatement. One relevant factor for this purpose is whether the requesting spouse significantly benefited, directly or indirectly, from the understatement. A significant benefit is any benefit in excess of normal support. Evidence of direct or indirect benefit may consist of transfers of property or rights to property, including transfers received several years after the year of the understatement. For example, if an innocent spouse receives property (including life insurance proceeds) from the nonrequesting spouse that is traceable to items omitted from gross income that are attributable to the

[8] *N.W. McGee*, 123 TC 314, Dec. 55,781 (2004).

[9] *E.D. Campbell*, 121 TC 290, Dec. 55,355 (2003).

nonrequesting spouse, the innocent spouse will be considered to have received significant benefit from those items. [Reg. § 1.6015-2(d)]. In *Albin*,[10] the Tax Court denied innocent spouse relief because the requesting spouse had reason to know of the understatement. Even though she was not involved with her husband's tax shelter investment or preparation of the return, she signed the return joint returns without questioning why the couple's deductions were so high.

Partial Relief Also Available

If an innocent spouse had no knowledge or reason to know of only a portion of an erroneous item, the innocent spouse may be relieved of the liability attributable only to that portion [Reg. § 1.6015-2(e)(1)].

> **Example 26-5:** H and W are married and file a joint income tax return. Thereafter, H is convicted of embezzling $2 million from his employer. H kept all of his embezzlement income in an individual bank account, and he used most of the funds to support his gambling habit. H and W had a joint bank account into which H and W deposited all of their reported income. H transferred an additional $10,000 from the individual account to H and W's joint bank account. W paid the household expenses using this joint account, and regularly received the bank statements relating to the account. W had no knowledge or reason to know of H's embezzling activities. However, W did have knowledge and reason to know of $120,000 of the $2 million of H's embezzlement income at the time she signed the joint return because that amount passed through the couple's joint bank account. Therefore, W may be relieved of the liability arising from $1,880,000 of the unreported embezzlement income, but she may not be relieved of the liability for the deficiency arising from $120,000 of the unreported embezzlement income of which she knew and had reason to know [Reg. § 1.6015-2(e)(2) Ex.].

.02 Separate Liability Election

Code Sec. 6015(c) provides for the separate liability election which enables qualifying innocent spouses to limit their liability for a deficiency related to a joint return to the amount of the income and deductions they actually generated [Reg. § 1.6015-3(a)]. Relief under this election is only available for unpaid liabilities resulting from understatements of liability. Refunds are not authorized [Reg. § 1.6015-3(c) (1)].

The separate liability election is only available if the requesting spouse can prove that:

1. At the time relief is elected, the requesting spouse is divorced, widowed, legally separated, or has not been a member of the same household as the nonrequesting spouse at any time during the 12-month period ending on the date an election for relief is filed [Code Sec. 6015(c) (3) (A) (i); Reg. § 1.6015-3(a)].[11]

   Members of the same household defined. Spouses are considered members of the same household during either spouse's temporary absences from the household if it is reasonable to assume that the absent spouse will return to the household, and the household, or a substantially equivalent household, is main-

[10] *W.H. Albin*, 88 TCM 340, Dec. 55,772(M), TC Memo. 2004-230; *R.H. Golden*, CA-6, 2009-1 USTC ¶ 50,101, 548 F3d 487.

[11] *D.C. Jonson*, CA-10, 2004-1 USTC ¶ 58,122, 353 F3d 1181.

tained in anticipation of such return. Examples of temporary absences may include absence due to incarceration, hospitalization, business travel, vacation travel, military service, or education away from home [Reg. § 1.6015-3(b) (3) (i)]. A husband and wife who reside the same dwelling are considered members of the same household. A husband and wife who reside in two separate dwellings are considered members of the same household if the spouses are not estranged or if one spouse is temporarily absent from the other's household [Reg. § 1.6015-3(b) (3) (ii)].

2. The innocent spouse applied for relief no later than 2 years after the date of the first IRS collection activity [Code Sec. 6015(c) (3) (B)].

3. The spouse seeking relief had no actual knowledge of the other spouse's item giving rise to the deficiency. This means that relief will not be available if the IRS can show that the spouse claiming relief knew or had reason to know of an improper item [Code Sec.6015(c) (3) (C)]. Knowledge of the receipt of the income is sufficient to establish actual knowledge of the item [Reg. § 1.6015-3(c) (2) (i) (A)].

If the separate liability election is made, items are generally allocated between spouses in the same manner as they would have been allocated if the spouses had filed separate returns [Code Sec. 6015(d) (3)]. This means that in the case of a deficiency arising from a joint return, a spouse would be liable only to the extent items giving rise to the deficiency are allocable to that spouse.

Relief Unavailable if Requesting Spouse Had Actual Knowledge

Relief under the separate liability election will be unavailable for the part of a deficiency attributable to an erroneous items of the nonrequesting spouse if the IRS shows that the innocent spouse had actual knowledge of that item at the time he or she signed the joint return [Reg. § 6015-3(c) (2)]. The IRS must establish, by a preponderance of the evidence, that the requesting spouse had actual knowledge of the erroneous item in order to invalidate the election.

> **Example 26-6:** Husband received $5,000 of dividend income from his investment in X Co. but did not report it on the joint return. Wife knew that Husband received $5,000 of dividend income from X Co. that year. She had actual knowledge of the $5,000 of unreported dividend income from X Co. and no relief is available under the separate liability election for the deficiency attributable to the dividend income from X Co [Reg. § 1.6015-3(c)(2)(i)(A)].

The innocent spouse's actual knowledge of the proper tax treatment of the item or how it was actually reported on the return is not relevant for purposes of demonstrating that the requesting spouse had actual knowledge of an erroneous item [Reg. § 1.6015-3(c) (2) (i)].

> **Example 26-7:** Assume the same facts as in the example above and assume further that Wife did not know Husband's dividend income from X Co. was taxable even though she knew that Husband received the dividend income. Relief is not available under the separate liability election because Wife had actual knowledge of the dividend income even though she did not know how it should be treated [Reg. § 1.6015-3(c)(2)(ii)].

In *Cook*,[12] the taxpayer qualified for innocent spouse relief under Code Sec. 6015(c) even though she prepared invoices for her husband's business based on information she received from him. The taxpayer did not, however, see the amounts he collected and did not see records of bank deposits or serve as a signatory on the husband's bank accounts. In addition, she was not in a position to insist on examining his business records, because he subjected her to physical and emotional abuse throughout their marriage.

An innocent spouse may not be granted relief for all eligible years if the facts fail to support the innocent spouse's claim for relief.

In *Cheshire*,[13] the Court of Appeals for the Fifth Circuit denied innocent spouse relief to an ex-spouse who knew her husband received a retirement distribution that was not included on their joint income tax return, even though she reasonably believed her ex-husband's assertion that he had consulted with an accountant and was advised that the portion of the distribution used to pay off the mortgage on their home was not taxable. Innocent spouse relief was denied because the wife had "actual knowledge" of the transaction giving rise to the omitted income.

In addition, to demonstrate that a requesting spouse had actual knowledge of an erroneous item at the time the return was signed, the IRS may rely upon the following factors:

1. Whether the requesting spouse made a deliberate effort to avoid learning about the item in order to be shielded from liability; and
2. Whether the spouses jointly owned the property that resulted in the erroneous item. Joint ownership is a factor supporting a finding that the innocent spouse had actual knowledge of an erroneous item [Reg. § 1.6015-3(c)(2)(iv)].

In *Culver*,[14] the Tax Court held that an innocent spouse qualified for separate liability election relief from joint liability under Code Sec. 6015(c) because the IRS failed to prove by a "preponderance of the evidence" that the requesting spouse had actual knowledge of the embezzled funds.

> ▶ **PRACTICE POINTER:** This case makes it easier for innocent spouses to qualify for separate liability election relief under Code Sec. 6015(c). As a result of the very tough burden of proof imposed on the IRS by the Tax Court in *Culver*, the IRS will have a difficult time proving that a taxpayer's has actual subjective knowledge by a preponderance of the evidence of an erroneous item at the time a tax return is signed. The IRS is allowed to rely on all of the facts and circumstances to establish actual knowledge including whether the spouse deliberately tried to avoid learning about an item in order to be shielded from liability [Reg. § 1.6015-3(c)(2)].

The portion of the deficiency for which the innocent spouse remains liable is increased (up to the entire amount of the deficiency) by the value of any disqualified assets transferred to him by the other spouse. Disqualified assets are assets trans-

---

[12] *C.G. Cook*, 89 TCM 753, Dec. 55,926(M), TC Memo. 2005-22.

[13] *K. Cheshire*, CA-5, 2002-1 USTC ¶ 50,222, 282 F3d 326, *cert denied*, 537 US 881.

[14] *M.G. Culver*, 116 TC 189, Dec. 54,294 (2001).

ferred for the principal purpose of avoiding tax or payment of tax. Any assets transferred after the start of the 12 month period before the mailing of the first letter of proposed deficiency would be presumed to be disqualified assets. The presumption would not apply to transfers of assets under a divorce, separate maintenance or child support agreement [Reg. § 1.6015-3(c)(3)].

Allocation Procedures

If an innocent spouse qualified for relief under the separate liability election, erroneous items are generally allocated to the spouses as if separate returns were filed. This means that income items would generally be allocated to the spouse who earned the income or who owned the investment or business producing it. If both spouses had an ownership interest in an investment or business, an erroneous income item from it would be allocated between them in proportion to their respective ownership interests. Personal deductions generally would be allocated 50 percent to each spouse, unless the evidence shows that a different allocation is appropriate [Reg. § 1.6015-3(d)(2)(iii)].

For example, erroneous items of income or erroneous deductions related to a business or investment are allocated to the spouse who was the source of the income or who owned the business or investment.

> **Example 26-8:** Husband and Wife file a joint income tax return and two years later a deficiency is assessed with respect to their return alleging: (1) unreported interest income, of which Wife had actual knowledge, from their joint bank account; (2) a disallowed business expense deduction on Husband's Schedule C; and (3) a disallowed Lifetime Learning Credit for Wife's postsecondary education, paid for by Wife. The couple later divorce and Wife timely elects to allocate the deficiency. The erroneous items are allocable as follows: (1) The interest income would be allocated 1/2 to Husband and 1/2 to Wife, except that Wife has actual knowledge of it. Therefore, Wife's election to allocate the portion of the deficiency attributable to this item is invalid, and she remains jointly and severally liable for it. (2) The business expense deduction is allocable to Husband. (3) The Lifetime Learning Credit is allocable to Wife.

.03 Equitable Relief Election

The third and final option for innocent spouses is to make an election for equitable relief under Code Sec. 6015(f). This remedy is available in special situations where the other two remedies discussed above are unavailable for whatever reason and where it would be inequitable to hold the innocent spouse liable for any unpaid tax or any deficiency. The IRS has the authority under Code Sec. 6015(f) to grant equitable relief when the innocent spouse's situation cries out for help [Reg. § 1.6015-4(a)]. A similar provision is available under Code Sec. 66(c) for married individuals with community property income. The IRS has the authority to grant equitable relief if, taking into account all the facts and circumstances, it would be inequitable to hold the innocent spouse liable for the taxes [Code Sec. 6015(f)].

In Rev. Proc. 2013-34[15] the IRS updated its equitable innocent spouse relief guidance which applies to spouses who request either equitable relief from joint and several liability under Code Sec. 6015(f), or equitable relief under Code Sec. 66(c) from income tax liability resulting from the operation of community property law. Rev. Proc. 2013-34 is effective for requests for relief filed on or after September 16, 2013. In addition, it is effective for requests for equitable relief pending on September 16, 2013 either with the IRS, the Office of Appeals, or in a case docketed with a federal court. Rev. Proc. 2013-34 provides that innocent spouse relief is available to a requesting spouse who satisfies the following threshold conditions:

1. The requesting spouse filed a joint return for the tax year for which he or she seeks relief.
2. Relief is not available to the requesting spouse under Code Sec. 6015(b) or (c).
3. The claim for relief is timely filed:
   a. If the requesting spouse is applying for relief from a liability or a portion of a liability that remains unpaid, the request for relief must be made on or before the date that the period of limitation on collection of the income tax liability expires under Code Sec. 6502. Generally, that period expires 10 years after the assessment of tax, but it may be extended.
   b. Claims for credit or refund of amounts paid must be made before the expiration of the period of limitation on credit or refund, as provided in Code Sec. 6511. Generally, that period expires three years from the time the return was filed or two years from the time the tax was paid, whichever is later.
4. No assets were transferred between the spouses as part of a fraudulent scheme.
5. The nonrequesting spouse did not transfer disqualified assets to the requesting spouse. [Code Sec. 6015(c)(4)(B)].
6. The requesting spouse did not knowingly participate in the filing of a fraudulent joint return.
7. The income tax liability from which the requesting spouse seeks relief is attributable (either in full or in part) to an item of the nonrequesting spouse or an underpayment resulting from the nonrequesting spouse's income. If the liability is partially attributable to the requesting spouse, then relief can only be considered for the portion of the liability attributable to the nonrequesting spouse. Nonetheless, the IRS will consider granting relief regardless of whether the understatement, deficiency, or underpayment is attributable to the requesting spouse if any of the following exceptions applies:
   a. If an item is attributable or partially attributable to the requesting spouse solely due to the operation of community property law, then for purposes of this revenue procedure, that item (or portion thereof) will be attributable to the nonrequesting spouse.
   b. If the item is titled in the name of the requesting spouse, the item is presumptively attributable to the requesting spouse. This presumption is rebuttable.

[15] Rev. Proc. 2013-34, IRB 2013-42.

c. If the requesting spouse did not know, and had no reason to know, that funds intended for the payment of tax were misappropriated by the nonrequesting spouse for the nonrequesting spouse's benefit, the IRS will consider granting equitable relief although the underpayment may be attributable in part or in full to an item of the requesting spouse. The IRS will consider granting relief in this case only to the extent that the funds intended for the payment of tax were taken by the nonrequesting spouse.

d. If the requesting spouse establishes that he or she was the victim of abuse prior to the time the return was filed, and that, as a result of the prior abuse, the requesting spouse was not able to challenge the treatment of any items on the return, or was not able to question the payment of any balance due reported on the return, for fear of the nonrequesting spouse's retaliation, the IRS will consider granting equitable relief even though the deficiency or underpayment may be attributable in part or in full to an item of the requesting spouse.

e. The IRS will consider granting relief notwithstanding that the item giving rise to the understatement or deficiency is attributable to the requesting spouse, if the requesting spouse establishes that the nonrequesting spouse's fraud is the reason for the erroneous item.

Streamlined Determinations

In Rev. Proc. 2013-34, the IRS provides that it will make streamlined determinations granting equitable relief under Code Sec. 66(c) or Code Sec. 6015(f), in cases where the requesting spouse establishes that the requesting spouse (a) is no longer married to the nonrequesting spouse; (b) would suffer economic hardship if relief were not granted ; and (c) the requesting spouse in Code Sec. 6015(f) cases knew or had reason to know that there was an understatement or deficiency on the joint income tax return, or did not know or have reason to know that the nonrequesting spouse would not or could not pay the underpayment of tax reported on the joint income tax return. If the nonrequesting spouse abused the requesting spouse or maintained control over the household finances by restricting the requesting spouse's access to financial information, and because of the abuse or financial control, the requesting spouse was unable to challenge the treatment of any items on the joint return, or to question taxes due on a joint return for fear of the nonrequesting spouse's retaliation, then the abuse or financial control will result in this factor being satisfied; or (d) the requesting spouse in Code Sec. 66(c) cases did not know or have reason to know of an item of community income properly includible in gross income, which would be treated as the income of the nonrequesting spouse.

Factors

In determining whether it is inequitable to hold the requesting spouse liable for all or part of the unpaid income tax liability and whether full or partial equitable relief should be granted, all the facts and circumstances of the case must be considered. Abuse or the exercise of financial control by the nonrequesting spouse is a factor that may impact other factors. The following factors should be considered:

1. *Marital status*. Whether the requesting spouse is no longer married to the nonrequesting spouse as of the date the IRS makes its determination.

2. *Economic hardship*. Whether the requesting spouse will suffer economic hardship if relief is not granted.
3. *Knowledge or reason to know*. Whether the requesting spouse knew or had reason to know of the item giving rise to the understatement or deficiency as of the date the joint return was filed. If the requesting spouse was abused by the nonrequesting spouse and because of the abuse or financial control, the requesting spouse was not able to challenge the treatment of any items on the joint return for fear of the nonrequesting spouse's retaliation; this factor will weigh in favor of relief. The facts and circumstances that are considered in determining whether the requesting spouse had reason to know include, but are not limited to, the requesting spouse's level of education, any deceit or evasiveness of the nonrequesting spouse, the requesting spouse's degree of involvement in the activity generating the income tax liability, the requesting spouse's involvement in business or household financial matters, the requesting spouse's business or financial expertise, and any lavish or unusual expenditures compared with past spending levels.
4. *Abuse by the nonrequesting spouse*. If the requesting spouse establishes that he or she was the victim of abuse, relief is favored. Abuse comes in many forms and can include physical, psychological, sexual, or emotional abuse, including efforts to control, isolate, humiliate, and intimidate the requesting spouse, or to undermine the requesting spouse's ability to reason independently and be able to do what is required under the tax laws. The impact of a nonrequesting spouse's alcohol or drug abuse is also considered in determining whether a requesting spouse was abused.
5. *Legal obligation*. Whether the requesting spouse or the nonrequesting spouse has a legal obligation to pay the outstanding Federal income tax liability.
6. *Significant benefit*. Whether the requesting spouse significantly benefited from the unpaid income tax liability or understatement. A significant benefit is any benefit in excess of normal support.
7. *Compliance with income tax laws*. Whether the requesting spouse has made a good faith effort to comply with the income tax laws in the years following the years to which the request for relief relates.
8. *Mental or physical health*. Whether the requesting spouse was in poor physical or mental health. This factor will weigh in favor of relief if the requesting spouse was in poor mental or physical health at the time the return or returns for which the request for relief relates were filed or at the time the requesting spouse requested relief.

New Evidence Considered in Equitable Relief Cases

The Tax Court can consider new evidence outside the scope of the administrative record in determining whether a taxpayer should receive equitable innocent spouse relief under Code Sec. 6015(f).[16] Therefore the court may consider "all the facts and circumstances" relevant to a taxpayer's petition. In Chief Counsel Notice 2013-011, the

[16] *K.M. Wilson*, CA-9, 2013-1 USTC ¶50,147, 705 F3d 980, *aff'g*, 99 TCM 155, Dec. 58,248(M), TC Memo. 2010-134 (*Acq.*); *R.E. Neal*, CA-11, 2009-1 USTC ¶50,216, 557 F3d 1262.

IRS provided that the Tax Court will apply a *de novo* standard of review when reviewing requests for Code Sec. 6015(f) relief. Therefore the spouse seeking relief will be allowed to introduce new evidence that didn't exist in the administrative record.

.04 How to Request Innocent Spouse Relief

A requesting spouse seeking any form of innocent spouse relief must file Form 8857, *Request for Innocent Spouse Relief,* or other similar statement signed under penalties of perjury, no later than two years after the IRS's first attempts to collect the tax. However, the instructions carve out an exception for equitable relief. The amount of time the taxpayer has to request equitable relief depends on whether the taxpayer is seeking relief from a balance due, seeking a credit or refund, or both.

This carve-out is consistent with Notice 2011-70[17] and Prop. Reg. § 1.6015-5(b)(2) which provides that individuals who request equitable innocent spouse relief under Code Sec. 6015(f) will no longer be required to submit the request within two years of the IRS's first collection activity against the requesting spouse. Instead the request must be filed with the IRS within the period of limitation in Code Sec. 6502 for collection of tax or the period of limitation in Code Sec. 6511 for credit or refund of tax. A similar rule was added for claims for equitable relief from the federal income tax liability resulting from the operation of state community property law [Prop. Reg. § 1.66-4(j)(2)(ii)].

Prop. Reg. § 1.6015-5(b)(2) explains that if a requesting spouse files a request for equitable relief within the limitation period on collection of tax, the IRS will consider the request, but any relief in the form of a tax credit or refund depends on whether the limitation period for credit or refund was also open as of the date the claim for relief was filed and the other requirements relating to credits or refunds are satisfied [Prop. Reg. § 1.6015-5(b)(2)]. If a request for equitable relief is filed after the expiration of the limitation period for a credit or refund of tax, the IRS is barred from considering this request [Prop. Reg. § 1.6015-5(b)].

The proposed regulations also clarify what constitutes collection activity for purposes of starting the two-year deadline that applies to innocent spouse relief filed under Code Sec. 6015(b) and Code Sec. 6015(c). A notice of intent to levy and right to request a CDP hearing (section 6330 notice) is a type of collection activity that will start the two-year period. The two-year period will start irrespective of a requesting spouse's actual receipt of the section 6330 notice, if the notice was sent by certified or registered mail to the requesting spouse's last known address [Prop. Reg. § 1.6015-5(b)(3)(ii)].

Situations in Which Relief Unavailable

Innocent spouse relief is unavailable in the following situations:

1. A court of competent jurisdiction has issued a final decision on tax liability in a prior proceeding and relief from joint and several liability was an issue in that proceeding, or the innocent spouse meaningfully participated in that proceeding and could have requested relief from joint and several liability.

2. The innocent spouse entered into an offer in compromise with the IRS.

[17] Notice 2011-70, IRB 2011-32, 135.

3. The innocent spouse entered into a closing agreement with the IRS that disposed of the same liability for which relief is sought.

Note that the IRS is required to inform the nonrequesting spouse (or former spouse) that innocent spouse relief or separation of liability had been requested and the nonrequesting spouse (or former spouse) must be given the opportunity to participate in the determination of the amount of relief from liability [Reg. § 1.6015-6(a)(1)].

The election to seek innocent spouse relief under the separation of liability procedures for a particular tax year may be made at any point after a deficiency has been asserted by the IRS for that tax year [Code Sec. 6015(c)(3)(B)]. A deficiency is considered asserted by the IRS at the time the IRS states that additional taxes may be owed. It is not required that an assessment be made, or that all administrative remedies be exhausted, in order for a taxpayer to request innocent spouse relief. The IRS is required to inform both spouses when attempting to collect tax liability from either spouse [Code Sec. 6103].

.05 Estate's Executor May Seek Innocent Spouse Relief

An executor of an estate (or duly appointed representative) may either pursue an existing Form 8857 claim for spousal relief made during a decedent's lifetime, or may file a Form 8857 on behalf of a decedent for spousal relief provided the decedent satisfied the eligibility requirements while alive.[18] For purposes of relief by separation of liability, the decedent's marital status is determined on the earlier of the date relief was requested or the date of death.

Right to Intervene Survived Death of Nonelecting Spouse

In *Fain*,[19] the Tax Court concluded that a nonelecting spouse's right to intervene in an innocent spouse relief case survived his death and passed to his estate under Code Sec. 6015(e)(4). Thus, the IRS was obligated to notify the deceased spouse's heirs, executors, or administrators of the decedent's right to intervene.

.06 Tax Court Review

In addition to any other remedy provided by the law, an innocent spouse may petition the Tax Court to determine the appropriate relief available to the spouse [Code Sec. 6015(e)(1)(A)].

After filing Form 8857, the taxpayer can generally ask the Tax Court to review a request for relief in the following situations: (1) The taxpayer disagrees with the IRS' final determination notice telling him the extent to which the request for relief has been denied; (2) The taxpayer does not receive a final determination notice from the IRS within six months from the date the Form 8857 was filed.[20] If the IRS has denied the requesting spouse's election for innocent spouse relief, he or she may petition the Tax Court for review of that decision.[21] The petition must be filed within 90 days after the date the IRS mails the taxpayer notice of its final determination with respect to innocent

---

[18] Rev. Rul. 2003-36, 2003-1 CB 849.

[19] *S.V. Fain*, 129 TC 89, Dec. 57,127 (2007).

[20] Treas. Dept., IRS Publication 971, "Innocent Spouse Relief and Separation of Liability and Equitable Relief" (2012 Ed.), p. 3.

[21] *M.B. Butler*, 114 TC 276, Dec. 53,869 (2000); *D. Fernandez*, 114 TC 324, Dec. 53,875 (2000), *acq.* 2000-1 CB xvi, *acq.* 2004-35; *F.L. Charlton*, 114 TC 333, Dec. 53,879 (2000), *supplemental opinion*, 81 TCM 1439, Dec. 54,290(M), TC Memo. 2001-76; *T.*

spouse relief [Code Sec. 6015(e)(1)(A)]. The Tax Court has statutory jurisdiction to review the IRS's denial of equitable innocent spouse relief in situations where the IRS has not asserted a deficiency against the taxpayer [Code Sec. 6015(e)(1)].

Credits and Refunds

If a determination is made that a taxpayer qualifies for innocent spouse relief, credits and refunds may be made by the IRS, the Tax Court, or any other court with jurisdiction [Code Sec. 6015(g)(1)].

.07 Res Judicata

The doctrine of res judicata provides that when a court of competent jurisdiction enters a final judgment on the merits of a cause of action, the parties to the action are bound by that decision as to all matters that were or could have been litigated and decided in the proceeding. Four conditions must be met to preclude relitigation of a claim under the doctrine of res judicata: (1) the parties in each action must be identical (or at least be in privity); (2) a court of competent jurisdiction must have rendered the first judgment; (3) the prior action must have resulted in a final judgment on the merits; and (4) the same cause of action or claim must be involved in both suits. Once these conditions are met, each party is prohibited from raising any claim or defense that was or could have been raised as part of the litigation over the cause of action in the prior case.

In *E. Koprowski*,[22] the Tax Court concluded that a husband was barred by res judicata from claiming innocent spouse relief because the husband's income tax liability had previously been determined in a deficiency case in which he and his wife elected to proceed under the small tax case procedures which was exempt from appellate review.

Exception in Innocent Spouse Cases

Under Code Sec. 6015(g)(2), determinations made in a final court decision in any prior proceeding for the same tax period are conclusive, unless a spouse qualifies for innocent spouse relief and that that relief wasn't an issue in the prior proceeding. But the exception will not apply if the court determines that the spouse participated meaningfully in the prior proceeding.[23] Therefore, res judicata would not bar a taxpayer's claim for innocent spouse relief where one of the two spouses (where both spouses were represented by the same attorney) did not meaningfully participate in the prior decision before the court.[24]

Waivers

Taxpayers electing innocent spouse relief or separate liability may execute a written waiver of formal notice of deficiency and agree to the tax liability and any adjustment under the innocent spouse provisions [Code Sec. 6015(e)(5)]. This waiver of formal notice under the innocent spouse provisions is similar to the waiver that applies to

(Footnote Continued)

Corson, 114 TC 354, Dec. 53,882 (2000); *K.A. King*, 115 TC 118, Dec. 53,994 (2000), *acq.* 2002-2 CB xiii, *supplemental opinion*, 116 TC 198, Dec. 54,302 (2001); *K. Cheshire*, CA-5, 2002-1 USTC ¶50,222, 282 F3d 326, *cert. denied*, 537 US 881.

[22] *E. Koprowski*, 138 TC No. 5, Dec. 58,938 (2012); *K. Haag*, CA-1, 2012-2 USTC ¶50,428, *aff'g*, 101 TCM 1392, Dec. 58,603(M), TC Memo. 2011-87.

[23] *T.F. Noons*, 88 TCM 388, Dec. 55,786(M), TC Memo. 2004-243; *I. Baranowicz*, CA-9, 2006-1 USTC ¶50,137, 432 F3d 972.

[24] *L.W. Harbin*, 137 TC 93, Dec. 58,764 (2012).

deficiency procedures under Code Sec. 6213(d) and disputes continuing from pre-levy administrative due process hearings under Code Sec. 6330(d)(1)(A) [Code Sec. 7463(f)].

.08 Determining Eligibility for Innocent Spouse Relief

Consult the following flowcharts below to determine whether you qualify for innocent spouse relief.[25]

[25] Treas. Dept., IRS Publication 971, "Innocent Spouse Relief and Separation of Liability and Equitable Relief" (2012 Ed.), pp. 16-18.

Flowcharts

The following flowcharts provide a quick way for determining whether you may qualify for relief. But do not rely on these flowcharts alone. Also read the earlier discussions.

Figure A. Do You Qualify for Innocent Spouse Relief?

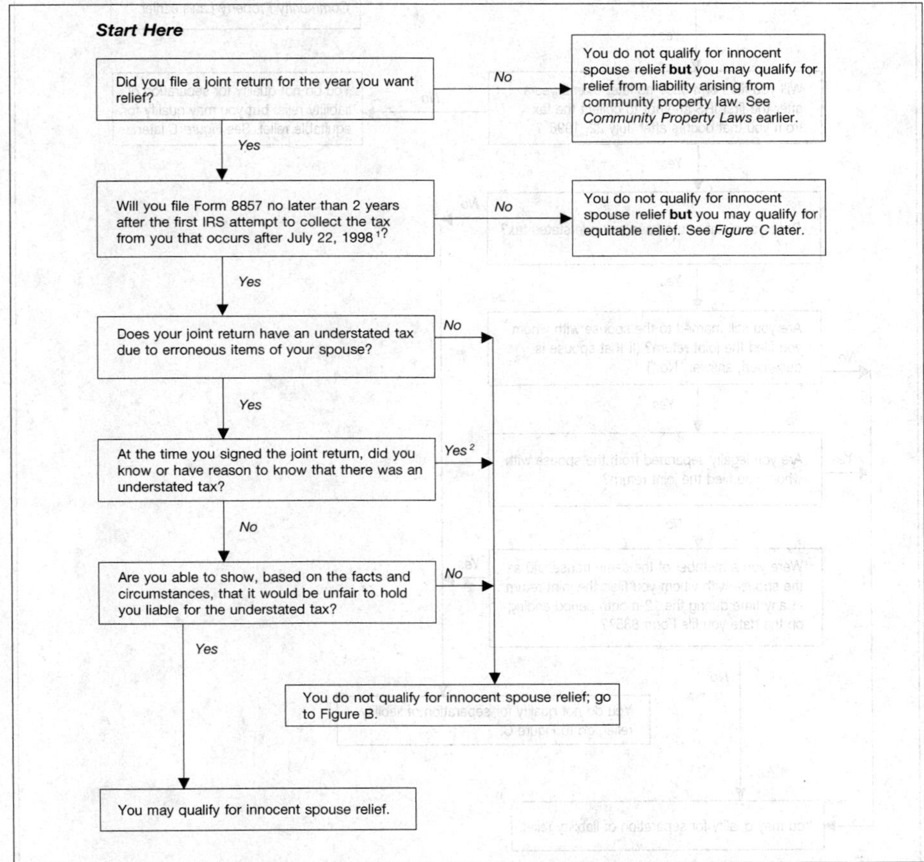

[1] Collection activities that may start the 2-year period are described earlier under *How To Request Relief*.

[2] You may qualify for partial relief if, at the time you filed your return, you knew or had reason to know of only a portion of an erroneous item.

Figure B. Do You Qualify for Separation of Liability Relief?

Start Here

Did you file a joint return for the year you want relief?

No → You do not qualify for separation of liability relief **but** you may qualify for relief from liability arising from community property law. See *Community Property Laws* earlier.

Yes ↓

Will you file Form 8857 no later than 2 years after the first IRS attempt to collect the tax from you that occurs after July 22, 1998*?

No → You do not qualify for separation of liability relief **but** you may qualify for equitable relief. See *Figure C* later.

Yes ↓

Does your joint return have an understated tax?

No → You do not qualify for separation of liability relief; go to Figure C.

Yes ↓

Are you still married to the spouse with whom you filed the joint return? (If that spouse is deceased, answer "No.")

No → You may qualify for separation of liability relief.

Yes ↓

Are you legally separated from the spouse with whom you filed the joint return?

Yes → You may qualify for separation of liability relief.

No ↓

Were you a member of the same household as the spouse with whom you filed the joint return at any time during the 12-month period ending on the date you file Form 8857?

Yes → You do not qualify for separation of liability relief; go to Figure C.

No → You may qualify for separation of liability relief.

*Collection activities that may start the 2-year period are described earlier under *How To Request Relief*.

Figure C. Do You Qualify for Equitable Relief?

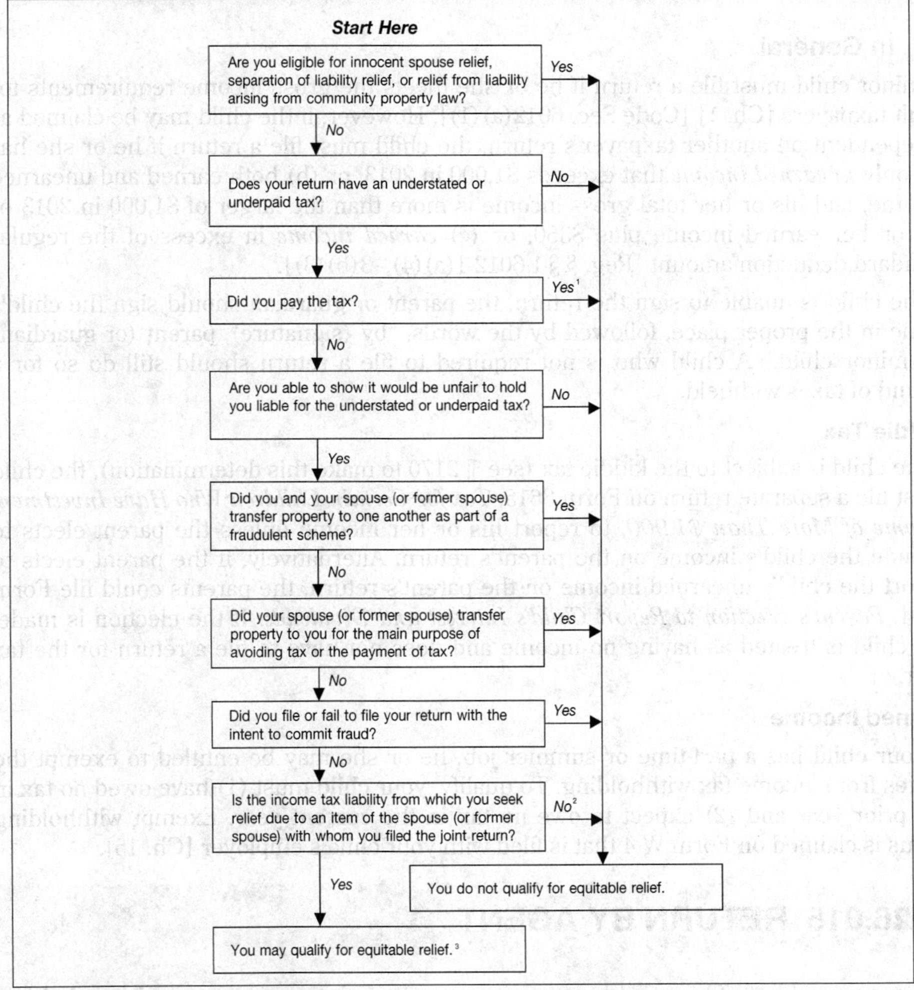

[1] You may qualify for equitable relief and receive a refund of certain payments made out of your own funds. See *Refunds* earlier.
[2] You may qualify for equitable relief if you meet any of the exceptions to condition (8) discussed earlier under *Conditions for Getting Equitable Relief*.
[3] You must file Form 8857 by the filing deadlines explained earlier in *Exception for equitable relief* under *How To Request Relief*.

Page 18 Publication 971 (September 2011)

¶26,010 RETURNS OF MINORS

.01 In General

A minor child must file a return if he or she meets the gross income requirements for adult taxpayers [Ch. 1] [Code Sec. 6012(a)(1)]. However, if the child may be claimed as a dependent on another taxpayer's return, the child must file a return if he or she has (a) only *unearned income* that exceeds $1,000 in 2013, or (b) both earned and unearned income, and his or her total gross income is more than the larger of $1,000 in 2013 or his or her earned income plus $350, or (c) *earned income* in excess of the regular standard deduction amount [Reg. §§1.6012-1(a)(4), -3(b)(3)].

If the child is unable to sign the return, the parent or guardian should sign the child's name in the proper place, followed by the words, "by (signature), parent (or guardian) for minor child." A child who is not required to file a return should still do so for a refund of taxes withheld.

Kiddie Tax

If the child is subject to the kiddie tax (see ¶2170 to make this determination), the child must file a separate return on Form 8615, *Tax for Certain Children Who Have Investment Income of More Than $1,900,* to report his or her income unless the parent elects to include the child's income on the parent's return. Alternatively, if the parent elects to report the child's unearned income on the parent's return, the parents could file Form 8814, *Parent's Election to Report Child's Interest and Dividends.* If the election is made, the child is treated as having no income and does not have to file a return for the tax year.

Earned Income

If your child has a part-time or summer job, he or she may be entitled to exempt the wages from income tax withholding. To qualify, your child must (1) have owed no tax in the prior year and (2) expect to owe no tax in the current year. Exempt withholding status is claimed on Form W-4 that is filed with your child's employer [Ch. 15].

¶26,015 RETURN BY AGENT

If you are unable to file your tax return, you may appoint an agent to make and sign a return on your behalf provided the return is accompanied by a power of attorney (or copy of one) authorizing the attorney to represent you in making, executing, or filing the return [Reg. §1.6012-1(a)(5)]. You or your authorized agent must sign your Federal income tax return in order for it to be a valid return [¶26,015] [Code Sec. 6061; Reg. §1.6061-1]. Form 2848, *Power of Attorney and Declaration of Representative,* giving the agent's power of attorney, should also be filed with your return [Code Sec. 6012(b); Reg. §1.6012-1(a)(5)]. A Form 1040 signed by an attorney on behalf of a taxpayer will not constitute a valid tax return if the taxpayer has not given the attorney a power of attorney to sign the return on his behalf.[26]

---

[26] *H.C. Elliott,* 113 TC 125, Dec. 53,498 (1999).

Most taxpayers can simply check a box on their tax return to authorize a paid preparer who signs the return to work directly with the IRS to fix return-processing problems. The box will not replace a power of attorney and thus will not permit preparers to represent or act on behalf of taxpayers.

¶26,020 RETURN BY FIDUCIARY

If an individual would be required to file a return [Ch. 1], a fiduciary acting for him must file one [Code Sec. 6012(b)(2)].

.01 Who Are Fiduciaries?

The term *fiduciary* means a guardian, trustee, executor, administrator, receiver, conservator, or any person acting in any fiduciary capacity for another person [Code Sec. 7701(a)(6); Reg. § 301.7701-6].

Fiduciaries required to file returns include the following [Code Sec. 6012(b)]:

- Guardian or a committee of an insane person [Reg. § 1.6012-3(b)(3)].
- Guardian of a minor unless the minor himself makes the return or has it made [Reg. § 1.6012-3(b)(3)].
- Guardian of a taxpayer who has disappeared. If his spouse is appointed guardian, she may file a joint return for herself and as guardian of her missing husband, if the other requirements are met.[27]
- Executor or administrator for decedent [Reg. § 1.6012-3(b)(1)].
- Trustee of a trust [Ch. 25].
- Trustee of an individual's bankrupt estate [discussed below].

> **Example 26-9:** The executor of a decedent's estate must file an income tax return for the estate on Form 1041 if the gross income from the estate is $600 or more [Ch. 25].

.02 What Return Form to Use

The guardian, executor or administrator must make the return for an individual on Form 1040, 1040A, or 1040EZ [Code Sec. 6012(b); Reg. § 1.6012-3(b)]. The return for an estate or trust is made on Form 1041.

How the Return Is Signed

Persons making the return must sign and indicate the capacity in which they are acting. If there are two or more joint fiduciaries, one can execute the return [Code Sec. 6012(b)(5); Reg. § 1.6012-3(c)].

[27] Rev. Rul. 80-347, 1980-2 CB 342, as modified by Rev. Rul. 82-189, 1982-2 CB 189.

.03 Fiduciaries Not Required to File

Receivers who are in charge of only a portion of the taxpayer's property need not make a return. Receivers who stand in place of an individual have a duty to file a return if the individual does not file it [Code Sec. 6012(b)(3); Reg. § 1.6012-3(b)(5)].

.04 Bankruptcy Estate

A bankruptcy trustee of an individual debtor's estate must file a return for the estate if its 2013 gross income is $10,000 (the sum of the exemption amount which in 2013 is $3,900 plus the basic standard deduction for a married individual filing a separate return which in 2013 is $6,100) [Code Sec. 6012(a)(9), (b)(4)]. However, the trustee of a partnership in a bankruptcy may not file a return for the income of a bankrupt partnership.[28] For corporations, see ¶ 26,030.

> **NOTE:** Although the estate of a partnership in bankruptcy is not treated as a separate entity, the trustee in bankruptcy must file annual information returns [¶ 26,180] for the partnership.

¶26,025 ELECTRONIC FILING OF TAX RETURNS BY INDIVIDUALS

.01 Mandatory E-Filing for Most Tax Return Preparers

Starting January 1, 2012, any tax return preparer who anticipates preparing and filing 11 or more Forms 1040, 1040A, 1040EZ and 1041 during a calendar year must use IRS *e-file* (unless the preparer or a particular return is administratively exempt from the *e-file* requirement or the return is filed by a preparer with an approved hardship waiver). Members of firms must count returns in the aggregate. If the number of applicable income tax returns is 11 or more, then all members of the firm generally must *e-file* the returns they prepare and file. This is true even if a member expects to prepare and file fewer than 11 returns on an individual basis.[29] In order to *e-file,* the tax return preparer must follow these three steps: (1) apply to participate in IRS *e-file* using the IRS *e-file* Application at IRS.gov by first creating an IRS e-services account, which facilitates electronic interaction with the IRS; (2) submit an IRS *e-file* application; and (3) pass a suitability check. These steps are described in detail in IRS Publication 3112, *IRS e-file Application and Participation.*

.02 Exemptions and Undue Hardship Waiver from E-Filing

In Rev. Proc 2011-25,[30] the IRS explained how certain classes of return preparers can obtain either an administrative exemption or an undue hardship waiver from e-filing. Exempt preparers include members of certain religious groups that are conscientiously opposed to its members using electronic technology; foreign preparers without Social Security Numbers; preparers ineligible for IRS e-file due to an IRS e-file sanction. Returns exempt due to the preparer's technological difficulties include: rejected returns that a specified tax return preparer attempted to e-file but was unable

---

[28] Senate Report No. 96-1035, p. 94, 96th Cong., 2nd Sess.

[29] IRS Pub. 3112, at 1 (2013).

[30] Rev. Proc. 2011-25, IRB 2011-17, 725.

to because the return was rejected; forms or schedules not supported by the preparer's software package; and other returns where the preparer experiences a short-term inability to electronically file due to some other verifiable and documented technological problem.

Return preparers should use Form 8948, *Preparer Explanation for Not Filing Electronically,* to explain why an individual income tax return that is able to be filed electronically was prepared and filed in paper format.

The IRS will grant undue hardship waivers only in rare cases. For example, the fact that a preparer doesn't have a computer or appropriate software or doesn't desire to obtain or use a computer or software doesn't, in isolation, constitute an undue hardship. An undue hardship waiver request based solely on this fact or personal desire, without any further explanation or justification (e.g., disability or financial hardship), will be denied. An undue hardship waiver is requested by submitting a signed and dated Form 8944, *Preparer e-file Hardship Waiver Request,* to the IRS between October 1 of the calendar year preceding the applicable calendar year and February 15 of the applicable calendar year, or within the timeframe specified in the instructions to Form 8944.

.03 Form 1040 IRS *E-File* Using Personal Computer

Taxpayers who have a computer, a modem and tax preparation software, which is available at a computer retailer or through web sites on the internet, can electronically file their tax return from their home computer through the IRS Web site at www.irs.gov.

In Publication 1345, *Handbook for Authorized IRS e-file Providers of Individual Income Tax Returns*, the IRS provides rules and requirements for participation in IRS e-file of individual income tax returns and related forms and schedules. Individuals can only electronically file tax returns with due dates in the current year. A taxpayer cannot electronically file an individual income tax return after the 15th day of October even if the IRS has granted an extension to file a return beyond that date. A return filed using IRS e-file may be a composite of electronically transmitted data and certain paper documents or be completely paperless. The paper portion of a composite return may consist of a paper transmittal Form 8453, *U.S. Individual Income Tax Transmittal* and other paper documents that cannot be electronically transmitted and must be attached to the Form 8453 and mailed to the IRS.

The following individual income tax returns and related return conditions cannot be electronically filed: (1) returns that are not current year tax returns; (2) tax returns with fiscal year tax periods; (3) amended tax returns; (4) returns containing forms or schedules that cannot be processed by IRS e-file other than those forms and schedules that are required to be submitted with Form 8453, *U.S. Individual Income Tax Transmittal for an IRS e-file Return*; (5) tax returns with Taxpayer Identification Numbers (TIN) within the range of 900-00-0000 through 999-99-9999. Exception: Adopted Taxpayer Identification Numbers (ATIN) and Individual Taxpayer Identification Numbers (ITIN) may fall within the range above. Valid ATINs contain the digits 93 in the fourth and fifth positions. Valid ITINs contain digits within a range of 70 through 88 in the fourth and fifth digits; and (6) Tax returns with rare or unusual processing conditions or that exceed the specifications for returns allowable in IRS *e-file.*

.04 Payment Options

Individual taxpayers have the following two electronic options for paying an income tax balance: (1) direct debit from a checking or savings account, or (2) charge on an American Express, VISA, Discover or MasterCard account. The direct debit method may be used if the taxpayer files electronically. The credit card option is available to taxpayers filing electronically or with a paper return. The IRS does not assess a fee for using either option. However, the credit card company may charge a user fee and could treat the charge as a cash advance subject to immediate interest charges.[31] See also ¶26,125.

CORPORATION TAX RETURNS

¶26,030 CORPORATION INCOME TAX RETURNS

Every corporation not expressly exempt must file an income tax return, even if it has no taxable income (including corporations in bankruptcy). Domestic corporations must file Form 1120, *U.S. Corporation Income Tax Return*, unless they are required to file a special return. The corporation must file returns for as long as it remains in existence [Code Sec. 6012(a)(2); Reg. § 1.6012-2(a)]. Returns must include identifying numbers [¶26,045] [Reg. § 301.6109-1(b)]. Corporations that received a charter, but have never perfected their organization, transacted business or received any income from any source, may be relieved of the duty of filing a return on application to the District Director [Reg. § 1.6012-2(a)(2)]. Receivers having possession or title to all or substantially all of the corporation's business or property must file the corporation returns, whether they are liquidating the corporation or operating its business. Trustees in dissolution and trustees in reorganization proceedings under federal bankruptcy laws have the same status as receivers [Code Sec. 6012(b)(3); Reg. § 1.6012-3(b)(4)].

.01 E-Filing Requirements

Corporations (including foreign corporations) and tax-exempt organizations with assets of $10 million or more and that file at least 250 returns during a calendar year, including income tax, information, excise tax, and employment tax returns, are required to e-file their Forms 1120, 1120-F and 1120-S income tax returns and Form 990 information returns. However, taxpayers may request a waiver of the electronic filing mandate.

The following chart reflects the e-filing requirements imposed on corporations, tax-exempt organizations, and private foundations:

[31] IRS Pub. 1345, at 23 (2012).

Entity	Form(s)	Applicable Date
Corporations, including electing small business corporations, with assets of $10 million or more that file at least 250 returns.	Form 1120, *U.S. Corporation Income Tax Return,* or Form 1120-S, *U.S. Income Tax Return for S Corporation.*	Tax years beginning November 14, 2007.
Tax-exempt organizations with assets of $10 million or more if they file at least 250 returns.	Form 990, *Return of Organization Exempt From Income Tax.*	Tax years beginning November 14, 2007.
Small tax-exempt corporations with gross receipts up to $50,000.	Form 990-N, *Electronic Notice (e-Postcard) for Tax-Exempt Organizations Not Required to File Form 990 or 990-EZ.*	Tax years beginning January 1, 2007.
Private foundations or section 4947(a)(1) trusts if they file at least 250 returns.	Form 990-PF, *Return of Private Foundation or Section 4947(a)(1) Nonexempt Charitable Trust Treated as Private Foundation.*	Tax years beginning November 14, 2007.

.02 How the 250 Return Determination Is Made

The determination of whether an entity is required to e-file because the entity files at least 250 returns is made by aggregating all returns, regardless of type, that the entity is required to file over the calendar year. Corrected or amended returns are not counted in determining whether the 250-return threshold is met. All members of a controlled group of corporations are required to file their Forms 1120 electronically if the total number of returns required to be filed by the controlled group of corporations is at least 250 [Reg. §§ 301.6011-5(d)(5), 301.6033-4].

.03 Electronic Filing Waviers

The IRS has issued guidance on the procedures that corporations, electing small business corporations, and tax-exempt organizations must follow to request a waiver of the requirement to electronically file Form 1120, Form 1120S, Form 990, and Form 990-PF.[32] Taxpayers can generally request waivers of the electronic filing requirement if they cannot meet those requirements due to technology constraints, or if compliance with the requirements would result in undue financial burden on the taxpayer. The waiver request must be submitted in written form and must contain the information prescribed by the guidance. The guidance also sets forth the circumstances under which electronically filed returns that are ultimately rejected will be considered timely filed.

[32] Notice 2010-13, IRB 2010-13, 327.

¶26,040 RETURN FOR SHORT TAX YEAR

Corporations in existence during any part of the tax year must file tax returns [Reg. § 1.6012-2(a)(2)]. The closing date of the first return of the newly organized corporation depends on whether it uses the calendar year or a fiscal year as its accounting period. A fiscal year may be adopted without permission of the IRS.

Example 26-10: If a corporation received its charter and began business on November 15, 2013, and wished to adopt the calendar year, its first return would be for the period November 15 to December 31, 2013, and subsequent returns would be for the calendar years following. If the corporation wished to adopt a fiscal year ending January 31, its first return would be for the period November 15, 2013, to January 31, 2014, and subsequent returns for the fiscal years following.

A return for a corporation from the date of incorporation to the end of its first accounting period is considered to be for a period of 12 months. It is not a fractional year return, and the income need not be put on an annual basis [Code Sec. 443(a)(2)]. Returns for periods of less than 12 months due to change of accounting periods must be put on an annual basis [Ch. 18].

Special rules apply to S corporations and personal service corporations that elect fiscal years [Ch. 18].

TAXPAYER IDENTIFICATION NUMBERS (TINs) AND PREPARER TAX IDENTIFICATION NUMBERS (PTINs)

¶26,045 PURPOSE OF THE NUMBER

The IRS automatic data processing (ADP) system analyzes returns and correlates information reported about every U.S. taxpayer. The key is the taxpayer identifying number that must be shown on every tax paper required to be filed—returns, statements or other documents. Entering the correct number cannot be over-emphasized since an omission or inaccuracy will impede the IRS in handling matters.

¶26,050 WHAT IS THE IDENTIFYING NUMBER?

.01 Individuals

The identifying number (TIN) for individuals and estates of decedents is the social security number [Code Sec. 6109(d); Reg. § 301.6109-1(a)(1)]. Some taxpayers may also have an employer identification number (EIN) if they are engaged in a trade or business [Reg. § 301.6109-1(a), (b)]. Thus, taxpayers may be required to use two numbers—one (TIN) for individual taxes and one (EIN) for business taxes.

Example 26-11: Mr. Johnson operates a retail business as a sole proprietorship. His income tax return includes his TIN number on the return form and most schedules, including the self-employment Schedule SE. He uses his EIN number on Schedule C, which shows profit or loss from the business.

Reporting Dependent's IDs

Individuals who claim personal exemptions (or the dependent care credit) for dependents or who have qualifying children and claim the earned income credit are required to provide taxpayer identification numbers (i.e., social security numbers) for such dependents or qualifying children, regardless of their ages or month of birth [Code Sec. 151(e)]. An otherwise valid dependency exemption will be denied unless the taxpayer reports the dependent's TIN on the return where the exemption is claimed. An incorrect TIN is treated as a mathematical or clerical error, allowing the IRS to summarily assess any additional tax due as a result of the denied exemption or credit [Code Sec. 6213(g)(2)(H)]. A penalty applies for failing to supply each TIN per return [Ch. 27][Code Sec. 6723].

.02 Other Taxpayers

Corporations, partnerships, trusts and estates, exempt organizations,[33] and investment clubs[34] use the employer identification number (EIN) [Code Sec. 6109; Reg. § 301.6109-1, 301.7701-11, 12].

NOTE: (1) A fiduciary filing for an individual includes the individual's TIN number and, if necessary, the EIN number; as noted, an estate or trust uses its EIN number. The fiduciary's own number is not used in either case. (2) Nonresident aliens and foreign corporations not doing business in the U.S. do not need identifying numbers [Reg. § 301.6109-1(g)].

.03 Tax Return Preparers

See ¶ 26,061.

.04 Household Employers Need Employer ID Numbers

The IRS requires that household employers include an employer identification number (EIN) on forms they file for their employees. This requirement applies to Forms W-2 and to Schedule H, Household Employment Taxes. If you are a household employer, you will need an EIN for Forms W-2 by January 31, and for Schedule H no later than the filing of your annual individual income tax return. If you are a household employer and need an EIN, you must complete and file Form SS-4, *Application for Employer Identification Number*. The instructions accompanying Form SS-4 explain how to apply for the EIN by mail or telephone.

.05 Aliens

Alien individuals who are not eligible to obtain social security numbers, may apply to the IRS for an Individual Taxpayer Identification Number (ITIN) for use in

[33] Rev. Rul. 64-8, 1964-1 CB 480.

[34] Rev. Rul. 63-247, 1963-2 CB 612.

connection with tax filing requirements [Reg. § 301.6109-1(d)(3)]. The application is made on Form W-7. The application on Form W-7 must be made far enough in advance of the taxpayer's first required use of the ITIN to permit issuance of the number in time for the taxpayer to comply with the required use (e.g., the timely filing of a tax return) [Reg. § 301.6109-1(d)(3)(ii)]. ITINs are intended to be used as proof of identity for nontax purposes (e.g., to obtain a driver's license, to claim legal residency, to seek employment in the United States, or to apply for welfare and health benefits). ITIN applicants must attach the original, completed tax return for which the ITIN is needed. A holder of a financial account generating income subject to information reporting or withholding requirements and applying for an ITIN must provide evidence that he has opened the account with the financial institution and has an ownership interest in the account.

¶26,055 PAYMENTS TO OTHERS

Returns filed for payments made to others (e.g., information returns [¶26,135] and employer returns on withholding [Ch. 15]) must include the payee's TIN number or EIN. This number must be furnished to the person filing the return when requested (and certified as correct in some cases). If the number is not obtained, payors must file an affidavit with their returns stating that the payees refused to give them their numbers.

¶26,060 HOW TO GET A NUMBER

Taxpayers without a taxpayer identification number, should apply for one. Applications (Form SS-5 for TIN number and Form SS-4 for EIN) are handled by any IRS or Social Security office. Applications should be made far enough in advance to permit its timely issuance [Reg. § 301.6109-1(d)].

> ▶ **OBSERVATION:** To obtain a TIN, the Social Security Administration requires an original birth certificate and another proof, such as a library card, report card, or immunization certificate. If a parent signs the application, then he or she will have to produce an original proof, such as a driver's license.

¶26,061 TAX RETURN PREPARER IDENTIFICATION NUMBERS

.01 PTIN Required

Tax return preparers may no longer use an SSN as a preparer identifying number unless specifically prescribed by the IRS [Reg. § 1.6109-2(a)(2)(i)]. Instead, a tax return preparer will be required to use a preparer tax identification number (PTIN) as the identifying number [Reg. § 1.6109-2(d)]. The tax return preparers must apply for a PTIN, renew the PTIN on a calendar-year basis, and pay the renewal fee of $63 for the 2013 filing season.[35] The initial application fee for a PTIN remains at $64.25. Tax return preparers can renew online. Preparers who fail to provide their identifying number are liable for penalties of $50 per return, up to a maximum of $25,000 for documents filed in a calendar year. All compensated preparers must register on the on-line registration system (on the Tax Professionals page at irs.gov) or submit a paper Form W-12, *Paid Preparer Tax Identification Number (PTIN) Application*.

.02 Competency Testing

As part of the process, all tax return preparers except CPAs, enrolled agents and attorneys are required to complete competency testing which could include a review of the preparer's history of compliance with personal and business tax filing and payment obligations [Reg. § 1.6109-2(f)]. CPAs, enrolled agents and attorneys must be active and in good standing with their respective licensing authorities to be exempt from competency testing. In addition, the IRS will require unenrolled preparers (individuals who are not CPAs, enrolled agents, or attorneys) to complete 15 hours of continuing professional education (CPE) each year and the classes must be taken from an IRS-approved provider.

The 15 hours of CE must include 10 hours of federal tax law, three hours of federal tax law updates and two hours of ethics each calendar year. Return preparers must provide their PTIN to the CE providers so it can be reported to the IRS. Non-signing preparers supervised by CPAs, attorneys or Enrolled Agents in law, accounting, and recognized firms also are exempt from the CE and test requirements, as are tax return preparers who do not prepare any Form 1040 series returns.[36] The chart below provides an overview of the various categories of individuals who may prepare federal tax returns for compensation and their responsibilities.

Category	PTIN	Tax Compliance Check	Background Check	IRS Test	Continuing Education	Practice Rights
Enrolled Agents*	Yes	Yes	Proposals Pending	Yes (Special Enrollment Exam)	72 hours every 3 years	Unlimited
Registered Tax Return Preparers**	Yes	Yes	Proposals Pending	Yes (RTRP Test)	15 hours per Year	Limited
CPAs***	Yes	Yes	Proposals Pending	No	Varies	Unlimited
Attorneys***	Yes	Yes	Proposals Pending	No	Varies	Unlimited
Supervised Preparers†	Yes	Yes	Proposals Pending	No	No	Limited

[35] IRS News Release IR-2012-103, Dec. 20, 2012.

[36] IRS News Release IR-2012-18, Feb. 10, 2012.

Category	PTIN	Tax Compliance Check	Background Check	IRS Test	Continuing Education	Practice Rights
Non-1040 Preparers‡	Yes	Yes	Proposals Pending	No	No	Limited

*__Enrolled Agents__ have passed a three-part, comprehensive IRS exam covering individual and business returns. They must adhere to ethical standards and complete 72 hours of continuing education courses every three years. EAs have unlimited practice rights before the IRS, which means they can represent clients for any tax matter.

**__RTRPs__ have passed an IRS test establishing minimal competency. The test covers only individual income tax returns (Form 1040). They must adhere to ethical standards. They must also complete 15 hours of continuing education each year. RTRPs have limited practice rights before the IRS, which means they can represent clients in only certain circumstances.

***__CPAs and Attorneys__ have unlimited practice rights before the IRS.

.03 Tax Return Preparer Defined

Reg. § 1.6109-2(g) provides that the term "tax return preparer" means any individual who is compensated for preparing, or assisting in the preparation of, all or substantially all of a tax return or claim for refund of tax. Factors to consider in determining whether an individual is a tax return preparer include:

- The complexity of the work performed by the individual relative to the overall complexity of the tax return or claim for refund of tax;
- The amount of the items of income, deductions, or losses attributable to the work performed by the individual relative to the total amount of income, deductions, or losses required to be correctly reported on the tax return or claim for refund of tax; and
- The amount of tax or credit attributable to the work performed by the individual relative to the total tax liability required to be correctly reported on the tax return or claim for refund of tax.

.04 Registered Tax Return Preparer (RTRP)

In Reg. § 1.6109-2(d), the IRS provides that attorneys, CPAs, enrolled agents, and registered tax return preparers (RTRP) who prepare all or substantially all of a tax return must obtain a PTIN. A RTRP is a new class of practitioner who (1) has successfully completed a written examination covering federal tax laws; (2) possesses a valid PTIN or other prescribed identification number; and (3) has not engaged in conduct that would, under Circular 230 justify suspension or disbarment of the practitioner.

In Notice 2011-6,[37] the IRS identified two additional groups of individuals who are eligible to obtain a PTIN: (1) specified individuals who are supervised by the attorney, CPA, enrolled agent, enrolled retirement plan agent, or enrolled actuary who signs the tax return or claim for refund prepared by the individual, and (2) individuals who certify they do not prepare all or substantially all of any tax return or claim for refund covered by a competency examination. Notice 2011-6 further provided after the competency examination is offered, only attorneys, CPAs, enrolled

[37] Notice 2011-6, IRB 2011-3, 315.

agents, RTRP, or the additional groups of individuals identified above will be eligible to obtain a PTIN.

In order to become a RTRP, applicants must pass an online one-time competency test by December 31, 2013 and pass a tax compliance check.[38]

TIME AND PLACE FOR FILING TAX RETURNS

¶26,065 WHEN RETURNS MUST BE FILED

Taxpayers must file their returns by the prescribed due date unless they have secured an extension to file [¶26,070]. Income tax returns are filed for a calendar year or for a fiscal year. Information returns [¶26,135 et seq.] generally are filed on a calendar year basis. A penalty is imposed for failure to file returns on time [Ch. 27].

The time for filing returns for taxes withheld by the payer are discussed at the following paragraphs: wage payments, Ch. 15; pensions, annuities, and other deferred income, Ch. 15; payments to nonresident aliens and backup withholding tax, Ch. 14; Ch. 15.

.01 Due Date on Saturday, Sunday, or Legal Holiday

If the due date for filing a return or performing any other prescribed act falls on a Saturday, Sunday or legal holiday, the act is timely if done on the next day that is not a Saturday, Sunday or legal holiday [Code Sec. 7503; Reg. §301.7503-1(a)]. *Legal holiday* includes any legal holiday recognized in an entire state where the act must be performed. The term also includes any District of Columbia holidays. If a legal holiday in D.C. falls on Saturday or Sunday, the preceding Friday or following Monday is treated as a holiday [Reg. §301.7503-1(b)].

.02 Filing by Mail—The Mailbox Rule

Taxpayers may file returns (and other claims including claims for refund, payments, documents or statements) by mail if properly addressed. If the envelope bears a U.S. postmark made by the U.S. Postal Service dated on or before the due date of the return (or within the required filing period for other claims or statements), it will be considered filed on time, even if it is received after the due date [Code Sec. 7502(a)]. This is known as the *timely mailed/timely filed rule*, or the mailbox rule. In other words, if a taxpayer mailed the return or tax payment on time, it is considered to be filed or paid on time even though it arrived at its destination late.[39]

Registered or Certified Mail to Prove Delivery of a Document

In Reg. §301.7502-1(e)(2), the IRS provides that other than direct proof of actual delivery, proof of proper use of registered or certified mail is the exclusive means to establish prima facie evidence of delivery of a document to the agency, officer, or office where the document must be filed. No other evidence of a postmark or of mailing will be prima facie evidence of delivery or raise a presumption that the document was delivered.[40]

---

[38] IRS News Release IR-2012-103, Dec. 20, 2012.

[39] *W.D. Blake*, 94 TCM 51, Dec. 57,001(M), TC Memo. 2007-184 (Proof of hand-delivery to U.S. Postal Service employee before deadline for filing sufficient under timely mailing/timely-filing rule even though arrived late).

[40] *Maine Medical Center*, CA-1, 2012-1 USTC ¶50,272, 675 F3d 110.

Refund Claim on Late-Filed Return

Reg. § 301.7502-1 permits a claim for credit or refund made on a late-filed original income tax return to be treated under Code Sec. 7502 as timely filed on the postmark date. Relief is available for refund claims on other late-filed original tax returns including Form 720, *Quarterly Federal Excise Tax Return,* and Form 706, *United States Estate (and Generation-Skipping Transfer) Tax Return.* A refund claim is generally considered timely if filed: (1) within three years from the time the return was filed or two years from the time the tax was paid, whichever is later, or (2) if no return was filed by the taxpayer, within two years from the time the tax was paid [Code Sec. 6511(a)]. See ¶ 27,125–¶ 27,130.

.03 Timely-Mailing/Timely Filing Rule Expanded to Foreign Postmarks

The IRS will accept as timely a federal tax return, refund claim, statement or other document required or permitted to be filed with the IRS or with the Tax Court that is mailed from and officially postmarked in a foreign country on or before midnight on the last date prescribed for filing, including any extensions [Code Sec. 7502].[41] The Tax Court held in *Boultbee,*[42] that the taxpayer's petition, which according to the U.S. Postal Service Track and Confirm service, entered the U.S. domestic mail service on the 147th day after the IRS mailed a deficiency to his Canadian address was timely filed before the 150-day deadline, even though it was received by the court on the 153rd day. According to the court, the U.S. Postal Service Track and Confirm service is functionally equivalent to a U.S. Postal Service postmark.

If the last date for filling falls on a Saturday, Sunday or legal holiday, the documents will be considered timely if postmarked on or before midnight on the next succeeding day which is not a Saturday, Sunday, or legal holiday [Code Sec. 7503]. Such returns will be deemed filed on the date the document was given to the designated delivery service, as recorded electronically on its database or marked on the cover in which the item is to be delivered pursuant to Code Sec. 7502(f)(2)(C).

.04 Electronic Postmark

The date of an electronic postmark given by an authorized electronic return transmitter will be deemed the filing date if the date of the electronic postmark is on or before the filing due date. If the electronic postmark is timely, the document is considered filed timely even if it is received by IRS after its due date [Reg. § 301.7502-1(d)(1)]. An electronic postmark is a record of the date and time (in a particular time zone) that an authorized electronic return transmitter receives the transmission of a taxpayer's electronically filed document on its host system. If the taxpayer and the electronic return transmitter are located in different time zones, the time in the taxpayer's time zone controls the timeliness of the electronically filed document [Reg. § 301.7502-1(d)(3)(ii)].

You may file your return at the last minute using certain qualifying private delivery services (PDS) other than the U.S. Postal Service and still qualify under the rule that a return or payment mailed on time is considered to be filed or received on time [Code Sec. 7502(f)].

---

[41] Rev. Rul. 2002-23, 2002-1 CB 811.

[42] *J.A. Boultbee,* 101 TCM 1031, Dec. 58,514(M), TC Memo. 2011-11.

The IRS has designated four PDS that you may use to file returns and make tax payments and have the assurance that they will be treated as filed on time if they are mailed on time.[43] The following private delivery services have been approved by the IRS:

- DHL Express (DHL)—DHL "Same Day" Service, DHL Next Day 10:30 am, DHL Next Day 12:00 pm, DHL Next Day 3:00 pm, and DHL 2nd Day Service.
- Federal Express (FedEx)—FedEx Priority Overnight, FedEx Standard Overnight, FedEx 2Day, FedEx International Priority, and FedEx International First.
- United Parcel Service (UPS)—UPS Next Day Air, UPS Next Day Air Saver, UPS 2nd Day Air, UPS 2nd Day Air A.M., UPS Worldwide Express Plus, and UPS Worldwide Express.

A delivery service not listed above does not qualify for the timely mailing rule.

Note that a registered mail date is treated as the postmark date, and registration is proof of delivery [Code Sec. 7502(c); Reg. § 301.7502-1(c)(2)].

For timely mailing by employers of tax deposits, see Ch. 15.

Short Tax Year for Corporations

A corporation must file returns for a period of less than 12 months [Ch. 18] within the same period after the close of the short period as if the short period were a fiscal year.[44]

.05 Individual Returns

If you are on a calendar-year basis, you must file income tax returns by April 15 of the year following the tax year involved. The 2013 federal income tax returns must be filed on or before April 15, 2014. If you use a fiscal year, you must file by the 15th of the 4th month following the close of the fiscal year [Code Sec. 6072(a); Reg. § 1.6072-1(a)].

Example 26-12: Ms. Brown is on a fiscal year ending April 30. She must file her return by August 15.

Joint Return by Surviving Husband or Wife

If a surviving spouse elects to file a joint return with the deceased spouse for the year the spouse dies, the time for filing the joint return is the same as if the death had not occurred.

Example 26-13: John Jones and his wife Mary are both calendar year taxpayers. If Mary dies during 2013, the joint return must be filed by April 15, 2014.

.06 Final Return for Decedent

The executor or administrator of a decedent must file the decedent's last return. It is due the same date a return would have been due had the decedent lived the entire tax year [Reg. § 1.6072-1(b)].

---

[43] Notice 2004-83, 2004-2 CB 1030.

[44] Rev. Rul. 71-129, 1971-1 CB 397.

.07 Corporate Returns

If your corporation is on the calendar-year basis, it must file its income tax returns by March 15. If your corporation is on a fiscal year, it must file its returns by the 15th day of the third month following the close of the fiscal year [Code Sec. 6072(b); Reg. § 1.6072-2(a)]. For payment dates, see ¶ 26,105.

A corporation that goes out of existence during its annual accounting period must file its income tax return by the 15th day of the third month after it ceased business and dissolved, unless the District Director grants an extension [¶ 26,070] [Reg. §§ 1.6071-1(b), 1.6072-2(a)].

.08 Foreign Corporations and Foreign Trusts

not having an office or place of business in the U.S. file their income tax returns by the 15th day of the sixth month following the close of the tax year [Reg. § 1.6072-2(b)].

.09 Tax Returns For Estates and Trusts

The fiduciary for an estate must file a return by the 15th day of the fourth month after the close of the tax year. Returns of trusts must generally be made on the calendar year basis [¶ 25,001]. Returns made on a calendar year basis must be filed by April 15 of the following year [Code Sec. 6072(a); Reg. § 1.6072-1(a)].

The last return of an estate or a trust must be filed by the 15th day of the fourth month following the closing of the estate or termination of the trust [Reg. § 1.6072-1].

.10 Exempt Organizations—Return of Unrelated Business Income

Return of unrelated business income on Form 990-T, *Exempt Organization Business Income Tax Return* (and proxy tax under Section 6033(e)), required of certain exempt organizations [Ch. 23] must be filed by the 15th day of the fifth month following the close of the tax year, if the organization is taxable as a corporation [Reg. § 1.6072-2(c)]. Domestic trusts, and foreign trusts having an office or place of business in the U.S., must file the return by the 15th day of the fourth month following the close of the trust's tax year [Reg. § 1.6072-1(a)]. Corporate exempt organizations may obtain an automatic 6 month extension to file Form 990-T by completing Form 8868, *Application for Extension of Time to File an Exempt Organization Return,* paying any tax due and signing the form.

¶26,070 EXTENSION OF TIME TO FILE RETURNS

.01 Six-Month Automatic Extension for Individuals

Taxpayers who expect to miss the April 15 tax return filing deadline, should file Form 4868, *Application for Automatic Extension of Time To File U.S. Individual Income Tax Return,* by April 15, to have an automatic extra six (four if out of the country) months, until August 15, to file that return Reg. § 1.6081-4(a)]. The best part about Form 4868 is that no questions are asked and taxpayers do not even have to sign the form. When Form 4868 is filed, taxpayers must:

1. Estimate to the best of their ability the total amount of their tax liability for the year;
2. Enter that amount on Form 4868; and
3. File Form 4868 by April 15. A taxpayer can request an automatic extension of time to file a U.S. individual income tax return in one of the following three ways: (1) file Form 4868 and pay all or part of estimated income tax due using the Electronic Federal Tax Payment System (EFTPS) or by using a credit or debit card; (2) file Form 4868 electronically by accessing IRS *e-file* using home computer or by using a tax professional who uses *e-file*; or (3) file a paper Form 4868. Taxpayers filing for an extension are not required to pay their tax but do so to avoid interest and penalties which begin to accumulate from the original due date of the return which generally is April 15.

▶ **WARNING:** When an individual, corporation, or private foundation gets an extension of time to file a tax return, the due date for filing the return is deferred six months, generally to October 15, but the time to pay the tax is not extended, unless the extension specifies otherwise [Reg. §§1.6081-1(a); 53.6081-1]. A properly filed Form 4868 avoids the failure to file penalty, but not the late payment penalty or interest. Interest and the late penalty run from the original due date of the return. If taxpayers send in at least 90 percent of the tax due on or before the original due date of the return (through wage withholding, estimated tax payments, or any payment accompanying Form 4868), they will be presumed to have met the reasonable cause requirement for avoiding the late payment penalty (0.5 percent per month) if the balance due is remitted with the return [Reg. §301.6651-1(c)(3)]. Note also that other important due dates are not deferred by filing Form 4868. For example, the due date for making IRA contributions is not deferred beyond the April 15 deadline.

.02 Automatic Six-Month Extension for Corporations

A corporation or an affiliated group of corporations filing a consolidated return will be allowed an automatic six-month extension of time to file its income tax return after the date prescribed for filing the return if the following requirements are met:

1. An application must be submitted on Form 7004, *Application for Automatic Extension of Time to File Certain Business Income Tax, Information, and Other Returns,*
2. The application must be filed on or before the date prescribed for the filing of the return of the corporation (or the consolidated return of the affiliated group of corporations) with the IRS office designated in the instructions.
3. The corporation (or affiliated group of corporations filing a consolidated return) must remit the amount of the properly estimated unpaid tax liability on or before the date prescribed for payment.
4. The application must include a statement listing the name and address of each member of the affiliated group if the affiliated group will file a consolidated return. Upon the timely filing of Form 7004, the six-month extension of time to file shall be considered as granted to the affiliated group for the filing of its consolidated return or for the filing of each member's separate return [Reg. §1.6081-3(a)].

No Extension of Time for the Payment of Tax

Any automatic extension of time for filing a corporation income tax return will not operate to extend the time for payment of any tax due on such return [Reg. § 1.6081-3(b)].

Termination of Automatic Extension

The IRS may terminate an automatic extension at any time by mailing a notice of termination to the corporation (parent corporation in the case of an affiliated group of corporations filing a consolidated return). The notice will be mailed at least 10 days prior to the termination date. It will be mailed to the corporation at the address shown on Form 7004 or to the corporation's last known address as defined in Reg. § 301.6212-2 [Reg. § 1.6081-3(c)].

.03 Overseas Extensions

U.S. citizens or residents may get an automatic two-month extension (until June 15) to file returns and pay tax if they: (1) maintain a tax home or live outside the U.S. and Puerto Rico or (2) serve in military or naval services abroad on the due date of the tax return [Reg. § 1.6081-5(a)(6)]. Your *tax home,* for this purpose, is defined the same as it is defined for purposes of the deduction for away-from-home travel expenses [See Ch. 10]. If you have no regular or principal place of business, then your regular place of abode in a real and substantial sense is considered your tax home.

If you otherwise qualify for the extension, you are not disqualified simply because you are physically present in the U.S. or Puerto Rico at any time, including the tax return due date [Reg. § 1.6081-5(e)].

> **NOTE:** This two-month extension does not apply to you if you are merely traveling outside the U.S. on the return due date [Reg. § 1.6081-5(f)].

If you use the two-month automatic extension, you need not file an application. But you must attach a statement to your return showing that you qualify for it [Reg. § 1.6081-5(b)].

> ▶ **OBSERVATION:** If you already had two extra months to file because you live or are serving overseas, you may still take advantage of the four-month extension discussed above. But you can only get two more months because both extensions run concurrently [Reg. § 1.6081-4(a)].

Suppose you expect to qualify as a bona fide resident of a foreign country [Ch. 28], but not until a date more than two months after the return's regular due date. You can use Form 2350, *Application for Extension of Time to File U.S. Income Tax Return,* to obtain an extension of time for filing your return. In general, the extension is for 30 days beyond the date on which you reasonably expect to qualify.

.04 Extension for Short Period Return

The time to file an income tax return for a short period may be extended by the IRS, if you show unusual circumstances [Reg. § 1.6071-1(b)].

.05 Automatic Filing Extension for Partnerships, Trusts, Estates and Pension Excise Tax Returns

Partnership Returns

A partnership required to file Form 1065, *U.S. Return of Partnership Income*, or Form 8804, *Annual Return for Partnership Withholding Tax,* is entitled to an automatic five-month extension of time to file if the partnership completes an application on Form 7004, *Application for Automatic Extension of Time to File Certain Business Income Tax, Information, and Other Returns,* on or before the later of the date prescribed for filing the return of the partnership, or the expiration of any extension of time to file. No additional extension will be allowed beyond the automatic five-month extension. An automatic extension of time for filing a partnership return of income does not extend the time for filing a partner's income tax return or the time for the payment of any tax due on a partner's income tax return [Reg. § 1.6081-2].

Estate or Trust Income Tax Returns

Any estate or trust required to file an income tax return on Form 1041, *U.S. Income Tax Return for Estates and Trusts,* will be allowed an automatic five-month extension of time to file the return if the estate or trust submits a complete application on Form 7004. No additional extension will be allowed beyond the automatic five-month extension [Reg. § 1.6081-6].

Bankruptcy Estate

A bankruptcy estate that is created when an individual debtor files a petition under either chapter 7 or chapter 11 of Title 11 of the U.S. Code that is required to file an income tax return on Form 1041, *U.S. Income Tax Return for Estates and Trusts*, and an estate or trust required to file an income tax return on Form 1041-N, *U.S. Income Tax Return for Electing Alaska Native Settlement*, or Form 1041-QFT, *U.S. Income Tax Return for Qualified Funeral Trusts* for any tax year will be allowed an automatic six-month extension of time to file the return after the date prescribed for filing the return if the estate files an application with the IRS and shows the amount properly estimated as tax for the estate or trust for the tax year. An automatic extension of time for filing a return granted will not extend the time for payment of any tax due on such return [Reg. § 1.6081-6(2)].

Pension Excise Tax Returns

An employer, other person, or health plan that is required to file a return on Form 8928, *Return of Certain Excise Taxes Under Chapter 43 of the Internal Revenue Code,* will be allowed an automatic six-month extension of time to file the return if the employer, other person, or health plan files an application on Form 7004. An automatic extension of time for filing a return granted will not extend the time for payment of any tax due on such return [Reg. § 54.6081-1].

¶26,075 WHERE TO FILE RETURNS

Unless the return is e-filed, taxpayers should file returns for income tax and self-employment tax in the Revenue District where they reside or have a principal place of business, or at the Service Center that serves that district. However, the IRS may designate special filing places for specific returns. Information returns generally are filed at a Service Center [¶26,135]. Amended returns also must be filed at a Service Center unless they are hand carried [Reg. §1.6091-2(e)]. For return of taxes withheld from wages, see Ch. 15. All taxpayers should consult the IRS website at www.IRS.gov to determine where to file tax returns.

¶26,080 USE OF AMENDED RETURNS

Taxpayers can correct an error in a return they have filed by filing an amended return. For this purpose, they must use Form 1040X and corporations Form 1120X. Other taxpayers may use a regular return form [Reg. §301.6402-3(a)]. The amended regular return can be filed on a return form for the same year as the return being corrected or another year's return if changed to show the correct year. The words "Amended Return" should be written or printed at the top of the regular return form. Taxpayers must explain the error that is being corrected. The IRS is not compelled to accept an amended return.

.01 When Is Tax Due?

If more tax is due because of a correction, taxpayers should pay the tax due with the amended return. Interest and penalties are imposed for delinquent returns [Ch. 27].

.02 Credit or Refund

If taxpayers are entitled to a credit or refund of income tax as a result of the correction, Forms 1040X, 1120X or the amended return (regular return form for taxpayers other than individuals or corporations) will serve as a claim for refund or credit. They must file the claim before the limitation period expires [Ch. 27].

.03 When to File Refund Claim

A refund claim is considered timely if filed: (1) within 3 years from the time the return was filed or 2 years from the time the tax was paid, whichever is later; or (2) if no return was filed by the taxpayer, within 2 years from the time the tax was paid [Code Sec. 6511(a)]. See Ch. 27 for further discussion.

¶26,085 SUBSTITUTE TAX FORMS

The IRS has established the general requirements and conditions for the development, printing, and approval of substitute tax forms and schedules.[45] You can file approved forms instead of official IRS-produced and distributed forms. The rules for all substitute forms are provided in Publication 1167, *General Rules and Specifications for Substitute Tax Forms and Schedules.*

The IRS also allows you to submit paper substitutes for Form W-2, and Form W-3. The information reported on Forms W-2 and W-3 is required to establish tax liability for employees and their eligibility for Social Security and Medicare benefits. A substitute Form W-2 and W-3 must conform precisely to IRS specifications. Employ-

[45] Rev. Proc. 2013-17, IRB 2013-11, 612.

ers will be assessed a penalty of $50 per Form W-2 that is not furnished to an employee on a form acceptable to the IRS (up to $100,000) [Code Sec. 6722]. The IRS publishes the requirements for the substitute forms.[46]

The IRS has also authorized the submission of a substitute Form W-9, but the IRS requirements must be closely followed in order for the substitute form to be accepted.[47]

SUPPORTING INFORMATION

¶26,090 ADDITIONAL INFORMATION THAT MUST BE FILED WITH THE RETURN

Income tax returns must be executed and filed in accordance with the regulations and the instructions with the return [Code Sec. 6011(a); Reg. § 1.6011-1]. Preparing and filing returns, therefore, involves more than merely reporting income and deductions, and figuring the tax. It may be necessary to include or attach to the return any required supporting information or statement.

¶26,095 HOW LONG TO RETAIN YOUR TAX RECORDS

Every person liable for tax is required to keep adequate books and records [Code Sec. 6001]. If are wondering what to do with all the receipts, notes, statements and other papers which you used in preparing your latest tax return, the easy answer is to just keep everything. Since this is not practical for everyone, the real answer is that you should keep documents for as long as the IRS has the legal authority to audit your tax return. If you are ever audited, it is mandatory for you to have adequate documentation of all entries on your return. The more papers you can show the IRS agent to support your position, the better.

.01 Tax Returns

In general, unless you have engaged in fraudulent activity, failed to file a return or understated a substantial amount of your income, the IRS can only come after you for the three years after you filed your return. For example, if you file your federal income tax return on the April 15 due date, the IRS could assess tax against you until April 15, three years later. If, however, you file your tax return late, the IRS has three years from the date you actually filed the return to come after you. Be forewarned, however, that the three-year period is extended to six years if you omitted more than 25 percent of gross income from your return. Neither the three nor the six year period begins to run, however, until a return is filed. If the IRS claims that you never filed a return for a particular year, they could come after you forever, unless of course you can prove that you did file a return. Obviously, you can only prove this if you have a copy of your filed tax return. We therefore recommend that you should keep your tax

[46] Rev. Proc. 2013-18, IRB 2013-8, 503.

[47] Rev. Proc. 96-26, 1996-1 CB 684; Announcement 96-77, 1996-35 IRB 15.

returns and all accompanying schedules and paperwork supporting your income and deductions for at least three years but to be on the safe side, we recommend retaining the records for six years.

.02 What Records to Keep

You have the flexibility to keep your records in any orderly manner that you choose. You can use:

- Checkbook record of deposits and expenses
- Receipts, sales slips and invoices
- Computerized records.
- Statement from bank or other financial institution
- Canceled checks or other proof of payment including your credit card bill.
- Brokerage house or mutual fund statements

The following table shows how long the IRS has to assess additional tax:

If You . . .	Then the Period Is . . .
1. Owe additional tax and (2), (3), and (4) do not apply to you	3 years
2. Do not report income that your should and it is more than 25 percent of the gross income shown on your return	6 years
3. File fraudulent return	No limit
4. Do not file a return	No limit
5. File a claim for credit or refund after you filed your return	Later of 3 years or 2 years after tax was paid
6. File a claim for a loss from worthless securities	7 years

If your financial picture involves or will involve any of the following situations you have added record-keeping responsibilities.

Carryforwards

If you claim carryforwards, keep the return and records for as long as necessary to claim the entire amount of the carryforward and then retain them in your records for an additional three years. For example:

1. Capital losses in excess of capital gains are limited to $3,000 against ordinary income. Excess capital losses can be carried forward indefinitely and used against future capital gains and up to $3,000 of ordinary income.
2. Passive activity losses are deductible only to the extent of passive income. Unused passive losses are suspended and are carried forward and used against passive income in later years. In the year that you sell the property, however, you will be able to claim all suspended passive losses.
3. Deductions for charitable contributions are limited by your adjusted gross income. Any unused charitable deductions are carried forward for up to five years. Retain copies of canceled checks, receipt from the organization, appraisals of property, detailed description of property and records of your out-of-pocket expenses.

4. Home office deductions are limited to the amount of income you earn from the business conducted in that home office. Any excess deductions can be carried forward for as long as you own the home and used against future income from the home office.
5. Investment interest in excess of net investment income may be carried forward indefinitely and used against net investment income.

Your Home

You should keep all records detailing how much you paid for a home or a vacation property for as long as you own it. This rule holds true even though as much as $250,000 ($500,000 for joint filers) of gain from the sale of your home can now escape tax [Code Sec. 121(b)(1); Ch. 7]. If you throw away all your records, where will you be if the exclusion provision is repealed or restricted? And what will you do if your gain exceeds $500,000? You never know what will happen to real estate values or to generous language in the Internal Revenue Code. To play it safe, keep the records.

Be sure to retain in your file all documents detailing your purchase of the property. This includes the mortgage documents and HUD-1 settlement sheet detailing the amount of real estate taxes, mortgage points, closing costs, commissions and other settlement costs that you paid at the closing.

Home Office

If you claim deductions for your home office, keep for at least six years every scrap of paper relating to maintaining your principal place of business at home. If you are claiming depreciation deductions, you will need to retain documentation of your basis in the home, which means keeping all settlement papers from the real estate closing. In addition, you will need to keep all your utility bills if you are also deducting a portion of these expenses as home office expenses. So retain these records for as long as your own the home.

Separation or Divorce

If you are separated or divorced, make copies of all tax returns and accompanying documentation. Remember that when you file a joint return with your spouse, you are each responsible individually and jointly for the entire tax liability, even if all the income was earned by only one spouse. This means that the IRS could come after you for the entire tax bill even if your spouse earned and spent all the money unless you qualify for innocent spouse relief as discussed in ¶26,005. Your records should also include copies of the divorce decrees or agreement of separate maintenance in order to support tax treatment of alimony and child support payments. Alimony is deductible by the spouse paying it and is included in the taxable income of the recipient spouse. Child support payments are neither income to the recipient nor deductible by the spouse paying the support. In addition any agreements or decrees regarding child custody are important because they could establish who is entitled to claim an exemption for each child. Records of the purchase of all jointly owned property are also important because they will help establish your basis in the property. Any property transferred to you by your spouse during your marriage as a result of a divorce will have the same basis in your hands as it did in your spouse's hands. This will be important when you sell the property.

IRAs and Pension Plans

Keep all records detailing additions to, withdrawals from, and loans from your tax-deferred IRAs, pension plans, and 401(k) plans. It is particularly important to retain records separating deductible and nondeductible contributions, since withdrawals from your deductible IRA will be taxed, whereas withdrawals from nondeductible IRAs will not be taxed because you have already paid income tax on those contributions. The IRS Form 8606 is filed each year that a nondeductible contribution is made to your IRA. You should keep this form indefinitely.

Stocks, Bonds, Mutual Funds

Keep records documenting your investments for as long as you own the investments. These records are needed to substantiate your basis in the investment as well as the amount of your capital gains and losses. It is also important if you own shares of stock or shares in mutual funds and are on dividend reinvestment to keep records of additional fractional shares purchased in order to accurately report your basis on any future sale of shares. Your investment records should enable you to determine your basis in the investment, the amount of your gain or loss, how much commission you paid, the date of the purchase and sale, and the amount of interest you paid to purchase the investment. Remember that investment interest in excess of net investment income may be carried forward indefinitely and used against net investment income down the road.

Gambling Winnings and Losses

You should keep an accurate diary of your gambling winnings and losses that include the following:

- Date and type of gambling activity,
- Name and address of the gambling establishment,
- Names of other persons present with you at the gambling establishment, and
- Amount you won or lost.

Medical Records

You should keep for at least three years all doctor and dentist bills, laboratory fees, hospital bills, prescriptions and bills for special medical aids such as wheelchairs and hearing aids.

Casualty or Theft Loss

If your home is destroyed by fire, or if your valuables are stolen or otherwise destroyed, you will want to claim a casualty or theft loss on your income tax return. To support this loss, you will need the police report as well as appraisals and pictures of valuables in your home. It is also a good idea to make a videotape of the rooms and furnishings in your home and to store it in a safe deposit box or fire-proof safe.

What to Do if Your Records Are Lost

If you need to reconstruct your financial records, you should call your attorney, accountant, real estate agent or title company to obtain copies of missing documents. If you did not retain a copy of your federal income tax return, you can request a copy from the IRS on Form 4506, *Request for Copy of Tax Return.* Form 4506-T, *Request for Transcript of Tax Return,* can be used to request tax return information. The IRS generally will not have copies of returns filed more than six years ago, but it should still have information regarding your filing status and a list of your income and deductions and the amount of taxes you paid.

.03 Electronic Storage of Records

All taxpayers are required to maintain books and records sufficient to establish the amount of gross income, deductions, credits, or other information that must be shown on any tax or information return [Code Sec. 6001]. If these records are all on paper, they become difficult for most individuals and businesses to store and retrieve. In an effort to relieve some of these overwhelming storage and retrieval burdens, the IRS has sanctioned the electronic storage of records and has outlined the requirements that taxpayers must meet to maintain their records on computer (machine-sensible records). In general, all Code Sec. 6001 requirements that apply to hardcopy books and records apply as well to machine-sensible books and records (i.e., data in an electronic format intended for use by a computer) and records maintained within an automatic data processing (ADP) system. An ADP system includes a mainframe, stand-alone or net-worked microcomputer system, data base management system, and a system that uses or incorporates electronic data interchange or an electronic storage system.

Taxpayers with assets of $10 million or more at the end of their tax year must comply with the record retention requirements established by the IRS.[48] A taxpayer's machine-sensible records must provide sufficient information to support and verify entries made on the taxpayer's return and to determine the correct tax liability. These records must reconcile with the taxpayer's books and returns. To meet this requirement, machine-readable records must reconcile with the taxpayer's books and taxpayer's return. A taxpayer must ensure that its machine-sensible records contain sufficient transaction-level detail so that the information and the source documents underlying them can be identified. Subject to exceptions, a taxpayer need not create any machine-sensible record other than that created either in the ordinary course of its business or to establish return entries. For example, a taxpayer who does not create, in the ordinary course of its business, the electronic equivalent of a traditional paper document (such as an invoice) generally does not have to construct such a record.

A taxpayer with assets of less than $10 million at the end of the tax year must comply with the record retention requirements if any of the following conditions exists:

- All or part of the information required by Code Sec. 6001 is not in the taxpayer's hardcopy books and records, but is available in machine-sensible records; or
- The district director notifies the taxpayer that machine-sensible records must be retained to meet the requirements of Code Sec. 6001.

A taxpayer's use of a third party to provide services relating to machine-sensible records does not relieve the taxpayer of its recordkeeping obligations and responsibilities under Code Sec. 6001.

---

[48] Rev. Proc. 98-25, 1998-1 CB 689; Rev. Proc. 97-22, 1997-1, CB 652.

Destroy Old Paper Records

The IRS has sanctioned the destruction of the original hardcopy books and records and the deletion of the original computerized records. You can destroy the paper records after you have completed your own testing of the electronic storage system and have instituted procedures that ensure its continued compliance.[49]

PAYMENT OF TAX

¶26,100 WHEN INDIVIDUAL TAX MUST BE PAID

You must pay income tax by the due date of the return [¶26,065]. You must pay any balance of the tax not collected through withholding on wages [¶15,001–¶15,045]or payments of estimated tax [¶14,200–¶14,220] by the 15th day of the fourth month after the close of the tax year (April 15 for calendar year taxpayers) [Code Sec. 6151(a); Reg. §1.6151-1(a)].

Example 26-14: Mr. Harris reports on the basis of a fiscal year ending on June 30. Payment of tax is due by October 15.

▶ **AUTOMATIC EXTENSION FOR FILING:** Individuals can obtain an automatic six-month extension to file their tax return. However, the automatic six-month extension of time to file does not extend the time to pay taxes due.

For further discussion of six-month automatic extension of time to file returns, see ¶26,070.01. For discussion of payment of tax on the installment plan, see ¶26,125.03. For discussion of offers in compromise, see ¶27,035. Individual taxpayers who owe delinquent federal income taxes may apply online for a payment agreement. For further discussion, see ¶26,125.

¶26,105 WHEN CORPORATE TAX MUST BE PAID

.01 In General

Full payment of corporate income tax is due by the 15th of the third calendar month following the close of the tax year. If your corporation is on the calendar year basis, it pays by March 15. If it uses a fiscal year and it ends, for example, on June 30, payment is due by September 15 [Code Sec. 6151(a); Reg. §§1.6072-2, 1.6151-1(a)].

Tax Must Be Deposited in Authorized Banks

Domestic corporations must deposit income and estimated taxes in a Federal Reserve bank or authorized commercial bank by the due date. The tax may be paid by one or more separate deposits, but a preinscribed Federal Tax Deposit Coupon Form must be presented for each deposit [Reg. §1.6302-1]. Checks or money orders should be drawn to the order of the bank where deposited. Depositories other than Federal Reserve banks are not required to accept checks drawn on other banks, but they may

[49] Rev. Proc. 97-22, 1997-1 CB 652.

do so. Corporations that do not receive the coupon deposit forms can call or write any IRS office (giving their name, identification number (EIN), and the month in which their fiscal year ends) in time to make the deposit [Reg. § 1.6302-1]. A penalty ranging from 2 percent to 15 percent may be imposed depending on when your corporation corrects the deposit [Ch. 27] [Code Sec. 6656(b)].

Except for deposits of $20,000 or more [Ch. 15], tax deposits mailed two or more days before the due date are timely filed even though they are received by the depositaries after due date. Usually, the registered or certified receipt is proof of the mailing date by a sender [Code Sec. 7502(c); Reg. § 301.7502-1(e)(i)].

Foreign Corporations

The tax for a foreign corporation having no office or place of business in the U.S. is due by the 15th day of the sixth month following close of the tax year [Code Secs. 6072(c), 6151(a); Reg. § 1.6072-2(b)]. Withholding agents may be required to deposit taxes [Ch. 15].

.02 Payments of Estimated Tax

Estimated tax payments are made by deposit with the preinscribed tax deposit coupon form. Unless a receipt is requested from the bank, your corporation must keep its own record of each payment.

Every corporation, including certain foreign corporations [Ch. 28] and insurance companies, may have to pay estimated tax. Estimated tax is the excess of the anticipated tax liability (including the alternative minimum tax (AMT) on Form 4626) [Ch. 16] less any credits [Code Sec. 6655]. Form 1120-W may be used as a worksheet to compute the estimated tax.

When Installment Payments Are Due

For calendar-year corporations, the due dates for estimated tax payments are:

Required installment	*Due date*
1st	April 15
2nd	June 15
3rd	September 15
4th	December 15

The estimated tax installments of corporations using fiscal years are due on the 15th day of the fourth, sixth, ninth and twelfth months of the tax year [Code Sec. 6655(i)]. If any due date falls on a weekend or legal holiday, the next regular workday is substituted.

Large corporations, defined as those with $1 million or more of taxable income in any of the three immediately preceding tax years, can use their last year's tax liability only for determining the first installment payment. They must use 100 percent of their current year's tax bills for calculating subsequent estimated tax payments. If a large corporation does use the last year's tax figure, though, the second payment must be adjusted to make up for any shortfall from using that method to calculate the first installment [Code Sec. 6655(d)].

Short Tax Year

Estimated tax need not be paid for a short period of fewer than four months [Prop. Reg. § 1.6655-5(b)(1)].

***De minimis* Exception**

Corporations with a tax liability of less than $500 need not make estimated tax payments.

.03 Penalty for Underpayment of Estimated Tax

If payments of estimated tax are not made when due, a penalty may be added to the tax [Ch. 27]. The penalty is figured on the amount by which any actual installment payment falls short of the required installment payment (see above) [Code Sec. 6655(a)].

Relief Provisions

There are two exceptions to estimated tax penalties: the annualized income exception and the seasonal income exception.

1. *The annualized income exception.* Under the annualized income exception, the amount required to be paid is computed by multiplying the "applicable percentage" for a given installment by the full tax on the annualized income for the "appropriate period" (in effect, the income for the period is projected over a whole year) and subtracting any prior payments. The applicable percentages are 25 percent for the first installment, 50 percent for the second, 75 percent for the third and 100 percent for the last installment [Code Sec. 6655(e)]. Schedules One or Two (as follows) must be elected for the entire year before the due date of the first estimated tax installment for the year for which the election applies. The three schedules have differing periods upon which the annualized income is based. The schedules are as follows:

Installment	Schedule One	Schedule Two	Schedule Three
First	1st 3 months	1st 2 months	1st 3 months
Second	1st 3 months	1st 4 months	1st 5 months
Third	1st 6 months	1st 7 months	1st 8 months
Fourth	1st 9 months	1st 10 months	1st 11 months

Example 26-15: Widget, Inc. is a calendar year corporation. It has $10,000 of taxable income in January, $15,000 of taxable income in February and $20,000 of taxable income in March. If Widget elects to use Schedule One, its annualized income for the April 15 estimated tax installment is $180,000 ($45,000 of taxable income for the first three months of the year, divided by three to get average income for one month and then multiplied by 12 to get annualized taxable income for one year). If Widget pays $45,000 (25 percent of $180,000) on or before April 15, it avoids an underpayment penalty for the first installment, regardless of how much income it has for the balance of the year.

▶ **IMPORTANT:** All corporations, large or small, can utilize the estimated tax safe harbor using the annualization method. However, once the annualization method is not used for an installment, your corporation must recapture any reduction in a prior installment caused by the use of the annualized income exception. The regular required installment is increased by the amount of the recapture.

▶ **WHAT TO DO?:** For a small corporation with a tax history, the safest thing to do is to base this year's estimated tax payments on 100 percent of last year's tax. New corporations (or large corporations to the extent they cannot use the 100 percent-of-last-year's-tax rule) will have to do some crystal ball gazing to comply with the tough rules. These corporations will have to make careful estimates of total tax liability for the year and gauge estimated tax payments accordingly—do not assume a payment based on annualized income will be sufficient.

2. *The recurring seasonable income exception.* Corporations that consistently earn a disproportionate amount of their income in one season of the year may annualize their income by assuming the income is earned in the current year and in the same pattern as in the preceding tax years. Thus, no penalty is imposed for an underpayment of any estimated tax installment if the payments for the tax year total at least 100 percent of the tax (see below) measured by a base period percentage of seasonal income [Code Sec. 6655(e)].

▶ **IMPORTANT:** Once your corporation stops using the seasonal income exception, you must recapture all of the savings resulting from using it for prior installments [Code Sec. 6655(e)].

Tax Computation for Seasonal Income

The tax against which the 100 percent floor (see above) is applied is figured as follows [Code Sec. 6655(e)]: (1) take the taxable income for every month of the tax year in which the installment must be paid; (2) divide that amount by the base period percentage (average percent which the taxable income for the corresponding months in the three preceding tax years bears to the taxable income for the three preceding tax years); (3) find the tax on the amount determined by basing the tax on the previous year's income, but at the current year's rate.

Multiply that tax by the base period percentage (as defined above) for the months in the tax year up to and including the month in which the installment is due. Note that this percentage, in all cases, must equal or exceed 70 percent of the total income for any six consecutive months of a tax year.

Rules for applying the relief provisions are on Form 2220. A claim that the penalty does not apply should be supported by a statement on Form 2220 filed with the return [Reg. § 1.6655-1(b)].

¶26,110 WHEN ESTATES AND TRUSTS PAY TAX

Payment of income tax is due by the 15th of the fourth calendar month after the end of the tax year. For a calendar-year estate or trust, the date is April 15.

.01 Estimated Tax

Estates and trusts file Form 1041-ES to pay estimated taxes. Estates and trusts use the same estimated tax payment schedule as individual taxpayers. Form 1041-T may be used to assign a trust's overpayments to beneficiaries [Ch. 14]. New estates, for their first two years, however, need not report and pay estimated tax [Code Sec. 6654(l)].

¶26,115 EXEMPT ORGANIZATIONS

Tax-exempt organizations must make quarterly estimated tax payments of the tax on unrelated business income, and private foundations must make quarterly estimated tax payments of the excise tax on net investment income. These estimated tax payments must be made under the same rules that apply to corporate income taxes [Code Sec. 6655(g)(3)]. A calendar year foundation's first quarter estimated tax payment is due on May 15th (or the fifteenth day of the fifth month of the tax year of fiscal year foundations).

¶26,120 EXTENSION OF TIME TO PAY TAX

The IRS may grant a reasonable extension for payment of the tax. An extension may exceed six months (12 months in the case of estate tax) only for persons abroad. [Code Secs. 6161(a)(1), 6165; Reg. §§1.6161-1(b), 1.6165-1].

▶ **OBSERVATION:** Interest will run during the extension period until payment is made. Reason: A payment due date is determined without regard to any time extension [Ch. 27].

.01 Online Extension Option

Individual taxpayers may qualify for a short-term agreement to pay their delinquent tax bill if they have: (1) filed all required tax returns; (2) owe $50,000 or less in combined tax, penalties and interest; and (3) can fully pay their taxes in 120 days or less. Taxpayers can submit their application for a payment agreement through the Online Payment Agreement application which is available at IRS.gov.

.02 File Form 1127

If you do not have enough cash to pay (not file the return) the taxes when they are due, you can apply for an extension of time to pay the tax on Form 1127, *Application for Extension of Time for Payment of Tax Due to Undue Hardship* [Reg. §1.6161-1]. When you file Form 1127, you will have to show the undue hardship that would result if the extension request were not granted. You can establish undue hardship if you can show that it would be more than just inconvenient for you to pay the tax when due. For example, if you can show that the only way for you to pay the taxes would be to sell property at a "sacrifice" price, you may qualify for the extension. You must be able to show that you do not have enough cash, above necessary working capital, to pay the tax. In determining cash available, the IRS expects you to include anything you can convert into cash and to use current market prices. In addition, you must be able to show that you cannot borrow to pay the tax, except under terms that will cause you severe loss and hardship. Form 1127 even asks you to complete the following sentence: "I can't borrow to pay the tax because:" If you can't answer this question honestly, don't file Form 1127.

In addition to establishing undue hardship, you will have to include a statement of your assets and liabilities and an itemized statement showing all receipts and disbursements for each of the three months immediately preceding the due date of the tax owed. This 6-month payment extension request will only be considered by the

IRS if you file it by the due date of your tax return. If you want to pay the amount you owe in installments, rather than delay full payment of the tax for 6 months, rather than complete Form 1127, you should complete Form 9465, *Installment Agreement Request,* which is discussed further in ¶26,125.

Interest on Underpayments and Overpayments

See ¶27,115.

Deficiency

If the IRS is satisfied that payment of a deficiency on the prescribed date will result in undue hardship, it may extend the time to pay it for not more than 18 months, and in exceptional cases, for a further period not over 12 months. However, no extension is granted to pay a deficiency that is due to negligence, intentional disregard of rules and regulations, or fraud with intent to evade tax [Code Sec. 6161(b); Reg. §1.6161-1].

Estimated Tax

An extension of time extends the time to pay estimated tax; but the penalty for underpayment of estimated tax [¶14,200] runs from the original due date for payment.

¶26,125 PAYMENT PROCEDURES

.01 Even Dollar Reporting

You may file your tax returns in whole dollar amounts, instead of showing cents. This is done by eliminating any amount less than 50 cents and increasing any amount between 50 cents and 99 cents to the next higher dollar. This method of reporting applies only to the total amounts to be shown on any line of the return. It cannot be used to figure the various items that have to be totaled to determine the final amount on the line. You cannot change your choice after the due date of your return [Code Sec. 6102; Reg. §301.6102-1].

.02 How to Pay the Tax

The IRS offers several payment options to assist taxpayers in meeting their tax obligations. Options include an installment payment plan, credit card payments and direct debit payments from a checking or savings account. Taxpayers may also enter into an offer in compromise as discussed in ¶27,035. Taxpayers who enter into installment agreements will be charged a fee to set up the agreements, interest and late-payment penalties. The penalty, usually 0.5 percent of the balance due per month, is reduced to 0.25 percent when the IRS approves the agreement for an individual taxpayer who timely filed the return and did not receive a levy notice.

If you're sending a check or money order, make it payable to "United States Treasury" and include your social security number, a daytime phone number, the year and type of form filed—for example, "2013 Form 1040." Use the Form 1040-V payment voucher if you have one and do not staple the payment to the tax return. Send any 2013 estimated tax payment separately.

While e-filing your return by computer or telefiling your return by phone, you may authorize the Treasury to electronically withdraw your tax payment from your checking or savings account on a specified date. This is similar to the electronic funds withdrawals many people have for their monthly mortgage, auto, utility or insurance payments, except this withdrawal for income tax is a one-time payment. There is no charge for this service. This scheduled payment option is available through April 15.

Electronic Funds Withdrawal

You may also authorize an electronic withdrawal when requesting an extension by phone. Use Form 4868 as a worksheet to prepare for the call, but don't mail it to the IRS. You will also need the adjusted gross income from your tax return to authorize the withdrawal. Those not making a payment with the extension request will not need the prior year tax information. You will receive a confirmation number at the end of the call for your records. The extension request line is open 24 hours a day until the filing deadline.

Creditor Debit Card Payments

You may also charge your taxes to an American Express, Discover Card, MasterCard or VISA account by calling or using the Web site of one of the two processors handling such payments. The tax instructions have details on accessing these services. Private sector companies process the credit card transactions and charge convenience fees. The IRS does not collect such fees, nor does the IRS receive or store the credit card numbers. The cardholder's account statement will show the tax payment and the fee separately.

You may use a credit card to pay the balance due on your income tax return, to make a payment related to an automatic filing extension request, to make estimated tax payments for next year, or to make an installment payment on taxes owed for prior or later years. If you make an extension-related credit card payment—which may be done only through one of the two commercial processors—you need not file Form 4868 or call the IRS extension line.

.03 Pay on the Installment Plan

The IRS has the authority to enter into a written agreement with a taxpayer that allows the taxpayer to make scheduled periodic payments (installment payments) of any tax liability if the IRS determines that such agreement will facilitate full or partial collection of the tax liability and the taxpayer owes $50,000 or less in tax [Code Sec. 6159(a); Reg. § 301.6159-1(a)]. When the IRS enters into an installment agreement, the IRS agrees to defer payment in return for the taxpayer's promise to pay the full amount of tax due. Penalties and interest will continue to accrue on the unpaid liabilities during the course of the agreement. Generally, during the period installment payments are being made, other IRS enforcement actions (such as levies or seizures) with respect to the taxes included in that agreement are held in abeyance.

A streamlined approval process is available if the amount due is not more than $10,000 and the taxpayer can pay the tax liability within a five-year period [Code Sec. 6159(c)(1)]. To ask for an installment plan, attach Form 9465, *Installment Agreement Request,* to the front of the tax return, listing the proposed monthly payment amount and date. Taxpayers who owe more than $50,000 must also complete Form 433F, *Collection Information Statement*. An electronic funds withdrawal program is also available. The IRS imposes a fee of $105 ($52 if payment made by electronic withdrawal) for entering into an installment agreement. If the taxpayer's income is below a certain level, the taxpayer may qualify to pay a reduced fee of $43 [Reg. § 1.300.1].

The fee for restructuring or reinstating an installment agreement is $45 [Reg. § 1.300.2]. The taxpayer entering into the installment agreement is the person liable for payment of the fee [Reg. § 1.300-1]. Taxpayers will also pay interest plus a late payment penalty.

The decision to accept or reject installment agreements lies within the discretion of the IRS. The Internal Revenue Manual provides guidance for determining how much a taxpayer should be able to pay in a partial payment installment agreement and how much should be set aside for the taxpayer's necessary living expenses. When the IRS evaluates a taxpayer's ability to pay, the agency classifies a taxpayer's expenses as either (1) necessary expenses, or (2) conditional expenses. The total necessary expenses establish the minimum a taxpayer and family needs to live on. If a taxpayer requests a partial payment installment agreement, then the taxpayer is allowed only necessary expenses; conditional expenses are disallowed. The necessary expense test has two prongs but only one must be satisfied in order for an expense to be considered "necessary." The expense must provide for either (1) the taxpayer's health and welfare, or (2) the taxpayer's production of income.

In *G. Thompson*,[50] the court found that an IRS settlement officer did not abuse her discretion when she denied a reduction of a taxpayer's monthly installment payments for back taxes based upon a tithing obligation to his church. The IRS classified an individual's church tithing expenses as "conditional expenses" for purposes of determining how much the taxpayer could pay in a partial payment installment agreement.

The installment agreement will automatically terminate and you will owe all unpaid taxes if any of the following events occur:

1. The information provided to the IRS in applying for the installment agreement proved to be inaccurate or incomplete;
2. You miss an installment payment;
3. You fail to respond to the IRS request for an update of your financial condition;
4. You fail to pay another tax liability when it is due; or
5. The IRS fears that collection of the tax that you owe is in jeopardy.

If the IRS fears that collection of the tax is in jeopardy, the IRS is required to give you 30 days notice before altering, modifying or terminating your installment agreement [Code Sec. 6159(b)(5)(A); Reg. § 301.6159-1(e)(4)].

.04 Fresh Start

Under the IRS's Fresh Start Initiative,[51] which was created to help struggling taxpayers, the threshold for using an installment agreement without having to supply the IRS with a financial statement is $50,000. The maximum term for streamlined installment agreements is 72 months. In order to qualify for the IRS Fresh Start Initiative, a taxpayer must agree to monthly direct debit payments.

[50] *G. Thompson*, 140 TC No. 4, Dec. 59,469 (2013).

[51] IRS News Release IR-2012-31, March 7, 2012.

.05 Partial Payment Installment Agreements

If the taxpayer has not made full payment by the collection statute expiration date, and the taxpayer has some ability to pay, the IRS will grant a partial payment installment agreement [Code Sec. 6159(a), (d)]. When a partial installment agreement is in place, the IRS is no longer restricted to seeking a payment agreement that will "satisfy the liability." Instead, the goal of the agreement is to have the taxpayer "make payments" in "full or partial" satisfaction of the liability. If the taxpayer cannot pay the tax liability in full by the collection statute expiration date, and the taxpayer has some ability to pay, a partial payment installment agreement (PPIA) may be granted. In many cases, taxpayers will be required to use any equity in assets to pay liabilities. A PPIA may, however, be granted if a taxpayer has no assets or equity in assets, or has liquidated available assets to make partial payment. In an asset case, a PPIA may be granted if the taxpayer does not sell or cannot borrow against assets with equity because the assets have minimal equity or the equity is insufficient to allow a creditor to loan funds [IRM 5.14.2.1.2 (9-26-2008)].

When the IRS enters into a partial payment agreement with a taxpayer, the agreement must be reviewed by the IRS at least every two years [Code Sec. 6159(d); Reg. § 301.6159(i)]. When conducting the two-year review, the IRS will consider the taxpayers income and expenses, as well as assets and equity, to determine if the balance can be fully paid, an adjustment to the payment amount is necessary, or if the agreement should continue without change [IRM 5.14.2.1.6 (9-26-2008)].

In Rev. Proc. 2002-26,[52] the IRS provides guidance on how it will apply a partial payment of tax, penalty and interest for one or more taxable periods. The guidelines apply to all taxes with the exception of alcohol, tobacco and firearms taxes and the harbor maintenance tax. Voluntary partial payments of assessed tax, penalties and interest will be applied as designated by the taxpayer in specific written directions or pursuant to the terms of offers in compromise [¶ 27,035]and collateral agreements. If no designation is made, the payments will be allocated by the IRS to periods in the order of priority that it deems will serve its best interest.

¶26,130 ELECTRONIC FEDERAL TAX PAYMENT SYSTEM (EFTPS)

.01 How to Use EFTPS

The Electronic Federal Tax Payment System (EFTPS) is a free service offered by the U.S. Department of Treasury which enables individual and business taxpayers to pay federal taxes electronically 24/7 using the Internet, or by phone using the EFTPS Voice Response System. EFTPS can be used to make all federal tax payments, including income, employment, estimated and excise taxes. Businesses can schedule payments up to 120 days in advance. Individuals can schedule payments up to 365 days in advance. Scheduled payments can be changed or cancelled up to two business days in advance of the scheduled payment date. Tax professionals/provid-

[52] Rev. Proc. 2002-26, 2002-1 CB 746.

ers can register for EFTPS and send up to 1,000 enrollments and 5,000 payments in one transaction.

.02 Penalties Imposed for Failure to Use EFTPS

In a particularly harsh decision, a district court held that an employer had to pay a 10-percent underpayment penalty for failure to make required deposits of payroll taxes under the EFTPS even though the taxpayer paid all required amounts on a timely basis by payroll deposits at its local bank which was an authorized governmental depository.[53] This was the first time that a court ruled that the penalty applied for failure to use the EFTPS, even where deposits were made on time.

INFORMATION RETURNS

¶26,135 INFORMATION RETURNS IN GENERAL

.01 In General

The government uses information returns to verify that persons receiving certain kinds or amounts of income report the income on their income tax return. The information return may report payments made to others, transactions during the year, the taxable status of the taxpayer or other facts. The procedures for reporting on information returns are handled by several variations of Form 1099. For example, dividends are reported on Form 1099-DIV. Most information returns are prepared on a calendar year-cash basis, even if the person filing the return is on a fiscal year-accrual basis. They are filed at an IRS Center. But Forms W-2 (or 1099-R) and W-3 must be filed with the Social Security office listed in the form instructions. Payors may apply for permission to file Forms 1099 and Form W-2 on magnetic tape or other media [Reg. § 1.9101-1].

.02 When to File

Information returns are filed annually for a calendar year by the last day of February of the following year. A summary Form 1096 is filed at the same time. In most cases a copy of the information return should be sent to the person named as payee. If not, a statement of the information reported must be delivered to the payee by the January 31 before the return is filed.

Due Date for Electronically Filed Information Returns Extended

The due date for payors to electronically send the IRS a copy of the information returns that they sent to the taxpayers for such items as dividends, partnership distributions, and interest paid during the calendar year, is March 31 of the year following the calendar year to which the return relates [Code Sec. 6071(b)].

Payors can request a 30-day extension to file an information return. The payor's application for an extension to file an information return is made to the IRS officer with whom the person files the return, or would be required to file an income tax

[53] *F.E. Schumacher Co.*, DC-OH, 2004-1 USTC ¶ 50,166, 308 FSupp2d 819.

return [¶ 26,075]. It must state the Service Center where the information return will be filed [Reg. § 1.6081-1(a)].

.03 Penalties Imposed for Non-Compliance With Information Return Reporting

The IRS will impose the following penalties for non-compliance with information return reporting:

- Returns filed up to 30 days after the due date: $30 per return with a maximum of $250,000 per calendar year ($75,000 for small businesses);
- Returns filed after 30 days following the due date, but on or before August 1: $60 per return, with a maximum of $500,000 per calendar year ($200,000 for small businesses); and
- Returns filed after August 1: $100 per return, with a maximum of $1.5 million per calendar year ($500,000 for small businesses).

For these purposes, a small business has gross receipts of less than $5 million.

.04 Guide to Information Returns

Consult the following guide to information returns to determine what to report, the amount to report, and the due date for the report.[54]

[54] Treas. Dept., 2013 General Instructions for Certain Information Returns (Forms 1097, 1098, 1099, 3921, 3922, 5498, and W-2G), pp. 20-23.

Guide to Information Returns (If any date shown falls on a Saturday, Sunday, or legal holiday, the due date is the next business day.)

Form	Title	What To Report	Amounts To Report	Due Date	
				To IRS	To Recipient (unless indicated otherwise)
1042-S	Foreign Person's U.S. Source Income Subject to Withholding	Income such as interest, dividends, royalties, pensions and annuities, etc., and amounts withheld under Chapter 3. Also, distributions of effectively connected income by publicly traded partnerships or nominees.	See form instructions	March 15	March 15
1097-BTC	Bond Tax Credit	Tax credit bond credits to shareholders.	All amounts	February 28*	On or before the 15th day of the 2nd calendar month after the close of the calendar month in which the credit is allowed
1098	Mortgage Interest Statement	Mortgage interest (including points) and certain mortgage insurance premiums you received in the course of your trade or business from individuals and reimbursements of overpaid interest.	$600 or more	February 28*	(To Payer/Borrower) January 31
1098-C	Contributions of Motor Vehicles, Boats, and Airplanes	Information regarding a donated motor vehicle, boat, or airplane.	Gross proceeds of more than $500	February 28*	(To Donor) 30 days from date of sale or contribution
1098-E	Student Loan Interest Statement	Student loan interest received in the course of your trade or business.	$600 or more	February 28*	January 31
1098-T	Tuition Statement	Qualified tuition and related expenses, reimbursements or refunds, and scholarships or grants (optional).	See instructions	February 28*	January 31
1099-A	Acquisition or Abandonment of Secured Property	Information about the acquisition or abandonment of property that is security for a debt for which you are the lender.	All amounts	February 28*	(To Borrower) January 31
1099-B	Proceeds From Broker and Barter Exchange Transactions	Sales or redemptions of securities, futures transactions, commodities, and barter exchange transactions.	All amounts	February 28*	February 15**
1099-C	Cancellation of Debt	Cancellation of a debt owed to a financial institution, the Federal Government, a credit union, RTC, FDIC, NCUA, a military department, the U.S. Postal Service, the Postal Rate Commission, or any organization having a significant trade or business of lending money.	$600 or more	February 28*	January 31
1099-CAP	Changes in Corporate Control and Capital Structure	Information about cash, stock, or other property from an acquisition of control or the substantial change in capital structure of a corporation.	Over $1000	February 28*	(To Shareholders) January 31
1099-DIV	Dividends and Distributions	Distributions, such as dividends, capital gain distributions, or nontaxable distributions, that were paid on stock and liquidation distributions.	$10 or more, except $600 or more for liquidations	February 28*	January 31**
1099-G	Certain Government Payments	Unemployment compensation, state and local income tax refunds, agricultural payments, and taxable grants.	$10 or more for refunds and unemployment	February 28*	January 31
1099-H	Health Coverage Tax Credit (HCTC) Advance Payments	Health insurance premiums paid on behalf of certain individuals.	All amounts	February 28*	January 31
1099-INT	Interest Income	Interest income.	$10 or more ($600 or more in some cases)	February 28*	January 31**
1099-K	Payment Card and Third Party Network Transactions	Payment card transactions.	All amounts	February 28*	January 31
		Third party network transactions.	$20,000 or more **and** 200 or more transactions		
1099-LTC	Long-Term Care and Accelerated Death Benefits	Payments under a long-term care insurance contract and accelerated death benefits paid under a life insurance contract or by a viatical settlement provider.	All amounts	February 28*	January 31

*The due date is March 31 if filed electronically.
**The due date is March 15 for reporting by trustees and middlemen of WHFITs.

Guide to Information Returns (Continued)

Form	Title	What To Report	Amounts To Report	Due Date	
				To IRS	To Recipient (unless indicated otherwise)
1099-MISC	Miscellaneous Income	Rent or royalty payments; prizes and awards that are not for services, such as winnings on TV or radio shows.	$600 or more, except $10 or more for royalties	February 28*	January 31**
	(Also, use to report direct sales of $5,000 or more of consumer goods for resale.)	Payments to crew members by owners or operators of fishing boats including payments of proceeds from sale of catch.	All amounts		
		Section 409A income from nonqualified deferred compensation plans (NQDCs).	All amounts		
		Payments to a physician, physicians' corporation, or other supplier of health and medical services. Issued mainly by medical assistance programs or health and accident insurance plans.	$600 or more		
		Payments for services performed for a trade or business by people not treated as its employees. Examples: fees to subcontractors or directors and golden parachute payments.	$600 or more		
		Fish purchases paid in cash for resale.	$600 or more		
		Crop insurance proceeds.	$600 or more		
		Substitute dividends and tax-exempt interest payments reportable by brokers.	$10 or more		February 15**
		Gross proceeds paid to attorneys.	$600 or more		February 15**
1099-OID	Original Issue Discount	Original issue discount.	$10 or more	February 28*	January 31**
1099-PATR	Taxable Distributions Received From Cooperatives	Distributions from cooperatives passed through to their patrons including any domestic production activities deduction and certain pass-through credits.	$10 or more	February 28*	January 31
1099-Q	Payments From Qualified Education Programs (Under Sections 529 and 530)	Earnings from qualified tuition programs and Coverdell ESAs.	All amounts	February 28*	January 31
1099-R	Distributions From Pensions, Annuities, Retirement or Profit-Sharing Plans, IRAs, Insurance Contracts, etc.	Distributions from retirement or profit-sharing plans, any IRA, insurance contracts, and IRA recharacterizations.	$10 or more	February 28*	January 31
1099-S	Proceeds From Real Estate Transactions	Gross proceeds from the sale or exchange of real estate and certain royalty payments.	Generally, $600 or more	February 28*	February 15
1099-SA	Distributions From an HSA, Archer MSA, or Medicare Advantage MSA	Distributions from an HSA, Archer MSA, or Medicare Advantage MSA.	All amounts	February 28*	January 31
3921	Exercise of an Incentive Stock Option Under Section 422(b)	Transfer of stock pursuant to the exercise of an incentive stock option under section 422(b).	All amounts	February 28*	January 31
3922	Transfer of Stock Acquired Through an Employee Stock Purchase Plan Under Section 423(c)	Transfer of stock acquired through an employee stock purchase plan under section 423(c).	All amounts	February 28*	January 31

*The due date is March 31 if filed electronically.
**The due date is March 15 for reporting by trustees and middlemen of WHFITs.

Guide to Information Returns (Continued)

Form	Title	What To Report	Amounts To Report	Due Date To IRS	Due Date To Recipient (unless indicated otherwise)
5498	IRA Contribution Information	Contributions (including rollover contributions) to any individual retirement arrangement (IRA) including a SEP, SIMPLE, and Roth IRA; Roth conversions; IRA recharacterizations; and the fair market value (FMV) of the account.	All amounts	May 31	(To Participant) For FMV/RMD Jan 31; For contributions, May 31
5498-ESA	Coverdell ESA Contribution Information	Contributions (including rollover contributions) to a Coverdell ESA.	All amounts	May 31	April 30
5498-SA	HSA, Archer MSA, or Medicare Advantage MSA Information	Contributions to an HSA (including transfers and rollovers) or Archer MSA and the FMV of an HSA, Archer MSA, or Medicare Advantage MSA.	All amounts	May 31	(To Participant) May 31
W-2G	Certain Gambling Winnings	Gambling winnings from horse racing, dog racing, jai alai, lotteries, keno, bingo, slot machines, sweepstakes, wagering pools, poker tournaments, etc.	Generally, $600 or more; $1,200 or more from bingo or slot machines; $1,500 or more from keno	February 28*	January 31
				To SSA	**To Recipient**
W-2	Wage and Tax Statement	Wages, tips, other compensation; social security, Medicare, and withheld income taxes. Include bonuses, vacation allowances, severance pay, certain moving expense payments, some kinds of travel allowances, and third-party payments of sick pay.	See separate instructions	Last day of February*	January 31

*The due date is March 31 if filed electronically.

Types of Payments
Below is an alphabetic list of some payments and the forms to file and report them. However, it is not a complete list of all payments, and the absence of a payment from the list does not indicate that the payment is not reportable. For instructions on a specific type of payment, see the separate instructions in the form(s) listed.

Type of Payment	Report on Form
Abandonment	1099-A
Accelerated death benefits	1099-LTC
Acquisition of control	1099-CAP
Advance health insurance payments	1099-H
Agriculture payments	1099-G
Allocated tips	W-2
Alternate TAA payments	1099-G
Annuities	1099-R
Archer MSAs:	
Contributions	5498-SA
Distributions	1099-SA
Attorney, fees and gross proceeds	1099-MISC
Auto reimbursements, employee	W-2
Auto reimbursements, nonemployee	1099-MISC
Awards, employee	W-2
Awards, nonemployee	1099-MISC
Barter exchange income	1099-B
Bond tax credit	1097-BTC
Bonuses, employee	W-2
Bonuses, nonemployee	1099-MISC
Broker transactions	1099-B
Cancellation of debt	1099-C
Capital gain distributions	1099-DIV
Car expense, employee	W-2
Car expense, nonemployee	1099-MISC
Changes in capital structure	1099-CAP
Charitable gift annuities	1099-R
Commissions, employee	W-2
Commissions, nonemployee	1099-MISC
Commodities transactions	1099-B
Compensation, employee	W-2
Compensation, nonemployee	1099-MISC
Contributions of motor vehicles, boats, and airplanes	1098-C
Cost of current life insurance protection	1099-R
Coverdell ESA contributions	5498-ESA
Coverdell ESA distributions	1099-Q
Crop insurance proceeds	1099-MISC
Damages	1099-MISC
Death benefits	1099-R

Type of Payment	Report on Form
Accelerated	1099-LTC
Debt cancellation	1099-C
Dependent care payments	W-2
Direct rollovers	1099-Q, 1099-R, 5498
Direct sales of consumer products for resale	1099-MISC
Directors' fees	1099-MISC
Discharge of indebtedness	1099-C
Dividends	1099-DIV
Donation of motor vehicle	1098-C
Education loan interest	1098-E
Employee business expense reimbursement	W-2
Employee compensation	W-2
Excess deferrals, excess contributions, distributions of	1099-R
Exercise of incentive stock option under section 422(b)	3921
Fees, employee	W-2
Fees, nonemployee	1099-MISC
Fishing boat crew members proceeds	1099-MISC
Fish purchases for cash	1099-MISC
Foreclosures	1099-A
Foreign persons' income	1042-S
401(k) contributions	W-2
404(k) dividend	1099-DIV
Gambling winnings	W-2G
Golden parachute, employee	W-2
Golden parachute, nonemployee	1099-MISC
Grants, taxable	1099-G
Health care services	1099-MISC
Health insurance advance payments	1099-H
Health savings accounts:	
Contributions	5498-SA
Distributions	1099-SA
Income attributable to domestic production activities, deduction for	1099-PATR
Income tax refunds, state and local	1099-G
Indian gaming profits paid to tribal members	1099-MISC
Interest income	1099-INT
Tax-exempt	1099-INT
Interest, mortgage	1098
IRA contributions	5498
IRA distributions	1099-R
Life insurance contract distributions	1099-R, 1099-LTC
Liquidation, distributions in	1099-DIV
Loans, distribution from pension plan	1099-R
Long-term care benefits	1099-LTC
Medicare Advantage MSAs:	
Contributions	5498-SA
Distributions	1099-SA
Medical services	1099-MISC
Mileage, employee	W-2
Mileage, nonemployee	1099-MISC
Military retirement	1099-R
Mortgage insurance premiums	1098

Type of Payment	Report on Form
Mortgage interest	1098
Moving expense	W-2
Nonemployee compensation	1099-MISC
Nonqualified deferred compensation:	
Beneficiary	1099-R
Employee	W-2
Nonemployee	1099-MISC
Original issue discount (OID)	1099-OID
Patronage dividends	1099-PATR
Payment card transactions	1099-K
Pensions	1099-R
Points	1098
Prizes, employee	W-2
Prizes, nonemployee	1099-MISC
Profit-sharing plan	1099-R
Punitive damages	1099-MISC
Qualified plan distributions	1099-R
Qualified tuition program payments	1099-Q
Real estate transactions	1099-S
Recharacterized IRA contributions	1099-R, 5498
Refund, state and local tax	1099-G
Rents	1099-MISC
Retirement	1099-R
Roth conversion IRA contributions	5498
Roth conversion IRA distributions	1099-R
Roth IRA contributions	5498
Roth IRA distributions	1099-R
Royalties	1099-MISC
Timber, pay-as-cut contract	1099-S
Sales:	
Real estate	1099-S
Securities	1099-B
Section 1035 exchange	1099-R
SEP contributions	W-2, 5498
SEP distributions	1099-R
Severance pay	W-2
Sick pay	W-2
SIMPLE contributions	W-2, 5498
SIMPLE distributions	1099-R
Student loan interest	1098-E
Substitute payments in lieu of dividends or tax-exempt interest	1099-MISC
Supplemental unemployment	W-2
Tax refunds, state and local	1099-G
Third party network transactions	1099-K
Tips	W-2
Transfer of stock acquired through an employee stock purchase plan under section 423(c)	3922
Tuition	1098-T
Unemployment benefits	1099-G
Vacation allowance, employee	W-2
Vacation allowance, nonemployee	1099-MISC
Wages	W-2

¶26,140 RETURN FOR BUSINESS PAYMENTS

.01 In General

Code Sec. 6041 provides that all persons engaged in a trade or business (including a partnership or nonprofit organization) that make certain payments in the course of that trade or business to another person of $600 or more in a tax year must file information returns reporting all payments and the name and address of the recipient. This filing requirement is commonly known as the "$600-or-more" rule. A separate return is required for each payee. Except for payments to employees [discussed below], returns are made on the appropriate Form 1099, with summary Form 1096, and filed by February 28 of the following year [Code Sec. 6041; Reg. § 1.6041-6]. The return requirement is met if a surviving business entity (i.e., a corporation, partnership, or sole partnership) following a merger or acquisition files a return with all the required information.[55]

What Is a Trade or Business

A "trade or business" is not limited to activities for gain or profit [Reg. § 1.6041-1(b)]. Tax-exempt organizations must file information returns if they make payments that qualify.[56] This applies to exempt as well as nonexempt trusts, to insurance companies making payments under any nontrusteed annuity plan, to trustees paying supplemental unemployment benefits from a trust created with employer contributions,[57] to self-employed retirement plans [Reg. § 1.6041-2(b)], to those making Medicare or Medicaid payments, and to those making direct payments to doctors or others providing health care services under certain insurance plans.

Who Is Subject to $600-or-More Rule

The reporting obligation applies if the total of all payments made by the payor in any tax year is $600 or more, even though the amount for any class of payment by itself is less than $600. Payments that must be reported include:

- Salaries, wages, commissions, fees, incentive awards and other forms of compensation;
- Interest, rents, royalties, annuities, pensions, and other gains, profits and income.

Reg. § 1.6041-1(d) lists the following payments that are specifically covered by the "$600-or-more" rule.

- Payments on life insurance, endowment, or annuity contracts have to be reported unless: (1) the payment is made due to an insured's death, (2) the payment is made as a result of the surrender or lapse of a policy other than one purchased under a qualified annuity plan or a tax-exempt employee trust, a tax-exempt organization, or a public school, or (3) the payment is a payment where a return is required by Reg. § 1.6047-1, relating to employee retirement plans covering owner-employees, or Reg. § 1.6052-1, relating to compensation in the form of group-term life insurance.
- Interest payments made on insurance policies.

[55] Rev. Proc. 99-50, 1999-2 CB 757.
[56] Rev. Rul. 56-176, 1956-1 CB 560.
[57] Rev. Rul. 62-54, 1962-1 CB 285.

- Fees paid in the course of a trade or business for the services of nonemployees, such as subcontractors, directors, or physicians.
- Prizes or awards paid in the course of a trade or business, such as winnings on television or radio programs, are reportable if they exceed $600.
- Gambling winnings of $600 or more ($1,200 or more from bingo or slot machine play and $1,500 or more from keno games) must also be reported.
- Amounts paid with respect to notional principal contracts, including embedded interest, generally are reportable payments. Reporting is not required if the payments are made to an exempt recipient, paid outside the United States (unless the payor has actual knowledge that the payee is a U.S. person), treated as effectively connected with a U.S. trade or business or paid by a non-U.S. payor or non-U.S. middleman.
- Distributions paid to shareholders by corporations in liquidation of the whole or any part of their capital stock.
- Rents collected by a rental agent on behalf of a property owner and welfare payments.

Exceptions

Payments made to the following entities are not required to file information returns under the Code Sec. 6041 "$600-or-more" rule: corporations, exempt organizations, governmental entities, international organizations, and retirement plans [Reg. § 1.6041–3(p)].

Fees Deducted from Payments

The amount to be reported as paid to a payee is the gross amount of the payment or payments before fees, commissions, expenses, or other amounts owed by the payee to another person have been deducted, whether the payment is made jointly or separately to the payee and the other person [Reg. § 1.6041-1(f)(1)].

Example 26-16: Attorney *P* represents client *Q* in a breach of contract action for lost profits against defendant *R*. *R* settles the case for $100,000 damages and $40,000 for attorney fees. *R* issues a check payable to *P* and *Q* in the amount of $140,000. *R* is required to make an information return reporting a payment to *Q* in the amount of $140,000 [Reg. § 1.6041-1(f)(2), Ex. 1].

Example 26-17: Assume the same facts as in Example 26-16, except that *R* issues a check to *Q* for $100,000 and a separate check to *P* for $40,000. *R* is required to make an information return reporting a payment to *Q* in the amount of $140,000 [Reg. § 1.6041-1(f)(2), Ex. 2].

Real Owner Must Be Disclosed

When anyone who is not the actual owner receives a payment for which an information return must be filed, he or she must supply the actual owner's name and address to the payor on demand [Reg. § 1.6041-5]. Failure to do so is punishable by a $25,000 ($100,000 for corporations) fine, one year in prison, or both [Code Sec. 7203].

Payments on Behalf of Another

A reportable payment may be made by one person on behalf of another person who is the actual source of the funds. In some cases, the "real payor" is required to report the payment, while in other cases, the "middleman" is required to do the reporting [Reg. § 1.6041-1(e)(1)]. Reg. § 1.6041-1(e)(1) makes it clear that a middleman must file an information return reporting a payment only if:

1. The middleman performs management or oversight functions in connection with the payment, rather than just administrative or ministerial functions. For example, a paying agent who merely writes checks at the direction of others is performing only an administrative or ministerial function and is not a payor for purposes of the information return requirements. On the other hand, a person who exercises discretion or supervision in connection with a payment is performing a management or oversight function and is a payor.
2. The middleman has a significant economic interest that would be compromised if the payment was not made. For example, a bank has a significant interest in a payment to a contractor when damage occurs to property securing a mortgage held by the bank.

Example 26-18: Community Bank provides financing to a real estate developer for a construction project. The bank puts the funds in an escrow account from which it makes disbursements for labor, materials, services, and other expenses relating to the project. The bank's services include approving payments to contractors and subcontractors; ensuring that loan proceeds are properly applied and that all bills are properly paid to avoid mechanic's or materialmen's liens; conducting site inspections to determine whether work has been completed; and evaluating and assessing costs of the project. Under Reg. § 1.6041-1(e)(1), Community Bank is treated as performing management or oversight functions and must file information returns for payments from the escrow fund.

Notice to Payees

Payors' information returns for business payments of $600 or more must be furnished to the person to whom the information relates [Code Sec. 6041(d)]. A penalty is imposed for failure to furnish such a statement [Ch. 27]. The separate mailing requirements with statements for payors of interest, dividends and patronage dividends who must give notice of information returns to payors have been eased.

.02 Payments to Employees

Employers report their employees' wages on Form W-2 [¶ 15,140]. In addition, employers must report all payments of compensation (whether or not subject to withholding) on Form W-2 if the total of these payments, such as group-term life insurance [¶ 26,160] plus wages, equals at least $600. At the employer's option, more than one Form W-2 may be used to report components of reportable amounts paid to each employee. Life insurance companies may report commissions paid to full-time life insurance salespersons and any taxable group-term life insurance premiums on Forms W-2 and W-3 [Reg. §§ 1.6041-2(a); 1.6052-1]. The time for filing Forms W-2 and W-3 is the same as for the reporting of withheld taxes [¶ 15,140]. When Form W-3 does not include any wages subject to withholding, it may be filed by February 28 of the following year [Reg. §§ 1.6041-2(a)(3); 1.6052-1(b)]. File returns on Forms 1096 and 1099 by the same date with the Revenue Service Center listed in form instructions. See also ¶ 26,075.

Taxpayers must use Form 1099-R, *Distributions from Pensions, Annuities, Retirement or Profit-Sharing Plans, IRAs, Insurance Contracts, etc.*, to report annuity and pension payments when the payments total $600 or more during the calendar year or when tax has been withheld on these payments. For those payments under $600 or not subject to withholding, use of the form is optional [Reg. § 31.3402(o)-2(f)]. Form 1099R must also be filed to report lump-sum distributions from profit-sharing and retirement plans.

> **NOTE:** Form 1099-R has been changed to reflect the fact that direct rollovers are exempt from 20 percent withholding that hits most other retirement plan payouts [Ch. 3]. There are new codes for reporting direct rollovers on Form 1099-R, and the IRS will assume it is entitled to a 20 percent cut of payouts that don't contain the code.

Payments totaling only $10 or more made to an owner-employee [Ch. 3] under a self-employed retirement plan must be reported on Form 1099-R. The first year contributions to the plan are made for him, the owner-employee must notify the trustee or insurer (for annuity contracts) of that fact not later than February 28 of the following year [Code Sec. 6047(b); Reg. § 1.6047-1].

Unemployment Compensation

Form 1099-G is used by payors who report payment of $10 or more of unemployment compensation during the calendar year [Ch. 5] [Code Sec. 6050B(a); Reg. § 1.6050B-1].

Electronic Tip Reporting Systems

For further discussion of reporting requirements regarding tips, see ¶ 15,015.

.03 Payments of Fees or Tax Refunds

Fees of $600 or more that are paid in the course of a taxpayer's trade or business to attorneys, public accountants, physicians, and members of other professions are reportable on Form 1099-MISC [Code Sec. 6041(a); Reg. § 1.6041-1(d)(2)]. Form 1099-MISC is also used for filing information returns for payments to health care service suppliers.

Report by Government Agencies

State and local agencies must file information returns on Form 1099-G, *Certain Government Payments*, as to income tax refunds, credits, and offsets aggregating $10 or more to any individual. Such information need not be furnished for individuals who do not claim itemized deductions on their federal income tax returns. When a return is required, the reporting agency must furnish the individual with a statement by the end of January of the year after the calendar year in which the refund was made or the credit or offset allowed [Code Sec. 6050E; Reg. § 1.6050E-1]. The appropriate federal officer must file information returns relating to social security and railroad retirement benefits and must furnish recipients with a copy of the statement [Code Secs. 6050F, 6050G].

Federal executive agencies must make information reporting on persons receiving federal contracts from the agency. However, the general information reporting requirements do not apply to: (a) contracts that are "classified" or (b) contracts involving a confidential law enforcement or foreign counterintelligence activity. These types of contracts are subject to a special form of reporting [Code Sec. 6050M].

.04 Payments of Fixed or Determinable Income

Taxpayer's must file Form 1099-MISC, *Miscellaneous Income*, for rent, services, prizes and awards, medical and health care payments, crop insurance proceeds, cash payments for fish purchased from anyone in the trade or business of catching fish, or generally the cash paid from a notional principal contract to an individual, partnership or estate, and other "fixed or determinable income" of $600 or more. Only payments in the course of a trade or business during the calendar year to an individual citizen or resident, a resident fiduciary, or a resident partnership, any member of which is a citizen or resident, must be reported [Reg. § § 1.6041-1(a), -3]. A resident partnership is one engaged in trade or business in the U.S. [Reg. § 301.7701-5]. Literary agents must report the gross amount of royalties received for their authors before deducting commissions, fees and expenses. See ¶ 26,145 for interest payments; ¶ 26,150 for dividends.

Example 26-19: Mr. Sloan works on straight salary for Agency Insurance, a partnership. He was paid $9,800 in commissions direct from insurance companies. He, in turn, paid the $9,800 to Agency. Sloan must file an information return for the payment. If Agency were a corporation, Sloan would not have to file.

Joint Payees

When a payment is made payable to joint payees, it may be considered "fixed and determinable income" to one payee even though the payment is not fixed and determinable income to another payee [Reg. § 1.6041-1(c)]. For example, when a payment in consideration for services is made payable to joint payees, one of whom is the service provider, an information return must be made showing the service provider as the payee if the payment is fixed and determinable income to the service provider, even if the payment is not fixed and determinable income to the other payee.

Rent Payments

Taxpayers must report rent paid directly to a landlord (other than a corporation) in the course of their trade or business on Form 1099-MISC if payments for the year amount to $600 or more. However, they need not make a report if they pay the rent to a real estate agent. The agent must file the information return if payments by the agent to the landlord (other than a corporation) during the year amount to $600 or more. The agent must report the gross amount collected for the landlord before deducting his commission or expenses. If the landlord is a corporation, no return is required from the tenant or the agent [Reg. § 1.6041-3(d)].

Royalties

Taxpayers must report payments made totaling $10 or more during a calendar year on Form 1099-MISC. Royalties required to be reported include payments for the right to exploit natural resources, such as oil, gas, coal, timber, sand, gravel, and other mineral interests, as well as payments for the right to exploit intangible property, such as copyrights, trade names, trademarks, books and other literary compositions, musical compositions, artistic works, secret processes or formulas, and patents [Code Sec. 6050N]. Payees who fail to supply TINs are subject to backup withholding rules [Ch. 14] [Code Sec. 3406(b)(3)(E)].

Pensions, Annuities, and Other Deferred Income

Employers, plan administrators, or other payors who withhold tax from pensions, annuities, and other deferred income [Ch. 15] must file information returns [Code Sec. 6047(d)]. Penalties are imposed for failure to comply [Ch. 27].

.05 Payments to Independent Contractors

If taxpayers pay an independent contractor for services performed in the course of their trade or business, they must file an information return if it's $600 or more for the year [Code Sec. 6041A(a)].

.06 Direct Sellers of Consumer Goods

Direct sellers who sell consumer goods on a buy-sell, deposit-commission or similar basis to a buyer who buys $5,000 or more in one year must file an information return 1099-MISC [Code Sec. 6041A(b)].

.07 Brokers

Code Sec. 6045(a) generally requires every person doing business as a broker to file an information return showing the name and address of the broker's customer and the customer's adjusted basis in the security sold and to identify whether any gain or loss is long-term or short-term. A broker is defined as a person who, in the ordinary course of a trade or business, stands ready to effect sales by others and includes a dealer, a middleman in a barter exchange, or any other person who acts as a middleman for consideration [Reg. § 1.6045-1(a)(1)]. The broker and any dealer acting as a middleman is required to make an information return for each sale effected by the broker in the ordinary course of the broker's trade or business. The sale must be reported on Form 1099-B, *Proceeds From Broker and Barter Exchange Transactions*, and must include the following sale information: (1) name, address, and taxpayer identification number of the customer; (2) property sold; (3) the Committee on Uniform Security Identification Procedures (CUSIP) number of the security sold (if known); (4) gross proceeds; (5) sale date; and (6) such other information as may be required by Form 1099 [Reg. § 1.6045-1(d)(2)].

The IRS has concluded that the information reporting requirements imposed on a broker who sells stock over the Internet do not differ from the reporting requirements imposed on other traditional sales of stock which are not over the Internet. Thus, the reporting requirements for a broker who sells stock over the Internet are the same as any other sale of stock not taking place over the Internet.

Brokers must furnish a statement of information reported to the IRS to the customer by January of the year after the year for which the return is filed. Failure to comply may be subject to a maximum penalty of $50,000 for the year [Code Sec. 6045; Reg. § 1.6045-1].

Farm managers are exempt from filing Form 1099-B for their farm management activities. This information must be filed by them on a Schedule F where it is provided in a more useful format [Code Sec. 6045(c)].

The IRS has said that a corporation redeeming its stock can report the redemption payouts on Form 1099-B. The corporation doesn't have to sort out which payments are taxed as dividends. The corporation should attach to each Form 1099-B an explanation stating that the corporation is using the form to report redemption payouts without classifying the proceeds as income or gain.

▶ **OBSERVATION:** Brokers must report securities and commodities sales transactions except for sales to exempt customers as defined in the regulations [Reg. § 1.6045-1]. Also, brokers must furnish customers with statements detailing certain in-lieu payments they receive on customers' securities that were transferred in a short sale open transaction. In addition, information return Form 1099 with transmittal Form 1096 must be filed annually for such brokers' statements.

Stock Basis Reporting Requirements

Code Sec. 6045(g) provides that in the case of a "covered security," every securities broker who is required to report the gross proceeds from the sale of the security under Code Sec. 6045(a) must also report the customer's adjusted basis in the security and whether any gain or loss with respect to the security is long-term or short-term. A "covered security" includes stock, notes, bonds, other evidences of debt, commodities, and derivatives.

The adjusted basis and type of gain must be reported:

- For most stock acquired on or after January 1, 2011;
- For stock in a mutual fund (regulated investment company or RIC) or a dividend reinvestment plan (DRP) acquired on or after January 1, 2012; and
- For other securities and options acquired on or after January 1, 2013 (extended to January 1, 2014).[58]

In general, stock basis is reported using the first-in, first-out (FIFO) method of specific identification method. The average basis method may be used by brokers or sellers for RIC stock or DRP stock in a corporation. Brokers have until February 15 to furnish certain information statements to customers and the IRS. Stock brokers and mutual fund companies will generally use Form 1099-B, *Proceeds from Broker and Barter Exchange Transactions,* to comply with the expanded year-end reporting requirements.

To enable brokers to satisfy these requirements for securities transferred between accounts, Code Sec. 6045A provides that a broker and any other person that transfers custody of a covered security to a receiving broker must furnish to the receiving broker a written statement that allows the receiving broker to satisfy the basis reporting requirements of Code Sec. 6045(g). The statement must be furnished within 15 days after the date of the transfer.

To enable brokers to satisfy the requirements of Code Sec. 6045(g) after a stock split, merger, or acquisition that affects basis, Code Sec. 6045B provides that an issuer must report to the IRS and to each stockholder a description of any such action and the quantitative effect of that action on basis. Form 8937, *Report of Organizational Actions Affecting Basis of Securities* should be used by issuers of a specified security to report any organizational action (such as a stock split, merger or acquisition) that affects the basis of stock.

---

58 Notice 2012-34, IRB 2012-21, 937.

Specific Identification of Securities

In general, a broker must report a sale on or after January 1, 2011, of less than the entire position in an account that was acquired on different dates or at different prices consistently with a customer's adequate and timely identification of the security [Reg. § 1.1012-1(c)]. If the customer does not provide adequate instruction, the broker must report the sale of any shares on a FIFO basis [Reg. § 1.6045-1(d)(2)(ii)].

Average Basis Method

The basis of RIC stock is computed using the average basis method which means that the costs of all shares in the account are averaged. Taxpayers may elect to use the average basis method for RIC stock acquired at different prices and maintained by a custodian or agent in an account for the periodic acquisition, redemption, sale, or other disposition of the stock [Reg. § 1.1012-1(e)(1)].

DRP Defined

A dividend reinvestment plan (DRP) is any written plan, arrangement, or program under which at least 10 percent of every dividend on any share of stock is reinvested in stock identical to the stock on which the dividend is paid. A plan that holds one or more different stocks may permit a taxpayer to reinvest a different percentage of dividends in the stocks held. A DRP may reinvest other distributions on stock, such as capital gain distributions, nontaxable returns of capital, and cash in lieu of fractional shares [Reg. § 1.1012-1(e)(6)(i)].

Stock is acquired in connection with a DRP if the stock is acquired under that plan or if the dividends and other distributions paid on the stock are subject to that plan [Reg. § 1.1012-1(e)(6)(ii)]. Shares of stock acquired in connection with a DRP include the initial purchase of stock in the dividend reinvestment plan, transfers of identical stock into the DRP, additional periodic purchases of identical stock in the DRP, and identical stock acquired through reinvestment of the dividends or other distributions paid on the stock held in the plan.

Election of Average Basis Method

A taxpayer makes an election to use the average basis method for shares of stock that are covered securities by notifying the custodian or agent in writing by any reasonable means including electronic format. A taxpayer may make the average basis method election at any time, effective for sales occurring after the taxpayer notifies the custodian or agent. The election must identify each account and each stock in that account to which the election applies. The election may specify that it applies to all accounts with a particular agent, including accounts the taxpayer later establishes with the agent [Reg. § 1.1012-1(e)(9)].

A taxpayer may revoke an election by the earlier of one year after the taxpayer makes the election or the date of the first sale of that stock following the election. An agent may extend the one-year period but a taxpayer may not revoke an election after the first sale of the stock. A revocation applies to all stock the taxpayer holds in an account that is identical to the shares of stock for which the taxpayer revokes the election. A revocation is effective when the taxpayer notifies the agent holding the stock to which the revocation applies in writing. After revocation, the taxpayer's basis in the shares of stock to which the revocation applies is the basis before averaging [Reg. § 1.1012-1(e)(9)(iii)].

A taxpayer may change basis determination methods from the average basis method to another method prospectively at any time by notifying the agent holding the stock in writing. A change from the average basis method applies on an account by account basis to all identical stock the taxpayer sells or otherwise disposes of on or after January 1, 2012 [Reg. § 1.1012-1(e)(9)(iv)].

Basis Computation

Reg. § 1.1012-1(e)(7) provides that average basis is determined by averaging the basis of all shares of identical stock in an account regardless of holding period. However, shares of stock in a DRP are not identical to shares of stock with the same CUSIP number if they are not in a DRP. The basis of each share of identical stock in the account is the aggregate basis of all shares of that stock in the account divided by the aggregate number of shares.

Order of Disposed Shares Sold or Transferred

In the case of the sale or transfer of shares of stock to which the average basis method election applies, shares sold are deemed to be the shares first acquired. If the number of shares sold or transferred exceeds the number of long-term shares in the account, the excess shares sold or transferred are deemed to be shares with a holding period of one year or less (short-term shares). Any gain or loss attributable to shares held for more than one year constitutes long-term gain or loss, and any gain or loss attributable to shares held for one year or less constitutes short-term gain or loss.

> **Example 26-20:** If a taxpayer sells 50 shares from an account containing 100 long-term shares and 100 short-term shares, the shares sold or transferred are all long-term shares. If, however, the account contains 40 long-term shares and 100 short-term shares, the taxpayer has sold 40 long-term shares and 10 short-term shares.

Reporting of Sales by S Corporations

Code Sec. 6045(g)(4) requires brokers to begin Form 1099-B reporting for S corporations (other than a financial institution) for sales of covered securities acquired on or after January 1, 2012.

Penalties Imposed for Failure to Comply

Code Sec. 6722 imposes a penalty on any transferor that fails to timely furnish a correct transfer statement under Code Sec. 6045A to the receiving broker. Soley for transfers of stock in 2011, the IRS will not assert penalties under Code Sec. 6722 for a failure to furnish a transfer statement under Code Sec. 6045A, and the transferred stock may be treated as a noncovered security upon its subsequent sale or transfer.[59]

Certain Realty Transactions

Information return reporting is required on Form 1099-S, *Proceeds From Real Estate Transaction* for transactions involving the sale or exchange of real estate including the following:

---

[59] Notice 2010-67, IRB 2010-43, 529.

- Improved or unimproved land, including air space.
- Inherently permanent structures, including any residential, commercial, or industrial building.
- A condominium unit and its appurtenant fixtures and common elements, including land.
- Stock in a cooperative housing corporation.

The party responsible for reporting both to the IRS and the seller is the *first* of the following who participates in the transaction: settlement agent (the person who prepares the statement); attorney for the buyer (the one who prepares documents transferring title); attorney for the seller (if he or she prepares the documents); the disbursing title or escrow company that disburses the most significant proceeds; mortgage lender; the seller's broker; the buyer's broker; and the buyer. The TIN of seller and total cash received must be listed on the Form 1099-S. Withholding is not required. Special rules apply to magnetic media reporting. The same filing dates apply here as do to other Forms 1099. The form is due to the IRS on February 28. It's unlawful for any real estate reporting person to separately charge any customer for complying with the information reporting requirements as to real estate transactions [Code Sec. 6045(e)(3)]. However, a real estate reporting person may take into account the cost of complying with Code Sec. 6045 reporting requirements when setting the service fees it will charge customers provided it does not list that cost as a separate charge.

An exemption from these reporting requirements exists for any sale or exchange of a residence of $250,000 or less for a single taxpayer (or $500,000 or less for a married taxpayer), if the real estate reporting person (generally, the person responsible for closing the transaction) receives written assurance, in a form acceptable to the IRS, from the seller that: (1) the residence is the seller's principal residence (as defined in Code Sec. 121); (2) if the real estate sale or exchange information requires disclosure as to whether there is federally subsidized mortgage financing assistance with respect to mortgages on residences, there is no such assistance with respect to the mortgage on the seller's residence; and (3) the full amount of the gain on the sale or exchange is excludable from the seller's gross income under Code Sec. 121 [Code Sec. 6045(e)(5)(A)]. Thus, information returns will generally not be required for sales of personal residences where the sales price does not exceed the amount eligible to be excluded from gross income under Code Sec. 121.

A real estate reporting person must obtain the following written assurances from the seller of a principal residence (including stock in a cooperative housing corporation) for that sale or exchange to be excepted from the reporting requirements of Code Sec. 6045(e):[60]

1. The seller owned and used the residence as the seller's principal residence for periods aggregating two years or more during the five-year period ending on the date of the sale or exchange of the residence.
2. The seller has not sold or exchanged another principal residence during the two-year period ending on the date of the sale or exchange of the residence.

---

[60] Rev. Proc. 2007-12, 2007-1 CB 354.

3. No portion of the residence has been used for business or rental purposes after May 6, 1997, by the seller (or by the seller's spouse or former spouse, if the seller was married at any time after May 6, 1997).
4. At least one of the following three statements applies:
   a. The sale or exchange is of the entire residence for $250,000 or less; or
   b. The seller is married, the sale or exchange is of the entire residence for $500,000 or less, and the gain on the sale or exchange of the entire residence is $250,000 or less; or
   c. The seller is married, the sale or exchange is of the entire residence for $500,000 or less, and (i) the seller intends to file a joint return for the year of the sale or exchange, (ii) the seller's spouse also used the residence as his or her principal residence for periods aggregating two years or more during the five-year period ending on the date of the sale or exchange, and (iii) the seller's spouse also has not sold or exchanged another principal residence during the two-year period ending on the date of the sale or exchange.
5. During the five-year period ending on the date of the sale or exchange of the residence, the seller did not acquire the residence in a like-kind exchange;
6. In cases where the seller's basis in the residence is determined by reference to the basis in the hands of a person who acquired the residence in a like-kind exchange, the like-kind exchange occurred more than five years prior to the date of the seller's sale or exchange of the residence.

The IRS has drafted a sample certification form.[61] Even though use of this form is recommended to be certain that all assurances required by the IRS are obtained, use of the IRS certification form is not mandatory.

Deadlines

The reporting person must obtain certifications any time on or before January 31 of the year following the year of the sale or exchange and the certification must be retained for four years after the year of the sale or exchange.

How to Avoid Penalties

Real estate reporting persons who rely on a certification that complies with IRS requirements will not be liable for penalties under Code Sec. 6721 for failure to file an information return or under Code Sec. 6722 for failure to furnish a payee statement to the seller. Penalties would apply, however, if the real estate reporting person had actual knowledge that any assurance is incorrect.

> ▶ **PRACTICE POINTER:** Qualifying for the exception to information reporting requirements does not excuse the seller from reporting sale of the home on Schedule D (Form 1040) of his or her federal income tax return [Ch. 7].

.08 Debt Reporting

Lenders (including the U.S. or a state) must report foreclosures or other acquisitions of property in full or partial satisfaction of a debt or debts on Form 1099-A. They

[61] Rev. Proc. 2007-12, 2007-1 CB 354.

must also report abandonments of secured property and must furnish statements to borrowers no later than January 31 of the following year. Reporting, however, is not required for consumer loans [Code Sec. 6050J]. Banks and other financial institutions must report the discharge of a borrower's debt of $600 or more. A copy of the information return must be provided to the borrower by January 31 of the year following the year of discharge [Code Sec. 6050P]. Financial entities must report discharges of debt of $600 or more on Form 1099-C and must specify the name, address, and taxpayer identification number of each person for which there was a debt discharge that constituted an "identifiable event" during the calendar year [Reg. § 1.6050P-1(d)(1)(i)]. Aggregation of multiple debt discharges of less than $600 is generally not necessary. Debt is considered discharged, and reporting is required, only if the following identifiable events occur: (1) a chapter 11 bankruptcy discharge of debt; (2) debt cancellation or extinguishment rendering the obligation unenforceable in receivership, foreclosure, or similar federal or state court proceedings; (3) debt cancellation or extinguishment upon the expiration of either the limitations period of collection or the statutory period for filing a claim or commencing a deficiency judgment proceeding; (4) debt cancellation or extinguishment pursuant to a creditor's election of foreclosure remedies that bars further collection efforts; (5) debt cancellation or extinguishment rendering the obligation unenforceable pursuant to a probate or similar proceeding; (6) a debt discharge at less than full consideration in accordance with an agreement between a financial entity and a debtor; (7) a debt discharge pursuant to a decision by the creditor, or the application of a defined policy of the creditor, to discontinue collection activity; or (8) the expiration of the nonpayment testing period.

.09 Exchange of Partnership Interests

A partner must notify the partnership if a partnership interest involving unrealized receivables or appreciated inventory is transferred. After notice, the partnership must file an information return that identifies the transferor and the transferee and furnish them a statement of the information shown on the return by January 31 of the following year [Code Sec. 6050K; Reg. § 1.6050K-1].

.10 Charitable Contributions

Donations of $250 or more must be substantiated by the charity for the donor to claim a deduction. However, the donor does not need the receipt if the charity files an information return that substantiates the amount of the contribution [Code Sec. 170(f)(8)(d)].

Information Return by Donee Relating to Dispositions of Donated Property

A charity must also file an information return if (1) it disposes of a property contribution within three years after receiving the property and (2) the donor has claimed a tax deduction in excess of $5,000. The return, which is filed on Form 8282, *Donee Information Return,* must identify the donor, the property and the sale [Code Sec. 6050L; Reg. § 1.6050L-1].

Disclosure Related to Quid Pro Quo Contribution

Charities are also required to inform donors in writing how much of the donor's contribution of more than $75 is deductible if the donor receives anything of more than token value in exchange for the contribution [Code Sec. 6115(a)].

Example 26-21: Donor makes contribution to ABC charity of $125 in exchange for theater tickets worth $60. ABC must inform donor either when gift is solicited or when it's received by donor that the deduction is $65. The charity is subject to penalties if it doesn't inform donors [Code Sec. 6714].

.11 Business Cash Receipts of $10,000 or More

Taxpayers who receive more than $10,000 cash or foreign currency in a lump sum in a 12-month period from one buyer as a result of a transaction in a trade or business must report the identity of the payor, the amount of cash received and the date and nature of the transaction to the IRS on Form 8300, *Report of Cash Payments Over $10,000 Received in a Trade or Business* [Code Sec. 6050I; Reg. § 1.6050-1]. Cash received in excess of $10,000 on the account of another must be reported by the business physically handling the cash.[62] Form 8300 may also be used to report cash transactions under § 5331 of the Bank Secrecy Act which requires any person who is engaged in a nonfinancial trade or business and receives more than $10,000 in coins or currency in one transaction (or two or more related transactions) to file a report with the Treasury Department's Financial Crimes Enforcement Network. Failure to comply with the reporting requirements may subject you to criminal as well as civil sanctions. If you intentionally disregard the reporting requirements you may be subject to a penalty equal to the greater of $25,000, or the amount of the cash involved (up to $100,000).

Taxpayers need not file Form 8300 if the transaction is not related to their trade or business. For example, if you own a jewelry store and sell your personal automobile for more than $10,000 in cash, you would not submit a Form 8300 for that transaction.

Cash includes U.S. coins and currency of the United States, as well as cashier's checks, traveler's checks, money orders and foreign coins and currency that circulates and is commonly accepted as money in the country in which it was issued.

If you are involved in what the IRS calls a *designated reporting transaction,* which is the retail sale of consumer durables, collectibles, or travel or entertainment, you are subject to the reporting requirements if you receive a cashier's check, bank check, bank draft, traveler's check or money order having a face amount of $10,000 or *less* in one or more related transactions. These cash equivalents are treated as cash and impose the cash reporting requirements on the recipient. This "$10,000 or less" provision works in conjunction with the duty imposed on the check or money-order issuer to report cash transaction of $10,000 or more, and is intended to eliminate duplicate reporting of the same transaction.

A *consumer durable* is a product that is:

1. Suitable under ordinary usage for personal consumption or use;
2. That can reasonably be expected to be useful for at least one year under ordinary usage; and
3. That has a sales price of more than $10,000.

For example, a $20,000 car is a consumer durable even if it is sold for business use, but a $20,000 dump truck or a $20,000 factory machine is not.

---

[62] LTR 200644017 (Aug. 1, 2006).

A collectible includes works of art, antiques, rugs, metals, gems, stamps, coins, and alcoholic beverages. A travel or entertainment activity relates to a single trip or event with a total sales price of more than $10,000 for the entire travel package.

Exceptions

A cashier's check, bank draft, traveler's check or money order received in a designated reporting transaction will not be treated as cash if it is really one of the following:

1. Loan proceeds;
2. Promissory notes or installment sales contracts;
3. Down payment plans.

Example 26-22: Don purchases gold coins from Marvin, a coin dealer, for $13,200. Don gives Marvin U.S. dollars in the amount of $6,200 and a cashier's check in the face amount of $7,000. Because the sale is a designated reporting transaction, the cashier's check is treated as cash. Therefore, because Marvin has received more than $10,000 in cash, Marvin must complete the report required by Code Sec. 6050I.

Example 26-23: Fran purchases a sapphire ring from a retail jeweler for $12,000. Fran gives the jeweler traveler's checks totaling $2,400 and pays the balance with a personal check in the amount of $9,600. Because the sale is a designated reporting transaction, the traveler's checks are treated as cash for reporting purposes. However, because the personal check is not treated as cash for purposes of Code Sec. 6050I, the jeweler has not received more than $10,000 in cash in the transaction and no report must be filed.

Example 26-24: Gus purchases a boat from Tom, a boat dealer, for $16,500. Gus pays Tom with a cashier's check in the amount of $16,500. The cashier's check is not treated as cash because the face amount of the check is more than $10,000. Tom need not file a report.

Receiving the Cash for the Account of Another

Cash in excess of $10,000 received by a person who in the course of a trade or business acts as an agent for someone else is also subject to the reporting requirements unless the agent uses all of the cash within 15 days in a second cash transaction which is: (1) reportable to IRS under Code Sec. 6050I, and (2) the agent discloses the name, address, and taxpayer identification number of the principal (the person for whom he received the money).

Example 26-25: Sam Black gives his attorney $75,000 in cash to purchase a piece of land on his behalf. Within 15 days the attorney purchases the property for cash from a real estate developer. The attorney discloses to the developer Sam's name, address, and taxpayer identification number. The attorney need not report the initial receipt of cash. If the facts are changed a little, the result would be different. For example, if the attorney pays the developer by means other than cash, or buys the property more than 15 days following receipt of the cash from Sam, or fails to disclose Sam's name, address and taxpayer identification number, or purchases the property from a person whose sale of the property is not in the course of that person's trade or business, the attorney would be required to report the receipt of cash from Sam.

When a clerk of a federal or state court receives more than $10,000 in cash as bail, the clerk must report the receipt on an information return [Code Sec. 6050I(g)(5)(B)]. If multiple payments are made to satisfy bail and the initial payment does not exceed $10,000, the initial payment and subsequent payments must be aggregated and the information return required by Code Sec. 6050I(g) must be filed by the 15th day after receipt of the payment that caused the aggregate amount to exceed $10,000. However, payments made to satisfy separate bail requirements need not be aggregated [Reg. § 6050I-2].

What Types of Transactions Are Covered

The reporting requirements arise only in a qualifying transaction. The term *transaction* includes but is not limited to the following: (1) A sale of goods or services; (2) A sale of realty property; (3) A sale of intangible property; (4) A rental of real or personal property; (5) An exchange of cash for other cash; (6) The establishment or maintenance of or contribution to a custodial trust, or escrow arrangement; (7) A payment of a preexisting debt; (8) A conversion of cash to a negotiable instrument; (9) A reimbursement for expenses paid; or (10) The making or repayment of a loan.

You may not divide a transaction into multiple transactions in order to avoid reporting requirements.

Related Transactions

Cash paid in "related transactions" will be aggregated for purposes of the reporting rules. The term *related transactions* means any transaction conducted between two parties in a 24-hour period. In addition, transactions between the same parties over more than 24 hours are related transactions if the recipient knows, or has reason to know that each transaction is one of a series of connected transactions.

How to Report

Cash transactions must be reported to the IRS on Form 8300 within 15 days after the date the cash was received. The return must contain the following:

(1) The name, address, and taxpayer identification number of the person paying the cash; (2) The amount of cash received; (3) The date and nature of the transaction.

A statement must be sent to anyone identified on Form 8300 as a cash payer by January 31 of the year following the year in which the cash is received. In addition, anyone required to file Form 8300 must keep a copy of each return filed for five years.

.12 Mortgage Interest of $600 or More

Taxpayers who receive mortgage interest (including points) of $600 or more in the course of a trade or business from individuals and reimbursements of overpaid interest must file Form 1098, *Mortgage Interest Statement.* The return must identify the payor/borrower and the aggregate amount of interest received. A written statement must be furnished to the payor by January 31 of the following year. The form is due to the IRS on February 28. Returns must also report the points paid and if these points were paid directly by the borrower [Code Sec. 6050H]. The reporting requirements apply to points payable in connection with any residential loan, regardless of whether the loan is a conventional loan, or is insured by the Federal Housing Administration or the Department of Veteran's Affairs. Excluded from the definition of reportable points are amounts paid to improve a taxpayer's principal residence. Points paid to refinance land contracts and similar forms of seller-financed transactions, however, should not be reported on Form 1098 because only points paid on the acquisition of the residence are reportable under the final regulations [Reg. § 1.6050H-1].

In addition, regulations require interest recipients to report certain reimbursements of overpayments on a mortgage [Reg. § 1.6050H-2(a)(2)(iv)].[63] For penalties, see Ch. 27.

If you sell your home and take back a mortgage (a so-called seller-financed mortgage), you do not have to file Form 1099-S. For seller-financed mortgages the seller and buyer must report each other's name, address and taxpayer identification number on his or her return.

.13 Long-Term Care Benefits

Any person paying long-term care benefits must file an information return disclosing the following: the name, address and taxpayer identification number (TIN) of each recipient; the name, address, and TIN of the chronically ill person on whose account the benefits were paid; the aggregate amount of benefits paid to each recipient during the calendar year; and whether the payments are made on a per diem basis or other periodic basis without regard to the actual expenses for that period [Code Sec. 6050Q]. A statement must be furnished to each recipient setting forth the name of the payor, its address, the telephone number of an information contact and the aggregate amount of reportable benefits paid during the calendar year. This statement must be furnished to the recipient on or before January 31 of the year following the year of payment.

Employers paying long-term care expenses should use Form 1099-LTC, *Long-Term Care and Accelerated Death Benefits,* to report the aggregate benefits paid and other information required under Code Sec. 6050Q. File Form 1099-LTC with the IRS. File Form 1099-LTC with the policyholder and file Form 1099-LTC with the insured.

.14 Payments to Attorneys

Any person engaged in a trade or business is required to report payments made to an attorney in connection with legal services (whether or not the services were performed for the payor) [Code Sec. 6045(f)]. The reporting requirement doesn't apply to the part of any payment that must be reported (1) under Code Sec. 6041(a) (trade or business payments of $600 or more reported on Form 1099-MISC, or that would have to be reported but for the $600 limit); or (2) under Code Sec. 6051 (wages reported on Form W-2) [Code Sec. 6045(f)(2)(B)].

Business taxpayers must report payments to attorneys and/or law firms in connection with legal services (whether or not such services are performed for the payor) on Form 1099-B, *Proceeds From Broker and Barter Exchange Transactions* [Code Sec. 6045(f)].

---

[63] Rev. Rul. 92-91, 1992-2 CB 49.

The only exception to this new reporting requirement is for payments reported on Form 1099-Misc. (reports of payments of income) or on Form W-2 (payments of wages). The exception in Reg. § 1.6041-3(c) from reporting any payments made to corporations does not apply to payments made to attorneys. The reporting requirements apply to payments made to attorneys regardless of whether the attorney is the exclusive payee. In addition, attorneys are required to promptly supply their TINs to persons required to file these information reports. Failure to do so could result in the attorney being subject to penalty under Code Sec. 6723 and the payments being subject to backup withholding.

> ▶ **PRACTICE POINTER:** Be sure there is no overlap of reporting payments for services rendered and payments to settle a case. For example, if two payments are simultaneously made to an attorney, one of which represents the attorney's fee and the second of which represents the settlement with the attorney's client, the first payment would be reported but the second payment would not because it represents the settlement with the client and no portion of its represents income to the attorney.

.15 Schools Receiving Student Loan Interest

An educational institution receiving payments of interest from students, if the interest may be deductible by the students, must report that interest to the IRS on Form 1098-E, *Student Loan Interest Statement*.

.16 Recipients of Federal Agency Contract Payments

Information reporting is required for persons receiving contract payments of $600 from a Federal executive agency [Code Sec. 6041A(d)(3)]. This reporting requirement applies to any person (including a corporation) who performed services for the Federal agency and received payments of $600 or more. An exception exists for certain classified or confidential contracts [Code Sec. 6041A(d)(3)(B)]. Note that this is a reduction from a prior $25,000 reporting threshold that existed in Reg. § 1.6050M-1(c)(1)(i).

.17 Payment Card and Third-Party Settlement Organizations (TPSOs)

Code Sec. 6050W requires credit card companies and third-party settlement organizations (TPSOs) to annually file with the IRS, starting with transactions in calendar year 2013, aggregate transaction reports listing their total annual payments to merchants that receive more than $20,000 and conduct more than 200 transactions each year [Code Sec. 6050W(e)].[64] The reporting requirement also applies to transactions settled through third-party payments networks, such as third-party organizations that settle online transactions [Code Sec. 6050W(b)]. A payment card includes, but is not limited to credit cards, debit cards, and most stored-value cards, such as gift cards [Code Sec. 6050W(d)(2); Reg. § 1.6050W-1(b)(3)].

Taxpayers must report, with respect to each participating payee, the gross amount of the aggregate reportable payment transactions for the calendar year and the gross amount of the aggregate reportable payment transactions for each month of the

[64] See General FAQs on Payment Card and Third Party Network Transactions (Feb. 21, 2013); Payment Card Transactions FAQs (Feb. 21, 2013); Third Party Network Transactions FAQs (Feb. 21, 2013).

calendar year [Code Sec. 6050W(F); Reg. § 1.6050W-1(a)(1)].[65] A participating payee, in the case of a payment card transaction, is any person who accepts a payment card as payment. In the case of a third-party network transaction, a participating payee is any person who accepts payment from a third-party settlement organization in settlement of the transaction.

Taxpayers should use Form 1099-K, *Payment Card and Third-Party Network Transactions,* to report the required information.[66] An insurance company or an affiliate administering a self-insured arrangement on behalf of an employer or other entity on a cost-plus basis or under an Administrative Services Only plan or an Administrative Services Contract plan will not be treated as a third-party settlement organization and therefore will not be subject to Code Sec. 6050W's reporting requirements.[67]

The return must be filed on or before February 28th (March 31st if filing electronically) of the following year [Reg. § 1.6050W-1(g)].

¶26,145 RETURNS FOR INTEREST PAID

.01 In General

File Form 1099-INT, *Interest Income,* for each person as follows: (1) if you paid interest in excess of $10 (except for the $600 limit for interest paid in the course of your trade or business) [¶26,140]; (2) for whom you withheld and paid any foreign tax on interest [¶26,185]; (3) from whom you withheld any Federal income tax under the backup withholding rules regardless of the amount of the payment. The return shows the amount paid and the payee's name, address and TIN. The payor can demand the name and address of the actual owner of the payment [Code Sec. 6041(a), (c); Reg. §§ 1.6041-1(a), -5]. Tax-exempt interest must also be reported on the tax return.

Report only interest payments made in the course of your trade or business including Federal, state, and local government agencies and activities deemed nonprofit, or for which you were a nominee/middleman. Report interest that is treated as original issue discount (OID) on Form 1099-OID, not on Form 1099-INT.

The return may be filed any time in the last quarter of the year after the final payment for the year is made. It must be filed at a Service Center by February 28 of the following year [Reg. § 1.6049-4(g)(1)].

Not Reported

You are not required to file Form 1099-INT for payments made to certain payees including the following: (1) a corporation; (2) a tax-exempt organization; (3) any IRA; (4) a U.S. agency; (5) a state; (6) the District of Columbia; (7) a U.S. possession; or (8) a registered securities or commodities dealer.

NOTE: Do not report tax-exempt or tax-deferred interest, such as interest on municipal bonds or interest that is earned but not distributed from an IRA.

---

[65] Notice 2011-88, IRB 2011-46; Notice 2013-56, IRB 2013-39, 262.

[66] LTR 201219013 (Jan. 30, 2012) (a company need not file Form 1099-K because not TPSOs (third-party settlement organizations) operating a third-party payment network. Therefore, no information reporting obligation.).

[67] Notice 2011-78, IRB 2011-41, 497.

An exempt-interest dividend from a regulated investment company (RIC), or a mutual fund, retains its tax-exempt status and is not reported on Form 1099-INT or Form 1099-DIV.

Notice to Payee

The payor must give the payee a statement that the payments are being reported to the IRS, with the amount and the payor's name and address. A copy of the return (Form 1099-INT) is used. The notice must be delivered by January 31 of the year following the year the payments were made. [Code Sec. 6049(c)].

.02 Interest Payment Defined

Generally, interest is paid when it is credited or set apart for a person without any substantial limitation or restriction as to the time, manner, or condition of payment. The interest must be made available so that it may be drawn on at any time and its receipt brought within the control and disposition of the person. For payments made on obligations subject to transactional reporting (e.g., savings bonds, interest coupons, and other demand obligations), interest is paid at the time the obligation is presented for payment. For example, interest on a coupon detached from a bond is paid when it is presented for payment.

.03 Successor/Predecessor Corporation

A successor corporation and a predecessor corporation may agree that the successor corporation will file one Form 1099-INT for each payee combining the reportable interest paid by both corporations. If the two corporations do not agree, or if other requirements described below are not met, the predecessor must file Forms 1099-INT to report the interest payments it made during the year, and the successor must file Form 1099-INT to report its own payments. The combined reporting procedure is available only when all the following conditions are met: (1) the successor corporation acquires substantially all the assets and assumes substantially all the liabilities of the predecessor corporation; (2) during the year of acquisition, but before the acquisition, the predecessor made reportable interest payments to payees; (3) during the year of acquisition, but after the acquisition, the predecessor did not make any reportable interest payments.

The predecessor and successor must agree that the successor assumes the predecessor's entire obligation to file Forms 1099-INT for reportable interest payments made in the year of acquisition. If they so agree and if the successor satisfies the predecessor's obligation, the predecessor does not have to file Forms 1099-INT. The Form 1099-INT filed by the successor for each payee must include the reportable interest payments made by the predecessor in the acquisition year and the reportable interest payments made by the successor in that year. Any backup withholding must also be combined on the form. When providing Form 1099-INT, or an acceptable substitute, to the interest recipient, the successor may include additional information explaining the aggregate reporting of the interest.

By the due date of the Forms 1099-INT, the successor must file a statement containing the following: (1) an indication that Forms 1099-INT are being filed on a combined basis; (2) the name, address, and employer identification numbers of both the successor and predecessor corporations.

.04 REMICs and Issuers of CDOs

The following taxpayers must file Form 1099-INT: real estate mortgage investment conduits (REMICs); issuers of collateralized debt obligations (CDOs); and, any broker or middleman who holds as a nominee a REMIC regular interest or CDO. The form is used to report interest of $10 or more, other than OID, accrued to a REMIC regular interest holder during the year or paid to the holder of a CDO. If you are also reporting OID, this interest and the OID can be reported on Form 1099-OID. You do not have to file both Forms 1099-INT and 1099-OID. You are not required to file or issue Form 1099-INT for exempt recipients including the following holders of REMIC regular interest or a CDO: (1) a corporation; (2) a broker; (3) a middleman/nominee; (4) a financial institution; (5) any IRA or MSA; and (6) a tax-exempt organization [Reg. § 1.6049-7(c)].

¶26,150 RETURNS FOR DIVIDENDS PAID

File Form 1099-DIV, *Dividends and Distributions,* to report the payment of dividends aggregating $10 or more in a calendar year to any person. In addition, file Form 1099-DIV if: (1) you have withheld and paid any foreign tax on dividends and other distributions on stock; (2) if you have withheld any federal income tax under the backup withholding rule [Ch. 14]; or (3) if you paid $600 or more as part of a liquidation.

The taxpayer identification number of the person to whom the dividends are paid and any amount of tax deducted and withheld from the dividends under the backup withholding rules of Code Sec. 3406, must also be shown on the forms [Reg. § 1.6042-2(a)(1)(ii)].

The corporation or broker paying the dividend and completing the Form 1099-DIV may demand the name of the actual owner, and failure to supply this name subjects the nominee to penalties. Some record owners who file a fiduciary return (Form 1041) that discloses the actual owner of the dividends need not file Form 1099-DIV. Nominees receiving dividends as custodians of mutual fund investment trusts file Forms 1096 and 1099-DIV unless the regulated investment company directly notifies the actual owners [Reg. § 1.6042-2(a)].

The return may be filed during the last quarter of the year after the final dividend payment. It must be filed at a Service Center by February 28 (March 31 if filed electronically) of the following year [Reg. § 1.6042-2(c)]. In addition to filing information returns with the IRS, payors must furnish statements (Form 1099-DIV) to the payees either in person or in a separate mailing by first-class mail. The time for furnishing the statement is after November 30 of the year and on or before January 31 of the following year, but not before the final dividend payment for the calendar year has been made [Reg. § 1.6042-4(c)].

If nontaxable dividends are paid by corporations that are not S corporations making actual distributions of previously taxed income, the dividends must be reported by the corporations on Form 5452, *Corporate Report of Nondividend Distributions.* This form should be filed with the corporation's income tax return. If the required information is not supplied, the distribution may be considered fully taxable.[68] A corporation making a nondividend distribution will be granted an extension of time to file Form 5452 if the corporation: (1) has not filed its tax return for the year, and (2) has not advised its shareholders that they have received nondividend distributions, and (3) is not requesting an extension beyond 9 months from the due date for filing its tax return (without extensions).

.01 Payments Not Reported

Taxpayers are not required to report on Form 1099-DIV the following:

1. Taxable dividends distributions from life insurance contracts and employee stock ownership plans are reported on Form 1099-R, *Distributions From Pensions, Annuities, Retirements or Profit-Sharing Plans, IRAs, Insurance Contracts, etc.*
2. Exempt-interest dividends from regulated investment companies retain their tax-exempt status but are reported on Form 1099-INT.
3. Substitute payments in lieu of dividends. These may be reported on a composite statement to the recipient with Form 1099-DIV.
4. Payments made to certain payees including a corporation, tax-exempt organization, any IRA, Archer MSA, or health savings account (HSA), U.S. agency, state, the District of Columbia, U.S. possession, or registered securities or commodities dealer.

.02 Patronage Dividends

Exempt farmers' cooperatives and corporations taxed as cooperatives [Ch. 23] must report patronage dividends and per-unit retain allocations [Ch. 23] of $10 or more on Form 1099-PATR, *Taxable Distributions Received From Cooperatives,* with the IRS by January 31 and send statements to the payees by February 28 [Code Sec. 6044; Reg. §§1.6044-2 and 1.6044-5]. Consumer cooperatives may apply on Form 3491, *Consumer Cooperative Exemption Application,* for exemption from reporting [Reg. §1.6044-4]. Information returns must be filed for reportable patronage dividends on which backup withholding tax [Ch. 14] was withheld, regardless of the amount. See ¶26,140.

Taxpayers are not required to file Form 1099-PATR for payments made to a corporation, tax-exempt organization including tax-exempt trusts (HSAs, Archer MSAs, and Coverdell ESAs), the United States, a state, a possession, or the District of Columbia [Reg. §1.6044-3(c)].

¶26,155 REPORTING REQUIREMENTS IMPOSED ON CORPORATIONS WHEN EMPLOYEES EXERCISE STOCK OPTIONS

Corporate employers must file information returns with the IRS regarding transfers of stock to employees within any calendar year if the transfer is (1) made in connection with the exercise of an incentive stock option, or (2) made under an

[68] Rev. Proc. 75-17, 1975-1 CB 677.

employee stock purchase plan where the option price is between 85 and 100 percent of the value of the stock [Code Sec. 6039(a)]. The corporation must continue to provide payee information to its employees regarding these stock transfers. The corporation must furnish each person it names in its information return with a written payee statement by January 31 of the following calendar year setting forth the information that the IRS may require [Code Sec. 6039(b)]. Failure to correctly provide this information may subject the corporation to a penalty [Code Sec. 6724(d)(2)(B)].

¶26,160 GROUP-TERM LIFE INSURANCE PREMIUMS

If a corporation pays group-term life insurance premiums that are taxable to an employee, the corporation must report the taxable amount for each employee on Form W-2 and the summary Form W-3 [Code Sec. 6052(a); Reg. § 1.6052-1(a)(1)]. Insurance companies must report the taxable amount for full-time insurance salespersons on the same or separate Form W-2 that reports an employee's tax withheld from wages. The employee's copy of Form W-2 serves as the statement that must be given to the employee by the January 31 preceding the filing date [Reg. § § 1.6052-1(b), -2(c)]. For further discussion of group-term life insurance see ¶ 2035, ¶ 15,015.01.

¶26,165 CERTAIN LIQUIDATIONS OR TERMINATIONS

A corporation in dissolution or liquidating any part of its capital stock, must file a report of the plan and the distributions made.

.01 Report on Plan

A corporation (or a farmer's cooperative) must file information Form 966, *Corporate Dissolution or Liquidation*, with the IRS office where it files its income tax return within 30 days after the adoption of a resolution or plan for dissolution of the corporation or for the liquidation of the whole or any part of its capital stock [Code Sec. 6043(a); Reg. § 1.6043-1(a)]. The return must be accompanied by a certified copy of the resolution or plan and all amendments to it [Reg. § 1.6043-1(b)(1)]. Exempt organizations and qualified subchapter S subsidiaries should not file Form 966.

.02 Return for Distributions

Information returns (Form 1099-DIV) must be filed for distributions in liquidation of $600 or more. They must be accompanied by Form 1096 and filed by February 28 of the year after the calendar year the distribution is made [Code Sec. 6043; Reg. § 1.6043-2(a)].

¶26,170 INFORMATION RETURNS FOR TAX-EXEMPT ORGANIZATIONS AND TRUSTS

Every tax-exempt organization must file an annual information return reporting items of gross income, receipts, disbursements and other information required by the IRS [Code Sec. 6033(a)(1)]. See also ¶ 23,106 for further discussion of reporting requirements imposed on tax-exempt organizations. Tax-exempt organizations must file Form 990, *Return of Organizations Exempt from Income Tax,* if gross receipts are greater than $200,000 and total assets are greater than $500,000. This return functions as the primary source of information about the organization's finances, governance, operations, and programs. Some members of the public rely on Form 990 as their primary or sole source of information about the tax-exempt organization.

Form 900-EZ, ***Short Form Return of Organization Exempt from Income Tax,*** may be filed if gross receipts are less than $200,000 and total assets are less than $500,000.

.01 Small Tax-Exempts May File e-Postcard

Small tax-exempt organizations may file the simpler Form 990-N, *Electronic Notice (e-Postcard) for Tax-Exempt Organizations Not Required to File Form 990 or 990-EZ,* rather than the standard Form 990 or Form 990-EZ if their annual gross receipts are $50,000 or less [Code Sec. 6033(i); Reg. § 1.6033-6].

An exempt foreign organization or exempt United States possession organization can submit Form 990-N if: (1) it normally does not receive more than $50,000 in annual gross receipts from U.S. sources; and (2) it has no significant activity in the United States including lobbying and political activity and the operation of a trade or business (excluding investment activity).

If at any time a tax-exempt organization no longer satisfies the requirements, the organization is required to file an annual return on Form 990 for the year in which it first ceased to qualify for relief and for all subsequent years in which the organization fails to qualify.

The annual gross receipts of an organization are normally not more than $50,000 if:

1. The organization has been in existence for one year or less, the organization's gross receipts, including amounts pledged by donors, are $75,000 or less during its first tax year;
2. The organization has been in existence for more than one year, but less than three years, the organization's average annual gross receipts for its first two tax years is $60,000 or less; and
3. The organization has been in existence for three years or more, the organization's average annual gross receipts for the immediately preceding three tax years, including the tax year for which the return is filed, is $50,000 or less.

This simplified reporting requirement does not apply to private foundations, Code Sec. 509(a)(3) supporting organizations, or political organizations exempt from income tax under Code Sec. 527.

.02 Tax Exempt Entity Reporting Requirements Expanded

The IRS may require that the annual information return filed by a Code Sec. 501(c)(3) charitable organization include information regarding the disaster relief activities conducted by the charity [Code Sec. 6033(b)(14)]. This includes the use of "qualified contributions" made by individuals to the charity which are not subject to the 50-percent contribution base deduction limitation for charitable contributions and the limitation on overall itemized deductions, as well as "qualified contributions" made by corporations to the charity which are not subject to the 10-percent of taxable income deduction limitation [Code Sec. 1400S(a)].

.03 Tax-Exempts Receiving Intellectual Property Contributions Subject to Strict Information Reporting Rules

Tax-exempt entities receiving donations of "qualified intellectual property" which includes certain copyrights, trademarks, trade name, trade secret, know-how, certain software, or similar intellectual property must file an information return with the IRS under Code Sec. 6050L if they sell or exchange those properties within three years after receipt [Reg. § 1.6050L-2(a)]. The return must contain information identifying the exempt organization, information identifying the donor, description of the intellectual property, the date of contribution, and the amount of income the exempt organization received during the tax year that is allocable to the intellectual property [Reg. § 1.6050L-2(b)]. Tax-exempts must report their receipt of intellectual property on Form 8899, *Notification of Income From Donated Intellectual Property.*

.04 Exemption from Filing

The following organizations are exempt from these filing requirements:

- Church, an interchurch organization of local units of a church, a convention or association of churches, or an integrated auxiliary of a church such as a men's or women's organization, religious school, mission society or youth group.
- A church-affiliated organization that is exclusively engaged in managing funds or maintaining retirement programs.
- A school below college level affiliated with a church or operated by a religious order.
- A mission society sponsored by or affiliated with one or more churches or church denominations, if more than half of the society's activities are directed at persons in foreign countries.
- An exclusively religious activity of any religious order.
- A state institution whose income is excluded from gross income.
- A government unit or affiliate of a governmental unit.
- A tax-exempt Code Sec. 501(c)(1) organization that is in instrumentality of the United States and organized under an Act of Congress.
- A political organization that is (a) a state or local committee of a political party; (b) a political committee of a state or local candidate; (c) a caucus or association of state or local officials; or (d) required to report as a political committee.
- An organization with gross receipts of $25,000 or less.
- A foreign organization, including organizations located in U.S. possessions, whose gross receipts from sources within the U.S. are normally $25,000 or less.

.05 Loss of Exempt Status for Failure to File Return or Notice

If a tax-exempt organization fails to file a required annual return or notice for three consecutive years, the organization's tax-exempt status will be considered revoked on and after the date set for the filing of the third annual return or notice. Any organization whose tax-exempt status was revoked must apply in order to obtain reinstatement of such status regardless of whether such organization was originally required to make an application. If the organization can show evidence of reasonable cause for the failure to file, the organization's exempt status may be reinstated effective from the date of the revocation [Code Sec. 6033(j)].

How Tax-Exempts Can Reinstate Lost Tax-Exempt Status

When tax-exempt organizations have their tax exempt status automatically revoked under Code Sec. 6033(j), Rev. Proc. 2011-36[69] provides a reduced user fee for reinstatement of that tax-exempt status. The reduced user fee applies only to small organizations that normally have annual gross receipts of no more than $50,000 in their most recently completed tax year.

In Notice 2011-43,[70] the IRS provided for retroactive reinstatement of tax-exempt status where a small exempt organization has had its exemption revoked for failure to file Form 990-N for three consecutive years. To regain its exempt status, the organization must apply for reinstatement and show reasonable cause for its consecutive filing failures. Small organizations that are eligible for the relief are also eligible for a reduced user fee of $100 for reinstatement of exempt status.

.06 Failure to File Certain Statements and Information Returns

A tax-exempt entity or an entity manager who fails to file a disclosure under Code Sec. 6033(a)(2) must pay $100 for each day the failure continues. The maximum penalty with respect to one disclosure must not exceed $50,000. The IRS may make a written demand, specifying a reasonable future date by which disclosure must be filed, on any tax-exempt entity subject to the penalty. Any person who fails to comply with such demand must pay $100 for each day after the expiration of the time specified in the demand during which the failure continues. The maximum penalty for failures with respect to any one disclosure must not exceed $10,000 [Code Sec. 6652(c)(3)].

Tax-exempt organizations and non-exempt charitable trusts are required to file Form 990, *Return of Organization Exempt From Income Tax,* to provide the information required by Code Sec. 6033. The penalty for failure to file Form 990 or for failure to include all required information on Form 990 is $20 for each day the failure continues. The maximum penalty per return is $10,000 or five percent of the organization's gross receipts, whichever is less. However, organizations with annual gross receipts exceeding $1 million are subject to an increased penalty of $100 per day, with a maximum penalty of $50,000 [Code Sec. 6652(c)(1)(A)]. No penalty is imposed if the filing failure in question is due to reasonable cause [Code Sec. 6652(c)(4)].

.07 Penalties Increased on Split-Interest Trusts

The penalties are increased for split interest trusts that fail to file Form 1041-A, *U.S. Information Return Trust Accumulation of Charitable Amounts,* as required by Code Sec. 6034. Penalties are generally increased from $10 to $20 per day, with a maximum penalty of $10,000, for any one return. Split interest trusts with gross incomes in excess of $250,000 face higher penalties of $100 per day with a maximum penalty of $50,000. An additional penalty may be assessed against a person required to file a Form 1041-A who knowingly fails to file the return [Code Sec. 6652(c)(2)(C)].

---

[69] Rev. Proc. 2011-36, IRB 2011-25, 915.

[70] Notice 2011-43, IRB 2011-37, 326.

¶26,180 PARTNERSHIP, FIDUCIARY, S CORPORATION, AND LIMITED LIABILITY COMPANY RETURNS

Information returns must be filed by a partnership, fiduciary, or S corporation. Trusts, estates, partnerships and S corporations must furnish copies of their information returns to beneficiaries, partners, or shareholders [Code Sec. 6034A, 6037(b)].

.01 Partnership Returns

The partnership return, Form 1065, is an information return of the partnership income and its distribution to the partners [¶24,020]. File Form 1065 by the 15th day of the fourth month following the close of the partnership tax year [Code Sec. 6031; Reg. §1.6031-1]. (If all partners are nonresident aliens, the return may be filed by the 15th day of the sixth month after the tax year. A partnership not engaged in U.S. trade or business and having no U.S. source income need not file a return.) Your partnership must furnish you and its other partners with copies of the information shown on its return. If your partnership has tax-exempt partners, it must supply them with information needed to compute what portion of its distributive share of income or loss is relevant to unrelated business income [Code Sec. 6031(b), (d)].

An electing large partnership must furnish Forms K-1 to its partners by March 15 following the close of the partnership's tax year [Code Sec. 6031(b)].

File Form 1065 with the District Director for the district where the partnership's principal office or place of business is located or, if none, with the Director, International Operations Division, unless instructions require filing elsewhere.

Partnerships with more than 100 partners must file their returns electronically [Code Sec. 6011(e)(2); Reg. §301.6011-3(a)]. Partnership returns filed electronically must consist of Form 1065, Schedules K-1, and related forms and schedules. Form 8453-PE, *U.S. Partnership Declaration for an IRS e-file Return,* will serve as the required signature document for the Form 1065 return. The telephone system (modem) is the only method of transmitting Form 1065 data electronically. All electronic Forms 1065 must be transmitted to the Tennessee Computing Center (TCC) in Memphis, TN. The following partnerships are excluded from having to file electronically: (1) fiscal year filers, (2) final year tax returns, (3) short year returns, (4) foreign-address partnerships, and (5) delinquent and amended returns.

Reg. §301.6011-3(b) permits the IRS to waive the electronic filing requirement if the partnership demonstrates that a hardship would result if it were required to file its return electronically. To request a waiver, a partnership must submit a written statement, signed under penalty of perjury by the tax matters partners, containing the following elements:

1. A notation at the top of the request stating, in large letters, "Form 1065 e-file Waiver Request: IRC Section 6011 (e)(2);"
2. The name, federal tax identification number, and mailing address of the partnership;
3. The tax year for which the waiver is requested;

4. A detailed statement which lists: (a) the steps the partnership has taken in an attempt to meet its requirement to file its return electronically, (b) why the steps were unsuccessful, (c) the hardship that would result, including any incremental cost to the partnership, of complying with the electronic filing requirements. Incremental costs are those costs that are above and beyond the costs to file on paper. The incremental costs must be supported by a detailed computation. The detailed computation must include a schedule detailing the costs to file on paper and the costs to file electronically;
5. A statement as to what steps the partnership will take to assure its ability to electronically file its partnership return for the next tax year; and
6. A statement signed by the Tax Matters Partner indicating: "Under penalties of perjury, I declare that the information contained in this waiver request is true, correct and complete to the best of my knowledge and belief."

.02 Return Requirements Imposed on U.S. Partners in Foreign Partnership

A U.S. taxpayer doing business with an interest in a foreign partnership must complete Form 8865, *Return of U.S. Persons With Respect To Certain Foreign Partnerships,* for any reportable event [Code Sec. 6046A, Reg. § 1.6046A-1(a)].

A *reportable event* is defined as:

1. An acquisition by a U.S. person of at least a 10 percent interest in a foreign partnership,
2. A disposition by a U.S. person of at least a 10 percent interest in a foreign partnership,
3. A change in a U.S. person's proportional interest in a foreign partnership that is equivalent to at least a 10 percent interest in the partnership [Reg. § 1.6046A-1(b)(1)].

A 10 percent interest means direct or indirect ownership of a interest equal to 10 percent of the capital interest or profits interest in a partnership, and an interest to which 10 percent of the deductions or losses of a partnership are allocated [Code Sec. 6046A(d)].

Form 8865 must be filed with the U.S. taxpayer's income tax return for the tax year in which the partnership's annual accounting period ends.

A U.S. taxpayer who transfers property to a foreign partnership must furnish certain information regarding those transfers [Code Sec. 6038B]. This information is required by the IRS to identify U.S. persons who contribute property to foreign partnerships and to ensure the correct reporting of those items.

Failure to properly report a transfer is subject to a penalty of 10 percent of the fair market value of the property of the property transferred with a cap of $100,000 unless the failure was intentional [Code Sec. 6038B(c)(1); Reg. § 1.6038B-2(h)(4)].

In addition, failure to report a contribution to a foreign partnership will result in gain recognition on the transfer as if the property had been sold.

.03 Fiduciary Returns

In addition to filing Form 1041 [¶26,020], a fiduciary must attach a separate Schedule K-1 to the form for each beneficiary of an estate or trust. This indicates each beneficiary's share of income, deductions and credits [Ch. 25]. The fiduciary should give Copy B to the beneficiary by the end of the month following the close of the tax year of the estate or trust.

Fiduciaries must give written notice of qualification as an executor or receiver, usually within 10 days from the appointment or authorization to act, to the District Director with whom the taxpayer was required to file returns. The notice must generally contain names and addresses of the taxpayer, the fiduciary, the court dealing with the proceedings along with certain dates [Code Sec. 6036; Reg. § 301.6036-1]. The notice can also be provided when the fiduciary files a notice of fiduciary relationship, Form 56 [Code Sec. 6903; Reg. § § 301.6036-1(c), 301.6903-1].

.04 S Corporation Returns

An S corporation [Ch. 21], must file an information return on Form 1120S for each tax year during its election [Ch. 21].

.05 Limited Liability Companies (LLC)

Most LLCs except single-member LLCs elect to be treated as a partnership for tax purposes [¶30,001]. As a partnership, the LLC will pay no federal taxes; rather each member will report his or her allocable share of LLC income and losses on his or her own individual tax return.

As discussed earlier, every partnership doing business in the United States is required to file Form 1065 for its tax year. This is an information return and must be signed by a general partner. If a LLC is treated as a partnership and files Form 1065, one of the company members must sign the return. Form 1065 generally must be filed on or before April 15 following the close of the partnership's tax year if its accounting period is the calendar year. A fiscal year partnership or LLC generally must file its Form 1065 by the 15th day of the 4th month following the close of its fiscal year.

¶26,185 RETURNS FOR FOREIGN ITEMS AND FOREIGN ORGANIZATIONS

For further discussion of information reporting requirements imposed on foreign items and foreign organizations, see ¶28,100–¶28,125.

TAX-SHELTERS

Even though the passive loss rules [¶13,090] have severely curtailed tax shelters as they originally appeared in the 80's, creative taxpayers have devised new and innovative tax shelters that have captured the attention of the IRS.

¶26,210 OBLIGATIONS IMPOSED ON TAX SHELTER PARTICIPANTS

Tax professionals, including attorneys, certified public accountants, enrolled agents, and enrolled actuaries, who practice before the IRS are subject to regulations found in Treasury Department Circular 230. In general, these rules govern who may represent taxpayers before the IRS, the duties and restrictions imposed on these representatives, the sanctions for any violation, and disciplinary proceedings. In particular, Circular 230 provides requirements that representatives must follow when issuing a tax shelter opinion (written advice regarding the federal tax aspects of a tax shelter). Practitioners who violate any of these rules of practice may be subject to censure, in addition to disbarment or suspension. The IRS may also impose monetary penalties for such violations in addition to, or in lieu of, suspension, disbarment, or censure. Employers, firms, and entities for whom a representative may be acting may also be subject to separate monetary penalties if the employer, firm, or entity knew, or reasonably should have known, of the representative's conduct. The amount of the monetary penalty imposed, however, cannot exceed the gross income derived from such conduct. For further discussion of Circular 230, see ¶27,040.

.01 Requirement to Disclose Reportable Transactions

Taxpayers must disclose on their tax returns certain information regarding each "reportable transaction" in which the taxpayer participates [Reg. § 1.6011-4(b)]. There are six categories of reportable transactions as follows:

1. *Listed transactions*—A listed transaction is a transaction that is the same as or substantially similar to one of the types of transactions that the IRS has determined to be a tax avoidance transaction and identified by notice, regulation, or other form of published guidance as a listed transaction.
2. *Confidential transactions*—A confidential transaction is a transaction that is offered to a taxpayer under conditions of confidentiality and for which the taxpayer has paid an advisor a minimum fee.
3. *Transactions with contractual protection*—A transaction with contractual protection is a transaction for which the taxpayer or a related party has the right to a full or partial refund of fees if all or part of the intended tax consequences from the transaction are not sustained. In Rev. Proc. 2007-20,[71] the IRS provides that certain transactions are not considered reportable transactions. The exception includes transactions where the refundable or contingent fee is related to: (1) the work opportunity credit, (2) the welfare-to-work credit, (3) the Indian employment credit, (4) the low-income housing credit, (5) the new markets tax credit, (6) the empowerment zone employment credit, (7) the renewal community employment credit, and (8) the employee retention credit.
4. *Loss transactions*—A loss transaction is any transaction resulting in the taxpayer claiming a loss exceeding specified amount. In Rev. Proc. 2013-11,[72] the IRS explained the types of losses that are not taken into account to determine if a transaction is a reportable transaction.

---

[71] Rev. Proc. 2007-20, 2007-1 CB 517.

[72] Rev. Proc. 2013-11, IRB 2013-2, 269.

5. *Patented transactions*—A patented transaction is a transaction for which a taxpayer pays (directly or indirectly) a fee in any amount to a patent holder or the patent holder's agent for the legal right to use a tax planning method that the taxpayer knows or has reason to know is the subject of the patent. A patented transaction also is a transaction for which a taxpayer (the patent holder or the patent holder's agent) has the right to payment for another person's use of a tax planning method that is the subject of the patent.
6. *Transactions of interest*—A transaction of interest is a transaction that is the same as or substantially similar to one of the types of transactions that the IRS has identified by notice, regulation, or other form of published guidance as a transaction of interest.

If a partner, shareholder of S corporations, or a trust beneficiary discover their participation in a reportable transaction from a Schedule K-1 received less than 10 calendar days before the due date of their return (including extensions), they will have 60 calendar days after the return due date to disclose the transaction to the IRS [Reg. § 1.6011-4(e)(1)].

In addition, if a transaction in which a taxpayer participates becomes a listed transaction or "transaction of interest" after the taxpayer files a return (including an amended return), the taxpayer is allowed 90 days from the date the transaction became a reportable transaction to disclose their participation. The disclosure statement must be made on Form 8886, *Reportable Transaction Disclosure Statement* [Reg. § 1.6011-4(e)(2)].

.02 Penalty for Failure to Disclose Reportable Transaction

A penalty is imposed on taxpayers who fail to disclose a reportable transaction [Code Sec. 6707A]. Under Code Sec. 6011 and its regulations, a taxpayer must file a disclosure statement on Form 8886, *Reportable Transaction Disclosure Statement*, for each reportable transaction in which the taxpayer participated. The taxpayer also must send a copy to the IRS Office of Tax Shelter Analysis (OTSA) at the same time. The penalty is in addition to any other accuracy-related penalties that may be imposed on the taxpayer [Code Sec. 6707(f)].

Reportable Transaction

A "reportable transaction" is any transaction with respect to which information must be included with a taxpayer's return or statement because the IRS has determined under regulations prescribed under Code Sec. 6011, that the transaction is of a type that has a potential for tax avoidance or evasion [Code Sec. 6707A(c)(1)].

Listed Transaction

A listed transaction is a reportable transaction that is the same as or substantially similar to a transaction that has been specifically identified by the Treasury as a tax avoidance transaction [Code Sec. 6707A(c)(2)]. In Notice 2009-59,[73] the IRS identified the transactions that it has determined to be "listed transactions" for purposes of the disclosure and registration requirements and associated penalties.

The penalty is equal to 75 percent of the decrease in tax shown on the return as a result of the transaction or which would have resulted if the transaction was

[73] Notice 2009-59, 2009-31, IRB 170.

respected for federal tax purposes [Code Sec. 6707A(b)(1)]. The minimum penalty is $10,000, or $5,000 in the case of an individual taxpayer [Code Sec. 6707A(b)(3)]. The maximum amount of the penalty is set by Code Sec. 6707A(b)(2) as follows:

	Reportable Transactions	Listed Transactions
Natural persons	$10,000	$100,000
All other taxpayers	$50,000	$200,000

A taxpayer incurs a separate penalty with respect to each reportable transaction that the taxpayer was required, but failed, to disclose within the time and in the form and manner required [Reg. § 301.6707A-1(c)(1)].

Example 26-26: Bob Smith and Mary Jones participate in a listed transaction through the SJ partnership formed for that purpose. Both partners, as well as the partnership, are required to disclose the transaction. All fail to do so. The failure by the SJ partnership to disclose its participation in a listed or otherwise reportable transaction is subject to the minimum penalty of $10,000, because income tax liability is not incurred at the partnership level nor reported on a partnership return. Bob and Mary, who also failed to comply with the reporting requirements of Code Sec. 6011, are each subject to a penalty based on the reduction in tax reported on their respective returns [Joint Committee on Taxation, *Technical Explanation of the Tax Provisions in H.R. 5297, the "Small Business Jobs Act of 2010"* (JCX-47-10), September 16, 2010].

Rescission of Penalties

The penalty cannot be waived with respect to a listed transaction. The IRS can rescind (or abate) the penalty only if rescinding the penalty would promote compliance with the tax laws and effective tax administration [Code Sec. 6707A(d)]. In making this determination, the IRS should consider the following factors:

- The taxpayer files a complete and proper Form 8886 after becoming aware it failed to make a timely disclosure;
- The failure to disclose the transaction resulted from an unintentional mistake of fact;
- The taxpayer has a established history of overall compliance and of properly disclosing other reportable transactions;
- The failure to include any information was beyond the taxpayer's control;
- The taxpayer cooperated with the IRS; and
- The taxpayer acted in good faith [Reg. § 301.6707A-1(d)(3)].

In determining whether to grant rescission, the IRS will not consider collectability of, or doubt as to liability for, the penalties (except that doubt as to liability to the extent it is a factor in the determination of reasonable cause and good faith may be considered) [Reg. § 301.6707A-1(d)(5)].

In Rev. Proc. 2007-21,[74] the IRS provides the exclusive procedures for requesting rescission of all or part of the penalties under Code Sec. 6707 (failure to disclose information on reportable transactions as discussed in ¶ 26,210.04) and Code Sec.

[74] Rev. Proc. 2007-21, 2007-1 CB 613.

6707A (material advisors' failure to file an information return for reportable transactions). The IRS describes the deadlines, the information required, and the factors it will consider in deciding whether to grant a rescission.

.03 Imposition of Accuracy-Related Penalty on Understatements With Respect to Reportable Transactions

A 20-percent accuracy-related penalty is imposed on any understatement attributable to an adequately disclosed listed transaction or reportable avoidance transaction [Code Sec. 6662A(a)]. The penalty is 30 percent if the transaction was not adequately disclosed [Code Sec. 6662A(c)]. The penalty applies only to the amount of the understatement that is attributable to the listed and/or reportable avoidance transactions without regard to other items on the taxpayer's return. The only exception to the penalty is if the taxpayer satisfies a more stringent reasonable cause and good faith exception (hereinafter referred to as the *strengthened reasonable cause exception*) [Code Sec. 6664(d)]. The strengthened reasonable cause exception is available only if the relevant facts affecting the tax treatment are adequately disclosed, there is or was substantial authority for the claimed tax treatment, and the taxpayer reasonably believed that the claimed tax treatment was more likely than not the proper treatment.

Undisclosed Transactions

If the taxpayer does not adequately disclose the transaction, the strengthened reasonable cause exception is not available (i.e., a strict-liability penalty applies), and the taxpayer is subject to an increased penalty equal to 30 percent of the understatement.

Determination of the Understatement Amount

The penalty is applied to the amount of any understatement attributable to the listed or reportable avoidance transaction without regard to other items on the tax return. For purposes of this provision, the amount of the understatement is determined as the sum of:

1. The product of the highest corporate or individual tax rate and the increase in taxable income resulting from the difference between the taxpayer's treatment of the item and the proper treatment of the item (without regard to other items on the tax return) and
2. The amount of any decrease in the aggregate amount of credits which results from a difference between the taxpayer's treatment of an item and the proper tax treatment of such item [Code Sec. 6662A(b)(1)].

.04 Tax Shelter Exception to Confidentiality Privileges Relating to Taxpayer Communications

Communications with respect to tax shelters are not subject to the confidentiality provisions that otherwise apply to a communication between a taxpayer and a federally authorized tax practitioner [Code Sec. 7525].

.05 Statute of Limitations for Unreported Listed Transactions

Code Sec. 6501(c)(10) provides that, if a taxpayer fails to disclose a listed transaction as required under Code Sec. 6011, the time to assess tax against the taxpayer with respect to that transaction will end no earlier than one year after the earlier of:

1. The date on which the taxpayer furnishes the information required under Code Sec. 6011, or
2. The date that a material advisor furnishes to the IRS, upon written request, the information required under Code Sec. 6112 with respect to the taxpayer related to the listed transaction [Prop. Reg. § 301.6501(c)-1(g)(1)].

If neither the taxpayer nor a material advisor furnishes the requisite information, the period of limitations on assessment will remain open, and thus, the tax with respect to the listed transaction may be assessed at any time.

Taxpayer Disclosures

To begin the one-year period, taxpayers must submit Form 8886 with a cover letter to the IRS Office of Tax Shelter Analysis unless the taxpayer also needs to provide the form to an IRS examiner or appeals officer.

Taxpayers that participated in one listed transaction over multiple years may submit one Form 8886 and one cover letter, identifying all of the relevant tax years. Taxpayers that participated in more than one listed transaction must submit separate Forms 8886 unless, the IRS explained, the listed transactions are the same or substantially similar. In that case, all of the listed transactions may be reported on one Form 8886 [Prop. Reg. § 301.6501(c)-1(g)(5)(i)(A)].

Taxpayers under examination or appeals consideration must also provide Form 8886 to the examiner or appeals officer. If the taxpayer does not, the one-year period under Code Sec. 6501(c)(10) will not begin until it provides the form to the examiner or appeals officer.

Pass-Through Entities

The limitations period generally remains open if a partner or S corp shareholder fails to disclose participation in a listed transaction even if the pass-through entity makes a disclosure. However, a pass-through entity's failure to disclose does not automatically apply Code Sec. 6501(c)(10) to all partners or shareholders [Prop. Reg. § 301.6501(c)-1(g)(4)].

Material Advisors

The one-year period begins when a material advisor provides list-maintenance and other information in response to an IRS request under Code Sec. 6112. The one-year period begins regardless of whether the material advisor furnishes the information within 20 days as required by Code Sec. 6708 [Prop. Reg. § 301.6501(c)-1(g)(6)]. However, the one-year period is not triggered in response to another IRS method of inquiry, such as an Information Document Request.

.06 Disclosure of Reportable Transactions by Material Advisors

Each material advisor to any reportable transaction (including any listed transaction) must timely file an information return with the IRS including:

1. Information identifying and describing the transaction;
2. Information describing any potential tax benefits expected to result from the transaction; and
3. Such other information as the IRS may prescribe [Code Sec. 6111(a)].

A *material advisor* is defined as any person who:

1. Provides material aid, assistance, or advice with respect to organizing, managing, promoting, selling, implementing, or carrying out any reportable transaction;
2. Provides material aid, assistance, or advice with respect to insuring any reportable transaction (and who derives gross income for such assistance or advice); and
3. Directly or indirectly derives gross income for such assistance or advice in excess of $250,000 ($50,000 in the case of a reportable transaction substantially all of the tax benefits from which are provided to natural persons) [Code Sec. 6111(b)(1)(A)].

Material advisors must provide a reportable transaction number to all taxpayers and material advisors for whom the material advisor acts as a material advisor. Material advisors are only required to report the identities of other material advisors who the material advisor knows, or had reason to know, acted in such a capacity with respect to the transaction [Reg. § 301.6112-1(b)(3)]. Potential material advisors who are uncertain as to whether a transaction must be disclosed may file a protective disclosure [Reg. § 301.6111-3(g)].

Penalty for Failing to Furnish Information Regarding Reportable Transactions

A $50,000 penalty is imposed on any material advisor who fails to file an information return, or who files a false or incomplete information return, with respect to a reportable transaction (including a listed transaction) [Code Sec. 6707(b)]. In the case of a listed transaction, the amount of the penalty is increased to the greater of:

1. $200,000 or
2. 50 percent of gross income received by the material advisor for any aid, assistance, or advice provided before the date the information return is filed. The penalty is increased to 75 percent of gross income for intentional disregard by a material advisor of the requirement to disclose a listed transaction [Code Sec. 6707(c)].

.07 Investor Lists and Modification of Penalty for Failure to Maintain Investor Lists

Each material advisor to a reportable transaction (including a listed transaction) is required to maintain a list that identifies each person who acted as a material advisor to the reportable transaction [Code Sec. 6112(a)].

Penalty for Failing to Maintain Investor Lists

A material advisor who is required to maintain an investor list and who fails to make the list available upon written request by the IRS within 20 business days after the request will be subject to a $10,000 per day penalty [Code Sec. 6708(a)]. The penalty applies to a person who fails to maintain a list, maintains an incomplete list, or has in fact maintained a list but does not make the list available to the IRS. No penalty will be imposed if the failure to make the list available is due to reasonable cause [Prop. Reg. § 301.6708-1(a)].

The 20-business-day period would begin on the first business day following the earlier of the date that the IRS: (a) mailed the request for the Code Sec. 6112 list by certified or registered mail to the person required to maintain the list; (b) hand delivered the request for the list directly to the person; or (c) left the request for the list at the last and usual place of abode or usual place of business of the person [Prop.

Reg. § 301.6708-1(b)]. In its discretion, the IRS may permit an extension of the 20-business-day response period. Before expiration of the 20-business-day period, the material advisor must show in writing that the material advisor cannot reasonably meet the deadline despite diligent efforts [Prop. Reg. § 301.6708-1(c)(3)].

.08 Penalty on Promoters of Abusive Tax Shelters

Under Code Sec. 6700, a promoter of an abusive tax shelter must pay a penalty in the amount of the lesser of $1000 or 100 percent of the gross income derived by that promoter. Code Sec. 6701 imposes a $1,000 penalty on any person who aids, assists, or advises in the preparation of a tax return knowing or having reason to believe that use of that advice would result in the understatement of another's tax liability. If the violation relates to the tax liability of a corporation, the penalty is increased to $10,000. In *Reiserer*,[75] the Court of Appeals for the Ninth Circuit concluded that the IRS could assess penalties against an attorney's estate for promoting an abusive tax shelter because the penalties were civil rather than penal in nature and thus survived the taxpayer's death.

.09 Substantial Understatement Penalty for Nonreportable Transactions

A corporate taxpayer has a substantial understatement if the amount of the understatement for the tax year exceeds the lesser of:

1. 10 percent of the tax required to be shown on the return for the tax year (or, if greater, $10,000) or

2. $10 million [Code Sec. 6662(d)(1)(B)].

.10 Actions to Enjoin Certain Conduct Related to Tax Shelters and Reportable Transactions

Code Sec. 7408 authorizes civil actions to enjoin any person from promoting abusive tax shelters or aiding or abetting the understatement of tax liability. Injunctions may also be sought with respect to the requirements relating to the reporting of reportable transactions [Code Sec. 6707] and the keeping of lists of investors by material advisors [Code Sec. 6708]. Thus, Code Sec. 7408 provides that an injunction may be sought against a material advisor to enjoin the advisor from:

1. Failing to file an information return with respect to a reportable transaction or

2. Failing to maintain, or to timely furnish upon written request by the IRS, a list of investors in each reportable transaction.

Injunctions may be sought with respect to violations of any of the rules under Circular 230, which regulates the practice of representatives of persons before the IRS.

---

[75] *K.H. Reiserer*, CA-9, 2007-1 USTC ¶ 50,412, 479 F3d 1160.

Assessment—Collection—Refunds 27

EXAMINATION OF RETURNS

General procedure . . . . ¶27,001
Examination procedure . . . . ¶27,005

PROCEDURE ON PROPOSED DEFICIENCY ASSESSMENT

The 30-day letter . . . . ¶27,010
District appeals office conference . . . . ¶27,015
The 90-day letter . . . . ¶27,020
Waiver by taxpayer . . . . ¶27,025
Appeals offices . . . . ¶27,030
Offers in compromise . . . . ¶27,035
Appearance at tax proceedings . . ¶27,040

ASSESSMENT AND COLLECTION OF TAX

When tax must be assessed and collected . . . . ¶27,045
Special limitation periods . . . . ¶27,050
When assessment period is reduced . . . . ¶27,055
When limitation period is suspended . . . . ¶27,060
Liability for tax of another taxpayer . . . . ¶27,065
How tax is collected . . . . ¶27,070
Whistleblower claims . . . . ¶27,071

PENALTIES

Overview . . . . ¶27,075
Document and information reporting penalties . . . . ¶27,080
Accuracy-related penalty . . . . ¶27,085
Tax return preparer, promoter, and protestor penalties . . . . ¶27,090
Delinquency penalties (failures to file or pay) . . . . ¶27,095
Other penalties . . . . ¶27,100
Penalty for underpayment of corporation estimated tax . . . . ¶27,105
Criminal penalties . . . . ¶27,110
Interest for failure to pay tax . . . . . ¶27,115

REFUNDS AND CREDITS

Overpayment of tax . . . . ¶27,120
Refund claims . . . . ¶27,125
Time for filing refund claims . . . . ¶27,130
Special periods for filing claims . . ¶27,135
Amount of refund limited . . . . ¶27,140
Form of refund claim . . . . ¶27,145
Filing the refund claim . . . . ¶27,150
Interest on refunds . . . . ¶27,155
Suit to recover tax . . . . ¶27,160
Quick refund for carrybacks . . . . . . ¶27,165
When limitation periods do not apply . . . . ¶27,170

THE UNITED STATES TAX COURT

Purpose of U.S. Tax Court . . . . . . ¶27,175
Appearance before Tax Court . . . . ¶27,180

Jurisdiction of Tax Court . . . . ¶27,185
Authority of regulations . . . . ¶27,190
How proceeding begins . . . . ¶27,195
The petition . . . . ¶27,200
The Commissioner's answer . . . . . ¶27,205
Petitioner's reply . . . . ¶27,210
Amended or supplemental pleadings . . . . ¶27,215
Judgment without trial . . . . ¶27,220
Time and place for hearing . . . . . . ¶27,225
How to take depositions . . . . ¶27,230
The Tax Court trial . . . . ¶27,235
The Tax Court opinion . . . . ¶27,240
Review of Tax Court decision . . . . ¶27,245

A filed income tax return is a self-assessment of how much tax a taxpayer owes for the year. The IRS first examines it for accuracy, completeness and correct form. All returns are then sorted and classified, and some are selected for examination. This chapter explains the procedure for examination, assessment and collection of deficiencies, refund of tax, and the work of the Tax Court. Collection of tax at the source (i.e., tax withholding) is covered in Chapter 15.

EXAMINATION OF RETURNS

¶27,001 GENERAL PROCEDURE

All business and individual tax returns are processed by an electronic data system that checks the accuracy of the return, the right to any refund claimed and inclusion of income reported on information returns [¶26,135–¶26,200]. The key to the system is the taxpayer identification number (TIN) [¶26,045–¶26,060]. All the information about the taxpayer is coordinated on magnetic tape by the IRS. The system also locates persons who do not file returns as required.

.01 Preliminary Examination

If a mathematical error is discovered in the taxpayer's figures—an amount wrongly transferred from one schedule to another or a mistake in addition, subtraction or multiplication—the IRS mails a notice of additional tax due to mathematical or clerical error (not a deficiency notice) to the taxpayer with a bill for any additional tax due. The taxpayer has no right to file a petition with the Tax Court for redetermination of the deficiency. If an overpayment resulted from the mathematical or clerical error, the excess is applied to future installments of tax [Code Sec. 6403] or is credited or refunded [Code Sec. 6402(a); Reg. § 301.6402-1].

.02 How Returns Are Selected for Examination

The criteria for selection include: returns reporting income above a designated level; returns showing substantial income not subject to withholding; returns with unusual dependency exemptions or disproportionately large deductions; and business returns that show a lower than normal gross profit ratio. Returns that call for large refunds receive a pre-refund review. Also, failure to answer inventory questions may trigger an examination.

The IRS also selects returns at random for its Taxpayer Compliance Measurement Program (TCMP). Every item on a return selected for a TCMP audit will be subject to verification. The purpose of this program is to furnish statistics on the type and number of errors that taxpayers are making and to provide a starting point for solutions to any problems uncovered. Some of the most common omissions that have turned up for individual returns are missing W-2 forms, incomplete or incorrect address or identifying number, incorrect blocks checked for dependents, entries on the wrong line, and failure to sign the return.

However, according to IRS, returns are primarily chosen for examination by use of a complex computer program known as the Discriminant Function System (DIF). The DIF process is essentially a mathematically oriented system that relies on a composite of "average taxpayer" figures based on previous returns. It assigns weights to entries on returns, and each return is given a score—the higher the score, the greater the probability of an error. Returns picked out by DIF are then screened manually and those items considered to have the highest error potential are selected for examination [¶27,005].

Other returns are selected by such methods as examining claims for credit or refund of previously paid taxes and matching information documents (e.g., Forms W-2 and 1099).

▶ **OBSERVATION:** An examination of a taxpayer's return does not suggest a suspicion of dishonesty or criminal liability. It may not even result in more tax. Many cases are closed without change in reported tax liability and, in many others, taxpayers receive refunds.

.03 Items That Invite Scrutiny

Although you face a very slim chance of being audited this year, you should be aware of certain red flags which will attract attention of the IRS computers that select the returns to be audited. The good news is that audits have declined to less than 1 percent of the 100 million individual income tax returns received by the IRS. The bad news is that your odds of being audited will rise sharply if you fit certain profiles. You should therefore take whatever steps you can to minimize an IRS audit, which can be aggravating, time-consuming and expensive.

Most audited returns are selected by computers that electronically scan and compare the return to a statistical average for taxpayers with similar income, number of children, professions and residences in certain parts of the country. The computer scores any discrepancies. The score, which is called the DIF or *discriminant function,* determines the likelihood that the return will be audited. An IRS examiner looks at the DIF scores and selects the highest 10 percent of DIF scores for audit review.

What Attracts IRS Attention

The IRS has focused its compliance in the following areas: (1) misuse of trusts and other pass-through entities to hide income; (2) claim of right scheme where taxpayer files a return and attempts to take a deduction equal to the entire amount of his or her wages; (3) phony, one-person religious organization; (4) offshore transaction; (5) employment tax evasion; (6) return preparer fraud; (7) abuse of the Americans with Disabilities Act; (8) slavery reparations; (9) home-based business; (10) EITC abuse; (11) use of complex and abusive corporation tax shelters to reduce taxes improperly; (12) inflated personal or business expenses; (13) false or bogus deductions; (14)

unallowable or bogus credits; (15) excessive exemptions; (16) preparing false Schedule Cs to claim deductions for nonexistent business expenses to offset income; (17) fraudulent Schedule Es; (18) offshore transactions used to avoid U.S. taxes by illegally hiding income in offshore bank and brokerage accounts or using offshore credit cards, wire transfers, foreign trusts, employee leasing transactions, private annuities, or life insurance to do so.

.04 Taxpayer Books and Records

Taxpayers (including foreign corporations, trades or businesses) are responsible for keeping books and records that are adequate for examination purposes [Code Sec. 6001; Reg. § 1.6001-1]. For further discussion of how long to keep tax records see Ch. 26. If taxpayers use an automatic accounting system, it should be set up so that records are available if the IRS requests them. In addition, at regular intervals, the general and subsidiary ledger balances should be printed out and income and expense account totals should be printed out and balanced with control accounts. For further discussion of electronic storage or records, see ¶ 26,095.

> **NOTE:** In the course of investigating a taxpayer's financial affairs, the IRS may issue a *summons* for the taxpayer's books and records from a bank, brokerage house, accountant, attorney, or other third-party record keeper. The IRS must provide you with reasonable notice before they contact third parties, such as your neighbors, banks, employers, or employees for books and records regarding your taxes [Code Sec. 7602(c)(1)]. This pre-notification is designed to prevent the IRS from making reputation-damaging inquiries about you and your business from third parties. The notice requirements do not apply: (1) to any contact that you have authorized; (2) if the IRS determines that the notice would jeopardize collection of any tax or the notice may involve reprisal against any person; or (3) in any pending criminal investigation [Code Secs. 7602(a), 7609]. For suspending statute of limitations for an unresolved dispute, see "NOTE," under "Wrongful levy" in ¶ 27,060.

The IRS may, however, serve a summons without court approval in a tax-shelter case. It did not matter that the records sought by the IRS include a list of investors whose names were not known.

¶ 27,005 EXAMINATION PROCEDURE

.01 In General

What can you expect if you are selected for an examination? Normally, it begins with a letter from the IRS. This will say whether additional information is needed for a correspondence examination. Or you may be called in for an office interview examination or be visited for a field examination.

If the examination is conducted by correspondence, you can simply mail in copies of any required information and usually settle the matter. If you are selected for review in an Internal Revenue office, you will be informed as to what areas of the return are being questioned and what records to bring to the interview. A field examination takes place where the books and records are kept (usually at your office or home, or the office of your accountant or attorney). Most often it is restricted to businesses and complex individual returns—and the examiner will check the entire return. A mutually satisfactory date will be set for an interview or field examination. [Reg. § 301.7605-1(b)].

Right of Disclosure

Early in the audit process, the IRS must distribute a comprehensive notice of taxpayer rights to every taxpayer it contacts regarding the determination or collection of tax. In clear, nontechnical language, the notice must explain your rights and IRS obligations during an audit; how to appeal IRS decisions; how to file claims for refunds; how to file complaints; and how the IRS can enforce tax laws through such means as liens, assessments and levies. This is generally accomplished by including a copy of IRS Publication 1, Your Rights as a Taxpayer, with the notice of examination.

Right to Representation

Any audit procedure must be suspended *immediately* if you clearly make known that you wish to be represented by anyone authorized to practice before the IRS (e.g., a lawyer, CPA, enrolled agent or enrolled actuary).

.02 Audits

Audits are scheduled on normal IRS workdays, during normal duty hours of the IRS. The IRS may schedule audits throughout the year. Although the IRS should try to minimize any adverse effects in scheduling the examination, there is no requirement that special accommodations be made on account of your busy season.

The IRS determines if an audit is to be conducted at an IRS office or in the field (that is, an audit conducted at your residence or place of business, or some other location other than an IRS office). The determination is based upon the facts of each case including the return's complexity, where your records are kept, any physical condition that makes it unreasonably difficult to travel and the physical safety of the IRS examiner.

Office audits are generally held at the IRS office within the assigned district that is closest to the address shown on your return. However, IRS agents are directed to be "reasonable" when scheduling examinations—taking distance into consideration. Field audits are generally conducted at the location where the original books, records, and source documents pertinent to the examination are maintained. This is usually your residence or principal place of business. Exceptions are made if the place of business is so small that you must close your business to accommodate the audit, or when it appears that the possibility of physical danger to any IRS personnel exists [Reg. § 301.7605-1].

.03 Limits Imposed on IRS Audits

The IRS is prohibited from using so-called "financial status audit techniques" or "economic reality examination techniques" to determine the existence of unreported income unless there is a reasonable indication that there is a likelihood of unreported income [Code Sec. 7602(e)]. This means that the IRS can no longer ask you about your educational background, where you go on vacation, where your children go to school, the number of cars you own and their makes and models, how much cash you have on hand, in a bank, hidden, or in a safe deposit box, whether you made any significant home improvements and what is the largest amount of cash you have ever had at any one time during the year. In addition, the IRS is prohibited from labeling a taxpayer as a "illegal tax protester" or any similar designation in its files.

.04 Third Party Notification Requirements

In an effort to stop IRS agents from threatening to embarrass you before business associates through third party notice, Code Sec. 7602(c)(1) requires the IRS to notify you prior to contacting third parties in connection with examining or collecting your taxes [Code Sec. 7602(c)(1)]. This beefed-up notification requirement does not apply to criminal tax matters. The IRS must also notify you prior to issuing summonses to third parties in connection with determining your tax liability [Code Sec. 7609(c)(1)]. As a result, you will now receive notice and have an opportunity to bring an action in the appropriate U.S. District Court to quash the summons. The purpose of this expansion is to afford you protection from the overly invasive and overbroad summonses that are often issued by the IRS to third parties, such as banks, credit union and neighbors, in connection with figuring out your unpaid tax bill. As a result of these changes, the IRS no longer has free rein to go on a fishing expedition in search of unreported income or overstated deductions.

Reg. § 301.7602-2(a) provides that no officer or employee of the IRS may contact any person other than the taxpayer with respect to the determination or collection of that taxpayer's tax liability without giving the taxpayer reasonable notice that such contacts may be made. A record of persons contacted must be made and given to the taxpayer both periodically and upon the taxpayer's request.

Reg. § 301.7602-2(b) defines third-party contact as a communication which—

1. Is initiated by an IRS employee;
2. Is made to a person other than the taxpayer;
3. Is made with respect to the determination or collection of the tax liability of such taxpayer;
4. Discloses the identity of the taxpayer being investigated; and
5. Discloses the association of the IRS employee with the IRS.

Initiation of Third-Party Contact by IRS Employee

An IRS employee initiates a communication whenever it is the employee who first tries to communicate with a person other than the taxpayer. Returning unsolicited telephone calls or speaking with persons other than the taxpayer as part of an attempt to speak to the taxpayer are not initiations of third-party contacts [Reg. § 301.7602-2(c)].

Example 27-1: An IRS employee receives a message to return an unsolicited call. The employee returns the call and speaks with a person who reports information about a taxpayer who is not meeting his tax responsibilities. Later, the employee makes a second call to the person and asks for more information. The first call is not a contact initiated by an IRS employee. Just because the employee must return the call does not change the fact that it is the other person, and not the employee, who initiated the contact. The second call, however, is initiated by the employee and so meets the first element [Reg. § 301.7602-2(c)(1)(ii), Ex. 1].

Example 27-2: A revenue agent trying to contact the taxpayer to discuss the taxpayer's pending examination twice calls the taxpayer's place of business. The first call is answered by a receptionist who states that the taxpayer is not available. The IRS employee leaves a message with the receptionist stating only his name, telephone number, that he is with the IRS, and asks that the taxpayer call him. The second call is answered by the office answering machine, on which the IRS employee leaves the same message. Neither of these phone calls meets the first element of a third-party contact because the IRS employee is trying to initiate a communication with the taxpayer and not a person other than the taxpayer. The fact that the IRS employee must either speak with a third party (the receptionist) or leave a message on the answering machine, which may be heard by a third party, does not mean that the employee is initiating a communication with a person other than the taxpayer. Both the receptionist and the answering machine are only intermediaries in the process of reaching the taxpayer [Reg. § 301.7602-2(c)(1)(ii), Ex. 3].

Person Other Than the Taxpayer and *Third Party* Defined

Reg. § 301.7602-2(c) (2) provides that the phrases *person other than the taxpayer* and *third party* are used interchangeably in this section, and do not include the following:

1. An officer or employee of the IRS acting within the scope of his or her employment;
2. Any computer database or web site regardless of where located and by whom maintained, including databases or web sites maintained on the Internet or in county courthouses, libraries, or any other real or virtual site; or
3. A current employee, officer, or fiduciary of a taxpayer when acting within the scope of his or her employment or relationship with the taxpayer. Such employee, officer, or fiduciary shall be conclusively presumed to be acting within the scope of his or her employment or relationship during business hours on business premises.

Example 27-3: A revenue agent examining a taxpayer's return speaks with another revenue agent who has previously examined the same taxpayer about a recurring issue. The revenue agent has not contacted a "person other than the taxpayer" within the meaning of Code Sec. 7602(c) [Reg. § 301.7602-2(c)(2)(ii), Ex. 1].

Example 27-4: A revenue agent examining a taxpayer's return speaks with one of the taxpayer's employees on business premises during business hours. The employee is conclusively presumed to be acting within the scope of his employment and is therefore not a "person other than the taxpayer" for Code Sec. 7602(c) purposes [Reg. § 301.7602-2(c)(2)(ii), Ex. 2].

Example 27-5: A revenue agent examining a corporate taxpayer's return uses a commercial online research service to research the corporate structure of the taxpayer. The revenue agent uses an IRS account, logs on with her IRS user name and password, and uses the name of the corporate taxpayer in her search terms. The revenue agent later explores several Internet web sites that may have information relevant to the examination. The searches on the commercial online research service and Internet web sites are not contacts with "persons other than the taxpayer" [Reg. § 301.7602-2(c)(2)(ii), Ex. 3].

Determination or Collection of Tax Liability Defined

A contact is "with respect to" the determination or collection of the tax liability of such taxpayer when it is made for the purpose of either determining or collecting a particular tax liability and when directly connected to that purpose. While a contact made for the purpose of determining a particular taxpayer's tax liability may also affect the tax liability of one or more other taxpayers, such contact is not for that reason alone a contact "with respect to" the determination or collection of those other taxpayers' tax liabilities.

Example 27-6: As part of a compliance check on a return preparer, an IRS employee visits the preparer's office and reviews the preparer's client files to ensure that the proper forms and records have been created and maintained. This contact is not a third-party contact "with respect to" the preparer's clients because it is not for the purpose of determining the tax liability of the preparer's clients, even though the agent might discover information that would lead the agent to recommend an examination of one or more of the preparer's clients [Reg. § 301.7602-2(c)(3)(ii), Ex. 1].

Example 27-7: To help identify taxpayers in the florist industry who may not have filed proper returns, an IRS employee contacts a company that supplies equipment to florists and asks for a list of its customers in the past year in order to cross-check the list against filed returns. The employee later contacts the supplier for more information about one particular florist who the employee believes did not file a proper return. The first contact is not a contact with respect to the determination of the tax liability of "such taxpayer" because no particular taxpayer has been identified for investigation at the time the contact is made. The later contact, however, is with respect to the determination of the tax liability of "such taxpayer" because a particular taxpayer has been identified. The later contact is also "with respect to" the determination of that taxpayer's liability because, even though no examination has been opened on the taxpayer, the information sought could lead to an examination [Reg. § 301.7602-2(c)(3)(ii), Ex. 3].

Disclosing Taxpayer's Identity

An IRS employee discloses the taxpayer's identity whenever the employee knows or should know that the person being contacted can readily ascertain the taxpayer's identity from the information given by the employee.

Example 27-8: A revenue officer seeking to value the taxpayer's condominium calls a real estate agent and asks for a market analysis of the taxpayer's condominium, giving the unit number. The revenue officer has revealed the identity of the taxpayer, regardless of whether the revenue officer discloses the name of the taxpayer, because the real estate agent can readily ascertain the taxpayer's identity from the address given [Reg. § 301.7602-2(c)(4)(ii), Ex. 1].

Example 27-9: A revenue officer seeking to value the taxpayer's condominium unit calls a real estate agent and, without identifying the taxpayer's unit, asks for the sales prices of similar units recently sold and listing prices of similar units currently on the market. The revenue officer has not revealed the identity of the taxpayer because the revenue officer has not given any information from which the real estate agent can readily ascertain the taxpayer's identity [Reg. § 301.7602(c)(4)(ii), Ex. 2].

Disclosing IRS Association

An IRS employee discloses his association with the IRS whenever the employee knows or should know that the person being contacted can readily ascertain the association from the information given by the employee.

Advance Notice to the Taxpayer

An officer or employee of the IRS may not make third-party contacts without providing reasonable notice in advance to the taxpayer that contacts may be made. The pre-contact notice may be given either orally or in writing. If written notice is given, it may be given in any manner which the IRS employee responsible for giving the notice reasonably believes will be received by the taxpayer in advance of the third-party contact. Written notice is considered reasonable when it is either:

1. Mailed to the taxpayer's last known address;
2. Given in person;
3. Left at the taxpayer's dwelling or usual place of business; or
4. Actually received by the taxpayer [Reg. § 301.7602-2(d)(1)].

Note that pre-contact notice does not need to be provided if it has already been provided under another statute, regulation or administrative process [Reg. § 301.7602-2(d)(2)].

Periodic Post-Contact Reports

A record of persons contacted must be reported to the taxpayer periodically, but no less frequently than once a year. The period of time between these periodic reports shall be called the *reporting period*. The periodic report must be mailed to the taxpayer's last known address [Reg. § 301.7602-2(e)(1)]. The record of persons contacted should contain information which reasonably identifies the person contacted. Providing the name of the person contacted fully satisfies the requirements of Reg. § 301.7602-2 but Reg. § 301.7602-2 does not require IRS employees to solicit identifying information from a person solely for the purpose of the post-contact report. The record need not contain any other information, such as the nature of the inquiries or the content of the third party's response. The record need not report multiple contacts made with the same person during a reporting period [Reg. § 301.7602-2(e)(3)].

Exceptions to Notification Requirements

In the following situations, the IRS need not provide the advance notice or annual reports required under Code Sec. 7602(c):

1. If the taxpayer has given the IRS explicit authorization to contact a third-party, the IRS need not provide advance notice or annual reports required under Code Sec. 7602(c). Such third-party contacts include people authorized to represent the taxpayer including attorneys, corporate officers, and executors [Reg. § 301.7602-2(f)(1)].
2. If the taxpayer's authorized representative approved the third-party contact.
3. If the IRS employee making a contact has good cause to believe that providing the taxpayer with either a general pre-contact notice or a record of the specific person being contacted may jeopardize the collection of any tax [Reg. § 301.7602-2(f)(2)].
4. If the IRS employee making a contact has good cause to believe that providing the taxpayer with either a general pre-contact notice or a specific record of the person being contacted may cause any person to harm any other person in any way, whether the harm is physical, economic or emotional. A statement by the person contacted that harm may occur against any person is good cause to believe that reprisals may occur. This section does not require the IRS employee making the contact to question further the contacted person about reprisals or otherwise make further inquiries regarding the statement [Reg. § 301.7602-2(f)(3)].

Example 27-10: A revenue officer seeking to collect unpaid taxes is told by the taxpayer that all the money in his and his brother's joint bank account belongs to the brother. The revenue officer contacts the brother to verify this information. The brother refuses to confirm or deny the taxpayer's statement. He states that he does not believe that reporting the contact to the taxpayer would result in harm to anyone, but further states that he does not want his name reported to the taxpayer because it would then appear that he gave information. This contact is not excepted from the statute merely because the brother asks that his name be left off the list of contacts [Reg. § 301.7602-2(f)(3), Ex.1].

Example 27-11: The same facts as Example 27-10, except that the brother states that he fears harm from the taxpayer should the taxpayer learn of the contact, even though the brother gave no information. This contact is excepted from the statute because the third party has expressed a fear of reprisal. The IRS employee is not required to make further inquiry into the nature of the brothers' relationship or otherwise question the brother's fear of reprisal [Reg. § 301.7602-2(f)(3), Ex. 2].

5. Code Sec. 7602(c) does not apply to criminal investigations by the IRS and other law enforcement bodies [Reg. § 301.7602(f)(4)].
6. Code Sec. 7602(c) does not apply when the employee making the contact has good cause to believe that providing either the pre-contact notice or the record of the person contacted would thereby identify a confidential informant whose identity would be protected under Code Sec. 6103(h)(4) [Reg. § 301.7602-2(f)(6)].

7. Code Sec. 7602(c) does not apply to contacts made in the course of a pending court proceeding [Reg. § 301.7602-2(f)(7)].

.05 Examination of Partnership Items

Procedural rules have been established for examining items of partnership income, deduction, gain, loss, or other items at the partnership level in a unified partnership proceeding rather than in separate proceedings with the partners. Small partnerships are excluded from these procedures but they may elect to be governed by them. For this purpose, small partnerships are those that have ten or fewer partners, and each partner is an individual (married couples count as one) other than a nonresident alien, a C corporation, or an estate of a deceased partner [Code Sec. 6231(a); Reg. § 301.6231(a)(1)-1].

The examination usually begins when the IRS notifies the partnership that its return has been selected for examination. The most important person in partnership audits is the tax matters partners (TMP). The TMP is defined as either: (1) the general partner who is specifically designated as the TMP by the partnership; or (2) if no general partners has been so designated, the general partner who holds the largest profits interest in the partnership at the end of the tax year subject to audit. If two or more general partners hold an equally large profits interest, the general partner whose name would appear first in an alphabetical listing must assume the role of TMP [Code Sec. 6231(a)(7)].

If there is no general partner and the IRS decides that it would not make sense to apply (2) above, the IRS will select the tax matters partner. Within 30 days of making this selection, the IRS must notify all of the partners entitled to received notice of the selected TMPs name and address [Code Sec. 6231(a)(7)]. The TMP will receive notice of the outcome of the examination (the notice of final partnership administrative adjustment). Also, the IRS will notify partners entitled to notice that an examination is under way at least 120 days before the notice of a final partnership administrative adjustment (FPAA) is mailed to the TMP. The IRS will notify the partners entitled to notice of the FPAA within 60 days of mailing the notice to the TMP.

Within 90 days after notice of adjustment, the tax matters partner (TMP) may file a petition for readjustment of partnership items with the Tax Court, U.S. District Court or U.S. Claims Court. However, if a petition is not filed by the TMP, then any notice partner (or any 5 percent group) may file the petition within 60 days after the 90-day period has expired [¶ 27,135] [Code Sec. 6226].

.06 Taxpayer Cooperation

If you receive examination notices, you should produce all records required by the examiners and cooperate with them in every way possible. Nothing is gained by placing obstacles in their way as they can compel that books and records be produced [Code Sec. 7602(a); Reg. § 301.7602-1(a)]. Failure to appear or produce records when a summons is issued is punishable by fine, imprisonment, or both [Code Secs. 7210, 7601(b); Reg. § 301.7604-1].

.07 Fraud Investigation

In cases involving possible charges of fraud, you should be more cautious. If the agent investigating the case is from the Criminal Division, a so-called Special Agent, or if the regular examiner does or says anything to indicate that this examination is not purely routine, you should get professional legal advice before giving the agent any information.

The IRS can examine books without showing probable cause if it suspects fraud, even if the year had been previously examined[1] or was otherwise closed by statute of limitations.[2] Evidence obtained by a routine tax investigation is not admissible in a fraud proceeding, unless you have been warned of your right to remain silent and your right to have representation by a lawyer[3] or accountant.[4]

.08 Examiner's Finding

After an examination, the examiner informs you of their findings either orally or by letter, and must indicate the amount of any proposed deficiency. A notice of deficiency must not only give an explanation of why the IRS claims additional tax is due, but it must also explain the basis for any tax penalties [Code Sec. 7522(a)]. The IRS is required to send an annual written notice to each taxpayer with a delinquent tax account. This notice must contain the amount of the tax delinquency as of the date of the notice. Taxpayers can no longer falsely assume that just because they have not heard recently from the IRS, their deficiency claim has been forgiven or forgotten [Code Sec. 7524].

You should contact your professional advisers if you receive proposed assessments for additional tax. If you agree with the examiner's findings, you may consent to a deficiency assessment on Form 870, *Waiver of Restrictions on Assessment and Collection of Deficiency in Tax and Acceptance of Overassessment*, or Form 4549, *Income Tax Examination Changes*, depending on the type of audit [¶ 27,025]. Such filing closes the matter. The findings will not be reopened to make adjustments unfavorable to you, unless (1) there is evidence of fraud, malfeasance, collusion, concealment or material misrepresentation; (2) there was substantial error based on an established IRS position existing at the previous examination; or (3) failure to reopen would be a serious administrative omission.

If you disagree with findings made after correspondence examinations, you can ask for an Appeals Office conference [¶ 27,015] within the period specified in the form letters sent to you that included the findings. After an office interview examination, you can ask for an immediate conference with an Appeals officer who has full authority to settle the tax dispute, or wait for the form letter with the examiner's findings and a statement of your alternatives available, including consideration of the findings by an Appeals Office.

> **NOTE:** You should confer with your tax consultants as soon as possible after you receive the examiner's findings. With a consultation, you may have the benefit of professional advice as to whether it is best to accept an examiner's finding. In some cases, the District Director or you can request technical advice from the National Office.

---

[1] *M. Powell*, SCt, 64-2 USTC ¶ 9858, 379 US 48, 85 SCt 248.

[2] *B.E. Ryan*, SCt, 64-2 USTC ¶ 9859, 379 US 61, 85 SCt 232.

[3] *R.T. Mathis, Sr.*, SCt, 68-1 USTC ¶ 9357, 391 US 1.

[4] *W. Tarlowski*, DC-NY, 69-2 USTC ¶ 9554, 305 FSupp 112.

Secret Deals with IRS Agents Discouraged

A taxpayer may now bring a civil action for damages against the United States in a U.S. district court if any officer or employee of the United States intentionally reduces the tax due from an attorney, certified public accountant or enrolled agent representing a taxpayer in exchange for privileged information about a taxpayer. This action for damages is the exclusive remedy for recovering damages resulting from such actions. The damages recoverable are equal to the lesser of $500,000 or the sum of the actual, direct economic damages sustained by the taxpayer as a result of the information disclosure [Code Sec. 7435]. The purpose of this new law is to dissuade IRS employees from enticing tax professionals to reveal their client's tax secrets in exchange for favorable treatment of the tax advisor's own taxes.

Taxpayer Assistance Order

If you are suffering or are about to suffer a "significant hardship" as a result of tax law administration, you may file an application with the Office of the National Tax Advocate and request that they issue a taxpayer assistance order (TAO) which will prevent the IRS from taking action against you or may require the IRS to release a lien from your property [Code Sec. 7811]. The following circumstances will be deemed to cause significant hardship in this situation:

- Where you face an immediate threat of adverse action,
- Where there has been a delay of more than 30 days in resolving your problem, or
- Where you will incur significant costs or face long-term harm if the order is not granted.

Use Form 911, *Request for Taxpayer Advocate Service Assistance (and Application for Taxpayer Assistance Order)*, to request this special relief. In lieu of Form 911, you may file a written statement that contains the information specified in Reg. § 301.7811-1(b)(1). The National Taxpayer Advocate has broad authority to take any action permitted by law with respect to taxpayers who would otherwise suffer a significant hardship as a result of the manner in which the IRS is administering the tax laws [Code Sec. 7811(b)(2)].

PROCEDURE ON PROPOSED DEFICIENCY ASSESSMENT

A deficiency is the difference between the actual correct tax liability for the year and the tax shown on your return for the year, decreased by rebates and increased by prior assessments (or amounts collected without assessment). This section outlines procedures involved in deficiency assessments.

¶27,010 THE 30-DAY LETTER

If you refuse to accept a deficiency finding after a field examination, or do not agree with the determination following an office examination, you will receive a *30-day letter*. This is a form letter which states the IRS's proposed determination (including a complete explanation of its basis for its findings), describes your further appeal rights and advises you that you have 30 days to inform the District Director of your course of action. You may then ask for a District Appeals Office conference.

If you decide to accept the examiner's finding at this point, you may file Form 870, limiting interest on the deficiency, and pay the deficiency. If you do nothing, you will receive a 90-day letter [¶27,020]. If the period for tax assessment is about to expire, a 90-day letter can be issued without the necessity of a 30-day letter even though the case may be in the examination stage.

¶27,015 DISTRICT APPEALS OFFICE CONFERENCE

If you disagree with the examiner, you may ask for a district Appeals Office conference. The procedure used to ask for the conference depends on whether there was an office or field examination [¶27,005]. An office conference is held at a District Appeals Office within an Internal Revenue Region. You may be represented by any person qualified to practice before the IRS.

.01 Procedure After Examination

After an office examination or correspondence audit, you need only request an Appeals Office conference when you receive the examiner's findings and the amount of the proposed deficiency. The protest doesn' t have to be written, regardless of the amount of the proposed adjustment.

Field Examination

An Appeals Office conference cannot be arranged after a field examination until you receive a 30-day letter [¶27,010]. A brief written statement is needed if the proposed adjustment is between $2,500 and $10,000. A formal written protest is required for adjustments over $10,000.

.02 Presenting the Case

If the facts are in dispute, you will have to present the correct facts as you see them. This can be done in writing, by documentary evidence, and by affidavit. Legal questions also should be submitted in writing so that authorities may be cited and analyzed.

> ▶ **OBSERVATION:** You should make your requests for a District Appeals Office conference in writing, and attach to it a statement of facts and authorities.

.03 Results of Conference on Proposed Deficiency

An Appeals Office conference on a proposed deficiency may result in an agreement or disagreement.

1. If the Appeals officer and you reach an *agreement* on an income tax case, you sign Form 870-AD, *Offer of Waiver of Restrictions on Assessment and Collection of Deficiency in Tax and of Acceptance of Overassessment.* Form 890 is used in estate and gift tax cases. An attorney or accountant representing you may sign for you, if a power of attorney has been filed. A memorandum is then prepared setting forth the exact grounds upon which the conclusion rests, and all the papers in the case are turned over to the District Director for assessment and collection. Form 870-AD does not stop the

running of interest when filed.[5] Only you have the option to offer to waive restrictions, and interest runs until 30 days after the IRS has accepted the offer. The case may be reopened after post-review (but only with the approval of the Regional Director of Appeals), if there was substantial error or there is evidence of fraud or misrepresentation.[6]

2. If the Appeals officer and you still disagree after the conference, the Appeals Office may issue a statutory notice of deficiency (the 90-day letter) [¶27,020]. If you file a petition with the Tax Court within 90 days, the case will be retained by the Appeals office and turned over to the appropriate district counsel to prepare for trial. If no petition is filed within this period, the case will be transferred to the District Director for appropriate action. To expedite Tax Court cases, the IRS may require a settlement conference when 90-day letters have not been issued.

.04 Results of Conference on a Refund Claim

An Appeals Office conference on a refund claim has two possible outcomes:

1. The Appeals officer and you reach an agreement. This is referred back to the District Director. After that, the procedure in ¶27,150 is followed.
2. The Appeals officer and you reach no agreement. You then may follow the course of action indicated in ¶27,150.

¶27,020 THE 90-DAY LETTER

.01 In General

The IRS may not assess a tax deficiency unless it has first mailed a deficiency notice to the taxpayer and allowed the taxpayer to petition the Tax Court for a redetermination [Code Sec. 6213(a)]. The 90-day letter is a formal notice of the tax deficiency owed by the taxpayer. It is sent by registered or certified mail, and may be received any time after the expiration of the period allowed in the 30-day letter, if the taxpayer and the Appeals officer could not reach an agreement. Mailing to your "last known address" or to your accountant[7] is sufficient [Code Sec. 6212(b)(1); Reg. §301.6212-1(b)].

Last Known Address Defined

A taxpayer's *last known address* is the one that appears on his or her most recently filed and properly processed federal tax return, unless the IRS is given clear and concise notification of a different address [Reg. §301.6212-2(a)]. The IRS is permitted to use an address obtained from the USPS's National Change of Address database as a taxpayer's last known address in the absence of a more recent address. USPS gets the change of address information from a properly submitted USPS Form 3575, *Official Mail Forwarding Change of Address Form,* which may be used by businesses and individuals [Reg. §301.6212-2(b)(2)].

---

[5] *N.E. Goldstein,* CA-1, 51-1 USTC ¶9352, 189 F2d 752.

[6] *Cleveland Tr. Co.,* CA-6, 70-1 USTC ¶12,649, 421 F2d 475, *cert. denied,* 400 US 819.

[7] *J. Delman,* CA-3, 67-2 USTC ¶9676, 384 F2d 929, *cert. denied,* 390 US 952, 88 SCt 1044.

For 90 days (150 days if the notice is addressed to a person outside the United States) after the 90-day letter is mailed, the IRS generally may not assess tax or begin collection proceedings. The details are usually given in an attached statement, with notice that within 90 days from the date of mailing (150 days for taxpayers located outside the U.S. or District of Columbia) you may petition the Tax Court for redetermining the deficiency. A deficiency notice may be withdrawn if the IRS and you reach an agreement [Code Sec. 6212(d)]. However, withdrawal of the notice does not affect any suspension of the running of the statute of limitations.

In a bankruptcy case, the 90- (or 150-) day period for filing a petition in the United States Tax Court is suspended for the period during which the debtor is prohibited from filing under bankruptcy law [¶27,055], plus 60 days after the bankruptcy proceeding [Code Sec. 6213(f)(1)]. During the same period, however, the IRS may file a proof of claim, request for payment, or take other action such as asking the bankruptcy court to determine the debtor's personal liability for nondischargeable taxes[8] [Code Sec. 6213(f)(2)].

Notice for Joint Return

When you and your spouse file a joint return, the notice of deficiency may be a single joint notice. However, if either of you notifies the IRS that you have separate residences, the identical joint notice must be sent to each of you[9] [Code Sec. 6212(b)(2); Reg. § 301.6212-1(b)(2)].

When There Is a Fiduciary

Fiduciaries assume the powers, rights, duties, and privileges of the taxpayer [Code Sec. 6903(a); Reg. § 301.6903-1]. Fiduciaries are required to give the IRS notice that they are acting in a fiduciary capacity [Code Sec. 6903(b)]. If this notice is not filed, the deficiency notice does not have to be sent to the fiduciary; it can be sent to your last known address (as defined above). Fiduciaries may be relieved from further liability by filing written notice and proof that their fiduciary capacity has ended [Reg. § 301.6903-1].

Ten-Day Notice

The following fiduciaries must file a notice within ten days of the time they qualify [Code Sec. 6036; Reg. § 301.6036-1]:

- Receiver or trustee in bankruptcy, or other persons in control of debtor's assets; qualified by appointment or authority to act. (If the Treasury Department is given notice of the proceeding under the bankruptcy law, a fiduciary notice is not necessary.)
- Receiver in receivership proceeding (including foreclosure) in any U.S. or state court; qualified by appointment, authority to act, or by taking possession of debtor's assets.
- Assignee for benefit of creditors; qualified on the date of assignment.

---

[8] Senate Report No. 96-1035, p. 109, 96th Cong., 2nd Sess.

[9] *M.A. Dolan*, 44 TC 420, Dec. 27,440 (1965).

Excise Taxes

The IRS issues a deficiency notice if it determines that a deficiency exists in excise taxes payable by a private foundation [Ch. 23], or payable on certain retirement plans [¶27,100], or payable by a real estate investment trust [Code Sec. 6212; Reg. §301.6212-1(a)].

.02 What Taxpayers Can Do

You have these choices if you receive a 90-day letter:

- You may do nothing. Then the deficiency is assessed after the 90-day (or 150-day) period expires and referred to the Appeals Office Collection Division.
- You may sign Form 870 consent agreement (thus limiting interest on the deficiency [¶27,025]). Then the deficiency is assessed and referred to the Appeals Office Collection Division.
- You may file a petition with the Tax Court before the 90 (or 150) days have passed.

Time for Filing Tax Court Petition

Each notice that the IRS mails to you must specify the last date on which you can timely file a petition with the Tax Court. You must file a petition with the Tax Court within 90 days (150 days if the address is outside of the United States) after the date that the notice of deficiency is mailed by the IRS. The IRS is required to specify the 90th day (or 150th day) by which you can timely petition the Tax Court. The day the notice is mailed is not counted in fixing the 90- or 150-day period, but the day the petition is filed is counted.[10] If the last day is a Saturday, Sunday or legal holiday in the District of Columbia, it is not counted as the 90th or 150th day [Code Sec. 6213(a); Reg. §301.6213-1]. A properly addressed petition mailed to the Tax Court is timely filed with a post office postmark dated on or before the due date [Code Sec. 7502; Reg. §301.7502-1]. A postmark from a private postage meter is acceptable, but it must be dated on or before the due date and received not later than the time a petition with a post office postmark would ordinarily be received. However, a mark dated before the due date (not a private postage meter mark) made by a private courier service and delivery of a petition after the statutory time were not acceptable although the courier received the petition for delivery within the statutory time[11] [Ch. 26].

Electronic Postmark

The date of an electronic postmark given by an authorized electronic return transmitter will be deemed the filing date if the date of the electronic postmark is on or before the filing due date. If the electronic postmark is timely, the document is considered filed timely even if it is received by IRS after its due date [Reg. §301.7502-1(d)(1)]. An electronic postmark is a record of the date and time (in a particular time zone) that an authorized electronic return transmitter receives the transmission of a taxpayer's electronically filed document on its host system. If the taxpayer and the electronic return transmitter are located in different time zones, the time in the taxpayer's time

---

[10] *R.W. Chambers*, CA-DC, 2 USTC ¶530, 41 F2d 299.

[11] *M. Blank*, 76 TC 400, Dec. 37,720 (1981); *D.H. Leith*, 47 TCM 255, Dec. 40,587(M), TC Memo. 1983-670.

zone controls the timeliness of the electronically filed document [Reg. § 301.7502-1(d)(3)(ii)].

.03 When Deficiency Is Assessed

The deficiency in tax will not usually be assessed nor collected during the 90- (or 150-) day period for filing a Tax Court petition. If a petition is filed during this period, the tax is not assessed until the Tax Court decision becomes final [Code Sec. 6213(a); Reg. § 301.6213-1(a)]. For further discussion of assessments, see ¶25,045.

Immediate Assessment

Assessment or collection before the 90- (or 150-) day period is allowed in the following situations:

- An insufficient payment due to a mathematical or clerical error on the return may be collected. Notice of an amount due because of the error is not treated as a notice of deficiency. An abatement of the assessment in the notice is allowed if you file a request within 60 days after notice is sent [Code Sec. 6213(b); Reg. § 301.6213-1(b)].
- A "jeopardy assessment" can be made when delay might prevent the assessment or collection of a deficiency. A jeopardy assessment may be made before the 90-day deficiency notice is sent, but a deficiency notice must be issued within 60 days of the assessment [Code Sec. 6861; Reg. § 301.6861-1].
- Termination assessments can be made in certain cases [¶27,055]:
    1. On appointment of a receiver and, in very limited circumstances, in bankruptcy proceedings [¶27,055] [Code Sec. 6871].
    2. When tax is paid. A payment made after a deficiency notice has been mailed will not deprive the Tax Court of jurisdiction over the deficiency determined without regard to the payment [Code Sec. 6213(b)(4); Reg. § 301.6213-1(b)].
    3. When a petition for review of the Tax Court's decision is filed with a Court of Appeals, unless a bond is filed with the Tax Court [¶27,245].

.04 In a Partnership Proceeding

In a partnership proceeding, any deficiency resulting from an administrative determination generally may not be assessed nor collected (1) until 150 days after mailing the FPAA notice [¶27,005], or (2) if a Tax Court proceeding has started, until the court decision is final [Code Sec. 6225(a)(1)].

¶27,025 WAIVER BY TAXPAYER

You may be asked to sign a "Waiver of Restrictions on Assessment and Collection of Deficiency in Tax and Acceptance of Overassessment." Form 870 is used for income tax purposes; Form 890 for estate and gift tax.

.01 Effect of Waiver

By signing the waiver form, you give up the right to have an assessment deferred until after the 90-day period provided in the formal notice of deficiency [¶27,020].[12] When an overassessment of tax has been made, you and the District Director can sign the waiver form as an agreement of overassessment. If more than one year or different taxes are involved, you may waive the restrictions on immediate assessment of a deficiency for one year or type of tax, while agreeing to an overassessment of another year's tax liability or type of tax. The waiver stops the interest (including compound interest) [¶27,115] on the deficiency during the period from 30 days after filing the waiver to the date of notice and demand for payment [Code Sec. 6601(c); Reg. §301.6601-1(d)].

▶ **OBSERVATION:** If you are entitled to a refund of interest as a result of the above provision, you should immediately file a claim for refund.

.02 Waiver as Closing Agreement

A waiver form does not bar a claim for refund[13] nor an assessment. Exception: The IRS may ask you to sign Form 870-AD, rather than Form 870. This type of waiver does bar the filing of a refund claim though carrybacks, such as of a net operating loss, would still be allowed.[14] However, provisions barring refund claims are valid when inserted in the form[15] [¶27,145].

¶27,030 APPEALS OFFICES

An Appeals Office is established in each of the seven Internal Revenue regions where district Appeals Office conferences are held. Each Appeals Office is headed by a Regional Director of Appeals.

.01 Jurisdiction and Function

The Appeals Office is the single agency for settling disputes between the District Directors and taxpayers. It has the authority to settle cases fully and its decisions are final insofar as the IRS is concerned. A District Appeals Office conference is arranged at the requests of taxpayers who fail to receive satisfaction after an office or field examination [¶27,015]. A conference is granted even if no written protest is filed. However, a protest is required if the case is a field examination case and the proposed additional tax is more than $10,000. Generally, a conference before the Appeals Office is not granted during the 90-day status [¶27,020] whether or not you exercised your rights to an Appeals Office conference.

▶ **OBSERVATION:** Both you and the IRS generally may be ready and willing to concede something to avoid the delay, expense, and uncertainty of a court appeal. The Appeals Office seeks to work out a settlement that will be acceptable to both the IRS and you. Where the Treasury would have a clear-cut case before any court, the Appeals Office will not offer any reduction. But according to the

[12] *R. Nichols*, 93 TCM 657, Dec. 56,806(M), TC Memo. 2007-5.

[13] *W.A. Morse*, DC-MN, 59-1 USTC ¶9359, 183 FSupp 847.

[14] *C.S. Payson*, CA-2, 48-1 USTC ¶9196, 166 F2d 1008.

[15] *V.L. Schaefer*, DC-HI, 51-2 USTC ¶9372.

degree of doubt as to the position that the courts might take upon the various points at issue, the Appeals Office will offer a reduction in the proposed deficiency.

.02 Settlement of Issues

In most Tax Court cases, the Appeals Office has exclusive settlement jurisdiction for four months after the cases are docketed. The settlement period may be extended, but normally not beyond the date of the trial calendar call. Within 45 days of the receipt of the case, Appeals must arrange a settlement conference with you. Appeals may enter a full or partial settlement with you. If a partial settlement is reached, Appeals will refer the unsettled issues to Counsel for disposition.

.03 Partnerships

In partnership proceedings, all partners can participate. A tax matters partner (TMP) may enter into a settlement agreement for partnership items. It is binding on all partners unless there is a showing of fraud, malfeasance, or misrepresentation of fact. Partners who are not entitled to notice of final adjustment (FPAA) may file a statement providing that the TMP has no authority to act on their behalf. If the IRS enters into a settlement agreement with any partner, it must offer the same terms of settlement to other partners who request it [Code Sec. 6224(c)(2)].

¶27,035 OFFERS-IN-COMPROMISE

An offer-in-compromise is an agreement between a taxpayer and the IRS that settles the taxpayer's tax liabilities for less than the full amount owed. In general, the IRS will not accept an offer in compromise if it believes that the liability can be paid in full as a lump sum or through a payment agreement. The IRS looks at the taxpayer's income and assets to make a determination regarding the taxpayer's ability to pay. OICs are subject to acceptance on legal requirements.

Tax claims can be settled by offers in compromise or closing agreements. An alternative is for the taxpayer and the IRS to enter into an installment agreement for payment of the taxes over a three-year period. For discussion of installment agreements and other tax payment options, see ¶26,125.

.01 Offers in Compromise

Taxpayers who wish to settle their dispute outside the courts or who are experiencing financial difficulties and don't have sufficient funds to satisfy their tax liability, should consider submitting an offer-in-compromise to the IRS. The IRS has authority to reduce or compromise a tax liability if taxpayers enter into an offer-in-compromise contractual agreement with them. Taxpayers may take advantage of the IRS offer-in-compromise program to settle civil or criminal tax cases including interest and penalties [Code Sec. 7122(a); Reg. §301.7122-1]. The IRS is receptive to offers-in-compromise because the program offers them an opportunity to reduce accounts receivable and to bring nonfilers back into the tax system. In essence, the program enables the IRS to collect monies it would never otherwise receive. In *T. Szekely*,[16] the Tax Court concluded that the IRS erroneously failed to consider the taxpayer's offer-in-compromise and proceeded too hastily in closing the case without taking it into consideration.

Taxpayers should consider submitting an offer in compromise, however, only after they have exhausted all alternative payment options including: extensions of time to pay, installment agreements, and delaying collection. The IRS suggests that taxpayers consider liquidating assets to satisfy their tax debt or obtaining a loan to satisfy their tax liability. Loan costs may be lower than the combination of interest and penalties imposed by the IRS.

Grounds for Compromise

An offer to compromise a tax liability should set forth one of the following legal grounds for compromise and should provide enough information for the IRS to determine whether the offer fits within its acceptance policies: (1) doubt as to liability; (2) doubt as to collectibility; or (3) promotion of effective tax administration.

Doubt as to Liability

Doubt as to liability exists where there is a genuine dispute as to the existence or amount of the correct tax liability under the law. Doubt as to liability does not exist where the liability has been established by a final court decision or judgment concerning the existence of the liability. An offer to compromise based on doubt as to liability generally will be considered acceptable if it reasonably reflects the amount the IRS would expect to collect through litigation. This analysis includes consideration of the hazards of litigation that would be involved if the liability were litigated. The evaluation of the hazards of litigation is not an exact science and is within the discretion of the IRS.

Doubt as to Collectibility

Doubt as to collectibility exists in any case where the taxpayer's assets and income cannot satisfy the full amount of the liability. An offer to compromise based on doubt as to collectibility generally will be considered acceptable if it is unlikely that the tax can be collected in full and the offer reasonably reflects the amount the IRS could collect through other means, including administrative and judicial collection remedies. This amount is the reasonable collection potential of a case. In determining the reasonable collection potential of a case, the IRS will consider the taxpayer's reasonable basic living expenses to determine if taxpayers are capable of paying more than the amount they offered.[17] In some cases, the IRS may accept an offer of less than the total reasonable collection potential of a case if there are special circumstances.

The IRS will reject an offer in compromise premised on doubts about collectability as long as it reasonably determines that more than the proferred amount may be collectable. In *A. Dalton*,[18] the Court of Appeals for the First Circuit reversed the Tax Court to concluded that the IRS properly rejected a married couple's offer in compromise because they had a nominee interest in real property that was held in trust for

---

[16] *T. Szekely*, 106 TCM 375, Dec. 59,653(M), TC Memo. 2013-227.

[17] *M.W. Keller*, CA-9, 2009-1 USTC ¶50,428, 568 F3d 710.

[18] *A. Dalton*, CA-1, 2012-1 USTC ¶50,411, 682 F3d 149, *rev'g*, 135 TC 393, Dec. 58,341 (2011); *S.J. Johnson*, 136 TC 475, Dec. 58,635 (2011).

their adult sons. The court found that the IRS's determination that the couple's interest in the property would enable it to collect more than the amount they offered was reasonable.

IRS Instructed to Consider Economic Troubles

IRS employees are permitted to consider a taxpayer's current income and potential for future income when negotiating an offer in compromise. The IRS will consider "real-world situations" and (1) revise the calculation for the taxpayer's future income; (2) allow taxpayers to repay their student loans; (3) allow taxpayers to pay state and local delinquent taxes; and (4) expand the Allowable Living Expense allowance category and amount.

IRS Manual Revised to Consider Future Income

The IRS has revised Section 5.8.5 of the Internal Revenue Manual (IRM) that provides guidance in the computation of the taxpayer's future income value during the evaluation of an offer in compromise. This section now defines future income as an estimate of the taxpayer's ability to pay taxes due based on an analysis of gross income, less necessary living expenses, for a specific number of months into the future. In general, a taxpayer's current income will now be used in the analysis of future ability to pay.

Revised IRM section 5.8.5 now provides taxpayers with specific examples of when the use of income averaging and/or a collateral agreement is appropriate as follows:

Example 27-12: *Unemployed*. The taxpayer is a construction worker and between jobs. A review of the taxpayer's previous annual income and/or income averaging may be the appropriate method to determine taxpayer's income for calculation purposes.

Example 27-13: *Underemployed*. If a taxpayer is a teacher but recently moved, and is currently at a lesser paying job until a teaching position becomes available, or has been hired and does not begin work until the school season begins, the taxpayer is considered to be currently underemployed. The taxpayer's anticipated income once the taxpayer is fully employed should be considered.

Example 27-14: *Long-term unemployed*. Taxpayer has been unemployed for over one year. There are currently no employment opportunities for the taxpayer and the household is living on one income. Use of the taxpayer's current income with a future income collateral agreement (as discussed further below) is appropriate.

Promotion of Effective Tax Administration

The IRS may accept a taxpayer's offer-in-compromise in order to promote effective tax administration where it determines that, although collection in full could be achieved, collection of the full liability would cause the taxpayer economic hardship, which is defined as the inability to pay reasonable basic living expenses [Reg. § 301.6343-1(d)]. The IRS is prohibited from rejecting an offer-in-compromise from a low-income taxpayer solely on the basis of the amount of the offer [Code Sec. 7122(d)(3)(A)]. The following key factors would support a determination of economic hardship:

1. The taxpayer is incapable of earning a living because of a long-term illness, medical condition, or disability, and it is reasonably foreseeable that taxpayer's financial resources will be exhausted providing for care and support during the course of the condition;
2. Although the taxpayer has certain monthly income, that income is exhausted each month in providing for the care of dependents with no other means of support; and
3. Although the taxpayer has certain assets, the taxpayer is unable to borrow against the equity in those assets and liquidation of those assets to pay outstanding tax liabilities would render the taxpayer unable to meet basic living expenses [Reg. § 301.7122-1(c)(3)].

Factors Undermining Compliance

The IRS will not accept an offer-in-compromise if compromise of the liability would undermine compliance by the taxpayers with the tax law. Factors supporting a determination that the compromise would undermine compliance include the fact that the taxpayer has:

1. A history of noncompliance with the filing and payment requirements;
2. Taken deliberate actions to avoid the payment of taxes; and
3. Encouraged others to refuse to comply with the tax laws [Reg. § 301.7122-1(c)(3)].

Example 27-15: The taxpayer has assets sufficient to satisfy the tax liability. The taxpayer provides full-time care and assistance to his dependent child, who has a serious long-term illness. It is expected that the taxpayer will need to use the equity in his assets to provide for adequate basic living expenses and medical care for his child. The taxpayer's overall compliance history does not weigh against compromise [Reg. § 301.7122-1(c)(3)(iii), Ex.1].

Example 27-16: The taxpayer is retired and his only income is from a pension. The taxpayer's only asset is a retirement account, and the funds in the account are sufficient to satisfy the liability. Liquidation of the retirement account would leave the taxpayer without an adequate means to provide for basic living expenses. The taxpayer's overall compliance history does not weigh against compromise [Reg. § 301.7122-1(c)(3)(iii), Ex.2].

Example 27-17: The taxpayer is disabled and lives on a fixed income that will not, after allowance of basic living expenses, permit full payment of his liability under an installment agreement. The taxpayer also owns a modest house that has been specially equipped to accommodate his disability. The taxpayer's equity in the house is sufficient to permit payment of the liability he owes. However, because of his disability and limited earning potential, the taxpayer is unable to obtain a mortgage or otherwise borrow against this equity. In addition, because the taxpayer's home has been specially equipped to accommodate his disability, forced sale of the taxpayer's residence would create severe adverse consequences for the taxpayer. The taxpayer's overall compliance history does not weigh against compromise [Reg. § 301.7122-1(c)(3)(iii), Ex.3].

In deciding whether or not to accept a taxpayer's offer-in-compromise the IRS will look at two factors:

1. How much the taxpayer's assets less encumbrances are worth, taking into account the quick sale or liquidation value, which is the amount that would be realized from the sale of an asset in a situation where financial pressure causes the taxpayer to sell in a short period of time. In addition, the IRS will scrutinize assets, which have been transferred to related parties.
2. How much can be collected from the taxpayer's future income. When the IRS calculates a taxpayer's reasonable collection potential, it will now look at only one year of future income for offers paid in five or fewer months, down from four years, and two years of future income for offers paid in six to 24 months, down from five years. All offers must be fully paid within 24 months of the date the offer is accepted.
3. The IRS uses the Allowable Living Expense standards in cases requiring financial analysis to determine a taxpayer's ability to pay. These standards provide consistency and fairness in collection determinations by incorporating average expenditures for basic necessities for citizens in similar geographic areas. These standards are also used when evaluating installment agreement requests.

Lump-sum offers. Unless a waiver applies, a lump-sum offer in compromise must be accompanied by a down payment of at least 20 percent of the amount of the offer [Code Sec. 7122(c)(1)(A)]. A lump-sum offer includes single payments as well as payments made in five or fewer installments. If the taxpayer makes a partial payment of less than the 20 percent required amount, the IRS may accept the offer for processing and solicit payment of the remaining portion of the 20 percent amount. If the taxpayer does not pay the balance of the 20 percent amount in a timely manner, the IRS may return the offer as nonprocessable unless the IRS determines that continued processing of the offer would be in the best interests of the government.

Periodic payment offers. Taxpayers submitting requests for a periodic-payment offer in compromise (one payable in six or more installments) must include the first proposed installment payment with their application and continue making payments under the terms proposed while the offer is being evaluated [Code Sec. 7122(c)(1)(B)]. Unless a waiver applies, a periodic payment offer in compromise will be returned as nonprocessable if the submission of the offer is not accompanied by the full amount of the first proposed installment [Code Sec. 7122(d)(3)(C)]. Taxpayers qualifying as low-income or filing an offer based solely on doubt as to liability can receive a waiver of the new partial payment requirements.

If a periodic payment offer has been accepted for processing and the taxpayer fails to make full payment of the second or subsequent proposed installment while the offer is being evaluated, the IRS may solicit payment from the taxpayer of the unpaid amount of the subsequent installment. Additionally, taxpayers who fail to make payments under the terms of a periodic payment offer will be deemed to have withdrawn their offers [Code Sec. 7122(c)(1)(B)].

Offers automatically deemed accepted. The IRS will deem an offer in compromise accepted that is not withdrawn, returned, or rejected within 24 months after receipt of the offer [Code Sec. 7122(f)]. The postmark date is irrelevant in determining when an offer is submitted. The date an offer is rejected is the date on which the IRS issues a written notice of rejection. When calculating the 24-month time frame, the IRS will disregard any time periods when a liability included in the offer in compromise is the subject of a dispute in any court proceeding.

IRS treatment of OIC required payment. The IRS will treat the required payments as payments of tax, rather than refundable deposits.

Voluntary payments. Voluntary payments submitted in connection with an offer in compromise, to the extent they exceed the payment or payments required under Code Sec. 7122(c)(1), will be treated as refundable deposits if they are not designated as tax payments by the taxpayer.

Taxpayer may specify how payment applied. The taxpayer may specify how any payment made in conjunction with an offer in compromise is to be applied to the assessed taxes, penalties, interest, etc. [Code Sec. 7122(c)(2)(A)]. The specification must be made in writing when the offer is submitted or when the payment is made. The specification should clearly indicate how the partial payment or partial payments (in the case of a periodic payment offer) are to be applied to specific tax years (or other taxable periods) or to specific liabilities (e.g., income taxes, employment taxes, and trust fund recovery penalties). Once the taxpayer specifies how a payment is to be applied, the specification cannot later be changed. In the absence of a specification, the IRS will apply the required payment or payments in the best interests of the government.

User fees. When submitting Form 656, *Offer in Compromise,* taxpayers must include user fee of $150 before January 1, 2014. The fee for processing an offer to compromise on or after January 1, 2014 is $186 [Prop. Reg. § 300.3(b)(1)]. No fee is imposed on a low-income taxpayer. A low-income taxpayer is an individual whose income falls below poverty levels based on guidelines established by the U.S. Department of Health and Human Services. Taxpayers claiming the low-income exception should use the worksheet to Form 656-A, *Income Certification for Offer in Compromise Application Fee and Payment*, to determine if they qualify.

Doubt as to Liability

Revised Form 656 no longer contains a category based on doubt as to liability. Instead, taxpayers must use Form 656-L where taxpayers indicate the amount that the taxpayer believes is the correct amount of tax liability after credits. The taxpayer also must attach a detailed statement and supporting documents explaining the reasons why the assessed tax is incorrect.

Beware of Offers in Compromise Scams

The IRS has issued a consumer alert advising taxpayers who are having difficulty paying their tax bills to beware of unscrupulous promoters who claim that tax debts can be settled for "pennies on the dollar" through the Offer in Compromise (OIC) Program. Apparently, the IRS has become aware of some dishonest tax advisers who are collecting fees from taxpayers after convincing them erroneously that they should file an OIC application with the IRS. In most of these situations, the taxpayers have no chance of satisfying the OIC Program's requirements and the promoter retains the fee.

.02 Closing Agreements

The IRS may enter into what is known as a closing agreement with you on Form 866, in order to settle your complete liability. Form 866, *Agreement as to Final Determination of Tax Liability,* is used to conclusively close the tax liability for a tax period ending prior to the date of the closing agreement. The agreement is final and conclusive except upon a showing of fraud, malfeasance or misrepresentation of a material fact [Code. Sec. 7121(b); Reg. § 301.7121-1(c)]. The agreement generally is used in cases where you have made concessions because of others made by the government, and it is necessary to bar further action by either party. It is also used when a fiduciary desires to be discharged by the court and when corporations are winding up their affairs.

.03 Installment Agreements

An alternative to the offer-in-compromise is for you to enter into a written agreement with the IRS providing that you will pay the IRS the taxes that you owe them including interest and penalties in installment payments. Keep in mind, that this option differs from the offer-in-compromise because an installment agreement does not reduce the amount of taxes, interest, or penalties owed. However, it does give you more time to pay your tax bill and forestalls the IRS enforcement actions which can include levies or seizures. Request an installment agreement by filing Form 9465, *Installment Agreement Request* with your tax return. You need not submit detailed financial statements with the form. For further discussion, see Ch. 26.

¶27,040 APPEARANCE AT TAX PROCEEDINGS

Attorneys and certified public accountants may represent you before the IRS by filing a declaration stating they are currently so qualified in a particular state, possession, territory or commonwealth of the U.S. or in the District of Columbia, and are authorized to act for the designated client.[19] Other persons generally must be enrolled as agents [discussed below] before they can practice.

However, appearance without enrollment is possible in some cases. An individual may appear on his or her own behalf; full-time employees may appear for their employer; corporate officers and partners may appear for their corporation or partnership; fiduciaries or their full-time employees may appear for the entity they act for; and return preparers may deal with an examining agent [discussed below].[20] The Internal Revenue Service can discipline and disbar any person who appears before it.[21]

The Tax Court has its own rules for admission to practice [¶ 27,180].

---

[19] Treas. Dept. Circular No. 230, Sec 10.3.

[20] Treas. Dept. Circular No. 230, Sec 10.7.

[21] Treas. Dept. Circular No. 230, Sec 10.5.

.01 Admission to Practice Before IRS

Persons other than attorneys or CPAs must pass a written examination and be enrolled before they can practice before the IRS. Practice includes preparation and filing of documents (except tax returns), communication with the Service and representing clients at conferences, hearings or meetings.[22] Attorneys and CPAs cannot enroll as agents.[23] Application for examination is made on Form 2587, *Application for Special Enrollment Examination.* Application for enrollment is made on Form 23, *Application for Enrollment to Practice Before the Internal Revenue Service.* A filing fee must accompany the form. Successful applicants receive a permanent registration card.[24] The requirements for admission to practice and the disciplinary procedures may be found in Department Circular No. 230, which is discussed in greater detail below.

.02 Persons Preparing Returns

Unenrolled persons who prepare tax returns, if properly authorized (see below), can represent you before the revenue agent or examining officer [¶27,005]as to returns they have prepared.[25]

.03 Power of Attorney Required

Practitioners should obtain a power of attorney from the taxpayer, covering all responsibilities they may be called upon to exercise for you before the IRS. Form 2848, *Power of Attorney and Declaration of Representative,* can be used for this purpose.

.04 Tax Information Authorization

If your representative is simply to receive confidential information, the representative must file Form 8821, *Tax Information Authorization.* The authorization is not a substitute for situations that require a power of attorney such as to receive a refund check or sign a return on your behalf [Reg. §§601.502, 601.504].

> ▶ **OBSERVATION:** Form 8821 is strictly limited to allowing the designated representative to receive and/or inspect tax information in an IRS office. If broader powers are needed, Form 2848 [discussed above] must be filed. Taxpayers may check a box on their tax return to authorize a paid preparer who signs the return to work directly with the IRS to fix return-processing problems. The "check box" replaces Form 8821 but only for return-processing issues. Once the IRS completes processing the return, the authorization ends. The new box won't replace a power of attorney and thus won't let preparers represent or act for taxpayers.

.05 Circular 230 Standards of Practice

Tax professionals including attorneys, certified public accountants, enrolled agents, registered tax return preparers, and enrolled actuaries, who practice before the IRS are subject to the rules found in Treasury Department Circular 230.[26] In general, these rules govern who may represent taxpayers before the IRS, the duties and restrictions imposed on these representatives, the sanctions for any violation, and disciplinary proceedings. In particular, Circular 230 provides requirements that representatives

[22] Treas. Dept. Circular No. 230, Sec 10.2.

[23] Treas. Dept. Circular No. 230, Sec 10.4.

[24] Treas. Dept. Circular No. 230, Sec 10.6.

[25] Treas. Dept. Circular No. 230, Sec 10.7.

[26] Treas. Dept. Circular No. 230, Sec. 10.3(f).

must follow when issuing a tax shelter opinion (written advice regarding the federal tax aspects of a tax shelter). Practitioners who violate any of these rules of practice may be subject to censure, in addition to disbarment or suspension. The IRS may also impose monetary penalties for such violations in addition to, or in lieu of, suspension, disbarment, or censure. Employers, firms, and entities for whom a representative may be acting may also be subject to separate monetary penalties if the employer, firm, or entity knew, or reasonably should have known, of the representative's conduct. The amount of the monetary penalty imposed, however, cannot exceed the gross income derived from such conduct.

The Circular 230 regulations on tax shelter opinion standards establish "best practices" standards for those practicing before the IRS and provide mandatory standards for practitioners who provide *covered opinions*. The regulations define covered opinions and explain the requirements for these documents, as well as disclosures, and other written advice.

Standards for Tax Returns and Documents, Affidavits and Other Papers

Under Reg. § 10.34(a)(1)(i) and (ii), a practitioner may not willfully, recklessly, or through gross incompetence, advise a client to take a position on a tax return or claim for refund, or prepare a portion of a tax return or claim for refund containing a position, sign a tax return or claim for refund that the practitioner knows or reasonably should know contains a position that: (a) lacks a reasonable basis; (b) is an unreasonable position; or (c) is a willful attempt by the practitioner to understate the liability for tax or a reckless or intentional disregard of rules or regulations by the practitioner as described in Code Sec. 6694(b)(2).

A practitioner is subject to discipline under Reg. § 10.34(a) only after willful, reckless, or grossly incompetent conduct. Multiple practitioners from the same firm may be disciplined if their conduct in connection with the same act(s) does not comply with the standard of conduct required under Reg. § 10.34.

Best practices for tax advisors. The best practices rules are defined as "aspirational." Thus, a practitioner who fails to comply with best practices will not be subject to discipline. Even though the best practices rules are solely aspirational, tax professionals are expected to observe them to preserve public confidence in the tax system. The tax advisors should provide clients with the highest qualify representation concerning federal tax issues by adhering to best practices in providing advice and in preparing or assisting in the preparation of a submission to the IRS. Best practices to be observed by all tax advisors include:

1. Communicating clearly with the client regarding the terms of the engagement. For example, the advisor should determine the client's expected purpose for and use of the advice and should have a clear understanding with the client regarding the form and scope of the advice or assistance to be rendered;
2. Establishing the relevant facts, including evaluating the reasonableness of any assumptions or representations, relating the applicable law and judicial doctrines and arriving at a conclusion supported by the law and the facts;
3. Advising the client regarding the import of the conclusions reached, including for example, whether a taxpayer may avoid accuracy-related penalties if a taxpayer acts in reliance on the advice;
4. Acting fairly and with integrity in practice before the IRS.

Tax advisors with responsibility for overseeing a firm's practice of providing advice concerning federal tax issues or of preparing or assisting in the preparation of submissions to the IRS are advised to take reasonable steps to ensure that the firm's procedures for all associates and employees are consistent with the best practices standards outlined above.

Requirements for covered opinions. Strict requirements are imposed on covered opinions which include written advice (including electronic communications) that concern one or more federal tax issue(s) arising from:

1. A transaction that is the same as or substantially similar to a transaction that the IRS has determined to be tax avoidance transaction and is identified by the IRS as a listed transaction in Reg. § 1.6011-4(b)(2);
2. Any partnership or other entity, any investment plan or arrangement, or any other plan or arrangement with a principal purpose of avoiding or evading any tax; or
3. Any partnership or other entity, any investment plan or arrangement, or any other plan or arrangement with a principal purpose of avoiding or evading any tax if the written advice is:
   - A reliance opinion which is defined as written advice that concludes at a confidence level of at least more likely than not that one or more significant federal tax issues would be resolved in the taxpayer's favor. Written advice is not treated as a reliance opinion if the practitioner prominently discloses in the written advice that it was not written to be used and cannot be used for the purpose of avoiding penalties imposed on the taxpayer;
   - A marketed opinion which exists if the practitioner knows or has reason to know that the written advice will be used or referred to by a person other than the practitioner in promoting, marketing, or recommending a partnership or other entity, investment plan, or arrangement of a taxpayer;
   - Subject to conditions of confidentiality which exist if the practitioner imposes on one or more recipients of the written advice a limitation on disclosure of the tax treatment or tax structure of the transaction and the limitation on disclosure is legally binding. A claim that a transaction is proprietary or exclusive is not a limitation on disclosure if the practitioner confirms to all recipients of the written advice that there is no limitation on disclosure of the tax treatment or tax structure of the transaction that is the subject of the written advice; or
   - Subject to contractual protection which exists if the taxpayer has the right to a full or partial refund of fees paid to the practitioner if all or a part of the intended tax consequences from the matters addressed in the written advice are not sustained, or if the fees paid to the practitioner are contingent on the taxpayer's realization of tax benefits from the transaction.

Excluded advice. A covered opinion does not include written advice provided to a client during the course of an engagement if a practitioner is reasonably expected to provide subsequent written advice to the client that satisfies the requirements outlined above. Similarly, written advice generally will not be treated as a covered opinion if it does not concern a listed transaction or a plan or arrangement having the principal purpose of avoidance or evasion of tax and the written advice contains this disclosure. In addition, a covered opinion does not include written advice that concerns qualified plan qualifications, is a state or local bond opinion, or is included in documents that must be filed with the SEC. Even though state and local bond opinions are excluded from the definition of covered opinions, they are addressed in a separate proposed regulation and are subject to Circular 230 standards relating to written advice.

Requirements for covered opinions. In order to ensure that taxpayers receive information that is necessary for them to evaluate and rely on a covered opinion, the final regulations impose strict requirements on covered opinions. A practitioner providing a covered opinion must comply with each the following requirements:

- Use reasonable efforts to identify and ascertain all relevant facts and not rely on and base an opinion on any unreasonable factual assumptions or representations. For example, it is unreasonable to assume that a transaction has a business purpose or that a transaction is potentially profitable apart from tax benefits. A factual assumption includes reliance on a projection, financial forecast, or appraisal. It is unreasonable for a practitioner to rely on a projection, financial forecast, or appraisal if the practitioner know or should know that it is incorrect or incomplete or was prepared by a person lacking the skills or qualifications necessary to prepare the projection, financial forecast, or appraisal.
- Relate the applicable law (including potentially applicable judicial doctrines) to the relevant facts rather than rely on any unreasonable legal assumptions, representations, or conclusion;
- Evaluate all significant federal tax issues and reach a conclusion, supported by the facts and the law regarding the likelihood that the taxpayer will prevail on the merits with respect to each significant federal tax issue; and
- Provide an overall conclusion as to the federal tax treatment of the tax shelter item(s) and the reasons for that conclusion. If the practitioner is unable to reach a conclusion with respect to one of these issues, the opinion must state that the practitioner is unable to reach a conclusion with respect to those issues. The opinion must describe the reasons for the conclusions, including the facts and analysis supporting the conclusions, or describe the reasons that the practitioner is unable to reach a conclusion as to one or more issues.

Required disclosures. The following disclosures must be made in covered opinions:

- Prominent disclosure of the relationship between practitioner and the shelter promoter and any compensation arrangement, such as a referral fee or a fee-sharing arrangement between the practitioner and any person involved in the promoting, marketing, or recommending the entity, plan, or arrangement that is the subject of the opinion;
- A marketed opinion must prominently disclose that it was written to support the marketing or promotion of the arrangement and that the taxpayer should seek advice based on his particular circumstances from an independent tax advisor.
- A limited scope opinion must prominently disclose that it is limited to the issue(s) addressed in the opinion, that additional issue(s) may exist that could affect the federal tax treatment of the arrangement addressed in the opinion, that the opinion does not consider or reach a conclusion on those additional issues, and that the

opinion was not written, and cannot be used by the recipient, to avoid penalties for those issues outside the scope of the opinion.

- A practitioner must disclose whether an opinion fails to reach a conclusion at a confidence level of at least more likely than not with respect to a significant issue(s) addressed by the opinion and that the opinion was not written, and cannot be used by the recipient to avoid penalties for those issue(s).

Requirements for other noncovered written advice. A tax practitioner may not give written advice (including electronic communications) if the practitioner: (1) bases the written advice on unreasonable factual or legal assumptions; (2) unreasonably relies upon representations, statements, findings, or agreements of the taxpayer or any other person; (3) fails to consider all relevant facts; or (4) takes into account the possibility that a tax return will not be audited, that an issue will not be raised on audit, or that an issue will be settled.

New oversight responsibilities. Practitioners with responsibilities for overseeing a firm's practice of providing advice on federal tax issues must take reasonable steps to ensure that the firm has adequate procedures in place for all members, associates, and employees.

ASSESSMENT AND COLLECTION OF TAX

¶27,045 WHEN TAX MUST BE ASSESSED AND COLLECTED

.01 In General

An assessment is an administrative recording of a taxpayer's liability and sets the collection process in motion. An assessment is made by recording the taxpayer's liability. The purpose of the formal assessment is to ensure that the IRS is maintaining proper records and that taxpayers receive a record of their tax liability.

Code Sec. 6501 provides that the IRS is generally required to assess tax (or send a notice of deficiency) within 3 years after the later of the date the tax return is filed or the due date of the tax return. The United States Supreme Court says that for S corporations, the three-year period begins when the shareholders file their returns and not when the S corporation files its return.[27] Code Sec. 6501(a), clarifies that the return that starts the running of the statute of limitations for a taxpayer is the return of the taxpayer, not the return of a person or entity from whom the taxpayer has received an item of income, gain, loss, deduction, or credit.

> **NOTE:** A tax assessed or collected after the statute of limitations has expired is treated as an overpayment. It will be credited or refunded to you if you file a timely refund claim [Code Sec. 6401; Reg. § 301.6401-1].

To determine whether the document filed by the taxpayer qualified as a valid return for purposes of tolling the three-year statute of limitations under Code Sec. 6501(a),

[27] *S.B. Bufferd*, 93-1 USTC ¶50,038, 506 US 523, 113 SCt 927.

the taxpayer must satisfy the following requirements listed by the court in *R.D. Beard*:[28] (1) the document must contain sufficient data to calculate tax liability; (2) the document must purport to be a return; (3) there must be an honest and reasonable attempt to satisfy the requirements of the tax law; and (4) the taxpayer must have executed the document under penalties of perjury. Perfect accuracy is not required for the document to constitute a return.

.02 Omission of Substantial Amount of Income Results in Extended Limitations Period

The period of limitations on assessments is extended from 3 years to 6 years when a taxpayer omits a substantial amount of gross income from an income tax return [Code Sec. 6501(e)(1)(A)]. A substantial omission is an amount that's greater than 25 percent of the amount of gross income stated in the return. For a trade or business, gross income means the total of the amounts received or accrued from the sale of goods or services (if such amounts are required to be shown on the return) prior to diminution by the cost of such sales or services [Code Sec. 6501(e)(1)(A)(i); Reg. § 301.6501(e)-1(a)(ii)]. The regulations provide that an understatement of gross income resulting from an overstatement of basis constitutes an omission from gross income for purposes of Code Sec. 6501(e)(1)(A) [Reg. § 301.6501(e)-1(a)(iii)].

Extended Statute of Limitations Applied When Accountant Embezzled Money

In *City Wide Transit, Inc.*,[29] the Court of Appeals for the Second Circuit reversed the Tax Court to conclude that the IRS could make an employment tax assessment after expiration of Code Sec. 6501(a) three-year statute of limitations because the taxpayer's accountant filed fraudulent tax returns in order to embezzle money owed to the IRS. Instead of filing correct returns that had been prepared by a third-party payroll company, the accountant prepared, signed and filed returns to which he added a fraudulent tax credit that reduced the company's tax liabilities. He then altered company checks made out to the IRS, deposited them in his own account and drafted new checks to cover the company's reduced tax liability. The court concluded that the accountant's fraudulent activity triggered an open-ended assessment period available to the IRS under Code Sec. 6501(c).

Six-Year Assessment Period Not Applicable to Overstated Basis Deficiency

In *Home Concrete & Supply, LLC*,[30] the U.S. Supreme Court resolved a split among the appellate courts and the Tax Court when it concluded that a taxpayer's overstatement of its basis in an asset that resulted in an understatement of gross income from the asset's sale did not trigger the extended 6-year limitations period under Code Sec. 6501(e)(1)(A) because a basis overstatement is not an "omission from gross income." The Supreme Court found that the court's prior decision in *Colony, Inc.*[31] controlled. In that case, the Court interpreted identical language and limited the statute's scope to situations where specific receipts were left out of the computation of gross income.

---

[28] *R.D. Beard*, CA-6, 86-2 USTC ¶ 9496, 793 F2d 139.

[29] *City Wide Transit, Inc.*, CA-2, 2013-1 USTC ¶ 50,211, 709 F3d 102.

[30] *Home Concrete & Supply, LLC*, SCt , 2012-1 USTC ¶ 50,315, 132 SCt 71, *aff'g*, CA-4, 2011-1 USTC ¶ 50,207, 634 F3d 249.

[31] *Colony, Inc.*, SCt, 58-2 USTC ¶ 9593, 357 US 28 (1958).

The court therefore held that Code Sec. 6501(e)(1)(A) does not apply to an overstatement of basis and concluded that the 6-year period did not apply.

Future of Regulation in Light of Supreme Court Decision

With this decision, the Supreme Court has effectively invalidated Reg. § 301.6501(e)-1(a)(1)(iii), which generally provides that an understated amount of gross income resulting from an overstatement of unrecovered cost or other basis constitutes an omission from gross income for purposes of Code Sec. 6501(e)(1)(A). We can expect to see the IRS to withdraw and rewrite this regulation in the near future to reflect the Supreme Court's decision in *Home Concrete*.

.03 Extended Limitations Period for Income Omissions Attributable to Foreign Assets

The limitations period is six years if there is an omission of gross income in excess of $5,000 and the omitted gross income is attributable to a foreign financial asset with respect to which:

- Information reporting is required under Code Sec. 6038D (see ¶ 28,085), or
- Would be required if Code Sec, 6038D were applied without regard to the $50,000 aggregate asset value threshold amount and any other exceptions provided by IRS regulations in the case of duplicative disclosure of certain classes of assets [Code Sec. 6501(e)(1)(A)].

Any resulting tax deficiency arising from the omission of income in excess of $5,000 attributable to a foreign financial asset may be assessed, or a court proceeding for collection of such tax deficiency may be begun without assessment, at any time within six years after the tax return was filed [Code Sec. 6501(e)(1)(A)]. The current exception providing for a six-year limitations period for substantial omission of an amount in excess of 25 percent of the all gross income reported on the return remains unchanged. The six-year limitations period for the omission of income attributable to foreign assets and for substantial omission of gross income also applies in the case of such omissions of income by partnerships [Code Sec. 6229(c)(2)].

The statute of limitations period will be suspended if a taxpayer fails to timely provide information with respect to foreign financial assets required to be reported under Code Sec. 6038D or information with respect to passive foreign investment companies (PFIC) required to be reported. Thus, the limitations period will not begin to run until the information required by these provisions has been furnished to the IRS. The rule for the suspension of the limitations period in the case of failure to provide required information on foreign transfers is also clarified to provide that such a rule applies to the limitations period for assessment of tax imposed with respect to any return, event or period to which the information required to be reported relates.

.04 Assessment without Prior Assessment

In the following situations, the tax may be assessed, or a proceeding in court for collection of such tax may be begun without assessment at any time: (1) filing a false or fraudulent return with the intent to evade tax; (2) willful attempt to evade tax; (3) failure to file a return; (4) agreement to extend time when tax may be assessed; (5) when private foundation status has been terminated; (6) where gift tax on certain gifts is not shown on the return [Code Sec. 6501(c); Reg. § 301.6501(c)].

The Supreme Court allowed tax to be assessed at any time even though a fraudulent filer submitted a voluntary nonfraudulent return after the original return.[32] An unsigned or incompletely signed return may be treated as no return at all.[33]

.05 Commencement of Criminal Tax Prosecution

A criminal prosecution results in criminal penalties punishable by a fine of up to $100,000 ($500,000 for a corporation) and/or up to five years' imprisonment, plus costs of prosecution. [See ¶ 27,110]. In order to convict someone of criminal tax evasion under Code Sec. 7201, the law requires the government to prove the following three elements beyond a reasonable doubt: (1) willfulness; (2) an affirmative act constituting evasion or attempted evasion of tax; and (3) the existence of a tax deficiency.[34] Keep in mind that shareholders can only be found guilty of criminal tax evasion if a tax deficiency exists as a result of the evasion.[35]

A criminal prosecution must generally be started within three years after the offense is committed [Code Sec. 6531]. When a taxpayer commits a series of evasive acts over several years after incurring a tax liability, the statute of limitations begins to run on the date of the last evasive act.[36] A six-year period applies in a case where there is: (1) fraud or an attempt to defraud the U.S. by conspiracy or otherwise; (2) a willful attempt to evade or defeat any tax or payment: (3) willful aiding or assisting in the preparation of a false return or other document; (4) willful failure to pay any tax or make any return at the time required by law; (5) a false statement verified under penalties of perjury or a false or fraudulent return, statement or other document; (6) intimidation of a U.S. officer or employee; (7) an offense committed by a U.S. officer or employee in connection with a revenue law; and (8) a conspiracy to defeat tax or payment [Code Sec. 6531].

.06 Suit to Collect Tax

The government may collect tax by levy [¶ 27,070] or by suit if a timely court proceeding is begun. So long as the tax is still collectible, the statute of limitations will not expire. A judgment against you does not change the period for collection by levy [Code Sec. 6502(a); Reg. § 301.6502-1]. The collection period may be extended by written agreement between you and District Director before the period ends. Collection time may be extended after the period ends, if a levy was made during the period, and the extension is agreed upon before the levy is released [Code Sec. 6502(a); Reg. § 301.6502-1(a)(2)].

Collection of Tax Liabilities After Assessment Under Code Sec. 6502

Pursuant to Code Sec. 6502(a)(1), the IRS generally has 10 years from the date of assessment to collect a timely assessed tax liability [Reg. § 301.6502-1(a)]. In addition, the Code contains several provisions that operate to toll (extend) the period of limitations on collection upon the occurrence of certain events. For example, Code Sec. 6331(k) operates in part to suspend the period of limitations on collection for the

---

[32] *E. Badaracco*, 84-1 USTC ¶ 9150, 464 US 386, 104 SCt 756.

[33] *J.U. Reaves*, CA-5, 61-2 USTC ¶ 9703, 295 F2d 336.

[34] *M.C. Sansone*, 65-1 USTC ¶ 9307, 380 US 343, 85 SCt 1004.

[35] *J. D'Agostino*, CA-2, 98-1 USTC ¶ 50,380, 145 F3d 69.

[36] *L.F. Anderson*, CA-10, 2003-1 USTC ¶ 50,237, 319 F3d 1218.

period of time during which an offer in compromise is pending, for 30 days after rejection, and while a timely filed appeal is pending. Similarly, Code Sec. 6503(h) operates to suspend the period of limitations on collection for the period of time during which the IRS is prohibited from collecting a tax due to a bankruptcy proceeding, and for six months thereafter. These statutory suspension provisions toll the period of limitations on collection even if the period of limitations on collection previously has been extended pursuant to an executed collection extension agreement.[37]

Collection After Assessment

In any case in which a tax has been assessed within the applicable statutory period of limitations on assessment, a proceeding in court to collect the tax may be commenced, or a levy to collect the tax may be made, within 10 years after the date of assessment [Reg. § 301.6502-1]. The IRS may enter into an agreement with a taxpayer to extend the period of limitations on collection in the following circumstances:

1. *Extension agreement entered into in connection with an installment agreement.* If the IRS and the taxpayer enter into an installment agreement for the tax liability prior to the expiration of the period of limitations on collection, at the time the installment agreement is entered into, they may enter into a written agreement to extend the period of limitations on collection to a date certain. A written extension agreement entered into under this paragraph shall extend the period of limitations on collection until the 89th day after the date agreed upon in the written agreement [Reg. § 301.6502-1(b)(1)].
2. *Extension agreement entered into in connection with the release of a levy under Code Sec. 6343.* If the IRS has levied on any part of the taxpayer's property prior to the expiration of the period of limitations on collection and the levy is subsequently released pursuant to Code Sec. 6343 after the expiration of the period of limitations on collection, prior to the release of the levy, the IRS and the taxpayer may enter into a written agreement to extend the period of limitations on collection to a date certain. A written extension agreement entered into under this paragraph will extend the period of limitations on collection until the date agreed upon in the extension agreement [Reg. § 301.6502-1(b)(2)].

Proceeding in court for the collection of the tax. If a proceeding in court for the collection of a tax is begun, the period during which the tax may be collected by levy is extended until the liability for the tax or a judgment against the taxpayer arising from the liability is satisfied or becomes unenforceable.

Effect of statutory suspensions of the period of limitations on collection if executed collection extension agreement is in effect. Any suspension of the period of limitations on collection tolls the running of the period of limitations on collection, as extended pursuant to an executed extension agreement for the amount of time set forth in the relevant statute.

Example 27-18: The IRS enters into an installment agreement with the taxpayer to provide for periodic payments of the taxpayer's timely assessed tax liabili-

[37] *K.M. Klingshirn*, CA-6, 98-2 USTC ¶ 50,538, 147 F3d 526.

ties. At the time the installment agreement is entered into, the taxpayer and the IRS execute a written agreement to extend the period of limitations on collection. The extension agreement executed in connection with the installment agreement operates to extend the period of limitations on collection to the date agreed upon in the extension agreement, plus 89 days. Subsequently, and prior to the expiration of the extended period of limitations on collection, the taxpayer files a bankruptcy petition under chapter 7 of the Bankruptcy Code and receives a discharge from bankruptcy a few months later. Assuming the tax is not discharged in the bankruptcy, Code sec. 6503(h) operates to suspend the running of the previously extended period of limitations on collection for the period of time the IRS is prohibited from collecting due to the bankruptcy proceeding, and for 6 months thereafter. The new expiration date for the IRS to collect the tax is the date agreed upon in the previously executed extension agreement, plus 89 days, plus the period during which the IRS is prohibited from collecting due to the bankruptcy proceeding, plus 6 months [Reg. § 301.6502-1(d)(2)].

Date when levy is considered made. The date on which a levy on property or rights to property is considered made is the date on which the notice of seizure required under Code Sec. 6335(a) is given [Reg. § 301.6502-1(e)].

.07 When Assessment Period Begins

If a return is filed before the due date, the assessment period generally runs from the due date of the tax return. If the return is for income or social security tax withheld from wages or tax withheld at source [Ch. 15] and is filed before April 15 of the next calendar year, the period runs from that April 15 date rather than the early filing date [Code Sec. 6501; Reg. § 301.6501(b)-1(b)].

Wrong Return Form

If a trust or partnership return is filed in good faith by an association that later is held to be a corporation, it is treated as the return of the corporation, and the limitation period starts to run with its filing [Code Sec. 6501(g)(1); Reg. § 301.6501(g)-1(a)]. A corporate return filed under an election to be taxed as an S corporation (Form 1120S) [Ch. 21] is treated the same way if the corporation is later found not qualified for the S corporation election [Reg. § 1.6037-1].

If a taxpayer in good faith files a return as an exempt organization, and later it is held to be a taxable organization or to have unrelated business income[38] [Ch. 23], the statute of limitations starts to run when the return is filed [Code Sec. 6501(g)(2); Reg. § 301.6501(g)-1(b)]. The taxpayer is still subject to penalties for failure to file a proper return or to pay tax.[39]

.08 Extension of Time

The period for assessment or collection may be extended if both the IRS and the taxpayer consent in writing to the extension (Form 872) [Code Sec. 6501(c)(4); Reg.

---

[38] Rev. Rul. 69-247, 1969-1 CB 303.

[39] Rev. Rul. 60-144, 1960-1 CB 636.

§ 301.6501(c)-1(d)]. Form 872-A is used instead of Form 872 if Appeals office consideration has been requested.[40]

> **NOTE:** Form 872, *Consent to Extend the Time to Assess Tax*, should not be confused with Form 870 discussed in ¶ 27,025.01. Form 870 permits a proposed deficiency to be assessed immediately and waives the right to file a petition with the Tax Court. Form 872 simply extends the time to make an assessment. The consent may be limited to particular unsettled issues.[41]

.09 Private Foundations

The assessment and collection of excise taxes imposed on private foundations generally must be made within the three-year period [Code Sec. 6501(a), (l); Reg. § 301.6501(n)-1].

¶27,050 SPECIAL LIMITATION PERIODS

Special limitation periods for assessment apply to sale of a home, involuntary conversion, transferee liability and some other situations. (Note that adjustments of tax may be allowed after the limitation period expires, under certain conditions [¶ 27,170]).

.01 Carrybacks

As to net operating losses and capital losses and general business credits—deficiency for tax year to which carryback is made (and attributable to carryback) may be assessed within period deficiency can be assessed for tax year carryback was created [Code Secs. 6501(h), (j), 6511(d)(4)(C); Reg. § § 301.6501(h)-1, 301.6501(j)-1].

Deficiency due to carryback of foreign tax credit may be assessed within one year after time to assess deficiency for year from which credit was carried; same rule for disallowed oil and gas extraction taxes [Code Sec. 6501(i)].

.02 Exploration Expenses

Deficiency due to election to use unlimited exploration expense deduction (or its revocation) can be assessed up to two years after election (or revocation) [Code Sec. 617(a)(2)(C)].

.03 Involuntary Conversion

If you elect not to recognize gain on involuntary conversion of property, time for assessing any deficiency runs for three years from date you notify IRS of replacement of converted property or of intention not to replace or of failure to replace within required time [Ch. 7] [Code Sec. 1033(a)(2)(C)(i); Reg. § 1.1033(a)-2(c)(5)].

.04 "Late" Joint Return

If a "late" joint return replaces separate returns, the limitation period cannot end less than one year after joint return is actually filed [Code Sec. 6013(b)(4); Reg. § 1.6013-2(d)].

---

[40] Instructions for Forms 872, 872-A.

[41] Rev. Proc. 68-31, 1968-2 CB 917, as modified by Rev. Proc. 77-6, 1977-1 CB 539.

.05 Last Minute Claims

If the IRS receives an amended return and the limitations period would expire within 60 days of such receipt, it has 60 days after the day it receives the amended return to assess any deficiency it discovers [Code Sec. 6501(c)(7)].

.06 Transfers to Foreign Corporations

Assessment period for Sec. 367 transfers runs three years from the date the IRS receives notice of the exchange [Code Sec. 6501(c)(8)].

.07 Partnerships

Time limit for assessment as to partnership items is three years from the return due date or date the return was filed (whichever is later) [¶27,135] [Code Sec. 6229(a)].

.08 Personal Holding Company

A special six-year period for assessment applies when a personal holding company (PHC) fails to furnish data on the special schedule of the corporate income tax return or a foreign PHC shareholder fails to report a constructive dividend [Code Sec. 6501(f); Reg. § 301.6501(f)].

.09 Transferee Liability

(1) Liability must be assessed against the first transferee within one year after the time for assessment against the transferor expires. (2) Assessment against a later transferee must be made within one year after the time to assess liability against the preceding transferee expires, but not later than three years after end of time to assess against the original transferor. (3) Time for assessing against a fiduciary expires the later of (a) one year after liability arises or (b) when the period for collecting tax expires [Code Sec. 6901(c)]. See ¶27,065 for further discussion of transferee liability.

.10 Gift Taxes—Special Valuation Rules for Transfers of Interests in Corporations, Partnerships, or Trusts

Special valuation rules apply for the gift tax on transfers of certain interests in corporations, partnerships or trusts. An unlimited assessment or collection period applies if there is an inadequate disclosure on the gift tax return. Thus, the statute of limitations does not run on an undisclosed or inadequately disclosed transfer. To adequately disclose a gift, attach a statement to the return in a manner sufficient to apprise the IRS of nature of the gift [Code Sec. 6501(c)(9)].

.11 Self-Employment Taxes

If a credit or refund claim relates to an overpayment of self-payment tax attributable to a Tax Court employment status proceeding under Code Sec. 7436 and the credit or refund is otherwise prevented by the operation of any Code provision except an offer in compromise under Code Sec. 7122, such credit or refund may be allowed or made if a claim is filed on or before the last day of the second year after the calendar year in which the Tax Court decision becomes final [Code Sec. 6511(d)(7)].

¶27,055 WHEN ASSESSMENT PERIOD IS REDUCED

The period for assessment of tax may be shortened by a request for prompt assessment. A quick assessment also can be made before the 90-day period [¶27,020] to prevent tax evasion.

.01 Request for Prompt Assessment

The assessment period may be shortened to 18 months after a request for prompt assessment is filed for a return of a decedent or a decedent's estate or a return for a dissolved or dissolving corporation. If there has been an omission amounting to over 25 percent of the gross income reported on the return, or if a personal holding company fails to file the required information schedule, the six-year period for assessment applies, despite the request for prompt assessment [Code Sec. 6501(d); Reg. § 301.6501(d)-1]. If fiduciaries distribute estate assets after 18 months and have no knowledge or reasonable belief a tax is due, they are not personally liable for the tax.[42]

.02 Termination Assessments

If taxpayers (including corporations in liquidation) intend, by immediate departure from the U.S. or some other way, to avoid the payment of the income tax, the IRS may immediately determine the income tax due and payable for the current or preceding tax year. However, the tax year is terminated only for tax computation so that the tax year continues until its normal end. The taxpayer may contest the assessment in the Tax Court in the same manner as a jeopardy assessment. The IRS must issue a deficiency notice within 60 days after the later of the return due date for the full tax year or the return filing date [Code Secs. 6851, 6867; Reg. § 1.6851-1].

Termination Assessments in Case of Political Expenditures

The IRS can make an immediate determination and assessment of income or excise tax against a charity if it has made political expenditures in flagrant violation of the prohibition against making political expenditures. Any tax assessed may be for the current or preceding year and becomes due and payable immediately. [Code Secs. 6852, 7409].

.03 Jeopardy Assessment

If a tax or deficiency (income, estate, gift or certain excise taxes) is jeopardized by delay, the IRS can immediately assess the tax and serve notice and demand for immediate payment. Also, this assessment procedure applies to someone who carries a large amount of cash and denies ownership of it. You may contest liability in the Tax Court [Code Sec. 6861, 6867; Reg. § 301.6861-1].

.04 Administrative and Court Review

The IRS must furnish a written detailed statement to you within five days following the jeopardy or termination assessment stating the reasons for the assessment. You have 30 days to request IRS to review. After the IRS review, you can bring a suit in an appropriate District Court [Code Sec. 7429(b)(2)(A); Reg. § 301.7429-1, 3]. If a jeopardy

---

[42] Rev. Rul. 66-43, 1966-1 CB 291.

assessment is made before a notice of deficiency has been sent, the IRS has 60 days to send one [Code Sec. 6861(b)].

.05 Bankruptcy

No immediate assessment [¶27,020] is permitted in bankruptcy proceedings except on (1) the bankruptcy estate or (2) the debtor if the bankruptcy court case determining the debtor's liability has become res judicata. An immediate assessment can be made on the appointment of a receiver [Code Secs. 6871(a), (b)].

The bankruptcy court determines any questions about the amount and validity of taxes of the bankrupt provided it has not been previously decided by a court of law (i.e., Tax Court). If a Tax Court proceeding is pending, however, you may still present your tax claims to the bankruptcy or receivership court for resolution [¶27,020] [Code Sec. 6871; Reg. § 301.6871-1]. No Tax Court petition may be filed or continued while a bankruptcy or receivership proceeding is pending. Bankruptcy law automatically stays the start of a Tax Court case until the stay is lifted, a discharge is granted or denied, or the bankruptcy case terminates. The stay applies if a deficiency notice has been issued and the time for filing the Tax Court petition has not expired.[43] When stayed, the 90- (or 150-) day period for filing is suspended [¶27,020]. The limitation period is tolled during the stay and is also tolled if the fiduciary fails to file a notice of appointment [¶27,060].

Under bankruptcy law, taxes due the U.S. or other governmental unit may be discharged except those for which (1) no return was filed, or if a return was filed, it had been due within two years before the case began; or (2) the debtor filed a fraudulent return or attempted to evade or defeat the tax in some manner; or (3) the federal law[44] has given a priority status.[45]

¶27,060 WHEN LIMITATION PERIOD IS SUSPENDED

.01 In General

Some periods are not counted in determining whether the three years, or other applicable period, for assessment and collection of tax has passed [Sec. 6503]. In effect, an equivalent period is added after what ordinarily would be the end of the limitation period [¶27,020].

Bankruptcy

Statute of limitations is suspended while an assessment or collection is prohibited under bankruptcy law [¶27,055], plus 60 days after (for assessment) and six months after (for collection) [Code Sec. 6503(h)].

Court Control of Assets

Statute of limitations is suspended while assets of the taxpayer are in control or custody of a court in any U.S. or state court proceeding, and for six months there after [Code Sec. 6503(b); Reg. § 301.6503(b)-1].

---

[43] 11 USC § 362(a)(8), (e), (d).

[44] 11 USC § 507(a)(6).

[45] 11 USC § 523(a)(1).

Deficiency Notice Issued

The statute of limitations is suspended while the IRS Commissioner is prohibited from making an assessment due to the issuance of a deficiency letter, and for 60 days after; but the final 60 days start to run on the date a waiver on Form 870 [¶27,025] is filed.[46] If the proceeding is placed on the Tax Court docket, the statute is suspended until 60 days after the decision of the Tax Court becomes final [Reg. § 301.6503(a)-1].

Failure to File Fiduciary Notice in Bankruptcy

In bankruptcy or receivership cases, when the fiduciary or receiver has to give notice to IRS of his appointment, the statute of limitations is suspended from the start of the proceeding until 30 days after receipt of the notice by IRS (but not over two years) [Code Sec. 6872; Reg. § 301.6872-1].

Foreign Expropriation Losses

Time to collect tax attributable to recovery of loss is extended for the time the tax payment is extended [Ch. 26] [Code Sec. 6503(e)].

Private Foundation—Retirement Plans

The limitation period on assessing or collecting excise or termination taxes on private foundations is suspended for one year or when the IRS extends the time for corrective action. Similar provisions apply to excise taxes [¶27,100] payable by certain retirement plans.

> **NOTE:** The one-year period allows the private foundation to take corrective action to avoid the penalty [Code Sec. 507(g)(2)].

Taxpayer Outside U.S.

The limitation period is suspended while the taxpayer is outside U.S. for six or more consecutive months. If fewer than six months of the collection period remains when he returns, collection is allowed up to six months after his return [Code Sec. 6503(c); Reg. § 301.6503(c)-1(b)].

Wrongful Levy

The 10-year limitation period for collection after assessment is suspended when money or other property of another person is wrongfully seized or received. The suspension runs from time the property is taken until 30 days after it is either voluntarily returned or judgment in suit to enjoin levy or recover the property becomes final [Code Sec. 6503(f); Reg. § 301.6503(g)-1].

> **NOTE:** If the dispute between the third-party recordkeeper and the IRS is not resolved within six months after the IRS issues an administrative summons, the statute of limitations is suspended until the issue is resolved [¶27,001] [Code Sec. 7609(e)].

Issuing Designated Summons by IRS

The statute of limitations is suspended for a corporation during the time the IRS issues a "designated summons" [Code Sec. 6503(k)(1)].

A *designated summons* is one that is issued to determine any tax imposed if it: (1) is issued at least 60 days before the assessment period expires (including any exten-

[46] Rev. Rul. 66-17, 1966-1 CB 272.

sions); and (2) clearly states that it is a designated summons for purposes of this rule [Code Sec. 6503(k)(2)].

A designated summons can be issued by the IRS only once for any tax year.

> **NOTE:** The statute of limitation can only be suspended for the issuance of a designated summons as to a corporation, not for individuals.

The statute of limitations is suspended for the period that begins when a lawsuit is brought in court to either enforce or quash the designated summons and ends on the date there is a final resolution of the summoned person's response to the summons [Code Sec. 6503(k)(3)].

> ▶ **OBSERVATION:** This rule is designed to preserve the IRS's ability to conclude the audit and assess any taxes that might be due regardless of the time it might take to obtain judicial resolution of the summons enforcement lawsuit.

These rules for suspending the statute of limitations also apply as to any summons issued during the 30-day period following the issuance of the designated summons.

IRS regional counsel must review any designated summons regarding a corporation's tax return prior to its issue [Code Sec. 6503(k)]. In addition, use of a designated summons is limited to corporations that are being examined as part of the Coordinated Examination Program [Code Sec. 6503(j)(1)]. The IRS is also required to submit an annual report to the taxwriting committees of all designated summonses issued each year [Code Sec. 6503(j)].

¶27,065 LIABILITY FOR TAX OF ANOTHER TAXPAYER

Transferee liability is generally assessed and collected the same way as the tax giving rise to the liability. However, special rules apply to the transferee. Unpaid assessments against children for compensation they earn can be made against the parents.

.01 Transferred Assets

Taxpayers who transfer property to others without adequate consideration, may result in the imposition of transferee liability on the transferee under Code Sec. 6901. Code Sec. 6901(a) does not create or define a substantive liability, but merely provides the IRS with a procedure to assess and collect from the property's transferee the transferor's existing liability. Substantive state law controls whether a transferee is liable for a transferor's tax liabilities.[47] Code Sec. 6901(a) provides that the liability of a transferee of a taxpayer's property may be "assessed, paid, and collected in the same manner and subject to the same provisions and limitations as in the case of the taxes with respect to which the liabilities were incurred." Thus, the transferee of the assets of an insolvent transferor is ordinarily liable for the accrued and unpaid taxes of the transferor. The same rule applies when assets have been transferred by a taxpayer who later died or by a corporation that later dissolved or terminated its existence without making adequate provision for tax liabilities, or when the transferor is made insolvent by the transfer.[48]

---

[47] *Frank Sawyer Trust of May 1992*, CA-1, 2013 USTC ¶50,253, 712 F3d 597.

[48] *S. Keller*, 21 BTA 84, Dec. 6423, *aff'd*, CA-7, 3 USTC ¶964, 59 F2d 499.

A *transferee* includes a donee, heir, legatee, devisee, and distributee [Code Sec. 6901(h); Reg. § 301.6901-1(b)].

Procedure

Transferee liability is assessed and collected the same as a deficiency [¶ 27,010 et seq.] [Code Sec. 6901; Reg. § 301.6901-1], but a special limitation period for assessment applies [¶ 27,050]. Retransfer of the assets after notice of liability is issued does not relieve the transferee from liability, unless he or she did not know about the original transfer.[49] Collection of a transferor's full tax from some transferees does not bar collection of another transferee's share, if those who paid file refund claims.[50] A transferee is not bound by a transferor's stipulation of tax liability not based on the merits of the case.[51]

> **NOTE:** The amount of the transferee's liability cannot be more than the assets received.

.02 Parent's Liability for Child

An assessment of tax against a child related to compensation the child earns has the effect of an assessment against the parent [Code Sec. 6201(c); Reg. § 301.6201-1(c)]. The government's collection remedies can be enforced against both the parent and the child.

.03 Child's Liability for Parent's Tax Debt

In *S.E. Rubenstein*,[52] the Tax Court concluded that under Code Sec. 6901(a), an individual who cared for his elderly father in his father's Florida condominium had transferee liability with respect to his father's unpaid income tax liabilities in an amount equal to the fair market value of the condominium as of the date that it was transferred to the taxpayer for token consideration.

.04 Successor Corporation Liable for Predecessor's Tax

The way out of financial difficulties is not to simply dissolve an old business and establish a new business with a different name. A new corporation will be held liable for the federal taxes, including employment taxes owed by its predecessor if the newly formed corporation is found to be merely a continuation of the original business.[53] In deciding whether a successor business is merely a continuation of the old business with a new name, the court will consider the following factors: (1) the continuity of management and control, (2) retention of executive and operating personnel, (3) operation in the identical location and space, (4) transfer of assets from the old business to the new, (5) operation of the same business enterprise.

In *D.R. Griffin*,[54] the Tax Court held that an individual who sold part of his corporation's assets in one transaction and all of his corporate stock in a second transaction was not liable as a transferee for the corporation's unpaid income tax liability because

[49] *R. Ginsberg*, CA-2, 62-2 USTC ¶ 9625, 305 F2d 664.

[50] *S.C. Holmes*, 47 TC 622, Dec. 28,385 (1967).

[51] *B. Joannes*, 26 TCM 622, Dec. 28,521(M), TC Memo. 1967-138.

[52] *S.E. Rubenstein*, 134 TC 266, Dec. 58,235.

[53] *Today's Child Learning Ctr*, DC-PA, 98-1 USTC ¶ 50,252, 40 FSupp2d 268.

[54] *D.R. Griffin*, 101 TCM 1274, Dec. 58,571(M), TC Memo. 2011-61. See also *Salus Mundi Foundation*, 103 TCM 1289, Dec. 58,969(M), TC Memo. 2012-61.

the overall facts of the case showed that the transactions were entered into separately and that they weren't fraudulent.

.05 Employment Tax Assessment Against Partnership Extends to General Partners

The IRS can collect a partnership employment tax liability from a general partner who is liable for partnership debts under state law without making an assessment of the liability against him individually.[55]

¶27,070 HOW TAX IS COLLECTED

The IRS can attach a lien to property for taxes owed, and can then seize or levy on the property to collect the taxes owed. Any tax due can be collected by levy against your property after a certain time period. The federal tax lien is probably the most important tool the IRS has for collecting from delinquent taxpayers.

.01 Private Debt Collection Agencies

The IRS has the authority to use private debt collection (PDC) agencies to locate and contact taxpayers owing outstanding tax liabilities of any type and to arrange payment of those taxes [Code Sec. 6306(a)]. In order to refer a taxpayer's account, the IRS must have made an assessment pursuant to Code Sec. 6201. PDCs are authorized to offer taxpayers who cannot pay in full an installment agreement providing for full payment of the taxes over a five-year period. If the taxpayer is unable to pay the outstanding tax liability in full over a five-year period, the PDC would obtain specific financial information from the taxpayer and provide that information to the IRS for further processing [Code Sec. 6306(b)].

In order to protect taxpayers, there are several restrictions on a PDC's operations. First, provisions of the Fair Debt Collection Practices Act [see ¶27,075] apply to the PDCs. Second, taxpayer protections applicable to the IRS and its employees are also specifically applicable to the PDCs. Third, a PDC may not use subcontractors to contact taxpayers, provide quality assurance services, or compose debt collection notices, and the IRS must approve any other service provided by a subcontractor. Fourth, PDCs are required to inform every taxpayer contacted of the availability of assistance from the National Taxpayer Advocate, whose orders would apply to the PDC in the same manner and to the same extent as to the IRS. Finally, the IRS must process all payments [Code Sec. 6306(b)(3)].

The provision creates a revolving fund from the amounts collected by the PDCs from which the PDCs will be paid, and payment of fees for all services is capped at 25 percent of the amount collected under a tax collection contract. In addition, the IRS is allowed to keep up to 25 percent of amounts collected by a PDC for collection enforcement activities. The provision also absolves the IRS from liability for damages for the acts or omissions of persons performing services under a qualified tax collection contract. However, the PDCs will be liable for unauthorized collection

---

[55] *A.C. Galletti*, SCt, 2004-1 USTC ¶50,204, 124 SCt 1548, *on remand from SCt, rev'g and rem'g DC*, CA-9, 2005-1 USTC ¶50,176, *on remand from SCt, rev'g and rem'g BC-DC*, DC-CA, 2005-1 USTC ¶50,177.

activities in the same manner and to the same extent as the IRS and its employees. Additionally, if the IRS determines that a PDC or an individual has engaged in unauthorized collection activities, they can be barred from performing services under any qualified tax collection contract.

Scam Warnings

The IRS has issued guidance outlining the protections in place for the private debt collection program.[56] The IRS warns that scamsters try a variety of tricks to impersonate the IRS in hopes of tricking taxpayers into divulging personal or financial information or even conning people out of cash. Scam artists try to impersonate the IRS in person, by phone, by e-mail and over the Internet. The following key elements of the private debt collection program will alert taxpayers they are part of this program and help taxpayers from being scammed by impersonators:

- *Taxpayer notification.* All taxpayers who will be part of the private debt collection effort will know they are in the program before they are contacted by a private collection agency. If taxpayers haven't previously heard that they are in the program, they should be wary of any bill collectors saying they are working on behalf of the IRS.
- *IRS letter.* All participants selected for the program will get a letter from the IRS, telling them they've been selected for the private debt collection program. The name of the company will be included in the letter.
- *Collection agency letter.* All participants will subsequently receive a second letter, this one from the collection agency, informing taxpayers they will be contacted soon regarding back taxes.
- *Money collected.* When paying a collection agency on behalf of the IRS, remember that the check will be made out to the U.S. Treasury—not to an individual or firm. The collection agency will provide the appropriate IRS coupon and mailing address for the payment. The collection agencies will never ask for cash or checks written to individuals.

In general, all taxpayers should keep in mind the IRS never asks people for the PIN numbers, passwords, or similar secret access information for their credit card, bank, or other financial accounts. If in doubt about someone claiming to be from the IRS or working on behalf of the IRS, call the agency's toll-free help line at 800-829-1040.

.02 Levy and Distraint (Seizure)

The IRS has the authority to levy (seize) upon a taxpayer's property and rights to property when a person liable to pay any tax neglects or refuses to pay within ten days of a notice and demand for payment [Code Sec. 6331; Reg. § 301.6331-1]. Before the IRS issues a notice of lien or levy or begins to levy or seize a taxpayer's property, they first must secure a supervisor's approval. The approval process requires the supervisor to review the taxpayer's information, verify the balance of the tax debt due, and agree that the collection action proposed is appropriate under the circumstances. The circumstances that the supervisor should consider include the value of the asset subject to the seizure as it relates to the tax debt due. In addition, the taxpayer must receive notice of administrative proceedings that are available before

[56] Announcement 2006-63, 2006-2 CB 445.

the IRS proceeds with collection [Code Sec. 6331(d)]. Code Sec. 6330 also restricts the IRS's ability to proceed with collection until the taxpayer has had an administrative review and, if dissatisfied, a judicial review. The following may be the subject of administrative or judicial review: (1) any relevant issues relating to the unpaid tax or proposed levy; (2) challenges to appropriateness of collection; (3) alternatives to collection. After the IRS has considered less intrusive means of collecting the tax debt, the IRS is not required to wait any additional time before collecting its tax debt.[57]

The IRS may levy upon a taxpayer's salary, wages, or other property only after sending the taxpayer an additional 30-day written notice. Since a levy on wages, salary, or nonmeans tested recurring federal payments, such as Social Security is continuous from the date served, the IRS must release the lien by notice when the tax is paid or as soon as the levy becomes unenforceable due to lapse of time, economic hardship, etc. [Code Secs. 6331(e), 6343].

If the IRS has determined that the levy is creating an economic hardship due to the financial condition of the taxpayer, the IRS must release a levy upon all, or part of, a taxpayer's property or rights to property [Code Sec. 6343(a)(1)]. The regulations provide that a levy is creating an economic hardship due to the financial condition of an individual taxpayer and must be released "if satisfaction of the levy in whole or in part will cause an individual taxpayer to be unable to pay his or her reasonable basic living expenses." [Reg. § 301.6343-1(b)(4)].

In *K.A. Vinatieri*,[58] the Tax Court concluded that the IRS's decision to proceed with a levy of a taxpayer's property was an abuse of discretion because the levy would create an economic hardship. The taxpayer's monthly income equaled her monthly expenses and she only possessed a small amount of cash and a car worth very little.

Any person in possession of property that has been levied upon must surrender it unless it is already subject to judicial process [Code Sec. 6332(a); Reg. § 301.6332-1(a)]. An insurer need not surrender a life insurance or endowment contract, but must pay over amounts that could be advanced to the taxpayer (generally cash loan value) up to 90 days after notice of levy. Automatic advances agreed upon to keep the insurance in force are not counted if the agreement was made before the insurer had actual knowledge of the levy [Code Sec. 6332(b); Reg. § 301.6332-2].

Persons (including corporate officers and employees and partnership members and employees) who fail to turn over property levied on are liable for the tax due up to the value of the property, plus costs and interest. They may also be liable for a penalty of 50 percent of this amount [Code Secs. 6332(d)(2), 6621; Reg. § 301.6332-1(b)(2)]. Surrender of the levied property to the IRS relieves them from liability to delinquent taxpayer (or insurance beneficiaries) for the property [Code Sec. 6332(e); Reg. § 301.6332-1(c)].

Enforcement of Tax Liens on Entireties Property

In *E.L. Hatchett*,[59] the Court of Appeals for the Sixth Circuit ruled that the IRS could levy on and sell property held by the taxpayer in a tenancy by the entirety with his spouse. The IRS had levied to collect deficiencies, penalties, and interest. This case is

---

[57] *J.B. Clawson*, 87 TCM 1251, Dec. 55,623(M), TC Memo. 2004-106.

[58] *K.A. Vinatieri*, 133 TC 392, Dec. 58,026 (2009).

[59] *E.L. Hatchett*, CA-6, 2003-1 USTC ¶ 50,504, 330 F3d 875, *cert. denied*, SCt, 124 SCt 2094.

significant because a tenancy by the entirety is a form of co-ownership where creditors cannot attach or levy the property to satisfy a debt. Nevertheless, the appellate court found support for its conclusion in the Supreme Court's ruling in *Craft*,[60] where the Supreme Court held that federal tax liens attach to property held in a tenancy by the entirety. All property of a delinquent taxpayer subject to a tax lien includes property held in a tenancy by the entirety, even though state law insulates the property from creditors of one spouse [Code Sec. 6321].

Property Exempt from Levy

The following property is exempt from IRS levy so taxpayers will not be deprived of sufficient assets to earn a living and pay for life's necessities [Code Sec. 6334]:

- Wearing apparel and school books [Code Sec. 6334(a)(1)].
- Fuel, provisions, furniture and other household personal effects, as well arms for personal use, livestock, and poultry worth up to $8,790 in 2013 [Code Sec. 6334(a)(2); Reg. § 301.6334(a)(2)].
- Books and tools necessary for a trade, business or profession worth up to $4,400 in 2013 [Code Sec. 6334(a)(3); Reg. § 301.6334(a)(3)].
- Unemployment benefits [Code Sec. 6334(a)(4)].
- Undelivered mail [Code Sec. 6334(a)(5)].
- Certain annuity and pension payments [Code Sec. 6334(a)(6)].
- Workmen's compensation [Code Sec. 6334(a)(7)].
- Judgments for support of minor children [Code Sec. 6334(a)(8)].
- Limited amount of wages, salary and other income equal to the sum of the standard deduction and allowable personal exemptions for the year divided by 52 [Code Sec. 6334(a)(9), (d)].
- Certain service-connected disability payments [Code Sec. 6334(a)(10)].
- Certain public assistance payments [Code Sec. 6334(a)(11)].
- Assistance under Job Training Partnership Act [Code Sec. 6334(a)(12)].
- Any of the following property to pay back taxes of $5,000 or less including penalties and interest:
  1. Real property used as a residence by the taxpayer or any nonrental real property of the taxpayer used by any other individual as a residence [Code Sec. 6334(a)(13)(A); Reg. § 301.6334-1(a)(13)];
  2. Any of your nonrental real property used by someone else as a residence [Code Sec. 6334(a)(13)(A)]; or
  3. Certain business assets including your tangible personal property or your nonrental real property used in your trade or business [Code Sec. 6334(a)(13)(B)]. Under Code Sec. 6334(e)(2), such property is not exempt from levy if an IRS district director or assistance district director personally approves the levy in writing, or the IRS finds that the collection of tax is in jeopardy. An official may not approve the levy unless he determines that the

[60] *S.L. Craft*, 2002-1 USTC ¶50,361, 535 US 274, 122 SCt 1414.

taxpayer's other assets subject to collection are insufficient to pay the amount due, together with expenses of the proceedings.

A principal residence is not exempt from levy if a U.S. district court judge or magistrate approves the levy of the residence in writing.[61] U.S. district courts have exclusive jurisdiction to approve such levies under Code Sec. 6334(e)(1)(B). Therefore judicial approval is required before levy of a taxpayer's principal residence. In addition, the taxpayer must be given notice and an opportunity to participate in the proceeding [Reg. § 1.301.6334-1(d)]. The IRS is required to exhaust all other payment options before seizing a taxpayer's business or principal residence. The IRS must consider installment agreements, offers-in-compromise, and seizure of other assets before taking collection action against a taxpayer's business or principal residence. If the residence to be seized is the taxpayer's principal residence, the IRS may not seize it without written approval of the U.S. district court judge or magistrate [Code Sec. 6334(a)(13)(B), (e)(1)]. Since Social Security benefits are not listed as exempt in Code Sec. 6334(a), the District Court in *M.E. Acevedo*[62] held that they were subject to levy.

Continuous Levy

The IRS has the authority to issue a "continuous levy" on "specified property." Continuous levies attach to property held on the date of the levy and to certain payments received after the date of the levy and up until the levy is released [Code Sec. 6331(h)(1)]. The continuous levy relieves the IRS of the burden of making successive additional levies against the same taxpayer's future wages and wage replacement payments. The IRS has implemented an official Federal Payment Levy Program (FPLP) which will be used in conjunction with the IRS's regular levy program.[63]

Federal payments to a delinquent taxpayer will not be included in this program in certain circumstances, for example, where a taxpayer is in bankruptcy, in a hardship situation, or if the taxpayer has applied for relief as an innocent or injured spouse. This levy program will not apply to certain types of federal insurance programs, including Black Lung benefits or SSI payments. A taxpayer whose federal payments are subject to levy under the FPLP may contact the IRS to resolve the issue by paying the tax bill, entering into an installment agreement or proposing an offer in compromise.

The use of the continuous levy is at the IRS's discretion and must be specifically approved by the IRS before the levy takes effect [Code Sec. 6331(h)]. The IRS has the authority under Code Sec. 6331(h) to issue a continuous levy on a taxpayer's salary and wages and up to 15 percent of any of the following "specified payments": (1) any federal payment other than a payment for which eligibility is based on the income or assets of both of a payee; (2) unemployment benefits; (3) workmen's compensation; (4) the minimum levy exemption amount for wages and life payments; (5) certain "means-tested" public assistance payments, and (6) certain railroad annuity, railroad pension or railroad unemployment benefits [Code Sec. 6331(h)(2)].

The continuous levy rate is 100 percent of any specified payment due to a vendor of goods or services sold or leased to the federal government [Code Sec. 6331(h)(3)].

---

[61] *M.W. Hansen*, DC-CA, 2013-2 USTC ¶ 50,452.

[62] *M.E. Acevedo*, DC-MO, 2013-1 USTC ¶ 50,291.

[63] IRS News Release IR-2000-45, June 29, 2000.

The Court of Appeals for the Second Circuit in *Moskowitz, Passman & Edelman*,[64] ruled that a law firm was obligated by the IRS's continuing levy on a partner's salary under Code Sec. 6331(e) to surrender to the IRS the funds it paid to the partner as draws.

Levy Restrictions

No levy may be made in the following situations:

- While a taxpayer's proposal of an installment agreement is pending with the IRS;
- For 30 days after rejection of a proposal;
- While an installment agreement is in effect;
- For 30 days after termination of an installment agreement by the IRS; and
- During a timely filed appeal by the taxpayer to the IRS Office of Appeals of a rejection or termination decision [Reg. § 301.6331-4].

The IRS cannot proceed with a levy to collect tax liabilities without first issuing a notice of deficiency, even if the IRS and the taxpayers had previously entered into a closing agreement on Form 906.[65]

.03 Collection by Suit

If any person liable to pay any tax fails to pay it when due, the tax, with interest and additions, may be collected by a suit in the U.S. District Court [Code Secs. 7402, 7403; Reg. § 301.7403-1].

.04 Liens

Under Code Sec. 6321, the IRS has a tax lien on all property and rights to property belonging to any person liable to pay any tax if he neglects or refuses to pay the tax after demand for payment has been made[66] [Code Sec. 6321; Reg. § 301.6321-1 et seq.]. When the tax is assessed, the lien arises and it continues until the tax liability giving rise to it is paid or becomes unenforceable by reason of lapse of time [Code Sec. 6322]. In *J.A. Prince*,[67] the Tax Court found that an IRS lien, in place before the taxpayer filed for bankruptcy remained in effect despite the taxpayer's discharge from personal liability for his tax debt.

In order for the lien to be valid against certain persons, the IRS must file a Notice of Federal Tax Lien (NFTL) in accordance with Code Sec. 6323. The tax lien then becomes one of the many possible claims competing to be first to be satisfied out of the taxpayer's property. In order for the IRS to establish priority rights to the taxpayer's property against other creditors, the IRS must file the NFTL. The IRS can file the NFTL only after the IRS assesses the liability and sends the taxpayer a notice and demand for payment and the taxpayer refuses or neglects to pay the debt in full within 10 days after notification.

In IRS New Release 2011-20,[68] the IRS announced that it will no longer file a lien where the aggregate unpaid balance of assessment for the taxpayer is less than $10,000.

---

[64] *Moskowitz, Passman & Edelman*, CA-2, 2010-1 USTC ¶50,371, 603 F3d 162.

[65] *B.F. Manko*, 126 TC 195, Dec. 56,490 (2006).

[66] *B.A. Mrizek*, DC-IL, 59-2 USTC ¶9678, 187 FSupp 830.

[67] *J.A. Prince*, 133 TC 270, Dec. 57,977 (2009); *V.L. Wadleigh*, 134 TC 280, Dec. 58,243 (2010).

[68] IRS News Release IR-2011-20, February 24, 2011.

A preexisting tax lien on property remains enforceable against that property even after an individual's personal liability has been discharged in bankruptcy.[69]

Discharge of Liens

The IRS will release a federal tax lien, no later than 30 days after the date on which the IRS finds that the entire tax liability has been fully satisfied or has become legally unenforceable [Reg. § 301.6325-1(a)(1)]. A lien can also be discharged if the IRS determines that their interest in the specific item of property has no value.

Code Sec. 6325(b) provides several procedures for discharging property subject to a lien. Under Code Sec. 6325(b)(2)(A), the IRS may issue a certificate of discharge pursuant to which the government is paid the value of its lien interest in the property to be discharged. Persons who request a certificate may not seek judicial review of IRS's valuation determination through (1) a refund action under 28 USC § 1346(a)(1) or (2) an action for substitution of value under Code Sec. 7426(a)(4).

Under a lien discharge procedure in Code Sec. 6325(b)(4), the owner of property subject to a federal tax lien (other than the person liable for the tax) has the right to obtain a discharge upon either depositing cash or furnishing a bond acceptable to the IRS in the amount it has determined to be the value of the U.S. lien interest [Code Sec. 6325(b)(4)(A)]. The IRS must refund the amount deposited or release the bond, to the extent that it determines that the taxpayer's unsatisfied liability giving rise to the lien can be satisfied from a source other than property owned by the third party, or to the extent that it determines that the value of the U.S. interest in the property is less than the IRS's prior determination of value [Code Sec. 6325(b)(4)(B)]. Any amount not used to satisfy the liability must be refunded to the property's owner [Code Sec. 6325(b)(4)(C)].

The owner has 120 days after the date the certificate of discharge is issued to file a substitution of value action in district court challenging the IRS's determination of the value of the U.S. lien interest [Code Sec. 7426(a)(4)]. Absent such a challenge, within 60 days after the expiration of the 120-day period, the IRS may apply the amount deposited or collect on the bond to the extent necessary to satisfy the liability secured by the lien.

In Rev. Rul. 2005-50,[70] the IRS ruled that a third party could not maintain a refund action against the government under 28 USC Sec. 1346(a) after making a deposit with the IRS, or an action for substitution of value under Code Sec. 7426(a)(4) if a deposit was not made.

Lien Notification Requirements

The IRS must notify any person subject to a lien of the existence of the lien within five days of the lien being filed. The notice of lien must be given in person, left at the taxpayer's home or place of business, or sent by certified or registered mail to the person's "last known address" [Code Sec. 6320(a)(2)]. The notice must explain in simple, nontechnical terms the following: (1) the amount of the unpaid tax, (2) the person's right to request a hearing during the 30-day period beginning on the sixth day after the lien is filed, (3) the available administrative appeals and their procedures, and (4) the procedures relating to the release of liens [Code Sec. 6320(a)(3)].

---

[69] *G. Iannone*, 122 TC 287, Dec. 55,618 (2004).

[70] Rev. Rul. 2005-50, 2005-2 CB 124.

Until notice of the lien has been properly filed, it is not enforceable against a purchaser, mechanics lienor, judgment lien creditor or holder of a security interest [Code Sec. 6323(a); Reg. § 301.6323(a)-1]. Even after the lien is filed, it may not be enforced against some persons who do not actually know about the lien or who have certain specific claims against the taxpayer's property [Code Sec. 6323(b); Reg. § 301.6323(b)-1].[71]

Superpriorities Against Liens

Subject to varying conditions that must be met in each case, a filed lien cannot be enforced against the following persons who do not have actual knowledge of the lien at the time: purchasers (or security holders) of securities (stocks, bonds, notes, etc.); purchasers of motor vehicles; purchasers in a casual sale of tangible personal property of less than $1,000 (e.g., household goods, personal effects, property exempt from levy); insurers who issued life insurance, endowment or annuity contracts (also protected for automatic advances [discussed above] after actual knowledge of lien); banks and building and loan associations (for deposit-secured loans). Specific claims protected against a filed tax lien, again subject to varying conditions in each case, are: possessory lien for repair or improvement of personal property; real property tax and assessment liens; mechanics' liens for repair and improvement of personal residence at contract price under $5,000; attorney's lien enforceable against a judgment or settlement; purchaser of tangible personal property at retail [Code Sec. 6323(b); Reg. §§ 301.6323(b)-1, 301.6323(h)-1].

> **NOTE:** A limited priority against filed tax liens also is granted under specified conditions for advances made under financing agreements entered into before the tax lien is filed, and certain security interests may be protected for disbursements made within 45 days after the filing before the holder has actual knowledge of the lien [Code Secs. 6323(c)(2), (d); Reg. §§ 301.6323(c)-1, 301.6323(d)-1, 301.6323(h)-1].

Pre-Bankruptcy Federal Liens

The IRS has greater powers [Code Secs. 6321-6326] to enforce its liens than those possessed by private secured creditors under state law. But the federal provisions do not transfer ownership of the property to the IRS.[72] Ownership is transferred only when the property is sold to a bona fide buyer at a tax sale [Code Sec. 6339(a)(2)]. Until there is a sale, the Supreme Court has ruled, the property remains the debtor's and is subject to the bankruptcy law turnover requirement [11 USC Sec. 542(a)] in the event of a bankruptcy petition.[73]

Indexing and Filing of Liens

The filing of a notice of federal tax lien is governed solely by the Internal Revenue Code and is not subject to any other state or federal law. A tax lien is treated as complying with the filing requirements only if it is recorded in an appropriate public index. Real property liens are filed in the office designated by the state where the property is located.

---

[71] Rev. Rul. 2003-108, 2003-2 CB 963.

[72] *L.M. Rodgers*, SCt, 83-1 USTC ¶ 9374, 461 US 677, 103 SCt 2132.

[73] *Whiting Pools Inc.*, SCt, 83-1 USTC ¶ 9394, 462 US 198, 103 SCt 2309.

NOTE: If, under the laws of the state in which real property is located, a deed is not valid as against a purchaser of the property who (at the time of purchase) does not have actual notice or knowledge of the existence of the deed unless the fact of filing of the deed has been entered and recorded in a public index, the notice of lien will not be valid against any purchaser, holder of a security interest, mechanic's lienor, or judgment lien creditor until the fact of filing is entered and recorded in the index [Code Sec. 6323(f)(4)].

Notices affecting personal property must be filed in the office designated by the state where an individual resides or a corporation or partnership has its principal executive office when the lien is filed. If a state fails to specify an office for filing, or designates more than one, the tax lien is filed with the clerk of the U.S. district court for the judicial district where the property is located (for realty) or where the taxpayer resides or has its principal office (for personalty) [Code Sec. 6323(f); Reg. § 301.6323(f)-1].

For a notice of lien to remain in effect, it must be refiled, within the required period, in the office in which the prior notice was filed [Code Sec. 6323(g)].

.05 Set-Off or Counterclaim

The IRS, within the applicable period of limitations, can set off or credit the amount of any overpayment (including interest on it) against liability for any internal revenue tax [Code Sec. 6402; Reg. § 301.6402-1]. Set-offs may also be used if taxpayers claim a refund or credit of one tax [¶ 27,125], and they are in default to the U.S. on another tax or contract.

.06 Payroll Deductions

The IRS allows employees to arrange payroll deductions to satisfy delinquent taxes. Form 2159, *Payroll Deduction Agreement*, is used.

.07 Suit to Prevent Collection

Generally, no suit to restrain the assessment or collection of any tax can be maintained [Code Sec. 7421]. This includes suits to restrain enforcement of the liability of a transferee or fiduciary or suits to prevent revoking tax-exempt status.[74] There are exceptions. Collection of the tax can be enjoined when you (1) did not receive a 90-day letter and did not file Form 870 [¶ 27,025]; (2) have filed a petition with the Tax Court [Code Secs. 6212(a), 6213(a); Reg. § 301.6213-1]; and (3) request judicial review of jeopardy assessment procedures [¶ 27,055]. It can also be enjoined when a case is in bankruptcy proceedings [see above] [¶ 27,020; ¶ 27,055; ¶ 27,060] [Code Secs. 6213(a), (f)]. An injunction also may be allowed when it is clear from the facts and law that the IRS could not win a suit to collect the tax and only an injunction can protect the taxpayer.[75]

Third Parties Contesting Levy on Property

In some situations, the IRS may file a lien and then levy on property owned by a third party. This may occur if the taxpayer and the third party own the property jointly. The IRS also might levy on the property of a third party in the mistaken belief that

---

[74] *Bob Jones University*, SCt, 74-1 USTC ¶ 9438, 416 US 725, 94 SCt 2038; *Americans United, Inc.*, SCt, 74-1 USTC ¶ 9439, 416 US 752, 94 SCt 2053.

[75] *Williams Packing & Navigation Co., Inc.*, SCt, 62-2 USTC ¶ 9545, 370 US 1, 82 SCt 1125.

the property belongs to the person who owed the taxes. The only judicial remedy available to third persons seeking to challenge a levy is a wrongful levy suit under Code Sec. 7426(a)(1). This suit must be filed within nine months of the levy [Code Sec. 7426(a)(1); Reg. §301.7426-1]. In Rev. Rul. 2005-49,[76] the IRS concluded that a wrongful levy suit is the only judicial remedy for a person asserting that her property was wrongfully levied upon by the IRS to satisfy the tax debt of another.

A limit applies on damages recoverable for a wrongful levy [Code Sec. 7426(b)(2)].

The IRS can withdraw a public notice of tax lien before payment in full by the indebted taxpayer without prejudice, and can return levied property in certain circumstances, including when it's in the best interests of the taxpayer and the government. In the case of an erroneous lien, the taxpayer could request that the IRS make reasonable efforts to notify major credit agencies and financial institutions. [Code Sec. 6323(j)(2)].

.08 Fair Debt Collection Practices Act Applies to IRS

The IRS must comply with the Fair Debt Collection Practices Act in their dealings with taxpayers. This means that in their communications with taxpayers in connection with any tax collection activity, the IRS must call taxpayers on the telephone between the hours of 8:00 a.m. to 9:00 p.m. unless the taxpayer agrees to calls before and after these times [Code Sec. 6304(a)]. The Fair Debt Collection Practices Act also requires the IRS to refrain from harassing, oppressing, or abusing taxpayers in connection with the collection of any unpaid tax. The following activities are no longer allowed: (1) using or threatening to use violence or other criminal means to harm the physical person, reputation, or property of any person; (2) using obscene or profane language; (3) causing a telephone to ring or engaging any person in telephone conversation repeatedly or continuously with intent to annoy, abuse, or harass any person at the called number; (4) placing telephone calls without disclosing the caller's identity [Code Sec. 6304(b)].

.09 How to Collect Damages for IRS Collection Activities

If any officer or employee of the IRS recklessly or intentionally disregards any statutory or regulatory provision in connection with the collection of federal tax with respect to a taxpayer, the taxpayer may bring a civil action for damages against the United States in a federal district court [Code Sec. 7433(a)]. A judgment for damages resulting from unauthorized collection actions will not be awarded unless the court determines that the taxpayer has exhausted the administrative remedies available within the IRS, including the filing of an administrative claim [Code Sec. 7433(d)(1)]. An action seeking an award for damages for unauthorized collection cannot be filed until the earlier of (1) the time a decision is rendered on the claim, or (2) six months from the filing date of the claim [Reg. §301.7433-1(d)(1)]. In any successful action brought to recover damages resulting from unauthorized IRS collection activities, the taxpayer will be entitled to specified damages. The amount of damages is equal to the lesser of:

---

[76] Rev. Rul. 2005-49, 2005-2 CB 125.

1. $1 million ($100,000 in the case of negligent actions of IRS officers or employees); or
2. The sum of the costs of the action and the actual, direct economic damages sustained by the taxpayer as a proximate result of the reckless or intentional actions of the officer or employee or the negligent actions of the officer or employee [Code Sec. 7433(b); Reg. § 301.7433-1(a)].

Civil Actions by Nontaxpayers

Nontaxpayers, such as business associates and family members who were inappropriately and adversely impacted by unauthorized IRS collection actions, including wrongful levies, may also sue for civil damages if an IRS officer or employer disregards the tax laws [Code Sec. 7426(h)(1)]. If a federal district court determines that any IRS officer or employee recklessly or intentionally, or by reason of negligence, disregarded the tax laws, the federal government can now be liable to the taxpayer in an amount equal to the lesser of $1 million ($100,000 in the case of negligence) or the sum of (1) the actual, direct, economic damages sustained by the plaintiff because of the reckless or intentional or negligent actions of the IRS official; and (2) the costs of the action [Code Sec. 7426(h)(1)].

¶27,071 WHISTLEBLOWER CLAIMS

Individuals who provide valuable information to the government relating to violations of the tax laws may be entitled to receive a reward from the IRS for their efforts under the whistleblower provisions found in Code Sec. 7623. For further discussion of the income tax treatment of whistleblower awards see ¶ 2015.03.

.01 IRS Whistleblower Office

The IRS is required to pay nondiscretionary whistleblower awards and to provide the Tax Court with jurisdiction to review whistleblower awards under the auspices of a Whistleblower Office within the IRS [Code Sec. 7623]. The Whistleblower Office administers the whistleblower program and analyzes information provided to it by individuals and determines whether to investigate the matter itself, or assign the matter to an appropriate IRS office.

To claim a reward, an informant must file and sign Form 211, *Application for Reward for Original Information* [Reg. § 301.7623-1(d)]. The IRS will not divulge the informant's identity to any unauthorized person [Reg. § 301.7623-1(e)].

Individuals who are IRS employees when they obtain information on tax law violations or when they divulge the information may not claim rewards. Other current or former federal employees may claim rewards provided they did not obtain the information in the course of their official duties [Reg. § 301.7623-1(b)(2)].

.02 Amount of Whistleblower Award

If the IRS proceeds with any administrative or judicial action based on information provided by an informant, the IRS is obligated to pay the individual a reward based on the amounts collected. The reward will be at least 15 percent, and no more than 30 percent, of the collected amount [Code Sec. 7623(b)(1)]. The award is reduced in certain circumstances. For example, the award is reduced where the whistleblower planned or initiated the actions that led to the underpayment of tax [Code Sec. 7623(b)(2)].

In addition, interest may be included when calculating the size of the reward [Code Sec. 7623(a)]. The award amount will be determined by the Whistleblower Office based upon the extent to which the information substantially contributed to the administrative or judicial action and recovery.

In situations where the Whistleblower Office determines that the IRS's actions were based on an individual's allegations (rather than specific information), and those allegations arose from: (a) a judicial or administrative hearing; (b) a governmental report, hearing, audit, or investigation; or (3) the news media, a lesser reward is appropriate and a maximum reward amount would be 10 percent of the recovered funds [Code Sec. 7623(b)(2)].

The Whistleblower Office will consider the significance of the individual's contribution to the information resulting in the recovery. The office may reduce a reward if it determines that the claim was brought by an individual who planned and initiated the actions that led to an underpayment of tax or violation of the tax laws. If the individual is convicted of criminal conduct arising from his or her role, then the Whistleblower Office will deny an award [Code Sec. 7623(b)(3)]. The size of any reward may be appealed within 30 days of its determination. The appeal should be made to the Tax Court, which is granted jurisdiction with respect to these matters [Code Sec. 7623(b)(4)]. Tax Court review of an award determination may be assigned to a special trial judge [Code Sec. 7443A(b)(6)]. In *R. Cohen*,[77] a whistleblower's petition to order the IRS to reopen his award claim was dismissed for failure to state a claim. The whistleblower sought relief that was unavailable because the IRS never instituted an action or collected any proceeds based on the information he provided. The whistleblower believed the information he provided was actionable; however, the IRS Whistleblower Office denied that he was eligible for an award under Code Sec. 7623(b) because no proceeds were collected.

If the whistleblower's information implicates an individual taxpayer, an award is available only if the individual taxpayer against whom they are made has a gross income in excess of $200,000 for any tax year involved in the administrative or judicial action. The IRS will only pay 15 percent to 30 percent of the "collected proceeds" if the tax, penalties, interest, additions to tax, plus any additional amounts in dispute exceed $2 million [Code Sec. 7623(b)(5)]. The term "collected proceeds" include penalties, interest, additions to tax, and additional amounts resulting from the action based on the whistleblower's information, or from any settlement in response to such action. A reduction of an overpayment credit balance used to satisfy a tax liability incurred because of the information provided is also included in the definition of "amounts collected" and "collected proceeds" for Code Sec. 7623 purposes [Reg. § 301.7623-1(a)(2)].

No award will be made unless the information submitted to the IRS is submitted under penalty of perjury [Code Sec. 7623(b)(6)(C)]. No contract with the IRS is necessary to receive such an award [Code Sec. 76(b)(6)(A)].

The Whistleblower Office will acknowledge in writing any claim received. All awards will be subject to current federal tax reporting and withholding requirements. Therefore, award recipients will receive a Form 1099.

---

[77] *R. Cohen*, 139 TC 299, Dec. 59,220 (2012).

When the Whistleblower Office has made a final determination regarding a claim, the claimant will receive correspondence regarding its final award determination. Final Whistleblower Office determinations regarding awards under Code Sec. 7623(b) may be appealed to the United States Tax Court within 30 days.

.03 Tax Court Jurisdiction

The Tax Court has jurisdiction to hear appeals of determinations made by the Whistleblower Office. In *W.P. Cooper*,[78] the Tax Court held that a letter sent by the IRS to a whistleblower denying his claims constituted a "determination" conferring jurisdiction on the Tax Court to review the denial of the claim under Code Sec. 7623(b)(4). The court expressly noted that the name or label of the written notice from the IRS did not control whether the document constituted a determination.

.04 Deduction Permitted

An above-the-line deduction is permitted for costs and attorney's fees paid in connection with any whistleblower award for providing information regarding violations of the tax laws. However, no such deduction shall exceed the amount includible in the taxpayer's gross income as a result of such award [Code Sec. 62(a)(21)]. See ¶2015.03 for discussion of income tax treatment of awards.

.05 Disclosing Return Information to Whistleblowers

The Whistleblower Office may determine that it needs the assistance of the whistleblower and that it has to disclose return information in order for the whistleblower to be able to provide assistance more effectively. These types of disclosures are authorized by Code Sec. 6103(n). Reg. §301.6103(n)-2(a) provides that an IRS officer is authorized to disclose return information to a whistleblower to the extent necessary in connection with a written contract with the IRS, the whistleblower, and, if applicable, the legal representative of the whistleblower for services relating to the detection of violations of the tax laws.

Disclosure of return information "shall be made only to the extent the IRS deems it necessary in connection with the reasonable or proper performance of the contract." Whistleblowers may not disclose return information and they are subjected to civil and criminal penalties for doing so. Reg. §301.6103(n)-2(d) provides that any whistleblower who receives return information must protect the confidentiality of the return information and prevent any disclosure or inspection of the return information.

Any whistleblower who receives return information must agree in writing, before any return information is disclosed to permit an inspection of the whistleblower's premises by the IRS. The whistleblower must also agree to dispose of all return information by returning the return information, including any and all copies or notes made, to the IRS, or to the extent that it cannot be returned, by destroying the information.

.06 When Whistleblower Claims Will Be Denied

The IRS has issued procedural guidance on how whistleblower claims will be processed and provides in the Internal Revenue Manual (IRM) pt. 25.2.2 (Dec. 30,

---

[78] *W.P. Cooper*, 135 TC 70, Dec. 58,265 (2010).

2008) that whistleblower claims will be denied where the information provided does not (a) identify a federal tax issue upon which the IRS will act; (b) result in the detection of an underpayment of taxes; or (c) result in the collection of proceeds.

PENALTIES

¶27,075 OVERVIEW

The tax law imposes various civil and criminal penalties when a taxpayer or his or her tax preparer fail to properly account to the IRS as required by the tax law. Unlike interest (which is an addition to tax intended to compensate the IRS for late payments), penalties are intended to punish the taxpayer for unreasonably failing to file or pay taxes. Interest paid on a tax deficiency is a personal interest expense that is not deductible, as with fines and penalties.

The penalty rules are organized into four categories:

- Document and information reporting penalty [¶27,080].
- Accuracy-related penalty [¶27,085].
- Preparer, promoter and protester penalties [¶27,090].
- Delinquency (failure to file or make timely deposits) penalties [¶27,095].

This chapter includes a run-down of the most common penalties and charges imposed on wayward and delinquent taxpayers.

¶27,080 DOCUMENT AND INFORMATION REPORTING PENALTIES

Penalties are imposed when taxpayers fail to file correct information returns with the IRS or fail to furnish payee statements to other taxpayers on or before the due date [Code Secs. 6721, 6722]. Certain taxpayers (e.g., banks, employers, etc.) must file information returns with the IRS. Examples of information returns are interest, dividend and wage statements (e.g., Form 1099, Form 1099-DIV, Form W-2) [Code Sec. 6724(d)(1)]. See ¶26,135.

A return or statement is also required for the following items: payment of interest, dividends or patronage dividends [Ch. 26]; stock transferred under stock options [Ch. 26]; employees' group-term life insurance [Ch. 26]; fishing boat operators' wages; withheld income taxes; and tips.

Information returns do not require the payment of tax by the person submitting the return. Instead, they exist solely for the purpose of enabling the IRS to determine whether taxpayers have properly reported income, deductions and credits.

.01 Penalty for Failure to File Correct Information Returns

There are three separate and distinct categories of penalties that apply to information returns and payee statements as follows:

1. Penalty for failing to file an information return or to include correct information on an information return under Code Sec. 6721;
2. Penalty for failing to file a payee statement or to include correct information on a payee statement under Code Sec. 6722; and
3. Penalty for failing to comply with other information reporting requirements (which includes all reporting failures not covered by the other two categories) under Code Sec. 6723.

The amount of the penalty imposed varies depending on when an information return was due to be filed. The graduated penalty structure gives taxpayers an incentive to correct their errors as soon as possible.

The following penalty amounts are imposed for each of the prescribed time periods:

- If a person files a correct information return up to 30 days after the required filing date, the amount of the first-tier penalty is $30 per return, with a maximum penalty of $250,000 per calendar year ($75,000 for small businesses) [Code Sec. 6721(b)(1), (d)(1)(B)].
- If a person files a correct information return more than 30 days after the prescribed filing date but on or before August 1 of the calendar year in which the required filing date occurs, the amount of the second-tier penalty is $60 per return, with a maximum penalty of $500,000 per calendar year ($200,000 for small businesses) [Code Sec. 6721(b)(2), (d)(1)(C)].
- If a correct information return is not filed on or before August 1 of any year, the amount of the third-tier penalty is $100 per return, with a maximum penalty of $1,500,000 per calendar year ($500,000 for small businesses) [Code Sec. 6721(a)(1), (d)(1)(A)].

.02 Small Business Relief

Lower maximum penalty amounts under Code Sec. 6721 are provided for small businesses. Small businesses are defined as firms having average gross receipts of less than $5 million for the most recent three tax years (fiscal or calendar) ending before the calendar year for which the information return is filed. "Firms" can include sole proprietorships, corporations, partnerships and trusts and estates that are required to file information returns.

The maximum penalty for failure to file or for failure to provide complete or correct information is $500,000 [Code Sec. 6721(d)(1)(A)]. The maximum penalty for returns corrected within 30 days of the filing date is $75,000 [Code Sec. 6721(d)(1)(B)]. If a corrected return is filed after 30 days following the filing date but on or before August 1 of the calendar year, the maximum penalty is $200,000 [Code Sec. 6721(d)(1)(C)].

Gross Receipts Test

For purposes of determining the amount of gross receipts, the rules of Code Sec. 448(c) apply [Code Sec. 6721(d)(2)]. Average annual gross receipts are computed by dividing the sum of the gross receipts for as many of the previous three tax years (not including the current tax year) as the taxpayer conducted business by the number of those tax years. If a corporation or partnership was not in existence for the entire three-year period, the computation is made on the basis of the period during which it was in existence. Gross receipts for any tax year of less than 12 months must be annualized by multiplying the gross receipts for the short period by 12 and dividing the result by the number of months in the short period. Gross receipts for any tax year must be reduced by returns and allowances made during the year [Temp. Reg. § 1.448-1T(f)(2)(iii)].

Gross receipts generally include:

1. Total sales, net of returns and allowances;
2. Any income from services, investments, and incidental or outside sources; and
3. All other income from all activities that is properly recognized in the tax year under the firm's method of accounting (e.g., cash or accrual).

Interest, dividends, rents, royalties, and annuities are also included in gross receipts regardless of whether or not the income is received in the ordinary course of a trade or business. Temp. Reg. § 1.448-1T(f)(2)(i) allows sales of capital assets and depreciable property to be reduced by the assets' or property's adjusted basis in computing gross receipts and, in the case of sales of ordinary income property, the regulations preclude a reduction for the cost of goods sold or for the property's adjusted basis. Also, repayments of loans are not treated as gross receipts for purposes of the regulations.

In determining whether a firm has average annual gross receipts of less than $5 million, the gross receipts of related entities are taken into account. Related entities include: (1) a parent-subsidiary group of corporations; (2) a brother-sister corporate group; and (3) a combined business group, including partnerships, under common control.

De Minimis Rule

There is a special relief rule from the penalty under Code Sec. 6721 for taxpayers who file a small number or *de minimis* of incorrect information returns. If corrections are made on or before August 1 to information returns that are incomplete or incorrect as originally filed, a *de minimis* number of those returns will be treated as filed correctly, and no penalty will be imposed. The rule applies, in any given calendar year, to the greater of (1) 10 returns or (2) one-half of one percent of the total number of information returns required to be filed by the taxpayer during the calendar year. In other words, if the total number of returns corrected by the taxpayer exceeds the *de minimis* threshold, only the number exceeding the threshold is subject to penalty [Code Sec. 6721(c); Reg. § 301.6721-1(d)].

> **Example 27-19:** DeSantis Welding Co. files 500 information returns on the last day of February as required. DeSantis Welding later discovers errors on 17 of the returns, and files corrected returns within 30 days of the due date. Result: DeSantis is subject to a $105 penalty (seven information returns in excess of the ten allowed under the de minimis rule, times $15 penalty for each late return).

Inconsequential Omissions and Corrections

The penalty is not imposed if an error or omission the failure does not hinder or prevent the IRS from processing the taxpayer's return [Reg. § 301.6721-1(c)].

.03 Intentional Disregard for the Rules

If a failure to file a correct payee statement is due to intentional disregard of the filing requirements, the taxpayer will not be allowed to take advantage of the three-tiered graduated system, the small business break, or the *de minimis* rule [Code Sec. 6721(e)(1)]. Instead the penalty imposed is a fixed amount depending on when the information returns were due to be filed and the penalty amount is $250 [Code Sec. 6721(e)(2)].

Intentional Disregard

The phrase "intentional disregard" means a knowing or willful failure to timely file an information return or furnish the correct information on an information return. Whether a person knowingly and willfully fails to timely file an information return where required or furnish the correct information is based on the facts and circumstances in each case. Facts and circumstances considered include but are not limited to:

- Whether the failure to file timely or the failure to include correct information is part of a pattern of conduct by the person who filed the return of repeatedly failing to file timely or repeatedly failing to include correct information;
- Whether correction was promptly made upon discovery of the failure;
- Whether the filer corrects a failure to file or a failure to include correct information within 30 days after the date of any written request from the IRS to file or to correct the error; and
- Whether the amount of the information reporting penalties is less than the cost of complying with the requirement to file timely or to include correct information on an information return [Reg. § 301.6721-1(f)].

A penalty under Code Sec. 6721 for the intentional disregard of applicable filing requirements may be imposed against attorneys who relying on the attorney-client privilege fail to disclose client identification information on Form 8300, *Report of Cash Payments Over $10,000 Received in a Trade or Business*, in accordance with Reg. § 1.6050I-1(a)(3).

.04 Penalty for Failure to Furnish Correct Payee Statements

The other component of the document and information reporting penalty applies to taxpayers who must furnish payee statements to other taxpayers. Those who fail to furnish a correct payee statement (e.g., Form 1099-DIV, Form W-2) to the recipient of the income on or before the due date are subject to penalties depending on when the payee statements are due [Code Sec. 6722].

Code Sec. 6722 establishes a three-tier penalty structure that provides for progressively higher fixed per-statement penalties and yearly maximum amounts based on prescribed periods in which: (1) the statement is actually provided, (2) omitted information is provided, or (3) correct information is provided.

The following penalty amounts are imposed:

- If a person furnishes a correct payee statement up to 30 days after the required due date, the amount of the first-tier penalty is $30 per statement, with a maximum penalty of $250,000 per calendar year ($75,000 for small businesses) [Code Sec. 6722(b)(1), (d)(1)(B)].

- If a person furnishes a correct payee statement more than 30 days after the prescribed filing date but on or before August 1 of the calendar year in which the required filing date occurs, the amount of the second-tier penalty is $60 per return, with a maximum penalty of $500,000 per calendar year ($200,000 for small businesses) [Code Sec. 6722(b)(2), (d)(1)(C)].
- If a correct payee statement is not furnished on or before August 1 of any year, the amount of the penalty is $100 per return (the "third-tier penalty"), with a maximum penalty of $1,500,000 per calendar year ($500,000 for small businesses) [Code Sec. 6722(a)(1), (d)(1)(A)].

"Small businesses" are defined as firms with gross receipts of not more than $5 million [Code Sec. 6722(d)].

.05 Penalty for Failure to Comply with Other Requirements

A taxpayer who is required and fails to (1) include a correct taxpayer I.D. number (TIN) on a return, or (2) furnish a correct TIN to another person, is subject to a $50 penalty for each failure up to a maximum amount of $100,000 per calendar year [Code Secs. 6723, 6724(d)(3)].

.06 Waiver of Penalty for Reasonable Cause

None of the above penalties apply if the taxpayer establishes that the failure is due to reasonable cause and not willful neglect [Code Sec. 6724(a)]. Reasonable cause can exist if significant mitigating factors are present, such as the fact that a taxpayer has an established history of complying with the information reporting requirements.

¶27,085 ACCURACY-RELATED PENALTY

The accuracy-related penalty is 20 percent of the portion of the "underpayment" attributable to one or more of the following [Code Sec. 6662(a), (b)]:

- Negligence or disregard of rules or regulations.
- Any substantial understatement of income tax.
- Any substantial valuation misstatement.
- Any substantial overstatement of pension liabilities.
- Any substantial estate or gift tax valuation understatement.
- "Underpayments" attributable to transactions lacking economic substance. For definition of underpayment for purposes of Code Sec. 6662(a) see Reg. § 1.6664-2 which has been approved by the Tax Court in *G.L. Snow*.[79]

  ▶ **OBSERVATION:** The accuracy-related penalty applies only to the portion of the tax underpayment resulting from the inaccuracy. This means that a slightly negligent taxpayer is treated more leniently than one who is more culpable.

[79] *G.L. Snow*, 141 TC No. 6, Dec. 59,646 (2013).

There is no "stacking" of the accuracy-related components. For example, if part of an underpayment is due both to negligence and a substantial understatement of income tax, the maximum penalty is 20 percent of that portion. Also, the penalty is coordinated with the fraud penalty. If part of the underpayment is due to fraud, the IRS treats the entire underpayment as due to fraud. However, the taxpayer can overcome the IRS position if he or she can establish by the preponderance of the evidence that the underpayment is not due to fraud [Code Sec. 6663(b)].

The IRS will waive the accuracy-related penalty for taxpayers that disclose tax shelters and other questionable items reported on their returns.[80] Timely disclosure results in waiver of the accuracy-related penalty attributable to the disclosed item and due to one or more of the following: (1) disregard of rules or regulations or (2) any substantial understatement of income tax.

.01 Negligence

Negligence is defined as any failure to make a reasonable attempt to comply with the tax law, and includes the careless, reckless, or intentional disregard of rules or regulations [Code Sec. 6662(c); Reg. § 1.6662-3(b)(1)]. Negligence can include any failure to make a reasonable attempt to comply with the provisions of the Internal Revenue Code, to exercise ordinary and reasonable care in the preparation of a tax return, to keep adequate books and records, or to substantiate items properly [Code Sec. 6662(c); Reg. § 1.6662-3(b)]. In general, the negligence standard as in the tort context is objective, requiring a finding of a lack of due care or a failure to do what a reasonable and prudent person would do under analogous circumstances.[81]

The following factors strongly indicate negligence [Reg. § 1.6662-3(b)(1)]:

- Failing to include on the tax return income shown on an information return (for example, a Form 1099).
- Failing to make a reasonable attempt to determine the correctness of a deduction, credit, or exclusion that seem to a reasonable and prudent person to be "too good to be true" under the circumstances.
- A partner who treats a partnership item on his or her own return inconsistently from the way it's treated on the partnership return (and fails to inform the IRS of the inconsistency).
- A shareholder who treats an S corporation item inconsistently from the way the corporation treated the item on its return (and fails to inform the IRS of the inconsistency).

Adequate Disclosure for Purposes of Disregard of Rules or Regulations

The penalty for disregard of rules or regulations doesn't apply if an adequate disclosure is made. A disclosure is considered adequate if it is made on a properly completed Form 8275, *Disclosure Statement.* For a position contrary to a rule or regulation, Form 8275-R, *Regulation Disclosure Statement,* must be filed. However, this disclosure exception only applies if the: (1) taxpayer keeps adequate books and

[80] Announcement 2002-2, 2002-1 CB 304.

[81] See, e.g., *J.Z. Schrum,* CA-4, 94-2 USTC ¶ 50,451, 33 F3d 426.

records and properly substantiates items and (2) has a reasonable basis for taking the disclosed position [Reg. §§1.6662-3(c), 1.6662-4(f)].

> ▶ **REASONABLE BASIS STANDARD:** Adequate disclosure can prevent an accuracy-related penalty for disregard of rules or regulations only if a taxpayer has a "reasonable basis" for taking the disclosed position. Reg. §1.6662-3(b)(3) provides that reasonable basis is a relatively high standard of tax reporting. This means a standard that is significantly higher than not frivolous or not patently improper. The reasonable basis standard is not satisfied by a return position that is merely arguable or that is merely a colorable claim. If a return position is reasonably based on one or more of the authorities such as the Code, regulations, court cases, revenue rulings and procedures, the return position generally will satisfy the reasonable basis standard even though it may not satisfy the substantial authority standard [Reg. §1.6662-4(d)(3)(iii)].

.02 Substantial Understatement of Income Tax

An understatement of income tax is basically the difference between the tax shown on your return and the correct tax due. The IRS has the authority to impose a 20 percent accuracy-related penalty if a return contains a substantial understatement of income tax [Code Sec. 6662(b)(2)]. The penalty rate is increased to 40 percent in certain cases of gross valuation misstatements. An understatement is *substantial* if it exceeds the greater of: (1) 10 percent of the tax required to be shown on the return, or (2) $5,000 [Code Sec. 6662(d)(1)(A)].

In the case of a corporation other than an S corporation or a personal holding company, there is a substantial understatement if the amount of the understatement exceeds the lesser of (1) 10 percent of the tax required to be shown on the return for the tax year (or, if greater, $10,000 or (2) $10,000,000 [Code Sec. 6662(d)(1); Reg. §1.6662-4(b)(1)].

The penalty can be avoided if the taxpayer can show that: (1) he or she acted in good faith and there was reasonable cause for the understatement; (2) that the understatement was based on substantial authority; or (3) if there was a reasonable basis for the tax treatment of an item and that the relevant facts affecting the item's tax treatment were adequately disclosed on the return as discussed further below, or disclosed in a statement attached to the return on Form 8275 or Form 8275-R (for return positions contrary to a regulation) [Code Sec. 6662(d)(2)(B); Reg. §1.6662-4(d); Reg. §1.6662-4(f)].

Reasonable Cause under Code Sec. 6664(c)(1)

A taxpayer who is otherwise liable for the accuracy-related penalty may avoid the liability if he can show, under Code Sec. 6664(c)(1), that he had reasonable cause for a portion of the underpayment and that he acted in good faith with respect to that portion. Reg. §1.6664-4(b)(1) provides:

> The determination of whether a taxpayer acted with reasonable cause and in good faith is made on a case-by-case basis, taking into account all pertinent facts and circumstances. * * * Generally, the most important factor is the extent of the taxpayer's effort to assess the taxpayer's proper tax liability. Circumstances that may indicate reasonable cause and good faith include an honest misunderstanding of fact or law that is reasonable in light of all of the facts and circumstances, including the experience,

> knowledge, and education of the taxpayer. An isolated computational or transcriptional error generally is not inconsistent with reasonable cause and good faith. * * * Reliance on * * * professional advice * * * constitutes reasonable cause and good faith if, under all the circumstances, such reliance was reasonable and the taxpayer acted in good faith.

Whether the taxpayer acted with reasonable cause and in good faith thus depends on the pertinent facts and circumstances, including his efforts to assess his proper tax liability, his knowledge and experience, and the extent to which he relied on the advice of a tax professional.[82]

Standards Applicable to Corporate Tax Shelters

A corporate taxpayer that participated in a tax shelter may no longer decrease the amount of a substantial understatement of tax and the attendant substantial understatement penalty by showing that it had substantial authority for the position it took on a return and reasonably believed that its treatment was more likely than not the proper treatment. Such taxpayers must satisfy the more stringent reasonable cause standard to avoid the substantial penalty on tax shelter items [Code Sec. 6662(d)(2)(C)]. Regulations provide guidance on the application of the reasonable cause exception to a substantial understatement penalty attributable to a tax shelter item of a corporation [Reg. § 1.6662-4(g)]. The regulations provide that a corporation's legal justification may be taken into account in establishing that the corporation acted with reasonable cause and in good faith in its treatment of a tax shelter item only if there is substantial authority for the treatment of the item and the corporation reasonably believes in good faith that such treatment is more likely than not the proper treatment. For this purpose, legal justification includes any justification relating to the treatment or characterization under the federal tax law of the tax shelter item or of the entity, plan or arrangement that gave rise to the item. Thus, a taxpayer's belief (whether independently formed or based on the advice of others) as to the merits of the taxpayer's underlying position is a legal justification.

Substantial Authority

The substantial authority standard is an objective one involving the law's analysis and application to relevant facts. There is substantial authority for an item's tax treatment only if the weight of the "authorities" supporting the treatment is substantial in relation to the weight of those supporting opposing treatment [Reg. § 1.6662-3(b)(1)]. "Authorities" are listed below. This standard is less stringent than the "more likely than not" standard, but stricter than the "reasonable basis" standard.

The types of "authorities" include the following: (1) Internal Revenue Code; (2) proposed, temporary and final regulations; (3) revenue rulings and procedures; (4) tax treaties; (5) federal court cases; (6) congressional committee reports; (7) General Explanation of tax legislation prepared by the Joint Committee on Taxation (the so-called Blue Book); (8) private letter rulings and technical advice memoranda (9) actions on decisions and general counsel memoranda; (10) IRS information or press releases; and (11) IRS notices, announcements and other administrative pronouncements [Reg. § 1.6662-4(d)(3)(iii)].

---

[82] *S.G. Woodsum*, 136 TC No. 29, Dec. 58,658 (2011); *NPR Investments, LLC*, DC-TX, 2010-1 USTC ¶ 50,251; *W.E. Gustashaw*, CA-11, 2012-2 USTC ¶ 50,591, *aff'g*, 102 TCM 161, Dec. 58,729(M), TC Memo. 2011-195; *D. Palmlund*, CA-DC, 2012-2 USTC ¶ 50,418, *aff'g*, 136 TC 67, Dec. 58,508 (2011).

NOTE: You have substantial authority for an item's tax treatment if the treatment is supported by the conclusion of a ruling or a determination letter issued to you. It also exists if the treatment is supported by a technical advice memorandum in which you are named, or by an affirmative statement in an IRS agent's report. However, a holding ceases to be authority if it is overruled or modified [Reg. § 1.6662-4(d)(3)(iv)].

When to Rely on the Advice of Others

If you rely in good faith on the advice (including an opinion) of a professional tax advisor you may be able to avoid the accuracy-related penalty of Code Sec. 6662. The advice must be based on all material facts (including, for example, your purpose for entering into the transaction) and must you relate the applicable law to such facts in reaching your conclusion. The advice must neither be based upon unreasonable factual or legal assumptions (including assumptions as to future events) nor unreasonably rely on any representations, findings or agreements of the taxpayer or any other person [Reg. § 1.6662-4(g)(4)].

Example 27-20: Taxpayers invested in tax shelters and claimed hundreds of thousands of dollars of ordinary losses from the program on their tax returns. The IRS disallowed the losses claimed by the investors and imposed negligence penalties. The Court of Appeals for the Fifth Circuit concluded that the taxpayers were not subject to the negligence penalty because they had relied in good-faith on professional advice.[83] The test for imposition of the negligence penalty is whether or not the taxpayer was acting reasonably in claiming the loss. The court concluded that the taxpayers had relied on the advice of their experts before investing in the tax shelter and cannot be expected to challenge their tax expert, seek a second opinion or to try to monitor the expert on the provisions of the Tax Code.

Who Qualifies as an Expert

Relying on the advice of a tax expert to support a return position and to nullify the substantial understatement of income tax penalty imposed by the IRS will only work if the tax adviser is a competent tax expert, the advice is formal, given in good-faith, and is based on complete and accurate information [Reg. § 1.6664-4(c)(2)]. In addition the adviser will only be accepted in the court's eyes as a competent tax expert if he or she is a reputable attorney or accountant experienced in federal tax matters.

To successfully claim reasonable reliance on a professional adviser, the taxpayer must show that: (1) the adviser was a competent professional who had sufficient expertise to justify the taxpayer's reliance on him or her, (2) the taxpayer provided necessary and accurate information to the adviser, and (3) the taxpayer actually relied in good faith on the adviser's judgment.

Courts have routinely held taxpayers liable for Code Sec. 6662 penalties where the taxpayer unreasonably relied upon a tax adviser's advice because he or she failed to take adequate steps to determine that the adviser had sufficient expertise or that his or

[83] *J.B. Durrett, Jr.*, CA-5, 96-1 USTC ¶50,040, 71 F3d 515.

her advice was sufficiently independent and was not an employee or agent of the taxpayer [Reg. § 1.6664-4(c)(2)].[84]

Adequate Disclosure for Purposes of Substantial Understatement of Tax

The accuracy-related penalty for substantial understatement of tax may be avoided by adequately disclosing on the tax return the facts relevant to the tax treatment of the item—provided a "reasonable basis" exits for the treatment of the disclosed item and you acted in good faith [Code Sec. 6662(d)(2)(B)].

There are two ways to make an adequate disclosure: (1) on the return; or (2) with a red flag.

On the return. The IRS periodically issues revenue procedures listing certain tax forms and schedules that, if properly filled out, are an adequate disclosure in order to reduce the understatement of income tax and to avoid: (1) the substantial understatement penalty under Code Sec. 6662(d); (2) the preparer penalty under Code Sec. 6994(a) for understatements due to unrealistic positions taken by a taxpayer on a return [Reg. § 1.6662-4(f)(2)].

In Rev. Proc. 2012-51[85] the IRS identifies circumstances when the disclosure on a taxpayer's income tax return with respect to an item or a position is adequate for the purpose of reducing the accuracy-related penalty for substantial understatement of income tax under Code Sec. 6662(d) and for the purpose of avoiding the tax return preparer penalty under Code Sec. 6694(a) for understatements due to unreasonable positions with regard to income tax returns.

> ▶ **PRACTICE POINTER:** If tax return preparers follow the guidance provided in Rev. Proc. 2012-51, they will be able to claim aggressive return positions without worrying about an audit provided they have at least a reasonable basis for the position taken on the return and have adequately disclosed the position taken on the return as described above. Keep in mind, however, that no amount of disclosure will help a return position that is frivolous or unsupported by the facts.

Red flag. The surest way to make an adequate disclosure is to give the IRS a statement that identifies the item being disclosed, the amount of the item and either the facts that would alert the IRS to the nature of the potential controversy or a description of the legal issue involved. The information is presented on a properly completed form attached to the return or to a qualified amended return. For an item or position (except for one that is contrary to a regulation), disclosure must be made on Form 8275 (Form 8275-R for a position contrary to a regulation) [Reg. § 1.6662-4(f)(1)].

> ▶ **OBSERVATION:** Although designed to set off alarms at the IRS, this disclosure method offers you the greatest penalty protection. Even if your position is rejected, the IRS can't assert a substantial understatement penalty—and the disclosure may serve as protection against a negligence penalty as well.

---

[84] *Neonatology Associates*, CA-3, 2002-2 USTC ¶50,550, 299 F3d 221; *D.J. Vincentini*, 96 TCM 400, Dec. 57,602(M), TC Memo. 2008-271; *Estate of E.F. Stiel*, 98 TCM 529, Dec. 50,010(M), TC Memo. 2009-278; *Seven W. Enterprises, Inc.*, 136 TC 539, Dec. 58,650 (2011); *SAS Investment Partners*, 103 TCM 1845, Dec. 59,081(M), TC Memo. 2012-159.

[85] Rev. Proc. 2012-51, IRB 2012-51, 719.

.03 Substantial and Gross Valuation Misstatements—In General

Valuing property is important in several areas of the tax law. Overstating the property's value can result in a tax liability's understatement.

Example 27-21: Ms. Forrest donates five acres of land to the Fairlawn Orphanage, and takes a full charitable deduction on her return. If valued at $100,000, Forrest gets a $35,000 tax savings in her 35 percent tax bracket. If valued at $150,000, however, the savings jumps to $52,500—a $17,500 difference.

Substantial Valuation Misstatement

The 20 percent accuracy-related penalty applies to the portion of an underpayment of tax that is attributable to a substantial valuation misstatement. A substantial valuation misstatement exists if:

- The value or adjusted basis of any property claimed on a return is 150 percent or more of the correct value or adjusted basis [Code Sec. 6662(e)(1)(A); Reg. § 1.6662-5(e)(1)]; or
- The price for any property or services (or the property's use) claimed on the return as to any transactions between certain related taxpayers (so-called "Sec. 482 adjustments") [Ch. 20] is 200 percent or more (or 50 percent or less) of the correct amount [Code Sec. 6662(e)(1)(B)].

Example 27-22: Mr. Post contributes a building to his closely held S corporation. The corporation says the building is worth $300,000 and claims a first-year depreciation deduction of $7,692. The correct value of the building is actually $100,000. If the correct valuation were used, the depreciation writeoff would be only $2,564—a difference of $5,128. Since the corporation's valuation statement of the building is at least 150 percent more than the correct valuation, the 20 percent penalty applies. If the understatement resulted in an underpayment of $1,500, the substantial valuation misstatement penalty would be 20% × $1,500 or $300.

NOTE: The substantial valuation misstatement occurs if a taxpayer's "net section 482 transfer price adjustment" exceeds the lesser of $5 million or more than 10 percent of the taxpayer's gross receipts for the year. A net transfer price adjustment is the net increase in taxable income for a tax year resulting from all Sec. 482 adjustments in the price for any property or services (or for the property's use) [Code Sec. 6662(e)(1)(B)(ii), (3)(A)].

Any portion of the net increase in taxable income due to a price redetermination is disregarded if the taxpayer can document that the original value was determined by reasonably applying a statutory valuation method. Alternatively, the taxpayer can document that the original value was determined using some other method that does a better job of accounting for income than any statutory method. Also, the threshold is disregarded if any part of that net increase is due to certain transactions among foreign corporations [Code Sec. 6662(e)(3)(B)].

Since valuation is often a subjective concept, this is a potential area for abuse. Therefore, the IRS and Congress have established several guidelines and accompanying penalties that apply.

Determining if there is a substantial or gross valuation misstatement on a return is made on a property-by-property basis. Assume, for example that Blackacre has a value of $6,000, but Mr. Ames claims a value of $11,000, and that Whiteacre has a value of $4,000, but Ames claims a value of $10,000. Since the claimed and correct values are compared on a property-by-property basis, there is a substantial valuation misstatement as to Whiteacre, but not as to Blackacre, even though the claimed values ($21,000) are 150 percent or more of the correct ($10,000) when compared on a combined basis [Reg. § 1.6662-5(f)(1)].

> **NOTE:** This 20 percent penalty applies to all taxpayers (not just individuals, personal service corporations and closely-held corporations, as under prior law). But it applies only if the amount of the underpayment attributable to a valuation misstatement exceeds $5,000 ($10,000 for corporations other than S corporations or personal holding companies) [Code Sec. 6662(e)(2)].

Gross Valuation Misstatement

The rate of the penalty is 40 percent for gross valuation misstatements. A gross valuation misstatement occurs where:

1. The value or adjusted basis of any property claimed on any return is 200 percent or more of the amount determined to be the correct valuation or adjusted basis, or
2. The price for any property or for its use or for services claimed on any return in connection with a transaction between persons described in Code Sec. 482 is 400 percent or more (or 25 percent or less) of the amount described in Code Sec. 482 to be the correct amount of such price, or
3. The net Code Sec. 482 transfer price adjustment for the tax year exceeds the lesser of $20,000,000 or 20 percent of the taxpayer's gross receipts [Code Sec. 6662(h)(2)(A)].

In *AHG Investments, LLC,*[86] the Tax Court concluded that a taxpayer may not avoid application of the Code Sec. 6662(h) gross valuation misstatement penalty merely by conceding on grounds unrelated to valuation or basis. In *N. Crispin,*[87] the Court of Appeals for the Third Circuit affirmed the Tax Court to uphold the 40 percent gross valuation misstatement penalty even though the taxpayer relied on a tax professional's opinion. The court found that opinion to be based on false representations made by the taxpayer. The court also noted that the taxpayer was a former CPA familiar with tax matters and he should have known better.

---

[86] *AHG Investments, LLC,* 140 TC No. 7, Dec. 59,485 (2013).

[87] *N. Crispin,* CA-3, 2013-1 USTC ¶50,202, 708 F3d 507, *aff'g,* 103 TCM 1349, Dec. 58,980(M), TC Memo. 2012-70.

.04 Substantial Overstatement of Pension Liabilities

A 20-percent penalty for substantial overstatement of pension liabilities is imposed if the actuarial determination of pension liabilities is 200 percent or more of the amount determined to be correct. Further, if a portion of the substantial overstatement to which the penalty applies is attributable to a valuation misstatement of 400 percent or more (a gross valuation misstatement), the penalty is doubled to 40 percent of the underpayment [Code Sec. 6662(b)(4), (f)(1) and (h)].

The amount of the underpayment to which the penalty applies is the taxpayer's actual tax less the actual tax reduced by taking into account the valuation overstatement. However, if the amount of the underpayment for the tax year attributable to substantial overstatement of pension liabilities is $1,000 or less, no penalty applies [Code Sec. 6662(f)(2)].

The purpose of this penalty is to discourage the overvaluation of the future liabilities of a defined benefit pension plan, which results in excess employer contributions to the plan and corresponding excess deductions. The provision is aimed at preventing unreasonable actuarial assumptions that can understate the expected earnings of the plan (for example, assumption of 5 percent yield where a reasonable assumption would be 9 percent). The provision is also intended to prevent overstatements of the amount needed to fund a future benefit (for example, assumption of an unreasonably high rate of inflation or an extended payout period for survivors' benefits where the plan participant is presently unmarried).

.05 Substantial Estate or Gift Tax Valuation Understatement

The 20 percent accuracy-related penalty applies if you value any property claimed on an estate or gift tax return at 65 percent or less than the correct valuation amount. The penalty applies only if the underpayment attributable to the understatement exceeds $5,000. The penalty is doubled to 40 percent if the valuation claimed is 40 percent or less of the correct amount [Code Sec. 6662(g)(1), (h)(2)(C)].

In *Estate of Thompson*,[88] the Court of Appeals for the Second Circuit held that an estate was not liable for an accuracy-related penalty because reliance on the appraisers was reasonable and in good faith.

.06 Underpayments Attributable to Transactions Lacking Economic Substance

A 20-percent penalty is imposed on an underpayment attributable to any disallowance of claimed tax benefits because of a transaction lacking economic substance, as defined in new Code Sec. 7701(o), or failing to meet the requirements of any similar rule of law [Code Sec. 6662(b)(6)]. For further discussion of the Code Sec. 7701(o) and the economic substance doctrine, see ¶ 24,003.

The penalty is increased to 40 percent for an underpayment attributable to a "nondisclosed noneconomic substance transaction" [Code Sec. 6662(i)(1)]. A nondisclosed noneconomic substance transaction is any portion of a transaction lacking economic substance with respect to which the relevant facts affecting the tax treatment are not

[88] *Estate of Thompson*, CA-2, 2010-1 USTC ¶ 60,589, 370 Fed Appx 141.

adequately disclosed in the return or in a statement attached to the return [Code Sec. 6662(i)(2)].

No exceptions, including the reasonable cause exception, are available to the imposition of the penalty for any underpayment, or reportable transaction understatement, attributable to a transaction lacking economic substance [Code Sec. 6664(c)(2), (d)(2)].

A claim for refund or credit that is excessive under Code Sec. 6676 due to its lacking economic substance or failing to meet the requirements of any similar rule of law is subject to a 20-percent penalty, and will be treated as lacking a reasonable basis for purposes of trying to avoid the penalty [Code Sec. 6676(c)].

.07 Reasonable Cause Exceptions

There is a reasonable cause exception for substantial valuation misstatements on charitable deduction property and for gross valuation misstatements on property for which a charitable deduction is not being claimed [Code Sec. 6664(c)(2)].

.08 Fraud Penalty

If the IRS establishes that any part of an underpayment of tax is due to fraud, the entire underpayment will be treated as attributable to fraud, and a 75 percent fraud penalty is imposed [Code Sec. 6663(a), (b)]. To prove that a taxpayer is liable for the penalty, the IRS must prove by clear and convincing evidence that (1) an underpayment of tax exists, and (2) some part of the underpayment is attributable to fraud [Code Sec. 6663(a)]. If the IRS proves that any part of an underpayment is attributable to fraud, then the entire underpayment will be treated as attributable to fraud unless the taxpayer shows by a preponderance of the evidence that a portion could not be attributable in this fashion [Code Sec. 6663(b)].

Because it is difficult to prove fraudulent intent by direct evidence, the IRS may establish fraud by circumstantial evidence, which includes various "badges of fraud."[89] These factors focus on whether the taxpayer engaged in certain conduct that is indicative of fraudulent intent, such as: (1) understating income; (2) failing to maintain adequate records; (3) offering implausible or inconsistent explanations; (4) concealing income or assets; (5) failing to cooperate with tax authorities; (6) engaging in illegal activities; (7) providing incomplete or misleading information to the taxpayer's tax return preparer; (8) offering false or incredible testimony; (9) filing false documents, including filing false income tax returns; (10) failing to file tax returns; and (11) engaging in extensive cash transactions. The existence of any one factor is not dispositive, but the existence of several factors is persuasive circumstantial evidence of fraud. Courts will also consider a taxpayer's intelligence, education, and tax expertise in deciding whether the taxpayer acted with fraudulent intent.[90] However, if the taxpayer can establish that part of the underpayment is not attributable to fraud, that portion is not subject to the 75 percent penalty, although it may be subject to the 20 percent accuracy-related penalty. The portion coming under the 75 percent fraud penalty is not also subject to the 20 percent accuracy-related penalty [Code Sec. 6663(b)].

---

[89] *J.A. Hatling*, 104 TCM 475, Dec. 59,228(M), TC Memo. 2012-293; *R.W. Bradford*, CA-9, 86-2 USTC ¶9602, 796 F2d 303.

[90] *E.S. Iley*, 19 TC 631, Dec. 19,400 (1952).

Example 27-23: Mr. Appleton understated his income tax liability by $100,000. The IRS establishes that some of the understatement is attributable to fraud. Appleton, though, establishes that $40,000 is not attributable to fraud, but agrees that it is attributable to negligence. Result: Appleton owes $45,000 under the fraud penalty ($60,000 × 75%) and $8,000 under the accuracy-related penalty ($40,000 × 20%).

Filing of Return Required

The accuracy-related and fraud penalties do not apply if you have not filed a tax return [Code Sec. 6664(b)]. That doesn't mean you're off the hook, though. There's an up-to-75 percent penalty for fraudulent failure to file a tax return [¶ 27,095] [Code Sec. 6651(f)].

¶27,090 TAX RETURN PREPARER, PROMOTER, AND PROTESTOR PENALITES

.01 Tax Court Proceedings

The Tax Court may impose a penalty on any party that (1) institutes or maintains a proceeding mainly for delay, (2) takes a position in such proceeding that is frivolous or groundless, or (3) unreasonably fails to pursue available administrative remedies. The penalty may be as high as $25,000 ($10,000 if the proceeding is in a court other than the Tax Court) [Code Secs. 6673(a)(1), (b)].

.02 Attorney's Liability

Attorneys and others who are admitted to practice before the Tax Court can be liable for excess costs, expenses, and attorneys' fees that are reasonably incurred because the attorney or other person unreasonably multiplied proceedings before the court. If the attorney is appearing on behalf of the IRS, the U.S. must pay such excess costs [Code Sec. 6673(a)(2)].

> **NOTE:** Regulations explain when a taxpayer is considered to have exhausted administrative remedies to be able to collect litigation costs from the IRS. Taxpayers do have to agree to extend the period for assessment and collection to meet this requirement [Reg. § 301.7430-1].

The IRS may have to pay the litigation costs of a taxpayer if the IRS position in the case is "patently erroneous" or "substantially unjustified."[91] If you feel that the IRS has stuck to a position that has no basis in law or fact, you may be able to force the IRS to pay your attorney's fees. Base your claim on Code Sec. 7430 which provides that attorney fees may be awarded in a court proceeding brought by or against the U.S. in connection with the determination, collection, or refund of any tax, interest, or penalty.

In order for taxpayers to recover attorney's fees, the government has the burden of proving that its position was substantially justified [Code Sec. 7430]. The taxpayer is still, however, required to have prevailed on the merits. A rebuttable presumption

[91] *R.B. Bouterie*, CA-5, 94-2 USTC ¶50,580, 36 F3d 1361.

exists that the IRS's position was not substantially justified if IRS employees failed to follow published IRS guidance. The maximum hourly rate for recoverable attorneys' fees is $190 in 2013 [Code Sec. 7430(c)(1)(B)(iii)]. The difficulty of the issues raised or the unavailability of local tax expertise are factors that may justify a higher rate. Reasonable attorneys' fees may also be awarded to specified persons who represent, on a pro bono basis or for a nominal fee, taxpayers who win their case. The award must be paid to the attorney or the attorney's employer [Code Sec. 7430(c)(3)(B)]. The amount of actual, direct economic damages recoverable by a taxpayer who has been the victim of reckless IRS collection action has been increased from $100,000 to $1 million and a taxpayer is not required to exhaust his or her administrative remedies before filing such a claim against the IRS [Code Sec. 7433(d)].

.03 Tax Return Preparer Penalty

Penalty for Understatement by Tax Return Preparer

Code Secs 6694(a) and (b) impose penalties on tax return preparers for conduct giving rise to understatements of liability on a return, amended return, or claim for refund. For positions other than those with respect to tax shelters and reportable transactions to which Code Sec. 6662A applies, the Code Sec. 6694(a) penalty is the greater of $1,000 or 50 percent of the income derived (or to be derived) by the tax return preparer for an understatement of tax liability that is due to an undisclosed position for which the tax return preparer did not have substantial authority or due to a disclosed position for which there is no reasonable basis.

Penalty for Understatement Due to Willful, Reckless, or Intentional Conduct

The Code Sec. 6694(b) penalty is the greater of $5,000 or 50 percent of the income derived (or to be derived) by the tax return preparer for an understatement of tax liability that is due to a willful attempt to understate tax liability or that is due to reckless or intentional disregard of rules or regulations [Reg. § 1.6694-1(a)]. This is also called the second-tier penalty. The preparer penalty for willful or reckless conduct must be reduced by the amount of any penalty imposed for an unreasonable position relating to the same underpayment [Code Sec. 6694(b)(3)].

A firm that employs a tax return preparer subject to a penalty under Code Sec. 6694(b) is also subject to penalty if:

- One or more members of the principal management of the firm or a branch office participated in or knew of the conduct proscribed by Code Sec. 6694(b).

- The corporation, partnership, or other firm entity failed to provide reasonable and appropriate procedures for review of the position for which the penalty is imposed; or

- The corporation, partnership, or other firm entity disregarded its reasonable and appropriate review procedures through willfulness, recklessness, or gross indifference (including ignoring facts that would lead a person of reasonable prudence and competence to investigate or ascertain) in the formulation of the advice, or the preparation of the return or claim for refund, that included the position for which the penalty is imposed [Reg. § 1.6694-2].

Tax Return Preparer Defined

The term "tax return preparer" means any person who prepares for compensation, or who employs one or more persons to prepare for compensation, all or a substantial portion of any return or any claim for refund of tax [Code Sec. 7701(a)(36)(A); Reg. § 301.7701-15(a)]. The preparation of a substantial portion of a return or claim for refund is treated as if it were the preparation of a return or claim for refund. The tax return preparer penalties also apply to preparers of estate and gift tax, employment tax, and excise tax returns, and returns of exempt organizations [Code Sec. 7701(a)(36)(A)]. In Rev. Proc. 2009-11,[92] the IRS lists the returns and claims for refund that are subject to the penalties for understatement of a taxpayer's liability by a tax return preparer under Code Sec. 6694 and for the tax return preparer's failure to sign the return or claim for refund under Code Sec. 6694(b).

A person is not be a "tax return preparer" merely because the person:

1. Furnishes typing, reproducing, or other mechanical assistance,
2. Prepares a return or claim for refund of the employer (or of an officer or employee of the employer) by whom he is regularly and continuously employed,
3. Prepares as a fiduciary a return or claim for refund for any person, or
4. Prepares a claim for refund for a taxpayer in response to any notice of deficiency issued to such taxpayer or in response to any waiver of restriction after the commencement of an audit of such taxpayer or another taxpayer if a determination in such audit of such other taxpayer directly or indirectly affects the tax liability of such taxpayer [Code Sec. 7701(a)(36)(B)].

Preparers are divided into two categories for purposes of the return preparer penalties: signing tax return preparers and nonsigning tax return preparers [Reg. § 301.7701-15(b)].

Signing Tax Return Preparer

A signing tax return preparer is the individual tax return preparer who has the primary responsibility for the overall substantive accuracy of the preparation of the return or refund claim [Reg. § 301.7701-15(b)(1)]. If there is a signing tax return preparer that individual generally will be considered the person who is primarily responsible for all of the positions on the return or claim for refund giving rise to an understatement unless, it is concluded based upon credible information that the signing tax return preparer is not primarily responsible for the position(s) on the return or claim for refund. In that case, a nonsigning tax return preparer within the signing tax return preparer's firm will be considered the tax return preparer who is primarily responsible for the position(s) on the return or claim for refund giving rise to an understatement [Reg. § 1.6694-1(b)(1)].

Nonsigning Tax Return Preparer

A nonsigning tax return preparer is a tax return preparer who is not a signing tax return preparer but who prepares all or a substantial portion of a return or refund claim with respect to events that have occurred at the time tax advice is rendered. Examples of nonsigning tax return preparers are preparers who provide oral or written advice to a taxpayer or to another tax return preparer when that advice leads

[92] Rev. Proc. 2009-11, 2009-3 IRB 313.

to a position or entry that constitutes a substantial portion of the return [Reg. § 301.7701-15(b)(2)].

In determining whether an individual is a nonsigning tax return preparer, time spent on advice that is given after events have occurred that represents less than five percent of the aggregate time incurred by such individual with respect to the position giving rise to the understatement is not taken into account. However, time spent on advice before the events have occurred will be taken into account if all of the facts and circumstances show that:

1. The position giving rise to the understatement is primarily attributable to the advice,
2. The advice was substantially given before events occurred primarily to avoid treating the person giving the advice as a tax return preparer subject to penalties, and
3. The advice given before events occurred was confirmed after events had occurred for purposes of preparing a return [Reg. § 301.7701-15(b)(2)].

Example 27-24: Attorney A, an attorney in a law firm, provides legal advice to a large corporate taxpayer regarding a completed corporate transaction. The advice provided by A is directly relevant to the determination of an entry on the taxpayer's return, and this advice leads to a position(s) or entry that constitutes a substantial portion of the return. A, however, does not prepare any other portion of the taxpayer's return and is not the signing tax return preparer of this return. A is considered a nonsigning tax return preparer [Reg. § 301.7701-15(b)(2)(ii), Ex. 1].

Example 27-25: Attorney B, an attorney in a law firm, provides legal advice to a large corporate taxpayer regarding the tax consequences of a proposed corporate transaction. Based upon this advice, the corporate taxpayer enters into the transaction. Once the transaction is completed, the corporate taxpayer does not receive any additional advice from B with respect to the transaction. B did not provide advice with respect to events that have occurred and is not considered a tax return preparer. [Reg. § 301.7701-15(b)(2)(ii), Ex. 2].

Who is not a tax return preparer. The following persons are not considered tax return preparers [Code Sec. 7701(a) (36) (B); Reg. § 7701-15(f)]:

1. An official or employee of the IRS performing official duties;
2. Any individual who provides tax assistance under a Volunteer Income Tax Assistance (VITA) program established by the IRS, but only with respect to returns prepared as part of the VITA program;
3. Any organization sponsoring or administering a VITA program established by the IRS, but only with respect to that sponsorship or administration;
4. Any individual who provides tax counseling for the elderly under a program established pursuant to section 163 of the Revenue Act of 1978, but only with respect to those returns prepared as part of that program;

5. Any organization sponsoring or administering a program to provide tax counseling for the elderly established pursuant to section 163 of the Revenue Act of 1978, but only with respect to that sponsorship or administration;
6. Any individual who provides tax assistance as part of a qualified Low-Income Taxpayer Clinic (LITC), but only with respect to those returns and refund claims prepared as part of the LITC program;
7. Any organization that is a qualified LITC;
8. An individual who provides only typing, reproduction, or other mechanical assistance in the preparation of a return or refund claim;
9. An individual preparing a return or refund claim of a taxpayer, or an officer, a general partner, member, shareholder, or employee of the taxpayer, by whom the individual is regularly and continuously employed or compensated or in which the individual is a general partner;
10. An individual preparing a return or refund claim for a trust, estate, or other entity of which the individual is either a fiduciary or is an officer, general partner, or employee of the fiduciary;
11. An individual preparing a return or refund claim for a taxpayer in response to a notice of deficiency issued to the taxpayer or a waiver of restriction on assessment after initiation of an audit of the taxpayer or another taxpayer if a determination in the audit of the other taxpayer directly or indirectly affects the tax liability of the taxpayer; or
12. A person who prepares a return or refund claim for a taxpayer with no explicit or implicit agreement for compensation, even if the person receives an insubstantial gift, return service, or favor.

Primary responsibility. An individual is a tax return preparer subject to Code Sec. 6694 if the individual is primarily responsible for the position(s) on the return or claim for refund giving rise to an understatement [Reg. § 1.6694-1(b)(1)]. A person who furnishes to a taxpayer or other preparer sufficient information and advice so that completion of the return or claim for refund is largely a mechanical or clerical matter is considered an income tax return preparer, even though that person does not actually place or review placement of information on the return or claim for refund [Reg. § 301.7701-15(a)(1)].

One preparer per position. There is only one individual within a firm who is primarily responsible for each position on the return or claim for refund giving rise to an understatement. In some circumstances, there may be more than one tax return preparer who is primarily responsible for the position(s) giving rise to an understatement if multiple tax return preparers are employed by, or associated with, different firms [Reg. § 1.6694-1(b)(1)].

Substantial portion. Reg. § 301.7701-15(b)(3) provides that only a person who prepares all or a substantial portion of a return or claim for refund shall be considered to be a tax return preparer of the return or claim for refund. Whether a schedule, entry, or other portion of a return or claim for refund is a substantial portion is determined based upon whether the person knows or reasonably should know that the tax attributable to the schedule, entry, or other portion of a return or claim for refund is a substantial portion of the tax required to be shown on the return.

A single tax entry may constitute a substantial portion of the tax required to be shown on a return. Factors to consider in determining whether a schedule, entry, or other portion of a return or claim for refund is a substantial portion include but are not limited to:

1. The size and complexity of the item relative to the taxpayer's gross income; and
2. The size of the understatement attributable to the item compared to the taxpayer's reported tax liability.

***De minimis* rule.** With respect to a nonsigning preparer of a schedule, entry, or other portion of a return or claim for refund, the schedule, entry or other portion is not considered to be a substantial portion if it involves gross income, deductions, or the basis of which credits are determined that are either:

1. Less than $10,000; or
2. Less than $400,000 and also less than 20 percent of the gross income as shown on the return or claim for refund (or, for an individual, the individual's adjusted gross income).

In applying this *de minimis* rule, all schedules, entries or other portions must be aggregated.

Defense to Penalties

A tax return preparer will be able to avoid the Code Sec. 6694(a) penalty if the tax return preparer can show:

1. The position taken has a "reasonable basis" and is "adequately disclosed;"
2. An undisclosed position is supported by "substantial authority" and is not a tax shelter;
3. The understatement was due to reasonable cause and the return preparer acted in good faith [Code Sec. 6694(a)(3)].
4. For a tax shelter or reportable transaction, if it is "reasonable to believe" that the position would "more likely than not" be sustained on its merits. This standard applies regardless of whether the position is disclosed.

Reasonable Basis Standard

The Code Sec. 6694(a) penalty will not be imposed on a tax return preparer if the position taken (other than a position with respect to a tax shelter or a reportable transaction to Code Sec. 6662A applies) has a reasonable basis and is adequately disclosed [Reg. § 1.6694-2(d)(1)].

For these purposes, "reasonable basis" has the same meaning as in Reg. § 1.6662-3(b)(3), relating to the accuracy-related penalty on taxpayers [Reg. § 1.6694-2(d)(2)]. Therefore, reasonable basis is a relatively high standard of tax reporting that is much higher than not frivolous or not patently improper. It is commonly interpreted as providing taxpayers with a 20 percent or greater chance of success. It is not satisfied by a return position that is merely arguable or that is merely a colorable claim. If a return position is reasonably based on one or more of the numerous authorities set forth in Reg. 1.6662-4(d)(3)(iii) (taking into account the relevance and persuasiveness of the authorities, and subsequent developments), the return position will generally satisfy the reasonable basis standard even though it may not satisfy the substantial authority standard [Reg. § 1.6662-3(b)(3)].

Adequate Disclosure Standard

Signing tax return preparers. For a signing tax return preparer, Reg. § 1.6694-2(d)(3)(i) provides that disclosure of a position for which there is a reasonable basis but for which there is not substantial authority is adequate in one of the following three ways:

1. The position may be disclosed on a properly completed and filed Form 8275, *Disclosure Statement*, or Form 8275-R, *Regulation Disclosure Statement*, as appropriate, or on the tax return.
2. Disclosure of the position is adequate if the tax return preparer provides the taxpayer with a prepared tax return that includes the appropriate disclosure.
3. For tax returns or claims for refund that are subject to penalties other than the accuracy-related penalty for substantial understatements, the tax return preparer advises the taxpayer of the penalty standards applicable to the taxpayer. This third rule is intended to address the situation when the penalty standard applicable to the taxpayer is based on compliance with requirements other than disclosure on the return.

Nonsigning tax return preparers. For a nonsigning tax return preparer, Reg. § 1.6694-2(d)(3)(ii) provides that disclosure of a position that satisfies the reasonable basis standard but does not satisfy the substantial authority standard is adequate if the position is disclosed in accordance with Reg. § 1.6662-4(f) (which permits disclosure on a properly completed and filed Form 8275 or Form 8275-R, as applicable, or on the return in accordance with an annual revenue procedure described in Reg. § 1.6662-4(f)(2)).

Advice to taxpayers. If a nonsigning tax return preparer provides advice to the taxpayer with respect to a position, disclosure of that position is adequate if the tax return preparer takes the following steps:

1. Advises the taxpayer of any opportunity to avoid penalties under Code Sec. 6662 that could apply to the position and of the standards for disclosure.

2. The tax return preparer must also contemporaneously document the advice in the tax return preparer's files. The contemporaneous documentation should reflect that the affected taxpayer has been advised by a tax return preparer in the firm of the potential penalties and the opportunity to avoid penalty through disclosure [Reg. § 1.6694-2(d)(3)(ii)(A)].

Advice to another tax return preparer. If a nonsigning tax return preparer provides advice to another tax return preparer with respect to a position, disclosure of that position is adequate if the tax return preparer takes the following steps:

1. Advises the other tax return preparer that disclosure may be required.
2. The tax return preparer must also contemporaneously document the advice in the tax return preparer's files. The contemporaneous documentation should reflect that the tax return preparer outside the firm has been advised that disclosure may be required. If the advice is to another nonsigning tax return preparer within the same firm, contemporaneous documentation is satisfied if there is a single instance of contemporaneous documentation within the firm Reg. § 1.6694-2(d)(3)(ii)(B)].

Requirements for advice. Each return position for which there is a reasonable basis but for which there is not substantial authority must be addressed by the tax return preparer. The advice to the taxpayer with respect to each position must be particular to the taxpayer and tailored to the taxpayer's facts and circumstances. The tax return preparer is required to contemporaneously document the fact that the advice was provided.

There is no general pro forma language or special format required for a tax return preparer to comply with these rules. A general disclaimer, however, does not satisfy the requirement that the tax return preparer provide and contemporaneously document advice. Tax return preparers may rely on established forms or templates in advising clients regarding the operation of the penalty provisions of the Code. A tax return preparer may choose to comply with the documentation standard in one document addressing each position or in multiple documents addressing all of the positions [Reg. § 1.6694-2(d)(3)(iii)].

Substantial Authority Standard

If a return position is reasonably based on one or more of the authorities set forth in Reg. § 1.6662-4(d)(3)(iii), which applies for purposes of the "substantial authority" standard for undisclosed positions, the return position will generally satisfy the reasonable basis standard. The authorities set forth in Reg. § 1.6662-4(d)(3)(iii) include:

1. Applicable provisions of the Internal Revenue Code and other statutory provisions;
2. Proposed, temporary and final regulations construing such statutes;
3. Revenue rulings and revenue procedures;
4. Tax treaties and regulations thereunder, and Treasury Department and other official explanations of such treaties;
5. Court cases;
6. Congressional intent as reflected in committee reports, joint explanatory statements of managers included in conference committee reports, and floor statements made prior to enactment by one of a bill's managers;
7. General Explanations of tax legislation prepared by the Joint Committee on Taxation (the Blue Book);
8. Private letter rulings and technical advice memoranda;
9. Actions on decisions and general counsel memoranda (as well as general counsel memoranda published in pre-1955 volumes of the Cumulative Bulletin);
10. IRS information or press releases; and
11. Notices, announcements and other administrative pronouncements published by the IRS in the Internal Revenue Bulletin.

Conclusions reached in treatises, and legal periodicals are not considered authority. Moreover, an authority is no longer an authority to the extent it is overruled or modified, implicitly or explicitly, by a body with the power to overrule or modify the earlier authority.

For undisclosed positions, a position is unreasonable if there is no "substantial authority" for a position. This is a higher confidence standard than the reasonable basis standard for disclosed positions. Until final regulations or other further guidance is issued, "substantial authority" has the same meaning as in Reg. § 1.6662-4(d)(2) of the accuracy-related penalty regulations according to Notice 2009-5.[93] In Notice 2009-5, the IRS provides further that the authorities considered in determining whether there is substantial authority for a position are the authorities described in Reg. § 1.6662-4(d)(3)(iii), as listed above.

The substantial authority standard is an objective standard involving an analysis of the law and application of the law to relevant facts [Reg. § 1.6662-4(d)(2)]. It is less stringent than the more-likely-than-not standard (which requires that there be a greater than 50-percent likelihood of the position being upheld), but more stringent than the reasonable basis standard. Typically it requires roughly a 40 percent possibility of success.

Verification of information furnished by taxpayer or other party. Reg. § 1.6694-1(e) provides that a tax return preparer generally may rely in good faith without verification upon information furnished by the taxpayer or by another advisor, another tax return preparer or other party (including another advisor or tax return preparer at the tax return preparer's firm). The tax return preparer is not required to audit, examine or review books and records, business operations, documents, or other evidence to verify independently information provided by the taxpayer, advisor, other tax return preparer, or other party.

The preparer, however, may not ignore the implications of information furnished to the tax return preparer or actually known by the tax return preparer. The preparer must make reasonable inquiries if the information as furnished appears to be incorrect or incomplete.

Reasonable Cause Exception

The Code Sec. 6694(a) understatement penalty will be imposed if, considering all the facts and circumstances, the understatement is due to reasonable cause and the tax return preparer acted in good faith [Code Sec. 6694(a)(3); Reg. § 1.6694-2(e)].

Reg. § 1.6694-2(e) provides that the factors to consider in determining reasonable cause and good faith, include the following:

1. *Nature of the error causing the understatement.* The error resulted from a provision that was complex, uncommon, or highly technical, and a competent tax return preparer of the type at issue reasonably could have made the error. The reasonable cause and good faith exception, however, does not apply to an error that would have been apparent from a general review of the return or claim for refund by the tax return preparer.

---

[93] Notice 2009-5, 2009-3 IRB 309.

2. *Frequency of errors.* The understatement was the result of an isolated error (such as an inadvertent mathematical or clerical error) rather than a number of errors. Although the reasonable cause and good faith exception generally applies to an isolated error, it does not apply if the isolated error is so obvious, flagrant, or material that it should have been discovered during a review of the return or claim for refund. Furthermore, the reasonable cause and good faith exception does not apply if there is a pattern of errors on a return or claim for refund even though any one error, in isolation, would have qualified for the reasonable cause and good faith exception.

3. *Materiality of errors.* The understatement was not material in relation to the correct tax liability. The reasonable cause and good faith exception generally applies if the understatement is of a relatively immaterial amount. Nevertheless, even an immaterial understatement may not qualify for the reasonable cause and good faith exception if the error or errors creating the understatement are sufficiently obvious or numerous.

4. *Tax return preparer's normal office practice.* The preparer's normal office practice, when considered together with other facts and circumstances, such as the knowledge of the tax return preparer, indicates that the error in question would occur rarely and the normal office practice was followed in preparing the return. Such a normal office practice must be a system for promoting accuracy and consistency in the preparation of returns or claims for refund and generally would include, in the case of a signing tax return preparer, checklists, methods for obtaining necessary information from the taxpayer, a review of the prior year's return, and review procedures. Notwithstanding these rules, the reasonable cause and good faith exception does not apply if there is a flagrant error on a return or claim for refund, a pattern of errors on a return or claim for refund, or a repetition of the same or similar errors on numerous returns or claims for refund.

5. *Reliance on advice of others.* For purposes of demonstrating reasonable cause and good faith, a tax return preparer may rely without verification upon advice and information furnished by the taxpayer and information and advice furnished by another advisor, another tax return preparer. The tax return preparer may rely in good faith on the advice of, or schedules or other documents prepared by, the taxpayer, another advisor, another tax return preparer, or other party (including another advisor or tax return preparer at the tax return preparer's firm), who the tax return preparer had reason to believe was competent to render the advice or other information. The advice or information may be written or oral, but in either case the burden of establishing that the advice or information was received is on the tax return preparer. A tax return preparer is not considered to have relied in good faith if

   a. The advice or information is unreasonable on its face;

   b. The tax return preparer knew or should have known that the other party providing the advice or information was not aware of all relevant facts; or

   c. The tax return preparer knew or should have known (given the nature of the tax return preparer's practice), at the time the return or claim for refund was prepared, that the advice or information was no longer reliable due to developments in the law since the time the advice was given.

6. *Reliance on generally accepted administrative or industry practice.* The tax return preparer reasonably relied in good faith on generally accepted administrative or industry practice in taking the position that resulted in the understatement. A tax return preparer is not considered to have relied in good faith if the tax return preparer knew or should have known (given the nature of the tax return preparer's practice), at the time the return or claim for refund was prepared, that the administrative or industry practice was no longer reliable due to developments in the law or IRS administrative practice since the time the practice was developed.

Tax Shelters and Reportable Transactions

Code Sec. 6694(a)(2)(C) provides that, for positions with respect to tax shelters or a reportable transaction, the return preparer penalty is imposed unless it is reasonable to believe that the position would "more likely than not" be sustained on its merits. Reg. § 1.6662-4(g)(1)(i) provides that tax shelter items of a noncorporate taxpayer will not be included in the understatement for the year if:

1. There is "substantial authority: for the tax treatment of that item;" and
2. The taxpayer reasonably believed at the time the return was filed that the tax treatment of that item was "more likely than not" the proper treatment.

Notice 2009-5 provides that a position with respect to a tax shelter will not be deemed an unreasonable position if there is substantial authority for the position and the preparer advises the taxpayer of the penalty standards applicable to the taxpayer if the transaction has a significant purpose of federal tax avoidance or evasion. The advice provided to the taxpayer must explain that, if the position has a significant purpose of tax avoidance or evasion, then:

1. There must be at a minimum substantial authority for the position.
2. The taxpayer must possess a reasonable belief that the tax treatment was more likely than not the proper treatment to avoid a penalty under Code Sec. 6662(d).
3. Disclosure will not protect the taxpayer from assessment of an accuracy-related penalty. The tax return preparer must also contemporaneously document the advice in his or her files.

Taxpayer's reasonable belief. Reg. § 1.6662-4(g)(4) provides that a taxpayer should reasonably believe that the tax treatment of an item is "more likely than not" the proper tax treatment if:

1. The taxpayer analyzes the pertinent facts and authorities and in reliance upon that analysis, reasonably concludes in good faith that there is a greater than 50-percent likelihood that the tax treatment of the item will be upheld if challenged by the IRS; or
2. The taxpayer reasonably relies in good faith on the opinion of a professional tax advisor, if the opinion is based on the tax advisor's analysis of the pertinent facts and authorities and unambiguously states that the tax advisor concludes that there is a greater than 50-percent likelihood that the tax treatment of the item will be upheld if challenged by the IRS.

.04 Tax Return Preparer Disclosure Requirement Penalties

There is a $50 penalty for each time a tax return preparer fails to (1) furnish a copy of a return or a claim for refund to the taxpayer, (2) sign the return or the claim for refund, (3) furnish an identifying number, (4) retain for three years copies or a list of returns and refund claims filed, or (5) file correct information returns. Maximum penalty: $25,000 per failure for each type of violation per calendar year. The penalty does not apply if it is shown that such failure was due to reasonable cause and not due to willful neglect [Code Sec. 6695; Reg. § 1.6695-1(a)(1)]. An income tax return preparer must manually sign the return or claim (which may be a photocopy) after it is completed and before it is presented to the taxpayer for signature [Reg. § 1.6695-1(b)(1)]. If a tax return preparer presents for a taxpayer's signature a return or claim for refund that has a copy of the preparer's manual signature, the preparer may either:

1. Retain a photocopy of the manually signed copy of the return or claim for refund, or
2. Use an electronic storage system meeting to store and produce a copy of the return or claim manually signed by the preparer [Reg. § 1.6695-1(b)(4)(1)].

NOTE: Tax return preparer penalties apply in addition to other penalties [Code Sec. 6696(a)].

.05 Penalties for Aiding and Abetting Understatement of Tax Liability

Code Sec. 6701 imposes a penalty on "any person who aids or assists in, procures, or advises with respect to, the preparation or presentation of any portion of a return, affidavit, claim, or other document, who knows (or has reason to believe) that such portion will be used in connection with any material matter arising under the internal revenue laws, and who knows that such portion (if so used) would result in an understatement of the liability for tax of another person."[94] The penalty applies with respect "to each such document," and is in the amount of $10,000 if the document relates to the tax liability of a corporation, and $1,000 if the document relates to the tax liability of any other person [Code Sec. 6701(b)]. The IRS may assess only one penalty under Code Sec. 6701 per document for a taxpayer for a taxable period or event.

The first element of Code Sec. 6701 requires assistance in return or document preparation. The second element requires that a person know, or have reason to believe, that the document will be used in any material matter. Although *material* has not been defined under Code Sec. 6701, it has been defined under a comparable criminal penalty, Code Sec. 7206.[95] The third element requires that a person "know" that, if so used, the document will result in an understatement of the tax liability of another person. Section 6701 applies regardless of whether the taxpayer whose tax is understated has knowledge of, or consents to, the actions which resulted in the understatement [Code Sec. 6701(d)].

---

[94] *F. Ogbazion*, DC-Ohio, 2013-1 USTC ¶ 50,293; *J.M. Sansom*, DC-FL, 88-2 USTC ¶ 9422, 703 FSupp 1505, *motion denied*, 707 FSupp 1296; *L. Baisden*, DC-CA, 2007-1 USTC ¶ 50,432. *See also D.H. Sanders*, DC-GA, 2007-2 USTC ¶ 50,673; LTR 200512016, Feb. 8, 2005.

[95] *D.R. Mattingly*, CA-8, 91-1 USTC ¶ 50,068, 924 F2d 785, 788 (observing that "[i]n connection with 6701, it appears that Congress specifically intended to create a provision to penalize aiding and abetting conduct similar to that conduct punished under 7206").

.06 Penalty and Disciplinary Action Imposed on Appraisers for Substantial and Gross Valuation Misstatements Attributable to Incorrect Appraisals

A civil penalty may be assessed against appraisers for certain types of valuation misstatements. A person who prepares an appraisal of property value must pay a penalty if: (1) he or she knows, or reasonably should have known, that the appraisal would be used in connection with a federal tax return or refund claim; and (2) the claimed value of the appraised property results in a substantial valuation misstatement related to income tax under Code Sec. 6662(e), a substantial estate or gift tax valuation understatement, or a gross valuation misstatement under Code Sec. 6662(h) [Code Sec. 6695A(a)]. The Code Sec. 6695A appraiser penalty is in addition to any other penalties provided by law. Deficiency procedures for income, estate, gift and certain excise taxes do not apply to the assessment or collection of the appraiser penalty.

The penalty thresholds for an income tax understatement due to a substantial or gross valuation misstatement is lower to the lesser of: (1) the greater of $1,000 or 10 percent of the tax underpayment amount attributable to the misstatement; or (2) 125 percent of the gross income received by the appraiser for preparing the appraisal [Code Sec. 6695A(b)]. However, no penalty is imposed if the appraiser establishes that the appraised value was more likely than not the proper value [Code Sec. 6695A(c)].

Disciplinary Actions Against Appraisers

The IRS has wider latitude to discipline appraisers because the requirement that the Code Sec. 6701 civil penalty for aiding and abetting a tax understatement must be assessed before the IRS may discipline an appraiser no longer exists. This means that the IRS may discipline an appraiser without first assessing the civil penalty for aiding and abetting in an understatement of another person's tax liability.

.07 Frivolous Tax Submissions: Penalty for Specified Frivolous Submissions

Taxpayers who file a federal tax return, including an original or amended return, based on positions that are the same as or similar to the listed positions are deemed to be frivolous and therefore subject to a $5,000 penalty under Code Sec. 6702(a) and a penalty under Code Sec. 6702(b) for filing a return based on a "specified frivolous submission." If a person withdraws a submission within 30 days after receiving notice from the IRS that it is a specified frivolous submission, the penalty will not be imposed [Code Sec. 6702(b)(3)]. Code Sec. 6702(d) authorizes the IRS to reduce the amount of the frivolous tax submission penalty assessed if the IRS determines that a reduction would promote compliance with and administration of the federal tax laws. In Rev. Proc. 2012-43,[96] the IRS described the limited circumstances in which a person may be eligible for a one-time reduction of any unpaid Code Sec. 6702 penalties. If the person satisfied the eligibility criteria, including filing all tax returns and paying all outstanding taxes, penalties (other than under Code Sec. 6702) and related interest, the IRS will reduce all unpaid Code Sec. 6702 penalties against that person to $500.

---

[96] Rev. Proc. 2012-43, IRB 2012-49, 643.

Specified Frivolous Submissions

A "specified frivolous submission" is a specified submission that either:

1. Is based on a position that the Secretary has identified as frivolous in his prescribed frivolous positions list; or
2. Reflects a desire to delay or impede the administration of federal tax laws [Code Sec. 6702(b)(2)(A)].

A "specified submission" is:

1. A request for a hearing after (1) the IRS files a notice of lien under Code Sec. 6320; or (2) the taxpayer receives a pre-levy Collection Due Process Hearing Notice under Code Sec. 6330; and
2. An application relating to (1) agreements for payment of tax liability in installments under Code Sec. 6159; (2) compromises under Code Sec. 7122; or (3) taxpayer assistance orders under Code Sec. 7811 [Code Sec. 6702(b)(2)(B)].

Frivolous Tax Positions

In Notice 2010-33,[97] the IRS updated its list of positions that are identified as frivolous and therefore subject to the "frivolous tax return" penalty imposed under Code Sec. 6702(a) and the penalty for a "specified frivolous submission" under Code Sec. 6702(b). Positions that are the same as or similar to those listed in the notice are considered frivolous.

¶27,095 DELINQUENCY PENALTIES (FAILURES TO FILE OR PAY)

.01 Failure to File Tax Return or Pay Tax

If a taxpayer who is required to file a tax return fails to timely file that return or if the tax is not timely paid, a penalty is imposed under Code Sec. 6651, unless the taxpayer shows that the delay resulted from "reasonable cause" rather than willful neglect [Code Sec. 6651(a)(1)]. The failure to file/pay penalty imposed under Code Sec. 6651 applies to all taxes for which a taxpayer is required to file a return, including income, estate and gift, and most excise taxes.

For any failure to file a return, the penalty is 0.5 percent for the first month of failure and an additional 0.5 percent for each month or part of a month thereafter, up to a maximum of 25 percent [Code Sec. 6651(a)(1); Reg. § 301.6651-1(a)]. It runs from the due date of the return until the date the IRS actually receives the late return. If the failure to file an income tax return extends for more than 60 days, the failure to file penalty may not be less than the lesser of $135 or 100 percent of the tax due on the return [Code Sec. 6651(a)]. Some relief from this penalty is provided in Code Sec. 6651(h) which allows for a reduction in the 5 percent penalty to 0.25 percent if an installment agreement is in effect. If an individual files a return of tax on or before the due date for the return (including extensions), the penalty will be reduced from 0.5 percent to 0.25 percent [Code Sec. 6651(h)]. In Service Center Advice Memorandum

[97] Notice 2010-33, IRB 2010-17, 609.

200135025,[98] the IRS concluded it could not reduce the penalty rate under Code Sec. 6651(h) until the installment agreement is in effect which occurs when the IRS performs an affirmative act to accept the agreement. Because the mere receipt of a proposed installment agreement does not involve any affirmative act by the IRS, an installment agreement is not accepted, or in effect, on the day that the taxpayer mails or the IRS receives the installment agreement proposal. The reduced rate is only available from the day the IRS accepts the installment agreement proposal.

Additional Tax for Failure to Pay After Notice and Demand

Code Sec. 6651(a)(3) provides that an additional penalty ranging from 0.5 percent a month to a maximum of 25 percent will be imposed for failure to pay a deficiency if within 21 days of the date of notice and demand (10 business days if the amount for which such notice and demand is made equals or exceeds $100,000), the taxpayer fails to pay the tax required to be shown on a return unless the taxpayer can show that the failure was due to reasonable cause and not due to willful neglect [Reg. § 301.6651-1(a)(3)].

Penalty Increased for Failure to Pay in Certain Cases

The penalty for failure to pay tax is increased from 0.5 percent to 1 percent a month on the earlier of the IRS's notice and demand for immediate payment or 10 days after a notice before levy is given. The IRS is required to give at least 30 days' notice of its intent to make a levy [Code Sec. 6651(d)].

.02 If Taxpayer Subject to Both Failure to File and Failure to Pay Penalties

If the taxpayer is subject to both penalties, the sum of both penalties may not exceed 5 percent per month [Code Sec. 6651(c)(1)]. The overall maximums of 25 percent, however, apply separately to each penalty. In other words, the combined penalty for failure to file and failure to pay is 5 percent of the unpaid tax liability for each month or part of a month that a return is late, but not for more than 5 months. The 5 percent penalty includes a 4.5 percent penalty for filing late, and 0.5 percent penalty for paying late. The 25 percent combined maximum penalty includes 22.5 percent for filing late and 2.5 percent for paying late. The 0.5 percent late payment penalty is not limited to 5 months and continues to increase to a maximum of 25 percent until the tax is paid in full. The maximum 25 percent penalty for paying late is in addition to the maximum 22.5 percent penalty for filing late, for a total penalty of 47.5 percent.

The Code Sec. 6651(a)(e) addition to tax for failure to pay a deficiency within the days allotted after notice and demand is not offset by the 5 percent failure to file penalty [Code Sec. 6651(c)]. The Code Sec. 6651 penalties do not apply to either an individual's or a corporation's failure to pay estimated taxes [Code Sec. 6651(e)].

.03 Penalty Imposed on "Net Amount Due"

The amount of the failure to file/pay penalty is computed based on the "net amount due," rather than on the gross amount of tax due [Code Sec. 6651(a)]. Thus, the amount of tax shown on the return is reduced by any amount of tax paid on or before the start of the month for which the tax is being computed. Credits against tax that may be claimed on the return are also subtracted from the amount shown to give the

[98] SCA 200135025 (July 24, 2001).

net amount. If the amount required to be shown as tax on any return is less than the amount actually shown as tax, the lower amount is used to figure the penalty [Code Sec. 6651(b), (c); Reg. § 301.6651-1(d)].

The "net amount due" is computed by reducing the taxpayer's correct tax liability for the tax period at issue by the amount of tax paid on or before the date prescribed for payment of the tax (and by the amount of any credit against the tax that may be claimed on the return). Thus, if part of the tax has been prepaid through payment of estimated tax or withholding on wages, the addition applies only to the amount that still has to be paid [Code Sec. 6651(b)(1); Reg. § 301.6651-1(d)]. As a result of this rule, a taxpayer who is owed a refund cannot be charged a late filing penalty.[99] But a taxpayer who didn't file because he mistakenly believed he owed no tax will be charged the penalty.[100] Returns that are filed late, but which show no tax due in excess of the taxpayer's withholding and/or estimated tax payments (and applicable credits) are not subject to the Code Sec. 6651(a)(1) late-filing penalty, since there is no net amount due on which such penalty can be imposed.

.04 Fraudulent Failure to File

The failure to file penalty is increased to 15 percent of the net amount due for each month the return is late, up to a maximum of 75 percent, if the failure to file is deemed to be fraudulent [Code Sec. 6651(f)]. The IRS has the burden of proving that the failure to file was fraudulent. To determine whether the taxpayers' failure to file is fraudulent, courts will consider the following factors: (1) failure to file income tax returns, (2) understatement of income, (3) concealing of assets, (4) failure to cooperate with taxing authorities, (5) making frivolous arguments, (6) failure to make estimated tax payment, (7) giving implausible or inconsistent explanations of behavior, (8) being convicted of willful failure to file an income tax return. In *R.E. Mason*,[101] the Tax Court held that the taxpayers were liable for the fraudulent failure to file penalty because of their failure to file returns, their failure to make estimated tax payments, their failure to cooperate with the IRS investigation, and their attempt to conceal assets.

.05 Filings That Constitute Valid Returns

Generally, taxpayers are required to file a return that conforms to the regulations and advised to use IRS-issued forms [Reg. § 1.6011-1(b)]. In *R.D. Beard*,[102] the court considered several Supreme Court decisions and developed a four-part test that is often relied on to determine what constitutes a valid return for purposes of the Code Sec. 6651 failure to file/pay tax penalties. Under the four-part *Beard* test, a document is sufficient for purposes of the statute of limitations if: (1) there is sufficient data to calculate the tax liability, (2) the document purports to be a return, (3) there is an honest and reasonable attempt to satisfy the requirements of the tax law, and (4) the taxpayer executes the return under penalty of perjury. In *M.R. Halcott*,[103] the Tax Court applied the *Beard* test and concluded that a taxpayer who timely filed his

[99] *C. Patronik-Holder*, 100 TC 374, Dec. 49,003 (1993), *acq.* 1993-2 CB 1.

[100] *H.L. Richardson*, 91 TCM 981, Dec. 56,475(M), TC Memo. 1991-258.

[101] *R.E. Mason*, 88 TCM 398, Dec. 55,790(M), TC Memo. 2004-247.

[102] *R.D. Beard*, 82 TC 766, Dec. 41,237 (1984), *aff'd*, CA-6, 86-2 USTC ¶ 9496, 793 F3d 139.

[103] *M.R. Halcott*, 88 TCM 286, Dec. 55,754(M), TC Memo. 2004-214.

federal income tax return reporting zero income, deductions, credits, and tax liability should be liable for failure-to-file penalties because his return did not constitute a "valid return" for Code Sec. 6651(a)(1) purposes.

.06 Reasonable Cause for Failure

A taxpayer may avoid the failure to file/pay penalty by showing a reasonable cause for the delay in filing or payment and the absence of willful neglect of the obligation to file or pay [Code Sec. 6651(a)(3)]. Neither "reasonable cause" nor "willful neglect" is defined in the Internal Revenue Code.

In *R.W. Boyle*,[104] the Supreme Court provided that the taxpayer bears the burden of proving both reasonable cause and the absence of willful neglect. In that case, the Court also defined "willful neglect" as "a conscious, intentional failure or reckless indifference" and explained that taxpayers should look to the regulations for guidance in defining these terms. The Court concluded in *R.W. Boyle*, that tardy action by hired accountants or lawyers did not constitute "reasonable cause" to excuse a taxpayer from paying the failure to file a timely return penalty.

Reg. § 301.6651-1(c)(1) provides that the failure to file is due to reasonable cause if the taxpayer exercised ordinary business care and prudence and was nevertheless unable to file the return within the prescribed time. A failure to pay is considered due to reasonable cause to the extent that the taxpayer shows that he exercised ordinary business care and prudence in providing for payment of his tax liability and was nevertheless either unable to pay the tax or would suffer an undue hardship if he paid on the due date. Undue hardship, in turn, means that "substantial financial loss, for example, loss due to the sale of property at a sacrifice price, will result to the taxpayer for making payment on the due date of the amount with respect to which the extension is desired" [Reg. § 1.6161-1(b)].

In determining whether the taxpayer was unable to pay despite ordinary business care and prudence, consideration is given to all the facts and circumstances of the taxpayer's financial condition, including the amount and nature of the taxpayer's expenditures in light of income (or other amounts) he could, at the time of such expenditures, reasonably expect to receive prior to the date prescribed for the payment of tax [Reg. § 301.6651-1(c)].

Thus, for example, a taxpayer who incurs lavish or extravagant living expenses in an amount such that the remainder of his assets and anticipated income will be insufficient to pay his tax, has not exercised ordinary business care and prudence in providing for the payment of his tax liability. Moreover, a taxpayer who invests funds in speculative or illiquid assets has not exercised ordinary business care and prudence in providing for the payment of his tax liability unless, at the time of the investment, the remainder of the taxpayer's assets and estimated income will be sufficient to pay his tax or it can be reasonably foreseen that the speculative or illiquid investment made by the taxpayer can be utilized (by sale or as security for a loan) to realize sufficient funds to satisfy the tax liability. A taxpayer will be considered to have exercised ordinary business care and prudence if he made

---

[104] *R.W. Boyle*, SCt, 85-1 USTC ¶ 13,602, 469 US 241, 105 SCt 687. See also *J. Shafmaster*, CA-1, 2013-1 USTC ¶ 50,184, 707 F3d 130; *E.J. Meehan*, CA-3, 2013-2 USTC ¶ 50,419; *J.A. Fonteneaux*, CA-5, 2013-2 USTC ¶ 50,491; *D.L. Nelson*, CA-11, 2013-2 USTC ¶ 50,522; *M. Leathers*, DC-KS, 2013-1 USTC ¶ 50,315.

reasonable efforts to conserve sufficient assets in marketable form to satisfy his tax liability and nevertheless was unable to pay all or a portion of the tax when it became due [Reg. § 301.6651-1(c)(1)].

In assessing ordinary business care and prudence, the IRS will examine the taxpayer's reason for failure to comply, whether the taxpayer has a history of complying with the tax law, the length of time between the event and the cited reason for the failure to comply, and whether the circumstances were beyond the taxpayer's control (Internal Revenue Manual (Handbook), I.R.M. 20.1.1.3.1.2, February, 2008). The IRS Manual provides the following examples of situations that constitute reasonable cause: (1) Ignorance of the law even though taxpayers have an obligation to make reasonable efforts to determine their tax obligations [I.R.M. 20.1.1.3.1.2.1, February, 2008]; (2) Mistake [I.R.M. 20.1.1.3.1.2.2, February, 2008]; (3) Forgetfulness [I.R.M. 20.1.1.3.1.2.3, February, 2008]; (4) Death, serious illness or unavoidable absence [I.R.M. 20.1.1.3.1.2.4, February, 2008]; (5) Inability to obtain records [I.R.M. 20.1.1.3.1.2.5, February, 2008].

.07 Failure to Make Timely Tax Deposits

Taxpayers are required to deposit taxes when the taxes owed the IRS reach a certain dollar amount. Code Sec. 6656 imposes a penalty for failure to make timely deposits of these taxes and the penalty applies in connection with employment taxes, backup withholding, the withholding of tax paid to foreigners, and certain excise taxes. The penalty is not applicable where it is shown that the failure was due to reasonable cause and not to willful neglect. In order to avoid the penalty, a taxpayer must make an affirmative showing of all facts alleged as a reasonable cause in a written statement containing a declaration that it is made under the penalties of perjury. The penalty may also be abated for first-time depositors. Whether a taxpayer's financial condition should be examined when determining reasonable cause for purposes of the penalties imposed for nonpayment of withholding taxes has been the subject of litigation resulting in a circuit split. In *Brewery, Inc.*,[105] the U.S. Court of Appeals for the Sixth Circuit used a bright line test and held that financial difficulties can never constitute reasonable cause to excuse penalties for failure to pay employment taxes. In *Fran Corp.*,[106] the U.S. Court of Appeals for the Second Circuit held that a case-by-case assessment is necessary. The U.S. Court of Appeals for the Third Circuit in *East Wind Industries, Inc.*,[107] and the U.S. Court of Appeals for the Ninth Circuit in *Van Camp & Bennion*,[108] agreed with the Second Circuit and held that all facts and circumstances of a taxpayer's financial situation must be examined.

The graduated penalty is assessed under Code Sec. 6656(b)(1)(A) as follows:

1. Two percent of the amount of the underpayment if the failure is for not more than five days;
2. Five percent of the amount of the underpayment if the failure is for more than five days but not more than 15 days;

---

[105] *Brewery, Inc.*, CA-6, 94-2 USTC ¶ 50,435; *S.J. Sebesta & Assoc.*, DC-Ohio, 2001-1 USTC ¶ 50,211.

[106] *Fran Corp.*, CA-2, 99-1 USTC ¶ 50,208.

[107] *East Wind Industries, Inc.*, CA-3, 99-2 USTC ¶ 50,968.

[108] *Van Camp & Bennion*, CA-9, 2001-1 USTC ¶ 50,446, 251 F2d 862.

3. 10 percent of the amount of the underpayment if the failure is for more than 15 days.

However, if the tax is not deposited on or before the earlier of (1) the day that is 10 days after the date of the first delinquency notice to the taxpayer or (2) the day on which notice and demand for immediate payment of tax is given in cases of jeopardy, the penalty will be imposed at the rate of 15 percent of the amount of the underpayment [Code Sec. 6656(b)(1)(B)].

For special rules regarding an employer's failure to deposit withholding and employment taxes, see Ch. 15.

The IRS may waive the penalty for failure to deposit payroll taxes for a person's inadvertent failure to deposit any employment tax if:

1. The depositing entity meets the net worth requirements applicable for an award of attorneys' fees generally, net worth may not exceed $2 million for individuals and $7 million for corporations [Reg. § 301.7430-5(f)];
2. The failure to deposit occurs during the first quarter that the depositing entity was required to deposit any employment tax; and
3. The employment tax return was filed on or before the due date [Code Sec. 6656(c); Reg. § 301.6656-1(a)].

Taxpayers may designate the application of a deposit of taxes to a period or periods within the return period to which the deposit relates. The designation must be made during the 90 days immediately following the date of an IRS penalty notice informing the taxpayer that a penalty has been imposed for the return period to which the deposit relates [Code Sec. 6656(e)].

¶27,100 OTHER PENALTIES

There are a number of individual penalties that can apply in addition to the general penalties above. A summary of other penalties follows:

- *Bad checks.* If tax is paid with a bad check (or money order), a penalty is imposed unless the check was tendered in good faith and with reasonable cause to believe it will be paid. The amount of the penalty is 2 percent of the check's amount (unless the check was for less than $1,250, in which case the penalty is the lesser of $25 or the amount of the check) [Code Sec. 6657; Reg. § 301.6657-1].
- *Partnership returns.* There is a per month penalty of $195 multiplied by the number or partners for late or incomplete returns unless due to reasonable cause [Code Sec. 6698(b)]. See ¶ 24,020. This penalty is in addition to criminal penalties [¶ 27,110].
- *Private foundations.* A penalty equal to 100 percent of initial and additional excise taxes is imposed on the foundation, its manager, a disqualified person or government official if (1) the violation was willful and flagrant, or (2) the person was liable for any such tax as to a prior violation with same or another foundation [Code Sec. 6684; Reg. § 301.6684-1].
- *Public charities.* A 25 percent excise tax is imposed on an electing charitable organization if it incurs excess lobbying expenditures to influence legislation [Code Sec. 4911].

- *Retirement plans.* A nondeductible 6 percent excise tax on excess contributions to individual retirement accounts (IRAs) [Code Sec. 4973]; also, a 10 percent penalty tax on premature distribution withdrawals from IRAs [Code Secs. 408(d), 72(t)]. A two-tier excise tax is imposed on employers' plans for underfunding [Code Sec. 4971].
- *Registered obligations.* An excise tax is imposed on the issuer of a registration-required obligation not in registered form. The tax is 1 percent of the principal multiplied by the number of years (or portions thereof) in the term of the obligation [Code Sec. 4701(a)(1)].
- *Notices by brokers to payors.* A $500 per failure penalty is imposed on any retail broker who intentionally fails to notify the payor that the payee is subject to withholding [Code Sec. 6705].
- *Penalty for Filing Erroneous Income Tax Refund or Credit Claims for Excessive Amounts.* Returns that make erroneous income tax refund claims or credit claims made for an ''excessive amount'' are subject to a penalty equal to 20 percent of the excessive amount. The penalty does not apply to claims for refunds or credits relating to the earned income credit, which is subject to its own set of rules [Code Sec. 6676(a)]. An ''excessive amount'' is the amount by which the refund or credit claim exceeds the amount allowable under the Code for the tax year [Code Sec. 6676(b)]. However, if it can be shown that the claim for the excessive amount has a reasonable basis, the penalty will not apply [Code Sec. 6676(a)]. The penalty does not apply to any portion of the excessive amount of a refund claim or credit which is subject to an accuracy-related penalty imposed under Code Secs. 6662 or 6662A, or under the fraud penalty provisions of Code Sec. 6663 [Code Sec. 6676(c)].

¶27,105 PENALTY FOR UNDERPAYMENT OF CORPORATION ESTIMATED TAX

Corporations are generally required to pay four installments of estimated tax equal to 25 percent of its "required annual payment." Installments are due by April 15, June 15, September 15 and December 15. For fiscal year corporations, the due dates are the 15th day of the fourth, sixth, ninth and twelfth months of the year [Code Sec. 6655(a); Reg. § 1.6655-1].

A penalty is imposed on the amount of underpayment for the period of underpayment [¶ 27,115]. The required annual payment, for corporations other than large corporations [discussed below], is the lesser of: 100 percent of the tax shown on the current year's return or 100 percent of the tax for the preceding year. (The last-year's-tax escape hatch remains intact for corporations eligible to use it; see below.)

.01 Exceptions

A corporation does not owe an underpayment penalty if it satisfies any of the following: (1) The corporation based its installment on its "annualized income"; (2) The corporation based its installment on its "adjusted seasonal income"; or (3) The corporation's tax for the year is less than $500 [Code Secs. 6655(e), (f)]. For further discussion of the exceptions, see ¶ 26,105.

¶27,110 CRIMINAL PENALTIES

Criminal penalties can be imposed as follows:

- Willful failure to pay the tax or estimated tax, make a return, or keep the records and supply the information required by the law and regulations—misdemeanor punishable by fine of $25,000 (or $100,000 for corporations), imprisonment for not over one year (5 years for willful failure to report large cash transactions as required by Code Sec. 6050I), or both [Code Sec. 7203].
- Willful failure to collect, account for, and pay over any tax by any person required to do so—felony, punishable by fine of $10,000, imprisonment for not more than five years, or both [Code Sec. 7202].
- Willful attempt to evade or defeat the tax—felony, punishable by fine of $100,000 (or $500,000 for corporations), imprisonment for not more than five years, or both [Code Sec. 7201].
- Willful making and subscribing of a return in which not every material matter is believed to be true and correct—felony, punishable by fine of $100,000 (or $500,000 for corporations), imprisonment for not more than three years, or both [Code Sec. 7206].
- Willful filing of any known false or fraudulent document, including an income tax return[109]—misdemeanor, punishable by fine of $10,000 (or $50,000 for corporations), imprisonment of not more than one year, or both [Code Sec. 7207; Reg. § 301.7207-1].
- Knowing or reckless disclosure by a tax return preparer or use by them of any information furnished to them for, or in connection with, the preparation of income tax returns for any purpose other than to prepare, or assist in preparing, the returns [Code Sec. 7216(a); Reg. § 301.7261-1(a)]. The offense is considered a misdemeanor punishable by fine of $1,000, imprisonment up to one year, or both. In Rev. Rul. 2010-4,[110] the IRS describes three scenarios in which tax return preparers may disclose or use tax return information without being subject to criminal penalties under Code Sec. 7216 and civil penalties under Code Sec. 6713. A tax return preparer may use tax return information to identify taxpayers affected by a change in the tax law, inform them of the change, advise whether it would be appropriate for them to file amended returns, and assist in the preparation and filing of any amended returns. A tax return preparer who is also an accountant may also use tax return information to determine who might be affected by a prospective tax rule change to contact potentially affected taxpayers for whom the accountant/preparer reasonably expected to provide accounting services (such as tax advice) in the next year. Finally, tax return preparers may disclose their taxpayer lists kept to a third-party service provider holding itself out as providing services that include creation, publication, and distribution of newsletters, bulletins, or similar communications to taxpayers whose tax returns the tax return preparers have prepared or processed containing tax information and general business and economic information or analysis for educational purposes, or for

---

[109] *M.C. Sansone*, SCt, 65-1 USTC ¶ 9307, 380 US 343, 85 SCt 1004.

[110] Rev. Rul. 2010-4, IRB 2010-4, 309.

purposes of soliciting additional tax return preparation services for the tax return preparer. In Rev. Rul. 2010-5,[111] the IRS discusses the circumstances under which tax return preparers would not be liable for criminal and civil penalties for disclosing return information to a domestic professional liability insurance carrier. Disclosures necessary for price quotes or to otherwise obtain or maintain professional liability insurance coverage will not result in penalties. Similarly, disclosures made to the insurance carrier as required for purposes of reporting and investigating claims or for the carrier's selection of an attorney to represent the return preparer will not result in penalties. Finally, a return preparer may make disclosures to the selected attorney related to the claim or potential claim or in seeking legal advice from an attorney who is not a representative of the carrier, without taxpayer consent.

.01 Limitation Period

The statute of limitations on these offenses is three years in some cases and six years in others, the latter applying mostly to attempts to defraud the government and willful attempts to evade or defeat the tax [Code Sec. 6531]. The six-year limitation period begins to run from the date a return is filed, or its due date, whichever is later.[112]

¶27,115 INTEREST FOR FAILURE TO PAY TAX

Code Sec. 6601 requires the payment of interest on any amount of tax that is not paid on or before the last date prescribed for payment of the tax. Code Sec. 6151 provides that the date for payment of tax is generally the date a taxpayer must file a return reporting the tax (determined without regard to any extension of time for filing the return). Code Sec. 6601(e) provides that interest shall be assessed, collected, and paid in the same manner as tax. Interest on tax underpayments begins to run (unless abated as discussed in ¶27,115) from the last day prescribed by law for payment of the tax [Code Sec. 6601]. By contrast, interest on penalties is imposed from the date of the notice and demand to the date of payment [Code Sec. 6601(e)]. The due date for payment of interest is determined without regard to any extension of time to file returns (including an automatic extension or installment agreement) [Ch. 26]. Interest runs during the period of the extension and until payment is made. If payment is demanded before the due date because of jeopardy, interest does not run before the prescribed due date [Code Sec. 6601(b)]. Interest on underpayment of accumulated earnings tax accrues from the due date of the income tax return for the year the tax is initially imposed [Code Sec. 6601(b)(4)]. Interest on a deficiency that is offset by a carryback of a net operating loss, net capital loss or general business credit [Ch. 14] runs from the original due date of the tax to which the deficiency relates to the filing date for the tax year in which the loss or credit arises [Code Sec. 6601(d); Reg. § 301.6601-1(e)]. If a net operating loss carryback eliminates the appropriate credit, no interest is payable on the tax originally offset by the credit.[113]

---

[111] Rev. Rul. 2010-5, 2010-4 IRB 312.

[112] *A.F. Habig*, SCt, 68-1 USTC ¶9243, 390 US 222, 88 SCt 926.

[113] *M.C. Miller*, CA-9, 2002-2 USTC ¶50,759, 310 F3d 640.

In general, interest is compounded daily. However, the daily compounding of interest does not apply to the penalty for underpaying estimated tax [Ch. 24].

Interest is also imposed on any assessable penalty, additional amount, or addition to the tax, if the additional amount is not paid within ten days from notice and demand for payment [Code Sec. 6601(e); Reg. § 301.6601-1(f)]. However, interest runs from the due date of the return (including extensions) if the penalty is assessed for the following: (1) failure to file a timely return [¶ 27,095]; (2) a substantial understatement of tax [¶ 27,085] and (3) a valuation misstatement [¶ 27,085].

The compounding of interest is suspended if the interest on deficiency is suspended after a waiver of restrictions on assessment has been filed [Code Sec. 6601(c)]. In addition, the interest-free period provided in Code Sec. 6601(e)(3) to taxpayers for payment of tax reflected in first notice and demand is extended from 10 to 21 calendar days for deficiencies of less than $100,000 (taxpayers with larger deficiencies have 10 business days to pay the tax) [Code Sec. 6601(e)].

The underpayment and overpayment rates are tied to the federal short-term interest rate:

- The overpayment rate is the federal short-term interest rate (AFR) plus three percentage points for individuals and AFR plus two percentage points corporations with overpayment no more than $10,000 (1/2 percentage point if more than $10,000).
- The underpayment rate is generally the AFR plus three percentage points (five percentage points for corporations exceeding $100,000) [Code Sec. 6621].

The interest rate is adjusted quarterly. It is determined during the first month of each quarter, and takes effect the following quarter. For example, the January AFR is the rate used to determine the interest to be charged on underpayments and overpayments for April, May, and June. The IRS determines the interest rate based on average market yield on outstanding U.S. marketable obligations with remaining maturity periods of three years or less [Code Secs. 6621(b)(3), 1274(d)(1)(C)]. If the tax is being paid in installments, interest on any portion of the tax not shown on the return runs from the due date of the first installment. For an unpaid installment of tax shown on the return, interest runs from the due date for that particular installment [Code Sec. 6601(b)(2); Reg. § 301.6601-1].

.01 Deposits to Suspend Running of Interest on Potential Underpayments

Code Sec. 6603 permits a taxpayer to deposit with the IRS cash that subsequently may be used to pay an underpayment of income, gift, estate, and generation-skipping or certain excise taxes. The purpose of the deposit is to suspend the accrual of underpayment interest while the IRS and a taxpayer dispute taxpayer liability. Interest will not be charged on the portion of the underpayment that is deposited for the period that the amount is on deposit. Generally, deposited amounts that have not been used to pay a tax may be returned to the taxpayer if the taxpayer so requests in writing.

The IRS must pay interest on a deposit that is returned to the taxpayer to the extent (and only to the extent) that the deposit is attributable to a disputable tax. The rate of interest is the federal short-term rate determined under Code Sec. 6621(b), compounded daily.

A *disputable tax* is the amount of tax specified at the time of deposit as the taxpayer's reasonable estimate of the maximum amount of tax attributable to disputable items [Code Sec. 6603(d)(2)(A)].

A *disputable item* is any item of income, gain, loss, deduction, or credit if the taxpayer:

1. Has a reasonable basis for its treatment of such item and
2. Reasonably believes that the IRS also has a reasonable basis for disallowing the taxpayer's treatment of such item [Code Sec. 6603(d)(3). If a taxpayer has been issued a 30-day letter, the amount of disputable tax is, at a minimum, the amount of the proposed deficiency specified in the letter [Code Sec. 6603(d)(2)(B)].

Using a Deposit to Offset Tax Underpayments

Any amount on deposit may be used to pay a tax underpayment. If an underpayment is paid in this manner, the taxpayer will not be charged underpayment interest on the portion of the underpayment that is paid for the period the funds were on deposit.

Return of Amounts

A taxpayer may request the return of any amount of deposit at any time. The IRS must comply with the withdrawal request unless the amount has already been used to pay tax or the IRS properly determines that collection of tax is in jeopardy. Interest will be paid on deposited amounts that are withdrawn at a rate equal to the short-term applicable federal rate for the period from the date of deposit to a date not more than 30 days preceding the date of the check paying the withdrawal. Interest is not payable to the extent the deposit was not attributable to a disputable tax.

Procedures for Making Deposits

In Rev. Proc. 2005-18,[114] the IRS established guidelines for taxpayers to follow when making, withdrawing, or identifying deposits in an attempt to stop the running of interest on potential tax underpayments under Code Sec. 6603. Taxpayers must send a check or a money order accompanied by a written statement designating the remittance as a deposit and identifying: (a) the type(s) of tax, (b) the tax year(s), (c) the amount of the disputed tax, and (d) the basis for the disputed tax.

A remittance that is not designated as a deposit (an "undesignated remittance") will be treated as a payment and applied by the IRS against any outstanding liability for taxes, penalties, or interest. Undesignated remittances treated as payments will be applied to the earliest tax year for which there is a liability and will be applied first to tax, then penalties, and finally to interest.

A taxpayer may elect to have a deposit that exceeds the amount of tax ultimately determined to be due applied against another assessed or unassessed liability. For example, a taxpayer under examination for several different years may request that a deposit made for one type of tax in one year be applied to another type of tax in another year. The request must be in writing and must be directed to the same office where the original deposit was made.

---

[114] Rev. Proc. 2005-18, 2005-1 CB 798.

A taxpayer may request the return of all or part of a deposit at any time before the IRS has used the deposit for payment of a tax. To request a return of a deposit, taxpayers must submit a written statement to the IRS requesting that the deposit be returned.

.02 Large Corporate Underpayments

The interest rate on corporate underpayments that exceed $100,000 or "Hot Interest" is the (Hot Interest) federal short-term rate plus 5 percentage points [Code Sec. 6621(c)(1); Reg. § 301.6621-3].

The $100,000 threshold includes the excess of the tax imposed exclusive of interest, penalties, additional amounts, and additions to tax. Thus, any payment made after the last date prescribed for payment (for example, by way of an amended return) won't affect the threshold amount. Different types of taxes are not combined for this threshold.

For the purpose of determining the period to which the large corporate underpayment rate applies, any notice or letter is disregarded if the amount of the deficiency, proposed deficiency, assessment or proposed assessment set forth in the letter or notice is not greater than $100,000 (determined by not taking in account any interest, penalties, or additions to tax) [Code Sec. 6621(c)(2)(B)(ii)].

This rate applies to periods after the 30th day following the earlier of the date the IRS sends: (1) the 30-day letter [¶ 27,010]; or (2) the 90-day letter [¶ 27,020] [Reg. § 301.6621-3(c)(2)].

.03 Interest Netting

A net interest rate of zero applies to equivalent amounts of overpayments and underpayments that exist for any period of mutual indebtedness by the same taxpayer and the IRS. This means that no interest for income taxes and self-employment taxes will be imposed to the extent that underpayment and overpayment interest run simultaneously on equal amounts paid by the same taxpayer [Code Sec. 6621(d)]. This is called *global interest netting* and it means basically that the interest rate for overpayments and underpayments of tax for any period of mutual indebtedness between taxpayers and the IRS has essentially been equalized.[115] Note that the zero net interest rate applies to all individual and corporate taxpayers even where the special rates for large corporate underpayments or overpayments in excess of $10,000 would apply. As a result of the global netting rule, it is now impossible for taxpayers to take advantage of the interest rate differential and delay paying back taxes so the higher underpayment interest charged would be available to offset any overpayments that the taxpayers were later assessed.

"Same Taxpayer" Requirement

Code Sec. 6621(d) authorizes interest rate netting only to "the same taxpayer" that made the equivalent overpayment and underpayment. In *Energy East Corp.*,[116] the Court of Appeal for the Federal Circuit affirmed the Court of Federal Claims to hold that interest netting was not available with respect to interest on a parent corpora-

[115] See *Exxon Mobil Corp.*, 136 TC 99, Dec. 58,538 (2011), *aff'd*, CA-2, 2012-2 USTC ¶ 50,511, 689 F3d 191.

[116] *Energy East Corp.*, CA-FC, 2011-1 USTC ¶ 50,460, 645 F3d 1358, *aff'g*, FedCl, 2010-1 USTC ¶ 50,291, 92 FedCl 29.

tions' deficiency and interest on overpayments made by two of its subsidiaries because the subsidiaries were separate and different taxpayers wholly unrelated to the parent corporation both at the time the underpayment was due and the overpayments were made.

Interest Netting Must Be Requested

Since the IRS does not currently have the ability to automatically apply the net rate of zero as provided in Code Sec. 6621(d), in order for you to ensure application of the zero net interest rate in all applicable situations, you should request that it be applied or request that the IRS recompute the net interest rate of zero if you disagree with the IRS's computation. Requests for application of the zero net interest rate should be made on Form 843, *Claim for Refund and Request for Abatement*.

.04 Interest Abatement

Code Sec. 6404(a) authorizes the IRS to abate an assessment of tax (including interest) if the assessment is excessive in amount, untimely, or erroneously or illegally assessed. Code Sec. 6404(b) precludes taxpayers from filing administrative claims for abatement with respect to income, estate, or gift taxes. For other types of tax, taxpayers may file an administrative claim requesting that the IRS abate an improper assessment [Reg. § 301.6404-1(c)].

Code Sec. 6404(e) permits the abatement of interest assessed on "any deficiency," or on the payment of any tax under Code Sec. 6212, that is attributable to unreasonable errors or delays caused by IRS employees performing managerial or ministerial acts. Managerial acts include extensive delays resulting from IRS loss of records, and IRS personnel actions including transfers, training, illness or leave. The term *any deficiency* includes income tax, estate and gift tax and the tax imposed on public charities.

In *M.C. Miller*,[117] the Court of the Appeals for the Ninth Circuit held that the IRS lacks authority to abate assessments of interest on employment taxes under Code Sec. 6404(e). In *Palihnich*,[118] the Tax Court concluded that the IRS abused its discretion by failing to abate interest that accrued due to the IRS's losing the taxpayer's amended tax returns for 11 years.

Abatement for Disaster Victims

If the IRS extends the due date for filing income tax returns and paying income tax for any taxpayer located in a federally declared disaster area, the IRS will abate the interest that would otherwise accumulate during the extension period [Code Sec. 7508A)]. Reg. § 1.301.7508A-1 clarifies the rules relating to the postponement of certain tax-related deadlines due to a federally declared disaster, terrorist, or military actions and allows the IRS to suspend interest, penalties, additional amounts, and additions to tax that normally accrue while a tax-related act is postponed. The regulation also clarifies that a postponement of time to perform a tax-related act does not extend the due date to perform the act, but merely allows the IRS to disregard a time period of up to one year.

---

[117] *M.C. Miller*, 79 TCM 2213, Dec. 53,930(M), TC Memo. 2000-196, *aff'd*, CA-9, 2002-2 USTC ¶ 50,759, 310 F3d 640.

[118] *N.J. Palihnich*, 86 TCM 488, Dec. 55,328(M), TC Memo. 2003-297.

Suspension of Interest Where IRS Fails to Contact Taxpayer

If an individual taxpayer files a Federal income tax return on or before the due date for that return (including extensions), and if the IRS does not timely provide a notice to that taxpayer specifically stating the taxpayer's liability and the basis for that liability, then the IRS must suspend any interest, penalty, addition to tax, or additional amount with respect to any failure relating to the return that is computed by reference to the period of time the failure continues and that is properly allocable to the suspension period [Code Sec. 6404(g)(1)(A)]. A notice is timely if provided before the close of the 36-month period beginning on the later of the date on which the return is filed or the due date of the return without regard to extensions [Reg. § 301.6404-4(a)(1)]. The suspension period begins on the day after the close of the 36-month period and ends 21 days after the IRS provides the notice [Reg. § 301.6404-4(a)(4)]. This suspension rule applies separately with respect to each item or adjustment [Reg. § 301.6404-4(a)(3)]. If, a taxpayer provides to the IRS an amended return or other signed written document showing an additional tax liability, then the 36-month period does not begin to run with respect to the items that gave rise to the additional tax liability until that return or other signed written document is provided to the IRS.

The general rule for suspension under Code Sec. 6404(g)(1) does not apply to any interest, penalty, addition to tax, or additional amount with respect to any listed transaction as defined in Code Sec. 6707A(c) or any undisclosed reportable transaction. [Reg. § 301.6404-4(b)(5)(i)].

The Tax Court has jurisdiction to review these interest and penalty abatement issues [Code Sec. 6404(h)(1)]. The Tax Court has jurisdiction to determine whether the IRS's failure to abate interest for an eligible taxpayer was an abuse of discretion [Code Sec. 6404(h)(1)]. In *J.F. Hinck*,[119] the Supreme Court held that the Tax Court is the exclusive forum for judicial review of an IRS decision not to abate interest.

An action to review an IRS decision not to abate interest must be brought within 180 days after the date the IRS mails its final determination not to abate interest [Code Sec. 6404(h)(1)]. To be eligible to apply for Tax Court review, a taxpayer must meet the same net worth and size requirements imposed with respect to awards of attorneys' fees under Code Sec. 7430(c)(4)(A)(ii)]. Generally, for individuals, net worth may not exceed $2 million; for businesses, net worth may not exceed $7 million [Reg. § 301.7430-5(f)].

Rev. Rul. 2005-4[120] extends the scope of the Code Sec. 6404(g) suspension rules for interest and penalties owed on additional taxes to those taxes that are voluntarily reported by taxpayers on amended returns or in written correspondence to the IRS.

In Rev. Proc. 2005-38,[121] the IRS describes how taxpayers may seek administrative relief if the IRS has assessed interest for periods during which interest should have been suspended under Code Sec. 6404(g). Although there is no prepayment right to administrative relief with respect to the abatement of interest assessed in violation of Code Sec. 6404(g), the guidance provides a permissive procedure for seeking such relief. Taxpayers may notify the IRS that interest was erroneously assessed by

---

[119] *J.F. Hinck*, SCt, 2007-1 USTC ¶ 50,496, 127 SCT 2011.

[120] Rev. Rul. 2005-4, 2005-1 CB 366.

[121] Rev. Proc. 2005-38, 2005-2 CB 81.

submitting Form 843, *Claim for Refund and Request for Abatement.* Notification to the taxpayer of the IRS's abatement determination does not, however, constitute a final determination letter from which the taxpayer can petition the Tax Court. If the IRS does not exercise its authority to abate interest alleged to have been assessed in violation of Code Sec. 6404(g), the taxpayer may pay the disputed interest assessment, file an administrative claim for refund, and if that claim is denied or not acted upon within six months from the date of filing, bring suit for refund.

REFUNDS AND CREDITS

¶27,120 OVERPAYMENT OF TAX

.01 Overpayment Interest

If an audit reveals that a taxpayer has overpaid taxes, the taxpayer is entitled to the amount of the overpayment, plus interest on the amount of the overpayment [Code Sec. 6611(a)]. This is referred to as "overpayment interest" and Code Sec. 6611(b) provides that the interest should be paid from the "date of the overpayment" to the date of the refund or credit. In *Ford Motor Co.,*[122] the Court of Appeals for the Sixth Circuit affirmed a district court to hold that interest owed to a taxpayer on an overpayment of tax should be calculated from the date that the taxpayer converted a tax deposit to a tax payment. The taxpayer had argued that the overpayment interest should be calculated from an earlier date when it first made the tax deposit.

Review Tax Return

Before filing a refund claim, taxpayers should review the entry for each item on the tax return for the year in question and recompute the tax to make sure if there is an actual overpayment of the entire tax. If this is not done, and the IRS finds errors from which you received an advantage, the amount of the overpayment may be reduced or entirely eliminated. An additional tax might even be assessed, if the statute of limitations has not run.[123]

.02 Refund Options Available to Taxpayers

Taxpayers who are due a tax refund from the IRS can receive that tax refund in a number of ways. Taxpayers should use Form 8888, *Allocation of Refund (Including Savings Bond Purchases),* to designate where the refund should be sent and to split their refund among several of the available refund options which include the following:

- Directly deposit the refund (or part of it) to one or more savings or checking accounts at a bank or other financial institution (such as a mutual fund, brokerage firm, or credit union) in the United States,
- Use the refund (or part of it) to buy up to $5,000 in paper series I savings bonds (the bonds can only be purchased in multiples of $50),

---

[122] *Ford Motor Co.,* CA-6, 2013-1 USTC ¶50,102, 508 Fed Appx 498, *cert. applied for* (07/24/2013).

[123] *E.P. Lewis,* SCt, 3 USTC ¶856, 284 US 281, 52 SCt 145.

- Directly deposit the refund (or part of it) into a retirement account such as an IRA, health savings account, Archer MSA, or Coverdell education savings account,
- Deposit the refund (or part of it) to a TreasuryDirect® online account to buy U.S. Treasury marketable securities and savings bonds.

With the savings bond option, taxpayers can designate who will receive a savings bond as well as the co-owner or beneficiary. In addition, Form 8888 was revised so that taxpayers no longer need to enter a pre-specified routing number for entering savings bond information. Now, they will simply enter the bond owner's name and the savings bonds will be mailed to the taxpayer or the person designated on the form.

.03 Offset of Overpayment

The IRS may, within the applicable period of limitations, offset any overpayment of individual, fiduciary, or corporate income tax (including interest on the overpayment) against:

1. Any outstanding liability for any tax (including any interest, additional amount, additions to tax or assessable penalty) owed by the taxpayer making the overpayment;
2. Any past-due child support;
3. Past-due and legally enforceable debt due federal agencies;
4. Past-due, legally enforceable state income tax debts [Code Sec. 6402(a)]; and
5. Unemployment compensation debts resulting from fraud [Code Sec. 6402(a) and (f)(1)].

For purposes of refund offsets to collect unemployment compensation debts, the definition of covered unemployment compensation debt includes past-due debts of an individual for erroneous payment of unemployment due to failure to report earnings, as well as those due to fraud [Code Sec. 6402(f)(4)(A)]. Thus, a covered unemployment compensation debt includes a past-due debt for erroneous payment of unemployment compensation due to a person's failure to report earnings which has become final under state law. Additionally, a covered unemployment compensation debt includes contributions due to a state's unemployment fund for which the state has determined the person to be liable, regardless of whether the liability is due to fraud. In either case, a covered unemployment compensation debt can include a debt that remains uncollected for more than 10 years [Code Sec. 6402(f)(4)(B)].

¶27,125 REFUND CLAIMS

Claims for refund fall into three classes: claims for taxes paid on the original return, for overpayments through withholding on wages or estimated tax paid, and for payments made on a deficiency notice. It is not necessary to pay the tax under protest to get a refund.

.01 Overpayment by Withholding or Estimated Tax

The excess of the tax withheld on wages and the estimated tax paid over the tax shown as due on the return will be refunded to you, or, at your election, will be credited against your next year's estimated tax, if any. However, the IRS may credit any overpayment of individual, fiduciary, or corporate income tax against any outstanding tax, interest or penalty owed by you [Reg. § 301.6402-3].

Adjustment for Corporate Estimated Tax Overpayment

A corporation overpaying its estimated tax (including alternative minimum tax) can apply for an adjustment on Form 4466, *Corporate Application for Quick Refund of Overpayment of Estimated Tax,* within two and a half months after the close of its tax year. Actual payments of estimated tax must exceed the current revised estimate of tax liability by at least 10 percent and by at least $500 [Code Sec. 6425(b)(3); Reg. § 1.6425-1(b)(1)].

.02 Payment of Assessed Deficiency

Taxpayers may prefer to pay deficiencies and avoid the interest charge. Then they can file a claim for refund, and if the claim is rejected, sue to recover. Or they, when the deficiency notice is received, may decide that an appeal to the Tax Court is useless. Later events, for example, a court decision, may change the situation. So a claim for refund still can be made, if it is filed in time.

.03 When Taxpayer Appeals to Tax Court

If a deficiency notice has been issued, and you appeal to the Tax Court, no refund or credit will be allowed and no suit for recovery of any part of the tax can be maintained in any court. There are three exceptions: (1) overpayment determined by a Tax Court decision that has become final; (2) an amount collected above the amount determined by the Tax Court decision; and (3) any amount collected after the period for levy or suit for collection has expired [Code Sec. 6512(a)].

¶27,130 TIME FOR FILING REFUND CLAIMS

.01 Three-Year Limitation

A refund claim is considered timely if filed: (1) within three years from the time the return was filed or two years from the time the tax was paid, whichever is later, or (2) if no return was filed by the taxpayer, within two years from the time the tax was paid [Code Sec. 6511(a); Reg. § 301.6511(a)-1]. If return was filed prior to the due date, the three-year period starts to run from the date the return was due [Code Sec. 6513(a); Reg. § 301.6513-1].

> **Example 27-26:** The due date of an individual return for the calendar year 2012 is April 15, 2013. If the taxpayer filed his return early on February 15, 2013, the three-year limitation period starts running from April 15, 2013, the due date rather than the filing date. If he filed on May 15, 2013, the limitation period starts from that date.

A claim is considered to be filed on the date postmarked [Code Sec. 7502(a)(1); Reg. § 301.7502-1]. If the due date falls on a Saturday, Sunday or legal holiday, the next business day is the due date. See ¶ 27,135 for discussion of special refund periods [¶ 27,135]. If the due date of a refund claim falls on a Saturday, Sunday or legal holiday and a taxpayer's return is filed on the next succeeding day that is not a Saturday, Sunday or legal holiday, the refund claim will be timely if it is filed within three years of the return's filing date according to Rev. Rul. 2003-41.[124]

> **NOTE:** Returns of taxes withheld from wages [Ch. 15] or withheld at source [Ch. 15]for a year filed before April 15 of the next year are considered filed and the tax paid on April 15 [Code Sec. 6513; Reg. § 301.6513-1].

.02 Two-Year Limitation

There is an exception to the three-year period. You can file a claim for refund within two years from the time the tax is paid, if the two-year period ends at a later date than the three-year period [Code Sec. 6511(a); Reg. § 301.6511(a)-1]. For this purpose, estimated tax [Ch. 14] and tax withheld at source [Ch. 15] are considered paid on the due date of the return (without extensions), and income tax withheld on wages is considered paid by the wage earner on the 15th day of the fourth month after the tax year it is allowed as a credit [Code Sec. 6513(b); Reg. § 301.6513-1(b)].

The Tax Court has said that a remittance is considered to be a "payment" that would start the two-year period running only when the taxpayer intends that the remittance satisfy an existing tax liability. If the remittance is merely a "deposit" with respect to a tax liability that is to be determined at some future time, the two-year period does not begin to run.[125]

A taxpayer cannot sue for a refund of taxes paid after the expiration of two years from the date of mailing by the IRS of a notice of disallowance of the claim. The two-year period can be extended if the parties execute Form 907, *Agreement to Extend Period of Limitations.* In *Kaffenberger,*[126] the Court of Appeals for the Eighth Circuit held that the IRS cannot extend the two-year statute of limitations for bringing a refund suit once the two-year period has expired.

.03 Time Extended by Waiver

The IRS sometimes asks you to file a waiver (Form 872) extending the time an assessment can be made against you. A waiver filed before the time to file a refund claim expires extends the time to file a claim [Code Sec. 6511(c); Reg. § 301.6511(c)-1]. The IRS may postpone the deadline for filing refund claims for up to one year (up from 90 days) for taxpayers affected by a federally declared disaster [Code Sec. 7508A(a)]. In Rev. Proc. 2007-56,[127] the IRS updated its list of time-sensitive acts that may be postponed under Code Sec. 7508A if a taxpayer is affected by a federally declared disaster or a terrorist or military action or, under Code Sec. 7508, if an individual serves in, or in support of, the U.S. armed forces in a combat zone or contingency operation. The list includes more than 200 time-sensitive deadlines.

.04 Refunds for Taxpayers Who Fail to File

The general rule is that the statute of limitations on filing a refund claim is the later of three years from the date the return was filed or two years from the date the taxes were paid. If taxpayers file the refund claim within three years of the filing of the return, then the refund amount is limited to amounts paid within three years

---

124 Rev. Rul. 2003-41, 2003-1 CB 814.

125 *R.B. Risman*, 100 TC 191, Dec. 48,902 (1993), *nonacq.*, 1996-2 CB 2, *nonacq.*, 1997-1 CB 1.

126 *E.J. Kaffenberger*, CA-8, 2003-1 USTC ¶ 50,164, 314 F3d 944.

127 Rev. Proc. 2007-56, 2007-2 CB 388.

preceding the refund claim. If taxpayers file the claim within two years of the time the tax was paid, then the refund is limited to the amount paid within two years preceding the claim date. If taxpayers fail to file a refund return as of the date the IRS mails a deficiency notice, the law provides that they may recover in the Tax Court taxes paid during the three years preceding the IRS mailing date. This means that a three-years look-back period has replaced the two-year look-back period established previously by the Supreme Court[128] for taxpayers who file returns after the IRS has mailed a notice of deficiency [Code Sec. 6512(b)(3)]. There no longer is a discrepancy between the late filers who benefited from the three-year look-back period and the nonfilers who were stuck with the two-year look-back period.

.05 Statute of Limitations Suspended During Disability

Under Code Sec. 6511(a), a taxpayer must file a claim for credit or refund of tax within 3 years after the date of filing a tax return or within 2 years after the date of payment of the tax, whichever period expires later. If no return was filed, the refund claim must be filed within 2 years from the time the tax was paid. A special exception in Code Sec. 6511(h) provides that the statue of limitations period will be suspended or tolled for filing a claim for credit or refund during any period that a taxpayer is considered to be "financially disabled."

An individual is considered to be financially disabled if he or she is under a medically determinable medical or physical impairment that:

1. Can be expected to result in death or which has lasted or can be expected to last for a continuous period of not less than one year, and
2. Renders the person unable to manage his or her financial affairs [Code Sec. 6511(h)].

In applying the medically determinable test, the IRS will evaluate whether a medical opinion that a physical or mental impairment exists has been provided by a person qualified to give an expert opinion on that particular type of impairment.

> ▶ **WARNING:** A person will not be treated as financially disabled during any period that a spouse or guardian is authorized to act on behalf of the person in financial matters [Code Sec. 6511(h)(2)].

In *Brosi,*[129] the Tax Court held that a taxpayer did not qualify for suspension of the refund limitation period on account of financial disability where his claim was based on caring for his disabled mother.

The IRS has outlined the information that must be submitted under Code Sec. 6511(h)(2)(A) in order to request suspension of the period of limitations for claiming a credit or refund of tax due to an individual taxpayer's financial disability.[130]

Basically, proof of the existence of the taxpayer's financial disability must be furnished to the IRS [Code Sec. 6511(h)(2). The following statements must be submitted along with your claim for credit or refund of tax due to financial disability:

1. A written statement by a physician qualified to make the determination that sets forth the following:

---

[128] *R.F. Lundy,* SCt, 96-1 USTC ¶50,035, 516 US 235, 116 SCt 647.

[129] *B.L. Brosi,* 120 TC 5, Dec. 55,013 (2003).

[130] Rev. Proc. 99-21, 1999-1 CB 960.

- The name and a description of the taxpayer's physical or mental impairment;
- The physician's medical opinion that the physical or mental impairment prevented the taxpayer from managing the taxpayer's financial affairs;
- The physician's medical opinion that the physical or mental impairment can be expected to result in death, or that it has lasted (or can be expected to last) for a continuous period of not less than 12 months;
- To the best of the physician's knowledge, the specific time period during which the taxpayer was prevented by such physical or mental impairment from managing the taxpayer's financial affairs; and

2. A written statement by the person signing the claim for credit or refund stating that no person, including the taxpayer's spouse was authorized to act on behalf of the taxpayer in financial matters during the period of financial impairment. Alternatively, if a person was authorized to act on behalf of the taxpayer in financial matters, the beginning and ending dates of the period of authorization.

¶27,135 SPECIAL PERIODS FOR FILING CLAIMS

The usual period for filing a refund claim may be extended for particular transactions as follows:

- *Bad debts and worthless securities.* A refund claim related to a deduction for a bad debt or a loss from a worthless security, or the effect of these deductions on the application of a carryover, can be filed within seven years from the date the return was due, instead of three years from the filing of the return. For a similar claim relating to a carryback, the period is seven years from the due date for filing the return for the year of the net operating loss which results in the carryback, or the period for a net operating loss carryback (see below), whichever ends later [Code Sec. 6511(d)(1); Reg. § 301.6511(d)-1].
- *Carrybacks.* A refund claim based on a general business credit carryback, net operating loss carryback, and capital loss carryback can be filed up to three years after the prescribed due date for filing the return (including extensions) following the end of the tax year in which the credit was earned or the loss incurred [Code Sec. 6511(d)(2)(A); Reg. § 301.6511(d)-2]. A beneficiary of an estate that has a net operating loss carryback, reducing distributable net income of a prior year, can file for refund under this provision.[131] In *Electrolux Holdings, Inc.,*[132] the Court of Appeals for the Federal Circuit held that the special capital loss exception to the general limitations period for filing a refund claim did not apply because the overpayment was not attributable to a carryback, as the exception requires.

If a claim for carryback refund is filed under this provision, or a timely application for carryback adjustment [¶27,165] is made, recovery of an earlier overpayment will be allowed even if it might otherwise be barred [Reg. §§ 301.6511(d)-2].

[131] Rev. Rul. 61-20, 1961-1 CB 248.

[132] *Electrolux Holdings, Inc.*, FedCl, 2007-2 USTC ¶50,583, 491 F3d 1327.

- *Partnerships.* A tax matters partner (TMP) must file a request for an administrative adjustment of partnership items that give rise to a credit or refund claim. The IRS may process it as a claim for credit or refund on partners' returns, conduct a partnership examination, or take no action. If no action is taken, a TMP may file a petition either with the Tax Court, a District Court, or the Claims Court. Request for an administrative adjustment must be made no later than three years from due date of the partnership return, or the date it was filed. A petition to the court must be filed within six months of the request for an administrative review, and before two years after the date of the request.

In addition, any partner may file a request for administrative adjustment (RAA) of partnership items for a partnership tax year by no later than three years after the return was filed (or due date, if later) and before mailing of a notice of FPAA to the TMP for such tax year. This effectively is an amended return and the IRS may process it as a claim for credit or refund on nonpartnership items, assess any additional tax resulting from the requested adjustments, conduct a partnership examination, or treat all partnership items of the partner as nonpartnership items. If any part of the RAA is not allowed, the same time limits that apply to a suit by a TMP also apply to suits by individual partners [Code Secs. 6227, 6228, 6230, 6511(g)].

- *Retirement plans.* Special period of limitation for refund or credit of amounts included in income and later recaptured on qualified plan termination. The three-year limitation period is extended for one year after recaptured amount is paid [Code Sec. 6511(d)(6)].
- *Taxes paid or credited.* Foreign taxes paid and overpayments credited to estimated tax may entitle taxpayers to a refund.
- *Foreign taxes.* If claim for credit or refund arises from payment or accrual of taxes to a foreign country or U.S. possession for which credit is allowed against the U.S. tax, time for filing claim is ten years from due date of return for which the taxes were actually paid or accrued [Code Sec. 6511(d)(3); Reg. § 301.6511(d)-3]. It also applies to credit or refund claims for correcting mathematical errors in figuring the foreign tax, discovering creditable taxes not reported when the tax return was filed, or any other adjustments to the amount of the credit, including those due to paying of additional foreign taxes.[133]
- *Overpayment applied to estimated tax.* An overpayment claimed as a credit against estimated tax for the following year [Code Sec. 6402(b)] is treated as a payment for the year the estimated tax is paid. Ordinarily no claim for credit or refund will be allowed for the year the overpayment was made, and the limitation period on refund or credit starts to run with the second year [Code Sec. 6513(d); Reg. § 301.6513-1(d)]. But see ¶ 27,125 for special refund rule applying to corporations.

¶27,140 AMOUNT OF REFUND LIMITED

If taxpayers file a refund claim during the three-year limitation period, the credit or refund cannot exceed the portion of the tax paid within the three years (plus

[133] Rev. Rul. 68-150, 1968-1 CB 564.

extensions of time granted to file the return) preceding the filing of the claim. If they do not file the claim within the three-year period but do file on time within the two-year period, the credit or refund cannot exceed the portion of the tax paid during the two-year period preceding the filing of the claim. If no claim is filed the limit on the amount of credit or refund is determined as if a claim was filed on the date the credit or refund is allowed [Code Sec. 6511(b); Reg. § 301.6511(b)-1].

Example 27-27: XYZ Corporation filed its 2012 return and paid $1,000 tax on March 15, 2013. Claim for refund of all or any part of the $1,000 tax must be filed by March 15, 2016.

Example 27-28: Assume the same facts as in Example 27-27. Assume also that on August 3, 2013, the government assessed an additional tax of $700 for 2011 and the taxpayer paid this amount on August 12, 2013. The taxpayer learned later that it neglected to take sufficient deductions in the 2011 return and for that reason overpaid its tax by $1,000. If the claim is filed by March 15, 2015 (within three years after the return was filed), the entire overpayment of $1,000 may be recovered. If the claim is filed after March 15, 2015, but by August 13, 2015 (within two years after the $700 assessment was paid), the refund may not exceed $700. If the claim is filed after August 13, 2015, the time will have expired and nothing may be recovered.

¶27,145 FORM OF REFUND CLAIM

Claims for refunds of overpayments of income taxes are made on original tax returns or amended tax returns. [discussed below]. Taxpayers usually make claims for refund of other taxes, interest, penalties, and additions to tax on Form 843 [Reg. §§ 301.6402-2, 301.6402-3].

NOTE: Corporations can receive expedited refunds (before filing their actual corporate tax return) of estimated tax overpayments for the prior year. Form 4466, *Corporation Application for Quick Refund of Overpayment of Estimated Tax* is used. To qualify, those tax payments must exceed the corporation's expected tax by at least 10 percent of the expected tax, and the overpayment must amount to at least $500.

The IRS may treat an informal refund claim as a valid claim provided such claim is later perfected by a formal refund claim. Form 870 or 890 series on which the taxpayer agrees to an overassessment of income taxes may be considered a valid claim for refund or credit.[134]

.01 Statement of Claim

Careful thought should be given to the preparation of the section on reasons advanced for the claim. If the claim is rejected and you sue on it, you will generally be

[134] Rev. Rul. 68-65, 1968-1 CB 555.

precluded from advancing grounds for recovery not stated in the claim.[135] Facts should be fully presented and verified [Reg. § 301.6402-2(b)]. Legal arguments should be outlined if the claim turns on points of law. An amended return is not necessary in filing a claim for refund based on the original return, but may be a way to establish the amount of the refund.

.02 Amending the Claim

Taxpayers can amend or supplement their claims during the time within which they could file a new claim. They cannot amend a claim to change the facts after the statute of limitations has expired;[136] but if the facts are not changed, an amendment may be allowed.[137]

.03 Amended Tax Returns as Claims

Individuals who have filed Forms 1040, 1040A, or 1040EZ should file their claim for a refund of income taxes on amended return Form 1040X. Corporations having filed Form 1120 should use Form 1120X. Other taxpayers file their claims on the appropriate amended income tax return; for , trusts use Form 1041 and exempt organizations use Form 990T [Reg. § 301.6402-3].

¶27,150 FILING THE REFUND CLAIM

The refund claim, together with appropriate supporting evidence, generally must be filed with the service center at which the taxpayer currently would be required to file a tax return for the type of tax to which the claim relates. If a taxpayer is required to file a claim for credit or refund on a particular form, then the claim must be filed in a manner consistent with such form and form instructions. If a taxpayer is filing a claim in response to an IRS notice, then the claim must be filed in accordance with the specific instructions contained in the notice regarding the proper address for filing [Reg. § 301.6402-2]. If the claim for refund is made on behalf of a deceased taxpayer, Form 1310, *Statement of Person Claiming Refund Due a Deceased Taxpayer* should be attached unless either of the following apply:

1. The taxpayer filing Form 1310 is a surviving spouse filing an original or amended joint return with the decedent, or
2. The taxpayer filing Form 1310 is a personal representative filing an original Form 1040, Form 1040A , Form 1040EZ, or Form 1040NR for the decedent and a court certificate showing the appointment is attached to the return.

.01 Administrative Procedure

If the claim is based on a return, the administrative procedure is substantially the same as in cases involving determination of a deficiency. An examiner is assigned when a field investigation is called for. If his report is unacceptable to you, you may

---

[135] *Felt & Tarrant Mfg. Co.*, SCt, 2 USTC ¶ 708, 283 US 269, 51 SCt 376.

[136] *M.S. Andrews*, SCt, 38-1 USTC ¶ 9020, 302 US 517, 58 SCt 315, *Garbutt Oil Co.*, SCt, 38-1 USTC ¶ 9021, 302 US 528, 58 SCt 320.

[137] *J.J. Caswell*, DC-CA, 61-1 USTC ¶ 9130, 190 FSupp 591.

have a district Appeals office conference [¶27,015]. A claim based on payment of a deficiency assessment on which conferences were held will usually be disallowed on the findings of the conferences.

.02 Decision on Claim

If the decision on a refund claim is in your favor, a certificate of overassessment is issued by the IRS. If the overassessment exceeds $1 million, it must be reported to the Joint Congressional Committee on Internal Revenue Taxation [Code Sec. 6405; Reg. §301.6405-1], except for an overpayment made by a corporation based on a tentative return. The amount involved is credited against any taxes owed by you for any year not barred by the statute of limitations [Code Sec. 6402]. Any balance is refunded.

If the decision is against you, you can sue to recover [¶27,160].

.03 Explanation of Claim for Refund Disallowance

The IRS is required to explain to you the specific reasons why a claim for refund is disallowed or partially disallowed. Claims for refund can be disallowed based on a preliminary review or on examination by a revenue agent [Code Sec. 6402(j)]. This means that you must receive one of the following:

1. A form explaining that the claim is disallowed for one of the following reasons: (a) the claim was filed late; (b) it was based solely on the unconstitutionality of the revenue acts; (c) it was waived as part of a settlement; (d) it covered a tax year or issues which were part of a closing agreement or an offer in compromise; (e) it was related to a return closed by a final court order.
2. A revenue agent's report explaining the reasons that the claim is disallowed.

¶27,155 INTEREST ON REFUNDS

If the government does not promptly mail your refund check, you are entitled to receive interest [Code Secs. 6611(a), 6621; Reg. §301.6611-1]. The interest is figured and compounded daily from the date of the overpayment to a date set by the IRS. This date cannot be more than 30 days before the refund check date [Code Sec. 6611(b)(2); Reg. §301.6611-1].

.01 Adjusted Rate

The overpayment rate, adjusted quarterly, is based on the federal short-term rate plus three percentage points. Similar to the underpayment rate, it is determined during the first month of each quarter [Code Sec. 6621(a)(1)]. For the rate on underpayments, see ¶27,115.

> **NOTE:** The IRS determines the interest rate (federal short-term) based on average market yield on outstanding U.S. marketable obligations with remaining maturity period of three years or less [Code Secs. 6621(b)(3), 1274(d)].

No interest is paid on refunds made within 45 days after the due date of returns filed on or before the due date or on refunds made within 45 days after a late return is filed [Code Sec. 6611(e)]. The 45-day grace period applies to refunds claimed for any type of tax on any return. The refund check's date (rather than the date the refund is allowed) reasonably determines whether a tax overpayment has been refunded within 45 days.[138]

NOTE: Inquiries about refund checks should state the taxpayer's identification number (TIN) and be addressed to the IRS Service Center that processed the claim, as indicated on the check.

.02 Credit for Overpayment

When an overpayment is credited against a later assessed deficiency instead of being refunded, interest runs from the date of overpayment to the due date of the deficiency[139] [Code Sec. 6611(b); Reg. § 301.6611-1(h)]. Penalties are offset against the overpayment before interest is computed.[140]

.03 No Review of Interest Allowed

In the absence of fraud or mathematical mistake, the allowance or failure to allow interest on any credit or refund cannot be reviewed by any administrative or accounting officer, employee, or agent of the U.S. [Code Sec. 6406].

.04 Special Provisions

There are special interest provisions for:

- *Carrybacks.* If the overpayment results from the carryback of a net operating capital loss, or foreign taxes paid, no interest is allowed for the period before the filing date for the tax year the loss or the foreign tax was paid or accrued [Code Sec. 6611(f), (g); Reg. § 301.6611-1(e)].
- *Excessive withholding or estimated tax.* If the claim is based on excessive withholding from wages or on an excessive estimated tax payment, interest is allowed from the date the final return was due even though the tax was paid earlier [Code Secs. 6513(d), 6611(d); Reg. § § 301.6513-(d), 301.6611-1(d)].

¶27,160 SUIT TO RECOVER TAX

.01 In General

A suit to recover refund may be started only if you have filed a claim [Code Sec. 7422(a)] and only if you have paid the entire tax, including any deficiency claimed by the IRS.[141] Interest on the tax need not be paid before suit.[142]

Proof

In a suit to recover, you have to prove that the tax was overpaid.[143] The suit must be based on the same grounds as the refund claim.[144]

---

[138] GCM 39772 (Apr. 12, 1985).

[139] For guides on how to figure interest when the period that interest is payable is restricted under the law, see Rev. Proc. 60-17, 1960-2 CB 942 as modified by Rev. Proc. 83-58 1983-2 CB 575 and Rev. Proc. 84-66, 1984-2 CB 637.

[140] *W.E. McDonald*, DC-TN, 66-2 USTC ¶ 9516.

[141] *W.W. Flora*, SCt, 58-2 USTC ¶ 9606, 357 US 63, 78 SCt 1079, *adhered to*, SCt, 60-1 USTC ¶ 9347, 362 US 145, 80 SCt 630.

[142] *Kell-Strom Tool Co., Inc.*, DC-CT, 62-2 USTC ¶ 9541, 205 FSupp 190.

[143] *R.E. Roybark*, CA-9, 55-1 USTC ¶ 9122, 218 F2d 164.

[144] *McKeesport Tin Plate Co.*, CA-3, 77 F2d 756.

.02 When to File

Taxpayers may not start a suit to recover until after six months from the date they filed the refund claim, unless a decision on the claim is made before then. They must start the suit before the end of two years from the date of mailing to them, by registered or certified mail, of a notice disallowing part or all of the claim [Code Sec. 6532(a); Reg. § 301.6532-1].

The period cannot be extended by filing a new refund claim, on the same grounds, after the disallowance.[145] A 30-day letter disallowing the claim is a decision on the claim.[146]

Extension of Time to File

If the last day of the period is a Saturday, Sunday or legal holiday, the time is extended to include the next business day [¶ 26,070]. The two-year period can be extended for any period agreed on in writing [Code Sec. 6532(a)(2); Reg. § 301.6532-1(b)].

Waiver of Notice

If taxpayers file a written waiver of the requirement that they be mailed a notice of disallowance of your refund claim, the two-year period for filing suit for recovery starts to run on the date the waiver is filed [Code Sec. 6532(a)(3); Reg. § 301.6532-1(c)].

.03 Where to File

Suit to recover taxes erroneously or illegally assessed or collected must be brought against the United States [Code Sec. 7422(f)]. You may institute the suit either in the U.S Claims Court at Washington, D.C., or in a Federal District Court.[147] The proper District Court is the court for the judicial district where an individual taxpayer resides or a corporation has its principal place of business or its principal office or agency.[148] Either party has a right to trial by jury.[149]

.04 When 90-Day Letter Is Issued

If taxpayers sue for a refund and a notice of deficiency is issued before the case is heard, appeals to the Tax Court would result in concurrent jurisdiction in both courts over the same case. To prevent this, the proceedings must be stayed for the 90-day period, so they can appeal to the Tax Court, plus an additional 60 days thereafter. Then, if they appeal to the Tax Court, the other court loses jurisdiction. If they do not appeal, the other court gets sole jurisdiction [Code Sec. 7422(e)].

.05 Appeal from Lower Court

Appeal from a District Court decision is to the U.S. Court of Appeals for the circuit in which the District Court is located. Decisions of the various circuits of the U.S. Courts of Appeal may be reviewed in the Supreme Court only on certiorari or certificate.

Decisions of the U.S. Claims Court may be appealed to the Court of Appeals for the Federal Circuit. Formerly, Court of Claims (now U.S. Claims Court) decisions were

---

145 *Cullman Motor Co.*, DC-AL, 60-2 USTC ¶ 9581.

146 *Register Publishing Co.*, DC-CT, 61-1 USTC ¶ 9246, 189 FSupp 626.

147 28 USC § 1346.

148 28 USC § 1402.

149 28 USC § 2402.

appealed to the Supreme Court by petition for certiorari or certificate.[150] Petitions for certiorari generally must be made within 90 days after decision is entered. If a good reason is shown, up to an additional 60-day extension may be granted.

.06 Recovery of Refunds Paid

The U.S. can sue to recover an erroneous refund if the suit is begun within two years after the refund (within five years if the refund was induced by fraud or material misrepresentation) [Code Sec. 6532(b); Reg. § 301.6532-2]. An alternative is a suit for recovery by the deficiency collection procedure [¶ 27,045]. In *Greene-Thapedi*,[151] the Court of Appeals for the Seventh Circuit concluded that the IRS's suit to recover refunds erroneously made to a taxpayer was not barred by the limitations period. The court held that the two-year limitations period under Code Sec. 6532(b) for the IRS to bring suit begins on the date the refund check clears the Federal Reserve Bank.

.07 Taxes on Private Foundations and Retirement Plans

Payment of the full amount of an excise tax imposed on a private foundation or payment of the special taxes imposed on retirement plans gives either payor the right to sue for refund, but not if the private foundation or the retirement plan has brought another suit or a Tax Court action for a deficiency as to any other excise or special tax imposed on it [Code Sec. 7422(g)].

.08 Tax Refund Even When Paying Another's Taxes

If you were forced to pay someone else's tax bill under protest in order to remove a lien on your property, you can sue for a tax refund, even though the taxes were originally assessed against the other person according to the United States Supreme Court.[152]

¶27,165 QUICK REFUND FOR CARRYBACKS

A net operating loss [Ch. 13; Ch. 20], corporate capital loss [Ch. 20], general business credits [Ch. 14], and amounts attributed to a claim of right adjustment [Ch. 18]for the current year may be carried back to one or more preceding years to reduce the tax liability reported for those years. Since examination of a refund claim usually takes time, a special procedure allows taxpayers to apply for a speedy refund or credit for an overpayment resulting from a carryback [Code Sec. 6411; Reg. §§ 1.6411-1—1.6411-3]. The application is not a refund claim [Reg. § 1.6411-1], so a separate claim may be advisable.

Corporations that expect a net operating loss may apply for an extension of time to pay the preceding year's tax [discussed below].

.01 Application

For a tentative carryback adjustment to get a quick refund is filed with the service center for the district where the tax was paid or assessed. It must be filed on or after the due date of the return (including extensions of time to file) for the tax year the

---

[150] 28 USC § 1295.

[151] *Greene-Thapedi*, CA-7, 2005-1 USTC ¶ 50,191.

[152] *L.R. Williams*, SCt, 95-1 USTC ¶ 50,218, 514 US 527, 115 SCt 1611.

loss or credit arises, and within 12 months after such tax year.[153] Corporations use Form 1139, *Corporation Application for Tentative Refund*; other taxpayers use Form 1045, *Application for Tentative Refund*. Corporations that filed Form 1138 for an extension of time to pay tax [discussed below] must file Form 1139 by the end of the month that includes the due date (plus extensions) of the return of tax to be deferred, for a further extension.

Since Form 1139 is filed after the close of the year the loss is incurred or credit earned, it is based on the exact figures of the tax return. The application must show the tax liability of the previous years affected by a loss carryback and the effect of the recomputation for the carryback[154] [Reg. § 1.6411-2]. For general business carrybacks, a schedule showing the carryback computation and a recomputation of the credit after the carryback must be attached to the application.

.02 Procedure on Claim

The IRS examines the application and credits or refunds any decrease in tax allowed for the carryback and claim of right adjustments [Ch. 18] within 90 days from the last day of the month in which the tax return due date falls (including extensions of time to file), or within 90 days from the time the application is filed, if that is later [Code Sec. 6411(b); Reg. § 1.6411-3].

> **NOTE:** The IRS can disallow any application that contains material omissions or mathematical errors that cannot be corrected within the 90-day period [Reg. § 1.6411-3(b)]. In most cases, the IRS allows the amounts shown in the application. If it is later found that the allowances were erroneous, the erroneous part of the allowance may be recovered and an adjustment made against the taxpayer [Code Sec. 6411(b)]. The taxpayer may file the usual claim for refund [¶ 27,145] and sue for recovery [¶ 27,160] if the claim is not allowed [Reg. § 1.6411-3(c)].

.03 Time to Pay Corporate Tax Extended

A corporation that expects operations for the tax year to result in a net operating loss carryback can apply on Form 1138 for an extension of the time for payment of a part of its taxes for the preceding tax year [Code Sec. 6164(a); Reg. § 1.6164-1].

¶ 27,170 WHEN LIMITATION PERIODS DO NOT APPLY

Improper tax results can be corrected in certain situations after the time for refund or assessment has passed. An "adjustment" by refund or additional assessment is allowed [Code Secs. 1311-1315]. Some adjustments can be made only when a determination of tax liability or refund is inconsistent with the treatment of the item in another year or as to another taxpayer [Code Sec. 1311(b)].

While the statute often works to the taxpayer's advantage, the issue should be given the most careful study before filing a claim for refund. A refund claim may open the way for assessing a deficiency otherwise barred.

---

[153] Instructions for Form 1139.

[154] Instructions for Form 1139.

.01 Inconsistent Determination Required

In these situations, determination of tax liability or refund in the later year must be inconsistent with the treatment in the year barred by the statute of limitations. For instance, a successful assertion that rent should be included in income for the year received is inconsistent with the original treatment, which included the item in the year of accrual.

Adjustment will be made in the following circumstances:

- *Double inclusion of income.* This occurs when there is included in one year income which erroneously has also been included in the income of a previous year now barred by the statute of limitations. Or, an item is included in the income of one taxpayer and erroneously has been included in the income of a related taxpayer [Code Sec. 1312(1); Reg. § 1.1312-1].

- *Double deduction.* This occurs if a deduction or credit is allowed in one year (or to one taxpayer) which erroneously has also been allowed in another year (or to a related taxpayer)[155] [Code Sec. 1312(2); Reg. § 1.1312-2].

  Example 27-29: On his tax return, a taxpayer claimed a casualty loss deduction. After he had filed his return and after the statute of limitations had expired, it was discovered that the loss actually occurred in a different year. The taxpayer, therefore, filed a claim for refund for the correct tax based upon the allowance of a deduction for the loss in that year, and the claim was allowed by the IRS. Here, it is the IRS that is barred from opening the original return and it is the taxpayer who is benefited by Code Sec. 1312(2).

- *Double exclusion of gross income.* This occurs if an item of income is included in one year, and then the taxpayer gets it excluded because it belonged in a prior year now barred [Code Sec. 1312(3)(A); Reg. § 1.1312-3].

  Example 27-30: In 2007, U.S. Motors, Inc. recovered a judgment against General Steel Co. for breach of contract. The judgment was paid, but Steel appealed to a higher court and the judgment was not affirmed until 2008. Motors erroneously included the recovery in its 2008 return instead of its 2007 return, and in February 2013 filed for refund of the 2008 tax. Since the statute of limitations prevented the IRS from assessing a deficiency against the 2007 return, Code Sec. 1312(3)(A) permits an adjustment.

- *Affiliated corporations.* If a deduction or credit of a corporation is treated in a manner inconsistent with the way the item is treated by an affiliated corporation, then an adjustment is allowed [Code Sec. 1312(6); Reg. § 1.1312-6].

- *Basis of property.* Adjustments are made if income, deductions and the like were incorrectly determined in prior years as to items chargeable to a capital account [Code Sec. 1312(7); Reg. § 1.1312-7].

---

155 Rev. Rul. 72-127, 1972-1 CB 268.

- *Trust items.* If an item of trust income or deduction is treated in a manner inconsistent with the way the item is treated in the hands of the fiduciary or beneficiary, as the case may be, then an adjustment is allowed [Code Sec. 1312(5); Reg. § 1.1312-5].

.02 Relief Without Inconsistent Determination

Two situations may arise when relief is possible without the later year being inconsistent with a prior position of the successful party [Code Sec. 1311(b); Reg. § 1.1311(b)-1]. If there is no deduction or inclusion made in the prior year, there is no positive action as to which the successful party in the dispute over the later year can be said to have taken a position. Compare this with cases where there is, in the prior year, positive inclusion of income or taking of a deduction.

Deduction or Credit Disallowed

An adjustment can be made to allow a deduction or credit to which the taxpayer (or related taxpayer) is entitled in a prior year now barred [Code Sec. 1312(4); Reg. § 1.1312-4]. However, the deduction or credit in the current year must not have been barred when the taxpayer formally claimed the deduction or credit for the year disallowed [Code Sec. 1311(b) (2) (B); Reg. § 1.1311(b)-2]. An adjustment is also allowed if a loss is erroneously treated as an ordinary or capital loss.[156]

> **Example 27-31:** The taxpayer is on the cash basis. He erroneously failed to deduct a payment made in 2008, and, instead, claimed the deduction in 2010. In 2011, a deficiency was assessed on the ground that the deduction in 2010 was erroneous, and the taxpayer replied in writing, claiming the deduction for 2008. In 2013, the Tax Court disallowed the deduction for 2008. The statute of limitations bars taking the deduction in 2008. Code Sec. 1312(4) permits an adjustment.

Unreported Income

An adjustment is allowed to exclude income not reported and on which tax was not paid, but which is includible in a prior year of the taxpayer (or of a related taxpayer) [Code Sec. 1312(3) (B); Reg. § 1.1312-3(b)]. However, the inclusion in the correct year must not have been barred at the time the IRS formally claimed the inclusion for the incorrect year [Code Sec. 1311(b) (2) (A); Reg. § 1.1311(b)-2].

THE UNITED STATES TAX COURT

¶27,175 PURPOSE OF U.S. TAX COURT

The Tax Court has the authority to review deficiencies asserted by the IRS against taxpayers for additional income, estate, gift, and self-employment taxes, as well as certain excise taxes on private foundations.

---

[156] Rev. Rul. 68-152, 1968-1 CB 369.

The outstanding feature of the United States Tax Court is that it affords you an opportunity to contest your tax liability for a proposed income, estate and gift tax deficiency *before* paying a penny of tax [¶ 27,185]. The court usually obtains jurisdiction only after a deficiency notice has been issued by the IRS and you file a timely petition for a hearing [¶ 27,020; ¶ 27,185]. Then the court tries the case and renders a decision anew on the evidence before it, rather than on a mere review of the evidence before the IRS.

.01 Place of Trial

The Tax Court or any of its divisions may sit at any place within the United States [Code Sec. 7445]. Consequently, you may ask that your case be tried at or near the city in which you are located [¶ 27,195]. Tax Court proceedings (except a small tax claim proceeding [discussed below]) are governed by the rules of evidence that apply in trials without a jury in the District Court of the District of Columbia [Code Sec. 7453; TC Rule 143(a)].

.02 Proving a Case

The Tax Court can consider only the evidence that the parties produce. Usually, the taxpayers have the burden of proof [but see ¶ 27,205]. They must present sufficient evidence to prove their case as stated in the petition, regardless of what evidence they have already presented to the IRS. However, the IRS must prove transferee liability, fraud, and the liability of a foundation manager for knowingly participating in an act of self-dealing, or engaging in certain wrongful acts [Code Secs. 6902(a), 7454; Reg. § 301.7454-2]. The Tax Court and the U.S. Claims Court may assess damages for a taxpayer's delay or for bringing a suit on frivolous grounds as well as award taxpayer litigation costs [Code Secs. 6673, 7430].

.03 Small Tax Case Procedure

The Tax Court has adopted simplified procedures to handle small tax cases. A *small tax case* is one in which neither the disputed amount of the deficiency nor the claimed overpayment exceeds $50,000, including additions to tax, for a tax year [Code Sec. 7463(a)]. Small tax case procedures may be used, at your request and with the concurrence of the Tax Court for income, estate, gift, certain employment, and certain excise taxes. The Tax Court's small case procedures are also available for innocent spouse relief redeterminations under Code Sec. 6015(e) and disputes continuing from pre-levy administrative due process hearings under Code Sec. 6330(d)(1)(A) [Code Sec. 7463(f)]. The proceedings will be conducted as informally as possible. You will not have to prepare briefs or deliver oral argument. You could either represent yourself (pro se) or be represented by someone admitted to practice before the Tax Court. You file your petition on Form 2 which you may obtain from the court clerk. The decision of the court is based on a brief summary opinion and is not reviewable on appeal and will not serve as a precedent for future cases. The court has discretion in applying rules of evidence and procedure. The result in a small tax case becomes final 90 days after the decision is entered [Code Sec. 7481(b)].

Authority of Special Trial Judges

The Chief Judge of the Tax Court is specifically authorized to assign the following categories of cases to special trial judges:

1. Declaratory judgment proceedings,
2. Proceedings under Code Sec. 7463 (involving small tax cases),
3. Proceedings in which the deficiency or claimed overpayment does not exceed $50,000 [Code Sec. 7443A(b)(3)],
4. Proceedings under Code Sec. 6320 (notice of lien filing) or Code Sec. 6330 (hearing before levy),
5. Proceedings under Code Sec. 7436(c) (involving employment status and employment taxes of $50,000 or less per calendar quarter),
6. Proceedings under Code Sec. 7623(b)(4) (appeals of whistleblower award determinations), and
7. Other proceedings which the chief judge may designate [Code Sec. 7443A(b)].

In the first six categories, the Chief Judge may assign the special trial judge not only to hear and report on a case, but also to decide it [Code Sec. 7443A(c)].

.04 Declaratory Judgments

A petition for a declaratory judgment [TC Rules 210-218] may be filed in the Tax Court to determine the validity of an IRS determination in the following situations:

1. To determine whether an organization is exempt under Code Sec. 501(c)(3) (charities and churches), Code Sec. 509(a) (private foundation), or Code Sec. 4942(j)(3) (private operating foundation) [Code Sec. 7428];
2. To determine whether a retirement plan is qualified;
3. To determine whether a prospective issue of government obligations is tax-exempt under Code Sec. 103(a);
4. To determine an estate's eligibility for installment payments under Code Sec. 6166; and
5. To challenge a final notice of redetermination of the value of a gift within the gift tax statute of limitations period [Code Sec. 7477].

¶27,180 APPEARANCE BEFORE TAX COURT

The Tax Court has its own rules of practice. Individuals may appear in their own behalf, and members of a partnership or corporate officers may appear on behalf of the partnership or corporation. Also, a fiduciary may represent an estate or trust [TC Rule 24]. A practitioner must be admitted to practice in the Tax Court before representing a client there.

.01 Admission to Practice

An applicant for admission to practice before the Tax Court must establish that he or she is of good moral character and repute and is possessed of the requisite qualifications to represent others in the preparation and trial of cases.

An attorney at law may be admitted to practice before the Tax Court upon filing a completed application accompanied by a fee and a current certificate from the clerk of the appropriate court, showing that the applicant has been admitted to practice before and is a member in good standing of the Bar of the Supreme Court of the United States, or of the highest or appropriate court of any State or of the District of Columbia, or any commonwealth, territory, or possession of the United States. A current court certificate is one executed within 90 calendar days preceding the date of the filing of the application.

An applicant who is not an attorney at law must file with the Tax Court a completed application accompanied by a fee. In addition, the applicant must give evidence of his or her qualifications by means of the Tax Court's written examination and possibly an oral exam. An application for admission must be on the form provided by the Tax Court. The application must be sponsored by at least two persons admitted to practice before the Tax Court and each sponsor must send a letter of recommendation directly to the Admissions Clerk of the Tax Court.

Upon approval of an application for admission and satisfaction of the other applicable requirements, an applicant will be admitted to practice before the Tax Court upon taking and subscribing the oath or affirmation prescribed by the Court. Corporations and firms will not be admitted to practice or recognized before the Tax Court [TC Rule 200].

.02 Application

An attorney, seeking admission to practice before the Tax Court, must file an application with the Admission Clerk. Applicants other than attorneys seeking admission by examination must have three individuals already admitted to practice before the court send letters of sponsorship directly to the court [TC Rule 200]. Also, the court may impose a periodic registration practice fee up to $30 a year on practitioners [Code Sec. 7475].

¶27,185 JURISDICTION OF TAX COURT

The Tax Court may hear appeals from Commissioner's notice of deficiency or liability of income tax, estate or gift tax, self-employment tax, excise taxes on private foundations, public charities, pension funds and real estate investment trusts, employment taxes,[157] as well as actions for certain declaratory judgments, [¶ 27,175] for disclosure actions under Code Sec. 6110, for the determination of employment status, and to determine the proper amount of employment tax under Code Sec. 7436(a) [Code Secs. 7428, 7436, 7442, 7436(a), 7476]. In addition, the Tax Court has the authority to enjoin levy actions

[157] *J.M. Philbin*, 26 TC 1159, Dec. 21,942 (1956); *C.E. Clarke*, 27 TC 861, Dec. 22,266 (1957).

during the period that the levy action is required to be suspended under the pre-levy administrative due process hearing procedures [Code Sec. 6330(e)(1)]. However, jurisdiction is not conferred to the Tax Court unless a timely appeal has been filed under Code Sec. 6330(d)(1) and then only with respect to the unpaid tax or proposed levy to which the appeal relates [Code Sec. 6330(e)].

.01 Items Subject to Review

The Tax Court has jurisdiction over and is therefore authorized to consider the following:

- Appeals involving constitutional questions;[158]
- Closing agreements;[159]
- Fraud penalties;[160]
- Failure to pay penalty;
- Statute of limitations[161] [Code Sec. 6214(a)];
- Whether the IRS abused its discretion in refusing to abate interest owed by a taxpayer who meets the Code Sec. 7430 net worth requirements [Code Sec. 6404];
- Refund or credit of any overpayments that were collected within the period during which the IRS is prohibited from collecting by levy or through a court proceeding [Code Secs. 6213(a), 6512(a), 6512(b)(1)];
- Refund or credit of an overpayment that is not contested on appeal [Code Sec. 6512(b)(1)];
- Declaratory judgments for estate tax installment payments where estate consists largely of interest in closely held business [Code Sec. 7479(a)];
- Declaratory judgments for gift tax revaluation [Code Sec. 7477(a)];
- Determination of wages and employment status in worker classification disputes[162] [Code Sec. 7436];
- IRS due process determination not to abate failure to pay penalty;[163]
- Jeopardy levies;[164]
- Challenges to liens against tax liabilities purportedly discharged in bankruptcy;[165]
- Overpayments that have been credited or refunded by the IRS;[166]
- IRS's denial of equitable innocent spouse relief in situations where the IRS has not asserted a deficiency against the taxpayer.
- Redetermination of additions to unpaid employment tax.[167]

---

[158] *Independent Life Ins. Co. of America*, 17 BTA 757, Dec. 5481, *aff'd*, CA-6, 67 F2d 470.

[159] *Holmes & Janes, Inc.*, 30 BTA 74, Dec. 8470.

[160] *Gutterman Strauss Co.*, 1 BTA 243, Dec. 97, *acq.* 1926-1 CB 3.

[161] *Troy Motor Sales Co.*, 14 BTA 546, Dec. 4631, *aff'd*, SCt, 2 USTC ¶737, 283 US 483, 51 SCt 549.

[162] *Evans Publishing, Inc.*, 119 TC 242, Dec. 54,930 (2002).

[163] *B.R. Downing*, 118 TC 22, Dec. 54,604 (2002).

[164] *J.W. Dorn*, 119 TC 356, Dec. 54,974 (2002), *supplemental opinion*, 86 TCM 5, Dec. 55,209(M), TC Memo. 2003-192.

[165] *H. Washington*, 120 TC 114, Dec. 55,072 (2003).

[166] *Sunoco, Inc.*, 122 TC 88, Dec. 55,530 (2004).

[167] *Charlotte's Office Boutique, Inc.*, CA-9, 2005-2 USTC ¶50,593, 425 F3d 1203.

- Consolidation of review of collection due process (CDP) cases [Code Sec. 6330(d)(1)].
- Deficiency arising from S corporation shareholder's inconsistent treatment.[168]
- To allow widow to pursue innocent spouse relief under *res judicata* exception.[169]
- To delete specific letter ruling terms.[170]
- To review the IRS's determination under Code Sec. 6330(g) that it would disregard the taxpayer's hearing requests.[171]
- Outside basis determination and application of 40 percent penalty.[172]
- Executor's challenges to estate and gift tax deficiencies.[173]
- IRS's determination that a single-member limited liability company's worker was an employee based on a Form SS-8, *Determination of Worker Status for Purposes of Federal Employment Taxes and Income Tax Withholding*, filed by the LLC employer.[174]

The Tax Court lacks jurisdiction pursuant to Code Sec. 6512(b)(4) to determine the following:

- Whether the IRS, under Code Sec. 6402(a) improperly credited married taxpayers' overpayment from one tax year to the husband's 24-year-old tax liability.[175]
- In a deficiency proceeding to redetermine an individual's liability for Code Sec. 6707A penalties for failure to report involvement in a listed transaction.[176]
- To determine the timeliness of the claims for credit for unused overpayments for tax years that were not properly before it.[177]
- The taxpayer's overpayment interest claim.[178]
- Over an interim partnership proceeding in which two lower level partnerships engaged in a Son of Boss transaction.[179]

.02 Deficiencies

In general, the Tax Court can review only proposed assessments of tax deficiencies. However, when the Tax Court assumes jurisdiction on a deficiency, it reviews your entire liability for the year at issue, and may find that there is an added deficiency or an overpayment [Code Sec. 6512(b); Reg. § 301.6512-1]. In addition, the Tax Court is empowered to do the following:

- Hear motions to restrain assessment and collection actions taken after a Tax Court petition has been filed but before the decision of the court is final.

---

168 *M.C. Winter*, 135 TC 238, Dec. 58,313 (2010).

169 *S.F. Deihl*, 134 TC 156, Dec. 58,138 (2010).

170 *Anonymous*, 133 TC 13, Dec. 58,112 (2010).

171 *J.B. Thornberry*, 136 TC 356, Dec. 58,602 (2011).

172 *Tigers Eye Trading*, 138 TC 67, Dec. 58,945 (2012).

173 *J. Widtfeldt*, DC-Neb., 2012-2 USTC ¶ 60,651.

174 *Staffmore, LLC*, 106 TCM 122, Dec. 59,607(M), TC Memo. 2013-187.

175 *S. Bocock*, 127 TC 178, Dec. 56,661 (2006).

176 *S.G. Smith*, 133 TC 424, Dec. 58,028 (2009).

177 *T.D. Porter*, 100 TCM 40, Dec. 58,272(M), TC Memo. 2010-154.

178 *Sunoco, Inc.*, CA-3, 2011-2 USTC ¶ 50,665, 663 F3d 181.

179 *Rawls Trading, L.P.*, 138 TC 271, Dec. 58,997 (2012).

- Review interest assessed by the IRS on tax deficiencies determined by the Tax Court.
- Order the IRS to cease any assessment or collection efforts until the court's decision is made final [Code Sec. 6213(a)].
- Order the IRS to pay a refund to a taxpayer who wins in Tax Court (although the Tax Court may not hear a suit for a refund) [Code Sec. 6512(b)].
- Determine whether a taxpayer's discharge in bankruptcy relieved him from the tax liabilities determined by the IRS on substitute returns that it had prepared.[180]
- Note that the Tax Court does not have jurisdiction to hear petitions filed during pending bankruptcy cases.[181]

Limitations in Case of Petition to Tax Court

If a taxpayer who receives a deficiency notice elects to file a petition with the Tax Court, then the Tax Court acquires exclusive jurisdiction to determine the existence of a deficiency or to award a refund for the tax years covered by the deficiency notice [Code Sec. 6512(a)]. The taxpayer may not bring a separate refund suit in any other court for recovery of any part of the tax at issue in the Tax Court case. The taxpayer is permitted to file a claim for credit or refund in another court for the same tax year only with respect to:

1. Overpayments determined by the Tax Court's final decision [Code Sec. 6512(a)(1)];
2. Any amount the IRS collects that is in excess of the tax computed in accordance with the Tax Court's final decision [Code Sec. 6512(a)(2)];
3. Any amount collected after the period of limitations for collection has expired [Code Sec. 6512(a)(3)];
4. Overpayments attributable to partnership items that are determined at the partnership level in a separate proceeding, [Code sec. 6512(a)(4)];
5. Any amount that was collected within the period during which the IRS is prohibited from collecting by levy or through a court proceeding under Code Sec. 6213(a) [Code Sec. 6512(a)(5)]; or
6. Any claim for credit or refund of an overpayment that is not contested on appeal which the IRS is authorized to refund under Code Sec. 6512(b)(1) [Code Sec. 6512(a)(6)].

.03 Issues Raised by Pleadings

The Tax Court is limited to the issues raised in the petition and other pleadings, and the evidence supporting them.[182]

.04 Jurisdiction Over Other Years

In redetermining a deficiency of income tax for any tax year or of gift tax for any calendar year or calendar quarter, the Tax Court can consider such facts with relation to the taxes for other years or calendar quarters as may be necessary correctly to redetermine the amount of such deficiency, but has no jurisdiction to determine

[180] *N. Swanson*, 121 TC 111, Dec. 55,280 (2003).

[181] *B. Drake*, 123 TC 320, Dec. 55,822 (2004); *C.L. Prevo*, 123 TC 326, Dec. 55,823 (2004).

[182] *Buffalo Wills-Sainte Claire Corp.*, 2 BTA 364, Dec. 657.

whether or not the tax for any other year or calendar quarter has been overpaid or underpaid [Code Sec. 6214(b)].

.05 Who Files Petition?

Petition to the Tax Court must be brought by and in the name of the person to whom the deficiency or liability notice was directed, or by and in the full descriptive name of his fiduciary. If there is a variance between the name in the deficiency or liability notice and the correct name, reasons for the variance must be stated in the petition [TC Rule 34(b)].

.06 Service of Papers

The petition is served on the Commissioner or the appropriate representative by the Clerk of the Tax Court. All other papers required to be served can be done by the parties if the originals, together with a certificate of service (Form 10), are filed with the Clerk. Service is complete on mailing (whether by registered or certified mail) or by hand delivery to a party or his counsel [TC Rule 21(b)].

¶27,190 AUTHORITY OF REGULATIONS

The Tax Court will be bound by the IRS regulations unless they are found to be unreasonable and inconsistent with the Code.[183]

¶27,195 HOW PROCEEDING BEGINS

A proceeding before the Tax Court is generally started by filing a petition.

.01 When to File Petition

You must file the petition with the Tax Court within 90 days after the notice of deficiency or liability was mailed to you. The period is 150 days for taxpayers "outside of the United States,"[184] or for the estate of a decedent dying abroad[185] [Code Sec. 6213(a); Reg. § 301.6213-1]. The IRS must include on each deficiency notice the last day on which you may file a petition with the Tax Court and have it be timely filed [Code Sec. 6213(a)]. The court cannot extend the time to file.[186] The IRS may postpone the deadline for filing a Tax Court petition for up to 120 days for taxpayers affected by a federally declared disaster [Code Sec. 7508A(a)].

---

[183] *Topps of Canada, Ltd.*, 36 TC 326, Dec. 24,850 (1961).

[184] *D.L. Smith*, 140 TC 48, Dec. 59,465 (2013) (Canadian resident was a person "outside of the United States").

[185] *P. Du Pasquier*, 39 TC 854, Dec. 25,998 (1963).

[186] *G. Joannou*, 33 TC 868, Dec. 24,042 (1960).

The Filing Period

The day the deficiency notice is mailed is not counted, but the day of filing the petition is counted.[187] The period begins to run from the date the deficiency notice is mailed. A second mailing of a notice generally does not start a new 90-day period, unless the first mailing was abandoned.[188]

E-Filing Mandatory in Tax Court

The Tax Court has announced that electronic filing of documents is mandatory for most parties represented by counsel in the Tax Court. An e-filer must send the judge assigned to the case a courtesy paper copy of an e-filed document that is longer than 50 pages. If no judge is assigned, the courtesy copy should be mailed to the Chief Judge. Any document required to be e-filed that is delivered to the Clerk's Office in paper form will not be accepted.

Mandatory e-filing does not apply to: (a) pro se taxpayers, including taxpayers assisted by low-income taxpayer clinics and Bar-sponsored pro bono programs that participate in Tax Court calendar calls; (b) practitioners who apply to the Court for and are granted relief from the requirement to e-file based on good cause; and (c) documents not eligible for e-filing in the Tax Court, such as petitions and sealed documents.

The Court may except from e-filing a practitioner who is counsel of record in a case and permit the practitioner to file in paper form if the practitioner files a motion with the Tax Court in paper form and is able to show good cause. Because a request for exception does not alter any preexisting deadlines, the practitioner should submit the document sought to be paper-filed along with the motion for exception.

Filing by Mail

The petition is considered to be filed on time when it is mailed, postage prepaid, to the proper office within the prescribed time as indicated by the postmark on the envelope. This applies even if it is received after the time has expired. Incorrect private postage meter dates must be corrected by the post office. If you send the petition by registered or certified mail, the date of registration, or the postmarked date on the certified mail receipt, is the date of mailing [Code Sec. 7502; Reg. § 301.7502-1].

Electronic Postmark

The date of an electronic postmark given by an authorized electronic return transmitter will be deemed the filing date if the date of the electronic postmark is on or before the filing due date. If the electronic postmark is timely, the document is considered filed timely even if it is received by IRS after its due date [Reg. § 301.7502-1(d)(1)]. An electronic postmark is a record of the date and time (in a particular time zone) that an authorized electronic return transmitter receives the transmission of a taxpayer's electronically filed document on its host system. If the taxpayer and the electronic return

---

[187] *R.W. Chambers*, CA-DC, 2 USTC ¶ 530, 41 F2d 299.

[188] *T. Boccuto*, CA-3, 60-1 USTC ¶ 9447, 277 F2d 549; *W.I. Tenzer*, CA-9, 61-1 USTC ¶ 9186, 285 F2d 956.

transmitter are located in different time zones, the time in the taxpayer's time zone controls the timeliness of the electronically filed document [Reg. § 301.7502-1(d)(3)(ii)].

If the last day for filing the petition falls on a Saturday, Sunday, or is a legal holiday in the District of Columbia, time for filing is extended to include the court's next business day [TC Rule 25]. Private delivery services (PDS) are now on parity with the U.S. Postal Service [Code Sec. 7502(f)]. As a result, taxpayers can rely on the postmark of PDS designated by IRS to prove that they timely mailed tax-related documents under Code Sec. 7502. The IRS has designated a number of PDS that you may use to file returns and have the assurance that they will be treated as filed on time if they are mailed on time.[189] The private delivery services approved by the IRS are listed at ¶ 26,065.

.02 Request for Place of Hearing

The petition should be accompanied by a request on Form 5 that the hearing on the case be held at or near the city more convenient for you [TC Rule 140(a), (b)]. In addition, in a declaratory petition involving revocation, the Commissioner in his answer must state the date on which he expects the action to be ready for trial (this enables the court to plan its calendars) and an estimate of the time involved [TC Rule 212].

.03 Filing Fee

A $60 filing fee must be paid at the time of filing of any and all the petitions in the U.S. Tax Court [Code Sec. 7451]. The filing fee may be waived entirely if, by affidavit, the taxpayer is unable to pay.

.04 Filing a Motion

If, after the Tax Court determines a deficiency, the IRS assesses and collects the deficiency with interest, within one year after the Tax Court decision becomes final, the taxpayer may file a motion on the Tax Court for a determination that he overpaid the interest [Code Sec. 7481(c)]. Comparable rules are provided where in the original Tax Court case, the court determines there was an underpayment. If the taxpayer disagrees with the IRS's computation of interest, then one year after the date the Tax Court's decision becomes final, he can file a motion in the Tax Court for a determination that the IRS had underpaid the interest.

> **NOTE:** A $60 filing fee is also required to file a petition by a partner for readjustments of partnerships items [Code Secs. 6226, 7451]. See also ¶ 27,135.

.05 Capacity to Sue

The taxpayer must have proper capacity to petition the Tax Court. In one case, the Tax Court ruled that a suspended corporate taxpayer lacked the proper capacity to file a petition with the court because the corporation's powers, rights and privileges were under suspension when the petition was filed.[190]

---

[189] Notice 2004-83, 2004-2 CB 1030.

[190] *David Dung Le, M.D., Inc.*, CA-9, 2002-1 USTC ¶ 50,112, 22 Fed Appx 837, *aff'g*, 114 TC 268, Dec. 53,859 (2000).

¶27,200 THE PETITION

An attorney or accountant preparing petitions to the Tax Court should bear in mind that it will consider only the issues that are set out in the petitions. The issues and the facts upon which they are based should be covered so completely that, when judges read petitions, they can tell immediately what the disputes are about and what the facts are. A good rule is to give such a complete presentation that the facts alleged can be proved and adopted as findings of fact by the court, and in sufficient detail to justify a decision in the taxpayer's favor.

.01 Form

The petition, including the petition for a declaratory judgment and for disclosure actions (and all other papers filed with the Tax Court), may be prepared by any process, provided the information is set out in clear and legible type and is substantially in accordance with Form 1 in style and content. It must also be properly signed.

.02 Deficiency of Liability Notice

A copy of the deficiency notice or liability must accompany the petition and each copy of it. If a statement accompanied the notice, the part of it that is material to the issues set out in the assignments of error must also be attached. If the notice referred to earlier notices from the Service that are necessary to explain the determination, the parts material to the issues raised by assignments of error must be attached.

¶27,205 THE COMMISSIONER'S ANSWER

The Commissioner has 60 days after service of a copy of the petition to file an answer, or 45 days for motions on the petition. If an amended petition is filed, the Commissioner has the same time after service to file an answer or for motions on the petition unless the court fixes a different time. Similar provisions apply to a petition for a declaratory judgment.

.01 Contents

The Commissioner's answer must fully and completely advise the petitioner and the court of the nature of the defense. It must contain a specific admission or denial of each material allegation contained in the petition or state that the Commissioner lacks knowledge or information to form a belief as to the truth of any allegation. The Commissioner may qualify or deny only part of an allegation. If special matters like res judicata, collateral estoppel, estoppel, waiver, duress, fraud, and statute of limitations are pleaded, a mere denial will not be sufficient to raise this issue. Moreover, the answer must state every ground on which the Commissioner relies and has the burden of proof.

¶27,210 PETITIONER'S REPLY

When the Commissioner's answer alleges material facts, you usually have 45 days after service of the answer to file a reply or 30 days for motions on the answer.

The reply must contain a specific admission or denial of each material allegation in the answer on which the Commissioner has the burden of proof. Lack of knowledge or information as to the truth of any allegation must be asserted. The reply must state every ground, together with supporting facts, on which the petitioner relies. If special matters like res judicata, collateral estoppel, estoppel, waiver, duress, fraud, and the statute of limitations are raised in the answer, a mere denial in the reply will not be sufficient to raise these issues.

¶27,215 AMENDED OR SUPPLEMENTAL PLEADINGS

Pleadings may be amended once as a matter of course at any time before responsive pleadings are served. If no responsive pleadings are permitted and the case has not been placed on the trial calendar, they may be amended within 30 days after they are served.

Supplemental pleadings may be permitted when a party wishes to indicate transactions or occurrences that took place after the pleadings. Permission may be granted even though the original pleadings are defective.

¶27,220 JUDGMENT WITHOUT TRIAL

Any case not requiring a trial for the submission of evidence (as, for example, where sufficient facts have been admitted, stipulated, established by deposition, or included in the record in some other way) may be submitted at any time after joinder of issue by motion of the parties filed with the Court. The parties need not wait for the case to be calendared for trial and need not appear in Court.

A case may be disposed of before trial by a motion for judgment on the pleadings or a motion for a summary judgment. Any party may move for a judgment on the pleadings, but the motion must be made within such time so as not to delay trial. A motion for summary judgment must be made at any time starting 30 days after the pleadings are closed, but it must also be made within such time so as not to delay trial. Any written response to the motion for summary judgment must be made not later than ten days before the hearing. A decision on the motion for summary judgment will be rendered only after every genuine issue of material fact has been disposed of.

> **NOTE:** An action for declaratory judgment, except for revocation and governmental obligation cases, may be disposed of before trial on the "administrative record."

¶27,225 TIME AND PLACE FOR HEARING

Upon joinder of issue (generally by filing of an answer or reply, where the answer raises affirmative issues), the court will set a calendar date and a city (generally the one requested by the petitioner [¶27,195]) for the hearing. No hearing is necessary if the facts are established by deposition.

.01 Postponement

If a case is set for trial and for any reason a postponement is desired, a motion should be made immediately on receipt of the notice setting the hearing. Usually, the court denies motions for continuance made on the day the case is called, or within 30 days of that date.

.02 Discovery

The parties are urged to obtain the required information through informal consultation or communication. If this can't be done, formal discovery procedures involving interrogatories and the production of documents or things should be followed. Upon the consent of all parties, depositions [¶27,230] may be used as a discovery device and may be taken of both party and nonparty witnesses.

.03 Admissions

Requests for admissions must be written and must be served and any motion to review the sufficiency of the response must be served no later than 45 days prior to the calendar call. The party making the request must file the original with the court at the same time that a copy of the request is served on the opposing party.

.04 Stipulations

Before the hearing date has been set, taxpayer's counsel may be asked to confer with the Regional Appeals Office and a member of the Regional Counsel's staff to try to settle the case. If the case is settled, a stipulation of settlement will be filed with the court and no trial is required. In addition, the court on its own motion, or at the request of either party, may schedule its own pretrial conference [TC Rule 110]. Rule 91 provides that specific rules for numbering the exhibits to be attached to stipulations of facts, and for exhibits to be introduced at trial. Rather than numbering the petitioner's exhibits, and lettering the respondent's exhibits, the parties must number the exhibits serially, placing after the number a "P" for a petitioner's exhibit, and a "J" for a joint exhibit [TC Rule 91]. For example, the first exhibits, if offered first by petitioner, second by respondent, with a third joint exhibit, would be labeled as follows: 1-P, 2-R, 3-J.

¶27,230 HOW TO TAKE DEPOSITIONS

Depositions can be taken by written interrogation, which is unusual, or by oral examination of the witness by both parties. An application (on Form 7) to take a deposition must be filed with the court at least 45 days before the trial date. The court supplies the application form.

¶27,235 THE TAX COURT TRIAL

The Tax Court is a trial court, and follows formal trial court procedure, except for small tax cases which are conducted as informally as possible. If the parties have reached a settlement and filed a stipulation to that effect, the court will enter decision accordingly. If, at the calendar date, no settlement has been reached, and both parties answer "ready," the judge or clerk will note the probable date of the trial.

.01 Burden of Proof

Under the Tax Court Rules, the taxpayer generally bears the burden of proof unless one of the following four exceptions apply:

1. Fraud with intent to evade tax;
2. The knowing conduct of a foundation manager, trustee, or of an organization manager;
3. Transferee liability, or
4. Unreasonable accumulation of earnings and profits.

If these four situations apply, the burden of proof is shifted to the IRS.

The Code also contains other provisions shifting the burden of proof to the IRS as follows:

1. In proceedings concerning required reasonable verification of information returns [Code Sec. 6201(d);
2. Review of jeopardy levy or assessment procedures [Code Sec. 7429(g)(1);
3. Property transferred in connection with performance of services [Code Sec. 83(d)(1);
4. Illegal bribes, kickbacks and other payments [Code Sec. 162(c)(1) and (2);
5. Golden parachute payments [Code Sec. 280G(b)(2)(B);
6. Expatriation [Code Secs. 877(e), 2107(e) and 25-1(a)(4)];
7. Public inspection of written determinations [Code Sec. 6110(f)(4)(A)];
8. Penalties for promoting abusive tax shelters [Code Sec. 6703(a)];
9. Income tax return preparer's penalty [Code Sec. 7427];
10. Status as employees (pursuant to the safe harbor provisions of section 530 of the Revenue Act of 1978).

Level of Credible Evidence Needed to Shift Burden of Proof to IRS

The burden of proof in a court proceeding may be shifted to the IRS where taxpayers present credible evidence with respect to a factual issue that is relevant to determining their tax liability [Code Sec. 7491(a)(1)]. Taxpayers must also satisfy several conditions discussed below.

First, the taxpayer must comply with the substantiation and recordkeeping requirements of the Code and regulations [Code Sec. 7491(a)(2)(A); Code Sec. 7491(a)(2)(B)]. In addition, the taxpayer must introduce credible evidence with respect to a factual issue that is necessary to determine the taxpayer's liability. Credible evidence, refers to the quality of evidence that, after critical analysis, a court would find to be sufficient to serve as the basis for its decision on the issue, absent any contrary evidence. Implausible factual assertions, frivolous claims, and tax-protestor-type arguments do not qualify as credible evidence. Further, evidence will not meet this standard if the court is not convinced that it is worthy of belief. If evidence from both sides has been introduced and it is equally balanced, the court should find that the IRS has not sustained its burden of proof.

The Committee Report also adds that substantiation requirements must be met, whether generally or specifically imposed, and that the substantiation requirements include any requirement in the Code or regulations that a taxpayer establishes an item to the IRS's satisfaction. If a taxpayer fails to substantiate any item, the taxpayer will not have satisfied all the conditions that are prerequisite to claiming an item on a tax return, and thus, the burden of proof provision will not apply.

.02 Argument

At the trial, petitioner's counsel makes an opening statement, and formally presents evidence, as would be done in a trial before a United States District Court. Any admissions or stipulations made or depositions taken must be introduced as evidence. Commissioner's counsel then presents the government's case. If the presentation on behalf of the Commissioner involves affirmative issues, petitioner's counsel has opportunity for rebuttal.

At the end of the trial, the court may ask the parties to make oral arguments and file citations of authorities referred to in the presentations. Unless otherwise directed, each party has 60 days after the conclusion of the hearing to file a brief on the issues on which he has the burden of proof. Within 45 days after a brief is filed, the opposing party may file a reply brief. Briefs or oral arguments are not required in small tax cases.

.03 Rehearing

Any motion for reconsideration of an opinion or findings of fact must be filed within 30 after a written opinion or ages of the transcript that contain findings of fact or opinion have been served, unless the court otherwise permits.

> ▶ **OBSERVATION:** A well-reasoned and well-researched brief is needed at the end of the tax court trial. The briefs filed by Commissioner's counsels in tax cases are uniformly good. If briefs for taxpayers are not equally good, their cases are jeopardized.

¶27,240 THE TAX COURT OPINION

After the trial, the Tax Court judge writes the findings of fact and opinion in a single discussion called an "Opinion." Note that this is not the court's decision. This is important for several reasons. The date of the decision determines the time for filing an appeal from the decision [¶ 27,245]. The decision is a specific order that:

- Finds the amount of the deficiency;
- Finds there is no deficiency; or
- Dismisses the case for any reason.

The decision is usually entered immediately after publication of the findings of fact and opinion if the court decides the deficiency or liability notice is correct. If it decides the deficiency should be revised, decision is entered after proceedings under Rule 155.

.01 Rule 155

Instead of itself determining the tax due, the court may direct the parties to compute the liability under TC Rule 155. Each party submits a computation of tax liability in the light of the court's opinion. If the parties cannot agree, the case may be set for argument on the settlement, and the court determines the tax due.

No new issues can be raised under Rule 155,[191] but the court may consent to raising an obvious issue; for example, the deficiency was barred by the statute of limitations.[192]

Declaratory Judgments

If the action is assigned to a "special trial judge" and he is authorized to make the decision, then he must submit his decision to the court's chief judge before service on the parties.

.02 Procedure After Decision

If the petitioner is satisfied with the Tax Court's decision, his counsel should, within 30 days of the serving of the Report, file a determination of the result under Rule 155. If he is dissatisfied with the Tax Court's decision, counsel has 90 days after the decision is entered within which to file a notice of appeal [Code Sec. 7483].

.03 Equitable Recoupment Doctrine in Tax Court

The U.S. Tax Court may apply the doctrine of equitable recoupment to the same extent as it may be applied in federal civil tax cases by the U.S. District Courts or the U.S. Court of Claims [Code Sec. 6214(b)].

¶27,245 REVIEW OF TAX COURT DECISION

The Tax Court has very little power to set aside or change its decision once it has become final[193] [Code Sec. 7481; Reg. §301.7481-1]. However, the Seventh Circuit Court holds that the Tax Court has jurisdiction to reopen such a decision on the grounds that fraud had been committed on the court.[194] Tax Court decisions can be reviewed by the Courts of Appeals to the same extent as decisions of the district courts in civil actions tried without a jury [Code Sec. 7482(a)]. The findings of facts made by a Tax Court judge and the factual inferences the Tax Court draws from the findings are binding, unless they are clearly erroneous. If the reviewing court has a firm conviction that a mistake was made, the Tax Court finding is "clearly erroneous."[195] Decisions in small tax cases are not reviewable [¶27,175] [Code Sec. 7481(b)]. Taxpayers seeking a redetermination of interest by the Tax Court may file a motion for redetermination, rather than petitioning with the court within a year after the decision becomes final [Code Sec. 7481(c)].

---

[191] *Bankers Pocahontas Coal Co.*, SCt, 3 USTC ¶998, 287 US 308, 53 SCt 150.

[192] *Excelsior Motor Mfg. & Supply Co.*, CA-7, 43 F2d 968.

[193] *B. Lasky*, SCt, 57-1 USTC ¶9482, 352 US 1027, 77 SCt 594.

[194] *W.H. Kenner*, CA-7, 68-1 USTC ¶9149, 387 F2d 689, *cert. denied*, 393 US 841, 89 SCt 121.

[195] *M. Duberstein*, SCt, 60-2 USTC ¶9515, 363 US 278, 80 SCt 1190; *A. Imbesi*, CA-3, 66-2 USTC ¶9481, 361 F2d 640.

.01 Appeals

Appeal from a decision of the Tax Court is usually made to the U.S. Court of Appeals for the circuit where the petitioner has his legal residence when the notice of appeal is filed. A corporation appeals to the circuit where its principal place of business or principal office or agency is located; if it has none, to the circuit where it filed the return [Code Sec. 7482].

You Can Appeal Failure to Refund

If the IRS fails to refund your overpayment and interest within 120 days after a Tax Court decision becomes final, the Tax Court may order the IRS to pay you. This order can be appealed as a final decision. The Tax Court does not, however, have the authority to decide the merits or validity of credits or offsets that would reduce or eliminate the refund to which you are otherwise entitled [Code Sec. 6512(b)(2)].

Time to File

A notice of appeal may be filed by either the Commissioner or the taxpayer within 90 days after the Tax Court's decision is entered. If it is filed by one party, any other party to the proceeding may file a notice of appeal within 120 days after the decision [Code Sec. 7483]. In certain cases, decisions of Courts of Appeals may be reviewed by the Supreme Court of the United States [¶27,160].

.02 Bond to Stay Assessment and Collection

Appeal from a Tax Court decision does not act as a stay of assessment or collection of the deficiency determined by the Court. The taxpayer, on or before the date of filing his or her notice of appeal, must file with the Court a bond not exceeding double the amount of the deficiency, or else a jeopardy bond [Code Sec. 7485].

.03 Effect of Courts of Appeals Decisions

It is well established that the Tax Court will follow decisions of the Court of Appeals for the same circuit to which the Tax Court decision can be appealed.[196]

---

[196] *J.E. Golsen*, 54 TC 742, Dec. 30,049 (1970), *aff'd*, CA-10, 71-2 USTC ¶9497, 445 F2d 985, *cert. denied*, 404 US 940, 92 SCt 284.

28 Foreign Income—Foreign Taxpayers

CREDIT FOR FOREIGN TAXES

Who can claim the foreign tax credit? ¶ 28,001

How to claim the foreign tax credit ¶ 28,005

Limitations on the foreign tax credit ¶ 28,010

Source rules for personal property sales ¶ 28,015

Adjustment to the credit for foreign tax refund ¶ 28,020

Credit for corporate shareholders in foreign corporations ¶ 28,025

FOREIGN TAXPAYERS

How foreign taxpayers are taxed ¶ 28,030

Resident aliens ¶ 28,035

Nonresident aliens ¶ 28,040

Foreign corporations ¶ 28,045

Foreign source income taxed at U.S. rates ¶ 28,050

What is U.S.-source income? ¶ 28,055

Tax treaty provisions ¶ 28,060

Tax on expatriation to avoid tax ¶ 28,065

U.S. INCOME FROM FOREIGN SOURCES

Earned income of citizens from sources outside U.S. ¶ 28,070

Allowances to U.S. government officers and employees in foreign service ¶ 28,075

Income from sources in U.S. possessions ¶ 28,080

When U.S. shareholders taxed on foreign investments ¶ 28,085

FOREIGN TRUSTS

Foreign trusts with U.S. owner ¶ 28,090

Foreign person as trust grantor ¶ 28,095

REPORTING REQUIREMENTS IMPOSED ON FOREIGN INVESTMENTS OF U.S. TAXPAYERS

FATCA reporting of specified foreign financial assets ¶ 28,100

Foreign bank and financial accounts (FBAR) reporting ¶ 28,101

Penalties for failure to file FBAR ¶ 28,102

Offshore voluntary disclosure program (OVDP) ¶ 28,103

Information returns required regarding U.S. ownership of foreign corporations ¶ 28,105

Information returns required of foreign-owned U.S. corporation or foreign corporation engaged in U.S. business ¶ 28,110

Information returns required of foreign interests in U.S. real property . . . . ¶28,115

Information returns required for transfer of property to foreign corporation . . . . ¶28,120

CREDIT FOR FOREIGN TAXES

¶28,001 WHO CAN CLAIM THE FOREIGN TAX CREDIT?

.01 In General

U.S. citizens, resident aliens, and domestic corporations are taxed on their worldwide income without regard to whether the income arose from a transaction outside the United States. To prevent double taxation—once by the foreign country where the income is earned and again by the United States—these taxpayers are allowed to reduce their U.S. tax liability on foreign-source income by the amount of foreign taxes paid on that income. The amount of credit that may be claimed is subject to several limits, including an overall limit designed to prevent the taxpayer from using the credit to reduce U.S. tax liability on U.S. source income [Code Sec. 904(a)]. This limit essentially caps the credit at the amount of U.S. tax that would have been paid on foreign-source taxable income. The calculation requires the taxpayer to determine its taxable income from foreign sources as a percentage of worldwide taxable income.

There are two foreign tax credit limitation categories or baskets: passive category income and general category income [Code Sec. 904(d)(1)]. Passive category income is defined as passive income and specified passive category income, while the general category includes income other than passive category income. Thus, all foreign tax credit limitation categories will be reclassified into either the passive or general limitation category. For purposes of maximizing the foreign tax credit limitation, the shrinkage in categories will make it more important to find exceptions to the category.

For purposes of the foreign tax credit limitation, passive income includes the following components of foreign personal holding company income under Code Sec. 954(c) [Code Sec. 904(d)(2)(B)(i)]:

- Dividends,
- Interest,
- Rents and royalties,
- Annuities,
- Net gain from certain property transactions,
- Net income equivalent to interest,
- Income from notional principal contracts,
- Payments in lieu of dividends,
- Payments in lieu of dividends from certain securities loans,

- Gain on a sale or exchange of stock in excess of the amount treated as a dividend, and
- Amounts received under a contract under which the corporation is to furnish personal services if some person other than the corporation has the right to designate the individual who is to perform the services or the individual who is to perform the services is designated in the contract and amounts received from the disposition of such a contract.

The passive basket does not include any of the following [Code Secs. 904(d)(2)(A)(iii)]:

1. Export financing interest which is interest derived from financing the sale or other disposition of certain property for use or consumption outside the United States. This includes property manufactured, produced, grown, or extracted in the United States by the taxpayer or a related person, if not more than 50 percent of its fair market value is attributable to products imported into the United States [Code Sec. 904(d)(2)(G)],
2. High-taxed income, which is income that would be passive income if the foreign income taxes paid or accrued by the taxpayer with respect to such income and the foreign income taxes deemed paid by the taxpayer with respect to such income exceeds the highest rate of tax specified in Code Sec. 1 or 11, whichever applies, multiplied by the amount of such income [Code Sec. 904(d)(2)(F)], and
3. Income other than passive income treated as separate baskets.

Taxpayers have full use of the AMT foreign tax credit in computing AMT. Note, however, that taxpayers must still apply the regular foreign tax credit limitations in computing the AMT-foreign tax credit. Once it is computed, it may offset AMT in full.

Holding Period for Claiming Credit for Taxes Withheld on Dividends

The holding period requirement for claiming foreign tax credits with respect to dividends has been amended to ensure that taxpayers can satisfy the holding period requirements when they purchase stock one day before the ex-dividend date. The revised holding periods are:

- **Foreign tax credit with respect to dividend income.** The stock must be held for 15 days or less within the 31-day period beginning 15 days before the ex-dividend date [Code Sec. 901(k)(1)(A)(i)]; and
- **Foreign tax credit for dividends on cumulative preferred stock.** The stock must be held for 45 days or less within the 91-day period beginning 45 days before the ex-dividend date [Code Sec. 901(k)(3)(B)].

With some exceptions, in order to claim a foreign tax credit for withholding taxes paid on gain or other income besides dividends, taxpayers will have to meet a holding period requirement with respect to the property producing the income. The holding period for the property is 15 days or less during the 31-day period beginning on the date which is 15 days before the date on which the right to receive the payment arose [Code Sec. 901(l)].

Pass-Through Entities and Allocation of Foreign Tax Credit

Partners in a partnership or beneficiaries of an estate or trust may be allowed their share of the credit for foreign taxes paid by the partnership, estate or trust [Code Sec. 901]. Partnerships must allocate foreign taxes in the same way that they allocate the income to which the taxes relate. Under Code Sec. 901(b)(5), foreign taxes paid by a partnership or other entity may now be attributed to persons who are members of a partnership or beneficiaries of an estate, rather than just to individual partners or beneficiaries. Thus, the rule covers both individual and corporate partners [Code Sec. 901(b)(5)].

Credit or Deduction?

Taxpayers may either claim a credit for the foreign taxes under Code Sec. 901 or take a deduction for them under Code Sec. 162 or 164, but they cannot take advantage of both [Code Sec. 275(a)(4)]. See Ch. 9. If they claim a standard deduction, however, they can still claim a foreign tax credit. If they choose to claim the credit, they must make an election in the manner specified below. They will generally benefit more from the credit than from the deduction. This is because the credit is a dollar-for-dollar offset against taxes that are due, but the deduction merely reduces a taxpayer's gross income.

> **Example 28-1:** Mr. and Mrs. Bundy have adjusted gross income of $120,000, $20,000 of which is dividends from foreign sources. They had to pay $2,000 in foreign income taxes on that dividend income. As an itemized deduction, the foreign income tax reduces their U.S. tax by $620. If, however, the Bundys choose to claim a credit for the $2,000 foreign tax, their U.S. tax will be reduced by the full $2,000. Therefore, they have an additional tax benefit of $1,380 by taking the credit.

Any unused foreign tax credit may be carried back for one year or carried forward for 10 years [Code Sec. 904(c)].

.02 Foreign Tax Credit Abuses

The IRS has announced that foreign tax credits will be disallowed if they were generated in transactions viewed by the IRS as abusive.[1]

The IRS stated that it would scrutinize abusive transactions designed to generate foreign tax credits using the substance over form doctrine, the step transaction doctrine, debt-equity principles, Code Sec. 269, the partnership anti-abuse rules of Reg. § 1.704-1 and the substantial economic effect rules of Reg. § 1.701-2. Moreover, the IRS will identify abusive foreign tax credit transactions as "listed transactions" for purposes of the tax shelter disclosure (Code Sec. 6011), disclosure of reportable transactions (Code Sec. 6111) and list maintenance requirements (Code Sec. 6112). See Ch. 26 for further discussion of tax shelters.

The IRS has released temporary regulations that attempt to stop U.S. companies from artificially generating foreign tax credit to reduce U.S. tax liability [Temp. Reg. § 1.901-2T(e) (5) (iv)]. The target of these new rules is U.S. businesses that engage in

---

[1] Notice 2004-19, 2004-1 CB 606.

artificially engineered, highly structured transactions with foreign companies to create a foreign tax liability when the basis of the underlying business transaction would result in little or no foreign tax. The foreign tax liability is then used to offset the taxpayer's actual tax liability.

In Notice 2004-20,[2] the IRS identified a transaction that involved the generation of foreign tax credits paid on gain that was not subject to tax in the United States. The transaction involved the purported acquisition of the stock of a foreign target corporation by a domestic corporation. An accompanying Section 338 election was made and a prearranged plan to sell the target corporation's assets generated a taxable gain for foreign, but not U.S. purposes.

¶28,005 HOW TO CLAIM THE FOREIGN TAX CREDIT

.01 In General

Individuals, nonresident aliens and estates and trusts compute the foreign tax credit on Form 1116, *Foreign Tax Credit (Individual, Estate or Trust)*. An individual with de minimis foreign tax credits may elect to be exempt from the foreign tax credit limitation rules [Code Sec. 904(j)]. An individual who makes the election is not required to file Form 1116; the credit is claimed directly on Form 1040. An individual is not required to file Form 1116 to claim the credit if (1) all of the individual's income is foreign source gross income in the passive category, (2) all income and foreign taxes paid were reported on a qualified payee statement, for example Form 1099-INT, and (3) total creditable taxes do not exceed $300 ($600 if married, filing a joint return). An individual who makes the election to be exempt from the foreign tax credit limitation will not be able to carryforward excess foreign tax credits to or from the year for which the election is made.

> **Example 28-2:** Taxpayer is single and earns $27,000. She is paid a dividend of $720 from a Japanese company through her investment in a mutual fund. The Japanese government withheld $103 in taxes on the dividend and reported the dividend to her on Form 1099-DIV. Taxpayer has no expenses for the year and claims a standard deduction. Since she has creditable foreign tax credits of less than $300, she can elect to calculate her foreign tax credit without using the foreign tax credit limitation or using Form 1116. Taxpayer will claim the $103 foreign tax credit directly on Form 1040. Because she has elected to be exempt from the foreign tax credit limitation, she will not be able to carryforward any unused foreign tax credits to the tax year.

Corporations file Form 1118, *Foreign Tax Credit, Corporations,* if the corporation elects the benefits of the foreign tax credit. Form 1118 must be attached to the taxpayer's tax return. A bond may be required if the foreign tax has not yet been paid [Reg. § 1.905-2]. The election applies to every foreign tax, but a taxpayer can change the election any time before the time to file a claim for credit or refund expires (for the foreign tax

[2] Notice 2004-20, 2004-1 CB 608.

credit, ten years) for the year the choice is made [Code Secs. 901(a), 6511(d)(3)(A); Reg. § 1.901-1(d)]. If a carryback or carryover is involved [¶ 28,010], the period is measured from the year from which the excess taxes may be carried.[3]

.02 When To Claim the Credit

If taxpayers use the accrual method of accounting, they must generally claim the credit in the tax year the foreign tax accrued. If they use the cash method, they can either take the credit in the tax year the foreign tax is paid or in the tax year it accrues. Once they claim the credit in the tax year the foreign tax accrues, they must continue to use this method [Code Sec. 905(a); Reg. § 1.905-1(a)]. In the year that they make the election, they can claim a double credit—once for the foreign taxes actually paid in that year and again for the foreign taxes accrued.[4]

Taxpayers can make or change their choice to claim the credit at any time during the period within 10 years from the due date for filing the return for the tax year for which they make the claim. They make or change their choice on their tax return (or on an amended return) for the year that their choice is to be effective.

.03 Foreign Taxes That Are Creditable

A foreign tax that operates as an income, war profits, or excess profits tax for most taxpayers is generally creditable. The foreign tax creditability depends not on the way a foreign government characterizes its tax but on whether the tax, if enacted in the U. S., would be an income, war profits, or excess profits tax [Reg. § 1.901-2(a)(1)(ii)]. Reg. § 1.901-2(a)(3)(i) provides further that a foreign tax's predominant character is that of a U. S. income tax "[i]f . . . the foreign tax is likely to reach net gain in the normal circumstances in which it applies." Three tests set forth in the regulations provide guidance in making this assessment [Reg. § 1.901-2(b)(1)]. The tests indicate that net gain consists of realized gross receipts reduced by significant costs and expenses attributable to such gross receipts. A foreign tax that reaches net income, or profits, is creditable. In *PPL Corp.*[5] the U.S. Supreme Court concluded that the United Kingdom's windfall profits tax on several companies that were privatized between 1984 and 1996 was a creditable excess profits tax for purposes of the foreign tax credit. Accordingly, the United States owner of a portion of one of the privatized companies was entitled to claim the foreign tax credit for its share of the company's windfall tax.

Not every levy by a foreign country qualifies for the foreign tax credit. Generally, to be so qualified, the foreign tax has to be imposed on *income* as that term is understood for U.S. income tax purposes [Reg. § 1.901-2(a)(1)]. This means that taxpayers cannot claim a credit for real or personal property taxes, sales taxes or gasoline taxes imposed by a foreign government. Also, the tax cannot be a payment for a specific economic benefit (such as user fees) that is not available to everyone who pays the country's income tax; nor does the tax qualify if there is no income tax to the general population. For example,

---

[3] Senate Report No. 1393, p. 16, 86th Cong., 2nd Sess.

[4] *J.V. Ferrer*, 35 TC 617, Dec. 24,618 (1961), *rev'd and remanded on other issue,* CA-2, 62-2 USTC ¶ 9518, 304 F2d 125.

[5] *PPL Corp.*, SCt, 2013-1 USTC ¶ 50,335, 133 SCt 1897, *rev'g*, CA-3, 2012-1 USTC ¶ 50,115.

the right to extract government-controlled oil would be considered a specific economic benefit [Reg. § 1.901-2 (a) (2) (ii) (B)].

.04 When Foreign Tax Credit Cannot Be Claimed

If a foreign country requires the taxpayer to participate in an international boycott as a condition of doing business within the country, the taxpayer may not be eligible to claim a credit for the income taxes paid to that country [Code Secs. 908(a), 999(b)]. The IRS has issued guidelines to determine participation in a boycott.[6]

Code Sec. 901(j) provides that taxpayers may not claim a foreign tax credit for taxes imposed by a country in the following situations:

1. The United States does not recognize the country;
2. The United States has severed relations with the country;
3. The United States does not conduct foreign relations with the country; and
4. The country has been designated by the Secretary of State as a country that repeatedly provides support for acts of international terrorism.

Code Sec. 901(j) no longer applies to a foreign country if: (1) the President determines that a waiver of the application of Code Sec. 901(j) to such foreign country is in the national interest of the United States and will expand trade and investment opportunities for U.S. companies in that foreign country; and (2) the President reports to Congress, not less than 30 days before the waiver is granted, the intention to grant the waiver and the reason for the waiver.

NOTE: Even though the taxpayer may not be able to take certain foreign taxes as a credit, they may still be taken as deductions if they are incurred in a trade or business or qualify as itemized deductions [Code Sec. 908(b)].

.05 Foreign Tax Credit Abuses

The IRS has announced that foreign tax credits will be disallowed if they were generated in transactions viewed by the IRS as abusive.[7]

The IRS scrutinizes abusive transactions designed to generate foreign tax credits using the substance over form doctrine, the step transaction doctrine, debt-equity principles, Code Sec. 269, the partnership anti-abuse rules of Reg. § 1.704-1 and the substantial economic effect rules of Reg. § 1.701-2. Moreover, the IRS will identify abusive foreign tax credit transactions as "listed transactions" for purposes of the tax shelter disclosure (Code Sec. 6011), disclosure of reportable transactions (Code Sec. 6111) and list maintenance requirements (Code Sec. 6112). See Ch. 26 for further discussion of tax shelters.

In Notice 2004-20,[8] the IRS identified as listed transactions for purposes of the tax shelter disclosure, registration, and list maintenance regulations a purported stock acquisition that involved the generation of foreign tax credits on gain that was not subject to U.S. taxation. The transaction involved the purported acquisition of the stock of a foreign target corporation by a domestic corporation. An accompanying

---

[6] Notice 84-1, 1984-1 CB 328; Notice 84-7, 1984-1 CB 338.

[7] Notice 2004-19, 2004-1 CB 606.

[8] Notice 2004-20, 2004-1 CB 608.

Section 338 election was made and a prearranged plan to sell the target corporation's assets generated a taxable gain for foreign, but not U.S. purposes.

.06 Structured Passive Investment Arrangements

In order to stop taxpayers, U.S. businesses, from engaging in artificially engineered, highly structured transactions with foreign companies solely to generate foreign tax credits, the IRS has released structured passive investment arrangement regulations [Reg. § 1.901-2(h)(2)]. The targeted transaction would be an ordinary financing arrangement between a U.S. person (or a portfolio investment of a U.S. person) and a foreign counterparty and create a foreign special purpose vehicle (SPV). The SPV is structured to create income for foreign tax purposes that is subject to foreign tax. Differences between U.S. and foreign tax law are exploited so the U.S. person can claim a foreign tax credit and the foreign counterparty claims a foreign tax benefit. The identified transactions can be grouped into the following three main categories: (1) U.S. borrower transactions, (2) U.S. lender transactions, and (3) asset holding transactions [Reg. § 1.901-2(e)(5)(iv)].

In U.S. borrower transactions, the U.S. person indirectly borrows funds from a foreign counterparty through an SPV. The lender's interest income is effectively isolated in the SPV. Both the borrower and the foreign lenders claim to have an interest in the SPV. This entitles the U.S. borrower to claim a tax credit for the foreign tax imposed on the SPV, and the foreign lender to receive tax-free distributions from the SPV [Reg. § 1.901-2(e)(5)(iv)(D), Exs. 1 through 3].

In U.S. lender transactions, the U.S. person indirectly loans funds to a foreign counterparty. Again, the loaned funds are channeled through an SPV, and the income from the foreign borrower is effectively shifted into the SPV. The U.S. person claims an equity interest in the SPV, and the income from the foreign borrower is effectively shifted into the SPV. The U.S. person claims an equity interest in the SPV, receives payments from the SPV and claims a credit for foreign tax imposed on the SPV's income. The credit eliminates all or most of the U.S. person's U.S. tax liability and, often, the U.S. tax that would be owed on the U.S. person's unrelated foreign source income [Reg. § 1.901-2(e)(5)(iv)(D), Ex. 5].

In asset holding transactions, the U.S. person moves an income-producing asset into an SPV in a foreign tax jurisdiction. The U.S. person's overall tax liability would not be affected, as the U.S. person would get a foreign tax credit for any foreign tax paid. However, a foreign counterparty also participates in the arrangement, and thereby shares the cost of the foreign tax, while also obtaining a foreign tax benefit. Thus, the U.S. person is better off paying the foreign tax instead of U.S. tax because it shares the foreign tax with the foreign counterparty. The foreign counterparty's participation allows it to obtain foreign tax benefits, for which it compensates the U.S. person [Reg. § 1.901-2(e)(5)(iv)(D), Ex. 9].

As a general rule, the regulations provide that an amount paid to a foreign country is not a compulsory payment and so is ineligible for the foreign tax credit if the foreign payment is attributable to a structured passive investment arrangement [Reg. § 1.901-2(e)(5)(iv)(A)].

A structured passive investment arrangement is an arrangement that satisfies the following six conditions [Reg. § 1.901-2(e)(5)(iv)(B)]:

1. A special purpose vehicle (SPV) is used and substantially all of the SPV's gross income (for U.S. tax purposes) is passive investment income, substantially all of its assets are held to produce passive investment income and the foreign tax payment is attributable to the entity's income. An entity includes a corporation, trust, partnership or disregarded entity [Reg. § 1.901-2(e)(5)(iv)(C)(3)] See Reg. § 1.901-2(e)(5)(iv)(D), Ex. 4;
2. A U.S. party would be eligible to claim a foreign tax credit for all or a portion of the foreign payment if the payment were an amount of tax paid;
3. The U.S. party's proportionate share of the foreign payments attributable to the entity's income is or is expected to be substantially greater than the foreign tax credits under Code Sec. 901(a) the U.S. party reasonably would expect to be eligible to claim if the U.S. party directly owned its proportionate share of the assets owned by the SPV;
4. The arrangement is reasonably expected to result in a foreign tax benefit for a counterparty or a person related to the counterparty;
5. The arrangement involves a counterparty; and
6. The arrangement is treated differently under the tax systems of the United States and the applicable foreign country.

These six requirements are common to arrangements that are intentionally structured to generate the foreign payment.

The SPV requirement in 1., above, will be met with respect to the passive investment income requirement if the income is foreign personal holding company income, described in Code Sec. 954(c), with the following modifications:

1. Passive investment income excludes personal service contract income described in Code Sec. 954(c)(1)(H);
2. The exception from foreign personal holding company income for dividends, interest, rents and royalties received from related corporate payors under Code Sec. 954(c)(3) is disregarded; and
3. The exception from foreign personal holding company income for payments received by a controlled foreign corporation (CFC) from another CFC under Code Sec. 954(c)(6) is disregarded [Reg. § 1.901-2(e)(5)(iv)(C)(5)(i)].

The determination of foreign personal holding company income and whether income can be excluded as qualified banking or financing income under Code Sec. 954(h) or qualified insurance income under Code Sec. 954(i) is made at the entity level, treating the entity as if it were a CFC.

.07 Notification of Foreign Tax Redetermination

Generally, a taxpayer that claims a foreign tax credit must notify the IRS when there has been a change in the taxpayer's foreign tax liability (referred to as a "foreign tax redetermination)" [Code Sec. 905(c)]. A taxpayer that fails to notify the IRS of a foreign tax redetermination is subject to penalty, unless the taxpayer can show that the failure was due to reasonable cause rather than willful neglect. The penalty is calculated, by adding to the deficiency attributable to the foreign tax redetermination, an amount equal to five percent of the deficiency if the failure does not exceed one month. An additional five percent is added for each month (or fraction of a month) that the failure continues [Code Sec. 6689; Temp. Reg. § 1.905-4T(e)(3)].

A foreign tax redetermination is defined as a change in foreign tax liability that can affect a taxpayer's foreign tax credit. Foreign tax redeterminations include: (1) accrued taxes that when paid differ from the amounts added to post-1986 foreign income taxes or claimed as credits by the taxpayer (e.g., as a result of corrections to overaccruals or additional payments); (2) accrued taxes that are not paid before the date that is two years after the close of the tax year to which the taxes relate; (3) taxes that are paid and then refunded in whole or in part; and (4) taxes taken into account when accrued, but translated into U.S. dollars on the date of payment, if there is a difference between the dollar value of the accrued tax and the dollar value of the tax paid attributable to currency fluctuations [Code Sec. 905(c)(1); Temp. Reg. § 1.905-3T(c)].

Where a redetermination of U.S. tax liability is required as a result of a foreign tax redetermination, a taxpayer must generally notify the IRS by filing an amended return, Form 1118, *Foreign Tax Credit—Corporations*, or Form 1116, *Foreign Tax Credit (Individual, Estate or Trust)*. In addition, a statement must be filed for the tax year for which a redetermination of U.S. tax liability is required. However, where a foreign tax redetermination requires an individual to redetermine his U.S. tax liability and as a result of the foreign tax redetermination, the amount of creditable taxes paid or accrued by him during the tax year doesn't exceed the applicable dollar limitation in Code Sec. 904(k), he isn't required to file Form 1116 with the amended return for the tax years if he satisfies the Code Sec. 904(k) requirements [Temp. Reg. § 1.905-4T(b)(1)(i)].

¶28,010 LIMITATIONS ON THE FOREIGN TAX CREDIT

.01 Limits Applicable

Taxpayers may claim a tax credit against their U.S. tax liability for income taxes paid or accrued to a foreign country or to a U.S. possession [Code Sec. 901]. The amount of the foreign tax credit is limited to the U.S. tax liability that can be attributed to the taxpayer's net foreign-source income [Code Sec. 904]. To determine foreign-source income, taxpayers must allocate and apportion their expenses [Code Secs. 862(b) and 863(a)].

This limitation treats all foreign income as a single unit and limits the tax credit to U.S. income tax attributable to the taxable income from all sources outside the U.S. Under this limitation, operating losses in one foreign country offset income from another foreign country. The maximum credit can thus be obtained by using the following formula:

$$\frac{\text{Total taxable income from sources outside U.S. (but not exceeding total taxable income)}}{\text{Entire taxable income from all sources}} \times \text{Pre-credit U.S. income tax on worldwide income}$$

Example 28-3: Bellis, Inc., a domestic corporation, had income of $50,000 from the U.S., $50,000 from country X and $50,000 from country Y. Bellis paid a tax of $19,000 to X and $21,000 to Y on the income from those countries. The tax is figured as follows:

Taxable income from U.S.	$50,000	
Taxable income from X	50,000	
Taxable income from Y	50,000	$150,000
U.S. tax on $150,000 income, before credits		$ 41,750
Limitation for X and Y combined ($100,000/$150,000 × $41,750)		27,833
Net tax payable		$ 13,917

Individuals with no more than $300 ($600 for married persons filing jointly) of creditable foreign taxes and no foreign source income except qualified passive income may elect to exempt themselves from the foreign tax credit limitation [Code Sec. 904(k)]. In general, the term qualified passive income refers primarily to investment income, such as dividends, interest, and rents, that is shown on a payee statement furnished to the individual. This means that they will be able to claim the foreign tax credit without using Form 1116. To qualify the following requirements must be met: (1) The taxpayer must be an individual; (2) The taxpayer's only foreign source income for the tax year must be qualified passive income (dividends, interest, royalties, etc.) reported on a payee statement (such as Form 1099-DIC or Form 1099-INT); (3) The taxpayer's creditable foreign taxes for the tax year are not more than $300 ($600 if filing a joint return); and (4) the taxpayer elected this procedure for the tax year [Code Sec. 904(k)].

NOTE: If taxpayers make this election, they may not carry back or carry over any unused foreign tax to or from this tax year.

.02 Apportionment and Allocation of Interest Expense

To determine net foreign-source income, a taxpayer must allocate and apportion interest expense. Code Sec. 864(e)(2) provides that allocation and apportionment of interest expense must be made on the basis of assets rather than gross income. Under the asset method, interest expense is apportioned among a grouping of gross income in proportion to the average total values of the assets within the group.

Taxpayers may elect to compute the value of their assets for purposes of allocating interest expense items based on the tax book value method or the fair market value method [Temp. Reg. § § 1.861-8T(c)(2), 1.861-9T(g)(1)(ii)]. Taxpayers using the tax book value method may elect to change to the fair market value method at any time.[9] Taxpayers that elect to use the fair market value method must continue to use that method unless expressly authorized by the IRS to change methods [Temp. Reg. § 1.861-8T(c)(2)]. Taxpayers may also apportion certain other expenses based on the comparative value of assets provided that such apportionment is made in accordance with the rules of Temp. Reg. § 1.861-9T(g).

The use of adjusted tax basis in assets to apportion interest expenses under the tax book value method may result in disparities between the bases of domestic and

[9] Rev. Proc. 2006-42, 2006-2 CB 931.

foreign assets because of the differences in depreciation methods applicable to those assets. For example, the tax book value of tangible property used in the United States generally reflects depreciation of that property pursuant to the modified accelerated cost recovery system (MACRS) which generally permits a taxpayer to depreciate tangible property (other than real property) under the 200-percent declining balance method, or the 150-percent declining balance method in the case of certain property. [See ¶11,030 for further discussion of MACRS.] MACRS also permits taxpayers to depreciate property over shorter recovery periods than a property's class life. In contrast, tangible property used predominantly outside the United States generally must be depreciated pursuant to the Alternate Depreciation System (ADS) which requires a taxpayer to depreciate tangible property using the straight line method of depreciation. [See ¶11,040 for further discussion of ADS.] Additionally, ADS generally requires taxpayers to use recovery periods equal to the property's class life resulting in longer depreciation periods than those used under MACRS.

As a result of accelerated depreciation under MACRS as compared to slower depreciation under ADS, an asset used in the United States generally will have a lower adjusted tax basis (i.e., tax book value) than if the same asset were used predominantly outside of the United States. The relatively higher tax book value for assets used predominantly outside the United States results in an increased apportionment of interest expense to foreign source income and a corresponding reduction in the taxpayer's foreign tax credit limitation.

Alternative Tax Book Value Method

Taxpayers may elect to take advantage of an elective alternative method of determining the tax book value of assets (the "alternative tax book value method") when apportioning interest expense between U.S. and foreign sources. Entities electing the alternative tax book value method may change to the fair market value method at any time for any open year, but IRS consent is required. The alternative tax book value method, which is elective, allows taxpayers to determine the tax book value of all tangible property subject to a depreciation deduction by using the straight-line method, conventions, and recovery periods of the alternative depreciation system (ADS). The alternative method is intended to minimize basis disparities between foreign and domestic assets of taxpayers that may arise when taxpayers use adjusted tax basis to value assets under the tax book value method of expense apportionment.

The alternative tax book value method allows a taxpayer to elect to determine the tax book value of tangible property subject to MACRS depreciation as though the property had been depreciated using the ADS during the entire period in which it has been in service [Temp. Reg. § 1.861-9T(i)(1)(i)].

The elective alternative to the existing tax book valuation method provides taxpayers with the option of determining the adjusted bases of both foreign and domestic assets under one consistent depreciation method for purposes of apportioning expenses under the asset method described in Reg. § 1.861-9T(g). A uniform depreciation methodology will help reduce the basis disparity between foreign and domestic assets that can occur under the existing tax book value method.

In Rev. Proc. 2006-42,[10] the IRS issued administrative procedures under which a taxpayer may obtain automatic consent to change from the fair market value method to the alternative tax book method of valuing assets for purposes of apportioning expenses pursuant to Temp. Reg. § 1.861-9T(g). Accordingly, taxpayers that change from the fair market value method to the alternative tax book value method pursuant to this revenue procedure will be treated as expressly authorized to change methods.

U.S.-Owned Foreign Corporations

If at least 10 percent of the earnings and profits of a U.S.-owned foreign corporation is attributable to U.S. sources, then a dividend or r interest payment is U.S.-source income to the extent it is attributable to sources within the United States. For this purpose, a foreign corporation is U.S.-owned if at least 50 percent of the total voting power of its voting stock or of the total value of its stock is held by U.S. persons [Code Sec. 904(g)].

.03 Foreign Tax Carryover and Carryback

Where taxes paid or accrued to any foreign country or U.S. possession for any tax year are more than the amount allowable as a credit under the overall limitation, the excess may be carried back and then carried forward. The excess foreign tax credit carryback period is one year and the excess foreign tax credit carryforward period is 10 years [Code Sec. 904(c)]. The same carryback and carryforward periods apply for excess foreign oil and gas extraction and foreign oil related taxes [Code Sec. 904(c)]. Unused foreign taxes are carried back to the earliest tax year, and then are carried forward [Reg. § 1.904-2(b)(1)].

Unused Taxes Carried to Deduction Year

A foreign tax credit may not be carried to a tax year in which a foreign tax deduction was claimed. The taxpayer must also reduce the carryback or carryforward by the amount it would have chosen to claim as a credit rather than a deduction in the tax year. For example, if a taxpayer claimed a deduction for foreign taxes paid in an earlier year, instead of a credit, any unused foreign taxes of the current year carried back to the "deduction" year are to be considered as used in the year of the deduction. However, no tax benefit will result either as a deduction or as a credit for taxes considered as "used in the deduction year." Rather, a foreign tax credit limitation is determined for the deduction year in order to reduce the amount of unused taxes that can be carried to another year. A taxpayer can avoid this outcome by timely filing an amended return, reversing his choice of deducting taxes, and claiming the tax credit instead. The ten-year period for claiming a credit or refund is determined by reference to the due date for the return in which the taxes are paid or accrued [Code Sec. 6511(d)(3)(A)].

Figuring the Foreign Tax Credit

In computing a taxpayer's taxable income for purposes of the foreign tax credit limitations, the taxpayer should omit personal exemption deductions for individuals, estates and trusts [Code Sec. 904(b)]. On joint returns, the taxpayer should apply the credit against both spouses' total tax and figure the limitation on the combined taxable income—but excluding personal exemption deductions. Reg. § 1.904-3(c)

---

[10] Rev. Proc. 2006-42, 2006-2 CB 931.

provides detailed explanations and examples of the special rules applicable to the computation of carrybacks and carryovers of unused foreign taxes paid or accrued to foreign countries by married couples filing joint returns.

.04 Treatment of Foreign Source Qualified Dividends and Gains

If a taxpayer received foreign sourced qualified dividends and/or capital gains (including long-term capital gains, unrecaptured Code Sec. 1250 gain, and/or Code Sec. 1231 gains) that are taxed in the U.S. at a reduced tax rate, the taxpayer must adjust the amount of foreign source income that is reported on the return to avoid the allowable foreign tax credit being significantly overstated and triggering a substantial underpayment penalty.

Code Sec. 904(b)(2) contains the special rules that apply to capital gains and losses and the adjustments that are required when calculating the foreign tax credit limitation [Code Sec. 904(b)(2), (3); Reg. § 1.904(b)-2]. Specifically, foreign source capital gains and losses are subject to (1) a capital gain net income limitation adjustment (i.e., U.S. capital loss adjustment) and (2) a capital gain rate differential adjustment. Under these rules, gains from the sale or exchange of a capital asset include gains under Code Sec. 1231 relating to property used in a trade or business [Code Sec. 904(b)(3)(C); Reg. § § 1.904(b)-1, 1.904(b)-2].

Capital Gain Net Income Limitation Adjustment

The numerator of the foreign tax credit limitation fraction (foreign source taxable income) must be adjusted in cases where the taxpayer has a net capital gain from foreign sources that exceeds net U.S.-source capital losses (excess of foreign source net capital gain over net capital gain from all sources). The adjustment is necessary because foreign gain is offset by domestic loss for U.S. taxpayers, and therefore, a portion of the gain is not subject to tax. Foreign source taxable income includes gain from the sale or exchange of a capital asset only to the extent of "foreign source capital gain net income" which is the lesser of (1) capital gain net income (or net capital gain) from foreign sources, or (2) capital gain net income (or net capital gain) from all sources [Code Sec. 904(b)(2)(A), (3)(A)]. Capital gain net income is the excess of capital gains over capital losses and net capital gain is the excess of net-long term capital gain over short-term capital loss [Reg. § 1.904(b)-1(f)(5)]. If foreign source capital gains do not exceed foreign source capital losses, there is no foreign source net capital gain and the adjustment is not required. The adjustment is also not required where foreign source capital gains do not exceed net capital gains from all sources.

For purposes of determining the numerator of the foreign tax credit limitation fraction (foreign source taxable income), foreign source capital gain net income is taken into account only to the extent of capital gain net income from all sources. Reg. § 1.904(b)-1(a)(1)(i) provides that foreign source capital gain net income is determined by taking into account all capital gain and loss items in the taxpayer's foreign tax credit separate limitation categories in the aggregate. Foreign source capital gain net income is then reduced to the extent the amount exceeds capital gain net income from all sources.

If the reduction is required and the taxpayer has only one separate foreign tax credit limitation category, the reduction is required for that category. If there are two or more categories, the reduction must be apportioned, pro rata, based on the amount of foreign source capital gain net income in each category. Where a capital gain rate differential adjustment must be made (see below), the reduction is apportioned among the different rate categories in each separate category [Reg. § 1.904(b)-1(a)(1)(ii)]. The capital gain net income limitation is determined using the following steps:

1. Determine foreign source capital gain net income based on all of the capital gain and loss items in the taxpayer's separate foreign tax credit limitation categories in the aggregate.
2. Determine the capital gain net income from all sources.
3. Determine the excess, if any, of foreign source capital gain net income over capital gain net income from all sources.
4. If there is one separate foreign tax credit limitation category, reduce the capital gain net income in the category by the amount in (3), above.
5. If there is more than one category, apportion the reduction between the categories, pro rata, based on the capital gain net income in each category.
6. If there is a capital gain rate differential adjustment, the reduction is apportioned among the different rate groups in each separate category.

Capital Gain Rate Differential Adjustment

Where there is a capital gains rate differential (e.g., capital gains are taxed at lower rates than ordinary income), adjustments must be made to capital gains and foreign source losses when calculating the numerator of the foreign tax credit limitation fraction. Capital gains, but not losses, are also adjusted in the denominator of the fraction. The adjustment is needed to take into account the difference between the maximum U.S. tax rate and the more favorable capital gains rates [Code Sec. 904(b)(2)(B); Reg. § 1.904(b)-1(b), (c), (d)]. Without these adjustments, the amount of pre-credit U.S. tax attributable to foreign source income would not be accurate. The capital gain rate differential adjustment for foreign source capital gains and losses must be made after the capital gain net income limitation adjustment (see above) [Reg. § 1.904(b)-1(c)(1)(i)].

For individuals, the capital gain tax rate differential exists for any tax year in which the taxpayer is subject to Code Sec. 1(h), relating to the maximum capital gains tax rate. For corporations, a differential exists if the corporate rate exceeds the alternative rate of Code Sec. 1201(a) [Code Sec. 904(b)(3)(D); Reg. § 1.904(a)-1(b)(1)]. Because the alternative rate of tax under Code Sec. 1201(a) is 35 percent, the same top rate as the corporate tax rate, the alternative tax does not currently apply. The rate differential portion is the excess of the highest applicable rate over the alternative rate over the highest applicable rate.

An individual taxpayer can elect not to make the rate differential adjustments if certain requirements are met. To elect out of the adjustment, the highest rate of tax imposed on the taxpayer's taxable income (excluding net capital gain and qualified dividend income) cannot exceed the highest rate of tax in effect under Code Sec. 1(h) *and* foreign source net capital gain, plus foreign source qualified dividend income must be less than $20,000 [Reg. § 1.904(b)-1(b)(3)].

An individual taxpayer with qualified dividend income for which the income tax rate of Code Sec. 1(h) applies must make a rate differential adjustment in a manner similar to the adjustments for capital gains. The special rules for taxpayers with U.S.

source net long-term capital losses do not apply. A taxpayer can elect out of the rate differential adjustment if certain requirements are met (see above) [Reg. § 1.904(b)-1(e)].

Steps for Determining Capital Gain Rate Differential Adjustment

The rules for determining the capital gain rate differential adjustment generally require that the following steps be taken:

1. First, for purposes of the foreign tax credit limitation numerator, determine whether the capital gain net income limitation adjustment is required, and if so, make the appropriate reductions.
2. Second, for purposes of the foreign tax credit limitation numerator, adjust foreign source capital gain net income in each separate category long-term rate group or apply the special rules in Reg. § 1.904(b)-1(c)(1)(ii), for taxpayers with a U.S. net long-term capital loss and short-term capital gain from either U.S. or foreign sources.
3. Third, for purposes of the numerator of the foreign tax credit limitation, net foreign source capital losses in each separate category rate group according to the ordering rules in Reg. § 1.904(b)-1(d).
4. Fourth, for purposes of the denominator of the foreign tax credit limitation, net all U.S. and foreign source capital gains and losses and adjust any remaining net capital gains based on the rate group.

Adjustments to Numerator of Foreign Tax Credit Limitation Fraction for Foreign Source Long-Term Capital Gains

Computation of foreign source taxable income for purposes of the numerator of foreign tax credit limitation requires adjustment of foreign source capital gain net income in each separate category long-term rate group. The rule also requires adjustment of foreign source net capital losses in each separate category rate group. Under Reg. § 1.904(b)-1(c)(1), foreign source capital gain net income in each separate category long-term rate group must be reduced by the rate differential portion of the capital gain net income.

U.S. Net Long-Term Capital Loss and Short-Term Capital Gains

Taxpayers with a U.S. source net long-term capital loss and either U.S. source or foreign source short-term capital gains must follow special rules, in lieu of the rules discussed above, for determining the capital gain rate differential adjustment. Under the rules, the foreign source capital gain net income in each separate long-term rate group is reduced by the rate differential portion of the applicable rate differential amount. The applicable rate differential amount is arrived at by (1) determining the U.S. long-term capital loss adjustment amount, and (2) determining the applicable rate differential amount. The taxpayer must first determine whether a reduction under the capital gain net income limitation is required (see above). The U.S. long-term capital loss adjustment amount is the amount by which the U.S. source net long-term capital losses exceeds the reduction of any foreign source long-term capital gain (i.e., due to the U.S. long-term capital loss adjustment (see above)). The long-term capital loss adjustment amount is apportioned on a pro rata basis to each separate category long-term rate group with capital gain net income. The rate differential adjustment under Reg. § 1.904(b)-1(c) applies to the amount remaining after the apportioned amount is subtracted [Reg. § 1.904(b)-1(c)(1)(ii)].

Adjustments to Numerator of Foreign Tax Credit Limitation Fraction for Foreign-Source Capital Losses

A taxpayer must make a rate differential adjustment for foreign source capital losses. A taxpayer with a net capital loss in a separate category rate group (excess of foreign source capital losses over capital gains in the separate category rate group) must reduce the net capital loss by the sum of the rate differential portions of the capital gain net income in each long-term rate group offset by the net capital loss. Ordering rules are provided for determining which capital gains are offset. The rules require adjustment of foreign capital losses that offset capital gains associated with different tax rates, as well as those that offset U.S. capital gains [Reg. § 1.904(b)-1(d)].

Adjustments to Denominator of Foreign Tax Credit Limitation Fraction

Taxable income from all sources for purposes of the denominator of the foreign tax credit limitation includes gain from the sale or exchange of a capital asset only in an amount equal to the capital gain net income less the sum of the rate differential portions of each rate group of net capital gain [Code Sec. 904(b)(2)(B)(ii); Reg. § 1.904(b)-1(c)(2)]. Thus, a taxpayer would net all U.S. source and foreign source capital gains and losses and adjust the remaining net capital gain, based on the rate group. Ordinary income from both U.S. sources and foreign sources is included in the denominator. Note that the denominator is the same for each category of income.

.05 Treatment of Foreign Losses

Code Sec. 904(f) provides that taxpayers with overall foreign losses greater than foreign income can reduce U.S. tax on U.S. income. The tax benefits from the deduction of excess foreign losses are subject to recapture. Under the general recapture rule, a portion of the foreign income earned is treated as derived from U.S. sources.

The coordination rules provide that U.S. source capital loss that reduces foreign source capital gains under the capital net income limitation (see above) is disregarded in determining the amount of a taxpayer's U.S. source taxable income for purposes of computing additions to the taxpayer's overall foreign loss accounts [Reg. § 1.904(b)-1(h)]. The rule prevents the double counting of capital losses from U.S. sources. A taxpayer's losses from U.S. sources, for purposes of Code Sec. 904(f)(5)(D), is the amount by which (1) the taxpayer's foreign source taxable income in the aggregate, after taking into account the capital gain differential adjustment, exceeds (2) the taxpayer's entire taxable income, after taking into account the capital gain differential adjustment. The rule prevents distortions to the foreign tax credit limitation fraction that would otherwise result from U.S. source capital gains and losses.

If U.S. income taxes were reduced because the taxpayer claimed an overall foreign loss (expenses exceeded income from all foreign sources), to insure that the taxpayer didn't enjoy a tax windfall, the loss is recaptured in later years when the taxpayer has taxable income from foreign sources. Generally, the recapture is accomplished by treating a portion of foreign-source taxable income in a later year as U.S.-source income. As such, it does not qualify for the foreign tax credit. The amount to be treated as U.S.-source income is the lesser of: the foreign loss or 50 percent of the foreign taxable income in the later year. The taxpayer can choose to have a greater percentage of the taxable foreign income treated as U.S.-source income [Code Sec. 904(f)(1)]. (The taxpayer may be inclined to opt for the higher percentage if he or she is claiming a credit rather than a deduction for the foreign tax.)

Example 28-4: Mr. West, a U.S. citizen, owns a manufacturing plant in Europe. He incurred overall losses of $30,000. In the following year, the plant had a profit of $25,000. The amount of the foreign taxable income that is recaptured and treated as U.S.-source income is $12,500 (50 percent of $25,000).

There is also recapture of a loss on business property used predominantly outside the U.S. that is disposed of prior to the time the loss is recaptured under the general rules. You are treated as having a recognized gain in the year you dispose of the property. The gain is the excess of the fair market value of the property disposed of over your adjusted basis in the property. In such cases, 100 percent of the gain (to the extent of losses not previously recaptured) is recaptured [Code Sec. 904(f)(3)].

¶28,015 SOURCE RULES FOR PERSONAL PROPERTY SALES

.01 Rules

The rules for determining the source of income are important since the U.S. acknowledges that foreign countries have the first right to tax foreign income, but the U.S. generally imposes its full tax on U.S. income.

The U.S. generally taxes the worldwide income of U.S. persons, and the source rules are primarily important for U.S. persons in determining their foreign tax credit limitation. A premise of the foreign tax credit is that it should not reduce U.S. tax on U.S. income, but only U.S. tax on foreign source income.

▶ **OBSERVATION:** The source rules also affect foreign persons. These rules are primarily important in determining the income over which the U.S. asserts tax jurisdiction. Foreign persons are subject to U.S. tax on their U.S.-source income and certain foreign-source income that is effectively connected with a U.S. trade or business [¶28,030 and ¶28,055].

Income from selling tangible or intangible personal property is generally considered as being from the country of the seller's residence. If personal property is sold by a U.S. resident, the income from the sale is generally treated as U.S.-source. If sold by a nonresident, the income is generally treated as foreign-source. For this purpose, a *U.S. resident* is a U.S. citizen or resident alien who has a tax home in the U.S., a nonresident alien who has a tax home in the United States, and any corporation, trust, or estate that is a United States person [Code Sec. 865(g)(1)(A)].

U.S. citizens and resident aliens whose tax homes are outside the U.S. will not be treated as nonresidents for a sale of personal property unless an income tax of at least 10 percent of the gain on the sale is paid to a foreign country [Code Sec. 865(g)(2)]. However, this rule does not apply to the sale of certain stock by taxpayers who were bona fide residents of Puerto Rico for the entire tax year. The stock must be in a corporation that is engaged in an active trade or business in Puerto Rico from which it derives more than 50 percent of its gross income for the three-year period ending with the close of the corporation's tax year immediately preceding the year of sale [Code Sec. 865(g)(3)]. Instead, the Puerto Rico residents benefit from the tax exemption that applies to Puerto Rico-source income [Code Sec. 933].

Inventory

Income from the sale of inventory property generally is sourced to the place where title to the property passes from seller to buyer [Code Sec. 865(b), Reg. § 1.861-7(c)]. However, there are instances when the location of title passage does not determine the source of the income. When a nonresident alien maintains an office or other fixed place of business in the United States, income from the sale of personal property (including inventory property) attributable to the United States office is sourced to the United States [Code Sec. 865(e)(2)(A)].

Intangibles

The term *intangible* means any patent, copyright, secret process or formula, goodwill, trademark, trade brand, or other like property [Code Sec. 865(d)(2)]. When intangibles are employed to generate income that is contingent on the intangibles' productivity, the source of the income is determined in accordance with the location of the intangible [Code Secs. 865(d)(1)(B), 861(a)(4)]. Thus, a U.S. copyright generates U.S. source income.

To the extent that a sale of an intangible generates payments that are not contingent on the productivity of the intangible, the source of the payments is determined according to the place of residence of the intangible's owner [Code Sec. 865(d)(1)(A)]. Thus, an outright sale of a U.S. copyright by a nonresident alien generates foreign source income. An exception to this rule exists if the owner of the intangible takes depreciation deductions with respect to the intangible [Code Sec. 865(d)(4)(A)]. The gain realized on the sale of the intangible, to the extent it does not exceed the depreciation deductions, is sourced to the United States in the same proportion as the U.S. depreciation deductions bear to the total depreciation deductions taken with respect to the intangible [Code Sec. 865(c)(1)(A)]. The gain in excess of the depreciation deductions is sourced based on the residence of the intangible's owner [Code Sec. 865(d)(4)(B)].

The general rule for sourcing income from the sale of goodwill not contingent on its productivity treats the income as from sources in the country in which such goodwill was generated [Code Sec. 865(d)(3)]. To the extent that goodwill may be depreciated, the amount of gain not in excess of the depreciation deductions is sourced as gain from the sale of the other intangibles.

Depreciation and Amortization

The residence-of-the-seller rule doesn't apply to income from the sale of depreciable personal property to the extent of prior depreciation deductions. The source of that income is determined under a recapture rule. If depreciation deductions have been allocated against U.S.-or foreign-source income, then gain from the sale of depreciable property must be similarly treated. Gain in excess of those deductions is treated as if the property were inventory property. If certain depreciable property is used predominantly within or outside the U.S. in a tax year, the allowable depreciation deductions are allocated entirely against either U.S.-or foreign-source income, respectively. Gain in excess of the depreciation deductions is sourced the same as inventory property; i.e., where title to the property passed. However, if personal property is used predominantly in the U.S., the gain from the sale, to the extent of the allowable depreciation deductions, is treated entirely as U.S.-source income. If the property is used predominantly outside the U.S., the gain, to the extent of the depreciation deductions, is treated entirely as foreign-source income [Code Sec. 865(c)].

Likewise, to the extent of previously allowed amortization deductions from the sale of intangible property, the source of the income is determined under the recapture rule. The recapture rule applies whether or not payments are contingent on the productivity, use or disposition of the property. When payments are contingent, the source of all payments should be determined under the recapture rule until the entire recapture amount has been recaptured, and any remaining payments are sourced under the general intangible rules. The source of gain from the sale of intangible property in excess of amortization recapture is determined under the residence-of-the-seller rule when the payments aren't contingent on the productivity, use or disposition of the property. When payments are contingent, the source rule for royalties applies to the gain [Code Sec. 865(d)(4)].

Income earned by U.S. residents from selling personal property and certain intangible property through an office or other fixed place of business outside the U.S. is treated as foreign-source if (1) the income from the sale is attributable to the business operations located outside the U.S. and (2) at least 10 percent of the income is paid as tax to the foreign country. If less than 10 percent is paid as tax, the income is U.S.-source [Code Sec. 865(e)].

¶28,020 ADJUSTMENT TO THE CREDIT FOR FOREIGN TAX REFUND

If taxpayers receive a foreign tax refund, they must file an amended U.S. income tax return immediately, so that their U.S. taxes can be redetermined. If the foreign tax is refunded without interest, their tax deficiency will not include interest. If the foreign tax refund is received with interest, their deficiency will include the interest received, but not exceeding the appropriate rate of interest on the U.S. tax due. Annual interest is charged from the date of the refund until the deficiency is paid.[11]

¶28,025 CREDIT FOR CORPORATE SHAREHOLDERS IN FOREIGN CORPORATIONS

A domestic corporation that owns at least 10 percent of the voting stock of a foreign corporation from which it receives dividends, may claim a credit for the taxes attributable to those dividends paid by the foreign corporation [Code Sec. 902(a); Reg. § 1.902-1(a)]. The following formula is used to figure taxes which the domestic corporation is considered to have paid (the "deemed-paid" foreign tax credit):

[11] Rev. Rul. 58-244, 1958-1 CB 265.

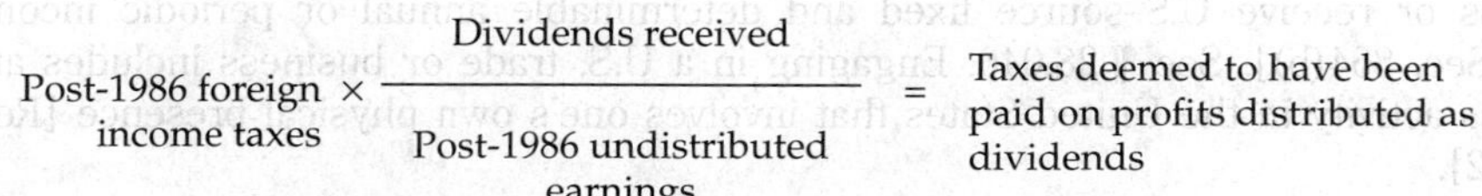

$$\text{Post-1986 foreign income taxes} \times \frac{\text{Dividends received}}{\text{Post-1986 undistributed earnings}} = \text{Taxes deemed to have been paid on profits distributed as dividends}$$

Example 28-5: A Corp. (a U.S. corporation) owns 50 percent of the voting stock of B Corp. (a foreign corporation). B Corp. earned $100,000 before taxes and paid a foreign income tax of $20,000. Out of the remaining $80,000 it paid a dividend of $40,000 to A Corp. A Corp. includes in income $50,000, which is the gross-up of the $40,000 dividend and the $10,000 of tax it is deemed to have paid, computed as follows:

$$\$20{,}000 \times \frac{\$40{,}000}{\$80{,}000} = \$10{,}000$$

The deemed-paid foreign tax credit of a U.S. corporation owning at least 10 percent of the voting stock of a foreign corporation is computed with reference to the pool of the distributing corporation's post-1986 accumulated earnings and profits and accumulated foreign taxes [Code Sec. 902(a)]. This is intended to prevent taxpayers from losing deemed-paid credits because the foreign corporation had a deficit in earnings and profits in some years that the IRS considered to reduce accumulated profits (for prior years in which foreign taxes were paid), reducing the amount of creditable taxes. This provision also limits the taxpayer's ability to average high-tax and low-tax years, resulting in a deemed-paid credit that reflects a higher than average foreign tax rate over a period of years.

The amount of dividends received for purposes of the deemed-paid credit may include earnings currently taxed to domestic corporations that own at least 10 percent of the stock in a controlled foreign corporation [¶ 28,085] [Code Sec. 960(a)]. In this case, the domestic corporation cannot claim a duplicate increase in the foreign tax credit limit when the earnings are actually distributed by the foreign corporation. However, the domestic corporation may be entitled to increase the limit by the amount of taxes paid directly on the distribution (such as withholding tax) [Code Sec. 960(b)]. The limit is simply increased by the direct taxes paid (but not more than the amount in a special "excess limitation account") [Code Sec. 960(b)].

FOREIGN TAXPAYERS

¶28,030 HOW FOREIGN TAXPAYERS ARE TAXED

.01 Resident and Nonresident Aliens

The U.S. taxes *resident* aliens in the same manner that it taxes U.S. citizens—their worldwide income, whatever its source, is subject to U.S. income taxes [¶ 28,035, ¶ 28,050]. But *nonresident* aliens and foreign corporations are taxed differently. The United States generally taxes nonresident aliens only if they engage in a U.S. trade or business or receive U.S.-source fixed and determinable annual or periodic income [Code Sec. 864(b)]. See ¶ 28,040. Engaging in a U.S. trade or business includes any business activity in the United States that involves one's own physical presence [Reg. § 1.864-2].

A nonresident alien engaged in a U.S. trade or business is taxed on income that is effectively connected with the conduct of that trade or business [Code Sec. 882(a)(1)]. See ¶ 28,050. Different rules are applied depending on whether or not the income is U.S.-source income. In the case of U.S.-source income that is effectively connected with a U.S. trade or business, a nonresident alien will be subject to the graduated tax rates applicable to U.S. residents.

In the case of U.S.-source income that is not effectively connected with a U.S. trade or business and consists of rents, dividends, royalties, or other fixed or determinable annual or periodic income, the nonresident alien will be subject to a flat 30-percent withholding tax. If a treaty applies, the withholding amount may be reduced.

Royalty income paid for the right to use intangible property generally is sourced where the property is used or is granted the privilege of being used [Code Secs. 861(a)(4) and 862(a)(4)]. For example, royalty income received for the use of trademarks in making foreign sales is sourced outside the United States.[12]

In *R. Goosen,*[13] the Tax Court concluded that a nonresident alien professional golfer's endorsement income was allocable both between U.S.-source and non-U.S.-source income and between personal service income and royalty income.

Exceptions

Expatriates from the U.S. may be subject to U.S. tax on all their U.S.-source income if they relinquished their citizenship to avoid tax [¶ 28,040].

Tax treaties between foreign countries and the U.S. may result in foreign taxpayers from those countries receiving special tax treatment for various income items [¶ 28,060]. United States tax treaties with many countries call for a reduction of the tax rate imposed by those foreign jurisdictions on income paid to U.S. citizens and businesses investing or operating in those countries. If the individual proves U.S. residency under some of these treaties, the host country will allow withholding of that country's tax rate at the treaty-reduced rate.

Taxpayers working or investing overseas who need proof of U.S. residence to qualify for lower treaty rates must use Form 8802, *Application for U.S. Residency Certification.* The Form replaces the previous procedure that required taxpayers to send the IRS a letter explaining why they were entitled to lower foreign tax rates.

Tax discrimination against U.S. citizens or corporations by a foreign country may lead to higher taxation of citizens and corporations of that country. In such cases, a Presidential proclamation can double the U.S. tax rate (up to 80 percent of taxable income) for citizens and corporations of the foreign country or impose the same discriminatory tax

---

[12] Rev. Rul. 68-443, 1968-2 CB 304.

[13] *R. Goosen,* 136 TC 547, Dec. 58,655 (2011); see also *S. Garcia,* 140 TC No. 6, Dec. 59,484 (2013).

on the U.S. income of citizens and corporations coming from the offending country [Code Secs. 891, 896].

.02 Withholding Requirements

Payments of U.S. source income to foreign persons create a number of withholding and information reporting obligations for both the payor and the recipient of these payments. Specifically, under Code Sec. 871(a), nonresident alien individuals are subject to a 30 percent tax (unless reduced under an income tax treaty entered into between the United States and the foreign country) on certain items of income they receive from sources within the United States that are not effectively connected with the conduct of a trade or business in the United States. Code Sec. 871(a)(1) taxes nonresident aliens on all "interest . . . , dividends, rents, salaries, wages, premiums, annuities, compensations, remunerations, emoluments, and other fixed or determinable annual or periodical gains, profits, and income" that are received from sources in the United States.

Gambling winnings paid to a nonresident alien fall within this provision, except for wagers placed in "blackjack, baccarat, craps, roulette, or big-6 wheel [Code Sec. 871(j)]. The IRS taxes nonresident alien gamblers differently from U.S. citizen gamblers. The IRS allows U.S. citizens to subtract losses from their wins within a gambling session to arrive at a per-session taxable win or loss. But, for non-resident aliens, the IRS applies a per-bet rule which means that a nonresident generally cannot deduct or offset gambling losses against gambling winnings [Code Sec. 873]. In *S.J. Park*,[14] the Court of Appeals for the D.C. Circuit reversed the Tax Court to hold that a nonresident alien who has gambling winnings in the United States must determine gain or loss on a per-session basis rather than on a per-bet basis.

> **Example 28-6:** A U.S. citizen who is playing slots first wins $100 but then loses the $100 before leaving the casino for the night. In that hypothetical, the U.S. citizen would have $0 in income to report because only gains measured over a single gambling session are subject to tax.

> **Example 28-7:** A nonresident alien also wins $100 and then loses $100. The nonresident alien has $100 in income to report (the $100 he won in the initial bet) because the IRS interprets the applicable provision to require non-resident aliens to pay taxes on gains *from each bet*.

The tax liability imposed under Code Sec. 871(a) on the payment of items of income is generally collected by way of withholding at the source pursuant to Code Sec. 1441(a). The withholding agent is generally the person who has control, receipt, custody, disposal, or payment of amounts that are paid to the foreign taxpayer. Withholding agents are generally required to report payments of such income to the IRS on Form 1042-S.

---

[14] *S.J. Park*, CA-DC, 2013-2 USTC ¶50,423, 722 F3d 384.

Exception for U.S. Source Income

Code Sec. 871(i)(2)(D) provides that the 30-percent withholding tax is no longer required on dividends of foreign corporations that are treated as U.S. source income under the 25-percent source rule of Code Sec. 861(a)(2)(B). If a foreign corporation derives 25 percent or more of its gross income as income effectively connected with a U.S. trade or business for the three-year period ending with the close of the tax year preceding the declaration of the dividend, then a portion of a dividend paid to its shareholders will be U.S. source income [Code Sec. 861(a)(2)(B)]. The portion of the dividend that is treated as U.S. source income is equal to the ratio of the gross income of the foreign corporation that was effectively connected income with its U.S. trade or business over the total gross income of the foreign corporation during the three-year period ending with the close of the preceding tax year.

U.S. Source Dividends Paid to Puerto Rico Corporations Subject to Reduced Tax and Withholding

U.S. source dividends paid to a Puerto Rico corporation are subject to U.S. taxation and withholding at a 10-percent rate [Code Secs. 881(b)(2)(A) and 1442(c)(2)(A)]. The 10-percent tax and withholding rate for U.S. source dividends paid to Puerto Rico corporations applies if: (1) at all times during the tax year less than 25 percent in value of the Puerto Rico corporation's stock is beneficially owned (directly or indirectly) by foreign persons; (2) at least 65 percent of the Puerto Rico corporation's gross income is shown to the satisfaction of the IRS to be effectively connected with the conduct of a trade or business in Puerto Rico or in the United States for the three-year period ending with the close of the tax year of the corporation; and (3) no substantial part of the income of the Puerto Rico corporation is used (either directly or indirectly) to satisfy obligations to persons who are not bona fide residents of Puerto Rico or the United States [Code Secs. 881(b)(2)(A) and 1442(c)(2)(A)].

.03 Withholding Agents May Obtain ITINs for Foreigners Claiming Treaty Benefits

The 30-percent withholding rate can be reduced under an income tax treaty entered into between the United States and the foreign country. A withholding agent may generally rely on a Form W-8BEN, *Certificate of Foreign Status of Beneficial Owner for United States Tax Withholding,* or Form 8233, *Exemption From Withholding on Compensation for Independent (and Certain Dependent) Personal Services of a Nonresident Alien Individual,* provided by, or for, the foreign individual certifying eligibility for a reduced rate of tax under an income tax treaty. Reg. § 1.1441-1(e)(4)(vii) generally provides that a taxpayer identifying number (TIN) must be furnished on a Form W-8BEN or Form 8233 in order for a foreign individual to obtain the benefit of reduced withholding under an income tax treaty [Reg. § 1.1441-6(b)(2)(ii)]. If a foreign individual receiving such an unexpected payment currently is unable to obtain a TIN prior to payment, the withholding agent would be required to withhold tax at the 30-percent rate, rather than the treaty rate, and the foreign individual would be required to file for a refund in order to obtain the benefits of the income tax treaty.

In order to reduce the burden on foreign individuals receiving unexpected payments, the IRS will permit certain withholding agents to enter into special acceptance agent agreements with the IRS that will allow those withholding agents, in their capacity as acceptance agents, to seek ITINs through an expedited process for these foreign individuals claiming treaty benefits [Reg. § 1.1441-6 (g) (1)]. It is anticipated that any withholding agent who qualifies as an acceptance agent under Reg. § 301.6109-1 (d) (3) (iv) and who anticipates making unexpected payments will be allowed to enter into such an agreement. However, the IRS will allow the use of the expedited process only when an application for an ITIN using the standard process will not generate an ITIN in time for the payment.

In limited circumstances, a withholding agent who has entered into such a special acceptance agent agreement may rely on a beneficial owner withholding certificate without regard to the requirement that it include a TIN. In order for a withholding agent to rely on a beneficial owner withholding certificate that does not contain a TIN, the withholding agent must be unable to obtain an ITIN for the foreign individual because the IRS is not issuing ITINs at the time of an unexpected payment to the individual or any time prior to the time of payment when the withholding agent had knowledge of the unexpected payment and the nature of the unexpected payment must be such that it cannot reasonably be delayed until the withholding agent could obtain an ITIN for the foreign individual through the use of the expedited process. The regulations further provide that the IRS must receive the foreign individual's application for an ITIN on the first business day following payment [Reg. § 1.1441-6(g) (2)].

Except as provided in these regulations or in Reg. § 1.1441-6(c), a foreign individual will continue to be required to provide a TIN on a beneficial owner withholding certificate (Form W-8BEN or Form 8233) in order to obtain the benefit of a reduced rate of withholding under an income tax treaty.

¶28,035 RESIDENT ALIENS

Generally, resident aliens are taxed the same as U.S. citizens [Reg. § 1.871-1]. This means that they are taxed on their worldwide income.

.01 Who Is a Resident Alien?

Code Sec. 7702(b) (1) (A) provides that an alien will be treated as a U.S. resident for federal income tax purposes if the individual:

1. Is a lawful permanent resident of the U.S. at any time during the year [Code Sec. 7702(b) (1) (A) (i); Reg. § 301.7701(b)-1(b)]. This is known as the "green card test."
2. Meets a "substantial presence" test [Code Sec. 7702(b) (1) (A) (ii); Reg. § 301.7701(b)-1(c)]; or
3. Makes the first year election under Code Sec. 7701(b) (4) [Code Sec. 7702(b) (1) (A) (iii)].

An alien who fails to satisfy these requirements will be treated as a nonresident alien for federal tax purposes [Code Sec. 7701(b) (1) (B)]. The rules are not intended to override any U.S. treaty obligation, even though they will govern determination of residency for U.S. tax purposes [Reg. § 301.7701(b) (1) (a)].

Green Card Test

An alien who has been lawfully given the privilege of residing permanently in the United States as an immigrant is deemed to be a lawful permanent resident of the United States unless the status has been revoked or judicially or administratively determined to have been abandoned. This also is referred to as the green card test [Reg. § 301.7701(b)-1(b)].

Lawful Permanent Resident

An individual whose expatriation date is on or after June 17, 2008, will cease to be treated as a lawful permanent resident if that individual: (1) begins to be treated as a resident of a foreign country under the provisions of a tax treaty between the United States and the foreign country, (2) does not waive the benefits of the treaty applicable to residents of the foreign country, and (3) notifies the Secretary of the commencement of such treatment [Code Sec. 7701(b)(6)].

Substantial Presence Test

An alien who is physically present in the United States for at least 31 days during the calendar year and a total of 183 days during the last three years meets the substantial presence test. For purposes of the 183-day requirement, each day present in the U.S. during the current calendar year counts as a full day, each day in the first preceding year as one-third of a day, and each day in the second preceding year as one-sixth of a day [Code Sec. 7701(b)(3)(A); Reg. § 301.7701(b)-1(c)(1)].

Days excluded under substantial presence test. Any day is excluded as a day of presence for purposes of the substantial presence test if the alien individual is physically present in the United States on that day and is an individual who is:

- Exempt,
- Physically unable to leave the United States because of a medical condition,
- In transit between two points outside the United States, or
- A commuter [Reg. § 301.7701(b)-3(a)].

Exempt individuals. For purposes of calculating days of presence, exempt individuals who may exclude days that they are present in the United States include certain foreign-government individuals (including full-time employees of an international organization), teachers or trainees, students and professional athletes [Code Sec. 7701(b)(5)(A); Reg. § 301.7701(b)-3(b)].

Teachers, trainees and students must substantially comply with relevant visa requirements to qualify as exempt. An individual is considered to have substantially complied with the visa requirements if he or she has not engaged in any activity prohibited by the Immigration and Nationality Act. That an individual's visa has not been revoked is irrelevant in determining substantial compliance [Reg. § 301.7701(b)-3(b)(6)]. The immediate family of a foreign government alien or an organization-related alien, and a teacher, a trainee or a student may also qualify for exemption [Reg. § 301.7701(b)-3(b)(2)].

Medical condition in transit. An individual will not be considered present on any day that the individual intends to leave but is unable to do so because of a medical condition or medical problem that arose while he or she was present in the U.S. [Reg. § 301.7701(b)-3(c)(1)]. A preexisting condition will not be considered to arise while an individual is in the U.S. if the problem existed prior to the individual's arrival in the U.S. and the individual was aware of the condition. Whether or not the individual sought treatment for condition is irrelevant to the determination of exemption of days in the calculation of presence [Reg. § 301.7701(b)-3(c)(3)].

Commuters. An individual who regularly commutes for business purposes from the U.S. to his or her residence in Canada or Mexico is not considered to be present in the U.S. on the days commuted to a place of employment and back to his or her residence within a 24-hour period [Code Sec. 7701(b)(7)(B); Reg. § 301.7701(b)-3(e)]. In order to be a regular commuter, the alien must commute to the United States on more than 75 percent of the workdays in the working period.

Crew members of foreign vessels. Regular crew members of foreign vessels engaged in transportation between the U.S. and a foreign country or U.S. possession are not considered present in the U.S. for purposes of the substantial presence test on any day that they are temporarily present in the U.S., unless they otherwise engage in trade or business on that day [Code Sec. 7701(b)(7)(D)].

Closer connection exception. An alien individual who otherwise meets the substantial presence test will not be deemed to be a U.S. resident if that person:

1. Has a tax home (as defined in Code Sec. 911(d)(3)];
2. Has a closer connection to a foreign country; and
3. Is present in the U.S. for fewer than 183 days during the current calendar year [Reg. § 301.7701(b)-2].

   Alien individuals meeting the closer connection exception must file a statement outlined at Reg. § 301.7701(b)-8 to prove that they satisfy the exception.

First Year Election

An individual alien who moves to the United States too late in the year to meet the substantial presence test under Code Sec. 7701(b)(3) and does not otherwise qualify as a resident, may elect to be a resident for part of that year. This election is effective for a portion of a single calendar year referred to as the election year. To qualify for the election, the alien:

1. Must not have qualified as a resident for the calendar year immediately preceding the election year;
2. Must qualify as a resident under the substantial presence test in the calendar year immediately following the election year;
3. Must be present in the U.S. for at least 31 consecutive days in the election year; and
4. Must be present in the U.S. for at least 75 percent of the number of days in the period beginning with the first day of the 31-day presence and ending with the last day of the election year.

In applying the 75-percent test, an individual will be treated as present in the U.S. for up to five days during which he or she was actually absent from the country [Code Sec. 7701(b)(4)(A)].

An alien individual who makes the election will be treated as a resident for that portion of the election year that begins on the first day of the earliest presence period that satisfies both the 31-day and 75-percent tests.

The election is made on the alien's tax return for the election year, but it may not be made before the individual has met the substantial presence test for the calendar year following the election year. Once made, the election can be revoked only with IRS consent [Reg. § 301.7701(b)-4(c)(3)(v)]. An alien individual may be required to file a statement to delineate the basis upon which he or she is claiming United States residency status. Thus, an alien individual who otherwise meets the substantial presence test must file a:

- Statement to explain the basis of the individual's claim that he or she is able to satisfy the closer connection exception under [Reg. § § 301.7701(b)-2, 301.7701(b)-8(a)(1)];
- An alien individual must file a statement to explain the basis of the individual's claim that he or she is able to exclude days of presence in the U.S. because he or she is either exempt or has a medical condition [Reg. § 301.7701(b)-8(a)2]; and
- A statement must be filed by an individual who is seeking to establish that a period of *de minimis* presence of ten or fewer days should be disregarded for purposes of the his or her residency starting or termination date [Reg. § 301.7701(b)-8(a)(3)].

The statement must be made on a fully completed Form 8840, *Closer Connection Exception Statement for Aliens,* or Form 8843, *Statement for Exempt Individuals and Individuals with a Medical Condition,* and attached to the alien individual's return for the tax year the statement is relevant [Reg. § 301.7701(b)-8(b)].

In the case of an individual seeking to establish a period of de minimis presence, the statement must also contain the following information:

1. The first and last day that the individual was present in the U.S. during the current year;
2. The dates of *de minimis* presence that the individual is seeking to exclude from his or her residency starting or termination dates;
3. Sufficient facts to establish that the individual has maintained his or her tax home in and a closer connection with a foreign country during a period of *de minimis* presence and following the individual's last day of presence in the U.S. during the current year or following the abandonment of his or her status as a lawful permanent resident during the current year;
4. The date that the individual's status as a lawful permanent resident was abandoned or rescinded; and
5. Sufficient facts (including copies of relevant documents) to establish that the individual's status as a lawful permanent resident has been abandoned or rescinded [Reg. § 301.7701(b)-8(b)].

An alien individual who is required to file a statement and who fails to do so may be required to include all days of presence in the U.S. This "penalty" will not apply if the alien individual can establish by clear and convincing evidence that he or she took reasonable steps to become aware of the filing requirements [Reg. § 301.7701(b)-8(d)].

.02 Tax on Resident Aliens

A resident alien must pay income tax on all income, whether it comes from inside or outside the United States. The resident alien may claim the same deductions that a U.S. citizen can, and similar personal and dependency exemptions. Also, the resident alien may claim the foreign tax credit [¶ 28,001] (which may be reduced if the home country does not provide a reciprocal credit) [Code Sec. 901(c)].

.03 Dual-Status Aliens

A taxpayer who is both a resident and nonresident alien in the same tax year (usually the years of arrival and departure) is taxed on income from all sources for the part of the year that he or she is a resident alien, but only on U.S.-source income for the part of the year that he or she is a nonresident alien. Form 1040 is filed with Form 1040NR used as an attachment.

¶28,040 NONRESIDENT ALIENS

A nonresident alien is generally subject to U.S. income tax at graduated rates only on income effectively connected to a U.S. trade or business and a 30 percent tax, or a reduced treaty rate, on certain U.S. source passive type income, known as fixed or determinable, annual and periodical income, or FDAP [Code Sec. 871(a); Reg. § 1.871-1(a)].

.01 Filing Exception for Nonresident Aliens

Generally, the requirement to file a return has been eliminated for nonresident aliens who earn wages effectively connected with a U.S. trade or business that are less than the amount of one personal exemption which is $3,900 in 2013.

.02 Who Is a Nonresident Alien?

A nonresident alien is an individual alien (including a fiduciary and a citizen of a U.S. possession) who does not meet the definition of a resident alien [¶ 28,035].

.03 Tax on Nonresident Aliens

A nonresident alien may not: (1) file a joint return (unless married to a U.S. citizen or resident) [Code Sec. 6013(g)], (2) use the Tax Table or Tax Rate Schedule for single individuals if married individuals filing separately, or (3) file head of household returns [Code Sec. 2(b)(3)(A)]. Nonresident aliens are not subject to the self-employment tax [Code Sec. 1402(b)].

> **NOTE:** If nonresident aliens are married to a U.S. citizen or resident, they can elect to be taxed as a resident to take advantage of the joint filing option. However, once this election is made, their world wide income is subject to tax, even though the income might have been otherwise exempt under a tax treaty [Reg. § 1.6013-6].

Deductions

Nonresident aliens are generally not allowed deductions from income that are not connected with their U.S. business activities. Except for personal exemptions and certain itemized deductions (i.e., certain contributions to IRAs or Keogh plans or self-employed health insurance costs), deductions are allowed only to the extent that they are related to effectively connected income. If nonresident aliens establish that they are in the U.S. on temporary assignment, they may be able to deduct ordinary and necessary travel expenses.[15]

Capital Gains and Losses

If effectively connected with U.S. trade or business [¶28,050], a nonresident alien's capital gains and losses are treated the same as those of U.S. citizens [Ch. 8]. All other capital gains are taxed at a flat 30 percent (or lower treaty) rate, but only if the nonresident alien spent a total of at least 183 days in the U.S. during the tax year [Code Sec. 871(a)(2)].

Interest

If a taxpayer receives interest on portfolio obligations issued after July 18, 1984, the interest is not subject to the 30 percent tax. However, this tax continues to apply to existing obligations subject to tax. Two types of portfolio debt are involved: (1) interest paid on certain obligations not in registered form (bearer debt) and (2) interest paid on an obligation in registered form (registered debt), for which a statement is filed that the beneficial owner is not a U.S. person [Code Sec. 871(h)]. See Ch. 15.

Contingent interest generally cannot qualify as portfolio interest and, therefore, generally cannot avoid the 30 percent tax. This includes interest contingent on the debtor's cash flow, the value of property or a dividend, partnership distribution or other payment made to the debtor. However, fixed-term debt issued or agreed on before April 8, 1993 is not affected by this new rule.

Earned Income Tax Credit

Individuals who are nonresident aliens for any part of the tax year will be ineligible to claim the earned income tax credit (EITC) unless they are covered by an election to be treated as a U.S. resident for that year [Code Secs. 6013(g), (h), 32(c)(1)(E)]. This change was made because nonresident aliens generally are not required to report their foreign-source income on their U.S. individual income tax returns. As a result it was possible for them to qualify for the EITC on the basis of low U.S. earned income even when their worldwide income exceeded the income phaseout limits for the EITC. The change prevents nonresident aliens from claiming the EITC unless they are married and agree to subject their worldwide income to U.S. individual income tax by virtue of making the election under Code Sec. 6013(g), (h).

.04 Returns and Payment of Tax

Nonresident aliens file Form 1040NR. They can claim the deductions and credits allowable to them only if they file accurate returns that contain the necessary information [Code Sec. 874(a); Reg. § 1.874-1(a)]. If they have wages subject to withholding, they must file returns and pay taxes at the same time and manner as U.S. citizens. If they do not have wages subject to withholding, they must file a return

[15] Treas. Dept., IRS Publication 519, "U.S. Tax Guide for Aliens" (2013 Ed.), p. 29.

and pay taxes by the 15th day of the sixth month after the close of the tax year. For withholding from nonresident aliens, see Ch. 15.

.05 Waiver for Foreign Taxpayers Filing Late Returns

A nonresident alien individual engaged in a trade or business within the United States will be taxed on income effectively connected with the conduct of the trade or business within the United States [Code Sec. 871(b)(1)]. Similarly, a foreign corporation engaged in a trade or business within the United States is taxed on its income effectively connected with the conduct of the trade or business within the United States [Code Sec. 882(a)(1)]. In determining the amount of effectively connected taxable income, both the nonresident alien individual and the foreign corporation (collectively, "foreign taxpayers") generally may deduct from effectively connected gross income expenses that are properly allocated and apportioned to that gross income. However, under Code Secs. 874(a)(1) and 882(c)(2), a foreign taxpayer generally is entitled to those deductions, and to allowable credits, only if it files a true and accurate U.S. income tax return including on the return all the information necessary for the calculation of the deductions and credits.

The filing deadlines may be waived if the nonresident alien individual establishes that he or she acted reasonably and in good faith in failing to file a U.S. income tax return (including a protective return). A nonresident alien individual will not be considered to have acted reasonably and in good faith if the individual knew that he or she was required to file the return and chose not to do so. In addition, a nonresident alien individual will not be granted a waiver unless the individual cooperates in determining his or her U.S. income tax liability for the tax year for which the return was not filed. The following factors in determining whether the nonresident alien individual, based on the facts and circumstances, acted reasonably and in good faith in failing to file a U.S. income tax return [Reg. § 1.874-1(b)(2)]:

i. Whether the individual voluntarily identifies himself or herself to the IRS as having failed to file a U.S. income tax return before the IRS discovers the failure to file;

ii. Whether the individual did not become aware of his or her ability to file a protective return by the deadline for filing the protective return;

iii. Whether the individual had not previously filed a U.S. income tax return;

iv. Whether the individual failed to file a U.S. income tax return because, after exercising reasonable diligence (taking into account his or her relevant experience and level of sophistication), the individual was unaware of the necessity for filing the return;

v. Whether the individual failed to file a U.S. income tax return because of intervening events beyond the individual's control; and

vi. Whether other mitigating or exacerbating factors existed.

Example 28-8: In Year 1, A is a nonresident alien individual who became a limited partner with a passive investment in a U.S. limited partnership that was engaged in a U.S. trade or business. During Year 1 through Year 4, A's U.S. partnership interest incurred losses. A's foreign tax advisor incorrectly concluded that because A was a limited partner and had only losses from A's partnership interest, A was not required to file a U.S. income tax return. A was aware neither of his obligation to file a U.S. income tax return for those years nor of A's ability to file a protective return for those years. A had never filed a U.S. income tax return before. In Year 5, A began realizing a profit rather than a loss with respect to the partnership interest and, for this reason, engaged a U.S. tax advisor to handle A's responsibility to file U.S. income tax returns. In preparing A's U.S. income tax return for Year 5, A's U.S. tax advisor discovered that returns were not filed for Year 1 through Year 4. Therefore, with respect to those years for which filing deadlines were not met, A would be barred from claiming any deductions that otherwise would have given rise to net operating losses on returns for these years, and that would have been available as loss carryforwards in subsequent years. At A's direction, A's U.S. tax advisor promptly contacted the appropriate examining personnel and cooperated with the IRS in determining A's income tax liability, for example, by preparing and filing the appropriate income tax returns for Year 1 through Year 4 and by making A's books and records available to an IRS examiner. A has met the standard for waiver of any applicable filing deadlines [Reg. § 1.874-1(b)(3), Ex. 1].

¶28,045 FOREIGN CORPORATIONS

.01 In General

Any corporation not organized or created in the U.S. is a foreign corporation [Reg. § 301.7701-5]. Foreign corporations, like nonresident aliens, are taxed generally only on U.S.-source income, but they are taxed at different rates depending on whether the U.S. income is business or nonbusiness connected (i.e., investment income).

Tax on Foreign Corporations

All U.S.-source income that is effectively connected with a foreign corporation's U.S. business [¶ 28,050] is taxed at the regular U.S. corporate rate [¶ 20,010] [Code Sec. 882]. In this connection, capital gains effectively connected with a U.S. business are taxed at the regular U.S. corporate rate [¶ 28,040]. U.S.-source nonbusiness investment income [¶ 28,050] generally is taxed at a flat 30 percent rate unless a lower rate is set by an applicable tax treaty [Code Sec. 881, 894(a)]. As in the case of nonresident aliens, however, interest paid to foreign corporations on certain debt instruments is not subject to the 30 percent tax [Code Sec. 881(c)]. For the treatment of gain from the disposition of U.S. real property and for an election to treat investment income from real property as business income, see ¶ 28,050.

Fixed or Determinable Annual or Periodical Income

Code Sec. 881(a) imposes a 30-percent tax on "fixed or determinable annual or periodical" (FDAP) income received from sources within the United States by a foreign corporation, "but only to the extent the amount so received is not effectively connected with the conduct of a trade or business within the United States." Taxes owed under Code Sec. 881(a) are generally supposed to be withheld at the source [Code Sec. 1442(a)]. Thus, in order for a company to be liable under Code Sec. 881(a) the amount received must be (1) FDAP income and (2) received from a U.S. source [Code Sec. 881(a)].

The rules in Code Sec. 861 to 863 are used to determine FDAP income's source. Two rules are especially important here. The first rule addresses interest and provides that the source of interest is the residence of the obligor [Code Secs. 861(a)(1), 862(a)(1); Reg. § 1.861-2]. The second rule addresses services and provides that the source of services is where the services are performed [Code Sec. 861(a)(3); Reg. § 1.861-4].

In *Container Corp.*,[16] the Court of Appeals for the Fifth Circuit affirmed the Tax Court to conclude that guarantee fees paid by a U.S. subsidiary corporation to its Mexican parent were not U.S. source income subject to the 30-percent tax on FDAP income. The guarantee fees were more closely analogous to a fee for services, which is sourced to where the services are performed (here, Mexico), than to a payment of interest, which is sourced to the residence of the obligor (here, the United States). The guarantee lacked a principal characteristic of a loan because the parent corporation in this case did not extend funds to its subsidiary. Moreover, the parent corporation was not directly liable on the loans, but would only be required to make good on them if the subsidiary defaulted.

Foreign Corporation's Interest Expense Deduction

A foreign corporation computes the amount of interest expense that is allocable under Code Sec. 882(c) to income effectively connected (or treated as effectively connected) with the conduct of its U.S. trade or business under Reg. § 1.882-5.

Reg. § 1.882-5 generally requires a foreign corporation to use a three-step calculation to determine the amount of interest expense that is allocable under Code Sec. 882(c) to income effectively connected (or treated as effectively connected) with the foreign corporation's conduct of a trade or business within the United States. These rules are intended to better reflect current practices in the foreign banking industry and to harmonize the deemed earnings repatriation from a foreign corporation's trade or business within the United States with the way in which dividends are repatriated from U.S. companies to their foreign shareholders.

Under the three-step process, the total value of the U.S. assets of a foreign corporation is first determined (Step 1). Reg. § 1.882-5(b)(2)(ii)(A) provides that a taxpayer should use fair market value rather than adjusted basis in valuing U.S. assets in Step 1.

Next, the amount of U.S.-connected liabilities is determined using fair market value rather than adjusted basis (Step 2). Finally, the amount of interest paid or accrued on U.S.-booked liabilities is adjusted for interest expense attributable to the difference between U.S.-connected liabilities and U.S.-booked liabilities (Step 3). Alternatively, a foreign corporation may elect to determine its interest rate on U.S.-connected liabilities by reference to its U.S. assets, using the separate currency pools method. In Step 3, Reg. § 1.882-5(d)(5)(ii)(B) provides that a foreign bank with excess U.S.-connected liabilities over U.S.-booked liabilities under the adjusted U.S. booked liabilities method

---

[16] *Container Corp.*, CA-5, 2011-1 USTC ¶ 50,351, *aff'g TC in an unpublished opinion, per curiam*, 134 TC 122, Dec. 58,131 (2010).

(AUSBL) can elect to use the 30-day London Interbank Offering Rate (LIBOR) to calculate interest on the excess U.S.-connected liabilities.

Branch Profits Tax

A 30 percent "branch profits tax" is imposed on profits of foreign corporations conducting business in the U.S. [Code Sec. 884(a)]. The base for the branch profits tax (the dividend equivalent amount) is the foreign corporation's effectively connected earnings and profits—reduced for an increase in U.S. net equity and increased for a decrease in U.S. net equity. *U.S. net equity* means U.S. assets (money and adjusted bases of assets) reduced by U.S. liabilities. Provisions are also made for coordinating the branch profits tax with the income tax treaty between the U.S. and a foreign country.

Earnings Stripping Rules

The earnings stripping rules prevent certain tax-exempt foreign corporations from claiming interest deductions through their U.S. subsidiaries. This situation usually arises when a U.S. subsidiary borrows money from a foreign parent corporation. If the subsidiary has too much debt, the earnings stripping rules say that the subsidiary is not allowed to deduct some or all of the interest paid to the parent. The disallowed interest may be carried forward for up to three years [Code Sec. 163(j)]. The earnings stripping rules apply to certain loans taken out by U.S. subsidiaries if the loans are guaranteed by a tax-exempt foreign parent corporation [Code Sec. 163(j)(3)].

Returns and Payment of Tax

Foreign corporations generally file Form 1120F. The returns are due (a) by the 15th day of the third month after the end of the tax year if the foreign corporation has an office or place of business in the U.S. or (b) by the 15th day of the sixth month if it is without an office or place of business in the U.S. [Ch. 26]. In either case, the tax is payable in full with the return [Ch. 26].

A foreign-controlled U.S. corporation or a foreign-controlled foreign corporation engaged in a U.S. trade or business must furnish certain information as to its transactions with any related party. Also, foreign-controlled corporations and U.S.-controlled foreign corporations must furnish information that the IRS requires for carrying out the installment sales rules.

¶28,050 FOREIGN SOURCE INCOME TAXED AT U.S. RATES

.01 Effectively Connected Income

Nonresident aliens and foreign corporations (i.e., foreign persons) are subject to U.S. taxation in the same manner as U.S. persons on income effectively connected with the conduct of a U.S. trade or business [Code Secs 871(b) and 882(a)]. The foreign source income will be subject to U.S. tax if the nonresident alien or foreign corporation has an office or other fixed place of business within the United States and the income specified is attributable to that place of business. The rule applies to three limited categories of foreign source income in certain situations where definite U.S. economic connections exist [Code Sec. 864(c)(4) and Reg. § 1.864-5]. Foreign source income that is deemed effectively connected under the rules of Code Sec. 864(c)(4)(B) must also meet the applicable effectively connected tests of Reg. § 1.864-4 (i.e., the asset-use test, the business-activity test, and the banking-activity test) as if the income were from U.S. sources [Reg. § 1.864-5(a)].

The foreign source income covered by the "effectively connected" rule includes:

1. *Rental and royalty income* received in the active conduct of a licensing business and derived from intangible personal property located outside the United States or from any interest in such property. This includes rentals and royalties for the use of, or for the privilege of using, outside the United States, patents, copyrights, secret processes and formulas, goodwill, trademarks, trade brands, and franchises. It also includes gains or losses from the sale of any such property. Rental or royalty income from real property or from tangible personal property is excluded [Code Sec. 864(c)(4)(B)(i) and Reg. § 1.864-5(b)(1)].
2. *Dividends or interest* derived from the active conduct of a banking, financing, or similar business within the United States, or received by a corporation that has as its principal business trading in stocks or securities for its own account [Code Sec. 864(c)(4)(B)(ii) and Reg. § 1.864-5(b)(2)).
3. *Foreign sales income* attributable to a U.S. office. This covers the foreign sales (i.e., outside of United States) of personal property which is either stock in trade (inventory items) or property held primarily for sale to customers in the ordinary course of business [Code Sec. 864(c)(4)(B)(iii) and Reg. § 1.864-5(b)(3)]. But it does not include property, which is sold for use, consumption, or disposition outside the United States if a foreign office or other place of business materially participated in the sale. However, in the case of products destined for the United States, the income will be treated as effectively connected with a U.S. business to the extent that the sales activities are carried on by the U.S. office. A foreign office or branch is considered to have materially participated in a sale if it (1) solicited the order which is the basis for the sale, (2) negotiated the contract of sale, or (3) performed significant services incident to the sale which were necessary for its consummation and were not subject to a separate agreement between the seller and the buyer. But a foreign office is not deemed to have materially participated in a sale merely because (1) the sale is made subject to the final approval of the foreign office, (2) the property sold was held in, and distributed from, such foreign office, (3) samples of the products are displayed, or (4) the foreign office performed merely clerical functions incident to the sale [Reg. § 1.864-6(b)(3)].

Exceptions

Foreign-source interest, dividends or royalties paid by a foreign corporation in which the recipient owns or is considered as owning more than 50 percent of the combined voting power of all classes of stock in the foreign corporation that are entitled to vote is not considered effectively connected income [Code Sec. 864(c)(4)(D)].

Foreign source income that may be treated as effectively connected income also includes the economic equivalent of the income described above in categories (1) through (3) [Code Sec. 864(c)(4)(B)]. Thus, foreign source income that is the economic equivalent of rents and royalties derived from intangible property could qualify as effectively connected income.

Example 28-9: ABL is a foreign corporation engaged in the conduct of a U.S. trade or business. ABL has an office in Seattle, Washington, where new computer software is developed. ABL enters into an agreement allowing BKR, a foreign corporation with no U.S. office, to use the software. BKR, however, will not pay ABL. Instead, BKR will forgive a portion of a loan owed to it by ABL. The cancellation of indebtedness income is the economic equivalent of rent or royalties paid for the use of the property outside of the United States. Thus, ABL must treat such foreign source income as effectively connected with the conduct of a U.S. trade or business because it is attributable to its office in the United States.

.02 Office or Fixed Place of Business in United States

In order for foreign source income to be considered effectively connected income, the nonresident alien or foreign corporation must have an office or other fixed place of business in the United States [Code Sec. 864(c)(4)(B) and Reg. § 1.864-7]. A facts and circumstances test is used to make this determination and foreign law is not controlling. The nature of the taxpayer's business and its physical facilities must be considered [Reg. § 1.864-7(a)]. Factors to consider include (1) fixed facilities, (2) management activities, (3) agent activity, (4) employee activity, and (5) office or other fixed place of business of a related person. As a general rule, an office or other fixed place of business is a fixed facility, i.e., a place, site, structure, or similar facility through which a nonresident alien or foreign corporation is engaged in a trade or business. Examples of an office or fixed place of business include a factory, store or other sales outlet, a workshop, or a mine, quarry, or other place of extraction of natural resources [Reg. § 1.864-7(b)].

The location of management activities is taken into account when determining if there is an office or fixed place of business. The place where top management decisions are made does not alone indicate where a foreign corporation has an office or fixed place of business. Reg. § 1.864-7(c) requires an examination of the day-to-day trade or business of the foreign corporation. An office or other fixed place of business of an agent is not considered a U.S. office unless the agent is a dependent agent operating in the ordinary course of his trade or business and either has the authority (regularly exercised) to negotiate and conclude contracts in the name of the nonresident alien individual or foreign corporation or has a stock of merchandise from which he regularly fills orders on behalf of the nonresident alien individual or foreign corporation. Authority is regularly exercised if it is exercised with some frequency over a continuous period of time [Code Sec. 864(c)(5)(A) and Reg. § 1.864-7(d)].

The office or fixed place of business of an independent agent will not be treated as the office or fixed place of business of the principal who is a nonresident alien or foreign corporation, irrespective of an authority the agent might have. An independent agent means a general commission agent, broker, or other agent of independent status acting in the ordinary course of his business in that capacity [Code Sec. 864(c)(5)(A); Reg. §§ 1.864-7(d)(2) and 1.864-7(d)(3)].

An employee of a nonresident alien or foreign corporation will be treated as a dependent agent if the employer does not have a fixed facility either inside or outside of the United States. If there is a fixed facility and the employee regularly uses the facility in the ordinary course of his duties carrying on the trade or business of the employer, the office is considered the office or fixed place of business of the employee, despite the rules discussed above for agents [Reg. § 1.864-7(e)]. For example, a foreign corporation that only has a U.S. showroom would have a U.S. office or fixed place of business due to the fact that it has employees in the United States that run the showroom even though the employees have limited independent authority [Reg. § 1.864-7(e), Ex.].

¶28,055 WHAT IS U.S.-SOURCE INCOME?

Aside from the obvious sources such as U.S. business profits, wages and salaries, U.S.-source income includes:

- *Interest from the United States,* such as interest on bonds, notes or other interest-bearing obligations. (This term does not apply to interest on deposits with persons carrying on the banking business, to interest on amounts held by insurance companies under an agreement to pay interest thereon or to interest on deposits with mutual savings banks, savings and loan associations and the like. Furthermore, the term does not include interest from an organization which derives most of its income from foreign sources.)
- *Dividends* from domestic corporations, except those that are allowed to exclude income from U.S. possessions or those which derive most of their income from foreign sources.
- *Wages* or other compensation received for personal services rendered in the United States.
- *Pensions and annuities* received from a domestic trust.
- *Rents or royalties* from property located in the United States.
- *Gain from the sale of real property* located in the United States.
- *Gain from the sale of personal property* purchased outside of the United States.
- *Social security benefits.*

.01 Source Rules

Generally, the rules for determining the source of income from sales of personal property are based on the residence-of-the-seller rule. If the sale is made by a U.S. resident, it's U.S.-source income; if made by a nonresident, its source is outside the United States. There are separate rules applicable to inventory, depreciable personal property, intangibles, sales through offices or fixed places of business and stock of affiliates.

Residency

A taxpayer's "tax home" is controlling. A U.S. citizen or resident alien is a U.S. resident if he or she does not have a tax home in a foreign country. A corporation, trust or estate is a U.S. resident if it is a U.S. person. The residency of partners in a partnership is determined at the partner level when possible. A U.S. citizen or resident alien won' t be considered a resident of another country for a sale of personal property unless a 10 percent income tax on the gain is paid to the country. A nonresident alien is a U.S. resident if he or she has a tax home in the United States. [Code Sec. 865(g)].

Source Rules for U.S. Possessions

A taxpayer must use the same rules for determining whether income is derived from sources within the United States to determine whether income is derived from sources within Puerto Rico, American Samoa, Guam, and the Northern Mariana Islands. An individual will only be considered a bona fide resident of a U.S. possession if: (1) the individual is physically present in the possession for 183 days during the tax year, (2) does not have a home for tax purposes outside the possession during the tax year, and (3) does not have a closer connection to the United States or another country than to the possession [Code Sec. 937(a)].

Reg. § 1.937-1(c)(1) provides that a United States citizen or resident alien individual will be treated as having satisfied the 183-day test if that individual:

1. Was present in the relevant possession for at least 183 days during the tax year;
2. Was present in the relevant possession for at least 549 days during the three-year period consisting of the tax year and the two immediately preceding tax years, provided that the individual was also present in the relevant possession for at least 60 days during each tax year of the period;
3. Was present in the United States for no more than 90 days during the tax year;
4. During the tax year had earned income in the United States, if any, not exceeding $3,000 as specified in Code Sec. 861(a)(3)(B) and was present for more days in the relevant possession than in the United States; or
5. Had no significant connection to the United States during the tax year.

In general, the principles for determining whether income is U.S. source income also apply to determine whether income is possession source. Similarly, the principles for determining whether income is effectively connected with the conduct of a U.S. trade or business apply to determine whether income is effectively connected to a possession trade or business [Reg. § 1.937-3(b)]. See ¶ 28,080.

Inventory

Income from the sale in the U.S. of personal property that is stock in trade or that is held primarily for sale to customers in the ordinary course of the taxpayer's trade or business ordinarily has its source within the U.S., regardless of the location of the taxpayer's tax home. Conversely, income from the sale of inventory property outside the U.S. (even though it was bought within the United States) has its source outside the U.S. [Code Secs. 861(a)(6), 865].

Depreciable Personal Property

For depreciable personal property, to determine the source of any gain from the sale, the taxpayer must first figure the part of the gain that is not in excess of the total depreciation adjustments on the property. This part of the gain is allocated to sources in the U.S. based on the ratio of U.S. depreciation adjustments to total depreciation adjustments. The rest of this part of the gain is considered to be from sources outside the United States. The source of gain from the sale of depreciable property that is in excess of the total depreciation adjustments on the property is determined as if the property were inventory property (see above) [Code Sec. 865(c)].

Intangibles

The source of payments from the sale of intangibles is determined as if they are royalties only to the extent the payments are contingent on the intangible's productivity, use or disposition. Payments from selling goodwill are considered to come from where they are generated [¶ 28,015] [Code Sec. 865(d)].

Offices or Fixed Places of Business

If a nonresident has a U.S. office or other fixed place of business, income from the sale of personal property (including inventory) attributable to the office is from a U.S. source. Exceptions: inventory sold for use, disposition, or consumption outside the U.S. if your office outside the U.S. materially participated in the sale and certain amounts are included in gross income under Code Sec. 951(a)(1)(A). Suppose a U.S. resident maintains a foreign office or other fixed place of business. Then, income from sales of personal property—other than inventory, depreciable property or intangibles—that is attributable to that foreign office or place of business is treated as being from sources outside the U.S. However, this rule does not apply unless an income tax of at least 10 percent of the income from the sale is actually paid to a foreign country [Code Sec. 865(e)].

Stock in a Foreign Corporate Affiliate

Income from the sale of stock in a foreign corporate affiliate by a U.S. resident is foreign-source income if the affiliate is engaged in the active conduct of a trade or business, and the sale takes place in the foreign country in which the affiliate derived more than 50 percent of its gross income during a three-year period [Code Sec. 865(f)].

¶28,060 TAX TREATY PROVISIONS

Tax treaties and conventions with foreign nations are designed to eliminate double taxation of income and to prevent tax evasion. Some income is exempt while other income is taxed or withheld at a lower than normal rate [Ch. 15; ¶ 28,030; ¶ 28,040; ¶ 28,045]. Similar provisions apply to the taxes of the other party to the convention. Generally, in the event of a conflict between a statutory provision and a treaty provision, the one that became effective later governs.

A tax treaty generally permits taxpayers to request competent authority assistance when they think that the actions of the United States, the treaty country, or both, result or will result in taxation that is contrary to the provisions of the treaty. The U.S. competent authority assists taxpayers with respect to matters covered in the mutual agreement procedure provisions of tax treaties. Competent authority assistance may also be available with respect to issues specifically dealt with in other provisions of a treaty. The IRS has released updated procedures by which a taxpayer may obtain assistance from the U.S. competent authority under the provisions of an income, estate, or gift tax treaty.[17] Taxpayers are urged to examine the specific provisions of the treaty under which relief is sought in order to determine whether relief may be available in their particular case. In general, requests for competent authority assistance should be submitted in accordance with this guidance. However, where a treaty or other published administrative guidance provides specific procedures for requests for competent authority assistance, those procedures will apply and the provisions of the IRS guidance will not apply to the extent inconsistent with such procedures.

¶28,065 TAX ON EXPATRIATION TO AVOID TAX

The expatriation rules found in Code Sec. 877 were enacted in 1966 in an effort by Congress to shut an escape hatch that allowed wealthy Americans to avoid paying federal income tax by expatriating or renouncing their United States citizenship in order to claim offshore tax havens as their home. Under Code Sec. 877, an individual who gives up U.S. citizenship and a long-term United States resident who terminates U.S. residency may be liable for federal income tax at graduated rates for ten years after expatriation or cessation of United States residency under an alternative tax regime.

Code Sec. 877 applies to individuals who relinquished their citizenship or ceased to be lawful permanent residents prior to June 18, 2008. Taxpayers who expatriate in order to avoid taxation must calculate their tax under two alternative methods for 10 years after expatriating. The taxpayers must calculate their tax on United States source income under the graduated rates or as nonresident aliens and default to the higher of the two alternatives.

Code Sec. 877A replaced the 10-year alternative income tax with a one-time deemed-sale tax imposed on covered expatriates who expatriate after June 18, 2008.

.01 Code Sec. 877A Tax Regime

Code Sec. 877A(a) imposes a mark-to-market regime on "covered expatriates" who include U.S. citizens and long-term residents who relinquish U.S. citizenship or cease to be lawful permanent residents of the United States on or after June 17, 2008. A long-term resident is a lawful permanent resident of the United States in at least 8 years of the 15 years preceding expatriation. The deemed-sale rules under the mark-to-market regime require a covered expatriate to treat all property as if sold on the day before the expatriation date for its fair market value. A taxpayer can use losses to offset gains but cannot report a loss. The wash sale rules of Code Sec. 1091 do not apply.

.02 *Covered Expatriate* Defined

Code Sec. 877A(g) (1) (A) defines the term "covered expatriate" to mean an expatriate who satisfies any of the following three tests:

1. Has average tax liability for the five preceding years that exceeds $155,000 in 2013 (the "tax liability test");
2. Has a net worth of $2 million or more on the expatriation date (the "net worth test"); or

[17] Rev. Proc. 2006-54, 2006-2 CB 1035.

3. Fails to certify, on Form 8854, *Initial and Annual Expatriation Information Statements,* that he or she complied with all federal tax obligations for the five preceding years (the "certification test").

There are two exceptions to an individual's classification as a covered expatriate under the tax liability test and the net worth test above. The first exception applies to an individual who was born with citizenship both in the United States and in another country provided that:

- As of the expatriation date, the individual continues to be a citizen of, and is taxed as a resident of, the other country; and
- The individual has been a U.S. resident under the substantial presence test of Code Sec. 7701(b)(1)(A)(ii) for not more than 10 years during the 15-year period ending with the year of expatriation.

The second exception applies to a United States citizen who relinquishes United States citizenship before reaching age 18½, provided that the individual was a resident of the United States under the substantial presence test for no more than 10 years before such relinquishment.

A U.S. citizen continues to be a United States citizen for tax purposes until the individual's citizenship is treated as relinquished. United States citizenship is relinquished on the earliest of the four following dates:

- The date the United States citizen renounces United States nationality before a diplomatic or consular officer of the United States;
- The date that the individual furnishes to the State Department a signed statement of voluntary relinquishment of United States nationality, confirming the performance of an expatriating act;
- The date that the State Department issues a certificate of loss of nationality; or
- The date that a United States court cancels a naturalized citizen's certificate of naturalization [Code Sec. 877A(g)(1)].

.03 Allocation of Exemption Amount

In 2013, the first $668,000 of net gain is excluded. This amount, which is adjusted for inflation annually, is termed the exemption amount [Code Sec. 877A(a)(3)]. The exclusion amount must be allocated among all built-in gain property that is subject to the mark-to-market regime and is owned by the covered expatriate on the day before the expatriation date, regardless of whether the covered expatriate makes an election to defer tax with respect to any such property pursuant to Code Sec. 877A(b). Specifically, the exclusion amount must first be allocated pro-rata to each item of built-in gain property by multiplying the exclusion amount by the ratio of the built-in gain with respect to each gain asset over the total built-in gain of all gain assets. The exclusion amount allocated to each gain asset may not exceed the amount of that asset's built-in gain. If the total Code Sec. 877A(a) gain of all the gain assets is less than the exclusion amount, then the exclusion amount that can be allocated to the gain assets will be limited to the total Code Sec. 877A(a) gain.

Each individual is eligible for only one lifetime exclusion amount. Thus, if a covered expatriate becomes a U.S. citizen or long-term resident, and then loses such citizenship or ceases to be a lawful permanent resident and thereby becomes a covered expatriate subject again to Code Sec. 877A, the individual's exclusion amount on the second expatriation is limited to the unused portion of his or her exclusion amount remaining (if any) after the first expatriation, as adjusted for inflation. For example, if a covered expatriate used one third of the exclusion amount for the first expatriation, he or she will have two thirds of the exclusion amount available, as adjusted for inflation, in the event of a second expatriation.

After allocating the appropriate amount of the exclusion amount among the gain assets, the covered expatriate must report gains and losses on the appropriate Schedules and Forms depending upon the character of each asset. Losses may be taken into account only to the extent permitted by the Code, except that the wash sale rules of Code Sec. 1091 do not apply.

.04 Property Defined

Property for purposes of the mark-to-market rules includes any interest subject to estate tax, plus beneficial interests in trusts that would not be included in the estate. The following types of property are excluded from the mark-to-market regime of Code Sec. 877A: deferred compensation, specified tax deferred accounts, and interests in a non-grantor trust of which the covered expatriate was a beneficiary on the day before the expatriation date. In the case of eligible deferred compensation, the payor is required to withhold 30 percent from the taxable payment made to a covered expatriate. A taxpayer payments if defined as a payment received by the covered expatriate that would have been includible in gross income has the expatriate continued to be subject to tax as a citizen or resident of the United States.

.05 Basis Adjustment

Taxpayers will have the benefit of a basis adjustment for the step-up attributable to the deemed sale. Therefore, when the property is eventually sold, the taxpayers will avoid double taxation. A taxpayer who owns assets prior to becoming a United States citizen or long-term resident can use the fair market value of the assets on the date he or she became a resident as the basis for the deemed sale. An individual also has the option of making an irrevocable election not to have this rule apply [Code Sec. 877A(a) and (h)(2)].

.06 Requirements of Code Sec. 6039G

Code Sec. 6039G requires any U.S. citizen who has renounced his or her United States citizenship or any long-term resident who has terminated his or her United States residence to provide a statement to the IRS for the tax year of expatriation that includes the following information:

1. The taxpayer's TIN;
2. The mailing address of the individual's principal foreign residence;
3. The foreign country in which the individual is residing;
4. The foreign country of which the individual is a citizen;
5. Information detailing the individual's income, assets, and liabilities;

6. The number of days during any portion of which that individual was physically present in the United States during the tax year [Code Sec. 6039G(a) and (b)].

All United States citizens who relinquish their United States citizenship and all long-term residents who cease to be lawful permanent residents of the United States must file Form 8854, *Initial and Annual Expatriation Statement,* to certify that they have complied with all federal tax law during the five years prior to the year of expatriation.[18] A penalty will be imposed if required information is not provided [Code Sec. 6039G].

.07 Form W-8CE

A covered expatriate must file Form W-8CE, *Notice of Expatriation and Waiver of Treaty Benefits,* on the earlier of:

1. The day prior to the first distribution on or after the expatriation date, or
2. 30 days after the covered expatriate's expatriation date if the covered expatriate had any of the following before their expatriation date:
   - A deferred compensation item,
   - A specified tax deferred account, or
   - An interest in a nongrantor trust with the relevant payor.

For detailed discussion of the revised expatriate alternative estate tax regime, the revised expatriate alternative gift tax regime, revised and gift tax imposed on transfers of stock in closely held foreign corporations, see ¶ 29,160.

U.S. INCOME FROM FOREIGN SOURCES

¶28,070 EARNED INCOME OF CITIZENS FROM SOURCES OUTSIDE U.S.

.01 In General

The worldwide income of a U.S. citizen or resident alien generally is subject to U.S. income tax regardless of where the taxpayer is living and without regard to whether the income arose from a transaction or activity originating outside the geographic borders of the United States. The taxpayer is subject to the same income tax return filing requirements that apply to U.S. citizens or residents living in the U.S. The U.S. citizen who earns income in a foreign country may also be taxed on that income by the foreign host country, thus leading to possible double taxation. In order to mitigate any potential inequity caused by the double taxation, a qualified individual may be able to:

- Claim a foreign earned income exclusion; and
- Claim a foreign housing exclusion [Code Sec. 911(a)].

In order for a taxpayer to qualify for the foreign earned income and the foreign housing exclusions, the taxpayer's tax home must be in a foreign country throughout the period

[18] Notice 2009-85, 2009-45 IRB 598.

that he or she establishes qualified residence in the foreign country through either the bona fide residence test or the physical presence test [Code Sec. 911(d)(1); Reg. § 1.911-2]. A foreign country is any territory, including airspace and territorial waters, under the sovereignty of a government other than the United States. The exclusions are unavailable if the taxpayer is present in a foreign country in which travel is generally restricted [Code Sec. 911(d)(8)].

The taxpayer must satisfy all of the following three requirements in order to claim the foreign earned income exclusion, the foreign housing exclusion, or the foreign housing deduction:

1. The taxpayer's tax home must be in a foreign country. An individual's tax home is the general area of his main place of business, employment, or post of duty regardless of where the taxpayer maintains his or her family home. It is the place where the taxpayer permanently or indefinitely works as an employee or self-employed worker. A taxpayer who is only temporarily absent from his tax home in the U.S. on business would not qualify for the foreign earned income exclusion. A taxpayer is not considered to have a tax home in a foreign country for any period during which his abode is in the U.S.

2. The taxpayer must have foreign earned income which includes wages, salaries, professional fees and other amounts received as compensation for personal services actually rendered when the taxpayer's tax home was located in a foreign country and the taxpayer met either the bona fide residence or physical presence test [Code Sec. 911(b)(1) and (d)(2); Reg. § 1.911-3]. Foreign earned income does *not* include [Code Sec. 911(b)(1)(B) and Reg. § 1.911-3(c)]:

   - Amounts paid by the United States or by a U.S. agency to its employees, even where the amounts are paid to the employees as salary and the United States or its agency is reimbursed by a foreign government [Reg. § 1.911-3(c)(3)];

   - Amounts received as a pension or annuity, including social security benefits [Reg. § 1.911-3(c)(2)];

   - Amounts included in income because of an employer's contributions to a nonexempt employee trust or to a nonqualified annuity contract [Reg. § 1.911-3(c)(4)];

   - Compensation received in the form of a distribution of corporate earnings profits [Reg. § 1.911-3(b)(1)];

   - Income received after the close of the tax year following the tax year in which the services were performed unless attributable to the prior year [Reg. § 1.911-3(e)];

   - Amounts included in income as a recaptured unallowable moving expense [Reg. § 1.911-6(b)(4)(ii)];

   - Allowances for meals or lodging furnished by an employer and excluded from the employee's gross income under Code Sec. 119 [Reg. § 1.911-3(c)(1)]; or

   - Income earned in a country with respect to which travel restrictions are in effect [Code Sec. 911(d)(8)].

3. The taxpayer must qualify as one of the following:
   - A U.S. citizen who is a bona fide resident of a foreign country or countries for an uninterrupted period that includes an entire tax year.
   - A U.S. resident alien who is a citizen or national of a country with which the United States has an income tax treaty in effect and who is a bona fide resident of a foreign country or countries for an uninterrupted period that includes an entire tax year.
   - A U.S. citizen or a U.S. resident alien who is physically present in a foreign country or countries for at least 330 full days during any period of 12 consecutive months.

In order for the taxpayer to claim these benefits, a taxpayer abroad must file a tax return and attach Form 2555, *Foreign Earned Income*. One who is only claiming the foreign earned income exclusion may be able to use the shorter Form 2555-EZ, *Foreign Earned Income Exclusion*. To avoid double taxation, once in the U.S. and once in the foreign country, the taxpayer may be able to claim a tax credit or an itemized deduction on his U.S. return for the foreign income taxes that he or she pays. Also, under tax treaties or conventions that the U.S. has with many foreign countries, the taxpayer may be able to reduce his foreign tax liability.

Foreign Earned Income Exclusion

A taxpayer whose "tax home" is in a foreign country and who qualifies under either the bona fide residence test or the physical presence test (discussed at ¶28,070.03) may exclude up to $97,600 in 2013 [Code Sec. 911(a)(1)]. Married individuals who both live and work abroad and meet either the bona fide residence test or the physical presence test can jointly exclude as much as $195,200 in 2013. Once the foreign earned income exclusion is elected, it remains effective for all subsequent tax years until the taxpayer affirmatively revokes the election. Once revoked, however, the taxpayer cannot make another Code Sec. 911 election for five years without IRS approval. The maximum foreign earned income exclusion limit must be reduced ratably for each day during the calendar year that the taxpayer fails to satisfy either the bona fide residence or physical present test. The exclusion is also limited to the excess of the individual's foreign earned income for the year over his or her foreign housing exclusion which is discussed at ¶28,070.05.

Foreign earned income does not include amounts paid by the U.S. or a U.S. agency to an employee of the U.S. or agency.

No Double Benefits

A taxpayer who claims the exclusion cannot claim any credits (including the foreign tax credit or earned income credit) or deductions with respect to the excluded income. For IRA purposes, the excluded income is not considered compensation and, for figuring deductible contributions when the taxpayer is covered by an employer retirement plan, the excluded income is included in his or her modified adjusted gross income

Income Earned in Foreign Countries Where Travel Prohibited

If travel to any foreign country is prohibited by law: (1) the foreign earned income exclusion may not be claimed for income received from sources within that country attributable to services performed during that period; (2) the foreign housing cost exclusion may not be claimed for any expenses allocable to such period for housing in that country, or for housing of the taxpayer's spouse or dependents in another country while the taxpayer is present in that country; and (3) an individual is not treated as a bona fide resident of, or as present in, a foreign country for any day during which the individual was present in that country during that period [Code Sec. 911(d)(8)(A)]. For example, in Notice 2006-84,[19] the IRS concluded that United States citizens and residents who earn income by performing services at the U.S. Naval Base at Guantanamo Bay, Cuba may elect to exclude their foreign earned income and housing costs from gross income, provided they meet the other requirements of Code Sec. 911 because travel to this location is not prohibited by U.S. law.

IRS Targets Frivolous Foreign Residence Argument

The IRS has targeted taxpayers attempting to reduce their federal tax liability by taking frivolous positions based on the argument that their wages or other income are excluded from gross income under Code Sec. 911 because the State, Commonwealth, or Territory of the United States in which they resided or performed services is a foreign country.[20]

Taxpayers reducing their federal tax liability by taking frivolous positions based on this argument will be liable for the actual tax due plus statutory interest. In addition, the IRS will determine civil penalties against taxpayers where appropriate, and those taxpayers also may face criminal prosecution. Promoters and others who assist taxpayers in engaging in these schemes also may be enjoined from doing so under Code Sec. 7408.

.02 *Foreign Earned Income* Defined

Foreign earned income is defined as income earned by the taxpayer as an employee or from a trade or business engaged in by the taxpayer in a foreign country [Code Sec. 911(b)(1)(A)]. The place of receipt of the earned income is not relevant. The term earned income includes wages, professional fees, commissions from sales of life insurance and other amounts received as compensation for personal services rendered, but does not include that part of the compensation derived for personal services rendered by the taxpayer to a corporation which represents a distribution of earnings or profits rather than a reasonable allowance as compensation for the personal services [Code Sec. 911(d)(2)(A)]. If the taxpayer is engaged in a trade or business in which both personal services and capital are material income-producing factors, no more than 30 percent of the taxpayer's share of the net profits of the business can be excluded [Code Sec. 911(d)(2)(B); Reg. § 1.911-2].

Foreign earned income does not include:

1. The value of meals or lodging excluded from gross income;
2. Pension or annuity payments, including social security benefits;
3. Payments from the U.S. or any agency or instrumentality of the of the U.S.;
4. Amounts included in gross income due to employer's contributions to a nonexempt employee trust or to a nonqualified annuity contract;

---

[19] Notice 2006-84, 2006-2 CB 677.

[20] Notice 2010-33, IRB 2010-17, 609.

5. Amounts included in gross income because moving expenses may not be deducted against excludable foreign income; and
6. Amounts received after the close of the first tax year after the tax year in which the services were performed [Code Sec. 911(b) (1) (B); Reg. § 911-3(c)].

.03 How to Qualify for Foreign Earned Income Exclusion

To qualify for the foreign earned income exclusion, a taxpayer must have a "tax home" in a foreign country and meet either the bona fide residence or physical presence test.

1. *Bona fide residence test.* The individual must be a "bona fide resident" of a "foreign country" for an uninterrupted period which includes an entire tax year (e.g., January 1 through December 31, for calendar year taxpayers) [Code Sec. 911(d) (1) (A)], or
2. *Physical presence test.* The individual must be physically present in the foreign country during at least 330 full days during 12 consecutive months [Code Sec. 911(d) (1) (B)]. The amount of foreign earned income excluded is the lesser of the foreign earned income in excess of the housing exclusion (see below) or the annual dollar limit multiplied by a fraction [Code Sec. 911(b) (2) (A)]. The numerator of the fraction is the number of qualifying days in the tax year in which the individual meets the 330-day test. The denominator is 365 (366 for leap years). If the individual has been a bona-fide resident for the entire tax year, the fraction is equal to one, which would result in the exclusion of all foreign earned income up to $97,600 in 2013.

Thus, a taxpayer must both (1) maintain a "tax home" in a "foreign country" and (2) either (a) establish a bona fide residency for an entire year or (b) be present in a foreign country during at least 330 full days in a 12-month period.

"Foreign Country" Defined

The term "foreign country" includes any territory under the sovereignty of a government other than that of the United States. It includes the territorial waters of the foreign country (determined in accordance with the laws of the United States), the air space over the foreign country, and the seabed and subsoil of those submarine areas which are adjacent to the territorial waters of the foreign country and over which the foreign country has exclusive rights, in accordance with international law, with respect to the exploration and exploitation of natural resources [Reg. § 1.911-2(h)]. Consistent with this regulation, the Tax Court has held that a U.S. taxpayer may claim the foreign earned income exclusion only with respect to wages earned while in or over foreign countries and not for wages earned in international airspace or in or over the United States.[21] In *W.D. Rogers*,[22] the Tax Court concluded that a flight attendant whose duties were performed in and out of the United States could not exclude all of her income

---

[21] *C.J. LeTourneau*, 103 TCM 1229, Dec. 58,951(M), TC Memo. 2012-45; *E.D. Clark*, 95 TCM 1265, Dec. 57,376(M), TC Memo. 2008-71 ("[I]nternational waters are not a 'foreign country' for purposes of Code Sec. 911, and income * * * earned while traveling in international waters is not 'foreign earned income' excludable from gross income.").

[22] *W.D. Rogers*, 105 TCM 1478, Dec. 59,482(M), TC Memo. 2013-77.

under the foreign earned income exclusion, but only that part allocated to services performed in a foreign country.

Tax Home Defined

An individual's "tax home" for Code Sec. 911 purposes is located either:

- At the individual's regular place of business, or
- If the individual has no regular place of business, then at his or her abode in a real and substantial sense [Reg. § 1.911-2(b)].

A taxpayer is not considered to have a tax home in a foreign country for any period during which his abode is in the U.S. [Code Sec. 911(d)(3)]. But, temporary presence in the United States does not necessarily mean that the individual's abode is in the United States during that time. Maintenance of a dwelling in the United States by an individual whether or not that dwelling is used by the individual's spouse and dependents does not necessarily mean that the individual's abode is in the United States [Reg. § 1.911-2(b)].

Numerous cases have addressed the meaning of "tax home" for Code Sec. 911 purposes and have defined "abode" as an individual's home, habitation, residence, domicile, or place of dwelling. If the taxpayer's ties to the United States remain strong, the courts have held that his or her abode remained in the United States, especially when his or her ties to the foreign country were transitory or limited.[23] For example, in *J.B. Harrington*,[24] the taxpayer resided in Texas with his family before he went to Angola on a work assignment. The court found that the taxpayer husband maintained strong ties to the United States while he was in Angola: he maintained a bank account in Texas and a Texas driver's license and had two vehicles registered in Texas. In contrast, the taxpayer's ties to Angola were almost nonexistent: he did not own land or vehicles, he did not travel, he did not bring his family with him (they were prohibited from accompanying him or staying with him), and he did not maintain a bank account in Angola. The court concluded that the taxpayer's ties to Angola were "severely limited and transitory," and held that the taxpayer husband's abode for purposes of Code Sec. 911 remained in the United States.

The IRS noted in a Generic Legal Advice Memorandum,[25] where it addressed the meaning of the term "tax home" for Code Sec. 911 purposes, that in most decisions, the courts have looked for the following factors when determining a taxpayer's tax home:

- A U.S. bank account,
- U.S. driver's license, and
- U.S. voter's registration,
- Whether the taxpayers had strong familial, economic and personal ties in the United States and only transitory ties in the foreign country where the taxpayers worked.

---

[23] *R.C. Bujol*, 53 TCM 762, Dec. 43,895(M), TC Memo. 1987-230, *aff'd without published op.*, CA-5, 842 F2d 328; *J.T. Lemay*, 53 TCM 862, Dec. 43,931(M), TC Memo. 1987-256, *aff'd*, CA-5, 88-1 USTC ¶ 9182, 837 F2d 681.

[24] *J.B. Harrington*, 93 TC 297, Dec. 45,989 (1989); see also *J.F. Daly*, 105 TCM 1850, Dec. 59,562(M), TC Memo. 2013-147.

[25] IRS Advice Memo, AM 2009-003 (April 10, 2009).

Example 28-10: The taxpayer is employed on an offshore oil rig in the territorial waters of a foreign country with works on a 28-day on/28/day off schedule. The taxpayer returns to his family residence in the United States during the off periods. The taxpayer is considered to have a tax home in the United States and does not satisfy the tax home test in the foreign country. Thus, the taxpayer cannot claim either the exclusion or the housing deduction.

Rare Taxpayer Victory for Yacht Captain and Chef

In *Struck*,[26] the Tax Court held that a married couple who lived and worked on a yacht outside of U.S. territorial waters did not have an abode in the U.S. and qualified for the foreign earned income exclusion because they spent at least 330 days during a consecutive 12 month period in a foreign country.

Example 28-11: The taxpayer is a marketing executive in the United States and his employer transferred him to London, England for a minimum of 18 months to set up a sales operation in Europe. The taxpayer retained ownership of his home in the United States but rented it to another family and placed his car in storage. The taxpayer moved his spouse, children, furniture and family pets to a home that the employer rented for him in London. Once in London, the taxpayer leased a car and obtained British driving licenses for himself and his spouse. The couple opened bank accounts with a London bank and secured consumer credit cars. The taxpayer's family all obtained library cards for the local public library and the taxpayer and his wife became active in the neighborhood civic association and worked for a local charity. The taxpayer's tax home is in London for the time that he lives there and he satisfies the tax home test in the foreign country and he qualifies for the tax benefits.

Waiver of Period of Stay in Foreign Country to Qualify for Foreign Income Exclusion

The 330-day physical presence requirement imposed by Code Sec. 911(d)(1)(B) in order for a taxpayer to qualify for foreign income exclusion will be waived if Americans working abroad could reasonably have been expected to meet the requirements but were required to leave the foreign country because of war, civil unrest or similar adverse conditions which precluded the normal conduct of business [Code Sec. 911(d)(4); Reg. § 1.911-2(f)]. An individual must establish that but for those conditions the individual could reasonably have been expected to meet the eligibility requirements. In Rev. Proc. 2004-17,[27] the IRS provided information for individuals who failed to meet the eligibility requirements to exclude foreign earned income and housing costs due to adverse conditions in a foreign country.

As a result, the eligibility requirements needed to claim an income exclusion are waived for purposes of Code Sec. 911. Therefore, any individual who left one of the foregoing countries on or after the specified departure date will be treated as a qualified individual with respect to the period during which that individual was a bona fide resident of such

[26] *M.R. Struck*, 93 TCM 928, Dec. 56,845(M), TC Memo. 2007-42.

[27] Rev. Proc. 2004-17, 2004-1 CB 562.

foreign country, if he or she would have satisfied the requirements but for those conditions.

The Court of Appeals for the Tenth Circuit concluded that individuals were not entitled to exclude from gross income compensation that they earned as employees of a demilitarization contractor on Johnston Island, a U.S. insular possession. The Section 911 foreign income exclusion was unavailable because Johnston Island is not a foreign country.[28]

.04 Amount Allowed

To figure the maximum amount excludable for any year, amounts received are taken into account in the tax year in which the services to which the amounts are attributable are performed [Code Sec. 911(b) (2) (B)].

Spouses are each entitled to an exclusion for their earnings. If community property states, the total amount excludable by the spouses for the tax year is the amount that would have been excludable if the income were not community income [Code Sec. 911(b) (2) (C)].

.05 Exclusion for Foreign Housing Expenses

In addition to the exclusion for foreign earned income, taxpayers who live and work abroad may elect to exclude from gross income a certain amount of foreign housing expenses provided by his or her employer [Code Sec. 911(a) (2); Reg. § 1.911-1(a)]. The maximum amount of an individual's foreign housing expenses that may be excluded from gross income is the excess of:

1. His or her reasonable "foreign housing expenses" for the tax year which include the reasonable cost of providing housing for the taxpayer and his family (including a second foreign household for the taxpayer's spouse and children if they do not reside with the taxpayer because of adverse conditions), reduced by
2. A "base housing amount" equal to 16 percent of the maximum foreign earned income exclusion amount for the calendar year, which is $97,600 in 2013, multiplied by the number of days of foreign residence or presence by the individual for the year (16 percent of $97,600 is $15,616 or $42.78 per day in 2013 [Code Sec. 911(c) (1) (B); Reg. § 1.911-4]. However, foreign housing expenses may be excluded only to the extent of the lesser of the expenses attributable to employer-provided amounts or the individual's foreign earned income for the tax year.

▶ **PLANNING POINTER:** The "reasonable" amount of foreign housing expenses of an individual that may be used in calculating a taxpayer's foreign housing exclusion is limited to 30 percent of the maximum foreign earned income exclusion amount for the year, computed on a daily basis and multiplied by the number of days of foreign residence or presence by the taxpayer for the year [Code Sec. 911(c)(2)]. Thus, the maximum amount of foreign housing expenses that may generally be used in calculating the foreign housing exclusion for 2013 is limited to $29,280 (30 percent of $97,600) or $80.22 per day.

[28] *E.N. Umbach*, CA-10, 2004-1 USTC ¶50,148, 357 F3d 1108; *A. Hautzinger*, 86 TCM 231, Dec. 55,259(M), TC Memo. 2003-236.

The IRS may adjust this limitation for specific geographic locations that have higher housing costs relative to the United States as illustrated in Notice 2013-31[29] where the IRS identified locations within countries with high housing costs relative to housing costs in the United States and provided adjusted limitations on housing expenses for individuals to use in determining housing expenses under Code Sec. 911(c)((2)(A). However, the taxpayer must actually reside within the geographic limits of the high-cost location identified by the IRS to claim the adjusted limit (the taxpayer cannot reside in a suburb of the location to claim the adjusted limit) [Code Sec. 911(c)(2)(B)].

"Housing Expenses" Defined

The term "housing expenses" means the reasonable expenses (not lavish or extravagant under the circumstances) paid or incurred in the tax year for housing in a foreign country for the individual and his or her spouse and dependents (if they reside with the individual) [Code Sec. 911(c)(3)(A); Reg. § 1.911-4]. Included are expenses attributable to housing such as rent, the fair rental value of employer-provided property, utilities (other than phone charges), insurance, nondeductible occupancy taxes, nonrefundable fees paid for securing a lease, rental of furniture, household repairs, and residential parking. Interest and taxes (including the share of interest and taxes of a member of a housing cooperative) are not included, however. Also not included are expenses for such things as house improvements, purchased furniture, the cost of domestic labor, mortgage payments, and reimbursed expenses which are excludable from income.

In certain instances, housing expenses eligible for the housing cost amount exclusion or deduction can include the cost of maintaining a second foreign household [Code Sec. 911(c)(3)(B)]. To qualify, the household must be maintained for the individual's spouse or dependents, and the individual must show that there are "adverse living conditions" at the individual's tax home (meaning that it is dangerous or unhealthful to live there). An individual is never allowed to deduct the cost of more than one second foreign household at the same time.

The housing exclusion applies when amounts are considered paid with "employer-provided" amounts. Employer-provided amounts are any amounts paid or incurred on behalf of the individual by the employer. The amounts must be paid in connection with foreign earned income that is taxable (before taking into account the foreign earned income exclusion). However, the housing costs do not need to be paid directly by the employer to qualify. For example, any salary paid by the employer to the employee is considered an employer-provided amount.

Work Camps

If a taxpayer is furnished lodging in a camp located in a foreign country by an employer, the camp is considered part of the employer's business premises. Thus, the employee may exclude from income the value of meals and lodging. To qualify as a camp, the lodging must: (1) be for the employer's convenience, (2) be located as near as practicable to the work site, (3) be in an area that's not available to the public, and (4) accommodate ten or more employees. The camp does not have to be in a hardship

[29] Notice 2013-31, IRB 2013-31, 1099.

area and need not constitute substandard lodging to qualify for the exclusion [Code Sec. 119(c)].

.06 Foreign Housing Cost Deduction

Only individuals who have self-employment income may claim the foreign housing deduction [Code Sec. 911(c)(4)(A)]. The deduction is taken "above-the-line," meaning that it is deducted from gross income and is not subject to the limits that apply to deductions from adjusted gross income. The housing deduction cannot exceed foreign earned income, less the foreign earned income exclusion and the housing exclusion. In addition, a housing cost amount deduction in excess of this limit can be carried forward one year, to the next tax year only [Code Sec. 911(c)(4)(C)(i)]. The amount carried forward can be deducted only to the extent that it is needed to come up with the maximum deduction allowed because of the limitation. In other words, the current year's housing cost amount deduction is taken before the carry forward is allowed.

.07 Rates of Tax Applicable to Nonexcluded Income for Citizens Living Abroad

To ensure that U.S. citizens living abroad are subject to the same U.S. tax rates as individuals living and working in the United States a "stacking rule" applies. Thus income that has been excluded from gross income as either foreign earned income or as a foreign housing allowance is included for purposes of determining the regular tax rate and the tentative minimum tax rate applicable to the nonexcluded income [Code Sec. 911(f)]. Accordingly, the regular tax is equal to the excess, if any, of the tax that would be imposed if the taxpayer's taxable income were increased by the excluded amount, over the tax that would be imposed if the taxpayer's taxable income were equal to the amount excluded [Code Sec. 911(f)(1)]. The tentative minimum tax is equal to the excess, if any, of the amount that would be the tentative minimum tax if the taxpayer's taxable excess were increased by the amount excluded, over the amount that would be the tentative minimum tax if the taxpayer's taxable excess were equal to the excluded amount [Code Sec. 911(f)(2)].

> **Example 28-12:** An individual with $80,000 of foreign earned income that is excluded under Code Sec. 911 who also has $20,000 in other taxable, nonexcluded income (after deductions), would be subject to tax on that $20,000 at the rate or rates applicable to taxable income in the range of $80,000 to $100,000 [Conference Committee Report (H.R. Conf. Rep. No. 109-455)].

For purposes of determining the applicable tax rates, the excluded amount is reduced by the aggregate amount of any deductions or exclusions disallowed under Code Sec. 911(d)(6), which denies a double benefit for those amounts that are properly allocable or chargeable to the excluded income [Code Sec. 911(f)].

.08 Returns Due Before Exclusion Established

Reg. § 1.911-7(a)(1) provides that in order to receive either exclusion provided by Code Sec. 911(a), a qualified individual must elect, separately with respect to each exclusion, to exclude foreign earned income and the housing cost amount. The election may be made on Form 2555, *Foreign Earned Income,* or on a comparable form. Each election must be filed either with the income tax return, or with an amended return, for the first tax year of the individual for which the election is to be effective. An election once made remains in effect for that year and all subsequent years unless revoked. Each election must contain information sufficient to determine whether the individual is a qualified individual.

The statement must include the following information:

1. The individual's name, address, and social security number;
2. The name of the individual's employer;
3. Whether the individual claimed exclusions under Code Sec. 911 for earlier years after 1981 and within the five preceding tax years;
4. Whether the individual has revoked a previously made election and the tax year for which such revocation was effective;
5. The exclusion or exclusions the individual is electing;
6. The foreign country or countries in which the individual's tax home is located and the date when such tax home was established;
7. The status (either bona fide residence or physical presence) under which the individual claims the exclusion;
8. The individual's qualifying period of residence or presence;
9. The individual's foreign earned income for the tax year including the fair market value of all noncash remuneration; and,
10. If the individual elects to exclude the housing cost amount, the individual's housing expenses [Reg. § 1.911-7(a)(1)].

Extensions

An individual needing an extension of time for filing Form 2555 may apply for an extension of time by filing Form 2350, *Application for Extension of Time to File U.S. Income Tax Return.* The application must set forth the facts relied on to justify the extension of time requested and must include a statement as to the earliest date the individual expects to become entitled to any exclusion or deduction by reason of completion of the qualifying period [Reg. § 1.911-7(c)(2)].

¶28,075 ALLOWANCES TO U.S. GOVERNMENT OFFICERS AND EMPLOYEES IN FOREIGN SERVICE

The following allowances are excluded from the gross income of U.S. government officers and employees in foreign service: (1) cost-of-living allowances received by government civilian personnel stationed outside the continental U.S., (2) certain Peace Corps allowances, (3) certain foreign areas allowances [Code Sec. 912; Reg. §§ 1.912-1, -2].

.01 Employees of Foreign Governments

Code Sec. 893 provides that compensation of employees of a foreign government or international organization received for official services is exempt from tax if (1) the employee is not a citizen of the United States; (2) in the case of an employee of a foreign government, the services are of a character similar to those performed by U.S. Government employees in foreign countries; and (3) in the case of an employee of a foreign government, the foreign government grants an equivalent exemption to U.S. Government employees performing similar services in the foreign country. Code Sec. 893(b) requires the Secretary of State to certify to the IRS information regarding the second and third conditions. However, in *Abdel-Fattah*,[30] the Tax Court held that Code Sec. 893 does not require the U.S. Department of State's certification as a condition of a claim of exemption by an employee of a foreign government.

In *R.E. Harrison*,[31] the Tax Court concluded that a German citizen, who was employed by the German Defense Administration located in the United States, was a permanent resident of the United States and a resident alien for tax purposes. As a resident alien, she was required to include compensation for services, such as wages, in her gross income unless she qualified for an exemption under either Code Sec. 893 or the North Atlantic Treaty Regarding the Status of Their Forces (NATO SOFA). The Tax Court concluded that her wages were not exempt under Code Sec. 893 because only two of the three conditions required for exemption were satisfied. The third condition, which required reciprocal treatment by the German government, was not satisfied because Germany did not exempt from German tax wages received by United States employees permanently residing in Germany and working for the United States government. Her wages were not exempt under the treaty because the exemption from tax provided by the treaty applied to a civilian component. Since she was a permanent resident of the United States, she was not part of the civilian component for purposes of the treaty.

¶28,080 INCOME FROM SOURCES IN U.S. POSSESSIONS

.01 Possession Exclusion for Residents of American Samoa

A possession exclusion is available to individuals who are bona fide residents of American Samoa for the entire tax year. The exclusion will apply to bona fide residents of Guam and the Northern Mariana Islands once an implementing agreement is entered into with the United States [Code Secs. 876(b)(1), 931].

.02 Tax Treatment of Guam, American Samoa, and the Central Northern Mariana Islands

Individuals who are bona fide residents of American Samoa, Guam, or the Commonwealth of the Northern Mariana Islands (CNMI) during an entire tax year are subject to U.S. tax in the same manner as a U.S. resident. However, in the case of a bona fide

---

30 *Abdel-Fattah*, 134 TC 190, Dec. 58,198 (2010), *acq*. Nov. 22, 2010.

31 *R.E. Harrison*, 138 TC 340, Dec. 59,042 (2012).

resident of one of these possessions, gross income does not include the income derived from sources within any U.S. possession and the income effectively connected with the conduct of a trade or business by such individual within any U.S. possession, except amounts received for services performed as an employee of the United States or any agency thereof [Code Sec. 931(a); Reg. § 1.931-1(a)]. An employee of the government of a U.S. possession will not be considered an employee of the United States or of an agency of the United States [Code Sec. 931(d)].

Example 28-13: D, a U.S. citizen, files returns on a calendar year basis. In April 2013, D moves to American Samoa, where he purchases a house and accepts a permanent position with a local employer. For the remainder of the year and for the following three tax years, D continues to live and work in American Samoa and has a closer connection to American Samoa than to the United States or any foreign country. D is considered a bona fide resident of American Samoa for 2013. Accordingly, D should exclude from his 2013 federal gross income any income from sources within American Samoa and any income that is effectively connected with the conduct of a trade or business within American Samoa [Reg. § 1.931-1(a)(2), Ex.].

For the possessions exclusion to apply there must be an implementing agreement in effect with the possession of the taxpayer's residence and the United States. Currently, only American Samoa has entered into an implementing agreement that has become effective. The possessions exclusion will apply to Guam and the CNMI once an implementing agreement becomes effective.

Deductions and Credits

In any case in which any amount otherwise constituting gross income is excluded from gross income, there will not be allowed as a deduction from gross income any items of expenses or losses or other deductions (except the deduction relating to personal exemptions), or any credit, properly allocable to, or chargeable against, the amounts so excluded from gross income [Reg. § 1.931-1(b)].

Bona fide residents of American Samoa, Guam, or the CNMI are required to file a U.S. return and pay taxes on a net basis if they receive income from sources outside the three possessions (either U.S. or foreign source income). A U.S. return is not required to be filed, however, if the possession resident's nonpossession source income is less than the amount that gives rise to a filing requirement under U.S. law. To the extent that income constitutes income from sources outside of the United States, a U.S. citizen who is a bona fide resident of a Code Sec. 931 possession may claim a foreign tax credit under Code Sec. 901(b).

The requirements necessary to establish bona fide residence in the U.S. possessions of American Samoa, Guam, the CNMI, Puerto Rico, or the Virgin Islands are provided in Code Sec. 937. The same rules used to determine income sourcing within the United States, including income effectively connected with the conduct of a trade or business in the United States, apply to determine income sourcing within American Samoa, Guam, the CNMI, Puerto Rico, or the Virgin Islands, including income effectively connected with a trade or business conducted within these possessions.

.03 Establishing Residence in U.S. Possession

Code Sec. 937(a) provides that in order to establish bona fide residence in Guam, American Samoa, the Northern Mariana Islands, Puerto Rico, or the Virgin Islands, a person must show that he or she:

1. Was present for at least 183 days during the tax year in the specified possession, and

2. Does not have a tax home outside such specified possession during the tax year and does not have a closer connection to the United States or a foreign country than to such specified possession.

In addition, Code Sec. 937(b) provides that rules similar to the rules for determining whether income is income from sources within the United States or is effectively connected with the conduct of a trade or business within the United States (source rules found in Code Sec. 864(c)) apply for purposes of determining whether income is from sources within a possession or effectively connected with the conduct of a trade or business within Guam, American Samoa, the Northern Mariana Islands, Puerto Rico, or the Virgin Islands.

The IRS has amended previously issued final regulations to add a new alternative to the presence test that is used to determine whether an individual is a bona fide resident of: Guam, American Samoa, the Northern Mariana Islands, Puerto Rico, or the Virgin Islands and therefore qualifies for exemption from tax in the United States. The previously issued regulations provide that an individual who is not present in a possession for at least 183 days during the tax year will nevertheless meet the presence test if during the tax year the individual: (1) spends no more than 90 days in the U.S.; or (2) earns no more than $3,000 from U.S. sources and spends more days in the possession than the U.S.; or (3) has no significant connection to the U.S. [Reg. § 1.937-1(c)]. A person is present in the possession for a particular day if he or she is physically present in the possession during any time during that day [Code Sec. 7701(b)(7)(A)].

Averaging Test Added

Reg. § 1.937-1 incorporates an alternative to the presence test that requires the individual to be present in the relevant territory for a simple nonweighted three-year average of 183 days per year, provided that a minimum of 60 days of presence is met in each of those three years. Thus, under this alternative, an individual will satisfy the presence test for a tax year if the individual is present in the relevant territory a minimum of 549 days during the three-year period that includes the current tax year and the two preceding tax years, so long as the individual is also present in the relevant territory for a minimum of 60 days in each year during that three-year period. This test is in addition to the existing regulatory alternatives to the statutory test and incorporates the existing rules for counting days. Presence in a possession for 549 days during a three-year period is equivalent to an average presence of 183 days during each tax year (183 × 3 = 549). This new test was created to provide sufficient flexibility to accommodate absences from the territory to pursue a range of activities.

Reason for Change

This 549-day averaging test is a welcome change to the regulations because it offers much-needed flexibility in satisfying the presence test when an individual needs to be outside of a possession for an extended period during the year for nonmedical family emergencies, charitable pursuits or business travel.

> **Example 28-14:** Harry, a U.S. citizen, is engaged in a profession that requires frequent travel. He spends 195 days of each of the years 2012 and 2013 in Puerto Rico. In 2014, Harry spends 160 days in Puerto Rico. Harry satisfies the presence test of Reg. § 1.197-1(c) with respect to Puerto Rico for tax year 2014. Assuming that in 2014 Harry does not have a tax home outside of Puerto Rico and does not have a closer connection to the United States or a foreign country, then regardless of whether Harry was a bona fide resident of Puerto Rico in 2012 and 2013, Harry is a bona fide resident of Puerto Rico for 2014 [Reg. § 1.197-1(g), Ex. 1].

A bona fide resident of American Samoa, Guam, or the CNMI who is a shareholder in a controlled foreign corporation in which:

1. At least 80 percent or more of the corporation's gross income for a preceding three-year period was from sources in, or effectively connected with the conduct of a trade or business in, one of the aforementioned possessions, *and*
2. At least 50 percent or more of the corporation's gross income for such period was derived from the active conduct of a trade or business in such possession

is not considered to be a U.S. person for purposes of applying certain reporting and taxation rules under Code Secs. 951-964 [Code Secs. 951(a), (b), and 957(c)].

Income Sourcing Rules for U.S. Possessions

For purposes of determining whether income, including income that is effectively connected to a trade or business conducted in a possession, is sourced within American Samoa, Guam, or the CNMI, rules similar to those for determining the sourcing of income within the United States will apply, including the rules sourcing income that is effectively connected with the conduct of a trade or business in the United States [Code Sec. 937(b)(1); Reg. §§ 1.937-2, 1.937-3]. In addition, income treated as U.S. source income, or treated as income effectively connected with the conduct of a trade or business within the United States, is not treated as income from within any of the possessions or as income effectively connected with the conduct of a trade or business within any of the possessions [Code Sec. 937(b)(2)].

Application of Expatriation Rules

A U.S. person who terminates U.S. citizenship or permanent residency and becomes a resident of a U.S. possession will be subject to U.S. tax from gains on the sale or exchange of property (other than stock or debt obligations) located in the U.S. during the 10-year period beginning when that person lost or terminated U.S. citizenship or residency [Code Sec. 866]. Individuals who expatriate, generally must file Form 8854, *Initial and Annual Expatriation Statement*, for each year they are subject to the Code Sec. 877 alternative tax regime. The form is (1) used to establish that an individual has ceased to be a U.S. citizen or terminated long-term residency (initial information statement) and (2) to comply with the annual information reporting requirements of Code Sec. 6039G, which requires detailed income, asset and liability information (annual information statement).

Reporting Requirements

In order to provide the United States and some "specified possessions" with adequate information to enable them to divide their net tax collections, a civil penalty of $1,000 may be assessed against a taxpayer who fails to file the information required by the IRS for this purpose. The "specified possessions" include Guam, American Samoa, the Northern Mariana Islands and the Virgin Islands. The penalty will be imposed on any individual who became, or ceased to be, a bona fide resident of Puerto Rico, Guam, American Samoa, the Northern Mariana Islands and the Virgin Islands and failed to file the notice required by Code Sec. 937(c). The civil penalty is in addition to the tax required to be shown on the return and also is in addition to any criminal penalty that may be assessed by law. The penalty, however, is not applicable if the taxpayer can show reasonable cause for failure to file the required notice or information [Code Sec. 6688].

.04 Filing Requirements for Income from Individuals in Puerto Rico, CNMI, U.S. Virgin Islands, and Guam

If a taxpayer has income from Puerto Rico, American Samoa, CNMI, U.S. Virgin Islands and/or Guam, the taxpayer will probably have to file a tax return with one of the possessions' tax departments. The taxpayer may even have to file two tax returns: one with the possessions' tax department and the other with the IRS.

Form 8898

The IRS has issued Form 8898, *Statement for Individuals Who Begin or End Bona Fide Residence in a U.S. Possession*, pursuant to Code Sec. 937(c) and Reg. § 1.937-1(h). Individuals with worldwide gross income of more than $75,000 must file Form 8898 for the tax year in which the individual becomes or ceases to be a bona fide resident of one of the following U.S. possessions: American Samoa, Guam, the Commonwealth of Northern Mariana Islands, the Commonwealth of Puerto Rico, or the U.S. Virgin Islands. Individuals must file Form 8898 by the due date (including extensions) for filing Form 1040, *U.S. Individual Tax Return*, or Form 1040NR, *U.S. Nonresident Alien Income Tax Return*.

Puerto Rico

The Commonwealth of Puerto Rico has its own separate tax laws. Thus, if the taxpayer is a U.S. citizen and also a resident of Puerto Rico for the entire year, the taxpayer must include income from worldwide sources on his or her Puerto Rican return. Wages and cost-of-living allowances paid to you by the U.S. government for working in Puerto Rico are subject to Puerto Rican tax. If the taxpayer reports U.S. source income on his or her Puerto Rican tax return, the taxpayer can claim a credit on against Puerto Rican tax, up to the amount allowable for income taxes paid to the United States. A U.S. citizen who is a bona fide resident of Puerto Rico for the entire tax year may exclude income from sources within Puerto Rico, except for amounts received as employees of the United

States. Deductions allocable to excluded income may not be claimed on the taxpayer's U.S. income tax return [Code Sec. 933(1)].

Guam

Guam has its own tax system based on the same tax laws and tax rates that apply in the United States. A U.S. citizen with income from sources in Guam and the United States must file an income tax return with either Guam or the United States, but not both. The return must include income from worldwide sources. A taxpayer who is neither a resident of Guam nor a resident of the United States at the end of the tax year should file with Guam if he or she is a citizen of the United States (born or naturalized in Guam). If the taxpayer is a U.S. citizen or resident but not otherwise a citizen or resident of Guam, the taxpayer should file with the United States.

Commonwealth of the Northern Mariana Islands (CNMI)

A U.S. citizen with income from the CNMI and the United States must file an income tax return with either the CNMI or the United States. Both need not be filed. If the taxpayer is a resident of the CNMI on the last day of the tax year, the taxpayer should file a tax return with Guam. If the taxpayer is a resident of the United States on the last day of the tax year, the taxpayer should file a return with the United States. If the taxpayer is neither a resident of the CNMI nor a resident of the United States at the end of the tax year, but is a citizen of the CNMI, the taxpayer should file with Guam.

U.S. Virgin Islands (USVI)

Individuals who qualify as bona fide residents of the USVI (or individuals who file a joint return with such bona fide residents) during the entire year must pay tax to the USVI under the mirror system on their worldwide income [Code Sec. 932(c); Reg. § 1.932-1(c)]. Income tax returns must be filed with the U.S. Virgin Islands Bureau of Internal Revenue (VIBIR). Bona fide residents of the Virgin Islands have no additional tax liability to the United States as long as they report all income from all sources and identify the source of each item of income on the return filed with the Virgin Islands [Code Sec. 932(c)(2)]. Code Sec. 932(c)(4) provides further that if a Virgin Island resident files a return with VIBIR, reports his or her income from all sources, identifies the source of each item shown on such return, and fully pays his or her tax liability to the Virgin Islands, the income is excluded from gross income for U.S. federal income tax purposes. Thus, these Virgin Island residents will have no additional U.S. federal income tax return filing obligation [Code Sec. 932(c)]. But if any requirement of Code Sec. 932(c)(4) is not satisfied, then the Virgin Island resident falls back into the federal tax reporting and payment system, because his/her income would no longer be excluded for purposes of calculating his/her U.S. tax liability.

Reg. § 1.6091-3(c) provide that income tax returns of an "individual citizen of a possession of the United States" (whether or not a citizen of the United States) who has no legal residence in the United States should be filed with the director of the service center designated in the instructions issued with that form. USVI taxpayers file their tax returns on the same Form 1040 that U.S. taxpayers use when they file their federal tax returns. In a footnote, the Form 1040 instructions state that "permanent residents of the Virgin Islands should use: V.I. Bureau of Internal Revenue, 9601 Estate Thomas,

Charlotte Amalie, St. Thomas, VI 00802" when filing their Form 1040 individual income tax returns.

In *A.I. Appleton*,[32] the Tax Court concluded that a U.S. citizen who was a permanent USVI resident and who filed income tax returns with the VIBIR for three consecutive years satisfied his federal income tax filing obligation. In addition, the Court found that the filing of U.S. Virgin Islands territorial tax returns started the running of the Code Sec. 6501(a) three-year period of limitations. See ¶ 27,045.

American Samoa

American Samoa has its own separate and independent tax system. Although its tax laws are modeled on the U.S. system, there are certain differences. A U.S. citizen and a resident of American Samoa must report gross income from worldwide sources on his or her Samoan tax return. If the taxpayer reports non-Samoan source income on the Samoan tax return, the taxpayer can claim a credit against Samoan tax liability for income taxes paid on that income to the United States, a foreign country, or another possession. If the taxpayer is a resident of American Samoa for part of the tax year and then leaves American Samoa, the taxpayer must file a tax return with American Samoa for the part of the year that he or she was present in American Samoa. Bona fide residents of American Samoa include military personnel whose official home of record is American Samoa.

A nonresident of American Samoa should report only income from Samoan sources on the Samoan tax return. U.S. citizens residing in American Samoa are considered residents of American Samoa for income tax purposes.

As discussed in detail above, a possession exclusion applies to individuals who are bona fide residents of American Samoa for the entire year. If the taxpayer qualifies for the possessions exclusion and all of his or her income is from sources in American Samoa, Guam, or the CNMI, or is effectively connected with a trade or business in these possessions, the taxpayer does not have to file a U.S. income tax return [Reg. § 1.931-1(b)(4)]. If the taxpayer qualifies for the possessions exclusion and has income from sources outside American Samoa, Puerto Rico, Guam, or the CNMI, the taxpayer must file a U.S. income tax return if his or her standard deduction (computed as discussed above) plus the minimum income level for filing a tax return [see Ch. 1] exceeds gross income from sources outside American Samoa, Guam, and the CNMI.[33]

¶28,085 WHEN U.S. SHAREHOLDERS TAXED ON FOREIGN INVESTMENTS

As a general rule, U.S. shareholders are not taxed on their foreign investments until they receive dividend payments when dividends are repatriated back to the parent corporation. However, certain "U.S. shareholders" who invest in a controlled foreign corporation (CFC) are taxed on certain kinds of corporate profits in the year the profits

---

[32] *A.I. Appleton*, 140 TC 14, Dec. 59,543 (2013).

[33] Treas. Dept., IRS Publication 570, "Tax Guide for Individuals With Income From U.S. Possessions" (2013 Ed.), pp. 10-11.

are earned, even if the income is not distributed until a later year [Code Sec. 951]. This accelerated tax timing rule applies to three kinds of earnings.

.01 *U.S. Shareholder* Defined

A U.S. shareholder is any United States citizen, corporation, partnership, estate or trust, or other "person" who owns (or is treated as owning) at least 10 percent of the stock, by vote, in a foreign corporation [Code Sec. 951(b)].

.02 *CFC* Defined

A foreign corporation is considered a CFC if more than 50 percent of the stock, by vote or value, is owned (directly or indirectly) by U.S. shareholders on any day in the corporation's tax year [Code Sec. 957(a)].

.03 What CFC Income Is Taxed

The U.S. shareholder must include in his income his or her pro rata share of the CFC's: (1) "subpart F income" (as defined below) for the year including previously excluded "subpart F income" withdrawn from investment in foreign base company shipping operations and from investment in less developed countries [Code Sec. 951(a)(1)(A)]; (2) earnings invested in "U.S. property" which include stock real estate, patents or copyrights, inventions, models, secret formula or processes which were acquired or developed by the CFC for use in the U.S. [Code Secs. 951(a)(1)(B), 956(c)].

.04 Definition of *Subpart F Income*

A CFC shareholder's *subpart F income* is defined in Code Sec. 952(a) as the sum of the following:

1. Income from insuring risks outside the CFC's home country [Code Secs. 952(a)(1), 953(a)(1)];
2. The foreign base company income [Code Secs. 952(a)(2), 954];
3. Income from countries subject to an international boycott [Code Secs. 952(a)(3), 999];
4. Income from certain illegal activities such as illegal brides, kickbacks, or other payments paid by or on behalf of the corporation during the tax year of the corporation directly or indirectly to an official, employees, or agent of a government; and
5. Income earned in countries that cannot qualify for the foreign tax credit [Code Sec. 952].

   NOTE: Income taxed currently under any of these provisions is not taxed again when actually distributed to the shareholders [Code Sec. 951].

The rules for constructive ownership of stock [Ch. 22] apply with modifications [Ch. 26]. A United States shareholder of a foreign investment company electing current taxation is not required to include a share of a CFC's income [Code Sec. 951(c)].

> **NOTE:** There is a restriction on what constitutes a permissible tax year for controlled foreign corporations with more than 50 percent of the total voting power or stock value owned by a U.S. shareholder. Tax years must generally conform to the tax year of the majority U.S. shareholder [Code Sec. 898].

.05 Returns

Taxpayers owning 10 percent of either total value of corporate stock or the total combined voting power of all classes of stock with voting rights must file an annual information return on Form 5471, *Information Return of U.S. Persons With Respect To Certain Foreign Corporations*. Failure to file the return will result in penalties [Code Sec. 6038; Reg. § 1.6038-2].

.06 Disposition of CFC Stock

Gain from the sale, exchange or redemption of stock in, or from the liquidation of, a foreign corporation is (to the extent of its post 1962 earnings and profits attributable to that stock) taxable as ordinary dividend income if:

1. The selling or exchanging shareholder is a U.S. citizen or resident, or a domestic partnership, corporation, trust or estate; and
2. The shareholder was a "U.S. shareholder" of the corporation at some time during the five-year period ending on the date of the sale, and
3. The foreign corporation was a CFC at some time during the five-year period that the shareholder was a "U.S. shareholder" [Code Sec. 1248(a)].

This dividend treatment may also apply to certain distributions or dispositions with respect to a domestic corporation, e.g., where the domestic corporation was formed or availed of principally for holding directly or indirectly stock of one or more foreign corporation [Code Sec. 1248(e), (f)].

This dividend treatment does not apply to Code Sec. 303 redemptions, amounts otherwise treated as dividends, ordinary income, short-term capital gains, or gains from sales made by non-U.S. persons [Code Sec. 1248(g)]. Nor does it apply to gifts or other transfers that do not result in recognized gain.

FOREIGN TRUSTS

¶28,090 FOREIGN TRUSTS WITH U.S. OWNER

.01 Tax Treatment of U.S. Owner of Foreign Trust

Any U.S. person who transfers property to a foreign trust that has a U.S. beneficiary is treated as the owner of the portion of the trust that is attributable to the transferred property [Code Sec. 679(a)(1); Reg. § 1.679-1(a)]. Accordingly, the income received by the trust with respect to such transferred property is taxable to the transferor under the grantor trust rules. For further discussion of grantor trust rules see ¶ 25,115.

If a foreign trust acquires a U.S. beneficiary in any tax year and has undistributed net income (accumulated income taxable to a beneficiary upon distribution) at the close of the tax year prior to the year that the beneficiary is acquired, the transferor of property is treated as having received additional income in the first tax year in which he becomes subject to the grantor rules. The amount of the additional income is equal to the undistributed net income attributable to the transferred property remaining in the trust at the end of the last tax year before the trust had a U.S. beneficiary [Code Sec. 679(b)].

Example 28-15: Alice, a U.S. citizen, transfers $20,000 to an existing trust in Canada on June 1. Alice's son, also a U.S. citizen, is a beneficiary of the trust. The transfer increases the trust's principal to $40,000. Alice reports her income on the calendar-year basis, and is required each year to report one half of the income earned by the trust.

These rules apply to transfers of property by any U.S. person, including transfers by U.S. citizens or residents, by domestic partnerships, by domestic corporations, and by estates or trusts that are not foreign estates or trusts. Employee trusts created and organized outside the United States and charitable trusts described in Code Sec. 6048(a) (3) (B) (ii) are specifically excluded [Code Sec. 679(a)].

Exceptions

Code Sec. 679 does not apply to the following four types of transfers:

1. A transfer to a foreign trust because the transferor died;
2. A transfer to a foreign pension or deferred compensation trust;
3. A transfer to a foreign charitable trust; or
4. A transfer to a foreign trust for fair market value [Reg. § 1.679-4].

A transfer is for fair market value only to the extent of the value of property received from the trust, services rendered by the trust, or the right to use property of the trust. For example, rents, royalties, interest, and compensation paid to a trust are transfers for fair market value only to the extent that the payments reflect an arm's length price for the use of the property or for the services rendered by the trust [Reg. § 1.679-4(b) (1)].

Foreign Trust Defined

A trust is treated as a domestic trust if:

1. A U.S. court (federal, state or local) exercises primary supervision over the administration of the trust (the court test); and
2. One or more U.S. fiduciaries have the authority to control all substantial decisions of the trust (the control test) [Code Sec. 7701(a) (30) (E)].

A trust that does not satisfy both these criteria is a "foreign trust." [Code Sec. 7701(a) (31)].

U.S. Beneficiary Defined

A foreign trust that has received property from a U.S. transferor is treated as having a U.S. beneficiary unless during the tax year of the U.S. transferor: (1) no part of the income or corpus of the trust may be paid or accumulated for the benefit of a U.S. person; and (2) if the trust terminated at any time during the tax year, no part of the income or corpus of the trust could be paid to, or for the benefit of, a U.S. person, either directly or indirectly [Reg. § 1.679-2(a) (1)].

A beneficiary is not treated as a U.S. beneficiary if the beneficiary first became a U.S. person more than 5 years after the date of the transfer of property to a foreign trust [Code Sec. 679(c) (3)].

A trust having a foreign corporation as a beneficiary may be treated under the attribution rules as "having a U.S. beneficiary" [Code Sec. 679(c) (2)].

Transfer Defined

Transfer is broadly defined as any direct, indirect or constructive transfer by a U.S. person to a foreign trust [Reg. § 1.679-3(a)]. If any portion of a trust is treated as owned by a U.S. person, a transfer of property from that portion of the trust to a foreign trust is treated as a transfer from the owner of that portion to the foreign trust. [Reg. § 1.679-3(b)].

> **Example 28-16:** In Year 1, Adam, a U.S. citizen, creates and funds *DT*, a domestic trust. Adam has the power to revest absolutely in himself the title to the property in *DT* and is treated as the owner of *DT* pursuant to Code Sec. 676. In Year 4, *DT* transfers property to *FT*, a foreign trust. Adam is treated as having transferred the property to *FT* in Year 4 for purposes of this section.

Transfers with a Principal Purpose of Tax Avoidance

A transfer to a foreign trust by any person (intermediary) to whom a U.S. person transfers property is treated as an indirect transfer by a U.S. person to the foreign trust if the transfer has a principal purpose of tax avoidance [Reg. § 1.679-3(c)(1)]. A transfer is deemed to have been made with a principal purpose of tax avoidance if:

1. The U.S. person is related (within the meaning of Reg. § 1.679-3(c)(4)) to a beneficiary of the foreign trust, or has another relationship with a beneficiary of the foreign trust that establishes a reasonable basis for concluding that the U.S. transferor would make a transfer to the foreign trust; and
2. The U.S. person cannot demonstrate that: (a) the intermediary has a relationship with a beneficiary of the foreign trust that establishes a reasonable basis for concluding that the intermediary would make a transfer to the foreign trust; (b) the intermediary acted independently of the U.S. person; (c) the intermediary is not an agent of the U.S. person under generally applicable United States agency principles; and (d) the intermediary timely complied with the reporting requirements of Code Sec. 6048 [Reg. § 1.679-3(c)(2)(i)].

Example of principal purpose of tax avoidance. In Year 1, Anna, a U.S. citizen, creates and funds *FT*, a foreign trust, for the benefit of her children, who are U.S. citizens. In Year 4, Anna decides to transfer an additional $1,000 to the foreign trust. Pursuant to a plan with a principal purpose of avoiding the application of Code Sec. 679, Anna transfers $1,000 to a foreign person who subsequently transfers that money to *FT*. Anna is treated as having made a transfer of $1,000 to *FT* under Reg. § 1.679-3(c)(1) [Reg. § 1.679-3(c)(5), Ex. 1].

Example of U.S. person unable to demonstrate that intermediary acted independently. Alan, a U.S. citizen, creates and funds *FT*, a foreign trust, for the benefit of his children, who are U.S. citizens. In Year 1, Alan transfers *XYZ* stock to his uncle, a nonresident alien. The uncle immediately sells the *XYZ* stock and uses the proceeds to purchase *ABC* stock. In Year 4, the uncle transfers the *ABC* stock to *FT*. Alan is unable to demonstrate that the uncle acted independently of him in making the transfer to *FT*. Under Reg. § 1.679-3(c)(1), Alan is treated as having transferred the *ABC* stock to *FT* [Reg. § 1.679-3(c)(1)]. Under paragraph (c)(3) of this section, the uncle is treated as an agent of Alan, and the transfer is deemed to have been made in Year 4 under Reg. § 1.679-3(c)(3) [Reg. § 1.679-3(c)(5), Ex. 2].

.02 Reporting Requirements for Foreign Trusts

The opportunity for tax avoidance from unreported transactions involving foreign trusts was so great, that lawmakers beefed up the information reporting requirements for certain transaction between U.S. persons and foreign trusts [Code Sec. 6048(a)]. As a result, anyone establishing a foreign trust (called a grantor) is now required to file information returns with the IRS when certain triggering events occur [Code Sec. 6039F].[34]

A responsible party is required to provide written notice of specified events within 90 days of their occurrence [Code Sec. 6048(a)]. U.S. persons and executors of the estates of U.S. decedents should file Form 3520, *Annual Return to Report Transaction with Foreign Trusts and Receipts of Certain Foreign Gifts,* to report certain transactions with foreign trusts and to report the receipt of certain large gifts or bequests from certain foreign persons. Form 3520 is due on the date the income tax return for the tax year is due, including extensions. Two transferors or grantors of the same foreign trust, or two U.S. beneficiaries of the same foreign trust, may file a joint Form 3520, but only if they file a joint income tax return.

The notice must include the amount of money or other property transferred to the trust in connection with the transfer and the identity of the trust and of each trustee and beneficiary of the trust [Code Sec. 6048(a)(2)]. Form 3520 requires information necessary to determine whether a purported gift is properly classified as a gift or income. The donee must provide limited information regarding: (1) whether the foreign donor is an individual, corporation, partnership or estate; and (2) whether the foreign donor was acting as a nominee or intermediary for another person. A brief description of the property received will be required, but the IRS does not expect that information regarding the identity of the foreign donor will be required unless the donor is a partnership or foreign corporation (or nominee of such an entity). Reporting is required only for gifts actually or constructively received by a U.S. person, and only if the U.S. person knows or has reason to know that the donor is a foreign person.

Reportable Events

Grantors of a foreign trust are required to file information returns with the IRS when the following "reportable events" occur [Code Sec. 6048(a)(3)]:

1. Creation of any foreign trust by a U.S. person;
2. Direct and indirect transfer of any money or property to a foreign trust, including a transfer by reason of death;
3. Death of a U.S. citizen or resident if any portion of a foreign trust was included in a decedent's gross estate; and
4. A U.S. person's (except certain tax exempt organizations) receipt of gifts or benefits from foreign sources totaling more than $14,723 in 2012 [Code Sec. 6039F(a)]. The

---

[34] Notice 97-34, 1997-1 CB 422, as superseded in part by Notice 2003-75, 2003-2 CB 1204 with respect to Canadian retirement plans.

definition of a reportable gift for this purpose excludes amounts that are qualified tuition or medical payments made on behalf of the U.S. person, and amounts distributed to a U.S. beneficiary of a foreign trust if such payments are properly disclosed under the above information reporting requirements.

The "responsible party" must file the written notice with the IRS on or before the 90th day after one of these "reportable events" occurs. A *responsible party* includes the: (1) grantor, for the creation of an inter vivos trust; (2) transferor, in the case of a money or property transfer (except by reason of death); or (3) executor of a decedent's estate [Code Sec. 6048(a)(4)].

.03 Definition of Beneficiary

The definition of beneficiary is important under the new reporting requirements because a U.S. beneficiary who receives a distribution, directly or indirectly, from a foreign trust must now report the name of the trust and the amount of the distribution if he knows or has reason to know that the trust is a foreign trust. The term *beneficiary* is defined very broadly to include any person that could possibly benefit, directly or indirectly, from a foreign trust at any time. This includes persons who could benefit if the trust were amended, whether or not the person is named in the trust instrument as a beneficiary or whether or not the person is eligible to receive a distribution in the current year.

.04 Sanctions for Noncompliance

A person who fails to provide the required notice or return for either: (1) the transfer of property to a new or existing foreign trust; or (2) a distribution by a foreign trust to a U.S. person, is subject to an initial stiff penalty equal to 35 percent of the gross reportable amount (generally the value of the property involved in the transaction) [Code Sec. 6677(a)]. An additional $10,000 penalty is imposed for continued failure for each 30 day period (or fraction thereof) beginning 90 days after the IRS notifies the responsible person. In no event can the total amount of penalties exceed the gross reportable amount [Code Sec. 6677(a)]. The penalties are subject to a reasonable cause exception [Code Sec. 6677(d)]. If a U.S. owner of a foreign trust fails to provide an annual reporting of trust activities under Code Sec. 6048(b) an initial penalty equal to 5 percent of the gross reportable amount will be imposed [Code Sec. 6677(b)].

If the U.S. person fails, without reasonable cause, to report the receipt of foreign gifts as required, the IRS is authorized to determine the tax treatment of the unreported gifts. In addition, the U.S. person is subject to a penalty equal to 5 percent of the amount of the gift for each month that the failure continues, but the total penalty cannot exceed 25 percent of such amount [Code Sec. 6039F(c)].

.05 Exceptions to Reporting Requirements

The following exceptions to the reporting requirements exist:[35] (1) A U.S. transferor is not required to report a transfer of property to a foreign trust if the transferor recognizes gain, and has less than 10 percent in the foreign transferee immediately after

[35] Notice 97-18, 1997-1 CB 389, as modified by Notice 97-42, 1997-2 CB 293 and Notice 98-17, 1998-1 CB 688.

the transfer; (2) No reporting is required on corporate or partnership distributions; (3) The penalty will not be imposed if the transferor reports the transfer by the due date of the income tax return for the year of the transfer.

Examples: Assume the following facts exist: A is a U.S. citizen. DC is a domestic corporation. DT is a domestic trust. FT is a foreign trust.

Example 28-17: *Contribution to FT.* A contributed cash to FT, through a broker, in exchange for units in FT. The value of the units in FT is disregarded in determining whether A has received fair market value. The contribution by A is therefore a gratuitous transfer and must be reported.

Example 28-18: *Interest payment to FT.* A borrows cash from FT, an unrelated foreign trust. Arm's-length interest payments by A will not be treated as gratuitous transfers. Thus, A is not required to report the interest payments.

Example 28-19: *Trust distribution to FT.* A created and funded DT. After A's death, DT distributes cash to FT, which is a beneficiary of DT. The trust distribution by DT is a gratuitous transfer. DT must report the distribution.

Example 28-20: *Dividend payment to FT.* A creates and funds FT, which owns stock of DC, a publicly traded company, which pays a dividend to FT. The dividend is not a gratuitous transfer and need not be reported.

¶28,095 FOREIGN PERSON AS TRUST GRANTOR

In an effort to stop foreign persons from using trusts to avoid U.S. income tax, foreign trusts with U.S. beneficiaries are subject to U.S. income tax and the U.S. beneficiaries must pay tax on distributions from these foreign trusts [Code Sec. 672(f)(5)].

A taxpayer will now be treated as the true grantor of a foreign trust and will be taxed on the income of the foreign trust if the taxpayer: (1) is the trust's beneficiary, and (2) made direct or indirect gifts to the supposed foreign grantor who otherwise would have been treated as the owner under the grantor trust rules. This rule applies, however, only to the extent it results, directly or indirectly, in income being taken currently into account in computing the income of a U.S. citizen or resident or a domestic corporation [Code Sec. 672(f)(1)]. Therefore, trust income from a foreign grantor trust will now be taxable to the U.S. beneficiary when distributions are made to the U.S. beneficiary, subject to the following exceptions:

- The grantor trust rules continue to apply to the portion of the trust where that portion of the trust is revocable by the grantor either without the approval of another person or with the consent of a related or subordinate party who is subservient to the grantor [Code Sec. 672(f)(2)(A)(i)].

- The grantor trust rules continue to apply to the portion of a trust where the only amounts distributable from that portion during the grantor's lifetime are to the grantor or the grantor's spouse [Code Sec. 672(f)(2)(A)(ii)].

There is a *de minimis* exception for distributions that do not aggregate more than the amount of the gift tax annual exclusion.

The IRS has issued regulations governing the tax treatment of U.S. persons who benefit from offshore trusts created by foreign trusts (inbound trusts) [Reg. § 1.672(f)-1]. The result is that many foreign trusts treated as grantor trusts under prior law will now be treated as nongrantor trusts, subjecting the beneficiaries to U.S. tax. The new rules subject beneficiaries to tax on amounts received directly or indirectly from a foreign trust and the proposed regulations cover the circumstances under which a distribution from a foreign trust received through an intermediary will be treated as having been received directly from the foreign trust. The amount will be deemed to have been paid directly by the foreign trust if one of the three following conditions is satisfied:

1. The intermediary is a related party to the US beneficiary or the foreign trust and transfers property received from the trust;
2. The intermediary would not have made the transfer except for receiving property from the trust; or
3. The intermediary received the property from the trust as part of a plan to avoid U.S. tax.

NOTE: The rule does not apply if the intermediary is the grantor of the portion of the trust from which the distribution was made.

REPORTING REQUIREMENTS IMPOSED ON FOREIGN INVESTMENTS OF U.S. TAXPAYERS

¶28,100 FATCA REPORTING OF SPECIFIED FOREIGN FINANCIAL ASSETS

The Foreign Account Tax Compliance Act (FATCA) was enacted to prevent tax evasion by U.S. citizens who use offshore bank accounts to avoid paying federal income tax. FATCA accomplishes this objective in the following two ways:

1. Requiring U.S. taxpayer to disclose on Form 8938, *Statement of Specified Foreign Financial Assets* any interest in specified financial assets that in the aggregate exceed $50,000;
2. Requiring U.S. persons who own a foreign bank account, brokerage account, mutual fund, unit trust, or other financial account to file Form TD F 90-22.1, *Report of Foreign Bank and Financial Accounts* (FBAR) if (a) the person has a financial interest in, signature authority, or other authority over one or more accounts in a foreign country, and (b) the aggregate value of all foreign financial accounts exceeds $10,000 at any time during the calendar year. See ¶ 28,101.

Under FATCA, single individuals with interests in a "specified foreign financial asset" during the tax year with an aggregate value over $50,000 on the last day of the year ($75,000 at any time during the tax year) (increased to $100,000 and $150,000, respectively for married joint filers) must disclose on their federal tax returns the name and address of the financial institution, the account number, and the maximum value of the asset during the tax year [Code Sec. 6038D(a)]. In the case of any stock or security, the disclosed information must include the name and address of the issuer and information necessary to identify the class or issue of the stock or security. In the case of any other instrument, contract, or interest, a taxpayer must provide any information necessary to identify the instrument, contract, or interest along with the names and addresses of all issuers and counterparties with respect to the instrument, contract, or interest.

.01 "Specified Foreign Financial Asset" Defined

For purposes of the Code Sec. 6038D reporting requirements, a "specified foreign financial asset" includes:

- Any depository, custodial, or other financial account maintained by a foreign financial institution, and
- Any of the following assets that are not held in an account maintained by a financial institution:
  1. Any stock or security issued by a person other than a U.S. person,
  2. Any financial instrument or contract held for investment that has an issuer or counterparty other than a U.S. person, and
  3. Any interest in a foreign entity [Code Sec. 6038D(b)].

The following examples of other "specified foreign financial assets" are provided in Temp. Reg. § 1.6038D-3T(d): stock issued by a foreign corporation; a capital or profits interest in a foreign partnership; a note, bond, debenture, or other form of indebtedness issued by a foreign person; an interest in a foreign trust; an interest rate swap, currency swap, basis swap, interest rate cap, interest rate floor, commodity swap, equity swap, equity index swap, credit default swap, or similar agreement with a foreign counterparty; and, any option or other derivative instrument with respect to any of these previously listed items or with respect to any currency or commodity that is entered into with a foreign counterparty or issuer.

.02 Who Must File Form 8938

The Foreign Account Tax Compliance Act (FATCA) requires specified persons who own "specified foreign financial assets" within an aggregate value exceeding $50,000 on the last day of the year ($75,000 at any time during the tax year) (increased to $100,000 and $150,000, respectively for married joint filers) to report those assets to the IRS on Form 8938, *Statement of Specified Foreign Financial Assets.* If a taxpayer is required to file Form 8938, this does not negate his or her requirement to file an FBAR (Form TD F 90-22.1, *Report of Foreign Bank and Financial Accounts*). See ¶ 28,101.

Difference Between FBAR and FATCA Requirements

Note that the FBAR requirement applies to a taxpayer's direct or indirect financial interest in, or signature authority (or other authority that is comparable to signature authority) over a financial account that is maintained with a financial institution located in a foreign country if for any calendar year, the aggregate value of all foreign accounts exceeded $10,000 at any time during the year.

FATCA is more broadly applicable to all of the taxpayer's "specified foreign financial assets" which include, as provided in Code Sec. 1471(d)(2), any depository or custodial account maintained by the financial institution as well as any equity or debt interest in the financial institution (other than interests which are regularly traded on an established securities market) with an aggregate value over $50,000 on the last date of the year or $75,000 at any time during the tax year [Temp. Reg. § 1.6038D-1T(7)]. These figures increase to $100,000 and $150,000 for joint filers.

A "specified person" must file Form 8938 when the value of his or her "specified foreign financial asset" is above the applicable reporting threshold. A taxpayer is a specified person if the taxpayer is a "specified individual" or "specified domestic entity" (definition reserved) [Temp. Reg. § 1.6038T-1T(1)]. A "specified individual must satisfy one of the following requirements in Temp. Reg. § 1.6038D-1T(2):

- A U.S. citizen;
- A resident alien of the United States for any part of the tax year;
- A nonresident alien who makes an election to be treated as a resident alien for purposes of filing a joint income tax return; or
- A nonresident alien who is a bona fide resident of American Samoa, Guam, the Northern Mariana Islands, the U.S. Virgin Islands or Puerto Rico.

.03 Reporting Thresholds

The IRS instructions accompanying Form 8938 describe the applicable reporting threshold for taxpayers living in the United States and taxpayers living abroad as follows:

- Unmarried taxpayers living in the United States satisfy the reporting threshold if the total value of the taxpayer's specified foreign financial assets is more than $50,000 on the last day of the tax year or more than $75,000 at any time during the tax year.
- Married taxpayers filing a joint return and living in the United States satisfy the reporting threshold if the value of their specified foreign financial assets is more than $100,000 on the last day of the tax year or more than $150,000 at any time during the tax year. The thresholds for married couples filing separate returns and living in the United States are $50,000/$75,000.
- A taxpayer who is a bona fide resident of a foreign country for an uninterrupted period that includes the entire tax year, or is present in a foreign country during at least 330 full days during any period of 12 consecutive months ending in the tax year satisfies the reporting threshold if the taxpayer is not filing a joint return and the value of the taxpayer's specified foreign financial assets is more than $200,000 on the last day of the tax year or more than $300,000 at any time during the tax year. A married couple residing abroad and filing a joint return would not file Form 8938 unless the value of specified foreign assets exceeds $400,000 on the last day of the tax year or more than $600,000 at any time during the year.

.04 FATCA Reporting and Withholding Obligations for Foreign Financial Institutions (FFIs)

Under FATCA, a foreign financial institution (FFI) is required to report to the IRS certain information about financial accounts held by U.S. taxpayers or by foreign entities in which U.S. taxpayers hold substantial ownership interests [Code Sec. 1471(b); Reg. § 1.1471-4]. A FFI is a foreign entity that accepts deposits in the ordinary course of a banking business, holds financial assets for the account of others as a substantial part of its business, or is an investment entity whose gross income is primarily attributable to investing, reinvesting, or trading in financial assets [Code Sec. 1471(d)(4); Reg. § 1.1471-5(d)]. A FFI meets the FATCA reporting requirements by:

- Identifying U.S. accounts it maintains in accordance with certain verification and due diligence procedures;
- Reporting certain information to the IRS regarding the U.S. accounts and accounts held by a U.S. person who is unwilling to provide the required information (recalcitrant account holders); and
- Deducting and withholding tax on any payment of U.S. source income by the FFI to a recalcitrant account holder or nonparticipating FFI [Code Sec. 1471(b); Reg. § 1.1471-4(a)].

In Notice 2013-43,[36] the IRS provides that if a FFI fails to meet the FATCA requirements, a U.S. withholding agent must deduct and withhold a tax equal to 30 percent on any withholdable payment made to the FFI after June 30, 2014, unless the withholding agent can reasonably rely on documentation the payment is exempt from withholding [Code Sec. 1471(a); Reg. § 1.1471-2(a)]. The withholding requirement applies without regard to whether the payee receives a withholdable payment as a beneficial owner or as a qualified intermediary. A withholdable payment includes any payment of U.S. source fixed or determinable, annual or periodical (FDAP) income, and for any sales or other dispositions occurring after December 31, 2016, any gross proceeds that can produce interest or dividends that are U.S. source FDAP income [Code Sec. 1473(a); Reg. § 1.1473-1(a)]. Withholdable payments do not include items of income effectively connected with a U.S. trade or business, payments of interest or original issue discount (OID) on short-term obligations, and other nonfinancial payments including not but limited to payments for services, leases of property, and interest payable from the acquisition of goods and services.

The IRS provides further in Notice 2013-43 that withholding is not required with respect to any payment under a grandfathered obligation or from any gross proceeds from the disposition of a grandfathered obligation [Reg.§ 1.1471-2(b)]. A grandfathered obligation is any legally binding agreement or instrument outstanding on July 1, 2014, such as a debt instrument, line of credit, derivatives transaction, life insurance contract, and immediate annuity contract. It does not include any legal agreement or instrument treated as equity for U.S. tax purposes or that lacks a stated expiration or term (for example, savings deposits, demand deposits, or deferred annuity contract). Similarly, it does not include brokerage agreement, custodial agreement, investment insurance or annuity contract, or similar agreement to hold

[36] Notice 2013-43, IRB 2013-31, 113.

financial assets in an account for another person. A material modification of a grandfathered obligation will result in the obligation being treated as newly issued and subject to withholding. A payment made under a grandfathered obligation does include a payment made to a flow-through entity such as a partnership or trust. This includes a payment made with respect to the entity's disposition of the obligation. A foreign pass-through payment does not include any payment made under a grandfathered obligation, or any gross proceeds from the disposition of such an obligation.

A U.S. withholding agent for this purpose includes any person in whatever capacity having the control, receipt, custody, disposal, or payment of any withholdable payment or foreign pass-through payment [Code Sec. 1473(4); Reg. § 1.1473-1(d)]. A U.S. withholding agent, participating FFI, qualified intermediary, or any other person that fails to withhold and deposit tax as required is liable for the tax and penalties, and is indemnified against claims and demands of anyone for the amount of the payments [Code Sec. 1474; Reg. § § 1.1474-1, 301.1474-1]. Form 1041 is used to report and pay taxes withheld during the tax year. In addition, an annual information return must be filed on Form 1042-S and a copy furnished to the recipient of the withholdable payment, including any qualified intermediaries, withholding foreign partnerships, and withholding foreign trusts. Both forms are due by March 15 of the calendar year following the year the withholdable payment was made to the recipient. In Notice 2013-43, the IRS provides that the first information return must be filed by March 31, 2015, with respect to the 2014 calendar year.

.05 Participating Foreign Financial Institution (FFI) Agreements

A foreign financial institution satisfies its reporting requirements under FATCA by: (1) entering into an FFI agreement with the IRS (participating FFI); (2) being deemed to comply with the FATCA requirements without the need to enter into a FFI agreement (a deemed-compliant FFI); or (3) being a resident in a country that executes a intergovernmental agreement (IGA) with the United States.

Identification Requirement

A participating FFI is required to identify and document the status of each holder of an account maintained by the FFI to determine if the account is a U.S. account, non-U.S. account, or an account held by a recalcitrant account holder or nonparticipating FFI [Reg. § 1.1471-4(c)]. A U.S. account is a financial account held by one or more specified U.S. persons or U.S.-owned foreign entity, including any depository or custodial account maintained by the FFI, and any equity or debt interest in the FFI other than an interest regularly traded on an established securities market [Code Sec. 1471(d); Reg. § § 1.1471-5(a), 1.1473-1(c)]. A specified U.S. person is any U.S. person *other than* a: dealer in securities, commodities, or derivative financial instruments; broker; publicly traded corporation; tax exempt organization, trust, or individual retirement plan; bank, real estate investment trust (REIT), regulated investment company (RIC or mutual fund), common trust fund or charitable remainder trust; or government entity.

An FFI must follow due diligence procedures for identifying and documenting account holders based on the value and risk profile of the account, and by permitting FFIs in many cases to rely on information they already collect [Reg. § 1.1471-4(c)]. Generally, accounts with a balance or value of more than $50,000 ($250,000 for a cash value insurance or annuity contract) but less than $1 million are only subject to electronic review of searchable data for indicia of U.S. status. Accounts with a balance that exceeds $1 million are subject to review of electronic and non-electronic files for U.S. indicia, including an inquiry of the actual knowledge of any relationship manager associated with the account. A preexisting account of an individual with a balance or value of $50,000 or less, as well as certain cash value insurance contracts with a value of $250,000 or less, are excluded from the due diligence review unless the FFI elects otherwise. Preexisting accounts of an entity with account balances of $250,000 or less are also exempt from review until the account balance exceeds $1 million.

Reporting Requirement

A participating FFI is required to report annually to the IRS the name, address, and taxpayer identification number (TIN) of each holder of a U.S. account which is a specified U.S. person. In the case of any account holder which is a U.S.-owned foreign entity, the participating FFI must report the name, address, and TIN of each substantial U.S. owner of the entity [Code Sec. 1471(c); Reg. § 1.1471-4(d)]. The FFI must also report the account number, the year-end account balance or value in U.S. dollars, and the gross amount and character of dividends, interest, or other income paid or credited to the account. This includes the gross proceeds from the sale or redemption of property paid or credited to the account. Special rules are provided for a participating FFI to report information regarding its recalcitrant account holders. If an FFI is prohibited by foreign law from reporting the required information with respect to an account, then it must close the account within a reasonable period of time or must otherwise block or transfer the account.

A participating FFI reports the required information on Form 8966 with respect to each account maintained at any time during the calendar year. The form must be filed electronically with the IRS by March 31 of the year following the end of the calendar year to which it relates. Form 8809 is used to request a 90-day extension. In Notice 2013-43, the IRS provides special reporting rules that apply for U.S. accounts and owner-documented FFI maintained during the 2014 calendar year if the effective date of the FFI agreement of the participating FFI is on or before December 31, 2014. As an alternative to filing Form 8966, the FFI may elect to be subject to the same reporting requirements of U.S. institutions. Thus, the institution must provide a full Form 1099 reporting for every account with a U.S. person or U.S. foreign entity as an account holder. As a result, both U.S. and foreign source amounts (including gross proceeds) are subject to reporting under this election regardless of whether the amounts are paid inside or outside the United States.

Withholding Requirement

An participating FFI is required to deduct and withhold 30 percent from any withholdable payment made by the FFI to an account held by a recalcitrant account holder or to a nonparticipating FFI after June 30, 2014 [Reg. § 1.1471-4(b)].[37] If an FFI is prohibited by foreign law from withholding as required with respect to an account, then it must close the account within a reasonable period of time or must otherwise block or transfer the account. A participating FFI is not required to deduct and

---

[37] Notice 2013-43, IRB 2013-31, 113.

withhold tax on a foreign pass-through payment made by the FFI to an account held by a recalcitrant account holder or to a nonparticipating FFI before the later of January 1, 2017, or the date final regulations are issued defining foreign pass-through payments. A participating FFI may elect not to withhold on any withholdable payments, but instead have a U.S. withholding agent withhold tax on payments the electing FFI receives which are allocable to a recalcitrant account holder or a nonparticipating FFI [Code Sec. 1471(b)(3)].

.06 FATCA Reporting and Withholding Obligations for Non-Financial Foreign Entities (NFFEs)

In Notice 2013-43, the IRS provides that under FATCA, if a non-financial foreign entity (NFFE) is the beneficial owner of a withholdable payment made to the NFFE after June 30, 2014, then the NFFE is required to report certain information to the withholding agent [Code Sec. 1472(b); Reg. § 1.1472-1(b)]. The reporting requirement is satisfied if the NFFE reports the name, address, and taxpayer identification number (TIN) of each substantial U.S. owner or if it certifies that it does not have any substantial U.S. owners. If the NFFE or other payee fails to meet the reporting requirement, then the withholding agent must deduct and withhold a tax of 30 percent from the withholdable payment.

A NFFE for this purpose is any foreign entity that is not a financial institution, meaning the entity does not accept deposits in the ordinary course of a banking business, does not hold financial assets for the account of others as a substantial part of its business, and is not engaged primarily in investing. A substantial U.S. owner is:

- In the case of a corporation, a U.S. person that owns, directly or indirectly, more than 10 percent of the corporate stock by vote or value;
- In the case of a partnership, a U.S. person that owns directly or indirectly, more than 10 percent of the capital or profits interests of the partnership; and
- In the case of a trust, a U.S. person treated as an owner of any portion of the trust under the grantor trust rules and any U.S. person holding more than 10 percent of the beneficial interests [Code Sec. 1473(2); Reg. § 1.1473-1(b)].

A withholding agent that receives information about any substantial U.S. owners of an NFFE must report the information to the IRS on or before March 15 of the calendar year following the year in which the withholdable payment is made [Code Sec. 1472(b); Reg. § 1.1472-1(e)]. This includes the name of the NFFE and the name, TIN, and address of each U.S. substantial owner.

So long as the NFFE and the withholding agent satisfy their reporting requirements, withholding is not required unless the withholding agent knows or has reason to know that any information provided about substantial U.S. owners is incorrect. A withholding agent is also not required to withhold taxes if the withholding agent may treat the payment as beneficially owned by an excepted NFFE. An excepted NFFE includes a publicly traded corporation and its related entities, a U.S. possessions entity, the government of a foreign country or U.S. possession, an international organization, or an active NFFE [Code Sec. 1472(c); Reg. § 1.1472-1(c)]. An active NFFE is any NFFE if less than 50 percent of its gross income for the calendar year is passive income, and less than 50 percent of its assets produce or are held for the production of dividends, interest, rents and royalties (other than those derived in the active conduct of a trade or business), annuities, or other passive income. In addition, entities which are by definition not financial institutions are considered excepted NFFEs, including certain holding companies, start-up companies, NFFEs that are liquidating or emerging from reorganization or bankruptcy, and certain hedging entities.

Withholding is not required with respect to any payment under a grandfathered obligation or from any gross proceeds from the disposition of such an obligation. A grandfathered obligation is any legal obligation outstanding on July 1, 2014, that produces or could produce a withholdable payment or pass-through payment. It does not include any instrument treated as equity for U.S. tax purposes or any legal agreement that lacks a definitive expiration or term [Reg. § 1.1471-2(b)].

.07 Penalties Imposed for Failure to Disclose Foreign Financial Assets

An individual who fails to file Form 8938, *Statement of Specified Foreign Financial Assets* and furnish the required information about "specified foreign financial assets" for any tax year at the prescribed time and in the prescribed manner is subject to a penalty of $10,000 [Temp. Reg. § 1.6038D-8T(a)]. An additional penalty may apply if the IRS notifies the individual by mail of the failure to disclose and the failure to disclose continues. If the failure to disclose the required information continues for more than 90 days after the day on which the notice was mailed, the individual is subject to an additional penalty of $10,000 for each 30-day period (or a fraction thereof) during which the failure continues after the expiration of the 90-day period. The additional penalty with respect to any failure may not exceed $50,000 [Code Sec. 6038D(d); Temp. Reg, § 1.6038D-8T(c)].

Example 28-21: Brian is notified by the IRS of his failure to disclose information related to specified foreign financial assets with respect to a single tax year. Brian takes remedial action on the 95th day after the notice is mailed. He therefore incurs a penalty of $20,000, consisting of the base amount of $10,000 plus $10,000 for the fraction (i.e., the five days) of the 30-day period following the lapse of 90 days after the IRS notice was mailed.

Example 28-22: Heidi is notified by the IRS of her failure to disclose information related to specified foreign financial assets with respect to a single tax year. She postpones remedial action until the 181st day after the notice is mailed. Heidi is therefore subject to the maximum penalty of $50,000, which consists of the base amount of $10,000 plus $30,000 for the three 30-day periods, plus $10,000 for the one fraction (i.e., the single day) of the 30-day period following the lapse of 90 days after the IRS notice was mailed.

The Code Sec. 6038D penalty is not imposed on any individual who can show that the failure is due to reasonable cause and not willful neglect [Temp. Reg. § 1.6038D-8T(e)(1)]. However, the fact that a foreign jurisdiction would impose a civil or criminal penalty on the taxpayer (or any other person) for disclosing the required information is not a reasonable cause [Code Sec. 6038D(g); Temp. Reg. § 1.6038D-8T(e)(3)].

The three-year statute of limitations for assessments of tax is extended to six years if there is an omission of gross income in excess of $5,000 attributable to a foreign financial asset, which may or may not be subject to information reporting under Code Sec. 6038D [Code Sec. 6501(e)(1)(A)]. The three-year limitations period is also suspended for failure to timely provide Code Sec. 6038D information reporting [Code Sec. 6501(c)(8)].

A 40 percent penalty is also imposed on any understatement attributable to an undisclosed foreign financial asset [Code Sec. 6662(j); Temp. Reg. § 1.6038T(f)(1)]. If a taxpayer fails to disclose amounts held in a foreign financial account, any underpayment of tax related to the transaction that gave rise to the income would be subject to the penalty provision, as would any underpayment related to interest, dividends or other returns accrued on such undisclosed amounts.

.08 Online FATCA Registration

The IRS has opened an online registration system for financial institutions needing to register with the IRS under FATCA.[38] By January 2014, financial institutions will be expected to finalize their registration information by logging into their accounts, making any necessary changes and submitting the information as final. As registrations are finalized and approved in 2014, registering financial institutions will receive a notice of registration acceptance and will be issued a global intermediary identification number.

¶28,101 FOREIGN BANK AND FINANCIAL ACCOUNTS (FBAR) REPORTING

Even if the accounts generate no taxable income, U.S. persons who own a foreign bank account, brokerage account, mutual fund, unit trust, or other financial account must file Form TD F 90-22.1, *Report of Foreign Bank and Financial Accounts* (FBAR) if: (1) the person has financial interest in, signature authority, or other authority over one or more accounts in a foreign country, and (2) the aggregate value of all foreign financial accounts exceeds $10,000 at any time during the calendar year.

The FBAR filing requirement is limited to a "United States person" who is defined to include: (1) a citizen or resident of the United States, (2) a domestic partnership, (3) a domestic corporation, or (4) a domestic estate or trust. The IRS has suspended permanently the FBAR filing requirement for persons who are not United States citizens, United States residents, or domestic entities (corporations, partnerships, trusts, or estates).

Beginning June 30, 2013, taxpayers must file FBARs electronically. Taxpayers who are unable to file electronically may contact the FinCEN Regulatory Helpline to request an exemption [FAQ-17]. The FBAR must be *received* (not just filed) with the IRS for each calendar year, on or before June 30, of the following year. The June 30 deadline may not be extended. Relief has been provided, however, to certain individuals with only signature authority over, but not financial interest in, foreign financial accounts.[39] The Financial Crimes Enforcement Network (FinCEN) has released new Form 114a, *Record*

[38] IR-2013-69, Aug. 19, 2013.

[39] FinCEN Notice 2012-2.

of Authorization to Electronically File FBARs, which allows FBAR filers to file the forms jointly with their spouses, as well as to submit them via third-party preparers.

.01 Tax Amnesty Program for U.S. Citizens Living Abroad

The IRS has announced a plan to help U.S. citizens who are low compliance risks and who are residing overseas (including dual citizens) file delinquent FBARs obligations without facing penalties or additional enforcement action.[40] The procedure became effective on September 1, 2012. Eligible individuals generally must have simple tax returns and owe $1,500 or less in tax for any of the covered years.

Taxpayers using the new procedures will be required to file delinquent tax returns along with appropriate related information returns for the past three years, and to file delinquent FBARs for the past six years. Taxpayers must also pay any federal tax and interest that is due. If a taxpayer presents higher compliance risk, he or she will be subject to a more thorough review and potentially be subject to an audit, which could cover more than three tax years.

¶28,102 PENALTIES FOR FAILURE TO FILE FBAR

.01 Civil Penalties for Failure to File FBAR

In Notice 2013-43, the IRS outlined the following civil penalties that could apply if taxpayers fail to file Form TD F 90-22.1 (Report of Foreign Bank and Financial Accounts, commonly known as an "FBAR"):

- A penalty for failing to file the Form TD F 90-22.1 (Report of Foreign Bank and Financial Accounts, commonly known as an "FBAR"). United States citizens and residents must annually report their direct or indirect financial interest in, or signature authority (or other authority that is comparable to signature authority) over, a financial account that is maintained with a financial institution located in a foreign country if, for any calendar year, the aggregate value of all foreign accounts exceeded $10,000 at any time during the year. Generally, the civil penalty for willfully failing to file an FBAR can be as high as the greater of $100,000 or 50 percent of the total balance of the foreign account per violation.[41] Nonwillful violations that the IRS determines were not due to reasonable cause are subject to a $10,000 penalty per violation.
- A penalty for failing to file Form 8938 reporting the taxpayer's interest in "specified foreign financial assets," including financial accounts, certain foreign securities and interests in foreign entities required by Code Sec. 6038D. The penalty for failing to file each one of these information returns is $10,000, with an additional $10,000 added for each month the failure continues beginning 90 days after the taxpayer is notified of the delinquency, up to a maximum of $50,000 per return.

---

[40] IR-2012-65, June 26, 2012.

[41] *J. McBride*, D. Utah, 2012-2 USTC ¶50,666, 908 FSupp2d 1186.

- A penalty for failing to file Form 3520, *Annual Return to Report Transactions With Foreign Trusts and Receipt of Certain Foreign Gifts.* Taxpayers must also report various transactions involving foreign trusts, including creation of a foreign trust by a United States person, transfers of property from a United States person to a foreign trust and receipt of distributions from foreign trusts under Code Sec. 6048. This return also reports the receipt of gifts from foreign entities under Code Sec. 6039F.The penalty for failing to file each one of these information returns, or for filing an incomplete return, is the greater of $10,000 or 35 percent of the gross reportable amount, except for returns reporting gifts, where the penalty is five percent of the gift per month, up to a maximum penalty of 25 percent of the gift.
- A penalty for failing to file Form 3520-A, *Information Return of Foreign Trust With a U.S. Owner.* Taxpayers must also report ownership interests in foreign trusts, by U. S. persons with various interests in and powers over those trusts under Code Sec. 6048(b).The penalty for failing to file each one of these information returns or for filing an incomplete return, is the greater of $10,000 or 5 percent of the gross value of trust assets determined to be owned by the United States person.
- A penalty for failing to file Form 5471, *Information Return of U.S. Persons with Respect to Certain Foreign Corporations.* See ¶ 28,105 for further discussion of this requirement. Certain United States persons who are officers, directors or shareholders in certain foreign corporations (including International Business Corporations) are required to report information under Code Secs 6035, 6038 and 6046. The penalty for failing to file each one of these information returns is $10,000, with an additional $10,000 added for each month the failure continues beginning 90 days after the taxpayer is notified of the delinquency, up to a maximum of $50,000 per return.
- A penalty for failing to file Form 5472, *Information Return of a 25% Foreign-Owned U.S. Corporation or a Foreign Corporation Engaged in a U.S. Trade or Business.* See ¶ 28,110 for further discussion of this requirement. Taxpayers may be required to report transactions between a 25 percent foreign-owned domestic corporation or a foreign corporation engaged in a trade or business in the United States and a related party as required by Code Secs 6038A and 6038C. The penalty for failing to file each one of these information returns, or to keep certain records regarding reportable transactions, is $10,000, with an additional $10,000 added for each month the failure continues beginning 90 days after the taxpayer is notified of the delinquency.
- A penalty for failing to file Form 926, *Return by a U.S. Transferor of Property to a Foreign Corporation.* See ¶ 28,120 for further discussion of this requirement. Taxpayers are required to report transfers of property to foreign corporations and other information under Code Sec. 6038B. The penalty for failing to file each one of these information returns is ten percent of the value of the property transferred, up to a maximum of $100,000 per return, with no limit if the failure to report the transfer was intentional.
- A penalty for failing to file Form 8865, *Return of U.S. Persons With Respect to Certain Foreign Partnerships.* United States persons with certain interests in foreign partnerships use this form to report interests in and transactions of the foreign partnerships, transfers of property to the foreign partnerships, and acquisitions, dispositions and changes in foreign partnership interests under Code Secs. 6038, 6038B, and 6046A.

Penalties include $10,000 for failure to file each return, with an additional $10,000 added for each month the failure continues beginning 90 days after the taxpayer is notified of the delinquency, up to a maximum of $50,000 per return, and ten percent of the value of any transferred property that is not reported, subject to a $100,000 limit.

- Fraud penalties imposed under Code Secs. 6651(f) or 6663. Where an underpayment of tax, or a failure to file a tax return, is due to fraud, the taxpayer is liable for penalties that, although calculated differently, essentially amount to 75 percent of the unpaid tax.
- A penalty for failing to file a tax return imposed under Code Sec. 6651(a)(1). Generally, taxpayers are required to file income tax returns. If a taxpayer fails to do so, a penalty of 5 percent of the balance due, plus an additional 5 percent for each month or fraction thereof during which the failure continues may be imposed. The penalty shall not exceed 25 percent.
- A penalty for failing to pay the amount of tax shown on the return under Code Sec. 6651(a)(2). If a taxpayer fails to pay the amount of tax shown on the return, he or she may be liable for a penalty of .5 percent of the amount of tax shown on the return, plus an additional .5 percent for each additional month or fraction thereof that the amount remains unpaid, not exceeding 25 percent.
- An accuracy-related penalty on underpayments imposed under Code Sec. 6662. Depending upon which component of the accuracy-related penalty is applicable, a taxpayer may be liable for a 20 percent or 40 percent penalty.

.02 Criminal Charges for Failure to File FBAR

A taxpayer who willfully fails to file an FBAR or willfully files a false FBAR will be subject to criminal penalties under 31 U.S.C. § 5322.[42] A person convicted of tax evasion is subject to a prison term of up to five years and a fine of up to $250,000. Filing a false return subjects a person to a prison term of up to three years and a fine of up to $250,000. A person who fails to file a tax return is subject to a prison term of up to one year and a fine of up to $100,000. Failing to file an FBAR subjects a person to a prison term of up to ten years and criminal penalties of up to $500,000.

¶28,103 OFFSHORE VOLUNTARY DISCLOSURE PROGRAM (OVDP)

.01 Requirements of OVDP

The IRS's prior Offshore Voluntary Disclosure Program (*2009 OVDP*), and Offshore Voluntary Disclosure Initiative (*2011 OVDI*), which closed on September 9, 2011 enabled the IRS to centralize the civil processing of offshore voluntary disclosures and to resolve many cases without examination. In FAQs Offshore Voluntary Disclosure Program Frequently Asked Questions and Answers (June 19, 2013) the IRS explained

[42] *J.A. Simon*, CA-7, 2013-2 USTC ¶50,480, 727 F3d 682.

that a new program that is similar to the previous programs is now available to taxpayers who wish to voluntarily disclose their offshore accounts and assets to avoid prosecution and limit their exposure to civil penalties but have not yet done so. There is no set application deadline. The objective of the program is to bring taxpayers who have used undisclosed foreign accounts and undisclosed foreign entities to avoid or evade tax into compliance with United States tax laws. In return, the taxpayer will avoid substantial civil penalties and eliminate the risk of criminal prosecution.

.02 Procedures

Under the terms of the OVDP taxpayers are required to:

- Provide copies of previously filed original (and, if applicable, previously filed amended) federal income tax returns for tax years covered by the voluntary disclosure.
- Provide complete and accurate amended federal income tax returns (for individuals, Form 1040X, or original Form 1040 if delinquent) for all tax years covered by the voluntary disclosure, with applicable schedules detailing the amount and type of previously unreported income from the account or entity (e.g., Schedule B for interest and dividends, Schedule D for capital gains and losses, Schedule E for income from partnerships, S corporations, estates or trusts and, for years after 2010, Form 8938, *Statement of Specified Foreign Financial Assets*).
- File complete and accurate original or amended offshore-related information returns (see FAQ 29 for certain dissolved entities) and Form TD F 90-22.1 (*Report of Foreign Bank and Financial Accounts*, commonly known as an "FBAR") for tax years covered by the voluntary disclosure.
- Cooperate in the voluntary disclosure process, including providing information on offshore financial accounts, institutions and facilitators, and signing agreements to extend the period of time for assessing liabilities and FBAR penalties.
- Pay 20 percent accuracy-related penalties under Code Sec. 6662(a) on the full amount of offshore-related underpayments of tax for all years.
- Pay failure to file penalties under Code Sec. 6651(a)(1), if applicable.
- Pay failure to pay penalties under Code Sec. 6651(a)(2), if applicable.
- Pay, in lieu of all other penalties that may apply to undisclosed foreign assets and entities, an offshore penalty computer by aggregating for each year the values of foreign accounts and other foreign assets. The penalty is calculated at 27.5 percent of the highest year's aggregate value during the period covered by the voluntary disclosure. If the taxpayer has multiple accounts or assets where the highest value of some accounts or assets is in different years, the values of accounts and other assets are aggregated for each year and a single penalty is calculated at 27.5 percent of the highest year's aggregate value.
- Submit full payment of any tax liabilities for years included in the offshore disclosure period and all tax, interest, accuracy-related penalties for underpayments related to offshore accounts and entities, and, if applicable, the failure to file and failure to pay penalties with the required submissions or make good faith arrangements with the IRS to pay in full, the tax, interest, and these penalties.

- Execute a Closing Agreement on Final Determination Covering Specific Matters on Form 906.

- Agree to cooperate with IRS offshore enforcement efforts by providing information about offshore financial institutions, offshore service providers, and other facilitators, if requested.

- If the taxpayer has a Canadian registered retirement savings plan (RRSP) or registered retirement income fund (RRIF), and did not make a timely election pursuant to the U.S.-Canada income tax treaty to defer U.S. income tax on income earned by the RRSP or RRIF that has not been distributed, they many make the election.

.03 Eligibility to Participate in OVDP

Taxpayers including entities, such as corporations, partnerships and trusts that have undisclosed offshore accounts or assets are eligible to apply for IRS Criminal Investigation's Voluntary Disclosure Practice and the OVDP penalty regime [FAQ-12]. If the IRS has initiated a civil examination, regardless of whether it relates to undisclosed foreign accounts or undisclosed foreign entities, the taxpayer will be ineligible to participate in the OVDP. Taxpayers under criminal investigation by CI are also ineligible.

A taxpayer who has properly reported all taxable income but learned that he or she should have been filing FBARs in prior years to report a personal foreign bank account or to report the fact that he or she had signature authority over bank accounts owned by his or her employer may come forward under the new OVDP to file the delinquent FBARs according to the FBAR instructions and include a statement explaining why the FBARs are filed late [FAQ-17].

.04 Possible Criminal Charges for Failure to Comply with OVDP

A taxpayer who fails to comply with requirement of the OVDP may face the following criminal charges:

- Tax evasion (26 U.S.C. § 7201),

- Filing a false return (26 U.S.C. § 7206(1))

- Failure to file an income tax return (26 U.S.C. § 7203).

.05 Inability to Pay Penalties

A taxpayer who is unable to pay the tax, interest, and accuracy-related penalty, and, if applicable the failure to file and failure to pay penalties with their OVDP submission should request the IRS to consider other payment arrangements. The burden will be on the taxpayer to establish inability to pay, based on full disclosure of all assets and income sources, domestic and offshore, under the taxpayer's control. Assuming that the IRS determines that the inability to fully pay is genuine, the taxpayer must work out other financial arrangements with the IRS, to resolve all outstanding liabilities, in order to be entitled to the penalty relief under this program.

¶28,105 INFORMATION RETURNS REQUIRED REGARDING U.S. OWNERSHIP OF FOREIGN CORPORATIONS

Information returns about foreign corporations must be filed on Form 5471, *Information Return of U.S. Persons with Respect to Certain Foreign Corporations,* with its appropriate supporting and separate schedules if a U.S. person owns 10 percent or more of the value of their stock, or if a U.S. person controls the corporations [Code Secs. 6038, 6046].

Information reporting on Form 5471 is required by the following persons:

1. A U.S. citizen or resident who becomes a director or officer of a foreign corporation if a U.S. person meets the 10 percent ownership threshold;
2. A U.S. person who, upon the acquisition of stock, meets the 10 percent ownership threshold if both the acquired stock and stock owned on the date of the acquisition are taken into account;
3. A U.S. person who acquires stock equal to or exceeding the 10 percent ownership threshold;
4. A person who becomes a U.S. person while meeting the 10 percent stock ownership threshold; or
5. A person who is treated as a U.S. shareholder [Code Sec. 6046(a)].

¶28,110 INFORMATION RETURNS REQUIRED OF FOREIGN-OWNED U.S. CORPORATION OR FOREIGN CORPORATION ENGAGED IN U.S. BUSINESS

Every domestic or foreign corporation that is engaged in a trade or business in the U.S. and controlled by a foreign person must file an information return on Form 5472, *Information Return of a 25% Foreign-Owned U.S. Corporation or a Foreign Corporation Engaged in a U.S. Trade or Business* [Code Sec. 6038A; Reg. § 1.6038A-1]. Reporting is required if at any time during a tax year a foreign person owns at least 25 percent of the reporting corporation's stock either by value or voting power [Code Sec. 6038A(c)(1)]. Form 5472 must be timely filed with a corporate income tax return, or filed separately when the return is due (including extensions) at the IRS Center where the corporation files its return.

> **NOTE:** A corporation subject to the reporting requirements must report its transactions with all related persons (as defined under Code Sec. 267(b); 482; or 707(b)(1)), not merely its transactions with corporations in its controlled group [Code Sec. 6038A(c)(2)].

¶28,115 INFORMATION RETURNS REQUIRED OF FOREIGN INTERESTS IN U.S. REAL PROPERTY

Information returns must be filed by foreign persons holding direct investments in U.S. real property interests. Foreign persons must file if they (1) did not engage in a U.S. trade or business during the year and (2) have direct U.S. real property interests that equal or exceed $50,000. The return must show the name, address, a description of all the U.S. real property interests, and such other information as the regulations may require [Code Sec. 6039C(a)]. For withholding on sales, see Ch. 15. Penalties are imposed for failure to comply [Code Sec. 6652(f)].

¶28,120 INFORMATION RETURNS REQUIRED FOR TRANSFER OF PROPERTY TO FOREIGN CORPORATION

.01 Who Must File

A U.S. citizen or resident, a domestic corporation, or a domestic estate or trust must file Form 926, *Return by a U.S. Transferor of Property to a Foreign Corporation*, with the IRS pursuant to Code Sec. 6038B. The purpose of Form 926 is to report an exchange or distribution of tangible or intangible property to a foreign corporation in the following situations:

1. Complete liquidations of subsidiaries;
2. Transfer to corporation controlled by transferor;
3. Exchanges of stock and securities in certain reorganizations;
4. Distribution of stock and securities of a controlled corporation;
5. Receipt of additional consideration;
6. Nonrecognition of gain or loss to corporations and treatment of distributions; or
7. U.S. person makes a liquidating distribution to a foreign person [Code Sec. 6038B(a)(1)(A)].

.02 Reporting Requirements

Any U.S. person required to report a transfer to a foreign corporation must provide the required information on Form 926, Form 926 and any attachments must be filed with the income tax return for the tax year in which the transfer occurred. Verification of Form (including attachments) occurs by signing the income tax return with which it is filed [Reg. § 1.6038B-1(b)(1)(i)]. This facilitates the electronic filing of Form 926 with the transferor's income tax return.

.03 Date of Transfer

The date of transfer is the first date on which title to, possession of, or rights to the use of stock, securities, or other property pass [Reg. § 1.6038B-1(b)(4)].

.04 Jointly Owned Property

For jointly held property, each transferor must comply with the reporting rules with respect to the particular interest transferred. However, a husband and wife who file a joint tax return may file one Form 926 with their tax return [Reg. § 1.6038B-1(b)(1)(iii)].

.05 Cash Transfers

A U.S. person that transfers cash to a foreign corporation must report the transfer to the IRS if:

1. Immediately after the transfer, the person holds, directly or indirectly, at least 10 percent of the total voting power or total value of the foreign corporation; or
2. The amount of cash transferred by the U.S. person or any related person to the foreign corporation during the 12-month period ending on the date of the transfer exceeds $100,000 [Reg. § 1.6038B-1(b)(3)].

.06 Transfers by Partnership

If the transferor is a domestic or foreign partnership, the domestic partners of the partnership, not the partnership itself, must comply with Code Sec. 6038B and file Form 926. Each domestic partner is treated as a transferor of its proportionate share of the property.

.07 Exceptions to Filing

Form 926 need not be filed in the following situations:

1. A U.S. person that transfers stock or securities under Code Sec. 367(a) is not required to file Form 926 if:

   a. The U.S. transferor owned less than five percent of both the total voting power and the total value of the transferee foreign corporation immediately after the transfer:

      (1) The U.S. transferor qualified for nonrecognition treatment with respect to the transfer; or

      (2) The U.S. transferor is a tax-exempt entity and the income was not unrelated business income; or

      (3) The transfer was taxable to the U.S. transferor and such person properly reported the income on its timely filed return; or

      (4) The transfer is considered to be to a foreign corporation solely by reason of Reg. § 1.83-6(d)(1) and the fair market value of the property transferred does not exceed $100,000.

   b. The U.S. transferor owned five percent or more of the total voting power or the total value of the transferee foreign corporation, taking into account Code Sec. 318 attribution rules, immediately after the transfer creates a potential ambiguity as to how many of the following four factors under Reg. § 1.6038-1(b)(2)(i)(B) must be satisfied:

      (1) The transferor properly entered into a gain recognition agreement under Reg. § 1.367(a)-8; or

(2) The transferor is a tax-exempt entity and the income was not unrelated business income; or

(3) The transferor properly reported the income from the transfer on its timely-filed tax return for the tax year that includes the date of the transfer; or

(4) The transfer is considered to be to a foreign corporation solely by reason of Reg. § 1.83-6(d)(1) and the fair market value of the property transferred does not exceed $100,000 [Reg. § 1.6038B-1(b)(2)(i)].

2. Reorganizations under Code Sec. 354. For exchanges of stock and securities in certain reorganizations under Code Sec. 354, a U.S. person does not have to file Form 926 if:

   a. The U.S. person exchanges stock or securities of a foreign corporation in a recapitalization described in Code Sec. 368(a)(1)(E); or

   b. The U.S. person exchanges stock or securities of a domestic or foreign corporation for stock of a foreign corporation under an asset reorganization described in Code Sec. 368(a)(1) that is not treated as an indirect stock transfer under Reg. § 1.367(a)-3(d) [Reg. § 1.6038B-1(b)(1)(i)]. This exception applies to Code Sec. 368(a)(1)(A) reorganizations, including triangular mergers under Code Sec. 368(a)(2)(D) and (E), and Code Sec. 368(a)(1)(G) reorganizations occurring on or after January 23, 2006 [Reg. § 1.6038B-1(g)(4)].

29

Gift and Estate Taxes

Fundamentals of estate and gift tax planning . . . . ¶29,001

Basis considerations . . . . ¶29,005

GIFT TAX

Nature and imposition of tax . . . . . ¶29,010

Transfers subject to gift tax . . . . . . ¶29,015

Transfers exempt from gift tax . . . . ¶29,020

Valuation of gifts . . . . ¶29,025

Valuation of gifts with retained interests . . . . ¶29,030

ESTATE TAX

Imposition of the estate tax . . . . . . ¶29,035

THE GROSS ESTATE

Gross estate . . . . ¶29,040

Property subject to dower or curtesy . . . . ¶29,045

Joint estates and qualified joint interest . . . . ¶29,050

Community property . . . . ¶29,055

Transfers with retained life estate . . . . ¶29,060

Revocable transfers . . . . ¶29,065

Transfers taking effect at death . . . ¶29,070

Life insurance . . . . ¶29,075

Transfers within three years of death . . . . ¶29,080

Transfers subject to a power of appointment . . . . ¶29,085

Transfers for insufficient consideration . . . . ¶29,090

Survivor annuities and other death benefits . . . . ¶29,095

Property for which marital deduction was previously allowed . . ¶29,100

VALUATION OF ESTATE PROPERTY

General principles . . . . ¶29,105

Alternative valuation methods . . . ¶29,110

DEDUCTIONS FROM GROSS ESTATE

Allowable deductions . . . . ¶29,115

Marital deduction . . . . ¶29,120

Charitable and similar transfers . . ¶29,125

Deduction for state death taxes . . ¶29,130

Estate and gift tax rate schedule . . ¶29,135

Applicable exclusion amount . . . . ¶29,140

Credit for foreign death taxes . . . . ¶29,150

Credit for tax on prior transfers . . . ¶29,155

Estates of nonresident noncitizens . . . . ¶29,160

Qualified family-owned business interest deduction . . . . ¶29,161

QUALIFIED DISCLAIMERS

Nature and benefits of disclaimers . . . . ¶29,165

GENERATION-SKIPPING TRANSFER (GST) TAX

Purpose of the GST tax . . . . ¶29,170
How GST works . . . . ¶29,175
Transfers subject to GST tax . . . . . ¶29,180
The GST exemption . . . . ¶29,185
Transfers exempt from GST tax . . ¶29,186
Trust severance for GST purposes . . . . ¶29,187
Computation and filing requirements . . . . ¶29,190

PROCEDURE ON RETURNS

Filing requirements . . . . ¶29,195
Payment of the tax . . . . ¶29,200
Estate tax deferral . . . . ¶29,205

¶29,001 FUNDAMENTALS OF ESTATE AND GIFT TAX PLANNING

The federal government considers it a privilege for you to be able to gratuitously transfer property to family members or friends during your lifetime and when you die. For this privilege, you are subject to a gift tax on lifetime transfers, an estate tax on transfers at death, and a generation-skipping transfer (GST) tax on transfers to grandchildren and great-grandchildren that the government thinks are too large. This chapter provides an overview of these wealth transfer taxes. For a more detailed discussion of the estate and gift tax, see the Estate and Gift Tax Handbook.

.01 Tax-Free Transfers

Fortunately, many transfers are entirely free of transfer tax. For example, unlimited amounts can be transferred free of transfer tax to your spouse [¶29,120] and to charities [¶29,125]. In addition, in 2013 and 2014 you can give $14,000 to an unlimited number of individuals without owing any gift tax [¶29,020]. You can also pay someone's tuition and medical expenses without being charged with gift tax [¶29,020]. The $14,000 annual gift tax exclusion ($28,000 if a married couple elects gift-splitting) is available in 2013 and 2014 for gifts of present interests in property made to an unlimited number of donees [Code Sec. 2503; ¶29,020].

.02 Estate Tax Legislation

Changes Made by EGTRRA

Under the provisions of the Economic Growth and Tax Relief Reconciliation Act of 2001 (P.L. 107-16) (EGTRRA), the estate and gift tax rules were gradually changed over an eight-year period. The estate tax exclusion rose from $2 million for decedents dying in 2006-2008, to $3.5 million in 2009. The estate tax was repealed by EGTRRA for people dying in 2010 only, however, EGTRRA provided that the gift tax would remain in place in 2010, with gift tax exclusion of $1 million and a maximum gift tax rate of 35 percent. In addition, in 2010, there was a significant change in the method used to determine the basis of all capital assets transferred at death—from "step-up in basis" to "modified carryover basis." Under this modified regime, a recipient's basis in property acquired from a decedent was the lesser of (1) the decedent's adjusted basis in property, or (2) the fair market value (FMV) of the property on the decedent's date of death. For further discussion of carryover basis, see ¶ 29,005.

The estate tax provisions of EGTRRA were scheduled to sunset at the end of 2010, and on January 1, 2011, estate and gift tax law would return to what it would have been under pre-2001 law as if EGTRRA had never been enacted. The unified estate and gift tax would be reinstated with a combined exclusion of $1 million per person. The maximum tax rate would rise from 45 percent in 2007-2009 to 55 percent (plus a 5 percent surtax) in 2011 and thereafter.

The Tax Relief Act of 2010 increased the unified credit exemption and the lifetime gift tax exemption to $5,120,000 in 2012. These increases allowed the estates of decedent dying in 2012 to avoid estate tax on an estate worth $5,120,000 and to make lifetime gifts of $5,120,000 ($10,240,000 if gift-splitting elected) free of gift tax. The Tax Relief Act of 2010 reunified the estate and gift tax and reduced the top estate and gift tax rate to 35 percent in 2012. In addition, the law increased the generation-skipping transfer (GST) tax exemption for generation skipping transfers to $5,120,000 and reduced the GST tax rate on transfers made in 2012 to 35 percent.

The Tax Relief Act of 2010 extended the estate tax provisions of EGTRRA two more years so that it was scheduled to sunset on December 31, 2012. The federal estate, gift, and GST tax changes enacted by EGTRRA and the Tax Relief Act of 2010 that were set to expire with respect to the estates of decedents dying and gifts and GSTs made after December 31, 2012 were made permanent for estates of decedents dying, gifts made, or GSTs after December 31, 2012. However, the maximum tax rate imposed under the federal estate and gift taxes will now be 40 percent with respect to the estates of decedents dying and gifts made in 2013 and later years, rather than 35 percent. The GST tax rate, which is tied to the maximum estate tax rate, will also be 40 percent. In addition, the five-percent surtax, formerly imposed on estates and gifts in excess of $10 million and up to $17,184,000, will not be imposed on the estates of decedents dying or gifts made in 2013 or later. The estates of decedents who die during 2013 have an applicable exclusion amount of $5,250,000 with this amount increasing to $5,340,000 in 2014.

The increase of the estate tax exclusion amount (which also serves as the estate tax return filing threshold) to $5,250,000 in 2013 and to $5,340,000 in 2014 will undoubtedly continue the decline in the number of federal estate tax returns filed and the corresponding revenue collected by the federal government. According to the IRS (http://www.irs.gov/uac/SOI-Tax-Stats-Estate-Tax-Statistics-Filing-Year-Table-1), the number of estate tax returns declined 87 percent from about 73,100 in 2003 to about 9,400 in 2012 primarily due to the gradual increase in the filing threshold. It is expected that they will drop even more in 2013 and 2014 as the exclusion amount increases and the estate tax affects fewer and fewer decedents.

.03 The Importance of Estate Planning

Estate plans should be reviewed now to consider the impact of the American Taxpayer Relief Act of 2012 on the estate plan. Regardless of the inevitable tax law changes, wills and trusts should be reviewed at least every five years to take into account life changes and shifts in one's financial situation. Changes that would mandate a review would include health changes, marriage, divorce, and a birth or a death in the family. Estate planning cannot be ignored because it is not just about saving estate taxes. For example, avoiding probate, providing for the disposition of assets to loved ones, avoiding conservatorship proceedings and establishing long-term trusts to preserve assets for future generations, are only some of important nontax reasons for engaging in estate planning.

¶29,005 BASIS CONSIDERATIONS

.01 Stepped-Up Basis Rules

The stepped-up basis at death rules of Code Sec. 1014 continue to apply generally to the property acquired from the estates of decedents dying before and after 2012. Under the stepped-up basis rules, the income tax basis of property acquired from a decedent at death generally is stepped up (or stepped down) to equal its value as of the date of the decedent's death (or on the date six months after the date of death, if alternate valuation under Code Sec. 2032 is elected on the decedent's estate tax return).

Under the stepped-up basis rules, the recipient of property is also generally deemed to have met the one-year capital gains holding period, regardless of how long the decedent had owned the property before death [Code Sec. 1223(9)]. Although the recipient of property acquired from a decedent generally receives a basis that is stepped up to its date of death value, there are exceptions to this rule:

- The income tax basis of property for which special use valuation has been elected will be equal to its special use value, as determined for estate tax purposes under Code Sec. 2032A [Code Sec. 1014(a)(2)].
- The basis of stock in a Domestic International Sales Corporation (DISC) acquired from a decedent must be reduced by the amount that would have been treated as ordinary income under Code Sec. 995 if the decedent had lived and sold the stock on the applicable estate valuation date [Code Sec. 1014(d)]. (This rule is to prevent the recipient of stock from escaping taxation on the DISC income attributable to the stock when the recipient disposes it.)
- A decedent's executor may elect to exclude from the taxable estate up to 40 percent of the value of land subject to a qualified conservation exclusion under Code Sec. 2031(c). To the extent that the value of such land is excluded from the decedent's taxable estate, the basis of the property is not stepped up to its date of death value [Code Sec. 1014(a)(4)].

Special Rule Applicable to Appreciated Property

Another special rule applies to appreciated property acquired by a decedent as a gift within one year of death if the property passes from the decedent to the original donor or to the donor's spouse [Code Sec. 1014(e)]. The basis of such property in the hands of the original donor (or his or her spouse) is the decedent's adjusted basis in the property immediately prior to death, rather than its fair market value on the date of death. The objective of this provision is to prevent individuals from transferring property in anticipation of a donee's death merely to obtain a tax-free step up in basis upon receipt of the property from the donee's estate.

.02 Mechanics of Carryover Basis Rule

The Code Sec. 1022 carryover basis election gives executors the power to apply modified carry basis treatment to property acquired from a decedent who died in 2010. When the election is made on Form 8939, *Allocation of Increase in Basis for Property Acquired From Decedent*, the estate will not be subject to federal estate tax and the estate does not need to file Form 706, even if the value of the estate exceeds the exemption equivalent. Executors will use Form 8939 to:

- Make the Code Sec. 1022 election for 2010 decedents;
- Report information about property acquired from a decedent; and
- Allocate basis increase to certain property acquired from a decedent.

Once made, the Code Sec. 1022 election is irrevocable.

For purposes of this election, an executor means the executor or administrator of the decedent's estate. If no executor or administrator is appointed, any person in possession of any property of the decedent is considered an executor under Code Sec. 2203.

The carryover basis rule of Code Sec. 1022 provides that the income tax basis of property acquired from a decedent will generally be carried over to the recipient. More specifically, the recipient of the property will receive a basis equal to the lesser of the:

1. Adjusted basis of the property in the hands of the decedent, or
2. The fair market value of the property on the date of the decedent's death.

Example 29-1: Mom dies in 2010, leaving her ABCo stock, which she purchased for $20 per share to Son. The executor for Mom's estate makes the election for application of EGTRRA rule to apply to the estate. At Mom's death, the stock has a fair market value of $45 per share. Under the new carryover basis rule, Son will receive Mom's basis of $20 per share in the stock. If Son later sells the stock for $50 per share, he will incur a $30 per share gain ($50 – $20). Under the old stepped-up basis rules, Son's basis in the stock would be $45 and his gain would only be $5 ($50 – $45).

.03 Exceptions to Carryover Basis

There are two exceptions to the "carryover" basis regime.

1. An executor of a decedent's estate will be able to increase the basis of assets owned by the decedent and acquired by the beneficiaries at death, up to a total of $1.3 million [Code Sec. 1022(b)]. This $1.3 million amount is increased by the amount of the amount of unused capital losses, net operating losses, and certain built-in losses of the decedent.
2. The basis of property transferred to a surviving spouse can be increased by an additional $3 million. This means that property transferred to a surviving spouse can be increased by a total of $4.3 million. Nonresidents who are not U.S. citizens will be allowed to increase the basis of property by up to $60,000.

.04 Property Subject to Carryover Basis

The modified carryover basis rule will only apply to "property acquired from a decedent," which is defined in Code Sec. 1022(e) as:

- Property acquired by bequest, devise, or inheritance, or by the decedent's estate from the decedent;
- Property transferred by the decedent during his lifetime to a qualified revocable trust or to any other trust with respect to which the decedent reserved the right to make any change in the enjoyment thereof through the exercise of a power to alter, amend, or terminate the trust; and
- Any other property passing from the decedent by reason of death to the extent that such property passed without consideration.

The implications of the new carryover basis rule will be very expensive for taxpayers who receive appreciated property from a decedent in 2010. Property acquired from a decedent will have the same basis in the hands of the recipient as in the hands of the decedent and will result in a greater gain when sold than if the old step-up basis were applicable. In addition, the character of gain on the sale of property received from a decedent's estate is carried over to the recipient. For example, real estate that has been depreciated and would be subject to recapture if sold by the decedent will be subject to recapture if sold by the recipient.

.05 Ineligible Property

The following types of property transfers will be ineligible for the basis increase [Code Sec. 1022(d)(1)(D)]:

- Property acquired by a decedent by gift from a nonspouse less than three years before death;
- Property that constitutes a right to receive income in respect of a decedent;
- Stock in foreign investment and personal holding companies;
- Stock or securities of a foreign personal holding company;
- Stock of a domestic international sales corporation (or former domestic international sales corporation);
- Stock of a foreign investment company; and
- Stock of a passive foreign investment company (except for which a decedent shareholder had made a qualified electing fund election).

.06 Ownership Rules

In general, the basis of property may be increased above the decedent's adjusted basis in that property only if the property is owned, or is treated as owned, by the decedent at the time of the decedent's death [Code Sec. 1022(d)(1)(A)]. The following ownership rules apply.

Joint Tenants with Surviving Spouse

Property held as joint tenants or tenants by the entireties with the surviving spouse, one-half of the property is treated as having been owned by the decedent and is thus eligible for the basis increase [Code Sec. 1022(d)(1)(B)(i)(I)].

Joint Tenants with Other Than Spouse

Property held as joint tenants with right of survivorship with anyone other than the surviving spouse is deemed to be owned by the decedent (and thus eligible for the basis increase) to the extent the property is attributable to consideration furnished by the decedent [Code Sec. 1022(d)(1)(B)(i)(II)].

Joint Tenants Acquired Interests by Gift, Devise or Inheritance

If multiple joint tenants acquired their interests by gift, devise or inheritance, and if their interests are not otherwise specified or fixed by law, the decedent joint tenant will be treated as the owner (and thus eligible for the basis increase) to the extent of the value of a fractional part to be determined by dividing the value of the property by the number of joint tenants [Code Sec. 1022(d)(1)(B)(i)(III)].

Qualified Revocable Trust

Property transferred by the decedent during his lifetime to a qualified revocable trust (under Code Sec. 645(b)(1)) is considered to be owned by the decedent and thus eligible for the basis increase [Code Sec. 1022(d)(1)(B)(ii)].

Powers of Appointment

The decedent will not be treated as the owner of property solely by reason of holding a power of appointment with respect to such property [Code Sec.1022(d)(1)(b)(iii)]. Therefore, property in a general power of appointment marital trust appears not to qualify for the $1.3 million basis adjustment at the surviving spouse's subsequent death, unless the spouse exercises the power of appointment to leave the assets to his or her estate.

Community Property

The decedent is treated as owning the surviving spouse's one-half share of community property if at least one-half of the whole of the community interest in such property is treated as owned by and acquired from, the decedent without regard to this clause [Code Sec. 1022(d)(1)(B)(iv)]. Thus, the decedent's one-half interest in the community property and the surviving spouse's interest in the community property are both eligible for the $1.3 million and $3.0 million basis adjustment.

.07 Rules Applicable to Basis Increase

Basis increase will be allocable on an asset-by-asset basis (e.g., basis increase can be allocated to a share of stock or a block of stock). However, in no case can the basis of an asset be adjusted above its fair market value. If the amount of basis increase is less than the fair market value of assets whose bases are eligible to be increased under these rules, the executor will determine which assets and to what extent each asset receives a basis increase.

.08 Penalties for Failure to File Required Information

1. Unless excused by a showing of reasonable cause, the executor or any person who is required to report to the IRS transfers at death of noncash assets in excess of $1.3 million in value under Code Sec. 6018(b)(1) and who fails to do so is liable for a penalty of $10,000 for each such failure [Code Sec. 6716(a)]. Additionally, a failure to file a return required under Code Sec. 6018(B)(2) (relating to appreciated

property acquired by the decedent within three years of death) will subject the executor or other person required to file to a penalty of $500 for each such failure [Code Sec. 6716(a), (c)].

2. Any donor required to provide to recipients of property by gift the information relating to the property that was reported on the donor's gift tax return (e.g., the fair market value and basis of property), with respect to such property, who fails to do so, is liable for a penalty of $50 for each failure to report such information to a donee [Code Sec. 6716(b)].

3. Note that no penalty is imposed with respect to any failure that is due to reasonable cause [Code Sec. 6716(c)].

4. If any failure to report to the IRS or a beneficiary is due to intentional disregard of the rules, then the penalty is 5 percent of the fair market value of the property for which reporting was required, determined at the date of the decedent's death (for property passing at death) or determined at the time of gift (for a lifetime gift) [Code Sec. 6716(d)].

▶ **PLANNING POINTER:** The modified carryover basis rules make it mandatory for taxpayers to maintain records of their original cost basis as well as the adjusted basis for some, if not all of their property. This adds a whole new level of complexity to the recordkeeping and retention rules imposed on taxpayers. Now taxpayers must retain records detailing the tax basis of all assets of significant value. From a planning perspective, it is easier to collect and retain this information when the purchaser is still alive, rather than trying to recreate the basis history many years from now after the original purchaser has died. Proving basis can be particularly nettlesome for assets, such as mutual fund shares that may have been purchased over a number of years. Under the carryover basis regime, record retention becomes very important for collectibles purchased over a lifetime, such as rare books, artwork, coins, and antiques. It will be difficult, if not impossible to recreate the basis history for these assets years after the original purchaser is dead and has given the property away. Moreover, in the absence of clear and complete records establishing the basis of the assets, the IRS will be forced to reconstruct the basis for the asset. You can be sure that they most likely will approximate a basis that will not be favorable to the taxpayer.

GIFT TAX

¶29,010 NATURE AND IMPOSITION OF TAX

.01 Gift Tax Rules

The following table illustrates the change in the gift tax rates and applicable exclusion amounts:

Table 1. Gift Tax Rates

	2011	2012	2013	2014
Gift Tax Exemption	$5 million	$5,120,000	$5,250,000	$5,340,000
Maximum Gift Tax Rate	35%	35%	40%	40%

Previously made gifts will "consume" part of the applicable exclusion amount, but at gift tax rates imposed at the time of the currently made gift. Thus, if a donor made a gift of $1 million in 2011 when the maximum gift tax rate was 35 percent, rather than 40 percent, the person should still be able to make $4,250,000 of additional gifts after 2011 and have such additional gifts "sheltered" from gift tax by the donor's remaining $4,250,000 applicable exclusion amount.

Make Tax-Free Gifts

Wealthy taxpayers can pass as much as $5,250,000 in 2013 (increasing to $5,340,000 in 2014) to younger generations with no current tax cost as a result of the increase in the lifetime gift tax exclusion amount. Married taxpayers can give away as much as $10,500,000 in 2013 (increasing to $10,680,000 in 2014). When selecting assets to give away, donors should look for assets that have the potential to appreciate in value because any income from and appreciation of the gifted property subsequent to the date of the gift will be transferred to the donee free of wealth transfer taxes.

Taxpayers who take advantage of gifting before year-end may realize the following benefits:

- *Removal of appreciation from estate*. The main objective for making gifts of appreciating property during a donor's lifetime is to remove from the donor's estate any income from and appreciation of the gifted property subsequent to the date of the gift because growth in the value of the gifted property is transferred to the donee totally free of gift and estate taxes. Even though the value of the gifted property is later added back to the donor's taxable estate as adjusted taxable gifts and factors into the donor's estate tax calculation, the appreciation and income on the gifted assets are not included in the estate tax calculation. This aspect of gifting appreciating property can be very beneficial and donors should try to make gifts of their most rapidly appreciating assets in order to take advantage of this tax-savings opportunity.

  Example 29-2: Dad makes a gift to his daughter of $250,000 worth of stock. As a result of the annual exclusion and the applicable credit amount in 2013 he pays no gift tax. Dad dies 15 years later when the value of that stock has increased to $1 million. All appreciation subsequent to the date of the gift (from $250,000 to $1 million) has escaped estate and gift tax. If Dad had instead held that stock until his death, all $1 million of value would have been subject to estate tax.

- *Gift tax removed from estate*. Under Code Sec. 2035(b) if the donor pays gift tax on gifts made during his or her lifetime, the gift tax is not included in the donor's estate unless the gift tax was paid on a gift made within three years of the decedent's death. Thus, if the decedent made gifts in excess of the exclusion amount and paid a gift tax, the gift tax paid is removed from the decedent's estate for estate tax purposes after three years from the date the gift was made.

- *Tax exclusive nature of gift tax.* Although the gift tax rate is the same as the estate tax rate, it is less expensive from a tax perspective to make a gift than to bequeath the same amount upon death. This is because gifts are tax exclusive (i.e., only the value of the property given as a gift is taxed), while the estate tax is tax inclusive (i.e., there is an estate tax on the estate tax, as well as on the bequeathed property). Therefore the effective rate of the gift tax is lower than the effective rate of the estate tax.
- *State estate tax avoidance.* Lifetime federal exclusion gifts will save the donor substantial state estate taxes because most states do not impose a gift tax on lifetime gifts or on prior gifts at death.
- *Income shifting.* Even with the Kiddie Tax, shifting income-producing assets to younger donees in lower income tax brackets will save income taxes. For further discussion of the Kiddie Tax see ¶ 2170.
- *No GST.* If the donor allocates generation-skipping transfer tax exemption to lifetime gifts, the gifts and future appreciation will avoid exposure to estate and generation-skipping transfer (GST) tax. The GST exemption amount in 2013 is $5,250,000 (increasing to $5,340,000 in 2014). See ¶ 29,170–¶ 29,190 for further discussion of GST tax.

Disadvantages of Lifetime Gifts

- *Carryover basis.* The basis of property acquired by gift is the same as it would be in the hands of the donor, increased by the amount of gift tax (if any) paid [Code Sec. 1015(a)]. For further discussion of carryover basis, see ¶ 29,005.
- *Donor loses income.* When donors give away income-producing property, they lose the right to receive that income. This may present insurmountable obstacles to some donors who are reluctant to give up assets that might otherwise be available to them in case of financial emergencies. One way to generate income for the donors even after the assets are gifted away is to make installment sales to grantor trusts which are discussed in more detail below.
- *Donor loses control.* Some donors may find it difficult to lose use and control over assets that they have spent a lifetime accumulating.

.02 The Gift Tax in General

The gift tax is imposed on lifetime gratuitous (or below fair market value) transfers made during the calendar year. The tax applies whether the transfer is in trust or otherwise, whether the gift is direct or indirect, and whether the property is real or personal, tangible or intangible [Reg. § 25.2511-1]. Interest-free loans (subject to certain exceptions) and forgiveness of debts are examples of indirect transfers that are subject to gift tax. If you meet certain requirements, you are not charged with making an indirect transfer when you refuse a gift or bequest from someone else. See discussion of qualified disclaimers at ¶ 29,165.

A "gift" is defined in Reg. § 25.2511-1(c) as "all transactions whereby property, or property rights or interests are gratuitously passed or conferred upon another, regardless of the means or device employed." Code Sec. 2511(a) provides further that the gift tax applies to all gratuitous transfers, whether direct or indirect, whether outright or in trust, and whether the property transferred is real or personal, tangible or intangible

[Reg. § 25.2511-1(a)]. The gift tax does not apply, however, to transfers made by a nonresident alien of property that does not have a United States *situs*.

You don't have to have *donative intent* (i.e., you need not be motivated by disinterested generosity) for a transfer to be subject to gift tax. And the donee need not be in existence at the time of the gift. For example, a transfer in trust for your grandchildren is a taxable gift even if you have no grandchildren at the time of the transfer.[1]

Code Sec. 2512(b) provides that "where property is transferred for less than an adequate and full consideration in money or money's worth, then the amount by which the value of the property exceeded the value of the consideration shall be deemed a gift." [Reg. § 25.2512-8]. In other words, the value of the gift for gift tax purposes is the amount that the value of the property transferred by the donor exceeds the value in money or money's worth of the consideration given for the property. When taxpayers sell property to family members, the IRS will closely examine all the facts and circumstances to see if a fair price was paid. Consideration not reducible to money or money's worth, such as love and affection, is disregarded. Similarly, the surrender of marital rights is not ordinarily regarded as consideration; but, special rules exempt property settlements from tax [¶ 29,020]. On the other hand, property sold in the ordinary course of business to an unrelated party is considered a transfer for full and adequate consideration-and therefore not subject to gift tax-even though it later turns out to be a bad bargain [Reg. § 25.2512-8].

Tax-Saving Exceptions

Taxpayers don't necessarily owe gift tax just because they make a taxable gift. Transfers to a spouse and transfers to charities can escape gift tax due to offsetting deductions. There also is a $14,000 per donee annual exclusion in 2013 and 2014 and exclusions for payment of someone else's medical expenses or tuition [¶ 29,020].

.03 Who Owes the Gift Tax?

The gift tax is imposed only on individuals, resident or nonresident [Code Sec. 2501]. But a gift by a corporation is considered a gift from the stockholders of the corporation. And a gift to a corporation generally is considered a gift to its stockholders. [Reg. § 25.2511-1(h)(1)].

The obligation to pay the gift tax owed on a gift is primarily the financial responsibility of the donor (i.e., the gift giver) [Code Sec. 2502(c); Reg. § 25.2502-2]. However, if the donor is short on cash (or simply so desires), a gift can be made on the condition that the donee (i.e., the recipient) pays the gift tax (called a "net gift"). In other words, the donee can contractually assume the responsibility of paying the gift tax on the transfer.[2]

The IRS ruled in Rev. Rul. 75-72[3] that if a donee agrees to pay the gift tax as a condition to receiving the gift, the gift tax will be imposed only on the net gift. The net gift is the value of the property less the gift taxes owed on the transfer. In order for the gift tax paid by the donee to be deducted from the value of the transferred property, the donee

[1] *M.B. Robinette*, SCt, 43-1 USTC ¶ 10,014, 318 US 184, 63 SCt 540; *H.W. Smith*, SCt, 43-1 USTC ¶ 10,013, 318 US 176, 63 SCt 545; *E.C. Dillingham Est.*, 88 TC 1569, Dec. 44,003 (1987), *aff'd*, CA-10, 90-1 USTC ¶ 60,021, 903 F2d 760.

[2] *V.P. Diedrich*, SCt, 82-1 USTC ¶ 9419, 457 US 191, 102 SCt 2414; Rev. Rul. 80-111, 1980-1 CB 208.

[3] Rev. Rul. 75-72, 1975-1 CB 310.

must be able to prove that the donee only received the gift because he or she agreed to pay the gift tax. If the obligation to pay the gift tax is illusory or too "contingent and speculative" as it was in *Estate of Armstrong*,[4] the donees cannot apply the net gift doctrine to reduce the value of the property.

.04 Nonresident Noncitizens

The gift tax also applies to nonresidents who are not U.S. citizens [Code Sec. 2501]. However, it applies only with respect to property situated in the United States; and it does not apply to intangible personal property, except in the case of a noncitizen who expatriated to avoid U.S. taxation [¶ 29,160] [Code Sec. 2501(a)]. The rate schedule applicable to citizens and residents also applies to a nonresident noncitizen. However, a nonresident noncitizen is not entitled to the unified credit [Code Sec. 2505(a)]. A special, limited credit of $13,000 (no inflation adjustment) (increased for residents of U.S. possessions and by treaty) [¶ 29,160] is applied only against the estate tax of a nonresident noncitizen [Code Sec. 2102(b)(1)]. Residents of possessions are entitled to a unified credit equal to the greater of $13,000 or $46,800 multiplied by the proportion of the decedent's gross estate situated in the United States [Code Sec. 2102(b)(2)].

¶29,015 TRANSFERS SUBJECT TO GIFT TAX

The gift tax reaches all gratuitous transfers of property except those that the law specifically excludes [¶ 29,020]. But the gift tax does not ordinarily apply unless the gift is complete-that is, not until the donor relinquishes control of the transferred property. Thus, the tax does not apply to a revocable transfer [Reg. § 25.2511-2]. On the other hand, a transfer with a possibility that the property will come back to the transferor does not make a gift incomplete. Such a transfer is subject to gift tax. However, the amount of the gift is reduced by this possibility of reverting back to the donor. Exceptions: There is no reduction where the possibility of reverter cannot be valued, or depends on a remote or speculative contingency.

> **Example 29-3:** Mr. Frank gives Blackacre to his nephew, Ben. The terms of the gift provide that Blackacre will revert to Frank if Ben dies first. The taxable gift is the value of Blackacre reduced by the value of the reversion.

.01 Below-Market Loans

Subject to certain exceptions, you can be charged with making a gift when you lend money to a family member or friend at no or low interest [Code Sec. 7872(c)(1)(A)]. Below-market loans also have income tax consequences [Ch. 2].

In one case, a mother's transfer of $100,000 to each of her two sons constituted taxable gifts rather than loans to the extent that they exceeded the annual gift tax exclusion applicable to that year.[5] The factors considered by the court in reaching a conclusion that a bona fide creditor-debtor relationship was not created included the following:

---

[4] *F. Armstrong Est.*, CA-4, 2002-1 USTC ¶ 60,427, 277 F3d 490.

[5] *E.B. Miller*, 71 TCM 1674, Dec. 51,105(M), TC Memo. 1996-3, *aff'd*, CA-9, 97-1 USTC ¶ 60,277.

- There was no real expectation of repayment.
- No interest was charged.
- There was no security or collateral for the note.
- There was no fixed maturity date for either note.
- Although the notes stated a due date for payment of the principal, neither child was aware of such date and the mother testified that she did not intend to demand payment on the stated due date.
- There was no discussion of the consequences, if any, that would result in the event either child defaulted on the note.
- There were no discussions of extensions of time for payment when both children failed to make the complete payment on their due dates.
- At the time that the notes were executed, the mother did not expect her children to ever pay her back.
- The children were not financially able to repay the notes.
- The taxpayer's records did not adequately reflect that the transfers were loans forgiven by the mother. Her designation of the character of the transfers as "loan" on the checks and any other actions relating to the transfers were not indicative of their substance.

.02 Loan Guarantees

You can even incur a gift tax liability if you pay off a loan you guaranteed for your child or someone else. In addition, the IRS has said that a parent's enforceable promise to guarantee a loan can itself be taxable.[6]

.03 Powers of Appointment

A power of appointment is a power granted by the donor enabling the donee to designate who shall take the property or benefit from its enjoyment. Your parent or another relative may have given you a power of appointment over property. The power could be a general power or a special power [¶ 29,085]. If it's a general power, you are charged with a gift when you exercise or release of the power [Code Sec. 2514(b)]. The lapse of such a power is also considered a transfer; but the transfer is taxable only to the extent the transferred property exceeds the greater of $5,000 or five percent of the value of the appointive property at the time of the lapse [Code Sec. 2514(e)].

.04 Joint Tenancies and Tenancies by the Entirety

Joint tenancy is a form of property ownership between two or more persons. See ¶ 29,050. Each joint tenant has the same interest and same rights in the property as the other co-tenant. The most important aspect of a joint tenancy is that it contains the rights of survivorship. This means that the interest of a deceased joint tenant does not pass in accordance with the provisions in a will, but passes directly to the surviving joint tenant. As a result of this survivorship feature, the joint tenancy form of property ownership functions as a means of probate avoidance because probate only applies to property that is titled in an individual's name alone.

---

[6] LTR 9113009 (Dec. 21, 1990).

A tenancy by entirety is a form of property ownership available only to a husband and wife as a marital unit. It's key feature is the right of survivorship—the survivor becomes the fee simple owner of the property when the other spouse dies. The tenancy is also terminated by transfer of the property or when the couple divorce. Entireties property is subject to the claims of the creditors of both spouses. The majority of jurisdictions that recognize tenancy by the entireties, so-called full bar jurisdictions, completely prohibit creditors from attaching entireties property to satisfy the debts of only one spouse. The other jurisdictions that recognize tenancy by the entirety, so-called modified or partial bar jurisdictions, permit creditors to attach one spouse's interest in entireties property for that spouse's debts only, subject to the rights of the nonliable spouse. The right of survivorship and the protection from separate creditors makes tenancy by the entirety an attractive and simple estate planning device. But couples with estates over the applicable exclusion amount, who use joint tenancies as their sole means of estate planning are failing to take advantage of estate tax savings techniques offered and sanctioned by the IRS.

The creation or termination of a joint tenancy can have gift tax consequences. The rules are different for joint tenancies between married persons (which may be treated as regular joint tenancies or as tenancies by the entirety, depending on state law) and those between unmarried persons and for joint tenancies involving spouses who are U.S. citizens and spouses who are not U.S. citizens. As a general rule, if one tenant furnishes more consideration than another, that first person is treated as having made a taxable gift to the other. If the donee is the donor's spouse and is a U.S. citizen, no gift tax has to be paid because of the unlimited gift tax marital deduction. The unlimited gift tax marital deduction is not available for donees who are not U.S. citizens [Code Sec. 2523(i)(1)]. However, such gifts are eligible for a special gift tax annual exclusion of $143,000 in 2013 (increasing to $145,000 in 2014) and lifetime exclusion [Code Sec. 2523(i)(2)]. If the joint tenancy or tenancy by the entirety is in real property and the spouse furnishing less than his or her share of the consideration is not a U.S. citizen, the creation of the joint tenancy or tenancy by the entirety will not be treated as a taxable gift; if the joint tenancy or tenancy by the entirety is in personal property, each spouse will be treated as having furnished one-half of the consideration [Code Sec. 2523(i)(3)]. If, during the lifetime of the tenants, the property is sold or the tenancy is otherwise terminated, a gift tax is imposed unless the proceeds are divided in proportion to the amount paid (or deemed paid) by each party for acquiring the property. But the marital deduction shelters the tax, unless the donee spouse is a noncitizen [Code Sec. 2523(i)(1)]. In that case, there is no marital deduction and the $143,000 annual exclusion available for gifts to noncitizen spouses in 2013 (increasing to $145,000 in 2014) applies. If the amount of the gift exceeds this exclusion, then gift tax liability arises but no tax is owed if the donor has available unified credit.

> **Example 29-4:** Frank and Maria are husband and wife. Both are U.S. residents, but Maria is a Brazilian citizen. In 1996, Frank bought real property entirely out of his own funds for himself and Maria as tenants by the entirety. The creation of the joint tenancy does not result in a taxable gift. In 2013, they sell the real property for $520,000, and Maria keeps all the proceeds. Result: In 2013, Frank is treated as making a gift of $520,000 to Maria, the first $143,000 of which is

sheltered by the annual exclusion. Note that if Maria were a U.S. citizen the entire gift would be sheltered by the marital deduction.

The creation of a nonspousal joint tenancy is a taxable gift to the extent that the funds furnished by one party exceeds the value of that person's interest. Note though that if the joint tenancy is in a bank account, the depositor who opens a joint bank account with his or her own funds generally is not considered to make a completed gift until the other joint owner makes a withdrawal without any obligation to account for the withdrawal. The termination of a nonspousal joint tenancy is a taxable gift to the extent the donor's share of the proceeds is less than the donor's interest in the property.

.05 Deemed Gifts and Indirect Gifts

Some transactions that are not ordinarily considered transfers have been taxed as gifts because they indirectly enriched others. For example, in one case the failure of a controlling shareholder to protect his right to annual preferred noncumulative dividends resulted in indirect gifts to minority common shareholders.[7] In another case, a controlling Class B preferred shareholder made taxable gifts to common shareholders as a result of his failure to convert Class A preferred stock when the corporation realized substantial earnings.[8]

.06 Disposition of QTIP Income Interest

Giving a spouse an income interest in a trust generally does not qualify for the gift or estate tax marital deduction unless the trust is a qualified terminable interest property (QTIP) trust or the spouse has a general power of appointment over the trust principal [¶ 29,020]. The marital deduction merely defers tax until the spouse dies or disposes of his or her interest. Under a special rule, a spouse who transfers any part of his or her life interest in a QTIP trust for which the marital deduction was allowed is charged with making a gift of the entire value of the property subject to the life estate, less any amount received on the disposition and any interest retained. The annual exclusion [¶ 29,020] is allowable for the income interest portion; no annual exclusion is allowable for the remainder interest because it is a future interest [Code Sec. 2519]. The value of the gift is reduced by the gift tax to be paid by the donee as determined under an interrelated computation [Reg. § 25.2519-1].

> **Example 29-5:** Paul Paulsen's will created a trust to pay all the income quarterly to his wife, Edna, for life, with remainder over to his daughter. Paul bequeathed assets worth $1 million to the trust. The QTIP election was made, and the marital deduction was allowed to Paul's estate. In 2013, when the trust is worth $1,214,000 and her life interest $200,000, Edna assigns her life interest to her sister. Edna made no other transfers to her sister that year. Result: In 2013, Edna makes a taxable gift of $1,200,000. The taxable gift consists of a life estate valued at $200,000 reduced to $186,000 as a result of the $14,000 present interest annual exclusion and the remainder interest worth $1,014,000. The life interest is taxed as a completed gift under Code Sec. 2511 and the remainder interest is taxed under Code Sec. 2519.

---

[7] LTR 8723007 (Feb. 18, 1987).

[8] LTR 8726005 (Mar. 13, 1987).

NOTE: Edna can recover the federal gift tax attributable to part of the transfer [Code Sec. 2207A]. Although the entire value of the trust assets less the $14,000 present interest annual exclusion is taxable to Edna [Reg. § 25.2519-1], she is entitled to reimbursement for the gift tax attributable only to the value of the remainder interest [Reg. § 25.2207A-1]. That amount of tax may be recovered by Edna from the trust [Reg. § 25.2207A-1(f), Ex.].

.07 Generation Skipping Tax Gross-Up

If a transfer subject to the gift tax is also subject to the generation skipping transfer (GST) tax as a direct skip [¶ 29,180], the amount of the gift is increased by the GST tax [Code Sec. 2515].

.08 Qualified Tuition Programs (Code Sec. 529 Plans)

Contributions of $14,000 in 2013 and 2014 ($28,000 in 2013 and in 2014 if married couple), to a qualified tuition program will be treated as a completed gift of a present interest from the contributor at the time of the contribution [Code Sec. 529(c)(2)]. As a result, these contributions will be eligible for the annual gift tax exclusion and are also excluded for purposes of the generation-skipping transfer tax. If the contribution exceeds $14,000 ($28,000 if married couple), the contributor may elect to have the contribution treated as if made ratably over five years beginning in the year the contribution is made [Code Sec. 529(c)(2)(B)]. See ¶ 5110 for a detailed discussion of college savings plan.

Example 29-6: In 2013, you make a $30,000 contribution to a qualified tuition program and elect to have it treated as five annual contributions of $6,000. You could make up to $8,000 in other transfers to the beneficiary each year without paying any gift tax.

According to this five-year averaging rule, a donor may contribute up to $70,000 every five years ($140,000 in the case of a married couple) with no gift tax consequences, assuming no other gifts are made to the beneficiary in the five-year period. A gift tax return must be filed with respect to any contribution in excess of the annual gift-tax exclusion limit, and the election for five-year averaging must be made on the contributor's gift tax return.

If a donor making an over-$14,000 contribution dies during the five-year averaging period, the portion of the contribution that has not been allocated to the years prior to death is includible in the donor's gross estate.

Example 29-7: Beth Bell makes a $65,000 contribution to a qualified tuition program in 2013 and elects to treat the transfer as being made over a five-year period. Beth dies the following year. $14,000 would be allocated to the year of contribution, another $14,000 would be allocated to the year of death, and the remaining $37,000 would be includible in the Beth's gross estate.

For estate tax purposes, the value of any interest in a qualified tuition program will be includible in the estate of the designated beneficiary.

¶29,020 TRANSFERS EXEMPT FROM GIFT TAX

Donors are only taxed on the total amount of taxable gifts made during the calendar year, less the marital and charitable deductions. But certain transfers are not counted as taxable gifts. These exempt transfers include the first $14,000 in 2013 and in 2014 of gifts (other than gifts of future interests in property) to an unlimited number of individuals. In 2013, the first $143,000 (increasing to $145,000 in 2014) of gifts to a spouse who is not a citizen of the United States (other than gifts of future interests in property) are not included in the total amount of taxable gifts made during that year. There is also an educational exclusion, a medical exclusion, and an exclusion for contributions to a political organization defined in Code Sec. 527(e)(1) [Code Secs. 2501(a)(5), 2503(b), (e), 2523(i)(2)].[9]

.01 Annual Exclusion

There is an annual per donee exclusion of $14,000 in 2013 (no change in 2014). If the value of all gifts made by a particular donor to a donee in a calendar year is less than the amount of the annual gift tax exclusion, the gifts are not taxable. If they total more than the amount of the annual gift tax exclusion, they are taxable only to the extent they exceed that amount. If not made by year-end, the annual per-donee per donee gift tax exclusion is lost forever. The benefits do not accumulate from year to year.

Unlimited Number of Donees

The exclusion applies to each donee on gifts from each donor. Thus, you can make gifts of $14,000 per year to as many people as you like without owing any gift tax. By taking advantage of the annual exclusion through a planned giving program spanning several years, you can substantially reduce your estate taxes. Not only do the annual exclusion transfers themselves get removed from your estate tax base, but the post-transfer appreciation in their value also gets removed.

Since you can make annual exclusion gifts of up to $14,000 in 2013 (no change in 2014) to an *unlimited* number of donees and still have the exclusion apply to each donee, if you can afford it and want to really reduce the amount of your taxable gross estate, you can make gifts of $14,000 in 2013 (no change in 2014) to each of your grandchildren and children and their spouses without owing any gift tax.

"Present Interest" Requirement

The annual gift tax exclusion is only available for gifts of a "present interest" in property. A *present interest* is a legal term which means that the enjoyment or possession of the gift must be immediate or in the present rather than off in the distant future. Gifts of *future interests*, which are gifts where possession or enjoyment of the property is postponed until some future time like after someone else dies (as is the case with a remainder interest in a trust), do not generally qualify for the gift tax exclusion unless special requirements are met.

---

[9] Rev. Rul. 82-216, 1982-2 CB 220.

Gifts of LLCs and Other Closely Held Business Interests

In order for the gift/transfer of an ownership interest in a business entity to qualify for the annual gift tax exclusion, the transfer must qualify as a present (rather than a future) interest in property. In the context of the transfer of an interest in an LLC, the court in *A.J. Hackl*[10] held that a husband and wife's gifts of units in a limited liability company (LLC) to their children and grandchildren failed to qualify for the annual gift tax exclusion because the donees did not have the immediate use, possession or enjoyment of the LLC units. The donees did not receive an "unrestricted and noncontingent" right to the immediate use, possession or enjoyment of the transferred property (or the income therefrom). The LLC operating agreement prevented the donees from obtaining a substantial economic benefit from the LLC units because the donees could not: (1) unilaterally withdraw their capital accounts; (2) sell or transfer their units without the consent of the LLC's manager; or (3) unilaterally effectuate a dissolution of the LLC. Moreover, the donees did not have the right to the use, possession or enjoyment of the income from the LLC units because there was no expectation that the LLC would produce immediate income and the distribution of any income that was generated was at the discretion of the manager. As a result, the donors were not entitled to the annual exclusions for their gifts of the LLC membership units.

In *Price*,[11] the Tax Court followed *Hackl* to conclude that the transfer of limited partnership (LP) interests by husband and wife donors to their adult children failed to qualify for the annual gift tax exclusion because the children did not have the unrestricted right to the immediate use, possession or enjoyment of their interests in the LP (or the income generated by the interests). In order to qualify as a gift of a present interest for purposes of Code Sec. 2503(b), the children were required to receive not just all of the donors' legal rights in the transferred property, but a "substantial present economic benefit" derived from ownership of the property. Pursuant to the LP agreement, the children were prevented from obtaining a substantial economic benefit from the LLC units because the agreement restricted their ability to transfer their interest. Further, the children were not even properly characterized as partners of the LP and were effectively only assigned a right to receive profits. The children were also not given an unrestricted right to the partnership income because income from the LP did not flow "steadily," nor could it be "readily ascertained." As a result, the donors were not entitled to Code Sec. 2503(b) annual exclusions for their gifts of the LLC interests.

In *J.W. Fisher*,[12] a husband and wife's transfer of membership interests in a limited liability company (LLC) to each of their seven children failed to qualify for the annual gift tax exclusion because the transfers were of a future interest in the underlying property. The couple gave each of their children a 4.76-percent membership interest in the LLC, whose primary asset was an undeveloped plot of lake-front property. Under the terms of the operating agreement, both the children's right to receive distributions as well as their right to transfer their membership interests was significantly restricted, preventing them from retaining a "substantial present economic benefit" in the prop-

---

[10] *A.J. Hackl*, CA-7, 2003-2 USTC ¶60,465, 335 F3d 664.

[11] *W.M. Price*, 99 TCM 1005, Dec. 58,103(M), TC Memo. 2010-2.

[12] *J.W. Fisher*, DC-IN, 2010-1 USTC ¶60,588.

erty. The court relied on *Hackl* and since the gifts were not gifts of a present interest in the LLC, they failed to qualify for the annual gift tax exclusion under Code Sec. 2503.

Limited Partnership Interest Gifts Qualified for Annual Gift Tax Exclusion

In *Estate of G.H. Wimmer*,[13] the Tax Court concluded that gifts of limited partnership interests made were gifts of present interests and thus qualified for the gift tax annual exclusion. Over a five-year period, gifts of limited partnership interests were made, pursuant to transfer restrictions prescribed in the trust instrument, to family members and a trust benefitting family members. The partnership's primary purpose was to invest in property on a profitable basis. The partnership was funded with publicly traded and dividend-paying stock. The partnership received dividends from the stock and made distributions to the limited partners. The purpose of the family limited partnership was to increase family wealth, control the division of family assets, restrict nonfamily rights to acquire family assets, and, by using the gift tax exclusion, transfer property to younger generations without fractionalizing family assets. In accordance with *A.J. Hackl*, to qualify as a present interest, the gift must confer a substantial present economic benefit by reason of the use, possession, or enjoyment of the property or the income from the property. The court concluded that the right to income was a present interest because the estate proved that on the date of each gift: (1) the partnership expected to generate income; (2) as a result of the fiduciary relationship between the general partners and the trustee of the grandchildren's trust, a portion of partnership income was expected to flow steadily to the limited partners; and (3) the portion of the income flowing to the limited partners could be readily ascertained.

▶ **PLANNING TIP:** To avoid the problems faced by the taxpayers in *Hackl, Price*, and *Fisher*, gifts/transfers of interests in limited partnerships or LLCs should be accompanied by grants of limited rights to withdraw income and principal similar to those granted in *Crummey* as discussed below. Another alternative is to transfer an LLC that generates income, a portion of which can flow through to the donees, thus creating the requisite present use and enjoyment of the gift.

▶**PRACTICE POINTER:** Several drafting suggestions will avoid running into problems like the Fishers:

- Don't include a prohibition on transfers but provide that any transferee will be subject to a right of first refusal, within reasonable time limits.
- Do not explicitly favor reinvestments over distributions in the partnership agreement.
- Make distributions annually and predictable.
- Mandate distributions of net cash flow.
- Specify that the general partner/manager owed fiduciary duties to the other partners/members.
- Give donees a *Crummey* withdrawal power with respect to gifts of limited partnership interests that would enable donees to withdraw fair market value of their limited partnership interests for a limited period of time after each

[13] *G.H. Wimmer Est.*, 103 TCM 1839, Dec. 59,079(M), TC Memo. 2012-157.

gift. This is obviously an unusual provision to be in a partnership agreement. Such a right would reduce or eliminate any discount for lack or marketability or control with respect to that portion of each gift that qualified for the annual exclusion, but, depending on the context, that may be a modest penalty to pay for the entire elimination of the gift tax on the first $14,000 of gifts to each donee in 2013 (no change in 2014).

- Give donee-partners a limited period of time to sell the interest to the partnership for its fair market value, determined without regard to the existence of the put right.

Crummey to the Rescue

Thanks to a famous case where the taxpayer's name was *Crummey*,[14] you can convert a gift made to a trust, which would otherwise qualify as a future interest and therefore ineligible for the gift tax annual exclusion, into a present interest by giving the donor the right to withdraw property from the trust, even though he or she does not actually exercise the withdrawal right. As long as the power to exercise a withdrawal right exists, the interest qualifies as a present interest and is therefore eligible for the Code Sec. 2503(b) annual gift tax exclusion. It doesn't matter that, as a practical matter minor children are unable to exercise the withdrawal right without the appointment of a guardian.

In a generous interpretation of *Crummey*, the Tax Court in *Cristofani*[15] held that a 15 days unrestricted demand right given by a grandmother to each of her grandchildren who only had contingent remainder interests qualified as a present interest in the corpus of the trust. The IRS has even issued a formal approval of the result in the case. This means that a trust beneficiary need not have a vested remainder interest in the trust corpus or income in order to qualify for the annual gift tax exclusion. Even though the IRS issued a formal approval of the result in the case,[16] they also issued a sternly-worded warning to overly creative estate planners.

Therefore, the IRS has approved *Crummey* withdrawal powers as short as 15 days in *Cristofani* for as long as 60 days[17] and 90 days.[18] However, a 3-day demand right was held to be insufficient in Rev. Rul. 81-7.[19] It is preferable for the lapse time of the withdrawal power to begin to run on the date of the gift transfer rather than the date of the notice.

In statements accompanying the approval, the IRS indicated that they intend to challenge aggressively gift tax exclusions arising out of the granting of *Crummey* powers. The IRS stated that it "does not contest annual gift tax exclusions for *Crummey* powers where the trust instrument gives the power holders a bona fide unrestricted legal right to demand immediate possession and enjoyment of trust income or corpus." However, the IRS intends to deny "the exclusions for *Crummey*

[14] *D.C. Crummey*, CA-9, 68-2 USTC ¶12,541, 397 F2d 82.

[15] *M. Cristofani Est.*, 97 TC 74, Dec. 47,491, *acq. in result*, 1992-1 CB 1. *See also L. Kohlsaat Est.*, 73 TCM 2732, Dec. 52,031(M), TC Memo. 1997-212.

[16] IRS Action on Decision (1996-010, IRB 1996-29 IRB 4).

[17] LTR 199912016 (Dec. 12, 1998).

[18] LTR 8044080 (Aug. 11, 1980).

[19] Rev. Rul. 81-7, 1981-1 CB 474.

powers, regardless of the power holders' other interests in the trust, where the withdrawal rights are not in substance what they purport to be in form."

This simply means that you can expect the IRS to take a closer look at your trust if you make contributions to trusts with multiply contingent beneficiaries having *Crummey* powers or with individuals having only *Crummey* powers and no other interests in the trust. They will look behind the mere form of the *Crummey* rights to see the true substance of the arrangement. For example, in Letter Ruling 200341002, the IRS ruled that a grantor was not entitled to the gift tax annual exclusion for gifts made to a trust subject to *Crummey* withdrawal powers in the hands of four charities. The IRS concluded that the charities' nonexercise of such powers indicated an implied understanding among the parties that no exercise was ever to occur. Thus, the IRS found the charities' *Crummey* powers to be illusory and denied annual exclusions on those grounds.

When Is Gift Effective?

A taxable gift is made when the donor has made a completed gratuitous transfer of property. The gift transfer is complete when the donor has relinquished sufficient dominion and control over the property so that it is no longer subject to the donor's will or the donor no longer has the power to change its disposition (whether for the donor's own benefit or the benefit of others) [Reg. §25.2511-2(b)]. In other words, a gift transfer is complete when a person has completely parted with and retains no strings over the property transferred in the gift.

> ▶ **PLANNING POINTER: Is a check a gift when it is given or cashed?** Year-end is a good time to be sure you have made your annual exclusion gifts. But don't wait until December 31 to give your grandchild the check. The IRS could argue that the gift was made the following year when the check cleared the bank, rather than in the year that you wrote the check and gave it your grandchild. The gift giver would then lose the opportunity to take advantage of his or her annual gift tax exclusion in the year of the gift and any subsequent gifts made the following year would exceed that year's quota.

The law provides that a gift made by check is not complete until the check is cashed, certified, or negotiated for value to a third person. As a result if you are giving a check and intend to claim an exclusion for the gift, allow enough time for the check to be cashed before the end of the year. Alternatively, consider giving a certified check which is as good as cash because it is considered a completed gift when you hand over the check.

When you make late year-end gifts by check it is important to figure out the year in which the gift is made. This determination is important for purposes of using up your annual gift tax exclusion. Any portion of the annual exclusion that is not used up by year-end cannot be carried over to the next year.

.02 Relation-Back Rule

When a check is delivered to a noncharitable donee, completion of the gift will "relate back" to the earlier of:

1. The date on which the donor parted with dominion and control under local law; or
2. The date on which the donee deposited, cashed or presented the check for payment if:[20]
   - The drawee bank paid the check when it was first presented,
   - The donor was alive when the bank paid the check,
   - The donor intended to make a gift,
   - Delivery was unconditional, and the check was deposited, cashed or presented in the calendar year in which the favorable gift treatment was sought and within a reasonable time of issuance.[21]

For example, if grandma gives grandson a holiday gift in the form of a check and it is drawn and presented for payment to the grandson's bank in December, but was not accepted until January of the following year, it was a completed gift in December. The relation-back doctrine will preserve the grandmother's annual exclusion gift in this situation if the grandmother is still alive at the time the check is presented for payment.

Example 29-8: Dad gives Son a $14,000 check on December 31. Dad wants the check to qualify as a an annual gift tax exclusion gift in the year he wrote the check. Son cashes the check early the following year while Dad is still alive. The check is considered a gift in the year that Dad wrote the check and gave it to his son, even though it wasn't cashed until the following year because: (1) Dad intended to make a gift; (2) Dad delivered the check unconditionally (e.g., there were enough funds in the account to cover the check and there was no understanding that Son would hold off on cashing the check); and (3) Son could have presented the check to the bank before the end of the year of the gift.

Exception to Relation-Back Rule

The relation-back rule does not apply when gifts are made to noncharitable donees and the donor dies before the checks are cashed.[22] This means that the value of checks drawn on a gross estate will remain part of the estate if they are cashed after the decedent has died because the decedent possessed, until death, the power to revoke the checks until accepted or paid by the drawee bank. Therefore, they were not completed gifts because the decedent maintained dominion and control over the amounts in the checking account against which the checks were written until death.

▶ **PLANNING POINTER:** Taxpayers who are elderly or seriously ill should make annual exclusion gifts as soon as possible rather than waiting until December 31. The courts have declined the invitation to extend the relation-back rule to noncharitable donees, where the checks did not clear during the decedent's lifetime. If you receive an annual exclusion gift from a wealthy friend or relative on his or her deathbed, you should cash the check immediately. Running to the bank with the check will be beneficial to both you and the donor. Why? When

[20] Rev. Rul. 96-56, 1996-2 CB 161.

[21] *A.F. Metzger Est.*, CA-4, 94-2 USTC ¶60,179, 38 F3d 118.

[22] *S.H. Newman Est.*, 111 TC 81, Dec. 52,811 (1998), *aff'd*, CA-DC, 99-2 USTC ¶60,358, 203 F3d 53; *M.R. Rosano Est.*, CA-2, 2001-1 USTC ¶60,401, 245 F3d 212.

the donor dies, his or her executor will be able to reduce the amount of the decedent's taxable estate by the amount of the gift. You will benefit because you will have access to the money sooner. Another suggestion for donors making deathbed annual exclusion gifts is to give the money in the amount of a certified check, which will be considered a completed gift upon receipt by the donee.

Split Gifts Available for All Spouses Regardless of Sex

Code Sec. 2513 allows a married couple to treat a gift to a third person as if each spouse had made one-half of the gift. In other words, when one spouse makes a gift to a third party with his or her own money, the nondonor spouse may join in the gift as if the nondonor spouse had put up the money for one-half of the gift. This is called gift splitting and it is a valuable estate planning tool that provides an opportunity for spouses to double the amount of the annual exclusion available for a gift. By engaging in gift splitting, a married couple can benefit from each spouse's annual gift tax exclusion. The gift-splitting provisions require the filing of an election for each calendar year in which a married couple split their gifts to third persons [Code Sec. 2513(a) and (b)].

Prior to the Supreme landmark decision in *E.S. Windsor*,[23] only married couples of the opposite sex were entitled to "split" gifts and double their annual gift tax exclusion ($14,000 for 2013, for a total tax-free gift of $28,000 with no increase in 2014). After *E.S. Windsor* and the IRS release of Rev. Rul. 2013-17,[24] where the IRS ruled that all legal same-sex marriages will be recognized for federal tax purposes, same-sex legally married couples can take advantage of gift-splitting. In the interest of achieving uniformity, stability, and efficiency in the application and administration of the tax laws, the IRS adopted a "state of celebration" rule in Rev. Rul. 2013-17. Accordingly, same-sex couples who were legally married in one state will always be treated as married for federal tax purposes even if they reside in a state or jurisdiction that does not recognize same-sex marriage. For further discussion of *E.S. Windsor*, and its impact on the marital deduction, see ¶29,120.

> **Example 29-9:** Spouse 1 gives $28,000 to Son in 2013. Spouse 2 consents to gift splitting. As a result, Spouse 1 is treated as if she gave Son $14,000 and Spouse 2 is treated as if she gave Son $14,000. No gift tax is owed that year because the annual per donee exclusion allowable to each spouse applies to the gift even though Spouse 1 supplied the all the funds for the gift.

Gift-Splitting Applies to All Gifts During the Year

Once consent to gift-splitting is agreed to by both spouses, it automatically applies to all gifts made during the calendar year. The spouses may not pick and choose which gifts to split during a particular calendar year [Reg. § 25.2513-1(b)]. Moreover, if both spouses make gifts in a year when they have agreed to gift-split, all gifts made during that year must be split.

---

[23] *E.S. Windsor*, SCt, 2013-2 USTC ¶60,667, *aff'g*, CA-2, 2012-2 USTC ¶60,654, *aff'd*, DC-NY, 2012-1 USTC ¶60,647, 833 FSupp 394.

[24] Rev. Rul. 2013-17, IRB 2013-38, 201.

How Do Spouses Signify Consent?

Reg. § 25.2513-2 provides that consent must be signified by both spouses. If both spouses file gift tax returns, each spouse must signify consent on his or her own return or on the other spouse's return, or both may signify consent on one of the returns. It is preferred for each spouse to consent on the other spouse's return.

Tax Return Required to Gift-Split

Married couples who make joint gifts must file a gift tax return on IRS Form 709. Each spouse must sign the return to show that he or she consents to treat the gifts as having been made one-half by each. If you neglect to consent to split gifts on a timely filed gift-tax return you may find your otherwise tax-free gift subject to tax.

In addition to making annual exclusions available for the spouse with less wealth, gift-splitting makes it possible to take advantage of his or her exemption equivalent of unified credit and sometimes results in a lower gift tax bracket. Both husband and wife must be U.S. citizens or residents. The donor spouse must not give the consenting spouse a general power of appointment over the transferred property. They must agree to split all gifts made during the calendar year as long as they are married to each other. And if they divorce, they must not remarry during the calendar year. When you split gifts, you and your spouse are jointly and severally liable for the tax on all gifts made during the calendar year [Code Sec. 2513]. If you make split gifts of future interests or gifts exceeding $28,000 during either 2013 or 2014, you and your spouse each must file a separate gift tax return.

Gifts to Minors

The present interest requirement for the annual exclusion could pose a problem when you want to make a gift to a minor but you don't want him or her to have immediate access to the funds. To solve this problem, the law provides that a gift of property to an individual under age 21 qualifies as a present interest eligible for the exclusion if:

1. The income from the gift may be spent for the benefit of the donee before he or she reaches age 21; and
2. To the extent not expended, the income (a) will pass to the donee on attaining age 21, or (b) will be payable to the donee's estate or as the donee appoints if the donee dies before reaching the age of 21 years [Code Sec. 2503(c)]. Transfers to custodial accounts under the Uniform Transfers to Minors Acts (and similar acts) satisfy these requirements. This is so even if final distribution has to take place when the donee reaches the age of 18 years because that is the age of majority under state law.[25]

▶ **OBSERVATION:** Don't name yourself as trustee or custodian of a gift to a minor. Rather, name your spouse or some other relative. The reason for this is that if you, the donor, die while serving as trustee or custodian over the gifted funds, the value of the property will be included in your gross estate and be subject to estate tax. This would defeat one of the advantages of making the transfer in the first place. The same problem could arise if you merely retain the power to appoint yourself to such position [Code Sec. 2038].[26]

---

[25] Rev. Rul. 73-287, 1973-2 CB 321.

[26] Rev. Rul. 70-348, 1970-2 CB 193.

.03 Giving Gifts Under a Durable Power of Attorney

A durable power of attorney authorizes someone to handle another person's financial affairs if that person becomes disabled or incompetent and are unable to act on his or her own behalf. The power is labeled "durable" because it is not revoked by incompetency and will continue in effect after incapacity, permitting continued management of a taxpayer's affairs without the expense or complexity of obtaining authority to act through judicial process. If properly drafted, a power of attorney can authorize the attorney-in-fact (the person designated to act on behalf of another) to make gifts on behalf of another. Thus the practice of making annual exclusion gifts can continue even after taxpayers become disabled provided the proper gift-giving language is used. Authorizing the person exercising the power to perform "any and all acts" without even specifically mentioning the power to make gifts, is not sufficient.

Keep in mind, however, when considering gift-giving under a durable power of attorney that the courts will be suspicious of gifts made by an agent under a durable power of attorney because of the opportunity for fraud and abuse. In fact, if the durable power of attorney does not expressly authorize making gifts, courts are reluctant to imply the existence of gift-giving privileges in the absence of a state statute authorizing such inference. If taxpayers intend for an agent to make gifts on their behalf after they have become incapacitated, they must make certain that the durable power of attorney includes language expressly authorizing them to execute gifts on behalf of another.

Taxpayers will not be able to rely on loose language in a bank-drafted power of attorney to support gift-giving privileges. The courts will only uphold gifts by agents pursuant to durable powers of attorney where the power of attorney expressly authorizes the agent to make the gifts or where state statute implied that such power existed.[27] To be sure that gift-giving made by a third-party will qualify for the annual gift tax exclusion, the power of attorney should specifically give the attorney-in-fact the authority to make gifts on another's behalf in order to take advantage of the annual gift tax exclusion. Be sure he or she is authorized "to make gifts in the pattern" used during the taxpayer's lifetime. Courts have upheld gifts by agents pursuant to durable powers of attorney only where the power of attorney expressly authorizes the agent to make the gift or where state statute implied that such power existed.

Keep in mind when creating gift-giving powers under a power of attorney that the IRS and the courts are inherently suspicious of gifts made by a donor who is dead and therefore unable to corroborate or deny the claim. This is especially true when the gift is made by an agent pursuant to a durable power of attorney and the opportunity for abuse and the conflict of interest exists. To ward off any claims of abuse, the power of attorney should expressly state that the agent has the authority to make gifts on behalf of the principal in order to take advantage of the annual gift tax exclusion. If the principal has engaged during his or her lifetime in making annual gift tax exclusion gifts, include in the power of attorney language authorizing the

---

[27] *A.J. Frank Est.*, 69 TCM 2255, Dec. 50,549(M), TC Memo 1995-132; *G.A. Townsend*, DC-NE, 95-1 USTC ¶60,192, 889 FSupp 369.

agent to make annual exclusion gifts in the pattern used during his or her lifetime. Failure to include these few sentences could have costly repercussions because gifts that fail to qualify for the annual gift tax exclusion will be included in the decedent's taxable estate.

For example, one court concluded that thirty-eight $10,000 deathbed gifts made under a durable general power of attorney were void because the authority to make the gifts was not expressly authorized in the document and therefore the gifts were includable in the decedent's gross estate under Code Sec. 2038(a)(2).[28]

.04 Medical and Educational Expenses

All qualified medical payments made on behalf of another person are gift-tax free. The payments for medical care (as defined in Code Sec. 213(d)) must be made directly to the provider of the medical care.

All amounts paid on behalf of an individual as tuition directly to a qualifying educational institution to be used exclusively for the education or training of designated individuals will be eligible for the unlimited gift tax exclusion [Code Sec. 2503(e)(2)(A)]. The tuition exclusion applies to tuition expenses of full-time or part-time students. The tuition must be paid directly to the educational organization providing the education [Reg. § 25.2503-6(b)(2)].

The exclusion for educational expenses applies to tuition for any educational organization, including nursery, elementary, secondary schools, colleges and universities. However, the exclusion does not cover books, rent, board, and other living expenses. The individual may be a full-time or part-time student [Reg. § 25.2503-6(b)(2)]. A qualifying educational organization is an organization with a regular faculty and curriculum and a regularly enrolled body of students in attendance at the place where the educational activities are carried on [Code Sec. 170(b)(1)(A)(ii)]. The school may be either domestic or foreign.

The payments must be made directly to the educational institution. Payments made by the donor to the donee who uses them (or is reimbursed) to pay for tuition at the school will fail to qualify for the gift tax exclusion.

Payments made to a trust with terms requiring the trustee to use the trust funds to pay tuition expenses will not qualify for the Code Sec. 2503(e) exclusion because the payments are not a direct transfer to an educational organization. Reg. § 25.2503-6(c), Ex. 2, considers a situation where a donor transfers $100,000 to a trust which requires the trustee to use the trust funds to pay tuition expenses for the donor's grandchildren. The example concludes that the donor's transfer to the trust is not a direct transfer to an educational organization and therefore fails to qualify for the unlimited gift tax exclusion available to taxpayers who pay for someone else's education.

▶ **PRACTICE POINTER:** Unlike the annual per donee exclusion, which is limited to $14,000 per year per donee in 2013 (no increase in 2014), no dollar limit exists on qualified educational expenses if payments are made directly to the school and are earmarked for the payment of a specific person's tuition Code Sec. 2503(e)]. This very effective and relatively easy estate reduction tool is a gift from Congress that taxpayers often overlook.

---

[28] *S.S. Swanson Est.*, CA-FC, 2001-1 USTC ¶ 60,408.

Example 29-10: Ralph and Rachel Richard have one granddaughter in college. Her total annual tuition is $40,000. The Richards can pay this amount free of gift tax. Had they transferred $40,000 to the grandchild's parents, only $28,000 would qualify for the annual exclusion with the remainder subject to gift tax in the year of the tuition payment.

NOTE: While the exclusion is particularly good for grandparents, parents, aunts, uncles and other relatives can take advantage of it. You don't even have to be related to the person on behalf of whom medical or tuition payments are made.

A contribution to a 529 college savings or prepaid tuition plan qualifies as a completed gift of a present interest to the designated beneficiary of the plan but does not qualify as a qualified transfer to an educational organization eligible for exclusion under Code Sec. 2503(e) [Code Sec. 529(c)(2)].

.05 Property Settlements

A transfer under a written agreement between husband and wife in settlement of marital, property or child support rights incident to divorce is exempt from gift tax if divorce occurs no more than one year before, or two years after, the agreement is entered [Code Sec. 2516].

.06 Pension Rights

Company retirement plans generally must provide a survivor annuity for the spouse of a married participant and bar other forms of payout unless the spouse consents [Ch. 3]. A spouse's consent to waive his or her right to receive an annuity theoretically could be regarded as making a gift. However, the law makes it clear that the waiver of a qualified joint and survivor annuity or qualified pre-retirement survivor annuity is not taxable as a gift. The waiver must be made before the death of the retirement plan participant [Code Sec. 2503(f)].

.07 Marital Deduction

Unlimited amounts can be transferred to your spouse free of gift tax by virtue of the gift tax marital deduction (unless your spouse is not a U.S. citizen). Outright transfers qualify without needing to meet any special requirements. Transfers in trust qualify only if special requirements are met. For example, a life income interest in a trust generally does not qualify unless the trust is a QTIP trust or the spouse has a general power of appointment over principal. These requirements are designed to ensure that the property will automatically be taxed when the spouse dies or disposes of the property. In other words, the marital deduction generally does not allow tax to be permanently avoided. Rather, it is aimed at providing tax-deferral. The requirements are discussed in greater detail in connection with the estate tax marital deduction, which is subject to similar rules [¶29,120]. The gift tax marital deduction is not allowed for transfers to a noncitizen spouse [though there is a $143,000 (increasing to $145,000 in 2014) annual exclusion in 2013 for gifts to noncitizen spouses, as discussed above] [Code Sec. 2523(i)(2)].

.08 Charitable Deduction

Transfers to charity are exempt from gift tax by reason of a charitable deduction [Code Sec. 2522]. There is also an estate tax charitable deduction. Requirements for both deductions are similar and are discussed at ¶29,125.

¶29,025 VALUATION OF GIFTS

The amount that is subject to tax is clear when money is transferred-it's simply the amount of cash given. But when property other than money is transferred, the amount subject to tax is the fair market value of the property at the time of the gift, less any payment made by the donee. The value of gifts can't be arrived at arbitrarily. Rather, it must be determined under principles prescribed by the IRS. These principles generally also apply for estate tax valuation purposes and are discussed in connection with estate tax valuation at ¶29,105. (Some special estate tax valuation rules like alternate valuation and special use valuation [¶29,105] do not apply for gift tax purposes.)

.01 What Constitutes "Adequate Disclosure" of Gifts

If a gift has been "adequately disclosed" on a gift tax return, the IRS cannot revalue the gift for gift tax purposes once three years have passed since the return was filed. The three-year gift tax statute of limitations does not start running until the gift is adequately disclosed on a gift tax return [Code Sec. 6501(c)(9)]. The IRS has issued guidelines on what constitutes "adequate disclosure" of transfers of property reported as gifts in Reg. § 301.6501(c)-1(f)(2)(i)-(v).

The IRS provides in Reg. § 301.6501(c)-1(f)(2) that a gift will be adequately disclosed on the gift tax return only if it is reported in a manner adequate to apprise the IRS of the nature of the gift and the basis for the reported value.

In lieu of describing the gift, Reg. § 301.6501(c)-1(f)(3)(i) permits taxpayers to submit an appraisal of the gift provided the appraisal satisfies the following requirements:

1. The appraisal is prepared by an appraiser who holds himself or herself out to the public as an appraiser or performs appraisals on a regular basis;
2. The appraiser is qualified to make the appraisals of the type of property being valued by virtue of the appraiser's qualifications, as described in the appraisal that details the appraiser's background, experience, education and membership, if any, in professional appraisal associations; and
3. The appraiser is not the donor or the donee or a member of the family of the donor or donee, or any person employed by the donor, the donee, or a member of the family of either.

Code Sec. 2001(f) relieves taxpayers of the recordkeeping burdens traditionally associated with gift-giving. Once the three statute of limitations has passed, taxpayers can rest assured that the value of a gift as disclosed on a gift tax return or on a statement attached to a return will not be challenged by the IRS for estate tax purposes. The final determination of a gift's value could be the value that is: (1) reported on a gift tax return (if not challenged by the IRS prior to expiration of the statute of limitations), (2) determined by the IRS (if not challenged by the taxpayer in court), (3) determined by a court, or (4) agreed upon by the taxpayer and the IRS in a settlement [Code Sec. 2001(f)].

.02 Amended Return Required if Gift Not Adequately Disclosed

In order to begin the running of the period of limitations on assessment for a gift that wasn't adequately disclosed on a gift tax return (Form 709), the donor must file an amended gift tax return for the calendar year in which the gift was made.[29] The amended return must identify the transfer and provide all of the information required under Reg. § 301.6501(c)-1(f)(2) that was not previously submitted with the original gift tax return. The amended return must be filed with the same Service Center where the donor filed the original return. The top of the first page of the amended return must have the words "Amended Form 709 for gift(s) made in (the applicable calendar year) in accordance with Rev. Proc. 2000-34." Why is this important? Adequate disclosure of gifts is crucial because gift taxes can only be assessed for the three year period from the return due date or filing date, whichever occurs later. This period will begin to run only if the donor submits the required information for the gift on an original or amended gift tax return.

¶29,030 VALUATION OF GIFTS WITH RETAINED INTERESTS

Gifts with a retained interest are generally valued at the full value of the property transferred (both common and preferred) minus the value of the interest retained by the donor. In many cases, the retained interest has no value which increases the gift tax costs of the original transfer of the junior interest (the common stock). Here's a closer look at some of the specific rules:

.01 Retained Interests in Corporations and Partnerships

Special valuation rules apply to determine the amount of a gift made when a parent, for example, transfers a junior equity interest in a corporation or partnership (e.g., common stock) to a son, for example, while also retaining a senior equity interest (e.g., preferred stock). The retained interests affected by these valuation rules are: (1) an "extraordinary payment right," which includes a put, call, conversion right, any right to compel liquidation, or any similar right, the exercise of which affects the value of the transferred interest [Reg. § 25.2701-2(b)(2)]; or (2) a "distribution right" (a right to receive distributions as to an equity interest) from a controlled corporation [Code 2701; Reg. § § 25.2701-1, 25.2701-2(b)(3)].

If the rules apply, then the amount of the gift is determined by subtracting the value of any retained interests and other nontransferred equity interests from the total value of family-held interests in the corporation or partnership. (Reg. § 25.2701-3(b) contains a method of valuing the gift.) Generally, in determining the value of any retained interest held by the transferor or applicable family member:

- Any extraordinary payment right is valued at zero;
- Any distribution right is generally valued at zero unless this right is a "qualified payment right" (generally, a fixed dividend or distribution payable on a periodic basis); and
- Any other right is valued as if any right valued at zero did not exist [Reg. § § 25.2701-1(a)(2), 25.2701-2(b)(6)].

[29] Rev. Proc. 2000-34, 2000-2 CB 186.

By according little or no value to the various retained rights and interests, the value of the gift is substantially increased.

These valuation rules do not apply if: (1) market quotations for the retained or transferred interest are readily available on an established securities market; (2) the retained interest is of the same class as the transferred interest (i.e., both are common stock); or (3) the retained interest is proportionately the same as the transferred interest [Code 2701(a); Reg. §25.2701-1(c)].

> **NOTE:** A transfer of a retained interest that was valued under Code 2701 rules is to be adjusted for estate, gift and generation skipping tax purposes to reflect the increase in value to the original transfer caused by the current rules [Code 2701(e)(6)].

.02 Trusts and Term Interests in Property

The value of an interest retained by a transferor or family member generally is zero unless the interest is a "qualified interest"-right to receive fixed amounts payable at least annually or a right to receive amounts at least annually that are a fixed percentage of the trust's assets [Code 2702; Reg. §25.2702-1, -2, -3]. Exception: These restrictive rules do not apply to a transfer of an interest in a personal residence (not necessarily a principal residence) inhabited by the holder of the term interest [Code 2702(a)(3)(A)(ii)]. In other words, personal residence GRITs still offer tax-saving opportunities. Transfers to individuals who are not considered family members, such as nephews and nieces, are also excepted from the restrictive rules [Code 2704(c)(2)]. For further discussion of qualified personal residence trusts, see your Estate & Gift Tax Handbook, ¶233(c).

.03 Lapsing Right and Restrictions

The lapse of a voting or liquidation right in a family-controlled corporation or partnership is either a transfer by gift or a transfer which is includible in the gross estate of the decedent, whichever is applicable. The amount of the transfer is the excess of the value of all interests in the entity held by the transferor immediately before the lapse over the value of the interests immediately after the lapse [Code 2704; Reg. §25.2704-1(d)].

Any restriction that effectively limits the ability of the corporation or partnership to liquidate is ignored in valuing a transfer among family members if: (1) the transferor and the family members control the corporation or partnership (generally, 50 percent or more ownership), and (2) the restriction either lapses after the transfer or can be removed by the transferor or family members. The rule does not apply to a commercially reasonable restriction that arises as part of a financing with an unrelated party or a restriction required under state or federal law [Reg. §25.2704-2].

ESTATE TAX

¶29,035 IMPOSITION OF THE ESTATE TAX

The federal estate tax is a tax imposed on the right to transfer property at death. The tax, reported on Form 706, *United States Estate (and Generation Skipping Transfer) Tax*

Return, is applied to estates for which the decedent's ''gross estate,'' exceeds the filing threshold. Included in the gross estate are real estate, cash, stocks, bonds, businesses, and decedent-owned life insurance policies. Deductions are allowed for administrative expenses, indebtedness, taxes, casualty loss, and charitable and marital transfers. The taxable estate is calculated as gross estate less allowable deductions. For further discussion of the "gross estate" see ¶ 29,040. For discussion of the valuation of estate property, see ¶ 29,105.

THE GROSS ESTATE

¶29,040 GROSS ESTATE

The gross estate is the starting point for figuring the decedent's estate tax liability. It includes all property owned at death and property transferred during life over which the decedent retained certain rights or controls. More specifically, the gross estate includes: certain property held jointly by the decedent and others [¶ 29,050]; community property [¶ 29,055]; property subject to a general power of appointment [¶ 29,085]; certain life insurance proceeds [¶ 29,075]; transfers reserving the income or the right to use or enjoy the transferred property [¶ 29,060]; transfers reserving the power to change, revoke or terminate the right to use or enjoy the transferred property [¶ 29,065]; survivor annuities, including those under pension and profit-sharing plans [¶ 29,095]; dower or curtesy of a surviving spouse [¶ 29,045]; certain property for which a marital deduction was previously allowed [¶ 29,100]; and certain transfers made within three years of death [¶ 29,080].

Various laws exempt from income taxation bonds, notes, bills and certificates of indebtedness of the federal government or its agencies. However, those statutes do not apply to the estate tax since this tax is an excise tax on the transfer of property and not a tax on the property transferred [Reg. § 20.2033-1]. A statutory exemption from tax does not apply to the estate tax (or the gift tax or generation-skipping transfer tax) unless it specifically references the Internal Revenue Code provisions.[30]

¶29,045 PROPERTY SUBJECT TO DOWER OR CURTESY

A spouse's dower or curtesy interest or statutory interest in place of dower and curtesy (i.e., a right to some portion of the deceased spouse's estate) is included in the gross estate [Code Sec. 2034; Reg. § 20.2034-1]. But they don't increase estate tax because they qualify for the marital deduction [¶ 29,120].

[30] P.L. 98-369, 641.

¶29,050 JOINT ESTATES AND QUALIFIED JOINT INTEREST

.01 In General

A joint tenancy with a right of survivorship is a form of ownership under which jointly held property passes to the survivor on the joint tenant's death. Except for spousal joint tenancies, however, the value of the entire property generally is included in the gross estate of the deceased joint tenant. Exception: If the nonspousal survivor can prove that he or she paid part of the property's cost, the portion representing the survivor's contribution is not included in the decedent's gross estate. The contribution does not include money or property acquired from the decedent.

Example 29-11: Harold Green uses his own funds to buy property in the names of himself and his son, Joseph, as joint tenants with right of survivorship. When Harold dies, the full date-of-death value of the property will be included in his gross estate.

Example 29-12: Frank Brown furnished $20,000 and his brother, Sam, supplied $60,000 to purchase a piece of property as joint tenants with the right of survivorship. Of Sam's $60,000, $10,000 was a gift from Frank. At the time of Frank's death the property was worth $160,000. Since Frank is regarded as having furnished $30,000 of the purchase price, $60,000 is includable in his gross estate, arrived at as follows: $160,000 × ($30,000 ÷ $80,000) = $60,000.

For property acquired by gift, devise or inheritance, only the value of the deceased tenant's fractional interest is included [Code Sec. 2040; Reg. § 20.2040-1].

NOTE: Joint tenancy should not be confused with tenancy in common. In a tenancy in common, the deceased can transfer his share to whomever he desires. The property does not automatically go the surviving joint tenant. Only the fractional interest of the decedent is included in his or her gross estate.

Example 29-13: The facts are the same as in Example 29-12, except that Frank and Sam took title as tenants in common. Since Frank held a 25 percent undivided interest in the property, $40,000 is includible in his gross estate ($160,000 × .25).

"Qualified Joint Interest" of Spouses

In general, regardless of who furnished the consideration, only one-half of a spouse's qualified joint interest is included in the deceased joint tenant's gross estate. *Qualified joint interest* means an interest held by only the spouses as tenants by the entirety or joint tenants with the right of survivorship [Code Sec. 2040(b)]. Because of the unlimited marital deduction [¶ 29,120], this property passes tax-free to the surviving spouse. Note that the cost basis for the property in the hands of the survivor is (1) the adjusted basis as to one half, plus (2) the estate tax value as to the balance [Ch. 6].

Example 29-14: Steven Black bought property with $50,000 of his own funds in the names of himself and his wife, Eve, as joint tenants with the right of survivorship. Steven dies when the property is worth $80,000. One-half of the date-of-death value ($40,000) of the property is includible in Steven's gross estate. And that one-half has a stepped-up basis (in years other than 2010) when Eve sells the property. Thus, her basis becomes $65,000 ($25,000 + $40,000).

A different rule applies in the case of joint tenancies created before 1977 if the decedent supplied all of the consideration for the property in question. Under these circumstances, the entire value of the property is includible in the decedent's gross estate. Further, the transferee of the property acquires a stepped up basis as of the date of the decedent's death.[31]

Example 29-15: Assume the same facts as in Example 29-14 except that the purchase was in 1976. The full $80,000 is included in Steven's estate and Eve would get an $80,000 basis.

.02 Pros and Cons of Jointly Held Property

Many couples have the misconception that they can avoid all other estate planning by simply titling all of their assets in joint names of husband and wife (including same-sex spouses). Married couples often prefer joint tenancies (called *tenancies by the entireties*) because they are a simple way of transferring property upon death. Upon the death of the first spouse, the property passes automatically, by operation of law to the surviving spouse. Jointly held property also avoids the often time-consuming and expensive state probate process. In addition, the property is protected from the creditors of only one spouse. But couples with estates over the applicable exclusion amount who use tenancies by the entireties as their sole means of estate planning are failing to take advantage of estate tax savings techniques sanctioned by the IRS and will end up paying in taxes the very money they had intended to leave to their loved ones. Ownership of excessive amounts of jointly owned property between husband and wife can result in what is called "overfunding" the marital deduction. This occurs when too much property is transferred to the surviving spouse causing an unnecessarily large estate tax at the surviving spouse's death. If property is jointly owned with rights of survivorship, no estate tax will be due at the death of the first spouse because of the unlimited marital deduction that allows all property to pass tax-free to a surviving spouse. But when the second spouse dies, the beneficiaries will be hit with a big estate tax bill because the first spouse's unified credit was wasted.

A simple solution to this problem is to sever all the joint tenancies so that each spouse has separate ownership of an amount at least equal to the applicable exclusion amount. Then take advantage of a simple device known as a bypass trust to shelter assets totaling up to twice the applicable exclusion amount from estate tax.

---

[31] *M.L. Gallenstein*, CA-6, 92-2 USTC ¶60,114, 975 F2d 286.

.03 Bypass Trusts in Estate Planning

A bypass trust is probably the most common estate planning trust because it is used to take advantage of the first spouse to die's applicable exclusion amount. In addition, if the trust is properly drafted, the trust funds will also escape estate tax upon the death of the surviving spouse. Most bypass trusts provide that the trust income will be used to provide the surviving spouse with a life income and upon the death of the surviving spouse, the property passes to the children. Normally, only the exact amount necessary to absorb the applicable exclusion amount, goes into the bypass trust because anything over that amount will be subject to tax in the estate of the first spouse to die.

The most common estate planning technique, which is called the split estate plan, requires equalizing the size of each spouse's estate so that each estate gets the benefit of low estate tax brackets and makes full use of the applicable credit amount. Then the applicable exclusion amount is left to nonspousal beneficiaries in a bypass trust and the balance is left to the surviving spouse. Principal and interest generated by assets in the bypass trust may be used for the surviving spouse's health, education, maintenance and support and after the surviving spouse's death the balance is distributed to the children of the marriage. Often the surviving spouse is given a limited power of appointment in order to change the final distribution of assets at his or her death. If structured properly, this scheme results in a zero tax bill. The amounts in the bypass trust are not taxed when the first spouse dies because they are sheltered by his or her applicable exclusion amount. They are not subject to estate tax when the second spouse dies because he or she did not own or have control over the assets at death. The amount passing to the surviving spouse qualifies for the unlimited marital deduction when the first spouse dies. This so-called marital share is not subject to estate tax in the surviving spouse's gross estate to the extent that it does not exceed the surviving spouse's own applicable exclusion amount.

Estate plans based on estate tax applicable exclusion amounts need to be reviewed periodically. In the past, bypass trusts have been funded with a formula disposition that leaves the applicable exclusion amount to nonspousal beneficiaries and the balance to the surviving spouse. For example, in the past, the language to fund the bypass trust has typically been tied into the applicable exclusion amount or the amount necessary to "reduce estate tax to zero," or "to eliminate any federal estate tax." In light of the increase in the applicable exclusion amount in years prior to 2010 when the estate tax is repealed, this language may serve to fund the bypass trust with 100 percent of a decedent's modest estate and unwittingly impoverish the surviving spouse because nothing will be left to fund the marital share. Drafters must ask whether the surviving spouse will have sufficient assets to maintain his or her lifestyle if most or all of the family assets go to fund a bypass trust for the benefit of children. The surviving spouse only has an income interest in the bypass trust as well as a limited power to invade for health, education, maintenance or support. These limitations exist to make certain that the amounts in the bypass trust escape gross estate tax in the estate of the surviving spouse. When funding the bypass trust, you will have to consider the decedent's estate planning objections and the financial needs of the surviving spouse.

▶ **PLANNING POINTER:** *Formula Clauses Need Periodic Review.* Formula clauses are clauses inserted in estate planning documents such as wills and trusts that express the beneficiary's interest in terms of a pecuniary or fractional formula. The use of formula clauses is frequently used by estate planners to ensure the proper division of property, but it is extremely important that formula clauses must be reviewed in light of legislative changes to make certain that they continue to implement the testator's long-term intent for his or her loved ones. A common problem is transferring too little or too much to the surviving spouse because of overfunding of the credit shelter trust in the typical split estate plan.

How Portability Impacts Credit Shelter Trusts

Prior to the adoption of portability which came into the law with the passage on the Tax Relief Act of 2010, the estate tax exemption of the first spouse to die was considered to be wasted unless the spouse (1) owned assets in his or her name alone equal to the exemption amount in the year of death and (2) left such assets to a beneficiary other than the surviving spouse or charity—such as the couple's children, or a "credit shelter" (bypass) trust for the life benefit of the surviving spouse. For additional discussion of portability, see ¶ 29,140.

The concept of portability, first introduced by the Tax Relief Act of 2010 permits a surviving spouse to use the unused portion of the deceased spouse's exclusion amount for estate and gift tax purposes but not for GST tax purposes [Code Sec. 2010(c)(4)]. Portability is now permanent and is available to a surviving spouse if the deceased spouse died after December 31, 2012.

Now that portability is a permanent concept, credit shelter trusts may no longer need to be created solely to avoid wasting the deceased spouse's exemption amount. With portability, any applicable exclusion amount that remains unused as of the death of the last deceased spouse who dies in 2013 and thereafter (the "deceased spousal unused exclusion amount" (DSUEA)) generally is available for use by the surviving spouse, as an addition to the surviving spouse's own applicable exclusion amount which is increased to $5,250,000 in 2013 (increasing to $5,340,000 in 2014). For a more detailed discussion of portability, see ¶ 29,140.

Why It Still Makes Sense To Create Credit Shelter Trusts

It still makes sense to create credit shelter trusts when the first spouse dies rather than rely on the portability provision because:

1. The unused exclusion from a particular predeceased spouse will be lost if the surviving spouse remarries and survives his or her next spouse,
2. Growth in the assets are not excluded from the gross estate of the surviving spouse unlike the growth in a bypass trust which is excluded,
3. There is no portability of the GST exemption, and
4. Bypass trusts offer asset protection, centralized management, and restrict transfers of assets by the surviving spouse. However, if everything is left outright to the surviving spouse and portability is relied on, the advantages are simplicity and a step-up in basis when the surviving spouse dies.

¶29,055 COMMUNITY PROPERTY

Arizona, California, Idaho, Louisiana, Nevada, New Mexico, Texas, Washington and Wisconsin have community property laws. Generally, community property is included in the decedent's gross estate only to the extent of the decedent's interest under state law. Community property qualifies for the marital deduction [¶29,120].

> ▶ **OBSERVATION:** Unlike the case of a qualified joint interest created after 1977, the basis of the entire community property-not just one-half-is stepped up to the estate tax value.

¶29,060 TRANSFERS WITH RETAINED LIFE ESTATE

The value of the decedent's gross estate includes the value of all property that the decedent transferred during his or her life (except in case of a bona fide sale for an adequate and full consideration) by trust or otherwise, under which he has retained for his life or for any period not ascertainable without reference to his death or for any period which does not in fact end before his death:

1. The possession or enjoyment of, or the right to the income from, the property, or
2. The right, either alone or in conjunction with any person, to designate the persons who will possess or enjoy the property or the income from the property [Code Sec. 2036; Reg. § 20.2046-1(a)].

"An interest or right is treated as having been retained or reserved if at the time of the transfer there was an understanding, express or implied, that the interest or right would later be conferred." [Reg. § 20.2036-1(c)(1)(i)].

> **Example 29-16:** Sally Simpson transfers property to her children, but reserves the right to receive the income from it, in quarterly payments, for life. However, the transfer document states that Simpson's estate does not get any income that accrues between the last quarterly payment and the date of her death. The value of the property is includible in Simpson's gross estate. Reason: The period for which the income was reserved is tied to her death.

In *Estate of Tehan*,[32] the Tax Court concluded that a decedent's estate included the value of a condominium unit that the decedent had purportedly transferred to his eight children in a series of fractional interest gifts during the three years preceding his death. The value of the condominium unit was includible in his gross estate because the decedent retained the right to possess and enjoy the residence during his life as evidenced by the fact that he continued to live there at all times after the purported transfers, paid all of the monthly expenses with respect to the unit, and at no time sought the permission of his children in order to have guests in the unit or to redecorate it.

---

[32] *T.J. Tehan Est.*, 89 TCM 1374, Dec. 50,045(M), TC Memo. 2005-128.

The retention need not be expressed. An implied retention causes the value of the transferred property to be included in the gross estate as well [Reg. § 20.2036-1(a)(ii)]. The IRS often seeks to use the implied retention rule to tax a residence transferred by a parent to a child when the parent continues to live in the residence after the transfer. And cases have gone both ways on this issue. One winner: A similar transfer by a father to his son and daughter-in-law was also excluded.[33]

A retained power to designate who shall possess or enjoy the transferred property or its income causes inclusion of the property subject to the power in the transferor's gross estate, even though the power is retained in a fiduciary capacity [Reg. § 20.2036-1(b)(3)]. A settlor-trustee's power to accumulate income is regarded as a power to designate enjoyment. The same is true of a settlor's power to appoint himself or herself as successor trustee having such power.[34]

▶ **OBSERVATION:** For the assets of an irrevocable trust to be included in the settlor's gross estate, the settlor must have retained an enforceable right to receive income. Giving an independent trustee absolute discretion to distribute income to the settlor is not enough. If the settlor is also a trustee, the discretion to invade principal for the beneficiaries is not considered a reserved right to designate who shall possess or enjoy the property if the discretion is limited by an ascertainable standard (e.g., the health, support, or education of the beneficiaries).[35]

Example 29-17: Harry Harrison created an irrevocable trust to pay the income to his sister for life with remainder over to her children. He named Family National Bank as trustee with power to accumulate income. Harrison retained the right to appoint a successor trustee. Since the trust instrument did not expressly state otherwise, Harrison could have appointed himself as successor trustee. Upon Harrison's death, the entire value of the trust assets is includible in his gross estate. Reason: Harrison could have made himself the successor trustee and determined whether the income would be paid to his sister currently or it would be accumulated for her children.

.01 Right to Vote Stock

Retention of voting rights in the stock of a "controlled corporation" is considered retention of the enjoyment of transferred property. A controlled corporation is a corporation in which the decedent and his or her relatives owned, or had the power to vote, stock having at least 20 percent of the total combined voting power of all classes of stock at any time after the transfer and during the three-year period ending on the date of the decedent's death [Code Sec. 2036(b)].

---

[33] *C.I. Diehl*, DC-TN, 68-1 USTC ¶ 12,506; Rev. Rul. 78-409, 1978-2 CB 234; Rev. Rul. 70-155, 1970-1 CB 189.

[34] *C.E. O'Malley*, SCt, 66-1 USTC ¶ 12,388, 383 US 627, 86 SCt 1123.

[35] *E.E. German Est.*, CtCls, 85-1 USTC ¶ 13,610, 7 CtCls 641; *L.T. Powell*, CA-10, 62-2 USTC ¶ 12,097, 307 F2d 821; *R.W. Wier*, 17 TC 409, Dec. 18,533 (1951), *nonacq.* 1966-2 CB 8; *M.M. Green Est.*, 64 TC 1049, Dec. 33,425 (1975), *acq. in result* 1976-2 CB 2.

.02 Reciprocal Trusts

You cannot get around the retained life interest rule by getting together with someone else, say your brother, and setting up identical trusts to benefit each other. If you do this, the value of your brother's trust is included in your gross estate and vice versa if the arrangement leaves each of you in about the same economic position as you would have been if you named yourselves as life beneficiaries.[36]

.03 Grantor's Power to Change Trustees Approved

The IRS has concluded that a grantor's (creator of a trust) reservation of the unqualified power to remove a trustee and appoint a new one, other than himself, is not a reservation of the trustee's discretionary powers of distribution that would cause the trust corpus to be included in the grantor's gross estate.[37] As a result, you can now create a trust and reserve the power to remove a trustee and appoint an independent one in the trust language and not have the trust assets included in your gross estate under Code Sec. 2036(a) and Code Sec. 2038(a)(1). The same result was reached by the Tax Court[38] where the court refused to take what it called a "quantum leap" in equating a grantor's trustee-removal power with retention by the grantor of the trustee's decision-making powers. In the absence of a side agreement between the grantor and the new trustee (which would be fraudulent), the grantor's retention of trustee-removal powers did not amount to the grantor retaining the power to determine who will enjoy the trust property which would result in the trust assets being subject to estate tax.

▶ **PRACTICE TIP:** When drafting a trust a trustee removal and replacement provisions should be included in all trusts. This will afford you the flexibility to remove a trustee and appoint a new one without having the trust assets included in your taxable gross estate.

¶29,065 REVOCABLE TRANSFERS

.01 In General

Property that the decedent transfers during life (except in the case of a bona fide sale for adequate and full consideration in money or money's worth) is included in the decedent's gross estate if at the time of death the decedent had the power to make a substantial change in the beneficial enjoyment of the property, or if the decedent gave up such power within three years of death. Unlike the reserved life estate rule [¶29,060], it is not necessary for the power to have been reserved by the decedent; it is immaterial when or from what source the decedent acquired the power [Code Sec. 2038(a)(1)]. It does not matter whether the power can be exercised by the decedent alone, or only with someone else, or even only with the consent of the trustee and a beneficiary.[39]

---

36 *I.P. Grace Est.*, SCt, 69-1 USTC ¶12,609, 395 US 316, 89 SCt 1730.

37 Rev. Rul. 95-58, 1995-2 CB 191.

38 *H.S. Wall Est.*, 101 TC 300, Dec. 49,330 (1993), *later proceeding,* 102 TC 391, Dec. 49,708 (1994).

39 *City Bank Farmers Tr. Co.*, SCt, 36-1 USTC ¶9001, 296 US 85, 56 SCt 70.

Trust Revocable by Beneficiary

When a beneficiary (or any person other than the decedent) has exclusive and sole power to revoke or terminate a trust, the trust property is not taxable in the gross estate of the person who set up the trust [Reg. § 20.2038-1(a)].

The value of the property transferred is not includible in the decedent's gross estate if the decedent can exercise the power to alter, amend, revoke or terminate only with the consent of all parties having a vested or contingent interest in the transferred property—and this power adds nothing to the decedent's rights under local law [Reg. § 20.2038-1(a)(2)]. In some states, such a power adds nothing because the settlor's creditors cannot reach the trust income or corpus. But in other states such a power exposes the trust income to the settlor's creditors. In that case, the transferred property is taxable.[40] The rationale is that the decedent, as creator of the trust, has an interest in property that can be reached by creditors much the same way as a power to appoint to one's creditors is taxable [¶ 29,085].

Nature of Power

Property that the decedent transfers and that is subject to a power to alter, amend, revoke or terminate is included in the decedent's gross estate, even if the decedent cannot use the power to benefit yourself,[41] or the power is exercisable only as custodian (such as under the Uniform Transfers to Minors Act)[42] or as trustee.[43]

Other lesser powers covered by the inclusion rule are (1) a power to change the beneficiaries,[44] (2) a settlor-trustee's power to invade corpus for the beneficiary, unless the power is limited by an ascertainable standard,[45] (3) a power to control income flows to a beneficiary, unless limited by an ascertainable standard[46] and (4) the right to use trust funds for a spouse's support (where obligation existed under state law to support spouse).[47]

Revocable Transfers versus Retained Life Interest

In the case of a transfer with retained life estate, the transferred property is not includable in the decedent's estate unless the decedent, expressly or by implication, reserve an interest in the property [¶ 29,060]. In the case of revocable transfers, on the other hand, all that is necessary for inclusion is that the decedent be in possession of the taxable power at the time of death.[48]

> **NOTE:** This rule does applies only when the power or control contemplated derives either from a direct reservation retained by the decedent at the time of the transfer from the decedent of the property contemplated or from the conditions of the original transfer from the decedent. It does not apply to a decedent

[40] *E.E. German Est.*, CtCls, 85-1 USTC ¶ 13,610, 7 CtCls 641.

[41] *E.J.Porter*, SCt, 3 USTC ¶ 1065, 288 US 436, 3 SCt 451; *H. Holmes Est.*, SCt, 46-1 USTC ¶ 10,245, 326 US 480, 66 SCt 257.

[42] Rev. Rul. 57-366, 1957-2 CB 618; Rev. Rul. 59-357, 1959-2 CB 212; Rev. Rul. 70-348, 1970-2 CB 193.

[43] *C.E. O'Malley*, SCt, 66-1 USTC ¶ 12,388, 383 US 627, 86 SCt 1123.

[44] *D.M. Crile*, CtCls, 76-2 USTC ¶ 13,161, 212 CtCls 97.

[45] Rev. Rul. 73-143, 1973-1 CB 407.

[46] *Irving Trust Co.*, CA-2, 45-1 USTC ¶ 10,182, 147 F2d 946.

[47] LTR 9122005 (Feb. 27, 1991).

[48] Rev. Rul. 70-348, 1970-2 CB 193.

who obtained such a power or control when property transferred was retransferred to the decedent, in an independent and unrelated transaction.[49]

.02 Revocable Living Trusts

A revocable living trust is used to manage assets including property, money and investments in case the taxpayer becomes mentally or physically disabled. It also is used to remove assets from probate. The trust is established during the taxpayer's lifetime with the taxpayer as trustee and another person or financial institution named as successor trustee. A revocable trust is appropriate for anyone who is expected to become incapacitated or experience decreased mental acuity as a result of illness or a disease. Someone diagnosed with Alzheimer's disease or with a terminal illness would be perfect candidates provided their gross estate is less than the applicable exclusion amount and saving estate taxes is not their prime concern. Just keep in mind that assets in a revocable living trust are fully includible in the taxpayer's gross estate upon death because the assets remain under the taxpayer's control.

In a revocable trust, the settlor or the creator of the trust reserves the power to revoke or cancel the trust at any time before death or disability. The living trust only becomes irrevocable (unchangeable) when the settlor dies or becomes disabled. At that time, the assets transferred into the trust are disposed of as provided in the trust agreement, which essentially becomes a will substitute.

A revocable living trust gives the taxpayer the opportunity to:

- Plan for the orderly disposition of wealth after death without the delay associated with probate proceedings;
- Preselect who will handle your financial affairs upon incapacity;
- Avoid the expense of a state court supervised guardianship or conservatorship proceeding;
- Dispose of property in private without public scrutiny;
- Avoid ancillary estate proceedings in those nondomiciliary jurisdictions where you own property subject to estate administration.

.03 Gifts Made from Revocable Trusts

Taxpayers who have established a lifetime program of making annual exclusion gifts to loved ones and have created a revocable living trust will be able to continue this policy even after becoming disabled. Code Sec. 2035 provides that a gift made from a revocable trust will be treated as a direct gift made by the person who originally created the trust [Code Sec. 2035(e)]. As a result, gifts from a revocable trust within three years of the trust creator's death will not be included in his or her gross estate. This important change codifies the conclusions reached by the courts that had addressed the issue.

> ▶ **DRAFTING TIP:** Be sure that the revocable trust includes language expressly authorizing the trustee to make annual exclusion gifts to designated beneficiaries. In the absence of the necessary language authorizing gift-giving from the revocable trust, the gifts will be included in the donor's gross estate.

---

[49] *J.P. Reed Est.*, DC-FL, 75-1 USTC ¶ 13,073.

.04 Revocable Trust Treated as Part of Estate

Executors can now make an irrevocable election to treat revocable trusts as part of the decedent's probate estate for income tax purposes [Code Sec. 645(a)]. Treating a revocable trusts as part of a deceased person's estate can save death taxes because estates receive more favorable tax-treatment than revocable trusts as follows:

1. Estates are allowed a charitable deduction for amounts permanently set aside for charitable purposes while post death revocable trusts are allowed a charitable deduction only for amounts paid to charities;

2. The active participation requirement imposed by the passive loss rules is waived in the case of estates for two years after the owner's death;

3. Estates can qualify for the amortization of reforestation expenditures under Code Sec. 194; and

4. Estates are not required to use calendar years. By electing to be treated as part of the estate, a revocable trust effectively can have a noncalendar tax year during that period and engage in income deferral to postpone the payment of taxes.

5. Another reason for making the election is to avoid the generation-skipping transfer tax. While the election is in effect, the trust is not subject to the generation-skipping transfer tax.

6. The election to combine the revocable trust and the estate can simplify the winding up process traditionally associated with settling an estate. It may even eliminate the need to file a separate income tax return for the revocable trust. See Ch. 25 for detailed discussion.

¶29,070 TRANFERS TAKING EFFECT AT DEATH

Property that the decedent transfers during life (except in a bona fide sale for full and adequate consideration) is included in the decedent's gross estate if (1) the decedent retained a reversionary interest in the property (i.e., a chance to get it back on the happening of a stated condition); (2) the reversionary interest, immediately before the decedent's death, is worth more than 5 percent of the value of the property; and (3) possession or enjoyment of the transferred property can be obtained only by surviving the decedent [Code Sec. 2037; Reg. § 20.2037-1]. The value of a reversionary interest is determined under IRS tables.

A reversionary interest includes the possibility that the transferred property may return to the decedent or the decedent's estate or may be subject to the decedent's power of disposition. (Note that it does not include the reservation of a life estate [¶ 29,060] or the possible return of, or power of disposition over, income alone from the property.) The value of the property transferred has to be included in the decedent's gross estate whether the reversionary interest arises by operation of law or by virtue of an express reservation in the instrument of transfer [Code Sec. 2037; Reg. § 20.2037-1].

¶29,075 LIFE INSURANCE

.01 In General

Life insurance is afforded many breaks under the tax laws. The inside build-up of policies with an investment component is not subject to current income tax and in most cases the recipient of death benefits paid on a policy doesn't have to pay income tax on them. Plus, with proper planning, life insurance proceeds can be kept free of estate tax.

Life insurance can be a valuable tool in the estate planning process and can be used to achieve the following goals:

1. Provide estate liquidity and avoid forced sales of illiquid assets at depressed prices to pay federal or state estate taxes and administration expenses;
2. Replace the lost income of the decedent and meet the immediate and future needs of the surviving family members;
3. Enlarge an existing estate or to create a sizable estate for decedents who otherwise would be leaving no estate or only a modest estate to loved ones; and
4. Provide a funding mechanism for buy-sell agreements, nonqualified deferred compensation agreements, and key-man insurance programs.

Role of Life Insurance in Estate Planning

Keep in mind that insurance exists to do more than just pay estate taxes. It can satisfy many other important financial needs and can serve other planning objectives. For example, it may provide funds needed by the insured's beneficiaries for their living expenses after the insured's death. It can be used to pay state death taxes. Moreover, life insurance is a tax-sheltered investment as a result of Code Sec. 101 which provides that insurance grows free of income tax.

Tax Treatment of Life Insurance

The proceeds of a life insurance policy on the decedent's life are included in the decedent's gross estate if the proceeds are payable to the executor or receivable by anyone for the benefit of the decedent's estate [Code Sec. 2042; Reg. § 20.2042-1]. Insurance payable to other beneficiaries is included in the decedent's gross estate if the decedent possesses any incidents of ownership in the policy at the time of the decedent's death or the decedent possessed any incidents of ownership in the policy within three years of the decedent's death. In other words, proceeds paid to named beneficiaries are free of estate tax only if all incidents of ownership of the policy were transferred more than three years before death. The decedent is deemed to possess incidents of ownership exercisable either alone or in conjunction with any other person [Code Sec. 2042(2)]. "Incidents of ownership" include the power, individually or as trustee, to change the beneficiary, to change the beneficial ownership in the policy or its proceeds, or the time or manner of enjoyment of the property, to surrender or cancel the policy, to assign the policy, to revoke an assignment, to pledge the policy for a loan, and to obtain from the insurer a loan against the surrender value of the policy [Reg. § § 20.2042-1(c)(2), 20.2042-1(c)(4)].

It is important to understand that the inclusion of life insurance in a decedent's gross estate differs from basic income tax principle of Code Sec. 101(a), which provides generally that the proceeds of life insurance are *excluded* from the gross income (not gross estate) of the recipient.

.02 Irrevocable Life Insurance Trust

Irrevocable life insurance trusts offer taxpayers a technique for removing life insurance proceeds from their gross estate as well as the estate of a surviving spouse, provided that the taxpayer and his or her spouse do not own the policy. An irrevocable life insurance trust is a trust that cannot be changed where the trust is both the owner and beneficiary of one or more life insurance policies. Creating an irrevocable life insurance trust is a valuable estate planning tool that can save you a substantial amount of estate taxes.

Disadvantages of Irrevocable Life Insurance Trust

By definition an irrevocable trust cannot be amended or modified in any way after execution. Modification through court proceedings can be difficult, if not impossible. In addition, taxpayers lose all control over the policy insuring their lives, including the right to borrow against the policy's cash value or to change the policy's beneficiaries. Taxpayers can retain no control over the assets owned by, or transferred to, the trust. They cannot serve as trustees or co-trustee of the trust because this would pull the life insurance proceeds back into your estate and would defeat the major purpose for establishing the trust [Code Sec. 2036].

They can, however, decide whether or not to provide the funds needed by the trustee to pay the life insurance premiums. If the premiums are not paid the policy would lapse and the irrevocable life insurance trust would in essence be revoked.

How Does the Trust Become Owner of the Policy?

BEST METHOD: First, establish the irrevocable life insurance trust, then have the independent trustee of the trust apply for the life insurance on the insured's behalf. The trust then becomes both the owner and beneficiary of the life insurance policy; and, upon the insured's death, the trustee will invest the insurance proceeds and administer the trust on behalf of the beneficiaries.

SECOND BEST: Transfer ownership of an existing life insurance policy to an irrevocable life insurance trust. This method will result in exclusion of the insurance proceeds from the insured's gross estate only if the insured survives the transfer by at least three years [Code Sec. 2035]. If the insured dies within the three-year period, the proceeds will be included in his or her gross estate.

The insured can even make annual gift-tax exclusion transfers ($14,000 in 2013 with no change in 2014) to the trust each year to pay for the premiums without causing the proceeds to be taxed in his or her estate under Code Sec. 2503(b). Here's how it's done: The insured should use a so-called *Crummey* power, which gives the holder a limited (at least 30 days) right to withdraw the premium funds transferred to the trust. This causes the transfer to qualify as a present rather than future interest [¶ 29,020]. The withdrawal power expires after about 30 days and is never expected to be exercised, although legally the beneficiary could exercise it. The trustee should never, however, engage in any written or oral communications to the effect that the powers are technical and not to be exercised.

> ▶ **PLANNING POINTER:** The courts have said that a policy purchased with funds furnished by the insured, but owned by another person, is not included in

the gross estate if the insured dies within the three-year period. That's because the insured never possessed any incidents of ownership.[50] And the IRS has announced that it will no longer litigate cases in this area.[51] The IRS has stated in Action on Decision 1991-012, after reviewing the statute and the three adverse court decisions that: "Although we continue to believe that substance should prevail over form and that such indirect transfers should be included in a decedent's gross estate, in light of the three adverse appellate opinions . . . , we will no longer litigate this issue."

NOTE: Unless the decedent's will provides otherwise, the executor can recover from a beneficiary any estate tax generated by insurance proceeds included in the gross estate and paid to the beneficiary [Code Sec. 2206].

.03 Incidents of Ownership

The decedent doesn't have to be the actual, legal owner of a policy to have an incident of ownership. Rather, the right to any economic benefits of the policy is considered an incident of ownership. These include the power to change the beneficiary, to surrender or cancel the policy, to assign it, to pledge it for a loan, or to borrow against the surrender value. Possession of any one incident of ownership causes the proceeds to be included in the gross estate of the insured. Incidents of ownership also include a reversionary interest in excess of five percent of the value of the policy, taking into account any incidents of ownership held by others. A reversionary interest includes the possibility that the proceeds will be paid to the decedent's estate. But the possibility that the decedent might inherit a policy on his or her life from someone else (e.g., a child bought insurance on the decedent's life and could die leaving it to the decedent) is not a reversionary interest or an incident of ownership. Incidents of ownership held by a corporation where the decedent is the sole or controlling shareholder are attributed to the decedent, if the proceeds are not payable to the corporation or are not payable for a valid business purpose [Reg. § 20.2042-1(c)(2)].

Example 29-18: At age 51, Frank Jackson assigns a policy on his life to a trust he created to pay the income to his sister, Edith, age 47, for her life. The trust will terminate upon Edith's death. At that time, the corpus, including the insurance policy, will revert to Frank, if alive, or be distributed to his surviving son. Frank is survived by Edith. The insurance proceeds are includible in Frank's gross estate because actuarially he had a reversionary interest in the policy in excess of five percent of its value [¶ 29,105].

Example 29-19: Assume the same facts as in Example 29-18, except that the trust instrument gives Edith the power to surrender the policy and obtain cash. Because of Edith's power to obtain the cash surrender value, Frank's reversionary interest does not amount to incidents of ownership.

---

[50] *J. Leder Est.*, CA-10, 90-1 USTC ¶ 60,001, 893 F2d 237; *E.L. Headrick Est.*, CA-6, 90-2 USTC ¶ 60,049, 918 F2d 1263; *F.M. Perry Est.*, CA-5, 91-1 USTC ¶ 50,283, 931 F2d 1044.

[51] AOD/CC-1991-012, July 3, 1991.

Insurance on Another's Life

The value of an insurance policy that a taxpayer owns on another's life is included in the taxpayer's gross estate.[52] The ownership of the policy determines who pays the tax, not the name of the insured.

.04 Second-to-Die Life Insurance Policies

A popular tool in life insurance planning is the second-to-die or survivorship life insurance policy. Here's how it works. Instead of buying individual life insurance for either a husband or wife, for example, the taxpayer purchases life insurance covering both spouses with the policy only paying a benefit after the second spouse dies. The premiums payable for second-to-die policies are lower than they would be for single life insurance policies because the death benefit on the second-to-die policy is delayed until after the second spouse dies, thus affording the insurance company more time to invest the premiums. The downside, however, is that even though the annual premiums may be smaller, they may be payable for a much longer time. Consider the following example: A 50-year-old man wants to purchase a $1 million individual universal life insurance policy. His annual premium from one insurance company would be $10,150. If however, he purchased a second-to-die policy covering him and his 50-year old wife, his annual premium would be reduced to $5,070.

Second-to-die policies make sense where life insurance proceeds are needed to provide liquidity to pay estate taxes at the death of the surviving spouse. This can be important in situations where the bulk of the estate consists of illiquid assets, such as a family business, farm, or an art collection, which otherwise would have to be sold to pay the estate tax. With the second-to-die policy in place, the estate taxes can be paid and the remainder of the estate left in tact for the heirs. Buying second-to-die policies also makes sense if one of the spouses is sick. The cost of buying life insurance once someone has become sick may be prohibitive, whereas spreading the risk over the lives of a healthy spouse and an unhealthy one will result in lower overall premiums.

As a result of the unlimited marital deduction, when the first spouse dies, the policy passes to the surviving spouse without paying estate tax. A trickier issue, however, is who should own the second-to-die policy. Ideally neither of the insureds should own the policy. The second-to-die policy should be applied for, acquired, and owned by someone or some entity (such as an irrevocable insurance trust) other than the insureds. The insured individuals should never have any control over the policy because control would constitute a taxable "incident of ownership" in the policy. If they do retain any ownership, the proceeds from the policy will be included in their gross estate, thus eliminating one of the benefits of the policy. The irrevocable life insurance trust is the recommended ownership vehicle because it affords the insureds the opportunity to control the disposition of the insurance benefits by means of the language in the trust documents. For discussion of the tax treatment of exchanges of second-to-die policies, see Ch. 6.

---

[52] *E.M. Donaldson Est.*, 31 TC 729, Dec. 23,405 (1959).

¶29,080 TRANSFERS WITHIN THREE YEARS OF DEATH

Even if the decedent has transferred away all "incidents of ownership" in a policy insuring his or her life, the insurance proceeds may still be included in his or her taxable estate under the so-called "three year rule," which brings the insurance proceeds back into the decedent's estate if the decedent made that transfer within three years of his or her death Code Sec. 2035(a).

The three-year rule also applies to transfers with retained life estate [¶ 29,060], revocable transfers [¶ 29,065] and transfers taking effect at death [¶ 29,070] [Code Sec. 2035(a)(2)]. The three-year rule taxes releases within three years of death of a retained interest that would cause inclusion if held at death. For example, if the decedent set up a trust and reserves the right to the income from the trust for his or her life, the trust property is included in his or her gross estate [¶ 29,060]. Under the three-year rule, inclusion is required if the life interest is released to someone else within three years of death.

.01 Revocable Transfers Included in Estate

A release of a power of revocation within three years of death also is included in a decedent's gross estate. There has been much confusion over whether withdrawals from a revocable trust within three years of death that ultimately go to a third party are includible in your estate under this complicated interplay of rules. This confusion was settled by enactment of Code Sec. 2035(e).

.02 Gifts from Revocable Trusts Within Three Years of Death

The value of property transferred to a donee from a decedent's revocable trust within three years of the decedent's death is not includible in the decedent's gross estate under Code Sec. 2038 because it is treated as having been made directly by the decedent [Code Sec. 2035(e)]. Nor is it includible in a decedent's gross estate as a proscribed transfer within three years of death. Gifts made by a trustee from a revocable trust are treated as if they were made by the decedent and are eligible for the annual gift tax exclusion [Code Sec. 2035(e)].

▶ **PRACTICE POINTER:** As a result of this rule that treats gifts from revocable trusts as if they were made by the decedent, gifts from a revocable trust will remove assets from the gross estate for estate tax purposes.

Example 29-20: Mom set up a revocable trust and gave the trustee the power to make annual gifts of $14,000 in 2013 to each of her children and grandchildren. Gifts from Mom's revocable trust are treated as if they were made by Mom and are eligible for the annual gift tax exclusion.

Purposes for Which Rule Applies

The value of other property given away within three years of death is not included in the gross estate for the usual estate tax purposes. However, it is included for purposes of making the following special estate tax computations [Code Sec. 2035(c)]:

- Determining eligibility for special use valuation [¶ 29,110].
- Determining eligibility for installment payment of estate taxes [¶ 29,200]. The requirement that more than 35 percent of the adjusted gross estate be an interest in a closely held business must be met both with and without the application of the three-year inclusion rule.
- Determining whether the estate meets the eligibility requirements for sale or exchange treatment on the redemption of certain closely held stock to pay death taxes [¶ 29,200].
- For purposes of imposing tax liens [Ch. 27].

Example 29-21: Sam Spock owns all of the stock in a closely held company. Its value in relation to his other assets is not sufficient to qualify for special use valuation or installment payment of estate tax, both of which require that the business consist of a certain percentage of his estate to qualify. So Sam makes lifetime gifts to his spouse and children of cash and other property. If Sam doesn't survive for three years after those gifts, they are included in his gross estate. And that could render the estate ineligible to use the special use valuation and installment payment of estate tax breaks.

NOTE: As is the case of all lifetime transfers, the three-year inclusion rules do not apply to property transferred through a bona fide sale for adequate and full consideration.

.03 Gross-Up of Gift Tax

Although gifts made within three years of death are not generally included in the gross estate, gift taxes paid on such transfers are included, whether paid by the donor or by the donor's estate and whether paid on gifts made by the donor or the donor's spouse. The gift tax paid by a donee as a condition of a gift made within three years of the donor's death is includable in the donor's gross estate because the gift tax is primarily the obligation of the donor.[53]

¶29,085 TRANSFERS SUBJECT TO A POWER OF APPOINTMENT

A power of appointment is a power to determine who will own or enjoy the property subject to the power. Powers are valuable in estate planning because they provide for flexibility to meet changing circumstances. For example, you may want to give your surviving spouse a power to give property to those of your children who are in the greatest need. Your spouse will be able to respond to the needs of different children as they arise. The estate tax consequences of powers vary depending on whether the power is a general power or a special power.

---

[53] *S.C. Sachs Est.*, CA-8, 98-2 USTC ¶13,781, 856 F2d 1158.

.01 General Powers

A general power of appointment is a power that is exercisable in favor of the holder, the holder's estate, creditors of the holder, or creditors of the holder's estate. A discretionary power to consume or to invade trust corpus for the benefit of the decedent is also considered a general power of appointment, unless it is limited by an ascertainable standard relating to the decedent's health, education, support or maintenance [Code Sec. 2041(b)(1)(A)]. A power to invade principal "as required for the decedent's *continued comfort*, support, maintenance, or education" was limited to an ascertainable standard and therefore not a general power.[54] The value of property subject to a general power of appointment at the time of death is includable in your gross estate. Even the mere existence of a general power of appointment, without its exercise, would result in inclusion of the trust proceeds in your taxable estate.

Property over which you have a general power of appointment is taxable, even if you are unaware of its existence.[55] However, any estate tax generated by property subject to a general power of appointment is recoverable from the recipient of the property in the absence of a contrary testamentary direction. A power to invade trust principal for a beneficiary who is also a trustee is not a general power of appointment if the power is discretionary and the beneficiary cannot participate as trustee in decisions to invade.[56]

Released and Lapsed Powers

In some situations, property over which the decedent has a general power of appointment may be included in the the decedent's gross estate even though the decedent releases the power during his or her lifetime. Inclusion is required where the property would have been included in the decedent's gross estate under Code Secs. 2035-2038 if the decedent had owned the property outright at death, instead of just having a general power of appointment, and similarly disposed of it.

> **Example 29-22:** Jim Johnson has a life income interest in a trust and a general power of appointment over the remainder. Less than three years before his death, Jim releases the power of appointment. The value of the trust is includible in his gross estate. Reason: It would have been includible as a transfer within three years of death if Jim were the owner of the trust assets [¶29,070]. Note that the release of the power would not result in any estate tax if Johnson did not have an income interest in the trust.

The lapse of a power by failure to exercise it is treated as a release only to the extent that the property that could have been appointed by exercising the lapsed powers exceeded in value greater of $5,000 or five percent of the value of the appointive property at the time of the lapse.[57] Powers designed to take advantage of this limitation are sometimes referred to as "five or five" powers.[58]

---

[54] *N.H. Vissering Est.*, CA-10, 93-1 USTC ¶60,133, 990 F2d 578.

[55] *J.C. Freeman Est.*, 67 TC 202, Dec. 34,099 (1976).

[56] *H. Garfield*, DC-MA, 80-2 USTC ¶13,381.

[57] Rev. Rul. 66-87, 1966-1 CB 217.

[58] *D.C. Crummey*, CA-9, 68-2 USTC ¶12,541, 397 F2d 82.

Example 29-23: Brian Brady created a trust for his wife, Marlene, and gave her a noncumulative power to make annual income withdrawals of $20,000. Marlene died three years later, without ever exercising her power. The trust income in the year of Marlene's death was $50,000. There was a lapse of $15,000 ($20,000 – $5,000), which is includable in Marlene's gross estate. Amounts attributable to lapses during the two prior years also have to be included in Marlene's gross estate.

NOTE: A qualified disclaimer of a power is not a release or lapse [¶29,165].

.02 Special Powers

A power of appointment that is exercisable in favor of a class of persons, not including the decedent, his or her estate, his or her creditors, or the creditors of his or her estate, is a special or limited power of appointment. Ordinarily, property subject to a special power of appointment is not includible in the holder's gross estate. However, the property is includible if the power is exercised to create another power which, under state law, can be exercised to postpone the vesting of property or an interest in property without regard to the date the first power was created.

Joint Powers

A power that is exercisable only in conjunction with the donor of the power or with a person having a substantial and adverse interest in the property that is adverse to exercise of the power in favor of the with the donee of the power is not considered a general power of appointment [Code Sec. 2041(b)(1)(C)].

Example 29-24: Hal Herbert created a trust to pay the income to Mary Oliver, whom he named trustee, for life. The trustee has the power to use the principal for the beneficiary as she sees fit. The power to access the principal of the trust, though, is exercisable only in conjunction with Hal. Mary did not have a general power of appointment because her power over the principal was exercisable only in conjunction with the donor of the power. So the trust is not includible in her gross estate.

Example 29-25: Gary Smith created a trust to pay the income to his brother, Joe, for life with the remainder over to his granddaughter, Nancy. Joe could demand distributions of corpus, but the trustee required Nancy's consent before he could make any distribution. Joe does not have a general power of appointment because his power is exercisable only in conjunction with Nancy, a person having a substantial and adverse interest.

¶29,090 TRANSFERS FOR INSUFFICIENT CONSIDERATION

The rules for including property transferred during the decedent's lifetime or subject to a general power of appointment do not apply to the extent full consideration was received for the transfer. Thus, gratuitous transfers are fully included in the gross estate. But in the case of transfers for insufficient consideration, only the excess of the fair market value of the property over the consideration received is included [Code Sec. 2043].

With regard to general powers of appointment, consideration is taken into account when it is furnished for the exercise or relinquishment of a power-not when it is furnished for the creation of the power.[59]

.01 Marital Rights

The relinquishment or promised relinquishment of marital rights, other than support rights, is not treated as consideration for this purpose. Marital rights include dower, curtesy, and any statutory estate created in lieu of such rights. However, any transfer under a written agreement in settlement of marital and property rights incident to divorce is considered to be made for full consideration if the agreement is made not more than two years before or one year after the divorce. The agreement need not be approved by the divorce decree [Code Secs. 2043(b), 2516].

A bona fide arm's length transfer made in the ordinary course of business without donative intent is deemed to be made for full consideration [Reg. §25.2512-8].

¶29,095 SURVIVOR ANNUITIES AND OTHER DEATH BENEFITS

A decedent's gross estate includes the value of any annuity or other payment receivable by someone else under a contract or agreement, as a result of surviving the decedent. At the time of death, the decedent must be receiving (or have the right to receive) payments, either alone or in conjunction with someone else, for the decedent's life or for any period not ascertainable without reference to the decedent's death or for any period that does not in fact end before the decedent's death [Code Sec. 2039]. Examples of items includible under this rule include retirement benefits, IRAs, amounts paid under an annuity contract and amounts paid under an employment contract calling for retirement and survivor benefits. The agreement need not be in writing.

The amount of survivor benefit included in the decedent's estate is proportionate to the contribution or consideration furnished by the decedent. In the case of an employee's annuity, an employer's contribution to an employee's plan is deemed consideration furnished by the employee.

> **Example 29-26:** Sam Richardson is receiving pension benefits from his former employer. Upon his death, Richardson's daughter Edith will receive survivor benefits for the rest of her life. The value of those survivor benefits, at the time of Richardson's death, will be included in his gross estate.

[59] *B. Steinman Est.*, 69 TC 804, Dec. 34,998 (1978).

Example 29-27: Bill and Beth Henderson purchased a joint and survivor annuity for $50,000. Each paid one-half of the cost. Beth's interest is worth $40,000 at the time of Bill's death. Since he paid for half of the annuity, half of its date of death value ($20,000) is included in his gross estate.

The survivor benefit provisions do not apply to life insurance. (For estate taxation of life insurance, see ¶ 29,075.) They apply only when the decedent was in actual receipt of, or had a right to receive, benefits (other than wages or salary or other employment compensation) during his or her life and a surviving beneficiary receives benefits under the same arrangement. A death benefit that is not taxable as a survivor benefit may be taxable as property owned by the decedent at death. A rule of thumb is that if the decedent has any enforceable right at the time of death and as a result payment is made to a survivor or to the estate, the amount is includible in his or her gross estate. The inclusion may come under either the rules for property owned at the time of death, a survivor benefit, a transfer taking effect at death, or other taxable life transfer. On the other hand, if the decedent has no enforceable right but his or her employer makes a voluntary payment or voluntary payments to the surviving spouse or children or to any other person, the death benefit is not taxable under any estate tax provisions.[60]

Death benefits payable to a surviving spouse usually qualify for the marital deduction. See ¶ 29,120 for discussion of the marital deduction.

Example 29-28: Gary Allen was an employee of Breadnut Corp. Every year Breadnut gives a bonus to a certain class of employees, of which Gary was one. To be eligible, the employee must be alive on the last day of the company's fiscal year. If an employee dies before the end of the fiscal year, the company has discretion to pay the bonus to the employee's widow or children. Gary died before the last day of the fiscal year, and the company paid the bonus to his daughter. Since Gary had no enforceable right to any part of the bonus on the date of his death, the amount paid to his daughter is not includible in his gross estate.

NOTE: Certain death benefits paid by the government are not includible because they are payable under statute rather than under contract or agreement. These include payments made under the Social Security Act, the Railroad Retirement Act, the Federal Coal Mine Health and Safety Act of 1969 and the Public Safety Officers' Benefit Act.[61]

¶29,100 PROPERTY FOR WHICH MARITAL DEDUCTION WAS PREVIOUSLY ALLOWED

Giving a spouse a life income interest in a trust generally does not qualify for the estate or gift tax marital deduction unless the trust is a QTIP trust or the spouse has a

[60] *W.E. Barr Est.*, 40 TC 227, Dec. 26,103 (1963).

[61] Rev. Rul. 81-82, 1981-1 CB 127; Rev. Rul. 60-70, 1960-1 CB 372; Rev. Rul. 76-102, 1976-1 CB 272; Rev. Rul. 79-397, 1979-2 CB 322.

general power of appointment over principal. These requirements are designed to ensure that the property will be taxed automatically when the spouse dies or disposes of the property. In other words, the marital deduction merely defers tax. If the spouse has a general power, the trust property will be taxed under the rules discussed at ¶29,085. If the trust is a QTIP, a special rule includes the value of the property in the spouse's estate unless he or she made a lifetime disposition of the income interest [Code Sec. 2044]. In that case, the lifetime disposition triggers a gift tax. Unless the decedent directs otherwise by will, the estate tax attributable to the inclusion of QTIP is recoverable from the remainderman [Code Sec. 2207A].

VALUATION OF ESTATE PROPERTY

¶29,105 GENERAL PRINCIPLES

.01 In General

Code Sec. 2031 provides that a decedent's gross estate includes the value, at the time of death, of all property owned by the decedent. Property is generally included in the gross estate at its fair market value (FMV) at the time of death unless the executor elects the alternate valuation date [Code Sec. 2032; Reg. §20.2032-1(a)] or special use valuation [Code Sec. 2032A; Reg. §20.2032A-3]. For further discussion of these alternative valuation methods, see ¶29,110.

Generally speaking, the fair-market value is the price that a hypothetical willing buyer would pay a hypothetical willing seller, with both persons having reasonable knowledge of relevant facts and neither person under a compulsion to buy or to sell [Reg. §20.2031-1(b)]. The particular characteristics of these hypothetical persons are not necessarily the same as those of any specific individual or entity and are not necessarily the same as those of the actual buyer or the actual seller. Nor are these hypothetical persons considered to be compelled to buy or sell the property in question. These hypothetical persons are considered to know all relevant facts involving the property. Each of these hypothetical persons also is presumed to be aiming to achieve the maximum economic advantage (i.e., maximum profit) from the hypothetical sale of the property. For property that is generally obtained by the public in the retail market, FMV is the price at which the item or a comparable item would be sold at retail. The price tangible personal property brings at auction or is advertised at in a newspaper is presumed to be the retail price.[62] If property is sold at an auction, its value is the bid price plus any premium paid to the auction house. An IRS determination of fair market value is accepted as correct until the taxpayer proves it is wrong.[63]

Events occurring after death are generally not considered in valuation unless they were reasonably foreseeable at the date of valuation or the time of death.[64] Keep in mind that the value of a decedent's interest in stock will be determined at the time of

---

[62] Rev. Proc. 65-19, 1965-2 CB 1002.

[63] *C.H. Napp*, DC-AL, 71-2 USTC ¶12,802; *J.P. Lyons Est.*, 35 TCM 605, Dec. 33,799(M), TC Memo. 1976-136.

[64] *V.C. Andrews Est.*, DC-VA, 94-1 USTC ¶60,170, 850 FSupp 1279.

his death and not at the time the stock passes to the estate.[65] Events that cause the price of the stock to change after death will therefore be disregarded. For example, post-death events cannot be considered when valuing a deduction for unpaid income taxes taken on an estate tax return[66] or when valuing a claim deducted on a federal estate tax return.[67]

Valuation Statement

If the IRS does not accept the estate's property values, the estate is required to furnish a valuation statement upon written request. The statement must explain the basis of the valuation or proposed valuation, displaying any computation and containing a copy of any expert appraisal made for the IRS. It must be furnished within 45 days after the request or after the IRS makes a determination or proposed determination, whichever is later [Code Sec. 7517; Reg. § 301.7517-1].

.02 Stocks and Bonds

The fair market value of listed securities, stocks and bonds that are publicly traded on national or regional exchanges is the average between the highest and the lowest published quotations for the valuation date. If there were no sales on the valuation date, the nearest sale dates within a reasonable period before and after the valuation date are used. The securities are valued at a weighted average of the mean between the highest and lowest prices on these dates [Reg. § 20.2031-2].

Example 29-29: Doris Doe died on Friday, June 15, leaving common stock in Rabbit Corporation. There were no sales on June 15. However, on June 13 the mean sale price per share was $10; it was $15 on June 20. These are the nearest dates before and after the valuation date on which there were sales of Rabbit stock, two trading days before and three after. The stock is includable in Doris's gross estate at $12 per share, arrived at as follows:

$$\frac{(3 \times 10) + (2 \times 15)}{3 + 2} = 12$$

NOTE: The value of listed securities established under these methods may be adjusted for extraordinary circumstances. For instance, if the transfer consists of a large block of securities, a discount factor may be applied under the blockage rule. This valuation rule takes into account the fact that flooding the market with a large number of shares for sale tends to depress the price. On the other hand, if the large block of securities furnishes voting control, a premium factor may be applied.

---

[65] *C.K. McClatchy Est.*, CA-9, 98-2 USTC ¶ 60,315, 147 F3d 1089.

[66] *E.M. McMorris Est.*, CA-10, 2001-1 USTC ¶ 60,346, 243 F3d 1254.

[67] *E.P. O'Neal Est.*, CA-11, 2001-2 USTC ¶ 60,412, 258 F3d 1265, *on remand*, DC-AL, 2002-2 USTC ¶ 60,448, 228 FSupp2d 1290.

Mutual Funds

The fair market value of mutual funds is the bid or redemption price.[68] For further discussion of determining basis and gain or loss of mutual fund shares, see Ch. 6.

.03 Valuing Closely Held Business Stock

The valuation of closely held nonpublicly traded stock is a complex task for the executor because the shares often have no ready market from which either sales or bid and asked prices may be obtained. Actual arm's-length sales on or close to the valuation date provide the best evidence of value. In the absence of actual sales, various factors, or a combination thereof, are used in arriving at fair market value. These factors include (but are not limited to) comparable sales, net worth, capitalization of earnings, price-earnings ratio, history of the enterprise, economic outlook of the particular industry, dividend-paying capacity, and good will.

Valuation Discounts

The following discounts are generally taken into consideration when computing the estate tax in a closely held corporation:

- Discount for lack of marketability to reflect the difficulty that closely held corporations often experience when trying to convert shares to cash;
- Discount for lack of control to reflect the absence of power to make decisions regarding the closely held corporation;
- Pending litigation or the possibility of a stockholder suit;
- Discount for built-in capital gains tax liability.[69]

The following cases illustrate the application of these discounts when valuing closely held corporate stock for estate tax purposes.

In *Estate of Noble,*[70] the court valued closely held stock at the price at which the stock was sold even though the sale took place more than a year after the owner's death. Even though sales of stock that occur before death are more commonly used for valuation purposes, the court used the subsequent sale because it gave the best indication of value.

In *J.L. Okerlund,*[71] the Court of Appeals for the Federal Circuit concluded that courts may, but are not required to consider subsequent events in valuing closely held stock. Closely held stock should be valued as of the valuation date on the basis of market conditions and facts on that date without regard to hindsight. The court concluded that conditions and facts arising after the valuation date should be used sparingly.

Discount for Built-in Capital Gains Liability

The rationale for the built-in hypothetical capital gains tax discount is to reflect an anticipated financial burden expected to impact future owners. A purchaser buying a corporation with appreciating assets will have to incur a second-level capital gains

---

[68] *D.B. Cartwright,* CA-2, 72-1 USTC ¶12,836, 457 F2d 567, *aff'd,* SCt, 73-1 USTC ¶12,926, 411 US 546, 93 SCt 1713.

[69] *F. Jelke III Est.,* CA-11, 2007-2 USTC ¶60,552, 507 F3d 1317; *B.E.J. Dunn Est.,* CA-5, 2002-2 USTC ¶60,446, 301 F3d 339.

[70] *H.M. Noble Est.,* 89 TCM 649, Dec. 55,903(M), TC Memo. 2005-2.

[71] *J.L. Okerlund,* CA-FC, 2004-1 USTC ¶60,481, 365 F3d 1044, *aff'g,* FedCl, 2002-2 USTC ¶60,447, 53 FedCl 341.

tax on future appreciation that a purchaser of directly-owned assets will not have to bear. As a result, prospective purchasers should have to pay less to purchase the stock subject to the capital gains tax on future appreciation and an adjustment should be made to the value of the stock to reflect the financial burden of built-in gains tax attributable to its future appreciation.

Using Buy-Sell Agreements for Valuation Purposes

Even though closely held stock may not have a ready market, the value of the stock may be established by a buy-sell agreement with the company and its shareholders. The agreement must have a bona fide business purpose and be binding on the shareholder during life and upon the shareholder's estate at death.[72]

Buy-sell agreements can be useful estate-planning tools because they provide for the contractual purchase of closely held business interests at a set price when a business owner dies. Unlike publicly traded corporations, closely held businesses typically do not have a market eager to purchase a owner's interest after death. This can present a cash-flow problem for family members. Here are some of the benefits associated with the buy-sell agreements:

- They can prevent an unwanted dilution of control that occurs when outsiders become shareholders or partners in a closely held business.
- They can prevent a sale of the business to unwanted third parties.
- They can provide cash for what may otherwise be an illiquid estate of a deceased closely held business owner. Often a closely held business interest is the most valuable asset in the decedent's estate. The buy-sell agreement can help establish a value for that asset and prevent a forced sale of business assets following the death of the owner to provide funds for payment of estate taxes and administration expenses.
- They can prevent inadvertent termination of an S corporate election or status as a professional corporation under state law.
- They can ensure a smooth transition of power or business ownership after the death, disability, or retirement of an owner.
- They can help avoid protracted disputes between business owners.
- They can establish the value of a deceased owner's interest for the federal estate tax return. The value of the business will also be important if the surviving owners want to sell the business and need to establish a purchase price.
- They provide certainty for the remaining business owners regarding the terms under which a deceased owner's interest will be purchased.

Code Sec. 2703 provides that buy-sell agreements created or substantially modified after October 8, 1990, may establish value for estate tax purposes only if the agreements are bona fide business arrangements, the terms are comparable to those of similar arrangements negotiated at arm's-length, and the agreements are not a testamentary device [Reg. § 25.2703-1(b)(4)]. The valuation price set out in the buy-sell agreement does not fix the value of shares or an interest for federal gift tax

[72] Rev. Rul. 59-60, 1959-1 CB 237, modified by Rev. Rul. 65-193, 1965-2 CB 370, and amplified by Rev. Rul. 80-213, 1980-2 CB 101 and Rev. Rul. 83-120, 1983-2 CB 170.

purposes. The existence of the agreement is one factor to be considered in determining the value of the interest.

In *Estate of True,*[73] the Court of Appeals for the Tenth Circuit concluded that the prices in buy-sell agreements based on tax book value were not controlling in valuing businesses for estate and gift tax purposes because the agreements were testamentary substitutes unsupported by adequate consideration. The buy-sell agreements at issue in *Estate of True,* however, were entered into prior to October 8, 1990, when Code Sec. 2703 was added to the law to clarify the use of buy-sell agreements for estate tax valuation purposes. If the same buy-sell agreements had been created after October 8, 1990, they would have been subject to Code Sec. 2703, which provides that buy-sell agreements created or substantially modified after October 8, 1990, may establish value for estate tax purposes only if the agreements are bona fide business arrangements, the terms are comparable to those of similar arrangements negotiated at arm's-length, and the agreements are not a testamentary device. Thus, Code Sec. 2703 imposes one new requirement on the previous criteria needed for the agreement to set a binding value for estate tax purposes-namely, the terms must be comparable to those of similar arrangements negotiated at arm's-length [Reg. § 25.2703-1(b)(4)].

Buy-sell agreement ignored. In *Estate of Blount,*[74] the Court of Appeals for the Eleventh Circuit held that a buy-sell agreement between the decedent and his closely held corporation must be ignored in determining the value of the corporate shares because the decedent's control over the corporation rendered the agreement not fixed and binding during his lifetime. In addition, the estate failed to establish that the terms of the agreement were comparable to those that would be entered into among unrelated parties

Buy-sell agreement fixed price of stock. In *Estate of Amlie,*[75] a buy-sell agreement restricting the sale of a decedent's stock in a bank fixed the fair market value of the stock in determining the value for estate tax purposes because the requirements of Code Sec. 2703(b) were satisfied as evidenced by the following:

1. The agreement reached between the prospective heirs fixed the value of all of the decedent's bank stock;
2. The agreement between the heirs and conservator was enforceable as proven by the court order approving the settlement and granting the conservator the authority to effectuate the terms and conditions of the agreement;
3. The agreement furthered a business purpose to serve the decedent's best interest by minimizing the risk to the decedent of holding a minority interest in a closely held bank;
4. The agreement was not a testamentary device as the decedent received significant consideration under the agreement; and
5. The agreement was similar to comparable arm's-length transactions.

---

[73] *H.A. True Jr. Est.,* CA-10, 2004-2 USTC ¶ 60,495, 390 F3d 1210.

[74] *G.C. Blount Est.,* CA-11, 2005-2 USTC ¶ 60,509, 428 F3d 1338.

[75] *P.I. Amlie Est.,* 91 TCM 1017, Dec. 56,482(M), TC Memo. 2006-76.

Minority Interest Discount

The minority interest discount is central to many estate planning techniques which involve the transfer of minority interests in limited liability companies, family limited partnerships and closely held corporations, to family members as part of a gift-giving program. If the IRS accepts the minority interest discount, it can result in a significant reduction in transfer taxes for the family. The minority discount is based on the premise that holders of minority interests have little influence or control over business policy and affairs, for example, with respect to the payment of dividends or compelling the sale of the business. Because the owner of a minority interest in a closely held company lacks these benefits, the theory behind this oft-used wealth transfer tax technique is that a hypothetical buyer of these shares will pay less per share to acquire a minority interest than the hypothetical buyer would pay to acquire a controlling interest. The discounts can range from a modest 20 percent to a more substantial 50 percent discount that is applied to the decedent's proportionate share of the asset value of the entire company.

When valuing transfers of minority interests of a closely held company to family members in Rev. Rul. 93-12,[76] the IRS did not aggregate the transferred shares to determine whether the family members were given a controlling interest in the company (which would result in a premium being added to the shares' value). As a result it was possible to transfer more stock to family members claiming a minority stock with a reduced estate or gift tax cost.

Example 29-30: Dad owns stock in a closely held business, which is worth $1 million on the books. When Dad dies the stock is divided among his four children. If the executor of the estate applies a minority discount of 50 percent when the estate tax return is filed, the estate will only owe tax on $500,000 rather than $1 million.

.04 Insurance

The value of an insurance policy payable in a lump sum on your death is the amount of the proceeds. If it is payable as an annuity, the value is determined by use of actuarial tables [Code Sec. 7520]. The value of an insurance policy owned by you on the life of another person is based on the replacement cost or the interpolated terminal reserve (i.e., an amount computed by interpolating between the initial and the terminal reserve) [Reg. § 20.2031-8(a)(2)]. This also holds in cases involving simultaneous deaths.[77]

.05 Business Interests

The fair market value of an interest in a business, whether a partnership or proprietorship, is determined by the willing-buyer-willing-seller test. All the business' assets-including the good will of the business and demonstrated earning capacity-are important factors in the valuation [Reg. § 20.2031-3]. Here too, a buy-sell agreement may determine estate tax valuation.

---

[76] Rev. Rul. 93-12, 1993-1 CB 202.

[77] *E.M. Wien Est.*, CA-5, 71-1 USTC ¶ 12,764, 441 F2d 32; *Old Kent Bk. & Tr. Co.*, CA-6, 70-2 USTC ¶ 12,703, 430 F2d 392; *H.H. Chown Est.*, CA-9, 70-2 USTC ¶ 12,702, 428 F2d 1395.

.06 Limited Interests-Annuities, Life Estates, Terms Certain, Remainders, and Reversions

Limited interests, such as an annuity or income interest for life or a term certain, a remainder interest or a reversionary interest, are valued under tables published by the IRS [Code Sec. 7520]. The actuarial factors in the tables are based on the most recent mortality experience and interest at 120 percent of the applicable federal midterm rate (compounded semiannually).

.07 Real Property

In general, the fair market value of real property is based on its highest and best use (but current use valuation is permitted under certain circumstances, as discussed below). Value can depend on various factors such as the type of property, its location,[78] the condition of the property, economic prospects in the community where the property is located, comparable sales, etc.

.08 Individual Retirement Accounts (IRAs)

An IRA account owned by a decedent at death is considered part of the decedent's estate for Federal estate tax purposes [Code Sec. 2039(a)]. Therefore, the estate must pay an estate tax on the value of the IRA. In addition, an income tax will be assessed against the beneficiaries of the accounts when the accounts are distributed [Code Sec. 408(d)(1); Code Sec. 691(a)(1)(B)]. To compensate (at least partially) for this potential double taxation, Code Sec. 691(c) grants the recipient of an item of income in respect of decedent (IRD)—an income tax deduction equal to the amount of Federal estate tax attributable to that item of IRD.[79] Therefore, decedent's beneficiaries will be allowed a deduction in the amount of Federal estate tax paid on the items of IRD included in the distributions to them from the IRA. The deduction is allowed in the same year the income is recognized—that is, when the IRA is actually distributed [Code Sec. 691(c)(1)(A)].

Discount for Beneficiaries' Income Tax Liability

In *Estate of Kahn*,[80] the value of two IRAs included in a decedent's gross estate was not reduced by the anticipated income tax liability that would be incurred by the beneficiaries upon distribution of the IRAs. For purposes of applying the willing seller-willing buyer test, the subject of a hypothetical sale was the underlying assets of the IRAs, not the IRAs themselves. The tax burden associated with distributing the assets in the IRAs would not be transferred to a hypothetical buyer. Therefore, the hypothetical buyer would not consider the income tax liability of the IRA beneficiary because the beneficiary, rather than the buyer, would pay the tax. In addition, it was not appropriate to apply a lack of marketability discount in valuing the IRAs because the underlying assets of the IRAs were marketable securities, unlike a situation involving (for example) closely held stock. No reduction in value was warranted because the hypothetical sale of the marketable securities would not transfer any built-in tax liability or marketability restriction to a willing buyer, who would receive the securities free of any such burden.

---

78 *A.P. Cockrell*, DC-MS, 73-1 USTC ¶12,919.

79 *L.R. Smith Est.*, CA-5, 2004-2 USTC ¶60,493, 391 F3d 621.

80 *D.F. Kahn Est.*, 125 TC 227, Dec. 56,195 (2005).

Moreover, there was no basis for supplementing the relief from double taxation granted in Code Sec. 691(c) by discounting the value of the decedent's IRAs for estate tax purposes. Because no discount applied, the IRAs were valued based on their respective account balances on the date of the decedent's death.

.09 Appraiser Penalty Applies to Substantial and Gross Estate or Gift Tax Valuation Misstatements

A civil penalty is imposed against appraisers for certain types of valuation misstatements that result in tax underpayments. The penalty amount is the lesser of: (1) the greater of $1,000 or 10 percent of the tax underpayment amount attributable to the misstatement, or (2) 125 percent of the gross income received by the appraiser for preparing the appraisal. However, no penalty is imposed if the appraiser establishes that the appraised value was more likely than not the proper value [Code Sec. 6695A(b) and (c)]. A person who prepares an appraisal of property value must pay the penalty if: (1) he or she knows, or reasonably should have known, that the appraisal would be used in connection with a federal tax return or refund claim; and (2) the claimed value of the appraised property results in a substantial valuation misstatement related to income tax under Code Sec. 6662(e), a substantial estate or gift tax valuation understatement under Code Sec. 6662(g), or a gross valuation misstatement under Code Sec. 6662(h) [Code Sec. 6695A(a)].

A gross valuation misstatement for estate and gift taxes occurs when the claimed property value is 40 percent or less of the correct amount [Code Sec. 6662(h)(2)(C)]. The appraiser penalty will be applied to situations where the claimed value of the appraised property results in a substantial estate or gift tax valuation understatement under Code Sec. 6662(g) [Code Sec. 6695A(a)]. For estate and gift taxes, a substantial valuation understatement occurs if the claimed value of any property on an estate, gift or generation skipping tax return is 65 percent or less of the amount determined to be the correct valuation amount [Code Sec. 6662(g)(a)].

Assessment

The appraiser penalty under Code Sec. 6695A must be assessed within 3 years after the return or claim for refund with respect to which the penalty is assessed was filed, and no proceeding in court without assessment for the collection of such tax may begin after the expiration of that period [Code Sec. 6696(d)(1)].

Claim for Refund

Any claim for refund of an overpayment of a valuation penalty assessed under Code Sec. 6695A must be filed within 3 years from the time the penalty was paid [Code Sec. 6696(d)(2)].

¶29,110 ALTERNATIVE VALUATION METHODS

.01 Special Use Valuation

There is a special or current valuation available for estates consisting substantially of farm or closely held business realty under Code Sec. 2032A. The purpose of Code Sec. 2032A was "to encourage the continued operation of family farms and other small family businesses by permitting real property used for the farm or business to be valued upon its present use, rather than upon its highest and best use."[81] Specifically, "Code Sec. 2032A relieves taxpayers from having to sell an eligible family farm or business when the income from its present use is insufficient to pay the tax calculated upon its highest and best use."[82] Real property located on a family farm or business might have an exorbitantly high fair market value if developed as a shopping center or otherwise put to its highest and best use. Because this could result in a very high estate tax to a family that did not plan to convert the property to its so-called highest and best use, the law allows this type of property to be valued at its current use. To ensure against abuse of current use valuation, the law contains a provision for recapture of the lost taxes if, within ten years, the property is no longer used for farming or closely held business purposes or is transferred to someone other than a family member or qualified heir. An executor may elect to value real property includible in a decedent's estate that is used for farming or for closely held business use on the basis of the property's actual use, rather than on the traditional basis of "highest or best" use, if certain conditions are met [Code Sec. 2032A].

Current use valuation cannot reduce the gross estate by more than $1,070,000 in 2013 (increasing to $1,090,000 in 2014). For example, if the highest and best use of farmland is for development, valued at $3 million, but its value as farmland is $1,070,000, the estate can only be reduced by $1,070,000 in 2013 [Code Sec. 2032A(a) (2)]. The executor may elect to determine special use valuation on the alternate valuation date.[83]

Special use valuation applies only to real property located in the United States and used for farming purposes or in a closely held business. To qualify for special use valuation, these conditions must be met [Code Sec. 2032A].

- The decedent was a U.S. citizen or resident;
- The real property is located in the United States;
- The adjusted value of real and personal property that was being used on the date of the decedent's death for a qualified use by the decedent or a member of the decedent's family and that was acquired from or passed from the decedent to a qualified heir is at least 50 percent of the adjusted value of the decedent's gross estate;
- At least 25 percent or more of the adjusted value of the decedent's gross estate consists of the adjusted value of real property that satisfies the following requirements: (1) it was acquired from or passed from the decedent to a qualified heir of the decedent and that and (2) during the eight-year period ending on the decedent of the decedent's death, there were periods aggregating five years or more during which the property was owned by the decedent or a member of the decedent's family and used for a qualified use by the decedent or a member of the decedent's family and there was material participation by the decedent or a member of the decedent's family in the operation of the farm or other business [Code Sec. 2032A(b) (1) (B)];

---

[81] *M. Schuneman*, CA-7, 86-1 USTC ¶13,660, 783 F2d 694.

[82] *Id.*

[83] Rev. Rul. 83-31, 1983-1 CB 225.

NOTE: Adjusted value is fair market value (without regard to the special use valuation) less any mortgage or other indebtedness against property in the estate. A surviving spouse's interest in qualified real property held as community property is taken into account for purposes of meeting the 50 percent and 25 percent tests, but not for purposes of reducing the $1 million limitation in 2010.[84]

- The real property must pass from, or be acquired from, the decedent by a member of the decedent's family, known as a qualified heir [Code Sec. 2032A(b)(1)(a)]. Family members who may be qualified heirs include the decedent's spouse, parents, children, siblings, nieces and nephews (but not aunts and uncles). A spouse of any family member is also a family member and may be a qualified heir [Code Sec. 2032A(e)(2)]. Qualified real property may pass to a qualified heir as a result of a qualified disclaimer[¶29,165].[85] Real property passing to a trust can qualify if the beneficiary has a present interest. If it is a discretionary trust (i.e., one in which distribution of income is left to the trustee's discretion), all the beneficiaries must be qualified heirs [Code Sec. 2032A(g)].
- The decedent or a family member materially participated in the farm or business operation in five out of the eight years ending on the date of the decedent's death [Code Sec. 2032A(b)(1)(C)]. If the decedent died disabled or retired and was receiving social security benefits, the eight-year period ends with the beginning of the disability or retirement [Code Sec. 2032A(b)(4)]. In the case of a surviving spouse, active management of the farm or business is regarded as material participation and can be tacked onto the material participation of the predeceased spouse [Code Sec. 2032A(b)(5)]. Active management means the making of business decisions other than daily operating decisions, and requires a lesser standard of involvement than material participation.

Example 29-31: Andrew materially participated in the operations of his farm from January 2004 through February 2009, when he became disabled. After he became disabled, his wife, Angela, actively managed the farm. Andrew died in 2012; Angela died in 2013. Andrew's and Angela's work constitute sufficient material participation to qualify the farm for special use valuation (assuming the other requirements are met) in both estates. Reason: Andrew materially participated for five out of eight years ending with the onset of his disability. Angela's three years of active management can be tacked onto Andrew's material participation.

How to Elect

The election for special use valuation must be made on a timely filed estate tax return (Form 706) or on a late-filed Form 706 as long as it is the first return filed after the due date [Code Sec. 2032A(d) (1); Reg. § 20.2032A-8(a)]. The election, once made, is irrevocable. In order to make a valid election, certain information is required to be included in the Notice of Election, and each person who has an interest in the property is required to sign an agreement consenting to the imposition of additional estate tax in the event of

[84] LTR 8014022 (Dec. 27, 1979).

[85] *G.L. McDonald*, CA-8, 88-2 USTC ¶ 13,778, 853 F2d 1494, *cert. denied*, 490 US 1005; Rev. Rul. 82-140, 1982-2 CB 208.

a failure to use the property for its qualified use within 10 years of the decedent's death. Both a notice of election and an agreement by heirs must be attached to the estate tax return. The Notice of Election must contain detailed information about the real property that is the subject of the special use valuation [Reg. § 20.2032A-8(a)(3)].

Right to Correct Mistakes

If an election is timely filed and (1) the Notice of Election does not contain all of the required information or (2) the signature of one or more persons required to sign the agreement is missing or the agreement does not contain all the required information, the executor may provide the missing information or signatures within 90 days of being notified by the IRS [Code Sec. 2032A(d)(3)].The executor may supply the missing information or signatures within 90 days of being notified by the IRS, without regard to compliance with the regulations.

Protective Election

A protective election may be filed if it is uncertain whether the estate qualifies for special use valuation so that if the requirements are met during audit, the election will be available [Reg. § 20.2032A-8(b)]. A protective election is made by a notice of protective election filed with the estate tax return stating that a protective election under Code Sec. 2032A is being made pending the final determination of values. The protective election must be made on a timely filed estate tax return. If you make a protective election, you complete the estate tax return by valuing all property at its fair-market value.

A protective election does not extend the time for payment of any amount of tax. If you wish to extend the time to pay the taxes, you should file IRS Form 4768 in adequate time before the return due date. If it is later determined that the estate qualifies for special use valuation, you must file a supplemental estate tax return within 60 days after date of this determination. Executors have a reasonable period of time to correct technical oversights in a filed election but must do so within 90 days after an IRS notice [Code Sec. 2032A(d)(3)]. To get this second chance, the executor must have "substantially complied" with the requirements the first time around. The IRS has taken a pretty tough stance on what constitutes substantial compliance but courts have been more lenient, saying a reasonable, honest mistake won't prevent an executor from showing he or she substantially complied with the requirements. If the executor submits a timely notice of election and recapture agreement, but the election or agreement does not contain all the required information or signatures, the executor may supply the missing information or signatures within 90 days of being notified by the IRS [Code Sec. 2032A(d)(3)].

Recapture of Estate Tax Benefits

The recapture tax is an additional estate tax that is imposed if within ten years after the decedent's death and before the death of the qualified heir, the real property is transferred to a nonfamily member or is not used for farming or other closely held business purposes [Code Sec. 2032A(c)(1)].[86] The qualified heir has a two-year period after the decedent's death to begin putting the real property to a "qualified use." The

[86] LTR 8350035 (Sept. 9, 1983).

ten-year recapture period is extended by the length of any grace period that is used before "qualified use" begins [Code Sec. 2032A(c)(7)]. No recapture tax is imposed if there is an involuntary conversion of qualified real property and the proceeds are used to purchase qualified replacement property at least equal in value to the amount realized on the conversion [Code Sec. 2032A(h)]. The cash lease of specially-valued real property by the surviving spouse or a lineal descendant of the decedent to a member of the family of the surviving spouse or lineal descendant, who continues to operate the farm or closely held business, does not cause the "qualified use" of the property to cease for purposes of imposing the additional estate tax [Code Sec. 2032A(c)(7)].

Filing Requirements and Payment of Additional Tax

The qualified heir must file Form 706-A, *United States Additional Estate Tax Return* and pay the additional tax within six months after a taxable disposition or cessation of qualified use unless an extension of time has been granted. The form must be filed if there is an early disposition, an early cessation of qualified use, an exchange, or involuntary conversion of specially valued property even if no additional tax is due. No tax is due on an early disposition to a family member who consents in writing to personal liability for any additional tax that may become due. And no additional tax is imposed on an exchange of specially valued property for "qualified exchange property" (i.e., property that will be used for the same qualified use) [Code Sec. 2032A(i)(1].[87]

Amount of Additional Tax

The amount of the recapture tax is the lesser of the following [Code Sec. 2032A(c)(2)]:

1. The difference between the estate tax liability and what the liability would have been had special use valuation not been elected (if the special use valuation affected more than just the property for which tax is now recaptured). Multiply the above by this fraction: difference between fair market value and special use value of the property, divided by the difference between the fair market value and special use value of all qualified property; or

2. The excess of the amount realized on the sale of the interest or its fair market value (if no sale) over the special use value.

The adjusted tax difference is the difference between the estate tax liability and what the liability would have been had special use valuation not been elected. The attributable amount bears the same ratio to the adjusted tax difference as the excess fair market value of the particular qualified property bears to the excess fair market value of all qualified property. In other words, the adjusted tax difference is multiplied by a fraction the numerator of which is the difference between the fair market value and the special value of the property and the denominator of which is the difference between the fair market value and the special value of all qualified property.

There is a special lien on all qualified property, including qualified replacement property. The lien continues until the tax benefits are recaptured or potential liability ends [Code Sec. 6324B].

> **NOTE:** A qualified heir may elect to increase the basis of specially valued real property to its fair market value on the date of the decedent's death or alternate

[87] LTR 8207050 (Nov. 19, 1981).

valuation date (if applicable) when the recapture tax is imposed. If the recapture event was a sale, the qualified heir's recognized gain is, therefore, reduced because the basis increase is deemed to occur immediately before the recapture event [Code Sec. 1016(c)].

.02 Alternate Valuation Method

Fair-market value of the decedent's assets for estate tax purposes is determined as of the date of death unless the executor elects the alternate valuation method to value the decedent's property [Code Sec. 2032(a); Reg. § 20.2031-1(b)]. If the value of the decedent's gross estate declines in the six months following the decedent's death and if electing to use the alternate valuation date for estate tax purposes would reduce the taxes due, the executor may elect under Code Sec. 2032 to value the assets of the estate as of the date six months after the decedent's death. If an executor elects the alternate valuation method under Code Sec. 2032, the property included in the decedent's gross estate on the date of his death is valued as of whichever of the following dates is applicable:

1. Any property "distributed, sold, exchanged, or otherwise disposed of" within six months after the decedent's death is valued as of the date on which it is first distributed, sold, exchanged, or otherwise disposed of;
2. Any property not distributed, sold, exchanged, or otherwise disposed of within six months after the decedent's death is valued as of the date six months after the date of the decedent's death;
3. Any property, interest, or estate which is affected by mere lapse of time is valued as of the date of the decedent's death, but adjusted for any difference in its value not due to mere lapse of time as of the date six months after the decedent's death, or as of the date of its distribution, sale, exchange, or other disposition, whichever date first occurs [Code Sec. 2032(a)(1); Reg. § 1.2032-1(a)].

The election, however, is limited. The alternate valuation can be made only if it results in a reduction in both the value of the gross estate and the sum of the estate and generation-skipping transfer taxes (reduced by credits allowable against these taxes) imposed on the estate for which the election is made [Code Sec. 2032(c)]. Reg. § 20.2032-1(b)(1) provides that the determination of whether there has been a decrease in the sum (reduced by allowable credits) of the estate tax and GST tax liability is made with reference to the estate tax and GST tax payable by reason of the decedent's death. This avoids the problem of not being able to determine whether the election will reduce the sum of the two taxes if the GST tax will not be imposed until later on (e.g., in the event of a later taxable termination or a taxable distribution).

Meaning of "Distributed, Sold, Exchanged, or Otherwise Disposed Of"

The phrase *distributed, sold, exchanged, or otherwise disposed of* comprehends all possible ways by which property ceases to form a part of the gross estate. For example, money on hand at the date of the decedent's death which is thereafter used in the payment of funeral expenses, or which is thereafter invested, falls within the term *otherwise disposed of*. The term also includes the surrender of a stock certificate for corporate assets in complete or partial liquidation of a corporation. The term does not, however, extend to transactions that are mere changes in form. Thus, it does not include a transfer of assets to a corporation in exchange for its stock in a transaction with respect to which no gain or loss would be recognizable for income tax purposes under Code Sec. 351. Nor does it include an exchange of stock or securities in a corporation for stock or securities in the same corporation or another corporation in a transaction, such as a tax-free merger, recapitalization, or reorganization under Code Sec. 368 where no gain or loss is recognizable for income tax purposes [Reg. § 20.2032-1(c)(1)].

When property is considered "distributed." Property may be "distributed" either by the executor or by a trustee of property included in the gross estate. Property is considered as *distributed* upon the first to occur of the following:

1. The entry of an order or decree of distribution, if the order or decree subsequently becomes final,
2. The segregation or separation of the property from the estate or trust so that it becomes unqualifiedly subject to the demand or disposition of the distribute, or
3. The actual paying over or delivery of the property to the distributee [Reg. § 20.2032-1(c)(2)].

Property may be sold, exchanged, or otherwise disposed of by:

1. The executor;
2. A trustee or other donee to whom the decedent during his lifetime transferred property included in his gross estate under Code Secs. 2035 through 2038, or Code Sec. 2041;
3. An heir or devisee to whom title to property passes directly under local law;
4. A surviving joint tenant or tenant by the entirety; or
5. Any other person [Reg. § 20.2032-1(c)(3)].

If a binding contract for the sale, exchange, or other disposition of property is entered into, the property is considered as sold, exchanged, or otherwise disposed of on the effective date of the contract, unless the contract is not subsequently carried out substantially in accordance with its terms. The effective date of a contract is normally the date it is entered into (and not the date it is consummated, or the date legal title to the property passes) unless the contract specifies a different effective date.

"Included Property" and "Excluded Property" for Alternate Valuation Purposes

If the executor elects the alternate valuation method, all property interests existing at the date of the decedent's death, which form a part of his gross estate are referred to as *included property*. Furthermore, such property interests remain included property for the purpose of valuing the gross estate under the alternate valuation method even though they change in form during the alternate valuation period by being actually received, or disposed of, in whole or in part, by the estate. On the other hand, property earned or accrued after the date of the decedent's death and during the alternate valuation period, which does not represent a form of included property itself or the receipt of included property, is excluded in valuing the gross estate under the alternate valuation method. Such property is referred to as *excluded property* [Reg. § 20.2032-1(d)].

The following types of property are considered included property for alternate valuation purposes:

1. Interest-bearing obligations, such as bonds or notes, may comprise two elements of included property at the date of the decedent's death, namely, (i) the principal

of the obligation itself and (ii) interest accrued to the date of death. Each of these elements is to be separately valued as of the applicable valuation date. Interest accrued after the date of death and before the subsequent valuation date constitutes excluded property [Reg. § 20.2032-1(d)(1)].

2. Leased realty included in the gross estate and with respect to which an obligation to pay rent has been reserved constitute included property. Any rent accrued after the date of death and before the subsequent valuation date is excluded property [Reg. § 20.2032-1(d)(2)].
3. With respect to noninterest-bearing obligations sold at a discount, such as U.S. savings bonds, the principal obligation, and the discount amortized to the date of death are property interests existing at the date of death and constitute included property. The obligation itself is to be valued at the subsequent valuation date without regard to any further increase in value due to amortized discount. The additional discount amortized after death and during the alternate valuation period is the equivalent of interest accruing during that period and, therefore, is not to be included in the gross estate under the alternate valuation method [Reg. § 20.2032-1(d)(3)].
4. Shares of stock in a corporation and dividends declared to stockholders of record on or before the date of the decedent's death and not collected at the date of death constitute included property of the estate. On the other hand, ordinary dividends out of earnings and profits (whether in cash, shares of the corporation, or other property) declared to stockholders of record after the date of the decedent's death are excluded property and are not to be valued under the alternate valuation method. If, however, dividends are declared to stockholders of record after the date of the decedent's death with the effect that the shares of stock at the subsequent valuation date do not reasonably represent the same included property of the gross estate as existed at the date of the decedent's death, the dividends are included property, except to the extent that they are out of earnings of the corporation after the date of the decedent's death. For example, if a corporation makes a distribution in partial liquidation to stockholders during the alternate valuation period, which is not accompanied by a surrender of a stock certificate for cancellation, the amount of the distribution received on stock included in the gross estate is itself included property, except to the extent that the distribution was out of earnings and profits since the date of the decedent's death. Similarly, if a corporation, in which the decedent owned a substantial interest and which possessed at the date of the decedent's death accumulated earnings and profits equal to its paid-in capital, distributed all of its accumulated earnings and profits as a cash dividend to shareholders of record during the alternate valuation period, the amount of the dividends received on stock includible in the gross estate will be included in the gross estate under the alternate valuation method. Likewise, a stock dividend distributed under such circumstances is included property [Reg. § 1.2032-1(d)(4)].

Value of Property Affected by Lapse of Time

In order to eliminate changes in value due only to mere lapse of time, Code Sec. 2032(a)(3) provides that any interest or estate "affected by mere lapse of time" is included in a decedent's gross estate under the alternate valuation method at its value as of the date of the decedent's death, but with adjustment for any difference in its value as of the subsequent valuation date not due to mere lapse of time. Properties, interests, or estates which are "affected by mere lapse of time" include patents, estates for the life of a person other than the decedent, remainders, reversions, and other like properties, interests, or estates. The phrase *affected by mere lapse of time* excludes obligations for the payment of money, whether or not interest-bearing, the value of which changes with the passing of time [Reg. § 20.2032-1(f)(2)].

Example 29-32: Henry died owning an income interest in a trust for the duration of the life of Wilma, his wife. On the date of Henry's death, Wilma was 47 years and five months old, and the trust assets were valued at $2 million. Six months later, the trust assets were valued at $1,950,000. Furthermore, the fact that Wilma is a half year older reduces the value of the income interest based on her life span. If Henry's executor uses the alternate valuation date, the reduction in the value of the life interest due to the mere lapse of time is not taken into account, but the lower value of the trust assets is used.

Valuation of Life Estates, Remainders, and Similar Interests

The values of life estates, remainders, and similar interests are determined by applying the methods prescribed in Reg. § 20.2031-1 (f) (2) (i), using:

1. The age of each person, the duration of whose life may affect the value of the interest, as of the date of the decedent's death, and
2. The value of the property as of the alternate date.

Valuation of Patents

To illustrate the alternate valuation of a patent, assume that the decedent owned a patent that, on the date of the decedent's death, had an unexpired term of ten years and a value of $78,000. Six months after the date of the decedent's death, the patent was sold, because of lapse of time and other causes, for $60,000. The alternate value would be determined by dividing $60,000 by 0.95 (ratio of the remaining life of the patent at the alternate date to the remaining life of the patent at the date of the decedent's death) and would, therefore, be $63,157.89 [Reg. § 20.2032-1 (f) (2) (ii)].

Keys to Alternate Valuation

1. All assets in the decedent's gross estate are affected by the election and must be valued as of the alternate valuation date [Reg. § 20.2032-1 (d)]. In other words, the executor cannot elect the alternate valuation date for some assets and not others [Reg. § 20.2032-1 (b) (2)]. The executor may elect alternate valuation and also elect special use valuation for real property.
2. The election is not available unless the valuation change will decrease both the federal estate tax (and the GST tax, where applicable) and the size of the decedent's gross estate [Code Sec. 2032 (c)].
3. Property that comes into existence after the decedent's death is not subject to the election. Thus, in general, most dividends declared to shareholders of record after the decedent's death generally are not included or valued under the alternate valuation method [Reg. § 20.2032-1 (d) (4)].

4. Under Code Sec. 2032(b), if alternate valuation is elected, deductions for losses are allowed only to the extent they are not reflected in the values used to determine the gross estate.
5. If the election is made and property is "distributed, sold, exchanged or otherwise disposed of" within the six-month period, the date of disposition is considered the alternate valuation date [Code Sec. 2032(a)(1)].

How to Elect

The election to use the alternate valuation method is made on the last estate tax return filed by the executor on or before the due date of the return (including extensions of time to file actually granted) or, if a timely return is not filed, the first estate tax return filed by the executor after the due date, provided the return is filed no later than one year after the due date (including extensions of time to file actually granted) [Code Sec. 2032(d)]. Once the election is made, it is irrevocable, provided that an election may be revoked on a subsequent return filed on or before the due date of the return (including extensions of time to file actually granted). The election may be made only if it will decrease both the value of the gross estate and the sum (reduced by allowable credits) of the estate tax and the generation-skipping transfer tax payable as a result of the decedent's death. If the election is made, the alternate valuation method applies to all property included in the gross estate and cannot be applied to only a portion of the property [Code Sec. 2032(d); Reg. § 20.2032-1(b)(1)].

Requests for extension of time to make the election. Estates that fail to make the alternate valuation election on the last estate tax return filed before the due date or the first return filed after the due date can request an extension of time to make the election or protective election pursuant to Reg. § 301.9100-1 and Reg. § 301.9100-3. The extension will not be granted unless the estate tax return is filed no later than one year after the due date of the return (including extensions of time actually granted) [Reg. § 20.2032-1(b)(3)].

Protective Elections

Estates may also make a protective election if, based on the tax return as filed, use of the alternate valuation method would not result in a decrease in both the value of the gross estate and the sum (reduced by allowable credits) of the estate/GST taxes due with respect to the property includible in the decedent's gross estate. A protective election may be made to use the alternate valuation method if it is subsequently determined that such a decrease would occur. A protective election is made on the decedent's estate tax return. The protective election is irrevocable as of the due date of the return (including extensions of time actually granted). The protective election becomes effective on the date on which it is determined that use of the alternate valuation method would result in a decrease in both the value of the gross estate and in the sum (reduced by allowable credits) of the estate tax and generation-skipping transfer tax liability payable as a result of the decedent's death [Reg. § 20.2032-1(b)(2)].

The estate tax return where the alternate valuation election is made must be filed on time and should be sent by registered or certified mail at a U.S. Post Office or one of the private delivery services (PDSs) designated by the IRS [Code Sec. 7502(c), (f); Reg. § 301.7502-1(c)]. You can use a private delivery services designated by the IRS to meet the "timely mailing as timely filing/paying" rule for tax returns and payments. For a list of the private delivery services approved by the IRS, see ¶ 26,065.

The IRS has been consistently unsympathetic to executors who are late in making the alternate valuation election. In *Estate of Eddy*,[88] the Tax Court denied an executor's ability to make this election because it was made more than one year after the deadline (with extensions) for filing the estate tax return.

In certain situations, however, executors may find relief in Reg. § 301.9100-1(c), which provides that the IRS may grant a reasonable extension of time to make a regulatory or statutory election (but no more than six months, unless the taxpayer is abroad). Reg. § 301.9100-3 provides that relief will be granted when the taxpayer provides evidence that he or she acted reasonably and in good faith and the grant of relief will not prejudice IRS interests. For example, in Letter Ruling 200302007, the IRS concluded that an executor was entitled to an extension to make an alternate valuation election when a law firm failed to advise the executor about the availability of the election. The IRS concluded that the executor had acted reasonably and in good faith when the executor's law firm had failed to advise about the alternate dates. Therefore, the IRS granted an extension of time to make the election.

After-Death Planning Strategies

The Code Sec. 2032 election allows you to reduce the amount of estate tax to be paid. However, its income tax consequences must be considered. Use of the election will result in a lower cost basis to the heirs and higher future income taxes.

If the executor must sell assets to meet the estate's cash requirements, the executor should make the sales during the six-month alternate valuation period. If the alternate valuation date is used, no loss is realized and recognized on the sale for income tax purposes. Usually, the estate tax savings from using the alternate valuation date are greater than the income tax savings resulting from the long-term capital loss that would be generated if the alternate valuation date were not used.

To minimize the estate tax value, the executor should not make any distributions during the six-month alternate valuation period. By making a distribution before the decline in value has occurred, the executor will forfeit the estate reduction that might be obtained by using the alternate valuation date.

DEDUCTIONS FROM GROSS ESTATE

¶29,115 ALLOWABLE DEDUCTIONS

The estate tax is imposed on the taxable estate, which is the gross estate reduced by the following deductions: funeral expenses, expenses of administering the estate, debts owed at time of death including claims against the estate and unpaid mortgages on property included in the gross estate, casualty and theft losses occurring during

[88] *E.H. Eddy Est.*, 115 TC 135, Dec. 54,004 (2000).

administration of the estate, charitable contributions made by the estate, and the unlimited marital deduction [¶ 29,130].

.01 Expenses and Losses

The executor is entitled to claim a deduction from the gross estate for funeral expenses, administration expenses, claims against the estate, certain taxes, unpaid mortgages or other debt incurred by the estate. To be deductible the expenses must be allowable under the local law governing the administration of the decedent's estate [Code Sec. 2053(a)]. If the executor does not know the exact amount of executor's commissions and attorneys' fees to be paid by the estate, an estimated amount should be deducted from the estate if it is ascertainable with reasonable certainty [Reg. § 20.2053-1(d)(4)(1)].

If the expense is for the administration of assets not subject to claims (i.e., nonprobate assets such as property in a trust established during the decedent's lifetime) it must be paid before the expiration of the period for assessing estate tax deficiencies (generally three years from the due date for filing) [Code Sec. 6501; Reg. § 20.2053-8].

A deduction under Code Sec. 2053(a) is allowed only for expenses actually and necessarily incurred in the administration of the decendents estate. A deduction will not be allowed for expenses incurred for the benefit of the beneficiaries individually. In *S.M. Davenport Est.*,[89] the Tax Court denied the estate of a 12-year-old a deduction for a lavish funeral luncheon because the estate failed to show sufficient proof of its reasonable relationship to the funeral.

Interest will only be deductible if the estate can show it needed the money because it either had no liquid assets or a sale of the illiquid assets would have resulted in significant losses. In *Estate of Gilman*,[90] the court permitted a deduction for estate tax purposes for interest and closing costs paid on a bona fide loan incurred by the estate to the extent that the loan was necessary to pay legitimately incurred obligations of the estate. The interest and closing costs associated with the portion of the loan used to pay nondeductible estate expenses were not deductible.

Administrative Expenses

The U.S. Supreme Court held in *Estate of Hubert*,[91] that the marital and charitable deductions must be reduced for administration expenses paid from income only if these payments would materially affect the interest of the charity or the surviving spouse. In addition, Code Sec. 2056(b)(4)(B) provides that a marital deduction bequest is reduced when it is encumbered in any manner or where the surviving spouse incurs any obligation imposed by the decedent with respect to the passing of the interest. For example, if the principal is charged with an administrative expense (even if the estate deducts the expense for income tax purposes and not for estate tax purposes) the value of the marital deduction bequest passing under Code Sec. 2056 receives a corresponding reduction.

---

[89] *S.M. Davenport Est.*, 92 TCM 324, Dec. 56,642(M), TC Memo. 2006-215.

[90] *H. Gilman Est.*, 88 TCM 627, Dec. 55,831(M), TC Memo. 2004-286.

[91] *O.C. Hubert Est.*, SCt, 97-1 USTC ¶ 60,261, 520 US 93, 117 SCt 1124 (1997).

In addition, the IRS has issued regulations addressing the effect of certain administration expenses on the valuation of property that qualifies for the estate tax marital or charitable deduction.

The regulations provide that for purposes of determining the marital deduction, the value of the marital share, which is the property passing from the decedent which is eligible for the marital deduction, will be reduced by "estate transmission expenses" paid from the marital share [Reg. § 20.2056(b)-4(d)(2)]. For further discussion of marital deductions, see ¶ 29,120.

"Estate transmission expenses" are expenses that would not have been incurred but for the decedent's death and the consequent necessity of collecting the decedent's assets, paying the decedent's debts and death taxes, and distributing the decedent's property to those who are entitled to receive it. Estate transmission expenses include all expenses that are not estate management expenses, and include "expenses incurred in collecting estate assets, paying debts, estate and inheritance taxes, and distributing the decedent's property to those who are entitled to receive it." Examples of these expenses include executor commissions and attorney fees (except to the extent specifically related to investment, preservation, and maintenance of the assets), probate fees, expenses incurred in construction proceedings and defending against will contests, and appraisal fees [Reg. § 20.2056(b)-4(d)(1)(ii)].

On the other hand, for purposes of determining the marital deduction, the value of the marital share shall not be reduced by the amount of "estate management expenses" attributable to and paid from the marital share. *Estate management expenses* are defined as "expenses incurred in connection with the investment of the estate assets or with their preservation or maintenance during a reasonable period of administration." Examples of these expenses could include investment advisory fees, stock brokerage commissions, custodial fees, and interest [Reg. § 20.2056(b)-4(d)(1)(i)]. However, pursuant to Code Sec. 2056(b)(9), the amount of the allowable marital deduction shall be reduced by the amount of these management expenses that are deducted on the decedent's federal estate tax return under Code Sec. 2053 [Reg. § 20.2056(b)-4(d)(3)].

The regulations do not provide a test based on what constitutes a material limitation, but rather focus on the character of the administration expenses.

▶ **PLANNING TIP:** Estate planners should maintain thorough records which adequately allocate their fees and charges for services between the following two categories: (1) estate transmission expenses (as defined above) which are expenses incurred for the administration of the estate, payment of taxes and distribution of assets; and (2) estate management expenses (as defined above) which are expenses incurred in connection with the investment, maintenance or preservation of the estate.

.02 Claims Against the Estate

The amount that may be deducted as claims against a decedent's estate are limited to amounts for legitimate and bona fide claims that:

1. Represent personal obligations of the decedent existing at the time of the decedent's death;
2. Are enforceable against the decedent's estate at the time of payment; and
3. Are actually paid by the estate in settlement of the claim [Reg. § 20.2053-4(a)(1)].

Events occurring after the date of a decedent's death may be considered when determining whether and to what extent a deduction is allowable against a decedent's estate [Reg. § 20.2053-4(a)(2)].

The amount an estate may deduct for claims against the estate is a frequently litigated issue because Code Sec. 2053(a) does not tell executors whether they should value a claim at its date of death value or whether to consider post-death events in valuing the claim. Even though many courts have addressed the issue, there is little or no consistency regarding the extent to which post-death events are to be considered in valuing such claims. To resolve the issue once and for all, final regulations provide that events occurring after a decedent's death should be considered when determining the deductible amount and the amount deducted is limited to amounts actually paid by the estate in satisfaction of deductible expenses and claims [Reg. § 20.2053-4(a)(2)]. Final court decisions regarding the amount and enforceability of the claim or expense are accepted in determining the deductible amount. In addition, a claim against the estate is deductible only if the value of the claim is "ascertainable with reasonable certainty, and will be paid" [Reg. § 20.2053-1(b)(3)]. A deduction is not allowed to the extent the expense or claim is compensated for by insurance or is otherwise reimbursed [Reg. § 1.2053-1(d)(3)].

In *G.H. Saunders Est.*,[92] the Tax Court held that a decedent's estate was only able to claim a Code Sec. 2053 estate tax deduction for the amount of a claim against the estate that was actually paid during the administration of the estate because this amount could be determined with absolute certainty.

In addition, no deduction may be claimed on an estate tax return for a claim that is potential, unmatured, or contested at the time the return is filed. If a contested or contingent claim cannot be resolved before the expiration of the limitations period for refund claims, the estate may file a protective claim to preserve its right to claim a deduction [Reg. § 20.2053-4(d)(2)]. When a claim against an estate lists multiple defendants, the estate may only deduct the decedent's portion of the liability [Reg. § 20.2053-4(d)(3)].

Claims and Expenses Involving Family Members

Claims by family members or beneficiaries of a decedent's estate will be strictly scrutinized to ensure that they are legitimate claims [Reg. § 20.2053-1(b)(2)]. Reg. § 20.2053-1(b)(2)(ii) provides the following list of factors indicative of the bona fide nature of a claim or expense involving a family member of a decedent, a related entity, or a beneficiary of a decedent's estate or revocable trust:

1. The transaction underlying the claim or expense occurs in the ordinary course of business, is negotiated at arm's length, and is free from donative intent
2. The nature of the claim or expense is not related to an expectation or claim of inheritance.
3. The claim or expense originates pursuant to an agreement between the decedent and the family member, related entity, or beneficiary, and the agreement is substantiated with contemporaneous evidence.

---

[92] *G.H. Saunders Est.*, 136 TC 406, Dec. 58,610 (2011); see also *Marshall Naify Revocable Trust*, CA-9, 2012-1 USTC ¶ 60,639, 672 F3d 620, *aff'g*, DC-CA, 2010-2 USTC ¶ 60,603.

4. Performance by the claimant is pursuant to the terms of an agreement between the decedent and the family member, related entity, or beneficiary and the performance and the agreement can be substantiated.

5. All amounts paid in satisfaction or settlement of a claim or expense are reported by each party for Federal income and employment tax purposes, to the extent appropriate, in a manner that is consistent with the reported nature of the claim or expense.

If a claim becomes unenforceable after the decedent's death, the estate may not deduct that claim [Reg. § 20.2053-4(d)(4)]. If a claim represents a decedent's obligation to make recurring payments that will likely continue for a period extending beyond the final determination of the estate tax liability, a deduction is allowed only as each payment is made, provided the period of limitations for claims for refund has not expired or the estate has properly preserved the claim for refund [Reg. § 20.2053-4(d)(6)]. Alternatively, a deduction is allowed for the cost of a commercial annuity purchased by the estate from an unrelated dealer in commercial annuities in satisfaction of that obligation.

Estate Entitled to Deduct Palimony

In *B. Shapiro Est.*,[93] the Court of Appeals for the Ninth Circuit concluded that an estate was entitled to a Code Sec. 2053 estate tax deduction for palimony paid by the estate. The court found that homemaking services were adequate consideration to support a contract under the applicable state law. However, pursuant to Code Sec. 2053(c)(1)(A), the claim was only deductible to the extent that the consideration was adequate and full in money or money's worth, which is a factual issue to be determined by the district court.

Post-Death Adjustments of Deductible Tax Liability

Post-death adjustments increasing a tax liability accrued prior to the decedent's death, including increases of taxes, will increase the Code Sec. 2053(a)(3) deduction for that tax liability. Similarly, any refund subsequently determined to be due to and received by the estate with respect to taxes deducted by the estate reduce the amount of the deduction taken for that tax liability under Code Sec. 2053(a)(3). Expenses associated with defending the estate against the increase in tax liability or with obtaining the refund may also be deductible under Reg. § 20.2053-3(d)(3). A protective claim for refund of estate taxes may be filed before the expiration of the period of limitations for claims for refund in order to preserve the estate's right to claim a refund if the amount of a deductible tax liability may be affected by such an adjustment or refund [Reg. § 20.2053-6(g)].

Example 29-33: Increase in tax due: After the decedent's death, the IRS examines the gift tax return filed by the decedent in the year before the decedent's death and asserts a deficiency of $100x. The estate pays attorney's fees of $30x in a nonfrivolous defense against the increased deficiency. The final determination of the deficiency, in the amount of $90x, is paid by the estate prior to the expiration of the limitation period for filing a claim for refund. The estate may

[93] *B. Shapiro Est.*, CA-9, 2011-1 USTC ¶ 60,614, 634 F3d 1055.

deduct $90x under Code Sec. 2053(a)(3) and $30x under Reg. § 20.2053-3(c)(2) or (d)(3) in connection with a timely claim for refund.

Example 29-34: Refund of taxes paid: Decedent's estate timely files D's individual income tax return for the year in which the decedent died. The estate timely pays the entire amount of the tax due, $50x, as shown on that return. The entire $50x was attributable to income received prior to the decedent's death. Decedent's estate subsequently discovers an error on the income tax return and timely files a claim for refund of income tax. Decedent's estate receives a refund of $10x. The estate is allowed a deduction of only $40x under Code Sec. 2053(a)(3) for the income tax liability accrued prior to the decedent's death. If D's estate had claimed a deduction of $50x on D's United States Estate (and Generation-Skipping Transfer) Tax Return (Form 706), the deduction claimed under Code Sec. 2053(a)(3) will be allowed only to the extent of $40x upon examination by the IRS.

The IRS has released Notice 2009-84[94] to provide a limited administrative exception to the IRS's ability to examine Form 706 in connection with certain protective claims. Pursuant to Notice 2009-84, if the period for limitations on assessment has expired and a timely-filed protective claim for refund has become ready for consideration, the IRS will refrain from reexamining each item on the 706. The IRS will instead limit its examination to the deduction under Code Sec. 2053 that was related to the protective claim. However, the IRS will recompute the estate tax liability based on its determination.

.03 Taxes

The value of a decedent's taxable estate will be determined by deducting from the gross estate the amount of any estate, inheritance, legacy or succession taxes actually paid to any state or the District of Columbia with respect to property included in the decedent's gross estate [Code Sec. 2058].

Taxes are deductible in computing a decedent's gross estate only as claims against the estate (except to the extent that excise taxes may be allowable as administration expenses) [Reg. § 20.2053-6(a)]. Deductible taxes include property taxes accrued as an enforceable obligation of the decedent at death, unpaid income taxes on income received by the decedent and includible in his or her income tax return during lifetime, unpaid gift taxes on gifts made by the decedent before death, and excise taxes incurred by the estate in selling the decedent's property, if the sale was needed to pay claims against the estate, preserve the estate, or effect distribution.

Post-death adjustments increasing a tax liability accrued prior to the decedent's death, including tax increases will increase the amount of the deduction claimed. Similarly, any refund subsequently determined to be due to and received by the estate with respect to taxes deducted by the estate will reduce the amount of the deduction claimed for that tax liability. Expenses associated with defending the estate against the increase in tax liability or with obtaining the refund may also be deductible. A protective claim for refund of estate taxes may be filed before the expiration of the period of limitations for

[94] Notice 2009-84, IRB 2009-44, 592.

claims for refund in order to preserve the estate's right to claim a refund if the amount of a deductible tax liability may be affected by such an adjustment or refund [Reg. § 20.2053-6(g)].

.04 Charitable Pledges

Pledges or subscriptions to charitable organizations are exceptions to the general rule that deductible claims must arise from obligations for which bona fide consideration was received. A pledge or subscription is deductible if the contribution would be deductible as a charitable bequest [¶ 29,125] [Reg. § 20.2053-5].

.05 Mortgage Deduction

A mortgage or other secured debt is deducted from the gross estate if the underlying property is included in the gross estate. If you were personally liable for the debt or it is enforceable against other estate property, the full value of the mortgaged property is included in your gross estate. Then a separate deduction is taken for the obligation on Schedule K of Form 706. If the estate is not liable, the mortgage is subtracted from the property's value. Only that net amount (i.e., the "equity of redemption") is included in the gross estate, and no separate deduction is allowed.

In other words, a full recourse debt requires full inclusion; a nonrecourse debt requires inclusion of the equity of redemption [Reg. § 20.2053-7]. Election of special use valuation for the property does not bar the full deduction.[95]

.06 Losses

A deduction is allowed for losses from theft and casualties (e.g., fire and storms) incurred during the administration of the estate [Code Sec. 2054]. An executor's inability to recover estate taxes from the beneficiary ultimately liable is not considered a loss.[96]

¶29,120 MARITAL DEDUCTION

.01 In General

A married taxpayer can transfer unlimited amounts to a spouse either during life or at death free of transfer tax if the spouse is a U.S. citizen. Lifetime transfers are shielded from tax by the gift tax marital deduction [¶ 29,020], and transfers at death are exempted by the estate tax marital deduction, which is our focus here. Both of the deductions are subject to many of the same requirements.

The unlimited marital deduction does not eliminate or reduce tax on the transfer of assets out of the marital unit, but merely postpones the payment of tax because property that qualifies for the marital deduction in the estate of the first spouse to die is includable in the estate of the surviving spouse unless it is spent or given away by the surviving spouse during his or her lifetime.

Transfers from one spouse to his or her surviving spouse, if these transfers satisfy the technical requirements listed below, will be deducted from the transferor spouse's

---

[95] Rev. Rul. 83-81, 1983-1 CB 230.

[96] Rev. Rul. 69-411, 1969-2 CB 177.

gross estate when his or her federal estate tax bill is computed. The deduction is mandatory [Code Sec. 2056(a)]. The marital deduction results in a deferral of the federal estate tax that would otherwise be due when the first spouse dies. The marital deduction may only be claimed for property interests that pass from the decedent to the surviving spouse and are included in the decedent's gross estate.

The following five requirements must be satisfied for the transfer of an interest in property to qualify for the unlimited estate tax marital deduction:

1. The decedent must be a citizen or resident of the United States at the time of death [Reg. § 20.2056(a)-1(a)].
2. The decedent must be survived by a spouse who is a citizen of the United States [Code Sec. 2056(d); Reg. § 20.2056(a)-1(b)(1)]. The citizenship status of a surviving spouse is determined at the time of the filing of the decedent spouse's federal estate tax return, including extensions [Code Sec. 2056(d)(4)]. A surviving spouse who at the time of the decedent's death is not a U.S. citizen may become a citizen within a permissible period, thereby fulfilling this requirement.
3. The interest in property must be included in the decedent's gross estate [Code Sec. 2056(a)]. For example, life insurance proceeds on the life of the decedent paid to the surviving spouse from a policy owned by the surviving spouse would not be included in the decedent's gross estate. Thus, the proceeds from such a policy would not satisfy the inclusion requirement.
4. The interest in property must pass from the decedent to his or her surviving spouse [Code Sec. 2056(a)]. The passing requirement is broadly defined to include interests transferred (passing) to the spouse by will, intestate succession, right of survivorship, the exercise of a power of appointment, and the designation of the surviving spouse as the beneficiary of an insurance policy owned by the decedent on the decedent's life [Reg. § 20.2056(c)-1].
5. The surviving spouse must not receive a terminable interest in property which is an interest that lapses after the passage of time, such as the right to income only for the spouse's life or for a stated number of years.

Same-Sex Spouse May Claim Marital Deduction

In *E.S. Windsor*,[97] the Supreme Court concluded that a surviving same-sex spouse was entitled to claim an unlimited estate tax marital deduction under Code Sec. 2056 and receive a full refund of the estate tax she paid as a result of the unconstitutional application of DOMA § 3 which had denied the marital deduction to the same-sex couple who were regarded as nonmarried under the federal tax laws. After *E.S. Windsor*, and the IRS release of Rev. Rul. 2013-17,[98] where the IRS ruled that all legal same-sex marriages will be recognized for federal tax purposes, same-sex legally married couples can take advantage of the estate tax marital deduction which is a valuable planning tool used to defer transfer taxes in larger estates until the surviving spouse dies. The IRS adopted a "state of celebration" rule in Rev. Rul. 2013-17 which

[97] *E.S. Windsor*, SCt, 2013-2 USTC ¶ 60,667, *aff'g*, CA-2, 2012-2 USTC ¶ 60,654, *aff'g*, DC-NY, 2012-1 USTC ¶ 60,647, 833 FSupp 394.

[98] Rev. Rul. 2013-17, IRB 2013-38, 201.

means that same-sex couples who were legally married in one state will always be treated as married for federal tax purposes even if they later move to or reside in a state or jurisdiction that does not recognize same-sex marriage.

▶ **PLANNING POINTER:** Same-sex legally married couples with large estates should revisit their estate plans to make certain that interests passing to the other spouse qualify for the marital deduction and other tax benefits. Amending returns may be an option for taxpayers who failed to claim the marital deduction because they were considered not married under federal tax law prior to Windsor. See ¶27,130 for rules on filing refund claims.

.02 Terminable Interest Rule

A marital deduction is not allowed for nondeductible terminable interests in property. A terminable interest in property is an interest which will terminate with the passage of time or on the occurrence of some contingency [Reg. § 20.2056(b)-1(b)]. Examples are life estates, terms for years, annuities, patents, and copyrights. The reason for the terminable interest rule is that the purpose of the marital deduction is to allow tax deferral not tax avoidance. If terminable interests were allowed to pass under the marital deduction, tax avoidance would result because the transferred property would escape tax in the estates of both spouses.

A terminable interest is nondeductible under the marital deduction if another interest in the same property passed from the decedent to some other person for less than full consideration in money or money's worth and, by reason of its passing, the other person becomes entitled to enjoy any part of the property after the termination of the spouse's interest [Reg. § 20.2056(b)-1(c)(1)].

Example 29-35: Bruce Harrison devised Blackacre to his wife, Mary, for her life with remainder over to his son, Albert. Mary's is a terminable interest because it will terminate upon her death. It is not deductible because upon its termination the remainder interest in Blackacre will pass to Albert who paid nothing for it.

Example 29-36: George O'Henry bequeathed his residuary estate to Alma, his wife, if living on the date of distribution of his estate. Alma was living on the date of distribution and received the assets of the residuary estate. No marital deduction is allowable because Alma's interest is a nondeductible terminable interest that could have been defeated by her failure to survive distribution. (But there is an exception for survival for limited period, see below.)

Example 29-37: Franklin Roberts is the owner of an annuity for a term of 40 years or the earlier death of the survivor of himself and his wife, Susan. He bequeathed the unexpired term to Susan. The marital deduction is allowable. Reason: Franklin passed his entire interest in the property to Susan, and no one else will get the annuity after her death.

.03 Exceptions to the Terminable Interest Rule

The marital deduction is available for the following terminable interests: (1) an estate trust, (2) qualified terminable interest property (QTIP), (3) a transfer conditioned on the spouse's survival for a limited period, (4) a life estate coupled with a general power of appointment, (5) life insurance or annuity payments with power of appointment in the surviving spouse, and (6) a qualified interest in a qualified charitable remainder trust.

.04 Estate Trust

The marital deduction is allowed for a bequest in trust to pay income to the surviving spouse for life with remainder over to the surviving spouse's estate. This device is known as an estate trust. It qualifies for the deduction, even if payment of income is discretionary. However, the accumulated income, as well as corpus, must be paid to the surviving spouse's estate.[99]

.05 Qualified Terminable Interest Property (QTIP)

Estate planning can become very complicated when taxpayers get married the second time around but have children from the first marriage. In these circumstances they should think about a valuable estate planning tool known as the qualified terminable interest property (QTIP) trust.

The QTIP trust was designed for taxpayers who have remarried, want to provide for their second spouse after the taxpayer dies, but don't want to disinherit children from the prior marriage. The QTIP trust accomplishes both objectives. It will enable the taxpayer, at death, to provide not only for a surviving spouse with income for his or her lifetime but also to pass money and property on to children from that earlier marriage. Estate taxes will be deferred until the death of the second or surviving spouse. The attractive feature of the QTIP trust is that the taxpayer can control what happens to his or her money from the grave since the terms of the trust control the ultimate disposition of assets. The QTIP trust also offers a way to manage money for a surviving spouse who lacks financial sophistication or has medical expenses that could deplete the estate leaving nothing for minor children or other dependents.

Another attractive feature of the QTIP trust is the flexibility it affords the executor because QTIP treatment is elected by the executor, rather than being automatic or mandatory. This flexibility affords the executor the discretion to elect out of QTIP treatment if the election would result in higher estate taxes when the surviving spouse dies. The executor would generally have 15 months after the date of death to make the final decision regarding a QTIP election. Another benefit is the fact that with the QTIP, the executor also has the option of making a reverse QTIP election, which results in the decedent (not the surviving spouse) being treated as the transferor for purposes of the generation-skipping transfer tax even though the QTIP is taxed in the estate of the surviving spouse.

Reverse QTIP Election

Code Sec. 2652(a)(3) gives an executor or trustee who is making the QTIP election to treat the property as if the QTIP election had not been made. As a result of this "reverse

[99] Rev. Rul. 68-554, 1968-2 CB 412.

QTIP election" the decedent remains, for GST tax purposes, the transferor of the QTIP trust or property rather than the surviving spouse. Thus, the decedent's GST tax exemption may be allocated to the QTIP trust or property even though the QTIP is taxed in the estate of the surviving spouse. The reverse QTIP election must be made on the same return that the QTIP election is made [Reg. § 26.2652-2(b)]. The election is irrevocable and must be made with respect to all the property in the trust to which the QTIP election applies [Reg. § 26.2652-2(a)]. The reverse QTIP election should be made when executors want to avoid wasting any of the deceased spouse's available GST exemption. This allows the executor to still be able to take advantage of the ability to reduce estate taxes to zero when the surviving spouse dies. [See Estate & Gift Tax Handbook ¶ 444 and ¶ 602(c)].

How to Undo Unneeded QTIP Election

In Rev. Proc. 2001-38,[100] the IRS provided relief for surviving spouses and their estates in situations where a predeceased spouse's estate made an unnecessary QTIP election that did not reduce its estate tax liability. If the appropriate steps are taken as detailed in the revenue procedure, the unneeded QTIP election will be treated as null and void for federal estate, gift and generation-skipping transfer tax purposes. To undo the QTIP election, the taxpayer will have to produce evidence that a QTIP election qualifies to be undone. The taxpayer should produce a copy of the estate tax return filed by the predeceased spouse's estate establishing that the election was not necessary to reduce the estate tax liability to zero, based on values as finally determined for federal estate tax purposes. This information, coupled with an explanation of why the election should be treated as void, should be submitted either with the Form 706 filed for the surviving spouse's estate, or with a request for a private letter ruling submitted at any time before filing that Form 706.

The following consequences of undoing the QTIP election will result: (1) QTIP property won't have to be included in the survivor's estate on her death under Code Sec. 2044; (2) if the spouse makes a gift of the income interest, she will not be treated as making a gift of the remainder interest under Code Sec. 2519; and (3) the spouse won't be treated as the transferor of the property for GST purposes under Code Sec. 2652(a).

How QTIP Trust Works

Property is left in a trust that pays income to your spouse for his or her lifetime. After he or she dies, the trustee distributes assets in the trust to your children from the first marriage. If children exist from the second marriage or if the second spouse has his or her own children, the remainder will be divided up in some agreed-upon manner. Assets held in the trust qualify for the unlimited marital deduction, and so escape estate tax in the estate of the first spouse to die. Estate tax will be deferred until the death of the second spouse.

Typically, the marital deduction is drafted into a document by means of what is called an optimum marital deduction formula. This means that the surviving spouse is left just enough but not more than is absolutely necessary to reduce the decedent's estate tax to zero. The objective here is to minimize estate tax when the surviving spouse dies

[100] Rev. Proc. 2001-38, 2001-1 CB 1335.

because amounts qualifying for the marital deduction are taxed in the estate of the surviving spouse. What you are looking for here is a formula designed to take full advantage of the annual exclusion amount and then reduce the decedent's estate tax to zero by making bequests qualifying for the marital deduction. For example, if Dad dies in 2005 with an optimum marital deduction formula, the exemption equivalent amount of $1.5 million in 2005 would be allocated to the credit shelter trust and would avoid taxation in the estates of both spouses. Any remaining assets would be allocated to the marital deduction disposition which would be drafted to reduce estate taxes to zero.

QTIP Requirements

An estate tax marital deduction is only available under Code Sec. 2056, for qualified terminable interest property if the following four requirements exist [Code Sec. 2056(b)(7)]:

1. The surviving spouse must be entitled to receive, for life, all the income from the entire interest or from a specific portion, payable annually or at more frequent intervals. (An annuity can qualify as an income interest.) The QTIP deduction will still be available even if the "stub income" is not distributed to the surviving spouse's estate [Reg. § 20-2056(b)-7(d)(4)]. Stub income is the income that accumulates between the time the surviving spouse dies and the date when the last quarter income payment from the trust must be distributed to beneficiaries. No QTIP deduction will be available if the trust is funded with a unproductive property (e.g., a future interest in timberland) unless the trust language permits the trustee to either make the property productive or convert it into productive property within a reasonable time [Reg. § 20.2056(b)-5(f)(4)].[101] A surviving spouse's income interest which is limited to the amount of income property for the spouse's health, maintenance, education, and support will not qualify for the QTIP marital deduction because the spouse's income interest was limited.[102]

   In Rev. Rul. 2006-26[103] the IRS described three situations where a surviving spouse would be considered to have a qualifying income interest for life in an IRA or other qualified plan and a trust, which was the named beneficiary of the IRA, for purposes of making a QTIP election to treat both as qualified terminable interest property. In the three situations, the income of the trust, excluding the IRA, and the income of the IRA would be determined separately regardless of the fact that the IRA distribution would be made to the trust. In addition, the surviving spouse would have the power to compel the trustee to withdraw from the IRA all the income earned on the IRA assets at least annually and distribute that amount to the spouse. In two of the situations, the income of the trust and IRA would be determined pursuant to applicable state law. In the other situation, applicable state law (common or statutory) would be applied to determine the amount of IRA income that the spouse could compel the trustee to withdraw in accordance with the requirements of Code Sec. 2056(b)(7)(B)(ii) and Reg. § 20.2056(b)-5(f)(1).

---

[101] LTR 9717005 (Dec. 18, 1986).

[102] *R.H. Davis Est.*, CA-9, 2005-1 USTC ¶ 60,497, 394 F3d 1294. *See also* LTR 200505022 (Nov. 8, 2004).

[103] Rev. Rul. 2006-26, 2006-1 CB 939.

2. No one-not even the spouse-may have a power to appoint the property to any other person during the spouse's lifetime [Code Sec. 2056(b)(7)(B)(ii)(II)].
3. The executor must make an irrevocable election on the estate tax return to claim a marital deduction for all or a portion of the property [Code Sec. 2056(b)(7)]. The QTIP device lets the decedent pass property to beneficiaries of his or her choice while at the same time providing for the surviving spouse during life.
4. The property funding the QTIP trust must "pass" directly from the deceased to the surviving spouse. The IRS has taken the view that where the executor has the discretion to decide whether to treat the property as QTIP property, the "pass" requirement is violated. The courts have taken an opposite view.[104] IRS regulations conform to the numerous court decisions and allow an estate tax marital deduction for a surviving spouse's interest in property that was contingent upon the executor making a QTIP election. In addition, the regulations clarify that the interest will not fail to qualify for the marital deduction because the portion of the property for which the QTIP election is not made passes to or for the benefit of persons other than the surviving spouse [Reg. § § 20.2044-1; 20.2056(b)-7(d)(3)].

How to Make QTIP Election

The QTIP election must be made by the executor on the last estate tax return (Form 706) filed by the due date or on the first return filed after the due date. [Reg. § 20.2056(b)-7(b)(3)]. Once made, the election is irrevocable. Your executor can make the election by simply listing the qualified terminable interest property on Schedule M on the estate tax return and deducting its value. Your will should instruct the executor to make the election. A protective QTIP election can be made if, at the time the estate tax return is filed, there is an issue concerning whether an asset should be included in the decedent's gross estate or the nature of the property to which the surviving spouse is entitled. [Reg. § 20.2056(b)-7(c)]. A partial election must be expressed as a percentile or fractional share. A specific number of shares of a block of stock, though not expressed as a percentile or fractional share, qualifies as a specific portion (i.e., a partial election), since any appreciation or depreciation in the value of the entire block of stock

[104] *A.M. Clayton Jr. Est.*, CA-5, 92-2 USTC ¶ 60,121, 976 F2d 1486; *W.E. Robertson Est.*, CA-8, 94-1 USTC ¶ 60,153, 15 F3d 779; *J.D. Spencer Est.*, CA-6, 95-1 USTC ¶ 60,188, 43 F3d 226; *W.E. Clack Est.*, Dec. 51,193 (1996), 106 TC 131, *acq.* 1996-2 CB 1.

will be reflected in the specific number of shares.[105] An annuity that is included in the decedent's gross estate qualifies as QTIP automatically; an election is necessary only to refuse acceptance of QTIP treatment for an annuity [Code Sec. 2056(b)(7)(C)]. The deductible interest is the specific portion of the property that (assuming the interest rate for valuing annuities) would produce income equal to the minimum amount payable annually to the surviving spouse [Reg. § 20.2056(b)-7(e)(2)]. For example, $200,000 of a $500,000 trust paying $20,000 a year to the surviving spouse for life is treated as a qualifying income interest, assuming that the applicable interest rate is 10 percent [Reg. § 20.2056(b)-7(h), Ex. 11].

IRS Issues Guidance on Late Reverse QTIP Election

In Rev. Proc. 2004-47,[106] the IRS released an alternate method for executors and trustees to make a late reverse QTIP election under Code Sec. 2652. The alternate method may be used in lieu of the letter ruling process. Relief for a late reverse QTIP is available under Rev. Proc. 2004-47 if the following requirements are met:

1. A valid Code Sec. 2056(b)(7) QTIP election was made,
2. The reverse QTIP election was not properly made because the taxpayer relied on counsel who failed to advise the taxpayer of the need or proper method to make a reverse QTIP election,
3. The decedent has a sufficient amount of unused GST exemption,
4. The estate is not eligible for an automatic six-month extension,
5. The surviving spouse has not made a lifetime disposition of any part of the qualifying income interest for life in the QTIP property,
6. The surviving spouse is alive or no more than six months have passed since the surviving spouse's death, and
7. The estate files a request for more time to make a reverse QTIP election. The request must have a cover sheet that states "Request for Extension Filed Pursuant to Rev. Proc. 2004-47."

.06 Transfer Conditioned on Survival for Limited Period

A bequest to a spouse on the condition that the spouse does not die within six months of the decedent qualifies for the marital deduction if the spouse in fact survives the six-month period. A bequest on the condition that the surviving spouse not die before a specified event will also qualify, provided the event is of such a nature that it could occur only within six months of the decedent's death and it did not in fact occur. If the condition is one that may occur either within or after the six-month period, the deduction will not be allowed, unless the condition relates to death as a result of a common disaster. However, a common disaster condition disqualifies the interest if state law can deprive the surviving spouse of the property interest at the time of final audit of the estate tax return [Reg. § 20.2056(b)-3].

---

[105] LTR 8435002 (Apr. 6, 1984), LTR 8602005 (Sept. 30, 1985).

[106] Rev. Proc. 2004-47, 2004-2 CB 169.

Example 29-38: Jason Johnson bequeaths 3,000 shares of stock to his wife, Helen, if she survives him by six months. If Helen does not survive him by six months, the shares are to go to his nephew. Jason dies on February 1, and on August 1 Helen is still living. The bequest qualifies for the marital deduction.

Example 29-39: Bette Josephson is the primary beneficiary of an insurance policy on the life of her husband, Donald. Their daughter, Daphne, is the contingent beneficiary. The policy provides that the interest of the primary beneficiary will fail if that beneficiary is not alive when the insurance company receives due proof of death of the insured. Donald dies, and the proceeds are paid to Bette. The insurance proceeds do not qualify for the marital deduction. Reason: Submission of proof of death could have occurred later than six months after the decedent's death.[107]

.07 Life Estate with Power of Appointment

The marital deduction is available for property in which you give your spouse a life estate coupled with a general power of appointment [¶ 29,085] if five conditions are met: (1) your surviving spouse must be entitled to all the income from the entire interest or a "specific portion" of it; (2) the income must be payable at least annually; (3) your surviving spouse must have the power to appoint the entire property or the specific portion to himself or herself or to his or her estate; (4) the power must be exercisable by your surviving spouse alone and in all events, whether by will or during life; and (5) the property interest must not be subject to a power held by anyone else to appoint the interest to any other person [Reg. § 20.2056(b)-5].

▶ **SPECIFIC PORTION DEFINED:** For marital deduction purposes, the term specific portion includes a portion based on a percentage or fraction of the transferred property; a fixed-dollar amount doesn't qualify. This rule is effective for gifts made and decedents dying after October 24, 1992 [Code Sec. 2056(b); Reg. § 20.2056(b)-5(c)(3)].

.08 Life Insurance or Annuity with Power of Appointment

The insurance exception is similar to the one for a life estate with power of appointment. However, in the case of this exception to the terminable interest rule, the payments must begin not later than 13 months after the decedent's death. The insurance contract must provide either that the proceeds be paid in installments or be held by the insurer subject to the payment of interest [Reg. § 20.2056(b)-6].

.09 Interest in Qualified Charitable Remainder Trust

The marital deduction is allowable for an interest in a charitable remainder annuity trust or a charitable remainder unitrust [Ch. 9]if the surviving spouse is the only noncharitable beneficiary of the trust [¶ 29,125] [Code Sec. 2056(b)(8)].

.10 Rules for Noncitizen Spouses-Qualified Domestic Trust (QDOT)

An estate tax marital deduction is unavailable for property transferred to a spouse who is not a U.S. citizen, unless the transfer is made to a qualified domestic trust

[107] Rev. Rul. 54-121, 1954-1 CB 196.

(QDOT). A tax, equivalent in amount to the foregone estate tax, is imposed on distributions of trust property from a QDOT. However, when the noncitizen spouse dies, a tax credit is allowed under Code Sec. 2013 (for tax paid on prior transfers) for any estate tax imposed because of the loss of the marital deduction and for any tax imposed on distributions from a QDOT. The credit is allowed regardless of how long it has been since the first spouse died [Code Sec. 2056(d)(3)].

The unlimited gift tax marital deduction is unavailable for transfers to a noncitizen spouse. Instead, only a $143,000 annual gift tax exclusion in 2013 (increasing to $145,000 in 2014) is available for transfers to noncitizen spouses. Bear in mind, however, that taxpayers with less than the amount of the exemption equivalent in assets need not be concerned with these special rules because they can pass that amount tax-free to anyone they want, no matter what their citizenship.

The reason that noncitizen spouses are singled out for different tax treatment under the law stems from the perception of Congress that opportunities for abuse existed when property was left by a decedent to a surviving spouse who was not a citizen of the United States. Lawmakers were afraid that, after the death of the first spouse, the surviving spouse who was not a U.S. citizen, would leave the country and their heirs would be able to avoid estate tax on everything the second spouse took with him or her. If the surviving spouse had been a U.S. citizen, when he or she died, Uncle Sam could have taken a large slice out of his or her estate. Congress enacted the QDOT laws to remedy this perceived abuse.

Requirements

In order to claim a marital deduction for property passing to a noncitizen surviving spouse, the property must pass to the surviving spouse in a qualified domestic trust (QDOT) [Code Sec. 2056(d)(2)]. Property passing from a decedent to the decedent's surviving spouse will be treated as passing to the surviving spouse in a QDOT if the property is transferred to such a trust before the date on which an estate tax return is filed or if the property is irrevocably assigned to a QDOT under an irrevocable assignment that is made on or before the date the estate tax return is filed and that is enforceable under local law. The determination whether a trust is a QDOT is made as of the date that an estate tax return is filed or, if a judicial proceeding is commenced on or before the due date (including extensions) for filing an estate tax return to change the trust to a QDOT, as of the time when changes pursuant to that proceeding are made [Code Sec. 2056(d)(5)].

To qualify as a QDOT, the trust must first have the characteristics of a trust that would qualify for a marital deduction if the surviving spouse were a citizen. This means that it must be either a QTIP trust, power of appointment trust estate trust, or charitable remainder trust with the surviving spouse as the only noncharitable income beneficiary. Legal arrangements that have substantially the same effect as trusts will be treated as trusts [Code Sec. 2056A(c)(3)].

The trust must satisfy the following requirements instrument of the QDOT provide the following: [Code Sec. 2056A(a); Reg. § 20.2056A-2]:

1. The trust must be maintained under the laws of a state or the District of Columbia, and the administration of the trust must be governed by the laws of a particular state or the District of Columbia. A trust may be established pursuant to an instrument executed under the laws of a foreign jurisdiction provided that

the foreign instrument designates the laws of a particular state or the District of Columbia as governing the administration of the trust and such designation is effective under the law of the designated jurisdiction.

2. The trust instrument must provide that at least one trustee must be a United States citizen or domestic corporation and that no distribution of corpus may be made unless the U.S. trustee has the right to withhold any estate tax imposed on the distribution [Code Sec. 2056A(a)(1)(A)].
3. The trust must meet additional regulatory requirements to ensure the collection of the postponed estate tax on the QDOT; and
4. The executor must elect to treat the property as QDOT property.

The IRS has released final regulations and a revenue procedure, which relate to the security arrangements necessary to ensure collection of the estate tax imposed on QDOTs as required by Code Sec. 2056A(a)(2).

Security Arrangements

The regulations impose additional requirements on QDOTs to ensure collection of the QDOT estate tax [Reg. § 20.2056A-2(d)(1)]. Different requirements are imposed depending on whether the QDOT has assets of $2 million or less or more than $2 million. If the fair market value of the QDOT's assets (determined without reduction for any indebtedness with respect to the assets) as finally determined for federal estate tax purposes is $2 million or less, the trust instrument must provide either that no more than 35 percent of the fair market value of the trust assets (determined annually on the last day of the trust's tax year will consist of real property located outside the United States or that the trust will meet any of the security arrangements imposed on QDOTs with assets in excess of $2 million [Reg. § 20.2056A-2(d)(1)(ii)]. If the value of foreign real property on the last day of the QDOT's tax year exceeds 35 percent of the fair market value of the trust's assets due to distributions of principal during that year, fluctuations in the value of the foreign currency in the jurisdiction where the real estate is located, or fluctuations in the fair market value of any asses held in the QDOT, the trust will have one year to comply with the 35 percent requirement or satisfy any of the security arrangements imposed on QDOTs with assets in excess of $2 million. The law provides that a QDOT that has assets with a fair market value in excess of $2 million, may alternate among the three following security arrangements, provided at least one of the following three arrangements is operative at all times [Reg. § 20.2056A-2(d)(1)(i)]:

1. The trust instrument must provide that whenever the Bank Trustee security alternative is used for the QDOT, at least one U.S. trustee must be a bank;
2. The trust instrument must provide that whenever the bond security arrangement alternative is used for the QDOT the U.S. trustee must furnish a bond in favor of the IRS in an amount equal to 65 percent of the fair market value of the trust assets (determined without regard to any indebtedness with respect to the assets), as finally determined for estate tax purposes; or
3. The trust instrument must provide that whenever the letter of credit security arrangement is used for the QDOT the U.S. trustee must furnish an irrevocable letter of credit issued by a bank incorporated and doing business in the U.S., a United States branch of a foreign bank, or a foreign bank with a confirmation by a bank incorporated and doing business in the U.S. for an amount equal to 65

percent of the fair market value of the trust assets (determined without regard to any indebtedness with respect to the assets) as finally determined for federal estate tax purposes.

Duration of Bond or Letter of Credit

The regulations provide that the security arrangement must remain in effect until the trust ceases to function as a QDOT. A taxpayer filing a notice of failure to renew a bond or letter of credit must mail the notice to the IRS at least 60 days prior to the end of the term of the bond or letter of credit. The notice must also be mailed to the U.S. trustee of the QDOT.

IRS Provides Sample Language

The IRS provides sample language that drafters can use in a QDOT instrument in order to satisfy the new security requirements imposed by the regulations.[108]

Personal Residence Exclusion

The value of the surviving spouse's personal residence and "related furnishings" up to a total value of $600,000 may be excluded in determining whether the $2 million threshold is exceeded [Reg. § 20.2056A-2(d)(1)(iv)(A)]. A personal residence is either the surviving spouse's principal residence or one additional residence [Reg. § 20.2056A-2(d)(1)(iv)(D)]. To qualify for the exclusion, a personal residence must be available at all times for use by the surviving spouse and may not be rented out to another party, even when not occupied by the surviving spouse. The term *related furnishings* means furniture, appliances, fixtures, decorative items and china. Rare artwork, valuable antiques and automobiles of any kind or class are specifically excluded [Reg. § 20.2056A-2(d)(1)(iv)(E)].

Annual reporting will be required where the residence that was previously subject to the exclusion is sold, or where the residence ceases to be used as a personal residence during the year.

Cessation of Use

If the residence ceases to be used as a personal residence of the surviving spouse, or is sold during the term of the QDOT, the exclusion may be transferred to another residence that is held in either the same QDOT or in another QDOT, provided such residence is used as a personal residence of the surviving spouse. If the residence is sold and less than the entire adjusted sales price is reinvested in a new residence, the amount of the exclusion equals the amount reinvested in the new residence plus any amount previously allocated to a residence that continues to qualify for the exclusion, up to a total of $600,000 [Reg. § 20.2056A-2(d)(1)(iv)(G)].

> **NOTE:** The marital deduction is allowed for a bequest to a noncitizen spouse who was a resident at the time of the decedent's death and becomes a citizen before the estate tax return is filed [Code Sec. 2056(d)(4)].

QDOT Tax

The tax treatment of the QDOT differs from the tax treatment afforded other marital trusts created for U.S. citizens. Normally marital trusts created for U.S. citizens enjoy freedom from tax until the surviving spouse dies. In sharp contrast, a tax, known as

[108] Rev. Proc. 96-54, 1996-2 CB 386.

the QDOT tax, is imposed on the value of distributions of principal (not income) made from a QDOT during the surviving spouse's lifetime (other than for hardship), and on all assets remaining in the trust when it ceases to qualify as a QDOT. These taxes are in addition to the tax imposed on those assets remaining in the QDOT at the surviving spouse's death. Don't expect to rely on the hardship exception to avoid the QDOT tax on principal distributions because the IRS will only grant a hardship exception in extraordinary circumstances.

The principal that is taken out of the QDOT trust is taxed as though it had been part of the estate of the first spouse to die. To make matters worse, the estate tax rate is calculated to include all prior distributions. As a result each successive withdrawal pushes the taxpayer into higher estate tax brackets.

Note, however, that there is no estate tax due on distributions of income from a QDOT. Only principal distributions are taxed.

In addition, payment of the tax on a distribution out of the trust is itself considered a distribution subject to the tax [Code Sec. 2056A(b)(3), (b)(2)].

Before determination of the tax on the decedent's taxable estate, QDOTs are taxed at the highest estate tax rate, and any overpayment is refunded with interest after the correct tax bracket is determined. Multiple QDOTs are taxed at the highest tax rate in effect on the date of the decedent's death; and no hardship exemption is allowed, unless the executor designates a U.S citizen or a domestic corporation that meets regulatory tax collection requirements and is responsible for filing all estate tax returns and paying all taxes imposed. The estate tax return on distributions is due April 15 in the year following the calendar year in which the distributions are made. The entire trust is subject to the tax if it ceases to be a QDOT [Code Sec. 2056A(b)].

> ▶ **TAX BREAK:** Distributions from a QDOT during the spouse's life receive carryover basis. And the basis is increased by the amount of estate tax allocable to appreciation after the decedent's death, but not above the fair market value of the property on the date of distribution [Reg. § 20.2056A-12].

¶29,125 CHARITABLE AND SIMILAR TRANSFERS

Taxpayers can transfer unlimited amounts to charities either during life or at death tax free of transfer tax. Lifetime transfers are shielded from tax by the gift tax charitable deduction [¶ 29,020] and transfers at death are exempted by the estate tax charitable deduction, which is our focus here. Specifically, a deduction is allowed for transfers to five types of beneficiaries for public, charitable, and religious uses [Code Sec. 2055(a)]:

1. To or for the use of the United States, any state, political subdivision of the state or the District of Columbia, for exclusively public purposes;
2. To or for the use of any corporation or association organized and operated exclusively for religious, charitable, scientific, literary or educational purposes, including the encouragement of art and the prevention of cruelty to children or animals, or to foster national or international amateur sports competition without providing athletic facilities or equipment;

3. To a trustee, or a fraternal society, order, or association operating under the lodge system, if the transferred property is to be used exclusively for religious, charitable, scientific, literary, or educational purposes or for the prevention of cruelty to children or animals;
4. To or for the use of any veterans' organization incorporated by Act of Congress, or any of its departments, local chapters, or posts; or
5. To an employee stock ownership plan if the transfer qualifies as a qualified gratuitous transfer of qualified employer securities within the meaning of Code Sec. 665(g).

The estate tax deduction is equal to the value of assets transferred to or for the use of a charitable organization operating exclusively for religious or charitable purposes [Code Sec. 2055(a)]. The charitable deduction is reduced by the amount of any federal and/or state death taxes payable out of the assets allocated to the charitable bequest [Code Sec. 2055(c)]. Only the value of assets actually going to the charity is eligible for the tax deduction.[109]

.01 Value of Restrictions Imposed on Charitable Bequests

The value of the taxable estate is determined by deducting from the value of the gross estate the amount of all bequests, legacies, devises, or transfers to or for the use of any corporation organized and operated exclusively for religious, charitable, scientific, literary, or educational purposes, including the encouragement of art. The estate may claim a charitable deduction provided: (1) no part of the contribution inures to the benefit of any private shareholder or individual; and (2) the contribution is not used to attempt to influence legislation or intervene in any political campaign on behalf of (or in opposition to) any candidate for public office.

Reg. § 20.2055-1(a) provides that a deduction is allowed under Code Sec. 2055(a) for the value of property included in the decedent's gross estate and transferred by the decedent to certain charitable entities. In general, the amount allowable as an estate tax charitable deduction is the fair market value of the property passing to charity without restriction. Under certain scenarios, however, this value may not be the same as the value included in a decedent's gross estate. For example, the imposition of restrictions or other limitations imposed on charitable contributions of property may result in a reduction in the value of the charitable bequest and consequently a reduction in the amount of the charitable deduction.[110] In these situations, property encumbered by some restriction or condition limiting its marketability or use must be valued in light of this limitation. Not all restrictions, however, that are imposed on donees will result in a reduction of the charitable deduction. Carefully drafted restrictions on charitable bequests will have no impact on the value of the charitable bequest.

.02 Qualified Conservation Easement

An executor may make an irrevocable election to exclude from a decedent's gross estate up to 40 percent of the value of land subject to a qualified conservation

[109] *M.P. Bradford Est.*, 84 TCM 337, Dec. 54,880(M), TC Memo. 2002-238.

[110] *Ahmanson Foundation*, CA-9, 81-2 USTC ¶ 13,438, 674 F2d 761; *M.M. Schwan Est.*, 82 TCM 168, Dec. 54,406(M), TC Memo. 2001-174; Rev. Rul. 85-99, 1985-2 CB 83.

easement. The applicable percentage is reduced (but not below zero) by 2 percentage points for each percentage point (or fraction thereof) by which the value of the qualified conservation easement is less than 30 percent of the value of the land (determined without regard to the value of such easement and reduced by the value of any retained development right). The values taken into account shall be such values as of the date of the contribution regardless of the values of the land and easement at the date of the creation of the easement [Code Sec. 2031(c)(2)].

The maximum amount that can be excluded is $500,000 [Code Sec. 2031(c)(3)]. The executor computes the value of the exclusion by multiplying the value of the land that is subject to a qualified conservation easement (excluding value of any structures on land) by the applicable percentage. The result may be excluded from the decedent's gross estate provided the exclusion amount is less than the exclusion limit for the year as provided in Code Sec. 2031(c)(3). The purpose of the qualified conservation easement is to encourage taxpayers to take a second look at conservation easements as a way not only to reduce estate taxes but also to preserve land without future development.

The irrevocable election is made by: (1) filing Schedule U with a timely filed Form 706 (including extensions); (2) including all required information; and (3) excluding the applicable value of the land that is subject to the easement on Form 706. The transferee of land subject to a conservation easement that is acquired at death receives a carryover basis, to the extent that the value of land is excluded from the taxable estate.

Keep in mind that the deduction for post-mortem conservation easements is limited to estate tax. This means that no income tax deduction is allowed to the decedent's estate or to the decedent's qualified heirs with respect to such a post-mortem conservation easement [Code Sec. 2031(c)(9)]. The exclusion is also reduced by the amount of any charitable deduction allowed under Code Sec. 2055(f) with respect to the land.

Definition of *Land* Subject to Easement

For estates of decedents dying after December 31, 2012, the exclusion for a qualified conservation easement will be available to any otherwise qualified real property that is located in the United States or any possession of the United States, that was owned by the decedent or a member of the decedent's family during the three-year period ending on the date of the decedent's death, and is subject to a qualified conservation easement granted by the decedent or a member of the decedent's family [Code Sec. 2031(c)(8)(A)]. Members of the decedent's family include the decedent's spouse; ancestors; lineal descendants of the decedent, of the decedent's spouse, and of the parents of the decedent; and the spouse of any lineal descendant. A legally adopted child of an individual is considered a child of the individual by blood [Code Sec. 2031(c)(8)]. In addition, the conservation easement must have been placed on the property by the decedent, a member of the decedent's family, the executor of the decedent's estate, or the trustee of the trust that holds the land subject to the conservation easement [Code Sec. 2031(c)(10)].

An interest in a partnership, corporation, or a trust will qualify for the exclusion provided at least 30 percent of the entity is owned, directly or indirectly, by the decedent [Code Sec. 2057(e)(3)].

For estates of decedents dying after December 31, 2012, the exclusion for a qualified conservation easement will be restricted to real property within 25 miles of a metropolitan area (as defined by the Office of Management and Budget), a national park, or a wilderness area (unless the land is not under significant development pressure as determined by the IRS) or 10 miles of an Urban National Forest (as designated by the Forest Service of the U.S. Department of Agriculture) [Code Sec. 2031(c)(8)(A)].

Date Used to Determine Values

The values used to calculate the applicable percentage, including the value of the property subject to the easement and the value of the easement, for estates of decedents dying after December 31, 2012, will be determined as of the date of contribution [Code Sec. 2013(c)(2)].

Qualified Conservation Easement Defined

A *qualified conservation easement* is a qualified conservation contribution of a qualified real property interest [Code Sec. 2031(c)(8)(B)]. A *qualified real property interest* means either:

1. The entire interest of the donor, other than a qualified mineral interest;
2. A remainder interest; or
3. A restriction granted in perpetuity on how the land may be used [Code Sec. 170(h)(2)]. The restriction must include a prohibition on anything more than a *de minimis* use of the land for commercial purposes [Code Sec. 2031(c)(8)(B)].

A qualified conservation contribution is a contribution of a qualified real property interest to a qualified organization exclusively for conservation purposes [Code Sec. 2031(c)(8)(B)]. The land subject to the conservation easement must be preserved for one of the following conservation purposes:

1. The preservation of land areas for outdoor recreation or education of the public;
2. The protection of a relatively natural habitat of fish, wildlife, or plants, or a similar ecosystem; or
3. The preservation of open space (including farmland and forest land) where such preservation is for the scenic enjoyment of the general public, or pursuant to a clearly delineated Federal, state, or local conservation policy and will yield a significant public benefit [Code Sec. 170(h)(4)]. Keep in mind that land subject to an historical easement is not eligible for the new exclusion.

Contributed Property Must Be Debt-Free

Debt-financed property is not eligible for the exclusion [Code Sec. 2031(c)(4)(A)]. Debt-financed property is property with an acquisition indebtedness on the date of the decedent's death. Acquisition indebtedness includes the unpaid amount of:

1. Indebtedness incurred by the donor in acquiring the property;
2. Indebtedness incurred before the acquisition of the property if such indebtedness would not have been incurred but for such acquisition;
3. Indebtedness incurred after the acquisition of the property if such indebtedness would not have been incurred but for such acquisition and the indebtedness was reasonably foreseeable at the time of acquisition; and

4. The extension, renewal, or refinancing of an acquisition indebtedness [Code Sec. 2031(c)(4)(B)].

Post-Mortem Easements

In the case of a qualified conservation contribution made after the date of the decedent's death, an estate tax deduction is allowed under Code Sec. 2055(f), but only if no income tax charitable deduction is allowed to any person with respect to the grant of the easement. [Code Sec. 2131(c)(9)].

.03 Bequests to Foreign Governments

The deduction is allowed for a bequest to a government for public purposes only if the government is the United States or a state or a political subdivision. However, the deduction is allowed for bequests to foreign governments for exclusively charitable or educational purposes or other deductible purposes. The will should expressly state the purpose of any bequest to a foreign government because no deduction is allowed if there is any possibility that it may be used for some other public purpose.[111]

.04 Split Interests

If you leave interests in the same property to both charitable and noncharitable beneficiaries (e.g., an income interest to one and the remainder to the other), special requirements must be met in order to get a charitable deduction. You cannot simply leave "all the income" to either party and be entitled to a charitable deduction. In the case of a charitable lead interest, it must be a guaranteed annuity or a unitrust interest (i.e., a fixed percentage of the fair market value of the property, determined and distributed yearly). In the case of a charitable remainder interest, it must be in a charitable remainder annuity trust, a charitable remainder unitrust, or a pooled income fund [Ch. 9] [Code Sec. 2055(e); Reg. § 20.2055-2].

In *E.C. Galloway*,[112] the Court of Appeals for the Third Circuit denied a decedent's estate a charitable deduction for the amount of trust principal that would eventually be distributed to two charitable beneficiaries from a split-interest trust. Even though the court characterized the result as "unfortunate," it felt compelled to follow the clear statutory language of Code Sec. 2055(e)(2) which disallows a charitable estate tax deduction where there is a split-interest between charitable and noncharitable beneficiaries and the property is not transferred in a qualifying form such as in an annuity trust, a unitrust, or a pooled income fund.

▶**PRACTICE POINTER:** The failure to carefully draft charitable provisions in a trust can have expensive, unintended consequences. Even though the court practically apologized for the decision in this case, they strictly followed the statutory language.

Special IRS tables [¶ 29,105] are needed to figure the amount of the deduction for these various charitable lead and remainder interests. The tables change monthly based on changes in interest rates. The deduction can be figured using the table for

---

[111] *E. Kaplun*, CA-2, 71-1 USTC ¶ 12,735, 436 F2d 799; *National Sav. & Trust Co.*, CtCls, 71-1 USTC ¶ 12,738, 436 F2d 458, 193 CtCls 775; *Old Colony Trust Co.*, DC-MA, 70-2 USTC ¶ 12,707, 313 FSupp 980, *aff'd*, CA-1, 71-1 USTC ¶ 12,734, 438 F2d 684; Rev. Rul. 74-523, 1974-2 CB 304.

[112] *E.C. Galloway*, CA-3, 2007-2 USTC ¶ 60,543, 492 F3d 219.

the month in which death occurs or the table for either of the two prior months, whichever produces the largest deduction.

Exceptions

The split-interest rule, requiring charitable split interests to be in specified forms,[113] does not apply to a transfer (not in trust) of a remainder interest in your personal residence or a farm or to an undivided portion of your entire interest in property [Reg. § 20.2055-2(e)(2)(ii)]. Perpetual easements and restrictive covenants do not have to be in the specified forms either. And a work of art and its copyright are treated as separate properties. Thus, a work of art can be transferred to certain charitable organizations and its copyright retained without following the split-interest rule.

NOTE 1: If the transfer of a charitable remainder interest in a personal residence or farm is in trust, the trust must comply with the split-interest rule.[114]

NOTE 2: The value of a qualified work of art on loan to certain charitable organizations at the time of death is not discounted to reflect the unexpired period of the loan. It is included in the gross estate at its full value as if the loan had not been made [Code Sec. 2503(g)].

Reformation

There are rules for reforming split-interest trusts that do not qualify for the charitable deduction. Reformation of a testamentary trust must be retroactive to the date of death and of an *inter vivos* trust to the date of its creation. Provision must be made for correcting any overpayment or underpayment to a beneficiary.

There are limits on the extent of the reformation. For example, the difference in actuarial values of the charitable interests in the unreformed and reformed trusts cannot exceed five percent of the actuarial value of such interest in the unreformed trust. A noncharitable interest in a charitable remainder trust must terminate at the same time both before and after the reformation. However, a noncharitable interest for a term of more than 20 years can be reduced to 20 years. For a charitable lead trust, the charitable interest must be of the same duration both before and after the reformation [Code Sec. 2055(e)(3)(B)]. If all the noncharitable beneficiaries die by the due date for filing the estate tax return (including extensions) and the property passes to the charity, the charitable deduction is allowed without reformation [Code Sec. 2055(e)(3)(F)].

▶ **TIME LIMITATION:** If the trust instrument does not provide for payments to noncharitable beneficiaries in specified dollar amounts or as a fixed percentage of fair market value, reformation proceedings must be commenced not later than 90 days after the due date of the estate tax return (including extensions) or, if no estate tax return is required, after the due date (including extensions) for the first income tax return of the trust [Code Sec. 2055(e)(3)(C)(iii)].

.05 Charitable Lead Trusts

A charitable lead trust is a useful tax strategy that commits income from property to charity for a fixed number of years, after which the remainder interest is distributed to noncharitable beneficiaries, usually the donor's children. There are numerous benefits to using the charitable lead trust in an estate plan. First, the decedent's estate

[113] Rev. Proc. 83-32, 1983-1 CB 723.

[114] Rev. Rul. 76-357, 1976-2 CB 285.

gets a charitable estate tax deduction, which will greatly reduce the estate tax bite. Second, if the property in trust appreciates in value, at the termination of the trust term, the beneficiaries will receive the property at its increased value, without paying tax on the appreciation. Finally, during the trust term when the charity has an income interest, the charity will put the income to good use.

The charitable lead trust saves taxes because only the "present value" of the family's remainder interest, rather than the entire value of the assets transferred to the trust, is considered a taxable gift. You can be a wizard and make the taxable remainder interest practically vanish by combining the right set of numbers. With a charitable trust term of 24 years and a rate of interest of 8 percent per year, the amount of tax savings is astounding. Let's assume the trust were funded with $150 million. In this case, the taxable gift made to the trust would only be about $30 million. A basic rule of thumb emerges after you begin working with the government's actuarial factors to compute the value of the remainder interest. The larger the income interest and the longer the trust term the more valuable the income interest becomes and the value of the taxable remainder interest diminishes and taxes are reduced.

The charitable lead trust is a great way to leave money or a business to family members if they do not need the money immediately. To qualify for tax savings, the charitable lead trust must be in the form of a unitrust or an annuity. Under a basic unitrust, the charity receives one or more yearly payments equaling a fixed percentage of the value of the asset, as that value is determined at the beginning of each year. With the annuity trust, the charity receives a yearly fixed payment equaling at least 5 percent of the value of the asset at the time the deferred-giving agreement was signed.

Charitable lead trusts offer a way for you to leave money to charity but also pass the bulk of your estate in tact to your family while saving a bundle on estate taxes. Furthermore, the charitable lead trust offers a way for the real estate or business to stay in the family.

The CLT saves wealth transfer taxes because only the "present value" of the family's remainder interest, rather than the entire value of the assets transferred to the trust, is considered a taxable gift. The amount of the taxable gift is computed by taking the fair market value of the assets transferred to the CLT and reducing it by the gift or estate tax charitable contribution deduction. A zeroed-out CLAT would be created when gift or estate tax is eliminated entirely. A zeroed out CLAT results when the term and guaranteed annuity payment provided under a CLAT are structured so that the present value of the charitable contribution deduction equals the fair market value of the assets transferred to the CLAT.

The IRS has released sample forms, annotations and alternate provisions for *inter vivos* and testamentary grantor and nongrantor charitable lead annuity trusts (CLATs).[115] The IRS has also released sample *inter vivos* nongrantor and grantor charitable lead unitrusts (CLUTs) forms in Rev. Proc. 2008-45[116] and a sample form testamentary charitable lead unitrust form in Rev. Proc. 2008-46.[117] Trusts that satisfy

[115] Rev. Proc. 2007-45, 2007-29 IRB 89; Rev. Proc. 2007-46, 2007-29 IRB 102.

[116] Rev. Proc. 2008-45, 2008-30 IRB 224.

[117] Rev. Proc. 2008-46, 2008-30 IRB 238.

the requirements outlined in the sample IRS forms and procedures may qualify for an IRS safe harbor.

.06 Charitable Remainder Trusts

The charitable remainder trust is a popular estate planning tool that allows taxpayers to enjoy the income from property during their lifetime but provide in a trust document that the property will eventually pass on to a charity after their death. Two types of charitable remainder trusts exist. There is a charitable remainder annuity trust (CRAT) and a charitable remainder unitrust (CRUT). A CRAT is a trust that must pay, at least annually, a fixed dollar amount equal to at least five percent of the initial value of the trust assets to a noncharitable beneficiary for the life of the children or grandchildren or for a term of years (not to exceed 20 years) with the remainder passing to charity. A CRUT is similar except that the amount of the annual payments is a fixed percentage of the trust assets, valued annually [Code Sec. 664(d)].

A charitable remainder trust distributes income to the beneficiaries, who typically are grandchildren, for their lifetime. After the younger generation dies, the assets in the charitable remainder trust pass on to the charity designated in the trust document. In the year of creation, the trust creator receives a charitable deduction equal to the fair market value of the charity's remainder interest. The deduction amount will be based on the age of each beneficiary and the percentage of the trust assets that will be paid to the beneficiaries annually.

Charitable remainder trusts are subject to a 100 percent excise tax on their unrelated business taxable income (UBTI). Charitable remainder trusts that have UBTI will not lose their tax-exempt status for the year; rather, an excise tax will be imposed in the amount of UBTI itself [Code Sec. 664(c)(2)(A); Reg. § 1.664-1(c)(i)]. The UBTI is considered income of the trust for purposes of determining the character of the distribution made to the beneficiary. The tax is treated as paid from corpus. The claim preclusion rule under Code Sec. 6212(c), which generally prevents the IRS from filing an additional deficiency notice once a taxpayer files a Tax Court petition challenging the deficiency, applies to this tax [Code Sec. 664(c)(2)(C)]. For further discussion of charitable remainder trusts, see the Estate & Gift Tax Handbook, ¶ 253.

.07 Charitable Deduction for Fractional Contributions of Tangible Personal Property

In general, a donor can claim a charitable deduction for income and estate and gift tax purposes for a contribution of a fractional interest in tangible personal property provided that the donor satisfies the requirements for deductibility and, in subsequent years, makes additional charitable contributions of interests in the same property.

The amount of the *income* tax charitable deduction for additional contributions of tangible personal property in which the donor had previously made a contribution of an undivided fractional interest (an initial fractional contribution) is equal to the lesser of (1) the value of the property used to determine the charitable deduction for the initial fractional contribution or (2) the fair market value of the property at the time of the additional contribution [Code Sec. 170(o)(2)]. See ¶ 9070 for further discussion.

Recapture Rules

Any income or gift tax charitable deduction allowed for contributions of undivided interests in tangible personal property will be recaptured (with interest) if:

1. The donor fails to contribute all of the remaining interests in the property to the donee (or another charitable organization if the donee is no longer in existence) before the earlier of the tenth anniversary of the initial fractional contribution or the donor's date of death; or

2. The donee fails to take substantial physical possession of the property or fails to use the property in a manner related to the donee's exempt purpose during the period beginning after the initial fractional contribution and ending on the earlier of the tenth anniversary of the initial contribution or the donor's date of death [Code Secs. 170(o)(3), 2522(e)(2)].

Furthermore, if an income or gift tax charitable deduction is recaptured, as described above, an additional tax will be imposed in an amount equal to 10 percent of the amount recaptured [Code Secs. 170(o)(3)(B), 1522(e)(2)(B)].

Both the income and gift tax charitable deduction will be allowed for the contribution of a fractional interest in tangible personal property only if the taxpayer, or the taxpayer and the donee, hold all interests in the property immediately before the contribution [Code Secs. 170(o)(1)(A), 2522(e)(1)(A)]. Therefore, if a person other than the taxpayer or donee holds an interest in the property, the deduction will be denied.

¶29,130 DEDUCTION FOR STATE DEATH TAXES

The state death tax deduction under Code Sec. 2058 has been made permanent for the estates of decedents dying after December 31, 2012. Accordingly, the estates of decedents dying after December 31, 2012, will be able to deduct state death taxes paid to a state or the District of Columbia from a decedent's gross estate. The state death tax credit allowed for estate, inheritance, legacy, or succession taxes paid to any state or the District of Columbia was permanently repealed for the estates of decedents dying after December 31, 2012.

¶29,135 ESTATE AND GIFT TAX RATE SCHEDULE

The maximum tax rate imposed under the federal estate and gift taxes is 40 percent with respect to the estates of decedents dying and gifts made in 2013 and later. The GST tax rate, which is tied to the maximum estate tax rate, is also 40 percent for GSTs made in 2013 or later. In addition, the five-percent surtax which was formerly imposed on estates and gifts in excess of $10 million and up to $17,184,000, will not be imposed on the estates of decedents dying or gifts made in 2013 or later. The following table shows the unified estate and gift tax schedule for 2013 and later:

Table 2. Unified Tax Rate Schedule 2013 and Later

(A) Amount subject to tax equal to or more than—	(B) Amount subject to tax less than—	(C) Tax on amount in column (A)	(D) Rate of tax on excess over amount in column (A)
			Percent
	$ 10,000		18
$10,000	20,000	$ 1,800	20
20,000	40,000	3,800	22
40,000	60,000	8,200	24
60,000	80,000	13,000	26
80,000	100,000	18,200	28
100,000	150,000	23,800	30
150,000	250,000	38,800	32
250,000	500,000	70,800	34
500,000	750,000	155,800	37
750,000	1,000,000	248,300	39
1,000,000		345,800	40

Surtax not imposed. The five-percent surtax that had been applied to estates and taxable gifts larger than $10 million and up to $17,184,000 prior to 2002 will not be imposed on the estates of decedents dying and taxable gifts made after December 31, 2012.

¶29,140 APPLICABLE EXCLUSION AMOUNT

.01 Unified Estate and Gift Tax Exclusion Amount

The applicable exclusion amount is the amount of property that each taxpayer is allowed to transfer free of transfer tax. Code Sec. 2010 operates to allow each estate an exemption in an amount equal to the applicable exclusion amount in effect in the year of the decedent's death. The estate tax applicable exclusion amount for decedents dying in 2013 is $5,250,000 with the amount increasing to $5,340,000 in 2014 [Code Sec. 2010(c)(2)(A)].

.02 Portability

The concept of "portability" of a deceased spouse's unused exclusion (DSUE) amount has been made permanent for the estates of decedents dying after December 31, 2012. Portability is available if the executor of the first deceased spouse makes an election on a complete and properly prepared estate tax return (Form 706), regardless of whether the decedent is otherwise required to file an estate tax return. Basically, the portability feature allows the surviving spouse of a decedent dying after December 31, 2012 to use the decedent's unused exclusion amount in addition to the surviving spouse's own exclusion amount ($5,250,000 in 2013 and increasing to $5,340,000 in 2014) for taxable transfers made during life or at death if the executor of decedent files a timely and complete estate tax return. Portability was designed to simplify estate planning by eliminating the need for spouses to retitle property and create credit shelter trusts solely to take full advantage of each spouse's basic exclusion amount.

The unused portion of a decedent's applicable exclusion amount may be utilized by the estate of the decedent's surviving spouse at his or her later death [Code Sec. 2010(c)]. The portability provision eliminates the cumbersome task of requiring spouses to create complicated wills with credit shelter trusts solely to take full advantage of each spouse's basic exclusion amount. Portability will also eliminate the need to track how much property is owned by each spouse individually which often forced couples to retitle property solely for estate planning purposes. See ¶29,050.

Making the Election

In order for a decedent's surviving spouse to take into account that decedent's deceased spousal unused exclusion (DSUE) amount, the executor of the decedent's estate must elect portability of the DSUE amount on a timely-filed Form 706, *United States Estate (and Generation-Skipping Transfer) Tax Return* [Temp. Reg. § 20.2010-2T(a)]. The return will be considered timely-filed if it is filed 9 months after the decedent's date of death or the last day of the period covered by an extension (if an extension of time for filing has been obtained) [Temp. Reg. § 20.2010-2T(a)(1)].

After the timely filing of a complete and properly-prepared estate tax return, an executor of an estate of a decedent (survived by a spouse) will be deemed to have elected portability of the decedent's DSUE amount unless the executor chooses not to elect portability [Temp. Reg. § 20.2010-2T(a)(2)]. The executor will not be considered to make the portability election if either of the following applies: (1) The executor opts out of the portability election by checking the box indicated on Form 706; or (2) The executor does not timely file an estate tax return [Temp. Reg. § 20.2010-2T(a)(3)]. A portability election is irrevocable, unless an adjustment or amendment to the election is made on a subsequent return filed on or before the due date of the return [Temp. Reg. § 20.2010-2T(a)(4)]. The portability election is effective as of the decedent's date of death, so the DSUE amount received by a surviving spouse may be applied to any transfer occurring after the decedent's death. Under Temp. Reg. § 20.2010-2T(a)(5), the executor of an estate of a nonresident decedent who was not a citizen of the United States at the time of death cannot make a portability election. If an executor is appointed, qualified, and acting with the United States on behalf of the decedent's estate, only that executor may make or opt out of a portability election.

Computing Exclusion Amount of a Surviving Spouse

Code Sec. 2010(c)(2) embodies the portability concept and provides that the estate tax applicable exclusion amount is (1) the "applicable exclusion amount" plus (2) for a surviving spouse, the "deceased spousal unused exclusion amount (DSUEA)."

Computing DSUEA

The "applicable exclusion amount" means the applicable exclusion amount of the last deceased spouse of the surviving spouse [Code Sec. 2010(c)(4)(B)(i); Temp. Reg. § 20.2010-2T(c)(1)(i)]. Generally, only the applicable exclusion amount of the decedent in effect in the year of the decedent's death will be known at the time the DSUEA must be computed and reported on the decedent's estate tax return. Amounts on which gift taxes were paid by a decedent are excluded from adjusted taxable gifts for the purpose of computing that decedent's DSUEA [Temp. Reg. § 20.2010-2T(c)(2)].

Last Deceased Spouse Limitation

If a surviving spouse is predeceased by more than one spouse, regardless of the sex of that spouse,[118] the amount of unused exclusion that is available for use by the surviving spouse is limited to the lesser of (1) the basic exclusion amount or (2) the basic exclusion amount of the surviving spouse's last deceased spouse over the combined amount of the deceased spouse's taxable estate plus adjusted taxable gifts.

Note the specific language—"the *last* deceased spouse's applicable exclusion amount." This means that surviving spouses with multiple ex-deceased spouses cannot pick and choose which deceased spouse's unused exclusion amount they want to use.

The term "last deceased spouse" means the most recently deceased individual who was married to the surviving spouse at that individual's death [Temp. Reg. § 20.2010-1T(d)(5)]. Remarriage alone does not affect who will be considered the last deceased spouse and does not prevent the surviving spouse from including in the surviving spouse's applicable exclusion amount the DSUEA of the deceased spouse who most recently preceded the surviving spouse in death. In addition, the identity of the last deceased spouse of the surviving spouse for purposes of portability is not affected by whether the estate of the last deceased spouse elects portability of the deceased spouse's DSUEA or whether the last deceased spouse has any DSUEA available [Temp. Reg. § § 20.2010-3T(a)(3), 25.2505-2T(a)(3)].

Example 29-40: Husband died in 2012 with a taxable estate of $3 million. An election is made on his estate tax return to permit Wife to use any of Husband's unused exclusion amount. Wife, who had not made any lifetime taxable gifts, dies in 2013 with a taxable estate of $10 million. The executor of Wife's estate computes her deceased spousal unused exclusion amount as the lesser of: (1) Wife's applicable exclusion amount of $5,250,000 or (2) Husband's basic exclusion amount ($5 million since he died in 2012) minus (3) the amount of his taxable estate ($3 million), or: $2 million. Accordingly, the total applicable exclusion amount available to Wife's estate is $7,250,000: her basic exclusion amount of $5,250,000, plus $2 million in deceased spousal unused exclusion from Husband's estate.

Authority to Examine Returns of Deceased Spouses

In determining the allowable DSUEA, the IRS may examine any one or more returns of each deceased spouse of the surviving spouse whose executor elected portability. Upon examination, the IRS may adjust or eliminate the DSUEA reported on a return. The ability of the IRS to examine returns of a deceased spouse applies to each transfer by the surviving spouse to which a DSUEA has been applied. The returns and return information of a deceased spouse may be disclosed to the surviving spouse or the surviving spouse's estate [Temp. Reg. § § 20.2001-2T(a), 20.2010-2T(d), 20.2010-3T(d) and 25.2505-2T(e)].

---

[118] *E.S. Windsor*, SCt, 2013-2 USTC ¶ 60,667; Rev. Rul. 2013-17, IRB 2013-38, 201.

Portability and Nonresidents Who Are Not Citizens

An executor of the estate of a nonresident decedent who was not a citizen of the United States at the time of death may not make a portability election on behalf of that decedent [Temp. Reg. § 20.2010-2T(a)(5)]. A nonresident surviving spouse who was not a citizen of the United States at the time of such surviving spouse's death may not take into account the DSUEA of any deceased spouse of such surviving spouse, except to the extent allowed under a treaty obligation of the United States [Temp. Reg. § § 20.2010-3T(e), 25.2505-2T(f)].

Examination of Prior Returns

To ensure compliance, the IRS is granted the authority to examine estate and gift tax returns of a predeceased spouse in order make determinations regarding the surviving spouse's claim to the unused portion of the predeceased spouse's exclusion amount [Code Sec. 2010(c)(5)(B)]. This authority extends even after the statutory period of limitations has expired under Code Sec. 6501.

▶PORTABILITY PRACTICE POINTERS:

- *Form 706 must be filed regardless of size of decedent's estate.* Executors of estates of decedents must timely file a complete Form 706 for the decedent's estate (even if the decedent's estate is under the annual exclusion amount and the executor is not otherwise required to file a Form 706 for that estate) in order to make the portability election and enable the surviving spouse to use the decedent's unused exclusion amount in addition to surviving spouse's own basic exclusion amount. To ensure the correct exclusion amount and tax rates, executors should use the Form 706 issued for the year of the decedent's death. Until IRS revises the Form 706 to expressly contain the computation of the deceased spousal unused exclusion amount, a *complete* and correct Form 706 will be deemed to contain that computation.

- *Portability election is irrevocable.* Once made, the portability election is irrevocable.

- *Election must be made within 9 months after decedent's death.* The executor must file Form 706 and therefore make the portability election within 9 months after the date of the decedent's death plus a possible extension of not more than 6 months [Code Sec. 6075(a)]. Executors may request the automatic extension of time to file Form 706 by timely filing Form 4768, *Application for Extension of Time To File a Return and/or Pay U.S. Estate (and Generation-Skipping Transfer) Taxes*.

- *Timing very important.* No portability election may be made if the Form 706 is filed after the time prescribed by law (including extensions) for filing a Form 706.

- *No portability of unused GST exemption of a predeceased spouse.* A surviving spouse may not use the unused GST tax exemption of predeceased spouse. It is also not available for a nonresident alien spouse [Code Secs. 2101(c)(2), 2102].

- *IRS exam rights.* The IRS may examine the return of a predeceased spouse even after the time has expired under Code Sec. 6501 for purposes of determining the DSUEA amount available for use by the surviving spouse [Code Sec. 2010(c)(5)(B)].

¶29,150 CREDIT FOR FOREIGN DEATH TAXES

The estate of a U.S. citizen or resident is allowed a credit for death taxes paid to a foreign country or its political subdivision or to a U.S. possession. The credit is allowed only for property situated in the foreign country and included in the gross estate. The amount of the credit may not exceed either of the following two limitations [Code Sec. 2014(b)]:

First limitation: The amount of the credit for a particular country's death tax is limited to the amount of the foreign death tax actually paid to that country multiplied by a fraction the numerator of which is the value of property in the foreign country subjected to foreign death tax, included in the decedent's gross estate, and for which no deduction is allowed under Code Sec. 2053(d) and the denominator of which is the value of all property subjected to foreign death tax.

Second limitation: The amount of the credit cannot exceed the gross federal estate tax, less the unified credit and credits for gift tax, multiplied by a fraction the numerator of which is the adjusted value of property situated in a foreign country and included in the decedent's gross estate and the denominator of which is the value of the decedent's entire gross estate, less charitable and marital deductions.

No credit is allowable for the Canadian tax on appreciation on a deemed disposition at death; but a deduction is allowable.[119] Generally, the credit must be claimed within four years of filing the estate tax return [Code Sec. 2014(e)].

¶29,155 CREDIT FOR TAX ON PRIOR TRANSFERS

A credit is allowed against the estate tax for all or a part of the estate tax paid with respect to the transfer of property (including property passing as a result of the exercise or nonexercise of a power of appointment) to the present decedent by or from a person (the "transferor") who died within 10 years before, or within two years after, the decedent ("transferee"—the decedent for whose estate the Form 706 estate tax return is filed) [Code Sec. 2013]. The credit is computed on Schedule Q of the Form 706 estate tax return after completing the worksheet provided in the Instructions for Form 706.

This credit can never be larger than it would be if the decedent had not received the property. No credit is available for any gift tax that may have been paid with respect to the transfer of property to the decedent. If the transferor predeceased the present decedent by more than two years, the credit allowable is reduced by 20 percent for each full two years by which the death of the transferor preceded the decedent's death. The idea here is to provide a break because the property was recently taxed in someone else's estate. Thus, if the marital deduction was allowed for the property received from the earlier decedent, the estate may not claim the credit. In the case of

119 Rev. Rul. 82-82, 1982-1 CB 127.

transfers to a surviving alien spouse for which the marital deduction was not available [¶29,120], the prior transfer tax credit is allowable regardless of the date of death of the first decedent [Code Sec. 2056(d)(3)].

The amount of the credit is the lesser of the specified percentage of the amount of federal estate tax attributable to the transferred property in the first decedent's estate or in your estate.

The property does not have to be identifiable in your estate. Any transfer of property that was included in another decedent's estate qualifies. Thus, the credit is allowable for a bequest of a life estate to you within the credit period.[120]

.01 How to Figure the Credit

The credit is calculated in two ways. The lesser of the two is the one allowed. Each imposes a different limit.

First Method

The credit cannot exceed the proportion of the transferor's estate tax that the value of the transferred property received by you bore to the total adjusted taxable estate of the transferor. The first trial credit is figured by the following formula:

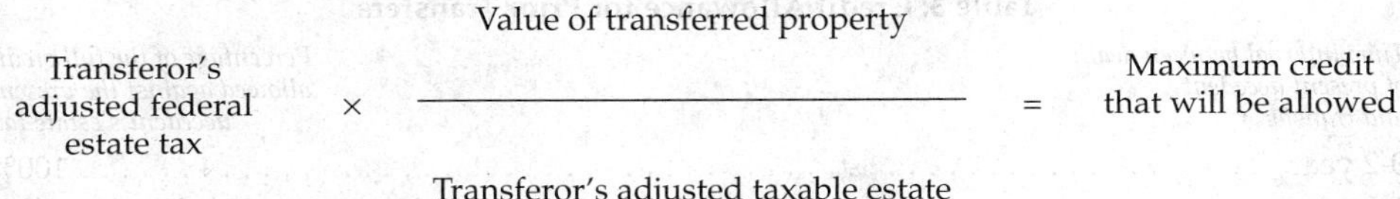

Value of transferred property
Transferor's adjusted federal estate tax
×
=
Maximum credit that will be allowed
Transferor's adjusted taxable estate

The *transferor's adjusted estate tax* is the federal estate tax paid on his estate, plus any credits for gift tax or tax on prior transfers allowed the estate. His *adjusted taxable estate* is his taxable estate, less all death taxes [Code Sec. 2013(b)].

> **NOTE:** The additional estate tax on the disposition of certain farm property or of closely held property is treated as "federal estate tax" for the credit [Code Sec. 2013(f).

Second Method

The credit cannot exceed the proportion of your estate tax that the value of the property received from the transferor bears to the total of your estate. The second trial credit is figured as follows: The estate tax on your taxable estate is figured (after deducting the unified credit and credit for gift taxes paid and foreign death taxes paid), without taking any credit for tax on prior transfers. From this figure is subtracted the estate tax that results when your estate is reduced by the value of the property transferred. The difference is the second trial credit [Code Sec. 2013(c); Reg. §20.2013-3]. In figuring this trial tax, any charitable deduction must be reduced. The amount is determined by multiplying the full charitable deduction by the ratio that the value of the transferred property bears to your gross estate less deductions for expenses and losses[121] [¶29,115][Code Sec. 2013(c)(1); Reg. §20.2013-3]. The marital deduction is the value of the property passing to the surviving spouse without any proportionate reduction and without limitation as to amount.[122]

---

[120] Rev. Rul. 59-9, 1959-1 CB 232.

[121] Rev. Rul. 61-208, 1961-2 CB 148.

[122] Rev. Rul. 90-2, 1990-1 CB 169.

In computing the two trial credits, the property transferred to you has the same value as it had in the transferor's estate for estate tax purposes. Specific property does not have to be identified. The value of property received from a transferor is presumed to be contained in your estate. But when the property transferred is encumbered in any way, or when you incur any obligation imposed by the transferor with respect to the property, its value is reduced by an equivalent amount.[123] The value of the transferred property is also reduced to the extent of death taxes (federal or state) imposed on the property and the marital deduction allowed in the transferor's estate [Code Sec. 2013(d); Reg. § 20.2013-4].

If the transferred property could not be valued by recognized principles at the transferor's death, no credit is allowed.[124]

.02 Amount of Credit Allowed

The credit is allowed in full if you die within two years after the death of the transferor. If you die later than that, the credit is reduced by 20 percent every two years, so that no credit is allowed after the 10th year. Table 3 shows the percentage of the credit allowed [Code Sec. 2013(a); Reg. § 20.2013-1(c)].

Table 3. Credit Allowance for Prior Transfers

Time interval between death of present decedent and transferor	*Percentage of the full credit allowed against the present decedent's estate tax*
0-2 year	100%
3-4 years	80%
5-6 years	60%
7-8 years	40%
9-10 years	20%
more than 10 years	0%

¶29,160 ESTATES OF NONRESIDENT NONCITIZENS

The gross estate of a nonresident alien consists of the same items as that of a citizen or resident. But a nonresident estate is subject to the tax only with respect to property having a United States situs [Code Sec. 2106]. Real property located in the United States has a U.S. situs. Stocks of domestic corporations have a United States situs, regardless of where the certificates are located. Debt obligations (e.g., bonds) of a United States person, including the United States, a state or political subdivision, are considered as situated in the United States [Code Sec. 2104]. There are certain exceptions relating to bank deposits [Code Secs. 2104(c)(2), 2105].

Situs rules are also provided in bilateral tax treaties. The tax law sections that include property transferred during life [Code Secs. 2035 through 2038] apply to nonresident aliens if the property is located in the United States at the time of the transfer or the decedent's death [Reg. § 20.2104-1(b)].

---

[123] Rev. Rul. 78-58, 1978-1 CB 279.

[124] Rev. Rul. 67-53, 1967-1 CB 265.

The estates of nonresident noncitizens are taxed at the same rates as those of citizens and residents. But they are allowed a unified credit of only $13,000 (no adjustment for inflation), unless they are entitled to a greater amount under a treaty [Code Sec. 2102]. See ¶29,101.04. They are allowed the marital deduction for property passing to a spouse who is a U.S. citizen; but deductions for expenses are available only in proportion to the amount of the gross estate situated in the United States. And the charitable deduction is allowed only for charitable uses in the United States [Code Sec. 2106].

In the case of estates of nonresident noncitizens, the phaseout of the unified credit for estates over $10 million is adjusted to reflect the lower unified credit available [Code Sec. 2101].

Estates of residents of U.S. possessions who become U.S. citizens because of their connection with the possession (e.g., birth there) are taxed only with respect to property situated in the U.S. The unified credit for such estates is the greater of (l) $13,000 or (2) $46,800 multiplied by a fraction the numerator of which is the value of the property situated in the U.S. and the denominator of which is the value of the gross estate worldwide [Code Sec. 2102].

.01 Expatriation to Avoid Estate and Gift Tax

The expatriation laws were enacted to shut a loop hole that allowed Americans to avoid paying the wealth transfer taxes by expatriating or renouncing their U.S. citizenship in order to claim offshore tax havens as their home. See ¶28,065 for discussion of expatriation to avoid federal income tax.

A gift tax is imposed on transfers of intangible property by a nonresident not a citizen of the United States if the donor is an expatriate and subject to the alternate tax regime set forth in Code Sec. 877(b) [Code Sec. 2501(a)(3)(A)].

Expatriation After June 3, 2004 and Before June 17, 2008

If a former citizen or long-term resident who is subject to the alternative tax regime of Code Sec. 877(b) dies within 10 years of relinquishment of citizenship or residency, an estate tax is imposed on the transfer of U.S.-situs property, including the decedent's pro rata share of the U.S. property held by a foreign corporation. The estate tax is computed on the taxable estate, as determined by Code Sec. 2106, using the same estate tax rate schedule used for the estate of a U.S. citizen or resident [Code Sec. 2107(a)].

The alternate tax retime of Code Sec. 877(b) applies to individuals who expatriate after June 3, 2004, if:

1. The individual had average annual net income tax liability in excess of $155,000 in 2013 (increasing to $157,000 in 2014) for the five-year period preceding the date of the loss of U.S. citizenship [Code Sec. 877(a)2)(A)];
2. The individual's net worth is $2 million or more on the date of the loss of U.S. citizenship [Code Sec. 877(a)(2)(B)]; or
3. The individual fails to certify under penalties of perjury, that he or she has complied with all U.S. tax obligations for the preceding five years and has provided evidence of compliance as required by the IRS [Code Sec. 877(a)(2)(C)].

Expatriation After June 17, 2008

For any individual whose expatriation date is on or after June 17, 2008, the alternative tax regime of Code Sec. 877 is replaced with a one-time mark-to-market tax under Code Sec. 877A [Code Secs. 877(h), 877A].

Code Sec. 877A(a) generally imposes a mark-to-market regime on expatriates who are covered by Code Sec. 877A, providing that all property of a "covered expatriate" is treated as sold on the day before the expatriation date for its fair market value. Any gain arising from the deemed sale is taken into account for the tax year of the deemed sale. Any loss from the deemed sale is taken into account for the year of the deemed sale, except that the wash sale rules. Under Code Sec. 877A(a)(3), the amount that would otherwise be includible in gross income by reason of the deemed sale rule is reduced (but not to below zero) by $668,000 in 2013 (increasing to $680,000 in 2014). The amount of any gain or loss subsequently realized will be adjusted for gain and loss taken into account under the mark-to-market regime without regard to the amount excluded. Pursuant to Code Sec. 877A(b), a taxpayer may elect to defer payment of tax attributable to property deemed sold.

A "covered expatriate" is any U.S. citizen who relinquishes citizenship and any long-term U.S. resident who ceases to be a lawful permanent resident of the United States, if the individual:

1. Has an average annual net income tax liability for the five preceding years ending before the date of the loss of U.S. citizenship or lawful permanent residency that exceeds $155,000 in 2013 (increasing to $157,000 in 2014) ("tax liability test");
2. Has a net worth of $2 million or more on that date ("net worth test"); or
3. Fails to certify under penalties of perjury that he or she has complied with all U.S. tax obligations for the preceding five years or fails to submit evidence of compliance as required by the IRS.

The date that the individual relinquishes his or her U.S. citizenship or in the case of a long-term U.S. resident, ceases to be a lawful permanent resident is the expatriation date [Code Sec. 877A(g)(1)-(g)(3); Code Sec. 877(a)(2)(A), (B) and (C)].

Exceptions. The net worth and tax liability tests described above will not apply to an individual if the individual:

1. Became, at birth, both a citizen of the United States and of another country, and continues to be a citizen of, and is taxed as a resident of that other country, and has been a resident of the United States for not more than 10 tax years during the 15-tax year period ending with the year during which the expatriation date occurs [Code Sec. 877A(g)(1)(B)(i)], or
2. The individual's relinquishment of United States citizenship occurs before the individual attains age 18½, and the individual has been a resident of the United States for not more than 10 years before the date of relinquishment of U.S. citizenship [Code Sec. 877A(g)(1)(B)(ii)].

Loss of lawful permanent residency. A long-term U.S. resident is defined as an individual who was a lawful permanent resident for at least eight out of the 15 tax years ending with the year the individual ceases to be a lawful permanent resident within the meaning of [Code Sec. 877A(g)(5)]. This covers an individual who lost his or her green card status in accordance with immigration laws, either through revocation or through procedures where he or she has been administratively or judicially determined to have abandoned such status [Code Sec. 877A(g)(3)(B)]. In addition, an individual ceases to be treated as a lawful permanent resident of the United States for all tax purposes if he or she commences to be treated as a resident of a foreign country under a tax treaty between the United States and that foreign country, and does not waive the benefits of the treaty applicable to residents of such foreign country, and notifies the IRS of the commencement of such treatment [Code Sec. 7701(b)(6)].

Relinquishment of U.S. citizenship. A citizen is treated as relinquishing his or her U.S. citizenship on the earliest of four dates:

1. The date the individual renounces his U.S. nationality before a diplomatic or consular officer of the United States in accordance with immigration laws (provided the State Department issues a certificate of loss of nationality to subsequently approve the renunciation);
2. The date the individual furnishes the State Department with a signed statement of voluntary relinquishment of U.S. nationality confirming the performance of an act of expatriation (provided also that the State Department issues a certificate of loss of nationality to subsequently approve the voluntary relinquishment);
3. The date the State Department issues to the individual a certificate of loss of nationality; or
4. The date a U.S. court cancels a naturalized citizen's certificate of naturalization [Code Sec. 877A(g)(4)].

The mark-to-market tax applies to most types of property interests held by the individual on the expatriation date, with certain exceptions. Code Sec. 877A(c) provides that the mark-to-market regime does not apply to deferred compensation items, specified tax deferred accounts, and interests in a nongrantor trust of which the covered expatriate was a beneficiary on the day before the expatriation date. If the covered expatriate is treated as the owner of any portion of a trust under the grantor trust rules on the day before the expatriation date, the assets held by that portion of the trust are subject to the mark-to-market regime.

Code Sec. 877A(d) provides alternative tax regimes that apply to "eligible deferred compensation items" and to other deferred compensation items ("ineligible deferred compensation items"). In the case of "eligible deferred compensation items," Code Sec. 877A(d)(1)(A) provides generally that the payor must deduct and withhold from any taxable payments to a covered expatriate with respect to such items a tax equal to 30 percent of the amount of those taxable payments. In the case of "ineligible deferred compensation items," Code Sec. 877A(d)(2)(A) provides that a covered expatriate generally is treated as having received an amount equal to the present value of the covered expatriate's accrued benefit on the day before the expatriation date.

Information required from individuals losing U.S. citizenship. Individuals who lose U.S. citizenship and long-term residents who terminate their residency in the U.S. are required to provide the U.S. government with information regarding their identities, foreign residence, and assets and liabilities for the year of expatriation. Unless excused by a finding of reasonable cause, an individual who fails to file this statement as required, is subject to a $10,000 penalty [Code Sec. 6039G(d)].

Individuals who are subject to the alternative tax regime of Code Sec. 877 and expatriate after June 3, 2004, or expatriate on or after June 17, 2008 and are subject to Code Sec. 877A are required to provide information detailing their annual income, assets and liabilities, TIN, the mailing address of their principal foreign residence, the foreign country of residence and the foreign country of citizenship. In addition, they must provide the number of days they were physically present in the U.S. during the tax year [Code Sec. 6039G(b)]. Information reporting is required on an annual basis for each tax year the individual is subject to an alternative tax regime [Code Sec. 6039G(a)].

In Notice 2009-85,[125] the IRS provides detailed guidance for expatriating taxpayers subject to the new mark-to-market regime of Code Sec. 877A and the corresponding reporting rules under Code Sec. 6039G.

.02 Inheritance Tax Imposed on Gifts and Bequests from Expatriates

A U.S. citizen or resident who receives property, directly or indirectly, by gift, devise, bequest, or inheritance from a covered expatriate after the date of expatriation must pay a tax equal to the value of the covered gift or bequest multiplied by the highest estate tax rate in effect under Code Sec. 2001(c) or, if greater, the highest gift tax rate in effect under Code Sec. 2502(a) [Code Sec. 2801(a) and (b)].

This special transfer tax applies only to the extent that the value of the covered gifts and bequests received by any person during the calendar year exceeds the annual gift tax exclusion amount in effect under Code Sec. 2503(b) for that calendar year ($14,000 in 2013 with no change in 2014) [Code Sec. 2801(c)]. The tax is reduced by the amount of any gift or estate tax paid to a foreign country with respect to such covered gift or bequest [Code Sec. 2801(d)]. This rule applies to covered gifts and bequests received on or after June 17, 2008, from transferors (or the estates of transferors) whose expatriation date is on or after June 17, 2008.

Covered gifts and bequests to a U.S. trust are also subject to the tax. If covered gifts are made to a foreign trust, distributions from that trust to a U.S. person are subject to the tax [Code Sec. 2801(e)(4)].

Exceptions to Covered Gift or Bequest

A covered gift or bequest does not include property that:

1. Is a taxable gift by a covered expatriate shown on a timely filed gift tax return [Code Sec. 2801(e)(1)];
2. Is included in the gross estate of a covered expatriate and shown on a timely filed estate tax return [Code Sec. 2801(e)(2)]; or
3. Would be eligible for an estate or gift tax charitable deduction or marital deduction if the transferor were a U.S. person [Code Sec. 2801(e)(3)].

> **Example 29-41:** A nonresident expatriate, died with a gross estate of $20 million, $5 million of which was situated in the United States as of the date of his death. He bequeathed his U.S.-situs property to his U.S. citizen cousin. The decedent's executor timely filed a federal estate tax return, reporting the prop-

[125] Notice 2009-85, IRB 2009-45, 598.

erty situated in the United States. As a result, the cousin does not have to pay the special transfer tax under Code Sec. 2801 upon receipt of the bequest.

Covered bequests. A "covered expatriate" is an individual who has either relinquished U.S. citizenship or any long-term U.S. resident who terminates U.S. residency, if such individual: (1) has an average annual net income tax liability for the five preceding years ending before the date of the loss of U.S. citizenship or residency termination that exceeds $155,000 in 2013 (increasing to $157,000 in 2014), as adjusted for inflation; (2) has a net worth of $2 million or more on such date; or (3) fails to certify, under penalty of perjury, that he has complied with all U.S. federal tax obligations for the preceding five years (or fails to submit such evidence of compliance as the IRS may require) [Code Sec. 877A(g) (1) (A)].

A covered expatriate does not include: (1) a former dual citizen who continues to be taxed as a resident of the other country of citizenship and who was a U.S. resident for not more than 10 years during the 15-year period prior to expatriation or (2) an individual who relinquished citizenship or long-term residency prior to reaching the age of eighteen and one-half years and was a resident of the U.S. for not more than 10 years prior to the date of expatriation [Code Secs. 2801(f), 877A(g) (a) (B)].

Transfers in trusts. A covered gift or bequest made to a domestic trust is subject to tax in the same manner as a U.S. citizen or resident described above and, as the recipient, the trust is required to pay the tax imposed [Code Sec. 2801(e) (4) (A)]. A covered gift or bequest made to a foreign trust is also subject to tax, but only at the time a distribution (whether from income or principal) is made to a U.S. citizen or resident from the trust that is attributable to the covered gift or bequest [Code Sec. 2801(e) (4) (B) (i)]. The recipient is allowed an income tax deduction under Code Sec. 164 for the amount of tax paid or accrued under Code Sec. 2801 by reason of a distribution from a foreign trust, but only to the extent the tax is imposed on the portion of the distribution included in the recipient's gross income [Code Sec. 2801(e) (4) (B) (ii)]. For purposes of Code Sec. 2801 only, a foreign trust may elect to be treated as a domestic trust [Code Sec. 2801(e) (4) (B) (iii)]. This election may be revoked with the consent of the IRS.

Example 29-42: If in the Example above, the decedent bequeathed the $5 million of U.S.-situs property to a foreign trust created for the benefit of his cousin, the trust would not be subject to tax on receipt of the covered bequest. Rather, the cousin must pay a tax upon receipt of each distribution that is attributable to the bequest and is allowed to take a corresponding income tax deduction to the extent that the taxed portion of the distribution is included in her gross income. However, if the foreign trust elects to be treated as a domestic trust, the tax is paid at the trust level.

NOTE: Form 8854, *Initial and Annual Expatriation Statement*, must be filed by every individual who loses U.S. citizenship or terminates long-term resident status.

¶29,161 Qualified Family-Owned Business Interest Deduction

The qualified family-owned business interest (QFOBI) deduction under Code Sec. 2057 has been permanently repealed because it was viewed as obsolete in light of the increased applicable exclusion amount.

.01 Additional Tax Continues for Recapture Events

Even though the QFOBI deduction was repealed, if an estate elected to claim the QFOBI deduction for the estate of a decedent dying prior to 2004, an additional estate tax would be imposed if specific recapture events occurred within 10 years of the decedent's death and before the death of the qualified heir, even if the event happened during the period that the deduction was repealed.

.02 Recapture Tax Events

An additional tax is imposed if any of the following recapture events occurs within 10 years of the decedent's death and before the qualified heir's death: (1) the qualified heir ceases to meet the material participation requirements; (2) the qualified heir disposes of any portion of his or her interest in the family-owned business, other than by a disposition to a member of the qualified heir's family or through a conservation contribution under Code Sec. 170(h); (3) the principal place of business of the trade or business ceases to be located in the United States; or (4) the qualified heir loses U.S. citizenship. The amount of the tax is based upon when the recapture event occurs in relation to the decedent's death.

If the recapture event occurs within the first six years of material participation, 100 percent of the reduction in estate tax attributable to the heir's interest, plus interest, is recaptured. Thereafter, the applicable percentage is 80 percent in the seventh year; 60 percent in the eighth year; 40 percent in the ninth year; and 20 percent in the tenth year. The total amount of tax potentially subject to recapture is the difference between the actual amount of estate tax liability for the estate and the amount of estate tax that would have been owed had the QFOBI deduction not been taken.

QUALIFIED DISCLAIMERS

¶29,165 NATURE AND BENEFITS OF DISCLAIMERS

Everybody likes to inherit property from a deceased loved one, but there are situations when it may make sense from a tax perspective to say "thanks, but no thanks." Disclaimers are the legal way to say "thanks, but no thanks" when you have inherited property under the terms of a will or trust from a decedent and want to pretend as if you never did in an effort to save wealth transfer taxes or reorder the disposition of assets. This may become necessary because of unexpected changes in the family dynamics or unexpected changes in the tax laws that occurred after the original documents were drafted.

A properly drafted disclaimer will ensure that a property interest passes as if the person making the disclaimer predeceased the decedent. Thus, the disclaimed assets will pass to a person not originally designated to receive that interest. The identity of this recipient will be determined according to the terms of the will or if the will is unclear, as provided in state law.

.01 Requirements for Valid Disclaimer

Under Code Sec. 2518(a), if a person makes a qualified disclaimer with respect to any interest in property, then for estate, gift, and generation-skipping transfer tax purposes, the disclaimed interest will be treated as if the interest had never been transferred to the disclaimant. Instead, the interest will be considered as having passed directly from the decedent to the person entitled to receive the property as a result of the disclaimer. The term *qualified disclaimer* means an irrevocable and unqualified refusal by a person to accept an interest in property, but only if:

1. The refusal is in writing;
2. The writing is received by the transferor of the interest, his or her legal representative, or the holder of the legal title to the property to which the interest relates, no later than nine months after the later of (a) the date on which the transfer creating the interest in the person is made or (b) the day on which the person attains the age of 21;
3. The person has not accepted the interest or any of its benefits; and
4. As a result of the refusal, the interest passes without any direction on the part of the person making the disclaimer and passes either (a) to the spouse of the decedent or (b) to a person other than the person making the disclaimer.

A qualified disclaimer cannot be made with respect to an interest in property if the disclaimant has accepted the interest or any of its benefits, expressly or impliedly, prior to making the disclaimer [Reg. § 25.2518-2(d)(1)]. Acceptance is manifested by an affirmative act that is consistent with ownership of the interest in the property. Acts indicative of acceptance include: using the property or the interest in the property; accepting dividends, interest, or rents from the property; and directing others to act with respect to the property or interest in the property. However, a disclaimant is not considered to have accepted the property merely because, under applicable local law, title to the property vests immediately on the decedent's death in the disclaimant.

The person doing the disclaiming is called the disclaimant under the disclaimer rules. For example, if Son disclaims property from Dad's estate, Son is the disclaimant and the property will pass under state law to whomever would take the property if Son had died intestate (without a will) immediately before Dad's death. The property is treated as if it was never transferred to Son who, although still very much alive, is treated for tax purposes as having died immediately prior to the event that caused the property to pass to him. As a result, the property is treated as going to someone else, usually the next beneficiary in line for the transfer, and the disclaimant is not regarded as making a gift to the person who receives the property provided the disclaimer is a qualified disclaimer under Code Sec. 2518(a) [Reg. § 25.2518-1(b)].

In order for the disclaimer to constitute a qualified disclaimer and avoid gift tax and/or GST tax liability, the following five requirements must be met [Reg. § 25.2518-2(a)]:

▶ **PRACTICE POINTER:** The disclaimant must satisfy all of these requirements, or he or she will be treated as having made a gift to the person to whom the disclaimed interest passes with resulting gift tax liability.

1. *Irrevocable and unconditional.* The disclaimant must make an irrevocable, unconditional refusal to accept an interest in property [Code Sec. 2518(b); Reg. § 25.2518-2(b)].

2. *Written refusal.* The disclaimer must be in writing and must be signed by either the disclaimant or the disclaimant's legal representative [Code Sec. 2518(b)(1)]. A written instrument manifesting the intent to disclaim an interest in property is required.[126]

The form of the disclaimer should conform to the standards set forth in state statute. Generally, the disclaimer should describe the property being disclaimed, the nature of the disclaimer, and its extent. In addition, the disclaimer may have to be witnessed and acknowledged. This will be provided in the state statute.

3. *Receipt/delivery requirement.* The written disclaimer must be received by the transferor of the property interest or his or her legal representative. The delivery must be completed no later than nine months after the later of: (1) the date on which the original transfer for Federal wealth transfer purposes was made [Reg. § 25.2518- 2(c)(3)]; or (2) the date nine months after the day on which the disclaimant attains the age of 21, or learned of the inheritance, whichever occurs later, if the beneficiary was a minor at the time of the transfer [Code Sec. 2518(b)(2); Reg. § 25.2518-2(c)]. Be sure to check local law to determine whether the disclaimer must be recorded or filed. Because a disclaimer must be made in a timely manner, the date of the original transfer is important. When the transfers occur differs depending on the type of transfer involved as illustrated in the following situations:

   - *Transfers made at death.* The nine-month period begins to run on the date of the wealth holder's death when the transfer occurs after someone has died. The starting date is not the date the will is admitted to probate.
   - *Transfers by gift.* The starting date for lifetime transfers is the date the transfer of property occurred.
   - *Transfers where transferor retained interest in the property.* If a lifetime transfer is included in the transferor's gross estate because the transferor retained an interest in the property (e.g., if a life income interest in a trust was retained), the person who received the interest in the property during the grantor's lifetime and another person who would receive an interest in the property on or after the grantor's death would each have nine months after the taxable transfer in which to disclaim.
   - *Transfers involving general power of appointment.* If your mother gave you a general power of appointment over property, you have nine months after the creation of the power to disclaim it. If your brother gets the property as a result of the disclaimer, your brother must disclaim the property nine months after you exercised your disclaimer [Reg. § 25.2518-2(c)(3)].

---

[126] *T.J. Chamberlain Est.,* CA-9, 2001-1 USTC ¶ 60,407.

• *Transfers involving special power of appointment.* In the case of a special or limited power of appointment (i.e., a power that specifically does not permit appointment so as to benefit the holder, directly or indirectly), the holder of the power, permissible appointees, and persons who take the property in default of appointment must disclaim within the nine-month period that begins at the time of the taxable transfer creating the power [Reg. § 25.2518-2(c)(3)].

When is the Disclaimer Considered Delivered?

A timely transmittal of your disclaimer will be treated as timely delivery if you mailed your disclaimer on time even though it arrived at its destination late [Code Sec. 7502; Reg. § 25.2518-2(c)]. You can even mail your disclaimer at the last minute using certain qualifying private delivery services (PDSs) other than the U.S. Postal Service and still qualify under the rule that a return or payment mailed on time is considered to be filed or received on time [Code Sec. 7502(f)]. You can use one of the IRS approved private delivery services designated by the IRS to meet the "timely mailing as timely filing/paying" rule for tax returns and payments. For the list see ¶ 26,065.

4. *Pass without direction.* The interest in the disclaimed property must pass without any direction on the part of the disclaimant to either: (1) the spouse of the decedent; or (2) a person other than the disclaimant without any direction on the part of the person making the disclaimer [Code Sec. 2518(b)(4); Reg. § 25.2518-2(e)]. A special exception exists for a disclaimer by a decedent's surviving spouse with respect to property transferred by the decedent [Reg. § 25.2518-2(e)].
5. *No acceptance of benefits.* The disclaimant can not accept or benefit, expressly or implicitly, from the disclaimed property in any way prior to the disclaimer [Reg. § 25.2518- 2(d)(1)]. If a person receives any form of consideration for disclaiming an interest in property, he or she is deemed to have accepted the property and a qualified disclaimer cannot be made. Acceptance is manifested by an affirmative act that is consistent with ownership. This means that the disclaimant cannot do any of the following: (1) use the property (except in a fiduciary capacity when the actions are directed towards preserving and protecting the property); (2) accept dividends, interest, or rent; (3) direct others to act with respect to the property; (4) receive any consideration in return for making the disclaimer; or (5) enter into any agreement, express or implied, in which the disclaimed property is transferred to a person at the direction of the disclaimant. Note that taking delivery of title to the property (without any further action) in an individual capacity does not constitute the acceptance of benefits [Reg. § 25.2518-2(d)]. In *Estate of Engelman,*[127] the Tax Court concluded that a disclaimer for the estate of trust property was not a qualified disclaimer because the decedent's exercise of the power of appointment document, which became effective on her death, was an acceptance of the property in trust under Code Sec. 2518 [Reg. § 25.2518-(2)(d)(4), Ex. 7].

The acceptance of one interest in the property will not, however, by itself constitute an acceptance of any other separate interests created by the transferor and held by the disclaimant in the same property [Reg. § 25.2518-2(d)(1)]. For example, all of the

[127] *L. Engelman Est.,* 121 TC 54, Dec. 55,242 (2003).

income interests beneficially owned by a trust beneficiary are considered as one interest, while the beneficial interest in the trust principal represents a separate interest. A beneficiary may accept benefits from the income interest without accepting a benefit from the interest in trust principal. The Court of Appeals for the Fifth Circuit held that disclaimers were not unqualified merely because the disclaimers were made with the expectation of a future benefit or an implied promise of gifts in the future.[128] Even though the beneficiaries expected to receive some future benefit from the decedent's husband if they disclaimed their bequests, there was no contractual agreement or formal obligation between the parties. The "mere expectation" or an "implied promise" was not sufficient to disqualify the disclaimer.

In Rev. Rul. 2005-36,[129] the IRS concluded that a beneficiary's disclaimer of an interest in a decedent's individual retirement account (IRA) is a qualified disclaimer under Code Sec. 2518 (if all other requirements are satisfied) although the disclaimant received the required minimum distribution (RMD) from the IRA for the year of the decedent's death. A qualified disclaimer may be made with respect to all, or a portion of, the balance of the IRA, except for the income attributable to the RMD. Specifically, a qualified disclaimer can be made if, when the disclaimer is made, the beneficiary entitled to receive the disclaimed amount is paid the disclaimed amount and the income attributable to such amount or the disclaimed amounts are segregated in a separate fund.

IRA Balance May Be Disclaimed by Beneficiary

In Rev. Rul. 2005-36,[130] the IRS concluded that a beneficiary's disclaimer of an interest in a decedent's individual retirement account (IRA) is a qualified disclaimer under Code Sec. 2518 (if all other requirements are satisfied) although the disclaimant received the required minimum distribution (RMD) from the IRA for the year of the decedent's death. A qualified disclaimer may be made with respect to all, or a portion of, the balance of the IRA, except for the income attributable to the RMD. Specifically, a qualified disclaimer can be made if, when the disclaimer is made, the beneficiary entitled to receive the disclaimed amount is paid the disclaimed amount and the income attributable to such amount or the disclaimed amounts are segregated in a separate fund.

.02 Partial Disclaimers

To make a partial disclaimer, you must refuse to accept an undivided portion consisting of a fractional or percentile share of the donor's entire interest [Code Sec. 2518(c)(1); Reg. § 25.2518-3(b)]. Severable property is property that can be divided and that, after division, retains a complete and independent existence. For example, you could claim one half of your interest in property, such as $300,000 of a $600,000 inheritance. If you inherited a farm, you could disclaim one half of your interest in the farm, but you could not disclaim just the second floor of the farmhouse. The disclaimer is a qualified partial disclaimer provided the disclaimer extends over the entire term of the disclaimant's interest in the property (and in other property into which the property is converted) and applies to each and every interest the disclaimant has in that property.

---

[128] *L.S. Monroe Est.*, CA-5, 97-2 USTC ¶ 60,292, 124 F3d 699.

[129] Rev. Rul. 2005-36, 2005-26 IRB 1368.

[130] Rev. Rul. 2005-36, 2005-26 IRB 1368; *See also* LTR 200616041 (Jan. 25, 2006).

A disclaimer of an undivided portion of a separate interest in property that satisfies the other requirements of a qualified disclaimer is a qualified disclaimer. Each interest in property that is separately created by the transferor is treated as a separate interest in property. An undivided portion of a disclaimant's separate interest in property must consist of a fraction or percentage of each and every substantial interest or right owned by the disclaimant in the property and must extend over the entire term of the disclaimant's interest in the property and in other property into which the property is converted [Reg. § 25.2518-3(b)].

Example 29-43: Sam Smith conveys Blackacre to her daughter, Lydia. Within nine months, before accepting any benefits from the property, Lydia properly disclaims one-half of her entire interest in Blackacre. The disclaimer is a qualified partial disclaimer.

Example 29-44: Same facts as in Example 29-43, except that Lydia disclaims her life interest in Blackacre, while retaining the remainder. The disclaimer is not a qualified partial disclaimer. So, if the life interest passes, it is a taxable gift from Lydia.

You can also make a partial disclaimer by refusing to accept an "undivided" interest in property consisting of a fractional or percentile share of each and every substantial interest or right given to you [Reg. § 25.2518-3(b)]. This means that a donee or disclaimant can disclaim a percentage or fraction of an income interest from a trust [Reg. § 25.2518-3(d), Ex. 15]. Similarly, the donee of an outright gift of realty or securities cannot carve out an income interest and disclaim the remainder [Reg. § 25.2518-3(d), Ex. (2)].

Partial Disclaimer of Only Part of Split-Interest Trust Not Qualified Disclaimer

In *Estate of Walshire*,[131] the Court of Appeals for the Eighth Circuit upheld the validity of Reg. § 25.2518-3(b), which provides that in order for a disclaimer to be valid, it must be made of an undivided interest in property and cannot be made of a remainder interest in the property while retaining a life estate. The decedent attempted to disclaim the remainder interest of his share of his deceased brother's residuary estate while reserving the income and use of the property for his life. The court concluded that the disclaimer was invalid because Reg. § 25.2518- 3(b) specifically precludes the decedent from dividing the property horizontally (i.e., retaining a life interest while disclaiming the remainder interest). Reg. § 25.2518-3(b) requires disclaimer of an "undivided portion" of the disclaimed property. An "undivided" interest encompassed all of the rights associated with a fee interest, and did not include an interest solely in the remainder. As a result, the court concluded that the decedent failed to make a qualified disclaimer and the value of the property was includible in his estate for federal estate tax purposes.

---

[131] *T.J. Walshire Est.*, CA-8, 2002-1 USTC ¶ 60,439, 288 F3d 342.

In *Estate of Christiansen,*[132] the Court of Appeals for the Eighth Circuit affirmed the Tax Court to hold that no deduction was allowed for any of the property passing to a charitable lead annuity trust as a result of a disclaimer by a decedent's daughter because she failed to disclaim the contingent remainder interest in the trust. The court noted that Reg. § 25.2518-3(b) provides that "A disclaimer of some specific rights while retaining other rights with respect to an interest in the property is not a qualified disclaimer of an undivided portion of the disclaimant's interest in property." The court said that the daughter's retaining a remainder interest while giving up present enjoyment fit neatly into this definition. The court found that the daughter's remainder interest was neither "severable property" nor "an undivided portion of the property." Thus the daughter could not disclaim the present enjoyment of partnership units that passed to the trust but retain a remainder interest in such units. The daughter was not permitted to disclaim a "horizontal slice" of her interest in the property—in other words, she could not disclaim the income interest and keep the remainder. A savings clause in the disclaimer did not change the result because, no matter how the clause operated, it would violate one of the requirements for a qualified disclaimer. Therefore, because the daughter did not make a qualified disclaimer as to any portion of the property passing to the trust, none of the property passing to the trust was eligible for a charitable deduction.

Disclaimer Trusts

If a taxpayer wants to disclaim an interest in property but still needs the income that the disclaimed property generates, a disclaimer trust could be used to satisfy both needs. As long as the decedent's will provides for the establishment of a disclaimer trust, any income-generating assets that the taxpayer wants to disclaim will pass into a disclaimer trust, which provides under the terms of the trust that the income is distributed to the disclaimer.

.03 Planning for the Disclaimer

Disclaimers should be fully considered in the estate planning discussions. For maximum flexibility, the possibility of a disclaimer trust should be anticipated and specifically provided for in the estate planning documents. Considering and planning for a disclaimer early on is very important because you have only nine months from the date of the property transfer or the date of the decedent's death to make a qualified disclaimer. In addition, significant tax savings can be lost if the disclaimant accepts the property or benefits from it in any way. Once this has occurred, the disclaimant is precluded from making a qualified disclaimer with respect to that property. The U.S. Supreme Court has held that an heir's disclaimer of his interest in an estate will not protect him from liens for federal tax taxes he owes.[133] This means that disclaimers cannot be used to thwart tax liens against the disclaimant's property from applying to the disclaimed interest. Consider using a disclaimer as an estate planning device in the following situations:

---

[132] *H. Christiansen Est.*, CA-8, 2009-2 USTC ¶ 60,585, 586 F3d 1061, *aff'g*, 130 TC 1, Dec. 57,301 (2008).

[133] *R.F. Drye Jr.*, SCt, 99-2 USTC ¶ 51,006, 528 US 49, 120 SCt 474 (1999).

- To postpone decisionmaking on property transfers until you have had time to determine the impact of the changes that have occurred from the time the estate plan was originally drafted and the date of death. Disclaimers in effect give you an alternate estate plan that you can fall back on if circumstances mandate it.
- To correct any drafting errors or omissions that existed in the original estate plan.
- To cure deficiencies in the existing estate plans.
- To reduce the size of a taxable estate.
- To increase the amount that will pass to others free of transfer tax.
- To create a QTIP trust.
- To fund the unified credit fully.
- To reduce generation-skipping transfer tax.
- To create, enlarge, or reduce charitable donations.
- To salvage a defective marital bequest.
- To avoid inadvertent termination of S corporation status by passing S corporation stock to a nonqualified trust (i.e., one that has more than one beneficiary).

Disadvantages to Disclaimers

There are three disadvantages to estate planning based on the surviving spouse disclaiming a portion of the amount received from the decedent.

1. There are specific requirements that must be satisfied in order for the disclaimer to be qualified for estate and gift tax purposes. The disclaimer by the surviving spouse must be made in writing within nine months after the decedent's death and before any benefits from the disclaimed assets have been claimed.
2. Surviving spouses may be reluctant to disclaim or give up assets that would otherwise be theirs to keep despite the wishes of their spouse. They may find it necessary in effect to disinherit their offspring in light of financial set-backs or the state of the economy or the stock market when their spouse dies.
3. Depending on disclaimer-based estate planning is never a good idea when there are children from a prior marriage. A surviving spouse may find it particularly difficult to disclaim large sums of money and see the money go to children from a deceased spouse's prior marriage.

GENERATION-SKIPPING TRANSFER (GST) TAX

¶29,170 PURPOSE OF THE GST TAX

The generation-skipping transfer (GST) tax may apply to you even if you are not super-wealthy. It may apply to the simplest trusts used by grandparents to pass wealth on to grandchildren. It can apply, for example, to simple trusts used by middle income taxpayers to pass wealth on to grandchildren. In an arrangement common among middle-class taxpayers, the GST tax would apply to a trust in which a grandparent's children enjoy lifetime income from property that is left in trust for the grandchildren, the grandchildren inheriting the trust assets when their parents die. Additionally, GST tax consequences must be considered any time a grandchild holds an interest in a life insurance trust. Suffice it to say that this monster may apply to you when you least expect it. It is foolhardy not to appreciate the impact of the GST tax on wealth transfers. Understanding the GST special vocabulary and appreciating when and how the tax applies will help you to take full advantage of the GST exemption in order to minimize exposure to this tax. Good GST planning can reduce or possibly avoid the tax completely.

The GST tax was created to close up a loophole in the estate and gift taxing system. For years wealthy individuals created dynasty-type trusts that passed wealth down through the generations without ever having paying a dime of wealth transfer taxes. These trusts were only limited by the rule against perpetuities and a lawyer's creativity. Here's how they worked. The parent placed the wealth in a trust in which the child and then the grandchild had the right to the income from the trust with the principal going to the great-grandchild. In this example, the parent would skip two generations of estate tax. No tax would be imposed at the child's level and no tax would be imposed when the grandchild died even though the child and grandchild had an income interest in the trust as well as substantial powers over the use, management, and disposition of the trust assets. While the tax advantages of generation-skipping trusts were theoretically available to all, in actual practice these devices were more valuable (in terms of tax savings) to wealthier families.

Example 29-45: Double taxation: Father leaves commercial real estate to Son when he dies. Son wills the land to his children. By the time the land reaches Grandchildren, it has been taxed in two estates—both Father's and Son's.

Example 29-46: Classic GST trust: In order to avoid this double taxation, lawyers draft a will for Father that puts the land in a trust. Son receives the trust income for his lifetime. When Son dies, the trust terminates and the land goes to Grandchildren. Without a GST tax, the land would be taxed in only one estate before reaching the grandchildren. Today this transfer would be subject to the GST tax.

Congress realized that generation-skipping was unfair because it enabled some families to pay these taxes only once every several generations, whereas other families who could not pay attorneys to create tax-saving trusts, paid these taxes every generation. Generation-skipping also reduced the progressive effect of the transfer taxes, since families with moderate levels of accumulated wealth might pay as much or more in cumulative transfer taxes as wealthier families who utilized generation-skipping devices.

The GST tax was enacted to ensure that transfers are taxed at least once for each generation where substantial amounts are being transferred [Code Sec. 2601]. GST tax-saving opportunities are available with the GST exemption which allows a taxpayer and his or her spouse to each make transfers free of the tax as a result of the GST exemption [Code Sec. 2631]. See ¶ 29,185 for further discussion of GST exemption. Married individuals who treat their gifts as made jointly can effectively double this exemption. The exemption acts to insulate generation-skipping transfers from the GST tax. In addition, you will not owe GST on most small gifts, tuition payments, and medical expense payments that skip a generation.

¶29,175 HOW GST WORKS

If a generation skipping transfer is fully subject to tax, the GST tax is computed by multiplying the amount of the transfer by the maximum federal estate tax rate effective at the time of the decedent's death. If part of your exemption has been allocated to a transfer, the calculation is more complicated. The amount transferred is multiplied by the maximum estate tax rate multiplied by the applicable fraction. This fraction is found by subtracting from the number one a fraction, the numerator of which is the amount of the exemption allocated to the gift and the denominator of which is the value of the property transferred [Code Sec. 2642].

> **Example 29-47:** Grandfather transfers $1 million in trust for his granddaughter and allocates $250,000 of the GST exemption to the trust. The inclusion ratio is .75 (1 minus $250,000/$1,000,000). The GST tax would be $300,000 (.75 multiplied by the maximum 40 percent estate tax for estates of decedents dying in 2013) multiplied by $1,000,000).

.01 Inclusion Ratio

When you allocate GST exemption to a direct skip or trust, the GST tax will be reduced or eliminated by the inclusion ratio which is the percentage of the outright transfer that exceeds the amount of GST exemption allocated to the transfer [Code Sec. 2642]. The inclusion ratio for any property transferred in a GST is 1 minus the "applicable fraction" determined for the trust from which a generation-skipping transfer is made or, in the case of a direct skip, the applicable fraction determined for such a skip [Code Sec. 2642(a)]. Simply stated, 1 minus the "applicable fraction" will equal your inclusion ratio. Your objective should be to get an inclusion ratio of zero because this will mean that the applicable rate of tax for the trust or transfer will be zero. You can accomplish this if the amount of GST exemption allocated to the trust or direct skip transfer equals the value of the trust or transfer at the time of the transfer even if the value of the assets appreciates over time.

> **Example 29-48:** Bill created a trust with income distributed to his son, Sam for life. When Sam died the trust was to be distributed to Sam's children. Bill transferred $1 million into the trust. On a timely filed gift tax return Bill allocated $1 million of his GST exemption to the trust. When his son died the value of the trust fund was $3 million. The inclusion ratio is zero because the GST exemption allocated to the trust is equal to the amount transferred even though the actual amount in the trust appreciated in value over time. The applicable rate is the maximum federal estate tax rate multiplied by the inclusion ratio of zero or zero percent. Therefore no GST tax is due on this taxable termination. If no GST exemption had been allocated to the trust, the applicable rate would be 40 percent, which is the maximum federal estate tax rate effective

in 2013, multiplied by the inclusion ratio of one. The tax would be $1,200,000 ($3 million times 40 percent).

.02 The Applicable Fraction

The numerator of the applicable fraction is the amount of the GST exemption allocated to the trust or the property transferred in the case of a direct skip not in trust [Code Sec. 2642(a)(2)(A); Reg. § 26.2642-1(b)(1)]. The denominator of the applicable fraction is the value of the property transferred to the trust (or involved in the direct skip) reduced by the sum of the following:

1. Any federal estate tax or state death tax actually recovered from the trust attributable to such property, and
2. Any charitable deduction allowed with respect to the property [Code Sec. 2642(a)(2)(B); Reg. § 26.2642-1(c)(1)].

Example 29-49: Grandfather gives $750,000 to Grandchild in a direct skip. If he allocates $750,000 of his GST exemption to this transfer and assuming there are no estate/death taxes and no charitable deductions, the inclusion ratio is zero, computed as follows: One minus $750,000/$750,000 equals zero. The tax rate on this transfer is zero and no GST tax is imposed [Reg. § 26.2642-1(c)(2)].

Example 29-50: Grandfather gives $750,000 to Grandchild in a direct skip. If he fails to allocate any GST exemption to the transfer, the inclusion ratio is one, computed as follows: One minus $0/$750,000 equals one. Therefore at the 2013 estate tax rate of 40 percent, a 40 percent GST tax is imposed on the transfer for a total GST tax bill of $300,000.

Example 29-51: Grandfather leaves $10 million in trust for the benefit of Grandchildren. At the time of the transfer in 2013, the full $5,250,000 GST tax exemption is allocated to the trust. Assuming there are no estate/death tax and charitable deductions, the calculation of the GST tax would be as follows: $5,250,000 divided by $10 million equals .525. The inclusion ratio equals .48 (one minus .525). The GST tax rate is the product of the inclusion ratio of .48 and the maximum federal estate tax rate in 2013, which is 40 percent. Thus the rate of tax on this transfer is 19.2 percent [Reg. § 26.2642-1(d), Ex. 1].

.03 Valuation Rules

If an allocation of GST exemption to any transfer of property is made on a timely filed gift tax return or is deemed to be made under Code Sec. 2632(b)(1) (lifetime direct skips) or under Code Sec. 2632(c)(1) (lifetime indirect skips), then:

1. The value of the property for purposes of calculating the inclusion ratio will be the value of the property as finally determined for gift tax purposes, and
2. The allocation will be effective on and after the date of the transfer. In the case of an allocation deemed to have been made at the close of an estate tax inclusion period (ETIP), the value of the property for inclusion ratio purposes will be the value at the

time of the close of the ETIP, and the allocation will be effective on and after the close of the ETIP [Code Sec. 2642(b)(1)].

An ETIP is any period after a transfer during which the value of the transferred property would be includible in the gross estate of the transferor if he or she died [Code Sec. 2642(f)(3)].

Similarly, the value of the transferred property for purposes of determining the inclusion ratio will be its value as finally determined for estate tax purposes. However, if the requirements respecting allocation of post-death changes in value are not met, the value of the property will be determined as of the time that the distribution occurred [Code Sec. 2642(b)(2)(A)].

¶29,180 TRANSFERS SUBJECT TO GST TAX

The GST tax applies to transfers that go directly to people who are two or more generations younger than you (called skip persons). The GST tax is imposed on three types of generation-skipping events: direct skip, taxable distributions and taxable terminations [Code Sec. 2601]. The GST tax is designed to be both a substitute transfer tax and a supplement to the estate tax system. It operates as a substitute transfer tax because the GST tax will not apply to taxable distributions and taxable terminations if the distribution or termination of the interest is otherwise subject to either the gift or estate tax. It operates as a supplemental tax in the case of a direct skip because the GST tax will be imposed in addition to the estate or gift tax imposed on a direct transfer to a skip person. The GST tax is imposed when you make non-exempt transfers to people who are two or more generations below your generation. In GST parlance, these are known as skip persons. If no skip persons are involved in the transfer, the trust is not subject to the GST tax. Drafting a trust so that skip-persons are intentionally avoided, if possible, could present an important planning opportunity.

.01 Skip Person Defined

A *skip person* is defined as an individual assigned to a generation that is two or more generations below that of the transferor [Code Sec. 2613(a)(1); Reg. § 26.2612-1(d)(1)]. For example, a grandchild is a skip person. A trust can be a skip person if: (1) all interests in property held in trust are held by skip persons, or (2) if there is no nonskip person holding an interest in the trust and no distributions can be made from the trust to nonskip persons [Code Sec. 2613(a)(2); Reg. § 26.2612-1(d)]. A person will not have an interest in the property held in the trust, as required in (1) above, merely because his or her support obligation may be satisfied by a distribution that is within the discretion of a fiduciary or pursuant to the Uniform Gifts/Transfers to Minors Act [Reg. § 26.2612-1(e)(2)(i)]. A trust meets the second part of this definition if the probability of a distribution to a nonskip person is "so remote as to be negligible," which the regulations define to mean that "it can be ascertained by actuarial standards that there is less than a 5 percent probability that the distribution will occur" [Reg. § 26.2612-1(d)(2)(ii)].

Example 29-52: Tom establishes an irrevocable trust for the benefit of his grandchild, Sam. The trustee has discretion to distribute property for Sam's support without regard to the duty or ability of Sam's parent to support him. Tom's child, Cathy, does not have an interest in the trust because the potential use of the trust property to satisfy her support obligation is within the discretion of a fiduciary. Cathy would be treated as having an interest in the trust if the trustee was required to distribute trust property for Sam's support [Reg. § 26.2612-1(f), Ex. 13].

.02 Nonskip Persons

A nonskip person is any person (including a trust) who is not a skip person [Code Sec. 2613(b)]. For example, a child is a nonskip person. For transfers to family members, generations are figured along family lines. All determinations are made relative to the transferor. That's why determining the identity of the transferor is so important. You, your spouse and siblings are in one generation. Children (including adopted children), nieces and nephews are in the first younger generation. Grandchildren, grandnieces and grandnephews are in the second younger generation, and so on. A child who is adopted is treated identically to those related by blood [Code Sec. 2651(b)(3)(A)]. For transfers you make to nonfamily members, generations are measured from the date of your birth. Individuals not more than 12½ years younger than you are treated as members of your generation; more than 12½ but not more than 37½ years younger, first younger generation, and so on a new generation every 25 years [Code Sec. 2651(d)]. However, anyone who has ever been married to you is always considered to be in your generation, regardless of age [Code Sec. 2651(c)]. If an estate, trust, partnership, or corporation is a beneficiary, the generation assignment is based on who owns the beneficial interest [Code Sec. 2651(f)(2)].

.03 Generation Assignment Where Intervening Parent Is Deceased—The Predeceased Ancestor Exception

The predeceased ancestor exception is a generation assignment rule in Code Sec. 2615(e)(1) that may apply to determine whether the recipient of a transfer is a skip person and therefore if the transfer is subject to GST tax. The predeceased ancestor exception will apply if you make a gift to your grandchild and at the time you made the gift, the grandchild's parent is dead. In this situation, for purposes of generation assignment, the predeceased ancestor exception provides that your grandchild is considered to be your child rather than your grandchild. Similarly, your grandchild's children will be treated as your grandchildren rather than your great-grandchildren. Thus, if the recipient's parents died before the transfer, the generational assignment of a person (who otherwise is a skip person) is redetermined by disregarding the intervening generation [Code Sec. 2651(e)(1); Reg. § 26.2612-1(a)(2)]. The "predeceased ancestor exception applies if both:

1. An individual is a descendant of a parent of the transfer (or the transferor's spouse or former spouse); and
2. The individual's parent who is the lineal descendant of the parent of the transferor (or the transferor's spouse or former spouse) died prior to the time the transferor is

subject to estate or gift tax on the transfer from which an interest of that individual is established or derived.

An individual satisfying these criteria is treated as though the individual were a member of the generation that is one generation below the lower of either:

a. The transferor's generation, or
b. The generation assignment of the individual's youngest living lineal ancestor of the individual who is also a descendant of the parent of the transferor (or the transferor's spouse or former spouse).

Example 29-53: Assume Grandfather makes a transfer to Grandson. Under the general rule, Grandson is a skip person because he is two generations below Grandfather. If Grandfather is Grandson's paternal grandfather and Grandson's father is deceased, the predeceased parent rule would assign Grandson to his father's generation. In that case, he would not be a skip person and this would not be a GST transfer. If Grandson's mother was deceased and his father was still living, however, Grandson would be a skip person and the predeceased ancestor exception would not apply.

Example 29-54: Mom transfers property to Child and Grandchild. Child (i.e., Grandchild's parent) is deceased at the time of the transfer. According to the predeceased ancestor exception, Grandchild will move up to the Child's generation so that the Mom's transfer will not be a direct skip subject to GST tax.

When Transferee's Interest in Property is Established

For purposes of the predeceased ancestor exception, an individual's interest in property or a trust is established or derived when the transferor is subject to the estate or gift tax. If the property is subject to transfer tax on the property on more than one occasion, then the individual's interest is considered established or derived on the earliest of these occasions. The interest of a remainder beneficiary of a trust for which a QTIP election under Code Sec. 2523(f) or Code Sec. 2056(b)(7) has been made, is deemed to have been established or derived, to the extent of the QTIP election, on the date when the value of the trust corpus is first subject to tax under Code Sec. 2519 or Code Sec. 2044. However, this rules does not apply to a trust to the extent that an election under Code Sec. 2652(a)(3) (reverse QTIP election) has been made for the trust because, to the extent of a reverse QTIP election, the spouse who established the trust will remain the transferor of the trust for GST purposes [Reg. § 26.2651-1(a)(3)].

Ninety-Day Rule

For assigning individuals to generations for purposes of the GST tax, any individual who dies no later than 90 days after a transfer occurring because of the death of the transferor is treated as having predeceased the transferor [Reg. § 26.2651-1(a)(2)(iii)]. A living person is not treated as having predeceased the transferor solely by reason of a provision of applicable local law; e.g., an individual who disclaims is not treated as a predeceased parent solely because state law treats a disclaimant as having predeceased the transferor for purposes of determining the disposition of the disclaimed property [Reg. § 26.2651-1(a)(2)(iv)].

Predeceased Ancestor Exception and Collateral Heirs

The predeceased ancestor exception applies to transfers to collateral heirs, provided that the decedent has no living descendants at the time of the transfer [Code Sec. 2651(e)(2)]. For example, the exception would apply to a transfer made by an individual (with no living lineal heirs) to a grandniece where the transferor's nephew or niece who is the parent of the grandniece is deceased at the time of the transfer. For the predeceased parent rule to apply to transfers to collateral heirs, only the transferor must have no living lineal descendants at the time of the transfer [Reg. § 26.2651-1(b)].

Application to Taxable Terminations and Taxable Distributions

The predeceased ancestor exception applies to taxable terminations and taxable distributions, provided the parent of the relevant beneficiary was deceased at the earliest time that the transfer (from which the beneficiary's interest in the property was established) was subject to estate or gift tax [Code Sec. 2651(e)(1)]. For example, when a trust was established to pay an annuity to a charity for a term of years with a remainder interest granted to a grandson, the termination of the term for years would not be a taxable termination subject to the GST tax if the grandson's parent (who is the son or daughter of the transferor) is deceased at the time the trust was created and the transfer creating the trust was subject to estate or gift tax.

Adoptions

An individual will be treated as a member of the generation that is one generation below an adoptive parent for purposes of determining whether a transfer from the adoptive parent to the adopted individual is subject to GST tax if the individual is: (1) legally adopted by the adoptive parent; (2) a descendant of a parent of the adoptive parent or the adoptive parent's spouse; (3) under the age of 18 at the time of the adoption; and (4) not adopted primarily for GST tax-avoidance purposes [Reg. § 26.2651-2(b)]. A legal adoption may create another generation assignment but will not substitute for the blood relationship.

Example 29-55: T establishes an irrevocable trust, Trust, providing that trust income is to be paid to T's grandchild, GC, for 5 years. At the end of the 5-year period or on GC's prior death, Trust is to terminate and the principal is to be distributed to GC if GC is living or to GC's children if GC has died. At the time of the transfer, T's child, C, who is a parent of GC, is deceased. GC is treated as a member of the generation that is one generation below T's generation. As a result, GC is not a skip person and Trust is not a skip person. Therefore, the transfer to Trust is not a direct skip. Similarly, distributions to GC during the term of Trust and at the termination of Trust will not be GSTs [Reg. § 26.2651-1(c), Ex. 1].

Example 29-56: On January 1, 2013, T transfers $100,000 to an irrevocable inter vivos trust that provides T with an annuity payable for four years or until T's prior death. When the trust terminates, the corpus is to be paid to T's grandchild, GC. The transfer is subject to gift tax and, at the time of the transfer, T's child, C, who is a parent of GC, is living. C dies in 2015. In this case, C was alive at the time the transfer by T was subject to the GST tax. Therefore, the predeceased ancestor exception do not apply. When the trust subsequently terminates, the distribution to GC is a taxable termination that is subject to the GST tax to the extent the trust has an inclusion ratio greater than zero [Reg. § 26.2651-1(c), Ex. 2].

.04 Direct Skip

The most common generation-skipping transfer is a direct skip. A direct skip is a taxable gift during life or transfer at death from a transferor directly to a skip person who is someone two or more generations below the donor's generation [Code Sec. 2612(c)].

A trust can also be a skip person and a direct skip gift to a trust is taxed like a direct skip gift to an individual. In the classic example, grandparent makes an outright gift to a grandchild or more remote descendant. This is treated as a direct skip because the grandparent has made a gift to someone two or more generations below his generation. The recipient of the gift is called a skip person. If the grandparent makes a transfer to a trust, this transfer is also a direct skip and the trust is considered a skip person if all the interests in the trust are held by skip persons. A direct skip is subject to both the generation-skipping tax and the estate or gift tax [Code Sec. 2612(c)(1)].

Example 29-57: Grandfather creates a trust under his will in the amount of $100,000 with income payable to Grandchild, Anna until age 25, remainder to his grandchild, Billy. This testamentary trust constitutes a direct skip and is subject to GST tax. This particular trust is a skip person since all interests in the trust are held by skip persons [Code Sec. 2613(a)(2)(A)].

.05 Taxable Termination

A *taxable termination* is the termination (by reason of death, lapse of time, release of power, or otherwise) of a beneficiary's interest held in trust if, immediately after the termination, all remaining interests are held by skip persons, unless at the time of the termination, a transfer subject to federal estate or gift tax occurs and a new transferor is determined for the property [Code Sec. 2612(a)].

A taxable termination will not occur if the probability of a distribution to a skip person is so remote as to be negligible. This means that "it can be ascertained by actuarial standards that there is less than a 5 percent probability that the distribution will occur" [Reg. § 26.2612-1(b)(1)(iii)].

Example 29-58: Grandfather's trust provides that income be paid to Child for life. When Child dies, the trust principal is to be paid to Grandchild. Since Child has an interest in the trust, the trust is not a skip person and the transfer to the trust is not a direct skip. If Child dies survived by Grandchild, a taxable termination occurs at Child's death because Child's interest in the trust terminates and thereafter the trust property is held by a skip person who occupies a lower generation than the child [Reg. § 26.2612-1(f), Ex. 4].

.06 Taxable Distribution

A *taxable distribution* is any distribution other than a direct skip or taxable termination of either income or principal from a trust to a skip person [Code Sec. 2612(b)]. If any portion of GST tax (including penalties and interest) imposed on a distributee is paid from the distributing trust, the payment is an additional taxable distribution to the distributee. The additional distribution is treated as having been made on the last day of the calendar year in which the original taxable distribution is made [Reg. § 26.2612-1(c)(1)].

> **Example 29-59:** Grandfather establishes an irrevocable trust under which the trust income is payable to Child for life. When Grandfather's grandchild attains 35 years of age, Grandchild is to receive one half of the principal. The remaining one half of the principal is to be distributed to Grandchild when Child dies. Assume that Child survives until Grandchild attains age 35. When the trustee distributes one half of the principal to Grandchild on his 35th birthday, the distribution is a taxable distribution because it is a distribution to a skip person and is neither a taxable termination nor a direct skip.

.07 Trust Defined for GST Purposes

A trust is generally defined as a legal relationship or arrangement under which an individual, who is called the settlor or grantor, transfers property to another person, who is called the trustee, so the property can be administered for the benefit of a third party, who is called the beneficiary. A trust is more broadly defined for GST tax purposes to include any arrangement (other than an estate) that has substantially the same effect as a trust [Code Sec. 2652(b)]. For example, arrangements involving life estates and remainders, estates for years, and life insurance and annuity contracts are considered to be trusts for GST tax purposes [Code Sec. 2652(b)(3); Reg. § 26.2652-1(b)(1)].

> **Example 29-60:** Grandmother transfers cash to an account in the name of Child, as custodian for Child's minor child, Grandchild, under a state statute substantially similar to the Uniform Gifts/Transfers to Minors Act. For GST tax purposes, the transfer to the custodial account is treated as a transfer to a trust [Reg. § 26.2652-1(b)(2), Ex. 1].

Generally, a trust will exist even where the identity of the transferee is contingent upon the occurrence of an event. For GST tax purposes, however, where the identity of the transferee is contingent upon an event that must occur within six months of the transferor's death, a trust does not exist [Reg. § 26.2652-1(b)(1)].

.08 Definition of *Trustee*

A *trustee* is defined for GST tax purposes as the person designated as trustee under local law or, if no such person is designated, the person who actually or constructively possesses the property held in trust [Code Sec. 2652(b)(2); Reg. § 26.2652-1(c)].

.09 Definition of *Executor*

For GST tax purposes, *executor* has the same meaning as it does for estate and gift tax purposes [Code Sec. 2652(d)]. Despite this generalization, executor is defined for GST purposes as the executor or administrator of the decedent's estate. However, if no executor or administrator is appointed, qualified or acting within the United States, the executor is the fiduciary who is primarily responsible for payment of the decedent's debts and expenses. If these is no such executor, administrator or fiduciary, the executor is the person in actual or constructive possession of the largest portion of the value of the decedent's gross estate [Reg. § 26.2652-1(d)].

.10 *Transferor* Defined

The GST tax analysis must begin with determining who is the *transferor* of the wealth that is subject to the GST tax. Determining the identity of the transferor is important because application of the GST tax depends on generation assignments which all begin with the "transferor." In general, the transferor is the person who most recently was subject to estate or gift taxes with respect to the property [Code Sec. 2652(a); Reg. § 26.2652-1(a)(1)]. For purposes of determining who is the transferor under the GST rules, it only matters if the taxpayer was "subject to" estate or gift taxes. Disregarded is the fact that no gift or estate tax is actually imposed as a result of an exclusion such as the annual per donee exclusion from gift tax or the exemption equivalent. The identity of the transferor is not affected just because some or all of the gift qualifies for an exclusion.

Example 29-61: Grandfather transfers $100,000 to a trust for the sole benefit of Grandchild. The transfer is a completed gift for gift tax purposes. For GST purposes, Grandfather is the transferor of the $100,000. It is immaterial that a portion of the transfer is excluded from the total amount of Grandfather's taxable gifts as a result of the annual gift tax exclusion. What matters is that the transfer is subject to gift tax making Grandfather the transferor [Reg. § 26.2652-1(a)(6), Ex. 1].

.11 Gift-Splitting

When a married couple elect under Code Sec. 2513 to treat a gift as made equally by both of them for federal gift tax purposes, they have agreed to a practice known as gift-splitting. This is a way for couples to reduce their taxable estate while they are still alive to see their children enjoy the money. In this situation, two spouses regardless of their sex[134] can give a total of $28,000 in 2013 (with no change in 2014) and each year thereafter to each child and/or grandchild. For GST purposes, each spouse is treated as the transferor of one half of the entire value of the property transferred, even though only one of them actually transferred all the property under state law [Reg. § 26.2652-1(a)(4)]. Gift-splitting allows married couples to utilize both GST exemptions even though only one spouse owns all the property.

---

[134] *E.S. Windsor*, SCt, 2013-2 USTC ¶ 60,667; Rev. Rul. 2013-17, IRB 2013-38, 201.

Example 29-62: Grandfather transfers $100,000 to a trust for the sole benefit of Grandchild. The transfer is a completed gift for gift tax purposes. Grandfather's spouse consents under Code Sec. 2513 to split the gift with him. For GST purposes, Grandfather and his spouse are each treated as the transferor of $50,000 to the trust [Reg. § 26.2652-1(a)(6), Ex. 2].

Generally, the transferor is the decedent in the case of a testamentary transfer. In the case of a transfer subject to gift taxes, the transferor is the donor. The two exceptions that will be discussed here are the special rule for certain QTIP trusts and the exception for certain nongeneral powers of appointment.

In the case of a QTIP trust, the spouse who creates the QTIP trust is the transferor initially, but the surviving spouse would become the transferor of the property held in the QTIP trust when he or she dies and the property becomes taxable in the surviving spouse's gross estate as is required under Code Sec. 2044 (provided no reverse QTIP election as discussed below is made) [Reg. § 26.2652-1(a)(1)]. Code Sec. 2044 provides that the gross estate of the surviving spouse in a QTIP trust includes the fair market value of the trust funds or property in which the spouse has a life estate as their value is determined when the surviving spouse dies.

Example 29-63: Husband transfers $100,000 to a trust providing that all the net trust income is to be paid to Second Wife for her lifetime and upon her death it should pass to his children from his first marriage. He elects under Code Sec. 2523(f) to treat the transfer as a transfer of qualified terminable interest property and he does not make a reverse QTIP election under Code Sec. 2652(a)(3). When Second Wife dies, the trust property is included in her gross estate under Code Sec. 2044. Thus she becomes the transferor at the time of her death [Reg. § 26.2652-1(a)(6), Ex. 3].

¶29,185 THE GST EXEMPTION

.01 GST Exemption

Each person may escape GST tax on a portion of their generation-skipping transfers by taking advantage of his or her $5,250,000 irrevocable GST exemption in 2013 (increasing to $5,340,000 in 2014) [Code Sec. 2631(a)]. A husband and a wife each have his or her own exemption. As a result, if a married couple elects to split a transfer and treat it as made one-half by each spouse pursuant to the gift-splitting rules of Code Sec. 2513, they can effectively avoid GST tax on $10,500,000 of wealth transferred to their grandchild in 2013 (increasing to $10,680,000 in 2014) [Code Sec. 2652(a)(2)]. Judicious allocation of each person's GST exemption is extremely valuable because it also insulates from the GST all future appreciation and accumulated income earned by the money or property which was the subject of the allocation. The following example highlights the need for wise allocation of each person's GST exemption.

Example 29-64: In 1988, Grandfather created a trust with income distributed to Son for life and then distributed to Grandchildren when Son dies. He transferred $1 million into the trust in 1988. Son dies in 2013 and at that time the value of the trust fund is $5,250,000. Grandfather failed to allocate GST exemption to the transfer. The tax imposed when Son dies in 2013 is $1,837,500 (35 percent × $5,250,000). If Grandfather's entire $1 million GST exemption had been allocated to the transfer of the $1 million into the trust on a timely filed gift tax return, no GST tax would have been due when Son died. Tax savings = $1,837,500.

Table 4 tracks the top GST tax rate and the GST exemption amount from 2009 through 2013.

Table 4. GST Tax: Exemptions and Rates

Taxable Events Occurring in:	Top Tax Rate	Exemption
2009	45%	$3.5 million estate
2010	0%	$5 million*
2011	35%	$5 million
2012	35%	$5,120,000
2013	40%	$5,250,000
2014	40%	$5,340,000

* The $5 million exemption applies whether not the estate of a decedent who died in 2010 made the election to apply the EGTRRA zero estate tax rule and carryover basis.

.02 Who Allocates GST Exemption

Only the transferor or his executor has the power to allocate GST exemption to any property [Code Sec. 2631(a); Reg. § 26.2632-1(a)]. This limitation is important because a change in the identity of the transferor will likewise change the persons who can allocate GST exemption. After the transferor has changed, any previous allocation of GST exemption becomes obsolete and only the new transferor or the new transferor's executor can allocate GST exemption to the transfer.

> **Example 29-65:** Husband transfers $1 million to a trust providing that all the net trust income is to be paid to his spouse for her lifetime and upon her death it should pass to his grandchildren. He elects under Code Sec. 2523(f) to treat the transfer as a transfer of qualified terminable interest property and he does not make a reverse QTIP election under Code Sec. 2652(a)(3). When the spouse dies, the trust property is included in her gross estate under Code Sec. 2044 and she becomes the transferor at the time of her death. It is up to her or her spouse to allocate some or all of her GST exemption to the trust. If the husband had previously allocated GST exemption to this trust, the benefits of the allocation are now lost.

.03 How the GST Exemption Allocation Is Made

The GST exemption is cumulative over life and at death. If a taxpayer fails to use up all of the GST exemption while still alive, it can be allocated by the executor of the decedent's estate to transfers taking place at the decedent's death. If the GST exemption is not allocated during life or at death, it expires and is unavailable to anyone else.

For generation skipping transfers made by will, the allocation is made by the estate's executor. The GST exemption may be allocated at any time from the date of the transfer and before the date for filing the individual's Federal estate tax return (including any extensions for filing that have been actually granted) [Code Sec. 2632(a)(1); Reg. § 26.2632-1(a)]. If no estate tax return is required to be filed, the GST exemption may be allocated at any time before the date a Federal estate tax return would be due if a return were required to be filed (including any extensions, actually granted).

The applicable fraction for a trust is redetermined whenever an additional exemption is allocated to the trust. The numerator of the redetermined applicable fraction is the sum of the amount of GST exemption currently being allocated to the trust plus the value of the nontax portion of the trust. The denominator of the redetermined applicable fraction is the value of the trust principal at the time of the redetermination. The nontax portion of the trust is determined by multiplying the value of the trust assets at the time of redetermination by the original applicable fraction.

In general, executors are not permitted to make retroactive allocations of increases in the GST tax exemption to previous transfers, including direct skips except in certain situations.

If property is held in trust, the allocation of GST exemption is made to the entire trust rather than to specific trust assets. If a transfer is a direct skip to a trust, the allocation of GST exemption to the transferred property is also treated as an allocation of GST exemption to the trust for purposes of future GSTs with respect to the trust by the same transferor [Reg. § 26.2632-1(a)]. An allocation of GST exemption by an individual or by the executor of the individual's estate is irrevocable [Code Sec. 2631(b)]. However, an allocation by an individual does not become irrevocable until after the due date (including any extensions for filing that have been actually granted) of the Form 709, *United States Gift (and Generation-Skipping Transfer) Tax Return* [Reg. § 26.2632-1(a)]. As a result, an allocation on a timely filed Form 709 may be amended if the amended allocation is also timely and identifies the transfer and nature and extent of the modification [Reg. 26. 2632-1(b)(2)(iii), Ex. 1].

Allocation of GST Exemption Made on Form 709

An allocation of GST exemption to property transferred during the transferor's lifetime, other than in a direct skip, is made on Form 709 [Reg. § 26.2632-1(b)(2)]. The allocation must clearly identify the trust to which the allocation is being made, the amount of GST exemption allocated to it, and if the allocation is late or if an inclusion ratio greater than zero is claimed, the value of the trust assets at the effective date of the allocation [Reg. § 26.2632-1(b)(2)].

Effective Date of Allocation of GST Exemption

An allocation of GST exemption is effective when the gift tax return (Form 709) is filed. A gift tax return (Form 709) is treated as filed on the date it is mailed for determining when a late allocation of the GST exemption is effective [Reg. § 26.2632-1(b)(2)(ii)].

Allocations After the Transferor's Death

After someone dies, his or her unused GST exemption is automatically allocated on the due date for filing the estate tax return (Form 706) to the extent not otherwise allocated by the executor on or before that date. The automatic allocation occurs whether or not a return is actually required to be filed [Reg. § 26.2632-1(d)(2)]. An allocation of GST exemption with respect to property included in the gross estate of a decedent is effective as of the date of death. A timely allocation of GST exemption by an executor for a lifetime transfer of property that is not included in the transferor's gross estate is made on a Form 709. A late allocation of GST exemption by an executor, with respect to a lifetime transfer of property, is made on Form 706 or Form 706NA and is effective as of the date the allocation is filed. An allocation of GST exemption to a trust is effective if the notice of allocation clearly identifies the trust and the amount of the decedent's GST exemption allocated to the trust [Reg. § 26.2632-1(d)(1)].

.04 Relief from Late GST Tax Allocation Elections

The IRS is authorized to grant extensions of time to make the election to allocate GST tax exemption and to grant exceptions to the time requirement [Code Sec. 2642(g)(1)]. This provision has been made permanent effective for estates of decedents dying, gifts made, or GSTs made after December 31, 2012. If relief from a late election is granted, then the value on the date of transfer to trust would be used for determining GST transfer tax exemption allocation. In determining whether to grant relief for late elections, the IRS should consider all relevant circumstances, including evidence of intent contained in the trust instrument or instrument of transfer.

Extension of Time To Make Allocation of GST Exemptions

In proposed regulations the IRS has identified the standards that will apply in determining whether to grant a transferor or a transferor's estate an extension of time under Code Sec. 2642(g)(1) to take any of the following actions:

1. Allocate GST exemption to a transfer;
2. Elect under Code Sec. 2632(b)(3) not to have the deemed allocation of GST exemption apply to a direct skip;
3. Elect under Code Sec. 2632(c)(5)(A)(i) not to have the deemed allocation of GST exemption apply to an indirect skip or transfers made to a particular trust; and
4. Elect under Code Sec. 2632(C)(5)(A)(ii) to treat any trust as a GST trust [Prop. Reg. § 26.2642-7(a)].

When Allocation is Effective

- If an extension of time to allocate GST exemption is granted, the allocation of GST exemption will be considered effective as of the date of the transfer, and the value of the property will determine the amount of GST exemption to be allocated
- If an extension of time to elect out of the automatic allocation of GST exemption is granted, the election will be considered effective as of the date of the transfer.
- If an extension of time to elect to treat any trust as a GST trust is granted, the election will be considered effective as of the date of the first (or each) transfer covered by that election [Prop. Reg. § 26.2642-7(b)].

The amount of GST exemption that may be allocated to a transfer pursuant to an extension is limited to the amount of the transferor's unused GST exemption as of the date of the transfer. Thus, if the amount of GST exemption has increased since the date of the transfer, no portion of the increased amount may be applied by reason of the grant of relief to a transfer taking place in an earlier year and prior to the effective date of that increase [Prop. Reg. § 26.2642-7(c)].

How to request relief. The transferor or the transferor's executor requesting relief needs to file a private letter ruling request following the procedures set forth in the Proposed Regulations and meeting the circumstances described therein. These circumstances include situations in which the transferor intended to allocate GST exemption or make an election and the failure to allocate or elect was inadvertent.

Basis for relief. Requests for relief under Code Sec. 2642(g)(1) will be granted when the taxpayer provides evidence to establish to the satisfaction of the IRS that the taxpayer acted reasonably and in good faith, and that the grant of relief will not prejudice the Government's interests [Prop. Reg. § 1.26.2642-7(d)(1)].

Reasonableness and good faith. The following nonexclusive list of factors will be used to determine whether a transferor or the executor of a transferor's estate acted reasonably and in good faith:

1. The intent of the transferor or the executor of the transferor's estate to timely allocate GST exemption or to timely make an election as evidenced in the trust instrument, instrument of transfer, or contemporaneous documents, such as Federal gift or estate tax returns or correspondence;
2. The occurrence of intervening events beyond the control of the transferor, or of the executor of the transferor's estate that caused the failure to allocate GST exemption to a transfer or the failure to elect;
3. The lack of awareness by the transferor or the executor of the transferor's estate of the need to allocate GST exemption to a transfer after exercising reasonable diligence, taking into account the experience of the transferor or the executor of the transferor's estate and the complexity of the GST issue;
4. Evidence of consistency by the transferor in allocating (or not allocating) the transferor's GST exemption, although evidence of consistency may be less relevant if there is evidence of a change of circumstances or change of trust beneficiaries that would otherwise support a deviation from prior GST tax exemption allocation practices; and
5. Reasonable reliance by the transferor or the executor of the transferor's estate on the advice of a qualified tax professional retained or employed by either (or both) of them, and the failure of the transferor or executor, in reliance on or consistent with that advice, to allocate GST exemption to the transfer or to make an election [Prop. Reg. § 26.2642-7(d)(2)].

Prejudice to government interests. For purposes of determining whether a transferor or transferor's estate is entitled to an extension of time to make allocations of GST exemption under Code Sec. 2642(g)(1), the following nonexclusive list of factors will be used to determine whether the interests of the government would be prejudiced:

1. The grant of requested relief would permit the use of hindsight to produce an economic advantage or other benefit that either would not have been available if the allocation or election had been timely made, or that results from the selection of one out of a number of alternatives (other than whether or not to make an allocation or election) that were available at the time the allocation or election could have been made timely;
2. If the transferor or the executor of the transferor's estate delayed the filing of the request for relief with the intent to deprive the IRS of sufficient time (by reason of the expiration or the impending expiration of the applicable statute of limitations or otherwise) to challenge the claimed identity of the transferor, the value of the transferred property that is the subject of the requested relief, or any other aspect of the transfer that is relevant for transfer tax purposes; and
3. A determination by the IRS that, in the event of a grant of relief, it would be unreasonably disruptive or difficult to adjust the GST tax consequences of a taxable termination or a taxable distribution that occurred between the time for making a timely allocation of GST exemption or a timely election and the time at which the request for relief was filed. [Prop. Reg. § 26.2642-7(d)(3)].

Situations where standard of reasonableness, good faith, and lack of prejudice to government not met. The IRS will not grant an extension when the standard of reasonableness, good faith and lack of prejudice to the interests of the government is not met. This standard is not met in the following situations:

1. The transferor or the executor of the transferor's estate made an allocation of GST exemption or an election under Code Sec. 2632(b)(3) or (c)(5), on a timely filed federal gift or estate tax return, and the relief requested would decrease or revoke that allocation or election;
2. The transferor or the transferor's executor delayed in requesting relief in order to preclude the IRS, as a practical matter, from challenging the identity of the transferor, the value of the transferred interest on the federal estate or gift tax return, or any other aspect of the transaction that is relevant for federal estate or gift tax purposes;
3. The action or inaction that is the subject of the request for relief reflected or implemented the decision with regard to the allocation of GST exemption or an election that was made by the transferor or executor of the transferor's estate who had been accurately informed in all material respects by a qualified tax professional retained or employed by either (or both) of them; or
4. The IRS determines that the transferor's request is an attempt to benefit from hindsight [Prop. Reg. § 26.2642-7(e)].

Period of limitations. A request for relief does not reopen, suspend or extend the period of limitations on assessment of any estate, gift, or GST tax under Code 6501. Thus, if the IRS requests that the transferor or the transferor's executor consent to an extension of the period of limitation on assessment or collection of gift and GST taxes for the transfers that are the subject of the request relief, the transferor may refuse to extend the period of limitations or limit the extension to particular issues or to a particular period of time [Prop. Reg. § 26.2642-7(f)].

.05 Automatic Allocation of GST Exemption for Direct Skip

If a direct skip occurs during your lifetime, any of your unused GST exemption will automatically be allocated to the transferred property (but not in excess of the fair market value of the property on the date of the transfer) [Reg. § 26.2632-1(b)]. You may prevent the automatic allocation of GST exemption by describing on a timely filed Form 709 the transfer and the extent to which the automatic allocation should not apply. In addition, a timely filed Form 709 accompanied by payment of the GST tax (as shown on the return with respect to the direct skip) is sufficient to prevent an automatic allocation of GST exemption with respect to the transferred property [Reg. § 26.2632-1(b)].

> **Example 29-66:** Tom transfers $50,000 to a trust in a direct skip. Tom does not file a timely gift tax return electing out of the automatic allocation. Tom and his spouse, Sally, file an initial gift tax return on which they consent to have the gift treated as if one half had been made by each. As a result of the election, which is retroactive to the date of Tom's transfer, Tom and Sally are each treated as the transferor of one half of the property transferred in the direct skip. Thus, $25,000 of Tom's unused GST exemption and $25,000 of Sally's unused GST exemption is automatically allocated to the trust. Both allocations are effective on and after the date that Tom made the transfer [Reg. § 26.2632-1(b)(2)(iii), Ex. 5].

.06 Automatic Allocation of GST Exemption for Indirect Skip

If any individual makes an indirect skip during his or her lifetime, any unused portion of such individual's GST exemption will be automatically allocated to the property transferred to the extent necessary to make the inclusion ratio for such property zero. If the amount of the indirect skip exceeds such unused portion, the entire unused portion will be allocated to the property transferred [Code Sec. 2632(c)(1)]. The unused portion of an individual's GST tax exemption is the portion of the exemption that has not previously been: (1) allocated by such individual; (2) treated as allocated under Code Sec. 2632(b) with respect to a direct skip occurring during or before the calendar year in which the indirect skip is made; or (3) treated as allocated under Code Sec. 2632(c)(1) with respect to a prior indirect skip [Code Sec. 2632(b)(2)]. This rule is similar to one that automatically allocates GST exemption to direct skips to GST trusts.

Those that do not want the automatic allocation to apply have the opportunity to elect out. Under Reg. § 26.2632-1(b)(2), a transferor who wishes to elect out of the automatic allocation rules for indirect skips would have the options of: (1) electing out for the specific transfer to the GST trust, (2) making a single election with regard to the trust that applies to the current transfer and all subsequent transfers made to the trust by that transferor, (3) electing out with respect to only certain designated future transfers to a trust, or (4) electing out with respect to all future transfers made by the transferor to any trust, whether or not the trust exists at the time of the election out.

Reg. § 26.2632-1(b)(2)(iii)(4) provides that the transferor may elect out with respect to future transfers although the transferor has not made a current-year transfer and is not otherwise obligated to file a federal gift tax return. In addition, a citation to the specific regulation section that authorizes an election is not required on the statement to elect out of the automatic GST allocation or to treat a trust as a GST trust.

The regulations clarify that an election out of the automatic allocation rules for future years is limited to automatic allocations relating to indirect skips made during the transferor's life and has no effect on the automatic allocation rules that apply after the transferor's death [Reg. § 26.2632-1(b)(2)(iii)(D)]. Moreover, an automatic allocation with respect to an indirect skip is effective as of the date of the transfer and is irrevocable on the due date for filing the federal gift tax return for the calendar year in which the transfer is made, regardless of whether a gift tax return is filed. An affirmative partial allocation of GST exemption will be treated as an election out of the automatic allocation rules with respect to the balance of that specific transfer. At any time before the due date of the gift tax return for the calendar year in which an estate tax inclusion period (ETIP) closes, a transferor may elect out of the automatic allocation rules for indirect or direct skips subject to an ETIP [Reg. § 26.2632-1(c)(1)(i)].

.07 Retroactive Allocation of Unused GST Exemption

An individual may allocate unused GST tax exemption to any previous transfer(s) made to a trust, on a chronological basis [Code Sec. 2632(d)]. This rule is designed to protect taxpayers when there is an "unnatural order of death" (such as when the second generation predeceases the first generation transferor) by allowing a transferor to allocate GST tax exemption retroactively to the date of the respective transfer to the trust.

Availability of Retroactive Allocation

An individual may make a retroactive allocation of GST tax exemption if:

1. A non-skip person has an interest or a future interest in a trust to which any transfer has been made;
2. Such person is a lineal descendant of a grandparent of the transferor or of a grandparent of the transferor's spouse or former spouse and such person is assigned to a generation below the generation assignment of the transferor; and
3. Such person predeceases the transferor [Code Sec. 2632(d)(1)].

Future interest. A person has a "future interest" in a trust if the trust permits income or corpus to be paid to such person on a future date or dates [Code Sec. 2632(d)(3)].

Retroactive allocation made in calendar year within which non-skip person's death occurs. If a transferor's retroactive allocation is made on a gift tax return (Form 709) that is filed on or before the date prescribed for gifts made within the calendar year within which the non-skip person's death occurred, then:

1. The value of such transfer(s) is determined as if such allocation had been made on a timely filed gift tax return (Form 709) for each calendar year within which each transfer was made;
2. Such allocation is effective immediately before such death; and
3. The amount of the transferor's unused GST tax exemption that is available for allocation is determined immediately before such death [Code Sec. 2632(d)(2)].

Example 29-67: Father created an irrevocable trust for the primary benefit of Son, who was age 21. The trust instrument provided that (1) the trustee has discretion to distribute trust income to Son during his lifetime and (2) one-third of the trust corpus is to be distributed to Son at age 27, one-half of the remaining corpus at age 30, and the remainder of the corpus at age 35 (which will terminate the trust). If Son dies before reaching age 35, the corpus is to be distributed in equal shares to Son's children. Father made a transfer to the trust but did not allocate any of his GST tax exemption to the transfers on the gift tax returns reporting the transfers. Before reaching age 27, Son died, thus resulting in a taxable termination for GST tax purposes. Father may retroactively allocate unused GST tax exemption to the prior transfer to the trust and thereby exempt the trust property transferred to Son's children from the application of the GST tax.

.08 Automatic Allocation After Death

After someone dies, his or her unused GST exemption is automatically allocated on the due date for filing the Form 706 or 706NA to the extent not otherwise allocated by the decedent's executor on or before that date. The automatic allocation occurs whether or not a return is actually required to be filed. Unused GST exemption is allocated pro rata on the basis of the value of the property as finally determined for estate tax purposes in the following order:

1. To direct skips treated as occurring at the transferor's death; and then
2. To trusts with respect to which a taxable termination may occur or from which a taxable distribution may be made [Reg. § 26.2632-1(d)(2)].

To prevent your executor from wasting your GST exemption after your death, the regulations provide that no automatic allocation of GST exemption will be made in the following circumstances:

1. To a trust that will have a new transferor with respect to the entire trust [Reg. § 26.2642-1(d)(2)]. The new transferor or his or her executor would be the only people able to allocate GST exemption to that trust;
2. To a trust if, during the nine month period ending immediately after the death of the transferor, no GST has occurred and at the end of the nine month period no future GST can occur [Reg. § 26.2642-1(d)(2)].

.09 Electing Out of GST Exemption Allocation

The IRS has provided taxpayers with procedures needed to make the Code Sec. 2632(c)(5)(A)(i) election not to have the automatic Code Sec. 2632(c)(1) GST exemption allocation of unused GST tax exemption apply for certain transfers to a GST trust, and the Code Sec. 2632(c)(5)(A) election to treat a trust as a GST trust Reg. § 26.2632-1].

A transferor who wishes to elect out of the automatic allocation rules would have the option of: (1) making the Code Sec. 2632(c)(5)(A)(i) election not to have the Code Sec. 2632(c)(1) deemed allocation of unused GST tax exemption for certain transfers to a GST trust; (2) making a single election that applies to the current transfer and all subsequent transfers made to the trust by that transferor; (3) electing out with respect to only certain designated future transfers; or (4) electing out with respect to all future transfers made by the transferor to any trust, whether or not the trust exists at the time of the election out [Reg. § 26.2632-1(b)(2)].

A transferor may elect out of future transfers although the transferor has not made a current-year transfer and is not otherwise obligated to file a federal gift tax return. A citation to the specific regulation section authorizing an election is not required on the statement to elect out of the automatic GST allocation or to treat a trust as a GST trust [Reg. § 26.2632-1(b)(2)(iii)(4)].

An election out of the automatic allocation rules for future years is limited to the automatic allocation rules under Code Sec. 2632(c), relating to indirect skips made during the transferor's life, and has no effect on the automatic allocation rules under Code Sec. 2632(e), which apply after the transferor's death [Reg. § 26.2632-1(b)(5)(D)].

Moreover, an automatic allocation with respect to an indirect skip is effective as of the date of the transfer and is irrevocable on the due date for filing the federal gift tax return for the calendar year in which the transfer is made, regardless of whether a gift tax return is filed. An affirmative partial allocation of GST exemption will be treated as an election out of the automatic allocation rules with respect to the balance of that specific transfer. At any time before the due date of the gift tax return for the calendar year in which an estate tax inclusion period (ETIP) closes, a transferor may elect out of the automatic allocation rules for indirect or direct skips subject to an ETIP [Reg. § 26.2632-1(b)(2)(D)].

Example 29-68: On December 1, 2013, T transfers $100,000 to an irrevocable GST trust. The transfer to the trust is not a direct skip. The date prescribed for filing the gift tax return reporting the taxable gift is April 15, 2014. On February 10, 2014, T files a Form 709 on which T properly elects out of the automatic allocation rules with respect to the transfer and allocates $50,000 of GST exemption to the trust. On April 15th of the same year, T files an additional Form 709 on which T confirms the election out of the automatic allocation rules and allocates $100,000 of GST exemption to the trust in a manner that clearly indicates the intention to modify and supersede the prior allocation with respect to the 2013 transfer. The allocation made on the April 15 return supersedes the prior allocation because it is made on a timely-filed Form 709 that clearly identifies the trust and the nature and extent of the modification of GST exemption allocation. The allocation of $100,000 of GST exemption to the trust is effective as of December 1, 2013. The result would be the same if the amended Form 709 decreased the amount of the GST exemption allocated to the trust [Reg. § 26.2632-1(b)(4)(iii), Ex. 1].

¶29,186 TRANSFERS EXEMPT FROM GST TAX

.01 Exclusion for Annual Code Sec. 2503(b) Gifts

You are entitled to an annual exclusion from gift tax of $14,000 per donee in 2013 (no change in 2014) for gifts of a *present interest* [Code Sec. 2503(b)]. Outright direct skip transfers that qualify as nontaxable annual exclusion gifts are not subject to GST tax. In addition, if you make direct skip transfers to a *qualified trust* and the transfer qualifies as a nontaxable annual exclusion gift because of the annual gift tax exclusion under Code Sec. 2503(b), the trust will have an inclusion ratio of zero and will thus not be subject to GST tax [Code Sec. 2642(c)].

The gift tax annual per donee exclusion operates by permitting the first $14,000 in 2013 (no change in 2014) in value of property or interest in property, other than future interests, that you transfer to any number of individuals to be excluded from current taxable gifts for federal gift tax purposes [Code Sec. 2503(b)]. There is no limit on the number of donees for whom an annual exclusion may be taken or the number of years in which it may be taken. Thus, as an estate planning tool, you can make an unlimited number of annual exclusion gifts each year without owing any gift tax. The per donee exclusion renews annually and there is no carryover of any unused amount.

The gift tax annual exclusion is only available for present, not future interests in property. The unrestricted right to the immediate use, possession, or enjoyment of property or income from property constitutes a present interest in property [Reg. § 25.2503-3(b)]. A future interest is a right to use, possess, or enjoy money or property that will not commence until a future date or time. As result gifts in trust and gifts of remainder interests will not qualify for the annual exclusion.

Qualified Trust Defined for GST Annual Exclusion Purposes

A direct skip in trust, which is a nontaxable gift because of the annual gift tax exclusion, will be subject to GST tax as a taxable direct skip, unless the trust is a qualified trust. A trust will be qualified for these purposes if it complies with the following requirements:

1. During the life of the skip person, the trust must be for the current benefit of the skip person only. This means that no portion of the corpus or income of the trust may be distributed to (or for the benefit of) any person other than the skip person; and

2. If the trust does not terminate before the skip person dies, the assets of the trust will be includable in the skip person's gross estate [Code Sec. 2642(c)(2); Reg. § 26.2642-1(c)(3)].

Example 29-69: *Gift entirely nontaxable.* On December 31, 2013, Grandfather transfers $14,000 to an irrevocable trust for the benefit of Grandson, who possessed a right to withdraw any contribution to the trust such that the entire transfer qualifies for the annual gift tax exclusion under Code Sec. 2503(b). Under the terms of the trust, the income is to be paid to Grandson for 10 years or until his prior death. Upon the expiration of Grandson's income interest, the trust principal is payable to Grandson or Grandson's estate. The transfer to the trust is a direct skip. Grandfather made no prior gifts to or for the benefit of Grandson during 2013. The entire $14,000 transfer is a nontaxable transfer. For purposes of computing the tax on the direct skip, the denominator of the applicable fraction is zero, and thus, the inclusion ratio is zero [Reg. § 26.2642-1(d), Ex. 2].

If the trust is partly taxable and partly nontaxable, it is divided into two parts as illustrated in the examples below. The nontaxable part has an inclusion ratio of zero and the taxable part has an inclusion ratio subject to the amount of GST exemption allocated to the transfer.

Example 29-70: *Gift nontaxable in part-GST tax exemption allocated.* Grandfather transfers $20,000 to an irrevocable trust for the benefit of Grandchild. Under the terms of the trust, the income to be paid to Grandchild for 10 years or until his prior death. Upon the expiration of Grandchild's income interest, the trust principal is payable to him or to his estate. Further, Grandchild has the right to withdraw $14,000 of any contribution to the trust such that $14,000 of the transfer qualifies for the annual exclusion under Code Sec. 2503(b). Solely for purposes of computing the tax on the direct skip, Grandfather's transfer is divided into two portions. One portion is equal to the amount of the nontaxable transfer ($14,000) and has a zero inclusion ratio; the other portion is $6,000 ($20,000 – $14,000). With respect to the $6,000 portion, the denominator of the applicable fraction is $6,000. Assuming that Grandfather has sufficient GST tax exemption available, the numerator of the applicable fraction is $6,000 (unless Grandfather elects to have the automatic allocation provisions not apply). Thus, assuming Grandfather does not elect to have the automatic allocation not apply, the applicable fraction is one ($6,000/$6,000 = 1) and the inclusion ratio is zero (1 – 1 = 0) [Reg. § 26.2642-1(d), Ex. 3].

Gift Splitting

If a spouse does not have sufficient funds to take advantage of his or her annual exclusion gift tax exclusion, his or her exclusion need not be wasted. The Code allows two spouses to treat a gift to a third person made by either spouse as a gift made one half by each spouse [Code Sec. 2652(a)(2)]. In other words, when one spouse makes a gift to a third party from his or her interest in property, the Code permits the nondonor spouse to join in the gift as if the nondonor spouse had made one-half of the gift [Code Sec. 2513]. Thus, if you transferred $28,000 to your son in 2013 and your spouse consents to gift splitting, the transfer is treated as made $14,000 by you and $14,000 by your spouse and no gift tax is owed because the annual per donee exclusion allowable to each spouse applies to the gift.

.02 Exclusion for Payment of Medical and Tuition Expenses

Direct skips made directly to schools or hospitals to provide for a skip person's tuition or medical expenses are excluded from GST tax [Code Sec. 2642(c)]. The good news is that, unlike the annual gift tax exclusion, no dollar limit exists on qualified educational or medical expense transfers.

Education Expense Exclusion

The exclusion for educational expenses is limited to tuition for any educational institution, including nursery, elementary and secondary schools. An educational organization is an organization with a regular faculty and curriculum and a regularly enrolled body of students in attendance at the place where the educational activities are carried on [Code Sec. 170(b)(1)(A)(ii)]. The educational organization may be domestic or foreign. The exclusion does not cover books, rent, board and other living expenses. The individual may be a full-time or part-student [Reg. § 25.2503-6(b)(2)]. The payments must be made directly to the educational institution. Payments to the donee who uses them (or is reimbursed) for education expense will fail to qualify for the exclusion. This restriction is very important. If you give the money directly to your family and tell them to pay the tuition and hospital bills with the money, you will lose the exclusion. It's that simple.

Example 29-71: Grandfather establishes a trust that will pay income and principal in the trustee's discretion to Grandfather's grandchildren. The trustee makes distributions from the trust directly to hospitals and schools to cover bills for medical and tuition, respectively. If Grandfather had paid the hospital and school bills directly, the payments would have qualified under Code Sec. 2503(e) for the annual gift tax exclusion, regardless of amount and would not have been subject to the GST tax. However, because the distributions from the trust are not direct skips, they are subject to the GST tax.

Medical Care Exclusion

Transfers qualifying under the medical expense exclusion [Code Sec. 2503(e)] are limited to medical care as defined under Code Sec. 213(d), more specifically, for the diagnosis, cure, mitigation, treatment, or prevention of disease, or for the purpose of affecting any structure or function of the body. Health care insurance premiums qualify. Amounts must be paid directly to the medical service or care provider and not an intermediary. The exclusion does not apply to amounts that are reimbursed to the donee by insurance [Reg. § 25.2503-6(b)(3)].

NOTE: While the educational or medical exclusion is particularly good for grandparents, other relatives, including parents, aunts, and uncles, can also take advantage of the exclusion. You don t even have to be related to the person for whom the medical or tuition payments are made because the education and medical exclusions exist without regard to the relationship between the donor and the donee.

¶29,187 TRUST SEVERANCE FOR GST PURPOSES

Practitioners are advised not to waste the valuable GST tax exemption on transfers that would not have been subject to GST tax in the first place. For example, it would be a waste of the GST tax exemption to allocate it to assets passing to non-skip persons or on transfers to charities that are not even subject to the GST tax. If a discretionary trust authorizes distributions to skip as well as non-skip persons, it would be wise to sever or split the single trust into two or more separate trusts with different beneficiaries.

If a trust is severed in a qualified severance, the resulting trusts are treated as separate trusts under Code Sec. 2642(a)(3). As a result, the inclusion ratio of each new resulting trust may differ from the inclusion ratio of the original trust. In many cases, a qualified severance of a trust will facilitate the most efficient and effective use of the transferor's GST tax exemption. According to the IRS, it will continue to "encourage" the reporting of each qualified severance to ensure that the GST tax provisions will be properly applied to the trusts. In notifying the IRS of the severance of a trust, the final regulations require that the words "Qualified Severance" appear at the top of Form 706-GS(T), *Generation-Skipping Transfer Tax Return for Terminations*.

A "qualified severance" is the division of a single trust and the creation of two or more trusts if: (1) the single trust is divided on a fractional basis; and (2) the terms of the new trusts, in the aggregate, provide for the same succession of interests of beneficiaries as are provided in the original trust [Code Sec. 2642(a)(3)(B)(i)]. If a trust has an inclusion ratio that is greater than zero and less than one, the trust must be severed in a specified manner that produces one trust that is wholly exempt from GST tax, and one trust that is wholly subject to GST tax [Code Sec. 2642(a)(3)(B)(ii)]. Each of the two new trusts created may be further divided into two or more trusts under Code Sec. 2642(a)(3)(B)(i). A trustee may elect to sever a trust in a qualified severance at any time [Code Sec. 2642(a)(3)(C)].

Because the post-severance resulting trusts are treated as separate trusts for GST tax purposes, certain actions with respect to one resulting trust will generally have no GST tax impact with respect to the other resulting trust(s). For example, GST exemption allocated to one resulting trust will not impact on the inclusion ratio of the other resulting trust(s); a GST tax election made with respect to one resulting trust will not apply to the other resulting trust(s); the occurrence of a taxable distribution or termination with regard to a particular resulting trust will not have any GST tax impact on any other trust resulting from that severance [Reg. § 26.2642-6(a)].

.01 Qualified Severance Requirements

A qualified severance must satisfy the following requirements provided in Reg. § 26.2642-6(d):

1. The single trust must be severed pursuant to the terms of the governing instrument, or pursuant to applicable local law.
2. The severance must be effective under local law.
3. The date of severance must be either the date selected by the trustee when the trust assets are to be valued in order to determine the funding of the resulting trusts, or the court-imposed date of funding in the case of an order of the local court with jurisdiction over the trust ordering the trustee to fund the resulting trusts on or as of a specific date. For a date to satisfy the definition in the preceding sentence, however, the funding must be commenced immediately upon, and funding must occur within a reasonable time (but in no event more than 90 days) after, the selected valuation date.
4. The single trust (original trust) must be severed on a fractional basis, so that each new trust (resulting trust) is funded with a percentage of the original trust, and the sum of those percentages is one hundred percent. For this purpose, the percentage may be determined by means of a formula (for example, that fraction of the trust the numerator of which is equal to the transferor's unused GST tax exemption, and the denominator of which is the fair market value of the original trust's assets on the date of severance).
5. The terms of the resulting trusts must provide, in the aggregate, for the same succession of interests of beneficiaries as are provided in the original trust. This requirement is satisfied if the beneficiaries of the separate resulting trusts and the interests of the beneficiaries with respect to the separate trusts, when the separate

trusts are viewed collectively, are the same as the beneficiaries and their respective beneficial interests with respect to the original trust before severance.

6. In the case of a qualified severance of a trust with an inclusion ratio of either one or zero, each trust resulting from the severance will have an inclusion ratio equal to the inclusion ratio of the original trust.
7. In the case of a qualified severance occurring after GST tax exemption has been allocated to the trust, if the trust has an inclusion ratio that is greater than zero and less than one, then the trust must be severed initially into two trusts. One resulting trust must receive that fractional share of the total value of the original trust as of the date of severance that is equal to the applicable fraction used to determine the inclusion ratio of the original trust immediately before the severance. The other resulting trust must receive that fractional share of the total value of the original trust as of the date of severance that is equal to the excess of one over the fractional share described in the preceding sentence. The trust receiving the fractional share equal to the applicable fraction shall have an inclusion ratio of zero, and the other trust shall have an inclusion ratio of one. If the applicable fraction with respect to the original trust is .50, then, with respect to the two equal trusts resulting from the severance, the trustee may designate which of the resulting trusts will have an inclusion ratio of zero and which will have an inclusion ratio of one. Each separate trust resulting from the severance then may be further divided in accordance with the rules of this section.

.02 How to Report a Qualified Severance

A qualified severance is reported by filing Form 706-GS(T), *Generation-Skipping Transfer Tax Return for Terminations.* Unless otherwise provided in the applicable form or instructions, the IRS requests that the filer write "Qualified Severance" at the top of the form and attach a Notice of Qualified Severance (Notice). The return and attached Notice should be filed by April 15th of the year immediately following the year during which the severance occurred or by the last day of the period covered by an extension of time, if an extension of time is granted, to file such form [Reg. § 26.2642-6(e)].

.03 When to Make a Qualified Severance

A qualified severance of a trust may occur at any time prior to the termination of the trust. Thus, provided that the separate resulting trusts continue in existence after the severance, a qualified severance may occur either before or after:

1. GST tax exemption has been allocated to the trust,
2. A taxable event has occurred with respect to the trust, or
3. An addition has been made to the trust.

Because a qualified severance is effective as of the date of severance, a qualified severance has no effect on a taxable termination or a taxable distribution that occurred prior to the date of severance. A qualified severance shall be deemed to occur before a taxable termination or a taxable distribution that occurs by reason of the qualified severance [Reg. § 26.2642-6(f)].

Example 29-72: *Severance based on actuarial value of beneficial interests.* T establishes Trust, an irrevocable trust providing that income is to be paid to T's child

C during C's lifetime. Upon C's death, Trust is to terminate and the assets of Trust are to be paid to GC, C's child, if living, or, if GC is not then living, to GC's estate. T properly elects, under Code Sec. 2632(c)(5), to not have the automatic allocation rules contained in Code Sec. 2632(c) apply with respect to T's transfers to Trust, and T does not otherwise allocate GST tax exemption with respect to Trust. Thus, Trust has an inclusion ratio of one. The trustee of Trust, pursuant to applicable state law, divides Trust into two separate trusts, Trust 1 for the benefit of C (and on C's death to C's estate), and Trust 2 for the benefit of GC (and on GC's death to GC's estate). The document severing Trust directs that Trust 1 is to be funded with an amount equal to the actuarial value of C's interest in Trust prior to the severance, determined under Code Sec. 7520. Similarly, Trust 2 is to be funded with an amount equal to the actuarial value of GC's interest in Trust prior to the severance, determined under Code Sec. 7520. Trust 1 and Trust 2 do not provide for the same succession of interests as provided under the terms of the original trust. Therefore, the severance is not a qualified severance [Reg. § 26.2642-6(j), Ex. 3].

.04 Consequence of Qualified Severance

If a trust is divided in a qualified severance into two or more trusts, the separate trusts resulting from the severance will be treated as separate trusts for GST tax purposes and the inclusion ratio of each new resulting trust may differ from the inclusion ratio of the original trust [Code Sec. 2642(a)(3)]. Because the post-severance resulting trusts are treated as separate trusts for GST tax purposes, certain actions with respect to one resulting trust will generally have no GST tax impact with respect to the other resulting trust(s). For example, GST exemption allocated to one resulting trust will not impact on the inclusion ratio of the other resulting trust(s); a GST tax election made with respect to one resulting trust will not apply to the other resulting trust(s); the occurrence of a taxable distribution or termination with regard to a particular resulting trust will not have any GST tax impact on any other trust resulting from that severance [Reg. § 26.2642-6(a)].

¶29,190 COMPUTATION AND FILING REQUIREMENTS

.01 In General

Executors determine the amount of GST tax multiplying the "taxable amount" by the "applicable rate" [Code Sec. 2602]. The taxable amount and who is responsible for paying the tax will change depending on whether the transfer is a direct skip, taxable distribution, or taxable termination [Code Sec. 2603].

Direct Skips

The taxable amount in the case of a direct skip will be the value of the property received by the transferee [Code Sec. 2623]. The donor or the transferor will be liable for the tax unless the direct skip is made from a trust, in which case the trustee will be liable for the tax [Code Sec. 2603(a)(2), (3)].

The direct skip is the most economical of the GST transfers because, unlike taxable distributions and taxable terminations, direct skips do not include the GST tax in their tax base. The tax due on a direct skip is imposed on a tax-exclusive basis. This means that the tax is imposed only on the amount actually received. The GST tax is not part of the tax base. When the transferor pays the GST tax, the GST tax is treated as an additional gift for gift tax purposes [Code Sec. 2515].

Example 29-73: Grandfather gives $2 million to Grandson in a transfer that constitutes a direct skip. Grandfather owes GST tax in the amount of $800,000 on the transfer (40 percent × $2 million in 2013) because no GST exemption was allocated to the gift. Grandfather's payment of GST tax on the transfer is treated as an additional gift for gift tax purposes. As a result, the amount of his gift to Grandson equals $2,800,000 ($800,000 and $2 million). Grandfather must pay the gift tax on that amount.

A federal gift tax return (Form 709) must be filed for any direct skip that occurs during the lifetime of the transferor [Reg. § 26.2662-1(b)(3)(i)]. It is due on April 15 of the year following the calendar year in which the gift is made (plus extensions). The transferor in the case of an inter vivos direct skip is personally liable for the tax and must file the return [Reg. § 26.2662-1(c)(1)(iii)]. A federal estate tax return (Form 706) or Form 706NA must be filed by the executor for any direct skip that occurs when the decedent dies [Reg. § 26.2662-1(b)(3)(ii)]. It is due nine months after the date of the decedent's death (plus extensions). The trustee in the case of a direct skip from an explicit trust or trust arrangement, or with respect to property that continues to be held in trust, is personally liable for the GST tax and must file the estate tax return [Reg. § 26.2662-1(c)(1)(iv)].

Taxable Terminations

The taxable amount in the case of a taxable termination will be the value of all property involved in the taxable termination, reduced by any deductions for expenses, indebtedness and taxes [Code Sec. 2622]. Form 706GS(T) must be filed for any taxable termination [Reg. § 26.2662-(1)(b)2]. In a taxable termination, the trustee is personally liable for the GST tax and must file the return [Reg. § 26.2662-1(c)(ii)].

The trustee of the trust which produced the taxable termination will be liable for the tax [Code Sec. 2603(a)(2)]. The GST tax on a taxable termination is determined by multiplying the taxable amount times the applicable rate [Code Sec. 2602]. But the taxable amount is computed differently from the way in which you determine the taxable amount on a direct skip. Taxable terminations are taxed on a tax-inclusive basis. This means that you compute the GST tax by including in the tax base the property used to pay the tax. This makes the taxable termination more expensive than the direct skip.

Taxable Distributions

The taxable amount in the case of a taxable distribution will be the value of the property received by the transferee reduced by any expenses incurred by the transferee in connection with the determination, collection, or refund of the GST tax [Code Sec. 2621]. The recipient of the wealth or the transferee will be liable for the tax [Code Sec.

2603(a)(1)]. If the trustee pays the GST tax (including penalties and interest) from the distributing trust, the payment of the tax will constitute an additional taxable distribution and is treated as having been made on the last day of the calendar year in which the original taxable distribution was made [Code Sec. 2621(b); Reg. § 26.2612-1(c)].

Like the taxable termination, the GST tax is imposed on a tax-inclusive basis. This means that the taxable amount includes the GST tax. As a result you compute the GST tax by including in the tax base the property used to pay the tax.

> **Example 29-74:** Grandfather established a trust which paid income and principal in the trustee's discretion to his child and then his grandson for 20 years and then to terminate in a final distribution to the grandson. The grandfather allocated no GST exemption to the transfer of $500,000 into the trust. In 2013, the trustee distributes $2 million to the grandson in a taxable distribution. The grandson is liable for the $800,000 GST tax (40 percent × $2 million) on the taxable distribution and he receives only $1,200,000 of the $2 million left for him by his grandfather.

Form 706GS(D) Must Be Filed for Any Taxable Distribution

The trust involved in a taxable distribution must file Form 706GS(D-1), *Notification of Distribution From a Generation-Skipping Trust*, which must be sent to each person receiving a distribution from the trust [Reg. § 26.2662-1(b)(1)]. In a taxable distribution, the transferee is personally liable for the GST tax and must file the return, unless the governing instrument specifically directs otherwise [Reg. § 26.2662-1(c)(1)(i)].

PROCEDURE ON RETURNS

¶29,195 FILING REQUIREMENTS

.01 Estate Tax Returns

An estate tax return, Form 706, *United States Estate (and Generation-Skipping Transfer) Tax Return*, must be filed for a decedent who was a U.S. citizen or resident if the amount of the decedent's gross estate exceeds the applicable exclusion amount, reduced by the amount of the decedent's adjusted taxable gifts [Code Sec. 6018(a)(1). An estate tax return must be filed for the estate of a decedent who was a nonresident alien if the portion of the decedent's gross estate situated in the United States exceeds $60,000, reduced by the amount of the decedent's adjusted taxable gifts [Code Sec. 6018(a)(2)]. The return must be filed within nine months after the date of death. Reg. § 20.6081-1(a) provides that the executor of a decedent's estate will be allowed an automatic 6-month extension of time to file Form 706 beyond the regular due date. The application for the automatic extension must be submitted on Form 4768, ***Application for Extension of Time To File a Return and/or Pay U.S. Estate (and Generation-Skipping Transfer) Taxes***, and filed with the IRS on or before the regular due date for filing the Form 706 [Reg. § 20.6081-1(b)]. It must include an estimate of the full amount of estate and generation-skipping transfer tax due [Reg. § 20.6081-1(b)(1)]. An automatic extension of time for filing the return does not extend the time for paying the tax. If an extension of time to file a return is obtained, but no extension of time for payment of the tax is granted, interest will be due on the tax not paid by the due date and the estate will be subject to all applicable late payment penalties [Reg. § 20.6081-1(e)].

The estate tax return on distributions to a noncitizen surviving spouse from a qualified domestic trust (QDOT) [see ¶ 29,120] is due on April 15 of the year following the calendar year in which the distributions are made Code Sec. 2056A(b)(5)].

.02 Gift Tax Returns—Form 709

You must file a gift tax return on Form 709, *United States Gift (and Generation-Skipping Transfer) Tax Return*, for gifts of present interests exceeding $14,000 in 2013 (no increase in 2014) in value to a donee for the calendar year and for gifts of future interests, regardless of the amount. However, you do not have to file a return for any transfer to your spouse that qualifies for the unlimited marital deduction, or any medical or educational related transfer that is exempt from gift tax.

You need not file a gift tax return for a donor who makes a gift to charity in excess of the annual gift tax exclusion if the entire value of the donated property qualifies for a gift tax charitable deduction [Code Sec. 6019(3)].

You must file the gift tax return on or before April 15 following the close of the calendar year in which you make the gift. If you are on a calendar year and you get an extension to file your income tax return you automatically also get an extension to file the gift tax return. If a donor dies during the calendar year the gift is made, the gift tax return is due when the estate tax return is due [Code Sec. 6075].

Requesting an Extension of Time to File Form 709

There are two methods of extending the time to file the gift tax return. Neither method extends the time to pay the gift or GST taxes. If an extension of time to pay the gift or GST taxes is necessary, the requests must be made separately [Reg. § 25.6161-1].

1. *By extending the time to file income tax return (Form 1040).* Any extension of time granted for filing the taxpayer Federal income tax return will also automatically extend the time to file the taxpayer's gift tax return. Income tax return extensions are made by using Form 4868 [see ¶ 26,070.01] or Form 2350, *Application for Extension of Time to File U.S. Income Tax Return* (for U.S. citizens and resident aliens who expect to qualify for special tax treatment). These forms may only be used to extend the time for filing the gift tax return if they are also being used to request an extension of time to file the taxpayer's income tax return.
2. *By filing Form 8892.* If the taxpayer does not request an extension for his or her income tax return, the taxpayer should use Form 8892, *Application for Automatic Extension of Time to File Form 709 and/or Payment of Gift/Generation-Skipping Transfer Tax*, to request an automatic 6-month extension of time to file the gift tax return. This form must be used instead of writing a letter to the Cincinnati Service Center to request an extension of time to file Form 709. In addition to containing an extension request, Form 8892 also serves as a payment voucher for a balance due on federal gift taxes for which the taxpayer has requested a filing extension.

   ▶ **CAUTION:** Even if the taxpayer was granted an extension to file the gift tax return, the taxpayer must still pay the tax due on the original due date.

.03 Split Gifts

If spouses split gifts [¶ 29,020], each spouse must consent to gift splitting on the gift tax return. If only one spouse has made gifts during the year, and the spouse consents to split the gift, the other spouse does not have to file a gift tax return as long as the total value of gifts made to any one person is not more than $28,000 in 2013 and the gift is not of a future interest.

.04 GST Tax Returns

The due date for filing GST tax returns generally coincides with the due dates for gift and estate tax returns [Reg. § 26.2662-1].

¶ 29,200 PAYMENT OF THE TAX

.01 In General

In general, any estate tax that is due must be paid within nine months after the date of the decedent's death unless an extension of time is granted or the estate has elected under Code Sec. 6166 to defer the payment of estate tax as discussed in ¶ 29,205. The executor may elect to pay the estate tax on a reversionary or remainder interest six months after the termination of the precedent interest or interests in the property. A further extension, not exceeding three years, may be granted for reasonable cause [Code Sec. 6163].

.02 Extension of Time to File Estate Tax Return

Use Form 4768, *Application for Extension of Time to File a Return and/or Pay U.S. Estate (and Generation-Skipping Transfer) Taxes,* to apply for an extension of time to file the following forms:

- Form 706, *United States Estates (and Generation-Skipping Transfer) Tax Return;*
- Form 706-A, *United States Additional Estate Tax Return* (used to report recapture of special use valuation);
- Form 706-D, *United States Additional Estate Tax Return under Code Sec. 2057*(used to report recapture of the qualified family-owned business deduction); and
- Form 706-QDT, *United States Estate Tax Return for Qualified Domestic Trusts.*

In addition, executors who are abroad may also request extensions beyond the automatic six-month period [Reg. § 20.6081-1(b)(2)].

The Court of Appeals for the Ninth Circuit held in *R.B. Baccei*[135] that late payment penalties were properly assessed against decedent's estate because the executor estate failed to properly complete Form 4768, requesting a six-month extension of time to pay estate tax.

When asking for an automatic 6-month extension, the taxpayer need not provide an explanation for the request. The executor must include with Form 4768 a check or money order that estimates the full amount of estate and GST tax due [Reg. § 20.6081-1(b)(1)]. An automatic extension of time for filing the return does not extend

[135] *R.B. Baccei,* CA-9, 2011-1 USTC ¶ 60,612, 632 F3d 1140.

the time for paying the tax. If an extension of time to file a return is obtained, but no extension of time for payment of the tax is granted, interest will be due on the tax not paid by the due date and the estate will be subject to all applicable late payment penalties [Reg. § 20.6081-1(e)]. The estate tax return on distributions to a noncitizen surviving spouse from a qualified domestic trust (QDOT) is due on April 15 of the year following the calendar year in which the distributions are made [Code Sec. 2056A(b)(5)]. See ¶ 29,120 for further discussion of QDOTs.

Reg. § 20.6081-1(c) provides that the IRS has the discretion to grant requests for an extension of time with the showing of good cause, even if the request is made after the due date. However, the IRS's decision regarding whether to grant an extension of time to file is subject to judicial review. In *P. Proske Est.*,[136] the district court found that the estate demonstrated good and sufficient cause for an extension and that the IRS had abused its discretion in denying the executor's request to extend the time for filing the estate tax return. The court concluded that there was no indication of bad faith on the part of the estate and no showing of how the IRS's interests would be prejudiced by granting the extension.

¶29,205 ESTATE TAX DEFERRAL

An executor may also elect to pay the estate tax attributable to a decedent's closely held business interest in two or more (but not exceeding 10) equal annual installments starting no later than five years after the regular due date for payment if: (1) a closely held business interest is included in the gross estate of a decedent who was a U.S. citizen or resident at the time of his death; and (2) the value of the business interest exceeds 35 percent of the decedent's adjusted gross estate [Code Sec. 6166]. If the executor takes advantage of the deferral provision, the payment of that portion of the decedent's estate attributable to the estate's interest in one or more closely held businesses may be deferred for up to 14 years with the estate making annual payments of interest only for the first four years and paying the balance in 10 equal annual installments. The deferral period is 14 years rather than 15 years because the due date for the last payment of interest coincides with the due date for the first installment of tax.

.01 Purpose of Deferral

Congress enacted Code Sec. 6166 to permit the deferral of the payment of federal estate tax when it would be necessary to sell the assets used in an on-going business to pay the estate tax at one time. The purpose of the deferral is to prevent a family-owned business from having to sell the business in order to raise the money required to pay the estate tax owed on that business. As a result of the deferral, family members have more time to save up the money from the profits generated by the family business to pay the estate tax. Deferral of tax is only available for the portion of the estate tax attributable to closely held interests in an active trade or business owned by the decedent at the time of death. The amount of estate tax attributable to the closely held business interest is determined by multiplying the tax imposed (minus credits) by a fraction. The numerator of the fraction is the value of the closely

---

[136] *P. Proske Est.*, DC-NJ, 2010-1 USTC ¶ 60,594.

held business interest included in the gross estate and the denominator is the value of the gross estate (reduced by expenses and losses) [Code Sec. 6166(a)(2)].

.02 Requirements

To qualify for the deferral, (1) the decedent must have been a citizen or resident of the United States; (2) the value of the decedent's interest in a closely held business at the time of death must equal at least 35 percent of the value of his or her adjusted gross estate for federal estate tax purposes, and (3) the executor must elect to pay the estate tax attributable to the closely held business interest in two or more (but no more than 10) equal installments [Code Sec. 6166(a)(1)].

.03 Special Rule for Interest in Two or More Closely Held Businesses

If the decedent held interests in two or more closely held businesses at the time of death, the interests are combined and are treated as an interest in one closely held business for purposes of the 35 percent test, if at least 20 percent or more of the total value of each business is included in the decedent's gross estate. Aggregation is available with respect to different types of interests in closely held businesses (e.g., a corporation and a partnership). The interest of the decedent's surviving spouse is treated as owned by the decedent in satisfying the 20-percent requirement if the decedent and the surviving spouse held the interest as community property, joint tenants, tenants by the entirety, or tenants in common [Code Sec. 6166(c)].

.04 Interests in Closely Held Businesses

To qualify for the deferral, the value of the decedent's interest in a closely held business must exceed 35 percent of his or her adjusted gross estate. An interest in a closely held business is defined for these purposes as:

- An interest as a proprietor in a trade or business carried on as a proprietorship;
- An interest as a partner in a partnership carrying on a trade or business if 20 percent or more of the total capital interest was included in the decedent's gross estate or the partnership had 45 or fewer partners effective for the estates of decedents dying after December 31, 2012; or
- Stock in a closely held corporation carrying on a trade or business if 20 percent or more in value of the voting shares of the corporation is included in the decedent's gross estate or the corporation had 45 or fewer shareholders effective for the estates of decedents dying after December 31, 2012 [Code Sec. 6166(b)(1)].

The determination as to whether an interest qualifies as an "interest in a closely held business" must be made immediately before the decedent's death [Code Sec. 6166(b)(2)(A)]. Thus, a decedent must own an interest in a closely held business immediately before death to be eligible for an extension of time for payment under Code Sec. 6166.

An interest in a closely held business includes the following:

- *Stock in qualifying lending and finance business interests.* For purposes of qualifying for an estate tax deferral, an executor may elect to treat any asset used in a "qualifying lending and finance business" as an asset which is used in carrying on a trade or business. A lending and finance business is a qualifying lending and finance business if (1) based on all the facts and circumstances immediately before the date of the decedent's death there was substantial activity with respect to the lending and finance business; or (2) during at least three of the five tax years ending before the date of the decedent's death, the business had at least: (a) one full-time employee, substantially all of whose services were the active management of such business, (b) 10 full-time, nonowner employees substantially all of whose services were directly related to such business, and (c) $5 million in gross receipts from those lending and finance activities [Code Sec. 6166(b)(10)(B)(i)].

The term *qualifying lending and finance business* does not include any interest in an entity, if the stock or debt of the entity or a controlled group of which the entity was a member was readily tradable on an established securities market or secondary market at any time within three years before the date of the decedent's death [Code Sec. 6166(b)(10)(B)(iii)].

.05 Attribution Rules

For purposes of determining whether a business is closely held, the following attribution rules apply:

- In determining the number of shareholders or partners, a stock or partnership interest is treated as owned by one shareholder or partner if it is: (1) community property, or (2) held by spouses as joint tenants, tenants by the entirety, or tenants in common [Code Sec. 6166(b)(2)(B)].

Property owned, directly or indirectly, by or for a corporation, partnership, estate, or trust is treated as owned proportionately by or for its shareholders, partners, or beneficiaries. For purposes of this rule, a person will only be treated as a beneficiary of a trust if the person has a present interest in the trust [Code Sec. 6166(b)(2)(C)].

- All stock and all partnership interests held by the decedent or by any member of his family will be treated as owned by the decedent [Code Sec. 6166(b)(2)(D)]. Members of the decedent's family include his siblings, spouse, ancestors, and lineal descendants [Code Sec. 267(c)(4)].
- For purposes of the 35 percent requirement, the interest in a closely held farm business includes an interest in the residential buildings and related improvements occupied on a regular basis by the owners, lessees, or employees operating or maintaining the farm [Code Sec. 6166(b)(3)].

.06 Holding Company Stock Election

Under a special rule, an executor may elect to treat the portion of any holding company stock as an interest in a closely held business. To qualify for this special treatment, the executor must elect to treat the portion of holding company stock representing direct ownership (or indirect ownership through one or more holding companies) by that company in a business company as business company stock [Code Sec. 6166(b)(8)]. A business company is a corporation carrying on a trade or business. This election applies only if all the shares (parent and subsidiary) involved are not readily tradable on the stock exchange effective for the estates of decedents dying after December 31, 2012 [Code Sec. 6166(b)(8)(B)]. For purposes of the 20-percent voting stock requirement, stock is treated as voting stock to the extent the holding company owns voting stock in the business company.

> **NOTE:** If the executor makes the holding company stock election, neither the five-year deferral of principal payments nor the lower interest rate are available [Code Sec. 6166(b)(8)].

.07 Deferral Unavailable for Passive Assets

The estate tax deferral under Code Sec. 6166 is unavailable for closely held business interests attributable to passive assets held by the decedent [Code Sec. 6166(b)(9)]. As a result, the decedent's ownership of passive investment property such as real estate will not count in determining: (1) the value of the closely held business, and (2) whether the 35-percent requirement is satisfied [Code Sec. 6166(b)(9)].

The term *passive asset* is defined in Code Sec. 6166(b)(9)(B)(i) as any asset other than an asset used in carrying on a trade or business. Thus, the estate tax deferral under Code Sec. 6166 is only available for interests held by the decedent in an active trade or business and the decedent's ownership of passive investment property such as real estate may not constitute ownership of a qualifying interest in a closely held business.

Active Trade or Business Requirement

In order for an interest in a business to qualify as an interest in a closely held business under Code Sec. 6166, a decedent must have conducted an active trade or business, or must have held an interest in a partnership, LLC, or corporation that itself carries on an active trade or business as distinguished from the mere management of investment assets. To determine whether a decedent's interest in real property is an interest in an asset used in an active trade or business, the IRS will consider all the facts and circumstances, including the activities of agents and employees, the activities of management companies or other third parties, and the decedent's ownership interest in any management company or other third party.

When Real Estate Interests Qualify for Deferral

A frequently contested issue between the IRS and taxpayers has been determining whether a decedent's real estate investments constitute an interest in an active trade or business for purposes of the estate tax deferral. After a series of rulings where the IRS concluded that the decedents' interest in real estate did not constitute an interest in a closely held business because the decedents' interest represented a mere investment, in Rev. Rul. 2006-34,[137] the IRS provided taxpayers with a list of six factors that the IRS will consider in determining whether a decedent' interest in real estate is an interest in an active trade or business so as to constitute an interest in a closely held business for purposes of an estate tax deferral under Code Sec. 6166.

Factors indicating real estate is active trade or business. The IRS will consider the following nonexclusive six factors in determining whether a decedent's interest in real property is an interest in an active trade or business:

1. The amount of time the decedent devoted to the trade or business;
2. Whether an office was maintained from which the activities of the decedent, partnership, LLC, or corporation were conducted or coordinated, and whether the decedent maintained regular business hours for that purpose;
3. The extent to which the decedent was actively involved in finding new tenants and negotiating and executing new leases;
4. The extent to which the decedent provided landscaping, grounds care, or other services beyond the mere furnishing of leased premises;

---

[137] Rev. Rul. 2006-34, 2006-1 CB 1171.

5. The extent to which the decedent personally made, arranged for, performed, or supervised repairs and maintenance to the property (whether or not performed by independent contractors), including without limitation painting, carpentry, and plumbing; and
6. The extent to which the decedent handled tenant repair requests and complaints.

In each situation, the real property interests are included in the decedent's gross estate and aggregate in value more than 35 percent of the decedent's adjusted gross estate within the meaning of Code Sec. 6166(b)(6).

Example 29-75: At the time of A's death, he owned a ten-store strip mall titled in A's name. A personally handled the day-to-day operation, management, and maintenance of the mall as well as most repairs. When unable to personally perform a repair, he hired a third-party independent contractor and reviewed and approved the work performed. A's activities went beyond those of a mere investor collecting profits from a passive asset. Moreover, even in situations in which A hired independent contractors to perform repairs that A could not perform personally, A was involved in the selection of the contractors and reviewed and approved the work performed. Under these circumstances, the use of independent contractors on occasions when A could not personally perform the work does not prevent A's activities from rising to the level of the conduct of an active trade or business. Thus, A's ownership of the strip mall qualifies as an interest in a closely held business.

.08 Time for Payment

The deferral of the estate tax (not the interest) is for up to five years from the original payment due date [Code Sec. 6166(a)(3)]. After the first installment of the estate tax is paid, the executor must pay the remaining installments annually by the date one year after the due date of the preceding installment payment. There must be at least two but no more than 10 equal annual installment payments [Code Secs. 6166(a)(1), 6166(a)(3)].

.09 Interest Owed on Deferred Estate Tax

A two-percent interest rate is imposed on the amount of deferred estate tax attributable to a farm or closely held business interest worth up to $1,430,000 in 2013 (increasing to $1,450,000 in 2014) [Code Sec. 6601(j)(2)]. Forty-five percent of the underpayment rate of interest, as determined under Code Sec. 6621, applies to the deferred estate tax attributable to the value of closely held business property that exceeds $1,430,000 in 2013 (increasing to $1,450,000 in 2014). The special two-percent interest rate is not available with respect to deferred estate tax payments on certain holding company stock and other non-readily-tradable business assets [Code Sec. 6166(b)(7)(A)(iii) and Code Sec. 6166(b)(8)(A)(iii)]. In these cases, the applicable interest rate is forty-five percent of the rate for underpayments of tax. No deduction is allowed for interest payments in this situation.

Interest Not Deductible

Interest on the unpaid portion of the tax is not deferred and must be paid annually. Interest must be paid at the same time and as a part of each installment payment of the tax. No estate tax administration expense deduction is allowed for any interest payment on any unpaid portion of the estate tax for the period during which an extension of time for payment of the tax is in effect under Code Sec. 6166 [Code Sec. 2053(c)(1)(D)]. This provision eliminates the need to file supplemental estate tax returns and make complex computations to claim an estate tax deduction for interest paid.

NOTE: No income tax deduction is allowable for any interest payable on any unpaid portion of the estate tax for the period during which an extension of time for payment of the tax is in effect under Code Sec. 6166 [Code Sec. 163(k)].

Interest Computation

Under Code Sec. 6601(j), the maximum amount of the estate tax that may be subject to the lower two-percent interest rate is the lesser of:

1. Estate tax owed on $1,430,000 in 2013 (increasing to $1,450,000 in 2014); or
2. The amount of the estate tax that is attributable to the closely held business and that is payable in installments.

.10 Acceleration of Payments

Under Code Sec. 6166(g), the estate tax deferral is generally lost if [Code Sec. 6166(g)]:

1. The executor fails to pay an installment of principal or interest by the due date of any installment [Code Sec. 6166(g)(3)]; or
2. 50 percent or more of the value of the decedent's interest in the closely held business is redeemed, sold, exchanged or otherwise disposed of or money and other property attributable to that interest is withdrawn from the business. However, a disposition does not include the transfer of an interest because of the death of the original transferee, or a subsequent transferee, if it is transferred to a family member of the last transferor [Code Sec. 6166(g)(1)(D)]. For example, if an interest for which an election had been made was inherited by a son and that son died, the transfer to a member of that son's family is not considered a disposition.

NOTE: A qualified redemption of stock under Code Sec. 303 to pay death taxes, funeral costs, and administrative expenses is not considered a distribution or withdrawal for purposes of accelerating payments, but the value of the interest in the closely held business is reduced by the value of the stock redeemed [Code Sec. 6166(g)(1)(B)].

The acceleration rules apply in the cases of the disposition of any interest in holding company stock, or any withdrawal of money or other property from the holding company, if the election to treat holding company stock as business company stock had been made. If the election was made, the acceleration rules apply to any disposition of the business company stock by the holding company, or any withdrawal of any money or other property from the business company attributable to its stock by the holding company owning that stock [Code Sec. 6166(g)(1)(E) and (F)].

.11 Time and Manner of Election

The executor makes the election by attaching a "Notice of Election" to a timely filed estate tax return on IRS Form 706 (including extensions) [Code Sec. 6166(d)]. The notice must contain the following information [Reg. § 20.6166-1(b)]:

1. The decedent's name and taxpayer identification number as they appear on the estate tax return;
2. The total amount of tax to be paid in installments;
3. The date elected for paying the first installment;
4. The number of annual installments, including the first installment, in which the tax is to be paid;
5. The properties shown on the estate tax return that make up the closely held business interest (identified by schedule and item number); and
6. Why the estate qualifies for installment payments.

If you do not include information for items 2, 3, and 4, the election is presumed to be for the maximum amount payable in installments and must be made in 10 equal installments, the first payment of which is due five years after the due date for paying the estate tax.

The IRS can require the estate to post a bond in an amount up to double the amount of the tax deferred as additional security for the payment of the deferred obligation [Code Sec. 6165]. An executor may elect a lien in favor of the United States [Code Sec. 6324A] in lieu of the bond under Code Sec. 6165. The executor makes such an election by filing a notice of election with the IRS office where the estate tax return is to be filed prior to the payment of the full amount of the deferred estate tax and any interest due plus any additions to tax, assessable penalties, and costs attributable to the deferred amount. The notice must be filed with a written agreement describing the property subject to the lien and signed by all persons with an interest in the property. The maximum value of the property that the IRS may require as lien property cannot exceed the sum of the amount of taxes deferred and the required interest amount [Code Sec. 6324A].

Mandatory Bond Requirement Nixed

In *E.P. Roski Est.*,[138] the Tax Court concluded that the IRS had abused its discretion by requiring that every estate provide a bond or special tax lien to qualify for the Code Sec. 6166 election. The court found that it was Congress's intent that the IRS would evaluate on a case-by-case basis whether the bond or special tax lien requirements were necessary. Thus, the court held that the IRS has no authority to require a bond or special lien in every case where an estate elects to pay the estate in installments under Code Sec. 6166. The court concluded that making the furnishing of security mandatory added a substantive requirement to Code Sec. 6166 that Congress had not intended.

Security Requirement

In light of the decision in *Estate of Roski*, the IRS announced a change in its policy in Notice 2007-90,[139] and provided interim guidance for estates making an election to pay all or part of the estate tax in installments until regulations are issued. The standards should be applied on a case-by-case basis to identify those estates making an election under Code Sec. 6166 in which the government's interest in the deferred estate tax and the interest thereon is deemed to be sufficiently at risk to justify the

[138] *E.P. Roski Est.*, 128 TC 113, Dec. 56,896 (2007).

[139] Notice 2007-90, 2007-2 CB 1003.

requirement of a bond or special lien. The regulations will implement those standards and related procedures.

In order to determine whether the government's interest in the deferred tax is adequately secured, the IRS will consider information contained in the estate tax return and attachments to the return. Estates that have filed returns that do not contain adequate information to make this determination may be contacted and required to provide additional financial information to the IRS for purposes of making this determination. The IRS may terminate an estate's election for failure to respond to such requests within a reasonable timeframe. If, after this individual evaluation and analysis, the IRS determines there is a sufficient credit risk regarding the government's collection of the estate tax payments deferred under Code Sec. 6166, the IRS will notify the estate that it must provide a bond or elect to provide a special lien in lieu of a bond. If the estate then refuses to provide a bond or a special lien, the IRS will terminate the estate's Code Sec. 6166 election. The estate may then seek reconsideration of the termination by the Office of Appeals and, if the Office of Appeals upholds the IRS's determination, the estate then will have the opportunity to petition the Tax Court for a declaratory judgment with regard to whether its Code Sec. 6166 election may be continued.

The IRS will consider the following factors in determining whether deferred installment payments of estate tax under Code Sec. 6166 pose a sufficient credit risk to the government to justify the requirement of a bond or special lien: (1) duration and stability of the business, (2) ability to pay the installments of tax and interest timely, and (3) compliance history.

Protective Election

You may make a protective election to defer payment of any part of the estate tax that is still unpaid when the values are finally determined (or agreed to, following an examination of the return). This protective election also covers any deficiencies attributable to the closely held business interest [Reg. § 20.6166-1(d)]. Extension of tax payments under this election depends on whether the final values meet the requirements for deferral under Code Sec. 6166. However, a protective election does not extend the time for paying the tax. Such an extension must be granted under Code Secs. 6161 or 6163.

You make a protective election by filing a "Notice of Protective Election" with a timely filed estate tax return on Form 706. Within 60 days after the values are finally determined or agreed to, you must send a letter containing a final "Notice of Election" with the required information to the IRS office where you filled the estate tax return. You must pay any previously unpaid tax and interest now due, plus any unpaid tax and interest that is not attributable to a closely held business and that is not eligible for further extension (or currently extended) under Code Sec. 6161 or 6163.

> **NOTE:** If an actual or protective election was not made, you can still elect to pay a portion of any deficiency in installments within 60 days after notice and demand for payment [Code Sec. 6166(h); Reg. § 20.6166-1(c)]. This election must contain the same information as a notice of election filed with the original estate tax return.

Deciding Whether to Make the Election

The clear advantage of an Code Section 6166 deferred payment of taxes is the availability of the low two-percent interest rate on deferred estate tax attributable to a farm or closely held business interest worth $1,430,000 in 2013 (increasing to $1,450,000 in 2014). The disadvantages of a Section 6166 election include:

1. The family cannot dispose of or withdraw cash out of the closely held business above certain levels without accelerating the full estate tax due.
2. If the business interest exceeds $1,430,000 in 2013 (increasing to $1,450,000 in 2014), interest must be paid at 45 percent of the current underpayment rate.
3. The estate may incur a bonding expense.

▶ **CAUTION:** Under Code Sec. 2002, liability for payment of the estate tax is imposed on the executor. If the unpaid portion of the estate tax bears a substantial relationship to the value of the closely held business interests and if the estate does not have other substantial assets, a risk exists that a decline in the profits of the business would leave the executor in a position where he or she would have to sell the business to meet the installment payments. A sale of the business during a period of declining profits might result in a loss leaving the personal representative holding insufficient funds to pay the balance of the estate tax. In this situation, the executor would be personally liable for the balance of the estate tax owed.

.12 Declaratory Judgment Relief

If the IRS finds that an estate is ineligible for installment payment of estate tax, the executor may seek a declaratory judgment before the Tax Court regarding the estate's eligibility for installment payments [Code Sec. 7479]. This provision applies to both the initial and continued eligibility to pay estate tax in installments. The Tax Court's jurisdiction to determine an estate's eligibility for the installment payment of estate taxes extends to the issue of which businesses that are includible in the decedent's gross estate are eligible for the deferral of tax [Code Sec. 7479(a)]. Provided the IRS's adverse determination is sent by certified or registered mail, a pleading for a declaratory judgment must be filed with the Tax Court within 90 days of the IRS mailing [Code Sec. 7479(b)(3)].

In order to be eligible for judicial review under Code Sec. 7479, the estate must show that it exhausted all administrative remedies within the IRS. A taxpayer is deemed to have exhausted all available administrative remedies if the IRS fails to make a determination within 180 days of a request for determination, provided all reasonable steps to secure such determination have been made [Code Sec. 7479(b)(2)]. In Rev. Proc. 2005-33,[140] the IRS provided guidance on exhausting administrative remedies before seeking a declaratory judgment pursuant to Code Sec. 7479 where an executor has made an election under Code Sec. 6166 to extend the time for payment of estate tax. To be deemed to have exhausted all administrative remedies, the applicant is required to complete the following steps:

1. The executor must timely file a Form 706 on behalf of the estate and attach the election to extend the time to pay pursuant to Code Sec. 6166(a); and

---

[140] Rev. Proc. 2005-33, 2005-1 CB 1231.

2. Within 30 calendar days after the mailing date of a preliminary determination letter from the IRS, the applicant must request, in writing, a conference with the IRS's Appeals Office and fully participate in the conference.

After these actions are completed and a reasonable time has expired for the IRS to issue a final determination letter subsequent to the appeals conference (which is deemed to have ended on the 61st day after the conference), an applicant is deemed to have exhausted all administrative remedies. An applicant will also be deemed to have exhausted all administrative remedies in the following situations: (1) upon the issuance of a final determination letter where a preliminary determination letter was not received, as long as the failure to receive a preliminary letter was not due to the actions or inactions of the applicant; (2) where the applicant has not received a preliminary or final determination letter after 180 days has expired from the date a request for determination was made, and the failure is not due to any action or inaction on the applicant's part; or (3) at least 61 days after an appeals conference was requested in response to a preliminary determination letter and the IRS has not responded.

Assessments

After the return is filed, it is examined by the proper officials in the IRS. If the return is found to understate the tax, the IRS notifies the executor that it will issue a deficiency notice unless the matter is settled. If a deficiency notice is issued, the executor may petition the Tax Court for a redetermination or pay the tax and apply for a refund from the IRS. If the refund is denied, the taxpayer may apply to the U.S District Court or the U.S. Claims Court. Collection is postponed during the pendency of the case, unless the assessment was a jeopardy assessment [Reg. §§301.6212-1, 301.6213-1]. The IRS ordinarily has three years from the date a return is filed to make an estate, gift, or generation skipping transfer tax assessment [Code Sec. 6501]. No proceeding in a court for the collection of an estate or gift tax can be begun without an assessment within the three-year period. If no return is filed, the tax may be assessed, or a suit commenced to collect the tax without assessment, at any time. If an estate or gift tax return is filed, and the amount of unreported items exceeds 25 percent of the amount of the reported items, the tax may be assessed or a suit commenced to collect the tax without assessment, within six years after the return was filed [Code Sec. 6501].

Refunds

Refund claims must be filed within three years of the return's due date or two years of the payment of the tax, whichever is later. It should state the amount of refund claimed and the grounds on which the claim is based [Code Sec. 6511].

Limited Liability Companies and Limited Liability Partnerships

DEFINITIONS

What is a limited liability company? . . . . ¶ 30,001

LLC filing requirements . . . . ¶ 30,002

Determining whether an LLC is appropriate business entity . . . . . . ¶ 30,005

ORGANIZATION OF LLCs

Articles of organization . . . . ¶ 30,010

Operating agreements . . . . ¶ 30,015

Bulletproof vs. flexible statutes . . ¶ 30,020

Comparisons of organizational attributes . . . . ¶ 30,025

MEMBERSHIP IN LLCs

Who can be LLC members? . . . . . . ¶ 30,030

Sole proprietors . . . . ¶ 30,035

Capitalizing by members . . . . ¶ 30,040

Characterizing a member's LLC interest . . . . ¶ 30,045

Assignment of a member's interest . . . . ¶ 30,050

Is an LLC membership interest a security? . . . . ¶ 30,055

PROFESSIONAL LIMITED LIABILITY COMPANY

Professional limited liability company (PLLC) . . . . ¶ 30,060

FOREIGN LLCs

Foreign LLCs . . . . ¶ 30,065

USURY

Is the defense of usury unavailable to an LLC? . . . . ¶ 30,070

TAXATION OF LLCs

Tax treatment of LLCs . . . . ¶ 30,075

Check-the-box to determine entity classification . . . . ¶ 30,080

How to make check-the-box election . . . . ¶ 30,085

Changing entity classification . . . . ¶ 30,090

LLCs and self-employment tax . . ¶ 30,095

LLCs and the payroll tax . . . . ¶ 30,100

APPLICABILITY TO SPECIFIC TYPES OF BUSINESS

Real estate investments . . . . ¶ 30,105

Manufacturing or service company converting to LLC status . . . . ¶ 30,115

The sole proprietor . . . . ¶ 30,120

OTHER TAX AND NONTAX FEATURES OF LLCs

State tax laws . . . . ¶ 30,125

LLC name . . . . ¶ 30,130

Formation of LLCs . . . . ¶30,135
LLC tax year . . . . ¶30,140
Method of accounting . . . . ¶30,145

MEMBERSHIP

Number of members . . . . ¶30,150
Membership in an LLC . . . . ¶30,155
Continuity of life . . . . ¶30,160
Powers of the LLC . . . . ¶30,165
Limiting liability . . . . ¶30,170
The operating agreement . . . . ¶30,175
Management . . . . ¶30,180
Voting rights . . . . ¶30,185
Contributions of members to an LLC . . . . ¶30,190
The allocation of LLC profits and losses . . . . ¶30,195
Distributions . . . . ¶30,200
Disassociation . . . . ¶30,205
Withdrawal, dissolution and winding up . . . . ¶30,210
Mergers and consolidations . . . . . . ¶30,215
Termination of an LLC . . . . ¶30,220

DEFINITIONS

¶30,001 WHAT IS A LIMITED LIABILITY COMPANY?

When small business owners are deciding which form of business entity would be appropriate for a business, consideration should be given to the limited liability company (LLC). The LLC, which is a legal business entity created under state law, has become an attractive entity for conducting a wide variety of businesses. Reason: The LLC is a hybrid entity that offers the best of both the corporate and partnership worlds and is easier to deal with than the S corporation which restricts many more aspects of operating the business including the number of shareholders allowed and their nationality just to name a few. See ¶21,010.

The LLC combines the limited liability benefit of conducting a business in the corporate form with the passthrough tax treatments associated with doing business as a partnership. Like a partnership, the LLC avoids tax at the entity level and passes through taxable income, losses and credits to the "member" level. In addition, since the LLC is taxed like a partnership, it may specially allocate items of income or expense provided the allocations have substantial economic effect [Code Sec. 704(b)]. In the LLC context, a *member* is the person who owns an interest in the LLC and is the functional equivalent of a partner or shareholder. The members of an LLC have the discretion to decide how they want to share profit and losses provided the agreement is reflected in the LLC's operating agreement or the articles of incorporation, which are filed with the state.

.01 Creation of the LLC

Since state law governs the formation and operation of LLCs, the first thing to do when establishing an LLC is to execute an operating agreement in accordance with the state statute where the business will operate. All 50 states, and the District of Columbia, have enacted LLC statutes. Most of these state LLC statutes permit the formation of a single-member LLC. Be aware, however, that since there is no uniform

LLC statute, significant variations exist from state to state. Taxpayers should carefully consult the statute in a state before deciding if the LLC is the best entity in that jurisdiction for their business. Although many states require that the operating agreement be in writing, there are some that do not mandate a written agreement. Nevertheless, we recommend that the members of the LLC execute a written operating agreement in order to craft a management structure that suits the business's individual needs. In addition, a written agreement may resolve potential trouble spots and obviate the need for attorneys down the road when disputes erupt.

.02 Default Statutes

Some states have a so-called default statute, which means that, in the absence of an LLC agreement, the state statute controls. In essence, if taxpayers fail to draft an LLC agreement or if they omit a necessary provision in the agreement the state will write their agreement for them.

.03 Advantages of LLCs

When properly drafted, the LLC offers the following advantages:

1. Limited liability—No member of a LLC is personally liable for the LLC's obligations in contract or tort. The LLC members are immune from any liabilities, debts or obligations of the LLC.
2. Conduit-type tax treatment—Like a partnership, the LLC avoids tax at the entity level and passes through taxable income, losses and credits to the member level and the members must report the income on their individual tax returns.
3. Preferable to a limited partnership because LLCs do not require the existence of a general partner who is subject to unlimited liability. All LLC members are eligible to participate in the management of the business while still receiving the benefits of limited liability. Limited partners, on the other hand, cannot participate in control of the limited partnership without risking loss of their limited liability.
4. Preferable to S corporations because S corporations limit the number and type of shareholders and impose special tax restrictions on allocations of income and loss. It is also easier to qualify a business as an LLC than as an S corporation. See ¶21,010.

.04 Disadvantages of LLCs

The disadvantages associated with operating a business as an LLC include the following:

1. The ability of the LLC member to deduct losses may be limited by the passive loss rules imposed by Code Sec. 469 or the at-risk limitations imposed by Code Sec. 465. See ¶13,090 for further discussion of the passive loss rules and ¶13,100 for further discussion of the at risk rules. Either or both of these provisions may eliminate or reduce the ability of LLC members to deduct losses passed through to them from the LLC.

   In *Assaf*,[1] the passive activity loss rules of Code Sec. 469 did not preclude a married couple from deducting leasing activity losses incurred by their LLC. The

---

[1] *F.A. Assaf*, 89 TCM 694, Dec. 55,915(M), TC Memo. 2005-14.

LLC, which owned the real property, also provided substantial support services to its attorney tenants, including answering phones, taking messages, clerking services, and other secretarial services. Thus, the payments made to the LLC were principally for the services provided, not for the space leased and, therefore, the taxpayers qualified for the extraordinary personal services exception to the passive activity rules. In addition, the wife spent a substantial amount of time on the leasing activities and legal support services and, therefore, materially participated in the LLC's activities. Therefore, because the LLC's activities were nonpassive, its losses could be netted against other income.

2. The IRS can collect unpaid employment taxes from an single member LLC under the Code Sec. 6672 trust fund penalty tax, which allows the IRS to personally assess and collect an LLC's unpaid employment taxes from the single member LLC's owner, if the owner is considered to be a responsible person. See ¶30,095 for further discussion.

¶30,002 LLC FILING REQUIREMENTS

.01 LLCs Classified as Partnerships

If an LLC has at least two members and is classified as a partnership, it generally must file Form 1065, *U.S. Return of Partnership Income*. An LLC classified as a partnership is subject to the same filing and reporting requirements that are imposed on partnerships. Only a member manager of an LLC can sign the partnership tax return and only a member manager can represent the LLC as the tax matters partner. A member manager is any owner of an interest in the LLC who, alone or together with others, has the continuing authority to make the management decisions necessary to conduct the business for which the LLC was formed. If there are no elected or designated member managers, each owner is treated as a member manager. For further discussion of the tax treatment of partnerships, see Chapter 24.

.02 LLCs Classified as Disregarded Entities

An LLC with only one member (single-member LLC) is treated as an entity disregarded as separate from its owner for income tax purposes under Reg. § 301.7701-3(f)(2) and the LLC reports its income, deductions, gains, losses, and credits on its owner's federal income tax return. For example, if the owner of the LLC is an individual, the LLC's income and expenses would be reported on the following Schedules filed with the owner's Form 1040:

- Schedule C, *Profit or Loss from Business* (Sole Proprietorship);
- Schedule C-EZ, *Net Profit From Business* (Sole Proprietorship);
- Schedule E, *Supplemental Income and Loss*; or
- Schedule F, *Profit or Loss From Farming*.

A single-member LLC that is classified as a disregarded entity for income tax purposes is treated as a separate entity for employment tax purposes and must use its name and employer identification number (EIN) for reporting and payment of employment taxes. The LLC will need an EIN if it has employees or if it will be required to file any excise tax forms.

A single-member LLC classified as a disregarded entity must use the owner's social security number (SSN) or (EIN) for all income tax purposes including all information returns and reporting related to income tax.

.03 LLCs Classified as Corporations

An LLC with either a single member or more than one member can elect to be classified as a corporation rather than classified as a partnership or as a disregarded entity under the default rules. To elect to be treated as an association taxable as a corporation, the LLC must file Form 8832, *Entity Classification Election*. After making this election, the LLC can file a Form 1120, *U.S. Corporation Income Tax Return*.

An LLC with either a single member or more than one member can elect to be classified as an S corporation by filing Form 2553, *Election by a Small Business Corporation*. LLCs electing classification as an S corporation are not required to file Form 8832 to elect classification as a corporation before filing Form 2553. By filing Form 2553, an LLC is deemed to have elected classification as a corporation in addition to the S corporation classification. An LLC making this election should file Form 1120S, *U.S. Income Tax Return for an S Corporation*. For further discussion of the tax treatment of S corporations, see Chapter 21.

¶30,005 DETERMINING WHETHER AN LLC IS APPROPRIATE BUSINESS ENTITY

Each organization employed for conducting business has unique tax benefits and pitfalls depending upon its ability to function within the requirements of the conditions mandated by the jurisdiction in which it was organized and the relevant provisions of the Internal Revenue Code and IRS regulations. The following chart is intended to provide an easy access to the similarities and differences between the various organizations used to conduct business. (See also Comparison table in Ch. 21.)

Table 1. Comparison of S Corporation, General Partnership, Limited Partnership and LLC

Comparison as to	S Corporation	General Partnership	Limited Partnership	LLC
a) Limited Liability	Shareholders have limited liability even if they participate in management.	General partners are jointly and severally liable for the obligations of the partnership.	Limited partners have limited liability protection. General partners are jointly and severally liable for the obligations of the partnership.	Members have limited liability protection.

Comparison as to	S Corporation	General Partnership	Limited Partnership	LLC
b) Participation	Managed by board of directors.	All general partners may participate in management.	Participation by general partners only. Limited partners will lose their limited liability protection if they participate in management.	All members may participate in management.
c) Transferability of Ownership Interests	Restrictions imposed by stockholder's agreement, if any.	Restrictions imposed by partnership agreement.	Restrictions imposed by partnership agreement.	Restrictions imposed by statute (bullet proof) or by operating agreement.
d) Number of Owners	1 to 100.	At least 2, no maximum.	At least 2, no maximum.	At least 2, no maximum. Some states allow one member.
e) Owner Qualifications	Ownership limited to U.S. citizens and residents, estates, and to certain U.S. trusts.	No restrictions.	No restrictions.	No restrictions.
f) Classes of Ownership Interests	Generally only one class of stock is permitted. However, voting differences are allowed.	Multiple classes allowed.	Multiple classes allowed.	Multiple classes allowed.
g) Continuity of Life	Yes.	Usually, no.	Usually, no.	Usually, no.
h) Taxation	Generally, only taxed at the shareholder level, but some S corporations are subject to tax on recognized built-in gains, and excess net passive income.	Taxed only at the partner level.	Taxed only at the partner level.	Taxed only at the member level.

Comparison as to	S Corporation	General Partnership	Limited Partnership	LLC
i) IRS Election Required	Must elect S status by filing Form 2553.	No filing required.	No filing required.	No filing required.
j) Special Allocation of Income and Loss	Special allocations are not allowed.	Special allocations are allowed but disregarded if without "substantial economic effect."	Special allocations are allowed but disregarded if without "substantial economic effect."	Special allocations are allowed but disregarded if without "substantial economic effect."
k) Deductibility of Loss	Shareholders may deduct their allocable share of the corporation's losses to the extent of the tax basis in their shares and loans to the S corporation. However, basis does not include the shareholder's share of corporate debt.	Partners may deduct their allocable share of the partnership's losses to the extent of the tax basis in their partnership interest, which includes their allocable share of the partnership debt.	Both limited and general partners may deduct their allocable share of the partnership's losses to the extent of the tax basis in the partnership interest, which includes their allocable share of partnership debt.	Members may deduct their allocable share of the LLC's losses to the extent of the tax basis in their LLC interest, which includes their allocable share of LLC debt.
l) Tax Treatment of Property Contributions	No recognition of gain on transfer of appreciated property only if the transferring shareholders are in "control" of the corporation (code section 351).	No recognition of gain on transfer of appreciated property by partner (i.e., no control requirement).	No recognition of gain on transfer of appreciated property by both general and limited partners (i.e., no control requirement).	No recognition of gain on transfer of appreciated property by members (i.e., no control requirement).
m) Liquidation	Distribution of appreciated property is taxable at the corporate level, and passed through to the shareholder.	No recognition of gain on a distribution of property (other than cash) until the partner sells the property.	No recognition of gain on a distribution of property (other than cash) until the partner sells the property.	No recognition of gain on a distribution of property (other than cash) until the member sells the property.

Comparison as to	S Corporation	General Partnership	Limited Partnership	LLC
n) Inside Basis Adjustments on Transfer of Interests	No adjustment in basis of corporate assets to reflect change in basis of transferred stock.	Special election available to adjust basis of partnership assets to reflect change in basis of transferred partnership interest.	Special election available to adjust basis of partnership assets to reflect change in basis of transferred partnership interest.	Special election available to adjust basis of LLC assets to reflect change in basis of transferred LLC interest.
o) Tax Year	Generally, calendar year.	Generally follows tax year of majority partner.	Generally follows tax year of majority partner.	Generally follows tax year of majority member.

▶ **OBSERVATION:** Taxpayers not desiring an LLC should be aware of IRS rulings[2] in which the IRS approved the creation of Subchapter S corporations joining together as partners in order to avoid complying with the maximum shareholder requirement to validate an S corporation election.[3]

▶ **OBSERVATION:** A C corporation does offer the same shield of limited liability as an LLC; however, the C corporation is subject to a double tax—first at the corporate level and second at the shareholder level upon the receipt of regular and/or liquidating dividends. Also, appreciation in corporate assets is subject to corporate tax, either on the sale of the assets or on the distribution of such assets in liquidation or upon redemption of corporate stock.[4]

▶ **OBSERVATION:** A personal service corporation (PSC) is a corporation that has as its principal business the performance of personal services substantially by employee-stockholders, typically doctors, lawyers, accountants, etc. See ¶20,010 for further discussion of PSCs. Generally, these corporations "strip" their income by having their professional employee-shareholders draw salaries leaving no taxable income in the corporation at year-end (otherwise subject to the maximum 35 percent corporate tax rate). The IRS has been upheld by the Tax Court which concluded that such salaries, when deemed excessive, should be treated as nondeductible disguised dividends.[5] Such excessive salary would, of course, make no difference if the entity were a PLLC or a LLP.

[2] Rev. Rul. 94-43, 1994-2 CB 198.

[3] LTR 9022024 (Feb. 28, 1990).

[4] *Pope & Talbot, Inc.*, CA-9, 99-1 USTC ¶50,158, 162 F3d 1236.

[5] *Richlands Medical Ass'n*, 60 TCM 1572, Dec. 47,064(M), TC Memo. 1990-660, *aff'd*, CA-4, 953 F2d 639 (unpublished opinion 2/3/92).

ORGANIZATION OF LLCs

¶30,010 ARTICLES OF ORGANIZATION

An LLC is organized simply by the filing of a document with the Secretary of State generally called "Articles of Organization" or a "Certificate of Formation." This document can be filed by one person; but, in order to secure favorable partnership tax treatment by the IRS, it must have at least two or more members in its operation.

¶30,015 OPERATING AGREEMENTS

In those jurisdictions having flexible LLC statutes, the LLC will have an "Operating Agreement" executed among its members which, like a partnership or corporate stockholders' agreement, sets forth the conditions by which the LLC will be operated, managed, terminated and otherwise function. The Operating Agreement is a private document, not open to public scrutiny, but subject to review by the IRS to insure that the LLC will be treated either as a corporation or partnership, depending upon the characteristics of continuity of life, limited liability, centralized management and free transferability of interests, as defined in the Operating Agreement.

¶30,020 BULLETPROOF VS. FLEXIBLE STATUTES

The states which have enacted LLC legislation are divided between those with "bulletproof" and those with "flexible" provisions.

.01 Bulletproof Statutes

Jurisdictions with bulletproof LLC statutes have mandatory provisions concerning limited liability, transferability of interests, centralized management and continuity of life, insuring that, if an LLC is organized under the statutes of those jurisdictions, the LLC will be classified as a partnership for federal income tax purposes.

.02 Flexible Statutes

In jurisdictions with flexible provisions, the LLC organizers have flexibility to structure the LLC according to the provisions contained in the operating agreement. This means that organizers have the leeway to be treated either as a corporation or a partnership. The flexible jurisdictions also contain "default" provisions in their LLC statutes which are triggered in the absence of an operating agreement executed between the LLC members. The default provisions generally insure partnership status. Accordingly, these jurisdictions permit the LLC to deviate from the statutory provisions when putting together their articles of organization and operating agreement; however, if the members fail to address a particular matter in these documents, then the statutory provisions take over.

¶30,025 COMPARISONS OF ORGANIZATIONAL ATTRIBUTES

An equity interest in a LLC is owned by a member (as compared to a stockholder or partner). It is governed by its members or a manager(s) (as compared to a board of directors or a general partner) and is created by "Articles of Organization" (as compared to a certificate of incorporation or a partnership agreement). The LLC is operated through the provisions contained in an "Operating Agreement" (as compared to corporate bylaws and/or a stockholders' agreement or the provisions of a partnership agreement).

MEMBERSHIP IN LLCs

¶30,030 WHO CAN BE LLC MEMBERS?

Members of an LLC can be corporations, individuals, trusts, pension plans, charitable foundations, nonresident aliens and, in fact, any kind of entity.

¶30,035 SOLE PROPRIETORS

There are a number of states which allow an individual to conduct business through an LLC. The IRS will not permit a single-member LLC to elect to be classified as a partnership but will permit a single-member LLC to elect to be classified as a corporation [Reg. § 301.7701-3(a)].

¶30,040 CAPITALIZING BY MEMBERS

Contributions by the members of an LLC to its capital may be made by cash, property, services rendered, a promissory note or other obligation evidencing a future contribution of cash, property or services—or any combination of the foregoing.

> **NOTE:** Be aware that, if you receive an LLC membership interest as payment for services, you will be subject to taxable ordinary income, the timing of which depends on whether the LLC membership interest is for past or future services [see Ch. 24].

¶30,045 CHARACTERIZING A MEMBER'S LLC INTEREST

A membership interest in a LLC is considered personal property; a member has no specific interest in the property of the LLC.

▶ **OBSERVATION:** A judgment creditor of a member has no right under LLC statutes to lien, levy or otherwise recover a judgment against property owned by the LLC. At best, a judgment creditor could obtain a charging order causing the payments made to the member by the LLC be directed toward payment of the judgment. Also, a member of an LLC who files for bankruptcy (either voluntary or involuntary) would generally trigger a dissolution of the partnership since bankruptcy of a member is one of the dissolution events. Presumably, a desperate creditor could conceivably use this tactic to obtain the member's allocable share of the LLC property received by the member upon LLC dissolution.

¶30,050 ASSIGNMENT OF A MEMBER'S INTEREST

Most default provisions allow the assignment of a member's interest, in whole or in part. The assignee is entitled only to share in the economic attributes of the assignor-member, i.e., to the distribution and allocation of profits and losses to which the assignor would be entitled. However, in the absence of the approval of at least a majority in interest of the members, the assignee is precluded from participating in the management of the LLC, which together with the economic attributes, represents a complete membership interest in the LLC.

¶30,055 IS AN LLC MEMBERSHIP INTEREST A SECURITY?

If an interest in an LLC as a member is treated as a security, then it cannot be offered or sold without registration or exemption therefrom under federal and/or state securities laws. If an LLC membership interest is treated as a security, then the LLC could have substantial disclosure obligations and create potential liability under the antifraud provisions of the applicable securities laws.

▶ **OBSERVATION:** In most cases involving the creation of PLLCs and PLLPs, there would be no attempt at public solicitation nor would such be the case in the typical manufacturing or service LLC. However, where solicitation of investments from outside interests is intended, it would be wise for the LLC organizers to obtain professional advice before entering into what could be a costly and unintended enterprise. Also, it is generally held that general partner interests do not constitute a security since general partners have the right to participate in management and do not rely on others with respect to their investment (as limited partners do). A member-managed LLC would appear to fit into this category.

PROFESSIONAL LIMITED LIABILITY COMPANY

¶30,060 PROFESSIONAL LIMITED LIABILITY COMPANY (PLLC)

The PLLC is an LLC with the added provision inherently required for personal liability by a professional: that is, he/she remains personally liable for his/her own acts of negligence and for the negligent acts of those under his/her own supervision. Thus, the PLLC is essentially the same as a professional corporation in the personal liability standard that it imposes on professionals such as lawyers, certified public accountants and other licensed professions. However, the PLLC, if structured properly, can provide tax treatment as a partnership rather than a corporation.

> **NOTE:** The nontax considerations for determining whether to be a shareholder in a professional corporation or an PLLC are essentially the same: i.e., limiting your liability for potential malpractice claims only to yourself and the negligence of those working under your supervision. The major consideration for opting for a PLLC is, therefore, rooted in tax savings and being subject to tax at only one level.

FOREIGN LLCs

¶30,065 FOREIGN LLCS

Organizations such as Germany's GmbH, Latin America's Limitada or France's SARL are forms of LLCs created in their countries of origin which, where authorized to conduct business in the USA, will be treated as LLCs by the state in which they are conducting business. Generally, LLCs formed under the LLC laws of other jurisdictions, including foreign countries, are permitted to register and be recognized by the jurisdiction in which they seek to conduct business. The LLC laws of the jurisdiction where they were formed govern its organization and internal affairs and the liability of its members and managers. Thus, a one-person LLC formed under the Texas LLC laws may register to conduct business in another jurisdiction which does not recognize one-person LLCs.

USURY

¶30,070 IS THE DEFENSE OF USURY UNAVAILABLE TO AN LLC?

A question has been raised, particularly among those engaged in real estate, as to whether an LLC can, where appropriate, use the defense of usury to mitigate the interest expense of a costly financing. Since usury is no defense to a corporation and the LLC is a creature of local law having both corporate and noncorporate characteristics, the question will have to be resolved on a local level by legislation, administrative directives or by the courts.

TAXATION OF LLCs

¶30,075 TAX TREATMENT OF LLCS

.01 Income Tax Treatment

In analyzing the federal tax liability of an LLC, the first consideration is whether an LLC is a single member LLC or a multi-member LLC. If the LLC is a multi-member LLC, the next consideration is whether the LLC is taxed as a corporation or a partnership as explained by the IRS in LTR 200235023.[6]

LLC Taxed as Corporation

If a multi-member LLC has elected to be treated as an association taxable as a corporation, the IRS would apply the general rules of corporate taxation to the LLC. This means that the LLC is taxed as a corporation and the members would be the equivalent of shareholders in the corporation. To satisfy either an income tax or employment tax liability, the IRS could file either a Notice of Federal Tax Lien against the LLC (not the members) and file suit to foreclose the federal tax lien or levy on the LLC assets. If the LLC incurs an employment tax liability, the IRS may assert the trust fund recovery penalty against a member who qualifies as a responsible person under Code Sec. 6672.

LLC Taxed as Partnership

If an LLC is taxed as a partnership, any income tax liability arising from an LLC's activities flows through to its members. If the IRS filed a Notice of Federal Tax Lien to collect the income tax liability, a partner's name as the taxpayer is listed on the lien.

In regard to employment taxes, an LLC, like a partnership, could incur an employment tax liability as the employer. In that case, if the IRS filed a Notice of Federal Tax Lien, the partnership would be listed on the Notice of Federal Tax Lien as the taxpayer.

A major difference, however, exists between a general partner's liability for the partnership's employment taxes and a member's liability when an LLC is treated as a partnership and incurs an employment tax liability: while each general partner is derivatively liable for the full amount of the employment tax liability under state law, no member of the LLC has any liability for the employment tax liability under state law. It must be emphasized that state law creates the difference in treatment between general partners and LLC members, not federal law.

When a partnership incurs an employment tax liability, under state law the general partners are liable for the tax, just as they are liable under state law for other debts of the partnership.

---

[6] LTR 200235023 (Oct. 11, 2005, re-released with additional information).

Since the members are not liable for the employment tax liability of the LLC taxed as a partnership, the IRS may consider asserting the trust fund recovery penalty.

Single-Member LLC

A single-member LLC (SMLLC) can elect to be taxed as one of the following entities under Reg. § 301.7701-3(a) of the check-the-box regulations:

1. Disregarded entity which is taxed as a sole proprietorship if it is owned by an individual,
2. Corporation (C corporation, personal holding company, personal services corporation, or professional corporation),
3. S corporation (status achieved if the LLC elects to be taxed as a corporation and then make an S corporation election by filing Form 2553, *Election by a Small Business Corporation*). See ¶21,010 for discussion of the S corporation election process,
4. Series LLCs are a series of a domestic series limited liability company, a cell of a domestic cell company, or a foreign series or cell that conducts an insurance business. The debts and other liabilities of each series are only enforceable against that series. Each series is recognized as a distinct entity for state law purposes and each series can have its own separate business purposes. A series can be terminated without affecting the other series of the LLC. Each series of a series organization (such as a series LLC) would be treated for federal tax purposes as an entity formed under local law, regardless of whether local law actually treats the series as a separate entity [Proposed Reg. § 301.7701-1(a)(5)].

If a SMLLC has made an election to have the LLC treated as an association taxable as a corporation for federal tax purposes, the LLC will be treated as a separate legal entity that may accrue its own tax liability, and the IRS may collect that liability only from the LLC rather than the individual member. This is the same result as when a multi-member LLC elects to be treated as a corporation. In that situation, the shareholders are not liable for the corporation's tax liability. Similarly, the single member of the LLC would similarly be insulated from the LLC's federal tax liability.

To recover a Form 941 employment tax liability, the IRS may assert the trust fund recovery penalty against any responsible person, which may in some situations include the single member owner. The single member owner, however, is not automatically a responsible person for employment tax purposes and the IRS must examine the facts and circumstances of each case to determine the responsible persons.

Multi-Member LLC

An LLC with two or more members can elect to be taxed as one of the following entities under Reg. § 301.7701-3(a) of the check-the-box regulations:

1. Partnership,
2. Corporation,
3. S corporation (status achieved if the LLC elects to be taxed as a corporation and then makes an S corporation election by filing Form 2553, *Election by a Small Business Corporation*). See ¶21,010 for discussion of the S corporation election process.

Disregarded LLC

If the single member owner has not elected on Form 8832, *Entity Classification Election,* to be treated as an association taxable as a corporation, the default provision of the check-the-box regulations provides that the LLC is to be disregarded as separate from its owner [Reg. § 301.7701-2(c)(2)(i)]. This means that the single member owner is treated like a sole proprietor, branch or division of the owner and is responsible for reporting tax liabilities arising from the operation of the LLC on Schedule C of the individual's Form 1040 [Reg. § 301.7701-2(a)]. A U.S. charity that wholly owns a disregarded entity must treat the operations and finances of the disregarded entity as its own for tax and information reporting purposes. For employment and certain excise tax purposes, an entity that is disregarded as separate from its owner is treated as an entity separate from its owner [Reg. § 301.7701-2(c)(2)(iv) and (v)]. In Notice 2012-52,[7] the IRS concluded that charitable contributions to disregarded domestic single-member limited liability companies (SMLLC) that are wholly owned and controlled by U.S. charities are treated as charitable contributions to a branch or division of the U.S. charity. The U.S. charity is the donee organization for purposes of the substantiation and disclosure requirements. To avoid unnecessary inquiries, the charity is encouraged to disclose, in the acknowledgment or another statement, that the SMLLC is wholly owned by the U.S. charity and treated by the U.S. charity as a disregarded entity. The guidance is effective for charitable contributions made on or after July 31, 2012. However, taxpayers may rely on the guidance prior to its effective date for tax years for which the period of limitation on refund or credit under Code Sec. 6511 has not expired.

A disregarded LLC owned by a corporation is treated as a direct operating division of the corporation, reportable on the corporation's Form 1120 or 1120S tax return. A disregarded LLC owned by a partnership is treated as a direct operating division of the partnership and is reportable on the partnership's Form 1065.

.02 Excise Tax Treatment

A single member entity that is disregarded as an entity separate from its owner for federal tax purposes is treated as a separate entity for the following excise taxes reported on:

- Form 720, *Quarterly Federal Excise Tax Return;*
- Form 730, *Monthly Tax Return for Wagers;*
- Form 2290, *Heavy Highway Vehicle Use Tax Return;*
- Form 11-C, *Occupation Tax and Registration Return for Wagering;*
- Excise tax refunds or payments claimed on Form 8849, *Claim for Refund of Excise Taxes;* and
- Excise tax registrations on Form 637, *Application for Registration (For Certain Excise Tax Activities)* [Temp. Reg. § 301.7701-2T].

[7] Notice 2012-52, IRB 2012-35, 317.

¶30,080 CHECK-THE-BOX TO DETERMINE ENTITY CLASSIFICATION

Even though there are no provisions in the Internal Revenue Code specifically addressing the federal tax treatment of LLCs, an LLC can elect how to be treated for federal tax purposes under the check-the-box regulations. All the LLC has to do is check a box on Form 8832, *Entity Classification Election,* indicating whether it selects tax treatment as an association (taxable as a corporation) or as a partnership [Ch 24]. The check-the-box regulations provide a simplified elective procedure for entities to be classified for federal tax purposes as partnerships, even if they have corporate characteristics [Reg. §§301.7701-1 through 301.7701-3]. The check-the-box regulations make it feasible for more entities to take advantage of the single-level taxation system available to partnerships rather than the double-level taxation system that applies to corporations [Ch. 20].

If a single-owner entity fails to make the election, it will be subject to the default sole proprietorship treatment in Reg. §301.7701-3(b)(1)(ii) which provides that the LLC will be disregarded as a separate entity and treated as a sole proprietorship for federal tax purposes.

.01 Automatic (per se) Corporations

Certain business entities are automatically classified as corporations and may not elect another classification under the check-the-box regulations. This list of "per se corporations" as set forth in Reg. §301.7701-2(b) includes:

1. A business entity organized under federal or state statute, or under a statute of a federally recognized Indian tribe, is a corporation if the statute describes or refers to the entity as incorporated or as a corporation, body corporate, or body politic. This category includes governmentally chartered corporations as well as business corporations (e.g., national banking associations, the Student Loan Marketing Association, and a private corporation established under federal law).
2. An association, as determined under Reg. §301.7701-3, is a corporation.
3. A business entity organized under a state statute is a corporation if the statute describes or refers to the entity as a joint-stock company or joint stock association.
4. An insurance company is a corporation.
5. A state-chartered business entity conducting banking activities is a corporation if any of its deposits are insured under the Federal Deposit Insurance Act (12 USC §1811 et seq.) or similar statute.
6. A business entity wholly owned by a state, a political subdivision of a state, a foreign government, or a business entity treated as a foreign government is a corporation. Nonetheless, the income of such entities may escape tax under Code Sec. 115.
7. A business entity that is taxable as a corporation under a specific Code provision (other than Code Sec. 7701(a)(3)) is taxed as a corporation. For example, publicly traded partnerships and taxable mortgage pools are taxed as corporations under Code Sec. 7704 and Code Sec. 7701(i), respectively.

8. Certain business entities formed in a foreign country or U.S. possession are classified as corporations [Reg. § 301.7701-2(b)(8)(i)]. Entities not treated as corporations are listed in Reg. § 301.7701-2(b)(8)(ii).
9. An entity with multiple charters is treated as a corporation if it would be treated as such under the rules of Reg. § 301.7701-2(b) in any of the jurisdictions in which it is organized, even though it would not be treated as a corporation in the other jurisdictions.

.02 Default Entities

In order to reduce the number of elections that will be needed, Reg. § 301.7701-3(b) includes default classification rules which provide that most eligible entities can select entity classification without filing an election. The default classification rules aim to match a taxpayer's expectations. The regulations adopt a pass-through default for domestic entities, under which a newly formed eligible entity will be classified as a partnership if it has at least two members unless the entity elects to be treated as an association. Similarly, a single-owner entity will not be regarded as an entity separate from its owner unless an election is filed to classify the entity as an association. If the business entity that has only a single member is not treated as an entity separate from its owner, it is considered a sole proprietorship, branch, or division of that owner.

.03 Default for Foreign Entities

The default for foreign entities is based on whether the members have limited liability. Thus a foreign eligible entity will be classified as an association (taxed as a corporation) if all members have limited liability. A foreign eligible entity will be classified as a partnership if it has two or more members and at least one member does not have limited liability. A foreign entity will be disregarded as an entity separate from its owner if it has a single owner and that owner does not have limited liability.

.04 Default for Existing Entities

The default classification for an existing entity is the classification that the entity claimed immediately prior to January 1, 1997. An entity's default classification continues until the entity elects to change its classification by means of an affirmative election.

¶30,085 HOW TO MAKE CHECK-THE-BOX ELECTION

An eligible entity can elect its classification by filing Form 8832, *Entity Classification Election.* The regulations require that the election be signed by each member of the entity or any officer, manager, or member of the entity who is authorized under penalties of perjury to make the election. An election will not be accepted unless it includes all of the required information, including the entity's taxpayer identifying number (TIN). In addition, a copy of Form 8832 must be attached to the entity's tax or information return if the entity is required to file such a return for the tax year for which an election is made. For entities that are not required to file a return, a copy of the form must be attached to the income tax or information return of all direct or indirect owners of the entity for the tax year of the owner that includes the date on which the election took effect. Although failure to attach a copy will not invalidate an otherwise valid election, penalties may be imposed against persons who are required to, but who do not, attach Form 8832 to their returns.

.01 Late Election Relief

In Rev. Proc. 2009-41,[8] the IRS extended relief with respect to a late entity classification election to both initial classification elections and changes in classification elections, and has extended the time for filing late entity classification elections. This guidance is the exclusive means for eligible entities to obtain relief for a late entity classification.

An entity must meet the following requirements for relief under Rev. Proc. 2009-41:

- The entity failed to obtain its requested classification as of the date of its formation or upon the entity's classification becoming relevant solely because Form 8832 was not filed timely, or
- The entity failed to obtain its requested change in classification solely because Form 8832 was not filed timely, and
- The entity has not filed a federal tax or information return for the first year in which the election was intended because the due date has not passed for that year's federal tax or information return, or
- The entity filed all required federal tax returns and information returns consistent with its requested classification for all of the years the entity intended the requested election to be effective and no inconsistent tax or information returns have been filed by or with respect to the entity during any of the tax years.

Relief must be requested before three years and 75 days from the requested effective date, and reasonable cause for the failure to timely make the classification election must be shown.

The IRS instructed taxpayers to write "Filed Pursuant to Rev. Proc. 2009-41" across the top of Form 8832 and attach both a declaration and the reasonable cause statement to the form. The declaration must state that the taxpayer qualifies for relief under Rev. Proc. 2009-41.Taxpayers must also explain their reason for failing to file a timely election. Applicants need not pay user fees.

¶30,090 CHANGING ENTITY CLASSIFICATION

.01 Conversion Options Available

Reg. § 301.7701-3(g) describes how elective changes in an entity's classification are treated for federal tax purposes. There are four possible elective changes in classification:

- A partnership can elect to be taxed as an association,
- An association can elect to be taxed as a partnership,
- An association (with a single member) can elect to be disregarded as an entity for tax purposes, and
- A disregarded entity can elect to be taxed as an association.

[8] Rev. Proc. 2009-41, IRB 2009-39, 439.

.02 Tax Implications of Conversions

The tax consequences of these switches are discussed below. The tax treatment of an elective change in classification is determined under all relevant Code provisions and general principles of tax law, including the step transaction doctrine, so that the tax consequences of an elective change will be identical to the tax results that would have occurred if the taxpayer had actually taken the deemed steps provided in the regulations [Reg. § 301.7701-3(g)(2)].

Partnership to Association

A partnership that elects to be classified as an association is deemed to have contributed all its assets and liabilities to the association in return for stock in the association. The partnership is subsequently deemed to have liquidated by distributing the stock in the association to its partners [Reg. § 301.7701-3(g)(1)(i)].

Association to Partnership

An association that elects to be classified as a partnership is deemed to have liquidated by distributing all of its assets and liabilities to its shareholders. The shareholders are then deemed to have contributed all of the assets and liabilities to the partnership [Reg. § 301.7701-3(g)(1)(ii)].

Association to a Disregarded Entity

An eligible entity that is classified as an association and elects to be disregarded as an entity separate from its owner is deemed to have distributed all its assets and liabilities to its single owner and to subsequently have liquidated [Reg. § 301.7701-3(g)(1)(iii)].

Disregarded Entity to an Association

The owner of an entity that is disregarded as an entity separate from its owner that elects to be classified as an association is deemed to have contributed all the assets and liabilities of that entity to the association in exchange for stock of the association [Reg. § 301.7701-3(g)(1)(iv)].

In two hypothetical situations, the IRS has explained the tax consequences when a single member domestic LLC that is disregarded for federal tax purposes as an entity separate from its owner under Reg. § 301.7701-3 becomes an entity with more than one owner that is classified as a partnership for federal tax purposes.[9]

In the first situation B purchased 50 percent of A's ownership in an LLC, but none of the purchase price was contributed to the LLC. The LLC was converted from a disregarded entity to a partnership. B's purchase is treated as the purchase of a 50 percent interest in each of the LLC's assets, which are treated as held directly by A. Immediately thereafter, A and B are treated as contributing their respective interests in those assets to a partnership in exchange for ownership interests in the partnership. A recognizes any gain or loss from the deemed sale of 50 percent of each asset. No gain or loss is recognized as a result of the conversion.

In the second situation, B contributed money to the LLC in exchange for a 50 percent ownership interest. The LLC is converted from a disregarded entity to a partnership.

---

[9] Rev. Rul. 99-5, 1999-1 CB 434.

B's contribution is treated as a contribution to a partnership in exchange for an ownership interest. A is treated as contributing all of the assets of the LLC to the partnership in exchange for a partnership interest. No gain or loss is recognized as a result of the conversion.

The IRS has also addressed by way of two hypotheticals the tax consequences of converting a multi-owner LLC classified as a partnership to a single-member LLC.[10]

In first situation, A and B are equal partners in AB, an LLC. A sells its entire interest in AB to B. The AB partnership terminates, and A must treat the transaction as the sale of a partnership interest and report any gain or loss. The AB partnership is deemed to make a liquidating distribution of all of its assets to A and B, and following this distribution, B is treated as acquiring the assets deemed to have been distributed to A in liquidation of A's partnership interest. Upon termination of AB, B is considered to receive a distribution of those assets attributable to B's former interest in AB, and must recognize any gain or loss on the deemed distribution.

In the second situation, C and D are equal partners in CD, an LLC. C and D sell their entire interests in CD to E. The CD partnership terminates and C and D must report gain or loss, if any, from the sale. The CD partnership is deemed to make a liquidating distribution of its assets to C and D. Immediately following this distribution, E is deemed to acquire, by purchase, all of the former partnership's assets.

- *Change in number of members.* If there is a change in the number of members of an association, the classification of an eligible entity as an association will not be affected. If an eligible entity classified as a partnership subsequently has only one member, the entity will be disregarded as an entity separate from its owner. If a single member entity that is disregarded as an entity separate from its owner subsequently has more than one member, the entity is classified as a partnership as of the date the entity has more than one member [Reg. § 301.7701-3(f)].
- *When changes become effective.* An election to change the classification of an entity is treated as occurring at the start of the day for which the election is effective. Any transactions that are deemed to occur as a result of the change in classification are treated as occurring immediately before the close of the day before the effective date of the election.

Example 30-1: If an election is made to convert from an association to a partnership effective on Jan. 1, the entity is treated as a partnership on Jan. 1 and the deemed transactions specified in the proposed regulations are treated as occurring immediately before the close of Dec. 31. As a result, the last day of the association's tax year will be Dec. 31 and the first day of the partnership's tax year will be Jan. 1 [Reg. § 301.7701-3(g)(3)].

Converting from Partnership to LLC

There are no tax consequences (no termination of partnership) upon the conversion of a partnership to an LLC where each partner retains the same percentage interest in profits, losses and capital as a member in the LLC.[11] Taxable gain will only occur where a partner's share of partnership liabilities is reduced as a result of the conversion by an

---

[10] Rev. Rul. 99-6, 1999-1 CB 432.

[11] Rev. Rul. 95-37, 1995-1 CB 130.

amount that exceeds his/her partnership basis. Moreover, the tax year of the converting partnership does not close with respect to any of the partners and the LLC retains the employer identification number of the partnership.

NOTE: An LLC files a Form 1065 when classified as a partnership and is required to confirm its LLC status by checking the appropriate box on Schedule B, item 1 of the Form 1065 and item A on the Schedule K-1.

▶ **OBSERVATION:** A C corporation or a Subchapter S Corporation subject to the built-in gains tax must be wary when converting to an LLC. In the case of a C corporation, there would be a double tax: first to the corporation on the liquidating distribution to its shareholders and then to the shareholders on the receipt of the distribution. The S corporation would suffer a corporate level tax. The tax price for the conversion may be too high.

Converting from Corporation to LLC or Limited Partnership

It may be advantageous for owners of a C corporation to convert to an LLC in order to retain limited liability and transferability of ownership but eliminate the double taxation of corporate earnings that occurs when operating as a C corporation.

Taxpayers who operate a business in the corporate form may find that converting to a limited partnership or an LLC will result in a tax savings for purposes of estate and gift taxes and state franchise taxes because many jurisdictions exempt LLCs and limited partnerships (not corporations) from state franchise taxes. The transfer taxes would be reduced because bigger discounts for lack of marketability and for minority transfers are available when transferring a limited partnership or LLC interest rather than transfers of shares of corporate stock.

▶ **PLANNING TIP:** Taxpayers desiring to convert from corporate form to a limited partnership or an LLC would typically treat the conversion as a liquidation of the corporation with resulting gain recognized at both the corporate and shareholder levels [Code Secs. 331(a) and 336(a)]. In order to avoid these taxes on the conversion, taxpayers should follow the procedure adopted by the taxpayers in three IRS-approved letter rulings. The taxpayers in these rulings made a timely check-the-box election, on the date of the conversion from corporate status to limited partnership or LLC status, to continue to be classified as an association taxable as a corporation. The conversion will qualify as a tax-free reorganization because it is merely a change in form [Code Sec. 368(a)(1)(F)]. The IRS has approved this technique as one without adverse tax consequences.[12]

Taxpayers who currently operate their business as an S corporation may find it advantageous to change to LLC status because unlike the S corporation, LLC statutes place no restrictions on the number of members or their national status. In addition, since the LLC can be taxed like a partnership, the LLC may specially allocate items of income or expense, provided these allocations have substantial economic effect [Code Sec. 704(b)]. The S corporation will not permit shareholders to make special allocations in this manner. Moreover, the LLC will not incur entity-level taxes, such as the S corporation's built-in gains tax and excess net passive income tax.

---

[12] LTR 200007011 (Nov. 16, 1999), LTR 199942009 (July 16, 1999), LTR 199947034 (Aug. 26, 1999).

.03 Start Date

A classification election takes effect at the start of the day for which the election is effective. Any transaction deemed to occur as a result of a change in classification is treated as occurring the day before. If a taxpayer elects to treat a stock purchase as an asset purchase under Code Sec. 338, an election to change the target corporation's classification cannot be effective before the day after the acquisition date of the target corporation.

.04 Signature Rule

To ensure that the taxpayers who recognize the tax consequences of a conversion election approve of the election, the election must be signed by every owner on the date of the deemed conversion transaction.

.05 Employer ID

An entity changing its classification need not obtain a new employer identification number, or EIN. The number used by the entity before the classification can continue to be used. Where an entity is disregarded, the owner's taxpayer identification number, or TIN, is used. If a disregarded entity elects a separate identity and it had an EIN, then that entity must use that EIN and not the owner's TIN. If that entity did not already have its own EIN, then it must apply for an EIN and not use the TIN of the single owner.

An eligible entity that makes an election to change its classification cannot make another election to change that classification within a 60-month period following the effective date of the original election. However, if there has been more than a 50 percent ownership change, the IRS can waive the application of the 60-month limit. If the election is made by all of the members of an electing entity, each person who is an owner at the time of the election must consent to the election.

¶30,095 LLCS AND SELF-EMPLOYMENT TAX

An individual owner of a single-member LLC classified as a disregarded entity is not an employee of the LLC. Instead, the owner is subject to tax on the net earnings from self-employment of the LLC which is treated in the same manner as a sole-proprietor for income tax purposes.

Code Sec. 1401 imposes a sole proprietor's tax on a sole proprietor's net earnings from self-employment.

Whether LLC members are liable for self-employment tax on their distributive shares of income from the entity is an important issue for the following two reasons: First, exposure to self-employment tax can be expensive. The self-employment tax is computed as follows [¶15,085]:

1. In 2013, a 12.4 percent tax is imposed on the first $113,700 of an individual's net earnings from self-employment for old-age, survivors, and disability insurance.
2. A 2.9 percent hospital insurance tax (Medicare) is imposed on *all* net earnings from self-employment.

As a result, in 2013, the first $113,700 of an individual's self-employment income is taxed at the full 15.3 percent and all self-employment income in excess of that amount is taxed at 2.9 percent. There is, however, a deduction allowed to the self-employed taxpayer for half of the self-employment taxes paid. In addition, self-employment tax is not imposed if an individual's net earnings from self-employment are less than $400 [Code Sec. 1401(b)(2)].

Second, participation in a qualified retirement plan, which affords participants valuable tax benefits, turns on whether they have all or a substantial portion of their income derived from their "net earnings from self-employment." Any income excluded from the definition of net earnings from self-employment will be excluded for purposes of calculating allowable contributions to qualified plans, which allow for tax-deferred retirement savings.

.01 Additional Medicare Tax on Self-employment Income

Beginning in 2013, an additional HI (Medicare) tax is imposed on wages and self-employment income above a certain threshold. Taxpayers other than corporations, estates, and trusts are subject to a 0.9 percent tax on self-employment income in excess of $200,000 ($250,000 in the case of a joint return, $125,000 in the case of a married taxpayer filing separately) for tax years beginning after December 31, 2012 [Code Sec. 1401(b)(2)]. The one-half of self-employment taxes that are deductible under Code Sec. 164(f) does not include the additional Medicare tax. Taxpayers who elect to reduce self-employment income by an amount equal to one half of the combined self-employment tax rate, pursuant to Code Sec. 1402(a)(12), do not include the additional Medicare tax in the rate used to make such computation [Code Sec. 1402(a)(12)(B)]. For further discussion, see ¶15,050.

.02 Who Must Pay Self-Employment Tax

Whether LLC members must pay self-employment tax turns on the tax treatment of the LLC member as follows:

- *LLC member taxed as corporation.* A member of an LLC that is taxed as a corporation will be subject to employment taxes on his salary, but not on dividends or distributions [Code Sec. 3101].
- *LLC member treated as general partner.* If an LLC member is treated for federal tax purposes as a general partner, the member will be subject to self-employment tax [Code Sec. 1402(a)].
- *LLC member treated as limited partner.* If the LLC is engaged in a trade or business, self-employment tax is not levied on the income allocated to a member designated as limited partners, except for guaranteed payments provided for remuneration for services rendered to the LLC as described in Code Sec. 707(c) [Code Sec. 1402(a)(13); Prop. Reg. § 1.1402(a)-2]. Guaranteed payments are payments made by the partnership to partners without regard to the partnership's income and are offset by a general partner's distributed share of a sustained loss. See ¶24,080 for further discussion of guaranteed payments.
- *Multi-member LLC.* A multi-member domestic LLC, unless an election is made to have it taxed as a corporation, is an entity that by default is classified as a partnership for federal tax purposes under Reg. § 301.7701-1. Generally, state law provides that general partners of a partnership are jointly and severally liable for

the partnership's obligations. Members of a multi-member LLC are generally not liable under state law for the LLC's debts including employment taxes. Thus, even if the multi-member LLC is classified as a partnership for federal tax purposes, the IRS cannot collect its employment tax from its members based on that classification.[13]

- *Single-member LLC.* LLCs owned by only one individual will be disregarded for federal tax purposes and taxed as proprietorships. All earnings from a proprietorship are subject to the self-employment tax therefore the sole owner of a single-member LLC will be personally liable for the employment taxes incurred by the LLC [Code Sec. 1401].[14]

.03 Definition of Self-Employment Income

Net income from self-employment, for purposes of determining liability for self employment tax, is defined generally as the gross income derived by an individual from any trade or business carried on by such individual. In the case of a partner in a partnership, the term includes a partner's distributive share (whether or not distributed) of net income or loss from a partnership engaged in a trade or business. The Internal Revenue Code distinguishes between general and limited partners for purposes of defining income from self-employment. A limited partner's distributive share of income or loss will not be counted as self-employment income, except for guaranteed payments (as defined in Code Sec. 707(c)) for a limited partner's services to the partnership. The reasoning behind this is that limited partners generally derive their income from capital, while general partners derive their income from the performance of services and should therefore be subject to self-employment tax.

.04 Functional Tests in Prop. Reg. § 1.1402(a)-2

The IRS has issued proposed regulations that establish functional tests for LLC members to apply in determining whether an individual is a limited partner and off the hook for self-employment tax. Prop. Reg. § 1.1402(a)-2(h)(2) defines limited partner for these purposes as an individual who:

1. Has no personal liability for the debts of or claims against the partnership;
2. Has no authority (under the law of the jurisdiction in which the partnership is formed) to contract on behalf of the partnership under the statute or law pursuant to which the partnership is organized; or
3. Participates in the partnership's trade or business for no more than 500 hours during the tax year.

An individual who holds more than one class of interest in a partnership and is not treated as a limited partner under the previous rule will be treated as a limited partner with respect to a specific class of partnership interest held by the individual if, immediately after the individual acquires that class of interest, both of the following requirements are satisfied [Prop. Reg. § 1.1402(a)-2(h)(3)]:

1. Limited partners own a substantial, continuing interest in that specific class of partnership interest.

---

[13] Rev. Rul. 2004-41, 2004-1 CB 845.

[14] LTR 200235023 (Oct. 11, 2005, re-released with additional information).

2. The individual's rights and obligations with respect to that specific class of interest are identical to the rights and obligations of that specific class of partnership interest held by those persons treated as limited partners of that specific class of partnership interest.

.05 Service Partner Exception

An individual who is a service partner in a partnership may not be a limited partner and thus may be exposed to self-employment tax [Prop. Reg. § 1.1402(a)-2(h)(5)]. A service partner is defined as a partner who provides services to or on behalf of a service partnership's trade or business. A service partnership is a partnership substantially all the activities of which involve the performance of services in the fields of health, law, engineering, architecture, accounting, actuarial science, or consulting. There is an exception, however, for those partners who provide only a de minimis amount of services to or on behalf of the partnership [Prop. Reg. § 1.1402(a)-2(h)(6)].

Example 30-2: Alice, Bob and Carol form an LLC to engage in a business. Alice does not perform services for the LLC. Each year Bob receives a guaranteed payment for 600 hours of services rendered to the LLC. Carol is elected manager of the LLC and has the authority to contract on behalf of the LLC. Only Alice avoids paying any self-employment tax in this example because she is the only one who is treated under the proposed regulations as a limited partner. She is a limited partner because (1) she is not liable personally for debts of or claims against the LLC; (2) she does not have authority to contract for the LLC under state law; and (3) she does not participate in LLC's trade or business for more than 500 hours during the year. Bob is a limited partner because he performs more than 500 hours of service during the tax year to the partnership and must pay self-employment tax only on the amount he received as a guaranteed payment. Carol must pay self-employment tax on her guaranteed payment and on her distributive share of LLC income because she has the authority to contract on behalf of the LLC and therefore is not treated as a limited partner [Prop. Reg. § 1.1402(a)-2(i) Example].

▶ PRACTICE TIPS:

- *How to limit exposure to self-employment tax.* The IRS will conclude that you are subject to self-employment tax if you are liable personally for debts of or claims against the LLC, have authority to contract on behalf of the LLC, or participate in the LLC's trade or business for more than 500 hours during the tax year. To avoid exposure to self-employment tax, draft the LLC articles so that LLC members fall just below these requirements.
- *Qualified retirement plan tip.* In addition, in order to maximize contributions to qualified retirement plans, the articles should provide for guaranteed payments for services to nonmanager members up to the maximum qualified compensation base. Although Code Sec. 1402(a)(13) provides that the guaranteed payments are subject to self-employment tax, the members could put away tax-deferred dollars for their retirement.

As mentioned above, a member of an LLC will be able to avoid paying self-employment tax if he or she is classified as a limited partner [Code Sec. 1402(a)(13)]. However, guaranteed payments made to the limited partner for services actually rendered to or on behalf of the partnership engaged in a trade or business are included in the individual's net earnings from self-employment and therefore are subject to self-employment tax. See Ch. 24.

¶30,100 LLCs AND THE PAYROLL TAX

Under Code Sec. 6672, personal liability is imposed upon the "responsible person" of an organization when he/she "willfully" fails to collect and pay over to the IRS employment taxes withheld from the employees' payroll. The personal liability is equal to the payroll taxes which have not been collected, or not accounted for and paid over [Ch. 15]. The responsible person can be generally described as the person(s) charged with the financial responsibility for running the LLC. The responsible person for nonpayment of employment taxes becomes "willful" when he or she makes a conscious choice to pay LLC creditors rather than the LLC payroll taxes. It is important therefore in allocating managerial responsibility among the members, managers, member-managers or nonmember managers, to provide, with specificity, in the written LLC operating agreement, the persons designated with the responsibility for financial management of the LLC. If no provision is made as to the allocation for this responsibility, the IRS can be expected to charge all member-managers and/or nonmember managers with joint and several liability for the delinquent employment taxes.

.01 "Check-the-Box" Regs. Upheld as LLCs' Sole Owners Held Liable for Employment Taxes

The Court of Appeals for the Sixth Circuit upheld the validity of the check-the-box regulations in *Littriello*,[15] and concluded that a taxpayer, who was the sole member of several LLCs which the regulations treated as disregarded entities under its default rule, was responsible for the LLC's employment tax. Similarly, in *McNamee*,[16] the Court of Appeals for the Second Circuit concluded that the owner of a single-member LLC who failed to treat the LLC as a corporation under the IRS check-the-box regulations was personally liable for the LLC's debts and liabilities including unpaid payroll taxes. The court rejected the taxpayers argument that the check-the-box regulations were invalid and concluded that the regulations, which allow the single-owner LLC to choose treatment as a corporation or as a sole proprietorship are "eminently reasonable." The court explained that the single-owner LLC has the option to choose to be treated as an association (i.e. a corporation) or to be disregarded as a separate entity. If an entity elects treatment as a corporation, its owner avoids personal liability if the LLC is disregarded. Since the owner of the single-member LLC in *McNamee* failed to elect treatment as a corporation, the court found the taxpayer to be personally liable for any debts and liabilities including payroll taxes.

---

[15] *F.A. Littriello*, CA-6, 2007-1 USTC ¶50,426, 484 F3d 372; *E.A. Kandi*, CA-9, 2008-2 USTC ¶50,599, 295 Fed Appx 873; *P.M. Comensoli*, CA-6, 2011-1 USTC ¶50,368; *C.P. Britton*, CA-1, 2010-2 USTC ¶50,584.

[16] *S.P. McNamee*, CA-2, 2007-1 USTC ¶50,515, 488 F3d 100.

In *Stearn & Co.*,[17] the sole proprietor of a company that was an LLC under state law was individually liable for unpaid employment taxes owed by the company. Since the owner did not elect to have the company treated as a corporation under the "check-the-box" regulations, the company was classified as a disregarded entity and treated as a sole proprietorship for federal tax purposes. The company's limited liability status under state law did not prevent the IRS from levying against the sole owner. He waived LLC protection and chose to have the company treated as a disregarded entity.

In *L&L Holding Co.*,[18] the district court held that entities that were the successive sole owners of a single-member LLC were liable for the company's unpaid employment taxes because the company failed to make an election to be treated as a corporation under the "check-the-box" regulations. Although the LLC was an employer for employment tax purposes, it was treated as a disregarded entity because of its failure to make the election under Reg. § 301.7701-3. Consequently, the IRS held the owners liable for the associated employment taxes and filed related tax liens against them.

APPLICABILITY TO SPECIFIC TYPES OF BUSINESS

¶30,105 REAL ESTATE INVESTMENTS

Many real estate investments have been structured as limited partnerships to provide maximum tax benefits to the investors through netting gross rental income against depreciation, real estate taxes, mortgage taxes and real estate operating expenses, so that the difference, whether it be taxable income or deductible loss, passes through directly on the investor's individual income tax return. Of course, there are still the tax issues of "passive losses" and "at risk" deductibility to be resolved [See Ch. 13].

In a limited partnership, the general partner retains general liability for partnership obligations and often must be independently capitalized. Further, limited partners who participate too actively in the conduct of the business of the partnership risk loss of limited liability, although this risk has been reduced in states, such as New York and Delaware, that have adopted the Revised Uniform Limited Partnership Act (RULPA). RULPA provides that a limited partner who participates in the conduct of the partnerships business will only be liable to creditors who reasonably believed, based on such limited partner's conduct that the limited partner was a general partner. Additionally, a substantial list of activities that may safely be engaged in by limited partners is provided. By virtue of these provisions, limited partners now may be substantially involved in decisions and activities of the partnerships without running the risk that their interests will be recharacterized.

In many real estate ventures structured as limited partnerships, the parties seek to combine limited liability and tax transparency by holding the bulk of their economic interests as limited partners and consolidating control of the partnership in or more corporate general partners.

---

[17] *Stearn & Co.*, DC-MI, 2007-2 USTC ¶50,676, 499 F Supp2d 899.

[18] *L&L Holding Co.*, DC-LA, 2008-1 USTC ¶50,324; *Medical Practice Solutions, LLC*, 99 TCM 1392, Dec. 58,208(M), TC Memo. 2010-98.

.01 Tax Benefits

Such an entity, if otherwise properly structured to qualify for pass-through tax treatment can provide the same benefits as an LLC with respect to the 99 percent interest held by the limited partners. However, this limited partnership structure suffers from several disadvantages.

- Two levels of governance are required, creating additional organizational complexity, legal fees and franchise tax liability.
- It may be necessary to capitalize the corporate general partner beyond its investment in the partnership. Such capital, plus any other assets of such general partner, will be at risk for the recourse obligations of the underlying partnership.
- The corporate general partner will incur entity-level tax, unless it is structured as a S corporation. As discussed below, S corporations create their own set of restrictions and issues.
- If the corporate general partner were determined to be undercapitalized, or if corporate formalities were not observed, it is possible (although remote) that its veil would be pierced, causing the limited partners who are its shareholders to face general liability.

.02 LLC Benefits

The LLC offers the same tax benefits as the limited partnership through pass-through taxation and, further provides the nontax benefit of preventing exposure of any member or manager to general liability and simplifies drafting problems by eliminating defining lines between general and limited partners.

It is not practical for most real estate investments to be structured as C corporations since investors are looking to obtain the benefits of depreciation, real estate taxes, mortgage interest and like operating expenses directly on their return (hopefully with passive loss and at-risk rules not applying) or, in the case of income, that it is taxed at only one level. Also, if the real estate has appreciated and is ripe for the sale, the shareholders will only obtain the fruit of their investment after it is squeezed twice—once at the corporate level and then again at the shareholder level, either in liquidation or redemption of their stock.

S corporations inhibit the promoters of a real estate investment because no more than 100 shareholders are permitted, only voting and nonvoting classes of stock are permitted; nonresident aliens, many trusts and corporations cannot be stockholders, and the possibility of inadvertent termination always lingers [Ch. 21].

Real estate investing is a business that is well suited to LLC creation or conversion since it permits both the tax and nontax benefits described above.

¶30,115 MANUFACTURING OR SERVICE COMPANY CONVERTING TO LLC STATUS

The typical manufacturing organization is a corporation, whether C or S, which incorporates to protect its stockholders from personal liability. It chooses a C or S, based upon the advice of its professional tax counsel, who then analyzes corporate and personal tax rates of the stockholders before making his/her recommendation.

The new manufacturing organization should consider forming an LLC in order to have the same personal liability protection and the opportunity to be subject to tax only once at the individual level and if there are losses to have such losses absorb other income reported on the Form 1040 (subject, of course, to the passive loss and at-risk rules).

However, the choice is not so simple in the case of an existing corporation since it may have unrealized gain among its assets. The cost of a conversion in such a case would be a double tax: once at the corporate level and then again at the shareholder level at liquidation. Therefore, those existing corporations considering conversion to an LLC must have their accountants make the calculations necessary to compare the tax cost of conversion by liquidation to the future tax savings anticipated in forming an LLC.

▶ **REMEMBER:** The tax-free rules allowing corporations to merge or otherwise reorganize do not apply to LLCs classified as partnerships. Not being corporations, they are not eligible to participate in a reorganization under the provisions of Code Sec. 368.

NOTE: In the case of a newly created service business, it is clear that the combination of limited liability and only one level of taxation make the formation of an LLC most attractive. However, care must also be taken in the case of converting a service corporation, by liquidating and forming an LLC. This follows because, while most service organizations may not have tangible assets with unrealized appreciation, they do carry, if successful in their field, goodwill and perhaps other intangibles. These intangibles have value and, as such, are subject to tax on liquidation therefore subjecting the corporate shareholders to a double tax—again at the corporate level and individual levels.

▶ **OBSERVATION:** A corporation that has operated as an S corporation during its entire existence is not subject to a tax on built-in gain.

¶30,120 THE SOLE PROPRIETOR

The sole proprietor faces all kinds of risks of personal liability. Historically, to avoid such risks, sole proprietors have chosen corporate status, either C or S, depending on the unique circumstances of the combination of corporate and individual income. Professionals, practicing as sole proprietors, also have chosen corporate status but are mandated by state law to incorporate as a personal service corporation, allowing clients and patients to sue them directly for malpractice but, at least, protecting them from commercial liability, such as breach of contract.

Sole proprietors may form an LLC under many enabling LLC state laws but the IRS refuses to treat them as partnerships for tax purposes.

A single-owner LLC cannot elect to be taxed as a partnership under the check-the-box regulations. It can either be classified as an association (taxed as a corporation) or be disregarded as an entity separate from its owner, thus rendering it a tax nothing. This means that single-owner LLCs will be treated under the check-the-box regulations as if they were conducted as a sole proprietorship, branch, or division of its owner [Reg. § 301.7701-3(a)]. See discussion in ¶ 30,080.

Achieving limited liability while limiting taxation to one level can be achieved for the nonprofessional through electing Subchapter S, or in the case of a professional, incorporating as a professional service corporation and eliminating the retention of corporate income through salary and fringe benefits (such as a pension plan).

OTHER TAX AND NONTAX FEATURES OF LLCs

▶ **OBSERVATION:** If the LLC is to operate in other states, its members must determine whether it will be treated as a corporation or a partnership in those states. Also, there may be city and other local taxes with which to contend. Therefore, LLC members must review with their attorneys and accountants both the tax and nontax considerations for operating out of the state of the LLC's formation.

¶30,125 STATE TAX LAWS

The tax and nontax features are interlocked in that an LLC has to conform to state laws as to formation, operation and dissolution. It also has to be formed to meet the particular tax needs of its members and the business (or nonprofit) activity in which it hopes to engage.

¶30,130 LLC NAME

Many state LLC laws require the LLC, when formed, to advise the public of its organizational status by including the term *limited liability company* or the abbreviation *LLC*. Also, some jurisdictions mandate that the name requested be distinguished from the name of any corporation, limited partnership, LLC or any other organization indicated on the records of the Secretary of State. If the LLC to engage in business in other jurisdictions, it is wise to confirm the name requirements of those other jurisdictions so as to avoid conflict and costly administrative or court proceedings.

¶30,135 FORMATION OF LLCs

An LLC can be formed for any lawful purpose by filing a document known generally as articles of organization with the Secretary of State. In many jurisdictions, one person can sign and file the articles of organization that person does not necessarily have to be a member (such as your lawyer or your accountant). Fees for filing the articles vary among the states. The LLC becomes a recognized legal entity at the time of filing with the Secretary of State who looks only to determine whether the Articles contain the information required by the state's LLC law and whether the filing fee has been paid. Most states have forms for filing. There are some jurisdictions, such as

New York, which require notice to the public of the filing within 120 days of filing, such notice to be published in two newspapers in the county in which the office of the LLC is located, etc.

▶ **COMMENT:** It is prudent to consult an attorney to arrange the filing so as to avoid the otherwise unnecessary costs which could follow by not adhering to the filing details of a particular jurisdiction.

NOTE: There is no indication in the filed certificates of formation available to the public as to names of the actual members of the LLC. That knowledge can only be obtained by reference to the LLC operating agreement which is a private document executed among the members either contemporaneous with or generally immediately subsequent to the filing of the Articles of Organization. Until some practice is adopted as to the filing of annual reports by LLCs with the states of their formation or operation, it is possible that members' names may not be available for public information.

¶30,140 LLC TAX YEAR

The tax year of an LLC depends on the classification of the LLC. If the LLC is classified as a partnership, its tax year is governed by Code Sec. 706(b) and it must adopt the tax year of one or more members having an aggregate interest in profits and capital in excess of 50 percent; if no such majority interest exists, then it must adopt the tax year of all its principal members (those having a 5 percent or more interest in LLC profits or capital).

NOTE: An LLC member cannot change to the tax year of an LLC unless he/she is a principal member. Also, it is clear that, in most cases, the individual members of the LLC will generally be on a calendar year.

If the LLC is taxed as a C corporation, it can choose any year end as the tax year end. If the LLC is taxed as an S corporation, it generally must use a calendar year end. A single-member's LLC required year end is the tax year of the owner.

¶30,145 METHOD OF ACCOUNTING

An LLC, like other taxpayers, is generally allowed to choose any accounting method that clearly reflects income and is regularly used in keeping the LLC's books [Code Sec. 448]. Professional service firms generally prefer to use the cash method because income does not have to be recognized until billed amounts are collected. However, Code Sec. 448(a) provides that the cash method of accounting is unavailable to (1) a C corporation, (2) a partnership which has a C corporation as a partner, or (3) a tax shelter. A personal service corporation is treated as an individual in Code Sec. 448(b)(2) and thus is eligible to use the cash method. However, the IRS has determined that an LLC that was classified as a partnership was allowed to use the cash method for computing its taxable income.[19]

[19] LTR 9432018 (May 16, 1994).

MEMBERSHIP

¶30,150 NUMBER OF MEMBERS

Jurisdictions are split as to the requirements for number of members to validate an LLC; there are those requiring at least two members and those allowing a single member. One might assume that in those jurisdictions requiring two members that, in the event one member dies, leaves or otherwise is removed from membership, an LLC will be forced to dissolve. However, many jurisdictions permit a "temporary failure" of the two member minimum to be cured by the admission of an additional member during the period generally contained in the LLC operating agreement between the event causing dissolution and the vote by members to continue the life of the LLC.

¶30,155 MEMBERSHIP IN AN LLC

Membership in an LLC is unrestricted, i.e., individuals, domestic and foreign corporations, trusts, nonprofit organizations, etc., are all eligible for LLC membership. In order for an assignment of a membership interest to be completely accomplished, it must fit the requirements of the LLC operating agreement and, generally, that requires the consent, either unanimously or by those holding a majority in interest of capital and profits, to permit the assignment.

In the absence of consent, the consequence of the assignment is to permit the assignee to succeed to the economic interest of the assignor-member's interest (his/her share of profits and losses) but without the ability to have a voice in the management of LLC activity. Further, the nonconsensual assignment does not generally preclude the assignor from continuing to participate in management since his membership has not been effectively terminated.

> ▶ **COMMENT:** Time and experience will no doubt bring changes to the LLC laws and the redrafting of LLC operating agreements. In this case, it does not make economic sense to the remaining members for a nonconsensual assignment to be made wherein the assignee has but an economic participation to profits while the assignor, who surrenders his/her economic stake, continues to have a say in the way an LLC conducts its business.

Another concern of a member is his/her right to withdraw from continuing in the LLC. In the absence of a provision in the LLC operating agreement providing for withdrawal (and, in most cases, good drafting would prevent this from happening), the default provisions take over. In New York, for instance, a member can only withdraw with the consent of 2/3 of the members in interest (excluding the withdrawing member). If the consent is not obtained, in the absence of an absolute prohibition in the operating agreement, the withdrawing member may, on six months prior notice, withdraw from membership. If, however, such a prohibition does exist in the operating agreement and nevertheless the withdrawing member leaves, he/she does face a potential lawsuit for breaching the operating agreement.

¶30,160 CONTINUITY OF LIFE

The LLC acts generally follow the revised uniform limited partnership laws and set forth events causing the dissolution of an LLC unless the members vote to continue. Many jurisdictions have omitted the 30-year limitation. Others, however, do limit the duration of LLCs and preclude perpetual duration. Finally, there are some states, such as Delaware, Florida and Texas, which expressly allow perpetual duration.

An LLC operating agreement might provide for dissolution of the LLC on the first of the following to occur:

1. The dissolution period indicated in the articles of organization; or
2. At the time or happening of events (e.g., death, disability, retirement, bankruptcy or expulsion of a member) unless within, e.g., 90 or 180 days, the LLC is continued either by the vote of the members or some other condition indicated by the operating agreement.

¶30,165 POWERS OF THE LLC

LLCs generally have the same power as an individual to do all things necessary or appropriate to carry out the LLC's business and purpose. Many states include a list of statutory powers derived from the stock corporation acts of that state. Most states do not require an LLC to include the powers to carry out its purposes in the Articles of Organization.

¶30,170 LIMITING LIABILITY

Limited liability is the most significant nontax attribute. Accordingly, LLC members, unlike sole practitioners or general partners, are not personally liable for the debts and obligations of the LLC; a member's liability is limited to his or her capital contribution. The LLC member(s) may still be economically compelled to be at risk, e.g., a bank loan or providing a personal guarantee to a recalcitrant landlord. Further, an LLC operating agreement may contain a provision imposing liability, e.g., restoring a negative capital account, an obligation which an outside creditor might be able to enforce.

¶30,175 THE OPERATING AGREEMENT

This is a most important document in operating as an LLC since it serves as the basis by which the members transact business with the public and among themselves. It serves as the framework for confirming, among other things, contributions to be made; how profits and losses are allocated; the nature and extent of membership in the LLC and the different classes of membership, if any; the conditions calling for dissolution or for departures of members, voluntary or involuntary, from continued membership; and, the basis for managing the conduct of LLC business. In short, the purpose of the operating agreements for LLCs, like any contract, is to prevent misunderstandings among the members as to operation and self governing conditions. Also, it allows dealing with the IRS to be easily transacted by allowing the IRS to look at a writing and determine the tax consequences stemming there from.

While there are jurisdictions which permit oral agreements among LLC members, it would be foolhardy to conduct a business on the convenience of memories afforded by oral exchanges; and, it would eventually lead to costly and time consuming litigation. Further, the absence of an operating agreement would cause the default provisions of a particular state to prevail, an unanticipated eventuality which could be in conflict with the intentions of the members.

> **NOTE:** Under bulletproof LLC state laws, members cannot change the requirement of unanimous consent required by the remaining members to permit an assignee to succeed to full membership (economic and management participation) or for dissolution to be avoided upon the disassociation of a member.

¶30,180 MANAGEMENT

Under the default provisions, the members are vested with management authority in running the LLC. However, if the operating agreement so provides, the members may elect managers to supervise business operations of the LLC, in much the same way that stockholders elect directors or general partners conduct a limited partnership. The members in the LLC operating agreement may authorize the limits of responsibility to the elected managers, who are not required to be LLC members, natural persons or residents of the state in which the LLC was formed. The managers are generally afforded exclusive authority to deal with the general public and have the obligation to act as fiduciaries in their dealings on behalf of the LLC and their dealings with LLC members. A manager who competes with the business of the LLC through direct or indirect association with a competitor of his/her LLC would probably face a lawsuit for breach of his/her fiduciary duties.

¶30,185 VOTING RIGHTS

An LLC operating agreement should set forth with clarity the voting rights of members and managers. Should voting to be on a per capita basis—one member, one vote? If so, there would be an unfair advantage over those members who made the larger contributions to the capital of the LLC or who have a higher stake in the sharing of profits and losses. On the other hand, giving such members a larger numerical vote count, would raise questions as to the timing of determining the contribution accounts of the members—at the date of contribution or the last financial statement filed covering the LLC's fiscal year or as of the end of the month preceding the vote being taken. Fairness among the members and good draftsmanship confirming with clarity the members' intentions can resolve the issue of measuring the voting rights of the members. In addition, it is imperative that actions of the LLC controlled by the voting be determined on the basis of unanimous consent or by a majority vote. Watch out for LLC state provisions which might contravene the operating agreement, e.g., in bulletproof states, unanimous consent is required to allow for the transfer of a membership interest.

¶30,190 CONTRIBUTIONS OF MEMBERS TO AN LLC

The LLC laws permit contributions by incoming members of cash, property or services rendered, or a promissory note or other obligation to contribute cash, or property or to perform services. Unless members have otherwise agreed, a member remains liable for his/her contribution obligations even if unable to perform because of death or disability. This means that the estate of a person who has failed to live up to his/her contribution obligation will be charged with paying it. Also, if a member fails to contribute the promised property or service, the LLC has the option to require that member to contribute cash to compensate for the difference.

> **NOTE:** It is likely that a member, and not just the LLC, might have a contractual right to sue the estate of a defaulting deceased contributor by arguing estoppel or the fact of his/her reliance on the commitment to contribute by the deceased contributor to the detriment of the suing member.

Also, defaulting members failing to make good on their contribution commitment might face sanctions under the operating agreement, such as forfeiting their membership interest, subordination of such interest to the interest of the nondefaulting members or a forced sale of their membership interest. Further, care should be taken as to creditors' rights which might allow a creditor to pursue remedies against the defaulting member if they extended credit in reliance on the defaulting member's commitment. In addition, any unpaid or unperformed contribution may not be compromised without the consent of all the members, unless otherwise provided among the members; and, in no case will a creditor be bound by the compromise.

¶30,195 THE ALLOCATION OF LLC PROFITS AND LOSSES

Many jurisdictions provide, in the absence of a provision in the operating agreement, that profits and losses will be allocated on a pro rata basis, based on the agreed value of member contributions (as shown on the LLC books) to the extent paid by and not returned to a member. While this might appear fair at first glance, it could prove unfair, particularly in a growing business where new members are added.

> **Example 30-3:** Jackson and Johnson each contribute $100 at the inception of the LLC. As a result of the success of the LLC, the value of the LLC business has increased in the next year to $500. Manning is invited to join at that time as an equal member and contributes $167 (1/3 of $500). Should Manning be entitled to a greater participation in profits based on his higher capital contribution? Drafting a provision to anticipate this eventuality or amending the operating agreement prior to Manning's becoming a member would prevent this problem from arising.

Also, be aware of the adverse influence of tax considerations as a factor in determining the profit and loss allocation. The tax concept of "substantial economic effect" must enter into a profit or loss allocation [See Ch. 24]. Simply stated, if an allocation is made to enhance the tax benefits of one partner as compared to the allocation, he/she would have received without consideration of the tax consequences to him/her, then such allocation could be challenged by the IRS.

¶30,200 DISTRIBUTIONS

Distributions, whether of cash or property, to members should be authorized by the provisions contained in the operating agreement. If the operating agreement is silent, distributions are generally to be allocated under the default rules based on the stated value of contributions made and not returned, or on the agreed allocation of profits and losses.

For distributions made during the course of the liquidation of the partnership, care should be taken with respect to creditors since distributions to members at the expense of creditors could provide a creditor with a remedy against the members or managers who participated in the preferential distribution.

¶30,205 DISASSOCIATION

Disassociation occurs upon an event giving rise to a member's termination from the LLC. Death, disability, bankruptcy represent some of the events leading to disassociation. Expulsion by unanimous consent of the other members is another such event which should however be supported by an enabling provision in the LLC Operating Agreement. The payment for disassociation should also be spelled out in the operating agreement; and, if not, many default provisions require payment to the withdrawing member or his estate of the "fair value of his interest." Fair value can be a very subjective factor and should be carefully addressed in the operating agreement without the intrusion of state default provisions.

¶30,210 WITHDRAWAL, DISSOLUTION AND WINDING UP

A typical state defaulting provision provides that an LLC dissolves and its affairs are to be wound upon the first to occur of the following:

1. Reaching the time limit set in the operating agreement, or if none, in 30 years;
2. Events set in the operating agreement;
3. The written consent of all the members;
4. The death, retirement, resignation, expulsion, bankruptcy or dissolution of a member or of any membership event, unless all members consent to continue within 90 days; or

5. Pursuant to a right to continue under the operating agreement, or pursuant to a judicial decree.

Generally, a court can order dissolution on application of a member or manager whenever it is not reasonably practicable to carry on the business in conformity with the operating agreement.

The distribution to be made in dissolution is also creditor sensitive (including those who are members and managers of the LLC). After creditors are paid, distributions are to be made to members and former members. Finally, members receive a return of their respective contributions and then a proportionate share of all remaining distributions. Sufficient funds should be set aside to settle claims and contingencies. A certificate of cancellation must then be filed with the Secretary of State.

¶30,215 MERGERS AND CONSOLIDATIONS

The LLC statutes permit mergers and consolidations of LLCs with any other *business entity* which is defined to include a corporation (both profit and nonprofit), a business trust or association, a real estate investment trust, a common-law trust, any other unincorporated business, including both general and limited partnerships and foreign LLCs. See ¶ 30,065 for discussion of foreign LLCs.

¶30,220 TERMINATION OF AN LLC

An LLC classified as a partnership is terminated in one of two ways:

1. When no part of the business, financial operation or venture of the LLC continues to be carried on by any of its members in the LLC format [Code Sec. 708(b)(1)(A)]; or
2. When 50 percent or more of the total interests in LLC capital and profits are sold or exchanged within a 12-month period [Code Sec. 708(b)(1)(B].

An LLC classified as a partnership is terminated when business activities are discontinued and its assets are distributed to members. If the LLC business is continued in a new form such as a corporation or sole proprietorship (not partnership form), Code Sec. 708(b)(1) provides that the LLC is terminated for tax purposes.

Termination of the LLC can result either from the cessation of all business and investment activities or from the removal of members or other change in the business entity that cause it to be classified as another entity (such as a corporation or sole proprietorship). In order to prevent inadvertent termination of LLC's which could occur when an LLC's business activities cease, the courts and the regulations provide that the LLC will continue as long as any of its business activities continue. Termination does not result merely because the LLC has abandoned its primary business purpose. Even a nominal amount of activity, such as holding property, can be sufficient to prevent a termination. In addition, the cessation of business activities and the termination of the LLC are considered to occur at the time of final distribution of assets to the members.

Reg. § 1.708-1(b)(1)(i) provides that an LLC member will continue to be treated as a member for tax purposes until the member's interest is sold or completely liquidated. When an LLC terminates as a result of ceasing to continue to carry on its business in a partnership, the date of termination is the date on which the winding up of the LLC's business affairs is completed [Reg. § 1.708-1(b)(1)].

Index

References are to paragraph (¶) numbers.

A

Accident and health plans, employer-provided . . . 4025–4025.06
. COBRA coverage in . . . 4025.04
. compliance penalties for . . . 4025.06
. employer contribution to . . . 4120.02
. nondiscrimination rules for . . . 4025.01; 4120.07
. reimbursements under . . . 4120.03
. renewability guarantee for . . . 4025.05
. shared cost of . . . 4025.03; 4120.06
. tax treatment of . . . 4025.02

Accountable plan for reimbursement employee business expenses . . . 9145.01; 10,015–10,015.01; 12,120.03

Accounting . . . 18,001–18,190

Accounting method . . . 18,001–18,050
. adjustments following change in, Section 481 . . . 18,050
. automatic change of . . . 18,005.03
. changing, process of . . . 18,005.02
. for multiple businesses . . . 18,001.02
. nonaccrual experience method . . . 18,080.02
. reasons to change . . . 12,010.05; 12,010.07; 17,045.03; 17,045.11
. record requirements for . . . 18,035
. reflective of income . . . 18,030–18,030.01
. safe harbors for . . . 18,001.04
. types of. *See also* individual types . . . 18,001–18,001.04
. types of changes of . . . 18,045.01

Accounting periods . . . 18,055.01
. automatic consent to change in . . . 24,070.05
. change in . . . 18,060–18,070.02
. general rules for . . . 18,055.01; 26,040
. natural business year one of . . . 21,016.03; 24,070.05–.06
. requesting change in . . . 18,065–18,065.01

Accrual basis accounting
. change from cash basis to . . . 18,045.03
. compensation for services under . . . 18,085.02
. deductions under . . . 18,130.02; 18,150
. deferred payments sales under . . . 19,055.01
. discounts under . . . 18,080.02
. for farming . . . 17,065.01; 18,025.01
. gross income inclusion under . . . 18,025; 18,080.02
. gross income reporting under . . . 18,080.02
. interest reporting for . . . 18,100.01; 18,155–18,155.04
. as one principal method of accounting . . . 18,001
. prepaid income under . . . 18,080.02; 18,115–18,115.02
. reporting gain on property sale under . . . 18,110.01
. reserves for expenses and losses under . . . 18,180.02
. tax deductions under . . . 18,160.02
. uncollectible amounts under . . . 18,080.02

Accrued benefits of qualified plan defined . . . 3020.03

Accumulated adjustments account (AAA) of S corporation . . . 21,050.02

Accumulated earnings and profits of S corporation . . . 21,050.02

Accumulated earnings credit . . . 20,150.03; 20,165.01
. disallowance of . . . 20,170–20,170.01

Accumulated earnings tax . . . 20,145–20,155.01
. avoiding . . . 20,155.01
. corporate liability for . . . 20,145.01
. income subject to . . . 20,150–20,150.03
. rate of . . . 20,155

Acquisition indebtedness . . . 23,175.03

Adjusted gross income (AGI)
. charitable contribution deduction limitations based on . . . 9075–9075.03
. computation of, for Roth IRAs . . . 3140.04
. computation of, for tax return . . . 8045.04
. deductions from . . . 1010.01
. expected . . . 14,215.02
. medical expenses deduction based on . . . 9100.01
. saver's credit for retirement based on . . . 14,130

Advance payments, inclusion in income of . . . 18,085.01; 18,085.04

Advanced lean burn technology motor vehicle credit . . . 14,195.03

Advanced nuclear facility business tax credit . . . 14,150

Adoption assistance program of employer . . . 4115.01

Adoption expense exclusion from wages . . . 4115–4115.10
. adoption assistance program . . . 4115.04
. adopted child needs identification number . . . 4115.07
. computation of MAGI for exclusion purposes . . . 4115.01
. double dipping prohibited . . . 4115.08
. eligible child . . . 4115.06
. employer-provided adoption assistance programs . . . 4115.01
. how to claim adoption exclusion . . . 4115.09
. income phaseout rules . . . 4115.02
. income tax withholding . . . 4115.10
. qualified adoption expenses . . . 4115.05
. special needs child defined . . . 4115.06

Adoption expenses credit . . . 13,015–14,015.10
. adopted child needs identification number . . . 14,015.06
. computation of MAGI for adoption credit purposes . . . 14,015.03
. dollar limitation . . . 14,015.01
. double dipping prohibited . . . 14,015.01
. eligible child . . . 14,015.06
. finality safe harbor . . . 14,015.07
. how to claim adoption credit . . . 14,015.09
. income phaseout rules . . . 14,015.02
. qualified adoption expenses . . . 14,015.06
. special needs child . . . 14,015.04
. timing of credit . . . 14,015.07

Advance payments . . . 18,085.04
. advance trade discount . . . 18,085.05
. inventoriable goods . . . 18,085.07
. prepaid gift cards . . . 18,085.06

Advertising expenses . . . 12,100
. deductible . . . 12,100.01; 18,150

References are to paragraph (¶) numbers.

Advertising expenses—continued
. nondeductible . . . 12,100.02

Agricultural chemicals security tax credit . . . 14,171

Aircraft, company-owned . . . 4015
. employer's deduction for . . . 4015
. entertainment use . . . 4015
. valuation of noncommercial flights on . . . 4015

Airline pilots, retirement benefits for commercial . . . 3040.01

Alcohol fuels credit . . . 14,170.02

Alimony
. recapture for excess front-loaded . . . 2150.02
. tax ramifications of . . . 2150.01

Alternate Depreciation System (ADS), electing . . . 11,040.06; 11,050.03

Alternate estate tax valuation . . . 29,110

Alternative energy property for residential alternative energy expenditures credit . . . 14,045.02

Alternative fueling stations, credit for installation of . . . 14,155–14,155.03

Alternative incremental research credit . . . 14,080.05

Alternative minimum tax (AMT) . . . 16,001–16,045
. adjustments and preference items under . . . 16,001; 16,001.04; 16,005–16,005.16
. annualizing income for . . . 14,220.02; 18,070.02
. child's tax return triggering . . . 2170.04
. computing . . . 16,001.03
. for corporations . . . 16,025–16,045; 20,010.03–.04; 20,070.03
. election to claim accelerated AMT and research credit in lieu of bonus depreciation . . . 14,157
. for estates and trusts . . . 25,100.04
. exemptions for . . . 16,015; 20,165.02
. exemption phase-out . . . 16,015.01
. exercise of ISOs as triggering . . . 2050.04
. offsets against . . . 16,001.05
. for personal holding companies . . . 23,001.01
. repealed for small businesses . . . 16,025.01
. for small business stock dispositions . . . 8105.09
. tax planning to avoid . . . 16,001.05
. tax rates for . . . 16,001.01

Alternative minimum tax credit
. for corporations . . . 16,045
. for individuals . . . 16,020.01–.04

Alternative minimum taxable income (AMTI)
. computing . . . 12,150.02
. corporate exemption from . . . 16,040
. in short tax year . . . 18,070.02
. tax rates applied to . . . 16,001.01

Alternative motor vehicle credit . . . 14,195.01–.05

Alternative tax regime . . . 29,160.01

Amended return . . . 26,080

American Samoa
. possession exclusion for residents of . . . 28,080.01
. tax treatment of . . . 28,080.02

Amortization
. change in . . . 18,045.01
. of excess business start-up expenses . . . 12,040.01
. of intangible property . . . 11,005.05
. of mining exploration costs . . . 12,195.01
. of reforestation expenditures . . . 12,215

Annuities . . . 5070–5080.05
. actuarial tables for . . . 5070.06
. employee . . . 5080–5080.05

Annuities—continued
. exclusion ratio for tax-free portions of . . . 5070.03; 5080.03
. expected return on . . . 5070.05
. joint and survivor . . . 3075.01; 3075.04; 5075
. private annuities . . . 5070
. purchased by tax-exempt organizations . . . 5080.03
. starting date of . . . 5070.02; 5080.05
. tax treatment of . . . 5070.01; 5080.01–.02
. tax-sheltered . . . 3165–3165.07
. taxation of distributions from . . . 3080.01
. types of . . . 5070.01

Annuity contracts
. cash value build-up of . . . 5070.01
. consolidation of . . . 6105.03
. distribution rules for . . . 3120.03; 5070.08
. employee contributions to . . . 5080.04
. funds received other than annuity from . . . 5070.07
. investment in . . . 5070.04
. limits for . . . 3040
. partial exchanges of . . . 6105.04
. premium payments for . . . 12,105.01
. sale or exchange of . . . 6105–6105.04

Anticonversion transactions for income . . . 8005.01–.10

Anticutback rules for qualified plans
. defined . . . 3020.04
. plan amendment subject to . . . 3035.03

Anti-*Morris Trust* provisions . . . 22,090.04

Appeals Office, IRS
. conference with . . . 27,015–27,015.04
. structure of . . . 27,030–27,030.03

Archer medical savings accounts (MSAs) . . . 9120–9120.06
. contribution limits for . . . 9120.02
. coverage under . . . 9120.04
. eligibility for . . . 9120.01
. establishing . . . 9120
. filing requirements for . . . 9120.05
. Medicare Advantage . . . 9120.06
. tax treatment of . . . 9120.04

Armed Forces
. compensation of members of . . . 2030.01–.05
. disability payments to members of . . . 5045.05
. mortgage interest deduction for members of . . . 9025.01
. moving expenses for members of . . . 9135.04
. reporting payments to . . . 15,140.02
. suspension of ownership period for principal residence of . . . 7010.02
. wages during military reserves leave for . . . 12,065.01

Assessments, tax. *See* Deficiency assessment, IRS

At-risk rules
. for partnership losses . . . 24,055.01
. for tax shelter losses . . . 13,100–13,100.13; 18,135

Athletic facilities operated by employer . . . 4080
. discrimination for use of, as permitted . . . 4080.02
. employee defined for . . . 4080.01

Attorneys, reporting payments for legal services of . . . 26,140.15

Audits of tax returns. *See also* Examinations, IRS
. items on returns that trigger . . . 27,001.03
. limits imposed on . . . 27,005.03
. records for . . . 26,095–26,095.03
. scheduling . . . 27,005.02
. types of . . . 27,005.02

References are to paragraph (¶) numbers.

Auto part remanufacturers and resellers, safe harbor accounting method for . . . 18,001.04

Average benefits test of qualified plan coverage . . . 3025.03

B

Bad debts
. advances to corporations by stockholders as . . . 13,150
. advances to relatives as . . . 13,145
. business . . . 13,125.01; 13,135–13,135.05
. deductible amounts for . . . 13,130; 18,175.01
. determining when debt becomes . . . 13,125.01
. losses distinguished from . . . 13,165–13,165.02
. on mortgage losses . . . 13,175
. nonbusiness . . . 13,140–13,140.03; 13,155
. overview of . . . 13,125
. recovery of, as income . . . 13,170–13,170.01
. worthless securities held by bank as . . . 13,160.01

Bankruptcy Abuse Prevention and Consumer Protection Act of 2004
. asset protection of Coverdell ESA assets under . . . 5115.09
. asset protection of 529 plan assets under . . . 5110.11

Bankruptcy estate
. home sale exclusion in . . . 7001.04
. tax return filing for . . . 26,020.04

Bargain purchases by employees, taxation of . . . 2005

Basis of property
. acquired by gift . . . 6030–6030.04
. acquired from a decedent . . . 6040; 29,005
. adjusted . . . 6001, 6001.02; 10,025.02; 11,065.03; 12,145.06; 12,200.02; 24,055.03; 24,095
. allocation of . . . 6080–6080.08; 11,015.02–.04
. appreciation affecting . . . 6025
. at time of death . . . 29,005; 6030
. carry-over . . . 6030.01; 6035; 6040.03; 29,005
. converted to business use . . . 6095.01–.02; 11,030.02
. of corporation . . . 20,020.02; 22,080
. of mutual fund shares . . . 6090
. cost . . . 6010–6025
. defined . . . 6001.01
. depreciable . . . 11,015–11,015.04
. in discharge of indebtedness . . . 2145.02
. to distributee-stockholder receiving securities . . . 22,070–22,075.02
. in divisive reorganizations . . . 22,115–22,115.01
. goodwill . . . 6080.06
. in installment sales . . . 19,025–19,025.06
. in inventory . . . 6100; 17,060
. in involuntary conversions . . . 7055.02; 7060–7060.07; 8060.05
. in like-kind exchanges . . . 6050.11
. for loss . . . 6030.02
. original . . . 6010
. in partial condemnation . . . 7060.06
. in partnership interest . . . 6115; 24,135–24,135.03
. in qualified small business stock . . . 8105.08
. received as payment for services . . . 6020
. received in exchange . . . 6015–6015.02
. received in subsidiary liquidation . . . 22,130
. recomputed in depreciation recapture . . . 8060.01
. step-up . . . 6040
. in transfers to corporations . . . 6075.05–.06; 22,085.04

Basis of stock in sales or exchanges . . . 2100–2100.01

Biodiesel fuels income tax credit and biodiesel mixture excise tax credit . . . 14,170.03

Bond premiums
. amortizable . . . 9155.01–.03
. amortizing capitalized expenses as part of . . . 9155.04
. of callable bonds . . . 9155.04
. of convertible bonds . . . 9155.04
. as miscellaneous itemized deductions . . . 9155
. for tax-exempt bonds . . . 9155.02
. for taxable bonds . . . 9155.01

Bond rights
. nontaxable . . . 2120.01
. taxable . . . 2120.02

Bonds
. alternative minimum tax . . . 5005.02
. arbitrage . . . 5005.01
. corporate issuance of . . . 20,090–20,090.05
. exclusion of interest on U.S. savings bonds . . . 2070.08
. insured . . . 5005.02
. interest on . . . 5005.01; 18,095.02
. as payment in installment sales . . . 19,010.01
. private activity . . . 5005.01; 5005.02
. savings bonds . . . 2070.08
. Series EE U.S. savings bonds . . . 2070
. Series I U.S. savings bonds . . . 2070
. sinking fund to pay . . . 20,030.02
. state and municipal . . . 5005–5005.02
. stripped tax-exempt . . . 5005.01
. U.S. savings bonds . . . 2070.08

Bonuses
. for accrual-basis taxpayer . . . 18,145.02; 18,205.01
. cost depletion deduction of . . . 12,180
. as deductible by employer . . . 12,065

Book inventories . . . 17,040

Boot
. affected in like-kind exchanges . . . 6050.06; 6055–6055.02
. nonqualified preferred stock treated as . . . 22,055.03
. in reorganizations exchanging securities . . . 22,055.02; 22,065.01; 22,110–22,110.02

Break in service for qualified plans
. defined . . . 3020.02
. disregarding certain years of service for . . . 3035.03

Brokers, information returns of . . . 26,140.07

Built-in loss, conversion transaction with property having . . . 8005.07

Business deductions . . . 12,001–12,220.02
. IRS challenges to . . . 12,001.03

Business energy credit . . . 14,055.03

Business expenses . . . 12,001–12,040.04
. capitalized. *See* Capital expenses
. compensation for services as . . . 12,045–12,085.04
. corporate takeover expenses . . . 12,005.02
. deductible . . . 12,001
. dissolution and liquidation . . . 12,005.02
. documentation of . . . 12,001.03
. for handicapped . . . 12,005.02
. of illegal business . . . 12,030–12,030.03
. incurred in trade, business, or profession . . . 12,001; 12,005
. loan origination costs . . . 12,005.02
. merger termination fee . . . 12,005.02
. ordinary and necessary . . . 12,001–12,001.01; 12,010.04; 12,100; 12,105.02; 12,135
. to produce future benefits . . . 12,010.07
. related to carrying on trade or business . . . 12,001

References are to paragraph (¶) numbers.

Business expenses—continued
. substantiation of . . . 12,001.03

Business insurance proceeds, tax treatment of . . . 2185
. death benefits . . . 2185.01
.

Business property
. dispositions of . . . 8055–8085
. insurance payments for . . . 12,105.02
. mid-quarter convention for . . . 10,025.02

Business start-up expenses . . . 12,040.01–.04
. amortization of . . . 12,040.01; 20,045.02–.03
. deduction maximum for . . . 12,040.01
. defined . . . 12,040.02
. eligibility for Section 195 deduction of . . . 12,040.02, 12,040.04
. examples of . . . 12,040.03

Buy-sell agreements
. to establish value for estate planning purposes . . . 29,105.03

C

Cafeteria facilities, employer-subsidized . . . 4050

Cafeteria plans of employee benefits . . . 4110–4110.09
. changing elections for . . . 4110.09
. defined . . . 4110
. health savings accounts in . . . 9115.01
. nondiscrimination rules for . . . 4110.08
. qualified benefits for . . . 4110

Capital account maintenance rules . . . 24,060.02

Capital assets . . . 8010–8010.13
. categories of . . . 8010
. defined . . . 8010
. depreciation recapture for . . . 8060–8060.05
. holding period for. *See* Holding period for capital assets
. items not considered as . . . 8010.12
. partnership interests as . . . 8010.06
. personal use property as . . . 8010.01
. property held for production of income as . . . 8010.04
. real property as . . . 8010.03
. residual method for allocation of . . . 8010.05
. securities as . . . 8010.01
. self-created musical works . . . 8010.07

Capital expenses
. asbestos removal . . . 12,010.03
. capitalized . . . 12,010.02; 12,010.05
. deductible . . . 12,010.01; 12,010.03
. distinction between repairs and . . . 12,011
. fees as . . . 12,075.03–.04
. intangibles . . . 12,010.05
. legal fees . . . 12,010.03
. losses distinguished from . . . 13,060–13,060.02
. for medical care . . . 9105.07
. repairs and improvements as . . . 12,011
. restorations . . . 12,011.09
. success based fees . . . 12,010.02
. takeover expenses . . . 12,010.03
. tax treatment of . . . 12,010–12,010.07

Capital gain distributions . . . 6090.01

Capital gains and losses
. carryover of . . . 8051.03
. of corporations . . . 20,075–20,080.01
. of estates and trusts . . . 25,045–25,045.05
. figuring . . . 8045–8051.03
. foreign-source . . . 28,010.04
. holding periods for . . . 8001; 8001.02

Capital gains and losses—continued
. individual's . . . 6001.04; 8001–8110.03
. long-term . . . 6090.02; 8001; 23,090.01
. net long-term . . . 8045.03
. net short-term . . . 6090.01; 8045.02; 9020.04
. offsetting . . . 6090.06; 8051.02
. on option sales . . . 8010.09; 8035–8035.04
. reporting . . . 8045.01–.04
. sale or exchange required to create . . . 8015
. short-term . . . 8001; 8105.06; 13,140.03
. on tax return . . . 8045.04
. tax treatment of . . . 8001.01; 16,001.01
. undistributed . . . 6090.01
. zero-percent tax rate on . . . 12,220.01

Capital gains dividends. *See* Dividends
. for automobile salespersons, exclusion rules for . . . 4010
. charitable contributions by . . . 9055.02; 4001–4010
. personal use of, valuation of . . . 4001.02; 4005–4005.05
. record requirements for . . . 4001.01
. value of, excluded from gross income . . . 4001

Capital structure of corporation, change in (Type E reorganization) . . . 22,035

Cars, deductions and credits for. *See* Vehicles

Cash balance plans . . . 3005.05

Cash basis accounting
. additions to reserves under . . . 18,180.01
. compensation for services under . . . 18,085.01
. deductions under . . . 18,130.01; 18,150; 20,070.01
. deferred payments sales under . . . 19,055.01
. entity types ineligible for . . . 30,095.02; 30,095.04
. expenses deducted when paid under . . . 18,020
. for farming . . . 17,065.01
. gross income for . . . 18,005; 18,080.01
. income recognized when constructively received under . . . 18,010–18,010.02
. interest and discounts under . . . 18,095.01–.03; 18,100.01; 18,155; 18,155.04
. for inventoriable items . . . 18,005.02
. method of payment affecting deductions for . . . 18,130.05
. as one principal method of accounting . . . 18,001
. reporting gain on property sale under . . . 18,110.01
. tax deductions under . . . 18,160.01

Cash contributions to charity . . . 9051

Cash incentives to purchase hybrids . . . 2005.01

Cash receipts exceeding $10,000, reporting . . . 26.140.12

Casualties and thefts
. business, netting of gains and losses for . . . 8065.01
. deducting losses from . . . 18,175.02
. of home . . . 9015.05; 12,125.07
. losses from, claiming . . . 13,020–13,030.02
. personal, netting of gains and losses for . . . 8065.02
. record retention for . . . 26,095.02
. separate returns to maximize deduction of . . . 26,005.04
. waiver of estimated tax penalties due to . . . 14,220.04

Certificates of deposit, reporting interest on . . . 18,095.03

Change in identity, form, or place of organization (Type F reorganization) . . . 22,040–22,040.01

Charitable contributions
. aircraft . . . 9052.06
. appraisals for . . . 9052
. appreciated property . . . 9052

References are to paragraph (¶) numbers.

Charitable contributions—continued
. benefits received from, tax treatment of . . . 9055–9055.02
. boats . . . 9052
. book inventory to public schools . . . 12,020
. carryover of . . . 9080.02; 9080.04
. cars . . . 9052
. cash . . . 9051
. claiming deduction for . . . 9085
. of computers . . . 12,020
. conservation easements . . . 9071
. corporate . . . 20,070–20,070.05
. current . . . 9080.01
. deduction for . . . 9050–9095; 18,170–18,170.01
. depreciation on business property in . . . 8060.03
. by estates and trusts . . . 25,035.03; 25,065.01
. of facade easements . . . 9072
. of food inventory . . . 12,020
. of fractional interests . . . 9070
. gift tax not imposed on . . . 29,020.08
. intellectual property . . . 9052
. inventory . . . 17,005.02
. lifetime . . . 29,125–29,125.06
. limitations on . . . 9075–9075.03; 9080.01–.04
. noncash . . . 9052
. nondeductible . . . 9050.01; 9050.03
. organizations qualified for deductions of . . . 9050.01
. of partial interests . . . 9065
. by partnership . . . 9055.02
. of property . . . 9052
. reporting . . . 9050.02; 9065.01; 9065.10; 26,140.11
. by S corporation . . . 9055.02
. split-interest . . . 29,125.04
. tax tips and questions and answers for . . . 9095
. for travel, meals, and lodging . . . 9060.01
. types of . . . 9050; 9055.02
. written acknowledgments of . . . 9055.02; 9065.03

Charitable lead trusts . . . 29,125.05

Charitable organizations
. lobbying expenses for . . . 12,035.01
. out-of-pocket expenses for . . . 9060–9060.02

Charitable remainder trusts . . . 29,125.06

Chauffeur services . . . 4001.03

Child support payments, tax treatment of . . . 2150.05

Child tax credit . . . 14,020–14,020.05

Children
. adopted . . . 4115–4115.06
. deficiency assessment against . . . 27,065.02
. family income splitting with S corporations to transfer business profits to . . . 21,002
. income reporting for. *See also* Kiddie tax . . . 2170–2170.04
. income shifting to . . . 12,045.01
. Roth IRA for . . . 3140.07
. services while employed by parent of . . . 15,060.04
. social security (FICA) taxes on . . . 15,050.05
. tax returns of . . . 26,010.01

Children of divorced or separated parents, dependency exemption for . . . 1060.04

Children, tax rate for . . . 2170.01

Circular 230 Standards of Practice . . . 27,040.05

Circulation expenses amortized for AMT . . . 16,005.11

Classification Settlement Program (CSP) for worker classification . . . 15,070.04

Clergy
. election for social security coverage by . . . 15,060.05

Clergy—continued
. exemption from self-employment tax for . . . 15,060.05
. mortgage interest deduction for members of . . . 9025.01
. payments considered income to . . . 15,105.06

Closely held corporations
. advances to . . . 2065.01
. compensation paid by . . . 12,050.0
. for passive loss rules . . . 13,090.02; 13,090.06

Closing agreements to settle tax claim . . . 27,035.01

Coal, Section 1231 treatment for gain or loss on sale of . . . 8080

Collapsible corporation rules, repeal of . . . 8090

Collateralized debt obligations (CDOs), interest reported by . . . 26,145.04

Collectibles, investing IRA savings in . . . 3130.03

College savings plan . . . 5110.01
. investment options . . . 5110

Combat zone, military personnel in . . . 2030.02

Commissions . . . 12,060–12,060.02

Commodity futures, short sales of . . . 8030.04

Commodity tax straddles . . . 8030.05

Common trust fund . . . 25,125–25,125.01

Commonly controlled business, qualified plan requirements for . . . 3050–3050.02

Communist organization employees exempt from social security coverage . . . 15,060.09

Community property income . . . 2001.03

Community property states
. election of S corporation status by spouses in . . . 21,010.03
. list of . . . 29,055
. support using community funds in . . . 1060.03

Community renewal provisions and incentives . . . 12,220–12,220.02

Commuting costs . . . 10,001.02... 10,001.02

Company cars and airplanes . . . 4001–4020; 10,020–10,020.03

Compensation
. cap on . . . 12,085–12,085.04
. of child employed by parent . . . 12,045.01
. gift versus . . . 2010; 2020.02
. of government employees . . . 2025
. of member of Armed Forces . . . 2030.01–.04
. noncash . . . 2035–2035.04
. paid in notes . . . 2005
. paid in state or local bonds . . . 2035.03
. for qualified plans defined . . . 3040
. reasonableness of . . . 12,050–12,050.04
. for Roth IRAs . . . 3140.02
. for services . . . 12,045–12,085.04; 18,085.01–.04
. taxability of . . . 2005
. types of . . . 2005.01
. unreasonable, deduction of . . . 12,001.03

Conservation easements . . . 9071
. protected in perpetuity . . . 9072.03
. valuation of . . . 9073

Conservation, transfers of property for . . . 9071–9073
. deductions of real property interests contributed as . . . 9071
. income interest in . . . 9074
. partial interests in . . . 9065

References are to paragraph (¶) numbers.

Conservation, transfers of property for—continued
. qualified organizations for . . . 9071
. remainder interest in . . . 9074
. right to use of property as . . . 9074

Consolidated returns of affiliated groups . . . 20,160–20,160.05
. extension of time to file . . . 26,070.02
. PHC tax rules for . . . 23,040

Constructive sales rules . . . 8030.02

Contested liabilities . . . 18,130.03

Continuing care facilities, loans to . . . 2065.02

Controlled corporations
. assets in divisive reorganization involving . . . 22,100.02; 22,105–22,115
. multiple tax limitations for . . . 20,165–20,165.04
. replacement of property by . . . 7065.01
. Section 351 exchanges to . . . 20,005.05–.06
. transfers of property to . . . 6045; 6075–6075.03; 6075.07; 22,085.02

Controlled groups . . . 20,165.03–.04

Conventions
. on cruise ships . . . 10,005.04
. foreign . . . 10,005.03

Conversion transactions . . . 8005.01–.10
. future commitment of funds in . . . 8005.08
. interest amount figured for . . . 8005.05
. ordinary income in . . . 8005.04
. property with built-in loss as part of . . . 8005.07
. recharacterization in . . . 8005.01
. reporting requirements for . . . 8005.10
. requirements for . . . 8005.02
. Section 1256 contracts not treated as . . . 8005.09
. source of funds for . . . 8005.06
. tax treatment of . . . 8005.03

Copyrights . . . 8010.07
. basis in . . . 6110

Corporate inversion transactions, identifying . . . 22,001.03

Corporate reorganizations *See* Reorganizations

Corporate tax . . . 20,001–20,175

Corporate-owned life insurance (COLI) policies . . . 12,110.02

Corporations. *See also* individual types . . . 20,001–20,175; 22,001–23,220.02
. accumulated earnings tax . . . 20,145
. adjusted current earnings of . . . 16,030–16,030.06
. affiliated . . . 20,160–20,160.05; 22,010.04; 22,130.02
. AMT for . . . 16,025–16,045
. asset acquisitions by . . . 20,110–20,110.02
. capital contributions . . . 20,020
. capital gains and losses of . . . 20,075
. charitable contributions . . . 20,070
. change in tax year of . . . 18,065.01
. change of ownership of . . . 12,080.03
. classification of businesses as . . . 20,001–20,001.02
. constructive ownership rules for . . . 22,175.06
. contributions to capital of . . . 20,020–20,020.02
. control of . . . 20,170.01; 22,030.02; 22,085.03; 22,160.03
. controlled. *See* Controlled corporations
. deductions . . . 20,040; 20,045
. deficiency assessment against . . . 27,065.03
. defined . . . 20,001
. disallowed deductions . . . 20,040
. dividends received from domestic corporations . . . 20,050

Corporations. —continued
. dividends received from foreign corporations . . . 20,055
. dividends on public utility preferred stock . . . 20,060
. division into multiple corporations of . . . 22,030.01
. domestic . . . 20,015; 20,035.01; 20,050–20,050.05; 21,001
. earnings and profits of . . . 20,105–20,105.06
. estimated taxes of . . . 20,005.02
. foreign . . . 20,015; 20,055–20,055.01; 23,020.03; 23,090.08; 23,170.01; 26,065.08; 26,105.01; 26,185.01; 27,050.06; 28,025; 28,045.01–28,065
. foreign-controlled . . . 26,185.01
. as generally exempt from interest allocation rules . . . 18,155.04
. income of . . . 20,015–20,030.02; 20,095; 20,175
. installment payment . . . 20,005.02
. liquidations of . . . 22,120–22,130.02; 26,165–26,165.02
. net operating losses of . . . 20,115–20,125
. organizational expenditures of, deduction of . . . 20,045.01
. principal purchase for creation . . . 20,040
. property distributions made by . . . 20,100–20,105.06
. property distributions received by . . . 20,025
. rate of tax imposed on . . . 20,010
. related, sale of stock to . . . 22,160–22,160.03
. reorganizations of . . . 20,140–20,140.03
. Schedule M-3 . . . 20,035
. securities exchanges by . . . 22,055.01–22,060
. securities of, transactions in . . . 20,085–20,110.02
. short tax year of . . . 26,065.04
. small . . . 16,025.02–.05
. tax evasion . . . 20,040
. tax returns . . . 20,005.03; 20,035
. tax treatment of . . . 20,005; 20,010
. taxation of . . . 20,001–20,010.04
. transfers of property to . . . 20,005.05
. transfers to joint ventures from . . . 12,080.03

Corporation's assets, transfer of (Type D reorganization) . . . 22,030.01–22,030.03
. liability assumption rules inapplicable in . . . 22,085.03

Corporation's property, acquiring another (Type C reorganization) . . . 22,025–22,025.04; 22,055.04–.05

Cosmetic surgery fees, tax treatment of . . . 9105.03

Cost allocation methods for inventory . . . 17,045.06–.07
. elective simplified . . . 17,045.08

Coverdell education savings accounts (ESAs) . . . 5115–5115.08
. assets remaining after education in . . . 5115.07
. bankruptcy protection of assets in . . . 5115.09
. converted to Roth IRA . . . 3140.05
. coordination of other higher education savings vehicles with . . . 5110.06, 5115.06
. distributions from . . . 5115.04; 5115.06
. eligibility for . . . 5115.01
. excess contributions to . . . 5115.08
. expenses covered by . . . 5115.05
. as nondeductible from gross income . . . 5115.02
. reporting contributions to and distributions from . . . 5115.03
. rollover to another account of family member of . . . 5115.07; 5115.08

Covered employment for social security taxes . . . 15,050–15,050.05

References are to paragraph (¶) numbers.

Credits *See* Tax credits

Cruise ships
. conventions on . . . 10,005.04
. luxury water transportation to business destination on . . . 10,005.05

D

Damages from IRS collection activities . . . 27,070.09

Damages from lawsuit, tax treatment of . . . 5045.04; 5065–5065.07
. for contract violations, allocation of settlements of . . . 5065.06
. for discrimination . . . 5065.01–.02
. interest portion of . . . 5065.05
. for interference with contracts . . . 5065.03
. punitive . . . 5065; 5065.04
. relating to personal or family rights . . . 5065.01
. structured settlements for . . . 5065.07
. wrongful death . . . 5065

Day care in home . . . 12,125.09
. meal expenses . . . 12,125.09
. standardized meal and snack expenses . . . 12,125.09

***De minimis* fringe benefits** . . . 4095–4095.02

Death benefits in gross estate . . . 29,095

Death of decedent holding QSBS, disregarded stock purchase upon . . . 8105.02

Death prior to retirement
. premature IRA distributions not penalized in cases of . . . 3135.02
. premature qualified plan distributions not penalized in cases of . . . 3085.01
. preretirement survivor annuity in case of . . . 3075.02

Debt collection agencies, use of private . . . 27,070.01

Debt instruments, reporting income from . . . 2070–2070.08

Decedent, final tax return of . . . 25,100.01

Decedent, stepped-up basis for property received from . . . 6040–6040.05
. alternate valuation date for . . . 6040.04
. carryover basis rule for . . . 6040.03
. exceptions to . . . 6040.02
. joint ownership affecting . . . 6040.04

Deductions, tax. *See also* Standard deduction
. for accrual-basis taxpayers . . . 18,130.02
. from adjusted gross income (AGI) . . . 1010.01; 2190.04
. business . . . 12,001–12,220.02
. by employers . . . 3040; 3060.01–.02; 3060.04
. capital loss . . . 8051–8051.03
. corporate . . . 20,040–20,070.05
. for cash-basis taxpayers . . . 18,130.01; 20,070.01
. for estates . . . 25,055–25,090; 29,115–29,125
. for estimated inventory shrinkage . . . 17,025.05
. for interest paid . . . 3095.04
. itemized. *See* Itemized deductions
. passed through to S corporation shareholders . . . 21,045
. personal . . . 9001–9165
. recapture of mine exploration expenditures . . . 12,195.01
. record retention for . . . 26,095.02
. recovery of tax benefit items from prior year's . . . 2190; 2190.03–.07
. for self-employment tax paid . . . 15,085.02
. state and local tax . . . 9030–9045; 25,045.05

Deductions, tax.—continued
. for tax-exempt organizations . . . 23,170.03
. travel and entertainment . . . 10,001–10,055.03
. for trusts . . . 25,055–25,090
. for tuition and fees . . . 9165

Deferred compensation plans, nonqualified . . . 3001; 3170–3170.06
. death benefits of . . . 3170.05
. defined . . . 3170.05
. distributions from . . . 3170.05
. popularity of . . . 3170.03
. reporting requirements for . . . 3170.05
. security in . . . 3170.06
. social security tax rules for . . . 15,075.06
. tax consequences to employees of . . . 3170.05
. tax consequences to employers of . . . 3170.04
. trust types for . . . 3170.06

Deferred payment sales . . . 19,055–19,055.03
. collections on discounted notes for . . . 19,055.02
. gain or loss in year of sale for . . . 19,055.01
. indeterminate market value for . . . 19,055.03
. not on installment plan . . . 19,055

Deficiency assessment, IRS . . . 27,010
. appeal to Tax Court of . . . 27,020.03; 27,125.03; 27,185.02
. assessment period for . . . 27,045.07–27,055.09; 27,170–27,170.02
. in bankruptcy . . . 27,055.05
. for child . . . 27,065.02
. collection of . . . 27,045.01–.03
. extension of limitation on assessments . . . 27,040
. immediate . . . 27,020.03
. jeopardy . . . 27,055.03–.04
. lawsuit to pursue . . . 27,045
. limitation periods for . . . 27,050–27,050.11; 27,060.01
. in partnership proceeding . . . 27,020.04
. payment of . . . 27,125.02
. payroll deductions for . . . 27,070.06
. period of assessment . . . 27,040
. request for prompt . . . 27,055.01
. termination . . . 27,055.02; 27,055.04
. for transferee liability . . . 27,065–27,065.04

Defined benefit plans
. adjustment of benefit rules for . . . 3040.01
. benefit accrual tests for . . . 3055
. combined plan limits for . . . 3040.03
. deduction limitation of defined contribution plan combined with . . . 3060.04
. excise tax on nondeductible contributions to . . . 3060.03
. excise tax on transfers from terminated . . . 3085.02
. fixed benefits from . . . 3005.01
. forfeitures in . . . 3035.03
. funding rules for . . . 3060.03
. in-service withdrawals prohibited for . . . 3075.03
. Keogh . . . 3155–3155.01
. limits on benefits from . . . 3040–3040.01
. liquidity requirement for . . . 3060.03
. maximum deduction for contributions to . . . 3060.02
. minimum participation requirements for . . . 3030.02
. top-heavy . . . 3045–3045.03

Defined contribution plans . . . 3005.02
. contribution limits for . . . 3040
. deduction limitation of defined benefit plan combined with . . . 3060.04
. employer contributions to . . . 3005.01
. ESOP . . . 3160
. Keogh . . . 3155–3155.01

References are to paragraph (¶) numbers.

Defined contribution plans—continued
. maximum benefits provided by . . . 3040.02
. money purchase plans . . . 3005.02
. top-heavy . . . 3045–3045.03
. transfers from terminated defined benefits plan to . . . 3085.02
. types of . . . 3005.01

Delivery services approved by IRS . . . 26,065.04; 29,165.01

Dependent care assistance plans . . . 4060
. exception for highly compensated employees in . . . 4060.01
. reporting payments of . . . 15,140.02

Dependent care credit . . . 14,001–14,001.06

Dependents
. birth or death during year of . . . 1055.02
. exemptions for . . . 1055.01–1070.02; 5085.03
. income of . . . 1060.03; 1070.01–.02
. medical expenses of . . . 9110.02
. requirements for filing individual return for . . . 1001.02
. standard deduction for . . . 1035.03

Depletion
. AMT treatment of . . . 16,010.01; 16,030.03
. basis for . . . 12,160.02; 12,170.02
. cost . . . 12,170–12,170.05
. deduction for . . . 12,155–12,180; 25,070–25,070.02
. defined . . . 12,155
. of timber . . . 12,185–12,185.02
. percentage . . . 12,175–12.175.04

Depletion allowance
. for life tenant . . . 12,160.03
. for partner . . . 24,135.03
. percentage . . . 12,175–12,175.04

Depletion reserve accounts . . . 12,190

Depreciable assets, dispositions of . . . 11,040.09

Depreciation. *See also* individual types . . . 11,001–11,065.03
. ACRS . . . 8060.02; 11,001; 11,055–11,055.03
. AMT treatment of . . . 16,005.06; 16,010.04; 16,030.01
. bonus first-year . . . 6055.04; 11,001.01–.02; 11,045.11; 16,005.06
. of business property . . . 12,125.07
. calculating . . . 18,045.01
. cap on . . . 10,025.03
. changing method of . . . 11,060.02; 18,045.01
. claiming . . . 11,010; 25,070–25.070.02
. date property placed in service as beginning . . . 11,020
. determinable useful life requirement for . . . 11,005–11,005.01
. general rules for . . . 11,001–11,001.02
. of listed property . . . 11,040.08
. methods for . . . 11,001
. MACRS. *See* Modified accelerated cost recovery system (MACRS)
. reporting requirements for . . . 11,025
. types of property not subject to . . . 11,005.02–.03
. types of property qualifying for deduction of . . . 11,005; 11,010.01–.03
. useful life. *See* Useful-life depreciation system

Depreciation recapture
. for capital assets . . . 9060–8060.05
. in installment sales . . . 19,030–19,030.02
. in like-kind exchanges . . . 6055.03

Designated Roth 401(k) contributions . . . 3150.06

Direct sellers, information returns of . . . 26,140.06

Disability
. premature IRA distributions not penalized in cases of . . . 3135.02
. premature nonqualified deferred compensation distributions in cases of . . . 3170.05
. premature qualified plan distributions in cases of . . . 3085.01
. QSBS purchased incident to . . . 8105.02

Disability benefits . . . 5045–5045.07

Disabled access credit . . . 14,090–14,090.04

Disaster Mitigation Payments Tax Treatment Act of 2005 . . . 5100.03; 7040.01

Disaster relief, exclusion for . . . 5100.03–.10

Discount obligations, deduction for high-yield . . . 20,090.05

Discounted notes, collections on . . . 19,055.02

Disputed income . . . 18,120

Disqualification of plans . . . 3015

Disqualified individuals for golden parachutes . . . 12,080; 12,080.05

Disqualified persons of private foundations . . . 23,130.01

Disqualified persons, prohibited and taxable transactions between qualified plans and . . . 3100
. defined . . . 3160.05
. excise tax imposed for . . . 3100.03
. transfers of plan assets one of . . . 3100.01

Disqualified tax advisor defined . . . 26,210.01

Distributable net income (DNI) for trusts and estates . . . 25,020–25,020.03
. beneficiary's share of each item of . . . 25,035–25,035.03
. exclusions from . . . 25,045.04

Distributions by estates . . . 25,030–25,030.07; 25,085.02

Distributions, corporate . . . 20,100–20,105.06

Distributions, designated . . . 15,040

Distributions of 529 plans . . . 5110.03

Distributions of property . . . 2080.02

Distributions of securities . . . 2095–2120.02
. divorce-related . . . 2150.04

Distributions of trusts . . . 25,025–25,030.07

Distributions, qualified plan . . . 3075–3085.01
. amount of . . . 3075.04
. commencement of . . . 3075.02
. death after commencement of . . . 3075.04
. exceptions to penalties for early . . . 3085.01
. lump-sum . . . 3075.01; 3075.04
. in-service . . . 3075.03
. installment . . . 3075.04
. premature . . . 3085.01
. rollover . . . 3080.02; 3085.01
. taxation of . . . 3080–3080.02
. types of . . . 3075.01
. withholding on . . . 15,040–15,040.04

Distributions, Roth IRA . . . 3140.06

Distributions, S corporation . . . 21,050–21,050.02

Distributions, SEP . . . 3145.08

Distributions, source of corporation's . . . 2075.02–.03

Distributions, tax-exempt and specially treated . . . 2090

Distributions to partners . . . 24,100–24,125.03

Distributions to partners—continued
. basis of property distributed in . . . 24,105; 24,105.02; 24,110.01–24,115.02
. holding period for . . . 24,105.01
. as sale or exchange . . . 24,125–24,125.03
. tax consequences of . . . 24,125.03
. as transferees . . . 24,110–24,110.03
. of unrealized receivables or inventory items . . . 24,120–24,120.05

Distributor's agreement, canceling . . . 8010.10

Dividends. *See also* Qualified dividends . . . 2075–2090
. automatic reinvestment of . . . 2080.03
. building and loan association . . . 18,090.02
. capital gain . . . 2080.04; 8001.03; 23,090.01
. consent . . . 2080.05
. constructive . . . 2085–2085.02
. corporate property sales to stockholders treated as . . . 2175; 22,070–22,075.02
. defined . . . 2075
. distinguishing loans from . . . 2085.01
. ESOP . . . 3160.03
. excluded from reduced tax rate . . . 2080.01
. extraordinary . . . 20,065.03–.04
. interest payments distinguished from . . . 9005.01
. on life insurance and endowment policies . . . 5035
. liquidating . . . 2130–2130.03
. matched to distribution source . . . 2075.03
. nondeductible . . . 12,050.01–.02
. ordinary . . . 6090.06
. passed through mutual and money market funds . . . 2080.03; 6090.01; 8001.02–.03
. patronage . . . 18,090.03; 23,220.02; 26,150.02
. payments in lieu of . . . 2080.01
. personal holding company . . . 23,020.02
. public utility preferred stock . . . 20,060
. received from domestic corporations . . . 20,050–20,050.05
. received from foreign corporations . . . 20,055–20,055.01
. reinvestment of . . . 6090.04; 6090.06
. reporting . . . 2075.04; 2080.01; 18,090–18,090.03; 26,150–26,150.02
. return of capital . . . 2125–2130.03
. stock. *See* Stock dividends
. stock value counted as . . . 2095.03
. tax-exempt mutual fund . . . 16,010.03; 23,090.02
. tax-exempt-interest . . . 6090.01
. taxation of . . . 2080.01; 8001.01; 15,105.01; 16,001.02
. withholding for . . . 15,045.02

Dividends-paid deduction . . . 20,150.02
. of RICs . . . 23,090.03

Dividends-received deduction
. foreign corporation distributions qualifying for . . . 20,055–20,055.01
. limitations on . . . 20,065–20,065.04
. of partnerships . . . 24,040.07
. qualifying for domestic . . . 20,050.05
. of RICs . . . 23,090.04

Divorce
. premature qualified plan distributions for QDRO upon . . . 3085.01; 3090
. property transfers incident to . . . 2150.03; 29,030.05
. QSBS purchased incident to . . . 8105.02
. record retention for papers associated with . . . 26,095.02
. stock redemptions related to . . . 2150.04
. tax ramifications of . . . 2150.01
. transfers of installment obligations incident to . . . 19,050.03

Dollar-value costing for inventory . . . 17,030.01

Domestic production activities, deduction for . . . 12,150.01

Domestic production gross receipts . . . 12,150.03

Double taxation of corporations . . . 20,005.01; 20,145

Double-extension method for valuing inventory . . . 17,030.01

E

Earned income credit (EIC) . . . 14,005–14,005.07; 27,001.03

Earned income, foreign . . . 28,070–28,070.08

Earnings and profits (E&P)
. defined . . . 2075.01
. distributions from current or accumulated . . . 2070.02; 2075.03
. distributions in excess of . . . 2075

Easement, property, basis reduced by . . . 8060.07

Economic Growth and Tax Relief Reconciliation Act of 2001 (EGTRRA)
. estate and gift tax changes of . . . 29,001.01–.02
. profit-sharing plan contribution maximum increased by . . . 3005.03
. sunsetting provisions of . . . 29,130.01

Economic interest in property . . . 12,160.01

Economic substance doctrine . . . 24,003

Education expense deduction
. deductible expenses for employed professionals . . . 12,130.03
. deduction for higher education expenses . . . 9165
. for ordinary and necessary expenses of employed professionals . . . 12,130–12,130.03
. for present job skills . . . 12,130.02
. for refresher courses . . . 12,130.01
. penalties imposed for failure to comply with . . . 24,003, 27,085
. qualified tuition and related expenses . . . 9165

Education IRAs. *See* Coverdell education savings accounts (ESAs)

Educational assistance, employer-provided . . . 4055.01
. to terminated employee . . . 4055.02

Educational tax incentives . . . 5085.03

Elderly and permanently disabled, credit for . . . 14,010–14,010.03

Electing small business trust (ESBT)
. conversion from QSST to . . . 21,014.06
. defined . . . 21,014.06
. election as . . . 21,014.06
. as S corporation shareholder . . . 21,014.06

Electric vehicle credit . . . 14,180

Electronic Federal Tax Payment System (EFTPS)
. payment options for . . . 26,130.02
. types of tax payments using . . . 26,130.01

Electronic filing of corporate tax returns . . . 26,030

Electronic filing of individuals' tax returns . . . 26,025.01–.05
. advantages of . . . 26,025.03
. antiabuse requirements for . . . 26,025.06
. electronic postmark for . . . 26,065.04
. form for . . . 26,025.01
. payment options for . . . 26,025.05
. registering to use . . . 26,025.04

References are to paragraph (¶) numbers.

Electronic postmark by authorized electronic return transmitter . . . 27,070.02

Electronic Tax Application (ETA), tax deposits and payments using . . . 26,130.02

Electronic withdrawal for e-filings . . . 26,125.02

Embezzled funds, repayment of . . . 13,010.04

Employee achievement awards . . . 4075; 15,080.01
. aggregation rule for amount of . . . 4075.03
. amount excluded for . . . 4075.02
. employee defined for . . . 4075.01
. limitations for . . . 4075.04

Employee benefits. *See* Fringe benefits

Employee business expenses
. list of . . . 12,120.02
. as miscellaneous itemized deductions . . . 9145.01
. as not considered wages . . . 15,080.03
. reimbursed . . . 12,120.03; 15,080.03
. reporting . . . 15,140.02

Employee discounts . . . 4070
. amount excluded from income for . . . 4070.01
. exception for highly compensated employees for . . . 4070.02

Employee stock purchase plans (ESOPs) . . . 3160
. abusive . . . 3160.06
. deemed owed shares in . . . 3160.05
. dividends paid from stock owned by . . . 3085.01
. employee tax benefits in . . . 3160.04
. employer common stock securities in . . . 3160
. employer tax benefits in . . . 3160.03
. excise tax on . . . 3160.05
. loans to . . . 3160.03
. put options received in lieu of securities in . . . 3160.02
. rollover of S corporation stock to IRAs from . . . 21,025.07
. S corporation stock ownership by . . . 3160.05
. voting rights for securities in . . . 3160.01

Employees
. defined . . . 15,010.01; 15,070.02
. misclassification as independent contractors of . . . 15,070.04
. record retention by . . . 15,150
. refunds and credits for . . . 15,155–15,155.01
. statutory, independent contractors versus . . . 15,010.02; 15,070.02–.03
. types of . . . 14,010.01

Employer identification number (EIN) . . . 15,050; 26,050

Employer securities, lump-sum distributions including . . . 3080

Employer social security credit on tips . . . 14,110

Employers going out of business, tax filing responsibilities of . . . 15,135; 15,140

Employers providing child care assistance for employees, tax credit for . . . 14,125

Employers providing differential wage payments to military personnel, tax credit for . . . 14,126

Employment exempt from social security (FICA) taxes . . . 15,060–15,060.11

Employment tax. *See also* Self-employment tax; Social security taxes
. deficiency assessment for . . . 27,065.04
. evasion of, audits triggered by . . . 27,001.03
. for household employees . . . 14,205.02
. Section 530 relief for . . . 15,070.04

Empowerment zone employment credit . . . 14,100.01–.02

Empowerment zones
. defined . . . 14,100
. low-income community in . . . 14,135
. maximum expensing deduction increased for . . . 11,045
. tax incentives in . . . 12,220

Energy conservation subsidies, tax-free . . . 5,095

Energy Tax Incentives Act of 2005
. clean renewable energy bonds (CREBs) credited by . . . 14,096
. qualified facilities added by . . . 14,095
. research tax credit modified by . . . 14,080.01

Energy-efficient appliances, manufacturer's tax credit for . . . 14,145–14,145.03

Energy-efficient commercial property deduction . . . 12,151

Energy-efficient new homes, tax credit for . . . 14,140

Enhanced oil recovery credit . . . 14,085–14,085.03

Enterprise zones, tax-free bonds issued by . . . 5005.01

Entertainment, business . . . 10,040–10,055.03
. allocation of expenses for . . . 10,040.02
. directly related to business . . . 10,040; 10,045–10,045.05
. of employees . . . 10,040.02
. exceptions to restrictions for . . . 10,045.05
. facilities used for . . . 10,045.03–.04
. gifts as. *See* Gifts
. limit of 50 percent for deducting . . . 10,040; 10,040.03; 10,045.04
. ordinary and necessary . . . 10,040, 10,040.02
. reporting requirements for . . . 10,055.02–.03
. scope of . . . 10,040.01
. substantiation of . . . 10,055.01

Entity types
. comparison table of . . . 21,005

Environmental clean-up expenses . . . 12,012

ERISA, qualified plan requirements under . . . 3015

Escrow, purchase price of property placed in . . . 18,110.03

Estate planning
. bypass trusts in . . . 29,050.03–.04
. with 529 plans . . . 5110.09
. importance of . . . 29,001.03

Estate tax . . . 29,035
. alternate valuation . . . 29,110
. credit for . . . 29,155–29,155.02
. deduction from gross estate of . . . 25,040.02; 25,080.01
. deferring . . . 29,205
. effects of repeal of . . . 29,001–29,001.01
. extension of time to file estate tax return . . . 29,200
. filing requirements for . . . 29,195.01
. imposition of . . . 29,035
. payment of . . . 29,200.01
. rates of . . . 29,135
. treatment of stock in RICs for . . . 23,090

Estates. *See also* Gross estate . . . 25,001–25,125
. claims against . . . 29,115
. deductions of . . . 25,055–25,090; 29,115–29,125
. defined . . . 25,010
. disclaimers for . . . 29,165–29,165.03
. election to treat revocable trust as part of . . . 25,005

References are to paragraph (¶) numbers.

Estates.—continued
. estimated tax payments of . . . 25,105
. expenses of . . . 29,115
. income tax return of . . . 25,100
. innocent spouse relief requested by executors of . . . 26,006
. joint . . . 29,050.01–.02
. nonresident noncitizens' . . . 29,160–29,160.0
. ordinary and necessary expenses of . . . 25,080.01
. retained life . . . 29,060–29,060.03
. revocable transfers to . . . 29,065.01–.04
. tax year of . . . 25,110.01
. taxable income of . . . 25,015–25,020.03
. taxation of . . . 25,001–25,001.02
. transfer of property to . . . 25,050.01–.02
. valuation of property in . . 29,105.01–29,110.02

Estimated tax . . . 14,200–14,220.04
. of corporations . . . 20,005.02; 26,105.02
. due dates for . . . 14,210.01
. of estates and trusts . . . 25,105; 26,110.01
. of farmers and fishermen . . . 14,210.02
. figuring . . . 14,215.01–.04
. procedures for paying . . . 14,200.01; 14,210.01
. of S corporations . . . 21,030.02
. tax base for . . . 14,210.03
. of tax-exempt organizations . . . 26,115
. taxpayers filing . . . 14,205.01–.03
. types of income requiring payment of . . . 14,200.01
. underpayment of . . . 14,205.03; 14,220.01–.04; 26,105.03
. when to pay . . . 14,210–14,210.02

Examinations, IRS
. cooperation of taxpayers in . . . 27,005.06
. findings of agents in . . . 27,005.08
. items on returns triggering . . . 27,001.03
. notification requirement for . . . 27,005.04
. of partnership items . . . 27,005.05
. preliminary . . . 27,001.01
. procedures for . . . 27,005.01–.08
. records for . . . 27,001.04
. selection of returns for . . . 27,001.02–.03

Exclusions from gross income . . . 5001–5120.04
. for annuities . . . 5070–5080.05
. basic rules for . . . 5001
. for disability benefits . . . 4120.07; 5045
. for government obligations . . . 5005–5010
. for life insurance . . . 5015–5040
. rules for gifts, inheritances, and damages used for . . . 5055–5065.07
. special rules applied for . . . 5085–5120.04
. types of tax-free income as . . . 5001

Exempt organizations. *See* Tax-exempt organizations

Expatriation to avoid tax . . . 28,065
. allocation of exemption amount
. . Code Sec. 877A tax regime . . . 28,065
. covered expatriate defined . . . 28,065

Expensing property. *See* Section 179 expensing of tangible personal property

Extensions of time for filing and payment of tax
. for individual taxpayers . . . 26,070

F

Fair market value
. of property defined . . . 6015.01

Family limited partnerships (FLPs) . . . 24,015.03

Farm activities, tax shelter passive . . . 16,005.09

Farm rental exception . . . 15,105.03

Farm-price inventory valuation method . . . 17,070.03

Farmers' expenses
. business, deductible and nondeductible . . . 12,205.01
. capital . . . 12,205.02
. deductions for prepaying . . . 18,185
. for estimated tax . . . 14,210.02
. poultry-related expenses . . . 18,185
. prepaid farm supplies . . . 18,185
. recreational . . . 12,205.03
. reporting . . . 12,205
. rules for costs of . . . 17,045.10

Farming income . . . 17,065.01–.04
. accrual accounting for . . . 17,065.01; 18,025.01
. income averaging for . . . 17,065.02

Farming syndicates . . . 12,205.04

FBAR . . . 28,085

Federal agency contract payments, information returns of recipients of . . . 26,140.17

Federal Insurance Contributions Act (FICA), OASDI and Medicare taxes established by . . . 15,050; 15,070

Federal Unemployment Tax Act (FUTA) (See also Unemployment taxes (FUTA))
. employers' payment of . . . 15,110–15,110.02
. FUTA tax credit . . . 15,115
. tax rate for . . . 15,110.01
. worker's compensation of . . . 15,070

Federally declared disaster areas
. assistance to taxpayers in . . . 5100.08
. casualty loss on demolished home in . . . 13,045.01
. due date for tax returns in . . . 26,070
. involuntary conversions of property in . . . 7040.01; 7040.03; 7055.03
. like-kind exchanges following . . . 6050.05
. reporting losses in . . . 13,020.03

Fees for attorneys, accountants, and professionals . . . 12,075
. as capital expenditures . . . 12,075.03
. in corporate takeover attempt . . . 12,075.04
. deductible . . . 12,075.01
. nondeductible . . . 12,075.02
. tax treatment of . . . 15,095.06

Fees for medical services, types of deductible and nondeductible . . . 9105.02

FICA. *See* Social security taxes

Fiduciaries for trusts and estates
. liability of . . . 25,005–25,001.01
. returns filed by . . . 25,001.02; 25,010.03
. will or trust instrument filed by . . . 25,100.03

Fiduciary tax returns . . . 26,020
. for bankruptcy estates . . . 26,020.04
. receivers not required to file . . . 26,020.03
. signature of . . . 26,020.02

Filing requirements for individual federal income tax . . . 1001–1001.06; 26,001–26,025.07

Filing status. *See also* individual types . . . 1020–1030.02

Film and television production costs . . . 12,152

Financial asset-securitization investment trusts (FASITs), interest reported by . . . 26,145.04

Financial counseling for employees as fringe benefit . . . 4085

Financial institutions, lost deposits in insolvent . . . 13,155–13,155.01

References are to paragraph (¶) numbers.

First-in, first-out (FIFO) inventory pricing method . . . 17,015
. LIFO versus . . . 17,020.01

First-time homebuyer credit . . . 14,047

First-time homebuyers, premature IRA distributions not penalized in cases of . . . 3135.02

Fishermen, estimated tax payments of . . . 14,210.02

Flexible spending accounts (FSAs)
. extended period allowed to spend amounts in . . . 4120.04
. reimbursements of medicines and drugs from . . . 4120.03

Foreclosures, mortgage, deduction of . . . 18,175.02

Foreign bank and financial accounts (FBAR) reporting . . . 28,101–28,102
. civil penalties for failure to file FBAR . . . 28,100.01
. criminal penalties for failure to file FBAR . . . 28,100.01

Foreign corporation reorganization . . . 22,046

Foreign corporations . . . 28,045
. branch profits tax . . . 28,045
. earnings stripping rules . . . 28,045
. fixed or determinable annual or periodical income . . . 28,045.01
. Form 5471, *Information Return of U.S. Persons with Respect to Certain Foreign Corporations* . . . 28,105
. Form 5472, *Information Return of a 25% Foreign-Owned U.S. Corporation or a Foreign Corporation Engaged in a U.S. Trade or Business* . . . 28,110
. information returns required of foreign-owned U.S. corporation or foreign corporation engaged in U.S. business . . . 28,110
. information returns required of foreign interests in U.S. real property . . . 28,115
. information returns required for transfer of property to foreign corporation . . . 28,120
. interest expense deduction . . . 28,045.01
. ownership information returns required if U.S. Shareholder . . . 28,105
. returns and payment of tax . . . 28,045
. tax on . . . 28,045.01

Foreign death taxes, credit for . . . 29,150

Foreign financial assets; information disclosure . . . 28,085
. Offshore Voluntary Disclosure Program (OVDP) . . . 28,103. *See also* Offshore Voluntary Disclosure Program (OVDP)

Foreign governments
. bequests to . . . 29,125.03
. employees of . . . 28,075

Foreign investments of U.S. taxpayers, tax rules for . . . 28,085
. controlled foreign corporation defined . . . 28,085
. difference between FBAR and FATCA requirements . . . 28,100.02
. FATCA reporting and withholding obligations for foreign financial institutions (FFIs) . . . 28,100.04
. FATCA reporting and withholding obligations for non-financial foreign entities (NFFEs) . . . 28,100.06
. FATCA reporting of specified foreign financial assets . . . 28,100
. Form 8938, *Statement of Specified Foreign* . . . 28,100; 28,100.02
. Form TD F 90-22.1, *Report of Foreign Bank and Financial Accounts* (FBAR . . . 28,100; 28,100.02
. online FATCA Registration . . . 28,100.08

Foreign investments of U.S. taxpayers, tax rules for—continued
. participating Foreign Financial Institution (FFI) Agreements . . . 28,100.05
. penalties Imposed for Failure to Disclose Foreign Financial Assets . . . 28,100.07
. reporting requirements for . . . 28,090.02
. reporting requirements imposed on . . . 28,100-28,120
. reporting thresholds . . . 28,100.03
. "specified foreign financial asset" defined . . . 28,100.01
. when U.S. shareholders taxed on . . . 28,085

Foreign person as trust grantor . . . 28,095

Foreign service, allowances for government officers and employees in . . . 28,075

Foreign source income . . . 28,050
. effectively connected income . . . 28,050
. office or fixed place of business in U.S. . . . 28,050

Foreign tax carryover and carryback . . . 28,010.03

Foreign tax credit . . . 28,001–28,025
. abuse of . . . 28,005
. AMT . . . 16,020.04
. carryovers of . . . 22,150
. claiming . . . 28,001.01; 28,005.01
. limitation categories for . . . 28,001.01
. limitations on . . . 28,010.01–.05
. for partnerships . . . 24,040.08; 24,040.10
. redetermination, notice requirements . . . 28,005
. for RICs . . . 23,090.03
. structured foreign investment arrangements . . . 28,005

Foreign taxpayers. *See also* individual types . . . 28,030.01–28,065
. taxation of . . . 28,030.01–.03

Foreign trusts, assets of nonqualified deferred compensation plan in . . . 3170.05

Forgiveness of debt. *See* Indebtedness

Form SS-5
. applying for EIN on . . . 15,050
. applying for TIN on . . . 26,060

Form SS-16, "Certificate of Election of Coverage," clergy election of social security coverage using . . . 15,060.05

Form TD F 90-22.1, foreign accounts reported using . . . 26,210.09

Form W-2
. copies required for . . . 15,140
. correcting . . . 15,140.05
. dependent care assistance reported on . . . 4060.01
. employer contributions to HSA reported on . . . 9115.01
. employer reimbursements for moving expenses reported on . . . 9125.04
. employer-paid life insurance premiums reported on . . . 26,160
. extension of time to file . . . 15,140.04
. filing . . . 15,140.05; 26,025.01; 26,135.01; 26,140.02
. filings for businesses sold or out of business of . . . 15,135.03; 15,135.07; 15,140.03
. information on . . . 15,140.02; 26,140.02
. magnetic media for . . . 15,130.02
. military pay reported on . . . 2030.02
. reporting rules for . . . 15,140.02; 26,050.04

Form W-2c, "Statement of Correct Income and Tax Amounts," errors corrected on . . . 15,140.05

References are to paragraph (¶) numbers.

Form W-2G, reporting bingo or slot machine winnings on . . . 2015; 2155

Form W-3, "Transmittal of Income and Tax Statements," filing with Form 941 and W-2 of . . . 15,135.03; 15,140.05; 26,160
. filing . . . 26,135.01

Form W-4
. additional allowances claimed on . . . 15,025.03
. amended . . . 15,030.03
. effective date of revised . . . 15,030.03
. exempting wages from withholding using . . . 1001.04; 15,025.01
. for new employee . . . 15,030.02
. questionable, employer's responsibility for . . . 15,030.01
. reporting requirements using . . . 15,030.01
. responsibility for . . . 15,030
. special withholding allowance claimed on . . . 15,025.02
. voluntary withholding by claiming fewer allowances on . . . 15,020.10
. worksheets for . . . 15,030.04

Form W-4P, "Withholding Certificate for Pension or Annuity Payments,"

Form W-5, "Earned Income Credit Advance Payment Certificate," advance EIC payment provided on . . . 14,005.05

Form W-8BEN, "Certificate of Foreign Status of Beneficial Owner for United States Withholding," withholding agent use of . . . 28,030.03

Form W-9. interest and dividends with TINs reported on . . . 14,225.01

Form 23, "Application for Enrollment to Practice Before the Internal Revenue Service," application using . . . 27,040.01

Form 706, estate tax reported on . . . 29,195.01

Form 706GS(D-1) for taxable distributions for GST . . . 29,190.01

Form 709, gift tax reported on . . . 29,195.02

Form 720, "Quarterly Federal Excise Tax Return," refund claims using . . . 26,065.02

Form 870, "Waiver of Restrictions on Assessment and Collection of Deficiency in Tax and Acceptance of Overstatement," income tax assessment using . . . 27,025–27,025.02

Form 870-AD, "Offer of Waiver of Restrictions on Assessment and Collection of Deficiency in Tax and Of Acceptance of Overassessment," agreement accepted using . . . 27,015.03

Form 872, IRS waiver on . . . 27,045.08

Form 890, estate and gift tax assessments on . . . 27,025–27,025.02

Form 926, "Return by a U.S. Transferor of Property to a Foreign Corporation" . . . 28,120
cash transfers . . . 28,120
. exceptions to filing . . . 28,120
. jointly owned property . . . 28,120
. reporting requirements . . . 28,120
. transfers by partnership . . . 28,120
. who must file . . . 28,120

Form 940, "Employer's Annual Federal Unemployment (FUTA) Tax Return" . . . 15,120; 15,130
. amended . . . 15,130
. unemployment taxes reported using . . . 15,130

Form 941, "Employer's Quarterly Federal Tax Return"
. filing . . . 15,135.03
. taxes withheld from employees reported on . . . 15,130.01

Form 941-M for monthly withholding tax payments . . . 15,135.04

Form 942, withholding for domestics using . . . 15,135.02

Form 943, withholding for agricultural workers using . . . 15,135.02

Form 945, "Annual Return of Withheld Federal Income Tax," for taxes withheld outside employment . . . 15,130

Form 966 for liquidating corporate distributions . . . 2130.04

Form 990-PF, "Return of Private Foundation"
. filing . . . 23,151

Form 990-T, unrelated business income tax return using . . . 23,180
. due date for . . . 26,065.10

Form 1040, filing requirements for . . . 1005–1005.01; 26,001–26,001.05

Form 1040 IRS *E-File* for electronic filing . . . 26,025.01–.03

Form 1040A (short form)
. eligibility for using . . . 1005.02
. filing requirements for . . . 1005

Form 1040-ES payment voucher for estimated tax . . . 14,210.01

Form 1040EZ
. eligibility for using . . . 1005.03
. filing requirements for . . . 1005

Form 1040NR, nonresident alien returns using . . . 28,065.04

Form 1040-V payment voucher . . . 26,125.02

Form 1040X, amended return for individuals on . . . 26,080

Form 1041
. estate fiduciary as remitting tax with . . . 25,001.02; 26,180.03
. estate tax return filed using . . . 25,100.02
. trust tax return filed using . . . 25,100.03

Form 1041-ES, estimated taxes filed using . . . 26,110.01

Form 1041-T, assignments of overpayments using . . . 26,110.01

Form 1042S information return for tax withheld for nonresident aliens or foreign entities . . . 15,135.06

Form 1065, information return of partnership or LLC using . . . 26,180.01; 26,180.05

Form 1096 transmittal form
. for information returns . . . 26,140.01
. for shareholder returns . . . 22,001.03

Form 1098, "Mortgage Interest Statement," reporting interest received using . . . 26,140.13

Form 1098-T, "Tuition Payment Statement," educational institution information return on . . . 14,025.07

Form 1099, business payments on variations of . . . 26,140.01

References are to paragraph (¶) numbers.

Form 1099-A, property acquisitions from debt reported using . . . 26,140.09

Form 1099-B, "Proceeds From Broker and Barter Exchange Transactions"
. payments for legal services reported on . . . 26,140.15
. redemptions of mutual fund shares reported on . . . 6090.06

Form 1099-DIV, "Dividends and Distributions"
. dividends reported on . . . 14,225.03; 26,150–26,150.02
. mutual fund distributions reported on . . . 6090.06
. mutual fund investment expenses reported on . . . 9140.03
. stock liquidations reported on . . . 26,165–26,165.02

Form 1099-E, "Student Loan Interest Statement," schools receiving interest reporting on . . . 26,140.16

Form 1099-G
. government reporting on . . . 26,140.03
. unemployment compensation reported on . . . 26,140.02

Form 1099-INT, interest payments on . . . 14,225.03; 26,145.01; 26,145.03–.04

Form 1099-MISC, payments and gains reported on . . . 14,225.01; 14,225.03; 26,140.03–.04

Form 1099-R, "Distributions from Pensions, Annuities, Retirement for Profit-Sharing Plans, IRAs, Insurance Contracts, etc."
. Coverdell ESA contributions reported on . . . 5115.03
. minimum payments triggering use of . . . 26,140.02
. mutual fund retirement distributions reported on . . . 6090.06

Form 1099-S, "Proceeds from Real Estate Transaction," realty transactions on . . . 26,140.07

Form 1116, "Foreign Tax Credit," claiming credit using . . . 28,005.01

Form 1120, "U.S. Corporation Income Tax Return," domestic corporations filing . . . 20,035.01

Form 1120S, S corporation return filed using . . . 21,010.05; 26,030; 26,180.04

Form 1120X, amended return for corporations on . . . 26,080

Form 1127, extension of time to pay tax using . . . 26,120

Form 1128, "Application to Adopt, Change, or Retain a Tax Year," applying for change using . . . 18,065
. by partnership . . . 24,070.06
. by S corporation . . . 21,016
. taxpayers not required to file . . . 18,065.01

Form 2106, employee business expenses claimed on . . . 12,120.02; 12,120.03

Form 2159, "Payroll Deduction Agreement," assessment settlement using . . . 27,070.06

Form 2210, "Underpayment of Estimated Tax by Individuals and Fiduciaries," worksheet for installments in . . . 14,220.02

Form 2350, extension of time for filing for residents abroad using . . . 26,070.03

Form 2441, "Child and Dependent Care Expenses," dependent care credit claimed on . . . 14,001.05

Form 2553, "Election by a Small Business Corporation," S corporation status elected using . . . 21,010; 21,010.03

Form 2587, "Application for Special Enrollment Examination," application for examination on . . . 27,040.01

Form 3115, "Application for Change in Accounting Method"
. changing accounting method using . . . 18,005.02; 18,045.02–.03
. changing depreciation method using . . . 11,060.02
. changing inventory valuation method using . . . 17,025.02
. electing special rules for farming costs using . . . 17,070.09
. filing . . . 18,045.02
. safe harbor without filing . . . 18,001.04

Form 3468, business energy credit claimed on . . . 14,055.03

Form 3520, "Annual Return to Report Transactions with Foreign Trusts and Receipt of Certain Foreign Gifts," foreign trust reporting using . . . 28,090.02

Form 3903, "Moving Expenses," foreign and domestic moving costs reported on . . . 9125.04

Form 4361, election out of social security coverage using . . . 15,060.05

Form 4506, "Request for Copy of Tax Return," obtained to make disaster election . . . 13,020.03

Form 4563, figuring depreciation deduction on . . . 11,025

Form 4684, "Casualties and Thefts," computation of both gains and losses on . . . 13,030.02

Form 4868, "Application for Automatic Extension of Time To File U.S. Individual Income Tax Return"
. requesting automatic extension using . . . 26,070.01
. telephoning for extension using . . . 26,070; 26,125.02

Form 4952, "Investment Interest Expense Deduction," figuring deduction on . . . 9020.07

Form 5213, "Election to Postpone Determination," electing to postpone profitability of activity using . . . 13,085.02

Form 5305-B, "Health Savings Trust Account," safe harbors for HSAs using . . . 9115.01

Form 5305-C, "Health Savings Custodial Account," safe harbors for HSAs using . . . 9115.01

Form 5305-R, "Roth Individual Retirement Trust Account," as model form for establishing IRA . . . 3140.08

Form 5305-RA, "Roth Individual Retirement Custodial Account," as model form for establishing IRA . . . 3140.08

Form 5329, "Additional Taxes on Qualified Plans (Including IRAs) and Other Tax-Favored Accounts," exceptions to penalty on . . . 3085.01

Form 5498, "IRA Contribution Information"
. Coverdell ESA contributions reported on . . . 5115.03; 6090.06
. IRA, SEP, and SIMPLE contributions reported on . . . 6090.06

Form 5500, "Annual Return/Report of Employee Benefit Plan," requirements triggering use of schedules for . . . 3060

Form 6765, "Credit for Increased Research Activities," research expense credit claimed on . . . 14,080.01

References are to paragraph (¶) numbers.

Form 7004, "Application for Automatic Extension of Time to File Corporate Income Tax Return," extension to file return using . . . 21,010.05; 26,070.02

Form 8233, "Exemption From Withholding on Compensation for Independent (and Certain Dependent) Personal Services of a Nonresident Alien Individual," agent filing of . . . 28,030.03

Form 8300, "Report of Cash Payments Over $10,000 Received in a Trade or Business," cash receipts reported using . . . 26,140.12

Form 8332, "Release of Claim to Exemption for Child of Divorced or Separated Parents," waiving dependency exemption on . . . 1060.04

Form 8452-OL, "U.S. Individual Income Tax Declaration for On-Line Filing," requirement to submit . . . 26,025.01

Form 8453, "U.S. Partnership Declaration and Signature for Electronic and Magnetic Media Filing," as signature document . . . 26,180.01

Form 8606, "Nondeductible IRAs"
. filed with tax return for nondeductible IRA contributions or distributions . . . 3105.06
. reporting Coverdell ESA distributions on . . . 5115.03

Form 8615, "Tax for Children Under Age 14 Who Have Investment Income of More Than $1,600," separate return using . . . 2170.04

Form 8633, "Application to Participate in IRS e-file," online application form used in lieu of . . . 26,025.04

Form 8716, Section 444 election using . . . 21,016.02

Form 8801, AMT credit figured on . . . 16,020.01

Form 8806, reporting acquisition or change in capital structure of corporation using . . . 22,001.03

Form 8814, reporting child's unearned income on . . . 2170.02–.03

Form 8821, "Tax Information Authorization," representative filing . . . 27,040.04

Form 8827, "Credit for Prior Year Minimum Tax—Corporation," alternative minimum tax liability credit claimed using . . . 16,045

Form 8829, home office use claimed on . . . 12,125.07

Form 8832, "Entity Classification Election"
. classification as association using . . . 21,010.03
. classification as partnership using . . . 24,001.02; 24,002
. taxation as corporation versus partnership using . . . 20,001.02
. taxation as S corporation elected using . . . 21,010

Form 8839, "Qualified Adoption Expenses," adoption expense exclusion or credit claimed on . . . 4115.09; 14,015.09

Form 8850, prescreening and certification request on
. for work opportunity credit . . . 14,065.02

Form 8854, "Initial and Annual Expatriation Information Statement," information return using . . . 28,065.03

Form 8855, "Election to Treat a Qualified Revocable Trust as Part of an Estate," election using . . . 25,010.03

Form 8857, "Request for Innocent Spouse Relief (and Separation of Liability, and Equitable Relief," relief for innocent spouse claimed using . . . 26,006.03

Form 8863, "Education Credits—HOPE and Lifetime Credits," election for credit on . . . 14,025.06; 14,030.03

Form 8865, "Return of U.S. Persons with Respect to Certain Foreign Partnerships,"
. reportable events on . . . 26,180.02

Form 8869, "Qualified Subchapter S Subsidiary Election," election for QSub using . . . 21,010.01

Form 8872, "Political Organization Report of Contributions and Expenditures," required reporting using . . . 23,109.02

Form 8885, "Health Insurance Credit for Eligible Recipients," HCTC claimed on . . . 14,035

Form 8887, "Health Insurance Eligibility Certificate," eligibility for HCTC shown on . . . 14,035

Form 8898, "Statement for Individuals Who Begin or End Bona Fide Residence in U.S. Possession" . . . 28,080.04

Form 8899, qualified donee income reported on . . . 9052

Form 8938, "Statement of Specified Foreign Financial Assets . . . 28,100
. reporting thresholds . . . 28,100
. specified foreign financial assets . . . 28,100

Form 8949, "Sales and Other Dispositions of Capital Assets" . . . 8045

Form 9779, "Business Enrollment Form," enrollment in EFTPS using . . . 26,130.02

Foster care payments
. foster care payments defined . . . 5125.03
. foster care payments excluded from taxation . . . 5125.01
. foster care must be provided in taxpayer's residence . . . 5125.04
. foster individual defined . . . 5125.02

401(k) plans (cash or deferred arrangements)
. catch-up contributions by year to, table of . . . 3150.01
. contribution limits for . . . 3150.01
. distributions from . . . 3150.04–.05
. early participation in . . . 3150.03
. elective deferrals for . . . 3150.03
. employer contributions to . . . 3150
. matching contribution requirement for . . . 3150.03
. nondiscrimination rules for . . . 3150.02–.03
. Roth 401(k) plans . . . 3150.06
. SIMPLE . . . 3175.04
. taxation of . . . 3150.05

Fraud investigation, IRS Criminal Division for . . . 27.005.07

Frequent flyer miles, tax treatment of . . . 4020

Fringe benefits . . . 4001–4115.10
. adoption assistance one of . . . 4115–4115.10
. athletic facility use one of . . . 4080–4080.02
. cafeteria plans one of . . . 4110–4110.09
. company cars and airplanes one of . . . 4001–4020
. as deductible by employer . . . 12,065.02
. dependent care assistance one of . . . 4060–4060.01
. education reimbursement one of . . . 4055–4055.02

References are to paragraph (¶) numbers.

Fringe benefits—continued
. employee achievement awards one of . . . 4075–4075.04
. employee discounts one of . . . 4070–4070.02
. employer-provided cell phones . . . 4090
. financial counseling one of . . . 4085
. information returns for . . . 26,070.09
. insurance benefits one of . . . 4025–4040.04
. meals and lodging one of, employer-provided . . . 4045–4050
. moving expenses one of . . . 4105
. no-cost services one of . . . 4065–4065.02
. payments not considered as wages, rules for . . . 15,080.05
. of S corporation shareholders . . . 21,002
. small . . . 4095–4095.02
. social security tax rules for . . . 15,075.01
. transportation one of . . . 4100–4100.06
. withholding rules for . . . 15,015.03
. working condition . . . 4090–4090.03

Fuel production credits . . . 14,170–14,170.03

Funeral expenses, deduction from estate or trust for . . . 25,055.01

G

Gain or loss. *See also* individual types
. AMT treatment of . . . 16,005.07
. from disposition of property . . . 15,105.05; 24,100–24,125.03
. factors in figuring . . . 6001–6001.04
. on installment payments for interest in partnership assets . . . 24,145.02
. ordinary versus capital . . . 8010.13
. recognition of . . . 6005.01–.02; 22,055–22,055.05
. from sale of options . . . 8010.09; 8035–8035.04
. on transfer of partnership interest . . . 24,130–24,130.05

Gambling gains and losses
. Casual gamblers . . . 13,080
. in trade or business . . . 13,080
. record retention for . . . 26,095.02
. taxation of . . . 2015; 2155; 13,080

Gasoline and special fuels, credits for certain uses of . . . 14,165

General business credit . . . 14,050–14,155.03
. carryover of . . . 14,050.01
. figuring . . . 14,050.01

Generation skipping transfer (GST) tax
. computing . . . 29,175–29,175.02
. exemption . . . 29,185–29,186
. extension of time to make allocation of GST exemption . . . 29,185
. filing requirements for . . . 29,180
. gross-up of . . . 29,015.07
. predeceased ancestor exception . . . 29,180
. purpose of . . . 29,170
. qualified trust defined . . . 29,186
. skip person for . . . 29,180.01
. taxable terminations for . . . 29,190.01
. transfers exempt from . . . 29,185.01–29,186.02
. transfers subject to . . . 29,180–29,180.11
. trust severance for GST purposes . . . 29,185

Gift cards . . . 18,085.06
. deferring income on prepaid . . . 18,085.06

Gift tax . . . 29,001–29,030.03
. annual exclusion from . . . 29,020.01
. basis in property increased for . . . 6030.04

Gift tax—continued
. EGTRRA as changing but not eliminating . . . 29,001.02
. extension of time to file gift tax return . . . 29,195.02
. filing requirements for . . . 29,195.02
. gross-up of . . . 29,080.03
. loans subject to . . . 2065.01; 2065.03
. nature and imposition of . . . 29,010.01
. taxpayers owing . . . 29,010.02–.03
. transfers exempt from . . . 29,020–29,020.08
. transfers subject to . . . 29,015–29,015.08
. valuation rules for . . . 27,050.10

Gift-splitting . . . 29,020.02; 29,180.11; 29,195.03

Gifts . . . 5055
. of appreciated property . . . 9052
. of art . . . 9052
. basis of property received as . . . 6030–6030.04
. business . . . 10,050; 29,010.02
. compensation versus . . . 2010; 2020.02
. deemed . . . 29,015.05
. depreciation for . . . 8060.03
. durable power of attorney for giving . . . 29,020.03
. employee . . . 5055.01
. gift bags received by celebrities . . . 2005.01
. indirect . . . 29,015.05
. lifetime, advantages of . . . 29,005; 29,090
. to minors . . . 5055.02; 29,020.02
. of property declined in value . . . 9052
. relation-back rule for . . . 29,020.02
. from revocable trusts . . . 29,065.03
. spousal . . . 6035; 29,020.07
. taking effect at death . . . 29,070
. valuation of . . . 29,025–29,030.03

Going concern, test of business commencing as . . . 20,045.03

Golden parachute payments
. avoiding limitations on . . . 12,080.04
. defined . . . 12,080.02
. for disqualified individuals . . . 12,080; 12,080.03
. tax consequences of . . . 12,080.01
. types of . . . 12,080.06

Goodwill
. antichurning rules for . . . 11,005.05
. basis in . . . 6080.06

Government employees
. defined benefit plans for . . . 3040.01
. disability benefits for . . . 5045.05
. social security coverage of . . . 15,060.11
. taxable compensation of . . . 2025

Government obligations, income in . . . 5005–5010; 6090.06

Gross estate . . . 29,040–29,100
. deductions from . . . 29,115–29,125
. in figuring decedent's estate tax liability . . . 29,040
. transfers includible in . . . 29,030.03
. valuation of property in . . . 29,105.01–29,110.02

Gross income
. of decedent . . . 25,040.02
. defined . . . 2001.01
. of dependent . . . 1070.01–.02
. determined to learn whether to file return . . . 1001
. of estates and trusts . . . 25,040.01
. exclusions from . . . 2030.02; 5001–5120.04; 23,170.02
. inclusions in . . . 2001–2190; 3170.05
. reporting . . . 18,080–18,080.02

References are to paragraph (¶) numbers.

Gross profit of business, figuring . . . 17,005–17,005.01
Gross receipts
. accounting method based on amount of . . . 18,005.02
. of small corporation for AMT . . . 16,025.02–.05
Group support . . . 1060.03
Group-term life insurance . . . 5040
. combined with permanent benefits . . . 4030.03
. employer-paid . . . 4030
. nondiscrimination rules for . . . 4030.02
. requirements for income exclusion of . . . 4030.01

H

Head of household status . . . 1030
. principal place of abode required for . . . 1030.02
. qualifying child for . . . 1030.01
Health coverage tax credit (HCTC) . . . 14,035–14,035.04
Health insurance premiums
. funded with qualified plan funds . . . 3010.05; 3085.01
. medical expense deduction for . . . 9100.02
. prepaid . . . 9100.04
. for self-employed individuals . . . 9100.03
Health insurance reimbursements, tax treatment of . . . 2190.03
Health reimbursement arrangements (HRAs), employer-provided. *See also* Accident and health plans, employer-provided . . . 4120.01–.07
. contributions to . . . 4120.01
Health savings accounts (HSAs) . . . 9115.01
Heartland Disaster Tax Relief Act of 2008 . . . 5100
. additional exemption for housing individual displaced by disaster . . . 5100
. casualty and theft losses . . . 5100
. charitable giving incentives . . . 5100
. earned income credit . . . 5100
. education credit . . . 5100
. IRAs and other retirement plans . . . 5100
. net operating losses . . . 5100
. recapture federal mortgage subsidy . . . 5100
. refundable child tax credit . . . 5100
. replacement period for nonrecognition of gain 5100
Hedging transactions, short sales rules for . . . 8030.04
High-deductible health plans (HDHPs)
. Archer MSAs requiring coverage under . . . 9120.03
. defined . . . 9120.03
. requirements of . . . 9120.03
Highly compensated employees for qualified plans . . . 3020.05
Historic absorption ratio election . . . 18,045.03
Hobby losses and expenses . . . 13,085–13,085.03
. aggregating activities . . . 13,085
Holders of qualified zone academy bonds, credit for . . . 14,185–14,185.02
Holding companies. *See* Personal holding companies (PHCs)
Holding period for capital assets
. change in . . . 8001.02
. figuring . . . 8020–8020.02
. by type of property or transaction . . . 8020.02
Holding period for QSBS . . . 8105.06
Holding period on short sales . . . 8030.01
Home, day care in . . . 12,125.09
Home office
. allocation of interest for . . . 9015.05
. deduction of expenses for . . . 12,125–12,125.10
. dwelling units for . . . 12,125.01
. of employee . . . 12,125; 12,125.05
. exclusive use for business of . . . 12,125.03
. as principal place of business . . . 12,125; 12,125.04
. record retention for . . . 26,095.02
. reporting expenses for . . . 12,125.07
. trade or business use required for . . . 12,125.02
. travel to other work sites from . . . 12,125.06
Home sale exclusion
. application to U.S. uniformed service members . . . 7010.02
. current exclusion amount for . . . 7001.01
. election out of . . . 7001.06
. general rule for . . . 7001
. qualifying for . . . 7001.04
. reporting requirements for . . . 7001.02
. treatment of gain exceeding $500,000 for . . . 7001.05
Homebuilder's credit for new energy-efficient homes . . . 14,140
Hope Scholarship credit . . . 5110.06, 5115.06; 14,025–14,025.07; 14,030.05
Horse breeding and showing, hobby losses from . . . 13,085.01
Household employees, employment taxes for . . . 14,205.02; 15,060.02
Hurricane relief . . . 5100.01
. amount deductible as personal casualty loss . . . 13,020.03
. employee retention credit . . . 14,156
. exemption for housing evacuees . . . 1040.01
. expenses for donated inventory . . . 12,020
. extension of time to file returns . . . 26,070
. look-back rule . . . 14,005, 14,005.02, 14,020
. low-income housing credit requirements suspended . . . 14,060.01
. nonrecognition replacement period extended . . . 7035, 7050.01
. retirement plans, borrowing and withdrawals liberalized . . . 3095, 3125, 3135.02
. tax relief for victims . . . 2145
. work opportunity tax credit . . . 14,065
Hybrid accounting method . . . 18,001.01

I

Illegal activities, taxation of income from . . . 2001.04
Income assignment . . . 18,015–18,015.02
Income forecast depreciation method . . . 11,065.03
Income in respect of decedent, taxation of successor for . . . 2160; 25,040.02
Income levels necessitating filing a federal income tax return . . . 1001.01
Income reconstruction by IRS . . . 18,040–18,040.04
Income replacement insurance policies . . . 5045.02
Income tax payments by employers
. deposits for . . . 15,135–15,135.01
. locations for submitting . . . 15,135.03
. quarterly . . . 15,135.02
Income tax, state and local . . . 9030–9030.03
Income tax treaty, requirements for . . . 2080.01
Indebtedness
. acquired by related party . . . 2145.05

References are to paragraph (¶) numbers.

Indebtedness—continued
. for business real property, cancellation of . . . 2145.07
. cancelled as gift . . . 2145.04
. corporation stock transferred to cancel . . . 2145.03
. discharge of . . . 2145.01; 2145.02
. mortgage, settled for less than face value . . . 2145.06
. qualified form or qualified real property business . . . 2145.02
. for student loans, cancellation of . . . 2145.08
. tax circumstance of cancelled . . . 2145.02

Independent contractors. *See* Self-employed individuals

Indian employment credit . . . 14,105

Indian reservation property, recovery periods for . . . 11,035.05

Indian settlement payments, tax treatment of . . . 2005

Individual Identification Number (ITIN) for tax filing by aliens . . . 26,050.05; 28,030.03

Individual retirement account (IRA) contributions
. catch-up . . . 3105.03
. deductibility of . . . 3105.04–.05
. excess . . . 3115
. investment opportunities for . . . 3130–3130.03
. maximum, by year, table of . . . 3105.03
. nondeductible . . . 3105.06

Individual retirement account (IRA) distributions
. automatic rollovers of mandatory . . . 3120.01–.02
. default rule for postdeath . . . 3120.03
. distributions to charities . . . 3135.01
. incidental benefit requirement for . . . 3120.03
. phased retirement plan . . . 3120.04
. premature, penalty tax for . . . 3135.02; 9105.10
. qualified charitable distributions from IRAs to charities . . . 3125.05
. reporting . . . 3120.03
. RMDs one type of . . . 3105.07; 3120.03; 3135.02; 3140.05
. rollovers of . . . 3125–3125.03; 3140.05
. rules for, for deemed IRA . . . 3105.07
. taxation of . . . 3120.03; 3135

Individual retirement accounts (IRAs). *See also* individual types . . . 3105–3140.10
. bankruptcy treatment of . . . 3105.10
. deemed . . . 3105.07
. designated beneficiary for . . . 3120.03
. eligibility for . . . 3105
. employer-sponsored, exception to early withdrawal penalty for . . . 3085.01
. for married couples . . . 3105.02
. record retention for . . . 26,095.02
. rollovers to . . . 3080.02; 3085.01; 21,025.07
. Roth 401(k) . . . 3150.06
. Roth IRA . . . 3140
. SIMPLE . . . 3175.04
. spousal . . . 3110
. trust as beneficiary of . . . 3120.03
. wash sale rules, application of . . . 3135.03

Individual retirement annuities . . . 3130.02

Infertility-related medical expenses, deductible . . . 9105.05

Information returns. *See also* individual return types . . . 26,135
. deadlines for . . . 26,140.01
. extension to file . . . 26,135.02
. Information disclosure of foreign financial assets . . . 28,085

Inheritances . . . 5060

Inheritances—continued
. depreciation recapture rules not applied to . . . 8060.03

Injuries to employees unrelated to work, tax treatment of receipts for . . . 4120.05

Innocent spouse relief
. backup withholding protection in . . . 14,225.06
. electing . . . 26,006

INS Form I-9, "Employer Eligibility Verification Form" for legal workers . . . 15,030.02

Insolvency reorganization (Type G reorganization) . . . 22,045.01

Installation of alternative fueling stations, credit for . . . 14,155–14,155.03

Installment agreements
. authorization of partial payment . . . 19,001.01
. to settle tax claim . . . 27,035

Installment obligations
. disposition of . . . 19,050–19,050.04
. pledges of . . . 19,040
. tax-free transfers of . . . 19,050.02

Installment plan for tax payments . . . 26,125.03

Installment sales . . . 19,001–19,050.04
. allowance of suspended losses with . . . 13,090.10
. AMT treatment of . . . 16,030.04
. computing gain in . . . 19,020–19,020.06
. contingent sale price for . . . 19,025–19,025.06
. defined . . . 19,001
. of depreciable property . . . 19,030–19,030.02
. electing not to use installment method for . . . 19,001.03
. figuring income from . . . 19,015
. in foreign currency . . . 19,025.05
. interest charge on deferred tax liability in . . . 19,035–19,035.04
. like-kind exchanges in . . . 19,020.05
. minimum payments required for using installment method for . . . 19,010–19,010.01
. payments received in . . . 19,020.04
. reporting, decision for use of . . . 19,001.02
. types of property eligible for installment method for . . . 19,005–19,005.01

Insurance premiums, employer-paid. *See also* Life Insurance . . . 2035.01; 12,105.01–.03

Intangible drilling and development costs, depletion of
. AMT treatment of . . . 16,010.02; 16,030.02
. depreciation versus . . . 12,170.03

Intangible property
. acquiring, costs of . . . 12,010.07
. amortization of Section 197 . . . 11,005.05; 18,190.01
. capitalization rules for . . . 12,010.07
. creating, costs of . . . 12,010.07
. defined . . . 18,190.01
. disposition of . . . 11,005.05

Intellectual property, charitable contributions of . . . 9052

Interest
. abatement of, for tax liability . . . 27,115.04
. accrued on bonds . . . 2055
. bank, savings and loan association, and credit union . . . 2090
. capitalization rules for . . . 17,045.11
. capitalized . . . 9005.04
. deduction of . . . 3095.04
. on deferred tax liability . . . 19,035–19,035.04
. dividends distinguished from . . . 9005.01

References are to paragraph (¶) numbers.

Interest—continued
. exempt . . . 2055.02
. for failure to pay tax . . . 27,115–27,115.04
. imputed . . . 2070.06–.07; 20,175
. loan . . . 2065; 15,105.02
. nondeductible . . . 9025–9025.06
. OID . . . 2070
. on overpayments of tax . . . 26,120
. points on mortgage as . . . 9015.09–.10
. REMIC . . . 23,100.01; 23,100.03
. tax-exempt . . . 16,005.10; 16,010.03; 26,135.01
. taxable . . . 2055.01; 18,095.01
. transfer of . . . 2065.03
. on underpayments of tax . . . 26,120
. on U.S. obligations . . . 5010
. on U.S. savings bonds, annual reporting of . . . 2070.08
. unstated . . . 2070.07

Interest expense
. apportionment and allocation of . . . 28,010.02
. capitalization of . . . 12,110.03
. reporting . . . 26,145–26,145.04

Interest expense deduction . . . 9005–9025.06
. allocation of . . . 18,155.04
. AMT treatment of . . . 16,005.05
. classification of expenses for . . . 9005.02
. for personal interest expenses . . . 9010–9010.02
. reporting . . . 9005.02
. requirements for . . . 12,110
. for student loan interest . . . 9005.04
. for tax deficiencies . . . 9005.03

Interest income . . . 2055–2070.08

Interest payment. *See* Interest expense

Internal Revenue Service (IRS)
. changes of S corporation requiring approval by . . . 21,016.01
. delivery services approved by . . . 26,065.04; 29,165.01
. election to have tax figured by . . . 1015.02
. income reconstruction by . . . 18,040–18,040.04
. levies by . . . 3135.02
. permission to change accounting method by . . . 18,045.02
. record retention rules of . . . 26,095.03
. representation of taxpayer by practitioner authorized to practice before . . . 27,040–27,040.05
. small plan actuarial program of . . . 3060.03
. web site of . . . 26,025.01
. worker classification determinations by . . . 15,070.04

Inventory . . . 17,001–17,070.09
. accrual accounting for . . . 18,005.02
. advance payment for . . . 18,085.04
. basis of . . . 6100; 17,060
. defined . . . 17,001; 24,120.04
. donated to charity . . . 17,005.02
. expenses for donated . . . 12,020
. farming . . . 17,070–17,070.09
. goods included in . . . 17,010
. goods withdrawn for personal use from . . . 17,005.03
. in gross profit of business . . . 17,005–17,005.01
. manufacture of . . . 17,050.03
. methods disapproved for valuing . . . 17,055
. methods of pricing . . . 17,015–17,020.02
. as not depreciable . . . 11,005.03
. rolling-average method of inventory valuation . . . 17,025
. shrinkage estimates for . . . 17,025.05
. uniform capitalization rules for basis in . . . 6100; 17,045–17,045.07; 17,045.09; 17,049.11
. unsellable goods in . . . 17,025.03

Inventory—continued
. transfers of partnership interests involving . . . 24,130.03
. valuation methods for . . . 17,025–17,060
. writing down goods in . . . 17,035

Inventory capitalization rules . . . 17,025.03

Inventory price index method . . . 17,030.01

Investment credit . . . 14,055–14,055.05
. credits composing . . . 14,055
. recapture of . . . 14,055.01

Investment expenses
. defined . . . 9020.05
. in miscellaneous itemized deductions . . . 9145.02

Investment interest expense
. allocation of . . . 9020.03
. carryforward of . . . 9020.06
. limitation on deduction of . . . 9020.01; 24,040.06
. for net capital gain or qualified dividends . . . 9020.04
. reporting deduction of . . . 9020.07

Involuntary conversions of property
. assessments for, deficiency . . . 27,050.03
. of business . . . 7040.01
. depreciation recapture rules for . . . 8060.05
. disposition of property in reclamation laws for irrigation projects as . . . 7035.05
. from persistent drought . . . 7035.04
. gain or loss from . . . 7040–7040.03; 7055–7055.04; 7065.03; 8065–8065.01
. general rule for . . . 7035
. from governmental seizure or condemnation . . . 7035.02
. insurance proceeds for . . . 7035.04
. of principal residence . . . 7030; 7040.02–.03
. replacement property following . . . 7035.06; 7045–7045.04; 7060–7065.03; 8060.05
. reporting . . . 13,010.05
. time limit on replacement of property following . . . 7050.01–.05

Iron ore, Section 1231 treatment for gain or loss on sale of . . . 8080

Irrevocable life insurance trust . . . 29,075.02

Itemized Deduction Reduction Worksheet . . . 9001.01

Itemized deductions. *See also* individual deductions . . . 1010.01; 2190.01; 2190.05
. AMT treatment of . . . 16,005.01
. based on AGI . . . 9001–9001.01; 9140–9140.03
. for charitable contributions . . . 9050–9095
. claiming . . . 9001.02
. for interest expense . . . 9005–9025.06
. for medical expenses . . . 9100–9120.06
. miscellaneous . . . 9140–9165; 10,020.01; 16,005.02
. for moving expenses . . . 9125–9135.04
. for taxes paid . . . 9030–9045

J

Job Creation and Worker Assistance Act of 2002, bonus depreciation under . . . 11,001.01

Job-related education costs . . . 4055

Jobs and Growth Tax Relief Reconciliation Act of 2003
. accumulated earnings tax reduced by . . . 20,145
. tax rates changed by . . . 16,001.01
. withholding on real property sales by foreign person under . . . 15,045.05

Joint and survivor annuity . . . 3075.01; 3075.04

References are to paragraph (¶) numbers.

Joint return for married couples . . . 1020.01; 26,005–26,005.05
. change in election to separate returns from . . . 26,005.02
. on death of spouse . . . 26,005.03; 26,065.05
. "late," replacement of separate returns with . . . 27,050.04
. liability of each spouse for . . . 26,005.01
. living separately . . . 1020.03
. income from property on . . . 2001.03

Joint tenancy . . . 29,015.04

Joint ventures between tax-exempts and for-profit organizations . . . 23,109.04

K

Keogh (H.R. 10) plans
. ancillary benefits of plans for . . . 3155.06
. contribution maximums for . . . 3155.01
. defined benefit and defined contribution types of . . . 3155
. earned income required for . . . 3155.08
. establishing . . . 3155.01
. forfeitures for . . . 3155.05
. loans from . . . 3155.07
. multiplication limits for . . . 3155.04
. net earnings from self-employment for computing contributions to . . . 3155.03

Key employees
. for cafeteria plans . . . 4110.08
. loans to, nondeductible interest for . . . 9025.04
. for top-heavy plans . . . 3045.01

Kiddie tax
. AMT exemption amount for . . . 16,015.02
. filing requirements for . . . 2170.01
. tax rate for . . . 26,010.01

L

Last-in, first-out (LIFO) inventories
. accounting method for . . . 18,045.03
. qualified liquidations of . . . 17,030.03

Last-in, first-out (LIFO) inventory pricing method . . . 17,020–17,020.02
. costing inventory under . . . 17,030–17,030.03
. for retail merchants, conversion to . . . 17,050.05
. simplified dollar-value . . . 17,030.02

Last known address . . . 26,125
. how to change taxpayer's . . . 26,125

Laundry allowances . . . 4090.02

Lease acquisition costs . . . 12,095

Lease agreement
. cancellation payments for . . . 12,095.02
. construction allowance specified in . . . 2140.04
. rent payments under . . . 12,095.03

Lease transactions, leveraged . . . 12,095.04

Leased property
. depreciation of . . . 11,010.02
. tenant replacement of . . . 7065.01

Leased property, improvements by lessee to . . . 2140–2140.01
. construction allowance exclusion for . . . 2140.04
. in lieu of rent . . . 2140.02
. MACRS recovery period for . . . 11,050.04
. treatment of abandoned . . . 2140.03

Leased vehicles, inclusion amount for . . . 10,030.01

Leaseholds as capital assets . . . 8010.08

Leave-sharing plans, tax consequences . . . 2005.01

Legal separation from spouse, effect on medical expense deduction of . . . 9110.01

Levies, IRS
. on IRAs . . . 3135.02
. restrictions on . . . 27,070.02
. types of . . . 27,070.02

Liens on property for taxes . . . 27,070–27,070.09

Life annuity with term certain as qualified plan distribution . . . 3075.01

Life insurance. *See also* individual types . . . 5015–5040
. cash value build-up of whole life . . . 5015–5015.02; 9025.03
. death benefits from employer-owned life insurance . . . 2185
. dividends on . . . 5035
. employer-paid premiums for . . . 2035.01; 12,105.01–.03; 15,075.07; 15,080.05; 26,160
. endowment contracts for . . . 5030; 5035; 6065
. in estate planning . . . 29,075.01
. exchange of policies for . . . 6045; 6065–6065.01
. group-term . . . 4030–4030.03; 5040; 12,105.01; 15,075.07; 15,080.05; 15,140.02; 26,160
. incidents of ownership of . . . 29,075.03; 29,080
. proceeds of . . . 5020–5020.05; 29,080–29,080.03; 29,120.08
. in qualified plans . . . 3010.04
. second-to-die (survivorship) . . . 6065.01; 29,075.04
. single premium, loan to buy . . . 9025.02
. split-dollar . . . 2035.02; 4035; 9050.03; 12,105.01
. surrender of policy for . . . 5025

Lifetime Learning credit . . . 5110.06, 5115.06; 14,030–14,030.06

Like-kind exchanges
. basis affected by . . . 6050.11
. boot affecting . . . 6050.06; 6055–6055.02
. character of property for . . . 6050.03
. characteristics of, examined by IRS . . . 6050.13
. deferred . . . 6050.08; 6055.04
. depreciation recapture in . . . 6055.03
. exchange of property required for . . . 6050.06
. of fractional property interests . . . 6050.03
. of insurance policies . . . 6045; 6065–6065.01
. MACRS property acquired in . . . 6055.04
. of mortgaged property . . . 6060.01–.02
. multiple property . . . 6050.07
. parking transactions to facilitate . . . 6050.08
. in partnership . . . 6060.02; 24,096
. principal residences acquired in . . . 7010.03
. qualifying for . . . 6050.02
. of related persons . . . 6050.10
. reporting requirements for . . . 6050.12
. requirements for property in . . . 6050.04; 6050.13
. safe harbors for . . . 6050.07
. Section 1245 gain in . . . 8060.04
. of securities . . . 6045; 6070–6070.02
. as tax deferral technique . . . 6050
. three-party . . . 6050.08; 6050.09
. time-limit requirement for . . . 6050.05
. types of . . . 6050.06; 6050.08
. types of exchanges with gain not deferred for . . . 6050.02

Limited liability companies (LLCs) . . . 30,001–30,215
. advantages of . . . 30,001.03; 30,100; 30,105
. allocation of profits and losses of . . . 30,095
. articles of organization for . . . 30,010
. changing entity classification . . . 30,090

References are to paragraph (¶) numbers.

Limited liability companies (LLCs)—continued
. check-the-box entity classification for . . . 30,085
. choice of entity for . . . 30,085
. contributions of members to . . . 30,040; 30,190
. converting from partnership to . . . 30,095
. creation of . . . 30,001.01; 30,100
. default statutes for . . . 30,001
. defense of usury for . . . 30,070
. defined . . . 30,001
. disadvantages of . . . 30,090
. disassociation of, causes of . . . 30,205
. distributions to members of . . . 30,200
. filing requirements . . . 30,002
. foreign . . . 30,065; 30,080
. formation of . . . 30,135
. governance of . . . 30,025; 30,180
. for manufacturing company . . . 30,115
. members of . . . 30,030; 30,045–30,055; 30,095.04; 30,150–30,155
. mergers and consolidations of . . . 30,215
. method of accounting . . . 30,145
. names of, rules for . . . 30,130
. operating agreements for . . . 30,015
. pass-through of income and losses of . . . 30,095; 30,195
. payroll tax . . . 13,100
. personal liability of members in . . . 30,170
. powers of . . . 30,165
. professional . . . 30,060
. for real estate investments . . . 30,205–30,105
. responsible person for financial management of . . . 30,095
. self-employment tax for members of . . . 30,095
. series LLCs . . . 30,075
. for service organization . . . 30,115
. single-member . . . 30,080; 30,095
. for sole proprietors . . . 30,035; 30,120
. state-level provisions for . . . 30,020; 30,080; 30,124
. Tax Matters Member of . . . 30,095
. tax year of . . . 30,140
. taxation of . . . 30,075
. usury and the LLC . . . 30.070
. voting rights for . . . 30,185
. winding up of . . . 30,210
. withdrawal, dissolution and winding up . . . 30,210

Limited liability company income reporting . . . 2165; 2165.03

Limited partners . . . 13,090.06; 13,090.07

Liquidations, corporate . . . 22,120–22,130.02
. complete . . . 22,125.02
. property distributions in . . . 22,125–22,125.05

Liquidations, subsidiary . . . 22,130–22,130.02
. carryovers in . . . 22,135.01

Listed property, depreciation of . . . 11,040.08

Livestock
. casualty or theft losses of . . . 13,055.03–.04
. destroyed by disease or drought . . . 7035.03
. gain or loss from sale of . . . 8075–8075.01

Loan guaranty
. gift tax on . . . 29,015.02
. loss from . . . 13,165.02

Loans
. below-market . . . 29,015.01
. compensation . . . 2065.01
. to corporations by stockholders . . . 13,150
. deduction of interest payments on . . . 18,155.04
. distinguishing debt from equity . . . 2060
. dividend . . . 2065.01
. dividends distinguished from . . . 2085

Loans—continued
. exempted . . . 2065.02
. gift . . . 2065.01
. interest-free and low-interest . . . 2065–2065.03
. to key employees, interest on . . . 9025.04
. life insurance purchased to obtain . . . 12,105.01
. nonrecourse . . . 13,100.09
. by officers or employees . . . 13,140.01
. payments on . . . 18,155.04
. personal liability for . . . 13,100.09
. from qualified plans . . . 3095–3095.04
. by stockholder . . . 13,140.02
. student loans, deductibility of interest paid on . . . 9005.04
. tax treatment of . . . 2060

Lobbying expenses . . . 12,035–12,035.01

Lodging costs for treatment as deductible medical expenses . . . 9105.06

Lodging, employer-provided . . . 4045; 4045.02
. excludable from income . . . 4045.03
. for partner . . . 4045.06
. by stockholder in rent-free property . . . 4045.04
. travel allowance for . . . 10,015.03

Long-term care benefits, information returns for . . . 26,140.14

Long-term care insurance . . . 4040–4040.04
. chronic illness for . . . 4040.03; 5105.03
. covered expenses in . . . 4040.02; 5105.01–.02
. employer plans including . . . 5105.05
. medical expense deduction for premiums for . . . 9105.04
. per diem benefits limitation of . . . 4040.04; 5105; 5105.04
. requirements for income exclusion of . . . 4040.01; 5105

Long-term contracts . . . 19,075.04
. look-back method for . . . 19,075.03
. midcontract change in taxpayers under . . . 19,075.04
. percentage of completion method for . . . 19,075.02
. special accounting methods for . . . 16,005.15; 19,075

Losses . . . 13,001–13,175
. abandonment . . . 13,050
. bad debt distinguished from . . . 13,165–13,165.02
. business or trade . . . 13,010–13,010.05
. capital expenditures versus . . . 13,060–13,060.02
. casualty . . . 13,020–13,020.06, 13,030–13,030.02
. deductible . . . 13,001.01–13,005; 18,175.02; 25,055.02
. deduction from gross estate of . . . 29,115.06
. for demolished buildings . . . 13,045–13,045.01
. disallowed . . . 13,065–13,105.05
. farming . . . 13,055–13,055.07
. for financial institution deposits . . . 13,155–13,155.01
. gambling losses . . . 13,080
. hobby losses . . . 13,085
. in for-profit transactions . . . 13,015–13,015.03
. foreign, recapture of . . . 28,010.05
. gambling . . . 2015; 2155; 13,080
. passed through to partners . . . 24,045–24,055.03
. passed through to S corporation shareholders . . . 21,045.01–.02
. passive activity . . . 13,090–13,090.11; 13,100.05; 16,005.09; 18,140; 24,055.02
. property . . . 13,020.01
. specified liability losses . . . 12,010.05; 13,110.05
. suspended . . . 21,045.01; 21,045.03
. suspended passive . . . 13,090.09–.10
. theft . . . 13,025–13,025.04
. unused S corporation . . . 21,045.03

References are to paragraph (¶) numbers.

Losses—continued
. for worthless stock . . . 13,040–13,040.05

Lottery winnings, taxation rules for . . . 2015; 2015.02

Low-income housing credit . . . 14,060.01–.03

Lump-sum distribution from qualified plan . . . 3075.01; 3075.04
. defined . . . 3080.02
. rollovers of . . . 3080.02
. taxation of . . . 3080.02

M

MACRS property. *See* Modified accelerated cost recovery system (MACRS)

Magnetic media, types of returns required to be filed using . . . 15,130.02

Manufacturers' and processors' pools for inventory . . . 17,030.01

Manufacturer's credit for energy-efficient appliances . . . 14,145–14,145.03

Marital deduction for transfers between spouses . . . 29,020.07; 29,100; 29,120.01–.10
. same sex couple, right to claim . . . 29,120

Marital rights, types of . . . 29,090.01

Mark-to-market (MTM) method to value securities
. elections to use, mandatory and discretionary . . . 8040.01; 8040.04
. exceptions to securities for . . . 8040.02; 8040.04
. extension of time to make election . . . 8040.05
. making election for . . . 8040.05
. safe harbor for . . . 8040.01
. for Section 1256 contracts . . . 8040.03
. for securities futures contracts . . . 8040.06

Market discount for OID bonds . . . 2070.02

Married couple
. exemptions for . . . 1050–1050.04
. filing jointly status for . . . 1020.01
. filing separately status for . . . 1030.01–.02
. living separately . . . 1020.03
. offsets of losses against ordinary income by . . . 8051.02
. ownership and use requirements for principal residence sale exclusion for . . . 7015.01

Material advisor for tax shelters, disclosures by . . . 26,210.04

Meals, deduction of, while away from home . . . 10,005.01

Meals, employer-paid . . . 4045–4045.01; 4095.01
. cash equivalents for . . . 4095.03
. for partner . . . 4045.06
. payments in kind for . . . 15,080.02
. substantiation of . . . 10,055–10,055.02–.03

Medical expenses. *See also* individual expenses
. AMT treatment of . . . 16,005.04
. deductible costs considered to be . . . 9105–9105.13
. deduction of . . . 9100–9120.06; 18,165; 25,055.0 1
. payments of, as gift-tax free . . . 29,020.04
. premature retirement plan distributions to pay . . . 3085.01; 3150.04; 9105.10
. recipients of deduction for . . . 9110–9110.02
. record retention for . . . 26,095.02
. reimbursement of . . . 4120.03; 5045.01; 9105.01
. separate returns to maximize deduction of . . . 26,005.04

Medical insurance reimbursements, tax treatment of . . . 2190.03

Medical savings accounts. *See* Archer medical savings accounts (MSAs); Health savings accounts (HSAs)

Medical supplies and equipment costs, deductibility of . . . 9105.11

Medicare Advantage MSA . . . 9120.06

Medicare benefits, exclusion for . . . 5090.03

Medicare premiums, Parts A and B . . . 9100.02

Medicare taxes
. additional medicare tax . . . 15,050.03
. established by FICA . . . 15,050
. paid by working seniors . . . 5090.01

Medicines and drugs as deductible medical expenses . . . 9105.04

Membership dues, prepaid . . . 18,115.02

Merchandisers' pools for inventory . . . 17,030.01

Mergers and acquisitions, reporting for . . . 22,001.02

Military Family Tax Relief Act of 2003, tax relief to members of military under . . . 2030.01

Mine Rescue Team Training Tax Credit . . . 14,128

Mines, wells, and other natural deposits, depletion of . . . 12,175.03

Mining expenses
. AMT treatment of . . . 16,005.14
. for development . . . 12,200–12,200.02; 16,005.14
. for exploration . . . 12,195–12,195.02; 16,005.14

Mining inventory, allocation of costs for . . . 17,050.04

Minority business investments, tax breaks for . . . 8110.01–.03

Mixed-use property
. basis allocation for . . . 6080.02
. home sale gain exclusion for . . . 7020
. for qualified business use of car . . . 10,025.05

Modified accelerated cost recovery system (MACRS) . . . 8060.02
. adjusted basis of vehicles under . . . 10,025.01
. antichurning provisions for . . . 11,035.01–.02
. determining depreciation allowance under . . . 11,030.02
. electing out of . . . 11,035.03
. figuring deduction for . . . 11,040.04
. general rules for . . . 11,030
. for personal property . . . 11,040–11,040.09
. for property placed in service after 1986 . . . 11,001; 11,030
. property under, acquired in like-kind exchanges . . . 6055.04
. for public utility property . . . 11,035.04
. rate table for . . . 11,040.04
. for real estate . . . 11,050–11,050.04
. reclassified property for . . . 11,030.01
. recovery periods for . . . 10,025.01

Modified AGI (MAGI)
. for adoption expense exclusion . . . 4115.03
. for adoption expenses credit . . . 14,015.03
. for Coverdell ESA contributions . . . 5115.01
. for Hope Scholarship credit . . . 14,025.03
. for Roth IRA income limitation . . . 3140.03–.04
. for social security benefits in provisional income . . . 5090.01

Money-purchase plans
. features of . . . 3005.01
. Keogh . . . 3155.01

References are to paragraph (¶) numbers.

Mortality tables for RMDs . . . 3120.03
Mortgage credit certificates (MCCs) . . . 14,175
Mortgage insurance premiums . . . 9015
. deduction . . . 9015
. qualified mortgage insurance defined . . . 9015
. reporting requirements . . . 9015
. simplified method for allocating prepaid mortgage insurance premiums . . . 9015
Mortgage interest . . . 9005; 9015–9015.10
. AMT treatment of . . . 16,005.03
. deduction from gross estate of . . . 29,115.05
. for home office . . . 12,125.07
Mortgage points . . . 9015
. deduction of points . . . 9015.09
. refinancing of points . . . 9015.09
. seller-paid points deductible by buyer . . . 9015.10
Moving expenses . . . 9125–9135.04
. claiming deduction for . . . 9125.03–.04
. distance requirements for deducting . . . 9120–9130.01
. nondeductible expenses for . . . 9125.01
. qualifying expenses for . . . 9125.01
. tax-free employer reimbursements of . . . 9125.02
. time test for deducting . . . 9135–9135.04
Municipal leases . . . 5005.02
Mutual funds *See* Regulated investment companies (RICs)

N

Nanny tax . . . 15,060.02; 14,205.02
Nazi persecution, restitution of victims of . . . 5120–5120.04
. basis of property received in . . . 5120.02
. eligible individual defined for . . . 5120.04
. eligible restitution payment defined for . . . 5120.03
. excludable restitution payments to eligible individual in . . . 5120.01
Net capital losses of corporation, carryovers of . . . 20,075.02–.03; 22,135.03–22,140; 22,150
Net earnings from self-employment
. calculating . . . 15,095.01–.02
. income earned abroad included in . . . 15,095.03
. for Keogh contributions . . . 3155.03
. types of income in . . . 15,095.04–.06; 15,105.03
. types of self-employment income not considered . . . 15,105–15,105.06
Net investment income tax . . . 15,170; 15,050
. computation of tax . . . 15,170.02
. taxpayers subject to tax . . . 15,170.01
Net operating loss (NOL)
. AMT deduction of . . . 16,005.12
. carryover of . . . 9080.04; 13,110.01–.05; 13,115.03; 13,120–13,120.01; 18,050; 20,125; 20,135.01; 20,140–20,140.03; 21,035.01; 23,095.07; 27,050.01; 27,165–27,165.03
. corporate . . . 20,115–20,140.03
. defined . . . 20,115
. deduction of . . . 13,110–13,110.03; 20,135–20,135.01; 25,075
. determining . . . 13,115–13,115.03
. of farmers . . . 13,055.07
. figuring . . . 20,120
. liquidations or reorganizations facilitating carryovers of . . . 22,135.03–22,145.01
. in short tax year . . . 18,070.02
. tax refund for . . . 20,046.02
New markets tax credit . . . 14,135
New medical therapies credit . . . 14,075
90-day letter from IRS of tax deficiency assessment . . . 27,020.01–.04
Nonaccrual experience (NAE) accounting method . . . 18,080.02
Noncash charitable contributions . . . 9052
Nonprofit organization employees exempt from social security coverage . . . 15,060.10
Nonqualified deferred compensation
. distributions of . . . 15,140.02
. tax treatment . . . 3170
. transfers incident to divorce of . . . 2150.03
Nonqualified plans . . . 3001; 3170–3170.06
Nonqualified preferred stock (NQPS)
. IRC Section 351 exchanges of . . . 20,005.05; 22,055.03; 22,110.02
. treated as boot . . . 22,110.02
Nonqualified stock options (NQSOs) . . . 2040.02; 2045
Nonresident alien . . . 28,040
. definition . . . 28,040
. filing exception . . . 28,040
. expatriation rules for . . . 28,065
. income tax paid by . . . 28,040; 28,040.03–.06; 28,050.01–28,065
. as ineligible for standard deduction . . . 1035.04
. returns and payment of tax . . . 28,040
. separate return required for spouse of . . . 1020.01
. waiver for foreign taxpayers filing late returns . . . 28,040
. withholding for . . . 15,045–15,045.05; 15,135.06
Nontaxable compensation, types of . . . 2005.01

O

Offers in compromise to settle tax claim . . . 27,035.01
Offshore Voluntary Disclosure Program (OVDP) . . . 28,103
. eligibility to participate in . . . 28,103.03
. inability to pay penalties . . . 28,103.05
. possible criminal charges for failure to comply with . . . 28,103.04
. procedures . . . 28,103.02
Oil and gas producing properties . . . 12,170.05; 12,175–12,175.04
. tax shelters of . . . 18,130.06
Online tax payment options . . . 26,125.05
Operating day depreciation method . . . 11,065.02
Options, gain or loss from sale of . . . 8010.09; 8035–8035.04
Original issue discount defined . . . 2070
Original issue discount instrument, interest on . . . 18,155.03
Original issue discount (OID) bonds
. application of rules to transactions for . . . 2070.06-.07
. corporate . . . 2070.02
. deferred payments for . . . 2070.06
. exceptions to rules for . . . 2070.02; 2070.06
. short-term . . . 2070.04
. stripped . . . 2070.05
. tax-exempt . . . 2070.02; 2070.05
Orphan drug credit . . . 14,075
Outplacement assistance for employees . . . 4090.01

References are to paragraph (¶) numbers.

Overtime expenses . . . 4095.01
Owner-employees
. defined . . . 3155.02
. nondeductible payments to . . . 18,075.02

P

Parachute payments. *See* Golden parachute payments
Parents
. child's unearned income reported by . . . 2170.02–.03
. as unit for support . . . 1060.03
Parking expenses, employer-provided . . . 4100.03; 4100.06
Parsonage allowance . . . 4045.05
Partial condemnation of property
. basis in . . . 7060.06
. severance damages in . . . 7075.01
. special assessment in . . . 7070
Partial payments of tax, IRS application of . . . 26,125.05
Partners
. basis for partnership interest of . . . 24,095–24,096
. capital interest in partnership received for services by . . . 24,090.02
. change of, partnership tax year closure upon . . . 24,075.01
. contribution of property to partnership by . . . 24,065
. distributions to . . . 24,100–24,125.03
. distributive share of gains and losses of partnership for . . . 24,040.02; 24,045; 24,060–24,060.02
. distributive share of tax credits of partnership for . . . 24,040.10; 24,060–24,060.02
. distributive share of taxable income or loss of partnership for . . . 24,050–24,055.03; 24,060–24,060.02
. foreign . . . 24,070.01
. guaranteed payments . . . 24,080.04
. partnership ownership of stock of . . . 22,175.02
. payments upon retirement or death of . . . 24,145–24,150.03
. remuneration for . . . 15,070.03; 15,095.04; 24,080.04–.06
. tax liability of . . . 24,035–24,065
. tax year of . . . 24,070.01; 24,070.04
. tax-exempt . . . 24,070.01
. transactions between partnerships and . . . 24,080–24,080.06
. transferee, basis of . . . 24,135–24,140.04
Partnership interests
. basis in . . . 6115; 24,135–24,135.03
. exchange of, reporting . . . 26,140.10
. gifts of . . . 29,030.01
. liquidation of . . . 24,145–24.150.03
. as mix of ordinary and capital assets . . . 8010.06
. transfer of . . . 24,130–24,140.04
Partnerships . . . 24,001–24,150.03
. anti-abuse regulations and rules of . . . 24,003
. Appeals Office contact for . . . 27,030.03
. change in tax year of . . . 18,065.01; 18,075
. charitable contributions by . . . 9055.02; 24,040.05
. check-the-box for entity classification . . . 24,002
. Code Sec. 754 election . . . 24,115
. . extension period . . . 24,115
. codification of economic substance doctrine . . . 24,003
. comparison with other entity classifications of . . . 30,085
. computation of income by . . . 24,025–24,030
. contributions to . . . 24,090–24,090.04
Partnerships—continued
. conversion from association to . . . 24,002.04
. converting to LLC from . . . 30,090.03
. deficiency assessment for . . . 27,020.04; 27,050.07; 27,065.04
. defined . . . 24,001
. depreciation recapture rules for . . . 8060.03
. division of . . . 24,075.03
. economic accrual principles applied to . . . 24,075.04
. economic substance doctrine . . . 24,003
. electing exclusion from treatment as . . . 24,010
. entity classification as, late . . . 24,002.03
. entity classification of, check-the-box . . . 24,002
. expensing depreciable property of . . . 24,040.04
. family. *See also* Family limited partnerships (FLPs) . . . 24,015–24,015.02
. features of, compared with C and S corporations . . . 21,005
. filing requirements . . . 24,115
. foreign . . . 26,180.02
. fracking income of publicly traded partnership . . . 24,005
. how to make election . . . 24,115
. income reporting by . . . 2165; 2165.02; 24,020.01–.06
. IRS examination of items of . . . 27,005.05
. liabilities of, partner's basis for . . . 24,096
. master limited. *See* Publicly traded partnerships (PTPs)
. merger of . . . 24,075.03
. mutual fund . . . 24,090.04
. nonrecourse liabilities . . . 24,096
. passive activity limitations for . . . 24,040.03
. purpose . . . 24,115
. recourse liabilities . . . 24,096
. relief for untimely election . . . 24,115
. separately stated items for . . . 24,040–24,040.10; 24,045
. sham transaction . . . 24,003
. start-up and organizational expenditures of . . . 24,020.06
. stock ownership by . . . 22,175.02
. tax credits of . . . 24,040.10
. tax year of . . . 24,070.01–.03; 24,070.05; 24,070.07–24,075.05
. termination of . . . 24,075.02
. tiered . . . 24,075.05
. transactions between partners and . . . 24,080–24,080.06
. transactions between related parties and . . . 24,085
. who must sign . . . 24,115
Pass-through entities. *See also* individual types
. 2 percent floor at investor level for allocable expenses of . . . 9140.03
Passive activity losses . . . 13,090
. material participation . . . 13,090.04
. passive activity defined . . . 13,090.03; 13,090.06
. real estate professionals . . . 13,090.07
. rental activities . . . 13,090.05
. self-rental rule . . . 13,090.05
Passive foreign investment company . . . 2080.01
Patents
. basis in . . . 6110
. as capital assets . . . 8010.11
. holding period for . . . 8020.02
Payment card and third party payment transactions . . . 26,140
. Code Sec. 6050W . . . 26,140
. Due dates . . . 26,140
. Form 1099-K . . . 26,140

References are to paragraph (¶) numbers.

Payment card and third party payment transactions—continued
. payment card defined . . . 26,140
. reporting requirement . . . 26,140

Payment of tax . . . 26,125
. by credit card . . . 26,125
. by electronic funds withdrawal . . . 26,125

Payroll tax. *See also* individual taxes . . . 15,130–15,160.02
. depositing and paying . . . 15,135–15,135.07
. information returns for . . . 15,130–15,130.02

Penalties . . . 27,075–27,115.04
. accuracy related types of . . . 27,085–27,085.06
. for charities furnishing false or fraudulent acknowledgment of contributions . . . 9090
. for claiming more withholding allowances . . . 15,160.02
. criminal, types of . . . 27,110–27,110.01
. delinquency types of . . . 27,095.01–.02
. document reporting types of . . . 27,080–27,080.06
. for excess distributions from Coverdell ESA . . . 5115.04; 5115.07
. for failure to deposit or remit payroll taxes . . . 15,135.04; 15,160–15,160.01
. for failure to disclose reportable transactions . . . 26,210.01
. for failure to file correct information returns . . . 15,160.01
. for failure to file returns on magnetic media . . . 15,130.02
. for failure to fulfill due diligence requirements for EIC claims . . . 14,005.06
. for failure to furnish information regarding reportable transactions . . . 26,210.04
. for failure to furnish wage and tax statement to employee . . . 15,160.01
. for failure to maintain investor lists in tax shelters . . . 26,210.05
. for failure to report interests in foreign financial accounts . . . 26,210.09
. for failure to use EFTPS for tax payments . . . 26,130.01
. for failure to withhold and pay over tax . . . 15,160.01
. for false information to avoid backup withholding . . . 14,225.05
. for foreign trust activities . . . 28,090.04
. for fraudulent withholding statement . . . 15,160.01
. for health care coverage portability and renewability noncompliance . . . 4025.06
. for intentional disregard of applicable filing requirements . . . 27,080
. knowing or reckless disclosure by tax return preparer or use by them of any information furnished to them in connection with preparation of return . . . 27,110
. other, general types of . . . 27,100
. for premature annuity payout . . . 5070.08
. for premature IRA distributions . . . 3135.02
. for premature withdrawal from bank certificate of deposit . . . 9150
. preparer, promoter, and protestor types of . . . 27,090.01–.06
. for promoters of tax shelters . . . 26,210.06
. for substantial understatement for nonreportable transactions . . . 26,210.08
. for transaction lacking economic substance . . . 27,085
. treble damages as . . . 13,010.03
. trust fund . . . 15, 160.01
. for underpayment attributable to listed transactions or avoidance transaction . . . 26,210.01

Penalties—continued
. for underpayment attributable to transactions lacking economic substance . . . 27,085
. for underpayment of estimated tax . . . 14,205.03; 14,220.01–.04; 26,105.03; 27,105–27,105.01

Pension fund payments, taxation rules for . . . 2020–2020.02

Pension plans
. record retention for . . . 26,095.02
. types of . . . 3005.01
. types of benefits from . . . 3005.03

Pension Protection Act of 2006 . . . 3060.03

Percentage test for qualified plan coverage . . . 3025.01

Periodic payments, exception to penalty for
. for IRAs . . . 3135.02
. for qualified plans . . . 3085.01

Personal exemptions for self, spouse, and dependents . . . 1010.01; 1040–1070.02
. amount of . . . 1040.01–.03
. deduction for dependents of . . . 1055.01–1070.02
. deduction for spouses of . . . 1050–1050.04
. for estates and trusts . . . 25,060
. as inflation-adjusted . . . 1050.01
. number of . . . 1040.02
. partial . . . 1045.01
. phaseout of . . . 1045; 14,215.03
. prorated deduction for . . . 1040.03

Personal holding companies (PHCs) . . . 23,001–23,070
. AMT for . . . 23,001.01
. deficiency assessments for . . . 27,050.08
. defined . . . 23,001.02
. election of RIC status by . . . 23,080.05
. income requirements of . . . 23,005–23,005.01
. stock ownership requirement for . . . 23,010

Personal holding company tax . . . 23,001
. corporations exempt from . . . 23,015
. dividend distribution in year following payment of . . . 23,030
. income subject to . . . 23,020–23,020.03

Personal property
. defined . . . 8030.05
. MACRS for . . . 11,040–11,040.09
. source rules for sales of . . . 28,015.01

Personal service corporation
. change in tax year of . . . 18,065.01; 18,075–18,075.02
. flat tax rate for . . . 20,010.02
. minimum distributions of . . . 18,075.01–.02
. passive loss rules for . . . 13,090.02; 13,090.06

Phased retirement . . . 3120.04

Physician recruitment, guidance on . . . 23,109.05

Pledge of installment obligations to secure loan . . . 19,040

Pledge of stock for cash, tax treatment of . . . 8015.01

Political contributions . . . 12,025

Political organizations, IRC Sec. 527 . . . 23,109

Pollution control facilities under AMT . . . 16,005.16

Power of appointment, transfers subject to . . . 29,095–29,085.02; 29,120.07–.08

Power of attorney
. durable . . . 29,020.03
. for taxpayer representative . . . 27,040.03

References are to paragraph (¶) numbers.

Prepaid expenses . . . 18,130.06
Prepaid income . . . 18,115–18,115.02
Prepaid tuition plans . . . 5100.03
Preparers, tax return
. fraud by . . . 27,001.03
. return signed by . . . 26,001.03
. preparer tax identification number . . . 26,061
Preretirement survivor annuity for married vested qualified plan participants . . . 3075.02
Preservation of land or resources, conservation donations for . . . 9071
Principal residence
. acquired in like-kind exchange . . . 7010.03
. defined . . . 7005
. depreciation recapture rules for . . . 8060.03
. exclusion rule for gain on sale of . . . 7001–7001.06; 7025–7025.06
. in federally declared disaster area, demolition of . . . 13,045.01
. first-time homebuyers of, tax credit for . . . 12,220.02
. improvements to, for medical care . . . 9105.07
. information reporting . . . 7001
. involuntary conversion of . . . 7030; 7035–7035.06; 7040.02–.03; 7055.03
. ownership and use requirements for . . . 7010–7015.01
. partial interests in . . . 7025.05
. as qualified residence . . . 9015.05
. record retention for . . . 26,095.02
. remainder interests in . . . 7025.06
. rented portion of . . . 9015.05
. repossession of . . . 19,065
Private debt collection agencies . . . 27,070
Private foundations
. contributions of stock to . . . 9052
. defined . . . 23,115–23,115.01
. excise tax on . . . 23,125.01; 27,045.09; 27,160.07
. filing requirements of . . . 23,115.04
. investment income of . . . 23,120
. program-related investmetns . . . 23,145
. prohibited acts for . . . 23,125–23,135.01
. status of . . . 23,115.02
. tax on excess business holdings by . . . 23,140
. tax on improper expenditures and excess benefit transactions by . . . 23,185
. tax on self-dealing involving . . . 23,130.01
. tax on speculative investments by . . . 23,145
. tax on undistributed income of . . . 23,135
. termination of status as, tax subsequent to . . . 23,115.03
. transfer of assets between . . . 23,115.04
Prizes, awards, and lotteries, taxation of . . . 2015–2015.02
Probate
. avoiding . . . 29,065.02
Produce, casualty or theft losses of . . . 13,055.03–.04
Profit-making activity, proving . . . 13,085.02–.03
Profit-sharing plans
. of affiliated corporations, joint . . . 3060.05
. allocating contributions to . . . 3005.03
. employer contributions to . . . 3060.02
. life insurance in . . . 3060.03
Public assistance payments, exclusion for . . . 5090.04
Public safety officers, payments to survivors of . . . 5100.07
Public utility preferred stock, dividends on . . . 20,060–20.060.01
Publicly traded partnerships (PTPs)
. grouping of PTPs . . . 13,090
. losses under AMT for . . . 16,005.09
. passive activity held through PTP . . . 13,090
. treatment as corporations of . . . 24,005
Put and call options, gain or loss from sale of . . . 8010.09; 8035–8035.04

Q

Qualified active business for new markets tax credit . . . 14,135
Qualified adoption expenses . . . 4115.05; 4115.06; 14,015.06
Qualified alternative fuel motor vehicle credit . . . 14,195.05
Qualified alternative fuel vehicle refueling property . . . 14,155.02
Qualified appreciated stock, contributions of . . . 9052
Qualified business use of personal vehicle . . . 10,025.05
Qualified charitable conservation organization, donations to . . . 9071
Qualified conservation easement . . . 29,125.02
Qualified disaster defined . . . 5100.03
Qualified dividends
. of REIT . . . 23,095.06
. taxation of . . . 2080.01; 6090.01; 6090.06; 8001.02; 9020.04; 25,125.01
Qualified domestic relations order (QDRO)
. alternate payee for . . . 3090.01–.02
. benefits of . . . 3090.01
. defined . . . 3090
. IRS model language for . . . 3090.02
. receipt of qualified plan benefits under . . . 3085.01; 3090
. requirements for valid . . . 3090.02
Qualified domestic trust (QDOT) for noncitizen spouses . . . 29,120.10
Qualified education loan defined . . . 9005.04
Qualified education savings bond, exclusion for interest on . . . 2070.08
Qualified electric vehicle . . . 14,180
Qualified elementary and secondary education expenses defined . . . 5115.05
Qualified employer plans for deemed IRAs . . . 3105.07
Qualified energy efficiency improvements for residential energy property credit . . . 14,040.01
Qualified energy property defined . . . 14,040.01
Qualified energy resource (QER) for renewable electricity production credit . . . 14,095
Qualified equity investment for new markets tax credit . . . 14,135.01; 14,135.03
Qualified exchange accommodation agreements (QEAAs) . . . 6050.08
Qualified expenses for dependent care credit . . . 14,001.02
Qualified facilities (QFs) for renewable electricity production credit . . . 14,095–14,095.03

References are to paragraph (¶) numbers.

Qualified family-owned business interest deduction . . . 29,161
Qualified foreign corporation, taxation of qualified dividends of . . 2080.01
Qualified fuel cell motor vehicle credit . . . 14,195.02
Qualified health insurance costs defined . . . 14,035.03
Qualified higher education expenses (QHEE)
. Coverdell ESA to fund . . . 5115.05
. defined . . . 5115.05
. early distributions from retirement plans to pay . . . 3135.02; 3150.04
. 529 plan to fund . . . 5110.04
. student loan interest deduction for . . . 9005.04
Qualified housing interest defined for AMT . . . 16,005.03
Qualified hybrid motor vehicle credit . . . 14,195.04
Qualified intellectual property . . . 9052
Qualified joint and survivor annuity . . . 3075.01
Qualified long-term care services . . . 5105.01
Qualified low-income community investments . . . 14,135.01
Qualified new energy-efficient home . . . 14,140
Qualified nonrecourse financing . . . 13,100.10–.12
Qualified parking . . . 4100.03
Qualified plans. *See also* individual types
. costs of operating . . . 3035.03
. coverage provided by . . . 3025–3025.03
. distributions from . . . 3075–3075.04; 25,040.02
. early retirement reduction for . . . 3040.01
. employee contributions to . . . 3020.04
. employer securities in . . . 3060.04
. employer tax consequences for . . . 3060.01–.06
. exclusive benefit rule . . . 3015
. features of . . . 3020.04
. in-kind contributions to . . . 3060.04
. incidental benefits of . . . 3005.04
. integrated with social security system . . . 3065
. key terms for . . . 3020–3020.05
. loans from . . . 3095–3095.04
. minimum participation standards for . . . 3030–3030.02
. prohibited transactions for . . . 3100–3100.03
. requirements for . . . 3015
. tax benefits of . . . 3001
. tax credit for start-up of . . . 14,115
. tax exemption for . . . 3070
. tax-free rollovers from . . . 3125
. termination of . . . 3085.02
. types of . . . 3005–3005.05
Qualified production activities . . . 12,150.01
Qualified production activities income . . . 12,150.02
. of pass-through entities . . . 12,150.02
Qualified real property interest . . . 9071
Qualified renewal community assets . . . 12,220.01
Qualified replacement plan for retirement benefits . . . 3085.02
Qualified research expenses for research tax credit . . . 14,080.02
Qualified residence defined . . . 9015.05
Qualified residence interest . . . 9015–9015.10
. acquisition debt as . . . 9015; 9015.01
. home equity debt as . . . 9015; 9015.02
. requirements for deduction of . . . 9015.04
. types of . . . 9015..08
Qualified revocable trust (QRT), treatment as part of estate of . . . 25,010.03
Qualified short-term gain . . . 6090.01
Qualified small business
. businesses ineligible to be . . . 8105.04
. defined . . . 8105.03
Qualified small business stock (QSBS)
. active business requirement for company offering . . . 8105.05
. AMT for dispositions of . . . 8105.09
. basis rules for . . . 8105.08
. defined . . . 8105.02
. in empowerment zone, IRC Sec. 1202 exclusion for . . . 8105.01
. exclusion on gain from sale or exchange of . . . 8105
. rollover of gain on, tax-free . . . 8105.10
. tax treatment of . . . 8105.06
Qualified sponsorship payment for tax-exempt organization . . . 23,165.02
Qualified subchapter S subsidiary (QSub)
. definition of . . . 21,012.02
. effects of election . . . 21,012.04
. election of . . . 21,012.03
. owned by S corporations . . . 21,014.05
. revoking election . . . 21,012.05
Qualified subchapter S trust (QSST)
. defined . . . 21,014
. income beneficiaries of . . . 21,014
Qualified terminable interest property (QTIP) . . . 29,120
Qualified transportation fringe benefits . . . 4100–4100.06
. eligibility for . . . 4100.04
. reporting . . . 4100.05
Qualified tuition and related expenses
. Hope Scholarship credit for . . . 14,025; 14,025.04
. Lifetime Learning credit for . . . 14,030.02
. scholarships as tax-free used for . . . 5085, 5085.02
Qualified tuition programs (Section 529 plans) . . . 5100–5110.13
. bankruptcy protection of assets in . . . 5110.11
. compared to other college savings vehicles . . . 5110.02
. coordination with other higher education savings vehicles . . . 5110.06; 5115.06
. disadvantages of . . . 5110.10
. distributions coordinated with other higher education savings vehicles . . . 5110.06
. eligible institutions for . . . 5110.05
. estate planning using . . . 5110.09
. expenses covered by . . . 5110.04
. gift tax exclusion for . . . 29,015.08
. popularity of . . . 5110
. rollovers among . . . 5110.07
. state tax benefits for investors in . . . 5110.08
. tax treatment of earnings and distributions of . . . 5110.03
. types of . . . 5110.01
. U.S. savings bonds contributed to . . . 5110.06
Qualified tuition reductions . . . 5085.03
Qualified zone academy bonds (QZABs)
. credit for holders of . . . 14,185–14,185.02
. maximum amount issuable of, by state . . . 14,185.02
Qualifying advance coal project credit . . . 14,055.04
Qualifying child
. age test for . . . 14,005.01; 14,020.03
. for claiming child tax credit . . . 14,020.03

Qualifying child—continued
. for claiming dependency exemptions . . . 1055.01
. for claiming earned income credit . . . 14,005.01
. for claiming head of household status . . . 1030.01
. gross income of . . . 1070.01
. relationship test for . . . 1065.01; 14,005.01; 14,020.03
. support test eliminated for . . . 1060.01; 14,005.01

Qualifying dividends defined . . . 20,050.04

Qualifying gasification project credit . . . 14,055.05

Qualifying newspaper distributors and carriers as direct sellers . . . 15,060.07; 15,070.03

Qualifying relative
. for claiming dependency exemption . . . 1055.01
. gross income of . . . 1070.02
. relationship test for . . . 1065.02
. support test required for . . . 1060.02

Qualifying small business for cash accounting . . . 18,005.02

R

Rabbi trusts . . . 3170.06

Railroad track maintenance tax credit . . . 14,127

Railroad workers exempt from social security coverage . . . 15,060.08

Ratio test for qualified plan coverage . . . 3025.02

Real estate
. MACRS used for . . . 11,050–11,050.04
. passive activity rules not applied to professionals working in . . . 13,090.07
. undivided fractional . . . 6050.04

Real estate investment trust (REIT)
. administrative requirements for . . . 23,095.02
. capital gains dividends of . . . 8001.03
. diversification of assets of . . . 23,095.05
. election of status as . . . 23.095.01
. gross income requirement for . . . 23,095.04
. liquidating . . . 23,095.11
. ordinary income treatment rules for . . . 23,095.10
. prohibited transactions for . . . 23,095.03
. record retention for . . . 23,095.08
. required distributions of . . . 23,095.06
. tax on . . . 23,095.01
. tax-free division of . . . 23,095.12
. for timber . . . 23,095.03
. types of . . . 23,095.01

Real estate mortgage investment conducts (REMICs) . . . 23,100–23,100.04
. general rules for . . . 23,100.01
. interest of . . . 23,100.01, 23,100.03; 26,145.04
. qualifying as . . . 23,100.02
. taxation of . . . 23,100.04

Real estate rental income . . . 15,105.03

Real estate sales, apportionment of taxes for . . . 9040.01

Real estate tax rebate, tax treatment of . . . 2190.02

Real estate taxes as itemized deduction . . . 9030.07–.08; 12,125.07

Real property, replacement
. like-kind test of . . . 7045.04
. time limit on obtaining . . . 7050.04

Real property (Section 1250 property)
. disposition of, gain from . . . 8060.02
. repossession of . . . 19,065
. sale in lots of . . . 19,070

Real property (Section 1250 property)—continued
. sales by foreign persons of . . . 15,045.05
. subdividing . . . 8100–8100.01

Recognition awards, taxation rules for . . . 2015.01

Record retention of tax returns . . . 15,150–15,150.02; 27,001.04
. electronic . . . 26,095.03; 26,130.01
. by employee . . . 15,150
. by employer . . . 15,125; 15,050
. by individuals . . . 26,095–26,095.03

Reforestation expenditures, amortizing . . . 12,215

Refunds
. amount of, limitation on . . . 27,140
. for carrybacks . . . 27,165–27,165.03
. claimed in innocent spouse relief . . . 26,006
. claiming . . . 15,165; 27,015.04; 27,125–27,125.03
. of excise tax . . . 27,160.07
. filing claim for . . . 27,150–27,150.03
. foreign tax . . . 28,020
. form of claim for . . . 27,145–27,145.03
. interest on . . . 27,155–27,155.04
. for overpayment of tax . . . 27,120.01; 27,125.02
. special periods for filing claims for . . . 27,135; 27,170–27,170.02
. state and local income tax, tax treatment of . . . 2190.01
. suit to recover . . . 27,160.01–.08
. when to file for . . . 26,080.03; 27,130.01–.05

Regulated investment companies (RICs)
. basis of shares in . . . 6090.03
. dividends of . . . 2080.03–.04; 2095.03; 6090.01; 6090.04–.06; 8001.02–.03; 15,045.02; 16,010.03; 23,080.04; 23,090.01–.08
. frequently asked questions about . . . 6090.06
. liquidating, earnings of . . . 23,090.07
. ordinary income rates for gains passed through from . . . 6090
. PHCs electing status as . . . 23,080.05
. qualifying as . . . 23,080.04
. records for transactions in . . . 6090.06; 26,095.02
. sale of shares in . . . 6090.02; 6090.06
. short-term losses in . . . 6090.06
. tax on . . . 23,075–23,090.09
. tax tips for . . . 6090.05
. tax-free transfers to . . . 25,125.01

Rehabilitation credit . . . 14,055.02

Related party
. at-risk amount of lender who is . . . 13,100.09
. debt acquired by . . . 2145.05
. deductions for transactions involving . . . 25,090
. entities considered to be . . . 19,045.04
. installment sales to . . . 19,045–19,045.05
. loss deduction disallowed for certain sales to . . . 13,075–13,075.06
. suspended losses with . . . 13,090.10
. transactions between partnership and . . . 24,085

Remainder interests
. basis allocation in sale of . . . 6080.05
. depreciation of property having . . . 11,010.03
. in principal residence, sales or exchanges of . . . 7025.06

Renewable electricity production credit . . . 14,095–14,096

Renewal communities, incentives for . . . 12,220.01

Renewal community employment credit . . . 14,100

Rent-to-own property, depreciation of . . . 11,005.04

References are to paragraph (¶) numbers.

Rental activities, passive loss rules for . . . 13,090.05–.07; 14,060.03

Rental income paid to corporate shareholders . . . 20,030.01

Rents
. alternative payments as . . . 2135.01; 2140.02
. attributable to deferred rental agreement . . . 18,105.02
. for cash versus accrual taxpayers . . . 18,105.01
. deductible by business tenants . . . 12,095–12,095.04
. deductions offsetting income from . . . 2135
. for home office . . . 12,125.07
. reporting payments for . . . 26,140.04

Reorganizations . . . 22,001–22,115
. business purpose of . . . 22,010.02
. carryover of benefits, privileges, elective rights, and obligations in . . . 22,135–22,150
. Code Sec. 336(e) election . . . 22,125.02
. continuity of business enterprise in . . . 22,010.03
. continuity of interest (COI) in . . . 22,010.04
. defined . . . 22,001
. divisive . . . 22,090–22,115.01
. foreign corporations . . . 22,046
. gain or loss in . . . 22,055–22,055.05
. general rules for . . . 22,001
. information reporting for . . . 22,001.03
. liabilities assumed in . . . 22,085.01–.05
. limitations on deductions of duplicate losses . . . 22,071
. limitations on loss importation . . . 22,072
. parties to . . . 22,005
. plan for . . . 22,010.01
. reporting requirements . . . 22,001
. stock received in . . . 6085.02
. stock sale subsequent to . . . 22,010.04
. tax consequences of . . . 22,001.01
. tax-free, qualifying as . . . 22,010–22,010.04
. types of. *See also* individual types . . . 22,001; 22,015.01–22,050

Repaid income
. for accrual basis taxpayers . . . 18,125.02
. for cash basis taxpayers . . . 18,125.01

Repossessions . . . 19,060–19,065
. of real property by seller . . . 19,065

Research and experimental expenditures . . . 12,145–12,145.07
. AMT treatment of . . . 16,005.13
. for computer software . . . 12,145.07
. deferred . . . 12,145.04–.05
. expenditures not qualifying as . . . 12,145.01
. realistic prospect test of . . . 12,145.02
. tax credit for . . . 12,145.01

Research grants in self-employment income . . . 15,095.06

Research tax credit . . . 14,080–14,080.06
. for purposes of orphan drugs . . . 14,075

Residence. *See* Principal residence; Vacation home

Resident aliens
. definition of . . . 28,035
. filing requirements for . . . 1001.06
. green card test . . . 28,035
. substantial presence test . . . 28,035
. taxation of . . . 28,030.01
. withholding for . . . 28,030.02–28,035.03

Residential alternative energy expenditures credit . . . 14,045–14,045.04

Residential energy property credit . . . 14,040

Restitution payments to human trafficking victims
. nature of tax exclusion . . . 5130.01
. purpose of exclusion . . . 5130.02
. victim's losses defined . . . 5130.03

Restricted property
. inclusion in income of . . . 18,085.03
. transferred to employee . . . 12,065.03

Restricted stock treated as outstanding . . . 12,080.03

Retail merchants, inventory valuation for . . . 17,050.05

Retirement plans. *See also* Qualified plans; individual types . . . 2001–2175.04
. active participants in . . . 3105.04

Retirement savings contribution credit . . . 14,130

Return of capital not considered income . . . 2001.01

Revocable trusts . . . 29,065.01–.04

Rolling-average method of inventory valuation . . . 17,025

Roth 401(k)s . . . 3150.06

Roth IRAs
. abusive transactions involving . . . 3140.09–.10
. contribution limits for . . . 3140.02–.03
. converting other plan accounts to . . . 3140.05
. establishing . . . 3140.07
. income limits for contributions to . . . 3140.03
. maximum contributions by year to, table of . . . 3140.02
. for minor children . . . 3140.07
. model forms for . . . 3140.08
. no distributions required from . . . 3120.03
. reconversion to traditional IRAs of . . . 3140.05
. traditional IRAs compared to . . . 3140.01
. withdrawals from . . . 3140.05

Royalties
. alternative payments as . . . 2135.02
. deductions offsetting income from . . . 2135
. minimum, for depletion . . . 12,160.02
. reporting receipt of . . . 26,140.04

S

S corporation income reporting . . . 2165–2165.01

S corporation shareholders
. copies of returns to . . . 21,010.05
. eligibility of . . . 21,010.01
. fringe benefits for . . . 21,003
. health insurance payments for . . . 12,105.03
. inactive . . . 21,015
. income of . . . 15,095.05
. loan guaranties by . . . 21,045
. loans to S corporation by . . . 21,002; 21,045
. maximum of 100 . . . 21,010.01
. pro rata share of income, losses, deductions, and credits to . . . 21,020; 21,040–21,040.02
. trusts eligible to be S corporation shareholders . . . 21,014
. weighted voting rights of . . . 21,015

S corporation status
. advantages of . . . 21,002
. in bankruptcy . . . 21,025.08
. defective election of . . . 21,010.04
. disqualification of . . . 21,025.01
. drawbacks of . . . 21,003
. election of . . . 21,001–21,025.08
. late election of . . . 21,010.03

References are to paragraph (¶) numbers.

S corporation status—continued
. procedures for electing . . . 21,010.02
. requirements of . . . 21,010.01
. revoking . . . 21,025.02
. terminating . . . 21,016; 21,025; 21,025.04; 21,045.03

S corporation stock
. adjustments to basis of . . . 21,055.01
. ESOP ownership of . . . 3160.05
. gifts of . . . 21,002
. increasing basis in . . . 21,045
. inherited, basis in . . . 21,055.01
. single class of . . . 21,010.01; 21,015
. synthetic equity based on value of . . . 3160.05
. worthless . . . 21,040.02

S corporations . . . 21,001–21,055
. basis adjustment to stock of S corp. . . . 12,055
. change in tax year of . . . 21,016
. charitable contributions by . . . 9055.02
. comparison with other entity classifications of . . . 30,085
. computation of income of . . . 21,025.06
. consent of shareholders for election . . . 21,010
. constructive ownership rules for . . . 21,015
. contribution to capital of . . . 21,045
. conversion of C corporations to . . . 21,030.05–.06; 22,125.05
. electing taxation as . . . 21,010
. eligible shareholders . . . 21,012
. family income splitting using . . . 21,002
. features of, compared with C corporations and partnerships . . . 21,005
. filing requirements . . . 21,011
. ineligible corporations . . . 21,011
. inventory of . . . 21,035.01
. late elections . . . 21,010
. natural business year of . . . 21,016.03
. number of shareholders . . . 21,013
. one class of stock requirement . . . 21,015
. partnership interests held by . . . 21,035.01
. passive activity losses of . . . 21,045.04
. passive income restriction on . . . 21,025.04; 21,030.03; 21,003
. payroll taxes . . . 21,051
. penalty for failure to file S corp return . . . 21,011
. posttermination transition period of . . . 21,045.03
. prior-year investment credit of . . . 21,030.04
. qualified QSubs . . . 21,012
. reasonable cause for late or inadvertent defective election . . . 21,010.04
. recognized built-in gain of . . . 21,035–21,035.01
. recognized built-in losses of . . . 21,035.01
. relief from late or inadvertent defective election . . . 21,010.04
. required payments by . . . 21,016.02
. requirement for taxation as . . . 21,011
. shareholder limit . . . 21,013
. stock requirement . . . 21,015
. subsidiaries (QSubs) owned by . . . 21,010.01
. tax year of . . . 21,016–21,016.03; 21,025.05–.06
. taxable income of . . . 21,020
. taxation of . . . 21,002; 21,030–21,030.05; 21,035
. transfer of assets from C corporation to . . . 21,025.02
. trusts eligible to be shareholders . . . 21,014
. wage compensation for S corporation officers . . . 21,050

Salary. *See* Wages

Sales tax, state and local . . . 9030.03

Saver's credit for retirement contributions . . . 14,130

Savings incentive match plan for employee (SIMPLE) plans . . . 3175–3175.05

Savings incentive match plan for employee (SIMPLE) plans—continued
. annual summary description of . . . 3175.05
. catch-up contributions by year to . . . 3175.02
. contributions to . . . 3175.04
. converted to Roth IRAs . . . 3140.05
. defined . . . 3175.01
. distributions from . . . 3175.04
. establishing, requirements for . . . 3175.03
. model forms and amendments for . . . 3175.05
. optional exclusion of employees from . . 3175.04
. reporting requirements for . . . 3175.05
. for small business owners . . . 3175
. when to establish . . . 3175.03
. withdrawals from . . . 3175.03

Schedule A (Form 1040)
. casualty and theft loss claimed on . . . 13,030.01
. charitable contributions claimed on . . . 9050.02
. gambling losses itemized on . . . 2155
. itemized deductions entered on . . . 9001.02; 9005.02; 9015.04; 9140; 13,125.01
. tax payments entered on . . . 9030.01
. travel expenses reported on . . . 10,010.03
. unreimbursed depreciation reported on . . . 11,025

Schedule C (Form 1040)
. business bad debt reported on . . . 13,125.01
. business travel expenses of self-employed individuals reported on . . . 10,010.03
. depletion reported on . . . 12,165
. depreciation of business property of self-employed individuals reported on . . . 11,025
. expenses reported on . . . 12,125.07
. false deductions on, audits triggered by . . . 27,001.03
. profit or loss of business or profession on . . . 15,105.04
. Section 198 expenses on . . . 12,010.06

Schedule D (Form 1120), corporate capital gains and losses reported on . . . 20,075.01

Schedule D, losses reported on . . . 13,015.03; 13,125.01

Schedule E
. claiming depreciation of rental property on . . . 11,025
. depletion reported on . . . 12,165
. fraudulent, audits triggered by . . . 27,001.03
. Section 198 expenses on . . . 12,010.06

Schedule EIC, earned income credit claimed on . . . 14,005

Schedule F, farming bad debt reported on . . . 13,125.01

Schedule H filed with employment taxes for household employees . . 15,060.02

Schedule J, Farm Income Averaging," three-year income averaging using . . . 17,065.02

Schedule K-1
. for estate or trust beneficiaries . . . 25,001.02; 26,180.03
. for partners . . . 26,180.01

Schedule M-3 (Form 1120), corporations filing . . . 20,035–20,035.02

Schedule R, "Credit for the Elderly or the Disabled," IRS calculation of credit on . . . 1015.02

Scholarships
. by employers . . . 5100.08
. for health professions . . . 5085.01
. not counted in students' support . . . 1060.05
. qualified expenses for . . . 5085.02
. tax treatment of . . . 5085; 5085.03

References are to paragraph (¶) numbers.

Section 179 expensing of tangible personal property
. advantages of . . . 11,045.11
. basis adjusted for . . . 11,045.01, 11,045.06
. electing . . . 11,045.09
. investment limit for . . . 11,045.02
. maximum annual permitted . . . 11,045.01; 18,005.02
. property ineligible for . . . 11,045.05
. recapture of . . . 11,045.08
. revoking election of . . . 11,045.10
. taxable income limit for . . . 11,045.03
Section 195 expenses . . . 12,040.02
Section 1231 assets
. installment sales of . . . 19,030.02
. netting of gains and losses on . . . 13,030
. sale or exchange of . . . 8055–8055.02; 8065.01–8085
Section 1245 property, gain from disposition of . . . 8060.01; 8060.04–8065.01
. by corporation . . . 20,080
Section 1250 property, gain from disposition of . . . 8060.02; 8060.04–8065.01
. by corporation . . . 20,080–20,080.01
Secured debt . . . 9015.06
Securities dealers, valuing inventory of . . . 17,050.01
Securities, exchanges of . . . 6045; 6070–6070.02
. basis allocation in . . . 6080.01; 6080.04
. issued as stock dividend . . . 8030.03
. in stock splits and dividends . . . 6080.04
Securities futures contracts . . . 8040.06
Securities lending arrangements . . . 8,015
Self-employed individuals
. annualizing income for . . . 14,220.02
. business travel expenses of . . . 10,010.03
. as carrying on trade or business . . . 15,090
. clergy as . . . 15,060.05; 15,090.01
. EIN required for . . . 15,050
. fees for right to practice of . . . 12,115.02
. filing requirements for . . . 1001.05
. health insurance premiums for . . . 9105.08; 12,105.03
. pros and cons of status as . . . 15,070.01
. record retention by . . . 15,050
. reporting business expenses of . . . 12,115
. reporting payments to . . . 26,140.06
. self-employment taxes of . . . 12,115.01
. services excluded for . . . 15,090.02
. statutory employees versus . . . 15,010.02; 15,070.02–.03
. tax advantages for . . . 15,090.03
. time test for deducting moving expenses for . . . 9135.02
. travel expenses of . . . 12,115.03
Self-employment income. *See* Net earnings from self-employment
Self-employment tax
. amount of self-employment tax . . . 15,085
. computing self-employment tax liability . . . 15,085
. deducting self-employment tax . . . 15,085
. deficiency assessment for . . . 27,050.11
. fiscal years . . . 15,085
. included in figuring expected taxes . . . 14,215
. for LLC members . . . 30,095.01
. overpayment of . . . 15,165
. purpose of . . . 15,085
. of self-employed individuals (independent contractors) . . . 15,070.01; 15,085–15,085.02
. wage base for . . . 15,085.01
Separate income tax returns for spouses . . . 1020.01–.02
. exemptions allowed for . . . 1050.03
. property taxation rules for . . . 2001.03
. when to use . . . 26,005.04
Separate maintenance payments
. recapture for excess front-loaded . . . 2150.02
. taxation of . . . 2150.01
Services provided at no additional cost to employees . . . 4065
. exception for highly compensated employees for . . . 4065.02
. reciprocal agreements with other employers for . . . 4065.01
Severance damages
. defined . . . 7075.01
. nonrecognition treatment of . . . 7075.02
Severance pay, deductible . . . 12,070
Sham sales, loss deduction disallowed for . . . 13,070
Short sales of commodity futures . . . 8030.04
Short sales of options . . . 8035.03
Short sales of stock . . . 8030
. holding period on . . . 8030.01
. kinds of property in . . . 8030
. process of . . . 8030
. successive . . . 8030.02
Sick pay
. not taxed as wages, rules for . . . 15,080.04
. social security tax rules for . . . 15,075.05
. withholding on . . . 15,020.07
Simplified employee pensions (SEPs)
. catch-up contributions for . . . 3145.03
. contribution deadlines for . . . 3145.07
. contribution limits for . . . 3145.03
. converted to Roth IRAs . . . 3140.05
. deduction limits for contributions to . . . 3145.05
. distribution rules for . . . 3145.08
. establishing . . . 3145.02
. limits on . . . 3040
. prohibited transactions for . . . 3145.06
. reasons to use . . . 3145.01
. requirements for contributions to . . . 3145.04
. types of businesses using . . . 3145
Single filers. *See* Unmarried individuals
Small business exclusion from accrual accounting . . . 18,005.02
Small business investment company (SBIC), active business requirement waived for . . . 8105.07
Small business investment company (SBIC) stock, short sale of . . . 8030.01
Small business pension plan start-up, credit for . . . 14,115
Small business (Section 1244) stock
. AMT treatment of gains on sale of . . . 16,010.05
. exclusion for gain on sale or exchange of . . . 8105–8105.12
. ordinary loss treatment for . . . 8095–8095.03
. rollover treatment for, electing . . . 8105.10–.11
Small construction contractors, cash accounting for . . . 18,005.01
Small corporations, exemption from AMT for . . . 20,010.04

References are to paragraph (¶) numbers.

Small employer health insurance tax credit . . . 14,120

Smoking cessation programs as deductible medical expenses . . . 9105.12

Social security number, obtaining . . . 15,050

Social security retirement benefits
. IRA deduction limit for recipients of . . . 3105.05
. qualified plan benefits integrated with . . . 3065
. retirement earnings test for . . . 5090.01
. as support . . . 1060.03
. tax treatment of . . . 5090.01; 14,210.03
. tiers of . . . 5090.01

Social security taxes . . . 15,050
. covered employment for . . . 15,050–15,050.05
. employee refund of . . . 15,165
. employer payment of . . . 15,075.02
. employment exempt from . . . 15,060–15,060.11
. partially covered employment for . . . 15,065
. on wages . . . 15,050–15,050.01
. for working seniors . . . 5090.01

Software, development costs of . . . 12,145.07
. commercial, case law for research tax credit applied to . . . 14,080.04

Soil and water conservation expenditures . . . 12,210
. for assessments . . . 12,210.05
. deductible . . . 12,210.01
. expensing versus capitalizing . . . 12,210.04
. limitations on deductions for . . . 12,210.03
. nondeductible . . . 12,210.02

Sole proprietors, LLCs for . . . 30,035; 30,120

Source taxing prohibited for qualified retirement benefits . . . 3001.01

Specialized small business investment company (SSBIC)
. capital gain exclusion for . . . 8110.03
. tax deferral for . . . 8110.01–.02

Specified liability losses . . . 12,010.05; 13,110.05

Spin-offs
. distribution of stock and securities in . . . 22,095–22,100.01
. as divisive reorganization . . . 22,090.01
. lapse of stock restrictions in connection with . . . 22,100.01
. to transfer control to subsidiary . . . 22,090.07–.08

Split-ups and split-offs as divisive reorganizations . . . 22,090.01

Sports franchises, allocation of basis for . . . 6080.08

Spouse, death of. *See also* Surviving spouse
. personal exemption in year of . . . 1050.04

Spouses
. change in tax year of . . . 18,065.01
. death of. *See* Surviving spouse
. dower or curtesy interest of . . . 29,045
. innocent spouse relief for. *See* Innocent spouse relief
. liability for taxes of . . . 26,006
. noncitizen, QDOT for . . . 29,120.10
. separate liability election for . . . 26,006
. social security (FICA) taxes on spouses working for . . . 15,050.05
. split gifts for . . . 29,020.02; 29,180.11; 29,195.03
. spousal IRAs for stay-at-home . . . 3110
. stock ownership by . . . 22,175.01
. transfers of property between . . . 6035; 29,120.06

Standard deduction
. additional, eligibility for . . . 1010.01; 1035.02
. amount of . . . 1035.01
. dependent's . . . 1035.03–.04

Standard deduction—continued
. individuals ineligible for . . . 1035.04
. as replacing claim of itemized deductions . . . 1010.01; 1035.01

Standard mileage rate for business miles driven . . . 10,020.02

State and local taxes, deductible and nondeductible . . . 9030–9045

State and municipal obligations, interest on . . . 5005–5005.02

State death taxes, deduction for . . . 29,130

State unemployment insurance (SUI) tax payments . . . 15,120.01–.02

Statistical sampling to substantiate business-related entertainment expenses . . . 10,055.03

Statute of limitations for unreported listed transactions . . . 26,210.03

Statutory merger or consolidation (Type A reorganization)
. disregarded entities in . . . 22,015.01
. forward triangular . . . 22,015.01
. qualifying as . . . 22,015.01
. reverse triangular . . . 22,015.01
. short-term notes exchanged tax-free in . . . 22,005.01; 22,055.01

Stock, affiliated group . . . 20,160

Stock as replacement property . . . 7060.07

Stock bonus plans
. of affiliated corporations, joint . . . 3060.05
. allocating contributions among participants in . . . 3005.04
. employer contributions to . . . 3060.02

Stock brokerage commissions, accrual method accounting for . . . 18,080.02

Stock certificates, donation to charity of . . . 18,170.01

Stock, corporate
. constructive ownership of . . . 22,175–22,175.08
. disposition of . . . 20,085

Stock distributions . . . 2100–2100.02

Stock dividends
. boot received in exchange for . . . 22,065.01
. defined . . . 2095.01
. holding period for . . . 8020.02
. as Sec. 306 stock . . . 22,065.01; 22,170.01–.04
. taxation of . . . 2095.02
. in Type D reorganizations . . . 22,030.03

Stock options, employee
. AMT treatment of . . . 16,005.08
. constructive ownership of stock by owning . . . 22,175.06
. corporation's reporting requirements for exercise of . . . 26,155
. defined . . . 2040; 2050
. included in decedent's estate . . . 25,040.02; 2050
. nonqualified . . . 2040.02; 12,065.03
. nonstatutory, AMT treatment of exercise of . . . 16,030.06
. qualified . . . 2040; 26,140.02
. tax treatment of . . . 2040; 2045.01; 2050.01
. transfers incident to divorce of nonstatutory . . . 2150.03
. valuation of . . . 12,080.05

Stock redemptions . . . 22,155–22,175.08
. attribution rules in . . . 22,155.06; 22,155.08–.09
. complete . . . 22,155.04

References are to paragraph (¶) numbers.

Stock redemptions—continued
. disguised dividends in . . . 22,155
. held by corporation . . . 22,155.07
. incident to divorce . . . 2150.04
. partial . . . 22,155.04
. to pay death taxes . . . 22,165.01–.02
. related corporation used in . . . 22,160–22,160.03
. substantially disproportionate . . . 22,155.03
. treatment as sale or exchange of . . . 22,155.01–.02

Stock rights
. basis in distribution of . . . 2110.01
. effect of receipt of nontaxable . . . 2110
. holding period of . . . 2110.02; 2115.01; 8020.02
. issuance of . . . 2105
. taxable, distribution of . . . 2115

Stock shares purchased at different prices, gain or loss on . . . 6085–6085.02; 8025

Stock shares sold through broker . . . 18,110.02

Stripped preferred stock . . . 2070.05

Structured passive investment arrangements . . . 28,005

Student defined for support . . . 1060.05

Student FICA exception . . . 15,060.06

Student living with taxpayer, deductible expenses for unrelated . . . 9060.02

Student loans
. cancellation of debt of . . . 2145.08
. deduction for interest owed on . . . 9005.04
. information returns of schools receiving interest on . . . 26,140.16

Subscriptions, prepaid . . . 18,115.01

Supplemental unemployment benefit (SUB)
. nondiscrimination testing of . . . 3040
. payments of . . . 2035.04

Supplemental wage payments, withholding on . . . 14,225.01; 15,015.01

Support of dependent, items considered for . . . 1060.03

Surviving spouse
. election to treat inherited IRA as one's own by . . . 3120.03; 3125.03
. estate trust for . . . 29,120.04
. joint return for year of spouse's death for . . . 1025; 26,005.03
. survivor annuity for . . . 29,020.06
. taxable payments by employer to . . . 2020.01

Survivor and disability benefits, early retirement reduction not applied to . . . 3040.01

T

Tangible personal property
. AMT treatment of contributions of . . . 20,070.03
. IRC Sec. 179 expensing of . . . 11,045–11,045.11

Target benefit plans . . . 3005.05

Tax assessment . . . 27,040
. extension of limitation on assessments . . . 27,040
. period of limitation . . . 27,040

Tax claims, settlement options for . . . 27,035–27,035.03

Tax computation for individuals, federal . . . 1010.01–1015.02

Tax Court, U.S.
. answer to petition by Commissioner for . . . 27,205–27,205.01

Tax Court, U.S.—continued
. appeal of assessment to . . . 27,020.03; 27,125.03; 27,185.02; 27,200–27,200.02
. appearance before and admission to practice before . . . 27,180–27,180.02
. as bound by IRS regulations . . . 27,190
. depositions for . . . 27,230
. hearing by . . . 27,225–27,225.04
. judgment without trial by . . . 27,220
. jurisdiction of . . . 27,185–27,185.05
. opinion rendered by . . . 27,240–27,240.03
. procedures in . . . 27,175–27,175.04; 27,195–27,195.05
. reply of taxpayer to . . . 27,210
. review of decision made by . . . 27,245–27,245.03
. supplemental pleadings to . . . 27,215
. trial by . . . 27,235–27,235.03

Tax credits. *See also* individual credits . . . 14,001–14,195.05
. adoption expenses credit . . . 14,015
. advanced nuclear facility business tax credit . . . 14,150
. agricultural chemicals security tax credit . . . 14,171
. alternative motor vehicle credit . . . 14,195
. carbon dioxide capture credit . . . 14,158
. cellulosic biofuel producer credit (renamed the second generation biofuel producer credit) . . . 14,170
. child and dependent care credit . . . 14,001
. child tax credit . . . 14,020
. clean renewable energy bond credit . . . 14,096
. in connection with passive activities . . . 13,090.12
. Code Sec. 36B premium assistance tax credit . . . 14,121
. credits for certain uses of gasoline and special fuels . . . 14,165
. disabled access credit . . . 14,090
. earned income credit . . . 14,005
. elderly and permanently disabled . . . 14,010
. election to claim accelerated AMT and research credits in lieu of bonus depreciation . . . 14,157
. employer social security credit on tips (FICA tip credit) . . . 14,110
. employer wage credit for activated military reservists . . . 14,126
. employers providing child care assistance for employees . . . 14,125
. empowerment zone and renewal community employment . . . 14,100
. enhanced oil recovery credit . . . 14,085
. estimated . . . 14,215.04
. first-time homebuyer credit . . . 14,047
. fuel production credits . . . 14,170
. general business . . . 14,050–14,155.03
. health coverage tax credit . . . 14,035
. homebuilder's credit for new energy-efficient homes . . . 14,140
. hope scholarship credit/american opportunity tax credit . . . 14,025
. indian employment credit . . . 14,105
. installation of alternative fueling stations . . . 14,155
. investment credit . . . 14,155
. lifetime learning credit . . . 14,030
. low income housing credit . . . 14,060
. manufacturer's credit for Energy-efficient appliances . . . 14,145
. mine rescue team training tax. . . 14,128
. mortgage credit certificate credit . . . 14,175
. new markets tax credit . . . 14,135
. orphan drug credit . . . 14,075

References are to paragraph (¶) numbers.

Tax credits. —continued
. personal . . . 14,001–14,047.04; 25,095
. plug-in electric drive motor vehicle credit . . . 14,180
. qualified zone academy bonds . . . 14,185
. railroad track maintenance credit . . . 14,127
. recovery in subsequent years of . . . 2190.06
. refunds for carrybacks of . . . 27,165–27,165.03
. renewable electricity production credit . . . 14,095
. research tax credit . . . 14,080
. residential alternative energy expenditures credit . . . 14,045
. residential energy property credit . . . 14,040
. retirement savings contribution credit . . . 14,130
. small business pension plan start-up expenses . . . 14,115
. small employer health insurance tax credit . . . 14,120
. in short tax year . . . 18,070.02
. therapeutic discovery tax credit . . . 14,055
. work opportunity tax credit . . . 14,065
. worker retention credit . . . 14,156

Tax deficiencies, interest on . . . 9005.03

Tax evasion, criminal . . . 27,045.01

Tax forms, requirements for substitute . . . 26,085

Tax liability computation
. expenses of, in miscellaneous itemized deductions . . . 9145.03
. option for IRS . . . 1015.02
. steps in . . . 1015.01

Tax preference items for AMT. *See also* individual items . . . 16,010–16,010.05
. in corporations . . . 16,035
. forms of . . . 16,010
. list of . . . 16,001.04
. of partnerships . . . 24,020.02

Tax rate schedules
. for alternative minimum tax . . . 16,001.01
. for capital gains . . . 8001.01
. for corporations . . . 20,010.01
. for dividends . . . 2080.01; 8001.01–.02
. for estates and trusts . . . 25,100.02; 29,135
. for provisional income . . . 5090.01
. for unemployment taxes . . . 15,070

Tax returns, corporation . . . 20,005.03; 26,030–26,040
. corporate existence for . . . 26,030.01
. due date for . . . 26,065.07–.08
. electronic filing of . . . 26,030
. extension of time for filing . . . 26,070.02
. for short tax year . . . 26,040

Tax returns, estate and trust . . . 25,100–25,100.05
. due date for . . . 26,065.09; 26,110
. filing requirements for . . . 29,195.01–.03
. payment of taxes with . . . 29,200.01

Tax returns, individual . . . 26,001–26,025.07
. additional information filed with . . . 26,090
. adjustments to basis for gains and losses on . . . 6001–6116
. agent appointed to submit . . . 26,015
. amended, rules for . . . 26,080–26,080.03; 27,050.05; 27,145.03; 29,025.02
. capital gains and losses on . . . 8001–8110.03
. deductions on, business . . . 12,001–12,220.02
. deductions on, personal . . . 9001–9165
. depreciation on . . . 11,001–11,065.03
. due date for . . . 26,065–26,065.06
. examination of IRS of. *See* Examinations, IRS
. extension of time for filing . . . 26,070–26,070.01; 26,070.03–.04
. fiduciary filing of . . . 26,020–26,020.04

Tax returns, individual—continued
. filing requirements for . . . 1001–1001.06; 26,001–.02
. final . . . 18,070.01; 26,065.06
. first . . . 18,070.01
. gross income on, exclusions from . . . 5001–5120.04
. gross income on, inclusions in . . . 1010.01; 2001–2190
. losses on . . . 13,001–13,175
. online tax payment options . . . 26,125
. payments for . . . 26,025.05; 26,100; 26,120; 26,125.02
. processing . . . 27,001
. retaining . . . 26,095.01
. signature on . . . 26,001.02–.04; 26,005.05; 26,015
. tax credits on . . . 14,001–14,195.05
. where to file . . . 26,075

Tax returns, limited liability company . . . 26,180.05

Tax returns, partnership
. due date for . . . 26,180
. fiduciary as managing . . . 26,180.03
. for taxpayers having interests in foreign partnerships . . . 26,180.02

Tax shelter
. abusing ratable basis recovery rules . . . 19,025.02
. abusive, audits triggered by . . . 27,001.03
. confidentiality privileges for taxpayer in . . . 25,210.02
. imputed principal amount of debt instrument in . . . 2070.06
. investor lists in . . . 26,210.05
. listed transactions for . . . 18,130.03; 26,210.03
. obligations of participants in . . . 26,210–26,210.09
. prepaid expenses of . . . 18,130.06
. promoters of . . . 26,210.06

Tax shelter farm activities . . . 16,005.09

Tax treaties
. provisions of . . . 28,060
. on withholding rates . . . 15,045.04

Tax years, calendar and fiscal . . . 18,055–18,075.01

Tax-exempt organizations
. change in tax year of . . . 18,065.01
. information returns of . . . 23,105–23,105.01; 26,170–26,170.08
. involved in tax shelters . . . 23,190
. joint ventures with for-profit organizations of . . . 23,109.04
. lobbying expenses for . . . 12,035.01; 23,107
. loss of exemption by . . . 23,115.02; 23,165.02
. organization types not qualifying as . . . 23,110.02
. political campaign activities prohibited for . . . 23,108
. requirement for tax-exempt hospital to remain tax-exempt . . . 23,110
. sanctions for . . . 23,108.01; 23,108.03
. self-dealing, estate administrative exception . . . 23,130
. taxed on unrelated business income . . . 23,105; 23,155–23,175.03; 26,065.10
. types of . . . 23,110.01

Tax-free exchanges of property. *See also* individual types . . . 6045–6075.07
. general rules for . . . 6045
. holding period for . . . 8020.02

Tax-free income. *See also* individual types . . . 5001
. business expenses allocable to . . . 12,015
. interest related to, as nondeductible . . . 9025.01

Tax-free reorganization (Type B reorganization) . . . 22,020
. sales disguised as . . . 22,090.04

References are to paragraph (¶) numbers.

Tax-sheltered (Sec. 403(b)) annuities . . . 3165–3165.07
. catch-up contributions to . . . 3165.06
. contribution limit for . . . 3165.06
. distributions from . . . 3165.08
. exclusion of employer contribution to . . . 3165.05
. investment choices for . . . 3165.07
. nondiscrimination requirements for . . . 3165.06
. qualifying employers for . . . 3165.04
. required minimum distributions from . . . 3165.08
. rollovers for . . . 3165.08
. salary reduction agreements for . . . 3165.07; 3165.06
. for tax-exempt organization employees . . . 3165

Taxable compensation . . . 2005.01

Taxable income
. adjusted . . . 20,150.01–.02
. determining corporate . . . 20,015.01
. determining individual . . . 1010.01
. determining S corporation . . . 21,030.01
. increased upon plan disqualification . . . 3015
. responsibility for tax liability for . . . 2001.02
. for short year . . . 18,070.02

Taxes paid, deduction of . . . 9030–9045

Taxpayer assistance orders (TAOs) . . . 27,005.08

Taxpayer identification number (TIN)
. for aliens . . . 26,050.05
. for EIC . . . 14,005.01; 14,005.07
. for household employers . . . 26,050.04
. for individuals . . . 26,050.01
. as key to processing returns . . . 27,001
. obtaining . . . 26,060
. for other taxpayers . . . 26,050.02
. for payees receiving payments . . . 26,055
. for preparers . . . 26,050.03
. purpose of . . . 26,045
. for recipients of long-term care benefits . . . 26,140.14
. for withholding . . . 14,225.01

Teachers, deduction of classroom material expenses of . . . 12,120.01

Teachers, education expenses of . . . 12,120

Terms interest sales, basis allocation in . . . 6080.05

Theft or casualty losses, tax treatment of deductions of . . . 2190.04

Thrift or savings plans as qualified plans . . . 3005.05

Timber, depletion of . . . 12,185–12,185.02

Timber, REITs for . . . 23,095.03

Timber, sale treatment given to cut . . . 8070
. for disposal under cutting contract . . . 8070.02
. election for . . . 8070.01

Tips
. adjusting tax reported on . . . 15,145.03
. employer FICA on . . . 15,075.03
. reporting . . . 15,140.02
. social security tax rules for . . . 15,075.03
. withholding rules for . . . 15,015.04

Top-heavy retirement plans
. benefits measured for . . . 3045
. key employees for . . . 3045.01
. minimum benefit requirements for nonkey employees in . . . 3045.03
. vesting accelerated in . . . 3045.02

Trade-in, basis of property acquired in . . . 6015.02

Transfers of property subject to power of appointment . . . 29,085–29,085.02

Transfers of property to corporation . . . 6045; 6075–6075.03

Transfers of property to corporation—continued
. basis of property in . . . 6075.05–.06
. determining corporate control in . . . 6045; 6075–6075.01
. disproportionate . . . 6075.02
. liability of shareholder assumed in . . . 6075.03
. reporting requirement for . . . 6075.07
. transfer of property to foreign corporation . . . 26,185

Transfers of property to investment company . . . 6075.04

Transit passes as fringe benefit . . . 4100.01

Transportation expenses
. defined . . . 10,001
. for medical treatment as deductible medical expense . . . 9105.05
. for production of income as deductible . . . 10,001

Transportation workers, rules for meals and lodging of . . . 10,005.01; 10,015.03

Travel allowance
. accountable plan for . . . 9145.01; 10,015–10,015.01; 12,120.03
. actual expenses exceeding . . . 10,015.02
. employer-designed . . . 10,015.04
. high-cost localities for, list of . . . 10,015.03
. per-diem . . . 10,005.01; 10,015.03; 10,015.05; 12,120.03

Travel expenses, deductible . . . 10,001–10,001.01
. of children and spouse . . . 10,001.03; 10,005.02
. education-related . . . 10,001.05
. foreign . . . 10,005.02; 10,005.03
. from home office to other work sites . . . 12,125.06
. incidental . . . 10,015.03
. investment-related . . . 10,001.06
. for job-related courses . . . 12,130.03
. personal travel mixed with . . . 10,001.03
. reporting . . . 10,010.03
. restrictions on . . . 10,005–10,005.05
. state legislators' . . . 10,005
. substantiation of . . . 10,010–10,010.02

Triangular reorganization . . . 22,045.01

Truck drivers' wages subject to social security taxes . . . 15,075.04

Truck tires, accounting method for costs of . . . 18,001.04

Trust instrument
. copy of, filed with fiduciary's statement . . . 25,100.03
. multiple trusts in single . . . 25,010.04
. of nonexempt trust . . . 23,151

Trusts . . . 25,001–25,125.01
. abusive schemes using . . . 25,010.05
. bypass . . . 29,050.03–.04
. charitable deduction of . . . 25,035.03; 25,065.01
. deductions of . . . 25,055–25,090
. defective grantor trust . . . 25,115.06
. defined . . . 25,010.01
. disclaimer . . . 29,165.02
. distributions to beneficiaries by . . . 25,085.01–.02
. estimated tax payments of . . . 25,105
. foreign . . . 26,065.08; 26,185.01; 27,001.03; 28,090.01–28,095
. for generation skipping transfer tax . . . 29,180.07–.09
. grantor . . . 25,115
. income interest in, as gift . . . 29,015.08
. intentionally defective grantor trust . . . 25,116
. material participation test for . . . 13,090.04
. misuse of . . . 27,001.03
. nonexempt, treatment as private foundations of . . . 23,151

References are to paragraph (¶) numbers.

Trusts—continued
. ownership of stock of beneficiaries by . . . 22,175.03
. as S corporation shareholders . . . 21,014
. tax year of . . . 25,110.02
. taxable income of . . . 25,015–25,020.03; 25,055; 25,115
. taxation of . . . 25,001–25,001.02
. term interests in property of . . . 29,030.02
. throwback rules for . . . 25,120
. transfer of property to . . . 25,050.01–.02
. trust decanting . . . 25,010

Tuition and fees deduction . . . 9165

Tuition payments as tax-free gifts . . . 29,020.04

20-factor test of whether workers are employees . . . 15,070.02

U

Unconventional sources, credit for production and sale of fuel from . . . 14,170.01

Undistributed personal holding company income . . . 23,020–23,020.03
. defined . . . 23,020.01
. dividends not deductible from . . . 23,020.02
. exceeding earnings, taxation of . . . 23,020.02
. tax rate on . . . 23,025

Unemployment benefits includible in gross income . . . 5090.02

Unemployment compensation, reporting . . . 26,140.02

Unemployment taxes (FUTA) . . . 15,110; 15,195
. calculating . . . 15,070
. credits for . . . 15,115
. due dates for . . . 15,135.02
. not paid by self-employed individuals . . . 15,070.01
. returns for and payment of . . . 15,120
. where to file . . . 15,120

Unharvested crops, gain or loss from sale of . . . 8075; 8075.02

Unified credit for gifts and transfers . . . 29,140

Uniform capitalization rules (UNICAP) for inventory basis . . . 6100; 17,045–17,045.07
. costs subject to . . . 17,045.05
. for interest . . . 17,045.11
. property excluded from . . . 17,045.04
. taxpayers excluded from using . . . 17,045.09
. taxpayers subject to . . . 17,045.01
. valuation of inventory in compliance with . . . 17,045.03

Uniform lifetime table for RMDs . . . 3120.03

Uniforms, laundry allowances for . . . 4090.02; 12,135

Unit of production depreciation . . . 11,065.01

Unit-livestock-price inventory valuation method . . . 17,070.04

U.S. income from foreign sources . . . 28,070.01–28,085.01
. bona fide residence test . . . 28,070
. foreign earned income defined . . . 28,070
. foreign earned income exclusion . . . 28,070
. foreign housing cost deduction . . . 28,070
. foreign housing expense exclusion . . . 28,070
. housing expense defined . . . 28,070
. physical presence test . . . 28,070
. tax home defined . . . 28,070

U.S. possessions, tax treatment of residents of . . . 28,080.01–.04
. establishing residence in U.S. possession . . . 28,080

U.S. possessions, tax treatment of residents of—continued
. filing requirements . . . 28,080
. possession exclusion for residents of America Samoa . . . 28,080
. tax treatment of Guam, American Samoa, Central Northern Mariana Islands . . . 28,080

U.S. savings bonds
. contributed to qualified tuition program . . . 5110.06
. for education, excluding from income interest on . . . 18,100.03
. interest reporting for . . . 18,100.01
. issued at discount . . . 18,100.01
. issued on current income basis . . . 18,100.02
. Series EE . . . 2070.08; 18,100.02

Unrelated business income (UBI) tax of tax-exempt organizations . . . 23,105; 23,160–23,175.03
. determining when sales are related to function in . . . 23,165.02
. exceptions for conventions and trade shows to . . . 23,165.01
. special rules for types of organizations for . . . 23,170.04
. unrelated business defined for . . . 23,165
. unrelated business taxable income defined for . . . 23,160
. unrelated debt-financed income subject to . . . 23,175–23,175.03
. tax rates for . . . 23,180
. tax returns for . . . 23,180
. types of income subject to . . . 23,170–23,170.04

Unrelated debt-financed income . . . 23,175–23,175.03

Useful life defined . . . 11,060.01

Useful-life depreciation system . . . 11,001
. depreciation methods under . . . 11,060.02
. salvage value of property under . . . 11,060.03

Usury for LLCs . . . 30,070

V

Vacant land, sale of . . . 7005.02

Vacation home
. as income-producing property, tax treatment of . . . 7005.01
. losses from . . . 13,105–13,105.05
. personal and rental (hybrid) use of . . . 13,105.04
. personal use ceiling for . . . 13,105.03
. planning for . . . 13,105.05
. profits from sale of . . . 7005.01; 13,105.05
. record retention for . . . 26,095.02
. as rental property . . . 13,105.05
. as qualified residence . . . 9015.07; 13,105.01

Vacation pay
. employer's deduction of . . . 18,145.01
. withholding on . . . 15,020.06

Vacations, employer-provided . . . 4090.03

Valuation methods for inventory . . . 17,025–17,060

Valuation of personal versus business use of company car
. cents-per-mile . . . 4005; 4005.04
. commuting use . . . 4005.05
. employer-selected . . . 4005; 4005.01
. fair market value . . . 4005; 4005.02–.03
. fleet-average rule . . . 4005.03
. fuel in . . . 4005.03
. IRS tables as safe harbor for . . . 4005.03

References are to paragraph (¶) numbers.

Valuation of personal versus business use of company car—continued
. for part-year use . . . 4005.03
Valuation of property in estate . . . 29,105.01–29,110.02
Vehicles
. adjusted basis of . . . 10,025.02
. allowance or reimbursement for expenses of . . . 10,035.04
. business use of personal . . . 10,020–10,020.03; 10,025.05–.06
. company-owned or provided . . . 4001–4020; 10,020.01; 10,025.05; 10,035.03; 15,015.03
. depreciation deduction for . . . 10,025–10,025.06; 11,040.08
. donations of . . . 9052
. electric . . . 10,025.03; 10,030.01
. employer FAVR reimbursement for employee's business use of personal . . . 10,020.03
. expensing . . . 10,025.04; 11,045.01
. leased . . . 10,030–10.030
. loans for, interest on . . . 10,020.01
. purchase of previously leased . . . 18,001.04
. recapture rule for deductions of . . . 10,025.05
. reporting requirements for deductions for . . . 10,035–10,035.04
. substantiating expenses of . . . 10,035.01–.03
. tires for . . . 12,010.02
Venture capital companies . . . 23,085
Vesting in qualified plans
. defined . . . 3020.04
. immediate, upon partial plan termination . . . 3035.03
. schedule types for . . . 3035–3035.03
. years of service required for . . . 3030.01
Viatical settlements of life insurance for terminally or chronically ill taxpayers . . . 5020.05
Victims of Terrorism Tax Relief Act of 2001 . . . 5100.03
. exclusions from gross income of assistance under . . . 5100.05–.06
Voluntary cancellation of debts . . . 13,165.01
Voluntary employee benefit associations (VEBAs), nondiscrimination testing for . . . 3040
Voluntary offshore disclosure program . . . 28,100
. reporting requirements . . . 28,100
. who must file Form 8938 . . . 28,100
Voluntary tip compliance programs . . . 15,015.04

W

Wage limitation for social security taxes . . . 15,050.01
Wages
. annualizing . . . 15,020.04
. average estimated . . . 15,020.09
. cash . . . 15,060.02
. constructive receipt of . . . 18,010.02
. defined . . . 15,015.01
. for employees of multiple employers . . . 15,020.08
. payments not taxed as . . . 15,080–15,080.06
. no payroll period for, withholding in cases of . . . 15,020.04
. subject to social security tax . . . 15,075–15,075.07
. subject to withholding tax . . . 15,015.01
Wash sales . . . 6005.02
. application to IRAs . . . 3135.03
. dealers exempted from rules for . . . 13,065.04
. holding period for . . . 8020.02; 13,065.02
. losses on . . . 13,065
. mutual fund . . . 6090.06
. securities in . . . 13,065.03
Whistleblower award
. tax treatment . . . 2015
Whistleblower claims . . . 27,071
. tax court jurisdiction . . . 27,071
Withholding
. adjustments to . . . 15,145–15,145.03
. on average estimated wages . . . 15,020.09
. backup . . . 14,225–14,225.06
. on deferred income . . . 15,040–15,040.04
. exempting wages from . . . 1001.04
. exemption from . . . 15,025.01
. federal income tax . . . 15,001–15,045.05
. FICA (social security) . . . 15,050–15,105.06
. figuring . . . 15,020–15,020.12; 15,030.05
. increased toward end of year when estimated tax is underpaid . . . 14,205.03
. on foreign corporate dividends . . . 28,030.02
. on foreign persons . . . 28,030.02–.03
. on fringe benefits . . . 15,015.03
. on insurance coverage . . . 15,015.05
. on lump-sum retirement distributions . . . 3125.02
. for nonresident aliens . . . 15,045–15,045.05; 15,155.02
. on nonwage payments . . . 15,020.12
. part-year employment method for . . . 15,020.05
. payments subject to . . . 15,015.01
. payor's liability for . . . 15,040.04
. percentage method for . . . 15,020.01
. purpose of . . . 15,001
. responsibility for . . . 15,005–15,005.03
. rules for . . . 15,020.03
. for sales of mutual fund (RIC) shares . . . 6090.06
. supplemental wages . . . 15,015.02
. taxpayers subject to . . . 15,010–15,010.02
. on tips . . . 15,015.04
. unemployment, federal and state . . . 15,110
. voluntary, claiming fewer allowances in . . . 15,020.10
. wage bracket method for . . . 15,020.02
. wages subject to . . . 15,015–15,015.07
Withholding allowances . . . 15,025–15,025.03; 15,160.02
Work clothes, deduction for . . . 4090.02; 12,135
Work opportunity tax credit (WOTC) . . . 14,065.01–.02
Worker retention credit . . . 14,156
Workers' compensation
. excluded from gross income . . . 5045.03
. FUTA for . . . 15,070
Working condition fringe benefits . . . 4090–4090.03
Working Families Tax Relief Act of 2004
. dependency exemption rules of . . . 1070.01
. depreciation under . . . 11,001.01
. qualifying child defined by . . . 1030.01; 1055.01; 14,020.03
. qualifying relative defined by . . . 1055.01
. research tax credit in effect for orphan drugs under . . . 14,075
. support test for qualifying child eliminated by . . . 1060.01
Worthless bonds . . . 13,150–13,160.01
Worthless stock . . . 13,040–13,040.05
Wrongful Death Damages . . . 5065

Y

Years of service
. break-in-service rules for disregarding . . . 3035.03
. counted for vesting . . . 3035.03
. defined for qualified plans . . . 3020.01